Yale Language Series

The Japanese Language Through Time

Samuel E. Martin

YALE UNIVERSITY PRESS

New Haven and London

Library of Congress catalog card number: 87–50521
International standard book number: 0–300–03729–5

Printed in the United States of America by Thomson-Shore, Inc.,
Dexter, Michigan

*The paper in this book meets the guidelines for permanence and durability
of the Committee on Production Guidelines for Book Longevity of the
Council on Library Resources.*

10   9   8   7   6   5   4   3   2

CONTENTS

i

Part Two: Intervocalic consonants and attested elisions

Part Three: Vowel distinctions

Part Four: Ryūkyū vowel developments

Part Five: Origins of the earlier vowels

Part Six: Reconstructing canonical shapes

Part Seven: Problems of reconstruction

Charts

Charts

Acknowledgments

This book was written over a ten-year period, during which I enjoyed the support and encouragement of many people and institutions. It would have been impossible for me to gather the information contained in this work without the opportunities made available by trips to Japan that were supported at various times by grants from the Sumitomo Faculty Research Funds of Yale University, the Japan Foundation, and the Ministry of Education. I have benefited from the libary and other resources of the National Language Research Institute (Kokuritsu Kokugo Kenkyūjo) and from consultations with various eminent Japanese scholars. In particular, I am grateful for the generous guidance and advice of Hattori Shirō, Hirayama Teruo, and Kindaichi Haruhiko; I have also learned much from Akinaga Kazue, Sakurai Shigeharu, and Uwano Zendō. The works of other scholars have been helpful, as can be seen from the frequent references to them throughout this work; among others, I would like especially to mention Fujiwara Yoichi, Haraguchi Shōsuke, Hayata Teruhiro, Hiroto Atsushi, Ishizuka Harumichi, Kobayashi Chieko (Oyama), Komatsu Hideo, Mabuchi Kazuo, Mochizuki Ikuko, Murayama Shichirō, Nakamoto Masachie, Nakasone Seizen, Okuda Kunio, Okumura Mitsuo, Ōno Susumu, Ōshima Ichirō, Shibata Takeshi, Takayama Michiaki, Tokugawa Munemasa, Tsukishima Hiroshi, Umegaki Minoru, and Yoshida Kanehiko. My research was also enriched by studying the works of a number of non-Japanese scholars, including Hugh D.B. Clarke, Bruno Lewin, G.B. Mathias, James D. McCawley, Roy A. Miller, W.E. Skillend, S. Starostin, Maner Thorpe, Timothy J. Vance, and Günther Wenck.

Under the working title "Earlier Japanese", the substance of the study was presented and discussed in Yale Graduate School seminars over several years, and I am grateful for the helpful comments of the students, especially Seungja Choi, Andrew Dillon, Jan Heikkala, Peter Hendricks, Karen Kay, J. Ross King, Alan Poul, S. Robert Ramsey, Karen Sandness, Rosalind Thornton, and J.M. Unger. Leon Serafim, who assisted my research for several years, made significant contributions to major parts of the work, and provided perceptive criticism of other sections. Helpful information was received also from Thomas Robb. The research in this work is built upon earlier study which owed much to insights received from working with Hamako Chaplin and from reading the published research of Bernard Bloch and his students.

The final version of the manuscript was prepared using a personally configured version of the word processor Spellbinder on a Victor 9000 computer, working with a NEC P-6 printer. I am grateful to those who created these technological aids and to those who helped me understand them and modify them as needed. In particular, Rufus Hendon generously provided essential information and wise counsel.

The book is fondly dedicated to Nancy Martin, without whose encouragement, patience, and love I would never have been able to complete it.

                                                                S.E.M.

January 1987.

Preface

This book is a reference work for those interested in studying the history of Japanese words and sounds. Chapter 1 traces the phonetic system of the language back to its prehistoric beginnings. Chapter 2 comprises an extensive study of the development of voicing and nasality as distinctive features of the consonants. Chapter 3 explains the development of several interrelated processes of compression and assimilation in verb and adjective forms. Chapter 4 is a comprehensive study of Japanese accent. And the last three chapters constitute a succinct etymological dictionary, supported by a thorough reconstruction of the morphological structures found in the principal parts of speech. Readings from the text have been effectively used in courses in the history of the Japanese language.

This work is an attempt to understand the sounds and shapes of earlier stages of the Japanese language. For that reason you will find the same word sometimes written in more than one way, depending on just which stage and just what problems are under discussion. At first this may seem annoying and even baffling to those accustomed to a particular way of seeing Japanese transcribed, but there should be no difficulty for those who read the sections through in order and follow the particular arguments advanced. The transcriptions are not intended to be "exact", for much of what passes as transcriptional exactitude is an illusion. At times we approximate the rough phonetic characteristics we are talking about; at other times we use a conventional spelling that derives from our analysis of the phonological structure.

It seems unlikely that we can ever find an "earliest" version of Japanese. Instead, what we reconstruct, going beyond the philological attestations, are successively earlier hypotheses about the shapes and meanings of words and the components that make them up. For some of our words the etymology is pursued to remote antiquity; other words have been left at much later stages, without further analysis, for a variety of reasons, particularly the scarceness or uncertainty of prerequisite data. In general, the older the hypothesized forms the less sure we can be of the details. All starred (= unattested) forms are to some extent suspect, and often even the unstarred forms rely heavily on specific philological interpretations that may be controversial. Some of our reconstructed forms are undoubtedly words that were not a part of a particular stage of Japanese at all; they are the shapes that would have existed had the word been a part of the language at that time. The asterisk (= star) is placed in front of any form that is unattested. There is a certain vagueness inherent in the notion "unattested". Sometimes it means a form that we have reason to reconstruct and that we believe must have existed; sometimes it means a form that does not occur and perhaps could not reasonably be expected to occur. But at other times it means that the form may very well occur though I have been unable to verify that it does; for such forms the asterisk is often preceded by a question mark.

Chapter 1. Syllables and their components.

Part One: Internal reconstruction of consonant distinctions

0. Introduction.

The Japanese language today is spoken in a number of quite different varieties, and some of them differ so much as to be mutually unintelligible. The spread of mass communication and education, however, is rapidly changing the habits of speech, even in remote areas, in the direction of the more limited variations found in "standard" speech, which takes the educated "uptown" Tōkyō patterns as a model. These patterns are far from homogeneous or stable and they are under constant pressure from other patterns on all sides, and especially those traditional to the "downtown" Tōkyō speakers. Tradition cites Shibuya as typically "uptown" and Asakusa as typically "downtown", with a true "Edo-kko" requiring at least three generations of residence in Tōkyō. Needless to say, these traditions correlate only in part with what is found in the linguistic data.

In seeking to find out all we can about earlier kinds of Japanese we must first consider our most authentic and extensive sources: the varieties of modern speech. Each variety offers us rich evidence in the form of alternations in the shapes of particular morphemes and groups of morphemes, the patterns of accent and juncture, and the competing forms. From such evidence we can deduce the earlier shapes with considerable confidence, especially when our hypotheses are well supported by other evidence. The other evidence is of two types: philological data, both direct and indirect, from texts dating back almost 1500 years; and the comparison of modern dialects with each other and with the philological data. Finally, with considerably less confidence, we can look to other languages for evidence of possible cognates or borrowings.

0.1. Kinds of evidence; internal reconstruction.

It is instructive to attempt the internal reconstruction of earlier forms of a language from a single modern variety, despite the obviously unnecessary and perhaps misleading limitations this imposes. As an introduction to the wider study that follows, we will begin by seeing what turns up in an examination of a particular variety of Japanese which is arbitrarily extrapolated from available descriptions of contemporary Tōkyō speech. Chart 1 displays the syllables that make up the shapes of words in this kind of Japanese. The transcription is broadly phonetic, with the symbol ḡ representing the velar nasal [ŋ] and capital F and V used to represent the bilabial fricatives [ɸ] and [β]. Those syllables in italics appear only in the shapes of recent loanwords or marginal words, such as interjections and mimetics, and speakers vary in the extent to which they make use of each of these unusual types. The syllables in parentheses are often heard in other versions: (Fu) is one way to say hu, now usual only when the u is unvoiced or dropped, as in Fu̥ta 'lid' or na'iFu̥ 'knife', and even these are often heard with the nonlabial pronunciation. The syllables "(hya hyu hyo hi)" are replaced by ša šu šo ši in downtown Tōkyō and in individual words they are sometimes confused by uptown speakers, as well. By starting with the merged version, which has only the [š] type syllables, we will learn a useful point about internal reconstruction, as shown below.

1

0.2. Syllables and moras.

The top of Chart 1 presents a set of one-mora syllables. But there are also syllables that consist of a one-mora syllable followed by a dependent mora to make a two-mora syllable, sometimes called a "heavy" syllable. There are three kinds of dependent moras. The oral T (also written "Q") is a nonsyllabic oral obstruent with its articulation determined by the following consonant, so that the result is a prolonged consonant; and that phenomenon is often identified with the final glottal catch that abruptly ends certain interjections and marginal items. The nasal N (also written "ñ") is a nonsyllabic mora pronounced when final as a nasal prolongation of the vowel; when nonfinal, it assimilates in place of articulation to the following articulation. This sound is also used initially in the traditional pronunciations of what is written (and often pronounced) "uma, ume, umo", as in Nmaˀ = umaˀ 'horse', Nme⁻ = ume⁻ 'plum', Nmoreˀg̊i⁻ = umoreˀg̊i⁻ 'bogwood'. These pronunciations are quite old, and they are represented by the spelling "mum···" in syllabic writing of the Nara and Heian periods. The early-18th century Japanese-Korean glossary Waye ˡyuhay = Wago-ruikai used the unusual Hankul configuration "ngmwu···" to transcribe the prothetic nasal: ngmwu.ma (2:22v) = m[u]ma 'horse', and ngmwu.mye (2:29r) = m[u]me 'plum'. In later sections of what you are reading you will find N written just "n", followed by a hyphen or an apostrophe when (as before a vowel or y) it might be mistaken for the onset consonant /n/. And T will usually be written as a gemination of the following consonant: -pp-, -tt-, -kk-, -ss-.

The third type of dependent mora is a nonsyllabic vowel extension — either homorganic, realized as a prolongation which yields a long vowel; or diphthongal, rising to i (and in recent loanwords perhaps also to u). In downtown speech the diphthongs are frequently reduced to monophthongs: both ai and oi become ee, and ui becomes ii. For takaˀi 'high' you hear takeˀe, sug̊oˀi 'dreadful' is sug̊eˀe, and waruˀi 'bad' is wariˀi; maˀiniti 'every day' is not differentiated from meˀeniti 'death anniversary'. And usui⁻ 'is thin' sounds like usii, not ušii, introducing an additional type of unusual syllable *si*, which we did not bother to put in our chart. At some earlier time the sound traditionally written as "ei" become monophthongized as long /ee/ in Tōkyō and many other parts of Japan, though not all; and the /ee/ version is heard even in verb forms such as maneˀete = maneˀite 'beckoning' and huseˀede = huseˀide 'defending'. Under the influence of the written standards, however, younger speakers even in Tōkyō sometimes replace /ee/ by /ei/, They also replace Nmaˀ by umaˀ, and some speakers will use a back rounded vowel for "su tu zu" instead of the traditionally centralized unrounded [ɨ]. For those syllables without a sibilant, Chart 1 indicates a rounded version, but the rounding is often weak; the older tradition has a back unrounded vowel [ï] (IPA inverted "m") in eastern Japan. (On these points, see Doi 1957:235, citing Kindaichi Haruhiko.)

Three-mora syllables seem to occur in certain marginal words such as mimetics and impressionistic forms (ooTpira niˀ 'openly', booTkire⁻ = bookire⁻ 'a stick') and recent loanwords; also perhaps in verb forms such as toˀoTte 'passing' and haˀiTte 'entering', and even kaˀeTte 'returning'. These "extra-heavy" syllables have shapes like CV:N (or CV:T-), CV:i, CViN (or CViT-); but they will readily break into two syllables CV-VN, CV-VT, CV-i, CV-iN, CV-iT-. Tōkyō Japanese does not permit the accentual locus to occur on a dependent mora, yet we find cases like meeˀn-šuu 'the state of Maine', sɨpeiˀn-kaze 'Spanish influenza', sɨpuuˀn-rui 'spoons', hooˀn-rui 'horns', rooˀN-zoku 'salary-loan victims', and booiˀ-boo 'bellboy cap' that suggest a syllable division. Accentual evidence can be adduced to establish that there are heavy (two-mora) syllables with ui: ᵈŽiNruˀi-g̊aku 'anthropology' rather than the *ᵈŽiNruiˀ-g̊aku that we would expect if ru and i were separate syllables.

The accentuation of osoꞌi ka 'is it slow?' (rather than *osoiꞌ ka) would appear to confirm the existence of heavy syllables with -oi, though there are few examples of oi within a morpheme except for recent loans; the syllables with ai and ui or ɨi appear in Chinese loanmorphs (taꞌi-i 'gist', yuꞌi-itsɨ 'unique', sɨꞌi-i 'the water level') as well as in adjective forms such as kuraꞌi ka 'is it dark?', nemuꞌi ka 'are you sleepy?', usɨꞌi ka 'is it thin?'. But tooiꞌ ka 'is it far?' has a syllable division before the -iꞌ.

0.3. Long vowels; rearticulated vowels.

We are following the established practice of writing long vowels as double. We assume that a word like booi⁻ 'bellboy' has the same number of moras as a word like aoi⁻ 'hollyhock' but that the former is pronounced as two syllables [bo:-i] and the latter as three [a-o-i], or possibly two with a different division [a-oi]. It is, however, quite possible to pronounce /oo/ as two syllables, as well as two moras, by rearticulating the vowel; you keep the quality constant but put a kind of squeeze in the middle, with a decrescendo-crescendo effect. There are Japanese linguists who claim that such a pronunciation is distinctive from the long-vowel pronunciation in differentiating certain cases where the word contains a morpheme boundary: goꞌ-oku 'five hundred million' pronounced as three syllables with vowel rearticulation, goꞌoku 'karma sufferings' as two syllables with a long vowel in the first; sato-oya⁻ 'foster parent' differentiated from satooya⁻ 'sugar dealer'. One way to handle this situation is to insert what we may call Hattori's Apostrophe: goꞌ'oku, sato'oya⁻. Hattori (1961) sets up a phoneme of simple vowel onset which he writes by placing on line the mark for "smooth breathing" (*spiritus lenis*) which the ancient Greeks put over an initial vowel to differentiate it from an initial h- which they wrote with the reverse mark, called "rough breathing" (*spiritus asper*): ὀ = o, ὁ = ho. Since the Japanese phonetic phenomenon is distinctive only medially, and then only at morpheme boundaries, it is probably better treated as a kind of juncture. I have the impression that this subtle distinction, like that of English *a name* vs. *an aim*, is normally neutralized in ordinary speech when the words are familiar and are said in context: sato(')oya⁻ 'foster parent' and satooya⁻ 'sugar dealer' both with the long [to:] and without the rearticulation. On radio broadcasts I have heard [niꞌdʒu: | go:kuꞌeN] 'two billion five hundred thousand Yen' with a long vowel across the morpheme boundary. Additional evidence for Hattori's Apostrophe is found in pairs like su'u(ꞌ) [sɨ-u] 'sips' and suꞌu [sɨ:] 'number', su'uta⁻ [sɨ-u-ta] 'concert performance of stage music' and suꞌuta [sɨ:-ta] 'several', su'ꞌuri [sɨ-uri] 'vinegar vendor' and suꞌuri [sɨ:ri] 'mathematical principle'; in these words the quality of the vowel changes as it undergoes rearticulation as a separate syllable. Here again, though, I believe the distinction is neutralized in ordinary speech, where su(')u sounds like [sɨ:]; and, said fast, even the word tuu'uN [tsɨ:-uN] 'transportation' may suppress its ordinary rearticulation and sound like [tsɨ::N]. We write the long vowels as geminates and when they are sometimes rearticulated we will separate the two by using the hyphen that indicates the boundary between syllables or, as appropriate, between morphemes. The distinctive hyphen we use to write Hattori's Apostrophe (in those cases when it is not neutralized) is a readily removable feast. It but rarely turns up within a morpheme and there are many longer words where it is never needed; moreover, even in those words where the boundary is called for, it readily drops. Japanese linguists will sometimes write /'/ to indicate morphophonemic boundaries that are not heard at the surface level: two morphemes comprise saꞌ'i 'difference', and the accent of sa'iꞌ-do 'degree of difference' as contrasted with that of saꞌido 'side' implies two one-mora syllables in the underlying form, but the word ordinarily sounds exactly the same as the saꞌi

that represents several one-morpheme words 'talent; wife; rhinocerus; ...'. The
Chinese binom sa-u '(left-right →) information, instructions', just like the single
morpheme sau 'aspect', has become so⌐o in modern Japanese, with the hiragana
spelling "so-u"; and a similar pronunciation is given by the Hankul guide to the
hiragana version "sa-u" cited in the 1676 Korean work Chep-hay sin-e (= Shōkai-
shingo): ngkwo.swo.wu.nwo.ta.myey (10:18v) = go-sou no tame 'for your guidance'.
Between the earlier (sa'u >) sau and modern so⌐o the monophthongized sɔɔ (written
"sǒ") is attested by the Japanese-Portuguese dictionary of 1603.

I assume that rapid speech will run VV together as a single syllable whenever
possible: aa, ee, ii, oo, uu; ai, ui, perhaps oi; ei will be replaced by ee. And
sometimes o'u is replaced by oo, for ko'uri⌐teN 'retail store' is often pronounced
koori⌐ten (cf. kooriya⁻ 'ice dealer', kooriteki⁻ 'utilitarian'). But whenever the
accentual locus is heard on what would otherwise be a dependent mora, I assume a
rearticulation: ši'iru 'seal' is three moras in two syllables but šii⌐ru 'forces' is
three moras in three syllables even though the morpheme division must be taken as
šii-ru; ha⌐-aku⁻ 'grasp(ing)', a Chinese binom, and ma⌐aku 'mark' are both usually
pronounced as three moras in two syllables. I have recorded šiN-koobe⌐-eki 'New
Kōbe station' with the syllable [be:]. Other examples of e-e where long [e:] has
been observed: kareeda⁻ 'dead branch', ise⌐ebi⁻ 'lobster', kaǧe⌐e 'shadow picture',
hamee-a⌐sobi 'jigsaw puzzle', ie⌐ e no | mitši⁻ 'the way home'. And of e-i: keeto⁻
= ke-ito⁻ 'wool', teere⌐ = te-ire⌐ 'care; repair', me⌐eša = me⌐-iša 'eye doctor'.
On evaluating negative judgments by Japanese on pronunciations of the latter sort,
we must keep in mind the fact that a number of standard speakers are under the
impression they never pronounce ee for ei even within a morpheme, and some of them
actually say /ei/ as the spelling indicates for Chinese loanwords like "teinei"
= te⌐enee 'polite', attempting to keep them distinct from English loanwords like
me⌐edee 'May Day', though these too, despite the kana spelling with the bar that
indicates the vowel elongation, may end up hypercorrected to /ei/, thereby sounding
more like the original English versions.

0.4. Syllable boundaries.

The view of surface-syllable boundaries taken here is that they are normally
predictable in terms of the particular mora strings and the accentual pattern of the
phrase. That is why, despite our earlier disclaimer, a syllable boundary may in fact
intrude within a morpheme in such words as šii⌐ru 'compels', mee⌐Nšuu 'the state of
Maine', and sɨpei⌐Nkaze 'Spanish influenza'. It should be borne in mind that many
Japanese words, especially those fancy terms resulting from the national addiction
to making up new Chinese-character compounds, are more often written than spoken;
when they are read aloud the underlying boundaries tend to surface for all but the
most familiar words. Conversation is not laden with such terms as to-oo⁻ 'going to
Europe', too-oo⁻ 'Eastern Europe', or ᵈzo⌐o-o 'hatred'; there are easier ways to say
the same things. When you would expect a sequence like /oo-o/ in speech it is often
reduced to just /oo/: ᵈzo⌐o (o) | mi⌐ro 'Look at the elephant', o⌐o(o) gozaimasɨ
'There are many'. On the other hand, the word zyo-o⌐o 'queen' is often conflated
into zyoo-o⌐o.

Some dialects of Japanese drastically shorten the dependent moras, so that the
"heavy" (two-mora) syllables sound much like the "light" (one-mora) syllables, or
like English syllables. These have been dubbed "syllabeme" dialects by Shibata; they
are found in northeast Honshū, Niigata, Shimane, southeast Kyūshū, Tokunoshima,
and Yonaguni (cf. the map in Iwanami Kōza Nihongo 5:135). Certain dialects, notably
those of Kagoshima and Amami-Ōshima, readily suppress final high vowels, permitting
unreleased consonants to close a syllable.

0.5. Unvoiced vowels.

There are syllables in which the vowel is unvoiced (as if whispered) or even dropped, but leaves behind in the consonant some trace of its palatal (i) or non-palatal (u, ɨ) quality. The vowel unvoicing occurs under largely predictable rules, though there is considerable variation between dialects and speakers and even for a single speaker within individual words that reflect certain shape types (such as hih···, ših···, huh···, sɨh···); these problems we will set aside. The common devoicing rules used in Tōkyō are given in Chart 1. It is hard to say just how old these rules are (cf. Miyajima 1961), but the devoicing of high vowels (ɨ ʉ) between voiceless consonants probably goes back at least five centuries, if not longer. Cf. Sakurai 1978b:11, who says also that the modern heavy syllables developed (by uniting two separate one-mora syllables) sometime during the Muromachi period. On the possibility of earlier subsyllabic moras, see §52.

0.6. Notations.

The notations of accent, described more fully in Chapter 4, are made by placing the hook mark (ᐟ) after the vowel before an inherent fall of pitch, i.e. at the end of the last high syllable. When two or more marks appear, the word allows variant accentuations; if one of the variants is atonic that is shown by putting a raised minus (⁻) at the end of the word. While atonic words can be left unmarked, we will overtly mark them by putting the raised-minus at the end (kaze⁻ 'wind'), so that when a form is cited with no marks it means we offer no information on the accentuation.

Korean forms are cited in the Yale romanization, modified for Middle Korean to allow for the now obsolete vowel written *o, which was probably pronounced like a somewhat unrounded [ɔ], and for the obsolete consonants -W- (probably [β]), -G- ([γ] or [ɦ]), and -z-. The Korean vowel u is unrounded [ɨ]; wu and wo are rounded [u] and [o] respectively, and for modern Korean the w can be omitted for wo, and after the labials for wu, since there are no surface contrasts with the unrounded u and o. Modern Chinese forms are cited in Pīnyīn romanization; earlier forms are in a very rough approximation to reconstructed Middle Chinese readings or to earlier Japanese interpretations of them. Other notational devices are explained as they turn up.

1. Mimetic reduplications.

Mimetic reduplications simply iterate the morpheme and usually locate the accent at the end of the first syllable. These initial consonants form mimetic sets:

t : d		toᐟn-ton	doᐟn-don	(tapping)
s : ᵈz		saᐟwa-sawa	ᵈzaᐟwa-zawa	(rustling)
k : g		keᐟra-kera	geᐟra-gera	(laughing)
h : p : b	haᐟta-hata	paᐟta-pata	baᐟta-bata	(slapping)

Only oral g (never nasal ḡ) is used in these morphemes. When ᵈz... is iterated, the fricative z is heard, rather than the affricate ᵈz. The two articulations are not in contrast: the affricate version is usual after juncture (as at the beginning of a word) and the fricative version is usual within a word, except in extremely slow or overarticulated pronunciations. The opposition of voiced vs. unvoiced obstruent is exploited for mimetic effect, lending connotational nuances to the words. A puzzle: Why is h- an additional member of the p : b set, though it shares no common feature (such as labiality or obstruence) with that pair of sounds?

2. Reduplication of noun or adjective.

Reduplicating a noun or adjective stem induces a change in the initial of the repeated morpheme in the following cases:

t : d	taka-daˀka	tokiˀ-dokiˉ	
ts : z			tsɨneˀ-zɨˀneˉ
s : z	samaˀ-zaˀmaˉ	soreˀ-zore	sᶖkiˀ-zᶖki
š₁: ž			šimaˀ-žima
tš : ž			tšᶖka-žikaˉ
k : ḡ	kataˀ-ḡata	kotoˀ-ḡoto	kuniˀ-ḡuni kiˀ-ḡi
h : b	haya-baˀya	hoso-boˀso	hiˀ-bi
F : b			Fu̯ka-buˀka
š₂: b			širo-biˀro šᶖtoˀ-bito

Excepted are morphemes that contain b, ḡ, d, z, or ž to begin with ("Lyman's Law", see Ch. 2), such as tabi-tabiˉ, taˀda-tada, tšᶖˀbi-tšibi, tsɨḡiˀ-tsɨḡi, kaˀdo-kado, kaˀzɨ-kazɨ, tsɨžɨˀ-tsɨžɨ. These structures are very old and the rules are found in the earliest forms attested. The rules are regular but in modern Japanese they are productive only in certain dialects (mostly in the Ryūkyūs). They were not applied to words borrowed from Chinese: ten-teˀnˉ 'points', teki-tekiˉ 'dripping', haˀN-haˀN 'half and half', kuu-kuuˉ 'empty, vacant', koˀ-ko 'every house, door-to-door', tšoˀo-tšooˉ 'butterfly', šoˀ-šo 'various places', šiˀ-ši 'lion'. There are a few apparent exceptions, such as šuˀ-žu 'various', saN-zaˀNˉ 'brutally'; but seˀe-zee 'to one's utmost' is a reduplication only by false analogy. The rule does not apply to terms for body parts (hoˀ-[h]o 'cheek', tšᶖtšiˀ 'breast', teˀ-teˉ 'handsy') or kin roles (haˀ-ha 'mother', tšᶖtšiˀ 'father'). Except for teˀ-teˉ 'handsy' it may not be obvious that each of these examples is a reduplication. The words for 'father' and 'mother' are presumed to reduplicate the morphemes that appear as related shapes in oˀ-ži 'uncle' and oˀ-ba 'aunt'. Short forms for 'cheek' and 'breast' appear in ho-ppeˀta 'cheek' and tšiˀ-busa 'breast, udder'; we assume that the first syllables in these two words represent the unreduplicated etymon and are not the result of truncation. Other reduplicated body parts include mi-miˀ 'ear(s)', moˀ-mo 'thigh(s)', and meˀ-me (babytalk) 'eye(s)'. All the body parts with reduplicated names come as anatomical pairs.

Puzzles: (1) Why do h··· and F··· reduplicate as b···? (2) Why does š(i)··· sometimes reduplicate as b(i)···? (3) Why does k··· reduplicate as a nasal ḡ rather than an oral g (unlike the mimetics)? Except for these problems, the opposition (given that z substitutes for ᵈz internally) is voiced obstruent vs. unvoiced. There are no colloquial examples for te, se, ke, or he; cf. §38. (The reduplication teraˀ-dera 'every temple' is attested in earlier literature, but without indicating whether the initial of the third syllable was d or t.

3. Puzzling alternations.

Notice that Tōkyō š₁ alternates with ž and Tōkyō š₂ alternates with b(i). In other dialects š₂ is pronounced [ç], a voiceless palatal spirant without the sibilant groove (hush), or — when the following i is fully voiced as in himaˉ free time' — even as [h], a nonysyllabic voiceless i̯. For such dialects /hi/ ([çi] or [hi]) is in contrast with /si/ ([ši]), and hiˀ-hi 'baboon' will not be a homophone of šiˀ-ši 'lion' (these are both loanwords from Chinese). But the puzzle remains. Why is h- in alternation with b- — and for the mimetics with p-, as well — even though a shared (common) phonetic feature is lacking?

4. Oral and nasal versions of "g".

In our variety of Tōkyō speech g is in contrast with ḡ = [ŋ]: se˺ngo 'after the war' has the nasal ḡ but se˺ngo '1,005' has the oral g; ooḡa˺rasi 'big crow' ≠ ooga˺rasi 'large pane'. For many morphemes there are two shape alternants, oral g··· at the beginning of a word, including a free word used as the second component of a compound with another free word (as in kootoo-ga˺kkoo 'high school'), and the nasal ···ḡ··· within a word. The second morpheme of ka˺i-ḡun 'navy' is the first morpheme of gun-kan⁻ 'warship'; ge˺-ḡe 'lowest' is a reduplication. An oral g with no nasal reflex appears in recent loanwords, even internally (purogu˺ramu 'program'), and in mimetic words. A nasal ḡ with no oral reflex appears internally in native morphemes: kaḡi˺ 'key', ko˺ḡ-u 'row', aḡar-u⁻ 'rise'.

Some speakers (cf. Shibata 1965:100) use a voiced velar fricative [γ] in place of the nasal [ŋ], and in rapid speech the sound may drop completely when between vowels: /suimase˺n/ can mean suḡimase˺n 'it does not exceed' as well as suimase˺n 'does not smoke/sip' and the unique abbreviation of su[m]imase˺n 'excuse me; thank you'. According to Komatsu 1981 (Nihon-go no sekai 7:256-7) a similar weakening of -b- to a voiced labial fricative [β] is heard in longish words (abunai⁻, sabisi˺i, abare˺ru, kabu˺ru, kobore˺ru) but not at morpheme boundaries (se˺-bire⁻, ka-bin, to-bu˺kuro˺⁻, ka-boso˺i, ko-ba˺nasi, ne-buka˺i, su-baya˺i).

In many dialects the two kinds of g fall together as a single phoneme, and it is pronounced in one of three ways:

(1) oral [g], as in most of the Ryūkyūs and Kyūshū, south Honshū, west Shikoku, the Bōsō peninsula (Chiba) and the Izu islands (including Hachijō), Niigata, ...;

(2) nasal [ŋ], as in parts of Wakayama (Zhs 4:369, 397) and in a small area from Hamana Lagoon to Toyohashi (Zhs 3:19);

(3) prenasalized oral [ŋg] or [ᴺg], with a shorter nasal than that found in standard [baŋ·gohan] ban-go˺han 'supper', heard in Wakayama and south Shikoku. There are islands with [-ŋ-] in the Ryūkyūs (Kikai, Yonaguni, ...), and a few isolated areas have [-g-] in northeastern Honshū (Kgg 113:83a) and elsewhere.

The dialect of Irabu (Miyako) replaces -g- by a glottal stop, which we write as -q-: *agari > aqaï 'east', *[w]aga > aqa 'my' (Hirayama 1967:300).

5. Attaching vowel-initial endings to consonant-final stems.

Verbs of the "consonant-stem" (*yo-dan*) conjugation attach the endings -i (infinitive), -u (imperfect predicative), and -a··· (negative, etc.):

···k-i	···k-u	···k-a···		···ḡ-i	···ḡ-u	···ḡ-a···
···tš-i	···ts-i	···t-a···		···n-i	···n-u	···n-a···
···š-i	···s-i	···s-a···				
···r-i	···r-u	···r-a···				
···b-i	···b-u	···b-a···		···m-i	···m-u	···m-a···
··· -i	··· -u	···w-a···				

We notice that -u appears as -i (high central unrounded) after ts and s; the two sounds are in complementary distribution, as we discover in looking at their occurrence within morphemes, where the central version always appears after the sibilant and the back version never appears there. (The back version is clearly rounded only when unvoiced, and many speakers fail to round their lips noticeably for any occurrence of /u/.) We deduce that an earlier back rounded vowel [u] has largely lost its rounding and has been moved forward to a central position in assimilation to the point of articulation of the sibilant [s] and, of course, the affricate [ts]. Alternations to examine: š (before -i) and s; tš (before -i) and ts (before -u [i]) and t; zero (before -i and -u) and w (before a).

6. Alternations of h- with p-.

Alternations of h- with p- are found in several sets of words:

(1) Related Chinese binoms, as in den-poo 'telegram' with hoo-koku 'report' and koꞋo-hoo 'official report'. In binoms containing at least one bound element (and usually both are bound), all Chinese-origin morphemes that begin with h··· in most environments will appear as p··· after a morpheme that ends in ···n. The version with p··· appears also after the ···T which is a reduction of ···tu or ···ti, as in ᵈzaT-pooˉ 'general news'; cf. ᵈzatsɨ-rokuˉ 'miscellaneous notes'.

(2) After the intensive infix -T- native morphemes appear with p··· instead of h···: yoTpodoˉ = yohodoˉ 'quite', yaTpaꞋri = yahaꞋri 'after all; also', karaTpetaˉ 'totally unskilled (hetaꞋ)', kuiTpaḡureˉ = kui-haḡureˉ 'missing a meal, loss of livelihood', ··· . See also (4) below.

(3) After the intensive prefix ma(T)-, as in maT-kuꞋro 'jet black' and maT-šiꞋro 'snow white' and maT-taꞋira 'quite flat', the p··· version will appear: maT-paꞋdaka 'stark naked', maT-piꞋruma 'broad daylight (hirumaꞋ)', maT-pṵtaꞋtsɨ = ma-hṵtaꞋtsɨ 'right in two', ...

(4) Etymological sets: haT-paˉ 'leaf' (apparently this is a reduplication of haˉ 'leaf'); kenkaTpayaꞋi = kenka-bayaꞋi 'quick (hayaꞋi) to quarrel (ken-kaˉ)'; dadaTpiroꞋi 'unduly wide (hiroꞋi)'; šišiꞋTpana = šišiꞋbana '(tiger nose =) a snub/pug nose (hanaˉ)'; karaTparaˉ = sɨkiTparaˉ 'empty stomach (haraˉ)'; mukaTparaˉ = mukabaraˉ 'anger' (cf. haraꞋ o tateꞋru 'get angry'); yoTpiteˉ 'all night long' < yoTpɨtoi < yoꞋ hɨtoꞋ-yo 'one night of night'; pɨkaꞋ-pɨka hɨkaꞋru 'flash with a flash'; nagaTposoꞋi 'long and slender (hosoꞋi)' (Hirayama); ... . The word aꞋTpaꞋreˉ 'splendid, bravo' is from an earlier apare = aware but that fact is not immediately relevant here.

(5) A number of h··· morphemes appear as p··· after contracted variants of verb infinitives (see RGJ 400):

hɨki/hɨT   hɨTpaꞋru 'pull' < hɨki-haꞋru, hɨTpaꞋḡ(aꞋs)u 'strip' < hɨki-haꞋḡu, hɨTpataꞋku 'slap' < hɨki-hataꞋku, ...

o[]i/oT   oTpazimeꞋru 'begin' < o[]i-hazimeꞋru, oTporidaꞋsu 'throw out' < o[]i-hooridaꞋsu, oTpesu 'press down' < *o[]i-heꞋsu (for *heꞋsu cf. heši-oru 'break, smash' and ošiaꞋi hešiaꞋi 'pushing and shoving'), ...

yo[]i/yoT   yoTparaꞋu 'get drunk' < yo[]i-haraꞋu.

(6) The prefix ko(T)- 'little' in koTpiꞋdoku = hiꞋdoku 'harshly'. Cf. kodaꞋkaku = taꞋkaku 'high', koḡitaꞋnakuˉ = kɨtaꞋnaku 'untidily', kozewaꞋšɨku = sewaꞋšɨku 'hurriedly', ...

(7) The suffix -Tpanaši (deꞋ) '(leaving) just as it is' from hanaꞋši 'leaving it' (infinitive of a transitive verb), making a sentence conversion. See RGJ 422-3.

7. Correspondence of dialect p- with standard h-.

In many dialects of the Ryūkyūs p··· corresponds to Tōkyō h···: Miyako pana = Tōkyō hanaꞋ 'flower'. In some parts of the Ryūkyūs F··· ("hw···") is found in part or much of this vocabulary: Shuri Faa = Miyako paa = Tōkyō haˉ 'leaf'. Kobayashi (1975:82 n.73) reports Fa Fe Fo for ha he ho — but [çi] not Fi for hi — from older speakers in Izumo, and Fe for he from older speakers in Yamaguchi (62 n.45).

In Shizuoka (Tashiro-buraku in Ikawa-mura of Abe-gun) p··· is reported for panasu = hanaꞋsu 'speak', pukee = hukaꞋi 'deep', puru = huꞋru 'rain' and hoꞋru 'dig'), etc. (Zhs 7:26-7, but no text examples 7:247ff, cf. Miyara 1954:173); this is reported (Zhs 7:27) also for the Hachijō islands off the Izu peninsula.

Sporadic relics of initial p··· occur in the Nakanogō dialect of Hachijō, including pare- = ha're- 'get clear', pikar- = hika'r- 'flash', and pur- = hu'r- 'fall' and hur-⁻ 'shake' (Kgg 43:56 (1961)). But Hirayama (1965:12) thinks these cases of an initial p··· (and others) are secondary results of mimetic factors or the loss of a prefix. Cf. Shin Nihongo-kōza 3:117. Initial p- is also reported from Sanbu-gun in Chiba prefecture (Hōgen-gaku kōza 2:286-7).

8. Initial w-.

The initial w(a) of Tōkyō Japanese does not normally alternate with ···p···, unlike the h··· : wa' 'wheel' ≠ ha' 'tooth'; wata' 'cotton; guts' ≠ hata' 'flag'; watasu 'pass it over' ≠ hata'su 'fulfill/accomplish it'; ... . Nor does w··· alternate with ···b···. The counter for birds (itŠi'-wa 'one bird', sa'n-ba 'three birds', ᵈŽi'p-pa 'ten birds') uniquely intrudes a w··· allomorph into what is basically the usual h/p/b alternation, as found in iT-piki' 'one animal', sa'n-biki 'three animals', go'-hiki 'five animals'. The counter for birds, sometimes used also to count rabbits, derives from the noun ha⁻ = hane⁻ 'feathers, wing' but it never actually appears in the shape -ha; a homophone counts bundles and shows the same alternations. On how the -w- came about, see the morpheme-internal examples in §14, §15.

9. Correspondence of dialect b- with standard w-.

In various parts of the Ryūkyūs initial b··· corresponds to Tōkyō w··· : the Miyako words bara 'straw' and baka- 'young' correspond to Tōkyō wa'ra and wa'ka-. The first-person pronoun wa'(-re) 'I/me' is pronounced ba(-) in Miyako and Yaeyama. Corresponding to wa'ru- 'bad' we find baru-(sa-an) in Yonaguni; baru-(sa-han) in Hateruma of the Yaeyama islands; bai- (Ikema) and baz- (Hirara) in Miyako. Wakasu 'boil it' is bagasun in the Ishigaki dialect of Yaeyama; waka'i 'young' is baki-san in the Sonai dialect of Yaeyama (the second vowel is unexplained).

10. Reconstruction of wi, we, wo.

In Tōkyō w··· occurs only before the vowel /a/. Ryūkyū b··· sometimes appears before other vowels, for which an earlier Tōkyō or Kyōto w··· is confirmed by the philological evidence reflected in the historical spelling (rekisi-teki kana-zu'kai):
    (1) o'no 'ax' (historical spelling "wono") is bunu in Yonaguni; oba 'aunt' ("woba") is buba; oTto 'husband' ("wo(T)to") is butu; oi 'nephew' ("wohi") is bui; o'r-i 'be' ("wori") is bu-n; ototo'i 'day before yesterday' ("wototohi") is bututi; onna' 'woman' ("womina") corresponds to bunya 'woman, aunt' in the Sonai dialect of Yaeyama. According to Hirayama, Yonaguni oddly has ugi (not *bugi) for 'bucket' ("woke") but Miyara 1930:C-131b has "[vu:g'i]" with a different initial from the [u-] he writes elsewhere; Taketomi (Yaeyama) has buuki and Nakasuji (Miyako) guki but bur[ï] 'be' ("woru") and butu 'husband' ("wo(T)to").
    (2) Yonaguni birun, Yaeyama biirun, Miyako byuu correspond to Shuri wiiyun and Tōkyō yc'[]-u 'get drunk', for which the historical spelling "wehu" suggests the development yo[w]- < yew- (the vowel assimilated to the following labial) < (w)ew- (the distinction of w was lost before mid vowels) < ··· .
    (3) In Miyako and Yaeyama bi[i]-(run) means 'sit' (corresponding to Shuri i-yun); this must be cognate with the stem of Tōkyō i-ru for which the historical spelling is "wiru" and the meaning 'sit' occurs in older texts.

We conclude that earlier Japanese had initial wi, we, and wo, as well as wa. There
is no evidence for wu as distinct from u. There are very few examples of wi and we,
but wo occurs at the beginning of some 25 or more words.

On the island of Kudaka (off Okinawa) gi corresponds to "wi/e" and gu to "wo"
(Hirayama 1966:119): gii-n 'sit' ("wi-"); guii-n 'get drunk' ("wef-"); guu 'cord'
("wo"), gu-n 'be' ("wor-"), gutu 'husband' ("wo(T)to"), guki 'bucket' ("woke"). But
"wa" appears as wa, not ga. Similar phenomena are reported also for Kikai (Amami);
cf. Nakamoto 1976:403.

In certain non-Ryūkyū dialects some interesting cases of b⋯ turn up. For the
verb stem ow- 'pursue' bow- is used throughout most of the northeast and also in
Gifu, Aichi, Kyōto, Hyōgo, Tottori, Shimane, and Hiroshima (according to Tōjō 1956);
examples are cited from Akita (Zhs 1:186-7), Gifu (Zhgs 3:264), Tango (Inokuchi
287), Kōchi (Doi 1957:366). Yet the southern Ryūkyūs (Yonaguni, Yaeyama, Miyako)
lack the expected b-, and Old Japanese clearly had o⋯ , so the b must be secondary,
probably a reflex of wo 'tail' (for which both buu and dzuu are reported in Yaeyama)
prefixed to ow- along the lines of owar- 'end' ("wo-har-") < wo har- 'stretch [to
the] tail'. In Takeno-gun of Tango (Kyōto prefecture) bor- 'pick fruit' is probably
a reduction from wori-tor- 'break off and take'; cf. Inokuchi 292. The pronunciation
woru for 'bend' ("wor-") is reported (Zhs 8:115) from a place in Toyama (Hira-mura
in Kamina-shi of Higashi-Tonami-gun) but is unclear whether this contrasts with
whatever is the reflex of oru 'weave' ("or-").

11. Prothetic h-.

In Kabira of Ishigaki (Yaeyama) an initial h- appears where other dialects have
a vowel, provided the following consonant is voiceless: hụci = utšiˉ 'inside',
hụsï = uši 'ox', hụkida = oˈkịta 'arose', hạsi = ase 'sweat', hụta = (w)oˈtta
'stayed', ... And a similar phenomenon is found in Nakijin in northern Okinawa
(Nakasone 1983). But these are not the relics of a lost initial; the prothetic "h-"
is simply a linguist's device to account for the devoicing of an initial vowel that
assimilates in voicelessness to the consonant. In the Kabira case (at least) we can
say that the zero initial (') counts as voiceless and the vowel is unvoiced under a
general rule that applies between voiceless consonants; the rule is exemplified by
kạta 'shoulder', as well as (h)ạsi 'sweat'. Cf. Zhs 11:42-3, 257.

12. Internal -h-.

Internal -h- does not appear except in reduplications (haˈha 'mother', hoˈho =
hoˈo 'cheek', Chinese loanword hiˈhi 'baboon'), the adverb yahaˈri (from ya-hari),
the noun ahiruˉ (apparently from a[si]-hiro 'broad of foot'), and the two verbs
ahureˈru < abure- 'overflow' (cf. the derivative abureˈru 'fail to find a job') and
hohuˈru 'slaughter' (= kiri-hahur-u), both of which seem to constitute etymological
doublets with hoˈoru 'fling; neglect' ("hahuru"). Words like ko-hadaˉ 'medium-sized
gizzard shad' and ko-hazeˉ 'clasp' are compounds. Morphemes of Chinese origin freely
occur with h⋯ within a word: hoo-hooˉ 'method' ("hauhahu"), moku-hyooˉ 'aim', ...
In discussing hoho-eˈmu 'smiles' vs. hoˈo 'cheek' (from hoˈho), SA 2652:45b says "In
the Edo period *haha* was correctly pronounced *hawa*. *Haha* is a return to the ancient
pronunciation of Heian times" — a slight distortion of the facts (Akinaga 1977a,
Ikegami 1949); an example that spells fawa-usi for fafa-usi 'mother cow' is dated
1206 (KggD 973a). The pronunciation fafa is attested in the Hankul transcription
hwa.hwan.cya.mwo.nwo (8:274) = fafa-dya-mono '(the one who is) the mother' occurring
in the Korean work Chep-hay sin-e (= Shōkai-shingo) of 1676.

The Japanese-Portuguese dictionary of 1603 gives both fafa and "faua" = fawa; it also has afiru 'duck'. The word for 'cheek(s)' is spelled "fô" = [Fo:] in the 1593 translation of Aesop's Fables; Komatsu 1981:312 suggests that the reduplication was restored by analogy with mimi⁷ 'ear(s)', mo⁷mo 'thigh(s)', and tšįtši⁷ 'breast(s)'. Notice that hanahada⁻ 'extremely' is not *hanawada, as we would expect, and "fanafada" is attested by the 1603 dictionary; for more on this word, see Ch. 5.

In the early 1500s the future emperor Gonara made a riddle: Ha⁷ha ni wa ni-do⁷ a⁷itare-do mo, titi⁷ ni wa iti-do⁷ mo a⁷wazu 'for mother they meet twice, for father not even once', the answer being Kutibiru⁻ 'The lips'. (This riddle is quoted by Komatsu 1981:310 in a slightly different form taken from Toyohara Sumiaki's Taigen-shō of 1512; cf. Satō 1977:640b quoting from Gonara-in gyosen nazo of 1516.) It would seem that in the mainstream of the language, centering on the capital cities, the syllable ha was pronounced Fa from as early as 800 till as late as 1600, at least initially. But internally (within a morpheme) -F- was replaced by -w- before the end of the Heian period. If we treat F as /hw/ we can describe this as simply dropping the h-, though that description skirts a historical problem that will be taken up later. The dropping of the labial element /w/ from the initial /hw/- began around 1600, at least before /a/ when people started saying ha instead of Fa; before /o/ and /e/ (and /i/?) the delabialization may have been somewhat earlier, even, but later than the time when wi, we, and wo were beginning to be confused with i, e, and o (which happened between 1000 and 1200). Still, Collado in 1632 wrote fe, fi, and fia (= /fya/). The Korean textbook of Japanese called Chep-hay sin-e (= Shōkai-shingo), published in 1676 but compiled by Kang Wuseng in 1636 (Yasuda 1980:148) or 1618 (Kim 1957), indicates a labial pronunciation before i, e, and ya, just as Collado did. These syllables were written with the Hankul symbols for phi, phye, and phya; the ph- spelling was the closest that Hankul could come to a labial fricative before the palatal syllables and it does not necessarily imply that a stop was heard. For the syllables now pronounced ha, ho, and hu the Korean work wrote hwa, hwo, and hwu; we cannot, of course, be sure that the "hw-" was a labial initial in the Korean syllables of the time, but it seems likely that it was. The later work Waye ˡyuhay (= Wago-ruikai, ?1700) uses Hankul h- for all these syllables, however, and that phoneme was not labial except possibly before wu = /u/: ha.lwu (1:2v:8) = ha⁷ru 'spring', hwo.ka (1:11v:3) = hoka⁻ 'outside', hwu.ywu (1:34:1) = huyu⁷ 'winter', hi (1:1r:1) = hi⁻ 'sun', hyey.lwu (2:32r:7) = her-u 'shrink'. The revised edition of Chep-hay sin-e (1781) wrote hi, he, hya, and ha, with no hint of the labial. In the 1492 Korean work Ilopha (= Irofa = Iroha) the symbol for the Korean intervocalic voiced labial fricative (which the Yale romanization writes -W-), the "light p", was used as a device to write the initials of fa, fo, fu, and fi, but for fe the "light ph" appears. In the few actual examples, fi is written phi (phi.two = fito 'one') and fu is written hwu (hwu.ta = futa 'two'). The symbol "light m", used to write a hypothetical (and unpronounced) -W in Sino-Korean words that ended in a postvocalic final -u (= -w) in Chinese, appears twice: once to write kywoW = kyoo 'capital; Kyōto' and once to write the syllable Wwu = u in the Iroha poem, despite the simple wu used in the appended example wu.ti = uti 'inside'. According to Hamada (1970:84-5) the labiality of f- began to erode around the end of the Muromachi period, as shown by Chinese transcriptions and the vacillation in the spellings of the 1492 Korean Ilopha. But the Japanese-Portuguese dictionary of 1603 regularly wrote "fa, fe, fi, fo, fu".

Throughout the history of the language there was undoubtedly an initial p- as well as F-, in mimetic and marginal words at least, but it seems to have been noticed only from the Edo period. The syllable hi is pronounced [Fi] in several dialects, e.g. Kashima in Satsuma-gun of Kagoshima (Zhs 9:20); Naka-mura Igo in

Suki-gun of Shimane (Zhs 9:20). The labial syllables [Fi] and [Fe] are still used in
Izumo city; in Hanawa-machi of Katsuno-gun of Akita prefecture; and in Takajō-machi
of Kita-morogata of Miyazaki prefecture (Hōgen-gaku gaisetsu 157). Both [Fa] and
[Fe] are found in dialects of northern Honshū (id. 62); and [Fa Fu Fo] are reported
for Sakuragawa-machi of Isawa-gun in Iwate prefecture, where /hi/ is [çi] and /he/
is [çe] or [še].

The erosion of the labial quality from the ancestors of the syllables with the
orthographic "h" and "w" has been going on for over a thousand years, though in the
Ryūkyūs at a slower pace. The syllables have been slower to change initially than
medially, where their historical traces are often masked by vowel crasis or by
contraction, as in the Ryūkyū koo for Tōkyō kawa⁷ 'river' < kahwa⁷ [kaFa]. The
syllable hu is still [Fu] for many Tōkyō-type speakers, and [Fʉ] is especially
common before a voiceless consonant. For citations in the following pages we will
simplify our transcription by writing lowercase "f" for the bilabial fricative. A
labiodental version is reported for certain dialects such as Matsue (Shin Nihongo-
kōza 3:214) and notoriously Miyako, which also has a [v].

Lacking evidence to determine the earlier phonetic quality of the kana symbols
for the ha⁷-gyoo, scholars in Japan have disagreed on just when the labial lost its
stop quality. Hashimoto and Arisaka thought p- had become f- "before early Heian"
(AD 800) but Okumura thinks it was somewhat later, especially in eastern Japan; cf.
Akinaga 1977a:86. A passage in Ennin's diary, stating that Sanskrit p(a) is like
the Japanese voiceless labial initial "but more labial" is taken by some (Komatsu
1981:265) to imply that the Japanese initial was f- in 842, but others (Kamei 1960)
interpret the critical words to mean "and all other syllables with this initial are
also labial" rather than "but more labial", citing the parallel descriptions of the
other Sanskrit initials, each of which is named by the appropriate syllable with the
vowel /a/. Ōno Tōru (1957) believes p- persisted until quite late but he feels we
can arrive at no certain date for the f- version; he thinks that appare and moppara
were always -p-. Also Ōno Tōru doubts there was a voiceless fricative stage in the
development of intervocalic -p- to -w-; he thinks the -w- was reached fairly early
(during the Heian period), but he discounts purported examples from as far back as
the Nara period. On the other hand, Kuranaka (1975:6-43, esp. 40) claims that -f-,
as he writes the intervocalic labial, started changing to -w- before the Nara period
and became institutionalized during that period, with examples proliferating by the
time the Heian period was well under way.¹ The Shuri verb corresponding to standard
yawarag- 'get soft' is yahwarak- so that we suspect that at least in the first
morpheme of that stem a voiceless intervocalic bilabial must have been present in
the ancestral form and has persisted right down to the present day; other Ryūkyū
dialects, however, have the expected reflex yaarak- from elision of the voiced
version -w-. But Nakijin has the adjective yapaara-sen 'is soft' and Kudaka has
yapara-θaŋ (Ryūkyū-hōgen 15:23; -saŋ on p. 31 must be a mistake); Chabana and
Ie-jima also have yapara-. Notice also Shuri qahwa- 'insipid, bland'.

Japanese philologists traditionally refer to the intervocalic pronunciation of
-w- for orthographic "-h-", and the historical change that represents, by the highly
opaque term "(ha⁷-gyoo) tenko⁷-on". Traditional kana spelling is not always a
reliable guide to whether a modern -w- has an authentically voiceless ancestor;
since the overwhelming majority of cases go back to the "-f-" group, there has been
a tendency to regularize with that spelling when in doubt. The noun tawaši 'scrub
brush' is traditionally spelled "tafasi" but early attestations are lacking and the
word may well be the lenited version of an earlier tabasi, which is the modern form
reported for the dialect of Iga (western Mie); the etymology is unclear but it
likely includes taba 'bunch'. The noun ta⁷wai⁻ 'substance' which appears in the

idiomatic ta'wai⁻ (mo/no) na'i 'is trivial, easy, silly' is the result of intruding
a labial guide between the geminated vowels of ta'ai, which is an idiosyncratically
conflated form of the Chinese loanword ta'i 'body, substance'. The personal name
Hideo < fide-wo 'excellent male' is often spelled "Hideho" and associated with the
etymology 'excellent grain-top'; the spelling "Hideyo" with the associated etymology
'excellent generation' results from intruding an epenthetic -y-. There are other
names that were originally ····-wo but have undergone similar reassocations: Kazuo <
Kazu-wo ('Number [One] male') is often written as if from Kazu-ho or Kazu-(')o,
with fanciful semantic associations that are limited only by parental ingenuity.
Sometimes you will hear a real -[h]- pronounced in such words.

13. Internal -w-.

Although Tōkyō allows no vowel but /a/ after w having only wa as a w-syllable,
within a word as well as initially, morphophonemic evidence can be found for a
labial glide before /e/ as well: ko'e 'voice' and kowa-iro⁻ 'tone of voice', ue⁻
'up' and uwa-be⁻ 'surface'. In the examples given you might suspect a semivowel
has been intercalated by lagging articulation of the preceding rounded vowel (o or
u), but not all cases are after those vowels: na'e 'seedling' and nawa'-ǰiro⁻ 'riceplant nursery bed'.

We here presume speakers who retain the distinction of awa ≠ aa and therefore
do not say bawai for ba-ai 'situation'. But many Tōkyō people today probably lack
this distinction; for them an intervocalic -w- may be phonologically conditioned,
so that morpheme-internal cases could be inferred only from other observations.

There appears to be no evidence for two kinds of intervocalic labial that would
correspond to the historical spellings -h- (representing [F] = /hw/) and -w- proper,
as in the pair a'wa 'millet' ("aha") versus awa' 'bubble, foam' ("awa" = abuku').
Instances of orthographic "-w-" are few; most cases of modern -w- go back to /hw/
= [F]. Verb stems that end in "morphophonemic w" — zero alternating with -w- in the
consonant stems — are all treated as "h" in the orthography: awa'nai, a'u, a'i,
ao'o, a'tte (Kyōto o'ote) 'meet' are traditionally spelled "ahanai, ahu, ahi, ahe,
ahau, ahite". In a number of dialects, notably those of the Ryūkyū islands, the
intervocalic -w- from whatever source weakened and coalesced with the surrounding
vowels.

The noun hiwada⁻ = hi'⁻[-no-ki] no ha'da' 'cypress bark' must be a fairly old
compound; if it were new, it would be pronounced *hi-hada. The pronunciation ke'wa'i⁻
'signs' is an old-fashioned version of ke'-ha'i⁻ in which the tenuous association of
the second part with the Chinese morpheme that is initial in hai-tats-⁻ 'delivery'
goes unacknowledged. Modern ke'-ha'i⁻ is a reading pronunciation, based on a false
etymology, for the word actually goes back to kewawi < ke-fafi ("spirit-extend"); cf.
Komatsu 1981:301. Ikegami 1949:48 observes that the word for 'cypress bark' was hiwada
in Gekan-shū (?1241), which also has niwo for ni[h]o 'grebe' and fiwiru for hi[h]iru
'moth'; later versions of these obsolete words with -h- are the result of reading
pronunciations. Ikegami also observes that Myōgo-ki (1268/75) has fotooto for foto-
foto 'almost' (modern hoto'ndo).

14. Earlier pronunciation of "-w-".

Can we find evidence for an earlier stop pronunciation of the ancestor(s) of
internal -w-? Among the mimetic adverbs there is s-pa'-s-pa 'puffing' (and Miyara 145
says papa 'babytalk for cigarette or pipe' comes from that); this is clearly

the root found in sɨwanai 'does not sip/smoke' (spelled "suhanai"). As was observed
above (§12), the Ryūkyū dialects of Chabana, Kudaka, and Ie-jima have yapara- 'soft,
easy', cognate with Tōkyō yawa˩-ra-ka ("yaharaka"); Nakijin in northern Okinawa also
has -p-. In the dialects of Miyako 'hard' is kupa-, cognate with Tōkyō kowa˩-i
'fearsome' (from kofa- 'strong'); and this is huPaa- (with automatically unaspirated
p) in Nakijin, and huba- on the island of Kikai. In dialects of Yaeyama a(p)pïra
corresponds to Shuri ahwiraa/ahwiru = standard ahiru 'duck', for which the Nakijin
form is haPiˠraˠa; and NE Honshū (Inoue 1968:87) has apï(ru), probably from earlier
*appï(ru). In Nase-Kominato (Amami) verbs that correspond to Tōkyō -w- as well as
those that correspond to -b- have a voiced stop: noburi˩ = nu[w]-u 'sew', araburi˩
= ara[w]-u 'wash', quthaburi˩ = uta[w]-u 'sing', waraburi˩ = wara[w]-u 'laugh';
thuburi˩ = tob-u 'fly'. (The conjugation: waraban = warawanai, warabi = warai,
waratɨ = waratte. Cf. koban = kawanai 'not buy', koburi, kobi, kotɨ.) Similarly
also Kobama in Yaeyama (Nakamoto 1976:398) has kobun = ka[w]-u 'buy', hobun =
ha[w]-u, nubun = nu[w]-u 'sew', qarabun = ara[w]-u 'wash', warabun = wara[w]-u
'laugh', and tšikabun = tuka[w]-u 'use'. For Tōkyō sɨ[w]-u 'sip, smoke' Kobama has
suppurun, Chabana on Yoron has supuyun, Shuri has sipuyun, and Nase-Kominato has
šiburyun. The Shuri stem for 'salty' is sipu-kara- (Nakijin siPu-karaa-), though by
itself the word for 'salt' (OJ sifwo) is reduced to syuu (Nakijin suu). The Chinese
binom tai-hu˩u 'typhoon' is pronounced [te:pu:] on Kudaka, off southeastern Okinawa
(Ryūkyū-hōgen 15:36). Miyako has min-sïpïsa for the old word mimi-si[f]i 'deaf
person'. For o˩ 'tail' ("wo") Takeno-gun of Tango (eastern Kyōto-fū) has (w)onbo,
a reduplication like Tōkyō oTpo˩ 'tail'; for utši˩wa 'fan' ("utiha") Takeno-gun
has (w)otšiba (Inokuchi 193). For Tōkyō ue-ru ("uweru") 'plant' (cf. uwar-u 'get
planted') Kurojima in Yaeyama has bii-run (Hirayama, Kgg 67:B-15); through all of
Yaeyama and Miyako ibi- is common. For a˩o- 'blue' ("awo") the dialect of Sonai in
Yaeyama has abossadaru. Yonaguni has kabarun for kawaru 'changes' ("kaharu") but kaa
for kawa˩ 'skin'; 'change' is kaparun or kafarun on Kobama (Yaeyama). A number of
dialects have asabura for asa-ura⁻ 'hemp-soled sandals' (NKD) and Shikoku dialects
have takubaeru for takuwae˩ru 'store' ("takuhaheru") (Doi 1957:80). The old noun uo⁻
(?< iwo) 'fish' ("uwo") is ibo in Himi in Toyama (Zhs 3:21). The word corresponding
to ku˩wa 'mulberry' ("kuha") is bantsïgi in Ikema and bankïgi in Hirara (both
Miyako), but the etymological connection is uncertain.

 The dialect of Izu-Ōshima has [b] for "w" internally, even for morphemes with
a w- (tyaban for tya-wan⁻ 'rice bowl', from Chinese) or an earlier Japanese -f-
(kasiba for kasiwa < kasi-fa 'oak[leaf]').

 Other evidence of -w- < -b- can be found in the OJ saba-myek- = modern zawa-
me˩k- 'murmur, buzz, clamor', cf. sawag- < OJ sawak- 'clamor'. The initial voicing
of zawa-me˩k- must be mimetic; if it had taken place before -b- > -w- the voicing
would be canonically anomalous (cf. Lyman's Law).

15. Earlier pronunciation of "-h-".

 Various pieces of evidence can be adduced to support the hypothesis that the
orthographic "-h-" (as distinct from the "-w-") was originally a stop, presumably
voiceless -p-. Tōkyō o˩o-[ku] 'much, big' ("oho-") is cognate with Miyako upu-[f]
and Yonaguni ubu. The suffix -Tpo˩-, as in mizɨ-Tpo˩-ku 'being watery', derives
from the same etymon.[2]

 The mimetic sa˩wa-sawa 'fresh' ("saha" not "sawa", which is 'rustling' — cf.
Ōtsuki, Shin-Genkai 682d) also appears as sa˩ba-saba and the morpheme is part of
sawa˩-ya-ka 'fresh' and the adverb saTpa˩ri 'cleanly, totally'. Perhaps the etymon

is somehow related to saˈya-ka (or saˈ-ya-ka?) 'clear' and saeˈ-ru 'it cools',
which has the literary form sayu[-ru]. Cf. also samaˈs-u 'awakes one, makes one
sober' and sameˈ-ru 'cools off; gets sober; wakes up'.

The word aˈTpaˈre⁻ is an adjectival noun 'splendid', which is also used as an
interjection 'bravo'; it is etymologically related to aˈware 'pity; feeling; alas'
("ahare").

16. Intervocalic -y-; epenthetic palatal and labial glides.

Intervocalic -y- occurs within morphemes: tsɨya⁻ 'gloss', tsɨˈyu 'dew',
haˈya-ku 'being quick', tsɨˈyo-ku 'being strong'. There is no distinction of ye
from e, nor of yi from i, either initially or internally. But for many verb stems
that end in ···Ve- or ···Vi- we find morphophonemic evidence for an underlying -yu-
that precedes the e or i; the -y- surfaces in derived forms, as shown by these
pairs of infinitives:

    koˈe 'get fat' : koyaˈši 'make fat'
    taˈe 'come to an end' : tayaˈši 'bring to an end'
    kuˈi 'regret' : kuyaˈmi 'regret'

All such verbs show the -y- also in their literary forms ···Vy-u[ru] corresponding
to colloquial ···Ve-ru or ···Vi-ru (depending on the infinitive). The monosyllabic
infinitive ni 'cook, boil' has literary finite forms that are identical with those
of the colloquial (ni-ru for both attributive and predicative) but a -y- shows up in
the related infinitive niyaši 'boil (with anger)', perhaps epenthetically inserted
as a glide from i to a.

Some dialects freely insert an epenthetic palatal glide -y- between any vowel
and /e/; other dialects insert a labial glide after /u/ or /o/ before any vowel,
including /e/. The verb ueru⁻ 'plant' is pronounced uweru in Shingū (Wakayama) but
uyeru in nearby Tanabe (Hirayama 1979:56). Notice the common aberrant romanized
spellings of the surnames Ōe and Ueda as Ohye and Uyeda, as well as the variants of
personal names such as Hide-yo < fide-[w]o (see §14). The standard Kyōto dialect of
the 16th century must have used the palatal glide, to judge from the romanized
spellings of the Portuguese missionaries, such as "vye" = uye for ue < ufe 'above',
"yuye" for yue < yuwe 'cause', and "maye" for mae < mafe 'front'. But there are
exceptions in polysyllabic words: "iqiuoi" (JP) = ikiwoi for ikioi < ikifofi
'force', "iuori" (Esopo 498) = iwori for iori < ifori 'hut', "iuai" (JP)= iwai <
ifafi 'celebrating'.

17. Voiced sibilants and affricates before high vowels.

The traditional orthographic syllables "zi di zu du" are called yotu-ḡana⁻, which might be facetiously translated as 'the kana Gang of Four'. The term dates from as early as 1697 (Kgg 113:79a) and came into being because of confusions in spelling as the older phonetic distinctions were lost. The differentiation of /di/ ("ti) from /zi/ ("si) and of /du/ ("tu) from /zu/ ("su) is still maintained in certain areas. In Kōchi on the island of Shikoku [dži] or (Shibata 1977:103) [di] represents earlier "ti and [ži] represents earlier "si, [dzɨ] is the pronunciation of earlier "tu and [zɨ] that of earlier "su. The distinctions are heard in such pairs as [kudzɨ] 'rubbish' and [kuzɨ] 'arrowroot', [midzɨ] 'water' and [mizɨ] 'not see'; [kidži] 'plain cloth' and [kiži] 'pheasant', [Fudži] 'wisteria' and [Fuži] 'Mt Fuji'. (These are not quite minimal pairs, for there is a difference of accent in each case, but that is irrelevant to the consonant contrast.) The old distinction persists also in parts of Kyūshū (Hirayama 1968b:100, Itoi 1984). In northern Kyūshū (around Ōno-gun in the old province of Bungo, which is now Ōita prefecture) "tu" and "du" are still pronounced without affrication as [tu] and [du]. Non-affricated stop versions of dental + high vowel are widely found in the Ryūkyūs, but no Ryūkyū dialect maintains the yotu-ḡana⁻ distinctions of "t¹/ᵤ ≠ "s¹/ᵤ. Hattori (in Hokama 1972:61) says the distinctions were maintained in Kyōto at least until the end of the Muromachi period. Affricates were transcribed as such by the Portuguese in the late 1500s. (Komatsu 1981:310, 311 notes confusions in some of their transcriptions.) The fact that the distinctions, as voiced affricates versus voiced fricatives, are strictly maintained in the Hankul notations of Chep-hay sin-e (= Shōkai-shingo) 1676, but not consistently in those of Waye ¹yuhay (= Wago-ruikai) ?1700, which writes mi.zu (1:10r) = mizu < midu 'water' — despite ma.cu (2:40v) = mazu < madu 'first' — and hi.zi or hin.zi (1:17r) = hizi < fidi 'elbow', indicates that the merger took place around the end of the 17th century. In 1695 a spelling primer was devoted to differentiating words easily confused because of the loss of these distinctions: appropriately it was called Kana-mozi-dukai Ken-syuku-ryoo-ko [= tidimi-sizimi - suzumi-tudumi] syuu. The merger probably took place in eastern Japan much earlier, for the letters of Nichiren, who died in 1282, reveal pertinent spelling confusions.

In parts of the old provinces of Ōmi, southern Kii, Etchū, and (Oku-)Noto the syllables [tu du ti di] lack affrication, and the voiced affricates [dži] and [dzɨ] represent "si and "su (Okumura 1975c:151). In Narada [tu] and [du] lack affrication, but [dži] representing earlier "ti is affricated; earlier "si is represented by [ži] and earlier "su by [ðu], with a voiced interdental fricative. Unaffricated versions of tu are reported from parts of Mie prefecture (Zhs 4:27-28); unaffricated versions of both tu and ti from Kami-kuwabara in Shimokitayama-mura of Yoshino-gun in Nara prefecture (Zhs 8:227) and from Tatsu-ga-sako in Ōtsuki-machi of Hata-gun in Kōchi prefecture (Zhs 8:321).

In Chart 1 we have written such modern syllables as ᵈzɨ and ᵈži, with the notion that they are pronounced as affricates when initial and as fricatives when medial. But it has been observed (Martin 1952:15, Komatsu 1981:120) that for Tōkyō itself the fricative version is the norm for zɨ (as well as za zo ze) when initial as well as medial, and the affricate version is the norm for dži (as well as dža, džo, džu, and the innovative dže).

18. Affrication and palatalization.

There is obvious complementary distribution of [ɨ] (after s-, ts-, z-, dz-) and [u] (elsewhere). The sounds [s] and [š] appear to be in contrast, but if we treat [ša] as /sya/ by analogy with /kya/ and [ši] as /si/ by analogy with /ki/ (which has a front k-), we can reduce the inventory of syllable components by saying that the palatal version is an allophone of /s-/ before -yV and -i. (We will have to ignore the reduction of usui⁻ 'thin' to [usi:] in certain kinds of substandard or dialect speech.) If we set aside the marginal sounds *tsa tso tse* we can treat [tsɨ] as /tu/, as it is phonetically in some of the modern dialects and was in the older language; and we can treat [tša] and [tši] as /tya/ and /ti/, provided we ignore the innovative syllable *ti* (as in *tii-pa*ʼ*atii* 'tea party'). An alternative solution that is favored by many Japanese linguists will permit the inclusion of the unusual syllables: a phoneme /c/ represents the affricates so that [tša] is /cya/ and [tši] is /ci/. The morphological structure of verb forms supports the interpretation of [ši] as /si/ and of [tši] as /ti/, of [sɨ] as /su/ and of [tsɨ] as /tu/:

	Imperfect	Infinitive	Negative	Hortative	Imperative
'write'	kaʼk-u	kaʼk-i	kak-aʼnai	kak-oʼo	kaʼk-e
'stand'	taʼts-ɨ	taʼtš-i	tat-aʼnai	tat-oʼo	taʼt-e
'stab'	saʼs-ɨ	saʼš-i	sas-aʼnai	sas-oʼo	saʼs-e

What about the voiced counterparts? There are no consonant stems that end in ···z- or ···d-. We find, however, the literary forms of such verbs as maʼzu(ru) with the infinitive maʼze forming the stem of modern mazeʼ-ru 'mix' and naʼzu(ru) with the infinitive naʼde forming the stem of modern nadeʼ-ru 'pat'. The historical spelling of 'pat' is nadu(ru) with kana ˝tu. From the Tōkyō pronunciation neži'r-u 'twist' there is no way for us to know that the historical spelling of the literary version neʼzɨ(ru) with the infinitive neʼži is with ˝t- rather than ˝s-, being nedu(ru) and nedi. And all verb stems that end in ···žir- were earlier ···dir- (˝ti, not ˝si) except for naziʼr- 'rebuke', but there is no way to tell this from the modern Tōkyō pronunciation. For oži'-ru (= ožike-ru⁻) 'take fright' with the infinitive oʼži, however, there is a hint in the related verb odosu⁻ (= odokasu⁻) 'frighten' with the infinitive odoši'. And the literary forms oʼzɨ(ru) and oʼži are spelled oʼdu(ru) and oʼdi.³ As it happens, there are no literary verb forms with ···˝s-, so that the [z] or [ž] heard when such forms are read aloud today always represents ˝t. But the colloquial verbal nouns in the structure VN-žiru have a pseudo-literary form VN-zɨ(ru) with infinitive VN-ži, in which the nigori form of sɨ(ru) 'does' (with the infinitive ši') appears: kan-žiʼ 'feel' (whence the derived noun kanži⁻ 'feeling') is spelled with ˝si.

What we conclude is that t affricates automatically before a high vowel, /i/ or [ɨ] = /u/, except for certain speakers in recent loanwords; similarly, s and t(s) palatalize before i except for certain speakers in recent loanwords. And the same conclusions apply to d and z (and the initial ᵈz- version of z-). Palatalization of s and t (affricated to [ts]) before original i is found throughout the Ryūkyūs; but affrication of the unpalatalized t (in reflexes of ˝tu˝) is not common there, and the pronunciations [tu] and [du] are found in dialects much farther north, as we have observed. Earlier Japanese must have had the pronunciations [tu] and [du] even for the mainstream dialects; when did the affrication set in? Apparently this began happening sometime in the 1500s, perhaps much earlier in the east (Kōza Kokugo-shi 1:125). The eastern (Azuma) dialect of Old Japanese was transcribed as having ˝si˝ for the Kyōto ˝ti˝ (Hōjō 1955:430), and also one example of -ᵗ/ₛu in a fixed epithet (utifyisaᵗ/ₛu) of unknown origin but probably containing the verb saʼsu.

While the affricates were so transcribed by the Portuguese in the late 1500s, the probably 15th-century Chinese work Rìběn Guān-yuèyǔ regularly indicates the affricate for "ti" but varies between affricate and stop for "tu": tu-ki = tuki 'moon' but tsu-tši = tuti 'earth'. Yet the 1492 Korean work Ilopha (= Irofa = Iroha) writes "ti" and "tu" as stops, both in the poem itself and in two further examples: i.twu = itu 'five', wu.ti = uti 'inside'.

The pronunciations [ši] and [tši], or more likely [t,i], a palatalized t with coarticulation, must go back earlier, presumably to proto-Japanese. Distinctions made in the Ryūkyūs between [si] and [ši] are the result of the later raising of vowels there: [su] and/or [se] > [si]. Similar is the origin of the distinction of [ti] from [tši] in the Ryūkyūs.

The centering of [u] to [ɨ] after sibilants and affricates seems to have taken place between the Hankul transcriptions of 1676 in Chep-hay sin-e (= Shōkai-shingo) and those of ?1700 in Waye ¹yuhay (= Wago-ruikai):

Kana spelling	1676 Hankul	?1700 Hankul
fitotu 'one'	phi.two.ccwu (1:18v)	hi.two.ccu (1:54v:5)
madu 'first'	man.cwu (10:15r)	ma.cu (2:40v:1)
suzu 'tin'	swun.swu (10:23v)	su.zu (2:8v:2)

Waye ¹yuhay writes the Hankul equivalent of [tsɨu] for the long vowel: cu.wu.zi (1:36r) = tuuzi 'interpreter'.

In citing Tōkyō forms we will regularize our notation to "su tu si ti zu zi".

19. Palatalization before /e/.

As indicated by the spellings Yen for En and Yedo for Edo, an initial palatal glide before /e/ has been noticed by various observers. In Kyūshū and the Ryūkyūs you will hear [yeigwa] for Tōkyō e¹eḡa⁻ 'movies'. Moreover, the palatalization of s to [š] occurs there not only before /i/ but also before /e/; the city of Sasebo in Kyūshū is called /sašeho/ by its residents. Not only are both [še] and [že] (as in kaže 'wind') widely reported in Kyūshū, they also occur in dialects located in a number of prefectures of Shikoku and Honshū: Ehime (Zhs 5:321), Tokushima (Zhs 5:261); Yamaguchi (Zhs 5:199), Shimane (Zhs 8:257, 289), Tottori (Zhs 5:25), Okayama (Zhs 5:105), Hyōgo (Zhs 4:305), Mie (Zhs 4:27, 28), Yamanashi (Zhs 1:204), Ishikawa (Zhs 3:87; Kōda on Noto island, Zhs 8:173), Niigata (Zhs 2:325); Sado island, Zhs 8:31, 59, 89), Akita (Zhs 1:175, ze = [dže]), ... And [še] is sometimes heard even in Ōsaka and Kyōto (Zhs 4:189, 229). The correlation in distribution of [še] and [že] with [ye], while often found in Kyūshū, does not hold everywhere: Tsushima has [še] and [že] but [e] (Zhs 9:121); the dialect of Itoshiro in Shiratori-machi of Gunjō-gun in Gifu prefecture has [ye] but [se] and [ze] (Zhs 3:259). Minamikata-mura of Higashi-Usui-gun in Miyazaki prefecture has not only [še] and [že] (and [ye]?) but also [tše] for "te" and [dže] for "de" (Zhs 6:411). Iikubo of Himi city in Toyama has palatalized versions of te, ne, and ke, as well as [še] and [že] (Zhs 3:25). Ryūkyū verb gerunds end in -tši, but that can be explained as an expected progressive assimilation of the reflex of earlier -te to the preceding infinitive ending -i- (which then often disappears). Hamada (1977:584) makes the intriguing observation that there is a tendency in Tōkyō and elsewhere to pronounce [si] for earlier [ši], perhaps following the pattern whereby earlier [še] became [se] — or perhaps just overreacting to the tendency for [hi] (< [Fi]) to become [ši]. It is possible that Tōkyō may eventually end up with [ši] as the normal version of the orthographic "hi" and use [si] for "si", thus superannuating the Hepburn usage of "shi" much as the ongoing change from [Fu] to [hu] is doing for Hepburn "fu".

In the romanization used by the Portuguese in the late 1500s and early 1600s "xe" = [še] was written for the syllable corresponding to modern se, and "je" or "ie" = [že] for that corresponding to modern ze: "caje" = kaže 'wind' (modern kaze⁻) and "jefi/iefi" = žefi 'right or wrong' (modern ze¹-hi).

20. Stop and spirant versions of "y"; copula forms.

The Yonaguni cognates for words with Tōkyō initial y··· have a voiced stop d··· as in dama 'mountain' (yama¹), dagu 'burn' (yaku); duu 'hot water' (yu⁻), duga 'floor' (yuka⁻); dumun 'read' (yo¹mu), duru 'night' (yo¹ru); duda 'branch' (eda⁻ < yeda < yoda); daa 'house' (ya = ie¹ < ife¹); ... . But d also appears for initial y- in Chinese loanwords such as dasai 'vegetables' (ya-sai⁻), for there is no initial /y-/. Medial -y- is kept distinct from -d-: uya 'parent' (oya¹), uyubi 'finger' < oyobi = yubi¹, mayu 'eyebrow' (ma¹yu); hadaga 'naked' (hadaka⁻), kadu 'corner' (ka¹do), adi 'flavor' (azi⁻ < adi).

In northern Japan [ž] is common for [y] and [ži] for [(y)i]. Yamagata residents call the place variously Zyamaḡata, Dyamaḡata, and Syamaḡata (Yamagata-jiten 715; cf. Miyara 1954:182). Fukushima has [z] for y- in zugi 'snow' = yuki¹, zebi 'shrimp' = (y)ebi⁻, according to Zhs 1:17; and also i[f]e¹ 'house' is zyee, yo¹ku 'well' is zyee, cf. yo¹[k]i (> i¹i 'good') in western dialects > yei > (y)ee. It is unclear whether this pronunciation is an innovation or a continuation of something old. But if 'shrimp' is the same etymon as Old Japanese 'grapes', as we will assume, the zebi form must be secondary and developed after older e- and ye- had fallen together as ye-, since the Old Japanese word is written with phonograms indicating e- not ye-.

The copula forms da¹ and (dialect) dya¹ [dža] and ya¹⁴ are immediate reductions from de¹ a(r···) and ultimately from ni¹-te a¹[ri]; the pronunciation /dea/ is heard in Suzu on the Noto peninsula (Hōgen-gaku kōza 3:39). The copula form na¹ is an old both attributive and predicative forms, according to Kobayashi 1975:95 (n.88): rippa ⁿda e¹ 'a good house', byoogi ⁿda no¹ 'the sick one' (standard byooki na¹ no). As she puts it, "the copula alternant na is replaced by da"; with precopular nouns like byooki⁻ the suppletive attributive form /no/ is used: byoogi no go = byooki no ko⁻ 'a sick child').⁶ And the Aomori copula, at least in the forms corresponding to da¹ and de¹, has peculiar accentual characteristics according to Vance 1980a in that it can be deleted without affecting the noun, unlike regular particles, which sometimes leave traces behind in the form of an altered pattern on the noun.

21. Alternations of y- with d-, t-, and n-.

A few etymological sets appear to involve the alternation of y with d and/or t, though the details are obscure; there are also a few cases of y and n. Examples:

ya¹m- 'ail' : ita¹m- 'hurt'.
yam-⁻ 'cease' and yame-⁻ 'quit it' : tomar-⁻ 'stop' (vi.) and tome-⁻ 'stop it' (cf. also tamar-⁻ 'stay, accumulate' and tame-⁻ 'amass'; yodo¹m- 'stagnate').
yak-⁻ 'burn it' : tak-⁻ 'burn it'.
yo¹bo-yobo = to¹bo-tobo 'tottering'.
taya¹s- 'cut it off' and ta¹[y]e- 'be cut off, end' : ta¹t- 'cut it off'.
mado¹w- = mayo¹w- 'get bewildered'.

yoᵀke- = doke-⁻ 'avoid' (= noke-⁻, but saᵀke- is surely unrelated). The OJ stem was upper bigrade y*okiy- (but only attested once) and the Heian stem was quadrigrade yok-. It is probably related to yoko 'side' and yoko-si(ma) = yoko-sa(ma) 'sideways; wayward', which might be compared with Korean yekh < nyekh 'direction'.

yoziᵀr- = neᵀzi- (→ neziᵀr-) 'twist' : yoḡos-⁻ 'dirty it' : niḡoᵀs- 'muddy it'.

Shuri has kaᵀca for kaya⁻ 'mosquito net'; in Kuse-gun of Kyōto-fu iᵀya 'no' is said as inzya, cf. iᵀna 'nay' (Inokuchi 302).

22. Proto-Japanese initial voiced stops.

In our reconstructions we will assume that proto-Japanese, just like modern Yonaguni, had voiced stops b- for later w- and d- for later y-, but the d- was surely palatalized and possibly affricated, [dᵧ-] or [dž-] and it would perhaps be more congenial to amend our notation d- to "j-", though we will not do so. Shibata (Kgg 104:83a and 1971:8) expresses doubt about the antiquity of the Yonaguni d-. It can be argued that an initial "fortition" has taken place in the southern Ryūkyūs, tightening the voiced semivowels w- and y- into stops b- and d- (with a subsequent dispalatalization of the latter), but a more natural hypothesis would have the main stream dialects lenite earlier stops. Evidence for w- < *b-, and even -w- < *-b- (cf §14), is better than that for y- < *d- (or *j-), and there is precious little to attest an earlier -d- (or -j-) for -y-. Still, in later sections of this work we will write *b and *d for the proto-Japanese ancestors of w and y both initially and medially. (The reader may reinterpret the notations if unhappy with them.)

If there was, indeed, an early b- and d- (or j-), what about a voiced velar stop g-? I have discovered a fair number of possible cognate pairs in which Korean has initial k- where Japanese has zero (vowel beginning), such as kam- : aᵐ/ᵦ(i)- 'bathe'. Within Japanese there is the alternation of k- and zero in the distal deictics ka-/a- 'yon'; the forms without the k- are said to be attested from the middle of the tenth century. Ōno Tōru 1978:303 takes a dim view of the notion that the distal deictic a- is simply the result of elision of the initial of ka-. He suggests an independent origin *[w]a-/wo-, the latter found in OJ wo-ti 'yonder', which fills out the paradigm of k*o-ti : s*o-ti : (*ka-ti) 'here : there : yonder'.

Chiba has hakori and haḡori for ha-ori⁻ 'half-coat' and ninaḡori for niḡaᵀ-uri 'balsam pear' (cf. Miyara 1954:65, 67) — dialects in Kyūshū have nigago(o)ri (NKD) and the word is gooyaa in Shuri; but these phenomena are probably unrelated, as is the peculiar epenthetic -g- in nigoi for nioᵀi in Toyama, Gifu, and Shizuoka (NKD; Okumura in Sakakura 1976:33). There is also the intrusive -ŋ- in the Hagiwara (Gifu) verb nuᵀŋu = nuᵀ[w]u 'sew' (but the gerund is nuᵀute; Tsuzuku 1941:180-1.)

23. Medial voiced stops (dakuon); prenasalization.

We are not associating the later medial -b-, -d-, -g-, or -ḡ- with our set of reconstructed b- (later w-), d- or j- (later y-), and perhaps ?g- (later zero). It is unclear whether the latter phonemes occurred medially, though we will have to account for later -w- and -y- within certain morphemes.

The sounds that are later voiced between vowels (medial dakuon) were probably at an earlier time PRENASALIZED, as shown by various kinds of evidence:

(1) In the formation of the verb gerund ···bi-te, ···mi-te, and ···ni-te all become ···nde, and ···ḡi-te becomes ···i-de; the copula gerund niᵀ-te > deᵀ is a special instance.

(2) Dialects of northeast Honshū, such as Sendai, have -˜d- (with the nasality located on the vowel) for orthographic -"t- and voiced -d- for the orthographic -t-, so that ma'do 'window' is pronounced [mằdo] and mato⁻ 'target' is pronounced [mado]. Similarly, the velar nasal -ḡ- = [ŋ] (as in Tōkyō) is used for the orthographic -"k- and voiced -g- for the orthographic -k-, so that kagi' 'key' sounds like the Tōkyō version [kaŋi] but kaki⁻ 'persimmon' is pronounced [kagi]. In Kōchi, and other parts of Shikoku, -d- and -g- are prenasalized, and in some areas so is -b- (Shibata 1977:107, Clarke 1973); Aomori in northern Honshū is said to have examples of -ᵐb-, too. Wakayama has -ⁿd- and -ᴺg- (cf. Miller 1967:161). South Kinki (Shima) offers sporadic [˜d], [˜b], and [˜z], as well as [˜g] (Shin Nihongo-kōza 3:152).

(3) Islands off western Kyūshū (Zhs 9:17; also Iki, Zhs 9:18-9) have a voiced intervocalic [d] for orthographic -t- and [g] for -k- (but not *-b- for older orthographic -h-); they have prenasalized [˜b] for -b-, [˜d] for -d-, and nasal [ŋ] for -g-. The situation is the same in Tanegashima, Yakushima, and Nakanoshima of the Tokara archipelago (Hirayama 1968a:14). Makurazaki at the southern tip of Kyūshū is said to use prenasalized [˜d] and [˜g] for orthographic -d- and -g- and voiced intervocalic [d] and [g] for orthographic -t- and -k- (Zhs 6:26), much like the dialects of northeastern Honshū. The velar nasal [ŋ] is also found on Kikai in the northern Ryūkyūs, Yonaguni (Miyara 1954:20), and Hatoma in Yaeyama (Zhs 11:51). Hirayama (1966:442a) thinks the velar nasals of Kikai and Yonaguni are independently new, but it is unclear how he came to that conclusion.

(4) Prenasalized [˜dz] is a rarer phenomenon, but it is reported for -z- in northeastern Honshū (e.g. Tappi, Clarke 1973) and southern Kinki, where kaze⁻ 'wind' is pronounced [ka˜dze]. Clarke (1973:109) reports [ᵃdz], [ᵃdᶻ], [ᵃdʰ] before /u/ in the Sakawa dialect (Kōchi).

(5) There are a fair number of words in the Kobama dialect of Yaeyama, as reported in Ryūkyū-hōgen 9/10:39-90 (I have normalized the transcription), which have a nasal preceding a voiced dental or velar obstruent. These include:
 kandu 'corner' (ka'do), nundu 'throat' (no'do), sïndi 'sleeve' (sode⁻), bundurun 'dance' (odoru⁻), mando:n 'be bewildered' (mado'u), sïndaci 'growing up' (sodati'), qundi 'arm' (ude'), pandaka 'naked' (hadaka⁻, menda < *myenda < *imyanda < imada 'not yet' (ma'da), yunda 'branch' (eda⁻ < yeda < yo-da), pindarïᵉ 'left' (hidari⁻);
 kanƺï/kanzi 'wind' (kaze⁻), anƺa 'birthmark' (aza'), kanƺa 'odor' (Shuri kaƺa), panzun/panƺun 'removes' (hazusu⁻);
 pangun 'peel off, strip' (ha'ḡu), isungun 'rush' (iso'ḡu), ningaun 'pray' (neḡau⁻), pïrungirun 'widen/spread it' (hiroḡeru⁻), qutangaun 'doubt' (utaḡau⁻), [q]angarun/[q]ako:run 'rise' (aḡaru⁻).
Secondary devoicing of the syllable (Nakamoto 1976:230) accounts for the obstruents in kançï 'number' (ka'zu), kinçï 'wound' (kizu⁻), and minçï 'water' (mizu⁻); but 'wound' is also cited (Ryūkyū-hōgen 9/10:77) as kinƺï and 'water' as minƺï in the compound baki-minƺï 'spring'. Other examples of the devoicing: pinçï 'elbow' (hizi'), qançï 'flavor' (azi⁻), tunçï 'wife' (to'zi). A similar rule of devoicing probably acounts for the unvoiced obstruent in hancimi:run 'begin it' (hazimeru⁻), tancinirun 'inquire' (tazune'ru), nankirun 'throw' (naḡe'ru), and perhaps mança:hun 'mix it' (maze'ru), and kankan (p. 77 = kangan Nakamoto 1976:231) 'mirror' (kaḡami'); also nnka- (Thorpe 264) 'bitter' (niḡa-).
 Even in Shuri there are words that point to prenasalization before obstruents:
 handiyun ← handir- A 'get removed' (hazureru⁻)
 hansyun ← hans- A 'remove' (hazusu⁻)
 mindasi-, miƺirasi- B 'rare' (mezurasi'i)

  mangwir- A 'get dizzy' (magureʼru)
  mingwir-, migur- A 'turn' (meḡuruˉ)
  qanda B 'oil' (aburaˉ)
  çinpee B 'spit' (tubakiʼ)
The Shuri development -nd- ⟨ *-nb- occurs in a number of words:
  qanzun ← qand- B 'roasts' (abuʼru)
  kanzun ← kand- B, kabuyun ← kabur- 'wears on head' (kabuʼru)
  kunzun ← kund- A 'strangle; tie up' (kubir-uˉ 'strangle')
  yandi, yaburi B 'loss; breakage' (yabureʼ)
  yandiyun ← yandir- B 'get torn, burst, break' (yabureʼru)
And from Nakijin in northern Okinawa:
  ˹qanbiʼn 'roast' (abuʼru)
  ᵇ/ʟanbiʼn 'wear on head' (kabuʼru)
  kuᵀan˹riʼn 'get tired' (kutabireʼru)
  šin˹riʼn 'slide' (subeʼr-u)
  man˹dži ʼn 'mix' (mazeʼru)
  ˹ninbiʼn 'sleep' (nemuruˉ, dialect neburu)
  ˹pandži ʼn 'slip out' (hazureruˉ)

(6) Rodriguez observed nd and ng for -d- and -g- in the speech of Kyūshū in the
late 1500s and early 1600s.

(7) An early 18th-century Korean glossary of Japanese, Waye ʼyuhay = Wago-ruikai,
writes the Hankul equivalent of mp, nt, and ngk ("ng" = [ŋ]) as syllable-embedded
digraphs for the voiced stops, both word-initially and internally, but z for the
sibilant — with the revealing exceptions of hin.ci.li (1:22) = hiʼziriˉ ⟨ fiziri
'saint', hin.zi/hi.zi (1:17r) = hiziʼ ⟨ fidi 'elbow', and hyeyn.ccu (2:36v) = hen-zu
⟨ fen-su(ru) 'change'. Yet, the glossary appended to Sin Swukcwu's 1501 Korean
travelog Haytong ceykwuk ki = Kaitō-shokoku-ki (compiled 1471?), which gives Hankul
transcriptions of Okinawan words, writes khan.cuy (4:5) 'wind' (Shuri kazi), pwun.ti
(6:8) 'brush' (Shuri hudi, Nakijin pudii), son.ta.sa (4:8) 'cool' (Shuri ḡida-sa-)⁷,
wu.sang.ki (6:2) 'rabbit' (Shuri qusazi ⟨ usagi)⁸, ywo.sam.puy (4:7) 'evening'
(*yosa[ra]-be → Shuri yusandi, Miyako yusarabi)⁹, etc. (Cf. Iha 1931; the text
is reproduced in Tōjō 1969.) The perhaps late 15th-century Chinese language guide
Rìběn Guān-yuèyǔ (= Nihon Kan-yakugo) often used Chinese phonograms with a final
nasal to transcribe Japanese syllables preceding a voiced stop or sibilant: the
equivalent of modern Beijing mín-zú (2r "people-foot") for midu ⟩ mizuˉ 'water',
kān-jié (1r "carve-node") for kazeˉ 'wind', sūn-tiē (12v "grandson-paste") for sodeˉ
'sleeve'), wū-sǎn-jí (6r "me-scatter-rush") for usaḡiˉ 'rabbit', máng-gè (9r "busy-
each") for maḡoʼ 'grandson'. A similar device of dissyllabic digraphs is used by
Chep-hay sin-e (= Shōkai-shingo), the early 17th-century Korean textbook of spoken
Japanese by Kang Wusen published posthumously in 1676ˉ (cf. Kim 1957): tang.ka.i.ni
(8:31r) = taḡai niʼ 'reciprocally', kwo.nwon.kwo.lwo.wa (9:1r) = kono-ḡoro waʼ
'lately'; tan.ta.i.ma.man.tye (10:34r) = tadaʼima made 'until just now';
hwa.lwum.p.lwu.nwo mi.ci.ni (7:13v) = farubaru (⟩ haruʼbaʼru) no miti niʼ 'on a
distant road'. But the tautosyllabic syllable-initial ngk- also occurs, notably in
the recurrent word ngkwo.za.lwu = gozaʼru 'be'; and there are occasional examples of
initial mp- (in common Chinese loanwords): mpan (2:18v, 10:20r) = banˉ 'evening',
mpye.zi.nwo (10:21r) = *bezi (→ beti) no = betu noʼ 'another'; wa.ta.ku.si.nwo
mpwu.tyo.wu.hwo.wu (6:6r-v) = watakusi no bu-tyou-hou (= bu-tyoʼohoo) 'my blunder';
mpwu.zyen mpwung.kwo (9:27r) = buʼzen buʼn-go 'the old provinces of Buzen and Bungo
(northwestern Kyūshū)'; mpan.zi (9:14r) = baʼn-zi 'all matters, everything';

sam.*mp*wu.kywo.wu (7:22r) = san bu-gyou (= san-bu˥gyoo) 'the Three Magistrates' and
other uses of the word for 'magistrate' (8:1r, 8:4r, 8:4v, 8:5r, 8:6v, 8:18r-v,
8:20v). And there is at least one example of nt-: *nt*wo.ci.nwo.ta.myey.ni.mwo (1:17v)
= do˥ti no tame˥ ni mo '(not) for anyone's sake'. The tautosyllabic clusters are
limited in this work to word-initial position;[10] internal *dakuon* are either
written with the dissyllabic digraphs or simply ignored: hwa.lwu.*pa*lwu (8:14v, 8:25r)
= hwa.lwu*m*.pa.lwu (6:1v, 7:13r, 8:30r-v) = farubaru (> haru˥ba˥ru) 'far distant',
ywo.lwo.kwo.*p*wu (8:14r) = yoroko˥bu 'rejoice', wan.za.ttwo (10:4v, 10:23v) = wa˥za
to 'on purpose'; i*n*.*c*wu (9:23r) = idu (> izu⁻) '(the old province of) Izu', ma*n*.*c*wu
(1:17v-18r, 10:15r, 10:30r) = madu (> ma˥zu) 'first', cwu.nye*n*.*c*wu.nye (3:15v) =
tune-dune (> tune˥zu˥ne⁻) 'constantly', si*n*.*c*wu.kka.ni (2:17r) = siduka (> si˥zuka)
ni 'quietly'. Internal -k-, -t-, and -s- are sometimes written with the Korean
geminates but often with the same simple obstruent symbols used also at times for
the *dakuon* syllables: wa.ta.*k*u.si (6:6r) = wa.ta.*kk*wu.si (6:65) = watakusi⁻ 'I/me';
zyey.phi.*t*wo.mwo = zyey.phi.*tt*wo-mwo (3:5v, 4:29r) = ze-fi (> ze˥hi) to mo 'by all
means'; phi.two.*cc*wu (1:18v) = fitotu (> hito˥tu) 'one', kwo.*cc*i.wo (2:10r) = ko˥ti˥
[w]o 'us'; ka.yo.wu.ni.kwo.*ss*wo (8:7v) = kayou (> kayoo) ni˥ ko˥so 'precisely thus'.
Yasuda 1977 suggests that prosodic factors may account for the geminate spellings,
which also include the inexplicable ⋯nnwo = nwo for the particle no˥ 'of', as in
wo.mwo.i.*nn*wo.hwo.ka.*n*wo.ngkwo.ci.swo.wu (9:3r) = omoi-no˥-hoka⁻ no go-ti-sou
(> go-ti˥soo) 'extraordinary feast', but his argument is unconvincing. Yet -f-, like
f-, was distinctively represented by hw(a), h(wu/wo), or ph(i/ye/ywo). Hankul simple
-p- represented either -b- or (after t) -p-: ki.kye.pa (4:21v) = kike˥ba 'when I
listen', it.pa.i (2:7r) = it-pai (> i˥p-pai) 'one cupful'. Japanese -pp- in nippo˥n
'Japan' was uniquely represented by an unusual syllable-initial cluster: ni.*pph*won
(2:8v and eight other examples),[11] which Hamada (1970:94, 96) suggests may have been
intended to represent niffon, found in romanized form in Collado. The word also
appears as ni-hwon (1:9v and eight other examples). When Hankul p- is found at the
beginning of a word it represents b- and should have been written mp-:
pan.wo.swu.lwu.mwo.mwo (4:27v) = ba˥n suru mono˥ 'someone to stand watch',
pan.wo.swu.lwu.ttwo.mwo (4:30r) = ba˥n [w]o suru to˥ mo 'though one stands watch',
pan.wo.sasi.la.lyey (4:29v) = ba˥n [w]o sasirare 'stands watch'. (There is no word-
initial p- in the Japanese text.) The triangle that served as the Hankul symbol for
the Middle Korean voiced sibilant transcribed the Japanese /z/ both initially and
medially, but medially we also find -n.s- and (doubly marked) -n.z-: ka.*z*yey
(10:20r) = kaze⁻ 'wind'; swu*n*.*s*wu (10:23v) = su˥zu 'tin'; ka.na.la*n*.*z*wu (10:17) =
kanarazu⁻ 'necessarily', na*n*.*z*wo = na˥zo 'why' — cf. na.*z*yey.ni (1:28v, 3:11r) =
na˥ze ni 'why', sa*n*.*z*wo (9.3v) = sa˥zo 'indeed', na.ni.two*n*.*z*wo (9:17r) = nani-tozo⁻
'please', sywo.wu*n*.*z*i.ki.ni (3:10v) = syou-ziki (> syoozi˥ki˥) ni 'seriously'. The
-n.z- device seems to be the spelling used for the negative ending -azu:
wo.ywom.pa*n*.*z*u (1:9r, 10:23) = oyobazu⁻ 'not reaching', mwo[.]wu.sa*n*.*z*u (2:16v,
10:30r) = mousazu (> moosa˥zu) < mausazu 'not (venture) to say/do', yey.kwu.wa*n*.*z*wu
(1:27v) = [y]e˥ kuwa˥zu 'unable to eat'. But there is at least one example with
-n.s-: na.nwo.mye.na.la*n*.*s*wu (9:7r) = nano˥me narazu 'is unusual'. The affricate -du
= [dzu] was transcribed -cwu (ambiguously also -ccwu) or -n.cwu; in the text there
is no initial du-, nor is there any di- or dy-. Occasionally the simple Hankul -s-
represents (ambiguously) -z-: sa.kwu.*s*i.ccwu (9:3r, 9:6v, 10:16r, 10:34) = saku˥-
zitu 'yesterday', mpan.*s*i (109:20r) = mpan.zi (2:18v) = ban-zi 'become night'. The
Hankul transcriptions were intended as a phonetic guide to the hiragana text they
flank, but that text itself fails to mark the *dakuon*, so they do not represent
"reading" pronunciations. A few of the Hankul versions of words imply a variant

of the Japanese word that is unattested in other sources: a.kwu.*mp*wu.wu (1:13v) =
*aku-buu = aku-huu⁻ 'ill wind'; wa*n.s*wu.lwu.lwu (2:17r) = *wazururu = wasururu (→
wasureru⁻) 'forget'; two.wu*n.t*wo.wu.mi (9:22v) = *toudoumi = "tootoumi" (NKD) <
tofotafumi < tofo[t]u af[a]-umyi 'distant lake (= Hamana Lagoon) → the Tōtōmi
region'; si.mwo.*mp*wu.sa (9:23r) = *simobusa = simo-[tu-f]usa > simoˈosaˈ⁻ 'the old
province of Shimōsa'; *z*wu.wa.wu (9:26r) = *zu-wau = su-ou = suˈoo 'the old province
of Suō'; *s*wu.i.pwun (1:32v) = *sui-bun = zuˈi-bun 'to the extreme'. But some of
these readings may be artificial, or mistakes — as "fesi" for "feti" = beti 'other'
in the hiragana of 10:21r must be. The Hankul transcriptions sometimes write a known
Japanese variant: hwa.*s*i.mye.tyey (1:34, 3:4v, 3:5r, 4:1r) = fasimete = fazimete >
hazimete⁻ 'beginning' (but -s- is found in a number of modern dialects); for the
hiragana "iya-iya" (5:12v) the transcription is i.ywo.i.ywo = iyoˈ-iyo 'more and
more'. The earlier work Ilopha (= Irofa = [Kōji go-nen Chōsen-ban] Iroha) of 1492
provides the first attestation of dissyllabic digraphs used to write the *dakuon*:
hwo*n.t*wo = fodo > hodo⁻ 'extent; because', ha*m.p*a = haba⁻ 'width'.

(8) Dialect forms and variants provide various other bits of evidence for the
prenasalized consonants:

  ušaŋgi (Ishigaki) = usaĝi⁻ 'rabbit'

  igoku (?= iĝoku) / inoku (dialects in Kyōto-fu, Inokuchi 318) = uĝoˈku 'move'

  manĝa iˈi = ma ĝa iˈi 'be fortunate'[12]

  tonĝaˈru = toĝaˈru 'get sharp/harsh'

  otonĝai (Izumo dialects, Shibata and Fukushima 1981:40) = otoĝai⁻ 'jaw'

  ⋯ tabi⁻ / tanbi⁻ 'every time that ⋯ '

  donzoko⁻ < do-soko 'the utter depths'

  donzumari⁻ < do-tumar- 'the upshot, the final stage'

  donziriˈ⁻ < do-siri 'the tail end' (cf. dekkaˈi < do-ika- 'huge')

  (me-no-tama >) mentamaˈ (slang, SA 2671:38b) = medamaˈ 'eyeballs'

  to-n[u]si 'door-master' > toˈzi (tuncï in Kobama) 'wife'; aˈru-n[u]si 'possess-
master' > aˈruzi 'owner'

  wara-n-kutu 'straw shoes' > wara(ĝ)utu/warandu > waradu > waradi > warazi 'straw
sandals'

  [wa˜tsɨka] is the Yamagata version of waˈzuka < waduka (cf. Yamagata-jiten 7)

  Shuri qangwee-ii = aĝura⁻ 'sitting crosslegged'

  eĝao < wem[i]-ka[f]o 'smiling face'

  saĝa 'character' < Middle Chinese .syang (> Beijing xiāng) 'appearance', for
which the standard Japanese versions became s(y)aɷ > s(y)au > s(y)ɔɔ > s(y)oo

  koozo 'paper mulberry' < kauzo ?< *kaɷzo < kam[i]-so ('paper hemp')

  Old Japanese fagat- = fanat- 'release' (Kōza Kokugo-shi 1:312; Arisaka 1955:170).

    The word naˈze 'why' is thought to be from na[ni-yue] zo, but perhaps it is
nan[i]-so 'do what' in which -so is equivalent to si[teˈ]; cf. doˈo-site 'how come,
why'. The old prohibitive command expression na V-i so 'don't V' is still used in a
remote village of Shizuoka, according to Miyara 1954:170: (naa) ki so 'don't come'
— the first element is optional, and seems to have become so early in the Heian
period. Notice the relationship between naˈzo 'riddle; why; or something' (with a
variant naˈnzo, at least in the last meaning) < naˈn[i]-so and naˈdo 'or something,
and whatnot' < naˈn[i]-to; also naˈnka 'or something, or the like' < naˈni-ka
'something'. In Ōsaka the particle zo attaches to the content-interrogatives to
make indefinites, like ka in Tōkyō: dare-zo⁻ = daˈre-ka 'someone'.

    The two adverbs tyoˈodo < tyɔɔdo < tyaudo 'exactly' and tyaˈnto 'correctly' are
thought to represent different outcomes of the same etymological source: probably
the loanmorph tyoo < tyɔɔ < tyau < *tyaɷ < Middle Chinese .tyeng followed by the
subjective essive (= adverbial) marker toˈ. Cf. Kamei 1969:12.

Clarke (265) observes that the loss of prenasalization appears to have taken place in the order: z, b, d, g. He cites evidence from the Gotō islands (near Nagasaki) for earlier prenasalized stops in these situations:

$$\cdots g^1/_u = [{}^{\eta}g] > [\eta]$$
$$\cdots b^1/_u = [{}^{m}b] > [m]$$
$$\Big\} \quad \cdots N$$

Was proto-Japanese like dialects of northeast Honshū and southernmost Kyūshū (and like Korean) in having voiced allophones (-d-,-z-, -g-, and perhaps -b-) for phonemes that were voiceless initially (t-, s-, k-, p-)? Or did the modern dialects each independently develop these voiced versions at later dates? We must assume that at least some varieties of proto-Japanese had voiceless -t- and -k-, since those are the versions preserved in the mainstream dialects spoken in Kyōto and Tōkyō, and they must go back to the earliest pronunciations, for there would be no phonetic motivation to explain a later devoicing. Perhaps at one early stage there was free variation between voiced and voiceless such that later the modern dialects happened to "jell" in various ways. It should be noted that in Aomori prefecture /k/ and /t/ are voiceless after voiceless vowels, after -n-, and after -T-: sịta 'below' (or 'tongue'), guntai 'troops', asaTte 'day after tomorrow'.

In Yonaguni -g- corresponds to the mainstream -k- and the velar nasal -ŋ- corresponds to standard -ḡ-, but after the syllable si- the earlier -k- is tensely deaspirated (we will symbolize this as -K- in place of Hirayama's Greek kappa or italic *k*) instead of voiced; the expected -gi < -ki, however, is replaced by -Ti, as in tuTi < toki 'time' (cf. sagi < sake 'wine').[13] Internal -t- remains voiceless and is tensely deaspirated (our -T-, Hirayama's Greek tau or italic *t*) while the initial t- is the usual slightly aspirated version, but it gets replaced by s- before an original u (but not u < o) and, in the allophone [š], before i (but not i < e), as in [šiKara] < tikara 'strength' and [šiKuŋ] < tuk- 'pound (rice)' but [ti:] < te 'hand' and [tuŋuŋ] < toḡ- 'polish'. The tensely deaspirated initials T-, C- = c-, K-, and rarely P- are mostly the result of dropping a high vowel between voiceless consonants and then reducing the consonant cluster: Taa < sita 'tongue' (the vowel length is automatic in monosyllabic free forms), Tii < tuki 'moon', caa [tsa:] < kusa 'grass', Kuuru < fukuro 'bag', ... And ci- is also the reflex of earlier si (but not si < se) and su (but not su < so): cici < susu 'soot' or, with different accent, < sisi 'flesh'; cima < sima 'island', haci < hasi 'chopsticks'; but asi < ase 'sweat' and suba < soba 'beside'. It is also the reflex of earlier fi (but not fe) — cii < fi 'fire' or (with different accent) 'day' but hii [çi:] < fe 'fart' — as well as earlier ti (but not te): cii < ti 'blood' but tii < te 'hand'.[14] In many dialects of the northern Ryūkyūs, such as Shodon in Amami and Nakijin in Okinawa, distinctively unaspirated initial consonants have developed from what were once just allophones before the high vowels. The lack of aspiration became distinctive when the mid vowels were raised (e > i, o > u) without suppressing the aspiration that characterized the preceding stops, so that [tʰe:] > [tʰi:] 'hand' was put in minimal contrast with [Ti:] 'breast'. Linguists in Japan have mostly treated the deaspirated versions as the marked phonemes; Martin 1970b treated the aspirated versions as the marked phonemes for Shodon.

24. Phonemic interpretation of the prenasalized obstruents.

Can we treat the prenasalized obstruents of earlier Japanese as dyads of nasal + oral to be written /np nt nk ns/? One argument that supports the idea is the fact that morphemic or etymological boundaries sometimes occur between the nasal and the oral, i.e. within the "nigori" itself or between the components of the later voiced reflexes. One well-known group of examples involves the negative forms of the verb, and another involves the predicating auxiliary for verbal nouns:

(1) **V-anu** is the attributive negative; the predicative finite and the infinitive are both **V-azu**, which comes from **V-an[i] su**, the infinitive of the old negative auxiliary which is found in uncontracted form in a few early examples such as sirani 'unknowing(ly)' (and is the source of -ḡateni 'unable' < V-i n[i] kate-), followed by the predicating auxiliary su(ru). **V-azi** is the negative hortative of literary Japanese 'will not do' (expressing determination: makezi = makenai 'I will not be defeated'), but in Yoron(-machi) of the Ryūkyūs kakazi is the ordinary negative 'does/will not write', equivalent to standard kaka⌐nai; a contracted form kaka[]i is used with the same meaning in Kametsu of Tokunoshima. **V-azi** comes from **V-an[i] si** with the same negative infinitive, here followed by the infinitive of su(ru).

(2) There are about 35 different shapes of bound verbal nouns coming from single morphemes of Chinese that cause voicing of the sibilant of the auxiliary, turning s- into z-, as in sin-zi 'trust' and kan-zi 'feel'. Most of the sibilant-voicing verbal nouns are morphemes which ended in a nasal in Middle Chinese (cf. Lewin 130); but a number of morphemes ending in a nasal do not voice the sibilant, e.g. han-su⌐ru 'oppose'. The final velar nasal of many Chinese morphemes turned into a high vowel in later Japanese, and the high vowel (i or u) in turn assimilated to create the modern long vowels "ei" (ee) and "ou" (oo). Moreover, a few of the morphemes that belong to the -zu(ru) > - ziru group never had a nasal in Chinese: too-zi⌐ru¯ < tou < .dhew 'throw', koo-zi⌐ru¯ < kau < .kaw 'get heightened/exaggerated', hoo-zi⌐ru¯ < fau < paw' 'report'. Eight of these verbal nouns do not come from Chinese at all; they are reductions of Japanese structures with a final syllable that begins with a nasal. Five come from the structure adjective stem + -mi (cf. RGJ 876-8):

  omon-zi⌐ru¯ ← omon-zu⌐ru¯ < omo-mi su(ru) 'value';
  karon-zi⌐ru¯ ← karon-zu⌐ru¯ < karo-mi su(ru) 'belittle' (karo- = karu- 'lightweight');
  aman-zi⌐ru¯ ← aman-zu⌐ru¯ < ama-mi su(ru) 'content oneself with';
  yasun-zi⌐ru¯ ← yasun-zu⌐ru¯ < yasu-mi su(ru) 'be contented with'
  uton-zi⌐ru¯ ← uton-zu⌐ru¯ < uto-mi su(ru) 'be cold toward'.

And three come from the structure noun + particle ni⌐:

  sakin-zi⌐ru ← sakin-zu⌐ru < saki ni su(ru) 'go ahead';
  soran-zi⌐ru ← soran-zu⌐ru < so⌐ra ni su(ru) 'memorize';
  gaen-zi⌐ru ← gaen-zu⌐ru < kae ni su(ru) 'consent'.

For more on these verbal nouns, see RGJ 876-8.

The structure A-mi su(ru) > A-n-zu(ru) seems to have been common in the late Heian period; the 11th-century Myōgi-shō attests natukas̄imuzu 'long for', in which the syllable "mu" represents either -m or the -N which merged -m with -n, in any event a compression of the ending -mi.

25. Sequential voicing *(rendaku)*.

Certain compounds are marked by a "nigori" device, called rendaku¯ 'sequential voicing'. It is tempting to consider the structure N-¨N (compound-noun nigori) as a reduction of N n[o] N when the first noun is subordinated to the second, and N n[i] N when it is coordinated, as in reduplications. Certain combinations of noun with verb or adjective also can perhaps be treated as containing n[o] or n[i]:

  N [no/ḡa] A-i → N-¨A-i, as in kyoomi-buka⌐i 'interesting' ← kyo⌐omi⌐ no/ḡa huka⌐i 'interest is deep', na-daka⌐i 'famous' ← na no/ḡa taka⌐i 'name is high', sinboo-zuyo⌐i 'patient' ← si⌐nboo no/ḡa tuyo⌐i 'patience is strong', ...

  N [no/ḡa] simi-ru → N-¨simi-ru, as in tosiyori-zi⌐mita seikatu 'the life of one old before his time', inakamono-zi⌐mite iru 'is countryfied', ...

  N [ni] ta⌐t-u → N-¨tat-u, as in me-da⌐tu 'be conspicuous', tabi-da⌐tu 'set off on a journey', yaku-da⌐tu 'be useful', saki-da⌐tu 'go ahead', ...

N [ni] tate⌐-ru → N-"tate-ru, as in zyunzyo-date⌐ru 'put in order', tituzyo-date⌐ru 'bring discipline to', kityoo-date⌐ru 'establish a basis', ...
   N [no/ga] tu⌐k-u → N-"tuk-u, as in iro-zu⌐ku 'take color', ki-zu⌐ku 'notice', ne-zu⌐ku 'take root', ...
   N [ni/o] tuke⌐-ru → N-"tuke-ru, as in iti-zuke⌐ru 'locate', imi-zuke⌐ru 'give significance to', genki-zuke⌐ru 'enliven', na-zuke⌐ru 'name', ...

Other structures of this sort will be found in RGJ 282-6. In attempting to explain *rendaku* as a reduction from a nasal syllable we do not, of course, claim to offer a synchronic description of the modern language, where the device is simply one way to mark compounds made up of elements at least one of which is free and not of recent foreign origination. Such compounds as denki-ḡo⌐tatu 'electric quilt' and kabusiki-ḡa⌐isya 'stock company' denote recent inventions, and the binoms of Chinese origin ko-tatu⁻ 'foot-warmer quilt' and kai-sya⁻ 'business company' are not of particularly early attestation themselves. Komatsu 1981:104-5 explains the *rendaku* phenomenon as the result of the fact that the distinctively voiced syllables (*dakuon*) could not stand at the beginning of a word in early Japanese, so that converting a voiceless initial to its voiced counterpart was a way of indicating that it was to be taken as the second part of a longer word; the words borrowed from Chinese and English were generally exempted from this process because they can begin with the distinctively voiced consonants. For more on *rendaku* see Ch. 2, §3, §5; on -ba Ch. 2, §4.1.

   Some Chinese loanmorphs with basically (or usually) unvoiced initials will frequently voice the initial when attached to a loanmorph that ends in a nasal, as when certain counters are attached to the numerals san- 'three', sen- 'thousand', man- 'ten thousand', and the native element nan- 'how many' (but not when attached to yon- 'four'): sa⌐n-ḡai 'three floors, third floor', se⌐n-bon 'a thousand slender objects', na⌐n-zoku 'how many pairs (of footwear)'; there are no examples with -t··· → -d··· . These are rather loose compounds; while the alternation is phonologically constrained it cannot be said that it is phonologically determined, for there are other counters which are not susceptible to the alternation: sa⌐n-kai 'three times', sa⌐n-pun 'three minutes', sa⌐n-satu 'three volumes'. In tighter compounds, for the most part old and sometimes semantically opaque, a similar but sporadic phenomenon can be observed: mon-do⌐o 'questions and answers', ren-ḡe⁻ 'lotus blossom', sa⌐n-ze⁻ 'three states of existence' — cf. the etymologically identical but later sa⌐n-sei 'three generations, third generation'. Some such compounds are standardized in the modern language with a voiceless initial but are found with the voiced version in dialects or older attestations: sen-taku⁻ 'laundry' is often heard as sendaku, and that form is attested by the Japanese-Portuguese dictionary of 1603, which has the entry "xendacu" = [šendaku] though a later note says that "xentacu" = [šentaku] is "better than xendacu". (The word zite⌐n-sya⁻ 'bicycle' is sometimes pronounced zide⌐n-sya⁻, perhaps influenced by the words zido⌐o-sya⁻ 'automobile' and de⌐nsya⁻, since there is no nasal before the dental stop.) In 1603 the word si⌐n-syaku 'considering' was pronounced as it is today, but in the text Sangō-shiiki of 1154 the pronunciation sim[u]-zyaku is attested (KggD 970a).
   As in the phenomenon exemplified by kan-zi⁻ 'feeling' (§24), the phonological constraint includes strings of Vu and Vi which go back, by way of nasal Vũ and Vĩ, to the Chinese velar nasal. That will account for examples such as these:
   (.tyung-kwok > tyuũ-koku >) tyu⌐u-ḡoku 'central provinces, China'
   (.tong-.sey > toũ-sai >) to⌐o-zai 'east and west'
   (.wang-'tsye > waũ-si > ɔɔ-zi >) o⌐o-zi 'prince'
   (.byang-'teng > byaũ-teũ >) "biðdô" = byɔɔ-doo > byoo-doo⁻ 'equality'
   (.myeng-.syang > myaũ-syaũ > myɔɔ-zyɔɔ >) myoo-zyoo⁻ 'bright star (= Venus)'.

Sometimes the phenomenon was falsely extended to loanmorphs with Vu that did not go
back to the Chinese velar nasal: the word that is now pronounced kooken⁻ 'efficacy'
is given the pronunciation kɔɔgen in the Japanese-Portuguese dictionary of 1603 and
(Wenck 4:235) the -g- is attested also by the Kagaku-shū of 1444; the first morpheme
is kau- < kaw˙ without a nasal final. The word (hhaw˙-/hyaw˙-.hwa(y) >) kyeu-kwe >
"qeôqe" = kyooke (NKD) > kyo˥oge (Mkz, NKD) 'propagating Buddhist thought' seems to
have voiced the initial of the second element rather late, perhaps under the popular
rule of thumb "If it's Buddhist give it an esoteric reading!".

In the modern language there is a rule which regularly replaces h- (< f-) by p-
in the second element of a Chinese binom made up of two bound morphemes — including
the obsolescent word ton-pi 'evasion', mistakenly given as an exception ("ton-hi")
in Martin 1952. The effect of the rule is to preserve the voiceless labial stop that
was originally the initial of the basic form for each of these morphemes. But some
of these words were earlier pronounced ···n-b··· : what is now ka˥npaku (< kanpaku⁻)
'chief adviser to the emperor' was noted as kwanbaku in the Ikyō-shū manuscript of
Setsuyō-shū (= Setchō-shū), thought to have been written perhaps as early as 1450,
and also in the Japanese-Portuguese dictionary of 1603, and it seems generally to
be assumed that this was the original version of the word, which was first attested
(but only in semantograms) in 887, according to Ōno. Hamada (1970:106-8) suggests
that the ···n-p··· version was competing with ···n-b··· in the 1500s. Both kwanbaku
and kwanpaku appear in Brinkley's dictionary (1896), but Hepburn's (1867) has only
kwanbaku. A similar example: si˥npu 'male parent, father' is found as sinbu in
Setsuyō-shū and the JP dictionary, only sinpu appears in Brinkley, but Hepburn has
go-sinbu-sama 'your father' in his English-Japanese "Index", though the word does
not appear as an entry in the Japanese-English dictionary itself, nor does either
sinbu or sinpu. Matters are further complicated by several factors:

(1) Some of the single loanmorphs are treated as free Japanese nouns, and they
are susceptible to the *rendaku* marking of native compound nouns.

(2) Some of the bound loanmorphs have developed fairly free uses in the voiced
version as suffixes or postnouns, such as (-⁻)bon⁻ 'text, book' and (-⁻)zyuu⁻ 'all
through (a time/place)', which contrasts with the etymologically identical morpheme
(-⁻)tyuu⁻ 'midst, among, while'. (Blinded by the traditional orthography, even good
textbooks of Japanese often fail to draw this distinction properly.)

(3) Some often appear with the voiced version also after a short vowel, as in
the words ka˥-zan 'volcano' and ge-zan⁻ 'descending the mountain' or (also ge-san⁻)
'returning from a temple retreat'.

(4) Some were borrowed from Chinese in two versions, so that the voiced-initial
pronunciation turns up also as the first element of certain compounds. For these
it is often difficult to say whether the initial voicing in the second element of a
binom is secondary or primary. Some of these doublet borrowings are so distributed
that either twin may (unpredictably) begin a compound but as a second element only
the voiced version occurs: si˥-sa 'suggestion', si-kyoo⁻ 'instruction'; zi˥-i
'demonstration'; hyo˥o-zi⁻ 'indication'. Some are used as free nouns in semantic
contrast: ti˥ means only 'earth, ground, land' but zi˥ (< di) also, and more
commonly, means 'material, (back)ground, ... '.

It is understandable that Japanese lexicographers have not always been clear
about these matters, partly because of the intrinsic difficulty, but mainly because
the entire subject of "reading Chinese characters" has been a can of worms from the
very beginning, and critical questions are easily avoided by simply using the graphs
— which are invested with the false prestige of being the "real language", without
revealing the intended pronunciation at all. Where we are fortunate enough to have
earlier indications of the phonetic facts, such as those provided by the Portuguese
romanizations of the 15th and 16th centuries, there are sometimes differences from

what is enshrined as the standard version today: si-zen⁻ 'natural' is "iinen" or
"jinen" = zi-nen⁻. The /zinen/ version is reported from Gifu prefecture (Tōjō 1954:
571), and is found in standard zinen-zyo⁻ 'Japanese yam' and zinen-zyoo⁻ '(growing)
wild'; southern Shikoku offers /zizen/ (NKD 8:551b). It is claimed that before the
"medieval period" the pronunciation was zinen in the meaning 'spontaneously' (and
also as a Buddhist term) but sizen in the meaning 'by any chance' (NKD 10:20b). The
spelling sinsen (?= sïzen) is found in a text dated 1184 (KggD 971b).

It has been claimed (KggD 974b) that *rendaku* in compounds of Chinese elements
is common AFTER a morpheme with the "going" tone (marked by dot at the upper right
corner of the character) but uncommon BEFORE such a morpheme. A clearcut correlation
of *rendaku* with accentual phenomena, however, has not been proven. (See Ch. 4.)

26. Sporadic examples of initial voiced obstruents.

Various dialects afford sporadic examples of initial voiced obstruents. For
hi⁷ru 'leech' Fukushima has biru (Miyara 1954:16) and dialects of Kyōto-fu (Amada,
Ikaruga, Kasa — Inokuchi 353) have biiru. For kaeru⁻ 'frog' Fukushima has geeru
(Miyara ibid.), Aomori gae⁷ro, Kagoshima gairo (with accent B), and dialects of
Kyōto-fu (Inokuchi 324) have gaeru. For kani⁻ 'crab' Fukushima has gani (Miyara
ibid.), as does the Tango area of Kyōto-fu (Inokuchi 280), cf. standard gani-mata⁻
'bowlegged'. Fukushima also has bati for hati⁻ 'bee', as do a number of other
dialects; the word is [badzï] in Tappi (Clarke 49). Other dialects have /game/
for ka⁷me 'tortoise' (Miyara 1954:17); gaya for kaya⁻ 'mosquito net' (Takeno-gun,
Inokuchi 280), gazyami (Amami) and gazyan (Okinawa) for ka⁻ 'mosquito' — the
suffix is a mystery; zuna for suna⁻ 'sand' (southern Kyūshū, Miyara 1954.17, Hattori
1973:381). Shodon (Amami) has gakyi(i) for ka⁷ki 'oyster' (Onna on Okinawa has
gaacii), dehe(e) for take⁻ 'bamboo' (Shuri daki), busyi(i) for husi⁷ 'node, joint',
ganyi(i) for kani⁻ 'crab', and gutyrya for kuzira⁻ (< kudira) 'whale'. Other initial
voicings: Shuri garaşi for karasu⁻ 'crow', guci for kuki⁷⁻ 'stalk', (zii-)bira
'onion' (cf. hi⁷ru 'garlic'); Kudaka gai for kai⁻ 'shell'; Yaeyama gui for ku⁷i
'stake'; Yaeyama (Ishigaki, Taketomi, Kobama) gusi for OJ kusi 'rice wine'.

Do these voiced initials mean that proto-Japanese had initial np-, nt-, nk-,
ns-? Probably not; they are more likely to be of secondary origin. In some words,
such as the names of plants and animals, the voiced-initial version may result from
the truncation of a compound in which the first element was dropped (perhaps *mitu-
n-pati 'honey bee' > mitu⁷-bati → [mitu⁷-]bati⁻ 'bee') or reduced to simple
nasality (perhaps *myi-takey 'honorable bamboo' > m[i]-take > ndake > dake > daki
'bamboo'). The noun ba⁻ 'place' can be accounted for as a truncation of any of the
many compounds like tati-ba⁷ 'standpoint' from a structure [V-i]-n-pa. Other modern
voiced initials result from dropping an initial syllable, often i-, as in [i]bara⁻
'rosebush', [i]da⁷su 'put out', [i]da⁷ku 'embrace'. But some are due to mimetic
factors of uncertain antiquity: ba⁷ᵤa-bata, pa⁷ta-pata, (fata-fata >) ha⁷ta-hata
'beating, slapping'. There are two such words in the Man'yō-shū: byisi-byisi ni
'snivelly' (M 892) and bu 'buzz (of a bee)' (inferred from a play on words in M
2991). And the majority of voiced initials are found in words known to be borrowed
from Chinese (boo⁻ 'stick', doku⁷ 'poison', ga⁻ 'moth') or English (ba⁷su 'bus' or
'bath', do⁷a 'door', ga⁷su 'natural gas'). It has generally been assumed that the
distinction of voiced (DAKU) syllables from voiceless (SEI) came in with Chinese
loanwords. At least two examples of these are found in Man'yō-shū poems: ga-ki
'hungry ghost' (M 608) and, ultimately of Indic origin, baramon 'Brahmana, Brahman'
(M 3856). Since, however, ga-ki was written with the original Chinese semantograms
and there is a question about the phonogram used to transcribe the initial stop of
baramon, we cannot be sure that the Man'yō-shū poets used the same voiced (or the
prenasalized voiced) initials as later became traditional for these two words.

The numeral go- 'five' also occurs in the Man'yō-shū (M 3827, M 3858) but only as
a semantogram, so we do not know how it was pronounced. Two Indic Buddhist names
came in by way of Chinese transcriptions: bisyamon⁻ 'Vaiśravaṇa' (attested 797)
and birusyana⁻ 'Vairocana' (attested 1107⁻). The earliest initial voiced sounds in
the native truncations are attested in 1020 (daite < idaki-te 'embracing') and 1169
(doko < iduko 'where', bara < ibara 'rosebush').¹⁵ On early voiced initials cf.
Okumura 1977:244.

There is considerable evidence for a feeling of "markedness" about initial
voiced sounds: they occur naturally — unmarked — in loanwords, both the old loans
from Chinese and the modern ones from European languages, but originally they were
not found in the native words, so that an initial b-, d-, z-, or g- marks a word as
a borrowing, a truncation, or in some other way "special". In mimetic words, for
example, the voicing is a connotative overlay (often meaning "excessive, vulgar,
undesirable") on the basic unmarked form: gera-gera is a more obtrusive laugh than
kera-kera. Komatsu 1981 points out that the native noun bara⁻ 'rosebush', a
truncation from ibara⁻, can be deemed a prickly plant, as when the word is written
in hiragana, or — perhaps more often — a lovely blossom, as when it is written in
katakana, which conveys images of stylish, new things from the western world, which
are supposed to be pleasant. On the other hand, when railroaders use the word gasen⁻
for ka-sen⁻ '(overhead) power lines' (made up of Chinese loanmorphs), it marks the
term as a technical word, and it has nothing to do with evaluative judgments, nor
with the earlier phonology (cf. Nakagawa 1978:55b).

27. Medial voiced obstruents reduced from nasal-initial syllables.

Certain examples of medial voiced obstruents can be etymologically accounted
for as reductions of a syllable with a nasal initial: tooḡe 'mountain pass' <
tauḡe < OJ tamukey; OJ kuga 'land' < kunu-ka < kuni-ka; tab(e)- 'eat' < tam[a]p-
'bestow' (Zdb 438c); suzuri 'inkstone' < sumi-suri; ... . A group of delimiters or
"restrictives" (see RGJ) attach with compound-noun nigori: ⁻bakari, - dokoro,
⁻ḡurai, ⁻ḡoro, ⁻dake, ⁻zoi⁻ ("so[f]i), ⁻zumi⁻ ("sumi), ⁻zumi⁻ ("tumi), ...
But in specific lexicalizations some have interesting variants: kore-kurai/- kkurai⁻
= kore-ḡurai⁻; korenbakari, koreppakari = kore-bakari; kore-kiri/- kkiri/ḡiri;
ari-ttake⁻; ... . The name of the old province of Kazusa comes from kam[i]-tu-[fu]sa
'the bunch above' in contrast with neighboring Simoosa⁻ < simo-[tu-f]usa 'the
bunch below' (cf. Shibata 1977:111); a similar pair of old provinces are called
Simotuke (now Ibaraki) < simo-tu-ke 'lower meal[-field]' and Koozuke (now Gunma)
< kauzuke < kam[i]-tu-ke[no] 'upper meal[-field]'.

Other examples: kandori⁻ < kazi-tori 'helmsman', kanbase/kaobase⁻ < kafo-base
'countenance' (cf. Hamada 1952); koozi < kaũdi < kamudati 'yeast' — cf. te-midu >
teũdu > tyoozu 'ablution', ka[n]i-mina > kam[i]na > kaũna → [ ]-gauna (cf. §26) >
goona (JP) 'hermit crab'. It is unclear whether nukinderu 'excel, surpass' contains
evidence of (i)nde- 'emerge' or whether it is a contraction of nuki n[i] deru. The
doublet tatta⁻ = tada 'but, just' suggests that a reduplication like *ta n[i] ta or
perhaps *tan-ta[n] may be the source of tada, but it seems likelier that the word
was an early borrowing from the same source as the later-borrowed tan < ¦dhan'
with an aberrant [d] for -n and an echo vowel or "neutral" epenthetic -a as in
certain other borrowings from Chinese. Although foto-foto > hoto-hoto⁻ is usually
taken as the earlier form of hotondo 'almost (all)', the nasal suggests that both
are variant reductions from *foto ni foto (cf. hotori⁻ 'vicinity'). The two unusual

old adjectives tokizi(-) 'untimely' and onazi(-) 'same' probably were contracted
from toki [ara]n[i] si ('time not be') and on[o ar]an[i] si 'self not be', with the
-azi structure accounted for in §24 as the infinitive of the negative auxiliary +
a predicating auxiliary. (But Miller has suggested that -si- was a "privative"
suffix.) There remain unanalyzable etyma with internal prenasalized obstruents:
*kanpi > kabi 'mildew', *anti > adi > azi 'flavor', *minki > miḡi 'right', *kanse
> kaze 'wind', ...

28. Doublets with m and b.

A number of words appear in modern dialects or in earlier attestations as
doublets, one variant having -m- and the other -b-. Examples:

(1) -b- = -m-	hibo	= himo⁻ 'cord'	
	kabi	= kamiꟼ 'paper' (Ryūkyūs)	
	keburi	= kemuri⁻ 'smoke' (Ritchō on Yoron hinbusi,	
	kubo	= kuꟼmo 'spider'	Jinrui-kagaku 10:166)
	sebi	= semi⁻ 'cicada'	
	sebai	= semaꟼi 'narrow'	
	tuburi	= tumuriꟼ 'head'	
	atuberu	= atumeꟼru 'gather'	
	neburu	= nemuꟼru 'sleep'	
	toburau⁻	= tomurau⁻ 'mourn'	
	tobosiꟼ⁻	= tomosiꟼ⁻ 'torch'	
	kibiꟼ···	= kimiꟼ ḡa waruꟼi 'feel bad'	
(2) -m- = -b-	kimi	= kiꟼbi 'millet'	
	amunai	= abunai⁻ 'dangerous'	
	samisii	= sabisiꟼi 'lonely'	
	eramu	= eraꟼbu 'select' (Hachijō yoramu)	
	kamuru	= kabuꟼru 'wear on one's head'	
	tattomu	= tattoꟼbu 'revere'	

Words like these differ from the many words which appear only with -m- or only with
-b-. It is puzzling that the philological attestations seem to indicate that some
cases of -m- come from -b- and conversely some cases of -b- come from -m-.
    Tsukishima (1969:386-9) discusses the fact that there was "a lot of alternation
between -b- and -m- during the Heian period". He finds pairs that are synchronic
doublets (maboru = mamoru 'guard', amaneku = abaneku 'extensively') and pairs in
which one seems to have developed from the other (tubafiraka > tumabiraka 'in full
detail', simara > sibara-ku 'a while'). He cites as synchronic doublets ayamati =
ayabati 'error', sonemu = sonebu 'envy', sainamu = sainabu 'torment', siramu =
sirabu 'investigate', tinamu = tinabu 'be connected (with)', fimo = fibo 'cord',
kamamisusi- = kamabisusi- 'noisy'.
    Arisaka (1955:550-62) lists nearly 25 words in which he says "-m- changed to
-b- in the Heian period", including kimi > kibi 'millet', emisi/emisu > ebisu
'Ainu', umara > ubara 'thorn', femi > febi 'snake', amu > abu 'gadfly', namu > nabu
'line up', ayumu > ayubu/ayobu 'walk', amusu > abusu 'douse with', samorafu >
saburafu 'serve' (cf. samurai 'warrior'). On the other hand, he cites a few words
in which he says "-b- changed to -m- during the same period", such as omobuku >
omomuku 'tend/go toward' and kasobu > kasumu(/kasobu) 'graze'. And he lists nearly
twenty words as synchronic doublets for which the historical antecedent is in doubt;

these include semi = sebi 'cicada', fimi = fibi '(skin) cracks', tami = tabi 'time =
occasion' (cf. modern tanbi), usomu = usobu and uso-muku = uso-buku 'whistle, howl'.
Also an example in initial position, muti = buti 'whip'.

    Matsumoto (1965) counsels us to explore separately the alternation in the
derivational suffixes marking verb stems, our "formants" of Ch. 6, suggesting that
there were different sources for what became modern -mu and -meru from what became
-bu, -beru, and -biru. The selection of one or more of the formants for a particular
derived stem was a matter of morphological choice rather than phonological change,
and competing forms survived. For the other words, Matsumoto claims that there were
two periods of phonological change: from the Nara into the Heian period the change
was from -m- to -b-, mostly in words with the vowel /a/; from the late-Heian "Insei"
period into the Kamakura period the change from -b- to -m- took place in quite
different words, mostly with the vowel /u/. But a few words that underwent the first
change had syllables with o or u and these took part again in the second change:
having gone from -m- to -b- they then went back to -m- again. It is not clear that
this explanation is justified by the small number of examples adduced. I would
prefer to say that virtually all such cases are the result of sporadic fallout,
variously attested or unattested, from earlier /-np-/, which should have yielded -b-
in all cases, just as virtually all cases of /-nt-/ became -d-. Unlike what happened
to the dental string, however, the labial results are more confusing. But so, in a
way, are those of the velar: earlier /-nk-/ became -g- or -ḡ- = [ŋ] more or less
consistently in a given dialect, but dialect mixture sometimes leads to confusion in
the treatment of individual items by a given speaker. (It must be kept in mind, of
course, that there was an original -m- separate from -np-, but there is no evidence
for an original -ŋ- distinct from -nk-.) Although the earliest phonograms give
omobuku and katabuku for what became later omomuku and katamuku, if the etymologies
include the verb muku 'turn toward' the forms with -b- are aberrant, unless (with
Unger) we assume the verb itself has initial *np-; the verb uso-buku/uso-muku
'whistle, howl', on the other hand probably has as its second element the verb fuku
< *puk- 'blow' and could be explained as *uso n[i] puk-. There are a number of
vexing problems with individual etymologies among these words with forms in -b- and
-m-. (Cf. the remarks by Yamaguchi Yoshinori, Kgg 116:77.)

    A few sets of etyma may show alternations of -d- and -n- perhaps parallel to
those of -b- and -m-: sonafe- 'equip' is written sodafe- in Bussokuseki-no-uta;
ide- 'emerge' and in- 'go away' have somewhat similar meanings, the first being used
to mean 'leave', but in- 'go away' may well be etymologically associated with sin-
'die' since they form a unique hybrid conjugation — like the vowel stems in the
finite forms inu(ru) and sinu(ru) but like the consonant stems in the subjunctive
(presumptive inamu and sinamu, etc.) and, mootly, in the infinitive (ini and sini),
for which we lack evidence to decide the proper assignment, since the tell-tale
vowel distinctions of Old Japanese were neutralized for the front vowels after
dentals. An example of -n- and -t- is OJ inadaki/itadaki 'hair on the head'. There
are also a few examples of initial d- alternating with n- in etymological sets:
damaˀru/domoˀru 'hush/stammer' : namaˀru 'speak in dialect, ... '; dokeru⁻/yokeˀru =
nokeru⁻ 'remove' and noku⁻ = doku⁻ 'step aside'. Notice the form with y-; yokeˀru
may be an unrelated synonym, but medial -y- and -n- turn up as variants in oyazi =
onazi⁻ 'same'. There are also the variant forms of the copula daˀ, zyaˀ, yaˀ, and
attributive naˀ — all presumably going back to niˀ aˀ[ri] or niˀ-te aˀri (see §20).
Komatsu 1981 suggests that d- ← n-, as in doku⁻ ← noku⁻ 'step aside' and dora-neko⁻
'stray cat'), comprises an unusual type of "expressive nigori".

29. Sibilant and affricate articulations.

The quality of the sound used for s- and z- (or ^{d}z-) varies in different areas. Kōchi (Shikoku) sometimes uses interdental fricatives [θ] and [ð], especially before i as in suθi for su'si' 'sushi' (Zhs 5:17, 371, 377). The island of Toshima, not far from Tōkyō, has θa θe θo for sa se so and ða ðe ðo for za ze zo (Zhs 7:21); Narada (Uwano 1976b) has the same set and also θu ðu for su zu (but ši ži for si zi). In Kyōto, too, [θ] is occasionally heard for s or h < s. Other cases of s-swallowing (deapicalization) include se/sye/Fe/he reported for Yamagata (Yamagata-jiten 716) as in four pronunciations of the word for 'back' (senaga = senaka); the labial version Fenaga) is particularly surprising, but it is probably due to analogy with cases of Fe that correspond to standard he < fe. On Kudaka, off southeastern Okinawa, a sound described as [θ] or [ᵗθ] is used for both s- and t- except in the syllables si-, ti-, and tu-; the sound forms a separate phoneme, for vowel changes have put s- and t-in contrast with it (Ryūkyū-hōgen 15:15).

Word families display alternations between t and s in dialects and in competing variants of words: hana'tu = hana'su 'release', subomeru⁻ = tubomeru⁻ 'make it narrow', kobo'tu = kobo'su 'shatter; spill', hutagu⁻ = husagu⁻ 'cover', kisana'i = kitana'i 'dirty', ta'ne/sa'ne 'seed' (sa'ne is semantically differentiated as 'core'), mattu'gu = massu'gu 'directly'; hita- 'unswerving, unceasing' and hisa-'longlasting'; perhaps mutu^b/mu⁻ 'be intimate' and musubu⁻ 'tie'; yature'ru 'get emaciated/gaunt/shabby' and yaseru⁻ 'grow thin/gaunt'; OJ sizim- < tidim- ← tizim-'shrink'; ... . But o-ta'kebi 'war cry' is not related to sakebi' 'yell', because the historical spelling shows o-ta'kebi to come from OJ wo 'male' + takye-biy, the infinitive of an upper-bigrade compound verb takye-biy- 'show bravery' made up of the lower-bigrade stem takye[y]- 'act brave' and a formant; see takebiru in Ch. 6. The Kyōto-fu dialects of Amada, Ikaruga, and Kasa (Inokuchi 339) have tamoso for tamoto' 'sleeve'; cf. suso⁻ 'skirt bottom'. For the word osorosi'i 'dreadful' the pronunciations o(t)torosi(i) are widely used in western Japan; the form is said as (w)otorosi in Takeno-gun of Kyōto-fu (Inokuchi 293). Perhaps related are od(o)-'fear' in odo(ka)su⁻ 'frighten' and odi(ke)ru > ozikeru⁻ 'take fright'. The Shuri word for husu'ma'⁻ 'opaque sliding door' is huçima [Futsima]; the verb stem waka't-'divide' is wakas- in Shuri. For si the Yonaguni dialect has unaspirated [tci] (c is a palatal stop): [tcima] = sima' 'island', [tcitci] = si'si 'flesh'; but Yonaguni reflexes of sa su so all have [s] and that suggests that the [tci] results from a fortition like what is said to have happened on Hachijō island where [tš] is used for s-. Yet Yonaguni replaces t- by s- in [ši] < ti (from earlier ti but not ti < te) and [su] < tu (from earlier tu but not tu < to). Hateruma has [kątši] for kaze⁻, 'wind', [kątsï] for ka'su 'dregs', putsï for hosi⁻ 'star'. In Tōkyō z- is pronounced [^dz] after juncture, e.g. word-initial. Japanese babytalk replaces s- with ty- [tš] or ts-, as in variants of the honorific title -san, -tsan, -tyan, and even (Kuse-gun of Kyōto-fu, Inokuchi 312) -yan. Perhaps relevant here are the Tōkyō pronunciations tittya'i = tiisa'i 'little' (though that could be a variant reduction from tip[i]-sa- rather than from ti[p]i-sa-), namattiro'i⁻ 'pale, wan' < na'ma 'raw' + siro'i 'white', nagattiri'⁻ 'overstaying one's welcome' < na'ga- 'long' + siri' 'buttock'. In this connection Ingram has made an interesting observation (quoted in Language 40:155): "[s] and [z] are even more difficult for the child to articulate than [š], [ž], [tš], or [dž]". It is relevant, perhaps, that Spanish has a phoneme [tš] but no [š]. The eastern (Azuma) dialect of Old Japanese is transcribed in the Man'yō-shū as using si for ti in a number of words, such as sisi for titi' 'father'. In compounds Old Japanese has (-)ti for 'wind; direction', as in koti 'east (wind)' and fayati 'gust'; as well as (-)si, as in nisi⁻ 'west; [Ryūkyū] north' and fimugasi > higasi'⁻

'east'. Cf. the modern Aomori oci⁻ (= oti⁻) for osi⁻ 'deaf' and hetyo⁻ for heso⁻
'navel'. Some linguists have assumed that Old Japanese — or perhaps proto-Japanese
or pre-Japanese — for the sound that is now "s" must have used the affricate sounds
[ts] and [tš] or even a palatal stop [c], made with the front of the tongue in a
single articulation, with the tip safely tucked away against the lower teeth. There
are those (e.g. Miller 1967:202) who assume the affricate version (for Miller [tˢ])
only before the back vowels u o a. The conclusions of a study by Kobayashi Akemi
1981 (Journal of Ōsaka University of Foreign Studies 52:63-80): sa was [tša] at
least until around the middle of the 9th century and became [ša] by c. 1100-1250;
so was [tšo] in the 8th century; swo and su were [šwo] and [šu]; si was [ši] in
the 7th century, se was [še] in the 8th century. Hamada (1977:583-4) thinks that
[š] and [ž] were the earlier pronunciations of s- and z- because of spellings like
"sugyauza" for Chinese loanwords like syugyo'o-zya 'ascetic'. Unger 1975a argues
that proto-Japanese had c- for all instances of what we spell as s-; he reconstructs
a proto *s- only for the morphemes which appear as doublets with and without an /s/
(§31), as in a'me 'rain' and ko-same⁻ 'shower'.¹⁶ Unless we accept Unger's view, we
will have to assume an /s/ at the earliest stage, which later (at various times and
in various places) developed allophones such as [ᵗs] for s- and modern [ᵈz] for z-.
From the standpoint of typological universals proto-Japanese would be unusual if it
had an affricate but no sibilant. Perhaps at the earliest stage there were competing
versions of /s/, one with the tongue tip up (grazing the upper teeth or the alveolar
ridge) and the other with the tongue tip down, touching the lower teeth in order to
make the hiss by creating turbulence around the blade.¹⁷

30. Alternation of z with d; of t or d with r; of n with r; of y with r.

    In addition to the automatic alternation of [ᵈz]- with -[z]- and of [ᵈž]- with
-[ž]- in modern Tōkyō, there are dialect alternations of /z/ and /d/. In the Kyōto-
fu dialects of Amada, Ikaruga, and Kasa nazeru is reported for nade'ru 'pat, pet'
(Inokuchi 359), mukaze for mukade⁻ 'centipede' (id. 348), nozo for no'do 'throat'
(id. 351). Nazeru is reported also for Hagiwara (Tsuzuku 1941:193). These look like
weakenings (lenition), but there are also reports of what look like hardenings
(fortition): nodoku for nozoku⁻ 'peek' (id. 351), hida for hiza⁻ 'knees' (id. 353),
dasiki for zasiki⁻ 'room' (Kuse-gun, id. 309), deni for zeni⁻ 'money' (id. 310).
There may be a relationship between the verb kizam-⁻ 'cut' and the obsolete words
kida 'a cut/division' and kida-kida = kiza-kiza 'mincing'; but notice also kizu⁻
'wound, flaw'. At first glance tozi'ru ("todiru") and toza'su⁻ 'close' seem to make
a promising pair, but the latter is said to be from to-¨sas- 'stick (= attach) the
door'. In Izu-Ōshima /da do de/ represent both ¨ta ¨to ¨te and ¨sa ¨so ¨se
(Shin Nihongo-kōza 3:116). In the Aden dialect of Kikai the three syllables za zu ze
are pronounced [da du de] (Hattori 1932, cf. Kgg 133:59).
    A possible alternation of t and r is found in ot(o)- of oto'su 'drop' and
oti'ru 'falls' as compared with or(o)- of oro'su 'lowers' and ori'ru 'descend'.
An alternation of s and r: nosoi = noro'i 'dull' in the Kyōto-fu dialects of Amada,
Ikaruga, and Kasa (Inokuchi), cf. osoi⁻ 'slow'. Confusion of -d- and -r- is widely
found in the Ryūkyūs and in parts of Kansai; cf. the dialect adjective stem
sindo- 'tired', derived from the Chinese binom sin-ro[o] 'heart work'.
    There are several examples of n alternating with r: seᵃ/zenaki = seseragi⁻ <
seᵃ/zeraki '(the sound of) rapids'; Tappi ku'zina for kuzira⁻ 'whale'; (NKD "Kishū"
= Kii =) Wakayama teneru = tere'ru 'feel awkward'; perhaps inari 'god of grain'
written as if *ina-ni 'rice bear[er]' but also suggested to be a contraction of
i[ne]-nari 'rice-yielding'; placenames ending ···rV spelled with phonograms ending
in -n such as Si'raḡi 'Shilla' (with phonograms sin-ra = Korean Sin-la), Su'ruḡa

(phonograms syun-ka), TuꞮruğa spelled with phonograms read ton-ᵏ/ğa and thought to
be from *tunwo ka 'horn deer', KaꞮra 'Mimana; ancient Korea or China; ... ' believed
to be from KaꞮn 'Korea, Han'; the phonogram FILL /man/ used as one way to write
the suffix -maro in male personal names — the scholar Kada no Azumamaro (1669-1751)
wrote his surname in phonograms (*on-yomi* ka MINT + *kun-yomi* ta 'field') but for his
personal name he used the semantically fanciful 'spring' for azuma and the phonogram
for -maro; the noun soroban 'abacus' is taken from an early Chinese version of what
is modern Beijing suàn-pan; ... . See Ōno Tōru 1957:132-3, who suggests that /r/ may
very well have come from a prenasalized [~r] and thus fit in with the "other" *dakuon*
(voiced obstruents), so that its failure to appear initially except in truncations
and Chinese loanwords is parallel to the *dakuon* restrictions. Possibly relevant is
the medial string in Nakijin (northern Okinawa) ꜛqinruꞮn for ireru⁻ 'put in'; cf.
Nakijin kuTanꜛriꞮn for kutabireꞮru 'get tired'. Shuri offers several examples of
-n- for -r- or -r- for -n-: kunabⁱ/ₐr- = kurabir- for kurabe-⁻ 'compare', tarum- for
tanoꞮm- 'request' (Yonaguni also has tarum-), kuner- (? < kore- < kor[af]e-) for
koraeꞮ- 'endure, restrain', kanagir- = karageꞮ- 'tie/tuck up'. The eastern (Azuma)
dialect of Old Japanese sometimes has /na/ where the central dialect had /ra/ (KggD
954b). We here set aside the assimilation of -rV- to a following nasal, as in the
casual wakaꞮnnai 'I dunno' for wakaraꞮnai 'I don't know' and suꞮn no 'gonna do it?'
for suruꞮ no 'are you going to do it?'. The Ryūkyū finite endings -n, -m, and -r are
probably not directly connected with either the alternations or the asssimilations
described here, but go back to morphologically distinct markers in proto-Japanese.
Examples of -ŋ for the ending -ru in main-island dialects, such as those of Okayama
and (Toguchi 1974) Ōaza Tsurusaki of Ōita-shi in Kyūshū, are all probably secondary
developments. Notice also -n for -ri in the adjectival noun sakan 'flourishing' from
the infinitive-derived noun sakari⁻.

     In Old Japanese the stems of certain intransitive verbs such as kaye[y]- =
kare[y]- 'leave, separate' occur as doublets with either -y- or -r-. These are
competing versions of originally complex stems containing two different formants,
reconstructed in Ch. 6 as *-da- and *-ra-. Often these formants are followed by yet
another formant *-Ci- to make the Old Japanese bound auxiliaries -ye[y]- < *-da-Ci-
and -re[y] < *-ra-Ci-.

31. Alternation of s- with zero.

     A number of examples can be adduced to demonstrate the alternation of s- with
zero, the most familiar being aꞮme 'rain' with its combining form -same in haru-
same⁻ 'spring rain', ko-same⁻ 'shower', etc. The traditional treatment has been to
dismiss the -s- as a form of the prefix sa- 'small' (etc.) but the semantics do not
particularly support that view and it seems odd to have the prefixed form often
chosen as the second element of a compound. Other examples of s- in alternation with
zero: ara-/sara- 'new' as in ara-/sara-yu⁻ 'newly drawn bath'; iꞮne and -sine as in
obsolete uru-sine = uruti⁻ 'nonglutinous rice'; aꞮ[w]o/-sa[w]o 'blue' as in maT-saꞮo
'pale' — but saꞮwo occurs as a free form in Old Japanese (M 3889), and that fact
may support the prefix explanation. There is the verb root sut-/ut-/us- 'lose' found
in usi-naw-⁻ 'lose', sute-⁻ 'reject', and uꞮse-⁻ 'lose' and variants. Also the verb
pair sin-⁻ 'die' and in-⁻ 'pass/go away', which form a uniquely hybrid conjugation
in older Japanese. In the early language the stem sin- would never take the perfect
auxiliary nu(ru), which is thought to derive from in-, but by Kamakura times forms
like sininu, sininiki, etc., were permitted (Satō 1973:96, 260). Other etymological
groups with (s)- include afa- > awaꞮ-i 'thin, dilute' and safas- > sawaꞮsu⁻ (Shimane
awasu) 'dilute the astringency (of persimmons); bleach; lightly lacquer' (the verb

is not attested before Edo); uwe- > ueru⁻ 'plant' and suwe- > sueru⁻ 'place, seat'
(cf. Korean se- 'stand'); OJ akare- and sakar- 'separate' (but I treat these stems
as unrelated); OJ amanesi, samanesi, and manesi 'universally, lots'; ... . Cf.
Hamada 1950. An Old Japanese word that might be thought to belong here is kata-sifa
'hard rock', but that is probably best treated as a contraction of kata-s[i] ifa
'it's hard — the rock', an example of the use of the predicative form in attributiv
position, not uncommon in fixed epithets (see §7). The Old Japanese metaphor kakifa
'eternal rock' is probably < ka[ta]-kyi [i]fa 'hard rock' with the attributive; two
variant forms katifa ?< kat[a(-)] ifa and kasifa ?< ka[ta]-si [i]fa are attested
(Zdb 178a).

The Ryūkyū dialects have a few words with a glottal initial for "s-": qu-ri
= so-re⁻ 'that', the mesial deictic which appears as sa-/so- and perhaps also in
saꞌr-⁻ 'go away' (cf. ka-/ko- for the proximal deictic and koꞌ- 'come'); quutu B
(Shuri) 'offing' = soto-uꞌmi 'outer sea' (Nakijin tuu A is either a truncation or
unrelated); qiba-, siba- = sema-, seba- 'narrow' (but the s- forms may be from *sa-
iba-). If the Ryūkyū forms went back to an initial *o- or *e- we would expect just
*u-ri and *uutu and *iba- with no initial consonant (or with a nondistinctive
semivowel onset, w- or y-). Perhaps OJ ore 'you' is from [s]ore.

I reconstruct a proto phoneme *z- for these etyma in which s- alternates with
zero, feeling that it will fit in with the reconstructed *b- for later w-, *d- for
later y-, and perhaps *g- for k- alternating with zero, at least in pre-Japanese,
as well as for the hiatus filler to be posited as just C (unspecified consonant) in
the derivation of certain verb stems and inflectional forms. But Unger rejects the
notion that the proto phoneme in question (if it existed) was voiced. He points to
the fact that when there is an alternation it is the -s- form that occurs between
vowels, an environment that offers no phonetic motivation for the devoicing that is
later evidenced: why should speakers turn off the voice in the middle of haru-same⁻
'spring rain'? Unger has reconstructed a voiceless affricate *c- for the large
number of words with a stable s- and claims that the small number of other cases,
such as those mentioned above, represent the original sibilant *s-. He may very well
be right, but we will continue to use the familiar notation "s-" for our earliest
reconstruction of the more frequent initial and the notation "*z-" or "*[z]" for the
unusual situation. The reader is invited to consider the notation to mean simply
"disappearing/alternating s" rather than a phonetically real voiced sibilant. The
small number of examples for our *z- (and perhaps for our problematic *g-, as well)
suggests that perhaps we are simply dealing with a sporadic initial elision that
occurred for unknown reasons. And some of the words may in fact preserve a prefix
s[a]-, as the conventional interpretation has it. The noun (-)swo = wo 'hemp' (cf.
swode 'sleeve' and so 'garment') could be a compression s[a]wo from sa-wo '(?true)
hemp' and that might be an apheretic form [a]sa-wo of the stem found in asawo-ra
'hemp(en cloth)' (M 3484 — Azuma). If OJ w- comes from earlier *b- the contraction
hypothesis would require either lenition (*-b- > -w-) or an otherwise unsupported
proto-syllable *bwo (koꞌo-type "bo").[18]

Finally, we should perhaps mention a more remote possibility. The -s- could be
the relic of a genitive marker, like the Middle Korean -s-, perhaps a variant of the
Old Japanese particle (-)tu (see Ch. 7, §7.3).

Part Two: Intervocalic consonants and attested elisions.

32. Intervocalic consonant elisions.

The location of the Tōkyō accent of the verb sii⁷ru 'compel' (cf. si⁷iru 'a seal') tells us that a consonant must have dropped between the two vowels, and the historical spelling informs us that the consonant was -f- ("h"), pronounced -w- at the time it dropped. In fact, we can safely conclude that virtually all cases of V-V must go back to VCV in proto-Japanese. Accordingly, adjective + -i must have some missing consonant between the stem-final vowel and the finite ending. This can be confirmed by two pieces of evidence: (1) the intensive or explicit form A-ku a⁷ri, and (2) the philologically attested earlier forms A-ki (adnominal, usually called "attributive") and A-si ("predicative"), marked by endings that are described and explained in Ch. 7. The presumptive (= hortative-tentative) verb ending -oo from the philologically attested -a(w)u must similarly have had at least -w- if not *-b-. And, from survival of -an as a presumptive, we know that the form was actually -amu, which is also attested. The [y] in -yoo, the modern alternant after vowel stems, is the result of an analogical reformation based on a conflation of s(i)yoo < se[m]u 'will do', as explained in Ch. 3, where elision is treated in detail.

33. "Onbin".

The term onbin⁻ refers to a variety of phenomena: syncope, a kind of internal weakening and loss of syllabicity; crasis (merging of vowels); monosyllabification; consonant assimilations; simplification of geminates; etc. The internal weakening of consonants, called lenition, may lead to total elision. Examples of VELAR elision are found not only in the adjective attributive (taka-ki > taka-[]i > taka⁷i, and for some dialects > ?takei > takee > take) and the Kansai version of the adjective infinitive (taka-ku > taka-[]u > takɔɔ > ta⁷koo > ta⁷ko), but also in individual items of vocabulary, especially in Chiba (Miyara 1954:64),[19] but sporadically found elsewhere:
   ka[k]i 'scratch' in kai-kur-⁻ 'reel hand-over-hand, turn pages', kai-tumande⁻ 'summarizing, in summary', kai-bori⁻ 'catching fish by draining the water', kai-aki⁻ 'sleeved coverlet', kai-dori⁻ = utikake⁻ 'long outer garment';
   tu[k]i 'collide' in tui-tate⁻ 'single-leaf screen';
   tu[k]i 'moon' in tui-tati⁷ 'new moon = first day of the month';
   hu[k]i 'blow' in hui-tyoo 'announcing, trumpeting' (-tyoo 'listening' < teu < teŋ < Middle Chinese .thyeng);
   ta[k]i 'burn' in ta⁷i-matu '(pine) torch';
   sa[k]i 'cape' in Sa⁷itama⁻ (placename);
   ka[k]i 'fence' in kai-ma-mi⁷ru 'peek (as through a fence)'.
Both voiceless and voiced velar stops elide in verb gerunds ···[k]i-te and ···[g̊]i-de, as explained in Ch. 3. Other cases of [g̊]i occur sporadically, especially in rapid speech. This is reminiscent of the softening of [g] to [γ] to zero in modern Turkish: da[ğ]a 'mountain', which may prove cognate with Japanese take⁷ 'peak' and ta⁷ka- 'high' (and perhaps yama⁷ 'mountain', if that is from *da[ga]-ma).
   The stages of LABIAL lenition are usually assumed to be -p- > -f- > -w/0-. This presumes a proto-Japanese internal (as well as initial) stop /p/ as the ancestor of OJ /f/, which may have been a voiced bilabial fricative [β] when intervocalic, since that would more naturally account for the later -w-. Arguments for the internal -p- as a stop are found in §14; to those we can add the eastern morphophonemic rules

that reduce ka[p]i-te to kaT-te 'buying' rather than the western koo-te < kɔɔ-te < kaw-te ("kaute") < kawi-te (?< kaβi-te < ?kabi-/kapi-te). If ya 'house' (in ya˥-ne 'roof' and the common Ryūkyū yaa) is to be related to i[p]e˥ 'house' (< "ifye" ← *ipey < *ipa-i, see §45 and Ch. 5), for which the Azuma form is attested as "ifa", we would have to assume a very early elision i[p]a or, equally unique, y[ip]a.

Lenition (to -w-) and elision of -m- is attested sporadically in the late Heian period. We have mentioned the verb presumptive (future) ending -a-mu > -a[m]u > -ɔɔ > -oo (> -o), on which more will be said in Ch. 3. There are also casual reductions of -[m]i- as in su[m]imase˥n 'excuse me; thank you' which may sound the same as su[w]imase˥n 'I don't smoke' and rapid-speech su[ḡ]imase˥n 'it does not exceed'.

More drastic reductions are found in -tyaw- < -ti[m]aw- < -te simaw- 'do all, complete doing' and the dialect forms -[tšoku] < -t[e]yoku < -te[y]oku (epenthetic glide) < -te oku 'does for now/later' (the standard contraction is -t[e]oku) and -[tšaru] < -t[e]yaru < -te yaru 'does as a favor'.

34. Elision of w-; merger of "-f-" with "-w-"; -y- and -w- in verb stems.

Some of the consonants that are attested for earlier Japanese have been dropped in the course of the development of the modern language. At one time the syllable /wi/ was distinct from /i/, /we/ was pronounced differently from /e/, and /wo/ was not the same as /o/. But eventually the w- dropped in /we/, while initial o- picked up a prothetic w-, so that the 16th-century Portuguese observed wo for both "o" and "wo", though that automatic w- later dropped, too, so that both syllables are now just o. (A prothetic y- was picked up earlier by the merged e- and it, too, was written by the Portuguese missionaries but has now disappeared in the standard language.) With modern loanwords new w- syllables are coming in (wi˥ndoo 'window', we˥tto 'wet', wo˥tuka 'vodka') but the older distinctions are totally lost. From the historical spellings we can list the principal words that once were pronounced with the distinctive w-:

WI	wi(-do) 'well'	wi-	(1) 'sit; perch; abate; settle; dock'
	wi(-no-sisi) 'boar'		(2) 'teeth get on edge from sour food'
	wi 'rush (plant)'		(3) 'lead' (= fiki-wi-)
	wiya = uya 'rite'		
	winaka 'country(side)'		
WE	we(-ba/-sa) 'bait'	we-n-ko, wenu 'puppy'	
	we = yuwe 'reason'	wef- 'get intoxicated'	
	we 'picture'	wer-, wegur- 'carve'	
	wegu '(a kind of sedge)'	werag- 'rejoice'	
	wem- 'smile'	wetak- 'gasp' (= afek-)	
WO	wo 'tail'	wodor- 'dance'	
	wo 'male; husband'	wodos- 'fasten armor plates'	
	wo 'hemp'	wok- 'invite'	
	wo 'peak; hill'	womek- = wamek- 'call'	
	wo- 'little'	wor- 'break, fold, bend'	
	wo(-ro) 'thong; string'	wor- 'be, stay'	
	woba 'aunt'	worogam- = wogam- 'worship'	
	wodi 'uncle'	woti- 'revert, return'	
	woka 'hill'	wosim- 'regret; prize'	
	woke 'bucket'	wowor- 'bend around; droop luxuriantly'	
	woko (na) 'stupid'	woye- 'get weak'	
	wori 'occasion, season'		

wosa 'head leader, elder'   wosa-na- 'juvenile'
wosa 'batten, (loom) read'   wo-si- 'dear, precious; bedgrudged'
woso = kafa-uso 'otter'   wokasi- 'amusing'
woti, woto 'yonder'

Between vowels, as initially, -w- is heard only before /a/ and many speakers ignore
it even there, or insert a -w- that is historically inappropriate for certain words,
such as ba-ai⁻ 'situation'.[20] It is uncommon to find a modern -h- within a native
morpheme, for the ancestor of modern /h/ — earlier f and still earlier p — merged
with /w/ internally. And the modern language makes no distinction of Ve ≠ Vye or of
Vi ≠ Vyi. That means that the following distinctions have merged:

m o d e r n	<	s o u r c e s		
Vwa		Vfa	Vwa	
Vo		Vfo	Vwo	
Vu		Vfu	V(w)u	
Ve		Vfe	Vwe	Vye
Vi		Vfi	Vwi	V(y)i

Below are lists of the principal words going back to each source. Not listed are
consonant-final verb stems ending in /w/, which are all from -f-; the following
vowel varies with the ending: af- 'meet' → afanu, afi, afu, afe.

-wa	awa 'bubble foam'	-fa	All cases not listed under -wa, including:
	siwa 'wrinkle'		afa 'millet'
	tawa 'saddle of mountain'		bifa 'loquat'
	iwasi 'sardine'		ifa 'crag'
	wawara-ba 'ragged leaves'		fifa 'siskin'
			kafa 'river; 'skin'; 'side'
			kifa 'edge' (and derivatives)
			nifa 'garden'
			safa 'swamp'
			tofa 'eternity'
			afabi 'abalone'
			afare 'dismay'
			kafara 'brick'
			kafaya 'toilet'
			kafazu 'frog'
			safara 'mackerel'
			tafasi 'swab, scrub brush'
			ufaki 'fickle'
			ufasa 'gossip'
			tafa-goto 'foolish talk'
	kawak- 'dry up'		kafar- 'change' (vi)
	sawag- 'make noise'		kofas- : kofare- 'break'
	suwar- 'sit'		mafar- 'revolve' : mafas- 'revolve it'
	tawam- 'bend; slacken'		safar- 'touch'
	uwar- 'be planted'		safas- 'dilute astringency; bleach; ... '
	wawak- 'tatter, rend'		kufafe- 'add' : kufafar- 'be added'
			tafake- 'fool around'
			osofar- 'be taught'
			...

-wo   awo 'green, blue'   -fo   kafo 'face'
       miwo 'channel'   nifo 'grebe (bird)'
       sawo 'pole'   sifo 'salt; tide'
       towo 'ten'   nafo 'furthermore'
       tawori 'saddle of   ifafo 'crag'
                mountain'   ikifofi 'force, vigor'
       towo(-wo/-towo) 'bending'
       kawor- 'smell'   kofor- 'freeze'
       mawos- 'humbly say'   nafor- : nafos- 'improve'
        > ma(w)us- > moos-   nifof- 'be fragrant'
       siwore- 'wither'   ofof- 'cover'
       towom- = tawam- 'bend'   tofor- : tofos- 'pass'
       toworaf- 'sway, bob'
       wowor- 'bend around;   ofo- 'big, much/many'
         droop luxuriantly'   tofo- 'distant'

-(w)u   All cases of Vu   -fu   afufi 'hollyhock' > aoi
        not listed as Vfu   afug- 'face up' > aog-
        are -(w)u.   afug- 'fan' > aog-
                                             afur- 'fan' > aor-
                                             afure- 'overflow'
                                             tafure- : tafus- 'topple' > taore- : taos-

-wi   awi 'indigo'   -fi   efi 'ray, skate'   -(y)i   kayi 'oar'
       nawi 'earthquake'   fafi 'ashes'   seyi 'height'
                                         kafi 'shell'
                                         nifi 'new'
                                         tafi 'red snapper'
                                         tofi 'water pipe'
                                         yofi 'night'
                                         afida 'interval'
                                         afiru 'duck'
       mawir- 'humbly go'   sifi- 'compel, force'   kuyi- 'regret'
       fiki-wi- 'lead'   fafir-21 'enter'   oyi- 'get old'
       moti-wi- 'use'

-we   kowe 'voice'   -fe   ife 'house'   -ye   faye = faya 'carp'
       yuwe 'reason'   mafe 'front'   fiye 'millet'
       suwe 'end'   nafe 'seedling'   fuye 'flute'
       tuwe 'stick'   nife 'sacrifice; gift'   saye 'chimera'
       tukuwe22 'desk'   ufe 'above'   saye 'dice'
                                         kafede 'maple'   tukuye22 'desk'
                                         kaferu 'frog'
       suwe- 'place'   afe- 'dress (vegetables)'   aye- 'spill'
       uwe- 'starve'   kafe- 'change it'   faye- 'grow'
       katuwe- 'starve'   ofe- 'end it'   fiye- 'get cold'
                                         sofe- 'append it'   foye- 'howl'
                                         atafe- 'give'   fuye- 'increase'
                                         kafer- : kafes- 'return'   iye- 'get well'
                                         furufe- 'shake it'   iye- 'get shot'
                                         kakafe- 'embrace, hold'   kiye- 'vanish'
                                         kamafe- 'construct'   koye- 'cross over'

kanafe- 'fulfill'
kazofe- 'count'
korafe- 'endure'
kotafe- 'answer'
osife- 'teach'
sarafe- 'rehearse'
sasafe- 'prop'
sonafe- 'provide, equip'
tagafe- 'violate'
tatafe- 'fill with, praise'
tatofe- 'liken'
tonafe- 'chant'
tugafe- 'put arrow to bow'
tukafe- 'be used; serve'
tukafe- 'be obstructed'
totonofe- 'arrange'
+ all other verbs
  not listed as Vye
  or Vwe.

koye- 'get fat'
kuye- 'crumble'
miye- 'get seen'
moye- 'bud; burn'
naye- 'droop'
saye- 'get clear'
suye- 'turn sour'
woye- 'get weak'
amaye- 'get sweet'
atuye- 'get grave'
ibaye- 'whinny'
kikoye- 'get heard'
midaye- 'be corrupt'
modaye- 'writhe'
nifoye- 'be red'
obiye- 'feel fear'
sakaye- 'prosper'
sinaye- 'wilt'
sobiye- 'tower'
tabaye- 'bundle'
tufiye- 'be wasted'
wakaye- 'be
  rejuvenated'
korofaye- 'get
  scolded'
(oboe- ‹) omofoye-
  'be thought'

By examining related forms, we see that many of the vowel-stem verbs ending in Vi and Ve can be shown to have an underlying -f- or -y- between the vowels. The -y- of the latter type can be heard in the literary forms: attributive (adnominal) Vyuru and predicative Vyu, regarded as synchronic contractions of Vy[$^1/_e$ s]uru in Martin 1975b. Some of these verbs have transivity-paired mates that attest the -y-:

fayas- : faye- 'grow'
fiyas- : fiye- 'cool off'
fuyas- : fuye- 'increase'
iyas- : iye- 'heal'
koyas- : koye- 'fatten'

moyas- : moye- 'burn'
tayas- : taye- 'end'
tuiyas- : tuiye- 'waste, collapse'
obiya(ka)s- : obiye- 'frighten : fear'
amayakas- : amaye- 'sweeten'

Some of the stems are clearly related to other words that attest the -y-:

kuyam- 'regret', kuyasi- 'regrettable' : kuyi- 'regret'
nayo-nayo 'drooping' : naye- 'wither, droop, weaken'
sayaka 'clear, bright' : saye- 'get clear/bright, get cold'
? oya˥ 'parent' : oyi- 'get old, age'

More complicated examples are the three stems niyas- : niye- : ni- 'cook, boil' and the pair kes- ‹ kiyas- 'extinguish' : kiye- 'vanish'.

Yet others afford no such handy evidence: hoye- 'howl', kikoye- 'get heard', koye-
(: kos-) 'cross over', miye- 'get seen', modaye- 'writhe', mukuyi- 'repay' (but cf.
RGJ 836 n.176), sakaye- 'prosper', suye- 'turn sour', ... You can tell that these
have the -y- only from the literary forms ···yu(ru). But such literary forms are
widely used for the colloquial ···e-ru regardless of its historical origin, for the
spelling has been confused. You will find that dictionaries often cross-list the
···yu(ru) spellings for the more legitimate "···huru" or "···uru". There are also
spelling mistakes that go the other way, with "···huru" for "···yuru"; see RGJ 837.
The Japanese-Portuguese dictionary of 1603 has "ye yuru yeta" for what was earlier
e u(ru) eta 'get', and the "yuru" is clearly analogical, even though it supports my
analysis of the finite forms as abbreviations: y[e s]uru.

The morphophonemic evidence for underlying -y- and -w- was noticed by Kamo
Mabuchi in his Goi-kō of 1769 (cf. Mabuchi Kazuo in Kōza Kokugo-shi 1:298-300).

35. Sporadic elision of initial consonants; doublets (m and n, f and k).

The lists in the preceding sections are a guide to consonants that have elided
between vowels. On the etymological distinction of -w- from -f- (< -p-) we might
look for evidence in words with the -T/N- intensifier that is found in haTki'ri,
bon'ya'ri, etc., for it yields -Tp- and -Nw-. But the only examples I have found are
yanwa'ri 'softly' (cf. yawa-ra'-ka < yafa-) and hunwa'ri 'wafting' (= hu'wa-huwa),
both spelled with "ha" in the traditional orthography.

Certain droppings of initial consonants are sporadic:

[w]a: OJ [w]are 'I/me', [w]akat- 'divide, share', [w]atari 'neighborhood'.

[y]u: Dialect usugu, isugu = yusug̃u⁻ 'wash out'— cf. igoku = ug̃o'ku 'move'.

[m]u: OJ [m]uzina 'badger; raccoon-dog'.

[n]i: inau = nina'u 'bear on the shoulders' in Kuse-gun of Kyōto-fu (Inokuchi
306); OJ [n]iham- 'throng, become full' (Zdb 51c, but the n··· form is not listed
in the body of the dictionary).

[n]u: OJ uruf- = nure[y]- 'get wet'.

[n]a: [n]ani 'how' (Miyara 1954:71) in Chiba, Hachiōji, Asakawa. This has often
been associated with Korean ani 'no', and in Amada, Ikaruga, and Kasa of Kyōto-fu
the word nani is used to mean iya 'no' according to Inokuchi 348. Standard na'ni
'what, anything, *(with negative)* nothing' is one of the indeterminates; Hachijō has
ani for 'what'. Also bear in mind the negative auxiliary (V-a -) na-, explained in
Ch. 6; the adjective na- 'lacking, nonexistent'; the literary interjection i'na
'nay'; and the Old Japanese prohibitive adverb na (V-i so) 'don't V'.

There are doublets that have mi for ni or ni for mi in various dialects:
mii-/nii- 'new'; mira/nira 'leek' (cf. Korean manul < manol 'garlic'); nigaku =
mig̃aku⁻ 'polish', nino = mi'no 'raincape' (Takeno-gun of Kyōto-fu, Inokuchi 291).
We are reminded of Ie-jima (off Okinawa) where mi- regularly becomes ni-, while pi-
(= standard hi- < fi-) regularly becomes ti- (but -bi- does not become di-) in an
unusual assimilation of consonant position to the modern high front vowel whether
that is from earlier *i or *e (cf. Nakamoto 1976:307). According to Yamaguchi (Kgg
116:77) there are two historic tendencies at work:

(1) nV > mV before a labial or velar syllable: nifo(dori) > mifo(dori) 'grebe',
nifofu > mifofu 'emit fragrance', nigir-u > migir-u 'grasp' — perhaps the source of
migi(ri) 'right' (Shuri niziri < nigiri), nigai > migai 'bitter', ... For possible
cases of n- > m- before a rounded vowel see the dialect reflexes for nizi 'rainbow'
and no 'field' in Ch. 5.

(2) mV > nV before a dental syllable: mina > nina 'snail', mino > nino 'raincape',
mira > nira 'leek', mitu(ru) > nitu(ru) 'fill', kumato > kunato 'dark corner', ...

Ryūkyūan naa or nyaa 'already, now' is from *[i]nya < *imya (by progressive palatal assimilation) < *ima; the labial nasal has assimilated to the following palatal, before or after the loss of the first syllable. The word is maa (?< *myaa) < [i]ma in Yonaguni and Hateruma. The standard version moo may have assimilated the vowel to the labial initial: [i]ma > ma(a) > mɔɔ (JP) > moo/mo[o]. But more likely it is the result of truncation from a compound.

The OJ umyi/una- 'sea' might suggest an m/n alternation but the forms could also be accounted for as variant reductions of something like *u-mina; on min(a) 'water' see §52.

A few sets of words show a labial that varies with a velar (cf. Kuranaka 79): fukum-/kukum-/fufum- 'embrace, include', fam-/kam- 'chew, eat'; nofokiri/nokokiri 'saw', kofor-/kogor- 'freeze'. The internal -f- may be spurious, for it could represent an epenthetic glide inserted between vowels left adjacent by elision of a velar: ko-[g]or- > kowor- spelled "kofor-", treating the word as a reduplication (*ko[ri] n[i] kor-) of kor- 'freeze'. And fufum- could be accounted for as fu[k]um- > fu(w)um-, but kukum- would remain a problem; perhaps two different etyma have been blended, as seems likely for the verbs kam- and fam- (cf. fame[y]- 'insert, fill in' and famar- 'be inserted, filled in').

Part Three: Vowel distinctions

36. Vowel systems.

The kana spelling that developed in Heian times reflects a five-vowel system. Certain modern dialects show EXPANDED systems, with additional vowels resulting from the crasis of diphthongs: ai and au > ɛ and ɔ; oi and ui > ö and ü. In the Ryūkyūs the raising of the mid vowels e and o to i and u respectively, together with certain shortenings of long vowels, has resulted in several different systems — some that are smaller than the five-vowel system, some that are larger (cf. Zhs 11:23).

Our consideration of vowels will start from the familiar Heian system, which is largely preserved in modern standard Japanese except for certain developments that led to the long vowels, described just below. Once these developments are taken care of, we proceed to consider pre-Heian vowels, first from the clues we find in the later system and then from philological evidence.

The vowel cluster /ei/ is kept distinct from the long /ee/ in the Ryūkyūs, in Kyūshū and southern Shikoku, and in the Kii peninsula area (Hirayama 1968b:95). The coexistence of se and sei 'shaggy hoof' (sei attested as early as 918) suggests that the long-vowel pronunciation of ee for ei may have been around for a long time in one area or another (cf. Endō 1974:37). Two kinds of long /oo/ are distinguished in the central area of Niigata prefecture (Kindaichi 1967b:148, KggD 129b); two kinds of long /ee/ are reported in other areas. In some cases these distinctions are of recent origin, but the historical distinction of long ɔɔ < au from oo < ou is still preserved in central Echigo (Niigata prefecture), the Akiyama district of Nagano, and on Sado island, while in Izumo ou > oo but au > aa (Kindaichi in Kōza Kokugo-shi 1:152). In parts of Nagano the open long [ɛ:] < ai or ae contrasts with [e:] < ie or ei, so that maita⁻ 'sowed' is pronounced [mɛ:ta] and mi˥eta 'appeared' is pronounced [me:ta]; the same dialects have [asɛ:] < asai⁻ 'shallow', [osö] < osoi⁻ 'slow', and [usü] usui⁻ 'thin', according to Shin Nihongo-kōza 3:106. The central-Niigata distinctions mentioned by Kindaichi apparently maintain the Muromachi-period Kyōto pronunciations of [ɔ:] < au and [o:] < ou (id. 3:97). In central and northern Kyūshū the Muromachi distinctions are observed but with the vowels raised: afita > aw[i]-ta > ɔɔta > oota 'met'. ofi-ta > ow[i]-ta > oota > uuta 'chased'; kura[k]u naru > kuroo naru 'gets dark', kuro[k]u naru > kuruu naru 'gets black' (id. 3:232-3).

A problem. Why do we find surviving /au/ and /ou/ in such verb forms as kau <
ka[f]u 'buy' and tou < to[f]u 'inquires' in Tōkyō and Kyōto, where we would expect
the long-vowel forms found in a number of dialects (e.g. Narada[23]) /koo/ < kɔɔ and
/too/? The spellings of the Japanese-Portuguese dictionary of 1603 clearly show the
standard pronunciations of that day were [kɔ:] and [to:]. Hamada 1977:585 thinks
that during the Muromachi period [ɔ:] and [o:] may have been sloppy or fast-speech
pronunciations that never completely displaced the clear versions [au] and [ou];
yet, if so, that would appear to be true only for the verb forms — cf. the Kansai
adjective infinitives asoo⁻ < asɔɔ < asa-[k]u 'shallow' and osoo⁻ < oso-[k]u 'slow'.
A likelier explanation is that the modern Kyōto forms are analogical restorations.
A third explanation would assume the survival of a different kind of juncture with
the ···[f]-u ending, and that assumption is implied by Hattori's Apostrophe in such
notations as ka'u and to'u. An explanation of that sort would have to claim that the
juncture, or apostrophe, achieved a true phonological status when the -[w]- < -f-
disappeared;[24] it should be kept in mind that w was never distinctive before u in
historic Japanese. For more on this problem, see Ch. 3.

In Kyōto the two monophthongizations ou > [o:] and au > [ɔ:] probably set in
around 1300, beginning with the Chinese loanwords and then extending to native
words, where often (as with the verb forms) there was a morpheme boundary before the
-u. Hamada (1951, 1970:86-7) says the monophthongization ou > oo took place in the
middle of the Muromachi period, i.e. around 1450. Perhaps we can say that it was
completed by that time. But Tsuzuku 1968 thinks the diphthongal version of "ou"
lasted much longer, pointing to remarks by Rodriguez and transcriptions by the
Chinese as well as the Koreans. It is unclear just how long, or in what areas,
speakers maintained the distinction of long open [ɔ:] versus long close [o:] that
the Portuguese of the late 15th century noted as "ŏ" versus "ô". The very earliest
indication of both merger and monophthongization appears to be an annotation of
1159, which spells "kotofuru" ?= /kotooru/ for kotafuru = /kotɔɔru/ < kota(w)uru <
kotafuru 'answer' (KggD 970a). Texts of 1246, 1252, and 1337 show confusion of /oo/
and /ɔɔ/ (KggD 975a, 976a, 979b). These and the 1159 example may represent dialect
or substandard speech, but they are at least precursors of the merger. One theory
(KggD 129) has it that the two vowels fell together at some point between 1615 and
1657, but somewhat earlier in the east, since the vowels were confused in spellings
found in manuscripts by Nichiren (1222-82) and Seami (1364-1443). Yet they were kept
apart by Ongyoku-gyokuenshū (1727); cf. Satō 1977:245a. The early 18th-century
Korean glossary of Japanese Waye ¹yuhay = Wago-ruikai (?1700) merges the two long
vowels and writes both usually as "wo.wu" = /oo/, as in kwo.wu.ngkwo.wu (1:35r) =
koogo¹o 'empress' and kywo.wu (1:4v) = kyo¹o 'today', but the spelling "wo.wo"
occurs for a few words: kwo.wo.kwo.wo (1:22r) = ko¹okoo 'filial piety', kwo.zwo.wo
(1:53r) = kozo¹o 'young priest', hwo.wozu.lwu (2:40r) = hoo-zu¹ru⁻ 'report',
wo.wo.two.ri (2:20v) = ootori⁻ 'Japanese stork', two.wo.ntwo.li (2:40r) = toodori⁻
'ringleader', wo.wo.wu (2:38v) = oo¹u⁻ 'shelter', ... It includes the verbs kwo.wu
(1:55v) = /koo/ 'buy', wo.wu (2:41r) = /oo/ 'meet', as well as the longer examples
wo.ngi.nwo.wu (2:32v) = /oḡinoo/ 'supplement' and wu.ta.ngwo.wu (1:29v) = /utaḡoo/
'doubt' and also hi.lwo.wu (1:30v) = /hiroo/ 'pick up' (where modern Kyōto has
hirau). One apparent exception is ha.wu = /hau/ 'crawl' in ha.wu.mwu.si (2:27v) =
ha¹u-musi 'crawling insects' but that may be a frozen compound, as implied by the
separate entry in NKD; another exception is na.zwo.la.wu = nazora¹u 'be like', for
which I have no good explanation.

Our account implies that the order of change was first monophthongization by
crasis (au > ɔɔ) and then, by raising, a merger with the monopthongized oo < ou.

The pre-merger stage is attested by Portuguese spellings with "ɔ̆" (= ɔɔ, the long open vowel) distinguished from "ô" (= oo, the long close vowel). The 1676 Korean textbook of Japanese Chep-hay sin-e (= Shōkai-shingo) writes the merged version with the equivalent of "ou", not "oo", but that is simply imitating the hiragana spelling for the long closed vowel, which continues to be "ou" even today except for cases of oo < o[w]o < ofo or owo. The polite auxiliary sa[f]ura[f]u > sɔɔrɔɔ > sooroˈo is compressed → soro in the Hankul spelling of the 1676 work; but a later edition in 1781 writes the Hankul equivalent of sooro, with compression of the last syllable only. The humble verb mausi > mɔɔsi > moˈosi 'say/do', which is written with a Chinese character in the midst of the Hankul transcription, is given a unique Hankul configuration that can be taken as a compression of the two syllables into one: mwo[.]wu.si. There are only three examples of the long o in the 1492 Korean work Ilopha (= Irofa = Iroha): mwo.wosi = moˈosi < mɔɔsi < mausi 'humbly say/do', two.wu = toˈ[w]o 'ten', and kywoW = kyoˈo 'capital; Kyōto'. These words probably had the same long vowel, despite the divergent spellings. We conclude that "ou" was a device to write "oo" (of either origin) as early as 1492; the "ow" indicated by the spelling "woW" in the last example is simply following the 15th-century Korean orthographic tradition for treating the Chinese syllable-final -u in Sino-Korean readings of the characters.

The Japanese-Portuguese dictionary usually wrote "ouo" = [owo] for words going back to ofo or owo, thus "vouoi" = [wowoi] 'are many' and "touori" = [towori] 'passing'; but some words are spelled both ways: "couori, côri" = [kowori, ko:ri] 'ice', ... The number 'ten' is spelled "touo" = [towo] but 'ten days' is "tôca" = [to:ka]. And ···o-[k]u is monophthongized: "vouô" = [wowo:] 'lots' ← ofo-[k]u.

37. Sources of modern long vowels.

In recent loanwords long vowels can be etymologically primitive. But in older vocabulary the modern long vowels are in most cases the result of either: (1) the secondary elongation of a simple short vowel, or (2) the crasis of two short vowels. The two short vowels may be in adjacent morphemes or within a single morpheme. We can find evidence for a lost consonant between the two vowels in most of the native Japanese words of that type and also in many of the morphemes borrowed from Chinese. Certain consonant elisions are peculiar to the initials of specific morphemes and do not occur WITHIN morphemes except sporadically: -[k]iˈ and -[k]uˈ of the adjective inflection, -aˈ[m]u of the verb inflection. From the historical spellings and/or comparison with Middle Chinese forms, as reflected in modern Cantonese or the loans in Korean, we obtain reliable information on many of the lost consonants together with other details about the earlier pronunciation. In the lists below, the Chinese loanmorphs are italicized; for some of the words a rough version of the Middle Chinese pronunciation is underlined and the Middle Korean version (of the fifteenth century) is given for comparison. Notice that final high vowels (i u) may go back to the Chinese nasal velar (-ng = [ŋ]) as well as to semivowels and also (in the case of -u) to -p. The rightmost of the Japanese forms below are posited as early Heian, but without indication of accent and with a few older features.

ii < i-i	ki-iro⁻ yellow'
< i-ki	osii⁻ 'precious' < wosi-ki⁻
< ye-i yo-i < yo-ki	iˈi 'good' < yeˈi < yoˈ-i < yoˈ-ki
< iw-i < if-i	iiˈ (wa sinai) 'say (not)' < iw-iˈ < if-i
< u-i < u-ki	dial. wariˈi 'bad' < waruˈ-i < waˈru-ki
< (s)i-u < (s)i-ku	dial. (yorosi <) yorosii 'satisfactorily' < yorosi-u < yorosi-ku⁻

uu < u-u

      < uu < *uꟷ

          < u-ku

          < u(w)-u < uf-u

yuu < *yuꟷ

    < yu[w]u < yuf-u

    < (y)iu < (y)i[w]u

        < (y)ifu

            < (y)i-u < (y)i-ku

                < (y)iw-u

aa < a-a

    < awa

        < afa

    < a(y)i (< ...)

    < au

yaa < ya-a

    < yawa < ya-wa

        < yafa

    < a(y)i (< ...)

    < yau

oo < owo

      < ofo

    < ou

      < *oꟷ

      < o-ku

      < ofu

      < o[w]-u < of-u

    < ɔɔ < a[w]u

           < *aꟷ

      < afu

      < a[w]-u < af-u

      < a-ku

      < amu

      < awa

          < afa

---

*hu*ꞌ*-un* 'misfortune', *aku*ꞌ*-un*⁻ 'bad luck' mizu-uꞌmi 'lake'²⁵

*ku*ꞌ*u* 'sky' < *kuꟷ (< .khung, MK kwong)

waꞌruu 'bad' < waꞌru-ku

kuꞌu 'eat' < kuꞌ(w)-u < kuꞌf-u

*tyu*ꞌ*u* 'middle' < *tyuꟷ (< .tryung, MK tywung)

yuu⁻ 'tie' < yu[w]-uꞌ < yuf-uꞌ

*kyu*ꞌ*u* 'nine' < ki[w]u (< 'kyew, MK kwu)

*zyu*ꞌ*u* 'ten' < zi[w]u < zifu (< zhip, MK sip)

oꞌokyuu 'big'< oꞌoki-u < oꞌoki-ku < *ofo-ki-ku

yuu⁻ 'say' < (y)iw-uꞌ < (y)if-u

ba-ai⁻ 'situation'< ba-afi; *ha*ꞌ*-aku*⁻ 'grasp'

dial. aa 'bubble' < awa

dial. aa 'millet' < awa < afa

dial. — Hiroshima, Yamaguchi, Shimane (Hirayama 1968b:153); Totsukawa (kaꞌate < kaꞌite < kaki-te 'writing'); Aichi, Shimane, Okayama, Kumamoto, Miyazaki (Shibata 1977:105).

dial. — parts of Tango and Tanba (Okumura in Shin Nihongo-kōza 3:151-2): kaata 'bought' < kauta (= kawta < kawita < kafi-t···), baazu 'bonze' < *bau-zu* < *baꟷ-zu*

*zya*ꞌ*-aku*⁻ 'evil'

tyaan⁻ < *tya-wan*⁻ 'rice bowl'

yaaraka < yawaraꞌka 'soft' < yafa-ra-ka

dial. — part of Tottori (Hirayama 1968b:158) Ine (Tango, Kyōto-fu) ippyaa < ip-pai 'full', simyaa < simai 'end' (Jugaku 1979:155)

dial. si-*yaa* ga nai (= si-*yoo* ga naꞌi) 'inevitable', providing evidence that yoo < yɔɔ < yau < *yaꟷ (< yang', MK yang)

toꞌo 'ten' < towo

too-⁻ 'far' < towo- < tofo-; hoꞌo 'cheek' < "fδ" = [Fo:] < fowo < fofo; ookiꞌi 'big' < "vôqij" = [wo:ki:] < (w)owo-ki-([k]i) < ofo-ki

koo- 'mouth' < kou (< 'kew, MK kwu)

*ko*ꞌ*o* 'public' < kou < *koꟷ (< .kung, MK kwong)

omoo⁻ 'heavy' < omo-u < omo-kuꞌ

*ko*ꞌ*o* 'kalpa' < kou < kofu (< kop, MK kep)

dial. koo 'beg' < kou < kow-u < kof-u

*ko*ꞌ*o* 'high' < kɔɔ < kau (< .kaw, MK kwo)

-*koo* 'river' < kɔɔ < kau < *kaꟷ (< .kyang, MK kang)

*ko*ꞌ*o* 'first Stem' < kɔɔ < kau (< kap, MK kap); oogiꞌ 'fan' < "wǒgui" = [wɔ:gi] < augi < afugi²⁶

dial. koo 'buy' < kɔɔ < ka[w]-u < kaf-u

taꞌkoo 'high' < takɔɔ < taꞌka-ku

kakoꞌo 'will write' < kakɔɔ < kakamu

dial. oo 'bubble' < ɔɔ < awa

dial. oo 'millet' < ɔɔ < awa < afa

ee < (y)e-e   iseˈ-ebi⁻ 'lobster', kare-eda⁻ 'dead branch'

   < (y)ei   *seˈe* 'generation' < sei (< <u>syey'</u>, MK syey)

       < *(y)eĭ   *meˈe* 'inscription' < mei < *meĭ (< <u>.myeng</u>,
                          MK myeng)

       < (y)ewi < (y)efi   meˈe 'niece' < meˈi < mewi < mefi; eˈe 'ray *(fish)'*
                        < eˈi < yewi < yefi

       < (y)e-i   meˈesya 'eye doctor' = meˈ-*isya*

       < o-i < o-ki   dial. kureˈe 'black' < kuroˈ-i < kuro-ki

       < εε < ai   dial. *neˈe* 'inside' < nεε < nai (< <u>nay'</u>, MK nay)

           < a-ki   dial. kuree⁻ 'dark' < kurεε < kura-i < kura-ki

           < awi   dial. eˈe 'indigo' < εε < ai < awi

               < afi   dial. hee⁻ 'ashes' < hεε < hai < fawi < fafi

               < awe < afe   dial. hee⁻ 'fly' < hεε < hae < fawe < fafe

       < (y)εε < yai < ya-ki   dial. haee 'quick, early' < hayee < hayεε < hayai <
                          faya-ki

            < -ai   dial. baee 'situation' < bayee < ba(y)εε < ba-ai[27]
                   (< ba-awi < ba-afi < ...)

yoo < you < *yoŭ   *yoˈo* 'use' < you < *yoŭ (< <u>yong'</u>, MK ywong)

    < (y)eu   *yoˈo* 'need' < (y)eu (< <u>yew'</u>, MK ywo);
                      myoˈo 'strange' < meu (< <u>myew'</u>, MK mywo)

       < (y)efu   *-yoo* 'leaf' < (y)eu < yefu (< <u>yep</u>, MK yep)

       < (w)ef-u   dial. yoo 'gets drunk' < yo(w)-u < (y)ew-u
                   < (w)ew-u < wef-u

       < yo-ku   yoˈo 'well' < yoˈu < yoˈ-ku

   < yɔɔ < yau < *yaŭ   *myoo-* 'next' < myɔɔ < myau < *myaŭ (< <u>'myᵉ/ₐng</u>,
                         MK myeng)

Where we might expect to find *<u>yap</u> > yafu > yau > yɔɔ > *yoo*, instead there is <u>yep</u> > yefu > yeu > you > *yoo*. Similarly *<u>yaw</u> > yau > yɔɔ > *yoo* does not occur; instead we find <u>yew</u> > yeu > you > *yoo*. The words kefu 'today' and *kyau* 'capital' were used as puns in a poem written c. 900 (Okumura 1977:232).

In the listings above we have left out of account the monophthongization of /ai/ to [æ:] reported from Okayama, Shimane, Mie, Aichi, and Gifu (Shibata 1977:105); the shortening to [e] of the long ee that results from monophthongization of ai is reported from Kagoshima, Miyakazi, Akita, Iwate, and Aomori (ibid.).

The form siyoo 'will do' could be accounted for as < siyɔɔ < si(y)-au < si-amu, but by assuming it is merely an expansion of syoo < s(y)e-u < se-mu, we can account for the literary semu at the same time, and that seems to be the correct explanation, as we will see in Ch. 3, §3. Cf. the bound auxiliary -masyoo < -mase-u < -mase-mu, for which we have surviving evidence in the negative -masen < -mase-nu.

38. Vowel frequencies; peculiarities of /e/.

When we count the frequency of vowels in the c. 42,000 syllables written with phonograms in the running text of the Man'yō-shū, we find the following ratios:

       .23 i   u .15

         .09 e   o .24

                  a
                 .29

The low frequency of /e/ is striking (Mathias 1973:2, Ōno 1974:156). And if we set aside the Chinese elements and recent loans a list of vocabulary shows us that:

(1) Few words have /e/ in the first syllable.

(2) The vowel /e/ appears at the end of a number of verb stems that are paired with other verb stems ending in /aC/ or just /C/, as in tome- : tomar- 'stop' (tr. : intr.), mo˹re- : mora˹s- 'leak' (intr. : tr.), ake- : ak- 'open' (tr. : intr.).

(3) A number of nouns that end in /e/ in isolation often appear in an alternate shape with final /a/ when used as the first member of certain compound words.[28] Yet other nouns never appear with the final /a/, they always end in /e/. Examples of each type (cited in historical spellings, but with modern Tōkyō accents):

e /a	e
me˹ 'eye', ma˹-buta 'eyelid'	me˹ 'female'
a˹me 'rain', ama˹-do 'shutters'	ka˹me 'tortoise'
ame⁻ 'gluten', ama-⁻ 'sweet'	kame˹ 'jar'
tume⁻ 'claw', tuma-saki⁻ 'toe-tips'	tame˹ 'sake, reason'
	ume⁻ 'plum'
	kabe⁻ 'wall'
	na˹be 'pan'
ko˹we 'voice', kowa-iro⁻ 'tone of voice'	tu˹we 'staff'
na˹fe 'seedling', nafa˹-siro⁻ 'seedbed'	ma˹fe 'front'
ufe⁻ 'above', ufa-be⁻ 'top'	fafe⁻ 'fly'
sake⁻ 'wine', saka-duki˹⁻	ike˹ 'pond'
take⁻ 'bamboo', taka-mura⁻ 'bamboo grove'	wo˹ke 'bucket'
suge⁻ 'sedge', suga˹-gomo 'sedge mat'	toge˹ 'thorn'
mune⁻ 'ridge', muna-gi⁻ 'ridge-pole'	mine˹⁻ 'peak'
mune˹ 'breast', muna-moto˹⁻ 'bosom'	sune˹ 'shank (lower leg)'
ta˹ne 'seed', tana-tu-mono 'seed'	ki˹ne 'pestle'
fu˹ne 'boat', funa˹-bito 'boatman'	tu˹ne 'always'
kane⁻ 'metal', kana-gu⁻ 'metal fittings'	kane⁻ 'bell'[29]
te˹ 'hand', ta-na-go˹koro 'palm'	
	ude˹ 'arm'
	se⁻ 'shoal'
	a˹se 'sweat'
kaze⁻ 'wind', kaza-simo⁻ 'downwind'	aze˹ 'levee'
mure˹ 'crowd', mura-su˹zume 'flock of sparrows'	fire˹⁻ 'fin'

There are, of course, many nouns that end in /a/ but never appear in a shape with final /e/. Accentuation will not account for the two types of words. Although Old Japanese orthography happens to distinguish two kinds of /e/ in the velar and labial syllables, as we will see below, both kinds appear in the right column above; the left column, however, contains only Type 2.

39. Peculiarities of /i/.

A somewhat similar situation is found for /i/ but there are far fewer cases:

(1) The vowel /i/ appears at the end of certain verb stems that are paired with other stems that end in /uC/ or /oC/: tuki˹- 'be exhausted' and tuku˹s- 'exhaust', sugi˹- 'exceed' and sugo˹s- (earlier sugus-) 'pass'; oki˹- 'rise' and oko˹s- 'raise' (and oko˹r- 'arise'), oti˹- 'fall' and oto˹s- 'drop', ori˹- 'descend' and oro˹s- 'lower', fi˹- 'get dry' and fo˹s- 'dry it'.

(2) A few nouns that in isolation end in /i/ have an alternate shape with final /o/ or /u/ when used as the first member of at least a few compounds: fiꜚ 'fire' and foꜚ-noꜚ-fo 'flame', kiꜚ 'tree' and koꜚ-datiˉ 'grove', tukiꜚ 'moon' and tuku-yo = tukiꜚ-yo 'moonlit night', kaꜚmi 'god' and kamu-oya 'ancestor (who has joined the gods)'. Most nouns that end in /i/ have no such alternate shapes.

When we look at the expected correspondences between the Ryūkyū dialects and those of the main islands, we find a fair number of anomalous sets that lead us to suspect two kinds of underlying /e/ and /i/ each; very scanty evidence also points to two kinds of /o/. Before looking at that evidence, however, we will examine some of the philological findings.

40. Vowel distinctions attested for Old Japanese.

In the Nara period the use of Chinese characters for phonetic value as a kind of kana (syllabic phonograms) was such as to indicate two values each for later e, i, and o in certain syllables:

$i_1 \neq i_2$	$e_1 \neq e_2$	Two kinds of front vowels after velars (k g) and labials (f b m).
	$o_1 \neq o_2$	Two kinds of back mid vowel after velars (k g), and dentals (t d s z n), r, y, and (Koji-ki) m.

The distinction of $mo_1 \neq mo_2$ was lost after the Koji-ki (712), which distinguished 88 syllables, and it does not show up in the Man'yō-shū or the Nihon-Shoki, which distinguished only 87. There is also evidence for two kinds of (')e, the syllable e itself; the two are usually interpreted as $e_1 = $ [ye] and $e_2 = $ [e]. This distinction was lost by 938 (Zdb A-21).

The assignment of a syllable to Type One (koꜚo "A") or Type Two (oꜚtu "B") is correlated with certain phonetic features. For the front vowels this is essentially PALATAL quality for Type "A" versus non-palatal or possibly labiovelar quality for Type "B". For the back vowel it appears that Type A was more rounded and perhaps higher (more like u);[30] it is believed that Type B was more central and less rounded than today's /o/, more like a shwa [ə]. When the phonetic distinction is neutralized in distribution (i and e after dentals; o after labials other than m and later after m), it is often assumed that the actual pronunciation was Type A for both the front vowels and the back vowels, but we have no way of knowing which — if either — was the "unmarked" version. From morphophonemic evidence we see that the distinction was sometimes present in an underlying way even where there was surface neutralization (cf. Murayama 1954). For example, the alternation of kaneˉ with kana- indicates that the final e belongs with the Type Two (oꜚtu) vowel, the nonpalatal variety. For this and other reasons, a number of scholars believe that at an earlier time the koꜚo-otu distinctions were more widely distributed, perhaps occurring after every initial. Evidence has been offered that purports to show that the distinction was maintained for the syllables fo, o, and si, but this has not been generally accepted. (For the evidence, see Mabuchi 1957.) Both Igarashi and Ōno recognize the distinction for fo, as we will do, but Zdb does not. Inukai 1978 concludes that originally there were two different kinds of fo but the phonological differences may have already disappeared; that the syllable o was represented in two ways, one of the kana probably being older and replaced later by the other; si was represented by two different kana, but they represented the same sound in Koji-ki, though earlier they may have been pronounced differently. Mabuchi's philological reconstruction of two kinds of syllable (')o- can perhaps be supported by a few examples in which Nase (Amami) has initial qo- instead of the expected qu-:

qomoyun 'think' corresponds to the o'tu type o- of Mabuchi 1957:87 but quti=run
'fall' corresponds to the ko'o type. Apparently being unaware of Mabuchi's study,
Starostin 272 makes precisely the opposite identification; frequency considerations
seem to support him, though he does not mention that (or anything else) as his
reason. Unfortunately the Old Japanese data are scant and there are few examples of
the Nase qo-; one example is found in qoni 'ogre', but regrettably that word is not
attested by Old Japanese phonograms. Hattori (1983:11 ff.) offers evidence that the
initials of oku-ka 'remote place', okur- 'send', and okure- 'be late' were ko'o type
as opposed to the common o'tu type in oto 'sound', omop- (> omof-) 'think',
and okos- 'raise'.

The major dictionary of Old Japanese (Zdb) puts a line to the right of the Type
A (ko'o-rui) syllables and to the left of the Type B (otu'-rui) syllables. It puts a
line to the right of those ancestors of later vowel-initial (')e that are assumed to
have been [e] and to the left of those assumed to have been [ye]. Unfortunately that
decision can cause confusion: for Ci and Ce the right-side line marks the palatal
type but for the two ancestors of modern (')e the type with the palatal onglide is
marked by a left-side line.

In romanization the usual practice is to put a dieresis (or umlaut ¨) over
vowels of the Type B syllables, making them look like phonetic symbols for back
unrounded ï and ë and front rounded ö (though that is not necessarily the intention
of those using the symbols), and leave unmarked the vowels of the Type A syllables.
That practice is unwise for it suggests that the neutralized and unknown cases go
with the Type A syllables and that the latter are the unmarked norm. Mathias has
wisely suggested writing:

(1) ĭ ė ȯ for Type A (ko'o-rui) vowels;
(2) ï ë ö for Type B (otu'-rui) vowels;
(3) i e o for neutral vowels (in positions where the distinction is not found.
(4) I E O for those vowels for which the distinction is unattested or unknown,
though they appear in positions where the distinction is found.

A structural interpretation suggests treating the palatal-type front vowels as
/Cyi/ and /Cye/. As a purely orthographic notation, but with some obvious phonetic
implications, I have proposed that the nonpalatal counterparts be written as Ciy and
Cey, leaving i and e for both the neutral and the unknown cases, and also for the
later version of the merged phonemes after the distinction was lost. As we will see
below, the nonpalatal front vowels originated as diphthongs (ey < ay, iy < oy or uy)
and the palatal mid vowel in at least some words had a similar origin (Cye < Cya).

The traditional way of looking at the vowel distinctions in Japan, where the
situation is referred to as (zyo'odai) tokusyu-kanazu'kai 'special kana spelling (of
the Nara period)', treats the ko'o-otu distinctions as secondary characteristics of
the affected syllables. We might think of these characteristics as vectors (the way
Joos once described the English semivowels in complex nuclei): Type A (ko'o-rui)
carries a kind of centrifugal force and is more tense with an articulation that is
more extreme (peripheral); Type B (otu'-rui) carries centripetal force or no force
and is more lax, with articulations that are centralized. The traditional view (that
of Hashimoto and Arisaka, cf. Matsumoto 1974:87) treated the Type A syllables as
unmarked ("pure, simple") and their Type B counterparts as marked. Yet Type A mid
vowels (our Cye and Cwo) are less common in the vocabulary than are the Type B (our
Cey and Co), while the opposite is true for the high vowel types (our Cyi is much
more common than our Ciy); cf. Matsumoto 1974:88 n.1. There are correlations in the
morphology of the verb that led to the assignment of ko'o or o'tu status to the
ancestors of both i and e in the same way:

	Stem	Infinitive	Imperative	Concessive
Consonant stems	C-	C-yi	C-ye!	C-ey (-do/-ba)
Vowel stems: upper bigrade	C-iy-	C-iy	C-iy (yo)!	C-ure[y] (-do/-ba)
lower bigrade	C-ey-	C-ey	C-ey (yo)!	C-ure[y] (-do/-ba)
upper monograde	Cyi-	Cyi	Cyi (yo)!	Cyi-re[y] (-do/-ba)
fiy-*, miy-**	Ciy-	Ciy	Ciy (yo)!	Ciy-re[y] (-do/-ba)

*'get dry; winnow; sneeze' **'turn' (obsolete)

Adjective forms include the attributive -kyi and other forms with -kye(-mu, -ba),
as well as the infinitive -ku, the predicative -si, the nominalizing -sa, and the
circumstantial -myi. The adjective stem sometimes ends in a derivative suffix -key-
(as in saya-key- 'cool; clear, pure', faru-key- 'far distant') or -si- (as in sita-
si- 'intimate' and kana-si- 'heart-moving; sad; beloved'), to which the inflectional
suffixes are added. (But -si-si is usually reduced by haplology to -si.) See Ch.7.

Many of the vowel stems are paired with related stems: those ending in CuC or
CoC are paired with upper bigrades (C-iy-) and those ending in CaC are paired with
lower bigrades (C-ey-): tukiy- with tukus-, okiy- with okos-, tomey- with tomar-.
We can detect derivational suffixes or formants that relate the partner verbs so as
to express whatever constitutes the difference in meaning, which is usually a matter
of transitivity.

In interpreting the two types of ancestor for the syllable (')e as "ye" ≠ "ey"
it looks as though we have put the traditional "B" type with the palatal "A" type we
are writing as Cye — at least, if we assume that the initial y- in "ye" was really
just a palatal glide and not, say, the nonpalatalized d- of Yonaguni (as we will
write it for proto-Japanese but not for Old Japanese). At an underlying level we
find that the syllable ye in some words must be yey just as some cases of te must be
tey, because the syllable ends a lower-bigrade stem, as in these paired examples:
   tayas- 'bring to an end' : taye[y]- 'come to an end'
   fatas- 'complete, accomplish' : fate[y]- 'reach completion'
But at the surface level of Old Japanese there was no contrast between morpheme-
initial /ye/ and /yey/, nor between initial /te/ (? ="tye") and /tey/ except insofar
as the monosyllable of te[y] 'hand' (assigned an underlying ey to account for its
alternation with ta-) can be regarded as both initial and final. The syllable ye
occurs within morphemes (fuye 'flute', saye 'dice', nuye 'chimera; thrush', fyiye
'millet', ...) and also initially, as in yeda 'branch; limbs (of the body)', which
comes from yo-n-ta (as indicated by Shuri yuda, Yonaguni duda) by vowel assimilation
of the same sort as that found in modern e'e 'yes; good' < ye'e < *yei < yo'-[k]i
'good', which further assimilates to standard i'i 'good'. To avoid confusion we
might choose to write initial ye as je (or even de), but we would then want to do
this also for initial ya yo yu. (There is no need for Cya Cyo Cyu in Old Japanese.)

Since e- merged with ye- during the early Heian period we have no way to know
the precise initial of later (y)e- words for which early attestations are lacking,
but some have likely etymologies that are indicative: era 'gills' probably comes
from agi-ra, by way of *a[g]ira > *eyra.

The lower bigrade stem e[y]- 'get' lacks an initial consonant: the infinitive
is e[y], the imperative e[y] yo!, the concessive ure[y] (-do/-ba); the predicative
is u, the attributive uru. In those environments where the two kinds of front vowels
are not distinguished, the bracketed y is posited as an underlying segment whenever
a -y- appears for the corresponding shapes of those forms that contain the critical
environment. Among the upper monograde stems of Old Japanese we find i- 'shoot',
with the infinitive i, imperative i (yo)!, and concessive i-re[y] (-do/-ba); the
predicative and the attributive are both i-ru. Since there is no distinction of the

syllables *yi ≠ *iy we have no direct way of knowing whether 'shoot' is parallel to
myi- 'see' or to miy- 'turn', so we just write i-, not *[y]i- or *i[y]-.

A knowledge of the ancient vowel distinctions may save us from etymological
blunders: kamyi 'above' (accent pattern 2.4, low-high in Old Kyōto) can hardly be
taken as the same etymon as kamiy 'god' or kamiy 'hair' (both 2.3, low-low in Old
Kyōto), though nothing but meaning keeps us from treating the latter pair as one.
(Yet ingenuity might attempt a rescue of the failed etymology: perhaps kamiy 'god'
is a contraction of *ka[myi no] miy 'body above'.) That tafey 'bark-cloth' will be
reconstructed as *tapa[C]i strengthens the suspicion that it might be a loan from
Polynesian tapa.

Except for the morphophonemic alternations mentioned above, common to all
dialects, there is no evidence for the ancient vowel distinctions outside the
Ryūkyūs, despite Miller's claims to find such evidence in the "Satsuma" dialect of
southern Kyūshū (on which see Aoki 1974).

It is usually assumed that there was no distinction in Old Japanese between
syllables such as (')i and yi or (')u and wu, and just "i" and "u" are written.
But Mōri Masamori (1983 ms.) is reported to claim that the semivowel initials were
distinctive in these syllables (Hattori 1983:7a).

Part Four: Ryūkyū vowel developments

41. Front vowels and their reflexes in the Ryūkyūs.

Almost all the Ryūkyū dialects seem to have undergone a general raising of the
mid vowels, e > i and o > u. Exceptionally, the islands of Aka and Keruma in the
Kerama group (off southwestern Okinawa) are said to preserve the earlier e and o
(Nakamatsu 1983:40). The vowel raising is thought to have taken place no earlier
than the 13th century.

If we look at the vowel quality only, and ignore any traces of the earlier
distinctions that may linger in the quality of adjacent consonants, we see that all
varieties of i and e fell together in Okinawa and in Yonaguni, but that the i of
Type A (ko'o-rui), our "yi", had a separate development in Miyako (except for Minna)
and Yaeyama, on the one hand, and in Amami (exemplified by Shodon),[32] on the other:

Old Japanese	Miyako, Yaeyama	Amami	Okinawa, Yonaguni, Minna
Cyi	ï	yi [i]	
Ciy			
Cey	> i	i [ɨ]	> i
Cye			

But in Okinawa traces of the palatal quality of the original Cyi can be found in the
palatalization of initial consonants. OJ kyi- 'wear' is ci- in Okinawa and that is
dispalatalized to çi- [tsi] in Yonaguni, while it is kyi- in Amami and kï- in Miyako
and Yaeyama; OJ okiy- 'arise' is uki- in Okinawa, Miyako, and Yaeyama (and probably
ugi- in Yonaguni, but data are lacking), while it is qukhi in Amami. Moreover, the
table above falsely claims that all Ryūkyū reflexes of OJ iy are the same; they are
not. As we have concluded from morphophonemic alternations, there are two underlying
sources for Old Japanese iy: ···uCi and ···oCi (with the attested Type B back mid
vowel that we mark with an underline).[33] Those words having an OJ ···iy that derives
from ···oCi do not palatalize a preceding velar: *koCi > kiy 'tree' has the Shuri
reflex kii; *okoCi- > okiy- 'arise' has the Shuri reflex quki-. On the other hand,
kiyri 'fog' has the Shuri reflex ciri (cf. Okumura 1977:251) and the palatalization
tells us that the source of the Old Japanese form must be *kuCiri. The fact that the
Shuri form for 'cedar' is şizi [sidži] shows that its ancestor must surely have been
*suguCi even though Old Japanese fails to provide a morpheme alternant *sugu- to

indicate whether the vowel absorbed into the last syllable of sugiy was *u or *o.
The palatalized reflex raises a problem for those etymologies that posit a *rendaku*
form of kiy 'tree' as a suffix in the four OJ nouns sugiy 'cedar', wogiy 'reed,
sugarcane', fagiy 'bushclover', and yanagiy 'willow'; cf. the expected reflex in
Shuri caagi 'black pine', probably cognate with keyaki 'zelkova', for which we lack
the pertinent OJ data. We have no attested evidence what the first syllable of kiba
'fang' may have been in Old Japanese, but Shuri ciiba tells us that the syllable
must have been *kiy and that it must have come from *kuCi not *koCi. It is obvious
that the Shuri forms cannot be directly derived from the 8th-century Nara forms,
which had already merged with earlier ···uCi, they must go back to some earlier
ancestor of both Old Japanese and Okinawan; cf. Hattori 1970 and 1981. This point
was brought to my attention in an unpublished paper by Leon Serafim, who explains —
correctly, I believe — the development in a way which I will adapt to my present
framework as follows. In the Ryūkyūs, and perhaps in parts of Kyūshū, the proto-
apanese ···oCi became [e] which fell together with the monophthongizations of
···aCi and ···iCa — and with original /e/ if it is true that proto-Japanese had that
additional vowel, as Unger (among others) believes — while the proto-Japanese ···uCi
merged with the original palatal /i/; but Old Japanese raised the descendant of
proto-Japanese ···oCi and merged it with the descendant of proto-Japanese ···uCi to
yield the nonpalatal vowel we are writing ···iy, which eventually merged with the
palatal vowel we are writing (for Old Japanese) ···yi. In this connection, we should
bear in mind the arguments of Hattori 1976a for placing the date for proto-Japanese
earlier than the attestations of the Nara period on the basis of morphological data
from Hachijō island as well as from the Ryūkyūs. Given that there were already two
dialects within the literary tradition of Old Japanese, that of the central area
(Yamato) and that of the east (Azuma), the conclusion hardly needs restating, yet it
seems to be often overlooked.

  If we set aside our knowledge of Old Japanese and merely compare the Amami
(Shodon) or Okinawa (Shuri) words with standard Japanese, we immediately see that in
the Ryūkyūs there has been a general RAISING of e to (y)i and of o to u. But there
are ragged sets of irregular correspondences which correlate fairly well with the
ancient *ko'o-otu* distinctions. For the high front vowels:

OJ -yi :	Shodon -yi	OJ -iy :	Shodon -i [ɨ]
kyi	kyi 'spirit'	kiy	khi 'tree'
ikyi	qyikyi 'breath'	okiy	qwihi 'arise'
okyi	qukyi 'offshore'	amiy	qami 'bathe in'
mugyi	mugyi 'barley'	oti[y]	quti[34] 'fall'
tabyi	taabyi 'journey'	ori[y]	quri 'descend'
tumyi	timyi 'sin'	? kagi	khagi 'key'
...	...	? negi	nigi 'onion'
...	...	? yeri	yiri 'collar'

Exceptionally, OJ myidu 'water' corresponds to Shodon midi (Shuri miʒi), fyiru
'garlic' corresponds to Shodon hwiryi (Shuri hwiru), and obyi 'girdle' corresponds
to Shodon uubi (Shuri uubi). The word for 'girdle' might be explained by deriving
the noun from the (later) bigrade version of the verb obiy- 'gird', since all upper
bigrade infinitives show the corrspondence given in the column on the right, as we
would expect, but Old Japanese attests only the quadrigrade version ob-. The words
for 'water' and 'garlic' require further study; they have been adduced as evidence
for a proto-vowel *e. See below, §50.

Amami has two sets of correspondences for the mid front vowels of Old Japanese:

OJ -ey	:	Shodon -i [ɨ]		OJ -ey	:	Shodon -e [ë]
key		khi 'hair'		kagey		khage 'shadow'
ikey		qyikhyi 'pond'		sakey		sehe 'wine'
ukey		qukhi 'receive'		takey		dehe 'bamboo'
mey		mi 'eye'		kaze[y]		khade 'wind'
yumey		qyimyi 'dream'		ate[y]		qathe 'address'
wokey		wihi 'bucket'		? kuse[y]		khse 'habit'
mamey		mami 'bean'		? ude[y]		quthe 'arm'
kamey		khami 'tortoise'		? yuge[y]		yuge 'steam'
tumey		tumi 'claw'				

We have no good explanation for the divergence. But if only the clearcut examples are taken, the Shodon -e version occurs after a velar preceded by an OJ low vowel and in that environment there appear to be no examples of the other correspondence.

There are very few examples of Old Japanese Cye except for the quadrigrade verb imperatives, for which the correspondence is OJ -ye : Shodon -i [ɨ]. (It is hard to find Ryūkyū cognates for the other examples in Old Japanese.) If we were to assume that the "neutral" versions were earlier Cye, we could say OJ -ye : Shodon -yi on the basis of kore : khuryi 'this one' and possibly *myise : myisyi 'shop'. But the latter word, unattested in Old Japanese, is probably a derivative of the infinitive of the lower bigrade stem myise[y]- 'show', for which we would expect Shodon *myisi [misɨ] except that the shape is subject to the progressive palatal assimilation rule because of the palatality of the first syllable. The vowel correspondences found in OJ kabye : Shodon khubi 'wall' are unexplained; the Shodon form would lead us to expect perhaps OJ ?kobey. (If there is a relationship with the verb kabaf- 'protect' we expect OJ ?kabey.) The Shodon -u- may be just an idiosyncratic assimilation to the following syllable: a > o (labialized by the following b) > u (in the general raising of mid vowels). There are a few examples of initial OJ ye- : Shodon yi-, as in ye : yi 'handle' (Shuri wii), yeri : yiri 'collar' (Shuri wiiri). Cf. OJ eybyi 'grapes; *shrimp' : Shodon qyibyi 'shrimp' (Shuri qibi).

The correspondences for the front vowels, then, are as follows:

OJ	:	Shodon
-ey		-i [ɨ] but -e [ë] when preceded by /a/ + velar
-ye		-i [ɨ] but the syllable ye- : yi-
-iy		-i [ɨ]
-yi		-yi

There are a few exceptions, such as OJ tukiy 'moon' : Shodon th(i)kyi where we expect *th(i)ki or *tihi but the cause of the anomaly may be the devoicing of the first vowel, whereby the /t/ is automatically replaced by /th/. We have mentioned earlier the problems of sugiy : sigyi 'cedar'. fagiy : hagyi 'bushclover', and wogiy 'reed' : wugyi 'sugarcane'; also the words for 'water', 'garlic', and 'girdle'.

Most cases of Ce = [Cë] in monosyllabic morphemes of Amami are the secondary result of crasis and contraction: me(e) < mafye 'front', ne(e) < nafey 'seedling', hwe(e) < fafey 'fly' or < fafi 'ashes', ... And most cases of o are secondary, also: qo(o)- < awo 'blue, green', kho(o) < kafa 'river', so(o) < sawo 'pole', ...

From the regular correspondences for words attested in Old Japanese we can
hypothesize about those cases which (1) are not attested as to the *ko'o-otu*
distinction (or are not attested at all), or (2) are neutralized in environment:

OJ e = *ey : Shodon -i [ɨ]

(1) kame : khami 'jar'

(2) te : thi 'hand' (Shuri tii)
     ne : ni 'root'
     negi : nigi 'onion'
     ane : qani 'older sister'
     fane: hani 'feather'
     fune : huni 'boat'
     fone : huni 'bone'
     mune : muni 'breast'
     swode : sudi 'sleeve'
     fude : hudi 'brush'

OJ i = *yi : Shodon -yi

kami : khamyi 'paper
sabi : sabyi 'rust'
kugi : kugyi 'nail'
migi : myigyi 'right'
ti : tyi 'blood' (Shuri cii)
fati : hatyi 'bee'
isi : qyisyi 'stone'
wasi : wasyi 'eagle'
nusi : nusyi 'master; owner'
wodi : wudyi 'uncle'
sudi : sidyi 'tendon'
yari : yaryi 'spear'
nori : nuryi 'seaweed'
tori : thuryi 'bird'
uri : wuryi 'melon'
tiri : tiryi 'dirt, dust'
wofi : wui 'nephew'

There is also kyizi : kyidyi = kizi⁻ 'pheasant', a compression of the OJ kyigyisi.
The correspondence of kuti : kutyi = kuti⁻ 'mouth' is troublesome; internal evidence
(kutu-wa 'bridle bit') seems to indicate that the proto-Japanese form was *kutu-Ci,
so that the OJ form should have been kuti[y] rather than kut[y]i, but in that case
we would expect the Shodon form to be kuti with the central [ɨ] allophone of /i/.
Hirayama 1966:365 gives [kɥtsï] as the pronunciation in Kametsu on Tokunoshima,
which has a vowel system similar to that of Shodon; but for Nase and Koniya on
Amami-Ōshima he has the palatal version of the final syllable.

42. Back vowels and their reflexes in the Ryūkyūs.

In general throughout the Ryūkyūs any o was raised to u. As a result, Okinawan
m̄usi means both 'insect' (Tōkyō musi⁻) and 'perchance, if' (Tōkyō mo'si). But for
certain of the syllables it is possible to tell whether a Ryūkyū /u/ came from an
earlier u or from an earlier o, just as it is possible to tell whether a Ryūkyū /i/
came from an earlier i or from an earlier e in certain syllables: a trace of the
quality of the earlier mid vowel is left in the consonant. Voiceless consonants
apparently had two allophones: an aspirated variety, with delayed voice onset for
the vowel, occurred before the more open vowels (e o a) and an unaspirated variety,
with immediate voice onset after the crisp release (sometimes mistakenly labeled
"glottalization"), before the close vowels (i u). With the raising of the mid (half-
open) vowels, the onset-release feature became distinctive, resulting in paired
voiceless obstruents, aspirated versus unaspirated. From what we have said it is
obvious that these pairs were distinctive only before the "new" close vowels that
had absorbed the old mid vowels, but the distinction spread to /a/ through marginal
words (mimetics, cute forms, borrowings) and contractions of various kinds. Not all
Ryūkyū dialects maintained the distinction; it was largely lost, for example, in
the standard Okinawan of Shuri and in the Miyako dialects. But in Shuri the earlier
/ki/ and /ti/ are distinguished from the earlier /ke/ and /te/ by an affricated

palatalization: ki 'spirit' > cii [tši:] but ke 'hair' > kii; ti 'blood' > cii [tši:], but te 'hand' > tii. And earlier /tu/ is distinguished from earlier /to/ by affrication (nowadays palatalized): tuki 'moon' > çici [tsitši] (> cici [tšitši]) 'moon' but toki 'time' > tuci [tʰutši]. On the other hand, Shuri /huni/ means both 'boat' < fune and 'bone' < fone, Shuri /hwii/ [Fi:] means both 'fire' < fi and 'fart' < fe. And in no dialect will it be possible to tell whether mu and nu are earlier mu or mo, nu or no; whether ru and yu are earlier ru or ro, yu or yo. Nor will it be easy to tell whether mi and ni are earlier mi or me, ni or ne; whether ri is earlier ri or re. But for these syllables, see the Shodon evidence at the end of §41. With the initial crisp vowel onset written as a glottal stop, (q)u can be from earlier (')u or (')o; but wu is only from earlier wo since there was no historic /wu/ as distinct from (')u.

In Amami we find the following expected correspondences:

OJ wo- : Shodon wu-

wono̲ : wunu 'ax'
       (Shuri uun)
wori : wuri 'stay, be'
       (Shuri un)
(woto̲) : wuthu 'husband'
wo : wu 'cord'
wototufyi : wutti 'day
  before yesterday'

OJ Co- : Shodon C-u

mono̲ : munu 'thing'
iro̲ : qyiryu 'color'
foso : hw(u)su 'navel'
ywo(ru) : yu(ru) 'night'

OJ (')o- : Shodon qu-

okyi : qukyi 'offshore'
       (Shuri quuki)
oni : qunyi 'ogre'
       (Shuri quni)
oto̲ : quthu 'sound'
       (Shuri qutu)
oya : uya 'parent'

OJ (')u- : Shodon qu-

uta : qutha 'song'
usi : qusyi 'ox'
umyi : qumyi 'sea'
uma : quma 'horse'
ura : qura 'reverse side'
ugufyisu : quguisi 'bush
              warbler'
usagyi : usaakyi 'rabbit'

OJ Cu- : Shodon Cu

inu : qyinu 'dog'
faru : haru 'spring'
yu : yu 'hot water'

But although the syllables so to do > su thu du as expected, the syllables su tu du (with a few exceptions) > si ti di [sɨ tɨ dɨ]. An exception to the correspondences above is uri : wuryi 'melon' which ought to be quryi (cf. Shuri qui), so it may be a mistake in Martin 1970b.

There are interesting irregularities in which Shodon retains /o/ for an earlier Co in a non-initial syllable, and a number of these correspond to the Old Japanese Type A syllables that we transcribe as Cwo:[35]

atwo : qatho 'footprint'
satwo : sat(h)o 'village'
fatwo : hat(h)o 'pigeon'
tutwo : tito 'straw wrapper'
myinatwo : myinyaato 'port'
itwokwo : qyithook(h)o 'cousin'
takwo : thoho 'octopus'
mwokwo/mukwo : muho 'bridegroom'
matwo : matho 'target'
madwo : mado 'window, opening'

iswo : qyisyo 'rock(y beach) : beach'
suswo : suso 'skirt bottom'
yadwo : yado 'shelter, lodging : door'
tunwo : tino 'horn'
kamwo : khamo 'wild duck'
kumwo : kumo 'cloud'
kyimwo : kimo 'liver'
mwomwo : mumo 'thigh'
kwo : khago 'basket' (second syllable)
iswog- : qyisyoogar- 'rush'

Of the above, the following are -o also in Tokunoshima: 'pigeon', 'cousin', 'horn', 'cloud', 'bridegroom'; in Miyako 'pigeon'; in Hateruma 'horn' and 'cloud'. The word for 'cloud' is fumo in Taketomi (Yaeyama) and fumoŋ in Shiraho, according to Miyara;

komo in Nase but kumu in Koniya, according to Hirayama. In Shodon the word for 'jaw'
or 'chin' is qago and the same form appears in Miyako and Hateruma; Old Japanese
attests only agyi 'upper jaw'. Other Shodon words with -o which correspond to Old
Japanese words with an o of uncertain value or to words unattested in Old Japanese:
mumo 'peach' (OJ momo), hyimo 'cord' (OJ fyimo), nuno 'cloth' (OJ nuno and Azuma
ninwo), khapto 'helmet' (OJ kabuto); huro 'bath' (OJ —), khaso 'bonito' (OJ —),
khao 'face' (OJ —, later kafo), s(i)ro 'falsehood' (OJ —).

But there are a few examples of Shodon -o from the *otu ⁷-rui* o̲, as well:
ko̲ko̲ro̲ > khohooro 'heart' (the same on Tokunoshima — also Hateruma?), ino̲ti >
qyinootyi 'life', to̲ko̲ro̲ > thuro 'place' (with syncope of the middle syllable),
usiro̲ > qusyryo 'behind', myino̲ (based on phonograms of a name) > myinyo 'raincape';
omo̲f- > qumoor- (< *omor-) 'think'. The Old Japanese evidence is unclear for the
ancestors of Shodon yatoor- < *yator- 'hire', mudoor- < *mudor-/modor- 'return', and
thaboor- < *tabor- 'save'. There is one example of a Shodon -o that corresponds to
standard Japanese -u but it reflects an Old Japanese doublet: maywo/mayu : mayo
'eyebrow', and mayo also in Nase, Chabana, and Ishigaki, according to Hirayama. We
expect the standard Japanese -u to be reflected as -u in Shodon and we expect the
otu ⁷-rui Co also to be reflected as -u: mo̲no̲ : munu 'thing', oto̲ : quthu 'sound',
(woto̲) : wuthu 'husband', wono̲ : wunu 'ax', iro̲ : qyiryu 'color' (the -y- in the
second syllable is due to progressive palatal assimilation).

Unexplained is the fact that there are also a few words with Old Japanese *ko ⁷o-
rui* Cwo in non-initial syllables that show up with -u in Shodon rather than the -o
mentioned above: fakwo : haku 'box', kuswo : kw(u)su 'dung'. The word for 'thread'
occurs only twice in Old Japanese with the proper notations to indicate the vowel
type, and the two occurrences give conflicting testimony: itwo/ito̲. Shodon has both
qyitho 'thread' (presumably from OJ itwo) and qyityu 'silk' (presumably from ito̲);
Shuri has both qiicu [i:t͡šu] and qitu [itʰu] for 'silk'.

Part Five: Origins of the earlier vowels

43. Interpretations of the earlier vowel distinctions

What we have written as postconsonantal -ye, -iy, and -wo are the unusual or
less common varieties; most instances of later -e, -i, and -o descend from what we
are writing as -ey, -yi, and -o̲. Starostin 275 is intrigued by the fact that few
words with Cye-, Cey-, Ciy-, and Cwo- have putative Altaic cognates; but that is not
surprising, for there are not very many such words to begin with. Our orthography
suggests that the *ko ⁷o-rui* Cwo might be interpreted as the *otu ⁷-rui* Co̲ with a labial
semivowel -w- inserted (or its color superimposed). We have left the simple e and i
as symbols to write the neutralized -ye/-ey and -yi/-iy after dentals (etc.) and o
to write the neutralized -wo/-o̲ after those consonants where the distinction is not
expected: m (except in Koji-ki); f (though perhaps, as Ōno and Mabuchi believe, fwo
≠ fo̲ in Koji-ki and also in Jōgū-Shōtoku-hōō-teꜯ/ꜯisetsu); b; initial w (probably <
*b-); and zero (though Mabuchi thinks there was a distinction). Following Lange,
Unger treats our -yi and -ey as the norm and writes them i and e; he writes -ye as
we do but he treats our -iy as "-wi", on which we will say more below. For Unger
these are not merely notational conventions; he analyzes the vowel structure of Old
Japanese as comprising five vowels (i e a o u) and two semivowels, which he appears
to identify with the initial y- and w-,[36] the initials that we suggest may earlier
have been *d- (or *j-) and *b-. (The *b- and *d- were first proposed by Ramstedt.)
Partly because of his identification of the semivowels with initial y- and w-, Unger
is suspicious of the validity of the *ko ⁷o-otu* distinction for the syllable yo, since

a phonetic [ywo] for Old Japanese strikes him as implausible; a distinction of /dwo/
≠ /do/ would, however, be in keeping with /two/ ≠ /to/. If Unger (1977c:22) is right
yo 'generation; bamboo segment' is not the exception to the norm of Cwo for free
monosyllables that has worried other investigators (see §44).

The contraction and crasis of vowels provide evidence that many if not all
cases of -ey come from diphthongs that were earlier dissyllabic -ai; and that nearly
all of the few cases of -iy (Unger's "-wi") are compressions of earlier -oi and -ui.
This explains — up to a point — the origin of the two types for each of the two
front vowels in Old Japanese and the peculiarly weak distribution of both types of
/e/, for earlier there may have been only four nuclear vowels: i a o u. But that
assumes that all cases of -e go back to diphthongs; on this point Unger, for one,
has doubts. For proto-Japanese he would set up five vowels, adding an original /e/,
in order to account for a small residue of intractable etyma (such as ter- 'shine'
and tera 'temple') without resorting to such explanations as borrowing or sporadic
vowel raising/lowering. And both of these systems assume that the peculiar ko'o-rui
o that we are writing Cwo was not present as a distinctive element in the vowel
system. But how are we to rid ourselves of the embarrassment of this Cwo?

44. Origins of Cwo.

It is often assumed that Cwo (the ko'o-rui o) resulted from monophthongizing
a diphthong. Perhaps by analogy with the front vowels, it has been suggested (by Ōno
Susumu, among others) that Cwo represents a contraction of Cua and Cuo. Pitifully
few good examples have been adduced to support this notion; the best appears to be
the Old Japanese doublet situ-ori / sitwori 'a kind of cloth'. Ōno (1977:190)
offers tudwof- 'gather' ⟨ tudu af- and kazwofey- 'count' ⟨ kazu afey-, and also
(1978:209) wor- 'be' ⟨ u-ar-. Unger notes kuwe- and kwoye- 'kick' (kwoye- is found
in agwoye = a[si]-"kwoye 'foot-kick' etc.) together with a few other pairs, but he
fails to come up with cases of Cau or Cao, as has sometimes been proposed. Starostin
(275) would derive Cwo from Cua for two reasons: (1) there is parallelism with the
ko'o-rui Cye ⟨ Cia; (2) the Ryūkyū word kwa 'child' is cognate with OJ kwo.[37] But it
is strange that this word alone should be the only case of Cwo to be preserved as
Cwa, and a different etymology (contraction of ko-ra ⟨ kwo-ra 'children') has been
advanced by Hirayama and others. (The contraction, if true, must have happened
early, in view of the widespread use of the morpheme as a diminutive suffix.)
Starostin (279) believes Cwo may have come also from Cau in some instances, since
the phonogram HIGH koo ⟨ kɔɔ ⟨ kau ⟨ .kaw is used as well as the phonogram OLD kwo ⟨
'ku/'wo. But there seems to be no particular correlation found with the pertinent
vocabulary items. Of the other initials, only /two/ has a similar "odd" phonogram
KNIFE: too ⟨ tɔɔ ⟨ tau ⟨ .taw. The sole phonogram for /mwo/ is HAIR moo ⟨ mɔɔ ⟨ mau
⟨ .maw. The Ryūkyū reflexes of OJ uma-gwo 'grandchild' — Shodon maga, Shuri qnmaga,
Yonaguni maaŋu — might be adduced in favor of *Cau, but the first two could also be
explained as the result of elision in the morpheme -k[w]a 'child' (perhaps ⟨ ko-ra ⟨
kwo-ra 'children'), and the Yonaguni -Cu as the normal raising of any -Co.

Paul Sato (1975 ms.) has a different theory. Like a number of others, he is
inspired by what is called "Arisaka's Law", which is simply the observation that
certain strings of syllables do not occur within the morphemes of Old Japanese.
Within a root Co and Cwo do not coexist; *CoCu and *CuCo do not occur; CoCa and
CaCo are uncommon (Ōno 1977:203-6). This can be seen from a table of relevant
dissyllabic nouns of Old Japanese:

tana 'shelf'	(toga 'blame')	swora 'sky'	tuma 'spouse'	sima 'island
(maro 'round')	tono 'mansion'	--- (*CwoCo)*	--- (*CuCo)	iro 'color'
matwo 'target'	--- (*CoCwo)	mwomwo 'thigh'**	tunwo 'horn'	sirwo 'white'
kasu 'dregs'	kosi 'loins'	swoni 'kingfisher'	kuni 'country'	isi 'stone'

* But cf. kwofo-si(-) = kwofiy-si(-) 'lovable'.
** The pattern CwoCwo occurs only in reduplications. Cf. Matsumoto 1974:92.

It has also been observed that most of the free monosyllables of the susceptible shapes are Cwo, not Co, and that the postposed particles and suffixes are Co, not Cwo; but there are exceptions (cf. Mabuchi 1976:9-10). Whenever words with Ciy have a morphophonemic or an etymological alternate shape that is later Co- it is never attested as *Cwo, only Co, so we may presume that the unattested cases also go back to Co; later we will reconstruct these words as Co-[C]i with a suffix. Paul Sato believes that the unusual Cwo was originally an allophone of the primordial (otu⁷-rui) /o/, the result of a prehistoric version of Arisaka's Law in which the normal allophone was not permitted to occur except in the first syllable of a morpheme, unless preceded by a syllable that contained the same kind of -o; to put it another way, [o] was replaced by [wo], assuming that was the phonetic value, in any non-initial syllable following a vowel other than [o]. He would explain the monosyllabic nouns, such as two 'door' and nwo 'field', as getting restructured by analogy with their (presumably more common?) occurrences as second members of compounds. With that restructuring, together with the lexical restructuring of morphemes and the breakdown of Arisaka's Law in other ways, the two kinds of o were put into direct opposition as separate phonemes, at least in certain environments. This ingenious theory will still have to contend with a fair number of dissyllabic and polysyllabic nouns and verbs with Cwo in the first syllable, for which we have no indication of a truncation or a dropped prefix, but Sato attempts to explain these. Matsumoto (1974: 140) points out that the norm for free monosyllables is Cwo with the exception of yo 'bamboo segment; interval'; perhaps we can reverse Sato's idea (truncation) to explain yo. A few words occur as doublets Cwo/Co; the most conspicuous are the verbs twor-/tor- 'take', twof-/tof- 'inquire', twok-/tok- 'untie', and swof-/sof- 'follow', all with dental initials. A perhaps similar case with a labial initial: mamwor- or mamor- 'guard' (see Ch. 6). Other relevant verb stems all begin with Co, including ko- 'come' and (*)so- 'do'. For monosyllables Matsumoto hypothesizes (74-5) that Co was the appropriate version in "dependent" situations (i.e. when bound or quasi-bound), including ko(-) 'tree', and Cwo was appropriate for the "independent" situations (when free). Matsumoto is troubled by the exception of ywo 'night' ≠ yo 'bamboo segment; interval' but perhaps the latter form, if not a truncation, may be an extension of the "dependent" version. Matsumoto conjectures that the free Cwo monosyllables were "somewhat lengthened" (like monosyllabic nouns in Kyōto and Shuri today) and that that is responsible for the development of a difference in the allophones. He believes (25-6) that Cico and CiCwo were simply in free variation (sometimes unattested) but that as the last syllable of a stem or a noun -Cwo was more common; piro(-) 'wide' and sirwo(-) 'white' have alternants pira- and sira-, cf. ito/itwo/ita 'very'. Mabuchi (1976:9) suspects that there may have been some difference of meaning between the forms with -Co/-Cwo and the forms with -Ca, citing ika-/iko- 'formidable', iya/iyo(-) 'more and more', sina-/sinwo- 'pliant', and sira-/-siro-/sirwo 'govern, control'.

    If we accept the major outline of Matsumoto's (or Sato's) hypothesis, we still must acknowledge that at least the central dialect of Old Japanese somehow managed to develop a limited distinction of Cwo ≠ Co, only to lose the distinction again within a hundred years or so. The Amami (Shodon) evidence cited earlier argues that the qualitatively different allophones antecedent to the phonemic differentiation were already present in proto-Japanese.

A fairly comprehensive list of common words with Cwo in Old Japanese is appended below, arrayed by syllable types.

two

two 'door; place; time'
two 'outside'
two 'whetstone'
two(-) 'sharp'
twog- 'sharpen'
twof-/t_of- 'inquire'
twom- 'be rich'
twoma 'rush-mat roof'
twora 'tiger'
twozi 'wife' (< two-nusi)
twonafey- 'chant, advocate'
satwo 'inhabited place'
tutwo 'straw wrapper'
atwo/at_o 'footprint, trace; behind'
fatwo 'pigeon, dove'

fotwo 'extent; a while'
itwo/it_o 'thread'
itwo/it_o 'extremely'
matwo 'target'
matwo(-) 'round'
itwo-ma 'leisure'
itwokwo 'beloved; (later) cousin'
sitwori = situ-ori 'kind of cloth'
n_ori-two 'Shinto prayer'
utwo(-) 'aloof'
futwo(-) 'grand; plump'
tafutwo(-) 'exalted, sacred'
tafutwom-/tafutwobiy- 'value'
matwof- 'get bewildered/perplexed'

dwo

kadwo 'gate'
madwo 'window'
kamadwo 'oven'
tudwof- 'gather, come together'
tudwofey- 'bring together'

sadwof- '? be bewildered'
tadwor- 'go visit'
k_ot_o-dwo ' ? '
tokofyi-dwo ' ? '
(-)dwoti 'fellow ⋯'

swo

swo! 'catch-the-horse!'
(-)swo 'hemp'
(-)swo: i-swo '50', ya-swo '80'
swora 'sky'
swoma 'wooded mountain, mountain trees'
swoni 'kingfisher'
swofyi 'pale red'
swokyi: swokyi-ita 'shingle'
swode 'sleeve'
swof-/s_of- 'follow'
swofey-/s_ofey- 'add, append'
swonaf- '? be fully arrayed/supplied'
swobaf- 'romp'
swoga-swoga-si(-) = suga-suga-si(-)
  'fresh, invigorating'
suswo 'skirt bottom, hem'

iswo 'rock(y beach)'
fiswo 'small logs ⋯'
kuswo 'dung'
fafaswo 'oak'
okyiswo 'sigh, breath'
iswo(-) 'diligent'
iswog- 'rush'
aswob- 'play'
kaswob- 'steal'
araswof- 'struggle'
naswofey- 'liken'
kaswo-key(-) 'faint, dim'
swoswok- 'ruffle'
aswoswo-ni '? faintly'
oswofyi '? roof-beam; ⋯'
uswo-ᵇ/◼uk- 'blow hard'

zwo

kazwofey- 'count'

nwo
nwo 'field'
sinwo(/sino̱ Man'yō-shū) '(bamboo)'
tunwo 'horn'
sinwo(nwo)-ni 'bedraggled, washed-out'
sinwof-/sinuf- 'yearn'
sinwog- 'block'
sanwokata '(plant name, ?= akebi)'
tanwo-si- 'enjoyable'

rwo
kurwo 'black'
sirwo 'white'
murwo 'room'
fukurwo 'bag'
farwo-farwo 'distant'
arwozi = aruzi 'owner'
maturwof- 'serve' (= maturaf-)
maturwofey- 'have one serve'
kagyirwo-fiy 'heat shimmer'

kwo
kwo 'silkworm'*
kwo 'child' (kwo-ra/-domo 'children')
kwo 'basket' (= myi-kwo)
kwo- 'little'
kwo(-) 'saturated; deep, thick'
kwok- 'excrete; thresh'
kwofi 'carp'
kwofiy- 'love'
kwofo-/kwofiy-si(-) 'lovable'
kwobiy- 'flatter'
kwos- 'make it pass over'
kwoye[y]- 'pass over'
kwom- 'be flooded'
kwofor- 'freeze'
kwofare[y]- 'burn, smolder'
kwomayaka 'finely beautiful'
kwoma(-) 'rich, fertile'
kwo-sakey 'unrefined rice wine'
kwomo 'kind of seaweed'
  * ?('child' cf. Igarashi 62 n.1

kwonata 'well-developed riceland'
kwonamyi 'first/main wife'
kwokumyi 'growth, excrescent flesh'
ukwo/wokwo 'stupid'
fyikwo 'prince'
nekwo 'cat'
takwo 'octopus'
mwokwo/mukwo 'bridegroom'
yama-byikwo 'echo'
manakwo 'pupil of eye'
miyakwo 'capital'
fakwo 'box'
fakwob- 'transport'
kasikwo(-) 'fearful'
kasikwom- 'be in awe'
nikwo(-) 'soft, gentle'
nikwom- 'get soft'
sukwosi(-) 'little'
kwogwo 'rub-rub!'

gwo
kwogwo 'rub-rub!'
agwo (< amyi-kwo) 'net bag'
isagwo 'sand'
nagwoya 'gentle'
managwo 'sand'
managwo 'beloved child'

misagwo 'osprey'
itibyigwo 'berry'
agwoye 'heel spur'
?agwora/agura 'high seat; crosslegged'
mugwofey ' ? '

ywo
ywo(ru) 'night'
⋯ ywo(ri) = yu(ri) 'along; from'
ywowa(-) 'weak'
ywob- 'call'
maywo (later mayu) 'eyebrow; cocoon'
aywofyi = ayufyi 'skirt cord ⋯'
naywo-/nayu-takey 'pliant bamboo'
kyiywo(-) 'clean'
kyiywomey- 'cleanse'
maywof-/mayuf- 'get lost; fray'
kaywof- 'move across'
isaywof- 'waver'
kagaywof- 'twinkle'
samaywof- 'moan; roam, wander'
aywok- 'quake'
tadaywof- 'drift, float'

The Chinese loan gwo(-wi) 'five (rank)' is written with a semantogram, so it is unclear why Zdb treats it as 'gwo'.

? **fwo** (cf. Ōno Tōru 907)
fwo 'ear of grain'
-fwo: i-fwo '500', ya-fwo '800'
fwok- 'pray'
fwo-si(-) 'desired'
fwodari 'wine jug'
fwotumwori 'bud'
sifwo 'tide' (in sifwo-se)
sifwo 'salt'
i-fwo '500'
ya-fwo '800'
nifwo(-dori) 'grebe (bird)'

?**bwo**
No examples have been suggested.

mwo
mwomwo 'thigh'
(momo ?<) mwomwo 'hundred'
mwoye[y]- (?< moye[y]- 'burn')
mwokwo 'partner; bridegroom'
mwozu 'shrike'
simwo 'down, below'
kamwo 'wild duck'
imwo 'younger sister; beloved girl'
kyimwo 'liver; heart'
kumwo 'cloud'
mamwor-/mamor- 'guard'
idumwo 'Izumo'

(')**wo**
See n.31.

45. Origins of Cey and Cye.

The common type of mid front vowel, the *otu'-rui* -ey is seldom found in the
first syllable of polysyllabic words, though there are several monosyllables such as
mey 'eye', key 'hair', and te[y] 'hand', each of which has an alternant form with -a
in certain compounds. A number of paired verbs are differentiated by an alternation
of Ca with Cey, as in akamu 'it will open' and akeymu 'I will open it'. But the
alternation is disguised in certain forms, where the /a/ drops: the infinitive
(ak-yi : akey), the predicative (ak-u : ak-u), the attributive (ak-u : ak-uru). In
toma-r-u 'it stops' : tomey-ru 'stops it' and in akey-ru 'it brightens' : aka-s-u
'(brightens =) reveals it' the suffixes preserve the final /a/ intact. As we will
see below, this alternation points to the derivation -ey < -ay < -ai < -aCi with the
elided consonant in most cases probably our lost voiced-velar stop as the initial
phoneme of a suffix (*⋯-gi).

The best guess on an unknown or indeterminate Ce is that it is Cey, because Cye
is relatively rare. A few examples: mye 'woman', fyimye 'princess', fyera 'spatula',
kyesa 'priest's robe', kyefu 'today', kakye 'chicken', ifye 'house' (however, the
variant ifa casts doubt on the *ko'o-rui* assignment of the final syllable — cf.
Matsumoto 1974:96 and the entry "ie" in Ch. 5), kafyer- 'return', simyes- 'reveal',
takye(-) 'brave', kye-si(-) 'weird', sikye-si(-) '?dirty', namye(-) 'impertinent',
namye(-raka) 'slippery', ... Sometimes Cye is the result of contraction from
C(y)i-a, especially in inflected forms: sakyeri 'is in bloom' < sakyi ari. We may
wonder whether all instances of Cye are not the result of similar compressions, hard
to spot when a consonant has been elided. Perhaps mye 'woman', for example, comes
from myi-na 'female-person' (by eliding the -n- and then monophthongizing), for
which we find support in wo-myina '[?little] woman' — and perhaps in the Hachijō
island word menarabe 'girl' ?< *mina-[wa]rabe (rather than *me-[no w]arabe), which
corresponds to Shuri miyarabi < me-warabe. Matsumoto 1974 mentions three sources for
OJ Cye: (1) foreign borrowings, such as kyesa 'priest's robe' and perhaps kakye
'chicken'; (2) sporadic (and unexplained) fronting of Cey to Cye, as in kafyer-
/kafyes- 'return'— which in Ch. 6 we treat as lowering from Azuma kafyir-/*kafyis-;
(3) sporadic lowering of Cyi, as Matsumoto (114) treats mye 'woman' < myi (M 4343),
with no independent motivation.

46. Origins of Ciy.

On the *otu¹-rui* high front vowel -iy, to quote Mathias (36): "There are very few cases of root-internal ï *[our -iy]*. Only two examples turn up in my list of some 3000 OJ words: kïr- *[kiyr-]* 'fog' and mïna *[miyna]* 'all'. Nine other words with ï before a consonant are on the list, but they are either compounds on 'fog' or analyzable at the ï." This could be taken to suggest that miyna is a compound, perhaps miy 'body; self, I/me' + na 'person' (or 'you'?), or a variant of mur(a)- 'cluster' + na. And kiyr- 'fog' (also 'breath-steam') might be contracted from a phrase, perhaps ku[mwo] ari or ku[m]ori. Starostin (275) assumes that OJ miyna < *muina/moina is the result of metathesis on the basis of "the old Kyushu dialect möne < mönia/mönai" but he does not say where he found this form. Starostin also assumes a metathesis in tukiy 'moon' "< *tukui < *tukyu" on the basis of Ikema [tsïttšu] and in kiyri 'fog' "< *kuiri < *kyuri" on the basis of Ikema [tšuu]. But the metathesis is unneeded; Ciy < *Cui (unlike Ciy < *Coi) often palatalizes the preceding Ryūkyū consonant, probably as the result of an intermediate stage *Cü in contrast with *Cöy < *Coi. (A variant development of Cöy to Cey instead of Ciy is perhaps responsible for odd forms like key = kiy 'tree'.)

Most of our examples of Ciy are in upper bigrade verbs, and often there is a paired stem that ends in u or o:

amiy- 'bathe in' : amus- 'bathe one in'
okiy- 'rise' : ok̲o̲s- 'raise'
ofiy- 'grow' : ofos- 'cultivate'
fiy- 'be drained' : fos- 'dry it'
y̲o̲kiy- 'avoid' : y̲o̲k̲o̲s- 'insult'
tukiy- 'be exhausted' : tukus- 'exhaust'
sugiy- 'pass' : sugus- > sugwos- 'let pass'
kwofiy- 'love' : kwof̲o̲-si(-) / kwofiy-si(-) 'lovable'

sabiy- 'get desolate/rusty'
sifiy- 'compel'
miy- 'turn'
wabiy- 'be disappointed'
mutubiy- 'get intimate'
nobiy- 'extend' (see Ch. 6)
nagiy- 'get still': nag- 'mow;
  ... ' : nagusam- 'get calm' :
  nagwo(-ya-ka) 'calm, still'

By morphophonemic analogy we can add oti[y]- 'fall' : ot̲o̲s- 'drop' and ori[y]- 'descend' : or̲o̲s- 'lower'. And we know that, despite the lack of needed attestation pertinent to the quality of the o, 'cultivate' and 'dry it' must be *of̲o̲s- and *f̲o̲s- because of the alternation with -iy, which does not alternate with Cwo. That fact strongly implies that nagwo(-ya-ka) is a secondary development from the /nagu/ found in nagusam- (perhaps the vowel was lowered in assimilation to that of the first syllable or perhaps a suffix was incorporated); notice that sugwos- is attested later than sugus-, though it is difficult to explain the motivation for /u/ > /wo/ in this word (dissimilation from the vowel of the first syllable? contamination with kwos-?). Lacking are morphophonemic alternants for kiy 'enclosure', kiy-kaf- 'pen up (and raise)'; k̲o̲kiyda 'lots' (but a variant is k̲o̲k̲o̲da and k̲o̲k̲o̲ 'nine' is probably related), fiywe- 'scrape', kiyr- 'mist up', kiyras- 'make it misty/cloudy'. The OJ stem y̲o̲kiy- (Heian quadrigrade yok-) 'avoid, dodge' is probably related to y̲o̲k̲o̲ 'side'; cf. yoko-si(ma) = yoko-sa(ma) 'sideways; wayward'.

Only a few nouns end in iy, and most of them sometimes appear as the first element of compounds in an alternate shape ending in -u or the *otu¹-rui* -o̲:

(1) -iy : -u
miy 'body; fruit' : mu-zane 'the real thing', mu-kafari 'hostage'
kamiy 'god' : kamu-oya 'ancestor (who has joined the gods)'
tukiy 'moon' : tuku-ywo 'moonlit night'
kukiy 'stalk, stem' : kuku-tati 'flower stalks, peduncles'
tubiy = tubu 'grain, granule'
tukiy 'zelkova' : tuku-yumyi 'zelkova-wood bow'
tukiy 'tribute' : tuku-naf- 'compensate'

(2) -iy : -o̲
  kiy 'tree' : ko̲-dati 'stand of trees, grove'
  fiy 'fire' : fo̲-no̲-fwo 'flame'
? miy- 'turn' : moto̲oru 'turn round' ‹ moto̲foru ?‹ *mo-to̲fo̲-r-;
                  motoru 'deviate' ?‹ *mo̲-to̲ru ‹ moto̲[fo]ru ‹ *mo̲-to̲fo̲-r-
  yomi ‹ *yo̲miy = yo̲mo̲-tu-kuni 'Hades, land of the dead'

    Of the nouns which lack an alternant shape, some seem to be compounds (fagiy 'bushclover', magiy 'pickerelweed', wogiy 'reed, sugarcane', and sugiy 'cedar' may incorporate kiy 'tree, plant', but cf. §41); fiy 'water pipe' and miy 'winnower' are not attested as the first element of a compound; kiy 'enclosure, stockade, fortress', if not from *ka[k]u-Ci with a contracted form of the root of the verb kaku-m- 'enclose, surround', may be a loanword; and yamiy 'darkness' may well be an etymological variant of *yo̲miy 'Hades' (yo̲mo̲-). The Ainu words múy 'winnower' and kamúy 'god' are either borrowed from the Japanese or are the source of these two words; in either case, they attest to the earlier pronunciation as a diphthong. If the Shuri word kaabui is directly cognate with kabiy 'mildew, mold' it seems to preserve the phonetic source of OJ -iy, as does the Kobama (Yaeyama) çïkui 'moon' (Ryūkyū-hōgen 9/10:82). (Nakamoto 1976:231 cites the Kobama form as "[tsɨ̈kɨ̈sɨ̈]". Cf. Miyara 1930:143a: çukui-nu-yuu 'moonlit night' Ishigaki and Kobama.)

    A number of nouns ending in -iy are clearly derived from the infinitives of verbs for which there is evidence of -u or -o̲ in the root: nagiy 'calm', wabiy 'simple taste; apology', kwofiy 'love'. ... .

Part Six: Reconstructing canonical shapes

47. Syllable structure; elision of intervocalic consonants.

    Syllables of the type CyV (the *kai-yo'o'on* syllables) and CwV (the *goo-yo'o'on* syllables) are thought not to have existed in Old Japanese except as an artifact of the analysis we have made above. Later CyV and CwV are largely limited to Chinese loanwords (more recently European loanwords also), marginal items, and contractions of CiV, CuV, or the like. It is usually assumed that the Chinese loanwords were pronounced with a separate syllable for the later -y- and -w- and then compressed, but that has been called in question and deserves further investigation.

    There is scant evidence for -T- (*soku'on*⌐) or -N- (*hatu'on*) in Old Japanese, except perhaps in interjections or contractions, nor for long vowels — though it seems possible that one-mora nouns were automatically lengthened, at least in isolation, as they are in Kyōto and Shuri today. As we will see in Ch. 4, vowel length may have been a factor in the accentuation of proto-Japanese.

    Not only were there no long vowels in normal etyma; there were no strings of VV except for a few cases of Vi which are usually, for that reason, interpreted as Vyi, as in kayi 'paddle; oar'. (Does kayi form a doublet with kadi 'oar', *kadi/*kanti?). If there was no VV, then the diphthongs that underlie iy, ey, and ye must go back to o̲Ci (or uCi), aCi, and iCa. What is the missing consonant? In the verb forms there appears to be a derivative suffix, a formant making transitive/intransitive forms, of the shape -Ci-; this has likely cognates in the Korean formant that makes lexical passives and causatives (-ki-, -khi-, -hi-, -i-) and probably points to an earlier *-gi- in Japanese. For the nouns it has been suggested that a "particle i", cognate with the Korean nominative-case marker i and the quasi-free noun meaning 'person' or 'one' or 'thing', might have been attached to certain nouns; see Yoshitake 1929, Murayama 1954. Another possibility is that there is a noun suffix *-gi, diminutive or vacuous in meaning; a parallel is found in the Korean suffixes -(a)ki, -(a)hi, etc., that are added to certain common nouns. Unger, examining the semantics of the nouns in question, suggests that the suffix may have been some kind of non-singular marker for words not easily unpaired or individualized; he speculates that the suffix might be cognate with Korean tul (Middle Korean ˙tᵘ/ₒlh) 'plural(ly)' and he reconstructs *-di for the Japanese suffix. But the possibility should not be overlooked that ˙tᵘ/ₒlh is a reduction from :twulh 'two' ?< .twu(-) ˙pulh; it has also been suggested as a cognate for the Japanese pluralizers tati and (-)dwoti.

48. Alternations of -Cey with -Ca: deverbative -a or root-final -[a]?

We have proposed that verb stems ending in ···ey- are derived from *···a-gi- or the like; what is the /a/? There are a number of noun or noun-like forms (such as adverbs) ending in ···a that are related to consonant-stem verbs:
  hora˥ 'cave' (= hora-ana⁻) : ho˥r- < for- 'dig'
  nawa˥ 'rope' < nafa : na˥w- < naf- 'plait' (verb unattested in OJ)
  uta˥ 'song' : u˥t- 'strike; perform'
? mata˥ 'crotch, fork' : ma˥t- 'await, expect'
? kuma˥ '(hidden) corner, recess; river bend' : OJ kum- 'entwine' (? → 'hide')
? o-nara⁻ 'crepitation' : nar-⁻ 'sound'
  se˥ka-seka 'fidgety' : se˥k- 'hasten'
  tu˥ka-tuka 'directly' : tu˥k- 'come in contact'
  te˥ra-tera 'shining' : te˥r- 'shine'
  u˥ka-uka 'absent-minded' : uk-⁻ 'float'
  ti˥ra-tira/-hora 'scattered' : tir-⁻ 'be scattered'
  supa˥-supa 'puffing' : suw- < suf-⁻ 'sip, suck, puff'
  OJ ko̲to̲saka '? severing relations' : OJ sak- 'separate' (cf. sakar-, sakey-)
  OJ tata-sa 'being vertical' : ta˥t- 'stand'
  tatazu˥m- 'pause, stop' ?< *tata ni su˥m- ('settle into stand')
  suta-fey 'coffin' [Ōno] ?< 'discard jar' (cf. sute[y]-⁻)
  kara-yama 'brown (treeless) mountain' (kare[y]-⁻ 'wither')
Two explanations have been proposed:
  (1) There is a suffix -a which derives nouns, perhaps the same morpheme as the subjunctive -a which underlies V-amu presumptive, V-anu negative, V-as- causative or honorific, V-are[y]-/-aye[y]- passive.
  (2) What appear to be consonant-final roots actually have the final ···a as part of the root; the /a/ disappears (is elided) when a vowel follows. The second view would appear to be correct, though it is possible that some or all of the nouns are to be taken as *···a-a with a derivational suffix that happens to be identical with the elided vowel that ends the root. See Ch. 6 and Unger 1975a on this problem.

In any event, we have assumed that ···a- roots underlie the stems ending in ···ey-. For some verb stems in the latter class there are related nouns or adverbs ending in /···a/ similar to those above:
  tuka˥ 'hilt' : tukey- 'attach' < *tuka-gi-
  ta˥ra-tara 'dripping' : tare[y]- 'droop' < *tara-gi-
  mura˥ 'village', mura- 'group' (as in mura-gar- 'throng') : mure[y]- 'form a group' < *mura-gi-
  OJ tura '(joining in) a row', tura-nar- 'form a row' : ture[y]-⁻ 'be accompanied by, bring along' < *tura-gi-
Perhaps oya˥ 'parent' : oyi[y]- 'age' (upper bigrade). On the vowel problem here, see oi˥ru in Ch. 6. Notice also hukura 'a swelling', nuruma-yu 'tepid water'.

In the Nara period V-a na (subjunctive + na, cf. namu) was used to express desires; also V-a ne. Cf. Satō 1973:2:155-6.

It is possible that final -a was originally the epenthetic vowel found in a number of early Chinese loans that ended in a final -p, -t, or -k, such as dika 'direct' for the etymon later re-borrowed as diki with the usual (and modern) epenthetic high vowel -Cu but -Ci after an original front vowel, as seen in such loanwords as oꞌku 'hundred million' and eꞌki 'station'. The latter phenomenon is similar to the progressive palatal assimilation found sporadically in the northern Ryūkyūs (Martin 1970b:101a) and for a few words as far south as Miyako and Yaeyama. Syllables beginning with a dental or velar consonant are thereby palatalized after a syllable with the high front vowel yi: Shodon hyidyaaryi 'left', myithya 'earth', qyisyo 'beach', kyinyu 'yesterday', syryaamyi 'louse', thykyaara 'strength', nyigyaaku 'bitter'. But there are exceptions: hyiru 'daytime' (cf. qyiryu 'color'), qyikhaada 'raft' (cf. qyikyaaryi 'anchor'), syka 'deer'. The Shuri word for 'person' qcu is from *p[i]cu < *pityu < *pito. The palatal "smear" may have been more widely prevalent in earlier days; cf. the standard kikyoo⁻ 'bellflower' from the Chinese loan kit(i)-kau.

49. Other views: stems, roots, formant suffixes.

In his dissertation Unger differs from the treatment offered here in several respects. He seems to assume that the neutral cases of Old Japanese Ce are to be equated with /Cye/, except for the syllables "we" and "(ꞌ)e", just as he takes the neutral cases of Ci to be /Ci/ = Cyi. As a result he often has to assume Cye < *Ce, as in /tye/ < *te 'hand' and /sye/ < *se 'back', because of the alternations (ta- and so-) that do not show the palatal element. Among the verb forms he has to posit /motye-/ < *mote-. It seems preferable to treat the neutral cases as equivalent to Cey, especially when there are alternants or internal structure (such as mote[y]- < *mota-gi-) that point to an ···a at the end of the root. While we cannot be sure of the source of unknown or neutralized Ci, Ce, and Co, the best guesses would appear to be as follows. In the absence of evidence that points to Ciy, which is relatively uncommon, it is wise to assume that Ci came from *Cyi (< proto-Japanese *Ci); in the absence of evidence that indicates Ce < *Cye, which is relatively uncommon, we do well to assume the more common *Cey < *CaCi (or from a loan). But in the absence of evidence indicating whether Co is from Cwo or from Co, it is unwise to make a choice except on the basis of canonical shapes, relying in part on "Arisaka's Law".

Unger also assumes that proto-Japanese had a phoneme /c-/, presumably the affricate [ts-], and reconstructs this for all cases of Old Japanese /s/ except when there is evidence for the "disappearing s", in which case he reconstructs */Ns/ or */s/, as appropriate. But after */N/ or between vowels the internal evidence is unclear as to *s or *c so Unger writes *s to conform with Old Japanese. Unger's *c- has merit, for it will explain the s/t variants, Ennin's description of Chinese sounds, and correspondences to s of Korean c/t/s. Notice also Unger's discussion of Yamaguchi's "disappearing initials", the complete list of which can be found in Kgg 98:1-15 (1974). In Unger's list of roots you will find only two examples of s- as an initial: sa- 'small' and si- (meaning unclear). From the assumptions he makes it is not obvious why these are not to be reconstructed with *c-.

We have observed that Unger treats our Ciy as /Cwi/, following Lange. The two versions are not necessarily incompatible; they merely imply a slightly different route of development from the sources of the diphthong:

Unger: oCi > oi
        uCi > ui   > wi   > i

Martin: oCi > oi > öi
        uCi > ui > üi   > üy > ɨy > i[y]

The advantage of the notations -iy : -yi is not merely that they parallel those of
-ey : -ye but that this way of writing both pairs of front vowels permits us to make
some statements about the verb morphology that otherwise would be more complicated.
I assume that throughout much of the Old Japanese period -iy was pronounced [ɨy]
though earlier it was [üy] or possibly [wi].

Following Ōno and others, Unger demonstrates convincingly that the bigrade verb
stems arose from the attachment of a derivative suffix -[g]i- to roots that end in
Ca, leading to the "lower bigrade" stems ⋯Cey-; or to roots that end in Cu
and Co, leading to the "upper bigrade" stems ⋯Ciy-. A few of these are shown below.

	Root	→	OJ verb stem	+ Formant	→	OJ derived verb stem
(1)	aka	ak[a]- >	ak- 'it open'	-gi-	aka-[g]i- >	akey- 'open it'
	toma-[38]	—		-gi-	toma-[g]i- >	tomey- 'stop it'
				-ra-	toma-r[a]- >	tomar- 'it stop'
(2)	noko	nok[o]- >	nok- 'leave it'	-ra-	noko-r[a]- >	nokor- 'remain'
				-sa-	noko-s[a]- >	nokos- 'leave it'
	tumo	tum[o]- >	tum- 'pile it up'	-ra-	tumo-r[a]- >	tumor- 'it pile up'
	oko	—		-gi-	oko-[g]i- >	okiy- 'arise'
				-sa-	oko-s[a]- >	okos- 'awaken'
				-ra-	oko-r[a]- >	okor- 'happen, ⋯'
(3)	kuku	kuk[u]- >	kuk- 'creep out'	-ra-	kuku-r[a]- >	kukur- 'leak out'
	amu	—		-gi-	amu-[g]i- >	amiy- 'bathe in'
				-sa-	amu-s[a]- >	amus- 'bathe one in'

These examples are only a taste of the problems in reconstructing proto-Japanese
roots; for more details, see Ch. 6 and Unger's dissertation. A different view from
that underlying the reconstructions in this study will be found in Wenck 1976-7.

Part Seven: Problems of reconstruction.

50. The proto-Japanese vowel system.

From what has been said about the vowel distinctions we conclude that proto-
Japanese apparently had only four vowel phonemes. Such a system looks skew if it is
arrayed by the ordinary set of articulatory parameters:

$$i \qquad\qquad u$$
$$o$$
$$a$$

But the four-vowel system can be arrayed symmetrically if we posit the pair
of oppositions back vs. non-back and rounded vs. unrounded:

$$i \qquad\qquad u$$
$$a \qquad\qquad o$$

Yet, at least three scholars — Hattori, Serafim, Unger — have independently argued that the proto-Japanese vowel system must also have had a mid front vowel phoneme /e/. It has been remarked that there are a few examples of Old Japanese Ce in neutralized environments that cannot be explained as Ce[y], which derives from something like proto-Japanese Ca[C]i, as we would like to do. These include ter- 'shine', sek- 'obstruct', se^b/ₐa- 'narrow; pressing'; seri 'parsley', se 'older brother', semyi 'cicada', nekwo 'cat', nezumyi 'rat', tera 'temple' (likely borrowed from Korean tyel), ... But even if we include with all such examples those Cye words for which we have but scant evidence of a derivation from Ci[C]a, the lexical frequency of /Ce/ would be very low. It has been suggested that perhaps a larger number of words originally had the mid front vowel but, under conditions far from clear, some of those mid front vowels backed to /o/ and some were raised to /i/. This is a tempting line of speculation, for it would help with certain etymologies, as in attempting to explain the relationship of Japanese sima 'island' to Korean syem and to "sema" in Nihon-Shoki, which is thought to be an attempt to write the word in its Paekche (Kudara) version *syema (cf. Toh 1981:29). Ramstedt, however, explained Korean syem as the result of a "breaking" of *i to *ye, and that view is supported by Lee Ki-Moon 1959. Some examples of the alternation of /e/ and /i/ are given in §51. The alternation of /e/ with /o/ can be found in OJ se/so 'back'; so is found in compounds like so-muk- 'turn one's back' and obsolete so-bira¯ '(flat of) the back'. It appears likely that se[y] is an irregular development from *so-Ci (which ought to give *si[y]), just as the old variant key for kiy 'tree(s)' is from *ko-Ci (see below).

Both Hattori and Serafim observe that the proto-Ryūkyū word for 'water' must have been *medu, to account for Shodon midi rather than *myidi. A similar case: *peru 'garlic' > Shodon hwiryi, OJ fyiru; cf. Hattori (1981), who would include the verb imperative as *V-e. Thorpe (233) reconstructs proto-Japanese-Ryūkyūan *e in these words and adds *kezu 'wound' and *edu 'which'; also (282) *memezu 'earthworm', on the basis of forms in Kyūshū and Hachijō island, but that may represent a variant reduction of moCi- > mey- instead of > miy-, if the etymology is a reduplication of moCi- (> miy-) 'turn' + -zu < -n-su, just as key 'tree(s)' in old placenames is a variant reduction of ko-Ci (> kiy). Aomori has [meme¹ℤi] for 'earthworm'.

Hattori (1979:21:98, 22:108) postulates a more elaborate scheme of proto-Japanese vowels, based on correspondences between the central dialect of Old Japanese and what he reconstructs as an earlier (1400-) version of Shuri. His system, taken literally, would have its own assymetries:

ü	i	u		üi	ui		ii	uu
	e	ə	o		əi			ee	əə	oo
	a			ai		au		aa

In Hattori's scheme *ə is the source of OJ "ö" (our Co) and *au is the source of OJ "o" (our Cwo). His proto-Japanese *o represents the correspondence between (central) OJ /u/ and the earlier-Shuri */o/; his *ü represents the correspondence of OJ "ö" (our Co) or u with an earlier-Shuri */o/ or */u/. He says that in the central dialect of Old Japanese /i/ (our Cyi) developed from the proto-Japanese *e, /u/ from *o, and /i, ii/ (our Ciy, Ci:y) from *əi, but that the changes did not occur in the eastern dialect, as partially reflected on modern Hachijō island, nor in Kyūshū. The correspondences Hattori cites deserve further study, as does his reconstruction of the earlier Shuri forms. But as a first approximation we can approach proto-Japanese with the assurance that four — or, at most, five — vowels will handle the bulk of the vocabulary, at least in rough form. The question of vowel length is taken up in Chapter 4, in connection with the accentual system.

51. Minor vowel variations.

A number of different kinds of vowel variation have been observed in related words; in particular instances some of these may point to earlier shapes of roots.

(1) Co̱/Ca, Cwo/Ca

-ko̱/-ka 'place' as in so-ko⁻ 'there', su˥mi˥-ka 'residence', a˥ri-ka˥⁻ 'location' (cf. hoka⁻ 'outside', na˥ka 'inside'); notice also -ku in iduku = iduko = do˥ko 'where'

ko̱(-)/ka- 'this' as in ko-re⁻ 'this', ka˥-ku 'thus' (cf. ko̱- 'come'); also perhaps ki- if kyesa 'this morning' is from *ki asa

ko-/-ka 'day' as in ko-yomi˥ 'calendar' and too-ka⁻ 'ten days'

S ko = S ka 'whether S' (cf. Inokuchi 331)

OJ kyiko̱s-/kyikas- 'deign to hear, partake, ··· '

ko-(<?*kwo-)/ka- 'slight(ly)' as in ko-su˥r- 'rub' and ka-su˥r- 'graze'

so̱(-)/sa 'that' as in so-re⁻ 'that', sa˥ = sa-yoo 'so'; cf. OJ si = so̱ 'that'

ma(-)/mo- 'true/truly' as in mo-naka 'midst' and perhaps motomo, mokoro, mofara, moyura (see Zdb)

sirwo 'white' and sira-ka 'white hair'

kurwo 'black' and kura(-) 'dark'

kuswo 'dung' and kusa(-) 'smelly'

The variants kogom- and kugum- for kagam- 'stoop; crouch' are not attested early, but kugum- is in the Japanese-Portuguese dictionary and kugumaru is in Myōgi-shō. In dialect examples from Kyōto-fu such as narob- = narab- 'line up' (Inokuchi 348) and tatom- = tatam- 'fold' (id. 272) the vowel may have assimilated to the following labial consonant; an odd countercase, however, is hiraw- for hirow- 'pick up'. One etymology for hodo⁻ < fotwo 'extent' identifies the first syllable with the verb stem he-⁻ < fey- 'pass, elapse' and assumes an assimilation of the vowel. The bound morpheme haka in soko˥-haka-to-na˥ku 'in a general sort of way; vaguely, somehow' is from hoka = sika 'except for'; cf. kore haka nai < kore hoka/sika na˥i 'there's only this' in Takeno-gun of Tango (Inokuchi 286, 291). The particle sae < safey 'even' is thought to be derived from swofey 'adding on'. Perhaps we can include here oi-mek- = wa-mek- 'wail' (mimetic variants?) and wor- 'break, fold, bend' : war- 'split', if that pair is etymologically related. A fairly long list of OJ words with the Co̱/Ca variants will be found in Murayama 1954:87. Cf. also Matsumoto 1974, esp. 128-36. And see the suggested derivation of the verb ogo̱ru from agaru in Chapter 6.

(2) Cu/Ca

OJ tura = turu '(bow)string'

OJ waku-gwo 'young person' : waka-kwo 'child'

tamure (Myōgi-shō) = tumure 'hill'.

usu(-) ?< *us(a)- 'thin' : asa(-) 'shallow'

use[y]- 'vanish' : ase[y]- 'fade'

(3) Cwo/Cu, Co̱/Cu

OJ no̱gwof- = nuguf- 'wipe'

OJ sugus- = OJ Azuma sugwos- = modern sugo˥s- 'exceed; let pass'

OJ sukwo-si(-) 'little', OJ suku-na- 'scant' (Kyōto-fu dialects sukenai)

OJ maro̱ = maru⁻ 'round'

OJ aka-to̱kyi = Hn aka-tukyi 'dawn'

Heian karo- = modern ka˥ru- 'lightweight' (cf. karo-n-zi(-) 'treat lightly'

moromati (Kyōto-fu dialects) = muro˥mati⁻ 'Muromachi'

osagi (Kyōto-fu dialects) = usagi⁻ 'rabbit'
tanoki (Kyōto-fu dialects) = ta⸀nuki 'raccoon-dog'
yoki (Kyōto-fu dialects) = yuki⸀ 'snow'
The particle su⸀ra 'even' has a Heian variant sora. There are a number of OJ dialect variants with Cwo/Cu: agwora/agura 'high seat'; arwozi/aruzi 'owner'; farwo-farwo, faro-ka/faru-ka 'distant'; kaswo-key(-), kasu-ka 'dim'; ma-swomyi/-sumyi 'true-reflecting'; maywo(/mayu) 'eyebrow; cocoon'; naywo/nayu 'pliant'; tanwosi-/tanusi-'delightful'; taywora/tayura (meaning unknown); twoga/tuga (placename). On the Old Japanese doublets, see Matsumoto 1974:142-3.

(4) C<u>o</u>/Ci, Cwo/Ci

OJ Azuma firif- = fir<u>o</u>f- 'pick up' (modern Kyōto hiraw-)
s<u>o</u>m- 'be dyed' = sim- 'be dyed, soak in'
toto [dialect] = titi⸀ 'father'; to⸀o-san, to⸀t-tsan, to⸀t-tyan 'dad'
tyoppi⸀ri 'a wee bit', ti⸀[f]i-sa- 'little', ti⸀bi 'midget'
OJ n<u>o</u>-sakyi 'the first load of tribute of the year' (and a few other compounds
    with n<u>o</u>-), ni⸀ 'load' (cf. n<u>o</u>r- 'be loaded', n<u>o</u>se[y]- 'load')
awo 'blue, green', awi 'indigo'; sawo 'blue', -sawi in adi-sawi (Myōgi-shō
    adusawi) 'hydrangea'
OJ iswo 'rock(y beach)', iso = isi⸀ 'stone' in tobi-iso (Hiroshima)
    'stepping stones' and naka-iso (Tokushima) 'midstream stone' (Tōjō 1954)
OJ k<u>o</u>kiyda, k<u>o</u>kyida-ku (anomalous -kyi-) = k<u>o</u>k<u>o</u>da 'lots' (cf. k<u>o</u>k<u>o</u>no 'nine')
huso (Tosa, Tottori) = husi 'node, joint'
kurwo 'black', kuri(-tuti) 'black clay'
Shuri inu(-) = ona-ˢ/zi(-) 'same', cf. on<u>o</u>- 'self'

(5) Ce/Ci

nenzin = ninzin⁻ 'carrot'
sirame = sirami⁻ 'louse'
ooke-na = o⸀oki-na 'large'
kase, kasi 'shackles'
OJ t<u>o</u>se, t<u>o</u>si 'years'
The -e results from partial assimilation of -i to the preceding vowel (except for the first example). That would also account for Hagiwara's aberu = abiru⁻ 'bathe in' but not sieru = sii⸀ru 'force, compel' nor older-generation Hagiwara seru = suru⁻ 'do' and serya = sure⸀ba 'if do' (Tsuzuku 1941:193).

(6) Ca/Ci

suma(kko) [dialect] = su⸀mi(kko) < sumiy '(inside) corner'
OJ kyitasi = katasi(fo) 'rock salt' < kata(-) 'hard' sifwo 'salt'
OJ kyitana- 'dirty' ?< kata-na- 'ugly' (?< 'lacking shape', cf. kata- zuke-
    'put in shape, tidy up' < *kata ni tukey-)

(7) Cu/Ci (Cf. 46.)

kusu-nuk- 'skewer it', kusi⸀ 'skewer' (< kusi[y] < *kusu-Ci)
OJ Azuma asi-fu = asi-fiy 'reed fire'

(8) (')yu/(')i

yuwo = uo⁻ 'fish' (Inokuchi 363), OJ iwo/uwo
yuwasi = iwasi⁻ 'sardine'
yume⸀ = OJ i-mey 'dream'
iku = yuku 'go' (a doublet found in the Man'yō-shū, perhaps originally
    from the prefix i- + uk-⁻ 'float up/off', see Ch. 6)

The Ryūkyū words for na'ni 'what' and da're 'who' are difficult to explain. In Amami, Okinawa, and Yonaguni 'what' is nuu (bringing to mind Korean nwu 'who'); in Ōra (Miyako) and Yaeyama the word is noo, and Miyara says that the archaic Yaeyama version is nayu; Ikema (Miyako) has nau, and Uechi (Miyako) noa — perhaps noa is a metathesis? What we have here, I believe, is a set of various reductions from *naru (Hateruma is given the variant nuru in Hirayama 1966) < *nadu < *na-do < *na-zo with the old emphatic particle zo, which turns up ubiquitously in the Ryūkyūs as modern du, leniting to ru in much of Okinawa. The word for 'who' is probably similar in its derivation: various contractions from taru < *tadu < *ta-do < ta-zo. But the results are somewhat different in the two cases, perhaps because the morphemes differ in accent type: 'who' is the high register (A) and 'what' is the low (B). 'Who' is taa in Shuri, parts of Yaeyama (Ōhama, Sonai, Hateruma), and Yonaguni. It is taru in other parts of Yaeyama (Ishigaki, Taketomi, and [tarï] Kurojima); in Amami, Kikai, Tokunoshima, Okinoerabu [taruu], Yoron; and in parts of Miyako (Ikema, Ōra). In other parts of Miyako we find tau (Nakasuji), too (Hirara), and toa (Uechi — again, metathesis?) Our explanation assumes a relatively early lenition of -d- to -r- in these two morphemes only, with further loss of -r- in many places. (The particle du < zo remains with a stop initial in many of the relevant dialects, though it is ru in much of modern Okinawa. The form taru ga 'who' is found in the 1711 Okinawan dictionary Konkōken-shu.) For 'who' Kametsu (Tokunoshima) and Hentona (Okinawa) have taŋ with an unexplained final nasal; perhaps this is a relic of *[nd] or *[nz]. Oniya (Amami) has nuŋ for 'what'.

52. Subsyllabic moras; final nasals; sequential initials (*renzyoo*).

Modern Japanese has several kinds of "heavy" syllables consisting of two moras. Some of these syllables have diphthongs or long vowels that resulted from dropping intervocalic consonants and monophthongizing the juxtaposed vowels; others were borrowed from Chinese (or English) syllable types. Certain of the long vowels in the modern dialects are reflexes of accentual phenomena, discussed in Chapter 4. Many dialects automatically lengthen the vowel of a basically one-mora noun; some do this in all positions, and others will do it at least when the noun is not followed by an enclitic. The lengthening of monosyllables is attested as early as 794, when Kegon-ongi shiki has both ka and kaa for 'mosquito' (Hamada 1951:397; Nakata in Doi 1957: 119, Tsukishima 1969:395). Shinsen-Jikyō (892) spells fii for fi 'shuttle' and tii for ti 'fish hook'; Engi-shiki (925) has wii for wi 'rush'; and Myōgi-shō (1081) writes nuu for nu 'marsh', tii for ti 'cogon (thatch)', waa for wa 'wheel', and yaa for ya 'spoke' (cf. Ch.4, §7), as well as mii for mi 'see'. Some long vowels are probably due to expressive or mimetic effects, as those in kinterms such as (o-)baa 'grandmother', (o-)nee 'older sister', etc. Notice also the placename Kii, thought to be from kiy (< *ko-Ci) 'tree(s)'.

In a few words the vowel /a/ appears to have been conflated not as long /aa/ but as /au/, notably *ya-ka > yauka > yɔɔka > yooka 'eight days' and perhaps [i]ma 'now' > ?*mau > mɔɔ > moo 'already' (cf. §35), unless that is a truncation of (mo-faya <) ma-faya, namely *maw[aya]. The /aa/ > /au/ process, if it is genuine, could provide a direct transition sa > soo 'like that', and even ka(-) > koo 'like this' and sika-site > sikoo-site 'thus', instead of the usual explanation of elision in ka-[k]u and sika-[k]u with sa-u formed by analogy. Cf. yooyoo < ya[k]u-ya[k]u < ya[k]u-yaku 'eventually', said to be Heian examples of velar elision but perhaps from yaya = iyoiyo (Ōno seems to allow both derivations). Somewhat disturbing to the notion of /au/ as just an unmotivated "vowel extension" (cf. Yoshida 1976:160) is the word muika ?< muyuka < *mu-ka 'six days'. In Ch. 5 it is suggested that the

morpheme for 'day' might have been *uka, but perhaps a better explanation would be
the pleonastic incorporation of the usual shape (-)ka 'day': *ya-fi-ka > *yawika >
*yaw[i]-ka = *yaw-ka, conflated to yau-ka. The puzzling muyuka 'six days' could then
be explained as *mu-fi-ka > *muwika > *mu[w]ika > *muyka conflating or blending with
a competing *muw[u]ka to yield muyuka.

The subsyllabic nasal mora N and the subsyllabic obstruent mora T also may be a
result of expressive or mimetic factors, as in anmari⁻ 'excessive(ly)' and yappa⁻ri
'moreover, after all'. More often they are due to the elision of a vowel, usually
i or u. A preceding nasal (m- or n-) loses its distinctive place of articulation and
assimilates to the phoneme that newly follows it, producing the mora N; a preceding
stop (t- or k- or basic p-) assimilates to the articulatory point of the following
phoneme, producing the mora T. Less commonly, a vowel will elide after /r/, which
then assimilates in manner and place of articulation, becoming N before a nasal and
T before an oral obstruent (see RGJ 288n). That perhaps explains Kyōto kon-/son-/an-
dake < kore-/sore-/are-dake and .aru⁻ no ya → .an⁻no ya → .an⁻nya/.an⁻ne (Kuno
1984:92). Evidence for the reductions of -rⁱ/ᵤm- and -rⁱ/ᵤn- to -Nm- and -Nn- has
been found in the orthographic omission of the "r" syllables as early as 935 (Nakata
in Doi 1957:124). I know of no explanation for the conflation in several Chinese
loanmorphs in particular words: si⁻i-ka 'poems'; sii-zi = sii-si (JP) = si⁻-zi 'four
seasons'; sii-toku (JP) = sitoku⁻ 'consummate virtue'; sii-su⁻ru (si⁻i-su) 'slay';
hu⁻u-hu 'husband and wife'; hi⁻-roo 'revealing'; nyo⁻o-boo 'wife', nyo⁻o-go 'court
lady', nyo⁻o-in⁻ 'empress dowager'; kei-si '(house-official =) chamberlain'. (A
counter-case of compression: ho⁻o-i > ho⁻-i 'ordinary dress; commoner'.) In modern
Japanese the one-mora morphemes ka(-) and do(-) are lengthened as abbreviations of
ka-yo⁻o⁻ 'Tuesday' and do-yo⁻o⁻ 'Saturday', as in kaa-moku-doo 'Tuesday-Thursday-
Saturday', so as to make them the same number of moras as the rest of the set (niti
'Sunday', getu 'Monday', sui 'Wednesday', moku 'Thursday').

Although some of the syllables CyV (*kai-yo⁻o⁻on*) and CwV (*goo-yo⁻o⁻on*) have
come into being through contraction of native dissyllables, most examples arose with
the onslaught of Chinese borrowings. It is commonly assumed that syllables like kyo
and kwa were first borrowed into Japanese as dissyllables (kiyo and kuwa) and then
compressed, but we are probably misled by the kana orthography on this point.[39] The
Chinese syllables with CwV were less successfully implanted than those with CyV. To
begin with, they were limited to kwa and gwa and even these were not differentiated
from ka and ga in parts of Kantō (eastern Japan) and in the Chūbu area (Okayama,
Hiroshima, etc.), where kwa⁻-zi 'conflagration' was never distinguished from ka⁻-zi
'family affairs' (Shibata 1977:101). The word kwa-syo 'a kind of passport' appears
c. 739 (M 3754); written in semantograms ("pass place"), it is generally thought to
have been pronounced as [kwaso], but there is evidence that it was actually [waso]
(Kuranaka 71, Takeda 11:165). Characters with the reading notations *kwi, kwe, kwen,*
and *gwen* are found in texts but there is no evidence that the -w- was articulated in
actual loanwords. In addition to the Ryūkyūs, where the syllables kwV, gwV, hwV, and
qwV are common and come from various sources, there are only isolated parts of the
main islands where the "historic" kwa and gwa survive: Tokushima (Zhs 5:261), Kagawa
(Zhs 5:289); Ishikawa (Zhs 8:149, 173), Chiba (Zhs 2:197), ... Handy maps of the
distribution of kwa and gwa in modern dialects can be found in Hirayama 1968b:99b
and Okumura 1969:40.

A number of Heian orthographic variants lead us to deduce that at the beginning
of a word the syllable u- was sometimes reduced to N before a nasal. The usually
cited examples of (m)uma 'horse' and (m)ume 'plum' are perhaps the result of a
prothetic nasal mora that grew upon early Chinese loanwords *ma and *mey. But not
all cases of orthographic (m)u- are prothetic. In (m)ubey 'quite true' there may be

a lexicalization of the nasal grunt meaning 'uh-huh' (see Ch. 2, §4.2). And in a few
words the orthographic (m)u may well represent an original mu- even before a nasal,
though the *m- of (m)unagi 'eel' is put in doubt by the initial glottal reflex
in Nakijin qunaazi and Shuri qnnazi.

    Apparently the Chinese words ending in -m and -n (like those ending in -p, -t,
and -k) were originally supplied with a final close vowel by the Japanese borrowers,
as we can see from such early loans as zeni 'money' and sami-sen[i?] 'three-string
(banjo)'. But when the internal -N- became available that mora came to be used also
in word-final position as a way of pronouncing the Chinese words ending in -n or -m.
And a few native words reduced their final nasal syllables to N as well: the court
rank asomi became ason = /asoN/ by late Heian times. Chinese words ending in the
velar nasal -ŋ were supplied with a final high vowel, probably nasal: [ĭ] after
the syllables with Chinese front vowels, [ŭ] elsewhere. (The kana spellings have
-i, -u, or nothing.) For more on -ŋ > -i/-u see Okumura, Kgkb 19:194-206.)

    From the spellings of the Japanese-Portuguese dictionary of 1603 it is clear
that five hundred years ago those Chinese loanmorphs which today end in -tu were
usually pronounced without a final vowel: suisat = suisatu⁻ 'conjecture', also found
in Chep-hay sin-e = Shōkai-shingo (10:17r "swu.i.sat") of 1676; fimit = himitu⁻
'secret'; hatmei = hatumei⁻ 'enlightenment'; xetna [šetna] = se˥tuna 'instant';
bet-i = be˥tui 'ulterior motive'; itpit = ippitu˥ 'one brush' (Chep-hay sin-e 10:33r
"it.pit"). The Korean work also has (2:7r) kwo.nwo it.pa.i man.tye = kono ip˥-pai
made 'just this one cupful'. A few doublet forms are cited by the 1603 dictionary:
butji/butçuji [but(tsu)ži] 'Buddhist mass', matçudai/matdai [mat(su)dai] 'all the
ages to come', qiatat/qiatatçu [kyatat(su)] 'stepladder'. And those morphemes which
today end in -ti often retained the final vowel: ichimen = iti˥men⁻ 'one side',
despite fatmen = hati˥men⁻ 'eight sides'; "fatgicu, better fachigicu" = hati˥ziku
'the eight volumes of the Lotus Sūtra'; connichi or connit = ko˥nniti 'today'; ... .
Some Chinese words were borrowed in two versions, one with -ti and the other with
-t[u]; both versions are attested in the Japanese-Portuguese dictionary for the two
words bechi/bet [bet(ši)] = modern betu⁻ 'other' and xendachi/xendat [šendat(ši)]
= modern se˥ndatu 'leader'. Compare the treatment of Chinese -k, which retains the
epenthetic vowel (yacusocu = yakusoku⁻ 'a promise', teqicocu = tekikoku⁻ 'enemy
country') except that /-kuk-/ usually reduces to /-kk-/ in binoms: gaccŏ [gakkɔ:] =
gakkoo⁻ 'school' < gak(u)-kau, acqi = a˥kki 'evil spirit'< aku-k[w]i. Although there
appears to be little agreement on the matter among Japanese scholars, it is likely
that the -t pronunciations go back to the original borrowings from the Chinese,
despite the kana orthography with "-tu". If, instead, we assume that the epenthetic
vowel attached early to the Chinese final -t in the same way it did to the -k, then
we have to account for the suppression of the final vowel in the pronunciations of
the 16th and 17th century texts (and also the attestations of the Korean texts) as
but a passing phenomenon which mysteriously affected only the loanwords and not the
native vocabulary. The fact that Shinran divided the "entering-tone" (= stop) finals
into two groups 'slow' and 'quick' and wrote the latter (-t) with the same notation
he used for -n has been taken as evidence that the stop-final pronunciation goes
back at least to the early days of the Kamakura period. Komatsu 1981:199 implies
that the articulation of the final vowel in Chinese loans ending in -t did not take
place before the Edo period. The Chinese loans with the final labial followed the
pattern of native words with intervocalic -p- ("f") > -w-: pap > "fafu" > fa[w]u >
"fŏ" = /fɔɔ/ > foo > "hwo.wu" (Waye ˥yuhay = Wago-ruikai ?1700) = hoo⁻ 'law' was
like *pap-u > "fafu" > fa[w]u > "fo" = /fɔɔ/ > foo > hoo 'crawl'; the verb was
analogically restored to ha-u in modern Kyōto, but probably not before the 1700s

(cf. §36), and some Ōsaka speakers again today say hou (Makimura 1956:641b).

Reductions of /VtunV/ to /VtnV/ are found in modern dialects: matnoki < matuno-ki 'pine tree' and ketne < kitune 'fox' in peripheral Kinki dialects (Kuno 1984: 99 n.3). This is common in parts of Kyūshū and the northern Ryūkyūs, as well.

In Old Japanese, we assume, subsyllabic moras did not exist. Yet certain of the Ryūkyū dialects offer evidence that there may have been a final nasal in a few nouns of earlier Japanese, perhaps reduced from a full nV syllable.[40] There are a fair number of words in Hateruma, southernmost of the Yaeyama islands that end in a velar nasal [ŋ], which we will write just -n: nan 'name' = na⁻ and, with a different accentuation, 'rapeweed' = na¹; min or miin 'eye' = me¹ < mey; nuun 'field' = no¹ < nwo; noozïn 'rainbow' = Ishigaki noogi, Shuri nuuzi (see nizi¹⁻ in Ch. 5); minan 'snail' (Thorpe 326) = mina > nina; qman or nman (Hirayama has just nma but cf. Miyara 1930) 'horse' = uma¹; humon 'cloud' = ku¹mo < kumo¹ < kumwo; pan (Hirayama paa but cf. Miyara 1930) 'tooth' = ha¹ < fa;[41] pin 'fart' = he¹ < fe; isyon 'sand' from iso⁻ < iswo 'rock(y shore)', sïken 'moon' = tuki¹ < tukiy. The Yaeyama dialect of Kokin on Iriomote island (Nakamoto 1976:404) has /kin/ for 'hair' = ke⁻ < key. Yonaguni has tidan 'sun' = Shuri tiida; cirun 'vine' = turu¹; cinan 'sand' = suna⁻; kanin 'metal'= kane⁻; nnun < *t[u]nun 'horn' = tuno¹ < tunwo; nugan 'bran' = nuka¹; and min 'water' = mizu⁻ < midu < myidu. The last example is especially interesting. We might argue that the Yonaguni word for 'water' is a truncation of proto-Japanese *mintu, but a more exciting possibility is that the proto-Japanese form was *mina (cf. Koji-ki song 101:42-3 myina kоworo kоworo ni 'the waters churned round and round') and -tu was a separate morpheme, perhaps with the meaning *'liquid' as narrowed in tu 'spit' and possibly in ti ?< *ti[y] ?< *tu-Ci 'milk' (ti¹) and with different accent 'blood' (ti⁻). (Does tu form a doublet with yu¹ < *du 'hot water'?) That would simplify such etymologies as migiwa¹⁻ 'water's edge' < *min[a] - kipa rather than, say *mi[ntu] -n- kipa. On the other hand it is conceivable that these southern Ryūkyū dialects have somehow added the -n to a few isolated words — as perhaps, in at least some cases, just an echo of the nasal that occurs in an earlier syllable. Surely secondary is the final velar nasal of Yonaguni siban 'worry' (cf. Shuri siwa < sewa¹ 'care, trouble'), for the word is apparently a binom made up of Chinese loanmorphs that was first attested in the 15th-century dictionary Kagaku-shū. The Hateruma form pïn 'day' may be a truncation, to judge from these forms found in other Yaeyama dialects: pinucï (Taketomi), pinici (Kurojima and Sonai), pinicu (Ōhama). We could take the two final syllables to be the Chinese loanmorph niti 'day', but notice that Sonai (Yaeyama) also has minci 'eye' (Hateruma min) which could not be so explained. The Hateruma word sipusin (supusin according to Hirayama) 'knees' comes from tubusi < tubu-[fu]si 'anklebone', carried by the 1603 Japanese-Portuguese dictionary as tu(bu)busi; cf. Kobama island (Yaeyama) cubusun, Shodon (Amami) tibuusyi/tibusy, Shuri cinsi, Ikema (Miyako) cigusi. Hateruma nubusin 'neck' is nubui in Ikema (Miyako) and nibui in Nakasuji or Tarama (Miyako); other places in the Ryūkyūs the etymon appears as nubi, and that word means 'throat' in Shodon. Hateruma paton 'pigeon' shows up as patuna in Sonai on Iriomote (Yaeyama), suggesting that the -n is a reduction from -na. At least some of our examples, such as 'pigeon', may be the result of retaining the old derivative suffix -ne/-na or of applying it in new formations. Yonaguni cinan 'sand' could be from sunago < sunagwo < *suna -n- kwo by truncation. A few of the words may be retaining the old nasal onset of a dakuon syllable (< -nC-): pan 'foot' = pagi < *panki; sïn 'spit' = tuba < *tunpa[ki] (not just tu). Compare hun 'nail' = kugi⁻ < *kunki; mun 'barley' = mu¹gi < *munki; qon 'fan' = oogi¹ < ɔ ɔgi < a[f]ugi < *apunki; qunan 'eel' = unagi⁻; kangan 'mirror' = kagami¹; sin- 'pour' = tug-⁻ < *tunk-; sïna 'sun' = tida (Shuri

tiida) ?< *tinta; pinari 'left' = hidari⁻ < *pintari and sunat- 'raise' = soda˥t- <
*sontat- ⁴². Hateruma putugin 'Buddha' = hotoke˥⁻ < fot<u>o</u>key must be secondary.

We have observed that Chinese -m and -n were taken into Japanese as -m^i/$_u$ and
-n^i/$_u$ but the epenthetic vowel came to be elided. It is thought that -m and -n were
kept distinct in pronunciation for a while, but eventually they fell together as -N,
apparently by the end of the Heian period. A remark that was written in the early
1100s indicates that -m and -n were generally distinguished at that time "except by
the easterners" (Okumura 1977:232). There are attestations of confusion of -m and -n
that are dated 1195; the two finals were, however, differentiated in Hōjō-ki of 1216
(though the particle namu and the presumptive -mu were written as -n) and Hōbutu-shū
of 1221 (but -n was left unwritten in non-Chinese words). But the nasal finals were
confused in Kokin mokuroku-shō of 1238. (Cf. KggD 972b, 973b, 974a, 975a.)

Traces of -m survived into modern times in the words sa˥nmi < sam-wi 'trinity'
(the same string of Chinese etyma also yield sa˥n-i 'third position') and onmyo˥o-
doo = on'yo˥o-doo⁻ 'the way of Yin and Yang (divination)' from onmyoo < om-yau < om-
yaũ = i˥n'yoo 'Yin and Yang' (JP "vonyo" = won-yɔɔ represents a separate strain of
development). This is the result of medial gemination of -m, -n, and rarely -t,
called renzyoo⁻ 'sequential initial' (Martin 1952:84); the technical term originated
with students of Sanskrit and until modern times it referred to any morphophonemic
adjustments at syllable boundaries. The first attestation is an example in Wamyō-shō
(934): sinmi-^{s}/$_z$oo (also si[n]mi-soo) < sinmi-saũ < sim-i[n]-saũ 'herpes blisters'.
The noun kannoo⁻ 'response' < kan-oũ 'response' was spelled kannou in a text dated
1185 (KggD 972a). The phenomenon became quite common in Middle Japanese and it was
probably an obligatory rule for the colloquial pronunciation of Muromachi times —
the dictionary Setsuyō-shū (= Setuyo˥o-syuu), compiled at the end of the sixteenth
century, was called Setchō-shū (= Settyo˥o-syuu). But since the 1600s the rule has
subsided in the standard language, leaving behind only a few lexical relics such as
these: kannon⁻ < kwan-on 'Kuan Yin, Avalokiteśvara', hannoo⁻ < fan-oũ 'reaction,
response', ginna˥n < gin-an 'ginkgo nut', unnun⁻ < un-un 'and so on', innen⁻ < in-
[y]en 'causality', ri˥nne < rin-we 'transmigration of the soul', tenno˥o < ten-waũ
'emperor', ...⁴³ There are two words with the geminated -t: se˥ttin < set[u]-in,
an obsolescent word for 'toilet', and kuttaku⁻ < kut[u]-waku 'worry, care; ennui',
which the orthography has reanalyzed by replacing waku with a character read taku.
The Korean glossary of Japanese Waye ˥yuhay = Wago-ruikai (?1700⁻) has an example of
the geminated -n: man.nici = ma˥n'iti 'perchance' (1:27v). A similar phenomenon can
be seen in the compensatory gemination that accompanies the syncope of the high
vowel of -C^i/$_u$yV- as in the pronunciation tossyori for tosiyori 'old person' and
(Kyōto) dossyaro for dosu yaro (= desu daro) = desyoo 'must be'.

In Chinese words attempts were made to write the final -n with katakana "i" or
"ni", though these were also used in the regular way; often the mora was just left
unwritten, as was -T. Kana "mu" was eventually used to write the merged N but it was
gradually displaced by a special symbol: the katakana version is probably a variant
of "ni", the hiragana version is a reduction of the phonogram mu 'not'. Competing
with these symbols to write N during the Heian period were a number of other signs
such as V and > and |/ (like katakana "re"), etc. (See Tsukishima 1977:10, 48, 50.)
Although -T was occasionally written with kana "tu" from the end of the eleventh
century, it was usually left unmarked and must be inferred; the regular use of "tu"
came in during the Muromachi period (id. 9), and it became common only quite late to
reduce the size ("ₜᵤ") from that used to write the syllable /tu/ itself.⁴⁴
Shinran's Kyōkō-shinshō (1234) wrote -T "tu" after /u/, otherwise "ti" (KggD 974b).

Chart 1. The Syllables of Tōkyō Japanese

Italicized syllables appear in recent loans and marginal words; most are innovations
not used by all speakers. Parenthesized syllables are also heard in variant versions
(Fu) also as hu; and (hya hyu hyo hi) also as ša šo šu ši but the latter two groups
are etymologically distinct and kept apart in standard speech.

a	wa	ma	na	ra	ta	*tsa*	da	ᵈza	sa	ka	ga	ḡa	ha	*Fa*	pa	ba	*Va*
ya		mya	nya	rya	tša			ᵈža	ša	kya	gya	ḡya	(hya)		pya	bya	
u		mu	nu	ru	tsɨ			ᵈzɨ	sɨ	ku	gu	ḡu	hu	(Fu)	pu	bu	*Vu*
yu		myu	nyu	ryu	tšu			ᵈžu	šu	kyu	gyu	ḡyu	(hyu)		pyu	byu	
o	*wo*	mo	no	ro	to	*tso*	do	ᵈzo	so	ko	go	ḡo	ho	*Fo*	po	bo	*Vo*
yo		myo	nyo	ryo	tšo			ᵈžo	šo	kyo	gyo	ḡyo	(hyo)		pyo	byo	
e	*we*	me	ne	re	te	*tse*	de	ᵈze	se	ke	ge	ḡe	he	*Fe*	pe	be	*Ve*
	ye				tše			ᵈže	še								
	wi				ti		di							*Fi*			*Vi*
i		mi	ni	ri	tši			ᵈži	ši	ki	gi	ḡi	(hi)		pi	bi	

Heavy (two-mora) syllables:

  One-mora syllable + T followed by t(s/š) s š k p and for some also d ᵈz ᵈž g b.

  One-mora syllable + N.

  One-mora syllable + vowel extension: aa   ai
                                           uu   ɨɨ   ui   ɨi
                                           oo   ʔoi
                                           ee   (ei)
                                           ii

Syllables with unvoiced vowels:

  A high vowel (i u) of a one-mora syllable with initial voiceless consonant
  (t ts tš s š k h p) is unvoiced (1) when followed by a syllable that begins
  with a voiceless consonant; (2) before juncture, provided there is a basic
  accent within the word and the preceding syllable has a voiced vowel. The
  rules are sometimes overridden by morpholexical boundaries and other factors.

  (1) kᵢkuˀ, tšᵢkaraˀ, gešu̞ku, hᵢtoˀri, kᵢTpuˀ, pᵢkaˀ-pᵢka, pᵢ/Ttaˀri, šᵢTkaˀri,
      enpᵢtsi⁻, baˀku̞hu, tšiˀšᵢki, isɨ toˀ but isɨ⁻;

  (2) aˀkᵢ, aˀraši, kaˀrasɨ, arimaˀsɨ, soˀo desɨ and soˀo desɨ ka but soˀo desɨ ḡa.

Some speakers unvoice the vowel of ka or ko when the syllable is repeated at the
beginning of a word (ka̞kaˀnai, ko̞koˀro) and some unvoice the vowel of ha or ho
when it is followed by k or s (ha̞kaˀ, ho̞kori⁻, ho̞soˀi).

Note: Not included in the chart of syllables are attempts to pronounce kana
        spellings that seek to capture the English syllables in such words as
        'two' and 'do', for these are normally converted to the usual values
        of Japanese "tu" and "zu". NHK gives [t]uˀudaˀun for the baseball
        term 'two-down' but other sources (such as NKD) have [ts]uˀudan.

Chart 2. Periods discussed by Japanese grammarians

zyo˺odai	Old Japanese	Na˺ra period	c. 700-800
tyu˺uko	Early Middle Japanese	Heian⁻ period	
tyu˺usei	Late Middle Japanese	Kamakura˺⁻ period 1200-1378 Muro˺mati⁻ period 1367-1573 }	1200-1600
ki˺nsei	Modern Japanese	Edo⁻ (= Toku˺gawa) period	1603-1867
ge˺ndai	Contemporary Japanese	Me˺izi 1867-1912 Taisyoo⁻ 1912-1925 } Syo˺owa⁻ 1925-	1867-

For phonological history Nakata divides the Heian period into four:

early Heian	795-859
mid Heian	859-947
late mid Heian	947-999
late Heian	999-1192

The period 1086-1192 is often referred to as the Insei⁻ period.

Yamada included Muromachi (= Muro˺mati) in ki˺nsei 'modern', and contrasted that with ko˺dai 'ancient'; others would divide the Muromachi period into earlier and later halves, so as to put the dividing line for 'modern' in the middle of the period, c. 1450. (Cf. Sakakura, Kōza Kokugo-shi 1:200-1.) The term zyoodai-go⁻ refers to Old Japanese (Nara period); the term kodai-go⁻ refers to Early Middle Japanese = "classical" Japanese of the Heian period. The term ko˺go is variously taken as pre-modern or pre-contemporary and often it can be translated as "older (Japanese)" or, in reference to a vocabulary item, "obsolete" or "archaism".

Chart 3. Chronology of data sources for earlier Japanese.

600	622-70, 672-710 Man'yō-shū I, II
700	?700 Jōgū-Shōtoku - hōō - te/aisetsu
	702 Koseki-chō *(census records)*
	711-33 Man'yō-shū III
	712 Koji-ki (= Ki *SPEECH radical*)
	714 Harima-fudoki
	720 Nihon-Shoki (= Nihon-gi = Ki *THREAD radical*)
	721 Hitachi-fudoki
	733 Izumo-fudoki
	733-59 Man'yō-shū IV
750	752 Bussokuseki-no-uta
	772 Kakyō-hyōshiki
	789-92 Takahashi-no-ujibumi
	794 [Sin'yaku] Kegon[-kyō] ongi shiki
	797 Shoku-Nihongi
800	807 Kogo-shūi
	822 [Nihon] Ryōi-ki
	?824- [Tōdai-ji] Fuju-monkō
	830 Konkōmyō-saishōō-kyō
	840 Nihon-Kōki
	841 Shoku Nihon-Kōki (songs)
850	858 Saitō-ki (Ennin's diary)
	859 Taketori-monogatari
	860- Ryō no shūge
	880 Shittan-zō (Annen)
	892 [Shinsen-]Jikyō
	893 Shinsen-Man'yōshū
900	900 Ise-monogatari
	905 Kokin-shū
	923 Honzō-wamyō
	927 Engi-shiki: Naizen-shiki
	934 Wamyō-[ruiju-]shō (Minamoto Shitarō)
	935 Tosa-nikki
	940 Utsubo-monogatari
	940 Shōmon-ki = Masakado-ki *(copied 1099)*
950	951 Kōsen-shū = Masakado-ki *(copied 1099)*
	960 Kagerō-nikki
	970 Ochitsubo-monogatari
	981 Kinka-fu
1000	1000 Makura-no sōshi
	1002 Genji-monogatari
	1010 Murasaki-Shikibu-nikki
1050	1059 Sarashina-nikki
	1079 Konkōmyō-saishōō-kyō ongi (= "Ongi")*
	1081 [Ruiju -] Myōgi-shō *(compiled, see Ch. 4)*
	1093 Han'on-Sahō (Meikaku/Myō^k/$_g$aku)
1100	1106 Konjaku-monogatari
1100	1107 Shittan-yōketsu (Meikaku/Myō^k/$_g$aku)
	1111+ Uchigiki-shū
	1135+ Daihannya-kyō ongi
	1136 Hoke-kyō tanji *(copy)*
1150	1180 Iroha-jirui-shō
	1181 Shittan-kuden (Shinren)

1200	1200 Sangō-shii-ki-chū = Sankyō-shi-ki-chū
	1204+ Gekan-shū (Fujiwara Sadaie/Teika)
	1205 Shin Kokinka-shū
	1212 Hōjō-ki (Kamo Chōmei)
	1216 [Shiza -] Kōshiki
	1218 Uji-shūi-monogatari
	1219 Heike-monogatari
1250	1251 Hèlín yùlù = Kakurin-gyokuro (Luó Dàjīng)
	1268 Myōgo-ki
1300	1305 [Kokin [-waka-shū]] Kunten-shō
	1330 Tsurezure-gusa
1350	1363+ Kanamoji-zukai = Gyōa/Teika kanazukai
	1365-70 Hoke-kyō ongi (Shinkū)
	1371 Taihei-ki
	1376 Shūshǐ hùiyào = Shoshi-kaiyō (Táo Zōngyí)
	1381 Sengen-shō *(Genji glossary)*
1400	1444 Kagaku-shū *(thesaurus)*
1450	1474 Setsuyō-shū = Setchō-shū
	1477 Shiki-shō
	1492 Ilopha = Irofa = [Kōji go-nen Chōsen-ban] Iroha
1500	1501 Haytong ceykwuk ki (= Kaitō-shokoku-ki) (Sin Swukcwu)
	1532 Omoro-sōshi 1 *(cf. 1613, 1633)*
	1549- Rìběn Guān-yuèyǔ (= Nihon Kan-yakugo), part of 13-volume Huá-yí yuèyǔ (= Ka-i yakugo)
	1593 Feiqe no monogatari; Esopo no fabulas
1600	1603-4 Vocabulario da lingoa de Iapam (JP dictionary)
	1608 Rodriguez: Arte da lingoa de Iapam
	1613 Omoro-sōshi 2 *(cf. 1532, 1633)*
	1632 Collado: Ars grammaticae linguae Iaponiae
	1633 Omoro-sōshi 3-22 *(cf. 1532, 1613)*
	1636- Ongyoku-gyokuenshū *(cf. 1727; Yasuda 1980:148)*
1650	1650 Katakoto (Yasuhara Teishitsu)
	1672 Chep-hay sin-e (= Shōkai-shingo)
	1687 Bunō-ki *(see Ch. 4)*
	1695 Waji-shōran-shō (Keichū)
1700	?1700 Waye ^{1}yuhay (= Wago-ruikai) *(cf. Yasuda 1980:150)*
	1711 Konkōken-shū *(Okinawan dictionary)*
	1712 Wa-kan sanzai zue (Terajima Yoshiyasu)
	?1727 Ongoku-gyokuenshū (Miura Tsuguyasu) *(cf. 1636)*
	1738 Arte de la lengua Japona (Oyanguren)
1750	?1750- ^{1}In.e taypang (= Ringo-taihō) *(textbook of Korean)*
	1777 Wakun-shiori
	1790-8 Kojiki-den (Motoori Norinaga)
	1798 Kanazukai oku-no-yamamichi (Ishizuka Tatsumaro)
1800	1801 Kogen-seidaku kō (Ishizuka Tatsumaro)
	1802 [Tōkaidō-chū] Hizakurige (Jippensha Ikkyō)
	1806 Honzō-kōmoku-keimō (Ono Ranzan) *(dialect glossary)*
	1809 Ukiyo-buro
1850	1867 J.C. Hepburn: A Japanese and English Dictionary
	1869 W.G. Aston: A Short Grammar of the J. Spoken Language
	1872 W.G. Aston: A Grammar of the J. Written Language
	1888 B.H. Chamberlain: A Handbook of Colloquial Japanese
	1889-91 Genkai (Ōtsuki Fumihiko) *(4-vol. dictionary)*
	1895 B.H. Chamberlain: Essay in Aid of a Grammar and Dictionary of the Luchuan Language

*Tsukishima 1971:17 misanalyzes 'Konkōmyō-saishō-ōkyō-ongi'.

Chart 4. Relative chronology of phonetic developments
The broken lines and dots indicate less evidence or more counter-evidence.

	700	750	800	850	900	950	1000	1050	1100	1150	1200	1500

```
                700      750    800    850     900     950  1000 1050 1100 1150 1200    1500

kiy ≠ kyi     ———————————————————————————————···········
key ≠ kye     ——————————————————————————·········
fiy ≠ fyi     ————————————————————————······
fey ≠ fye     ———————————————————————·········
two ≠ to      —————————————————·········
kwo ≠ ko      ———————————————————————————····················
mwo ≠ mo      —————————···············
o ≠ wo¹       ———————————————————————————————————————— — — — — — — — — — ··
e ≠ ye²       —————————————————————————————————————————————————————·····
e ≠ we        —————————————————————————————————————————————————————————————····
i ≠ wi        —————————————————————————————————————————————————————————————····
-fa ≠ -wa     ————————————————————————————————————————————————————————————————
-fo ≠ -wo     —————————————————————————————————————————·········
-fe ≠ -we
-fi ≠ -wi  }  ——————————————————————————————————————————————————————————····
-fu ≠ -u
-we ≠ -ye³ }  ——————————————————————————————————————————————————————————····
-wi ≠ -i   }
kwa ≠ ka                                          ————————————————————————————————————————————————
? kwi ≠ ki }                          ——————————————————————————————————————————————····
? kwe ≠ ke }
/-T/, /-N/                  — — ——————————————————————————————————————————————————————————
-[k]i                          —————————————————————————————————————————————————————————————
-[k]u                              —————————————————————————————————————————
b- d- g- z- }
r-          } ( — — — —) ——————————————————————————————————————————————————
tu › tsu  }                                                                                ———
ti › tši  }
```

¹ Orthographic variants appear to indicate that /o/ and /wo/ fell together as [wo], and that is what is attested by the 1603 JP dictionary; the delabialized [o] of today probably developed in the 1700s. The earliest example of kana "o" used for "wo" is dated 883 (Tsukishima 1977:19). Later the two kana symbols were used by some writers to indicate pitch differences, as explained in Ch. 4 (cf. Tsukishima 1977:20). Even today the version with labial semivowel is occasionally heard after the nasal mora -N; also in reading pronunciations of the accusative particle wo, which is the only word still spelled with kana "wo" in the official orthography.

² It is usually assumed that /e/ and /ye/ merged as [ye] and that is the form attested by the 1603 JP dictionary. The dispalatalized [e] of modern standard Japanese had developed by 1775 (Nakata in Doi 1957:136), though it may have been in existence earlier, at least in eastern Japan. But since even the eastern dialects have yow- ‹ [w]ew- 'get intoxicated', probably the earlier versions of the merged syllable pairs in those dialects were also [ye] and [wo]. It seems more natural to assume that we › e at some point before e › ye, even if the transition period were short (i.e. the labial onset was lost and then the palatal glide developed), though attestations indicate we › ye directly. At that time the "Ce" syllables all probably were palatal [Cye] like the "Ci" syllables. The version with the palatal onglide [ye] is still found in Kyūshū and other places; after the mora -N the palatal onglide is sometimes heard even in Tōkyō speech, as in seN-[y]eN̄ '¥1,000'. Those speakers with initial ye- also often have sye- [še] for se. The JP dictionary wrote "xe" [še] for what is modern /se/, "ie" = "je" for modern /ze/, "ye" for modern /e/. But Rodriguez noted the pronunciations [se] and [ze] in the east at the time (Komatsu 1981:314).

³ An early pun of tayezu 'not end' with tafezu › ta[w]ezu › tayezu 'not endure' is attested in 923 (KggD 961b).

Notes to Chapter 1.

¹ It might be argued that the Hokekyō-tanji accent notation (of 1136) ˙so˙ro‥fu for the verbs sorou and soroeru represents s̲o̲r̲o̲bu, a rather late remnant of an earlier [-b-] version of the intervocalic labial (the ancestor of modern -b- was perhaps still prenasalized -nb- at the time), but the accent pattern is surprising to begin with, since dialect comparison would lead us to expect *s̲o̲r̲o̲[f]u.

² For proto-Ryūkyūan Thorpe 61 reconstructs *UQpo- 'much', *koQpa-/*kowa- 'hard', *yaQpara-/*yawara- 'soft', etc., and suggests that some cases of -w- come from *-p- with the -Q- as perhaps an expressive infix.

³ The modern language treats nezi⌐r-u 'twist' and ke⌐r-u 'kick' as consonant stems, but earlier they were vowel stems nezi- and ke-, as witnessed by compound verbs still in use: nezi-komu 'screw in', ke-tobasu 'kick away'. Just the opposite switch is shown by modern standard kari-ru ← kar-u 'borrow' and tari-ru ← tar-u 'suffice'. Kamei 1969:13-4 suggests that a confusion of forms of 'borrow' with those of 'buy' may have been responsible for the shift of 'borrow'. In western Japan katta means 'borrowed' and koota 'bought', but in eastern Japan 'bought' is katta and 'borrowed' is, in modern times, karita.

⁴ This is a Kansai version, attested in print from the second half of the Edo period. It is conceivable that ya⌐ might derive from [n]i a[r]- rather than de a[r]- ← n[i]te a[r]-; on elision of the initial nasal ···[n]i in Kansai dialects, see RGJ 49, 406, 742. The Okinawan copula yan ⟨ ya a- probably has a different origin; see RGJ 88.

⁵ Adnominal use of zya is attested from 1643 in expressions with -zya-mono and -zya-hito/-bito 'the person who is ··· '.

⁶ The final vowel was mistranscribed as "u". For the correct vowel, see Miyara 1930:213b.

⁷ Use of Hankul so (probably pronounced something like [sə] at the time) provides evidence that the Okinawan change of su ⟩ *sɨ ⟩ şi (later merging with si [ši]) had taken place by the early 1800s.

⁸ Assuming that the Chinese jí 'rush' was pronounced with an affricate at the time, this attestation indicates that the Okinawan change of -gi ⟩ -zi (= [dži]) had probably taken place by 1600.

⁹ The Hankul attestation may provide a hint that the Okinawan change -bVr- ⟩ -nd- (as in abura ⟩ qanda 'oil') was paralleled by a change -rVb- ⟩ -nd-, probably to be dated before 1700. The Korean vowel (puy instead of pi) suggests a Ryūkyū [ɨ] or [ï] on the way from /e/ to /i/.

¹⁰ With an ocasional exception: ngkwo.sa.i.mpan.wo.mwot.tyey (8:23r) = go-sa⌐i-ban [w]o mo⌐tte 'by adjudication'; kwon.mpan (10:22r) = ko⌐n-ban 'tonight'; sa.kwu.mpan (1:30r, 10:1r, 10:3r) = saku⌐-ban 'last night'; syem.mpan (10:9r) = sen-ba⌐n 'a thousand myriads'; tyey.i.sywu.mpwu.li (9:7r) = tei-syu - buri⁻ 'like a tavern-keeper'. And the revised edition of 1781 provides other examples: sa.nta.myey.tyey (1:12v) = sada⌐mete 'definitely'; cf. the first edition san.ta.myey.tyey (1:12r).

¹¹ The unusual spellings phi.phpan (5:28r) and pi.pphan (4:20v), for which the revised edition of 1781 has hi.pan, represent some version of the word hi⌐han⁻ ⟨ fi-fan 'criticism'; Hamada thinks there was confusion with piphan, the Korean version of this Chinese binom. The totally aberrant initial spelling in pphyywo.wu.cywu.wu (3:34) = byou-tyuu (= byo⌐o-tyuu⁻) 'the midst of illness' must be a graphic mistake for "mp-" (cf. Hamada 1970:107).

¹² The expansion of -g̃- to -ng̃- [-ŋːŋ-] could be regarded as an example of what I have elsewhere called CONFLATION, rather than a retention of an earlier /n/, but few of the instances of -n- before the other consonants could be thought of that way; two examples are tanbi = tabi < [tǎbi] 'time, occasion' and tonbi = tobi < [tǒbi] 'kite *(bird)*'. The -n- allomorph of the intensive infix (-T/N-) must be treated differently, for it occurs also before ···y··· (bon'ya⁷ri, hin'ya⁷ri) and ···w··· (yanwa⁷ri, hu⁷nwaka), as well as before voiced obstruents.

¹³ And the expected -ŋi from -gi is replaced by -di (nidi < nigi = migi 'right', kudi [older] < kugi [now used by younger speakers] 'nail') but [usaᴺgi] for 'rabbit' with conflicting versions in Nakamoto 1976: -g- (199), -ᵐg- (419). Cf. Ch. 2, §1.2.

¹⁴ In a practical orthography for Yonaguni I would suggest writing the initial tense consonants as geminates pp- tt- cc- kk- and the medial cases, which are automatic, with simple -p- -t- -c- -k-. There is, however, no contrast between tense cc- and aspirated c-, for the affricate is always tense, so we simplify the orthography to c-. Similar remarks apply to Nakijin, but there are a few marginal contrasts of aspirated affricate, so we will follow Nakasone's overdifferentiated notation and distinguish each unaspirated Nakijin stop in all environments (see Ch. 4, §16, n. 2).

¹⁵ According to Komatsu 1981:94 the first syllable of do⁷re 'which one', do⁷no 'which ··· ', and do⁷nna 'what sort of ··· ' is the result of analogy with do⁷ko; and tare 'who' was attracted by this group of words, voicing its initial to da⁷re, a form apparently not attested before the 1800s. Shibata 1977:107 wonders whether early spellings with ¹/ₐd- and ¹/ₐb- may have represented nasality [-d-] and [-b-], noting the pronunciation [ndaku] 'embrace' on the Shimabara peninsula of Nagasaki prefecture. The verb uba⁷u 'seize by force' is spelled ubafu, mubafu, and just bafu in the 11th-century Myōgi-shō; the Japanese-Portuguese dictionary of 1603 cites the infinitive as both ubai and bai, and the version with b- survives in modern dialects, including that of Shuri.

¹⁶ Ōno Susumu suggested that the original Chinese sound of the phonograms used in the Nihon-Shoki songs for the *o⁷tu*-type syllable "so" (= so̲) indicates that the pronunciation was [tso]. Ōno Tōru (1957:132) says the same logic would lead to the conclusion that the *ko⁷o*-type, which we will write below as swo, was [so] and he finds that unlikely. But if the *ko⁷o*-type was indeed /swo/ that would fit in with Ōno Tōru's notion that from an original [ts-] the fricative version [s-] happened first with -i and then -u (the high vowels); when it happened with -u it may well have happened also with -wo but not with -o̲, which perhaps was articulated in a more central position and with less rounding. (See n.18.)

¹⁷ Cf. Kamei Takashi (1975:10): "I imagine that originally Japanese had three phonemes /t/, /ts/, and /s/ which contrasted with one another, and the phoneme /s/ disappeared without any trace left in the writing." Ibuki-jima has an affricate initial in tiso for standard siso 'perilla' (Uwano 1985:127).

¹⁸ The difference between the *ko⁷o*-type and the *o⁷tu*-type vowels in our notations Cwo ≠ Co̲, Cye ≠ Cey, Cyi ≠ Ciy is elucidated in subsequent sections.

¹⁹ According to Ōshima (Shin Nihongo-kōza 3:92) in Chiba the elision of -k- takes place in the environments a/o/u···i/e/u (between a back vowel and a front or high vowel), yielding such forms as ka⁷[k]u, o[k]u⁻, de[k]i⁷ru, o[k]i⁷ru. From what he observes (93, 114), there seems to be an intermediate lenition of -k- to -h- in parts of Chiba and in Izu-Ōshima; this phenomenon is familiar in several dialects of the Ryūkyūs.

[20] Some dialects insert a -y-: bayai < ba-ai 'situation'. This is a back-formation
← bayee (with epenthetic palatal glide) < ba-ee < ba-εε < ba-ai (< ...). In the
case of kiya for kiwa 'brink', attested 1216 (KggD 973b) and that of kiyamari for
kiwamari 'extreme', attested 1277 (id. 977b), the glide -y- can be regarded as an
extension of the palatal quality of the preceding vowel. Similar: kiyamete for
kiwamete 'extremely', attested 1477 (Iwanami Kōza-Nihongo 5:278). With kowe > ?ko[w]
> koye (spelled "coye" by the Portuguese) 'voice' there occurs the usual development
of the syllable we > ye for which we infer an intermediate stage [e] that is not
attested (see Chart 4, n.2); cf. "couairo" = kowa-iro 'tone of voice'.

[21] The historical spelling often uses -(y)i- instead of -fi-; for the verb 'enter'
Kindaichi Kyōsuke lists both "fa(y)iru" and "fafiru" in Jikai. Since the stem is
reduced from the compound verb fafi-(y)ir-, either spelling is well motivated.

[22] Wamyō-shō spells tukuwe but there is an early-Heian example of tukuye; see
Ōno 851c and the entry tukue in Ch. 5.

[23] Uwano 1976b offers Narada examples: koo 'buy', moo 'dance'; hoo 'crawl', koo
'raise (animals)', oo 'meet', noo 'braid'. But polysyllabic stems in Narada retain
/au/: arau 'wash', morau 'receive', utau 'sing', warau 'laugh', ... ; tikau 'pledge',
ubau 'seize by force', ...

[24] The usual Tōkyō accentuation of ooˀi < o[f]o-[k]i may be said to support this,
though there are people who say oˀoi; cf. RGJ 17 n.3. The notion of lenition of [F]
to a subminimal phoneme of juncture (the medial occurrence of Hattori's Apostrophe),
is similar to what Kim Chin-wu (Kim Cinwu) and Toh Soo-hee (To Swuhuy) have proposed
to account for boundaries in Middle Korean that are orthographically retained long
after the apparent elision of a velar or labial consonant. I have maintained that
the Korean orthographic device wrote a real phoneme, a voiced fricative (either
velar or laryngeal) that neutralized the velar and labial stops that were lenited
but remained part of the consonant system at least through the 16th century.

[25] The junctured version is [mizɨuˀmi] /mizuˀuˀmi/; with dropped juncture this
would be [mizɨˀ:mi] /mizuˀumi/ but it is uncertain whether this version actually
occurs in Tōkyō, though it is reported for older speakers in Hakata.

[26] But aoˀgu 'fan' < "awogu" = awogu < afugu, aoi¯ 'hollyhock' < "auoi" = awoi <
*auwi < afufi, and taoˀre¯ 'collapse' < "tauore" = tawore < tafore escaped the
crasis and monophthongization that took place sometime before the late 1500s (cf.
Komatsu 1981:293).

[27] The dialect form bayai is a back-formation. See n.20.

[28] In Old Japanese the form ending in /a/, which is to be regarded as the basic
shape, sometimes appears also as the second member of a compound or by itself.
Cf. Matsumoto 1974:94.

[29] But 'bell' is probably just a semantic extension of 'metal'. Cf. suˀzu < suzu¯
'tin' and suzu¯ 'jingle-bell'.

[30] But Shibata believes it was lower [ɔ]; see Shibata and Mitsuishi 1979. In our
subsequent notations we use Cwo for Type One (koˀo-rui), Co̲ for Type Two (otu ˀ-rui),
and Co for those cases that are unknown, neutralized or later (merged) versions.
Shibata was apparently unaware of the fact that his view of the phonetic character
of these Old Japanese vowels coincided with that of Yoshitake 1929 (the conclusions
were reached on different grounds). Perhaps that is not surprising in view of the
fact that the name Yoshitake has been been totally (deliberately?) ignored by the
Japanese academic community, for reasons that I hope some sociologist or academic
historian will someday elucidate. Even such a devoted researcher as R.A. Miller was
unable to confirm that the given name is (as I have put it) Saburō. In any event,
fond though I am of my friend Shibata and the unknowable Yoshitake (and the amicable
Miller, for that matter), I am reluctant to embrace this view of the vowels.

[31] We would like to claim that the literary adverb e˺(-) 'can(not ⋯)' is from yo˺[ku] 'well', the adjective infinitive which (with velar elision only) became the Kansai yo[k]u ⟩ yoo and is used in the modern Kansai yoo V-an 'can't very well V', but there is a problem. Fujiwara Tameie's extant version of the Tosa-nikki, which scrupulously preserves the kana of 935, distinguishes this e(-) from the ye- of words like yeda 'branch' (Ōno 1977:163). Man'yō-shū examples use phonograms for "ey", which supports identifying the adverb with the infinitive 'get'.

[32] The Shodon words are cited in basic form, the shape that appears before the particle m ⟨ mo; in most environments a conflated or compressed alternant is heard. The notation follows Martin 1970b except that the accent has been omitted. Aspirated consonants are written Ch-, and q- represents the glottal stop.

[33] The C represents an elided consonant, probably -y- ⟨ -ɣ- ⟨ -g-, which we posit on the basis of the structure of syllable and syllable string. Other linguists may be happier with just ⋯ui and ⋯o̲i; if so, they are invited to ignore the C, the arguments for which will be given elsewhere.

[34] We would expect quthi, and Uemura gives the apirated version; Martin 1970b may be mistaken on the aspiration. The En dialect of Tatsugō-chō, in northern Amami-Ōshima, has the aspirated version (Ryūkyū-hōgen 14:39).

[35] Cf. Hattori 1968, repr. Hokama 1972:60; Shibata 1981. The parenthesized h in the Shodon citations represents divergences between Hattori's observations and my notes on the same dialect (Hattori's versions have the aspiration).

[36] Mabuchi (1976:13-4) points out that when (')e and (')ye fell together the merged version was [ye] and the merged version of (')o and (')wo was [wo]; he thinks this indicates that -ye and -wo were the "proper" phonetics (the norm) for the -e and -o rows of the syllabary.

[37] A third argument can be adduced in favor of Starostin's theory: the particle ⋯ safe 'even' is thought to derive from swofey 'adding', so that if our "swo" were [swa] it would simply be a matter of dropping the semivowel. Shibata believes that the Ryūkyū vowel raisings favor treating Cwo as [-ɔ]; see n.30.

[38] Unger further analyzes this as from to-ma- with another formant -ma-.

[39] If so, we will have to explain the old Shizukuishi [miyágu] 'pulse' (Uwano 1982-3:16) as a later conflation of myaku, rather than myaku as a compression of an earlier miyaku. Perhaps there was a lot of variation, with both compressed and conflated forms as the unusual Chinese shapes came into the language at different periods.

[40] Ryūkyū paradigmatic forms suggest that the first-person pronoun wa ⟨ *ba may have been *ban (or even *banu): Shodon wan 'I' or 'me'. wanu m 'also/even I'; but waa ga 'I (as subject)', waa mun 'mine', waa-khya 'we'. Welcome news though this may be for Altaicists (cf. Turkish ben 'I'), it should be noted that the Ryūkyū forms could also be explained as the result of incorporating the genitive-nominative marker n[u] ⟨ n̲o, a development which is not implausible but for which I find no immediately supporting evidence. though the hypothesis could perhaps serve also as an explanation for the anomalous final nasal found in certain nouns (discussed immediately below).

[41] Ainu hǎm 'leaf' might be a borrowing from a similar shape in some Japanese dialect, but the only nasal-final form attested in Japanese dialects is for 'tooth' and not 'leaf' — both OJ fa ⟨ *pa but with different accentuations.

[42] These two continue the initial voicelessness through the vowel and the nasal.

[43] Yet in the new word tyuunna˺ppu '(car engine) tune-up' renzyoo still lives.

[44] Myōgi-shō used the "entering-tone" mark (a dot in the lower-right corner or slightly higher) to indicate the -T in the two verbs uttafu(ru)/uttafey 'sue; appeal; complain of' and nottoru 'conform to; model after'; see Chapter 4.

Chapter 2. Voicing distinctions.

0. The sei-daku contrast.

All modern dialects of Japanese make use of a phonemic opposition traditionally called SEI vs. DAKU. These terms come from the traditional philology of China, where the ancestor of the word SEI 'clear' had a voiceless unaspirated initial and that of DAKU 'muddy' had a voiced aspirated initial (some believe it was merely voiced and not aspirated), so that the words were chosen as technical terms for iconic as well as impressionistic reasons. For Japanese the opposition is usually, but somewhat inaccurately, translated as "voiceless vs. voiced". For the phonetics of certain dialects, such as that of Hiroshima, the usual translation is accurate enough if we bear in mind that DAKU does not refer to all voiced initials but only to those for which there is a contrasting SEI. For the phonetics of other dialects, in various ways, the English terms are misleading. When we take into account all varieties of Japanese, there is a confusing overlap of phonetic manifestations for SEI and DAKU, for some of the traditional SEI sounds have voiced allophones and some of the DAKU sounds are nasal or preceded by a nasal. The chart at the end provides a rough guide to the situation. For each of four representative "types" of dialect, the major allophones of the phonemes in question are represented phonetically.[1] On the left is the reconstruction of the proto-Japanese phonemes; we have left undecided the question whether the voiceless phonemes were nondistinctively aspirated. Next is an attempt to show the categories represented by the Old Japanese orthography, with capital letters representing the sensitive initials and diacritics marking the features DAKU (") and SEI ('). These marks are based on the marks used by early Japanese scholars to represent both the sei-daku distinctions and the high-low distinctions of pitch accent; the device was taken from somewhat similar marks that were put on the four corners of Chinese characters by Chinese linguists from as early as the T'ang period.[2] Next in the chart are the morpheme-initial and morpheme-internal allophones of the reflexes of the proto-Japanese phonemes in each of the dialect types. A semicolon separates information from different dialects of the same type. (Through most of the Old Japanese period the phonetic manifestation of 'P was probably a bilabial f- in the mainstream dialects that are represented in the later documentation, though that is a matter of controversy.)

It is clear that the morpheme shapes of Old Japanese maintained the sei-daku distinctions much as the later dialects did, but the phonogram evidence is not always clearcut in particular instances and we must sometimes rely on evidence from the Heian period and later to determine whether a given occurrence of a particular phonogram is to be taken as SEI or DAKU. The problem of ambivalent and ambiguous phonograms has been treated at length by Ōno Tōru 1962 and 1978, who also takes up delicate questions of the homogeneity of orthography in different works and (in the case of Nihon-Shoki) even within different parts of a single work. In a number of situations, Old Japanese differs from some or all later versions of the language with respect to the sei-daku distinctions. It is useful to divide the discussion into: (1) single morphemes and opaque compounds so heavily lexicalized that they resemble single morphemes; (2) various types of compounds and contrasting syntactic structures — which from the clear cases can give us rules to apply to the doubtful cases; (3) a few particles and endings for which there is conflicting evidence or conflicting interpretations of the evidence.

In virtually all cases, the divergence consists of a SEI syllable in Old Japanese that corresponds to a DAKU syllable in later Japanese. The historical development that this implies and the synchronic morphophonemic replacement of an underlying SEI by a surface DAKU have both been called *nigori* (or *dakuon-ka*) 'muddying'. Within morphemes this is sometimes referred to as "sporadic voicing", and it has been suggested that such unpredictable outcomes might either be due to the influence of dialects which had voiced intervocalic allophones for the SEI consonants or result from a rather natural assimilation to the voicing of the surrounding vowels; these explanations are not necessarily in conflict with each other, but they ignore the problem of nasal versions of the DAKU outcomes. There remains the possibility that some of what are assumed to be SEI syllables in Old Japanese were actually DAKU syllables that were underdifferentiated by the orthography for one reason or another, perhaps because:

(1) The syllable is contiguous to a nasal syllable so the DAKU quality is easy to ignore. Ōno Susumu 1953:124-5, following Hashimoto (cf. Skillend 172), suggests a kind of "postnasal drip" in the orthography; but Ōno Tōru 575 rejects the notion. And SEI syllables can occur contiguous to nasals, too: 'nu'ka 'forehead', 'mu'si 'insect'. 'ni'fyi 'new', .ma'tu 'pine tree', .na.fa 'rope', ...

(2) In the kun-chū (reading notes to Chinese passages) of the Nihon-Shoki the iterative nigori — a repeat of a SEI syllable as DAKU — was ignored, and the same SEI phonogram was usually repeated. Or so it is claimed; the only examples I have seen are two that repeat the ambivalent phonogram BEAN: yaso-tu[¨]tukyi 'eighty (= many) spans of time', tatu-[i¨]tu '? stand [and] leave'. Maybe this happened elsewhere, too.

(3) In the case of compounds and certain syntactic structures it is possible that the syllable was pronounced DAKU (phonemically) but represented an underlying SEI (morphophonemically).

In the examples cited below, many taken from Nishimiya 1970, attestations of earlier periods are given for Old Japanese from Omodaka et al. (Zdb) and from Iwanami kogo jiten (Ōno [Susumu et al.]). The later attestations are mostly from [Ruiju -] Myōgi-shō (Mg) of 1081, as found in the Mochizuki index of 1974, and from the Japanese-Portuguese dictionary (JP) of 1603. A blank for Mg means there is no example with tone marks; Myōgi-shō has many kana-written words with no accent indications. The discussions in Zdb and Ōno refer loosely to the Nara period (Nr), the Heian period (Hn), the Kamakura period (Km), the Muromachi period (Mr), and the Edo period (known as the Tokugawa period to the political historian). The kana orthography of most periods usually ignored the sei-daku distinctions but scholarly notations and glossaries provide information — to varying degrees reliable — on these distinctions together with information on the accent. In citations from Mg the accent-and-voicing marks are indicated by putting dots before the initial consonant: ¨C distinctively voiced high, 'C distinctively voiceless high (and all other high syllables that are not ¨C); ..C distinctively voiced low, .C distinctively voiceless low (and all other low syllables not ..C). Some words in Mg lack marks altogether; they are irrelevant for this discussion. Other words lack marks on some of the syllables; this means the citation does not give information on either the pitch or (for sensitive syllables) the voicing: ka may represent 'ka, .ka, ¨ka (high-pitched ga), or ..ka (low-pitched ga). Except for these citations from Mg, a syllable written like ka below is to be taken as having a voiceless initial. When attempting to cite the accents reconstructed for proto-Japanese or Old Japanese, the notation of Mg is simplified: a dot is placed high or low before the initial of the syllable, and for the double-low types (Type 2.5) a final dot represents the latent fall of pitch as

in .sa˙ru. 'monkey'. Tōkyō forms are cited from Shin Meikai-jiten (Mkz) whenever
possible; otherwise from Meikai akusento jiten (Mka) or other sources, such as Nihon
kokugo dai-jiten (NKD). The accent of modern Tōkyō forms is marked by ˈ after the
vowel before the distinctive drop in pitch. If there is no accent mark, the word is
atonic, specifically shown by a raised minus at the end. If there is more than one
pattern, variant versions are reported; if one of the variants is atonic, a raised
minus (⁻) is attached at the end of the word. The JP citations have been normalized
in transcription: tu [tsu], du [dzu], di [dži], zi [ži], ti [tši], si [ši].
In the OJ citations Cyi, Cye, and Cwo represent kō-type syllables; Ciy, Cey, and C̲o
represent the otsu-type. Vowels of syllables that are neutral or unknown as to type
are written -i, -e, -o; these letters represent the later vowels, too. Brackets hold
the ellipted material of contractions or enclose optional elements.

   In discussing the OJ distinctions we resort to a conventional orthography in
which ¨P is represented by b, ˈP by f; ¨T by d, ˈT by t, ¨S by z, ˈS by s; ¨K by g,
and ˈK by k. There may have been a period when the major allophones were not far
from what the orthography suggests. But it seems likely that through much, if not
all, of the OJ period:
   (1) the DAKU sounds were prenasalized, and the nasality only gradually disappeared
in different dialects — probably after the OJ period — in the order z, b, d, g.
(See Clarke 1973:265.)
   (2) the phonemes s and z were (nondistinctively) affricated before at least some
of the vowels, and perhaps all.
   (3) the apical pairs t/d and s/z were palatalized before OJ -(y)i, though this may
not have occurred until -yi and -iy had fallen together, and that happened around
800, but at least a century earlier for apicals — before Man'yō-gana attestations.

   Discussions and dictionaries by Japanese grammarians are sometimes misleading
because they write with the same symbols those syllables that have unvoiced initials
(SEI) and those for which we lack reliable attestation of the voicing distinctions.
Unless we are indicating both SEI and DAKU by the marks ˈ and ¨ (as in the citations
from Mg), we will write syllables that are not attested as to sei-daku with capital
letters; in such citations, the lowercase p (or f), t, s, and k are to be used only
for those syllables attested as SEI. A caution is in order here. As Komatsu 1981:66-
7 warns us, while the double dot in Myōgi-shō unambiguously marks the initial as
DAKU (in addition to marking the syllable as high or low) the single dot does not
necessarily mean the initial is SEI. The single dot is used to mark the pitch but it
is noncommittal with respect to the sei-daku distinction.

1. Reverse nigori: apparent loss of voicing.

   Only a few words appear to have had a DAKU syllable in the earlier language but
the corresponding SEI syllable later. Seventeen of these are discussed below.

   (1) An example often cited is taki 'waterfall' (Mg ˈta˙ki; JP taki), for which the
earlier meaning was 'rapids', the OJ word for 'waterfall' being taru-myi. It has
been suggested (by Ōno and by Maruyama 1975:24) that the OJ form of the etymon may
have been tagyi, on the basis of the verbs tagyir- 'seethe' (Mg —; JP tagir-) and
tagyit- 'seethe', for which Zdb (413d) suspects a doublet takyit-, on the basis of
tyakyitu(-se) 'rapids' (JP takitu 'falling water'). Probably Zdb is quite correct to
assume that the ancestor of taki 'waterfall' was takyi 'rapids' with the unvoiced
stop, and that the verbs had doublet forms with both -k- and -g-. The voiced -g-
version could be due to mimetic devices or to interdialect borrowing. (Cf. n.4.)

(2) kufosa 'profit' is cited by Ōno as kubosa but Zdb decides on -f- because of the Mg variant 'ku'fu.sa. It is unclear what Ōno bases his -b- on; NKD cites the romanization in Hepburn's Japanese-English dictionary, and Brinkley's dictionary also has kubosa. The word is missing in JP and carried by later dictionaries only as an archaism; Kōjien has kuhosa, which looks suspect because of its morpheme-internal -h- where we would expect -[w]-.

(3) (toko)toba ni 'everlastingly': Mg 'to'kotofa; JP —; Mkz tokotowa⁻, to'wa ni (with the historical spelling "ha"). Miller, taken with the etymology *toko-tu-ifa 'everlasting rock', treats the occurrence in Bussokuseki-no-uta 10:3 as -f- despite the fact that the phonogram here (as in M 183) is GRANNY rather than WAVE and Ōno (920a) says there are DAKU marks in the Jakue-bon Kokin-shū; cf. Ōno Tōru 653. In order to explain the modern -w- we need an earlier -f-, all right; probably the best explanation is either a genuine doublet in OJ or an artificial "-w-" introduced from the orthography into later Japanese once the word was no longer part of the live vocabulary.

(4) kabyi 'ears of rice (etc.)', kamu-kafyi 'food offered to gods', Mg 'ka¨fi; JP — . Ōno dissociates kamu-kafyi from kabyi, suggesting that it perhaps contains the verb 'raise, nurture' (i.e. 'what will nourish the gods'). Could kabyi have been a prehistoric contraction of kam[u-ka]pyi 'nourishment (for the gods)'?

(5) fyi-no-gure[y] 'sunset'; Mg — ; JP — ; Mkz hi-no-kure⁻. The modern version may be a new formation; or, the OJ -g- may be due to the preceding nasal syllable. Cf. fiᵏ/gure (Hn); Mg — ; Mkz higure⁻.

(6) kadura 'wig' (probably from kamyi 'hair' + tura = turu 'vine'), kaduraku 'wear as a wig', kadurakyi-yama (placename); Mg .ka¨tu.ra; JP kadura; Mkz katura⁻. In view of Mg and JP attestations, the modern version appears to be late — perhaps a genteel or reading pronunciation? — but the OJ phonogram (BEAN) is not always unambiguously -du-, so there may have been a doublet, one reflecting the nasal of kamyi and the other not.

(7) sitadaru 'drip': Mg .si.ta¨ta.ru, .si.tataru; JP sitadaru; Mkz sitata'ru. Ōno says this has the same root as sitamu 'let it drip' (Mg .si.ta'mu); Mkz says it comes from "down" + "droop". A new formation? But perhaps an old doublet; the OJ phonogram evidence is not clear.

(8) aburu(ru) / abure[y] 'overflow' (abusu₁ 'let remain, leave'); Mg 'a¨fu.ru; JP afururu / afure; Mkz ahureru⁻. The modern -h- is highly suspect within a morpheme; we expect -w- or zero. Perhaps this is a reading pronunciation, or mimetic factors are at work; cf. abu(ru) / abiy 'bathe in' (abusu₂ = amusu 'douse with'); Mg —; JP abi / aburu, abiru; Mkz abiru⁻ (abiseru). The Shuri version qand(-ir-,-as-) is from *anbur-.

(9) izaru 'fish', izar[y]i-FI (Ōno: -byi) 'fishing fires'; Mg — ; JP isari(-bi); Mkz isari(-bi). The -z- looks authentic and there is no early evidence for an Old Japanese variant, yet the best explanation for the later -s- would seem to be an early doublet.

(10) agyi (placename) (Ōno: "anciently -g-"); Mg — ; PJ — ; Mkz a'ki. Perhaps the modern -k- is but the result of a reading pronunciation based on the Heian hiragana orthography, which failed to indicate the sei-daku distinctions. If that is not what happened, there must have been an earlier doublet.

(11) Ōno Tōru 553 would have obobosi- 'indistinct, vague' become later ofofosi-; Zdb lists the OJ word as ofofosi- because the majority of examples have clearly SEI phonograms, but there is one example (M 3899) with phonograms indicating obofosi- or (if the iterative nigori was ignored) obobosi-. The word does not appear in Mg, but the etymon is probably present in .o..fo.roke 'scant(?-perceived)', modern oboro(-ge) 'vague'. Ōno [Susumu] gives -b- but says "maybe ofofosi in Nr, not to be taken as

'big' because accent is wrong, instead cf. obore[y] 'drown'". Both for this item and for the next two, we may raise the question whether the syllable /bo/ was adequately represented by the phonogram orthography; the question arises again below for tufo 'jar' (91), ofotukana- 'vague' (90), and sofotu 'get soaked' (84).

(12) For 'drown' Zdb gives obofore[y] / oboforu(ru) but suggests there may have been a doublet with ofofore[y]; Ōno gives -b- but says "maybe -f-"; Mg 'o¨fo'fo.ru, o¨foforu; JP wobore / woboruru and Mkz obore¹ru are contractions (by haplology?). See also (11) above.

(13) Ōno Tōru 554 would have a verb ofod̲o̲re[y] / ofod̲o̲ru(ru) 'towsle' become later ofotore[y]; Mg has 'o¨fo'to're-¨ka'sira 'towsled head', but Ōno Tōru suspects that the nigori on the labial is a mistake. Ōno [Susumu] has obotor- (basing his <u>yo-dan</u> conjugation on the perfect attributive obotoreru of M 3844) and obotore- (oForeTaru of Makura-no-sōshi), with -b- assumed because of the Mg citation. Mg also has ofotoru with no diacritic marks. The phonograms in M 3855 are KEEP (normally /fo/) and CLIMB (normally /to/); perhaps Ōno Tōru justifies his /do/ on morphophonemic grounds, seeing the structure as a N-V compound with the verb toru 'take'. Cf. (11).

(14) Ōno Tōru 563 would correct the usual interpretation of the early family name fata to fada, on the basis of a passage in Kogo-shūi. Mkz has ha¹ta, but the modern version is probably a reading pronunciation.

(15) It is said (by Ōno Susumu and by Nakata but not by Zdb) that the placename Musashi (Mka mu¹sasi) was "anciently" muzasi (based on what?); notice the nasal initial of the preceding syllable.

(16) The form kaswobyi 'stealing' appears in Senmyō 19 only, and Ōno [Susumu] thinks the phonogram (FIELD-)HELP is confused in reading, but Ōno Tōru 1977:151 says the phonogram must represent /byi/; elsewhere the verb is always kaswof-. "Relationship with kasum- is unclear" (Zdb). The only clear Mg example (Kn Butsu-ka moto 65:3) is written .ka‥so'fu, which may be why Mochizuki has it listed among the examples of kazofey / kazofu(ru) 'count'.

(17) The compound noun hara¹kara⁻ 'sibling(s)' appears as faragara in Senmyō 25, and that is why Zdb and NKD cite the word as -g-; Ōno and Nakata cite it as -k-. For more on this word, see §3.5.1.

2. Acquired voicing in morphemes.

In the mainstream of the language there are only a few words which have later DAKU on an initial syllable that was SEI earlier:

(18) kama 'bulrush'; Mg 'ka'ma; JP gama; Mkz ga¹ma⁻.

(19) tani 'tick'; Mg 'ta.ni; JP tani; Mkz dani¹.

(20) t̲o̲y̲o̲mu 'clamor'; Mg ‥to.yo'mu; JP doyomu; Mkz doyo¹mu. Ōno "doyomu from Hn" but he ignores Shuri tuyum-.

Example (20) may involve mimetic factors; (18) and (19) are perhaps truncations of compounds or a dialect intrusion. A number of words for animals and plants turn up with voiced initials in dialects, probably as the result of truncating compounds; see Ch. 1, §26.

In two cases, the historical development may have been consonant metathesis rather than nigori:[3]

(21) tuda-tuda 'into pieces'; Mg .tu‥ta.tu‥ta; JP tudatuda; Mkz zu¹tazuta.

(22) azasa (a yellow flower); Mg 'a¨sa'sa, 'a'sa¨za; JP —; NKD asaza⁻ 'Nymphoides peltata'. Since metathesis in Japanese usually involves a whole syllable, not just a component of the syllable, example (22) is more convincing than (21), which may instead reflect the mimetic factors so frequently encountered in reduplications.

Examples of nigori within morphemes are listed below, grouped by the consonant type, which is given in the margin.

K (23) afukyi 'fan' (but there is some uncertainty about the phonograms); Mg .a.fu.ki (noun), .a.fu"ku (verb); JP awogu; Mkz oogi⌐ (noun), ao⌐gu (verb).

(24) akafu 'indemnify, buy'; Mg .a.ka'fu; Ōno "-g- after Hn"; PJ — ; Mkz aga-na⌐u.

(25) afeyku 'gasp' (Ōno "till Hn"); Mg 'a'fe.ku (accent irregular?); Ōno "Mr afeku, afegu"; JP ayegu; Mkz ae⌐gu. The Ōno reference spells with standard kana for the second syllable; the -fe- would have been pronounced -we- in late Hn and -ye- by Mr.

(26) uka (no myi-tama) 'food received'; Mg .u.ka; JP — ; NKD u⌐ga.

(27) ukatu 'bore a hole', ukey / uku(ru) 'a hole opens', ukey-gutu 'shoe with a hole'; Ōno "-g- late Hn"; Mg .u..ka'tu; JP ugat-; Mkz uga⌐tu.

(28) kasiku 'cook rice'; Mg .ka.si'ku; Ōno "kasigu Mr"; JP kasik-; Mkz kasi⌐gu.

(29) sirakiy 'S(h)illa (Sinla)'; Mg .si.ra.ki-.ko.to 'Silla harp'; JP — ; Mkz — ; Mkz si⌐ragi. Cf. Ōno Tōru 562, 764 n.64.

(30) tafusaki (< tafu-sakyi) 'loincloth'; Mg 'ta'fu'sa'ki, 'ta'fu'sa"ki; NKD toosagi, dialect toosaki.

(31) myi-tukyi '(something given in) tribute'; Mg 'mi'tuki-mono, 'tu..ki-.no-'nu'no, 'tu'ku-'no-fu.ne; JP — ; Mkz mitugi(-mono) "was -k- till Mr". Ōno [Susumu] would derive this word from 'attach' (tukey), but there is no lower bigrade form (*tukiy) for this verb, despite his statement.

(32) fwoku 'bless' (toyo-fwoku, koto-fwoku, fwokyi-uta); Mg — ; JP kotobuki; Mkz kotoho⌐gu, kotobu⌐ku, koto⌐buki; Ōno "kotofwokyi in later ages [i.e. from c. 1600] was kotobuki, kotohogi".

(33) fyimorokyi 'platform/gift for gods'; Mg 'fi"fo'ro'ki; JP fimorogi.

(34) fuseku 'defend', Ōno "till [?= through to the end of] Nanboku-chō [1336-92]"; Mg .fu.se'ku; JP fusegu; Mkz huse⌐gu.

(35) misasaki 'mausoleum' (Zdb "tentatively"); Ōno "misazaki till Heian, and then misasagi" (from his notation you might think this was myisazakyi but that is because he neglects to differentiate unknowns from ko⌐o-type syllables); Mg 'mi'sa"sa'ki; JP — ; Mkz misasagi⁻ ("anciently misazaki").

(36) marokasu, marokare[y] / marokaru(ru) 'form a clod (an entity)'; Mg .ma'ro'ka'su, 'ma'rokasu (first accent unreliable?); JP — ; Mkz marogasu⁻.

(37) yatukare 'humble I/me' (< ya-tu-kwo [w]are); Mg .ya:tu'ka'rᵉ/¹; Mkz yatugare⌐⁻.

(38) yukyi 'arrow quiver'; Mg .yu'ki, .yu"ki; JP — ; Mkz yu⌐gi.

(39) yuraku, yurakasu 'clink, jingle' < mimetic yura(-yura); Mg — ; JP — ; Mkz yura⌐gu⁻ 'swing, sway, shake'.

(40) yokir-u 'pass by' (?< yor[y]i kyir-); Mg 'yo'ki.ru; JP yogir- (Ōno "yogiru from Mr"); Mkz yogi⌐r-u.

(41) fituki 'coffin' (Ōno: "< fyitu kiy 'lidded-box fortress'; -k- till Mr") — also just ki; Mg 'fi'tuki, 'fi'to'ki; JP fitsukigome, fitsuki no kome 'second crop of rice' (?); Mkz hitu⌐gi⁻.

(42) wakaturi 'gimmick' < wakaturu / wokoturu 'deceive' (cf. wok- 'invite'); Mg 'wa"ka'tu'ri, 'wa'ka'tu.ru, '[w]o'ko'tu.ru (on the difference between noun and verb see note, Zdb 814a); JP — ; Mkz — . Nishimiya implies that the -t- was later -d-; is that a mistake?

(43) turugyi, turukyi 'sword' (thought to be a doublet); Mg .tu.ru..ki, .tu.ru.ki; JP turugi; Mkz turugi⌐.

The following set of verbs is confusing:

Zdb		Ōno	Mg	JP	Mkz
(44a) susuku	'rinse'	susugu	'su'su.ku, 'su'su.ku	susug-	susuguˉ
(44b) sosoku	'rinse'	} sosoku	} 'so'so.ku, .so.so..ku	—	soso'guˉ
	'ruffle'				
	'pour'	sosogu			

For 'ruffle' we see from the infinitive-derived noun swoswokyi 'being all ruffled up' that "so" must have been /swo/. (It is poorly attested in phonograms.) Ōno derives 'ruffle' from so̲so̲ (not swo!), a mimetic for the sound of wind. For 'pour' the set epithet mina-so̲so̲ku 'water-pouring' (if that is what it means) has so̲.

(45) fak- 'fletch an arrow': Zdb fag-, Ōno "anciently fak-"; Mg (.)fa..ku; JP —.

K-N (46) tukunofu 'compensate' ("till Mr"); Mg .tu.ku'no.fu; JP tukunoi / tukunoo; Mkz tuguna'u. Ōno would derive this from tukiy 'tribute' + a variant of -naf-.

(47) tukumu 'close mouth'; Mg .tu.ku'mu; JP — ; Mkz tugu'mu.

N-K (48) nikyi 'smooth, soft' (opposite of ara 'rough'), nikyibiy / nikyibu(ru) 'smoothe'; Ōno nigi "Hn and after"; Mg 'ni'ki-'ta'fe 'smooth cloth', ? 'ni"ki.me 'seaweed'; JP niki 'mild times of the year', nikoyaka ni 'mildly', niginigi sita 'lively'. Perhaps related to nikwo (Mg :ni'ko); cognate with Korean nik- 'ripen'?

(49) fyimukasi 'east'; Mg 'fi'mu"ka.si; JP figasi; Mkz higasi'ˉ.

(50) — 'supplement, supply'; Mg 'o'ki'nu.fu; oginufu (Mr), oginofu, oginafu; JP woginoi / woginoo; Mkz ogina'u. Ōno thinks this is a compound of 'put' and 'sew'.

T (51) ata 'enemy'; Mg 'a'ta; JP ata no kataki; Ōno "ada from Edo"; Mkz ada'.

(52) atasi- 'alien' (Ōno "anciently"); Mg 'a.ta.si; JP adasi; Mkz adasi- (in the compound nouns adasi-o'toko and adasi-go'koro).

(53) fotwo 'extent; a while'; Mg — ; JP fodo; Mkz hodo.

(54) fota-kufyi 'half-burned stake'; Hn fota 'fuel wood'; Mg 'fo'takufi; JP fota; Mkz ho'taˉ 'sticks for burning'.

(55) fotofasir-u 'jump with joy'; Mg 'fo"to'fa'si.ru, 'fo'to"fasiru; Ōno "fodobasiru late Mr"); JP fodobasiru; Mkz hotobasi'ru ("anciently hodoᵇ/basir-").

N-T (56) matwo, madwo 'window' (Zdb); Ōno only madwo; Mg .ma"to, .ma'two; JP mado; Mkz ma'do.

(57) matwo 'round' (whence matwo 'target' says Zdb); Mg 'ma'to 'target', .ma'to (nari) '(is) round', .ma"to-ka (ni) 'round'; Ōno "also matoka, JP matoka na fito".

(58) muratwo 'kidney; heart'; Mg 'mu'ra"to; JP — ; Mkz — ; Ōno "-d- from end of Heian to beginning of Edo".

(59) yotari 'drivel'; Mg 'yo"ta'ri; JP —; Mkz yodare.

(60) momyit- ("Nr") 'leaves turn color' (from Ōno's romanization you might think mwo... but that is because he neglects to differentiate the unknown from the ko'o-type syllables) > momidi[y] / momidu(ru) Hn.

(61) momyit[y]i-ba 'leaves turned in color' > .mo.mi..ti[y]-.ba (Mg); JP momidi; Mkz mo'mizi, momizi'-ba.

(62) na-muti 'you' ("Nr"); Ōno na-mudi "Nr -t-"; Mg 'na:mu"ti; JP nandi; Mkz na'nziˉ.

(63) muti 'whip'; Wamyō-shō "muti popularly said as mudi"; Shinsen-Jikyō buti; Mg .mu.ti-utu, ..fu.ti(-utu); JP muti, buti; Mkz mu'ti.

(64) namita, namida 'tear', Ōno "both, but from late Man'yō-shū times only -d-" (?); Mg .na.mi"ta; JP namida, nanda; Mkz na'mida.

(65) myitufa 'water god' ("Nr"); Ōno "myi-tu-fa later -du-"; Mg 'mi"tu'fa; JP —.

(66) myituti 'dragon' (Ōno compares Korean milu and J [woro]ti); Mg 'mi'tu'ti; JP — ; Mkz mi'zutiˉ.

(67) matwofu 'get bewildered' ("anciently"); Mg .ma..two'fu; JP madoi ariku; Mkz mado˥u.

(68) mutukaru 'fret' ("from Nr"), mutukasi- 'difficult' (Hn); Mg —, ˙mu˙tukasi; JP mutukaru, mutukasi-; Mkz muᵗ/ᵤuka˥ru, muᵗ/ᵤuka˥si-.

(69) mutumasi- 'intimate'; Mg ˙mu˙tumasi; mutumasi-/mutumazi- "from Mr"; JP mutumasi-, Mkz mutuma˥zi-. The word is from mutubu (Mg ˙mu˙tu..fu) 'get intimate', related to musubu (Mg ˙mu˙su..fu) 'knot together'.

-N (70) wotudu ni (all examples are Man'yō-shū poems by Yakamochi, with ni), wotutu = ututu 'reality; present'.

(71) watatumyi 'ocean' (<— wata -tu myi 'ocean's spirit'); Mg ˙wa˙ta.tu.mi; JP —; > watatu-umyi (misreading by false analogy) > watadu-umi in Ekirin-bon Setsuyō-shū of 1469 or earlier; Mkz watatumi⁻, "wadatumi is a latterday [= post-1600] change".

(72) *fyi-tumey 'hoof'; Mg .fi.tu˙me, ˙fi˙tu˙me; JP fizume; Mkz hi˥zume⁻.

S (73) kas̲o̲ 'father' (Ōno "Nr") — paired with ir̲o̲ 'same mother' (whence ira-tu-mye 'young lady'); Mg ˑka¨so 'parents' (= kazo-iro[fa], Ōno).

(74) misasaki 'mausoleum': see (34).

(75) kasikey- 'get numb/weak'; Mg ˙ka˙si.ku; JP kasike, kazike; Mkz kazikeru⁻.

S-N (76) fasama 'valley, gap' ("till Hn" — noun from fasam-?); fazama "Mr"; JP faza(-ma) 'space or time'; Mkz hazama˥⁻, NKD dialect haza 'gap, interval; furrow'.

N-S (77) naswofey / naswofu(ru) 'imitate'; Mg ˙na¨su˙ra.fu; JP nazoraye/nazorayuru; Mkz nazorae˥ru.

(78) nos̲o̲ku 'eliminate' (Ōno "Nr"); Mg .no..so'ku; Mkz nozoku⁻.

P (79) tukufa (*placename*) "Nr"; Mg — ; JP — ; Mkz tuku˥ba.

(80) ifukaru 'doubt', ifukasi- 'doubtful'; "-f- or -b- in Hn"; Mg .i:fuːkaru/ .i..fu.karu, .i.fu.ka'si/.i..fu.ka'si; JP —, ibukasi-; Mkz ibuka˥ru, ibuka˥si-.

(81) kakyi-tu-fata 'fence flag = iris' (M 3291), Wamyō-shō); Mg ˙ka˙ki˙tu¨fa.ta; JP — ; Mkz kakitu˥bata.

(82) kofotu, kofore[y] / koforu(ru) 'spill' (vt., vi.) "till Km", kobotu, koboruru "from Mr"; Mg .ko..fo'su, .ko..fo'ru and .ko.fo'tu, .ko.fo'ru (was there a difference in meaning?); JP kobosu, kobore / koboru; Mkz kobo˥su, kobore˥ru. (Shuri kuus- < *kofos- 'take apart; tear down'.)

(83) su-fye, su-bye 'means' (OJ doublet); Mg —; JP sube; Mkz su˥be˥.

(84) sofotu 'get soaked' — Nr has only one example s̲o̲foTi but that probably represents s̲o̲foti[y] / s̲o̲fotu(ru); Mg — ; JP — ; Hn "both quadrigrade and upper bigrade"; "later" (but when? Ōno lists it) sobot-, cf. modern sobo-nure˥ru 'get drenched', sobo-hu˥ru 'drizzle'. Was /bo/ inadequately represented in the Old Japanese phonograms? See (11).

(85) fafuru 'slaughter' (Ōno faburu); faburu 'bury, cremate' > Mg .fa.uːfu.ru > Mkz hoomu˥ru; fabura[ka]su 'throw away'; fafuri 'assistant priest' (Ōno faburi), Mg ˙fa˙fu˙ri — cf. fafi 'ashes' (Mg .fa.fi and ˙fa˙fi) ?< *fafiy < *fafu-gi 'that which is burned away' or *fafu-kiy 'burnt-up wood'.

(86) fitafuru ni 'intently' (presumably fi... = fyi... but phonogram evidence is available only in kun-chū; Zdb "no evidence for -b-", but Ōno has fitaburu); Mg .fi.ta'fu.ru; JP — ; Mkz hitaburu⁻.

(87) fotofori 'getting feverish/angry' (noun from verb infinitive); Mg .fo.toforu, .fo.to'wo.ru; JP fotowor-; Mkz hotobori˥⁻ 'lingering warmth'.

(88) musefu 'choke up' ("Nr"); Mg ˑmu˙se..fu; JP musebu = muse / musuru; Mkz musebu⁻.

(89) yurufu 'relax', "modern -b-" (?); Mg .yu.ru'fu; JP yurumu; Mkz yuru˥mu.

(90) ofotukana- 'vague' (Zdb, because the M 1952 phonogram is KEEP, but see 11 on the question whether the syllable /bo/ was adequately represented); Ōno obotukana-; Mg ofotukana- (no marks); JP wobotukanai; Mkz obotukana˥i⁻.

(91) tufo, tufu 'jar' (Ōno "perhaps -f- in Nr"); Mg ˈtu¨fo; JP tubo, Mkz tubo⁻.
Yonaguni cibu C. The phonogram is KEEP /fo/ in M 1444, MARK /fu/ in Shoki kun-chū;
but the latter is a hapax and the former may be an underrepresentation — see (11).
   (92) erafu 'choose' ("Nr"); Mg .eˈra..fu; JP erabu; Mkz eraˈbu.
   (93) utufo 'hollow'; Mg ˈuˈtuˈfo; JP — ; Mkz utubo⁻. Ōno: "from mid-Heian -w-,
rarely -b-". Yonaguni cibu A < ?*[u]tubo.

P-N (94) turufamyi 'a kind of oak (kunugi); acorn'; Ōno turubamyi — no OJ phonograms,
but WAVE (fa) in Wamyō-shō and Shinsen-Jikyō; Mg .tu.ru.fa.mi (corrected from
.tu.ru.fa.yu). Ōno Tōru cites M 4109 with WAVE.

N-P (95) tubafira-ka, tubafirake- (< tubafirakey-) 'in clear detail'; Mg
.tu..ma.fiˈraka (?= tubafiraka); tumafira-ka "Km"; JP tumabiraka; Mkz tumabiˈraka.
   (96) inafa (*placename*, cf. Ōno Tōru 561); Ōno inaba; Mka iˈnaba.
   (97) In Nr the verb sinwofu 'yearn' (Mg —) was kept apart from sinobiy /
sinobu(ru) 'suffer' (Mg ˈsiˈno..fu) but these came to be confused in Hn and fell
together. In JP the verb is quadrigrade: sinobi / sinobu / sinooda. The modern
language has sinob⁻- ("newly sinoˈb-") but the idiomatic structure V-ruˈ ni
sinobiˈnai reflects the earlier upper bigrade conjugation; cf. RGJ 837. The phonogra
DEAD-MOTHER /byi/ is used to write /fyi/ in sinwofyi 'yearn' in M 465, but
that is thought to be because the author is mourning his mother (Ōno Susumu 1977:
184); the Kyōto University text has the phonogram COMPARE /fyi/.
   (98) noforu 'climb' (K 58, 59, 71, 99 phonogram WORRY; M 4011 phonogram KEEP),
listed by Zdb and Ōno as -b- but see Ōno Tōru (503-4, 559-60) for the argument
that this was -f- (as Igarashi lists it); Mg ˈnoˈfo.ru, ˈnoˈforu and twenty-seven
citations with -b-; JP, Mkz noboru⁻.

   The following set of words may be examples of the iterative nigori:

(99) kukufyi 'swan'; Ōno kugufyi ("also kofu [Wamyō-shō], kofi, kubyi");
Mg .ku.kuˈfi, .kukuˈfi; JP kugui; Mkz kuˈgui⁻.
(100) kukuru 'dart/crawl through; dive, evade'; Mg .ku.kuˈru, .ku..kuˈru; Ōno
"kuguru Mr"; JP kuguru; Mkz kuguˈru.
(101) ukakafu 'spy; seek out; inquire; visit' (Ōno "Nr"); Mg ˈuˈkakafu, ˈuˈka¨ka.fu;
JP ukagɔɔ; Mkz ukagaw⁻-.
(102) tutuku 'continue' (Zdb "hard to decide"); Ōno tuduku; Mg ˈtu¨tuku; JP tuduku;
Mkz tuzuku⁻.
(103) sasa-namyi 'wavelets' (Ōno "anciently" = Hn); Mg — ; JP saza-nami; Mkz
sazanami⁻.

   But these two words have SEI sounds in JP, so the DAKU must be after 1600:

(104) kakayaku 'shine, glisten'; Mg ˈkaˈkaˈya.ku; JP kakayaku; Ōno "-g- early
modern"; Mkz kagayaˈku.
(105) sitoto '(a kind of bird)'; Mg .siˈtoˈto; JP sitoto; Mkz — ; Kōjien "anciently
sitoto" (NKD sitodo "from kiˈnsei" = sometime after 1600).

   And the following is also doubtful:

(106) fyifyiku, fyifyiraku 'sting, smart' (cf. modern hiˈri-hiri, piˈri-piri);
Mg ˈfiˈfiˈra.ku; Ōno "Mr -b-"; Mg — . Cf. (? >) fyibyiku 'echo'; Mg :fi..fiˈku;
JP fibiku; Mkz hibiˈku.

   Two words treated as OJ -g- by Zdb and Ōno may have had doublet forms:

(107) kugi 'nail' is so treated despite ambivalent phonograms "for the time being
because of Mg"; Mg has both ˈku¨ki and ˈkuˈki, but the single dot may be marking
only the tone here.

(108) usagyi 'rabbit' is so treated despite ambivalent phonograms because of Azuma
wosagyi and Myōgi-shō. The Mg citation for 'rabbit' itself lacks a mark on the velar
(.u˙saki) and in the other two words cited by Mg the morpheme is before a nasal
syllable and the markings are not unambiguous: ˙u˙sa˙ki-no-miti, ˙u˙sa¨ki-no-miti
'rabbit path' (?); ˙u˙sa¨ki-˙mu˙ma, ˙u¨sa¨ki-˙mu.ma 'donkey'.

JP and Mkz usagi and kugi seem to point to earlier -g-, as do the forms reported by
Clarke for three peripheral dialects. But there is also Ryūkyū evidence that points
to -k-. For these two words the Yonaguni dialect has the oral -g- that corresponds
to OJ -k- rather than the velar nasal -ŋ- that corresponds to OJ -g-;[4] the southern
Amami dialect of Shodon has usaakyi/usak < usakyi 'rabbit', but kugyi/kuk < kugyi
'nail' (Martin 1970). Yet the Shuri forms are palatalized versions of earlier -g-,
and the Miyako forms also are from an earlier -g-. Shuri and Yaeyama yagamasi-
corresponds to standard yakamasi- 'noisy', an adjective not attested before 1600.

3. Acquired voicing in compounds: rendaku.

3.1. Nigori constraints; Lyman's Law.

In certain types of compound the second member replaces a SEI initial with its
DAKU counterpart, either obligatorily or optionally, subject only to the constraint
that two DAKU syllables are not permitted within a morpheme, so that the nigori
process is vacuous when a non-initial syllable of the second member is OJ b, d, z,
or g. OJ had no morphemes with initial DAKU syllables except a few truncations, the
loanwords from Chinese, and perhaps several suffixes and suffixed particles which
etymologically were originally SEI. In later Japanese the nigori process is, of
course, vacuous before an initial DAKU as well as nasals, y, w, and r, which are
voiced phonetically but neutral as far as the sei-daku distinction goes. This
constraint has been called Lyman's Law; it was presented in Japanese by Ogura
Shinpei (cf. Martin 1952:48-9), who was taken to task by Ōno Tōru 761 n.17 for
the presumption that Benjamin Smith Lyman had discovered it, quoting (540) from
Motoori Norinaga's Kojiki-den a clear statement of the essence of Lyman's Law.
    We will consider several situations, taking much of our data from Ōno Tōru's
study, checked against the sources. The situations involve verbal structures (3.2),
noun-incorporating verbs (3.3), adjectival structures (3.4), and noun structures
(3.5).

3.2. Verbal structures.

3.2.1. Verb infinitive + verb.

In OJ a verb infinitive followed by another verb is sometimes to be taken as
two syntactic units 'do V₁ and do V₂', as in tukiy fa kyi[y] fey yuku 'the months
come and pass away' (K 29); in the modern colloquial language the corresponding
structure is V-te V (< V-[y]i te[y] V) but the older pattern V-[y]i V is also used,
especially in written Japanese. There are times, however, when the OJ structure is
V-yi - V, forming a single compound verb. The later language treats the compound
verb as a single accentual unit, but in Heian times — and presumably earlier — the
second verb was given a separate accentuation, so that we must assume a juncture.
Yet, despite the juncture, the compound verb replaced an initial SEI in the second
verb by its DAKU counterpart. For certain compounds the DAKU forms are attested in
early phonograms; for others the DAKU is either unattested or counterindicated, and

for some there are also conflicting attestations with SEI, which either reflect a differing treatment (syntactic vs. lexical) or are morphophonemic representations which simply ignore the DAKU. Examples:

  i-yor[y]i - datas[y]i 'deigns to lean upon' (K 105).
  ofiy - dat[y]eru 'grown luxuriant' (K 58); cf. ofiy - tat[y]i '(?) growing' (M 4111), ide[y] tat[y]i te[y] 'leaving' (K 54), fure[y] tatu 'quivering' (K 75).
  ifyi - durafyi 'say this and that, equivocate' (M 3300).
  yukyi - guras[y]i 'get there within the day' (M 4011).
  sukyi - banuru 'digs out' (K 100).
  akyi - darazu 'is unsatisfactory' (M 4176) — "usually treated mistakenly as -t-" (Ōno Tōru 546); Mg .a.ki.ta'rasu, .a.kitaru; JP akidarazu, akidaranu, akidaru; Mg akitarinai⁻.
  yukyi - gafyer[y]i 'go and return, make a round trip' (M 3978, 4490); Ōno Susumu "-k-, but -g- in Nr"; Zdb segregates these into separate entries but there are no phonograms for the assumed -k- version.

     A few expressions seem to have had both treatments: mukafyi - dat[y]i (M 4127 with phonogram FAT), mukafyi tat[y]i (M 4430 with phonogram MANY) 'stand facing' (Zdb has -t- but fails to give the source or the meaning); tat[y]i - zakayuru 'grow thickly, luxuriate' (K 92), tat[y]i - sakayuru (NS 53).

3.2.2. Verb infinitive + auxiliary.

     Auxiliaries are usually pronounced as separate words: V-yi Aux, as in V-yi kate[y] / katu(ru) 'can V'. But the fossilized negative infinitive of this auxiliary takes nigori: V-yi - gate[y]n[y]i 'unable to V'. Apparently it was confused with V-yi - gata ni 'being difficult to V', which is an adverbialization from V-yi - gata- 'difficult to V', with the verb+adjective compound treated in the same manner as a compound of noun + adjective (see §3.1). V-yi kane[y] / kanu(ru) 'cannot V' is written with phonograms for /ga/ in the Azuma songs only (e.g. M 3442); cf. Zdb 205c, Ōno Tōru 538.

3.2.3. Typically verbal prefixes.

     A verb does not acquire nigori by attaching a typically verbal prefix, such as i-, which is semantically obscure: i-kyiramu 'will cut' (K 52), i-tworamu 'will take' (K 52), i-kumyi 'intertwine' (K 91), i-swofyi woru 'is by my own side' (K 40), i-fafyi 'crawl' (M 199), i-kogyi 'row' (M 4408); other examples lack phonograms. An apparent exception, according to Ōno Tōru, is i-gafyer[y]i komu 'will come back' (K 86) with the phonogram CONGRATULATE, which is usually /ga/ in Koji-ki though ambivalently /ka/ or /ga/ elsewhere; Ōno Tōru 614 admits that this phonogram — like BEAN /du/, GRANNY /ba/, and [FIELD-]HELP /byi/ — is sometimes used for a SEI syllable in Koji-ki too, but he treats that as a scribal mistake for ADD /ka/ (the top part of the graph CONGRATULATE), as the others are treated for CAPITAL /tu/ (though there is no apparent similarity in graph), WAVE /fa/ (top part of GRANNY), and COMPARE /fyi/ (bottom part of [FIELD-]HELP). But the Nihon-Shoki version of the poem (NS 70) writes the phonogram HUNGER, which unambiguously represents /ga/, so that i-gafyeri is the proper reading. I believe this means that the traditional etymology is wrong: this word is not a verb with the prefix i- but something else, probably a contraction of *ikyi-gafyeru = yukyi-gafyeru 'go and return'; iku is attested in the Man'yō-shū as a colloquial version of yuku, then as now.

3.2.4. Intensive prefixes.

A few verb infinitives — kakyi 'scratch', os[y]i 'push', ut[y]i 'hit', ar[y]i 'stay' — are often used as intensive prefixes, and then they do not induce nigori:

kakyi-fyiku 'pluck' (K 75), kakyi-tuku 'land on' (K 98); ... .

os[y]i-teru 'completely illuminate' (M 4360), os[y]i-farafyi 'drive away, get rid of' (? — NS kun-chū with GRANNY phonogram), ... ; in NS 17 we come across os[y]i-byirakane[y] 'please open' with unambiguous /byi/ (phonogram SLEEP) but in NS 96 and elsewhere we find os[y]i-fyirakyi with the phonogram [FIELD-]HELP, which represents /byi/ occasionally in Koji-ki but is usually /fyi/ in Nihon-Shoki.

ut[y]i-kyitamasu 'deign to punish' (NS 112), ut[y]i-farafyi 'shake it off' (M 3625), ... Exception: ut[y]i-zinofyi 'unwittingly yearn' (M 4196) — "usually treated mistakenly as -s-" (Ōno Tōru 546, cf. Ōno Susumu 167a); see (97) in §1.2.

ar[y]i-sar[y]i te[y] 'managing to keep on living' (M 3933), ar[y]i-tamotofor[y]i 'keep walking around' (M 4008), ... In M 145, 3992, 4002 we find ar[y]i-gaywofyi 'keep going and coming' but in K 2 ar[y]i-kaywofase[y] 'deign to set out'. Zdb suggests a doublet for the former.

In Old Japanese there are few (if any) examples of fyikyi 'pull' as an intensive prefix; that became common in Heian times and later.

3.2.5. Other prefixes.

Certain other items listed as prefixes by dictionaries are attached with nigori of the initial syllable of the verb. These are probably all derived from nouns, though some of the etymologies are uncertain:

ta-basir[y]i 'splashing' (M 4298, phonogram GRANNY); ? ta-bakaru 'plan, consider; dupe' (no phonograms); ? ... . Perhaps (ayufyi/aywofyi) ta-dukuru 'tie on (a skirt-cord for carrying provisions)' (NS 105, M 4008), ta-basamyi 'grasping (arrows — in hand or armpit)' (M 3885, 4465).

sa-gamyi ni kamyi 'chew and chew' (K preface kun-chū phonogram CONGRATULATE, NS kun-chū phonogram EGO); ? sa-gumoru 'cloud up' (no phonograms); ? ... .

kwo-dakaru 'be somewhat elevated' (K 101); ? ... .

3.2.6. Adverb + verb.

A verb does not acquire nigori when preceded by an adverb or an adjective stem used adverbially: toyo fwokyi 'richly blessing' (K 40), tofo sokyinu 'has become far separated' (M 3389, 4258), futwo sir[y]i (M 4469) = futwo sikyi (M 36, 199) 'sturdily erecting', taka sir[y]i 'nicely manage' (M 38), ... Exceptions: faya-gufyi 'eating fast' (K 97, phonogram TOOL — but faya kufyi in the corresponding NS 75, with phonogram GROUP), iya-zakar[y]i 'getting farther and farther away' (M 3412, phonogram SHOOT), tika-duku 'come close, approach' (M 877, phonogram BEAN), ... The "exceptions" can be handled as lexicalizations, indicated by our hyphen.

3.3. Noun-incorporating verbs.

3.3.1. Incorporating the subject.

A number of compounds are reduced from the structure N [ga/no]⁸ V, with an obligatory nigori:

kumwo-banare[y] / -banaru(ru) 'clouds part' (K 56, M 3691).
kamwo-dwoku, -duku 'wild ducks alight' (K 9, NS 5).
fyi-deru 'sun shine' (K 100).
fyi-gakeyru (K 100) 'the sun beams' — listed as -kageyru by Zdb, but the long discussion admits that the phonograms call for -gakeyru.
ne-daru 'roots spread out' (K 100).
ne-bafu 'roots extend' (K 100) — for some reason missing in Ōno.
ura-gare[y] 'branches wither' (M 3436).
tuma-gomoru 'the-wife-is-confined' (fixed epithet; NS 94).
sita-deru '[flower below] shines beautifully' (M 4059).
ama-zakaru 'heaven-is-distant' (fixed epithet; M 880) — also /sa/ (NS 3, ...).
fye-datu 'get separated' (M 866, 1522), cf. fye-date[y]/-datu(ru) 'separate' (M 4073, 4076); Mg .fe..ta'tu .
kamu-dumaru 'gods gather' (M 894).
ko-daru 'grow lush' (M 3433).
ikyi-doforu 'get indignant' (M 4154) — but Shoki kun-chū and Shinsen-Jikyō write this with the phonogram STOP /to/; Mg .i.ki..to'wo.ru, ikito'fo.ru, .i.kitoforu .
a-gaku '(foot-scratch =) paw, flounder' (M 1141); Mg .a..ka'ku .
akyi-duku 'show signs of autumn' (M 2160, 3655, 4111).
iro-duku 'take on color' (M 3699).
yufu-duku 'become night' (M 3820 but no phonograms).
ywo-gutatu '(night rots =) night grows late' — phonograms only in the infinitive-derived noun ywo-gutat[y]i 'late at night'.
Compare the usual ellipsis of [ga/no] without lexicalization: nisi fukyi 'the west wind blows' (K 56), kumwo tat[y]i 'clouds arise' (K 21), tukiy tatanamu (← tat[y]inamu, with assimilation of the second vowel) 'the moon will have risen' (K 29), myidu tamaru 'water accumulates' (K 45), fanatiru 'flowers scatter' (M 822), kamu fwokyi 'god blesses' (K 40 — notice that instead of kamiy this uses the older form kamu, which we would not expect outside a compound), ... Some expressions seem to have had both treatments: kuti fyifyiku (K 13), kuti-byifyiku (NS 14) 'the mouth smarts'; cf. Ōno Tōru 542.

3.3.2. Incorporating the direct object.

A number of compounds are reduced from the structure N [wo] V, with obligatory nigori:

ikyi-duku 'breath; pant' (K 43, M 1520); Mg .i.ki¨tu.ku .
koto-date[y] 'declaration' (NS 46 has the only phonogram), derived noun < (morphemically written) koto-date[y]/-datu(ru) 'declares'.
koto-dofu 'converse' (M 3510 — other citations SEI); koto-dofyi 'conversing' (M 884, 4125).
na-duke[y]/-duku(ru) 'name' (M 4078); Mg 'na¨tu.ku .
kosi-dukurafu 'gird one's loins' (NS 106).
ya-doru 'lodge, take shelter' (M 7); Mg .ya..to'ru .
fye-date[y]/-datu(ru) 'separate' (M 4073, 4076), cf. fye-datu 'get separated' (M 866, 1522); Mg .fe..ta'tu .

uma-daku '? rein in (? or spur on) a horse' (M 4154).

ma-baru 'watch' (Bussokuseki-no-uta, phonogram GRANNY); Mg .ma¨fa.ru .

fyi-dasu 'raise (children)' (from "add days"); Zdb lists as -t- but notes that
Jōgū-ki has -d-. The intransitive counterpart fyi-daru appears only in semantograms.

ama-derasu 'deign to shine heaven' (M 4125); Ōno "-d- in Nr"; Zdb suggests a doublet
for this word.

   Compare the usual ellipsis of [wo] without lexicalization: tati fakeymasi 'I
would gird you with a sword' (K 30), kyinu kyise[y]masi 'I would clothe you with a
garment', sawo tor[y]i 'to take the boat-pole' (K 51), sibyi tuku 'harpoons the
tuna' (K 111), ...
Problematic: nuka-Tuku 'kowtow', for which Ōno has -d- but Zdb gives -t- on the
basis of Mg 'nu˙ka˙tu˙ki-'mu˙si 'click-beetle (elaterid)' but there are no old
phonograms; JP nukaduku; Mkz nukazu˥ku. The verb saigyiru 'block, obstruct' (pre-
Heian kun-chū) is believed to be derived from sakyi [wo/ni] kyir-u 'cut [the/in]
advance' through an unusually early instance of velar elision sa[k]yi; the Mg
attestation is 'sa˙i¨ki.ru, but the prior component was confused with 'sa.fe[y] /
'sa.fu / 'sa˙fu.ru 'obstruct' so that from Kamakura times the form safe-giru is
seen; JP sayegiru; Mkz saegi˥r-u.

3.3.3. Incorporating other objects.

   A few compounds are reduced from the structure N [ni] V, with an
obligatory nigori:
   sakyi-dat[y]eru '(which) stood ahead' (K 17) — but sakyi-tati in Bussokuseki-no-
uta (phonogram MANY).
   (awokakyi -)yama-gomor[y]eru 'enclosed in (green-hung) mountains' (a fixed
epithet; K 31).
   kum[w]o-gakur[y]i 'hide in the clouds' (M 4011).
   myiyama-gakur[y]i te[y] 'vanished from sight in the deep mountains' (K 113).
   sima-gakuru 'hides in the islands' (M 3597); sima-gakure[y] / -gaku(ru) (M 3692).
   kata-dukyi 'adjoin on one side' (M 4207).
   myi-duku 'is soaked in water' (NS 95, M 4340); but M 4094 has -tuku (phonogram
CAPITAL).
   mwomwo-daru '(suffices to be a hundred =) is much, are many' (K 1010).
   mwomwo-dutafu 'far-off' (fixed epithet; K 43, 112).
   sima-dutafyi 'follow the island' (M 4408, 4414).
   iswo-dutafu 'follows the rocky beach' (K 38).
   ifa-basiru 'rock-splashing' (fixed epithet, M 3617).
   sita-bafey / -bafu(ru) 'secretly feels' — no phonograms but -b- based on the
phonogram in the derived noun sita-bafey (M 3371).
   ta-basamyi 'grasping (arrows — in hand or armpit)' (M 3885).
   ta-dukur[y]i 'tie on' (NS 106, M 4008).
There appear to be few, if any contrastive examples of simple ellipsis of [ni]. For
that reason, Ōno Tōru would correct ama-sosor[y]i 'soars in the sky' (M 4003) and
ama-teru 'it-shines-in-the-sky' (fixed epithet, M 3650) to ama-zosor[y]i and ama-
deru respectively. The phonograms are FORMERLY, usually /so/, and the Japan-made
kokuji "BOW-ONE" (perhaps originally a variant of HEAVEN), usually /te/. Ōno Tōru
(544) would also correct momotarazu (NS 53) to -d- though it is written with the
phonogram MANY, usually /ta/. But we might consider this instead to be a type of
structure different from that of the verb mwomwodar- (← mwomwo ni tar-): like the
later restrictive ¯ta˥razu 'inadequate for ... ', the second part could be regarded
as a separate word.

3.3.4. Incorporations of uncertain derivation.

A few nouns appear to be derived from N [ ] V-yi but the underlying structures are not always clear. Some show nigori or doublet forms, others not:

ta-banare[y] 'parting' (M 3569) must ultimately come from ta (= te[y]) wo fanare[y] 'separate the hands'; Mg — ; JP — ; Mkz — .

tu-fakyi 'spit' < tu [wo] fakyi (phonogram WAVE in Shinsen-Jikyō); Mg 'tu.fa.ki; Ōno "Mr tubaki, tuwaki"; JP tu, tubaki; Mkz tuᴵbaᴵ, tubakiᴵ.

ko-tat[y]i (NS 105), ko-dat[y]i (M 867, 4026) 'grove' < ko (= kiy) [no] tat[y]i 'tree stand'; Zdb "doublet?"; Mg — ; JP kodati; Mkz koᴵdati⁻.

kuka-tat[y]i 'trial by holding hot water' perhaps < *kuka 'hot broth' (cf. kuka-fey 'vessel used in trial by hot water', Korean kwuk 'broth') + [ ] tat[y]i; Mg —; JP —; Mkz kukatati⁻ (obviously an archaism). In Nihon-Shoki kun-chū the -ta- is written with the phonogram PULL, and that seems to be the basis for treating it as SEI. This phonogram is "mostly SEI" in Nihon-Shoki, according to Ōno Tōru 684. Ōno Susumu 1953:279 and 301 casually neglects to differentiate the use of the phonogram as -da-, though three of his examples on 301 are elsewhere in his work (in the text and in the word index) so marked: nadasu 'deign to stroke', yeda 'branch', and wodate 'small shield (also placename)'. The kun-chū sakyitaturu on 222 is of undetermined meaning and structure, apparently treated as -t- because the phonogram is usually SEI.

3.3.5. Nigori acquired at later periods.

There are a few N-V compounds which did not show early nigori but at some later time acquired it:

ta-kuru 'wind (with the hand)'; Mg .ta.kuru; JP takuru; Mkz taguᴵru.

ma-tataku 'blink (the eye)'; Mg .ma..taːta.ku; JP matataku, madataku; Mkz matataᴵku.

3.4. Adjectival structures.

3.4.1. Noun-incorporating adjectives.

An adjective stem takes obligatory nigori when a noun is prefixed. Most N-A structures are derived from N [ga/no] A but a few are N [ni] A and some are unclear: ka-gufasi 'is fragrant' (K 44); fana-gufasi '(its flower) is beautiful' (NS 67); ko-dakaku te[y] 'tree growing tall' (M 4209); sita-gataku 'so the bottom is firm' (K 106); ni-gurwokyi 'dark red' (K 43); ura-ganasi 'is sad at heart' (M 3584); ura-gufasi 'is beautiful to one's mind' (NS 77, M 3993); ura-gwofiysi (M 3993), -gwofwosi (K 111) 'is beloved to one's heart'; kokoro-ganasi 'is sad at heart' (M 3639), kokoro-gusi (< ku[ru]si) 'is troubled of soul' (M 3973); ma- gufasi 'is beautiful to the eye (M 3424), ?mey-gusi 'is unbearable (to the eye); is cute' (M 4106); yama-dakamyi 'the mountain being high' (K 79, NS 69); ... .

In omofyi-ganasi 'is sad of thought' (M 3686) and omofyi-gurusi 'is pained at heart' (M 3481) the noun is derived from a verb infinitive. The nigori rule includes adjectival nouns derived from noun + adjective stem: fa-byiro 'broad-leafed' (K 58), ne-zirwo 'radish-white' (K 62), ... Because of the rule, Ōno Tōru 549 says 'hand' (or prefix) + 'great' cannot be the correct etymology for tafutwo- 'exalted, sacred'; cf. ta-dofo- 'far'. But no other etymology has been proposed. Apparent exceptions to the rule are ma-tika- '(interval) near', written with the phonogram KNOW in M 3524, and ma-tofo- '(interval) far', written with

the phonogram CLIMB in M 3522 and the phonogram EQUAL (GROUP) in M 3522; Ōno blandly
writes -d- with no explanation. If -t- is correct, as the phonograms indicate, I
believe the explanation is that the etymology is wrong for the two passages written
in phonograms, which are to be construed as containing the prefix 'truly' (§3.2)
rather than the noun 'interval'.[6]

The following three adjectives are derived from N-V structures: ikyi-doforosi
'is indignant' (NS 30), ikyi-dukasi 'is sighful' (M 3547), namyita-gumasi 'is
tearful' (K 63, M 449).

3.4.2. Prefix + adjective stem.

When a prefix is attached to an adjective stem, nigori is usually in order:
myiti wo ta-dofomyi 'because the way is far' (M 3957); afyidu-ne no kuni wo sa-
dofomyi 'because the land of Afyidu-ne is far away' (M 3426); ("myina no wata")
ka-gurwokyi kamyi 'hair that is black ("as a snail's guts")' (M 804); ... . But
the prefix (or adverb?) ma- attaches without nigori (cf. Ōno Tōru 549): ma-kanasi
'truly poignant' (M 3348, 3366, 3567, 4413, and without phonogram 532); ma-tofo-
'quite distant' (M 3441, 3463,3522); ... . The adjectival noun ma-sirwo 'pure white'
(M 4155) could be taken as prefix + noun.

3.4.3. Adverb + adjective.

Clearcut cases of adverb + adjective are not found (Ōno Tōru 547); perhaps an
example is ya-gataku (K 103 with phonogram CONGRATULATE), if taken as iya 'very' +
kataku 'firmly', or rather as an adverbial conversion of (?*) iya kata- 'so as to be
very firm'.

3.4.4 Verb infinitive + adjective kata- 'hard'.

The adjective kata- 'hard' can be readily attached as an auxiliary to a verb
infinitive, with an obligatory nigori: ar[y]i-gatasi '(hard to exist =) is rare'
(M 4011); e[y]-gataku are[y]-ba 'as it is difficult to obtain' (Bussokuseki-no-uta
18, phonogram CONGRATULATE); e[y]-gatakyi kagey 'shade that is hard to get' (M 3573)
in which the phonogram is CAN /ka/ but Ōno Tōru 631 would correct that to EGO /ga/
on the basis of what he calls *koden-bon* — presumably meaning "old manuscript(s)",
not otherwise identified.

3.5. Noun structures.

3.5.1. Noun compounds: noun + noun.

As in the later language, some noun compounds of OJ exhibit nigori but others
do not. Coordinative compounds (cf. Martin 1952:49) never have nigori: yama-kafa
'mountains and rivers' (M 4468) — contrast the descriptive compound yama-gafa
'mountain river' (NS 113); titi-fafa 'father and mother, parents' (M 4346); omo-titi
'mother and father' (M 4402); kusa-kiy 'plants and trees' (M 4314); ... . These
coordinative ("dvandva") compounds were probably differentiated by accent and/or
juncture from the direct juxtaposition of nouns by the casual ellipsis of some
coordinating particle such as to 'and'; cf. RGJ 158-9.

In other types of N-N compound it is difficult to find semantic correlations:

siba-kakyi 'twig fence' (K 108, 110)   ana-dama 'jewel with hole' (K 7)
afa-fu 'millet field' (K 12)   ina-gara 'rice stalks' (K 35)
asi-fara 'field of reeds' (K 20)   tokoro-dura 'yam vines' (K 35)
asa-fyi 'morning sun'   nwo-byiru 'wild rocambole' (K 44)
mura-tori 'flock(ed) birds' (K 5)   nifwo-dori 'grebe' (K 39)
suga-tatamyi 'sedge mat' (K 20)   yama-gafyi⁷ 'mountain valley' (M 3867)
tatamyi-komo 'mat rushes' (K 32)   ...
ko-kufa 'wooden hoe' (K 62)
...

Some words may have occurred as doublets: 'plank door' is ita-two in K 2 and M 804 (both with the phonogram DIPPER/MEASURE) and NS 96 (phonogram PLAN) but ita-dwo in M 3467 (phonogram TIMES), which is — perhaps significantly — an Azuma song (cf. Ōno Tōru 539); 'mountain field' is clearly yama-da in K 79 and NS 69, but Shōsō-in kana (ko-)monjo has yama-ta with the phonogram MANY, according to Zdb 770c, where the question is not raised whether the meaning might be different ('mountains and fields'). In JP and later works both words have nigori. The OJ word kafa-dwo 'river ferry(-place)' (M 859) is written kafa-two in an Azuma song (M 3546), and for some reason that is the citation in Zdb; cf. Ōno Tōru 539. It is assumed that the word for 'baby deer' was the doublet ka-kwo (as in kun-chū) and ka-gwo (as in Wamyō-shō, in the Nihon-Shoki version of the Koji-ki name [Prince] Kagosaka, and also in the compound ma-kagwoya 'deer-shooting arrow'), Mg .ka.̈ ko. The old word 'seaship' sifo-fune[y] (M 3450, 4389), sifo-bune[y] (M 3556, 4368) is said by Zdb to have probably had both forms; Ōno lists only -b-. The OJ word for 'orange' is attested tatiᶠ/ᵦana, a doublet according to Ōno: tatifana (NS 125), fana-tatibana (NS 35).

Four old compounds with the bound element -kara are troublesome:

ya-kara 'family' (Wamyō-shō, phonogram ADD); Mg .ya.ka.ra; JP yakara, Mkz and NKD ya˺kara˺.

u-gara 'clan, family, kin(smen)' (NS kun-chū, phonogram EGO); Mg 'u'ka.ra; JP — ; Mkz u˺kara⁻. This is said to be from u[myi]-kara (cf. RGJ 47n); perhaps the elided nasal left a temporary trace?

fara-gara 'siblings', so listed by Zdb apparently because of the phonogram WHAT in Senmyō 25, despite the phonogram ADD in Ryō no shūge and Shinsen-Jikyō; Ōno -k-; Mg — ; JP farakara; Mkz (Mka, NHK) hara˺kara⁻.

tomo-gara 'companion', so listed by Zdb despite the phonogram ADD in Bussokuseki-no-uta 12 and Shinsen-Jikyō; Mg 'to'mo¨ka'ra; JP tomogara; Mkz tomogara˺⁻. While we share the concern of Miller 1975 over this word, we will not so severely scold our Japanese colleagues for their obtuseness; as the citations from Mg and JP above show, Miller is unfair in saying that "modern standard J tomogara is the sole basis for their interpretation of the Old Japanese form" (129a). Nor should it escape our attention that the preceding syllable is nasal.

3.5.2. Compound-noun nigori acquired in later Japanese.

These compound nouns have nigori in later times, but not in Old Japanese:

ama-kum[w]o 'raincloud' (M 800, 3409); Mg — ; JP amagumo; Mkz amagu˺mo.

utu-fari 'beampost' < uti far[y]i (N [ ] V) 'inside stretch' (kun-chū, Shinsen-Jikyō, Wamyō-shō); Mg 'u'tu'fa'ri; JP utubari; Mkz utubari⁻.

ufa-fye '(surface) cordiality' (M 631); Mg — ; JP — ; Mkz uwabe⁻ 'surface'.

yufu-fye 'evening' (M 3767); Mg :yu'fu¨fe (accent irregular); JP yuube; Mkz yuube˺.

k<u>o</u>-tati/-dati 'grove' (a doublet); Mg — ; JP kodati; Mkz ko˺dati⁻.

woka-sakyi 'tip of hill' (NS kun-chū); Mg — ; JP — ; Mka oka˺zaki *(placename)*.
Ōno says there was a popular dance tune in "early modern" times called wokazaki; he
apparently refers to the "lion-dance tune of early Edo" mentioned in Kōjien 285a.

kuti-fyiru 'lip' (kun-chū), Zdb "tentatively -f- because no clear evidence of -b-
in Nr"; Ōno -b-; Mg 'ku'ti¨fyi.ru; JP kutibiru; Mkz kutibiru⁻.

kafyeru-te[y] '"[its leaf is like a] frog hand" > maple' (M 3494); Ōno gives -d-
but Zdb notes correctly that the uncontracted form was -t-; Mg .ka.fi.ru'te-.no-.ki,
.ka.fe..te-no-ki, .ka.fe¨te; JP "caide" = kaide; Mkz kaede˺.

ta-fyito 'traveler' (NS 104), contraction of tabyi-fyito (Wamyō-shō) — Ōno 1975
gives ta[byi]-byito, but his 1953 reading of NS 104 was tafyito; Mg 'ta¨fi¨fi'to;
JP tabyuuto, tabibito; Mkz tabibito⁻.

musu-fyi (n<u>o</u> kamiy) 'mysterious procreative power' (K text, Wamyō-shō), derived
from musu, Mg .mu'su '(moss etc.) grow' — whence musu-kwo 'son' and musu-mye
'daughter' (Mg .mu'su'me) but umu 'give birth' is apparently unrelated because of
the conflicting accent (Mg 'u.mu) and the unexplainable -s- on the intransitive;
"later mistakenly associated with musubyi 'linking'".

ta s<u>o</u> kare 'Who he?'; Mg — ; JP taso 'who?', tasokare-doki 'twilight'; Mkz
tasogare⁻. This was lexicalized, apparently in Muromachi times, to mean 'twilight
(when dusk makes it hard to recognize people)'.

Similar, but unattested for OJ is the compound noun ko-tama 'tree spirit; echo';
Mg .ko'ta.ma; JP kotama; Mkz kodama⁻; ... .

3.5.3. Obligatory nigori in Old Japanese noun compounds.

According to Ōno Tōru, certain OJ nouns usually or always have nigori as the
second member of certain kinds of N-N compound:
kata 'beach; the bay (of placename)': Examples?
ti 'the road (to/through placename)': sasanamyi-di 'the Sasanami road' (K 43).
Exception: tagyima-ti 'the Tagima road' (K 78, NS 64).
kafa 'the river (of placename)': sawi-gafa 'the Sawi river' (K 21), yamasir<u>o</u>-gafa
'the Yamashiro [= Kizu] River'.
(fey/)fye in N-n<u>o</u>-bey/-bye 'direction/vicinity of N': tok<u>o</u>-no-bye 'bedside' (K 34,
M 904, M 3927) = tok<u>o</u>[¨]fye = tok<u>o</u>-bye (M 4331); yama-n<u>o</u>-bye ('mountainside', a
placename in NS 79) ?= yama-bye (a person's name in K kun-chū and M 1516); kafa-n<u>o</u>-
bye (NS kun-chū) = kafa-n<u>o</u>-bey 'riverside' (K 58, phonogram DOUBLE) — but Ōno and
others treat this as kafa n<u>o</u> fey, or even kafa n<u>o</u> [u]fey. The version "kafa-bye"
(M 16, 3820) is written with semantograms, but kafa-fey appears in NS 117. There is
also kafa-biy (M 20, 4309), which may be a variant of (-)miy 'around, in the bend of'
(from the verb miy- 'turn around'). Cf. the discussion of the problem in Ōno Tōru
623, 763 n.51.

3.5.4. Prefix + noun.

After certain prefixes a noun always has nigori: wo-date 'small shield' (K 43),
wo-bune[y] 'little boat' (K 53), wo-dani 'little valley' (K 112), sa-wo-basi
'bridge' (NS 24), ... (This makes 'little tree' a plausible etymology for wogiy
'reed'.) The prefix sa- induces nigori in sa-gor<u>o</u>mo 'garment'(M 3398), sa-giyri
'fog' (NS kun-chū), and perhaps sa-gufa 'hoe' (Harima-fudoki but the noun is
written with a semantogram so the -g- must be imputed).

The prefix kwo- 'little' often induces nigori, as in kwo-bu⌐suma 'bedding' (M 3454), `ko..si.u.to-`mye 'sister-in-law' (Mg), and these nouns (Mkz): kogoe⁻ 'quiet voice', ko-guti⁻ 'small mouth', ko-gata⁻ 'small type'. ko-gata⌐na⌐ 'dagger', ko-guma⁻ 'little bear', ko-za⌐kura 'small cherry'. ko-za⌐iku 'handicrafts' — many of which occur earlier but without OJ phonograms. But some occurrences of kwo- do not induce nigori: kwo-saru 'the little monkeys' (NS 107); (Yama-no-bye no) Kwosima-kwo 'Miss Little-Island (of Mountainside)' (NS 79) — cf. 4.3; .ko.te 'forearm, gauntlet (Mg); kotori⁻ 'bird' (Mkz); kosio⁻ 'small tide' (Mkz); ... . Zdb 285a lists a number of non-nigori examples from Shinsen-Jikyō and Wamyō-shō along with some which are presumably part of the OJ vocabulary but do not appear as entries of the dictionary.

As prefixes wo 'male' and mye 'female' do not induce nigori: wo-fiy 'nephew', mye-fi[y] 'niece'; mye-ka 'female deer, doe' (Wamyō-shō, which lists sa-wo-sika for 'male deer, stag'); wo-fyito (Ryō no shūge), wo-futo (Shinsen-Jikyō, Wamyō-shō) 'husband'; ... . Apparently exceptional are mye-dori 'hen' (K 59; Mg .me̤.to.ri; JP medori, mendori) and wo-dori 'rooster' (Wamyō-shō, but Kinka-fu wo-tori; Mg — ; JP wodori). Perhaps these are contractions of ···-n[o]-tori; cf. modern mendori⁻ and ondori⁻. The words wo-su 'male' and m[y]e-su 'female' are surprisingly late in attestation; they are not in JP. The -su may be related to the suffix in names of birds, such as karasu 'crow', fototogyisu 'cuckoo', ugufyisu 'bush warbler' and the word for 'pheasant': kyigyisu (Wamyō-shō), Mg `ki̤`ki̤`su — with the variants kyigyisi (K 2) and KiSi (Honzō-wamyō), JP kizi, Mkz kizi⁻.

After the honorific prefix myi- a noun never has nigori: myi-kyi 'wine' (K 40), myi-kamiy 'god' (K 40), ... After the prefix ma- 'true, complete' a noun usually takes no nigori:

  ma-kam[w]o 'wild duck' (M 3524); Mg — ; JP — ; Mkz ma⌐gamo⁻.
  ma-kane[y] 'iron' (M 3560); JP magane; Mkz ma⌐gane⁻.
  ma-sofo 'cinnabar' (M 3560); Mg — ; JP — ; Mkz —.
  ma-kusa 'fodder' (Kōtai-jingū gishiki-chō); Mg `ma`ku`sa; JP makusa, magusa;
Mkz magusa⌐⁻.
Exceptionally ma-de[y] 'both hands' is distinguished from (?*)ma-te[y] 'hand' (cf. ma-kai and ma-kadi 'both oars') but the word does not appear in phonograms; the form is deduced from the use of the same configuration of semantograms as a rebus writing of the particle ma⌐de, on which more will be said below.

The old prefix yu- 'sacred' was attached without nigori: yu-ka 'a kind of jar' (Shōsō-in [ko-]monjo), yu-kiy '(those lands supplying grain for) festive wine' (kun-chū). (The OJ word for wine was myi-kyi; for -kiy in compounds see Ōno 349a.) There are examples attested only by semantograms: yu-sasa 'unsullied bamboo-grass' (M 2336), yu-tane 'purified (rice-)seed' (M 1110), ...

3.5.5. Adjective stem + noun.

In OJ an adjective stem could directly precede a noun without inducing nigori. It is unclear whether such a structure is to be treated as a phrase or a word, but the occurrence of the bound variant sira- for sirwo- 'white' perhaps favors the latter interpretation, at least for some cases:
  sira-tama 'white jewel (= pearl?)' (K 3, NS 92), sira-tuyu 'white dew' (M 4312), sira-kum[w]o 'white cloud' (M 866); sira-ka 'white hair' (= sirwokyi kamyi/key) — Ōno writes this -g-, as in JP siraga and Mkz siraga⌐, but Zdb notes that it is -k- in Shinsen-Jikyō and the word was used in Shoku-Nihongi in writing the name of the emperor Sirakabe (which could not be -gabe because of Lyman's Law).
  kurwo-kwoma 'black pony' (NS 81), kurwo-kamyi 'black hair' (M 4331), ...

awo-kakyi 'green hedge' (K 31).
taka-kiy 'high fortress' (K 10).
ofo̱-kyimyi 'great lord' (K 29), ofo̱-kafara 'big river' (K 37), ofo̱-takumyi 'carpenter', ofo̱-tati 'big sword' (NS 89), ...
naga-fyito̱ 'long-lived person'(K 74).
two-kama 'sharp sickle' (K 28).
But there are also a few examples with nigori: aka-dama 'red jewel (= coral?)' (K 8); asa-di(-fara) '(field of) low reeds' (M 3603); asa-zinwo(-fara) '(field of) low bamboo' (K 36); ... . And later, nigori was quite common: ofo-ti 'highway' became JP wooti but Mkz o⌐ozi; sirwo-kane[y] 'silver' was Mg .si.ro˙ka˙ne and JP sirokane but Mkz sirogane⁻.

3.5.6. The structure N -tu N.

The structure N -tu N usually has no nigori, and in the early stages of the language it can be accorded the same treatment as N no̱ N. Later some of the forms were lexicalized and survived as compound nouns. Examples: nifa -tu to̱ri 'barnyard fowl' (K 2), okyi -tu to̱ri 'bird of the offing (= wild duck)' (K 5), sima -tu to̱ri 'island bird (= cormorant)' (K 15); mafye -tu two 'front door' (K 23); sakey -tu sima (name of an island) (K 54); ... . (In fama -tu tidori 'beach plover' nigori is precluded by Lyman's Law.) The lexicalization of Numeral -tu N in myitu-guri 'a chestnut threesome' (K 43) may be a reflex of a double genitive -tu -n[o̱]. For more on this, see Ch. 7, §7.3.

3.5.7. Reduplications.

There appears to be no nigori with certain reduplications of Old Japanese:
to̱fo̱-to̱fo̱si 'is distant' (K 2).
taka-taka ni 'expectantly, with high expectations' (M 4107).
suku-suku to 'vigorously' (K 43).
tura-tura (ni) 'intently, thoroughly' (M 54, 56); Mg .tu˙ra-XY; JP turatura; Mkz tu⌐ratura.
kure-kure to 'all dark and dismal' (M 888, 3237).
komo-komo 'reciprocally' (no phonograms); Mg ˙ko.mo- XY.
sika-sika 'thus and thus' (no phonograms); Mg — ; JP sika-sika to; Mkz sika⌐zika. Ōno says the nigori dates from Edo times.
fo̱to̱-fo̱to̱ 'almost' (M 1979, 3772); Mg .fo.to.fo..to; fotowoto (Iroha-jirui-shō); JP fotondo; Mkz hoto⌐ndo — the nasal requires explanation.
The word to̱kyi-to̱kyi (NS 68, M 4323) is apparently to be taken as meaning 'at set times, each' rather than 'sometimes', for which the clear attestations as toki-doki do not appear until JP, which draws a semantic distinction between the two words. The word farwo-farwo 'distant' (NS 109, M 866) appears as farwo-barwo in M 4398 (with phonogram GRANNY); Mg —; JP farubaru; Mkz haru⌐ba⌐ru. (From the discussion in Ōno Tōru 317 you might get the idea that in M 4398 the third syllable was written with WAVE, but see 338:n.59, which makes it clear that the phonogram is GRANNY.)
However, nigori turns up in sakyi-zakyi 'each and every promontory [? or: destination]' (K 6), ko̱to̱-go̱to̱ 'all things' (K 9), ko̱ti-go̱ti 'various places' (K 91, M 213), kuni-guni 'lands' (Zdb index but no example; Mg — ; JP kuniguni; Mkz kuni⌐guni), kusa-gusa 'various kinds' (no phonograms; Mg, JP — ; Mkz kusa⌐gusa), ... And there is always the possibility that the other OJ reduplications, such as sima-sima 'islands' (NS 40; Mg — ; JP simazima; Mkz sima⌐zima) were being written

morphophonemically. Yet we may do well to stick closely to the text orthography,
in view of the JP evidence on toki-toki, although that might be explained as a
contraction of toki [to] toki as opposed to, say, toki n[i] toki for the nigori
version.

3.5.8. Verb + noun.

There are a few examples of nigori in V-yi - N, such as uwe[y]-gusa '(rooted)
plants' (K 37), katar[y]i-goto 'what is said' (K 2), ... The two words 'silkworm'
and 'egg (or shell)' are differentiated by Zdb and Ōno on the basis of Mg marks,
despite the fact that the last syllable of each is written with the phonogram OLD
in the Wamyō-shō (for 'silkworm' also in Shinsen-Jikyō):
  kafyi-kwo 'silkworm' < 'raise child' (V-yi - N); Mg .ka'fi.ko; JP kaiko, kaigo;
Mkz ka'iko.
  kafyi-gwo 'egg, shell' < 'shell child' N - N; Mg .ka.fi.ko, .ka.fi'ko; JP kaigo;
modern Ryūkyūan kuuga < kooga.
There is at least one example of a verb predicative prefixed to what is probably
a noun: yosu-ka 'a (place to) hold' (M 3862, Bussokuseki-no-uta 18) from yose[y] /
yosu(ru) 'bring' + (-)ka 'place'; Mg —; JP yosuga; Mkz yo'suga⁻.

4. Voicing in particles, endings, and bound auxiliaries.

A number of OJ particles, endings, and bound auxiliaries begin with consonants
that are sensitive to the sei-daku distinctions. Most of these are attested always
as SEI: kara, koso,[8] safey, si [mo], sura, fye, ... The genitive-nominative
marker ga is always DAKU,[9] as is the desiderative ga-na that is built upon it; the
interrogative particle ka is always SEI, as are ka-mo, ka-na, and the Heian ka-si
that are built upon it. The bound auxiliary goto 'like' and the bound auxiliary
adjective goto-si 'is like' that derives from it are always DAKU. It is generally
assumed that goto(-ni) 'each, every' was voiced (as the phonogram in M 4000 has it),
so that in moto [¨]koto ni 'on every tree' (NS 114) with the phonogram DITCH the
distinction is orthographically underdifferentiated. Similar underdifferentiation
of the dental stop occurs for the particle dani 'even', written [¨]tani with the
phonogram MANY in NS 107 and NS 127; the same use of MANY is also found in ye[¨]ta-
ye[¨]ta 'every branch' (NS 125).
  For a few of these grammatical elements we find both SEI and DAKU attestations,
and that has led some to question whether there were also early SEI versions of what
were later DAKU syllables in: (1) -ba; (2) bey-(si); (3) -do [mo]; (4) zo; (5) -zu,
-zi; (6) made. We will examine the arguments and the evidence.

4.1. The focus particle (-)fa, -ba.

The focus particle fa is always SEI after a noun: ko-no myi-kyi fa wa ga myi-
kyi narazu 'this wine is not my wine' (K 40). It is SEI after a nominalization, as
in yuku fa 'the one who goes' (K 55), and usually when following a particle:
  N ywori fa: asu ywori fa 'from tomorrow on' (K 113, NS 86).
  N ywo fa: fama ywo fa yukazu 'does not go along the beach' (K 38).
  N ni fa: ywo ni fa ... fyi ni fa 'of days ... of nights ... ' (K 27, NS 26); afa-
fu ni fa 'in the millet field' (K 12, NS 13); asa-two ni fa 'at the morning door'
(K 105); okyi-fye ni fa 'in the offing' (K 53); fye ni fa 'to the shore' (NS 4);
tama-key ni fa 'in the rice tub' (NS 94); kuni ni fa 'in my homeland' (NS 82); ... .
  N ni si[y]-te[y] fa: M 35.

··· to͝ fa: makamu to͝ fa 'thinking to embrace' (K 28), nakazi to͝ fa '(saying) that
you will not cry' (K 5).

N fa mo͝: K 25, NS 28, ...   N fa ya: K 7, 23, 34; ... .   N fa yo͝: NS 10, ...
But for wo-ba only DAKU is attested (K 2, 5, 96, 101; NS 97; ...). This is true
even, contra Miller 1975, in Bussokuseki-no-uta 19:4 (phonogram GRANNY). And for
certain other situations we find conflicting attestations:

The particle sequence ko͝so͝-ba is written with phonogram GRANNY in six[10] Man'yō-
shū examples (M 52, 217 twice, 1629,[11] 3577, 3956) and with WAVE in two (M 1782,
3522). It is written with kun-gana phonograms for /fa/ (or perhaps /ba/) in two
other Man'yō-shū examples (M 1, 1990); and in one example (M 3330) the uncommon
phonogram THIN, here /ba/ (Ōno Tōru 487), is used. In three Koji-ki examples (K 6,
73, 78) the phonogram is WAVE and in one (K 78) it is GRANNY; NS 62 has WAVE, too,
but Ōno Tōru 561 believes the WAVE writings are all mistakes for GRANNY (which has
WAVE as its top component), like the examples of WAVE used for the -ba of wo-ba in
M 552 and M 3570, for the latter of which the Ruiju-koshū text has GRANNY.

V-a-ba 'if V'[12] is recorded only as DAKU in Koji-ki: kakura-ba 'if it hide' (K 4),
ina-ba 'if they go away' (K 5), ko͝fasa-ba 'if she asks' (K 10), uta-ba 'if we
strike' (K 11), sasa-ba 'if I mark her as my possession' (K 44), naka-ba 'if she
cries' (K 83), fabura-ba 'if they exile' (K 86), ifa-ba 'if they say' (K 90), sane[y] te[y]-ba 'if one has slept' (K 80), makazukye-ba 'if I had not embraced'
(K 62), ar[y]is[y]e-ba 'if it had existed' (K 30), sir[y]is[y]e-ba 'if I had known'
(K 76), ... — all with the phonogram GRANNY. In the Nihon-Shoki orthography GRANNY
is usually fa, but it is used (by mistake?) to write one example of V-a-ba: tataba
'if it will rise' (NS 116). Except for kyise[y]-["]fa (NS 81) with SOW, all of the
other examples in the Shoki songs are written with phonograms that are ambivalently
ma or ba: POLISH in ko͝fasa-ba 'if she begs' (NS 7*b*), taye[y]-ba 'if it snap in
two' (NS 46 according to Ōno's interpretation), nara-ba 'if it be' (NS 92); DEVIL
in yo͝r[y]i ko͝-ba 'if it starts to shake' (NS 91); FINE/QUERY in ko͝fasa-ba 'if she
begs' (NS 7*a*), saka-ba 'if it blooms' (S 45), meyde[y]-ba 'if we prize it' (NS 67),
naka-ba 'if she cries' (NS 71), nara-ba (NS 103 twice), and the morphologically more
complex forms makazukye-ba 'if I had not embraced' (NS 58 — probably < makazu
[ar[y]i]-kyi [ar]-a-ba) and nakye-ba 'if he be missing' (NS 80 — probably < nakyi
[ar]-a-ba); variant form of TIE in kwosa-ba 'if we convey' (NS 19 — Nihon koten
bungaku zenshū 1:405 has a wrong character for sa).

V-ey-ba 'V and so/then' is written in Koji-ki only once with the phonogram WAVE:
no͝fo͝re[y]-ba 'since she climbs' (K 71) but the same word recurs in K 58 and K 59
with the phonogram GRANNY. All other Koji-ki occurrences are written with GRANNY:
tatas[y]ere[y]-ba (K 2), are[y]-ba (K 3, 5, 111), imase[y]-ba (K 5, 43), tatakafey-
ba (K 15), sare[y]-ba (K 22), fure[y]-ba (K 29), yukey-ba (K 37), myire[y]-ba (K 42,
54, 77, 109), tumey-ba (K 55), t[w]ofey-ba (K 78), myidare[y]-ba (K 80). With the
single exception of tokane[y]-["]fa (NS 127) with WAVE, Nihon-Shoki always writes
V-ey-ba with phonograms that are ambivalently ma or ba: POLISH in tatakafey-ba (NS
12), yukey-ba (NS 83); FINE/QUERY in myire[y]-ba (NS 34, 55, 87, 102), no͝fo͝re[y]-ba
(NS 53, 54), kwo͝yure[y]-ba (NS 61), twofe[y]-ba (NS 64), imase[y]-ba (NS 75),
tatase[y]-ba (NS 75), myise[y]-ba (NS 97), and the morphologically more complex
myiye[y]ne[y]-ba 'since it is invisible' (NS 30). There are no occurrences of V-a-ba
in Bussokuseki-no-uta and only two of V-ey-ba, both written with GRANNY: mature[y]-
ba (16:2), are[y]-ba (18:2). Since /fa/ is written consistently with WAVE elsewhere
in that work (6:4, 7:2, 8:4, 19:6) we reject Miller's interpretation of GRANNY as
/fa/ both here and in the much-maligned word mabar[y]i (16:2). (Cf. Skillend 65:
"corruption of ba [GRANNY] to fa [WAVE] more likely than the other way around".)

In the Man'yō-shū WAVE is usually /fa/ but in the first 13 volumes there are
eight places where it writes V-a-ba: tafusaba (36), kafey-ba (285), kyis[y]e-ba
(2148), yukyer[y]is[y]e-ba (1497), sigeykye-ba (1910 — probably < sigeykyi [ar]-a-
11), siramase[y]-ba (468), aramase[y]-ba (603), myimase[y]-ba (1658). And there are
an equal number of examples of V-ey-ba written (in at least some manuscripts) with
WAVE: yukyere[y]-ba (1442), fukyinure[y]-ba (2677), ? se[y]se[y]-ba (38), yukyisika-
ba (1443), arane[y]-ba (1525), afane[y]-ba (3297). In the later volumes of the
Man'yō-shū, which contain many dialect forms, there are a number of examples of
V-a-ba written (in at least some manuscripts) with WAVE: fyika-ba (3364, 3416),
yuka-ba (3687), ara-ba (4124, 4125), inora-ba (4392), fura-ba (4423), ofiy-ba
(3452), fiy-ba (4034), yuturina-ba (3355), fiyna-ba (3710), wakare[y]na-ba (3989,
4379), sir[y]is[y]e-ba (3545-a,b), fukyis[y]e-ba (3616), watas[y]era-ba (4126),
tofokye-ba (3969). And also of V-ey-ba: wore[y]-ba (3896a,b), itare[y]-ba (4011),
tate[y]-ba (4033), sare[y]-ba (4393, written with SOW in 3907), fyikey-ba (3397),
tate[y]re[y]-ba (3443), ine[y] tuke[y]-ba (3459), kafyesafey-ba (4129), tokey-ba
(3483), nagare[y]-ba (3491), omofey-ba (4300); afanafye-ba (3524), sane[y]nafye-ba
(3466, -nafye = standard OJ -ne[y] izen-kei of negative auxiliary), arane[y]-ba
(4125); nar[y]inure[y]-ba (4434); aramase[y]-ba (3524); kwofiysika-ba (3376). In
these later volumes there are also examples of WAVE used to write ba in tubara-
tubara ni 'thoroughly' (4065, first ba only), koko-ba 'a lot' (4684), wo-bayasi
'woods' (3538), sita-bafeysi 'yearned in secret' (3381), nuba-tama no 'jet black'
(3598, 3651), siba 'brushwood, twigs' (4158, 4286). According to Ōno Tōru WAVE was
used to write ba in sayuri-bana 'lily blossom' (4088) though Zdb shows this as (or,
corrects this to?) GRANNY; sakura-bana 'cherry blossom' (4395), written with GRANNY
in 829 and 4077; tanabata 'weaver-maid' (3900), written with GRANNY in K 7 and NS 2;
and tatibana 'orange' (3574, 4058 twice, 4341, 4371, 4471), written with SOW /fa/ in
NS 125 but with FINE/QUERY /ba/ in fana-tatibana 'flowering orange' in NS 35 (and
with GRANNY in the corresponding song K 44) — but Ōno Susumu treats 'orange' as an
OJ doublet tatif/bana.

On the other hand, the focus particle in V-a-zu fa 'not V but rather/instead'
— which occurs in only one passage of the songs, itade ofa-zu fa 'not undergo the
wounds ... but rather' — is written with the phonogram WAVE in K 39 and BREAK in NS
29. It is written with WAVE in M 3630 (yukazu fa), 3711 (torazu fa), 4003 (taye[y]-
zu fa), 4408 (afyi myizu-fa). Similar is naku fa (M 4113).

4.2. The modal auxiliary bey-.

The modal auxiliary adjective bey- 'ought, must, may, can, likely will, ... '
is often written with semantograms in Old Japanese. It does not appear in the Koji-
ki songs (except for K 84:4) and only once in those of Nihon-Shoki: ku bey-kyi
'(when) he is supposed to come' (NS 65). There it is written with the phonogram
DOUBLE, which elsewhere often represents /fey/: ufey 'above' (NS 60, 76), sima-fey
'island shore' (NS 126), tafey 'bark cloth' (NS 74), tukafey 'serve' (NS 78),
torafey 'hold on to' (NS 31), nifey 'offerings (to gods etc.)' (NS kun-chū), sabafey 'May-fly' (NS kun-chū); funa-no-fey 'prow of a ship' (NS kun-chū) — or
should this be funa-no-bey (see §4.3)? But in kaga-nabey te[y] 'adding day on day'
(NS 26) and ubey si ka mo 'indeed true!' (NS 103), the phonogram DOUBLE is read
/bey/ by Ōno 1953 (and others) — though that is not obvious from his syllable index
on p. 317 or the character index on pp. 279-80. An occurrence of ubey in NS kun-chū
is written with the phonogram EACH, which elsewhere represents /mey/ (as in NS 82,
85, 86 twice, 96 twice, 108) but never /fey/.

In the Man'yō-shū the phonogram DOUBLE is used ambivalently to write /fey/ or /bey/, and sometimes even /fo/, according to Ōno Tōru 651. It is used to write the paradigmatic forms of the modal auxiliary in the following poems:

   bey-si 18, 128, 795, 798, 811, 832, 1635, 1999, 3578, 3784, 3951, 4165, 4408, 4467, 4509.
   bey-kyi 166, 422,1044, 1522, 2865, 3365, 4043.
   bey-ku 199, 817, 829, 851, 1478, 1525, 1532, 3581, 3712, 3739, 3935, 4080, 4096, 4164.
   bey-myi 3468.

And the phonogram EVIL (elsewhere /fey/) is used to write bey-kyi in M 4364. According to Yoshida 1973 there are 203 examples of the auxiliary in Koji-ki, Nihon-Shoki, and Man'yō-shū; but most are written with semantograms.

In Bussokuseki-no-uta there are three occurrences of the auxiliary, two written with the phonogram SHUT (sutu bey-si 19:5, odu bey-k[u] arazu ya 20:6) and one with the phonogram DOUBLE (sutu bey-si 19:6). Miller 1975 would treat the latter as bey- but the others as fey-, probably because SHUT is used to write /fey/ in wofeymu 'I will end' (14:5, 14:6) and tukafey 'serve' (13:6); he contends that the adjacent lines 19:5 and 19:6 are using the phonetic difference for rhetorical effect. But Ōno Tōru says DOUBLE is here used in its voiced value. The phonogram SHUT is used to write bey-kyi in Senmyō 14; it was once thought to be used also in the word akarabey 'brighten = show delight' (Zdb), but this was corrected by Ōno Tōru (610) to akarafey and that is what you will find in Ōno 1974. In Nihon-Shoki SHUT is used for non-initial fey in two kun-chū words farafey-tu-mono '(a religious vessel)' and mugwofey (meaning unknown), and in two verb forms of the songs: afey ya mo (NS 68) and [o]mofey do (NS 43 twice). In Koji-ki SHUT is used in omofey-do (K 28) and its apheretic form [o]mofey-do (K 52 twice), in fafeykyeku (K 45), and in tamafey (K 73); wagyifey (K 59) is written with EVIL. For ubey na (K 29 iterated) and ubey si koso (K 73) the phonogram DOUBLE is used.

The most widely accepted etymology (see Yoshida 1973:852) treats bey- as an apheretic form of ubey 'quite true, right of course, surely', a predicable adverb which could be followed by the particles mo (M 1452), si (K 73, NS 103), or na (NS 63), as well as the predicator nar- < ni ar-. This word was also spelled mubey (Saibara with phonogram mu, Mg 'mu"fe) and may have been pronounced [m:be] during at least part of its lifetime. The etymology of ubey is uncertain; Ōno suggests the interjection u (= mu = [m:]) 'uh-huh' followed, perhaps, by afey 'make agree' (or, taken as izen-kei, 'agreed'?) The grunt of assent (mu) is first attested in early Kamakura times (Uji-shūi-monogatari 77), but it was undoubtedly around from the beginning of the language — if not, indeed, of all mankind! If bey- is a truncated form of [m]ubey (or even mufey, though no one has suggested that reading) then it seems unlikely that the initial was pronounced voiceless. The only cases of muf··· are number-noun phrases (mu - fasira 'six gods' and mu - fo 'six hundred') and all sequences of mVf are rare except for obvious compounds such as those with the honorific prefix myi-. There are the nouns myifwo = nifwo 'grebe', mafye 'front', mofyi 'drinking cup', and the verbs maf- 'dance', tamaf- 'give', omof- 'think'. And nVf is limited to nifey 'offering' and the verbs naf- 'braid', nuf- 'sew', and perhaps nofor- 'climb'.

4.3. The concessive structure (-)to mo, -do [mo].

Both (-)to mo and -do [mo] occur with the meaning '(even) though'. From the evidence in the songs of Koji-ki and Nihon-Shoki it is obvious that the distribution of the SEI and DAKU versions were determined by syntactic criteria: -do [mo] is used (like -ba) after the *izen-kei* (V-ey ...) and (-)to mo is used elsewhere. The phonograms used in Koji-ki are CLIMB /to/ and SHUTTLE (now read *zyo*) /do/. In the Shoki songs /to/ was written with CLIMB, EQUAL, MOSS (now *tai*), or RISE (now *too*), and /do/ was written with ENDURE (now *tai* — used also for /de/ in the Shoki songs) and with "PARTICLE" (now *dai/nai* — the shape is RUNNING-WEST). In examining the examples below, bear in mind that only Koji-ki distinguishes mo from mwo, so that we write "mo" for the other sources. The data:

V-u to mo:	RISE	wataru to mo (NS 119)
	CLIMB	ifu to mo (K 5), wor[y]i to mo (K 11, 56, 66 twice)
	MOSS	wor[y]i to mo (NS 89)
V-azu to mo:	CLIMB	nukazu to mo (NS 89)
A-ku to mo:	EQUAL	kasikwoku to mo (NS 45)
V-ey-do [mo]	ENDURE	ifey-do (NS 6), [o]mofey-do (NS 43 twice)
		yore[y]-do mo (NS 4, with unique phonogram for /re/)
	PARTICLE	kyikoye[y]sika-do (NS 37)
		ifey-do mo (NS 11)
	SHUTTLE	fyikare[y]-do (K 8); sure[y]-do, omofey- do (K 28);
		[o]mofey-do (K 52 twice)
		kyikoye[y]sika-do mo (K 46)

There are no occurrences of V-ey-do [mo] with a phonogram that is elsewhere treated as SEI in Koji-ki. But the Shoki songs have four examples written with RISE: kakamey-do mo (NS 90), sakey-do mo (NS 114), nar[y]ere[y]-do mo (NS 125), ne[y]sika-do (NS 110). We would be tempted to decide that the basic reading of the phonogram is /do/ and that the one occurrence as /to/ (NS 119) is a mistake, if it were not for the occurrence of RISE as /to/ elsewhere in the Shoki songs: tob- 'fly' (NS 60), tok- 'untie' (NS 127), tor- 'take' (NS 108), toko-yo 'eternal' (NS 112), tono 'lord' (NS 16, 17); koto 'harp' (NS 109), fyito 'person' (NS 110, 111, 115), moto 'bottom; root; (counter for trees)' (NS 114), yamato 'Japan' (NS 106).

The phonogram CLIMB /to/ is used to write narane[y]-do mo (M 1860 written with semantograms before -do); note the surrounding nasality. Otherwise it represents the syllable /do/ only in dialect poems:
  ama-wotomye-domo (M 3890), su-dori (M 3993), kafa-tidori (M 4147), todomuru (M 4036), todomeymu (M 4085), todomyi (M 850), yodose (M 3907), (yukamu) tadokyi (M 3696), (tabyi no) yadori (M 3643).
  V-ey-do: are[y]-do (M 3891), myire[y]-do (M 3901, M 3978), mate[y]-do (M 4253), tagufyere[y]-do (M 3978), ? nomey-do (M904), kyitare[y]-do (M 3901); fur[y]inure[y]-do (M 3919); ? wosika-do (M 3969); itofane[y]-do (M 3904).
  V-ey-do mo: are[y]-do mo (M 4000, M 4008), sakey-do mo (M 4323), myire[y]-do mo (M 3993, M 4003), sikare[y]-do mo (M 3948), todomyi kane[y]-do mo (M 850, both syllables).

The phonogram RISE /to/ is used to write the syllable /do/ in several non-dialect songs:
  yodo (M 490, M 2712), nado (M 509), todokofor[y]i (M 492), adomofyi (M 1780).
  V-ey-do: ar[y]ikyere[y]-do (M 308), ? nare[y]-do (M 486); and various examples which write the preceding elements in semantograms (M 131, M 135 twice, M 207, M 297; M 3865, M 3857).
In the dialect poems RISE usually represents /do/, including V-ey-do mo: myire[y]-do mo (M 4111 with semantogram SEE/ken), okey-do mo (M 4111), myiture[y]-do mo (M 4112). For the exceptions where it represents the usual /to/, see Ōno Tōru 650. RISE also writes /do/ in one Shoku-Nihongi kun-chū, sakey-do mo.
    The kun phonogram [a]t[w]o (FOOTPRINT/seki) is once used to write /do/ in myire[y]-do (M 36).
    The only example of V-ey-do in Bussokuseki-no-uta is are[y]-do (15:2), and it is written with the phonogram EQUAL, which appears in only one other place (2:3), where it writes /to/ in yaswo kusa to 'with the Eighty Signs', so that Miller 1975 assumes the expression must have been pronounced /areto/.[18] It should be noted that there are no occurrences of /do/ otherwise in these poems and that other occurrences of /to/ are written with the phonogram STOP, including the particle in utur[y]i saru to mo 'even though it will change and pass' (10:2), sin[w]ofye to 'esteem him, I tell you!' (7:5, 6), watasamu tamey to 'intending for them to hand it on' (13:4), forobu to so ifu 'they say indeed that they wear away to nothing' (17:5), nosoku to zo kyiku 'we hear indeed that they are removed' (17:6).
    The poems of the Man'yō-shū generally maintain the distinctions shown above. But, as often happens elsewhere in the vocabulary, basically SEI phonograms are occasionally used to write DAKU syllables — from carelessness, perhaps, just as nigori marks are casually (and meaninglessly) omitted at times right down to the present day; or, perhaps in an attempt (not necessarily successful) to capture regional features of pronunciation. According to Ōno Tōru's study, there are only three non-dialect poems where the phonogram EQUAL /to/ is used to write what must have been pronounced /do/: todomyi ni (M 1780) involves both iterative nigori and a prenasal position; are[y]-do (M 2, M290) is written with a semantogram (POSSESS/yuu) for are[y]. In the dialect poems we find that EQUAL is used to write /do/ in the following situations:
  todomyi kane[y] (M 804); yodo fa yodomu to mo (M 860, three syllables written with EQUAL); tidori 'plover' (M 4146); ama-wotomye-domo 'fisher girls' (M 3597); kwodomo 'children'[14] — following the semantogram CHILD/si in M 4094 and M 4487 and following the semantogram INFANT/zi in M 3962 but the phonogram OLD /kwo/ in M 853.
  V-ey-do: kure[y]-do (M 4344), fukey-do (M 4353), fofomare[y]-do (M 4387), ifey-do (M 4410), are[y]-do (M 4255, following the semantogram POSSESS/yuu; M 903, the semantogram STAY/zai), (tabyi) tofey-do (M 4388), omeyfo-do (= omofey-do) (M 4343).
  V-ey-do mo: are[y]-do mo (M 894, M 4378), inure[y]-do mo (M 4351), myire[y]-domo (M 4001, following the semantogram SEE/ken), aswobey-do mo (M 828, M 836).
    Incidentally, Skillend 174 raises the possibility that the province of Kazusa may have had prenasalized realizations of the DAKU initials while Shimōsa's were just "voiced"; this is based on the Man'yō-shū evidence that the particle ga is written as "ka" in songs from Shimōsa five times but only twice as "ga", while songs from Kazusa wrote the particle six times as "ga" and only once as "ka". That might, of course, reflect phonemic variants in the shape of the particle, rather than dialect differences in the phonetic system itself.

4.4. The emphatic particle zo, so.

A common emphatic particle of Old Japanese is written with either the phonogram
NARRATE zo (now read zyo) or the phonogram FORMERLY so (now read soo):

	zo	so
N —	K 3, 40	K 7, 85, 97, NS 108 (— mo ya), 109, 110
N si —	K 45	
wo si —	K 47 (— mo); NS 38	
V-a-mu —	K 5, 86	
V-a-mu to —		K 22 (fukamu to —)
V-a-zu —		K 52
V-u —		K 10 (inogofu —)

In the Shoki songs there are a few other phonograms. For so: PLACE (now read syo),
STRATUM (now syoo). For zo: PLOW, PREFACE, and BOIL (all now read zyo). The data:

N —		NS 99 (PLACE), 32 (STRATUM)
V-azu —		NS 43 (STRATUM)
V-azi —	NS 124 (BOIL)	
V-a-mu —	NS 70 (PLOW)	
V-a-mu to —	NS 124 (BOIL)	
V-yi te[y] —	NS 50 (PREFACE)	

In later Japanese there is virtually no evidence for the SEI shape, except for
JP ta so 'who', which is thought to be a descendant of OJ tare so (K 98, with the
phonogram FORMERLY); and Mg .i.ka.ni'so — also, unmarked ikaso (?= *.i.ka..so) —
which is thought to be ika-ni + the emphatic particle, just as nazo 'why' (M 3373,
Mg 'na..so) is thought to be a contraction of nani + the particle.

In the songs of Koji-ki and Nihon-Shoki the phonogram NARRATE is used only to
write the particle zo. The only other word that contains the syllable zo[16] is
kozo 'last year' written with the phonogram EXIST (now read zon) in K 79 and with
the phonogram SPEAR-TANG (now obsolete) in NS 70, where it is immediately followed
by the particle koso, which uses FORMERLY used to write the syllable so.

Ōno Tōru assumes (620) that FORMERLY was simply "used for NARRATE" in writing
this particle, but since FORMERLY appears elsewhere as /so/ and the particle is also
written with PLACE and STRATUM in the Shoki songs, it seems best to posit a doublet
and follow the phonograms in each passage. Ōno [Susumu] believes the particle was
originally so (perhaps derived from the deictic 'that') but from fairly early times
developed the DAKU variant zo as a "precursor" of what eventually became the only
pronunciation. However, Ōno Tōru (554-7) argues that the particle had a single
shape zo and that the use of FORMERLY to write this common word was no more than a
conventional substitution, which should not to be taken as actually representing a
voiceless version. He points out that both in the Koji-ki and Shoki songs the SEI
phonograms are not noticeably more frequent than the DAKU in writing the particle,
and in the Man'yō-shū the phonogram FORMERLY is overwhelmingly preferred: in the
non-dialect songs, 249 instances as against only 35 for NARRATE and 8 for PREFACE;
in the dialect songs, 112 instances as against only 5 for NARRATE. These statistics
do not particularly support the chronological development so > zo that Ōno Susumu
postulates as happening during the OJ period. If we follow him (and now, apparently,
Miller) in taking the phonograms for this particle at face value, then the shape in
Man'yō-shū days was almost always so, but in the more primitive times of Koji-ki it
was almost equally common as zo, which once again became the common form from Heian
on: zo/so > so(/zo) > zo. And the zo form won out not only in the main islands, but
also throughout the Ryūkyūs, where the particle is a common feature of colloquial
speech in modern reflexes such as /du/ and (Okinawan) /ru/.

4.5. The negative forms V-a-zu and V-a-zi.

The negative forms V-a-zu and V-a-zi are generally assumed to have had DAKU syllables in Old Japanese; when phonograms where chosen to write them, usually the unmistakably DAKU type was selected. In the Koji-ki songs -zu is always written with the phonogram RECEIVE (K 5 twice, 6, 10, 36, 39, 40, 43, 47, 52, 61, 71, 73, 78, ...). In the Nihon-Shoki songs RECEIVE is used in NS 66; BABY (now read *zyu*) is used nine times (NS 7, 15, 29, 32, 64, 67, 81, 86, 96, 111 twice) and CONFUCIANIST (now *zyu*) is used thirteen times (NS 11, 14, 32, 38, 43, 49, 58, 63, 82, 83, 89, 110, 115). But there are a few places where the phonogram NECESSARILY, basically representing /su/, is used instead. Bussokuseki-no-uta 3:4 uses the SEI phonogram in writing e[yi] myi-zu te[y] 'we cannot see'. Miller 1975 would read that /emyisute/ and refers his readers to Miller 1971:272-3, where he lists seven examples of V-azu written with NECESSARILY. The list seems to have been taken from Ōno Tōru 1962:640 but printed with an obvious misnumbering of the seventh example as "4943" for "4043" (there are only 4516 poems in the collection). The list:

    (1) afazu 'not meeting' (M 809)
    (2) tirazu 'not falling' (M 845)
    (3) mono̱-[i]fazu 'saying nothing' (M 4337)
    (4) ifazu 'saying nothing' (M 4364)
    (5) kwofiyzu 'not loving' (M 4371)
    (6) kafyer[y]i-myizu 'not looking back' (M 4372)
    (7) kyi[y] nakazu 'come and not be crying' (M 4043 — but only the Kan'ei-bon text

has the SEI phonogram, the other manuscripts have DAKU).

Ōno Tōru points out that examples 3-6 are dialect poems; he suspects the first three examples contain scribal mistakes for DAKU phonograms. Also cited (758) is tamafazu 'not giving' written with the phonogram NECESSARILY in Shōsō-in kana-monjo A. There are three examples of NECESSARILY used to write /zu/ in the Shoku-Nihongi, one in Senmyō 28 and two in Senmyō 3. But the DAKU phonogram RECEIVE (now read *zyu*) is used in Senmyō 26 and 45. (See Ōno Tōru 608.)

It will be noticed that the syllable in question in the Bussokuseki-no-uta example is preceded by a nasal syllable. The middle syllable of the word nezumyi 'rat' (Mg .ne¨su'mi, JP nezumi, Mkz nezumi⁻) is written with the phonogram NECESSARILY in Kakyō-hyōshiki and Saibara (Zdb, Ōno Tōru 755) and in Wamyō-shō (Zdb); here the syllable is flanked by a nasal syllable on either side. Ōno Tōru (670, 736) observes that the syllable /zu/ in the name Kuzumaro is written with NECESSARILY in the prose of M 786, 789, and 791, yet in Shoku-Nihongi it is also written with phonograms that are clearly to be read /ku(n)zumaro/.

V-a-zu is the negative counterpart of V-u (when predicative) or V-yi, and V-a-zi is the negative counterpart of V-a-mu 'will': ko̱mu ka ko̱zi ka 'whether I will come or not' (M 1922). This point is very well argued by Yoshida 1973, who also discusses the various etymologies that have been proposed. The most plausible one assumes a contraction from the infinitive of the bound negative auxiliary verb -(a)n- + forms of the verb 'do': -an-[y]i su > -azu, -an-[y]i si[y] > -azi. The form V-a-de, which began appearing in Heian times as a substitute for V-azu te[y], is thought by some to be a contraction from an unattested *V-an-[y]i te[y]. Cf. Ōno 1974:1457b.

There are few occurrences of -zi: wasure[y]-zi is written with SCHOLAR (now read *si*) in K 9 and K 13; EAR-ORNAMENT is used in NS 5 to write wasure[y]-zi and in NS 124 to write ara-zi.

DAKU syllables resulting from a contraction of nasal + SEI syllable are found in a number of etymologies that have been proposed, such as those of Hashimoto quoted by Ōno Tōru 571: simo-tu-ye > siduye, kamyi-sas[y]i > kazasi, yuymyi-turu > yuduru, yumyi-key > yugey, yumyi-tuku > yuduku. But Ōno Tōru, who takes a dim view of postnasal drip as an explanation for nigori, thinks these cases can be explained simply as compound nigori that is independent of the contraction process.

4.6. The particle made [ni].

The expression ··· made [ni] '(to) the extent of; till' is not particularly common in Old Japanese. There seem to be no examples in the Koji-ki songs, and only one in the songs of Nihon-Shoki (NS 78), where the syllable /de/ is written with the phonogram MUD, which always represents a DAKU syllable — as it does, for example, in ide[y] tatasu 'deign to emerge' (NS 102). The Man'yō-shū has a number of examples written with phonograms that always represent /de/: MUD in M 4122 and 4075, CLAY in M 4513. But there are also examples written with phonograms that basically represent /te/: BOW-ONE in M 485, 1809, 2028, 3056, 3264, and 3742; variant of LOW in M 892. The phonogram LIFT, used in M 876, represents only /de/ in the non-dialect poems, but it is ambivalent in the dialect poems, where it writes the second syllable of the noun swode 'sleeve' in M 3389 as well as of the particle made [ni] (M 804, 839, 844, 876, 3448), yet it is also used to write the gerund particle te[y] and a few other words containing the syllable /te/. (See Ōno Tōru 646-7.) In the Shoki songs, LIFT represents /de/. The phonogram BOW-ONE writes only the syllable /te/ in the non-dialect poems of the Man'yō-shū, except for the handful of occurrences where it writes the second syllable of swode 'sleeve', nade[y] 'pat', and ide[y] 'emerge'. In Shoku-Nihongi it is used for the second syllable of the particle in Senmyō 1 (twice), 4, 5, 7, 13 (three times), and 25; otherwise BOW-ONE writes /te/.

In Bussokuseki-no-uta BOW-ONE writes the syllable /te/ six times. The remaining two occurrences are in the particle: tada ni afu made ni, masa ni afu made ni 'till we meet directly, till we meet face to face' (6:5-6). Miller 1975 claims that this must have been pronounced /mateni/ and is the "older form" of made ni, which he says developed by the "same processes of contraction and voicing" by which ni-te became modern de; in saying this, he ignored the difference in the order of the oral and nasal syllables, for which I believe there is in fact no parallel case. It is true that ma-de 'both hands' (> 'completely') has been proposed by Ōno as the origin for the particle — cf. the rebus representation LEFT-RIGHT in M 420 and M 1134 — so that ultimately the noun te[y] 'hand' may be involved. Though Miller's methodological assumptions are left unstated, he apparently presumes that what is sometimes written with a SEI phonogram and sometimes with the DAKU counterpart must have had two variant pronunciations.[18] On the other hand, scholars in Japan have generally taken the position that when there is clear attestation of a DAKU syllable in some of the ocurrences, those attestations written with basically SEI phonograms are also to be taken as DAKU. As Ōno Tōru puts it: "It was the usual thing in uncontrived popular orthography to use basically voiceless phonograms for the voiced ones too" — but not the other way around! He also says that even in more formal, studied orthography the basically SEI phonograms were chosen to write the DAKU syllables when those were (1) the result of compound marking (rendaku); (2) in partial reduplications (such as tuduk- 'continue'); (3) in enclitic particles.

In the string /madeni/ the syllable in question is flanked by nasal syllables, so that not only prenasal drip but also postnasal drip could be held responsible for the Bussokuseki-no-uta orthography. Even when ni does not follow, we still have the preceding nasal syllable. But perhaps Ōno Tōru is right in assuming that this all belongs to part of the larger insouciance which the Japanese display in allowing themselves to use SEI syllables to represent DAKU (but not vice-versa!) — not only in early days, but even now, when "kabushiki kaisha" (or at least "K.K.") is the romanization often seen for what is pronounced kabushiki-gaisha, yet geisha is never seen as "keisha". If we were to apply Miller's tacit assumptions about Old Japanese orthography to the habits of modern Japanese, we would have to surmise that a well-known scholar who appears in Miller's bibliography as "Nakada Norio" had changed his name sometime between 1957 when the revised edition of the book he coauthored with Doi Tadao (Nihon-go no rekishi) appeared with the appropriate furigana given in the colophon, and 1972, when volume 2 of Kōza Kokugo-shi not only carries contradictory furigana in its colophon but even informs us in elegant romanization that the book is copyrighted by "N. Nakata". (Will the real Mr Infield please rise and tell us how to pronounce his name?)[17] Perhaps it is unfortunate that the romanization forces a definite decision on voiced vs. voiceless where in the kana orthography the nigori mark often serves as no more than a REMINDER of voicing — or of permissible voicing. (I have seen it next to a Chinese character in a neon sign advertising a Shinjuku hotel with the name Ie-jima, to remind us not to pronounce 'island' as shima.)

At the same time, we do well to remember that the language has doublets such as gurai and kurai, which are not exactly free variants in speech, though people often write kurai for what they pronounce as gurai. Other sei-daku doublets still alive include mutukasii/muzukasii 'difficult', in which the preceding nasal syllable may or may not be responsible for the voicing but the voiceless version is also used.[18] Ōno Susumu assumes OJ doublets when (and, presumably, only when) there is evidence in the later attestations for the voiceless versions — as with the so/zo particle. Given the facts we have examined, that seems the most reasonable attitude. Yet even though we assume that both SEI and DAKU versions existed for the emphatic particle, it does not follow that every ocurrence written with a basically SEI phonogram was necessarily pronounced /so/. There may have been more than one "Mr Nakata" in Nara days who wrote /so/ but said /zo/.

And perhaps none of this is too surprising. English is rife with intervocalic voicings of recent origin — some regional, others widespread: congratulate, significant, electricity (either or both), ... I still recall my surprise on discovering, many years ago, that a well-known avenue in Berkeley, California, is spelled "Shattuck" rather than "Shadick". And I have yet to come across written acknowledgment that the ambiguity of the statement "I wonder what they had to eat" is usually resolved in the present "I wonder what they have to eat", which means "I wonder what they have available [for someone] to eat" with /-vt-/ but "I wonder what they are forced to eat" with /-ft-/. (Similarly /-zt-/ vs. /-st-/ in "has to eat".) A case of "reverse nigori" in English is found in the widely heard pronunciation of -t- for -d- in the name Wimbledon, the site of tennis tournaments in England.

5. Rendaku in later Japanese.

5.1. Modern compound nouns.

Many modern compound nouns are of recent origin. But the nigori device is sometimes activated by analogy with earlier formations: ama⁷-ŋutu 'galoshes' were not around until sometime after 1912 but treating kutu⁷ as -ŋutu is by analogy with other compounds, such as wara⁷-ŋutu 'straw footgear', which goes back well over a thousand years. A remark was made in §25 of Chapter 1 about the recentness of such inventions as denki-ŋo⁷tatu 'electric quilt' and kabusiki-ŋa⁷isya 'stock company' and the fact that the two Chinese-origin binoms ko-tatu⁻ 'foot-warmer quilt' and

kai-sya⁻ 'business company' are themselves not of particularly early attestation.
Words of Chinese origin that are treated as free nouns often prove susceptible to
rendaku: oo-ŋe˥nka 'big quarrel' and huuhu-ŋe˥nka 'domestic dispute', tati-ŋe˥iko
'rehearsal', ko-ŋi˥yoo 'clever', yuki-ŋe˥siki 'snow scene', soo-da˥isyoo 'commander-
in-chief', mori-da˥kusan 'lots and lots', oo-da˥iko 'big drum'; yasu-bu˥sin 'cheap
construction', manga-bon⁻ 'comic book'; oo-zo˥n 'big loss', ate-zu˥iryoo 'guess',
murasaki-zu˥isyoo 'amethyst', uta-za˥imon 'ballads sung by itinerant priests', asa-
zi˥e 'shallow wisdom', tamari-zyo˥oyu 'a kind of soy sauce'. There are two kinds of
delicious siso⁻ 'perilla, beafsteak-plant' (which, despite its accent, is a Chinese
binom): ao-zi˥so 'green perilla' and aka-zi˥so 'red perilla'. Among the kinds of
syasin⁻ 'photograph' there is one type called ao-zya˥sin 'blueprint'. Various other
examples will be found in Martin 1952, interspersed with examples of bound morphemes
of Chinese origin that have apparently undergone rendaku in individual lexical
formations. The process is not productive for even the binoms, however, and the
principal new formations are with certain recurring elements that might best be
regarded as suffixes or postnouns in the modern language: (-)bon⁻ 'book', -ŋa˥isya
'company', ... (Compare the words called "restrictives" and "quasi-restrictives" in
Martin 1975.)

The word ti˥nŋin 'wages' is usually written as if a compound of the Chinese
loans ti˥n 'wage' and ki˥n 'money; gold', offering a unique example of rendaku for
the latter noun; but the actual etymology of the word is probably gi˥n 'silver;
money'. This is a modern word, first attested in 1698, and it may well represent two
etyma, for Hepburn 1886 gives "chinkin" and Brinkley 1896 has both "chinkin" and
"chingin", with examples under the latter. The version with -kin may be a reading
pronunciation (based on the character falsely used) or it may represent a competing
compound with the morpheme (-)kin rather than (-)gin.

5.2. The productivity of rendaku.

In fact, the process of rendaku is not freely productive for native elements,
either. Compounds undergo the process as the result of specific analogy to other
compounds with the same element. A few native nouns of the susceptible shape types
have never appeared with voicing of the initial and probably never will. I believe
these are valid examples: kita˥⁻ 'north', ka˥su 'dregs', ka˥se 'shackles', tuti⁻
'earth', hama˥ 'beach', hasi⁻ 'edge', hima⁻ 'leisure', hi˥me 'princess', and tuya
'gloss'; for sita˥ 'below' Gakken kokugo dai-jiten 835 gives an obsolete example
tana-zita 'below [= at] the counter, storekeeping' but NKD has tana-sita. Failure to
indulge in rendaku may be accidental: some nouns make few compounds, and others
offer only a single rendaku example, often obsolete or archaic. The noun tame˥ 'the
sake (of)' undergoes rendaku in one word, ryoo-dame⁻ 'mutual benefit', and kuso˥
'dung' undergoes it only in ma-ŋuso˥ 'horse droppings'. There are not many kinds of
tawasi⁻ 'scrub-brush' but one of them turns out to be kamenokoo-da˥wasi 'a brush to
scrub tortoise-shells'. Certain morphemes that, in modern Japanese, are not free
nouns also fail to offer an example of rendaku: kiki-⁻ 'hear; take effect'; ko⁻
'this' (cf. so⁻ 'that' which takes rendaku in sore˥-zore 'respectively'), ki˥-
'come' (cf. ki-⁻ 'wear' which readily forms compounds as -ŋi '···wear, garb for
···'); ? ... . The verb si-⁻ 'do' takes rendaku after certain verbal nouns (see Ch. 1,
§25) and also as the initial element of si-ai⁻ 'athletic tournament' in hoonoo-zi˥ai
'festival tourney', rensyuu-zi˥ai 'practice meet', etc. The verb ke˥- ⊁-ke˥r-
'kick' has rendaku in one word, asi˥-ŋe˥ 'kicking'.

The fact that certain words with -m- fail to show rendaku is probably because they were earlier -b- (or, rather, -mb-) and therefore were subject to the block of Lyman's Law: himo⁻¹⁹ 'cord', kemuri⁻ 'smoke', ... (Contrast these with kimo⁷ 'liver', never attested with the -b-, and do-ŋimo⁻ 'one's "guts" = fortitude'.) Similarly, hasi⁻ 'edge' forms a doublet hasi/hazi; cf. hazime⁻- 'begin it'. It is unclear whether an earlier -b- might account for the failure of hima⁻ 'leisure' to show rendaku; the word is not attested in a dakuon version (*fiba) but the noun ma⁻ 'space' may just form a doublet with ba⁻ 'place'. By itself ko⁷ 'flour' does not undergo voicing; but rendaku is usual when ko⁷ is part of the more common noun kona⁷ (>-ŋona). In the meaning 'tide' sio⁷ seems never to undergo the process, but as 'salt' sio⁷ shows rendaku: ama-zio⁻ 'light salting'. That rendaku is still alive is evident in the lexicalization of ki-ka⁷e⁷ru 'change (clothes)' to kiŋa⁷e⁷ru, which has taken hold since around 1960 or so. No other instance of the construction V-i-kaeru 'change V-ing; change the N that one V-s' has done this. Foreign loanwords of the past 400 years or so appear to be unsusceptible to rendaku, though there may be occasional exceptions, such as iroha-ŋa⁷ruta 'kana cards' from ka⁷ruta < Portuguese carta 'card'. The noun kiseru⁻ 'pipe' (thought to be from Cambodian [Khmer] khsier) undergoes rendaku: kuwae-ŋi⁷seru 'handfree pipe-smoking', natamame-ŋi⁷seru 'flat-tubed pipe', nobe-ŋi⁷seru 'all-metal pipe', ban-ŋi⁷seru 'long coarse pipe for everyday use', nanban-ŋi⁷seru 'broomrape (plant)'.

5.3. Exceptions to Lyman's Law.

Finally, we have the problem of exceptions to Lyman's Law. There are a very few isolated examples, such as rei-de⁷ŋami/-te⁷ŋami 'letter of thanks' and waka-zi⁷raŋa/ -si⁷raŋa 'prematurely white hair', which are listed by dictionaries in two versions. The name Saburo⁷o⁻ ('Boychild Three') is sometimes -za⁷buroo in compound names (Syooza⁷buroo, Kanza⁷buroo, ...), but the first part of this word goes back to the Chinese borrowing sam(¹/ᵤ) (later san) with a final nasal mora; it is the originally nasal final mora in the preceding element (syoo < seű < SHENG; kan; ...) that is responsible for the rendaku. The truly perplexing case is hasiŋo⁻ 'ladder', which occurs in quite a few compounds as -ba⁷siŋo, e.g. nawa-ba⁷siŋo 'rope ladder'. One explanation would be a variant *hasiko at some stage, but that is not attested, even in dialects. The noun is first attested in the Muromachi period, and the etymology is uncertain, but it is probably a diminutive (with the suffix -ko/-ŋo) of hasi⁷ 'bridge; ladder'. The Japanese-Portuguese dictionary of 1604 offers fasigo "or fasino( )ko". The exception hun-ziba⁷ru ← fumi-sibar- 'tie up' (not attested before 1500) is probably the result of associating an unattested *hun-zimar- ← *fumi-simar- with sibaru. (This is another effect of the -b/m- confusion mentioned in §5.2.)

5.4. Unusual cases of rendaku.

There are a few Myōgi-shō notations in which the rendaku affects not the first but the second syllable: ˈsiˈta-.ku…tu 'undershoes'. These might simply be mistakes, but they probably reflect contracted forms of the second element: where Zs Mg has ˈsiˈta-.ku…tu 'undershoes' Kn Mg has :siˈta-u…tu with the annotation "KU" beside the last syllable. (Cf. Komatsu 1977a:381.) The Japanese-Portuguese dictionary has kami-gakura for kami-kagura 'sacred dances'; Morita 1977:28 suggests that this is the application of rendaku which then forces a "clearing" (devoicing) of the initial of the syllable -gu-. He calls our attention to the modern variants hara-zutumi = hara-tuzumi 'drumming one's belly' and sita-zutumi = sita-tuzumi 'clicking one's tongue'.

But those oddities could be explained as resulting from syllable metathesis, which happens sporadically under other circumstances. (Morita's example ato-zisari "< ato-sizari" may be unjustified; see siˢ/ₐzaru in Ch. 6.)

Of etymological interest are several examples of -uzi for usi 'ox'. Myōgi-shō has .ti-.u..si 'milk cow' and .a.me-.u..si 'a kind of ox'. There are examples of oso-uzi 'slow ox' (Muromachi) and perhaps ?iki-uzi = iki-usi 'live ox', ?ko-uzi = ko-usi 'calf', and ?wo-uzi = wo-usi 'bull', forms cited by Ōno without textual references. Modern dialects attest the word beeko-uzi (Tanba) or beko-zi (Mie), a compound that incorporates the dialect noun beko 'ox', which is thought to be a loan from Ainu pekó 'ox'. It seems we must reconstruct at least a doublet usi/uzi from *u(n)si, a form that could be a compound of unknown u(-) and -si 'animal' (cf. si-ka = ka 'deer' and perhaps sisi 'flesh; animal'), with optional genitive -(n)- (cf. hituzi < fyituzi < *pitunsi 'sheep'). Further research on these etyma will need to take into account -su/-so 'animal, bird, thing', as nominalizer (dialect) 'thing, one, fact', perhaps to be associated with the Middle Korean nominalizer so/to); mi 'serpent' < miy < *m[u]si, Ryūkyū iki-musi 'animal'; oso = (Muromachi) kafa-uso/-woso = (Wamyō-shō) woso 'otter'; and Middle Korean 'sywo 'ox'.

5.5. Functional load and orthographic negligence.

In the Nara period, separate sets of characters were used to write dakuon and seion syllables. But there were ambivalent phonograms, such as BEAN for both /tu/ and /du/.[20] And voiceless Man'yō-gana symbols were used for voiced in the Shōsō-in letters (before 762); cf. Wenck 1959:215. When katakana and hiragana came into existence, during the Heian period, the dakuon syllables were not distinguished in writing from the corresponding seion syllables; it was only with the advent of reading marks to indicate the accent that a device was sometimes used to indicate the dakuon, leading to the modern "double dot" dakuoʼn-ten, which even now people often neglect to write. The Heian indifference toward the voicing distinctions can be attributed to two factors: the low functional load of the distinction in the non-Chinese vocabulary and the development of kana-maʼziri writing, with the Chinese elements always written in Chinese and only native particles and the like written in kana.[21] (Cf. Hamada 1971.) These same factors are at work today, discouraging the Japanese from paying attention to writing the distinction or, indeed, worrying about it in any way.

Chart. Phonetic realizations of SEI-DAKU distinctions.

This chart is just a rough guide. For Yonaguni there are a number of special developments, here irrelevant; see Ch. 1, §23. Vowels are noted phonemically.

proto-J	Old J	Type 1 dialects (Tōkyō, Kyōto, Hiroshima, ...)	Type 2 dialects (northern Honshū, western Kyūshū)	Type 3 dialect (Miyako)	Type 4 dialect (Yonaguni)
b-	w-	wa ∅-	wa ∅-	b-	b-
-b-	-w-	-wa -∅-	-wa -∅-	-∅-	-∅-
( )	(¨P-)	b-	b-	b-	b-
-np-	-¨P-	-b-	-˜b-	-b-	-b-
p-	˙P-	fu çi h-	fu çi h-	pʰ-	fu çi h-
-p-	˙P-	-wa -∅-	-wa -∅-	-∅-	-∅-
d(y)-	y-	y-	y-; ž-	y-	d-
-d(y)-	-y-	-y-	-y-; -ž-	-y-	-y-
( )	(¨T-)	dzu dži d-	dzu dži d-	d-	d-
-nt-	-¨T-	-zu -ži -d-	-˜dzu -˜ži -˜d-	-d-	-d-
t-	˙T-	tsu tši tʰ-	tsu tši tʰ-	tʰ (tši tsï)	tci tʰ-
-t-	-˙T-	-tsu- -tši- -tʰ-	-dzu- -dži- -d-	-tʰ- (tši tsï)	-tci- -t- [1]
( )	(¨S-)	dži dz-	dži dz-	d- (dži dzï)	d-
-ns-	-¨S	-ži- -z-	-ži -z-; -˜ži -˜z- [2]	-d- (dži dzï)	-d-
(t)s-	˙S-	ši s-	ši s-	ši s-	ši s-
?(t)ši					
( )	(¨K-)	g- [3]	g-	g-	g-
-nk-	-¨K-	-ŋ- -g- --	-ŋ- -ŋg- -˜g-	-g-	-ŋ-
k-	˙K-	kʰ-	kʰ-	kʰ-	kʰ-
-k-	˙K-	-kʰ-	-g-	-kʰ-	-g-

[1]Both unaspirated.   [2]Tappi dialect (Clarke).

[3]But the nasal velar is used initially as well as medially in towns on Hamana
   Lagoon and part of Toyohashi city, according to Shin Nihongo-kōza 3:108.

Notes to Chapter 2.

¹ Dialect data can be found in several sources; the most helpful are Hirayama's several monographs on the Ryūkyūs and Clarke's 1973 dissertation on dialects of northern Honshū, southern Shikoku, and islands west of Kyūshū.

² According to KggJ 533b (and KggD 495-6) attestation for attaching tone marks to characters can be found in the work Kuāngmǐu zhèngsú by Yán Shī-gǔ, who died in 648, and in the work Shǐjì zhèngyì zìlì (introduction dated 736) by Zhāng Shǒujié. Use of tone marks in Japan began around 950 (before 897 according to Mabuchi, Kōza Kokugo-shi 1:277) and kana began showing the marks in the 11th century, with extant examples in a text (Dainichi-kyō kōdai jōju giki) of 1072 (or possibly 1059? —Tsukishima 1969:394, who cites a single example from the 987 work Kongō-kai giki). Marking DAKU syllables with paired circles is earliest found in the Seidai-ji book Goma-mikki (1035). A distinction between horizontally paired circles (ₒₒ) and vertically paired circles (⁚) appears in annotations of 1166-9 (called Shishu-sōi-so Ninnan-ten) to the work Bunkyō-hifu-ron by Kūkai (= Kōbō-daishi 774-835), and in old sūtra-chanting notes of the Tendai and Shingon sects. (Cf. Kindaichi 1974.) The horizontal pair, called hondaku¹-ten 'original-DAKU mark', was used to mark intrinsically DAKU syllables which were always DAKU. The vertical pair, called sindaku¹-ten "new-DAKU mark", marked DAKU syllables as morphophonemic variants of syllables that were basically SEI. (The term sindaku⁻ appears in Hoke-kyō tanji 1136 cf. Okumura 1952 n.13.) The "tone marks" (syo¹o-ten) continued in use for the DAKU syllables after they were no longer used to show pitch accent; the paired mark was eventually called dakuten⁻ and the single mark fell into disuse except for special purposes such as indicating that a syllable of the f- (later h-) column was to be read as p-, the source of the single circle called handaku¹-ten "half-DAKU mark" which came into use during the Edo period. (The term handaku⁻ was first used by Monnō in Waji-taikan-shō 1754; cf. Satō 1979:36.) Komatsu 1981:71 calls the single mark hudaku¹-ten 'non-DAKU mark' and says it was used in some of the manuscripts of the 1400s and 1500s to mark a SEI syllable that it was feared might be misread as an unmarked DAKU, not only for the f- syllables, but also for t-, s-, and k-. It was fairly late before the DAKU marks were generally moved to the upper right of the kana symbols, where there is no danger of their being misinterpreted as intended also to indicate the high/low pitch shown by the upper/lower position on the left. The modern position appears in manuscripts of Seami (1353-1433) and "verbatim notes" on the Kokin-shū dated 1481. This was well after the distinction of the "going tone" (LH = rise) had been lost, thus freeing the upper right corner where that tone had been marked; and perhaps more importantly it was after the dot system of marking tones found in Myōgi-shō had been replaced by the marks used in the scores (bokufu⁻) of the sūtra-chanting guides called syo¹omyoo⁻: KAKU ⁻ low, TI \ high (Bumō-ki). On the history of the nigori marks see Wenck 1959:233-7, Komatsu 1981:54-73.

³ Perhaps also in these: te-tudaf- (JP tetdai) 'aid'; sitadami 'periwinkle' (if this is from [i]si-tatami). Both have Yaeyama reflexes with -d-, (Miyara), as in the forms cited.

⁴ But Nakamoto 1976:198 treats Yonaguni -gi- as the regular reflex and says -ni comes only from -ŋe (Tōkyō ge-/-ŋe). Hirayama 1964 gives [usaᴺgi] with a unique segment but [kugi] ("older speakers also /kudi/"); cf. [kaŋi] < kage 'shadow'. Notice that Yonaguni tagi 'waterfall' then points to proto-Japanese *tagi rather than *taki, but the Yonaguni accent (B) is incongruent, so the form may be a borrowing. NKD cites osaki from Hida and usaki from Ōsumi for 'rabbit'. In [kyaŋgi] 'black pine' and [haŋgi] 'sumac' the last part seems to be a reduction of -no-ki.

⁵ The notation of particle ellipsis here may be misleading. There are, to be sure, examples of ga marking the subject of subordinate clauses in the Man'yō-shū, but in main clauses (without auxiliaries) the subject was left unmarked.

⁶ A later exception is omo-hayui 'embarrassing', JP (w)omo-fayui, which NKD claims as "also -b- in medieval and modern language" (i.e. Muromachi and Edo periods).

⁷ Mkz yamakai⁻ is probably an archaism; Mg — ; JP — .

⁸ But in Late Middle Japanese there are attestations of goso, on which (along with sooroo/zooroo and sama/zama) see Yasuda 1977:34; cf. Kamei 1969:12.

⁹ The phonogram ADD /ka/ writes the particle in M 4343, but we assume that this is a mistake for CONGRATULATE, so that only the last word in the phrase wa ga myi = wa ga mye 'my wife' is a dialect variant. The same mistake occurs in K 19, where wa ga is written with ADD though in K 20 the correct phonogram CONGRATULATE is used. This type of scribal error results from writing only the top part of the phonogram; a similar mistake is the writing of WAVE /fa/ for GRANNY /ba/, mentioned below.

¹⁰ According to a note by Ōno Susumu on M 52 (Nihon koten bungaku taikei 4:335) there are seven, but I have been unable to locate the seventh.

¹¹ Two texts (Kishū-bon, Ruiju-koshū) have WAVE. Zdb cites the passage both ways: koso-fa 772b, koso-ba 840a.

¹² Ōno thinks V-a-ba must have developed later than V-ey-ba and Zdb 571d suggests that it may have come from V-a-m[u] fa. The distinction between the two forms is alive in the Ryūkyūs. According to Matsumura (in Doi 1957:244) the form V-a-ba disappeared from the standard language after the beginning of the Edo period.

¹³ Miller (141b) presumes a doublet with -do the "no doubt later form" and says "writings with unambiguous tö [= to] are by no means rare elsewhere in the Old Japanese corpus". From the listings here, the reader can judge for himself the rarity. Ōno 1975 derives -do mo from the deictic to 'that' (perhaps an old variant of so?) and the focus particle mo, suggesting that the voicing was not original; from the frequency in early texts he believes V-ey-do mo was the earlier version, contracting somewhat later to V-ey-do, which became more popular in Heian times.

¹⁴ Ōno Tōru 649 suggests there may be semantic overtones from the graph, which not only means EQUAL but also GROUP (with the kun reading -ra).

¹⁵ The Koji-ki songs lack the syllables zwo, bwo, bo; Shoki songs lack the same syllables and also gye. (Cf. Ōno Tōru 614, 673-4.)

¹⁶ Miller apparently assumes that the Bussokuseki-no-uta orthography (at least) wrote vowel sequences morphophonemically — presumably they pronounced myi-at[w]o as /myeto/? — but represented phonemically the initial consonants of particles etc.

¹⁷ Three distinguished Japanese linguists assured me in Tōkyō in May 1976 that the scholar in question pronounces his name Nakata, yet Kokugo nenkan 1980:128b tells us to read it "Nakada" and the Shōgakkan dictionary Kogo dai-jiten 1984 tells us the work was copyrighted in the name of "N. Nakada" and coauthors. From the information on p. 163 of Sakuma Ei 1972 (Nihon-jin no sei) we conclude that the 80,000 persons bearing that surname ("mostly in western Japan") pronounce it Nakada; yet p.21a of P.G. O'Neill 1972 (Japanese Names) leads us to believe the name is always pronounced Nakata. (Nakata/Nakada Norio was born in Nara; he now resides in Tōkyō.) Finally, E.A. Fol'kman's Slovar' yaponskikh imeni i familiy offers not only a choice of Nakata or Nakada, but also Uchida! Perhaps Miller was hasty in scolding Doi for miswriting Yanagita Kunio's surname as Yanagida; many a library has his works so alphabetized. Incidentally, the reason we drive "Toyota" cars made in a place originally called Toyoda is not, as I once thought, because of a feeling of superfluousness or ugliness in the double-dot diacritic that marks the dakuon, but because a numerologist consulted by the Toyoda family in 1937 advised them that eight was their lucky number and so they changed the katakana version of the name

from TO-YO-¨TA which has ten strokes to TO-YO-TA which has eight strokes; or so it
is claimed in Business Week 2750:50 (1982:8:2). I have been told that the city of
Toyoda has changed its name officially to "Toyota" to match that of the automobile.
The problem is not confined to surnames, as anyone who has been to the prefecture of
Iba˥raki/Iba˥ragi can testify. When in 1945 I first visited the port of Sasebo in
Kyūshū I was surprised to hear the residents calling the place Sasyeho. The local
folk of Karu˥izawa⁻ pronounce the town's name with -s- (Komatsu 1981:211); in Nagano
the pronunciation is Karuisawa⁻, but younger speakers have hybridized it as both
Karuizawa⁻ and Karu˥isawa (Kudō 1978:20-1). The isolated mountain enclave called
Totsukawa (that seems to be the approved version) is also called Totsugawa, and both
versions appear in NKD. Americans should not be surprised to learn that the river
that flows through Toyokawa city in Aichi prefecture is known as the Toyogawa
(Nakagawa 1966:311a); after all, the "Arkansas River" is called the /arkɛnzəs/ when
it passes through Arkansas City, Kansas, and becomes the /árkənsɔ̀/ when it gets
into the state of Arkansas (= "Arkansaw"). Tōkyō's well-known Akiha˥bara used to be
called Akiba˥-hara or Akiba˥-ppara; the name was taken from the shrine Akiba-zi˥nzya
named for Akiba-no-yama in Shizuoka. (The pronunciation Akiwabara is also reported.)
Cf. Akinaga 1977c. Nor is the problem confined to names. Certain variant versions of
common vocabulary have gone unnoticed for years: the word yuugata⁻ 'evening' is
pronounced yuukata by older speakers in parts of northern Tōkyō, and the
pronunciation yukkata is also reported. The word spelled "gipusu" is usually
pronounced gi˥busu 'plaster cast', and the word "tihusu" is widely pronounced
ti˥busu 'typhus'; though the latter has been noted by a few lexicographers, the
former remains neglected. Among the nouns created from Chinese loans, such popular
pronunciations as sendaku for sentaku⁻ 'laundry' and zide˥n-sya for zite˥n-sya
'bicycle' have gone ignored, though tuudatu⁻ for tuutatu 'notification' has been
picked up. Morphophonemic analogies are sometimes apparent. It is understandable
that many a kenkyuu-zyo˥⁻ 'research institute' romanizes its name as -syo or -sho;
the director of the institute, after all, bears the title of syo-tyoo⁻.

   [18] The SEI form mutukasii (and the verb mutukaru 'fret') is the Kansai version,
the DAKU form muzukasii (and muzukaru) the Kantō version, according to Tai 107. The
pronunciation matudake for matutake 'mushroom' (first attested in the Japanese-
Portuguese dictionary of 1603) is said to be "elegant", and mattake is considered
"dialect". Apparently yomi˥-kuse˥ or yomi˥-guse⁻ 'one's peculiar (or corrupt)
pronunciation' are simply variants. It remains to be explained why nobori˥-guti⁻
'bottom of stairs' is always -g- but ori˥-kuti⁻ 'head of stairs' is usually -k-
rather than the variant ori-guti under which it is listed in Kenkyusha's Japanese-
English dictionary; the JP dictionary has both for the latter word but does not list
nobori˥-guti⁻. It gives -k- for agari-guti⁻/agari˥-kuti⁻ 'main entrance' (listed
with the less common -kuti by Kenkyusha) and iri-guti⁻/iri-kuti⁻ (listed with
the more common -guti by Kenkyusha and only with -guti by Mkz); JP does not carry an
entry for a word equivalent to modern de˥-guti 'exit'. The DAKU form a˥da˥kamo for
the adverb a˥ta˥kamo 'just as if' was first attested in Hepburn 1867. The DAKU
manᵃ/ₒgareru for manuᵏ/ᵧgareru 'escape' can be found in Brinkley 1896 and an early
(940) attestation is cited in NKD from Utsubo-monogatari; the other attestations
(including Shinsen-Jikyō, Myōgi-shō, and JP) are all SEI.

   [19] Nakagawa 1966:313 thinks there may be Man'yō-shū examples of -bimo. I wonder.

   [20] Perhaps related is the erroneous assumptions in borrowing foreign loanwords
today, where decisions on voiced vs. voiceless are made without undue concern for
the source language: kuroozu-a˥ppu 'close-up', ru˥uzu na 'loose', ...

   [21] As Skillend (184) points out, scribal disregard of the sei-daku distinction had
started already in the Man'yō-shū, beginning with the mid rounded vowel, and it came
to be gradually generalized.

Chapter 3. Syncope and elision.

1. The verb gerund: variant forms.

All dialects of Japanese make a verb form we call the gerund by attaching to
the infinitive (-i) a suffix. In the southern Ryūkyūs (Yaeyama and Yonaguni) many
of the gerund forms are made by attaching a reflex of si-te 'doing', the gerund of
si 'do', with various reductions. There seems to be no evidence of this structure
elsewhere in the Ryūkyūs, nor does any dialect of the main islands require that
explanation. All other gerunds are assumed to have developed, like those of Literary
Japanese, from the infinitive + -te, itself the infinitive of the perfect auxiliary
tu(ru). Tsushima has a competing form that attaches -tu, -tsu, -tši, or -q; this is
thought to be a relic of the use of the auxiliary tu(ru) as a kind of "connective
particle" (cf. Zhs 9:151).

In Heian Japanese the auxiliary tu(ru) and its infinitive te were set off from
the preceding infinitive by a juncture. Presumably the loss of the juncture is what
triggered the contractions and assimilations that characterize many of the modern
formations and are part of what is called *onbin*. Apparently the juncture was slower
to disappear in the gerunds of vowel verbs; that may indicate that the infinitives
were pronounced with a long vowel (···e-i, ···i-i), ignored in the kana spellings,
where the consonant verbs had infinitives with a short vowel (··· C-i). The gerunds
of the vowel-stems remained uncontracted (···e-te, ···i-te) and did not undergo the
onbin reductions. It should be noted that a number of verbs have switched classes —
from vowel stem to consonant stem or from consonant stem to vowel stem, both in
classical times and later. A familiar example is the verb 'borrow', kariru⁻ in
Tōkyō but karu⁻ in Ōsaka.

Our description of the gerund as simply the infinitive of the perfect auxiliary
tu(ru), while historically correct, may be misleading. Even in the Nara period the
element te[y] had acquired special characteristics that set it apart from the verbal
auxiliary, so that it is usually treated as a "particle" by the grammarians and the
lexicographers. Individual examples of velar elision in gerund forms appear fairly
early (810, according to Tsukishima 1969:365) and sporadic examples are found also
in nouns. In Myōgi-shō the gerund forms apparently have a juncture, for the (-)te
is assigned an independent accent; yet there and in earlier Heian texts there are
examples of the shortened shapes, such as oi-te for oki-te, so that some of the
processes had already begun — perhaps as free variants — by early in the 11th
century, but these did not supplant the unshortened forms in the spoken language
until sometime after 1200. According to Komatsu 1981:179-80 the reduced forms were
relaxed variants (like modern san for the honorific sama or aˀnta for anaˀta 'you')
which coexisted with the more formal versions for many years and may have been
present in colloquial speech from much earlier than the attestations would lead us
to believe; we might draw an analogy with the coexistence of the forms "can't" and
"cannot" in English.

The Chart for Ch. 3 presents a series of ordered phonetic developments that
will account for most of the common dialect forms, excluding peculiarly Ryūkyūan
developments, with each form starting from a "source", the phonetic shape assumed
for proto-Japanese. Hypothetical intermediate forms which do not turn up in any
known dialect are preceded by an asterisk (*). The following assumptions have been
made about proto-Japanese phonology:

(1) Stops were voiceless initially; they were nondistinctively aspirated, at least
initially before nonhigh vowels. The aspiration is here noted by -h-. The gerund
ending -the[y] is aspirated because the stop is initial after a juncture.

(2) Stops were nondistinctively voiced after the nasal phoneme -n; they were optionally voiced between vowels. Some modern dialects retain the voicing; most have the unvoiced version.)

(3) There was no distinction of i and yi. We will write yi so that i is available to note the later development in certain Ryūkyū dialects of a non-palatal(izing) high front vowel, created from the raising of e or the fronting of u.

There is an order to the numbering of the postulated stages of development, but a given later form is not required to go through each process, since the chart is a composite picture to account for forms in many dialects and it should be viewed as if in three dimensions. The Tōkyō form yo¹nde 'reading' is the result of applying Process 13 ("dental assimilation") directly to the output of Process 4 (*yomyde), and khatte 'buying' results from the same application to the output of Process 2 (*khapyte). Processes 8 and 9 are troublesome. In Process 8, "labial vocalization", we include the formation of *···wt··· from *···pyt··· and of *···wd··· from *···myd··· in order to account for the derivationally later forms that are attested. But a string *···nyd···, which occurs only in the stems šin- 'die' and in- 'depart', is assumed to undergo a separate "palatal vocalization" (Process 9). This might be regarded as simply an elision of the dental nasal, but we choose to put the formation of a postulated *···yd··· with the attested ···yt··· from ···çt··· (from ···št···). Another approach would assume the dropping of the reduced nasal syllables *-ny- and *-my- with compensatory lengthening. That would imply that amyi-the 'knitting' will yield (?)a:de in the dialects that have yo:de from yomyi-the 'reading'; if, instead, they have (?)o:de < *ɔɔde, that would be an argument favoring the stage *awde (< *amyde) which the chart postulates. In this connection, it is instructive to examine the forms found in the Japanese-Portuguese dictionary of 1603 and other works published by the Portuguese missionaries; for the most part the dictionary forms are given in the perfect "-ta" form, but the rules are the same as for the gerund on which that form is based.

	Infinitive	-t··· form	Meaning
(1)	ami	onda	'knit'
	cami = kami	cŏda = kɔɔda	'bite'
	fami	fŏda = fɔɔda	'eat'
	yami	yŏda = yɔɔda	'stop, cease'
	fasami	fasŏda = fasɔɔda	'put between'
	qizami = kizami	qizŏda = kizɔɔda	'carve'
	sainami	sainŏda = sainɔɔda	'torment'
	manabi	manŏda = manɔɔda	'learn'
	yerabi	yerŏda = yerɔɔda	'choose'
	voyobi = woyobi	woyŏda = woyɔɔda	'reach'
(2)	comi = komi	côda = kooda	'enter'
	momi	môda = mooda	'rub'
	tobi	tôda = tooda	'fly'
	yobi	yôda = yoda	'call'
	asobi	asôda = asooda	'play'
	corobi = korobi	corôda = korooda	'roll'
(3)	yemi	yende	'smile'
	sonemi = sonyemi	soneôda= sonyooda	'envy'
	saqebi = sakyebi	saqeôda = sakyooda	'yell'

(4) umi   unda   'give birth to'
     fumi   funda   'tread on'
     sumi   sunda   'live'
     casumi = kasumi   casunda = kasunda   'mist up'
     fukumi   fucũda = fukunda   'embrace'
     nusumi   nusũda= nusunda   'steal'
     susumi   susunda   'advance'
     yurumi   yurunda   'relax'
     musubi   musunda   'tie'

(5) voximi = wošimi   woxiũda = wošuuda   'spare, grudge'
     chigimi = tšidžimi   chigiũde = tidžuude   'shrink'
                             chigiũda = tidžuuda
     ayaximi = ayašimi   ayaxũda = ayašuuda   'doubt'
     canaximi = kanašimi   canaxiũda = kanašuuda   'be sad'
     curuximi = kurušimi   curuxiũda = kurušuuda   'suffer'

(6) xini = šini   xinda = šinda   'die'
     ini   inda   'depart'

There are two entries in the main dictionary that are given with what look like
irregular forms, but those must be misprints, for the regular forms appear in the
supplement of 1604:   Dictionary   Supplement

 yomi   yŏda = yɔɔda   yŏda = yooda   'read'
 yorocobi = yorokobi yorocŏda = yorokɔɔda yorocŏda = yorokooda 'rejoice'

The same misprint as the first also occurs in Rodriguez (28) but later on the same
page and on the following page the correct form yŏda (identical with 'called')
appears. And yorocŏde = yorokonde appears in Esopo (413, 417).
     The form "onda" for 'weave' is of particular interest, for it starts with "o-"
rather than "vo-" = wo-, as was usual for those words with historical o- as well as
those with wo-. This may have been an attempt to write the pronunciation [ɔŏda] or
[onda]. Elsewhere initial "ŏ-" represents ɔɔ- < au, as in ŏ = ɔɔ < a[w]u (< afu)
'meet' and ŏta = ɔɔta < a[w]ita (< afita) 'met'. In Esopo this verb is spelled vŏ
(463) = wɔɔ and vŏte (473) = wɔɔte, but yŏ··· in compounds after the infinitive:
yuqiyŏte (470, 479, 500), canaximiyŏta (453), yyŏta (464; < i-afita), ariyŏta
(425), deyŏte (446, 461, 501). The last two compounds are given by the Japanese-
Portuguese dictionary as "ariai, ariŏ, ariŏta" (it is unclear whether "riŏ" is to
be taken as /riɔɔ/ or as /ryɔɔ/) and "deai, deuŏ" (= dewɔɔ), "deŏta" (= deɔɔta for
there was no *dyɔɔ, only "jŏ" = [džɔ:]). But the dictionary also reports "deqiai,
deqiyo [→ deqiyŏ], deqiyŏta" = dekiai, dekiyoo, dekiyoota. The Portuguese nasal
vowel ũ is written for at least two of the longer stems ending in /m/; perhaps
"fukũda" was an attempt to write [fukuũda]. Both stems appear with -un- in Esopo
(412): fucunde = fukunde, nusunde. The dictionary also has tçuxxinde = tsuššinde
'humbly' (tutusinde); the supplement lists tçutçuximi = tsutsušimi 'humility'.
     Other forms in the dictionary:
(7) cogui = kogi   coida = koida   'row'
     fegui = fyegi   feida = fyeida   'pare/peal/strip down'
     auogui = awogi   auoida = awoida   'fan; gaze upward'
(8) caqi = kaki   caita = kaita   'write'
     iqi/yuqi = iki/yuki   iita/yuita   'go'
     vodoroqi = wodoroki   vodoroita = wodoroita   'be startled'
     fataraqi = fataraki   fataraita   'work'

(9)	caxi = kaši	caita = kaita	'lend'
	fataxi = fataši	fataita	'accomplish, fulfill'
(10)	cari = kari	catta = katta	'mow'
	catari = katari	catatta = katatta	'tell'
(11)	cai = kai	côta = koota	'buy'
	mucai = mukai	mucôta = mukoota	'face'
(12)	soi	sôta = soota	'follow'
	firoi	firôta = firoota	'pick up'
(13)	nui	nŭta = nuuta	'sew'
(14)	iy/yui = ii/yui	yŭta = yuuta	'say'
(15)	yoi(/yei)	yôta = yoota	'get drunk'

The altered forms of the infinitive were used in the sixteenth century not only before -te and -ta, but also before the old ending -tu, which meant the same thing as the representative -tari and was pronounced (by the late 1500s) with affrication as -tsu and -dzu: vodottçu fanetçu = wodottsu fanyetsu 'leaping and jumping' (Esopo 413), tattçu itçu = tattsu itsu 'standing up and sitting down' (Collado 45), caitçu iôzzu = [kaitsu yo:dzu] 'writing and reading' (Collado 45). A few verb forms with -tu are preserved in the modern language as literary clichés, pronounced in accordance with the conventions of reading classical spellings with the regular infinitive. But the idiom ku'nzu (< kundu < kumi-tu) hogu'retu 'grappling and separating = repeatedly clashing' preserves the pronunciation of the 16th century. Cf. xixiuo funzzu qetçu (Esopo 500) = šiši wo funzu kyetsu (← fumi-tu ke-tu) 'trampling and kicking the tiger').

The chart implies that velar elision took place after syncope, for that seems to be the best way to account for the voicing of the dental initial of the gerund ending (-te → -de) when it is attached to a consonant stem that ends in a basic g; we presume that the voicing took place between the two stages.[1] We must assume that the Tōkyō form kasite is two syllables [khašte], though three moras, as a result of devoicing the i. There are problems with this explanation, however, as well as with the assumption that "hushing" did not precede syncope. As observed in Chapter 1, we have no reason to doubt that the Japanese mora si was pronounced [ši] from the very beginning. In all dialects of Japanese at least some of the gerund forms of the consonant stems take shapes that reflect some of the processes shown in the chart, but certain forms appear to have survived intact without undergoing any of the processes. In the Oki islands the form for 'went' is ekita without velar elision (Hirayama 1968b:159 where it is unclear whether the middle vowel is unvoiced),[2] and western Tanba (in Kyōto prefecture) has /ikita/ according to Shin Nihongo-kōza 3:171, which points out (168, 171) that in Kyōto itself 'went' is ita, presumably a shortening from the expected iita, which is attested in the 16th century and still survives in Suzu-gun of Oku-Noto; in Tōkyō the irregular form itte is but a forlorn relic of the original Kantō-type pattern for all of the velar-final verb stems, holding out against the elision pattern which has come in from the Kansai area to overwhelm the other stems. In parts of Izumo ikite is reported (by Shibata and Fukushima 1981:61). From the orthography one might assume that yet another intact survivor is Tōkyō's kasite 'lending', but here we have accounted for the pseudo-syllable si as an artifact of the preferred treatment of the phenomenon of vowel unvoicing.

The chart of verb gerunds does not include certain forms of interest from Yamaguchi. According to Kobayashi 1975:64 (cf. n.47) the forms ka'ita < ka'ki-ta 'wrote' and da'ita < da'sita 'put out' have variants ka'ata and da'ata. Presumably this is the result of the development aa < a(y)i mentioned in Ch. 1, §37. It might

be thought that a similar case is also found in Izumo kaata < ka[f]i-ta 'bought'
(Kobayashi 88) but in that dialect ka'[k]ita 'wrote' > ka'eta/ke'eta and da'[s]ita
'put out' > da'eta/de'eta, so that (as shown in §37 of Ch. 1) Izumo kaata 'bought'
is an example of aa < au. According to Kobayashi (70-1, n.57) the Izumo dialect
completely drops the adjective-infinitive ending -ku, yielding forms like siro' naa
'becomes white' < siro'-ku na'ru; siro'-te 'is white and' < siro'-ku-te; aka-te 'is
red and' < aka-ku-te. (Does the -ku drop in the negative -ku na-i, too?)

   In eastern Japan the reinforcement of the adjective gerund -ku-tte may have
arisen from pressure to preserve the unvoiced [t] after the original juncture before
it dropped, in one of those dialects which would otherwise pronounce /···kute/ as
[···gude]. The pronunciation [gu] for -ku is usual in such dialects, but -kute is
apparently always [kute] "because of two voiceless consonants and medial high vowel
which is also voiceless" according to Kobayashi 1975:106 (describing Aomori). This
is interesting in that it suggests that either the intervocalic voicing of the
obstruents is secondary or, alternatively, the vowel devoicing must have set in
early. It is tempting to speculate that -tte < -ti-te (and -ri-te and -pi-te) must
have developed in the same way, with the consonant simply dropping rather than
assimilating: the geminate -tt- resulted from an attempt to preserve an appropriate
voiceless allophone even when the juncture drops. This is particular attractive for
explaining the development of -tte from -pi-te since that is limited to eastern
Japan, while the developments from -ti-te and (less so) from -ri-te are more widely
located. Pertinent forms are reported from Hachijō island (Shin Nihongo-kōza 3:54-5),
where -ti-te stays intact but -ki-te and -si-te both become -tte (compare Tōkyō's
irregular itte from iki-te 'going'), and both -gi-te and -bi-te become -dde (in one
dialect -nde).

   It is a puzzle that modern Kyōto has kau 'buy' and omou 'think' for what was
recorded four centuries ago by the Portuguese as cǒ = kɔɔ and omô = omoo. (There
are exceptions, notably hoo 'crawl', which Umegaki 1946:80 attributes to the analogy
of hoota 'crawled' — but why for this verb only? Notice also omoo to = omou to
'when one thinks', Zhs 4:242.) Hamada 1970:377b suggests that the versions with au
and ou may have come in, or have been restored, as reading pronunciations with the
spread of literacy after the Meiji restoration. He notes that the dialect versions
of hirau, tugunau, and tukurau (for standard hirou, tugunou, and tukurou) may have
come about by analogy with the more common -au type of verbs; cf. his note (501)
which adds oginau < "okinufu".

   The modern gerund forms for the consonant stems are usually described — or
dismissed — as examples of that catch-all category "onbin" (see Ch. 1, §33). This
word looks like a translation of the western term "euphony" but as a technical term
in the field of kokugogaku it was first used by Motoori Norinaga, who included in
its scope the problem of sei-daku distinctions (Ch. 2) as well as the four types of
reduction known as "i", "u", "N", and "T". (The term had also been used by Keichū.)
So far as I know, there has been little attempt to explain why the forms came into
being, though hints turn up here and there in the literature. In Heian times a
distinction is observed to develop between the SYLLABLE and the MORA; by 1200, long
vowels and diphthongs, as well as -N and -T, were an obvious part of the colloquial
language. With the loss of juncture in attaching -te to the infinitive, a pressure
must have made itself felt to shorten the gerund forms of the consonant stems so
that they would have the same number of syllables as the other major forms of the
paradigm. This was accomplished by syncope: the high vowel i (representing the
infinitive ending) lost its syllabicity before -te, with subsequent adjustments as
shown by the chart. But if okyi te[y] > oite 'putting' why did okiy te[y] > okite
'rising'? It seems likely that the juncture may have been retained after the

infinitives of the vowel stems, perhaps owing to the unwritten length of the vowel,
which resulted from absorbing the infinitive ending -i. In any event, the gerunds of
the vowel stems really required no syncope, for they were already the same length in
syllables as other forms of the paradigm, except — perhaps — for the infinitive
itself. Put another way: the gerunds dropped one syllable, but for the vowel-stem
verbs this was the unwritten length of the infinitive, so that the written result
looks as if nothing happened.[3]

The velar elision -[k]i took place sporadically in ordinary nouns, as well as
in infinitive-derived nouns and gerunds:

  kisai < kisa[k]i (Genji) 'empress';
  tuigaki < tuikaki (JP, Mg) < tu[k]i-kaki 'mud fence';
  tuizi < tuidi < tui[fi]di < tu[k]i-fidi (Mg) 'mud fence';
  suigai < suika[k]i < su[k]i-kaki (JP) 'lattice fence';
  yaito (Ōsaka: Makimura 722a) / yaitoo (NKD, JP) < "yaitofu" (Mg) < yaito <
ya[k]i-to 'moxibustion' — cf. modern Ōsaka yai NKD) 'moxibustion'
  saitu^k/ₒoro (Mg) < *sa[k]i-tu koro 'the other day'; ... .
But the elision is productive today only for the gerunds (ki[k]ite 'listening' ≠
kikite 'listener'), and new verb stems ending ···k- are not being created. Notice
also the velar elision in the attributive form of the adjective -[k]i; see §2 of
this chapter.

More complicated examples of *onbin* phenomena are found in these words:
  koobasi-/kanbasi- 'fragrant' < kɔɔbasi-/kanbasi- (JP) < kaubasi- (Mg) /
kam[u]basi- (kana notes of 910) = kaűbasi- < ... < kagufasi- < ka (n) kufa-si-
'odor be fine'.
  kanmuri 'crown', kaburi 'the head [shaken in dissent]' < kamuri, kaburi (JP) <
kauburi (Mg) = kaűburi < ... < kagafuri (?< ka-n-kapur- reduplication).
  imooto, imoto (JP) 'younger sister' < imouto (Mg) < ... < imwo-fyito̲.

What is often treated as sibilant elision -[š]it··· apparently took place by
way of dissibilation to -ç[i̜]t··· with a voiceless palatal fricative, as attested in
Wakayama by forms such as "hanahita" (Okumura 1968:35a) = hanaçta. The fricative
quality then weakened to leave only the palatality, which was realized as the voiced
glide -y-. In modern dialects this phenomenon is less common with shorter stems,
where there is more danger of homophone clashes, and rare with stems of accent type
A;[4] it does not occur for toosu 'let pass' and moosu 'humbly say', nor for causative
V-asite < V-asete. Cf. Okumura 1958:516, 1969:35-6. In sixteenth-century Kyōto the
shorter forms seem to have been regular for all sibilant-final stems but one,
to judge from the Japanese-Portuguese dictionary, which has "touoita" = towoita for
toosita 'let pass' but "mõxita" = mɔɔsita for moosita 'humbly said'. (Causatives in
the dictionary are "V-axete" = V-ašete.) Okumura 1969:34b says that Kyōto started
losing the rule that converted verb forms with "···sit···" (-št-) to "···it···" (-yt-)
fairly early, well before the two conjugationally hybrid verbs sinu(ru) 'die' and
inu(ru) 'depart' were regularized as consonant stems. That change had happened in
Edo by around 1760 but it was not attested in Kyōto until later (KggD 76a). As
Kyōto reverted to the earlier forms still used in eastern Japan (hanašta 'spoke'),
it was to some extent on a case-by-case basis, for individual verbs continued with
the -yt··· version even after the bigrade conjugations (-uru/-e and -uru/-i) were
generally simplified to the monograde conjugation (-eru/-e and -iru/-i) — for Kyōto
perhaps only after 1760,[5] and after the period when yobi-te and yomi-te became youde
> yoode (around 1550?). In addition to the verb gerunds, there are several other
examples of the elided sibilant, which may have originated in a different way:
ona[s]i-dosi '(of) the same age', ate < atai < ata[s]i < [w]atasi < [w]ata[ku]si
'I/me' (on the coexistent pronoun forms cf. Komatsu 1981:179-80), ...

2. Velar elision in adjective forms.

In western Japan two paradigmatic forms of the adjective were shortened one syllable by dropping -k- and reducing the final close vowel to a subsyllabic mora; these forms are the attributive -[k]i and the infinitive -[k]u. The juxtaposed vowels resulting from the velar elision in the infinitive were subject to crasis, whereby ···o-u > ···oo, ···a-u > ···ɔɔ, ···i-u > ···yuu, and ···(y)e-u > ···yoo. The same crasis also occurred for the imperfect forms of verb stems ending in a basic oral labial, an earlier ···p- or ···f- that had become ···w- and then was elided: in the 16th century Kyōto speakers said koo for ko[w]-u 'beg', kɔɔ for ka[w]-u 'buy', and yoo for yo[w]u 'get drunk'. Modern Kyōto speakers have restored the -u versions; but yuu[6] remains the modern pronunciation of i[w]-u.

There are only a few "short" adjective stems, and many are quite long. The proliferation of this late-blooming class of conjugated words, often created by formants such as -si-, probably led to pressure to shorten the forms. It is unclear whether accentual factors may have been at work, as well. It seems odd that Tōkyō elided the velar in the attributive -[k]i but not in the infinitive -[k]u.[7] The use in Tōkyō of the elided form -[k]u before gozaima˧su and zonzima˧su — but not before gozaimase˧n or zonzimase˧n — must be a fairly late borrowing from Kyōto speech, as are the elisions of -r- in the polite-stylizations of the honorific verbs goza[r]ima˧su, irassya[r]ima˧su, nasa[r]ima˧su, and ossya[r]ima˧su.

Adjective infinitives with elided velar -[k]u can be found as early as 1020, and Murasaki Shikibu's diary (1010) contains many -[k]i examples (cf. KggD 964b).[8] The velar elision was earlier and more widespread for A-si-ku than for A-ku. Sakurai 1965a:46 says there are three reasons: the words are long; the preceding vowel is /i/; and the structure is "more tightly joined" (presumably the result of the other two factors[9]). The text forms in Genji are in the following ratios:

A-ku	.81	A-siku	.42
A-u	.19	A-siu	.58

The elision is two or three times more common for the -si- adjectives, and if you take just lexical items (individual adjectives), the percentage of A-u is still lower, since ita-[k]u 'painfully, terribly, very' accounts for a fifth of the cases of A-[k]u.

Sakurai observes that the adjective was originally (i.e., in proto-Japanese) just the stem. The infinitive is the stem + an element -ku (also attached to verb stems as a nominalization),[10] which agglutinated early — as shown by the Heian accent — and had many uses. Later, in the main islands only, the elements -( )ki (attributive) and -( )si (predicative) were attached loosely, as indicated by the unusual Heian accents with final high-fall of pitch. Sakurai thinks the element -si was originally identical with the emphatic particle si and probably also with the retrospective attributive (V-i)-si. But the -si- that forms emotive adjectives must have been attached very early, to judge from stem-vowel alternations and the Ryūkyū forms, presumably before -ku was attached (A-si-ku). The attributive A-si-ki perhaps came into being later than A-si; see the discussion in Ch. 7 of early uses of the predicative for the attributive, notably in fixed epithets. The A-ki element was apparently identical with the retrospective (V-i)-ki, which is predicative except in the nominalization -keku < -kyeku < *-ki aku.

The velar-elided ending -[k]u is spelled with kana "-u", but the pronunciation is subject to vowel crasis and reduction, the geminate vowels forming a single long syllable. This can be illustrated as follows, with some of the examples accompanied by the spellings of the Japanese-Portuguese dictionary of 1603.

```
S o u r c e       R e s u l t                E x a m p l e s

···-u-[k]u    →    ···uu                     su-[k]u → suu ("sǔ") 'sour'
                                             karu-[k]u → karuu ("carǔ") 'lightweight'

···i-[k]u     →    "···iu" = ···yuu          ooki-[k]u) → ookyuu ("vôqiǔ) 'big'
                                             osi-[k]u → osyuu ("voxǔ") 'dear'

···o-[k]u     →    "···ou" = ···oo           yo-[k]u → yoo ("yô") 'good'
                                             oso-[k]u → osoo ("vosô") 'slow'

···a-[k]u     →    "···au" = ···ɔɔ › ···oo   na-[k]u → nɔɔ ("nǒ") › noo 'lacking'
                                             ama-[k]u → amɔɔ ("amǒ") › amoo 'sweet'
```

Four adjectives ending in ···(y)e- in Kyōto of the early 1600s are obsolete today:[11]

```
···(y)e-[k]u  →    "···eu" = ···yoo          sige-[k]u → sigyoo ("xigueô") 'dense'
                                             take-[k]u → takyoo (?"taqeô")[12] 'brave'
                                             amane-[k]u → amanyoo ("amaneô")[13] 'general'
                                             ··· be-ku → byoo ("beô") 'must'
```

In modern dialects the shortened -[k]u often coexists with the original -ku. The two versions may compete; the unshortened version -ku may be used for particular adjectives or classes of adjectives; or, they may be complementary in syntax, as when the Tōkyō speaker says ta'koo gozaima'su but ta'kaku gozaimase'n. According to Kitahara 1967:32 the elided version -[k]u is most common for adjectives ending in /i/ (hence all the longish stems in ···-si-);[15] is rare for those ending in /u/; is more common for ···a- than for ···o- or (a small group at best) ···e-. The Japanese-Portuguese dictionary gives "womô" = /womoo/ ← omo-[k]u 'being heavy', but Esopo (1593) has "womoqutomo" (413) = womo-ku to mo 'even being heavy'. For goto- 'like' the Portuguese attest only the fossilized forms gotoqu(-ni) = goto-ku (ni) and gotoqi-no = goto-ki no. The expected forms *gotoi ← goto-[k]i and *gotoo (*"gotô") ← goto-[k]u somehow never developed.

The long vowels are sometimes shortened, especially when followed by the gerund ending -te or by na'ru/suru 'become/make': usu-te 'being thin', amo na'ru 'become sweet'. There are shortenings in other situations, too, such as the familiar o-hayo for o-hayoo (gozaima'su) 'Good morning!'. The shortening seems to be more common for longer adjectives, as we would expect. There are dialects, both those with -ku a: those with -[k]u, in which the entire syllable drops when -te or na'ru/suru follows, as in Nagoya (Minami 1975:257): ta'ka[-ku]-te, na'[-ku]-te; ta'ka[-ku] na'ru/suru. Also Hiroshima (Ōhara 1937:72): ta'ka[-ku]-te. And, in free variation, in Arita and Shingū of Wakayama prefecture (Hirayama 1979:64): ama na'ru, amo na'ru 'get sweet'. Adjectives with the formant -si- often shorten -si-[k]i → -si[i], so that the imperfect form falsely sounds as if it were the literary predicative form, the haplological -si[-si]. This seems to happen in a number of dialects, e.g. Matsue (Ōhara 1937:75). Some speakers in Kyōto (Martin 1975b:392) assimilate the vowel in ···syuu (← ···si[k]u) → ···sii, and this is often shortened to ···si, so that the pronunciation /yorosi/ may represent either the imperfect yorosii ← the attributive yorosi-[k]i or the infinitive yorosii ← yorosii ← yorosi-[k]u.

A good map of the dialect distribution of the -[k]u phenomenon is found in Hirayama 1968b:106. The dialects preserving -ku are those of eastern and northern Honshū (and Hokkaidō), of Shimane prefecture, and of the west-coast area of Kyōto prefecture. Not indicated on the map is the widespread use of the elided form in an area centering on Nagoya; cf. Sakurai 1965b.

3. Reductions of the presumptive form of the verb.

Modern Japanese has a form we will call the "hortative", which is constructed by attaching -oo to consonant stems and -yoo to vowel stems; the ending is sometimes shortened to just -(y)o. Common English translations are 'let's do it' or '(I think) I'll do it, let me do it': Kaero'(o) 'Let's go home'; Tyo'tto miyo'o 'Let me have a look at it'; Norimasyo'o ka 'Let's get aboard, shall we' or 'I'll/We'll get aboard, OK?'; Neyoo to omoima'su 'I think I'll go to bed'; Kaki-naoso'o ka to omo'tte imasu ga ... 'I'm wondering whether to (whether I should) rewrite it'; Akeyo'o ka ne' 'I wonder if I/we should open it'; ... . With this meaning of intention or invitation, the action must be something that is voluntary or can be controlled, and the subject is first-person, singular or (more often) plural. Another meaning is found in the structure V-(y)oo to suru '(am/is/are) about to V' or 'sets out to V, tries to V'. This pattern permits any subject, and sometimes involuntary actions are acceptable: hi ga deyo'o to suru/sita toki' ni 'when the sun was about to come up'; uru'sa'ku naro'o to site ita tokoro' 'just as it was about to become annoying'; ... .

In colloquial Japanese there is another structure, which we will call the "tentative"; it is made by adding daro'(o) or desyo'(o) to the finite forms of verb, adjective, or copula, but N [da'] daro'(o)/desyo'(o) 'it is probably N' obligatorily drops the imperfect copula da', though the perfect copula is retained in N da'tta daro(o)/desyo(o) 'it was probably N'. The tentative means 'probably, likely; I think; don't you think; would (in all likelihood); will (probably)': A'me ga | hu'ru daroo 'It will probably rain', A'me ga | hu'ru | daro'o 'It will rain, I think'; Omosiro'i | desyo'o? 'Don't you find it fun?'; Rainen desyo'o ka 'Will it be next year?'. The structure -ta daro'o is often shortened to -ta [da]ro'o: Tomodati ga ka'etta [da]roo 'My friend must have left'; Kane ga na'katta [da]roo 'I guess there was no money'; Ga'n datta [da]ro 'Musta been cancer'; Omosi'ro'katta | [da]ro'? 'I bet it was fun, wasn't it'.[15]

In synchronic descriptions the hortative ending itself is sometimes treated as basically -yoo, with the /y/ dropping automatically after a consonant (yom-yoo → yomoo) just as the consonant of the imperfect ending -ru drops (yom-ru → yom-u). But the dropping of y cannot be treated as automatic, since the syllable type Cyo(o) exists. And the two phenomena result from different historical processes. Perhaps a better approach is to describe the -y- of -yoo as an epenthetic glide inserted after /i/ or /e/; the polite -⁻masyo'o is irregular. But that description is historically misleading, too, as we will see.

Since involuntary actions do not permit the hortative interpretation, for those verbs that refer to such actions written Japanese often uses the hortative forms instead of the tentative structure: A'me ga huro'o/hurimasyo'o = A'me ga hu'ru daroo/desyoo 'It will probably rain'; Mondai mo aro'o/arimasyo'o = Mondai mo a'ru daroo/desyoo 'There will be problems'. In place of N daro'o/desyo'o the uncontracted structure N de aro'o/arimasyo'o is used; and for the adjective the contracted form A-karo'o ← A-ku aro'o is found. Certain dialects use A-karo'o as a colloquial form, in place of the standard A-i daro'o; but I have not come across ?*A-karimasyo'o. There is also A-i de aro'o/arimasyo'o.

These structures go back to a single form of Literary Japanese which we will call the "presumptive", made by attaching -(a)mu to the verb stem: yom-amu 'will read', kaf-amu 'will buy', age-mu 'will give', e-mu 'will get', forobi-mu 'will get ruined', mi-mu 'will see', ke-mu 'will kick'; and the irregular ko-mu 'will come' and se-mu 'will do'. Sometime between the Heian period and the Edo period, the nasal consonant eroded, and the ending was pronounced first -(a)ũ with a nasal vowel and then -(a)u with no nasality. That left two vowels juxtaposed; crasis set in, as we can tell from the forms written in Roman letters by the Portuguese around 1600:

yoma[m]u	"iomǒ" = yomɔɔ	'will read'
kafa[m]u	"cauǒ" = kawɔɔ	'will buy'
age[m]u	"agueô" = agyoo	'will give'
e[m]u	"yǒ" = yoo	'will get'
forobi[m]u	"forobeô" = forobyoo[16]	'will get ruined'
mi[m]u	"meô" = myoo	'will see'
ke[m]u	?"qeô"= kyoo[17]	'will kick'
ko[m]u	"cô" = koo	'will come'
se[m]u	"xô" = šoo (= syoo)	'will do'

The reduction to a nasal vowel -ũ probably took place by the end of the 12th century.[18] The nasal vowel, in turn, suffered two different fates. In one version the nasality dropped but the vowel quality remained; in the other the vowel quality dropped and the nasal remained, so that there was a contrast between sem[u] 'will do' and sen[u] 'will not do'. The Heian contrast between -m and -n was eventually neutralized into the subsyllabic mora -N.[19] One structure which became quite common in the Muromachi period is the presumptive + su(ru) 'do'; the basic meaning of the structure was virtually the same as the original meaning of V-(a)mu 'intend to, will' or 'probably (will)'. The auxiliary verb was voiced ··· zu(ru) as it was when attached to Chinese verbal nouns ending in a nasal (Ch. 1, §24), but the usual orthography failed to show distinctive voicing until fairly late. The Japanese grammarians usually describe the structure ···n - su(ru) and ···u - zu(ru) as an abbreviation of ···mu-to-su(ru) with the particle to ˀ (the subjective essive); but the particle must have been ellipted before the loss of nasality in the version ···u - zu(ru), for otherwise it would be difficult to account for the voicing of the sibilant.[20]

There are modern dialects which have syoo for siyoo 'let's do it', as in the area of Tanba and further west in Hyōgo prefecture; that looks like a relic of the 16th-century form. But in Kōchi prefecture syuu is reported (Kōza Kokugo-shi 1:162) and in parts of central and southern Honshū myuu is used for miyoˀo 'let's see it' and okyuu for okiyoˀo 'let's get up'. These may be the result of raising the long vowel of the standard forms (assimilating in tongue height to the preceding /i/) and later compressing the form: miyoo > *miyuu > myuu.

The modern standard forms are thought to have started from a conflation of the Muromachi form syoo into siyoo. And the other vowel stems, which by now were all restructured as monograde so that aguru 'give' was ageru and okuˀru 'rise' was okiˀru, attached -yoo either by analogy or by contraction of the structure V-i [si]yoo, as suggested by Martin 1975b:613 n.15. There it is implied that the V-yoo forms of the 16th century are the result of inserting an epenthetic glide into an underlying form V¹/ₑ-a[m]u. But that would make it difficult to explain why the 16th-century forms have the closed vowel /-yoo/ rather than the open vowel /-yɔɔ/ that we would expect from a crasis of iau; cf. the assimilated Chinese loanwords "yǒ" = /yɔɔ/ 'manner' < yau (< YANG) ≠ "yô" = /yoo/ 'need' < yeu (< YEW). Since the syllable se was probably pronounced še = /sye/ at least from the middle of the Heian period, when e- and ye- fell together as ye-, it would be possible to account for the closed vowel by adopting the explanation that the forms all developed by way of infinitive + semu = /syemu/ > /syeu/ > /syoo/. What is ellipted is shown by the brackets of ···[¹/ₑ s]yeu, and the crasis then sets in, yielding forms like "caqeô" = /kakyoo/ < kak[e s]yoo < kake syeu (< syeũ < syemu). This may seem to amount to the same thing as saying that "all the vowel-stem presumptives are made by analogy with syoo < semu" but I believe the processes by which the forms developed can be more clearly seen through the other presentation. It is tempting to try to explain

the form /syemu/ itself as < si-amu, but it seems more likely that the form was
originally /semu/ < *so-mu with -mu attached to the original stem *so from which
the various irregular forms of the verb are derived (see Ch. 6). Another and simpler
explanation for the verbs with ···e infinitives is this: just as se was /sye/, so
probably the other cases of Ce were /Cye/[21] and -mu was attached directly to the
stem: kakye-mu > kakye-u > kakyoo 'will hang it'. But then we would expect mi-mu >
mi-u > myuu 'will see' and sikodi-mu > sikodi-u > sikodyuu 'will falsely report';
myuu 'will see' occurs as a modern dialect form and is said to be attested earlier
than the 16th-century myoo (where? — cf. the quotation from Fujitani Akira in
Yoshida 1971:158). The Iki islands have kyuu 'will wear' and okyuu 'will rise'
(Yoshida 1971:156); these probably go back directly to ki-[m]u and oki-[m]u. The
16th-century forms such as "meô" = /myoo/ 'I will see' etc.[22] would have to be
taken as analogical restructuring.

The explanation of modern forms like kake-yoo will have to involve analogy in
any event, for if they were simply expansions of the 16th-century forms they would
appear as ···i-yoo rather than ···e-yoo. The 16th-century versions merged the upper
(···i) and lower (···e) grades of bigrade verbs when forming the presumptive ···yeu
> ···yoo. It has been suggested that the ···i-yoo and ···e-yoo forms developed in
the east, where the form ki-yoo for ko-yoo 'will come' is found in dialects and is
attested from the Meiji period (Yoshida 1971:154). The historically expected form
for 'come' is koo (< kou < komu), as recorded by the Portuguese ("cô") and found in
modern dialects (Yoshida 1981:154), including Ōsaka — where, however, ko'(o) may be
a contraction of koyo'o just as syo(o) may be a contraction of siyoo (Martin 1975b:
610) rather than a relic of the sixteenth century.

As the forms for 'come' (ko-mu) and 'do' (se-mu < *so-mu) show, the presumptive
auxiliary -mu was attached directly to the stem, as was the negative auxiliary -nu:
ko-nu 'not come', se-nu < *so-nu 'not do'. With the "consonant-final" stems there is
an intervening -a- which has been explained either as part of the "ending" or as a
separate morpheme (which I have called the "subjunctive") that is used in attaching
the causative and passive auxiliaries, too; either explanation will require a rule
to elide the -a- after a vowel. But both explanations are historically misleading,
for it appears that the basic forms of the "consonant" stems of Old Japanese are
best reconstructed as ending in a vowel, most commonly /a/. See Ch. 1, §§48-9.
Accordingly, the historical structure for the presumptives can be indicated by
writing yoma-mu rather than yom-amu (or yom-a-mu). Because of the various kinds of
contractions that took place between the time of proto-Japanese and that of Old
Japanese, for the language of the Nara period there are good reasons to set up the
dichotomy of consonant-final versus vowel-final stems, and both of the synchronic
explanations offered above are adequate for that system of conjugation, but not for
the older — and deeper — structure.

In the standard colloquial language of today neither the hortative nor the
tentative occurs adnominally, but both are sometimes adnominalized in the written
style (Martin 1975b:740-1); and in earlier Japanese, including the language spoken
in the 1500s, the presumptive was adnominalized with no change of form.

The modern polite auxiliary -⁻ma'su is irregular in the negative -⁻mase'n and
the hortative -⁻masyo'o. These forms, together with the provisional -⁻masu'reba, are
often used as criteria for classifying the auxiliary as *sagyoo-he'nkaku* "irregularly
conjugated like suru". The -⁻ma'su form is the old predicative; the attributive
-⁻masu'ru is sometimes used in adnominalizations, and the provisional based upon it,
-⁻masu'reba, is heard in speeches. The negative is a contraction of -⁻mase'nu. The
hortative preserves the form found in the 16th-century "-maraxô" = -marasyoo;
the modern auxiliary -⁻ma'su is a contraction of -marasu(ru).

Another structure with the same meaning as the tentative (and the tentative uses of the presumptive) is expressed as ⋯ ⁻be¹e, ⋯ ⁻nbe¹(e), and ⋯ ⁻ppe¹ in various modern dialects (Martin 1975b:609, 943-4). This goes back to the auxiliary adjective be-[k]i, with the infinitive be-[k]u, and the literary predicative be-si; the word had a wide range of meaning, including permission ('may') and necessity ('must').²⁸ In the days when the predicative forms were distinguished from the attributive for the vowel stems, the predicative was used before this auxiliary, and Rodriguez follows that practice in citing the forms "agubequ, agubeqi, agubesi" = agu beku, agu beki, agu besi. Even when he cites the colloquial contraction be[k]i he uses the predicative of the preceding verb: "agubei" (111v) 'will give'. The contracted forms bei ⟨ be-[k]i and "beô" = /byoo/ ⟨ be-[k]u are found in Esopo (1593): "xicarubei" = sikaru bei '(who) would be such' (454), "arubeômo" = aru byoo mo 'that it would even exist' (462). Rodriguez has "xicarubeô" = sikaru byoo (12).

The tentative conversion of modern Japanese can be applied to negatives: A¹me ga hura¹nai daroo 'It probably won't rain'. The negative corresponding to the hortative is the structure V-ru ⁻ma¹i 'let's not do it' or '(I think) I won't do it', but that is uncommon in everyday speech, being replaced by circumlocutions such as V-anai yo¹o ni siyoo 'let's decide not to do it', V-ru¹ no o yameyoo 'let's give up (the idea of) doing it', or V-anai yo¹ 'I won't do it!'. But V-ru ⁻ma¹i turns up in the written style or in more formal speech, especially in larger structures such as quotations or balanced expressions where it is paired with the corresponding affirmative. And in earlier Japanese ma¹i carried the meaning of imperfect tentative negative 'probably won't'. The word ma¹i is a contraction, either ma[z]i or ma[zi]i from mazi-[k]i, the Muromachi contraction of the earlier attributive. In the Heian period the predicative form was mazi, which is to be explained as an obligatory haplology of *mazi[-si] in order to account for the infinitive mazi-ku and the attributive mazi-ki. The -zi- of this word is thought to be the same as the -zi of make[y]-zi 'I will not be defeated!' and to come from -n[i] - si, the infinitive of the negative auxiliary + the infinitive of su(ru) 'do'. The element masi- has been explained in two ways (cf. Yoshida 1973:828-33). The first explanation says it is the auxiliary masi, which attaches to the stem (with -a- for the consonant-final stems) and imparts the meaning 'it is likely that'; for that, several etymological explanations have been offered (Yoshida 1973:403-4), of which the best incorporates the presumptive -mu. The second explanation says that it is a truncation of [u]masi, the predicative form of the adjective uma- 'good, pleasing, satisfactory', so that the original structure would carry meanings something like 'do not [that] it is satisfactory'; that might account for the prohibitive use ('it is not all right to do it'), which serves as the negative counterpart of the permissive use of the auxiliary be-si (be-ki, be-ku) to mean 'it is all right to do it'.

In modern Japanese ⁻ma¹i is attached to the attributive form of the verb (yo¹mu ⁻ma¹i, ageru ⁻ma¹i, mi¹ru ⁻ma¹i, ku¹ru ⁻ma¹i, suru ⁻ma¹i) but the word's ancestor in the Heian period (mazi) followed the predicative form (yomu mazi, agu mazi, miru mazi, ku mazi, su mazi — and also the morphologically "true" predicative of the existential verb aru mazi); forms such as ku¹ ⁻ma¹i and su ⁻ma¹i survive — and are prized — in modern usage, where I treat them as contractions of the more colloquial ku¹ru ⁻ma¹i and suru ⁻ma¹i (Martin 1975b:943). During the Muromachi period it was common to attach the auxiliary to the stem (with -a- for the consonant-final stems): yoma-mai, age-mai, mi-mai, ko-mai, se-mai (⟨ *so- + ...). Of these Muromachi V-mai forms, ko-ma¹i and se-ma¹i survive in modern dialects, which also have ki-ma¹i and si-ma¹i. And there are modern dialects in which the ending is attached to consonant-final stems as -omai: ikomai = iku ⁻ma¹i, aromai = a¹ru ⁻ma¹i. Cf. Martin 1975b:943; Yoshida 1971:305-6.

Notes to Chapter 3.

¹ Ignored here are forms such as khoynde (spelled "koinde") that are reported for
southern Kinki dialects (Okumura 1969:36a), Tanba, and Matsumoto (Kōza Kokugo-shi
1:166). This appears to be a development from Stage 4 (*khoŋyde) before Stage 6 (and
12, which for the -g- and -k- stems has skipped 6). Quite puzzling is the Hagiwara
development ⋯ŋi-te > ⋯i-te as in iso¹ŋu iso¹ite 'rush' and tu¹ŋu tu¹ite 'pour'
(Tsuzuku 1941:183); this cannot be explained as simply devoicing the -d- by partial
assimilation to the voiceless consonant of the preceding syllable, for there is also
the example mo¹ŋu mo¹ite 'pluck'. Yet it is difficult to believe that the -t- was
never voiced in these forms. According to Tsuzuku (1941:180) some speakers say
no¹ŋita 'doffed' (= nu¹ida) — and he gives without comment (185) iso¹ida 'rushed'.
Other forms: kaza-ka¹ite 'smell an odor' (← kaŋ-), to¹ita 'whetted' (← to¹ŋ-).

² According to Ōhara 1937:161 in Matsue the gerund of yuk-/ek- 'go' uniquely
escapes velar elision and the vowel is unvoiced: yuki̧te.

³ Komatsu 1975:14a thinks that oite and okite are the result of their different
accentuations, all-high versus low-low-high, pointing to similar cases of velar
elision in high-atonic nouns: tu[k]ikaki, tu[k]ifidi. But each of the two accent
patterns, the low-register stems and the high-register stems alike, occurs in both
conjugations of verbs so that the accent alone cannot be the answer. Ōno 1977:213
claims that the 8th-century vowel distinctions are responsible for the difference:
okyi te > oite 'put' vs. okiy te > okite 'arise' (and akey te > akete 'open it').
But the vowels had merged before the elision. There is a Kyūshū dialect (Ōita-shi
Ōaza Tsurusaki) which reduces o¹tite → o¹tte 'falling' and presumably o¹rite →
o¹tte 'descending' (as well as attested karite¹ → katte¹ 'lending' and tarite¹ →
tatte¹ 'sufficing'); cf. Toguchi 1974:11. This appears to be a late development,
independent of the Hachijō island patterns otte ← otite 'falling', itte ← ikite
'living', and tute ← turete 'bringing as company' (Kindaichi 1967a:44a, 1977:103).
There are not many upper bigrade stems, to begin with, and some are of shapes not
susceptible to the elision: oyi[y]- 'get old', kuyi[y]- 'regret', ... (cf. Komatsu
1981:183).

⁴ According to Tsuzuku 1941:182-3 in the Hagiwara dialect of Gifu prefecture the
tonic verbs (Type B) are ⋯[s]ite and the atonic (Type A) are ⋯site, but educated
people apparently correct some of the tonic forms so as to retain the sibilant:
oto¹ita → oto¹sita 'dropped'.

⁵ But there are attestations of sugiru (← suguru) and sakaferu (← sakafuru) in
the work Sangō-shii-ki-chū = Sankyō-shi-ki-chū (as index-listed by KggD despite
the furigana on 172d), c. 1200; yabureru (← yabururu) in Kinkai-[waka-]shū, 1213;
and kuiru (← kuyuru) in the Kōzan-ji text of Rongo, 1303. Cf. KggD 175b, 973a.
The simplification seems to have progressed faster for the -uru/-i verbs than for
the -uru/-e verbs, which are at least five times as numerous; and the provisional-
concessive form (*izen-kei*) was later than the merged predicative-attributive, so
that forms like sugireba ← sugureba and akereba ← akureba are attested later than
forms like sugiru ← suguru and akeru ← akuru. The Japanese-Portuguese dictionary
of 1603 has the bigrade conjugation for 'sleep' (ne, nuru, neta) and 'get' (ye,
yuru, yeta < e, uru, eta; notice that the prothetic y- is retained even before the
/u/), and either bigrade or monograde for 'pass' (fe, furu or feru, feta), though
only feru is used in the examples and it appears also in Esopo (463) of 1593. It
should be noted that the -uru forms persist in a number of modern dialects, and
inuru 'depart' and sinuru 'die' occur in many areas of western Honshū, Shikoku, and
Kyūshū (cf. Kyūshū hōgen no kiso-teki kenkyū 187). There are parts of Kyūshū (the
Buzen area of Fukuoka, the Bungo area of Ōita, and northeastern Miyazaki) where the

old upper bigrade conjugation is said to have been absorbed by the more populous lower-bigrade conjugation: okuru oki 'arise' → okeru oke (ibid. 154-5). But that description is perhaps misleading, for it is possible that the Kyūshū forms may be retaining a different development from one of the ancestors of the Old Japanese vowel Ciy < C̲o̲-i or Cu-i. Compare the old variant key = kiy 'tree' < *ko̲-Ci.

⁶ The pronunciation yuu for i[f]u 'say' is attested as early as 1221 (KggD 974a).

⁷ The velar-elided infinitive can be found in dialects that are of the Tōkyō type with respect to accentual patterns, such as the northern Kyūshū dialect reported by Toguchi 1974:115 and dialects of the Chūgoku area such as Okayama. There may be a correlation between the preservation of the velar in -ku and the relatively unrounded articulation of /u/ that prevails in eastern Japan. It has occasionally been observed that the eastern dialects have "strong" consonants, exemplified by geminations such as a'sa kkara 'from morning on', while the western dialects have "strong" vowels as shown by the automatic lengthening to two moras of the one-syllable nouns. The weakest vowel is /u/ and in rapid speech it often drops in situations that have largely escaped the ears of phoneticians, such as the common pronunciation [kokŋo] for kokugo 'national language'. Sakurai 1965b attempts to explain the fact that the elision in -[k]i pervades all the modern dialects (except Hachijō) though -ku fails to elide the velar in eastern Japan. He assumes a phonetic difference in the accent patterns, such that while the -ku syllable was low-pitched in Kyōto of the late-Heian period (a̅k̅a-ku 'red' vs. siro̅-ku 'white') it had already changed in the dialects of the east to a later pattern (a̅k̅a-ku vs. siro̅-k̅u, as found in modern Hakui) while, by way of a̅k̅a-k̅u vs. si̅ro-k̅u (as in the patterns reported by Kindaichi for Nozaki on Noto island), en route to the modern Tōkyō a̅k̅a-k̅ vs. si̅ro-ku. (See Ch. 4, §15.) Sakurai assumes that the later pattern, with high pitch on -ku for adjectives of both A and B accent types, took hold in eastern Japan quite early, before the velar elision. Since there are, however, dialects of the Tōkyō type which elide the velar in -[k]u (notably those of the Chūgoku area) he must assume that the accentual development in these dialects lagged behind that of the east, although following a parallel course. An alternative explanation would postulate some later influence from a Kyōto-type grammar that was superimposed on the existing accentual patterns; perhaps that would also account for the use of the elided form in an area centering on Nagoya. For more on the accent of the adjective forms, see Ch. 4, §9.

⁸ The earliest examples: 897 kufasiu su and 948 tadasiu su (Sakurai 1966a).

⁹ Or a semantic factor. Komatsu 1981:171-2 says that in the Heian period siroki mono meant any 'white thing' but siroi mono meant only 'face powder', equivalent to the modern o-siroi; he also points to women's names like Takai-ko and Akirakei-ko in Kokin-shū and Ise-monogatari.

¹⁰ Some scholars take the basic form to be aku, because that will simplify the description for some of the forms; but other scholars scorn the notion. This matter is taken up elsewhere.

¹¹ Old Japanese had name- 'overfamiliar, rude' and a number of forms with the suffix -key- such as sidu-key- 'quiet' and akira-key- 'bright'. In the Heian period se- 'narrow, cramped' and afatuke- 'superficial, flippant' are attested. The phrase sigyoo ueru 'plant them densely' has been reported from "an area in Shikoku" (Kawakami Shin, Nihon Bungaku Ronkyū 24:95 (1965)).

¹² I have not yet found an attestation but perhaps one will turn up.

¹³ The Japanese-Portuguese dictionary also has the fossilized amanequ = amaneku 'generally', which is still alive today.

¹⁴ The only adjective stems that end in /i/ are the emotive stems with the formant -si- except for o'oki- < o[f]o-ki nari 'big' and i- < yo- 'good'. The Japanese-Portuguese dictionary has vôqina = wooki-na 'big' and vôqini = wooki-ni 'greatly',

as well as vouoi = wowoi < ofo-ki 'much/many' with the infinitive vouô = wowoo <
ofo-ku, but the 1593 Esopo (485) has vouoquno = wowoku-no < ofo-ku no 'much/many',
as well as vôquina (412) and vôquini (413). (The dictionary simplifies the spelling
"qui" to "qi".)

[15] I take modern -taroo to be new, rather than a direct development from -taramu
(< -te aramu); two examples of -ta de aroo are cited by Yoshida 1971:364-5. The case
for -karoo < -karamu is better, but I suspect there was a later contraction there,
too. Cf. Martin 1975b:606 n.4.

[16] From Esopo, which offers two other examples of upper bigrade verbs:
"xicogiô" = šikodžoo = /sikodyoo/ 'will falsely report/accuse'; "deqeô" = dekyoo
'will be made' (JP "deqi decuru deqita" = deki dekuru dekita). The form "mochiyô" =
/motiyoo/ 'will use' is from the upper monograde stem "mochij mochiiru mochiita" =
motii motiiru motiita. There is also an example of atayô = atayoo 'will give' from
the lower bigrade verb ataye atayuru (→ ataeru); and a causative xemesaxerareô =
šemesašeraryoo 'will cause to attack' ← ···-rare -raruru (→ -rareru). Collado 10
says the form for tate- 'build' is "tateô or tachô" = /tatyoo/ pronounced (perhaps
optionally?) [tatšo:]. See n.20.

[17] No attestation has come to my attention.

[18] There are examples from as early as 1142 (Gokuraku-negai ōjō-shū: wakareu
'will depart') and 1184 (Sangō-shii-ki-chū = Sankyō-shi-ki-chū), and a kana reading
note may date a century earlier (Yoshida 1971:152, citing a study by Tsukishima).
Examples dated 1215 and 1216 are cited in KggD 973b.

[19] The negative attributive form was generally written "-nu", simply ignoring the
colloquial reduction to -N. When "-N" was written, it was intended to represent the
colloquial version of -mu.

[20] There is a single attestation of semu do su in Myōgi-shō (Kn Hō-ka 39:7), as
well as of semu to su (Kn Sō-chū 49:8). Earlier the expression seems to have been
consistently -mu to su as in kaze fukamu to su (K 21:5) 'the wind is about to blow'.

[21] Cf. the adjective infinitives sigyoo < sigye[k]u, takyoo < takye[k]u, amanyoo <
amanye[k]u in §2. Independent evidence that the syllables ke and me were /kye/ and
/mye/ are the kana spellings "keu" and "meu" — and the Portuguese spellings "ceô" =
kyoo and "meô" = myoo in the two Chinese loanmorphs keu 'teach' and meu 'strange',
which go back to Chinese KYAW and MYAW; the assimilation of the low vowel /a/ to the
palatal quality of the preceding /y/ may have taken place along the borrowing trail,
for Korean has kywo[W] and mywo[W]. Yet although /ti/ had become affricated [tši],
as attested by the Portuguese "chi", and /tya tyo tyu/ had also become affricates as
shown by the spellings "cha cho chu", there is no indication that /te/ was also
affricated (the Portuguese did not write "che"), with possibly one exception:
Collado's note that the presumptive of tate- 'build' is "tateô or tachô" (cf.
n.15). Notice that the Portuguese wrote sikodyoo 'will falsely report/accuse' as
"xicogiô", showing an affricate pronunciation [džo:], but dekyoo 'will be made'
is written "deqeô", not *ie··· or *gie··· or *ge···, so the pronunciation must have
been [de-] as it is today.

[22] There are not many verb stems that end in /i/. The only ones that I have found
attested for the presumptive are mi- 'see' and the four stems that are mentioned in
n.15. A few others may turn up in texts. Rodriguez spells "miô" for 'will see';
there was no difference in pronunciation between the spellings "Ceô" and "Ciô".

[23] The velar-elided forms bei and beu are attested from around 1000; there are
examples of both in Genji (cited in Ōno:1147, 1148 — cf. Tsukishima 1969:533).
Takamatsu 1969 finds 85 examples of bei in ten Heian texts; most of them follow the
verb of existence (a[ru] bei) and its derivatives. In addition to the forms that are
mentioned here, the obsolete adjective form be-mi < bey-myi is also found in early
texts. For more on the modal auxiliary bey-, see Ch. 2, §3.2.

P r o c e s s e s   u n d e r l y i n g   t h e   v e r b   g e r u n d   f o r m s

	'die'	'call'	'read'	'row'
0. *Source*	*syinyi-the	*yombyi-the	*yomyi-the	*khoŋgyi-the
1. *Syncope*	*syiny -the	*yomby -the	*yomy -the	*khoŋgy -the
2. *Aspiration suppression*	*syinyte	*yombyte	*yomyte	*khoŋgyte
3. *Cluster reduction*		*yomyte	*yomyde	*khoŋyte
4. *Automatic voicing*	*syinyde	*yomyde	*yomyde	*khoŋyde
5. *Hushing*	*šinyde			
6. *Velar elision*				<u>khoyde</u>
7. *Dissibilation*				
8. *Labial vocalization*		*yowde	*yowde	
9. *Palatal vocalization*	šiyde			
10. *Monophthong-ization*	ši:de	yo:de[2]	yo:de[2]	
11. *Vowel raising* (ɔ: > o:)				
12. *Vowel shortening*	šide	yode[5]	yode[5]	
13. *Dental assimilation*	<u>šinde</u>	<u>yonde</u>	<u>yonde</u>	khonde[6]
14. *Oral assimilation* (denasalization)	?šidde	yodde[7]	yodde[7]	khodde[7]
15. *Stop shortening*	(šide) =11	(yode) =11		

[1] Okayama (Kgg 34:84, 55:64), S. Mie (Umegaki 1962:120-2), Fujitsu in Saga (Hirayama 1951a:90-1), Ōita (Toguchi 1974:108), S. Kyūshū (id. 250-1); Fukui (id. 233); Muromachi Kyōto (Kgg 104:79b); JP. For a good map of the dialect distribution see Okumura 1969:41. The s-elision is said to be quite old (cf. Haguenauer 340) with attestations from around 900, slightly later than the earliest examples of k-elision.

[2] Parts of Nara prefecture (Umegaki 1962:330), S. Mie (id. 120-2), rarely Fukui (id. 233); Fujitsu in Saga (Hirayama 1951a:901); Tamana in Kumamoto (ibid.); ... . The form yo:de 'calling' would appear to be attested, in the spelling you[˝]te, as early as 1165 (cf. KggD 970b); but it is quite possible that the kana 'u' represents a nasal -m- or -ɱ, as it probably does in the 1002 spelling tuu[˝]te ← tumi-te 'pinching' (cf. Tsukishima 1969:461). There is a 1085 attestation of yonde 'calling' in the spelling yomu[˝]te (Tsukishima 1969:463). Incidentally, a report of the form [nom·dari] < nomi-tari in Igo of Oki island (Zhs 8:267), would appear to confirm the ordering I proposed in Language 43:255 n.15 and repeat above; cf. Tsuzuku 1970.

'write'	'lend'	'borrow'	'buy'	
*khakyi-the	*khasyi-the	*kharyi-the	*khapyi-the	0. Source
*khaky -the	*khasy -the	*khary -the	*khapy -the	1. Syncope
				2. Aspiration suppression
				3. Cluster reduction
				4. Automatic voicing
	*khašte			5. Hushing
khayte				6. Velar elision
	(*)khaçte			7. Dissibilation
			*khawte	8. Labial vocalization
	khayte[1]			9. Palatal vocalization
			khɔ:te[3]	10. Monophthong-ization
			kho:te[4]	11. Vowel raising (ɔ: > o:)
			khote[5]	12. Vowel shortening
khatte[7]		khatte	khatte	13. Dental assimilation
				14. Oral assimilation (denasalization)
	khate[8]		khate[8]	15. Stop shortening

[3] Old Kyōto, Portuguese Kyūshū, etc.

[4] Modern Kyōto etc.

[5] S. Mie, Tamana in Kumamoto; Kagoshima (Kgg 44:82).

[6] N. Nara (Umegaki 1962:329), S. Mie and the Shima peninsula (Kōza Kokugo-shi 1:166); northern Nagano (Kudō 1978:155); parts of Hokkaidō (by a different rule? Kgg 34:3-4).

[7] Southern Izu islands (Hirayama 1951a:177, 203). This is the traditional Kantō-type pattern, now replaced by the Kansai-type except for the single case of itte 'go' (Kindaichi 1977b:103). In the Hachijō islands itte ← ikite 'live' (id. 104, Zhs 7:196); the stem is apparently iki-, as in the standard language, and not the pre-Kamakura ik-.

[8] Kawachi in Ōsaka; N. Nara; Harima in Hyōgo (Umegaki 1962:520).

Chapter 4. Accentual distinctions.

1.0. Accent phrases and pitch patterns.

Japanese is spoken in phrases, and each phrase carries a tune, a pattern of pitch that is demarcated by boundaries we refer to as junctures. In a few dialects these patterns are not distinctive; the pitch assignment is automatically determined by the location of the junctures and the shape of the phrase. But most dialects have at least two distinctive patterns, and some have as many patterns as there are syllables in the phrase plus one additional pattern. For simpler and shorter words the choice of pattern cannot be predicted from other features of the phonology or the grammar; the pattern must be listed in the lexicon as part of the makeup of the word, just like the syllables with their consonants and vowels. Compound words and phrases carry accent patterns than can be predicted on the basis of the underlying patterns of the component parts, provided those underlying patterns are indicated in the lexicon. Predictable patterns are assigned by rules that are relatively simple in those dialects with few distinctive patterns to begin with, but there are many subtle details in the more complicated dialects, such as those of Tōkyō and Kyōto. We have a great deal of information on the assignment of pitch patterns in Tōkyō speech and a fair amount on a number of other dialects. Only information directly relevant to major problems of reconstruction will be presented in this work.

The distinctive pitch patterns are usually referred to as ACCENT, and the assignment of a pitch pattern to a given word is described in terms of the ACCENTUATION (basic accent) of the components together with a set of rules which, when properly applied, will yield the pattern heard. This is a broad use of the term ACCENT; below we will find reason to restrict the term to the locus of change of pitch (usually a fall from high to low) and refer to certain basic assignments of pitch level as REGISTER. We have left out of our discussion the use of pitch contours and modifications of accentual patterns to express sentence intonation, for here we assume a starting point that is more abstract than the raw utterance.

In the sections that follow, the phonetic pitch patterns are stated in terms of high and low and they are represented with a line above or below the syllable; when a fall occurs within a syllable the mark `\` is placed on the vowel and when a rise occurs the vowel carries the mark `/`. (Some books place the diacritic ´ over a vowel to indicate the locus, especially in representations of standard Tōkyō Japanese.)

The locus at which a high pitch stops and a low begins is marked by the symbol ˈ
(called kagiˈ 'hook') at the mora boundary. The syllables themselves are spelled in
a conventional orthography which ignores a number of details that are not directly
relevant to the discussion, such as the suppression of final high vowels in certain
of the Kagoshima forms. Junctures are indicated by | (minor) and ‖ (major); these
are enclosed in brackets when suppressed or cancelled. Charts 1-4 show the types of
accent phrase found in certain representative dialects. Each chart of types is
accompanied by a chart of example phrases, followed by a list of tag translations.

1.1. Types of accent phrase: Shuri.

Chart 1:1 displays the accent types found in phrases of from two to seven moras
in the Shuri dialect of Okinawa. This dialect has no one-mora phrases, and the one-
mora nouns of Tōkyō (such as na 'name') correspond to two-mora words with a
lengthened vowel (na͞: or na͞a, as we will usually write it). Words of this type can
probably be considered basically one-mora in Shuri, too, since when they turn up in
compounds the vowel is often short (na͞-nui 'adult personal name'). The lengthening
of the vowel makes these words indistinguishable — both in isolation and when a
particle is attached — from words with basically long vowels that come from separate
syllables deriving from earlier diphthongs, such as those in many Chinese loanwords;
such words with basically long vowels lack the short alternants. (It should be
mentioned that there are other Ryūkyū dialects in which this historical difference
has been lost, such as that of Shodon, where vowel length is a feature of canonical
shape and there are long and short alternants for both types of words.) One-mora
morphemes which are never lengthened are either grammatical elements, such as
endings and particles, or Chinese elements that fail to occur as free nouns.

Shuri has two types of accent phrase, which we will call TONIC and ATONIC. The
tonic words are marked "1" in the dictionary Okinawa-go jiten and the atonic words
are marked "0", but we will substitute "A" and "B" respectively, to accord with
Hirayama's notation for Kagoshima. The tonic phrases ("A") are marked by a fall of
pitch from high to low (a locus) at the end of the second mora unless that is the
last mora or is dependent (vowel prolongation as simple length or as nasality), in
which cases the locus comes at the end of the first mora. Put another way, the first
mora is pitched high and the high extends through the second mora when that is
neither final nor dependent. The atonic phrases ("B") cannot easily be characterized
as either "high" or "low": they rise gently at the end, so that you clearly hear the
juncture between two atonic phrases. In a string between junctures, each successive
phrase — whether tonic or atonic — is pitched lower, like descending stairsteps.

1.2. Types of accent phrase: Kagoshima.

The Kagoshima accent phrases (Chart 2:1) are quite similar to those of Shuri,
except that the locus of the tonic words is always on the penultimate (next-to-last)
syllable; if there is only one syllable, the locus is heard as a fall of pitch
within that syllable (ò). On the other hand, the atonic phrases of Kagoshima have a
nondistinctive high on the last syllable so that the earlier syllables are clearly
heard as low, but apparently there is no rise of pitch on a one-syllable phrase so
that it is not clearly high or low. The phonetic realization of the atonic phrases
is simply an exaggerated version of the Shuri rendering. Although we illustrate the
Kagoshima phrases with one-mora syllables, the two-mora syllables (CVC, usually a
reduction of basic CVC¹/ₙ, or CV: or CVn) are treated the same way, so that the
chart applies to syllables, not to moras as such. You will notice that the phonetic
manifestations of pitch in Kagoshima are dependent on the length of the phrase.
Although the choice of "A" or "B" pattern is always determined by the intrinsic
accentuation of the first word in the phrase, the actual tune of a word will vary
depending on whether other words are attached in the phrase: the word for 'wind'
is high-low by itself (ka̅ze) but low-high when followed by a monosyllabic particle
(ka̅ze̅ ga) and low-low when followed by a dissyllabic particle (kaze ma̅de̅) or two
monosyllabic particles (kaze n̅i̅ mo).

1.3. Types of accent phrase: Tōkyō.

For dialects like that of Tōkyō, unlike Shuri and Kagoshima, it is important
to know not only WHETHER the phrase has a locus but WHERE, for the position of the
locus is not fixed by the length of the phrase, but is determined by the intrinsic
accents of the words that make up the phrase. The patterns that result are displayed
in Chart 3:1. The ratio of accent types to moras is n+1, where the "plus-one"
represents those phrases which have no locus but are atonic. Since these correspond
historically to the TONIC phrases of Shuri and Kagoshima, we will try to keep our
bearings constant by noting them as "A". The "A" group of words are atonic in
Tōkyō — and, as we will see, in Kyōto — because they are unmarked by a locus;
they are tonic in Shuri and Kagoshima because they have a distinctive locus, though
the position of that is automatically determined. In Meikai-kokugo-jiten and its
revision Shin Meikai-kokugo-jiten, the locus of an entry word is noted by number,
counting moras from the beginning of the word, with the atonic words given the
notation "0". The Tōkyō "0" words correspond to our "A" (unlike the "0" words of

the Okinawan dictionary, which correspond to our "B"); the Tōkyō prototonic words, those with an initial accent ("1"), correspond to our "B" (but words marked "1" in the Okinawan dictionary correspond to our "A"). Tōkyō words marked with the number "2" and higher numbers correspond historically to both the "A" and the "B" types in individual ways which result from loss of the accentual feature of initial register, found still alive in dialects like that of Kyōto, as we will see below. Such words include the "oxytonic" with a final basic accent that is heard only when a particle is attached (so that you can hear the low on the mora following the locus) and the "mesotonic" with the locus at one of the moras other than the one that begins or ends the word.

Tōkyō speech is characterized by long plateaus: except for the first syllable, the stretch of high pitch extends until it is relieved by a locus. The first mora is automatically low for all phrases that are neither prototonic nor monosyllabic. This is a kind of "warm-up" for the vocal cords, and after it the voice rises and stays up on a high pitch, to be brought down only by a locus. Certain accentually similar dialects, such as that of Aomori, extend the initial automatic low, and rise gently to the last high-pitched syllable, or rise only for that syllable. You can think of these dialects as having a slow "warm-up".[1] Within a phrase the locus is determined by the component words; typically once an intrinsic locus has occurred all later loci are ignored (cancelled). But within a word, and in certain types of syntactic phrases, more complicated rules apply. The intrinsic accent of a compound noun, for example, is determined by the basic type of the second component, with certain adjustments, as explained below (§3).

A short atonic phrase is often run right onto a following phrase, dropping the juncture: kono [|] hati 'this bee' has the same tune as tomodati 'friend' and iku [|] umi 'the sea we go to' has the same tune as mizuumi 'lake'. After a tonic phrase the juncture sometimes drops in rapid speech if the following phrase is quite short, and especially when it is atonic, but the normal phrasing keeps the juncture: dono | hati (daroo ka) 'what bee (can it be)?', aru | umi (e | ikimasita) '(we went to) a certain sea'. But whenever the juncture is minor ("|"), as in our examples, the later plateau of "high" pitch is reduced to a lower level than the plateau of the preceding phrase; if it is at the same or a higher level, the speaker is using a major juncture ("‖"), perhaps in order to lend special emphasis to the following phrase (as would happen if it replaced the minor juncture in our examples).

Tōkyō Japanese has both "light" syllables that contain only one mora and "heavy" syllables that are made up of two moras. The second mora of a heavy syllable must be one of three types:

(1) an anticipation of the following oral consonant, heard as an abrupt moment of silence in -pp- -tt- -kk- but by a lengthening of the hiss in -ss- and of the hush in -ssy- (and of the pharyngal breathiness in the -hh- of recent loanwords such as Bahha 'Bach');

(2) a nasal elongation of the vowel — an = [a˜], in = [i˜], un = [u˜] or after the sibilant [ɨ˜], en = [e˜], on = [o˜]) with the nasal assimilating in position of articulation to a following consonant (-np- = [mp], -nt- = [nt], -nk- = [ŋk]);

(3) an oral elongation of the vowel in the same position — aa = [a:], ii = [i:], uuu = [u:] or after the sibilant [ɨ:], oo = [o:]) — or as a higher glide (ai oi ui; occasionally ei; rarely, in recent loanwords, au).

The accentual locus never occurs at the end of the second mora of a heavy syllable of Types 1 and 2: when expected in that position, the locus moves back a mora: kike'n-do 'degree of danger' (cf. manzoku'-do 'degree of satisfaction'). Heavy syllables of the third type have two different origins. Some are intrinsically (basically) heavy and never permit the locus to fall at the end of the second mora; others are reduced from two one-mora syllables, often with a morpheme boundary between them, and are pronounced as two syllables when the locus is expected after the second mora: sai'-do 'degree of difference' from sa'-i 'difference' normally pronounced the same as sa'i 'talent'. (Cf. sa'i-do 'repeated time', pronounced the same as sa'ido 'side'.) When the accentuation rules call for a locus at the end, an extra-heavy syllable of three moras even within a morpheme is split into two syllables, light + heavy or heavy + light depending on the mora structure: ko'in 'coin', koi'n-syoo 'coin dealer'; guri'in 'green', gurii'n-sya 'Green Car'; booi 'bellboy', booi'-tyoo 'bell captain'.

1.4. Types of accent phrase: Kyōto.

The dialect of Kyōto is like that of Tōkyō in that some phrases are tonic, having a locus (a fall of pitch) and some are atonic, without a locus; it is also like Tōkyō in that the position of the locus within the phrase is distinctive. But Kyōto nearly doubles Tōkyō's number of phrase types by making a distinction of initial REGISTER: it makes a difference whether a phrase begins high or low. Chart 4:1 displays the phrase types in the two registers so as to show how the

various patterns mirror each other. In Tōkyō the first syllable of a phrase,
unless it is marked by a locus, is automatically low, but in Kyōto the initial low
is always distinctive, as is the low that sets in after a locus. In Kyōto it is the
HIGH pitch that is nondistinctive, and the last mora of a low atonic word is
automatically high; for some Kinki-dialect speakers the rise indicated by this
phrase-final high or by the high before a locus in a low-register tonic word is a
gradual climb that extends from the beginning of the low stretch.[2] Notice these
characteristics of the system:

(1) Some phrases have two stretches of low pitch, one assigned by the initial
register and the other marking the locus.

(2) The stretch of low pitch may be of any length — before or after a locus,
or with no locus.

(3) a stretch of high pitch may be of any length only if it is a continuation of
initial high pitch, for in a low-register word the high pitch is confined to a
single syllable, either the one that precedes the distinctive locus or —
nondistinctively — the last of the phrase.

In Chart 4:2 the examples of high-register phrases are displayed with the
phonetic high-pitch span marked (by an overline); the unmarked stretches are low
and always occur after the locus (marked ˺). The examples of low-register phrases,
however, are displayed in the opposite fashion: the low-pitch spans are marked (by
an underline) and the high-pitched mora, whether the mora before the distinctive
locus or the nondistinctively high final mora of an atonic phrase, is left unmarked.
Kindaichi (1951:87 and elsewhere) has made a good argument for treating the initial
low as a special case of the locus. In his view the low-register words have a locus
(the onset of low pitch) at the very beginning — they are "preaccented" just as
Tōkyō's oxytonic nouns are "postaccented" — and they may or may not have a second
locus at a later point. The synchronic argument for this interpretation, by which
kabuto 'helmet' is treated as ˺kabu˺to and usagi 'rabbit' is treated as ˺usagi,
is based on the economy of distinctive units (one "accent" device accounts for both
register and locus), and on the uniformity of phonetic manifestation: the onset of
low pitch is always distinctive, and that constitutes the marking feature. But there
are few if any morphophonemic phenomena to offer in support of the equation of

the initial low pitch of register with the low pitch of locus. McCawley offered the
behavior of the particle mo 'also/even', which always attaches low, so that k̄āzē ḡā
contrasts with k̄āzē mo, which can be treated as /kaze ⁷mo/. But Haraguchi 1977:92-5
turns the argument around by claiming that when the particle is cited in isolation,
meaning "the particle mo" it is treated as high. Since bound linguistic forms cited
in isolation as technical terms are quite often given artificial (or "reading")
pronunciations, Haraguchi's argument is weak. The "preaccent" of mo and of certain
other emphatic particles is probably the result of an earlier juncture, as we will
see below. The historical advantage of Kindaichi's treatment is that it allows him
to explain many of the Tōkyō forms as the result of a right shift — a delay or lag
in realization by one syllable — of the initial onset of the low pitch: thus Kyōto
⁷hune > Tōkyō hu⁷ne 'boat', Kyōto ⁷kabu⁷to > Tōkyō ka⁷buto 'helmet' (with automatic
cancellation of the second locus), etc. On this historical explanation, see §15.
In our phonemic notations we will adopt the convention of marking Kyōto's initial
low register with a dot, treating it as a marking device that is different from the
locus (marked, as it is for Tōkyō, with ⁷).

   In Tōkyō the locus is not permitted to occur after the second mora of a"heavy"
syllable, and the Chūgoku dialects (e.g. Hiroshima) are like Tōkyō in this respect.
But certain Tōkyō-type dialects (cf. Hiroto 1961:164) have no such restriction: for
example, Okayama and Yamaguchi and southwestern Shikoku, where in the dialect of Hat
(Doi 1952:25-6) we find such patterns as koōmori for Tōkyō k̄oōmori 'bat' and tenki
for Tōkyō tenki 'weather'. Nor is there any such restriction in Kyōto, for Tōkyō's
sinnē⁷n-kai 'New Year's party' is Kyōto's .sinnen⁷-kai and Tōkyō's yuubi⁷n-kyoku
'post office' is Kyōto's yuubin⁷-kyoku. The application of accentuation rules to
compounds of differing constituencies leads to such contrasts as those found in
sinkee⁷-syoo 'neurosis' and sin-se⁷ehu 'new government' (McCawley 1977:282),
.hibai⁷-hin '(something) not for public sale' and .mi-ka⁷ihatu 'undeveloped'. But
within a morpheme or simple word the locus seldom if ever appears at the end of the
second mora of a heavy syllable; .kon⁷-ban 'tonight' is a compound. The Kyōto accent
of nouns like sek⁷kai 'interference', kak⁷koo 'cuckoo', sak⁷ka 'writer', rok⁷kaa
'locker', nip⁷pon 'Japan' (= ni⁷hon), .suit⁷ti 'switch', (.koohii-)pot⁷to '(coffee-)
pot', etc., appears to be exceptional, but that is an artifact of the analysis, for
we are following Hirayama in positing the locus directly before the first low mora
rather than after the last high mora, and the silent moras (represented by the cover
symbol -T- or -Q-) can be heard neither as high nor as low. But these words belong

typologically with the group that includes guˈntai 'troops', koˈoka 'effect',
raˈitaa 'lighter', .sutaˈato 'start', and hiˈnto 'hint'; accordingly, we would do
well here to adjust our notations to seˈkkai, kaˈkkoo, saˈkka, roˈkkaa, niˈppon,
.suiˈtti, poˈtto, etc., and give the appearance of conforming to the interpretation
underlying Umegaki's notations in Nihon-kokugo-daijiten. One anomaly in the NKD data
is yotˈtu for 'four [as adverb]' in contrast with yoˈttu 'four [as noun]' and yaˈttu
for 'eight'; Hirayama is consistent in his notation for the words (yotˈtu, yatˈtu).
But Umegaki also has ikˈ-kai 'one time [as noun]', zatˈ-to 'roughly', and a few
other anomalous markings.[3] Other apparent exceptions are .kaiˈko 'silkworm' (an
ancient compound), .tenˈde ni 'respectively' (from a reduplication), and obvious
compounds such as .zuiˈ-mushi 'pearl moth', .sanˈ-ri 'three leagues', .senˈ-ri 'a
thousand leagues', .senˈ-getu 'last month', .tooˈ-zi 'that time', .dooˈ-sya 'the
said company'; .tooˈ-miti 'far road'. But there are also Chinese binoms of less
obvious constituency: .kooˈkoo 'filial piety', .hooˈkoo 'service', .nooˈgyoo
'agriculture'; and the place name .ooˈu 'Ōu = Mutsu and Dewa, the northeast'. And
in Ōsaka we find onˈna 'woman' for which the Kyōto form (according to Umegaki) is
oˈnna. There are occasional anomalies in the treatment of the heavy syllables in the
Kyōto accent data found in Hirayama 1960 and in NKD: Umegaki has .tahen-ˈkei for
Hirayama's taheˈn-kei; Hirayama has .zyo-tenˈin where the rules seem to call for
.zyo-teˈn'in. Hirayama has hoosoˈo-kyoku for Umegaki's hoosooˈ-kyoku, though both
have hoosooˈ-hoo. The following are anomalous in both sources: .sinbuˈn-si/-sya,
.kikaˈn-si/-sya, unteˈn-syu, ... Perhaps the anomalies are due to Tōkyō influences.

1.5. Types of accent phrase: other dialects.

Certain dialects have developed systems of accent that are peculiar when viewed
from the perspective of the dialects we have described, but these odd developments
are thought to be relatively recent. According to Uwano 1976a the Hirosaki dialect
has an accent system which is the "mirror image" of the Tōkyō system, for the low
pitch is distinctive and the high is determined. (For more on the Hirosaki dialect,
see §10:5.)

In Narada the locus is at the end of the last low mora, BEFORE a high. Atonic
words have no last low (because an attached particle continues as low), and the last
low of an oxytonic word can be ascertained only before a particle other than /no/,
being neutralized otherwise, so that there is no way to tell whether it is really
"last" or not: oxytonic a̅s̲i̲ g̅a̅ carries a different tune from atonic u̅s̲i̲ g̲a̲, but

a̅si no 'of the leg' has the same tune as u̅si no 'of the ox'. The initial high is
always nondistinctive, like the initial low in Tōkyō; the locus is before the
distinctive high that can appear later. The Narada locus can be said to be the
same as Tōkyō's in POSITION but different in REALIZATION: a point of rise rather tha
a point of fall. Some of the high-low-high tunes that result sound odd to the Tōkyō
ear. See Ch. 5, §5.5, for the patterns.

From the viewpoint of synchronic typology there are four kinds of accentual
systems in Japanese dialects, according to Uwano (1977b:318):

the mirror-image types of Tōkyō vs. Hirosaki and also Shizukuishi-machi in Iwate
prefecture, which is very similar to Hirosaki;

the type represented by Narada, and Hasuda in Saitama prefecture, in which the
locus is determined at the syllable before the high pitch (= the last low syllable);

the type represented by Kyōto, and by two places in Mie prefecture, Atawa in
Minami-Muro county Kanayama-chō of Kumano city, where both the first onset of low
pitch and the onset of high pitch, or the point before it, are distinctive.

Two other types, the "accentless" dialects, should be mentioned. The single-
pattern dialects use pitch patterns only to demarcate phrases, not to differentiate
words: the tune helps you locate the junctures. In the dialect of Miyakonojō (in
southern Kyūshū) the last syllable of a phrase is always high; in the dialect of
Shimagawa (southern Shikoku) the first syllable is always high. In Sendai the last
two syllables are high-low and all preceding syllables are high except the first.
There are also dialects in which tunes fluctuate in free variation, but do not
distinguish words from each other; the accent of these dialects — called "vague"
(aimai) by Hirayama — are thought to have resulted from relatively recent loss of
distinctive patterns.

Akinaga (1966) has made interesting observations on the distribution of certain
typological characteristics of accent found in dialects:

(1) Dialects in which the segmental phonology has no influence on the locus of the
accent: Kyōto-type dialects; Okayama; southwest Kyūshū.

(2) Dialects in which the accentual locus shifts away from dependent moras (long
vowels, diphthongs, -N-, -T-): Tōkyō-type dialects in the east and the north;
Tottori, Shimane, Hiroshima, Yamaguchi, northern Kyūshū.

(3) Dialects in which not only the dependent moras but also the high-vowel
syllables (-i, -u) cause the accentual locus to shift away: Hokkaidō and the

northern parts of Honshū; part of Chiba (the Bōsō peninsula); Toyama and Ishikawa (including the Noto peninsula); the Takamatsu area of Shikoku; Matsue, the Shimane peninsula, Oki island; Tsushima.

Another set of characteristics:

(1) Dialects which have a pitch-fall within a "syllable" (= mora): Kyōto- type dialects except most of those of Shikoku; Toyama, Ishikawa, Noto peninsula, parts of northern Honshū and southernmost Hokkaidō.

(2) Dialects which have both pitch-fall and pitch-rise within a "syllable" (= mora): the Takamatsu area of Shikoku; Shimokita peninsula, northernmost Honshū; an area near Morioka.

1.6. Oxytonic words in Kyōto.

Kyōto's oxytonic pattern is peculiar in several ways. It occurs only in low-register nouns of two syllables like saru 'monkey' and mado 'window' and in a very few three-mora nouns with a dependent middle mora: minna 'all' (but minna in Ōsaka), noppo 'a gangly person', matti 'matches', gittyo 'a left-hander', makka 'crimson'; and according to Hirayama deppa 'buck teeth' (for which Umegaki gives deppa). At an underlying level it may be possible to treat the final syllable as long: saruu, madoo, minnaa, ... In Kyōto the length is always curtailed before a juncture but the fall of pitch persists; when a particle is attached the length is totally suppressed and the fall is heard as low pitch on the particle: saru ni. In Kōchi both the length and the fall are both totally suppressed even before a juncture, so that in isolation the noun saru 'monkey' with its distinctive final high is heard with the same tune as hune 'boat' with its nondistinctive final high; but they are different morphophonemically, as can be seen from hune nī 'to the boat' and saru ni 'to the monkey'. If our description assumes the underlying length, that means we predict identical pronunciations for such pairs as madoo | akeru (with ellipted particle) and mado o | akeru 'I'll open the window'; the prediction for Kyōto will be mado [|] akeru and mado o | akeru. That is, we assume that ···V̄ᴵ: shortens to ···V̇(:) regardless of its origin; the notion is borrowed from Shibata 1955. It is unclear what happens to honoo 'flame', historically three syllables; we would expect the natural pronunciation to be hono in Kyōto and hono in Kōchi, but literacy or other factors may prevent this from being true. Shibata (1980:417) says that hato 'pigeon' is phonetically like ketoo 'damn white-man'

(but Umegaki has k̄etoo for that word). Similar problems are posed by the final
long vowel of a few Chinese binoms and foreignisms, such as hoh̄ee 'infantry',
pur̄ee 'play', sut̄aa 'star', and a number of examples with conflicting data from
Hirayama (unmarked) and Umegaki (U):

  tasu̅u 'majority' (U t̄asuu), zyoo̅o 'queen' (U z̄yooo), zyoroo 'whore' (U z̄yoroo /
  zyoroō), kas̄oo 'house physiognomy' (U k̄asoo), ses̄oo 'state of the world' (U s̄esoo)

Umegaki has also koz̄oo / k̄ozoo 'bonze', for which Hirayama gives only the latter
version. With these words compare boró 'rag, scrap', yabó 'uncouth', buyó 'gadfly',
sutó 'strike'; hisyó 'escaping the heat' (U hi̅syo) or 'secretary' (U h̄isyo),
tohó 'walking' (U toh̄o), tiká 'subway' (U ti̅ka).
Some of the missing oxytonic patterns are found in paradigmatic forms of verb stems
in modern Kyōto, but they are peculiar in that both the length and the accent are
totally suppressed before juncture, including those junctures that themselves are
later suppressed:

  kak̄u ḡa 'write but'   kak̄u 'write'   kaku | teḡam̄i 'letter to write'
                                               kaku [|] h̄ito 'man to write'
                                               kaku | oz̄iisan 'gaffer to write'
  okir̄u ḡa 'rise but'   okir̄u 'rise'   okiru [|] t̄oki 'when I rise'
  kakurer̄u ḡa 'hide but'   kakurer̄u 'hide'   kakureru | tok̄oro 'place to hide'

   In the late-Heian texts nouns such as mat̄u and sarú were usually treated as
identical in accent: both behaved like modern Kōchi's low atonic matu except before
the adnominal particle /no/, where both were like modern Kōchi's low oxytonic saru.
But in the texts there are also numerous examples of a special marking for the final
fall of these oxytonic nouns (like modern Kyōto sarú), as well as some of the verb
and adjective forms.

1.7. Oxytonic words in Tōkyō.

   In Tōkyō the distinction between oxytonic and atonic words is generally
neutralized before juncture (though the fall may persist with heavy syllables);
the final accent is suppressed, much as in Kōchi:

  kod̄omo ḡa | kot̄ori w̄a | ot̄oko ga | hut̄ari w̄a |
  kod̄omo | kot̄ori | ot̄oko | hut̄ari |

1.8. Adjacent accent phrases with a suppressed juncture.

The nondistinctive low pitch which is heard on the initial mora of non-prototonic words of all Tōkyō-type dialects disappears (i.e. is smoothed to high) when the preceding juncture is suppressed. The juncture usually persists when both words are tonic, i.e. have a locus. The nondistinctive high pitch which is heard on the final mora of the low atonic words of Kyōto disappears (i.e. is smoothed to low) when the following juncture is suppressed. The juncture persists when both words are low in register. When the juncture is suppressed the resulting accent pattern is often identical with one of the patterns of simplex words. But some of the resulting patterns do not occur for simplex words; those must always contain at least one underlying juncture that will break the string into occurring simplex patterns.

	T ō k y ō	K y ō t o
'this bee'	kono [|] hati	kono [|] hati
'friend'	tomodati	tomodati
'this rock'	kono [|] iwa(ga)	kono [|] iwa
'thunder'	kaminari(ga)	kaminari
'this boat'	kono [|] hune	kono [|] hune → kono hune
'umbrella'	amagasa	(amagasa, amagasa)
'bush warbler'	(uguisu)	uguisu
'this monkey'	kono [|] saru	kono [|] sarù → kono saru
'a certain bee'	aru	hati	aru [	] hati
	---	---
'a certain rock'	aru	iwa(ga)	aru [	] iwa
	(asagata, asagata)	asagata
'a certain boat'	aru	hune	aru	hune
Cf. 'sky blue'	(sorairo)	sorairo
'a certain monkey'	aru	saru	aru	sarù

The juncture may drop after the final accent has been suppressed; Tōkyō oxytonics are then treated like atonics, for that is what they have become:

kodomo [ga] | kimasita   →   kodomo [|] kimasita   'A child came.'

otoko [ga] | kimasita   →   otoko [|] kimasita   'A man came.'

hutari [wa] | kimasita   →   hutari [|] kimasita   'Two (people) came.'

hana [o] | mita   { → hana [|] mita   } 'I looked at flowers.'
                      → hana [|] mita

hana [o] | mita   →   hana [|] mita   } 'I looked at noses.'

(The first version of 'I looked at flowers' results from dropping the juncture, thereby suppressing the accent of the verb, BEFORE the ellipsis of the particle, so that the oxytonic accent of the noun survives.)

Polysyllabic words with a "heavy" (two-mora) final syllable move the locus back from the weak (dependent) mora so that the fall of pitch normally is not lost except before a suppressed juncture. The common suppressed-juncture situation is with adverbs:

kinoo | kinoo wa | kinoo | kimasita → kinoo [|] kimasita 'came yesterday'

takusan | takusan wa | takusan | kaimasita → takusan [|] kaimasita 'bought lots'

But heavy monosyllables are treated as prototonic, not oxytonic:

kyoo | kyoo wa | kyoo | kimasita (*kyoo [|] kimasita) 'came today'

The way the locus retreats, rather than drops, in these heavy-ended polysyllables is reminiscent of the Kyōto treatment of oxytonic nouns like saru in isolation.

2.0. Pitch patterns of inflected stems.

An important class of words is made up of inflected STEMS to which paradigmatic
ENDINGS are attached: these are the verbs and the (predicated) adjectives. The
pitch pattern of a given paradigmatic form, or of such a form with an enclitic
particle attached, is predictable provided we have certain information about the
stem. We must know whether the stem belongs to one or the other of two underlying
patterns which, following Hirayama, we will label A and B. The actual realization of
the pitch patterns varies considerably in different dialects, but that is not our
immediate concern. The accentuation of verb stems, compound verbs, and infinitive-
derived nouns is taken up in §8, where the reader will find details omitted in the
following sections. As we have seen, the dialect of Shuri and that of Kagoshima use
only two distinctive patterns for ALL phrases, so that the various verb forms are
like noun phrases of equivalent length in the accentuations that distinguish them;
we can omit the details.

2.1. Tōkyō verb patterns.

The way the two types of pitch pattern are realized in Tōkyō verb forms can
be illustrated with a representative sample of stems and endings. We will consider
the nonpast or imperfect form, which ends in -ru or -[r]u; the infinitive, which
ends in -i or -[i]; and the past or perfect form, which attaches the ending -ta
(derived by contraction from earlier -t[e] a[r-]) to the infinitive with various
adjustments of elision, syncope, and assimilation as explained in Chapter 3.

A	'wear'	'put'	'insert'	'change'	'begin'	'doubt'
	ki-ru	ok-u	ire-ru	kawar-u	hazime-ru	utaga-u
	ki < *ki-i	ok-i	ire	kawar-i	hazime	utaga-i
	ki-ta	oi-ta	ire-ta	kawat-ta	hazime-ta	utagat-ta

B	'see'	'write'	'rise'	'think'	'join'	'rejoice'
	mi-ru	kak-u	oki-ru	omo-u	awase-ru	yorokob-u
	mi < *mi-i	kak-i	oki	omo-i	awase	yorokob-i
	mi-ta	kai-ta	oki-ta	omot-ta	awase-ta	yorokon-da

In Tōkyō a low initial syllable followed by high pitch is nondistinctive; the low pitch is distinctive only when it sets in after a high, i.e. when there is a fall. Certain Tōkyō-type dialects — Sapporo and Akita (Hirayama 1960), Morioka (Kindaichi Kyōsuke 1935), Tsuruoka (KKK 1953), Tottori (Hiroto and Ōhara 1953) — lack the "high plateau" that characterizes Tōkyō speech, and in those dialects only the syllable immediately before the fall is clearly high: awaseru, yorokobu. For Tōkyō-type dialects in general the syllable before the fall to low pitch is often referred to as the "accented syllable", and words without such a fall are referred to as unaccented or ATONIC words. Accordingly we can describe Tōkyō verb stems as atonic (Type A) and tonic (Type B), but we must take care that using these terms does not mislead us when we take up other dialects and when we consider the earlier patterns of the language.

When an enclitic particle is attached to a verb form the particle is low:

A   ki-ru ga   ok-u ga   ire-ru ga   kawar-u ga   hazime-ru ga   utaga-u ga
    ki wa   ok-i wa   ire wa   kawar-i wa   hazime wa   utaga-i wa
    ki-ta ga   oi-ta ga   ire-ta ga   kawat-ta ga   hazime-ta ga   utagat-ta ga

B   mi-ru ga   kak-u ga   oki-ru ga   omo-u ga   awase-ru ga   yorokob-u ga
    mi wa   kak-i wa   oki wa   omo-i wa   awase wa   yorokob-i wa
    mi-ta ga   kai-ta ga   oki-ta ga   omot-ta ga   awase-ta ga   yorokon-da ga

From the isolated forms it would be difficult to claim that one pattern is marked ("accented") and the other not. But from the behavior with particles and endings we can say that the stems of Type A are unmarked (or ATONIC) and those of Type B are marked (or TONIC); we mark the accent at the locus of the fall, which is predictable for a given form. We say that a word with a fall of pitch has an overt accent, a word without has none. Monosyllabic endings and particles are tonic in underlying form, as we can detect when something is attached without juncture: ··· ni wa, ···-ru ga, ···-ru kara, etc. But some of the underlying patterns are obscured by various surface adjustments that cause an intervening juncture to drop after it has done its job, letting atonic words run directly onto the following word(s). The particle to¹, meaning 'that ··· (end-quote)' or 'if/when', attaches with or without underlying juncture, depending on the speaker, so that you will hear both ok-u to and ok-u to, both oi-ta to and oi-ta to. The version that pitches the

particle high is like the structure of adnominalized verb + noun, for which an
underlying juncture is posited; a surface cancellation prevents us from hearing the
juncture in no͞ru ⌈|⌉ kuruma 'the car one rides' and no͞ru ⌈|⌉ hiko͞oki 'the plane one
rides', but the juncture is implied by what we hear in ori͞ru | kuruma (ma͞de) '(up to)
the car one leaves' and ori͞ru | hiko͞oki 'the plane one leaves', in which the lower
plateau of the second high stretch tells us that the juncture is of the lesser type
called minor juncture. The phrase a͞ku to͞ mo means either 'also/even the door that
will open' with the noun to¹ 'door' or 'also/even [saying] that it opens' with the
particle, but a͞ku to mo has only the second interpretation.

One surprising exception in Tōkyō — though regular in certain Tōkyō-type
dialects (cf. Terakawa et al. 1951:393, 409, etc.; Kudō 1978:116-9) — is that the
particle ni '(in order) to' is pitched high after the infinitive of a Type-A stem:
o͞k-i ni (i͞ku) '(goes) to put it', ka͞tar-i ni (ku-͞ru) '(comes) to tell it'.
A possible explanation was offered in Martin 1975b:404, where I suggested that
the pattern indicates a dropped juncture resulting from an ellipsis, but it is
difficult to maintain the validity of the ellipsis in view of the antiquity of
purpose expressions such as V-i ni iku, which occur in the Koji-ki songs of the
eighth century. Yet, compare the very similar phenomenon in Kyōto (below, §2.2).

The situation in the Tōkyō-type dialect of Hagiwara is unusual: ka͞u ga
'buys but' (unlike Tōkyō's ka͞u ga) yet kat͞ta ga 'bought but' (< *ka͞p⌈i⌉-ta ga);
to͞bu ga 'flies but' yet to͞nda ga 'flew but' (< *to͞nb⌈i⌉-ta ga); and na͞ku ga
'cries but' yet na͞ita ga 'cried but' (< *na⌈k⌉i-ta ga). From the explanation in
Tsuzuku 1941:187 we would conclude that ga is attached without an immediately
underlying juncture, and that the imperfect of Hagiwara's Type-A verbs is now
atonic and no longer oxytonic as it is in Tōkyō. What about the behavior of
the other particles in Hagiwara? On this, information is lacking.

Since the perfect (or "past") and gerund forms are made by attaching -ta and
-te respectively to the infinitive, with appropriate shape adjustments, we would
expect the forms in the third row of Type A shown above to show the pattern V-ī-ta͟.
And there are Tōkyō-type dialects, such as those of Nagoya and Totsukawa, that
have either o͞ita or ō͞ita, the latter version resulting from an automatic retreat
of the accentual locus to the first mora of the heavy syllable, so that the surface
realization coincides with the pattern found for Type B verbs such as ka͞ita. This
information provides a welcome explanation for the otherwise puzzling fact that
Tōkyō accentuates the contraction of oite [i]ta 'was putting' (or 'had put') as

oīteta but the contraction of oite [i]ru 'is putting' (or 'has put') as oīteru
(Martin 1975b:514). The underlying form for 'was putting', expressed in terms of
locus, must earlier have been o[k]i¹-te | i[i¹]-ta which led to oi¹-te | i-ta and
then in Tōkyō oite[¹] | i¹ta with the juncture cancelling the final accent of the
gerund and afterward dropping to yield oite i¹ta > oite¹ita > oite¹ta. Whereas
oite[¹] | iru¹ simply contracted: oite iru¹ > oiteru¹. The remaining puzzle is why
the uncontracted form is now oite ita¹ rather than *oite i¹ta. Probably that is new
and due to a back-formation which has recreated the model for the contraction on
the basis of the separate later form, as found in the focused conversions: oite¹
wa/mo [|] ita¹. Aside from the focused conversions, the uncontracted form had likely
died out in the spoken language except (perhaps with the juncture) as an emphatic
version. For more on these problems, see below, §8.3.

        We leave unexplained the two forms mi-ta and mi-te in the Tōkyō-type dialect
of Hagiwara (Tsuzuku 1941:195). The corresponding forms for the verb kuru 'come'
look superficially like the Tōkyō forms that result from the probably late devoicing
of the first syllable (ki-ta, ki-te) but the explanation must be different.

2.2. Kyōto verb patterns.

        Kyōto-type dialects have verb-stem classes that correspond to the two types of
A and B, but most of the longer stems belong to Type A. That is because the Kyōto
Type-A class has absorbed original Type-B stems of the following kinds: all of the
consonant stems ("yo-dan" verbs) of two or more syllables except for aruk- 'walk',
hair- 'enter', mair- 'come/go', kakus- 'conceal', and a few others (listed in §8);
all stems of three or more syllables except for kakure- 'be hidden' and a few others
(listed in §8). The resulting patterns for Kyōto itself:

A	'wear'	'put'	'insert'	'change'	'begin'	'doubt'
	ki-ru	ok-u	ire-ru	kawar-u	hazime-ru	utaga-u
	kī < kī-i	ok-i	īre < *īre-i	kawar-i	hazīme < *hazīme-i	utaga-i
	kī-ta	oi-ta	ire-ta	kawat-ta	hazīme-ta	utago[o]-ta

B	'see'	'write'	'rise'	'walk'	'hide'
	mi-ru	kak-u	oki-ru	aruk-u	kakure-ru
	mī < mi-i	kak-i	okī < *okī-i	aruk-i	kakure < *kakure-i
	mī-ta	kai-ta	okī-ta	arui-ta	kakure-ta

For Kyōto, unlike Tōkyō, low pitch is distinctive on the first syllable as well
as when it occurs after a high pitch. But the high pitch, on the other hand, is
nowhere distinctive except when it ends at the locus before a low (as in Tōkyō).
When enclitic particles are attached the Kyōto patterns are these:

A ki-ru ga   oku ga   irer-u ga   kawar-u ga   hazime-ru ga   utaga-u ga
   ki wa   ok-i wa   ire wa   kawar-i wa   hazime wa   utaga-i wa
   ki-ta ga   oi-ta ga   ire-ta ga   kawat-ta ga   hazime-ta ga   utago[o]-ta ga

B mi-ru ga   kak-u ga   oki-ru ga   aruk-u ga   kakure-ru ga
   mi wa   kak-i wa   oki wa   aruk-i wa   kakure wa
   mi-ta ga   kai-ta ga   oki-ta ga   arui-ta ga   kakure-ta ga

     The stems of Type A are unmarked with respect to accent: they are high atonic.
The stems of Type B are marked by distinctive initial low, which continues till the
point where the ending is attached: they are low atonic. Both -ru and -i attach as
high, and in isolation that will sound exactly the same as the nondistinctive rise
acquired automatically in Kyōto by an otherwise all-low phrase. But when you attach
an enclitic particle after the ending, the particle is low, so that the phrases of
Type B behave like the Tōkyō atonic verb form + particle: Kyōto kaku ga 'writes
but' has about the same tune as Tōkyō oku ga 'puts but' except that the initial
low is perhaps more prominent. From the forms given we can predict the word pitch
pattern if we say there is a basic, i.e. morphophonemic, accent (the locus before
the low) on the infinitive ending -i and the various -t··· forms that are reduced
from attachments to the infinitive: -i¹-ta with a delay of one mora in realizing the
accent when the mora that represents the infinitive is absorbed into the preceding
syllable of the contraction. But the accent of the imperfect form with an attached
particle is a puzzle: if we assume -ru¹, that will explain kaku ga 'writes but'
yet it will make us predict *oku ga for oku ga 'puts but'. And it is interesting
that that is the pattern we find for oku no 'putting' or 'the one to put', according
to the data in Kobayashi 143 and Umegaki 1963 (and for Kōchi, Doi 1952:30).[1]
For the Type-B verbs the pattern is that of tatu no wa (the Kōchi version of Doi
1952:31) 'the one to stand' or 'standing'. A number of the Tōkyō-type dialects
attach the word /no/ as a tonic noun with an underlying juncture implied:
oku [|] no wa rather than oku no wa, as in Hata (Doi 1952:30), Yamaguchi (Kobayashi
1975:59 n.42), and Nagano (Kudō 1978:51-2). It is unclear for Yamaguchi and Nagano

what happens with a tonic verb — whether it is k̄aku | n̄o wa or, as in Tōkyō,
k̄a̲k̲u̲ no wa; but Hata is like Tōkyō (Doi 1952:31).

It appears that we must assume that Kyōto has a juncture before certain of the
particles, such as ga 'but', ka 'question', to 'when/if' or 'that … (unquote)',
si 'and', … , after the Type-A imperfect only. From the data in Kobayashi, we must
also assume a juncture before ni 'in order to' in those purpose expressions that
are made on the infinitive of the Type-A verbs: a̅k̅e̅ ̅n̅i̅ ̅(̅i̅k̅u̅) '(go) to open it' and
not *ak̲e̲ ni̅. With a tonic-verb infinitive we could assume an underlying juncture
that is dropped at the surface level: aru̲k̲i̲ [|] n̅i̅. But such phrases can also be
accounted for without the juncture. Compare the similar problem in Tōkyō mentioned
earlier; are there Kyōtō type dialects which differ from Kyōto in the treatment
of these expressions? It is a mystery just how these phenomena — the accentuation
of atonic imperfect + ga (etc.) and of atonic infinitive + ni — came about. A
possibly related mystery: why does the imperfect -ru[1] attach as high to Type-A stems
whereas the infinitive -i[1] attaches as low?[2] Is this because the modern imperfect
form derives from the earlier adnominal (*rentai-kei*)? But then the Type-B form is
a puzzle. Kindaichi thinks the predicative ending (*shūshi-kei*) was earlier -ūu̲,
as in huk̅ūu̲ 'it blows', which shortened to -ū when it was adnominalized, as in
hu̲k̲u̅ ̅kaze 'the wind that blows'. But in view of the remodelling of the longer
vowel-stem (bigrade) forms, other factors may be at work.

And yet another puzzle presents itself. Although the -t… forms that are
contracted from -t[e] a[r]-, such as the perfect in our examples, will attach to the
Type-A stem infinitive (with appropriate adjustments) as low, the gerund form
itself, though a contraction from -i te, is high throughout just like the imperfect:
k̅i̅-te, o̅i̅-te, i̅r̅e̅-te, k̅a̅w̅a̅t̅-te, h̅a̅z̅i̅m̅e̅-te, u̅t̅a̅g̅o̅[o̅]-te. Kindaichi tells me that
these versions represent the gerund in close juncture with a following auxiliary;
when a phrase-final juncture follows ('does and') the accent is what we would
expect from the earlier forms: k̅i̅-t̲e̲, o̅i̅-t̲e̲, etc.[3] That explanation leaves us with
a different problem, the accent of the close-juncture forms. As suggested by
Kindaichi, the patterns here may be accounted for in some manner related to the
"shortening" rules by which the adnominal forms for Type-A verbs lose the fall of
pitch on the -(r)u ending.

When we account for the pattern of kak̅-u̅ g̲a̲ 'writes but' and oki-r̅u̅ g̲a̲ 'rises
but' as the result of a locus that terminates the ending, we imply that certain of

the paradigmatic forms are basically oxytonic. But Kyōto, unlike Tōkyō, lacks the
category of oxytonic nouns. Yet it may be possible for us to reinterpret the vexing
"double-low" nouns like sarù 'monkey' and amè 'rain' as oxytonic (see §7.3), for
sarū ga and amē ga have the same pattern as kak-u ga. But then we are left with the
following problems:

(1) Before juncture (i.e. in isolation, without the particle) these "oxytonic"
nouns of Kyōto preserve a phonetic manifestation of the accent by putting a fall on
the last syllable, perhaps to be reinterpreted as long, at least phonemically:
sarù = sarūu. (See §7.3.) But when the verb forms occur before juncture they
suppress the locus: kak-u 'writes, kak-u [|] tegami 'the letter one writes',
kak-u [|] hito 'the person who writes'. In the last two examples the final syllable
of the verb form fails to show the automatic rise appropriate before a juncture (cf.
kak-u | tee 'the hand that writes' and kak-u | oziisan 'the gaffer who writes'),
so we know the juncture is suppressed, yet we can tell that there is an underlying
juncture in the first example from the tune alone, for Kyōto does not allow more
than a single syllable to be high after the initial low, so that pitch patterns with
a longer stretch of high after a low must consist of two phrases at an immediately
underlying level. Both the synchronic description and the diachronic explanation
will require separate rules to account for the oxytonic nouns (if that they be) and
the oxytonic verb forms of Kyōto. But in some of the other Kinki dialects, such as
that of Kōchi, the rules are more uniform, since before juncture those dialects
suppress the accentual locus of the oxytonic noun, too. And that makes the pattern
for a noun like sarū for Kyōto's sarù distinct from that for a noun like matu
'pine tree' only at the morphophonemic level; the distinction is heard only when a
particle is attached: sarū ga has a different tune from matu ga.

(2) Oxytonic words, whether nouns or verbs, are limited to phrases that begin with
low pitch. Where we might expect a locus at the end of a high (Type-A) verb form,
the locus retreats one syllable, as in the infinitives *kawar-i ⁷ → kawa'r-i
'change' and *hazime ⁷ → hazi'me 'begin', with which we can contrast the infinitive
*kakure-ī ⁷ → kakure ⁷ (wa) 'hide' with no retreat beyond that resulting from the
monophthongization of vowel string. There may be good reason for the discrepancy in
the system of canonical shapes permitted the accent phrases. In Chart 4:1 we see
that the ratio of Kyōto accent phrase types to moras is 2n-1 and the "minus-one" is
just because there is no oxytonic low to balance the prototonic high. Our missing
category is partially filled at the morphophonemic level by words like .saru ⁷ (ga)

'monkey', .kak-u¹ (ga 'writes but') .minna¹ (ga) 'all' (= Ōsaka .min¹na), .okiru¹
(ga) 'rises (but)'; ---, .kakureru¹ (ga) 'hides (but)'; ---, .kakuresasu¹ (ga)
'lets one hide (but)'.

(3) Oxytonic ("double-low") nouns are largely limited to nouns of two syllables.
One exception is .minna¹ = minná 'all' and that is .min¹na = minna in Ōsaka.
Perhaps there was a historical process which led the oxytonic accent to retreat in
longer phrases; can we find further evidence to support this notion?

The patterns for the verb infinitives are displayed in our chart with the
particle wa attached; we could have used the particle mo instead but that would be
deceptive for Kyōto where the particle mo is always pitched low: kaze wa 'as for
the wind', kaze mo 'even/also the wind'. Although Ōsaka has a similar HHL pattern
for nouns like otoko 'man', in Kyōto such words are HLL (otoko) and there are
only a few compounds like iti-ri 'one league' which share the pattern of kaze mo.
The fact that the particle wa is low in ok-i wa 'arise' and in kak-i wa 'write'
cannot be predicted from its behavior with nouns. The following particles are always
low (in McCawley's view "preaccented") for the Kyōto dialect: mo 'even/also',
e 'to', sika 'save', hoka 'save', to 'that ··· (unquote)', yori 'than', yara 'and',
ya 'and', and the copula forms ya 'is' and yatta 'was'; perhaps a few others, too,
on which the sources are less clear (zo 'indeed', made 'until/even', ...).

I suspect that a number of the pitch assignment rules for particular forms of
the paradigm have developed fairly late in certain dialects, such as that of Kyōto,
where various factors have worked to obscure the originally simpler patterns.
Such suspicions deepen when we observe that certain otherwise anomalous patterns
such as kawat-ta 'changed', with the low pitch setting in one mora earlier than in
the infinitive, are regular in Kōchi: kawat-ta. (Cf. Kyōto otoko and Kōchi otoko
'man'.) Kōchi also has the expected kai-ta for Kyōto's anomalous kai-ta 'wrote'.
Yet Kōchi has anomalies of its own: omou for Kyōto's omou 'thinks', okiru for
okiru 'rises'. These, however, are relics of the accent patterns of the Muromachi
and early-Edo periods, used in Kyōto itself at least up to three or four hundred
years ago (KggJ 994). Unfortunately we lack detailed information on the paradigmatic
forms, with and without enclitics, for certain other dialects that would likely show
patterns more representative of earlier Kyōto speech.

3. Initial register; compound nouns; atonic and tonic patterns; tonic types.

If we were reconstructing solely on the basis of the inflected forms discussed in the preceding section, we would need to posit only two accentual features, based on the pitch of the first syllable: Type A for those with high initial in Kyōto and Type B for those with low, since these correspond respectively to what we are calling "A" and "B" words in Kagoshima and Shuri. This assignment of initial REGISTER as we will call it, is part of the basic makeup of individual lexical items, and its origins go back deep into the prehistory of the language.[1] In general an etymological group shares the same register: if a given verb is Type B, then derivationally related verbs — and often nouns, as well — are also Type B.[2] For Kagoshima and for a number of the Ryūkyū dialects (but not all) the accent of each noun can be fully accounted for in terms of initial register or direct later reflexes of it. In these dialects[3] the accent of a compound noun is simply a reduction of the accents of a syntactic phrase: the register of the compound is the same as that of the first member.

In Kyōto, too, the accent of a compound noun has the same initial register as the first member. But there are additional complications. If we leave aside certain older compounds and special problems (see §7), the productive rules for a compound of two free nouns are as follows.

(1) When there is no inherent fall of pitch in the second noun, a fall is placed after the first mora:

A+A seezi 'politics' + kyooiku 'education' → seezi-kyooiku 'political training'
B+A katee 'home' + kyooiku 'education' → katee-kyooiku 'home training'
A+B huzin 'woman' + mondai 'problem' → huzin-mondai 'woman problem'
B+B zidoo 'child' + mondai 'problem' → zidoo-mondai 'child problem'

(2) When there is a fall of pitch in the second noun, that locus is ignored (the fall is cancelled) and a new fall is placed after the first mora; but this rule will appear to apply vacuously with Type-A nouns that have a fall, since these will be found mostly to locate the fall after first mora to begin with (Ōsaka onna for Kyōto onna 'woman' and otoko for Kyōto otoko 'man' form a small group of unusual pattern):

A+A sugí 'cedar' + hayasi 'grove' → sugi-bayasi 'cedar grove'

     kyoo 'Kyōto' + onna / ōnna 'woman' → kyoo-onna 'Kyōto woman'

A+B daikon 'radish' + hatake 'field' → daikon-batake 'radish field'

B+A matú 'pine' + hayasi 'grove' → matu-bayasi 'pine grove'

B+B mugí 'barley' + hatake 'field' → mugi-batake 'barley field'

(3) However, if the second noun is itself a compound — and these are McCawley's
"long" nouns — an accentuation has already taken place; the accent of the second
member stays:

   yamato 'Yamato' + mono-gatari 'tale' → yamato-monogatari 'Tales of Yamato'

   isoppu (= isoppu) 'Aesop' + mono-gatari 'tale' → isoppu-monogatari 'Aesop's Fable

The compound noun mono-gatari is derived from the noun mono 'thing' + the verb
infinitive katar-i 'tell'; this type of formation follows the same accentuation
rules as noun + noun (with certain exceptions). The notation isoppu, which is an
interpretation of Hirayama's marking, represents an underlying pattern isoppu
(like irogami 'colored paper'), which manifests the high pitch on the preceding
voiced mora; see §1.4.

   Except for a number of minor details, the rules for accentuating noun compounds
in Tōkyō are similar to those of Kyōto. But an important difference is that in a
true compound — as contrasted with a syntactic reduction — the accent of the first
member is completely ignored: the accentuation of Tōkyō compound nouns is entirely
determined by the second member, which retains its locus of fall (= its accent) if
that is situated after any mora other than the last; if the accent is not retained,
then a new fall is assigned to a locus after the first mora. In both Tōkyō and Kyōto
the locus generally retreats one syllable if the second noun is no longer than one
or two moras; this accounts for the open-ended class of "preaccentuated suffixes".
There are also a certain number of suffixes which defy the rules and leave the
compound with no fall of pitch; these are called the "atonicizing suffixes" and form
an essentially closed class.

   From this broad overview we conclude that it is necessary to recognize two
quite different features that are realized by the same phonetic device of pitch
contours: initial REGISTER, and LOCUS of fall. The latter device we will refer to as
"accent", speaking of those words with an inherent basic accent as "tonic" and of
those words without a basic accent (with no inherent fall of pitch) as "atonic". For
Kagoshima, Shuri, and similar dialects, there are no tonic words and no distinctive

accent in this narrow sense of the word; there is only distinctive register, and where a fall of pitch is heard it is a manifestation of the register.

Although we often speak of "tonic" and "atonic" verbs in Tōkyō and Kyōto, what we really refer to is initial register: Type A with high-initial pitch in Kyōto and with no basic fall of pitch in Tōkyo, versus Type B with low-initial pitch in Kyōto and with a basic fall in Tōkyō. The pitch patterns of individual paradigmatic forms are obtained by rules working from these two basic types. If we look at nouns we find a deceptively large number of "tonic" types in both Tōkyō and Kyōto. In a representative list of 446 two-syllable native nouns only .31 do not have a basic fall of pitch after one syllable or the other. But this is because both Tōkyō and Kyōto have taken an important accentual class that was originally low atonic and merged it with a rather small class of high tonic; the missing class, which is easy to establish because the nouns are all Type B in Kagoshima, constitutes .28 of the list. When we treat that missing class (to be labeled "2.3") as historically low atonic and add it to the high atonic group, the total of all atonic nouns comes to .59 of our list. Comparable figures, as we might expect, obtain for the three-syllable nouns: .37 high atonic + .29 low atonic = .61 atonic nouns. For monosyllables there is a 50-50 split between A and B in Kagoshima, but Type-B nouns appear to have been tonic in earlier Japanese, so that only .33 of the monosyllables turn out to be originally atonic. (But see §7 for a revised view of the "B" monosyllables.)

I strongly suspect that these two features, REGISTER (high vs. low initial pitch) and ACCENT (locus of fall of pitch) are to be accounted for historically in quite different ways, despite their superficial similarity in phonetic realization. Moreover, as we will see below, the notion of accent as locus of "fall" may well have to modified for earlier Japanese to locus of "change" of pitch.

4. Reconstructing noun accent types on the basis of modern dialects.

Using only the modern dialects it is possible to reconstruct with fairly sure confidence the major "accent types" of earlier Japanese and to assign words to their original accent classes, despite later mergers that have often obscured the earlier situation. As a preliminary sorting device we will assign a numerical code to designate each of the classes posited for the ancestral language. But we must bear in mind that these classes are to be considered in terms of two kinds of feature — initial register and locus (of fall or change of pitch) — and our choice of numbers which follows the tacit assumptions made by Japanese linguists who have worked on these problems, is designed to allow us easily to display the register distinctions as well as distinctions of locus or "accent" in the narrow sense; the code is far from arbitrary.

From the data provided by the dialects it is clear that we must posit at least three proto classes for one-syllable nouns; these are designated "1.1, 1.2, 1.3".[1] Two-syllable nouns require at least five proto classes ("2.1—2.5") and the three-syllable nouns require at least seven ("3.1—3.7"). Some linguists would expand this requirement to ten by splitting three of the classes: 3.2a and 3.2b, 3.5a and 3.5b, 3.7a and 3.7b. (The additional classes are not directly supported by philological evidence; they assume a proto system somewhat earlier than the extant notations of the eleventh and twelfth centuries.) It has also been argued that an additional class is required for two-syllable nouns, splitting 2.2 into 2.2a and 2.2b. We will accommodate these additional classes in our scheme despite various doubts about them, for they can easily be regrouped. (Komatsu 1959 posits seven types for two-syllable nouns, thirteen for three-syllable nouns; that is on the basis of evidence for rise and fall within syllables. See below, §7.4.) Many four-syllable nouns are compounds and the reconstruction of their accentual patterns is difficult; we will consider the accent of words of four or more syllables in connection with phrase types (§11) and with rules for accentuating compound nouns (§10), summarizing the philological evidence in §12.

From a comparison of the Tōkyō accent of over four hundred two-mora nouns with the corresponding register patterns (A and B) of Kagoshima, we find at once four classes, shown below with examples and the pitch patterns both in isolation and with a typically monosyllabic enclitic (ga) attached.

Class Tag	Tōkyō type	Tōkyō form	Kagoshima form	Kagoshima
2.1 'bottom'	atonic	soko, soko ga	soko, soko ga	
2.2 'sound'		oto, oto ga	oto, oto ga	} A
2.3 'color' }	oxytonic	{ iro, iro ga	iro, iro ga	
2.4 'boat'	prototonic	hune, hune ga	hune, hune ga	} B

Although Kagoshima has only two patterns and there are but three in Tōkyō, the correspondence of the Tōkyō oxytonic words to Kagoshima Type A in some cases and to Type B in other cases tells us that the ancestral language had an additional type.

When we compare either or both of these dialects with the Kyōto dialects — or some similar dialect, such as that of Kōchi — we find it necessary to set up an additional proto class "2.5" in order to account for words like saru 'monkey' and ame 'rain', which differ from matu 'pine' and hune 'boat' in the Kyōto patterns:

Class Tag	Tōkyō	Kagoshima	Kyōto	Nouns	Percent
2.1 'bottom'	soko, soko ga	soko, soko ga	soko, soko ga	139	.32
2.2 'sound'	oto, oto ga	oto, oto ga	oto, oto ga	58	.13
2.3 'color'	iro, iro ga	iro, iro ga	iro, iro ga	125	.28
2.4 'boat'	hune, hune ga	hune, hune ga	hune, hune ga	73	.16
2.5 'rain'	ame, ame ga	ame, ame ga	ame, ame ga	51	.11
Total				446	1.00

What we have been considering are correspondences of relatively high frequency: each proto class contains a respectable number of examples. There are also several correspondences of much lower frequency. Instead of accounting for these by assuming a larger number of original classes, we presume that for one or more of the dialects the particular words have — often for unknown reasons — slipped individually out of their original classes and become historically irregular. In some cases a word has a competing variant that is regular; in other cases, related dialects preserve an earlier pattern, so that it is important to check the related dialects when that information is available. Below are listed some of the major irregularities among the dissyllabic nouns; at least thirteen are irregular in Tōkyō, four in Kyōto, and four in Kagoshima.

Class	Tag	Tōkyō	Kagoshima	Kyōto
2.2 (a)	'eagle'	wasi, wasi ga	wasi, wasi ga	wasi, wasi ga
	'stem'	miki, miki ga	miki, miki ga	miki, miki ga
		miki, miki ga		
2.2 (b)	'fang'	kiba, kiba ga	kiba, kiba ga	kiba, kiba ga
	'rudder'	kazi, kazi ga	kazi, kazi ga	kazi, kazi ga
2.3 (a)	'rose'	bara, bara ga	bara, bara ga	bara, bara ga
	'beam'	keta, keta ga	keta, keta ga	keta, keta ga
2.3 (b)	'god'[2]	kami, kami ga	kami, kami Oa	kami, kami ga
	'cloud'[3]	kumo, kumo ga	kumo, kumo ga	kumo, kumo ga
	'octopus'	tako, tako ga	tako, tako ga	tako. tako ga
	'bushclover'	hagi, hagi ga	hagi, hagi ga	hagi, hagi ga
		hagi, hagi ga		
		hagi, hagi ga		
2.4 (a)	'other'	hoka, hoka ga	hoka, hoka ga	hoka, hoka ga
	'here'	koko, koko ga	koko, koko ga	koko, koko ga
2.4 (b)	'brushwood'	siba, siba ga	siba, siba ga	siba, siba ga
		siba, siba ga		
2.2 (c)	'husk'	kara, kara ga	kara, kara ga	kara, kara ga
2.2 (d)	'chin'	ago, ago ga	ago, ago ga	ago, ago ga
2.3 (c)	'shore'[4]	kisi, kisi ga	kisi, kisi ga	kisi, kisi ga
(d)	'ball'	tama, tama ga	tama, tama ga	tama, tama ga
2.1 (a)	'ant'	ari, ari ga	ari, ari ga	ari, ari ga
2.3 (e)	'design'	aya, aya ga	aya, aya ga	aya, aya ga
2.4 (c)	'awl'	kiri, kiri ga	kiri, kiri ga	kiri, kiri ga
(d)	'raincape'	mino, mino ga	mino, mino ga	mino, mino ga

There are difficult cases:

2.? 'ax' ōno, ōno ga ōno, ono ga ono, ono ga

If we take the accentuations of Kagoshima and Kyōto as regular this word belongs
to the proto class 2.1. But Kōchi differs from Kyōto: its pattern ono ga ought to
correspond to Kyōto *ono ga and if we take that with Tōkyō as the regular reflexes
the proto class is 2.4. But other Tōkyō-related dialects differ from Tōkyō: Sapporo
and Hiroshima have ono ga, as does Ōita. If we take the Tōkyō reflex as aberrant the
correspondence betwen the Kagoshima pattern and those of Sapporo and Hiroshima (but
not Ōita, which merges 2.2 with 2.1) indicates the proto class 2.2. Yet on the basis
of philological evidence we conclude that Kyōto and Kagoshima are just as aberrant
as Tōkyō, and only Ōita, Hiroshima, and Sapporo correctly reflect the original
accentuation, which turns out to be 2.3, as indicated unambiguously by the Yonaguni
pattern. Our three key dialects all have aberrant accents for this noun.

In the case of the word for 'loquat' we cannot decide whether the proto class
was 2.4 or 2.5, because the crucial Kyōto form is aberrant:

2.4/5 'loquat' bīwa, bīwa ga biwa, biwa ga biwa, biwa ga

But in Kōchi, according to my notes, 'loquat' is biwa, biwa ga, so the word must
be 2.4. (The one citation in Myōgi-shō indicates the uncommon pattern rise-low,
bíwa, which Kindaichi would interpret as biīwa. It is conceivable that this was a
way of writing — or a development from — biwà or biwaa. On the anomalous rise,
see §7.1.) Compare the similar word for 'lute'; it has an aberrant accent in Tōkyō:

2.3 (b) 'lute' bīwa, bīwa ga biwa, biwa ga biwa, biwa ga

These two words are early borrowings from Chinese, where they were identical in form
and probably also in origin, for the lute has the shape of a loquat.

And there are misleading cases. From examining just the three dialects we would
assume that geta 'clogs' was 2.1 with Kyōto (getā, geta gā) aberrant; the Kōchi form,
according to my notes, is gēta, gēta ga, confirming the assignment. But it turns out
that both Tōkyō (geta ga) and Kagoshima (gēta, geta ga) are aberrant for this word,
which belongs in class 2.4 since the dialects of Okinawa indicate Type B (2.3/4/5),
and Tōkyō-type dialects of NE Kyūshū have gēta (Hirayama 1951a). Kōchi is aberrant:
Kyōto preserves the correct reflex. The word appears to be first attested in the
16th century, but it may be older.

Most modern dialects have merged certain of the original accent classes. Only one modern dialect preserves the entire set of five distinctions for two-syllable nouns. This is the dialect of Ibuki-jima, an island in Kagawa prefecture, described by Wada Minoru (1966b) in two varieties, that of a 70-year old (*a*) and that of a junior high school student (*b*). (For the notation of 2.3, see the discussion below. The mark ˋ represents a high fall.)[5]

		Ibuki-jima (*a*)	Ibuki-jima (*b*)
2.1	'neck'	kubí, kubi ga	kubi, kubi ga
2.2	'sound'	ōto, ōto ga	otò, ōto ga
2.3	'color'	? īro, īro ga / īro ga	īro, īro ga
		? iro, iro ga / iro ga	
2.4	'pine'[6]	matū, matu ga	matū, matu ga
2.5	'monkey'	sarū/sarù, sarū ga	sarù, saru gà

Wada points out that the tune of type 2.3 could be treated either as HIGH-MID or as MID-LOW but must be kept distinct from the HIGH-LOW of 2.2 in Dialect (*a*). We will probably be happier with the MID-LOW interpretation, which treats the older dialect as a transitional stage between the 12th-century version (LOW-LOW) and that of Dialect *b* (HIGH-LOW). For a detailed study of the Ibuki-jima accent, see Uwano 1985. Uwano interprets the accent system in terms of three initial registers (High, Fall, Low) and a locus ˈ that marks the mora boundary before a DISTINCTIVELY lower pitch within a register. The resulting notation for the two-syllable nouns:

2.1	HØ	2.4	LØ
2.2	H1	2.5	L2
2.3	FØ		

(Satō Eisaku 1985 takes a similar approach.)

There are dialects which have five or even six kinds of pattern for two-mora nouns but these reflect only four underlying types. The extra patterns correlate with segmental shape-type and depend on whether the final vowel is close (i u) or not. The island of Sanagi (Kagawa prefecture) exemplifies this: see Hayata 1978 and the references therein.

5. Philological evidence for earlier accent types.

In Heian sources such as the classified glossary of Chinese characters called
[Ruiju -] Myōgi-shō, compiled in 1081, and in certain reading notes to early texts
a handy system of "tone marks" (syo'o-ten) was employed both to mark the SEI-DAKU
distinctions (described in Ch. 2) and also to mark the pitch patterns of the words.
From that information we can surmise the pronunciations used in the eleventh and
twelfth centuries in Kyōto, and this is sometimes called the "Old Kyōto dialect".
Although that is certainly not the earliest Japanese, there seem to be virtually no
accentual distinctions made in later dialects that cannot be described as if they
stemmed from the patterns found in these materials of the late Heian period. The
marks are dots, placed (predominantly) at the lower or upper left of a written
character that represents a syllable; conveniently enough the lower and higher
positions apparently correspond to the actual low and high pitch, respectively,
though the terminology is based on that of the Chinese tone marks which the system
took as its model: hyo'o(-syoo) or he'i(-sei) 'even (tone)' for the low pitch and
zyo'o(-syoo/-sei) 'rising (tone)' for the high. (We are uncertain about the earlier
phonetic value of the tones in the various dialects of Chinese which, directly or
indirectly, may have influenced the Japanese traditions. On traditional values for
tones in China and in Japan for Chinese readings, cf. Kindaichi 1951b:686- 97: also
Ting 1975, 1983.) It is difficult to interpret the exact intentions of the persons
adding the dots to the texts — for some were ignorant, some were careless — and a
number of subtleties remain matters of controversy among those studying the data.
yet we have a fairly clear picture of the main patterns, which look to be directly
ancestral to the later patterns of the Kyōto-type dialects.[1] The body of data in
Myōgi-shō has been made readily accessible by the 1974 publication of Mochizuki's
painstaking index of the markings in four manuscript copies. The four versions are
the Zusho-ryō [- bon], also called Tosho-ryō [- bon], of 1081 and three popular
revisions compiled before 1178, which are less reliable in their markings but more
extensive in their coverage of vocabulary: the Kōzan-ji [- bon], the Kanchi-in
[- bon], and the Chinkoku-shukoku-jinja [- bon]. Mochizuki also includes citations
from Wamyō-[ruiju-]shō (931-8), Hoke-kyō tanji (ms 1136), [Maeda - bon] Iroha-jirui-
shō (1177-81), and [Iwasaki - bon] Jikyō (ms of Kamakura period). Other important
Heian-period accent notations can be found in old manuscripts (ko-sya'hon) of and
commentariess (si'-ki) on Nihon-Shoki and in Konkōmyō-saishōō-kyō ongi, a guide to
pronouncing the Chinese version of Suvarṇa-prabhāsa-uttamarāja-sūtra.

One matter of controversy is whether for earlier Japanese we are justified
in differentiating class 2.5 from 2.4. The distinction of these two accent types is
usually taken as the critical diagnostic to determine whether a given dialect is of
the "Kyōto type", for only dialects of the Kyōto type are said to have this peculiar
distinction. And the distinction is maintained even in non-contiguous territory, as
pointed out by Okumura 1969 (cf. his map on p.39), for certain dialects of the Noto
peninsula and Sado island keep the distinction though they are cut off from other
Kyōto-type dialects except for sea traffic, as is true also for the Kyōto-type
dialects of Shikoku. Words of both classes are marked identically in most of the
isolated citations of Myōgi-shō: low-high. A number of the Kyōto-type dialects of
today fail to differentiate the two types when nouns are said in isolation; the fall
of 2.5 is heard only when a particle is attached. According to Ōhara 1951a:416, the
distinction of 2.5 from 2.4, in slow speech at least, is marked by the fall of pitch
in Kyōto but not, except when followed by a particle, in Kōchi. Ōhara (who provides
comprehensive lists of relevant words on 417-8) says the difference between the two
patterns can be heard before a number of particles (ga, wa, o, ni, no): umi ḡa 'sea'
(2.4) has a different tune from saru ga 'monkey' (2.5). But the difference is not
heard before the always-low particles mo, e, or yori: umi mo and saru mo have the
same pattern, as if 2.4 were merged into 2.5 in these environments. (Though quite
unconnected, this is reminiscent of the neutralization of the oxytonic and atonic
polysyllables in Tōkyō in two environments: before an immediately underlying
juncture, and before no[1] unless the resulting phrase is followed by an overt
juncture. Cf. Martin 1970a.) A number of linguists assume that what is true of Kōchi
today may have been true also of the dialect spoken in eleventh-century Kyōto and
that the modern Kyōto habit of putting a fall on the last mora of the 2.5 nouns in
isolation developed only later. Yet we must reconstruct the class, however it was
pronounced, in order to account for the words which fall into this category. While
2.5 is the least populated of the five major classes of dissyllables, it is hard to
believe that Kyōto "created" it simply by segregating certain nouns from 2.4 in some
unexplained way. At most, Kyōto extended the differentiation to the words also when
pronounced in isolation, if they were not earlier so differentiated, and perhaps
extended membership in the class to a number of words that appear not to have been
original members, in particular a number of the low atonic nouns such as mame 'bean'
and kame 'tortoise', a question requiring further consideration. We will see below
that there are corresponding classes of "double-low" nouns and phrases of three

syllables (nouns of Type 3.7) and also of longer nouns and phrases, too. The best
arguments for the idea that Type 2.5 may have developed, or at least expanded,
secondarily are found in the dialect of Wakayama, where the double-low pattern has
become productive as a kind of semantic marker, according to Ogawa 1942. The pattern
imposes a connotation of oddness or cuteness to nicknames, terms for animals and
plants, and it also characterizes a number of truncations, such as these:[2]
matè 'razor-clam' taken as an abbreviation of mate-gai, mayù 'eyebrow' of mayu-ge
(or mayu-gē); omò 'face, surface' as an abbreviation of omote, imò 'younger sister'
of īmooto (< Edo īmooto < Heian imouto). The Wakayama data are reminiscent of the
"changed tone" that marks diminutives in Cantonese.

A number of nouns with (C)V:, (C)Vn, and similar heavy syllables which are
prototonic in Tōkyō and Hiroshima probably go back to a pattern with the accent on
the second mora, as shown by other dialects which permit the locus to occur on (= at
the boundary after) the second element of a heavy syllable, e.g. Hata (Doi 1952:25):
koo˩mori 'bat', sin˩setu 'kindness', sen˩bei 'rice crackers', soo˩men 'vermicelli',
tan˩popo 'dandelion', nii˩san 'older brother', yuu˩rei 'spirit', on˩gaku 'music',
gen˩kan 'entryway', kon˩-ban 'this evening', ai˩satu 'greeting', ... Patterns that
are similar occur in Yamaguchi-shi (Hiroto 1961:164, cf. Okuda 135n): ai˩satu
'greeting', sen˩sei 'teacher', zin˩rui 'mankind', un˩tin 'transport charges',
sin˩setu 'kindness', tyuu˩gaku 'middle school', and even endoo˩ 'peas' — all are
prototonic in Hiroshima except that sensei 'teacher' is atonic (and in Tōkyō it is
sense˩i).

.   .   .

Our interpretation of earlier Japanese as including the double-low accent class
2.5 is in part based on the assumption that at least certain particles attached to
nouns as enclitics, without juncture, as they do today in all dialects. But most of
the linguists who have struggled with the philological evidence have been led to the
conclusion that the farther back one goes the fewer the particles that were attached
as enclitics; most are thought to have been given independent accentuations and, we
must presume, independent phrasings at an earlier time. Wenck 1959:403 says that the
particles at the Myōgi-shō stage of the language were attached for the most part
with independent pitch patterns as follows:

HIGH   1.1 ḡa, n̄ī, w̄o, ē (< f̄e)[3]; w̄a (< f̄a), ȳa, k̄a, s̄ī; t̄o 'with';
             A-s̄ī/-z̄ī (predicative)[4]; V-i t̄e (gerund)
        2.1 k̄ara, s̄a[f]e, ḡa-nī; V-i t̄utū
        2.2 k̄oso, n̄omi; V-a m̄asi
        3.1 V-i n̄agara
        3.2 b̄akari

LOW   1.3 mo[5], zo; (na V-i) so 'don't!'; to 'that ··· (unquote)', V-e do
             'though'; V-a ba 'if'; V-a de 'not doing'; A-ki (attributive, *n.4*).
        2.3 V-a zaru

UNUSUAL 2.x ȳori after LOW, yori after HIGH
        2.x n̄ari / narī (free variants?)
        1.x n̄o after HIGH, no after LOW

Wenck's conclusions are based on the study of Tsukishima 1951 (data reflecting the
Kyōto patterns of some period between 1200 and 1500 acording to Tsukishima) and on
Ōhara 1951. Sakurai (1964:30b, 33-44, 35-6, 37b; 1965c:184, 223 n.4) offers similar
data from manuscripts of Nihon-Shoki[6] and adds to 2.2 the particle strings d̄o-mo
and k̄a-mo; he treats mò, zò, yò, and sì as FALLING; he treats kosò as LOW-FALL
(like a 2.5 noun); and he says /to/ ('with' ?) has reverse tonicity (like yori).
Mochizuki 1973 argues that the particles ni and wo were said with the RISE (nī⌉,
woō) and voices the suspicion that wa and ga (and even /no/, p. 47-8) may also have
had the rise, even though, unlike ni and wo, these particles are not attested with
the GOING-tone mark; Kindaichi 1973 is unconvinced.

    During the early-Edo period (Okumura 1981:276) Kyōto treated the following
particles as always low: e 'to', to 'that ··· (unquote)', ya 'and', si 'indeed'; ka
'question', zo 'indeed', mo 'even/also', ya 'question', ya 'hey', yo 'I tell you',
na 'you see'; yori 'than; from', site 'and', sa[f]e 'even', si-mo 'indeed', da- ni
'even', made 'till; even', ka-si 'indeed'; nando 'or something, and the like, and
others' (also ··· n̄ando). According to Maeda 1949, the following particles are
always low in modern Ōsaka: e 'to', ka 'question', mo 'even/also', yo-ka (= yori)
'than', made 'till; even', dake 'only', hodo 'as much as', bakkari 'only, just', and
yori-mo 'even than'. (In the early-Edo period hodo and bakari were like ga, wa, o,

and ni, attaching high after high and low after low.[7]) Kobayashi lists the following
particles as always low in modern Kyōto: e 'to', mo 'even/also', yori 'than',
made 'till; even', sika 'save', yara 'and the like'; nen 'you see' (sentence-final);
ya/na (copula), nara 'if it be', yatta 'was' and other copula forms except for de
and /no/. (But, unlike Maeda's Ōsaka report, dake 'only' is given as "unaccented" —
like ga; and hodo 'as much as' is not mentioned.) For Kōchi the following patterns
are listed by Kobayashi as always low: e 'to', mo 'even/also', yori 'than', made
'till; even', sika 'save', yara 'and the like', ya 'and', yo 'indeed', sae 'even',
si 'and', ki(ni) 'because'; copula forms except de and /no/. (Both dake 'only' and
hodo 'as much as' are treated as "unaccented", like ga and kara.) The Wakayama low
particles are e, mo, made, sika ('save; rather'), ya 'and', ya 'is', and (no no →)
no 'the one of ⋯ ' (Yukawa 1984:2:20).

Ōhara 1951:421 observes that in a manuscript of a commentary (si '-ki) on the
Nihon-Shoki annotated with tone marks "though wo and ni are usually written HIGH"
there are examples of: .a˙me .ni 'in heaven', .a˙me .wo 'heaven (direct object)';
.ma˙fe .ni 'in front'; .sa˙ra .ni 'anew', .su¨te .ni 'already', .ta¨ta .ni 'simply,
only', .ma˙sa .ni 'directly', .tu˙fi .ni 'finally'. (The last two are also in
Kunten-shō; Akinaga 1974:343a, 203a.) And in Kokin-kunten-shō (= [Kokin - [waka-
shū]] Kunten-shō) he finds examples of markings that he interprets as aki koso
'precisely autumn', kage bakari 'just shadow', tuyu wo 'dew (direct object)',
faru wo 'spring (direct object)', yofa ni ya '(whether) at night', but he also finds
examples such as yoru wo 'night (as direct object)'; these findings are all
confirmed in Akinaga 1974. Moreover, the markings of old manuscripts of Nihon-Shoki
thought to date from mid-Heian times do not distinguish nouns of 2.4 from 2.5 even
with particles attached (Ōhara 1951:423).

Ōhara reaches the conclusion that the distinction of class 2.5 from 2.4 (in
any environment) was not original but somehow developed for dialects of the Kyōto
type, apparently in late Heian times, though this point is unclear. (Disagreeing
with both Ōhara and Ogawa: Hattori, Kindaichi, Komatsu, and earlier Sakurai; but
Sakurai 1975:91-103 reverses his position.) I prefer a different interpretation.
Those who annotated the texts followed overly slow "reading pronunciations" as
annotators are apt to do today, and under such circumstances junctures unnatural to
speech are to be expected.[8] The idea is not original with me; see Sakurai 1965c and
1966de for a clear and balanced view of the problem. He suggests that the enclitics

enjoyed varying degrees of cohesiveness: some particles, such as /no/, were always
stickier than others, such as /koso/. In modern Tōkyō the dissyllabic enclitics
(especially sa'e, de'-mo, ma'de 'even', and the like) are often set off by juncture
for special emphasis. This is less common for the monosyllabic enclitics, but I have
recorded the following from TV news: ··· i'ma no | na'ikaku ‖ ga' ‖ ··· 'the present
cabinet'; soo iu na'ka | de' ‖ ··· 'in the midst of all this'; ··· kyoodan ni ta'tu
no mo ‖ raisyuu gu'rai kara ‖ ni' ‖ nari-so'o desu 'will be getting back to the
lecture platform starting perhaps next week, it appears'. An insistent ··· ‖ wa' ‖
is often heard in public speeches.

   Without a particle the nouns of 2.5 were written with the same low-high pattern
as those of 2.4, and they may even have been pronounced that way, as in Kōchi today.
But another possibility is that a real but subtle phonetic distinction of FALL from
HIGH was simply ignored by those putting on the marks. Mochizuki 668-9 believes that
the Zusho-ryō Myōgi-shō intended the position of to'o(-syoo/-sei) 'East (tone)'
or hyo'o-kei/he'i-kei = hyo'o-syoo/he'i-sei [no] karu 'even-tone light' — slightly
higher than the low position of the "even" mark — for some of the 2.5 nouns, as
well as certain other morphemes, and that this is to be interpreted as a fall within
the syllable: .a··fu = abù 'gadfly'; .ko·we = kowè 'voice'; .na··fe = nabè 'pan';
.tu··fi 'ni = tufì nì 'finally'; .tu·ne 'ni = tunè nì (and 'tu·ne 'ni = tunè nì)
'always'. This notion stems from Komatsu 1959 (and later works); a few examples are
also found in Konkōmyō-saishōō - kyō ongi (1079).

   If we separate the feature of initial register from the notion of accent and
treat the latter as a locus — not of "fall" (as it is later for most of the modern
dialects) but of "change" — then we can speak of those particles that attach with
no change as ATONIC and those that attach with a reversal of pitch level as TONIC.
Myōgi-shō provides information mostly on words in isolation, but there are a few
short phrases which offer data of the following sort:
TONIC PARTICLE (switches pitch from preceding syllable)
   'mo   ware ni mo arazu 'in spite of oneself'; nikumi suru wo mo 'even though
          hating'; sika mo 'moreover'; cf. wefi mo sezu (Ongi
          Iroha) 'not even drunk'.
   'to   makusa to suru ni kafu 'a substitute for fodder' (not the verb kaf-u);
          semu to sù/su 'want to do'; firu yoru to 'night and day' (NS 100a).
          Exceptional: fito to naru 'become adult' — we expect fito to naru.

? 'ga   yé ga fara '(epidemic belly =) colic'.

  'yori   katī yori yuku 'goes on foot'; moto yori 'originally'; siri yori kutī yori koku yamafi '(ailment that breaks from bottom and from mouth =) cholera', kafa yori 'by way of the river' (NS 104a), kafa-fune yori (NS 104b) 'by riverboat'; ya["]furema yori morī te (NS 99a) 'filtered through the decayed places'. The last syllable of the particle yori is always low; in terms of the conclusions reached below (§14) this could be accounted for if the basic shape is posited as ending with a long vowel (yorii).[9]

ATONIC PARTICLE (continues on pitch of preceding syllable)

  ni[10]   tomo nī 'together'; ware nī mo arazu 'in spite of oneself'; ana ni sumu 'live in a hole'; kore nī o[k]i te 'at this'; ima nī 'any minute now'; koko nī 'here'. (Is to nī kaku nī 'anyway' to be explained by junctures?)

  tu[11]   simo tu kata '(direction) below'; simo tu fige 'beard'; uti tu miya 'interior palace' (NS 115b)

  no   tori no wata 'bird craw/entrails'; take no kafa 'bamboo bark'; kane no sabi 'metal rust'; take no kusi 'bamboo skewer'; kani no ko 'crab spawn'; sake no utufamono 'wine utensil'; koromo no kubi 'neck of gown'; koromo no suso 'hem of gown'; kuruma no wa 'wagon wheel'; to no kagi 'door key'; ti no miti 'blood vessel', wi no ko 'pig', di no yamafi 'hemorrhoid ailment'; iwo no kasira̡ no fone 'fishhead bone'; kamo no kuso 'duck droppings'; eyami no oni 'plague devil'; fafagata no mefi 'maternal niece'; oni no yagara 'devil's-shaft (= Phlomis umbrosa)'; wono no ye 'ax handle'; ka no waka-duno 'young horn of deer'; tati no kabuto 'sword hilt'; kaku no gotoku 'like this'; tanogofi no fako 'handkerchief box'; ki no utufo no midu 'water in the hollow of a tree'; foko no saki 'halberd tip' (Ongi).

There are apparent exceptions, such as sude ni 'already'. And nine nouns that are thought to belong to class 2.4: afa no urusine 'nonglutinous millet' (also annotated as afa no — or perhaps afà no?), fune no kadi / nome 'boat rudder / caulking', ima no wotoko 'present (= later) husband', ine no kafi 'rice hulls', kata no fone 'shoulder bone', kibi no moti 'millet cake', kinu no siri / kubi 'bottom/neck of garment', mugi no kasu 'barley bran', uri no sane 'melon seed', zeni no fatamono 'money forge'. A tenth example: karī no 'of a wild goose' (NS 126a).

According to Ōhara 418, kibi 'millet' is treated as 2.5 in some parts of the Kinki
area (see also the suggestion of a FALL notation on the last syllable, in Mochizuki
671); and so are awa (< afa) 'nonglutinous millet', and yado 'shelter, lodging'
(Ōhara 417). Ōhara lists a few words as belonging with 2.5 that Hirayama's Kyōto
accents do not confirm, but Umegaki's data in NKD support Ōhara: koto 'harp'
(Hirayama "0"), soba 'buckwheat' ("1"), toga 'blame' ("1"). Terakawa gives the Ise
accent of 'now' as i͞ma (2.4) / imà (2.5). Perhaps the other nouns listed above
(ine 'rice', fune 'boat', kata 'shoulder', kinu 'silk; garment', mugi 'barley', uri
'melon', and zeni 'money') were also of Type 2.5 at an earlier time. If so, the
behavior of the particle /no/ would be in no way exceptional. But what troubles
Ōhara (420, 423) is that the attested behavior of ALL nouns that (according to the
accentuation of the modern dialects) belong to Type 2.4 and Type 2.5 appears to be
identical: nouns of both types act as if "2.4" before most particles (ga, fa, wo,
ni[12]) and as if "2.5" before the particle /no/ only. I suspect that the original
class 2.5 may have been larger than is indicated by the evidence of later dialects
and that through the years 2.4 has been acquiring members of 2.5; but that runs
contrary to the usual view (to which we will return in §14). If this suspicion is
correct, the lack of attestation for *LH-H with an "original" 2.4-no must be due
either to the paucity of data or to a rule that neutralized the 2.4-5 distinction
before this particle only, a kind of prosodic adjustment, such as that by which
Kindaichi would explain the peculiar behavior of 3.5 and 4.7 with attached /no/:
*(L)LLHH → (L)LLHL.[13] The asterisked types are attested in Myōgi-shō for nouns
that (see §12) I am labeling Type 4.7 (LLHH) and Type 5.8 (LLLHH), e.g. ko͞foro͞gi
'cricket' and ikusa͞bune 'warship'; but only three compounds have turned up as
examples of the latter. To be on the safe side I propose to assign nouns to the
proto class 2.5 only when there is overt evidence in at least one modern dialect.
Unless (or until) such evidence turns up for ine, fune, kinu, mugi, uri, and zeni,
they will be treated as 2.4. On the wider problems raised by the phonetic "rise-
fall" or "double-low" of Type 2.5 (and of Type 3.7), see §14.

The system of "tone dots" used in Myōgi-shō and other Heian texts is simple
and consistent. More elaborate notations are found in the later chanting guides,
known as (husi-)haˈkase, but these have been interpreted by Kindaichi as systems
consistent with the Heian notations. In certain texts using the so-called Teika-
kanazuˈkai, the spelling system devised by Fujiwara Sadaie/Teika in the thirteenth

century, Ōno Susumu (1950) discovered that the kana symbols for earlier /o/ and /wo/ were kept distinct not to indicate the segmental syllables — for these had fallen together as [wo], but to mark pitch differences: the o-kana was used for the "even-tone" (low) syllable [w̲o̲] and the wo-kana was used for the "rising-tone" (high) syllable [w̄ō].[14]

   Earlier, Kindaichi 1947 found that the Wa-kun (Japanese glosses) in the text of Konkōmyō-saishōō - kyō ongi (1079) used pairs of phonograms, i.e. Man'yō-gana, for a number of the syllables according to whether the tone was high or low, and the marking accords both with those instances in which there are confirming tone marks added and in other instances with Myōgi-shō notations or dialect comparisons. (Kindaichi notes that Ōya Tōru had earlier discovered the same thing.) He raised the question (48a) whether there may be other such texts. For over thirty years that question remained unanswered. Then in 1981 Takayama Michiaki published his important discovery of a statistical correlation between the accent patterns of dissyllabic nouns found in Myōgi-shō and the traditional Chinese tones of the Man'yō-gana phonograms used to write poems in parts of Nihon-Shoki. (See Takayama 1981, 1982, 1983, 1984.) The correlation is amply confirmed by the tones of the phonograms used to write other nouns in the poems, and also the verb and adjective forms. All of the evidence provided by these phonograms (and those in the Ongi) is included with the data of Chapters 5, 6, and 7. The accent patterns are based on treating the Chinese "Even" tone as LOW and all the other tones as HIGH.[15] The accent patterns that are interpreted from the phonogram tones must be evaluated with caution, since they appear to be accurate to varying degrees in different parts of the work; in general, they cannot be relied upon to disprove patterns that are elsewhere overtly attested by tone marks. There seems to have been a deliberate effort to choose the phonograms to accord with the accent patterns; why then, we may ask, is the correlation only statistically maintained? One answer might be corruption of the orthography as the text got copied by scribes who did not realize why the particular characters were originally chosen and substituted characters they found more congenial. Perhaps the original writers chose to mark the accents only when it struck their fancy, often preferring an overwhelmingly common phonogram even when it was counter-indicated by the tone; scribal carelessness may have been a factor. There is also the possibility that the scribes, especially if they were non-Japanese, may have miswritten some of the accents because their command of the spoken language (or of Chinese) was flawed.

6. Mergers of older accent classes.

The earlier classes of two-syllable nouns have merged in several different ways in modern dialects, as shown by the representative examples below.

	2.1	2.2	2.3	2.4	2.5
Myōgi-shō	...	...	...	...()...	
Ibuki-jima	...	...	...	...	...
Kyōto	...	....		...	...
Tōkyō	...	....		....	
Ōita	....		...	....	

| Sapporo, Hakodate, Aomori, Hirosaki, Akita, Niigata | { .... (final vowel close: i u) |
| | { .... (final vowel open: a e o) |

| Matsue, Izumo | { .... (final vowel close: i u) |
| | { .... (final vowel open: a e o) |

| Kagoshima | .... |

Ryūkyūs: (1)   ....   Amami (Koniya, Shodon); Kikai (Onotsu), Okinawa (Shuri); Miyako (Tarama); Yaeyama (Ishigaki)

   (2)   ....   Amami (Nase); Kikai (Keraji); Yoron (except Mugiya); Miyako (Ikema); Yaeyama (Kurojima)

   (3)   ....   Tokunoshima (Kametsu); Okinoerabu (except Tamina); Yoron (Mugiya); N.Okinawa (Nakijin), Naha; Yaeyama (Sonai); Yonaguni

   (4)   ....: ... :........   Okinoerabu (Tamina); Ie-jima
        :........:

The Matsue and Izumo data are from Hiroto and Ōhara; the tunes are LH-H, LH-L, and (for 2.4/5¹/ᵤ) HL-L. There is a disconcerting misprint in Kindaichi 1958a (Introduction:14), which might mislead us into thinking that one Tōkyō-type dialect distinguishes 2.5 (with close final vowel) from 2.4; the mistake is corrected in the revised edition (1981), where hasi 'chopsticks' is correctly given as HL-L. Like Ryūkyū (2) above, Fukuoka merges 2.1/2/3 ≠ 2.4/5.

Kindaichi and Hirayama believe the Kyūshū and Ryūkyū patterns stem from a common matrix that corresponds to the Ōita pattern (cf. Kindaichi 1975:137):

2.1/2	2.3	2.4/5
LH-H	LH-L	HL-L

It is true that all the way from morthern Kyūshū to Yonaguni 2.1 and 2.2 are merged, but one dialect (Nakanoshima in the Tokara archipelago) maintains a morphophonemic distinction between them and instead merges 2.3 with 2.4/5 (Tajiri 1975; see below). (Thorpe 131 rejects this "Ōita hypothesis" on the origin of the Ryūkyū accent. He thinks the Kantō area was settled by migrants from Kyūshū; cf. §14, §15.)

More unusual mergers of accent classes are reported for Kyōto-type systems by Yamaguchi 1976:7-9. Two dialects of Wakayama (Shingū and [Higashi-Muru-gun] Hongū-machi) have 2.1/4, 2.2/3, 2.5; in Tenkawa-mura (Nara) the division is 2.1 vs. 2.2/3/4/5 and in Nishi-Yoshino-mura Nishi-Hiura (Nara) it is 2.1/4 vs. 2.2/3/5, as it is also (Kindaichi 1977a:148) in Tarui-machi of western Gifu. In Akō (Hyōgo) and in Takahama (Fukui) the division is 2.1/4, 2.2/3, 2.5 (id. 152), as in the two Wakayama dialects. Sekigahara-machi of western Gifu has a two-way division of 2.1/4/5 as HH vs. 2.2/3 as HL (id. 148). Certain dialects in Kagawa have merged the atonic high (2.1 and 3.1) and the atonic low (2.3 and 3.4) types, as least for the dissyllables, e.g. Marugame, Niihama, Takamatsu (id. 160-2). On Takamatsu and Hiruma-machi, see Hirayama 1957b. A similar merger took place in Suzu, but only for three-syllable nouns (3.4 → 3.1). Most unusual is the division 2.1/5, 2.2, 2.3, 2.4 reported (Nakai 1984) for five islands in the Bisan Straits of Seto Inland Sea: Manabe, Sanagi, Iwaguro, Hiro, Shishi.

Interesting complications are afforded by certain Ryūkyū dialects:

(1) A number of words in class 2.4/5 with final open vowel in Old Japanese have shifted to 2.3: kasa 'umbrella', kata 'shoulder', ita 'board', ase 'sweat', ame 'rain', kado 'corner', ... This makes no difference in Shuri, where 2.3/4/5 are all merged as B; in Nakijin and Yonaguni these words have the accent type B rather than the expected C.

(2) Most of the words ending in a modern close (= high) vowel, whether from an Old Japanese close vowel (i u) or half-open (= mid) vowel (e o), that are in 2.4/5 stay with their group but many of them lengthen the preceding vowel, and occasionally both vowels are lengthened. (Yet the short vowel usually turns up in compounds.) Examples from Shuri:

*u   maaçi 'pine' < matu 2.4; quuşi 'mortar' < usu 2.4; şiişi 'soot' < susu 2.5; saaru 'monkey' < 2.5; kuubaa 'spider' < kumo 2.5 (Shuri -aa may be a suffix).

*o   yaadu 'lodging' < yado 2.4; quutu 'offing' ?< soto 'outside' 2.4; quuku 'deep inside' < oku 2.4; qiicuu 'thread' < ito 2.4; muuku 'son-in-law' < muko 2.5; maadu 'opening' < mado 2.5

*i   nuusi 'owner' < nusi 2.4; haai 'needle' < fari 2.4; haasi 'chopsticks' < fasi 2.4; uubi 'girdle' < obi 2.4; qiici 'breath' < iki 2.4; taabi 'sock' < tabi 2.5

*e   naabi 'pan' < nabe 2.5; kaagi 'shadow' < kage 2.5; wuuki 'bucket' < woke 2.5

There are also examples of 2.3: haaci 'large bowl' < hati 'pot' 2.3; kaami 'jar' < kame 2.3; kaamii 'tortoise' < kame 2.3; guusi 'skewer' < kusi 2.3; maai 'ball' < mari 2.3; maami 'bean' < mame 2.3; maaku 'curtain' < maku 2.3; muutu 'source' < moto 2.3; wuun (Yonaguni bunu) 'ax' < wono 2.3, and maybe qiibi 'finger' < yubi 2.3 (< oyobi 3.4). The word for 'horse' is qnma (< uma 2.3) in Shuri, but nuuma in dialects of Miyako (Ikema, Uechi, Nakasuji) and nnma in two dialects of Yaeyama (Kurojima, Taketomi).

It remains to be explained why other nouns failed to lengthen the vowel. Short vowels are found in the Shuri reflexes of:
   mugi 'barley', tumi 'sin', umi 'sea', uri 'melon' (all 2.4); kaki 'oyster' and negi 'onion' (2.5);
   fune 'boat' (but long in nagari-buunii 'boat ride', cf. Tokunoshima fuuni), ine 'rice', tane 'seed' (2.4); ase 'sweat', ame 'rain' (2.5);
   tubu 'grain' (2.4); firu 'leech', yoru 'night' (2.5);
   ato 'footprint', kado 'corner', miso 'beanpaste', mino 'raincape' (2.4); koto 'harp' > kutuu with FINAL long vowel, momo 'thigh(s)' (2.5).

Also to be explained: the length in naaka 'inside' < naka 2.4; uusa 'yarn guide' < wosa 2.4, hwiira 'moldboard; spatula' < fera 2.4, and naada/maada 'not yet' < mada 2.4; there is also saataa 'sugar' < *satau (> standard satoo), probably 3.4. And: saazi 'heron' < sagi 2.1, yuuci 'small ax' < yoki (?2.3/?2.4 < 2.1), wiiri 'collar' < eri 2.2b, ciiba 'fang' < kiba 2.2b. See §14, §15.

Some of the words with short vowels in Shuri listed above turn up with long vowels in other dialects of Okinawa: the word for 'sea' is quumi in Ishikawa (= Qisicaa) and Higa (= Hwiza), according to Kindaichi 1975:140. And 'leech' is biiru in dialects of Kyōto-fu (Inokuchi 353). Hattori (1978-9:21, 22) cites quite a few additional examples from the Okinawan dialect of Onna:
   (2.5) tuuyu 'dew', qaasii 'sweat', qaamii 'rain', gaacii 'oyster', maayuu 'eyebrow', muumuu 'thighs', yuuruu 'night';
   (2.4) puuni 'boat', qaawaa 'millet', qiicaa 'board', kaasaa 'umbrella', kaataa 'shoulder', nuumii 'chisel', muuzii 'barley', waaraa 'straw';
   (2.3) nuumi 'flea', paama 'beach', puuni 'bone', qaanaa 'hole', qinnuu 'dog', suumii 'ink', taamaa 'ball/jewel', tuunuu 'horn', naamii 'wave', nuukaa 'bran', paazii 'shame', paanaa 'flower', miimii 'ear', yuumi ("?") 'bow', qiimii 'dream', waataa 'guts'. Hattori (22:108) also calls attention to long-vowel forms in two dialects of the island of Yakushima, just south of Kyūshū: haasi 'chopsticks',

haai 'needle', kaaŋe 'shadow', saaru 'monkey', and ooke 'bucket' (Miya-no-ura);
maatsu 'pine' (Onoma). And (11:109) he mentions that Uwano Zendō has found haari
'needle', naabe 'pan', and maatu 'pine' (with the appropriate voiced allophone of
-t-) in six locations on the northeast coast of Iwate. NKD reports yooru (Fukuoka)
'night' and yooki (Hida) 'small ax' (Shuri yuuci B but Myōgi-shō yoki HH = 2.1).
Kusakabe 1968 reports long vowels in a number of northern Okinawa dialects,
including yaamaa for 'mountain' (2.3) in Kin and uunuu for 'ax' (2.4) in Kusigwa
and Sukuta.

7.0. Accent patterns of shorter nouns.

We can reconstruct the proto-Japanese accent types for perhaps 800 nouns of
one, two, and three syllables (= moras). In Chart 5 the patterns are arrayed
according to our numerical code and also according to certain features of contour
that cross the three word-length classes. Both the number of examples thought to
belong to each type and the corresponding percentage of the total are intended as
tentative figures to be read as "about ... ". (The total number of items in the
corpus examined varies in different sections of this study, but the percentages
remain largely unaffected by that.)

For each accent type a chain of correspondences is shown on the basis of six
dialects. From north to south these are Tōkyō, Kyōto, Kagoshima, Shodon (Amami),
Shuri (Okinawa), and Yonaguni. Data from the three Ryūkyū dialects are unavailable
for a number of words but the correspondences are fairly clear.

The accent patterns of Tōkyō and Kyōto are cited by digit. The numerals refer
to the last HIGH syllable for Tōkyō (so that 0 means there is no fall and 1 means
the second syllable is low) but they refer to the onset of a LOW syllable for Kyōto:
0 means all syllables are high; 1 means the first syllable is low; 1:3 means the
first syllable is low and there is another low on the third syllable, but it is
represented by a fall within the second syllable when that is the last before a
juncture — in Hirayama 1960 the dissyllables are noted as "1;25". Kagoshima words
of Type A have a fall of pitch, those of Type B have no fall; Shodon and Shuri are
similar, but the automatic location of the fall differs. These notations are all
taken from Hirayama and I have adapted his system to note the three-way distinctive
patterns of Yonaguni: words marked A are all-low (hence end-low), those marked B
are end-high, and those marked C are end-fall.

The patterns for Myōgi-shō, representing the Kyōto accent of the 11th and 12th
centuries, are given after the type number and stated in terms of high (H) and low
(L). Included are certain hypothetical additions proposed by Hayata (2.2a and 3.2a),
Hattori (3.5a), and McCawley (3.7a). The Myōgi-shō patterns for these hypothetical
types are preceded by an asterisk: we assume they fell together with the following
"(b)" types before the time of Myōgi-shō, though it is thought that 3.5a may be
attested. The notations after the hyphen represent assumptions about the pitch of an
attached monosyllabic enclitic. Not all particles behave the same way; what is shown
is the behavior of the "atonic particles", which simply continue on the same pitch
as the preceding syllable. For this reason we differ from certain other linguists in
writing LL-L for 2.3 (instead of LL-H), LLL-L for 3.4 (instead of LLL-H) and LLH-H
for 3.5b (instead of LLH-L — and this implicitly rejects the distinction between
3.5a and 3.5b). Where our notation seems to show a change of pitch on the enclitic,
as in LH-L for 2.5 and *LHH-L for 3.7a — we presume a morphophonemic peculiarity of
the last syllable of the noun (i.e. an oxytonic accent): whether in isolation saru
'monkey' was spoken with the low-high tune of matu 'pine', as in modern Kōchi, or
with a high fall on the second syllable, as in modern Kyōto, we believe that the
underlying form inherently has both the high and the low on that syllable. A Kōchi-
type pronunciation results from suppressing the low in isolation; a Kyōto-type
pronunciation results from blending the low with the preceding high to yield the
high fall. And similar presumptions hold for the H-L of Type 1.2 and the L-H of Type
1.3: the unaccented particle is attached to the underlying form of the nouns, which
has the low and the high combined in a single syllable. The modern Kyōto version
lengthens the vowel of all one-mora nouns;[1] the extension simply continues the high
pitch of 1.1 (ēe 'handle') and serves to carry the pitch fall for 1.2 (hāa 'leaf')
and the rise for 1.3 (teē 'hand'). According to Umegaki 1946:47 "there is a strong
tendency for a following one-syllable particle to lengthen also: naa noo, kaa gaa,
kii oo". Kobayashi 1975 (150, 153) says one-mora nouns are short in Kōchi before a
particle but long in isolation, while in Kyōto they are long in all environments.
When the Kyōto or Ōsaka speaker tries to shorten the noun in .té .mo = /teēmo/ the
speaker is forced to say either /temō/ or /tēmo/, dropping one or the other of the
"preaccents"; cf. Kindaichi 1944:216, Wada 1959:17b.

But there is something wrong with our class 1.3. Though the modern dialects
require the reconstruction of only three accent types for monoysyllabic nouns, both
evidence from Myōgi-shō and structural considerations indicate that earlier kinds
of Japanese must have had four types.[2] The high that is heard in Kyōto as a rise in
isolation (with lengthened vowel) or as a high on an attached particle is clearly

nondistinctive: the nouns are simply low-register atonic. Kindaichi has suggested
that these nouns were originally just low (cf. Okumura 1972:145), with the rise
developing later. And for the few which appear with an attached atonic particle in
Myōgi-shō we find not the "L-H" of our chart, but "L-L": ka no waka-duno 'young
horn of deer'; te no aka [?= aya] 'fingerprint'; me no mafe '(before one's eyes =)
while still alive'; ki no take 'tree fungus', ki no mimi 'tree-ears (a kind of
fungus)'. These nouns are all marked with the HEI "even" tone (= low) in isolated
citation. But certain other nouns are marked with the KYO "going" tone (a dot on the
upper right corner) and they were apparently pronounced with a rise from low to high:
mé 'female'; mó 'garment'; ná 'exorcism'; sú 'nest' (and the compound suu-ya
'nest, den' attested from 1116, Tsukishima 1969:396), sú 'reed screen' cf. su
'vinegar'); wí 'rush'; wé 'bait'; fá 'tooth'; fí 'cypress', fí 'shuttle' (cf. fi
'ice, hail'); yá 'building'; yú 'citron'. The word for 'hemp' wó is marked with a
rise; the probably related word for 'cord' is marked high in the three citations in
Mochizuki, but Okumura 1972:147 also cites a rise notation from a different version
of Myōgi-shō. (Modern Kyōto and Tōkyō treat 'cord' as Type B, a reflex of 1.3; but
Kagoshima and Shuri treat it as Type A, a reflex of 1.1 or 1.2.) The word meaning
'marsh' is listed both as monosyllabic nú and dissyllabic nuu; the word ni 'load'
is marked low in Myōgi-shō but rise in Iroha-jirui-shō; and the word fi 'fire' is
listed both as low and as high — as is fi 'sun; day', which the dialect comparison
puts in 1.2, though in the meaning 'day' this word when adnominally modified is
treated by the Tōkyō speakers at Type B, tonic. Okumura 1972:147 adds the following
rise citations to those carried in Mochizuki's index: mí 'a fish — perhaps the
dace?' (Wamyō-shō), ná = naní 'what' (Myōgi-shō), sí 'rumex' (Wamyō-shō), and
sé 'shaggy hoof' (Wamyō-shō), for which Mochizuki offers one rise citation from the
Iroha-jirui-shō. (Of this list the only item found with an attached particle is mé
'female' in me no warafa 'girl', and that does not confirm the rise.)³ Endō 1974:
36-7 thinks the monosyllabic nouns with the "going" tone were heavy syllables with
two moras, the second being a lengthening of the vowel; monosyllabic nouns with the
other tones he thinks were one-mora syllables, with short vowels. The two moras
are attested for nuu 'marsh' in two citations from Myōgi-shō, and the phonograms
for 'shuttle' in Shinsen-Jikyō (892) indicate it was pronounced fii (Zdb 603a); in
Honzō-wamyō (918) the word for 'shaggy hoof' is written both se and sei, which
suggests that the pronunciation was probably see and that orthographic "ei" was
used to represent long /ee/ earlier than is usually thought (Endō 1974:37).

In any event, from the interpretation in §12 it is obvious that we need a low-register type (L-L) for nouns with underlying one-shape syllables as well as each of the longer types. We can call this Type 1.3a; it apparently absorbed the "rise" word of 1.3b by making the rise automatic and thus extending it to the nouns of 1.3a, which we believe originally stayed low.

It should be noted that in the formulas of Chart 5 (and elsewhere) the data for Tōkyō come strictly from the modern dialect. For that reason a few of the patterns cited differ from the "Tōkyō-type" (proto-)pattern cited by Kindaichi and others on the basis of information from related dialects. For example, the fact that the modern dialects of Sapporo, Matsumoto, Numazu. Hiroshima, and Ōita all have namīda where Tōkyō has namida indicates that the "1" for Tōkyō in the formula of Type 3.5b must earlier have been "2". (Cf. Okuda 1975 n.13; Kindaichi 1943:72-5, 1958b:62b; Watanabe 1975:186-7.) According to Mase Yoshio (Kudō 1978:223a) parts of Nagano preserve the "older" Tōkyō pattern of "1" for modern "0" in words of Type 3.6 such as usagi 'rabbit'. The Kyōto forms, similarly, are cited from modern Kyōto.

7.1. Words with initial rise.

We have remarked that a number of monosyllabic nouns were marked with the kyo[1] = kyo-syoo/-sei "going(-tone)" dot in the upper right corner, generally interpreted as a rise from low to high pitch within the syllable.[4] Okumura 1972 cites a number of other words marked with the rise on the first or only syllable:

   (1) the interjection á 'oh'; the predicative verb forms ú 'gets', kú 'comes', fú 'passes'; the verb infinitives é 'get', kí 'come', fé 'pass', mí 'see'; the subjunctive form kó- '[not/will] come';

   (2) the adverbs fóbo / fóbo 'about', mádu (also mādu) 'first', mósi 'perchance', yáya 'a bit'; the adjective infinitives tóku 'early', náku 'lacking', yóku 'well'; the adjective -mi forms námi 'lack', yómi 'good'.
On the -ku and -mi forms of the adjectives see §9. The verb forms are apparently the result of contraction, for the ending has been absorbed into the stem syllable; in underlying form the stem is simply low (i.e. Type B) and the ending is high, as with the longer stems (§8). There are also a few dissyllabic nouns marked with rise on the first syllable; the rise had no reflex in later developments, so for the purposes of our lists we have classified them as if they were initial low. The notations probably represent a transitional stage in which the first syllable had free variants, one with a long vowel and rising pitch, the other with a short vowel and low pitch, though there is only one example ('shank') that is clearly attested with the long vowel:

Dissyllabic nouns with initial rise in Myōgi-shō

yúri = *yuúri / *yurí 'lily' (> yurī; but Nakijin C, Shuri B)

yúsi = *yuúsi / *yusī '(a spinous evergreen)'

síme = *siíme / *simē 'sparrow'

fára = *faára / *farā 'trumpet (horn)'

tísa = *tiísa / *tisā 'lettuce'

kíˢ/za = *kiíˢ/za / *kiˢ/zā 'elephant'

kúko = *kuúko / *kukō 'Chinese matrimony vine'

fémi = *feémi / *femī / fenbíˢ 'snake'

bífa = *biífa / *bifā 'loquat' — but bífa in Iroha-jirui-shō and Wamyō-shō
                              (Numoto 1979:29)

fági = faági / fagī 'shank'

yúfi[n] = *yuúfi / *yufī 'mating (of livestock)'

yási = *yaási / *yasī 'palm tree'

góma⁶ = { ? *goóma / *gomā } 'sesame'
         { ? *goóma / *gomā }

{ fíme = *fiíme / *fimē } 'hawfinch, grosbeak'
{ fíme⁷ = *fiíme / *fimē }

The list of dissyllabic nouns given above is believed to be comprehensive.
There are also a few longer compounds with mé- 'female' such as mé-gafara
'female (= concave) tile', mé-katura 'a kind of cinnamon (called yabu-nikkei =
Cinammomum penduculatum)', mé-kemono 'female animal', mé-tamasifi/-tamasifī
'female spirit', mé-biru 'small leek', and probably médo-gúsa 'Sericea lespedeza
(= medo-hagi)'. Hayata 1977a observes that the rise-high contour is found also in
a few longer Chinese binoms such as físui 'jade', rúban 'pagoda roof' (= roban),
síwoni 'aster' (= sion), s[i]yáko (Kn Mg) = syáko (Zs Mg, one version of Wamyō-shō
[Numoto 1979:283]) 'giant clam'. Some of these are spelled with heavy (two-mora)
syllables: konzen 'marigold (= kinsen-ka)', s[i]yúuro (syúro in the Wamyō-shō
[Numoto 1979:28] and in the Iroha-jirui-shō súro) 'hemp palm'(= syuro), noúseu
'trumpet flower (= roosyoo-ka = noozen-kazura)', taúk[u]wes[i]yaku 'peach-blossom

stone = white stone with pink dots'. The high-low contour is found in the Chinese
binoms zísyaku 'magnet, compass' — also sísyaku (Zs Mg), sísiyaku (Kn Mg) — and
tókati 'cloth of cotton blended with rabbit fur'. The noun é-yami 'epidemic' is
thought to begin with the Chinese loanmorph (y)eki 'war'. And Kindaichi 1964a:351
cites ídure[-mo] 'which[-ever]', becoming Kamakura ídure.

In accounting for these contours we will take a hint from Kindaichi's neat
interpretation of the rise as a two-mora sequence of low + high and say that the
words were in the process of contraction at the time of Myōgi-shō; once the two-
mora syllable was thoroughly contracted into one mora the rise simply stayed low.
Uwano perceptively proposed the free variation of long and short patterns shown
above, though most of the assumed variants without the rise are not attested.
Certain more obvious contractions may conceal a nasal mora (see Endō 1974), an -n
reduced from -nV: názo (Kn Mg) < *naní-ª/zo 'why' — cf. ikázo / íka-ní-so (both
Kz Mg); omó- from omo-fí 'think' in omó miru and omó fakaru (both Zs Mg) = omo[m]-
< *omop[i]-.

Mochizuki 1972 (and see also Mochizuki 1971) makes the astute observation that
we cannot be sure that the group of earlier rise words is limited to those attested
with the "going" tone dot; some of the low-initial and high-initial words may well
have had a rise at the beginning, and especially those attested both ways. In making
compounds and derivatives the rise is treated as if low — that is, the compound or
derivative belongs on the low pitch register — but sometimes it is treated as if it
were high-register (Mochizuki 1972:2b). Perhaps we can find hidden members of the
fraternity of initial-rise words by looking for compounds or derivatives which
irregularly have the opposite register from the initial element as marked by the
sources.

According to Numoto 1979 the well-assimilated Chinese loanwords normally began
with the low register and are marked by Wamyō-shō and Myōgi-shō with the "even" or
the "going" tone unless they are syllables that ended in a final stop in Chinese
(-p -t -k) and are marked "entering" tone. He believes that the examples given as
initial high, with the "rising" tone, either go back to an earlier initial rise (the
"going" tone) or are newly created reading pronunciations. Numoto says the initial
syllable of these assimilated loanwords preserved an original system of three tones
— "even", "going", "entering" — that characterized the early colloquial (Go-on)
versions of Chinese loanmorphs, but that the tones of the later syllables of the
words show little reflection of the basic tones of the loanmorphs they represent.

7.2. Words with initial fall.

In Konkōmyō-saishōō - kyō ongi the word for 'rainbow' is attested with an
initial fall of pitch, marked by the to'o-ten or "east dot" (slightly raised at the
lower left corner of the syllable symbol):[8] nízi = *nīizi / nīzi (Kn). There is
dialect evidence for a long vowel in the first syllable; the original shape of the
etymon is unclear but perhaps it was *ni-musi 'red/beautiful *snake' (cf. ma-musi
'viper'). The ancestor of the Kyūshū placename Hyūga is noted as fímuka in old
manuscripts of Nihon-Shoki (Sakurai 1964:35a), and the etymology reflected by the
traditional characters is 'sun' (Heian fí = fīi) + the verb-root 'face' muk(a);
a similar etymology for higasi 'east' will be found in Ch. 5.

7.3. Words with final fall.

In the modern Kinki dialects certain words have an intrinsic fall of pitch on
the last syllable but this fall is not heard in all dialects, except as a high pitch
when an enclitic follows on low pitch. The classic examples are nouns of Type 2.5
which are kept distinct from those of 2.4 before pause or particle: Kyōto sarú
'monkey' unlike matū 'pine', sarū ga unlike matu ga. Although for many words
the Heian notations fail to differentiate the 2.5 pattern from that for 2.4, a
number of words are thought to bear the to'o-ten "east-dot" notation on the final
syllable, as we have remarked earlier. There are a few similar words with three
moras (listed in Hirayama as "1;35"): mattí 'matches', deppá 'buck teeth' (but
Umegaki has deppā), gittyó[9] 'a left-hander', noppó 'a gangly person', makká
'crimson', minná 'all' (in Ōsaka and Kōchi minna). One phonemic solution is to
regard the final "fall" as indicating a two-mora "heavy" syllable, as we have
observed in §1.6: sarūu, minnāa. This implies a purely phonetic contraction,
such as that which makes mado o 'window (as direct object)' sound the same in
rapid speech as madó (with no particle or a "dropped" particle); similarly, in fast
speech maē e 'to the front' sounds like maé 'front'. But the contraction becomes
phonemic when a particle not made up of the vowel of the preceding syllable is
attached: madō e, maē o, minnā ga (in Ōsaka and Kōchi minna ga). By "contraction"
we imply that the underlying form in Kyōto has a long final syllable, but that does
not necessarily mean the length is of ancient origin. In other Kinki dialects there
occur words with low initial and final for which the Kyōto patterns differ:
Kameyama kyoó 'today' (as noun), hoó 'law, way'; tikamé 'nearsighted', yuubé 'last
night', kuisinbó 'greedy person' (Hattori 1929); kuronbó 'black man' (Kindaichi

1944:196). Cf. Kindaichi 1964a:331, 345. Wada 1942:11 mentions also mukasí '(days of) yore'[10] and settù 'Settsu (placename)' "or at least mukasī ga and settū ga". Wada also reports, as "emphatic", ué no 'above' and sītà no 'below'; cf. Kindaichi 1964a:337. The latter two words belong to the small class of dissyllabic nouns that are normally atonic in Tōkyō but oxytonic when modified by adnominal phrases — and in Nagano oxytonic even when unmodified (Kudō 1978:48-52), yet never oxytonic in Narada or Kōfu (Uwano 1976:9 n.); other members of the class are uti 'inside' (or 'home') and hito 'person', for which the Kinki dialect of Akō has hītò (Kindaichi 1944:200). The Heian markings would lead us to class these nouns all as 2.2, but I have put them in 2.2a along with a few nouns like kita 'north' which have competing variants (oxytonic and atonic) in Tōkyō, and I assume the earlier accentuation was ōò for this class of words (2.2a). But hi 'day' and tokoro 'place' behave in a similar fashion in Tōkyō: normally atonic, they are oxytonic (and for hi this is equivalent to prototonic) when adnominal phrases precede them. I have not given hi 'day' a separate class — it is, with 'sun', 1.2 — and I have left tokoro with 3.1 (high atonic) but perhaps it should go with 3.2a, or it calls for a class 3.1a. On classing these words as originally having a final fall, cf. Komatsu 1971:610, Kindaichi 1964a:346 ("tokorò ?"); see also Hattori 1933:35.

If we set up a class "3.1a", as exemplified by tokoro 'place', and define it so as to include those words for which Tōkyō has competing accentuations of atonic and oxytonic, the following seven nouns will belong: hideri 'drought', hokora 'shrine', katami 'keepsake' (see Hirayama 1960 for the oxytonic variant), migiwa 'waterside', yasuri 'file'; and hesaki 'bow of boat' (for which the "3.1" may be in question, since Kagoshima has B and there are no philological attestations) and mimoto 'divine/noble location' (for which all the evidence is scant). If we extend the definition to include nouns that are unexpectedly oxytonic in Tōkyō but la the atonic variant the category may also include humoto 'foot of mountain' (which is philologically 3.1/2 but the dialects point to 3.4) and kakine 'fence' (which is philologically 3.1/3.2, but Tōkyō oxytonic/mesotonic, and Tōkyō-type dialects oxytonic/atonic). If we include those nouns which are oxytonic or oxytonic/atonic in at least one Tōkyō-type dialect, a number of additional members can be found:

hatisu 'lotus', hitai 'forehead', hunori 'glue plant', ikari 'anchor', karada 'body', kotori 'bird', kousi 'calf', koyama 'hill', kutuwa 'bridle bit', mamusi 'viper', mikata 'ally', minami 'south', miyama '(deep) mountains', mukasi 'yore', yodare 'drivel'; and hizume 'hoof' (philologically 3.5a/b and 3.1, Tōkyō atonic/ prototonic) and mukuro 'body' (philologically 3.1/3.2 and perhaps 3.4).

If we were to include in the criteria for this category "3.1a" the irregular Kyōto
reflex "2 < 3" = HLL < HHL, as found for hitai 'forehead' (Umegaki), mamusi 'viper',
and minami 'south' in the lists above, we can add these nouns:

> ebisu 'Ainu' (Tōkyō prototonic/atonic, Hiroshima mesotonic), hisio 'a kind of
> beanpaste; salted meats', hyuuga 'turning toward the sun; Hyūga *(placename)*',
> kawaya 'toilet' (Kagoshima B), kuize 'stump; stake', okubi 'belch' (Umegaki).

There are also a number of nouns otherwise assigned to "3.1" for which, irregularly,
the Tōkyō accent is protonic or mesotonic, and/or for which Kyōto has "1" (low
atonic) and Kagoshima or Ryūkyūan has "B" (low register). In addition to a few of
the items in the lists above, these include:

> akubi 'yawn', akuta 'trash', azami 'thistle', azana 'alias', haniwa 'red-clay
> burial objects', hitugi 'coffin', hokori 'dust' (Yonaguni B), hutuka 'two days',
> ikada 'raft', kabura 'turnip; arrow whistle', kizuna 'fetter', kuruma 'car(t)',
> madara 'spots', masago 'sand', misao 'fidelity', muika 'six days', namae 'name'
> (Shuri B), otto 'husband', yagura 'tower', yaziri 'arrowhead', yooka 'eight days'.
> Also perhaps minato 'port' (Shodon and Nakijin B).

Finally, there are a few infinitive-derived nouns that we list as "3.1" but which
are marked by one or more of the criteria mentioned above: kasumi 'mist', kazari
'decoration', kudari 'descent' (HHL in Zusho-ryō Myōgi-shō, assuming that the form
is not intended to be the infinitive itself), kusari 'a chain', mukai '(facing)
opposite', tikai 'vow, pledge', tukai 'errand; servant' (Yonaguni B). For details on
each of the items that may belong to "3.1a" see the individual entries in Ch. 5.

  Komatsu (1974:113) claims toʼo-ten "east-dot" evidence for a type of noun with
final fall that includes the following three words: mizu < *mĭdù 'water', *mīzò
'ditch', tubo < *tŭfò (? = tŭwò) 'jar'. The evidence is based on the persistence
of the final fall in compounds: hi-mizu < fi-midù 'ice water', tukuri-mizu <
tukuri-midù 'boiled (and cooled) water', ase-mizu < ? ase-midù 'sweat flowing like
water', konzu < ko-mizu < ko-mudù / ko-midù '(thick water =) broth from boiling
rice'; ase-mizò '(?) rivulet of sweat'; hasitubo < fasi-tubò 'jar for chopsticks',
sumitubo < sumi-tubò 'ink jar'. Komatsu believes the class may have been larger but
was dying out at the time of the notations (i.e., late Heian). There is little
evidence from modern dialects; but Yonaguni has a final fall on cibu, the reflex
for tubo 'jar', putting it in accent type C rather than the expected type A. And one
version of Kyōto simizu 'clear water' is simīzu (see Ch. 5). Nakanoshima (in the
Tokara archipelago south of Kyūshū) puts both mizu 'water' and miti 'road' with

2.2 (m̄i̱ẕu, miz̄u ga) as contrasted with 2.1 (ūs̱i̱, us̄ī g̱a̱); see Tajiri 1975. (This
dialect has a three-way morphophonemic distinction for dissyllabic nouns 2.1 ≠ 2.2
≠ 2.3/4/5, but in isolation the distinction between 2.1 and 2.2 is neutralized.)
According to Kusakabe 1968:40 the dialects of Kunigami and Ōgimi (northern Okinawa)
treat the reflexes of both mizu and mizo as low register (B) and accord the same
treatment to the reflexes of the following nouns of Type 2.1:

> eda 'branch', hane 'feather', hosi 'star', kugi 'nail', miti 'road' (cf. the
> Nakanoshima treatment as 2.2), momo 'peach', musi 'insect', nuno 'cloth', o[t]to
> 'husband', suna 'sand', take 'bamboo', tume 'claw', yome 'bride'.

There is other evidence to put some of these words in the class "?2.1a". Hattori
1973 cites Kōchi 'insect' as mu˹si (= 2.2 or 2.3) and the Ibuki-jima accent is the
reflex of 2.3; 'sand' is suna˹ (= 2.2 or 2.3) in parts of the Ida area of Gifu
(Okumura 1976c:289) and optionally in dialects of Shizuoka, Nagano, and Yamanashi
(Kindaichi 1943); and Shodon puts the reflex of take 'bamboo' in the low register B.
Notice that the Shuri reflex of mizo 'ditch' is (n)nzu B, with optional length on
the first syllable and Nakijin has the two variants mizu C and (mi)zuu A. On the
Wakamatsu peninsula (of northern Kyūshū) the reflex of tume 'claw' is given the
accentuation corresponding to Type 2.3. In addition to the nouns listed above,
certain of the nouns listed as "2.1" might be suspected to be members of the group
"2.1a" on the basis of several irregularities in the reflexes found in modern
dialects. The irregular reflexes involve a fall of pitch (Tōkyō 1 or 2, Kyōto 2)
or indications of low register (Kyōto 1 or 1:3, Kagoshima B, Ryūkyū B or C). The
nouns that are likely candidates:

> ami 'tiny shrimp', ari 'ant', asi 'reed', hata 'rim' (Kagoshima/Nakijin B, Ibuki-
> jima F = 2.3), heta 'calyx', hire 'fin; scarf' (Tōkyō 0/2, Ibuki-jima F = 2.3),
> hisi 'water-chestnut', huki 'bog-rhubarb', kabi 'mildew' (Shizukuishi 2, Nakijin
> C, Shodon/Shuri B), kasa 'sore', komo 'wild rice', mama 'as is', moti 'holly',
> moti 'rice-cake' (Shodon B), neya 'boudoir', nie 'new rice', nogi 'awn; fishbone',
> sade 'scoop net', sagi 'heron' (Tōkyō dialects 2, Ibuki-jima H1 = 2.2), saki
> 'ahead' (Hiroshima 0/2, Ibuki-jima H1 = 2.2), sama 'appearance; direction; ... ',
> siba 'turf' (Myōgi-shō HH/HL), sina 'quality, goods' (Myōgi-shō HH/HL), siro
> 'thing; ... ', siwa 'wrinkle', sugi 'cedar' (Shodon B), suso 'skirt bottom'
> (Shodon B), suzu 'bell' (Shodon B), suzu 'tin', taka 'height; quantity', taka
> 'hawk' (Shuri B), taki 'waterfall', tama 'occasional' (Kagoshima B), tomo
> 'companion; together', toti 'horse chestnut', tuki 'ibis', tumi 'sparrow-hawk',
> tura 'line' (Myōgi-shō HH, Nihon-Shoki HL), tutu 'pipe, tube', ure 'branch,
> twig', yatu 'eight', yotu 'four'; perhaps buta 'pig'. And the infinitive-derived
> nouns mane 'mimicry', suke 'support pillar', tomi 'riches', ture 'companion',
> wabi 'simple taste; apology'.

Sakurai has questioned whether the compounds adduced by Komatsu are behaving according to the appropriate rules of compound-noun accentuation as he had earlier formulated them, but Hayata 1977a devised a set of rules that call for retention of the locus represented by the "fall" (see §10.1). Sakurai also calls attention to a couple of compounds with a final monosyllabic noun, though it cannot be said that these support his compound-noun rule: aoto < awo-tó (Zs Mg) / awo-tō (Kn Mg) 'bluegray grindstone' and hiro-me < firo-mè 'broad-leaf seaweed (= konbu)'. (On the latter see also Komatsu 1971:610.) Kindaichi 1964a:350 cites hito-e < fito-fè 'single-layer' from the Zusho-ryō Myōgi-shō (other Mg citations are fito-fē) and also ta-makì (for which Mochizuki has only ta-makī) 'arm ornament, elbow-guard', maedare < mafedarè), and faturù 'a garment comes unsewn or gets frayed' (cited from Zs Mg, faturū in Kn Mg); he cites akidù 'dragonfly' from one text of Nihon-Shoki and suggests also honoo < ? fonofò 'flame'.

If we set up a category "3.4a" to take care of akitu < akidu 'dragonfly', aoto 'bluegray grindstone', hirome 'broad-leaf seaweed', hitoe 'single-layer', temaki 'arm ornament', and perhaps honoo 'flame', we may find reason to include also a number of nouns that are (for the most part) philologically attested as LLL but show irregular reflexes in certain dialects, particularly oxytonic/atonic variants in the Tōkyō-type dialects, high register in Kagoshima or Ryūkyū dialects, or the oxytonic C pattern of Yonaguni. Nouns that perhaps fall into this group ("?3.4a"):

aima 'interval', asida 'clogs', asita 'tomorrow', himusi 'moth' (Kindaichi "Heian LLF?"), hotoke 'Buddha', ikusa 'battle', imina 'taboo name', iori 'hut', kabati 'cheekbone', kasuri 'splashed pattern', kawara 'tile', kemono 'animal', konusi 'fist', kotoba 'word', muzina 'badger', nanae 'seven/many layers' (Kindaichi "Heian LLF"), nagae 'long handle', nagisa 'beach', nakago 'center', nakama 'companion', namasu 'thin-sliced raw fish', namazu 'catfish', naname 'aslant', naniwa 'Naniwa (= Ōsaka)', nanoka 'seven days', nemoto 'root', nikibi 'pimple', nuime 'seam', suzuri 'ink-slab', tadati 'at once', tamoto 'sleeve', toriko 'captive', turugi 'sword', tuzumi 'drum', unazi 'nape', uroko 'fish scale', usio 'tide', utiwa 'fan', uzura 'quail', warabi 'bracken', yakara 'family', yasiro 'shrine', yuube 'last night'.

This raises the question whether there might not be a group of "2.3a" (either independent of or perhaps identical with 2.5) to include those nouns which show high-register reflexes or pitch-fall in modern dialects: asa 'hemp', awa 'bubble, foam', hone 'bone' (Yonaguni C), husa 'bunch', ike 'fishpond', kame 'jar', kame 'tortoise', kimo 'liver; heart', kiwa 'brink', nomi 'flea' (Nakijin and Yonaguni C), nori 'seaweed' (Hiroshima 1, Nakijin C), tubi 'vulva' (Shuri and Nakijin A 'arse'), ude 'arm'; perhaps huti 'rim; cliff' (if that is not 2.4); and quite a few others,

including those that (like kame 'tortoise', kaki 'oyster', and nae 'seedling') are
attested as LL in Myōgi-shō but have the 1:3 pattern in some modern Kyōto-type
dialects, though it is usually assumed that the modern accent pattern developed
secondarily. There are also a few words of types 2.4 and 2.5 that are irregularly A
in Ryūkyū reflexes: 2.4 sumi 'corner' (Shodon, Nakijin, Shuri A); ?2.5, ?2.4 soba
'buckwheat' (Shodon, Nakijin A); 2.5 turu 'crane' (Shuri, Nakijin A).

7.4. Rises and falls.

Leaving aside the specific nouns mentioned above, Kindaichi 1964a:411-2 points
to the fact that some of the patterns with falls are called for by certain phrases
or inflected forms of Heian Japanese. What was said as k̄aze mo 'wind even/too' in
the Kamakura period (and later) he presumes to have been k̄aze mó (?< *k̄aze [|] m̄oo)
in the Heian period; and what was āma-ki 'sweet ⋯ ' in the Muromachi period had
been āma-kí (?< *āma [|] k̄ii, cf. Sakurai 1962c) not only in the Heian period but
also during the Kamakura period, retaining its final fall under the pressure of such
forms as taka-kí 'high ⋯ '. See §9.1. Sakurai 1978b:90-1, noting that words with a
terminal fall predominantly end in high vowels (-i, -u), would like to treat the
fall as some sort of conditioned "allophone" of the high pitch.

Endō 1974 explains the "going-tone" dot as representing LENGTH and NASALITY,
regardless of — or independently from — the accent. It is interesting that the
upper-right corner is the position to which the double-dot of the nigori (dakuten)
eventually gravitated when the dots were no longer used to mark pitch. (Cf. Okumura
1952, Sakurai 1966c.)

A dot at the lower right corner of a character was used to mark the Chinese
"entering" tone (nissyoo/nissei), and a slightly raised version represents nissei/
nissyoo no karu 'the "light" entering tone'; it is also called toku-sei/-syoo. The
entering-tone words of Chinese ended in a final stop (-p, -t, -k) so that the pitch
of the tone was nondistinctive. There are three examples of the entering tone used
to write the second mora of a verb corresponding to modern uttaeru 'sues': utt̄afu
(twice), utt̄afur̄u. And one example of the "light" entering tone is used to write
the second mora of the verb n̄ottoru 'model on, follow'. On final -t in Chinese
loanwords, see Ch. 1, §52.

8.0. The accent of verbs.

Each of the paradigmatic forms of the verb in modern Japanese has a pattern of pitch that can be predicted according to:

(1) the register (the initial pitch) of the STEM, which can be reinterpreted for Tōkyō as either "tonic" (Type B, with Kyōto low register) or "atonic" (Type A, with Kyōto high register);

(2) the presence or absence of an underlying locus of pitch change (an accent) in the attached ENDING(S).

Essentially similar factors account for what we know of the corresponding forms in eleventh-century Kyōto and, presumably, in proto-Japanese. It is difficult to find adequate data in the early sources for some of the paradigmatic forms, but the general picture is clear.

8.1. The accentuation of verb forms in 11th-century Kyōto.

The following lists exemplify the patterns for the predicative form with the tonic ending -'u; the attributive form (mostly unattested in Myōgi-shō) with the tonic[1] ending -(u)ru; the infinitive with the tonic ending -'i; and the infinitive-derived noun with the atonic ending -i (for which there are a number of individual exceptions).[2] A few other forms are cited without special comment. The patterns I expect for proto-Japanese are these:

subjunctive V-a[3]   + -'mu 'will'
                            -n[i] si > -zi 'will not'
                            -n[i] su > -'zu 'do not'
                            -nu ' ⋯ which do not'
infinitive V-'[y]i   + [s]u → V-'u predicative 'do'
                            [s](ur)u → V-(ur)u attributive ' ⋯ which do'
                            a → V-'ye > V-'e imperative 'do!'

The provisional-concessive (*izen-kei*) form V-(ur)'ey (-ba/-do) is a contraction from the attributive + a noun /i/, as explained in Ch. 6, where the imperative is also accounted for. In these notations the mark (') represents a CHANGE of pitch level (high after low, low after high) which then continues until a juncture or another mark. Also cited are examples of the gerund: this consists of the infinitive + te', which is given a separate accentuation (HIGH probably from earlier FALL) and for that reason is taken to be set off from the preceding infinitive by a juncture. Although syntactic function early distinguished this particle from its source, the infinitive of the high-register perfect auxiliary (V-i) tu[ru], the separated phrasing appropriate to the structure infinitive + auxiliary was retained until sometime after 1200. The modern rules for compound verbs do not go back to proto-Japanese, as we will see in §8.3.

The verb register types are marked as A or B; the digit in front represents the number of syllables not of the stem but of the predicative imperfect that ends in -ʔu, for that is the paradigmatic form found most often in Myōgi-shō. In assuming that for 2-B and 3-B verbs this ending is simply high, rather than a fall, I am following Mochizuki 1975 (Kgg 102:31-49) on the basis of the most reliable sources for the tone marks: Zusho-ryō Myōgi-shō and Konkōmyō-saishōō-kyō ongi. Our lists include a few unattested forms (preceded by an asterisk) that are deemed useful to illustrate the expected patterns; an exclamation-point precedes attested exceptions. A "+" means that the expected form is attested. The notation "< 3" assumes that the 2-syllable vowel stem goes back to an earlier 3-syllable stem, which we reconstruct for proto-Japanese.

List of verb forms found in Myōgi-shō

	-ʔu	-(ur)u	-ʔi teʔ		-ʔi	-i
V-2-A	H-L	H-H	H-L H		H-L	H-H
oku 'put'	+	*ōku	ōki te,		*ōki	*ōki
			ōi te, ōi te			
fiku 'pull'	+					
kiku 'hear'	+					
maku 'roll'	+				māki	
naku 'cry'	+					
nuku 'remove'	+					
tuku 'poke'	+					
yuku 'go'	+	yūkū				
ifu 'say'⁴	+					
kafu 'buy'	+					
ofu 'pursue'	+				ōfi	
?sofu 'attach' vi.	+					
yufu 'tie'	+		yūfi te			
osu 'push'	+		! ōsi te			
kasu 'lend'	+					
kesu 'extinguish'	+					
masu 'increase' '	+					

	H-L	H-H	H-L H	H-L	H-H
faru 'stretch'	+				
fer-u 'shrink' vi.	+				
karu 'mow'	+				
naru 'sound'	+				
nuru 'paint'	+				
noru 'ride'	+				
sir-u 'know'	+				
tir-u 'scatter' vi.	+				
uru 'sell'	+			ūr<u>i</u>	
waru 'split' vi.	+				
yaru 'send'	+				
tugu 'succeed'	+		! t͞ui d͞e	tug͟i	
tobu 'fly'	+				
kumu 'dip'	+				
momu 'rub'	+			mom͟i	
tumu 'accumulate'	+				
umu 'give birth'	+				
yamu 'stop' vi.	+				
sinu 'die'[5]	+	*s͞inur͞u[6]		*s͞in͟i	*s͞ín͟i

V-2-A < 3	H-L	HH-H[7]	H-L H	H-L	H-H
odu 'fear'	+	*od͞uru	ōd͟i te	*ōd͟i	*od͞ī
yodu 'twist'	+		yōd͟i te		
kobu 'flatter'	+			kob͟i	kob͞i
negu 'appease'	+			neg͟i	
kafu 'change it'	+				
sutu 'throw away'	+		s͞ut͟e te		
iru 'put in'	+		īr͟e te		
karu 'wither'	+			kar͟e	
nuru 'get wet'	+				
agu 'raise'	+		ag͟e te		
hagu 'attach, ...'	+				
magu 'bend it'	+				

V-2-B	L-H	L-L	L-H H	L-H	L-L
amu 'knit'	+	*amu	*ami te	*ami	ami
kumu 'assemble'	+				kumi
sumu 'live; end'	+				
komu 'enter'	? +		kom[u] de		
yamu 'fall ill'	+				
yomu 'read'	+				
afu 'meet'	+				
kufu 'eat'	+				? kufi[8]
faku 'wear'	+				
fuku 'blow'	+				
maku 'sow'	+				
tuku 'reach'	? +		tui te		
fitu 'be steeped'	+		fiti te		
katu 'win'	+				
matu 'wait'	+				
motu 'hold'	+		mo[ti] te	moti...	
tatu 'stand'	+			tati...	
fosu 'dry it'	+				
sasu 'point'	+			sasi...	sasi, sasi
fagu 'strip'	+			? fagi...[9]	
kogu 'row'	+				
nugu 'doff'	+				
furu 'rain; fall'	+				
foru 'dig'	+				
karu 'hunt, drive'	+				! kari
kir-u 'cut'	+				
ner-u 'knead'	+				? neri[10]
soru 'shave'	+				
suru 'rub'	+				
toru 'take'	+				

V-2-B < 3	L-H	L-LL	L-H H	L-H	L-L
simu 'freeze'	+	*simuru	simī te	*simī	*simi[11]
todu 'close it'	+			(*?)todī	! todī
oku 'arise'	−		! (w)okī te (mistake?)		

komu 'put in'	? +		kome te		
foyu 'bark'	+				
fuku 'deepen'	−		fuke te		

V-3-A	HH-L	HH-H[12]	HH-L H	HH-L	HH-H
kataru 'tell'	+	*kataru	! katarī te[14]	*katari	*katarī
kazaru 'adorn'	+				kazari
ikaru 'get angry	+		! īka[ri] te[13]		īkarī
kitaru 'come'	+				
saguru 'grope for'	+				
fodasu 'shackle'	+				fodasi
itasu 'bring'	+				
nurasu 'wet it'	+				
sakebu 'yell'	+				
sukumu 'crouch'	+		sukum[u] de		

V-3-A < 4	HH-L	HH-HH	HH-L H	HH-L	HH-H
fazimu 'begin it'	+	*fazimuru	fazime te	*fazime	fazime
kasanu 'layer it'	+		kasane te		kasane
sasafu 'support'	+				
tuidu 'order'	+				tuide
umaru 'get born'	+				
osafu 'press'	! osafu,				
(< ōs[i] afu)	osafu				

V-3-B	LL-H	LL-L	LL-H	H	LL-H	LL-L
tutumu 'bundle'	+	*tutumu	*tutumi̅	te	*tutumi̅	tutumi
uramu 'resent'	+					urami
agaku 'paw'	+		agai̅	te		
we-kaku 'draw'	+		we-kai̅	te		
omofu 'think'	+					omofi
yosofu 'garb'	+		yosofu̅	te		
yurufu 'loosen it'	+		yurufi̅	te		
afugu 'fan'	+					
fuker-u 'addicted'	+					
mabaru 'look at'	+					
mamoru 'guard'	+					
modir-u 'twist'	+					
fitasu 'steep'	+					
kakusu 'hide it' !	kakusu̅, kaku̅su					

V-3-B < 4	LL-H	LL-LL	LL-H	H	LL-H	LL-L
afasu 'join them'	+	*afasuru	afase̅	te	*afase̅	*afase

V-4-A	HHH-L	HHH-H	HHH-L	H	HHH-L	HHH-H
adifafu 'taste'	+	*adi̅fafu	*adi̅fafi̅	te	*adi̅fafi̅	adi̅fafi
okonafu 'act'	+					
sitagafu 'follow'	+		sitagafi̅	te		
utagafu 'doubt'	+					utagafi̅
itadaku 'crowned'	+					itadaki̅
kakayaku 'shine'	+		kakayai̅	te		
kuturogu 'relax'	+					
okotaru 'shirk'	+					

V-4-B	LLH-L[16]	LLL-L	LLH-L H	LLH-L	LLL-L
ayamatu 'err'	+	*ayamatu	ayamati te	ayamati	
ayamaru 'err'	+			ayamari	
itufaru 'busy'	+		itufari te		
kotowaru 'reject'	+				
matagaru 'straddle'	+				
mazifaru 'mingle'	+			mazifari	
tatakafu 'fight'	+				
tukurofu 'mend'	+				
odoroku 'surprised'	+				
sirizoku 'retreat'	+				
yorokobu 'rejoice'	+				yorokobi

V-4-B ‹ 5	LLH-L[16]	LLL-L	LLH-L H	LLH-L	LLL-L
kam(u)gafu 'think'	+	*kam(u)gafuru	*kam(u)gafi te	*kam(u)gafe	*kam(u)gafe

There are also a few verbs with one-syllable infinitives, for which some of the forms are available with early accent notations. These are listed below according to type. (On lengthening the vowel of monosyllabic infinitives, see §2, n.3.)

	Predicative	Attributive	Infinitive	Gerund
fu 'pass'	fú (= fuu)	*furu	fé (= fee)	fe te
ku 'come'	kú (= kuū)	*kuru	*kí (= kiī)	
su 'do'	sū[17]	suru	*sī ‹ *sì = sīi	sī te
kiru 'wear'	kīru	*kīru	*kī ‹ *kì = kīi[18]	ki te[19]
niru 'resemble'	nīru	*nīru	*nī ‹ *nì = nīi	---[20]
iru 'shoot; cast'	īru	*īru[21]	*ī ‹ *ì = īi	
firu 'winnow'	fīru[22]	*fīru	*fī ‹ *fì = fīi	
firu 'dry'	fīru[22]			
miru 'see'	mirū[23]	*mirū[24]	mí (= mii) › mī[25]	

And there are a few citations of longer verbs in Myōgi-shō; we presume that
the accentuation of the paradigmatic forms will be similar to those of the shorter
verbs. In Type V-5-A we find both obiyakasu 'intimidate' and tukasadoru 'manage',
with HHHH-L for the predicative; but exceptionally tukamaturu 'serve' suggests a
contraction from a compound verb — and it is tukamaturu in Kōzan-ji Myōgi-shō,
tukamaturu in Nihon-Shoki (tukamaturu according to Okada). In Type V-5-B, with the
predicative LLLH-L, Myōgi-shō has amanetasu 'extend widely', firugaferu / firugaferu
'flutter', kasikomaru 'humble oneself', and titifakuru 'break out with measles'.
But the anomalous pattern LLL(-)L-H is found in kokoro-miru 'try', kaferi-miru
'look back', and kaferi-utu 'revenge'; the pattern of the final verb dominates,
and the first element is atonicized.

8.2. Accent patterns of verb stems.

Only two basic categories, here called A and B, are needed to account for the
accentual behavior of Japanese verb stems, provided we set aside certain special
developments. The special developments are as follows.

(1) A few stems such as aruk- 'walk' and kakus- 'hide it', together with some of
their derivatives, had a "third" pattern of LH-L (aruku) for the predicative and
the infinitive in the 11th century. They retain this pattern in modern Toyama and
Takamatsu (Kindaichi 1942:170). A few Kinki dialects, notably Kōchi and Tanabe,
retain the Muromachi pattern LH-H that is reflected in Bumō-ki (kakusu). But Kyōto
and other Kinki dialects now use the pattern LL-H (aruku) and that is in contrast
with the larger number of three-syllable consonant stems such as ugok- 'move' which
had the 11th-century pattern LL-H (ugoku 'move') but were later absorbed into the
HH-H class of modern Kyōtō (→ ugoku) while changing to a pattern HL-L (ugoku)
for the Muromachi accent reflected in Bumō-ki and for modern Kōchi, Tanabe, and
Akō; and to the modern Toyama pattern LH-L (ugoku) that neutralizes the three-way
distinction of the earlier language. At least 19 verbs of this "third" pattern,
which we will label Type B′ (LH-L in Myōgi-shō), were absorbed into Type A by
Kyōto (as if the earlier form had been LL-H):

 aburu 'roast'; erabu 'choose'; harau 'sweep'; kaburu 'put/wear on head'; kegasu
 'soil'; kegar[er]u 'get soiled'; kezuru 'comb'; kizuku 'build'; kogasu 'scorch'[26];
 morasu 'let leak'; neburu 'lick'; negau 'request'; nogar[er]u 'escape'; ogamu
 'worship'; sagaru 'descend' (B′ in Iroha-jirui-shō but no Mg examples); taosu
 'topple it'; taor[er]u 'get toppled'; terau 'show off (skill)'; tukar[er]u 'weary'.

The group of stems of modern Kyōto Type B that go back to Type B´ of the 11th century contains the following verbs:

aruku 'walk', kaka[er]u 'embrace', kakur[er]u 'hide', kakusu 'hide it', mair-u 'humbly come/go', moti[ir]u 'use', sasa[er]u 'prop', tora[er]u 'catch'.

Also the following verbs according to Umegaki, but not Hirayama (who has A):

kakag[er]u 'raise', mood[er]u 'go to worship', motag[er]u 'lift', sasag[er]u 'hold up, offer'. (For Kyōto early in the Edo period kakag[er]u and sasag[er]u are attested as B´. What are the Kōchi forms?)

These verbs are all thought to have originated as compounds or derivatives made on an initial verb of Type B; the unusual accentuation of Type B´ is the result of contracting two separate verb forms. In addition, modern Kyōto Type B includes the following longish verbs that are unattested for the 11th century:

barasu 'reveal', butukaru 'hit', damaru 'be silent', hair-u 'enter', ikedoru 'capture alive', kakawaru 'be concerned (in)' (Bumō-ki LHHH = B´), kodawaru 'oppose', koraeru 'endure/restrain', motenasu 'treat hospitably', moteamasu 'have too much', motehayasu 'laud', obuu 'carry piggyback', toraseru 'give', tukaeru 'obstruct/support'.

Also the following verbs according to Hirayama but not Umegaki (who has A):

iradatu 'get irritated', kosikakeru 'sit', kozir-u 'wrench', kozireru 'get wrenched', nomasu 'make/let drink', nomer-u 'stumble', tutaeru 'transmit', tutawaru 'get transmitted'.

And the verbs kakumau 'shelter' and sabireru 'deteriorate, get desolate' according to Umegaki, but Hirayama has A. (Hirayama's Kyōto B for niseru 'imitate' must be a mistake; other sources and other dialects treat this verb as consistently A, like its related intransitive niru.) Umegaki has B also for gutir-u 'complain', said to be from the Chinese binom gu-ti (for which Umegaki has low atonic but Hirayama high atonic); Hirayama does not list the verb. Umegaki has B for dookeru 'jest' but Hirayama has A, yet the noun dooke is low atonic for both sources; despite the traditional etymologies this word may very well not be of Chinese origin. Umegaki has B for kanguru 'surmise hidden motives' (from Chinese kan 'account' + kuru 'wind it'); Hirayama lacks the item. The group of Type B stems in modern Kyōto also includes the following verbs which were regular Type B in 11th-century Kyōto and thus ought to have joined the other longish verb stems as modern Kyōto Type A:

kotaeru 'answer', kuwaeru 'add', kuwawaru 'be added', yaburu 'tear', yabureru 'be torn', obosu/obosimesu 'deign to think'.

And according to Hirayama but not Umegaki (who has A for these) also narasu 'tame',
tukamu 'grasp' (perhaps an Umegaki misprint, cf. tukamaru 'is caught, cling' B, yet
tukamaseru 'make catch' A), and tukuru 'make'; for Umegaki and Ōhara 1932-3 also
ureeru 'grieve' (but Hirayama has A). Umegaki also has B for tasinameru 'reprove'
but that must be a misprint, since A is cited for the literary form (NKD 13:27b).
To this irregular group (modern Kyōto B), Kyōto has added certain verbs that were
earlier Type A, including koru 'harden' (also B in Tōkyō) and these longer stems:

> asobu 'play'[27], sakeru 'avoid', useru 'vanish', u[zu]meru 'bury', u[zu]maru /
> u[zu]moreru 'be buried', wabiru 'apologize'; according to Umegaki also sasou
> 'entice, invite' (but Hirayama has A).

And, according to Hirayama but not Umegaki (who has A), also these ten verbs:

> hirau = hirou 'pick up', horeru 'love', kagu 'smell', kaku 'lack', masu 'increase'
> saru 'depart', sou 'follow', suteru 'discard', ueru 'plant', uwaru 'be planted'.

The verb stem ue- 'plant' was Type A in Kyōto perhaps as late as 1687, when it was
so treated in Bumō-ki (cf. Tsuzuku 1951:402, Sakurai 1977:851b "uyu"), though the
accents in that work are thought to reflect an earlier period; both ue- 'plant' and
sute- 'discard' are A in other Kinki dialects (Hyōgo, Toyama, Suzu, Kōchi, Sakawa).
This appears to be true of some of the other verbs, as well; cf. Kindaichi 1942.169
(which is divergent with respect to a few of the modern Kyōto forms that he cites).
Five verbs that were Type A in 11th-century Kyōto (and are Type A in Kagoshima) have
become B in both Kyōto and Tōkyō:

> koru 'harden', kuwadateru 'plan' (but Umegaki has A for Kyōto), turanaru 'join
> in a row', turanuku 'pierce through', and (Tōkyō optionally A) takuwaeru 'save/
> store up' (but Umegaki has A for Kyōto).

The verbs yozir-u 'twist', yozireru 'get twisted', and kaker-u 'soar' were A in
Myōgi-shō but are B in Tōkyō, Kyōto, and Kagoshima. (The verb emu 'smile' was A
earlier but NKD gives B for Tōkyō and Kyōto, though the verb is now in disuse.) The
verb tottuku 'obsess', Type B in Kyōto and either A or B in Tōkyō, is a contraction
of the compound tori-tuku, based on a B infinitive; the derived noun tottuki means
'approach; beginning'. The verb ker-u < ke-ru 'kick' is B in most modern dialects,
but A in Kyōto, Hyōgo, and Kōchi (B in Toyama), and Myōgi-shō has evidence for both.

(2) The stem [w]or- 'be, stay' is accentually irregular in a number of modern
Kinki dialects, such as Kōchi o͞ru with the unique pattern H-L (Hattori 1931-3:2:
178), but not in Kyōto, where it is regular Type A (o͞r͞u with the pattern H-H), as

it is in the corresponding reflexes of Kagoshima and Shuri. In Tōkyō and the Chūgoku
dialects the verb is unexpectedly Type B, with paradigmatic irregularities in at
least one dialect, that of Okayama; cf. Kindaichi 1964a:369-7 (and see Chart 9).[28]
But oru 'be' is Type A in the Tōkyō-type dialects of Hata (Doi 1952:29), Hattō,
Matsue, and Izumo; in the enclave of Totsukawa; and also in NE Kyūshū (Hirayama
1951a:180). Kindaichi believes the irregular developments come from an unusual type
in the proto language (we can call it Type A´), which he thinks had the pattern *H-L
for all forms of this verb, including the attributive that is the source of the
modern imperfect: *w̄oru (koto) instead of *wor̄u (koto). (Such a view lends support
to the hypothesis that this verb was originally a compound: *w̄i- ar-.) If Kindaichi
is correct, that means that Modern Kyōto (and perhaps even Kyōto of the eleventh
century, for which we lack the needed attestation) regularized the forms as normal
Type A. The stem or- 'weave' is irregularly B in Kyōto according to Hirayama but
Umegaki has regular A; the stem is irregularly B in Tōkyō (but A is "permissible"
according to Kindaichi 1958a), yet apparently it is A in other Tōkyō-type dialects
(Narada, Hamada, Matsue, Izumo). The Kagoshima verb is irregularly B, unless that
is a misprint in Hirayama, but the derived noun is A.

The stem ok- 'put' is unexpectedly Type B ōku in dialects of Shizuoka, Nagano,
and Yamanashi (Kindaichi 1943:2:13a) but regular Type A in Tōkyō, Hiroshima (and
the entire Chūgoku area), and Ōita.

And the stem um- 'give birth' is Type B in Sapporo, Akita, and the Kun[i]naka
section of Yamanashi (Watanabe 1957:188); also in Chiba, where Kindaichi (1977a:142)
says that ko o u'mu replaced the earlier ko o na'su for 'bear a child' and, being
new, was simply given the prevailing-type accent pattern for verb stems.

(3) The verbs sinu 'die' and inu 'pass away' are regular consonant stems of Type
A in modern dialects, but they are the only stems that end in the dental nasal /n/.
Earlier they were ambivalent (consonant/vowel) stems of a hybrid conjugation with
such forms as sinu (predicative), sinuru (attributive), sini (infinitive), sinure-
[ba/-do] (hypothetical/concessive), sina-[ba/mu] (subjunctive/future), and sine (the
imperative). Kindaichi believes these verbs originally had a FALL (instead of just
LOW) on the ending of the predicative *s̄inù[29] and that of the infinitive *s̄inì,
like verbs of Type B (with FALL instead of HIGH): consonant stems such as tat-
'stand' with the forms tatù and tatì (also hypothetical tatè-); vowel stems such
as uk(e)- 'receive' with the forms ukù and ukè (but hypothetical *uk̄ure-).

(4) In Tōkyō the vowel dyad is treated as a single syllable in verbs such as
t̄oosu, k̄aer-u, and k̄aesu; these verbs are regular (to͞osu, kaer̄-u, kae͞su) in certain
accentually similar dialects, such as those of the Chūgoku area. But the two verbs
m̄air-u and h̄air-u stay prototonic in places like Nagoya, Hiroshima, etc., unlike
the other verbs (kae͞ru, too͞ru, ...); they have a different history, as can be seen
from the way Kyōto treats them. Cf. Kindaichi 1977b:464. Yet in NE Kyūshū these verb
are ma͞ir-u and ha͞ir-u according to Hirayama 1951a:183. The dialects of the Tōkyō typ
described by Hiroto and Ōhara offer irregular data. Hattō and Goka-mura have too'su
but Hamada and Izumo have to'osu, while Matsue uses both versions; all have to'oru
except for too'ru in Goka-mura; moo'su is reported for Hattō and Goka-mura, but
mo'osu for Hamada, Matsue, and Izumo. Yet kae'r-u and kae'su are the only versions
reported for all five dialects.

     Also in Tōkyō the devoicing of high vowels will shift the basic locus of accent
to the right (so that it gets realized on a voiced syllable) either optionally or
obligatorily in certain verbs, such as tuk̄u (ga) 'arrives (but)', yet the underlying
accent is often revealed by paradigmatic forms not subject to the vowel devoicing:
t̄uita 'arrived'. And the accent remains as expected (t̄uku) in dialects such as those
of the Chūgoku area, where vowel devoicing is less prevalent. In general we will
ignore these presumably late innovations in the surface forms of Tōkyō verbs.

(5) The assignment of a verb stem to Type A or Type B in a modern dialect is not
always a reliable guide to the earlier assignment. In particular, the absorption
into Type A of Kyōto longer stems that were originally Type B requires us to check
elsewhere before we can be sure which of the longer stems were originally Type A.
Kagoshima is a safer guide, but exceptional assignments turn up there, too, as can
be seen when all the other dialects, including Shuri, are in joint disagreement with
the Kagoshima type. When the 11th-century accentuation is attested, usually that
will settle a question of assignment, but there may be a few stems that Myōgi-shō
assigned differently from the proto language: azukeru 'put in trust' is A in Myōgi-
shō and modern Kyōto but B in Tōkyō, Kagoshima, and Shuri; kuwadateru < kufatateru
'raise one's toes (in anticipation), undertake, plan' is A in Myōgi-shō, but B in
Tōkyō and Kagoshima — and (according to Hirayama but not Umegaki) in modern Kyōto.
(The verb is not reported for the Ryūkyū dialects.) Most of the verb stems that have
conflicting type assignments will be found in the lists of Charts 9, 10, and 11.
Notice that Tōkyō speakers tend to assume that an unfamiliar or little-spoken verb
is tonic, like the majority of familiar verbs (Kindaichi 1972:424), and that will
account for a number of the variants.

(6) Among the Tōkyō-type dialects, that of Goka-mura on Oki island appears to be unique in shifting longer verbs of Type B into Type A: arasou, atumaru, atumeru, azukaru, azukeru, tazuneru, ... This is reminiscent of what Kyōto does, but there is a difference, for Kyōto merges Type B stems into Type A when the infinitive is three or more syllables so that both sodati 'grow up' and sodate 'raise' become Type A, but Goka-mura merges the Type B stems into Type A when the imperfect is four or more syllables, so that sodatu remains B while sodateru is A. (Similarly, awasu is B but awaseru is A.)

(7) At least four verb stems had the unusual pattern of HLH- in the 11th century; they are thought to be contractions of two words each, the first a Type A infinitive or noun and the second a Type B verb.

The verb osaeru 'restrain, press back/down', attested in Myōgi-shō as ōsaf̄u and ōsafu (the latter is also found in Kamakura and Muromachi attestations), is probably contracted from the infinitive ōsi 'press' + the Type B stem af(e)- 'join'; the modern Kyōto and Kagoshima type is A, but Tōkyō has B, and the Kyōto type in the early-Edo period is attested as B.

The verb hos-su(ru) < fos-su(ru) 'desire', attested in Myōgi-shō as fo[s]su, is from *fori su[su] with the infinitive of the old Type A stem for- < *por- 'desire'; hos-suru is Type B in modern Kyōto and Kagoshima, A or B in Tōkyō, following the canonical patterns of bound verbal nouns.

The obsolete verb modasu 'keep silent; do not speak', attested in Myōgi-shō as m̄odasù and m̄odas̄u and modasu, and in Iroha-jirui-shō as módasu, is thought to be sù = s̄u[u] 'do' attached to the Old Japanese verbal noun moda 'not speaking' (the accent is unattested), which may be cognate with the Korean negative adverb mo:t 'not possibly'.[30] (The stem is attested as m̄odas- in Shiza-Kōshiki of the Kamakura period and in Heike-mabushi of the early-Edo period.)

The verb simesu 'show, indicate', given in Myōgi-shō as s̄im̄es̄u / s̄imesu > s̄imesu (attested in both the Kamakura and the early-Edo periods) > (?) simes̄u > simes̄u > (modern Kyōto) s̄imes̄u, with Kagoshima A and Tōkyō either A or B, is perhaps from the infinitive *s̄i[i] 'do' + mesù = mes̄u = mes̄u[u] 'see', as Ōno suggests, or from an otherwise unexplained noun *s̄ime + sù = s̄u[u] 'do', as Kindaichi suggests. But, though hos-su(ru) retains the irregular conjugation of su(ru) 'do' and (according to Kindaichi 1954) modasu retained that conjugation till Kamakura times, simesu has been treated as a consonant stem ending in /s/ throughout historic times. The shift of ⋯-su(ru) → ⋯s- is quite common all through the history of the language, however, as can be seen from modern zoku-sanai/-sinai 'does not belong' (cf. RGJ 378, 873).

In addition, Mochizuki gives Kōzan-ji Myōgi-shō citations of RLH/LLH for turubu 'mate' (the first pattern is odd) and of Rxx/LHL for makaru 'humbly go/come (to report)'.

8.3. Accent patterns of compound verbs.

Our two basic accentual categories are Type A and Type B. Stems of Type A begin with a HIGH pitch in Myōgi-shō and in modern Kinki dialects; those of Type B begin with a LOW pitch. Derived stems such as the passive and the causative are normally accentuated as A or B in accordance with the inherent accentuation of the underlying stem. But in Kyōto the longer stems become A: motas[er]u, mitasu, and tarasu are A though motu, mitiru, and tareru are B; sasaru 'be stuck' is A though sasu 'stick' and its regular passive sasareru are B. As an exception, Hirayama gives narasu as B (like nareru) but Umegaki has A for narasu. There are also exceptions like the verb meiwaku-garu 'find it a nuisance', which retains the B register of the adjectival noun meīwaku.

A compound verb consists of a verb infinitive attached to a following verb. In some of the compound verbs, the second member is used as an auxiliary. In others, the first member has lost most of its meaning and is used as a kind of prefix (uti- 'hit and' just intensifies). But in many compounds both verbs contribute fully to the meaning of the resulting form, which may or may not carry the grammar (the valences) of one or the other of the component verbs, or of both.

In the dialects of southern Kyūshū and the Ryūkyūs and in those of the Kinki area, ompound verbs maintain the accentual category of the first verb. If the compound begins with the infinitive of a verb of Type A, it will be accentuated as Type A; if the compound begins with the infinitive of a verb of Type B, it will be accentuated as Type B.[31] In 11th-century Kyōto the verbs of Type A began HIGH and continued that pitch through the stem; the verbs of Type B began LOW and continued that pitch through the stem. (But when an ending was attached to a 3-syllable stem to make a 4-syllable form, the final low metathesized with the basic high of the ending: yorokob- + -ū → yorokōbu 'rejoice'. Similarly

for stems of four and five syllables.) In the Ryūkyūs and in southern Kyūshū what
corresponds to the initial high is a fall to low pitch. In the Shuri dialect the low
pitch sets in early, typically after the first or second syllable. In the Kagoshima
dialect the high pitch that marks all words of Type A is placed on the next-to-last
syllable of the word (within a monosyllable a fall is heard); words of Type B put an
automatic high on the last syllable, and that high automatically moves over when a
particle is attached.

The modern Kyōto dialect resembles the 11th-century system found in Myōgi-shō,
but the modern dialect has let Type A, with its high initial, absorb all the Type B
simple verbs of three or more syllables except for the irregular ones like kakure-
mentioned earlier; and Type A has also absorbed all Type B consonant verbs of two
or more syllables: u̅gok- ← ugok- 'move', y̅orokob- ← yorokob- 'rejoice'.[32]
Exceptions such as aruk- ← a̅ru̅k-, as earlier mentioned, are thought to be the
result of contracting compound verbs.[33] In saying that the "simple" verbs were
absorbed, we mean to include causatives and passives (kak̅u̅ 'write', k̅akaseru̅ 'cause
to write', k̅akareru̅ 'get written' — Okumura 1975c:168); according to Hirayama
1960:19 kakaseru̅ and kakareru̅ also occur but they are less common. (Hirayama cites
yomaseru, nomaseru, kuwaseru, and sasareru as B, but Umegaki gives them as A.
Kuwaseru 'feed, ... ' is attested as B for Kyōto in the early-Edo period.) But we do
not mean to include compound verbs, for they are regularly accentuated according to
the (modern) type of the initial member. Any "long" stem with the accentual pattern
of Type B must, therefore, be one of these compounds, such as kaki-naos- 'rewrite',
aruki-tuzuke- 'continue to walk', aruki-mawar- 'walk around', nage-sute- 'throw
away', and uke-tamawar- 'humbly hear'. If the initial verb is one that originally
was Type B but has become modern Kyōto Type A, the modern accentuation prevails:
k̅angae-naos- 'rethink', k̅angae-tuzuke- 'continue to think', k̅angae-das- 'recall',
from k̅angae- ← k̅anga[f]u̅.

The absorption into Type A of the longer Type B verbs did not take place in
some of the other Kinki dialects such as Kōchi, which retains a "B" category that
is marked by a low on the second syllable of 3-syllable verbs (u̅goku 'move',
i̅kiru 'live') and on the third syllable of 4-syllable verbs (y̅orokobu 'rejoice',
atuumeru 'gather'); this is the pattern of Kyōto in the Muromachi period (as
attested in Bumō-ki) and in the early-Edo period (as attested in Heike-mabushi).
The accentuation of compound verbs in all Kinki dialects is like that of Kyōto:
it follows the accent type of the verb that is the first member of the compound.

The Tōkyō rules for compound verbs, however, have some interesting twists. As in the other dialects, in Tōkyō the first verb determines the accentuation of the compound. Formations such as the causative and the passive are given the same accent as the verb stem at the beginning; this is true of all Tōkyō-type dialects. Those stems of historical Type A are atonic, with non-distinctive lowering for the first syllable and high pitch throughout the stem, and into the ending, and the same is true of the derived forms:

ki= 'wear', ur= 'sell', ake- 'open it', susum- 'advance', tuzuke- 'continue it', hatarak- 'work', ... ; ur-ase- 'make one sell', ur-ase-rare- 'be made to sell'.

Those stems of historical Type B are tonic, with the accent realized as a fall to low pitch after the last syllable of the stem, and the pitch of the other syllables automatically determined; the derived forms are similar:

mi- 'see', kak- 'write', tabe- 'eat', hanas- 'speak', yorokob- 'rejoice', mi-rare- 'get looked at', tabe-sase-rare- 'be made to eat', yorokob-ase- 'gladden'

In polysyllabic vowel stems the accent retreats one syllable when endings are attached that begin with /t/, namely the gerund and forms derived by amalgamation with it: tabe-te, tabe-ta, tabe-tara, tabe-tari; tabesaserare-te, ... The retreat occurs in Tōkyō and Hiroshima, in Hata on Shikoku (Doi 1952:30), in Yamaguchi, and in NE Kyūshū (Hirayama 1951a:181,184); but not in Izumo or Aomori (Kobayashi 1975:78, 100), nor in Nagoya (Tsuzuku 1941:386).[34]   And in Niigata (Hirayama 1953:109) the accent retreats only from unvoiced /i/: okite 'arising' but nigete 'fleeing'. The "retreat" version tabe-te must be older than the paradigm-regularizing version tabe-te because it preserves the accent of the infinitive (tabe) and is in regular correspondence with the Kyōto tabe-te just as Tōkyō's kabuto 'helmet' is in regular correspondence with Kyōto's kabuto; cf. Tsuzuku 1951:386.

In Tōkyō the oxytonic accent basic to infinitives of atonic stems is cancelled when the gerund ending -te is attached: ate (wa) + te → atete (wa) 'applying', kasane (wa) + te → kasanete (wa) 'layering', wasure (wa) + te → wasurete (wa) 'forgetting'. But in Totsukawa, most of Owari, and most of Gifu (Tsuzuku 1941:186, 1951:390) the basic accent of the infinitive survives (atete, kasanete, wasurete), and southwestern Shikoku is said to be similar; this is true also for the perfect: Hata aketa (Doi 1952:30). In a part of Tōkyō metropolis, Ōme-machi in Nishi-Tama-gun, ateta and ateta are in free variation (Tsuzuku 1951:390). In one dialect of Chiba, Kitajō of Tateyama-shi, the suspensive use of the gerund ('does and')

preserves the infinitive accent (atete) but when an auxiliary follows, the accent
is lost (atete iru), as is true for the perfect (ateta); Tsuzuku (ibid.) does not
say what happens when a focus particle is attached but I would expect it to be like
Tōkyō (atete wa). From the literature it is unclear whether the above remarks hold
also for the one-syllable infinitives, ? nite for Tōkyō nite (wa) 'resembling', and
for the consonant stems: ? kasite for Tōkyō kasite (wa) 'lending', ? kiite for
kiite (wa) 'hearing', ? kaide for kaide (wa) 'smelling', ? yonde for yonde (wa)
'calling', ? sinde for sinde (wa) 'dying', ? katte / koote for katte (wa) 'buying',
? katte for katte (wa) 'mowing'. We would expect the accent to shift in some of
these forms because of the weak syllable/mora before the -te; if the accent shifts
forward, to the right, the forms end up identical with the Tōkyō versions. Tsuzuku
(1951:411) cites his own Hagiwara (Gifu) oita 'put' and suggests that it comes from
earlier o[k]ita, like Totsukawa oita.

   With the Tōkyō compound verbs, too, it is the infinitive at the beginning that
determines the accent of the compound. For older speakers the accentuation of the
compound is the result of a polarity-reversing (or "alpha-switch") rule: regardless
of the accent type of the second verb, if the first verb is Type A the compound is
Type B; if the first verb is Type B the compound is Type A. This can lead to the odd
result that the accent type shifts back and forth each time an additional auxiliary
is attached, as described in RGJ 440. But younger speakers make all compound verbs
tonic, regardless of the components. Except for the passives and causatives, which
follow the older rules (akesaserare- 'be made to open' for old and young alike), few
longish atonic verb forms will be heard from younger speakers. At first glance we
wonder whether the polarity-switch rule for accentuating compound verbs might be
telling us something about an older stage of the language, but a closer look reveals
that an important part of this rule for the "older" speakers may actually be little
more than a hundred years old (cf. Akinaga 1967). To begin with, when the initial
infinitive is tonic and more than two syllables long, there is often an alternative
old-fashioned Tōkyō version which treats the compound as a syntactic reduction that
keeps intact the accent of the infinitive itself: omoi-dasu for omoi-dasu (younger
omoi-dasu) 'recall', kaziri-tuku for kaziri-tuku (younger kaziri-tuku) 'bites
into'. The formal expressions osore-iru and osore-irimasu 'excuse me; thank you'
apparently occur ONLY in this version, for the younger as well as the older Tōkyō
speakers; we would expect to hear (?*)osore-iru and (?*)osore-iru and certainly

(?*)o̲sore-iri-ma̲su, since the polite auxiliary (V-i-)m̄as-u is unique in dominating the accent of the infinitive to which it is attached. (There is at least one example with a shorter infinitive: k̄oki-tukeru 'drive one hard'.) According to Ōhara 1942:103, in the Tōkyō-type dialects of the Chūgoku area of Honshū and also in southwestern Shikoku, this syntactic-reduction pattern is used whenever the first infinitive is tonic, whether long or short: t̄ori-dasu 'take out' for Tōkyō tor̄i-dasu (younger tori-da̲su), n̄age-tukeru 'throw and hit' for Tōkyō nage-tukeru (younger nage-tuke̲ru), as well as oyo̲gi-mawaru 'swim around' for the usual Tōkyō oyogi-mawaru (younger oyogi-mawa̲ru). Tsuzuku 1951:963 says the same thing is true for eastern and northern Gifu, Ina-machi in Shinano, Hata in Shikoku, and Ōme-machi in the western part of Tōkyō metropolis. Kindaichi reports similar patterns for Yamanashi, Nagano (cf. Kudō 1978:218), and Gunma prefectures (Akinaga 1967:136). This pattern (the syntactic reduction) seems to be the earlier treatment for all the Tōkyō-type dialects; it represents a stage that is later than that of the days when the two verbs were pronounced not yet as a compound but as loosely joined phrases, with separate accentuations for the infinitive and the following verb.

But our present-day evidence applies only to the tonic infinitives. How did the atonic infinitives come to make tonic compounds? According to Tsuzuku 1951, in the Chūgoku areas mentioned above and in Gifu and the other areas a compound verb retains the basic oxytonic accent[35] of the infinitive of an atonic stem: yob̄i-dasu, nor̄i-mawasu, sagas̄i-dasu, hakobi-dasu, hiro̱i-atumeru, hataraki-hazimeru. This is true also of the Tōkyō-type dialects of Hattō and Goka-mura (Hiroto and Ōhara).[36] In Izumo (Tsuzuku 1951:396, with the notation adjusted), the accent type of the compound is the same as the accent type of the first verb: tori-da̲su from t̄or-i · 'take' but yob̄i-dasu from yob̄-i 'call'; oyogi-mawaru from oyog-i 'swim' but yob̄i-yoseru 'call over' from yob̄-i 'call'. In this respect Izumo resembles the two-pattern dialects of southern Kyūshū and the Ryūkyūs, as well as Kyōto; but the phonetic realization of the accent types follows that of the Chūgoku dialects, which are Tōkyō-type.[37]

Tsuzuku suggests that the Tōkyō tonic accentuation for the compounds with an atonic initial verb (such as yob̄i-dasu, hakobi-da̲su, and hataraki-hazime̲ru) developed from an earlier version like that used in Gifu and in the Chūgoku area (yob̄i-dasu, hakob̄i-dasu, hataraki-hazimeru); Tōkyō speakers retained the tonicity

of the infinitive when tightening the compound, rather than cancel it (together
with its realization as the oxytonic accent) before dropping the juncture, but then
realized the resulting tonic verb according to the canonical patterns for tonic
simple verbs or single-stem derivatives such as ugoku, atumeru, kokokorozasu,
atumesaseru, tabesaserareru, atumesaserareru, kokorozasaserareru, ...
In Tsuzuku's native dialect of Hagiwara (Gifu prefecture, Tsuzuku 1951:399),
longish forms of compound verbs have the option of following the tonic canonical
patterns: nage-tukeru or nage-tukeru, ugoki-hazimeru or ugoki-hazimeru,
hataraki-hazimeru or hataraki-hazimeru. And this includes longish forms of
compound verbs that in shorter paradigmatic forms do not enjoy the option:
tori-dasan or tori-dasan 'won't take out' but presumably only tori-dasu and not
*tori-dasu. (Tsuzuku is unclear on this point, but his "longish" apparently means
at least five syllables long.) This is the rule now followed by the younger Tōkyō
speakers, on a regular basis rather than optionally, for all compound verbs.
Tsuzuku (1951:397) suggests that the older-generation Tōkyō development of earlier
tori-dasu to the atonic tori-dasu was due to a feeling that there is something odd
about prototonic words in general, and he compares more recent atonicizations such
as densya > densya, but I share Akinaga's distrust of this explanation, since that
would not account (except perhaps by analogy) for the fact that oyogi-hazimeru
developed into oyogi-hazimeru, and in any event prototonic accents are freely
maintained in forms like tabete and tabetara despite paradigmatic pressures to
regularize them to tabete and tabetara, as in some of the other Tōkyō-type dialects.

    There was probably a time lag in tightening the compounds with the infinitives
of tonic (Type B) stems, as compared with those made on the oxytonic infinitives of
atonic stems. During that period of lag, the polarity-reversing rule set in and at
least briefly flourished, only to be replaced by an extension of the "tonicizing"
rule that was a part of it. The lag is partly reflected in the oldest attested
pattern we have for Tōkyō: omoi-dasu, hakobi-dasu; tori-dasu, yobi-dasu. We can
explain three of these four patterns as follows: yobi[ˈ|]daˈsu → yobidaˈsu,
hakobi[ˈ|]daˈsu → hakobidaˈsu, omoˈi[|]daˈsu → omoˈidasu. The last stage of
the fourth form is the puzzle: toˈri[|]daˈsu → toˈridasu → toridasuˈ. A rather
similar situation with a time lag can perhaps be discerned in contemporary speech,
where kono neko 'this cat' is usually said as a single phrase but dono | neko
'which cat' is said as two phrases, with reduced accent on the second; similarly,
notta hikooki 'the plane I boarded' but orita | hikooki 'the plane I got off'.

In Heian times V-i V was pronounced with separate accentuations of the two
verbs. The phrase juncture is not always obvious from the notation, but we can
safely follow Kindaichi in assuming it for cases like sasí ōku and ide masu by
analogy with the clear cases like fíki wíru and seme tóru (cf. Sakurai 1960:73b
n.6.) Notice that the phrase (or accentual) juncture does not necessarily drop
immediately with the various syllable reductions, lenitions, and assimilations known
collectively as "onbin" which developed during the Heian period: ōki te, oi te, and
ōite coexist in Myōgi-shō.[38] We can see something similar today in the juncture
that we infer from the retained but reduced accent of the second component of such
contracted constructions as [hanaš:tokīmaš:ta] = hana'sit[e] | okima'sita.[39]
From the documentary evidence Sakurai (1960:69a) concludes that the compound verbs
(perhaps starting with verb + the gerund particle te?) were tightened into single
phrases during the "chūsei" period of Late Middle Japanese (1200-1600), beginning
with early-Kamakura examples found in Shiza-Kōshiki. A comparable tightening can be
seen in the contemporary Tōkyō treatment of certain gerund-auxiliary expressions:

  (1) the loss of accent by motte 'holding' in expressions of "bringing/taking"
with verbs of movement (RGJ 513-4) as contrasted with recent syntactic reductions
such as mite-toru 'grasp, take in';

  (2) the initial accent acquired by the /t/-ending forms of the auxiliary oku
after atonic gerunds (RGJ 539), as in utatte oita and utatt oita 'got it sung';

  (3) the retention of the basic accent of the atonic gerund when the initial i- of
the /t/-ending forms of iru 'be' is elided (RGJ 914-5), as in utatte ta contracted
from utatte ita 'was singing'.

Similar, and perhaps more extensive, phenomena are reported (by Tsuzuku) for Nagoya
and Gifu and (by Kindaichi) also for Shimoda and Hamamatsu; see Akinaga 1967:136.
Tsuzuku (1951:387-8) observes that in Nagoya the expression of purpose V-i ni iku
'go to V' is run together as a complex atonic phrase, and that is true not only of
asobi ni iku 'go to play' (which is the same in Tōkyō though related dialects have
the expected asobi ni | iku) but also of otosi ni iku 'go to drop it' where Tōkyō
has otosi ni | iku. It is unclear what happens to these Nagoya expressions when a
focus particle is intruded; in Tōkyō the particle imposes a juncture but that does
not affect the irregularly cancelled accent of the oxytonic infinitive of an atonic
stem: asobi ni wa | ikimasen 'I won't go to PLAY', otosi ni wa | ikimasen 'I won't
go to DROP it'. In Nagoya and Gifu (id. 388) the gerund-auxiliary expressions
V-te kuru, V-te iku, V-te aru, and V-te yaru are run together, with the gerund

losing its accent: huite kuru 'it starts to blow' (Tōkyō huite | kuru); tatetaru ←
tatete aru 'it is built' (Tōkyō tatete aru). Tsuzuku (ibid.) cites an example of a
double auxiliary from Itō-machi in Shizuoka: mite kite miru 'I'll try going to have
a look at it'. The gerund-auxiliary expressions are often reduced to a single phrase
in Tōkyō but the auxiliary then loses its accent after the gerund of a tonic verb:
tabete miru = tabete | miru 'I'll try eating it'. The bound polite auxiliary -masu
is given a dominant tonic accent in Tōkyō: agemasu from ageru 'give' as well as
tabemasu from taberu 'eat'. But for the older speakers in Hagiwara, the former is
agemasu — and we would expect the latter to be (?) tabemasu. The Kinki dialects use
regular compound-verb patterns: Kyōto agemasu ← ageru, tabemasu ← taberu.[40]

For an overview of compound verbs, see Chart 12.

8.4. Accent patterns of infinitive-derived nouns.

In dialects like those of Kagoshima and Shuri, which have only two accentual
patterns, the accent of the derived noun is identical with that of the infinitive.
There appear to be only a few exceptions, e.g. Kagoshima has Type B accent for oi
'the old' but Type A for the verb 'get old'. (Nakijin and Yonaguni also give the
same accents to the derived noun and the infinitive.)

In 11th-century Kyōto the derived noun was atonic high for stems of Type A and
atonic low for stems of Type B, while the infinitive was marked by a change of pitch
from that of the stem:

kobi 'flatter', kobi 'flattery'; fazime 'begin', fazime 'the beginning'.

kumi or kumi (*kumii) 'assemble', kumi 'a set'; nokori or nokori (*nokorii)
'remain', nokori 'what remains'; (*ayamat-i →) ayamati 'make a blunder',
ayamati 'a blunder'.

But the noun sometimes fails to atonicize: the Maeda text of Nihon-Shoki has umi no
'of birth' (Ishizuka 1978:133a).

Modern Kyōto has a change of pitch at the end of the infinitive form, such that
it can be heard only when another element is attached:

iki˥ wa sen 'will not go', iki˥-soo ya 'is about to go';

yomi˥ wa sen 'will not read', yomi˥-soo ya 'is about to read';

kakusi˥ wa sen 'will not hide it', kakusi˥-soo ya 'is about to hide it'.

When the infinitive appears before juncture at the end of a phrase, as a substitute
for the gerund meaning 'does and' (the "suspensive" use), the accent of consonant-
stem infinitives retreats one syllable provided that syllable is not the first of a

low-register word: i'ki 'goes and', aga'ri 'rises and', kaku'si 'hides it and';
but yomi' 'reads and' and kake' 'hangs and' do not let the accent retreat. From what
Kobayashi says (unfortunately without examples), the retreat does not occur with
vowel stems: ake' not ?*ake 'opens it and', hazime' not ?*hazi'me 'begins it and',
kakure' not ?*kaku're 'hides and', nomisugi' not ?*nomisu'gi 'overdrinks and'.
(In my treatment, which differs from Kobayashi's interpretation, the infinitives of
both Type A and Type B are basically oxytonic but in phrase-final position the
realization of the final accent is anticipated — moved left — by one syllable.)

Nouns derived from infinitives of verbs that are Type A in modern Kyōto are
regularly atonic high: iki (ga) 'outbound journey', kasi (ga) 'lending, renting
out', ake (ga) 'opening, dawn', tuzuki (ga) 'continuation', hazime (ga) 'beginning',
matomari (ga) 'orderly assemblage', akogare (ga) 'longing'. But nouns derived from
infinitives of Type A verbs that were originally Type B usually lower all but the
first syllable: ha'nasi 'talk', ya'sumi 'rest period', na'gare 'stream'. In Kōchi
only the last syllable is low (hana'si, yasu'mi, naga're) and this was the accent
pattern in Kyōto four centuries ago; the development is the same as for the low
atonic otoko 'man' > oto'ko (Kōchi, early-Edo Kyōto) > o'toko (modern Kyōto) and
resulted from the loss of the low atonic types (cf. §10, n.1). There are quite a few
exceptions and individual or dialectal variations among Kinki speakers, as shown in
Charts 6:1 and 6:2. Two-syllable nouns derived from infinitives of Type B, which
remain Type B in modern Kyōto, also lower the last syllable, but in compensation
they also raise the first syllable, paralleling the development of the low atonic
yama > ya'ma with the loss of the low atonic types, so that the tune of a dissyllabi(
noun is just the reverse of that of the Type B infinitive from which it is derived:
   yo'mi 'reading' < yomi' 'read'; ni'ge 'flight' < nige' 'flee'; a'mi 'net' < ami'
   'knit'; ho'ri 'ditch' < hori' 'dig'; to'mi 'riches' < tomi' 'be rich'.
(The irregular Tōkyō accent of to'mi where we expect *tomi' must be the result of
borrowing from a Kyōto-type dialect.) There are a few exceptions, such as obi ga)
for *o'bi — which happens to be, irregularly, the Tōkyō form and might be expected
to turn up in one or another of the Kinki dialects — 'girdle' from the infinitive
obi' (wa sen) '(does not) gird oneself'; hate (ga) 'reaching the end' for *ha'te
from hate' (wa sen) '(does not) reach the end'; ... . The noun nuki (ga) 'omission'
< nuki' (wa sen) '(does not) omit' is regular within the Kyōto system, and the verb
is Type A in Myōgi-shō, but it is odd that Kagoshima has Type B for both noun and
verb and Tōkyō has the irregular nu'ki for the noun (but ··· nuki used as a quasi-

restrictive after a noun) though the Tōkyō verb is atonic, as expected. Perhaps
there has been contamination with the Type B stem nug- 'remove'; the Okinawan
reflexes of these two verbs overlap in meaning, and they may be the same original
etymon. There are a few other irregularities in Tōkyō or Kyōto versions of two-
syllable nouns derived from tonic infinitives; these are set forth in Chart 8.

Nouns derived from the infinitive of compound verbs are ATONIC; whether Type A
or Type B (for those dialects with initial-register distinctions) depends on the
register of the compound verb, which in turn depends on the initial infinitive:
Kyōto i̅ki̅sugi̅ (ga) 'going too far' ← i̅ki̅-sugi̅ ⌐ (wa sen) '(does not) go too far';
nomisugi̅, nomisugi ga̅ 'overdrinking' < nomi-sugi̅ ⌐ (wa sen) '(does not) overdrink';
kakinaosi̅, kakinaosi ga̅ 'rewriting' < kaki-naosi̅ ⌐ (wa sen) '(does not) rewrite'.
We find that certain anomalies are brought about by lexicalization.[41] The noun
mikomi̅, mikomi ga̅ 'expectation' would lead us to think that Kyōto treats the
underlying infinitive as being from a compound verb made on the Type B stem mi-
'see, look'. But compounds made on monosyllabic tonic infinitives are absorbed into
Type A, as we have seen in the preceding section on the accent of compound verbs, so
that the infinitive of 'expect' is mikomi̅ ⌐ (wa sen) '(does not) expect' or miko⌐mi
(···) 'expect and (···)'; similar is miai̅, miai ga̅ 'interviewing' with the infinitive
of 'interview' given the accent mia̅i ⌐ (wa sen) '(does not) interview', mia⌐i (···)
'interviews and (···)'. The accent of these nouns must have been inherited intact
from an earlier period, before the contraction of the infinitive mi-i̅ > mi̅ led to
the absorption. (According to Kindaichi 1964:401 the mi̅ form had taken hold by the
early part of the 13th century.) The accentuation of the noun otituki̅, otituki ga̅
'calming down' indicates that the underlying infinitive is from a compound verb,
as does the fact that the infinitive is accentuated oti-tuki̅ ⌐ (wa sen) '(does not)
calm down' and oti-tu⌐ki (···) 'calms down and (···)'. Similarly mitome̅, mitome ga̅
'recognition' and mi-tome̅ ⌐ (wa sen) '(does not) recognize' indicate an underlying
compound verb. Yet in the latter case we would expect the compound to be absorbed
into Type A (*mi̅-tome̅-) along with other compounds made on mi̅ < mi-i̅. This accent
must have been lexicalized before contraction of the infinitive led to absorption
of the other compounds into Type A. Compare mi̅tuke̅ 'observation post' < mituke̅ ⌐
(wa sen) '(does not) discover': the accent of the noun follows that of the verb,
which has been absorbed into Type A, though originally a compound verb of Type B.
Was the noun mituke created more recently than the noun mitome? In Kagoshima both
noun and verb are regular (Type B), with no accentual indication of lexicalization.

In Tōkyō the atonic accent of both words (mituke, mitukeru) is what we would expect
from a compound verb but the lack of a tonic variant for the younger speakers
(*mituke'ru) tells us that the verb was lexicalized well before their rule came into
being. The verb asobu 'play' has been removed by Kyōto (and also Hyōgo and Suzu)
from the historical category of Type A and put with the Type B′ verbs; the derived
noun is accordingly treated as atonic low: asobi, asobi ga 'game' < asobi' (wa sen)
'(does not) play'. But Kōchi keeps the verb with Type A, so presumably the Kōchi
derived noun is atonic high: (?) asobi (ga) < asobi' (wa sen).

    Since Tōkyō has lost the initial-register distinctions, the derived nouns of
all compound verbs are simply atonic: mikomi, mitome, mituke, miai, and otituki
could each indicate either a compound verb or a simple atonic stem. The lack of a
tonic-stem version of the infinitives mitome' (wa sinai), mituke' (wa sinai),
and otituki' (wa sinai), is all that tells us these former compounds have been
lexicalized with respect to accent. On the other hand, the younger speakers have
mi-ko'mi (wa sinai) and mi-a'i (wa sinai) for the older mi-komi' (wa sinai)
and mi-ai'i (wa sinai), so we know that these are being treated as compound verbs.

    In further derivations it is not always clear whether we confront noun +
infinitive or noun + infinitive-derived noun (when such a derived noun is otherwise
attested). Note that mika["]to - wo["]kami su 'do obeisance to the court' (NS 101b
[11:144-K]) has an appropriate compound-noun accentuation; but mi-KADO mawiri su
'attend court' (NS 132b[14:420-K) poses a problem.

9. The accent of adjectives.

Like the verbs, the stems of predicated adjectives too are marked by initial register but not by accentual locus. The majority of the stems are the low-initial Type B and accordingly they are tonic in Tōkyō; long stems were always Type B and a number of modern dialects, such as Nagoya (Shibata 1958:178, 160), treat all adjectives as Type B, removing the distinction of register from this category of words. Inflectional paradigms for the adjective appear to have developed somewhat later than those for the verb (see Ch. 7). In the Nara period and in modern dialects of the Ryūkyūs the raw stem, without an ending, can serve as an adnominal, but the mainstream literary language limits this to certain types of compound noun. For the historical stages of earlier Japanese we must take account of five paradigmatic forms that are made by suffixing the endings -'ku, -'k[y]i, -'si, -'sa, and -'m[y]i. Elsewhere I have suggested that the predicative -si and the attributive -k[y]i may derive from prehistoric contractions of -sa ar-[y]i and -ku ar-[y]i, respectively, with the auxiliary 'be' used to predicate the abstract -sa '-ness' and the factual -ku '-ing'; but we will set that controversial notion aside for a moment (see Ch. 7) and speak of a paradigm of five forms for the adjective throughout early Japanese. Other forms also appear, especially by Heian times; they are the result of later contractions of -ku ar- (and in the Ryūkyūs also of -sa ar-) as well as a few other structures, such as -k[y]i-a-mu (or possibly -k[y]i a[ra]mu) > -k[y]emu 'will/would be'. (The distinction of Cye from Cey and of Cyi from Ciy was lost before the time of Myōgi-shō and that is why the y is put in brackets.)

Evidence for the accentual patterns of the adjective forms is neither plentiful nor easy to interpret; we must rely on other sources in addition to Myōgi-shō to help fill the gaps (cf. Mochizuki 1972). I believe the underlying patterns for at least part of the 11th century and for earlier periods are based on the following rules. (The quasi-bound adjective goto- 'like', however, has unique patterns: ḡot̲o̲-s̲i̲, ḡot̲o̲-k̲i̲, ḡot̲o̲-k̲u̲.)

The rules:

(1) The initial pitch continues through the stem. A change of pitch occurs when one of the endings is added, since each is marked by an accent, but the accent is sometimes ignored, especially with the attributive.

-'si[1]   —   na-sī 'is lacking'

    kata-si 'is hard'   taka-sī 'is high'

    ayafu-si 'is dangerous'   mizika-sī 'is short'

    kanasi[-si] ⎫   fisasi[-sī] ⎫
    *kana[si]-si ⎬ 'is precious'   fisa[si]-sī ⎬ 'is longlasting'

                                             namagusa-sī 'is fishy'

                                          medurasi[-sī] ⎫
                                          medura[si]-sī ⎬ 'is rare'

-'k[y]i[2]   —   na-kī 'lacking'

    *ama-ki → ama-kī 'sweet'[3]   siro-kī 'white'; asi-kī 'bad'[4]

    *ayafu-ki 'dangerous'   tifisa-kī, tifisa-ki 'little'

    *kanasi-ki 'precious'[5]   *fisasi-kī, fisasi-ki 'longlasting'

                                            *namagusa-kī 'fishy'

                                          *medurasi-kī 'rare'

(2) But when -'ku or -'mi is attached to a Type B (low) stem, the change of pitch to high occurs on the last syllable of the stem, which is the only syllable of the five monosyllabic adjectives: na- 'lacking', yo- 'good', to- 'sharp', ko- 'thick(ly saturated)', su- 'sour'. The vowel in each of the monosyllabic adjective stems was probably lengthened automatically in these forms, to pick up the locus, as indicated by the "going-tone" rise notation put on a few forms (§7.1), at least in one Heian dialect.[6] Since with a Type B stem the pitch on the endings itself usually reverts to the low of the initial register, we can describe this phenomenon as a surface metathesis of high and low realizations on the last two syllables.

-'ku   —   *na-ku → (naā-ku >) na-ku 'being lacking'

    *ama-ku 'being sweet'[7]   *waka-ku → waka-ku 'being young'[8]

    tayasu-ku 'being easy'   *fitosi-ku → fitosi-ku 'being equal'[9]

-'m[y]i   —[10]   *na-mi → (naā-mi >) na-mi 'being lacking'

                                            *waka-mi → *waka-mi 'being young'[11]

(3) When -'sa is attached to a Type B (low) stem, the change to high pitch sets in on the last syllable of the stem, just as it does when -'ku or -'mi is attached; but, at least for the shorter stems, the pitch stays up through the endings, so that we consider this a retreat of the locus itself, rather than a surface metathesis of the actual pitches.

```
-'sa           —                              na-sa → (*naa-sa = *ná-sa >) na-sa 'lack'
           *ama-sa 'sweetness'               *taka-sa → taka-sa 'height'
                                             *firo-sa → firo-sa 'width'
```

Some of the asterisks above constitute predictions that the forms may yet turn up in tone-marked texts. (I have not put an asterisk in front of na-sa; although it lacks a Heian attestation, Akinaga 1974:160a cites the Kamakura example su[¨]fe [= sube] na-sa 'lack of means'.) The asterisks also tacitly assume that it is from the postulated patterns that we can most easily account for the development of the accentual patterns that characterize the paradigmatic forms in later Japanese. But modern Japanese shows considerable variation in the accentuation of the forms in question and it may prove difficult to isolate the many factors behind some of the modern accents; cf. Martin 1967, 1968.

Yet the development of the patterns for the adjective forms of modern Tōkyō and of Kyōto from at least the Muromachi period can be neatly described in terms of the forms we have assumed, since there is a parallel development for certain noun types exemplified by azuki 'red bean', inoti 'life', and kabuto 'helmet'. If we accept the prevalent view of a final fall in Heian-Kamakura -kí (= -kíi), however, we find what looks like a temporary diversion (perhaps in Kyōto only?), as shown between brackets in the chart below.

	Heian	Hn-Kamakura	Muromachi	Edo	Kyōto	Tōkyō
A	azuki				a'zuki	azukí' (ga)
	kata-ki	[kata-kí]	kata-i	kata-i	(→ ka'ta-i)[12]	kata-í' (ga)[13]
	kata-ku	kata-u		kato-o	(→ kato'-o)	kata-kú' (wa)[14]
B	kabuto				kabu'to	ka'buto
	taka-ku	taka-u		tako-o	tako'-o	ta'ka-ku
	inoti		inoti		i'noti	ino'ti (> i'noti)[15]
	taka-kí	[taka-kí]	taka-i		ta'ka-i	taka'-i

10.0. The accent of compound nouns.

The accentuation of compound nouns in the modern dialects, especially that of Tōkyō, has been explored in considerable detail by Akinaga 1968, Hirayama 1960, McCawley 1968 and 1977, Okuda 1975, and Martin 1975b. From the available literature (especially Okuda 1975) it appears that the Tōkyō-type dialects follow the same general rules as Tōkyō, except for the treatment of specific elements (such as particular "suffixes") within the categories to which the rules refer. For those rules which are (in essence) shared by Tōkyō and Kyōto, there is a fair agreement on the membership in the various categories. Exceptional cases, both within the individual dialects and in the cross-dialect comparison, will call for historical explanations. In the material below we examine a number of these cases; but much research on the history of the exceptional cases remains to be done.

A study of the noun compounds in Myōgi-shō reveals certain regularities that can be accounted for in terms of: (1) the initial pitch of the first of the two nouns compounded, (2) the existence of a change of pitch (a locus) somewhere in the second noun, (3) the relative length of the compound. Reflexes of each of these factors can be found at work in the accentuation rules for compound nouns in later dialects, and something similar must have been available to speakers of proto-Japanese. From these rules and other facts we have seen, it is clear that Kyōto speakers in the eleventh century used initial pitch (what we are calling REGISTER) in one way and change of pitch on later syllables (what we are calling LOCUS) in quite another way; this too surely carries on a difference that must have been characteristic of proto-Japanese.

What happened to the later language is this. The Kagoshima-type dialects lost accentual locus distinctions (and rules), while retaining register. The Tōkyō-type dialects obscured the register distinctions, except for verbs and adjective stems, where the locus was never distinguished, and retained only rules of "accent" (= locus) — reinterpreting the verb and adjective stems; the Kyōto-type dialects, while heavily eroding the low register by absorbing its atonic words of Type 2.3 into the tonic high-register Type 2.2 (as did Tōkyō but not all of the Tōkyō-type dialects), maintained distinctions both of register and of accent, together with rules pertaining to them. But instead of the accent surfacing as a CHANGE of pitch (up or down), both Kyōto and Tōkyō came to realize the accentual locus only in terms of FALL of pitch, with the rise from low to high becoming automatic and nondistinctive for both dialects (in different ways); this is clear from the modern rules for accentuating noun compounds.

The question arises: can we reconstruct the accent of a given compound noun from the modern dialects? In general, the answer is no. A major reason for the irregularity of cross-dialect correspondence of many nouns that are three or more syllables in length is that they are compounds. Some of the compounds are heavily lexicalized and quite old, so that in some or all of the dialects the accent is inherited in those reflexes appropriate to simple nouns. But others are new creations, and still others are old compounds that have been remodelled to conform with the accentuation of the new compounds that are freely made up with the modern rules for each dialect. The rules have changed and the factors that went into the original rules have been simplified and/or obscured. For example, we might expect that we could establish the age of a compound that begins with a noun of Type 2.3: in Kyōto the noun would have been low-initial before 1300 but became high-initial (Type 2.2) at some time during the following century and a half (i.e. by about 1450), so we could look for compounds beginning low and regard these as definitely "old" for that reason. A search of the data is disappointing: y̅a̅ma < yama 'mountain' yields only high-initial compounds except for yama-si 'mountaineer, mountebank' and Umegaki gives the accentuation y̅a̅ma-si for that. (There are also a few proper names which are assigned accent according to different rules: Hirayama lists yama̅guti, yama̅zaki, and yama̅sita but Umegaki has y̅a̅maguti, y̅a̅mazaki, and y̅a̅masita. Kagoshima is irregularly Type A for the first two.) There are several low-initial compounds with m̅i̅mi < mimi 'ear', but most are high-initial. The low examples found are mimi-k̅a̅ki 'earpick', mimi-k̅u̅so 'earwax', mimi-d̅a̅re 'discharge from the ear', mimi-t̅a̅bu 'earlobe'; and Hirayama has mimi-k̅a̅zari for Umegaki's m̅i̅mi-ka̅zari 'ear ornament'.

.   .   .

I have found a fair number of discrepancies between the Kyōto accentuations reported by Hirayama in Zenkoku-akusento-jiten and by Umegaki in Nihon-kokugo-daijiten. For verb stems and infinitive-derived nouns these discrepancies are indicated in Charts 4-11, and Chart 14 summarizes the more striking discrepancies for the nouns. Other discrepancies will be discovered in the following sections. With compound nouns there appear to be a number of factors at work to produce variant accentuations in the Kinki dialects: canonical shapes and frequency of patterns; degree of lexicalization; the general erosion of the low register which has been in slow but cumulative progress since 1300;[1] and the influence of other dialects, especially the modern standard speech with Tōkyō patterns.

10.1 The accentuation of compound nouns in Kyōto and other Kinki dialects.

In the Kinki dialects the register of a compound noun (A with high-pitched initial, B with low-pitched initial) is determined by the first member, but there are a fair number of exceptions, especially when the first member is monosyllabic; some of these are treated together with noun "prefixes" in §10.2. McCawley 1977:281 calls attention to the fact that several Chinese binoms are listed as Type A by Hirayama despite the fact that the compounds made with them as first member are of Type B. He offers three such words (kootoo 'high-grade', gaˈimu 'foreign affairs', and giˈmu 'compulsory work') and I have found a number of others. But Umegaki offers conflicting data for a number of the examples:

kootoo¯ (H), .kootoo¯(U)	::	.kootoo-gakˈkoo (H) = .kootoo-gaˈkkoo (U)
gaˈimu (H), .gaiˈmu (U)	::	.gaimu-ˈsyoo (HU), .gaimu-daˈizin (HU)
zeˈimu (H), .zeiˈmu (U)	::	.zeimu-ˈsyo (HU)
hoˈomu (H), .hooˈmu (U)	::	.hoomu-ˈsyoo (HU), .hoomu-daˈizin (HU)
koˈomu (H), .kooˈmu (U)	::	.koomu-ˈin (HU)
kyoˈogi (HU)	::	.kyoogi-ˈkai (H), kyoogi-ˈkai (U)

In at least four cases, however, Umegaki agrees with Hirayama:

giˈmu (HU)	::	.gimu-kyoˈoiku (HU)
koˈzi (HU)	::	.kozi-ˈin (HU)
zyoˈsi (HU	::	.zyosi-daˈigaku, .zyosi-dai¯ (H)
koˈori (HU)	::	.koori-syuˈgi (HU)

I believe the first three may have come from putative earlier versions (?).giiˈmu, (?).koˈzi, (?).zyooˈsi with a lengthening of the short monosyllabic first morpheme similar to that in siˈi-ka 'poems' and a few similar words. The fourth noun earlier may have been (?).kooˈri. A possibly similar case:

koˈozi (HU)	::	.koozi-ba¯ (H), but koozi-ˈhi (H)

The noun .gosyoˈ-gaki '(a kind of persimmon)' would appear to offer another example but that is owing to a false etymology; according to NKD the first element is a corruption of a placename (Gose) and not goˈsyo 'palace', as the kanji would have it. There are a few compound nouns with low register (Type B) in Kyōto despite the fact that the first element is a Type A native noun, e.g. .isiˈ-bai 'lime', .isiˈ-dan 'stone steps', .isi-keˈri 'hopscotch', and .isi-naˈge 'stone throwing' from iˈsi (2.2b). And mizu¯ 'water' (2.1a) yields a few low-register compounds: .mizu-boˈosoo 'chicken pox', .mizu-deˈppoo 'water pistol'; and according to Hirayama the compounds

.mizu-bu⌐kure 'water blister', .mizukake⌐-ron 'futile discussion', .mizu-iro⁻ 'light blue', and .mizu-e⁻ 'watercolor painting' — but these are all of the high register according to Umegaki. Umegaki has the high register for akane-iro⁻ 'madder red', consistent with akane⁻ 'madder', but Hirayama gives .akane-iro⁻ (and does not list akane⁻ 'madder') despite akane-zome⁻ 'madder dyeing, madder-dyed cloth'. Umegaki's .kawa-bata⁻ 'river-side' and .kawa-uso⁻ 'otter' must be misprints; and Hirayama has high register for these. Most compounds with hana⁻ 'nose' (2.1) are Type A, but the following are Type B both in Hirayama and Umegaki:

.hana-betya⁻ 'flat-nosed', .hana-ga⌐mi 'kleenex', .hana-go⌐e 'nasal voice', .hana-ta⌐re 'nasal drip'; and for Hirayama .hana-uta⁻ 'humming' (hana-uta⁻ U), .hana⌐-ge 'nostril hairs' (hana⌐-ge U); Umegaki also has .hana-daka⁻ 'high-nosed'.

The infinitive-derived noun yaki 'baking/broiling; baked/broiled thing' is Type A (2.1) but it begins a number of compounds that are listed as Type B by Hirayama and Umegaki alike:

.yaki-imo⁻ 'roasted yam', .yaki-so⌐ba 'chow mein', .yaki-ba⁻ 'crematorium' (but Umegaki has yaki-ba⁻ for 'place to burn something'), .yaki-mi⌐so 'toasted beanpaste', .yaki-me⌐si 'toasted (frizzled) rice', .yaki-mo⌐ti 'toasted rice cake; jealousy'.

Umegaki has Type A for Hirayama's .yaki⌐-tori 'broiled chicken', .yaki-ha⌐maguri 'broiled clams', .yaki-bu⁻ 'toasted *fu* (wheat-gluten bread)', .yaki-bu⌐ta 'roast pork', and .yaki-ri⌐ngo 'baked apple', and lacks information on .yaki-za⌐kana 'broiled fish' while giving yaki-doo⌐hu for Hirayama's .yaki-do⌐ohu 'toasted bean curd', ya⌐ki-nori for Hirayama's .yaki-nori⁻ 'toasted seaweed', and either ya⌐ki-guri or yaki-gu⌐ri for Hirayama's .yaki-gu⌐ri 'roasted chestnuts'. Other compounds with yaki- are Type A in both sources but Umegaki has yaki-gu⌐si and yaki⌐-gote for Hirayama's yaki-gusi⁻ 'skewer' and yaki-gote⁻ 'hot iron'. The noun yamome⁻ 'widow' is high atonic for Umegaki, but Hirayama gives .yamome⁻ (low atonic), and 'widow's life' is accordingly .yamome-gu⌐rasi for Hirayama but yamome-gu⌐rasi for Umegaki; the Myōgi-shō attestations for 'widow' are HHH (like Umegaki's modern version) and HHL, both indicating Type A, yet Kagoshima makes the noun (and its compound) Type B.

There are also a few examples where the compound is Type A despite the fact that the first element is a native noun of Type B.[2] All examples with .haru 'spring' are low except haru-same⁻ 'spring rain' (B in Kagoshima and "Kamakura LLLH" according to NKD); similarly with .aki 'autumn' except aki-k/ɡusa⁻ 'autumn plants' and aki-zora⁻ 'autumn sky', and Hirayama has aki-go⁻ for Umegaki's .aki-⌐go 'autumn

silkworm'. All compounds with .amè 'rain' are low in register and so are those with
its combining form .ama- except for ama-gu⁻ 'raingear', ama-do⁻ 'rain-shutters',
ama-ˈmizu 'rain-water', ama-yaˈdori 'shelter from the rain', and ama-gi⁻ (U) /
aˈma-gi (H) 'raincoat', all Type B in Kagoshima. The noun .hune⁻ 'boat' has the
combining form huna- in compounds; for Kyōto these are all B in Hirayama but A
according to Umegaki. Occasionally Hirayama has B for a compound made up of Type A
noun + verb infinitive but Umegaki has A:

  kosi⁻ (HU) :: .kosi-aˈge (H), kosi-age⁻ (U); .kosi-maˈki (H),kosi-maki⁻ (U);
  .kosi-kaˈke (H), kosi-kake⁻ (U) — compare the verb (← N+V) .kosikakeru (H),
  kosikakeru (U).

Yet there are similar compounds that are listed as Type A:

  kosi-maˈwari (HU); kosi-nage⁻ (HU); kosi-nuke⁻ (HU); kosi-tuˈki (H),
  kosi-tuki⁻ (U).

For at least one such example Hirayama has the compound Type A, as expected, but
Umegaki has it Type B:

  miya⁻ (HU) :: miya-maˈiri (H), .miya-maˈiri (U).

    The accentual locus, if there is one, is determined by the second member of the
noun compound — to which any, all, or none of the following three rules may be
applied: (1) the accent is cancelled; (2) an accent is newly imposed (with the locus
at the end of the first syllable of the second member); (3) the accent, whether
basic and retained or newly imposed, retreats one syllable. We can illustrate the
application of the rules to compounds of two dissyllabic nouns by examining the
materials in Umegaki 1963:42-7, which represent the results of a study by Maeda
Isamu called "Ōsaka-akusento no hukugō-hōsoku: yon-onsetsu mukatsuyō-go no baai",
Kinki-hōgen 19:9-17 (1953), which is — as Umegaki says — "not easily seen" today.
Umegaki's categories "A" - "L" are recapitulated below, with a schematic diagram
that ignores the register of the second member — and, for that matter, of the first
also — with the applicable rules marked "+". But probably it would be simpler to say
that all accents (= loci) are cancelled; "E" and "F" then have newly imposed accents
(at the same locus as the one cancelled), and "F" further undergoes a retreat of the
new accent. For longer second elements, an accent will stay without retreating; the
imposed accent will always be at a locus between the first and second syllables of
the second element.

Kyōto compound nouns

	N-N	Cpd N	Accent: (1) cancelled	(2) imposed	(3) retreats
A G }	oo-oo	oooo			
B H }	oo-oo	ooo'o		+	
C I }	oo-oo	oo'oo		+	+
D	oo-o'o	oooo	+		
E	oo-o'o	ooo'o			
F	oo-o'o	oo'oo			+
J	oo-oò	oooo	+		
K	oo-oò	ooo'o	(+	+)*	
L	oo-oò	oo'oo	(+	+)*	+

* But if we assume that the falling accent here represented by ò (= ò)
  is treated as the oxytonic version of the locus "¬"
  we can say that the accent merely retreats.

The population of Umegaki's categories "A" – "L" can be attributed partly to earlier accent patterns, partly to other factors, but many assignments appear to be without historical motivation, i.e. arbitrary. Below are listed the nouns Umegaki assigns to each category listed according to their historical types. Those preceded by "ᵛ" are infinitive-derived nouns. Those preceded by "⁺" are assumed to belong to the type despite the lack of Heian attestation.

A ...- oo
   2.1 azi 'flavor', ari 'ant', ⁺boo 'club, stick', hako/-bako 'box', hata/-bata 'side, rim', hana/-bana 'nose', hiza 'lap, knees', huta/-buta 'lid', huda 'tag', hude 'brush, pen', ᵛiri 'with ⋯ in it', ⁺isu 'chair', kabi 'mildew', kabu 'stump', kabe 'wall', kane/-gane 'metal', kane/-gane 'bell', kara/-gara 'characteristic', ᵛkari/-gari 'borrowing', ᵛkasi/-gasi 'loan', kayu 'gruel', kuwa/-guwa 'hoe', mune 'ridge of a roof', niwa 'garden', ᵛnuri 'varnish', saki/-zaki 'tip; cape', sara/-zara 'plate', soko/-zoko 'bottom', sode 'sleeve', tana/-dana 'shelf', ᵛtome/-dome 'stop', tori/-dori 'bird', tubo 'jar', tume/-zume 'claw', tuya 'gloss', usi 'ox', wage = mage 'topknot', ᵛyaki 'fry', yabu 'bush, thicket', yari 'spear', yome 'bride', ⁺zyun 'order'.   (⁺ = 0-0-A.)
   2.2a sita 'below'.
   2.2 < 2.3 kuso 'dung'.
   2.5 < 2.3 kaki/-gaki 'oyster'.
   2.x: 0-0-B betu 'separated (by ⋯)', hei/-bei 'wall', hitu '(large) lidded box', syaku 'stomach/chest pain';
            1/2-0-B koya/-goya 'shed';
            1-1-B dai 'fee';
            0-1-A zen 'tray-table'.

G ...- .oo
   2.4 ato 'footprint', hune/-bune 'boat', ita 'board', ito 'thread', obi 'girdle',
kazu 'number', kami/-gami 'above', kinu/-ginu 'silk; garment, geta 'clogs', miso
'beanpaste', ᵛmuki 'facing, destined for' (also J), naka 'middle', nusi 'owner',
saya/-zaya 'sheath; price-gap', sora/-zora 'sky', taba 'bunch'.
   2.4 < 2.3 ana 'hole', kawa/-gawa 'skin; fur; bark', tama/-dama 'ball; gem; coin',
⁺sin 'pith', ⁺mori 'guard', ⁺un 'fate'. (⁺ = 1-1-B.)
   2.4 < 2.2 kara/-gara 'shell, husk'.
   2.4 (?< 2.5) yado 'lodgings'.
   2.x: 0-1-B tan 'phlegm'.

B ...- oo
   2.1 haba 'width', ᵛhari/-bari 'stretching', ᵛhiki/-biki 'pulling', hue/bue
'whistle', kago 'basket', kao/-gao 'face', kubi 'neck'; ᵛage 'raising', ᵛire
'putting in', ᵛkai/-gai 'purchase', ᵛkari/-gari 'hunting', ᵛmaki 'rolling', ᵛnuki
'removing', ᵛturi/-zuri 'fishing'.

H ...- .oo
   2.4 hari/-bari 'needle', kado 'corner', siru/-ziru 'juice', suzi 'tendon;
authority', usu 'mortar'.

C ...- oo
   2.1 ame 'rice gluten', ban 'evening', hae/-bae 'housefly', hati/-bati 'bee', hige
'beard', huki/-buki 'bog-rhubarb', kaki/-gaki 'persimmon', kaze 'wind', kawa/-gawa
'side', kizu 'wound', kiri 'paulownia', kiri/-giri 'fog', kuni/-guni 'country',
kuti/-guti 'mouth', ᵛmai 'dance', ᵛmake 'defeat', miti 'road', mizu 'water', musi
'bug', moti 'rice-cake', saba 'mackerel', sake/-zake 'wine', sasa/-zasa 'bamboo
grass', take/-dake 'bamboo', yuri 'lily'.

I ...- .oo
   2.4 ⁺ban 'number', ⁺dai 'platform', iki 'breath', iti 'market', kasa/-gasa
'umbrella', kuzu 'trash', mugi 'barley', ⁺tin 'wages', tubu 'grain', umi 'sea',
uri 'melon'. (⁺ = 1-1-B.)

D ...- oˡo
   2.2a aza 'birthmark', ⁺an 'bean-jam', hata/-bata 'flag', hito/-bito 'person',
⁺heya/-beya 'room', iwa 'rock', kaki/-gaki 'fence', (kata/)gata/-gata 'type, shape',
kawa/-gawa 'river', kuse(/-guse) 'bad habit', kui(?/-gui) 'stake', mune 'breast',
⁺siki 'type', ⁺sumi/-zumi 'India ink', tako/-dako 'callus', ⁺turu(?/-zuru) 'vine',
⁺turu(/-zuru) 'bowstring', yaku 'public service', ziku 'scroll'.
   2.2b bin 'bottle', isi 'stone', kasa 'bulk', numa 'marsh; lake', tera/-dera
'temple', tie/-zie 'wisdom'.
   2.2 < 2.3 aka 'dirt', ami 'net', asi 'foot', bara 'rose', desi 'apprentice', hazi
'shame', hana/-bana 'flower', hama 'beach', hara 'belly', hone/-bone 'bone', huku
'garment', huti/-buti 'rim', huro/-buro 'bath', ike 'pond', imo 'yam', inu 'dog',
iro 'color', kagi 'key', kami/-gami 'god', ᵛkire/-gire 'cut', kisi/-gisi 'shore',
kuki/-guki 'stalk', kumo/-gumo 'cloud', kura/-gura 'storehouse', kusa/-gusa 'grass',
kusi/-gusi 'comb', kutu/-gutu 'shoes', maku 'curtain', ᵛmise 'shop', mono 'thing',
moto 'origin', nawa 'rope, line', neko 'cat', niku 'meat, flesh', nuka 'bran', oni
'ogre', ᵛori 'fold', oya 'parent', sabi 'rust', sio 'salt', sima/-zima 'island',

sita 'tongue', sumi/-zumi 'charcoal', ᵛtuke 'attached'/-zuke 'dated', tuti 'earth', tura/-zura 'face', ude 'arm', uma 'horse', ura 'reverse (side)', waza 'trick', yama 'mountain', yami 'darkness'; perhaps -ᵛai of imi-ai etc.

  ?2.2 < 2.3 ⁺ᵛkoe(?/-goe) 'fertilizer', mozi 'written character'.

  2.1 ᵛmane 'mimicry', siwa 'wrinkle', ⁺syoku 'meal'.

  2.x: 1-2-A kizi 'material', pan 'bread', sisi 'lion'.
           1-2-B hon/-bon 'book', mitu 'honey', zin 'camp, encampment'.
           1-1-A en 'porch'.

E ...- o˥o

  2.2 oto 'sound'; ⁺kega 'mishap; injury; wound, damage', ⁺kiti 'luck'. (⁺ = 2-2-B.)

  2.2 < 2.3 kuri/-guri 'chestnut', mari 'ball', sao/-zao 'pole', susi/-zusi 'sushi', tai/-dai 'sea bream'; ᵛhori/-bori 'dig', ᵛhosi/-bosi 'dry', ᵛhuri/-buri 'rain', ᵛkiri/-giri 'cut', ᵛkori/-gori 'harden', ᵛmesi '(eat) food', ᵛmori 'leak', ᵛsasi/ -zasi 'point', ᵛsuki/-zuki 'like', ᵛtare/-dare 'drip', ᵛtori/-dori 'take'.

  2.2 ?< 2.3 baba 'old woman' (1/2-2-A); tuba 'spit' (1/2-2-B).

  2.2/2.5 < 2.3 mame 'bean' (also J).

F ...- o˥o

  2.1 saki 'ahead' (≠ 'tip; cape').

  2.2 hasi/-basi 'bridge'; ⁺take/-dake 'extent' (2-2-B).

  2.2 < 2.3 kai/-gai 'shell', kiku/-giku 'chrysanthemum', sune 'shin', toki/-doki 'time', ⁺ᵛuti 'hit'; ᵛhare/-bare 'clear weather' (also Kt > 2.5).

  ?2.2 kazi 'fire' (1-2-B); sei 'characteristic' (2-2-A).

J ...- .oò

  2.3 kase/kasi 'shackles'

  2.5 ayu 'sweetfish', hato/-bato 'pigeon', hebi 'snake', kumo/-gumo 'spider', mado 'window', mae 'front', momo 'thigh', muko 'son-in-law', nabe 'pan', turu/-zuru 'crane', ⁺z(y)ako 'small fishes' (1-1:3-B).

  2.5 < 2.3 mame 'bean' (also E).

  2.5 < 2.4 ago 'chin'

  ?2.5 < 2.1 ᵛmuki 'facing, destined for' (also G).

  ?2.5 moya 'mist' (1-0[H]/1:3[U]-B).

K ...- .oò

  2.5 kage 'shadow', kiᵇ/ₘi 'millet' (Kt > 2.4), kobu 'seaweed', koe/-goe 'voice', oke 'bucket', saru/-zaru 'monkey', soba 'buckwheat', toi 'waterpipe', tuyu 'dew'.

L ...- .oò

  2.5 ame/-same 'rain', sake 'salmon'.

It is difficult to make general statements about the shorter noun compounds, but longer compounds follow productive rules. For both Tōkyō and Kyōto a locus after any non-final syllable is preserved in a polysyllabic second member of a compound; when there is no preservable locus, a new accent is imposed after the first mora of the second element. But the locus, whether preserved or imposed, will retreat (i.e. be anticipated) by one syllable —in Kyōto one mora — if the second element is a single morpheme of one mora, or of two moras provided the second is dependent or consists of a voiceless consonant + i or u. That is, the retreat occurs on two-mora morphemes with the canonical shapes (C)V:, (C)Vi, (C)Vn, CVk[1]/u, CVt[1]/u[3] (all common in Chinese loanmorphs); less often CVs[1]/u; rarely (if ever) CVh[1]/u. That statement accounts for the patterns of these phrases:

	K y ō t o			T ō k y ō
(1)	ka'motu no eki →	kamotu'eki	: kamotu'eki ←	ka'motu no e'ki
(2)	i'e no .nusi →	ie'nusi	: ie'nusi ←	ie' no nu'si
	(→ ie no .nusi)		:	(→ ie no nu'si)
(3)	aomo'no no .iti →	aomono'iti	: aomono'iti ←	aomo'no no i'ti
(4)	anraku na isu →	anraku'isu	: anraku'isu ←	a'nraku na isu
(5)	saiboo no ma'ku →	saiboo'maku	: saibo'omaku ←	saiboo no maku'

> MEANINGS: (1) 'freight station', (2) 'houseowner', (3) 'vegetable
> market', (4) 'easy-chair', (4) 'cell membrane'.

Exempted from the retreat are recent loans:

(6)	tennen no ga'su →	tennenga'su	: tennenga'su ←	te'nnen no ga'su
(7)	kankoo no ba'su →	kankooba'su	: kankooba'su ←	kankoo no ba'su

Compare:

(8)	kankoo no kyaku →	kankoo'kyaku	: kanko'okyaku ←	kankoo no kyaku

But both treatments are reported for certain loanwords:

(9)	ke'eburu no ka'a →	keeburu'kaa	: keeburu'kaa ←	ke'eburu no ka'a
		keeburuka'a	: keeburuka'a	
(10)	wa'nman no ka'a →	wanman'kaa[4]	: wanma'nkaa[5] ←	wa'nman no ka'a
		wanmanka'a[6]	: wanmanka'a[7]	

> MEANINGS: (6) 'natural gas', (7) 'sightseeing bus', (8) 'sightseers',
> (9) 'cable-car', (10) 'one-man (operated) car'.

There are a number of other exceptional cases, and with compound nouns of four syllables or less the accentuation(s) in use are hard to predict. For the compounds of two dissyllables studied by Maeda and Umegaki, we can say that certain of the second-element classes (C/I, F, L; most of B/H, E and K) exemplify the rules for the longer compounds. But classes A/G, D, and J create atonic nouns, and often this turns out to be true of their longer compounds as well as the shorter ones. A and G consist mostly of atonic nouns, and many nouns in D go back to the earlier atonic

low (2.3); the J words are all the "oxtyonic" or double-low type in modern Kyōto
and most of them go back to 2.5. It has been widely noted that the atonic patterns
are favored by four-mora nouns, especially Chinese binoms made up of two-mora
morphemes (and usually written with two kanji). Not only in Kyōto but also in other
Kinki dialects there appears to be a trend toward the HIGH atonic pattern for many
words of four moras. Several examples of the ongoing erosion of the low register
(cf. §10, n.1) are found in Yamana 1965: Kyōto .mimiku'so 'earwax' is mimiku'so in
Kōchi, Matsuho, and Naruto; Kyōto .nokogi'ri 'saw' is nokogi'ri in Kōchi (older
speakers say noko'giri, Doi 1952:35) and Matsuho, noko'giri in Naruto. On the other
hand, where Kōchi has .miso'siru and Naruto .misosi'ru 'beanpaste soup' (as we
expect from .miso 'beanpaste'), Kyōto has misosi'ru and Matsuho miso'siru. (But it
seems strange that Kōchi should have .yuki'guni 'snow country' since yu'ki is high
register and always was so; the Matsuho-Naruto version yukigu'ni and the atonicized
yukiguni of Kyōto are what we expect.) The low register of .mugiwara 'barley straw'
in Kyōto and Matsuho is predicted from that of .mugi 'barley', yet Kōchi and Naruto
have mugiwara. The word for 'thunder' must have been low-register earlier, since
Kagoshima has it Type B and the first element kami was Type 2.3 (low atonic), but
in Kyōto, Kōchi, and Matsuho the word is kaminari, and Naruto has atonicized it to
kaminari. The word itazura 'idle; prank' is resolutely high atonic throughout its
entire attested history, and it is treated that way for Kōchi, Naruto, and Matsuho
by Yamana and for Kyōto by Umegaki, yet Hirayama has .itazura, which — if it is not
a misprint — suggests an unusual change from the high register to the low, bucking
the general trend. There are many discrepancies in the data offered by Hirayama and
Umegaki, and there seem to be Tōkyō-type influences in some of the variants:
Hirayama's koomoriga'sa '(bat-shaped) umbrella' looks as if it were retaining the
prototonic Tōkyō accent of ka'sa (whence Tōkyō koomori-ga'sa) but Umegaki gives
koomori'gasa which is more what we would expect from Kyōto .kasa; and Hirayama's
garasuma'do 'glass window' must be influenced by Tōkyō garasu-ma'do from ma'do
'window', for Umegaki's garasu'mado is consistent with Kyōto's .mado. Both sources
give garasu'bati 'glass pot' (Tōkyō garasu'bati) from the Type-2.3 noun (earlier
hati) that is now ha'ti in Kyōto and hati' in Tōkyō. In general, it is the modern
accent type that determines the behavior. Tōkyō's niwaka-a'me 'a sudden shower'
retains the prototonic locus of a'me 'rain', but that is oxytonic .ame in Kyōto
and the newly imposed accent of the compound retreats: .niwaka'ame. A similar
case: Tōkyō ka'su 'dregs' retains its locus in abura-ka'su 'oil dregs', for which
the corresponding Kyōto word is abura'kasu with a retreat of the accent that is
newly imposed because Kyōto's .kasu is atonic.

10.2. Noun prefixes in Kyōto and Tōkyō.

When the first element of a compound noun is a monosyllabic noun the compound is accentuated according to the same rules as when the first element is longer, but the initial low-register is sometimes lost. For example, a good many compounds with .te 'hand' (1.3) as the first element fail to begin low as expected; instead, these words are absorbed into the high register, perhaps as part of the general erosion of the low register that we have commented on above. But in Kagoshima, with very few exceptions, compounds with monosyllabic first elements of Type B retain that reflex of the low register, despite the fact that the phonetic manifestation of the reflex is now toward the end of the word.

Charts 15:1 to 15:4 display the Kyōto accentuation of compound nouns with the first elements .te 'hand', .me 'eye' and its combining form ma-, .ki 'tree' and its combining form ko-, .hi 'fire' and its combining form ho-. (The word for 'hand' also has a combining form ta- but there are few compound nouns in which it appears.) By attaching the form at the top of each column to the forms listed below it you can obtain the appropriately accentuated compound: te⌐- + -aka = te⌐aka 'hand grime', te- ⌐ + -ka⌐gen = teka⌐gen 'knack', te- ⁻ + -gami⁻ = tegami⁻ 'letter', .te- ⁻ + -aki = .teaki⁻ 'task-free', .te- ⌐ + -ma⌐ri = .tema⌐ri '(hand) ball'. The raised minus at the end of a form is a reminder that the lack of a locus mark ⌐ means the form is atonic. Set aside are a number of problems of constituency and derivation, such as whether a second element is the verb infinitive or the infinitive-derived noun and whether in such compounds the form is directly derived from a N+V compound; these questions are of little consequence here. Included are examples of -AN "with an adjectival noun for second element" and -A "with an adjective for second element" though these are not immediately relevant to this section. It will be noticed that a large number of compounds are given different accentuations by Umegaki from those given by Hirayama. Umegaki's versions are marked "U", Hirayama's "H"; the unmarked words are accentuated identically by both. Like the variation shown in Chart 13, the differences between the two sources may be of register, of locus, or of both. For some of the words one or the other of the sources will have two versions and both are marked; where a source lacks data on a form this is marked with "x": "U x" for Umegaki's omissions, "H x" for Hirayama's.

Certain short elements seldom or never occur as free nouns but are attached as prefixes to free nouns and bound Chinese-loan nouns. These too generally follow the compound-noun accentuation rules and presumably each prefix has a register assigned

to it. In charts 16:1 to 16:5 we examine compounds with some of the more productive
of these prefixes. The basic register assignment of oo- 'big' (16:1) should be low
according to Ryūkyū data (all the attested Shuri forms with the reflex quhu- are
Type B) and Heian attestations, yet both Kagoshima and Kyōto have an overwhelming
majority of the words in Type A (high register), especially the longer examples.
The prefix ko- 'little' is clearly high register, probably identical with the noun
ko 'child' (Type 2.1), but there are a few examples that are low register in Kyōto,
and even more that are Kagoshima B. The Chinese prefix soo- 'all' makes compounds
that are all Type B in Kagoshima, yet the majority of the compounds in Kyōto are
high register. The Chinese prefix syo- 'several' is clearly high register: there are
no examples that are low in Kyōto or Type B in Kagoshima. The Chinese prefix zyo-
'female' is A in Kagoshima, with no exceptions, but there are a number of words for
which Kyōto has low register in one or the other of our sources. The term "Chinese
prefix" refers to a morpheme anciently borrowed from China, along with its graphic
representation. It is is sometimes difficult to characterize these loanmorphs from
Chinese as clearly "bound" or "free"; in Japanese many can be said to be only quasi-
free and for purposes of making binoms they are like the bound elements of Greek and
Latin origin in English, such as "hydro-, proto-, pro-, post-, ante-, ..." or "-ize,
-ism, -ate, -oid, -al, -ic". The loan morphemes ta 'many' and ta 'other' (Chart
16:5) are sometimes used as free nouns and given the accentuation A in Kagoshima and
high-falling in Kyōto; but they begin a number of compounds which are low register
in Kyōto though these are all A in Kagoshima. Many of the "compound nouns" listed in
the charts are binoms made up of essentially bound elements at both ends: they are
heavily lexicalized. A set of negative prefixes, however, is quite productive with
free nouns as well as bound loanmorphs; these are displayed in Charts 17:1 to 17:5.
The prefix hi- 'non-, un-' has uses as a free noun with high atonic accent in Kyōto
(Type 1.1) and the corresponding Type A accent in Kagoshima. This prefix, unlike the
other negative prefixes, is often given separate phrasing as one of the pseudo
adnouns discussed in RGJ 750-1. The separate phrasing is used for emphasis — like
English "UN-economical" — and in pronouncing new or unfamiliar combinations. The
prefix hu- 'not' produces compounds that are virtually all A in Kagoshima, but
Kyōto has many of these compounds in the low register; as a productive prefix with
longish free nouns, hu- is mostly treated as high by Umegaki but low by Hirayama,
though there is one contrary example (H hu-zyuꞏubun, U .hu-zyuꞏubun 'insufficient').
The prefix bu- 'not, un-', originally a variant of mu- but orthographically somewhat
confused with hu- (cf. RGJ 390), is mostly high register in Kyōto but usually B in

Kagoshima, with a few exceptions in both. The productive prefix mu- 'lacking, un-,
-less' makes compounds that are mostly A in Kagoshima and high register in Kyōto,
but there are a number of exceptions listed as low by one or both of our sources. As
a free noun mu is high atonic in Kyōto and A in Kagoshima. The prefix mi- 'not yet,
un-⋯-en' is fairly productive with verbal nouns and those bound morphemes that were
verbs in Chinese; most of the compounds are low register in Kyōto, but in Kagoshima
they are all Type A. And no examples are listed for Shuri, raising the question of
how early the prefix came into use. The honorific prefix mi- is common in Shuri, but
limited to set expressions in the main-island dialects; it yields only high-register
compounds (A in Kagoshima and Shuri). Compounds with the prefix ma- 'true, truly'
are A in Kagoshima, Shuri, and Yonaguni; but in Kyōto they are all B except for
⁻mappa˺daka and ⁻massyo˺oziki.

The honorific prefix o- makes compounds that are Type B in Kagoshima, are low
atonic in Kyōto, and are atonic in Tōkyō. The accentuation is consistent with the
etymology of the prefix, which is a contraction of the adjective stem oo- < o[f]o-
< *opo- 'big'; this was low and atonic in 11th-century Kyōto. The regular treatment
can be seen from the following examples; all are atonic in Tōkyō, low atonic in
Kyōto and B in Kagoshima. The dot marks the register, of no relevance to Tōkyō.
We omit the atonic-reminder notation " ...⁻ ".

   .o-me, .o-yu, .o-tya, .o-rei, .o-kyuu; .o-ie, .o-uti, .o-uma, .o-kane, .o-kuni,
   .o-saki, .o-satu, .o-sato, .o-soba 'near', .o-miya, .o-kayu, .o-huda, .o-sezi,
   .o-zigi; .o-megane, .o-itoma, .o-miyage, .o-zasiki, .o-aiso[o], .o-seibo,
   .o-syooyu, .o-tanzyoo, .o-bentoo, .o-tyuugen, .o-boo-san; ... .

And nouns derived from infinitives (of diverse types):

   .o-hure, .o-make, .o-kaesi, .o-kaeri, .o-iwai, .o-azuke, .o-kawari 'change' [see
   below for other meaning], .o-kuyami, .o-yasumi, .o-kotae, .o-aturae, .o-kotozuke,
   .o-mazinai, .o-ide, .o-mori; .o-sirusi, .o-maturi, .o-mamori; ... .

But having said that the honorific prefix o- makes low atonic compounds, we must
allow for numerous exceptions; cf. RGJ 332-6, the starting point for this study.
The exceptions can be grouped into the following categories. (Where two versions are
separately cited, the Tōkyō form precedes the colon.)

1. Tōkyō and Kyōto both have a fall of pitch and the locus of that fall is the
same in both dialects. In each word with the fall after the second syllable the
pitch pattern is virtually the same in Tōkyō and Kyōto, but in Tōkyō the low pitch
on the first syllable is nondistinctive (and less noticeably low) while in Kyōto the
initial low is distinctive. The forms are cited with an initial dot that can be
ignored in reading the Tōkyō forms.

1a.   .o-ya¹tu, .o-mo¹tya, .o-me¹si (= .omesi-ti¹rimen), .o-ha¹gi, .o-ba¹ke,
.o-hi¹ya, .o-to¹mo, .o-hi¹ru, .o-mu¹tu, .o-sa¹tu (= satuma-imo : satuma-¹imo),
.o-hu¹ro (according to U [but not in NKD] though H has o-hu¹ro : .o-huro),
.o-de¹ki, .o-tu¹mu, .o-tu¹ya, .o-tu¹yu, .o-de¹n, .o-se¹wa, .o-su¹si; .o-te¹nki,
.o-te¹gami, .o-ta¹huku, .o-da¹butu, .o-ku¹ruma, .o-ku¹motu, .o-so¹matu-sama;
.o-ka¹a-san, .o-to¹o-san, .o-zi¹i-san, .o-ba¹a-san, .o-ni¹i-san, .o-ne¹e-san,
.o-hi¹me-san, .o-zyo¹o-san — but .o-boo-san is atonic.
Nouns derived from verb infinitives: .o-ha¹ziki; .o-ma¹wari 'making one's rounds;
turning/whirling around' [see below for other meanings]; .o-ko¹ge; .o-sya¹re.

1b.   .o-tu¹gi but Tōkyō also o-tugi¹; .o-siti¹ya but Tōkyō also atonic
o-sitiya.

1c.   Tōkyō o¹-tu̜kisama or o-tu̜ki¹sama : Kyōto .o-tu¹kisama, o-tu̜ki¹ai :
.o-tu¹kiai. (The accent shift is due to the vowel devoicing in the second
syllable of the Tōkyō forms.)

1d.   .o-huto¹n, .o-huta¹kata, .o-tyaga¹si, .o-hanaba¹take. In these the
phonetic pattern differs in the two dialects. The Tōkyō tune automatically rises
to a plateau beginning with the second syllable, but the Kyōto initial stays low
until the syllable before the locus, which alone is high.

2. Kyōto has the locus one syllable later than Tōkyō.

2a.   o-si¹goto : .o-sigo¹to, o-te¹huki : .o-tehu¹ki; o-se¹kkai : .o-sek¹kai
(but this is an artifact of the analysis, see §1.4). And nouns from verb
infinitives: o-ni¹giri : .o-nigi¹ri, o-ne¹dari : .o-neda¹ri, o-hi¹tasi :
.o-hita¹si, o-su¹wari : .o-suwa¹ri, o-ma¹wari : .o-mawa¹ri 'policeman; side-
dishes with rice' [see above for other meanings], o-a¹mari : .o-ama¹ri,
o-mu¹subi : .o-musu¹bi, o-sya¹buri : .o-syabu¹ri, o-sya¹beri : .o-syabe¹ri,
o-ka¹wari : .o-kawa¹ri 'second helping' [compare .o-kawari 'change'].

2b.   Tōkyō o-hi¹neri or atonic o-hineri : Kyōto .o-hine[¹]ri [see 5],
o-hito¹yosi or atonic o-hitoyosi : .o-hitoyo¹si.

3. The Tōkyō version is the expected atonic, but Kyōto has a locus:

o-siri : .o-si¹ri, o-tera : .o-te¹ra, o-hatu : .o-ha¹tu; o-daizi : .o-da¹izi,
o-hayasi : .o-ha¹yasi; o-hi-sama : .o-hi¹-sama, o-ikutu : .o-iku¹tu (compare
i¹kutu : .iku¹tu : Kg B), o-ikura : .o-iku¹ra (compare i¹kura : .ikura : Kg A),
o-hukuro : .o-huku¹ro, o-hyakudo : .o-hyaku¹do; o-kinodoku : .o-kinodo¹ku,
o-matidoosama : .o-mati¹doosama. And nouns from verb infinitives: o-tuki :
.o-tu¹ki, o-soroi : .o-soro¹i.

4. The Kyōto version is the expected atonic, but Tōkyō has a locus.

4a.   o-zyu¹u : .o-zyuu (= zyuubako), o-bo¹n : .o-bon, o-ka¹mi : .o-kami,
o-ta¹ma : .o-tama (= tamazyakusi or tamago), o-te¹dama : .o-tedama, o-na¹sake :
.o-nasake, o-tyu¹uniti : .o-tyuuniti, o-se¹nbe[e] : .o-senbe[e]. And nouns from
verb infinitives: o-yo¹bare : .o-yobare, o-yu¹zuri : .o-yuzuri.

4b.   Tōkyō is optionally atonic: o-ha[¹]ri : .o-hari, o-hu[¹]se : .o-huse,
o-to[¹]gi : .o-togi (according to Hirayama but Umegaki has .oto¹gi), o-me[¹]dama
: .o-medama, o-so[¹]ozai : .o-soozai, o-da[¹]tin : .o-datin.

5. Miscellaneous nouns from verb infinitives:

o-hi[ˈ]neri : .o-hine[ˈ]ri (H) / .o-hineri (U)
o-hi[ˈ]raki : .o-hiraˈki (H) / .o-hi[ˈ]raki (U)
o-kiˈmari : .o-kimari (H) / o-kimaˈri (U)
o-simeri : .o-simeˈri (H) / .o-simeri (U)
o-naˈgare : .o-nagare (H) / .o-nagaˈre (U).

6. In Kagoshima all the above words are regularly Type B with the exception of the
following, which Hirayama lists as Type A:

.o-moˈtya, o-deˈn, .o-taˈhuku, .o-zyoˈo-san, .o-tamazyaˈkusi,
o-kaˈmi : .o-kami, o-da[ˈ]tin : .o-datin.
Type A also includes .o-tenba 'tomboy, hussy', regular in Kyōto and Tōkyō.

Adjectival nouns are like nouns: the regular accent of o-AN is low atonic but
there are numerous irregular forms; in particular, a prototonic locus is apt to be
retained in Tōkyō. A list of the irregular forms is unavailable at this time.

.   .   .

When o- is attached to a paradigmatic form of a verb (always the infinitive) or
of an adjective (any form), the Tōkyō accent is atonic. In Kyōto the accent is low
atonic for the verb infinitive:

hatarakiˈ wa sen 'I will not work', hataraˈki 'I work and ⋯ ' (see §2.2);
o-hataraki naharu 'will deign to work'
.arukiˈ wa sen 'I will not walk', .aruˈki 'I walk and ⋯ '; .o-aruki naharu
'will deign to walk'.

But a Kyōto adjective form retains its underlying (historical) locus:

.hayoˈo → .o-hayoˈo, .takaˈku → .o-takaˈku (= .takoˈo → .o-takoˈo)
(.hayaˈ[k]i >) haˈyai → .o-hayaˈi (Tōkyō/Kagoshima B)
(.yasuˈ[k]i >) yaˈsui → .o-yasuˈi
(amaˈ[k]i >) aˈmai → .o-amaˈi
(.sitaˈsi[k]i >) sitaˈsii → .o-sitaˈsii
(yasaˈsi[k]i >) yasaˈsii → .o-yasaˈsii

Compare Tōkyō's atonic o-medetoo and o-yakamasyuu with Kyōto's .o-medetoˈo and
.o-yakamasyuˈu.

10.3. Noun suffixes in Kyōto and Tōkyō.

When the second element of a compound noun is a monosyllabic noun (of one or
two moras) or a dissyllabic noun of the canonical shape (C)VÇ^i/$_u$, in which Ç is a
voiceless consonant, the accentuation rules impose a locus immediately before that
element. Stated the way we have looked at it above, an accent imposed (as with the
longer nouns) at the end of the first mora of the second element is obliged to
retreat one syllable. In Kyōto the locus retreats one MORA, though in some of the
available data there is confusion on the treatment of "heavy" syllables. For Kyōto
both the locus imposition and the retreat are in terms of moras, but in Tōkyō the
retreat is in terms of syllables, since the locus is not allowed to follow the
second mora of a heavy syllable.

What is true of monosyllabic nouns (and dissyllables of the proper shape) is
true of all Chinese loan morphemes, since these are limited to the appropriate
shapes. Many of the Chinese elements are bound, others are barely free; yet, they
are highly productive in making compounds, so we call them "suffixes" even though
the meaning they impart to the compound may be quite substantial, and they often
constitute the semantic head of the compound. There is no need to list the "preaccented" suffixes as such, for they are members of an open set and the accentual
locus in their compounds is predicted by the general rule for all noun compounds.
But there is another set of "atonicizing suffixes" that is essentially closed,
though apparently growing in membership. Only atonic compounds are created by
suffixes such as -teki '-ic' (a device for making abstract adjectival nouns) or -sei
'-ness, characteristic' (a device for making abstract [pure] nouns) or -siki 'type'
(compare -^{7}siki 'ceremony' or 'formula'), and the like, as well as a number of
syntactically quasi-free native elements like -gata 'model' or 'shape' and -mono
'one characterized by being ⋯ ' (but -mono 'thing; act; person' follows more
idiosyncratic rules). Membership in the class of atonicizing suffixes is much the
same in all dialects that have distinctive locus, but Tōkyō appears to be extending
the class by offering an atonic option to compete with the regular preaccentuation
for a number of suffixes, such as -[^{7}]sya 'vehicle' and -[^{7}]kin 'money'. A fairly
comprehensive list of atonicizing suffixes will be found in Chart 18, which also
lists minor types of exceptional suffixes, such as that of -zyo^7 (with no retreat)
varying with -zyo (atonicizing) 'place'.

It should be emphasized that the rules of register assignment work from the
beginning of a compound and the rules of locus work from the end. When any further

compounding takes place, the pattern will remain the same, and the constituency of
the larger compound is irrelevant. However long the word, and whatever may be its
constituency, you can tell its register by checking the first element and its locus
by finding the last point in the word where a compound rule could be applied.
Infinitive-derived nouns are treated as simplex units even when derived from a
compound verb, since those deriving from a compound verb already had an atonic
pattern assigned by the derivation process itself.

10.4. The accentuation of noun compounds in 11th-century Kyōto.

In the following pages you will find examples culled from Myōgi-shō (and
occasionally other sources) that seem to follow certain rules of compound-noun
accentuation. (For other studies of a similar sort, see Sakurai 1958a and Hayata
1977a.) As in the modern language, there are exceptions to the rules. Some of these
"exceptions" may represent nothing more than mistakes in the manuscripts; others
may be the result of morphophonemic notation or of treating the compounds as simple
syntactic reductions (preserving the patterns of the components),[8] and undoubtedly
some are due to factors beyond our ability to discover. Rules 1 and 2 could well be
collapsed into a single rule — or, rather, a general statement: initial register
persists until changed by a locus. The locus of the accent placed by Rule 3 is
sometimes the last syllable, sometimes the next to last; the place of realizing
the locus may have varied freely or perhaps it was determined by factors yet to be
discovered. The rules for accentuating compound nouns ($N_1 + N_2$):

1. If N_1 begins high, the compound will be HH··· (at least) and often HHH··· .
An exception: kara 'husk; handle' + sawo 'pole' → karasafo = karasawo 'flail'.
And this will be an exceptional case even if we choose an alternative etymology
kara- 'of Chinese/foreign origin' for the first element, for while the initial low
is thereby explained, Rule 5 is disregarded. The accent of the word for 'husk;
handle' is anomalous in modern Kyōto: low atonic kara, kara ga.

2. If N_1 begins low, the compound will be LL··· (at least) and often LLL··· .
There seem to be no exceptions.

3. When there is a CHANGE (i.e. an accentual locus) in N_2, such as LH or HL,
there will usually be a change (a locus) on the last or next-to-last syllable of
the compound, which may or may not coincide with the original locus of N_2. There
are a number of exceptions: tabibito; ifebato, inagi, inamura, kotowaza, nafasaba,
tamagusi, tukigoro, umabiyu, warabuta, amagufa, ...

4. When the compound is five syllables or longer there will usually be a change (an accentual locus) at the next-to-last or last syllable, whether N₂ itself has an original locus or not: k̄īzu + t̄ōkōrō → k̄īzudōkōrō 'wound', ofo- + oyobi → ofooyobi 'thumb', ... Some exceptions: nikimibana 'pimply nose', yamakagami 'Ampelopsis japonica', ...

5. For compounds of four syllables or fewer, when N₂ is atonic, either HH[H] or LL[L], the compound is usually atonic:

mimi + kuso → mimikuso 'earwax'   n̄īfa + t̄ōrī → n̄īfatōrī 'chicken'
fama + f̄īsī → famabisi 'burnut'   t̄ōrī + ami → t̄ōrīami 'bird net'
wāra + f̄ūta → warabuta 'straw seat-mat' f̄ītō + t̄ōmō → f̄ītōdōmō 'people'
muḡī + nafa → muginafa 'cruller'   f̄āta + foko → fatafoko 'flag spear'

But there are a number of exceptions:

kafa + m̄ūsī → kafam̄ūsī 'caterpillar'   ur̄ī + fafe → urifafe 'melon fly'
yama + m̄omō → yamamomo 'wild peach'   ine + kuki → inaguk̄ī 'rice stalk'
tama + k̄īzu → tamak̄īzu 'gem flaw'   kas̄ū + kome → kasugome 'wine lees'
yama + kak̄ī → yamagak̄ī 'wild persimmon' wāra + kutu → waragutu 'straw shoes'
m̄ītī + f̄ātī → m̄ītībat̄ī 'honey bee'   asa + k̄āfo → asagafo 'morning-glory'
tura + fone → turafone 'face bone'
fama + kuri → famagur̄ī 'clam'   wo + fone → wobone 'tail bone'
asi + kasi → asiᵏ/ɡas̄ī 'shackles'   no + tati → nodat̄ī '(dagger)'
....
kut̄ī + fas̄ī → kut̄ībasi 'beak of bird'   īfa + koke → īfagoke 'rock moss'
as̄ī + nafa → as̄īnafa 'reed rope'   f̄ūmi + f̄āko → f̄ūmibako 'box for letters'
as̄ī + wata → as̄īwata 'reed tips growing īsi + kan̄ī → īsigani 'rock crab'
                      like cotton'   k̄āfa + t̄āke → k̄āfatake 'river bamboo'
f̄ā + k̄ōrōmō → f̄āgōrōmo 'feather gown'

Examples of N₁ + N₂ compounds from Myōgi-shō. Exceptions are marked with ⁺.

2.1 HH   +   1.1 H   →   HHH
    fana 'nose'   ti 'blood'   fanati = fanadi 'nosebleed'
                      ke 'hair'   fanage-··· 'nostril hair'
                  2.1 HH   HHHH
    kasa 'sore'   futa 'lid'   kusabuta 'scab'
    nifa 'garden'   tori 'bird'   nifatori 'chicken'
    kuti 'mouth'   fasi 'edge'   ⁺ kutibasi 'beak of bird'   ⁺HHHL

	2.2	HL			HHHL	
sake 'wine'			tuki 'cup'		sakaduki 'wine cup'	
kane 'metal'			mari 'bowl'		kanamari 'metal bowl' (also ⁺HHHH?)	
	2.3	LL			HHHH	
fata 'loom; cloth'			mono 'thing'		fatamono 'loom'	
kane 'metal'			kuso 'dung'		kanakuso 'slag'	
tori 'bird'			ami 'net'		toriami 'bird net'	
kubi 'neck'			kasi 'shackles'	⁺	kubikasi 'cangue, pillory' ⁺HHHL	
	2.4	LH(-H)			HHHL	
turi 'fishing'			fune 'boat'		turibune 'fishing boat'	
kane 'metal'			tuti 'hammer'		kanaduti 'hammer'	
			tuwe 'staff'		kanaduwe 'metal staff'	
			fasi 'chopsticks'		kanabasi 'metal chopsticks'	
	2.5	LH(-L)			HHHL	
kane 'metal'			nabe 'pan'		kananabe 'metal pan'	
kuti 'mouth'			fibi 'cracks'		kutifibi 'chapped lips'	
	3.1	HHH			HHHHL	
kizu 'wound'			tokoro 'place'		kizudokoro 'wound'	
kasa 'sore'			tokoro 'place'		kasadokoro 'sore'	
kane 'metal'		HHx	fodasi 'shackle'		kanafodasi 'metal foot-shackle'	
	3.4	LLL			HHHHL	
take 'bamboo'			fakari 'yardstick'		takebakari 'bamboo yardstick'	
tori 'bird'		LLx	afase 'matching'		toriafase 'cockfight'	
	3.5a	LLH(-H)			HHHHL	
sake 'wine'			abura 'grease'		sakaabura 'unstrained sake'	
fana 'nose'			fasira 'pillar'		fanabasira 'bridge of nose'	

2.2	HL		+	1.1	H		→	HHH	
	? aza 'birthmark'			na 'name'				azana 'alias; falsehood'	
					1.3	L(-H)		HHL	
	sita 'below'			mo 'garment'				sitamo 'lower garment'	
					2.1	HH		HHHH	
	fito 'person'			tomo 'together'				fitodomo 'people'	
	kafa 'river'			take 'bamboo'			⁺	kafatake 'river bamboo'	⁺HHLL
	fumi 'letters'			fako 'box'			⁺	fumibako 'box for letters'	⁺HHLL
	isi 'stone'			kani 'crab'			⁺	isigani 'rock crab'	
					2.2	HL		HHHL, HHLL (no examples?)	
	tabi 'journey'			fito 'person'			⁺	tabibito 'traveler'	⁺HHHH⁹
					2.3	LL		HHHH	
	fata 'flag'			foko 'spear'				fatafoko 'flagged spear'	
	kafa 'river'			kame 'tortoise'			⁺	kafagame 'river tortoise'	⁺HHLL
	isi 'stone'			kame 'tortoise'			⁺	isigame 'terrapin'	⁺HHLL
	ifa 'rock'			koke 'moss'			⁺	ifagoke 'rock moss'	⁺HHLL
					2.4	LH(-H)		HHHL	
	kami 'paper'			zeni 'money'				kamizeni 'paper money'	
					2.5	LH(-L)			
				Examples lacking.					

	3.1	HHH		HHHHL	
kafa 'river'		yanagi 'willow'		kafayanagi 'purple willow'	
isi 'stone'	HHx	tatami 'mat'		isidatami 'stone paving'	
	3.4	LLL		HHHHL	
fito 'person'		kasira 'head'		fitogasira 'weathered skull'	
	3.7	LHL		HHHHL	
ifa 'rock'		kusuri 'drug'		ifakusuri 'lendrobium'	

2.3	LL	+	1.1	H	→	LLL (Examples?)	
	toki 'time'			yo 'world'	⁺	tokiyo 'era'	⁺LLH[10]
			2.1	HH		LLLL	
	fama 'beach'			fisi 'caltrop'		famabisi 'burnut'	
	nafa 'rope'			saba 'mackerel'		nafasaba 'dolphin'	
	kafa 'skin'			musi 'bug'	⁺	kafamusi 'caterpillar'	⁺LLHL
	kuso 'shit'			musi 'bug'	⁺	kusomusi 'gold bug'	⁺LLHL
	tama 'gem'			kizu 'wound'	⁺	tamakizu 'gem flaw'	⁺LLHL
	yama 'mountain'			momo 'peach'	⁺	yamamomo 'wild peach'	⁺LLHL
	yama 'mountain'			suge 'sedge'	⁺	yamasuge 'wild sedge'	⁺LHLL
	yama 'mountain'			kaki 'persimmon'	⁺	yamagaki 'wild persimmon'	⁺LLLH
	yumi 'bow'			fazu 'notch'	⁺	yumufazu 'bowstring notch'	⁺LLLH[11]
			2.2	HL		LLLH	
	fama 'beach'			kuri 'chestnut'		famaguri 'clam'	
	yama 'mountain'			nasi 'pear'		yamanasi 'wild pear'	
	siri 'butt(ock)'			fone 'bone'		siribone 'tail bone'	
						LLHL	
	mame 'bean'			kara 'shell'		mamegara 'bean pod'	
	yumi 'bow'			turu '(bow)string'		yumiduru 'bowstring'	
	nafa 'rope'			semi 'cicada'		nafaᵃ/ᵤemi 'female cicada'	
	yumi 'bow'			tuka 'hilt'		yumiduka 'bow-hilt'	
					⁺	LLLL (Rule 3 disregarded.)	
	tama 'gem'			kusi 'skewer'		tamagusi 'sprig of sakaki'	
	tuki 'moon'			koro 'time'		tukigoro 'the past few months'	
			2.3	LL		LLLL	
	mimi 'ear'			kuso 'dung'		mimikuso 'earwax'	
	tuti 'earth'			kura 'storehouse'		tutigura 'cellar'	
				muro 'room'		tutimuro 'cellar'	
	fana 'flower'			kame 'jar'		fanagame 'flowerpot'	
				fusa 'bunch'		fanabusa 'calyx'	
	kame 'jar'			fara 'belly'		kamebara '(an ailment)'	
	yama 'mountain'			kufa 'mulberry'		yamagufa 'wild mulberry'	
			2.4	LH(-H)		LLLH(, LLHL?)	
	kafa 'skin'			kinu 'garment'		kafaginu 'fur garment'	
	fara 'belly'			obi 'belt'		faraobi 'bellyband'	
					⁺	LLLL (Rule 3 disregarded.)	
	uma 'horse'			fiyu 'amaranthus'		yamabiyu '(plant name)'	
			2.5	LH(-L)		(LLLH — No examples?)	
						LLHL	
	kufa 'mulberry'			mayu 'cocoon'		kufamayu 'silkworm'	
						LLHH	
	tuti 'earth'			nabe 'pot'		tutinabe 'earthenware pot'	

	3.1	HHH		LLLHL
mimi 'ear'		kusari 'chain'		mimigusari 'ear pendant'
	?	futagi 'plug(ging)'		mimifutagi 'ear plug'
fama 'beach'		sasage 'cowpea'		famasasage 'Caesalpinia japonica'
kafa 'skin'		koromo 'gown'		kafagoromo 'fur gown' (also ⁺LLLL)
	3.2	HHL		LLLHL
yama 'mountain'		ubara 'rosebush'		yamaubara 'wild rose'
	3.4	LLL		LLLHL
ofo- 'big'		oyobi 'finger'		ofooyobi 'thumb'
yama 'mountain' (?)		kagati 'gr. cherry'		yamakagati 'wild ground cherry'
				LLLLH
kuso 'dung'		fukuro 'bag'		kusobukuro 'stomach'

2.4 LH   +   1.1 H   →   LLL
naka 'inside'		ko 'child'		nakago 'center'
	1.3	L(-H)		LHL
usu 'mortar'		fa 'tooth' (1.3b)		usuba 'molar tooth'
ine 'riceplant'		ki 'tree' (1.3a)	⁺	inagi 'drying pole ··· ' ⁺LLL
	2.1	HH		LLLL
wara 'straw'		futa 'lid'		warabuta 'straw lid'
uri 'melon'		fafe 'fly'	⁺	uribafe 'melon fly' ⁺LLLH
zeni 'money'		kasa 'sore'	⁺	zen(i)gasa 'ringworm' ⁺LLHL
	2.2	HH		LLHL
mugi 'barley'		kara 'shell'		mugigara 'barley husk'
naka 'inside'		koro 'time'		nakagoro 'midway'
			⁺	LLLL (Rule 3 disregarded.)
ine 'riceplant'		mura 'bunch'		inamura 'rick'
	2.3	LL		LLLL
mugi 'barley'		nafa 'rope'		muginafa 'cruller'
ine 'riceplant'		kuki 'stalk'	⁺	inaguki 'rice stalk' ⁺LHHL
kasu 'dregs'		kome 'rice'	⁺	kasugome 'wine lees' ⁺LHHH
wara 'straw'		kutu 'shoes'	⁺	wara(g)utu 'straw shoes' ⁺LLLH
	2.4	LH		LLLH
kinu 'silk'		kasa 'umbrella'		kinugasa 'silk umbrella'
		ita 'board' LLxH		kinuita 'fulling block'
mugi 'barley'		kasu 'lees'		mugikasu 'barley bran'
	2.5	LH(-L)		
		(Examples lacking.)		
	3.1	HHH		LLLHL
wara 'straw'		fumide 'brush'		warafumide 'straw brush'
	3.4	LLL		LLLHL
ine 'riceplant'		turubi 'mating'		inaturubi 'lightning'

2.5 LH(-L)   +   1.2 H(-L)   →   LLH
asa 'morning'		fi 'sun'		asafi 'morning sun'
	1.3	L(-H)		LLH or LHL (Examples?)
			⁺	LLL (Rule 3 disregarded.)
nama 'raw'		su 'vinegar'		namasu 'sliced raw fish'
koto 'harp'		wo 'cord'		kotowo 'harp-string'

		2.1	HH		LLLL *(Examples?)*[12]	
	asa 'morning'		kafo 'face'	+	asagafo 'morning-glory'	+LLHL
		2.2	HL		LLLH	
	tate 'vertical'		isi 'stone'		tateisi 'upright stone'	
		2.3	LL		LLLL	
	mayu 'eyebrow'		sumi 'charcoal; ink'	mayuzumi 'eyebrow paint'	
		2.4	LH		LLLH	
	ame 'rain'		kinu 'clothing'		amaginu 'raincoat'	
		2.5	LH(-L) *(Examples lacking.)*		

3.1	HHH	+	2.1	HH	
	tamari < vb.			midu 'water'	tamari<u>midu</u> 'stagnant water'
			2.3	LL	
	fituzi 'sheep'			kusa 'grass'	fituzi<u>gusa</u> 'waterlily'

3.4	LLL	+	2.1	HH	
	kasira 'head'			kasa 'sore'	kasira<u>gasa</u> 'scalp sore(s)'
			2.3	LL	
	itati 'weasel'			kusa 'grass'	itati<u>gusa</u> 'forsythia'
			2.4	LH	
	ikusa 'battle'			fune 'boat'	ikusa<u>bune</u> 'warship'

3.5	LLH	+	2.2	HL	
	yamato 'Japan'			uta 'song'	yamat<u>outa</u> 'Japanese song'[13]
			2.3	LL	
	abura 'oil'			wata 'cotton'	abura<u>wata</u> 'hair-oil cotton'
				tuno 'horn'	abura<u>duno</u> 'wheel-oil container'
			2.5	LH(-L)	
	yamato 'Japan'			koto 'harp'	yamato<u>koto</u> 'Japanese harp'[14]

3.6	LHH	+	2.1	HH	
	tumuzi 'whirl'			kaze 'wind'	tumuzi<u>kaze</u> 'whirlwind'
			2.2	HL	
	okina 'gaffer'			hito 'person'	okina<u>bito</u> 'old person'[15]
			2.3	LL	
	usagi 'rabbit'			(m)uma 'horse'	u<u>sagimuma</u> 'donkey'
			2.4	LH	
	karasu 'crow'			uri 'melon'	karasu<u>uri</u> 'snakegourd'[13]
				mugi 'barley'	karasu<u>mugi</u> 'oats'[14]
			2.5	LH(-L)	
	karasu 'crow'			femi 'snake'	karasu<u>femi</u> 'black snake'

3.7	LHL	+	2.1	HH	
	tubaki 'camellia'			momo 'peach'	tubaki<u>momo</u> 'nectarine'

4.5	LLLL	+	1.3	L(-H)	
	nof/kogiri 'saw'			fa 'tooth'	nokogiri-ba, nokogiriba⁻ 'sawtooth'

4.9	LLHL	+	3.4	LLL	
	yumiduru 'bowstring'	fukuro 'bag'			yumi<u>durubukuro</u> 'bowstring bag'

11. Accent patterns of longer nouns.

The earlier accent patterns of nouns of one, two, and three syllables can be reconstructed on the basis of the modern dialects, as we have seen in §4, and these reconstructions generally coincide with types attested for 11th-century Kyōto in Myōgi-shō and other sources; but it is difficult to use dialect information to reconstruct the accentuation of longer nouns, for many of these are compounds and their patterns have been remodelled in the later dialects. Below are listed the patterns of longer nouns for which examples can be found in Myōgi-shō. Some of the words are only partially attested, for not all of the syllables carry marks; these examples are preceded by a question mark and assigned types by extrapolation from similar structures or from dialect comparisons. Not all of the examples in §10 are recapitulated here; the list is comprehensive but not exhaustive.

4.1 HHHH   tomodati 'friend', futokoro 'bosom', ifamuro 'stone cellar', itadura 'idle; prank', kamudati (> kaudi, *kaudu > koozu) 'malt, yeast', katabami 'wood sorrel, oxalis', minamoto 'source', misazaki 'mausoleum', murasame 'passing shower', nifatori 'chicken', orimono 'textile', sakasama 'upside-down', siutome 'mother-in-law', sofemono 'addition', tabibito 'traveler', tomogara 'companion', toriami 'bird net', yukusaki 'destination, future'; ? kedamono 'animal', ...

4.2 HHHL   fobasira 'mast', futatabi 'twice', inisife 'yore', kamizeni 'paper money', kanaduti 'hammer', konokata 'thenceforth', manaita 'chopping board', morotomo 'together', ? musasabi 'flying squirrel', sakaduki 'wine cup', takumamo 'bulrush', turibune 'fishing boat', ukifasi 'floating bridge', wineburi = inemuri 'dozing', ...

4.3 HHLL   fatusimo (= fatu simo 2.1 + 2.3) 'first frost', fumibako 'box for letters', isigame 'terrapin', isigani 'rock crab', katagayu 'firm-cooked rice', kurenawi 'crimson', midukane 'mercury', nayoᵗ/ᵭake 'pliant bamboo', ...

4.4 HLLL   mitokoro 'three places/points', mizakari 'at its height', ...

4.5 LLLL   awouri '(melon)', awosaba 'mackerel', ? fanabira 'petal', ifebato 'domestic pigeon', imouto 'younger sister', (? kaminari 'thunder' *unattested in Mg*), kamizori = kamisori 'razor', kam[u]zasi 'hairpin' (also kanzasi 4.6), kasumomi 'craw of bird', katabiwo 'podocarp (= maki)', kotowaza 'proverb', kudamono 'fruit', kurogane 'iron', mayuzumi 'eyebrow paint', mimisifi 'deaf', ofogasa 'big umbrella', ofotori 'big bird', otouto 'younger brother', ofokaze 'big wind', ofogane 'big money', tugomori 'last day of month', urusine 'nonglutinous rice', waromono = warumono 'rascal'; ... .

4.6 LLLH   amaginu 'raincoat', famaguri 'clams', faraobi 'bellyband', irokudu 'gills', kanzasi 'hairpin' (= kam[u]zasi 4.5), karauri 'cucumber', kamouri 'winter melon', katafara 'side', katim[u]do 'pedestrian' (< *kati-n[o] pito), kinugasa 'silk umbrella', neriito 'scoured thread', sirouri 'white muskmelon', sitadami 'periwinkle', tateisi 'upright stone', umisiru 'pus'; ? maborosi 'phantom', ...

4.7 LLHH   amabiko 'echo', karakago 'croaker *(fish)*', karakura 'saddle', koforogi 'cricket', komeˢ/ᵤzaki 'broken rice', noramame 'wild beans', senbei 'rice crackers' (< Ch), sirokane = sirogane 'silver', toneriko 'ash tree', tutinabe 'earthenware pot', ...

4.8 LHHH   arui-fa = aruiwa 'or, perhaps', kasugome 'wine lees', ofobune 'big
boat', otogafi 'lower jaw', sensai = senzai 'garden plantings' (< Ch), tuzurame
'widened/surprised eyes', ...
4.9 LHHL   karibito 'hunter' (= kariudo = karyuudo), murasaki 'purple', tatibana
'orange', tuᶠ/ᵦubusi 'anklebone', tubunaᵏ/ᵧi 'anklebone', ...
4.10 LHLL   fasibami 'filbert', kasasagi 'magpie', kasesaba 'hammerhead shark',
namekuti = namekuzi 'slug', orifusi 'occasion', tuwamono 'weaponry', yusabari
'swing'; ikubaku 'how much' (or 4.9?), ? yamabato 'turtledove' (or 4.5?); sukosiki
'little', sibaraku 'for a while' (or 4.11?); ... .
4.11 LLHL   asagafo 'morning-glory', fukigawa 'bellows', ikaruga 'grosbeak,
Japanese hawfinch', kafabori (= koomori) 'bat', karaefi = karei 'flatfish', kayaguki
'lark', mamegara 'bean pod', nakagoro 'midway', tanasoko 'palm of hand', tanasuwe
'fingertips', uguisu = ugufisu 'bush warbler', ...
Also four-syllable adjectival nouns with the endings ···ka ···yaka, or ···raka:
atataka 'warm', awoyaka 'blue', azayaka 'clear', fanayaka 'gorgeous', fogaraka
'cheerful', komayaka 'dense', matoyaka 'round', madaraka 'striped', mameyaka
'serious', meduraka 'rare', ogosoka 'solemn', sukuyoka (= sukoyaka) 'healthy',
sumiyaka 'swift', tawoyaka 'pliant', yafaraka 'soft'.

5.1   HHHHH   fataorime 'weaver-girl', maturigoto 'government', onodukara 'self',
... .
5.2   HHHHL   akaaduki 'red bean', akamagusa 'Eupatorium lindelyanum', awogaferu
'tree frog', fanagenuki 'nostril tweezers', fitogasira 'weathered skull', fituzigusa
'waterlily', isidatami 'stone paving', kafayanagi 'purple willow', kasadokoro
'sore', ? katatuburi 'snail'[1], kizudokoro 'wound', kosiguruma 'parade float',
kutisakira 'lips; bill', sukumomusi 'peat-bug', takabakari 'bamboo yardstick',
teratutuki 'woodpecker', toriafase 'cockfight', ...
5.3   HHHLL   kafarafudi 'river wisteria', magarikane 'carpenter's square',
tamarimidu 'stagnant water', tumuzikaze 'whirlwind', ...
5.4   HHLLL   arakazime 'beforehand', yomezukae 'boudoir attendant', ...
5.5   HLLLL   ikumidake (NS) 'luxuriant bamboo', ? ... .

5.6   LLLLL   aburaduno 'wheel-oil container', fakarikoto 'scheme', famafukura
'Carpesium abrotanoides', fitotubiru 'garlic bulb', kokorozasi 'hope', niofiuma
'packhorse', uguromoti 'mole (rodent)', warafayami 'intermittent fever', ...
5.7   LLLLH   aburatuki 'lamp', fitofeginu 'unlined garment', kusobukuro 'stomach',
oyobinuki 'thimble', tatibukuro 'sword bag', ...
5.8   LLLHH   ikusabune 'warship', naribisako 'gourd', rokurogana 'lathe', ...
5.9   LLHHH   kasikigate 'hodgepodge', ofotudumi[2] 'large drum', ?
yamatokoto[3] 'Japanese harp', ...
5.10   LHHHH   katatagafi 'disarray', uᵃ/ᵤagim[u]ma[4] 'donkey', utimidari 'a kind of
fancy box', ...
5.11   LHHHL   ayamegusa 'sweetflag', karasuuri 'snakegourd', m[u]mago-mefi/-wofi
'grand-niece/nephew', tubunegusa 'Asarum nipponicum', ...
5.12   LHHLL   karasumugi 'oats' (also 5.11), suzumidaka 'female sparrow-hawk', ...
5.14   LLHHL   ofounaᵗ/ᵈe 'the Great/Grand Canal', umatunagi 'horse depot',
yamatouta 'Japanese song', ...
5.15   LLHLL   kuromanako 'black eyes', yamakagati 'huge snake', yamautugi
'Clerodendron trichosomum', yukafabira 'unlined bathrobe', ...

5.16 LLLHL   aburabiki 'oil brush', fafakibosi 'comet', inabikari 'lightning', inaturubi 'lightning', itatigusa 'forsythia', kagamikake 'mirror stand', kakuremiti 'secret passage', karasufemi 'black snake', kasiragasa 'head wound', kotodomori 'stammering', mugisukufi 'barley scoop', ofooyobi 'thumb', sironamari 'lead', sisibisifo 'salted chopped meat', warafumide 'straw brush', and five-syllable adjectival nouns ending -raka: tubafiraka/tumabiraka 'in clear detail', ...

6.1 HHHHHH   noborikudari (?= 3.1 + 3.1) 'ascent and descent', tafaburegoto 'prank', ...
6.2 HHHHHL   kaburamimizu 'a kind of earthworm', katafarabone 'ribs', koromotutumi 'clothes bundle, furoshiki', minasikogusa 'Cynanchum atratum', watasibune 'ferry boat', yatumekabura 'whistling arrow (···)', ...
6.3 HHHHLL   agekasugafi 'latch for a push-up door', asifaragani 'a kind of crab', nifakunaburi 'wagtail (bird)', ...
? 6.4 HHHLLL   --- ;   ? 6.5 HHHLLL   --- ;   ? 6.6 HLLLLL   ---

6.7 LLLLLL   ? ikufatokoro 'target mound' (or 6.22?), yamasirogafa (NS) 'the Yamashiro River', ...
? 6.8 LLLLLH   --- ;   ? 6.9 LLLLHH   ---
6.10 LLLHHH   kamiokosina 'common thistle', ? netamasigafo (Kn Mg) = netamasikafo (Ck Mg) 'jealous face', ofo-mu-fusuma (NS) 'august bedding', ofo-mu-takara (NS) 'the (common) people, the peasantry', ? ... .
6.11 LLHHHH   yamatokauti 'Yamato and Kawachi = east and west', ...
? 6.12 LHHHHH   ---
6.13 LHHHHL   fisikoiwasi 'anchovy', ofonemusi 'rice weevil', tufamonogura 'armory', utikake^k/ginu 'a kind of long garment', ...
? 6.14 LHHHLL   yubaribukuro 'bladder' (LHxHLL), ? ... .
? 6.15 LHHLLL   --- ;   ? 6.16 LHLLLL   ---
6.17 LLHHHH   ofoyakegoto 'public affairs', ? yamadorikusa 'barrenwort', ...
? 6.18 LLHHLL   --- ;   ? 6.19 LLHLLL   ---
6.20 LLLHHL   kaminoyagara 'Gastrodia elata', ofomitegura 'offerings to gods', ...
6.21 LLLHLL   anafazikami 'ginger', ? ikusaguruma 'war chariot', imo^s/ziutome 'wife's sisters', kataminasigo 'half-orphan', ...
6.22 LLLLHL   kamakirimusi 'longhorned beetle', kokoromadofi 'bewilderment', komuragaferi 'leg cramp', kugutumafasi 'puppeteer', sagarifusube 'drooping wart/ wen', sitadeyubari 'urine drip', ...
6.23 LLLLLH   asidaka^k/gumo (= asidaka-no kumo) 'daddy-longlegs', ? ... .

... (Unattested types are not listed.)
7.2   HHHHHHL amak/gutinedumi 'house mouse', kafakumatudura 'spindletree'.
7.3   HHHHHLL karasukutinafa 'black snake'.
? 7.10 LLLHHHH ? itatihazikami 'Japanese pepper tree', ? ofomiatuomono (NS) 'august broth'.
7.11 LLLLHHH ofoutadokoro (Km waka notes) 'Imperial Poetry Bureau'.
7.14 LHHHHHH tatematurimono 'offering to a superior; ··· '.
7.16 LHHHHLL tikirikauburi 'head kerchief'.
7.21 LLLLLHL ooziga-huguri (= 4.7 + 3.2) 'a lump of praying-mantis eggs', sirokanedukuri 'made of silver', yumidurubukuro 'bowstring bag'.
7.30 LLLLHLL inaofosedori '(a bird)', kukutuboosi 'a kind of cicada'.

12. Phrase types and word types.

When an enclitic particle is attached to a noun the resulting phrase will have a pitch pattern identical to that of one of the groups of nouns of the appropriate number of syllables. To use examples from Myōgi-shō, the phrase t͞i n͞o 'of blood' (N 1.1-p) has the phrase pattern heard in the noun k͞ane 'metal' (N 2.1); the phrase k͞ane n͞o 'of metal' (N 2.1-p) has the pattern of k͞oromo 'gown' (N 3.1); the phrase k͞oromo n͞o 'of the gown' (N 3.1-p) has the pattern of t͞omodat͞i 'friend' (N 4.1); and so on. Paradigmatic forms of the verb and adjective also fall into patterns available for the equivalent number of syllables forming a noun or a noun + particle: k͞ataru 'tells' (V 3.A-ru) and k͞atasi 'is hard' (A 3.A-si) have the same tune as ad͞uki 'red bean' (N 3.2); mam͞oru 'protects' (V 3.B-ru) and takas͞i 'is high' (A 3.B-si), at least as we have treated them, share the melody of inot͞i 'life' (N 3.5); (*wakak͞u →) wakak͞u 'being young' (A 3.B-ku) carries the same pattern as kab͞uto 'helmet' (N 3.7) and kib͞i no 'of millet' (N 2.5-p); (*yorokob͞-u→) yorok͞obu 'rejoices' (V 3.B-ru) and uguf͞isu 'bush warbler' (N 4.11) are both LLHL; and so on. We can distinguish between basic WORD (or STEM) patterns and PHRASE patterns; the phrase patterns include all the word/stem patterns but expand the number as additional syllables are added by attaching endings and particles. Among the word patterns the stems of verbs and adjectives can be categorized with only the two registers high (A) and low (B), provided we account for a few minor exceptions, but a number of nouns require us also to take into account a locus of change (the "accent" as narrowly defined).

Kindaichi 1974:74-5 sets out to state the makeup of phrase patterns (which he calls the *gun*) in terms of word types (which he calls the *rui*). In Chart 13 I have tried to refine and elaborate Kindaichi's basic concept. This chart differs from Kindaichi's description in a number of details that mostly have to do with the interpretation of the patterns found in inflected forms[1] and with the decisions on the relative closeness with which particles were attached. In showing the makeup of phrase types in the chart, "-p" represents a one-mora atonic particle attached without an intervening juncture. I have not included the tonic particles posited in §5 because the paucity of data raises questions as to the validity of the category; and it is quite likely that ˈmo and ˈto (along with the other particles that are intrinsically low in modern Kinki dialects) were separated from the noun by an underlying juncture in at least some of their occurrences. I have also excluded from the chart a few other forms, including the unusual (B´) verb type exemplified by

a̱rī̱ku̱ / a̱rūku̱ 'walks', discussed elsewhere. Nor have I included the gerund structure
V-i t̄e, since t̄e was set off by juncture and given the independent accentuation
inherited from its origin as the infinitive of the auxiliary t̄u(ru). (If we were to
ignore the juncture and include the gerunds we would have to add a few unusual
patterns that allow a rise of pitch after a fall: Īre t̄e 'putting it in' would be
HLH and f̄azīme t̄e 'beginning it' would be HHLH, patterns that are anomalous and not
otherwise needed.) Also omitted are phrases with a string of particles (⋯ ni fa,
⋯ wo mo) because the sparse data hardly permit reliable conclusions at this time.
A number of the patterns undoubtedly contained other kinds of phrases, in addition
to those shown. As the phrases grow longer, the number of patterns increases, but
some of these patterns — as indicated by the question marks — are either poorly
attested or seemingly unattested. The designation for verbs and adjectives includes
a digit that represents the number of syllables in the stem + a one-syllable ending,
such as the usual "dictionary" forms V-ru and A-si. For longer adjectives only the
ending -ku is shown; the ending -si is subject to haplology when attached to those
adjective stems that end with the formant -si-, so that we find conflicting accent
patterns depending on which syllable /si/ is considered the omitted one (cf. §9).

    As in modern Kyōto, one-syllable nouns isolation were probably lengthened to
fit into the two-syllable classes, as if a particle were attached:

N 1.1	→ 2.1	tῙ → t̄ῙῙ	'Blood.'
N 1.2	→ 2.2	fà → f̄aa̱	'Leaf.'
N 1.3b	→ 2.4	fá → fa̱ā	'Tooth.' *(See n.2.)*

The length provides a mora to carry the fall (N 1.2) or rise (N 1.3b) of pitch.[2]
For a few words the extra mora is clearly attested, e.g. k̄Ῑi̱ (nari) 'yellow' in
Chinkoku-shukoku-jinja Myōgi-shō. It seems likely also that nouns of Type 2.5 were
lengthened in isolation so as to fit into the phrase pattern 3.7: sa̱rú was probably
pronounced sa̱rūu̱ in isolation ('Monkey.'), with the same tune as sa̱rū no̱ 'of the
monkey'. That is why our chart does not display a column for one-syllable phrases.
Although basic underlying shapes of a single syllable characterized several types of
nouns, we presume that one-syllable PHRASES did not exist — with the possible
exception of quasi-bound phrases after minor junctures, such as the gerund particle
⋯ | t̄e, but that too may have been pronounced long (t̄ee or t̄ee̱). Various particles
and endings are monosyllabic, as are five adjectives and a few verb stems.

13. Realization of register and accent in earlier Japanese.

We have a fairly clear picture of the accentual patterns of 11th-century Kyōto. Were these very different from those of 8th-century Nara, or from those of proto-Japanese? The only philological evidence available is in the kun readings of Koji-ki, where the character ZYOO ("rising [tone]") marks 32 words and KYO ("going [tone]") marks one word. The examples are given below with rough translations borrowed mostly from Philippi. The character ZYOO is transcribed with the asterisk "*" and KYO with the exclamation point "!".

(1) toyo kumwo * nwo [no] kamiy "Abundant-clouds-field deity'[1]
(2) u fyidi ni * [no] kamiy '[?]-mud-clay deity'
(3) su fyidi ni ! [no] kamiy 'Sand-mud-clay deity'
(4) aya * kasikwone [no] kamiy 'Ah-how-awesome deity'
(5) e * wotokwo wo 'What a fine lad!'
(6) e * wotomye wo 'What a fine maid!'
(7) futwomani ni * urafey te[y] 'divining by deer shoulder-bone cracks'
(8) e * fyimye 'What a fine princess!'
(9) ofo nwo-de[y] * fyimye 'Great-plain-hand princess'
(10) ofo tama-*-ru wakey 'Great-[?]'
(11) amey no fukyi * wo [no] kamiy 'Heavenly [roof-]thatching male deity'
(12) ofo yama * tu myi [no] kamiy 'Great-mountain-spirit deity'
(13) ma saka yama * tu myi [no] kamiy 'True-hill mountain-spirit deity'
(14) oku yama * tu myi [no] kamiy 'Interior mountain spirit deity'
(15) ina sikomey * sikomeykyi '[?] is frightful'
(16) soko tu wata * tu myi [no] kamiy 'Bottom sea-spirit deity'
(17) naka tu wata * tu myi [no] kamiy 'Middle sea-spirit deity'
(18) ufa[2] tu wata * tu myi [no] kamiy 'Upper sea-spirit deity'
(19) itikyi sima * fyimye [no] myikoto 'Ichiki-island princess goddess'
(20) fiy * [no] kafa 'the river Fiy'
(21) = (12)
(22) asi * nadu ti[y] 'Foot-stroking elder [deity]'
(23) te[y] * nadu ti[y] 'Hand-stroking elder [deity]'
(24) amey no tudofey tine * [no] kamiy 'Heavenly-congregating-[?] deity'
(25) fute myimyi * [no] kamiy 'Large-ear deity'
(26) sasi kuni ofo * [no] kamiy 'Great deity of the land of Sashi'
(27) ofo yama * kufyi[3] [no] kamiy 'Great-mountain-stake deity'
(28) (iro se) itu se [no] myikoto * '(Sibling) Five-rapids prince'
(29) u * kafyi ga tomo 'Cormorant-keepers group'
(30) suga-kama * yura dwomyi 'Suga-(ka)ma Yura female' (placenames?)
(31) tori * mye [no] myikwo '[Bird ?] princess'
(32) mwozu no myimyi * fara 'Mimihara [Ear-field] in Mozu'
(33) myimyi * [no] myikwo 'Prince of Mimi'

The passages raise two questions: (1) Why were only these few expressions chosen for the "tone" marking? (2) What phonetic realizations do the marks represent? Neither question has found a satisfactory answer. Most of the expressions are names derived from phrases that could be taken in more literal meanings; following an idea that originated with Keichū, it has been suggested that the mark is perhaps intended to indicate that in the names the usual accent is overridden. (Cf. Komatsu 1973:388, 1977a:364; and, most explicitly, 1981:237-40.) Kindaichi once offered the suggestion that the marks are intended to apologize for using Chinese characters that would have the "wrong" tone if read in the traditional Chinese. (Cf. Wada 1952.)

As we can see, the philological evidence available is scant and unrevealing. In the absence of evidence to the contrary, we can only assume that the accent system of 8th-century Nara differed little from that of 11th-century Kyōto. What about the earlier accent of the ancestral language, proto-Japanese? This is something we must reconstruct on the basis of the correspondences in the modern dialects and the attestations of 11th-century Kyōto, together with later attestations of the same area. With the possible exception of the additional subcategories proposed by Hayata and Hattori — and, perhaps, the distinction of 1.3a vs. 1.3b proposed earlier in this work — the correspondences in the main require no categories not attested i: Myōgi-shō.[4] Working algebraically, it is possible to derive all of the accentual categories of the modern dialects from those in that work. But accounting for the phonetic manifestations of the categories is a more difficult problem. Various attempts have been made to show how, for example, the Tōkyō-type dialects have simply shifted the locus of fall by one syllable (to the right). As McCawley points out, repeated one-syllable shifts of locus appear to have happened frequently — and independently — in various dialects. Most scholars assume that the pitch patterns o proto-Japanese, from which the rules would derive the modern accentuation of the dialect forms, are essentially those of 11th-century Kyōto. Kindaichi, for example, would derive the Tōkyō-type accents from the Kyōto type.[5] And Hirayama 1968:41 posits a kind of typological evolution: Kyōto-type → Tōkyō-type → Kagoshima-type. The simplest way to state the developments in a general way appears to be roughly as follows (cf. McCawley 1977):

(1) Kagoshima-type dialects retain the initial-register distinctions (A and B) and lose the locus distinctions. (But certain Ryūkyū dialects, such as Nakijin and Yonaguni, retain a reflex of the low tonic patterns as a kind of additional register, which we mark as "C".)

(2) Tōkyō-type dialects obscure the initial-register distinctions by shifting the locus of change, which — now as FALL from HIGH — becomes the only manifestation of accent. (But further developments then took place in such unusual dialects as Narada and Hirosaki, with a phonetic redefinition of the locus.)

(3) At some point the low plateau representing the "low atonic" categories became incompatible for both Tōkyō and Kyōto. Perhaps independently, they shifted 2.3 (LL) into 2.2 (HL); and Kyōto shifted 3.4 (LLL) into 3.3 (HLL) while Tōkyō put a locus on the final syllable.[6] (At the same time, or perhaps earlier, our 1.3a became part of 1.3b.) One result of all this was that the Kyōto high pitch on the final syllable of 2.4 (LH) and 3.6 (LHH, later LLH[7]) became nondistinctive except to mark juncture, serving as a cue to confirm the initial low register. Another result was that in Kyōto, as in Tōkyō, the distinctive locus was now always a FALL of pitch.

There remain many problems in plotting the phonetic developments found in the modern dialects and in accounting for the various mergers of accent types (§6). We will put these problems aside for future work. Meanwhile, let us turn our attention to the phonetic nature of initial register in proto-Japanese. From the accent of the modern dialects it would appear that this involved pitch level, as it does in Kyōto today. But the suggestion has been offered (Martin 1975a) that the primary phonetic manifestation of the "low" register may have been VOWEL LENGTH. That hypothesis was inspired by the number of otherwise unexplained long vowels found in Shuri, and to a lesser extent in other Ryūkyū dialects, in nouns of Types 2.3, 2.4, and especially 2.5. This notion is attractive, I believe, but perhaps the claim is too bold. Still to be explained is why the majority of low-register nouns did not maintain the vowel length and why so few verb stems seem to manifest the reflex.[8] If we were to apply the comparative method quite strictly, it would be necessary to reconstruct vowel length independently of the initial-register distinctions, leaving unexplained the preference of long-vowel words for the low register. Usually what is done is just to ignore the Ryūkyū long vowels, presuming that they can somehow be explained as secondary developments.[9] Either way, I feel that we are missing something important about the earliest form of the language.

Kindaichi (in Tōjō 1953:152) calls our attention to interesting phenomena from the southern part of the Noto peninsula of Ishikawa prefecture. According to Iwai Ryūsei (in Tōjō 1961:3:94-8) the dialect of Oshimizu in Hakui-gun of Ishikawa prefecture has a long first syllable in almost all words of Type 2.4 (such as kama 'sickle' and umi 'sea') and quite a few in Type 2.5 (such as aki 'autumn' and huna 'crucian carp'), with the pattern L:L or L:H in free variation; there are also some

examples of L:LL such as karasu 'crow' (Type 3.6). (As in Tōkyō, Type 2.3 has merged
into 2.2.) This would seem to be excellent independent evidence of the antiquity of
vowel length for the "low" pitch.[10]   It is disturbing that the Komatsu dialect has
vowel length in the first syllable of those words of Type 2.2 (hasi 'bridge', mati
'town', hiru 'daytime') and Type 2.3 (asi 'foot', kutu 'shoes', mimi 'ear') that end
in a high vowel, the pattern being H:L. But this is perhaps an independently arising
phenomenon; possibly it is a shape-restricted retention of the earlier vowel length
we assume for Type 2.3 extended to the less-populated Type 2.2 with the merger of
the two types, even though the pattern of the merged type does not begin with a low
pitch. Kindaichi favors the view that vowel length arose independently in these Noto
dialects and in the Ryūkyūs under similar influence of the accent and the [modern]
high vowel in the final syllable; but in the Ryūkyūs there are a few examples also
with final low vowel, such as Shuri naaka for naka 'inside' (Type 2.4), as well as
examples with final modern high vowels that come from earlier mid vowels. The ease
with which vowel length is lost — independently, sporadically, or under canonical
restrictions — can be seen in the compression of vowel length that is heard in many
kinds of modern Japanese. According to Kindaichi (in Tōjō 1953:151) long vowels
shorten optionally and sporadically in many of the Kinki and Shikoku dialects,
regularly in ("Kita-Oku" =) Hokuō (which means the northern part of Mutsu and thus
presumably Aomori and Iwate prefectures) and "Satsu-Gū" (= Satsuma and Ōsumi, i.e.
Kagoshima prefecture), and even in Tōkyō under certain shape restrictions.

Okumura 1972:139-74 argues that the accentual system must have been uniform for
all Japanese dialects until fairly late, at least up through the time that the loans
from Chinese ("Kango") were penetrating the spoken language, because he finds cross-
dialect classes for two-mora one-morpheme nouns in the borrowed material. Though not
without problems, this is a promising argument that deserves further exploration.
Notice that the traditional marking for the tones of Chinese characters when read in
isolation is often different from that found in genuine borrowings. According to
Kindaichi 1951b:700 the tradition for the Kan-on readings was just the opposite of
that for the Go-on readings: what was "even" in Kan-on is usually marked "rising"
or "going" in Go-on.

14. Double-accent nouns.

Certain of our word types have patterns in the Kyōto-type dialects (and also in the reconstructed earlier language) that first rise in pitch and then fall. The examples below illustrate this; where the modern Kyōto form differs from the earlier pattern, the development is shown in parentheses.

2.5   sarú(:) 'monkey', asá(:) 'morning'

3.7a   kusúri 'drug';   3.7b kabúto 'helmet'

4.9   murásaki 'purple' (> murásaki)

4.10   kasásagi 'magpie', sibáraku 'a while'

4.11   mamegára 'bean pod' (> mamegára), sumiyáka 'swift' (> sumiyáka)

5.11   karasuúri 'snakegourd'

5.12   karasúmugi, also karasumúgi 5.11 (> karasúmugi) 'oats'

5.16   inabíkari 'lightning' (> inabíkari)

A number of longer words that, in earlier Japanese, began with strings of more than two low syllables followed by high pitch and then a reversion back to low (such as 'lightning' above) have raised the initial low string to high in modern Kyōto. (The examples in Hirayama's dictionary with the notations "1;5" = LLLHL and the like are almost all the result of the modern compound-noun rules.) Perhaps this will help account for the fact that longer verbs and all adjectives (except those few with monosyllabic stems) have become high-initial (Type A) in Kyōto. Modern Tōkyō speakers, on the other hand, tend to make all the longer verbs "tonic", i.e. Type B.

With the longer nouns it is far from certain that what we detect in the notations of Myōgi-shō as distinctive patterns (LHLL 4.10 ≠ LLHL 4.11; LHHHL 5.11 ≠ LHHLL 5.12 ≠ LLLHL 5.16) were actually used to distinguish nouns in the eleventh century, for variant markings of the same word are sometimes found, as can be seen in the example 'oats' above. I suspect that the little-populated categories of 4.9 and 4.10 are probably to be put with the large and productive category 4.11. And probably 5.11 and 5.12 are to be taken as nondistinctive variants of (or even scribal mistakes for) the category 5.16. If that is true, we are left with the following patterns: 2.5   3.7   4.11   5.16

                                     LH(L)   LHL   LLHL   LLLHL

What sets a pattern of this group apart from all the rest is that it is marked not just in one way (by initial register) as are 2.1 and 2.3, 3.1 and 3.4, 4.1 and 4.5, 5.1 and 5.6, etc.; nor just in two ways (by initial register and by locus of change)

as are the rest. A pattern of this group is marked in THREE ways: the initial low
register, a locus of change, and a reversion to low pitch. One way of looking at
this is to say that there are two loci of change and that the nouns accordingly have
two "accents" in addition to the initial register. This view would appear to be
supported by the fact that most of the longer nouns involved are compounds, some
with pitch patterns that are the obvious results of the compound rules stated in
§10.4; the second accent could be explained as assigned by a rule of compounding or
as a remnant of the pitch pattern of one of the components. But doubt is cast on
that interpretation by the considerable number of simple two-syllable nouns of Type
2.5.¹ Let us look at the matter from a different point of view. Notice that the
reversion to low pitch is always located immediately after the locus of change to
high. We might be tempted to think that when the register is low the accent perhaps
manifests itself only as a momentary change of basic pitch level; yet that would be
untrue of phrase types like 3.6 (u̅s̅a̅g̅i̅ 'rabbit'), 4.7 (k̅o̅f̅o̅r̅o̅g̅i̅ 'cricket'), or 4.8
(o̅t̅o̅g̅a̅[f̅]i̅ 'lower jaw'). Instead, it appears that whatever was at work in the first
place to make the initial register low is once again operating immediately after the
accent in these words. Now, it was suggested in §13 that earlier vowel length was
what led to the initial low register; can we extend that hypothesis to include the
low pitch that repeats after the accent? Suppose we put the symbol ' before the
syllable that carries the abstract accent (locus) represented by change-of-pitch and
put a colon (:) after the vowel at the onset of low register or reversion thereto —
NOT, mind you, the onset of "low pitch", for when that occurs in a high-register
word it is part of the cues for the locus of change, telling us that the "accent" is
on the preceding syllable. Our examples will look like this:

2.5   sa:'ru: 'monkey', a:'sa: 'morning'
3.7   ku:'suri: 'drug', ka:'buto: 'helmet'
4.11   ma:me'gara: 'bean pod'
5.16   i:nabi'kari: 'lightning'

But now it is immediately apparent that the locus of pitch change is predictable,
given the location of the vowel length. The words can be written sa:ru:, a:sa:,
ku:suri:, ka:buto:, ma:megara:, i:nabikari:. Structurally — and earlier perhaps
phonetically, as well — these types are simply a special kind of atonic noun.

An alternative hypothesis deserves consideration. Suppose we assume that long
vowels occurred in the first syllable of 2.5 words only. Then we could state a rule
that "low pitch reverts immediately after the accent provided the first syllable is
long".

The rationale would be that the vowel length somehow reinforced the basic register; the reversion would be nondistinctive if we pinned the distinctiveness on the initial vowel. But such a view would obscure the beauty of separating the initial register from the locus. If you look at our chart of phrase types you will see that the types below the line in the chart are mirror images of the types above the line, provided we leave aside the double-accent categories. What we are saying is that the heavily populated categories of 2.1, 3.1, 4.1, etc., are simply "high-register" with no accent; the corresponding categories of 2.3, 3.4, 4.5, etc., are simply "low-register" with no accent. If the latter group, the low atonic phrases, are treated as the marked category, and the marking is written as (or as if) vowel length, the results will look like this:[2]

1.1	2.1	3.1	4.1
ki 'spirit'	hana 'nose'	katati 'shape'	minamoto 'source'

1.3a	2.3	3.4	4.5
ki: 'tree'	ha:na 'flower'	a:tama 'head'	ku:damono 'fruit'

The remaining types will pair off according to locus of accent:

1.2	2.2	3.2	3.3
ha' 'leaf'	ha'si 'bridge'	azu'ki 'red bean'	ti'kara 'strength'
[h͞a_ = h͞a͞a]	[h͞asi͟]	[a͞zuki͟]	[t͞i͞kara]

1.3b	2.4	3.5	3.6
ha:' 'tooth'	ha:'si 'chopsticks'	su:da're 'screen'	u:'sagi 'rabbit'
[ha͞⁻ = ha͞a͞]	[ha͟si͞]	[sudar͞e]	[u͟sagi͞]

The pitch patterns attested in Myōgi-shō, shown in brackets, can be derived from the forms by a set of rules that seem strange to us only because we are used to thinking of the accentual locus as a fall of pitch in the modern dialects.

The view of early Japanese accent presented above differs from that of other investigators in a number of ways. The particular implications can be summed up:

(1) The notion of "accent" is restricted to refer to a marking device that operates at most only once in a phrase.

(2) Something over 60 percent of the nouns of two and three syllables are atonic. If we distinguish 1.3a as an atonic low class, the same percentage prevails for the monosyllabic nouns as well. (This provides an independent argument in favor of making that distinction.)

(3) The number of tonic types available is equal to the number of syllables in the phrase; but some of the types theoretically available for longer phrases may have been little used and perhaps merged with the more common types.

(4) There is no need for a notion of "preaccented" nouns.

(5) In the earliest retrievable form of the language, vowel length (:) was probably the distinguishing characteristic of what we have called low register. The low pitch, if present, was a determined feature. Provided we reject Types 4.10, 5.12, and 7.17b (as suggested above), the distinctive vowel length could occur on the first syllable of a word, or on the first and last, but never on the last syllable alone, nor on any medial syllable.

The notion of vowel length as the distinguishing characteristic may well be questioned, especially with respect to the longer nouns. But it must be remembered that we can hardly hope to reconstruct many nouns longer than three syllables; most of the longer nouns, and indeed many of the shorter ones, are compounds made up in later days and their pitch is to be assigned according to the rules and phonetic manifestations of the time they came into being. Not all instances of our final ":" can be assumed to exist in proto-Japanese, if we think of that as a real language, for it is possible that by the time i:nabi'kari: and ma:me'gara: were created the vowel length may have lost its distinctiveness, replaced by the pitch cues. Yet it is interesting that the Shuri form for the compound noun 'bean pod' is maamigaraa (accent type B), which preserves much of the form we would like to posit for early Japanese. But our mu:'rasaki: 'purple' (of unknown etymology) corresponds to Shuri murasaci (accent B), and not *mu:rasaci: — perhaps because the close vowels have retained earlier length with less vigor, perhaps because of the open vowel in the second syllable, or maybe because only a minority of all the words retained vowel length into historic times in any event. (Another possibility is that the word is a loan from main-island Japanese.)

Hattori would reconstruct long vowels for part of the vocabulary of 2.3, 2.4, and 2.5. He finds that the long vowels will be needed also for one or two nouns of Type 2.2: kiba 'fang' and kusi 'skewer', but neither is a clear case, since kusi should rather be classified as 2.3 and kiba seems to be a compound. The length of Puusi (with distinctively unaspirated initial) 'star' (2.1) in the Kushi dialect of Okinawa is left unexplained. And Hattori overlooks the Shuri examples of yuuci B 'small ax' (Myōgi-shō yoki HH = 2.1; Hida yooki), saazi A 'heron' (sagi 2.1), and wiiri B 'collar' (eri 2.2). Hattori (22:111) hypothesizes that the Old Kyōto

low-register atonic nouns had final vowel prolongation with a rise in pitch which
later became the only cue once the vowel shortened. Independently of the accentual
phenomena, Hattori would reconstruct proto-Japanese long /oo/ for the ancestor — or
phonetic representation? — of Old Japanese *koo*-type "o", our (C)wo, e.g. *soodai
for swode 'sleeve'. And either /ee/ or /ai/ for the non-palatal version of the Old
Japanese syllable "ey", reconstructing *eebi or *aibi for eybyi 'shrimp'. He also
(22:107) reconstructs *aapaa 'millet' but *kapaa 'skin' and 'river' because the
medial labial consonant of 'millet' is preserved as -w- in Shuri (qawa), Yonamine
(qaawaa [?= Nakijin qawaa]), and Onna (qaawaa), whereas it is lost in the other two
words: Shuri kaa, Yonamine haa, Onna khaa. Apparently Hattori postulates a separate
proto-Japanese class for those nouns that turn up as CV:CV in Onna (or similar
dialects) from those that turn up as CV:CV:, with long vowels in both syllables.
The data are spotty, however, and for the moment it seems better to assume sporadic
compression or conflation of the final syllables; the pervasive lengthening of final
syllables in the Yonamine dialect certainly appears to be secondary, as are the
various lengthenings and shortenings of the Shodon dialect (see Martin 1970b and
Serafim 1984). It should be borne in mind that each of the morphemes (including the
monosyllables), that appears with a long vowel also has an allomorph with the short
vowel, as found in many compounds; and this is true whether the length is automatic
(as in the monosyllables) or distinctive. It is true for all the dialects that seem
to offer evidence for earlier vowel-length distinctions.

15. The historical development of modern accent patterns.

According to the prevailing view established by Kindaichi the accent patterns
of each of the modern dialects can be accounted for by a series of developments from
patterns like those of 11th-century Kyōto. Certain words show exceptional patterns
that are explained as due to such factors as the monosyllabification of separate
syllables into two-mora "heavy" syllables that in some dialects will not permit a
locus on the second mora (Tōkyō kaʾi < kaiʾ 'shell'); other syllable weakenings,
such as vowel devoicing, which shift the manifestations of the locus to an adjacent
stronger syllable; and analogy with homophones that earlier belonged to different
patterns. But the developments themselves are described in terms of a one-syllable
shift of locus that either anticipates or delays the phonetic realization of the
locus, which is usually a fall of pitch, and sometimes repeated shifts (to left or
right) are required to account for later forms. Kindaichi has neatly explained many

of the modern Tōkyō-type patterns by assuming a right-shift of the locus: o⌐to ›
oto⌐ 'sound' (2.2), ⌐matu › ma⌐tu 'pine' (2.4) and ⌐sarụ = ⌐saru⌐(u) › sa⌐ru (2.5).
This will attribute the loss of the low-register distinction to the right-shift of
the "preaccent" (representing the register) onto the first syllable, and the loss
of the "double-accent" of 2.5 to the right-shift of the second accent (representing
the locus) onto the boundary of a nonexistent syllable.[1]

   But in saying "We can regard the Tōkyō accent system as having split off from
the Kyōto system of the period of [Ogino Chiichi's 1776] Heike-seisetsu[2] = Heike-
mabushi" Kindaichi (1971:934) implies a surprisingly late date for the shifts. If in
fact the accent patterns of the Tōkyo-type dialects are derived from something like
the Kyōto-type patterns, then the divergence must have preceded Kyōto's merger of
Type 2.3 (yama › yāma) with 2.2 (ōto), since a number of the Tōkyō-type dialects
either (as in Ōita) preserve a distinctive 2.3 or (as in Akita and Sapporo) merge
it in a different way: with 2.1/2 only if the final vowel is i or u, otherwise with
2.4/5. Tōkyō's merger of 2.3 must have taken place independently of Kyōto's,
yet early enough for the "right shift" to operate uniformly on both classes. (Notice
also the merger of 2.3 with 2.1 in certain of the Kyōto-type dialects of Shikoku;
see the end of this section].) The loss of the atonic low-register class in Kyōto
took place between 1300 and 1450; see §10 n.1.

   Chart 21 outlines one attempt to derive the modern patterns of both Kyōto and
Tōkyō from those of 11th-century Kyōto. A series of stages is posited to account
for the necessary changes, but both the number and the chronology of the stages are
far from clear, especially with respect to Tōkyō.[3] Kindaichi 1975:72 assumes a
series of nine stages, with intermediate changes that are intended to account for
the patterns found in a variety of modern dialects on the Noto peninsula which seem
to be intermediate between "Kyōto-type" and "Tōkyō-type". Of particular interest
are his 6th stage, whereby āme ga 'rain' (2.5) becomes modern Hakuchi ame gā⌐ in
contrast with kasa ga 'umbrella' (2.4); his 8th stage, whereby modern Nozaki has
developed an initial high that is nondistinctive in āme gā but distinctive in
k̄asa ga; and his 9th stage, whereby modern Kōda (and Tōkyō) merge the two patterns
by dropping the final high of 2.4 so that the initial high becomes distinctive:
āme ga, k̄asa ga. Cf. Sakurai's explanation of the lack of velar elision in
eastern Japan for the adjective infinitive forms with the suffix -ku (Ch. 3, §2.)

   A number of scholars, however, have felt uneasy with Kindaichi's conclusion
that the Tōkyō patterns derive from patterns like those of Kyōto; they would feel

happier if it could be shown to be the other way around. More than fifty years ago
Hattori (1933:61, 70 n.5) pointed out that the dialect geography indicates that the
Tōkyō-type dialects must reflect the "older" patterns. Perhaps it would be possible
to consider an opposite development from what Kindaichi has proposed, and argue for
a left-shift in Kyōto from earlier patterns (of Old Kyōto or at least of proto-
Japanese) more like those of Tōkyō. That would explain the low register in Kyōto-
type dialects as a development that results from a shift of the locus to a position
BEFORE rather than after the first mora of a word, thereby lowering the pitch at the
beginning. (To be sure, this would leave still unexplained the distinction of the
least frequent type 2.5, which is distinguished only in the Kinki dialects; but on
that problem see Sakurai 1978a.) An explanation of this sort has been proposed by
Ramsey 1978 on the basis of morphophonemic phenomena; he suggests that something
like the Tōkyō pitch patterns were characteristic not only of proto-Japanese, but
also of the 11th-century "Old Kyōto" dialect, for he would reinterpret the tone
marks of Myōgi-shō and other sources with phonetic values that are just the reverse
of those hitherto assumed: the "even-tone" mark at the lower left of a character is
reinterpreted as high pitch and the "rising-tone" mark at the upper left as the low
pitch. The contrary attestations of the Muromachi period are attributed to a major
change in the Kyōto dialect during the Kamakura period, when the "low" atonic types
were lost (cf. §10 n.1). Ramsey's interpretation has appeal to those of us who find
it hard to believe that important — and similar — changes could take place in the
various peripheral dialects while the speech of the cultural and economic center of
the country (the Kinki area) remained remarkably stable, except for isolated pockets
in the mountains of southern Nara prefecture, which have patterns like those of
Tōkyō. Ramsey bases his reinterpretation on the pitch shapes of certain types of
noun when it serves as second member of a noun + noun compound[4] (would that perhaps
help explain the emergence of the class of "atonicizing suffixes"?), and on the
behavior of types corresponding to the Tōkyō oxytonic patterns when the enclitic
/no/ is attached. We will take a closer look at the latter phenomenon below.

   With the exception of certain dialects of Shikoku (see below, at the end of
§15), where 2.3 joins 2.1 (HH), and Ibuki-jima, all Kyōto-type dialects merge Type
2.3 (LL) with 2.2 (HL) so that both the earlier 2.2 and 2.3 are pronounced HL. A
similar merger takes place in some, but not all Tōkyō-type dialects: 2.3 is kept
apart from 2.2 (which falls together with 2.1 as atonic) by Ōita; by Niigata and
Hirosaki; and (except when the final vowel is i or u) by Akita, Sapporo, Matsue,

and Izumo. In Tōkyō and Hiroshima the merged type 2.2/3 is pronounced LH; the words are oxytonic, that being defined as the class of all words of more than one syllable that have a basic locus on the last syllable. In Narada, an unusual Tōkyō-type dialect, the underlying final accent of these oxytonic words is realized by putting the high on the first syllable of an attached particle; at the same time, a nondistinctive high is put on the initial syllable, so that what the Tōkyō speaker with his nondistinctive initial low pronounces as yama ga (2.3) and oto ga (2.2) is realized by the Narada speaker as yama ga and oto ga which have a nondistinctive high initial and delay the realization of the accentually distinctive high by a lag of one syllable.

Tōkyō has a rule which cancels the final accent of oxytonic nouns, of any length, before the enclitic /no/. For our purposes this cancellation can be treated as optional; what triggers it is situations under various syntactic conditons which usually produce a fairly tight-knit phrase, with close juncture after the enclitic. The cancellation takes place for ALL oxytonic nouns, including those of historical types 2.2 and 2.3, as well as longer nouns. From that we could draw either of two conclusions: (1) the rule postdates the merger of 2.3 with 2.2; or, (2) the rule originally applied only to 2.2 but was extended to 2.3 after that type merged with 2.2. Not all Tōkyō-type dialects have the cancellation rule, for it appears to be lacking in Yamaguchi (Kobayashi 1975:54), Aomori (id. 99), and Izumo (id. 72); the situation in Nagano is unclear (Kudō 1978:51 conflicts with id.:123-4). Yamaguchi and Aomori, like Tōkyō, merge 2.3 with 2.2 as oxytonic, but Izumo merges 2.1 with 2.2 as LH(-H) and keeps 2.3 distinct as oxytonic LH(-L). Narada retains the rule: Tōkyō's (2.2) yuki no | ⋯ → yuki no ⋯ 'of the snow' and (2.3) uma no | ⋯ → uma no ⋯ 'of the horse' are realized in Narada as yuki no | ⋯ → yuki no ⋯ and uma no | ⋯ → uma no ⋯ . So the rule must predate the split of the Tōkyō and Narada systems, but we still do not know whether it predates the merger of 2.3 with 2.2. The rule of oxytonic cancellation is also absent in the dialects of Hokkaidō (Hirayama 1951b:11, 12). According to Kyūshū-hōgen no sōgō-teki kenkyū 203- in dialects of Fukuoka both 2.3 and 2.2 are merged with 2.1 as LH, in contrast with 2.4 and 2.5 merged as HL. Nouns of the merged class 2.1/2/3 are oxytonic when an enclitic is attached (sake ga, oto ga, yama ga) but if that happens to be /no/ the final accent is cancelled: sake no, oto no, yama no. (But the dialect recorded as "Fukuoka city" in Kindaichi 1958:Introduction:14 is like Ōita with three types of dissyllables: 2.1/2, 2.3, 2.4/5.) A similar situation is reported by Kindaichi 1975: 30-1 for "most of Buzen and Bungo, and Itoshima-gun of Fukuoka prefecture"; in those areas of northeastern Kyūshū, however, 2.3 is kept distinct from 2.2 precisely (and only?) when the enclitic /no/ is attached:

2.3-ga   =   2.2-ga LH-L, but HL-L if noun shape is $(C)^e/o/_a(C)^i/_u$

2.3-no LH-H ≠   2.2-no LH-L, but HL-L if noun shape is $(C)^e/o/_a(C)^i/_u$

Kindaichi 1975:31 also reports a two-pattern dialect in parts of Nagasaki in which the merged low classes of 2.3/4/5 ("B") are LL-H when particles such as /ga/ are attached but LL-L when /no/ is attached.

Now, some interesting facts turn up in the Kyōto-type dialects. According to Okuda 1975:24-5 (to whose notations I have added junctures) the dialect of Ōsaka changes a prototonic high noun HL(L) to atonic high HH(H) before the particle /no/ but only in those cases where the prototonic high happens to correspond to the Tōkyō oxytonic type:

Tōkyō   Ōsaka

(1) yama no | ie →   yama no | ie →

    yama no ie (ga)   yama no ie

(2) uma no | asi →   uma no | asi →

    uma no asi (ga)   uma no asi

(3) hana no miyako →   hana no | miyako →

    hana no miyako   hana no miyako

(4) hikari no | hayasa →   hikari no | hayasa →

    hikari no hayasa   hikari no | hayasa

(5) takara no | motigusare →   takara no | motigusare →

    takara no motigusare   takara no | motigusare

MEANINGS: (1) 'mountain house', (2) 'horse's leg', (3) 'glorious capital',
(4) 'speed of light', (5) 'useless possession of treasure'.

But those Ōsaka prototonic nouns which do NOT correspond to Tōkyō oxytonics fail to undergo this change before the particle /no/:

(6) a̅sahi no | hi̅kari̅ (ga)   a̅sahi no | hi̅kari

(7) i̅noti no | oya̅ (ga)   i̅noti no | o̅ya

(8) zyo̅gakkoo no | se̅nsei   zyo̅gakkoo no | se̅nsei

> MEANINGS: (6) 'light of morning sun', (7) 'preserver of one's life',
>
> (8) 'women's college teacher'.

At first glance it would appear that the shrewd Ōsakan mysteriously knows just when a word will be oxytonic in Tōkyō, but the puzzle is deeper, for there are Tōkyō oxytonics which do NOT correspond to Ōsaka prototonics and these fail to undergo the change in Ōsaka:

(9) hasa̅mi̅ no | kireazi̅ →   hasa̅mi no | kireazi̅
    hasa̅mi no kireazi̅

> MEANING: (9) 'sharpness of scissors'.

What the Ōsakan is recognizing is only those words which correspond in the two dialects HISTORICALLY, and from Okuda's examples (all of which are 2.3 or 3.4) it would appear that the Ōsaka rule might be restricted to those words which earlier were low atonic. If this were true we would not expect an Ōsaka reflex of the Tōkyō cancellation in yuki̅ no ⋯ → yuki̅ no ⋯ 'of the snow' because the word for 'snow' is 2.2 (HL) in Myōgi-shō. But Kobayashi 1975:142 cites the rule as working for such Kyōto 2.2 nouns as u̅ti no → u̅ti no 'of the house, ours' and yo̅so no → yo̅so no 'of someone else'. (Kobayashi notes that the rule "may apply to three-syllable nouns with initial high accent, though less regularly than in dissylabic nouns", a cryptic reference to the situation that Okuda describes for Ōsaka.) Kobayashi 1975:165 gives examples from Kōchi of 2.2 and 2.3 nouns, and also three-syllable nouns. In Kōchi the nouns in phrases such as atama̅ no → atama̅ no 'of the head' and oto̅ko no → oto̅ko no 'of the man' have the accent one syllable later than in Kyōto and Ōsaka; they are not prototonic but follow the same rule. These nouns belong to Type 3.4; other examples cited by Kobayashi (222) are Kōchi kata̅na 'sword', koto̅ba 'word', kasi̅ra 'head', i̅tigo 'strawberry', musu̅me 'daughter', hana̅si 'story', suzu̅ri 'inkstone', tuku̅ri 'making', tasu̅ke 'help'. This class includes those nouns regularly derived from low-initial ("B") verb infinitives such as the last two examples. (Doi 1952:33 limits the Kōchi rule to dissyllables.)

Okuda is puzzled by the fact that Ōsaka has the accent change for k͞okoro
'heart' (as in k͞okoro no | ͞oku → kokoro no ͞oku 'the bottom of one's heart')
where Tōkyō has kok͞oro (and kok͞oro no | ͞oku), but a competing version "in some
areas" of Tōkyō according to Kindaichi 1958a is kok͞oro (ga) and speakers with
that version will presumably pronounced kok͞oro no | ͞oku → kokoro no ͞oku.
Okuda is also puzzled by the appearance of the accent change with ͞abura 'oil',
as in ͞abura no | b͞in → abura no b͞in 'oil bottle', for abura is atonic in Tōkyō
and the phrase abura no b͞in requires dropping only the juncture. Both abura
and kokoro belong to Type 3.5 (LLH) in Myōgi-shō, as do inoti 'life' and namida
'tear'. In Tōkyō a few nouns of this type are atonic rather than the expected
prototonic and for this reason the class is split into 3.5a (abura), with the
assumption that their pattern was originally LLH-H, and 3.5b (inoti), assumed to
have been originally LLH-L. Unfortunately, we lack data on how other members of 3.5
behave when /no/ is attached in Ōsaka. Umegaki 1963:63 cites Kyōto ͞it͞iri no | m͞iti
→ ͞it͞iri no m͞iti 'a one-league road'. HHL is an unusual pattern for a Kyōto noun
(cf. Kobayashi 1975:130); examples are a few other numeral-counter compounds like
͞it͞i-do 'one time' and ͞roku-z͞i 'six o'clock', and words with -T/N- such as ͞onna
'woman' and k͞it͞te 'stamp' (on which there are questions of interpretation and
notation). From Umegaki's Kyōto example and the Kōchi examples we can surmise that
a more general statement of the rule for Kyōto-type dialects is as follows:[5]

> A high atonic phrase HH(H)-H will result from attaching the enclitic /no/
> to those prototonic nouns which are reflexes of the earlier accent types 2.2
> (HL oto 'sound'), 2.3 (LL yama 'mountain'); 3.2b (HHL azuki 'red bean'), 3.3
> (HLL tikara 'strength'), 3.4 (LLL atama 'head'), 3.5a (LLH[-H] abura 'oil').

In Tōkyō there will be a corresponding atonic phrase LH(H)-H for these types but
the rule cancelling the oxytonic accent is vacuous for the last type (3.5a); it
yields atonic forms in Tōkyō so that no change occurs when /no/ is attached.[6] The
effect of the /no/-attachment rule for all the dialects where it is reported seems
to be that it creates an ATONIC phrase where otherwise there would have been a
phrase with an accentual locus. The rule appears most widely with reflexes of the
old low atonic types 2.3 and 3.4. But in 11th-century Kyōto the particle /no/
generally attached as low after low and as high after high (Sakurai 1976:305) so
that there resulted such forms as t͞ake no 'of bamboo' (2.1) and k͞uruma no 'of the
wagon' (3.1), on͞i no 'of the ogre' (2.3) and ͞ikusa no 'of the battle' (3.4); ͞ifa no
'of the stone' (2.2), ⋯ ͞sak͞iri no 'of mist' (3.2) and unfound *t͞ikara no 'of the

strength' (3.3); fiziri no 'saintly' (3.7a = *LHH > LHL); unfound *fidari no 'left'
(3.6) and *kabuto no 'of the helmet' (3.7b). But when /no/ was attached to native
nouns of the pattern LH (2.4/5) or LLH (3.5) it was pitched low: umi no 'of the
sea' (2.4), ame no 'of heaven' (2.5), kokoro no 'of the heart' (3.5). Sakurai's rule
amounts to this:

> In a low-register word the enclitic /no/ mirrors the initial register
> unless at least two high syllables intervene.

This rule, he says, was lost sometime between early Kamakura (1200) and Edo (1500),
after which the enclitic /no/ was treated like the other particles. (But the latter
statement requires qualification, as we have just seen from the modern data, and
also from attestations of the accent of Kyōto in the early-Edo period.) For Chinese
loanwords the register-mirror rule was inoperative and /no/ just continued the pitch
of the syllable to which it was attached; Sakurai (197-8) explains this anomaly by
assuming that Chinese binoms marked "L-H" and "L-LH" were pronounced with long and
rising syllables [RH] and [LRH], structurally equivalent to /LHH/ and /LLHH/ (as
found in native words), so that the environment calling for the rule was lacking.

      According to the treatment in Martin 1970a and 1975b the oxytonic nouns and
adverbs of Tōkyō cancel the final locus before juncture and the juncture may then
disappear. (This is one way to account for oxytonic/atonic alternants of adverbs.)
At the time such a cancellation became a rule the particles and the copula must have
been separated from nouns with no juncture, or at most a weaker juncture. Pertinent
data from other dialects are yet to be found, so that the relative age of this rule
remains a question. The only Kyōto examples that seem to be similar:

N o u n	A d v e r b
.amaˈ ri [H], aˈ mari [U] 'excess'	.amari⁻ 'overly'
issaˈ tu [U] 'one (book)'	issatu⁻ '(the extent of) one (book)'
.ittoˈ o 'first class'	.ittoo⁻ [U] 'most, best'
ikˈ -kai [U] (?= iˈ kkai) 'one time'	ik-kai⁻ 'once'
otoˈ toi 'day before yesterday'	ototoi⁻ '(on) the day before yesterday'
.dandaˈ n 'steps'	.danˈ dan [U] 'by steps, gradually'

Somewhat odder: Umegaki's mittu⁻ and muttu⁻ for the adverbial use of miˈ ttu 'three'
and muˈ ttu 'six'; Umegaki also has "adverbial" yotˈ tu for yoˈ ttu 'four' but that is
an anomalous locus (see §1.4) and he has only yaˈ ttu for 'eight'. (Hirayama gives

but one version for these numbers: mit'tu, mut'tu; yot'tu, yat'tu. The locus is regular according to his notational conventions.)

We have mentioned that certain dialects of Shikoku join 2.3 with 2.1 (HH), notably the dialect of Hakuchi in Samachi-mura, Miyoshi-gun, Tokushima prefecture (Ikuta 1951), and that of Takamatsu and adjacent areas of Kagawa prefecture. The resulting pattern for Takamatsu is cited as HH by Kindaichi 1944:200; as LH by Kindaichi 1958:14; and as "both LH and HH" in the 1981 revised edition of the latter. Takamatsu also merges the low atonic three-syllable nouns with the high atonic class (Kindaichi 1944:203). In this connection, it is of interest to examine the remarks of Konparu Zenpō in his 1455 work Mōtan-shichin-shō (cf. Kindaichi 1974:233 and Sakurai 1976:403). Below is a translation of the relevant passage:

> 'Dog' as īnu is Kyōto speech; as inu it is the dialect pronunciation of Bandō (the East) and Chikushi (Kyūshū). As īnu it is the Shikoku dialect. However, even in Kyōto the Shikoku dialect version is heard in īnu-o-monō 'mounted archery practice with moving dogs as targets'; the pattern of the accent is adjusted to what comes after, and it is said as īnu-o-mono [i.e. the Kyōto version has high pitch on the last two syllables where Shikoku has it only on the final syllable]. For īnu-bāba 'dog target rink' and īnuwī-hikime 'a kind of arrow [depicted in NKD 2:299c]' it is the same thing.

According to Kindaichi (1974:233) īnu is the modern pattern in an area from western Kagawa to Tokushima prefecture, the "Mima Miyoshi" area. The Kyōto version in the compound is superficially similar, but it is attributed to a morphophonemic adjustment. Just what was the adjustment? The expression is probably reduced from īnu no | o[f]ī-mono → īnu no [|] oīmono (atonicization rule) → īnu [no] oīmono (ellipsis) → īnu | o[i]mono (juncture reintroduced, marked by lowering the pitch of the second phrase).[7] The "Shikoku" version for the second phrase is identical with modern Kyōto low atonic (usagī with nondistinctive high on the last syllable of the phrase) but that does not mean it merged with the low-atonic category of that time and place. The last sentence seems to imply īnu no |bāba → īnuno [|] bāba → *īnu [no] bāba (etc.) but this could be handled as the noun-compound accentuation rule at work, rather than the more elaborate mechanism required for the first situation.

16. Developments in northern Okinawa: Nakijin.

The dialects of the northern part of the island of Okinawa resemble those of
southern Amami (such as Shodon) and that of Yonaguni in several ways. They have
developed a distinction between aspirated and unaspirated consonants. They have
obscured the etymological shapes of words by processes that I call compression and
conflation,[1] whereby some syllables are shortened or dropped and others are expanded
by lengthening the vowel. In Shodon and Nakijin (and probably other dialects of the
northern areas) the compressed or conflated forms correlate with accent types.
Shodon, like Shuri, has only two accent types, and these correspond to the historic
registers. Dialects of northern Okinawa and of Yonaguni, on the other hand, have
three accent types. The A type corresponds to the historical category of the high
register, both atonic and tonic (for dissyllables, 2.1 and 2.2). The low register
is represented by two types: B corresponds to the low atonic pattern (2.3) and C to
the low tonic (2.4 and 2.5).

The publication in 1983 of Nakasone's dictionary of the Nakijin dialect has
made available an invaluable source of lexical and accentual information, which I
have tried to incorporate in later chapters of this book.[2] The accent carefully
described by Nakasone for his native speech comprises quite a few phonemically
distinct patterns, as a result of compound boundaries, conflation or compression of
syllables, and other secondary happenings. But for historical purposes these can be
reduced to the three types mentioned above. The phonetic realization of the three
historic types can be stated as follows:

A is basically an all-high plateau. But a low pitch, which originally must have
been nondistinctive, is put on the first syllable of words that are 3, 4, or 5 moras
long; and a similar (originally nondistinctive) low is put on the last syllable of
4-mora and 5-mora words: HH, LHH, LHHL, LHHHL. (There are, to be sure, a few longer
words that are all-high throughout, but their patterns are the result of special
circumstances.)

B is low-high, and the initial low spreads: LH, LLH, LLLH (when the second vowel
is long), LLHH (when the final vowel is long or a diphthong).

C is high-low: HL, HLL. For longer words, the situation is a bit unclear, but we
will treat as "C" those patterns that spread the initial low: LLHL and LLLHL/LLHHL,
in contrast with the "A" patterns of LHHL and LHHLL(/?LHHHL). Notice the variant
forms kasaa HLL = kaasaa LLHL 'sore', both C.

Monosyllabic nouns are lengthened to two moras in Nakijin:

1.1/2 → 2.1/2   A   1.1 HH (Cii 'blood'), 1.2 HH (Pii 'day')
1.3a/b → 2.3   B   1.3a LH (Pii 'fart'), 1.3b LH (Pii 'fire')
1.3b → 2.4/5   C   1.3b HL (Pii 'water pipe')

Most originally dissyllabic nouns lengthen to three moras, but some remain two:

2.1 HH tui 'bird', qai 'ant'.
     But qamii 'gluten', panaa 'nose' 3.1 HHH.
2.2 HH Cuu 'person', haa 'well', nii 'breast'.
     But qisii 'stone', paTaa 'flag' HHH 3.1.

2.3 LH qmaa 'horse', naa 'rope', soo 'pole', nai 'fruit'.
     But qamii 'net', panaa 'flower', yamaa 'mountain' 3.4 LLH)

2.4 HL pai 'needle'.
     But maCi(i) 'pine', puni(i) 'boat', naha(a) 'inside' 3.7 HLL before nu (= no).
2.5 HL hui 'voice'.
     But huki(i) 'bucket', muhu(u) 'bridegroom' 3.7 HLL before nu (= no).

In similar fashion, most three-syllable nouns are lengthened to four or

five moras, but some remain three:

3.1 LHH kazai 'decoration', kaCuu 'bonito', tunai 'neighbor', piCee 'forehead'.
     But kaTaaCi 'shape', saKaana 'fish', paziimi 'start' 4.1 LHHL.
3.2 LHH pugui 'scrotum'. But saKuura 'cherry', kusaabi 'wedge' 4.1 LHHL.
3.3 LHH ---.
     But ˢ/ciKaara 'power', ᵏ/ʰugaani 'gold' 4.1 LHHL.

3.4 LLH haara 'tile', qoozi 'fan', qumui 'thought', piCai 'light'.
     But puTuKii 'Buddha', kuyumii 'calendar', tanumii 'request', peesii 'musical
     accompaniment' 4.5 LLHH; taKaara 'treasure', haTaana 'ax', huTuuba 'words',
     puKuuru 'bag' 4.6 LLLH.
     And paKaamaa 'man's skirt', pasaamii 'scissors', kagaamii 'mirror', waraabii
     'bracken', quraamii 'regret' 5.6 LLLHH.
3.5 LLH nadaa 'tear(drops)', sidee 'reed screen'.
     But qinuCii 'life', qanᵈ/ᵣaa 'oil', pasiraa 'pillar', maqKaa 'pillow', pooCii
     'broom' 4.5 LLHH; kuKuuru 'heart', nasiibi 'eggplant', nasaaKi 'sentiment'
     maCiigi 'eyelash' 4.6 LLLH.
     And qawaarii 'sympathy', yamaaTuu 'Yamato', (y)iihacii 'artist' 5.6 LLLHH.
3.6 LLH ---.
     But husaazi 'rabbit', garaasi 'crow', maKuuTu 'truth', qunaazi 'eel' 4.6 LLLH.
     And haTaadii 'one hand' 5.6 LLLHH.

3.7 HLL Cigaa 'measure'.
     But kabuuTU 'helmet', paTaaKi 'field', siziiKa 'quiet', yuTaaKaa 'rich' 4.6
     LLLH; kukuCii 'feeling', manTaa 'eyelid' 4.5 LLHH.
     And namaarii 'lead', mii-kusuu 'eye gum' 5.6 LLLHH.

And so on, for nouns of four and five syllables.

There are two main accent types for Nakijin verbs, with these patterns for the citation form (the imperfect):

HH nan 'sound', sun 'do'

LHH tubin 'fly', naCun 'weep'

HHHL hoorun 'buy', muirun 'burn'

LHHHL kazaarun 'decorate',
    hasiibin 'play';
    paziimin 'begin'

LH nan 'become', sun 'shave'

LLH numin 'drink', haCun 'write'

LLHL huirun 'bark', tuurun 'pass'

LLLHL quduruCun 'be startled',
    tanuumin 'request';
    siraabin 'check'

And there are two accent types for the adjectives, with these patterns for the citation form (the imperfect):

HHHL kuusen 'saturated',
    qoosen 'unripe'

LHH(H)L haCi(i)sen 'thick'

LHHHL qaKaasen 'red', qamaasen 'sweet'

LHHHL qangasen 'dangerous'

LHHHHL muCiiKasen 'difficult',
    yagaamasen 'noisy'

LLHL tuusen 'far', peesen 'early',
    nukusen 'warm', sabisen 'lonely'

HHLL waqsen 'bad', yaqsen 'cheap'

LL(L)HL haCi(i)sen 'hot', puru(u)sen 'old'

LLLHL nagaasen 'long', yutaasen 'good'

LLHLL paziKasen 'ashamed',
    qinCasen 'short'

LLLHLL huTuurusen 'horrible',
    hasaamasen 'disgusting'

LLHHLL uigoosen 'itchy'

LLLHHLL qumusiruusen 'fun',
    munumizirasen 'rare'

LLLLHHLL namaagusaasen 'fishy'

The phonetic melodies of the Nakijin accent patterns, which tend to obscure the original registers, are much like the prosodic tunes of Shodon which I have treated as nondistinctive (Martin 1970:112), having heard their highs and lows within a narrower range than I heard the patterns of high and low that distinguish the registers.

17. Unresolved problems.

As we have seen, there are Ryūkyū dialects (such as Nakijin and Yonaguni) which require a third register "C" to account for patterns reflecting the low tonic patterns of earlier Japanese. This register differs from the other two in being dynamic: the phonetic realization is a fall of pitch at or toward the end of the word, at a predictable location given the shape of the word in the particular dialect. We have suggested that it would be possible to apply a similar concept to account for the anomalous final falls in pitch described in §7.3. We have hesitated because the number of examples seems small and we would like to account for them in other ways, if possible. But if we allow certain anomalous accents in the modern dialects as evidence for a "C" register that otherwise left few traces, the number

increases considerably. When the only evidence is an unusual reflex in just one
dialect, we may well disregard that as a sporadic irregularity, to be explained on
an individual basis — perhaps the result of borrowing from another dialect or of
morphophonemic confusion between atonic and oxytonic patterns, which is fairly
common. Individual words, after all, sometimes slip out of the pattern to which they
belong. (In my native dialect of southeastern Kansas the words *thing* and *hang* rime
with the name of the velar nasal symbol *eng*, yet words like *ring* and *sang* remain in
their historic categories.) But when there are similar reflexes in several dialects,
especially if they are located quite far apart, a more general explanation probably
is called for.

Uwano claims that the description of certain modern dialects requires yet
another dynamic register (we can call it "D") to account for otherwise unaccountable
rises; I have not touched upon this question. But it should be noted that the
additional registers posited by Uwano for synchronic descriptions do not reflect the
earlier rises and falls that concern us here; they are reflexes of earlier types
that are within the simpler frame of reference requiring only two registers and one
locus. The initial rises described in §7.1 could be described with a "D" register,
but from the small number of examples and the canonical shapes involved, I suspect
that such a register — if needed — was a transient phenomenon brought about by
ongoing processes of COMPRESSION and CONFLATION. We find these two processes at work
today, especially in the northern Ryūkyūs, lengthening some kinds of words and
shortening others. In many cases the final falls may be the result of compressing
two syllables into one; that is, the "F" is really "HL" and at an earlier time the
patterns were one syllable longer. These processes may account for the emergence of
the double-low Type 2.5.

Why do verb stems have only two historic patterns but nouns have many patterns?
We have mentioned one hypothesis: the verb stems were originally compounds that
incorporated some sort of auxiliary (perhaps the ancestor of the infinitive *-Ci)
and lost the locus distinctions they might earlier have had. But another explanation
is possible. Perhaps in origin many of the noun stems are compounds, or truncations,
or truncations of compounds. The many nouns that end in ...ey (the *otu*-type "e")
are to be reconstructed as ...a-i < *...a-Ci, and the -Ci was probably some sort of
suffix or marker (cf. Morishige 1984). We might account for the double-low pattern
of Kyōto's amè = amee 'rain' as *ama i, a low-high stem followed by a low morpheme.
But there is no particular evidence that the suffix *-Ci was, in fact, low: tume

'claw' is from tumey < *tuma-Ci and k̄an̄e 'metal' is from kane[y] < *kana-Ci but they have no fall of pitch. (However, notice that tume is irregularly Type B in northern Okinawan dialects of Kunigami and Ōgimi and it has the reflex of Type 2.3 on the Wakamatsu peninsula of Kyūshū.) Perhaps Kyōto's a̱sá = a̱s̄a̱a (the accent is unattested in Myōgi-shō) is a truncation of *asam, as suggested to Polivanov by the Korean a'chom. And *asam might in turn be a contraction of *a̱s̄a-m̱a, a low-high noun + a low noun; yet the attested pattern for ma 'interval', presumed to be the last syllable of the dialect word asama, is high.

There are two prejudices which lead investigators to support opposite views on some of the issues raised here. One is the somewhat romantic notion that earlier systems must have been simpler than later systems: life, and culture, keeps getting more complicated. The other is the entropy-inspired view that earlier systems must have been more complicated: people are sloppy, they tend to lose distinctions. In particular instances evidence can be found to support either viewpoint. Thus the proliferation of modern Cantonese tones can be shown to have developed from a simpler system, and the now complicated word-accentuation rules of English are a blend of the very simple systems of Germanic and Romance; yet Polish and Czech seem to have developed a predictable (word-demarcating) accent out of a more complex system, and dialects in different parts of Japan (e.g. Kumamoto, Ibaraki) appear to have lost earlier accentual distinctions altogether. The evidence indicates that there are no universal trends in language change, just recurrent types of change that may complicate or simplify specific structures depending on particular historic circumstances.

Chart 1:1.   Shuri accent phrases: types.

O.-jiten	Type	Mark	1	2	3	4	5	6	7	moras
1	A	TONIC		o͞o	o͞o͞o	o͞o͞o͞o	o͞o͞o͞o͞o	o͞o͞o͞o͞o͞o	o͞o͞o͞o͞o͞o͞o	
				ō:	ō:o	ō:oo	ō:ooo	ō:oooo	ō:ooooo	
0	B	ATONIC		oo	ooo	oooo	ooooo	oooooo	ooooooo	

Chart 1:2   Shuri accent phrases: examples.

1	2	3	4	5	6	7	moras
	'kazi	'sakura	'kasabuta	'kani-butuki	'qinaka-sudaci	'kugani-kamisasi	
		'kazi nu	'sakura nu	'kasabuta nu	'kani-butuki nu	'qinaka-sudaci nu	
	'cii	'taaçi	'naasati	'ciiru-kabi			
		'cii nu	'taaci nu	'naasati nu	'ciiru-kabi nu		
	mimi	katana	karakasa	waka-winagu	wikiga-warabi	ciyaciyaa-bui	
	tii	mimi nu	katana nu	karakasa nu	waka-winagu nu	wikiga-warabi nu	

MEANINGS: 'kazi 'wind', 'cii 'blood', mimi 'ear', tii 'hand', 'sakura 'cherry', ··· nu 'of ···',
'taaçi 'two', katana 'sword', 'kasabuta 'scab', 'naasati 'day after tomorrow', karakasa 'umbrella',
'kani-butuki 'metal Buddha', 'ciiru-kabi 'yellow-paper offering', waka-winagu 'young woman', 'qinaka-sudaci
'bringing up on the farm', wikiga-warabi 'boy', 'kugani-kamisasi 'golden comb', ciyaciyaa-bui 'drizzle'.

Chart 2:1.   Kagoshima accent phrases: types.

Type	Mark	1	2	3	4	5	6	7	syllables
A	TONIC	ó	o̅o̲	o̲o̅o̲	o̲o̲o̅o̲	o̲o̲o̲o̅o̲	o̲o̲o̲o̲o̅o̲	o̲o̲o̲o̲o̲o̅o̲	
B	ATONIC	o	o̲o̅	o̲o̲o̅	o̲o̲o̲o̅	o̲o̲o̲o̲o̅	o̲o̲o̲o̲o̲o̅	o̲o̲o̲o̲o̲o̲o̅	

Chart 2:2   Kagoshima accent phrases: examples.

1	2	3	4	5	6	7	syllables
'ti\	'kaze	'sakura	'kasabuta	'kodomo-beya	'inaka-kotoba	'Minami-Amerika	
	'ti ga	'kaze ga	'sakura ga	'kasabuta ga	'kodomo-beya ga	'inaka-kotoba ga	
	'ti ni mo	'kaze ni mo	'sakura ni mo	'kasabuta ni mo	'kodomo-beya ni mo		
te	yama	atama	mamegara	nezumi-iro	murasaki-iro	gozyuuen-dama	
	te ga	yama ga	atama ga	mamegara ga	nezumi-iro ga	murasaki-iro ga	
	te ni mo	yama ni mo	atama ni mo	mamegara ni mo	nezumi-iro ni mo		

MEANINGS: 'ti 'blood', te 'hand', 'kaze 'wind', ··· ga (subject), yama 'mountain', 'sakura 'cherry',
··· ni mo 'also to/at ···', atama 'head', 'kasabuta 'scab', mamegara 'bean pod', 'kodomo-beya
'children's room', nezumi-iro 'gray', 'inaka-kotoba 'rustic word', murasaki-iro 'purple',
'Minami-Amerika 'South America', gozyuuen-dama '¥50 coin'.

Chart 3:1.   Tōkyō accent phrases: types.

Hirayama	Type	Mark	1	2	3	4	5	6	7	moras
0	A	ATONIC	ō	oo	ooo	oooo	ooooo	oooooo	ooooooo	
(= n)	: :	OXYTONIC	[ō]	oo_	ooo_	oooo_	ooooo_	oooooo_	ooooooo_	
6	: :								ooooooo	
5	: :							oooooo	ooooooo	
4	: :						ooooo	oooooo	ooooooo	
3	: :					oooo	ooooo	oooooo	ooooooo	
2	: :				ooo	oooo	ooooo	oooooo	ooooooo	
1	B	PROTOTONIC	ō_	oo	ooo	oooo	ooooo	oooooo	ooooooo	

Chart 3:2   Tōkyō accent phrases: examples.

1	2	3	4	5	6	7	moras
ti	kaze	sakana	tomodati	kodomo-beya	murasaki-iro	gozyuuen-dama	
	ti ga'	kaze ga'	sakana ga'	tomodati ga'	kodomo-beya ga'	murasaki-iro ga'	
	iwa'	otoko'	imooto'	o-syoogatu'	zyuuiti-gatu'	nihyakutooka-go'	
						Nisi-Ogikubo-'syo	
						zyuuiti-gatu' ga	
					aiai-ga'sa	Ikebukuro-'eki	
					o-syoogatu' ga	aiai-ga'sa ga	
					tatami-o'mote	kodomo-a'tukai	
				niwaka-a'me	niwaka-a'me ga	niwaka-a'me made	
				imooto' ga		nama-a'rukooru	
			mizuu'mi	natu-ya'sumi	hito-ma'ziwari	hito-ma'ziwari ga	
			otoko' ga	mizuu'mi ga	natu-ya'sumi ga	o-te'tudai-san	
		koko'ro	ugu'isu	o-se'kkai	o-ma'wari-san	o-ma'wari-san ga	
		iwa' ga	koko'ro ga	ugu'isu ga	o-se'kkai ga	o'kusama-tati	
te'	sa'ru	i'noti	ko'omori	o'-tuki-sama	o'kusama-tati	(A'mano-hasidate)	
	te' ga	i'noti ga	i'noti ga	ko'omori ga	o'-tuki-sama ga	o'kusama-tati ga	
		sa'ru ga	sa'ru made	i'noti made	ko'omori made	o'-tuki-sama made	

MEANINGS: ti 'blood', te' 'hand', kaze 'wind', iwa' 'a rock', sa'ru 'monkey', sakana 'fish', otoko' 'man', koko'ro 'heart', tomodati 'friend', imooto' 'younger sister', mizuu'mi 'lake', ugu'isu 'bush-warbler', ko'omori 'bat', kodomo-beya 'children's room', o-syoogatu' 'New Year's', niwaka-a'me 'shower', natu-ya'sumi 'summer holiday', o-se'kkai 'meddlesome', o'-tuki-sama 'moon', murasaki-iro 'purple', zyuuiti-gatu' 'November', aiai-ga'sa 'shared umbrella', tatami-o'mote 'mat front', hito-ma'ziwari 'social mixing', o'kusama-tati 'ladies', o-ma'wari-san 'patrolman', gozyuuen-dama '¥50 coin', nihyakutooka-go' 'after the autumn typhoon', Nisi-Ogikubo-'syo 'Nishi-Ogikubo stationhouse', Ikebukuro-'eki 'Ikebukuro station', kodomo-a'tukai 'treating as a child', nama-a'rukooru 'raw alcohol', o-te'tudai-san 'housekeeping help', A'mano-hasidate 'Amanohashidate'.

Chart 4:1.   Kyōto accent phrases: types.

U	H	2	3	4	5	6	7	moras
1	2	o̅o̲	o̅o̲o̲	o̅o̲o̲o̲	o̅o̲o̲o̲o̲	o̅o̲o̲o̲o̲o̲	o̅o̲o̲o̲o̲o̲o̲	
2	3		o̅o̅o̲	o̅o̅o̲o̲	o̅o̅o̲o̲o̲	o̅o̅o̲o̲o̲o̲	o̅o̅o̲o̲o̲o̲o̲	
3	4			o̅o̅o̅o̲	o̅o̅o̅o̲o̲	o̅o̅o̅o̲o̲o̲	o̅o̅o̅o̲o̲o̲o̲	
4	5				o̅o̅o̅o̅o̲	o̅o̅o̅o̅o̲o̲	o̅o̅o̅o̅o̲o̲o̲	
5	6					o̅o̅o̅o̅o̅o̲	o̅o̅o̅o̅o̅o̲o̲	
6	7						o̅o̅o̅o̅o̅o̅o̲	
0	0	o̅o̅	o̅o̅o̅	o̅o̅o̅o̅	o̅o̅o̅o̅o̅	o̅o̅o̅o̅o̅o̅	o̅o̅o̅o̅o̅o̅o̅	

                    H I G H
·· } ATONIC
                    L O W

U	H	2	3	4	5	6	7	moras
0	1	o̲o̅	o̲o̲o̅	o̲o̲o̲o̅	o̲o̲o̲o̲o̅	o̲o̲o̲o̲o̲o̅	o̲o̲o̲o̲o̲o̲o̅	
6	1;7						oooooo̲o	
5	1;6					oooooo̅	oooooo̅o	
4	1;5				ooooo̅	oooo̅oo	ooooo̅oo	
3	1;4 (1;3⁵)	(oo̲ò)	oooo̅	ooo̅oo	oooo̅oo	ooooo̅oo	
2	1;3 (1;2⁵)	(o̲ò)	oo̅o	oo̅oo	oo̅ooo	ooo̅ooo	oooo̅ooo	

U = Umegaki's notation (in Nihon-kokugo-daijiten). This marks the last high
    syllable before a low; the numeral is enclosed in a square for high-
    register words, in a circle for low-register words.

H = Hirayama's notation (in Zenkoku-akusento-jiten). This marks the syllable
    on which a low pitch sets in. Hirayama puts all notations in a circle,
    so that his circled zero (for high atonic) is in conflict with Umegaki's
    circled zero (for low atonic).

Both notations count from the left (the beginning of the phrase).

Chart 4:2.   Kyōto accent phrases: examples.

H	2	3	4	5	6	7	moras
2	ī'wa	o'toko	sī'itake	dā'idokoro	dā'ikkirai	dā'iku-san-tati	
	nā'a 'name'	ī'wa ga	a'sagao	sī'itake ga	dā'idokoro ga	o'toko-san-tati	
	(nā' ga)	nā'a ga	o'toko ga	o'toko ni wa	sī'itake ni wa	sī'itake (']yatta	
	(tī 'mo)	(tī 'yori)	nā'a ni wa	nā'a made wa	o'toko made wa	dā'idokoro ni wa	
3		itī-'ri	bake'mono	mi-go'sirae	bake'mono ga	bake'mono ni wa	
		sak'ka	ugu'isu	ugu'isu ga	itī-'ri (']yatta	itī-'ri (']yattara	
		kaze 'mo	kaze 'yori	itī-'ri ni wa	ugu'isu ni wa	ugu'isu (']yatta	
		tīī 'mo	tīī 'yori	sak'ka ni wa	mi-go'sirae ga	mi-go'sirae ni wa	
4			kamina'ri	Kirisi'tan	?take-no'kogiri	Kirisita'n-tati	
			sakana 'mo	natu-ya'sumi	natu-ya'sumi ga	natu-ya'sumi ni wa	
			kaze ni 'mo	Doitu-'zin	kamina'ri ni wa	sakana 'yattara	
			tīī ni 'mo	sakana 'yori	sakana 'yatta		
5				hanasi-go'e	tatami-o'mote	kodomo-a'tukai	
				tomodati 'mo	Amerika-'zin	tomodati 'yatta	
6					oogane-mo'ti	kamikiri-ba'sami	
					kodomo-beya 'mo	hyakuen-dama 'yori	
7						undoo-sen'syu	
						hyakuen-dama 'mo	
0	kaze	sakana	tomodati	kodomo-beya	hyakuen-dama	gozyuuen-dama	
	tīī 'blood'	kaze ga	sakana ga	tomodati ga	kodomo-beya ga	hyakuen-dama ga	
	(tī ga)	tīī ga	kaze ni wa	sakana ni wa	tomodati ni wa	kodomo-beya ni wa	

· ·

1	.hune	.usagi	.sora-iro	.nezumi-iro	.murasaki-iro	.syotokuzei-komi	
	.tee	.hune ga	.usagi ga	.sora-iro ga	.nezumi-iro ga	.murasaki-iro ga	
	(.te ga)	.tee ga	.hune ni wa	.usagi ni wa	.sora-iro ni wa	.nezumi-iro ni wa	
1:7						.murasaki-iro 'mo	
1:6					.aiai-ga'sa	.nanohana-ba'take	
					.nezumi-iro 'mo	.aiai-ga'sa ga	
1:5				.unagi-me'si	.niwaka-me'kura	.soori-da'izin	
1:4			.iroga'mi	.abura-'musi	?.ito-no'kogiri	.abura'musi-tati	
			.minna'a	.mugi-ba'take	.abura-'musi ga	?.ito-no'kogiri ga	
			.minna' ga	.usagi 'yori	.iroga'mi ni wa	.iroga'mi yatta	
			.usagi 'mo				
(1:3□		.minnà)	.hune ni 'mo				
1:3		.saru'u	.nade'siko	.ka-ha'nsuu	.tyuu'gakusei	.o-te'ntoo-sama	
		.saru' ga	.kabu'to ga	.o-zi'i-san	.nade'siko ni wa	.tyuu'gakusei ga	
		.kabu'to	.tee 'yori	.kabu'to ni wa	.ka-ha'nsuu ga	.ka-ha'nsuu ni wa	
		.hune 'mo					
		.tee 'mo					
(1:2□		.sarù)					
(1:2		.té 'mo)					

(Chart 4:2 continued)

MEANINGS: i'wa 'rock', o'toko 'male', si'itake 'shiitake mushroom', da'idokoro 'kitchen',
da'ikkirai 'much disliked', da'iku-san-tati 'carpenters', na'a 'name', a'sagao 'morning-glory',
o'toko-san-tati 'males', na' = na'a 'name', ti = tii 'blood', (']yatta 'it was', iti-'ri 'one
league', bake'mono 'ghost', mi-go'sirae 'outfit, dress', sak'ka 'writer', ugu'isu 'bush warbler',
kaze 'wind', tii 'blood', kamina'ri 'thunder', Kirisi'tan 'Kirishitan (early Japanese Christian)',
?take-no'kogiri 'bamboo saw', Kirisita'n-tati 'the Kirishitans', sakana 'fish', natu-ya'sumi 'summer
holiday', Doitu-'zin 'German', (')yattara 'if it was', hanasi-go'e 'speaking voice', tatami-o'mote
'mat front', kodomo-a'tukai 'treating as a child', tomodati 'friend', Amerika-'zin 'American',
oogane-mo'ti 'billionaire', kamikiri-ba'sami 'barber scissors', kodomo-beya 'children's room', undoo-
sen'syu 'athlete', taisyuu-sak'ka 'popular writer', hyakuen-dama '¥100 coin', gozyuuen-dama '¥50 coin':
.hune 'boat', .usagi 'rabbit', .sora-iro 'sky blue', .nezumi-iro 'gray', .murasa.i-iro 'purple',
.syotokuzei-komi 'including income tax', .te = .tee 'hand', .aiai-ga'sa 'shared umbrella',
.nanohana-ba'take 'a field of rape-blossoms', .niwaka-me'kura 'suddenly blind', .soori-da'izin
'prime minister', .iroga'mi 'colored paper', .abura-mu'si 'cockroach', ? .ito-no'kogiri
'jigsaw, fretsaw', .abura'musi-tati 'cockroaches', .minna' = .minnà = .minna'a 'all',
.saru' = .sarù = .saru'u 'monkey', .nade'siko 'a pink (Dianthus superbus)', .ka-ha'nsuu
'majority', .tyuu'gakusei 'middle-school student', .o-te'ntoo-sama 'the sun', .kabu'to 'helmet',
.o-zi'i-san 'grandfather'.

Chart 5.   Accent patterns of shorter nouns.

1.1 H-H ti 'blood' 0-0-A A-A-A 15 =.*33*	**2.1 HH-H** kaze 'wind' 0-0-A A-A-A 139 =.*31*	**3.1 HHH-H** katati 'shape' 0-0-A A-A-A 110 =.*37*
		3.2a *HHH-L>HHL-L tokage 'lizard' 0-1:3-A A-A-(C) 7 =.*02*+
		3.2b HHH-L azuki 'red bean' 3(/0)-2-A A-A-(A) 7 =.*02*+
	2.2a *HH-L>HL-L hito 'person' 0(/2)-2-A A-A-A 8 =.*02*	
1.2 H-L ha 'leaf' 0-2-A A-A-A 8 =.*17*	**2.2b HL-L** isi 'stone' 2-2-A A-A-A 50 =.*11*	**3.3 HLL-L** hatati 'twenty' 1(<2)-2-A A-A-A 11 =.*04*⁻

....

(1.3a L-L) → 1.3b	**2.3 LL-L** yama 'mountain' 2-2-B B-B-B 125 =.*28*	**3.4 LLL-L** kagami 'mirror' 3-2(<3)-B B-B-B 87 =.*29*
		3.5a LLH-H sudare 'reed screen' 0-2-B B-B-B 5 =.*02*⁻
		3.5b LLH-H (?<*LLH-L) namida 'tears' 1(<2)-2-B B-B-B 27 =.*09*
1.3b L-H te 'hand' 1-1-B B-B-B 23 = .*50*	**2.4 LH-H** matu 'pine' 1-1-B B-B-C 73 =.*16*	**3.6 LHH-H** usagi 'rabbit' 0-1-B B-B-(C) 27 =.*09*
		3.7a *LHH-L>LHL-L kusuri 'drug' 0-1:3-B B-B-C 9 =.*03*
	2.5 LH-L saru 'monkey' 1-1:3-B B-B-C 51 =.*11*	**3.7b LHL-L** kabuto 'helmet' 1-1:3-B B-B-C 11 =.*04*
	———	———
793	46 =.*06* 446 =.*56*	301 =.*38*

Charts 6:1-3.
   Kinki accent of nouns derived from infinitives of verbs that were originally Type B but are now Type A in Kyōto.

The nouns are cited with the Tōkyō patterns, and ꞌ marks the vowel just before the locus; two or more marks show accentual variants and the raised minus (⁻) at the end of a form indicates an atonic version. The regular Tōkyō pattern is oxytonic but the locus may move back one syllable/mora when a string of two vowels comes at the end. Forms with irregular versions in Tōkyō are preceded by the mark # and are treated in Charts 7:1-2. All nouns and verbs listed are Type B in Kagoshima unless otherwise marked. Kinki data sources: H = Hirayama's Kyōto data in Zenkoku akusento jiten; U = Umegaki's Kyōto data in NKD; O = Ōhara Hidetsugu's data for Ōsaka-Kōbe and Akashi-Himeji in Ōhara 1937.

Chart 6:1   Three-syllable derived nouns.

Group	Kinki accent patterns			
	ō꜔oo	.oo꜔o	.oo꜔o	ooo
hanasiꞌ, hibikiꞌ, hikariꞌ, kumoriꞌ, nagameꞌ, nagareꞌ, tutomeꞌ, tutumiꞌ, #kaꞌmaꞌeꞌ, #oꞌrosiꞌ; suꞌmaꞌi	H U	O		
konomiꞌ, koyasiꞌ, nigoriꞌ, nioꞌi, nokoriꞌ, sadameꞌ, sodatiꞌ, todokeꞌ, tooriꞌ, tukuriꞌ, yasumiꞌ; #saꞌwagi; homareꞌ⁻, tuzuriꞌ⁻.	H U			
negaꞌi¹, sakebiꞌ, sirabeꞌ, wakareꞌ; #kaꞌgiriꞌ	U	O		H
inoriꞌ, iwaꞌi, suzumiꞌ, tamesiꞌ, tatoꞌe, uramiꞌ, yurusiꞌ; #haraꞌi(?⁻)²	U			H
kaesiꞌ, oboꞌeꞌ, sonaꞌeꞌ, tooriꞌ, utusiꞌ; #sabakiꞌ	H			U
kobosiꞌ (H x)			U	U
toosi	U		H	
#saꞌgariꞌ	U		U³	H U
#taꞌnomiꞌ	U			H U
tasukeꞌ		O		H U
hasamiꞌ, yabureꞌ		O	H U	
kotaꞌeꞌ		O	H U	
awaseꞌ				H U O
#tumugi⁻; #haꞌnareꞌ; yatoꞌi			H	U
hasiriꞌ; #sigokiꞌ⁻			U	H
siboriꞌ			H U⁴	
amariꞌ, hakariꞌ 'scales', hatakiꞌ, soroꞌiꞌ; #doꞌmori, #taꞌyori, #moꞌguri			H U	
mayoꞌi, nagekiꞌ, naraꞌi		O		H U
ayumiꞌ, azukeꞌ, hagemiꞌ, hakariꞌ 'measure', hineriꞌ, isogiꞌ, kaeriꞌ, koboreꞌ, kuguriꞌ, kusariꞌ, kuyamiꞌ, kuzureꞌ, magireꞌ, mamoriꞌ, modoriꞌ, nayamiꞌ, togameꞌ, ugokiꞌ, uturiꞌ; kuruꞌiꞌ; #kaꞌsegiꞌ, #neꞌtamiꞌ, #siꞌnogiꞌ, #suꞌberiꞌ; #osameꞌ⁻, #sudatiꞌ⁻, tigiriꞌ⁻; #taꞌtari				H U
aseriꞌ, damasiꞌ, kubariꞌ, kisimiꞌ				H⁵

¹Verb: B' - B-A-B.   ²Verb: B' - B-A-B.   ³In .o-sagaꞌri 'rainfall'.
⁴Only as 'red-and-white mix (of flowers)'.   ⁵Data lacking for U.

(Chart 6:1 continued)

· · ·   · · ·   · · ·

Oddities, such as disparity between infinitive and derived noun;
see also Chart 10.

Group	ō꜒oo	oo̅꜒o	oo̅꜒o̲	.o̅o̅o̅	.o̲o̲o̲	Verb type
tagai'⁻					H U	B - B-A-B
tigiri'⁻			H U			A - B-A-B
sakebi'	U		H			A - B-A-B
nazuke' (Kg A)			H U			B - B-A-A
#maga'i(?⁻) (Kg A)			H U			B - B-A-A
#magure' (Mg ooo)			U	H		x - B-A-(B)
kota'e'		O	H U			B - B-B-B
#ha'ziki'			H U	U		B - B-A-B
kakusi'		U	H			B´- B-B-B
#si'mari			H	H U		x - B-A-B
oyogi'			H	U		B - B-A-B
tubomi' (Kg B!)			H U O			x - A/B-A-A
tumami' (Kg A)		H		U		x - A-A-A
mukai⁻ (Kg A)	H U				U	A - A-A-A
yogore⁻ (Kg A)	H				U	x - A-A-A
kimari⁻					H U	x - A-A-A
mawari⁻ (Kg A)			H U			x - A-A-A
sasa'e'⁻ (Kg A)					H U	B´- A/B-B-A
#kugiri'⁻			H		U	x - B-A/B-x (U)
tuka'e' 'obstruction; support'					H U	x - B-A-B (H)

Chart 6:2.   Four-syllable derived nouns.

Group	ōōō'o̲	ō'o̲o̲o̲o̲	ooo'o̲	oooo	.o̲o̲o̲o̲	Verb type
kanga'e, kokoro'e, tukuro'i	H U					
tetuda'i, #uzu'maki		H U				
#asira'i⁻, #aki'na'i		H		U		
samuga'ri'			H U			
otoro'e'			H U	U		
akirame'⁻, anado'ri'⁻, araso'i⁻, atuma'ri', ayama'ri', ayama'ti', azuka'ri', ganbari'⁻, hakara'i⁻, haradati'⁻, hazira'i⁻, hetura'i, hirame'ki', hiyaka'si', hokoro'bi', ikigo'mi'⁻, irodo'ri'⁻, kanasi'mi'⁻, katamu'ki'⁻, katayo'ri'⁻, kokoro'mi'⁻, kuturo'gi'⁻, matiga'i, maziwa'ri'⁻, mokuromi'⁻, narawasi'⁻, nigiwa'i, omomu'ki'⁻, osama'ri'⁻, sitata'ri'⁻, takurami'⁻, tasina'mi'⁻, tikazuki'⁻, tutusimi'⁻, uragi'ri'⁻, urana'i; #hagemasi'⁻, #hanikami⁻, #iradati⁻, #kusuburi'⁻ (U x)				H U		

Oddities:

Noun	ōōō'o̲	ō'o̲o̲o̲o̲	ooo'o̲	oooo	.o̲o̲o̲o̲	Verb type
ikedo'ri'⁻				U	H	x - A/B-A-x (U) / A/B-B-B (H)
kuwada'te'⁻				U	H	x - B-B-B (H) / B-A-x (U)
kakawari'⁻				H U		x - A/B-B-B
kodawa'ri'⁻				H U		x - A/B-B-A
kosika'ke'	U	H				x - B-A-A (H) / B-B-x (U)
motenasi'⁻				H U		x - A/B-B-B
kosirae⁻	H			U		A - A-A-A
ukagai⁻	H			U		A - A-A-A

Chart 6:3   Five-syllable derived nouns.

Noun	oooo'o̲	ooooo	.o̲o̲o̲o̲o̲	Verb type
ikidoori'⁻		H U		B - B-A-B
kokorozasi'⁻	U	H U		x - B-A-B
moteamasi⁻ (H x)			U	B+A - A/B-B-B
moteasobi⁻ (H x)			U	B+A - A/B-B-B

Chart 7:1.   Tōkyō accent patterns for three-syllable nouns derived from tonic infinitives.

The usual pattern is o͟o͞o⌐¹ (→ o͟o⌐¹o͟ if the final syllable is dependent), sometimes with an alternant that is prototonic (ō⌐¹o͟o͟) or atonic (o͟o͟o͟), and a few have only the prototonic version. Items in the last group are subclassed by the Kinki patterns shown in Chart 6:1.

Group	Tōkyō accent patterns			
	o͟o͞o⌐¹	o͟o͞⌐¹o͟	o͞⌐¹o͟o͟	o͟o͟o͟
hanare, haziki, kagiri, kasegi, magure, orosi¹, sabaki, sagari², sinogi, suberi³, tanomi	+		+	
sumai		+	+	
kotae, kurui, oboe, sonae, soroi	+	+		
harai⁴, iwai, mayoi, negai, nioi, tatoe, yatoi; magai⁵		+		
kamae⁶	+	+	+	
sasae (Verb: B´ -A/B-B-A)	+	+		+
domori, sawagi, simari, tatari, tayori; moguri			+	
ikari, kugiri, netami, sigoki, sudati, tigiri, tumugi, tuzuri; osame; homare	+			+
hanasi, hibiki, hikari, kumori, nagame, nagare, tutome, tutumi; konomi, koyasi, nigori, nokori, sadame, sodati, todoke, toosi, tukuri, yasumi; sakebi, sirabe, wakare; inori, sagari, suzumi, tamesi, urami, yurusi; tasuke; kaesi⌐¹, kobosi⌐¹, toori⌐¹, utusi⌐¹; hasami, yabure; awase; hasiri; sibori; hakari, hataki; nageki, narai; amari, ayumi, azuke, hagemi, hakari (both meanings), hineri, isogi, kaeri, kobore, kuguri, kusari, kuyami, kuzure, magire, modori, nayami, togame, ugoki, uturi; aseri, damasi, kubari, kisimi; kakusi; oyogi; ···	+			

¹As 'wholesale' either o'rosi or orosi'; as 'wind blowing down' only o'rosi; as 'lowering' only orosi'.
²With sa'gari only as 'wrestler's apron', though o-sa'gari has other meanings.
³But su'beri only as abbreviation of kata-su'beri 'figure-skating'.
⁴Listed as also atonic by H; the verb is B - B-A-B.
⁵Listed as also atonic by H; the verb is B - B-A-A.
⁶All three versions in NHK.

Chart 7:2.   Tōkyō accent patterns for four-syllable nouns
                  derived from tonic infinitives.

The usual pattern[1] is o͟ooo⒈ freely varying with o͟oo⒈o (and only the
latter if the final mora is dependent), with or without an oxytonic variant
(o͟oooo), but some of the nouns are always either oxytonic (o͟ooo⒈) or atonic (o͟ooo).

Group	Tōkyō accent patterns		
	o͟oo⒈o	o͟ooo⒈	o͟ooo
akirame, anadori, ikigomi, irodori, katamuki, katayori, kuturogi, osamari, sitatari, tasinami, uragiri; kokoromi	+	+	+
atumari, ayamari, ayamati, azukari, hirameki, hiyakasi; kosikake; hokorobi, samugari; otoroe	+	+	
rasoi, hakarai, hazirai; asirai	+		+
heturai, matigai, nigiwai, uranai; kangae, kokoroe, tetudai, tukuroi	+		
ganbari, haradati, mokuromi, narawasi, takurami, tikazuki, tutusimi; kakawari[2]; ikedori[3]		+	+

Oddly atonic only:
hagemasi, hanikami, iradati, kusuburi;
 motenasi[3]
| | | | + |

Oddities:

	o͟oo⒈o	o͟ooo⒈	o͟ooo
	aki͞⒈nai	akina͞⒈i	
	uzu⒈maki		
	huru⒈mai	huruma⒈i	huruma͞i

[1]The pattern of oxytonic varying with retracted oxytonic (i.e. with the locus of the accent before rather
than after the final syllable) is also found for a number of nouns of four or more syllables: kamina'ri'
'thunder'; kinodo'ku' 'pitiful', wagama'ma' 'willful'; also, compounds with -mo'no' such as tabe-mo'no'
'food'. But tate'-mono 'building' and iki'-mono 'living creature' show another pattern of variation, and
yomi'-mo'no' 'something to read' combines both. Many such words have an atonic variant: otosi-mo'no'⁻
'something dropped', takara-mo'no'⁻ 'treasure', kangae-mo'no'⁻ 'something to think about'. The atonic
variant is probably new and may not be found in all dictionaries. The oxytonic version of each of these words
seems to be the oldest, and that is what would be predicted by the rules for the nouns derived from tonic
infinitives: cf. Kawakami 1973:69.

[2]The verb is A/B-B-B, and the same pattern is shown by the related verb kakaeru, for which Myōgi-shō
has kakafu LHL = Type B'.

[3]The verbs: A/B-B-B, unattested in Myōgi-shō.

Chart 8.   Tōkyō and Kyōto accent variants in nouns
                derived from two-syllable verb infinitives.

Noun	Tōkyō			Kyōto				Verb type
	ōō	ōō'	ō'o	ōō	ō'o	.ōō	.ōŏ'	
huse 'ambush'		+			U	U	H	B - B-B-B
kui 'regret'		+	+		U	H		x - B-B-B
nui 'sewing' (H x)		+	+		U			B - B-B-B
yoi 'intoxication'		+	+	H	U			B - B-B-B
hare 'being clear'		+	+		U		H	B - B-B-B
wake 'dividing, ...'			+			H	U	B - B-B-B
koi$_1$ 'love'			+	H	U			B - B-B[U]-(B)
koi$_2$ 'begging'		?+	+					B - B-B-B
kui 'eating'		+	+					B - B-B-B
ue 'hunger'		+	+	H	U			B - B-B-B
aki 'weariness'		+		H	U			B - B-B-B
kati 'victory'		+		H	U			B - B-B-B
kari 'hunting' (Mg LH)			+	H	U			x - A/B-A-A
maki 'roll'			+	U	H			A - A-A-A
obi 'girdle' (Mg LH, Kg B)			+	H	U			x - A/B-B-A
tomi 'riches'			+	H	U			x - B-B-A
muki 'facing toward'			+			H	U	x - A-A-A
nuki 'omission'			+	U	H	U		A - A-A-B
kuke 'blindstitch'	+			H	U			x - A-A-B
tuki 'attendant'			+	H	U			B - B-B-B
tugi$_1$ 'next' (Mg HL)			+		H	U		A - A-A-A
tugi$_2$ 'patch'	+			H	U			
hagi 'patch'	+				H	U		x - A-B-A
hure 'touch'			+	H	U[1]			B - A-B-A
deki 'make; yield'	+			H	U			x - B-A-B
toi 'inquiry'	+			H	U			A - A/B-A-B
oi 'the old' (Kg B)	+		+	H	U			B - B-A[H]/B[U]-A
hate '(reaching) the end'			+	H	U[2]			x - B-B-B
mane 'mimicry' (Sr B)	+			U	H			x - A-A-A
sage 'lowering'		+[3]			H	U		x - B-A/B-B
koge 'getting scorched'			+			H	U	x - B-B-A
kori 'hardening, freezing'			+		H	U		A - B-B-A
mori 'guard'			+	U[4]		H		x - B-A-(?B[5])
zure 'discrepancy, lag'			+		H	U		x - B-A[U]/B[H]-A
sori 'warp'			+		H	U		x - B-B-A
nagi 'calm'			+		H	U		x - B-B-A
nari 'sound'	+	+[6]		H	U			A - A-A-A[6]
yake '(burning), despair'	(+)		+	U			H	A - A-A-A
tate$_1$ 'shield'			+		H	U		B - B-B-B
tate$_2$ 'vertical'			+			H	U	B - B-B-B
seki$_1$ 'cough'			+		U	H		B - B-B-B
seki$_2$ 'dam; barrier' (Kg A)			+		H	U		B - B-B-B

[1] But .o-hure⁻ (H), .o-hu're (U) 'official communication', Tōkyō o-hu're or o-hure'. See §10.2.

[2] But Edo ha'te HL.   [3] But o-sa'ge (a hairstyle), cf. Kyōto .o-sa'ge.

[4] As 'babysitter' .mori'; for the Tōkyō form NHK has o-mo'ri but H and K have the expected atonic variant o-mori⁻. The verb (Km B) is now used only in dialects.

[5] The verb is not listed in H but the derived noun is B.

[6] H has B for both Tōkyō and Kagoshima: other sources all have the expected A for Tōkyō.

Chart 9.   Problematic correspondences: infinitives
                of one or two syllables.

Type	Stem: Ng - Tk-Kt-Kg	Sd-Sr-Yn	Verb	Noun	Noun: Ng - Tk-Kt-Kg Sd-Sr-Yn
A	A - A-A-A	(A)-A-x	maku 'roll'	maki	x - 1-A[U]/2[H]-A (A)-A-x
	A - A-A[U]/B[H]-A	x-A-x	kaku 'lack'	—	
			horeru 'love'	—	
			[1]suteru 'discard'	—	
		A-(A)-x	kagu 'smell'	kagi	x - A-x-x x-x-x
		A-A-A	[2]sou 'follow'	soi	x - A-A[U]-x
		x-x-x	masu 'increase'	masi	x - A-A-A
	A - A-B-A	x-A-x	umeru 'bury'	—	
		x-x-x	wabiru 'apologize'	wabi	x - A-A[U]/B[H]-A
			ueru 'plant'	—	
	A - (A/)B-A[U]/B[H]-B	x-A-A	oru 'weave'	ori	x - A[H]/B-A[U]/2[H]-A x-x-x
	x - A-A-A	x-x-x	maneru 'mimic'	mane	A - A-A[U]/2[H]-A x-B-x
	A - B-B-x	x-x-x	emu 'smile'	emi	x - B/1-A-A x-x-x
?A	A - A-A-B	x-A-A	saku 'bloom'	—	
			[3]tuku 'soak' (vi.)	—	
			[4]nuku 'remove'	nuki	x - 1-A[U]/2-B x-A-x
		x-(B)-x	[5]kamu 'blow nose'	—	
		x-A-x	haku 'wear'	—	
			hakeru 'let wear'	—	
			huku 'thatch, cover'	—	
	A - A/B-A[U]/B[H]-A	x-x-x	saru 'depart'	—	
	A - A/B-A-B	x-A-x	tou 'inquire'	toi	x - A-A-B x-x-x
	A - B-B-A	x-x-x	koru 'harden, freeze'	kori	x - B-2-A x-x-x
			sakeru 'avoid'	—	
			useru 'vanish'	—	
	A - B-A-A	B-B-x	iru 'shoot'	—	
		x-A-x	oziru 'fear'	—	
	A - B-A-B	x-x-x	iru 'cast metal'	—	
	x - B-A[U]/B[H]-A	x-x-x	zureru 'slip'	zure	x - B-2-A x-x-x
?A/B	x - B-A[H]/B[U]-A	x-x-x	megeru 'succumb'	—	
	B - A/B-A-x	x-x-x	taderu 'poultice, foment'	—	
?A'	A - B-A[H]/A'[U]-A	A-A-A	[6]oru 'be'	—	
?B	B - B-A-A	x-x-x	eru 'get'	—	
			suberu 'control'	—	
	B - B-A[H]/B[U]-A	x-A-x	heru 'pass'	—	
		x-?B-x	mogu 'pluck'	—	
		x-B-B	yamu 'ail'	—	
			oiru 'age'	oi	x[7] - A/1-A[H]/2[U]-B x-x-x
		x-x-x	nosu 'stretch it'	—	
	B - A/B-A-A	x-x-x	karu 'hunt'	kari	LH - 1-A[H]/2[U]-A x-x-x
	A/B - A-B-A	x-x-x	museru 'choke up'	—	
	B - A-B-A	A?-A?-x	[8]abiru 'bathe in'	—	
		x-B-x	[9]ou 'bear'	—	
			hureru 'touch'	hure[10]	x - A[H]/B[U]-A[H]/2[U]-B x-B-x

(Chart 9, p. 2)

(?B)

	x - A-B-A	A?-A?-x	[11]hagu 'patch'	hagi	x - A-2-B x-x-x	
	B - B-A[H]/B[U]-B	x-B-B	hagu 'peel off'	—		
		x-x-x	nosu 'iron'	nosi	x - B-2-B x-B-x	
	x[12] - B-A-(B)	x-A-x	moru 'guard'	mori	x - 2-A[U]/B[H]-B x-B-x	
	B - B-B-A	x-B-x	imu 'shun'	imi	x - B-2-x x-B-x	
		x-B?-x	kau 'raise'	—		
		B-B-B	saku 'rip it'	—		
			sakeru 'get ripped'	—		
		x-B-x	haneru 'jump'	hane	x - B-2-A x-B-x	
			kareru 'wither'	—		
			sogu 'chop off'	sogi[12]	x - B/1-x-x x-x-x	
		x-x-x	bokeru 'dote'	—		
			ieru 'heal' (vi.)	—		
			saeru 'get cold/serene'	sae	x - B-2-A x-x-x	
			simeru 'occupy'	—		
			ueru 'hunger'	ue	x - B/1-2-A x-x-x	
B	B - B-B-B	x-B-x	akiru 'weary'	aki	x - B-A[H]/2[U]-B x-x-x	
			hateru 'reach the end'	hate	x - B-A-B x-B-x	
			togeru 'attain'	—		
			ir-u 'roast'	iri	x - B-2-x x-x-x	
		B-B-B	katu 'win'	kati	B - B-A[H]/2[U]-B x-B-x	
	x - B-A-B	x-B-x	[13]keru 'kick'	—		
		x-A?-x	yosu 'stop it'	—		
	x - B-B[U]-B	x-(B)-x	[14]kou 'love'	koi	B - B/1[15]-2-B x-B-x	
	B - A/B-B-B	x-B-x	kutiru 'rot'	—		
	x - B-A/B-B-B	x-B-x	sageru 'lower'	sage	x - B-2-B x-(B)-x	
	(B) - A/B-B-A	x-x-x	obiru 'gird'	obi	LH - 2-B-B B-B-x	
	x - B-B-A	x-x-x	[16]himeru 'conceal'	—		
			kogeru 'get scorched'	koge	x - B-1:3-A x-x-x	
			koneru 'knead'	—		
			nagu 'mow; get calm'	nagi	x - B-2-A x-x-x	
			takeru 'excel'	—		
			taberu 'eat'	—		
		x-B?-x	hazeru 'burst open'	—		
			ureru 'ripen'	—		
?A	x - B-B-A	x-x-x	tomu 'be rich'	tomi	A - 1-2-A x-x-x	
?A/B[17]	x - A/B-B-A	x-x-x	aseru 'get shallow; fade'	—		
B<B+B	x - B-A-B	x-B-x	dekiru 'get produced'	deki	x - A-A-B x-x-x	

[1]Cf. intransitive sutaru A - A-A-B, noun sutari x - A-A-B; variant sutareru A - A-A-B.
The modern passive suterareru and causative sutesaseru are like suteru. The compound verb
sute-oku is A-B-A according to H but A/B-A-x according to NKD. Compound nouns with sute-
as the first element show ragged correspondences in modern dialects:

0-0[U]/1[H]-A	sute-ba, -bati, -isi, -inu, -mi, -uri
0-0[U]/1[H]-B	sute-gane, -ne
3/4-5-B	sute-dokoro
0-1:3-A	sute-go
3-4[U]/1:4[H]-B	sute-zerifu

NKD also has sute-buti, sute-mono, sutare-mono, sutari-mono (all 0-0-x) and sute-huda
0/4-0/3-x. Shuri has şitiyun (= suteru) A, but şitariyun (= sutareru) B.

[2]Also 'be added/attached'; cf. the derived transitive soeru 'add' A - A-A-A x-A-x.

[3]Cf. tukeru 'soak it' (A) - A-A-A x-A-x, but B in Narada.

[4]Kg confuses nuku with nugu B - B-B-B x-B-B. Narada nuku B = nugu 'remove'.
Cf. nukeru 'be removed' (A) - A-A-A x-A-x.

[5]Mochizuki omits the third tone mark of Mg fana kamu HHHx. Probably a misprint.

[6]Type A´ may be contracted from an early compound of A+B (wi - ar-). Oru < woru is
A throughout the Ryūkyūs but the cognate of aru 'be' uniquely seems to be Type A´ in
Yonaguni; everywhere else, and earlier, aru is B.

[7]Km A is attested in Akinaga 1972:42a.

[8]Abiru is A in Narada.

[9]"Hn A or B; Km and Edo B" says NKD, but Mg has only B. Cf. ou 'pursue' A - A-A-A x-A-x.

[10]And o-hure 3/4-1[H]/1:3[U]-B.

[11]The Ryūkyū cognate means 'distribute; build a boat'.

[12]Abbreviation of sogi-i'ta¯.

[13]"Hn A" says NKD, but the verb is not in Mochizuki. (NKD: "Mg kuyu, koyu.") Modern Tk ker-u.

[14]The verb is not listed by H. Compound nouns with koi as first element are Kt A but Kg B.
Koi-kogareru 'burn with love' is probably to be taken as noun + verb (cf. Mkz ko'i kogare'ru)
but Mka has koi-kogare'ru¯ as if verb + verb; NKD gives A/B-B-x but H has A/B-A-x. Compare
koi-suru 'love': H gives koi-su'ru - ko'i-suru - B, but NKD has ko'i-suru - A - x, Mka both.

[15]The oxytonic version (koi'), found only in NKD, probably represents a Tōkyō-type dialect,
and not Tōkyō itself.

[16]Cf. hisomeru B - A/B-A-B x-x-x; hisomaru x - B-A-x x-x-x.

[17]But the adjective stem asa- 'shallow' is A.

Chart 10.   Problematic correspondences:
             infinitives of three syllables.

Type	Stem: Mg - Tk-Kt-Kg	Sd-Sr-Yn	Verb	Noun	Noun: Mg - Tk-Kt-Kg Sd-Sr-Yn
A	λ - λ-λ-λ	x-λ-x	[1]kataru 'tell'	katari	x - λ-λ-λ x-x-x
			mukau 'face'	mukai	x - λ-λ[U]/2[HU]-λ x-λ-x
			oyobu 'reach'	[2]oyobi	x - λ/1-1-λ x-x-x
		B-λ-x	musubu 'tie'	musubi	x - λ-λ-λ x-x-x
		x-λ-λ	yakeru 'get burned'	yake	x - λ/2-λ[U]/1:3[H]-B x-x-x
	x - λ-λ-λ	x-x-x	[3]kimaru 'be decided'	kimari	x - λ-B-λ x-x-x
		x-λ-x	konasu 'grind; handle'	konasi	x - λ/B-λ-λ x-x-x
			mawaru 'go round'	mawari	x - λ-2-λ λ-λ-x
			yogoreru 'get dirty'	yogore	x - λ[U]/2[H]-λ x-λ-x
		x-B-x	abareru 'rampage, rage'	—	
	λ - λ[K]/B[H]-λ-λ	x-λ-x	[4]kudasu 'lower; defeat'	kudasi	x - λ-λ-x x-λ-x
	λ - λ-λ[U]/B[H]-λ	x-x-x	[5]uwaru 'get planted'	—	
		λ-λ-x	hirou, hirau 'pick up'	—	
	λ - λ/B[U]-λ[U]/B[H]-λ	x-λ-x	tutaeru 'transmit'	tutae	x - λ/B-2-x x-λ-x
	x - λ-λ-λ/B	x-x-x	kasumu 'get misty/dim'	kasumi	λ - λ-λ-λ/B x-x-x
	λ - λ[H]/B-λ-λ	x-λ-x	hikaeru 'wait; jot down'	hikae	x - λ/2/3-λ-λ x-λ-x
	λ - λ/B-λ-λ	x-x-x	[6]itaru 'reach'	itari	x - λ/B-λ-λ x-x-x
			itasu 'cause; do'	—	
			[7]kagameru 'bend/tilt it'	—	
			kurau 'eat, drink, get'	—	
			minoru 'bear fruit'	minori	x - λ-λ-λ x-x-x
			matou 'put on, wear'	matoi	x - λ-λ-λ x-x-x
			okasu 'commit; defy'	—	
			[8]satosu 'admonish'	satosi	λ - λ-λ-λ x-x-x
			[9]sitau 'love; follow'	—	
			sosogu 'pour'	sosogi	x - λ-λ-λ x-x-x
			[10]tikau 'vow, pledge'	tikai	x - λ/2-λ/B-λ x-x-x
			turaneru 'put in a row'	—	
			yuwaeru 'tie up'	—	
		x-λ-x	horobiru 'go to ruin'	—	
			isameru 'admonish'	isame	x - λ/B-λ-λ x-x-x
			[11]masaru 'excel, surpass'	—	
			maturu 'celebrate'	maturi	λ - λ/B-λ-λ x-λ-x
			motureru 'get entangled'	moture	x - λ/B-λ-λ x-λ-x
			obieru 'fear'	obie	x - λ/B-x-x x-x-x
			tadareru 'get inflamed'	tadare	x - λ-λ-λ x-λ-x
			tumoru 'pile up; estimate'	tumori	x - λ-λ-λ x-λ-x
			yugamu 'get warped'	yugami	x - λ/B-λ-λ x-λ-x
			yugameru 'warp, bend'	—	
		x-(λ)-x	oboreru 'drown'	—	
			osou 'attack'	—	
		x-(B)-x	tuieru 'get spent'	—	
	λ - λ/B[new]-λ-λ	x-λ-x	nozomu 'hope/look for'	nozomi	λ - λ/B-λ-λ x-λ-x
			saguru 'search/grope for'	saguri	x - λ/B-λ-λ x-x-x
			[12]satoru 'realize'	satori	λ - λ-λ-λ x-x-x
	x - λ/B[new]-λ-λ	x-x-x	subomu 'get narrow'	subomi	x - λ-x-x x-x-x
	λ - λ[old]/B-λ-λ	x-x-x	[13]ikaru 'get angry'	ikari	λ - λ/B-λ-λ x-x-x

(Chart 10, p. 2)

(A)

	x - A(/B[H])-A-A	x-x-x		konareru 'be digested'	konare	x - A-A-A x-x-x
	x - A/B-A-A	x-x-x		amaeru 'seek favor'	amae	x - A-x-x x-x-x
				hezuru 'pare down'	—	
				kuberu 'fuel/stoke with'	—	
				sosoru 'arouse, excite'	sosori	x - A/B-A-A x-x-x
				yuragu 'swing, shake'		
		x-A-x	[14]akasu 'reveal; spend night'	akasi	x - A-A-A x-x-x
	x - B-A-A	x-A-x		tagir-u 'seethe'	tagiri	x - B-x-x x-x-x
		x-(A)-x		motoru 'deviate'	—	
				soyogu 'rustle'	soyogi	x - B-A-A x-x-x
		x-(x)-x		norou 'curse'	noroi	x - A/B-A-A x-x-x
?A/B	x - A/B-A-A	x-B-x	[15]kasamu 'grow in bulk'	—	
			[16]tubomu 'get narrow'	tubomi	x - B-A-B x-B-x.
				mukumu 'swell/puff up'	mukumi	x - A/B-A-B x-x-x
				owasu 'burden with'	—	
	x - A/B-A-x	x-x-x		tonaru 'neighbor'	tonari	A - A-A-A A-A-x
A<B+A	A - A/B-A-x	x-x-x		kitaru 'come'	—	
				kitasu 'bring'	—	
	A - A[U]/B[H]-B	x-x-x		mitomeru 'recognize'	mitome	x - A-A[U]/B[H]-B x-x-x
A+A	x - A-A-B	x-x-x		simau 'finish; close up'	simai	x - A-A-A x-x-x
?A+A	B' - B'-B-B	x-B-x		mair-u 'humbly come/go'	—	
A+B	x - B-A-A	x-A-x		niau 'befit'	niai	x - A-A-A x-x-x
	HLF - A/B-A-A	x-x-x		simesu 'show, indicate'	simesi	x - A/B-A-A x-x-x
	HLH/HLL - B-A-A	x-(A)-x		osaeru 'restrain'	osae	x - 2/3-A-A x-x-x.
	HLF/HLH/RLL - B-A-x	x-x-x		modasu 'be silent'	—	
	HL (fo[s]su) - A/B-B-B	x-x-x		hos-suru 'desire'	—	
?A	A - A-A-B	x-x-x	[17]sutaru 'get disused'	sutari	x - A-A-B x-x-x.
	x - A-A-B	x-x-x		kawasu 'exchange'	—	
				sioreru 'droop'	—	
?A/B	x - A-A-B	x-x-x		simesu 'dampen/wet it'	simesi	x - A-x-x x-x-x
		(B)-B-x	[18]simer-u 'get damp'	simeri	x - A-A-B x-x-x
	A - A-B-A	x-A-x		sazukeru 'grant; teach'	—	
			[19]umeru 'bury; fill'	—	
			[19]umoreru 'get buried'	—	
		x-x-x	[19]umaru 'be buried'	—	
		x-B-x		uzumeru 'bury; fill'	—	
	A - B-A-B	x-x-x		aegu 'pant'	aegi	x - B-A-x x-x-x
				ahureru 'overflow'	—	
				awaremu 'pity'	—	
				habukeru 'be excluded'	—	
				habuku 'exclude, curtail'	—	
				hiideru 'excel'	—	
				korasu 'concentrate'	—	
			[20]kuziku 'sprain, dislocate'	—	
				sakebu 'yell'	sakebi	x - B-A[H]/1[U]-B x-x-x
				sonemu 'envy'	sonemi	x - B-A-B x-x-x
			[21]suguru 'select'	—	
				tigir-u 'pledge'	tigiri	LHL - A/B-A-B x-A-x
				tonaeru 'chant'	tonae	x - 2/3-A-x x-x-x

(Chart 10, p. 3)

(?A/B   A - B-A-B)

		x-B-x	tamotu 'keep, maintain'	—	
	A - A/B[U]-A-B	x-x-x	kubir-u 'strangle'	—	
		x-A-x	kubireru 'be constricted'	—	
	A - B-A-A	x-x-x	habamu 'hinder, obstruct'	—	
			22hokoru 'take pride, boast'	hokori	x - A/B-A-A x-x-x
			idaku 'embrace'(= daku AAA)	—	
			kakotu 'offer pretext'	—	
			kibamu 'turn yellow'	—	
			kobamu 'resist'	—	
			modaeru 'writhe, agonize'	modae	x - 2/3-A-A x-x-x
			tawameru 'bend it'	—	
			tawamu 'bend, yield'	—	
			23todomeru 'stop it'	todome	x - B-A-B x-x-x
			24totugu 'become a wife'	totugi	A - x-x-x x-x-x
		x-A-x	sugureru 'excel'	—	
			25tukusu 'exhaust; work'	—	
	A - B-A-A	x-B-x	sosir-u 'slander, blame'	sosiri	x - B-A-A x-B-x
			tataru 'curse'	tatari	x - 1/A-A x-B-x
		x-(x)-x	nazukeru 'name'	nazuke	x - B-A-A x-B-x
	A - A/B-A-B[?]	x-(A)-x	26isamu 'show spirit, prance'	isami	x - A-x-x x-(A)-x
	A - A/B-A-B	x-(x)-x	mukuiru 'reward; requite'	mukui	x - A/B-A-B x-A-x
		x-x-x	27kasumeru 'steal, ...'	—	
	A - B-A-x	x-x-x	hodasu 'shackle'	hodasi	A - A/B-A-x x-x-x
	A - A/B[new]-A-B	x-A-x	sugaru 'cling; depend'	—	
?B	B - B-A-A	x-B-x	agameru 'respect; worship'	—	
			husegu 'protect, defend'	husegi	x - B-A-A x-x-x
			ikou 'relax'	28ikoi	x - A/2-A-A x-B-x
			itou 'hate; grudge'	itoi	x - 2/3-x-x x-x-x
			kanau 'be suitable'	—	
			kaneru 'combine; cannot'	—	
			karameru 'entangle'	—	
			29mamoru 'guard'	mamori	x - B-A-A x-B-x
			30okoru 'arise, occur; anger'	okori	x - B-A-A x-B-x
			taguru 'pull/reel in'	—	
			ubau 'seize by force'	—	
			yadoru 'lodge'	yadori	(B) - B-A-A x-x-x
			yodomu 'stagnate; stammer'	yodomi	B - A/B-A-A x-x-x
		B-B-x	yatou 'hire'	yatoi	x - 3-A[U]/1:3[H]-A x-x-x
		x-(B)-x	karamu 'tangle; be tangled'	—	
			kawaku 'get dry'	kawaki	x - B-A-A x-x-x
		x-B-B	31hedateru 'set apart'	hedate	x - B-A-A x-B-x
			mozir-u 'twist'	moziri	x - B-A-A x-x-x
		x-(B)-B	mayou 'get bewildered'	32mayoi	x - 2-A-A x-x-x
		x-x-B	madou 'get bewildered'	madoi	x - A/2-A-A x-x-x
		x-x-x	agaku 'paw'	agaki	x - B/1-A-A x-x-x
			idomu 'challenge'	idomi	x - B-x-x x-x-x
			33iyasu 'cure'	—	
			magau 'be confused (with)'	magai	x - A/2-A-A x-x-x
			kanaderu 'play (harp)'	—	

(Chart 10, p. 4)

```
(?B     B - B-B-A              x-x-x)
                                         nakasu 'entrust'                —
                                         sinau 'bend, be pliant'         —
                                         tukaneru 'bundle'         tukane   B - x-x-x x-x-x
                                         ugatu 'dig, bore; wear'         —
                              x-x-x  [34]hatasu 'accomplish'            —
                                         kiou 'strive; compete'          —
                                         mamieru 'have audience with'    —
                                         mazieru 'mix; exchange'         —
                                     [35]natuku 'get familiar/fond'      —
                                         nazumu 'cling'                  —
                                         ninau 'shoulder'                —
                                         tunoru 'collect; intensify'     —
                                         tuzumeru 'contract'             —
                                         urumu 'get wet'                 —
       (B) - B-A-A            x-x-x      kanaeru 'grant (request)'       —
       (B) - B-A-A       x-A[new?]-x     otoru 'be inferior, lag'        —
       B - B-A-x              x-B-x      tagau 'differ; violate'   tagai    LHH - A-B-B x-B-A[36]
                                         takumu 'plan, devise'     takumi   x - A/1-A-B x-x-x
                              x-x-x      hatureru 'ravel, fray'          —
       x - B-A-B              x-B-x      tuner-u 'pinch, nip'            —
       x - B-A-A              x-B-x  [37]harasu 'clear, dispel'          —
                                         nasuru 'rub, smear'             —
                              x-x-x      nazimu 'get familiar'     nazimi   x - B-2-A x-x-x
                                         sasaru 'be stuck/embedded'      —
?A/B   x - B-A-A              x-A-x      sawagu 'clamor'           sawagi   x - 1-2-A x-(A)-x
                                     [38]sugosu 'get beyond; overdo'     —
                              x-B-x      tutuku 'peck; nudge'            —
                              x-x-x  [39]akasu 'weary; satiate'          —
                                         aoru 'flap, fan'          aori     x - B-A-A x-x-x
                                         boyakeru 'get dim/blurred'      —
                                         daber-u 'chatter'               —
                                         doyasu 'hit on back; roar'      —
                                         guzuru 'grumble, fret'          —
                                         hadakeru 'bare'                 —
                                         iburu 'smolder'           iburi    x - B-x-x x-x-x
                                         ibusu 'smoke'             ibusi    x - A/B-A-A x-x-x
                                         kager-u 'get obscure'     kageri   x - B-x-x x-x-x
                                         kamosu 'brew'                   —
                                         kasigeru 'tilt it'              —
                                         kisou 'compete'                 —
                                         nagomu 'calm down'              —
                                         namakeru 'shirk'                —
                                         seou 'carry on one's back'      —
                                         sirakeru 'get white'            —
                                         sobieru 'tower'                 —
                                         tadoru 'grope; trace'           —
                                         taker-u 'rage, roar'            —
                                         tawakeru 'fool around'    tawake   x - B-1:3-A x-x-x
                                         tayoru 'rely'             tayori   LHL - 1-1:3-A x-B-x
                                     [40]tinamu 'be connected with' tinami  A - A/B/1-A-A x-x-x
```

(Chart 10, p. 5)

```
(?A/B  x - B-A-A              x-x-x)
                                      tobokeru 'look blank: dote'  —
                                      tozasu 'shut/close it'       —
                                      yudaneru 'entrust'           —
       x - B-A-A             x-x-x  41zurasu 'slip/shift it'       —
       A/B - B-A-B           x-B[Lit.]-x  sibaru 'bind, tie'       —
       B - A[H]/B-A-A        x-x-x    yosou 'dress/equip oneself'  yosoi   B - 2-A-A x-x-x
       B - B-A-A?            x-B-x    nokosu 'leave (behind/over)' —
                                      tagaeru 'violate'            tagae   x - B/2-x-x x-x-x
                                      tugumu 'shut (mouth)'        —
       B - B-A-x             x-A-x    nogasu 'let escape'          —
                             x-A[new?]-x  todaeru 'cease,halt'     —
B      x - B-A-B             x-x-x    donaru 'yell, roar'          —
                                      hosoru 'dwindle'             —
                                      hoter-u 'flush, feel hot'    hoteri  x - B-A-B x-x-x
                                      hurasu 'let/make it rain'    —
                                      mezameru 'wake up' (vi.)     mezame  x - B-A-B x-x-x
                                      mezasu 'aim'                 mezasi  x - B-x-x x-x-x
                                      nigasu 'let escape'          —
                                      sibireru 'get numb'          sibire  x - B-A[U]/1:3-B x-x-x
                                      simaru 'be shut/tight/firm'  simari  x - 1-A[H]/1-B x-B-x
                                      tigir-u 'tear off, pluck'    —
                             x-B-x    azukeru 'give in trust'      azuke   x - B-A-B x-x-x
                                      ikasu 'let live; ...'        —
                                      kuyamu 'regret; lament'      kuyami  x - B-A-B x-B-x
                                      nagameru 'gaze at'           nagame  x - B-2-B x-B-x
                                      sorou 'be complete/regular'  soroi   x - B/2-1:3-B x-B-x
                                      tamesu 'try'                 tamesi  x - B-A-B x-B-x
                             x-B[new]-x  ibaru 'swagger'           —
                             x-(B)-x  kazir-u 'gnaw'               —
                                      namaru 'speak in dialect'    namari  x - B-2-B x-x-x
                             B-B-B    kusaru 'spoil, rot'          kusari  x - B-A-B x-x-x
       x - B-A/B-B           x-x-x    kugir-u 'mark off'           kugiri  x - A/B-A[H]/1[U]-B x-x-x
       (B) - A/B-A-B         x-x-x    hitaru 'get soaked'          —
       B - A/B-A-B           x-x-x  42hisomu 'lurk; scowl'         hisomi  x - B-x-x x-x-x
                                      hitasu 'soak (in)'           hitasi  x - B-A-B x-x-x
                                      tuzuru 'write: bind'         tuzuri  x - A/B-1-B x-x-x
                             x-B-x    asaru 'forage, hunt, fish'   asari   x - A-A-B x-x-x
       B - A[old(?)]-A-B     x-x-x    tomosu 'burn (light)'      43tomosi  x - A/B-A-x x-B-x
       (B) - A[old(?)]-A-B   x-B-x    tomoru 'be alight, burn'     —
       B - B-A-A/B           (B)-B-(B)  okosu 'raise; arouse'      —
       B - B-A-B             B-B-B    nagareru 'flow'              nagare  x - B-2-B x-B-x
                                      oyogu 'swim'                 oyogi   x - B-A[H]/1[U]-B x-B-x
                             x-B-B    amaru 'be excessive'         amari   B - B-1:3-B x-B-x
                                      narau 'learn; copy'          narai   x - 2-A-B x-B-x
                                      nokoru 'remain, be left'     nokori  B - B-2-B x-B-x
                                      tasukeru 'help; save'        tasuke  B - B-A-B x-B-x
                                      yurusu 'allow; forgive'      yurusi  B - B-A[H]/2[U]-B x-(B)-x
```

(Chart 10, p. 6)

(B   B - B-A-B)

	B-B-x	hikaru 'shine'		hikari	B - B-2-B x-B-x
		⁴⁴hiromeru 'spread it'		—	
		kaesu 'return it'		kaesi	x - B-A[H]/2-B x-B-x
		tooru 'pass by/through'		toori	x - B-A[U]/2[H]-B x-B-x
	x-B-x	aogu 'fan'		oogi<aogi	B - B-2-B B-B-x
		awaseru 'put together, mix'		awase	x - B-A-B x-(B)-x
		haziku 'flip, snap; repel'		haziki	x - 1/3-1:3/1[U]-B x-x-x
		hibiku '(re)sound; echo'		hibiki	B - B-2-B x-B[new?]-x
		hiner-u 'twist; pinch'		hineri	x - B-A-B x-x-x
		komoru 'be confined/fraught'		—	
		kuzureru 'collapse'		kuzure	x - B-A-B x-x-x
		midareru 'be disturbed'		midare	x - B-A-B x-B-x
		mookeru 'gain as profit'		mooke	x - B-2-B x-B-x
		nikumu 'hate'		nikumi	x - B-A-x x-?B-x
		osameru 'obtain: subdue'		osame	x - A[H,NHK]/B[K]-A-B x-x-x
		toosu 'let pass by/through'		toosi	x - B-2[U]/1:3[H]-B x-x-x
		wakareru 'get separate'		wakare	x - B-A[H]/2[U]-B x-B-x
		yasumu 'rest'		yasumi	x - B-2-B x-B-x
		yasumeru 'put at ease'		—	
	x-B[new]-x	inoru 'pray'		inori	B - B-A[H]/2[U]-B x-x-x
	x-?B-x	kamaeru 'set up; assume'		kamae	x - B/1/2-2-B x-A-x
		naburu 'tease, ridicule'		naburi	x - B-x-x x-x-x
	x-A-x	hiraku 'open'		hiraki	x - B-A-B x-x-x
		yatureru 'get shabby/gaunt'		yature	x - B-A[U]/2[H]-B x-x-x
	x-x-x	hataku 'dust, beat, slap'		hataki	x - B-1:3-B x-x-x
		iwau 'celebrate'		iwai	x - 2-A[H]/2[U]-B x-B-x
		kagir-u 'limit'		kagiri	B - B/1-A[H]/2[U]-B A-B-x
		koboreru 'fall, drop'		kobore	x - B-A-B x-x-x
		kobosu 'spill; grumble'		kobosi	x - B-A/1:3-x x-x-x
		nadameru 'soothe, placate'		—	
		netamu 'envy'		netami	x - A/B-A-B x-x-x
		nizir-u 'crawl'		niziri	x - B-x-x x-x-x
		sumau 'reside'		sumai	x - 1/2-2-B x-B-x
		yatusu 'dress shabbily, ...'		—	
?B - B-A-B	x-x-x	siger-u 'grow thick/dense'		—	
x - B-A-B	x-B-x	nagasu 'let flow; float'		nagasi	x - 1/3-2-B x-B-x
		nobasu 'extend; defer'		—	
	x-x-x	komaru 'be distressed'		—	
		konomu 'like'		konomi	x - B-2-B x-x-x
		magireru 'be confused'		magire	x - B-A-B x-x-x
		midasu 'disturb: corrupt'		—	
		moguru 'dive'		moguri	x - 1-1:3-B x-x-x
		mookaru 'profit'		—	
		nadareru 'slope'		nadare	x - A/B-2-B x-x-x
		niburu 'get dull/blunted'		—	
		tamukeru 'offer (tribute)'		tamuke	x - B-A-B x-x-x
(?A/)B - B-A-B	x-x-x	hubuku 'heavily blow/storm'		hubuki	x - 1-2-B x-x-x
x - B-A[U]-(B)	x-x-x	magureru 'get dizzy, faint'		magure	x - B-B/1-A[U]/B[H]-B x-x-x

(Chart 10, p. 7)

?A/B	x - B-B-A	x-A-x	tukaeru 'get choked'	tukae	x - B/2-1-A x-A-x
		x-x-x	barasu 'lay bare: dismantle'	—	
			obuu 'carry piggyback'	—	
	x - B-A[U]/B[H]-A	x-x-x	sorasu 'bend/avert it'	—	
	x - B-A-B	x-A-A	damasu 'cheat'	damasi	x - B-A-B x-x-x
	x - A/B-A-B	x-x-x	izaru 'crawl (on knees)'	izari	x - A-A[H]/B[U]-B x-x-x
			kogoeru 'get frozen'	kogoe	x - B[NKD]-x-x x-x-x
			kusasu 'disparage'	—	
			nedaru 'importune, ask for'	—	
			[45]sikaru 'scold'	sikari	x - A-A-B x-x-x
B′	B′ - B-B-B	x-B-x	kakureru 'hide oneself'	—	
			kakusu 'hide/conceal it'	kakusi	x - B-A[H]/1:3-B x-B-x
	B′ - A/B-A-B	x-B-x	kegareru 'get soiled'	kegare	x - A/B-2-B x-x-x
			taoreru 'collapse; succumb'	taore	x - B-x-x x-x-x
	(B′) - A/B-A-B	x-B-x	taosu 'topple'	—	
	B′ - A/B-B-B	x-x-x	kakaeru 'hold in arms'	kakae	x - A-B-B x-x-x
	B′ - B-A-B	x-B-x	aburu 'roast'	aburi	x - B[NKD]-x-x x-x-x
			harau 'sweep; clear: pay'	harai	x - 2(?/A)-A[H]/2[U]-B x-B-x
			kaburu 'put/wear on head'	kaburi	x - B/1(/A[H])-A-B x-x-x
			nogareru 'flee, escape'	—	
			sagaru 'go/come down'	sagari	x - B/1-A/2[U]/1:3[U]-B x-x-x
		x-x-B	negau 'request, desire'	negai	x - 2-A[H]/2[U]-B x-x-x
		x-B-B	erabu 'choose'	erabi	x - B-x-x x-x-x
			ogamu 'worship'	—	
		x-x-x	kegasu 'soil'	—	
			morasu 'let leak: omit'	—	
	B′ - B-A-x	x-x-x	yubiku 'boil'	—	
?B′	B′ - A/B-B-A	x-x-x	sasaeru 'support; prop'	sasae	x - A/B-2-1-A x-x-x
	B′ - A/B-A[H]/B[U]B	x-B-x	motageru 'lift, raise'	—	
	B′ - B-B-A	x-x-x	toraeru 'capture'	—	
			torawareru 'get captured'	toraware	x - A/B-B-A x-x-x
	B′ - B-A-A	x-x-x	hohuru =*hoburu 'slaughter'	—	
			kizuku 'build'	—	
	B′ - (B-A-A) x-x-x		[46]kogasu 'burn; yearn for'	—	
	(B-A-A)		makaru 'humbly go/come ····'	—	
			terau 'show off; pretend'	terai	x - A/2-A-A x-x-x
	B′ - B-A-A	x-A-x	kogareru 'be burning'	—	
			tukareru 'get weary'	tukare	x - B-2-A x-x-x
	B′ - A[Mkz]/B-A[U]/B[H]-B x-x-x		[47]mooderu 'go to worship'	—	
	B′ - A-A-B	x-x-x	[48]kezuru 'comb'	—	
	B′ - A/B-A-A	x-x-x	megumu 'bestow; bless'	megumi	x - A-A-A x-B[Lit]-x
	B′ - A-A-A	x-x-x	sasageru 'hold up, offer'	—	
	B - B-B-B	x-B-x	kotaeru 'answer'	kotae	x - B/2-1:3-B x-x-x
		x-(B)-x	yaburu 'tear/break it'	—	
			yabureru 'get torn; burst'	yabure	x - B-1:3-B x-(B)-x
	B - A/B-B-B	x-B[Lit]-x	kuwaeru 'add; inflict'	—	
	B - B-A[U]/B[H]-B	x-B-x	narasu 'train/inure; level'	narasi	B - 1-A-B x-x-x
	x - B-B-B	x-A-x	damaru 'hush, be silent'	—	
	x - B-B-B	x-B-x	koraeru 'endure; restrain'	—	
B+A	B′=B+A - A/B-B-B	x-x-x	motiiru 'use'	—	
	x - B-B-B	x-x-B	hair-u 'enter'	—	
B+B	x - A-B-B	x-x-x	butukeru 'hurl; bump, hit'	—	

(Chart 10, p. 8)

[1]But Narada inexplicably has B for kataru.

[2]Cf. Mg oyobi LLL (= B) 'finger' > yubi LL - 2-2-B.

[3]Cf. the transitive counterpart kimeru x - A-A-A x-x-x, with the derived noun kime x - A-A-A x-x-x.

[4]Cf. kudaru 'descend' A - A-A-A x-x-x, with the derived noun kudari x - A-A-A x-A-x: kudasaru 'give me/us' x - B-A-A x-x-x.

[5]Cf. ueru 'plant' A - A-B-A A-x-A, which lacks a (free) noun from the infinitive ue.

[6]Itaru is B in Narada.   [7]Only H gives Tōkyō B; cf. kagamu A - A-A-A x-A-x.   [8]Sitau is B in Narada.

[9]Satosu is B in Narada.   [10]Tikau is B in Narada.   [11]Masaru is B in Narada.

[12]Satoru is B in Narada.   [13]Ikaru is B in Narada.

[14]According to Mkz the verb akasu is A in the meaning 'explain, prove' in Tōkyō but B as 'see the night through'; the derived noun (A) means 'proof' or 'lantern'.

[15]But kasamu must be A; cf. kasanaru, kasa 'bulk'.

[16]In the general meaning 'narrow, close up' (intransitive), a synonym (variant?) of subomu, the verb tubom is A in Tōkyō; in the meaning 'have a blossom about to open' the verb is B (K 1958) or A/B (Mkz): the derived noun (B-A-B x-B-x) means 'a bud about to open'. The derived transitive tubomeru is x - A-A-A x-x-x, but the intransitive tubomaru is x - A[K]/B[H]-A-A x-(B)-x; subomaru is x - A/B[new]-A-A x-x-x and subomeru is x - A/B[new]-A-B x-x-x (unless the Kagoshima report is a misprint).

[17]Cf. the transitive counterpart suteru A - A-A[U]/B[H]-A A-A-x, which lacks a (free) noun from the infinitive sute.

[18]But simer-u is Hiroshima B (Okuda 280); Tōkyō must be aberrant. Proto-Japanese B.

[19]Kyōto B must be a later innovation.   [20]Narada has A for kuziku.

[21]Cf. sugureru 'excel' A - B-A-A x-A-x: Narada, Hattō, and Hamada B, but Matsue and Izumo A.

[22]For Tōkyō, NKD has only A but NHK and H give A/B for hokoru.

[23]Cf. todomaru A - A/B-A-A x-A[Lit/new]-x, lacking a derived noun from the infinitive todomari: like Tōkyō, Matsue is A/B but Hattō, Hamada, and Izumo are B. Is Kg B for todome a misprint?

[24]If the etymology with two 'gate' (1.1) is correct, totugu must be A.

[25]But the intransitive tukiru is A - A/B-B-B x-x-x. Narada has B for tukusu.

[26]Narada has B for isamu. Is Kg B a misprint or mistake? — cf. isameru Kg A. Shuri has qisami- (< isame-) A.

[27]And since the compound verb kasume-toru (x - B-A-B) is not given an older Tōkyō version as Type A, the stem should not go back to B.

[28]For Tōkyō NHK has ikoi A, Mkz 2, Mka both.   [29]Cf. the intransitive okiru x - B-B-B B-B-B.

[30]Both verb and noun are B in Shuri.

[31]Cf. the intransitive hedataru x - B-A-A x-B-x, noun hedatari x - A/B-A-A x-x-x.

[32]Only NHK carries both Tōkyō versions for mayoi.

[33]Cf. the intransitive ieru B - B-B-A x-x-x.

[34]Is Kg A a misprint or mistake? — cf. the intransitive hateru B - B-B-B.

[35]Kōchi natuku B shows that Kg A must be anomalous.

[36]The Yonaguni reflex has an oral (rather than nasal) g, and that indicates a borrowing.

[37]But the intransitive hareru is B - B-B-B x-B-B, with the noun hare x - B/2-2[U]/1:3[H]-B x-x-x.

[38]Cf. sugiru B - B-B-B B-B-x.   [39]But akiru B - B-B-B x-B-x.

[40]For Tōkyō, NHK gives tinami A/1, NKD has B (tinami¹).

[41]Cf. the intransitive zureru x - B-A[U]/B[H]-A x-x-x.

[42]Cf. hisomeru B - A/B-A-B x-x-x; hisomaru x - B-A-x x-x-x.   [43]The compound tomosi-bi is A.

[44]Cf. hiromaru B - B-A-A x-B-x; Hamada A/B but Hattō, Matsue, and Izumo B. Synonyms hirogaru and hirogeru are A - A-A-A x-A-x (but only the intransitive in Mg) and noun hirogari is x - A-A-A x-x-x. The adjective hiroi 'wide' is B - B-B-B B-B-B.

[45]The Tōkyō tonic version of sikaru is in H.

[46]Cf. the intransitive kogeru x - B-B-A x-x-x, noun koge x - B-1:3-A x-x-x.

[47]Mg maude(te) LHL(H), maudu LHL; B' in Nihon-Shoki, too.

[48]Cf. kezuru 'sharpen' A - A-A-A x-x-A.

Chart 11.   Problematic correspondences:
             infinitives of four or more syllables.

Type	Stem: Mg - Tk-Kt-Kg	Sd-Sr-Yn	Verb	Noun:	Mg - Tk-Kt-Kg Sd-Sr-Yn
λ	λ - λ-λ-λ	x-λ-x	[1]hirogaru 'spread out'	hirogari	x - λ-λ-λ x-x-x
			ukagau 'visit; hear; watch'	ukagai	x - λ-λ[U]/4[H]-λ x-x-x
		x-x-x	kosiraeru 'make'	kosirae	x - λ-λ[U]/4[H]-λ x-x-x
	λ - x-λ-x	x-λ-x	okoturu 'deceive; flatter'	(—)	
	λ - x-x-x	x-λ-x	modoroku 'get spotted/confused'	—	
	λ - x-λ-x	x-x-x	marokasu 'lump it'	—	
			modorokasu 'make spotted/confused'	—	
	λ - x-λ-x	x-x-x	wakaturu 'deceive'	—	
	x - λ-λ-λ	x-λ-x	yogoreru 'get dirty'	yogore	x - λ-λ[U]/2[H]-λ x-λ-x
λ	λ - λ/B-λ-λ	x-λ-x	habakaru 'shrink from; spread'	habakari	x - λ-λ-λ x-x-x
			horobosu 'ruin, destroy'	—	
			okotaru 'shirk'	okotari	x - λ-λ-λ x-x-x
			todokooru 'stagnate; ...'	todokoori	x - λ-λ-λ x-λ-x
			wazurau 'worry; ...'	wazurai	λ - λ-λ-λ x-λ-x
			[2]yasinau 'nurture; foster'	yasinai	x - λ-λ-λ x-(λ)-x
		x-λ[Lit/new]-x	[3]todomaru 'halt; stay; ...'	—	
		x-λ-λ	utagau 'doubt; suspect'	utagai	λ - λ-λ-λ x-λ-x
		x-x-x	aziwau 'taste'	aziwai	x - λ/3-λ-λ x-λ-x
			hodokosu 'give (alms); do'	hodokosi	x - λ/B-λ-λ x-x-x
			mazinau 'charm'	mazinai	x - λ/3-λ-λ x-x-x
			usuragu 'get thin/pale, abate'	—	
	λ - λ[H]/B-λ-λ	x-x-x	kagayaku 'shine'	kagayaki	x - B/3-λ-λ x-x-x
	λ - λ/B-λ-λ	x-(B)-x	tuiyasu 'spend; waste'	—	
	x - λ/B-λ-λ	x-λ-x	nagusameru 'comfort; amuse'	nagusame	x - λ/B[H,NHK]-λ-λ x-λ-x
	x - λ/B-λ-λ	x-x-x	amayakasu 'indulge, pamper'	amayakasi	x - λ-x-x x-x-x
			[4]otozureru 'visit'	otozure	x - λ/B[NHK]-λ-λ x-x-x
			usureru 'get thin'	—	
			wazurawasu 'trouble, vex'	—	
	λ - B-λ-λ	x-λ-x	azamuku 'dupe, deceive'	—	
			[5]katarau 'talk together'	katarai	x - x-λ/3-λ-λ x-λ-x
			tanabiku 'spread out'	—	
			tattobu, tootobu 'revere'	—	
		x-B[Lit]-x	uyamau 'respect, honor'	uyamai	x - λ-λ-λ x-x-x
		x-x-x	ayabumu 'feel anxiety ...'	ayabumi	x - B/3-λ-λ x-x-x
			azaker-u 'deride'	azakeri	x - B-λ-λ x-x-x
			hagukumu 'sit/brood over'	—	
			hurumau 'behave'	hurumai	λ - λ/2/3-λ-λ x-x-x
			kanasimu 'grieve'	kanasimi	x - x-λ/B/3-λ[U]-x x-x-x
			katadoru 'model after, copy'	—	
			kazikeru 'get numb'	—	
			masaguru 'grope'	—	
			matuwaru 'coil, wreathe'	—	
			muragaru 'flock, throng'	muragari	x - λ-λ-λ x-x-x
			musaboru 'covet; indulge in'	—	
			nazoraeru 'liken; imitate'	—	
			saegir-u 'intercept, interrupt'	—	
			saezuru 'sing, chirp; prattle'	saezuri	λ - B-λ-λ x-x-x
			sasurau 'wander, roam'	sasurai	x - λ/B[K]-λ-λ x-x-x
			siitageru 'oppress'	—	

(Chart 11, p. 2)

(A	A - B-A-A	x-x-x)			
			tabakaru 'plan; dupe'	—	
			⁶tairageru 'flatten; subdue; ...'	—	
			tawameru 'bend it'	—	
			tawamureru 'frolic, dally'	tawamure	A - A/B-A-A x-B[Lit]-x
			tiribameru 'inlay'	—	
			todoroku 'roar; throb'	todoroki	x - B-A-A x-x-x
			todorokasu 'let resound/throb'	—	
			tuibamu 'peck at'	—	
			tukasadoru 'rule'	—	
			⁷wananaku 'shudder, quiver'	wananaki	x - B/3-A-B x-x-x
	(A) - B-A-A	x-(A)-x	obiyakasu 'intimidate'	—	
	A - A[WHK]/B-A-A	x-x-x	azawarau 'deride'	azawarai	x - A/3-A-A x-x-x
	A - A[WKD,H]/B-A-A	x-x-x	nonosir-u 'revile, denounce'	nonosiri	x - A/B-A-A x-x-x
	A - B-A-x	x-x-x	segukumaru 'hunch (up/over)'	—	
			waganeru 'bend into a circle/ring'	(—)	
	A - B-x-x	x-x-x	tobasir-u 'splash'	tobasiri	x - A/B-B-x x-x-x
	A - A[Mkz,Hiroto]/B-A-A	x-x-x	tomurau 'mourn for'	tomurai	x - A-A-A x-x-x
	x - B-A-A	x-x-x	migomoru 'get pregnant'	—	
	x - B-A-A	x-x-x	sakadatu 'bristle'	—	
			sakarau 'oppose, run counter (to)'	—	
			samayou 'wander, prowl'	—	
			tumadatu 'stand tiptoe'	—	
A+A	A(=A+A) - B-A-A	x-A-x	oginau, oginuu 'make up (for)'	oginai	x - A/3-A-A x-x-x
?A	A - A-A-B	x-x-x	tumazuku 'stumble, trip'	tumazuki	x - A-A-B x-x-x
	A - B-B-A	x-x-x	turanaru 'stand in a row'	—	
			turanuku 'pierce; attain'	—	
	A - A-B-A	x-B-x	uzumaru 'get buried/filled'	—	
	x - B-B-A	x-x-x	obusaru 'ride piggyback'	—	
	x - B-A[U]/B[H]-A	x-x-x	kosikakeru 'sit'	kosikake	x - B/3-1:4[H]/2[U]-A x-x-x
	x - B-A-A	x-x-x	doyomeku 'resound'	doyomeki	x - A-A-A x-x-x
			gomakasu 'cheat; ...'	gomakasi	x - A/B/3-A-A x-x-x
			itukusimu 'love; pity'	itukusimi	x - A/B-A-x x-x-x
			kanzuku 'suspect, realize'	—	
			karakau 'tease'	—	
			kebadatu 'get nappy/fluffy'	—	
			kirameku 'glitter'	—	
			kurumaru 'be bundled'	—	
			madoromu 'doze off'	madoromi	x - A-A-A x-x-x
			musibamu 'get worm-eaten'	—	
			sazameku 'make an uproar'	sazameki	x - A/B-A-A x-x-x
			siitageru 'oppress'	—	
			sinadareru 'droop'	—	
			sobiyakasu 'raise (shoulders)'	—	
			sobohuru 'drizzle'	—	
			tabidatu 'set off on a journey'	tabidati	x - A/B-A-A x-B-x
			tetudau 'help, assist'	tetudai	x - 3-2-A x-x-x
			tibasir-u 'get bloodshot'	—	
			tubuyaku 'mutter, grumble'	tubuyaki	x - A/B-A-A x-x-x
			ugomeku 'wriggle, squirm'	—	
			yobawaru 'yell'	yobawari	x - A-x-x x-x-x
			yokogir-u 'cross, traverse'	—	

(Chart 11, p. 3)

?A	?A/B - x - B-A-A	x-x-x			
			yoromeku 'stagger, totter'	yoromeki	x - A-A-A x-x-x
			yosoou 'adorn/equip oneself'	yosooi	x - B-A/3-A-A x-x-x
			zawameku 'murmur, stir'	zawameki	x - A/B-A-A x-x-x
	x - A[K]/B[H]-A-A	x-(B)-x	ᵉtubomaru 'get narrow'	—	
		x-A[Lit]-x	nagaraeru 'live on/long'	—	
	x - A/B-A[H]/B[U,O]-A	x-x-x	kakageru 'put up, hoist'	—	
	A - A/B-B-A	x-A-x	takuwaeru 'store, save'	takuwae	x - A/B-3-1-A x-x-x
	x - A/B-B-A	x-x-x	kodawaru 'show prejudice, oppose'	kodawari	x - A/B/3-B-A x-x-x
			kuturogu 'relax'	kuturogi	x - A/B/3-A-B x-x-x
	A - B-A-B	x-A-x	yawarageru 'soften it'	—	
			yawaragu 'get softened'	—	
	x - B-A-B	x-A-x	asirau 'treat, manage'	asirai	x - A/3-A[U]/2-B
			sazukaru 'be blessed/taught'	—	
	A - B-A-B	x-x-x	anadoru 'despise'	anadori	x - A/B/3-A-B x-x-x
			hizamazuku 'kneel'	—	
			kutugaer-u 'get overturned'	—	
			kutugaesu 'overturn it'	—	
			minagir-u 'overflow'	—	
			tadayou 'drift'	—	
			tadayowasu 'set/carry adrift'	—	
?A/B	B - B-A-A	x-A-x	ayakaru 'enjoy similar good luck'	—	
		x-x-x	akinau 'deal in, sell'	akinai	B - 2/3-2-A x-B-x
			ayasimu 'doubt; wonder'	ayasimi	x - A/B-A-x x-x-x
			ayaturu 'manipulate, work'	ayaturi	x - A/B/3[NHK]-A-x x-x-x
			habikoru 'spread, overgrow'	—	
			heturau 'flatter'	heturai	x - 3-A-A x-x-x
			hirameku 'flash; flutter'	hirameki	x - A/B/3-A-A x-x-x
			hirugaer-u 'turn over, flutter'	—	
			hirugaesu 'reverse/wave it'	—	
			itawaru 'show compassion; ...'	itawari	x - A/B/3-A-A x-x-x
			izanau 'entice; invite'	izanai	B - A/B-A-x x-x-x
			maᵈ/ṭataku 'wink; flicker'	matataki	x - B/2-A-A x-x-x
			mutiutu 'whip'	—	
			tamerau 'hesitate, waver'	tamerai	x - a-A-A x-x-x
			totonoeru 'arrange; procure'	—	
			tugunau 'compensate for'	tugunai	x - A/3-A-A x-x-x
			tuzumaru 'shrink; be condensed'	—	
	B - B-A-x	x-x-x	honomeku 'glimmer (dimly)'	honomeki	x - B/3-x-x x-x-x
	x - B-A-A	x-x-x	honomekasu 'hint; show faintly'	—	
?B	B - A/B-A-B	x-x-x	unagasu 'bend neck; urge, press'	—	
			unazuku 'nod, bow head'	—	
			utubuseru 'lay/lie face down'	utubuse	x - A-A-B x-x-x
			utubusu 'lie face down'	utubusi	x - A-A-B x-x-x
	x - A/B-A-B	x-A-x	utumuku 'look down'	utumuki	x - A-A-B x-x-x
		x-x-x	hagurakasu 'parry, dodge'	—	
	x - A/B[K]-A-B	x-B-x	utumukeru 'face it down'	utumuke	x - A-A-B x-x-x
	x - B-A[U]/B[H]-B	x-x-x	iradatu 'get irritated'	iradati	x - A-A-B x-x-x
	?A/B - B-A-B	x-B-x	hakarau 'arrange, contrive'	hakarai	x - A/3-A-B x-B-x
	B - B-A-A	x-(B)-x	sizumaru 'calm down, subside'	—	

(Chart 11, p. 4)
  (?B)

	B - B-A-A	B-B-B	odoroku 'get surprised'	odoroki	x - B/3-A-A x-x-x
		B-B-x	maziwaru 'mingle' (vi.)	maziwari	x - A/B/3-A-A x-B-x
		x-B-x	arasou 'dispute, argue over'	arasoi	x - A/3-A-A x-x-x
			arawareru 'appear'	araware	x - B/3-A-A x-x-x
			arawasu 'express; author'	—	
			hiromaru 'spread' (vi.)	—	
			odorokasu 'surprise'	—	
			⁹sakidatu 'precede'	sakidati	x - A-A-x x-A-x
			sokonau 'harm, spoil'	—	
			totonou 'be arranged, be in order'	—	
	B - B-A-A	x-x-x¹⁰	ibukaru 'be curious/indignant'	—	
			itonamu 'perform, conduct'	itonami	x - A/B/3-A-A x-B[Lit]-x
			omomuku 'tend (toward)'	omomuki	B - A/B/3-A-A x-B-x
			omoner-u 'flatter'	—	
			sainamu 'torment; reproach'	—	
			uruou 'get damp/moist'	uruoi	B - A/3-A-A x-B-x
	B - A/B-A-A	x-x-x¹⁰	imasimeru 'admonish'	imasime	B - A/B[NHK]-A-A x-B-x
	(?B) - B-A-A	x-B-B	tagayasu 'till, cultivate'	—	
	x - B-A-A	x-B-x	aganau 'atone/pay for; buy'	aganai	x - A/3-A-A x-B-x
			¹¹hedataru 'is apart, distant'	hedatari	x - A/B-A-A x-x-x
			kasabaru 'be bulky; be piled up'	—	
		x-B?-x	karamaru 'get entangled/wound'	—	
		x-(B)-x	¹²kakumau 'shelter'	—	
	B - B-A-B	x-A-x	otoroeru 'get weak, decline'	otoroe	x - B/3-A[U]/4[H,U]-B x-x-x
			tutusimu 'be careful/discreet'	tutusimi	x - A/B-A-B x-A-x
B	x - A/B-B-B	x-x-x	kuwawaru 'participate; grow'	—	
	B - B-A-B	x-B-x	aturaeru '(custom-)order'	aturae	x - B/3-A[U]/4[H]-B x-B-x
		x-x-x	manug/ᴋareru 'escape, be saved'	—	
	(B) - B-A-B	x-x-x	kusuburu 'get smoky; smolder'	kusuburi	x - A/B[Mkz]-A-B x-x-x
	x - B-A-B	x-x-x	ganbaru 'try hard; persist'	ganbari	x - A/B-A-B x-x-x
			hanikamu 'be shy/bashful'	hanikami	x - A/B-A-B x-x-x
			haradatu 'get angry'	haradati	x - A/B-A-Bx-x-x
			hazirau 'feel shy/bashful'	hazirai	x - A/B-A-B x-x-x
			hiyakasu 'poke fun at; browse'	hiyakasi	x - B/3-A-B x-x-x
			ikigomu 'be spirited'	ikigomi	x - A/B/3-A-B x-x-x
			katayoru 'lean; be partial'	katayori	x - A/B/3-A-B x-x-x
			kokoroeru 'understand'	¹³kokoroe	x - B/3-4-B x-B-x
			kokorozasu 'aspire to'	kokorozasi	x - A/B-A/4[U]-B x-x-x
			korasimeru 'chastise'	—	
			kotozukeru 'send as a message'	kotozuke	x - A/B-A-B x-x-x
			kusarasu 'spoil it, let it rot'	—	
			mabataku 'wink, blink'	mabataki	x - 2-3-B x-x-x
			temadoru 'take time' (sic)	tematori	x - A/B/3-4-x x-x-x
			temaneku 'beckon'	temaneki	x - 2-3-B x-B-x
			uragir-u 'betray'	uragiri	x - A/B/3-A-B x-x-x
			uzumaku 'whirl, swirl'	uzumaki	x - 2-2-B x-x-x
	x - B-A-B	x-B-x	hakadoru 'make progress'	—	
			hodokeru 'come loose'	—	
			katamuku 'be inclined, slant'	katamuki	x - A/B/3-A-B x-B-x
			kutabireru 'get tired'	kutabire	x - B/3-A-B x-B-x
			matigaeru 'mistake, blunder'	—	
			matigau 'be wrong/mistaken'	matigai	x - 3-A-B x-B-x

(Chart 11, p. 5)

(B	x - B-A-B	x-B-x)			
			mokuromu 'plan, envisage'	mokuromi	x - A/B-A-B x-B-x
			tasikameru 'ascertain, confirm'	tasikame	x - A-A-B x-x-x
	B - x-A-x	x-x-x	tuzusir-u 'mouth, mumble'	—	
	B - B-A-B	B-B-B	kangaeru 'think'	kangae	x - 3-4-B x-B-x
		x-B-B	atumaru 'gather, assemble'	atumari	x - B/3-B-A x-x-x
		B-B-x	azukaru 'take in trust'	azukari	x - B/3-A-B x-x-x
		x-B-x	ayamaru 'err; apologize'	ayamari	(B) - B/3-A-B x-B-x
			¹⁴osamaru 'be at peace; ...'	osamari	B - A/B/3-A-B x-x-x
			tikazukeru 'bring near'	—	
			tikazuku 'draw near'	tikazuki	x - A/B-A-B x-x-x
			tukurou 'mend; adjust'	tukuroi	x - 3-4-B x-x-x
		x-(B)-x	takuramu 'scheme, plan'	takurami	x - A/B-A-B x-x-x
	(B) - B-A-B	x-B-x	narawasu 'train; teach'	narawasi	x - A/B-A-B x-B-x
	B - B-A-B	x-x-x	akirameru 'make clear; ...'	akirame	x - A/B/3-A-B x-x-x
			ayamatu 'err, mistake'	ayamati	(B) - A/B-A-B x-B-x
			hagemasu 'encourage'	¹⁵hagemasi	x - A/B-A-B x-x-x
			hokorobu 'come unsewn'	hokorobi	x - B/3-A-B x-x-x
			ikidooru 'get indignant'	ikidoori	x - A/B-A-B x-x-x
			irodoru 'color'	irodori	x - A/B/3-A-B x-B-x
			kasikomaru 'humble oneself'	—	
			kokoromiru 'try'	kokoromi	B - A/B/3-A-B x-x-x
			nigiwau 'be lively, bustling'	nigiwai	x - 3-A-B x-x-x
			sitataru 'drip'	sitatari	x - A/B/3-A-B x-x-x
			tasinameru 'make suffer: reproach'	—	
			tasinamu 'suffer; relish; ...'	tasinami	x - A/B/3-A-B x-B-x
			uranau 'divine, foretell'	uranai	x - 3-A-B x-B-x
			urayamu 'envy'	—	
			wakimaeru 'discern'	wakimae	x - 3-A/4-B x-x-x
?B′	x - A/B-B-B	x-x-x	kuwawaru 'be added'	—	
B+B	x - A/B-B-B	x-B-x	moteamasu 'have too much'	moteamasi	x - A-B[NKD]-x x-x-x
		x-x-x	motehayasu 'extol; value'		
			motenasu 'treat, entertain'	motenasi	x - A-B-B x-x-x
	x - A-B-B	x-x-x	butukaru 'run into; collide; face'	—	
	x - A/B-A[U]/B[H]-B	x-x-x	ikedoru 'capture alive'	ikedori	x - A/B-A[U]/1[H]-B x-B-x
B+A	B+A - A/B-B-B	x-B-x	moteasobu 'play with'	moteasobi	x - A-B[NKD]-x x-x-x
		x-x-x	¹⁶tatematuru 'offer: do'	—	
	?B′(=B+A) - A[U]/B[H]-B x-x-x		sasageru 'hold up, offer'	—	

¹See Chart 10, note 44.   ²The Tōkyō B version for yasinau is given by H and NHK.
³Cf. the transitive todomeru A - B-A-A x-x-x, derived noun todome x - B-A-B x-x-x: Kg misprint?.
⁴NKD gives the Tōkyō A version for otozureru.
⁵Cf. kataru A - A-A-A x-A-x (but Narada B!), derived noun katari x - A-A-A x-x-x.
⁶Cf. the adjectival noun taira LLH - 0-1-B x-(x)-x; perhaps Shuri /too/ A is cognate.
⁷Cf. ononoku A - A-A-A x-x-x, which lacks a derived noun.   ⁸See Chart 10, note 16.
⁹Kanchi-in Mg LLxx but Kamakura (Shiza-Kōshiki) A. We expect *A from saki 2.1. Shuri is a puzzle.
¹⁰These two groups would belong under the proto '?A/B' group above except for other evidence (clear
etymologies, Ryūkyū or other dialects) that indicates B.
¹¹Cf. hedateru B - B-A-A x-B-B, derived noun hedate x - B-A-A x-B-x.
¹²Cf. kakumu = kakomu A - A-A-A x-A-x, derived noun kakomi x - A-A-A x-x-x: kakou A-A-A x-A-x, derived
noun kakoi x - A-A-A x-A-x.   ¹³For Tōkyō, NHK has B/3, H has A/B (misprint for B/3?).
¹⁴Cf. the transitive osameru B - B-A-B x-B-x, derived noun osame x - A/B[NHK]-A-B x-x-x.
¹⁵The Tōkyō atonic version for hagemasi is given only by Mkz.
¹⁶The Tōkyō atonic version for tatematuru is from H

Chart 12.   Accent patterns of compound verbs.

Stem types:	A—B	A—A	A—B	A—A	B—B	B—A	B—B	B—A
Example:	uri-dasu	uri-mawaru	hakobi-dasu	hakobi-mawaru	kaki-dasu	kaki-mawaru	aruki-dasu	aruki-mawaru
Tōkyō:								
younger	oo̅-o'o	oo̅-oo'o	ooo̅-o'o	ooo̅-oo'o	oo̅-o'o	oo̅-oo'o	ooo̅-o'o	ooo̅-oo'o
older	oo̅-o'o	oo̅-oo'o	ooo̅-o'o	ooo̅-oo'o	oo̅-oo[']	oo̅-ooo[']	ooo̅-oo[']	ooo̅-ooo[']
oldest	oo̅-o'o	oo̅-oo'o	ooo̅-o'o	ooo̅-oo'o	oo̅-oo[']	oo̅-ooo[']	oo̅'o-oo	oo̅'o-ooo
Chūgoku, Gifu, ···	oo̅'-oo	oo̅'-ooo	ooo̅'-oo	ooo̅'-ooo	o̅'o-oo	o̅'o-ooo	oo̅'o-oo	oo̅'o-ooo
Izumo	oo̅-oo	oo̅-ooo	ooo̅-oo	ooo̅-ooo	oo̅-o'o	oo̅-oo'o	ooo̅-o'o	ooo̅-oo'o
Kyōto:								
now	oo̅-oo[']	oo̅-ooo[']	ooo̅-oo[']	ooo̅-ooo[']	.oo-oo[']	.oo-ooo̅[']	.ooo-oo[']	.ooo-ooo̅[']
1100	oo̅ .oo̅	oo̅ ooo̅	ooo̅ .oo̅	ooo̅ ooo̅	.oò .oo̅	.oò ooo̅	.ooò .oo̅	.ooò ooo̅
Kagoshima	'oo-oo̅	'oo-ooo̅	'ooo-oo̅	'ooo-ooo̅	oo-oo̅	oo-ooo̅	ooo-oo̅	ooo-ooo̅
Shuri	'oo̅-oo	'oo̅-ooo	'ooo̅-oo	'ooo̅-ooo	oo-oo	oo-ooo	ooo-oo	ooo-ooo

High pitch is overscored; low is unmarked; ` marks a fall in pitch.

[1] *locus (not shown for 1100 Kyōto),* ' *Type A (Kagoshima and Shuri),*   . *low register (for Kyōto).*

Chart 13.   Phrase types and word types.

```
2.1  N 2.1        3.1  N 3.1        4.1  N 4.1-p      5.1   N 5.1       6.1    N 6.1
HH   N 1.1-p      HHH  N 2.1-p      HHHH N 3.1-p      HHHHH N 4.1-p     HHHHHH N 5.1-p
     N<V2.A-i          N<V3.A-i          N<V4.A-i
     V 2.A-ru N        V 3.A-ru N        V 4.A-ru N   5.2   N 5.2       6.2    N 6.2
     ?A 2.A-sa         (A 3.A-ki)                     HHHHH V 5.A-i,-ru HHHHL

                  3.2  N 3.2        4.2  N 4.2        5.3   N 5.3       6.3    N 6.3
                  HHL  V 3.A-i,-ru  HHHL V 4.A-i,-ru  HHHLL N 4.2-p     HHHHLL N 5.2-p
                  HHL  A 3.A-si,-ku,      A 4.A-ku
                          (-ki),-mi,                  5.4   N 5.4       6.4    --
                          ?-sa       4.3  N 4.3       HHLLL N 4.3-p     HHHLLL N 5.3-p
                                    HHLL N 3.1-p

2.2  N 2.2        3.3  N 3.3                                            6.5    --
HL   N 1.2-p      HLL  N 2.2-p      4.4  N 4.4        5.5   N 5.5       HLLLLL N 5.4-p
     V 2.A-i,-ru        A goto-si,   HLLL N 3.3-p      HLLLL N 4.4-p
     A 2.B-ku,-mi          -ki,-ku                                     6.6    --
     A 2.B-ku,-mi                                                      HLLLLL N 5.5-p

------------------------------------------------------------------------------------------
2.3  N 2.3        3.4  N 3.4        4.5  N 4.5        5.6   N 5.6       6.7    N 6.7
LL   [N 1.3a-p]   LLL  N 2.3-p      LLLL N 3.4-p      LLLLL N 4.5-p     LLLLLL N 5.6-p
     N<V2.B-i          N<V2.B-i          N<V4.B-i     5.7   N 5.7
                      V 3.B-ru N                     LLLLH V 5.B-i,-ru  6.8    --
                      (A 3.b-ki)   4.6  N 4.6              A 5.B-ku     LLLLLH A6.B-ku
                                   LLLH A 4.B-ku     5.8  (N5.8)?       6.9    N 6.9
                  3.5  N 3.5                         LLLHH N 4.6-p     LLLLHH (N 5.8)?
2.4  N 2.4        LLH  V 3.B-i,-ru  4.7  N 4.7                          6.10   N 5.7-p
LH   N 1.3-p           A 3.B-si,(-ki) LLHH N 3.5-p    5.9   N 5.9       LLLHHH N 6.10
     V 2.B-i,-ru                                     LLHHH N 4.7-p      6.11  (N 5.9-p)?
     A 2.B-si,-ki  3.6  N 2.4-p      4.8  N 4.8                         LLHHHH N 6.11
                  LHH  N 3.6        LHHH N 3.6-p      5.10  N 5.10      6.12   --
                      A 3.B-sa                       LHHHH N 4.8-p     LHHHHH N 5.10-p

- - - - - - - - - - - - - - - - - - - - - - - - - - - - - - - - - - - - - - - - - - - - -
                                                                      6.13   N 6.13
                                                                      LHHHL
                                                                      6.14   N 6.14
                                    4.9  N 4.9        5.11  N 5.11     LHHHLL N 5.11-p
                                    LHHL             LHHHL             6.15   --
                                                                      LHHLLL N 5.12-p
2.5  N 2.5                                                            ?6.16   --
LHL  ?→ 3.7       3.7  [N 2.5]?      4.10  N 4.10      5.12  N 5.12     LHLLLL (N 5.13-p)?
(LF)             LHL  N 3.7         LHLL  N 3.7-p     LHHLL N 4.9-p     6.17   N 6.17
                      A 3.B-ku                                         LLHHL
                                    4.11  N 4.11      5.13  N 5.13    ?6.18   --
                                    LLHL V 4.B-i,-ru  LHLLL N 4.10-p   LLHHLL (N 5.14-p)?
                                                                     ?6.19   --
                                                     5.14  N 5.14     LLHLLL (N 5.15-p)?
                                                     LLHHL             6.20   N 6.20
                                                                      LLLHLL N 5.16-p
                                                     5.15  N 5.15     6.21   N 6.21
                                                     LLHHL N 4.11-p    LLLLHL
                                                     5.16  N 5.16     6.22   N 6.22
                                                     LLLHL N 4.11-p    LLLLLH A 7.[si]-si
```

Chart 14.   Kyōto accentuation of nouns: discrepancies in data.

There are quite a few differences between the data in Hirayama's Zenkoku akusento jiten and Umegaki's data in
NKD. Most of the examples cited below are simple nouns, with the addition of a few compounds, adverbs, etc.
The examples are arranged in categories of contour and register and subgrouped according to number of moras.
The notations follow Hirayama except that the colon (:) is substituted for his semicolon (;) and type 1:3 is
extended to include his '1:25'. On the right are two columns of data for some of the words elicited from
two Kansai speakers: N = Nakayama Yukihiro (born 1947 in Takatsuki), T = Takayama Masaaki (born 1958 in Ōsaka).

Nouns with register differences (one source LOW, the other HIGH):

H	U	Examples	N	T		H	U	Examples	N	T
0	1	ho 'ear of grain'				1	0	ba 'place'		
								ya 'building'		
		emi 'smile'								
		kaba 'bulrush'	0	0				kai 'result, effect'		
		kasa 'sore'	0	0				kuwa 'hoe' (Ise 0/1)	1	1
		kati 'walking'						kayu 'gruel' (= o-kai)		
		kati 'victory'	2	2				tumi 'sin'	1	1
		abata 'pockmark'						aona 'greens'		
		agura 'crosslegged'						basue 'outskirts'		
		akasi 'light; proof'						hunani 'cargo'		
		azami 'thistle'						mukasi 'long ago'		
		igata 'mold, matrix'						nagae 'long handle'		
		ikada 'raft'	0	0				natume 'jujube'	0	0
		irori 'hearth'						sisai 'details'		
		kirara 'mica'						taira 'flat'	1	1
		miburi 'gesture'								
		minari 'attire'								
		nazuna 'shepherd's purse'								
		robata 'fireside'								
		sozoro 'involuntarily'								
		susuki 'eulalia'	1	1						
		tihiro '1000 spans'								
		ukiyo 'evanescent world'								
		ariake 'morning moon'						akagane 'copper'		
		hatagoya 'inn'						amagumo 'raincloud'		
		sensai 'plantings'						ikenie 'sacrificial offering'		
		syakunage 'rhododendron'						inamura 'rick'		
								itazura 'prank: idle'		
								kurogane 'iron'		
								mamegara 'bean-straw'		
								mattaku 'perfectly'		
								nengoro 'cordial'		
								sirogane 'silver'		
								takenawa '(at its) height'		
								yomibito 'poet'		
0	0/1	aima 'interval'								

Nouns with differences of register and locus:

H	U	Examples	N	T	H	U	Examples	N	T
0	1:3	gake 'cliff'			1:3	0	uso 'lie, falsehood'		
		mura 'mottled'							
		same 'shark' (= huka)	1:3	1:3					
		arawa 'overt'					kurage 'jellyfish'	1:3	1:3
		haniwa 'burial objects'	0	0			naname 'aslant'	1:3	0
		iruka 'dolphin'	0	0			otori 'decoy'	0	0
		menoo 'agate'							
		yosuga 'means'							
		kotosara 'especially'					misasage 'mausoleum'		
0	1/3	siratuti 'white clay'			1/3	0	—		
0	0/1:4	sakasama 'upside-down'			0/1:4	0	—		
2	1:3	buti 'spotted'			1:3	2	hato 'pigeon'	1:3	1:3
		haze 'goby'	1:3	1:3			hina 'chick'	1:3	1:3
		ho[h]o 'cheek' (= hoppeta)	1:3	1:3			kobu 'knarl, lump'	1:3	1:3
		kiba 'fang'	2	2			mame 'bean'	1:3	1:3
		mozi 'letter'	2	2			ubu '(by) birth: naive'	1:3	1:3
		mozu 'shrike'	1:3	1:3					
		toge 'thorn'	2	2					
		mati 'sewn-in strip'							
		sugu 'straight(way)'							
		tui (ni) 'finally'	2	2					
		tuto (ni) 'early'							
		koto (ni) 'especially'							
		mabuti 'rim of eyelid'					amari 'excess' (n.)	1:3	1:3
		magusa 'fodder'	0	1:3			hisoka 'secret'	1:3	3
		monzi 'letter'	0	0			hitoe 'single-layer'		
		nagisa 'beach'	0	0			kenuki 'tweezers'		
		natane 'rape (weed)'					koziki 'beggar'		
		serihu 'words, lines'					masa-ni 'really'	1:3	1:3
		tokusa 'scouring rush'					nakaba 'middle, half'		
							nakama 'companion'		
							tanuki 'raccoon-dog'		
							yonaka 'midnight'		
2	2/1:3	mata 'crotch'	2	2					
2/1	1:3	—			1:3	2/1	simizu 'clear water'	0	0
3	1:3	tyanto 'correctly'			1:3	3	komaka 'fine, detailed'		
							hanage 'nostril hair'	3	1:3
							hutatu 'two'	1:3	1:3
							tadati 'at once'	1:3	1:3
		hotondo 'almost (all)'					teguruma 'hand cart'		
		kedamono 'animal'	0	0			tobiuo 'flying fish'		

H	U	Examples	N	T	H	U	Examples	N	T
3	1:4	—			1:4	3	amagoi 'prayer for rain' koetago 'manure bucket'		
4	1:4	yadorigi 'mistletoe'			1:4	4	kutibiru 'lips' mizukaki 'web: paddle'	1:4	1:4
							hutagokoro 'duplicity' ominaesi 'Patrinia'		
5	1:4	—			1:4	5	watasibune 'ferryboat'		
2	1	sono 'garden' sube 'means'	2	x	1	2	kuwa 'mulberry' (Ise 2) tama 'jewel: ball'	2	2
		suasi 'barefoot'					asase 'shallows' hitai 'forehead'	0	0
							rokuro 'pulley: lathe' siwasu 'the 12th month' tedori 'capture' tegata 'bill, note'		
							kurokami 'black hair'		
3	1	—			1	3	nagame 'long rain' sizuku 'drop'		
		osidori 'love-birds'	1:3	0			hayabusa 'falcon' sibagaki 'twig fence'		

Nouns with only locus differences — LOW register:

H	U	Examples	N	T	H	U	Examples	N	T
1	1:3	kibi, kimi 'millet'			1:3	1	aka 'red'		
		nazo 'riddle'	1:3	2			ani 'older brother'	2	1:3
		soba 'buckwheat'	1:3	1:3			ao 'blue'		
		toga 'blame'	1:3	1:3			mado 'window'	1:3	1:3
		tuba 'sword-guard'	1:3	2			mayu 'eyebrow'	1:3	1:3
							'cocoon'	1:3	2
							susu 'soot'	1:3	1:3
							uzi 'grub'	1:3	1:3
		hadae 'flesh'	1	1			izumi 'spring, source'		
		hisyaku 'ladle'					mayuge 'eyebrow'		
		mogura 'mole'					yubune 'bathtub'		
		naniwa 'Naniwa (= Ōsaka)'							
		otona 'adult'	1	1					
		nagaame 'long rain'					kagerou 'heat haze' katasaki 'shoulder'		
1	1:4	kakurega 'hiding place'			1:4	1	ainiku 'unfortunate' gekokuzyoo 'hierarchy reversal'		
1:4	1:3	yooyaku 'gradually'							
2	1	ebosi 'a kind of cap'			1	2	—		

Nouns with only locus differences — HIGH register:

H	U	Examples	N	T		H	U	Examples	N	T
0	2	ake 'red'				2	0	hame 'panel'		
		era 'gill(s)'						hogu = hogo 'wastepaper'	2	x
		kari 'wild goose'	2	2				hoo 'law, way'	0	0
		kase 'shackles'						huke 'dandruff'	0	2
		kawa 'skin'	1	1				miko 'prince'	2	2
		kera 'mole-cricket'						muro 'room, shed, cellar'	2	2
		kisi 'shore'	2	2						
		kosi 'riding-platform'								
		momi 'fir'	2	2						
		moti 'holly'								
		sagi 'heron'	2	2						
		sata 'tidings'								
		tade 'knotweed'								
		tiba 'Chiba'								
		tigo 'baby'	2	2						
		atara 'alas, regrettably'						komura = kobura 'calf (leg)'	0	1:3
		hakaze 'wing-flapped breeze'						konomi 'fruit, nut'	0	0
		hiziki 'brown seaweed'						nigori 'muddiness'		
		honemi 'bones and flesh'						sibahu 'lawn'		
		hubako 'box for letters'						sokoi 'ulterior motive'		
		ikesu 'fish crawl'						tamuro 'encampment'		
		inori 'pryaer'						tasuki 'sleeve-tie'	3	3
		iraka 'tile'						tobira 'door(-panel)'	0	0
		kaina 'upper arm'						yaiba 'forged blade'		
		katura 'Judas-tree'	2	2						
		kawaya 'toilet'	0	0						
		komiti 'path, alley'								
		kousi 'calf (of cow)'	0	0						
		koyomi 'calendar'	2	0						
		mamusi 'viper'	0	0						
		misoka '30th day'								
		musiro 'rather'								
		mutuki 'diaper'								
		nakai 'parlormaid'								
		okute 'late rice'								
		oomi 'Ōmi (place)'								
		sakaki 'sacred tree'	2	2						
		sango 'coral'								
		sigure 'shower'								
		simoyo 'frosty night'								
		timata 'crossroads'	0	0						
		umaya 'horse-stable, barn'	0	0						
		katakoi 'onesided love'						akinai 'commerce'		
								koorogi 'cricket'	2	2

0	0/2	kogane 'gold'	0/2	0	—
		kawabe 'riverside'			

2	0/2	uzura 'quail'	0/2	2	—

0	3	humoto 'foot of mountain'	3	0	—

hanabusa 'calyx'
hitoe-ni 'intently'
humiobako 'box for letters'
katasumi 'one corner'
katawara 'side'
kawagiri 'river fog'

0/3	2/3	—	2/3	0/3	moromi 'unrefined sake/soy'	3	0

2	3	nedoko 'alcove'	3	2	—

tamasii 'spirit'

aonori 'green laver'
hobasira 'mast'   3   3
kakehasi 'hanging bridge'
ototosi 'year before last'   3   3
uguisu 'bush-warbler'   3   3
yamadori 'mountain bird'   3   3

0	4	amaneku 'extensively'	4	0	asiato 'footprint'		
		asatte 'day after tomorrow'			ninniku 'garlic'	0	1:4
		hatukari 'first wild goose'			tomosibi 'torch'		

hakarigoto 'scheme'
kokorozasi 'hope'   —
maturigoto 'government'

4	2	atakamo 'just as if'	2	4	kokonotu 'nine'

4	3	monoii 'speech: dispute'	3	4	—

4	5	nisikihebi 'python'	5	4	aounabara 'wide blue sea'
					noborikudari 'ascent and descent'

For 'ladle' (Hirayama .hisyaku) Umegaki offers the unusual pattern 1:2 .hi᷄syaku,
which we interpret as four-mora 1:3 .hii̅syaku.

There are only a few infinitive-derived nouns and longer compounds in the lists above, but
similar accentual differences can be found in many examples of those word classes. Some of that
information will be found in other parts of this work.

Charts 15:1-4.   Kyōto accent of compound nouns with
                      monosyllabic first elements.

Patterns marked "H" are from Hirayama, those marked "U" from
Umegaki (NKD). The unmarked patterns are found in both.

Chart 15:1.   Compounds with .te¯ 'hand' as first element.

Except as shown below, the compounds are all low (and Kagoshima B):
.te-ami¯, .te-dama¯, .te-zuri¯, ... ; .te-ma'ri, .te-a'buri H =
.teaburi¯ U, ... All longer adjectives are reflexes of the earlier
B class (now initial high but with a locus), and that accounts for te-a'rai
(cf. te-arai¯ N < N+V), -a'tui, -ba'yai, -bi'roi, -go'wai, -hi'doi,
-ka'tai, -nu'rui, ...

te¹-	te-¹	te-¯	.te-¯	.te-¹
-ma¹				
-aka				
-asi²				
-ate				
		-bata¯	.te-bata¯	
H -buri		U -buri¯		
H -dai		U -dai-		
H -dori³		U -dori¯	H .te-dori¯²	
-date				
		-duru¯		
		-gami¯		
-gara		-giwa¯		
-guti				
-hai				
U -hazu		H -hazu¯		
-hon				
-ire				
-kizu				
U -kuda			.te-kuda¯	
-kuse				
		-mae¯		
-mane				
-moto				
		-nami¯		
H -oi		U -oi¯		
-oti				
		H -sio¯	U .te-sio¯	
H -sita		U -sita¯		
-suri				
-tuki⁴				
		U -zao¯ (H x)		
		-arai¯		
H -asobi (U x)				
	U -ba'nare	H -banare¯		
		-banasi¯ ⁵		
		-bikae¯ ⁶		

(Chart 15:1, p. 2)

te¹-	te- ¹	te- ¯	.te- ¯	.te- ¹
-bukuro				
	-da'suke			
Ħ -gakari	U -ga'kari			
	-gi'rei (AN)			
-gotae	U -go'tae			
	U -gu'soku (Ħ x)			
	U -ha'zime	Ħ -hazime¯		
	Ħ -ho'doki	U -hodoki¯		
	-ka'gen			
	U -ka'gami			Ħ .te-ka'gami
	-ma'neki⁷			
	Ħ -ma'wari	U -mawari-		
	-mu'kai⁸			
-no-hira	-no'-hira⁹			
				.te-no'-koo
				Ħ .te-no'-suzi (U x)
			Ħ .te-no-uti¯	U .te-no'-uti
	-nugui¯			
	-okure¯			
U -saguri	Ħ -saguri¯			
-tudai¹⁰ Kg A				
		-watasi¯¹¹		
U -zukuri				Ħ .te-zu'kuri

¹Also tema-si'goto and tema¹-tin. But Ħ .tema-zon¯, U tema-zon¯. Umegaki has tema-do'ri, with the verb tema-doru¯; Hirayama does not list the noun.

²Edo HHL (tea'si).

³Hirayama differentiates 'receipts' (te'dori) from 'capture' (.tedori¯); Umegaki has tedori¯ for both.

⁴Cf. te-tuke¯.

⁵The verb is tebanasu¯.

⁶The verb is tebikaeru¯.

⁷But the verb is temaneku¯, according to Hirayama. (NKD has no entry for the verb.) Longer verbs are almost all A in Kyōto.

⁸But the verb is temukau¯. See the preceding note.

⁹Edo HLLLL (te'nohira). For Umegaki's .te-no'-ura Hirayama has .te-no-u'ra.

¹⁰The verb is tetudau¯.

¹¹The verb is tewatasu¯.

Chart 15:2.   Compounds with .me⁻ 'eye' as first element.

Except as shown below, the compounds are all low (and Kagoshima B).

me¹-	me-¹	me-⁻	.me-⁻	.me-¹
H -do				U .me-dò
-ate				
-gane				
		H -hana⁻	U .me-hana⁻	
U -hasi		H -hasi⁻		
-isya				
		H -kago⁻	U .me-kago⁻	
-kata				
-mai				
U -maze		-maze⁻		
		-mie⁻		
-moto				
-saki				
		-sita⁻		
		-ue⁻		
		H -zaru⁻	U .me-zaru⁻	
		-doori⁻		
-gusuri				
U -kusare (H x)¹				
		-zamasi⁻		
	-za¹wari			
	-bu¹nryoo			

ma¹-	ma-¹	ma-⁻	.ma-⁻	.ma-¹
	-ba¹taki²			
				.ma-bu¹ta
H -buti				U .ma-bu¹ti
-na-ko Kg A				
		-tataki⁻³ Kg A		
		-zirogi⁻		
	-no-a¹tari			

¹Also mekusare-¹gane.

²The verb, of course, like most longer Kyōto verbs, is A: ma-bataku⁻. Other such verbs are me-gakeru⁻ and me-zasu⁻. The compound .me-zasi⁻ is not the derived noun of me-zasu⁻: it is N + V infinitive from me o sasi[ta mono] '(string of fish that are) skewered together through the eyes (for drying)'. Longer adjectives are all a reflex of the earlier B class (now initial high but with a locus), and that accounts for me-za¹toi, me-zama¹sii, me-maguru¹sii, and ma-ba¹yui.

³The verb is ma-bataku⁻, Kagoshima A.

Chart 15:3.   Compounds with .ki⁻ 'tree, wood' as first element.

Except as shown below, the compounds are all Kagoshima B.

ki¹-	ki- ¹	ki- ⁻	.ki- ⁻	.ki- ¹
ki¹-do¹				
ki¹-gi				
H ki¹-me			.ki-me⁻	
			.ki-bori⁻	
			.ki-gata⁻	
			.ki-gire⁻	
			.ki-gumi⁻	
			.ki-gutu⁻ Kg A	
			.ki-hada⁻	
			.ki-hen⁻	
			H .ki-kuzu⁻	U .ki-ku¹zu
ki¹-no-ko				
U ki¹-no-me	H ki-no¹-me			
			.ki-no-mi⁻	
	H kido¹-ban		.kido-ba¹n	
	H kido¹-guti			U .kido¹-guti
	H kido¹-sen		.kido-se¹n	
U ki¹-nobori	U ki-no¹bori		H .ki-no¹bori	

ko¹-	ko- ¹	ko- ⁻	.ko- ⁻	.ko- ¹
		ko-dama⁻		
		ko-dati⁻		
		ko-guti⁻²		
		kokage⁻ Kg A		
ko¹-no-ha				
H ko¹-no-mi		U ko-no-mi⁻³		
		U ko-ppa⁻	H .ko-ppa⁻	

¹ But U .kidò as 'garden-gate: theater entrance'.

² Cf. ko¹-guti 'little mouth/entry'.

³ Kamakura LLH.

Chart 15:4.   Compounds with .hi⁻ 'fire' as first element.

Except as shown below, the compounds are all Kagoshima B.

hi¹-	hi-_¹	hi-_⁻	.hi-_⁻	.hi-_¹
U hi¹-asi			H .hi-asi⁻	
				.hi-ba¹na
hi¹-basi¹				
hi¹-bati				
			.hi-dane⁻	
			.hi-guti⁻	
			.hi-hen⁻	
U hi¹-moti			H .hi-moti⁻	
U hi¹-moto			H .hi-moto⁻	
U hi¹-no-ke				H .hi-no¹-ke
hi¹-no-ko				
hi¹-no-mi				
hi¹-no-te				
U hi¹-asobi				H .hi-a¹sobi
U hi¹-basira				H .hi-ba¹sira
	U hi-bu¹kure			H .hi-bu¹kure
	U hi-da¹ruma			H .hi-da¹ruma
	U hi-no¹-ban		H .hi-no¹-ban	
U hi¹-no-moto			H .hi-no¹-moto	

ho¹-	ho-_¹	ho-_⁻	.ho-_⁻	.ho-_¹
U ho¹-ya (H x)				
U ho¹-kage		H ho-kage⁻ Kg A		
U ho¹-kuti		U ho-kuti⁻ (H x)		
U ho¹-mura		U ho-mura⁻ (H x)		
				.ho-no¹-o²

¹Heian LLH.   ²Kamakura LLH, Edo HLL.

Charts 16:1-5.   Kyōto accent of compound nouns with prefixes.

Chart 16:1.   The prefix oo- 'big'.

The compounds are all Kagoshima B. Attested Shuri reflexes (with quhu-) are all B.

o¹o-	oo¹-	oo- ¹	oo- ‾	.oo- ‾	.oo- ¹ .oo¹-
U -de			H -de‾		
				-ne‾	
	U -ya				H -ya
	U -ame	H -a¹me			
			U -ana‾	H -ana‾	
	U -are		H -are‾		
		U -a¹ri	H -ari‾		
		U -a¹se	H -ase‾		
				-azi‾	
		-ba¹ka			
				-ban‾¹	
				-beya‾	
		U -bu¹ne³	H -bune‾		
		U -bu¹ri	-buri‾²		
				-haba‾	
		U -i¹ri	H -iri‾		
		U -de¹ki	H -deki‾		
	U -gane		H -gane‾		
		-gara‾			
		-gata‾			
		U -go¹to	H -goto‾		
		U -go¹syo	H -gosyo‾		
			U -guti‾⁴	H -guti‾	
H -gyoo			U -gyoo‾		
-hasi					
-kami 'wolf'					
			-kata‾⁵		
U -kawa		H -ka¹wa			
U -kaze	H -kaze				
	H -kazi	U -ka¹zi			
			U -kura‾ (Hx)⁶		
				-maka‾	
			-make‾		
				-mata‾	
U -mizu	H -mizu				
		U -mi¹e	H -mie‾		
				-mono‾	
				-mozi‾	
U -mori			H -mori‾		
		U -mo¹te	H -mote‾		
		-mo¹to	U -moto‾		
					-mugi
			U -mune‾⁷	H -mune‾	

(Chart 16:1, p. 2)

o˥o-	oo˥-	oo- ˥	oo-‾	.oo-‾	.oo- ˥	.oo˥-
U -nami			H -nami‾			
				H -sazi‾ (U x)		
			-sio‾			
			H -suzi‾			
				-taba‾		
				-tubu‾		
		U -u˥ke	H -uke‾			
	U -umi	H -u˥mi				
		H -u˥so (U x)				
			-yoso‾			
	H -yuki	U -yu˥ki				
	U -zake	H -za˥ke				
				H -zara‾		U ˥-zara
-zei						
-zeki						
		U -zo˥n	H -zon‾			
			-zora‾			
U -zume			H -zume‾			
		-a˥gura				
		-a˥kubi				
		-a˥rasi				
		-a˥tari				
		-a˥wate				
		-bu˥kuro				
		U -da˥iko	H -daiko‾			
		U -da˥nna	H -danna‾			
		-do˥koro				
		U -do˥ogu (H x)				
		-do˥ori				
				-gakari‾		
		-ge˥nka				
		-go˥e				
		-ha˥rai				
		-hi˥roma				
		-i˥bari				
		-i˥sogi				
		U -mawari‾	H -mawari‾			
		-me˥dama				
		-mi˥soka				
		-mo˥oke				
		-mu˥kasi				
		-mu˥koo				

(Chart 16:1, p. 3)

o꜒o-	oo꜒-	oo- ꜔	oo- ꜉	.oo- ꜉	.oo- ꜔ .oo꜒-
		U -o꜒toko			H -o꜒toko
			-ppira⁻		
		-sa꜒wagi			
		H -si꜒goto (U x)			
		-so꜒ozi			
		-te꜒mon			
		-te꜒suzi			
		-ti꜒gai			
		H -to꜒rii (U x)			
			-utusi⁻		
		-wa꜒rai			
		-wa꜒rawa			
		H -ya꜒kedo (U x)			
		-zi꜒dai			
			U -zikake⁻	H -zikake⁻	
		-zi꜒nusi			
		H -zi꜒sin (U x)			
		-zu꜒moo			
		-zyo꜒tai			
			-zukami⁻		
		H -da꜒sukari			U -da꜒sukari
		-ma꜒tigai			
			U -miyabito⁻		U -miya꜒bito
		-so꜒odoo			
		-u꜒nabara			
		-u꜒ridasi			
		H -wa꜒ribiki (U x)			
		-wa꜒zurai			
		U -ya꜒suuri⁸			
		-yo꜒rokobi			

Relevant words: ooki-na, ooki-i B-B-A 'big', oo-i B-B-B 'many/much': Sd (qu)hu(u)-, hwii- A 'big': Sr quhu-san A 'many/much' ('big' is magi-san A); Yn ubu- B 'big'. Heian B: ofo[k]i nari, o[f]o (- N) 'big; many/much'. Notice also Kyōto oo-ra꜒ka.

[1]Umegaki also has high atonic oo-ban⁻₂ 'old palace-guard'.

[2]Umegaki: oo-bu꜒ri 'deluge', .oo-buri⁻ 'big gesture'. Hirayama has only oo-buri⁻ 'deluge'.

[3]Heian LLLH oobune.   [4]Heian ooguti LLHH ooguti.   [5]Edo high atonic HHHH ookata.

[6]Cf. ookura-꜒syoo, ookura-da꜒izin.   [7]Heian low atonic LLLL oomune.

[8]Hirayama has a mesotonic version oo-yasu꜒uri and that, if not a mistake, suggests the structure oo-yasu + uri, but perhaps it reflects one of the Tōkyō patterns. In any event, the example is different from oo-date꜒mono and oo-nagina꜒ta, which preserve the accents of the second members, tate꜒-mono and nagi-na꜒ta.

Chart 16:2.   The prefix ko- 'little'.

Except as shown below, the compounds are all Kagoshima A.

ko'-	ko- '	ko- ¯	.ko- ¯	.ko- '
		-na¯ 'petty' (H-x)[1]		
		-te¯[2]		
		-ya¯ Kg B		
-ban Kg B				
		-bana¯		
		-bata¯		
		-bito¯ Kg B		
		-bune¯		
		-buri¯[1,2]		
		-dasi¯ Kg B		
		-eda¯		
		-gane¯ 'sun'		
		-gara¯		
		-gata¯		
		U -gire¯	H -gire¯ Kg B	
		-goe¯ Kg B		
		-goto¯ Kg B		
		-guna¯		
U -guti		H -guti¯		
		-haba¯		
		-haze¯ Kg B		
		-hiza¯		
		-iki¯		
		-isi¯		
		-inu¯		
				-ke'si¯[3] Kg B
			-nane¯ Kg B	
		-nata¯		
-nati				
		U -natu¯ (H x)[4]		
		-nini¯		
		-niti¯		
		-nono¯ Kg B		
		-nozi¯		
-nugi				
		-nuka¯		
		U -sai¯	H -sai¯	
U -saku		U -saku¯[5]	H -saku¯ Kg B	
		U -sane¯	H -sane¯	
			H -sazi¯ (U x)	
U -sode		H -sode¯		
		U -syaku¯	H -syaku¯	

(Chart 16:2, p. 2)

ko'-	ko-'	ko-¯	.ko-¯	.ko-'
		-tori¯ Kg B		
U -tubu		H -tubu¯		
		-ume¯		
		-uri¯ Kg B		
U -usi[6]		H -usi¯		
		U -wake¯	H -wake¯	
		-waki¯		
U -yagi		-yagi¯		
		-yama¯[7] Kg B		
		-yami¯		
U -yoo		H -yoo¯		
-yubi				
		-yuki¯[8]		
		-zeni¯		
		U -ziwa¯	H -ziwa¯	
-zoo				U -zo'o
-zuti		U -zuti¯		
	-a'kinai			
	-aki'ndo			
	-ba'nasi			
		-basiri¯		
		-butori¯		
	-bya'kusyoo			
	H -da'nuki (U x)			
				-gata'na[9]
U -gitte	-ga'wase			
	-gi'tte			
	-iti'ri			
	-ki'zami			
		-musume¯		
ko'ozi[10] Kg B				
	-ni'motu			
	-ni'nzu(u)			
	U -o'dori			H -o'dori
	H -o'toko	U -otoko¯		
	-ri'koo			
	-ri'kutu			
		H -ryoori¯ (U x)		
	H -se'gare	U -segare¯		
	-tesaki¯ Kg B			
	U -yo'ozi			
	-za'kana			
	U -za'kura (H x)			
	-ze'riai			

(Chart 16:2, p. 3)

ko¹-	ko- ¹	ko- ⁻	.ko- ⁻	.ko- ¹
-zukai Kg B				
	-zu¹kuri			
-zutumi Kg B				
	-zyu¹uto			
	-bya¹kusyoo			
	H -ha¹nniti[11]			
	H -ha¹ntoki[12]			
	U -na¹maiki	H -namaiki⁻		
	-ya¹kunin			
	U -ryoori¹ya			
	-zappa¹ri			
	-itizi¹kan			
	H -ryoori¹ten (U x)			

[1]But H .koma-zu¹kai = U koma-zu¹kai. The adjectival noun koma is obsolete, replaced by the extended form koma-ka, which underlies the adjective komaka- 'fine, detailed'.

[2]The Kagoshima accent is A, but kote-nage⁻ and kote-si¹rabe are B: cf. ko-tesaki⁻ Kg B.

[3]And .kokesi-ni¹ngyoo Kg B.

[4]Hirayama lacks the simplex, but has the compound komatu-na⁻.

[5]Cf. (HU) .kosaku¹-nin = U ko-saku¹-nin⁻.   [6]Heian HHH koyama.

[7]Perhaps it would be better to treat the first element of ko-usi 'calf' as the noun ko 'child' (0-0-A): cf. ko-ma 'colt' (1/2-1-A), ko-buta 'piglet' (0-0-A), ko-neko 'kitten' (2-0-A). The prefix and the noun are probably the same etymon, and the adjective meaning came first: 'child' ← 'little [one]'.

[8]Meaning 'light snowfall'. Cf. ko-yu¹ki 'powder snow'.

[9]And .kogatana-za¹iku.

[10]This is koozi < koudi < koůdi < ko-m[i]ti 'alley'.

[11]Umegaki has -han¹niti and -han¹toki.

Chart 16:3.   The prefix soo- 'all'.

The compounds are all Kagoshima A. Cf. .soo¹-zite A 'generally'.

so¹o-	soo- ¹	soo- ‾	.soo- ‾	.soo- ¹
			-.de‾	
-ki				
-ri				
		-dai‾		
U -gaku		H -gaku‾		
			-gawa‾ (U x)	
	U -¹giri		H -giri‾	
		-goo‾		
U -in		H -in‾		
		-kai‾		
		-kaku‾		
		-kan‾		
H -kei		U -kei‾		
			-name‾		
		-ran‾		
U -ron		H -ron‾		
-ryoku				
		-ryoo‾		
		-sai‾		
		-setu‾		
		-sin‾		
U -suu		H -suu‾		
		-syoo‾		
		-tai‾		
U -ten		H -ten‾		
U -toku		H -toku‾		
H -tyoo (U x)				
		H -zai‾	U -zai‾	
		-zyoo‾		
			-zime‾	
			-gakari‾	
	-ho¹nke			
				H -i¹reba (Ux)
			-kuzure‾	U -ku¹zure
			-makuri‾	
			H -matome‾ (U x)	
	U -ni¹kai			H -ni¹kai
	-se¹nkyo			
	-yo¹san			
			-zarai‾	U -za¹rai
	-zi¹syoku			

(Chart 16:3, p. 2)

so¹o-	soo- ¹	soo- ⁻	.soo- ⁻	.soo- ¹
	-da¹isyoo			Ħ -da¹isyoo
	-do¹oin			
	-ho¹nzan			
	-kes¹san = -ke¹ssan			
	-ko¹ogeki			
	-mo¹kuroku			
	-syu¹unyuu			
	-ton¹suu			
	Ħ -sire¹i-bu (U x)			
	Ħ -sire¹i-kan,			
	U -sirei¹-kan			

Chart 16:4.   The prefix syo- 'several'.

The compounds are all Kagoshima A.

syo¹-	syo- ¹	syo- ⁻	(.syo- ⁻	.syo- ¹)
			None.	*None.*
-ha				
-hi				
-ka				
-si				
-sya				
-syu				
-syo				
-ten				
-zi				
-hoo				
-kun				
-koku				
		-ron⁻		
-setu				
-soo				
-syuu				
	-do¹ogu			
	Ħ -ga¹ikoku (U x)			
	Ħ -mo¹ndai (U x)			
	Ħ -zap¹pi (U x)¹			

¹Kagoshima s̄ȳo | zappī.

Chart 16:5.   The prefix zyo- 'female'.

The compounds are all Kagoshima A.

zyo¹-	zyo- ¹	zyo- ‾	.zyo- ‾	.zyo- ¹
-i				
-si¹				
-zi				
U -kan			H -kan‾	
			-ketu‾	
U -koo			H -koo‾	
			-kyuu‾	
U -nan			H -nan‾	
U -oo				H -o¹o
		U -roo‾	U -roo‾	H -ro¹o
			-ryuu‾	
		-sei‾ 'sex'		
		U -sei‾₂ 'voice: ···'	H -sei‾₂	
U -soo			H -soo‾	
-syoku				
		U -syoo‾	H -syoo‾	
		U -syuu‾	H -syuu‾	
		-tyuu‾		
				-zyuu‾
				-kyo¹osi
	U -se¹ito			H -se¹ito
-gakusei				
				-kyo¹oin
	U -te¹n-in		H -ten¹-in (?)	

¹But .zyosi-dai‾ and .zyosi-da¹igaku (both Kagoshima A).

Chart 16:6.   The prefix ta- 'many'.

The compounds are all Kagoshima A. As free noun: ta 1-2-A.

ta¹-	ta- ¹	ta- ‾	.ta- ‾	.ta- ¹
-ka				
-zi				
			-ben‾	
			-boo‾	
-bun 'portion'				
			-dai‾	
			-doku‾	
		U -gaku‾₁ 'learn' (H x)	-gaku‾₂ 'amount'	
		U -gen‾₁ 'words' (H x)	-gen‾₂ 'dimension'	
U -hoo (H x)			-kan‾	
		U -koo‾ 'luck'	H -koo‾	
			-nan‾	
		-nen‾₁,₂,₃		
			-ryoo‾ 'quantity'	
			-sai‾₁,₂.₃	
			-saku‾	
			-san‾	
		U -suu‾		
	H -su¹u			
		-syoo‾		
			-yoo‾	
		U -zei‾	H -zei‾	
		-zyoo‾		

			(-he¹n-kei.
			U -hen¹-kei)¹
			(-kaku¹-kei)¹
			(-kes¹-situ)¹

(-me¹n-tai)¹

-sin-kyoo‾

¹The locus is due to the added suffix: if the simpler forms occurred, we would expect the patterns to be .ta-hen, .ta-kaku‾, .ta-ketu‾, ta-men‾.

Chart 16:7.   The prefix ta- 'other'.

The compounds are all Kagoshima A. As free noun: ta 1-2-A.

ta¹-	ta-¹	ta-¯	.ta-¯	.ta-¹
-ke	None.			None.
-zi				
		-bun¯ 'hear'[1]		
		-gon¯/-gen¯		
U -hoo		H -hoo¯$_{1,2}$		
U -ka 'section' (H x)				
H -koku			U -koku¯	
U -koo 'school' (H x)				
			-kyoo¯	
		-nen¯$_2$		
		-nin¯		
U -riki		H -riki¯		
U -ryoo 'dominion' (H x)				
		-ryuu¯		
			-satu¯	
		-sen¯$_{1,2}$	H -sen¯$_1$	
-son				
		U -syoo¯$_{1,2,3}$	H -syoo¯$_{1,2}$	
		U -yoo¯ (H x)		
-zitu				

[1] The compound means 'publicity, reaching others' ears'.

Charts 17:1-5.   Kyōto accent of compounds with
                        negative prefixes.

Chart 17:1.   The prefix hi- 'non-, un-'.

Except as shown, the compounds are Kagoshima A. Free noun: 1-0-A.

hi ˈ-	hi- ˈ	hi- ‾	.hi- ‾	.hi- ˈ
			-ban‾ Kg B	
			-bon‾ Kg B	
		U -boo‾ (H x)		
			-doo‾ Kg B	
			-goo‾	
		U -hoo‾	H -hoo‾	
		U -koo‾	H -koo‾	
-nan				
			-nin‾ Kg B	
		U -sai‾	H -sai‾	
			-zyoo-₁ Kg B	
			'ordinary'	
		U -zyoo‾₂	-zyoo₂ 'feeling'	
	U -goˈori (H x)[1]			
	U -eˈisei (H x)			
	U -gooˈhoo			H -gooˈhoo
	U -kiˈnzoku			H -kiˈnzoku
	U -koˈkumin			H -koˈkumin
	U -koˈokai			H -koˈokai[2]
				H -koˈonin (U x)[2]
	U -koˈosiki			H -koˈosiki

[1]Compare:

        U hi-goori - syuˈgi   H .hi-goori - sei‾ (U x)
                                           H .hi-goori - syuˈgi
                                           H .hi-goori - teki‾ (U x)

[2]Kagoshima: hi‾ | kookai‾, hi‾ | koonin‾.

Chart 17:2.   The prefix hu- 'not'.

Except for hu-sidara and hu-syuugi, the compounds are Kagoshima A.

hu¹-	hu- '	hu- ⁻	.hu- ⁻	.hu- '
-bi				
-gi				
H -gu				U -gù
			-i⁻	
H -ka			U -ka⁻	
-ki				
-ri				
-ryo				
U -si			H -si⁻	
H -ti 'curable'			U -ti⁻	
H -wa (U x)				
H -zi₁ 'time'			U -zi⁻₁	
H -zi₂ = -ti			U -zi⁻₂ = -ti⁻	
			-an⁻	
			-batu⁻	
-bin₁,₂,₃				
			U -bin⁻₄ 'quick' (H x)	
-ben				
-dan₁				
¹H -dan₂			U -dan⁻₂	
U -deki			H -deki⁻	
		U -doo⁻	H -doo⁻	
U -ete				H -e'te
			-hatu⁻	
			-hei⁻	
			-hoo⁻	
		U -hyoo⁻	H -hyoo⁻	
			-kai⁻ (Kg x)	
			-kaku⁻	
			U -kati⁻ (H x)	
			-kitu⁻	
			-kutu⁻	
			-kei⁻	
			-ketu⁻	
			-man⁻	
			-mei⁻	
			-metu⁻	
			-min⁻	
		U -mon⁻	-mon⁻	
			-moo⁻	
U -muki			H -muki⁻	
U -nare			H -nare⁻	
U -nen			H -nen⁻	
			-noo⁻	
				-nyo'i

(Chart 17:2, p.2)

hu'-	hu-'	hu- ‾	.hu- ‾	.hu-'
		U -rin‾	H -rin‾	
U -saku			H -saku‾	
U -rati			H -rati‾	
			-ryoo$_1$ 'good'	
U -ryoo$_2$ 'catch'			H -ryoo$_2$ 'catch'	
		U -san‾	H -san‾	
H -sin$_3$		U -sin‾$_{1,2,3}$	H -sin‾$_{1,2}$	
			-sei‾	
		-sigi‾		
		-soku$_1$ 'enough'		
		U -soku‾$_2$ 'measure'	H -soku‾$_2$ 'measure'	
			-syoo‾$_1$ 'worthy'	
		U -syoo‾$_2$ 'zeal'		
-syoo‾$_2$ 'zeal'				
	U -syu'bi			H -syu'bi
			-tei‾$_{1.2}$	
			-teki‾$_{1,2}$	
			-too‾	
			-tuu‾	
			-tyaku‾	
			-tyoo‾	
			-yoo‾	
	-zen‾			
	U -zai‾		H -zai‾	
	U -zimi‾		H -zimi‾	
	U -zui‾		H -zui‾	
			H -zyoo‾	
	U -zyun‾$_{1,2}$		H -zyun‾$_{1,2}$	
	U -do'oi			H -do'oi
	U -go'ori			H -go'ori
	U -gu'ai (H x)			
	U -ʰ/ba'rai			H -ʰ/ba'rai
	U -ho'n'i			H -ho'n'i
	U -ka'gen (H x)			
				-ka'kai
				H -ka'ketu
	U -ka'bun		U -kabun‾	H -ka'bun
	U -ka'noo		U -kanoo‾	H -ka'noo
	U -ka'sigi		H -kasigi‾	
	U -ka'tte (H x)			
	U -ke'iki			H -ke'iki
	U -ki'soku		H -kisoku‾	
				-kyo'ka
	U -ma'zime			H -ma'zime
	U -ne'nka			H -ne'nka
	-ni'ai			
				H -ni'nka

(Chart 17:2, p.3)

hu¹-	hu-¹	hu-¯	.hu-¯	.hu-¹
	U -ri¹eki			H -ri¹eki
	U -ri¹koo			H -ri¹koo
	U -sa¹nka			H -sa¹nka
	U -senme¹i³			H -senme¹i³
	U -si¹dara			H -si¹dara Kg B
	U -si¹matu			H -si¹matu
	U -si¹zen			H -si¹zen
	U -syo¹oka			H -syo¹oka
	U -syo¹oti			H -syo¹oti
	U -syo¹ozi			H -syo¹ozi
U -syuugi				H -syu¹ugi Kg B
	U -syo¹zon			H -syo¹zon
	U -ta¹sika			H -ta¹sika
	U -te¹giwa			H -te¹giwa
	U -te¹iki			H -te¹iki
	U -to¹doki			H -to¹doki
	U -to¹kugi			H -to¹kugi
	U -to¹kui			H -to¹kui
	U -tu¹goo			H -tu¹goo
	U -tu¹tuka	H -tutuka¯		
	U -tyu¹ui			H -tyu¹ui
	U -wa¹tari	H -watari¯		
	U -yo¹oi			H -yo¹oi
H -yukai	U -yu¹kai			
-zaiku				
H -ziyuu	U -zi¹yuu			
	U -zo¹roi			H -zo¹roi
	U -zyo¹ori			U -zyo¹ori
	U -a¹nsin (H x)			
	U -byo¹odoo			H -byo¹odoo
	U -go¹okaku			H -go¹okaku
	U -gyo¹oseki		H -gyooseki¯	
	U -gyo¹ozyoo (H x)			
				-hi¹tuyoo
	U -hyo¹oban			H -hyo¹oban
	U -ka¹nzen		H -kanzen¯	
				H -kap¹patu =
				U -ka¹ppatu
				H -ke¹izai,
				U -kei¹zai
	U -ke¹nkoo			H -ke¹nkoo
	U -ke¹nsiki			H -ke¹nsiki
				H -ke¹nzai (U x)
	U -ko¹ohei			H -ko¹ohei
	U -ma¹nzoku			H -ma¹nzoku
	U -me¹n b/moku			H -me¹n b/moku
				H -ni¹nsyoo²,
				U -nin¹syoo²

(Chart 17:2, p.4)

hu¹-	hu- ¹	hu- ⁻	.hu- ⁻	.hu- ¹
	U -ryo'oken			H -ryo'oken
	U -sa'nsei			H -sa'nsei
	U -se'ikaku			H -se'ikaku
	U -se'ikoo			H -se'ikoo
	U -se'iritu			H -se'iritu
	U -se'isyutu			H -se'isyutu
	U -se'ssei			H -ses'sei
				H -si'nmin (U x)
	U -si'nkoo			H -si'nkoo
	U -si'nsetu			H -si'nsetu
	U -si'n'yoo			H -si'n'yoo
	U -si'nzin			H -si'nzin
	U -so'o'oo			H -so'o'oo
	U -syo'oziki			H -syo'oziki
				H -te'kikaku (U x)
	U -te'isai			H -te'isai
	U -te'kinin			H -te'kinin
	U -te'kitoo			H -te'kitoo
	U -te'ttei			H -tet'tei
	U -to'kusaku			H -to'kusaku
	U -to'oitu			H -to'oitu
	U -to'omei			H -to'omei
	U -yo'ozyoo			H -yo'ozyoo
	H -zyu'ubun *sic!*			U -zyu'ubun *sic!*
	U -ko'koroe			H -ko'koroe
	U -yu'kitodoki, -yukito'doki			

¹Hudan 'usually' and 'uninterrupted' are etymologically the same, though often written with different characters. An atonic Tōkyō variant is given by K only for 'uninterrupted'. For that meaning, U gives only a low atonic Kyōto version, differentiating it from the high prototonic pattern for 'usually', but H gives the latter for both meanings.

²But the H version mistakenly implies the constituency .hu-ni'nsyoo 'non pregnancy-disorder' whereas the U version reflects the correct constituency .hunin'-syoo 'non-pregnancy disorder': the word means 'barenness'.

³The locus is a puzzle, since the adjectival noun senmei 'fresh' is high atonic for both H and U. We would expect *hu-se'nmei or *.hu-se'nmei. Perhaps the word was earlier *senme'i or *.senme'i, later atonicized.

Chart 17:3.   The prefix bu- 'not, un-'.

The compounds are Kagoshima A.

bu¹-	bu-¹	bu-¯	.bu-¯	.bu-¹
		U -zi¯	H -zi¯	
-kimi				
			-kotu¯	
U -nan		H -nan¯		
		-nin¯		
			-rai¯	
		-ryoo¯		
		-sata¯		
U -sui		H -sui¯		
-syoo				
U -zama		H -zama¯		
		-zei¯		
	-ki'ryoo			
	-ki'yoo			
	-sa'hoo			
	U -si'tuke		H -situke¯	
	-a'nnai			
	-hu'uryuu			
	U -ka'kkoo =			
	H -kak'koo			
		-kittyo[o]¯		
	-tyo'ohoo			
	-yo'ozin			

Chart 17:4.   The prefix mu- 'lacking, un-, -less'.

Except as noted, the compounds are Kagoshima A. Free noun mu 1-0-A.

mu¹-	mu-¹	mu-‾	.mu-‾	.mu-¹
		-da‾		
-ga				
U -ge		H -ge‾		
-hi				
-i				
U -ki 'season' (H x)				
H -ki 'term; organic'[1]			U -ki‾ 'term; organic'	
-ku				
-mi				
-ni				
-ri				
-ryo (H x)				
-si 'regard'			U -si‾ 'regard'	
-si 'self'				
U -si 'beginning' (H x)				
-ti₁,₂				
				-tyà
-zi (< -di)				
		U -boo‾₁,₂	H -boo‾₁,₂	
-byoo				
U -dai₁,₂		H -dai‾₁,₂		
		-dan‾		
U -doku		H -doku‾		
U -doo		H -doo‾		
-eki				
		-en‾		
		-gai‾ 'lid'		
U -gai 'harm'		H -gai‾ 'harm'		
-gaku				
U -gei		H -gei‾		
		-gen‾		
		-gon‾		
		U -hoo‾	H -hoo‾	
		U -huu‾	H -huu‾	
	H -i¹gi			U -¹gi
	H -i¹mi			U -i¹mi
		H -kei‾	U -kei‾	
		-kin‾		
U -kizu		H -kizu‾		
		H -kon‾ 'root'	U -kon‾ 'root'	
		U -kon‾ 'trace' (H x)		
			-koo‾	
-kuti				
		-kyuu‾		

(Chart 17:4, p.2)

mu¹-	mu-¹	mu-⁻	.mu-⁻	.mu-¹
			-mei⁻ 'name'	
		U -mei⁻ 'inscribe' (H x)		
		-nen⁻		
			-noo-	
		H -ri'si		U -ri'si
		-ron⁻		
		-rui⁻		
		-ryoo⁻₁,₂		
-ryoku				
U -sai 'talent'		H -sai⁻ 'talent'		
		U -sai⁻ 'wife' (H x)		
U -saku		H -saku⁻		
		-san⁻		
		-sei⁻₁,₂		
-seki₁,₂				
		-sen⁻₁,₂		
		-sin⁻₁,₂		
		-soo⁻₁,₂		
		-suu⁻		
-syoku₂				
		-syoo⁻₁,₂		
		-syuu⁻		
U -tai		H -tai⁻		
		-teki⁻	U -teki⁻	
		-tin⁻		
		-too⁻₁,₂,₃,₄		
		-tuu⁻		
-yoku				
		-yoo⁻	H -yoo⁻	
-zai				
		-zan⁻₁,₂		
U -zihi	H -zi'hi			
	-zi'ko			
		-zin⁻₁,₂		
	-syu'mi			
-zitu				
-zyaki				
		-zyoo⁻₁,₂,₃		
	U -bo'obi			H -bo'obi
	H -i'siki			U -i'siki
				-ki'gen
				-ki'mei
				-ki'ryoku
				-syo'zoku
	U -me'nkyo			H -me'nkyo
	-ri'kai			
	U -ri'soku			U -ri'soku

(Chart 17:4, p.3)

mu¹-	mu- ¹	mu- ⁻	.mu- ⁻	.mu- ¹
	-sa¹betu			U -sa¹betu
	-ta¹npo			
	U -to¹doke			H -to¹doke
	-zi¹kaku			
	-zo¹osa			
	U -ha¹itoo			H -ha¹itoo
	U -ho¹osyuu			H -ho¹osyuu
	-hu¹nbetu			U -hu¹nbetu
	U -hyo¹ozyoo			H -hyo¹ozyoo
	H -ka¹nkaku			
	H -ka¹nkei			U -ka¹nkei
	-ka¹nsin			
	H -kyo¹oiku			U -kyo¹oiku
				-no¹oryoku
	-se¹igen			
	-se¹kinin			
	H -ses¹soo = U -se¹ssoo			
	-si¹nkei			
	-syu¹ukyoo			
	-te¹ikoo			
	-te¹itoo			
	H -tep¹poo = -te¹ppoo U			
	-to¹nᵗ/zyaku			
	H -tya¹kuriku, U -tyaku¹riku			
	H -zi¹nzoo			U -zi¹nzoo
	-zyo¹oken			

---

¹ But .muki-hi¹ryoo, -ka¹gaku, -tyo¹oeki: H .muki-en¹ki (despite mu¹ki!) and U mu¹ki-enki (despite .muki!).
Notice also .muki .kagoo¹-butu (Hirayama's '1:3:6'), where muki(-) serves as a pseudo adnoun (RGJ 750-2).

Chart 17:5.   The prefix mi- 'not yet, un-...-en'.

The compounds are all Kagoshima A. No Shuri examples. Newish?

mi¹-	mi- ¹	mi- ⁻	.mi- ⁻	.mi- ¹
-ti¹				
			-hai⁻	
			-kai⁻	
			-kan⁻₁.₂	
			-ken⁻	
U -ketu			ʮ -ketu⁻	
			-kon⁻	
		ʮ -man⁻	U -man⁻	
			-mei⁻	
			-noo⁻	
-rai				
U -ren		ʮ -ren⁻		
			-ryoo⁻	
			-sai⁻	
			-syoo⁻	
				ʮ -syo¹ti (U x)
			-tei⁻	
			-too⁻₁.₂	
			-tyaku⁻	
U -zen			-zen⁻	
				-zo¹u
			U -harai⁻	ʮ -ha¹rai
	U -so¹siki			ʮ -so¹siki
				ʮ -se¹iri (U x)
				ʮ -hak¹ken (U x)
				ʮ -hak¹koo (U x)
	U -ha¹ppyoo			ʮ -hap¹pyoo
				ʮ -hat¹tatu (U x)
				-ka¹ihatu
				-ka¹iketu
				-ka¹itaku
	U -ke¹iken			ʮ -ke¹iken
				-se¹inen

¹But .miti¹-suu.

Chart 18.   Atonicizing suffixes of Chinese origin.   *(Nine pages.)*

Suffix	Tōkyō			Hiroshima			Kyōto-Ōsaka		
	`_‾`	`‾_`	`_‾`	`_‾`	`‾_`	`_‾`	`_‾`	`‾_`	`_‾`
-ban 'guard' ban 1-1-B < .phywan	`-‾`	`‾_`		`-‾`				`‾_`	
-ban 'disk; board' ban 1-1-B < .bhwan	`-‾`			`-‾`				`‾_`	
-ban 'board' (han/ban) < 'pan	`-‾`			`-‾`				`‾_`	
-ban 'edition' han 1-2-B < 'pan	`-‾`			`-‾`				`‾_`	
-ban 'seal; size' han 1-1-B < phwan'	`-‾`			`-‾`				`‾_`	
-ben 'dialect' ben ?1-2-A < 'bhyan	`-‾`			`-‾`			`-‾`	`(‾_)`	
-ben 'valve' ben ?1-2-A < bhen'	`-‾`	`‾_`		`-‾`			`?`		
-betu 'difference, classified by ··· ' betu 0-0-B < bhyet	`-‾`			`-‾`			`-‾`		
-bin 'mail; transport' bin 1-2-B < bhyan'	`-‾`	`‾_`		`-‾`				`‾_`	
-bin 'bottle' bin 1-2-A < .bh(y)eng		`‾_`		`-‾`	`‾_`		`-‾`	`‾_`	
-bon 'tray' bon 0-1-A < .bhwen		`‾_`		`-‾`				`‾_`	
-bon 'book' hon 1-2-B < 'pwen	`-‾`			`-‾`					`-‾`
-bun 'sentence' bun 1-2-A < .m(b)ywen	`-‾` /	`‾_`		`-‾`				`‾_`	

-bun: (1) 'portion,
  'quantity, content'
    (2) 'part;
  status, relation'
bun 1-2-B
< bhywen'
	`-‾`
	
	`?-‾`
		`?‾_`
		
		`‾_`
				`-‾`
				
					`‾_`
							`?`
							
								`‾_`	

(Chart 18, p. 2)	Tōkyō	Hiroshima	Kyōto-Ōsaka
-byoo 'illness' (byoo) < bhyang˙	-‾	-‾	˥_
-dai 'charge, expense' dai 1-1-B < dhay˙	-‾ / ˥_	_˥	-‾
-dai: (1) 'stand, seat' (2) 'level' dai 1-1-B < .dhay	-‾ / ˥_ ˥_	-‾ ˥_	˥_ ˥_
-dai 'size' dai 1-0-B 1-0-B	-‾	-‾ ˥_	˥_
-dai 'university' ← daigaku 0-0-A < dhay˙-hhak	-‾	-‾	-‾
-doo 'hall; press' doo 1-1-B < .dhang	-‾	-‾	-‾
-en 'inflammation' (en) < .hhyam	-‾ ˥_	-‾	˥_
-ga 'drawing, picture' (ga) < hhwa(y)˙	-‾	-‾	˥_
-gan 'eye' (gan) .ngan	-‾ / ˥_	-‾	˥_
-gi 'spirit' ki 0-0-A < khyey˙	-‾ ˥_ _˥	-‾ _˥	-‾ ˥_
-go 'after' (go) < ˙hhew	-‾ _˥	-‾ _˥	-‾ ˥_
-go 'language; word' go 1-0-B < ˙ngyo	-‾	_˥	-‾
-ha 'group' (?) ha 1-x-x < phay˙	-‾	_˥	-‾
-han 'meal; rice' (han) < ˙pan	-‾	-‾	-‾
-hen 'vicinity' hen 0-2-A < .p(y)en	-‾	-‾	?
-hen '(left) radical' hen 0-0-A < .phyan	-‾	˥_	-‾

(Chart 18, p. 3)	Tōkyō	Hiroshima	Kyōto-Ōsaka
-hin 'commodity' hin 0-1-B ‹ phyem˙	-‾ / ˥-	-‾	˥-
-hoo 'law; way, method' hoo 0-2-A ‹ pywap	-‾ / ˥-	?-‾ ?˥-	˥-
-hu 'record; score' musical score' hu 0-0-A ‹ po˙	˥-	-‾	˥-
-huu: (1) 'style' (2) 'wind' huu 1-2-A ‹ .pyung	-‾ -‾ / ˥-	-‾ -‾	-‾ ˥-
-hyoo 'list, chart' hyoo 0-0-A ‹ ˙pyaw	-‾	-‾	-‾
-hyoo 'criticism' hyoo 0-2-A ‹ .bhyang	˥-	-‾	˥-
-hyoo 'vote' hyoo 0-0-A ‹ .phyew	-‾	-‾	˥-
-hyoo 'signpost' (hyoo) ‹ .pyew	-‾	-‾	-‾
-ka 'person' (ka) ‹ .ka	-‾	-‾	-‾
-ka '-ize; -ization' (ka) ‹ hwa˙	-‾ / ˥-	-‾	˥-
-ka 'section' ka 1-1-B ‹ khwa˙	-‾	˥-	˥-
-ka 'specialty' (ka) ‹ .khwa	-‾	˥-	˥-
-kan 'tube' kan 1-1-A ‹ ˙kwan	-‾	-‾ ˥-	. ˥-
-kan 'can' kan 1-1-A ‹ kwan˙	-‾	-‾	˥-
-kan 'warship' (kan) ‹ hham˙	-‾ / ˥-	˥-	˥-
-ke 'family of ⋯ ' (ke) ‹ .ka	-‾ / ˥-	˥-	-‾

(Chart 18, p. 4)	Tōkyō	Hiroshima	Kyōto-Ōsaka
-kei 'meter' (kei) < kei'	-‾ / ⌐‾	-‾	⌐‾
-kei 'shape, model' (kei) < .hhyeng	-‾	-‾	-‾
-kei 'system' (kei) < hhey'	-‾ / ⌐‾	-‾	-‾
-kei 'lineage; clique' (kei) < hhey'	-‾ / ⌐‾	-‾	?-‾ / ⌐‾
-ken 'ticket' ken 1-2-B < khywan'	⌐‾	-‾	⌐‾
-ken 'dog' (ken) < 'khwen	-‾	-‾	⌐‾
-kin 'bacteria' kin 1-2-A < kyun' (/ .kyun)	-‾ / ⌐‾	-‾	⌐‾
-kin 'muscle' (kin) < .kyen	⌐‾	-‾	⌐‾
-kin 'money; metal; gold' kin 1-2-A < .kyem	-‾ / ⌐‾	-‾	⌐‾
-koo 'incense' koo 1-2-B < .hyang	-‾	-‾	-‾
-koo 'worker' (koo) < .kᵘ/₀ng	-‾ / ⌐‾	-‾	⌐‾
-kyoo 'sūtra' kyoo 0-0-B < .kyeng	-‾	-‾	-‾
-kyoo 'mirror; lens' (kyoo) < kyang'	-‾	-‾	-‾
-kyoo 'religion' (kyoo) < kyaw'	-‾	-‾	-‾
-kyoo 'maniac' (kyoo) < .ghywang	-‾	-‾	-‾
-kyuu 'class' kyuu 1-2-A < kyep	-‾	-‾	⌐‾

(Chart 18, p. 5)	Tōkyō	Hiroshima	Kyōto-Ōsaka
-kyuu 'salary' (kyuu) ‹ <u>kyep</u>	-‾(/ ˥-)	˥-	˥-
-mai 'rice' (mai) ‹ <u>m(b)ey'</u>	-‾	-‾	-‾
-mi 'taste, touch' (mi) ‹ <u>m(b)ywey'</u>	-‾ ˥-	-‾ -˥	-‾
-nin 'person' (nin) cf. -zin ‹ <u>.nhyen</u>	-‾ ˥-	-‾ -˥	-‾ ˥-
-ri 'within' (ri) ‹ <u>'li</u>	˥-	˥-	-‾
{ -riki -ryoku } 'power' { (riki/ryoku) ‹ <u>.lyek)</u>	-‾ ˥- ˥-	-‾ -˥	-‾ ˥- -‾
-ritu 'stand, establish' (ritu) ‹ <u>.lyep</u>	˥-	-‾	-‾
-ryoo 'fee' (ryoo) ‹ <u>lyew'</u>	˥-	-‾	-‾
-ryuu 'style' (ryuu) ‹ <u>.lyew</u>	-‾	-‾	-‾
-san 'acid' san 1-2-A ‹ <u>.swan</u>	-‾	-‾	˥-
-san 'product' (san) ‹ <u>'s(r)an</u>	-‾	-‾	?-‾ ?˥-
-san 'silkworm' (san) ‹ <u>.dzham</u>	-‾ ˥-	-‾	?
-sei (1) 'life' (2) 'student' sei 1-2-A ‹ <u>.sreng</u>	-‾ ˥-	-‾ ?˥-	-‾ ˥-
-sei 'system' sei 1-2-B ‹ <u>tsyey'</u>	-‾	-‾	-‾
-sei 'nature; gender' sei 1-2-A ‹ <u>sye/ang'</u>	-‾	-‾	-‾
-sei 'manufacture' (sei) ‹ <u>tsyey'</u>	-‾	-‾	-‾

(Chart 18, p. 6)	Tōkyō	Hiroshima	Kyōto-Ōsaka
-sen 'line' sen 1-2-A ‹ syen˙	-¯(/ ˥-)	-¯ ˥-	˥-
-sen 'gland' (sen) ‹ *syen˙	-¯ / ˥-	-¯	˥-
-sen 'war, battle' (sen) ‹ tsyen˙	-¯ / ˥-	?	˥-
-sen 'ship' (sen) ‹ .dzhywen	-¯	-¯	˥-

-siki (1) 'style'
    (= hoosiki)
   (2) 'ceremony'
    (= gisiki);
    'formula'
    (= suusiki)
siki (2‹)1-2-B
‹ syek
	-¯
	
	˥-
		-¯
		
		?˥-
			-¯
			
			˥-

-soo 'grass, herb' (soo) ‹ ˙tshaw	-¯	-¯	-¯
-sui 'water' (sui) ‹ .syuy	˥-	-¯	˥-
-syo 'place' (syo) cf. -zyo ‹ ˙sro	-¯ (˥-) -˥	-˥	˥-
-syo 'office' syo 1-0-A ‹ zhyo˙	-¯ (˥-) -˥	-¯ -˥	˥-
-syo 'writing; book' syo 0-0-A ‹ .syo	-¯ / ˥- / -˥	˥-	˥-
-syoo 'warrant, license' (syoo) ‹ tsyeng˙	˥-	˥-	-¯
-syoo 'illness' (syoo) ‹ tsyeng˙	-¯ / ˥-	˥-	˥-
-syoo 'victory' (syoo) ‹ syeng˙	-¯	?	(-¯/) ˥-
-syoo 'nature' syoo 1-2-B ‹ sye/ang˙ cf. sei	-¯ ˥- -˥	˥-	˥-

(Chart 18, p. 7)

	Tōkyō		Hiroshima		Kyōto-Ōsaka	
-syu 'wine' (syu) < ˙tsyew	‾	˥‾	‾	˥‾		˥‾
-syu(u)/-si 'group' syuu 1-2-A < tsyung˙	‾		‾	˥‾	?	
-tai 'group; troops' tai 1-2-A cf. tei < twey˙ (dhwey˙)	‾		‾			˥‾
-tai 'body; style' tai 1-2-A < ˙they	‾	˥‾	‾			˥‾
-tai 'belt; zone' (tai) < tai˙	‾		‾		‾	˥‾
-tan 'coal' (tan) < than˙	‾		‾			˥‾
-tei 'appearance' tei 1-0-A cf. tai 'body' < ˙they	‾		‾		‾	
-tei 'boat' (tei) < ˙th(y)eng	‾		‾		‾	
-tei 'pavilion; cottage' (tei) < dh(y)eng	˥‾		‾		?	
-tei 'embankment' (tei) < .tey	‾		‾		‾	
-tei 'mansion' (tei) < ˙tey	‾		‾		‾	
-teki '-ic, -ish' (teki) < t(y)ek	‾		‾		‾	
-ten 'store, shop' (ten) < t(y)em˙	‾	˥‾	‾			˥‾
? -tetu 'iron' tetu 0-2-A < thyet *Examples all truncations?*	‾	˥‾	‾	˥‾	‾	˥‾
-ti 'earth; place' ti 1-1-B cf. zi < dhi˙	˥‾		˥‾		‾	
-tin 'fare, charge' (tin) < n(d)ryem˙	˥‾		‾˥		˥‾	
-too 'light' (too) < .teng	‾		‾		‾	

(Chart 18, p. 8)	Tōkyō	Hiroshima	Kyōto-Ōsaka
too 'tower; stupa' too 1-2-B ‹ thap	-¯	-¯	-¯
-too 'island' (too) ‹ ˈtaw	-¯	-¯	-¯
-too 'sugar' (too) ‹ .dhang	-¯	-¯	-¯
-too 'sword' (too) ‹ .taw	-¯	-¯	-¯
-too 'political party' too 1-2-B ‹ ˈtang	-¯	-¯	-¯
-too 'tube' (too = doo) ‹ .dhung	-¯	-¯	-¯
-too 'hot water' (too) ‹ .thang	-¯	-¯	-¯
-tuu 'expert' tuu 1-2-A ‹ .thung	-¯ ⌐-	-¯	⌐-
-tuu 'pain' (tuu) ‹ .thung	-¯ ⌐-	-¯	-¯
-tyoo 'bird' (tyoo) ‹ ˈt(y)ew	-¯	-¯	-¯
-tyoo 'style; tune' (tyoo) ‹ tyewˈ (dhewˈ	-¯	-¯	⌐-
-tyoo 'album; register' (tyoo) ‹ tyangˈ	-¯	-¯	-¯
-tyoo 'court' (tyoo) ‹ .dh(r)yew	-¯(/) ⌐-	⌐-	⌐-
-tyuu 'midst' tyuu 1-1-B cf. -zyuu ‹ .t(r)yung	-¯	-¯	-¯
-tyuu 'insect' (tyuu) ‹ .dh(r)yung	-¯ ⌐-	-¯	⌐-
-yaku 'translation' yaku 1-2-B ‹ yᵃ/ek	-¯ ⌐-	-¯	⌐-
-yaku 'role, post' yaku 2-2-B ‹ ywayk	-¯ ⌐-	-¯	⌐-

(Chart 18, p. 9)   **Tōkyō**   **Hiroshima**   **Kyōto-Ōsaka**

-yoo 'style, appearance' -¯   ?   -¯
(yoo)
‹ yang'

-yoo 'use'   -¯   -¯   -¯
yoo 1-2-B
‹ yong'

-yu 'oil'   -¯   ˥-   -¯   -¯
(yu)
‹ .yew

-za 'seat; theater;
     constellation'   -¯   -¯   -¯
za 1-1-B
‹ dzhwa'

-zai 'crime; sin'   -¯   ˥-   ˥-   ˥-
(zai)
‹ 'dzhwey

-zai 'drug; dose'   -¯   ˥-   ˥-   ˥-
(zai)
‹ dzhey'

-zi 'material'   -¯   -˥   -¯
zi (‹ di) 0/1-1-B cf. ti
‹ dhi'

-zi 'character, letter'   -¯ (˥-)   -˥   -¯
zi 1-1-B
‹ dzhyey'

-zin 'person'   ˥- (-˥)   -¯   -˥   ˥-
(zin) cf. -nin
‹ .nhyen

-zon 'loss'   -¯   ˥-   -˥   -¯   -¯   ˥-
son 1-2-B
‹ 'swen

-zyo 'place'   -¯   ˥-   -˥   -˥   ˥-
(syo) cf. -syo
‹ 'sro

-zyoo 'place'   -¯   -¯   ˥-
(zyoo)
.dh(r)yang

-zyoo 'on; over; anent' -¯   -¯   -¯
zyoo 1-2-B
‹ zhyang'

-zyoo 'letter, document' -¯   ˥-   -¯   ˥-
(zyoo)
‹ dzh(r)ang'

-zyoo 'state, condition' -¯   -¯   -¯
(zyoo) ?abbr ‹ zyootai
‹ dzhryang'

-zyun 'sequence, order' -¯   -¯   -¯
zyun 0-0-A
‹ zhywen'

-zyuu 'throughout'   -¯   ˥-   -¯
tyuu 1-1-B cf. -tyuu
‹ .t(r)yung

Chart 19.   Atonicizing suffixes not of Chinese origin.   *(Four pages.)*

The more productive patterns are shown; for a fair number of items there are various lexical exceptions. When more than one pattern is indicated the variation may be partly conditioned by the shape or accent of the first element; it may be due to conflicting reports; or it may be random. What appears to be free variation is indicated by the slash "/". Parentheses enclose less common alternatives. Not included are verb infinitives or nouns derived from them (including those which may be "quasi-restrictives" as described in RGJ 133), many of which are included in Okuda's Hiroshima list. Most of the suffixes are dissyllabic nouns of types 2.3 and 2.2 (LH˥ in Tōkyō and Hiroshima, H˥L in Kyōto) but a few are of the other types.

Suffix	Tōkyō			Hiroshima			Kyōto-Ōsaka		
	-‾	ˈ‾	-ˈ	-‾	ˈ‾	-ˈ	-‾	ˈ‾	-ˈ
-ana 'hole' ana 2.3	-‾	(ˈ‾)		?			-‾		
-ba 'place' ba 1.3a	-‾		-ˈ	-‾		-ˈ	-‾		
-bara 'belly' hara 2.3	-‾			?			-‾		
-bata 'side' hata 2.1	-‾			-‾			-‾		
-beri 'rim' heri 2.3	-‾			?			-‾		
-beta 'clumsy' heta 2.3	-‾			-‾			-‾		
-beya 'room' heya 2.3	-‾			-‾			-‾		
-bone 'bone' hone 2.3	-‾			-‾			-‾		
-buro 'bath' huro 2.3	-‾(/) ˈ‾			-‾			-‾		
-busi:									
(1) 'folksong'	-‾			-‾			-‾		
(2) 'dried fish' husi 2.3	-‾			?			-‾	ˈ‾	
-buti 'rim' huti 2.3	-‾			-‾			-‾		
-dama 'ball; bullet; coin' tama 2.3	-‾			-‾			-‾		
-dani 'valley' tani 2.3	-‾			-‾			-‾		
-de 'hand' te 1.3a cf. -te	-‾		(/-ˈ)	-‾			-‾		
-dera 'temple' tera ?2.2a	-‾			?			-‾	ˈ‾	-ˈ
-doki 'time' toki 2.3	-‾		(/-ˈ)	-‾			-‾	ˈ‾	

(Chart 19, p. 2)	Tōkyō	Hiroshima	Kyōto-Ōsaka
-gami 'hair' kami 2.3	-‾　⌐-	?	-‾　(⌐-)　-⌐
-gami 'paper' kami 2.2b	-‾　⌐-	?	-‾　⌐-　-⌐
-gao 'face' kao 2.1	-‾ (/⌐-)(/-⌐)	?	⌐-　-⌐
-gara: (1) 'hull, husk'	-‾	-‾	-‾
(2) 'stem; handle'	-‾	-‾	-‾
(3) 'character' kara 2.2b	-‾	-‾	-‾
-gata₁: (1) 'shape'	-‾	-‾	-‾
(2) 'type' kata 2.2b	-‾	-‾	-‾
-gata₂ 'direction; time/place; person' kata 2.2b	-‾　(⌐-)	?	-‾　(⌐-)
-gata₃ 'persons' kata 2.2b	-‾ / ⌐- / -⌐	?	⌐-
-gawa 'side' (gawa 2.1 ⟨) kawa ?2.2b	-‾	-‾　　-⌐	(-‾/) ⌐-
-giwa 'edge, brink' kiwa 2.3	-‾　　(/-⌐)	-‾　　-⌐	-‾
-goto (1) 'fact' (2) 'words' koto 2.3	-‾　　(/-⌐)	-‾　　-⌐	-‾
-goya 'hut' koya 2.3	-‾	-‾	-‾
-gura 'storehouse' kura 2.3	-‾	-‾	-‾
-gusa (1) 'grass' (2) 'sort' kusa 2.3 cf. -kusa	(-‾) ⌐-		⌐-
-guse 'habit' kuse 2.2b cf. -kuse	-‾	-‾	-‾
-guti 'mouth, opening, entry' kuti 2.1 cf. -kuti	(-‾) ⌐-	?	(-‾) ⌐-
-gutu 'shoes' kutu 2.3	-‾ ⌐-	?	-‾ ⌐-
-hada 'temperament' hada 2.4	-‾ / ⌐-	⌐-	-‾ ⌐-
-imo 'potato' imo 2.3	-‾	-‾	-‾
-iro 'color' iro 2.3	-‾	-‾	-‾

(Chart 19, p. 3)	Tōkyō			Hiroshima		Kyōto-Ōsaka	
-kata:							
(1) 'direction; time/place; person' cf. -gata	-⁻	(¹-)	-¹	-⁻		-⁻	
(2) V-i-kata 'way to V' kata 2.2b	-⁻	¹- / -¹		-⁻	-¹	-⁻	
-ke 'an air of' ke ?1.1	-⁻		-¹	-⁻	-¹	-⁻	¹...-
-ko 'flour, powder' ko 1.3a	-⁻	¹-	-¹	-⁻	-¹	-⁻	
-kusa 'grass' kusa 2.3 cf. -gusa	-⁻	(¹-)		?		-⁻	
-kuse 'habit' kuse 2.2b cf. -guse	-⁻	¹-	-¹		-¹	-⁻	
-kuti 'mouth, opening, entry' kuti 2.1 cf. -guti	-⁻	¹-		?		-⁻	
-ma 'room, space' ma 1.1	-⁻	(¹-)	-¹	-⁻		-⁻	
-mae 'front; portion' mae 2.5	-⁻			-⁻		-⁻	
-mame 'bean' mame 2.3	-⁻	¹-		?		-⁻	(¹-) (-¹)
-me 'eye; point' me 1.3a	-⁻		-¹	-⁻	-¹	-⁻	
-mesi 'meal; rice' mesi 2.3	-⁻	¹-		-⁻	¹-	¹-	-¹
-mi '-ness' Cf. RGJ 911.	-⁻		-¹	-⁻	-¹	-⁻	
-mono 'thing; act; person' mono 2.3	-⁻	¹-	-¹	-⁻	¹-	-⁻	
-moto 'root; source; around' moto 2.3	-⁻		-¹	-⁻	-¹	-⁻	
-mura 'village' mura 2.2b	-⁻			-⁻		-⁻	
-nami 'average; each (in a row); of the order of' nami 2.3	-⁻			-⁻		-⁻	
-nawa 'rope' nawa 2.3	-⁻			-⁻		-⁻	
-ne 'price' ne 1.2	-⁻	¹-		-⁻	¹-	-⁻	
-neko 'cat' neko ?2.3, ?2.5	-⁻		-¹		-¹	-⁻	

(Chart 19, p. 4)	Tōkyō		Hiroshima		Kyōto-Ōsaka	
-no 'moor' no 1.3a	-⁻		-⁻		-⁻	
-numa 'swamp' numa ?2.2b	-⁻		-⁻		-⁻	
-oya 'parent' oya 2.3	-⁻		-⁻		-⁻	
-saki 'destination' saki 2.1	-⁻	(-⁷)	-⁻		-⁻	
-sima 'stripe'; 'island': *see* -zima						
-sita 'under' sita 2.2a	-⁻	(-⁷)	-⁻		-⁻	
-sita 'tongue': *see* -zita						
-soko 'bottom' soko 2.1 cf. -zoko	-⁻		?		-⁻	
-te 'hand; ··· ': (1) V-i-te 'person who V-s' (cf. K 1954:344)	-⁻	-⁷	-⁻	-⁷	-⁻	
(2) other te 1.3a cf. -de	-⁻	-⁷	-⁻	-⁷	-⁻	
-(t)tura 'face' tura 2.3 cf.-zura	-⁻		?		-⁻	
-tuti 'earth, clay' tuti 2.3	-⁻		-⁻		-⁻	
-ura 'reverse' ura 2.3	-⁻		-⁻		-⁻	
-waza 'work; trick' waza 2.2b	-⁻	⁷- -⁷	-⁻		-⁻	
-ya 'shop; house; person; dealer' (cf. ie 2.3)	-⁻		-⁻		-⁻	
-yama 'mountain' yama 2.3	-⁻		?		-⁻	
-yu 'hot water' yu 1.3a	-⁻		-⁻		-⁻	
-zaka 'slope' saka 2.3	-⁻		-⁻		⁷-	
-zata 'news' sata 2.3	-⁻		?		-⁻	⁷-
-zima 'island' sima 2.3	-⁻		?		-⁻	
-zita 'under': *see* -sita						
-zita 'tongue' sita 2.3	-⁻	⁷-			-⁻	
-zoko 'bottom' soko 2.1 cf. -soko	-⁻		-⁻		-⁻	
-zura 'face' tura 2.3 cf. -(t)tura (RGJ 129)	-⁻		-⁻		-⁻	

Chart 20.   Chronology of data sources for earlier accent.

This is a rough guide for quick reference. Dates reflect the earliest
year of composition, publication, or copying; accent markings are not always
of the same period. The list is limited to works that are frequently cited.
More information can be found in Tsukishima 1969:613-32, Kindaichi 1974:225,
and Kokugo-gaku dai-jiten.

700		
	712	Koji-ki
	720	Nihon-Shoki (= Nihon-gi), ko-shahon [old manuscript copies]:
		1000 Iwasaki - bon Kōgyoku-ki
		1142 Zusho-ryō (= Tosho-ryō) - bon Nihon-Shoki
		1150 Maeda - bon Nintoku-ki, Yūryaku-ki, Keitai-ki, Bidatsu-ki
		1150 Kitano - bon Nihon-Shoki
		1303 Kamakura - bon Nihon-Shoki
800		
	830	Tōdai-ji Fuju-monkō
	830	[Saidai-ji - bon] Konkōmyō-saishōō-kyō (Suvaṛa-prabhāsa-uttamarāja-sūtra)
850	850	[Ishiyama-dera - bon] Daihannya-kyō ongi. *See 1286.*
	892	[Shinsen-]Jikyō
900		
	905	Kokin[-waka]-shū. *See 1226.*
	934	Wamyō-[ruiju-]shō
	940	Shōmon-ki (= Masakado-ki). *See 1099.*
950		
1000	1000	*See 720.*
	1040	Daihannya-kyō jishō
1050		
	1079	Konkōmyō-saishōō - kyō ongi
	?1081	[Ruiju -] Myōgi-shō:
		?1081-1100 Zusho-ryō (= Tosho-ryō) - bon ~
		?1179 Kōzan-ji - bon ~
		1241, 1251 Kanchi-in - bon ~
		?1350 Chinkoku-shukoku-jinja - bon ~
	1099	Shinpuku-ji Shōmon-ki. *See 940.*
1100		
	1136	Hoke[-kyō] tanji *(copy)*
	1142	*See 720.*
1150	1150	*See 720.*
	?1179	*See 1081.*
	1180	Iroha-jirui-shō
1200		
	1216	Myōe shōnin: [Shiza -] Kōshiki
	1216	Fujiwara Sadaie/Teika: Teika-kanazukai
	1223	Kusha-ron ongi-shō
	?1226	Date-ke - bon Kokin-waka-shū. *See 905.*
	?1241	Fujiwara Sadaie/Teika: Gekan-shū. *Copy 1280.*
	1241	*See 1081.*
	1268/75	Myōgo-ki I/II *(Kindaichi 1964a:338 has '1270'.)*
	?1270	Butsuyuigyōkyō. *Reflects accent of Insei or early Kamakura (Sakurai 1976:110-31).*
	1278-93	Nihon-gi shi-ki *(Eight commentaries on Nihon-Shoki. Copies 1427, 1428.)*
	1286	[Tenri-toshokan - zō] Daihannya-kyō ongi. *See 850.*

1300	13--?	hyōhyaku: Mie[i]-ku ~ , Daihannya ~ , ··· . *List in Sakurai 1975:225 n.22.*
	1303	*See 720.*
	1305	Watarai [brothers] Enmei (= 'Nobuaki', *Kindaichi 1974:216*) and Ensei (?= Nobumasa): [Kokin- [waka-shū]] Kunten-shō. *Present text later. See Kindaichi 1964a:322 n.3.*
	?1310	Hasso saimon: other saimon (Mie[i]-ku ~ , Myōjin-kō ~). *See Sakurai 1976:107. Cf. 1675.*
	1333	Jōben: [Jōben - bon] Shūi[-waka]-shū. *Early-Kamakura accent.*
1350	?1350	*See 1081.*
	1363	Gyōa: Kanamoji-zukai
	1381	Emperor Chōkei: Sengen-shō
1400	14--?	rongi[-sho] = zō-shōmyō. *Chanting guides that reflect early-Kamakura accent.*
	1427/60	Nihon-gi *(Nihon-Shoki)* shi-ki: Mikanagi - bon ~ . *Early-Kamakura accent. See 1278-93.*
	1428	Nihon-gi *(Nihon-Shoki)* shi-ki: Ōei - bon ~ . *Early-Kamakura accent. See 1278-93.*
1450	1455	Konparu Zenpō: Mōtan-shichin-shō. *Dialect accent.*
1500	1500	Tōin Sanehiro: Myōmoku-shō. *Also referred to as Kai-gō Myōmoku-shō.*
	1563	Daishō-hyakujō [dai] san-jū yomikuse
1600		
	1608	Rodriguez: Arte da lingoa de Iapam
1650		
	1675	Busshōe saimon, Mie[i]-ku saimon. *Cf. ?1310.*
	1687	Bumō-ki.[1] *Late-Muromachi or early-Edo accent.*
	?1690	'Kyōdai - Heike' = Kyōto-dai[gaku] - bon Heike-monogatari. *Early-Edo accent.*
	1695	Keichū: Waji-shōran-shō.
	1697	Keichū: Waji-shōran-tsūbō-shō. *Kamakura accent?*
1700		
1750		
	1754	Monnō(/Bunnō): Waji-taikan-shō.
	1777	Ogino Chiichi [kengyō]: Heike-seisetu/-mabushi[2]
	1778	Fujitani Nariakira: Ayui-shō
	1785	Motoori Norinaga: Kanji-san'on-kō
1800		

[1]Also called Humō-ki, Hōbō-ki, and Bibō-ki. The now-standard reading Bumō-ki dates from the mid-1930s.

[2]See §15 n.2.

Chart 21. Historical development.

Modern Kyōto 4 Edo 3 Mr 2 Km 1 circa 1100   1 ? 2 ? 3 ? Modern Tōkyō

```
                              ō-o                    → o-o
t̄i(:) ga                      1.1 ti 'blood'                      ti ga

                              ōo-o                   → oo-o
k̄aze ga                       2.1 kaze 'wind'                     kaze ga

                              ōoo-o                  → ooo-o
k̄atati ga                     3.1 katati                         katati ga

                              ō¹-o              → ᵗō-o¹ → o-ō 1.1
h̄a¹(:) ga                     1.2 ha 'leaf'                 ↑  ha ḡa 1.1

                              ō¹o-o ?← ᵗōo¹-o   2.1          hito ga 2.1,
h̄ī¹to ga                    ↓ 2.2a hito 'person'  ↑↓          hito¹ ga 2.2b
                        2.2b  ō¹o-o             2.2b → ᵗoo¹-o → ...
ī¹si ga                       2.2b isi 'stone'                    isi¹ ga

                              ōo¹o-o ?← ᵗoo¹-o   3.1
.tōka¹ge ga 3.7b ↓ ¹ōo¹o-o ← 3.2a tokage 'gecko'  ↑          tokage ga 3.1
              3.7b            ōo¹o-o            → ᵗooo¹-o → ...
ā¹zuki ga 3.3   ↓ ō¹oo-o ←    3.2b azuki 'redbean'                azuki¹ ga
              3.3
                              ō¹oo-o                         ↓
h̄a¹tati ga                    3.3 hatati 'twenty' 3.7b          h̄a¹tati ga 3.7b
--------------------------------------------------------------------------------
                              ¹o-o ← ᵗ¹o-o
.te(:) ḡa 1.3b             ↓  1.3a te 'hand'  ↓                  te¹ ga 1.3b
                    1.3b   ¹o-ō              1.3b → o¹-o
.su(:) ḡa                     1.3b su 'nest'                     su¹ ga
                2.2b
              ↑ ō¹o-o ←       ¹oo-o          → oo¹-o → ...  2.2b
ȳa¹ma ga 2.2b                 2.3 yama 'mountain'            ↑ yama¹ ga 2.2b
         3.3 ō¹oo-o ← ōo¹o-o ← ¹ooo-o  → ᵗo¹oo-o → ōoo¹-o 3.2b
k̄a¹gami ga 3.3 ↑             3.4 kagami 'mirror'             ↑ kagami¹ ga 3.2b
              3.3 ō¹oo-o ←    ¹ooo-o          3.1
ā¹bura ga 3.3     ↑           3.5a abura 'oil'  ↑                abura ga 3.1
                              ¹ooo-o ?← ¹o¹oō¹-o → oō¹o-o → ō¹oo-o ↓
n̄a¹mida ga 3.3               3.5b namida 'tears'          3.7b n̄a¹mida ga 3.7b
                              ¹oo-ō                → ō¹o-o
.matu ḡa   ¹oo-ō̄ ← ¹oo-ō ←   2.4 matu 'pine'                    n̄a¹tu ga
                              ¹ooo-ō               3.1
.usagi ḡa  ¹ooo-ō̄ ← ¹ooo-ō ← 3.6 usagi 'rabbit'  ↑             usagi ga 3.1
                              ¹oo¹-o              → ō¹o-o 2.4
.sarū¹(:) ga                  2.5 saru 'monkey'          ↑      sa¹ru ga 2.4
                          ↓   ¹oo¹o-o ?← ᵗ¹ooo¹-o 3.1
.kusu¹ri ga 3.7b      3.7b    3.7a kusuri 'drug'  ↑             kusuri ga 3.1
                              ¹oo¹o-o             → o¹oo-o
.kabu¹to ga                   3.7b kabuto 'helmet'              ka¹buto ga
```

Notes to Chapter 4.

Notes to Chapter 4, §1.

¹ On the pronunciation of atonic phrases as all-low "in rapid speech" in Tōkyō-type dialects of northern Honshū (e.g. Morioka) and Hokkaidō (e.g. Sapporo), see Hirayama 1955:54a. The Kyōto-type dialects of Toyama and Suzu also have a low flat tune: see Ch. 5. It has been observed that the Tōkyō initial low is not quite so noticeably low as the distinctive Kyōto initial low; also, that Tōkyō's prototonic high is not so markedly high as the later distinctive high in the other tonic types.

² And Kindaichi 1955b:335 observes that Ōsaka may be in the process of eliminating the rise altogether, leaving all-low stretches instead. On the "gentle rise" version of the low stretch, cf. Okumura 1975c.156, 157.

³ Sakurai 1967 and 1978b:76, on the basis of earlier notations of the accent, concludes that -T- formed a single syllable with the preceding mora "up to the Muromachi period", though Vn and V: were treated as two syllables; but aside from the analyst's artifact the only evidence for a later separate-syllable status must be the notoriously unreliable but much beloved "native speaker's intuition". On the intuition that the locus occurs on the silent mora, cf. Haraguchi 101-3. I account for it on the basis of canonical types. See also Okuda 1975:136n. Yukawa 1984:2:19 wisely concludes that (for Wakayama) the -T- is to be treated as low except when it is immediately between two highs.

Notes to Chapter 4, §2.

¹ And for o̅k̅u̅ na 'don't put!' according to the Ōsaka data of Maeda and Makimura; cf. kak̅u̅ na. Kindaichi 1964a:339-40 claims that modern Kinki dialects have the pattern (?)o̅ku na "because it is from the predicative rather than the attributive", but the stated pattern is otherwise unconfirmed, so I have questioned it.

² Apparently unique among the Kyōto-type dialects, Takamatsu (and vicinity) treats dissyllabic Type-A imperfects as they were treated in 12th-century Kyōto: o̅ku 'put'. Trisyllabic Type-A imperfects are similar, but the first syllable is unexpectedly lowered: ire̅ru 'insert'. The trisyllabic Type-B imperfects follow the pattern of originally low-atonic nouns (Type 3.4) in merging with the high atonic (3.1), as happened for these verbs (but not the nouns) also — and independently — in Kyōto. The dissyllabic Type-B stems are like those of Kyōto: kak̅u̅ 'write'. See Hirayama 1957b:249-51.

³ Monosyllabic infinitives are often lengthened before -te in dialects of Shikoku (Doi 1958:188, 276). Kindaichi (1963:93, 103) says "in the dialect of Kyōto in the Heian period" gerunds like mi-te "were trisyllabic, with a long initial syllable".

Notes to Chapter 4, §3.

[1] Nouns are distinguished by locus as well as register; why are the verb stems distinguished only by register? Serafim has made the suggestion that perhaps this is because the stems were all originally compounds that include an auxiliary, such as wi[y]- 'be', and there is a general rule that the locus of the first element drops, i.e. is irrelevant to the locus in the accent of the compound. But since a majority of shorter nouns do not have distinctive locus, either, perhaps the locus in the minority that have it owes to something else that we are overlooking.

[2] Kindaichi 1973:79 calls our attention to four groups of exceptions:

(1) The verb stems hiroge- 'widen it' and hirogar- 'get widespread' are A, but the adjective stem hiro- 'wide' is B in most dialects and in Heian attestations; yet dialects of Niigata and further north indicate that the earliest accent for the adjective stem must have been A and it was probably absorbed into the "majority" type accent for adjectives.

(2) The adjectival noun akiraka (Heian aki͞raka) 'bright, clear' is B but other derivatives of ak- 'open; dawn' are A, as is the verb stem itself; all four-syllable adjectival nouns ending in -ka, -yaka, or -raka are assigned a canonical accent pattern which overrides the etymological register.

(3) The color name aka 'red' is B (aka̍ in Kyōto) but the adjective stem aka- 'be red' is A; the noun probably shifted its accent by analogy with siro 'white' and kuro 'black' (siro̍ and kuro̍ in Kyōto), which form adjective stems of Type B. The adjectives kura- 'be dark' and siru- 'be quite clear' are A but it is not certain that they are etymologically related to 'black' and 'white'; the verbs kure- 'get dark' and sir- 'know' are both A.

(4) Although kore 'this' and sore 'that' are A (in Kyōto k͞ore and s͞ore), the related words koko 'here' and soko 'there' are B in Kyōto as far back as the Heian period (ko͞ko and so͞ko) and they are B also in Kagoshima; yet Tōkyō gives them the same accent as kore 'this' and sore 'that'. No explanation has been offered; but notice the Tōkyō homophone clash with soko 'bottom', which Kyōto avoids.

[3] With the unusual exception of Oki island; see Uwano 1984b.

Notes to Chapter 4, §4.

[1] Although only the Kyōto-type dialects distinguish 1.2 from 1.1 (just as only they distinguish 2.5 from 2.4) there is evidence that a three-way division of monosyllables must predate the split between these dialects and those of the Tōkyō type. In the Tōkyō-type dialects of Okayama, type 1.1 is kept distinct from 1.3 everywhere (as in Tōkyō, Ōita, and Kagoshima) and 1.2 goes with 1.1 in some areas (as it does in Tōkyō and Kagoshima) but with 1.3 in other areas. Cf. Mushiaki 1954. Kindaichi 1977b:465 cites evidence from other Tōkyō-type dialects, e.g. Totsukawa.

² Although Sapporo is like Tōkyō for 'god', Hiroshima has the expected regular accent ka̅m̅i̅, ka̅m̅i̅ ga. Tōkyō and Sapporo are both aberrant, but the older Tōkyō form is regular, like the Hiroshima form. A similar example is haha 'mother'; both haha 'mother' and kami 'god' were low-high in Tōkyō at the end of the Edo period (i.e. late 19th-century), according to Akinaga 1967:142.

³ Sapporo has the expected regular accent ku̅m̅o̅, ku̅m̅o̅ ga. Apparently Hiroshima, too, has the regular accent (Okuda 1975:291); Hirayama 1960:36 gives the Tōkyō irregularity also for Hiroshima but that may be a misprint. According to Hattori (1931-3:2:20) about twenty dissyllabic nouns in Hiroshima prefecture differ from the Tōkyō accent, including kumo 'cloud', kiba 'fang', tako 'kite', and tako 'octopus'.

⁴ The expected regular accent k̅i̅si, k̅i̅si ga is found in Kōchi. Kyōto is aberrant.

⁵ For more details on the accent of Ibuki-jima see Senoo 1966 and Wada 1966a. I am indebted to Thomas Robb for calling my attention to misprints in Wada 1966b and to several interesting facts about this material.

⁶ The word for 'sea' (umi) is aberrant in both dialects; there are a few other words listed by Wada as aberrant in one dialect or in both, and they are all two-syllable nouns with a close final vowel but display no pattern that would account for the aberrancies.

Notes to Chapter 4, §5.

¹ The earliest syo'o-ten date from 897, but Ennin may have used them a bit earlier (Tsukishima 1977:58-9).

² It is unclear whether the slight "oddness" felt about the Tōkyō prototonic patterns may be related; note the initial accent of dissyllabic family names, female personal names, and Chinese two-mora binoms, as well as mimetic reduplications.

³ Kindaichi distrusts the evidence for assigning e (< fe) to 1.1. On the basis of the Edo attestations and the modern dialects, he would place it in 1.3 as e (< f̅e̅).

⁴ But Kindaichi (1964a:405ff) would treat the adjective endings as -s̅i̅i̅/-z̅i̅i̅ and -k̅i̅i̅. (This is based on Kamakura materials and research by Tsukishima and Komatsu.) Cf. §9 n.1, n.2.

⁵ But in Kamakura materials, at least, m̅o̅ attached high after an atonic low; cf. Okumura 1975a, and notice Kz Mg koto m̅u̅ (= m̅o̅) nas̅i̅ (Mochizuki 215a). Kindaichi, on the basis of Komatsu's findings, would treat this particle as m̅o̅o̅ — as, in effect, would Sakurai (see below). Kindaichi 1960b:16-7 suggests that those particles which are intrinsically low (or "preaccented") in modern Kinki dialects had a fall in Heian times; he adduces examples of yo̖ = y̅o̅o, and ka̖ = k̅a̅a, as well as mo̖ = m̅o̅o̅.

⁶ Examples of f̅a̅: f̅i̅to f̅a̅ 'persons' (NS 114a), s̅u̅w̅e̅-fye f̅a̅ 'the top part' (70b), fayabusa f̅a̅ 'the falcon' (73c); k̅y̅i̅y̅i̅s̅i̅ f̅a̅ 'the pheasant' (83b), k̅u̅n̅i̅ ni f̅a̅ 'in the country' (81c), wa̅r̅e̅ f̅a̅ 'I' (74c), ka̅k̅ye f̅a̅ 'the rooster' (83b), moto-f̅y̅e̅ f̅a̅ 'at the

bottom' (70b), ... Examples of w̄o: tati w̄o 'sword' (NS 130a), fara-kara w̄o 'one related to us' (107a), f̄yito w̄o 'the people' (91b), s̄uwe-fye w̄o b̄a 'the top part' (83c), kokoro kimo w̄o '(with) their whole hearts' (132b); k̄yimyi w̄o 'lord' (70b), k̄uti w̄o 'horses' bits' (126a), watari w̄o 'the crossing' (87b), katati w̄o 'the state of affairs' (108b), ware w̄o 'me' (74c), imo w̄o 'the loved one' (70b), moto-f̄ye w̄o b̄a 'the base part' (83c), ...

[7] But Nihon-Shoki has this particle always high: n̄a ḡa 'you' (NS 73a, 76b), s̄i ḡa 'he/it' (79c), ono ["]k̄a mono k̄ara 'on account of his own things' (95a), far̄i ḡa ȳeda 'alder-tree branch' (95a); wa ḡa 'I' (passim), it̄uk̄yi ḡa ūfey no 'of [the area] above the second grove' (73c).

[8] But Kindaichi (1964a:336-7) observes that versions like īsi ga are more common in Kamakura texts while those of the earlier Insei (or late-Heian) period mostly have versions like īsi ḡa = īsi | ḡa. He takes this as evidence for a diachronic change in phrasing habits.

[9] Okumura (1975a:96) thinks the original pattern was yòri (= ȳoori). A phrase like ima mate ni 'by now' in the Maeda text of Nihon-Shoki (Ishizuka 1977:100b, 103a) must have had a juncture after the first word. Perhaps yori is not unique; cf. (Ishizuka 1977:95a) ono ["]k̄a mono k̄ara 'on account of his own things'.

[10] Cf. sifasu ni 'in the last month of winter' (NS 110b). All other examples in Nihon-Shoki are after high pitch: m̄yit̄i ni 'on the way' (81a), n̄ifa ni 'in the courtyard' (74b), k̄afa ni [sic] 'into the river' (94c), f̄uye n̄i tukur̄i 'making it into a flute' (83c), wat̄ari n̄i 'at the crossing' (70a); kōko ni 'here' (70b), sōko ni 'there' (70b), ofo k̄yimȳi n̄i 'to the great lord' (75c, 76c, 79b), ware n̄i 'to me' (83a), imo n̄i 'to my loved one' (83a).

[11] There seem to be no examples after low pitch.

[12] Cf. kōto n̄i tukur̄i 'making it into a harp' (NS 83c).

[13] The explanation (Kindaichi 1964a:438) is that a stretch of low plateau followed by a high plateau was avoided "perhaps because it sounded like a sequence of two words", and the shorter LH-no and LLH-no were similarly adjusted (to LH-L and LLH-L) by analogy with the longer stretches. Kindaichi says the phonetic sequence LLHH is found only in Nagoya and Tokushima of the modern dialects; but it is also found in northern Okinawa (Nakijin).

[14] The ordering of entries in the 12th-century Iroha-jirui-shō kept high-pitched "wo" = [w̄o] distinct from the low-pitched "o" = [wo] (Komatsu 1977:369), and that distinction was maintained in a number of other texts (Tsukishima 1977:20).

[15] My interpretation of the relevant Chinese tones differs from Takayama in a few instances of minor consequence. A number of the phonograms are traditionally assigned to more than one tone class. This causes no difficulty except when the

"Even" tone is involved. The phonograms assigned to both the Even tone and the
Rising (or "Raised") tone are ambivalent, and I have marked the ambiguous accent of
these as "Ḟ" (for the Chinese graphs see Ōno 1953:278-80):

> te CLAN-ONE (also te BOW-ONE ?< CLAN-ONE), byi and myi BOW-YOU (Takayama has
> this as Even only and myi WATER-BOW-YOU as Even-or-Raised but we treat that as
> Raised only); ru DRAG (left side of NUMBER) and zi MUSHROOM belong with this
> group but each appears in two kun-chū only.

A similar intepretation of "Ḟ" is given to phonograms that are assigned to both the
Going tone and the Even tone:

> fey/bey DOUBLE (Takayama has only H), ma/ba FINE/QUERY, ma/ba POLISH (Takayama:
> Raised only), mo EXPECT, myi/byi BOW-YOU, ro RUGGED MAJESTY, sa STONE-DISCREPANCY,
> sa SHED, ta/da HORSE LOAD, wa HARMONY, wa MUDDY WATER, wa EXCEED, wi DO; za STORE
> (= zau) and si THINK belong with this group but are normally used for L only;
> su TRANSPORT and zu BABY belong here but are normally used for H only.

A number of phonograms that belong here are used very little: te TOPIC, de DAUB,
nwo/nu ANGER (also dwo in Ōno's list but with no examples), na DIFFICULT.
Takayama puts ku BENT and ku COUPLET here, but I treat them as just Raised (= H);
the same is true of ma RUB.

There are three clearly ambivalent phonograms that belong to three traditional tone
classes (Even, Raised, and Going), and these are treated as ambiguous "Ḟ":

> fyi COMPARE, sa WATER-LITTLE-WOMAN (Takayama: Even only), wi ENTRUST.

With Takayama, I treat na THAT/WHAT as just Even (= L); and yo GIVE can be treated
as just High. A few other three-tone phonograms are ambivalent but predominantly
used for the Low pitch:
ne/de/di MUD, du STONE ARROWHEAD, si GIVE ALMS, se EQUAL/RADICAL-210.
But MUD and STONE ARROWHEAD are little used.

Notes to Chapter 4, §6. *(There are no notes to §6.)*

Notes to Chapter 4, §7.

¹ The "lengthened" monosyllables are pronounced the same as geminate vowels from
other sources, such as the joining of two morphemes. Thus the minimal threesome:
t͞i(i) 'blood', t͟i(i) 'earth', t͞i-i 'position'.

² Hattori 1951:55-6 set up a fourth type for ha 'tooth' and [w]e 'bait' to account
for the fact that the Kyōto forms are high-low (i.e. fall), hence marked "2" in our
notation, rather than the low-high (i.e. rise) that we mark as "1". These two words
are apparently the only examples; hi 'fire', ni 'load', su 'reed screen', and su
'nest' are low-high in Kyōto. Since all of these words all have the low-high (rise)
notation in Myōgi-shō (but 'fire' and 'load' only by inference, see below) we will
treat them as 1.3b and leave the Kyōto accents of 'tooth' and 'bait' as unexplained
anomalies: the nouns have slipped out of their historic categories. But Kindaichi
1964a assumes that 'nest' was *LH-H and 'tooth' was *LH-L making a "monosyllabic"

parallel to 2.5; see also Kindaichi 1983. Under our interpretation of "double-low" patterns it is hard to see how this type could be accounted for. One reason for assuming that proto-Japanese had initial L for 'nest' and 'tooth' and other nouns of Type 1.3b is that they are B in Kagoshima and the Ryūkyūs. In the same paper Hattori rightly rejects segregating na 'name' and hi 'sun; day' from Type 1.2 merely because of the irregularity implied by Myōgi-shō markings as low rather than high; and Mochizuki carries one Myōgi-shō version of hi 'sun; day' that is marked with the expected high.

³ Cf. yanofe < ya-no [u]fe 'rooftop'; but also sú-no | ko 'narrow slat of wood'.

⁴ Kindaichi 1951b:684 argues that the upper-right dot is to be interpreted as representing a rise from low to high because it occurs only on the first syllable of a word, allowing patterns like LHH(H) or LH(H)L, but *HL(L)H would be unusual within a word. Phonetic patterns of HLHL are found in certain modern dialects (e.g. Narada, Goka-mura on Oki island, dialects of the Izu islands) but at least one of the high pitches is always non-distinctive. Cf. Sakurai 1963:20a, 30a n.1.

⁵ See Endō 1974:42a. (But his notation LHL appears to be a misprint for LHH; cf. Mochizuki 1974a:482-3.)

⁶ This is ugoma, ugoma, and ogoma in Kanchi-in Myōgi-shō (Mochizuki 82b, 108b) and ugoma in Wamyō-shō (Asayama 1943:426) but in one version also "lately ugóma" (Numoto 1979:27). Compare Shuri quguma B.

⁷ Iroha-jirui-shō.

⁸ This dot represents what is called to'o-sei/-syoo 'the "east" tone' or hyo'o-syoo / he'i-sei no karu (also hyoosyoo-/heisei-kei) 'the "light" [version of the] even tone'.

⁹ According to Umegaki (NKD); Hirayama fails to list gittyò, but the same accentuation is cited by Kindaichi 1944:195 for Wakayama. Wakayama also has kottè 'bull' and otonbò 'youngest son' (Yukawa 1984:2:18).

¹⁰ In Maizuru mukasì, according to Kindaichi 1944:195; he also gives Maizuru yamazarù 'mountain monkey', Akō tunbò 'deaf-mute' (Kyōto tunbo), and Akō and Maizuru sarù 'monkey' (Kyōto sarù). These are examples of the ongoing erosion of the low register which started before 1300 (§10, n.1). Wakayama has kakkò 'looks' < *kakkoo (Kyōto kakkoo) and hanbù 'half' < *hanbun (Kyōto hanbun).

Notes to Chapter 4, §8.

¹ I make the bold assumption that the attributive was originally atonic for all verbs, but the Kamakura markings (as in Shiza-Kōshiki) indicate a tonic ending for Type-B stems, such that the pattern is identical with that of the predicative: matu ni, miru ni, firaku [koto], nagasu [mono]; but it is, of course, one syllable longer in the case of bigrade stems such as naguru ni which has the predicative

nagu. The tonic ending is also indicated for Type-A bigrade (polysyllabic) stems: naduru [koto], kofuru [koto]. The expression omofu ni looks like an exception, but it is noted as omofu ni in Zusho-ryō Myōgi-shō; the late-Heian accentuation of these attributives was apparently like that of the Kamakura notations, as can be seen also in firumu yamafi 'paralyzing ailment' in Kanchi-in Myōgi-shō. And the Maeda text of Nihon-Shoki has fafu musi mo 'even a creeping insect' (Ishizuka 76b), fanatu ya 'the arrow he lets fly' (129b), taturu kotodate 'the announcement that one makes' (71a), isaturu koto 'weeping' (130b); yet also fomuru kowe (= kowe) 'praising voices' (98, 99). See also the following note.

² Many of the exceptions are simply the same as the infinitive, as if the "atonicizing" process that is used to mark the derivation of noun from infinitive had failed to be applied. The attributive atonicization may be a similar kind of derivational process, also with frequent failure to apply, as in the preceding note. The atonicizing process can be observed in nouns reduced from phrases, such as fitotonari 'character, nature, disposition' ← *fito to nari 'become as a person'; the attested phrase fito to naru 'become adult' is partially atonicized already.

³ The attested accent patterns of subjunctive forms are not as consistent as we would like, but reflexes of the expected patterns can be found. For A-stems:
se["]su (NS 96b, 116b), kyikazu (NS 74b), kyikoyezu (NS 81b), ki["]sara["]su (NS 96b); ifamu (NS 117a), oyo["]famu to (NS 106a), watarafamu (NS 108a); è sezi (Mg), sikazi (Mg), kayofa["]si (NS 121a); senu ka (Mg).
And for B-stems:
afamu ka mo (NS 72a), kakeymu yo (NS 80a), afe tamafamu to (NS 128a); omofazu ni (Mg); yurusa["]si to (NS 103b); aranu (Mg), mitanu ka (Mg).
But most attestations of the B-stem forms with -zu seem to show a metathesis of the pitch of the ending with that of the last syllable of the subjunctive:
(?*arazu →) arazu (Mg), yurusa["]su (NS 103b), tamafa["]su (NS 92b, 105a).
And most attestations of A-stems with -mu seem to atonicize the pattern:
(?*semu →) semu (Mg, NS 95a), semu to (NS 116b) = semu to (NS 113b), siramu (NS 94a), siramu ya (NS 91b), ifamu ya (Mg), narabeymu (NS 79b), maturamu to (NS 79b), yasinafamu (NS 70c, 71a).
Similar attestations appear in the Kamakura materials (Km W):
ara["]su, mise["]su; semu, yaramu, wataramu.
These materials also atonicize a number of A-stem examples with -nu, the negative attributive: senu, siranu, sutenu, somenu, itaranu, yamanu ka. A few examples are found earlier: kyikosanu (NS 81b), maturanu (NS 108b), mitibikanu ka (Mg). At some still earlier stage of the language, I suspect, there was probably a juncture that separated the auxiliaries -mu and -nu (with its infinitive -ni) from

the subjunctive, which was perhaps simply the stem; if so, then our "ending" -a would have to be treated as either a reanalysis (an emerging morpheme) or a fictive device. In addition to the presumptive -mu and the negative -nu, the passive, the causative, and the subject-exaltation (honorific) auxiliaries attach to this form, too: tukafa-su 'deign to send on a mission' (NS 127a), tukafa-sa-re te 'being sent on a mission' (93b), tukura-simu 'have them make it' (115b).

⁴ Also ife domo.

⁵ An aberrant version sinu appears in the Nihon-Shoki notes (NS 131a [14:401-KW]). Similar: inu (mistake for *inu?) 'depart', attributive inuru, infinitive *ini; imperative ine. These two verbs are uniquely a blend of consonant-stem (yo-dan) and vowel-stem (ni-dan) conjugations. Cf. inu (mistake for inu?) 'sleep', unattested attributive *inuru, infinitive ine.

⁶ Attested: sinuru tumi 'a crime to die for' (NS 107b).

⁷ Cf. si ga tukuru made ni 'until it is spent' (NS 79a [14:314-M]); the bigrade stem tuki[y]- 'get exhausted' is Type A in the Nihon-Shoki, as is its transitive counterpart tukus- (NS 133a [14:426-K]).

⁸ It is unclear whether kufi-mono 'stuff to eat' contains the infinitive or the derived noun.

⁹ There are two versions attested for 'strip and tear': fagi yaburu, fagi-yaburu.

¹⁰ Apparently meaning 'burin' (?).

¹¹ Perhaps *simi > simo 'frost'?

¹² Cf. nani ni ka tukafu 'for what is it used?' (NS 110b); the attributive is called for by the preposed interrogative particle. Also: tukafu koto 'its use' (NS 110b) vs. tukafu 'use them' (NS 101b, 111a).

¹³ Mochizuki 1974a:612a.

¹⁴ This is probably a scribal error; we expect *katari te.

¹⁵ When an ending was attached to a 3-syllable stem to make a 4-syllable form, the final low metathesized with the basic high of the ending. Similarly with the longer stems. But in Nihon-Shoki (Okada) the following verbs are marked LLL-H: unagasu 'urge', obofosu (= omofosu) 'deign to think', kitamasu 'deign to chastise', "tukurafu" (= tukurofu) 'mend', toyomosu 'make it resound', and "mokoyofu" = mogoyofu (A in Myōgi-shō) 'wriggle along'. Two of these (obofosu and tukurofu) are cited as LLL-L in Ishizuka; at least the first is the attributive form, as predicted in the chart.

¹⁶ But with V-(a)-simu 'cause to V' the pattern is LLL-H: suma-simu 'cause to dwell', obi-simu 'cause to wear (around the waist)', ka(u)bura-simu 'cause to wear (on the head)'. With Type-A verb: se-simu 'cause to do'.

17 For Kindaichi s̲u̲u̲.

18 Attested as k̅i̅i̲ kufu = k̲i̲ ku̲f̅u̲ 'wear and eat' (Kanchi-in Mg).

19 Mochizuki 1974a:181a, 612b. Kindaichi thinks this ought to be k̅i̅te̲ or k̅i̅i̲ t̅e̲.

20 Related forms: n̅i̅-ta̲ri̲/-ta̅r̅i̲/-t̲a̅r̅i̲; for Kindaichi n̅i̅ta̲r̅i̅i̲

21 Attested: yu̲mi̲ i̅r̅u̲ ko̲to̲ no̲ (NS 101b).

22 Iroha-jirui-shō f̲i̲r̅u̲.

23 Also: m̲i̲-r̅e̲b̲a̲.

24 For the citations mi̲r̅u̲ n̅i̅ (Kanchi-in and Chinkoku-shukoku-jinja Mg), see n.1.

25 Examples: mí a̲gur̅e̅b̲a̲, mí / m̅i̅ u̲ka̲g̅a̅f̅u̅, me̲ mí f̅a̅r̲u̲. Kindaichi thinks the single m̅i̅ citation is a textual mistake in Kanchi-in Mg.

26 Like ko̲g̲e̅r̅u̲ 'get scorched'. The longer kogareru 'burn (= yearn)' is absorbed into Type A in Kyōto; the stem kogare- is attested in Myōgi-shō only as the first member of a couple of compounds, but the predicative form (kogaru) appears with the pattern LLL in Shiza-Kōshiki (Kamakura period). The Myōgi-shō verb ne̲y̲a̲su̲ 'knead' is Type B´ but it does not survive in the modern dialects. The verb sasageru 'hold up, offer' is B´ in Myōgi-shō but all modern dialects treat it as A. Okada cites Nihon-Shoki ko̲y̲a̲su̲ 'deign to lie flat' and o̲b̲a̲su̲ / o̲ba̲su̲ 'deign to gird'.

27 The verb asobu is treated this way also in Ōsaka and in Kameyama (Kindaichi 1942:169), and in Hyōgo and Suzu (Hirayama). The accent is a̲s̅o̅b̅u̲ in Kōchi and a̲s̲o̅b̅u̲ in Takamatsu according to Kindaichi 1942:169; but the Kōchi version in Hirayama is regular high atonic a̅s̅o̅b̅u̲, and Hattori 1931-3:2:179 says the Kōchi form is Type B (a̲so̲b̲u̲), like aruku 'walk', so that there appear to be several subvarieties of Kōchi accent for this verb. The verb ugoku 'move' is u̲g̲o̲k̲u̲ in Kōchi, Tanabe, and Akō, and u̲g̲o̅k̅u̲ in Shingū; elsewhere, the Kinki-type pattern is high atonic (u̅g̅o̅k̅u̲) as in Kyōto. The dialects of Kōchi, Tanabe, Akō, and Shingū, while converting the low-initial verbs of original Type B with infinitives of three or more syllables into high-initial stems, still keep them a different type ("tonic Type A") from the stems of "atonic Type A", with which they have merged in Kyōto. Longer examples: Kōchi t̅a̅s̅u̲ke̲ru̲, o̲d̲o̲r̅o̅k̅u̲, ... for Kyōto's t̅a̅s̅u̅keru̅, o̅d̅o̅roku̅, ... The Kyōto enlargement of the atonic (Type A) class of verb stems occurred after the first part of the Edo period (cf. Hattori 1931-3:3:16), perhaps in the early 1700s.

28 The "B" accentuation of Nagoya — and, presumably, that of Tōkyō too — is probably the result of Kinki phonetic influence; earlier in this eastern area the verb oru 'be' was not in use, being replaced by iru.

29 Kanchi-in Myōgi-shō has both s̅i̅nu̲ and s̅i̅n̲u̲, but only i̅n̅u̲.

30 It is tempting to relate the initial rise of the Iroha-jirui-shō notation, if that is real, with the long rising accent of Middle Korean mwo̲:t. The Korean

accent might reflect a dropped final vowel, such as the Japanese -a. The modern
Korean spelling (mos) is an analogical restructuring by which only verb stems are
allowed to end in /t/. The /s/ appears morphophonemically in the noun calmos(-ita)
'(it's) a mistake', derived from cal mot(-hanta) 'can't (do) well'. To be kept in
mind: the Chinese etyma m(b)ywet 'don't!' and m(b)ek/?m(b)ok 'be silent'. Old
Japanese moda is also predicated with ar- and wor- 'be': moda wor[y]i te[y] (M 350),
nakanaka ni moda aramasi wo (M 612), moda mo aramu (M 3976).

³¹ But the Kyōto dialect (and probably all the other Kinki dialects) absorbed
into Type A those compound verbs made on monosyllabic Type B infinitives, namely de
'emerge', ki 'come', and mi 'see'. There are only a few dictionary examples of the
first two: ki-awaseru, ki-kakeru; de-au, de-baru, de-mawaru, de-mukaeru, de-sakaru.
The third offers many examples: mi-au, mi-ataru, mi-naosu, mi-sokonau, mi-tukeru,
mi-tumoru, ... These verbs all follow the regular compound pattern in Tōkyō and
in Kagoshima. But mitomeru 'recognize' (from mi-tomeru, see note 33) has been
lexicalized as Type A for all Tōkyō speakers (mitomeru), though that is the regular
accentuation only for speakers following the older rules; we would expect the
younger speakers to say *mitomeru if they were treating it as a compound, and
that is indeed the accentuation found in NE Kyūshū and in Hamada, Matsue, and
Izumo, though Hattō is like Tōkyō. The Kyōto form is irregular in that it is NOT
absorbed into Type A, but gets the same treatment as compounds made on dissyllabic
tonic infinitives: mitomeru thus joins kakureru 'hide' as Type B; other simple
stems of three or more syllables are all absorbed into Type A. Other Tōkyō
lexicalizations include:
    mitukeru 'find' with no younger *mitukeru — though that is the form found in
Hattō, Hamada, Matsue, and Izumo;
    otituku 'calm down' with no younger *otituku — though that is the form found in
Hamada, Matsue, and Izumo, but Hattō is like Tōkyō;
    mihoreru 'lose oneself in looking at' with no younger *mihoreru;
    kaerimiru 'look back' with no older *kaerimiru;
    tukiau 'associate (with)' with no older *tukiau (cf. RGJ 440 n.36).
The reason the Kyōto dialect has treated the compounds made on these monosyllabic
B-stem infinitives as Type A is that the infinitives themselves are pronounced as if
they were from Type A verbs: as a result of contraction, the infinitive kī < ki-i
'come' sounds the same as kī < kī-i 'wear'. The infinitive of i- 'shoot an arrow'
is treated as Type B (tonic) in Tōkyō, where it is often replaced by a consonant-
stem conjugation with the infinitive īri (RGJ 393), but that accentuation is a
Tōkyō irregularity; the stem is historically Type A, so that Kyōto's ī-korosu
'shoot to death (with an arrow)' is the regular compound-verb accentuation and

corresponds to Kagoshima pattern A. Tōkyō treats i-korosu as A or, newly, B; Hattō, Matsue, and Izumo have A; Hamada has B; and Goka-mura has i-ko˥rosu (?< *i˥-korosu). Contraction of infinitives such as mi-ī > mí (Myōgi-shō) > mī had taken place by Kamakura times (Kindaichi 1964a:401).

[32] One result is that the Kyōto accentuation obscures the relationship between pairs of verbs such as kakeru 'hang it' (two-syllable infinitive kake˥) and kakaru 'it hangs' (three-syllable infinitive kakari˥ with the locus retreating to kaka˥ri before underlying juncture). A similar, but slightly different situation is found in the Tōkyō-type dialect of Goka-mura (on Oki island); see §8.3, (6). The modern Kyōto treatment of longer B stems as Type A appears to be independent of the superficially identical situation in Takamatsu (and elsewhere in Kagawa prefecture), where the merger seems to have been part of the merger of the earlier low atonic pattern (noun types 2.3, 3.4, and 5.6) with the high atonic patterns (2.1, 3.1, 5.1). See Hirayama 1957b:249-51.

[33] If mitome- 'recognize', now Type B in Kyōto, were attested in Myōgi-shō it would presumably be as two accentual phrases: the infinitive mí (= miī) and the attributive tomuru. The obsolete stem tom(e)- 'pursue, inquire after' is given the gloss of 'recognize/acknowledge' in the predicative tomu that is cited by Myōgi-shō. (Do not confuse this with the Type A stem tom(e)- 'stop'.)

[34] But the retreat occurs even in such forms as ō˥kiru and ka˥keru in dialects of Shizuoka, Yamanashi, and Nagano, according to Kindaichi 1943:2:13a, who also cites (14a) naga˥reru and (Yamanashi) a˥ruku. On the last verb, cf. Watanabe 1957:189, who attributes to monophthongization of diphthongs the retreat "in parts of Yamanashi" for the verbs a[r]iku (= aruku), hair-u, mair-u, and kaer-u; but he also cites ka˥kusu without explanation (is the vowel unvoiced?). The Narada dialect of Yamanashi has the reflex of the Tōkyō prototonic in ariku 'walk' and hair-u 'enter' (Uwano 1976b:19), but kakusu 'hide it' and mair-u are the reflexes of the Tōkyō mesotonic pattern (id. 21); on the peculiar patterns of Narada, see §1.5 and §5.7.

[35] Since inflected forms so often occur without an attached particle, the basic oxytonic accent of certain of the forms, such as the infinitives of atonic stems, is cancelled much of the time. For that reason, it is easy to jump to the conclusion that these forms are simply atonic, like the stems, and attribute the accent heard when a particle is present to the particle itself, saying something like "a particle has an accent which retreats one syllable when the particle is attached to an atonic inflected form". (Very similar to the rule for "preaccented" noun suffixes.) But this sort of description will obscure the fact that the particles do not behave that way when they are attached to a noun (or a noun + a particle): cf. the Tōkyō pronunciation of susumi wa˥ 'as for the advance' with susumi˥ wa (sinai) '(I will not) advance'. In Izumo an oxytonic accent is usually cancelled (or right-shifted?)

when a particle is attached to a word ending in a high vowel, whether verb or noun, according to Ōhara 1937:65a: kagami⁷ 'mirror', kagami ga⁷. Since the infinitive ends in -i, presumably Izumo will fail to make a distinction between the derived noun and the infinitive of atonic verbs, except for those vowel stems ending in /e/, for they have absorbed the ending. (Cf. Kobayashi 68, n.51.) From Kobayashi's description, it would appear that Izumo has lost all trace of the oxytonic forms of atonic verbs, so that for this dialect the forms may properly be described as atonic.

³⁶ But in Goka-mura the basic locus that marks one-syllable infinitives of A verbs is delayed so as to fall on the first syllable of the second verb: si-harau 'pay off'. Cf. the infinitives of B verbs: mi-sokonau 'mistake'.

³⁷ Matsue and Hamada are similar to Izumo. In areas intermediate between Izumo and Chūgoku all compound verbs are said to be tonic, as with the younger Tōkyō speakers. Good Izumo examples can be found in Ōhara 1942:103; see also Hiroto and Ōhara 1953.

³⁸ Myōgi-shō examples of juncture despite onbin: no[ri] tabu = /not tabu/ 'deign to say', no[ri] toru = /not toru/ 'conform', tum[i] saku = /tun zaku/ 'rend'.

³⁹ In emphatic or reading pronunciations, longish inflected forms are sometimes broken into two phrases, probably without influence from the junctures deeply buried in the contractions that led to the forms. That may be the best explanation for the Kyōto version of too⁷kara⁷zu 'not far distant' cited in Hirayama, though that could be treated as a contraction of too⁷k[u] ara⁷zu. (Umegaki cites the Kyōto form as tookarazu.)

⁴⁰ When citing the finite verb-forms (···-ru, ···-ta) we will follow the common practice of ignoring the oxytonic accent that (in most of the dialects discussed) is basic to these forms when they are made on atonic stems; the accent is cancelled by a juncture — which, in turn, may disappear — but it will be heard when a particle is attached with no intervening juncture.

⁴¹ There is no need to list as an exception the noun sasitukae 'hindrance' (x - A-B-B) from the verb sasitukaeru ([B+?] - A/B-B-B). The verb is a compound, following the regular rules for Tōkyō (reverse tonicity of the first infinitive for older speakers, tonic for the younger), as well as for Kyōto and Kagoshima, where a compound verb preserves the register of the first infinitive. The second verb of the compound, tukaeru 'get obstructed', in Kagoshima is irregularly of Type A, as is its derived noun tukae; the Shuri forms are also Type A. We assume that these dialects have assimilated the accent to that of the verb tukaeru 'serve' (A - A-A-A), but it is possible that the Type B accentuation of Tōkyō and Kyōto is the irregularity, from unknown causes, and that the Kagoshima and Shuri accentuation preserves the proto-Japanese version. We lack an 11th-century attestation; yet if the etymology is from tuk- 'poke, stab' we would expect the accent to be Type A. (Tukaeru 'serve' is derived from tukau 'use', Type A.) According to Hirayama, Kyōto

treats tukiau̅ 'associate (with)' (← B+B) as a compound verb, but — unless NKD has
a misprint — Umegaki accentuates the verb as a lexicalization t̅ukia̅u, merging it
with the A group just as Kyōto treats longer B-stem verbs in general; yet both
Umegaki and Hirayama treat the derived noun as B (tukia̅i). Tōkyō treats the verb
as a lexicalization tuki̅au (with no older-generation *tuki̅au reported); the derived
noun is given by most sources as only atonic tuki̅ai (as if from a compound verb) but
NHK reports also a tonic version tuki̅ai which I too have observed, so that the noun
is exemplifying the Tōkyō options available for those four-syllable nouns derived
from tonic infinitives that end in vowel dyads, such as arasōi̲ / arasoi̅ 'struggle'
(see RGJ 884).

Notes to Chapter 4, §9.

[1] The established opinion, based on Komatsu's research, treats this ending as
-si̷ = -si̅i̲, which might be interpreted as -⸜si⸝ with two loci; cf. Sakurai 1959b
but also the criticism of Mochizuki 1972. Sakurai 1962b:23 says the -si̷ forms
maintained the fall into the Kamakura period for the Type B (low) adjective stems
but not for the Type A (high) stems; he thinks -si̷ and -ki̷ were accentuated as
separate phrases until after the Kamakura period had begun, though the -ku (and
-siku) forms were agglutinated earlier. He says (54b) that the velar elision of
-[k]u became general around the 10th century but that of -[k]i only around the 13th
century. On the velar elision see Ch. 3.

[2] According to the established view -k[y]i̷ = -k̅[y̅]ii̲ (see n.1). This view may be
supported by examples which mark -ki as low or (perhaps) with the slightly raised
"east-dot" mark, such as these: ayasi-ki 'strange' (NS 116b, 126a), fisasi-ki
'longlasting' (NS 120a), asi-ki 'evil' (NS 109b, 111b), take-ki 'brave' (NS 127b).
And, similarly: fisa-si (? fisa-si̷) 'is longlasting' (NS 125b), aya[si]-si 'is
strange' (NS 97b).

[3] And ara-ki̅ kokoro 'wild heart' (NS 123b). But: kata-[k]i̲ koto 'firmness'
(NS 121a).

[4] And ofo-[k̅]i ikusa no ki̅mi 'great warlords' (NS 123b).

[5] And atarasi̅-kyi 'the much-to-be-regretted ··· ' (NS 79c), y̅orosi-kyi 'excellent
··· ' (NS 77b).

[6] Cf. the lengthening of monosyllabic infinitives of verbs (§2 n.3).

[7] Cf. k̅ata-ku 'being hard' (NS 79b, 93a).

[8] And yowa̅-ku 'being weak' (NS 117b). But the example asi-ku 'being bad' (NS 127b)
is either an exception or a mistake.

[9] And kurusi̅-ku 'being distressing' (NS 112b), kasik̅wo-ku tomo 'though full of
awe' (NS 71a).

[10] Kamakura: usu̅-mi 'being thin' (W).

¹¹ Kamakura: taka-mi 'being high' (S).

¹² The Type A adjectives, kept distinct in early-Edo Kyōto as in modern Kōchi (kata-i : taka-i), fell together with the larger class of Type B adjectives in Kyōto and a number of the other Kinki dialects at some point during the past two or three hundred years. The dialects of Tsu, Yamada, and Wakayama are like Kōchi in that they preserve the distinction: atui 'thin', atui 'hot' (Ōhara 1932-3:77b).

¹³ Owing primarily to the syllable structure, a surface readjustment yields katai ga for this and similar forms; but when -i forms a separate syllable the underlying pattern is unchanged: too-i ga 'is far but'.

¹⁴ For reasons as yet unexplained (perhaps analogy, perhaps syllable weakening), kata-ku wa is a newer version in competition with kata-ku wa. Compare the gerund forms kata-ku-te and taka-ku-te, which competes with a newer version taka-ku-te, according to Akinaga (in Kindaichi 1958a).

¹⁵ This is a later development in Tōkyō; related dialects have inoti.

Notes to Chapter 4, §10.

¹ The time of the merger of the low atonic classes into high-register classes in Kyōto has been pinned down by Sakurai as follows: "The change began between 1241 (the death of [Fujiwara] Teika) and 1293 (the birth of Gyōa)" (Sakurai 1976:393). "The change was completed [with Type 3.5 > 3.3] between 1449 (Myōmoku-shō) and 1455 (Mōtan-shichin-shō)" (id. 404) — i.e. mid-Muromachi. "The change was 150 years in progress, 1293-1449, from late Kamakura to early Muromachi" (id. 412).

² The loanword for 'gasoline' is low register (.gasori'n according to Hirayama, .gaso'rin according to Umegaki) but the compounds are given as high-register by Umegaki (Hirayama lists none), including gasorin-ka'a 'gasoline-fueled car'. The Tōkyō versions are atonic gasorin and either gasorin-ka'a or gasori'n-kaa, according to NKD.

³ But at least one canonical shape (CVki) does not provoke the accent retreat in certain dialects, e.g. Nagano (Kudō 1978:9), where presumably 'freight station' would be said as kamotu-e'ki. We might call the Tōkyō version of dissyllables of this type "quasi heavy monosyllables"; the final vowel is voiceless in Tōkyō except when a voiced sound immediately follows.

⁴ Hirayama.   ⁵ Mkz.   ⁶ Umegaki.   ⁷ NKD.

⁸ The example tori sisi wo 'birds and beasts (as object)' from the Maeda text of Nihon-Shoki (Ishizuka 1977:115b) was probably pronounced as three phrases. Similar: asa + nuno → asa nuno 'hemp cloth', siro (adjective stem) + kane → siro kane 'silver'.

⁹ Is Rule 1 overriding Rule 3?

¹⁰ This could be a syntactic reduction toki yo.

¹¹ Also (Ck Mg) LLHH, which could be a syntactic reduction.

¹² There are no good examples. The noun sirokane LLHH 'silver' is a syntactic reduction 2.3 + 2.1 (see n.8); the first element is the adjective stem, not the noun siro 2.5. Probably kurogane LLLL is be treated in a somewhat similar way, but with lexicalization: 2.3 + 2.1 → LLLL (= 4.5).

¹³ These four words look to be syntactic reductions (cf. §11 n.3). The two Myōgi-shō citations of yamatouta in Mochizuki are conflicting; I reinterpret them.

¹⁴ Rule 4 has been disregarded.

¹⁵ Also LLLLL.

Notes to Chapter 4, §11.

¹ Written as if HHLHL, however; so perhaps to be taken as HH|LHL 2.1 + 3.7, a syntactic reduction of adjective stem ('hard') + noun ('head'). The accent of the ·noun is not separately attested. See the next two notes.

² Written LLHHH, however; so perhaps to be taken as LL|HHH 2.3 + 3.1, as a syntactic reduction of the adjective stem 'big' + noun 'drum'.

³ Written LLHLH, however; so perhaps to be taken as LLH|LH 3.5 + 2.4/5. Yamatokoto could thus be accounted for as a syntactic reduction — as in Komatsu 1977:381, who cites as similar the words siraki-koto LLL-LH 'Silla harp' and kutara-koto LLL-LH 'Paekche harp', but we lack attestations for the isolated accent of those placenames.

⁴ The -z- is probably a mistake in the (Chinkoku-shukoku-jinja) Myōgi-shō notation.

Notes to Chapter 4, §12.

¹ Forms with "intrasyllabic" rise and fall are excluded from the chart, since I assume that they are contractions from longer forms or otherwise to be explained. Certain of the paradigmatic forms therefore end up in a different category from where Kindaichi would put them.

² But in saying that (at least in Myōgi-shō) Type 1.3b had a rise of pitch we imply two moras in the underlying form (faā). If we now allow the monosyllabic nouns of 1.3a (such as ki 'tree') to have an automatic length as well, the two classes will fall together unless 1.3a is kept apart by retaining low pitch on the second mora (kii 'tree'), which is what we have implied for the earlier (pre-Mg) basic form (§7, n.2). Kindaichi (1964a:327-9) thinks monosyllables (at least L-H) were not lengthened in the Muromachi period, but probably in Heian were long in isolation yet short with a particle, since a phrase LL would have become HL in the later language (as happened to N 2.3). But Kindaichi 1960b suggests that in the Heian period and earlier all syllables were "unmarked" as to vowel length and freely fluctuated between short and long, with the phonemic distinction setting in later so as to distinguish the SHORT vowels (a clipping of the vowel, as it were) from the newly

emerging long vowels that were created by reducing diphthongs, perhaps about the time the "*onbin*" reductions of verb and adjective forms seem to hint at a faster articulatory stance in general: a speed-up of tempo which, I believe, would also serve to explain what happened to the "falling" accents, especially in forms of the verb and adjective.

Notes to Chapter 4, §13.

[1] The Shinpuku-ji text misplaces the ZYOO so that it follows nwo, and that is the version in Wada 1952; cf. Fujii 1944:23, Sakurai 1970:75.

[2] Or ufey?

[3] Or -gufyi?

[4] This statement presumes that at least some of the nouns of Type 2.5 are marked differently from those of 2.4; see §4. We are also putting aside the question of whether certain modern irregularities of correspondence might substantiate a few additional "final-fall" classes such as 2.1a, 3.1a, etc. See §2.3.

[5] See Kindaichi 1975:49-81. Polivanov took a similar position in the 1920s.

[6] Kindaichi's view is that that Kyōto first changed LLL into HHL and then to HLL and that Tōkyō went from a stage HHL to HHH(-L). He says (1955a:29) that the loss of an initial low string in Kyōto in the course of the second half of the 14th century (cf. §10 n.1) strengthened the "word demarcation" role (i.e. the function as a cue to juncture) while weakening the "morpheme [or word] differentiation" role.

[7] Kyōto may have undergone the change LHH > LLH before Ōsaka. According to Sakamoto (1983:35b), words like usagi were LHH in Ōsaka of the late 17th century and became the modern LLH between 1700 and 1750. On the basis of Heike-mabushi, Okumura thinks LHH and LLH were in free variation in the early Edo period, but Sakamoto says there is no evidence for the variation in the Ōsaka materials of the late 17th century. An interesting thing I noticed in these materials is that several of the originally high atonic nouns of three syllables are given the double-low pattern LHL: agito, akuta, aziro, ... Are there any similar cases in modern Kansai dialects?

[8] Verbs perhaps showing the expected reflex: kuuzun = kogu 'row', uuyun = oru 'bend, break', qaakiyun = wakeru (or sakeru?) 'split', ... Hirayama suggests that there may be Ryūkyū dialects which retain vowel length in a larger number of words. Kindaichi observes that influences of the main-island dialects during the Tokugawa period may be responsible for the loss of vowel length in some of the words where we would expect to find it.

[9] See now Kindaichi 1975:140-3.

[10] Okumura 1975a:151 remarks on "similar phenomena" in Yaku-shima, Koshiki(-jima), Shimabara [Hida], and Oki island, as well as the Ryūkyūs.

Notes to Chapter 4, §14.

[1] A number of the 2.5 nouns, such as negi 'onion' and oke 'bucket', can be shown
to be COMPOUNDS, and it is quite possible that even those which are not known to be
more than a single morpheme were nonetheless at an earlier stage more complex,
perhaps incorporating a suffix of some sort. It has been noted that certain semantic
groups are well represented in 2.5, especially zoological and botanical names. But
those groups are also represented in the other types. If there was a suffix, it need
not have been segmental, of course; recall Ogawa's 1942 observation that the final
fall in Wakayama is a semantic marker (§4). Another possibility, first proposed by
Polivanov, is that nouns of 2.5 are TRUNCATIONS: the final fall is the last gasp of
a dropped phoneme (or phoneme string), which might or might not constitute a suffix.
What first led Polivanov to this notion, I believe, is the fact that the putative
Korean cognate for Japanese asa 2.5 'morning' has a final -m (Middle Korean a'chom);
he was also alert to the final nasal that southern Ryūkyū dialects have for a few
words that historically end in vowels (see Ch. 1, §52), though the examples do not
correlate with any particular accent types. For a recent view of these questions,
see Whitman 1984. See also §17.

[2] The segmental phonemes are given in modern guise; the appopriate 11th-century
shapes are with f- for h-, and aduki for azuki. Since our accent is representing a
yet earlier Japanese, presumably proto-Japanese, the shapes will be different still,
e.g. p- for f- and -nt- for -d-. See Ch. 1 for this information.

Notes to Chapter 4, §15.

[1] At least one Kyōto-type dialect, Akō, in Hyōgo prefecture, lacks distinctions of
initial register; in free variation the first syllable is always either high or (as
in Tōkyō) somewhat lowered (Uwano 1977b:292, 318). Kindaichi (1977:72, 78) calls
such border dialects "pseudo-Kyōto type".

[2] The reading in the English summary of Kindaichi 1959. Doi Tadao (KggJ 184b)
gives the reading Heike-shōsetsu; Akinaga 1977:94 and Uwano 1977b:314 read the
name as Heike-mabushi; and other sources (e.g. Kamei Takashi, KggJ 841b) do not
bother to inform us. The "-mabushi" reading of the name was recently established as
authoritative by Kindaichi, who found it used by three blind minstrels who were
preserving the Nagoya tradition of Ogino Chiichi, but the title is generally read as
"-seisetsu" by the uninitiated; "-shōsetsu" is pedantic. The lengthy study of
Okumura 1981 nowhere tells us how he pronounces the name, not even in the colophon,
but the order of the entry in the index is incompatible with the reading "-mabushi",
so I assume the author intended the name to be pronounced "-seisetsu", though the
"-shōsetsu" version would also be compatible with the order of the index entry.

[3] With the nondistinctive lowering of the initial syllable in Tōkyō (Stage 3) the pattern of 3.3 yields the pattern found in ko̧mu̅ˈgi 'wheat' and this coincides with the pattern of 3.5a that emerges from Stage 1 as found in i̧to̅ˈko 'cousin'. But the words for 'wheat' and 'cousin', which exemplify the regular Tōkyō-type pattern, are exceptional in Tōkyō itself; the majority of the 3.3 and 3.5b words are shifted to 3.7b, so that ha̅ˈtati ga 'twenty' (3.3) and na̅ˈmida ga 'tear(drops)' (3.5b) have the same tune as ka̅ˈbuto ga 'helmet' (3.7b) in Tōkyō, though Tōkyō-type dialects have ha̧ta̅ˈti ga and na̧mi̅ˈda ga.

[4] According to Ramsey, certain compounds in which the second noun is Type 2.4 or 2.5 (thus prototonic in Tōkyō) are accentuated in modern Kyōto with a locus that coincides with that of Tōkyō and is the same as the locus of the second noun in Tōkyō but not in modern Kyōto. He concludes that Kyōto must be maintaining an earlier pattern for the noun when it is in the compounds. Unfortunately we lack pertinent data from other Kyōto-type dialects and our two sources of Kyōto data are often in conflict, especially with regard to compounds. For instance, Ramsey's k̅o̅o̅mori-ga̅ˈsa is taken from Hirayama (1960) but Umegaki (NKD) accentuates the compound as k̅o̅o̅moriˈ-gasa, putting Ramsey's point in doubt. Kyōto seems to be preserving a form of the rule stated in §10.4, in which there is an anticipation of the locus by one syllable: "When the compound is five syllables or longer there will usually be a change (an accentual locus) at the next-to-last or last syllable [*modern: third-from-last or next-to-last*], whether N₂ has an original locus or not." With four-syllable compounds, the same variation is found when the second noun is tonic (has a locus): the accentuation of the compound is at the last or next-to-last syllable, which may or may not coincide with the original locus of the second noun. The position of the locus in the compound appears to be rather independent of its position in the second noun, as can be seen from these Myōgi-shō examples:

Compound accent is the same as N₂:		*Compound accent differs from N₂:*	
t̅uki 'cup'	saka-d̅uki 'winecup'	---	
k̅ara 'shell'	mame-g̅ara 'bean pod'	n̅asi 'pear'	yama-nasi̅ 'wild pear'
---		fasi̅ 'chopsticks'	kana-basi̅ 'metal ···'
ka̅sa 'umbrella'	kinu-ga̅sa 'silk ···'	ma̅yu 'cocoon'	kufa-ma̅yu 'silkworm'

Survivors from this list are optionally atonic in Tōkyō: saka-zukiˈ⁻, mame-garaˈ⁻; yamaˈ-nasi⁻, kinuˈ-gasa⁻. Both Kyōto sources agree on s̅aka-zu̅ki and disagree on the register of mame-gar̅a (Hirayama) vs. mame-gara̅ (Umegaki). Only Umegaki lists y̅ama-nasi (as a common noun) and k̅inu-gasa.

⁵ The rule in Wakayama is optional (Yukawa 1984:2:20):
I̅nu no | e̅sa → i̅nu no e̅sa 'dog food', I̅nu no | tyawan̅ → i̅nu no tyawan 'dog's bowl'; a̅tama no | naka → atama no naka 'inside one's head'; o̅okaze no | hi̅i → o̅okaze no hi̅i 'a day of high wind'.

⁶ There are only a few longer oxytonic nouns in Tōkyō. Apparently they too cancel the accent when /no/ is appropriately attached: o̲tooto no → o̲tooto no 'of younger brother', i̲mooto no → i̲mooto no 'of younger sister', o̲syoogatu no → o̲syoogatu no 'of New Year's'; z̲yuuitigatu no → zyuuitigatu no 'of November'. Only the last-mentioned has a corresponding Kyōto form that we might expect to show the change, but I lack data on whether z̲yuuitigatu no → ?zyuuitigatu no happens in Kyōto or not.

⁷ The "modern" rendering of the word is inuo'omono, according to NKD, which gives the historical spelling "ohu" for the long vowel. It is unclear whether: (1) the spelling represents /o[w]u/ ← /owi/ (<"ofi") by assimilation of the second vowel; (2) the lengthening is secondary; or, (3) Konparu shortened the vowel, though the mainstream tradition did not, or simply ignored the vowel length in his transcription.

Notes to Chapter 4, §16.

¹ There are a few examples of these phenomena in Tōkyō Japanese. Conflation occurs in a few words like kaa-moku-doo 'Tuesday-Thursday-Saturday'. In addition to well-known lexical variants such as ari'gato[o] 'thanks', sayo[o]na'ra 'good-bye', and ikimasyo'[o] 'let's go', a casual shortening of final length is often heard in words with more than one heavy syllable: kooto[o]-ga'kko[o] 'high school', sense'[e] 'teacher, doctor', ningyo[o]⁻ 'doll' (cf. ni'ngyo 'mermaid'). The *onbin* phenomena are examples of compression, and the emergence of the -yoo ending for the tentative forms si-yoo 'let's do', tabe-yoo 'let's eat', etc., is an example of conflation.

² I have modified Nakasone's phonetic transcription while carefully preserving the distinctions he makes, even in environments where these are neutralized. A voiceless obstruent is always unaspirated when medial within a morpheme. The unaspirated consonants are written with capital letters (P T K) where Nakasone uses Greek letters, and for consistency I have written C for his "c", since the affricate is normally unaspirated, there being only a few examples of the contrasting aspirated version (which Nakasone writes as "ç"). I have written "q" both for the glottal initial (including qm- and qn-) and for the geminating postvocalic mora that Japanese linguists like to write as "Q"; notice that maqKaa 'pillow' counts as four moras, but qmaa 'horse' as two.

Chapter Five: Nouns.

5.0. Introduction.

This chapter presents a list of about 4200 nouns. The column at the left identifies the accent class(es) to which we propose assigning the noun on the basis of the evidence shown. Then comes the modern form, by which we have alphabetized the list, and various earlier versions, either attested or inferred. The meanings that are given as glosses are merely intended as tags to help identify the forms. The array of accent correspondences following the gloss begins with 11th-century Kyōto. These are mostly citations from Myōgi-shō (Mg); when unspecified usually at least the Kanchi-in text (Kn); other citations are from from the Zusho-ryō (Zs), Kōzan-ji (Kz), and Chinkoku-shukoku-jinja (Ck) texts of Myōgi-shō and from three other sources included in Mochizuki's index: the Maeda text of Iroha-jirui-shō, Hoke-kyō tanji, and the Iwasaki text of [Shinsen-]Jikyō. (Data on late-Heian accent from sources not included in Mochizuki's index are given at the end of the array.) Next in the formula, after a spaced dash, are the three dialects of Tōkyō (Tk), Kyōto (Kt), and Kagoshima (Kg); then, following a space, the three Ryūkyū dialects of Shodon (Sd), Shuri (Sr), and Yonaguni (Yn). For a good many of the entries further historical and dialect data are provided. Where we lack data or where the etymon is thought to be absent from the dialect, the symbol "x" replaces the accent notation. Underlined accent notations are irregular according to the correspondences assumed, but longer patterns are underlined only when an irregularity of register is noticed or when one of the attested patterns differs from the accent-class number that is assigned. Earlier versions of many words are not attested but must be reconstruct the reconstructed or inferred forms are preceded by an asterisk (meaning "unattested as such") and the asterisk is put in parentheses when the components of a compound are attested but the compound as a whole is not. For each entry the rightmost form is the earliest we attempt to reconstruct, but for some words that is simply the modern form and for others, which may not have been a part of the language during earlier stages, the reconstructions may well be ghosts. Where an etymology includes the notation "(< ...)", further derivational information will be found under the separate entries. Words thought to be loans from some earlier version of Chinese are given etymologies marked "< Ch" followed by a rough approximation of a likely Middle ("Ancient") Chinese pronunciation of the 6th or 7th century A.D., with the tones indicated by dots placed before or after the syllable in a higher or lower position according to the traditional scheme (.☐ Even, '☐ Rising, ☐' Going, ☐. Entering) but the Entering tone is left unmarked since it is obvious from the final -p, -t, or -k.

The list includes a number of the longer nouns attested in our sources. Many of these are compounds, for which it is difficult to reconstruct a "proto" accent. The accent assignments proposed are based on the attestations for the late-Heian accent, except when those are unavailable, and a few such words are assigned classes on the basis of apparent correspondences across dialects. When there is considerable question about the assignment a question-mark precedes the notation; a number of entries are assigned to more than one category to reflect conflicting data. The questionable assignment of certain nouns to the atonic "final fall" subclasses (2.1a, 3.1a; 2.3a, 3.4a) proposed in Ch. 4 §7.3 is not shown as such, but each relevant entry includes the dialect data adduced to support the assignment.

5.1. Accent notations; sources.

In the accent notations a slant line separates variants (competing versions): "A/B" means that we find reports of both the accent type symbolized by "A" and that symbolized by "B". Some of the Kyōto variants are peculiar to one or the other of our two major sources, "[H]" = Hirayama Teruo 1960 (Zenkoku akusento jiten) and "[U]" = Umegaki Minoru, who provided the Kyōto data in Nihon kokugo dai-jiten (NKD); where there are differences, the source is noted. For earlier periods the accents are stated explicitly in patterns of H (High) and L (Low) for each syllable; F means "Fall" (HL in one syllable) and R means "Rise" (LH in one syllable). An "x" in the schema indicates that the syllable lacks a mark in the attestation: in "HxL" only the first and third syllables carry tone marks. When an accent formula is queried in its entirety an online question-mark precedes it: "?LLL" means "Was this pronounced with the low atonic pattern?" or "Is there an attestation that should be interpreted as LLL?" When the pitch of only a single syllable is queried, a raised question-mark is placed before the symbol: "L?LH" means "Was the second syllable low?" or "Is the mark placed on the second syllable to be interpreted as in the low position?"

Information on the Kamakura-period accent is taken from "(S)" = Kindaichi 1964a (Shiza-kōshiki no kenkyū) and from "(W)" = Akinaga 1974 (Kokin-waka-shū shōten-bon no kenkyū: sakuin-hen). but the accent of three sources in the latter (W 18, 19, 20) belong to the Muromachi period and are so treated. The historical judgments made by Kindaichi in NKD are cited after "K:" but only when this will add to information given earlier in the entry or differs from that. The periods for which Kindaichi offers judgment are Heian ("Hn"), Kamakura ("Km"), Muromachi ("Mr"), and Edo, but notice that Edo refers to the Kyōto accent of the early Edo (= Tokugawa) period, and not the accent of the city of Edo which became modern Tōkyō. (Accent information preceded by "Edo" alone is taken from Okumura 1981.) The citations of "1700 Ōsaka" accent are taken from Sakamoto 1983 and pertain to attestations of the late 17th century; these accents are cited only when they supplement (or vary from) the "Edo" citations. I have translated "... -rai" as "... and since", or "... and later". From NKD it is unclear just when Kindaichi's historical judgments are based the attestations for a given period (and just which attestations) and when they are based on inference from earlier and later periods; some of these judgments, along with possible misprints, are queried. NKD gives "Edo LH" for virtually all cases of nouns of Type 2.3, but that does not necessarily mean that an attestation is found in the early Edo materials for each such noun. Kindaichi consistently treats Kyōto monosyllables as long; Okumura's R and F are the same as Kindaichi's LH and HL, respectively, when the noun is a monosyllable.

The Heian accents found in notations of the Maeda text of Nihon-Shoki (NS) are cited by page and column of Ishizuka 1977; to ease the finding of certain items they are located in greater detail, following Ishizuka's numbers, which refer to text page, and with appended -K for katakana and -M for Man'yō-gana. Where Okada 1956 presents Nihon-Shoki accents that supplement or differ from those in Ishizuka, they are added as "NS (Okada)". Similarly, "Km (Okada W)" shows where Okada 1956 differs from or supplements Akinaga on data in the Kokin-kunten-shō. Differing Nihon-Shoki accents in Sakurai 1964 are cited as "NS (Sakurai)". Accents marked "NS (T)" are cited from Takayama 1983; those marked "NS (T+)" are Martin's interpretation of the rest of the NS phonogram vocabulary (in a few instances emendations of Takayama). The patterns, to be treated with caution, are based on treating the Chinese "Even" tone as LOW and all other tones as HIGH. (For certain monosyllables the "Going" tone may represent RISE instead of HIGH, as individually indicated.)

5.2. Segmental notations; pronunciations.

Segmental forms are cited only when of special interest or in giving the source
of the attestations. The Shodon forms are cited from Martin 1970b and the Shuri
forms are mostly from Okinawa-go jiten (but "j-" is changed to "y-", "N" is written
as "n", and "Q" is represented by "-t-" or a geminate). For Shuri the letters "s",
"c", and "z" write the traditionally palatalized sounds , which might better be
transcribed as "sy, cy, zy", while their (formerly distinctive) non-palatalized
counterparts are written with a cedilla: "ş, ç, ʒ". For those dialects where it
is distinctive (such as Shodon and Shuri), the glottal stop is written as "q-". The
Yonaguni forms are cited mostly from Hirayama 1964 and 1967, with discrepancies
between the two works noted, but there are a few citations from other sources, as
indicated. The orthography used for the Yonaguni forms is a simplified version of
Hirayama's: "ç" is rewritten as "c"; distinctively unaspirated stops are written
with capital letters ("T-") but, as in Hirayama 1967 unlike 1964, with lowercase
letters ("t-") when they occur in a position that will neutralize the phonemic
opposition with the aspirated stops. Nakijin forms are from Nakasone 1984, with
notational adjustments (see Ch. 4, §16). Forms of other dialects are mostly cited
from NKD unless otherwise noted. Etymological notes are cautiously taken mainly from
NKD or from Ōno Susumu (et al., Iwanami Kogo-jiten) but some are taken from other
sources and a few are original to this work.

The pronunciation shown for each period is an orthographic representation that
requires interpretation. Although "-f-" is used to reflect the medial occurrence of
kana ha ʔ-gyoo syllables in the Heian and later periods, the phoneme was probably
never pronounced as a voiceless fricative in non-initial position. In Kyōto after a
certain time during the Heian period the phoneme was pronounced -w- and earlier it
may have been -b- (or optionally -b-/-p-) as an allophone of /p/; this was at a
time when the later "-b-" was still phonetically [-mb-], which we phonemicize as
/-np-/. Our initial "f-" was earlier p- but it is a matter of controversy just how
early the fricative version set in; after all, in parts of the Ryūkyūs the sound
remains a stop today (Chapter 1, §7). We have chosen to use the notation *d- for the
ancestor of the initial y-, but perhaps "*j-" — to be interpreted as the voiced
affricate [dž] or as the palatalized voiced stop [dy] — would have made a better
choice, being the IPA notation of y-, in any event. (On the ancestral pronunciation
of later y-, see Ch. 1, §22.) We use the notation *b- for the ancestor of later w-
and believe it was a voiced stop. For our notation of the vowel distinctions of the
Nara period, see Ch. 1, §40. Those instances of Old Japanese "Co" which are known to
be of the otsu-type in contrast with the kō-type, here shown as /Cwo/, are marked
with an underline: kok̲o̲r̲o̲. (The underline corresponds to the rigorous use of the
dieresis in other works: kökörö.) The remaining instances of "Co", left unmarked,
are those in neutralizing environments or for which the polar value is unknown
because the syllable is recorded ambivalently or in semantograms rather than in
phonograms. (A number of Japanese linguists, including Ōno, misleadingly use the
dieresis as a default notation when the vowel is not known to be of the kō-type.)
When both types of o are clearly indicated as variants, the notation may be C(w)o,
as in t(w)or- = twor- in competition with to̲r- 'take'. In general we rely on the
entry notations of Zdb (= Omodaka et al. 1967) as the main authority for the vowel
distinctions, but Igarashi 1969 is required for decisions on /fo/.

5.3. Compound nouns; junctures.

In proto-Japanese, those compound nouns that were made up of two free elements were probably pronounced with a juncture between the elements, i.e. said as two words, and that accounts for the use of a space rather than a hyphen in citing the earliest forms. The accent assigned the compound as such is assumed to date from whenever the two-word phrase was tightened into one word by dropping the juncture; for longer words, the accent type is simply the earliest attested. Myōgi-shō often attests as two words, with inferred juncture, what was later treated as a compound. The expressions m̄iti ăto 'rut' and m̄idu ūmi 'lake' are taken as 2.1 | 2.4 because of the pattern HLH, which does not appear within a word; another example is ūti t̄o 'inside and out', which is 2.2 | 1.1. The modern Tōkyō accent of miz̄uu¹mi 'lake' is unusual for having the locus on the second of two like vowels, and that indicates a morpheme boundary. Since the pattern is the same as that of kon̄o u¹mi 'this sea' (cf. d̄o¹n̄o | ū¹mi 'which sea'), we might be tempted to assume a suppressed juncture: mizu [|] u¹mi. But missing is the analogy of N | N structures in which the juncture is clearly suppressed, except for the elliptical N [no]| N (Martin 1975:1048-9).

For many of the earlier accent patterns we are justified in suspecting that they contain dropped junctures, with the location depending on the constituents. The pattern of the "compound" is simply that of its parts; unless there are two points of fall in a string (such as HLHL), we have no ready way to know whether the stretch was being treated as one word or two words, just as our ears alone cannot detect the difference between the Tōkyō patterns of tom̄odati 'friend' and kon̄o [|] hati 'this bee'. The possible constituents of pattern types are displayed in §6 below. In the longer formulas "1.1" includes 1.2, and "2.4" includes 2.4, on the assumption that those contrasts were neutralized.

5.4. Incorporated genitives.

The earlier forms reconstructed for certain compound nouns contain a "genitive" (an adnominalizer) in the form of the marker -n-, sometimes clearly a reduction of the particles no or ni, both of which also occur, as does na. There is another such marker, -tu, and it sometimes occurs in combination with -n- as a kind of "double genitive". The function of -tu has been described by some as "locative-genitive". We regard the counter "-tu" as a specialized use of this genitive; it appears likely that "-ti" < -tu-Ci is an extended version. Rarely the "genitive" appears after the attributive (= adnominal) form of a verb or adjective; cf. RGJ 659. It is unclear to what extent the phonological bonding obliges us to put a hyphen before and/or after these markers. The structures were originally phrases but that is not always obvious from the accent types given, especially for the longer nouns, since these are taken from late-Heian or Kamakura sources, and by those times many of the compound nouns had been lexicalized.

Examples of -tu in various combinations:
(1) N -tu N: ama-tu-hitugi, asatuki, hatuse, hatusigure, [hetuhi], hinatume, hotue, katatukata, miketumono, miya-tu-ko, niwatutori, notutori, ototoi < wototufyi, simotukata, sirituto, sitatumiti, tanatumono, tokotukuni, totukuni, totu-kuniguni, utitu-kuni, utitu-miya, wata^t/$_z$umi, yamatumi, yomo-tu-kuni. Also yakko < ya-tu-ko; karayatuko. Cf. katuuri, sitodati, yatugare, yatukorama; tokotowa, ... (The examples are from the entries of §5.9 and that accounts for the inconsistent hyphenation.)
(2) N -tu [N]: si^t/$_z$u, yatu 'damn guy', ?... .
(3) A -tu N: too-tu oya, ...

(4) V -tu N: [mukatuo], ?... .
(5) V-ru -tu N: kurutuhi, ?... .
(6) Numeral -tu: hitotu, hutatu, kokonotu, mi(t)tu, mu(t)tu, nanatu, ya(t)tu,
yo(t)tu; ikutu; ?itu. Perhaps also hatu(-) 'first', hatuka, hutuka, ituka, yooka.
?(7) Numeral -tu -tu: ? itutu.
?(8) Numeral -ti ?< -tu-Ci (or ?< to[s]i): hatati, misoti, ...
?(9) Numeral -n- -tu: yorozu.
?(10) Numeral -n- -ti ?< -tu-Ci (or ?< to[s]i): yasozi, ...
(11) N -n- -tu N: ikazuti, ikisudama < ikizutama, tezukara, ?... . And perhaps
kedamono and kudamono; but Iwate [kiđago 2/3] = 'soybean flour' (= ki-na-ko)
contains the local form of the adnominalized copula, corresponding to standard da.
(12) N -n- -tu [N]: akitu < akidu.
(13) N -tu -n- N: ?hituzi, kakitubana, kakitubata, matuge, simatuᵗ/đori, ...
(14) Numeral -tu -n- N: yatugi, yotuziro, ...

5.5. Accent notations for dialects.

In addition to the six dialects in the schematic formulas, data from other
dialects will be found for certain of the entries, especially when deemed helpful
in evaluating the patterns of closely related dialects. Data for the Tōkyō-type
dialects of Hattō, Hamada, Matsue, Izumo, and Goka-mura are from Hiroto and Ōhara
1955; data for Hata, a Tōkyō-type dialect at the southeast corner of Shikoku, are
from Doi 1952. Data for Tappi (a Tōkyō-type dialect in northern Honshū) and for
Sakawa (a Kyōto-type dialect in Kōchi prefecture of Shikoku) are from Clarke 1973.
The Tōkyō-type dialect cited as "NE Kyūshū" is from Hirayama 1951a:172-85; the
specific dialect is that of Shirakawa village of Miyako district in Fukuoka
prefecture. The Tōkyō-type accent of the Wakamatsu peninsula (Fukuoka) is from
Soeda 1975. The Narada information is from the excellent study of Uwano 1976. Our
notation follows Uwano in writing the number of the low syllable that occurs right
before the distinctive high, so that the notations directly represent the reflexes
of the Tōkyō forms even though the phonetic tunes sound quite different. Below is
a table of the phonetic patterns represented by the notations, together with the
historical types of which they are reflexes.

Phonetic patterns	Narada notation	Historic types
ō-o̲	(1 -) 0	1.1
o̲-ō	1	1.2, 1.3
ōo-o̲	(2 -) 0	2.1
o̲ō-o̲	1	2.4, 2.5
ōo̲-ō	2	2.2, 2.3
ōoo-o̲	(3 -) 0	3.1, 3.5a, 3.6, 3.7a
o̲ōo-o̲	1	3.3, 3.7b
ōo̲ō-ō	2	3.5b
ōo̲o-ō	3	3.2, 3.4

Data for Ōsaka and Ise are cited from Terayama and Kusaka 1944; Toyama and Suzu are from Hirayama 1960. The notations for these and other Kyōto-type dialects represent essentially the same phonetic tunes as those of Kyōto, but the unusual notation "1:2" is a flat low tune that lacks the nondistinctive rise on the phrase-final syllable that is characteristic of "1". This is the reflex of Types 1.3, 2.4, and 3.6 in both Suzu and Toyama and in Toyama it is also the reflex of Types 1.1, 2.1, and 3.1.

The Tōkyō-type dialects of Matsue and Izumo are cited in the notations of Hiroto and Ōhara; essentially the tunes are the same as those represented by the corresponding notations for Tōkyō. But these facts must be kept in mind when the notations are read:
 (1) Unlike Tōkyō, which merges 2.2 with 2.3, Matsue and Izumo merge Type 2.2 with 2.1, as "0".
 (2) It follows that "2" is the normal reflex for Type 2.3, as it is in Tōkyō.
 (3) Like all Tōkyō-type dialects, Matsue and Izumo merge Types 2.4 and 2.5, with the expected reflex "1". But for these two dialects when the final vowel is open (*e a o*) the merged Type 2.4/5 further merges with 2.3, as "2". Only when the final vowel is close (*i* or *u*) will the merged Type 2.4/5 be kept distinct, as "1".

> Note: The dialect shown as "Matsue" on p. 14 of the introduction to Kindaichi 1958 differs from that described by Hiroto and Ōhara in the following way: nouns ending in i or u of Type 2.5 are the only ones with the tune HL-L (= "1") and all other nouns ending in i or u merge with the tune LL-H, in isolation LH, which is an allophonic variant of LH-H (= "0"). The segregation of even a subset of the nouns of Type 2.5 would raise a problem in classifying this version of "Matsue" as a Tōkyō-type dialect. But apparently the 1958 chart was mistaken on this point, as indicated in the revised edition of 1981, which treats the patterns in the same way that Hiroto and Ōhara do.

The Tōkyō-type dialect of Goka-mura on Oki island is cited from Hiroto and Ōhara, but I have changed certain of their phonetic notations ("1:3, 1:4") for longer words to "0", so as to conform with the phonological notation these authors use for two-syllable atonic nouns. Atonic words of three and four syllables in this dialect have a nondistinctive high pitch on the first and third syllables (s̄ak̄an̄a 'fish', k̄anemōtī 'rich man'); and the atonic words of five or more syllables have a nondistinctive high pitch on the first and fourth syllables (t̄akaramōno 'treasure', h̄itokat̄amari 'one (clump)'). An atonic noun of two syllables has a nondistinctive lowering of the first syllable, as in Tōkyō, but when you attach a particle the resulting three-syllable phrase is given the appropriate seesaw tune of the three-syllable atonic noun (kaz̄e 'wind' but k̄aze ḡa like s̄ak̄an̄a). Yet the addition of a particle to an atonic noun of three or four syllables does not change the original tune of the noun (s̄ak̄ana ḡa, k̄anemōti ḡa).

> This analysis follows the description in Hiroto and Ōhara. The version of Goka-mura reported by Uwano (1975) has k̄anemōtī ḡa; but for the nouns of five syllables, he reports t̄akaramōno ḡa rather than the *t̄akaramōno ḡa that his treatment of the four-syllable nouns might lead us to expect.

In isolation the dissyllabic words marked "2" have their distinctive high pitch moved back one syllable (yam̄a ḡa but yām̄a 'mountain') and thus will be expected to sound the same as the dissyllabic words marked "1" (āme 'rain, āme ḡa) but, at least when the words are spoken slowly, the tunes are kept apart by a rise in pitch on the last syllable: amé(:), ame ḡá, not to be confused with the atonic pattern (k̄aze ḡa, s̄ak̄an̄a). Cf. Hiroto and Ōhara 168, Uwano 1975:76. From the descriptions I suspect that the distinction of "1" from "2" is neutralized in dissyllabic words when they occur in isolation. We can compare the continuing controversy over whether

the Tōkyō oxytonic dissyllables ("2") have the same pattern in isolation as the
atonic dissyllables ("0"); the underlying morphophonemic patterns can be kept
distinct in slow or reading pronunciations, such as are often used by experimental
phoneticians, but they are not distinguished at normal speech tempos, though the
underlying patterns may leave influences on the juncture reductions at a near-
surface level. The phonological accent types of Goka-mura merge the historic noun
categories as follows:

Goka-mura type	Historic pattern types
0	2.1, 2.2; 3.1, 3.2, 3.4, 3.5a, 3.7a
2	2.3; 3.3, 3.5b
1	2.4, 2.5; 3.6, 3.7b

As in other dialects, there are a number of irregular reflexes, especially for the
three-syllable nouns. Hiroto and Ōhara report difficulty hearing a distinction
between the two types of one-syllable nouns, as we might expect in isolation, and
cite them all as "1". so I have omitted data from Goka-mura for the monosyllables.

   Goka-mura verbs of Type A are here noted as "0"; in Hiroto and Ōhara those of
three or four syllables are noted "1:3", those of five or more "1:4". The verbs of
Type B are noted as "1" (kaku 'write') or "2" (aruku 'walk', hanasu 'talk'). But
the longer verbs of original Type B have merged into Type A, so that atumaru
'gather' is listed as "0" (Hiroto and Ōhara "1:3") just like the Type-A verb
ōkonau 'act', and similarly we note "0" for takuwaeru 'store, save'. Three-syllable
verbs of Type B that have consonant-final stems maintain their distinctive tonic
accent, but the three-syllable verbs that have vowel-final ("ni-dan") stems all
merge as Type A. This means that sodatu 'be raised' ("2") is Type B, in contrast
with the pattern of susumu 'advance' ("0") of Type A, but sodateru 'raise' ("0")
has the same Type-A pattern as susumeru 'promote'. Since word types 3.1 and 3.4
fall together, nouns derived from infinitives of three syllables should all be
atonic, whether the verb is A or B: the noun hanasi 'talk' ("0") is derived from
the infinitive of hanasu ("2" = B) and nemuri 'sleep' ("0") is from the infinitive
of nemuru ("0" = A). Yet a good many of these derived nouns, from both A and B
infinitives, turn out to be pronounced prototonic ("1"). This appears to be the
result of simply dropping the later nondistinctive high, so that the middle stretch
no longer sags and the word stays low, with the result that the initial high now
becomes distinctive. (A few of the nouns have both treatments.) Examples:

hazime; nagusame; owari, izari, kaori, kazari, nioi, nerai, amari, oyogi, tayori;
hazimari, atumari, ayamari, arasoi, utagai, okonai, katamari, kotowari, mazinai,
tanosimi, maziwari, wazurai, ...
   Both treatments ("1/0"): tutome or tutome, negai or negai, takuwae or takuwae.

A similar explanation probably accounts for certain other long atonic nouns that
are listed as irregularly "1".
   The accents of the Kyōto-type dialect of Ibuki-jima ("Ib") are cited from
Uwano 1985, whose notations have been modified by dropping zero in the formulas for
the atonic patterns of the three registers (H high, L low, F falling) and explicitly
writing the register for the high tonic monosyllables ("H1") even though there is no
low counterpart (*L1). Each notation is equated with the historic type(s) to which
it pertains: H = 1.1, 2.1, 3.1, or 4.1 according to the length of the noun; L = 1.3,
2.4, 3.6, or 4.6; F = 2.3, 3.4, or 4.5; etc. See Ch. 4, end of §4.

5.6. Homonymous surface patterns of words and phrases (in Myōgi-shō).

In Ch. 4, §12 and Chart 13, we have seen how a given accent pattern may represent a string of several different combinations of underlying patterns, depending on the constituency of the particular compounds or phrases that are marked by the pattern. Below is a list of surface patterns for words of two, three and four syllables that shows the possible underlying strings.

o̅o̅	2.1	=	o̅ o̅	1.1 + 1.1	ò̅ o̅	1.2 + 1.1		
o̅o̲	2.2	=	o̅ o̲	1.1 + 1.3	ò̅ o̲	1.2 + 1.3		
oo	2.3	=	o̲ o̲	1.3 + 1.3				
oo̅	2.4	=	o̲ o̅	1.3 + 1.1				
oò	2.5	=	o̲ ò	1.3 + 1.2				

---

o̅o̅o̅	3.1	=	o̅ o̅o̅	1.1 + 2.1	o̅o̅ o̅	2.1 + 1.1		
o̅o̅o̲	3.2	=	o̅ o̅o̲	1.1 + 2.2	o̅o̅ o̲	2.1 + 1.3		
o̅oo	3.3	=	o̅ oo	1.1 + 2.3	o̅o̲ o̲	2.2 + 1.3		
ooo	3.4	=	o̲ oo	1.3 + 3.3	oo o̲	2.3 + 1.3		
ooo̅	3.5	=	o̲ oo̅	1.3 + 2.4	oo o̅	2.3 + 1.1		
oo̅o̅	3.6	=	o̲ o̅o̅	1.3 + 2.1	oo̅ o̅	2.4 + 1.1		
oo̅o̲	3.7	=	o̲ o̅o̲	1.3 + 2.2	oo̅ o̲	2.4 + 1.3		

---

o̅o̅o̅o̅	4.1	=	o̅ o̅o̅o̅	1.1 + 3.1	o̅o̅ o̅o̅	2.1 + 2.1	o̅o̅o̅ o̅	3.1 + 1.1
o̅o̅o̅o̲	4.2	=	o̅ o̅o̅o̲	1.1 + 3.2	o̅o̅ o̅o̲	2.1 + 2.2	o̅o̅o̅ o̲	3.1 + 1.3
o̅o̅oo	4.3	=	o̅ o̅oo	1.1 + 3.3	o̅o̅ oo	2.1 + 2.3	o̅o̅o̲ o̲	3.2 + 1.3
o̅ooo	4.4	=	o̅ ooo	1.1 + 3.4	o̅o̲ oo	2.2 + 2.3	o̅o̅o̅ o̲	3.3 + 1.3
oooo	4.5	=	o̲ ooo	1.3 + 3.4	oo oo	2.3 + 2.3	oooo̲ o̲	3.4 + 1.3
ooo̅o̅	4.6	=	o̲ ooo̅	1.3 + 3.5	oo oo̅	2.3 + 2.4	ooo o̅	3.4 + 1.1
oo̅o̅o̅	4.7	=	o̲ o̅o̅o̅	1.3 + 3.6	oo o̅o̅	2.3 + 2.4	ooo̅ o̅	3.5 + 1.1
oo̅o̅o̲	4.8	=	o̲ o̅o̅o̲	1.3 + 3.1	oo̅ o̅o̅	2.4 + 2.1	oo̅o̅ o̅	3.6 + 1.1
oo̅o̅o̲	4.9	=	o̲ o̅o̅o̲	1.3 + 3.2	oo̅ o̅o̲	2.4 + 2.2	ooo o̲	3.6 + 1.3
oo̲oo	4.10	=	o̲ ooo	1.3 + 3.3	oo̲ oo	2.4 + 2.3	ooo̲o̲ o̲	3.7 + 1.3
ooo̲o̲	4.11	=	o̲ ooo̲	1.3 + 3.7	oo o̅o̲	2.3 + 2.2	ooo̅ o̲	3.5 + 1.3

5.7. List of abbreviations.

A	high atonic (stem or derived noun) or reflex of high atonic
A´	special class of high stems
adj	adjective (= adjective stem)
adj -si-	adjective stem with the suffixed formant -si-
aux	auxiliary
B	low atonic (stem or derived noun); or reflex of low atonic
B´	special class of low stem
Bm	Bumō-ki (Muromachi accent)
bnd	bound
Ch	Chinese (= some version of earlier Chinese, perhaps 6th century A.D.)
Ck	Chinkoku-shukoku-jinja text of Myōgi-shō
dial.	dialect
Edo	Edo-period Kyōto language (from around 1600)
F	fall (from high to low pitch, within a syllable)
H (formulas)	high pitch
H (citations)	Hirayama Teruo (1960 unless otherwise noted)
Hn	Heian period (c. 800-1200)
Ib	Ibuki-jima (from Uwano 1985)
inf	infinitive (= ren'yō-kei)
Ir	Iroha-jirui-shō (1180)
JP	Japanese-Portuguese dictionary, Vocabulario da lingoa de Iapam 1603-4
K	Kindaichi Haruhiko (esp. data in NKD and Mka)
K 1 - 113	Koji-ki songs (by number, as in Philippi)
K kun(-chū)	phonogram translation notes in Koji-ki
...-K	katakana (in NS references)
Kg	Kagoshima
KggD	Kokugo-gaku dai-jiten
Km	Kamakura period (1200-1378)
Kn	Kanchi-in text of Myōgi-shō
Kt	Kyōto
kun(-chū)	phonogram translation note (in Nihon-Shoki or Koji-ki)
Kz	Kōzan-ji text of Myōgi-shō
L (formulas)	low pitch
...-L	"left" (in Ishizuka's NS references)
[Lit.]	literary
M	Man'yō-shū songs (cited by number, M 1 — M 4516)
...-M	Man'yō-gana (in NS references)
Mg	Myōgi-shō = Ruiju Myōgi-shō
mim	mimetic element/adverb/etymon
Mka	Meikai kokugo akusento jiten (Kindaichi 1958)
Mkz	Shin Meikai kokugo jiten (1972)
Mochizuki	Mochizuki Ikuko (the 1974 index, unless otherwise noted)
Mr	Muromachi period (1378-1573)
Nakata	Nakata Norio et al.: Kogo dai-jiten (1983)
NHK	Nippon-Hōsō-Kyōkai: Nihon-go hatsuon akusento jiten (1966)
Nk	Nakijin (Okinawa; from Nakasone 1983)
NKD	Nihon kokugo dai-jiten (1972-6)
Nr	Nara period (c. 700-800)
NS	Nihon-Shoki (from Ishizuka 1977)
NS (Okada)	Nihon-Shoki (from Okada 1956)

NS (T)	Nihon-Shoki (from Takayama 1983)
NS (T+)	Nihon-Shoki (Martin's additions/emendations to Takayama)
Okuda	Okuda Kunio 1971
Ongi	[Shōreki-bon] Konkōmyōsaishōō-kyō ongi. Text (Komatsu's index).
Ongi (Iroha)	The Iroha poem in Ongi.
Ongi-m	Man'yō-gana in Ongi that is assumed to reflect the accent.
Ongi-n	Inserted notes in Ongi.
Ōno	Ōno Susumu (etymologies cited from Iwanami Kogo-jiten)
Ōtsuki	Ōtsuki Fumihiko (etymologies cited from NKD or Daigenkai)
R (formulas)	rise (from low to high pitch, within a syllable)
RGJ	A Reference Grammar of Japanese (Martin 1975)
S	Shiza-kōshiki (Kamakura accent; from Kindaichi's index)
Sd	Shodon (Amami; from Martin 1970b)
Sr	Shuri (Okinawa; from Okinawa-go jiten)
Sz	Shizukuishi (Iwate; from Uwano 1982-3)
(T)	= NS (T)
(T+)	= NS (T+)
(T+ kun)	= NS (T+ kun)
Tk	Tōkyō
U	Umegaki Minoru (Kyōto accent data in NKD)
Unger	Unger, J.M. 1975/77: Studies in early Japanese morphophonemics.
v, vb	verb
vi	intransitive verb
vt	transitive verb
W	Kokin-waka-shū shōten-bon (mostly Kamakura accent; Akinaga's index)
...W-	"wari[-chū]" = interlinear note (in Ishizuka's NS references)
x	unknown; data unavailable
Yn	Yonaguni
ygr	younger speakers
Yoshida	Yoshida Kanehiko (etymologies in Yoshida 1976, 1979)
Zdb	Omodaka et al. 1967: Jidai-betsu kokugo dai-jiten, jōdai-hen.
Zs	Zusho-ryō text of Myōgi-shō

5.8. Dialect location list.

Accentuations are cited from dialects in the following places, among others, with the dialect accent type as shown. (The geographical designations are not always precisely defined.)

Place	Tk-type	Kt-type	Other
Aichi prefecture	+		
Akō, western Hyōgo prefecture		+	
Akita prefecture/city	+		
Aomori city (mostly from Uwano 1984)	+		
Chiba prefecture/city	+		
Chūgoku area (= Hiroshima etc.)	+		
Fukuoka prefecture/city	+		
Gifu prefecture/city	+		
Goka-mura, Oki island, Shimane prefecture	+		
Hachijō (islands), off the Izu peninsula	+		
Hagiwara, Gifu prefecture	+		
Hakata (= Fukuoka city, from Hayata 1985)	+		
Hamada, Shimane prefecture	+		
Hata, southwestern Shikoku (Ehime prefecture)	+		
Hattō(-mura), Tottori prefecture	+		
Hida = northern Gifu prefecture	+		
Himeji, Hyōgo prefecture		+	
Hiroshima prefecture/city	+		
Hyōgo prefecture		+	
Ibuki-jima, Kagawa prefecture		+	
Ie-jima, Ryūkyū islands			+
Ise, Mie prefecture		+	
Iwami = western Shimane prefecture	+		
Izumo = eastern Shimane prefecture; city	+		
Kagoshima prefecture/city, southern Kyūshū			+
Kameyama, Mie prefecture		+	
Kōbe, Hyōgo prefecture		+	
Kōchi prefecture/city, Shikoku		+	
Kun(i)naka, Yamanashi prefecture	+		
Matsue, Shimane prefecture	+		
Matsuho, Seitan-chō, Awaji island, Hyōgo prefecture		+	
Matsumoto, Nagano prefecture	+		
Mino = southern Gifu prefecture	+		
Miyako [island(s)], southern Ryūkyū islands			+
Nagano prefecture/city	+		
Nagoya, Aichi prefecture	+		
Nakanoshima, Tokara-rettō, south of Kyūshū			+
Narada, Yamanashi prefecture	+		
Naruto, Tokushima prefecture		+	
NE Kyūshū = Shirakawa(-mura), Fukuoka	+		
Numazu, Shizuoka prefecture	+		
Ōita prefecture/city, northern Kyūshū	+		
Okayama prefecture/city	+		
Okushiri island, Hokkaidō	+		

P l a c e	Tk-type	Kt-type	Other
Onna, Okinawa, Ryūkyū islands			+
Ōra (= Upura), Miyako, Ryūkyū islands			+
Ōsaka		+	
Sakawa, Kōchi prefecture, Shikoku		+	
Sapporo, Hokkaidō	+		
Shimane prefecture	+		
Shimoda, Shizuoka prefecture	+		
Shizukuishi, Iwate prefecture (Uwano 1982-3)	+		
Shizuoka prefecture/city	+		
Shodon, Amami Ōshima, Ryūkyū islands			+
Shuri, Okinawa, Ryūkyū islands			+
Suzu, Noto peninsula, Ishikawa prefecture		+	
Takamatsu, Kagawa prefecture, Shikoku		+	
Tappi, Aomori prefecture	+		
Toyama prefecture/city		+	
Wakamatsu paninsula, northern Fukuoka	+		
Wakayama prefecture/city		+	
Yaeyama [islands], southern Ryūkyū islands			+
Yamaguchi prefecture/city, southern Honshū	+		
Yonaguni, southern Ryūkyū islands			+

5.9. List of nouns.

1.2   a(-) < [k]a(-) ?< *ga. 'that *(distal)*'. Edo F (= HL). Northern Okinawan
dialects have qa-/ha- in free variation; Miyako, Yaeyama, Yonaguni have only
ka- (Nakamoto 1983:175-7). *See* aa, anata, ano, are, asoko, ati, ati-ra, atti.

1.3b   a (= aa). 'oh!' *(interjection)*. R - 1-0-A̲ x-A̲-x.

*2.1   aa < a(-)₁.₂ *(lengthened by analogy with koo)*. 'that way, like that
(distal)'. x - 0/1-0-A x-x-x. Cf. soo. Not attested before Meiji?

3.1   abara < *anpara. 'ribs'. x - 0-0-(A) x-x-x. *(Kg A inferred from
abarabone.)* Goka-mura 1̲; Hattō, Hamada, Matsue, Izumo 0.

3.1   abara < *anpara (cf. abareru). *(1)* 'sparse, having many gaps' *(adj-n)*;
(2) (= abara-ya) 'an open pavilion, a gazebo, a dilapidated (run-down) house'.
HHH - 0-0-x x-x-x. Sz 0. Cf. mare.

5.1   abarabone < *anpara₃.₁ -n- pone₂.₃ (< ...). 'rib (bone)'. x - 0-0-A
x-x-x. Sz 0.

4.1   abaraya < *anpara₃.₁ da₁.₃ᵦ. 'an open pavilion, a gazebo; a dilapidated
(run-down) house'. HHHH - 3̲-0-B̲ x-A[Lit.]-x. Sz 0/4̲.

3.x   abata (?< Sanskrit arbuda 'scab'). 'pockmark'. x - 0-0[H̲]/1[U]-B x-x-x.
Sz 0/2. Dial. (Iyo) agata. (Yaeyama azari.)

-          abe-: *see* ae-.

2.5   abu < amu(?/abu) < *anpu. 'gadfly, horsefly'. LH/L̲L̲ - 1-1:3-A x-x-x.
Ongi LF. NS (76b [14:123-M]) L̲L̲; NS (T 75) LH. Matsue 0; Narada, Hattō,
Hamada, Izumo, Goka-mura 1. Ib *(rare)* L2 = 2.5. Nk B.

4.6   abukuma ?< *anpu?(₂.₅) kuma₂.₁. 'Gadfly Bend' (a river name: ~ gawa).
x - 0-x-x x-x-x. Km (W) LLLH (≠ afu kuma LH|HH/LH).

3.4   abumi < abumyi < *a[si]₂.₃ -n- pum[a-C]iₐ ('foot tread'). 'stirrups'.
LLL - 0̲-0̲-x. Edo HHL. Sz *(rare)* 0̲. Sr qabui B *(but we expect *qanzi B)*.

6.22   abumigawara < abumigafara < abumyi ₃.₄ (< *a[si₂.₃] -n- pum[a-C]iₐ) -n-
kapara₃.₄ ('stirrup tile'). 'a kind of roofing tile'. LLLLHL (Ck) / LHL|LLH
(Kn) - 4-x-x x-x-x.

5.16   abumizuri < abumyi₃.₄ (< *a[si₂.₃] -n- pum[a-C]iₐ) -n- sir[a-C]iₐ.
'(the callus) where stirrups chafe the horse'. LLxHL - x-x-x x-x-x.

3.5a/b   abura < *anpura. 'oil; grease'. LLH - 0-2-B B-B-B. Edo HLL. Sapporo,
Akita, Goka-mura, Hakata, Ōita 1; western Mino (= SW Gifu) 1/2; Narada, Hata,
Wakamatsu, NE Kyūshū 2; Numazu, Hida (= northern Gifu), Hattō, Hamada, Matsue,
Izumo, Hiroshima 0; Tappi, Aomori 3̲. Hyōgo, Kōchi 2; Toyama, Suzu 2̲ *(we expect
1:3)*; Ib F̲ = 3.4. Yn anda B. Cf. aburu.

5.16   aburabiki < *abura-ᶠ/ᵦyikyi < *anpura₃.₅ₐ (-n-) pik[a-C]iₐ. 'oil brush'.
LLLHL - x-x-x x-x-x.

5.7   aburaᵗ/₂uki < *abura-ᵗ/ᵤukyi < *anpura₃.₅ₐ (-n-) tuk[a-C]iᵦ. 'lamp'.
LLLLH - 3-5-x x-x-x.

5.16   aburawata < *anpura₃.₅ₐ bata₂.₃. 'cotton for applying oil to the hair'.
LLLHL - 3-4-x x-x-x.

5.6   aburazuno < aburaduno < *anpura₃.₅ₐ -n- tunwo₂.₃. 'wheel-oil container'.
LLLL - x-3-x x-x-x.

?5.6   aburimono < *anpur[a-C]iᵦₒ mono₂.₃. 'grilled/broiled food'. LLLxx -
0/4/5-0-x x-x-x.

2.2a   ada < ata < *a(n)ta. *(1)* 'foe'; *(2)* 'empty, vain':   HH - 2-2-A x-A-x.
NS (124a, 124b) HH; Aomori *(rare)*, Sz 0̲. Ib H = 1.1. Km (W) *(1)* HH, *(2)* HL —
and these are the patterns in Heike-mabushi (Okumura 1976a:217); but 1700
Ōsaka has HL for 'foe'. Mg has ada HL with the semantogram 'tall wave' — is

that for [n]ada? If -d- did not appear "till mid Edo" (NKD), how come it is in
the Ryūkyūs too? Waye ¹yuhay (?1700) has "a.nta" for 'foe' (2:40r). Dial.
atan, antan (Hizen), attan. Cf. aza(-na), ada-si, aᵗ/ₐam-, atar-. See Ch. 2.

4.1   adabana < *a(n)taₛ.ₛ♭ -n- panaₛ.ₛ. 'abortive blossom'. HHHx - 0-0-A x-x-x.
K: Hn HHHH.

4.1   adabara (Mg), atabara (JP) < *a(n)taₛ.ₛ♭ -n- paraₛ.ₛ. 'stomach cramp'.
HHHH - 0-0-x x-x-x. NKD: "Also -fara."

3.1   adana: see azana.

3.3   adasi < atasi < *a(n)ta-si(-). (1) 'other' (adnoun, cf. onazi); (2) 'vain,
empty' (adj):   (1) HLL - 1-0̲-x x-x-x. NS (Okada) HLL. See ada. Said to have
only -si and -siku forms, but NKD 1:295d gives an example of -siki.

6.2   adasi-ᵏ/₉okoro < *a(n)ta-si (-n-) ko̲ko̲ro̲. 'fickle heart'. x - 4-x-x x-x-x.
Km (W) HHHHHL (Kunten-shō), LLLxxx. (JP -k-)

?2.4 < *2.3 ae < afey < *apa-Ci[-Ci]ₛ. 'feast, treat, banquet'. LH(-tamafu) - 2-x-x
x-x-x.

4.5   aemono < afemono < *afey-mo̲no̲ < *apa-Ci[-Ci]ₛ mo̲no̲ₛ.ₛ. 'food dishes
dressed with various sauces'. LLLL - 2-0[U]/3[H]-B x-x-x.

?6.2   ae-/abe-tatibana < afey-tatibana ?< *apa-Ci[-Ci]ₛ tatibana₄.₉ (< *tatiₛ.₄
(-n-) panaₛ.ₛ). 'a bergamot (orange)'. HHHHxx - x-5-x x-x-x. K: Hn HHHHHL.

4.6   aezuki < afeduki < *afeydukyi < *apa-Ci[-Ci]ₛ -n- tukiₛ.ₛ♭. 'a bowl heaped
with dressed foods'. LLLH - 2-0-x x-x-x.

5.x   aezukuri < afedukuri < afey-dukuri < *apa-Ci[-Ci]₇ₛ.₄‹ₛ.ₛ⁺ₛ -n- tuku-r[a-
C]iₛ. 'a bouillabaise (of fish or fowl)'. LHHxxx - x-x-x x-x-x.

3.4   agata (< ?). 'local land belonging to the Court; countryside, rural
areas'. LLL - 1̲-2-x x-x-x. NS (Okada) LLL. Km (W) LLL.

4.1   agebari (Zs Mg — the dakuten on ba is smudged and looks as if it were a
seiten) < *agey-ᶠ/♭ari < *anka-Ci[-Ci]ₐ (-n-) par[a-C]iₐ. 'a kind of tent or
canopy'. HHHH 0-0-x x-x-x. Cf. hirabari.

6.3   agekasugai < age-kasugafi < *agey (< *anka-Ci[-Ci]ₐ) kasugafyi₇₄.₉ (< ...).
'latch for a push-up door'. HHHHLL (Ck, "ake-") - x-x-x x-x-x.

4.7   agemaki < ageymakyi (probably derived noun < *agey makyi HL|HL < *anka-
Ci[-Ci]ₐ mak[a-C]iₐ). 'a kind of hair-style'. LLHH - 2-2-x x-x-x. Register
incongruent with etymology.

2.2a   agi < agyi < *anki. 'jaw; gill'. HL - x-2-x x-A-x. Km x. Sr qazi A.

3.1   agito < *agyi-to < *ankiₛ.ₛₐ toₛ.ₛ. 'jaw(s); gill(s)' (= era). HHH - 0-0-A
x-x-x. Km (S) HHH. 1700 Ōsaka L̲H̲L. Cf. agitouₐ.

2.2b   ago < *anko. 'chin, lower jaw'. x - 2-1̲:3̲-A A-x-x. Aomori, Narada, Hamada,
Goka-mura 2; Matsue, Izumo 2̲ (= 2.3); Hattō 1̲; Hakata 1̲, ygr 0/2. Kōchi 2
[Martin]; Ib H1 = 2.2. (?< ag[iₛ.ₛₐ-t]o₇₁.₁)

3.4   agoe < agwoye < *a[siₛ.ₛ] -n- koye[y]ₛ.ₛ (/ kuwe[y], see ker-uₛ; 'foot-
kick'). '(?) spurs of rooster; bird's claw'. LLL - x-x-x x-x-x. NS (119b) LLL.

3.5a   agura ?< *a[siₛ.ₛ] -n- kuraₛ.ₛ♭. 'high seat; (sitting) cross-legged'. LLH -
0-0̲[H]/1̲[U]-A̲ x-(B)-x. NS (76a [14:121-M]) agwora LLH(-H); NS (T+ 75) L̲H̲L̲.
Aomori, Hakata 0; Narada 3̲. Ib L̲ = 3.6. Sr qangwee-ii/-dui B.

?3.4   ahiru < afiru/afiro ?< *a[siₛ.ₛ] piroₐₐⱼ ₛ. 'duck'. x - 0̲-0̲-B x-B-x.
Narada 3; Goka-mura 1̲; Aomori, Sz, Hattō, Hamada, Matsue, Izumo, Hakata 0̲.
Ib F = 3.4. The word may be Muromachi; cf. Akinaga 1977:74-5. But apï(ru) ?<
*appïra in NE Honshū (Gengo-kenkyū 52:87) and a(p)pï in Yaeyama argue for
an earlier origin.

-        ahuri < afuri: see aori.

?2.4 ?< 2.3   ai < afyi < *ap[a-C]iₛ. 'meeting, encounter; alternate hammering (by
two smiths)'. LH - 1-2-x x-x-x.

2.5   ai < awi < *abiy < *[z]abo̱(-)Ci. 'indigo'. x - 1-1:3-B B-B-B. Ib F̱ = 2.3,
L2 = 2.5. Cf. ao.

3.2b   aida < afyida < *apinta (< *api-n-ta ?= ap[a-C]i*ᴮ* -n- ta*ı.ₛₐ*). 'interval'.
HHL - 0-0̱-A Ḇ-A/Ḇ-x. NS (95a) HHL; NS (T+ 118) LᴴH. Km (S) HHL. Edo HHL.
Tk 0 ?< 3 (cf. konoaida⁷, Tsuzuku 1941:407); Narada 3 (= ai 2); Tappi, Aomori,
Akita, Nagano (Kudō 124), Hamada 3; western Mino (= SW Gifu) 0/3. Suzu, Hyōgo,
Kōchi, Sakawa 0̱; Toyama 1̱:2̱; Ib F̱ = 3.4. Nk qeezaa B; Sr qweeda A/Ḇ, qeeza B.

4.x   [aikui] < afikufi < *afyi kufyi < *ap[a-C]i*ᴮ* kup[a-C]i*ᴮ*. 'alternate
hammering' (= ai). xxHH (? *LH|H, *LL|LL) - x-x-x x-x-x.

?3.4   aima < afyi-ma < *ap[a-C]i*?ₐ.₄‹ₐ.ₛₑᴮ* ma*ı.ı*. 'interval'. x - 0̱/3-0̱(/1[U])-B
x-A̱-x. Sz 3. Nk qeema HHL (= A̱); Sr qweema A̱.

4.6   aimuko < afimuko < *afyi-mukwo < *ap[a-C]i*ᴮ* mukwo*ₐ.₄*. '(?) brother-in-law;
nephew-in-law'. LLLH - 3-4-x x-x-x.

4.11   ainbe < "afimube" < *afyinbey < afyi (< *ap[a-C]i*ᴮ*) n[i]fey*ₐ.ₗₐ* (< ...).
'a kind of autumn harvest festival'. LLHL - x-x-x x-x-x. Cf. nie.

4.1   ainiku < ayaniku (?= aya*ₐ.ₛ* niku*ₐₐⱼ ᴮ but register incongruent*).
'unfortunately'. HHHH - 0-1̱:4[H]/1̱[U]-Ḇ x-x-x. Sz 0.

4.6   aisiru < awi*ₐ.₄* - siru*ₐ.₄* < *abo̱(-)Ci siru. '(extract from) a brew of
indigo leaves; (liquid) indigo dye'. LLLH - x-x-x x-x-x.

5.16   ai-tutuzi < ai (?< *a[k]i*ₐ.ₛ* 'autumn', ?< *a[f]i*ₐ.ₓ* 'valley') tutunsi
('wisteria' < ?). 'azalea' (= satuki). LLLHL - 4-x-x x-x-x.

4.7   aiyome < afiyome < *afyi-yome*ₐ.ₗ* < *ap[a-C]i*ᴮ* yome*ₐ.ₗ* (< ...). 'sister-
in-law'. LLHH (Kz) - 0/2-0-x x-x-x. K: "Hn LLHL" (mistake?).

2.3   aka (?< ak[ut]a). 'dirt'. H̱L/LL - 2-2-B x-B-x. K: Hn LL. Ib F = 2.3.
Sr qaka B 'dirt soiling hair/clothes, grime'.

?2.5 < 2.1   aka. 'red'. x - 1-1:3[H]/1̱[U]-A̱ A-A-A. Tokushima 2̱; Izumo 1/2̱;
Hamada, Matsue, Hiroshima 1. Kōchi (Doi 1952:22), Ōsaka, Ise 1:3. Ib L2 = 2.5.
Nk (h)akaa Ḇ. Cf. aka*ₐₐⱼ ₐ*; akaru*ₐₐⱼ ᴮ*; akasu*ₐ*, akeru*ₐ*; aku*ₐ*; akiraka.

5.2 (= 2.1|3.2)   akaazuki < akaadukyi < *aka*ₐₐⱼ ₐ* antuki*ₐ.ₐₑ*. 'red bean'.
HH(|)HHL - 3-1:3-x x-x-x.

5.3 (= 2.1|2.3)   akaenba < aka*ₐₐⱼ ₐ* wem[u]ba*?ₐ.ₛ* (< ...). 'red dragonfly' (=
akatonbo). HH(|)HLL - x-x-x x-x-x.

4.1 (= 2.1|2.1)   akagane < *aka*ₐₐⱼ ₐ* -n- kana-Ci*ₐ.ₗ*. 'copper'. HH(|)HH -
0-0[U]/1̱[H]-A x-A̱-x. Sr qakugani A (-u- unexplained).

4.1   akagari (< ?). 'skin cracks, chaps' (= akagire). HHHH - 0-0-x x-x-x.

?5.1,?5.2 akahadaka < aka-fadaka < *aka*ₐₐⱼ ₐ* panta-ka*ₐ.₆*. 'stark naked' (*adj-n*).
HHHHH - 3-1:4-A x-A̱-x. But Hoke-kyō tanji HHHHL.

5.3   akakagati < *aka*ₐₐⱼ ₐ* kagati*ₐ.ₗ* (< ...) 'bladder/ground cherry' (= kagati
= hoozuki). HHHLL - x-x-x x-x-x. NS (T+ kun) LHHLL.

3.2a   aka*ᵏ/₉*o < *aka*ₐₐⱼ ₐ* (-n-) kwo*ₐ.ₗ*. x - 0-1:3-A x-x-x. 'baby; (= yurimimizu)
a kind of tubificid *(worm)*'. Aomori 2̱. Attested late 11th century.

?3.1   akama. 'bulrush' (= gama). HHH-··· - x-x-x x-x-x.

5.2   akamagusa < *akama*?ₐ.ₗ* -n- kusa*ₐ.ₛ*. 'Euopatorium lindleyanum' (=
sawaararagi = sawahiyodori). HHHHL - 4-4-x x-x-x.

?3.1, ?3.2x   akana < *aka*ₐₐⱼ ₐ* na*ı.ₛₐ*. 'a kind of red turnip'. x - 0-x-x x-Ḇ-x.
Sr qakana Ḇ 'beefsteak plant'.

?3.1, ?3.2x   akane < *aka*ₐₐⱼ ₐ* na-Ci*ı.ₛₐ*. 'madder (Rubio cordifolia)'. HHx (?=
HHH, ?= HHL) - 0-0-(A) x-x-x. K: Hn HHH.

4.11   akaraka < *aka*ₐₐⱼ ₐ* -ra-ka. 'radiant' (*adj-n*). LLxx - x-x-x x-x-x.
NS (120a) LLHL.

3.1   akari < *aka-r[a-C]i*ₐ*. 'light; torch; a bright/public place'. x - 0-0-A
x-A̱-x. NS (107b) ··· ḺH̱H̱ (?= *HHH). Sr qakai 'translucent shōji'.

4.1   akasama(-ni) < *aka-ₐ samaₛ.ₛₐ‹ₛ.₁. 'sudden(ly)' (= akara-sama). x - 0-x-x
x-x-x. NS (125b[14:282-K]) HHHH(-H). *(Okada misprints "akakama".).*

3.1   akasi < *aka-s[a-C]iₐ. 'light, lantern; proof, explanation; clarification,
enlightenment'. x - 0-0-A x-B̲-x. Nk x; Sr qakasi B̲ 'torch', qakasi-mun B̲
'riddle; something to think about'.

4.1   akatuki < akatᵘ/₀kyi < *aka(-)ₐ tokiₛ.ₛ. 'dawn'. HHxx - 0-0-A A-B̲-x.
NS (106a) HF̲HH = HHHH. Km (S) HHHH. Nk x.

3.2a   akaza ?< *akansa (< *akaₛₐⱼ ₐ + ?). 'Chenopodium album' *(the ashes are
used for dye)*. HHL - 0-1:3-x x-x-x.

2.1   ake < akey < *akaₛₐⱼ ₐ -Ciₛᵤf. 'red (color); red gown; (= akane) madder'.
HH - 0-0[H]/2̲[U]-A x-x-x.

?3.7a ?< 3.3   akebi (< ?). 'Akebia quinata' *(a vine)*. HLL - 0-1:3-B x-x-x.
Yamaguchi, Izumo (Kobayashi), Aomori (usually [agũ̃bi]), Sz 0. Kōchi 1:3
(Kobayashi). If Mg is right, then the modern dialects are all aberrant.

4.1   akebono < akeybono < *aka-Ci[-Ci]ₐ -n- po-no₍ₛ.ₛ. 'dawn, daybreak'. x -
0-0-A x-x-x. NS (106a) HHHH. Cf. honoka.

?*2.3   aki < *akyi (?< [w]akyi < *bak[a-C]i 'divide, distribute', cf. sabaku).
'barter; trade, peddling'. x - x-x-x x-x-x. Cf. akindo; akinau, agau.

2.5   aki < akyi < *aki. 'autumn'. LH - 1-1:3-B B-A̲-x. Km (W,S) LH. Edo LF.
K: Km-Edo LF. Toyama 2 *(expected reflex)*; Suzu 1̲ *(we expect 2)*; Ib L2 = 2.5.
Verbal origins suggested: ak[a]-ᵦ 'be satiated = suffice'; ak[a]-ₐ 'redden,
dawn; open, clear'.

-       akibito: *see* akindo.
-       akida: *see* akita.

?4.5   akinai < akinafyi = (*)akyi-nafyiᵦ (Zdb) < *aki₍ₛ.ₛ (< ...) -na-p[a-C]i.
'commerce'. LLxx - 2/3-0[U]/2[H]-A̲ x-B-x. Narada 4; Sz, Hattō, Matsue, Izumo
3; Hamada 2; Hakata 0, ygr 2. Sr qacinee B.

4.6   akindo, akyuudo < akibito < akyibyito̲ < *aki₍ₛ.ₛ -n- pito̲₍ₛ.ₛₐ. 'trader,
peddler, merchant'. LLLH - 2-1:3-A̲ x-B-x. Sz 2. Sr qacoodu B. Chep-hay sin-e
(Shōkai-shingo 1676) a.ki.wun.two (10:24a) = akiundo.

4.11   akiraka < akyiraka < *ak[a-C]iₐ -ra-ka. 'clear' *(adj-n)*. LLHL - 2-4-B
x-B-x. Km x. K: Mr HLLL.

?3.7 (= 2.4|1.3) / 3.4   akitᵗ/ₐa < akyi-[?"]ta *(no phonogram)* < *aki₍ₛ.ₛ (-n-)
taₗ.ₛₐ. 'autumn field; *(placename)*'. x - 1-1:3-B x-x-x. Km (W) LH(|)L / LLL.

?3.6, ?3.4a   akitu < akidu < akyidu < *akintu (?< *aki₍ₛ.₄ -n- -tu musi₍ₛ.₁ 'autumn
insect'). 'dragonfly' (= tonbo, enba). x - 0-1-B x-B-x. NS (76b [14:124-M])
LLL; Zs NS LLF (K 1964a:350); NS (T+ 75) F̲HH ?= H̲H̲H̲. Sz [ageẑu] 1̲. Nk
haKeedya B. Sr qaakeeẓuu B, but qakeẓu- in compound. See Ch. 4, §7.3 (p. 189).

?5.6   akitusima < akyidu-sima < *akintu₍ₛ.₆,₍ₛ.ₛᵦ (< ...) simaₛ.ₛ. 'the land of
Akidu = *(placename in Nara, extended to refer to)* Yamato; Japan'. NS (74b
[11:302-NM], 74c[11:305-M]) H̲L̲L̲|H̲L̲; (76b [14:125-M]) LLLLL; NS (T+ 62) L̲L̲H̲|L̲H̲,
(T+ 63) LHH|LL, (T+ 75) F̲LR-LL.

?3.7a, ?3.6   akome < *akomey ?< *a[fyi]-komey < *ap[a-C]iᵦ koma-Ci[-Ci]ᵦ. 'a
garment between underwear and outerwear'. LHL (Kn) / LHH (Ir) - 0-0̲-x x-x-x.

2.1   aku. 'lye'. x - 0-0-A x-A-x. K: Hn HH *(attested?)*. Km (W) HH. Narada,
Hiroshima 0. Ōsaka, Ise 0; Ib H = 2.1.

2.1   ... *aku. 'place/fact': k̄at̄ar̄[ū] ̄ak̄u (Zs), ītām̄[ū] ̄ak̄ū f̄ā (Zs); t̄am̄af̄āk̄ū
(NS 103b), t̄am̄af̄āk̄ū (NS 91a, 101a); m̄aūs̄āk̄ū (NS 110a). See K 1964a:459. But
note the doubt cast on the hypothesized noun itself in Yoshida 1973:457-519.

3.1   akubi (< ?; cf. okubi). 'yawn'. HHH - 0-0-B̲ ?B̲-A-A. Sapporo, Akita 2̲;
Aomori, Narada, Goka-mura 1̲; Hakata 1̲, ygr 0. Toyama 1:2 *(expected)*; Suzu 1:2
(we expect 0); Ib L2̲ = 3.5/7. Nase A; Nk haKuubi A.

3.1   akuta. 'trash, garbage, refuse'. HHH - 0/1-0-B x-B-x. 1700 Ōsaka LHL.
       Sz 3 (but usual word is gomi 2). Cf. aka.
-          akyuudo: see akindo.
2.5   ama(-) < *[z]ama. 'rain'. See ame.
2.5 (?< 2.3)   ama(-). 'heaven'. NS (91a [11:7-K], 92b [11:15-K] ama-tu LL-L.
       NS (T+ 3; 102) LL; NS (T+ kun) ama-no LL-L. See ame.
2.3   ama. 'fisher(woman)'. LL - 1-2-B x-x-x. NS (95a) LL. Km (W) LL/HL.
       1700 Ōsaka HL. Hattō, Matsue, Izumo, Wakamatsu 0; Hamada 1/0; Goka-mura 1.
       Ib L = 2.4 (also L2 = 2.5), H1 = 2.2.
2.4   ama. 'nun'. LH - 1-1-B x-x-x. Edo LH. Hattō, Matsue, Izumo 0; Hamada 1/0;
       Goka-mura 1. K: Hn-Edo LF (attestations?). Ib (rare) L = 2.4, H1 = 2.2.
4.7   amabiko < *ama-byikwo < *ama$_{2.5}$ -n- pikwo$_{2.1}$ (< pi$_{1.2}$ kwo$_{1.1}$). 'echo'.
       LLHH - 2-0-x x-x-x. Km (W) LLHL.
4.11   amadori < *[z]ama$_{2.5}$ -n- tori$_{2.1}$ ('rain bird'). 'a white-rumped swift
       (Apus pacificus)' (= amatubame). LLHL - 2-3-x x-x-x.
5.16   amagaeru < amagaferu < *amagafyeru < *ama$_{2.5}$ -n- ?kapiru$_{3.6}$. 'tree frog,
       hyla'. LLLHL - 3-1:4-B x-x-x.
3.1   amagi ?< *amagiy ?< *ama$_{adj\ A}$ -n- ko-Ci$_{1.3a}$. 'licorice' (= kanzoo).
       HHH - x-x-x x-x-x.
4.6   amaginu < *ama-gyinu < *[z]ama$_{2.5}$ -n- kinu$_{2.4}$. 'raincoat'. LLLH - 0/3-0-x
       x-x-x.
4.11   amagoi < amagofi < *ama-gofyi < *[z]ama$_{2.5}$ kop[a-C]i$_B$. 'praying for
       rain'. LLHL - 0/2/3-3[U]/1:4[H]-B x-B-x. Sz 3.
4.5   amagumo < ama-^{k}/$_g$umwo < *[z]ama$_{2.5}$ (-n-) kumwo$_{2.3}$. 'raincloud'. x - 0/3-
       0[U]/1[H]-B x-(B)-x. Km (W) LLLL. Sr qamigumu B < *ame-gumo.
?3.1   ama[h]i < amafi = amani ('clematis'). HHx (Ir) - x-x-x x-x-x. The spelling
       probably represents ama(w)i < ama[n]i.
7.2   amakutinezumi < ama^k/$_g$uti-nezumyi < *ama$_{adj\ A}$ (-n-) kuti$_{2.1}$ nensumi$_{3.6}$
       (< ...). 'house mouse'. HHHHHHL - 5-6-x x-x-x.
3.1   amana < *ama$_{adj\ A}$ na$_{1.3a}$. (1) 'sweet greens' (such as nazuna 'shepherd's
       purse'); (2) 'Tulipa edulis'; (3) (= amadokoro) 'Polygonatum japonicum' (=
       yamaemi); (4) (= narukoyuri) 'Polygonatum falcatum' (= yamaemi); (5) (=
       hunabara-soo) 'Cynanchum atratum' (= minasikigusa); (6) (= giboosi) 'plantain
       lily, hosta'; (7) (= maoo) 'mahuang, Ephedra sinica' (= katunegusa); (8) (=
       kanzoo = wasuregusa) 'day lily, Hemerocallis fulva'; (9) (= amani) 'clematis'.
       HHH - 0-0-x x-x-x.
3.1   amani (< ?). 'clematis' (= botanzuru). HHH - x-x-x x-x-x. Also ama[h]i <
       amafi (Ir), amana (Kn, Wamyō-shō).
5.16 = 2.3-no|2.2   amanogawa < amano^k/$_g$afa < *ama$_{2.5}$ (?< 2.3) no kapa$_{2.2a}$
       ('heaven river'). 'the Milky Way'. LLL(|)HL - 3-4-B x-x-x.
3.4   amari < *ama-r[a-C]i. 'excess; excessive(ly)':
       (1) Noun: LLL - 3-1:3[H]/2[U]-B x-B-x; NS (T+ 41) LLL; Km (S) LLL; Edo HHL;
       (after numerals) momoamari no (NS 94a), yo yoro["]su amari (NS 102b).
       (2) Adjectival noun: x - 3/2-0-x x-x-x.   (3) Adverb: x - 0-0-x x-x-x.
       Aomori 2 (adv. o), Hattō, Hamada, Matsue 3; Izumo 3/0; Goka-mura 1 (?< *0
       expected reflex). Ib noun F = 3.4, adverb anmari F = 4.5.
4.11   amasaku (< ?). 'feather cockscomb, Celosia argentea' (= umasaku = no-
       geitoo). LLHL - x-x-x x-x-x. Misprinted as "amakusa" in NKD 16:5b:13.
5.16   amasidari ?< ama$_{2.5}$ (< *[z]ama) si[ta]dari (< *sin[a]-tar[a-C]i$_{?B}$).
       'raindrop(s)'. LLLHL - 3-x-x x-x-x. Cf. sitataru < sitadaru; sidariyanagi.
3.5b   amata < ama-$_{(B)}$ -ta$_{?suf}$. 'extremely (much/many)'. LLH - 1-2-B x-x-x.
       NS (T+ 66) LLL. Edo HLL. Cf. amaru, amari.

6.10 = 2.3-tu|3.1   ama-tu-hituqi < ama₂.₅ (?<2.3) -tu fyi-tugyi (< *pi₁.₂ₐ tunk[a-
    C]i_A). 'the succession to the throne'. x - x-x-x x-x-x. NS (91a, 96b) LL-L|HHH,
    (92b) LL-L|LHH.

?5.16 < 6.22 (= 2.5-no | 3.2) amazakume, amanosakume < amanosagumye < *ama₂.₅ no
    sanku[ra-u_B] mye₁.₃ᵦ (< *miCa₁.₃ < ...). 'Heaven's Grasping Woman' (name of an
    evil goddess). "LLHLH" (?= *LLLHL) < LLL|HHL - x-x-x x-x-x.

4.2 (= 2.1|2.2)   amazura < amadura < *ama_adj A -n- tura?₂.₂ᵦ ('sweet vine').
    'Parthenocissus tricuspidata' (= totoki = tuta = natuzuta). HHxx ?= *HH(|)HL -
    0-x-x x-x-x.

2.1   ame < amey < *ama_adj A -Ci_suf. 'gluten'. HH - 0-0-A A-A-A. Ib H = 2.1.

2.5   ame < amey < *ama-Ci < *[z]ama-Ci. 'rain'. ?LL - 1-1:3-B B-B-B̲. NS (Okada)
    LH; NS (T 72) LL; (T+ 82) LH. Km (S) LH. Edo LF. Ib L2 = 2.5. Nk qamii B̲; Onna
    qaamii B. K: Hn-Km-Edo LF. Cf. (ko/haru/hi/mura)-same; abiru/amiru 'bathe'; ame
    'heaven'.

2.5   ame < amey < *ama-Ci. 'heaven'. ?LF - 1-2̲-x x-(B)-(B̲). NS (73b [11:254-M],
    73c [11:261-M]) LH; (93b [11:31-K, 132a[14:418-K]) ame-no LL-L. NS (T 60) LL,
    (T 2) LH. Km (W) L?H, amano- LLL. Edo LF. Hiroshima 1. Ōsaka, Ise 2̲. Yn ami-
    nu-myaa B 'rainbow' (< 'heaven-snake one').

?4.1   ameuˢ/₂i < *amey₂.₁ (< *ama-Ci₂.₁) u(n)si₂.₁. 'a gluten-colored ox (which
    was highly valued); (= me-usi) a cow'. LLLL (Kn, -z-) = *HHHH (etymology
    confused?) - 0-0-x x-x-x.

2.3   ami < amyi < *ami < *am[a-C]iᵦ. 'net'. LL - 2-2-B x-B-B. NS (T 3) LL.
    Edo HL. Ib F = 2.3.

?2.1   ami. 'a kind of tiny shrimp'. HH - 2̲-2̲-A x-x-x. (Related to ebi?)
    Hiroshima 2̲. Ōsaka, Ise 0.

?2.4   amo = omo. 'mother'. x - x-x-x x-x-x. ? NS (81b [14:439-M]) LH; NS (T 82)
    LH. The NS passage: a̅m̅o̅ n̅i̅ k̅o̅s̅o̅ 'only to mother', but the second syllable is
    also taken as a graphic abbreviation using MOTHER /mo/ for EACH /mey/, hence
    'in heaven only'. K: "Hn LF?"

-            amo- = ame 'heaven'.

-            amu: see abu.

-            amuˢ/₂iro: see aziro.

?4.1   amututi ?= antuti ?< *an[ta]₂.₂ᵦ tuti₂.₃ ('foe turf'). 'archery target
    mound' (= azuti). HHxx - x-x-x x-x-x.

-            amuziti: see anziti.

2.3   ana. 'hole'. LL - 2-1̲-B x-B-B. Km (S) LL. Narada 2; Hiroshima 1̲/2.
    Ōsaka 1̲; Ise 1̲/2; Ib L̲ = 2.4. Onna qaanaa B.

4.5 (= 2.3|2.3)   anadama < *ana₂.₃ -n- tama₂.₃. 'a jewel with a thread-hole'.
    x - x-x-x x-x-x. NS (Okada) LL(|)LL; NS (T+ 2) LH|LH.

4.10   anagati (< ?). 'necessarily, wholly' (adv). LHLL - 0-3-x x-x-x. Mr (Bm)
    HHLL. K: Edo HHLL/HLLL.

6.21   anahazikami < ana₂.₃ - fazikami?₄.₁ (< ...). 'ginger' LLLHLL - x-x-x
    x-x-x.

4.11   anahira < anafira < *ana-fyira < *a[si]₂.₃ -na- (?< -no) pira?₂.₂ᵦ.
    'the instep'. LLHL - x-x-x x-x-x.

?3.2b, ?3.3 anata < kanata < *kan[o k]ata < ?*ga no kata. 'that direction/way,
    over there; you'. x - 1/2-2-A x-x-x. Km (W) HHL/HLL. Mr (Bm) HHL. 1700 Ōsaka
    HHL. Aomori (rare), Hiroshima 3; Sz, Narada, Hattō, Hamada, Matsue, Izumo,
    Goka-mura, Wakamatsu 2. Ōsaka, Ise ('there') 3 / ('you') 2.

4.11   anaura < *a[si]₂.₃ -na- (?< -no) ura₂.₃. 'the sole of a foot'. LLHL -
    0-0-x x-x-x.

2.1   ane ?< *an[y]e < *ani mye (< *miCa ?= *mina). 'older sister'. x - 0-0-A
A-x-x. Edo HH. Hamada 0/<u>1</u>; NE Kyūshū, Narada <u>1</u> (cf. ani). Ib H = 2.1. Yn ati
C < ?. K: Hn-Edo HH. Dial. anne (cf. Korean enni).

2.4   ani ?< [n]ani*2.4*. 'how possibly?!' *(rhetorical)*. LH - 1-2-x x-x-x.
NS (71c [11:179-M]) <u>LL</u>; NS (T+ 49) LH. Attested as anni in 1184 (KggD 971b).

?2.5   ani. 'older brother'. x - 1-1:3[H]/1[U]-<u>A</u> x-x-x. Edo LF. 1700 Ōsaka
ani-go LHH. Ib L2 = 2.5.

?2.1   ano < [k]a-n<u>o</u> (?< *ga-n<u>o</u>). 'that ··· ' *(adnoun)*. x - 0-0-A A-A-(x). Ib <u>F</u>
= 2.3. Yn kanu A. K: Edo HL. ("Began to be used for kano in mid-Hn", Ōno.)

-         anziro = amu^s/_ziro: *see* aziro.

4.5   anzitⁱ/_u < amuziti (< Ch .am-ŝyet). 'hermit's cell' (modern ansitu).
LLxx - 0-0-x x-x-x. K: Hn LLLL.

2.5   ao < awo < *abo < ?< *zab<u>o</u>. 'blue, green'. (L)-1-1:3[H]/<u>1</u>[U]-B <u>A</u>-(<u>A</u>)-
(<u>A</u>/B). Okushiri island <u>2</u>; Izumo <u>1</u>/2; Matsue <u>1</u> *(we expect 2)*. Ib L2 = 2.5.
Nk qoo <u>A</u>; Yn au-cici <u>A</u>, aun B. Cf. ao*adJ B*, massao; ai. Note: Several compounds
are attested with high-register patterns incongruent with the etymologies.

4.5   aobie < awo^f/_bie ?< *awo fiywe[y] < *[z]abo*adJ B* (-n-) p^u/_oCi-baCi[-Ci]
(see hieru). 'a dagger made of green bamboo'. LLLL - x-x-x x-x-x.

?4.7   aobuti < awo-buti < *[z]ab<u>o</u>*adJ B* -n- puti*?2.4*. 'the yawning deep (blue)'.
<u>HHLL</u> *(odd)* - 0-<u>1</u>-x x-x-x.

?5.2, ?5.7   aogaeru < awogaferu < *awo-gafyeru < *[z]ab<u>o</u>*adJ B* -n- ?kapiru*3.6*.
'tree frog, hyla'. <u>HHHHL</u> - 3-1:4-B x-x-x. Sz 3. Mg register incongruent with
etymology. Cf. amagaeru.

?4.1   aoguro < awo-guro < *awo-gurwo < *[z]ab<u>o</u>*2.5 / adJ B* -n- kurwo*?2.5*.
'greenish black'. HHxx - A-x-x x-x-x. Register incongruent with etymology.

4.11   aohaka < awo-faka < *[z]ab<u>o</u>*adJ B* paka*2.3*. 'Green Tumulus' *(placename)*.
x - x-0-x x-x-x. NS (129b [14:383-K]) LLHL.

3.1   aoi < afufyi < *apupi. 'hollyhock'. HHx - 0-0-A x-x-x. K: Hn HHH. Aomori
(rare) <u>2</u>; Narada, Hiroshima, Hakata 0. Ōsaka, Ise 0; Ib H = 3.1. Cf. [karaoi].

?4.2, ?4.11   aomusi < awomusi < *[z]ab<u>o</u>*adJ B* musi*2.1*. 'green insect (caterpillar,
grub)'. HHHL *(odd)* - <u>2</u>-<u>1:3</u>-A x-x-x. Sz <u>0</u>. The Mg register is incongruent with
the etymology.

?3.4 (= 2.3|1.3)   aona < awona < *[z]ab<u>o</u>*adJ B* na*1.3a*. 'greens; (= kabu) turnip'.
xxL - <u>0</u>/<u>2</u>-<u>0</u>[U]/<u>1</u>[H]-<u>A</u> x-x-x. K: Hn LLL. Hakata 2, ygr 0.

4.11   aonori < awo-n<u>o</u>ri < *[z]ab<u>o</u>*adJ B* n<u>o</u>ri*2.3*. 'green laver (seaweed)'.
LLHL - 2-3[H]/2[U]-B x-A/B-x. Sz 0.

3.4   aori < afuri ?< *a[si]*2.3* pur[a-C]i*B* ('feet-touch'). 'mudguards hanging on
either side of a horse'. LLL - 3-<u>0</u>-x x-x-x.

?4.3   aosaba < awosaba < *[z]ab<u>o</u>*adJ B* sanpa*2.1*. 'mackerel'. <u>HHLL</u> *(odd)* - 2/0-x-x
x-x-x.

?3.4a   aoto < awo(-)two < *[z]ab<u>o</u> two (< ?). 'blue(-gray) grindstone'. LLF (Zs)
/ LLH (Kn) - <u>0</u>-<u>0</u>-x x-x-x. K: LLF"?". See Ch. 4, §7.3.

?5.1   aotuzura < awo-tudura < *[z]ab<u>o</u>*adJ B* tuntura*3.5a* (< ...). 'Simonemium
diversifolium/acutum' (= tuzurahuzi); *("mistaken usage")* 'Cocculus trilobus'
(= kamiebi). x - x-x-x x-x-x. Km (W) HHHHH. Km register incongruent with
etymology.

2.5|4.6   ao-unabara < awo*adJ B* unafara*4.6* (< ...). 'the wide blue sea'. LH|LLLH
(Zs) - 3/4-4[U]/5[H]-B x-x-x. K: Hn HHHHLL *(attested?)*.

?4.6   aouri < awouri < *[z]ab<u>o</u>*adJ B* uri*2.4*. 'a kind of melon'. LLLH - 2-1:3-x
x-x-x. K: Hn HHHL *(misprint?)*.

?4.2   aoyagi < awo-yagiy < *[z]ab<u>o</u>*adJ B* yanagiy*3.1* (< ?*dana*2.1* -n- k<u>o</u>-Ci*1.3a*).
'a green willow'. x - 0-0-B x-x-x. Km (W) HHHL, HHLL, HLLL (incongruent).

4.11   aoyaka < awoyaka < *[z]abo$_{2.5}$ / adj B -da-ka. 'blue'. LLHL - 2-x-x x-x-x.
-      ?*-apu = *pu = *pi 'day': see kyoo.

2.5   ara(-) 'new': see sara; arata.

2.2a   ara. 'chaff, bran; offal'. HL - 2-2(/0[U])-A x-A-x. Aomori 0; Hiroshima 2.
Ōsaka, Ise 2; Ib H2 = 2.2. Cf. araku, areru.

*2.3   [a]ra < *ara-$_B$. 'what exists; the existent; the manifest (vivid, real);
thing, one; amount': see -ra, -re. Cf. -ri; arawa.

?4.9   araara < *ara$_{adj A}$ - ara$_{adj A}$. 'rough(ly)' (adj-n, adv). LHxL (?= *LHHL) -
3-0-x x-x-x.

4.3   arabako < *ara$_{adj A}$ -n- pakwo$_{2.1}$ ('coarse[-holed] box'). 'a sieve for
winnowing grain'. HHLL - x-x-x x-x-x.

4.7   arahito < ara-fyito < *ara$_B$ pito$_{2.2a}$: (~ -gamiy < *-n- kamu-Ci$_{2.3}$)
'(a god of) visible men'. x - x-x-x x-x-x. NS (117a[14:109-K]) LLHH.

4.1   ara^k/$_g$ane < ara-kane < *ara$_{adj A}$ kana-Ci$_{2.1}$. 'ore, unrefined/unwrought
metal'. HHHH - 0-0-x x-x-x. Ongi HHHH.

5.4   arakazime (?< *arak[u] (< ar[a-u]$_B$ attr aku$_{*1.x}$) fazimey$_B$ inf (< *pan[a]-
si(-)ma-Ci[-Ci]). 'beforehand' (adv). HHLLL (Ck) - 0-0[U]/1[H]-A x-x-x. Mr (Bm)
LHLLL. Sz 0.

5.16   [arakazura] < ara-kadura < *ara$_{adj A}$ kantura$_{3.2}$. '? a rough-woven fence'.
LLLHx ?= *LLLHL (Kn, Bamboo Radical missing from 2d character) - x-x-x x-x-x.
Register incongruent with etymology. Only occurrence is Kn Butsu-ka moto 9:7.

3.2b   arame < *ara$_{adj A}$ me$_{1.x}$ (< ...). 'Eisenia bicyclis (a seaweed)'. HHx -
0/2-2-A x-x-x. Edo HLL. K: Hn HHL (inferred?).

4.1   aramoto < *ara$_{adj A}$ moto$_{2.3}$ ('coarse base'). 'unpolished rice with
unhulled rice (or other grain) mixed in'. HHHH - 0-0-x x-x-x.

4.2 (= 2.1|2.2)   araoda < ara-woda < *ara$_{adj A}$ woda$_{?2.2}$ (< ?bo-$_{?1.1}$/?[k]wo-$_{1.1}$
-n- ta$_{1.3a}$). 'a rough (untouched) field; (?) a newly opened field'. x - 3-0-x
x-x-x. Km (W) HH(|)HL.

?4.9   araragi < *araragiy < *ara-[a]ra$_{?4.9}$ (< ...) -n- ko-Ci$_{1.3a}$. 'wild leek
(= nobiru); Japanese yew (= itii)'. LHHx (?= *LHHL) - 0-0-x x-x-x. Cf. sawaararagi.

3.1   arare ?< *ararare[y] < *ara$_{adj A}$ - ara$_{adj A}$ -Ci. 'hail; rice-cake cubes'.
HHH - 0-1-B x-x-x. Hakata 2; Wakamatsu 3.

?3.4   arasi < *ara$_{adj A}$ si$_{1.x}$ ('rough wind'). 'storm'. LLL - 1-2-A x-A-B.
Mr (Bm) HHH. Edo HHL(/...). 1700 Ōsaka HHL. Ōita 3; Matsumoto, Numazu,
Hiroshima 1(/0 [Terakawa]); Sapporo, Aomori, Akita, Narada, Hattō, Hamada,
Matsue, Izumo, NE Kyūshū 0; Hakata 0, ygr 1; Goka-mura 0 (expected reflex).
Ōsaka 1:3, Ise 2; Ib F = 3.4. Nk qaraasi A; Yn arasi B (H 1964:71b). The Mg
register is incongruent with etymology.

3.1   arata < *ara$_{adj A}$ ta$_{1.3a}$. 'wild/rough field'; ? 'new(ly opened) field'.
Hn (Kn, Shinsen-Jikyō) LLL, (Kz) HLL - 0-0-x x-x-x. K: ('new field') "Hn LLL".

3.4   arata ?< *[z]ara-ta (cf. sara). 'new' (adj-n). LLL - 1-2-B x-x-(B).
Km (S) LLH. Yn aran B 'be new'.

4.1   aratama < *ara$_{adj A}$ tama$_{2.3}$. 'rough (uncut) gemstone'. HHHH - 0-0-x x-x-x.

3.1   arato < *ara$_{adj A}$ two$_{1.3a}$. 'rough grindstone' (cf. mato). HHH - 0-0-x
x-x-x.

3.7a/b   arawa < arafa < *ara-pa (?< *ara-$_B$ -pa-). 'overt, clear, apparent' (adj-
n). x - 0/1-0[H]/1:3[U]-B x-x-x. NS (107a) LHL. NS (T+ kun) arafa-ni LLH-H.
K: Hn LHH (where attested?). Cf. arawasu, aru.

2.2a   are < [k]are < ?*ga-raCi (see -re). 'that'. (HL) -0-2-A A-A-(x). Edo HL.
1700 Ōsaka HL. Aomori 0. Ib HL = 2.2. Yn kari A. ("First used for kare
in mid-Heian.")

2.3   are < *ara-Ci. 'barley flour stuck on rice cake'. LL - x-x-x x-x-x.

2.4   are < [w]are (< ...). 'I/me'. x - x-x-x x-x-x. NS (71a [11:160-M]) LH.
   NS (T 45, 126) LH. Km (Okada W) LH.

?2.1a   ari. 'ant'. x - 0-0-B̲ (A)-A-(C̲). Edo HH. Narada, Hiroshima, Goka-mura,
   Izumo 0; NE Kyūshū, Kurayoshi (Tottori), Matsue, Hattō, Hamada 1̲; Hakata 1̲,
   ygr 0. Ōsaka, Ise 0; Ib H = 2.1. Sd anyi A; Nk qai A = qaikoo C̲; Sr qai A̲ =
   qaikoo B (child's word); Kobama (Yaeyama) aara; Yn aya C (?< *ari -a). Cf.
   arikusa. The northern Ryūkyūs show reflexes of *ani (Shodon, Kikai) and *ami
   (Tatsugō and Ongachi on Amami, Isen on Tokunoshima). Miyako has reflexes of
   *aka ari 'red ant'.

?4.8, ?4.9   ariake < ariakey < *ar[a-C]iʙ aka-Ci[-Ci]ₐ. '(the latter half of the
   lunar month when it becomes) daybreak with the moon still up; morning moon; ...'
   LHxx - 0-0[H]/1[U]-B x-x-x.

3.4   arika < ariᵏ/ga < *ar[a-C]iʙ (-n-) kaₗ.ₓ ('be place'). 'location'. LLL -
   1̲/0̲/3-2-B x-x-x. Km (W) LLL. Sz 1̲/2̲.

?4.2; ?4.3 (= 2.1|2.3)   arikusa < *ariₑ.₁ₑ kusaₑ.ₛ (? 'ant grass'). 'a kind of
   globe thistle, Echinops setifer' (= higotai). HHHL (Kn) / HH(|)LL (Ck) - x-x-x
   x-x-x.

3.4   ario < ariwo < *ar[a-C]iʙ boₗ.ₗ. 'a (veritable/real) hill'. x - x-x-x
   x-x-x. NS (76c [14:135-M]) LLL; NS (T+ 76) L̲H̲L̲.

4.5   arisama < *ar[a-C]iʙ samaₐₑ.ₑₑ. 'appearance'. LLLL - 2/0-1:3[H]/3[U]-B
   x-B[Lit.]-x. K: Edo HHHL.

?3.5a, ?3.6   ariso < *ar[a]-iswo < *araₑ₂.ₛ iswoₑ.ₗ (or < *ar[a-C]iʙ [i]swoₑ.ₗ).
   'rocky shore'. x - 0-0̲-x x-x-x. Km (W) LLH/LHH (ar̄iso | um̄i). The etymology
   araₑₐⱼ ₐ iswoₑ.ₗ is incongruent in register.

?4.1, ?4.2   arizuka < ariduka < *ariₐₑ.₁ₑ -n- tukaₑ.ₑₑ. 'anthill, ant heap'.
   HHxx - 0-3-x x-x-x.

4.8   aruiwa < arui-fa ?< *ar[a]-uʙ ₐₜₜᵣ iₗ.ₓ paₚₒₗ. 'perhaps; or'. LHHH -
   2-1:3-B x-x-x.

3.5b   aruzi < *aru-n[u]si < *ar[a]-uʙ ₐₜₜᵣ nusiₑ.₄. 'owner'. xxH - 1-2-B x-x-x.
   Edo HLL. Aomori (rare), Narada 1. Ib H̲1̲ = 3.3, F̲ = 3.4. The form arwozi (M
   4498) probably has the Azuma dialect version of the attributive marker -(r)u;
   see Ch. 7, §4.

2.3   asa. 'hemp'. LL - 2-1̲-B B-A̲-x. NS (94a [11:42-K], 96a [11:72L-K, 11:72-K])
   LL. Km (W) LL. Edo L̲H̲. Hattō, Goka-mura, Wakamatsu 1̲; Hamada 0̲; western Iwami,
   Hiroshima, Yamaguchi (cf. Hiroto 1961:152), Narada, Matsue, Izumo 2. Sakawa 1̲;
   Ōsaka 0̲/1̲:3̲; Ise 2; Ib L̲ (= 2.4). Nk qasaa C̲. (Perhaps < *awo-so; cf. ma-wo.)

2.5   asa (?< as[it]aₐₑ.₄; ?< asuₑ.₄ with 2d vowel assimilated to first).
   'morning'. x - 1-1:3-B (x)-B-(x). Edo H̲L (cf. asu). Matsue, Izumo 1 (we expect
   2; influenced by asu?). Ib L2 = 2.5, L̲ = 2.4. Nk hasaa- (bound).

4.11   asabaka < *asaₐₑⱼ ₐ -n- paₗ.ₛₐ ('shallow place') -kaₛᵤf. 'shallow' (adj-
   n). LLHL - x-x-x. Traditionally "< *asa (-n-) pakaₑ.ₛ" but compare
   asabayaka.

?5.16   asabayaka < asaₐₑⱼ ₐ -n- paₗ.ₛₐ ('shallow place') - da-kaₛᵤf. 'shallow'
   (adj-n). LLLLH (Ir) ?= *LLLHL - x-x-x x-x-x.

5.11   asaborake ?< *asa-byirakye < *asa-byirakyi < *asaₑ.ₛ -n- pira-k[a-C]iʙ;
   ?< *asaₑ.ₛ [o]bor[o]ₛ.ₓ akeyₑ.ₗ (< aka-Ci[-Ci])ₐ. '(twilight at) dawn'.
   x - 0/3-0-x x-x-x. Km (W) LLLHL. Cf. asake.

4.11   asagao < asagafo < *asaₑ.ₛ -n- kapoₑ.ₗ. (1) 'morning face'; (2) 'morning
   glory'. (1) x - 0-3-x x-x-x; (2) LLHL - 2-2-B x-x-x. Sz 3; Narada, Hata, Hakata
   2. Kōchi 3.

3.5b   asahi < asa-fyi < *asa$_{2.5}$ pi$_{1.2}$. 'morning sun'. LLH - 1/2-2-B x-x-x.
NS (Okada, kunchū) LLL. Edo HLL. Sapporo, Tappi, Aomori, Akita, Nagano (Kudō
129), Numazu, Narada, Hida (= northern Gifu), western Mino (= SW Gifu), Hattō,
Hamada, Matsue, Izumo, Goka-mura, Hiroshima, Hata, Wakamatsu, Ōita 2. Ib H1 =
3.3.

3.4   asaka (< ?). 'Asaka' (placename). x - x-x-x x-x-x. Km (W) LLL: asaka no
numa 'Asaka marsh'.

5.16   asakasiwa < asa-kasifa < *asa$_{2.5}$ kasipa$_{3.2a}$ (< kasi$_{?2.5}$ pa$_{1.2}$). 'an oak-
tree in the morning'. x - 3-x-x x-x-x. Km (W) LLLHL.

?5.16; ?5.14, ?5.9   asakayama < *asaka$_{3.4}$ dama$_{2.3}$. 'Mount Asaka'. x - 0-x-x x-x-x.
Km (W) LLLxx, xLLxx (?= *LLLHL); LLHHL, LLHHH.

?3.4, ?3.5x   asake < asa-[a]key < *asa$_{2.5}$ aka-Ci[-Ci]$_A$. 'dawn, daybreak'.
x - x-x-x x-x-x. Km (W) LLL/LLH. Cf. asaborake.

4.7 (= 2.3|2.1)   asanuno < *asa$_{2.3}$ nunwo$_{2.1}$. 'hemp cloth, linen'. LL(|)HH - 0-1-x
x-B-x.

?3.4   asari < *asar[a-C]i$_B$. 'fishing, clamming, seeking; a kind of bivalve'.
x - 0-0-B x-x-x. Edo HHH. Aomori, Sz 0. Ib H = 3.1.

3.1 (= 2.1|1.1)   asase < *asa$_{adJ A}$ (< ...) se$_{1.1}$ (< ...). 'river shallows,
ford'. x - 0-1[H]/2[U]-A x-x-x. Km (W) HH(|)H. Sz 0/2.

?4.6   asatte (JP) < "asate" (Hn) ?< *asite (second vowel assimilated to first)
< *asite[y] < *asita-Ci. 'day after tomorrow'. LLH - 2-0[H]/4[U]-B B-B-C.

4.1 (= 2.1-tu|1.1)   asatuki < ?*asatukiy < *asa$_{adJ A}$ -tu$_{pcl}$?kiy$_{1.1}$ ('light/mild
onion'). 'chives'. HHH(|)H - 2-3-x x-x-x.

?3.6, ?3.1   asaza < asaza (Ir) / azasa (Kn) ?< *ansasa (< ?). 'water fringe,
Nymphoides peltata'. HHH (Ir) / LHH (Kn) - 0-0-x x-x-x.

?3.5x < ?*3.1   asazi < asa-di < *asa$_{adJ A}$ -n- ti$_{?1.2}$ (< tu-Ci). 'low-stemmed cogon
(= thatching grass)'. x - 0-0-x x-x-x. Km (W) LLH.

3.5   asazi < asadi < ?*asanti (< ?, cf. azi). 'Zacco platypus (= oikawa)'
(fish). LLH - x-x-x x-x-x.

5.2   asazihara < asadi-fara < *asa-di$_{?*3.1(>3.5)}$ (< ...) para$_{2.3}$. 'a field of
cogon (thatching grass)'. x - x-x-x x-x-x. NS (Okada) HHHHL; NS (T+ 85) LHHHL.

?4.6   asazuma < asaduma < *asa$_{2.5}$ -n- tuma$_{2.2a}$ ('morning spouse'). 'Asazuma'
(placename). x - 0-x-x x-x-x. NS (T+ 50) LHHF; NS (71c [11:180-M]): ~ no
LLLH-L.

2.5   ase (< ?). 'sweat'. LH - 1-1:3-B x-B-B. Km (S) LH-L. Edo LF. K: Hn-Km-Edo
LF. Toyama 1:3; Suzu 1:3 (we expect 1); Ib L2 = 2.5. Onna qaasii B.

3.4   ase^b/$_■$o ?< ase-[i]bo < ase$_{2.5}$ (< ?) ibo$_{2.5}$ (< ...). 'heat rash'. LLL -
3-1:3-B x-B-x. Sz, Hattō, Hamada, Matsue, Izumo 3; Goka-mura 0.

?4.6a   asemizo < ase$_{2.5}$ (< ?) myizo$_{2.1a}$ (< ...). 'rivulet of (= heavy) sweat'.
LLLF - 1/3-1:3-x x-x-x. Cf. asemizu.

?4.6a   asemizu < asemyidu < ase$_{2.5}$ (< ?) myidu$_{2.1a}$ (< ...). 'sweat flowing like
water'. ?*LLLF - 1-1:3-x x-x-x. See Ch. 1, §7.3.

2.1 (?> 2.4/5).   asi. 'reed'. HH - 1-1-B x-x-x. Edo HH. Aomori, Sz, Hiroshima 1.
Ōsaka, Ise, Kameyama 1:3; Ib F = 2.3.

2.3   asi. 'foot'. LL - 2-2-B (A)-(B)-x. NS (Okada) LL; NS (T+ kun) LL. Km (W)
LL. Mr (Bm) HL. 1700 Ōsaka HL. Suzu 1.; Ib F = 2.3.

4.6 (= 2.3|2.4)   asiato < *asi$_{2.3}$ atwo$_{2.4}$. 'footprint'. LL(|)LH - 3-0[U]/4[H]-B
x-x-x. Narada 3.

?3.1, ?3.3   asibe < asi-f/$_b$ye < *asi$_{2.1}$ -n- piCa$_{1.x}$. '(place) where reeds grow'.
x - 0/3[K]-1-B x-x-x. Km (W) HHH/HHL. On -f/$_b$- see Ch. 2.

4.1   asibiki 'mountain': see asihiki.

4.11   asibuti < asi-ʰ/ᵦuti < *asi₂.₃ (-n-) puti₂.₂. 'a horse with all four legs white from the knee down' (= yotuziro). LLHL - 0-0-x x-x-x.

3.4/3.5x asida (?< *asi₂.₃ -n- [i]ta₂.₄, ?< *asi₂.₃ -n- [si]ta₂.₂ₐ, ?< *asi₂.₃ -n- ta[ka]ₐdⱼ ᵦ). 'wooden clogs (geta)'. LLL/LLH - 0-0[H]/1[U] B-B-B. 1700 Ōsaka LHL. Aomori 3; Narada 2. Kōchi 0 (Doi 1952:24); Ib (rare) F = 3.4. Sd qaddya(a) B, Sr qasiza B, Yn acida B.

6.23 (=4.5|2.5) < 4.5-no̱|2.4   asidaka-gumo < asidaka*₄.₅ -no̱ kumo₂.₅ < *asi₂.₃ -n- taka ₐdⱼ ᵦ no̱ kumwo ₂.₅ ('leg-tall spider'). 'daddy-longlegs'. LLLL(|)LH < LLLLL|LH - 5-x-x x-x-x.

4.2 (=2.1|2.2) asigaki < asi-kakyi < *asi₂.₃ kaki₇₂.₂ₐ. 'a reed-woven fence'. x - 2-0-x x-x-x. Km (W) HH(|)HL.

5.16   asiganae < asiganafe < *asiganafey < *asi₂.₃ -n- kana-paCi₃.₁ (< kana₂.₁ pa-Ci₁.₁). 'a tripod kettle'. LLLHL - 3-4-x x-x-x. K: "Hn/Km HHHHL" (misprint?; mistake?).

4.11   asigasⁱ/ₑ, asikasⁱ/ₑ < *asi₂.₃ (-n-) kasi₂.₃. 'foot-cangue, shackles'. LLHL - 0-0-x x-x-x.

4.6   asiginu < *asigyinu ?< *asiₐdⱼ ᵦ -n- kinu₂.₄ ('bad silk'). 'rough silk cloth'. HHHL - 0/1-3-x x-x-x. Km (S,W) x. K: Km LLLH (where attested?). The register is incongruent with the etymology; cf. Komatsu 1977:406.

6.3   asiharagani < asifara-gani < *asi₂.₁ - para₂.₃ -n- kani₂.₁ ('reed-field crab'). 'a kind of crab'. HHHHLL - 4-x-x x-x-x.

4.1   asiʰ/ᵦiki < asifyiki (< ?, see NKD, Zdb). 'mountain'. x - 0-0-x x-x-x. NS (Okada) HHHH; NS (T+ 50) LLHH. (The register is incongruent with etymologies containing asi₂.₃ 'foot'.)

3.1   asii < asiwi < *asi₂.₁ bi₁.₃ᵦ. 'Arthraxon hispidus' (= kobunagusa). HHH - x-x-x x-x-x.

?3.2x   asika. 'sea lion, hairseal'. HHL - 0-0̱-B x-x-x. Sz 3.

4.5   asimaki < *asi-makyi < *asi₂.₃ mak[a-C]i ₁ₐ. 'leg wrappings, leggings, gaiters; (= asigarami = hariganemusi) wireworm, hairworm'. LLLL - x-x-x x-x-x.

?4.7, ?4.5   asinabe < asi-nabey < *asi₂.₃ nanpaCi₂.₅. 'a small tripod kettle'. LLHH (Kn) / LLLL (Ck) - 0-x-x x-x-x.

4.5   asinae < asinafey < *asi₂.₃ napa-Ci[-Ci]₇ᵦ. 'becoming lame; a lame person'. LLLL - 0-0-x x-x-x.

4.2   asinawa < asinafa < *asi₂.₁ napa₂.₃. 'a reed rope'. HHHL - x-1-x x-x-x.

3.4   asio < asiwo < *asi₂.₃ bo₁.₃ₐ. 'hawk jess(es)'. LLL - 0/2-x-x x-x-x.

?3.4   asita. 'tomorrow'. LLL - 3-0̱-B A̱-B-C̱. Km (S) LLL. Edo HHL. Narada, Hata 0̱; Hakata 0, ygr 3. Kōchi 0̱; Ib F = 3.4, Ḻ = 3.6, earlier aisa F = 3.4 (cf. koisa = koyoi). Sd athya(a) A̱; Nk haCaa B; Sr qaca B; Yn atta C̱. K: "Hn-Km LLH" (misprint?). Edo HHL. On Kansai dialects with high oxytonic see Ch. 4, §7.3.

4.5   asiwake < *asi-wakey < *asi₂.₃ baka-Ci[-Ci]ᵦ. 'leg-removable': ~ no tuku(w)e 'a desk with removable legs'. LLLL - x-x-x x-x-x.

4.2   asiwata < *asi₂.₁ bata₂.₃. 'reed tips growing like cotton'. HHHL - 0-0-x x-x-x.

4.1   asizuno < asiduno < *asi-dunwo < *asi₂.₁ -n- tunwo₂.₃. 'young reeds' (= asika[b]i = asiwaka). HHHH - 0-1:4-x x-x-x.

?2.4, ?2.3   aso (?< a[se] wo!; ?< [w]a so (< se), cf. seko; ?< aso[n] < ase-omi < ...). 'my dear fellow'. x - x-x-x x-x-x. NS (Okada) LH; NS (T 29, 62; T+ 28) LL. Edo ason HHH.

3.x   asoko < *a-₁.₂ (< ...) so̱-ko₂.₁ (< ...). x - 0-1[U[/1:3[H]-A x-x-x. Aomori, Sz 3. Ib asiko L2 = 3.5/7. Attested 10th century.

2.3   asu. 'morrow'. LL - 2-2-B x-(B)-x. NS (Okada) LL; NS (T+ 86) LL. Edo HL.
Narada 1. Ib *(rare)* F = 2.3. Sr qaca B (= asa) < *asita. (?< *a[ka-]s[a-]u*A*
[pi*1.2J* '[sun/day] that will dawn'; ? original form of asa 'morning', which has
assimilated the second vowel; ?< *as[a-no-p]u < *asa*2.5* no_ pi*1.2* 'morning's
day', cf. kyoo.)
3.5a   asuka ?< *asu ka ('morning fragrance'). 'Asuka' *(placename)*: ~ no kafa
'the Asuka river' (= asukagawa). x - 0-0_-x x-x-x. Km (W) LLH-L.
5.16; 5.14 (= 3.5|2.2); 5.10, 5.9 asukagawa < asuka-gafa < *asuka*3.5* (< ...) -n-
kapa*2.2a*. 'the Asuka River'. x - 3-4-x x-x-x. NS (T+ 118) LLHHLH. Km (W) LLLHL;
LLH(|)HL, LLHHH, LHHHH.
-            ata··· : *see* ada(···).
3.1   atai < atafyi < *atap[a-C]i*A*. 'value'. HHH (Kn) / HHL (Kn) - 0-0-A x-x-x.
Ib H = 3.1.
4.10   atakamo < *ata[-ra-*A*] ka*Pcl* mo*Pcl*. 'just as if' *(adv)*. LHLL - 1/2-2[U]/
4[H]-B x-x-x.
3.4   atama. 'head'. LLL - 3-2-B B-B-x. Hiroshima atamo (vowel assimilated to
labial nasal?). NS (114a) atoma LHL. Sapporo 2; Hata 3. Kōchi 3; Ib F = 3.4.
3.1   atara (? < *atara-*A*). 'alas; regrettably' *(adv)*. HHH - 0(/2[H])-0[H]/2[U]-
A x-B_-x. NS (79b, 80a) HHH; NS (T+ 78, 80) LLL.
?3.2b < 3.1   atari ?< *atar[a-C]i. 'vicinity'. HHL - 1_-2-A x-B_-x.
NS (72c [11:201-M] HHL; NS (T+ 54) LLH. Edo HHL. Narada, Goka-mura 1; Aomori,
Hattō, Hamada, Matsue, Izumo, Hiroshima 0. Ōsaka 3; Ise 2; Ib H1 = 3.3, H2 =
3.2, = 3.1. Nk hatai B 'nearby field', A 'portion, allotment'.
4.11   atataka < *ata-[a]ta-ka ?< *atu*adj B* - atu*adj B* -ka*suf*. 'warm' *(adj-n)*.
LLHL - 2/3_-4-B x-x-x. K: Edo HLLL. (Cf. placename Atami < *ata-umi 'warm sea'.)
2.1   ati 'yon(der) ··· ': *see* atti.
3.4   atiki. ' ? '. Hoke-kyō tanji (19v:4) LLL - x-x-x x-x-x. A gloss for the
Chinese character EKI 'increase, profit, ... '.
-            atikoti < ati*2.1* (< ...) ko_ti*2.1* (< ...). 'here and there'. x - 2/3-
1:3(/1:4 [U] 'topsy-turvy')-A x-x-x. Sz 3. Attested 1257 (KggD 976b).
3.1   ati-ra < *(k)ati-ra < *ka*1.1* (?< *ga) ti*?1.1* [a]ra*2.3*. 'yon(der) way/
direction'. x - 0-1_-A x-x-x. Sz 0.
2.4   ato < atwo ?< *a[si]*2.3* to_*1.x*. 'footprint, trace; behind'. LH - 1-1-B
x-B-C. NS (132a) LH; NS (T+ 96) LL. NS (T+ kun) atwo fye LH(|)H 'at one's
feet/heels'. Km (W,S) LH. Edo LH. Matsue, Izumo 2; Narada, Hattō, Hamada,
Goka-mura 1. Ib L = 2.4. Nase qato(o) A (H 1967:212); Nk qa(t)too H(H)LL (= C)
/ qatu-. (On /to_/ and /two/ see Zdb.)
3.4   atori ?< *a[kyi]-to_ri < *aki to_ri ('autumn bird'). 'mountain finch,
brambling (which migrates over from Siberia in October)'. LLL - 0-0_-x x-x-x.
K: "Hn HHH" *(misprint?)*.
3.1 < 2.1 atti < ati < *(k)ati < *ka*1.1* (?< *ga) ti*?1.1*. 'yon(der) way/direction'.
x - 2(→3)-1-A x-x-x. 1700 Ōsaka HL. Aomori, Sz 3.
4.5 < 2.3|2.3 atumono < *atu*adj B* mo_no*2.3*. 'hot broth'. LL(|)LL - 0-0-B x-x-x.
Cf. oon-atumono.
-            au*k*/*g*o: *see* oo*k*/*g*o.
2.3   awa < "afa" = awa < *aba. 'bubble, foam'. LL - 2-2-B x-B-B. Km (W) LL.
Edo HL. Nagano 1 (Kudō 1978); Hakata 1, ygr 2; Sz, Narada, Hattō, Hamada,
Matsue, Izumo, Goka-mura, Hiroshima 2. Hyōgo 1:3; Toyama, Suzu 1:3 *(expected)*;
Ib F = 2.3. Sr qaa B = qabuku B; Onna qaawaa B; Yn anbuku B (H 1964:71b).
Dial. aba (Shimane, Sanagi); awa-boko, a(n)buku, abu, abuki.

?2.5 < 2.4   awa < afa < *apa. 'millet'. LH - 1-1-B B-B-B. 1700 Ōsaka LH. Nagano
    (Kudō 1978), Hattō, Hamada, Goka-mura, Hiroshima 1; Matsue, Izumo 2. Ōsaka,
    Ise 1:3; Ib L = 2.4. Ohara 1951a:417: "LF in parts of Kansai", cf. Ch. 4, §7.3.
3.3   awabi < afabyi < *apanpi. 'abalone'. HLL - 1(<*2)-2-A/B x-x-x. NS (Okada)
    HLL; NS (T+ 92) ƎLH. Aomori 0; NE Kyūshū 1; Sapporo, Tappi, Akita, Matsumoto,
    Narada, Numazu, western Mino (= SW Gifu), Hattō, Hamada, Matsue, Izumo,
    Hiroshima, Goka-mura, Yamaguchi, Wakamatsu 2; Hakata 2, ygr 1; Ōita 3. Kg B
    according to Hirayama but A according to Kobayashi. Ib aobi H1 = 3.3. Nk qaabi
    B. Dial. a(a)bi, anbi.
4.11   awagara < afagara < *apa?2.5 -n- kara2.2(?a/b) ('millet stalk'). 'cornet
    fish, flutemouth' (= yagara). LLHL - x-x-x x-x-x.
?3.7a   awai < afafi < *afafyi < *apa-p[a-C]iв. 'border (area); interpersonal
    relationship, (friendly) relations; coloring, tint; juncture, gap, time,
    opportunity'. LHx /LHL (Ir) - 0/2-x-x B-x-x. Sd qawe(e) B 'time left'.
3.4   awaki < afaki < afakyi < *apaki (< ?). 'a tree: perhaps oak, holly, or
    laurel'. LLL - x-x-x x-x-x. NS (T+ kun) LLL.
3.5b ?< 3.4   aware < afare < *apare[y] < *aparaCi (?= *apa-ra-Ci[-Ci]в).
    'sympathy, pity'. LLH - 1(<*2)-2-B x-B-x. Km (S) LLH. Edo HLL. As interjection
    this was probably pronounced appare: NS (105a) LLL; NS (T+ 20; 104; 94) LLH.
    Km (W) LLL. K: Hn LLF (interj), Km LLF (noun); Edo HLL. Aomori, Hattō, Matsue,
    Izumo 2; Hakata 2, ygr 1; Narada [Lit.], Hamada 1. Ib H1 = 3.3. Cf. awaremu.
3.4   awase < afase[y] < *apa-sa-Ci[-Ci]в. 'lined garment'. LLx - 3-0-B x-(B)-x.
    Edo HHL. K: Hn-Km LLL (attested?). Ib F = 3.4.
4.5 (= 2.3|2.3)   awasio < awasifo < *awa-sifwo < *aba2.3 sipwo2.3. 'refined salt,
    table salt' (as opposed to katasio 'rock salt'). LL(|)LL - 0-0-x x-x-x.
3.4   awata < afata < *apata (?< *a[si2.3] pata2.1 'leg fin'). 'kneecap,
    patella' (= hizakabura). LLL - x-x-x x-x-x.
?2.1, ?2.3   aya ?< *[k]aya (< ...). 'Aya, descendants of early Chinese
    immigrants to Japan' (= aya-hito). x - 2-x-x x-x-x. Cf. ayahatori, ayabe.
2.3   aya < *ada. 'design'. LL - 2-2-A x-B-x. Km (W) LL. Narada, Hiroshima 2;
    Hakata 1, ygr 2. Ōsaka, Ise 0; Ib ?F = 2.3.
2.3   aya < *ada. 'strange': aya-ni 'strangely, oddly, for no good reason'.
    LL-H - x-x-x x-x-x. NS (T+ 33) LL-H; (T+ 77) LH-H. Cf. ayabumu.
?3.4 (?= 2.3|1.3)   ayabe < ayabye ?< aya?2.1,?2.3 (< ...) bye?1.3 (< ...). 'the
    Aya (= weavers) guild'. x -1-x-x x-x-x. NS (129b) LLL.
5.1   ayahatori < aya?2.1,?2.3,?2.5 fat[a]-ori?3.1<4.1 (< ...). 'an Aya
    (Chinese-descendant) weaver'. x - x-x-x x-x-x. NS (128a) HH(|)HHH.
?3.4, ?3.6   ayame < *ayamey < *ada2.3 ma-Ci1.3a (?< 'design eye'). 'design, ... ;
    (= ayamegusa) sweetflag'. x - 0- 1[H]/0[U]-A x-x-x. Km (W) LLL. 1700 Ōsaka
    LHH. Aomori 2 (expected); Narada 2. Hiroshima, Hakata 0. Ōsaka, Ise 0,
    ('sweetflag') 1; Ib L = 3.6.
5.11   ayamegusa < *ayamey-gusa < *ayamey3.6 (< *ada2.3 ma-Ci1.3a) -n- kusa2.3.
    'sweetflag'. LHHHL - 3-1:3-x x-x-x. Km (W) LHHHL/... .
5.12   ayametamu < *ayamey3.6 (< *ada2.3 ma-Ci1.3a) tamu2.1. 'a burnet,
    Sanguisorba officinalis' (= waremokoo). LHHLL (Zs) - x-x-x x-x-x.
2.5   ayu < *adu. 'sweetfish'. LH - 1-1:3-B x-x-x. NS (T 27:126) LH. Kt ai 1:3;
    Toyama, Suzu 1:2 (we expect 2); Ib L2 = 2.5. K: Hn LF.
3.7a   ayui < ayufi < aywofyi/ayufyi ?< *a[si]2.3 dup[a-C]iᴀ ('leg-tie'). 'a cord
    attached to one's skirt (to tie things on for carrying along)'. x - 0-0-x
    x-x-x. NS (Okada) LHL; NS (T+ 73 ayufyi) LLH, (T+ 74, 106 aywofyi) LLƎ.

2.2a   aza < *ansa. 'birthmark'. HL - 2-2-A A-A-A. Aomori, Sz 0. Hakata 1, ygr 2.
Ib H1 = 2.2. Sr qaza A; Yn ada A. Dialect versions: ada, adya, andya.
2.2b   aza < *ansa. 'village section'. x - 1-2-A x-x-x. Sz, Hiroshima 1. Ōsaka,
Ise 2; Ib H1 = 2.2.
-           aza (modern truncation) = azana.
?3.1   azami < azamyi < *ansami (< ?). 'thistle'. HHx - 0-0[H]/1[U]-B x-x-x.
Aomori, Sz 0. Ib L = 3.6. Nk qazaama B.
3.1   azana (= adana) < *ansa-na (?= a(n)taz.zb naɪ.z). 'alias; falsehood'.
HHH (-z-) - 0-0-B x-A-x. 1700 Ōsaka HHL. Sz 0. Ib H2 = 3.3.
4.11   azayaka < *ansa-da-ka ?< *a[ra-Ci]B -n- sa(-)da-ka (> sayaka). 'clear'
(adj-n). LLHL - 2-4-B x-x-x. Sz 3.
2.3   aze < *anse < ?*anse[y] < *ansaCi. 'levee'. x - 2-2-B x-x-x. Sz 0 (not the
usual word); Goka-mura 1; Hattō, Hamada, Matsue, Izumo 2.
2.1   azi < adi < *anti. 'flavor'. (x) - 0-0-A A-A-A. NS (T+ kun) LH. K: Km HH
(inferred from adifaf- HHHH in S?). Ib H = 2.1.
2.2b   azi < adi < *anti. 'saurel (fish)'. HL - 1-2-A x-x-x. Aomori, Narada,
Hakata 1; Hiroshima, Hattō, Hamada, Goka-mura, Yamaguchi 2; Matsue, Izumo 0 (=
2.1-2), but Kobayashi has Izumo 1. Ib H = 2.2.
3.2x   azika ?< azi[ro]ɜ.x ka[gwo]z.ɪ (?< *am[a-C]iB - siroz.ɪ kan-kwo). 'woven
basket'. HHL - x-x-x x-x-x. If the etymology with aziro (x - 0-0-x x-x-x) is
correct, the low register of am- was ignored at some point.
4.7   azimame < adi-mamey < *antiz.ɪ mamaCiz.ɜ. 'Egyptian kidney bean' (= huzi-
mame). LLHH - 0-4-x x-x-x. Register incongruent with etymology.
3.1 < 4.1 aziro < am[u]ziro < amuᵇ/ziro < *a[siz.ɪ] m[u]siroɜ.₄. 'a rough-woven
(loose-weave) mat of rush or bamboo; a kind of fish-weir'. "HLHH" (Kn -z-) /
HHHH (Ck -s-) - 0-0-x x-x-x. Edo HHL. 1700 Ōsaka LHL. (The traditional
etymology < ami 'net' or 'weave' is incongruent in register.)
4.1   [aziroi] < "adirowi" (Hoke-kyō tanji 64v:8) ?< aziro-[m]i 'a shallow
basket made of ajiro matting' (Brinkley 14a), ?< aziro-[w]i. 'rush'. HHHH -
x-x-x x-x-x.
?4.8   azisai < adusawi (Mg) < adisawi (Man'yō-shū) (< ?; perhaps adusa [a]wi
'catalpa indigo'?). 'hydrangea'. LHHH - 0/2-0-A x-x-x. Sz 3.
3.2b   azuki < adukyi < *antuki. 'red bean'. HHL - 3-2-A B-x-x. Sapporo, Tappi,
Aomori, Akita, Izumo, NE Kyūshū, Ōita 0; Matsumoto, Numazu, Narada, Hiroshima,
Hata 3; Hakata 2, ygr 3. Kōchi, Sakawa 1:3; Ib L2 = 3.5/7. Ainu antuki.
?3.4, ?3.7b   azuma < aduma < *antuma. 'Azuma' (placename). x-1-1:3-A x-x-x.
Km (W) aduma-uta LLL(|)HL, LLLLL, LHLLL. Edo LHL. K: Hn/Km LLL. Aomori 1.
4.5   azumatu < aduma-tu < *antuma?ɜ.₄,?ɜ.7b [pi]toz.za. 'a person from the
rural areas of the east (Azuma); the rural areas, frontier areas'. LLLL -
x-x-x x-x-x.
4.5 (=3.4|1.3) azumaya < aduma-ya < *antuma?ɜ.₄,?ɜ.7b daɪ.ɜb. 'rustic house, ... '.
x - 3-1[H]/1:4[U]-A x-x-x. K: "Hn LLLL" (confused with azumatu?).
3.4   azusa < adusa < *antusa. 'catalpa (tree)' (= yoguso-minebari). LLL -
0/2-1:3-x x-x-x. NS (70c[11:53-M]) LLL.
5.6 (= 3.4|2.3)   azusayumi < adusa-yumyi < *antusaɜ.₄ dumiz.ɜ. 'a catalpa-wood
bow'. x - 3-4-x x-x-x. NS (Okada) LLL(|)LL; NS (T+ 43) LHₑ|LH.
3.1   azuti < aduti < *antuti ?< *an[ta]z.zb tutiz.ɜ ('foe turf'). 'archery
target mound'. HHH - 0-0-x x-x-x. Cf. amututi.

1.3a   ba (?< *[ ] -n- pa, ?< *n[i]pa*2.1*). 'place'. L - 0-1[H]/0[U]-B x-B-x. Sz 0
            (1 in sono ba). Kōchi 1 (Doi 1952:20). Ib L = 1.3. Sr baa B 'situation, time;
            reason'. K: Hn LL, Edo LH.
2.x   baba < ba-*bud n* (< Ch m(b)a') ba*1.3a* (< ...). 'horse-training (racing)
            ground'. x - 1-2-B   x-x-x.
2.4   baka = hakka < fakka (JP) (< Ch bhak-.hha). 'mint'. LH - 0-1-B x-B-x.
2.1   ban (< Ch 'm(b)ywen). 'evening'. x - 0-0-A x-x-x. Sz *(rare)* 0 (1 in sono
            ban); Narada 0. Ib H = 2.1.
2.3   bara < [i]bara < *inpara. 'rosebush'. x - 0-2-B B-x-x. Ib H1 = 2.2.
?3.4   basyoo < ᶠ/baseu (< Ch .pa-.tsyew). 'plantain, Japanese banana plant'.
            x - 0-0-A B-B-x. Sz 0. See haseo.
4.8   basyooba < ᶠ/baseu*3.4* (< Ch .pa-.tsyew) -n- pa*1.2*. 'plantain (banana)
            leaf'. x - x-4-x x-x-x. See haseoba.
2.3   bati (?< Ch pwat). 'plectrum, drumstick'. LL - 2-2-B B-A-x. Aomori 0; Sz,
            Narada 2. Ib F = 2.3. Nk bacii B.
?1.3x   (-)be < (-)bye (?< Paykcey version of Ch bhew' 'section'). 'hereditary
            guild'. Sr -bi. See ayabe, karazukuribe, ...
1.x   -be < -bye < *-n- piCa: see (-)he.
2.4   beni (?< *bey-ni < *npaCi-ni; ?< *bo-ni < *npo-ni). 'rouge'. LH - 1-1-B
            B-B-x. Cf. hani, hena. Izumo 2; Narada, Hattō, Hamada, Goka-mura 1. Ib L =
            2.4.
2.x   bira (?< *[ ] -n- pira*?2.2b*). 'handbill, placard'. x - 0(1[H])-1:3-A x-x-x.
            Sz 0. Ib L2 = 2.5. ("Confused with English 'bill'.")
2.4 < 3.7b   biwa < bifa < biifa (< Ch .bhyey-.bha). 'loquat'. RL (= LHL) - 1-0-B
            x-B-x. Wamyō-shō, Iroha RH (Numoto 1979:29). Km (W) HH. Aomori, Sz 2. Kōchi 1
            [Martin]; Ib H = 2.1.
?2.3   biwa < bifa (< Ch .bhyey-.bha). 'lute'. LL - 1-2-B x-x-x. Edo HL. Sz 2.
            Kōchi 2 [Martin]; Ib H1 = 2.2.
-           boke: see moke.
2.1   bon (< Ch .bhwen). 'tray'. x - 0-0-A x-A-x. Sz, Hiroshima 0. Ōsaka 1; Ise
            0; Ib H = 2.1. As abbreviation of Ura-bon 'Feast of Lanterns': x - 1-1-x x-B-x;
            Hiroshima 1; Ōsaka, Ise 1; Ib L = 2.4.
2.1   boo < bou(?/bau)(< Ch 'bong). 'stick, club'. x - 0-0-A A-B-x. Sz, Narada,
            Hattō, Hamada, Matsue, Izumo, Hiroshima 0; Goka-mura 2. Ōsaka, Ise 0; Ib H =
            2.1. Nk C.
2.x   bora. 'mullet'. x - 0-1-x x-x-x. Km x. Sz 0. Ib L2 = 2.5.
2.2a   boro (?< *[ ] -n- poro). 'rag, scrap'. x - 1-1:3-A x-x-x. Aomori, Matsue,
            Izumo 2 *(Hiroto and Ōhara corrigenda)*; Sz, Hattō, Hamada, Goka-mura 1. Ib L2
            = 2.5. Ōhara: "Kt 2 but Ōsaka, Nara, Kōbe, Himeji 1."
?2.1   buta. 'pig'. x - 0-1:3-A x-x-x. Narada, Hattō 0, Hamada 0/1; Goka-mura,
            Iwami, Hiroshima, Yamaguchi 1 (Hiroto 1961.166); Hakata 1, ygr 0. Aomori, Sz,
            Matsue, Izumo 2. Ib L2 = 2.5. (Sr qwaa B < ?; cf. Hateruma quwa). Earliest
            citation in NKD is 1764. Etymology: perhaps < *puto- 'fat', cf. Sr buta-san A
            'is obese'. But maybe borrowed from Mongolian boduŋ 'wild boar' (Lessing 110b)
            or '3-4 year old boar' (cf. Ramstedt 1935:48b), Khalkha "bodon" = bodəŋ,
            Kalmuck bodŋ; also Mongolian boda 'unit of livestock' (Lessing 108b):
            information courtesy of J. Street. Cf. buu-buu 'oink-oink!' — which came
            first, the pig or the grunt?
?2.2x, ?2.1   buti < "-futi" < *(n)puti (or *[ ] -n- puti). 'spots, dapple, mottle;
            spotted, dappled, mottled'. HH-⋯ - 1-1:3[U]/2[H]-A x-x-x. Aomori ?2/?1; Sz 1.
            Ib H1 = 2.2. Cf. asibuti (with accentuation that favors 2.2 for this noun).
2.3   buti(/muti) < *nputi. 'whip'. LL - x-x-x x-B-x. Sr buci B. See muti.

4.1   butiuma < butim[u]ma < *(n)puti$_{?2.2x,?2.1}$ uma$_{2.3}$. 'dappled horse'. HHHH -
     0/2-x-x x-x-x.
?2.5   buto (< ?, cf. abu). 'gadfly, horsefly' (= buyu). LH - 1-1:3-x x-x-x.
?2.5   buy°/u (< ?, cf. abu). 'gadfly, horsefly' (= buto).

-         da (miswritten?) = ta 'who'. NS (T+ 40) da ka HL. See dare.
2.3   [dai] < dafi (< Ch n(d)ap). 'shroud; monk's robe' (= noo). LL - x-x-x
     x-x-x.
3.6   dan-go (< Ch .dhwan + kwo$_{1.1}$ 'child' or kwo$_{1.3a}$ 'flour'). 'dumpling'.
     x - 0-1-B x-B-x. Aomori 3 (?< *2); Goka-mura 1; Hattō, Hamada, Matsue, Izumo 0.
     Ib L = 3.6. Sr daagu B.
?2.2a, ?2.5   dani < tani (JP, Mg) < ?*(n)tani. 'tick'. HL - 2-1:3-B x-x-x. Km x.
     Sz, Hattō, Hamada, Goka-mura 2; Izumo 0 (= 2.1-2); Matsue 0/2 (= 2.1-2/2.3).
     Ib H1 = 2.2.
2.1   dare < tare (?< *ta-re[y] < *ta-raCi). 'who/someone'. (x) - 1-0-A (x)-A-A.
     Km (S,W) HH. Mr (Bm) HH. Nagano (Kudō 32), Hattō, Hamada, Matsue, Izumo, Hata
     (Doi 1952:29), Wakamatsu 0; Aomori, Narada, Goka-mura, Yamaguchi 1. Ib H = 2.1
     but dare ka L2 = 3.5/7. Ōsaka dare zo (HHH) 'someone' (= dare ka).
     Cf. Ryūkyū taru, *ta[r]u > too, taa < *ta-du < *ta-do (= ta-zo). Modern d- is
     by attraction to other indeterminates (doko, ...); it was not attested before
     the 19th century, except for the single example da ka (NS 40), which is assumed
     to be a miswriting of ta ka.
2.3   desi (< Ch dhey'-'tsyey). 'apprentice'. LL - 2-2-B x-x-x. Edo HL.
     Ib F = 2.3.
?2.1   dobu (< ?). 'gutter'. x - 0-1:3-A x-x-x. Aomori, Narada, Hattō, Hamada,
     Matsue, Izumo 0; Goka-mura 1. Ib L2 = 2.5.
?2.1 < 3.6   doko < idoko < iduko/iduku < ?*int^u/$_o$ko (see izuko). 'where'.
     x - (1)-0-(B) (x)-x-x. K: Edo HH. 1700 Ōsaka HH. Narada, Goka-mura 1; Nagano
     (Kudō 32), Hattō, Hamada, Hata (Doi 1952:29), Wakamatsu 0; Matsue, Izumo 0/2;
     Aomori 2. Ib H = 2.1. Idoko attested 1277; doko 1169 (?), 1309. The variants:
     iduku ← iduko (the last vowel assimilated to the preceding vowels) → idoko
     (the second vowel assimilated to the last). Ōsaka doko zo (HHH) 'somewhere'
     (= doko ka).
2.3   doku (< Ch dhok). 'poison'. LL - 2-2-B B-B-B. Edo HL. Aomori, NE Kyūshū
     0; Narada, Hattō, Hamada, Matsue, Izumo, Hiroshima 2. Ib F = 2.3.
?2.x   dono < do[re]-no < idure no (< ...). 'which ... '. x - 1-0-A x-x-x. Ib H
     = 2.1. K: Edo HH. Attested 1264.
?2.1 < 3.6   dore < idure < ?*int^u/$_o$re[y] < ?*int^u/$_o$-ra-Ci. 'which one'.
     x - (1)-0-(/2[U])-A B-B-(A). Hattō, Hamada 0, Matsue, Izumo, Hata 0/2; Goka-
     mura 1. Ib H = 2.1. Attested 1216. Usual explanation: o ← u by analogy with
     kore, sore. But cf. doko.
2.3   doro < *ntoro (< ?). 'mud'. x - 2-2-B B-B-B. Myōgo-ki (1270) LL (cf. K
     1964:338). Sz, NE Kyūshū 0; Hattō, Hamada, Matsue, Izumo, Hiroshima (Okuda) 2.
     Ib F 'dirt' = 2.3.
?2.1   dote (< Ch 'tho-.tey or 'tho + ta-Ci$_{1.3a}$ 'hand'). 'dike'. x - 0-0-B
     x-x-x. Narada 0. Ib H = 2.1.
?2.1 < 3.7b   doti < iduti < *int^u/$_o$-ti$_{3.7b}$ (see izuti): see dotti.
?3.1   dotira < doti$_{2.1}$ < iduti < *int^u/$_o$-ti$_{3.7b}$, see izuti) -ra (?< *[a]ra$_B$).
     'which way, where'. x - 1-1-A x-x-x. Hattō, Hamada, Matsue, Izumo, Hata 0.
     Attested 1259. Usual explanation: o ← u by analogy with koti, soti. But cf.
     doko.

?3.1 < 3.7b   dotti < doti < iduti < *intʷ/o-ti*3.7b* (*see* izuti). 'which way, where'. x - 1-1-A x-x-x. 1700 Ōsaka HHL. *See* dotira.

1.1   e < ey < *aCi. 'hackberry' (= e-no-ki). x - 0-0-x x-x-x.
?1.1   e < ey < *aCi. 'perilla' (= e-goma). H - x-2-x x-x-x.
1.1   e < ye (?< *daCi/*diCa, ?< *do). 'handle' (?< 'branch'). H - 0-0-A x-A-x.
Km (W) H. Edo H. Ib H = 2.1.
?1.1   e < ye (?< *daCi/*diCa, < ?*do). 'inlet' (?< 'branch'). H - x-0-x x-x-x.
NS (Okada) H. K: Km HL (attested? S,W x).
?1.2   e < ye (?< ye[da], *see* eda). 'branch'. x - x-2-x x-x-x. NS (T+ 35) "R" ?=
H. (T+ 23) L. K: Hm H (attested? S,W x).
?1.2   e < ye (?< [s]e, ?< ife-se). 'older [sibling]'. x - x-2-x x-x-x. K: Km HH
(attested? S,W x). Cf. Mg eiwoti LHHH 'father's older brother', finoe LLH
'(fire's older brother =) 3d of the 10 Heaven's Stems'.
1.3a   e < we (?< *be, ?< Ch hhway'). 'picture'. L - 1-1-B B-B-x. Ib L = 1.3.
1.3b   e < we < *be (< ?). 'bait' (= esa). R - 1-2-B x-x-x. Hiroshima 1. Kōchi
(Doi 1952:21), Ōsaka, Ise 2; Ib H = 1.1. K: Hn HL (misprint for LH?).
1.3b   e < ye < ye[ki] (< Ch ywa(y)k). 'epidemic' (= eyami). R - x-x-x x-x-x.
2.1   ebi < eybyi (?< *anpi, ?< *onpi). 'shrimp; (= ebi-zuru/-kazura) wild
grapes/grapevine'. HH - 0-0-A A-A-x. Ib H = 2.1. Nk qibii A 'crayfish', see C
(?< *sai ?< *sa-e[bi]) '(small) shrimp'. Cf. ei, kar[a]-ei.
5.2 (= 2.1|3.2)   ebikazura < *eybyi*2.1* (< ...) kadura*3.2* (< ...). 'wild grapes/
grapevine'. HHxxx - 3-4-x x-x-x. K: "Hn HHHHL" = HH(|)HHL.
3.7a   ebira < *yebyira (?< *yabyira < *da*1.2* -n- pira*2.2b*; ?< *ye[y]byira <
*daCi -n- pira). 'arrow quill'. LHL - 0-0-x x-x-x. Edo LHL.
?3.1   ebisu < eybyisu < *aCinpisu. 'Ainu' (= emisi/emisu). HHH··· - 1/0-2-x
x-x-x. Edo HHL. Hiroshima 2. Ōsaka 3; Ise 2.
6.2   ebisugusuri < *eybyisu-gusuri < *aCinpisu*?3.1* -n- kusuri*3.7a* ('Ainu
drug'). 'peony' (= syakuyaku). HHHHHL (Ir, -k-) - x-0-x x-x-x.
4.2   ebisume < *eybyisu-me < *aCinpisu*?3.1* me*1.x* (< ...). 'seaweed *(konbu)*'
(= hirome). HHHL - x-x-x x-x-x. K: Hn HHHF.
4.1   ebisune < *eybyisu-ne < *aCinpisu*?3.1* na-Ci*1.3a* ('Ainu root'). 'burnet'
(= waremokoo). HHHH - x-0-x x-x-x.
?3.1   eburi < *ye*1.1* (< ...) -n- pur[a-C]i*ʙ*. 'a kind of hoe'. HHx - 0-0-x x-x-x.
2.1   eda < yeda < *yoda < *do*1.1* -n- ta*1.3a* ('four arms/limbs'). 'branch'.
HH - 0-0-A A-A-A. NS (77a) HH; NS (T 76) HL; NS (T+ 125) yeda yeda HL|HL.
Edo HH. Ib H = 2.1. Dial. yoda. Nk yudaa A; Sr yuda/ida A; (northern Okinawa)
Kunigami, Ōgimi B; Yn duda A.
3.4 (?< 4.10)   edati < yedati < ye[ki]*1.x (?1.3b)* (< Ch ywa(y)k) -n- tat[a-C]i*ʙ*.
'conscripted labor; war(fare)'. x - x-x-x x-x-x. NS (123a [14:226-K]) LLL.
Cf. eyami.
1.3b-ga | 2.3   egahara < ye ga fara < *ye[ki]*1.3b* (< ...) ga para*2.3* ('epidemic
belly'). 'colic'. R-L|LL - x-x-x x-x-x.
4.5   ehasito < efasito [NS kana kun-chū] (< ?). 'lady'. NS (Okada) LLLL.
(Perhaps < *yo*adj ʙ* fasi*adj x* [fyi]to*2.2a* 'nice beautiful person'? Or "from
an old Korean word" (NKD) — but just WHICH old Korean word?)
?2.2b   ei < efi < ?*efyi (?< *yepyi < *depi < ?; ?< *api, ?< *opi). 'ray' *(fish)*.
x - 1-2-A x-x-x. Km (S,W) x. Sz 1. H1 = 2.2. Cf. ebi, kar[a]-ei.
?3.4, ?3.5b   ekaki < wekakyi < *we*1.3a* (< ...) kak[a-C]i*ʙ*. 'artist; painting,
drawing'. x - 3-2-B x-B-x. NS (96b, 122a) LLH. Matsue 2, Izumo 2/0.

?3.2b   ekubo < wekubo < *be[ma-Ci]_A (< ...) kunpo?₂.₁. 'dimple'. HHL - 1-2-B
    x-x-x. Sapporo, Aomori, Sz, Matsumoto, Numazu, Hamada, Hiroshima 1; Akita,
    Hattō, Goka-mura 2; Izumo, Ōita 0. Toyama 2 (we expect 1:3); Suzu 1 (expected);
    Ib H1 = 3.3.

2.1   emi < wemyi < *bem[a-C]i_A (< ... ; see emu). 'smile'. x - 1(/2[K])-
    0[H]/1[U]-A x-x-x. Km (S,W) HH. Mr (Bm) HH. Edo HH. Sz 1. Ib H1 = 2.2.

4.2   emigusa < wemi-gusa < *wemyi-gusa < *bem[a-C]i_A (< ...) -n- kusa₂.₃.
    (1) (= amadokoro) 'Polygonatum japonicum' (= amana); (2) (= ooemi = yamaemi =
    narukoyuri) 'Polygonatum falcatum' (= amana); (3) (= botanzuru) 'clematis';
    (4) (= rindoo) 'gentian'. HHHL - 2-x-x x-x-x.

3.2x   emisi/emisu < eymyisi < (3d vowel assimilated to 2d) < *eymyisu/eybyisu <
    *aCinpisu. 'Ainu' (= ebisu). x - x-x-x x-x-x. NS (109a) HHL; NS (T+ 11) HHL.

?3.1, ?3.2x, ?3.3   enba < wenba < wemufa ?< *bem[a]-u_A (< ...) pa?₁.₂ ('smiling
    wings'). 'dragonfly' (= akizu = tonbo). x - x-x-x x-x-x. See aka-enba, ki-enba.

3.2x   enisu < wenisu (?< wenzyu < Ch .hhwey-žyu'). 'Japanese pagoda tree,
    Sophora japonica' (= enzyu). HHL - x-x-x x-x-x.

3.2a   enoki < enokiy (= e-no-kiy) < *aCi₁.₁ no ko-Ci₁.₃ₐ. 'hackberry, Chinese
    nettle-tree'. HHL - 0-0-A x-x-x. Aomori (rare), Sz 2. Ib 'straw mushroom' H1 =
    3.3. Dial. yu-no-ki, yo-no-ki (vowel assimilation) < ye-no-ki < enoki. Sr bingi
    B is a puzzle.

3.1   enoko < wenoko < (*)we[nu]-no-kwo < *wenu₂.₁ (< ...) no kwo₁.₁.
    'puppy'. (x) - x-x-x x-x-x.

5.2   enokogusa < *we-no-kwo (< ...) -n- kusa₂.₃. 'foxtail, Setaria viridus'
    (= enokoro-gusa). HHxxx (= *HHHHL) - 3-x-x x-x-x.

2.1   enu < wenu ?< *wo-?₁.₁ (< ...) inu₂.₃. 'puppy-dog'. HH - x-2-x x-x-x.

4.8   eozi < e?₁.₂ -wodi₂.₁, eiwoti (Mg)< *e(i) bo-?₁.₁ (or [k]wo-₁.₁) -n-
    ti?₁.₃. 'father's older brother' (cf. otoozi). LHHH - x-x-x x-x-x.

?2.2a, ?2.3   era (?< a[g]i-ra < *anki₂.₂ₐ [a]ra*₂.₃; ?< ira₂.₃ 'thorn'). 'gill(s)'
    (= agito). x - 0-0[H]/2[U]-B x-x-x. Matsue 2; Hakata 0, ygr 2; Aomori, Sz,
    Hattō, Hamada, Izumo 0; Goka-mura 1. Ib F = 2.3, perhaps also H1 = 2.2.

2.2b   eri (?< *yeri ?< *yori < *dori; < (y)eri < [f]eri, see heri). 'collar'.
    x - 2-2-A A-B-x. 1700 Ōsaka HL. Dial. (Echigo) eeri. Sr wiiri B. Aomori, Sz,
    Hattō, Hamada, Goka-mura 2; Matsue, Izumo, Wakamatsu 2 (= 2.3). Ib F = 2.2.

2.3   esa < wesa (?< *weso < *beso < ?). 'bait' (= e). x - 0/2-2-B B-x-x. Km x.
    Hattō, Hamada, Matsue, Izumo 2. Ib H1 = 2.2. Sado ezo, Shizuoka yosa, Wakayama
    eso ?< *yoso < *yeso < *eso < *weso.

4.2   essai < etisai (< ?). 'the male sparrow-hawk (tumi)'. HHLL - x-x-x x-x-x.
    Perhaps borrowed from Korean e(n)chi-say 'jay'?

3.1   eturi < ye?₁.₂ (< ...) turi (< tur[a-C]i_A) ('branch hang'). 'split wood
    or bamboo tied to serve as underlay for roof or wall; roof/wall underlay'.
    HHH - x-0-x x-x-x. NS (T+ kun) LLH.

3.4 < 4.10   eyami < yeyami < ye[ki]₁.₃ᵦ (< Ch ywa(y)k) yami?(₂.₃) (<
    *dam[a-C]i_B). 'epidemic'. RLL/LLL - 0-0-x x-x-x. See §7.1. Cf. edati.

5.16   eyamigusa < yeyami₃.₄<₄.₁₀ (< ...) -n- kusa₂.₃. 'gentian (= rindoo);
    Atractylodes japonica (= okera)'. LLLHL - 3-4-x x-x-x.

?1.1   ga (< Ch .nga). 'moth'. x - 0-0-B x-x-x. Sz 0. Ib H = 1.1.

2.3   gaki (< Ch nga'-'kywey). 'hungry ghost, preta; glutton'. LL - 2-2-B
    x-B-x. Aomori 2. Ib F = 2.3. Sr gaci B. Zdb assumes OJ gakiy, taking the
    second semantogram as also phonetic.

2.1 (?< 3.1) (?> 2.4)   gama (?< *(n)kama) < kama (Mg) ?< [a]kama. 'bulrush'.
    HH - 0/1-1-B x-x-x. Sz, Hattō, Hamada, Matsue, Izumo, Goka-mura 0. Ib (rare)
    L2 = 2.5. Also kaba (?< *kanpa), akama.

?2.3   (-)gane < *-n- kane[y]2.3 (< *kana-Ci[-Ci]B). 'in order to, so as to'
    (postadnominal); 'something for the purpose of, material for'. See osuigane.
    A competing etymology: ··· gaPcl ne1.3a (< *na-Ci) 'root of ··· '.

2.1 < ?2.2b   gawa < *[ ] -n- kapa?2.2b. 'side, direction'. x - 0-0-A x-x-x. Ib L =
    2.4. See kawa.

2.4   geta ?< [sita]-geta < *-n- keta2.4 (< ?). 'clogs'. x - 0-1-A A-B-x. Aomori
    2 (expected); Tappi, Hida (= northern Gifu), Narada, Hattō, Hamada, Matsue,
    Izumo, Hiroshima 0; Goka-mura, NE Kyūshū 1. Kōchi 0 [Martin's notes]; Ib L =
    2.4. Although attested only from Edo, as a humble equivalent of asida the term
    may be older. Cf. Yoshida 1979:168-95.

2.4   geta 'square': see keta.

2.2b   gin (< Ch 'ngyen). 'silver'. x - 1-2-A x-x-x. Km x. Hattō, Hamada, Matsue,
    Izumo 1; Shimoda (K 1943), Goka-mura 2. Hakata 0, ygr 1. Ib H1 = 2.2.

2.2b   giri (< Ch ngye'-'lyey). 'duty'. x - 2-2-A A-A-x. Aomori 1; Hattō, Hamada,
    Goka-mura 2; Matsue, Izumo 2 (= 2.3).

1.3b   go (< Ch dial. version of .ghyey < ghyeg). 'the game of Go'.
    R - 1-2(/0[U])-B x-B-x. (Zs 148 R not in Mochizuki.) Km (W) H. Sz 1; Aomori,
    Hattō, Hamada, Matsue, Izumo, Hata 0. Kōchi 0 (Doi 1952:21); Ib H = 1.1.

?1.3b   go (< Ch dial. version of .ghyey < ghyeg). 'time; moment of death; limit'.
    H (Ir) - 1-0-B x-x-x. Km (W) L (afu go LH L). Sz 1. Ib L = 1.3.

?1.3b   go (?< Ch .hho). 'soybean mash; soybean milk; ... '. ?R (Ir) - 1-0-x x-x-x.

?2.1 < 3.6   goma < ᵘ/₀goma (< Ch .hho-.ma). 'sesame'. Rx - 0-0-B A-(B)-x.
    Sz, Narada, Hattō, Hamada, Matsue, Izumo, Hiroshima 0; Goka-mura 1; Hakata 1,
    ygr 0. Ōsaka, Ise 0; Ib H = 2.1. Nk qiguuma B; Sr quguma B. Wamyō-shō RH
    (Numoto 1979:27). See Ch. 4, §7.1.

2.3   gomi ?< *gomyi < *nkomi < *[ ] -n- kom[a-C]iB. 'rubbish, trash'. x - 2-2-B
    B-B-x. Sz, Hattō, Hamada, Goka-mura, Hiroshima 2; Matsue, Izumo 0; Hakata 0,
    ygr 2. Ib F = 2.3.

3.5x/3.6   gugusa (Mg) < kukusa (?< ku-? kusa2.3). 'Gleditsia japonica (honey
    locust)'. LLH/LHH - x-x-x x-x-x.

4.10   gyooyoo < gyau-yefu (< Ch 'hhyang-yep 'apricot leaves'). 'a decorative
    medalion attached to a horse saddle; a crest with paired apricot leaves' (cf.
    wabira). RLL = LHLL - 0-x-x x-x-x.

?1.1   ha(-) < fa(-) < *pa 'mother': see haha, oba, uba.

?1.1   ha(-) < fa(-) < *pa(-) 'red; ? bright': see hani2.1. Cf. hade?2.1;
    ? [hasi-]adj A , ? hana2.3; hareruB.

1.1   ha < fa < *pa 'jar': see he, utuwa.

1.1   ha < fa < *pa 'beginning, edge': see hatu(-)2.1, hana?2.1, haᵃ/zi2.1,
    haᵗ/date3.1, hazimeruA; soba2.4.

?1.2   ha < fa < *pa. 'feather' (= hane). H - 0-0-x x-x-x. K: Hn-Edo HL (all
    attested?). Hiroshima 0. Ōsaka, Ise 0.

1.2   ha < fa < *pa 'leaf'. H - 0-2-A A-A-A. Km (S,W) H-L. Edo F = HL. Aomori 0;
    Hakata 0, ygr 1. Ib H1 = 1.2.

1.3a   [ha] < fa < *pa. 'place': see ba, niwa.

1.3b   ha < fa < *pa. 'tooth'. R - 1-2-B B-B-B. Km x. Edo F = HL. Aomori,
    Narada, Hattō, Hamada, Matsue, Izumo, Okayama, Hiroshima, Yamaguchi 1. Kōchi
    (Doi 1952:21), Ōsaka, Ise 2; Ib H1 = 1.2. Hateruma pan (see Ch. 1, §52).

1.3b   ha ‹ fa ‹ *pa. 'blade'. x - 1-2-B B-B-B. Narada 1; Hakata 0, ygr 1. Ib H1 = 1.2. K puts this in 1.3b because (like ha 'tooth' and e 'bait') in Kt it is irregularly 2; the same HL (= F) accent is attested for 1700 Ōsaka (Kgg 135: 33b). No Mg data but the compound noun nofogiri-ba LLLLR could be regarded as a confirmation. Yet the rule for compound nouns would lead us to expect *LLLHL or LLLLH and the latter pattern is also attested in Myōgi-shō.

2.1   haba ‹ faba ‹ *panpa. 'width'. x - 0-0-A A-A-x. Sz 0. Ib H = 2.1.

3.7a ‹ 4.9 (= 2.3|2.2)   habaki ‹ fabakyi ‹ *pan[ki] pak[a-C]i. 'leggings, gaiters'. LHL (‹ *LH|HL)- 0-0-x x-x-x. Edo LHL.

2.4   hada ‹ fada ‹ *panta. 'skin, flesh'. x - 1/2-1-B B-B-x. NS (Okada) LH; NS (T 69) HH. Km x. 1700 Ōsaka LH. Hattō, Yamaguchi 1; Tappi, Hamada, Goka-mura 2; Matsue, Izumo 2 (expected reflex). Kōchi (Kobayashi) 2; Ib L = 2.4.

3.4   hadae ‹ fadafe (?‹ *fada - fye ‹ *panta$_{2.4}$ piCa$_{1.x}$; ?‹ *fada - [u]fey ‹ *panta$_{2.4}$ upa-Ci$_{2.2a}$). 'flesh'. LLL - 3/0/2-1[H]/1:3[U]-B x-x-x. Km (S) LLL. 1700 Ōsaka HHL.

3.6   hadaka ‹ fadaka ‹ *panta-ka (?‹ *panta$_{2.4}$ [a]ka$_{?2.5}$; ?‹ *panta$_{2.4}$ -ka$_{suf}$. 'naked'. LHH - 0(?‹1)-1-B x-B-C. Edo LHH (K: "LLH" mistaken). Narada, Goka-mura 1; Aomori (expected) 2; Akita, Ōita 2; Sapporo, Hattō, Hamada, Matsue, Izumo, Wakamatsu, Hakata 0. Ib L = 3.6.

3.4   hadake: (1) 'brush': see hake, uma-hadake. (2) 'psoriasis': see hatake.

3.1   hadare ‹ fadar^e/$_a$ ‹ *pantara(-Ci) ?‹ *pa[ra]$_{ala}$ n[i] tara-$_B$. 'with snow scattered about'. x - 0-0-x x-x-x. Km (W) HHH. Cf. harahara / barabara 'scattered' ?‹ *pa$_{1.3a}$ [a]ra-$_B$ 'place exist' or ... [a]ra$_{adj}$ $_A$ 'place sparse'.

3.6   hadasi ‹ fadasi ‹ *panta$_{2.4}$ [a]si$_{2.3}$. 'barefoot'. LHH - 0-1-B x-x-x. Edo LHH. Aomori 2 (we expect 1); Narada, Goka-mura 1; Hattō, Hamada, Matsue, Izumo, Wakamatsu, Hakata 0. Ib L = 3.6.

3.1   hadate: see hatate.

4.5 › 3.4 [hadauma]: see hazuma.

?2.1   hade ‹ fade (‹ ?). 'gaudy' (adj-n). x - 2-0-A x-x-x. Sz 2. Ib H1 = 2.2. Not attested before 17th century; thought to be from a samisen term (Kōza Nihon-go goi 3:158-67).

2.1   hae ‹ fafey ‹ *papaCi. 'fly' (insect). HH - 0-0-A A-A-x. Ongi HH. Ib H = 2.1.

2.3   hae ‹ faye (?‹ *pada with last vowel raised by -y-; ?‹ *pada-Ci). 'a kind of carp, Zacco platypus (= oikawa); dace (= ugui)' (fish). LL - 1-2-x x-x-x. Cf. haya.

2.x (? 2.3)   hae ‹ (JP) faye ?‹ *faye[y] ‹ *pada-Ci. (Kyūshū, Shikoku, Chūgoku) 'south wind'; (Ryūkyū) 'south wind; south'. x - x-x-x B-B-B. Hakata 0. Sd hwe(e) B, Sr hwe B, Yn hai B.

3.5b   haegi ‹ fafe^k/$_g$i ‹ *fafey-^{k}/$_g$iy ‹ *papa-Ci[-Ci]$_B$ -n- ko-Ci$_{1.3a}$. 'a kind of rafter (= taruki); ? the gable rafters'. LLH - x-0-x x-x-x. NS (96b) LLH.

5.2   haeharai ‹ fafe[y] - faraf[y]i ‹ *papa-Ci$_{2.1}$ para-p[al-C]i$_A$. 'a fly-haser; an insect-repellent; a kind of weapon'; ka no ~ 'a deer's tail'. HHHHL - 3-x-x x-x-x.

4.2   haetori ‹ fafe[y] - tori ‹ *papa-Ci$_{2.1}$ tor[a-C]i. 'fly-catching; fly-catcher'. HHHL - 3/4-3-x x-x-x.

2.2b   haga ‹ faga ‹ *panka ?‹ *pa$_{1.2}$ -n- kwo$_{1.3a}$ (2d vowel assimilated to the first). 'bird snare'. HL - 2-x-x x-x-x. Modern/dialect variant hago (x - 2/0-x-x x-x-x). NKD: "Also -k-" (merely orthographic?).

?2.3 ‹ 3.7b   hagi ‹ fagyi ‹ *panki. 'shank (= lower leg)'. RL/LL - 2-2-B B-x-C. Km (W) HL, HF, LL-H. Hiroshima 2. Ōsaka, Ise 2. Yn han C; Yaeyama pan. See Ch. 4, §7.1.

2.3   hagi < fagiy < *pan-koCi (?< *pan[a]*2.3* ko-Ci*1.3a*). 'bushclover,
lespedeza'. LL - 2/0/1-2 B-x-x. Aomori 1; Sz 1 (?/0); Narada 2(/1); Hiroshima
2. Ōsaka, Ise 2; Ib H1 = 2.2 *(plant is alien)*.

?2.2a < 2.3   hagi < (?*)fagyi < *pank[a-C]i. 'patch(ing)'. x - 0-2-A x-x-x. Sz 0.
(See Ch. 4, Chart 9.)

4.9 > 3.7a   [hagihaki]: *see* habaki.

?3.2a   hagusa < fagusa < ?*fak/ɡusa < *pa(n)-kusa < ? + kusa*2.3*. 'paddy weeds,
tare'. HHL - 1/0-x-x x-x-x. (Ir -k-.)

?2.1; ?2.3, ?2.4   haha (← fawa) < fafa < *pa-pa. 'mother'. HH/LL/LH - 1/2-2-A
x-A[Lit.]-x. Km (S,W) LH, Hx. Edo LH/(HL). 1700 Ōsaka LH. Sz, Narada, Hamada
1; Hattō, Goka-mura 2, Matsue, Izumo 0. Tk 1 < 2 (cf. Hiroto 1961:160). Ib H1
= 2.2. Most compounds indicate 2.1: haha-oya 'mother' x - 0-0-A x-A[Lit.]-x.

?4.1; ?4.5   haha-kata < fafa-gata (Mg) < *pa-pa*?2.1* -n- kata*2.2b*. 'mother'.
LLLL (?= *HHHH) - 0-0-A x-A[Lit.]-x.

-        hahaki: *see* hooki.

?3.1   hahako (← fawako) < fafa-kwo < *pa-pa*?2.1* kwo*1.1* ('mother and child').
'Artemisia keiskeana' (= inuyomogi). LHH/LxH (?= *HHH) - x-x-x x-x-x.

?4.2, ?4.1   hahakuri < faf/ᵥwakuri < *pa-pa*2.1* kuru-Ci*2.3* ('mother chestnut').
'Fritillaria verticallata, a kind of lily' (= baimo). HHHL (Ir) - x-4-x x-x-x.
K: Hn HHHH (cf. compound-noun accentuation rules, Ch. 4, §10.4).

4.1   hahakuso < fafa-kuswo (? or -kurwo) < *pa-pa*?2.1* kuswo*2.3* (?kurwo*2.5*).
'mole (on the skin)'. HHHH - x-x-x x-x-x.

3.1   hahaso (← fɔɔso < fawaso) < fafa-swo < *pa-pa*?2.1* swo*?1.1* (? 'mother
hemp/cloth'). 'oak'. HHH - 0-0-x x-x-x. Km (W) HHH. (Cf. hiso, soma, sobo.)

3.6   hahuni < fafuni (< Ch pak-'pywen). '(rice-)powder used as face whitener'.
LHH - x-0-x x-x-x.

2.1   hai < fafi (?< *fafiy < *fa[te]-fiy < *pata-Ci[-Ci]*B* po-Ci*1.3b* 'exhausted
fire'). 'ashes'. HH(/HL) - 0-0-A A-A-x. Ib H = 2.1. (Yn higun B ?< *fi-gomi
'fire trash'.)

5.16   haimayumi < fafi-mayumyi < *pap[a-C]i*B* ma-dumi*?3.1*. 'Eucommia ulmoides (=
totyuu); spindle-tree, Euonymus japonica (= masaki)'. LLLHL - x-x-x x-x-x.

4.10   haitaka ?< fa[s]itaka < *pasi (< ?) taka*2.1*. 'sparrow hawk, accipiter'.
LHLL (-s-) - 0/1-0-x x-x-x.

2.3   haka < faka < *paka. 'grave'. LL - 2-2-B B-B-B. NS (103a) LL. Edo HL.
Ib F = 2.3.

2.3   haka < faka < *paka. 'alloted amount; aim, intention; progress'. x - 2-2-A
x-x-x. Sz 1. Cf. hakaru, hakadoru; hakanai.

3.4   hakama < fakama < ?*paka-ma < *paka-*A* mo*1.3b*. 'man's skirt'.
LLL 3-2(<*3)-B x-B-B. NS (114b) LLL; NS (T+ 74) LLL. Edo HHL. Sapporo 2.
Kōchi, Sakawa, Hyōgo 3; Toyama 1:4; Suzu 0; Ib F = 3.4. Yn hagama B (H
1964:71b). The register is incongruent with the etymology.

3.4   hakari < fakari < *paka*(2.3)* -r[a-C]i*B*. 'weighing; scales'. LHL - 3-1:3
('scales')/0-B x-B-(B). Aomori, Sz 2; Wakamatsu, NE Kyūshū 1; Narada 3;
Hakata ('scales') 1, ygr 3. Ib L2 = 3.5/7. See Ch. 4, Chart 6:1.

5.6   hakarigoto < fakarikoto < *paka*(2.3)* -r[a-C]i*B* (-n-) koto*2.3*. 'scheme'.
LLLLL - 0/4/5-0[H]/4[U]-B x-B-x. Mr (Bm) HHHHL. Sz 4. (Sr -r- anomalous.)

?3.4   hakase (= hakusi) < fakase (< Ch pak-'dhryey). 'an expert (authority)'.
LLL - 1-1-B x-x-x. Edo HHL. Hattō 1; Goka-mura 2; Hamada, Matsue, Izumo 0.

2.3   hake < fake < fa[da]key < *pantaka-Ci[-Ci]*B*. 'brush'. x - 2-2-B x-B-x.
Km x. K: Hn LL *(attested?)*. Ib F = 2.3.

4.6   [hakikuzu] < fakikudu < *pak[a-C]i*B* kuntu*2.4*. 'sweepings'. LLLH - x-x-x
x-x-x. (Not in NKD; attested only in Mg?)

4.1   hakimono < fakimono < *fakyi-mono < *pak[a-C]i$_A$ mono$_{2.3}$. 'footwear'.
x - 0-0-B x-x-x. Mr (Bm) faimono HHHH. Sz 0.
-          hakka 'mint': see baka.
2.1   hako < fakwo < *pakwo (?< *p[ut]a$_{2.1}$ kwo$_{1.3a}$ 'lidded basket'). 'box'.
HH - 0-0-A A-A-A. Ongi HH. Edo HH. K: Km HH (attested?). Ib H = 2.1.
4.2   hakomono < fakomono (?< *pakwo$_{2.1}$ mono$_{2.3}$). 'bamboo basket'. HHHL - x-x-x
x-x-x.
2.3   hama < fama < *pama. 'beach'. LL - 2-2-B B-B-x. NS (Okada) LL; NS (T 48)
HH, (T+ 4) HH ?= HL; NS (T+ kun) LL. Km x. Edo HL. Ib F = 2.3. Onna paama B.
5.16   hamaakana < fama - akana < *pama$_{2.3}$ aka-na$_{?3.1,?3.2}$ (< ...). 'Bupleurum
falcatum' (= Misima-saiko). LLLHL - x-x-x x-x-x.
4.5   hamabisi < famabisi < *fama-byisi < *pama$_{2.3}$ -n- pisi$_{2.1}$. 'Tribulus
terrestris (a kind of burnut)'. LLLL - x-2-x x-x-x.
4.6   hamaguri < famaguri < *pama$_{2.3}$ -n- kuru-Ci$_{2.3}$ ('beach chestnut'). 'clam'.
LLLH - 2-2-B x-x-x. Sz 3; Izumo 4; Goka-mura 0; Narada, Hattō, Hamada, Matsue,
Hata, Hakata 2. Kōchi 2.
4.6 (= 2.3|2.4)   hama-hai < fama faf[y]i < *pama$_{2.3}$ pap[a-C]i$_B$ inf (= 2.4).
'Vitex rotundifloria (= hanagoo); fruit of Vitex cannabifolia (namae-no-ki =
ninzinboku = hananasu)'. LL(|)LH - x-x-x x-x-x.
5.16, 5.6 hamahukura < fama-fukura < *pama$_{2.3}$ puku-ra$_{3.1}$. 'Carpesium abrotanoides'
(= yabu-tabako). LLLHL (Kn), LLLLL (Ir) - x-x-x x-x-x.
3.5x (= 2.3|1.1)   hamamo < fama-mo < *pama$_{2.3}$ mo$_{?1.1}$. 'beach seaweed; (=
hondawara) sargasso, gulfweed'. x - 0/2-x-x x-x-x. NS (Okada) LL(|)H;
NS (T+ 68) LLL.
?5.8 (= 2.3|3.6)   hamanigana < fama$_{2.3}$ (< *pama) nigana$_{3.6}$ (< *ninka$_{adj B}$ na$_{1.3a}$.
'Siler divaricatum' (= hamasugana). LL(|)LHH (taken as two phrases by NKD) -
x-4-x x-x-x.
?4.7   [haman(i)si, hamazi] ?= fama(n)si < *pama$_{2.3}$ (-n-) si$_{1.3b}$. ? (plant name).
(Ch characters NYOU-KA 'brushwood flower'.) Cf. yama^s/zi.
5.16   hamasasage < famasasage < fama$_{2.3}$ (< *pama) sasage$_{?3.6}$ (< ...).
'Caesalpinia japonica' (= zyaketu-ibara). LLLHL - 3-4-x x-x-x.
5.16   hamasugana ?< famasuga$_{4.1}$ (< *pama$_{2.3}$ suga[-Ci]$_{2.3}$)na$_{1.3a}$. 'Siler
divaricatum' (= hamanigana). LLLHL - x-x-x x-x-x. (Or fama$_{2.3}$ *suga-na$_{3.x}$?)
?4.5, ?4.6   hamasuge < fama - sugey < *pama$_{2.3}$ sunka-Ci$_{2.3}$. 'nut grass, coco
grass' (= kugu). x - 2-3-x x-x-x. Cf. hamasugana.
?2.2b   hami < fami (?< *pa-m[us]i < *pa[p[a-C]i$_B$] m[us]i$_{2.1}$). 'viper' (= mamusi).
HL - 1-2-x x-x-x.
2.3   hami < fami < *famyi < *pami. (1) 'Phlomis umbrosa'; ?(2) 'dead/blind
nettle' (= odori-kosoo); ?(3) '*chestnut/acorn/filbert/oxalis' (see hasibami,
turubami, katabami) — cf. Korean :pam 'chestnut', kay-am < kay'Gam ?< *kay-
'kam, ?< *kay-'pam 'filbert'). LL - x-2-x x-x-x.
2.3   hami < fam[y]i < *pam[a-C]i. 'eating; adding in; foodstuff; (= kutubami)
a bridle bit'. LL - 1/2-2-x x-(B)-x. Sr hami B '(livestock) feed'.
2.5   hamo < famo < *pamo. 'eel'. x - 1-1:3-A x-(x)-x. Km x. Aomori 1 (we expect
2, unless the word is treated as /hamu/). Ib L2 = 2.5. Sr habu A 'snake'.
2.1   hana < fana < *pana. 'nose'. HH - 0-0-A A-A-(A). Km (W) HH. Mr (Bm) HH.
Edo HH. Ib H = 2.1. Yn hanaburu A.
?2.1   hana < fana < *pana (?< *pa$_{1.1}$ -na$_{suf}$). 'edge, end (point), extremity;
verge; outset, beginning'. x - 0/1-0/1:3-B x-A-x. Sz 1. Ib H = 2.1. Cf.
ha^s/zi$_{2.1}$, hata$_{2.1}$, hazimeru$_A$.

2.3   hana < fana < *pana. 'flower, blossom'. LL - 2-2-B B-B-B. NS (T 35, 67;
114) LL. Km (W) LL. Mr (Bm) HL. Edo HL. Ib F = 2.3. Onna paanaa B. (Perhaps,
despite register, < *pa[si*adj A*] na*1.3a* 'red/bright/beautiful *plant'.)

5.2   hanabasira < fanabasira < *pana*2.1* -n- pasira*3.6a*. 'bridge of nose'.
HHHHL - 0/3-0[H]/4[U]-A x-x-x. Sz 0.

?4.5   hanabira < fana-byira < *pana*2.3* -n- pira*2.2b*. 'petal'. LLxx - 3/4/0-4-B
x-B-x. K: Hn LLLL. Sz 2. Sr hanabira B 'shaved-fish flakes'.

4.5 < 2.3|2.3 hanabusa < fanabusa < *pana*2.3* -n- pusa*2.3*. 'calyx'. (LL)(|)LL -
0[H]/3[U]-B x-x-x.

3.4   hanada < fanada < *pananta (< ?). 'dark blue' (= hanada-iro). LLL -
0-0-(B) x-x-x.

4.5   hanagame < fanagame < ?*fana-gamey < ?*pana*2.3* -n- ka-n- pey*2.3*
(< ka*?1.3a* -n- pa-Ci*1.1*). 'flowerpot'. LLLL - 2-4-x x-x-x.

3.2a   hanage < *fana-gey < *pana*2.1* -n- ka-Ci*?1.1*. 'nostril hairs'.
x - 0-1:3[H]/3[U]-A x-A-x. Km x. Sz 0.

5.2   hanagenuki < *fanagey*3.3a* (< *pana*2.1* -n- ka-Ci*?1.1*) nukyi (< nuk[a-C]i*A*).
'tweezers'. HHHHL - 3-x-x x-x-x.

3.2a   hanagi < fana-giy < *pana*2.1* -n- kQ-Ci*1.3a*. 'nose-ring for an ox'. HHL -
0-0-x x-x-x.

4.2   hanahada < fanafada < ?*pana*?2.1* - pan[a] *?2.1* ('edge-edge') -ta*suf*.
'very, extremely' *(adv)*. HHHL/HHLL - 0-0-A x-x-x. NS (107a) HHHL. Km (S) HHHL.
Mr (Bm) HHHL. K: Hn HHLL, Km HHHL, Mr HHHH. Heian kunten-shō have examples of
fana-fana (Akinaga 1977c:73).

3.4   hanami < fana-myi < *pana*2.3* mi[-Ci]/miC[a-C]i*B*. 'flower-viewing'. LLL -
3-2-B x-B-x. Km x. 1700 Ōsaka HLL. Sz, Narada 3; Aomori 2̲. Ib F = 3.4.

3.4   hanasi < fanasi < *pana-s[a-C]i*B*. 'talk; tale'. x - 3-2/3̲-B B-B-B. 1700
Ōsaka HLL. Aomori, Sz, Narada 3. Ib F = 3.4. See Ch. 4, Chart 6:1.

4.5   hanatumi < fana-tumi < *fana-tumyi < *pana*2.3* tum[a-C]i*A*. 'picking
flowers; a flower picker, a person who picks flowers'. x - 3-0[U]/4[H]-A x-x-x.
Km (W) LLLL.

4.11   hanayaka < fanayaka < *pana*2.3* -da-ka. 'gorgeous'. LLHL - 2-4-B x-x-x.
K: Edo HLLL.

3.1   hanazi < fanadi < *pana*2.1* -n- ti*1.1*. 'nosebleed'. HHH - 0-0-A A-A-A.
Km x. Edo HHH. Hakata 2, ygr 3̲. Ib H = 3.1. Yn hanadi A (H 1964:71b).

4.2   hanazura < fana*t*/*d*ura < *pana*2.1* (-n-) tura (?= tura*2.2b* = turu*2.2b*
'vine'). 'ox halter'. HHHL - x-x-x x-x-x.

2.1   hane < fane < *pa*?1.2* -ne*suf* (?< *-ne[y] < *-naCi). 'feather'. HH - 0-0-A
A-A-A. Km x. Ib H = 2.1. Nk panii A; Kunigami, Ōgimi (northern Okinawa) B̲.

4.2   hanegaki < fanegaki < *fane-gakyi < fane*2.1* (< ...) -n- kak[a-C]i*B*. 'the
flapping of wings'. x - x-0-x x-x-x. Km (W) HHHL.

4.5   haneuma < fane[y]-m[u]ma < *pana-Ci[-Ci]*B* uma*2.3*. 'leaping/jumping horse'.
LLLL - 0/2-0/1̲-x x-x-x.

2.1   hani < fani < *pa(-)ni ?< *pa*adj A* n[a-C]i*1.3a* (also fane < *fa-ne[y]
< *pa na-Ci). 'red clay'. HH - 1̲-2̲-x x-x-x. Km x. (Modern accents artificial?
Cf. haniwa 3.1; but hanima ?3.5a.) Cf. hena, ? beni.

?3.5x   hanima < fani-ma < fani*2.1* (< ...) [u]ma*2.3*. 'a horse of clay'. x - x-x-x
x-x-x. NS (126b) LLH (register incongruent?).

3.1   haniwa < fani-wa < fani*2.1* (< ...) wa (< ba*1.3a*). 'haniwa (red-clay burial
objects)'. HHH - 0-0[H]/1:3[U]-A x-x-x. Narada 1̲. Ib H = 3.1, *(rare)* L = 3.4.

3.2x   hanizi < fanizi < *pa(-)n(i)si (< ?) = haze ('sumac'). HHL - x-x-x x-x-x.

3.1   haori < fa(w?)ori ?< *pa?₁.₂ (w?)or[a-C]i; ?< fafuri < *papur[a-C]i₄.
'coat'. x - 0-0-A x-A-x. Km x. Aomori, Sz O. Ib H = 3.1. Etymology: see NKD.

2.3   hara < fara < *para < *paru (the second vowel assimilated to the first).
'field'. LL - 1-2-B x-B-x. NS (102b, 115a) LH. Km x. Hattō, Goka-mura,
Hiroshima 1; Hamada, Matsue, Izumo 2. Ōsaka, Ise 1. Sr haru B (-u also in
Shimabara, Ōita?). Cf. haru, haruku, hareru.

2.3   hara < fara < *para. 'belly'. HL (Kn) - 2-2-B x-A-x. NS (96a) LL. Km x.
Edo HL. Hiroshima 2. Ōsaka, Ise 2. Hiroshima 2. Ib F = 2.3. Cf. haramu; wata.

?2.4 < ?3.6   hara < fara < *para. 'trumpet (horn)' (= hara no hue). RH - x-x-x
x-x-x. Km x. Cf. hora. See Ch. 4, §7.

5.6 (= 3.4|2.4)   haraegoto < farafey-goto < *para-pa-Ci[-Ci]₈ -n- koto₂.₃.
'words of prayer'. LLLL(|)LL - x-0-x x-x-x.

3.6   haraka < faraka < *para₂.₃ [a]ka₈dJ ₄ ('belly red'). 'croaker (= nibe);
trout (= masu)' (fish). LHH - x-1-x x-x-x. K: Hn-Km LHH (Km attested?). Also
farako (Kagaku-shū).

4.5   harakara < farakara < faragara < *para₂.₃ -n- kara₂.. 'sibling(s)'. x -
0/2-0-B x-x-x. NS (107a) LLLL. (The -g- is from the phonogram in Senmyō 25.)

4.6   haramaki < fara-makyi < *para₂.₃ mak[a-C]i₄. 'bellyband'. LLLH - 0/3-1:4-B
x-x-x. Sz 3.

3.4 (= 2.3|1.3)   harame < fara₂.₃ (-) mye₁.₉b < *para miCa (?= *mina). 'pregnant
woman'. LLL - x-x-x x-x-x.

4.6 (= 2.3|2.4)   haraobi < fara₂.₃ (-) obyi₂.₄ < *para onp[a-C]i₈. 'bellyband'.
LL(|)LH - 3(/0[H])-1:4-B x-B-x. Edo farubi HLL. Sz 3.

4.5   harawata < fara₂.₃ wata₂.₃ < *para bata. 'intestines, guts'. LL(|)LL -
4/0-4-B x-x-x. Sz 4.

2.3   hare < fare[y] < *para-Ci[-Ci]. 'fair/clear weather'. LL - 2(/1)-1:3[H]/
2[U]-x x-x-x. Km x. Edo HL. Narada, Hamada 1; Matsue 1/2; Hattō, Izumo, Goka-
mura, Hiroshima 2. Ib L = 2.4.

?2.2b, ?2.1   hari < fari < *par[a-C]i₄. 'opening up land; cultivated land'.
HL/HH(/LL) - x-x-x x-x-x.

2.3   hari < fari < *pari. 'crossbeam' (cf. utubari). x - 2-2-B x-x-x. Hiroshima
0. Ōsaka, Ise 2; Ib H = 2.1.

2.4   hari < fari < *pari ?< *pari[y] < *paru-Ci (Iwate haru < Azuma OJ faru).
'needle'. LH - 1-1-B B-B-C. Ongi-m LH. Km (W) LH. Edo LH. Izumo 2. Ib L = 2.4.
Sr haai B.

2.4   hari < fari < *pari. 'black alder' (= han-no-ki). x - x-2-x x-x-x.
NS (77a) LH; NS (T 14:76) LH.

4.1   harimati < farimati < *parimati. 'small yellowtail (buri)' (fish = hamati;
dial. inada, kanpati). HHHH - (0)-x-x x-x-x. Tk hamati 0 < ha[ri]mati.

3.7x   hario < fari-wo < *pari₂.₄ bo₁.₃ₐ ('needle tail'). 'saury' (fish) (=
sayori). LHL - x-x-x x-x-x.

2.5   haru < faru < *paru. 'spring (season)'. LH - 1-1:3-B B-B-x. Km (S) LF,
(W) LH. Mr (Bm) LH. Edo LF. Kōchi, Hyōgo, Ōsaka, Ise 1:3; Toyama, Suzu 2
(expected reflex).

?5.13   harugasumi < faru-kasumi < faru kasumyi < *paru₂.₅ kasu-m[a-C]i₄ (< ...).
'spring mist'. x - 3-4-x x-x-x. Km (W) LHLLL. Mr (W 18, 20) LHHHH, (19) LHHHL.

3.4   haruhi < faru-fyi < *paru₂.₅ pi₁.₂. 'a spring day'. x - x-x-x x-x-x.
NS (82c [17:111-M]) LLL; (T+ 94, 96) HH-E.

3.7b   haruka(-ni) < faruka < *paru-ka. 'way distant'. LHL(-H) - 1-1:3-B x-x-x.
Km (S) LHL(-L). Mr (Bm) LHL. Edo LHL. Ib L2 = 3.5/7. Cf. haru-baru.

4.6   harusame < farusamey < *paru*z.s* [z]ama-Ci*z.s*. 'spring rain'. x - 0-0-B
x-x-x. Km (W) LLLH. Sz 0.

-           hasama: *see* hazama.

3.4   hasami < fasamyi < *pa(n)sa-m[a-C]i*z*. 'scissors; pincers'. LLL - 3-1:3-B
B-A-C. Sapporo 2 (Uwano 1978:52b has Tk 3/2); Hakata 0, ygr 2/3. Kōchi, Sakawa
3 (but Doi 1952:24 has Kōchi 1:3); Ōsaka, Kōbe 3/1:3; Toyama 1:3 *(expected)*;
Suzu 1 *(we expect 0)*; Ib F = 3.4. Nk pasaamii B.

3.6   haseo < fase-wo < fase[u]*zs.a* (< *paseu < Ch .pa-.tsyew) wo*z.sb* (< *bo
'hemp'). 'banana plant' (= basyoo). LHH - x-x-x x-x-x. Sr (basyuu B =) uu B
'banana-fiber plant' *(see* o), basyaa B 'abaca cloth' (= basyoo-hu). Sd basya(a)
B 'banana plant'. Dial. (Iga) hasyo.

4.8 (?= 3.6|1.2)   haseoba < fasewo-ba < *fase-wo*zs.s* (< ...) -n- pa*z.z*. 'banana
(plantain) leaf'. LHHH (Kn) / xHHH(Ck) - x-4-x x-x-x Km (W) LHHH, HHHH, HHHL.

2.1   ha*ª*/zi < fa*ª*/zi < *pa(n)si (?< *pan[a]*z.z* si*z.x* 'edge direction'). 'edge'.
HH - 0-0-A x-(A)-x. Km (W) HH. Mr (Bm) HH. Edo HH. Narada hadži 0; cf. hazime,
hana. Ib H = 2.1. Sr hasibasi A 'edges'.

2.2b   hasi < fasi < *pasi. 'bridge, ladder'. HL - 2-2-A A-A-A. Ongi HL.
NS (102a) HL. Km x. Mr (Bm) HL. Edo HL. Aomori 0; Hakata 1, ygr 2. Toyama 2;
Suzu 1 *(we expect 1:3)*; Ib H1 = 2.2.

2.4   hasi < fasi < *pasi. 'chopsticks'. LH - 1-1-B B-B-C. Mr (Bm) LH. Edo LH.
Hata 1. Kōchi 1; Ib L = 2.4. Sr haasi B. Etymologies: ?< *fa[ya]si < *pa[da]-
si 'they are fast' (like Chinese kuàizi; ?< *pas[am]i 'scissors'; ?< *[taka-
Ci no] pasi 'ends [of bamboo]'. Ainu pasuy, if a loan (the Karafuto word is
sahka), suggests *pasi[y] < *pasuCi, perhaps *pasu[m]i < *pasami?

?4.10   hasibami < fasibamyi ?< *pasi (< ?) -n- pami*z.s*. 'filbert'. LHLL - 0-1-x
x-x-x. K: Hn-Km LHLL *(Km attested?)*.

4.1   hasidate '(setting up) a ladder': *see* hasitate.

3.5x   hasiha < fasifa < *pasipa (< ?). 'pyramid-shaped gemstone'. LLH - x-x-x
x-x-x. (The register is incongruent with Ōno's etymology of hasu 'aslant'.)

3.6   hasike < fasike (< ?). 'barge'. x - 0-1-B x-x-x. Aomori 0 (we expect 2);
Wakamatsu 0. Ib H = 3.1. Earliest example 1895?

3.5a/b   hasira < fasira < *pasira. 'pillar'. LLH - 0(/3[Mkz])-2-B (A)-(B)-B/C.
NS (96b) LLH. Km x. Edo HLL. Goka-mura, Sapporo, Wakamatsu, NE Kyūshū, Ōita 1;
Hakata 1, ygr 0/3. Matsumoto, Narada 2; western Mino (= SW Gifu) 1/2; Aomori,
Akita 3; Izumo 3 (Kobayashi), 0 (Hiroto and Ōhara); Numazu, Hiroshima 0. Nara,
Ōsaka 2; Kōbe, Himeji, Kōchi 1:3 (Ōhara 1932-3); Toyama 2 *(we expect 1:3)*;
Suzu 1:4 *(we expect 1:3)*; Ib L2 = 3.5/7. Nk pasiraa B = payaa C. Yn hira B
(H 1964:72a) / C (H 1964:185b, 1967:290a).

3.5a   hasita < fasita < *pasita. 'fragment, part; incomplete, partial, halfway;
unsatisfactory'. LLH - 0-1-B x-x-x. Edo HLL. Aomori, Sz 0. Ib L = 3.6.

4.10   hasitaka 'sparrow hawk': *see* haitaka.

4.1   hasit/date < fasi-tate < *pasi*z.zb* tat[a-C]i*z* '(setting up) a ladder'.
x - x-x-x x-x-x. NS (73c [11:271-M]) HHHH; NS (T+ 95) HHLI.

?4.6a   hasitubo < fasitubo [Mg] < ?*fasitufo < *pasi*z.a* tupo*z.zª* (*see* tubo).
'a chopstick jar, a jar for chopsticks'. LLLF - 2-3-x x-x-x. See Ch. 4, §7.3.

?2.3   has°/u < fas°/u < *pas°/u. 'a kind of carp' *(fish)*. LL, LH [Ir] - x-x-x
x-x-x. Km x.

2.1 < 3.1 hasu < ha[ti]su < fatisu < *pati-su. 'lotus'. HH(-no mi HH) - 0-0-A x-x-x.
Km x. Ib H = 2.1.

2.1   hasu < fasu < *pasu. 'aslant'. x - 0-0-A x-x-x. Km x. Ib H = 2.1.

-           [hasyoo] 'banana': *see* haseo, basyoo.

2.1   hata < fata < *pata. 'side, rim'. HH - 0-0-B̲ x-A-x. Km x. Sz 0; Matsue
0/2̲. Ib F = 2.3. Nk pataa B̲. Matsumoto 1974:96: < *pa-ta; cf. hana, haᵃ/ᵤi.

2.1   hata < fata < *pata. 'fin; fish'. HH - x-0-x x-x-x. Km x. Ib H = 2.1.

2.2x   hata(-) < fata < *pata. 'twenty'. HL (~ nana LL 'twenty-seven') - x-x-x.

2.2a   hata < fata < *pata. 'flag'. HL - 2-2-A A-A-A. Km x. Mr (Bm) HL. Edo HL.
Aomori 0; Hiroshima 2. Ōsaka, Ise 2; Ib H1 = 2.2. Yn hata A (H 1964:71a).

2.2a   hata < fata < *pata. 'loom; cloth'. HL - 2-2-A x-(x)-x. NS (106b) HL.
Km x. Aomori 0; Hiroshima 1̲/2. Ōsaka, Ise 2; Ib H1 = 2.2.

2.4   hata < fata < *pata. '(dry) field'. LH - 2/2̲-1-A̲ x-x-x. Km x. Matsue,
Izumo 2; Hattō, Hamada, Goka-mura, Hiroshima 1. Ōsaka, Ise 1. Cf. hatake.

4.1   hataasi < fata-asi < *pataₛ.ₗ asiₛ.ₛ. 'the end of a fluttering banner'.
HHHH - 0-x-x x-x-x.

4.1   hatabari < fatabari < *pataₛ.ₗ -n- par[a-C]i_A. 'width; sway, power'.
x - x-0-x x-x-x. Mr (Bm) HHHH.

3.2x   hatae < fataye < *pataₛ.ₛₒ yeₗ.ₗ (< ?). 'the handle/shaft of a halberd'.
HHL - x-x-x x-x-x. Cf. hatahoko.

3.7a   hatago < fatago < *pata (= ?) -n- kwoₗ.ₛₐ. 'a travel pack of provisions;
food at a wayside inn'. LHL - 0-1̲-x x-x-x.

4.1   hatahoko < fatafoko̲ < *pataₛ.ₛₒ pokoₛ.ₛ. 'flagged halberd (spear)'.
HHHH - x-0-x x-x-x. K: Edo HHLL.

?3.4/?3.7a   hatake < faᵗ/ᵈake < fatakey < *pa(n)takaCi (?< *pantaₛ.ₐ kak[a-C]i_B
'skin scratch'). 'pityriasis; psoriasis; scabies'. LLL (-d-)/ LHL (-t-) -
0-1:3-B x-x-x.

3.7a/b   hatake < fatakey < *pataₛ.ₐ -ka-Ciₗ.ₓ ('place' + suffix; or is pata a
truncation of pata-ka?). 'field'. LHL - 0-1:3-B B-B-C. NS (100b) LHL. Km x.
Matsumoto, Numazu, Hattō, Hamada, Matsue, Izumo, Hiroshima, Hakata 0; Hida (=
northern Gifu), Narada, Goka-mura 1; Sapporo, Aomori, Akita, Ōita 2̲; Wakamatsu
3̲. Kōchi 3̲; Suzu 1̲ (we expect 0); Ib L2 = 3.5/7. Yn "A" (H 1964:185a) mistaken
(cf. H 1964:71b, H 1967).

4.1   hatamono < fatamono (= fata-mo̲no̲) < *pataₛ.ₛₒ mo̲no̲ₛ.ₛ. 'loom; cloth'.
HHHH - x-x-x x-x-x. Km x.

?4.1   hataori < fata-ori < *pataₛ.ₛₒ or[a-C]i_A. 'weaver'. x - 2/3-4-A x-x-x. Sz 0.

5.1   hataori-me < fata-oriₜₐ.ₗ (< ...) myeₗ.ₛₒ (< ...). 'weaver girl, female
weaver'. HHHHH (Zs) /LH?HHH (Kn) - x-x-x x-x-x.

3.1   haᵗ/ᵈate < faᵗ/ᵈate ?< *paₗ.ₗ (-n-) tata-Ci[-Ci]_B. 'brink, edge, limit'.
x - 0-x-x x-x-x. NS (Okada) HHH.

3.3   hatati < fatati < *fatati[y] (?< *pata-tu-Ci, ?< *pata - to̲[s]iₛ.ₛ).
'twenty; twenty years old'. x - 1(<*2)-2-A x-A-A. Km x. Edo HLL. Sapporo,
western Mino (= SW Gifu), Hiroshima, Wakamatsu 2; Hakata 2, ygr 1. Aomori
2(?/3); Tappi, Akita, Matsumoto, Numazu, Narada 0̲. Ib H1 = 3.3. Yn hataci A
(H 1964:76b). Cf. hatuka.

2.3   hate < fate < fate[y] < *pata-Ci[-Ci]. 'end; limits'. x - 2-0-B x-B-x.
Km (W) LL. Edo HL. Ib F = 2.3.

?2.1a   hati < fati < *pati. 'bee'. HH - 0-0-A A-A-C̲. Km x. Edo HH. Ib H = 2.1.
Nk pacii A. Many dialects have /b-/, e.g. Tappi badzï (Clarke 49); this may be
from [mitu-]bati '[honey-]bee' or the like, i.e. < *[ ] -n- pati (Ch. 1, §26.)
According to Nihon-Shoki, four crates of honeybees were sent in 647 from Kudara
(Paekche) to be kept at Miwa-yama.

2.3   hati < fati < *pati (< Ch pwa̲t ?< Sanskrit pātra, cf. Korean pali).
'(begging-)bowl; (flower-)pot'. LL - 2-2-B x-B-x. Ongi LL. Edo HL. Ib F = 2.3.
Sr haaci B.

3.1   hatisu < fatisu < *patisu (?= *patiₛ.ₗ suₗ.ₛₒ 'bee nest'). 'lotus'. HHH -
0-0-x x-x-x. Narada 3̲. Ib (rare) H = 3.1. Km (W) hatisu-fa HHHL 'lotus leaf'.

2.3   hato < fatwo < *patwo. 'pigeon, dove'. x - 1-1:3[H]/2[U]-B B-B-C.
NS (Okada) LL; NS (T 71) LL. Km x. Edo HL. Narada, Hattō, Izumo, Goka-mura, and
one place in Nagano (K 1943) 2; Hamada, Matsue, Hiroshima (Okuda) 1; Hakata 0,
ygr 1. Ib F = 2.3. Nk pooTuu B; Sr hootu B; Yn hatu C (H 1964 — but A on p.71a).
Compounds: 2.3, not 2.5. Hateruma paton and Iriomote-Sonai patuna < *pato-na.
2.1   hatu(-) < fatu < *pa₁.₁ -tuₚcₗ. 'first': see hatukari, ... Sr haçi- A.
2.1|4.6   hatuhanazome < hatu-hanazome (NKD: hatuhana-zome) < fatu-fanazome <
fatu₂.₁ (< *pa₁.₁ -tuₚcₗ) pana₂.₃ -n- soma-Ci[-Ci]ₐ. '(what is) dyed with the
season's first saffron'. x - x-x-x x-x-x. Km (W) HH|LLLH.
3.1   hatuka < fatuka < *patu-ka (?< *pat[a]-uka; ?< *pa[ta] -tu ka). 'twenty
days'. x - 0-0-A B-A-x. Km x. K: Edo HHH. Hakata 1, ygr 0/3. Ib H = 3.1. Nk
paCiika A. Cf. hatati.
4.3   hatukari < fatu₂.₁ - kari₇₂.₄ (< *pa₁.₁ -tu) kari₇₂.₄. 'first wild goose
of autumn'. x - 3-0[H]/4[U]-A x-x-x. Km (W) HHLL.
?3.1, ?3.4   hatuko < fatuko < *patu₂.ₓ (< ?) kwo₁.₁. 'descendants'. LLL (Zs) /
HHx (Kn) - x-x-x x-x-x. K: Hn HHH. Cf. mikohana.
-          hatuma: see hazuma.
2.1|1.3a   hatu-o < fatuwo < fatu-fo < fatu₂.₁ (< *pa₁.₁ -tu) pwo₁.₃ₐ. 'first ear of
rice'. HH(|)L, HH|R - 0-0-A x-x-x.
3.1 = 2.1-tu|2.1   hatuse < fatuse ?< *pa₁.₁ -tu se₁.₁ (< ... ; 'edge [= mooring]
shoal'). (placename) (= hase). x - 1-1:3-x x-x-x. NS (77b [14:153-M, 155-M],
83c [17:121-M]) HHH; NS (T+ 97) HHH, (T+ 77) HLH. Km (W) HHH.
?5.1, ?5.2   hatusigure < fatu₂.₁ (< *pa₁.₁ -tu) sigure₃.₇ₐ (< ?). 'the first
late-autumn shower'. x - 1[H]/3[K]-4-A x-x-x. Km. (W) HHHHx.
4.3 = 2.1|2.3   hatusimo < fatu₂.₁ (< *pa₁.₁ -tu) simo₂.₃ (< ...). 'the first frost'.
HH(|)LL - 0-0-A x-x-x. Km (W) xxHx.
2.1|3.7   hatu-umago/-m[u]mago < fatu₂.₁ (< *pa₁.₁ -tu) uma-gwo₇₃.₁ (< *uma₇ₐₑ₁ ₑ
-n- kwo₁.₁). 'first grandchild'. HH|LHL - x-x-x x-A-x. Sr haçiqnmaga A.
-          hawa: see haha.   hawaki: see hooki.
?2.3   haya < faya < *pada (?< adj B). 'dace (= ugui); a kind of carp, Zacco
platypus' = oikawa (fish). x - 1-2-B x-x-x. Ib F = 2.3. Sz 1. Cf. hae.
?2.5   haya < faya < *pada. 'early; already' (adv). x - 1-1-B x-(x)-x. NS (T+ 12)
HL. Km (W) LH(-L). K: Hn LF (attested?). Sr hwee-ku A, hwee-san B 'early'.
4.7   haya-bune 'fast boat': see haya-hune.
4.5   hayabusa < faya-busa < *padaₐₐⱼ ₑ (-n-) pusa₂.ₓ (< ?). 'peregrine
(falcon)'. x - 0-1[H]/3[U]-B x-A-x. NS (73b [11:260-M]) LLLL; NS (T+ 59a) HHHH,
(T+ 59b) LLHH. Sz 4/2. Nk pensaa B; Sr hwensa A.
6.21   hayahito-gusa < *fayafyito₇₄.₅ (< *pada - pito) -gusa (< -n- kusa₂.₃).
'convolvulus' (= hirugao). LLLLHL - x-x-x x-x-x. Cf. hayato.
4.7   haya-ʰ/ᵦune < faya-bune (Mg) < *padaₐₐⱼ ₑ -n- puna-Ci₂.₄. 'fast boat'.
LLHH - x-3-x x-x-x.
3.4   hayasi < fayasi < *padasi (?< *pada-s[a-C]iₑ; ?< *padaₑ + ?). 'forest,
grove'. LLL - 3/0-0[H]/2[U]-B x-x-x. Km x. Mr (Bm) HHL. Sapporo, Hiroshima,
Ōita 0; Akita, Matsumoto, Numazu, Narada 3. Hyōgo, Kōchi 3; Toyama 1:3
(expected reflex); Suzu 0 (expected reflex); Ib F = 3.4.
3.4   hayati < faya-ti < *payaₐₐⱼ ₑ ti₁.ₓ ('fast wind') = faya-te (last vowel
partially assimilated to the first two?). 'wind storm'. LLL - 0/3-2-x x-x-x.
*3.4 < ?*4.5   hayato < haya[hi]to < fayafyito₇₄.₅ < *padaₐₐⱼ ₑ pito₂.₂ₐ. (?*LLLL)
- x-x-x x-x-x. 'the Hayato people (of ancient Kyūshū)'.
3.4   hazama < fazama < (Hn) fasama < *pasa-ma-ₑ (or *pasa-ₑ -ma₁.₁). 'gap,
valley'. LLx (Ck), HLx (Kn) - 0-0-x x-x-x. NS (Okada) LLL; NS (T+ kun) LHL.
Edo HHL. Dial. haza 'gap; interval; furrow'.

?2.2b < 2.3   haze < faze (?< faze[y] < *pansa-Ci[-Ci]ʙ). 'goby' *(fish)*.
   x - 1-2(/1:3[U])-A x-x-x. Km x. Hattŏ 2; Izumo, Goka-mura 2 *(= 2.3)*; Hamada
   1/2; Matsue 1/2 *(= 2.4-5 / 2.3)*; Sz 1.
?2.2b < 2.3   haze < faze *(2d vowel partially assimilated to the first)* < fazi <
   *pansi ?< *pan[i]si. 'sumac'. LL - 1-2(/1:3[U])-x x-A-x. NS (T+ kun) LH. Km x.
   Edo fazi HH. Ib L2 = 2.5. Sr hazi(gi) A; Yn hangi x (Hōgen kenkyū sōsho
   4:179b). Cf. hanizi; hani.
2.3   hazi < fadi < *fadi[y] < *pantu-Ci[-Ci]. 'shame'. LL - 2-2-B B-B-x. NS
   (133b) LL. (Sakurai 1978b:90 cites Ongi as LF but that is a mistake; the Ongi
   form is the verb predicative fadu.) Km x. Edo HL. K: HL "Mr and since". Ib F =
   2.3. Onna paazii B. Cf. hazukasi-ₐₐⱼ ʙ.
?4.1   hazikami < fazikami < fazikamyi < *pansikami (?< *pan[a]ₛ.₁ sikam[a-C]iₐ
   'nose pucker'). 'Japanese pepper (= itatihazikami = sansyoo); ginger (=
   anahazikami = syooga)'. HHHH-··· - 0-1-x x-x-x. NS (T+ 14) HHHH.
6.2   hazikamiuo < fazikami-u(w)o/i(w)o < *pansikamiₚ₄.₁ (< ...) iwoₛ.₁ (< ...)
   ('pepper fish'). 'salamander' (= hanzaki = sansyoo-uo). HHHHHL (-iwo) - x-x-x
   x-x-x.
3.1   hazime < fazimey < *pan[a]-si(-)ma-Ci[-Ci]ₐ. 'beginning, first'.
   HHH - 0-0-A x-A-A. Km (S, Okada W) HHH. Mr (Bm) HHH. Edo HHH. Goka-mura 1.
   Ib H = 3.1. Yn hadimi A (H 1964:71b).
2.1   hazu < fazu < *pansu. 'arrow notch; expectation'. HH - 0-0-A A-A-x. Km x.
   Ib H = 2.1.
2.2x   hazu < fazu (< Ch .pa-dhew'). 'croton'. HL - 1(Kenkyusha)-x-x x-x-x.
?5.1, ?5.2   hazukuroi < fa-ᵗ/ᵈukurofi < *paₚ₁.₂ (-n-) tuku-ra-p[a-C]iʙ (*see*
   tukurou). 'unruffling its feathers; arranging one's attire'. HHHxx - 2-3-x
   x-x-x.
3.4 < 4.5 hazuma < faᵗ/ᵈuma < fad[a]-uma < *pantaₛ.₄ umaₛ.ₛ. '(riding) a bareback
   horse'. LLL/LLx (-d-) - x-x-x x-x-x.
?1.1   he < fey < *pa-Ci. 'door(s), household(s)' (< 'oven/hearth' not 'house').
   H - x-x-x x-x-x.
?1.1   he < fey < *pa-Ci. 'oven': fey -tu fyi 'hearth spirit'. x - x-x-x x-x-x.
1.1   he < fey < *pa-Ci. 'jar, pot'. H - x-x-x x-x-x. Cf. kame, kanae; utuwa;
   nabe; (?) ue. (Ōno: perhaps < Korean pyeng 'bottle'.)
1.1   he < fey < *paCi (?= paₛ.₁ -Ciₛᵤf 'edge'). 'bow of boat' (cf. hesaki);
   'side' (*see* kawabe). H - x-0-x x-x-x. NS (T+ kun) funa-no fey LL-L|H. Km x. K:
   Hn HH/HL, Edo HH. (Has been compared with Korean pay < 'poy 'boat'; cf. hune.)
1.3a   he < fe (< ?). 'fart'. L - 1-1-B B-B-B. Km x. K: Edo LH. Ib L = 1.3.
   Hateruma pin (see Ch. 1, §52).
?1.3b   he < fe ?< *fey < *pa(-)Ci[-Ci]ʙ. *(1)* 'the shed (= shedding device) of a
   loom'; *(2)* (= heo < fe-wo) 'a foot-cord for a falcon' (*see* hemaki). L - x-0-x
   x-x-x.
?1.3x   he(-) < fye(-) < *piCa (?= *pinaₛ.ₛ but the register is incongruent).
   'separate, apart'. Cf. heya, hedatu, henaru.
1.x ?= 1.1   (-)he < fye < ?*piCa (?= *pina). 'shore, boundary; vicinity; side,
   direction': *see* inisie, katae, kawabe, moto-he, mae, nobe, sirie, sube, sue-
   e, uwabe, yamanobe, yamabe (§5.10), yorube. NS (Okada) H. NS (T+ 4) H; NS
   (T+ kun) atwo fye LH(|)H, makura·fye LHL|H; NS (T+ 126) sima-fye FL(|) = LL|H.
   Km (Okada W) H.
1.x   (-)he < fye < *piCa (?= *piraₚₛ.ₛb, see hira). 'layer'. *See* hitoe, hutae,
   nanae, kawabe, yae; ? hadae. Thorpe 257 relates this word to ofiy- < *opo-Ci-
   'get big, grow', noting words for 'quantity, some' in Ryūkyū dialects; cf.
   Nakamoto 1983:171.

2.5 ?< 3.6   hebi < fenbi/femi < feymyi (?< *paCimi ?= *papimi < *pap[a-C]i𝐵
m[us]i𝟮.𝟭, cf. mi𝟭.𝟮; ?< *paCinpi; ?< *ponpi). 'snake'. RH (femi) / LHH (fenbi)
- 1-1:3-B (A)-B-x. Km x. Goka-mura 0. Kōchi 1 (Hattori 1973).
Sr hwiibu B (cf. habu). Cf. Korean paymi < 'poyyam. On the accent: Ch. 4, §7.1.

?2.3   hedo < fedo (?< fendo < *fando < Ch 'pywan-'tho; ?< *feydo < *fa[k]ido <
*fakyi-do < *pak[a-C]i𝐵 -n- to[koro𝟯.𝟭𝐚]𝟳𝟭.𝟭. 'vomit'. ?LL-⋯ - 1(<2)-2-A
x-x-x. Sz 1. Ib H1 = 2.2.

2.x   hei < fei < ?*pe[k]i (< Ch peyk). 'wall'. x - 0-0-B B-(?B)-x. Sz, Narada,
Hiroshima 0; Hakata 1, ygr 0 (= 2.1/2). Ōsaka, Ise 0. Ib H = 2.1.

?3.6   hemaki < fe-maki < ?*fey𝟭.𝟵𝒃 (< *pa(-)Ci[-Ci]𝐵) makyi (< mak[a-C]i𝐴).
'the reel for a falcon's foot-cord'. "HLH" (?= *LLH) - x-x-x x-x-x.

2.2b   hemi < femi (< ?). 'Viburnum tomentosum, a kind of honeysuckle' (=
komatuzura = yabudemari). HL - x-x-x x-x-x.

-         hemi 'snake': see hebi.

2.x   hena < fena ?< *fey-na < *pa(-)[n]i𝟮.𝟭 (< ...) na*𝟳𝟭.𝟯𝐚. 'mud, earth'.
x - 2-x-x x-x-x. (The etymology implies two occurrences of *na, one buried in
*fey; cf. hani and variant hane.)

?3.1   henoko < fenoko (?< *finako < *pina𝟮.𝟮𝒃 kwo𝟭.𝟭; ?< *fyenokwo < *pi[n]a𝟮.𝟮𝒃
no kwo𝟭.𝟭 'chick egg'). 'testicle; penis'. HHH - 1-2-x x-x-x.

2.3   heo < fe-wo ?< *fey𝟭.𝟵𝒃 wo𝟭.𝟯𝐚 < *pa(-)Ci[-Ci]𝐵 bo𝟭.𝟯𝐚. 'a foot-cord for a
falcon'. LL - x-x-x x-x-x.

2.4   hera < fyera ?< *piCara ?< *pira𝟮.𝟮𝒃 (first vowel partly assimilated to
the second). 'moldboard; spatula'. LH - 1-1(/2[U])-B B-B-C. Km x. Ib L = 2.4.
Sr hwiira B. U distinguishes the two meanings by accent. ("Loan from Korean?")

2.3   heri < feri (< ?). 'rim, brink'. Ib F = 2.3. LL - 2-2-B x-B-x. Shimane,
Tottori heeri.

?3.1   hesaki < fey - sakyi < *paCi𝟭.𝟭 saki𝟮.𝟭. 'bow of boat'. x - 3/0-0-B x-x-x.

2.1   heso/hozo < feso/foso < *foso < *poso. 'navel'. HH - 0/1-0-A A-A-A. Km x.
Tappi fetyo 1; Hattō, Hamada, Matsue, Izumo 0. Ib heso H = 2.1. Cf. toboso.
(The etymology assumes o → e before s; or vowel dissimilation. Alternatively,
feso > foso with assimilation of the first vowel to the labial initial and to
the second vowel.)

?2.1   heta < feta (?< variant of fata < *pata𝟮.𝟭 'side'). 'calyx, stem (of
fruit)'. x - 0-0-B x-x-x. Hiroshima 0. Ōsaka, Ise 0; Ib F = 2.3.

2.3   heta < feta (?< [umi]-feta 'near the shore' < variant of fata < *pata𝟮.𝟭
'side'). 'clumsy, unskillful'. x - 2-2-B x-B-x. Sz, Hiroshima 2. Ōsaka, Ise 2;
Ib F = 2.3.

3.1   hetima < fetima (< ... , see NKD 17:638c). 'snake gourd'. x - 0-0-A x-x-x.
Aomori, Hamada, Wakamatsu 3; Sz, Hattō, Matsue, Izumo 0. Ib L = 3.6. (The
plant was introduced after 1500.)

-         [hetuhi]: see he𝟳𝟭.𝟭, hi𝟭.𝒙.

2.3   heya < feya ?< *fye-ya < *piCa𝟳𝟭.𝟯 da𝟭.𝟯𝒃. 'a room'. x - 2-2-B B-x-x.
Sz 2. Ib F = 2.3. Chiba heeya; Kumamoto hen'ya (note nasal!).

1.1   hi < *fyi < *pi (< Ch .pye). 'monument'. L (Ir) - 0-0-A A-A-A. Km x.
Ib H1 = 1.2.

1.2   hi < fyi < *pi. 'sun; day'. H/L - 0(/1)-2-A A-A-A. NS (132b) H-L; NS
(T+ 26) 𝐅-L. Km (S,W) H-L. Mr (Bm) H-L. Edo F = HL. Tk 0 but 1 when modified;
Aomori 0 (but 1 in sono hi). Ib H1 = 1.2 (also modified). Yn cii A. K: F = HL
"Hn and since". Hateruma pïn 'day' is probably a truncation: cf. (Yaeyama)
Taketomi pinucï, Kurojima and Sonai pinici, Ōhama pinicu ?< *pi-niti.

1.3a   hi < fyi < *pi. 'ice; hail'. L - x-0-x x-x-x. Km x. K: Hn LL. Is Kt
artificial? But cf. hisame. Verb stems hi[y]e[y]- (< *pi -da-Ci-) and
hiyas- (< *pi -da-sa-) are B. Cf. Sr hwii- B, Yn hii- C 'cold'.

1.3a   hi < fi (< ?). 'blurred (purblind) vision'. L - 1-x-x x-x-x.

1.3b   hi < fiy < *po̲-Ci. 'fire'. H/L/R - 1-1-B x-B-B. NS (115b) L. Km (W) L,
(S) L-H. Mr (Bm) L-H. Edo R. Ib L = 1.3. Yn cii B. K: Hn-Km LL, "Mr and since"
LH. Old eastern dialects have pu; cf. remarks on °/ᴜ in Ch. 7, §4.

1.3b   hi < fiy < *pª/o̲Ci. 'water pipe' (= toi). R - 1-0-x x-(B)-x. NS (T+ kun)
R ?= H (or really R = LH?). Km x. Hiroshima 1. Ōsaka, Ise 0. Sr hwiizaa B
'conduit pipe' < *fii-g(y)awa (< ...). Cf. kake-hi.

1.3b   hi < fyi < *pi. 'cypress' (= hi-no-ki). R - x-0-x x-x-x. NS (82b) R; NS
(T+ 96) "R" ?= H (or literally R = LH). K: Hn LH. Km x. Cf. kuro-be/-bi
(< *kurwo -n- pi) 'Japanese arborvitae'.

1.3b   hi < fyi/f[y]ii < *pi. 'shuttle'. R - 1-0-x x-(x)-x. Km x. K: Hn LH, Edo
HH. Sr hwizici B 'shuttle' < ?. Shinsen-Jikyō fii.

1.x   hi < fyi < *pi. '(divine) spirit, supernatural power': fey -tu fyi
'spirit of the hearth'. x - x-x-x x-x-x.

3.6   hibari < fyibari < *pinpari. 'skylark' (bird). LHH - 0(?<1)-1-B x-x-x.
Km x. Edo LHH. Aomori 2 (we expect 1); Tappi, Akita, Izumo 1 (expected?);
Sapporo, Wakamatsu, NE Kyūshū, Ōita 1; Hiroshima, Narada, Hattō, Hamada,
Matsue, Goka-mura 0; Hakata 1, ygr 0. Suzu 1 (we expect 1:2); Toyama 1:2
(expected); Ib L = 3.6.

3.5b   hibasi < fibasi < *fiybasi < *po̲-Ci₁.₃b -n- pasi₂.₄. 'firetongs'. LLH -
1(<*2)-2-B x-B-(A). Km x. Narada, western Mino (= SW Gifu), Hattō, Hamada,
NE Kyūshū 2; Goka-mura 1 (?< *2); Matsue, Izumo 0; Hakata 2, ygr 1. Ib F =
3.4. Yn cibasan A < *pi-basami (H 1964:72a).

2.3   hibi < fib/ᴍi < *fyib/ᴍyi < ?*pi-n-pi. 'skin cracks; cracks'. LL - 2-2-B
x-x-x. Km x. Sz 2. Ib F = 2.3.

3.4   hibiki < fyibyikyi < *pinpik[a-C]i₈ (< ... , see hibiku). 'echo'. LLL -
3-2-B x-B-x. Km (S) LLL. 1700 Ōsaka HHL. Sapporo 2. Ib F = 3.4. Nk x; "Sr word
new?" Cf. ibiki.

2.3   hida < fida < ?*fyida < ?*pinta. 'pleat'. LL - 1-2-B x-B-x. Hattō,
Hamada, Goka-mura 1; Matsue, Izumo 2. Ib F = 2.3. Sr hwiiza B. Aichi kida.

3.4   [hidame] < fidame < *fyidamey < *pinta₂.₃ ma-Ci₁.₃b. 'pleat'. LLL - x-x-x
x-B-x.

3.6   hidari < fyidari < *pinta(-)ri. 'left'. LHH (-t-) - 0(?<*1)-1-B B-B-C.
Km S (S) LHH. Edo LHH (K "LLH" mistaken). NE Kyūshū 2; Narada, Goka-mura,
Wakamatsu 1; Hakata 1, ygr 0. Ib L = 3.6. Yn ndai C. Hateruma pinari. NS (109a)
fi["]ta-no-kata LL-L-HL. Cf. migi(ri).

3.1   hideri < fyideri < *pi₁.₈ -n- ter[a-C]i₈. 'drought'. HHx - 0/3-0-A x-A-x.
Km x. Aomori, Narada 3. Ib H = 3.1.

2.1   hie < fyiye (?< *fyide[y] < *pidaCi; ?< *fyid[y]e < *pidiCa; ?< *piyo <
*pi - do, cf. Korean co < cwoh). 'barn-millet'. HH - 0(/1[H])-0-A x-x-x.
Hamada 2. Ib H = 2.1. Cf. kibi = kimi.

4.2   hiedori < hi[y]e-dori < hiyodori < *fyiyo-dori < ?*piyo (-n- tori) <
*pido. 'bulbul' (bird). HHHL - 0/2-1:3-B x-x-x. Modern Tk is hiyo(-dori).
Cf. sawa-hiedori.

3.2b < 4.2   higasi < fi(n)gasi < fimugasi < fyi-muka-si < *pi₁.₈ muka-ᴀ si₁.ₓ
('sun-face wind'). 'east'. HHHL (fimugasi) - 3/0-2-A A-(A)-x. Mr (Bm) HHL.
Tappi, Aomori (= azuma 1), Narada, western Mino (= SW Gifu), Hamada, Hattō 3;
Sapporo, Numazu, Matsue, Izumo, NE Kyūshū 0; Ōita 2. Ōsaka, Ise 2; Ib H2 = 3.2.

2.1   hige < fyigey < *pin-? (?< *pi -n-) ka-Ci*71.1*. 'beard'. HH - 0-0-A A-A-A.
Km x. Edo HH. Ib H = 2.1. Yn ngi A. Cf. hituzi.

4.2   higurasi < fyigurasi < *pi*1.2* -n- kura-s[a-C]i*A*. (1) 'passing the day, all
day long'; (2) 'beanpaste'; (3) 'an evening cicada (Tanna japonensis)'; (4)
'Prunella vulgaris, self-heal (= utubo-gusa)'. HHHL ('cicada') - 0-0-A x-x-x.

3.5x   higure < figure < *fyigure < *pi*1.3b* < *pi*1.3b* -n- kure*2.3* (< ?).
'a cypress plank or stave'. LLH - x-0-x x-x-x.

-          hii 'shuttle': see hi.

?2.4   hii < fiwi (?< *fyiyi < *pipi; ?< *fiyyi < *p*m*/*2*Cidi). 'baby's pubic
area'. LH - x-2-x x-B-x. Sd hwyi(i) B < *fi 'vulva'. K: "Hn LF?"

3.x < 2.1 hiiki < fiiki < fyikyi < *pik[a-C]i*A*. 'popularity, partiality'. x - 1-1-A
x-B-x. Sz 2/1; Goka-mura 2; Hattō, Hamada, Matsue, Izumo, Hakata 1. Ib H1 =
3.3. Sr hwiici B. (On the emphatic lengthening, cf. Hamada 1951:395.)

4.x < 3.x hiimago (x - 1-4-A x-x-x) = himago (x - 1-3-A x-x-x; Sz 0) < ?*fyi-magwo <
*pi (< ?) uma -n- kwo. 'great-grandchild'.

4.x < *5.x hiiragi < fyifyiragiy < *fyifyira[kyi]-giy ('smarting tree') < *pipi-
ra-k[a-C]i*A* -n- ko-Ci*1.3a*. 'holly tree'. LLxx - 1-2-A x-x-x.

?3.5x   hiiru < fifiru ?< *pipiru. 'moth(s)'. x - x-0-x x-x-x. K: Hn LLH (where
attested?). Cf. hiir-u 'flutter up'.

3.1   hikage < fyikagey < *pi*1.2* kanka-Ci*2.3*. 'shady place; (= hikage no kazura)
Lycopodium clavatum, club moss'. HHH - 0-0-A x-x-x. ₱HH = HHH.

3.4   hikari < fyikari < *pika-r[a-C]i*B*. 'flash'. LLL - 3-2-B x-B-x. Km (S) LLL.
Mr (Bm) HHL. Sapporo 2. Ib F = 3.4.

?2.1   (-)hiki ?< *fyikiy < *pik*m*/*2*-Ci (?< *piko- 'pull'). 'counter (numeral
auxiliary) for lengths of cloth, for animals (and later for insects and
fishes), ? for people'. x - 3(?<*2)-2-B x-(x)-x. Cf.(-)ki. Sr -hwici.

?2.3   hiki < *fiki < ?*fyikiy < *pik*m*/*2*-Ci. 'toad' (= hikigaeru). LL - 2-1:3-x
B-x-x. Sd byikyi(i)/byikkya B. Cf. (-)hiki*?2.1*, (-)ki*71.1*.

4.2   hikiobi < fiki-(w)obi < *fyikyi (< *pik[a-C]i*A*) ob[a-C]i*B*. 'small belt'.
HHHL - x-4-x x-x-x.

3.4   hikiri < fikiri < *fiy-kyiri < *po-Ci*1.3b* kir[a-C]i*B*. 'striking a fire;
a fire stick'. LLL - 3-1:3-x x-x-x.

3.1   hikite < fikite < *pik[a-C]i*A* ta-Ci*1.3a*. '(door) knob, handle'.
HHH - 0-0-A x-x-x.

?5.16·5.2 hikiyomogi < fikiyomogi ?< *fyikiy (< ?*pik*m*/*2*-Ci) yomogiy*3.6* <
?*pik[a-C]i*A* domo -n- ko-Ci ('pull- mugwort'). 'Styphonostegia chinensis'.
LLLHL (Kn), HHHHL (Ir) - 3-x-x x-x-x.

2.2a   hiko < *fyikwo < *pi (< ?) kwo*1.1*. 'great-grandson' = hi(i)- mago.
HL - 0-x-x x-x-x. Sz 0.

?2.1   hiko < *fyikwo < *pi*1.2* kwo*1.1* ('sun child'). 'prince; male god'.
x - x-x-x x-x-x. Cf. amabiko.

-          hikobae: see [hikobaeru] (Ch. 6). Cf. hituzi, oroka-oi.

?4.2   hikobosi < (Nr) fyikwo-fosi < *pi kwo (-n-) posi. 'Altair, the Herdboy
star'. HHHx/HHLL (?= *HHHL)- 2-3-x x-x-x.

2.1   hima < fima < ?*fyima < ?*pi (= ?) ma*1.1*. 'gap; leisure'. HH - 0-0-A
A-A-x. Km (S,W) HH. Edo HH. Ib H = 2.1. For *pi, see NKD 16:573c.

-          himago: see hiimago.

2.2b   hime < fyimye < *pi*1.2* miCa*1.3b* (?= *mina) ('sun woman'). 'princess;
lady'. HL -1-2-A x-x-x. NS (72c, 115b) HH, ····-HL, HH-···. NS (T+ 56) HH.
Edo HL. Aomori, Narada, Hiroshima 1. Ib H1 = 2.2.

2.3   hime < fime (truncation) = fime-ifi*4.5* < fyimye*2.2b* (< ...) ifyi*2.3*
(< ...). 'oven-cooked rice, as opposed to rice cooked in a steamer (kosiki)'.
LL - x-2-x x-x-x.

?2.4 ?< 3.6   hime = sime 'hawfinch, grosbeak' *(bird)*. RH(/RL [Ir]) - x-x-x x-x-x.
K: Hn RH.

?5.11   himekagami < *fyimye*s.sb* (< ...) kagami*s.s* (< ?) ('princess Metaplexis
japonica'). 'Pycnostelma paniculatum' (= suzusaiko).

5.2   hime^k^/ɢomatu < fime-komatu < *fyimye*s.sb* (< ...) kwo-matu*s.s* (< ...).
'a small pine'. HHHHL - x-4-x x-x-x.

4.2/4.3   himematu < fime-matu < *fyimye*s.sb* matu*s.s*. 'a small pine'. x - 2-3-A
x-x-x. HHHL/HHLL.

4.3   himemiko < fime-miko < fyimye*s.sb* (< ...) myi-kwo*s.s* (< ...). 'empress'.
x - x-x-x x-x-x. NS (96a [11:71-K]) HHLL *(Okada misprints "hitomiko")*.

4.7   himetone < fyimye*s.sb* (< ...) tone*?s.s* (< ...) 'female officials (in the
palace); princesses and ladies (of the inner and outer circle)'. x - x-x-x
x-x-x. NS (107b [11:277-K]) HHLL (? or HFLL).

3.5x < 4.x   himizu < fimidu (= fyi-myidu) < *pi*s.sa* mintu*s.sa* (< ...).
'icewater'. LLF (Zs) / xxH - x-0-x x-x-x. See Ch. 4, §7.3.

2.1   himo < fibo < fyimo < *pinpo. 'cord'. HH - 0-0-A A-A-x. NS (Okada) HH;
NS (T 66) HL, (T 127) FH ?= HH. Km (S,W) fibo HH. 1700 Ōsaka HH. Narada hibo
0. Ib (formerly hibo) H = 2.1. Sd himo(o) A.

4.1   himorogi < fib/ɢoroki < fyib/ɢorokyi < *pinporoki (< ?). 'tree/place for
the gods to descend; offerings to the gods'. HHHH - 0-0-x x-x-x. NS (T+ kun)
FHHL. Various etymologies have been offered, none convincing; for the latest
see Yoshida 1979:103-29.

-    himuka: *see* hyuuga.

?3.4   himusi < fyi-musi < *pi[piru]*?s.sa/b* musi*s.s*. 'moth; silkworm moth'. x -
1-2-x x-B-x. NS (71b) LLL; NS (T+ 49) H-HH. K: "Hn LLF?" Sr hwiimusi B 'sweet-
potato worm'. Cf. hiiru.

?2.2b, ?2.1   hina < fyina < *pina (?< *pi [= ?: cf. hima; Ch 'pyuy < pyweg
'countryside' na*?s.sa*; ?< Ch .pyen 'region' [> fen > hen]). 'remote place'.
x - 1-2-x x-x-x. NS (132b [14:418L-K) HH; NS (T 3) HH. Km (W) HH/HL. Cf. inaka.

?2.2b   hina < fina < ?*fyina < ?*pina. 'chick'. HL/HH - 1-1:3[H]/2[U]-B x-(B)-x.
Km x. Sz, Hattō, Hamada, Goka-mura 1; Matsue, Izumo 2 *(= 2.3)*. Ib L2 = 2.5.
Sr hwina-gata B 'a model'.

4.1   hinasaki < finasaki < ?*fyina*s.sb* (< ?*pina) sakyi*s.s* (< *saki) ('chick
tip'). 'clitoris'. HHHH - x-x-x x-x-x.

?3.3   hinata < finata < *fyi-nata < *pi*s.s* [no ka]ta*s.sb*. 'toward the sunshine;
a sunny place'. x - 0-2-A x-x-x. Aomori, Sz, Hattō 2; Hamada, Matsue, Izumo 0.
Ib H1 = 3.3.

4.2   hinatume < fyina-tu-mye < *pina*s.sb* -tu miCa*s.sb* (?= *mina). 'a country
girl'. x - x-x-x x-x-x. NS (Okada) HHHL.

?2.5   hine < fiyne (?< fu[ru] ine < *pu[ru]*edj B* [z]ina-Ci*s.s*). 'late rice,
stale grain; ... '. x - 1-1:3-x x-x-x.

4.11   hinezumi < finezumi < *fiy - nezumyi < *po-Ci*s.sb* ne(n)sumi*s.s* (< ...).
'the Fireproof Rat (a mythical beast of ancient China)'. LLHL - x-1:3-x x-x-x.

3.6   hinoe < finoe < *fiy*(s.sb)* (< *po-Ci) no ye*?s.s* (< ...). '(fire's older
brother =) third of the Ten Heaven's Stems'. LLH - 0-2-B x-B-x. Sr hwinii B.

3.5a/b   hinoki < finoki < (*)fyi-no-kiy < *pi*s.sb* no ko-Ci*s.sa*. 'cypress'.
x - 1/0-2-B x-B-x. Aomori, Sz, Hattō, Matsue, Izumo 2; Hamada, Goka-mura 1.
Ib H1 = 3.3.

3.7x   hinoo < fyinowo < *pi*s.sb* no bo*s.sa*. *(placename)*. x - x-x-x x-x-x.
Mr (Bm) LHL.

3.6   hinoto < finoto < *fiy$_{1.8b}$ (< *po-Ci) no [o]to$_{8.x}$. '(fire's younger
brother =) fourth of the Ten Heaven's Stems'. LLH - 2-2-B x-B-x.

?2.3   hio < fyiwo < *pi$_{1.3a}$ ibo/iCo$_{8.1}$ ('ice fish'). 'whitebait' (fish). LL -
1-2-x x-x-x. K: Hn-Km LL (Km attested?).

2.x   [hio] < fiwo < *fyiwo < *pibo. 'a paper mulberry' (= kozoo). x - x-x-x
x-x-x. Cf. [katabio].

4.11   hiomusi < fiwomusi ?< *fyiwo$_{(?8.3)}$ musi$_{8.1}$. 'dayfly, ephemera'. LLHL -
x-x-x x-x-x.

2.1   hira- (adj stem) 'flat, ordinary': see following compounds, hira$_{adj}$ A.

?2.2b   hira < fyira < *pira (< *pira$_{adj}$ A). 'sheet; petal'. HL - 1-2-x x-(A)-x.
NS (T+ kun) LL. Km x. Sr hwiraa 'flat thing'. Cf. bira; (-)he; hera.

4.1   hirabari < firabari (Zs) < *fyira-bari < *pira$_{adj}$ A -n- par[a-C]i$_A$.
'a kind of tent/canopy'. HHHH - O-x-x x-x-x. Cf. agebari.

3.2x   hira^b/$_{mi}$ < firami = fyirabyi < fira-[o]byi < fyira$_{8.1}$ (< *pira$_{adj}$ A)
obyi$_{8.4}$ (< onp[a-C]i$_{8}$). 'a kind of garment'. HHL - x-0-x x-x-x.

3.1   hirada < firada < ?*fyirada (?< *pira$_{adj}$ A -n- [i]ta$_{8.4}$). 'flat-bottomed
boat'. HHH (Ir) - O-O-x x-x-x. ("Also -t-; hirata-[bune].")

?3.1   hirade < fyirade ?< *pira$_{adj}$ A -n- ta-Ci$_{1.3a}$ ('flat hand'). 'an offertory
bowl, an oak-leaf cup'. HHx - x-x-x x-x-x. NS (T+ kun) LLH.

4.3   hiragane < firagane < *fyira-gane < *pira$_{adj}$ A -n- kana-Ci$_{8.1}$. 'sheet of
metal'. HHLL - x-x-x x-x-x. Km x. ("Also -k-.")

3.1   hirage < fira-ge ?< *fyira-gey < *pira$_{adj}$ A -n- kaCi$_{1.3a}$ (< ...) ('flat
[= ordinary] meal'). 'ordinary/usual [fare]': ~ no kame 'a jar for everyday
use'. HHH - x-x-x x-x-x.

3.1   hiraka < fira^k/$_{ga}$ < fyira-ka < *pira$_{adj}$ A (-n-) ka$_{?1.3a}$. 'an earthenware
plate': ama-no firaga 'a kind of ceremonial plate'. HHH - x-x-x x-x-x.
NS (T+ kun) LHH.

3.2x   hirami 'a kind of garment': see hirabi.

4.2   hiranabe < firanabe < *fyira$_{8.1}$ - nabey$_{8.5}$ < *pira$_{adj}$ A nanpaCi$_{8.6}$.
'a shallow flat pan'. HHL - x-0-x x-x-x.

5.2   hirasirage < firasirage < *fyira-siragey < *pira$_{adj}$ A sira-n[a]-ka-Ci[-
Ci]$_{8}$. (~ no yone)'unpolished/brown rice' (= kurogome). HHHHL - x-x-x x-x-x.

3.1   hirate < firate < *fyira-te < *pira$_{adj}$ A ta-Ci$_{1.3a}$ ('flat(-opened) hand').
'a hand clap (of invocation)' (= kasiwade). HHx - x-x-x x-x-x. K: HHH.

4.1   hirazima < firazima < *fyira-zima < *pira$_{adj}$ A -n- sima$_{8.3}$. 'a flat little
island'. HHHH - O-O-x x-x-x.

2.1   hire < fyire < ?*piraCi (? < *pira$_{?8.2b}$ -Ci). 'fin; scarf'. HH - 0/2-0-A
x-A-x. NS (T 100; 101), (T+ kun) FH. Km x. Aomori, Narada 2; Hakata 1 (we
expect 0), ygr 0/2. Ib F = 2.3.

2.3   hiro < firo < ?*fyiro < *piro. 'fathom'. LL - 1-2-x x-B-x. Km x.
Hiroshima 1. Ōsaka, Ise 2.

?3.4a   hirome < firome = fyiro-me < *piro$_{adj}$ B me$_{1.x}$ (< ...). 'seaweed (konbu)'
(= ebisume). LLL (Zs) / LLH (Kn) - x- 2/0-x x-x-x. K: "LLF"; cf. Komatsu
1971:632. See Ch. 4, §7.3.

3.6   hirosa < fyiro-sa < *piro$_{adj}$ B -sa$_{suf}$. 'width'. LHH - 0-1-B (B)-(B)-(A/C).
Km x. Aomori 0; Narada, Goka-mura 1. Ib L2 = 3.5/7, L = 3.6. Yn caan (< *piro-
sa a-) 'is wide' A [H 1964] / C [H 1967].

3.5a = 2.3|1.1 hirose < fyiro-se < *piro$_{adj}$ B se$_{1}$ (< ...). 'wide river shallows/
ford; Hirose (placename)'. x - 0-2-x x-x-x. NS (Okada) LL(|)H. Km (W) LL(|)H.

2.5   hiru < firu < ?*fyiru < *piru. 'leech'. LH - 1-1:3-B x-x-x. Ongi LF.
Narada, Hamada, Matsue, Izumo, Hiroshima 0; Hakata biru 1. Ōsaka, Ise 1:3; Ib
(rare) L2 = 2.5. Amada, Ikaruga, Kasa biiru ?< *[ ]-n- piru (see Ch. 1, §26).

2.1 (?< *2.3) hiru < fyiru < *piru (?< *peru). 'garlic'. HH - 1-1:3-x A-A-x. NS
(T 35) ᵽL. Km x. Sd hwiryi A; Sr hwiru A. Cf. kobiru, mebiru; nobiru. Perhaps
related: Sr (zii)bira 'onion' ?< *gibira ?< *[ ] -n- ki₁.₁ - pira?; the word
appears in a Hankul transcription "king.pi.na" = kibina, or perhaps kibira,
in the 1501 Ryūkyūan vocabulary of Haytong ceykwuk-ki.

2.2b   hiru < fyiru < *pi₁.₂ -ru?ₛᵤf. 'daytime'. HL - 2-2-A A-A-A. NS (100a) HL.
Km x. Edo HL. Narada 1. Ib H1 = 2.2. Yn cuu A (H 1964:71b, Shibata 1959:114)
but cuuma B < *piru-ma (H 1964:183a).

3.1, 3.2x hirume < firu-me < fyiru₂.₂ᵦ (< ...) mye₁.ₛᵦ (< ...). 'Day(light) Female'
(goddess name) = Amaterasu-ōmikami'. x - x-x-x x-x-x. Km (W) HHH, HHL. Also
firumi (?< *pi-ru mi[Ca]; last vowel assimilated to the others?).

5.7   hirumusiro < firu-musiro < *piru₂.ᵧ musiro₃.₄ ('leech mat'). 'Potamogeton
distinctus (franchetii/polygonifolius); (= hamazeri) Cnidium japonicum'.
LLLLH - 4-x-x x-x-x.

4.1 (= 2.1|2.1)   hirusaki < firusaki < *fyiru - sakyi < *piru₂.₁ saki₂.₁.
'a garlic bud'. HH(|)HH - x-x-x x-x-x.

?2.4, ?2.5   hisa < fyisa < *pisa. 'longlasting' (adj-n). x - x-x-x x-x-x.
Km (W) LH. K: Km "LF?". Cf. iku-hisasa; hita(-); hisasi-.

3.6   hisago < (Mr) fisa(-)ᵏ/ₔo ?< *pisa₊₂.₄ (kwo₁.₁). 'gourd, calabash'. LHH
(one Kn example of HHH) - 0-0-B x-x-x. NS (101a) ···HHL. Cf. nari ～ , niga ～ .
Later > hisyaku 'ladle, dipper' x - 0- 1[H]/1:2[U]-B x-x-x.

4.2   hisakaki < fi[me]-sakaki < *fyimye₂.₂ᵦ (< ...) sakakiy?₃.₄ (< ...).
'Eurya japonica'. HHHL - 2-x-x x-x-x.

-      hisaku: see hisyaku.

5.7   hisaku-gata < fisaku₃.₆ (< fisa(-)ᵏ/ₔo < ...) -n- kata₂.₂ᵦ. 'a ladle-
shaped thing; a flame-attached jewel attached on top of the 9th tier of a
pagoda'. LLLLH - x-x-x x-x-x.

3.1   hisame < fyi-samey < *pi₁.₃ₐ [z]ama-Ci₂.₅. 'hail, sleet; freezing rain'.
x - 0-0-A x-x-x. Register anomalous? Cf. hi[y]eru, hiyasu; hi.

3.1   hisasi < fyisasi < *pi₁.₂ sas[a-C]i₈. 'eaves'. HHH - 0-0-A x-x-x. Km x.
Narada 0/3. Toyama 1:3 (we expect 1:2); Ib (rare) H = 3.1, H1 = 3.3.

2.1   hisi < fyisi < *pisi. 'water-chestnut, caltrop'. HH - 0-0-A x-x-x. Km x.
Edo HH. Narada 2; Hiroshima 0. Ōsaka, Ise 0; Ib (rare) ?F = 3.3.

?3.6   hisiko < fisiko (< ?). 'anchovy'. LHH··· - 0-x-x x-x-x.

6.13/6.12 (= 3.6|3.1)   hisikoiwasi < fisiko₃.₆ iwasi₃.₁ (< ?). 'anchovy'.
LHHHHL (Kn) / LHH(|)HHH (Ck) - 4-x-x x-x-x.

?3.1   hisio < fi-sifo < ?*fiy-sifwo < ?*po-Ci[Ci]ₐ sipwo₂.₃ ('dried salt[ed]').
'a kind of beanpaste; (= sisi-bisio) salted meats'. HHH (Ck) - 0-2-x x-x-x.
Km x. Proposed etymology incongruent with Mg register.

2.3   hiso < fyiswo < *pi₁.ₛᵦ swo? (< ?; ?< s[a]wo₂.₃). 'small logs, typically
cypress, used as ceiling rafters'. LL - x-2-x x-x-x. Km x. (Cf. soma < swoma;
sobo; hahaso < fafaswo 'oak', so < swo 'hemp'.)

3.7b   hisoka < fisoka ?< *fyiso̲-ka < *piso-ka. 'secret' (adj-n). LHL - 1/2-
1:3[H]/2[U]-B x-x-x. NS (121b) HHx. Km (S) LHL. Mr (Bm) LHL. Edo LHL. Tk 2
due to vowel unvoicing. Cf. misoka, Mg misoka-[nusubito] LHH-/LLL-; hisomu.

?3.4a   hisui < fisui < *pi(i)sui (< Ch pywey'-tshywey'). 'kingfisher' (bird);
jade'. RHH - 1/2/0-1-A x- x-x. Km x. Ib L = 3.6. See Ch. 4, §7.3.

3.6   his(y)aku < fis(y)aku < fisa(-)ᵏ/ₔo (< ...). 'ladle'. x - 0-1:2[U]/1[H]-B
x-x-x. The unusual 1:2 is interpreted as hi͡isyaku. Sz [hiyagu] 2. See hisago.

?2.4   hita(-) < fyita(-) < *pita (cf. hisa). 'straight; unswerving, unceasing'.
See hitasura, hitaburu; hitao; hitati; cf. hito̲(-) 'one'. Sr hwita-ni B
'intently' (= hitasura).

4.11   hitaburu < fitafuru ?< *fyitafuru < *pita*s.4* (n[i]) pur[a]-u*A*. '(being) intent, unswerving; dauntless hero'. LLHL/LLxx - 0-x-x x-x-x.

3.1   hitai < fitafi < ?*fyitafyi < ?*pitapi. 'forehead'. HHH - 0- 1[H]/2[U]-A A-A-A. Km x. Edo HHH. Narada 0/3. Ib hitai/hutae H = 3.1. Yn Tai A < *p[i]tai.

5.2   hitaibiro < fitafi-byiro < ?*pitapi*s.1* -n- piro*adj* *B*. '(being) broad-browed' (adj-n). HHHHL - x-x-x x-x-x.

3.4   hitaki < fitaki < *fiytakyi < *po-Ci*1.sb* tak[a-C]i*A*. 'burning (bon)fires; place for burning fires'. LLL - 3-2-x x-x-x.

4.5 = 3.4|1.3 hitakiya < fitakiya < *fiytakyi*s.4* (< ...) ya*1.sb* (< *da). 'fire-guard's hut'. LLL(|)L - x-x-x x-x-x.

3.4   hitao < fyita-wo < *pita*?s.4* bo*1.1*. '(nothing but) straight hills, all (unbroken) hill country'. x - x-x-x x-x-x. NS (Okada) LLL; NS (T+ kun) LLL.

6.21   hita-omo^b/**muki** < fyita (?< *pita*?s.4*) omo^b/**mukyi** (< *omo*s.4* muk[a-C]i*A*. '(being) intent' (adj-n). LLLHLL - x-1/1:4-x x-x-x. K: Hn LLLLLL.

-         [hitari] < fyitari < *pit[o*?s.4,?s.s*] ar[a-C]i*B*. 'one person'. NS (T+ 11) fyidari = fyitari (cf. Tsuchihashi 1976:52) LLH. See hitori.

2.4|2.4   hitasura < fitasura < fyita-sura ?< *pita*s.4* sura-*B* ('straight grind'). 'intent(ly)' (adj-n, adv). LH|LH - 2/0-0-B x- (B)- x. Sr hwita-ni B.

?3.4   hitati < fitati (?< *fyitati < *pita*?s.4* ti*?1.1* 'straight road'). 'Hitachi' (placename). x - 2-2-A x-x-x. Km (W) hitati-uta LLL(|)HL.

3.1   hitira < fiti-ra (< Ch pit-.la). 'a kind of rice cake'. HHL - x-x-x x-x-x.

4.5   hitiriki (< Ch pyet-lyet). 'fipple flute, flageolet'. LLLL - 0/2-2-x x-x-x.

2.2a   hito < fyito < *pito. 'person'. HL - 0/2-2-A A-A-A. NS (79c, 91b, 108a, 114a, 127b, 133a, 134a) HL; (128b) ?HF; (84b [14:127-M]) HH. NS (T 42) HL, (T 6; 71) HH, (T 9, 11; 23, 27; 79; 93; 110, 111; 115) FH. Km (S,W) HL. Mr (Bm) HL. Edo HL. Tk 0 but 2 when modified. Okayama, Hiroshima, Yamaguchi 2 (Hiroto 1961:159); Narada, Hattō, Goka-mura 2; Hamada, Matsue, Izumo, Hakata 0. Ib H1 = 2.2 (also modified). Yn Tuu A < *p[i]tu < *pito.

?2.4, ?2.3   hito(-) < fyito(-) < *pito(-) 'one': see hitori, hitotu, ... Cf. hita(-).

5.2   hito-damai: see hito-tamai.

4.1   hitodomo < fito-domo < *fyito-domo < *pito*s.sa* -n- tomo*s.1*. 'people'. HHHH - x-x-x x-x-x. Km x.

?3.4a   hitoe < fyito-fye < ?*pito*?s.4* piCa*1.x*. 'one layer'. LLF/LLH(-L) - 2-3-B x-x-x. NS (T+ 127) FL-H. Km (S) LLH. 1700 Ōsaka LHH. Aomori, Sz, Narada, Hattō, Hamada, Matsue, Izumo 2. Ib F = 3.4, L2 = 3.5/7. See Ch. 4, §7.3.

5.7   hitoeginu < fitofeginu < *fyitofye*?s.sb* (< ...) -gyinu (< *-n- kinu*s.4*). 'unlined garment' (= fitofe-no koromo). LLLLH - x-x-x x-x-x.

4.11 = 3.4a-ni hitoe-ni < fitofe-ni < *fyitofye*s.sb* (< ...) ni. 'earnestly, intently'. LLH-L - 2-0[H]/3[U]-B x-x-x. Mr (Bm) HLL-L.

5.2   hitogasira < fyitogasira < *pito*s.sa* -n- kasira*s.4*. 'weathered skull'. HHHHL - 3-x-x x-x-x. Km x.

4.1   hitogoto < fyitogoto < *pito*s.sa* -n- koto*s.s*. 'what people say; repute, reputation'. x - 0-0-A x-x-x. Km (W) HHH. Sz 0.

?3.5b   [hitoi] < hito-hi < (*)fyito-fyi < *pito*?s.4* pi*1.s*. 'one day'. x - 2-2-x x-x-x. NS (121a) LLH, (132a) LHL (or LHF?). Km x. Edo HLL.

?5.14, ?5.16 hitokasane < *fyito*?s.4,?s.s* (< *pito) kasane[y]*s.1* (< kasa-na-Ci[-Ci]*A*). 'a pair'. LLHHL (?= *LLLHL, cf. hitokusari) - 2-x-x x-(x)-x. Sr cukasabi B < *fito-kasabe.

4.1   hitokazu < fyito-kazu < *pito*s.sa* kansu*s.4*. 'number of people'. HHHH - 0-0-A x-x-x.

4.1   hitokusa < fyito̱-kusa < *pito̱ₛ.ₛₐ kusaₛ.ₛ. 'the masses, the people'.
HHHH - x-x-x x-x-x. NS (T+ kun) ꟼHHH = HHHH.

4.11 (?= 2.3|2.2b)   hitokusa < fyito̱-kusa < *pito̱₇ₛ.₄,₇ₛ.ₛ kusa₇ₛ.ₛₑ. 'one kind'.
LL(|)HL - 2-3-x x-x-x.

5.16   hitokusari < *fyito̱₇ₛ.₄,₇ₛ.ₛ (< *pito̱) kusariₛ.₁ (< *kusar[a-C]i₄). 'a
pair'. LLLHL - x-x-x x-B-x. Sz 4. Sr cukusai B < *fito-kusari 'a set; together'.

3.1   hitomi < fitomi < ?*fyito̱-myi < ?*pito̱ₛ.ₛₐ mi[-Ci]/mi[C[a-C]iₛ. 'pupil
of eye'. HHH - 0/2-0-A x-x-x. Aomori 0; Sz 0/2.

4.10 (?= 2.4|2.3) hitomozi < fyito-modi < *pito̱₇ₛ.₄,₇ₛ.ₛ montiₛ.ₛ. 'one moji
(weight measure unit = mise = 1.2 kg) of cloth'. LH(?|)LL - x-x-x x-x-x.

?4.5, ?4.10   hitomura < fyito̱ₛ.₄,₇ₛ.ₛ (< *pito̱) muraₛ.₁. 'a cluster, a clump, a
mass'. x - 2-1-x x-x-x.

7.21   hitomura-susuki < fyito̱-mura₇₄.ₛ,₇₄.₁₀ (< ...) susukiₛ.₆ (< ...). 'a
cluster/clump of eulalia'. x - x-x-x x-x-x. Km (W) LLLLLHL.

3.7b   hitori < fyito̱ri < *pito̱₇ₛ.₄,₇ₛ.ₛ -ri (< *[a]r[a-C]iₛ). 'one person'.
LHL - 2̲-3̲-B (B)-B-C. NS (111b) LHx. Km (S,W) LHL. Edo LHL. Narada 1; Aomori,
Hattō, Hamada, Matsue, Izumo, Goka-mura, Wakamatsu 2̲. Ib L2 = 3.5/7.

4.2   hitosasi < fitosasi (no oyobi) < *fyito̱-sasi < *pito̱ₛ.ₛₐ sas[a-C]iₛ.
'index finger'. HHHL - x-x-x x-x-x.

5.2   hito-ᵗ/ₐamai < fito-tamafi < fyito̱ tamafyi < *pito̱ₛ.ₛₐ tama-p[a-C]iₛ.
'carriages lent to the attendants' (= soeguruma). HHHHL - 3-x-x x-x-x.

5.1   hitotonari < fyito̱tonari < *pito̱ₛ.ₛₐ to̱ₚₒₗ nar[a-C]iₛ. 'character,
nature, temperament; (body) build, physique'. HHHHH - 0-0-A x-x-x. Sz 0.

3.7b   hitotu < fyito̱tu < *pito̱₇ₛ.₄,₇ₛ.ₛ -tu. 'one'. LHL - 2̲-3̲-B (B)-B-C.
NS (T+ 27) ꟼH-R; (T+ kun) LLL. Km (S,W) LHL. Mr (B) LHL. Edo LHL. Narada 1;
Aomori, Wakamatsu 2̲. Kōchi 1:3 (Doi 1952:29); Ib L2 = 3.5/7. Sr tiiçi <
*puteetu, cf. the lack of palatalization on ti- and Hachijō teecu (Hattori
1979:21:112).

5.6   hitotubiru < fitotubiru < *fyito̱tu-byiru < *pito̱ₛ.₇ᵦ -tu -n- piruₛ.₁.
'garlic bulb'. LLLLL - x-x-x x-x-x.

4.11   hitotue < fyito̱-tuwe < *pito̱ₛ.₄,₇ₛ.ₛ tuweₛ.₄ (< ...). 'one tsue (= 10
feet)'. x - x-x-x x-x-x. NS (110b) LLHL.

3.1   hitoya < fyito̱ya < *pito̱ₛ.ₛₐ da₁.ₛᵦ. 'jail'. HHH - 0-2̲-x x-x-x.

?3.7x (?= 2.4|1.3) hitoyo < fyito̱-ywo < *pito̱₇ₛ.₄,₇ₛ.ₛ dwo₁.ₛₐ. 'one night'.
1700 Ōsaka LHL. x-2̲-3̲-x x-(B)-x. NS (Okada) LHL; NS (T+ 13) ꟼH-H. Sr cuyuru B
< fit(y)o-yoru.

4.11   hitoyori < fitoyori < *fyito̱ - yo̱ri < *pito̱₇ₛ.₄,₇ₛ.ₛ do̱r[a-C]iₛ. 'one
twist'. LLHL - x-3-x x-x-x.

2.1   hitu ?< *fyitu < *pitu. '(large) lidded box'. HH - 0-0-B̲ x-x-x. Sz 0.
Ib H = 2.1.

3.1   hitugi < fitᵐ/₀ki < *fyitᵐ/₀kiy < *pitᵐ/₀ (?= hituₛ.₁) ko̱-Ci₁.ₛₐ.
'coffin'. HHH - 0-0-A x-x-x. Km x. Narada 1̲. Ib H = 3.1. For -g-, see Ch. 2.

3.1   hitugi < fyi-tugyi < *pi₁.ₛ tunk[a-C]i₄. '(ama-no/-tu ~) the Imperial
Dignity (= role, position); the Emperor's successor'. x - 0-2-x x-x-x. NS (91a
[11:7-K], 96 [11:74-K] HHH, (92b)n [11:15-K]) LHH.

3.1   hituzi < fyituzi < *pitunsi. 'sheep'. HHH - 0-0-A (B)-A(/B)-(C). Narada
0/3̲. Ib H = 3.1. Yn hibida C. K: Hn-Km HHH (Km attested?). (?< *pi -tu -n-
[u]si 'bearded ox' like Korean yem-so < 'yem-'sywo 'goat'; cf. hige.)

3.1   hituzi < (Mr) fituᵗ/ₐi < (Hn) fituti (< ?). 'sprouting (anew, after being
cut)' (= hikobae). HHH - x-0-x x-x-x. Km (W) fituti HHH. Cf. oroka-oi.

5.2   hituzigusa < *fyituzi-gusa < *pitunsiₛ.₁ -n- kusaₛ.ₛ. 'waterlily'. HHHHL -
3-x-x x-x-x.

?2.5   hiwa < fifa < *pipa. 'a siskin *(bird)*; (= hiwa-iro) light (yellowish)
green'. x - 1-1:3-x x-x-x.

3.7b   hiyaka < fyiyaka < *pi-da*ʙ* (< *pi*ı.ʒa* -da) -ka* suf*. 'cold' (= hiyayaka,
adj-n). LHL - 1-1:3-B x-(B)-(C). Sr hwii- B, Yn hii-san C 'cold'. Cf. hieru.

3.7x   [hiyase] < fiyase < fyi-yase[y] < *pi*ı.ʒ* dasa-Ci[-Ci]*ₐ*. 'partial eclipse
of the sun'. LHL (Kn) - x-x-x x-x-x. The register is incongruent with the
etymology, but Kn Mg lists hi 'sun' as "L", perhaps meaning "F"?

?2.1   hiyo < *fiyo < ?*fyiyo < ?*pido 'bulbul' *(bird)*: *see* hiedori.

4.2   hiyodori: *see* hiedori.

-         hiyodori-zyoogo 'Solanum lyratum': *see* komatuzura, horosi, ...

3.1   hiyoko < fiyoko < *fyiyo - kwo < *pido*ᵐᵢ* kwo*ı.ı*. 'chicken'. x - 0-1-A
x-x-x. 1700 Ōsaka LHH. Goka-mura 1; Aomori, Sz, Hattō, Hamada, Matsue, Izumo 0.
Kōchi 0 (Doi 1952:23); Ib H = 3.1.

3.1   hiyori < fiyori < ?*fyiyori < *pi*ı.ʒ* do̲r[a-C]i. 'good weather'. x -
0/3-0-A x-x-x. Ib H = 3.1. (Cf. yoru*ʙ* 'select', yorosi*adj ₐ* 'satisfactory',
yorokobu*ʙ* 'rejoice'. Or: yoru*ₐ* 'approach'?)

?2.4, ?2.5   hiyu < ?*fyiyu < ?*pidu. 'amaranthus'. LH - 1-2-x x-x-x. Km x.

2.1   hiza < fyiza < *pinsa. 'lap; knees (= hiza-gasira/-kozoo)'. HH - 0-0-A
A-A-x. Ongi Hx. Km x. Mr (Bm) HH. Edo HH. Ib H = 2.1. Sd hyida(a) A 'lap';
Sr hwisya A 'foot, leg' — but Nakamoto 1983:64 would associate Ryūkyū *pisa
'foot' with *pira 'flat'; cf. hagi, sune.

5.2   hizakabura < fyiza-kabura < *pinsa*ʒ.ı* kanpu-ra*?ʒ.ı* (< ...) ('knee
stump'). 'kneecap, patella' (= awata = hizagasira = hizakozoo). HHHHL - x-x-x
x-x-x. Kn Mg "fisa(ra)kafara": *In Mochizuki the interpolated "ra" is written
with the top stroke missing, but it is not be read as "hu".*

4.1   hizatuki < fizatuki < *fyizatukyi < *pinsa*ʒ.ı* tuk[a-C]i*ʙ*. 'a small carpet
to keep knees from getting soiled (while kneeling); a present given upon
assuming an apprenticeship in the arts'. HHHH - x-x-x x-x-x.

2.2b   hizi < fyidi < *pinti (?< *pinta < *pinta < *pin[a] ta, cf. kaina).
'elbow'. HL - 2-2-A x-(A)-(A/C). Km x. Edo HL. Aomori 0. Ib H1 = 2.2.
Yn cidinka < *pidi-n[u]k[ur]a A (H 1967) / C (H 1964). Hattori *pedi (cf. p. 68).

2.3   hizi < fyidi < *pinti. 'mud'. LL - x-x-x x-x-x. Km x. Cf. hiziriko, uizi,
suhizi.

4.2   hiziita < fidiita < *fyidi*ʒ.ʒb* (< *pinti) ita*ʒ.₄*. 'an ancon (?)'. HHHL -
x-x-x x-x-x. Km x.

?3.2a   hiziki < fidiki < *fyidi*ʒ.ʒb* (< *pinti < ...) kiy*ı.ʒa* (< ko̲-Ci) ('elbow
wood'). 'wooden brace'. x - 0-0̲-x x-x-x. K: Hn HHL *(attested?)*.

?3.4   hiziki < fiziki < fizuki (̄< ?). (= fiᵃ/ᶻuki - mo) 'a kind of brown algae
(seaweed)'. x - 1̲-0̲[H]/2[U]-B x-x-x. Aomori, Sz 2. Ib H̲ = 3.1.

4.5   hizikimo < fiᵃ/ᶻuki*ʒ.₄* (< ?) - mo*?ı.ı*. 'a kind of brown algae (seaweed)'.
LLLL - x-x-x x-x-x.

4.2   hizimaki < fidimaki < *fyidi - makyi < *pinti*ʒ.ʒb* (< ...) mak[a-C]i*ₐ*. 'a
bracelet' (= kusiro). HHHL - x-x-x x-x-x.

3.7a/b   hiziri < fyiziri < *pi*ı.ʒ* -n- sir[a-C]i*ₐ* (? 'sun-knower'). 'saint'.
LHL/H̲H̲L̲ - 1/0-0̲-B x-x-x. NS (131b) FHL. (Okada) HHH. Edo LHL. K: Hn-Km-Edo LHL
(Km attested?).

4.5   hiziriko < fidiriko (= Nr fyidi-no̲-kwo) < *pinti*ʒ.ʒ* (-ri) kwo*?(ı.ı)*
(the -ri is unexplained). 'mud'. LLLL - x-0-x x-x-x. Cf. ko-hizi.

4.6   hizisame < fidisame (Mg) < fitisame < *fyiti-samey < *pit[a-C]i*ʙ* [z]ama-
Ci*ʒ.ʒ*. 'heavy/drenching rain; *(? by mistake)* cold rain (= hi-same)'. LLLH -
x-x-x x-x-x. (From the -d- version the etymology 'mud rain' also suggested.)

?2.4   hizu < fidu ?< *fyi(< *pi*₁.ₛₐ*) -du (< Ch .dhew) ('ice-head'). 'edible soft
bone of salmon head'. LH - 0-0-x x-x-x.

?3.5a/b, ?3.1 hizume < fidume < fitume < ?*fyi-tumey < ?*pi[ra]*?ₛ.ₛ♭* tuma-Ci*ₛ.₁.*
'hoof'. LLH (Zs) / HHH (Kn) - 0/1-0-B x-x-x. Km (S) HHH. 1700 Ōsaka HLL.
Matsue 0/3; Goka-mura 1; Aomori, Sz, Hattō, Hamada, Izumo 0. Ib H = 3.1. If
the suggested etymology is correct, the Zs and Kg versions are incongruent in
register. NKD has only -z- but Mg shows -t-; see Ch. 2.

1.1   ho < fo < *po. 'sail'. H - 0-1-0-A A-A-A. Km (S) H-H. Sapporo, Akita,
Hamada, Matsue, Izumo, Hiroshima [Terakawa], Ōita 0; Matsumoto, Narada,
Hiroshima [H] 1; Hattō 0/1. Ōsaka, Ise, Kōchi, Suzu 0; Toyama 2; Ib H = 1.1.

?1.3b   ho < fwo < *pwo. 'prominent one/thing'. x - x-x-x x-x-x. Km (W) H-L (but
fo-tu-ye 'top branch' LLL). Thought to be the same etymon as 'ear of grain'.
Mochizuki 1971:22 suggests that 'prominent one/thing' was 1.3b (R).

1.3a   ho < fwo < *pwo. 'ear of grain'. L - 1-0[H]/1[U]-A B-B-B. NS (T+ 34) fo mo
L-H. Km (W) L. Mr (W [18]) L-H. Edo R. Aomori 0; Sapporo, Akita, Matsumoto,
Numazu, Narada, Hattō, Hamada, Matsue, Izumo, Hiroshima, Ōita 1. Hyōgo, Ōsaka 0;
Ise 0/1; Kōchi 1; Toyama, Suzu 1:2; Ib L = 1.3. Yn huu B (H 1964:64a).

1.3b   ho- < fo- < *po- 'fire': see hi < fiy < *po-Ci.

1.x   -(h)o < -fo < *-po 'hundred' (= momo): see [mio].

3.5x   hobara < fofara < *popara (?< *po[so]*ₐ*ⱼ*ₐ* ₚ para*ₛ.₃*). 'the swim (= air)
bladder of a fish'. LLH - x-x-x x-x-x.

4.2   hobasira < fobasira < *po*₁.₁* -n- pasira*ₛ.₅ₐ*. 'mast'. HHHL - 4/2-3[H]/2[U]-
A x-B-x. Sz, Hakata 2.

?2.2a < 3.6   hobo < fobo < *ponpo (?= *pon[o] po[no]). 'approximately, mainly'
(adv). RL/RH -1-2-A x-x-x. Km (S) HH. Mr (Bm) HH. K: Hn RH. Ib H1 = 2.2.

2.2a   hodo < fotwo ?< *po(n)two, ?< *pe-(n)-two 'interval, degree'. x - 0/2-0-A
x-A-x. Km (W) HL. Edo 2 but when adverbial 0 (Okumura 1976). Aomori 0; Narada
2. Ib H = 2.1. Sr hudu A 'height, stature', hutu A 'for the time being'.

4.1   hodozura < fododura < *ponto (< ?) -n- tura*ₛ.ₛₐ*. 'Stemona japonica' (=
byakubu). HHHH - x-4-x x-x-x.

?5.14   [hogai-hito] < fokafi-fito < fwokafyi fyito < *pwoka-p[a-C]i*?ᵦ* pito*ₛ.ₛₐ*.
'a person saying a prayer for compensation; a praying beggar'. LLHxx ?=
*LLH(|)HL - x-x-x x-x-x. K: "Hn LLLLL".

4.11   hogaraka < fogaraka < *ponka-ra-ka. 'cheerful' (adj-n). LLHL - 2-4-B
x-x-(B). Mr (Bm) HLLL. Yn hugarasa B is borrowed. Sz 3.

3.2a   hogeta < fogeta < *po*₁.₁* -n- keta*ₛ.₄* (< ...). 'sailyard, boom'. HHL -
0/1-0-A x-x-x.

?2.3   hogu < fogu/fogwo(-) < *ponku/ponkwo (?< Ch 'pan-ko'). 'wastepaper'. LL -
2/1-2[H]/0-A x-B-x. Sz, Hiroshima 1. Ōsaka 0; Ise 1. Nk hugu C.

?3.4   [hogusi] 'a digging stick': see hokusi.

2.3   hoho 'cheek': see hoo.

4.2   hohodori < fofodori ?< *popo (= ?) -n- tori*ₛ.₁*). 'owl' (= hukuroo).
HHHL - x-x-x x-x-x.

2.4   hoka < foka < *poka. 'other; outside'. LH -0-1-B B-B-A. Km (W) foka-fe
xLL. Mr (Bm) LH. Edo LH. Narada, Goka-mura 1; Aomori (we expect 2), Hattō,
Hamada, Matsue, Izumo 0. Ib L = 2.4. Nk huKaa B.

-         [hokai-hito]: see [hogai-hito].

5.15   [hokaki-gai] < fokaki-kafi (< ? + kaki*ₛ.₄/₅* - kapi*ₛ.₃*). ? 'a kind of
shellfish'. LLHLL (Ck) - x-x-x x-x-x. Only one attestation?

2.3   hoko < fok̲o̲ < *pok̲o̲. 'halberd'. LL - 1-2-A x-x-x. Ongi LL. Km x. Mr (Bm)
HL. 1700 Ōsaka HL. Sz 1. Ib F = 2.3.

4.9   hokodati < fokodati < *pok<u>o</u>*ₛ.ₛ* -n- tat[a-C]i*ₛ*. 'door/gate pillars' (=
hoodate). LHHL - x-x-x x-x-x.
3.1   hokora < fokora < fokura < *pwo*ₗ.ₛₐ* kura*ₛ.ₛ* ('rice-ear granary').
'shrine'. HHH - 0/<u>3</u>-0-A x-x-x. NS (T+ kun) <u>HHL</u>. Km x. Matsue <u>3</u>; Goka-mura <u>2</u>;
Hattō, Hamada, Izumo 0.
3.1   hokori < fokori < ?*po-[o]k<u>o</u>ri (< *po*ₜ* ok<u>o</u>r[a-C]i*ₛ* '? - arise').
'dust'. x - 0-0-A (x)-A-<u>B</u>. Km x. Ib H = 3.1. Nk puKui A.
4.7 = 2.3|2.1 hokosaki < fokosaki < *fok<u>o</u>-sakyi < *pok<u>o</u>*ₗ.ₛ* saki*ₛ.ₗ*. 'spearhead'.
LL(|)HH - 0/3/4-0-A x-x-x.
4.5   hokotori < fokotori < *pok<u>o</u>*ₛ.ₛ* t(w)or[a-C]i*ₛ*. 'wielding a halberd; a
halberd-wielder'. LLLL - 3/4-4-x x-x-x.
?3.4   [ho*ᵏ*/*ᵍ*usi] <(-)fokusi < *fo[ri]-kusi < *por[a-C]i*ₛ* kusi*ₛ.ₛ*. 'a digging
stick'. *See* hu*ᵍ*/*ₖ*usi.
3.7b   ho*ᵏ*/*ᵍ*usi < fokusi < *p<u>o</u>*ₗ.ₛ₆* (-n-) kusi*ₛ.ₛ*. 'a bonfire stake/post'. LHL
(Ir) - 1-x-x x-x-x.
-          [hokura] < fokura: *see* hokora.
?3.4   hokuso < fokuso < *p<u>o</u>*ₗ.ₛ₆* kuswo*ₛ.ₛ*. 'tinder'. LLL (Ir) - <u>1</u>-x-x x-x-x.
2.3   hone < fone (?< *pon[y]e < *poniCa, ?< *pone[y] < *ponaCi). 'bone'. LL -
2-2-B B-B-<u>C</u>. Km x. Edo HL. Sz 2. Ib F = 2.3. Nk puni <u>C</u>; Onna puuni B.
?2.3   hono(-) < fono < *po-n<u>o</u> 'faint, slight':   *see* honogiku, honomeku;
honogura-; hodokeru, hodoku; hono-ka; ? akebono; ? hodo.
3.7b   honoka < fonoka < *pono-ka. 'faint, dim'. LHL - 1-1:3-B x-x-x. Km x.
?3.4a   honoo < fon<u>o</u>fo < *p<u>o</u>*ₗ.ₛ₆* n<u>o</u> pwo*ₗ.ₛₐ* ('grain-ear of fire'). LLL/HHH -
1/<u>2</u>-1:3-B x-x-x. Ongi-m LLH. NS (127b) LLH. Km (S) LLH. Edo HLL. 1700 Ōsaka
LHH. Aomori *(rare)* <u>2</u>; Hakata <u>2</u>, ygr 1; Narada 1. Ib <u>H1</u> = 3.3. K: Km LLF, Edo
HLL. See Ch. 4, §7.3. Cf. Kindaichi 1964:350.
?2.2a   hoo < fafu/fofu < *p*ª*/*ₒ*pu (< Ch <u>pywap</u>). 'law, way'. <u>LL</u> - 0-<u>2</u>[H]/0[U]-A
x-A-x. Km x. Edo HH. Sz <u>1</u>; Narada 0. Ōsaka, Ise 0; Kameyama <u>1:3</u>. JP fɔɔ/foo.
2.2b   hoo < fofo < *popo. 'Magnolia hypoleuca' (= f̄ōf̄o-no-ki = fofogasifa [no
ki]): ~ no kawa (< kafa < *kapa*ₛ.ₛ*) 'magnolia bark (used in herbal medicine)'.
HL(-) - x-x-x x-x-x.
2.3   hoo, hoho < fowo < fofo < *po-po. 'cheek(s)'. LL - <u>1</u>-2[H]/<u>1:3</u>[U]-<u>A</u> x-B-x.
NS (T+ kun) L*ᴾ* = LL. Km x. Sz *(rare)* <u>1</u>. Ib hoho <u>L</u> = 2.4. Cf. kao < kafo <
*kapo*ₛ.ₗ*; mimi.
5.2   hoogasiwa < fofogasifa < *poponkasipa?< *[o]po*ᴮ* pa*ₗ.ₛ* -n- kasipa*ₛ.ₛₐ*
(< ...) ('big-leafed oak'). 'Magnolia hypoleuca' (= hoo). HHHHL(-no ki -L L) -
3-x-x x-x-x.
3.5a/b   hooki < fauki < fawaki < fafakyi < *papaki < *pa[ka]*ᴮ* pak[a-C]i*ₛ*. 'broom'.
LLH - 0/1-2-B x-B-x. Ongi LxH. Hamada, Matsue, Izumo 0; Aomori, Narada (haaki),
Goka-mura, Hakata 1; Hattō 2. Ib <u>F</u> = 3.4.
5.16   hookiboosi < fauki-bosi < fawaki-bosi < fafakyi-bosi < *papaki*ₛ.ₛₐ/b*
(< ...) -n- posi*ₛ.ₗ*. 'comet'. LLLHL - 3-4-B x-(B)-x. Sr hooci-bu⁷si (= B|A).
4.5/4.6   hoosuke < fofo-suke[y] < *po-po*ₛ.ₛ* suka-Ci[-Ci]*ₐ*. 'a kind of formal
military helmet'. LLLL (Zs) / LLLH (Kn) - x-x-x x-x-x.
4.9(/4.11)   hoozuki < fofoduki ?< *fofo-dukyi < *po-po*ₛ.ₛ* -n- tuk[a-C]i*ₐ*.
'bladder/ground cherry, Chinese lantern plant' (= kagati, Physalis alkekengi).
LHHL/LLHL (cf. Sakurai 1978b:13) - 0-1:4-<u>A</u> x-x-x. Sz 1.
?2.1, ?2.4   hora < fora < *pora. 'cave'. x - 1/<u>2</u>-1/<u>1:3</u>-x x-x-x. Km (S) HH. Edo
HH. Cf. horu 'dig'.
?2.5   hora < *fora < *(n)pora (?< Ch). 'trumpet(-shell); bragging'. x - 1-1:3-<u>A</u>
x-<u>A</u>-x. Km x. Sz <u>0</u>; Hattō, Hamada 1; Matsue, Izumo <u>2</u>. Ib L2 = 2.5. Nk buraa <u>B</u>;
Sr bura <u>A</u> ?< *[ ] -n- pora (see Ch. 1, §26). Cf. hara. Earliest citation 1764.

4.1 horaana < fora-ana < *pora?ɛ.ı anaɛ.ɜ. 'cave'. x - 0-0-A x-x-x. Sz 0.

2.3 hori < fori < *por[a-C]iв. 'ditch'. x - 2-2-B x-x-x. K: Edo HL. Ib (rare)
F = 2.3.

3.4 horie < fori-ye < foriɛ.ɜ (< ...) ye?ı.ı (< ...). 'canal'. x - 0-0-x
x-x-x. NS (100b [11:126-K] placename) LLL. Km (W) LLL/LHH.

(?3.1) < 4.5 horike < hori[i]ke < fori-ike < foriɛ.ɜ (< ...) ikeyɛ.ɜ (< ...).
'a man-made pond'. x - 2-x-x x-x-x. Mr (Bm) HHH.

2.2b horo < foro < *poro. 'underwing feathers of a bird': foro-no fa (Ir).
HL (Ir) - x-x-x x-x-x.

3.3 horo-ha < foro-fa < *poroɛ.ɜb pa?ı.ɛ. 'underwing feathers of a bird'.
HLL - x-x-x x-x-x.

3.2x horosi < forosi < *porosi (< ?). 'Solanum lyratum' (= hiyodori-zyoogo).
HHL - x-x-x x-x-x.

3.x horosi < forosi < *porosi (< ?). 'hives, nettle rash'. x - x-x-x x-x-x.
Cf. kaza-ᵇ/вorosi.

2.1 hosi < fosi < *posi. 'star'. HH - 0-0-A A-A-A. NS (99a) HH. Km (S) HH.
Edo HH. Ib H = 2.1. Nk pusii A; Kunigami, Ōgimi (northern Okinawa) B.

4.5 hosi-uo < fosi-iwo < *pos[a-C]iв i(w)oɛ.ı (< ...). 'dried fish'. LHL -
2-3-B x-x-x.

- hoso 'navel': see heso.

?4.2 hosodati < fosodati < *posoadʲ в -n- tatiɛ.ɜ. 'a kind of sword'. HHHL -
0/2-x-x x-x-x. Accent incongruent with etymology?

?4.1 hosodono < fosodono < *poso -n- tonoɛ.ɜ. 'corridor'. HHHH - 0-0-x x-x-x.
Accent incongruent with etymology?

?3.4 hosoki < fosokiy < *posoadʲ в ko-Ciı.ɜa (?< 'slender tree'; ? not <
foso [dial.] 'oak'). 'Fagara mandshurica (= inu-zansyoo); Japanese pepper
tree, Zanthoxylum piperitum (= itati-hazikami = sansyoo)'. LLx - x-x-x x-x-x.
NS (T+ kun) LLH. K: Hn LLL.

4.6 hosokuzu < fosokudu < *po[-ku]swo?ɜ.₄ kuntuɛ.₄. 'sparks; (= hokuso)
'tinder'. LLLH (Ir, -t-) - x-4-x x-x-x.

?4.7, ?4.6 hosomiti < fosomiti < *foso-myiti < *posoadʲ в mitiɛ.ı. 'a narrow
road' (= hosozi). x - 2-1:3-B x-x-x. Sz (rare) 0/3.

?3.6, ?3.7x hososi < fososi < *pososi (< ?). '(?) stake, door-stop'. LHx (?=
*LHH/LHL) - x-x-x x-x-x. Attested only by Mg?

6.1, 6.2 hosotanigawa < foso-tanigafa < *posoadʲ в taniᵏ/вapa₄.? (< taniɛ.ɜ (-n-)
kapaɛ.ɜа). 'a narrow valley river'. x - x-x-x x-x-x. Km (W) HHHHHH, HHHHHL.
Km register incongruent with etymology?

?3.5b < ?4.7, ?4.6 hosozi < fosodi < *poso-nti < *posoadʲ в mitiı.ı. 'narrow road'
(= hosomiti x - 2-1:3-B x-x-x). LLH - 2-1-x x-x-x.

3.1 hosozi: see hozoti.

3.5b hotaru < fotaru < *potaru (< ?). 'firefly'. x - 1(<*2)-2-B x-(B)-x.
Km x. Mr (Bm) HLL. 1700 Ōsaka HLL. K: Hn "?LHH". Aomori, Narada, Hattō, Goka-
mura, Yamaguchi, Wakamatsu, Hakata 1; Hamada, Matsue, Izumo 0; NE Kyūshū, Hata
2. Ib L2 = 3.5/7. Sr hutaru-bi B 'tiny fire'. Etymologies: ?< *poı.ɜb 'fire' +
tar[a]-ₐ or ter[a]-в 'shine'; ?← Korean panti < 'pantoy 'firefly'.

2.2a hoto: see hodo.

?2.3 hoto < foto < ?*po-to. 'vagina'. x - x-x-x B-B-A. Sd hwyi(i) B; Nk poo C;
Sr hoo B; Yn hii A.

4.2 [hotodori] < fotodori < *potoɛ.x -n- toriɛ.ı. 'cuckoo' (= hototogisu).
HHHL - x-x-x x-x-x.

?3.5x hotogi < fotoki (< ?). 'a jug (for hot or cold water)'. LLH - x-0-x x-x-x.
Mr (Bm) LHL.

3.4   hotoke < fotokey (?< *pot_o_-kaCi). 'Buddha'. LLL - 3/0-0-B x-B-B/_C_.
Km (S) LLL. Mr (Bm) HHL. Edo HHL. Sapporo, Tappi, Akita, Numazu, Narada, Hattō,
Izumo, Hiroshima, NE Kyūshū 3; Hamada, Matsue 3/0; Matsumoto, Ōita 0. Kōchi
0; Hyōgo 3; Ib F = 3.4. Nk puTuKii B; Yn hutugi B (H 1964:71b) / _C_ (185b).
Ōno says -key is a suffix 'appearance', but it is more likely this is borrowed
directly from the -h- of Korean pwuthye.

?4.5   hotondo < fotondo < (Hn) fotowoto/fotofodo < foto-foto < *poto poto (cf.
hotori, hodo). 'almost (all)'. LLLL - 2-3[H]/1:3[U]-A x-x-x. Mr (Bm) HHLL.
K: Edo LHLL.

3.7a   hotori < fotori < *potori. 'vicinity'. LHL - 0/3-0-B x-x-x. NS (119b,
134b) LHL, (118b) HHL. Km x. Edo HHL/LHL. K: Mr "?HHL". Sz 2; Aomori, Hattō,
Hamada, Matsue, Izumo, Goka-mura, Wakamatsu 0. Ib L2 = 3.5/7.

5.16   hototogisu < fot_o_togyisu < ?*poto_mim_ to_pci_ n[a]ki_imf_ (< *nak[a-C]i_A_)
su_i.x_. 'cuckoo'. LLLHL(/LLHHL) - 3-4-A x-x-x. Sz 4. Hakata 4, ygr 3.

3.4   hotue < fwo-tu-ye < *pwo_1.3a_ -tu ye_?1.2_. 'top branch(es)'. x - x-x-x
x-x-x. NS (T+ 35) HHH. Km (W) LLL.

2.2b   hoya < foya < *poda. 'seasquirt'. HL - 1-2-x x-x-x. Sz 0.

2.2x   hoya < foya (Mg) < foy_o_ < *pod_a_/_2_. 'mistletoe' (= yadorigi). HL - x-2-x
x-x-x.

-          hozo 'navel': *see* heso.

3.1   hozoti < fos_o_di (?< *fos_o_-oti[y] < *pos_o_2.1 ot_o_-Ci[-Ci]_B_ 'navel drop').
'the falling off of a navel cord; a ripe melon'. HHH - x-0-x x-x-x.

3.1   hozuna < foduna < *po_1.1_ -n- tuna_2.3_. 'halyard'. HHH - 0-2-x x-x-x.

1.x   hu < fu < *pu (?< *pu[si]_2.3_). '(woven) stitch, mesh, weave, knit, knot'.
x - x-x-x x-x-x. *See* ya-hu.

1.x   hu < fu (?< *[o]fu_B pred_ < ... ; ?< *f[ay]u_B pred_ < ... ; ?< *p[ar]u
'field'). 'place where things grow' (cf. sonou): siba-hu 'turf, greensward,
lawn' x - 0-2[H]/0[U]-A x-x-x; [awa-hu] < awa-fu 'millet patch' NS (T+ 13)
LL-H; kasi no fu 'a growth of oaks' NS (T+ 39) LL L H H.

?3.3 < 4.3, ?3.2x < 4.2 hubako < fubako < fu[mi]bako < *fumyi-bakwo < *pumi_2.2b_
-n- pakwo_2.1_. 'a box for letters'. x - 0/1-0[H]/2[U]-A x-x-x; Edo HLL.

2.1 < 3.1 < 4.1   huda < fuda < funda < fum[u]_t_/_da_ < *fumyi -[i]ta< *pumi_2.2b_
ita_2.4_. 'card'. HH, HHH - 0-0-A x-A-x. Km x. Edo HH. Ib H = 2.1.

2.1 < 3.1   hude < fude < funde < fum[u]de < fumide < *fumyi -te < *pumi_2.2b_
ta-Ci_1.3a_. 'writing brush'. HH - 0-0-A A-A-x. Km x. Edo HH. Ib H = 2.1.

2.1   hue < fuye < *pude (< ?*pudaCi, ?*pudiCa). 'whistle, fife, flute'.
HH - 0-0-A B-x-x. NS (83c, 87a, 87b) HH; NS (T 97, 98) HH. Km x. Edo HH.
Ib H = 2.1. (The register is incongruent for the etymology < fu[kyi]_B_ ye_1.2_
'blow branch'.)

4.2   huehuki < fuye-fukyi < *pude_2.1_ (< ...) puk[u-C]i_B_ (< puk[a-C]i_B_). 'flute
player, piper'. HHHL - 3/4-4-x x-x-x.

?2.5   hugu < fuku < *pu(n)ku. 'blowfish'. x - 1-1:3-_A_ x-x-x. Km x. Sz 1.

3.2b   huguri < fuguri < *punkuri. 'testicles; scrotum'. HHL - 1-0-x A-A-A. Km x.
Sd huguuryi/hugur A 'penis'; Sr hugui A 'scrotum'; Yn ngui A 'testicles'.

5.1/5.2   hugurizuki < fuguri-duki < (Mg) fuguri-tuki (?< *fuguri-tukyi <
*punkuri_2.2b,?3.3_ tuk[a-C]i_B_). 'a horse ailment (with rumbling in the lower
belly)'. HHHHH (Kn) / HHHHL (Ck) x-x-x x-x-x.

?3.4   [hugusi] 'a digging stick': *see* [hukusi].

?3.1   [huhuki] < fufuki < ?*pupukiy < ?*pupukiy < ?*pupu (= ?) k_o_-Ci_1.3a_. 'bog
rhubarb, butterbur' (= huki). Hxx - x-0-x x-x-x. K: Hn HHH. Cf. mizu-hubuki,
yama-bu[hu]ki, uma-hu_h_/_buki.

3.x < 4.11   huigo < fuigoo < fuigɔɔ < fuigau < fuki-gafa < *puk[u-C]i*ᵦ* (?<
*puk[a-C]i*ᵦ*) -n- kapa*ₐ.ₛ* ('blow skin'). 'bellows'. LHLL - 1/0-1[H]/1:3[U]-A
x-(B)-x. Aomori, Sz 3; Goka-mura 0; Hattō, Hamada, Matsue, Izumo 1. Ib L2 =
3.5/7. Sr huuci B < *fuki[-gafa].

2.1   huka < fuka < *puka. 'shark' (= same). HH - 0/2[new]-0-A x-A-x.
Narada 1; Hattō, Hamada, Matsue, Izumo, Hiroshima 0; Aomori, Goka-mura 2.
Ōsaka, Ise 0; Ib H = 2.1.

4.6   hukagutu < *fuka-gutu < *puka*ₐₐⱼ* *ᵦ* -n- kutu*ₐ.ₛ*. 'foul-weather boots'.
LLLH - 0/2-1-x x-x-x.

?5.16   hukami-ᵏ/ₐusa < fukami-kusa ?< *fukamyi (< *pukami < ?) kusa*ₐ.ₛ*. LLLxx
(?= *LLLHL) - 3-4-x x-x-x. 'peony (= botan); spearflower (= yabu-koozi)'.

4.5   hukatumi < fukatumi < ?. 'Ranunculus sceleratus, cursed/ditch crowfoot'
(= ta-garasi). LLLL - x-x-x x-x-x.

?2.1, ?2.3   huke < fuke < ?*fu-key < ?*pu (= ?) ka-Ci*?₁.₁*. 'dandruff'.
x - 2[H]/0[K]-0-B x-x-x. Km x. Sz 2; Aomori, Hattō, Hamada, Matsue, Izumo,
Goka-mura 0. Ib F = 2.3.

?2.1   huki < fuki ?< *pukiy < ?*pu (= ?) ko̱-Ci*₁.ₛₐ*; ?< *fukyi < *puk[a-C]i*ᵦ*
('wipe', because the leaf was used as toilet paper). 'bog rhubarb, butterbur'.
x - 0-0-Ḇ x-x-x. Aomori, Sz, Hiroshima 0; Hakata (expected) 1, ygr 0. Ōsaka,
Ise 0; Ib Ḻ = 2.4. Cf. huhuki.

4.11   [hukigawa] < fukigafa 'bellows': see huigo.

2.3   huku < fuku < *puku (< Ch bhyuk). 'clothes, garment(s)'. x - 2-2-B B-x-x.
Sz, Hattō 1; Hamada 1/2, Matsue, Izumo, Goka-mura, Hiroshima 2. Ōsaka, Ise 2.
Ib H1 = 2.2.

3.6   hukube < fukube (< ?). 'blowfish' (= hugu). LHH - x-x-x x-x-x.

3.7x   hukuge < fukuge < *fuku-gey < *puku (= ?) -n- ka-Ci*₁.₁*. 'chick down, baby
down (fine hairs)'. LHL - x-2(bukuge)-x x-x-x.

3.1   hukura < fukura < *puku-ra(-). 'swelling; (= soyogo) a kind of holly
(Ilex)'. x - x-x-x x-x-x. Cf. Sr -bukkwa 'swollen place' (as in cii-bukkwa B
'breasts') < *-bukura.

3.4   hukuro < fukurwo < *pukurwo. 'bag'. LLL - 3-2-B B-B-B. Ongi-m LLL. Km x.
Edo HHL. Izumo 0̱; Goka-mura 0 (expected reflex); Sapporo, Wakamatsu 2̱; Akita,
Matsumoto, Numazu, Narada, Hattō, Hamada, Matsue, Hiroshima, Ōita 3; Hakata 0,
ygr 2/3. Suzu 1̱ (we expect 0); Ib F = 3.4. Yn Kuru B.

-      hukuro 'owl' (x - 2/3-x-x x-x-x): see hukuroo.

4.5/4.11 hukuroo < fukuroᶠ/ₖu < *pukuroᴾ/ₖu (< ?). 'owl'. LLLL/LLHL - 1/2-1:3-B
x-x-x. Ongi LLHL. Sz 1; Hata 2. Kōchi 1:4. (Cf. mimizuku; Sr sikuku B, taka-
ikuku A, mayaa-zikuku B.)

?3.4   [huᵏ/ₐusi] < fukusi < fokuse/(-)fokusi < *fo[ri]-kusi < *por[a-C]i*ᵦ*
kusi*ₐ.ₛ*. 'a digging stick (made of bamboo)'. x - x-x-x x-x-x. Also
[hoᵏ/ₐusi]. Cf. kana-bukusi.

2.2b   humi < fumi (?< *fumyi < *pumi; ?< Ch .m(b)ywen). 'writings'. HL -
2/1[new]-2-A x-x-x. NS (Okada) HL. Edo HL. Aomori (rare) 1̱. Ib (rare) H1 = 2.2.

?4.3, ?4.2 humibako < fumibako < *fumyi-bakwo < *pumi*ₐ.ₐᵦ* -n- pakwo*ₐ.₁*. 'a box for
letters'. HHLL (?= *HHHL) - 2-0[H]/3[U]-A x-x-x. Cf. hunbako.

4.3   humibitu < fum[u]-bitu < fumi*ₐ.ₐᵦ* (< ...) fitu*ₐ.₁* (< ...). 'a book box;
a letter box'. x - x-3-x x-x-x. Ongi HHLL.

3.1 (> 2.1)   [humida] > huda 'card': see huda.

3.1 (> 2.1)   [humide] < fumide < *fumyi-te < *pumi*ₐ.ₐᵦ* ta-Ci*₁.ₛₐ*. 'writing brush'.
HHH - x-0-x x-x-x. See hude.

5.2   humizukue < fumi-duku(w)e < *fumyi*ₐ.ₐᵦ* (< *pumi) -n- tukuye*ₐ.₁* (< ...).
'writing desk'. HHHxx (= *HHHHL) - 3-4-x x-x-x.

?3.1, ?3.4   humoto < fumot<u>o</u> < *pu[m[a-C]i] m<u>o</u>to*s.s* (cf. Kuranaka 104). 'the foot
of a mountain'. HHH/<u>HHL</u> - 3-0[H]/2[U]-B x-x-x. Edo HHL. Sapporo <u>2</u>; Goka-mura <u>1</u>
(we expect 0). Aomori, Akita, Matsumoto, Numazu, Narada, Hattō, Hamada, Matsue,
Izumo, Hiroshima, Wakamatsu, NE Kyūshū, Ōita 3; Hakata 0, ygr 3 (= 3.4). Kōchi
0; Toyama <u>1:3</u> (we expect 1:2); Ib F = 3.4.

2.4   huna(-) 'boat': see hune. NS (T+ 70) funa-amari <u>HL|LLH</u>. NS (T+ kun) huna-
n<u>o</u> fey LL-L|H.

2.5   huna < funa < *puna ?= *pu (< Ch) na*1.sa*. 'crucian carp' (fish). LH -
1-1:3-B x-x-x. Km x K: Hn LF. Toyama <u>1:2</u>; Suzu 1 (expected); Ib L2 = 2.5.

4.5   hunabata < funabata < *puna*s.4* -n- pata*s.1*. 'the side of a boat'.
xxLL (= *LLLL) - 0-0[U]/1[H]-B x-x-x.

?4.5   hunadana < funadana < *puna*s.4* -n- tana*s.1*. 'a stepping-board on a dugout
canoe'. LLLx - 0/4-0-x x-x-x.

4.1   hunadoko < funadoko < *puna*s.4* -n- t<u>o</u>ko*s.1*. 'a hurdle spread over the
bottom of a boat; the hold of a boat'. LLLL - 0-0-x x-x-x.

3.7x   hunako < funakwo < *puna*s.4* kwo*1.1*. 'boatman'. LHL - x-<u>2</u>-x x-B-x.

3.4   hunani < funani < *puna*s.4* ni*1.3b* (< *n<u>o</u>-Ci). 'cargo'. LLL - <u>0</u>/2-<u>0</u>[U]/
<u>1</u>[H]-B x-x-x.

?3.6   hunato < funatwo (< ?). 'a crossroads (god)' (= kuna*t*/*do*). LHH - x-x-x
x-x-x. NS (T+ kun) funatwo no kamiy LLL-L LL.

5.16   hunayakata < funa-yakata < *puna*s.4* da-kata*s.5a/b* (< ...). 'shelter on a
boat'. LLLHL - 3-3-x x-x-x.

5.16   hunayamoi < funayamofi (4th vowel assimilated to labial consonants) <
funa*s.4* - yamafyi*s.7b* < *puna*s.4* dama-p[a-C]i*s*. '(getting) boatsick, seasick'.
LLLHL - x-x-x x-x-x.

3.4   hunayu < funa-yu < *puna*s.4* du*1.3a*. 'bilge(water)'. LLL - x-<u>0</u>-x x-x-x.

?4.3, ?4.2   [hunbako] < fum[u]bako < fumibako (< ...). 'a box for letters'.
HHLL (Kn) / HHHL (Ck). See humibako.

-        [hunbitu] < fum[u]bitu: see humibitu.

2.4   hune < fune < *pune[y] < *puna-Ci. 'boat; tub'. LH - 1-1-B B-B-C. Ongi LH.
NS (127b) <u>HH</u>, (71c [11:190-M], 94a) LH; NS (T 51) RL = <u>HL</u>. Km (S,W) LH. Edo LH.
Hata, Hakata 1. Kōchi 1; Ib L = 2.4. Onna puuni B; Yn nni C. K: Hn-Km-Edo LH.

3.1   hunori < fun<u>o</u>ri < *pu (= ?) nori*?2.3*. 'glue plant, Gloiopeltis furcata'.
HHH - 0-0-A x-A-x. Km x. Narada <u>3</u>; Hakata <u>1</u>, ygr 0. Ib H = 3.1. Sr hunui A.

4.1/4.2 hunzuki < funduki ("fumuduki") < fumi-dukyi ?< *fumyi-dukyi < *pumi*?(s.sb)*
(-n-) tuku-Ci*s.s*. 'the 7th lunar month'. x - x-2-x x-x-x. Km (W)
HHHH/HHHL. Also fu-*t*/*z*uki.

2.3   huro < furo < *puro (? *purwo). 'bath'. LL - <u>1</u>/2-2-B B-(B)-x. Km x.
Sz, Hattō, Hamada, Matsue, Izumo, Goka-mura, Hiroshima (Okuda) 2. Ib F = 2.3.
Sd huro(o) B.

3.4   huroba < furo-ba < *puro*s.s* -n- pa*1.3a*. 'bathroom'. x - 3-2-B x-x-x. Km x.
Aomori 3.

3.1   hurui < furufi < furufyi < *puru-p[a-C]i*A*. 'sieve, sifter'. HHH - 0-0-A
x-x-x. Aomori <u>2</u>. Ib H = 3.1.

3.x   huruya < furu-ya < *puru*adj B* da*1.3b*. 'an old house'. x - 2-1-x x-B-x.
Km (W) LLH. Sr huruyaa B.

2.3   husa < fusa < *pusa. 'bunch'. LL - 2-2-B <u>A</u>-<u>A</u>-x. Km x. Aomori <u>0</u>. Ib <u>H1</u> = 2.2

?2.1   husi < fusi < *pusi. 'brushwood (= siba); fence, fencing, fenceboard'.
HH - x-<u>2</u>-x x-x-x. NS (T+ kun 'fence') HH. Km x. K: Hn x, Km HH.

2.3   husi < fusi < *pusi ?< *pusi[y] < *pus<u>o</u>Ci. 'node, gnarl, bamboo joint'.
LL - 2-2-B B-B-x. Km x. Edo HL. Sd busyi(i) B ?< *[ ] -n- pusi (see Ch. 1, §26).
Dial. (Kōchi, Tottori) huso.

4.1   husizuke ‹ fusiduke ‹ *fusidukey ‹ *pusi₇₂.₁ -n- tuka-Ci[-Ci]. 'catching fish with a weir (during winter)'. HHHH - x-0-x x-x-x.

3.5x   husube ‹ fusubey (‹ ?). 'skin blemishes (marks/growths)'. LLH - x-1-x x-x-x. Cf. sagari-husube.

3.4   husuma ‹ fusuma ‹ *pusuma (?‹ *pu(-)s[a-]uв mo₁.₃b 'garment to lie down in'). 'fusuma (= opaque sliding door); bedding'. LLL - 3/0/2-2-B x-B-x. Km x. Ib H = 3.1, (older) F = 3.4.

2.1   huta ‹ futa ‹ *puta. 'lid'. HH - 0-0-A A-A-A. Km x. Edo HH. Ib H = 2.1. Yn Taa A.

?2.1, ?2.2x   huta ‹ futa ‹ *puta 'two'. NS (T+ 2) HL, (T+ 40) ₣L ?= HL. futa nagara (Kn) 'both' HH HHH. *See* hutatu, hutari, ...

3.2a/b   hutae ‹ futa-fye ‹ *puta₇₂.₁,₇₂.₂ piCa₁.ₓ. 'double'. HHL - 3/2-1:3[H]/ 2[U]-A x-x-x. NS (71a, 130a) HHL, (71b) LHL; NS (T+ 47, 49) HL|H. Edo HLL. Narada 3; Matsue, Izumo, Goka-mura 0; Aomori, Hattō, Hamada 2. Ib L = 3.6, L2 = 3.5/7.

5.2   hutagokoro ‹ futa - kokoro ‹ *puta₇₂.₁,₇₂.₂ (-n-) kokoro₃.₅b. 'duplicity'. HHxxx - 3/0-1:4[H]/1[U]-A x-(A)-x. Km (S) HHHHL. K: Edo LLHHH. Sz 0.

5.2   hutamaᵏ/ɢami ‹ futamagami (Mg) ‹ *putama(n)kami (‹ ?). 'Asarum nipponicum' (= tubunegusa = kan-aoi). HHHHL - x-x-x x-x-x.

4.1   hutamata ‹ futamata ‹ *puta₇₂.₁,₇₂.₂ mata₂.₃. 'fork(ed thing)'. HHHH (Zs) - 0/4-1-A x-(A)-x. Sr tamatagaki A "sitting on the fence" ‹ *futa-mata - gake.

3.2a/b   hutari ‹ futari ‹ *puta₇₂.₁,₇₂.₂ -ri (‹ *[a]r[a-C]iв). 'two people'. HHL - 3-1:3-A (B)-A-A. NS (74a) HHL; NS (T+ 61) H₣H = HHH. Km (W) HLL. Edo LHL. Sapporo, Akita, Matsumoto, Numazu, Narada, Wakamatsu, Ōita 3; Aomori, Hiroshima 0; Hakata hutaari 2, ygr 3. Ib L = 3.6. Yn Tainitu A (H 1964:72a) ‹ *f[u]ta[r]i n[o f]ito.

4.2   hutatabi ‹ futa-tabyi ‹ *puta₇₂.₁,₇₂.₂ tanpi₂.₂b. 'twice; again'. HHHL - 0-3-x x-x-x. Km (W) HHHL. Mr (Bm) LHLL. K: Edo LHLL. Sz 0.

5.4 = 2.1|3.4 hutatamura ‹ futa-tamura ‹ *puta₇₂.₁, ₇₂.₂ tamurᵃ/o₃.₄ (‹ ...). 'two companies'. x - x-x-x x-x-x. NS (134b) HH(|)LLL.

4.1   hutatose ‹ futatose ‹ *futa-tose ‹ *puta₇₂.₁,₇₂.₂ tose (?‹ tosi₂.₃). 'two years'. HHHH - x-x-x x-x-x. Sr tatu A ‹ *futa-to[se].

3.2a/b   hutatu ‹ futatu ‹ *puta₇₂.₁,₇₂.₂ -tu. 'two'. HHL - 3(/0)-1:3[H]/3[U]-A (B)-A-A. NS (T+ 113) HLL. Km (S) HHL. Edo HHL/LHL. 1700 Ōsaka LHL. Akita, Matsumoto, Numazu, Narada, Ōita 3; Sapporo, Aomori, Hiroshima 0; Hakata hutaatu 2, ygr 3. Kōchi 3 (Doi 1952:29), 1:3 (H). Ib L = 3.6. Yn Taci A. K: Mr HHL/LHL. Hattori (1979:21:112): length in Sr taaçi A by analogy with 'one'; see hitotu.

?2.4   huti ‹ futi ‹ *puti. 'rim; cliff'. LH - 2-2-B B-A-x. NS (111b) LH. Km x. Edo LH. Sz 1; Hattō and Goka-mura ('cliff') 1, ('rim') 2; Narada, Hamada 2; Matsue, Izumo 2 (*expected reflex*). Ib ?F = 2.3. Sr huci A 'cliff'.

4.1   hutokoro ‹ futukoro / hutukuro ‹ *putᵘ/okᵘ/oro (‹ ?). 'bosom'. HHHH - 0-4-A x-B-x. Km x. Sz, Narada 0. Sr hucukuru B has unexplained palatalization.

?4.2   hutomugi ‹ futomugi ‹ *futo-mugyi ‹ *puto₅dʲ в munki₂.₄. 'barley' (= oomugi). HHHL x - 3/1:3-x x-x-x. Register incongruent with the etymology.

3.1   hutuka ‹ futuka ‹ *putuka(?‹ *puta₂.₁ ka₇₁.₃ₐ, ?‹ *put[a] uka; ?‹ *pu[ta]₂.₁ -tu ka₁.₃ₐ). 'two days'. HHH - 0-0-A B-B-x. Edo HHH. Hakata 0, ygr 3 (= 2.3). Ib H = 3.1. Nk puCiika A.

?2.5   hutu-ni ‹ futu ni ‹ *putu₅ᵢв ni. 'with a slice(-through); (= hutuku-ni ‹ futu-ku ni) totally, all' (adv). LH-x x-x-x x-x-x.

2.2a   huyu ‹ fuyu ‹ *pudu (?‹ *pid[a-]uв ‹ ...). 'winter'. x - 2-2-A A-A-A. Km x. K: Edo HL. Hakata 0, ygr 2 (= 2.3). Toyama 1.3; Suzu 1:3 (*expected reflex*); Ib H1 = 2.2.

3.2a   huyuge < fuyuge < *fuyu-gey < *pudu*s.sb* -n- ka-Ci*?1.1*. 'winter fur'.
HHL - 0-0-x x-x-x.

3.1   huyugi < fuyu-ki < *pudu*s.sb* ?kiy*1.1* (< ...). 'winter onion, Allium
fistulosum' (= wake-gi 'Welsh onion'). HHH - x-0-x x-x-x.

4.1   huyukawa < fuyu-kafa < *pudu*s.sb* (< ...) kapa*s.sb*. 'winter river, the
river in winter'. x - x-0-x x-x-x. Km (W) HHHH.

4.2   huyukusa < fuyu-kusa < *pudu*s.sb* (< ...) kusa*s.s*. 'winter plants/grasses'.
x - x-0-x x-x-x. Km (W) HHHL.

2.1   huzi < fudi < *punti. 'wisteria'. Hx - 0-0-A A-A-x. Km x. Edo HH.
K: Hn-Edo HH. Ib H = 2.1.

2.3   huzi < fudi < *punti (< ?) '(Mount) Fuji' (*placename*). x - 1-2-A x-x-x.
Km (W) LL. Sz, Hattō, Hamada, Matsue, Izumo, Wakamatsu 1; Goka-mura 2.
Ib H1 = 2.2.

5.2   huzibakama < fudi-bakama < *punti*s.1* -n- pakama*s.4* (< ...) ('wisteria
skirt'). 'chrysanthemum' (= kiku). HHHxx (?= *HHHHL) - 3/5-4-x x-x-x. Sz 0(/4).

4.2, 4.1 huzigawa < fudi-gafa < *punti*s.s* (< ?) -n- kapa*s.sb*. 'the Fuji River'
(*placename*). x - 0-0-A x-x-x. Km (W) HHHL, HHHH. The Km register is incongruent
with the etymology.

5.2   huzigoromo < fudi-goromo < *punti*s.1* -n- koromo*s.1*. 'a garment made of
rough-spun vine cloth; mourning wear'. HHHHL - 3-4-x x-x-x. K: Hn-Km HHHHL.

3.1   huzina < fudina < *punti*s,1* na*1.sa*. 'dandelion' (= tanpopo). HHH - x-x-x
x-x-x.

?3.1, ?3.2x   hyuuga < fimuka < (*)fyi-muka < *pi*1.s* muka(-)*A*. 'turning toward the
sun; Hyūga (*placename*)'. x - 1-2-A x-x-x. NS (Okada) LLL; NS (Sakurai) FLL.
(*The etymology indicates high register.*) Sr hwiza A 'Higa' (*placename*), hiza-
hoo B 'toward the east'. Cf. higasi.

1.1   i < wi (< Ch hhywey'). 'stomach' (= i-bukuro). x - 0-2-A x-(B)-A. Km x.
Ōsaka, Ise 0; Kōchi 0 (Doi 1952:20), 2 (Kobayashi); Ib H = 1.1. Nk qii A;
Sr qii B is thought to be "new" yet the etymon is found throughout the Ryūkyūs.

?1.1   i < wi < *bi. 'dam' (= iseki). x - (1)-x-x x-x-x. *See* igui.

?1.2, ?1.1   i < wi < *bi. 'boar' (= i-no-sisi). H - 0-2-A x-A-x. Km x. Edo H. Sz
1. Ōsaka, Ise 0/2. Ib H = 1.1. Sr ii A. K: "Hn HH" = 1.1, but Kt indicates 1.2.
In favor of 1.1 are wi-no asi 'boar's foot' and wi-no ko 'pig' but we lack clear
examples of 1.2-no N to show whether 1.2 merges with 1.1 before the particle
(as 2.5 merges with 2.4), though Mg fi-no i["]turu (= iduru) 'sun rise' may
argue against the merger. Modern Kt i'-no-sisi indicates 1.2; what do other
Kyōto-type dialects have? Cf. sai*s.1* 'wild boar'.

1.3a   i < wi < *bi. 'well' (= i-do). L - 1-0-x x-x-x. Km (W) L.

1.3a   i. 'gallbladder'. L - 1-2-x x-x-x. Km x. Aomori, Sz 0. Ib H = 1.1.

?1.3a   i. 'sleep': *see* ineru; ime; uma-i. Km (W) L.

*1.3a   i(-). 'sacred': *see* iwau, inoru, imu; itu, ituki, ituku, itukusi-. Also
yu(-).

1.3b   i < wi < *bi. 'rush' (*plant*). R - 1-2-x x-B-x. Km x. Aomori, Sz 0. Ib H =
1.1. Sr ii B. Engi-shiki wii. (Cf. modern i-gusa.)

1.x   ··· i. 'fact (that); that (which)': *see* aruiwa, mukuiru.

1.x   ··· i < *fiy < *p*ᵁ*/*o*Ci. 'niece/nephew': *see* mei, oi.

3.2a   ibara < mu*f*/*b*ara < u*?b*/*m*ara < ?*unpara. 'thorn; bramble; (= bara)
rosebush'. HHL - 0-1:3-B x-x-x. Sz 0; Izumo 2; Goka-mura 1. Km x. ⌷ mubarano-
mi < *u*b*/*m*ara no miy < *unpara*s.sa* no mu-Ci*1.1*. 'wild rose blossoms, used in
traditional medicine' (= eizitu: Kn Hō-ka 53:8 omits the second character of
the binom). "HHH- L|H" (Kn) ?= *HHL-L|H.

2.2x ibi < yubi < *dunpi. 'night heron'. HL - x-x-x x-x-x.

3.4 ibiki ?< ikyi [fyi]byikyi < *iki*2.4* pinpik[a-C]i*B*, ?< [f]ibiki*3.4* (< ...). 'snore'. x - 3-2-B x-x-x. Narada, Hattō, Hamada *(Hiroto and Ōhara corrigenda)* 3; Matsue, Izumo <u>0</u>; Goka-mura 0 *(expected reflex)*; Ib F = 3.4. Dial. (Aichi, Wakayama, and Kasika-gun of Kyōto) hibiki.

2.5a < 3.5a ibo < i[fi]bo < ifyi*f*/*b*o (Mg LLL/LLH) < *ipi*?2.3* (- n-) pwo*1.3a*. 'rice grain; wart'. x - 1-1:3-B x-x-x. Km x. Aomori 2 *(expected)*. Ib L2 = 2.5.

4.2 ibokai < ibokafi < *i[fyi]*f*/*b*o (< ...) kapi*3.3*. 'a purple conch': uma no ~ 'the noon trumpet(-shell)'. (LL-L|) HHHL (Kn) - x-x-x x-x-x.

5.16 ibomusi = ibomusiri < *i[fyi]bo*3.5<3.3* - musiri < *ipi*3.3* -n- pwo*1.3a* musir[a-C]i*B*. 'a praying mantis' (= kamakiri). LLLHL - 3-1:3-x x-x-x.

3.5a = 2.3|1.1 ideya < ide (?< id[ur]e*3.6* < ...) ya*Pcl*. 'well; nay; ... ' *(interj)*. LL(|)H - <u>1-1</u>-x x-x-x.

2.5 ido < wido < *bi*1.3b* -n- two*1.1*. 'well'. x - 1-1:3-B x-x-x. Km x. Kōchi 1:3; Ib L2 = 2.5.

2.3 ie < ifye (?< *ifey < *ipa-Ci; ?< *ipiCa; ?< *ipo [*see* io]). 'house'. LL - 2-2-B x-x-x. NS (92a) LL; NS (T 111) <u>LH</u>, (T 124 L<u>H</u> ?= LL. Km (S) LL. Mr (Bm) HL. Edo HL. Ib F = 2.3. Cf. ya (?< *i[w]a < *ipa). Azuma OJ ifa, one example of ifi, maybe variant reductions of *ipa-Ci or *ipiCa (? = *ipi-da?).

4.5 iebato < ifebato < *ifye*3.3* (< ...) - batwo (< -n- patwo*3.3*). 'domestic pigeon'. LHLL - 0-1:4-x x-x-x.

3.4 iei < ifye-wi < *ifye*3.3* (< ...) b*a*/*o*-Ci[-Ci]. 'staying/living at home; home, house'. x - <u>0-0</u>-x x-x-x. Km (W) LLL.

?4.10 ienire < ifenire < *ifye*3.3* (< ...) nire*3.2a* (< ...). 'Eranthis pinnatifida (= setubun-soo); Ulmus japonica (= harunire)'. ?LHLL (Kn: *Mochizuki 71c looks as if LLLL but the second-syllable dot is definitely high in the Kn Mg text*) - 2-0-x x-x-x. K: Hn LLLL.

2.2b iga < *inka. 'bur'. HL - 2-<u>1:3</u>-x x-x-x. Km x. Narada, Hiroshima 2. Ōsaka <u>1</u>; Ise <u>1:3</u>; Ib H1 = 2.2.

3.1 igata < i-kata < *i[-Ci] kata. 'mold, cast, matrix'. HHH - 0-0[H]/<u>1</u>[U]-A x-A-x. Sr qikata A. *Is Kt 1 [U] a misprint?*

(2.2b) [ige] (JP) < *(the second vowel assimilated to the first)* iga < *inka. 'bur; unhusked grain'. x - x-x-x x-x-x.

2.3 ige 'a rush-woven lunchbox': *see* ike.

?3.2x igui < [w]igu[w]i < wi-gufyi < wi*?1.1* -n- kupi*3.3b*. 'support stakes for stone-filled baskets used to protect river banks'. x - x-x-x A-x-x. NS (T+ 36) <u>HH</u><u>H</u> ?= HHL. Sd qyigui A 'stake' *(omitted in Martin 1970)*.

3.1 igisu (< ?). 'a kind of purple seaweed' (= igisu-nori). HHH - <u>1</u>-0-x x-x-x.

2.3 ii < ifyi < *ipi. 'cooked rice'. x - <u>1</u>-2-x x-x-x. NS (98a, 98b, 98c) LL; NS (T 104) L<u>H</u> ?= LL. Km x. Cf. iine, iibo; motii.

3.4 iibo < ifibo < ifyi*f*/*b*i < *ipi*?3.3* (-n-) pwo*1.3a*. 'rice grain; wart'. LLL - x-<u>0</u>-x x-x-x. *See* ibo.

3.5x iine < ifyine < *ipi*3.3* [z]ina-Ci*3.4*. 'cooked rice'. LLH - x-x-x x-x-x.

5.16 iisitami < ifisitami < *ifyi-sitami < *ipi*3.3* sitami*3.6* (< ?). 'a bamboo basket laid on the bottom of a rice steamer'. LLLHL - x-4-x x-x-x.

4.1 ii*t*/*d*oyo < ifidoyo (Mg) < *ifyi-doyo < *ipi*3.3* -n- t*o*do*?3.3* ('rich in food'). 'owl' (= hukuroo). LLLL - x-0-x x-x-x.

4.5 iiue < ifi-uwe < *ifyi - uwe[y] < *ipi*3.3* uba-Ci[-Ci]*?B*. 'hunger; being famished/starved'. LLLL - x-x-x x-x-x.

2.1 ika. 'cuttlefish'. HH - 0-0-A x-A-x. Km x. Ib H = 2.1.

2.2b   ika: ika(-ni). 'how'. HL(-?H) - 2-2-A (A)-A-x. NS (95c [11:68-K]) HL-L;
NS (T+ 99) HL|H. Km (S,W) HL-L. Mr (Bm) HL-L. Edo HL. Nagano 1 (Kudō 1978:92).
Sd qyikhya- and Sr caa A < *ik(y)a. K: Hn HL-H, Km HL-L; if so, in Heian the
particle was set off by juncture.

?2.2b   ika(-)··· 'mighty' (? = ika 'how [much]'): see ikazuti, ikamesi-, ...

3.1   ikada < *ikanta (?< *i-_pre_ [u]ka_A_ -n- [i]ta_s.4_ 'float board'; ?< *ika_s.sb_
-n- [i]ta_1.4_ '*mighty board'). 'raft'. HHH - 0-0[H]/1[U _misprint?_]-A B-x-x.
Hakata 2, ygr 0. Ib H = 3.1. Yn karuŋun A, anka B (H 1964:72a) < ?.

?3.4   ikaga < *ika_s.sb_ n[i]_pcl_ ka_pcl_. 'how'. LLL (Kn) - 2-1:3-A x-A-x.
Nk Caa ga A, Sr caa ga A (< *ikyaa ga).

?4.1   ika-hodo (< ...). 'how much'. x - 0-0-A (B)-(B)-x. Sd qyikhyaahwi(i) B, Sr
cahwi/cappi (< *ca(a)-quhwi) B < *ik(y)a-ofe < *ika_s.sb_ opo_adj_ _B_ ('how big').

-         ika-ni: see ika.

3.1   ikao = ikaho < ikafo < *ikapo (?< Ainu). 'Ikaho' (_placename_). x - 0-x-x
x-x-x. Km (W) HHH (ik͞afo n͞o numa).

3.1   ikari. 'anchor'. HHH - 0-0-A B-A-x. Narada 3; Hakata 1, ygr 0. Ib H = 3.1.
Nk qikaari A.

4.1   ikarii < ikari-wi < *ikari_s.1_ (< *ika-r[a-C]i_A_ bi_71.s._ 'an enraged boar'.
x - 3-0/4-x x-x-x. NS (117b) HHHH. K: "Km HHHH".

5.1   ikarizuna < ikari-duna < *ikari_s.1_ -n- tuna_s.s._ 'anchor line'. HHHHH -
3-3-x x-x-x.

4.11   ikaruga < *ikarunka (< ?). 'grosbeak, Japanese hawfinch' (_bird_) (= ikaru,
a later truncation?). LLHL - 0-0-x x-x-x. NS (78a _as name_) LLHL; (T+ kun) HLHH.

4.1   ikazuti < ikaduti < *ika_s.sb_ -n- -tu ti_1.1_ ('mighty spirit'). 'lightning'.
HHHH - 0-0-x x-x-x. NS (119a) xHHH. Ōno Tōru 1978:49, suspicious of the double
particle, suggests the etymology *ika_s.sb_ -n- tuti_s.4_ (< ...) 'mighty hammer'.

2.3   ike < ikey < *ika-Ci[-Ci]_B_ ('keep them alive'). '(fish-)pond'. LL - 2-2-B
B-B-(A). NS (84a) LL; NS (T 97) LL, (T 36) LH. Km x. Mr (Bm) HL. Edo HL.
Ib F = 2.3. Yn icitarai A. Nakanoshima treats ike as 2.1 (Tajiri 1975:47).

2.3   ik_k/g_e < wi-_k/g_e[y] < *bi_1.sb_ ka(-)Ci_71.s,71.1_. 'a rush-woven lunchbox'.
LL (-g-) - x-x-x x-x-x.

4.5   ikenie < ikenife < *ikey_?(2.3)_ (< *ika-Ci[-Ci]_B_) nifey_s.1a_ (< *nipi_s.1_
apa-Ci[-Ci]_B_). 'sacrificial offering'. LLLL - 0/4-0[U]/1[H]-B x-x-x. Sz 0.

3.4   ikesu < ikesu (Ck) /ikezu (Kn) < *ikey-_s/z_u < *ika-Ci[-Ci]_B_ (-n-) su_1.sb_
('screen'). 'a fish crawl; a device/place for keeping seafood alive in water'.
LLL-0/3-2[U]/0[H]-B x-x-x. Aomori 3. Ib F = 3.4.

2.4   iki < ikyi < *iki (?< *ik[a-C]i_B_, see ikiru). 'breath'. LH - 1-1-B B-B-C.
NS (Okada) LH. Km (S) LH(-H). Mr(Bm) LH. Edo LH. Toyama 1:2 (_expected reflex_);
Suzu 2; Ib L = 2.4. Sr qiici B; Yn iti C (Uemura 1959:126b, Shibata 1959:118,
H 1964:179a), ici C (H 1964:71a, 98).

?4.6, ?4.11   ikigusa < ikikusa < *ik[a-C]i (-n-) kusa_s.s._ 'an orpine, Sedum
erythrosticum' (= benkei-soo). LLLL (Kn) - 2-0/1-x x-x-x. K: Hn LHLL.

(?4.5)   ikioi: see ikiou (Ch. 6).

5.16   ikisudama < ikizutama (Mg) = *ik[a-C]i_B_ -n- -tu tama_?s.s._ 'a wraith, an
apparition (of a living person)'. LLLHL - 3-0-x x-x-x.

?2.2b   iku- = ika- 'how (much); ? mighty': ikubaku, ikura, ikutu, iku-hisasa.

?4.10   ikubaku < *ika_s.sb_ -n- paka_s.s_ (cf. bakari). LHLL - 0-1-B x-x-x. Km (W)
LHLL; Mr (W [20]) HHLL, LHLL.

?3.5x   ikuha < ikufa ?< *i[-Ci]_?A_ kupa(-)_B_. 'archery target'. LLH (Ir _as surname_)
- x-x-x x-x-x. NS (101b _as surname_) LLH.

?6.7, ?6.22   ikuhadokoro < ikufa_?s.s_ (< ...) -n- tokoro_s.1_. 'the target mound'
(= azuti). LLLLLL - x-5-x x-x-x. K: "Hn LLLLHL" (_inferred?_).

?5.11, ?5.10   iku-hisasa < iku-bisasa (Mg) < *iku₂.₂ᵦ -n- pisa?₍₂.₄₎-[pi]sa. 'for quite a (long) while'. LHHHL (Kz) / LHHHH (Kn) - x-x-x x-x-x. NS (T+ 15) iku-fyisa LH-HH. Register incongruent with etymology?

5.5   ikumidake < ikumyi-dakey < *i-_pre_ kum[a-C]i₈ -n- taka-Ci₂.₁. 'luxuriant bamboo'. x - x-x-x x-x-x. NS (83b [17:122-M]) HLLLx = (Okada) HLLLL; NS (T+ 97) HHHHL.

3.3   ikura < *iku₂.₂ᵦ -ra (< *[a]ra∗₂.₃). 'how much'. HLL - 1-1-A x-x-A. Edo LHL. 1700 Ōsaka HLL. K: Km LHL (attested?). Goka-mura 1; Hattō, Hamada, Hiroshima 0; Matsue, Izumo 3; Sz 2 (but nanbo 3 is usual). Ōsaka, Ise 1:3. Yn igurati A.

3.4   ikusa. 'battle; troops'. LLL - 3/0-1:3-B B-B-x. NS (94a, 122b [14:218-K], 130b) LLL. Km x. Edo HHL. Wakamatsu, NE Kyūshū, Matsue, Izumo 0; Goka-mura 0 (expected reflex); Narada, Hattō, Hamada 3. Ib F = 3.4.

5.8   ikusabune < *ikusa₃.₄ -n- puna-Ci₂.₄. 'warship'. LLLHH - 3-1:5-x x-B-x. Sr qikusabuni B "new?".

5.16   ikusagimi < ikusagyimyi < *ikusa₃.₄ -n- kimi₂.₁. 'battle leader, general'. LLLHL - x-x-x x-x-x. Cf. ikusa no kimi (NS 123b [14:240L-K]) LLL-L(|)HH.

?6.21   ikusaguruma < *ikusa₃.₄ -n- kuruma₃.₁. 'war chariot'. LLLH?LL - 4-x-x x-x-x.

3.7b   ikutu < *iku₂.₂ᵦ -tu. 'how many'. x - 1-1:3-B B-B-A. Km x. 1700 Ōsaka LHH. Goka-mura 1; Sz (but nanbo 3 is usual), Hattō, Hamada, Matsue, Izumo 2. Nk hiKuqCii B; Yn iguci A.

?2.4, ?2.5   ima. 'now'. LH - 1-1-B (B)-B-c. NS (100b, 103a) LH; NS (T 10, 12) LH, (T+ 116) LH. Km (S,W) LH. Mr (Bm) LH-L. Edo LH. Matsue 1 (we expect 2); Izumo 2. Ise 1/1:3; Ōsaka 1; Ib L = 2.4. Yn nai C. K: "Hn and since" LH/LF.

3.5b   imada (?< *ima₂.₄ -n- -ta_suf_). 'not yet'. LLH - 1-2-B (B)-(B)-(C). NS (83b [17:118-M]) LLL; NS (T+ 127 "imata") LLL, (T+ 96) LLH. Km (S) LLH. Nk x (cf. naa C 'already, soon' < im[y]a, naaCaa HHHL 'next day'); Sr naada/maada B; Yn maadi C. K: "Hn LHH/LLH?, Mr-Edo HLL".

?4.11   imamiti < *ima-myiti < *ima₂.₄ miti₂.₁ ('now road'). (name of a road). x - 2-x-x x-x-x. Km (W) LLHL, LLHH. Mr (W [20]) HHxx.

2.3 (?= 1.3|1.3) ime < i-mey < *i₁.₃ₐ ma-Ci₁.₃ₐ ('sleep eye'). 'dream' (= yume). L(|)L - x-x-x x-x-x. Sr qimi B.

5.16   imeawase < ime-afase < *ime₂.₃ (< i-mey < ...) apa-sa-Ci[-Ci]ᴮ. 'reading a dream'. x - x-x-x x-x-x. NS (106a [11:249-K]) LLLHL.

3.4   imina < imi-na < *imyi-na < *im[a-C]i₂.₃₊ᴮ na₁.₂. 'real name (as a grownup); posthumous name'. LLL - 0/2- 0/3-x x-x-x.

2.3   imo < imo/umo ?< *imwo. 'yam'. Lx - 2-2-B x-B-x. Km x. Ib F = 2.3. Sd ?*qyimo(o) B (cf. Shibata 1981).

?2.4, ?2.5   imo < imwo. 'male's sister; beloved girl'. x - 1-2-x x-x-x. NS (70b, 83a, 83a) LH; NS (T 5, 40, 43, 96, 113; 114) LH. Km (S) LH(-H). K: Hn LF (where from?). Cf. wagimo.

?4.5, ?4.6, ?4.11   imogara < *imwo₂.₃ -n- kara₂.₂ᵦ. 'yam stalks; dried yam stalks' (= imoᵃ/ₓi). LLLL (Kn) / xLLH (Ck) - 0-0-x x-x-x. K: "Hn LLHL" (attested?).

3.4   imoi < imofi (?< imafyi < *ima-p[a-C]i?ᴮ (but the extended verb is not attested). (= mono-imoi) 'purifying oneself; vegetarian food'. LLL (Ir) - x-x-x x-x-x.

4.5   imooto < imouto < *imwo-futo < *imwo?₂.₄ pito₂.₂ₐ. 'younger sister'. LLLL - 4-0-B x-B-x. Sz, Hata, Narada 4. Kōchi 4 (Doi 1952:26). 1700 Ōsaka imoto HHL. K: Edo HHHL.

3.4   imoᵃ/ₓi < *imwo₂.₃ (-n-) si₁.₃ᵦ. 'yam stalks; dried yam stalks' (= imogara). LLL (Ir) - x-x-x x-x-x.

6.21   imozyuutome < imoᵃ/ᵢiutome < *imwo₇₂.₄ (-n-) sifyito͟-mye₄.₁ (< ...).
'wife's sisters'. LLLHLL - x-x-x x-x-x.
?*2.1   ina. 'neigh!' *(sound of horse)*: see inaku, inanaku, ibaeru.
2.4   ina(-) 'riceplant': see ine.
2.4   ina. 'nay; disagreement'. LH - 1-3-x x-x-x. NS (T+ kun) L̲L̲. Km (S) LH.
?3.7a/b = 2.4|1.3; ?3.2b   inaba ?< *[z]ina₂.₄ ba₁.₃ₐ (< ...). 'Inaba' *(placename)*.
x-1-2-x x-x-x. Km (W) LH(|)L, HHL. Hamada, Goka-mura 1; Izumo 0; Hattō 3̲.
4.5   inabana (< ?). 'usual (events)'. LLLL - x-x-x x-x-x.
5.16   inabikari < *inabyikari < *[z]ina₂.₄ -n- pika-r[a-C]i₃.₁₊ₐ ('riceplant
flash'). 'lightning'. LLLHL - 3-4-B x-x-x. Ongi-m LLLHL. Nagano (Saku city,
Kgg 133:109b), Narada 1̲; Izumo 2; Hattō, Hamada 3; Sz, Matsue 4; Goka-mura,
Hakata 0. Cf. inazuma, inaturubi.
4.6   inabune < *[z]ina₂.₄ -n- puna-Ci₂.₄. 'a grain boat; ... '. x - 0/3-0-x
x-x-x. Km (W) LLLH.
3.4   inagi < *inagiy < *[z]ina₂,₄ -n- ko͟-Ci₁.₃ₐ. 'drying pole (⋯)'. LLL -
0̲/2̲-0̲-x x-x-x.
?3.1   inago < *inagwo (?< *ina (= ?) -n- kwo₁.₁). [dial.] 'sand' (= isago,
manago, masago, masunago). x - x-x-x x-x-x.
4.9   inaguki < *ina-gukiy < *[z]ina₂.₄ -n- kuku-Ci₂.₃. 'rice stalk'. LHHL -
0/2-3-x x-x-x. (NKD: "inakuki".)
?4.5   inagusa 'rice stalks/ears': see inakusa.
3.1   inaka < winaka < *bina(-)ka. 'country(side)'. (H) - 0-0-A A-A-A. Mg
winaka-bito HHHHx 'country person'. Km x. Edo HHH. Ib H = 3.1. Yn inaga A
(H 1964:71b). Cf. hina.
4.9 = 2.4|2.2 [inakui] < inakufi < ina-kufyi < *[z]ina₂.₄ kupi₂.₂ᵦ. 'rice stalks/
ears' (= inakusa). LH(|)HL (Ir) - x-x-x x-x-x.
?4.5   inaᵏ/ᵍusa < *[z]ina₂.₄ (-n-) kusa₂.₃. 'rice stalks/ears'. LLxx - 0-x-x
x-x-x.
4.5   inamura < *[z]ina₂.₄ mura₂.₁. 'rick'. LLLL - 0-1[H]/0[U]-B x-x-x.
7.30   inaoosedori < inaofosedori < *[z]ina₂.₄ opo-sa-Ci[-Ci]ᵦ -n- to͟ri₂.₁.
'a bird: perhaps the wagtail (= sekirei), the crested ibis (= toki), or the
sparrow (= suzume)'. LLLLLHL - x-x-x x-x-x.
5.7   inatabari < *[z]ina₂.₄ tanpari₂.ₓ. 'a bunch of cut rice plants'. LLLLH -
x-4-x x-x-x. K: "Hn LLLHL" *(mistake?)*.
4.6   inatubi < *ina-tubiy < *[z]ina₂.₄ tunpu-Ci₂.₄. 'a grain of rice' (=
inatubu). xxLH (= *LLLH) - x-x-x x-x-x.
5.6   inaturubi < *ina-turubyi < *[z]ina₂.₄ turunp[a-C]i₂. 'lightning'. LLLLL -
x-x-x x-x-x. Km x. Cf. inabikari, inazuma.
4.5   inazuka < inaduka < *[z]ina₂.₄ -n- tuka₂.₃. 'rick' (= inamura). LLLL -
0-x-x x-x-x. (NKD: "Also inatuka.")
?4.11   inazuma < inaduma < *[z]ina₂.₄ -n- tuma₂.₃ₐ ('spouse of rice').
'lightning'. xxHL (?= *LLHL) - 2/0-0-B x-x-x. Km x. Sz 2. Hakata 0.
?4.5   inazumi < inadumyi < *[z]ina₂.₄ -n- tum[a-C]iₐ. 'a rick of rice; a bunch
of rice plants'. LLxx - 0-x-x x-x-x.
2.4   ine < *ine[y] < *ina-Ci < ?*[z]ina-Ci (cf. kati-sine, kuma-sine, nori-
sine, uru-sine). 'riceplant'. LH - 1-1-B B-B-B̲. Km (W) LH. 1700 Ōsaka LH.
Kōchi 1; Ib L = 2.4. Yn nni B̲ 'rice'. Cf. yone (HH); iine.
4.2   inemuri < wineburi < *wi[y] - ne[y]buri < *bᵃ/ₒ-Ciₐ na-Ciₐ - (n[i]) -
pu-r[a-C]i₇ₐ. 'dozing'. HHHL - 3/4-1:4-B x-A-x. Sr iinibui A.
4.2   inisie < inisi[w]e < inisi-fye < *in[a-C]iₐ -si*ₐₜₜᵣ ₚₑᵣf* piCa₁.ₓ
('direction that is gone'). '(days of) yore, bygone times (days/years/ages)'.
HHHL - 0-0-A x-x-x. Sz 0.

4.3   inoasi ‹ wi-no-asi ‹ *bi₁.₂ no asi₂.₃ (‘boar leg’). ‘the cloth-roller on
a loom’. HHLL - x-0-x x-x-x.

5.x   i-no-huguri ‹ wi-no-fuguri ‹ *bi₁.₂ no punkuri₂.₂ᵦ. ‘boar testicles’.
x - 3-x-x x-x-x. Km x. K: Hn HHHHL (inferred?).

3.1   inoko ‹ wi-no-kwo ‹ *bi₁.₂ no kwo₁.₁. ‘offspring of wild boar; (= inosisi)
wild boar; (= buta) pig’. HHH - x-2-x x-x-x.

3.4   inori ‹ inori ‹ *inor[a-C]iᵦ ‹ *i-ₚᵣₑ nor[a-C]i₄. ‘prayer’. Lxx - 3-0[H]/
2[U]-B B-B-x. Km x. Edo HHL. Ib F= 3.4.

3.5b   inoti. ‘life’. LLH - 1(‹*2)-2-B B-B-C. NS (79b) LLH, (80a) LHH, (95b) xLH,
133a) LLx; NS (T+ 78, 81) LLH, (T+ 23) HLL. Km (S,W) LLH. Mr (Bm) HLL. Edo HLL.
Sapporo, Tappi, Aomori, Akira, Numazu, Narada, Hida (= northern Gifu),
Mino (= southern Gifu), Hattō, Hamada, Matsue, Izumo, Goka-mura, Hiroshima,
Yamaguchi, Wakamatsu, NE Kyūshū, Ōita 2. Ib F̲ = 3.4. Nk qinucii B; Yn nuti C̲
(H 1964:72a). (?‹ i[ki]₂.₄ no [u]ti₂.₂ₐ; ?‹ i[ki]₂.₄ no ti₇₁.₁).

4.10   insaki ‹ “imu-sakyi” = insakyi ?‹ *im[a]₂.₄ sakyi₂.₁; ? ‹ in[a-C]i₄ (or
just *in[a]-₄) saki₂.₁. ‘formerly’. NS (113b [14:34-K]) L⁷HLL (or L⁷FLL).
x - x-x-x x-x-x.

2.3   inu. ‘dog’. LL - 2-2-B B-B-B. Km x. Edo HL. Matsue, Izumo 1̲/2. Ib F = 2.3.
Onna qinnuu B.

2.1   io ‹ iwo ‹ *ibo. ‘fish’: see uo.

2.3   io ‹ ifo ‹ *ipo. ‘hut’ (= iori; cf. ie, iwa). LL - 1̲/2-0̲-x x-x-x. Km x.
K: “Hn-Km LL”. Hiroshima 0̲. Ōsaka, Ise 0̲.

2.3   io ‹ ifo ‹ *i-po. ‘five hundred’. x - x-2-x x-x-x. NS (79a, 90b) LL;
NS (T+ 78) LL.

3.1   iome ‹ “ifome” = /iwome/ ‹ *iwo-mey ‹ *ibo₂.₁ ma-Ci₁.₃ₐ. ‘fish eye(s)’.
HHH - x-x-x x-(B̲)-x. Sr qiyu-nu-mii B̲ ‘plantar warts’ (but qiyu A ‘fish’).

3.6   ioo ‹ yuɔɔ ‹ yuwau (?‹ yuwawa ‹ yu(w)awa ‹ “yu [no̲] afa” ‹ *du₁.₃ₐ no̲
aba₂.₃; ? Korean version of Ch .lyew-.hhwang). ‘sulfur’. LLH (Kn) / “LH” (Zs,
with H on Ch character) - 0-1-B B-B-x. Km x. Aomori 2 (also eo 2); Narada
(yuwoo), Hiroshima 0. Ōsaka, Ise 1; Ib L = 3.6. Sd yuwa(a) B; Sr yuuwaa B.
Cf. yu-no-awa.

3.4 (› 3.1)   iori ‹ ifori ‹ *ipor[a-C]iᵦ ‹ *ipo₂.₃ -r[a-C]i. ‘hut; armed camp’.
LLL - 0̲-0̲-A x-x-x. Ongi LLL. NS (108b, 122b) LLL. Mr (Bm) HHL. 1700 Ōsaka HHL.

4.2   iotori ‹ “ifotori” = /iwotori/ ‹ *ibo₂.₁ t(w)or[a-C]iᵦ. ‘fisher(man)’.
HHHL - x-3-x x-B̲-x. Nk qyuutui HHHL (= A) ‘fishing’, qyuutuyaa LLLHL (= C̲)
‘fisherman’; Sr qiyutuyaa B̲ ‹ *iwotori -a.

4.2   iozuki ‹ “ifozuki” /iwozuki/ ‹ *iwo-zukyi ‹ *ibo₂.₁ -n- suki₂.₁ (‹ suk[a-
C]i₄) (‘fish plow’). ‘dyer’s grape, pokeweed, Phytolaeca esculenta’ (= yama-
goboo). HHHL - x-0-x x-x-x.

2.3   ira. ‘thorn, spine’. LL - x-2-x x-x-x. Km x. Cf. ire.

3.5a   iraka ‹ ira-ka. ‘roof tile (ridge)’. LLH - 0-0[H]/2[U]-B x-B-x. Edo HLL.
Wakamatsu 0. Sr qirica (progressive palatal assimilation in second and third
syllables). K: Mr HLL. An inconclusive discussion of exogenous sources for
this word is found in Miller 1979 (Journal of Korean Studies 1:645).

3.6   irara ‹ ira₂.₃ - [i]ra₂.₃. ‘thorns; (= ira-kusa) nettle; (= karasu-no-
ndoo) vetch, Vicia sativa’. LHH - x-x-x x-x-x.

4.1(?/4.3)   irehimo ‹ irefimo ‹ *ire-fyiᵇ/ₘo ‹ *ira-Ci[-Ci]₄ pinpo₂.₁. ‘a kind
of collar-tie’. x - 0-x-x x-x-x. Km (W) HHHH/HHLL.

?4.1   iriai ‹ iriafi ‹ *iri-afyi ‹ *ir[a-C]i₄ ap[a-C]iᵦ. ‘sunset; the sunset
bell’. HHxx - 0-0-A x-x-x.

3.4   iriko ‹ *ir[a-C]iᵦ ko₁.₃ₐ. ‘dried sea-cucumber’. LLL - 3/2̲-0̲-x x-x-x.

2.3   iro̲. 'color'. LL - 2-2-B B-B-B. Ongi (Iroha) LL. NS (120a) LL. Km (S,W)
LL. Mr (Bm) HL. Edo HL. Ib F = 2.3.

?2.3, ?2.2b   iro̲/ '(same) mother' (= iro-fa LLH). x - x-x-x x-x-x. Km x. See
irome, iroᵗ/ᵈo.

3.2x   iroe < irofe[y] < *iro̲ₛ.ₛ -pa-Ci[-Ci]ₑ. 'inlaying color; decorating,
decoration'. HHL (Zs) - x-x-x x-x-x.

?3.4   iroko (> uroko) ?< *iroku (the third vowel assimilated to the second) <
*iroku[du] (< ... , see irokuzu). 'scale(s) on fish'. LLL (0/1-2-B) x-B-x.
Sr qirici (the later syllables underwent palatal assimilation to the first,
so the reflex is not *qiyuku). Kobama (Yaeyama) iraki, vowels unexplained.

4.6   [irokuzu] < irokudu < *irokuntu (?= iro̲ₛ.ₛ kuntuₛ.ₐ 'color scrap-paper').
'scale(s) on fish'. LLLH - x-3-x x-x-x. Mr (Bm) HHLL. Cf. iroko, uroko.

?2.2b|1.3b   irome ?< *iro̲ₛ.ₛ₆ myeₗ.ₛ₆ (< ...). '(a male's) younger sister by
the same mother' (= iro̲-mo). x - x-x-x x-x-x. NS (96a) HL|H (?= *HL|R).

3.4   irori ?< ir[i-t]ori < *ir[a-C]iₑ t(w)or[a-C]iₑ. 'bonito stock (broth)'.
LLL - x-0̲-x x-x-x.

?3.6, ?3.7x   irori < wirori (< ?). 'hearth'. x - 0-0̲[H]/1[U]-B x-x-x. 1700 Ōsaka
LHH. Goka-mura 1. Nara, Ōsaka 3̲; Kōbe, Himeji 3̲/0̲ [Ōhara].

?2.2b|1.3b (< ?2.3) iroᵗ/ᵈo ?< *iro-do < *iro̲?ₛ.ₛ₆ -n- [o]to̲ₛ.ₛ. 'younger sibling
(with same mother)'. Lxx - x-0̲-x x-x-x. NS (91b, 93a, 95b) HL|H (?= *HL|R).
K: "Hn LLL" (attested?).

3.1   iruka. 'dolphin'. x - 0-0̲[H]/1̲:3̲[U]-A x-x-x. Km x̲. K: Hn-Edo HHH. Sz 0.
Murayama says this is borrowed from Ainu [i]riku 'whale' (Karafuto), 'white
meat of whale' (Hokkaidō).

4.1   irukase ?< yurukͩ/ᵍase ?< *duru-(n[a]-)ka-sa-Ci[-Ci]. 'neglected'.
HHHH (Zs, -k-) - x-0̲-x x-x-x. Register incongruent with etymology.

?2.1   isa. 'whale' (= isana = kuzira). x - x-x-x x-x-x. Cf. isamu.

2.4   isa: see iza.

3.1   isago < isagwo ?< isa (= ?) -n- kwo̲ₗ.ₗ. 'sand' (= masago, masunago,
inago). HHH - 0-0̲-x x-x-x. NS (T+ 28) HHH. Km x. Mr (Bm) HHH. Edo HHH.
Cf. suna, sunago; iso.

3.1   isami < isamyi < *isa-m[a-C]i?ₐ/ᵦ. '(brave) spirit, bravery'. x - 0̲-0̲-x
x-(A)-x. NS (101b) HHH.

?3.1   isana < *isaₛ.ₗ naₗ.ₛₑ ('whale fish'). 'whale' (= kuzira). x - 0̲-x-x
x-x-x.

5.2   isanato̲ri < *isana?ₛ.ₗ (< isa?ₛ.ₗ naₗ.ₛₑ) to̲r[a-C]iₑ. 'whaling'.
x - 3-4-x x-x-x. NS (Okada) HHHHL; NS (T+ 68) HᵻL-HR = HHH|HL.

4.1   isͩ/ᵤarai < "wizarawi" < *wi[y]-ˢ/ᵤarafyi < *bͩ/ₒ-Ci[-Ci]ₐ (-n-) sara-p[a-
C]iₐ. 'one's seated bottom'. HHHH - 3-x-x x-x-x.

3.1   isari < wisari (< ?). 'plowshare (of a Chinese plow)'. HHH - x-0̲-x x-x-x.

4.x   isasaka (?< i[to]ₛ.ₛ₆ sasa[ya]kaₑₐ.ₗₗ < ...). 'a little, somewhat;
slight' (adv, adj-n). LLH?H?H - 2-0-B x-x-x. Km x. Mr (Bm) HLLL. K; Km LLHL
(where attested?), Mr-Edo HLLL. Cf. [isasake-]ₐdⱼ ᵦ.

?2.1   ise. 'Ise' (placename). x - 1̲-2̲-A x-x-x. NS (Okada) HH/HL; NS (T 8) LL,
(T 78) LH̲. Km (W) HH/HL. K: Edo HL. Ib H1̲ = 2.2.

2.2b   isi. 'stone'. HL - 2-2-A A-A-A(/?B). Km (S) HL. Edo HL. Nagano (Kudō 200),
Matsue, Izumo 0; Hattō, Hamada, Goka-mura 2. Ib H1 = 2.2. Yn ici-bugu A (H 1964:
71b) / B (H 1964:179a mistake?), ici A 'ox-dragged stone to harden field soil'.
Cf. iso, isago.

?4.1   isibai < isibafi < *isiₛ.ₛ₆ -n- fafiₛ.ₗ (< ...) ('rock ash'). 'lime'.
?HHHx - 0/2̲-1̲:3̲-A x-A-x.

4.2   isibasi < *isiₛ.ₛ₆ -n- pasiₛ.ₛ₆. 'stone bridge'. HHHL - 0-2-A x-A-x.

4.7   isibusi < *isi*ₐ.ₐᵦ -n- pus[a-C]i. 'a kind of goby *(fish)* resembling a
bullhead'. LLHH - 0-x-x x-x-x. Register incongruent with etymology.

5.2   isidatami < isi-datamyi < *isi*ₐ.ₐᵦ -n- tatami*ₐ.ₗ* (< tatam[a-C]i*ₐ*). 'stone
paving'. HHHHL - 3(/5)-4-A x-x-x. Sz 0.

4.3   isigame < *isigamey < *isi*ₐ.ₐᵦ -n- kamaCi*ₐ.ₐ*. 'terrapin'. HHLL - 0-0/1-x
x-x-x. K: Hn HHHH *(misprint?)*.

4.3   isigani < *isi*ₐ.ₐᵦ -n- kani*ₐ.ₗ*. 'rock crab'. HHLL - 0-0-x x-x-x.

5.2   isihaziki < *isi*ₐ.ₐᵦ pansik[a-C]i*ᵦ*. 'catapult; stone-tossing (game)'.
HHHHL - 3-1:4-x x-x-x.

?4.1   isikoro < isi*ₐ.ₐᵦ* - koro*ₐ.ₓ* ?< isi-kwo*ₐₐ.ₓ* -ro*ₛᵤf* (< -ra, *last vowel
assimilated to 3d vowel*). 'a piece of stone; rubble'. x - 3-0-A x-x-x. Sz 0.
Dial. isi-gora/gara. (Miller has an Altaic etymology for koro.) Cf. isi-kure.

?4.1   isikure < *isi*ₐ.ₐᵦ* kure*ₐ.ₓ* (< ...). 'a piece of stone; rubble' (=
isikoro). x - 0/3-0-x x-x-x.

4.1   isimoti < *isi*ₐ.ₐᵦ* m̲o̲t[a-C]i*ᵦ*. 'a kind of croaker
(fish)'. HHHH - 0/3/4-1/4̲-x x-x-x.

4.4 (= 2.2-n̲o̲ 1.3)   isinoti < *isi*ₐ.ₐᵦ* n̲o̲ ti*ₗ.ₐₐ* (? < *tu-Ci) ('stone milk/
teat'). 'stalactite'. HLLL - x-x-x x-x-x.

?*4.3 < ?5.4   *isi-tuti = isi-tutui ?< isi*ₐₐ.ₐᵦ* tutu-[C]i*ₐₐ.ₐₐₐ.ₐ*. 'sword with a
stone-head haft'. x - x-x-x x-x-x. NS (T+ 9) HHLL. Cf. kubu-tuti.

4.1   isizue < isizuwe < *isi*ₐ.ₐᵦ* -n- suwe[y]*ₐₐ.ₗ* (< *suba-Ci[-Ci]*ₐ* <
?*zuba-···*ₐ*). 'cornerstone, foundation'. HHHH - 0/3̲/4̲-0-A x-A-x. Sr qisizi A.

2.1   iso < iswo. 'beach; rock'. x - 0-0-A A-x-x. Km (W) HH. Edo HH. Aomori,
Hakata 0. Ib H = 2.1. Hateruma isyon 'sand' (see Ch. 1, §26). Cf. isi, isago.

-        isu(-no-ki):   *see* yusi.

?3.1   isuka (< ?). 'crossbill, grosbeak' *(bird)*. x - 0-0-x x-x-x.

2.4   ita. 'board'. x - 1-1-B B-B-B̲. Ongi-m LH. Km (S) LH. Edo LH. Hattō,
Hamada, Hiroshima 0̲; Narada, Goka-mura 1; Matsue, Izumo 2 *(expected reflex)*.
Ib L = 2.4. Nk hiCaa B̲; Onna qiicaa B.

3.4/3.5x   itabi < itafi (< ?; cf. itigo). 'Japanese fig' (= itabi-kazura). LLL/LLH -
x-x-x x-x-x. NS (T+ kun) LLH.

?3.4   itade < *ita*ₐₐⱼ ᵦ* -n- ta-Ci*ₗ.ₐₐ*. 'wounded hand'. x - 0̲-0̲/1̲-B x-x-x.
NS (T+ 29) ita["]te LLₑ. Sz 3.

3.4   itado < ita-ᵗ/ₐwo < *ita*ₐ.ₐ* (-n-) two*ₐ.ₗ*. plank door'. x - 2-1[U]/1:3[H]-B
x-x-x. NS (82c[17:113-M]) LLL; (Okada 2:45) HHH *(misprint?)* / (Okada 1:60a)
LLL; NS (T+ 96) LLL.

4.9   itadori ?< *itamitori < *ita-m[a-C]i*ᵦ* t(w)or[a-C]i*ᵦ* ('pain take').
'Japanese knotweed'. LHHL - 0/1-1:4-B x-x-x.

3.4   itai < ita-wi < *ita*ₐ.ₐ* bi*ₗ.ₐₐ*. 'a plank(ed) well'. x - 1-x-x x-x-x.
Km (W) LLL.

3.4   itami < itamyi < *ita-m[a-C]i*ᵦ*. 'pain'. (LLH *inf*) - 3-0̲-x x-x-x. Mr (Bm)
HHL. Edo H̲H̲H̲. Aomori 3. Izumo 0̲; Goka-mura 0 *(expected reflex)*. Ib F = 3.4.

3.4   itati. 'weasel'. LLL 3/0̲-2-B x-x-x. Km x. Narada 3; Sapporo, Akita, Ōita
2̲; Matsumoto, Numazu, Matsue, Izumo, Hiroshima 0̲; Hamada 3/0̲; Goka-mura 1̲ *(we
expect 0)*. Kōchi, Sakawa 1̲:3̲; Ib F = 3.4.

5.16   itatigusa < *itati*ₐ.ₐ* -n- kusa*ₐ.ₐ*. 'forsythia'. LLLHL - x-4-x x-x-x.
'forsythia'. LLLHL - x-4-x x-x-x.

5.7   itatihaze < itati-faze < *itati*ₐ.ₐ* faze*ₐ.ₐᵦ* (?< *pansaCi) ('weasel
sumac'). 'forsythia' (= itatigusa = rengyoo). LLLLH (Ir) - 3-5-x x-x-x.

?7.10 = 3.4|4.1   itatihazikami < itati-fazikamyi < *itati*ₐ.ₐ* pansikami*ₐₐ.ₗ*
(< ...). 'Japanese pepper tree, Zanthoxylum piperitum (= sansyoo);
Macrocarpium officinale (= sansyuu)'. LLLxxxx - 4-x-x x-x-x.

?3.4   itaya < *ita*2.4* da*1.3b*. 'shingle roof; shingle-roofed house; shingle
merchant; (= itaya-kaede) maple'. (LLL-···) - 0/2-1-x x-x-x. Edo HHL.
5.7   itayagai < *itaya*73.4* (< *ita*2.4* da*1.3b* -n- kapi*2.3* ('shingle-roof
shell'). 'a kind of bivalve'. LLLLH (Kn, Ck) - 3-4-x x-x-x. K: "Hn LLLHL"
(mistake?).
?4.5   itazuki < itatuki ?< *ita*adj B* tuk[a-C]i*B* ('painful contact'). 'a kind of
sharp-pointed arrowhead'. LLLx - x-0-x x-x-x. K: Hn HHHH *(mistake? register
incongruent)*. Cf. itazuku.
4.1   itazura < itadura < *itantura(< ?). 'prank, mischief; idle'. HHHH -
0-1[H]/0[U]-A x-A-x. Mr (Bm) HHHH. Sz 0.
2.4   iti. 'market'. LH - 1-1-B x-x-x. Km x. Ib L = 2.4. Perhaps < *iti[y] <
*itu-Ci (based on M 513); cf. Kawabata 1966:136, Zdb 83a (itu-siba).
3.7a   itibi (< ?). 'Indian mallow'. LHL - 0[Mkz]-1:3-x x-x-x. Cf. itigo.
-           itibiko: *see* itigo.
3.7a/b < 4.9 itigo < iti[bi]go < itibyigwo < itibyikwo (?< *it¹/*u*-n-pi kwo*1.1*).
'strawberry'. LHL - 0/1-1:3-B B-B-x. NS (T+ kun) itibyikwo LHHL. Matsue 0/3;
Narada, Yamaguchi, Hattō, Hamada, Hiroshima 0; Izumo 0 (Hiroto and Ōhara),
3 (Kobayashi); Nagano (Kudō 53), Tappi, Aomori 1; Hakata 2/1, ygr 0. Kōchi
(Kobayashi) 3; Ōsaka, Ise 1:3; Ib L2 = 3.5/7. Sr qicubi B.
4.5   itigura < *iti*2.4* -n- kura*2.3*. 'a kind of market warehouse (in Nara and
Heian times)'. LLLL - 0/2-0-x x-x-x.
?3.4   itii < itiwi (= "itifyi" < ?). 'Japanese yew, Taxus cuspidata' (=
araragi). LLL - 2/0-3-x x-x-x. NS (T+ kun) itifyi LLL. Km x. (Said to be
iti-wi 'grade one' < Ch yet-hhyuy'.)
5.11   itikomame < witiko-mame[y] < *bitiko*3.x* (< ?) mamaCi*2.3*. 'a round jewel-
like bean'. LHHHL - 3-4-x x-x-x.
2.4   ito (?< ito/itwo). 'thread'. LH - 1-1-B B-B-C. Km (W) LH. Matsue, Izumo
2; Hattō, Hamada, Hiroshima (Okuda) 0. Ib L = 2.4. Sd qyitho(o) B 'thread',
qyithyu(u) B 'silk'. Sr qiicuu B.
?2.2b   ito < ito/itwo. 'extremely' *(adv)*. HL - 1-2-x x-x-x. NS (128b) HL,
(Okada) LL. Km (S) HL. K: Edo HH. Cf. iyo; itaru*A*; ita*adj B*.
2.x   [ito] < itwo. *(prefix/adnoun)* 'young, lovable'; *(noun)* 'beloved child'.
x - x-x-x x-x-x.
2.x   ito(-) < itwo(-) *(bnd n)* 'interval': *see* itoma; itonamu.
3.5b   itoko < itokwo < *itwo*2.x* kwo*1.1* ('beloved child'). 'cousin'. LLx - 2-2-B
B-B-C. NS (T+ 28) LLL. Km x. Edo HLL. 1700 Ōsaka HHL. Tk 1/2 according to
Hiroto and Ōhara, and Mkz; but Aomori, Narada, Hattō, Hamada, Matsue, Izumo,
Goka-mura, Yamaguchi, Hata, NE Kyūshū, Wakamatsu and Hakata are all 2. Ib H2 =
3.2. Nk hiCi(i)Kuu B.
3.4   itoma < itwo*2.x* - ma*1.1*. 'leisure; furlough'. LLL - 3/0-0-B x-(B)-x.
Ongi-m LLL. NS (122a) LLL. Km x. Mr (Bm) HHH. Edo HHL. K: Mr-Edo HHL. Narada,
Hattō, Hamada, Izumo 0; Goka-mura 0 *(expected)*; Matsue 3. Ib *(rare)* F = 3.4.
3.7x   itori (?= i-tori; ?< *i-tu ari (< *ar[a-C]i*B*)). 'five people'. LHL - x-3-x
x-(B)-x. Also itutori, itutari, whence Sr qiçitai B.
4.6   itosuzi < ito*2.3* sudi*2.4* (< ...). 'thread(- line); (harp) string; course
(of events)'. LLLH - 2-3-x x-x-x.
?2.3   itu(-) (?< i -tu, cf. iso, i[f]o). 'five'. *See* itu-ka, itu-tu; cf. itori.
?2.3   itu(-) ?< i*1.3a* -tu*pcl*. 'sacred'. NS (T+ kun) LL. *See* ituku, itukusi-;
cf. yu, imu, ika-.
?2.4, ?2.5   itu. 'when; sometime'. LH - 1-1-B A-A-A. Km (W) LH. Edo LH. K: Hn-Km-
Edo LF. Hakata 0 but itu ka 1. Ib L = 2.4. Nk hiCii B. Ōsaka itu zo (LLH)
'sometime' (= itu ka).

3.4   ituka < itu₇₂.₃ (?= i -tu) -ka₇₁.₃. 'five days'. x - 3/0-2(adv 0)-x B-x-x.
     Edo HHL. Ib F = 3.4 (also adverbial).
3.7b = ?2.4/5|1.3   itu( )ka < itu₇₂.₄/₅ - ka_Pcl ₁.₃. 'sometime'. LHL - 1-1:3-A
     A-A-A. Hakata 1. Nk hiCii-Ka A.
?3.7a   ituki < itukyi < *i₁.₃ₐ tuk[a-C]i_B. 'place of ritual purification; place
     to celebrate a god, sacred grove'. x - 0/2-0-x x-x-x. NS (83c [11:261-M]) LHL;
     NS (T+ 60) LHL.
?3.5b, ?3.4   itutu < itu₇₂.₃ -tu (?= i -tu -tu). 'five'. LLL - 2-2-B (B)-B-B.
     NS (98b) LLL. Km (S) LLH(-H). Mr (Bm) HLL. 1700 Ōsaka HLL. Sapporo, Tappi,
     Aomori, Akita, Matsumoto, Numazu, Narada, Hiroshima, Hata, Wakamatsu, Ōita 2.
     Toyama 1:3 (expected reflex); Suzu 1:3 (we expect 0); Ib F = 3.4.
     Mg itutu wo fa/ba, junctures before the particles? Cf. iso, i[f]o; ituka.
2.2a   iwa < ifa < *ipa. 'crag, rock'. HL - 2-2-A A-A-x. NS (71a) HH(-···), (72c,
     105a) HL. NS (T 107, T+ kun) LL; (T 32, T+ 56, T+ kun) LH, (T 45) HH. Km (W)
     HL. Edo HL. Aomori 0. Ib H1 = 2.2.
4.2   iwabasi < ifabasi < *ipa₂.₂b -n- pasi₂.₂b. 'stepping-stone bridge; stone
     bridge'. HHHL - 0-x-x x-x-x.
4.2   iwagoke < ifa-gokey < *ipa₂.₂b -n- kokey₂.₃ (< *ko₁.₃ₐ ka-Ci₇₁.₁).
     (1) 'rock moss'; (2) (= iwatake) 'a kind of mushroom'; (3) (= iwahiba)
     'selaginella'. HHHL ('selaginella') - 2-0-x x-x-x.
4.2   iwagumi < ifagumyi < *ipa₂.₂b -n- kum[a-C]i_B. (1) 'a pile of rocks';
     (2) (= iwagoke = iwahiba) 'selaginella'; (3) (= hitotuba) 'Pyrrhosia lingua';
     (4) (= kokemono) 'curberry, bilberry'. HHHL - 0-0-x x-x-x.
5.6   iwaiuta < ifafi-uta < *ifafyi₂.₃ (< *ipap[a-C]i_B) uta₂.₂b. 'a celebratory
     song'. x - 2/3-4-x x-x-x. Km (S) LLLL.
5.2   iwaᵏ/ɡusuri < ifakusuri < *ipa₂.₂b (-n-) kusuri₃.₇ₐ. 'dendrobium' (=
     sekkoku). HHHHL (Ir, -k-) - 3-4-x x-x-x.
4.1   iwamuro < ifamuro (= ifa - murwo) < *ipa₂.₂b murwo₂.₃. 'stone cellar'.
     HHHH - 0-0-x x-x-x.
3.2a   iwane < ifane < *ipa₂.₂b na-Ci₁.₃ₐ. 'the base of a rock; a large rock'.
     x - 0-0-x x-x-x. NS (Okada) HHL. Km x. 1700 Ōsaka HHL.
2.2-no 2.3 iwa-no-kawa < ifa-no kafa < *ipa₂.₂b no kapa₂.₃ ('rock hide').
     'Pyrrhosia lingua' (= iwagumi = hitotuba). HLLLL - x-4-x x-x-x.
3.1   iwao < ifafo < *ipa₂.₂b pwo₁.₃b. 'crag'. HHH - 0-0-A x-x-x. Km x. 1700
     Ōsaka HHH. F = 3.4. K: Mr HHL.
3.1   iware < ifare < *ipa-ra-[C]i_A. 'reason, explanation'. Hxx - 0-0-A x-x-x.
     Edo HHH. K: Mr-Edo HHH. Sz 0.
3.1   iwasi (< i[wo₂.₁ yo]wa-si_adj B pred 'fish is weak'< ...). 'sardine(s)'.
     HHH - 0-0-A x-x-x. Km x. Narada yuwasi. Ib H = 3.1.
5.3   iwasimizu < ifasimidu < *ipa₂.₂b si-myidu₃.₆ (< ...). 'water from a rock
     spring'. HHHLL - 3-4-x x-x-x. Km (W) HHHLL.
5.2   iwatutuzi < ifa-tutuzi < *ipa₂.₂b tutunsi₇₃.₃ (< ?). (1) 'bilberry,
     Vaccinium praestans';   (2) 'Rhododendrum yedoense' (= renge-tutuzi);
     (3) 'wisteria growing around rocks'. HHHHL - 3-4-x x-x-x. Km (W) HHHHL.
3.1   iwaya < ifa-ya < *ipa₂.₂b da₁.₃b. 'grotto'. HHH - 0-0-A x-x-x. Km (S) HHH.
     Edo HHH.
?2.1   iya (< *ida) = iyo ('more and more; very'). HH-··· - x-x-x x-x-x.
     NS (T+ 36) LH, (T+ 40)L.
?2.2x,?2.1   iya < wiya 'respect': see uya. Cf. [iyabiru].
5.2   iya-itoko < *ida₇₂.₁ itwo-kwo₃.₅b. 'parent's cousin's child'. HHHHx -
     3-4-x x-x-x. K: Hn HHHHL.

?4.3   iya-iya < *ida$_{?z.1}$ ida$_{?z.1}$. 'more and more' (= iyo-iyo). HHxx (?= *HHLL) -
x-x-x x-x-x.

5.9   iyasibito < iyasi-fyito̲ < *ida-si$_{edj A}$ (-n-) pito̲$_{z.za}$. 'low-class people,
menials'. x - x-x-x x-x-x. NS (113a) LLHHH. Register incongruent with etymology

?2.1   iyo < *ido. 'gradually intensifying, more and more; extreme(1y), very'
(adverb, prefix). HH-··· - x-x-x x-x-x. Also iya. Cf. ito 'very'.

4.3   iyo-iyo < *ido$_{?z.1}$ ido$_{?z.1}$. 'more and more (= iya-iya); truly, for sure,
surely; at any moment now' (adverb). HHLL - 2-2-A x-x-x. Km x. Mr (Bm) HHLL.

4.11   iyoyoka (Mg) < iyoyaka < *ido$_{?z.1}$ -da-ka. '(trees) standing tall/majestic;
being bright, clear, distinct' (adj-n). LLHL - x-x-x x-x-x.

2.4   iza < i^a/$_z$a (< ?). (1) -s- 'well let me think (= I really can't say, I
don't rightly know)'; (2) -z- 'hey (come on) let's do it!' (interjection). LH -
1-2-A x-x-x. NS (T+ 28, 29, 35) L̲L̲; (T+ kun) HH but iza-wa LH-F̲. Cf. izanau.

-        izarai: see isarai.

?4.5   izayoi < isayofi < isaywofyi$_{?B}$ (< ...). 'wavering'; (= ~ no tuki) the
16th night of the lunar month'. x - 0̲-0̲-A̲ x-x-x. Km (W) LLLL, LHHH, HHLL.

-        izu-··· < idu- < *int^a/$_o$ (?< *entu, cf. Thorpe 233): see izuko, izure,
izuti.

3.6   izuko < iduko/iduku < ?*int^a/$_o$ko. 'where' (= doko). LHH - 1/0-1[U]/1̲:3̲[H]-
uA x-x-x. NS (105b, 118a) LHH. Km (W) LHH. Edo LHH. See doko.

?4.2   izumai < wi-zumafi < wi[y]-zumafyi < *b^a/$_o$-Ci[-Ci]$_A$ -n- suma-p[a-C]i$_B$.
'one's way of sitting; (seated) appearance'. HHxxx (?= *HHHL) - 0/2-3-A x-x-x.

?3.7a ?< 3.4   izumi < idumyi < *int[a]-u$_B$ mi[na]$_{z.1}$ ('it emerges, water'). '(well)
spring'. LLL - 1[new]/0-1:3[H]/1̲-B x-B-x. Mr (Bm) HHL. Narada, Wakamatsu,
Hakata 0. Ib F = 3.4.

3.6   izure < idure < ?*int^a/$_o$-re[y] ?< *int^a/$_o$-ra-Ci. 'which one' (= dore);
'sometime'. (?RHH/)LHH-0-1-A̲ B-B-A̲. NS (106b) LHH. Km (S) LHH. Mr (Bm) LHH.
Edo LHH. Yn ndi A. Aomori (rare) 0̲ (we expect 2); Ib L = 3.6. See dore; §7.1.

3.7b   izuti < iduti < *ind^a/$_o$-ti. 'which way, where (= doti[-ra]). LHL - 1-1̲-x
x-x-x. Km (W) LHL - 1-1̲-x x-x-x. Km (W) LHL — also i["]tura LHH?< *idu[ti]-ra.
Edo LHH. See doti(ra).

1.1   ka. 'mosquito'. x - 0-0-A (B̲-B̲-C̲). Ongi kaa HH. Edo H. Ib H = 1.1.
Sd gadyaami B, Nk gazaami B, Sr gazan B, Yn kadanku C: etymologies uncertain,
but the ga- may be < *[ ] -n- ka··· (see Ch. 1, §26). Cf. kaya.

1.1   ka. 'fragrance'. H - 0/1-0-A x-x-x. NS (120a 'oil of orchid') H. NS (T+
kun) ka kunomiy H|LLH 'fragrant fruit', ka tabu 'give incense' H(|)LL. Km (W)
H(-H). Ib (rare) H = 1.1. Cf. [kaza]; kagu$_A$, [kabu]$_A$, kaguwasi$_{edj A}$.

?1.1   (-)ka. 'hair' (= ke): see siraga. Cf. kawa 'skin; fur', kami 'hair (on the
head)', ...

1.2   ka(-). (1) (?< *ga) 'that (distal)' (= a-): see kanata/anata, kano/ano,
kare/are, kasiko/asoko; kayoru. NS (105b [11:236- K], 110b [11:337-K]) H.
Km (W) H. Edo F. (2) 'this (proximal)' (= ko̲-): see kaku/koo. Cf. ko-, so-.

1.3a   ka. 'deer' (= sika). L - x-0-x x-x-x. NS (T+ kun) a ka 'my deer' L(|)L.
Km x. Cf. kago. (K: "Hn-Km x.")

?1.3a   (-)ka. 'plate (to heap food on); utensil, jar': see mika$_{z.zb}$, hiraka$_{z.1}$,
kame$_{z.s}$; ke$_{?1.2,?1.1}$ 'container'.

?1.3a   (-)ka. 'day': see hatuka$_{z.1}$, ituka$_{z.4}$, muika$_{z.1}$, nanoka$_{z.4}$, tooka$_{?z.1}$,
yooka$_{z.1}$; koyomi$_{z.4}$; ke$_{1.za}$ 'days'; ?-uka.

(?1.3b >) 2.4 ka < kwa < "kuwa" (< Ch .hwa): ~ no kutu 'a kind of formal leather
shoe'. LH(xLL) - x-x-x x-x-x.

1.x   (-)ka. 'place': *see* arika, inaka, naka, sumika, yaka; kado; kakurega, tutuga, yosuga; yake, hatake; (-)ko. Cf. toko, tokoro, koro.

2.1   kaba = kama/gama (?< *kanpa). 'bulrush'. HH - 1-0[H]/1[U]-A x-(A)-x. Sz, Hattō, Hamada, Matsue, Izumo 0. Sr kaba-(yaci) A. Is Kt U a misprint?

?2.5 < 3.2a   kaba ?< kanifa (Mg) < *kanipa. 'birch'. HHL - 1-1:3-x x-x-x. Aomori 0. Ib *(rare)* H1 = 2.2. Ōno cites Ainu kari-npa from Kindaichi Kyōsuke; cf. karínpa 'cherrytree' in Hattori 1964 (Ainu hōgen jiten).

3.1   kabane < *kanpane < ?*kara𝑧.₂ᵦ (-n-) pone𝑧.𝑠 (< ...). 'corpse'. HHH - 0-0-x x-x-x. Km (S) HHH. Edo HHH. Narada 3. Ib *(rare)* F = 3.4 (?/H = 3.1). Cf. si-kabane; kara, karada; hone.

5.2   kabanegusa < *kanpane (< ...) -n- kusa𝑧.𝑠. *(1)* 'Paederia scandens' (= heso-kazura); *(2)* 'Alpinia kumatake' (= kawanegusa = kumatake-ran). HHHHL - 3-x-x x-x-x.

?3.4   kabati < "kafati" (Mg) ?= /kawati/ , kamati < *kanpati (< ?). 'cheekbone(s); side-railings on a wagon; frame(work); [dial.] head'. LLx - 0/3-0-A B-B-B.

2.1   kabe < *kabey < *kanpaCi. 'wall'. HH - 0-0-A A-A-x. Km x. Ib H = 2.1. Sr kubi A: the first vowel has perhaps assimilated to the following labial, but Miyako (Hirara) kuubi implies proto-Ryūkyūan *ko(o)be. Cf. kaba[f]i < *kanpap[a-C]i 'shelter, protect' (*see* kabau).

2.1   [kabi/kai] < (*)kabyi/kafyi < *ka(n)pi ?< *kam[i i]pi ('top rice'). 'sprout, shoot; (top of) unhusked ear of grain'; *(Heian confusion with kamyi)* 'handle'. HH - x-x-x x-x-x. Kabyi is attested only in ta-kabyi (NS kun-chū), a Heian confusion with ta-kamyi 'sword handle'.

2.1   kabi < kabiy < *kanpᵃ/ₑ-Ci (? < verb inf 'sprout'). 'mildew, mold'. (x) - 0-0-A x-B-x. Km x. Sz 2; Hiroshima 0, Ōsaka, Ise 0; Ib H = 2.1. Nk haabui C, Sr kaabui B (?< ka[fa]-bᵃ/ₑri B 'skin-[?]'). Cf. koozi < kamu-dati.

2.1   kabu < *kanpu. 'stump; (= kabura) turnip'. (x) - 0-0-A x-x-x. Ib H = 2.1.

?*2.3   kabu < *kanpu. 'head'. x - x-x-x x-(B)-x. Sr kabu B 'part of hairpin'. Cf. kabu-tuti; kaburu𝐵, kabus(er)u𝐵; kami𝑧.𝟺; koomuru𝐵, koobe?𝟹.𝟼,?𝟹.𝟽; kao𝑧.₁.

?3.1   kabura < kabu-ra < *kanpu𝑧.₁ - [a]ra∗𝑧.𝑠. 'turnip'. x - 0-1-A x-x-x. 1700 Ōsaka LHH. Ib L = 3.6. Cf. abura-na.

?3.1   kabura < *kanpura (?< *kanpu𝑧.₁ - [a]ra∗𝑧.𝑠 'turnip'). 'a whistle attached to the end of an arrow'. (HHH-···) - 0-1-x x-x-x. Edo HHH.

5.2   kaburaeri < kabura-weri < *kanpura𝑠.₁ (< ...) ber[a-C]i𝐵 (< ...). 'a bent-tip chisel (originally used to carve out arrow-whistles)'. HHHHL - x-x-x x-x-x.

6.2   kaburamimizu < *kanpura?𝟹.₁ ?mimi(n)su𝑠.𝟼 (< ...). 'a kind of earthworm'. HHHHHL - x-x-x x-x-x.

3.6   kaburo ("after Edo also kamuro"; < ?). 'a child's hair-style, a child with the kaburo hair-style; bald (head); treeless'. LHH - 0-1-x x-x-x. Edo LHH.

3.4   kabuti (< ?). 'bitter orange (= daidai); Japanese nutmeg (= kaya = kae)'. LLL - x-x-x x-x-x.

3.7b   kabuto (dial. kamuto, kanputo) < ?*kanputo (?< *kan-puta < *kan[pu]?∗𝑧.𝑠 puta𝑧.₁ 'head lid'). 'helmet'. LHL - 1-1:3-B x-B-x. Edo LHL. Tappi, Aomori, Hakata 1. Toyama 1:4 *(expected)*; Suzu 2 *(we expect 1)*; Ib L2 = 3.5/7.

-        kabu-tuti < *kanpu𝑧.₁ tutu-Ci𝑧.𝟺?<∗𝟹.𝟻. 'sword with a knob-head haft' (= kubu-tuti/-tutui). x - x-x-x x-x-x. NS (T + 9) HHHH.

?2.2b   kado < kadwo ?< *ka-n- two₁.₁ (?'great door', cf. [i]kᵃ/ₑ-, Middle Korean ˈha- and ˈkhu-). 'gate'. HL - 1-2-B x-x-x. Km (W) HL. Edo HL. Narada 1. Ib H1 = 2.2. Matsumoto 1974:120 suggests ka- 'place' for the first element; cf. yaka.

2.4   kado < kadwo < *kantwo (?< *kan[a] two 'one door'*1.1* or 'one keen'*adj B*).
'corner; ability; item, point, charge, grounds'. LH - 1-1-B x-B-B̲. NS (92a
[11:12-K]) LH. Ib L = 2.4. Nk ᵇ/ₖaduu B̲.

?3.1   kadobi < kadwobiy < *kantwo*?2.2b* (< ...) -n- po̲-Ci*1.3a*. 'ceremonial fire
in front of gate'. LLx - 2̲-0-x x-x-x. (The Mg register is incongruent in this
and the adjacent entry niwabi.).

?4.2   kadomori < *kadwomori < *kantwo*2.2b* (< ...) mor[a-C]i*7B*. 'gate guard'.
HHHL - x-x-x x-x-x.

3.1   kadoya < *kadwoya < *kantwo*2.2b* (< ...) da*1.3b*. 'gate-house'. HHH - x-x-x
x-x-x.

2.3   kae < kafe (< ?). (1) 'cypress (and similar trees)' (= hinoki-ka);
(2) 'Japanese nutmeg tree (= kaya) or its fruit (= kae/kaya no mi)'. LL - x-0̲-x
x-x-x.

3.6 < 4.1 kaede < kafede < kafyeru-te < kafiruᵗ/de*4.1* < *kapiru*2.6* (-n-) ta-Ci*1.3a*
('frog-hand [shape leaf]'). 'maple'. LHH - 0-1-B x-x-x. Km x. Aomori 3̲ (we
expect 2); Sz 0. Ib F = 3.6. Register incongruent with etymology?

5.6 = 3.4|2.3 kaerigoto < kaferiᵏ/goto < kafyeri-ᵏ/goto̲ < *kapi-r[a-C]i (-n-)
koto̲*2.3*. 'reply; report'. x - 0-0-x x-x-x. NS (103b [11:182-K], 106b [11:251-
K]) LLL(|)LL, (104b [11:212-K] mistake or misprint?) HLLLL. K: Edo HHHHL.

3.5x   kaeru < kaferu < *kafyeru < *kapir[a]-u (directly nominalized vi.). 'a
two-year-old hawk (that has moulted [and returned to shape])'. LLH - x-x-x
x-x-x. Cf. katagaeri.

3.6   kaeru < kafyeru < ?*kapiru (cf. kairude). 'frog' (= kawazu < kafadu <
*kapantu). x - 0-1-B x-x-x. Km x. K: Hn LHH (attested?). Aomori (usually gɛro
1), Narada (kaaru), Goka-mura 1; Hattō, Hamada, Matsue, Izumo, Hiroshima,
Yamaguchi, NE Kyūshū, Hakata 0. Ōsaka, Ise 1; Ib gyaaru L = 3.6. Kg gairo B;
Amada, Ikaruga, Kasa gaeru ?< *[ ] -n- kaeru (see Ch. 1, §26).

-        [kaerute] > kaede 'maple': see kaede.

2.5   kaga(-) 'shade, shadow; sunshine, light': see kage.

3.4   kagami < kagamyi < *kankami < *kanka*2.8* mi[-Ci]/mi[Ca-Ci]*B*. 'mirror'.
LLL - 3-2-B B-B-B. Km x. Mr (Bm) HHL. Edo HHL. Sapporo 2̲; NE Kyūshū 0̲. Kōchi 3;
Ib F = 3.4. Hateruma kangan. Cf. kage, kagayaku.

3.4   kagami (< ?). 'Ampelopsis japonica' (= kagamigusa). LLL (Ir) - x-x-x x-x-x

3.5x   kagami (< ?). 'Metaplexis japonica' (= gagaimo). LLH - x-x-x x-x-x.

5.16   kagamikake < *kagamyi-kakey < *kankami*2.4* (< ...) kaka-Ci[-Ci]*B*. 'mirror
stand'. LLLHL - 3-4-x x-x-x. K: Hn LLLLLL (misprint?). NKD Kt accent unclear.

3.1   kagari (?< *kanka-r[a-C]i). 'bonfire' (= kagari-bi). HHH - 0-0-x x-x-x.
Narada 3̲. Ib 'lamp charcoal'.

-        kagasi 'scarecrow': see kakasi.

?3.1   kagati < *kankati ?< *kanka*2.8* ti*?1.2* (?< ti[y] < *tu-Ci) ('shining
thistle'). 'bladder/ground cherry, Chinese lantern plant' (= hoozuki, Physalis
alkekengi)'. x - x-x-x x-x-x. Cf. akakagati, yamakagati, accent of yamautugi.

-        kagato 'heel': see kakato.

?2.3, ?2.4   kage < ka-gey < *ka*1.3a* -n- ka-Ci*1.1*. '"deer(-color) hair" = a horse
color'. x - 1-2-x x-x-x.

2.5   kage < kagey < *kanka-Ci (?< *ka n[i] ka, cf. ka 'day', kagayaku 'shine').
'shade, shadow; (in derivatives) sunshine, light, figure, silhouette'. LH -
1-1:3-B B-B-C. NS (T 72) LH. Km (S,W) LH(-L). Edo LF. Tappi, Matsue, Izumo 2̲.
Toyama 1̲; Suzu 1 (expected reflex); Ib L2 = 2.5. Sr kaagi/kazi B. K: Hn LF.

4.9   kageroo < kagerou < kagerofu < kagirofu < kagirofi < kagyirwofiy ?=
kagyir-uₛ fiy*1.3b* (< ... 'glimmer fire' with Azuma version of the attributive
marker -(r)u, or with assimilation to vowel height in adjacent syllables).
'heat haze; dayfly'. LHHL - 0/2-1[U]/1:3[H]-B x-x-x.

2.3   kagi (?< *kagiy < *kank^u/₂Ci; ?< *kagyi < *kanki). 'key; hook'. LL - 2-2-B
B-x-x. Km x. Mr (Bm) HL. 1700 Ōsaka HL. Ib H = 2.1. The etymology *kan[a]$_{2,1}$
k[ug]i$_{2,1}$ or *ka[na$_{2,1}$ ku]gi$_{2,1}$ 'metal nail' is appealing but the register is
incongruent; perhaps *kana is 'one'?

?3.4   kagiri < kagyiri < *kankir[a-C]i$_{8}$ (< ...). 'limit'. LLL - 3/1-0[H]/1[U]-B
x-B-x. Ongi LLL. NS LHL. Km (W) LLL/LHL. Edo HHL.

2.1   kago < *kan- kwo (?< *ka-n kwo$_{1,9a}$ 'big basket', cf. kado 'gate').
'basket' (= ko). x - 0-0-A A-(A)-x. Km x. 1700 Ōsaka HH. Ib H = 2.1. Sd
khago(o) A. Sr kuu A < ko < kwo '(bird)cage', kagu A 'palanquin'. Km x.
No early examples.

3.5b   kagura < *kam[u]-gura < *kamu-[Ci]$_{2,9}$ (-n-) kura$_{2,2b}$. 'sacred music'.
LxH - 1-2-A x-x-x. Km x. Hattō 1/0; Narada, Hamada, Goka-mura 1; Aomori,
Matsue, Izumo 3. Ib H1 = 3.3.

-        kahati: see kabati.

2.1   [kai] 'ear of grain': see [kabi/kai].

2.1   kai < (*)kwai (< Ch .hhwey). 'ascarid, roundworm' (= kaityuu). LL - x-x-x
x-x-x.

2.1   kai < kafi ?< kafyi < *kapi$_{8,1}$ < *kap[a-C]i$_{A}$. 'valley'. HH - 1-2-x x-x-x.
Km (W) HH. Cf. ma-na-^k/₉ai < ma-na-kafyi 'between the eyes'.

2.1   kai < kafi < *kafyi < *kap[a-C]i$_{A}$. '(good) result, effect (< recompense <
trade)'. x - 0-1[H]/0[U]-A x-x-x. Km (W) ?HH, (Okada W) LH. Edo HH. K: Km-Edo
LH. Hiroshima (Okuda) 0. Ib L = 2.4.

2.3   kai < kafyi < *kapi. 'shell; (= kaigo) egg, eggshell; spoon'. LL - 1-2-B
B-B-x. Km x. Edo HL. Narada, Shimoda, Goka-mura, Yamaguchi 2; Hattō, Hamada,
Matsue, Izumo, Hiroshima 1 (the accent retreat is due to monosyllabification).
Ib F = 2.3. Kudaka gai ?< *[ ] -n- kai (see Ch. 1, §26).

2.4   kai < *kaCi. 'paddle, oar'. x - 1-1-B x-B-x. Km (W) LH. Ib (rare) L = 2.4.
Sr kee B (borrowed?). K: Hn LH (attested?). Cf. kaku$_{B}$ 'scratch', kogu$_{A}$ 'row';
kazi$_{2,2b}$ 'rudder'.

4.6   kaidako < kafi-dako < *kapi$_{2,9}$ -n- tako$_{2,9}$. (1) 'paper nautilus' (= aoigai
= takobune); (2) 'octopus' (= ii-dako). LLLH - x-3-x x-x-x.

4.8   kaigane (< ?). 'shoulder blade, scapula' (= karigane-bone = ka[f]igara-
bone). LHHH - x-0-x x-x-x. Perhaps *kafyi[na] ga ne (< ...) 'upper-arm root'.

3.4/3.5x kaigo < kafyi-gwo < *kapi$_{2,9}$ -n- kwo$_{1,1}$. 'egg'. LLL/LLH - x-3-x x-x-x.

3.7b   kaiko < kafyi-kwo < *kap[a-C]i$_{8}$ kwo$_{1,1}$ ('child/egg to raise'). 'silkworm'.
LHL - 1-1:3-B B-x-x. NS (118b) LHL. Km x. Narada 2; Hakata 1. Toyama 2 (we
expect 1:4); Suzu 1 (expected); Ib L2 = 3.5/7. Cf. kogai.

3.4   kaina < ka[k]i-na < *kak[a-C]i$_{8}$ na$_{1,9a}$ ('scratch [= dye] greens' ?).
'Arthraxon hispidus, var. brevisetus' (= gobunagusa). LLL (Ir) - x-x-x x-x-x.

3.5a/b   kaina < kafyina < *kapina ?< *ka[mi]$_{2,4}$ pina (see hizi$_{2,9}$). 'upper arm'.
LLH - 0/1-0[H]/1[U]-B x-B-x. Edo HLL. 1700 Ōsaka HHL. Aomori (rare) 3; Sz 1.
Ib (rare) ?F = 3.4.

4.1   kairude < kafiru^t/₄e < kafyiru-^t/₄e[y] < *kapiru -n- ta-Ci. '(~ no ki)
maple' (= kaede). HHHH-L|L - x-x-x x-x-x.

3.1 < 4.2 kaizi < kafi-di < ka[ywo]fyi-di$_{A}$ < *ka(-)dwop[a-C]i$_{A}$ -n- ti$_{1,1}$. 'commuting
route' (= kayoizi). x - x-x-x x-x-x. Km (W Okada) HHH.

?3.5a   kakasi < ka^k/₉asi < *kankasi (?= *kanka-si 'it is smelly'). '(smelly)
scarecrow; animal scare'. x - 0-1-B x-x-x. 1700 Ōsaka HHL. Aomori, Sz, Narada,
Hattō, Hamada, Matsue, Izumo 0; Goka-mura 2; Hakata 0/1. Ib (-g-) L = 3.6.

?3.6   kakato (Hiroto and Ōhara: kagato). 'heel'. x - 0-0-B x-x-x. Km x. Sz,
Hattō, Hamada, Matsue, Izumo 0; Goka-mura 0/2; Hakata 2 (kagato), ygr 0.
Ib (-g-) L = 3.6. (New? See k¹/₄bisu).

2.4   kake < kakye (?< *kakiCa$_{?min}$; ?< Ch *.ka-.k(y)ey 'house fowl'). 'chicken'.
x - x-2-x x-x-x. NS (83b) LH; NS (T 96) LL. Cf. ka-kei (NKD 4:460a).

4.6   kakehasi < kakey-fasi < *kaka-Ci[-Ci] pasi$_{2.2b}$. 'suspension (hanging)
bridge; ladder, makeshift bridge'. LLLH - 2-2[U]/3[H]-B x-x-x.

3.x   kakehi, kakei < kakefi (JP) < *kakey-fiy < *kaka-Ci[-Ci]$_B$ p^a/$_o$Ci$_{1.3b}$.
'drain-pipe'. x - 0-0-B x-x-x.

4.11   kakenawa < kakey-nafa < *kaka-Ci[-Ci]$_B$ napa$_{2.3}$. 'bridle-rope for a horse'.
LLHL - x-x-x x-x-x.

3.5x   kakezi < kake-di < *kakey-di < *kaka-Ci$_B$ -n- ti$_{?1.1}$. 'a stony (and
precipitous) mountain road; a wooden viaduct along a ledge'. LLH - x-2-x x-x-x.

2.1   kaki (?< *ka-kiy < *ka- (= ?) ko-Ci$_{1.3a}$; ?< *kakyi < *kaki). 'persimmon'.
HH - 0-0-A x-x-x. Km x. Edo HH. Ib H = 2.1. Etymological speculations:
[a]ka-kyi '[one] that is red'; [a]ka-kiy < *aka ko-Ci 'red tree/plant'.

?2.2a   kaki < kakyi < *kaki (?< *kak[a-C]i$_A$). 'fence; hedge'. HL - 2-2-A B-A-x.
NS mi-kaki (118b) HHL, (99a) HHH; NS (T+ 88) HH, (T+ 13, 14) kakyi (-) moto
HL|HH. Km (W) mi-kaki HHL. 1700 Ōsaka HL. Narada 0; Matsue 1; Izumo 2 (= 2.3);
Hattō, Hamada, Hiroshima 2. Ōsaka, Ise 2; Ib H1 = 2.2. Sd khangyi B; Nk haCii A
Possible etymologies include kak[om]-i, kak[of]-i, kak-i; all are incongruent
in register.

?2.4/5 < 2.3   kaki < kakyi < *kaki. 'oyster'. LL - 1-1:3-A B-x-x. Km x. Narada,
Hiroshima 1. Ōsaka, Ise 1:3; Ib L2 = 2.5. Sd gakyi(i) B, Onna gaacii B ?<
*[ ] -n- kaki (see Ch. 1, §26).

3.2x   kakiho < kakyi-fwo < *kaki$_{?2.2a}$ (< ...) pwo$_{?1.2}$. 'fence (top)'. x - x-3-x
x-x-x. Km (W) HHL.

?3.1, ?3.4   kakina < *kakyina < *kak[a-C]i$_B$ na$_{1.3a}$ ('scratch [= dye] greens'?).
'Arthraxon hispidus, var. brevisetus' (= kaina = gobunagusa). HHH (Kn, *mistake
for LLL?*) - 0/2-x-x x-x-x.

?3.1   kakine < *kakyi -ne < *kaki$_{2.2b}$ -na-Ci (?). 'fence; hedge'. x - 2/3-0-A
x-x-x. Km (W) HHH/HHL. Aomori, Sz, Goka-mura, NE Kyūshū 0; Hattō 3/0; Narada,
Hamada, Matsue, Izumo 3. Ib F = 3.4.

5.2   kakitubana ?< *kaki$_{2.1/2.2b}$ (< ...) -tu -n- pana$_{2.3}$ ('persimmon blossom'
or 'fence blossom'?). 'Arisaema ringens' (= Musasi-abumi). HHHHL - x-4-x x-x-x.
Register incongruent with etymologies containing kak- 'scratch [= dye]'. See
following entry.

5.2   kakitubata < "kakitufata" ?< *kaki$_{2.1/2.2b}$ (< ...) -tu (-n-) pata$_{2.2b}$
('persimmon flag' or 'fence flag'?). 'a kind of iris'. HHHHL - 3-4-A x-x-x.
Sz 4. It may be that -bata is a corruption of -bana and that kakitubata and
kakitubana have a common etymology.

3.1   kakiwa < kakifa ? < *ka[ta]-kyi$_{adj A attr}$ ifa$_{2.2b}$ (< *ipa) ('hard rock').
'a steadfast rock'. HHH - 0-0-x x-x-x.

2.4   kako (< ?). 'a belt buckle/clasp'. LH - 1-2-x x-x-x.

?2.5   kako < kakwo (?< ka[kyi]-kwo < *kak[a-C]i$_B$ kwo$_{1.1}$ 'rowing child'; ?<
ka[di]-kwo < *ka[nti]$_{2.2b}$ kwo$_{1.1}$ 'rudder child', but register incongruent).
'rower, oarman, boatman'. LF/LH - 1-2-x x-A-x. NS (93b) LLL. Km x. Nk x; Sr
kaku A (borrowed?).

2.2b   kaku < ka-ku (?< *ga-ku). 'thus, this way, so' (> koo). HL - 2-2-A x-x-x.
NS (76b) HL; NS (T+ 72) LL, (T+ 102, 123). Cf. toni-kakuni, to^a/$_z$ama-koo^a/$_z$ama.

6.2   kaku-bakari < *ka-ku$_{2.2b}$ -n- paka-r[a-C]i$_B$. 'to that extent, so much'.
HHHHHL - x-x-x x-x-x.

5.2   kakumagusa < *kakuma (= ?) -n- kusa$_{2.2b}$. (1) 'goldthread, Coptis japonica'
(= ooren); (2) 'mahuang, Ephedra sinica' (= katunegusa = amana = maoo). HHHHL -
x-4-x x-x-x.

4.5   kakurega ‹ *kaku-ra-Ci[-Ci]ᴮ⁻ -n- ka₁.₃. 'a hiding place; a place to hide (oneself or things)'. x - 3-1[H]/1:4[U]-B x-x-x. Km (W) LLLL. Sz 4.

5.16   kakuremiti ‹ *kakure[y]-myiti ‹ *kaku-ra-Ci[-Ci]ᴮ⁻ mi(-)ti₂.₁. 'hidden passage'. LLLHL - x-x-x x-x-x.

2.1   kama = kaba ('bulrush').

2.1   kama. 'pot'. x - 0-0-A A-(B̲)-x. Km x. Edo HH. Ib H = 2.1. Nk hamaa A; Sr kama-nta B ‹ *kama-buta 'pot lid', ncama B ‹ *mi-kama A 'pot'; ?kama A 'oven' (cf. kamado). Aomori gama. K: Hn HH *(attested?)*.

2.4   kama. 'sickle'. LH - 1-1-B B-A̲-x. Km x. 1700 Ōsaka LH. Kōchi 1; Ib L = 2.4. Nk hamaa A̲; Sr kama A̲ (borrowed?).

4.1   kamaboko (‹ *kama₂.₁ -n- pwo₇₁.₂ kwo₁.₁ 'bulrush-tops' or *kama₂.₁ -n-poko₂.₃ 'bulrush halberd'). 'fish paste/pudding'. x - 0-0-A x-A-A. Sz 0.

3.1   kamado ‹ kamadwo ‹ *kama₂.₁ -n- two₁.₁. 'oven'. x - 0-0-A (x)-(x)-x. Km (W) HHH. Ib H = 3.1.

4.5   kamasisi (?‹ *kamo₇*₂.₃ sisi₂.₃ ‹ ?). 'a serow; a goral' (= kamo-sika). LLLL - x-3-x x-x-x. NS (Okada) LLLL; NS (T+ 107, kun).

?3.4   kamati: *see* kabati.

2.3   kame ‹ kamey ‹ *kamaCi. 'tortoise'. LL - 1̲-1:3̲-B B-B-B. Ns (T+ kun) LL. Km (W) LL. Edo HL. Sr kaamii B. Tappi 0̲; Narada and Matsue are aberrant 1̲ (like Tōkyō) but Hattō, Hamada, Izumo, Goka-mura, Hiroshima, and NE Kyūshū have 2 and, in competition with the aberrant accent (K 1943), so do dialects in Shizuoka and Nagano. The Kyōto (and Ōsaka) accent is aberrant, as is Ibuki-jima (L̲2 = 2.5), but Ise has regular 2. Dial. game ?‹ *[ ] -n- kame (see Ch. 1, §26).

2.3   kame ‹ ?*kamey ‹ ?*ka₇₁.₃ₐ -n- pa-Ci₁.₁ (*see* he). 'jar'. LL - 2-2-B B-B-C̲. Km x. Narada, Hattō 1̲; Hamada 0̲; Matsue, Izumo, Goka-mura, Hiroshima 2. Ōsaka, Ise 2. Ib H1 = 2.2. Nk hami C̲; Yn kami C̲ (H 1964:71a). Cf. kanae.

4.5   kamebara ‹ ?*kamey-bara ‹ ?*kamey ₂.₃ (‹ ?*ka₂.₃ -n- pa-Ci₁.₁) -n- para₂.₃ ('jar belly'). 'a kind of ailment'. LLLL - 0-1-x x-x-x.

2.2a   kami ‹ *kamyi/kabyi ‹ *kanpi. 'paper'. HL - 2-2-A A-A-A. Km x. Mr (Bm) HL. Edo HL. Aomori 0; Hakata *(expected)* 1, ygr 2; Toyama 2; Suzu 2̲ *(we expect 1:3)*. Ib H1 = 2.2. Sr, Yn kabi A.

2.3   kami ‹ kamiy ‹ *kamu-Ci. 'god; (= naru kami) thunder'. LL - 1̲-2-B x-B-B. NS (101a, 119a) LL; NS (T 112) LL, (T 37) LR = L̲H. Km (W) LL. Mr (Bm) HL. Edo HL. Sapporo, Aomori *(rare)*, Akita, Numazu, Matsue, Izumo, Wakamatsu, Ōita 1̲; Nagano (Kudō 40), Narada, Matsumoto, Hattō, Hamada, Goka-mura, Hiroshima 2. In Yamanashi the older variant is regular 2 (Watanabe 1957:184-5). Ib *(rare)* F = 2.3. Borrowed from/into Ainu kamúy? (Speculation: Is *kamu a metathesis of kuma₂.₃ 'bear'? Cf. kumasine.)

2.3   kami (?‹ kamyi₂.₄[-key₇₁.₁] 'top hair'; ? ka[m]i › key₇₁.₁ › ke, but cf. siraga). 'hair (on the head)'. LL - 2-2-B x-x-x. Ongi LL. Km (S) LL. Edo HL. Ib F = 2.3. Hakata 0, ygr 2. Sr karazi B, kantu A (?‹ kabuto); Yn karan, kanan A — the etymologies are unclear.

2.4   kami ‹ kamyi ‹ *kami. 'above'. LH - 1-1-B x-(B)-x. NS (Okada) LH; NS (T 32 'governor') L̲L, (T 94) R̲ ?= H̲L. Km (S) LH, (W) LL/LH/HH. Mr(Bm) L̲H-L. Edo LH. Hattō 0̲. Ōsaka 1; Ise 1/1:3̲; Ib L = 2.4.

4.5   kamiage ?‹ *kamiy-agey ‹ *kamu-Ci₂.₃ anka-Ci[-Ci]ₐ ('god giving'), but said to be ‹ "kamuimake" (› kan-imake) ‹ *kamu₂.₃ ima₂.₄ key₁.₃ₐ (‹ ...) ('god now meal'). 'a court ceremony to sacrifice old rice'. LLLL - x-x-x x-x-x.

4.5   kamigaki 'hair pin/stick': *see* koogai.

4.5   kamigaki (‹ ?). 'a kind of banner' (= onigasira). LLLL - x-x-x x-x-x. (Unique to Kn Mg?)

4.5   kamikaze, kamukaze < *kamu[-Ci]*2.3* kansa-Ci*2.1*. 'divine wind'. x - 2-0[H]/
3[U]-B x-x-x. NS (79a) LLLL; NS (T+ 8) LLLH, (T+ 78) LH|LH.

6.22   kamikirimusi < *kamyikyiri-musi < *kam[a-C]i*B* kir[a-C]i*B* musi*2.1*.
'longhorned beetle'. LLLLHL - 4-1:5-x x-x-x. Sz 5.

?3.3   kamina ?< *ka[ni]*2.1* mina*2.3* ('crab snail'), ?< *ka[ri]*2.1* (< *ka[ra-Ci]*A*)
mina*2.3* ('temporary snail'). 'hermit crab' (= yadokari). HxL (?= *HLL) x-x-x
x-x-x.

4.11 (?= 2.3|2.2)   kaminaga < *kami*2.3* (< ...) nanka*B*. 'having long hair; (being)
longhaired'. x - x-x-x x-x-x. NS (97b) LLHL.

-          kaminaki: see kannagi.

?4.5   kaminari < *kamiy-nari < *kamu-Ci*2.3* nar[a-C]i*A*. 'thunder'. x - 3/4-4-B
x-B-B. Km (W "kamunari" = kannari) LLLL. Sz 4; Narada 0; Hata 3; Hakata 0,
ygr 3. Kōchi 4. Yn kannari B.

4.5 = 3.4 (= 2.3-no)|1.3   kaminone < *kami*2.3* (< ...) no na-Ci*1.3a* ('hair root').
'a hair (of the head)'. LL-L(|)L - x-x-x x-x-x.

6.20 = 3.4 (= 2.3-no)|1.3   kaminoyagara < *kamiy*2.3* (< *kamu-Ci*2.3*) no ya-gara*3.2a*
(< *da*1.2* -n- kara*2.2b* 'god/thunder's arrowshaft'). 'Gastrodiaelata' (=
oninoyagara). LL-L(|)HH - x-x-x x-x-x.

6.10   kamiokosi-na < *kami*2.3* (< ...) okos[a-C]i*B* na*1.3a* ('hair-raise plant').
'common (plumed) thistle' (= himeazami). LLLHHH - 5-x-x x-x-x.

4.2   kami*a*/*z*eni < *kamyi-*a*/*z*eni < *kanpi*2.2b* (-n-) seni*2.5*. 'paper money'.
HHHL - x-x-x x-x-x.

4.5   kamitoki < kamiy-tokyi < *kamu-Ci*2.3* tok[a-C]i*B*. 'thundering' (=
kamitoke). LLLL - x-x-x x-x-x. Also: kantoki.

5.2, 5.1; 5.16 kamiyagawa < kami-ya*?3.3* (< *kanpi*2.2* da*1.3b* 'paper-maker') -n-
kapa*2.2a*. 'the Kamiya River' (placename). x - 3-x-x x-x-x. Km (W) HHHHL, HHHHH;
LLLHL.

4.5   kamizori = kamisori < *kamyi-*a*/*z*ori < *kami*2.3* (-n-) sor[a-C]i*B*.
'razor'. LLLL - 3/4-4-B x-B-x. Narada 4, Hakata 0.

2.1   kamo. 'woolen cloth'. HH - x-2-x x-x-x.

2.3   kamo. 'a metal tube inside the hub of a wheel (= karimo); a metal ring for
rosary beads'. LL - x-1-x x-x-x. K: "Km LL".

?2.5 < 2.3   kamo < kamwo. '(wild) duck'. LL - 1-1:3-B A-B-C. NS (Okada) LL.
Narada, Hamada, Yamaguchi 1; Matsue 1 (we expect 2); Izumo 2 (expected reflex);
Hattō, Goka-mura 2; Hakata 0, ygr 1. Kōchi (Kobayashi) 1:3; Ib L2 = 2.5.
Sd khamo(o) A; Nk kamuu A. K: Km LL (attested?), Edo (Keichū) HL.

3.6   kamome < ?kamame < *kam*a*/*o*-mey < *kam*a*/*o*-m[ur]ey < *kam*a*/*o*
(< *kamwo*?2.5<2.3*) -mey (< *mure[y]*2.1* < *mura-Ci[-Ci]*A*). 'seagull'.
LHH - 0-1-B x-x-x. Km x. Edo LHH. Goka-mura 1; Narada, Hattō, Hamada, Matsue,
Izumo, Hakata 0; Aomori 2 (also gome 1). Ib L = 3.6. Dial. ka(a)gome, kagame
(?< *kanka-···).

4.6   kamouri ?< *kamwo*2.3* uri*2.4*. '"winter melon", wax gourd' (= toogan).
LLLH - x-1:3-x x-x-x.

2.3   kamu(-) 'god': see kami, kagura, kamikaze; koogoosi*adj B*.

-          kamu··· : see kan··· .

4.1 (> 3.1)   kamudati = kandati (> kaudi > koozi) ?< *kan[p*a*/*o*-Ci]*2.1* (-n-)
tat[a-C]i*B* ('mold rise'). 'malt, yeast'. HHHH - x-x-x x-x-x. Cf. kabi.

2.1   kana(-) 'metal': see kane.

2.1   kana ?< ka[ri]*2.1* (< kar[a-C]i*A*) na*1.3*; ?< Sanskrit ka[ra]na. 'syllabary
writing'. x - 0-1-A x-A-x. Km x. 1700 Ōsaka karina. Ib H = 2.1. (Unger proposes
an etymology based on *kana 'one' but the register may be incongruent.)

?2.3 *kana(-). 'one' (cf. kaneru, kanau, kanaeru, kazoeru); 'a little, a bit, slightly' (cf. kagir-u 'glimmer'). Cf. kata(-).

2.3 (> 3.4) kana (> kanna) ?< *ka[ka-Ci]ₐ naₗ.ₓ 'scratch blade'). '(carpenter's) plane'. LL - x-x-x x-B-x. Km x.

4.2 kanabasi < *kanaₐ.ₗ -n- pasiₐ.₄. 'metal chopsticks'. HHHL - x-x-x x-x-x.

4.2 kanabata < *kanaₐ.ₗ -n- pataₐ.ₐ₆. 'metal loom'. x - x-x-x x-x-x. NS (73b, 73c) HHHL, NS (T+ 59) HLLL.

5.2 kanabukusi < *kanaₐ.ₗ -n- pukusiₐ₃.₄ (< ...). 'a digging stick made of metal'. HHHHL - x-x-x x-x-x.

3.1 kanae < kanafe < *kana-fey < *kanaₐ.ₗ pa-Ciₗ.ₗ. 'tripod kettle'. HHH - 0-0-x x-x-x. Km x. Mr (Bm) HHH.

4.1 kanagaki < kanakaki (Mg) < *kanaₐ.ₗ kak[a-C]iₐ. 'a kind of harrow (rake)'. HHHH - x-x-x x-x-x.

?3.1 kanagu < *kanaₐ.ₗ guₗ.ₓ (< Ch ghyu'). 'metal fixture'. x-0-2-A x-A-x. Aomori 2. Ib H2 = 3.2. Earliest citation JP.

5.2 kanahodasi < kanafodasi < *kanaₐ.ₗ ponta-s[a-C]iₐ/ₐ. 'metal foot-shackle'. HHHHL - x-4-x x-x-x.

4.1 kanakuso < *kanaₐ.ₗ kuswoₐ.ₐ. 'slag'. HHHH - 0-0-x x-A-x. Sr kan¹/ₐkusu A.

?4.2,?4.1 kanamari < *kanaₐ.ₗ mariₐ.ₐ₍₇₆₎. 'metal bowl'. HHHL/?HHHH - x-x-x x-x-x.

3.1 kaname ?< kanome < *kanomey < *kan[iₐ.ₗ n]o ma-Ciₗ.ₐₐ ('crab's eye'). 'pivot (of folding fan, etc.)'. x - 0-0-A x-A-x. Sz 0. Ib F = 3.6. Sr kanami A 'greeting (as a social pivot)'.

4.2 kananabe < *kana-nabey < *kanaₐ.ₗ nanpaCiₐ.₆. 'metal pan'. HHHL - x-x-x x-x-x.

?3.2b, ?3.1 kanata ?< *ka-n[oₐ.ₐ₆ k]ataₐ.ₐ₆ < ?*gaₗ.ₐ no kataₐ.ₐ₆. 'that way/ direction, over there (= anata)'. x - 1/2-2-A x-x-x. Km (W) HHH(-L), HHL, HLL. Edo HHL.

5.1 kanaᵗ/ᵤunai < kanaduna-wi < *kanaₐ.ₗ (-n-) tunaₐ.ₐ biₗ.ₐₐ. 'a well sweep with iron chain'. HHHHH - x-x-x x-x-x.

4.2 kanazue < kanaduwe < *kanaₐ.ₗ -n- tuweₐ.₄ (< ...). 'metal rod/staff'. HHHL - x-4-x x-x-x.

4.2 kanazuti < kanaduti < *kanaₐ.ₗ -n- tutu-Ciₐ.₄. 'hammer'. HHHL - 3/(0[H]/ 4[U])-4-A x-B-x. Sz 0; Hakata 2. Nk haniiyuCi A; Sr kan¹/ₐzicaa B (but kani 'metal' A).

4.2 kanbase/kaobase < kafo-base ?< *kapoₐ.ₗ -n- pasa-Ci[-Ci]. 'countenance, face'. HHHL - 0-0-x x-x-x.

4.2 kanbata (NKD: kan-hata) < "kamubata" (Mg) < kanifata < *kaniₐ.ₗ pataₐ.ₐ₆ ('crab loom'). 'a thin silk brocade'. HHHL - x-0-x x-x-x. Mr (Bm) HHHH.

4.7 = 2.3|2.1 kandomo < kamudomo (Mg) < *kamuₐ.ₐ tomoₐ.ₗ. 'shrine manager' (= kanbe). LL(|)HH - x-x-x x-x-x.

2.1 kane < *kane[y] < *kana-Ci. 'metal; bell'. HH - 0-0-A A-A-A. Km x. Edo HH. Ib H = 2.1. Yn kanin A, Hateruma kanin; cf. Ch. 1, §52.

2.1 kani. 'crab'. HH - 0-0-A A-A-C. Km x. Narada gani 0. Ib gane H = 2.1. Sd ganyi A; Nk gai A = ganii A; Sr gani A; Yn kanna C (with suffix?). Iwate (etc.) ganni. Forms with g- may be truncations < *[ ] -n- kani (see Ch. 1, §26).

3.2x (> ?2.4) kaniwa < kanifa < *kanipa (> kaba). 'birch'. HHL - x-x-x x-x-x. Km x. See kaba.

6.2 kaniwazakura < kanifa-zakura < *kanipaₐ.ₐ -n- sakuraₐ.ₗ. '(= kaba-zakura) types of cherry tree with bark resembling birch; especially Prunus grayana (= uwami-zakura)'. x - x-x-x x-x-x. Km (W) HHHHHL.

3.4 < 2.3 kanna < kana. '(carpenter's) plane'. (x) - 3-2-B x-(B)-x. NE Kyūshū 1; Narada 3. Ib F = 3.4. Sr kana B. Dial. (Wakayama, etc.) kana.

4.6   kannagi < kam¹/ₐnaki < kamiy-naki < *kamu-Ci*ₛ.ₛ* + ?. 'shrine maiden
(spirit medium)'. LLLH - 3/0-0-x x-x-x. Cf. mi-kannagi, as surname also
Mikanagi.

5.16   kannazuki < kam[u]na-duki = kamina-duki < *kamiy-na-dukiy < *kamu[-Ci]*ₛ.ₛ*
na (?= na*ₐdⱼ ᵦ*) -n- tuku-Ci*ₛ.ₛ*. 'the tenth month of the lunar calendar'.
x - 1-2-x x-x-x. NS (113b) LLLHL.

4.5   kannie < "kamunife" (Ck), "kamunibe" (Kn) < *kamu*ₛ.ₛ* nifey*ₜₛ.₁ₐ* (< ...).
'harvest festival' (= kanna^b/ₐe). LLLL - x-x-x x-x-x.

4.5   kanniwa < "kamunifa" < *kamu[-Ci]*ₛ.ₛ* nipa*ₛ.₁*. 'the Celestial Court'.
x - x-x-x x-x-x. NS (123a [14:229L-K, 14:230-K]) LLLL.

2.2b   kano < ka-n**o** ?< *ga-n**o**. 'that ⋯ (distal)' (= ano). x - 2-2-A (x-x-x).
NS (105b, 110b) HL. Km (S) HL.

6.22   kanonigegusa < *ka₁.ₛₐ n**o** nige*ₛ.ₛ* (< ...) -n- kusa*ₛ.ₛ* ('deer's-cud
grass'). 'ginseng'. LLLLHL - x-x-x x-x-x.

4.6/4.5   kanzasi (LLLH - 0-2-B x-B-x) = kam[u]zasi (LLLL) < *kamyi-*ᵃ/ᵤasi <
*kami*ₛ.ₛ* (-n-) sas[a-C]i*ᵦ*. 'hair-pin, hair ornament'. Km (W) LLHH/LLHL. Sz 3;
Hata 0. Kōchi 4. Sr kamisasi B (borrowed?).

4.11 = 2.3|2.2 kanzemi < "kamusemi" < kan*ₜₛ.ₛ* (< Ch .hhan) semi*ₛ.ₛₐ* (< ...). 'early
autumn cicadas' (= kansen). LL(|)HL - 1-x-x x-x-x.

-        kanziki: *see* kaziki ('snowshoes').

2.1   kao < kafo < *kapo. 'face'. HH - 0-0-A A-A-x. NS (119b,120a) HH. Km (W)
?HH. Edo HH. K: Hn-Km-Mr HH. Ib H = 2.1. On Man'yō-shū orthography that might
be taken to indicate *kawo, see Miyajima 1944:29-30 and Zdb 216:bc.

-        kaobase: *see* kanbase.

?5.2; ?2.1|3.1 kaokatati < kafo-katati < *kapo*ₛ.₁* katati*ₛ.₁* (< ...). 'countenance,
facial features'. HHHHx (?= *HHHHL, ?= *HH|HHH) - 0/4-4-A x-x-x. Cf. Seki
1977:72, 173-4.

3.1   kaori < kawori < *ka₁.₁ bor[a-C]i*ᵦ*. 'fragrance'. HHH - 0-0-A x-x-x.
Mr (Bm) HHH. Goka-mura 1.

2.2a   kara. 'husk, shell; (body) trunk; stem, stalk, handle; characteristic'.
HL - 2-1-A A-A-x ('characteristic' x - 0-0-A x-x-x). Km x. Mr (W 18, 19)
LH(-H). Aomori, Sz 0. Ōsaka 1; Ise 1:3; Kōchi ?2 [Martin's notes]; Ib L2 = 2.5.
Cf. karada, kabane.

2.2b   kara. 'empty' (< 'shell'). x - 2-1-A x-A-x. Aomori, Sz 0. Ōsaka, Kōchi 1;
Ise 1/1:3; Ib L2 = 2.5.

2.x (?2.2b)   kara. 'clan, family' (?< 'trunk'). Cf. yakara, harakara, u^k/ₐara;
Korean kyelo**y**.

2.5   kara. 'Han': (1) = Imna (= Mimana), a state in south Korea from the third
to the sixth centuries A.D. (2) 'Korea; China; foreign'. x - 1-1:3-(A) x-(B)-x.
Km (W) LL-⋯ . Ōsaka, Ise 1:3; Ib H1 = 2.2. Cf. kaya, aya.

5.16   karabakari: *see* karahakari.

3.1   karada ?< *kara*ₛ.ₛ* n[i] ta₁.ₛₐ 'trunk and limbs'; ?< *koro*ₜ*ₜₛ.₁* n[i]
ta₁.ₛₐ 'body *(cf. mukuro)* and limbs' *with the first two vowels assimilated to
the last vowel. '*body'. x - 0-0-A x-A-x. Aomori, Sz 0; Narada 3; Hakata
(expected) 2, ygr 0. Ib H = 3.1. Sr karata A = kara A.

4.6 (> 3.5b)   kar[a]ei (= karei) < kara-efi (< ?). 'flatfish'. LLLH - x-x-x x-x-x.

4.6   kara-ginu: *see* kara-kinu.

4.11, 4.5 karahagi < kara-fagi[y] < *kara*ₜ(ₛ.ₐ)* pan-koCi*ₛ.ₛ* (< ...). '(a kind of)
bushclover'. x - x-1:3-x x-x-x. Km (W) LLHL, LLLL.

5.16   kara^ᵇ/ᵦakari < kara-^f/ᵦakari < *kara*ₜₛ.ₛ* (-n-) pakari*ₛ.₄* (< *paka-r[a-
C]i*ᵦ*). 'weighing scales'. LLLHL - x-x-x x-x-x.

-        karahoi: *see* [karaoi].

4.6 karakagi < *kara*s.s* kagi*s.s* (< ...). 'door bolt/lock'. LLLH - x-1:4-x
x-x-x.

4.7 karakago < *karakanko (< ?). 'croaker' *(fish)*. LLHH - x-x-x x-x-x.
NKD "-ko" but Mg has -go.

4.6 kara-ᵏ/ᵨinu < *kara-kyinu < *kara*s.s* kinu*s.4*. 'a kind of outer garment
worn by court women'. LLLH - 2/3-1-x x-x-x.

4.6 karakoto < *kara*s.s* k*o̲t̲o̲*s.s*. 'a Chinese harp'. x - x-x-x x-x-x. Km (W
placename) LLLH.

4.5 karakumi < *kara*s.s* kumyi*s.s* (< kum[a-C]i*s*). 'a kind of braid'. LLLL -
0-1-x x-x-x.

4.5 karakuni < *kara-kuni[y] < *kara*s.s* kunu-Ci*?s.s,?s.sa*. 'the Han country =
Korea (also = China, = foreign country)'. x - x-1-x x-x-x. NS (87b, 93b) LLLL;
NS (T+ 100, 101) LLLH, (T+ 99) LL(|)HH.

4.7 karakura < *kara*s.s* kura*s.sb*. 'saddle'. LLHH - x-x-x x-x-x. NKD has -gu-
but -ku- in the compounds.

?4.1, ?4.5 karakusa < ?*kara[mi]-kusa < *karam[a-C]i*?s* kusa*s.s*. 'a design of
intertwined vines; an arabesque'. HHHH (Ir) - 2̲-2̲-x x-x-x.

4.5 karamomo < *kara*s.s* momo*s.s*. 'apricot' (= anzu). LLLx (= *LLLL) - 2-1:3-x
x-x-x.

4.5 karamusi < *kara*s.s* musi*s.s*. 'ramie (Boehmeria nivea), Chinese silk plant;
ramie fabric, grass cloth'. LLLL (Kn, -z-) - 0/2-2-x x-x-x.

4.6 karanasi < *kara*s.s* nasi*?s.sa*. *(1)* 'a kind of apple' (= aka-ringo);
(2) 'Chinese quince' (= karin). LLLH - 0/2-1:4-x x-x-x.

4.11 [karaoi] < "karawofi" < kara-fofi (Shinsen-Jikyō) < kara-afufi < *kara*s.s*
apupi*s.s*. 'hollyhock, Althaea rosea' (= tati-aoi). LLHL - x-x-x x-x-x.

4.8, 4.7, 4.11 karasaki < *kara-sakyi < *kara (= ?) saki*s.s*. 'Cape Kara'
(placename). x - 0/2-x-x x-x-x. Km (W) LHHH, LLHH, LLHL.

4.6 karasao < "karasafo" = karasawo < *kara (= ?) sabo*s.s*. 'flail'. LLLH -
0-3-x x-x-x. NKD "also -za-". (Etymology and accent of kara: Ch. 4, §10.4.)

3.7a/b karasi (?< kara-si*adj ?s pred* 'it is pungent'). 'mustard'. LHL - 0-1:3-B
x-B-x. Narada, Wakamatsu 1; Aomori 2̲; Hakata 1, ygr 0/3. Ib L2 = 3.5/7.

3.6 karasu < *kara-su. 'crow'. LHH - 1-1-B B-B-C. Edo LHH. K: Hn LHH/LHL.
Yamaguchi 0; Hamada 0/1; Narada, Hattō, Goka-mura, Wakamatsu, Hakata 1; Aomori,
Matsue, Izumo 2̲. Ib L = 3.6. Sd, Sr, Yn g- ?< *[ ] -n- karasu (Ch. 1, §26).

5.16 karasuheᵇ/ᵨi < karasufemi < *karasu*s.s* (< ...) feymyi*s.s* (< ...). 'black
snake'. LLLHL - 3-1:4-x x-B-x. Sr garaşihwiibaa B.

7.3 karasukutinawa < karasu-kutinafa < *kara-su*s.s* kuti[y]-nafa*4.s* (< kutu-
Ci*s.s* napa*s.s*). 'black snake' (= karasuhebi). HHHHHLL - x-x-x x-x-x.

5.11/5.12 karasumugi < *karasu-mugyi < *kara-su*s.s* munki*s.4*. 'oats'. LHHHL/LHLLL -
3-1:4-x x-x-x. Sz 4.

6.22 karasunameri < *karasu-nameyri < *kara-su*s.s* nama-Ci-r[a-C]i*?s*. 'a cramp
in (the calf of) the leg, a leg cramp'. LLLHL - x-x-x x-x-x. ("Also karasu-
naferi." Probably either /-naweri/ < na[m]eri or -na["]feri = -naberi.)

5.11 karasuuri < *kara-su*s.s* uri*s.4*. 'snakegourd'. LHHHL - 3-1:4-x x-x-x. Sz 4.

4.5 karatati < *kara*s.s* tati[bana]*s.s* (< ...). 'a trifoliate orange; (=
sarutori = ibara) a smilax'. LLLL - 0-0-B x-x-x.

4.6 karauri < *kara*s.s* uri*s.4*. 'cucumber' (= kyuuri). LLLH - 2-x-x x-x-x.

4.6 karausu < *kara*s.s* usu*s.4*. 'a kind of mortar'. LLLH - 3-1-x x-x-x.

5.16 karayatuko < *kara*s.s* ya-tu-kwo*s.sa* (< *da*s.sb* -tu kwo*s.s*). 'Korean
slaves'. x - x-x-x x-x-x. NS (125b) LLLHL.

4.5/4.11 karazake < karasake < *kara-sakey < *kara*adj s* saka-Ci*s.s* ('pungent
wine'). 'vinegar' (= su). LLLL (Kn) / LLHL (Ck) - x-x-x x-x-x.

2.2b   kare ?< *ga-ra-Ci. 'he; that one *(distal)*' (= are). HL - 1-2-A x-x-A.
    Edo HL. K: Hn-Mr-Edo HL. Hattō, Hamada, Matsue, Izumo, Goka-mura, Wakamatsu 1.
    Ib H1 = 2.2. 1700 Ōsaka kare-ra HLL.

2.3   kare < *ka (< ... 'thus') are[y] (< *ara-Ci*в*[-n- pa]) *(= koo da kara)*.
    'the reason'. x - x-x-x x-x-x. Edo HL.

4.5   [karehizi] < karefidi (< ?). 'snowshoes' (= ka(n)ziki, warigo). LLLL -
    x-x-x x-x-x.

3.4 < 4.x karei < karewi < karefyi < kare[y]-ifyi < *kara-Ci[-Ci]*в* ipi*z.z*. 'dried
    (cooked) rice to be taken along as food for a journey'. LLL - x-x-x x-x-x.

3.5b < 4.6   karei < karewi < karefi < kara-efi (< ?). 'flatfish'. LLH - 1-2-B
    x-x-x. Matsumoto, Ōita 1; Sapporo, Aomori, Akita, Hiroshima [Terakawa] 2;
    Numazu, Hiroshima (H) 0; Hakata 2, ygr 0/1; Ōsaka, Ise 1:3; Suzu 1:4 *(we
    expect 1:3)*; Toyama 1:3.

5.6   kareituke < karei*z.4* (< ...) tuke[y] (< *tuka-Ci[-Ci]*в*). 'a rope on the
    ring at the back of a saddle (originally used to attach provisions of dried
    rice)'. LLLLL - x-x-x x-x-x.

4.10   kare-koti < ka-[a]re ko̲-ti ('reason thus' < 'such-be this way').
    'therefore'. LHLL - x-x-x x-x-x. Attested only in Mg?

2.1   kari. 'a kind of dice' (= tyobo). HH - x-x-x x-x-x.

2.1   kari < *kar[a-C]i*A*. 'temporary, ephemeral' *(adj-n)*. x - 0-0-A x-A-x.
    Km (S) HH. Mr (Bm) HH. Sz 0. Ib H = 2.1.

2.4   kari. 'barb of a fish-hook'. LH - x-x-x x-x-x. Only in Mg (Kn, Ck)?

2.4 (?< *2.1) kari < *kar[a-C]i*A*. 'mowing; a "cut" of rice *(measure for bundles of
    cut grain, used to state field size or yield)*'. LH (?< *HH) - x-x-x x-x-x.

?2.4 < 2.3   kari < *kar[a-C]i*?в*. 'hunting'. LH - 1-0̲[H]/2̲[U]-A x-x-x. NS (108b,
    113b, 115b, 117a, 117b) LH. ?Km (W) LL/LH. Edo HH. Sz 1; Hamada 1/0̲; Izumo 2̲;
    Hiroshima (Okuda) 0. Ōsaka, Ise 1; Ib H̲ = 2.1.

?2.4   kari. 'wild goose'. LH - 1-0̲[H]/2̲[U]-A̲ x-x-x. NS (74b, 74c, 126a) LH;
    NS (T 62, 63) HH. Km (W) LH(-H), HH, LL(-L). Edo LH. Ib H̲ = 2.1.

4.8 = 3.6 (= 2.4-ga) | 1.1   karigane < *kari*z.4* ga*pcl* ne*z.z* (< ...). 'cry of the
    wild goose; a wild goose'. x - x-x-x x-x-x. Km (W) LHHH = LH-H H; (Okada)
    kafigane *(misprint?)* HHHL.

4.6   kariginu < *kari*?z.4<z.з* (< *kar[a-C]i*?в*) -n- kinu*z.4* ('hunting garb').
    'nobleman's attire' (= karigoromo). LLLH - 2/3-0-x x-x-x.

4.1   karigomo: *see* karikomo.

?5.7   karigoromo < kari*k*/*g*oromo < *kari*?z.4<z.з* (< *kar[a-C]i*?в*) (-n-) ko̲ro̲mo̲
    ('hunting gown'). 'nobleman's attire' (= kariginu). x - 3-4-x x-x-x. Km (W 5)
    LLxxx (?= *LLLLH), (W 17) HHHHL *(register incongruent)*.

3.7a   kariko < *kari*?z.4<z.з* (< *kar[a-C]i*в*) kwo*z.z*. 'a beater (for hunting
    game)'. LHL - 0-0̲-x x-x-x.

4.1   kari*k*/*g*omo < *kari-ko̲mo̲ < *kar[a-C]i*A* komo*z.z*. 'cut water-oats; straw
    matting'. x - x-x-x x-x-x. Km (W) HHHH, HHHL.

4.1 = 2.1|2.1 karimiya < *kari*z.z* (< *kar[a-C]i*A*) myi-ya*z.z* (< *mi-*z.z* da*z.зa*).
    'a temporary palace'. HHHx = *HH(|)HH - 0-0-x x-x-x.

*3.4   karite 'provisions': *see* kate.

4.1   kariyosu (?< kariyo [= Kwolye] su[ru]*A* or so/su 'thing'). 'music
    from Koryŏ Korea'. HHH (Ir) - x-x-x x-x-x.

4.2   karuisi < *karu*adj A* isi*z.zb* ('lightweight stone'). 'pumice'. HHHL - 0-0-A
    x-B̲-x. Sz 3. Nk haru(u)isi C̲; Sr karasi B̲.

4.9   karyuudo < kariudo/karibito < *kari-byito̲ < *kari*?z.4<z.з* (< *kar[a-C]i)
    -n- pito̲*z.za*. 'hunter'. LHHL-1(/2)-1:3-B x-x-x. NS (115a) LLLx, (117b) LHxx.
    Sz 2.

?2.1   kasa. 'sore, ulcer'. HH - 0-0[H]/1-A x-B-x. Km x. Narada 2; Hiroshima 0.
   Ib (rare) H = 2.1. Nk ka(a)saa C. ("?< Sanskrit khasa" but does that exist?)
2.2b   kasa. 'bulk'. x - 2-2[H]/1[U]-A x-x-x. Km x. Aomori, Narada, Hiroshima 2.
   Ōsaka, Ise 2; Ib H1 = 2.2. Dial. (Sendai, Sz, Buzen = Fukuoka, Kishū = Kii =
   Wakayama, Tsushima) gasa ?< *[ ] -n- kasa (see Ch. 1, §26). Cf. kasanaru.
2.4   kasa. 'umbrella'. LH - 1-1-B B-B-B. Km (W) LL-···, mi-kasa HHH.
   1700 Ōsaka LH. Kōchi 1; Ib L = 2.4. Nk hasaa B; Onna kaasaa B; Yn kasa B
   (H 1964:65a, 71a, 71b).
4.10   kasabiru < ?*kasa-byiru < *kasaₛ.₄ -n- piruₛₗ.ₛ ('umbrella leech').
   'a land leech' (= yamabiru). LHLL - x-x-x x-x-x.
4.1   kasabuta < kasaᶠ/ᵦuta < *kasaₚₛ.ₗ (-n-) putaₛ.ₗ. 'scab'. HHHH (-f-) -
   0-0-A x-A-x. Ib H = 4.1. Sr kasabuta/kasanta A.
5.2   kasadokoro < *kasaₚₛ.ₗ -n- tokoro. 'a sore'. HHHHL - x-4-x x-x-x.
4.5   kasamoti ?< *kasaₛ.₄ mot[a-C]i ('having umbrella'). (1) 'Angelica
   dahurica' (= sawaudo = yoroigusa); (2) 'Nothosmyrnium japonicum' (= sawaudo =
   koohon). LLLL - 0/4-1:3-x x-x-x.
4.10   kasasagi, kasasaki (Ck Mg) ?< *kasasaᵏ/ₛyi < ?*kasasa(n)ki. 'magpie'.
   LHLL (Ck) - 0-0-x x-x-x. Sz (rare) 0.
?4.5, ?4.6, ?4.11   kasatori (Okada: kasadori) < *kasaₛ.₄ t(w)or[a-C]i ('umbrella
   hold'). 'Eleagnus crispa (= akigumi); Mount Kasatori (placename)'. x - 0-x-x
   x-x-x. Km (W) LLLH, LLLL, LLHL, LH|LH. Mr (W 18, 19) HLLL.
?2.3   kase ?< kasi (2d vowel partially assimilated to first). (1) 'shackles';
   (2) 'skein frame/reel' (cf. ogase). x - 1-0[H]/2[U]-x x-B-x. (The two meanings
   are usually treated as having separate etymologies.)
?2.4, ?2.5   kaˢ/ₑe, [dial.] gaze (< ?). 'sea-urchin' (= uni). LH (Ir -z-) - x-x-x
   x-x-x.
4.10   kasesaba < *kaseₚₛ.ₛ (?< kasi) sanpaₛ.ₗ ('reel mackerel'). 'hammerhead
   shark' (= syumoku-zame). LHLL - x-x-x x-x-x.
4.9, 4.10   kaseyama < *kaseₛ.ₓ (< ?) damaₛ.ₛ. 'Mount Kase' (placename).
   x - 0-2-x x-x-x. Km (W) LHHL, LHLL.
4.6   kasezue < kase-duwe < *kase (?< kasi) -n- tuwe (< ...) ('shackle rod').
   'a walking stick (with prong or crotch on the end)'. LLLH - 3-4-x x-x-x.
2.3   kasi. 'shackles'. LL - 1-0-B x-x-x. Cf. kase.
?2.5 < 2.3   kasi. 'oak'. LL - 1-1:3-B x-x-x. NS (T+ kun) LL. Aomori 0; Sz,
   Hamada, Matsue, Hiroshima 1; Hattō, Izumo, Goka-mura 2. Ōsaka, Ise 2;
   Ib H = 2.1.
5.9   kasikigate < *kasik[a-C]i -n- kate (< ...). 'hodgepodge (of rice and
   vegetables)'. LLHHH - x-x-x x-x-x. Cf. Sr kasicii B < *kasiki-ifi 'steamed
   glutinous rice'.
3.3   kasiko ?< *ka-so-ko (?< *ga-so-ko). 'there, that place (distal)' (=
   asoko). HLL - 1-1-x x-x-x. 1700 Ōsaka HLL.
3.4   kasira. 'head; chief'. LLL - 3-2-B x-B-x. Km (W) LLL. Mr (Bm) HHL. Edo
   HHL. Narada 3. Ib F = 3.4.
5.16   kasiragasa < *kasiraₛ.₄ -n- kasaₚₛ.ₗ. 'scalp sores'. LLLHL - x-x-x x-x-x.
3.2a   kasiwa < kasifa < *kasiₛ.ₛ paₗ.ₛ ('oak leaf' >) 'oak'. HHL - 0-1:3-A/B
   x-B-x. NS (71c, 103b) HHH, (104a placename) HHL. Aomori 1; Narada 0/3; Hakata
   2, ygr 0. Ib L2 = 3.7. Kg A in Hirayama, but B according to Kobayashi. Sr
   kaasya B 'food-wrapping leaf'. The register is incongruent with the etymology.
4.1   kasiwade < kasifa-te < *kasifaₛ.ₛₐ (< *kasiₚₛ.ₛ paₗ.ₛ) (-n-) ta-Ciₗ.ₛₐ
   ('oak-leaf hand'). 'a court cook; (later) hand-clap'. HHHH - 0[H]/3-0-A x-x-x.
   Sz 0/4.

4.2   kasiyone < * kas[a-C]i_A yone_{?2.1, ?2.4} (< ...). 'washed rice (for a
sacrificial offering)' (= kasigome). HHHL - x-x-x x-x-x.
-          kaso 'father': see kazo.
2.4   kasu. 'dregs, lees'. LH - 1-1-B B-B-B̲. Ongi LH. Yamagata gasu ?< *[ ] -n-
kasu (see Ch. 1, §26). Matsue, Izumo 2̲. Ib L = 2.4. Nk ʰ/ₖasii B̲; Yn kaci B̲.
3.3   kasuga < *kasunka (?< kasum[u]_A (< ...) (-)ka_{?1.3a or 1.x} 'misty days [of
spring]' or 'misty place'). 'Kasuga' (placename). x - 1-2-x x-x-x. NS (82c
[17:111-M]) HLL; NS (T+ 94, 96) HL|H; NS (T+ kun) HHL. Edo HLL.
?4.3   kasugai < kasugafyi (?< *ka[na]_{2.1} sunka-p[a-C]i). 'latch'. ...-HHLL -
0/2-1:3-A x-x-x. Cf. age-kasugai. Sz 0.
4.8   kasugome < *kasu-go̲mey < *kasu_{2.4} -n- ko̲maCi_{2.3}. 'wine lees'. LHHH -
x-x-x x-x-x.
3.7b   kasuka < kasu-ka. 'dim' (adj-n). LHL - 1-1:3-B x-x-x. Km (S) LHL. Edo LHL.
3.1   kasumi < kasumyi < *kasu-m[a-C]i_A. 'mist'. HHH - 0-0-B̲/A x-x-x. Km (W)
HHH. Edo HHH. Sapporo 2̲; Narada 3̲. Ib H = 3.1.
3.5x   kasumo < *kasu_{2.4} [o]mo_{2.4}. 'freckle' (= soba-kasu). LLH - x-x-x x-x-x.
4.5   kasumomi ?< *kasu-momyi < *kasu_{2.4} mom[a-C]i_A. 'lees-soaked meat' (?).
LLLL - x-1-x x-x-x.
?3.4   kasuri (< ?). '(cloth with) splashed pattern'. x - 0̲/3-2-B x-x-x. Aomori,
Sz, Hamada, Matsue, Izumo, NE Kyūshū 0̲; Goka-mura 1̲ (we expect 0); Narada,
Hattō 3. Kōbe 1:3̲; Himeji 0̲ (Ōhara 1932-3); Ib H̲ = 3.1.
2.1 (= A)   kata(-) (adjective stem). 'hard'. (A - A-A-A A-A-A.)
2.2b   kata. 'direction'. HL - 2-2-A x-x-x. NS (109a) HL; NS (T 21) LL. Km (W)
HL(-H) / LL(-H). Edo HL. Aomori ('person') 2; Narada 1̲. Ib (rare, 'person') H1
= 2.2. (?< kata_{?2.3} 'one side')
2.2b   kata. 'shape' (= katati_{3.1}). x - 2-2-A x-A-x. NS (76b) HL; NS (T 75) LL.
Km (W) Hx. Edo HL.
2.2b   kata. 'beach; lagoon'. HL - 2-2-x x-(A)-x. Km (W) HL(-H) / LL(-H). Sr
kata-baru A 'shoal'.
?2.3   kata(-). 'one side (of two), one (of a pair); one person; unlined;
incomplete, half-; inclined toward; (do) intently'. See katane, kataomote,
katasumi, katatoki, katate, katawara, katawaki; katanaru, katanasu, kateru.
Cf. kana(-). Etymology: ?< *ka[na] - ta 'one hand/limb', cf. eda; ?< kata_{2.4}
'shoulder'; [Ōno] < Mongolian kaltas, Tungusic kaltaka 'half'.
2.4   kata. 'shoulder'. LH - 1-1-B B-B-B. Edo LH. Kōchi 1; Ib L = 2.4. Onna
kaataa B; Yn kata B (H 1964:65a, 71a), kataburuci B (H 1964:180a).
4.1   katabami < *katabamyi ?< *kata_{2.2b} -n- pami_{2.3}. 'wood sorrel, oxalis'.
HHHH - 0-0-B x-x-x.
4.5   [katabio] < katabiwo ?< *kata_{2.2b} -n- pibo_{2.x}. 'podocarp (tree)' (= maki).
LLLL - x-x-x x-x-x.
4.5   katabira < *kata-byira < *kata_{?2.3} -n- pira_{2.2b} 'unlined garment; ... '.
LLLL - 0/3/4-0-x x-x-x. Cf. yukatabira.
3.6   katae < (*)kata-fye < *kata_{2.3} pe_{1.x} (< ...). 'one of a pair; a part,
half; one side, a person to one side; a companion, a cohort; a remote place,
the countryside'. LHH - 0/2-x-x x-x- x. Edo LHH.
3.6   katae < kata-ye < *kata_{?2.3} ye_{?1.2} (< ...). 'the branch(es) on one side'.
x - x-x-x x-x-x. Km (W) LHH.
5.2   katagaeri < katagaferi ?< *kata_{2.2b} n[i] kafyeri_B (< *kapir[a-C]i_B)
('shape return'). 'a two-year-old hawk that has moulted once' (= katane).
HHHHL (Kn, Ck) - x-x-x x-x-x. Shinsen-Jikyō LLLHL.
4.3   katagayu < *kata_{adj A} -n- ka-du_{2.1} ('hard[-cooked] gruel'). 'firm-cooked
rice (as contrasted with sirukayu = modern kayu)'. HHLL - x-x-x x-x-x.

3.3   katagi: *see* kata^k/gi.

3.7a   katai < kata-wi < *kata?ₐ.ₛ bᵘ/ₒ-Ci[-Ci]ₐ ('be to one side'). 'beggar;
leper'. x - 0-1:3-x x-x-x. NS (T+ kun) LHL. K: Hn LHL *(where attested?)*.

5.16   katakasiki < *kata-kasikyi < *kataₐ.ₛ kasik[a-C]iₐ: ~ no ii (< ifyi <
*ipiₐ.ₛ) 'half-cooked (firm) rice'. LLHL(-L|LL) - x-x-x x-x-x.

3.3   kata^k/gi < katagi (Mg) < *kata-giy < *kataₐ.ₛb -n- koₒ-Ciₗ.ₛₐ. 'pattern
board, printing board; model'. HLL - 0-0-x x-x-x.

3.4   kataki ?< *katakyi (< ?). 'enemy'. LLL - 3-2-B x-B-B. Edo HHL. Akita 2.
Kōchi 3; Ib F = 3.4. Yn katati B (H 1964:71b). (Ōno: < 'one-side man', cf.
okina.)

4.5   katakoi < kata-kwofiy < *kataₐ.ₛ kwopoₒ-Ci[-Ci]ₐ.ₛ₊ᴮ. 'one-sided love'.
x - 0-0[H]/2[U]-B x-x-x. Km (W) LLLL.

4.x   katakuna (?< *kataₐdⱼ ₐ -kuₗₐf -na- (< *naₐdⱼ ᴮ) ('deficient with respect
to being hard'). 'obstinate'. x - 0-1[H]/0[U]-x x-x-x.

5.16   katakuzure < kata-kudure < *kataₐ.ₛ kuntu-ra-Ci[-Ci]ᴮ. 'collapsing
partially (on one side or in various places)'. LLLHL - x-x-x x-x-x.

3.1   katami < katamyi < *kataₐ.ₛb mi[-Ci]/mi[Ca-C]iᴮ ('shape see'). 'keepsake'.
?HHH - 0(/3[H])-0-ᴮ x-A-x. Km (W) HHH. Edo HHH. Aomori 3; Sz 0(?/2); Hattō,
Hamada, Matsue, Izumo, Hiroshima 0; Goka-mura 2. Ōsaka, Ise 0; Ib F = 3.4.

3.2a   katami (?< *kataₐdⱼ ₐ am[a-C]iₐ.ₛ₊ᴮ). 'bamboo basket'; variants katama,
katuma. HHL/HHH - 0-0-x x-x-x. Sr -katami 'counter for shoulder-loads' is from
the infinitive of a verb stem katami(r)- 'to shoulder'.

?3.4   katami < *kata-miy < *kata?ₐ.ₛ mu-Ciₗ.ₗ. 'one side of the body'. x - 0-0-x
x-x-x. Sz 2. Ib L = 3.6.

?3.5b, ?3.7b katami < *kata-miy < *kataₐ.₄ mu-Ciₗ.ₗ ('shoulder body'). 'upper
torso — representing a feeling of pride/smallness (hiroi/semai)'. x - 1-0-B
x-x-x. Hiroshima, Goka-mura 0. Ōsaka 0/1:3; Ise 1/1:3.

6.21   kata-minasigo < kataₐ.ₛ - miynasigwo₄.ₐ (< *mu-Ciₗ.ₗ na-siₐdⱼ ₐ pred -n-
kwoₗ.ₗ). 'a half-orphan, a child bereft of one parent'. LLLHLL - x-x-x x-x-x.

3.4   katana < *kata?ₐ.ₛ -naₗ.ₓ ('side blade'). 'sword, knife'. LLL - 3/2-2-B
B-B-C. Mr (Bm) HHL. Edo HHL. Sapporo, Wakamatsu, NE Kyūshū, Hakata, Ōita 2;
Hattō, Hamada, Matsue, Izumo, Narada 3; Goka-mura 0 *(expected reflex)*. Kōbe
(Robb) 1:3; Ib F = 3.4. Nk haTaana B 'ax'.

4.7 (= 2.3|2.1)   kata-naki < *kataₐ.ₛ - nakyiₐ.ₗ (< nak[a-C]iₐ). 'weeping alone,
unshared tears; half-crying; all-out weeping'. x - x-x-x x-x-x. NS (71c
[11:181M]) LL(|)HH; NS (T+ 50) HLLL, (T+ 69) HH|LH.

3.1   katane < *kataₐdⱼ ₐ neₗ.ₛₐ (< *na-Ci) ('hard root'). 'carbuncle'. HHH -
0-1-x x-x-x.

3.4   katane < *kataₐ.ₛ neₗ.ₗ (< *na-Ci[-Ci]ₐ). 'sleeping on one side without
turning over; numbness in legs/feet or arms/hands (as with paralysis); a two-
year-old hawk that has moulted once (= katagaeri)'. LLL - x-x-x x-x-x.

?3.7x, ?3.2a   katano < *kata-nwo ?< *kata?ₐ.ₛ nwoₗ.ₛₐ. 'Katano' *(placename)*.
x - 0-x-x x-x-x. Km (W) LHL, HHL.

5.16   kataomote < *kata?ₐ.ₛ omo-teₐ.₄ (< *omoₐ.₄ ta-Ciₗ.ₛₐ). 'one surface/face'.
LLLHL (Kz) - x-x-x x-x-x.

4.11   katasaki < kata-sakyi < *kataₐ.₄ sakiₐ.ₗ. 'upper shoulder'. LLHL -
0/4-1[U]/1:3[H]-B x-B-x. Sr katasaci B 'length of cloth from fingertips to
opposite shoulder'.

5.16   katasigiri < *kata[a]si-gyiri < *kata?ₐ.ₛ [a]siₐ.ₛ -n- kir[a-C]iᴮ.
'hopping (on one foot)' (= kataasi). LLLHL - x-4-x x-x- x.

?6.22   katasiro-gusa < *kataₐ.₄ - sirwoₐdⱼ ᴮ -n- kusaₐ.ₛ ('shoulder-white
plant'). 'lizard's-tail' (= hangesyoo). LLLLxx (?= *LLLLHL) - x-5-x x-x-x.

4.6 (= 2.3|2.4)   katasumi < *kata-sumyi < *kata?₂.₃ sumi₂.₄. '(a rope holding
down) one corner'. LL(|)LH (Hoke-kyō tanji) 0/3-0[H]/3[U]-B x-B-x.

5.10   katatagai < katatagafi < *kata?₂.₃ tagafyi₂.₆ (< tankapi₂.₄₊ᵦ < ...).
'disarray; being uneven or out of order'. LHHHH - x-x-x x-x-x.

?3.6   katate < *kata?₂.₃ ta-Ci₁.₃ₐ 'one hand'. x - 3/0-0-B x-x-x. Edo HHL.
Sz, Narada 3. Ib F = 3.4.

3.1   katati (?< *kata₂.₂ᵦ ti?₁.₁ 'spirit of shape'). 'shape'. HHH - 0-0-A
A-A-A. NS (120a, 126b) HHH. Km (S) HHH. Mr (Bm) HHH. Edo HHH. Goka-mura 2.
Ib H1 = 3.3.

?4.5 (= 2.3|2.3)   katatoki < *kata-tokyi < *kata₂.₃ toki₂.₃. 'half a spell, a
short while'. x - 0/4-4-B x-B[Lit.]-x.

?5.16 (= 2.3-tu|2.4)   katatukata < *kata₂.₃ -tu kata₂.₂ᵦ. 'one of a pair, one
end/side/direction, one of the two'. LLL|HL - x-x-x x-x-x.

2.1|?3.7 kata-tumuri = kata tuburi (Mg) < *kata∫ₐₐⱼ ₐ tunpuri?₃.₇ ('hard head').
'snail'. HH|LHL - 3-4[H]/1:4[U]-B x-x-x. Narada 3. Sakawa 1:4 (borrowed?
[= denden-musi]).

4.6   katawara < katafara < *kata₂.₃ para₂.₃. 'side'. LLLH - 0/3-0[H]/3[U]-B
x-B-x. Sz 4. Sr katahara B. K: Edo HHHL.

6.23   katawarabone < katafara-bone < *kata-fara₄.₆ (< *kata₂.₃ para₂.₃) -n-
pone₂.₃ (< ...). 'rib(s)'. LLLLLH - x-x-x x-x-x.

4.1   katazake < *kata-zakey < *kata∫ₐₐⱼ ₐ -n- saka-Ci₂.₁. 'unrefined sake'.
HHHH - x-x-x x-x-x.

2.3   kate < ka[ri]te < kar[efy]i₂.₄ (< ...) [a]te[y]ₐ (< ...). 'provisions'.
x - 1/2-2-B x-x-x. Km x. Mr (Bm) LH. K: Hn LL (attested?). Aomori, Sz 2.
Ib F = 2.3. See karei.

2.3   kati < *kat[a-C]i₈. 'victory'. LL - 2-0[H]/1[U]-B x-B-(B). Matsue 2/1;
Narada, Hattō, Hamada, Izumo, Goka-mura, Hiroshima 2. Ōsaka, Ise 2; Ib (rare)
H = 2.1. F = 2.3.

2.3   kati, katin (< Ch hhat). 'rough wool cloth; (= kati-ginu) a rough wool
garment; (= kati-iro) dark blue(-black)'. LL - 1-2-x x-x-x. Edo HL. K: Km LL.
Cf. tokati.

?2.4   kati. 'walking'. LH - 1-0[H]/1[U]-B x-B-x. Edo LH. K: "Hn ?LH, ?LF".
Hiroshima 1. Ōsaka, Ise 1/2.

4.5   katigata < *kat[a-C]i₈ -n- kata₂.₂ᵦ ('pound shape'). 'barley' (= oomugi).
LLLL - x-x-x x-x-x.

5.16   katiikusa < *kati?₂.₄ ikusa₃.₄. 'footsoldier'. x - x-x-x x-x-x. NS (122b)
LLLHL.

4.6   katindo = katim[u]do < *kati₂.₄ -n- pito₂.₂ₐ. 'pedestrian'. LLLH - x-3-x
x-x-x. K: "Hn ?LLLH, ?LLLF".

4.6   katisine < *kati (< *kat[a-C]i₈) [z]ina-Ci₂.₄. 'unhulled rice, rice to be
pounded' (= momi[-gome]). LLLH - x-x-x x-x-x.

3.1 (< *4.1)   katori < *kat[a]-ori < *kata₂.₁ or[a-C]i₄ ('hard weave'). 'a kind of
tight-woven cloth'. HHHH - x-0-x x-x-x.

?[2.5] < 3.7b katu < katuu < *kat[a-Ci]-u ('uniting'). 'moreover; and'. x - 1-2-A
x-x-x. Km (S) katuu-fa LHL-L. Edo katuu LHL.

4.11   katugime < *katugyi-mye < *katunk[a-C]i₈ miCa₁.₃ᵦ (?= *mina). 'a woman
diver' (= kazukime). LLHL - x-0-x x-x-x.

5.11   katunegusa < *katune (= ?₍ᵦ₎) -n- kusa₂.₃. 'mahuang, Ephedra sinica' (=
kakumagusa = amana = maoo). LHHHL - x-x-x x-x-x.

3.1   katuo < katuwo ?< *kat[a]-uwo (?< *kat[a]₂.₁ ibo₁.₁). 'bonito'. HHH -
0-0-A A-B-A. Aomori 0. Ib H = 3.1. Sd khaso(o) A; Nk kaCuu A; Sr kaçuu B;
Yn katu A (H 1964:72a).

5.2   katuomusi < katuwo*s.1* (< ...) musi*s.1*. 'drosophila (= nuka-ka); water
strider/skipper (= amenbo)'. HHHHL - x-x-x x-x-x.

3.1   katura. 'judas-tree' (= oka*t*/*z*ura). HHH - 0-0[H]/2[U]-A x-x-x. NS (T+ kun)
HHH. Km (W) HHH. Aomori *(rare)*, Hakata 1. Ib kazura L2 = 3.5/7.

3.7a   katura/kazura < *ka(n)tura < kam[i]*s.s* tura*ʔs.sb*. 'head-dress'. LHL -
0-2-B x-x-x. Km (W) HHL. 1700 Ōsaka HLL. Aomori [kažira], Sz 3; Wakamatsu 1;
Hakata -z- 1, ygr 0. Ib -z- L2 = 3.5/7. Mg -du-; *see* Ch. 2.

4.1   katuragi, kazuraki < kadurakiy ?< *kanturas.*sb* (< ...) kiy*1.sa* (< ...)
('vine fortress'). 'the western part of Nara prefecture; (name of mountain)'.
x - 0-0-x x-x-x. NS (72c [11:201-M]) HHHH; NS (T+ 84) HHL|H (incongruent).
Km (W) HHHH.

4.6   katuuri ?< kan (< Ch .hhan 'cold') -tu uri*s.4*; ?< ka[ra]*s.s* -tu uri*s.4*.
'winter melon = wax gourd, Benineasa hispida' (= toogan). LLLH - x-x-x x-x-x.

2.2a   kawa < kafa < *kapa. 'river'; (Ryūkyū) 'well'. HL - 2-2-A A-A-A.
NS (72a, 94b) HH, (73a, 101a, 104a) HL; NS (T 97) HL, (T 53, 56; 83) HH,
Km (S) HL. 1700 Ōsaka HL. Ib H1 = 2.2. K: Edo HL.

?2.2b   kawa < kafa < *kapa. 'side, direction'. x - 2-2-x x-x-x. *See* gawa.

2.3   kawa < kafa < *kapa. 'skin, fur'. LL - 2-0[H]/1[U]-B B-B-B. Edo HL.
Hiroshima 2. Kōbe (Robb), Ōsaka 1/1:3; Ib F = 2.3 ('peel, rind' L = 2.4).

3.2b   kawabe < kafabe < *kafa-bye < *kafa (-n-) fye/fey < *kapa*s.sa* -n-
piCa*1.x*/*paCi*1.1*. 'riverside'. x - 0/3-0-A x-x-x. NS (T+ 117) kafa fey HH L.
Igarashi 49a n.3: N fey 'side of N', N fye 'N and vicinity'.

3.4   [kawabe] < kafabe (?< *kapa*s.s* -n- piCa*1.x* 'skin layer'; ?< *kafa-bey
< *kapa*s.s* -n- [u]pa-Ci*s.sa* 'skin surface, *see* ue). 'skin'. LLL - x-x-x x-x-x.

4.2   kawabune < kafa-bune < *kapa*s.sa* -n- puna-Ci*s.4*. 'river-boat'. x - 0/3-0-x
x-x-x.

4.3   kawagame < "kafakame" = kafagame < *kafa-gamey < *kapa*s.sa* -n- kamaCi*s.s*.
'snapping turtle'. HHLL - x-x-x x-x-x. (NKD: "-kame".)

4.6   kawaginu < kafaginu < *kafa-gyinu < *kapa*s.s* -n- kinu*s.4*.
'fur garment'. LLLH - 0/3-1:3-x x-x-x.

4.2   kawagiri < kafa-giyri < *kapa*s.sb* k*ª*/*o*Ciri*s.1*. 'river fog'.
x - 0/2-0[H]/3[U]-A x-x-x. Km (W) HHHL.

5.16/5.6 kawagoromo < kafagoromo < *kafa-goromo < *kapa*s.s* -n- koromo*s.1*.
'fur gown'. LLLHL/LLLLL - 3-1:3-x x-x-x.

?4.2   kawahone < kawa-fone (> koofone > kofone > kohone*s.2*) < *kafa*s.sb*
(< *kapa) fone*s.s* (< ...) ('river bone'). 'candar, Nuphar japonicum'.
HHxx - 0-0-x x-x-x. K: Hn HHHL.

4.1   kawa*k*/*g*uma < kafa*k*/*g*uma < *kapa*s.sa* (-n-) kuma*ʔs.s*. 'river bend'.
x - x-x-x x-x-x. NS (110a) HHHH; NS (T+ 53) HL|LH. Km x.

7.2   kawakumatuzura < kafakuma*4.1* (< ...) - tudura*s.s* (< *tuntura). 'a
spindletree (= mayumi); a wingèd spindletree (= nisikigi)'. HHHHHHL - x-6-x
x-x-x.

4.10   kawamusi < kafamusi < *kapa*s.s* musi*s.1* ('fur insect'). 'caterpillar' (=
kemusi). LLHL - x-x-x x-x-x.

3.1   kawana < kafa-na < *kapa*ʔs.sa* na*1.sa*. 'edible river-weeds'. HHH - 0/2-0-x
x-x-x.

5.2   kawanagusa < kafa-na*s.1* -gusa (< -n- kusa*s.s*). 'edible river-weeds'.
x - 3-4-x x-x-x. Km (W) HHHHL.

4.1   kawanaka < kafa-naka < *kapa*ʔs.sa* naka*s.4*. 'midstream'. x - 0-0-x x-x-x.
NS (125a) HHHH.

5.2   kawanegusa (?< kafane-gusa < *kapa*s.sa* na-Ci*ɐ1.sa* -n- kusa*s.s*; ?< kabanegusa). *(1)* 'Alpinia kumatake' (= kabanegusa = kumatake-ran); *(2)* 'willow'.
HHHHL - 3-x-x x-x-x.

?3.1 (< *4.1), ?3.2x   kawara < kafara < *kapa$_{?2.2a}$ para$_{2.3}$. 'riverbed'. x - 0-0-A
(x)-A-x. NS (94b, *placename?*) HHL. Edo HHH. Narada kaara 0. Ib kaara H = 3.1.
The traditional etymology, given above, may be wrong; Akinaga 1977:67 makes
a good case for -ra as a suffix.

3.4   kawara < kafara < *kapara. 'tile'. LLL - 0-2-B x-B-C. Edo HLL. Akita,
Hamada, Matsue, Izumo, Hiroshima, Hakata 0; Goka-mura 2 *(we expect 0)*; Sapporo,
Sz 2; Aomori 3; Matsumoto, Numazu, Narada, Hattō, Hida (= northern Gifu),
Wakamatsu, Ōita 1. Suzu 1:3 *(we expect 0)*; Ib kaara H = 3.1. Nk haara B; Sr
kaara B; Yn kaara C (H 1964:71b). *H 1960:(46) is mistaken on Tk, see id.:147a.*
(Ōno says the word is borrowed from Sanskrit kapāla.)

3.5x (?< ?3.1, ?3.2x)   kawara < kafara < *kapara. ? 'Kawara' *(placename)*, or just
'the River' (esp. the Kamo[-gawa] River). x - x-x-x x-x-x. NS (118b [14:148-K])
kawara no sima *(this accent for* sima$_{2.3}$ *post-Km?)*. NS (T+ kun) HHL. Cf.
simakawara.

5.3   kawarahuzi < kafara$_{?3.1,?3.2}$ (< ...) - fudi$_{2.1}$ (< *punti) ('riverbed
wisteria'). *(1)* 'honey locust' (= saikati); *(2)* 'Caesalpinia japonica' (=
zyaketu-ibara). HHHLL - 3-x-x x-x-x.

6.2   kawarayomogi < kafara$_{2.4}$ (< ...) - yomogiy (< *domo$_?$ -n- ko-Ci$_{1.3a}$.
'chrysanthemum (= kiku); ... '. HHHHL - x-x-x x-x-x.

?4.1   kawa-^{s}/$_z$iri < kafa-^{s}/$_z$iri < *kapa$_{2.2a}$ (-n-) siri$_{2.3}$. 'lower streams; mouth
of a river'. x - 0-0-x x-x-x. NS (100b) HL(|)LH *(anomalous pattern)*.

4.3   kawatake < kafa-takey < *kapa$_{2.2a}$ taka-Ci$_{2.1}$. 'river bamboo'. HHLL -
2/0-0-x x-x-x.

6.3   kawatisanoki < kafatisa-no-ki < *kafa-tisa$_{4.x}$ (< *kapa$_{2.2a}$ tisa$_{2.x(<3.6)}$)
no ko-Ci$_{1.3a}$. 'Lilium concolor' (= santan-ka). HHHHLL - x-x-x x-x-x.

3.1 (< *4.1)   kawawa < kafa-wa[da] < *kapa$_{2.2b}$ banta$_{?2.3}$. 'river bend; Kawawa
(placename)'. HHH (Ir) - x-x-x x-x-x.

3.1   kawaya < kafa-ya < *kapa$_{(2.2)}$ da$_{1.3b}$ (? 'river$_{2.2a}$ house', ? 'side$_{2.2b}$
house'). 'toilet'. HHH - 0-0[H]/2[U]-B x-x-x. Km x. Sz 0. Ib *(rare)* H = 3.1.

5.2   kawayanagi < kafa$_{2.2a}$ (< *kapa) yanagiy$_{3.1}$ (< ?*dana$_{?2.1}$ -n- ko-Ci$_{1.3a}$)
('river willow'). 'purple willow'. HHHHL - 3-4-x x-x-x.

-         kawa-ziri: *see* kawa-siri.

4.1   kawazoi < kafa-^{s}/$_z$ofi < kafa-swofyi < *kapa$_{2.2b}$ swop[a-C]i$_A$. 'along the
river'. x - 0-0-A x-x-x. NS (Okada) HHHH.

3.6   kawazu < kafadu < *kapantu. 'frog'. x - 0-1-A x-x-x. 1700 Ōsaka LHH.
Sz *(rare)* 0. Cf. kaeru, hiki.

2.1   kaya < *ka$_{1.1}$ da$_{1.3b}$. 'mosquito net'. x - 0-0-A x-(x)-x. Hakata 0, ygr
2/1. Ib H = 2.1. Dial. (Takeno-gun) gaya ?< *[ ] -n- kaya (see Ch. 1, §26).

?2.3   kaya ?< *kaye *(second vowel assimilated to the first)* < ka[f]e (< ?).
'Japanese nutmeg'. x - 1-0-x x-x-x. Hiroshima 1. Ōsaka, Ise 1. *See* kae,
kabuti.

2.4   kaya < *kada. 'thatch'. LH - 1-0-B x-B-x. NS (96b, 110b) LH. Edo LH.
Aomori 2/0. Ōsaka, Ise 1; Ib L = 2.4. Cf. tigaya.

?2.5   kaya (?< *gada). 'Imna (Mimana), a state in south Korea during the third
to sixth centuries AD' (= kara$_{2.5}$). x - 1-x-x x-x-x. Cf. aya.

4.11   kayaguki ?< *kayagukyi < *kada$_{2.4}$ -n- kuk[a-C]i$_{?B}$ ('dart through thatch').
'lark'. LLHL - x-0-x x-x-x. NKD: "-ku-" (but both Mg and Ir have -gu-). Also
kaya-kuguri.

4.1   kayaribi < *kayari-biy < *ka$_{1.1}$ dar[a-C]i$_A$ -n- po-Ci$_{1.3b}$. 'smudge fire
(against mosquitoes)'. x - 3-4-A x-x-x. Km (W) HHHH. K: Hn-Km HHHH.

4.5   kayaziri < *kada$_{2.4}$ -n- siri$_{2.3}$. '(roof-)thatch edges'. x - x-x-x x-x-x.
NS (97a, 99a) LLLL.

4.2 kayoizi < kayofi-di < kaywofyi-di < *ka(-)dwop[a-C]i_A -n- ti_?1.1.
'commuting route' (= kayoimiti). x - x-x-x x-x-x. Km (W) HHHL.

2.1 kayu ?< *ka_1.1 du_1.3a ('scent hot-water'); ?< *ka[Ci]_1.3 du_1.3a (= key yu
'meal hot-water' *but the register is incongruent*). 'gruel, porridge'. HH(/HL) -
0-1[H]/0[U]-B x-A-x. Hiroshima 0. Ōsaka, Ise 1; Ib L = 2.4. Cf. katagayu.

2.1 kaza(-) 'wind': *see* kaze.

2.1 [kaza] < *kansa (= 'wind'). 'odor, scent'. x - x-x-x A-A-A. Attested 1268;
found in many Honshū dialects (NKD). Nk hazaa A 'stench' (≠ habaa A 'aroma');
Sd khada A; Sr kaza A; Yn kada(i) A. Kobama (Yaeyama) kanza. Cf. ka; kagu,
[kabu].

5.2 kaza-ᵏ/borosi < kaza-ᶠ/borosi < *kansa_2.1 (-n-) porosi_3.x. 'a fever rash'.
HHHHL - x-x-x x-x-x. (" -ᶠ/b- from Mr".)

4.1 kazakiri < *kaza-kyiri < *kansa_2.1 kir[a-C]i_B. 'flight 'remex/remiges =
flight feather(s)' (= kazakiri-bane). HHHH - 0/4-x-x x-x- x.

3.3 kazami (< Ch hhan'-.sram). 'a kind of garment (originally a sort of
sweat-suit)'. HLL (Ir) - x-0-x x-x-x. K: "Hn LLL" *(mistake?)*.

3.1 kazari < *kansa(-)r[a-C]i_A. 'ornament'. HHH - 0-0-A x-A-A. Akita 3 (verb
B); Goka-mura 1 (verb A); Narada 0. Ib H = 3.1. Yn kadai/kadari A (H 1964:71b).

3.4 kazasi < kanzasi < kamu^a/zasi < *kami_3.4 (-n-) sas[a-C]i_B. 'hair-pin, hair
ornament'. LLL - 0-0-B x-B-x. Sr kamisasi B.

2.1 kaze < *kaze[y] < *kansa-Ci. 'wind'. HH - 0-0-A A-A-A. NS (121a) HH.
Km (S,W) HH. Edo HH. Ib H = 2.1.

?2.4, ?2.5 kaze 'sea-urchin': *see* kase.

?2.1 kazi < kadi < *kanti < "kanuti" (NS kokun) < *kan^a/e-uti (cf. Kuranaka 93)
< *kan[a_2.1 u]t[a-C]i_B ('metal hit'). 'smith(ing)'. LH (Kn) / HH (Ck) - 2-2-x
x-B-x. Nk hanzaa C; Sr kanzaa B (< *kanzi -a) 'smith'.

?2.1, ?2.2b kazi < kadi < *kadi[y] < *kantu-Ci (M 3432: kadu). 'paper mulberry'.
HH - 1-2-x x-x-x. K: Hn HL *(where attested?)*. Cf. kozoo 'paper mulberry', kami
'paper'. (?< kazi_3.3b 'rudder', "because the leaf resembles a rudder".)

2.2a kazi < kadi < *kanti. 'rudder'. HL - 1-2-A A-B-x. NS (Okada) HL; NS (T 39)
LL. Hattō, Hamada, Goka-mura 2; Matsue, Izumo 0 (= 2.1-2); eastern Iwami
(Hiroto 1961:162), Tappi (Clarke 56), Aomori, Sz 1. Ib H1 = 2.2. Nk hazii A.
Cf. kai.

3.4 = 4.5 kaziki = kanziki (x - 0(/4[Mkz]-0[H]/3[U]-A x-x-x) ?< *ka[ka-Ci]_B -n-
sik[a-C]i_A. 'a kind of snowshoe'. LLL - x-x-x x-x-x. Cf. warigo.

4.2 kazitori < kadi-tori < *kanti_3.3b t(w)or[a-C]i_B. 'steering a boat;
helmsman'. HHHL - 2-4-A x-A-x. Sz 3.

2.4 kazo < kaso. 'father'. LH - x-1[U]-x x-x-x. NS (129a) LH; NS (T+ kun) LL.
Km x. Cf. iro.

2.4 kazu < *kansu. 'number'. LH - 1-1-B B-B-C. NS (96a[11:72-K]) LH. Edo LH.
Narada kazo [kao] 1; Matsue, Izumo 2. Ib L = 2.4. Yn kadi C (H 1964:65b, 71a).
Cf. kazoeru, kana(-).

3.2b kazura < kadura < *kantura (?*tura_?2.3b = turu_2.3b). 'vine, creeper'.
HHx - 0-2-A x-B-x. Km (W) HHL. Sz *(rare)* 0; Hakata 1, ygr 0. Nk hanza B; Sr
kanda B. Cf. kuzukazura; katura.

?3.7a kazura 'head-dress': *see* katura.

- kazuraki < kadurakiy: *see* katuragi.

?1.3a ?*ke- 'this' (= ko): *see* *ki-.

?1.1 ke < key (< ?). 'signs, appearance, feel'. x - 0/1-0-x x-x-x. Cf. ki.
Aomori 0; Hiroshima (Terakawa) 1, (Okuda) 0. Ōsaka, Ise 1; Ib L = 1.3.

?1.1 ke < key < *ka-Ci. 'hair'. H - 0-2-A A-A-A. Km (S) H(-x). Aomori, Narada,
Hattō, Hamada, Matsue, Izumo, Okayama, Hiroshima (etc.) 0. Toyama, Suzu, Hyōgo,
Ōsaka, Ise 2; Kōchi 0 (Hattori 1931:176, 1973:377; Doi 1952:20); Ib H = 1.1.

Cf. K 1964a:332 "Okayama, southeast Hiroshima, most of Shikoku, and early Km Busshō-e-saimon 0". K: Hn-Km-Edo HL. Cf. kemono; kami, siraga, saoge. Note: Kobayashi lists Izumo 1 but Hiroto and Ōhara have 0.

?1.2, ?1.1   ke < key < *kaCi (?< *ka-Ci, cf. ka$_{1.3a}$ 'plate ... ' but also uke). 'container (tray, box)'. H - x-0-x x-x-x. K: Hn HL. Cf. i^k/$_g$e, sara^k/$_g$e.

?1.3a   ke < key < *ka-Ci. 'days'. x - x-x-x x-x-x. Cf. ko-yomi$_{3.4}$; (-)ka.

1.3a   ke < key (?< [u]key < *uka-Ci '*food'; ?< *kaCi = ka[m]i < *kam[a-C]i). 'meal': myi-key 'exalted meal (as offering)', key-koto 'eating'; later asa-ge 'morning meal', yufu-ge 'evening meal', ke-^{k}/$_g$o 'lunch box'. x - x-x-x x-x-x. Edo ke-doki HLL 'mealtime'.

1.3a   ke < *key < *kaCi. 'everyday, informal, private', as contrasted with hare 'special(-occasion), formal, public'. L - 0-1-x x-x-x.

1.3b   ke < kye < *kiCa. 'strange' (adj-n): kye-naru NS (118a) R-LL; kye-ni (Kn) R-x.

-        -ke < key (= kiy) < *ko-Ci 'tree(s)': see ki.

?2.1   keba ?< *key$_{?1.1}$ (< ...) -n- pa$_{1.1}$ ('hair feathers'). 'nap, shag, fluff'. x - 0-0-x x-x-x. Sz 0. Cf. kebadatu.

4.1   kedamono < keydamono (= keyda-mono) < ?*ka-Ci$_{?1.1}$ -n- ta$_{1.3a}$ mono$_{2.3}$ ('hairy-limbed thing'). 'animal'. HHHx - 0-3[H]/1:3[U]-A x-x-x. Km (W) HHHH. Mr (W 20) HHHL. Hakata 2, ygr 0. Cf. kemono. (The usual etymology treats -da- as -ta- and considers it a variant of -tu 'of'.)

3.7b   kedasi < keydasi (< ?). 'probably; perhaps' (adv). LHL - 1-0[H]/1:3[U]-A x-x-x. On the etymology see Yoshida 1979: ?< key$_{?1.1}$ ita-si$_{adj\ B\ pred}$ 'the appearance is extreme'.

2.3   kega < *kenka (< ?). 'mishap; wound, damage'. x - 2-2-B x-B-x. 1700 Ōsaka HL. Aomori 2. Ib F = 2.3. Earliest attestation Mr? Cf. kegasu.

?2.3, ?2.4   kego < ke-^{k}/$_g$o < *key$_{1.3a}$ (< ...) -n- kwo$_{1.3a}$. 'a lunch box'. LL (Kn, -k-) / LH (Ck, -g-) - x-x-x x-x-x.

3.4   kemono < keymono (= key-mono) < *ka-Ci$_{?1.1}$ mono$_{2.3}$ ('hair thing'). 'animal'. LLL - 0-2-A x-x-x. Sz, Aomori, Narada, Hattō, Hamada, Matsue, Izumo, Wakamatsu 0; Goka-mura 0 (= 3.1 or 3.4); Hakata 0 (= 3.4). Kōchi (Kobayashi) 1:3; Kōbe (Robb) 0; Ib H = 3.1. Register is incongruent with the etymology; perhaps contaminated with ikimono < *ik[a-C]i$_B$ mono$_{2.3}$ (but cf. kedamono).

3.1   kemuri < keburi (?< *keyburi < ?*k^a/$_o$Cinpu-r[a-C]i$_A$). 'smoke' (= kemu, kebu). HHH - 0-0-A x-A-(A). NS (98b) LHH, (99b) HHL, (98a, 132a) HHH. Km (S) HHH. Edo HHH. Mr (Bm) HHH. Goka-mura 2. Ib ke^m/$_b$uri H = 3.1. Sr cimuri A [Lit.] = kibusi A. Yn kibunci A.

4.x   kengozi < "kenikosi" (< Ch .khen-.ngyew-'tsyey). 'morning-glory' (= asagao). x - x-x-x x-x-x. Km (W) LHHH, LHHL, LHL, LH|LH. Mr (W 19) LHLL.

3.2b   kenuki < *key-nukyi < *ka-Ci$_{?1.1}$ nuk[a-C]i$_A$. 'tweezers'. HHL - 3/0-1:3[H]/2[U]-A x-x-x. Sapporo, Aomori, Akita 0, Matsumoto, Numazu, Narada, Hiroshima 3. Kōchi, Sakawa 3; Ib H = 3.1.

2.3   kera (< ?). 'mole cricket'. LL - 0-0[H]/2[U]-B x-x-x.

2.1   kesa (< Ch .ka-.sa < Sanskrit kaṣāya). 'priest's robe, surplice'. HH - 0-0-B x-x-x. Edo HH. Ib F = 2.3. Hakata 0. (NKD "kaṣsya" is a misprint.)

2.4   kesa < kyesa < *ki-$_{?1.3}$ asa$_{2.3}$. 'this morning'. LH - 1-1-B x-x-x. Km (W) LH(-H). Edo LH. Ōsaka, Ise 1; Ib L = 2.4. (On a suspicion this may have been LF = 2.5, see Sakurai 1975:91-2.)

2.4   keta (< ?; cf. ita, kida). 'rafter, beam; lath, slat; row'. LH - 0-0-B x-B-x. Km x. Hakata 1, ygr 0. Narada, Hattō, Hamada, Matsue, Izumo 0; Goka-mura 2. Ib F = 2.4.

2.4   keta, geta (Kn Mg) (?< 'rafter', cf. Yoshida 1979:190-3). 'square' (adj-n). LH - x-x-x x-x-x. Cf. kata, kado. (Ōno: "Mg keda" mistake?)

3.5a   keyaki (< *keya-kiy < *k···a? ko-Ci). 'zelkova (tree)'. x - 0-2-B x-x-x.
Hattō 3; Hamada, Matsue, Izumo, Goka-mura 0. Ib F̲ = 3.4. First attested JP?
Cf. Sd khyaagi A, Sr caagi A, Yaeyama kyaangi, Yn kyangi 'black pine'; Yn
kidaki 'ebony'.

?5.6   kezuribana < *keydur[a-C]i?ʙ´ (< ...) -n- panaʂ.ɢ. 'an open-petal flower
shape whittled from the end of a log'. x - x-0-x x-x-x. Km (W 15) LLLLL, (W 14)
xxxLL; (W 17) HHHHH (register incongruent with etymology).

1.1   ki (?< *kiy < ?). 'onion' (= negi, cf. nagi). H - x-0-x x-x-x.

1.1   ki < ?*kiy (< Ch khyey´). 'vapor; spirit'. x - 0/1̲-0-A A-A-x. Km x.
Hiroshima 0. Ōsaka, Ise 0; Ib H = 1.1. Cf. iki 'breath', ke 'signs, ... '.

?1.1   (-)ki < kiy ?< *[fyi]kiy ?< *piko-Ci_A. 'counter (numeral auxiliary) for
lengths of cloth, for horses, (?) for people'. x - x-x-x x-x-x. NS (T+ 79) H.
See yatugi, (-)hiki.

1.2   ki(-) < kii (Mg) < *kiy < *kᵘ/₂-Ci. 'yellow' (adj-n). HL - 0/1̲-0-A
x-(A)-(A). Sz 0; Hiroshima kii-na 0. Ib H̲ = 1.1. Sr ci-iru A 'yellow',
Yn kiru-cici A 'is yellow'. (The Shuri palatalization suggests *ku-Ci rather
than *ko-Ci, but then we must explain ko-gane.)

?1.2   ki < *kiy < *kᵘ/₂Ci. 'fang' (= kiba HL). L̲ - x-x-x (A)-(A)-x. (Probably
*kuCi rather than *koCi. See kiba.)

1.3a   ki < kiy < *ko-Ci. 'tree; shrub; plant'. L - 1-1-B B-B-B. NS (72b [11:197-
M], 73a [11:215-M], 11:216-M]) L; NS (T+ 41, 53, 56) H̲. Km (S) L(-H). Edo R.
Ib L = 1.3. Cf. takigi; hinoki, keyaki, kusunoki, sakaki; hiiragi, kunugi,
miyatukogi, ogi, sugi, yanagi, yomogi. OJ variant *ko-Ci > key: Zdb 257d.

?1.3a   ki < kyi < *ki. 'pestle' (= kine). x - x-x-x x-x-x. Must be L because kine
is 2.4. Cf. kiuta.

?1.3a   *ki- 'this' (= ko): see kesa, kyoo. Or is this *ke-? Cf. Azuma Ce for
Co and also (Ch. 7, §4) sometimes for Ci.

?1.3a   (-)ki < kyi < *ki. 'inch'. L - x-x-x x-x-x. Cf. kiza, kida LL 'notch',
kizamu; Korean ´chi 'inch'. Mg uses the same semantogram to gloss kida-kida
(LLxx).

?1.3a   ki < kiy (< ?). 'enclosure, stockade, fortress'. x - x-x-x x-x-x. NS (90b)
ifo ki '500 fortresses' LL L; NS (T+ 100, 101) kiy no [u]fey ni 'atop the
fortress' L L L H; NS (T+ 7) taka kiy 'high fortress' LL L = (T+ 84) taka-kiy
LHH 'high fortress', (T+ 116) ima-kiy LꟼH = LHH. Cf. ki-t̄uku 'build' (B´ <
1.3|A). Miller 1979 (Journal of Korean Studies 1:16) and 1976 (cited in Miller
1979) follows Japanese scholars in claiming this is a borrowing from an "old
Paekche" word *kuy; for the Paekche word, see Toh 1981:27. But the Japanese
etymon may be a noun *ka[k]u-Ci made from the root of the verb stem kaku-m[a]-
'enclose, surround' (Ch. 6: kakomu).

1.x   ki (?< *kiy < ?). 'coffin'. x - x-x-x x-x-x.

1.x (?1.3x)   ki(-). 'natural, unspoiled, pure'. x - 1-1-x x-x-x. Sz 1. Compounds A
in Kg; B in Kt except ki-ito 2 (Ib H1 = 2.2); but few. Probably late; thought
to be [i]ki 'live' < iki[y] < iki[y] ← ik-i (restructured) < *ik[a-C]iʙ.

1.x (?1.3x)   (-)ki < kyi < *ki (< ?*k[am]i < *kam[a-C]iʙ 'brew', cf. kamosu).
'wine'. See miki. Kawabata (Kokugo-kokubun 407:6) notes that kurwo-ki 'dark
wine' and sirwo-ki 'light wine' are written with the phonogram for kiy (but the
attestations date from after 900), and he suggests kiy < *kuCi ?= ku[s]i
'wondrous elixir = rice wine'. If he is right, it will be necessary to explain
the second vowel of myi-kyi as assimilated to the first. Notice also NS (kun)
yu-kiy 'sacred wine > Number-One land of grain tribute'.

1.x   -ki(-) < -kyi(-) < *ki. 'man, male': see okina. Cf. kamiy-rᵘ/ₒ-kyi 'god
(title)'; -mi(-).

2.2b   kiba < *kiyba < *k^m/$_o$Ci -n- pa$_{1.2}$. 'fang, tusk'. HL - 1-2[H]/1:3[U]-A
A-A-x. Hiroshima 2; Matsue, Izumo 0 (= 2.1-2); Narada, Hattō, Goka-mura,
Wakamatsu 1. Kameyama, Ise 2; Ōsaka 1:3; Ib H1 = 2.2. Unaspirated Kwiiba A in
Kusigwa (Kusakabe 1968:46), palatalization of Sr ciiba A, and Yaeyama gïï-baa
(Shiraho gïï-ban), indicate the first etymon is *kuCi rather than *koCi.

?4.5   kibatisu: see kihatisu.

?2.4   kibi < kyibiy < *kinp^m/$_o$Ci (< ?). 'Kibi' (placename). x - 1-x-x x-x-x.
NS (T 40) HH. Km (W) LH.

2.5   kibi < *kyibyi = kimi < kyimyi < *ki-n-pi (< ?, cf. hie). 'millet'. LH/LF
- 1-1[H]/1:3[U]-B B-x-x. Izumo 2. On Kt 1:3 see Ōhara 1951:418 ("some places
also 1"). Ib (new?) L = 2.4. (Sr maazin A < *ma-gimi < *ma -n- kimi.) Cf. hie.

3.2a < 4.x   kibisu. 'heel'. HHL - 0-2-x x-x-x. Sz 0/2; Hakata (kibisy^a/$_o$,
kibisu) 1. See kubisu.

?3.5a   kibone ?< *kyi-bone < *ki$_{?1.2}$ -n- pone$_{2.3}$ (< ...) ('fang bone'). 'lower
jawbone'. "HRL", xHx = *HHL - 0-x-x x-x-x.

?2.3   kida < kyida < *kinta. 'a cut, a notch (= kiza < *kinsa); a unit of
measure'. (LL-) - x-x-x x-x-x. Cf. ki 'inch', kir-u 'cut'.

2.5   kido < *kiy-dwo < *koCi$_{1.3a}$ -n- two$_{1.1}$. 'wicket, gate'. x - 1-2/1:3-B
x-x-x. Sz 2. Ib L = 2.3.

4.1/4.3   kienba < kiwemufa < *kiy$_{1.2}$ (< *k^m/$_o$-Ci) wemufa$_{?3.1,?3.2}$ (< ...). 'a
yellow dragonfly' (= ki-tonbo). HHHL/HHLL - x-x-x x-x-x.

3.2a   kigawa < kigafa < *kiy-gafa < *k^m/$_o$-Ci$_{1.2}$ -n- kapa$_{2.3}$ ('yellow skin').
'orange peel'. HHL - 0-0-x x-x-x.

3.1   kihada < kifada < *kiy-panta < *k^m/$_o$-Ci$_{1.2}$ panta$_{2.4}$ ('yellow bark').
'cork-tree'. HHH - 0-0-x x-x-x.

?4.5   ki^h/$_b$atisu < (*)kiy-batisu < *ko-Ci$_{1.3a}$ -n- patisu$_{3.1}$ (< ...) ('tree
lotus'). (1) 'cotton/Confederate rose, Hibiscus mutabilis' (= huyoo);
(2) (Mg) 'rose of Sharon, alth(a)ea' (= mukuge). LLxx - x-x-x x-x-x.

?2.3 (< 1.3a) kii < kiy (← 'trees' < ko-Ci). 'the land of Kii (= Wakayama)'.
x - 1-2-A x-x-x. Sz 1. Ib H = 2.1.

2.3   kiku (< Ch kyuk). 'chrysanthemum'. x - 2-2-B B-B-x. Km (W) LL. 1700 Ōsaka
HL. K: Hn LL. Ib F = 2.3.

3.4   kikugi < ki-kugi < kiy (< *ko-Ci$_{1.3a}$) kugi$_{2.1}$ (< ...). 'peg, wooden
stopper'. LLL - 1/2-1:3-x x-B-x.

-            kikyoo 'bellflower': see kitikoo.

2.1   kimi < kyimyi < *kimi. 'lord'. HH - 0-0-A x-A-x. NS (70b, 71b, 92b, 92b,
94b, 104b, 113a, 114a, 118a, 123b, 127a, 134a) HH; NS (T 6, 128) HH, (T 68,
104) HL, (T 43, 123) HL ?= HH. Km (W) HH. Edo HH. Narada 2; Goka-mura 1.

?2.5   kimi 'millet': see kibi.

2.3   kimo < kyimwo < *kimwo. 'liver; heart'. LL - 2-2-A x-B-(B). NS (132b) LL.
Km (S) LL. Edo HL. Ib F = 2.3. Nk Cimuu B. Yn cimuɲuti A < *kimo-guti 'breast'
(no accent in H 1964:183 but A in H 1964:71), cimu B (Shibata 1959:113, 116).

3.1   kimono < *kyi (< *ki[-Ci]/ki[Ca-Ci]$_A$) - mono$_{2.3}$. 'garment'. x - 0-0-A
x-A-x. Km x. Aomori 3; Sapporo, Matsumoto, Hattō, Hiroshima, NE Kyūshū,
Wakamatsu 2. Ib kimon H = 3.1. Sr ciimun B 'winter kimono'. Cf. kinu.

2.2b   kin (< Ch .kyem). 'gold; money'. x - 1-2-A A-A-x. Km x. Shimoda (K 1943)
and Narada 2; Hakata 0, ygr 1. Ib H1 = 2.2.

2.4   kine < kyi(-ne) < *ki (- ?na-Ci$_{1.3a}$ 'root'). 'pestle'. x - 1-1-B x-x-x.
Ongi-m LH. Km x.

3.5b   kinoko < *kiy-no-kwo < *ko-Ci$_{1.3a}$ no kwo$_{1.1}$. x - 1-2-B x-B-x. 'mushroom'.
Hamada 1; Sz, Narada, Hattō, Matsue, Izumo, Goka-mura, Wakamatsu 2; Aomori 3.
Ib F = 3.6. Sr cinuku B (the palatalized initial indicates this is a borrowing;
the older term is found in Nk nabaa C).

?3.4, ?3.2b   kinoo < kyinofu < *kinopu (? < *ki < ... 'come', pu = pi 'day').
'yesterday'. HHx (Kz) - 2-2-A B-B-A. Ongi-m LLL. NS (97a kinefu) HHL, (Okada)
HHH. Edo HHL. Hattō, Hakata 2; Goka-mura, Hiroshima 0/2. Aomori, Hamada, Matsue,
Izumo, NE Kyūshū 0; Narada kinyoo 3. Ōsaka, Ise 3; Ib kinyoo H1 = 3.3. Sd B
but Nase kinu A. Yn nnnu A. Is the Tk accent (2<*3) due to monosyllabification?

2.4 < ?2.5   kinu < kyinu < *kinu. 'silk; garment'. LH(-L) - 1-1-B B-B-x.
NS (T 27) LL. Km (W) LH(-L). Edo LH. Izumo 1/2. Kōbe (Robb) 1/1:3; Ib L = 2.4.
Sr cin B. Suggested etymologies are incongruent in register: ki[ru]ᴀ nu[no]ₐ.ₗ
'cloth to wear', ki-[mo]noₐ.ₗ (< ...) with vowel assimilation.

4.6   kinugasa < kyinu-gasa < *kinuₐ.₄ -n- kasaₐ.₄. 'silk umbrella'. LLLH -
3/2-0-x x-x-x. Ongi LLLH.

4.8   kinuginu < *kyinu-gyinu < *kinuₐ.₄ n[i] kinuₐ.₄. 'sorting out the garments
of lovers after a night together; the morning after a night of love; leaving
each other, separating'. x - 0/2-0-x x-x-x. Km (W) LHHH.

?4.6 (> 3.4)   kinuita < *kyinu-ita < *kinuₐ.₄ itaₐ.₄. 'fulling block'. LLxH (Zs) -
x-x-x x-x-x. K: Hn LLL (from Kn? — see next entry).

3.4 < ?4.6   kinuta < kinu[i]ta (< ...). 'fulling block'. LLL (Kn)- 1-1:3-x
x-x-x.

3.6 < ?4.6   kirara ?< *kyirara < *kira -[a]ra ('glitter stuff'). 'isinglass;
mica'. LHH - 0-0[H]/1[U]-A x-x-x.

2.1   kiri < ?*kyiri < ?*kiri. 'paulownia'. HH - 0-0-A A-A-x. Ib H = 2.1.

2.1   kiri < kiyri < *kuCiri. 'fog'. HH - 0-0-A A-A-A. Km (S) HH. Edo HH. Ib H =
2.1. The palatalized initials of Shuri and Yonaguni ciri A indicate *kuCiri
(not *koCiri) and the /u/ is confirmed by Hachijō kuri. Unexplained: Benoki
(northern Okinawa) khooraa A; Taketomi (Yaeyama) kiruri A; Ishigaki kïru.

2.4   kiri < kyiri (?< *kir[a-C]iᴮ). 'awl'. LH - 1-1-A (x)- (B)-(B). Izumo 2.
Ib L = 2.4. Sr qiri B, Yn iri B ?< *i[gi]ri; Yaeyama i(i)ri, iru, iirasi,
iirasï; Kumamoto igiri ?< i- (= ?) -n- kiri.

?5.2, ?5.11   kirigirisu < *kyirigyiri-su < *kiriₐₘₐ n[i] kiriₐₘₐ -suₗ.ₓ
(< ...). 'cricket' (= koorogi). HH[HH]L (Kn) / Lxxxx (Ck) - 3-1:4(/4[U])-B
x-x-x. Km (W) HHHHL, LHHHL. Sz 4.

4.5   kirikui < kiri-kufi < *kyiri kufyi < *kir[a-C]iᴮ kupiₐ.₂ᵦ. 'a wooden
stake' (= ki no kirikui). LLLL - x-x-x x-x-x.

4.5   kirimimi < *kyiri - myimyi < *kir[a-C]iᴮ mi-miₐ.₃. 'a chopped-off
(severed) ear'. LLLL - x-x-x x-x-x.

2.3   kisa (?< *kiy-sa < *ko-Ciₗ.₃ₐ sa[ma]ₐₐ.₂ₐ). 'grain (of wood)'.
LL - x-2-x x-x-x. Km x.

2.3   kisa = kisa-kafyi (? 'notch shell'). 'ark shell' (= modern akagai).
LL - x-x-x x-x-x.

?2.3   *kisa(-). 'shaving, scraping' (see kisageru); ?'notch' (= kiza, see kisa
'ark shell').

2.x ?< 3.6   kiᵃ/₂a. 'elephant'. RH - x-x-x x-x-x. See §7.1.

3.4   kisage < *kisagey < *kisaₐₐ.₃ -n[a]-ka-Ci[-Ci]ᴮ. 'a tool for polishing
metal or stone; a scraper'. LLL - A-x-x x-x-x.

3.7a/b   kisai < kisaki (< ?). 'empress'. x - 0/2(?<*1)-2-x x-x-x. K (W) LHL.
?Mr (W 19) HHH(-L). Edo LHL.

4.11   kisaragi (< ?). 'the second month of the lunar calendar'. x - 0-0-B x-x-x.
NS (111a) LLHL. Km x.

2.3   kisi < kiysi (?< *kᵃ/₂Cisi, ?< *ku-isi). 'cliff; shore'. LL - 2-
0[H]/2[U]-B B-A-x. Km (S) LL. Edo HL. Aomori, Matsumoto, NE Kyūshū 1. Kōchi,
Toyama 2; Suzu 1; Ib F = 2.3. Nk x; Sr [Lit.] cisi A. Cf. Korean ˙kis,
kiˑsul(a)k, earlier :kos < *koˑco.

?2.3   kisi < kyisi < *kisi. '(Paekche) Korean lord': Ati kisi 'Lord Achi'
(descendant of Achiki), Wani kisi 'Lord Wani'. *See* ko[ni]kisi.

2.x   kiso < kyiso̲ < *kiso̲. 'last night'. x - x-x-x x-x-x. Cf. kinoo, kozo.
(NKD: "It is unknown whether the last syllable was -so or -zo.")

2.2a   kita < kyita < *kita. 'north'. HL - 2/0-2-A x-x-x. Km (S,W) HL. Mr (Bm)
HL. Edo HL. Narada, Hamada 0; Hattō, Goka-mura 2. Toyama 1:3 *(expected)*; Suzu
1; Ib H1 = 2.2.

?3.1, ?3.2x   kitai < kitafi < *kyitafyi < *kita-p[a-C]i*ₐ* (?< *kata-p[a-C]i).
'fish/meat dried whole'. HHH/HHL - x-x-x x-x-x. Cf. kitaeru.

4.11   kitakisu (< ?). 'burdock' (= goboo). LLHL - x-x-x x-x-x.

4.7   kitikoo < kitikau (< Ch kit-'kang). 'Chinese bellflower, balloon-flower'.
x - x-0-x x-x-x. Km (W) LLHH. → kikyoo x - 0-1-B x-x-x; Aomori 2; Ib L = 3.6.

3.6   kitune < kyitune (< ?). 'fox'. LHH - 0(?<1)-1-B B-A̲-x. Km x. Edo LHH.
Tappi, Akita, NE Kyūshū, Ōita 1; Aomori 1 *(we expect 2)*; Sapporo 2; Hiroshima,
Hida (= northern Gifu), Hattō, Hamada, Matsue, Izumo 0; Hakata 2, ygr 0. Ib L =
3.6. Nk x; Sr çiçini A̲ must be borrowed. Cf. kutune.

?5.16   kitunegusa < *kyitune*ₛ.₆* (< ?) -n- kusa*ₛ.ₛ*. 'Chloranthus serratus' (=
hutarisizuka). LLLLx (?= *LLLHL).

3.6   kiuta < kyi-uta < *ki*ₗ.ₛₐ* uta*ₛ.ₛᵦ*. 'pestler's song' (= kine-uta). LHH (Ir)
- x-x-x x-x-x.

2.3   kiwa < kyifa < *kipa. 'brink'. LL - 2-2-B B-A̲-x. Km (W) LL. Edo HL. Aomori
0̲; Narada 2. Ib F = 2.3. Nk Ciwaa B; Sr ciwa A is probably borrowed (we would
expect *caa).

?2.3   kiza < *kyiza < *kinsa. 'a cut; a notch' (= kida). x - x-x-x x-x-x.
Cf. kizamu, kizu; kisa, *kisa(-).

-           kiza 'elephant': *see* ki*ˢ*/*ᵤ*a.

?3.x < ?4.x   kizaya < kiza-ya < ?*ki(n)sa*ₛ.ₓ<ₛ.₆* da*ₗ.₃ᵦ* ('elephant house').
'animal shed'. RHx - x-x-x x-x-x.

2.1 (< 3.1)   kizi < kyigyisi < k[y]ig[y]isu < *ki-n-ki*?ₘᵢₛ* -su*ₗ.ₓ*. 'pheasant'.
HH - 0-0-A A-x-x. NS (83b, 108b) HHH; NS (T+ 96, 100) HHH. Km (W) HH. Ib F̲ =
2.4 *(the bird is alien)*.

2.1   kizu < kyizu < *kinsu. 'a wound; a flaw'. HH - 0-0-A x-A-A. NS (111a) HH.
Ib H = 2.1.

5.2   kizudokoro < *kyizu-dok̲o̲r̲o̲ < *kinsu*ₛ.₁* -n- tok̲o̲r̲o̲*₃.₁*. 'a wound'. HHHHL -
x-x-x x-x-x. Km x.

?3.1, ?3.4   kizuna < kiduna (?< *kyiduna < *k[ub]yi-duna; ?< *kiy-duna <
*ku[by]i-duna) < *kunpi*ₛ.₁* -n- tuna*ₛ.ₛ*. 'fetter, leash'. HHH - 1̲/0-2̲-B x-x-x.
Km x. Edo HHL. Ib H̲ = 3.1.

1.1   ko < kwo. 'child'; also (= tamago) 'egg' and (= kaiko) 'silkworm'.
H - 0-0-A A-A-(x). NS (71b, 74b, 81b [14:439-M], 97a, 133a, 133b) H; NS (T+ 23,
48, 74, 88, 91, 121, 127) H. Km (S,W) H. Edo H. Ib H = 1.1. Sd kwa(a) A (as a
suffix often -ggwa); Sr kkwa A; Yn aga-ŋa A (?< *aka-gwa). Used as a suffix in
dialects: -ko, -kko, -go; (Ryūkyū) -(k)kwa, -(g)gwa ?< *kora < *kwo -ra.

1.1   ko- < kwo(-). 'little'. H-··· . See Chart 16:2. (Etymologically identical
with 'child'?) Sr kuu-san A 'is little'; cf. komaka.

1.1   ko (< Ch .hho). 'arc'. x - 1̲-0-A x-x-x. Ib H̲1 = 1.2.

1.1   ko̲. 'this'. H - 1̲-0-(A) (A-(A)-A. Km (W) H. Edo H. Tōkyō and Kyōto accents
as found in ko wa ika-ni. Yn kuu A 'this one'. Cf. koko*ₛ.₄*.

1.2   ko(-) 'yellow': *see* ki.

1.3 (= B)   ko(-) < kwo*ₐₔⱼ ᴮ*. 'saturated, thick'.

1.3a   ko̲(-) 'tree' = ki. NS (T+ 12) ko̲ no̲ ma 'through the trees' LLH. Km (W) L.

1.3a   ko < kwo. 'flour'(= ko-na). L - 1-1-B x-B-B. Km x. Ib   L = 1.3.

1.3a   ko < kwo. 'basket' (= ka-go). L - 1-0-x x-A-x. Km x. Nk x; Sr kuu A.
     Cf. warigo, kego; sisiriko; mokko < moti-ko 'basket for carrying dirt/rubbish'.

1.3a   ko (< ?). 'sea-cucumber' (= nama-ko). L - x-0-x x-x-x. Km x.

1.x   (-)ko 'place': *see* koko, soko, doko; (< -kwo) miyako; (-)ka. Cf. toko,
     tokoro, koro.

3.3   kobiru < *kwo-byiru < *kwo$_{1.1}$ -n- piru$_{8.1(?<2.3)}$. 'wild leek' (= nobiru);
     'garlic' (= hiru = ninniku). HLL - 0-x-x x-x-x.

2.1   kobu ?< *konpu < "komu" = [koũ] < Ch .kong. ?'metal tube inside the hub
     of a wheel' (= kamo). Attested only in Mg? HH - x-x-x x-x-x.

?2.5, ?2.3   kobu < *ko(n)pu. 'gnarl, lump' (?< kobu[si]). x - 2-1:3[H]/2[U]-B
     x-B-x. Hattō, Hamada, Matsue, Goka-mura, Hata, NE Kyūshū 1; Hakata 1, ygr 2;
     Izumo, Hiroshima 2; Aomori, Sz 0. Kōchi (Doi 1952:22), Ōsaka, Ise 1:3; Ib L2 =
     2.5 → koburo L = 3.6. Sr guuhu B, ganaa B < ?.

2.5 < 3.7b   kobu < *konpu (= konbu 3.7b). 'seaweed'. x - 1-1:3-B x-B-x. Aomori
     (rare), Hiroshima 1. Ōsaka, Ise 1:3; Ib L2 = 2.5. Sr kuubu B.

-      kobura = komura: *see* siri-kobura = siri-ta▪/ᵦura.

3.4   kobusi (< ?*konpusi). 'fist'. LLL - 0/1-2-B x-x-x. Km x. Edo HHL.
     Hattō, Hamada, Goka-mura, Hiroshima 1; Matsue, Izumo 2; Sapporo, Aomori, Sz,
     Wakamatsu, Ōita 0; Akita, Matsumoto, Numazu 3. Ōsaka, Kōbe, Himeji 1:3 (Ōhara);
     Ib F = 3.4. *H 1960:(46) is mistaken on Tk, cf. id.:262b.*

3.7a   kodama < kotama < *ko$_{1.3a}$ (?-n-) tama$_{?8.3}$. 'tree spirit; echo'. LHL -
     0-0-A x-x-x. Km x. 1700 Ōsaka LHH. Aomori 0. Ib [Lit.] H = 3.1.

3.5a/b   kodati < ko-ᵗ/ᴅati < *ko$_{1.3a}$ (-n-) tat[a-C]i$_{8}$. 'grove, stand of trees'.
     x - 0/1-0-B x-x-x. NS (T+ 105 -t-) LLH. 1700 Ōsaka HHH. (Sr kikaci A < ?.)

3.1   kodomo < kwo-domo < *kwo$_{1.1}$ -n- tomo$_{8.1}$. 'child(ren)'. x - 0-0-A x-x-x.
     NS (121a) H?HH. Km x. Edo HHH. Wakamatsu 2. Ib H = 3.1.

2.3   koe < *kwoye[y] < *kwo-da-Ci[-Ci]$_{B}$. 'fertilizer, manure'. x - 2-2-B x-B-x.
     Ib F = 2.3. Sr kwee B.

2.5   koe < kowe[y] < *kowa-Ci (?< *koba-Ci; ?< *ko(w)aCi < *koCa-Ci). 'voice'.
     LH/LF - 1-1:3-B B-B-C. NS LL. Km (S,W) LH(-L). Edo LF. Hyōgo, Ōsaka, Ise, Kōchi
     1:3; Toyama 2; Suzu 1 *(expected)*; Ib L2 = 2.5. Sd khwii B; Sr kwii B; Yn kui C.

2.3   koga < *konka (< ?). 'barrel, vat, tub; bucket'. LL (Ir) - x-x-x x-x-x.
     (Widely found in modern dialects; see NKD.)

3.1   kogai < kogafi < *kwo-gafyi < *kwo$_{1.1}$ -n- kap[a-C]i$_{8}$. 'sericulture,
     keeping silkworms'. HHH - x-B-x x-x-x. Kt B[U] *misprint?*. Cf. kaiko.

3.1   kogame < *kwo-gamey < *kwo$_{1.1}$ -n- kamaCi$_{8.3}$. 'a small tortoise; a
     (snapping) turtle'. HHH - 0-0-x x-x-x.

?3.1   kogame < *kwo$_{1.1}$ -n- ?kamey$_{8.3}$ (< ...). 'a little jar (?)'. x - 0-x-x
     x-x-x. Km (W) HHH. Mr (W 20) HHH, (W 19) HHL, (W 18) HLx.

3.3   kogane (?< kugane) < *kᵘ/ₒ$_{1.8}$ -n- kana-Ci$_{8.1}$ ('yellow metal'). 'gold'.
     HLL - 1(<*2)/0-0-A (B)-A-A. Km x. Edo HLL. Narada 2; Sapporo, Tappi, Sz *(rare)*,
     Akita, Matsumoto, Numazu, Hiroshima 0; western Mino (= SW Gifu), Hida (=
     northern Gifu), Ōita 3. Hyōgo 2; Kōchi, Suzu 0; Toyama 1:3 *(expected reflex)*;
     Ib H = 3.1. Yn kugani A (H 1964:66b, 71b).

2.3   koge < *kwonka-Ci[-Ci]$_{B}$. 'scorched (thing)'. x - 2-1:3-A x-x-x.

3.1   koguso < koᵏ/ᵍuso < *kwo$_{1.1}$ (-n-) kuswo$_{8.3}$. 'silkworm excrement (used for
     manure)'. HHH - x-0-x x-x-x. Cf. kaiko.

3.6   kohada < kofada < *ko$_{1.3a}$ panta$_{8.4}$. 'tree bark'. LHH - x-x-x x-x-x.

3.1   kohagi < *kwo-fagiy < *kwo$_{1.1}$ pan-koCi$_{8.3}$. 'small bushclover'.
     x - 0/1-2-x x-x-x. Km (W) HHH.

?2.3 < 3.7x   ko-hi < ko-fi < kou-fi (< Ch .hhew-.pi). 'sore throat'. LL (Ir)/ RL
     (Kn) ?< *LHL - x-x-x x-x-x.
3.4   ko-hizi < ko-fidi < *kwo*adj B* pinti*g.3* ('thick mud'). 'mud' (= hiziriko).
     LLL - x-0-x x-x-x.
3.2a   kohone, koohone < kofone (Mg) < koofone < kaufone < *kaw[a]-fone <
     *kapa*g.2a* pone*g.3* ('river bone'). 'candock, Nuphar japonicum'. HHL - 0-0-x
     x-x-x.
?2.3   [koi] 'sore throat': see ko-hi.
2.3   koi < kwofiy < *kwopo-Ci[-Ci]*B*. 'love'. LL - 1-2-B x- B-x. Km (S,W) LL.
     1700 Ōsaka HL. Aomori, Narada, Wakamatsu 1 (as in Tōkyō the accent retreat is
     likely due to monosyllabification; Hiroshima 2. Ōsaka 1/2; Ise 1; Ib F = 2.3.
2.5   koi < kwofi (?< *kwofyi [Ōno] < *kwopi). 'carp'. LH - 1-1:3-B B-(B)-x.
     Km x. Aomori, Izumo (Kobayashi), Hiroshima, Yamaguchi 1. Kōchi (Kobayashi),
     Ōsaka, Ise 1:3; Ib L2 = 2.5. Sr kuu-qiyu B (?'little-fish'). K: Hn LF.
3.3   kokaze < *kwo-kaze < *kwo*1.1* kansa-Ci*g.1*. 'a (slight) breeze'. HLL -
     0/1-x-x x-x-x.
2.3   koke < kokey < *ko*1.3a* ka-Ci*?1.1* ('tree hair'). 'moss'. LL - 2-2-B x-x-x.
     Km x. Edo HL/HH. 1700 Ōsaka HL. Tk also 0 ("new"); Narada, Hiroshima 2;
     NE Kyūshū 1. Ōsaka, Ise 2; Ib F = 2.3.
4.5   kokenori < *kokey*g.3*(< *ko*1.3a* ka-Ci*?1.1*) nori*g.3*. 'seaweed'. LLLL -
     x-x-x x-x-x. Attested only in Kn Mg?
3.5a   kokera ?< *kokey[du]ra < *ko*1.3* keydura-*A* (< ?) ('wood whittle'), ?<
     *ko-[ka]keyra < *ko*1.3a* kakeyra*?3.1* (< ... §5.10; 'wood splinters'). 'wood
     chip(s); shingle'. LLH - 0-0-x x-x-x.
3.4   kokisi (?= *kogisi) < koni-kyisi < *kon[i]-kisi (= Paekche-Korean ko-n
     [i] 'big [one]' + kisi 'lord'). 'king (of Paekche Korea)'. x - x-x-x x-x-x. NS
     (108a, 130b, 131b) LLL. Note: "koni" may have represented just /kon/ 'big ··· '
     (later Korean kh[u]-wo-n); cf. konami.
2.4   koko < ko-ko. 'here, this place'. LH - 0-1-B x-x-x. NS (70b, 122a) LH;
     NS (T 43) LL. Km (S,W) LH. Edo LH. Register incongruent with ko(-) 'this'.
     Goka-mura 1; Hakata 1, ygr 2/0; Narada 0; Hattō, Hamada, Hiroshima 2; Matsue,
     Izumo 0/2. Ōsaka, Ise 1; Ib L = 2.4.
3.4   kokome < *koko*?* - mye*1.3b* (< *miCa ?= *mina). 'an ugly woman' (= sikome).
     LLL (Kz) - x-x-x x-x-x.
4.11   kokonotu < kokono -tu (?= koko*?2.3* no*pcl* tu*pcl*). 'nine'. LLHx - 2-2[H]/
     4[U]-B (A/B)-B-B. Km (W) kokono LLH. Mr (Bm) HLLL. Hattō, Hamada 2; Sz, Matsue,
     Izumo 3; Hata 2; Hakata 3, ygr 2. Kōchi 2 (Doi 1952:29). Cf. OJ kokoda 'lots'.
?3.5b   kokoro. 'heart'. LLH - 2/3-2-B B-B-B. NS (70b, 105b, 121b, 123b, 132b,
     133a) LLH. NS (T+ 43) LLH, (T+ 36) HHH. Km (S) LLH, (W) LLL. Mr (Bm) HLL.
     Edo HLL. Tappi, Numazu, Narada, Hattō, Hamada, Goka-mura, Yamaguchi, Hata,
     Wakamatsu, NE Kyūshū, Ōita 2; Sapporo, Aomori, Akita, Matsue, Izumo 3;
     Hakata 2, ygr 3. Ib F = 3.4.
5.6   kokorobae < kokoro-bafey < *kokoro*3.5b* -n- papa-Ci[-Ci]*B*. 'temper; view,
     attitude, (set of) mind'. x - 0-0-x x-x-x. NS (130b) LLLLL.
?5.16   kokorobase < *kokoro*3.5b* -n- pasa-Ci[-Ci]*?B*. '(the working of) one's
     mind/heart'. ?LLLHL - 0-0-x x-x-x. K: Edo HHHHH.
5.7   kokorobuto ?< *kokoro*3.5b* -n- putwo*adj B*. 'agar-agar' (= tengusa);
     white radish (= daikon); gelidium jelly (= tokoroten)'. LLLLH - x-0-x x-x-x.
     The traditional etymology relates the word to koru*A* 'freeze'.
5.6, 5.7, ?5.16   kokorogae < kokorogafe < *kokoro-gafey < *kokoro*3.5b* -n-
     kapa-Ci[-Ci]*A*. 'exchange of hearts'. x - x-x-x x-x-x. Km (W) LLLLL, xxxLH
     (= *LLLLH), xxxHL (?= *LLLHL).

5.15 = 3.5|2.3   kokorogimo < kokoro-kyimo < *kokoro₂.₅ₑ kimwo₂.₃. 'spirit,
     (heart and) soul; thought'. x - x-x-x x-x-x. NS (132b) LLH(|)LL.
6.22   kokoromadoi < koromadofi (Mg) < *kokoro-matwofyi < *kokoro₂.₅ₑ
     matwop[a-C]i₇ₑ. 'bewilderment'. LLLHL - x-5-x x-x-x.
5.6   kokorozasi < *kokoro₂.₅ₑ -n- sas[a-C]i₅. 'hope, aspiration'. LLLLL -
     0/5-0[H]/4[U]-B x-B-x. Sz 0. Cf. kokorozasu.
3.x   kokoti ?< *kokoti < *koko[ro mo]ti < *kokoro₂.₅ₑ mot[a-C]i₅. 'feeling'.
     x - 0-0-A x-B-x. 1700 Ōsaka HHL. Attested 10th century.
3.4   kokuwa < kokufa < *ko₁.₃ₐ kupa₂.₁. 'a wooden hoe'. x - x-2-x x-x-x.
     NS (73a, 73b) LLL; NS (T+ 57) HLL, (T+ 58) HHL.
?3.4   kokuwa < kokufa (< ?). 'Actinidia arguta' (= sarunasi). LLx - x-2-x x-x-x.
     K: Hn LLL.
2.1   koma < kwo-ma < *kwo₁.₁ [u]ma₂.₃. 'colt; horse'. HH - 0/1-1[H]/2[U]-A
     x-x-x. NS (80a) HH; NS (T+ 103) HL ?= H|L, (T+ 81, 115) HL ?= H|L. Km (W) HH.
     Sz, Narada 0.
?2.2b   koma. 'cyprinodont (tropical killifish), Orizia latipes; (= ei) ray'
     (fish). HL - x-x-x x-x-x. Attested only in Mg? Cf. kome.
2.3   koma. 'Koguryŏ (Kokwulye), an ancient Korean state'. x - 1-2-x x-x-x.
     NS (122a) LLL.
2.3   koma < *koma. '(toy spinning) top' (< Koma = Koguryŏ, the ancient Korean
     state whence it came). x - 1-1-A x-x-x. Aomori, Sz 0; Narada, Hattō, Hamada,
     Hakata 1; Matsue, Izumo, Goka-mura 2. Kōchi (Kobayashi) 1; Ib goma L = 2.4.
(*2.3)   koma(-) < *kwo-ma. (adj stem, adj-n) 'small, fine'. See komaka.
4.5/4.6   komabue < komabuye < *koma₂.₃ -n- pude₂.₁ (< ...). 'a kind of flute
     (which came from Koma = Koguryŏ)'. LLLL (Kn) / LLLH (Ck) - 2/3-x-x x-x-x.
?3.6   komai < komafyi < komafyi[kyi] ?< *ko₁.₃ₐ ma- fyikyi*₃.₁ (< ma-₁.₁
     pik[a-C]i₄). 'lath'. LHx (?= *LHH) - 1-0-x x-x-x.
3.7b   komaka ?< *kwo-ma₍ₐdⱼ ₐ₎-ka. 'fine, small, detailed' (adj-n). LHL -
     1/2/3-1:3[H]/3[U]-B x-x-x. Sz 3. Cf. Sr guma- B 'small', kuu- A 'little,
     young'; Yn kuma- B 'fine'.
?3.1   komatu < *kwo₁.₁ matu₂.₄. 'a (small) pinetree'. x - 0/1-0-x x-x-x.
5.1, 5.2   komatunagi < *kwoma₂.₁ (< *kwo₁.₁ [u]ma₂.₃) - tunagyi (< *tu[ra]-na-n[a]-
     k[a-C]i). 'tying a pony': ~ (kusa) (1) 'indigo plant'; (2) 'Potentilla
     cryptotaeniae' (= mitumoto-soo); (3) 'herb bennet' (= daikon-soo). HHHHH-xx
     (Kn), HHHHL-xx (Kz) - 3-x-x x-x-x.
5.7   komatuzura < komatudura ?< *kwo-ma₍ₐdⱼ ₐ₎ tuntura₃.₅ ('small wicker').
     (1) 'Viburnum tomentosum' (= hemi); (2) 'Zelkova serrata' (= keyaki);
     (3) 'Solanum lyratum' (= horosi = hiyodori-zyoogo). LLLLH - x-x-x x-x-x.
4.11   komayaka < kwomayaka < *kwo-ma₍ₐdⱼ ₐ₎ -da-ka. 'dense(ly growing)' (adj-n).
     LLHL - 2-4-B x-x-x. NS (119b) LxHL. K: Edo HLLL.
2.3   kome < komey < *komaCi. '(hulled) rice'. x - 2-2-B x-B-x. NS (Okada) LL;
     NS (T 107) LL. Km x. Hakata 0, ygr 2. Ib F = 2.3. Cf. Nk mee A, Miyako maz,
     Yn mai A. Perhaps ko- 'plant', -mey 'sprout' or 'eye' if not from Ch m(b)ei'.
2.3   kome ?< *koma-Ci. 'ray (= ei); ? cyprinodont (tropical killifish), Orizia
     latipes' (fish). LL - x-x-x x-x-x.
4.7   komeᵃ/ᵤzaki < *komey-ᵃ/ᵤzakyi < *komaCi₂.₃ (-n-) sak[a-C]i₇ₑ. 'broken
     rice'. LLHH(-z-) - x-4-x x-x-x.
2.3   komi < kwomyi < *kwom[a-C]i₅. 'paddy flooding (letting the water into a
     ricefield)'. x - x-x-x x-x-x. NS (100b [11:126-K]) LL.
?3.1, ?3.2x   komira < kwo-myira < *kwo₁.₁ mira₂.₃. 'leek' (= nira). Hxx (?= *HHH)
     x-3-x x-x-x. K: Hn HHL (attested?).
3.3   komiti < *kwo₁.₁ miti₂.₁. 'alley'. HLL - 1(<*2)/0-0[H]/2[U]-A x-x-x.
     Hattō 2; Hamada, Matsue 0/2; Izumo 3; Goka-mura 1.

4.11   komizu: *see* konzu.

2.1   komo. 'water-oats, wild rice (= ma-komo); straw matting'. HH - 0-2-A x-x-x
NS (T+ 94) HH. Sz, Narada, Hattō, Hamada, Matsue, Izumo, Goka-mura 0. Ib (rare)
H = 2.1.

2.3   komo < kwomo < *kwo*adj B* mo*?1.1*. 'eelgrass, Zostera japonica' (= ko-amamo).
LL - x-x-x x-x-x.

5.2   komobuturo < *komo*B.1* -n- puturo*?* (< ?). 'a kind of edible fungus ··· '
(= komozuno). HHHHL - x-x-x x-x-x.

4.5   komoriku < komori-ku < *koma-r[a-C]i*B* -ku*1.x*. 'a secluded (mountain-
girt) place'. x - x-0-x x-x-x. NS (77b [14:153-M, 14:155-M], 83b [17:120-M])
LLLL; NS (T+ 77, 99) HHHH.

4.1   komozuno < komo-duno < *komo*B.1* -n- tunwo*B.3*. 'a kind of edible fungus
that grows on water-oat (wild-rice) stalks'. HHHH - x-x-x x-x-x.

3.3   komugi < (*)kwo-mugyi < *kwo*1.1* munki*B.4*. 'wheat'. HLL - 2-2-A A-x-x. Edo
HLL. Sapporo, Aomori, Matsumoto, Narada, western Mino (= SW Gifu), Hakata 2;
Hida (= northern Gifu) 0/3; Tappi, Aomori, Akita, Numazu, Izumo [Kobayashi],
Hiroshima, Yamaguchi, Ōita 0. Hyōgo, Kōchi 3; Toyama 1:3 (expected reflex);
Suzu 0 (we expect 1:3); Ib H2 = 3.2.

3.5x   komura < *ko*1.3a* mura*B.x*. 'a stand of trees, a grove'. LLH - x-x-x x-x-x.

3.5a/b   komura < (*)kwomura [Zdb ta-kwomura] / kobura < ?*kwonpura. 'calf of leg'.
LLH - 0/1-2[H]/0[U]-A x-B-x. NS (114b)LLL. Sr kunda B < *kubura (< *kobura).
Cf. siri-kobura = siri-ta*/*bura.

6.22   komuragaeri < kwo*/*bura-gafyeri (< *-gafyiri) < ?*kwonpura*3.5a/b* -n-
kapi-r[a-C]i*B*. 'leg cramp(s)'. LLLLHL - 4-5-A x-(B)-x. Sr kundaqagayaa B (<
*komura-agari-a).

5.15, 5.14 (= 1.3|4.9)   komurasaki < *kwo-murasakyi < *kwo*adj B* murasaki*4.9* (< ?).
'deep/dark purple'. x - 3-3-A x-x-x. Km (W) LLHLL, L(|)LHHL. Mr (W 18) LLLLL,
(19) HLLxx.

?2.3, ?2.4   kona < *kwo*1.3a* -na*suf*. 'flour, powder' (= ko). x - 2-1-B x-(B)-x.
(Sr kuu B < ko.) Except in konagaki the dissyllable is not attested before Mr.
Sz 2; Hattō 1; Hamada 1/2; Matsue, Izumo, Goka-mura 2. Ib L = 2.4.

4.2   kona*k/*gaki < *kwona-*k/*gakyi < *kwo-na*?2.3,?2.4* (-n-) kak[a-C]i*B*. 'soup
with rice flour stirred in; rice-starch potage; (= zooni) rice cake boiled with
vegetables'. HHHL (Ck) - x-x-x x-x-x.

3.1   konami (?< Paekche-Korean *ko-n *a/*emi 'big mother'). 'first wife (under
polygamy)'. HHH - x-0-x x-x-x. NS (T+ 7) HHH.

4.3   konasubi < *kwo*1.1* nasunpi*3.5b*. 'small eggplant (JP); (= inu-hoozuki)
morel, (black) nightshade (Mg)'. HHLL - 2-x-x x-x-x.

?3.2a   konata ?< *ko-n[o*B.1* k]ata*B.2b*. 'this way/direction, here'.
HHx -1(/2[U])-2-A x-x-x. Km (W) HHL/HLL. 1700 Ōsaka HHL.

3.4   konata < kwonata ?< *kwo*adj B* -na (?= no) ta*1.3a*. 'well-developed
riceland (paddy)'. LLL - x-0-x x-x-x. (The etymology offered by Zdb and NKD is
incongruent in register: < *kona-s[a]-*A*.)

3.7b   konbu < *konpu. 'seaweed' (< kobu*B.B*). x - 1-1:3-B x-(B)-x. Sz 1. Ib L3 =
3.5. *See* kobu.

?2.3   koni ··· ?< Paekche-Korean ko-n [i] 'big [one], great': koni-kyisi >
kokyisi 'Paekche king', [koni-]oruku 'Paekche queen'. Note: "koni" may have
represented just /kon/ 'big ··· ' (later Korean kh[u]-wo-n); cf. konami.

3.6   konisi ?< *[kaῖ-sui] (< Ch .hyang-.syuy). 'coriander' (= koendoro). LHH -
x-x-x x-x-x.

4.5 (?= 3.4)   konnyaku < "koniyaku" (Mg) = konyaku (< Ch 'k[y]o'-nhyak).
'devil's-tongue'. LLLL (?= LLL) - 3/4-4-B x-B-x. Sz 4. Sr kon-yaku B.

2.1   kono < ko_{1.1} -no_{pcl}. 'this ⋯ ' (adnoun). HH - 0-0-A A-A-A. NS (105b)
H?H; NS (T+ 15, 13, 32, 33, 84) H(|)L, (T+ 32) L(|)L. Km (S) HH, (W) HH/HL.
Mr (Bm) HH/HL. Ib H = 2.1.

?4.2 (= 2.1|2.2), ?4.1 (= 2.1|2.1) konogoro < ko-no_{2.1} koro_{?2.2b,?2.1}. 'lately'.
HH(|)HL - 0-0-A x-A-x. NS (105b) H?HHH. Km x. See koro.

?4.3, ?2.1|2.4 konokami < kwo-no kamyi < *kwo_{1.1} no_{pcl} kami_{2.4}. 'the elder brother'.
HHxx - x-3-x x-x-x. NS (106b) HHLH (?= *HHLL, ?= HH|LH); (114b, 133b) H?HL?L.
K: "Km HHLL".

4.2 (= 2.1|2.2)   konokata < ko-no_{2.1} kata_{2.2b}. 'thenceforth'. HH(|)HHL - 2-3-x
x-x-x.

3.5b   konomi < konomiy < *ko_{1.3a} no_{pcl} mu-Ci_{1.1}. 'fruit'. LLH - 1-2-[H]/0[U]-B
x-x-x. Km (S) LHH. Edo HLL.

3.1   konori (< ?). 'male sparrow hawk'. HHH - 1-0-x x-x-x.

4.5   konosiro (< ?). 'gizzard shad'. LLLL - 2/3/4-0-x x-x-x. NS (T+ kun) HLLL.

4.7   konosita < ko_{1.3a} no_{pcl} sita_{2.2a}. 'under a tree'. x - 1-x-x x-x-x.
NS (Okada) LLHH.

3.5a   konzi < *kon-si (< Ch .kon/.kyen-'tsyey): see kozi 'scarf'. LLH - x-x-x
x-x-x.

?3.5b< 4.11   konzu < ko-mizu < "ko-mudu" < kwo-myidu < *kwo_{adj B} mintu_{2.1a}
(< ... 'thick water'). 'broth from boiling rice'. LLF (< *LLHL) - x-0-x x-x-x.
See Ch. 4, §7.3.

2.2b   koo < koo (JP) < kau < kaku_{2.2b} (< ka -ku < ...). 'thus, this way, so'.
(HL) - 1/0(=*2)-0-A x-x-x. Ib H = 2.1. Cf. to^s/_zama-koo^s/_zama.

?3.6, ?3.7a/b koobe < koobe < kaube < *kamyi-fye < *kami_{2.4} piCa_{1.x}. 'head'. LHH -
1/3/0-2-x x-x-x. 1700 Ōsaka LHH.

4.5   koogai < kaugai (?< [kaŭgai]) < kami-gaki < (*)kamyi-gakyi < *kami_{2.4}
(-n-) kak[a-C]i_{B}. 'hair pin/stick'. LLLL - 3/0[H]-2-B x-x-x. Narada 4; Hakata 0.
-        koohone: see kohone.

4.5   kooketi < kauketi (?< kafu-keti < Ch kap-kyet). 'a kind of tie-dyeing
practiced in early Japan'. LLLL - 0-0-x x-x-x.

4.11   koomori < koomuri/*koo^b/_mori < kau^b/_mori < kafabori ?< *kapa_{2.2a} mor[a-
C]i_{?B}/por[a-C]i_{?B} ('river guard'). 'bat'. LLLL - 1(?<*2)-2-B x-B-x. Hata 2;
Sz, Narada, Ōita (Toguchi 1974:24) 1. Kōchi 2; Hakata 1(/2). Sr kaabuyaa B <
?*ka[w]ab^a/_o[r]i-aa (why not > *ka(a)nzaa?). For the -^b/_- forms, see Kishida
1976:28, 44.

3.1   koono < ko-wono < *kwo_{1.1} bono_{2.3}. 'small ax'. HHH - x-0-x x-x-x. Km x.

3.1   koori < kofori (?< *kofari < *kopa-r[a-C]i_{A} 'freeze'). 'ice'. HHH - 0-0-x
x-x-x. Km (W) ⋯-xHL. Edo HHH. Hakata 1, ygr 0. Ib H = 3.1. Sr kuuri A 'sugar
candy; [new] ice'.

3.4   koori < kofori < *kopori (?< Korean kwo'wolh < kwo[p]wolh). 'district,
county'. LLL - 1-x-x x-x-x. Edo HHL. Hiroshima 0. Ōsaka, Ise 3. (Zdb is
cautious about /ko/, doubting that the attestation is the Japanese word.)

4.7   koorogi < "koforogyi" (?= /koworogyi/ < *koworo-na[a]-k[a-C]i, cf.
kororoku). 'cricket'. LLHH - 1-2[H]/0[U]-B x-x-x. Nagano 0 (Kudō 133); Sz,
Narada 1; Hakata 0, ygr 2/1. Register incongruent with kororoku.

?4.2   kooyobi < *kwo- oyobyi < *kwo_{1.1} odonpi_{3.4} (< ...). 'little finger' (=
koyubi). HHxx - x-3-x x-x-x. K: Hn HHHL (attested?).

3.1 < 4.1 koozi < kaudi (?< [kaŭdi]) < kam[u]dati (?< *kanp[^a/_o-Ci] tat[a-C]i_{B}
'mold rise'). 'malt, yeast'. HHHH - 0-0-A x-A-x. Goka-mura 1; Hakata 1, ygr 0.
Ib H = 3.1. Cf. kabi.

?3.2b   koozo < kauzo (?< [kaŭzo]) < kami-so < *kanpi_{2.2b} swo_{?1.1} ('paper hemp').
'paper mulberry'. x - 0-2-x x-x-x. See kazi.

2.1   kore < ko̱ -re < ?*ko̱*ı.ı* [a]ra-Ci*ɛ.ɜ*. 'this (one)'. HH - 0-0-A A-A-(x).
   Km (W) HH. Mr (Bm) HH. 1700 Ōsaka kore-ra L̲H̲L. Goka-mura 1̲. Ib H = 2.1.

?*2.1   koro. 'self; (by) oneself; *body': koro ni/to. Cf. korodatu, korohusu,
   koromo, mukuro.

?2.2a, ?2.1   ko̱ro. 'time'. x - 1̲-2-A x-A-x. NS (99b) HH. Km (W) HL. Edo HL.
   Aomori *(rare)*, Narada 0; Hiroshima (Okuda) 2. Ib H1 = 2.2. Cf. konogoro.

2.x   (-)koro 'lump' (?< '*body'): *see* isi-koro. Cf. kure*ɛ.x*.

3.1   ko̱ro̱mo̱. 'gown'. HHH - 0-0-A x-A-x. NS (71a, 71b) HHH; NS (T+ 47, 49)
   L̲H̲E̲; NS (T+ kun) HHH. Km (W) koromo-["]te HHHH. Edo HHH. Ib H = 3.1.
   Etymology: ?< *koro*?ɛ.ı* mo*ı.ɜb* 'body garment'; or, with the first vowel
   assimilating to the second, < kiro [Azuma attributive, Ch. 7 §4] = kiru*A attr*
   mo*ı.ɜb* / mo̱[no*ɛ.ɜ*] 'garment/thing to wear'; *see* kiru*A*, kiseru*A*. Matsumoto 1974:
   123 takes ko̱- to be the original root of the verb 'wear' (cf. kuru 'come'), witl
   kyi- a secondary formation, perhaps after the fashion of kyi(i) < *ko̱-Ci 'come'
   (infinitive). extended from the infinitive to other forms.

6.2   koromozutumi < koromotutumi < *koromo-ᵗ/ɟutumyi < *koromo*ɜ.ı* -n-
   tutum[a-C]i*ʙ* (< ...). 'clothes bundle, furoshiki'. HHHHHL - 4-5-x x-x-x.

4.1   koro-oi < ko̱ro-fofi ?< *ko̱ro [a]fafyi *(the next-to-last vowel assimilated*
   to the adjacent labials) < *ko̱ro*?ɛ.ɛb,?ɛ.ı* apa-p[a-C]i*ʙ*; ?= "ko̱ro-fofi" =
   koro*?ɛ.ɛb,?ɛ.ı* ap[a-C]i*ʙ*. 'time'. HHHH - 0/3-0-A x-x-x. Cf. koro-ai.

4.1 = 2.1|2.1   koru-moha < koru*(ɛ.ı)* (< *kor[a]-u*?A attr*) mo-fa*ɛ.ı* (< mo*ı.ı* pa*ı.ɛ*)
   ('seaweed that jells'). 'agar-agar' (= tengusa). HH(|)HH - x-x-x x-x-x.

3.1   kosame < kwosamey < *kwo*ı.ı* [z]ama-Ci*ɛ.ɜ*. 'a fine rain'. xHH - 0-0-A
   x-x-x. K: Hn HHH.

2.3   kose (< ?). 'eczema; prurigo' (= kose-gasa). LL - x-x-x x-x-x. Cf. kusa.

2.1   ko̱si. 'loins'. HH - 0-0-A A-A-A[H 1964]/B̲[H 1967 *misprint?*]. NS (71c) HH;
   NS (T 106) HH, (T 51) H̲L̲. Km x. 1700 Ōsaka HH. Ib H = 2.1. Nk husii A.

2.2b   ko̱si. 'shoulder-borne riding platform'. HL - 1̲-0̲[H]/2[U]-A x-x-x. Km x.
   Edo HL.

2.2b   ko̱si. 'story/level of a building' (< 'platform'). HL - 1̲-2-x x-x-x.

?2.3   kosi < kwosi (< ?). 'Koshi' *(placename)*. x - 1̲-2-x x-x-x. Km (W) LL.

?5.7, ?5.8   kosiabura < *kwosi (< *kwo-s[a-C]i*A*) anpura*ɜ.ɜe* ('filter oil').
   'Acanthopanax sciadophylloides: a tree (or its sap)'. LLLLH (Zs) / LLLHH (Kn)
   3-2-x x-x-x. Register incongruent with etymology.

4.2   kosibone < *kosi*ɛ.ɛb* -n- pone*ɛ.ɜ* (< ...). 'tailbone'. HHHHL - 0-0-A
   x-A-x. Sz O. Sr kusibuni A 'backbone' ('tailbone' is gamaku-buni A).

5.2   kosiguruma < *ko̱si*ɛ.ɛb* -n- kuruma*ɜ.ı*. 'parade float'. HHHHL - 3-4-A
   x-x-x.

3.5b   kosiki (< ?). 'a wooden vessel for steaming rice or beans; [from its
   similar shape] the hub of a wheel'. LLH - 1-0̲-x x-B-x. Edo HLL. Sr kusicii B.

3.5x (?= 2.3|1.1)   kosizi < kwosi-di < *kwosi*ɛ.ɜ* -n- ti*?ı.ı*. 'the Koshi road; the
   north'. x - x-x-x x-x-x. Km (W) LL(|)H. Edo HLL.

3.4   kosuki < *ko̱*ı.ɜe* sukyi*ɛ.ı* (< *suk[a-C]i*A*). 'an all-wood spade; a snow
   shovel'. LLL - x-x-x x-x-x.

3.1 = 1.1|2.1   kosuzu < *kwo*ı.ı* sunsu*ɛ.ı* (< ?). 'little bells'. x - 0-0-x x-x-x.
   NS (Okada) H(|)HH; NS (T+ 73) H̲E̲E̲ ?= H(|)HH.

2.1   kote < *kwo-te[y] < *kwo*ı.ı* ta-Ci*ı.ɜe* ('little hand'). 'gauntlet'. HH -
   0-0-x x-x-x. Narada, Hakata 0. Ib F̲ = 2.3.

2.1   koti (< *ko̱*ı.ı* ti*?ı.ı*) 'this way/direction': *see* kotti.

?2.3   koti < ko (= ?) + ti*ı.x*. 'east (wind)'. x -1-2-x B-B-x. Hakata 1̲.
   Sd khtyi B; Nk x; Sr kuci B. In Amami dialects ko-/ku- (Shibata 1981:46).
   Attested 10th century.

3.1   kotira ‹ koti*ᵦ.₁* (*ko*₁.₁* ti*₇₁.₁*) -ra (‹ *[a]ra*ᵦ.ᵧ*). ‘this way/direction;
I/me, we/us’. x - 0-1-A x-x-x. 1700 Ōsaka HLL.

2.3   koto. ‘fact, thing; words, saying’. LL - 2-2-B (x)-B-(x). NS (75c
[14:118-M], 91b [11:8-K], 101b [11:143-K], 121a [14:191L-K] LL. NS (T 109) LL,
(T 99) LH, (T+ 70) HH. Km (W,S) LL. Mr (Bm) HL. Edo HL. Ib F = 2.3.

2.5   koto. ‘harp’. LH(-L) - 1-0[H]/1:3[U]-B B-B-x. NS (83c) LH(-H); NS (T 41)
LH, (T 75, T+ kun) LL, (T 70; 97) HH. Km (W) LH(-x). Mr (Bm) LH. Edo LF.
Narada, Hattō, Hamada, Hiroshima 1; Matsue, Izumo 1 *(we expect 2)*; Goka-mura 2;
Hakata 0, ygr 1. Ōsaka, Ise 1:3; Ib L2 = 2.5, L = 2.4. Sr kutuu B. (On Kt 1:3
cf. Ōhara 1952:417.)

?2.5   koto. ‘different; special’: koto ni/naru. LH-L - 2-2[H]/1:3[U]-B x-B-x.
NS (125b) L?F-L (or L?H-L); (120a) koto fumi ‘another book’ LHxx. Km (W,S) LH-L.
(For ‘special’ H has Tk 1.) Goka-mura 2. Sr kuutu B ‘other than, besides’.

3.4   kotoba ‹ *koto*ᵦ.ᵧ* -n- pa*₁.₂*. ‘word(s)’. LLL - 3-2-B B-B-A. Km (W) LLL
= koto-no-fa LLLH. Mr (Bm) HHL. Edo HHL. Ib F = 3.4. Nk huTuuba B.

?4.5   kotobuki ‹ kotofokyi ‹ *koto*ᵦ.ᵧ* pok[a-C]i*₇ᵦ*. ‘congratulations; a long
life, longevity’. x - 2-2-B x-B-x. Sz 3.

4.5   kotodate ‹ *koto*ᵦ.ᵧ* -n- tata-Ci[-Ci]*ᵦ*. ‘announcement, pronouncement’.
x - x-x-x x-x-x. NS (71a [11:173-M]) LLLL; NS (T+ 46) LHHₚ.

5.16   kotodomori ?‹ *koto*ᵦ.ᵧ* -n- toma-r[a-C]i*ₐ* (*see* domoru). ‘stammering’.
LLLHL - x-4-x x-x-x.

4.5   kotogami ‹ koto-gamyi ‹ *koto*ᵦ.ᵧ* -n- kami*ᵦ.₄*. ‘the head/proximity of a
Japanese harp’. x - x-x-x x-x-x. NS (-k-) LLLL; NS (T+ 92 -g-) HL-HH.

3.4   kotoi ‹ kotofyi ‹ *koto*ᵦ.ᵧ* [o]p[a-C]i*₇ᵦ* (‘special burden-bear’). ‘a
large and sturdy ox’ (= kotoi-usi). LLL - x- 0/1-x x-(x)-x. Wakayama kotte 1:3.
Nk kuTii B (= kuTii-husii B) ‘bull’; Sr kutibusi A ‘sturdy-ox song’, kutiiqusi
B ‘bull’. Dial. kottoi, gottoi, kote, kottee.

3.4   [kotoo] ‹ koto-wo ‹ *koto*ᵦ.ᵧ* bo*₇₁.ᵧᵦ*. ‘harp string’. LLL - x-0-x x-x-x.

3.1   kotori ‹ *kwo*₁.₁* tori*ᵦ.₁*. ‘bird’. x - 0-0-A x-x-x. Narada 3. Km x. Ib H =
3.1.

3.4   kotori ‹ ko[to]-tori ‹ *koto*ᵦ.ᵧ* tor[a-C]i*ᵦ*. ‘assistant head bodyguard to
emperor; transport manager; head puppeteer’. LLL (‘bodyguard’) - x-x-x x-x-x.

4.10 / 2.4|2.4 kotosara ‹ *koto*₇ᵦ.ᵧ* sara*ᵦ.ᵧ*. ‘especial(ly); intentional(ly)’ *(adj-n,
adv)*. “RLL” (Kn) = LHLL / LH|LH (Ck) - 0/2-0[H]/1:3[U]-B x-x-x.

3.1   kotosi ‹ ko-tosi ‹ *ko*₁.₁* tosi*ᵦ.ᵧ*. ‘this year’. HHH - 0-0-A x-A-x. Km x.
Edo HHH. Hattō, Hamada 3; Narada, Matsue, Izumo, Goka-mura 0. Ib H = 3.1.

4.10 (?= 2.5|2.3)   kototae(-ni) ‹ kototafe ?‹ *koto-tafey ‹ *koto*₇ᵦ.ᵧ* tapa-Ci[-Ci]*ᵦ*
(? ‘withstanding the different’). ‘on purpose’. x - x-x-x x-x-x. NS (117a) LHLL.

4.5   kotowaza ‹ *koto*ᵦ.ᵧ* bansa*ᵦ.ᵧᵦ* (‘word [and] deed’). ‘proverb’. LLLL -
0/3-0-B x-x-x. Sz 4.

3.4   kotozi ‹ koto-di ‹ *koto-nti (?‹ *koto*ᵦ.ᵧ* m[i]ti, ?‹ *koto*ᵦ.ᵧ* -n- ti*₇₁.₁*).
‘harp bridge’. LLL - 2/0-0-x x-x-x. Km x. K: Mr LHL. Cf. kurazi ‹ kura-di.

4.6   kotozute ‹ koto-ᵗ/ᵤute (“from Mr”) ‹ *koto*-tute ‹ *koto*ᵦ.ᵧ* tut[a-C]i*ₐ*.
‘message’ (= tutegoto). x - 0/3-0-B x-x-x. Km (W) LLLH (LLHL infinitive). Sz 4.

3.1   kotti ‹ koti ‹ *ko*₁.₁* ti*₇₁.₁*. ‘this way/direction; I/me, we/us’.
x - (1/)2(→3)-1-A x-x-x. 1700 Ōsaka (H)HL. Aomori 3. Ib F = 3.4.

?3.1, ?3.5x   kotuo ‹ kotuwo (‹ ?; cf. katuo). ‘shark’ (= same). HHH (Kn), LLH
(Ck) - x-x-x x-x-x.

3.1   kousi ‹ kwousi ‹ *kwo*₁.₁* usi*ᵦ.₁*. ‘calf’. HHH - 0-0[H]/2[U]-A x-x-x.
Matsumoto 3; Hattō, Hiroshima 2; Hakata *(expected)* 2, ygr 0. Toyama 1:3 *(we
expect 1:2)*. Ib H = 3.1. (For Tōkyō Hiroto and Ōhara give 0/1.)

2.5   kowa(-) ‘voice’: *see* koe.

4.7   kowadaka < *kowa$_{2.5}$ -n- taka$_{adj\ B}$. 'a high/loud voice'. LLHH - 0-1-B
x-x-x.

5.13   [kowakunegi] < kofa-kuneki ?< *kopa$_{adj\ B}$ kuneki$_{3.4}$ (< ...). '? a sturdy
thread-winder stick (bobbin)'. LHLLL (Zs) - x-x-x x-x-x. See kunegi.

3.2x   kowasi < *kwo$_{1.1}$ basi$_{?2.2a}$. 'small eagle'. HHL - x- 0-x x-x-x.

2.3   koya < kwoya < *kwo$_{1.1}$ da$_{1.3b}$. 'shed, shack hut'. LL - 2/0-0-B x-x-x.
Sz 0; Hattō, Hamada, Matsue, Izumo, Goka-mura, Hiroshima (Okuda), Hata 2. Kōchi
2; Ib F = 2.3. Dial. (Hida) kooya. Register incongruent; maybe 2.3 ← *2.1?

3.1   koyama < (*)kwo-yama < *kwo$_{1.1}$ dama$_{2.3}$. 'hill'. HHH - 0-0-A x-x-x. Km (W)
koyama-tera HHHxx. Narada 3.

3.1   koyoi < koyofyi < *ko$_{1.1}$ dopi$_{2.1}$ (?< *ko dwo-pi with Cwo assimilating to
Co). 'tonight'. HHx - 0-0-A x-A-x. NS (105b [11:235-K]) HHH; NS (T+ 65)
LHH. Km (W) xHH. Edo HHH/HLL/LHH. 1700 ōsaka HHH. Hattō 3; Goka-mura 2; Narada,
Hamada, Matsue, Izumo 0. Ib L = 3.4 (older koisa L2 = 3.7, cf. aisa = asita).

3.4   koyomi < *koyomyi < ?*ka$_{?1.3b}$ dom[a-C]i$_B$ (or < ?*key-yomyi < *ka-Ci$_{?1.3b}$
dom[a-C]i$_B$. 'calendar'. LLL - 3-0[H]/2[U]-B B-B-B. Aomori, NE Kyūshū, Hakata
0; Izumo 0/3; Hattō, Hamada, Narada (etc.) 3. Goka-mura 0 (expected
reflex). Kōchi 3 (> Kt 2). Ib F = 3.4. Yn kuyumi B (H 1964:71b).

5.6 (= 3.4|2.3)   koyosimono < *koyosi-mono (< *koda-s[a-C]i$_{?B}$ mono$_{2.3}$.
'jelly; jellied meat/fish'. LLL(|)LL - x-x-x x-x-x.

3.5x   kozake (Mg), kosake < kwo-sakey < *kwo$_{adj\ B}$ (-n-) saka-Ci$_{2.1}$ ('thick
wine'). 'overnight brew(ed sake)'. LLH - x-2-x x-x-x. K: "Hn LLL" (mistake?).

3.1   kozaru < kwo-saru < *kwo$_{1.1}$ saru$_{2.5}$. 'little/baby monkey'. x - 0-0-x
x-x-x. NS (Okada) HHH; NS (T+ 107, T+ kun) HHH.

2.4 < 3.5x   kozi < konzi < *konsi (< Ch .kon/.kyen-'tsyey). 'a cloth wrapped
around the back of the hair to make it stand up tall; a scarf, a kerchief'.
LH - x-2-x x-x-x.

4.6   kozigata < kozikata (Mg) < *konsi$_{2.4}$ (< ...) kata$_{2.2b}$. 'the peak of a
head-dress; a [similarly shaped] door-stop'. LLLH - 0-x-x x-x-x.

3.4   koziki < ko[tu]-ziki (< Ch khyet-džhyek). 'beggar'. x - 3-1:3[H]/2[U]-B
x-x-x. Aomori, Sz, Narada, Hattō, Hamada 3; Matsue, Izumo, Wakamatsu, NE
Kyūshū 0; Goka-mura 2. Ib F = 3.4. The Japanese word is cited as kwocuciki (=
kotu-t/ziki) in the Korean work Waye ¹yuhay (1:15) of ?1720⁻, but that may be a
reading pronunciation; over a century earlier, JP has "cojiqi" = koziki.

3.1 = 1.1|2.3 kozima < kwozima < *kwo$_{1.1}$ -n- sima$_{2.3}$. 'little island'. x - 0-0-A
x-x-x. NS (79b [14:321-M]) H(|)HH. Km (W) HHH/HHL. Mr (Bm) HLL.

3.4   koziri < *ko$_{1.3a}$ -n- siri$_{2.3}$ ('wood butt'). 'chape, sheath-tip, scabbard-
point'. LLL - 0/3-0-x x-x-x.

2.4   kozo < *konso. 'last year; tonight or (= kyiso) last night'. LH - 1-2-x
x-B-x. NS (Okada) HL (mistake?); T (69) HH. Km (W) LH(-H). Edo LH.

3.4   kozue < kozuwe < *ko$_{1.3a}$ -n- suwe$_{2.1}$ (< ...). 'twig'. LLL - 0-0-A x-x-x.
Km x. Edo HHL. Aomori (rare) 0; Hattō, Matsue, Izumo 3; Goka-mura 0 (= 3.4 or
3.1). Ib [Lit.] H = 3.1. The dialects should reflect the low accent of 'tree';
perhaps the first syllable was reinterpreted as kwo- 'little'? Or, the compound
became opaque; but Hn LLL > Mr HHL would not yield Kt 0, nor Kg A. Ōno says
kozuwe is a Heian replacement for konure < ko$_{1.3a}$ n[o] ure$_{?2.1}$ (?< *ura-Ci).

3.1   kozuno < koduno < *kwo-dunwo < *kwo$_{1.1}$ -n- tunwo$_{2.3}$. 'hard bone inside the
tip of an ox-horn'. HHx (= *HHH) - x-0-x x-x-x. K: Hn HHH.

?4.1   kozyuuto < koziuto < kozifuto < kwozifyito < *kwo$_{1.1}$ -n- si-pito$_{3.1}$.
'husband's brother(s); wife; brother(s) or sister(s)'. "LLLL" (?= *HHHH) -
0/2/4-3-A x-x-x.

?4.1|1.3b kozyuutome < koziuto-me < *kozifuto-me < kwozifyito₇₄.₁ (< *kwo₁.₁ -n-
si-pito₉.₁) mye₁.₉ᵦ (< *miCa₁.₉ᵦ ?= *mina). 'husband's sister(s); wife's
sister(s)'. "HLLL|H" (?= *HHHH|R) - 0/4-3-x x-x-x.

1.x (-)ku 'place': see izuko < izukᵘ/ₒ, komoriku. Cf. kuni, (-)ko.

1.x -ku. This suffix makes derived adverbs and attaches to an adjective stem
to make the infinitive (cf. Ch. 4, §9; Ch. 7). See sakeku (< sakyi-ku), ...
Cf. aku; (-)ko; koto.

2.1 kubi < kubyi < *kunpi. 'neck; head'. HH - 0-0-A A-A-x. NS (121a) HH. Km x.
Ib H = 2.1. On Yn nubi C see nodo. The -byi is based on a single phonogram in
[Shinshaku] Kegon ongi shiki, thought to be late-Nara or early-Heian. But kubututi[y] (NS 29) = kubu-tutu[C]i (NS 9) 'sword with a knob-head haft' suggests
that the etymon may have been *kubiy < *kunpu-Ci, unless the first vowel of the
compound assimilated to the others and the form is a variant of kabu-tutu[C]i <
*kanpu 'head'.

4.2 kubikase < kubikasi < *kubyikasi < *kunpi₈.₁ kasi₈.₃. 'neck cangue'.
HHHL - 0-0-A x-x-x.

3.2b kubiki < *kubyi-kiy < *kunpi₈.₁ ko̱-Ci₁.₉ₐ ('neck wood'). 'a crosspiece in
front of the shaft-handles of a wagon'. HHL - 0/3-0̱-x x-x-x.

5.2 kubiooi < kubi-ofofi < kubyi ofofyi < *kunpi₈.₁ opo-p[a-C]i₈. 'a neck
cover (shawl) for a horse or an ox'. HHHHL - x-4-x x-x-x.

3.2a < 4.x kubisu, kibisu, kufisu < kufyifyisu (< ?). 'heel'. HHL - 0-2̱-A x-x-x.
Edo HLL. Hn kubyifyisu/kufyibyisu; JP kubisu, kibisu. (Replacement by kakato
late?)

3.6 kubiti ?< *kubyiti < *kunpi₈.₁ t[(w)ora-C]i ('neck take'). 'a (rat-)trap'.
LHH - x-x-x x-x-x. Attested only in Mg?

?4.1 kubizuna < kubi-duna < *kubyi-duna < *kunpi₈.₁ -n- tuna₈.₃. 'a neck rope,
a leash'. HHxx - 0-x-x x-x-x.

?2.1 kubo < *kunpo. 'hollow'. x - 1̱/0-1:3-x x-(A)-x. Cf. kubomu.

3.7b kuboka < *kunpo₇₈.₁ -ka. 'hollow, sunken' (adj-n). LHL - x-1:3-x x-x-x.
(Assigned not to 3.7x but to 3.7b because that is the pattern for CVCV-ka.)

3.2x kubosa < kufusa (Mg) < ?kufosa < *ku(n)posa (< ?). 'profit, interest'.
HHL - x-x-x x-x-x. On -b- see Ch. 2.

3.1 kubote ?< *kunpo₇₈.₁ ta-Ci₁.₉ₐ. 'a kind of basket for presenting offerings
to the gods'. HHH - x-x-x x-x-x.

?2.1, ?2.2 kubu-: see kubututi, kubi.

- kubura = komura 'calf of leg'.

?*4.6 kubututi (< kubututi[y] < kubu-tutu[C]i) = kubututui (unmonophthongized) <
kubu-tutu[C]i < *kunpu₇₈.₁,₇₈.₈ tutu-Ci*₄.₆›₃.₄. 'sword with a knob-head haft'.
x - x-x-x x-x-x. NS (T+ 29 kubututi) HL|HH, (T+ 9 kubututui) HH(|)LLL. The -i
has also been regarded as a particle: kubu-tutu[Ci] i. Alternative etymology:
(the first vowel assimilated to the other vowels) < kabu-tuti/*-tutui <
*kanpu₈.₁ tutu-Ci₃.₄‹*₃.₅.

2.4 kuda < *kunta. 'tube, pipe(; whistle; spool)'. LH - 1-1-B B-B-(x). Ib L =
2.4. Perhaps Yn nda B 'rice-thresher (tool)'?

4.5 kudamono < *kuntamono̱ (?< *ko₁.₉ₐ -n- -ta [= -tu] mono̱₈.₃; ?< *ko̱₁.₉ₐ -n-
ta[npa-p[a]-uᵦ] mono₈.₃). 'fruit'. LLLL - 2-3-B x-x-x. Km x. Narada, Hattō,
Hamada, Matsue, Izumo, Hata, Hakata 2; Goka-mura 0. Kōchi 4 (Doi 1952:26); Kōbe
(Robb) 1:3. Another etymology: -ta < ta[na(-)]₈.₄ 'seed'.

3.5x/3.6 kudani: see kutani.

3.4 kudara < kutara. 'Paekche (Paykcey), an ancient Korean state'. LLL(-)··· -
1̱-1:3-x x-x-x.

5.7 (?= 3.4|2.5) kudara-goto < kutara*s.4* -n- k<u>o</u>to*s.s*. 'a "Kudara" (= Paekche)
harp' (= kugo). LLL(|)LH - 3/4-1:4-x x-x-x. K: "Hn LLLLF?".

?5.16 = 3.4|2.2; ?5.14 kudara-humi < kutara-fumi < *kutara*s.4* pumi*s.sb*. 'the
Paekche Record'. x - x-x-x x-x-x. NS (131a) LL?L(|)HL, (Okada) LLHHL.

3.1 kudari < *kunta-r[a-C]i*A*. 'descending, descent'. <u>HHL</u> *(inf?)* - 0-0-A x-A-x.
NS (T+ 120 'ebb') HHH *(Tsuchihashi takes this as v inf, despite the preceding
particle /no/).* Aomori, Sz O. Ib H = 3.1. Cf. nobori-kudari.

2.3 kudo < *kunto (< ?). 'the smoke-hole of an oven; an oven; a hearth'.
LL - x-2-x x-x-x.

2.1 ?< *3.1 kuga < (Mg) "kumuka" (= /kunga/) < kun^i/<u>u</u>-ka < *kunu(-Ci)*?s.1,?s.sa*
ka*1.x*. 'dry land'. HH (Hoke-kyō tanji), HHH (Mg) - <u>1</u>-<u>2</u>-x x-x-x. Ongi HH.
Edo HH.

4.5 kugatati: *see* kukatati.

2.1 kugi (?< *kugyi < *ku(n)ki; ?< *kugiy < *ku(n)k<u>u</u>/<u>o</u>Ci). 'nail'.
HH(/LL/LH *Mg errors*) - 0-0-A A-A-A. Edo HH. Ib H = 2.1. Nk KuCii A; (northern
Okinawa) Kunigami, Ōgimi <u>B</u>. Hateruma hun. On the second consonant, see Ch. 2.

3.1 kugo, kuugo (?= [kuûgo]) (< Ch .khung-.hhew). 'a kind of harp'. HHH -
<u>1</u>-<u>2</u>-x x-x-x. K: "Hn RH" *(mistake based on kuko?).* (NKD: "also -k-", *but is this
merely orthographic?*)

2.1 kugu (< ?). 'nut-grass, coco grass; Cyperus rotundus'. HH - <u>1</u>-0-x x-x-x.
Km x.

3.5a/b kugui < kugufi (Kn) / kukufi (Ck) < *kukufyi < *ku(n)kupi. 'swan'. LLH -
0/1-1-x x-x-x. Km x.

?3.1 kuguse < *kunku- (?= *kunku[ma-Ci]*A*) se*1.s* (< s<u>o</u>). 'rickets; a hunchback
(humpback)'. (LLH/)HHH - x-0-x x-x-x. Also kutuse, segutu, semusi.

3.5a/b kugutu (?< Korean :kwang'tay < ?). 'puppet'. LLH - 0/1-<u>1</u>-x x-x-x.

6.22 kugutumawasi < kugutu*s.sa/b* (< ...) mafasi (< *mapa-s[a-C]i*A*).
'puppeteer(s)'. LLLLHL - 4-x-x x-x-x.

2.2a kui < kufyi < *kupi. 'stake'. HL - <u>1</u>-<u>2</u>-B B-A-x. Km x. Tōkyō and Wakamatsu
<u>1</u> < *2 due to monosyllabification; Shimoda 2; Aomori (kue) O. Ib H1 = 2.2.
Nk Kui B; Sr kwii A. Sd gwi <u>B</u> or qyigui A (< OJ wi-gufyi), *omitted in Martin
1970;* Yaeyama gui ?< *[ ]-n- kui (see Ch. 1, §26).

2.3 kui < kufi (< ?). 'green caterpillar' (= imomusi). LL - x-x-x x-x-x.

4.5 kuimono < kufimono < *kufyi-m<u>o</u>no < *kup[a-C]i*B* m<u>o</u>no. 'food; preparing
food, cooking'. LLxx - 3/4-3-B x-(x)-x. K: Edo HHHL. Sr kwee-mun B < kura[f]i-.

3.4 kuina < kufyina < *kupina (< ?). 'water rail, mud hen'. LLL - 0-<u>1</u>-x x-x-x.

3.1 kuize < kufize < *kufyi-z[uw]e < *kupi*s.sb* -n- suwe*s.1* (< ...). 'a tree
stump; (= kui) a stake'. HHH - 0-<u>2</u>-x x-x-x. Km (S) HHH. Mr (Bm) HHL.

4.5 ku^k/_gatati < kukatati ?< *kuka*?s.s* (?< Korean kwuk 'broth') tat[a-C]i*B*.
'trial by boiling water; hot water for ritual purification'. x - 0/4-x-x x-x-x.
NS (Okada) LLLL; NS (T+ kun) LLLH.

2.1 kuki < kukyi < *kuki. 'mountainside cave; peak'. HH - x-<u>2</u>-x x-x-x.
NS (T+ kun) <u>HL</u>. Km (S) HHH. Mr (Bm) HHL.

2.3 kuki < kukiy < *kuku-Ci. 'stalk; stem (cf. miki)'. LL - 2/<u>0</u>-2-B B-B-x.
Narada, Hattō, Hamada, Matsue, Izumo 2. Ib F = 2.3. Sr guci B ?< *[ ] -n- kuki
(Ch. 1, §26).

?2.4 < 3.6 kuko (< Ch 'kew-'ko/'kyey). 'Chinese matrimony vine, Lycium
chinense'. RH (= LHH) - <u>2</u>-<u>2</u>-x x-x-x.

3.4 kukumi < ku^k/_gumi < *kukumyi < *kuku-m[a-C]i*B*. 'holding in the mouth;
a gold or silver plate around a sword handle or sheath; a bridle bit'. LLL -
x-x-x x-x-x.

- kukusa: *see* gugusa.

?4.5   kukutati < *kuku*s.s* tat[a-C]i*s*. '(turnip/rape/...) peduncles (= flower
stalks)'. LLxx - x-x-x x-x-x. K: Hn LLLL. Cf. kuki.

?2.1 > ?2.3   kuma. 'nook, (hidden) corner, recess; river bend'. HH - 2-2-B x-x-x.
NS (T+ 56) LH. Hoke-kyō tanji HL. Km (W) HH(/HL). Aomori, Sz O. Ib F = 2.3.

2.3   kuma. 'bear'. x - 2-2-B B-B-x. Km x. Edo HL. K: Hn-Km LL (attested?).
Ib F = 2.3. See kami 'god', kumasine.

-        kumadaka: see kumataka.

?4.3   kumaguma < *kuma*?s.s<s.1* n[i] kuma*?s.s<s.1*. 'river bends'. x - 2-x-x
x-x-x. NS (73a) HHLx (?= *HHLL); NS (T+ 56) LH|LH.

4.6   kumasine ?< *kuma*s.s* [z]ina-Ci*s.4*, ? (metathesis) < *kamu*s.s* [z]ina-Ci*s.4*.
'washed rice offered to the gods'. LLLH - x-0-x x-x-x.

4.5   kuma*t*/*d*aka < *kuma*s.s* -n- taka*s.1* ('bear hawk'). 'crested eagle'. LLLL -
2-2-x x-x-x.

5.7   kumatuzura < kuma-tudura < *kuma*s.s* tuntura*s.s* (< ?). 'Verbena
officinalis'. LLLLH - 3-x-x x-x-x.

2.3   kumi < kumyi < *kum[a-C]i. 'set'. LL - 2-2-B x-B-x. Ib F = 2.3.

4.6   kumikaki < kumyi-kakyi < *kum[a-C]i*s* kaki*s.ss* (< ...). 'a fence woven of
bamboo or wood'. x - 3-4-x x-x-x. NS (Okada) LLLH; NS (T+ 90b) LHHH, (T+ 90a)
HHHH.

4.5   kuminawa < kuminafa < *kumyi-nafa < *kum[a-C]i*s* napa*s.s*. 'a plaited rope'.
LLLL - 0/2-x-x x-x-x.

2.3   kumo < kumwo. 'cloud'. LL - 1-2-B B-B-B. NS (Okada) LL; NS (T 116) LL.
Km (S,W) LL. Mr (Bm) HL. Edo HL. Like Tōkyō, Hiroshima and Wakamatsu are
prototonic 1; but Sapporo, Aomori, Akita, Matsumoto, Numazu, Hattō, Hamada,
Matsue, Izumo, Goka-mura, Hata, NE Kyūshū, and Ōita are regularly oxytonic 2.
The oxytonic is a variant in dialects of Shizuoka, Nagano, Yamanashi (K 1943);
in Yamanashi it is the older accent (Watanabe 1957:184-5). Hakata 0 (expected),
ygr 1. Hyōgo, Kōchi 2; Toyama 1:3 (expected); Suzu 1; Ib F = 2.3. Yn nmu B;
Hateruma humon (Ch. 1, §52).

2.5   kumo < ?*kunpo < ?*konpo. 'spider'. LH - 1-1:3-B A-B-B. NS (T 65) LH.
Km (W) LH(x). Hata 1. Kōchi 1:3; Akō 2 (K 1944:200) — by analogy with
'cloud'?; Ib L2 = 2.5. Nk hubu C; Sr kubu/kuubaa B. Hattori 1967:55
reconstructs *koobu/*koomu on the basis of Kyūshū kobu, koobu, koobi.

3.5b   kumotu (< Ch .k[y]ung-m(b)[y]wet). 'offering'. x - 1-2-B x-x-x.

?3.6   kuna*t*/*d*o (< ?) = hunato 'a crossroads (god)'. x - x-x-x x-x-x.

3.4   kunegi [dial. 'support stake for plants; windbreak grove'] < kuneki ?<
*kuni[y]*s.ss* (< *kunu-Ci 'land') kiy*s.ss* (< *k*o*-Ci 'wood'). '(?) a thread-
winder stick (bobbin)'. LLL (Kn = Zs kofa ~) - x-x-x x-x-x.

-        kuneki: see kunegi.

?2.1, ?2.2a   kuni ?< *kuni[y] < *kunu-Ci; ?< ku*s.x* ni*?s.sb*. 'nation, land'. HH -
0/2-0-A B-A-x. NS (81c, 82c, 98a, 98b, 123a) HH; (74b [11:303-M], 74c [11:306-
M], 76c [14:126W-M], 92a) HL; (107a, 122a, 123a, 123a, 131b) H?L (or H?F);
NS (T 75, 82) HH, (T 96; 22, 34, 54, 62, 63) LH. Km (W) HH. Hamada 2; Hattō,
Goka-mura 0; Hakata 0 (we expect 1), ygr 0. Ib H = 2.1. Nk kunii A. Sd accent
mistaken? Cf. kuga, (-)ku.

?4.4   kuniguni < *kuni*?s.1,?s.ss* n[i] kuni (< ...). 'various countries'.
x - 2-3[H]/1:3[U]-A x-x-x. NS (98b [11:95-K]) H?LLL.

4.2   kunimagi < kuni-magyi < *kuni*?s.1,?s.ss* (< ...) mank[a-C]i*?A*. 'searching
for a likely home territory'. x - x-0-x x-x-x. NS (Okada) kuni-maki HHHL;
NS (T+ kun) HHFL ?= HHHL.

3.4   kunugi < ?*kunugiy < ?*kunu- (= ?) k*o*-Ci*s.ss*. 'oak (Quercus serrata)'.
LLL - 3/0-0-B x-x-x. NS (109b) LLL. Aomori (rare) 2. Ib F = 3.4.

2.2b   kura. 'seat, saddle'. HL - 2-2-B A-A-A. NS (80a) HL; NS (T 81) HL. Km x.
Edo HL. Aomori 2. Ib (rare) F = 2.3. Yn hura A (H 1964:71a).

2.3   kura. 'storehouse'. LL - 2-2-B B-B-B. Km x. Mr (Bm) HL. Edo HL. Aomori 2.
Ib F = 2.3. Yn kura B (H 1964:71a).

4.1   kurabone < *kura₂.₂b -n- pone₂.₃ (< ...). 'a saddle frame'. HHHH - 0/4-0-x
x-x-x.

3.1, 3.2x kurabu ?< *kura^b/₌a < *kura₂.₂b [u]ma₂.₃ ('saddle horse'). 'Kurabu'
(placename). x - x-x-x x-x-x. Km (W) HHH, HHL.

5.2, 5.1 kurabuyama < *kurabu₃.₁,₃.₂ (< ...) dama₂.₃. 'Mount Kurabu (= Kurama)'.
x - x-x-x x-x-x. Km (W) HHHHL, HHHHH.

?3.7a/b   kurage < kuragye < *kurankiCa (< ?). 'jellyfish'. LLL (Kz) - 1/0-1:3[H]/
0[U]-B x-x-x. Km x. Aomori 2; Sz 0. L2 = 3.5/7.

3.1   kurai < kurawi < *kura-bi < *kura - bi[y] < *kura₂.₂b bª/₂-Ci[-Ci]_A.
'position'. HHH - 0-0-A x-A-x. NS (92b, 94b) HHH. Km (S) HHH. Mr (Bm) HHH.
Edo HHH. NE Kyūshū 3. Ib H = 3.1. Cf. motoi.

3.6   kurara (< ?). 'Sophora angustifolia'. LHH - 0-1-x x-x-x. Said to be <
*kura-[ma-_A] [a]ra₂.₃ 'dizzying stuff [it is so bitter]' but the register is
incongruent.

6.3 (?= 5.2|1.3x)   kurazukuri-be < kuradukuri₇₄.₂ (< kura₂.₂b -n- tuku-r[a-C]i_B
bye₇₁.₃ (< ...). 'the guild of saddlers'. x - x-x-x x-x-x. NS (121b) HHHHLx =
(Okada) HHHHL(|)L.

2.1   kure < *kure[y] < *kura-Ci[-Ci]_A. 'dark; end (of day/year)'. HH - 0-0-A
x-x-x. NS (T+ 120) LH(-L). Km x. 1700 Ōsaka HH. Ib H = 2.1.

?2.1   kure (< ?). '(the state of Wu in ancient) China'. x - 1-2-x x-x-x.
NS (T 103) HH. K: Hn HH. Cf. kure-hatori, kurenai, kuretake, kuretuzumi.

2.3   kure (< ?). 'a plank or stave'. LL - x-2-x x-B-x. Sr kuri B 'stave'. Cf.
higure.

2.x (?2.3)   kure ?< ku[zu]re (< ...). 'lump, clod'. See isi-kure, tuti-kure;
cf. -koro.

5.2   kure-hatori < kure₇₂.₁ (< ...) hatori₇₃.₁ (< ...). 'weavers/weaving from
(Wu) China'. x - 3-x-x x-x-x. NS (Okada) HHHHL. (NKD: "Also -hadori.")

4.3   kurenai < kurenawi < *kure₇₂.₁ n[o] awi[y]₂.₃ (< *[z]abo(-)Ci₂.₅)
('China indigo'). 'crimson'. HHLL - 2/3/0-0-A x- x-x. K: Edo HHLL. Sz 0.

4.3   kuretake < *kure₇₂.₁ taka-Ci₂.₁ ('China bamboo'). 'black bamboo' (=
hatiku). HHLL - 2-0-x x-x-x.

5.1   kuretuzumi < kuretudumi < *kure - tudumyi < *kure₇₂.₁ tuntumi₇₂.₃ ('China
drum'). 'a kind of drum'. HHHHH - 3-4-x x-x-x.

2.3   kuri < *kuri[y] < *kuru-Ci. 'chestnut'. LL - 2-2-B x-(x)-x. NS HL (cf.
kur^i/₌-kuma 'Chestnut Corner' [11:146-K] LLHH). Matsue 1; Narada, Hattō,
Hamada, Izumo, Hiroshima (etc.) 2. Kōchi, Ōsaka, Ise, Toyama 2; Suzu 1:3;
Ib F = 2.3. Cf. kuru-su 'chestnut grove'; OJ dialect kuzi.

2.4   kuri. 'black clay' (= kuri-tuti). LH (Zs) / LL - x-2-x x-(x)-x. Km x.
(Sr kuri B 'squid ink', see kuromi.) Cf. kurwo and a[w]o : a[w]i.

4.5   kurituti < *kuri₂.₄ tuti₂.₃. 'black clay; (= kuri-iro) 'black'. LLLL -
x-0-x x-x-x.

3.4   kuriya < *kuri₂.₄ da₁.₃b (?< '[smoke-]black place'). 'kitchen'. LLL -
0-0[H]/2[U]-B x-x-x.

?2.5, ?2.3   kuro < kurwo. 'black'. x - 1-1:3-B B-B-x. NS (80a) LL(?-···). Km x.
1700 Ōsaka HL. Narada, Hattō, Hamada, Hiroshima 1; Matsue 1 (we expect 2);
Izumo 1/2. Ōsaka, Ise 1:3; Ib L2 = 2.5. Nk Kuruu LHL (?← B = LLH, ?← C =
HLL). Cf. kuro_adj B. Is kuro : kuri like a[w]o : a[w]i? (But cf. kuro : kura-
and siro : sira-.)

4.6 kurodai < kurodafi < *kurwo*adj* *B* -n- tapi*2.3*. 'a black porgy' (fish).
LLLH (Kn) - 0-1:3-B x-x-x. (Ck -t-.)

4.5 kurogane < kurwogane < *kurwo-gane[y] < *kurwo*adj* *B* -n- kana-Ci*2.1*.
'iron'. LLLL - 0-1[H]/0[U]-B x-B-x. K: Edo HHHH. Sr kurukani B.

4.5, 4.6 kurokami < kurwo-kamyi < *kurwo*adj* *B* kami*2.3* (< ...). 'black hair'.
Sz 3/4. x - 0[H]/2[K]-1[H]/2[U]-B x-x-x. Km (W) LLLL, LLLH.

4.7 (?= 2.3|2.1) kurokoma < *kurwo*adj* *B* kwo-ma*2.1* (< *kwo*1.1* [u]ma*2.3*). 'black
colt'. x - x-0-x x-x-x. NS (80a [14:340-M, 341-M]) LL(|)HH; NS (T+ 81) LL(|)HḤ.

4.5 (?= 2.3|2.3) kurokusa < *kurwo-kusa < *kurwo*adj* *B* kusa*2.3*. 'Echinops setifer
(= higotai); Cynanchum atratum (= hunabara-soo)'. LL(|)LL - x-1-x x-x-x.

5.15 kuromanako < *kurwo*adj* *B* manakwo*3.5b* (< ...). 'black eyes'. LLHLL - x-4-x
x-x-x.

3.4 kuromi < kurwo-myi < *kurwo*adj* *B* -mi*suf*. 'blackness; black/dark powder;
octopus/squid ink'. LLL ('ink') - 3-1-x (x)-x-x. Sr kuri B 'squid ink'.

3.4 kuromi < kurwo-miy < *kurwo*adj* *B* mu-Ci*1.1*. 'dark meat/fish'. x - 3-1-x
x-x-x.

4.6 kuromugi < *kurwo-mugyi < *kurwo*adj* *B* munki*2.4*. 'buckwheat (= soba);
blighted barley'. LxLH/LLxx = *LLLH - 3-3-x x-x-x.

4.x kuroodo < kuraudo < *kura*2.3* -n- pito*2.2a*. 'a Treasury employee; a female
rank (in the Heian court)'. x - 2-3-x x-x-x. K: Edo HHLL.

4.x kurooto < kurouto < *kurwo*adj* *B* pito*2.2a*. 'an expert'. x - 1/2-1-B x-x-x.
Sz 2. Cf. sirooto.

4.5 kurotori < *kurwo*adj* *B* tori*2.1*. 'a black bird; (= kurogamo) black scoter'.
LLLL - 0-3-x x-x-x.

4.5 (?= 2.3|2.3) kurotuti < *kurwo*adj* *B* tuti*2.3*. 'black earth; rich loam/soil;
(fire-)blackened earth'. LL(|)LL - 0-1-B x-x-x.

2.3 kuru(-) 'chestnut': see kuri.

4.x (?4.5) kuru-busi (JP) < *kuru*2.3* -n- pusi*2.3* ('chestnut joint'). 'anklebone'
(= tubu-husi, tubuna*k*/*gi*). x - 2-0[H]/2[U]-B x-x-x. Sz 2. Kōbe (Robb) 3/1:3.

4.5 kurukusa ?< *kuru*2.3* kusa*2.3* ('chestnut grass'). 'a woad, a pastel' (=
hatokusa = taisei). LL(|)LL - x-x-x x-x-x.

3.1 kuruma. 'car(t)'. HHH - 0-0-A B-B-A. Km x. Edo HHH. Hakata 1 (?< *2), ygr
0. Ib H = 3.1. Nk Kurumaa B; Yn kurima A (the -i- is unexplained).

5.1 kurumazaki < *kuruma-zakyi < *kuruma*3.1* -n- sak[a-C]i*?B*. 'tearing asunder
between chariots'. HHHHH - x-x-x x-x-x.

3.6 kururi (< ?). 'a kind of double-headed arrow (used to catch fish or
aquatic birds)'. LHH - x-2-x x-x-x.

?4.2; ?4.11 kurutuhi < kuru-tu-fyi < *[a]kuru (< *ak[a-Ci]-uru*A*) -tu pi*1.2* (or
< *k[o]-uru*B* *attr* ...). 'the next day'. x - x-x-x x-x-x. NS (102a [11:144-K])
HHHL, (103a) HL H(|)H(-L), (105b [11:235-K]) LLHL.

?2.2b kusa. 'seed, source; variety, kind, sort'. HL - 2-x-x x-x-x. NS (120a
kusa-kusa) HL. Cf. hito-kusa.

2.3 kusa. 'grass'. LL - 2-2-B B-B-B. Km (W) LL. Edo HL. Ib F = 2.3. Yn caa B.

2.3 kusa. 'eczema'. x - 2-2-B x-B-x. Sr kusa 'filariasis'. Cf. kose.

3.x kusaba < *kusa*2.3* -n- pa*1.2*. 'leaves of grass'. x - 0/2-0-B x-x-x. Edo
HLL.

?3.3 kusabi (< ?). 'wedge'. HLL - 0-0-B x-A-x. Goka-mura, Hakata 1; Aomori, Sz,
Hattō, Hamada, Matsue, Izumo 0. Nk kusaabi A.

?4.5 kusabira < *kusa-byira < *kusa*2.3* -n- pira*?2.2b*. (1) 'edible greens';
(2) 'mushrooms'. LLxx - (1/)0(/2)-1:3-x x-x-x. K: Hn LLLL.

3.6 kusabu (< ?). 'hedgehog' (= harinezumi). LHH - x-x-x x-x-x.

3.6　　　kusagi ‹ kusa-giy ‹ *kusa*adj* *B* -n- ko̲-Ci*1.3a* ('smelly tree').
(1) 'Clerodendron trichotomum';　*(2)* 'Orixa japonica' (= ko-kuragi);
(3) 'Premna japonica' (= hama-kusagi). LHH (Zs)- 0-0̲-x x-x-x.

5.16　　　kusainagi ‹ kusawi-nagi (‹ ?; cf. i). 'wild boar' (= i, inosisi). xLLHL =
*LLLHL - x-3-x x-x-x.

4.x ‹ 5.16　　　kusamoti ‹ kusamoti[w]i ‹ kusa-motifi ‹ *kusa*B.3* mot[i]-ipi*3.1*
(‹ ...). 'a rice cake with herbs (mugwort etc.) mixed in'. x - 2-3-B x-x-x
‹ LLLHL x-x-x x-x-x. Sz 3. (Sr huuci|mu˺ci B+A.)

?4.5, ?4.10　　　kusamura ‹ *kusa*B.3* mura*B.1*. 'a patch of grass/weeds. a grassy
place'. LLxx - 0/4-0-B x-x-x. Ongi-m LHLL. Sz 4; Hata 4. Kōchi 4.

3.1　　　kusari ‹ *kusar[a-C]i. 'chain'. HHH - 0-0-A A-A-x. Km x. 1700 Ōsaka LHH.
Aomori, Akita 3̲; Hakata 1̲, ygr 0. Toyama 1:2 *(expected)*; Suzu 1̲ *(we expect 0)*;
Ib F̲ = 3.4.

4.1　　　[kusawai] ‹ kusa-fafyi ?‹ *kusa*B.2b* -pa-p[a-C]i. 'all kinds of things'.
x - x-x-x x-x-x. NS (103a) HHHH.

3.4　　　kusaya ‹ *kusa*B.3* da*1.3b*. 'a grass hut, a thatched hut; a hay barn/loft'.
LLL (Ir) - 2̲-1̲-x x-x-x.

2.2a　　　kuse (?‹ *kuse[y] ‹ *kusaCi. '(bad/any) habit'. x - 2-2-A A-A-x. Km x.
1700 Ōsaka HL. Aomori 0; Sz 0 (but 2 in ··· no kuse ni).

2.3　　　kusi. 'comb'. LL - 2-2-B B-B-B. Km x. K: Edo HL. Hyōgo, Kōchi, Toyama 2;
Suzu 1̲; Ib F = 2.3. (?← kusi 'skewer'; cf. mu-gusi, o-gusi 'hair; head'.)

2.3　　　kusi ‹ kusi[y] ‹ *kusu-Ci. 'skewer'. x - 2-2-B x-B-x. Km x. Aomori,
Matsue, Izumo 0̲. Ib F = 2.3. Sr guusi B ?‹ *[ ] -n- kusi (see Ch. 1, §26).
Cf. [kusunuku]*4* in Ch. 6 (the register is incongruent).

2.x　　　kusi ?‹ kusi[y] ‹ *kusuCi (?= *kusu-Ci, ?= *kusu[r]i). 'wondrous elixir
= rice wine'. x - x-x-x x-x-x. NS (T+ 32) LL. Yaeyama (Ishigaki, Taketomi,
Kobama) gusi ?‹ *[ ] -n- kusi (see Ch. 1, §26). Cf. kusu, kusu(-), kusudama,
kusuri, kususi; (-)ki 'wine'. Also taken to be a direct nominalization of the
predicative form of the old adjective kusi[-si] 'is strange, wondrous, rare'.

3.x　　　kusiro̲ (?‹ Korean kwu˺sul, ?← kusari*3.1*). 'bracelet'. x - 2-2-x x-x-x.
Variant (Shinsen-Jikyō) kuziri.

2.3　　　kuso ‹ kuswo. 'dung'. LL - 2-0̲-B B-B-x. NS (T+ kun) kuswo maru LL|LH
'defecate'. Km x. Ib F = 2.3. Somehow related: kusa*adj* *B* 'smelly', kusaru*B*
'rot'. Is the pair kuso : kusa- like kuro(-) : kura- and siro(-) : sira-?

5.7　　　kusobukuro ‹ (*)kuswo-bukurwo ‹ *kuswo*B.3* -n- pukurwo*3.4*. 'stomach'.
LLLLH - 3-4-x x-x-x.

?5.7　　　kusokazura ‹ kuso-kadura ‹ *kuswo*B.3* kantura*3.2*.　'Paederia chinesis'
(= hekuso-kazura). "LH|LLH" ?= *LLLLH - x-x-x x-x-x.

5.16　　　kusomayumi ‹ *kuswo*B.3* mayumyi*?3.1* (‹ *ma- dumi). 'wingèd spindle-tree
(euonymus)'. LLLHL - x-x-x x-x-x.

4.11　　　kusomusi ‹ (*)kuswo*B.3* musi*B.1* (‹ ...). 'gold bug' (= mar*u*/o-musi).
LLHL - 2-x-x x-x-x.

4.5　　　kusotobi ‹ "kuso-˺/ᵈofi" (?= kuso-tobi) ‹ *kuswo*B.3* ?tonpi*?2.5,?2.1*.
'buzzard' (= nosuri). LLLL - x-x-x x-x-x.

?2.4　　　kusu(-) 'medicine' (?= 'camphor'): *see* kusudama; kusi; kusuri, kususi.

?4.8　　　kusudama ‹ *kusu*(?2.4)* -n- tama*B.3*. 'festive ball or sachet (to ward off
evil or impurity)'. x - 0-1-B x-x-x. Sz 4. K: Km LHHH *(where attested?)*.

4.10　　　kusunoki ‹ *kusunokiy ‹ *kusu*?2.4* no̲ ko̲-Ci*1.3a*. 'camphor (tree)'.
LHLx = *LHLL - 2-1:3-B x-B-x. Sz 1. The -su- (for -şi-) of Sr kusunuci B
perhaps is a secondary assimilation or indicates borrowing.

3.7a   kusuri. 'drug'. LHL - 0-1:3-B B-B-C. Mr (Bm) LHL. Edo LHL. Goka-mura, Totsukawa, Ōita 1; Sapporo, Aomori, Akita, Wakamatsu 2; Hakata 2, ygr 0; Narada, Numazu, Hattō, Hamada, Matsue, Izumo, Hiroshima, NE Kyūshū 0. Ib L2 = 3.5/7. Yn cuuri C. Cf. kusunoki, kususi, kususi-*adj*.

3.6   kususi < kusu[ri]-si ?< *kusuri*ₛ.₇ₐ* siri (< *sir[a-C]i*ₐ*) ('know drugs'). 'doctor, physician, healer'. LHH - 2-1-x x-x-x. Cf. umagususi.

?3.2b, ?3.3   kusyami < kusame (< ?). 'sneeze'. x - 2-2-A x-x-x. Sz, NE Kyūshū 3; Narada 1. Ib H1 = 3.3.

3.5x/3.6   ku^t/ₐano < kutani (< ?). 'a plant, perhaps the gentian (= rindoo) or the peony (?= botan)'. x - x-x-x x-x-x. Km (W) LLH/LHH. Mr (W 19) HHL, (W 18) xHx.

2.1   kuti < *kuti[y] < *kutu-Ci (cf. kutuwa). 'mouth'. HH - 0-0-A A-A-A. NS (117a, 126a) HH; NS (T+ 14) HH. Km x. Mr (Bm) HH. Ib H = 2.1. Hakata 0 *(we expect 1, ygr 0; cf. hati 'bee')*. Yn Tii A < *kuti), Tibuni A (< *kuti-pone).

2.1   kuti. 'hawk'. HH - x-x-x x-x-x. NS (T+ kun) LL. According to NS this is a Paekche (Kudara) word; cf. Kanazawa, Chōsen-Gakuhō 11:33 (1957), and Toh 1981: 27. Cf. kotu 'peregrine falcon' (= hayabusa, NKD). For a lavish discussion of kuti see Miller, Journal of Korean Studies 1:36-42 (1979).

?2.2a   kuti, guti < *kuti. 'yellow corvina; Sciaena schlegeli' *(fish)*. HL - 1-1:3-x x-x-x. K: Hn HH (mistake?). The guti form ?< *[ ] -n- kuti (Ch. 1, §26).

3.x   kutiba < *kuti[y]*ᴮ* (< *kutu-Ci[-Ci] < *kuta-Ci[-Ci]) -n- pa*₁.₂*. 'dead leaves'. x - 0/2-0[H]/2[U]-B x-x-x. Edo HLL.

4.2   kutibase < *kutu-Ci*ₛ.₁* -n- pasa-Ci[-Ci]*ᴮ*. '(the look of) the mouth'. HHHL - x-x-x x-x-x.

4.2   kutibasi < *kutu-Ci*ₛ.₁* -n- pasi*ₛ.₁* ('mouth edge'). 'beak'. HHHL - 0-1:4-A x-x-x. Ongi HHHL. Narada, Hattō 4; Sz, Hamada, Matsue, Izumo, Goka-mura 0; Hakata 2, ygr 0. The low register in Kyōto is odd, but both H and U report it.

4.2   kutibiru < ?*kuti[y]-byiro < ?*kutu-Ci*ₛ.₁* -n- piro*adj ᴮ*. 'lips, beak'. HHHL - 0-1:4[H]/4[U]-A x-x-x. Ongi HHHL. Km (S) HHHL. Narada, Hattō 4; Hamada, Matsue, Izumo, Goka-mura 0. Dialect kuti-biri, -biro, -buro, -bera, -pera, -peru, -pero. NKD "anciently -f-?" (cf. ahiru 'duck').

4.2   kutibuto < *kuti[y]*ₛ.₁* (< *kutu-Ci) buto*ₛ.ᴮ* (< *nputo). 'mosquito; gadfly, horsefly'. HHHL - 0-x-x x-x-x.

4.2   kutihibi < kuti-fibi < *kutu-Ci*ₛ.₁* ?pi-n-pi*ₛ.ₛ*. 'lip cracks, chapped lips'. HHHL - x-4-x x-x-x.

4.5   kutinawa < kuti-nafa < *kutu-Ci*ₛ.₁* napa*ₛ.ₛ* ('mouth rope'). 'snake' (= hebi). LLLL - 0-1:4-x x-x-x. K: Edo LHLL. Wakayama kutinaa 1:4. Accent shows the etymology should be *kutu-Ci-*ᴮ* … 'rotten rope' (Murayama 1988:264).

4.1 (= 2.1|2.1)   kutisaki < *kuti[y] - sakyi < *kutu-Ci*ₛ.₁* saki*ₛ.₁*. 'lips'. x - 0-0-A x-A-x. Sz 0. Sr kucisaci A 'upper lip'.

5.2   kutisakira < kutisakyi*₄.₁* (< *kutu-Ci*ₛ.₁* saki*ₛ.₁*) -ra*suf* (< *[a]ra*₊ₛ.ₛ*). 'the edge/rim of the mouth, lips; the bill of a bird'. HHHHL - x-0-x x-x-x.

4.2   kutisubo < *kutu-Ci*ₛ.₁* sunpo*?ᴮ* (?< *sunpa*?ᴮ*, see subom⋯*ₐ*). 'pursed mouth; a utensil shaped like a pursed mouth'. HHHL - x-x-x x-x-x.

4.2(/4.1) kutitori < *kutu-Ci*ₛ.₁* t(w)or[a-C]i*ᴮ*. 'the role of holding a bridle rope on either side of a horse'. HHHL (Kn) / HHHH (Ck) - 3/4-4-x x-x-x.

4.1   kutiwaki < *kuti[y]*ₛ.₁* - wakyi*ₛ.ₛ* < *kutu-Ci*ₛ.₁* bak[a-C]i*ᴮ*. 'the sides of the mouth'. HHxx/xxHH = *HHHH - 0-x-x x-x-x.

2.1   kutu(-) 'mouth': see kuti.

2.3   kutu. 'shoes'. LL - 2-2-B B-x-B. Km x. Wakamatsu 1; Hakata 1, ygr 2. Goka-mura 0. Toyama 1:3; Suzu 1; Ib F = 2.3. Yn kutu B (H 1964:71a). K: Edo HL. Korean kwutwu is a modern borrowing from Japanese.

4.5   kutubako < *kutu-bakwo < *kutu*ₛ.ₛ* -n- pakwo*ₛ.₁*. 'a box for shoes'. LLLL - x-x-x x-x-x. Attested only in Kn Mg? Cf. getabako.

4.1   kutubami < kutu-bamyi < *kutu$_{2.1}$ -n- pam[a-C]i$_B$. 'a bridle bit' (= kutuwa). HHHH - x-x-x x-x-x. Km x. Mr (Bm) HHHH.

4.5   kutubiki < kutu-fyikyi < *kutu$_{2.3}$ (?-n-) pik[a-C]i$_A$. 'a foot-cord on a loom'. LLLL - x-x-x x-x-x.

4.6   kutugata < *kutu$_{2.3}$ -n- kata$_{2.2b}$. 'a wooden form for making shoes; a (shoeform-shaped) tile ornament fixed to either end of the roof beams on a palace or temple'. LLLH - 0-x-x x-x-x.

3.2x = 2.1|1.3 kutuko < kutu^k/$_g$o < *kutu$_{2.1}$ (-n-) kwo$_{1.3a}$. 'a feed-basket inserted in the mouth of a horse or an ox'. HH(|)L - x-x-x x-x-x.

7.30   kutukutuboosi < kutukutu - bo[f]usi < *kutu-kutu$_{8ib}$ -n- popu-si (< Ch pywap-.sri). 'a kind of cicada, Meimuna opalifera' (= tukutuku-boosi). LLxxLHL (= *LLLLHL) - 5-x-x x-x-x.

3.3   kutune = kitune$_{3.6}$ 'fox'. HLL (Kn) - x-x-x x-x-x.

3.4   kutuo < kutu - wo < *kutu$_{2.3}$ bo$_{1.3b,?1.1}$. 'shoestring, bootlace'. LLL - x-x-x x-x-x.

3.1   kutuwa < *kutu$_{2.1}$ ba$_{1.3a}$ ('mouth ring'). 'bridle bit'. HHH - 0-0-B̲ x-A-x. Aomori *(rare)*, NE Kyūshū 3̲. Toyama 1:2 *(expected reflex)*; Suzu 1̲ *(we expect 0)*; Ib F̲ = 3.4. Sr kutiba A.

5.2   kutuwazura < kutuwa$_{3.1}$ (< ...) -dura (< -n- tura$_{?2.1,?2.2b}$). 'the side-lines of a horse's bit'. HHHHL - x-x-x x-x-x.

2.1   kuwa < kufa < *kupa. 'hoe'. HH - 0-1̲[H]/0[U]-A x-A-x. Km x. Aomori 2̲; Ise 0/1̲; Nara 0; Ōsaka (Terakawa) 1̲; Ōsaka, Kōbe, Himeji 2̲ (Ōhara 1932-3); Ib H = 2.1. Sr kwee A < *kupai — cf. Miyako pai (Nakamoto 1983:13-4).

*2.1   kuwa(-) < kufa < *kupa. 'heel'. *See* kuwatateru 'stand tiptoe', kuwayugi 'fetlock'. Cf. kubisu.

2.3   kuwa < kufa < *kupa. 'mulberry'. LL - 1̲-1̲[H]/2[U,Ōhara 1932]-B B-B-x. NS (118b) H̲x. Km x. Narada, eastern Nagano (Kudō 147-8), Hattō, Matsue, Izumo, Goka-mura, NE Kyūshū 2; Hamada, Wakamatsu 1̲; Hiroshima 0̲. Ōsaka (Terakawa), Kōbe (Ōhara 1932) 1̲; Ōsaka (Ōhara), Nara, Himeji, Ise 2; Ib F = 2.3. Sr kwaa B. Mg kufa-no mi LLL(|)H 'mulberry (the fruit)'.

-        "kuwa" (< kwa): *see* ka.

4.x (?4.1)   kuwabira < kufabira < *kufa-byira < *kupa$_{2.1}$ -n- pira$_{2.2b}$. 'the flat of a hoe; the front of the foot (beyond the ankle)'. x - x-x-x x-x-x.

4.10   kuwamayu < kufa-mayu/-maywo < *kupa$_{?2.3}$ ma-dwo$_{?2.3}$ ('mulberry cocoon'). 'silkworm' (= kuwa-^{k}/$_g$o). LHLL - x-x-x x-x-x.

4.5 = 3.4|1.3 kuwasime < kufasi - mye < *kupasi[-si]$_{adj B pred}$ miCa$_{1.3b}$ (?= *mina). 'beautiful woman'. x - x-0-x x-x-x. NS (82c [17:112-M]) LLL(|)L.

4.2   kuwayugi < kufayu^k/$_g$i < *kufa-yu^k/$_g$yi (?< *kufa [a]yu^k/$_g$yi < *kupa$_{*2.1}$ adwu(n)k[a-C]i$_B$; ?< *kufa$_{2.1}$ yugi/yukyi (< ...) 'arrow quiver'). 'fetlock (joint) of horse' (= karasu-gasira). HHHL - x-A-x x-x-x.

?2.3, ?2.4   kuzi (?< *kunsi). 'lottery (chance)'. x - 1-2-B x-B-x. Aomori 1; Matsue, Izumo 0̲; Hattō, Hamada, Goka-mura, Hiroshima (Okuda) 2; Sz 2 (< kunzu 3). Hiroto and Ōhara, Mkz have 1/2 for Tōkyō. Ib F = 2.4. First attested Mr?

?3.2x, ?3.3   kuzika < kun$_{?2.1}$ (< Ch .kywen) sika$_{2.3}$. 'the fanged roe deer (= kiba-noro, hornless and smaller than the usual roe deer)'. HHL/HLL - x-x-x x-x-x.

?3.7a/b   kuzira < kudira < *kuntira. 'whale'. LHL - 0-1:3-B B-B-C. NS (T+ 7) LHL. 1700 Ōsaka LHL. Sapporo, Tappi (kuzina), Aomori, Akita, Numazu, Narada, Hattō, Goka-mura, Hata, Wakamatsu, NE Kyūshū, Ōita 1; Matsue, Izumo 3̲; Hamada, Hiroshima 0; Hakata 1, ygr 0. Kōchi 2̲ (Doi 1952:23); Ib L2 = 3.5/7. Sr, Sd g-··· ?< *[ ] -n- kudira (or *m[i]-kudira).

2.5   kuzu < *kunsu. 'arrowroot'. (L) - 1-1:3-B x-(B)-x. Km (W) LH(-x). Hakata 1. Ib L̲ = 2.4. Sr kuʒi B 'arrowroot flour'.

2.4   kuzu < kudu < *kuntu ?< *kunta *(the last vowel assimilated to the first,*
cf. kudasu). 'trash'. LH - 1-1-B x-x-x. Km x. Ib L = 2.4.

2.x   kuzu < kun[i]-su. 'aboriginal peoples (of Japan)'. x - 1-x-x x-x-x. Edo
HL. For etymologies, see NKD.

5.16   kuzukazura < kuzukadura < *kunsu$_{s.s}$ kantura$_{?s.7s}$ (< kam[i]-tura).
'arrowroot'. LLLHL - 3-x-x x-x-x.

?2.4, ?2.5   kyoo < kyefu ?< *ki-apu; or ?< *kyefyi < *ke-pi (or < keypu < *keypi
if the phonograms of M 4330 and M 4047 are taken as /key/, cf. Matsumoto 1974:
116) ?< *ko$_{1.1}$ (or *ka) pi$_{1.s}$ ('this day'). 'today'. LH - 1-1-B B-B-C. Ongi
(Iroha) LH. Km (S,W) LH. Edo LH. Ise, Kameyama 1:3; Ib L = 2.4. Yn suu C.
Matsue and Izumo 1 because of original final high vowel.

?3.5b   kyuuri < ki-uri (< ?*kiy - uri < *k^u/$_o$-Ci uri$_{s.4}$ 'yellow melon').
'cucumber'. LLH - 1(<*2)-2-B B-(B)-x. Km x. Goka-mura, NE Kyūshū, Wakamatsu,
Hakata 1; western Mino (= SW Gifu) 1/2; Tappi, Aomori (kiuri), Narada, Hattō 2;
Hamada, Matsue, Izumo 0. Toyama, Suzu 2 *(we expect 1:3)*; Ib F = 3.4

1.1   ma. 'room, space; *place (cf. ba)'. x - 0-0-B x-x-x. Km (W) H(-H).
Ib H = 1.1.

?1.1   ma(-). 'true, truth'. (H) - 0-0-x x-x-x. Sz 0. Ib H = 1.1. As noun, atonic
in Tōkyō, high atonic in Kyōto. Prefix: Kt B, the others A (Ch. 4, Chart 16:5.)

1.3a   ma(-) 'eye': *see* me.

1.3x < 2.3   ma(-) 'horse': *see* uma.

?4.10   maborosi < *manporosi (< ?). 'phantom'. LLxx - 0-0-B x-x-x. Ongi-m LHLL.
K: Edo HHHH. Sz 0.

3.4   mabusi (?< *ma$_{1.3a}$ (-n-) pus[a-C]i$_s$. 'a hunter's blind; (lying in) ambush'.
LLL - 3-x-x x-x-x.

3.7b   mabuta < *ma$_{1.3a}$ -n- puta$_{s.1}$. 'eyelid'. x - 1-1:3-B x-x-x. Sz, Hattō,
Hamada, Goka-mura, NE Kyūshū, Hakata 1; Matsue, Izumo 3; Aomori 1/3. Ib L2 =
3.5/7. (Sr miigaa$_s$ < me-gawa 'eye-skin'.) 1720- Waye ¹yuhay 1:16 "myey-hwu.ta"
or "ma.pu.ta". Earliest attestation Edo? Earlier manabuta.

2.4 < 3.5b   mada < imada (LLH) < *imanta. '(not) yet'. LH - 1-1-B B-B-C. Km (W)
LH. Ib L = 2.4. Sr maada B; Yn maadi C. Yaeyama meeda (Ishigaki, Taketomi),
menda (Kobama) — cf. mee 'already' C < *myee < *[i]myaa < *ima 'now'.

3.1   madara < *mantara/*montoro (cf. modoroku). 'spots'. HHH - 0-1:3-B x-x-x.
Sz 0.

4.11   madaraka < *mantara$_{s.1}$ -ka$_{suf}$. 'striped, mottled'. LLHL - x-4/1:4-x x-x-x.

5.2   madaramaku < *mantara$_{s.1}$ maku$_{s.s}$. 'a mottled curtain'. HHHHL - 4-1:4-x
x-x-x.

5.2   madarauri < *mantara$_{s.1}$ uri$_{s.4}$. 'yellow-speckled melon'. HHHHL - 3-1:4-x
x-x-x.

2.5   mado < madwo < *ma$_{1.3a}$ -n- two$_{1.1}$. 'window, opening'. LH - 1-1:3[H]/1[U]-B
B-B-x. Km (S) LH(-L). Edo LF. K: Hn-Mr LF. Ib L2 = 2.5.

3.7b   madoka < mat/$_d$o-ka < *mato$_{?s.s}$ -ka$_{suf}$. 'round'. LHx (?= *LHL) - 1-1:3-B
x-x-x. K: Mr LHL.

4.11   madoyaka < matoyaka < *mato$_{?s.s}$ -da-ka$_{suf}$. 'round'. LLHL - x-3-x x-x-x.

2.5   mae < mafye < ?*ma$_{1.3a}$ piCa$_{1.x}$ ('eye side', opposite of siri-fye).
'front'. LH - 1-1:3-B B-B-A[H 1967]/C[H 1964]. NS (T 24) LH. Ongi-m LL. Km x.
Edo LF. Hata 1. Kōchi 1:3; Ib L2 = 2.5, 'previously' H1 = 2.2. Nk mee C.

?4.6a   maedare < mafet/$_d$are < *mafye$_{s.s}$ (< ...) -t/$_d$are[y] (< (-n-) tara-Ci[-
Ci]$_s$). 'apron'. LLLH, LLLF - 0-1:4-B x-x-x. See §7.3; cf. K 1964a:355.

?2.1   maga < *manka (< ?). 'something bad; disaster'. x - x-x-x x-x-x.

?4.1   magagoto < *manka?₂.₁ -n- koto₂.₅. 'untoward event, disaster; mistaken
or wrongheaded talk, fallacy'. HHxx - 0-x-x x-x-x.

3.7b   magaki < magakyi < *ma (= ?) -n- kaki₂.₅b. 'rough-woven fence' (= masegaki
= mase). LHL - 1-0-x x-x-x. Km (W) LHL. Edo LHL. (Is ma from [u]ma 'horse'?)

3.1   magari < *manka-r[a-C]i₄. 'a kind of cake' (= magari-motifi). HHH - x-0-x
x-A-x. Sr magai A 'curve, something curved; bay'.

5.3   magarikane < *manka-r[a-C]i₄ kana-Ci₂.₁. 'carpenter's square'. HHHLL -
x-x-x x-x-x. Sz 0. NKD: -ᵏ/ɡane.

2.3   mago < [u]ma-gwo (< ? [m]uma-gwo) < *uma₅dⱼ ₈ ('worthy child').
'grandchild' (see umago).   (x) - 2-2-B B-B-C. Edo HL. 1700 Ōsaka mago-ko LHH.
Narada, NE Kyūshū, Wakamatsu 1; Hakata 1, ygr 2; Hiroshima 2. Ōsaka, Ise 2.
Nk qmaaga B; Sr qnmaga B; Yn maanu C. Mg: mumago-mefi/-wofi LHHHL 'grand-
niece/-nephew'.

?3.6   maguro (?< ma₁.₈₅ -n- kurwo₂.₅ 'eye black'; ?< ma?₁.₁ -n- kurwo₂.₅ 'true
black'; ?< man[a]?₂.₁ kurwo₂.₅ 'fish black'). 'tuna' (fish) (= sibi). x - 0-1-B
x-x-x. Narada, NE Kyūshū 3. Hattō, Goka-mura 1; Aomori, Sz, Hamada, Matsue,
Izumo, Wakamatsu, Hakata 0. Ib L = 3.6.

3.2b   magusa < makusa < ma?₁.₁ kusa₂.₅ ('true grass'). 'forage'. HHL - 0/3-2[H]/
1:3[U]-B x-x-x. Km x. Hamada 0/3; Sz, Matsue, Izumo 0; Goka-mura 1. Nk
qmanKusaa B = qmaanu-kusaa LLH-HHH. (The high register is incongruent for the
etymology *[u]ma₂.₅ kusa₂.₅ 'horse grass', or *[u]ma₅dⱼ ₈ kusa₂.₅ 'worthy/tasty
grass', but note Kt [U], Goka-mura, and Kg.)

3.7a   magusa < *mankusa (< ?). 'lintel'. LHL - 0/3-0-x x-x-x. Km x. K: Edo HLL.

-           ma-hito: see mooto.

2.1   mai < mafyi < *map[a-C]i₄. 'dance'. (x) - 0-0-A x-A-x. Edo HH. Ib H = 2.1.
Sr mooi A.

?2.3   mai < mafyi < *mapi (?< *map[a-C]i₄₈). 'offering, gift'. Cf. mainai,
mainau, tamau. x - x-x-x x-x-x. Note: Km (W) mafi(-nasi) HH(- H-H) ?= ma-bi <
*ma₁.₁ -n- pi₁.₈ 'respite day'.

?4.5   mainai < mafyinafyi < *mapi₂.₅ -na-p[a-C]i. 'bribe'. Lxxx - 0-0-x x-x-x.
See mainau.

?4.5   makabura < *ma₁.₈₅ kanpu-ra-₈ ('eye wear'). 'around the eye(lids) or
eyebrows'. x - x-x-x x-x-x.

?6.12, ?6.22   makabura-ᵗ/ɡaka < makabura?₄.₅ (< ...) (-n-) taka₅dⱼ ₈. 'being high-
rowed'. LHHHHH (Kn -t-) / LLHLHL (?= *LLLHL) (Kz -d-) - x-x-x x-x-x.

4.2   makayaki (< ?). 'great trumpet flower, Campsis chinensis' (= noozen-
kazura). HHHL - x-x-x x-x-x.

2.1   maki (?< following entry). 'firewood, brushwood'. x - 0-0-A x-x-x. Sz,
Narada, Hiroshima 0. Ōsaka, Ise 0; Ib H = 2.1.

?2.1, ?2.2b   maki < ma-kiy < *ma?₁.₁ ko-Ci₁.₈₅. (1) 'true wood; real tree;
timber'; (2) 'podocarp, Chinese black pine, Torreya nucifera'. HH - 1-2-x
x-x-x. NS (T 96) HH; NS (T+ kun) FH. Hiroshima 1. Ōsaka, Ise 0; Ib H = 2.1.

4.2   makiita < makyi-ita < *mak[a-C]i₄ ita₂.₄. 'a board for winding cloth
(around)'. HHHHL - x-0-x x-x-x.

4.2   makikusa ?< maki₂.₁ (< ...) kusa₂.₅. 'broom cypress' (= hooki-gusa).
HHHL - x-3-x x-x-x.

3.6   makoto < ma₁.₁ koto₂.₅. 'truth'. LHH - 0(?<1)-1-B x-B-A. Km (S) LHH.
Mr (Bm) LHH(-H). Edo LHH. Narada, Ōita 1; Akita 2; NE Kyūshū 3 (H 1951:177);
Sapporo, Aomori (rare), Hiroshima, Wakamatsu 0. Ib H1 = 2.2. Nk maKuuTu B.
K: Hn LHH/HHH; Km LHH, (mistaken) LLH.

2.3   maku (< Ch m(b)ak). 'curtain'. LL - 2-2-B x-B-x. Ib H1 = 2.2. Nk maKuu B;
Sr maaku/maku B.

4.11   makunagi < ma^k/gunaki < magunakyi < *ma(n)kunaki (?< *ma*1.3a* kuna(n)k[a-
C]i? 'brush eyes'). 'a kind of mosquito (= nuka-^k/ga); annoying insects such as
mosquitos, gadflies, etc.'. LLHL - x-3-x x-x-x. (K: "Hn LHHL" *misprint?*.)

3.5a/b   makura (? < *mak[a-]u*A* [a]ra*2.3*, but register incongruent). 'pillow'.
LL?H - 1(<*2)-2-B B-B-B. NS (83a[17:117-M]) LLH; NS (T+ 37) LLL, (T+ 96) HLL,
(T+ 94) LHL. Km (S) LLH. Edo HLL. Sapporo, Goka-mura, Hakata, Ōita 1; western
Mino (= SW Gifu) 1/2; Matsumoto, Narada, Hata, Wakamatsu, NE Kyūshū 2; Tappi,
Aomori, Akita 3; Numazu, Hida (= northern Gifu), Hattō, Hamada, Matsue, Izumo,
Hiroshima 0, Toyama 2 *(we expect 1:3)*; Suzu 1:4 *(we expect 1:3)*. Ib F = 3.4.
Sr makkwa B; Yn magura B (H 1964:71b).

6.x   makurakotoba < makura*s.5b* (< ...) kotoba*s.4* (< ...). 'a "pillow word"
(= fixed/conventional epithet)'. x - 4-5-B x-x-x. Km (W) HHHLLL; "HHHLHL";
LHL··· , LLL··· .

2.1   mama < ma-ma (< ?). 'as it is, undisturbed'. HH - 2-0-A x-B-x. Km x. Edo
HL. Sz 0. Ib H = 2.1. Nk ma(a)maa H(H)HL.

4.2   mamahaha < mama-fawa (JP) < mama-bafa (Mg) < *mama*?(2.1)* (-n-) papa*?2.1*,
?2.3, *?2.4*. 'stepmother'. HHHL - 0-0-A x-(x)-x. Sz 0. Cf. Akinaga 1977c:70.

?4.2, ?4.1   mamatiti < *mama*?(2.1)* titi*s.4* (< ...). 'stepfather'. ?HHHH/?HHHL -
0-0-x x-(x)-x.

4.1   mamayumi < mama-yumyi ?< *[u]ma*s.3* [u]ma*s.3* dumi*s.3* ('horse horse bow').
'a kind of polo'. HHHH - x-x-x x-x-x. Attested only in Mg?

2.1   mame ?< *mamey < *ma*?1.1* ma-Ci*1.3a* ('true eye'). 'sincere' *(adj-n)*.
x - 0-0-B x-x-x. Km (W) HH. Sz 0. Cf. mameyaka.

2.3   mame < mamey < *mamaCi (?< *ma*1.3a* - ma-Ci*1.3a* 'eye-eye'; register
incongruent for the etymology *ma*1.1* maCi*1.3a* 'true sprout'). 'bean'. LL -
2-2[U]/1:3[H]-B B-B-B. Ise, Kōchi 2 (Doi 1952:22); Ōsaka 1:3; Ib F = 2.3.
Sr maami B; Ōhama maamii B.

4.11   mamegara < *mamey-gara < *mamaCi*s.3* -n- kara*s.2b*. 'bean straw'. LLHL -
0/4-1[H]/0[U]-B x-B-x. Sr maamigaraa B.

4.6 ?= 3.4 (= 2.3-no)|1.1 mamenoha < mamenofa < *mamey-no-fa < *mamaCi*s.3* no
pa*1.3*. 'Acer distylum' (= maruba-/hitotuba-kaede). LLL(|)H - x-x-x x-x-x.

4.11   mame^t/zuki < mame-^t/duki < *mamey-^t/dukyi < *mamaCi*s.3* (-n-) tuk[a-C]i*A*.
'soybean flour' (= kinako). LLHL - x-x-x x-x-x.

4.11   mameyaka < *mamey*s.1* (< ...) -yaka (< -da-ka*suf*). 'serious' *(adj-n)*.
LLHL - 2-4-B x-x-x. K: Edo HLLL.

?3.4   mamori < *ma-mor[a-C]i(< ...). '(protective) amulet'. x - 3-0-A x-B-x.
Km (W) LLL. Sz, Wakamatsu 0. The verb is B - B-A-A x-B-x (Wakamatsu x). Zdb
has mamworu but mamori, moru, sakyi-mori, Ōno has "mamwori" and "sakyi-mwori"
(based on Azuma -muri?), but since his notation fails to distinguish Cwo from
unknown Co it is unclear which he intends.

3.2b   mamugi < *ma-mugyi < *ma*?1.1* munki*s.4*. 'wheat' (= komugi). HHL - x-2-x
x-x-x.

?3.1   mamusi < ma*1.1* musi*s.1* (< ...). 'viper'. x - 0-0[H]/2[U]-A x-x-x. Km x.
Aomori, Sz 0; NE Kyūshū 3; Hakata 1/2, ygr 0.

?2.1   mana (< *ma*?1.1* na*1.3a* 'true side-dish'). 'fish'. x - 1-x-x x-x-x. Cf.
manaita, sakana; maguro.

?2.2b   mana. 'don't!'. HL - x-x-x x-x-x. Km x. This is a Heian form used in
explicating Kanbun texts. Cf. V-u na (earlier na V-i so) 'don't'; Korean
:mal- 'refrain, desist; cease'.

4.11   manabuta < *mana(n)puta < ?ma*1.3a* no puta*s.1*. 'eyelid' (= mabuta*s.7b*).
LLHL - 0-0-x x-x-x.

3.1 (?< 4.x)   manago < managwo ?< *ma*71.1* [su]na-(n-)kwo*73.1,73.4*. 'sand' (=
masago, inago, isago, masunago). HHH - x-0-x x-x-x.

4.2   manaita < mana*72.1* ita*8.4* ('fish board'). 'chopping board'. HHHL - 4/0/3-
1:3[H]/2[U,Kuno]-A x-x-(x). Narada, Hattō, Hamada 4; Sz, Matsue, Izumo, Goka-
mura 0; Hata 3. Kōchi, Naruto, and Matsuho 3 (Yamana 1965), but Doi 1952:35
has 3 only for younger Kōchi and 0 for older. Yn nmanuta B.

3.5b   manako < manakwo < ?*ma*1.3a* n<u>o</u> kwo*1.1*. 'eye(ball)'. LLH - 1(<*2)-2-B
x-(B)-x. NS (119a) LLH. Km (S) LLH. Mr (Bm) HLL. Edo HLL. Tappi, Aomori,
Akita, Matsumoto, Numazu, Narada, Hattō, Hamada, Matsue, Izumo, Goka-mura,
Hiroshima, Hakata 2; Ōita 1; Wakamatsu, Sapporo <u>0</u>. Ib (rare) <u>H1</u> = 3.3. Sr
manuku B 'between the brows'.

4.11   manaziri < manasiri < ?*ma*1.3a* n<u>o</u> siri*2.3*. 'corner of eye (raised in
anger)'. (LLHx/xxHL =) LLHL - 0/2/3-0-A x-x-x. Km (S) LLHL.

2.1   mane < *mane[y] < *mana-Ci[-Ci]*A*. 'mimicry'. HH - 0-0[U]/<u>2</u>[H]-A x-<u>B</u>-x.
Edo HL. Hattō, Hamada <u>2</u>; Matsue, Izumo, Goka-mura 0. Ib <u>H1</u> = 2.2.

3.4   maneki ?< manekyi ('beckon') < *manek[a-C]i*8*. 'a loom treadle' (= humi-
gi). LLL - x-<u>0</u>-x x-B-x. Sr manuci B, cf. manik-/manuk- B 'invite' [Lit.]. No
phonograms for the noun, but Zdb takes it as mane-kiy, with 'wood'.

2.1   mara(-). 'rare': see mare, maroodo. Cf. abara.

2.3   mara. '(evil;) penis'. LL - 2-2-x x-B-B. (Said to be from Sanskrit māra,
but confused with verb maru < *mara-*B* 'excrete'.)

4.6   marazaya < *mara*8.3* -n- sada*8.4*. 'mare's vulva'. LLLH - x-x-x x-x-x.

2.1   mare < *mara-Ci. 'rare' (adj-n). HH - 0/<u>2</u>-0-A x-A-x. Edo HH. Ib <u>L2</u> = 2.5.
Cf. maroodo; abara.

3.2x   marera < *mara-Ci*8.1* [a]ra*8.3*. 'being few/rare'. HHL - x-x-x x-x-x.

2.2b   mari. 'bowl'. HL - x-2-x x-x-x.

2.3   mari (?< *mari[y] < *maru*8.1* -Ci despite register incongruity). 'ball'.
LL - 2-2-B x-B-x. Hattō, Hamada, Matsue, Izumo, Wakamatsu, NE Kyūshū <u>1</u>;
Narada, Goka-mura 2. Ib F = 2.3. Sr maai B. Is Sd maryi(i) B
'buttocks' cognate?

?2.4   maro. '(male name, name-suffix); I/me'. x - x-x-x x-x-x. NS (Okada) LH;
NS (T+ 39) LH. There are various etymologies, none convincing.

2.1   maro (?< *maru). 'round' *adj-8*). HH ('cut round') - x-x-x x-x-x.
Cf. maru*adj A*.

?4.1, ?4.2   maroodo < marauto < marafyit<u>o</u> < *mara*8.1* pito*8.2a* ('rare person').
'guest'. HHx - 2-3-x x-x-x. Cf. mare.

2.1   maru ?< mar<u>o</u> (?< (*)maru, the second vowel partially assimilated to the
first). 'round (thing)'. x - 0-0-A (A)-A-(A). Km x.

?2.3   maru < *mar[a]-u*8*. 'chamberpot, commode' (= o-maru). x - <u>0</u>-2-x x-x-x.

5.2   maruganae < maroganafe < *mar<u>o</u>*8.1* (< ...) -ganafey (< -n- kanafey*8.1* <
...). 'tripod kettle with round bottom'. HHHHL - x-x-x x-x-x.

4.2   mar*a*/<u>o</u>-musi ?< mar<u>o</u>*8.1* (< ...) musi*8.1* (< ...). 'gold bug' (= kuso-musi).
HHHL - x-x-x x-x-x.

2.5   masa(-ni). 'truly'. LH(-L). 1-1:3[H]/<u>2</u>[U]-<u>A</u> x-x-x. Km (S) LH(-L). Mr (Bm)
LH(-L). Cf. masasi*adj 8*, Sr masasi- B 'wonder-working'.

?3.1 (?<4.x)   masago < *masagwo ?< *ma*71.1* s[un]a-(n-)kwo*73.1,73.4*). 'sand' (=
manago, inago, isago, masunago). x - 0-0-<u>B</u> x-x-x. Km (W) xHH. Edo HHH.

3.4   masai < ma-safyi < *ma*71.1* sapi*72.1*. 'a sharp sword'. x - x-x-x x-x-x.
NS (Okada) LLL; NS (T+ 103) L<del>HH</del> ?= LLL. Register incongruent with etymology.

4.5   masakari, (dial.) masa*k*/*g*iri (?< *masa*8.3* kir[a-C]i*8* 'truly cut'). 'timber
ax'. LLLL - 2-2/4-x x-x-x. Sz 3.

?3.4, ?3.1   masaki < masakyi < *ma?1.1 sak[a-C]i𝐴 ('truly flourish'). 'Euonymus
     japonicus'. x - 0-0-x x-x-x. Km (W) LLL(/HLL).
5.2 = 3.1|2.2 masakizura < masakyi?3.4,?3.1 (< ...) -dura (< -n- tura?.?b).
     'Trachelospermum asiaticum' (= Teika-kazura). x - x-x-x x-x-x.
     NS (83a [17:117-M]) HHH(|)HL; NS (T+ 96) ₣HHHL ?= HHH(|)HL.
2.3   mase (< ?). 'rough-woven fence' (= masegaki, magaki). LL - 1-2-x x-A-x.
     Nk x; Sr [Lit.] masi A̲ 'tight fence of bamboo/wood'.
?2.4, ?2.3   masi. 'monkey' (= saru). x - x-x-x x-x-x. Km (W) masi-ra LH-L, LH-H,
     LL-H. The word must be quite old, for in the Man'yō-shū the MONKEY character
     is used as a phonogram for the particle masi; this word appears in a number of
     modern dialects, but information on how they accentuate it is unavailable.
2.1   masu. 'trout'. HH - 2̲-0-A x-x-x. Km x. Sz, Hiroshima 0. Ōsaka, Ise 2̲;
     Ib L̲2 = 2.5 (the fish is alien).
2.3   masu. 'measure'. LL - 2-2-B x-A̲-x. Km x. Matsue 1/2; Narada, Hattō, Hamada,
     Izumo, Goka-mura, Hiroshima 2. Kōbe (Robb) 0̲; Ōsaka, Ise 2; Ib F = 2.3.
     Sr maṣi A̲.
4.3   masumasu < *mas[a-]u𝐴 mas[a-]u𝐴 ('add add'). 'more and more, increasingly'
     (adv). HHxx - 2-1:3-A x-x-x. Km (S) HHLL, Mr (Bm) HHLL.
?4.1   masunago < *masunagwo < *ma?1.1 sunagwo?3.1,?3.4 (< suna?2.1 -n- kwo1.1).
     'sand' (= masago, isago, manago, inago, suna). x - x-x-x x-x-x.
4.2   masurao < masura-wo < *masura (< ?) bo1.1. 'brave/masterful man, hero;
     master'. HHHL - 0/4-0-x x-x-x. Probably < *masa-ra-𝐴 'excel', despite Miller's
     claims that it is borrowed from a hypothetical "Old Paekche" form that is of
     questionable pedigree, Journal of Korean Studies 1:9-17 (1979). The -u- is a
     problem in either etymology.
2.2a   mata. 'again'. HL - 0/1-2-A x-A-A. NS (114a, 133a) HL; NS (T+ 114) ₣L ?=
     HL. Km (S,W) HL. Mr(Bm) HHLL. Sz 0. Ib H1 = 2.2.
2.3   mata. 'crotch'. (L) - 2(/1:3[U])-B x-B-x. Km x. K: Hn LL. Ib F = 2.3.
4.5   mataburi < *mata?.? -n- puri (?< *pur[a-C]i𝐴, or -buri = ure?2.1). 'a
     forked branch'. LLLL - x-0-x x-x-x. Mataburi-gusa (LLLLxx) is a plant, perhaps
     the hydrangea (= modern azisai).
?4.4 < 2.2|2.2   matamata < mata?.?a mata?.?a. 'again and again, repeatedly'.
     x - 0/2-2:4[H]/2[U]-"AA" x-x-x. (Hirayama's notations for Kt and Kg represent
     two accent phrases.)
2.3   mate ?< *mate[y] < *mataCi. 'razor-clam' (= mate-gai x - 2-1:3-x x-x-x).
     LL - 1-1:3-x x-x-x. In Wakayama 1:3 but Ogawa 1942 attributes this to the
     assignment of a "contraction"-marker usage of the rise-fall contour, treating
     the word as an abbreviation of mate-gai.
2.2a   mati. 'field (sector/measure); town, market'. HL - 2-2-A A-B̲-A. Km (W) HL.
     Edo HL. Aomori 0; Goka-mura 1̲; Hakata 0̲, ygr 2 (= 2.3). Toyama 2; Suzu 1 (we
     expect 1:3); Ib H1 = 2.2. Nk maCii B̲.
?2.5   mati. 'sewn-in strip (in hakama etc.)'. x - 1-2[H]/1:3[U]-B x-x-x.
     Hiroshima 1. Ōsaka, Ise 1:3.
4.3   mati-mati. 'varied'. HHxx - 2/0-1:3-B x-x-x. Km (S) HHLL. Mr (Bm) HHLL.
     Cf. (< mati?.?b) 'various towns' x - 2-3-x x-x-x.
2.1   mato < matwo. 'target'. HH - 0-0-A A-A-x. NS (101b) HH. Km x. Edo HH.
     Goka-mura 2̲. Ib H = 2.1. Sd matho(o) A.
2.1   mato < *ma?1.1 two1.?a. 'fine grindstone'. HH - 0-0-x x-x-x.
?2.5   mato. 'round'. LH (?= *LF) - x-x-x x-x-x. Cf. madoka, madoyaka; maru.
     Zdb has /two/ but cites no evidence.
-       matoyaka: see madoyaka.

2.x   *matu. 'fire, torch' (?< 'pine', cf. taimatu). Sd qumaati/qumat B, Sr
qumaçi B 'fire' ?< *o-matu.

2.4   matu. 'pine'. LH - 1-1-B A-B-C. NS (T 27) LH. Km (W) LH(-x). Edo LH. Izumo
2; Matsue 1/2. Toyama 2 (we expect 1:2); Suzu 1:2; Ib L = 2.4. Nk mati C; Sr
maaçi B.

?3.5b   matuge < *ma1.3a -tu -n- ka-Ci?1.1 (see ke). 'eyelashes'. HHL/LxH - 1-2-B
x-B-C. Hattô, Hamada, Wakamatsu, Hakata 1; Aomori, Narada, Goka-mura 2.
Matsue, Izumo 3. Kôbe (Robb) 1:3; Ib L2 = 3.5/7. Nk maCiigi B. Yn mangi C.

4.1 ?< *4.5   matumuro < *matu2.4 murwo2.3. 'Matsumuro' (surname). Mr (Bm) HHHH.

3.1   maturi < *matur[a-C]i (< ...). 'festival'. A - 0/3-0-A x-A-x. Sz, Narada,
Hattô, Hamada, Matsue, Izumo 0. Sr maçiri A is probably borrowed (as revealed
by the -r-); cf. qumaçii B 'harvest festival' < *o-maturi.

5.1   maturigoto < *matur[a-C]i -n- koto. 'government'. HHHHH - 0-0[H]/4[U]-A
x-x-x. NS (133a) HHHHH. Sz (rare) 0.

4.11   matuyama < *matu2.4 dama2.3. 'a pine-covered mountain; Matsuyama
(placename)'. x - 0/2-2-B x-x-x. Km (W) LLHL.

4.11   mawatasi ?< *ma1.3a bata-s[a-C]iA (*ma?1.1 is incongruent in register).
'ceiling boards; covering a gap, making do'. LLHL (Zs) / LLLx (Kn) - 2-0-x.

?2.5   mayu < maywo < *madwo < *ma1.3a dwo?. 'eyebrow; cocoon'. LH - 1-1:3[H]/
1[U]-A B-B-B. Km x. Mr (Bm) LH. 1700 Ôsaka LF. Ib 'eyebrow' L2 = 2.5, 'cocoon'
H = 2.1. Sd mayo(o) B; Nk mayuu B; Onna maayuu B.

4.6; ?4.9 = 2.4|2.2 mayuage < *maywo-agey < *madwo?2.3 anka-Ci[-Ci]A. 'glaring,
scowling'. LLLH (Kz), LHxL ?= *LH(|)HL (Kn) - x-x-x x-x-x.

?3.1   mayumi < mayumyi < *ma?1.1 dumi2.3. 'euonymus, spindletree (used to make
archers' bows)'. (HLH =) *HHH - 1/0-0-x x-x-x. NS (70a, 70c) HHH; NS (T+ 43)
LLH. Km (W) HHH. Cf. haimayumi, kusomayumi.

4.5   mayuzumi < mayu-zumyi < *maywo-zumyi < *ma - dwo?2.3 -n- sumi2.3. 'eyebrow
paint'. LLLL - 2-1-B x-x-x. Sz 3.

?2.2b < 3.7b   mazu < madu < *mantu. 'first of all'. RL/HL - 1-2-A x-A-x. Km (S) HL.
Sz 1. Ib H1 = 2.2.

?1.1 < 2.1   -me < -mey < *m[ur]ey < *mura-Ci[-Ci]A. 'bird (< flock)'. See kamome,
sime, suzume, tubame. Cf. -su.

?1.3b   -me ?< *-mye (< *miCa ?= *mina 'female'). 'damn person': yatu-me, baka-me.

1.3a   me < mey < *ma-Ci. 'eye'. L - 1-1-B B-B-B. NS (T+ 29, 123) L.
Km (W) L(-H?)/L(-L). Edo R. Ib L = 1.3.

1.3a   me < mey ?< *maCi (? 'eye'), ?< moye[y] < *moda-Ci[-Ci]. 'sprout, bud'.
NS (T+ 13) L; (T+ kun) R ?= L (or really R = LH?). Km (W) ko-no-me LLL.
Ib L = 1.3. Cf. moeru, moyasu; kome.

1.3b   me < mye < *miCa (?= *mina [= *mi-na]). 'female'; cf. -mi-. (Azuma "myi"
?= mi.) R - x-0-x x-(B)-(B). NS (82c [17:112-M, 113-M]) ... L(-H); NS (T+ 3,
57, 58, 96) "R" ?= H or really R (= LH) but cf. mi 'fruit' ("R" = H). Km x.
Edo H. K: Hn LH, Edo HH. Sr mii-(mun) B; Yn mii-mita B 'hen'. Cf. me-su.

1.x   me (?< mo; ?< *mo-Ci). 'seaweed'. x - x-x-x x-x-x. Cf. arame, ebisume,
hirome, mirume, nigime, wakame.

1.3b|2.3   mebiru < ?*mye-byiru < *miCa1.3b (?= *mina) -n- piru2.1(?<*2.3) ('female
garlic'). 'a small leek'. R(|)LL - x-x-x x-x-x.

?2.4 < ?3.5x   medo (< ?). '(= medo-hagi) Sericea lespedeza; (= medo-ki) [a set of
50] divining sticks'. x - 1-x-x x-x-x. Km (W"?") LH/HH. See Ch. 4, §7.1.

?2.5   medo < me-do < *meydo < *ma-Ci1.3a -n- to[koro2.1]?1.1. 'aim; the eye
of a needle'. x - 1-2[H]/1:3[U]-A x-x-x. Km x.

?4.9 < 5.11   medogusa < *medo*s.4* (< ?) -n- kusa*s.s*. 'Sericea lespedeza' (= medo-
hagi). RHHL - x-x-x x-x-x. See Ch. 4, §7.1. Mochizuki 538a is mistaken in the
second Chinese character, which should be ZITU 'fruit': the text of Kn (Hō-ka
53:8) omitted a dash after the character of the preceding entry.

3.7b(/3.4)   medori < mye-dori < *miCa*1.sb* (?= *mina) -n- tori*s.1*. 'hen' (=
mendori x - 0-0-B x-x-x; Sz 4). LHL (Kn) / LLL (Ck) - 1-2-x x-B-x. NS (73c
[11:254-M] *as name*) LHL; NS (T+ 59 -t-) "R-HR" ?= HHH or R (= LH) | HH.

2.3   mega 'female deer': *see* meka.

3.5b   megane < *mey-gane[y] < *maCi*1.sa* -n- kana-Ci*s.1*. 'eyeglasses'. x - 1-2-B
x-(x)-x. 1700 Ōsaka HLL. Sz, Narada, Hattō, Hamada, Goka-mura, Hata, Wakamatsu,
NE Kyūshū, Ōita (Toguchi 1974:121) 2; Hakata 2, ygr 1; Aomori, Matsue, Izumo 0.
Ib H1 = 3.2. Sr mii-kagan B. Attested in JP.

1.3b|3.4 megawara < *mye-gafara < *miCa*1.sb* (?= *mina) -n- kapara*s.4*. 'female (=
concave) tile'. R(|)LLL - x-3-x x-B-x. Sr miigaara B.

4.11   me-haziki < me-faziki < *mey fazikyi < *ma-Ci*1.sa* pansik[a-C]i*s* (< ?).
'blinking'; [Mg] 'Leonurus sibiricus (= zyuui)'. LLHL - x-x-x x-x-x.

2.3   mei < myefi < *mye-fiy [cf. oi] < *miCa*1.sb* (?= *mina) -p*ʷ*/*o*Ci*1.x*.
'niece'. LL - 1-2-A B-(A/)B-x. Km x. Aomori 0. The Tōkyō accent retreat is
due to monosyllabification; Narada, Shimoda 2. Ib H = 2.1. Nk mii-ui C (*both
elements bound*) 'nieces and nephews'.

2.3   me*ᵏ/ga* < *mye-*ᵏ/ga* < *miCa*1.sb* (?= *mina) (-n-) ka*1.sa*. 'female deer,
doe'. LL - x-x-x x-x-x.

1.3b|3.1 mekatura < *mye-katura < *miCa*1.sb* (?= mina) katura*s.1*. 'a kind of
cinnamon, Cinnamomum japonicum pendulatum' (= yabu-nikkei). R(|)HHH - x-x-x
x-x-x.

1.3b|3.4 mekemono < mye (< *miCa*1.sb* ?= *mina) key-mono*?s.1,?s.s* (< *ka-Ci*?1.1*
mono*s.s*). 'female animal'. R(|)LLL - x-4-x x-x-x.

3.4   mekoma (< ?). 'raccoon-dog' (= tanuki). LLL - x-x-x x-x-x.

3.7x   mekura < *mey-kura < *ma-Ci*1.sa* kura*adj A*. 'blind, sightless'. x - 3-1:3-B
x-B-B. Goka-mura 0; Aomori, Narada, Hattō, Hamada, Matsue, Izumo 3; Hakata 0,
ygr 3/1. Ib F = 3.4. Sr mikkwa B. Yn miKwaa B. Cf. mesii.

?3.7b < 3.4 = 1.3|2.3   mekuso < *mey-kuswo < *ma-Ci*1.sa* kuswo*s.s*. 'eye discharge'
(= meyani). L(|)LL (Kz) - 1-1:3-B x-B-x. Km x. Aomori 3/1; Sz 1. Ib F = 3.4.

4.6 = 2.3 (= 1.3-no) | 2.4 menomae < menomafe < *mey*1.sa* (< *ma-i*1.sa*) no mafye*s.s*
(< ma*1.sa* piCa*1.x*). 'before one's eyes'. L-L|LH - 3-3[U]/1:3[H]-B x-B-x. Sz 3.
K: Edo HHLL.

3.4   menoo < menau (< Wu version of Ch 'm(b)a-'ndaw). 'agate'. LLL - 1/2-0[H]/
1.3[U]-A x-x-x.

?3.1, ?3.4   menoto < myenoto (?< *mye-no [o]to < *miCa*1.sb* (?= *mina) no oto*s.s*
'younger sister'). 'wet-nurse'. HHH (Kz) - 1/2-2-x x-x-x. Edo HHL. 1700 Ōsaka
HLL. Kz register is incongruent with the proposed etymology; a mistake for LLL?

5.16   me-no-warabe (Zs), mye-no-warafa < *miCa*1.sb* (?= *mina) no barapa*s.sb*[-
f/bye < ...]. 'girl'. LLLHL - x-x-x x-(B)-x. Sr miyarabi B 'unmarried farm girl'.

?2.3   meri < *mer[a-C]i < Ch myat (by way of Sino-Korean myel?). 'diminishing;
weakening'. x - 2/0-1-x x-x-x. If the Chinese etymology is wrong, then perhaps
< *(n)per[a-C]i; cf. her-u*A*.

2.3   mesi < myesi < *miCa-s[a-C]i*s*. 'food, rice'. x - 2-2-B B-(B)-x. Edo HL.
Aomori, Sz 2; Hattō, Matsue, Izumo 1. Ib F = 2.3. Sr misi-wan B 'rice bowl'.

?3.4   mesii < mesifi < *mey-sifiy < *ma-Ci*1.sa* sip*ᵘ*/*o*Ci[-Ci], or < *mey-sifyi
< *ma-Ci*1.sa* sip[a-C]i*?A*. 'blind, sightless'. LLL - 2-1:3-x x-x-x.

2.3   mesu < mye-su < *miCa₁.ₛ♭ (?= *mina) -su₁.ₓ (< *su/so). 'female (animal)'.
     x - 2-2-B x-x-x. Sz 1; Hattō, Hamada, Izumo, Goka-mura 1; Matsue 0/1. Ib H1 =
     2.2. Fukuoka mezo. Not in JP; earliest NKD citation is late Edo. Sr mii-mun B.
1.3|?4.5,?4.6 metamasii < *mye₁.ₛ♭ (< *miCa₁.ₛ♭ ?= *mina) tamasifyi?₄.₈,?₄.₆ (<
     *tama₂.₃ sipi?). 'female spirit. R|LLLL, R|LLLH (?= R|LLLF) - x-x-x x-x-x.
3.4   meuma < me-muma/-uma < *mye-uma < *miCa₁.ₛ♭ (?= *mina) uma₂.₃. 'mare,
     female horse'. LLL/LxL - 0/1-x-x x-x-x.
3.4   meyani < *mey-yani < *ma-Ci₁.₃ₐ dani₂.₃. 'eye discharge' (= mekuso).
     x - 3-1:3-B x-x-x. Aomori 2/3; Sz 3. Ib F = 3.4.
4.11   mezuraka < meyduraka < *meyd[ey]-u♭ -ra-ka (< ... ; see mederu). 'rare,
     precious' (adj-n). LLHL - 2-3-x x-(B)-x. Sr minda-syan B. Cf. mezurasi₂dⱼ ♭.
?1.1   mi- < myi- ?< *mi[na]. 'water': see migiri, migiwa.
?1.1   mi- < myi- < *mi- ?< *[i]mi < *im[a-C]i?♭ ('shun'). 'exalted, honored'.
     Cf. oon-. See Ch.4, Chart 17:5, and (in this list): mike, mikado, mikage, miko,
     mimaya, mine, misakari, misora, mitama, mitani, mitugi, miya, miyama. Other
     examples from NS: mi-ikari (112b) 'rage'; mi-ikusa (123b) 'royal army'; mi-ime
     (101a) 'royal dream'; mi-kaki (99a) = mi-kaki (118b) 'palace enclosure';
     mi-katati (91a) 'exalted face'; mi-kokoro (99a, 114a, problematic 122a)
     'exalted heart/mind'; mi-kokoro["]sasi (99a) 'august impulses'; mi-koto (115b,
     142a) 'exalted words'; mi-kura (100a) 'the Treasury'; mi-kurawi (122a) 'rank of
     Emperor'; mi-masikyi (99a) '(bed-)mat'; mi-me (120a) 'royal concubine'; mi-me
     (119a) 'royal eyes'; mi-mono["]katari (112a) 'exalted conversation' (Okada
     HHHHHH); mi-mune (95a) 'exalted breast'; mi-nari (120b) '(her) exalted form':
     mi-ne, (?) mi-ne (112b) 'royal slumber'; myi-obyi 'august girdle' NS (T+ 93,
     97) H|LH; myi-osufyi-gane (73c) '(material) for the august cloak'; mi-sato
     (102b) 'capital'; mi-su["]kata (91a) 'exalted form'; mi-ta (93a) 'official rice-
     lands'; mi-tu["]ki (92b) 'royal succession'; mi-we (117b) 'royal laugh';
     mi-yake (130b) 'official granary; jurisdiction'; mi-yo (93b) 'august time/era';
     mi-yu (112a) 'bath'; mi-yuka 'imperial couch'. Edo mi-su HH 'reed screen',
     mi-ura HHH 'divination', mi-uti HHL 'nobleman', mi-yuki HHL/HLL 'august going'.
?1.1   mi(-) < myi(-) < *mi(-). 'three'. (x - 1-1-x x-A-x.) See mikka, mi(t)tu.
1.1   mi < miy < *mu-Ci. 'body'. H - 0-0-A x-(A)-x. Km (S,W) H(-H). Edo H.
     Ib H = 1.1. Sr misigara A. NS (124b, 131b mi use-nu 'died') H.
1.1   mi < miy < *mu-Ci (?= 'body'). 'fruit'. H - 0-0-A A-A-A. Km (W) H(-H).
     NS (T+ 7) H. Yn mii A (H 1964:64a).
?1.2   mi (?< *myi ?< [fey]myi (see hebi); ?< miy [Zdb] < *mu[s]i₂.₁). '(sign of
     the) snake (6th of the 12 Branches); *worm, insect (cf. simi, nomi, sirami)'.
     x - 0-2-A x-A-(x). K: Km HH (where attested?). Sz 1. Ib H = 1.1. Cf. Yn
     aminumyaa B 'rainbow' < ami-nu-mi-aa 'heaven's-snake thing'.
?1.3x   (-)mi(-) < myi < *mi. 'woman': see me < mye < *miCa (?= *mina = mi-na);
     onna < womyina < *bomina (?= *bo- mi-na); omina < omyina < ?*[o]po mi-na.
     Cf. kamiy-r²/₀-myi 'goddess (title)'.
?1.3a   mi < myi (?< *[i]m[a-C]i♭ 'shun'). 'god, spirit'. See yamatumi, watatumi.
1.3a   mi < miy < *m²/₀Ci. 'winnower'. L - 1-1-B x-(B)-x. Km x. K: Edo LH.
     Narada, Hattō, Hamada, Matsue, Izumo, Hiroshima 1. Ōsaka 0; Ise 1; Ib L = 1.3.
     Sr miizookii B (← sooki B).
?1.3b   (-)mi ?< *miy < *mo-Ci. 'garment': see uwami; koromo.
-          "midame" (Mochizuki 513b) → yumidame (Kn text).
4.5   midarao(-no uma) < midarawo (?< *myidara-wo < *minta-ra-♭ bo₁.₃ₐ
     'disordered tail'). 'dappled-gray (horse)'. LLLL - x-x-x x-x-x. NS (126a) HHLL
     ?= Okada (misprint?) mitatiwo 'swift horse' HHHL.

3.2a   midori < myidori < *mintori. 'green'. HHL - 1-1:3-B x-(x)-x. Km (Okada W)
HHL. Mr (Bm) HHL/LHL. Edo HHL. Matsumoto, Numazu, Hamada, Goka-mura 0; Matsue
0/2; Sapporo, Aomori, Akita, Narada, Hattō, Izumo, Hiroshima 2; Matsumoto,
Numazu, Narada, Wakamatsu, Hakata, Ōita 1. Hyōgo, Kōchi, Toyama 1:3; Suzu 0 (we
expect 1); Ib H = 3.1, L2 = 3.5/7. Nk midurii B 'new buds' (*'green'). The Hn
accent looks authentic (two citations from Zs Mg). An etymology midu*s.1a* iro*s.3*
'water color' has been suggested, presumably by metathesis → *mid[u]-ori but
that would lead to /dwo/ instead of the attested /do/, unless *miduiro >
*midi[y]ro → midori is assumed. Also possible: *min[a] tori 'water bird', with
an extended meaning or perhaps as a truncation 'water-bird [color]'.

2.2b   mie < mife < *myi-fye < *mi*1.1* piCa*1.x* ('three layers'). 'Mie'
(placename). HL (Ir) - 1-2-A x-x-x.

3.2x   migara (?< *min[a]*s.1* kara*s.2b* 'water husk'). 'small insect in well water
(?= mosquito larva)'. HHL - x-x-x x-x-x.

2.x   mige < *myigey ?< *mi-*s1.1* 'exalted' [or 'three'?] (-n-) key*1.3a* (< ...
'meal'). 'ox/sheep stomach (or urine/excrement)'. Cf. nige; mike.

2.1   migi, (Kn Mg) miki (< ?). 'right (hand)'. HH - 0-0-A A-x-A. NS (109a) HH.
Edo HH. Ib H = 2.1. Yn nidi ?< *nigiri*A*. We lack attestations to verify the
palatal status of either syllable. One suggested etymology is nigir-i;
'grasping [one]', but the -ri has also been taken as analogic to hidari 'left',
perhaps because the form migiri is not attested early.

3.x (?= 3.1)   migiri = migi. 'right (hand)'. x - x-x-x A-A-x. Sr niziri A < *nigiri.

3.4   migiri < myigyiri < *min[a]*s.1* kir[a-C]i*s*. 'eave-trough stones/tiles to
catch the raindrops; yard, confines; time; (= migiwa) waterside'. LLL - 0/3-0-x
x-x-x. Km (S) LLL. Edo HHH.

3.1   migiwa < migifa < *myigyifa < *min[a]*s.1* kipa*s.s*. 'the water's edge, the
waterside'. HHH - 0/3-0-A x-x-x. Km x. Edo HHL. 1700 Ōsaka HLL. Narada 3. Ib
(rare) H = 3.1.

-       miguri: see mikuri.

-       [miizu] = "miwizu" (Mg) < mi[m]izu 'earthworm': see mimizu.

2.2b   mika < myika < *mi-ka (?< *mi[na]*s.1* ka*s1.3a*). 'a large jar (for storing
water or sake)'. HL - x-x-x x-x-x.

4.3   mikabati < *mika*s.x* (< ?) -n- pati*s.1*. 'horntail' (= kibati). HHLL - x-x-x
x-x-x.

3.1   mikado < myi-kadwo < *mi-*s1.1* kadwo*s2.2b* (< ...). 'emperor'. (H) - 0-0-A
x-x-x. NS (94a, 101b, 120b, 129b) HHH. Km (W) HHH. Edo HHH. Ib (rare) H = 3.1.

5.2   mikadomori < *myikadwo-mori < *mi-kadwo*s.1* (< ...) mor[a-C]i*s*. 'palace
guard'. HHHHL - x-x-x x-x-x.

6.2   mikado-ogami < myi-kadwo*s.1* (< ...) wogamyi*s'* (< ...). 'obeisance to the
emperor' [Aston]. x - x-x-x x-x-x. NS (101b [11:144-K]) HHHHHL.

3.1   mikage < myikagey < *mi-*s1.1* kanka-Ci*s.s* (< ...). 'image (of a departed
soul), spirit, soul'. HHH - 0/2-0-x x-(x)-x. Km (W) HHH/HHL. Sr mikazi A =
ncaagi B 'your form'.

3.1   mikata < myi-kata < *mi-*s1.1* kata*s2.s* ('honorable side'). 'ally; imperial
forces'. HHH - 0-0-B x-A-x. Km x. Edo HHH. Hamada 3; Narada, Hattō, Matsue,
Izumo, Goka-mura, Hiroshima, Hakata 0. Ōsaka, Ise 0; Ib H = 3.1.

3.1   mikawa < myikafa < *mi*s1.1* kapa*s.2b* ('three rivers'). 'Mikawa'
(placename). x - 1/3-0-A x-x-x. Km (W) HHH.

5.3   mikawamizu < mikafa-midu < *myi-kafa*s3.1* myidu*s.1a* < *mi-*s1.1* kapa*s.2b*
mintu*s.1* (< ...) ('honorable-river waters'). 'a kind of artificial stream in
palace gardens'. x - 3-4-x x-x-x. Km (W) HHHLL.

2.1   mike ‹ myikey ‹ *mi-?*1.1* key*1.3a* (‹ ...). ‘meal (offered to gods)’.
Kn (?) HH - 0-x-x x-x-x. Hiroshima 0. Ōsaka, Ise 0.

5.2   miketumono ‹ myi-key*3.1* -tu*pc1* mono (‹ ...). ‘dishes of food (offered to
gods)’. x - x-x-x x-x-x. NS (127a, 129b) HHHHL.

2.1   miki ‘right’: *see* migi.

2.2a   miki ‹ myi-kyi ‹ *mi-?*1.1* ki*1.x* (‹ ...). ‘wine’. x - 0/1-2-A x-x-x.
NS (T 32, 33) LH = LH, (T 15) ꟼH ?= HH. Km x. 1700 Ōsaka HL. Cf. miwa.

2.2a   miki (‹ ?). ‘trunk’. x - 0/1-2-A A-x-x. Km x. Sz 0; Aomori, Hattō,
Hamada, Matsue, Izumo, Goka-mura, Hata 1. Kōchi 0 (Doi 1952:22). Ib F = 2.3.
NKD citations 1716, 1764. (Said to be from *miy-kiy ‹ *mu-Ci*1.1* ko-Ci*1.3a*
‘body tree’.)

3.1 ‹ 2.1 mikka ‹ *myi(k)ka ‹ *mi?*1.1* -ka?*1.3*. ‘three days’. x - 0-0-A A-A-x.
Edo HHH. Narada 0; Hakata 0 *(we expect 2, ygr 0)*. Ib H = 3.1.

2.1   miko ‹ myi-kwo ‹ *mi-?*1.1* kwo*1*. ‘prince’. HH - 0/1-2[H]/0[U]-A x-x-x.
NS (92a, 94a) HH; NS (T 127) HH, (T 88) ꟼH ?= HH. Km (W) HH.

4.1   mikohana ‹ myikwo-fana ‹ *mi-*3.1* kwo pana?*(3.3)*. ‘progeny, descendants’.
x - x-x-x x-x-x. NS (Okada) HHHH. Cf. hatuko.

?3.2b   mikosi ‹ myi-kosi ‹ *mi-?*1.1* kosi*3.3b*. ‘palanquin’. HHL - 0/1-2-x x-x-x.
Narada 1. Ib L = 3.6, F = 3.4.

3.1   mikoto ‹ myi-koto ‹ *mi-?*1.1* koto*3.3* (‘exalted affair’). ‘lord/god;
prince’. x - 0-0-x x-x-x. NS (116a, 118a) HHH; NS (T+ kun) HHH. For the same
etyma with the meaning ‘exalted words’, see mi-, mikotonori.

5.1   mikotomoti ‹ myi-koto moti ‹ *mi-koto*3.1* (‹ ...) mot[a-C]i*B*.
‘governor’. x - x-x-x x-x-x. NS (110a, 122b [14:218-K]) HHHHH, (120a) HHHxx.

5.1   mikotonori ‹ myi-koto nori ‹ *mi-koto*3.1* (‹ ...) nor[a-C]i*A*. ‘the
emperor’s words’. NS (115b) HHHH[H], (120b) xxxHL.

?3.1   mikura ‹ myi-kura ‹ *mi-?*1.1* kura*3.3b*. ‘the emperor’s seat/position’.
See taka-mikura.

3.1   mikura ‹ myi-kura ‹ *mi-?*1.1* kura*3.3*. ‘the Treasury’. x - 0-x-x x-x-x.
NS (100a) HHH. Edo HHH.

?3.1   mikuri, (Mg) miguri ‹ *myi-*k*/*g*uri[y] ‹ *mi?*1.1*(-n-) kuru-Ci*3.3* (‘triple
chestnut’). ‘a bur reed’. HHx - 0-x-x x-x-x.

3.1   mikusa ?‹ *myi[du]*3.1a* (‹ ...) kusa*3.3*; ?‹ *myigusa *(no phonograms)* ‹
*min[a]*3.1* kusa*3.3*. ‘aquatic plants, water grass/weeds’ (= mizukusa). x - x-x-x
x-x-x. Km (W) HHH.

3.2x   mimana(-no-kuni) ?‹ *nim(a)*3.x* - na?*1.3a* (‘land of nim = Korean king’).
‘Imna (= Mimana), an old Korean state’ (also: kaya, kara). x - 1-0-x x-x-x.
NS (120a) HHL(-L-LL); NS (T+ kun) HLL.

4.1   mimasaka (‹ ?). ‘Mimasaka’ *(placename)*. x - 2-0-x x-x-x. Km (W) HHHH.
Etymological possibilities: ‘slope of nim [= Korean king]’ (cf. mimana);
‘slope of the esteemed horse or (*mima[ya]-saka) stable’.

3.1   mimaya ‹ *myi-maya ‹ *mi-?*1.1* [u]ma-ya*3.4* (‹ uma*3.3* da*1.3b*. ‘the stable of
an esteemed person’. HHH - x-x-x x-x-x.

2.3   mimi ‹ myimyi ‹ *mi-mi. ‘ear(s)’. LL - 2-2-B B-B-(B). NS (T+ kun) LL.
Km (S) LL. Edo HL. Ib F = 2.3. Onna miimii B; Yn mintahu B *(see* mimi-tabu).
K: Hn LL, Km-Edo HL *(mistaken on Km?)*.

4.x   mimiaka ‹ *myimyi-aka ‹ *mi-mi*3.3* aka*3.3*. ‘earwax’ (= mimikuso). x - 0/4-
0-B x-x-x. Sz 4.

4.2   mimidare ‹ mimidari ‹ *myimyi-dari ‹ *mi-mi*3.3* tar[a-C]i*B*. ‘discharge from
ears’. HHHL - 0-1:4-B x-(B)-x. Sr minzai B (‹ *mimidari), miminutai B.

5.16   mimigusari ‹ *myimyi-gusari ‹ *mi-mi*3.3* (-n-) kusari*3.1* (‹ ...). ‘ear
pendant’. LLLHL - x-4-x x-x-x. NKD -k-, but Zs Mg -g-.

5.16   mimihutagi < mimifutagi < *myimyi-futagyi < *mi-mi$_{s.s}$ puta-n[a]-k[a-C]i. 'earplug'. LLLHL - x-4-x x-x-x. NKD: "also -husagi".

4.5   mimikuso < *myimyi-kuswo < * mi-mi$_{s.s}$ kuswo$_{s.s}$. 'earwax' (= mimiaka). LLLL - 2-1:4-B x-B-x. Sz 2.

4.6   mimi^{s}/$_{z}$ese < *myimyi-sese < *mimi$_{s.s}$ se-se ('ear back' *with iterated* se$_{i.s}$ < ...). 'the root of the ear': ~ no fone 'the mastoid bone behind the ear'. xxLH (K -z-) = *LLLH - x-x-x x-x-x.

4.5   mimisii < mimisifi < *myimyi-sifiy < *mi-mi$_{s.s}$ sip^{u}/$_{o}$-Ci[-Ci], or < *myimyi-sifyi < *mi-mi sip[a-C]i$_{?A}$. 'deaf'. LLLL - x-4-x x-x-x. Ongi LxLL. Cf. mesii.

4.6   mimi-tabu/-tabi (Mg) < *myimyi-ta^{f}/$_{b}$u/-ta^{f}/$_{b}$i < *mi-mi$_{s.s}$ -ta(n)pu(-Ci)$_{?}$. 'earlobe'. LLLH - 3-1:4-B x-B-B. Mg also mimidari LxHL. Sz 3; Hakata 3, ygr 0. Sr mincabaa B 'ear' < *mimi-tabu-a. Yn mintahu B 'ear'. Dial. -tabo, -tabura: cf. siri-ta^{b}/$_{m}$ura.

3.6   mimizu ?< *miymiyzu (?< *memezu) < *mo-Ci-$_{?A}$ mo-Ci-$_{?A}$ -n- -su$_{i.r}$. 'earthworm'. LHH - 0(?<1)-1-B B-B-x. Goka-mura, Wakamatsu, Ōita 1; Hakata 1, ygr 0; Sapporo, Tappi, Aomori (memeźi), Akita 2; Narada, Hattō, Hamada, Matsue, Izumo, Hiroshima 0. Ib mimi^{z}/$_{do}$ L = 3.6. Cf. "miwizu" (Mg) = [miizu]. On the etymology and reconstruction, cf. Thorpe 282.

?6.3   mimizukara < mi-midukara: *(1)* < *miy$_{i.i}$ miydukara$_{4.s}$ (< ...) '(one)self'; *(2)* < *myi-$_{?i.i}$ miydukara$_{4.s}$ (< ...) 'an esteemed person himself'. LHHxxx (?= *HHHHLL) - x-x-x x-x-x.

?4.11   mimizuku < mimiduku < ?*myimyiduku ?< *mi-mi$_{s.s}$ (-n-) tuku$_{?s.s}$. 'owl'. xxHxx - 1/2-1:3-B x-x-x. Km x. K: Hn LLLL. Cf. hukuroo, zuku.

3.4   mimono < *myi-mono < *miC[a-C]i/mi[-Ci] mono. 'something worth seeing; taking a look'. LLx (= *LLL) - 3-0-B x-B-x. Sz 3.

?3.1   mimoto < myi-moto < *mi-$_{?i.i}$ moto$_{s.s}$. '(at/near) where a divine/noble being is located'. Hxx (Kz) - 0/3-x-x x-x-x. Sz 0/3.

?2.1, ?2.2a   mina(-) < myina(-) < *mina. 'water': *see* mizu; mina-ai, minamata, minamoto, minasita, minato; minagir-u, minagirau. NS (T+ 95) myina sosoku HL LLH.

2.2b ?< 2.1a   mina < miyna < *m^{u}/$_{o}$Cina (?< *mor[a-C]i$_{A}$ na$_{i.s}$ 'heap person', ?< *moro-Ci na 'many [+ suffix] persons'). 'all; everyone; everything'. HL - 2(/1/0)-2-A x-A-x. NS (T 35) HL. Km (S) HL. Edo HL. Wakamatsu 2 *(= 2.3, since this dialect regularly merges 2.2 with 2.1)*. Ib *(rare)* H1 = 2.2. On the accent, see Ch. 4, §7.3; on the vowel, Ch. 1, §46.

2.3   mina. 'snail' (LL - x-0-x x-x-x): *see* nina.

?*2.3   *mina (?= *mi-na) 'woman'. *See* me, onna.

4.1   mina-ai < mina-afi < *myina afyi < *mina$_{s.i}$ ap[a-C]i$_{s}$. 'confluence, river junction' (= mizu-ai, oti-ai). HHxx (?= *HHHH) - x-x-x x-x-x.

4.1   minamata < *myina-mata < *mina$_{?s.i}$ mata$_{s.s}$. 'fork(ing) of the water/stream'. HHHH - x-0-x x-x-x.

3.1 (?3.1a)   minami < myinamyi < *minami (< ?). 'south'. HHH - 0-2-A B-A-x. Km x. Mr (Bm) HHL, minnami HHHL. Edo HHH/HHL. 1700 Ōsaka HLL. Ōita 2; Hakata *(expected)* 2, ygr 0; Aomori, Hamada 3 (with Kt 2 this would suggest 3.2b, but Mg indicates 3.1); Sapporo, Akita, Matsumoto, Numazu, Narada, Hattō, Matsue, Izumo, Goka-mura, Hiroshima 0. Kōbe (Robb) 3/1:3; Kōchi 0; Ib H2 = 3.2.

4.1   minamoto < myinamoto < *mina$_{?s.i}$ moto$_{s.s}$. 'source'. HHHH - 0-0-A x-x-x. K: Hn-Mr HHHH. Sz 0.

*3.2x   minari < *miy-nari < *mu-Ci$_{i.i}$ nar[a-C]i$_{s}$. 'one's appearance/attire'. x - 1-1[U]/0[H]-B x-x-x. NS (120b) HHL. Hattō, Hamada, Matsue, Izumo, Goka-mura 0; Sz 3.

4.1   minasibo < *miynasibwo < *mu-Ci*1.1* na-si*adj B pred* -n- pwo *1.3a* 'an empty
ear of grain'. HHHH - x-x-x x-x-x.

4.2   minasigo < miynasigwo ?< *mu-Ci*1.1* na-si*adj B pred* -n- kwo*1.1*. 'orphan'.
HHHL - 3/0-1:4[H]/4[U]-A x-x-x. K: Hn-Edo HHHL. Sz 4/0.

6.2   minasikogusa ?< *miynasikwo-gusa < *mu-Ci*1.1* na-si*adj B pred* kwo*1.1* -n-
kusa*2.3*. 'Cynanchum atratum' (= hunabara-soo). HHHHHL - x-x-x x-x-x. Cf. amana.

4.1   minasita < myina-sita < *mina*?2.1* sita*2.2a*. 'under the water'. x - x-x-x
x-x-x. NS (84a) HHHH; NS (T+ 97) HL|HL.

4.1   mina*s*/*z*oko < myina-soko < *mina*?2.1* soko*2.1*. 'bottom of the water, deep
in the water' (= mizusoko). x - x-x-x x-x-x. NS (70c) HHHH; NS (T+ 44) HLLL.
Km (W) HHHH.

3.1   minato < myinatwo < *mina*?2.1* two*1.1*. 'port'. HHH - 0-0-A B-A-x. NS (102a)
HLL (?); NS (T+ 120) HL|H. Km (W) HHH. Edo HHH. Ib *(rare)* H = 3.1. Nk naaTu B;
Sr nnatu A.

?2.1, ?2.2a   mine < myine < *mi-*?1.1* ne*?1.1* (?<naCi). 'peak'. HH - 0/2-0-A x-x-x.
NS (115a) HH. Km (S) HH. Edo HH. Kōbe (Robb) 2; Ib H = 2.1.

?3.7b (> 2.2b?)   minna = mina. 'all; everyone; everything'. x - 3(/0)-1:4[H]/
1:3[U](/1)-A x-x-x. Hiroshima 3 (adv 0). Kōchi (Hattori 1973), Ōsaka, Ise 1:3;
Ib H2 = 3.2.

2.4   mino < myino < *mino (?< *min[a]*?2.1* [s]o*?1.1*). 'raincape'. LH - 1-1-A
B-B-x. Km x. K: Hn-Km LH. Narada, Hiroshima 1. Ōsaka, Ise 1. Sr nnu B; Ib L =
2.4. Identifying the second syllable as no is based on phonograms of a name
also written (in 702) with semantograms suggesting the word for 'raincape';
but Sd myinyo(o) B indicates *myinwo. (NKD gives etymologies with *miy-.)

4.5   minowata < *myi-no-wata < *mi*1.1* no bata*2.3*. 'the Three Foci (Vital
Spots): chest and upper and lower abdomen' (= sansyoo, one of the roppu
'Six Viscera'). LLLL - x-3-x x-x-x. Register incongruent with etymology.

?2.2a, ?2.1   mio < myiwo < *mi-bo < *mi[na]*?2.1* bo*?1.3b* ('water cord' not 'water
tail'). 'channel'. (Hx) - 0/1-2-x x-x-x. Mg miwo-biki (no fune) HHHH(-H LH).
Km (W) HL/HH.

2.2b   mio 'grebe': *see* nio.

2.2b   [mio] < mi-fo < *myi fo < *mi po. 'three hundred'. HL - x-x-x x-x-x.

2.3   mira < myira. 'leek'. *See* nira (x - 0/2-2-B x-x-x).

6.21   miranonegusa < *myira-no-ne - *k*/*g*usa < *mira*2.3* no na-Ci*1.3a* (-n-)
kusa*2.3*. 'a kind of wild ginger, Asiasarum heterotropoides' (= usuba-saishin).
xxxLHL (= *LLLLHL) - x-x-x x-x-x.

2.4   miru < myiru < *miru (?= *npiru). 'a kind of seaweed' (= mata-miru).
x - 1-2-x x-B-x. Sr biiru B. Cf. Korean mi(yek) 'wakame seaweed'.

3.7x (?= 2.4|1.3)   mirume < myiru-me < *miru*2.4* me*1.x* (*?1.3*) (< ...). 'a kind of
seaweed'. x - x-x-x x-x-x. Km (W) LHL (?= LH|L).

3.1   misago < myisagwo < *mi-sankwo (< ?). 'osprey'. HHH - 0-0-x x-x-x. Km x.

4.4   mi*s*/*z*akari < *myi-sakari < *mi-*?1.1* (< ...) saka-r[a-C]i*s.1←4*. 'at its
height/peak/liveliest' *(adj-n)*. HLLL - x-x-x x-x-x.

3.3   misaki < myi-sakyi < *mi-*?1.1* saki*2.1*. 'promontory'. HLL - 1/0-0-A x-A-x.
NS (T+ kun) HHL. Km x. Sapporo, Akita, Goka-mura 2; Matsumoto, Numazu 1;
Narada, Hiroshima, Ōita 0; Hakata 0, ygr 1; western Mino (= SW Gifu), Hida (=
northern Gifu), Sz *(rare)*, NE Kyūshū 3. Kōchi, Sakawa 2; Ib H1 = 3.3.

3.1   misao < myisawo (< ?). 'fidelity'. HHx - 0-0-A x-x-x. Km x. Mr (Bm) LHH.
Ōita 2. Kōchi 1; Ib *(rare)* H = 3.1. Zdb associates isa-wo-si- 'brave, diligent'
(= ?*mi-isa-bo); Ōno treats the word as 'sacred/exalted blue' (= *mi-[z]abo).

4.1   misasagi < misa*/zaki (< ?, *palatal status of mi and gi unknown*).
'mausoleum'. HHHH - 0-1:3[H]/0[U]-A x-x-x. Km x.

2.3   mise < myise[y] < *mi-sa-Ci[-Ci]ₐ. 'shop, (sales) display'. x - 2-2-B
B-x-x. Km x. Ib F = 2.3. Said to be a truncation of mise[-dana] 'display
shelf'.

2.1   miso < myi-so < *mi-ᵧ₁.₁ soₗ.ₗ. 'clothes, garment'. x - x-x-x x-A-x.
NS (94a, 96a) HH. Sr nsu A. (Ōno has "-so" = -swo or unknown -so; Zdb bases
-so on a phonogram.) Cf. so, misokake. ("Also mizo.")

2.2b   miso < myi-swo < *miᵧ₁.₁ -swoₗ.ₓ. 'thirty'. HL - 1-2-x x-x-x. Km (W)
HL/HH.

2.4   miso (< ?). 'beanpaste'. LH - 1-1-B B-B-x. Km x. Ib L = 2.4. (Perhaps Ch;
see NKD.) Cf. Korean mye'cwu 'soy malt'.

?4.1, ?4.2   miso-hagi < *misoᵧ (< ?) fagiyₑ.₂ᵦ (< pan-koCi). '(purple)
loosestrife, Lythrum anceps'. HHxx - 0-3-x x-x-x.

4.2   misok/gake < *myi-so kake[y] < *mi-soₑ.ₗ (< ...) kak[a-C]iₑ. 'clothes-
hanger'. x (= *HHHL) - x-x-x x-x-x.

?3.2a   misok/gi < misok/gyi (?< *miy-soki < *mu-Ciₗ.ₑ [so]sok[a-C]iₐ.
'ablution'. HHx ?= *H(|)HL - 0-0-x x-x-x. Km (W) HHL. Cf. sosogu.

3.1   misora < myi-swora < *mi-ᵧ₁.₁ sworaₑ.₄. 'the sky'. x - 0/2-0-A x-x-x.
NS (Okada) HHH; NS (T+ 102) H(|)LL.

3.x   misoti < myi-swoₑ.₂ᵦ -tiₗ.ₓ < ... . 'thirty; thirty years old'. x - x-x-x
x-x-x. *See* -ti.

?2.3   [mita] < *myita < *mita. 'earth, (dry) land'. x - x-x-x B-B-B. Sd myithya
B. Sr nca B. Yn nta B. Cf. [muta]; Korean mwuth 'dry land', mith 'bottom'.

3.1   mitake < *myi-takey < *mi-ₗ.ₗ taka-Ciₑ.ₑ. 'peak, mountain'. HHH - 0-0-x
x-x-x.

3.1   mitama < *myi-tama < *mi-ᵧ₁.₁ tamaₑ.ₑ. 'spirit'. HHH - 0-0-x x-x-x.
NS (131a [14:404-K]) HHH; NS (T+ kun) HLL (ara ~), ₣LL (saki ~), HL₣ = HLL
(kusi ~), LL₣ (ukano ~).

?3.4, ?3.1   mitani < *myi-tani < *mi-ᵧ₁.₁ taniₑ.ₑ. 'valley'. x - x-x-x x-x-x.
NS (Okada) LLL, register incongruent with etymology (cf. miyama, mitake);
NS (T+ 2) LLH.

3.2x   mitari < *myi-tari < *miᵧ₁.₁ -tariₑ.ₓ (<*-t[u]ₚ𝒸ₗ ar[a-C]iᵦ). 'three
people'. x - 1-x-x(A/B)-A-x. Km (W) HHL. 1700 Ōsaka LHH.

4.2   mitegura < myi-tegura < *mi-ᵧ₁.₁ ta-Ciₗ.ₑₐ -n- kuraₑ.ₑᵦ ('exalted hand-
seat'). 'offerings to the gods'. HHHL - 0-x-x x-x-x. Cf. oomitegura.

2.1   miti < myiti < *miti (?= *miᵧ₁.₁ tiᵧ₁.₁). 'road, path, way'. HH - 0-0-A
A-A-A. NS (71c, 81a, 122b, 134a) HH; NS (T 35, 50, 82) ₣H ?= HH, (T 64) ₣L ?=
HL, (T 37, 38]) LL. Km (S,W) HH. Edo HH. Hakata 0 *(we expect 1, ygr 0)*.Ib H
= 2.1. Nk miCii A; Kunigami, Ōgimi (northern Okinawa) B; Yn amiti A ?< *a[si]-
miti. Nakanoshima treats as 2.2.

2.3   miti 'honey': *see* mitu.

2.1|2.4   miti-ato < *myiti atwo < *mitiₑ.ₗ atwoₑ.ₒ (< ...). 'rut'. HH|LH - x-x-x
x-x-x. (Attested only in Mg?)

5.2 = 2.1|3.2 mitikurabe < miti-kurabe[y] < *mitiₑ.ₗ kura-n[a-]pa-Ci[-Ci]ₐ. 'a kind
of parcheesi (game)'. xxHHL = HH(|)HHL - x-x-x x-x-x.

?2.2x, ?2.1   mito < myi-two < *mi[na]ᵧₑ.ₗ twoₗ.ₗ. 'port' (= minato). x - 0/1-0-x
x-x-x. NS (134b[14:440-K]) ···HL. K: "Hn HH".

4.4   mitokoro < *myi-tokoro < *miᵧ₁.₁ tokoroₑ.ₗₐ. 'three places/points'.
HLLL (Kz) - 2-3-x x-x-x. Km x.

4.2   mitosagi < mito-sagi (?< *myido[riₑ.ₑₐ] sagiₑ.ₗ). 'heron, Ardea cinerea'
(= aosagi). HHLL - x-x-x x-x-x. *(Kenkyusha typo: "Adrea".)*

3.1   mitose < myi-tose < *mi?ı.ı to̲si̲ɜ.ɜ *(final vowel partially assimilated to
o̲). 'three years'. x - 1̲-0-x x-A-x. NS (98a, 99b) HHH. 1700 Ōsaka LHL. Sr
mitu/micu A.

?3.2b < 2.2b   mittu < *myi-tu < *mi?ı.ı -tuı.x. 'three'. HL - 1-2-x (A/B)-A-A. Km
(S,W) HL. Mr (Bm) HL. Edo HL. Aomori 0. Sd myit(i) A; Sr, Yn miiçi A.

2.3   mitu < miti (< Ch my̲et). 'honey'. LL - 1-2-B x-B-x. Ib H = 2.1.

4.6   mitubati < mitibati < *miti̲ɜ.ɜ -n- pati̲ɜ.ı. 'honey bee'. LLLH - 2-1:3-B
x-x-x. Wamyō-shō LLHH (Numoto 1979:30).

?3.1   mitugi < mituki < myitukiy < ?*mi-?ı.ı tuku-Ci̲ɜ.ɜ. 'tribute'. x - 0-0-x
x-x-x. NS (100a, 103a, 129a) HHH; (103a) HxH; (101b, 108b, 111b, 122a) HHL.
Km (W) HHH. Sg *(rare)*, Hiroshima 0. Ōsaka, Ise 0. For -g- < -k-, see Ch. 2.

5.1   mitugimono < myitukiy?ɜ.ı (< ...) mo̲no̲ɜ.ɜ. 'tribute'. HHxxx - 0-0-A x-x-x.
NS (131b) HHHHH. Sz *(rare)* 0/4.

4.1   mitumata < *myitu-mata < *mi-tuɜ.ɜb (= mi?ı.ı -tu) mataɜ.ɜ. 'three forks/
branches; three-pronged'. HHHH - 0/2-1-A x-x-x.

3.2x   mituna = mituno < *myi-tunwo < *mi?ı.ı tunwoɜ.ɜ. 'three-horn(ed)':
NS (103b) mi̲-tu̲na ka̲sifa > mitunagasiwa = mituno-kasiwa 'ceremonial oak-leaves'

2.2b   miwa < myiwa < *mi(-)ba (< ?). 'wine offered to the gods'. HL - 0/1-x-x
x-x-x. cf. miki.

3.6   "miwizu" (Mg) = mi[m]izu 'earthworm': LHH (Kn)/ HHH (Ck). *See* mimizu.

2.1   miya < myi-ya < *mi-?ı.ı daı.ɜb. 'shrine'. (H) - 0-0-A x-A-x. NS (72b,
72c, 113a, 115b) HH; NS (T 54, 55, 73) ₤L ?= H̲L, (T 84) ₤H ?= HH. Km (W) HH.
Edo HH. Ib H = 2.1. (Sr borrowed?)

4.11, (5.16)   miyabi(ya)-ka < myiyabiy-(ya-)ka < *myiyabiy?A/B (< *mi-daɜ.ı
-npᵃ/₂-Ci[-Ci]) -(da-)ka. 'elegant; courtly'. LLHL, LLLHL - 3-4-x x-x-x.
Cf. miyabiru.

?4.1a = 2.1|2.2a   miyabito < myiyaɜ.ı (< *mi-?ı.ı daı.ɜb) -fyito̲ɜ.ɜ (< *pito̲).
'shrine-keeper'. x - x-x-x x-x-x. Km x. NS (Okada) HHHL. K: Hn HHHF.

3.1   miyako < myiyakwo < myiyaɜ.ı (< *mi-?ı.ı daı.ɜb) -kwoı.x ('shrine place').
'capital'. HHx - 0-0-A x-A-x. NS (119b) xHH. Km (W) HHH/LHH. Mr (Bm) HHH. Edo
HHH. Ib *(rare)* H = 3.1. Ōno says -kwo is a variant of -ko̲ 'place' with the
vowel assimilated because of the preceding /a/ (?).

3.1   miyama < myi-yama < *mi-?ı.ı damaɜ.ɜ. '(deep) mountains'. x - 0-0-A x-A-x.
NS (T+ 86) myi-yama - gakuri te HHH(|)HLH|₤. Km (W) HHH. Narada 3. Ib *(rare)*
H = 3.1. (The first syllable is the honorific infix, not [huka]-mi as implied
by the kanji of the usual orthography.) Cf. mitake, mitani.

2.1-tu|1.1   miya-tu-ko < myi-yaɜ.ı (< *mi-?ı.ı daı.ɜb -tu kwoı.ı. 'government
(public) servants; *(name of a court rank)*'. HH-L|H (Ir) - x-x-x x-x-x.

5.2   miyatukogi < myiya-tu-kwo - giy < *myi-ya (< *mi-?ı.ı daı.ɜb) -tu kwoı.ı
-n- ko̲-Ciı.ɜɜ. 'elder(berry) tree' (= niwatoko). HHHHL - x-x-x x-x-x.

5.7   mizikaginu < *myizikagyinu < *minsi-kaₐdⱼ ₆ -n- kinuɜ.ɜ. 'a short gown'.
LLLLH - x-x-x x-x-x.

3.3   miziro < *miy-zirwo < ?*mu-Ciı.ı -n- sirwoɜ.ɜ. 'white-grained':
mi̲ziro-no̲ ine 'rice with grains still pale'. HLL - x-x-x x-x-x.

?2.1a   mizo < myizo̲ < *minso̲ (?< *min[a]?ɜ.ı s(w)op[a-C]iₐ). 'ditch'. HF/HH -
0-0-A x-B̲-A. Km x. Edo HH. Aomori, Sz, Narada, Hattō, Hamada, Matsue. Izumo.
Hakata 0. Ib H = 2.1. Nk mizu C = mizuu A = zuu A; Kunigami, Ōgimi (northern
Okinawa) B̲; Sr (n)nzu B; Yn midu A. Sakurai (Kgkb 336:22) takes Mg HF
as a scribal error for HH.

3.1   mizore < *misore [Shinsen-Jikyō] < ?*myiᵃ/₂ore < ?*mi(n)sore. 'sleet'.
x - 0-0-A x-x-x. Km x. K: Hn HHH *(attested?)*. Hakata 0. Ib H = 3.1. The precise
value of the first two syllables is unknown. The suggested etymology midu-arare
should yield *myidworare.

?2.1a   mizu < myidu < *mintu (?< *min[a]?ₛ.₁ tu₁.₃ₐ 'water *liquid'), ?< *mentu
            (?< *men[a] ...). 'water'. HF/HH - 0-0-A A-A-A. NS (T 83) HH, (T 36) ꬺH ?= HH;
            NS (T+ 118) HL. Km (W) HH. Edo HH. Hakata 0̲ (we expect 1, ygr 0; cf. kizu
            'wound'). Sd midi A; Nk mizii A; Kunigami, Ōgimi (northern Okinawa) B̲; Sr miẓi
            A; Yn min A; Hateruma min. Cf. simizu. (The evidence for *me... is midzi on
            Ie-jima, where me > mi but mi > ni.)

?2.4   mizu < myidu < *mintu or *mi(n)tu. '(being) young and vigorous; virtue;
            good omen, favorable sign'. x - x-x-x x-x-x. NS (97a, 97b) LH; NS (T+ kun) ꬺL
            ?= LL. Cf. mizumizusi- ₐdⱼ ᵦ.

4.1   mizuai < midu-afi < *myidu-afyi < *mintu₂.₁ₐ (< ...) ap[a-C]iᵦ.
            'confluence, merger of streams' (= mina-ai). HHHH - x-0-x x-x-x.

?4.2 < ?5.2   mizubuki < mizu-hubuki?ₛ.₂ < midu (< ...) fufuki (< ...). 'prickly
            water-lily' (= oni-basu). x - 3-x-x x-x-x.

5.2   mizuburui < midu-furufi < *myidu-furufyi < *mintu₂.₁ₐ (< ...) puru-p[a-
            C]iₐ. 'water filter/strainer'. HHHHL - 3-4-x x-x-x.

?4.6   mizugaki < midukaki < myidu-kakyi < *mintu/mi(n)tu?ₛ.₄ kaki₂.₂ᵦ (< ...).
            'fence around a shrine or palace'. LLLH (Kn) / HHHH (Ck) - 3/4-4-x x-x-x.

4.3   mizugane: see mizuᵏ/ₐane.

3.1   mizuha < midufa < myitufa < *mi(n)tupa (?< *min[a]?ₛ.₁ tu₁.₃ₐ pa?). 'god
            of water'. HHH - x-x-x x-x-x. Cf. (fey -tu) fyi < *pi 'spirit (of hearth)'.

?5.2   mizu-hubuki < midu-fufuki < *mintu₂.₁ₐ (< ...) ?pupukiy?ₛ.₁ (< ...).
            'prickly water-lily' (= mizubuki = oni-basu). (HH)HHx (?= *HHHHL) - x-4-x.

?4.1/4.2 mizukaki < midukaki < *myidu-kakyi < *mintu₂.₁ₐ (< ...) kak[a-C]iᵦ.
            'paddle; web (foot)'. (HH)HH (Kn) / HHHL (Ir) - 3/4-4[U]/1̲:4̲[H]-A x-x-x.
            Hakata 0̲ (we expect 2).

?4.6   [mizukaki] 'fence ... ': see mizugaki.

4.3   mizuᵏ/ₐane < midu-kane < *myidu - kane[y] < *mintu₂.₁ₐ (< ...) kana-Ci₂.₁.
            'mercury, quicksilver'. HHLL - x-0-x x-B-x. Sr miẓigani B 'mercury' ≠
            miẓikani B 'lead'.

4.3   mizukara < midukara < *miydukara < *mu-Ci₁.₁ (-n-) -tu kara₂.₂(?ₐ/b).
            'self'. HHxx - 1-2-A x-x-x. Km (S) HHLL. Mr (Bm) HHLL. K: Edo HHLL.

4.1, 4.2 mizuᵏ/ₐuki < myidu-kukiy < *mintu₂.₁ₐ (< ...) kuku-Ci₂.₃ ('water
            stalks'). 'hand(writing) traces; a letter of tidings; a writing brush'.
            x - 0-0-x x-x-x. Km (W) xxHH = *HHHH, xxHL = *HHHL.

6.1, 6.2 mizukukiburi < myidukukiy₄.₁,₄.₂ - buri(₂.₁) < *mintu₂.₁ₐ (< ...) kuku-
            Ci₂.₃ -n- pur[a-C]iₐ. (name of a poem). x - x-x-x x-x-x. Km (W) HHHHHH, HHHHHL.

5.3   mizukuroi < midukurofi < miy-dukurofyi < *mu-Ci₁.₁ (-n-) tuku-ra-p[a-C]iᵦ.
            'attiring oneself; arranging one's appearance'. HHHLL - 2-3-A x-x-x. Sz 0.

3.7x   mizuo < miduwo < *meydo?ₛ.₃ (< *ma-Ci₁.₃ₐ -n- to₁.₁) wo?₁.₃b (< *bo)
            ('needle's-eye strap'). 'stirrup strap'. LHL - x-x-x x-x-x.

?3.6   mizura < myidura < *mintura (?< *mi-m[i]₂.₃ tura_A 'ear dangle'). 'an
            ancient hair-style'. LHx (?= *LHH) - 0/1-0̲-x x-x-x. (Hn also bidura.)

3.1   mizuti < mituti < *myi[du]₂.₁ₐ (*min[a] tu) -tu ti?₁.₁ or *myi[na]?₂.₁
            -tu ti?₁.₁ (the form with -zuti may represent retained -n- of *mina rather
            than the influence of the initial nasal) ('water spirit'). 'sea serpent'.
            HHH - x-0-x x-x-x. NS (111b) HHH.

?3.1   mizuto < miduto < *myidu-two < *mintu₂.₁ₐ (< ...) two₁.₁. 'floodgate'.
            HHx (?= *HHH) - x-x-x x-x-x.

4.1   mizutuki < midutuki ?< *myidu-tukyi < *mintu₂.₁ₐ (< ...) tuk[a-C]iᵦ.
            'a bridle-bit strap'. HHHH - x-x-x x-x-x.

2.1|2.4   mizuumi < miduumi < *myidu umyi < *mintu₂.₁ₐ (< ...) umi₂.₄. 'lake'.
            HH|LH - 3-3-A x-x-x. K: Edo HHLL. Hakata 2/3; Sz, Narada, Hattō 3; Hamada,
            Matsue, Izumo, Goka-mura 0.

?1.2   mo. 'seaweed'. L̲ - 0-0̲(/2[U])-A x-A-x. NS (T+ 7) "R" = H. Km (W) H.
    K: Edo HL. Aomori, Akita, Numazu, Hiroshima, Ōita 0; Sapporo, Matsumoto,
    Narada 1̲. Kōchi 0̲; Toyama, Suzu 2. Ib H1 = 1.2. Cf. moha, me.

?1.1   mo. 'mourning; distress, misfortune'. L̲ - 0-0-A x-x-x. Aomori, Sz 0.
    Ib H = 1.1.

1.3b   mo < *mo̲. 'garment'. R - 0-0-x x-x-x. Km (S) L/H(-L). Cf. uwami; koromo.

?1.3a < 2.4   mo < [o]mo𝘴.𝟺 (= omo-te𝘴.𝟺). 'surface'. x - x-x-x x-x-x. Km (W) L/H.

2.2x < 3.6   moda (< ?). 'silence, not speaking'. HL-/RL- - x-x-x x-x-x.
    See modasu; Ch. 4, §8.2.

3.x   moegi < moye-gi < *moda-Ci[-Ci]ᴮ kiy𝘪.𝟸 (< kᵘ/₂-Ci). 'a yellow-green
    color'. x - 0-0-A x-x-x. Cf. moyogi.

?6.22   [moe-hazikami] < moye-fazikami < *moda-Ci[-Ci]?ᴮ pansikami?𝟺.𝟷 < ...
    'sprouting ginger'). '"purple ginger", a kind of ginger'. LLxxxx ?= *LLLLHL -
    x-x-x x-x-x.

4.1   moeᵏ/ᵍui < moekufi < *moye-kufyi < *moda-Ci[-Ci]ᴬ kupi𝘴.𝟸ᵇ. '(fire)brand,
    embers'. HHHH - x-x-x x-x-x.

-      mogosi: see mokosi.

?3.7a   mogura < *monkura (< ?). 'mole (rodent)' (= uguromoti). x - 0-1:3[U]/1[H]-
    B x-x-x. Aomori, Sz 1̲. Ig L̲ = 3.6. Variant mugura.

2.1   moha < mo-fa < *mo?𝟷.𝟷 pa𝘪.𝟸. 'seaweed'. HH - x-2-x x-x-x.

3.3 (< 4.3)   mohara < mofara = moppara < *mo(-t-)para ?< *mo-ₚᵣₑ (?< *ma-?𝟷.𝟷)
    paraᴬ 'exclusively': mohara HLL - x-2-x x-x-x, Km (W) HLL/"HLH" (odd);
    moppara x - 0/1-0-B x-A-x, Km (S) HHLL.

3.3   mohaya < mo-faya < *mo-ₚᵣₑ (?< *ma-, ?< *[i]ma𝘴.𝟺) pada?𝟸.𝟹. 'already'.
    x - 1-2-A x-x-x. Km x.

2.2b   moi < mofyi < *mopi. 'cup; water'. HL - x-x-x x-x-x. Km x. (Ōno fails to
    distinguish unknown Co from Cwo; there is no evidence for *mwopi or *mo̲pi.)

?2.5   moke = boke < *m(b)o[k]-k[w]a (second vowel partially assimilated to
    first) (< Ch m(b)uk-.kwa). 'Japanese quince, Chaenomeles lagenaria'. LH - 1-
    1:3-A x-B-x. Ib L2 = 2.5. Sr buki[-qiru] B 'pink (color)'.

2.5   moko < mwokwo: see muko.

3.5x   moᵏ/ᵍosi ?< *mo̲[to̲]𝘴.𝟹 kosi𝘴.𝟸ᵇ ('bottom floor'). 'a casket room on the
    lowest tier of a pagoda'. LLH - x-x-x x-x-x.

4.5   mokurani (Kn), mokuran (Ir) (< Ch m(b)uk-.lan). 'magnolia' (= mokuren).
    LLxx (Kn), LLLL (Ir) - x-x-x x-x-x.

2.1   momi (?< momyi < *mom[a-C]iᴬ 'pound'). 'unhulled rice'. HH - 0-0-A x-A-x.
    Km x. Ib H = 2.1.

?2.1   momi < *mom[a-C]iᴬ. 'cloth rub-dyed solid red'. x - 1-0-x x-x-x. Km x.
    Hiroshima 1. Ōsaka, Ise 2̲. Cf. momizi (but the register is incongruent).

?2.2b   momi (< ?). 'fir'. HL - 1-0[H]/2[U]-A x-x-x. Km x. Sz, Hattō, Hamada,
    Matsue, Izumo, Hiroshima 1̲; Goka-mura 2. Ōsaka, Ise 2.

?2.2b   momi < momyi < *momi. 'tree frog, hyla; flying squirrel (dial. momo, cf.
    musasabi)'. HL - x-x-x x-x-x. Km x. Ib H1 = 2.2 (the creature is alien).

3.4   momizi < momidi < momyiti < *momit[a-C]i𝘴. 'autumn colors'. (L) - 1-2-B
    x-A-x. Km (W) LLL. Edo HHL. Sapporo, Aomori, Akita, Matsumoto, Numazu, Narada,
    Nagano (Kudō 199b), Hida (= northern Gifu), Hattō, Hamada, Matsue, Izumo,
    Goka-mura, Hiroshima, Wakamatsu, NE Kyūshū, Ōita 2; Hakata 1. Toyama 1:3
    (expected); Suzu 1̲:3 (we expect 0); Ib H = 3.2. On -d- ← -t-, see Ch. 2. §2.

2.1   momo (< ?). 'peach'. HH - 0-0-A A-A-x. Km x. Hakata 0 (we expect 1, var
    0). Ib H = 2.1. Nk muumuu B̲; Kunigami, Ōgimi (northern Okinawa) B. Sd mumo(o)
    A indicates *-mwo.

2.3   momo < mwomwo (< ?; cf. -ho). 'hundred'. LL - 1-2-x x-B-x. NS (94a) LL;
NS (T+ 11, 53, ?85) LL. Km (W) LL···. Edo HL. Hiroshima 1. Ōsaka, Ise 2. Km x.
Sd mumo(o) B; Onna muumuu B.

2.5   momo < mwomwo (< ?). 'thigh(s)'. LH - 1-1:3-A B-B-B. Km x. 1700 Ōsaka LF.
Hiroshima 1. Ōsaka, Ise 2; Ib L = 2.4. Sd mumo(o) B; Nk mumuu B; Onna muumuu B.

4.11   momosi^k/$_g$i < momosikiy < mwomwo$_{2.3}$ si-kiy$_{2.x}$ (< ...). '(the precincts of)
the Imperial Palace'. x - x-x-x x-x-x. Km (W) LLHL, LLLH. Mr (W 18) HLLL.

?3.2a, ?3.7b   monaka < *mo-pre (?< *ma-$_{?1.1}$, cf. mannaka) naka$_{2.4}$. 'the very midst;
a bun with jam in the middle'. x - 1-1:3-A x-x-A. Km x. Sz 2. Ib L2 = 3.5/7.
Yn nnaga A.

2.3   mono. 'thing; person'. LL - 2-2-B A-B-B. NS (71c, 72c, 95a, 104b, 105b,
119a) LL; NS (T 84 'thing'; 50, 94 'person') HL. Km (S,W) LL. Mr (Bm) HL.
Edo HL. Ib F = 2.3. Sd may be a mistake (or A/B), cf. Nase B; Nk munuu/mun B.

4.5   [monohami] < monofami < *mono-famyi < *mono$_{2.3}$ pam[a-C]i. (kani no ~)
'the mouth parts (of a crab)'. LLLL - x-x-x x-x-x.

?3.3   monzi (< Ch .m(b)ywen-'tsyey). 'writing, written character(s), letter(s)'.
x - 1-2[H]/1:3[U]-A x-x-x. Edo LHL. Wakamatsu 1.

5.16 = 3.4|2.2 mooke-kimi < maukey$_{2.3←B}$ (< ... ; see mookeru) kyimyi$_{2.1}$ (< *kimi).
'crown prince' (= maukey no kyimyi NS 134a). x - x-x-x x-x-x. NS (92b)
LLL(|)HL.

?3.2x   mooto < mauto < mafuto < ma-fyito (?< *ma$_{?1..1}$ pito$_{2.2a}$, ?< *[u]ma$_{adj}$ $_B$
pito$_{2.2a}$. 'nobleman'. HHL (Kn) / HHH (Kz) - x-x-x x-x-x. Cf. uma-hito.

-         moppara: *see* mohara.

2.1   mori (?< *mor[a-C]i$_A$; cf. mure (§5.10), Korean mey < :mwoyh < *mwo'lih
'mountain'). 'woods, wooded place/hill; shrine woods'. HH - 0-0-A x-A-x.
Km (W) HH. Edo HH. Ib H = 2.1. Hakata 0 (we expect 1, ygr 0). Nk mui A
'(wooded/barren) hill'; Sr mui A. Matsumoto 1974:100 suggests *mori[y] <
*moro-Ci on the basis of OJ myi-moro 'place/grove where a god descends' and
fyimorokyi 'platform/gift for gods'.

?2.2a   mori (< ?). 'harpoon'. x - 1/0-2-x x-x-x. Km x. Aomori, Sz 0. Ib F = 2.3.

?2.1   moro(-). 'various, several'. HH-···: *see following entries*. Sd muru B
'all'; Nk muruu A, Sr muru A 'all, completely'. Sz 1. Ib L2 = 2.5.

4.1   morobito < moro-byito < *moro$_{?2.1}$ (-n-) pito$_{2.2a}$. 'many people, all the
people'. x - 0-0-x x-x-x. NS (128b) HHHH. Km x. JP -b-; "anciently [= Heian]
also -f-" (NKD).

3.4   moromi ?< *moro-miy < *moro$_{adj}$ $_B$ mu-Ci$_{1.1}$. 'unrefined sake or soy sauce'.
LLL - (2[H]/)3(/0[K])-2-B x-B-x.

4.1 = 2.1|2.1 moromoro (-no) < moro$_{?2.1}$ moro$_{?2.1}$. 'various, all (kinds of)'.
HHxx - 0-0-A x-x-(A). Km (S) HHHH(-H).

?4.2   moronari < *moro-nari < *moro$_{?2.1}$ nar[a-C]i$_B$ ('various births').
'oleaster' (= gumi). HHxx (?= *HHHL) - x-x-x x-x-x.

4.2   morotomo < moro$_{?2.1}$ tomo$_{2.1}$. 'together'. HHHL - 0-0-A x-A-(A). NS (133a)
HHHx. Km (W) xxHH. K: Edo HHHH.

2.2b < 3.3   mosi. 'perchance'. RL - 1-2-A x-A-x. Mr (Bm) HL. K: Hn RL, Km HL.
Ib H1 = 2.2. See Ch. 4, §7.1.

?3.1   mosio < mosifo < *mo-sifwo < *mo$_{?1.1}$ sipwo$_{2.3}$. 'seaweed salt'. x - 0-2-x
x-x-x. Km (W) HHH, LHH. Sr maasyu B 'salt' is thought to be from ma-sifo 'true
salt' despite the register incongruity.

3.7x = 1.3|2.2 mos/$_z$ita < *mo$_{1.3b}$ (-n-) sita$_{2.2a}$. 'underwear': ~ no tafusagi
'loincloth; underpants'. L(|)HL - x-x-x x-x-x.

3.1   mosoro (?< *mo[ro] siru, with vowel assimilation). 'thin/light sake (=
siru); unrefined sake (= moromi)'. HHH - x-x-x x-x-x.

3.4   motai < "motawi" (Zs) < motafi (Kn, Ck) < ?. 'a sake jar'. LLL - x-0-x
x-x-x.

2.1   moti (?< *mot[a-C]i_A). 'holly, Ilex (= moti-no-ki); birdlime made from
holly bark'. HH - 1-0[H]/2[U]-A x-A-x. Aomori 0; Sz (later learned), Hiroshima
1; Hakata (expected) 1, ygr 0/2. Ōsaka, Ise 2; Ib H = 2.1.

2.1 (?< 3.1)   moti (< motii < motifyi < *mot[a-C]i_A ipi_ɛ.ɜ). 'rice cake'.
HH - 0-0-A B-A-x. Km x. 1700 Ōsaka HH. Aomori, Narada, Hattō, Hamada, Matsue.
Izumo, Hiroshima 0; Hakata 1, ygr 2. Ōsaka, Ise 0; Ib H = 2.1. Nk muuCii C.

?4.2   motiawa < moti-afa < *moti_ɛ.ı (< ...) apa_ɛ.ɜ. 'glutinous millet'.
xxHL (= *HHHL) - 0-0-x x-x-x.

3.1 (< 4.x)   motii < motifyi < *mot[a-C]i_A ipi_?ɛ.ɜ ('sticky rice'). 'rice cake'.
HHH - x-0-x x-x-x. Cf. moti.

?4.1   motinawa < moti-nafa < *moti_ɛ.ı (< ...) napa_ɛ.ɜ. 'a rope smeared with
birdlime'. HHxx - 0/2-x-x x-x-x.

4.7   motizuki < moti-dukiy < *myiti-dukiy (the first vowel assimilated to the
initial labial) < *mit[a-C]i_B -n- tuku-Ci_ɜ.ɜ. 'the full moon (on the 15th day
of the lunar month), especially that of the 8th month'. LLLH - 2-2-x x-x-x.

2.3   moto. 'root; under; original'. (1) 'root': LL - 2/0-2-B x-B-x. NS
(Okada) LL; NS (T 13, 114; T+ kun) LL, (T 126) HL. Km (S,W) LL. Mr(Bm) HL.
Narada 0. Sr muutu B. (2) 'under': LH/LL - 2/0-2-B x-B-x. K: Hn-Km-Edo LF.
(3) 'original': LL - 1-2-B x-B-x. K: Edo HL. Narada 0; Hiroshima (Okuda)
2. Sr mutu B. According to Kindaichi 'under' would have been 2.5 in Heian (and
into Edo, for Heike-mabushi has 1:3 for this meaning, Okumura 1976:217).
but all three meanings surely go back to a single etymon with the low atonic
pattern (2.3). Ibuki-jima has F = 2.3 for all three meanings.

?4.5   motoara < *moto_ɛ.ɜ ara_adj A. 'sparsely growing trees'. x - x-x-x x-x-x.
Km (W) LLLL, LLLH, LLHH, LH|LH. Mr (W 19) HHHH.

4.5   motodori < motodori < *moto -n- t(w)or[a-C]i_B. 'topknot; (hair) queue'.
LLxx - 0/4-0-x x-x-x. Ongi LLxL. K: Edo HHHL.

3.5x ?= 2.3+1.1   moto-he < moto fye < *moto_ɛ.ɜ ?piCa_ı.x. 'bottom-side, base'.
x - x-0-x x-x-x. NS (70b, 83b) LL(|)H; NS (T+ 43) FLH ?= LL(|)H, (97) LHH.
K: "Hn LLF?".

3.4   motoi < motowi < *moto-wi[y] < *moto_ɛ.ɜ b^u/_o-Ci[-Ci]. 'basis'. LLL -
2(/3[H])-0[H]/2[U]-B x-x-x. Cf. kurai.

?3.3, ?3.4   mottomo < motomo (?< moto-mo[to] < *moto_ɛ.ɜ moto_ɛ.ɜ: ?< moto_ɛ.ɜ
mo_pcı). 'sensible, right; most, extremely'. HLL/LLL - x-0-x x-x-x. Mr (Bm) HLL.

?2.5   moya (< ?). 'haze, fog, mist'. x - 1-0[H]/1:3[U]-B x-x-x. Narada, Hattō,
Hamada, Goka-mura, Hakata 1; Matsue 1 (we expect 2); Aomori 0; Sz 2; Izumo 2.
Ib L = 2.4.

3.x   moyogi < moye-gi < *moda-Ci[-Ci]_?B -n- kiy_ı.ɜ (< *k^u/_o-Ci). 'a yellow-
green color'. x - 0-x-x x-x-x.

?2.2b < 3.3   mozi < monzi (< Ch .m(b)ywen-'tsyey). 'writing, character(s),
letter(s)': x - 1-2-A x-B-x. Km (W) HL. Edo HL. Cf. monzi. Sz 1. Ib H1 = 2.2.

2.3   mozi < modi < *monti[y] < *monto-Ci[-Ci]_B. '(= mozi-ori = moziri-ori)
crepe (fabric); muslin, sackcloth'. LL - 1-x-x x-x-x. Cf. mozir-u.

2.3   mozi < modi < *monti(< ?). 'moji, a unit for measuring weight of silk or
cotton' (= mise = 1.2 kg). LL (Ir) - x-x-x x-x-x.

3.7x = 1.3|2.2 mozita 'underwear': see mo^s/_zita.

4.5   mozizuri < modi-zuri < *monto-Ci[-Ci]_B -n- sur[a-C]i_B. 'an impression of
hare's-foot fern (= mozizuri-gusa = nezibana) on cloth, or its depiction in a
print; Spiranthes sinensis (lady's-tresses)'. x - 0/2-0-x x-x-x. Km (W) LLLL.

?2.4, ?2.5   mozu < mwozu ?< *mwom[wo] -su, ?< *mwo (-n-) -su. 'shrike' *(bird)*.
LH - 1-2/1:3[U]-A̱ x-(B)-x. NS (111a, 111b) LH. Km (W) xL (?). Aomori, Sz 1;
Goka-mura 2̲. Ib L2 = 2.5. Nk x; Sr moo-tui B 'thrush' spelled "mau-" in
Konkōken-shū (1711).

?1.1   mu(-) 'six' (x - 1-2-x x-A-x): *see* muika, mu(t)tu.

1.1   mu- 'fruit', 'body': *see* mi.

3.2a   mubara: *see* ibara.

-    mubatama = nubatama.

2.1   mube 'indeed': *see* ube.

2.3   mube (< ?). 'Stauntonia hexaphylla'. LL - 1/2-1-x x-x-x. Also "ube",
"umube".

2.1   muda ?< *mun(t)a (?< *mun[a]₂.₁ ta₁.₃ₐ 'empty hand'). 'useless, vain'.
x - 0-0-A x-A-x. Km x. Sr nna A 'empty'. Cf. muna-(si-)'empty'; the Chinese
characters are arbitrary.

2.4 (?< 2.5)   mugi < mugyi < *munki. 'barley'. LH - 1-1-B B-B-B. Km x. Hata 1.
Matsue 1/2̲; Izumo 2̲. Kōchi 1. Ib L = 2.4. Nk muzii B; Onna muuzii B; Yn mun B
(H 1964:65b, 21a).

4.11   mugigara < *mugyi-ᵏ/ᵧara < *munki₂.₄ (-n-) kara₂.₂(?ₐ/)ᵦ. 'barley husk'.
LLHL - 0-0-x x-x-x. Sz [muŋikara] 2.

4.6   mugikasu < *mugyi-kasu < *munki₂.₄ kasu₂.₄. 'barley bran'. LLLH - 2-0-x
x-x-x.

4.5   muginawa < muginafa < mugyi-nafa < *munki₂.₄ napa₂.₃. 'cruller'. LLLL -
0-0-x x-x-x. Shinsen-Jikyō has a verb muginafu 'make a cruller'.

5.16   mugisukui < mugisukufi < *mugyi-syukufyi < *munki₂.₄ sukup[a-C]i₄. 'barley
scoop'. LLLHL - 3-x-x x-x-x.

?3.7a   mugura < *munkura (variant of mogura 'mole'). 'creepers, trailing plants'.
x - 0-0-x x-x-x. Cf. yae-mugura. Also ugura, mogura.

3.1   muika ?< muyuka < ?*mudu?₂.₁ -ka₁.₃ₐ. 'six days'. x - 0-0-A B-x-x. Km x.
Edo muyuka HHH. Ib H = 3.1.

3.2a   mukade < ?*mukan-taCi (< ?). 'centipede'. HHL - 0-1:3-A x-B-C.
Aomori, Sz 0; Hida (= northern Gifu) mukaze 1/3; Hattō, Hamada 3; Goka-mura 1.
Ib mukaze L2 = 3.5/7. Nk muKaazi B; Yn nkadi C (H 1964:71b).

3.6   mukago, (Mg) nukago < ᵃ/ₘuka (< ?) -n- kwo₁.₁. 'brood bud, budlet,
propagule'. LHH - 0-1-x x-x-x.

3.1   mukai < mukafyi < *muka-p[a-C]i₄. '(facing) opposite'. x - 0-2-A x-A-x.
Mg mukafi-me HHxx-. Km (W) HHH. Aomori, Sz 2. Sr nkee A. Edo HHH.

3.1 (?3.1a)   mukasi. 'yore; long ago'. HHH - 0-1[H]/0[U]-A A-B-A. Km (S) HHH,
(W) mukasi-fe HHHL. Mr (Bm) HHH. Edo HHH. Aomori 0; Kurayoshi (Tottori).
Hamada, Hattō 3̲. Kōchi 1:3; Toyama 0 *(we expect 1:2)*, Suzu 0; Ib L = 3.6.
Nk muKaasi B; Yn nkaci A (H 1964:71b). Cf. Ch. 4, §7.3.

4.2   [mukatuo] < muka-tu-wo < *muka₄ -tu₍ₚ𝒸ₗ bo₁.₁. 'the hills beyond, yonder
hills'. x - x-x-x x-x-x. NS (Okada) HHHL; NS (T+ 108) HHLL.

2.5   muko < mwokwo. 'bridegroom, son-in-law; partner, companion'. LH - 1-1:3-B
B-B-C. NS (70a[11:46-M]) LL; NS (T+ 42 mokwo) LL. Km x. Edo LF. K: Hn-Edo LF.
Aomori (mogo) 2 *(expected reflex)*. Sd muho(o) B; Sr muuku B / muku-.

?3.2b   mukoo < mukafu < *muka-p[a-]u₄. 'over there, yonder; beyond'.
x - 2̲[NHK](?< *3)/0̲-2-A x-(A)-x. 1700 Ōsaka HHL. K: Mr HHH. Aomori 0; Narada 0
("but usually muken 0" ?< muka[f]i-n[i]). Ib H = 3.3. Sr mukoo A 'forehead'
(but 'over there' in compounds, borrowed?); cf. nkee < muka[f]i.

?2.5   muku. *(1)* 'a kind of yew, Aphananthe aspera (= muku-no-ki), or its fruit';
(2) 'gray sparling' (= muku-dori, *bird*). x - 1-1:3-x x-x-x. Km x. Edo HH.
Hiroshima 1. Ōsaka, Ise 1:3.

?2.5   muku. 'shaggy hair' (= muku-ge). x - 1-1:3-x x-x-x. Km x. Sz 1.
4.x   mukudori < *muku?ₛ.ₛ -n- tori₂.₁. 'gray sparling' (bird). x - 2/0-1:3-B
   x-x-x. Sz (rare) 3.
?3.7a   mukuge < *mukugey < *muku?ₛ.ₛ -n- ka-Ci?₁.₁. 'shaggy hair'.
   x - 0-1:3[H]/1-B x-x-x. Km x.
5.x (?5.10)   mukuge-inu < *mukugey?ₛ.₇ₐ (< ...) inuₛ.ₛ. 'shaggy dog' (= muku-inu).
   x - x-1-x x-x-x. K: Hn LHHHH (where attested?).
4.x   mukuinu < muku?ₛ.ₛ inuₛ.ₛ. 'shaggy dog'. x - 0-1-B x-B-x.
4.x = 5.16   mukurezi = muku-renizi (< Ch m(b)uk .lien-'tsyey). 'Koelreuteria
   paniculata (goldenrain, Chinese bladdernut)': ~ no ki. LLLHL - x-x-x x-x-x.
3.1   mukuro < mu-kuro ?< *mu[-Ci]₁.₁ kara[da]ₛ.₁ (with progressive vowel
   assimilation; or ... koro?*ₛ.₁). 'body; torso; corpse; dead tree-trunk'.
   HHH (Kn) / HHL (Kz) - 3/0-0-B x-x-x. NS (111a) LLL. Km x. Edo HLL.
-         mum··· : see um··· .
2.1   muna(-) 'empty, vain': see muda; cf. muna-si-ₐdⱼ A.
2.1   muna(-) 'ridge': see mune.
2.2b   muna(-) 'breast': see mune.
?4.1   munabone < *munaₛ.ₛb -n- poneₛ.ₛ (< ...). 'breast bone, sternum'.
   HHHx (?= *HHHH) - x-x-x x-x-x.
3.1   munagi 'eel': see unagi.
2.1   mune < *mune[y] < *muna-Ci (?< *mu-[Ci]₁.₁ na-Ci?₁.₁ 'body peak').
   'ridge (of roof)'. HH - 2[H]/0[K]-0-A x-A-x. Km x. Sz 2. Narada ('roof'),
   Hattō, Matsue, Izumo, Hiroshima 0; Hamada 0/2. Ōsaka, Ise 0. Ib H = 2.1.
   Cf. une.
2.1   mune ('ridge = high point' >) 'gist, purport'. HH - 2-2-A x-x-x.
   Km (S) HH. Edo HH. Ib H1 = 2.2. (Tk/Kt accent influenced by mune 'breast'?)
2.2a   mune < *mune[y] < *muna-Ci (?< mu-[Ci]₁.₁ na-Ci?₁.₁ 'body peak', cf.
   semine). 'breast'. HL - 2-2-A A-A-x. Km (S,W) HH. Edo HL. K: Hn-Km-Edo HL.
   Aomori 0. Ib H1 = 2.2.
?2.1   mura. 'mottle(s); motley'. x - 0-0[H]/1:3[U]-A x-x-x. Km x. Sz 0;
   Hiroshima 2. Ōsaka, Ise 1:3; Ib L2 = 2.5.
2.1   mura(-). '(being) a group, a cluster, a mass'. x - 2-0-x x-x-x. Cf. mure,
   mureru; hitomura, inamura, sisimura, takamura.
2.2b   mura (?< *mura-[Ci-]ₐ, cf. mure). 'village'. HL - 2-2-A A-A-A.
   NS (100b) HL; NS (T+ kun: ukati no mura) HL. Km x. Goka-mura 1; Hiroshima 2.
   Ōsaka, Ise 2; Ib H1 = 2.2.
3.1   murado < muratwo. 'kidney; heart'. HHH - x-0-x x-x-x. Mg -d-; "-d- from
   the end of Heian to the beginning of Edo [i.e. 1200-1500]" (Ōno).
4.9   murasaki < murasakyi (?< mura(-)ₛ.₁ sak[a-C]iₐ 'cluster bloom'). 'a
   gromwell, Lithospermum erythrorhizon; purple' (kodai ~ 'dark purple', Edo ~
   'light purple'); (= murasaki-nori) 'laver'. LLHL - 2-1:3-B x-B-x. Narada 1;
   Sz, Hata, Hakata 2. Kōchi 1:3.
4.1   murasame < murasamey < ?*mura?ₛ.₁ [z]ama-Ciₛ.ₛ. 'passing shower'. HHHH -
   0-0-A x-x-x.
3.1   murazi < *muransi (?< *muraₛ.ₛb nusiₛ.₄). 'one of the ancient rank titles
   (kabane)'. HHH (Ir) - 1-x-x x-x-x.
2.1   mure < *mure[y] < *mura-Ciₛ.₁ or *mura-Ci[-Ci]ₐ. (1) 'flock'. x - 2-0-A
   x-x-x. Ib H = 2.1. Cf. -me 'bird(s)'. (2) 'mountain': omure < wo-mure 'little
   mountain' (placename) — but Sr mui A is from mori.
2.3   muro < murwo. 'room, shed, cellar'. LL - 2-0[H]/2[U]-B x-x-x.
   NS (110b) LL. Km (S) LL. Mr (Bm) HL. Edo HL. Ib F = 2.3.

?4.5   murotumi < murwo-tumi < *murwo*ₑ.* ?tum[a-C]i*ₐ*. 'roadside inn'.
LLxx (?= *LLLL) - x-x-x x-x-x.

4.2   musasabi < musasabyi (< ?). 'flying squirrel'. HHHL - 2(/0[H])-1:3-A
x-x-x. Km x. Sz *(rare)* 4/2. NKD: "anciently *[i.e. Hn]* also muzasabi".

2.1   musi. 'insect, bug; *snake (*see* mi, nizi, yamakagasi)'. HH - 0-0-A A-A-A.
NS (76b) HH; NS (T 75) HH. Km (W) xH. Edo HH. Kōchi 2 (Hattori 1973); Ib F =
2.3. Nk musii A; Kunigami, Ōgimi (northern Okinawa) B. Cf. Ryūkyū iki-musi
(> Sr qicimusi B) 'animal'.

2.3   musi (?< Korean mwosi). 'ramie, Chinese silk plant, Boehmeria nivea;
(= musi-tareginu) a ramie veil on the back of a woman's hat'. LL - x-x-x x-x-x.

4.5   musimono < *musimono < *[u]mus[a-C]i*ₑ* mono*ₑ.ₛ*. 'a steamed dish, steamed
food'. LLxx (= *LLLL) - 2-3-x x-(B)-x. Sr qnbusii B.

3.4   musiro. 'straw mat'. LLL - 3-2-B x-B-B. Km (W) sa-musiro HHHL. Mr (Bm)
HHL. Edo HHL. Sapporo, Ōita 1; Matsue 3/0; Izumo 0; Goka-mura 0; NE Kyūshū 2.
Suzu 1 *(we expect 0)*; Ib F = 3.4. Yn musu B (H 1964:72a). Cf. aziro.

3.7b   musiro (?< mosi*ₑ.ₛb* ro*ₚcₗ*; ?< *a[ra*ₑ*]-mu si*ₚcₗ* ro*ₚcₗ*). 'rather' *(adv)*.
LHL - 1-0[H]/2[U]-B x-x-x. Mr (Bm) LHL. Aomori, Sz 1.

3.1   musuko < musukwo < *mu-s[a]-u*ₓₐ* *ₐttr* kwo*ₓ.ₓ* ('grow child'). 'son'.
x - 0-0-A x-x-x. Hakata 1 *(we expect 2)*, ygr 0. Ib H = 3.1.

?3.2b   musume < musumye < *mu-s[a]-u*ₓₐ* miCa*ₓₓ.ₓb* (?= *mina) ('grow female').
'daughter'. LHL (Kz) - 3-2-A x-x-x. Km (W) HHL. Edo HHL. Narada, Hattō, Hamada
3; Aomori, Matsue, Izumo, Goka-mura, Yamaguchi, NE Kyūshū (H 1951:178) 0;
Hakata 1 (*(we expect 2)*, ygr 3. Ib H2 = 3.1. K: Hn-Km-Edo HHL.

?2.1   [muta]. 'swamp, marshland; (Miyako) land'. x - x-x-x A-x-x. Sd mutha A
'swamp' ≠ myithya B 'earth'. Cf. [mita]; [nuta]; Korean mwuth 'dry land', mith
'bottom'.

2.x   -muti ?< *muti[y] < *mutu-Ci (cf. mutu- 'intimate'). 'esteemed and beloved
··· ' (usually suffixed to proper names). *See* nanzi. Cf. Kokugo-kokubun 416:7-8
(Kawabata); uti.

2.3   muti/buti/huti ?< *nputi (cf. Asayama 1943:4). 'whip'. (LL) - 1-2-A x-B-x.
Ongi LL. Km x. Edo HL. Aomori, Sz, Wakamatsu, Hakata 1. Ib F = 2.3. Sr buci B.

?3.2b   muttu < mu*ₓ.ₓ* (-t-) -tu. 'six'. x - 3-3-A (x-x-x). Km x. 1700 Ōsaka HLL.
Aomori 0; Narada 3. Ib H2 = 3.2 *(also adverbial)*. Kt 0 when adverbial [U].

2.2b   mutu < mu*ₓ.ₓ* -tu. 'six' (= muttu). HL - x-x-x (A/B)-A-A. Km x. Mr (Bm)
HL. Sr, Yn muuçi A.

3.5b   mutuki (< ?). 'diaper(s); loincloth'. LLH - 1-0[H]/2[U]-B x-x-x. Km x.
Perhaps < [fi]mo-tuki < *fyimo-tukyi < *pinpo tuk[a-C]i. Cf. Yoshida 1979:270.

?5.2   mutuoyobi < mu-tu*ₑ.ₑb* (< ...) oyobi*ₛ.ₐ* (< ...). 'a person born with an
extra finger'. HHHxx (?= *HHHHL)- x-x-x x-x-x.

?2.1, ?2.2x   muyu(-) < *mudu(-). 'six'. HH (Kn) x-x-x x-x-x. NS (125b) HL-···
'six [slaves]'. Cf. muika.

2.x   -muzi < -muti: *see* namuzi, nanzi.

3.4   muzina < muzina/uzina (?< *unsina < ?). '(= anaguma) badger; (= tanuki)
raccoon-dog; (= huigo) bellows'. LLL - 0/3-1-A x-x-x.

2.3   myaku (< Ch m(b)ayk). 'pulse, vein'. x - 2-2-B B-B-x. Ib F = 2.3. Sr myaku
B, naku B. Sz 2 = older [miyagu] 2.

1.1   na (V-i so). 'don't (V)!' NS (101a) na uka["]fase so 'let them not rise
to the surface!', (107a) na tori so 'take it not!', (128b) na ku["]farasime so
'let them have no concern with it!' Cf. na*ₐdⱼ* *ₑ*, -na- (neg. aux.), nani.

1.2   na. 'name; person (see onna, omina, okina, ?otona, ?mina)'. L (Kn) -
0-2-A A-A-A. Km (S,W) H(-L). NS (114a) H(-L). Edo F = HL. Aomori. Narada,
Hiroshima 0. Ōsaka, Ise 2; Ib H1 = 1.2. Hateruma nan (cf. Ch. 1, §52).

1.3a   na. 'rape(weed); greens; side-dish food (to eat with rice), including fish
(see sakana, isana, mana[ita]; cf. huna); ?*plant (cf. kamiokosina, hana)'.
x - 1-1-B B-B-A. NS (T+ 7 'greens', kun 'fish') L. K: Edo LH. Narada, Hiroshima
1. Ōsaka, Ise 1; Ib L = 1.3. Hateruma nan (cf. Ch. 1, §52).

?1.3a   *na. 'earth, ground; root'. (L) - x-x-x x-x-x. Cf. nai*₇₈.₄*; nae*₈.₃*,
ne*₁.₃ₐ*, takanna*₄.₂*; nezumi*₈.₆*; ni*₇₁.₃ᵦ*; (-)una 'sea'; neru < *na-Ci-₄ 'lie down';
nara*₈.₂ᵦ* 'Nara'; Paekche *ra/*na 'land' (Toh 1981:28).

1.3a   na 'inside' (= naka). x - x-x-x x-x-x. NS (T+ kun) L. Cf. nuna.

1.3b   na (< Ch .n(d)a). 'exorcism'. R - x-x-x x-x-x. Km x.

1.3b   na(-) ?= /nan/ < nan[i]. 'wh(at)'. R: na-ˢ/₂o R|L 'why', na-ˢ/₂o mo RH|L.
Cf. nazo, nani; Sd, Sr, Yn nuu (?< *noo < *na-[d]u < *na-do = na-zo); Miyako
noo (Ōra), nau (Ikema); Yaeyama noo, (archaic) nayu.

?1.3x   na 'you' (= nare); 'I/me' (Ōno, Zdb, but open to question). (x) - x-x-x
B-A-(A). NS (62 [11:303-M]) L, (73a [11:219-M], 76b [14:125- M]) H. NS (T+ 57.
75) na ga L H, (T+ 90) na wo L L, (T+ 62) na koso fa L LL L, (T+ 62a) na fa
L H. See nare, nanzi, nami, namu(-); nabito, nanimo, nase.

1.x   *na 'blade': see katana; kana 'plane'. Cf. nata, ono; nomi 'chisel'.

2.5   nabe < nabey < *nanpaCi ?< *na*₁.₃ₐ* -n- pa-Ci*₁.₁* ('food pot'). 'pan'. LH -
1-1:3-B B-B-C. Km x. K: Hn-Km LF. Hata 1. Kōchi 1:3; Ib L2 = 2.5. Sr naabi B.
(Borrowed from/into Korean nampi?) Cf. NS (T+ kun) myi-nafey ₣-LH = H|LH
'esteemed pan', wo-nabye L-LH [last vowel anomalous].

4.11   nabiyaka < *nabyiyaka < *nanpi-ya-ka (see nabiru). 'pliant, limp, lithe;
(JP) pretty' (adj-n). LLxx (= LLHL).

?2.2b   nada (?< *na[mi*₈.₃* api]nta*₈.₈ᵦ*, ?< *nam[i*₈.₃*] ta[ka*ₐₐⱼ ₛ*], ?< *nam[i*₈.₃*]
ta[t[a]-u*ₐ*] but register incongruent; ?< Ch). 'rapids, rough sea'. x - 1-2-A
x-B-x. Hattō, Hamada, Goka-mura, Hiroshima (Okuda) 1; Matsue, Izumo 2 (= 2.3).
Ib F = 2.3. Nk (obsolete) nadaa B.

4.11   nadaraka < *nanta-ra-ka 'smooth' (adj-n): ~ nari, ~ {ni} su. LLHL -
2-4-B x-x-x. Cf. naderu; nameraka, namer-u.

4.10   nadesiko < nadesikwo (< ?). 'wild pink, Dianthus superbus' (= tokonatu).
LHLL - 2-1:3-B x-x-x. Sz 2; Hata 2. Kōchi 1:3.

2.3 (?< 2.5)   nae < nafey < *napa-Ci (?< *na-pa-Ci; ?< *[i]na*₈.₄* -pa-Ci).
'seedling'. LL - 1-1-B B-B-x. Ongi-m LL. Km (W) LL. Mr (Bm) LH. Matsue, Izumo
2; the accent retreat found in other dialects (Tk, Narada, Hattō, Hamada,
Goka-mura 1) may be due to monosyllabification. Kōbe (Robb) 1:3; Ib L = 2.4.

3.4   nagae < naga-ye < *nanka*ₐₐⱼ ₛ* daCi/diCa*₁.₁*. 'a long handle'.
LLL - 0-0[U]/1[H]-A x-x-x.   ·

4.5   nagahito < naga-fyito < *nanka*ₐₐⱼ ₛ* pito*₈.₈ₐ*. 'a long-lifed (or long-
lived) person'. x - x-x-x x-x-x. NS (74b) LLLL; NS (T+ 62) LHHH.

4.1 = 2.3|2.3 nagakusa < *nanka*ₐₐⱼ ₛ* kusa*₈.₃*. 'pasqueflower, Pulsatilla cernura'
(= okinagusa). LL(|)LL - x-x-x x-x-x.

3.4   nagame: see nagameru (Ch. 6).

?3.5b < *4.6 (< 2.3|2.5) nagame < naga-amey < *nanka*ₐₐⱼ ₛ* [z]ama-Ci*₈.₃*. 'a long
(spell of) rain'. LLH - → naga-ame 3-1[H]- A x-B-x. The uncontracted modern
form is an etymological reversion (Komatsu 1977:385).

?3.6   nagara (< ?). 'Nagara' (placename). x - 1/0-x-x x-x-x. Km (W) LHL/LRL,
(W 17) LHH(-H).

3.4   nagare < *nagare[y] < *nanka-ra-Ci[-Ci]. 'flow, stream'. x - 3-2-B x-B-x.
Km (S,W) LLL. Mr (Bm) HHL. Edo HHL. Ib F = 3.4.

3.6   nagasa < *nanka*adj B* -sa*suf*. 'length'. LHx - 1(/0"new")-1-B (B)-(B)-(C).
Km (S) LHH. Narada, Hattō, Goka-mura 1; Hamada 0/1; Izumo 0; Matsue 0/3. Ib L2
= 3.5/7, L = 3.6. Yn naan C 'long'.

?4.5   nagatati < *nanka*adj B* tati*s.s* (< ...). 'a long sword'.
LLLx = *LLLL (Kn), LLHx (Ck)- 2/3-x-x x-x-x.

4.11   nagatuki < naga-*t*/*d*ukiy < *nanka*adj B* tuku-Ci*s.s*. 'the 9th month of the
lunar calendar'. x - 2-2-A x-x-x. Km (W) LLHL.

2.3   nage < nagey < *nanka-Ci[-Ci]*B*. 'throwing'. x - 2-2-B x-x-x. Ib F = 2.3.

3.4   nageki < nageyki*B* < *nanka*adj B* ik[a-C]i*B*. 'lament'. x - 3-0-B x-x-x.
Km (S,W) LLL. Edo HHL. 1700 Ōsaka HLL. Ib F = 3.4.

2.2b   nagi < nagiy < *nank*w*/*u*-Ci[-Ci]. 'calm'. x - 2-2-A x-x-x. Hattō 1/2,
Hamada, Goka-mura 2; Matsue, Izumo 2 (= 2.3). Ib H1 = 2.2. Cf. nagu; nago-yaka,
nagomu; nagusa(m-).

?2.1, ?2.3   nagi < *nagiy < *nan-? ko̲-Ci*1.3a*. 'a kind of black pine'. HH (Ir) -
1/2-x x-x-x. Km x. Edo HL.

2.3   nagi < nagiy < *nan-? ko̲-Ci*1.3a*. 'pickerelweed' (= mizuaoi). LL - x-2-x
x-x-x. NS (T 126) HL. Km x.

?4.2   naginata ?< *nagiy (< *nank*w*/*u*-Ci[-Ci] *?A/B* nata*s.1* 'mow ax'). 'a bayonet-
like weapon'. x - 4/3-4-A x-x-x. K: Edo HHHL. Sz 4/0; Narada, Hattō, Hamada,
Izumo 4; Matsue 3; Goka-mura, Hakata 0.

3.4   nagisa < nagyisa < *na(n)kisa (< ?). 'beach'. LLL - 3/0-2[H]/1:3[U]-B
x-x-x. Km x. Edo HHL. Aomori (rare) 3/0; Narada 3; Wakamatsu 0. Ib F = 3.4,
H̲ = 3.1. (Perhaps < *nag[a]*adj B* - isa; cf. isago, iso.)

?3.4   nago̲ri ?< *nam[i*s.s* no̲]ko̲r[a-C]i*B* ('wave remain'). 'aftertraces,
memory'. x - 3/0-0-A x-B-(x). Km (W) LLL. Edo HHL. Sz 3. Nk nagurii B. Is Yn
nanui A 'sound' cognate? (Cf. ne.)

?2.4, ?2.5   nai < nawi < ?*na-wi[y] ('earth sit/live') < *na*1.3a* b*u*/*o*-Ci[-Ci]*A*.
'earthquake'. LH - 1-2-x B-B-x. NS (Okada) LH; NS (T 91) L̲H̲ ?= LH. K: Hn LF
"?". Sr nee B.

2.4   naka (?< *na*1.3a* -ka*1.x*). 'inside'. LH - 1-1-B A-B-C. NS (102b) LH;
NS (T 35) LL. Km (S,W) LH. Mr (Bm) LH(-H). Edo LH. Ib L = 2.4. Sd naha(a) A:
Nase naa A̲ (H 1967:220). Sr naaka B / naka-. Yn naga C (H 1964:184, but 71a
has B (mistake?)) 'friendly relationship', C (H 1967) 'inside'.

?3.5a   nakaba < *naka*s.4* (< ...) -n- pa*1.3a*. 'middle; half'. LxL - 0/2/3-
2[U]/1:3[H]-B x-B-x. NS (129a) xLL, (Okada) LLH. Sz 2.

?3.4, ?3.7a   nakago < *nakagwo < *naka*s.4* -n- kwo*1.1*. 'center, core'. LLL - 2/0-
1:3-x x-B-x. Sr nakaguu B.

5.8   nakago-gati < *nakagwo*?3.4,?3.7a* (< ...) -n- kat[a-C]i*B*. 'being pithy'.
LLLHH - x-x-x x-x-x.

4.11   nakagoro < *naka*s.4* (< ...) -n- koro*s.2b*. 'midway'. LLHL - 0/2-0-B x-B-x.
K: Edo HLLL.

4.11   naka-hi*t*/*d*aa < naka-fi*t*/*d*aa < ?*naka*s.4* (< ...) pi(n)ta*s.s* ('center pleat').
'the very center/core'. LLHL - x-x-x x-x-x.

3.4   nakama < *naka*s.4* (< ...) ma*1.1*. 'companion'. x - 3-1:3[H]/2[U]-B x-x-x.
Aomori, Narada, Hattō, Hamada 3; Matsue 3/0; Izumo 0. Ib F = 3.4, H1 = 3.3.

3.x   nakara < *naka*s.4* -ra (< *[a]ra*s.s* < *ara-*B*). 'middle'. x - 1/0-2-x x-B-x.

?4.5   nakayama < *naka*s.4* (< ...) dama*s.s*. 'Nakayama' (placename). x - 0-1:3[H]-
B x-B-x. Km (W) LLLL. Sr nakeema B.

2.5   nama. 'raw'. x - 1-1:3-B B-B-C. Km x. Ib L2 = 2.5.

3.1   namae < na-mafe < *na mafye < ?*na*1.s* ma-piCa*s.s*. 'name'. x - 0-0-A x-B-x.
Hakata 1 (we expect 2), ygr 0. Ib H = 3.1. Nk x.

5.7   namaenoki < *namaye-no-kiy < *nama$_{g.g}$ ye$_{?1.g}$ no ko-Ci$_{1.ga}$ ('raw-branch
tree'). 'Vitex cannabifolia (used to make arrowshafts)' (= modern ninzin-boku).
LLLLH - x-x-x x-x-x. Cf. hama-hai.

3.6   namai < namawi < *nama$_{g.g}$ bi$_{1.gb}$. 'arrowhead (plant), Sagittaria trifolia'
(= modern omodaka). LHH - x-1-x x-x-x.

?3.2b   namako < *nama-$_g$ ko$_{1.ga}$ ('slippery sea-cucumber', *see* namer-u). 'sea-
cucumber'. x - 3/2-2-A x-x-x. Km x. Aomori, Sz 3; Hattō, Hamada, Matsue. Izumo
2; Goka-mura 0. Ib H1 = 3.3. Register incongruent with etymology?

3.7a   namari (< ?). 'lead'. LHL - 0-1:3-B x-B-x. Aomori 2; Narada, Hattō,
Hamada, Matsue, Izumo, Goka-mura, Hiroshima, Wakamatsu 0; Hakata 1, ygr 0.
Ōsaka, Ise 1:3; Ib L2 = 3.5/7.

3.4   namasu (?< *nama$_{g.g}$ su[k[a-C]i]$_B$ 'raw slice'). '(a salad of) thin-sliced
raw fish'. LLL - 3/0-2-B x-B-x. NS (115b) xxL. Km x. Aomori. Hattō, Hamada,
Matsue, Izumo 3. Ib F = 3.4.

4.5   namazii < namazifyi < *nama$_{g.g}$ (-n-) sip[a-C]i$_{?A}$ (cf. [siu]), Ch.6).
'half-hearted, unsatisfactory, rash, indiscrete' *(adv, adj-n)*. LLLL - 0-1-A
x-x-x. (In modern Japanese an adverb, namazi.)

3.4   namazu < namadu < *namantu (?< *nama-$_g$ 'slippery'). 'catfish'. LLL - 0-2-B
x-x-x. Narada, Matsue, Izumo 0; Goka-mura 0 *(expected reflex)*; Hattō, Hamada 3.
Ib F = 3.4, L = 3.6.

2.1   name (< ?). 'diarrhea'. HH - x-2-x x-x-x.

4.10   namekuzi < namekuti (Ck) / namekudi (Shinsen-Jikyō) < *name[y] - ku(n)ti
?< *nama-Ci[-Ci]$_B$ kutu-Ci$_{g.1}$ ('slippery mouth'). 'slug'. LHLL - 3/4-4-x x-x-x.
Sz 4; Hakata 3/2. Also namekuzi-ra/-ri.

4.11   nameraka < *namyeraka < *nanpiCa-ra-ka. 'smooth, slippery' *(adj-n)*. LLxx
(= *LLHL)- 2-4-B x-x-x. Cf. nadaraka; namer-u; [name-], [nabero-].

2.1   nami 'you': Sd nam[yi] A ?< na-m[ut]i. *See* namu(-), nanzi; na. nare.

2.3   nami < namyi < *nami. 'wave'. LL - 2-2-B B-B-B. Km (S,W) LL. Edo HL. Izumo
0; Narada, Hattō, Hamada, Matsue, Goka-mura, Hiroshima (etc.) 2. Ib F = 2.3.
Onna naamii B. Cf. naori; namu$_A$ 'line up' (but register incongruent); Paekche
*namu/*nami 'sea' (Toh 1981:28).

3.5b   namida < namyi^t/$_d$a < *nami(n)ta (< ?). 'tear(drops)'. LLH - 1(<*2)-2-B
x-B-B. Km (S) nanta (= nanda) LLH. Edo HLL. Sapporo, Numazu, Nagano (Kudō
1978), Narada, Hamada, Goka-mura, Hiroshima, Wakamatsu, NE Kyūshū. Ōita 2:
Hakata 1, ygr 2; western Mino (= SW Gifu) 1/2; Hattō 2/0; Hida (= northern
Gifu), Matsue, Izumo 0; Tappi, Aomori, Akita 3. Hyōgo, Kōchi 2; Toyama, Suzu 2
(we expect 1:3); Ib F = 3.4. Yn nuda B. See Ch. 2.

5.6   namidatari < namitatari (Mg) ?< *namyi^t/$_d$a-tare < *nami(n)ta$_{g.gb}$
tara-Ci[-Ci]$_B$. 'an acupuncture point 2 cm. below the eye'. LLLLL - x-x-x x-x-x.

3.7x   namomi (< ?). 'cocklebur' (= [w]onamomi). LHL - x-x-x x-x-x.

2.1 < 3.1 namu(-). 'you'. *HH < na-mu[ti] HHH. Cf. na, nami, nanzi, nare.

?4.5, ?4.1   namu-^{t}/$_d$ati < na-mu[ti] -tati. 'you all'. HLLL/HHxx - x-x-x x-x-x.
Km (S) nandati HHLL.

3.1   na-muzi = na-mudi < na-muti: *see* nanzi.

2.3   nana(-). 'seven'. LL-... - 1-2-B (x)-B-(x). Km (W) nana-se 'many rapids'
LL-H. Sz 1/2. Ib H1 = 2.2. Cf. nana-tu, nana-so, nanoka, nana-tokoro.

?3.4, ?3.5x   nanae < nana-fye < *nana$_{g.g}$ piCa$_{1.x}$ (?pira$_{?g.gb}$). 'seven/many layers'.
x - 2-3-B x-x-x. NS (Okada) LLL; NS (T+ 74) LL(|)H. K: Hn LLF.

?3.7b, ?3.4   naname, (Hn /) nanome (< ?). 'aslant'. LLL - 2-1:3[H]/0[U]-B x-(B)-x.
Edo HHH. Aomori, Narada, Hattō, Matsue, Izumo, Goka-mura, Hakata 2. Ib
F = 3.4, H2 = 3.2. Sr nanbeei B < verb nanbeer- ← nanbee- ?< *nanV-(n-)pap-i.
Cf. nadareru; nazo[f]e 'aslant', na^s/$_z$oeru 'cut aslant' ?< *nan[a]- swopa-Ci-.

4.2   nanariso (< ?; cf. Ch 'tsaw 'seaweed'). 'gulfweed, sargasso' (= modern
hondawara). HHHL - x-x-x x-x-x.

?3.5x   nanaso < nana$_{s.s}$ -swo$_{1.x}$. 'seventy'. LLH-⋯ - x-x-x x-x-x.

5.16   nana-tokoro < *nana$_{s.s}$ tokoro$_{s.1a}$. 'seven [storehouses]'. x - 2-4-x x-x-x.
NS (113a) LLLHL.

?3.5b   nanatu < *nana$_{s.s}$ -tu$_{1.x}$. 'seven'. x - 2-2-B (A/B)-B-B. Mr (Bm) HLL.
Edo HLL. Aomori, Sz, Hata, Hakata 2. Ib F = 3.4.

?4.8   nanbito < *nani fyito < *nani$_{s.4}$ pito$_{s.se}$. 'who'. (x) - 0-1-B x-x-x.
Km (S) LHHH.

2.4   nani. 'what; something'. (LH) - 1-1-B (B)-(B)-(A). NS (95b, 105b, 110b) LH;
NS (T 114, 116) LH, (T 128) HH. Km (S,W) LH(-H). Mr (Bm) LH(-H). Edo LH. Hakata
nan 0. Ib L = 2.4. Sd, Sr, Yn nuu: see na(-). Ōsaka nan[i] zo (LLH) 'something'
(= nani ka).

4.8   nanigoto < *nani$_{s.4}$ koto$_{s.s}$. 'what (event/thing)'. x - 0-1-B x-x-x.
Km (S) LHHH. K: Edo LLHH. Sz 0.

4.8   nanimono (= nani-mono) < *nani$_{s.4}$ mono. 'what (thing)'. x - 0-1-B x-x-x.
Km (S) LHHH. K: Edo LLHH.

3.4   naniwa < nanifa < *nanipa (< ?). 'Naniwa' (an old name for Ōsaka). x - 0-
1[H]/1:3[U]-A x-x-x. NS (71b) LLL; (71c [11:189-M]) nanifa(-)fvito LLL(|)HL.
NS (T+ 48, 51) LHH, (T+ 101) LHL. Km (W) LHH. K: "Hn LLL?; Km LLL or LHH?".

4.5 = 3.4(|)1.3, ?4.6   naniwazu < nanifa-du < *nanipa$_{s.4}$ -n- tu$_{1.3a}$. 'Naniwa port'
(old placename). x - 0-0-x x-x-x. Km (W) LLL(|)L, LLLH, LHHH.

3.4   nanoka, nanuka (?< *nanwo-ka; ?< *nana-uka; ?< *nana-[t]u$_{s.sh}$ ka$_{?1.3a}$).
'seven days'. x - 3/0-2-x B-(B)-x. Edo HHL/HHH. 1700 Ōsaka HHL. Aomori 0/3.
Narada 0. Ib F = 3.4. Sr nanka B 'weekly Buddhist memorial service'.

3.1   nanzi < nandi < na-m[u]di < *na$_{1.1}$ -muti$_{s.x}$ (?< *mutiy < *mutu-Ci). 'you'.
HHH - 0/1-2-A x-x-x. Km (S) HHH, nandi-ra 'you all' HHH-H. Mr (Bm) HHH.
Edo HHH. Hiroshima 1. Ōsaka 3; Ise 0.

?2.4, ?2.5   nao < nafo < *napo. 'straight; ordinarily; furthermore; better'.
LH/LL - 1-1-A x-x-x. Km (S) nao-si LH-L, (W) nao-koso LH-LL. Mr (Bm) LH.
K: "Km and since" LF (misleading? cf. Kt). Ib L = 2.4. Cf. sunao; [nao-]$_{adj B}$;
naoru, naosu.

?3.4   naobi < nafo^b/$_{m}$i ?< *nafobyi < *napo$_{adj B}$ -n[a]-p[a-C]i (inf of lost
verb?). 'restoring regularity, change of bad to good, change from disaster to
fortune)': ~ no kami 'the god who restores regularity'. See oo-naobi.

3.1   naori < na-wori ?< *na[myi] wori < *nami$_{s.s}$ bor[a-C]i$_{s}$. 'wave upon wave'.
x - x-x-x x-x-x. NS (Okada) HHH; NS (T+ 87) LLH. Register incongruent with
etymology.

2.3   nara. 'Japanese oak'. LL - 1-2-A x-x-x. Km x. Sz 1. Ib H = 2.1.

?2.2b   nara. 'Nara' (placename). x - 1-2-A x-x-x. Km x. NS (72b) HL; NS (T 95)
HH, (T 54) LL. Km (W) HL/LL. K: Edo HL. Ib H1 = 2.2. Perhaps borrowed from
Korean na'lah 'nation'; one phonogram version (NS 95) could be taken as naraku.
Cf. Lee Ki-Moon 1980 ("Ewen swucey"); Paekche *ra/*na 'land' (Toh 1981:28).

3.4   narai < narafyi < *nara-p[a-C]i$_{s}$. 'custom, practice'. (x) - 2-0-B x-B-x.
Km (S) LLL. Sr naree B. Edo HHL.

?2.5, ?2.4   nare < *na -re (?< *na$_{1.1}$ [a]ra-Ci$_{s}$). 'you'. x - 1-1-x x-x-x.
NS (Okada) LH. NS (T 104) HH — This accords with Ōno's text; the phonogram
is PRESS. Aiso has THAT/WHAT (na L); so does Tsuchihashi, but he may have
inadvertently switched phonograms with the syllable that begins the next word
(narikyeri). Km (W) LH(-L)/HH(-H). K: Hn-Km LF "?". Cf. na, namu, nami, nanzi.

2.3   nari < *na-r[a-C]i$_{s}$. 'shape; appearance'. LL - 2-2-B x-B-x. NS (118b) LL.
Km (W) LL. 1700 Ōsaka HL.

5.8   narihisago < narif/ɓisako < *nar[a-C]iᴮ fisa(-)ᵏ/ɑo (< ...). 'gourd,
calabash'. LLLHH - 3/4-x-x x-x-x.

4.5   nariwai < narifafyi < *nar[a-C]iᴮ (-)pap[a-C]iʙₑₐ v. 'livelihood;
occupation; farming'. LLLL - 0/3-1-x x-x-x.

3.5a/b   nasake (?< *naₐdⱼ ᴮ -saₛᵤf keyᵧₗ.ₗ (< ?) 'feeling of absence').
'sentiment, sympathy'. LLH (Zs) / LHH - 3/0/1-2-B x-B-x. Km (S) LLH, Edo HLL.
Narada 2; Aomori, Hattō, Hamada, Matsue, Izumo, Wakamatsu 3; Goka-mura 0;
Hakata 0, ygr 1. Ib F = 3.4.

?2.2a   nasi. 'pear'. HL - 2-2-A x-x-x. Km (W) HL. 1700 Ōsaka HL. Narada 0:
Yamaguchi (Kobayashi, also Hōgen to hyōjun-go 302), Goka-mura 1; Hamada,
Hattō 2. Toyama 2; Suzu 2 (we expect 1:3); Ib H1 = 2.2.

2.5   nasu (? truncation of nasubiₐ.ₒb). 'eggplant'. x - 1-2-B x-(B)-x. Tappi,
Sz, Narada, Hata, Wakamatsu 1. Kōchi 1:3 (Doi 1952:22); Ib H1 = 2.2.

3.5b   nasubi (< ?). 'eggplant'. x - 1-2-B x-B-x. Km x. 1700 Ōsaka HLL. K: Hn
LLH (where attested?). Aomori 2; Hakata 2, ygr 1. Ib L = 3.6. Sr naaṣibi B.

2.1   nata. 'hatchet'. x - 0-0-A B-x-x. Km x. Sz 0. Cf. na, ono, katana.

?3.5a   natane < *naₗ.ₛₐ tana-Ciₐ.₄ (< ...). 'rape(weed)' (= abura-na). x - 2-
2[U]/1:3[H]-B x-x-x. Aomori 3; Hattō, Hamada, Wakamatsu 2; Hakata 2, ygr 0;
Matsue, Izumo 0; Goka-mura 1.

2.2a   natu. 'summer'. x - 2-2-A A-A-A. Km (W) HL(-x). Edo HL. Okayama 1 (Hōgen
to hyōjun-go 302). Aomori 0. Toyama 2; Suzu 1 (we expect 1:3); Ib H1 = 2.2.

3.1   natume (?< natuₐ.ₒb [u]meyₐ.ₗ (< ...) 'summer plum'). 'jujube (fruit/
tree)'. HHH - 0-1[H]/0[U]-A x-x-x. Aomori 0; Sz 2.

4.1   natumusi < *natuₐ.ₒb musiₐ.ₗ. 'summer insects; firefly'. x - 2-3-x x-x-x.
NS (71b [11:178-M]) HHHH(-no̯ H); NS (T+ 49) LHHH. Km (W) HHHL.

2.3   nawa < nafa < *napa. 'rope'. LL - 2-2-B B-B-x. Ongi LL. Km (W) LL. 1700
Ōsaka HL. Ib F = 2.3. Yn nna B < *tuna. Cf. nau < nafu < *napa-ᴮ 'twist,
weave into rope'.

2.3   nawa(-) < nafa(-) < *napa 'seedling': see nae.

4.5   nawasaba < nafasaba < *napaₐ.ₛ sanpaₐ.ₗ (or "nafasaba" = nawasaba <
*na[m]aₐ.ₛ sanpaₐ.ₗ, cf. Ir namasa["]fa). 'dolphin' (= iruka). LLLL - x-1-x
x-x-x.

3.4   nawate < nafa-te[y] < *napaₐ.ₛ ta-Ciₗ.ₛₐ ('rope hand'). '(hand)line,
rope'; (?< *nafaₐ.ₛ tiᵧₗ.ₗ < ... 'seedling path') 'footpath between rice
fields'. LLL - 0-2-x x-x-x. Edo HHL.

4.11   nawazemi < nafaᵃ/ₓemi < *napaₐ.ₛ (-n-) semiₐ.ₛₐ (< ...). 'female (= mute)
cicada' (= o[o]si-zemi). LLHL - x-x-x x-x- x. NKD: "also -sebi".

3.2x   nayosi (?< naₗ.ₐ yo-siₐdⱼ ᴮ ₚᵣₑd 'is fortunate in name' [cf. ōno]). 'grey
mullet fingerling' (fish) (= ina). HHL - x-x-x x-x- x.

4.3   nayoᵗ/ₐake < naywo-takey < *nadwo₍ᴮ₎ (-n-) taka-Ciₐ.ₗ. 'pliant bamboo'.
HHLL - x-x-x x-x-x. Km (W) HHLL. Cf. naeru, nayo-nayo.

3.1   nazasi < *naₗ.ₐ (-n-) sas[a-C]iᴮ. 'designation; naming/name'. HHH - 0-0-A
x-A-x.

?2.5 < ?3.7b   nazo̲ < na[a]ₗ.ₒb ᵃ/ₓo (or < *nan[i]ₐ.₄ soₚ𝒸ₗ). (1) 'why' (= naze).
R(|)L - 1-1:3-x x-x-x; Km (S nanzo, W) HL; Narada 2; Sz 1 (= na-site 1).
(2) 'riddle'. x - 0/2[Mkz, Hiroto]-1[H]/1:3[U]-A x-x-x; Tappi, Hattō, Hamada,
Matsue, Izumo, Hakata 0; Sz, Narada, Goka-mura 2; Aomori 2 (expected) = older
nanzyo 1. Ib L2 = 2.5. Mg: nazo mo RH-L, nazo ya xL-H.

3.4   nazuki < nadukyi < *na(n)tuki (< ?). 'brain; [NE dial.] head, forehead'.
LLL - x-0-x x-x-x. Edo HHL.

3.5a   nazuna < naduna < ?*nantuₐ.ₓ naₗ.ₛₐ. 'shepherd's purse'. LHx (?= *LHH) -
0-1[U]/0[H]-B-x x-x-x.

3.x < 4.9 = 2.4|2.2 nazure < *nan[i]₂.₄ sure[y] *(2.2)* (< *s[o]-ura-Ci_A): ~ so RHL-H,
~ ka RHx-x 'Why?'.
?1.1   ne ?< *na-Ci (cf. muna/mune < *mu[-Ci] na-Ci). 'peak'. x - x-1-x x-x-x.
Km (W) H/L. Cf. mine, yane.
1.1   ne < *ne[y] < *naCi (?< na[r]i*₂.₁ < *nar[a-C]i_A; ?< na[k]i₂.₁ <
*nak[a-C]i_A; ?< *na-Ci (cf. naku, naru, nasu). 'sound; crying, weeping'.
x - 0-1-A x-A-(A). Km (W) H(-L). Edo F = HL. Sz, Hiroshima 0. Ōsaka, Ise 1.
Ib L = 1.3, *figurative* H = 1.1. Yn naŋui A (cf. naŋori).
1.2   ne ?< *ne[y] < *naCi. 'price'. x - 0-2-A x-A-x. K: Edo HH. Sz, Hiroshima 0.
Ōsaka, Ise 2; Ib H1 = 1.2.
?1.2   ne ?< *ne[y] < *naCi. '(sign of the) rat'. x - 0-2-A x-B-x. Km (S.W) x.
K: Km LL *(where attested?)*, Edo HL. Ib H = 1.1. Cf. nezumi, nora-ne.
1.3a   ne < *ne[y] < *na-Ci. 'root; ?*earth, ground'. L - 1-1-B B-B-B. NS (Okada)
L; NS (T+ 83; 57, 58) L, (T+ 13) H. Km (W) L(-H). Edo R. Ib L = 1.3. Cf. nai:
ni; takanna.
3.4   nebiru < nwobyiru < *nwo₁.₃ₐ -n- piru₂.₁*(?<₂.₃)*. 'wild rocambole' (= nobiru). LLL - 0/1-x-x x-x-x. NKD: "also -f-".
3.1   ne^b/ₘuri < *na-Ci_A - (n[i]) - pu-r[a-C]i*?_A*. 'sleep(iness)'. HHH - 0-0-A
x-A-(A). Hattō 3 (verb B). Yn nindun A 'sleeps'. Km (S) HHH.
3.2b < 4.2   nedoko < ne-doko[ro] < *na-Ci_A -n- tokoro₃.₁ₐ. 'sleeping place,
alcove'. HHxx (Kn) - 3-2[H]/3[U]-A x-x-x. Hattō 3; Aomori, Hamada, Matsue,
Izumo, Goka-mura 0.
3.4   negai < negafyi < neg[iyr]afyi < *nenk^u/₀-Ci-ra-p[a-C]i < *nank^u/wo
-Ci-ra-p[a-C]i₈. 'request'. (L) - 2-0[H]/2[U]-B x-B-(B). NS (129a) LLL. 1700
Ōsaka HHL. Narada, Hamada 3; Aomori, Hattō, Matsue, Izumo 2; Goka-mura 0/1. The
Tk accent is due to monosyllabification. Ib F = 3.4. Yn niŋun B 'request; pray'.
2.5   negi (?< *ne-gi < *na-Ci₁.₃ₐ -n- ki₁.₁ (< ...), *na-gi < *na₁.₃ₐ -n-
ki₁.₁ (< ...) 'root/earth onion'; ? < *nwogi < *nwo₁.₃ₐ -n- ki₁.₁ (< ...)
'field onion'). 'onion'. x - 1-1:3-B x-x-x. Km x. Sz, Hakata 1; Goka-mura 2.
Ib H1 = 2.2. Earliest citation in NKD is 1764. (Cf. nagi₈.₃ 'pickerelweed'.)
4.1   negigoto < *negiy-goto < *nenk^u/₀-Ci[-Ci] -n- koto₂.₃. 'prayer; what is
prayed for'. x - 2-0-x x-x-x. Km (W) HHHH.
3.1   negoto < *ne[y]-goto < *na-Ci[-Ci]_A -n- koto₂.₃. 'sleep-talking'.
HHH - 0-0-A x-A-x.
?2.3, ?2.5   neko < ne*ₘⁱₘ* kwo₁.₁. 'cat'. x - 1-2-B x-x-x. Edo HL. Narada, Hattō,
Hamada, Hiroshima, Hata, Wakamatsu, Hakata 1; Matsue, Izumo 2. Ōsaka [Makimura]
2; Kōchi 1:3 (Doi 1952:22), Kameyama 1:3. The first syllable is thought to be
mimetic; cf. nyao 'miaow'. Similarly mimetic: Sr mayaa/mayuu B, Yn maayu C.
3.4   nemoto < *ne[y]-moto < *na-Ci₁.₃ₐ moto₂.₃. 'root'. x - 3-1:3-B x-B-C.
Km/Mr x.
2.1 (< 3.1)   nemu: nemu-no-ki = nemuri-no-ki x - 1-2-x x-x-x = neburi-no-ki
HHH-··· - x-x-x x-x-x. 'silk tree, Albrizzia julibrissia'. Sz 1. Ib H1 = 2.2.
4.10   nemugoro < nemo^k/ₘgoro: *see* nengoro.
3.1   nemuri: *see* ne^b/ₘuri; (~ no ki) *see* nemu.
5.16   nenasigusa < nenasi-^k/ₘgusa < *ne₁.₃ₐ (< *na-Ci) na-si*adj B pred* (-n-)
kusa₂.₃. 'duckweed'. LHHHL (-g-)/ LLHHL (-k-)- 3-1:4-B x-x-x.
6.21   nenasikazura < nenasi-kadura < *ne₁.₃ₐ(< *na-Ci) na-si*adj B pred*
katura₃.₁. 'dodder, lovevine, Cuscuta japonica'. LLLLHL - 4-x-x x-x-x.
4.10   nengoro(-ni) < nemugoro < nemo^k/ₘgoro (< ?). 'cordial(ly)'. LHLL(-H) -
0-1[H]/0[U]-B x-x-x. Mr (Bm) LHLL.
2.3   neri < *ne[y]r-i < *nay[a]r-i < *nada-r[a-C]i < *nado-r[a-C]i₈.
'tempering, hardening, scouring (thread)'. LL - 2-2-B x-x-x. Km x. Ib F = 2.3.

4.6   neriito < *ne[y]r-i*g.g* (< ...) ito*g.4*. 'scoured thread'. LLLH - 3/0-3-x
         x-x-x.
?6.9, ?6.22   netamasigao < netamasi-ᵏ/ᵍafo < *netamasi[-si]*adj* *B* *pred* (-n-)
         kapo*g.1*. 'a jealous/envious face'. LLLLHH (Kn, -g-) / LLL?LHL (Ck, -k-) -
         0-x-x x-x-x.
?2.1   neya < *ne[y]-ya < *na-Ci[-Ci]*A* da*1.9b*. 'boudoir'. HH - 1-2-x x-x-A.
         Yn nida A.
2.3   nezi < nedi < *nedi[y] < *nentⁿ/ₒ-Ci[-Ci]. 'screw'. x - 1-2-B x-x-x.
         Km x. Sz, Matsue 1; Hattō, Hamada, Izumo, Goka-mura 2.
3.6   neziro < ne-zirwo < *na-Ci*1.9a* -n- sirwo*adj* *B*. 'white-rooted'.
         x - 0-x-x x-x-x. NS (73b) LHH; NS (T+ 58) LHH.
3.6   nezumi < nezumyi (?< *ne(n)-zumi < *na-Ci*1.9a* (n[i]) sum[a-C]i*B*
         'dwell in/on ground'); ?< *nonsumi < *nwo*1.9a* n[i] sum[a-C]i*B* 'dwell in field').
         'rat'. LHH - 0-1(?<1)-B B-x-x. Km x. Ongi LHx. Edo LHH. Matsumoto, Numazu,
         Narada, Hattō, Hamada, Matsue, Izumo, Hiroshima 0; Goka-mura, Wakamatsu,
         NE Kyūshū, Ōita 1; Hakata 1, ygr 0; Sapporo, Aomori *(we expect 1)*, Akita 2.
         Ib L = 3.6.
1.3b   ni < *ni[y] < *no̱-Ci. 'load, burden'. L/R - 1-1-B x-B-x. Km x. 1700
         Ōsaka LH = R. Aomori 0̱. Ib L = 1.3. Cf. nosaki*?9.4*; notori; also (despite
         register incongruity) noru*A*, noseru*A*.
?1.3b   ni. 'earth, dirt; red clay; red, beautiful; *odor'. L - x-x-x x-x-x. Km x.
         Cf. hani, beni; kuni; *na, ne 'root; ...'; Sr niibi B 'hard red earth'; nioi,
         nisiki, nizi. Mochizuki 1971:23 thinks this was 1.3b (R).
?2.3   nibe (< ?). 'croaker *(fish)*; fishglue'. LL - 1/2-0-x x-x-x. Sz 1/2. Ib F =
         2.3. Cf. nikawa.
?2.1a   nie < nife < nifey ?< *ni[fyi - a]fey < *nipi*g.1* (?mipi) apa-Ci[-Ci]*B*.
         'sacrifice of new rice'. HH - 1/2-1-x x- x-x. NS (T+ kun) HH. Km (W) HH.
         Cf. nii(-), niiname, ainbe, niwanoai.
5.8 = 2.3|3.6   nigahisago < "nigabiⁿ/ᵤako" < *ninka*adj* *B* ?pisa-kwo*g.6*. 'gourd.
         calabash'. LL(|)LHH - 3-x-x x-x-x.
3.6   nigana < *ninka*adj* *B* na*1.9a*. 'lettuce; (= rindoo) gentian'. LHH - 0-0-x
         x-x-x. Cf. hama-nigana.
?4.5, ?4.6   nigatake < *niga-takey < *ninka*adj* *B* taka-Ci*g.1* ('bitter bamboo
         [shoots]'). 'Phylostachys bambusoides (= madake); Pleioblastus simonii (=
         medake)'. x - 2-3-x x-B-x. Km (W) LLLL, LLLH, Sr nzaᵗ/ᵤaki B < *nigya-take.
2.3   nige (< ?; cf. niga*adj* *B*'bitter', ke*1.9a* 'meal'). '? cud'. LL - x-x-x
         x-x-x. Cf. nige-ᵏ/ᵍamu *(var. nirekamu)*; mige; kanonigegusa.
2.x   nigi < *nigyi < *ni(n)ki. 'lively': *see* nigiyaka; nigiwau, nigiwasu:
         niginigisi-.
2.1   nigi(-) < nikyi(-) < *niki (?< *nikwo with vowel assimilation). 'soft'.
         See following entries.
?3.2x, ?3.1   nigime < nikyi-mey < *niki*?g.1* ?mo[-Ci]*1.x*. 'a kind of seaweed' (=
         wakame). HHx (K: "HHL")- x-0-x x-x-x.
4.11   nigiraka < *nikyi-raka < *niki*?g.1* -ra-ka. 'oily smooth, sleek'. LLHL -
         x-x-x x-x-x.
-        nigiri: *see* migiri.
4.1   nigitae < (Hn) nikitafe < nikyi tafey < *niki*?g.1* tapaCi*?g.1* ('soft bark-
         cloth'). 'fine-woven cloth'. HHHH (K: "LLLL" *misprint?*) - x-0-x x-x-x.
4.11   nigiyaka < *nigyi-yaka < *ni(n)ki -da-ka. 'lively, bustling' *(adj-n)*.
         x - 2-4-B - x-x-x. Sz 3. Earliest attestation 13th century.
3.4   nigori < nigor-i < *ni(n)ko̱-r[a-C]i*B* (< ...). 'muddiness'.
         LLL - 3-2[H]/0[U]-B x-B-x. Km x. Sr mingwi B.

5.6   nigorizake < (*)nigori-ᵃ/₂akey< *ni(n)ko̲-r[a-C]i (-n-) saka-Ci₂.₁.
'unrefined sake'. LLLLL (-s-) - 3-4-B x-x-x.

4.5   niguruma < *ni₁.₃ₐ (?< *no̲-Ci) -n- kuruma₃.₁. 'wagon, cart'.
x - 2-1:3[H]/0[U]-B x-B-x. NS (122b) LLLL. Sz 2.

2.1   nii(-) < nifyi < *nipi (?< *mipi). 'new'. HH - 0-0-A A-A-x. Sd, Sr mii- A.
See Ch. 1, §35.

5.2 = 2.1|3.2 niimagusa < nifimagusa ?< *nifyi-makusa *(despite NKD)* < *nipi₂.₁
(?*mipi) makusa₃.₃ₐ (< ma-₂₁.₁ kusa₂.₃) ('new forage'). 'Euphorbia adenochlora,
a kind of spurge'. HH(|)HHL - x-x-x x-x-x.

?4.1, ?4.2   niiname < nifiname ?< nifyi-nafey < *nipi₂.₁ (? *mipi) n[o̲]
apa-Ci[-Ci]ᴮ. 'the court ceremony of sacrificing new rice' (= niwanoai).
HHHH (Kn) / HHHL (Ck) - 0-x-x x-x-x.

3.1   nikawa < nikafa < *ni[-Ci]/ni[Ca-Ci]ₐ kapa₂.₃ ('boil skin'). 'glue'.
HHH - 0-0-A A-A-A. Ongi HHH. K: Hn-Mr HHH. Ib H = 3.1.

?2.1   niki(-) (?< nikwo) 'soft': *see* nigi(-); [nikibiru]. [nikimu].

3.4   nikibi, [dial.] nikubi/nikumu < nikimi (Hn) < *nikuᵇ/ₘyi (with vowel
assimilation) < *nikunpi (?= *nikumi < *niku -m[a-C]iᴮ). 'pimple'. LLL-⋯ -
1̲-2-B x-B-x. Sz 2; Hattō 2/3; Hamada 1; Matsue, Izumo 0; Goka-mura 0 *(expected
reflex)*; Ib F = 3.4.   Sr nikun B.

5.6   nikimibana < *nikunpi/?nikumi₃.₄ (-n-) pana₂.₁. 'pimply nose'. LLLLL -
x-x-x x-x-x.

?2.1/?2.4 niko(-) < nikwo(-). 'soft'. HH (Kz) / LH (Kn) - x-x-x x-x-x. Cf. nigi- <
niki-?₂.₁; nikoge₃.₂ₐ.

3.2a   nikoge < (*)nikwo-gey < *nikwo?₂.₁ -n- ka-Ci?₁.₁. 'down(y hair)'. HHL -
0-0̲-x x-x-x.

2.3   niku (< Ch nhyu̲k). 'meat'. x - 2-2-B B-B-B. Km x. Sz 2. Kōchi 0 (Hattori
1973); Ib H̲1 = 2.2.

2.3   niku (< Ch nhyo̲k). 'a wool mattress/blanket'. LL - x-2-x x-x-x.

3.5b   nimotu < *ni₁.₃ₐ (< ...) (-)motu. 'baggage'. x - 1(<*2)-2-B x-B-x. Narada,
Hattō, Hamada, Yamaguchi, Wakamatsu, NE Kyūshū, Hakata 1; Aomori, Sz, Matsue,
Izumo, Goka-mura 2. Ib H̲1 = 3.3. Is -motu from Ch m(b)[y]wet 'thing' or from
mo̲t[a-]uᴮ '[that which] holds'?

2.3   nina < myina < *mina. 'snail'. LL - 2-2-x ?B-x-x. Sd myinyaa B 'shell'.
(Sr nna A 'empty' is from muna; *see* muda.)

4.x < 3.x ninniku, "also niniku" (?< *ni[ku]-niku₄ₐdⱼ ᴮ 'hateful [smell]'; ?< *ni₁.₃ₐ
niku₄ₐdⱼ ᴮ '*odor hateful'). 'garlic'. x - 0-4[H]/0[U]-B x-x-x. Km x. Sz 0.
Usually said to be < ninniku-faramitu (< Ch) 'kṣānti pāramitā = forbearance,
third of the six ascetic practices'. Not attested before 1700s?

?3.7a   ninuri < *ni₁.₃ₐ nur[a-C]iₐ. 'varnishing with red; a red-varnished thing'.
LHL - 0-0̲-x x-x-x.

2.2b   nio < nifwo/myifwo < (*nipwo/)*mipwo. 'grebe' (= kaituburi, *bird*). HL -
1-2-x x-x-x. Km x. Dialect miyo, myoo, muyo.

?4.1, ?4.2   niodori < nifodori < nifwo/myifwo-do̲ri < *(nipwo/)mipwo₂.₂ₐ -n-
to̲ri₂.₁. x - x-3-x x-x-x. NS (T+ 29) HHHH. Km (W) HHHL.

3.4   nioi < nifofyi < *ni?₁.₃ [o]po-p[a-C]iᴮ *or* *ni?₁.₃-pa-p[a-C]i. 'odor;
showing red, being beautiful'. (L) - 2̲(<*3)-2-B x-B-x. Km (W) LLL. Mr (Bm) HHL.
Edo HHL. Aomori, Hamada 2; Narada, Hattō 3; Matsue, Izumo 0 (verb A); Goka-
mura 1̲ (verb B). The Tk accent retreat is due to monosyllabification. Ib F =
3.4, L̲ = 3.6.

5.6   nioiuma < niofyiuma < *ni₁.₃ₐ op[a-C]iₐ uma₂.₃. 'packhorse'. LLLLL - x-x-x
x-x-x.

?4.1, ?A|3.6   ni(-)omoi ‹ ni-omof[y]i ‹ *ni[-Ci]/ni[Ca-Ci]*ᴀ* o- (‹ *o[po]*adj B*)
mopi*s.2b* ('boiled esteeemed-water'). 'boiled drinking water'. "HLHH" (?= *HHHH,
?= H|LHH) - x-3-x x-x-x. K: Hn HHHH.

2.3   nira ‹ myira ‹ *mira. 'leek'. x - 0/2-2-B x-x-x. Mg name-mira HHxx.
Sz, Matsue 1; Izumo, Hattō, Hamada 2; Goka-mura 0. Ib F = 2.3. Cf. oonira.

2.2a   nire (‹ nure ‹ *nure[y] ‹ *nura-Ci[-Ci]*ᴀ* 'be slippery-sticky'). 'yew
(tree)'. x - 0/1-2-A x-x-x. Km x. Sz 1. Ib F = 2.3. Awaji nure, Hida nere.

2.1   nisi. 'west; (Ryūkyū) north'. HH - 0-0-A A-A-A. Km (S) HH. Mr (Bm) HH.
Edo HH. Ib H = 2.1.

4.1   nisigawa ‹ nisigafa ‹ *nisi*s.1* -n- kapa*s.2b*. 'the Katsura river in the
west of Kyōto (as contrasted with the Kamo river in the east)'. x - 0-x-x
x-x-x. Km (W) HHHH. Mr (W 18) HHHL. Sz 0.

3.5b   nisiki ‹ nisikyi ‹ *ni*?1.5b* sik[a-C]i*ᴀ*. 'brocade'. LHH - 1(‹*2)-2-B x-B-x.
NS (Okada) LLH; NS (T+ 66) HLH. Km x. Edo HLL. 1700 Ōsaka HHL. Tappi, Aomori,
Akita, Hattō, Goka-mura 2; western Mino (= SW Gifu) 1/2; Sapporo, Matsumoto,
Numazu, Narada, Ōita 1; Hakata 1/0; Hiroshima 0; Matsue, Izumo 0/3. Ib H1 = 3.3.

5.16   nisikihebi ‹ nisikifemi ‹ *nisikyi*s.5b* feymyi*s.6* (‹ ...). 'Indian python;
rock snake'. LLLHL - 4-4[H]/5[U]-B x-x-x. Sz 4.

4.5   nitutuzi ‹ *ni*?1.3* tutunsi*?3.3*. (1) (= yama-tutuzi) 'Rhododendron
obtusum'; (2) (= miyama-sikimi) 'Skimmia japonica'. LLLL - x-x-x x-x-x.

2.1   niwa ‹ nifa ‹ *nipa (?= *ni*?1.5b* pa*1.3a* but register is incongruent).
'yard; garden'. HH - 0-0-A A-A-x. NS (74b [14:26-M], 83b [17:118-M]) HH; NS
(T 74, 96) HH. Km (W) HH. Mr (Bm) HH. Edo HH. Ib (rare) H = 2.1. Cf. ba, ma.

?3.1   niwabi ‹ nifabi ‹ *nifa-biy ‹ *nipa*s.1* -n- po-Ci*1.5a*. 'yard torch, garden
light'. LLx (odd, as is the following Mg entry; see kadobi) - 0-0-x x-x-x.
K: Hn HHH (inferred? cf. Ch. 4, §10.4, Rule 5).

3.7b   niwaka ‹ nifaka ‹ nipa-ka (‹ ?; cf. nii). 'sudden'. LHL - 1-1:3-A x-x-x.
Km x. Mr (Bm) LHL. Edo LHL. Aomori, Sz 2. Ib L2 = 3.5/7.

6.3   niwakunaburi ‹ nifa-kunaburi (‹ *nipa*s.1* + ?). 'wagtail' (= sekirei,
bird). HHHHLL - x-0-x x-x-x.

4.1/4.2   niwakusa ‹ nifa-kusa ‹ *nipa*s.1* kusa*s.3*. 'yard grass; (= hooki-gi)
broom(-tree)'. HHHH (Ir) / HHHL (Kn) - 0-0-x x-x-x. K: Hn HHHH.

-           niwanai: see niwanoai.

5.4   niwanoai ‹ nifano-afyi ?‹ *nif[yi]-a[fey] no afyi ‹ *nipi*s.1* (?mipi)
apa-Ci[-Ci]*B* no ap[a-C]i*B*. 'the court ceremony of sacrificing new rice'.
x - x-x-x x-x-x. NS (107b) HHLLL.

3.1   niwaso ‹ nifa-so ‹ *nipa*s.1* so/swo*?1.1* ('yard cloth [= cover]'). 'spurge,
euphorbia'. HHH (Ir)- x-0-x x-x-x.

5.2   niwatazumi ‹ nifatadumyi ‹ *nifa-tatu-myi ‹ *nipa*s.1* tat[a]-u*B* mi[na]*s.1*
(or mi[ntu]*s.1a* ‹ ...). 'standing water (floodwater, rainwater); puddle'.
HHHHL - x-4-x x-x-x.

4.1   niwatori ‹ nifatori (= nifa -tu tori) ‹ *nipa*s.1* tori*s.1*. 'chicken'.
HHHH - 0-0-B x-B-x. Km x. K: Edo HHHH. Sz 0; Hakata (expected) 2, ygr 0.

5.1   niwatutori ‹ nifatutori ‹ *nipa*s.1* -tu*pcl* tori*s.1*. 'yardbird, chicken'.
x - x-x-x x-x-x. NS (83b [187:118- M]) HH-H(|)HH; NS (T+ 96) HH-L|HH.

4.2   niwa-tuzu/-tutu ‹ nifa-tuᵗ/ᵈu ‹ *nipa*s.1* tu(n)tu*?* (‹ ?). 'Cantharis,
Spanish fly' (= tuti-hanmyoo, a kind of beetle). HHHL - x-x-x x-x-x.

5.2   niwazakura ‹ nifa-zakura ‹ *nipa*s.1* -n- sakura*s.1*. 'Prunus glandulosa'.
HHHHx (?= *HHHHL) - 3-x-x x-x-x.

?2.2a ‹ ?3.3   nizi ‹ ?*ni(i)nsi (?‹ ni*?1.5b* m[u]si*s.1* 'red/beautiful *snake').
'rainbow'. HL (?FL, see Ch. 4, §7.2) - 2/0[new]-2-A x-(B)-x. Ongi FL. Tappi,
Goka-mura 2; Aomori, Narada [nodži] 0; Hattō, Hamada, Matsue, Izumo, NE

Kyūshū 1; Hakata *(expected)* 1, ygr 0. Ib F = 2.3, formerly myoozi H2 = 3.1.
Sr nuuzi B ?< *nogi. Dialect: Iwate no[o]zi, Akita nogi, Ōita myoozi, Fukuoka
meuzi, Tottori nyoozi, Shizuoka and Shimane neezi. K 1977a:143 says the accent
variation is due to the variety of forms used for the word: /nizi/ was adopted
late and given the "prevailing-type" accent. OJ variant nwozi (Ōno, but his
ambiguous notation may mean just nozi?) or nuzi (Zdb). The -g- forms are a
puzzle. On the final nasal of Hateruma noozïn see Ch. 1, §52.

1.3a   no̲. 'arrow bamboo, bamboo for making arrows; arrowshaft'. L - 1-x-x x-x-x.
K: Hn LL, Edo LH.

1.3a   no < nwo. 'field'. x - 1-1-B x-(B)-B. NS (79a [14:313-M], 83b [17:119-M])
L; NS (T+ 78) L, (T+ 35) H. Km (W) L(-H). Edo R. Ib *(rare)* L = 1.3. Nk moo C
'hill, field, moor', Sr moo B; Yn nuu B (H 1964:64a). Hateruma nuun (cf. Ch. 1,
§52). (Nk and Sr moo a puzzle; cf. Middle Korean 'moyh 'uncultivated field'.)

?1.3b   no (? < [nu]no < *[nu]nwo$_{2.1}$). 'counter for lengths of cloth; a length of
cloth'. x - x-0-x x-x-x. Km x. K: Hn LL *(where attested?)*, Edo LH. (Kt accent
artificial?)

1.3b   no̲-. 'burden'. *See* ni.

4.5   noasobi < (*)nwo-aswobyi < *nwo$_{1.3a}$ a(-)swonp[a-C]i$_A$. 'an excursion to the
moors; a picnic'. x - 1-1:3-x x-B-x. NS (113b) LLLL. Sr mooqaşibii B.

-         nobara: *see* nohara.

2.3   nobe < nobey < *nonpa-Ci[-Ci]$_B$. 'stretching; what is stretched out (flat);
... '. (*LL)- 1/2-2-B x-B-x. Km x. Sz 1. Ib H1 = 2.2.

?2.4 (?= 1.3|1.1), ?2.5   nobe < nwo-["]fye [semantograms only] < *nwo$_{1.3a}$ (-n-)
piCa$_{1.x}$. 'field'. x - 1-2-B x-x-x. Km (W) LH(-L [no]). Edo LF.

?2.4, ?2.5   nobi < (*)nwo-biy < *nwo$_{1.3a}$ po-Ci$_{1.3b}$. 'wild/field fire'. x - 1-2-B
x-x-x. Km (W) LH. Sz, Hiroshima 1. Ōsaka, Ise 1/1:3.

?3.7a/b   nobiru < *nwo-f/ʙyiru < *nwo$_{1.3a}$ (-n-) piru$_{2.1(?<*2.3)}$. 'wild leek' (=
kobiru, araragi). x - 0/1-1:3-x x- x-x. Km x. Sz *(rare)* 0/1. Hiroshima 0/2.
Ōsaka, Ise 1:3. ("Also nef/ʙiru, nubiru.")

3.1   nobori < nofori < *nopor[a-C]i$_A$. 'climb'. (H) - 0-0-A x-A-x. Km x. Edo
HHH. On -b- see Ch. 2. Sz 0; Hakata 1 *(we expect 2)*, ygr 0. Ib H = 3.1.

6.1 = 3.1|3.1   noborikudari < nofori$_{3.1}$ kudari$_{3.1}$ < *nopo-r[a]C]i$_A$ kunta-r[a-C]i$_A$.
'ascent and descent, up and down'. HHH(|)HHH - 0/4-4[U]/5[H]-A x-A-x.

3.5b   nodati < *nwo$_{1.3a}$ (-n-) tati$_{2.3}$ (< ...). 'a kind of dagger'. LLH - 1-0-x
x-x-x.

2.4 < 3.5x   nodo < nom[u]do < nomido < nomyi-do < ?nomyi-two < *nom[a-C]i$_B$
two$_{1.1}$. 'throat'. LLH (nomido) - 1-1-B (B)-B-C. Km x. Edo LH. 1700 Ōsaka HL.
Sd nubi (-b- ?< -md-) B; Nk nudii/nuduu B; Sr nuudii B; Yn nudu C. Ib F = 2.3.
Sd nubi B 'throat' is probably a different etymon, 'neck': Hateruma nubusin,
Ikema (Miyako) nubui, Nakasuji (Miyako) nibui. (The forms are unexplained, but
Nakamoto 1983:53 takes nubi → nubui as a blend of nudu and kubi.)

4.6   nodobue < "nom[u]dobuwe" = /nondobu[w]e/ < nomyi-do$_{(2.4<)3.5}$ (< ...)
fuye$_{2.1}$ (< *pude < ?). 'whistle'. xLLH (= *LLLH) - 2/3-1:3-B x-x-x.

3.4 = 1.3|2.3   nogai < nwo-gafyi < *nwo$_{1.3a}$ -n- kap[a-C]i$_B$. 'pasturing animals:
(being raised) wild, undomesticated'. x - 0-1:3-x x-x-x. Km (W) LL(|)L.

?2.1   nogi (< ?). 'awn; fishbone'. HH - 0/1-2-x x-x-x. Km x. Sz 0; Hiroshima 1.
Ōsaka, Ise 2̲.

?2.2a   nogi [dial.] 'rainbow': *see* nizi.

3.7b   nohara, nobara, noppara < *nwo$_{1.3a}$ (-n-) para$_{2.3}$ (< *paru). 'field, plain,
moor'. x - 1-1:3-B x-x-x. Narada, Hattō, Hamada, Goka-mura 1; Aomori, Sz,
Matsue, Izumo 2. JP -b-.

2.1   noki ?< *nokyi < *nok[o-C]i ('exclude'), ?< *nobiy-kiy < *nonpo-Ci[-Ci]
(< ...) ko-Ci*1.3a* ('extend wood'). 'eaves'. HH - 0-0-A A-x-x. 1700 Ōsaka HH.
Ib H = 2.1.

4.2   nokizuke < noki-*s*/*z*uke ?< noki*s.1* (< ?) sukey*s.1* (< *suka-Ci[-Ci]*A*).
'a cross-board at the end of a rafter'. HHHL - x-0-x x-x-x.

2.5   noko. 'saw' (= nokogiri). x - 1-1:3-B x-x-x. Km x. Sz 1. Hakata 0, ygr 1.
Ib F = 2.3. Is noko a truncation of nokogiri?

4.5   nokogiri < nofogyiri < *nok*k*/*n*o -n- kir[a-C]i*B*. 'saw'. LLLL - 3/4-1:4-B
x-B-B. Km x. Tappi, Sz, Narada, Izumo 4; Matsue, Hata 3; Goka-mura 0. Kōchi 3,
younger 4 (Doi 1952:35). Nk noozirii B; Sr nukuziri B; Yn nuqudi B. It is
unclear whether the doublet is the result of *-p- assimilating to k-, or of
-k- assimilating to the labial vowels on both sides. Perhaps this is an early
example of velar lenition, no[k]o- > nowo- (spelled "nofo-") and the second
consonant was never *-p- at all, just an epenthetic glide -w-. The dialect form
yokogiri (Iwate, Hachijō) suggests an etymology 'side cut' but 'side' (2.1) is
the wrong register. Cf. yoki 'small ax'.

?5.7   nokogiriba < *nokogyiri-ba < *nokogyiri*4.8* (< *noko*s.s* -n- kir[a-C]i*B*)
-n- pa*1.3b*. 'sawtooth'. LLLLH/LLLLR - 3-1:5-x x-x-x.

5.6 = 3.4|2.3 nokorimono < (*)nokori-mono < *noko-r[a-C]i mono*s.s*.
'leftovers'. x - 0/3/4-0[H]/4[U]-B x-B-x. NS (100a) LLL(|)LL.

5.7 = 3.4|2.4 nokorisine < (*)nokori-sine < *nokor[a-C]i*B* [z]ina-Ci*s.4* (*see*
ine). 'rice with hulls that survived pounding'. LLL(|)LH - x-x-x x-x-x.

2.2b   noma, nome, nomi (?< *noma[-Ci]*B*, *nomey < *noma-[C]i*B*, *nomyi <
*nom[a-C]i*B*). 'boat caulking'. HL - x-x-x x-x-x. Km x.

2.3   nomi (?< *nomyi < *nom[a-C]i*B* '*bite' or < *nomiy < *no[myi]-mu[s]i <
*nom[a-C]i*B* musi*s.1* '*bite insect' [cf. mi*?1.8*]). 'flea' LL - 2-2-B B-B-C.
Km x. Matsue 1; Narada, Hattō, Hamada, Izumo, Goka-mura, Hiroshima 2. Ōsaka,
Ise 2; Ib F = 2.3. Nk numi C; Onna nuumi B. (If '*bite' ← 'swallow' seems
farfetched, perhaps < *nwomiy < *nwo mu[s]i 'field insect'.)

2.4   nomi < nomiy < *nom*a*/*o*Ci ?< *na*1.x* mu-Ci*1.1* ('blade body'). 'chisel'.·
LH - 1-1-B x-B-x. Km x. Izumo 2; Narada, Hattō, Hamada, Matsue, Goka-mura.
Hiroshima 1. Ib L = 2.4. Onna nuumii B.

3.4   nomusi, nomuzi < *nwo*1.3a* musi*s.1*. 'field insects; (= kikui-musi)
grain/wood borer; (= simi) clothes moth'. LLL - x-x-x x-x-x.

2.3   noo < nofu (< Ch n(d)ap). 'shroud; monk's robe' (= dai). LL - x-x-x x-x-x.

3.1   noosa: noosa-noosa < *nafusa nafusa (< ?; cf. nao). 'as much as one can.
to one's utmost'. HHH-... - x-x-x x-x-x.

?2.3   nora < *nwo-ra < ?*nwo*1.3a* [a]ra*s.s*. 'brambles; moors. fields'. x - 2-
1:3-x x-x-x. Km (W) LL. Mr (W 18) HL. Hattō 1; Hamada 1/2; Matsue. Izumo 2.

2.3   nora(-). '(roaming) wild; laziness; scoundrel'. LL··· - 1-1:3-(A) - x-x-x.
(Same etyma as preceding entry?)

4.7   noramame < *nora-mamey < *nora*s.s* mamaCi*s.s*. 'wild beans'. LLHH - x-1:4-x
x-x-x.

3.4   norane < nora*s.s* ne*?1.8*. 'shrewmouse' (= zi-nezumi). LLL - x-1-x x-x-x.

2.2b   nori ?< *no(-)r[a-C]i*A* ('tell'). 'law'. HL - 2-2-x x-x-x. NS (133a) HL.
Km x. Mr (Bm) HL.

?2.3   nori. 'seaweed'. x - 2-2-B x-(B)-x. Km x. Hiroshima (and Chūgoku in
general) 1 — distinguished from 'paste' (Hiroto 1961:161); Matsue. Hattō,
Hamada, Wakamatsu 1; Hakata 1, ygr 2; Narada, Izumo 2. Ib F = 2.3. Nk nui C
'blue-green algae', su-nui B 'a seaweed, *mozuku* (Nemacystus decipiens)'; Sr
nuuri B 'moss' (but the retained -r- is a problem); cf. kokenori.

2.3   nori. 'paste; starch'. x - 2-2-B B-B-x. Km x. Matsue, Goka-mura 1: Sz,
Narada, Hattō, Hamada, Izumo, Hiroshima 2. Ib F = 2.3. Nk. Sr nui B.

4.1   norigoto < nori-koto < *nor[a-C]i*ₐ koto*ₐ.ₐ*. 'the emperor's words'.
x - x-x-x x-x-x. NS (122b [14:221-K]) LHLx, (Okada) HHHH.

4.6   norisine < *nori-sine[y] < *nori? (< ?) [z]ina-Ci*ₐ.₄* (see ine).
'"red" rice (with hulls mixed in)'. LLLH (Shinsen-Jikyō) - x-x-x x-x-x.

?3.4   nosaki < no-sakyi < *no*ₗ.ₛᵦ* saki*ₐ.ₗ*. 'first crop of the year (sent as
tribute to the court)'. x - x-x-x x-x-x. Cf. ni. ("Also nozaki.")

2.3   nosi < *no(-)s[a-C]i*ₐ*. 'noshi *(dried sea-ear ceremoniously attached to
the wrapping of a gift)*; iron (for smoothing cloth)'. ?LH - 2-2-B x-B-x.
K: Hn LL. Hattō, Hamada, Matsue 1; Izumo, Goka-mura, Narada 2. Ib H1 = 2.2.

?2.4   nosi 'aster': *see* nozi.

4.6   nosigata < *nosi*ₐ.ₐ* (< ...) -n- kata*ₐ.ₐᵦ*. 'noshi/iron shape': nosigata
no kugi (*also, mistakenly?,* kugi) 'a nail with a head, a hobnail'. LLLH -
x-x-x x-x-x.

2.3   noti. 'later'. LL - 2/0-0-0 x-x-x. NS (97b, 132a) LL. Km (S,W) LL. Edo HL.
K: "Mr and since" HL. Hattō 0; Matsue 1; Narada, Hamada, Izumo, Goka-mura 2.
Ib F = 2.3.

4.1   notogoto < no[ri]to-goto < *nor[a-Ci]*ₐ* - to (< ?) -n- koto*ₐ.ₐ*. 'Shintō
prayer'. HHHH - x-x-x x-x-x.

4.7 = 1.3a-tu|2.1   notutori < *nwo*ₗ.ₐₐ* -tu tori*ₐ.ₗ*. 'wild fowl, especially the
pheasant'. x - x-x-x x-x-x. NS L-L(|)HH.

3.7b   nowaki < (*)nwo-wakyi < *nwo*ₗ.ₐₐ* bak[a-C]i*ₐ*. 'the autumn typhoon' (~ no
kaze). LHL-1/3-1:3-B x-x-x. Edo LHL.

3.6   nozeri < *nwo*ₗ.ₐₐ* (-n-) seri*ₐ.ₐ* (< ...). 'wild parsley; (= nodake)
angelica'. LHH - 1-1:3-x x-x-x.

?2.2a < ?3.3   nozi < ? nwozi < *nwonsi 'rainbow': *see* nizi. Hateruma noozïn (cf.
Ch. 1, §52).

?2.4   nozi ?< *nwo*ₗ.ₐₐ* si[woni]*ₐ.ₐ* (< ...) or ?< *nwo*ₗ.ₐₐ* si*ₗ.ₐᵦ* ('field
Rumex'). 'aster' (= sioni). LH - x-x-x x-x-x. (NKD: "Also nosi.")

2.x   nozi < no-di < *nwo*ₗ.ₐₐ* (-n-) ti*ₗ.ₗ*. 'a road through the moor(s)'.
x - 1-2-B x-x-x. Edo LF. K: Km LF (where? S,W x).

3.1   nozomi < nozomyi < *nonso-m[a-C]i*ₐ*. 'view; hope'. HHH - 0/3-0-A x-A-x.
Km (S) HHH. K: Hn-Edo HHH. Hamada 3 (verb B); Narada, Hattō, Matsue, Izumo,
Goka-mura 0. Ib H = 3.1.

1.3b   nu. 'marsh' (= nuu LH, numa); R(/LH) - x-x-x x-x-x. NS (T+ kun) nu na L L
'inside a marsh'.

?1.1, ?1.3x   *nu 'cloth': *see* nuno, nusa, kinu; cf. nuu < *nupa-*ₐ* 'sew', no*ₐₗ.ₐᵦ*
'a length of cloth'.

4.1   nubatama < *nunpa*ₐₐ.ₗ* tama*ₐ.ₐ*. 'the round black seed of the blackberry
lily; black'. x - x-0-x x-x-x. NS (80a [14:340-M]) HHHH; NS (T+ 81) LHLₗ =
LHLL. Km (W) [ª/ₘ]ubatama HHHH, HHHL, HHLL; ... .

3.7a/b   nubiru = nobiru 'wild leek'.

2.1 < 3.1 nude < nu[rⁱ/ₘ]-de < *nur[a-C]i*ₐ* -n- ta-Ci*ₗ.ₐₐ* ('paint hand'). 'sumac'.
HH - x-0-x x-x-x. Km x.

2.1   nude < nute 'wooden bell': *see* nute.

?2.2b   nue < nuye (< ?). 'chimera; thrush' *(bird)*. HH (Kn, Ck) / HL (Shinsen-
Jikyō) - 1-2-x x-x-x. Km x. Edo HH.(Tk 1 ?< *2)

4.5   [nuikinu] < nufikinu < *nufyi-kyinu < *nup[a-C]*ₐ* kinu*ₐ.₄*. 'a sewn garment:
a garment with seams'. LLLL - x-x-x x-x-x. (Attested only in Mg? Not in NKD.)

3.4   nuime < nufyi-mey < *nup[a-C]i*ₐ* ma-Ci*ₗ.ₐₐ*. 'seam'. LLL - 3-2-B x-B-C.
Ib F = 3.4. Nk noimii B; Yn nuimi C 'thread'.

4.5 = 2.3|2.3 nuimono < nufimono < *nufyimono < *nup[a-C]i*ₐ* mono*ₐ.ₐ*. 'needlework,
embroidery'. LL(|)LL (num[u]mono) - 1/3/4(/0[H])-3-B x-B-x.

?2.1   nuka. 'forehead' (= hitai). HH - 2-2-x x-x-x. Related to muka[f]i <
*muka-p[a-C]i*A* or just *muka-*A*? Cf. Sr mukoo A 'forehead' (but that may be
borrowed, for we expect nk···). Tk and Kt accent artificial and from 'bran'?

?2.3   nuka ?< *nuka-*B/?A* ka[pa]*s.s* 'remove skin' with haplology, or *nu[ka]-
ka[pa]); ?= nuka- *(the stem itself used as a noun).* 'bran'. HL - 2-2-B B-B-A.
Km x. Mr (Bm) HL. K: Hn LL *(where attested?).* Ib F = 2.3. Nk nuKaa B: Onna
nuukaa B; Yn nugan A (H 1964:71b; for -n see Ch. 1, §52).

3.4   nukae < *nuka - ey < *nuka*?s.s* aCi*?1.1* ('bran perilla'). 'beefsteak plant'
(= siso). LLL - x-x-x x-x-x. Km x.

4.1   nukagaki < *nukagakyi < *nuka*?s.1* -n- kak[a-C]i*B* ('forehead hang').
'bridle front'. HHHH - x-x-x x-x-x.

4.1   nukagami < *nukagamyi < *nuka*?s.1* -n- kami*s.s*. 'forelocks, hair on the
forehead'. HHHH - x-x-x x-x-x.

3.6   nukago: *see* mukago.

6.1   nukazukimusi [Brinkley] < nukatuki-musi < *nuka*?s.1* tuki*s.s* (< tukyi <
tuka-Ci*B*) musi*s.1*. 'click beetle, elaterid' (= kometuki-musi).

2.1   nuki < nukyi < *nuk[a-C]i*A*. 'woof, weft (= nuki-ito); brace'. HH - 0-0-x
x-x-x.

5.2   nukikaburi < *nukyi-kaburi < *nuk[a-C]i*s.1+A* kanpu-r[a-C]i*B'*. 'spinning-
wheel'. HHHHL - x-x-x x-x-x.

2.3   numa (?< *nu[ra]-*A* ma*s.1* 'wet/sticky place', ?< *nu*1.sb* ma*s.1*). 'marsh,
swamp, bog'. x - 2-2-A x-x-x. Km (W): asaka-no-numa, ikafo-no-numa *(placenames)*
Narada 2; Hakata 0, ygr 3 *(= 2.3).* Ib H1 = 2.2. Cf. nu, nuu. (The dialects
indicate 2.2b, but the compound noun numamizu begins low.)

4.5, 4.6 numamizu < numamidu < *numa-myidu < *numa*?s.s* (< ...) mintu*s.1a* (< ...).
'marsh water'. x - 2-3-x x-x-x. Km (W) LLLL, LLLH.

5.16   numigusuri < *numi (?< *nomi*s.s* 'flea',?< *nom[a-C]i*B* 'drink') -n-
kusuri*s.7a*. 'peony (= syakuyaku); Chinese matrimony vine' (= koku). LLLHx (?=
*LL(|)LHL) - x-x-x x-x-x.

-         nuna = nu na 'inside a marsh': *see* nu.

2.1   nuno < *nunwo (?< *nu*?1.1* nwo*?1.sb*). 'cloth'. HH - 0- 1[H]/0[U]-A A-A-A.
Km x. Mr (Bm) HH. Edo HH. Aomori 2; Ib *(rare)* H = 2.1. Sd nuno(o) A: Nk nuunuu
B = nunuu A; Kunigami, Ōgimi (north Okinawa) B. Azuma niwo. Cf. *nu, no*?1.sb*,
nuu < *nupa-*B*, kinu*s.4*.

4.1   nunobiki < *nunwo-byikyi < *nunwo*s.1* (< ...) -n- pik[a-C]i*A*. 'stretching
cloth out (to let it bleach in the sun); ... ; Nunobiki *(name of a waterfall)*'.
x - 0-0-x x-x-x. Km (W) HHHH.

4.2   nunoobi < *nunwo*s.1* obyi*s.4* (< onp[a-C]i*B*). 'cloth belt/girdle'. HHHL -
x-4-x x-x-x.

?3.1   nuride 'sumac': *see* nurude. NS (T+ kun) LHF.

3.1   nurite 'wooden bell': *see* nute.

?3.1(> 2.1)   nurude, nuride (> nude) < *nur[a-]u*A*/nur[a-C]i*A* -n- ta-Ci*s.sa* ('paint
hand'). 'sumac'. x - 0-1-x x-x-x. Km x.

?2.3, ?2.4   nusa. 'paper/cloth offering'. LL (Zs) / LH (Kn) - 1-2-x x-x-x. Km (W)
LL, Hx; Mr (W 19) HH. Cf. *nu, nuno, kinu. For a sometime suspicion this word
may have been HF (2.1a), see Sakurai 1975:91-2. But Komatsu 1960 (Kɡg 40:56)
treats it as LF (2.5).

?2.4, ?2.5   nusi. 'master; owner'. x - 1-1-B B-B-x. Mr(Bm) LH. Edo LH. Ōsaka,
Ise 1:3; Ib nosi L2 = 2.5, L = 2.4. Sr nuusi/nusi- B.

?4.11, ?4.5   nusubito = *nusu-byito̲ ?< *nusu(-)m[a-C]i*B* (-n-) pito*s.sa*, ?< *nusu*s.x*
-n- pito*s.sa*. 'thief'. LLLL/LLHL - 0-0[H]/3[U]]-B x-B-B. Mr (Bm) HHHL. Sz 4. Sr
nusudu B; Yn nusitu B (borrowed? cf. nicimun 'steals'). 1720- Waye ⁱyuhay 1:15
"nwu.su-hi.two".

2.3   nuta (?< *nu[ma]$_{2.2b}$ ta$_{1.3a}$, ?< *nu$_{?1.3}$ ta$_{?1.3a}$). 'mud(dy soil); a kind of bouillabaisse'. x - 2-2-x x-x-x. Ib F = 2.3. Cf. [muta]; nutafata LLLH 'deerhorn marking'.

2.1   nute (> nude) < nurite (< ?). 'wooden bell'. HH (-d-) x-0-x x-x-x. NS (T 85) LH. Km x. (Koji-ki -t-.)

2.4   nuu 'marsh' LH (= nu R).

-   nuzi 'rainbow': *see* nizi.

1.x   o- < on- < oon- < ofom[u]- < ofo-myi- < *opo$_{adj}$ $_B$ mi-$_{pre}$ (< ...). 'exalted' (honorific prefix). The shortest form first appears in Heian, before /m/ only (NKD 3:307b n.). See Ch. 4, §10.2.

1.x   [-o] < -fo < *-po. 'hundred': *see* [io], [mio], [yao]; Mg also has [muo] '600' and [kokonoo] '900' but without accent marks. Cf. momo.

1.1   o(-) < wo(-) < *bo(-). 'male': wo-no warafa (Zs) 'boy'. H - x-0-x x-x-x. Cf. osu, yamoo, sosanoo; oosi$_{adj}$ $_B$. Register incongruent: osu, odori, otakebi.

?1.1   o- < wo- (?< *bo-, cf. hono(-), ?< *[k]wo-). 'little'. Cf. Hōjō Tadao 1951:87. Cf. enu; osi$_{adj}$ $_A$.

1.1   o < wo < *bo. 'hill' (= oka). x - x-x-x x-x-x. If [w]o is taken as a truncation of [w]oka, perhaps that could be wo-[ta]ka 'litle height'. The accent of [mukatuo] suggests 1.3 rather than the 1.1 we have inferred from oka.

1.3a   o < wo < *bo. 'tail'. L - 1-1-A x-x-x. Km (S,W) L(-H). Edo R. Ib L = 1.3.

?1.3b   o < wo < *bo. 'hemp'. R - x-0-x x-B-A. NS (97a [11:77L-K]) R. Km x. Nk, Sr uu B 'banana-fiber plant'; Yn buu A 'hemp(-thread)' — *see next entry*.

?1.3b, ?1.1 o < wo < *bo. 'cord'. H - 1-1-A B-A-A. NS (T+ 125 'thong') L. (T+ 18 'cord [of life]') L. Km (W) H/R. Edo H. Narada, Hiroshima 0. Ōsaka 1; Ise 0; Ib H = 1.1, 'umbilical cord' L = 1.3. Nk, Sr uu A. (Probably from 'hemp'.)

2.1   oba < woba < *bo-$_{?1.1}$ (or [k]wo-$_{1.1}$) -n- pa$_{?1.1}$. 'aunt'. HH - 0-0-A A-A-x. Km (W) HH. 1700 Ōsaka HL. Ib H = 2.1.

?2.5   oba < o[fo]-ba < *opo$_{adj}$ $_B$ -n- pa$_{?1.1}$ (> o-baa). 'grandmother; old woman'. (LL-...) - 0-0-1:3-x x-x-x. K: "Hn LF?, Km HL?"

4.11   obaoba < oba$_{?2.5}$ - woba$_{2.1}$ < *o[fo]-ba wo-ba < *opo$_{adj}$ $_B$ -n- pa$_{?1.1}$ bo-$_{?1.1}$ -n- pa$_{?1.1}$. 'great-aunt'. LLHL - x-x-x x-x-x.

4.6   obasima (< ?). 'railing, handrail, banister'. LLLH - 0-0-x x-x-x.

4.1, 4.2 obayasi < wo-bayasi < *bo$_{?1.1}$ (or *[k]wo$_{1.1}$) -n- padasi$_{3.4}$ (< ...). 'grove'. x - x-x-x x-x-x. NS (Okada) HHHH, HHHL; NS (T+ 111, kun) LLHH.

2.4   obi < obyi < *onp[a-C]i$_B$. 'belt, girdle'. LH - 1-1-B B-B-x. Edo LH. Ib L = 2.4. Sr quubi B; Yn Tun A (?< *kiki-obi).

5.7   obibukuro < (*)obyi-bukurwo$_{(2.4)}$ < *onp[a-C]i$_{(B)}$ -n- pukurwo$_{3.4}$. 'a beltbag (for carrying provisions on a journey)'. LLLLH - 3-4-x x-x-x.

4.6   obikawa < (*)obyi-kafa$_{(2.4)}$ < *onp[a-C]i$_{(B)}$ kapa$_{2.3}$. 'a leather belt'. LLLH - 0-0-B x-x-x. NKD: "also -gawa".

3.4   obisi < *obyi$_{(2.4)}$-si[bari] < *onp[a-C]i$_{(B)}$ sim[a]-pa-r[a-C]i$_{?A/B}$. 'the small of the back (near where the obi is tied)'. LLL - x-x-x x-x-x.

5.16   obisibari < *obyi$_{(2.4)}$ - sibari$_{3.x}$ < *onp[a-C]i$_{(B)}$ sim[a]-pa-r[a-C]i$_{?A/B}$. 'the small of the back (near where the obi is tied)' (= obisi). LLLHL - x-x-x x-x-x.

4.6   obitori < *obyi$_{(2.4)}$ - t(w)ori < *onp[a-C]i$_B$ t(w)or[a-C]i$_B$. 'sheath buckle'. LLLH - x-x-x x-x-x.

3.5b   obone < wobone < *bo$_{1.3a}$ -n- pone$_{2.3}$ (< ...). 'tailbone'. LLH - 2-1-x x-x-x.

4.6   obukuro < wobukuro < *wo-bukurwo < *bo$_{1.3a}$ -n- pukurwo$_{3.4}$. 'a (horse-)tail holder'. LLLH - x-x-x x-x-x.

3.5x   obune < wo-bune < *bo-?1.1 (or *[k]wo-1.1) -n- puna-Ci8.4. 'little boat'.
           LLH - x-x-x x-x-x. Modern kobune.

3.4   obusa < wobusa < *bo1.3a -n- pusa2.3. 'a bird's tail spread out (like a
           bunch)'. LLL - 1-x-x x-x-x.

?2.2x   oda < wo-da < *?bo-?1.1 (or *[k]wo1.1) -n- ta1.3a. '(little) rice paddy'.
           x - 1-x-x x-x-x. Cf. araoda. 'a (horse-)tail holder'. LLLH - x-x-x x-x-x.

4.11   odaika < odafyika < *onta-pi (< ?) -ka. 'calm, quiet, smooth' (adj-n) (=
           odayaka). LLHL - x-x-x x-x-x. Cf. [odaisi-]adj.

3.1   odate < wo-date < *bo-?1.1 (or ([k]wo-1.1) -n- tate8.4 (< ...). 'small
           shield'. x - x-x-x x-x-x. NS (72b [11:200-M]) HHH; NS (T+ 54) LLͰ.

3.1   odori < wodori < *bontor[a-C]iA (< ?). 'dance'. (H) - 0-0-A (x)-A-A. Ib H
           = 3.1.

3.4 (= 3.1?) odori < wo-tori < *bo1.1 tori8.1. 'male bird, (= ondori) rooster';
           soldier'. x - 1-x-x x-A/B-x. NS (122a) LLL (register incongruent). Sr uudui
           A/B. ◖ ondori x - 0-0-A x-x-x.

3.2a   odoro < *ontoro (< ?). 'bush, thicket' (= yabu). HHL - 0-0-x x-x-x. Km x.
           Mr (Bm) HHH.

?3.4   ogase < wo-k/ɡase < *bo?1.3b (-n-) kase?2.3 (?< kasi). 'skein of linen (or
           the skein frame/reel); tangle(d)'. x - x-x-x x-x-x. Cf. saruoɡase.

4.1   ogatama < wok/ɡatama/wokadama ?< *boka-?A (-n-) tama?2.3 ('invoke spirit').
           'Magnolia/Michelia compressa'. x - 0-(0)-x x-x-x. Km (W) HHHH. "HHLH".

4.5 = 1.1|3.4 ogawara < wo-gafara < *bo1.1 -n- kapara8.4. 'male (= convex) tile'.
           HLxL = *H(|)LLL - 2-3-x x-B-x. Sr uuɡara B. K: "Hn LLLL?"

?2.3   ogi < wogiy < *bo?1.1 -n- ko-Ci1.3a. 'a reed, Miscanthus sacchariflorus:
           sugarcane'. LL (Kn -k-) - 1-2-x B-B-x. Sr uuzi B; Ōra buuɡï. On the Shuri
           palatalization see Ch. 1, §41.

4.11   ogimusi < wogi-musi ?< *wogiy?2.3 (< ...) musi8.1. 'a measuring worm, an
           inch worm' (= syakutori-musi). LLHL - x-x-x x-x-x.

?3.3, ?3.7x   ogiro < ogyiro < *onkiro (< ?). 'vast' (adj-n). x - x-1:3-x x-x-x.
           Km x. Mr (Bm) HLL.

2.x   ogo (< ?) 'a kind of reddish seaweed' (= ogo-nori). JP wogo, wogonai.
           x - x-x-x x-x-x.

3.6   ogoma = ugoma 'sesame'. LHH - x-x-x x-x-x.   See ɡoma.

4.11   ogosoka < *onko(-)so-ka (< ?). 'solemn, majestic' (adj-n).

3.x   ohagi/uhagi < ufaɡyi (< ?). 'aster, starwort' (= yomena). Lxx - x-x-x
           x-x-x.

4.1 < ?*5.1   oharano < o(o)fara-no < *opoadj B para8.3 (< *paru) nwo1.3a ('ɡreat-
           field moor'). 'Oharano' (shrine name). x - 0-0-x x-x-x. Km (W) HHHH. Reɡister
           incongruent with etymology.

2.3|2.3   [ohumono] < "ofumono" (Zs 163:4) = obu mono < *onp[a-]uB mono8.3
           ('thing to gird with'). 'jingle-bell jewel on belt'. LL(|)LL - x-x-x x-x-x.
           Cf. onmono.

2.1   oi < wofiy < *bo1.1 -pu/oCi1.x. 'nephew'. HH - 0-0-A A-(B)-(A). Edo HH.
           1700 Ōsaka HL. Ir H = 2.1. (Sr "literary"; Yn buiha A 'nephew/niece'.) Cf.
           mei.

2.3   oi < o[y]i[y] < *odo-Ci[-Ci]B (?< *oda-Ci[-Ci]). 'being old; old person'.
           x - 0/1-0[H]/2[U]-B x-x-(B). Km (W) LL. 1700 Ōsaka HH. Hiroshima 0. Ōsaka,
           Ise 2; Ib (rare) H = 2.1. Yn uiTu (< *oyi-pito) B. Cf. oya.

2.3   oi < ofi < *ofyi < *op[a-C]iB. 'a wooden back-pack'. x - 1-2-x x-x-x.
           Edo HL (< *LL).

4.5 = 2.3|2.3 oikake < o[y]i[y]-kakey < *odo-Ci[-Ci]B (< ...) kaka-Ci[-Ci]R.
           'horsehair side pieces on the hairdress of a military officer ··· '.
           LL(|)LL - 0-0-x x-x-x.

2.1   oka < woka ?< *bo₁.₁ -ka₁.ₓ ('hill place'). ?< *wo[ta]ka < *bo-?₁.₁ (or
*[k]wo-₁.₁) taka_adj ʙ) ('little height'). 'hill; land, shore'. HH - 0-0-A
x-x-x. NS (Okada) HH. Km (W) HH. Edo HH. Ib H = 2.1.

5.2   okatotoki < woka₂.₁ (< ...) totoki₃.ₓ (< ?). 'bellflower, balloonflower'
(= kikyoo). HHHHL - x-x-x x-x-x.

4.1 = 1.1|3.1   oka^t/zura < wo-katura < *bo₁.₁ ('male') katura₃.₁. 'judas-tree'.
HxHx = H(|)HHH - x-x-x x-x-x.

2.5   oke < wokey < wo-key < *bo?₁.₃ᵇ kaCi?₁.₂ (< ...) ('hemp container').
'bucket'. LH - 1-1:3-B B-B-C. K: Hn-Km LF. Ib L2 = 2.5. Nakanoshima treats oke
as 2.1 (Tajiri 1975:47). Sr uuki B; Yn ugi C. Dial. (Gifu, Iga) ooke.

?4.4 = 1.1|3.4 okemono < wo-kemono < *wo₁.₁ (< *bo₁.₁) key-mono₃.₄ (< *ka-Ci?₁.₁
mono₂.₃). 'male animal'. "LLLL" ?= *H(|)LLL - x-x-x x-x-x.

3.2a   okera < wokera (< ?). 'Atractylodes japonica'. HHL - 0-0-x x-x-x.

2.3   oki < okyi < *oki. 'offshore'. x - 0-0-B B-B-x. NS (Okada) LL; NS (T 4; 5)
HH. Km (W) LL(/LH). Edo HL. Narada ('north'), NE Kyūshū 0; but Hattō, Hamada,
Matsue, Izumo, Goka-mura, Hiroshima (and Chūgoku in general, Fujiwara 1972:89)
2. Ōsaka 0; Ise 2; Kōbe, Himeji 2 (Ōhara 1932-3); Ib F = 2.3. Sr quuci B.
Cf. oku.

?3.1   okibi < okiy-fiy < *oko-Ci[-Ci]ʙ (or *oko[-sa]-Ciʙ) po-Ci₁.₃ᵇ. 'blazing
fire'. x - 0-0-x x-x-x. Km (W) HHH. K: "Hn HHH" (mistake for Km?). Register
incongruent with etymology.

3.6   okina < okyina < *o-ki-na?< *o[po]_adj ʙ ki₁.ₓ na₁.₂. 'old man, gaffer'.
LHH - 0/1/2[K]-0[U]/1:3[U]/2[H]-A x-x-x. 1700 Ōsaka LHH. Aomori (rare) 1 (we
expect 2); Narada 1; Hakata 2, ygr 1. Cf. omina.

5.16   okinabito < *okyina-byito < *okina?₃.₅ₐ/ᵇ (< ...) -n- pito₂.₂ₐ. 'old
man'. LLLHL - x-x-x x-x-x.

5.16   okinagusa < *okyina-gusa < *okina?₃.₅ₐ/ᵇ (< ...) -n- kusa₂.₃.
'pasqueflower, Pulsatilla cernua'. LLLHx (= *LLLHL) - 3-4-x x-x-x.

3.4 = 2.3|1.3; 3.5x, 3.6 okitu < okyi-tu < *oki₂.₃ tu₁.₃ₐ ('offshore port').
'Okitsu' (placename): ~ no fama (name of a beach near Ōsaka). x - 0-x-x x-x-x.
Km (W) LL(|)L; LLH, LHH.

3.4   oko^s/zi < woko^s/zi (< ?). 'stingfish, scorpion fish' (= okoze < wokoze).
LLL - 2-2-x x-x-x.

5.7   okosigome < *okosi-gomey < *okosi?₍ʙ₎ (< ?) -n- komaCi₂.₃. 'a sweet
rice-cake concoction' (= okosi x - 2-1:3-A x-x-x). LLLLH - 3-1-x x-x-x.

?2.3   oku. '(deeply) interior' (≠ oku/ou < Ch). LL - 1-1-B (A)-B-B. Edo LH.
1700 Ōsaka HL. Aomori, Narada, Hamada, Goka-mura, Hiroshima, Yamaguchi 1;
Hakata 1 (expected); Hattō, Matsue, Izumo 2. Kōchi (Kobayashi) 1; Ōsaka, Ise 2;
Toyama 2 (we expect 1:2); Suzu 1:2. Sr quuku; Yn uku B (H 1964:70a, 71a).
Cf. oki.

?3.1   okubi. 'belch'. x - 0-0[H]/2[U]-B x-x-x. JP wokubi. Kn akufi HHL, okufi
(no accent marks); cf. akubi HHH 'yawn'. Perhaps from *wo-akubi 'little yawn'?

?3.4, ?3.5x, ?3.6   okute ?< *oku?₂.₃ ta-Ci₁.₃ₐ ('interior hand'). 'late rice'.
x - 0/3-2[U]/0[H]-B x-x-x. Km (W) LLL, LLH, LHH. K: Hn LLH. Ib H1 = 3.2. (An
etymology that derives oku from oku-[re-]ₐ 'late' is incongruent in register.)

?4.11   okuyama < *oku?₂.₃ dama₂.₃. 'deep mountains'. x - x-x-x x-x-x. Onqi
(Iroha) LLHL.

2.2b   oma < woma < *bo₁.₃ₐ [u]ma₂.₃. '(male) horse, stallion' (= o-uma). HL -
x-x-x x-x-x.

4.11   omeasi ?< *omey (< *omaCi[-Ci]?ʙ) asi₂.₃ ('fear[ful] leg'). 'a beriberi-
like ailment' (= koi). LLHL - x-x-x x-x-x.

4.11   omemusi < *omey (< *omaCi-[Ci]?ʙ) musi₂.₁ ('fear[ful] insect'). 'sow bug,
wood louse' (= warazi-musi). LLHL - x-x-x x-x-x.

2.3   omi < omyi (?< *o[fo-i]myi < *opo im[a-C]i_B 'great taboo'). 'minister (to
a god/lord)'. x - x-x-x x-x-x. NS (70c, 74b) LL; NS (T 91, 127) LL, (T 74, 88)
RE ?= HL, (T+ 44, kun) LH.

3.x < 4.7 / 4.6   omiki < o[fo]-miki < *ofo_{2.3} - myikyi_{2.2a} < *opo_{adj B} mi-_{?1.1}
ki_{1.x} (< ...). '(offertory) wine'. ofomiki LLLH (Ck) / LLHH (Kn) → o-miki
0-1-B x-x-x.

?3.6   omina < omyina < *o-mi-na ?< *o[po]_{adj B} mi_{1.x} na_{1.2}. 'old woman, gammer'.
x - x-x-x x-x-x. Cf. okina; onna.

?5.2   ominaesi, omina^b/mesi < wominafesi ?< womyina_{2.2b} (< ...) fyesi_A ('push'
< ...). 'Patrinia scabiosaefolia; ... '. x - 3-4[U]/1:4[H]-B x-x-x. Km (W
-"f"- ?= -b-) HHHHL. NKD says -b- appeared in Km, -m- in Mr. Sz 3.

2.x (?2.4)   omo. 'mother'. x - x-x-x x-x-x. NS (T+ kun) LH. See amo, omoharakara;
omonoki.

2.4   omo. 'surface; face' (= omo-te). x - 1-2-x x-x-x. Km (W) LH/LR(-H).

?2.5   omo. 'important'. x - 1-1:3-A x-x-x. Km x. Sz, Hiroshima 1. Ōsaka, Ise
1:3; Ib L2 = 2.5. Cf. omo_{adj A} 'heavy', o[p]o_{adj B} 'big'.

?4.10 (?= 2.4|2.3)   omodaka < omo[]taka < *omo_{2.4} -n- taka_{adj B} ('face high').
'Sagittaria trifolia, arrowhead (plant)'. LHxx ?= *LH(|)LL - 0-1:3-x x-x-x.

4.5   omogai < omoga[k]i < *omo-gakyi < *omo_{2.4} n[i] kak[a-C]i_B ('face hang').
'headstall' (= omozura). LLLL - x-x-x x-x-x.

6.22   omohahakuso < *omo fafa-kuswo < *omo_{2.4} papa_{?2.1} - kuswo_{2.3} (?← kurwo_{2.5})
('face mother-dung/-black'). 'a mole on the face'. LLLLHL - x-x-x x-x-x.

6.21   omoharakara < omo-farakara < *omo_{?2.4} faragara_{4.5} (< *para_{2.3} -n-
kara_{2.x}). 'siblings (with the same mother)'. x - x-x-x x-x-x. NS (Okada)
LLLHLL.

3.4   omoi < omofyi < *omo-p[a-C]i_B. 'thought'. LLL - 2-2-B B-B-(B). Km (S)
LLL. Edo HHL. Aomori, Matsue, Izumo 2; Narada, Hattō, Hamada 3. Goka-mura 0
(expected reflex). The Tk (etc.) accent retreat is due to monosyllabification.

?3.1   omoni < *omo_{adj A} ni_{1.3b} (< ...). 'a heavy burden'. x - 0-1(/0[U])-A
x-A-x. Km (W) HHH, LHH. Sr qnbunii A.

3.1/3.4   omosi < *omo-si_{adj A pred}. 'a weight'. HHH/LLL - 0-0-A x-A-x. Aomori, Sz
0. Ib H = 3.1. Sr qnbusi A. (Folk etymology omo-isi 'heavy stone'.)

3.4   omote < *omo_{2.4} ta-Ci_{1.3a}. 'surface'. LLL - 3-2-B x-B-x. NS (Okada) LLL;
NS (T+ kun) LLL. Km (S) LLL. Mr (Bm) HHL. Edo HHL. Kōchi 3; Ib F = 3.4.

3.4 < 4.5 = 2.4|2.4 omoto < o[fo]-moto < *opo_{adj B} [mi-]moto_{2.3}. 'august presence'.
x - 1-1:3-x x-x-x. NS (120b) LLL.

4.6   omozura < omo-dura < *omo_{2.4} n[i] tura(-)_A ('face-at hang'). 'headstall'
(= omogai). LLLH - x-x-x x-x-x.

?3.7x   omura < wo-mura < *bo_{1.1} mura_{2.1} ('crowd of hills; many ridges').
'? Omura (placename)' (or fixed epithet?): womura no takey ni 'to the peak of
Omura (or "of-the-many-ridges")'. x - x-x-x x-x-x. NS (75c [14:118-M]) LHL;
NS (T+ 75) LHL. The register is incongruent with the etymology.

?3.5a   ona^s/zi(-ku/-to) < ona-si(-)_{adj B}. 'same(-like)'. LLH(-L) - 0-1-B x-(x)-x.
NS (96a) LLL. Km (S) LLH(-L), (W) HLL(-H). K: Hn LLF, Km LLL(-H), Edo HHL(-L).
Aomori, Sz (= o(n)nasu 3) 3. Ib L = 3.6. Kt onnasi. Cf. onore, onozukara. It is
unclear whether/how Sr inu(-) B 'same' is related.

3.5x   onbe < o[f]onbe < *opo_{adj B} n[i]pey_{?2.1a} (< ... , see nie). 'sacrifice of
new rice; new-rice festival'. x - x-x-x x-x-x. Km (W) LLH.

2.3   oni (?< in/on 'hidden' < Ch 'yen/?'wen). 'ogre'. LL - 2-2-B B-B-x. Km x.
Edo HL. K: Mr-Edo HL. Narada, Hattō, Hamada, Goka-mura, Izumo 2; Matsue 1.
Ib F = 2.3.

?3.4   onibi < *oni-*f*/biy < *oni*g.g* (-n-) po-Ci*1.3b*. 'will-o'-the-wisp, fox fire
(= ignis fatuus)'. x - 2-3-x x-x-x. Sz 3. K: Hn LLL *(where attested?)*. Km x.

?5.14 = 2.3|3.2; ?5.9 = 2.3|3.1   oniyarai < oni*g.g* yarafi (< *yarafyi <
*dara-p[a-C]i*A*). 'dispelling the demons (of epidemic), exorcism'. LLHHx (?=
*LL(|)HHL, ?= *LL(|)HHH) - 3-4-x x-x-x.

4.5 = 2.3|2.3 onmono < "om[u]mono" (< obyi-m*o*no) < *onp[a-C]i*B(=2.3)* mono*g.g*.
'belt, girdle'. LL(|)LL - x-0-x x-x-x. Cf. [ohumono].

3.2b   onna < "wom[u]na" < womyina < *bo-*?1.1* (or [k]wo-*1.1*) mina*?*g.g* (< ...).
'woman'. HHx - 3-3[H]/2[U]-A A-A(/B)-x. Km (W) HHL. Edo HHL. Sapporo, Aomori,
Matsumoto, Numazu, Narada, Hattō, Hamada, Matsue, Izumo, Hiroshima, Hata, Ōita
3; Akita, Goka-mura, NE Kyūshū O. Kōchi 3; Ib H1 = 3.3, but usually onago H2 =
3.2.   Cf. me.

3.6   onna < "om[u]na" < omyina < *o-mi-na ?< *o[po]*adj B* mi*1.x* na*1.g*. 'old
woman, gammer'. LHH - x-x-x x-x-x.

5.2   onna-domo < wom[u]na-tomo < *womyina*g.gb* (< ...) t*o*mo*g.1>g.g*.
'maidservants; womenfolk; one's wife'. x - 3/4- x-x x-x-x. NS (106b) HHHHL.

6.22   onnakazura < "om[u]na-kadura" < omyina*g.g* (< ...) kadura*g.g* (< ...)
('gammer vine'). 'Cnidium officinale' (= senkyuu).

?4.1   onname < "wom[u]name" < *womyina-mye < *womyina*g.gb* (< ...) miCa*1.gb*
(?= *mina). 'concubine, mistress'. HxHH (Kn) / "HLHx" (Kz) - x-3-x x-x-x.

2.1   on*o* (?< *ona). 'self': NS (95a) ono ["]ka HH-H; NS (T+ 18) HH(-H),
(T+ 125) LL-H. Edo HH. *See* onore, onozukara; onazi.

2.1   ono < wo-nwo < *bo-*?1.1* (or *[k]wo-*1.1*) nwo*1.ga*. '(small) field/moor'.
x - 0-0-x x-x-x. NS (117a[14:127-K]) HH. Km (W) HH. Hattō, Goka-mura 1.

2.3   ono < won*o* < *bon*o* (?< *bo-*?1.1* (or [k]wo-*1.1*) na*1.x*/na[ta]*g.1* 'small
blade/hatchet' *but register incongruent*). 'ax'. (Cf. yoki.) LL - 1-0-A B-B-B.
Km (W) LL. Sz, Matsumoto, Wakamatsu 1; Numazu 0; Sapporo, Aomori, Akita,
Hiroshima, Ōita 2. Hyōgo 0; Toyama, Suzu, Kōchi 1; Ib *(rare)* H = 2.1. Nk
uunuu B; Kusigwa and Sukuta (northern Okinawa) uunuu B (Kusakabe 1968:55);
Sr uun B; Yn bunu B. Cf. tyoona (< "teuna") < *te-ona 'adze'.

3.7a, 3.6   onoe < wonofe < wo-n*o* [u]fey < *bo*1.3a* n*o* upa-Ci*?g.ga* ('tail top').
'mountaintop; Onoe *(placename)*'. x - 0-x-x x-x-x. Km (W) LHL, LHH (written
'tail-top', register incongruent with o*1.1* 'hill' but see the discussion under
that entry).

?3.3, ?3.2x   onoko < wo-n*o* kwo < *bo*1.1* n*o* kwo*1.1*. 'boy; man'. HLL - 1-x-x x-x-x.
NS (119b [14:169L-K]) HHL. Km (W) HLL(-)/HHH(-). Edo HHL. Kn M*a* also has
wonoko-go xxxHL.

?4.3 (?< *4.1) onoono < *ono*g.1* ono*g.1*. 'each, respectively; you all'. x - 2-1:3-A
x-x-x. Km (S) HHLL. Mr (Bm) HHLL. K: Edo HHLL.

3.1   onora < *ono*g.1* (?< *ona) [a]ra*g.g*. 'we/us; you (to an inferior)'.
HHH (Ir) - x-x-x x-x-x.

?3.2x, 3.1   onore < on*o*-re (< ?*ona-re < *ona*g.1* [a]ra-Ci*g.g*). 'self'. HHL -
0-0-B x-x-x. NS (?115b, 130b) HHL, (Okada) HHH. Mr (Bm) HHH. Edo HHH. Narada 0.
Ib H = 3.1.

3.4 = 2.3|1.3 onote < wono-te < *bono*g.g* ta-Ci*1.ga*: ofo ~ '(Great-)Ax-Hand' *(name)*.
x - x-x-x x-x-x. NS (130a) LL(|)L.

5.1   onozukara < on*o*dukara < *ono*g.1* (?< ona) -(n-)tu- kara*g.gb*. 'by itself'.
HHHHH - 0/2-0-B x-x-x. Mr (Bm) HHHHH. Sz 3.

2.3 = B   oo(-) < of*o*(-) < *op*o*(-) 'big; much': *see Ch. 4, Chart 16:1*. Cf. omo.

4.6   ooani < ofo-ani < *opo*adj B* ani*?g.g* ('big brother'). 'name of a bird,
perhaps the white pheasant or the kite'. LLLH - x-x-x x- x-x. Attested Mg only?

5.8, 5.16 ooaraki < ofo-arakiy < *opo_adj B ara-kiy?3.1 (< *ara_adj A kiy1.3a (< ?)
'rough fortress'). 'a temporary casket for a deceased nobleman; the casket
period (in the Nara era about a year); Ōaraki (placename)'. x - x-x-x x-x-x.
Km (W) LLLHH, LLLHL.

4.6/4.7   oobako < ofoba-ko < *ofoba-kwo < *opo_adj B -n- pa1.2 kwo1.1 ('large-leaf
child'). 'a broad-leafed plantain'. LLLH/LLHH - 0-1-B x-x-x.

4.8   oobune < ofobune < *opo_adj B -n- puna-Ci2.4. 'big boat'. LHHH - 0-1-A
x-x-x. Km (W) LLLH. K: Edo HHHH (if so, how come Kt returns to low atonic?).

4.5   oodaka: see ootaka.

4.5   oodake < ofodake < *ofo-dakey < *opo_adj B -n- taka-Ci2.1. 'black bamboo'
(= hatiku). LLLL - x-x-x x-x-x.

?4.11   oodati < ofodati < *opo_adj B -n- tati2.3 (< ...). 'a large sword'.
x - 1/0-1:3-x x-x-x. NS (Okada) LLHL.

4.5   oodoko < ofodoko < *opo_adj B -n- toko2.1. 'casket, coffin'. xxLL (=
*LLLL) - x-x-x x-x-x.

4.5   ooemi < ofowemi < *ofo_adj B (< *opo) wemyi2.3 (< ... B). 'Polygonatum
falcatum' (= emigusa = narukoyuri). xxLL (= *LLLL) - 0-1:3-x x-x-x.

3.4   ooga < ofoga (< ?). 'spinning wheel'. LLL - x-0-x x-x-x.

4.5   oogame < ofogame < *ofo-gamey < *opo_adj B -n- kamaCi2.3. 'big turtle'.
LLLx (= *LLLL) - x-x-x x-x-x.

4.5   oogane < ofogane < *opo_adj B -n- kana-Ci2.1. 'big money; big bell'.
LLLL ('bell') - 0(/4 'money')-0 ('money')/2 ('bell')-A x-x-x Km x.

4.6   oogasa < ofogasa < *opo_adj B -n- kasa2.4. 'big umbrella'. LLLH - 3-1-x
x-x-x. Km x.

3.4   oogi < afukyi < *apu(n)k[a-C]i_B. 'fan'. LLL - 3-2-B B-B-x. Km x. Edo HHL.
Aomori (rare), Akita, NE Kyūshū 0; Narada 3. Kōbe (Robb) 0; Toyama 2 (we expect
1:3); Suzu 2 (we expect 0); Ib F = 3.4. On -g- < -k-, see Ch. 2. Hateruma gon.

-          oogimi: see ookimi.

3.4   oogo: see ooko.

?4.6   oohara < ofo-fara < *opo_adj B para2.3 (< *paru) ('big field'). 'Ōhara'
(placename, surname). x - 0/1-2-B x-x-x. Km (W) LLLH, Mr (W 19) HHLL.

-          ooharano: see oharano.

3.4   ooi < ofofi < ofofyi < *opo-p[a-C]i_B. 'cover'. LLL - 1/2/0-2-A x-x-x.

3.4 = 2.3|1.3   ooi < ofo-wi < *opo_adj B bi1.3b. 'bulrush' (= huto-i). LLx (=
*LL(|)L) - x-x-x x-x-x.

?3.5b   ooi < ofo-wi < *opo_adj B bi1.3a. 'big well'. x - 1-x-x x-x-x. Km (W) LLH.

3.7a   ooi < ofofi (< ?). 'medic, bur(r)/snail clover' (= umagoyasi). LHL - 0-2-x
x-x-x.

?4.11   ookami < ofokami ?< *ofo kamiy ('big god' < *opo_adj B kamu-Ci2.3). 'wolf'.
LLxx - 1-2-A x-x-x. Km x. K: Hn LLHL (attested?). Sz 1; Narada, Goka-mura 2;
Hattō, Matsue, Izumo 0; Hamada 0/1.

4.x   ookata < ofo-kata < *opo_adj B kata?2.3. 'the main part; ... '. x - 0-0-B
x-A-x. K: Edo HHHH.

4.5/4.7   ookawa < ofo-kafa < *opo_adj B kapa2.2b. 'big river'. x - 1-4-B x-x-x.
Km (W) LLLL/LLHH.

4.5   ookaze < ofokaze < *opo_adj B kansa-Ci2.1. 'big wind'. LLLL - 3/4/0-
3[H]/2[U]-A x-B-x. Sz 4; Wakayama 3 (Yukawa 1984:2:18).

?4.7 (?= 2.3|2.1)   ook/gimi < ofo-kyimyi < *opo_adj B kimi2.1. 'great lord/prince;
emperor'. (x) - 0/3-0-A x-x-x. NS (72b [11:197-M], 74b [11:304-M], 75b [14:120-
M], 76b [14:124-M], 79b [14:314-M], 84a [17:126-M], 112a) LL(|)HH; NS (T+ 63,
93, 97, 103) LL(|)HH, (T+ 70) LL(|)HĤ ?= LL(|)HH (Tsuchihashi writes BOW-YOU
myi L but Ōno has WATER-BOW-YOU myi Ƒ), (T+ 53) LL(|)LƑ ?= LLLL, (T+ 102)
LLLH, (T+ 75, 76, 78, 90) HL|HH. Km (W) LL(|)HH.

?6.18 = 4.7(=2.3|2.1)|2.3   ookindati ‹ "ofokim[u]-dati" ‹ *ofokyimyi-tati ‹ ofo-
kyimyi₄.₇ (‹ *opo₈dj ₈ kimi₈.₁) tati₇₈.₃. 'great lords/princes'. LL(|)HH(|)LL
(Kn), LLLH(|)LL (Ck) - x-x-x x-x-x.

3.4   ook/₈o ‹ auk/₈o ‹ afuko ‹ *apuko (‹ ?). 'a shoulder-pole'. LLL - x-2-x
x-x-x.

4.5   ookubi ‹ ofokubi ‹ *ofo-kubyi ‹ *opo₈dj ₈ kunpi₈.₁. 'a large collar
(···)'. LLLL - x-1:3-x x-x-x.

4.6   ook/₈uti ‹ ofo-kuti ‹ *opo₈dj ₈ kutu-Ci₈.₁. 'big mouth/opening': ~ no
fakama 'a kind of underpants'. LLLH - 1-0-A x-x-x. K: Hn LLHH misprint?.

?4.7, ?4.9   oomae ‹ ofo-mafye ‹ ofo₈dj ₈ (‹ *opo) mafye₈.₈ (?‹ ma₁.₃₈ piCa₁.ᵪ).
'august presence'. x - 0/2-0-x x-x-x. NS (75c [14:119-MW]) LLHH, ([14:119-M])
LHHL; NS (T+ 72) LL-ᶠH ?= LL(|)LH, (T+ 75) HLᶠH (incongruent).

-    oomi-: see oon-.

3.5b   oomi ‹ afumyi ‹ af[a]-umyi ‹ *apa₈dj ₈ umi₈.₄ ('sweet-water lake'). 'Ōmi'
(placename). x - 1(?‹*2)-0[H]/2-B x- x-x. NS (87a[17:276-M]) LLH(-L). Km (W)
LLH. Edo HLL.

5.9 (?= 2.3|3.1)   oomi-hune ‹ ofo-myi - fune ‹ *opo₈dj ₈ mi-₇₁.₁ puna-Ci₈.₄.
'the emperor's boat'. x - x-x-x x-x-x. NS (71c [11:190-M]) LL(?|)HHH.
The accent suggests the constituency is oo-mihune (‹ ofo - myi-fune) rather
than the traditional treatment of omi- as a compound prefix.

4.6/4.7   [oomiki] ‹ ofomiki (Mg): see omiki (offertory rice wine).

4.5   oomira ‹ ofomira ‹ *ofo-myira ‹ *opo₈dj ₈ mira₈.₃. 'scallion: shallot'.
LLxx (= *LLLL) - x-0-x x-x-x.

6.20   oomitegura ‹ ofo-mitegura ‹ *opo₈dj ₈ myi-tegura₄.₂ (‹ ...). 'offerings
to the gods'. LLLHHL - 4-0-x x-x-x.

4.5   oomiti ‹ ofo-miti ‹ *ofo-myiti ‹ *opo₈dj ₈ mi(-)ti₈.₁. 'highway, main
road'. LLLL - x-3-x x-x-x. Cf. oozi.

4.6   oomiya ‹ ofo-myiya ‹ *opo₈dj ₈ mi-da₈.₁ (‹ ...). 'palace'. x - 0-0-x
x-x-x. NS (94b) LLLH.

4.11   oomizi ‹ afumi-di ‹ *afumyi₈.₈ (‹ ...) -n- ti₇₁.₁. 'the road to Ōmi'.
x - 3-x-x x-x-x. Km (W) LLHL.

?4.8, ?4.11   oomono ‹ ofo-mono ‹ *opo₈dj ₈ mono₈.₃. 'the great(est)/best thing;
(the emperor's) food, rice'. x - 0-1-A x-x-x. NS (98b) LHHH, (127a) LLHL. Sz O.

4.7   oomoto ‹ "ofu-moto" ‹ ofo-moto ‹ *opo₈dj ₈ [mi-]moto₈.₃. 'the emperor's
august presence; the court'. x - x-x-x x-x-x. NS (95b, 104a, 130a) LLHH.

4.5(/4.11)   oomune ‹ ofo-mune ‹ *opo₈dj ₈ muna-Ci₈.₁. 'main purport; in the
main'. LLLL(/LLHL) - 0-0[U]/1[H]-B x-x-x.

3.4   oon- ‹ ofom[u]- ‹ ofo-myi- ‹ *opo₈dj ₈ mi-₇₁.₁ (‹ ...). 'exalted,
august'. x - x-x-x x-x-x. NS (98a, 98b, 99a, 99b, 100a, 120b, 133b) LLL-.
Later oon- › on- › o-.

5.16   oonaobi ‹ ofo-nafob/ₘi ?‹ *ofo-nafobyi ‹ *opo₈dj ₈ napo-n[a]-p[a-C]i₈.
'festival of Naobi-no kami (the god who restores regularity/fortune)'.
x - x-x-x x-x-x. Km (W) LLLHL.

?7.10   oon-atumono ‹ ofomyi-atumono ‹ *opo₈dj ₈ mi-₇₁.₁ atu-mono₄.₈ (‹ ...).
'august broth'. x - x-x-x x-x-x. NS (99a) xLxHHHH ?= *LLLHHHH.

4.7 = 2.3|2.1   oonbe ‹ "ofom[u]be" ‹ *opo n[i]bey (‹ ...): see oonie. LL(|)HH -
x-x-x x-x-x.

3.7x, 3.4 = 2.3|1.3 oone ‹ ofo-ne ‹ *opo₈dj ₈ na-Ci₁.₃₈ ('large root'). 'the giant
white radish' (= daikon). LHL (Kn), LLL (Ck) - x-0-x x-B-x. NS (73a [11:218-
M], 73b [11:221-M]) LHL; NS (T+ 57, 58) LL(|)L. Sr qu(h)uni B (= deekuni B).

5.11   oonemusi ‹ ofo-[i]nemusi ‹ *opo₈dj ₈ [z]ina-Ci₈.₄ - musi₈.₁. 'rice weevil'
(= inamusi). LHHHL (Kn), HHHHL (Ck) - x- x-x x-x-x.

6.10   oon-husuma ‹ ofom[u]-fusuma ‹ *ofomyi-fusuma ‹ *opo*adj B* mi-*?1.1* (‹ ...)
pusuma*s.4* (‹ ...). ‘august bedding’. x - x-x-x x-x-x. NS (99a, 99b) LLLHHH.

4.6/4.7 = 2.3|2.1   oonie ‹ ofo-nife ‹ ofo*adj B* (‹ *opo) nifey*?2.1a* (‹ ...).
‘sacrifice (offering) of new rice; new-rice festival’. LLLH - x-x-x x-x-x.
NS (94b) LLLH, (105b) LL(|)HH. Also oonbe, onbe.

5.8, 5.10 oon-koto ‹ "ofom[u]-koto" ‹ ofo-myi- koto ‹ *opo*adj B* mi-*?1.1* koto*s.3*.
‘the emperor’s words/commands’. x - x-x-x x-x-x. NS (120b) LLLHH, (Okada) LHHHH

5.16   oon-kutu ‹ "ofom[u]-kutu" ‹ *ofo-myi- kutu ‹ *opo*adj B* mi-*?1.1* kutu*s.3*.
‘(the emperor’s) august shoes’. x - x-x-x x-x-x. NS (98b) LLLHL.

4.6   oon-ma ‹ "ofom[u]-ma" ‹ *ofo-myi- [u]ma ‹ *opo*adj B* mi- *?1.1* uma*s.3*.
‘the emperor’s horse’. x - x-x-x x-x-x. NS (?115b) LLLH.

?6.10   oon-takara ‹ "ofom[u]-takara" ‹ ofo-myi takara ‹ *opo*adj B* mi-*?1.1*
takara*s.4* (‹ ...) (‘august treasure’). ‘the (common) people, the peasantry’.
LL?HHHH (Kn) - x-x-x x-x-x. NS (98a, 100a, 133b) LLLHHH, (91b *mistake?*) LHHHHH,
(112a) LLxHHH. NS (Okada) has ofo-takara LL(|)HHH.

?6.17, ?6.20   oon-yamai ‹ "ofom[u]-yamafi" ‹ *ofo-myi- yamafyi ‹ *opo*adj B* mi-*?1.1*
dama-p[a-C]i*?B*. ‘the illness of the emperor’. x - x-x-x x-x-x. NS (132a)
LLHHHHL, (Okada) LLLHHL.

4.6   oon-zo ‹ "ofom[u]-so" ‹ *ofo-myi-swo ‹ *opo*adj B* mi-*?1.1* swo*?1.1*.
‘august garment(s)’. x - x-x-x x-x-x. NS (99a, 99b) LLLH, (98b) LxxH.

?4.11   oooba: *(1)* ‹ ofo*adj B* woba*s.1* (‹ *opo bo/[k]wo- -n- pa). ‘great-aunt’.
"LHLH" (Kn, Kz "-oba") ?= *LLHL - 1-3- x x-x-x. K: Hn LLHL. *(2)* ‹ ofo*adj B*
oba*s.8* (‹ *opo o[po] -n-pa). ‘great-grandmother’. x - x-x-x x-x-x. K: Hn LLHL
(attested?).

5.7   ooozi ‹ ofo*adj B* - ofodi*s.8b* ‹ *opo*adj B* opo*adj B* -n- ti*?1.3a* (‹ ...).
‘great-grandfather’. LLLLH/"LHLLH" *(mistake?)* - x-x-x x-x-x.

?7.x   ooooziozi ‹ ofoofodi*s.7* - wodi*s.1* ‹ *opo*adj B* opo*adj B* -n- ti*?1.3a*(‹ ...)
wodi*s.1* (‹ ...). ‘great-great-uncle’. "LLLLH|LH" (Ck) - x-x-x x-x-x.

5.16   oooyobi ‹ ofooyobi ‹ *ofo-oyobyi ‹ *opo*adj B* odonpi*s.4* (‹ ...).
‘thumb’. LLLHL - x-3-x x-x-x. Km x.

4.11   ooroka ‹ oforoka ‹ *opo*adj B* [o]ro-ka*s.2*. ‘careless, absent-minded’
(adj-n). x - x-4-x x-x-x. NS (72b) LLHL; NS (T+ 56) HLLL.

4.7 (= 2.3|2.1), 4.8   oosawa ‹ ofo-safa ‹ *opo*adj B* sapa*s.1*. ‘Great Swamp’: ~ no
ike *(placename)*. x - 0-0-x x-x-x. Km (W) LL(|)HH, LHHH.

5.15   oosazaki ‹ ofo-sasa*k*/*g*i ‹ ofo-sazakyi ‹ *opo*adj B* sa(n)saki*s.4* (‘great
wren’). ‘Ōsazaki’ *(name of an emperor)*. x - 3-x-x x-x-x. NS (90a) LLHLL.
Km (W) LLLHL, LLHLL, LLHHL.

3.1   oosi ‹ ofusi ?‹ *opo-si*adj B pred* (but register incongruent). ‘whole’
(adnoun), ‘wholly, generally’ *(adverb)*. NS (101a) HHH··· .

3.1 › 2.1 oosi ‹ ousi ‹ ofusi (?‹ *opus[a-C]i*?*). ‘(deaf-)mute’. HHH - 0-0-x x-x-x.
Ongi HHH. Modern osi.

3.5x   oosi ‹ ofo-*s*/*z*i ‹ *opo*adj B* (-n-) si*1.3b* (‘big Rumex’). ‘rhubarb’ (= kara-
daioo). LLH - x-x-x x-x-x.

4.5   oo*t*/*d*aka ‹ ofo-taka ‹ *opo*adjB* taka*s.1*. ‘goshawk’. LLLL - 0-0-x x-x-x.

5.9 = 2.3|3.1 ootakara ‹ ofo-takara (‹ ...): *see* oon-takara.

3.x   oote ‹ ofo-te ‹ *opo*adj B* ta-Ci*1.3a*. ‘front gate (of castle); ... ’.
x - 1-1-x x-x-x.

5.15 = 2.3|2.3 "ootikara" (NKD): *see* oozikara.

4.11 (?4.5 = 2.3|2.3)   ootono ‹ ofo-tono ‹ *opo*adj B* tono*s.3*. ‘great palace’.
LLHL (Kn) / LL(|)LL (Ck) - 0-0-x x-x-x. NS (90b, 104a[11:205-K], 119b; ?99b.
?104a [11:202-K]) LLHL.

4.5   ootori ‹ ofo-tori ‹ *opo*adj B* tori*s.1*. ‘big bird’. LLLL - 0-x-x x-x-x.

4.5 ootubo < ofo-tubo < *ofo-tufo < *opo_adj B tupo2.1a. 'a large jar; a chamberpot'. LLLL - 0-3-x x-x-x.

5.9 = 2.3|3.1 ootuzumi < ofotudumi < *ofo-tudumyi < *opo_adj B -n- tuntumi?3.1. 'a large drum'. LL(|)HHH - 3-4-x x-B-x.

5.14 oo-una^t/de < ofo - una-^t/de < *opo_adj B una-[i]de[y]3.x (< una?2.3 inta-Ci[-Ci]B). 'the Great/Grand Canal'. x - x-x-x x-x-x. NS (102a) LLHHL, (Okada, *misprinted "ofoutena"*) LLHHH.

7.11 ooutadokoro < ofouta-dokoro < *ofo-uta?4.6 (< *opo_adj B uta3.2b) -n- tokoro3.1a. 'the Imperial Poetry Bureau'. x - x-x-x x-x-x. Km (W) LLLLHHH.

3.4 = 2.3|1.3 oowa < ofo-wa < *opo_adj B ba1.3a. 'big wheel'. LL(|)L - x-x-x x-x-x.

4.6 oowasi < ofo-wasi < *opo_adj B basi ?2.2a. 'great eagle'. LLLH - 0-x-x x-x-x.

3.x ooya < ofo-ya < *opo_adj B da1.2. 'big arrow'. x - 1-x-x x-x-x.

?4.5, ?4.9 ooyake < ofo-yakey < *opo_adj B da-ka-Ci?2.3. 'public, open'. LLxx/LxLx (?= *LLLL) - 0-0-B x-x-x. NS (T+ 94 *placename*) LLHL. Sz 0.

6.17 ooyakegoto < *ofo-yakey?4.5 (< ...) -n- koto2.3. 'public affairs; ... '. LLHHHL - 0-0-x x-x-x.

4.7 = 2.3|2.1 ooyome < ofo_adj B (< *opo) yome2.1 (< ...). 'older brother's wife'. LL(|)HH - x-x-x x-x-x.

?4.11 = 2.3|2.2 (> 3.4) ooyoso < ofo-yoso ?< *opo_adj B doso2.2b. 'roughly; approximately' *(adverb)*. LLxL ?= *LL(|)HL - 0-0-B x-x-x. Kōbe (Robb) 1. Cf. oyoso.

3.5b oozi < ofodi < *opo_adj B -n- ti?1.3a. 'father's father, paternal grandfather; old man'. LLH - 1-2-x x-x-x. Edo HLL.

3.x oozi < ofo-^t/di < ofo-ti ("till mid-Mr") < *opo_adj B ti1.1). 'main road, highway'. x - 1-2-x x-x-x. Cf. oomiti.

7.21 = 3.5b-ga|3.2b ooziga-huguri < ofodi3.5b ga fuguri3.2b < *opo_adj B -n- ti?1.3a (< ...) -n-ka_pcl punkuri3.2b ('old man's scrotum'). 'a lump of praying-mantis eggs'. LLH-H|HHL - 5-x-x x-x-x.

4.5 = 2.3|2.3 oozika < ofo-zika < *opo_adj B -n- sika2.3 (< ...). 'large deer'. LL(|)LL - 0-0-x x-x-x. NS (Okada) LL(|)LL.

5.15 = 2.3|3.3 oozikara (NKD: "ootikara") < ofodikara (Kn, Ir) < *opo_adj B -n-tikara3.3 (< ...) ('great strength'). 'a kind of grain levy; regional tax grain'. LL(|)HLL - x-x-x x-x-x.

5.6/5.16 ooziozi < ofodi3.5b (< *opo_adj B -n- ti?1.3a) wodi3.1 (< *bo/[k]wo- -n-ti (< ...)). 'great-uncle'. LLLLL (Kn) / LLLHL (Kn, Ck) - x-x-x x-x-x.

4.7 (= 2.3|2.1) / 4.11 oozume < ofodume < *ofo-dumey < *opo_adj B -n- tuma-Ci2.1. 'crab's claws'. LL(|)HH / LLHL - 0/3-4-x x-x-x.

?2.3 ori < wori < *bori. 'cage'. x - 2-2-B x-x-x. Km x. Aomori 2. Ib H1 = 2.2.

4.10 orihusi < wori-fusi < *bor[a-C]i_B pusi2.3 ('bend joint'). 'occasion; (point in) time; just then; occasional(ly), now and then'. LHLL - 2-1-x x-x-x. K: Edo LHLL. For a suggestion this word might be LH|LL (2.4|2.3), see Seki 1977:72, 173-4.

4.1 orimono < *or[a-C]i_A mono2.3. 'textile'. HHHH - 2/3/0-0-A x-x-x. Sz 4, older 0.

3.2b oroka < *oro-ka. 'trifling; slapdash; stupid' *(adj-n)*. HHL - 1-2-B x-B-x. Mr (Bm) HLL. Edo HHL. Sz 2. Cf. ooroka.

5.1 oroka-oi < oroka-ofi < *oro-ka3.2 ofiy (< opo-Ci[-Ci]B). 'aftergrowth of grain on cut stalks (or from spilled seeds)' (cf. hikobae, hituzi). HHHHH - x-x-x x-x-x.

4.11 orosoka < *oro-so-ka. 'simple; sparse; negligent, remiss' *(adj-n)*. LLHL - 3-4-B x-x-x. Mr (Bm) HHLL.

3.5b   oroᵗ/ᵣi < woroti (< ?). 'a huge serpent'. LLH - 1-2-x x-x-x. Sz *(rare)* 2.

3.x   oruku = koni-oruku. '(Paekche) Korean queen'. x - x-x-x x-x-x.

?2.4, ?2.5   osa < wosa < *bosa. 'yarn guide'. LH - 1-0-x x-B-x. Km (W) LH(-H).
Sr uusa B. Perhaps < [w]o sa[si] < *boɪ.₃b sas[a-C]iₐ 'hemp point(er)'.

?2.4, ?2.5   osa < wosa < *bosa. 'elder, leader, chief'. LH - 1-0-x x-x-x. Km x.
Cf. osameru < wosamey- < *bosa-ma-Ci-ᵣ 'rule, suppress'.

?2.4, ?2.5   osa < wosa < *bosa. 'interpreting; interpreter'. LH - x-x-x x-x-x.
NS (122a [14:201-K]) LH. Km x. Kn Mg has -z-. For a suspicion that this word
may have been LF (2.5), see Sakurai 1975:91-2.

5.6 = 3.4|2.3 osamemono < wosamey-mono < *bosa-ma-Ci[-Ci] monoₛ.ₛ. 'imposts, tax
levies'. x - 4/5-0-x x-x-x. NS (112a) LLL(|)LL.

2.1   osi < wosi < *bosi. 'mandarin duck; lovebirds' (= osi-dori x - 2-3[H]/
1[U]-A x-A-x; Sr qusintui must be a borrowing, unless the glottal initial is
a mistake). HH - 1-x-x x-x-x. NS (T 113) LH. Perhaps a truncation of wosi-dori
?< *bo-si(-)ₐdⱼ ?ₐ -n- toriₛ.ₗ 'dear bird'.

2.1 < 3.1 osi < o[o]si < o[f]usi (?< *opus[a-C]i). '(deaf-)mute'. x - 0-0-A x-x-x.
Hakata *(expected)* 1, ygr 0. Ib H = 2.1.

4.2   osikawa < wosikafa (?< *bos[a-C]i?ₐ kapaₛ.ₛ). 'tanned skin, leather'.
HHHL - x-x-x x-x-x.

5.1   osimazuki < osimaduki < *osimadukyi ?< *osi-ma[si] -n- tuki < *os[a-C]iₐ
mas[a-C]iₐ -n- tuk[a-C]iₐ or ᵦ ('push; sit; poke or contact'). 'elbow-rest:
table, desk'. HHHHH - x-0-x x-x-x.

?2.3   oso < woso (< ?; cf. usi). 'otter' (= kawa-uso). x - 1-2-x x-x-x.
Wamyō-shō LL.

3.1   osoi < osofyi < *os[a-Ci]ₐ op[a-C]iᵦ. 'cover(ing); (= uwa-osoi) outer
garment; frame of a folding screen; saddle of a horse; roof-plank cover'.
x - x-x-x x-x-x. Cf. yosoi, osui. The relationship of OJ oswofyi '? roof beam'
is unclear.

3.4   osore < *osore[y] < *oso-ra-Ci[-Ci]ᵦ. 'fear'. (L) - 3-2-B x-x-x. Mr (Bm)
HHH. Edo HHL. Ib F = 3.4.

4.1   osouma < *osoₐdⱼ ₐ umaₛ.ₛ. 'a slow horse'. HHHH - x-x-x x-x-x.

2.3   osu < wo-su < *boɪ.ₗ -suɪ.ₓ (< su/so). 'male (animal)'. x - 2/0-2-A x-x-x.
Km x. Dial. (Fukuoka) ozo. Not in JP. See mesu. Goka-mura 2; Sz, Hiroshima,
Hattō, Hamada, Izumo 1; Matsue 0/1. Ōsaka, Ise 2; Ib H1 = 2.2. The register
is incongruent with the etymology.

3.1   osui < osufyi ?< osofyi < os[a-C]iₐ op[a-C]i?ᵦ. 'outer garment' (= osoi).
x - x-x-x x-x-x. See osuigane.

5.2   osuigane < osufyi-gane < osufyiₛ.ₗ (< ...) (-)ganeᵣₛ.ₛ (< ...).
'material for an outer garment': myi - NS (73c [11:255-M]) HHHHHL, NS (T+ 59)
H|LLH-Hᵉ.

5.2   osumedori < *osumeₛ.ₓ (< ?) -n- toriₛ.ₗ. 'Japanese night heron' (=
mizogoi). HHHHHL - 3-x-x x-x-x.

?2.1   oti < woti < *boti (?< *boti[y] < *boto-Ci < *boɪ.ₗ to-Ci?ₗ.ₗ 'male
spirit'). 'youthful/virile vigor'. x - x-x-x x-x-x. NS (117b [14:131-K])
woti-naku HHHF 'lacking vigor'. Cf. oto(-).

?2.2x, ?2.1   oti < woti < *bo? ti?ₗ.ₗ (or, Murayama 1954:80, *boti[y] < *boto-Ci).
'distant place, yon(der) way'. x - x-x-x x-x-x. Km (W) HL, HH. Cf. ati-ra,
atti, oto-.

2.2x   oti < woti < *boti. 'rape(weed), Brassica campestris' (= abura-na).
HL - x-2-x x-x-x. Perhaps *bo-?ₗ.ₗ (or *[k]wo-ₗ.ₗ) ti[sa]ₛ.ₓ<₃.ₛ 'small lettuce'
(or ti ?< *tu-Ci?ₗ.ₛ 'miscanthus').

4.1   otikata < woti-kata < wo-ti₇₂.₂,₇₂.₁ (< *bo₇ ti₇₁.₁) kata₂.₂ₕ. 'way over there (in the distance); a distant time; abroad, overseas'. x - x-2-x x-x-x. NS (Okada) HHHH; NS (T+ 28, 110, kun) LHHL.

2.2a   oto. 'sound'. HL - 2-2-A A-A-A. Km (S,W) HL. Edo HL. Aomori 0; Goka-mura 1/2. Ib H1 = 2.2. Yn utu A (H 1964:71a, Uemura 1959:136b). Dialect (Iga) ota; (Gifu, Iwate, Toyama) uto.

?2.3   oto(-) 'lower, lesser, younger': see otogai, otooto, oto-ozi, otoyome, menoto; cf. otoru, otosu.

?2.3   oto(-) < woto(-) < *boto(-). (1) ? 'young adult': see otoko, otome, ? otona; cf. oti 'youthful/virile vigor'. (2) 'yester-': see ototoi, ototosi. Murayama 1954:80 takes this as the stem of oti < woti.

?4.4   otodosi 'year before last': see ototosi.

?4.9   otogai < otogafi < ?*otogafyi < ?*otonkapi (?< *oto -n- kap[a-C]i 'lower joining'). '(lower) jaw'. LHHx - 0-1:3-A x-x-x. K: Hn LHHL. Sz 2.

3.4   otoko < wotokwo < *boto₇₂.₃ kwo₁.₁. 'male, young man'. LLL - 3-2-B x-x-x. NS (T+ kun) LHL. Km (W) xxL. Edo HHL. Kōchi 3; Ib F = 3.4.

6.22   otoko-ᵇ/ᵤakari < woto-kwo₂.₄ (< *boto₇₂.₃ kwo₁.₁) sakari₂.₁ (< saka-r[a-C]i₄). 'full bloom of manhood'. x - 4-5-B x-x-x. NS (91a) LLLLHL.

3.7a   otome < wotomye < *boto₇₂.₃ miCa₁.₃ᵦ (?= *mina₇₄₂.₃). 'female, maiden'. LHH - 3/0-1:3-B x-x-x. NS (70c[11:158-M], 119b, 131b) LLH; NS (T+ 44) LLH, (T+ 64, kun) LHH, (T+ 35, 71) HHH, (T+ 37) HHL. Km (W) HHH. 1700 Ōsaka LHL. Wakamatsu 2.

3.7b   otona ?< oto-na (?< *woto-na < *boto₇₂.₃ na₁.₃). 'adult'. x - 0-1/1:3[U]-B B-x-x. Edo LHH. Aomori, Hattō, Hamada, Hata, Wakamatsu, NE Kyūshū. Hakata 2; Matsue, Izumo 0; Narada (otuna), Goka-mura, Ōita (Toguchi 1974:123) 1. Kōchi 1 (Doi 1952:23); Ib L = 3.6. Not attested before Km/Mr? (Another etymology: *o[po₃dⱼ ᵦ - pi]to₂.₂ₐ na[-r[a-C]i]ᵦ 'large person become'.)

4.2   otonai < otonafyi < *oto-na-p[a-C]i₇₄. 'a sound (being audible); the sound of things; inquiring; repute, gossip'. x - x-x-x x-x-x. NS (Okada) HHHL; NS (T+ kun) LHHḶ

4.5   otooto < otouto < *oto-futo < *oto₇₂.₃ pito₂.₂ₐ. 'younger brother' — cf. oto(fyi) 'young person; younger brother/sister'. LLLL - 4-0-B x-B-B. NS (133b) LLLL, (106b) LLxL, (114b ototo) LLL. Km (W) LLLL/LHHL/HLLL. Edo ototo HHL. Sz, Narada, Hattō, Hamada, Matsue, Izumo, Hata 4: Goka-mura 0. Kōchi 4 (Doi 1952:26). Sr quttu B, Yn ututu B.

4.11   oto-ozi < oto-wodi < *oto₇₂.₃ wodi₂.₁ < *bo-₇₁.₁ (or *[k]wo-₁.₁) -n-ti₇₁.₃). 'father's younger brother' (cf. e-ozi). LLHL - x-x-x x-x-x.

3.4 (= 3.1?)   otori 'male bird; soldier': see odori.

3.7a   otori < wo-tori (?< *bo[k[a-C]i]₇₄ tori₂.₁ 'invite bird'). 'decoy'. LHL - 0/3-1:3[H]/0[U]-A x-x-x. Hamada 0/2; Hattō, Matsue, Izumo, Wakamatsu 0; Goka-mura 1. Ib L = 3.6.

?4.4   ototoi < wototofi < wototufyi/*wototofyi < *boto₇₂.₃ -tu pi₁.₂. 'day before yesterday'. x - 3-3-A B-B-C. Km x. K: Edo HHHL. Sz 3; Narada 4; Hakata 2. Sd wutti B, Sr wuttii B, Yn bututi C. The Tk accent retreat is due to monosyllabification.

?4.4   otoᵗ/ₐosi < wototosi < *boto₇₂.₃ tosi₂.₃. 'year before last'. x - 2-3[H]/2[U]-A x-x-x. Km x. K: Edo HHLL. Sz 3; Hattō, Hamada 4; Matsue, Izumo 0.

4.7   otoyome < *oto₇₂.₃ (< ...) yome₂.₁ (< ...). 'younger brother's wife'. LLHH - 2-0-x x-x-x.

3.1 (?< 3.1a) otto < wotto < wofuto/wofyito < *bo₁.₁ pito₂.₂ₐ. 'husband'. HHH - 0-0-A A-A-A. NS (106b woto) LL (cf. otoko). Km x. Edo HHH. 1700 Ōsaka HLL. Narada 1. Ib H = 3.1. Nk uqTuu B = quTuu A. Kunigami, Ōgimi (northern Okinawa) B; Sr utu A; Yn butu A.

3.1   owari < wofari < *bo(-)pa-r[a-C]i₄. 'end(ing)'. HHH - O-O-A x-B-x. Km (S)
HHH. Aomori 2; Goka-mura 1 (verb A). Ib H = 3.1. Nk qwai A; Sr quwai B may be
borrowed, for the initial glottal is anomalous, as is also the accent (the verb
is quwar- A).

2.3   oya < *oda. 'parent'. (LL) - 2-2-B B-B-B. NS (91b. 134a) LL; NS (T 104)
LH. Km (W) LL. Edo HL. Ise 2/1:3; Ib F = 2.3. Cf. oi < o[y]i[y].

3.6   oyako < oya-kwo < *oda₈.₃ kwo₁.₁. 'parent and child'. x - 1-1-B x-B-x. Edo
HLL. 1700 Ōsaka LHH. NE Kyūshū, Yamaguchi, Narada, Hattō, Hamada 1; Aomori 2
(expected); Matsue, Izumo, Goka-mura, Aomori 2; Hakata 2, ygr 1. Kōchi 1 (Doi
1952:23).

3.4 > 2.3   oyobi < *oyobyi < *odonpi < *odonp[a-C]i₄ *(register incongruent)*.
'finger' (> yubi). LLL - (x-x-x x-x-x). Km x. Cf. oooyobi. Murayama 1978
(Nihon-go keitō no tankyū 12) would reconstruct this word as *oyobiy.

5.7   oyobinuki < oyobyi-nukyi < *odonpi₈.₄ (< ...) nuk[a-C]i₄ ('finger poke').
'thimble' (= yubinuki). LLLLH - x-O-x x-x-x.

3.4 < 4.11   oyoso < o[f]oyoso < ?*opo₈d₃ ₈ doso₈.₈b. 'roughly, approximately'
(adverb). (x) - O-O-A x-x-x. Km (S,W) LLL. *See* ooyoso.

3.4   ozasi < wozasi < *bo₁.₈₈ -n- sas[a-C]i₈. 'fish dried on a skewer'. LLL -
2-1:3-x x-x-x.

2.1   ozi < wodi < *bo-₈₁.₁ (or [k]wo-₁.₁) -n- ti₈₁.₃. 'uncle; old man'. HH -
O-O-A A-(B)-x. NS (Okada) HH; NS (T 107, kun) LH. Km x. Edo HH. Ib H = 2.1.

3.6   oziro < woziro < *wo-zirwo < *bo₁.₈₈ -n- sirwo₈.₈. 'white-tailed'. LHH -
O-1-x x-x-x.

(1.2)   *pu (?< *apu) = *pi 'day':   *see* kinoo, kyoo.

?1.3x < *2.3   -ra ?< *[a]ra₈.₃ ('the existent') < *ara-₈. 'thing, amount, some;
(plural)'. H (Kn, Ck) - (x-x-x x-x-x). *See* ikura, makura, sakura, takara,
tatara, ... ; atira, dotira, kotira, sotira. Cf. -re, -ri, -tari.

(3.1←) 3.5a rakuda (< Ch lak-.dha). 'camel'. LLH - O-O-A x-x-x. Wamyō-shō LLH
(Numoto 1979:30). Aomori O; Sz 1.

?2.2b   rati (< Ch lywat). 'corral-fence'. LL - 1-2-A x-A-x. Ib H1 = 2.2. Wamyō-
shō LL.

?1.3x < *3.4   -re ?< *-re[y] < *-raCi < *[a]ra-Ci₈. 'thing, person'. *See* are,
dore, kare, kore, sore; dare, tare; nare, ware; -ri, -tari. Cf. -ra.

3.1   renizi (< Ch .lien-'tsyey). 'lattice-work' (= renzi). HHH - x-2-x x-x-x:
(renzi O-O-x x-x-x). Wamyō-shō HHH.

?1.3x < *3.4   -ri ?< *[a]r[a-C]i₈ ('the existent'). 'person': *see* hitori, hutari;
(*-t[u] ar[a-C]i) mitari, yo(t)tari. Cf. Old Turkish er 'man', er- 'be';
Chuvash ar 'man', Mongolian er(e) 'man'.

?4.8   rindoo < rintau/riutamu (?= riũtaũ (< Ch .lyong-'tam). 'gentian, autumn
bellflower' (= ryuutan). x - 1-2-x x-x-x. Sz 1.

3.4 < 4.5 ringo < riukou ?= riũkoũ (< Ch .lyem-.ghyem). 'apple'. LLLL - O(<*3)-2-B
x-x-x. Wamyō-shō LLLL. Aomori O; Sz, Narada 3. Ib H1 = 3.3.

1.1   ro (< Ch .lo). 'oar'. H (Ir) - O-O-A x-A-x. H = 1.1.

?1.1 < 1.3x   ro (< Ch .lo). 'hearth, fireplace'. L (Ir) - O-O-A x-x-x. Aomori, Sz
O. Ib H = 1.1. Cf. rohen O-O[H]/1[U]-A = robata O-O[H]/1[U]-B 'fireside'.

3.6   rokuro (< Ch lok-.lo). 'pulley, windlass, turning wheel'; (= rokuro-gana)
'lathe'. LHH - 1(/3[H]-2[U]/1[H]-B x-x-x. Aomori *(rare)* 3/1. Ib L = 3.6.

5.8   rokurogana < *rokuro (< Ch lok-.lo) -n- kana₂.₃. 'lathe'. LLLHH - x-x-x
x-x-x.

2.3   roo < rafu < *rapu (< Ch lap). 'wax'. LL - 1-2-B x-x-x. Aomori, Sz, Narada
0; Shimoda 2; Tk accent retreat due to monosyllabification. Ib F = 2.3.

?3.6 < 4.8   ruban < rufan (Kn, Ck) / ruban (Ir) ?< *ruu-ᵇ/ₚan (< Ch lo'-.bhwan).
'pagoda roof'. RHH (?< *LHHH) - 0-0-x x-x-x.

1.x   sa- (prefix): see saoge₂.₄/₃.₅, saosika₄.₁, ... ; ? sayodoko₄.₁.
Cf. sa₍ₐdⱼ₎ ₐ = se₍ₐdⱼ₎ 'narrow, small', sa-ˢ/ᵤa.

?1.1   sa- (prefix) 'early (spring)': see sanae₂.₁, samomo₃.₁; sawarabi 'bracken
sprouts', satuki 'fifth lunar month'. (?< sa[u] < Ch 'tsaw; ?< [ba]-sa <
*ba[ka]-sa, cf. wase)

?1.1   sa- (prefix) ?'true': see sai₂.₁ 'wild boar', sayo₂.ₓ 'night',
sayonaka?₄.₁ 'midnight', ...

?1.1   *sa(-) ?'arrow' (= *so-): see sati, satiya, satuya, soya; ? ikusa. Cf.
Korean 'sal.

?1.3a   sa(a) ?< s[ik]a₂.₃. 'so'. x - x-x-x x-x-x. Km (W) L. Modern ("literary")
relics: sa-hodo 0-0[H]/1[U]-A x-A-x; sa-made 1-2[H]/1:3[u]-A x-x-x; sa-mo 1-2-A
x-x-x; sa-nomi 1-2-x x-x-x.

2.1   saba < *sanpa (?< *sa₍ₐdⱼ₎ ₐ -n- pa₁.₃ᵦ 'small teeth'). 'mackerel'; (Sr)
'shark'; 'dolphin' (see nawasaba). HH - 0-0-A A-(A)-x. Km x. Aomori sanma 0.
Cf. sawara (x - 0-2-x) 'Spanish mackerel' (?< *sanpa [a]ra).

2.3   sabi < (*)sabiy < *sanpu-Ci[-Ci]ᵦ. 'rust'. LL - 2-2-B B-B-x. Km x. Ib F =
2.3. Cf. sabiru.

3.4   sadame < sadamey < *santa-ma-Ci[-Ci]ᵦ. 'decision; rule'. x - 3-2-B x-B-x.
Edo HHL. K: Mr HHL. Ib F = 3.4.

4.2   sadatami < *sa₍ₐdⱼ₎ ₐ -n- tatam[a-C]i₂.₁₊ₐ. '(floor) mat'. HHHL - x-x-x
x-x-x.

2.1   sade ?< *sa₍ₐdⱼ₎ ₐ -n- ta-Ci₁.₃ₐ. 'a scoop net'. HH - 2-2-x x-x-x.

5.6   saenokami < safe-no-kami < *safey no̲ kamiy < *sapa-Ci[-Ci]₂.₁₊ₐ no̲
kamu-Ci₂.₃. 'boundary god (to keep evil spirits out)'. LLLLL (miswritten
"-kaa") ?< *HH-H|LL - 3-x-x x-x-x.

?2.3, ?2.4   saga (? < Ch syang'). 'omen'. x - 1-x-x x-x-x. NS (97a, 106a) LL.
Edo HL(?/HH).

?2.4   saga (?< Ch syang' or sya(y)ng'). 'characteristic; fate, ... '. x - 1-1-x
x-x-x. Km x. K: Edo HL. Tsukishima 1977:50-1 doubts the Chinese etymology.

3.4   sagari < *sanka-r[a-C]iᵦ ('lowering'). 'a wide-brimmed pot into which
things were dangled to cook'. LLL - x-x-x x-x-x.

5.6, 5.7 sagarigoke < *sagari-gokey < *sanka-r[a-C]iᵦ kokey₂.₃ (< ...).
'Lycopodium clavata (= yamakazura = hikage-no-kazura); or perhaps (= saru-
ogase) usnea, Spanish moss'. LLxxx - 3-4-x x-x-x. Km (W) LLLLL, LLLLH.
Mr (W 19) "HHHLH".

6.22   sagarihusube < sagari₅.₄ (< *sanka-r[a-C]iᵦ) fusube₂.₅ (< ?). 'a drooping
wart or wen'. LLLLHL - x-x-x x-x-x.

?2.3   sage < sagey < *sanka-Ci[-Ci]ᵦ. 'lowering, ... '. x - 2-2-B x-(B)-x.

2.1   sagi ?< *sagyi < *sanki (note Sr palatalization, assuming the Sr form is
old). 'heron'. x - 0(/1[H])-0[H]/2[U]-A x-A-x. Km x. Aomori, Narada, Hattō 1;
Hamada, Matsue 0/1; Izumo, Goka-mura, Hiroshima 0; Hakata 1, ygr 0 (= 2.1).
Ōsaka, Ise 0; Ib (rare) H1 = 2.2. Sr saazi A. K: Hn-Edo HH (attested?).

2.1   sai < sa-wi < *sa-?₁.₁ bi?₁.₂,?₁.₁. 'wild boar'. x - x-x-x x-x-x. NS (76a)
HH.

?2.4, ?2.1   sai < safi < safyi < *sapi (?< Korean sap < 'salp; cf. Sino-Korean sap < Ch tsrhap). 'spade; (= ura-sai) sword'. x - x-x-x x-x-x. NS (Okada) HH. Cf. saizue.

?2.4   sai (< Ch 'sey). 'rhinoceros'. LH (Ir) - 1-2-A x-x-x. Kn Mg "lately xR" (?= LH). Sz 1. Ib H1 = 2.4.

?4.9   saibara ?< *sai-ba-raku (< Ch .tshwey-'mba-lak). 'saibara (song)'. LHHL (Ir) - 1/0-0-x x-x-x. K: Hn LLHL, Edo HHLL.

4.2   saigusa < sai-kusa < *sa[k]yi kusa < *saki_{?2.1,?2.2a} ?< *sak[a-C]i_A kusa_{2.3} ('lucky plant').   (1) 'a stem having three branches';   (2) (= hinoki) 'cypress';   (3) (= okera) 'Atractylodes japonica'.

3.5b   saisi (< Ch .tsrhay-'tsyey). 'a hairdress decoration'. LLH - 1-x-x x-x-x.

5.1 = 2.1-tu|2.2   saitu^k/_goro < *sa[k]yi -tu ^k/_goro < *saki_{2.1} -tu (-n-) koro_{2.2b}. 'the other day, a little while back'. HH-H(|)HL - x-x-x x-x-x.

4.1   saiwai < saifafi < sa[k]yi-fafyi < *saki_{?2.1,?2.2a} (< *sak[a-C]i_A) (-)pa-p[a-C]i. 'happiness, good luck'. HHHH - 0-0-B x-A-x. Km (S) HHHH. K: Edo HHHH. Sz 0.

4.5   saizue < safiduwe (Kn) / saituwe (Ck) < *safyi-^t/_duwe < *sapi_{?2.4} (-n-) tuwe_{2.4} (< ...). 'a kind of plow'. LHHL (Ck)/ LHHx (Kn) - x-x-x x-x-x.

2.1   saka(-) 'wine': see sake.

2.1   saka(-). 'backward; opposite (direction)'. x - 1-x-x x-A-x. Nk A. Cf. saka-sa[ma], sakanoboru, ...

2.3   saka. 'slope; (= sakai) boundary'. LL - 2-2-B A-(x)-x. Km (W) LL. K: Edo HL. Tk 2 but 1 "in some areas" (K 1958), "in old shitamachi [downtown]" (Kudō 1978:78) — see Akinaga 1977b:78; Matsumoto 1; Sapporo, Akita, Numazu, Narada, Hattō, Hamada, Matsue, Izumo, Hiroshima, Ōita 2. Ib F = 2.3. Nk sakaa A (new).

2.3   saka (= to[ri]-saka). 'cockscomb, crest'. LL - x-2-x x-x-x.

5.2   saka-abura < *saka_{2.1} anpura_{3.4a}. 'unrefined sake; sake lees'. HHHHL - x-4-x x-x-x.

3.4   sakai < sakafyi < *saka_{2.3} -p[a-C]i_B. 'boundary'. LLL - 2-2-B B-B-B. NS (107b) LLL. Km (S) LLL. Edo HHL. Matsumoto, Numazu, Narada, Hattō, Hamada, Ōita 3; Aomori, Matsue, Izumo 2; Goka-mura 0 (expected reflex). The Tk accent retreat is due to monosyllabification, cf. N-za'kai ← *sakai' (Akinaga 1958). Ib L = 3.6. Yn sagai B (H 1964:71b).

?3.4, ?3.1   sakaki < sakakiy < *saka_{2.3} ko-Ci_{1.3a} (? 'boundary tree'). 'sacred tree (Sakakia ochnacea)'. LLL - 0-0[H]/2[U]-A x-x-x. Km x. Hattō, Hamada 2; Sz (rare), Matsue, Izumo, Goka-mura 0. Cf. hi-sakaki.

3.1   sakan < sakari_{3.1} < *saka-r[a-C]i_A. 'flourishing, vigorous'. HHx - 0-0-A x-x-x. Km (S) HHH. K: Hn HHH.

3.1   sakana < *saka_{2.1} na_{1.3a} (? 'wine side-dish'). 'fish'. HHH - 0-0-A x-(x)-x. Ib H = 3.1. Cf. uo.

3.1   sakari < *saka-r[a-C]i_A. 'prospering'. HHH - 0-0-A x-x-x. Ongi HHH. Km (W) HHH. Mr (Bm) HHH. Edo HHH. Aomori 2. Ib H = 3.1.

4.1   sakasama < *saka_{2.1} sama_{2.2a}. 'upside-down'. HHHH - 0-0(/1:4[U])-A x-(A)-x. NS (127b) HHHH. Km x. Sz 0. Ib sakasa H = 3.1. Sr saka A, Nk sakaasama A (LHHLL).

4.1   sakasima < *saka_{2.1} sima_{?*2.2b}. 'contrary; ? treasonous; (= saka-sama) upside-down'. x - 0-0-x x-x-x. NS (133b) HHHH.

5.2   sakayomoi < sakayamofi < *saka-yamaf[y]i < *saka_{2.1} dama-p[a-C]i_B. 'illness from overdrinking; a hangover'. HHHHL - 3-x-x x-x-x.

4.2   sakazuki < sakaduki < sakadukyi < *saka_{2.1} -n- tuki_{2.2b}. 'winecup'. HHHL - 0/4-4-A B-A-x. Km x. Narada, Hamada 4, Hattō 3; Sz, Matsue, Izumo, Goka-mura 0; Hakata 0, ygr 3/4. Nk x.

2.1   sake < sakey < *saka-Ci. '(rice) wine, sake'. HH - 0-0-A A-A-A. Km (W) HH.
Sakawa 2 (Clarke 118 *but perhaps a misprint, since 145 has 0*); Toyama 1:2 *(low
flat, the expected reflex)*; Suzu, Ise, Ōsaka 0.
2.3   sake < *sakey < *sakaCi. 'owl'. LL - x-x-x x-x-x. Cf. saka*adj B* 'wise'.
?2.3, ?2.5   sake ?< sukey < *s*ª*/*u*kaCi (? from [Chishima] Ainu). 'salmon'. LL(/LH
'sweetfish'?) - 1-1:3-A x-x-x. Km x. Narada, Hattō, Hamada, Goka-mura,
Hiroshima, Hakata 1; Matsue, Izumo 1 *(we expect 2)*. Ōsaka, Ise 1:3; Ib syake
L2 = 2.5.
3.2x   sakeku < sakyiku < *saki*?2.1* (< *sak[a-C]i*A*) -ku. 'safely, in good
health'. HHL - x-x-x x-x-x. Nakata "sakyeku" but Zdb treats the word as an
Azuma variant of sakyiku, and that OJ dialect did not maintain the distinction
of Cye ≠ Cey: the phonograms have both kye (M 4372) and key (M 4368).
3.4   sakeme < *sakey-mey < *saka-Ci[-Ci]*B* ma-Ci*1.3a*. 'crevice, crack, rift' (=
wareme). LLL - 3-0-x x-x-x.
2.1   saki < sakyi < *saki. 'ahead'. HH - 0-0-A A-A-x. Ongi HH. NS (92a, 109a)
HH. NS (T+ kun) sakyi [ ]taturu HL|LHH. Km (S) HH; (W) HH/HL. Mr (Bm) HL. Edo
HL/HH. 1700 Ōsaka HL. Narada 0; Hiroshima 0/2. Ōsaka, Ise 0; Ib H1 = 2.2.
2.1   saki < sakyi < *saki. 'tip; cape' (?< 'ahead'). HH - 1-2-A A-A-A. NS (T
48) FL ?= HL. Ongi HH. NS (71b) HH. Km (W) HH. Hiroshima 0/2. Ōsaka, Ise 2;
Ib H = 2.1. Kt 2 dates back at least to 1777; cf. Okumura 1976:217. Yn sati A.
?2.1, ?2.2a   *saki < sakyi < *sak[a-C]i*A*. 'good luck/fortune (= sati), happiness'.
x - x-x-x x-x-x. NS (T+ kun) sakyi myi-tama HL(|)F-LL. Cf. saiwai, saiwau;
saigusa.
5.2   sakibarai < sakyibarafyi < *saki*B.1* n[i] para-pa-*B*'. 'clearing the way for
a nobleman or lord; paying in advance'. HHHHL *(first meaning)* - 3-0-A x-x-x.
3.4   sakide < sakiyde = *sakey-de < *saka-Ci[-Ci] *?B* -n- ta-Ci*1.3a*. 'chapped
(skin-cracked) hands'. x - 0-0-x x-x-x. NS (Okada) LLL; NS (T+ 108) HHF. K:
"Hn LLL/LLH?" On sakiy- = sakey- cf. Tsuchihashi 1976:337.
3.5x   sakugi < saku-giy < saku*B.3* (< syaku < Ch tšhyak 'footrule' *as euphemism
for hwet 'tablet'*) -n- ko-Ci*1.3a*. 'wood for a royal memorandum tablet'. LLH -
x-x-x x-x-x.
5.16   sakunanza < "sakunam[u]za" (< Ch zhyak-.nam - 'tshaw = syaku/seki-nan -
soo). 'rhododendron' (= syakunage x - 0-0[H]/1[U]-B x-x-x). LLLHL - x-x-x x-x-x.
3.2a (> 3.1)   sakura (?< *sak[a]-u*A* [a]ra*B.3+B* 'bloom thing'). 'cherry'. HHL -
0-0-A B-A-x. NS (Okada) HHH; NS (T+ 67) HLL. Km x. 1700 Ōsaka HHH. Aomori 0;
Hakata 1, ygr 0. Toyama 1:2 *(we expect 1:3)*; Suzu 0 *(we expect 1)*; Kōchi 0;
Ib x. Nk saKuura A. (No modern Kyōto-type dialect with 1:3? Is Mg mistaken?)
3.4   sakuri. 'hiccough'. LLL - x-1:3-x x-x-x. = syakkuri x - 1-1:4-B x-(B)-x.
Sr sakkoobi B.
?3.5x, ?3.4   sakuzu < sakudu < early Ch tsag (> 'tsaw) dug (> dhew'). 'a bath-
soap powder made of red-bean (azuki) flour'. LxH - x-x-x x-x-x. K: Hn LLL.
?2.2a ?< 2.1   sama. 'appearance; direction; ... '. x - 2-2-A x-A-A. NS (110b
[11:338-K]) HH. Km (W) HH. Ib H = 2.1. Sr zama A, Yn dama A (< *[ ] -n- sama);
cf. Tk zama 2 'plight' (Ib F = 2.3). Cf. *sima.
2.1   same < samey < *samaCi. 'shark'. HH - 0(/2[H])-0[H]/1:3[U]-A x-A-x.
Narada 1; Hamada 2; Hattō, Goka-mura 0/1; Izumo 0. Ib L2 = 2.5.
3.1   samomo < *sa-*?1.1* momo*B.1*. 'early peach; (= su-momo) plum; (= sanzasi)
hawthorn'. HHH - x-2-x x-x-x.
4.7 = 2.3|2.1   samukaze < *samu-kaze[y] < *samu*adj B* (< sanpu) kansa-Ci*B.1*. 'cold
wind'. x - 2-x-x x-x-x. NS (113b) LL(|)HH.
3.1   sanae < sanafe[y] < *sa-*?1.1* napa-Ci*B.3*. 'rice sprouts'. HHx - 0-2-0-A
x-x-x.

?3.2a   sanagi (< ?). 'chrysalis, pupa'. x - 0-1-A x-x-x. Aomori, Sz 2; Hattō 3;
      Hamada, Matsue, Izumo, Goka-mura 0; Ib L2 = 3.5/7. Not in JP.

?2.3   sane ?< *sane[y] < *sanaCi(?< *sa-?1.1 na-Ci1.3a 'true root'). '(large)
      seed, core'. LL - 1-2-x x-A-x. Km (W) HH. Sz 1/2. Ib F = 2.3. Nk sanii A.
      Cf. tane.

4.7   sanebuto < *sane-butwo < *sane?2.3 (< ...) -n- putwoadj B. 'Zizyphus
      vulgaris, jujube' (= sanebuto-natume). LLHH - x-x-x x-x-x.

5.2   sanekazura < sane-kadura < *sane?2.3 (< ...) kanturas.s. 'Cercidiphyllum
      japonicum (= Kadsura japonica), katsura tree'. HHHHL - x-x-x x-x-x. Register
      incongruent with etymology?

3.5b   sango < "sam[u]go" (< Ch .san-.hho). 'coral'. LLH - 1-0[H]/2[U]-A x-B-x.
      Hamada 0; Sz, Hattō, Matsue, Izumo 1; Goka-mura 2. Ib H1 = 3.3.

2.3   sao < sawo < *sabo (?< *sa[si - mi-]wo < *sas[a-C]iB mi-bo?2.2a,?2.1
      (< ...). 'pole'. LL - 2-2-B B-B-B. NS (Okada) LL — see saotori. Edo HL. Tappi
      (and all Tk-type dialects) 2. All Kt-type dialects have the expected reflex,
      including Ib F = 2.3. Yn suu B (H 1964:71a, 98).

?3.4, ?3.5x   saoge < sawoge < *sa-1.x bo-?1.1 -n- ka-Ci?1.1. 'small fine hairs'.
      LLL (Kn) / LLH (Ck) - x-x-x x-x-x.

4.1   saosika < sa-wo-sika < *sa-1.x/?1.1 bo-1.1 sikas.s (< ...). 'male deer,
      stag'. HHHH - x-x-x x-x-x. NS (Okada) HHHH. NS (T+ kun) HLHL.

4.6 = 2.3|2.4   saotori < sawo-twori < *sabos.s twor[a-C]iB (1sf = 2.4). '(boat)
      poleman'. x - x-x-x x-x-x. NS (70a [11:45-M]) LL(|)LH; NS (T 42) HLLH = HL|LH.

?4.2, ?4.5; ??4.1   saoyama < safoyama, *sapos.x (< ?) damas.s. 'Mount Sao'
      (placename). x - 0-x-x x-x-x. Km (W) HHHL, LLLL; xxHH.

2.1   sara ?< Sanskrit śarāva. 'plate'. HH - 0-0-A A-A-A. Ib H = 2.1. Yn sara A
      (H 1964:70b). (With Yn suri B compare Sr suurii B 'medium-sized plate' and
      suri 'hamper'.)

2.5   sara ?< *zara. 'new(ly)' (adj-n). LH(-L) - 1-1:3-A x-(B)-x. Km (S) LH-L.
      Mr (Bm) LH-L. Hiroshima 1. Ōsaka, Ise 1:3. Sr sara-··· B 'new'. Cf. ara, arata.

3.1   sarai < sarafi < *sarafyi < *sara-p[a-C]i4. 'rake, pitchfork'. HHH -
      0-1:3[U]-x x-x-x.

?3.4, ?3.3   sarak/ge < sara-key (< ?). 'a shallow jar (used in making sake)'.
      LLL (Kn -g-) / ?HLL (Ir -k-) x-x-x x-x-x. If the etymology includes sara
      'saucer' or *[a]sa [a]ra 'shallow thing', the register should be A (3.3);
      key < *kaCi?1.2,?1.1 (< ...) 'container'.

?4.2, ?4.5   sarayama < sara-yama < *saras.x (< ?) damas.s. 'Mount Sara'
      (placename). x - 0-x-x x-x-x. Km (W) HHHL, LLLL, LLxx.

2.5   saru. 'monkey'. LH - 1-1:3-B B-B-C. Km x. 1700 Ōsaka LF. Ib L2 = 2.5.
      K: Hn-Mr LF. Sr saaru/saru(-) B.

5.16   saruogase < saruwokase < *saru2.3 wo-kase?3.4 (< ...) ('monkey tangle').
      'usnea, Spanish moss'. LLLHL - x-x-x x-x-x.

2.1   sasa. 'bamboo-grass'. HH - 0-0-A x-x-x. NS (Okada) HH; NS (T+ kun) HH.
      Km (W) HH/LL. Ib H = 2.1.

?2.1, ?2.3   sa-a/za < *saadj A (-n-) saadj A. 'small, little' (adj-n, prefix).
      x - x-x-x x-x-x. See saa/zara, saa/zare(-isi), sasage, saa/za-nami.

?4.3   sasagane ?< sasas.1 gapcl ne1.3a (< ... 'root of bamboo-grass'), < sasa-
      gani (< ... 'little crab'). '[spider of the] ···' (fixed epithet/attribute of
      spider). x - x-x-x x-x-x. NS (Okada) HHLL; NS (T+ 65) HLHL. Km (W) sasagani
      HHLL. (The later version is -gani.)

?3.6, ?3.1   sasage < sasagey (?< *sa-sa?2.1,?2.3 -n- kaCi?; ?< *sasagiy?3.1 <
      *sa-sa?2.1,?2.3 -n- ko-Ci1.3a). 'cowpea'. LHH (Zs) / HHH (Kn) - 0-1-x x-x-x.
      NS (T+ kun) FLHH. Aomori 2. Ib sasagi L = 3.6. Cf. hama-sasage.

3.4   sasagi 'wren': *see* sazaki.

4.2   sasaguri < *sa-sa?₂.₁,?₂.₃ -n- kuru-Ci₂.₃. 'a small chestnut' (= sibaguri).
HHHHL - 2-4-x x-x-x.

?3.6   sasame (? < sasami < sasa₂.₁ mi[no]₂.₄ *but register incongruent*). 'grasses
used to weave straw raincapes (mino)'. L?Hx - x-x-x x-x-x.

?4.1   saˢ/za-nami < *sa-ˢ/za?₂.₁ namyi₂.₁ < *saₐdⱼ ₐ (-n-) saₐdⱼ ₐ nami₂.₁.
'little waves, wavelets' (= saˢ/zara-nami). x - 0-0-A x-x-x. Sz 0.

?3.7a, ?3.1   saˢ/zara < *sa-ˢ/za?₂.₁,?₂.₃ (< ...) [a]ra*₂.₃←ᵦ. 'small(-pattern)'.
x - x-x-x x-x-x. NS (84a) LHH(-L); NS (T+ 97) ?H ?= H(|)LL.

5.1 ?= 3.1|2.1 saˢ/zara-nami < *saˢ/za-ra?₃.₇ₐ,?₃.₁ (< ...) namyi₂.₁ (< nami).
'little waves, wavelets'. Also saˢ/zare-nami, saˢ/za-nami.

?3.7a, ?3.1   saˢ/zare < *sa-ˢ/za?₂.₁,?₂.₃ [a]ra-Ci*₂.₃←ᵦ. 'small, little (=
saˢ/zara); pebble (= saˢ/zare-isi)'. x - x-x-x x-x-x.

5.2 ?= 3.1|2.2 saˢ/zare-isi < *saˢ/zare₃.₇ₐ,?₃.₁ (< ...) isi₂.₂ᵦ. 'pebble'.
HHH(|)HL - 3-4-x x-x-x. Km (W) HHH(|)L.

5.1 ?= 3.1|2.1 saˢ/zare?₃.₇ₐ,?₃.₁ (< ...) namyi₂.₁ (< nami). 'little waves,
wavelets'. x - x-x-x x-x-x.

2.1   sasi (?< *saₐdⱼ ₐ [u(n)]si?₂.₃ 'little grub'). 'maggot'. HH - 1-x-x x-x-x.

?2.2b, ?2.3   sasi (?< Korean 'cas). 'castle'. x - x-x-x x-x-x. NS (123b) HL,
(131a) LL.

3.6   sasibu (< ?). 'Vaccinium bracteatum' (= syasyanpo < *sa-sa -n- po).
x - x-x-x x-x-x. NS (123b) HL, (131a) LL.

?4.5   sasigusi < *sas[a-C]i₈ -n- kusi₂.₃. 'ornamental comb'. LLL?L (Kn) / LHLL
(Ir) - 2-3-x x-x-x.

3.4   sasimi < *sas[a-C]i₈ miy₁.₁ (< *mu-Ci) ('slice meat'). 'sliced raw fish'.
x - 3-2-B x-B-x. Aomori, Sz, Narada 3. Ib F = 3.4.

4.7   sasinabe < sasi-nabey < *sas[a-C]i₈ nanpaCi₂.₃. 'a small spouted jug to
heat sake in'. LLHH - x-x-x x-x-x. Also sasunabe.

?3.6, ?3.7a/b sasori (?< *saswori < *sas[a]-u₈ ari₂.₁ₐ 'sting ant'). 'scorpion'.
LHH (Kn, Ck) / LHL - 0-1-0-A x-x-x. Aomori 0 (*we expect 1*); Sz, Wakamatsu 0.
Kōbe (Robb) 1:3/0; Ib F = 3.4.

3.4   sasue ?< *sas[a]-u₈ ye₁.₁ (< ...) ('attach handle'). 'a utensil (cup) with
a handle made of a warped layer of wood'. LLL - x-x-x x-x-x. Also sasae ?<
*sasa[-u] ye, or assimilation of second vowel to first.

?4.7, ?4.5, ?4.11   sasunabe < sasu-nabey < *sas[a-]u₈ nanpaCi₂.₃. 'a small spouted
jug to heat sake in' (= sasinabe). LLHH (Ck), LLHL/LLLL (Kn) - x-x-x x-x-x.

2.3   sata (< Ch .sra-thay'). 'tidings, news'. LL (Ir) - 1/2-0[H]/2[U]-B x-B-x.
Edo HL. Ib HL = 2.4.

?2.1   sati < *sati[y] < *satu-Ci (or *sa-?₁.₁ tu-Ci?₁.₁ 'arrow spirit').
'hunting device (or its spiritual power); abundant game/catch; good luck,
lucky'. HH - 1-2-A x-x-x. NS (T+ kun) HL. Km x. Ib F = 2.3. Cf. saki, saiwai;
soya; satu-ya, ? ikusa, Korean 'sal 'arrow'.

2.1   sato < satwo. 'village'. HH - 0-0-A A-(A)-x. NS (100b) HH. Km x. 1700
Ōsaka HH. Aomori 2. Ib (*rare*) H = 2.1, F = 2.3. Sd sato(o) A.

4.1   satobito < satwo-byito < *satwo₂.₁ -n- pito₂.₂ₐ. 'villager(s)'. x - 0-0-A
x-x-x. NS (Okada) HHHH; NS (T+ 73) HHHH.

?3.4   satoo < satɔɔ < satau (< Ch .sra-.dhang). 'sugar'. x - 2-2(<*3)-B x-B-C.
Narada 3; Hattō, Hamada, Matsue, Izumo 2; Goka-mura 1 (?< *0); Hakata 0, ygr
2. Ib H = 3.1. Nk saataa C; Sr saataa B; Yn sata C (H 1967:284).

3.1   satori < satwori ₐ < *satwoₐdⱼ ₐ -r[a-C]i₄. 'enlightenment, becoming
enlightened'. HHH - 0-0-A x-(x)-x. NS (91b, 95b, 109b, 133a) HHH. Mr (Bm) HHH.
Ib H = 3.1.

2.1   sawa < safa < *sapa. 'swamp, bog; valley; lots, much/many'. HH - 2-2-A
x-x-x. NS (Okada 'lots') LL; NS (T+ 20 'lots') HL, NS (T+ 9 'lots') safa ni
LH-L. Km (W) LL-H. Sz 2. (Tk and Kt as if from 2.3.) Sr suku A 'valley, swamp;
bottom' is from soko 'bottom' ('bottom land') and Sd/Sr saku 'valley, lowland'
might be a variant of that, but it is more likely related to a dialect word
sako; cf. the discussion under sakumu, Ch. 6.

?2.4   sawa(-) < *saba₈ᵢₐ: see sawa-sawa-, sawagu.

6.2   sawaararagi < safaₛ.₁ (< *sapa) arararagi[y] (< *ara-[a]ra₇₄.₉ -n-
ko-Ci₁.₉ₐ). 'Eupatorium lindleyanum' (= akamagusa = sawahiyodori). HHHHHHL -
x-4-x x-x-x.

?6.2   sawahiyodori < safa (< *sapa) f[y]iyodori₄.₂ (< *pido -n- tori) ('swamp
bulbul'). 'Eupatorium lindleyanum' (= sawaararagi = akamagusa). x (?*HHHHHL) -
4-x-x x-x-x.

3.1   sawari < safari < *sapa-r[a-C]i_A. 'hindrance'. HHH - 0-0-A x-(x)-x.
Mr (Bm) HHH. Ib H = 3.1.

?2.4|2.4   sawa-sawa, zawa-zawa < *saba₇₂.₄ saba₇₂.₄. 'clamorous'. x - 1-2-A/B x-x-x.
NS (73a) LH|LH; NS (T+ 57) HḶ-HḶ.

?5.2   sawasorasi < safaₛ.₁ (< *sapa) sorasi₃.ₓ (< ...). 'Nothosmyrnium
japonicum' (= kasamoti = koohon). HHHHx (Ir) - x-x-x x-x-x.

?4.1   sawaudo < safa-uᵗ/dₒ < *sapaₛ.₁ u(n)toₛ.₉. 'Angelica dahurica' (= kasamoti
= yoroigusa). x - x-x-x x-x-x.

2.4   saya < *sada (?< *sa[sa-Ci]_B da₁.₉ᵦ 'insert house'). 'sheath'. LH - 1-1-B
B-A/B-B. Edo LH. Hattō, Hamada 1; Matsue, Izumo 2; Yamaguchi prefecture 1/2
(Hiroto 1961:167). Ib L = 2.4. Nk sii B; Sr saya A/B, ṣii B; Yn saya B (H
1964:71a).

?2.4   saya < *sada. 'pod; legume' (?= 'sheath'). x - 1-1-x x-x-x. K: Hn "HH?"
(misprint for LL ?), Edo LH. Kōbe (Robb) 2/0; Ib L = 2.4.

3.7b   sayaka < *sada-ka₇ᵦ (cf. saeru). 'clear, bright'. LHL - 1-1:3-B x-B-x.
NS (105a) LHL. Km (W) LHL.

2.x   sayo < sa-₇₁.₁ ywo₁.₉ₐ. 'night'. x - 1/0-(2)-x x-x-x.

4.1   sayodoko < *sa-₁.ₓ ywodokoₛ.ₓ (< *dwo₁.₉ₐ -n- tokoₛ.₁). 'bed'. x - 1-x-x
x-x-x. NS (71a [11:175-M]) HHHH; NS (T+ 47) LHHL.

3.5x   sayomi < *sa-yomyi < *saₐdⱼ A dom[a-C]iᵦ ('narrow[-thread] count' but
register incongruent). 'fine-woven cloth' (sayomi-no nuno). LLH - x-x-x x-x-x.

?4.1, ?4.2   sayonaka < sa-ywonaka < sa-₇₁.₁ ywo-naka₇₃.₄ (< *dwo₁.₉ₐ naka₈.₄).
'the very middle of the night; midnight'. x - x-x-x x-x-x. Km (W) HHHH, HHHL.

?2.1, ?2.3   sa-za 'small, little': see sa-ᵃ/₂a.

?3.5b   sazae, sazai (< ?). 'wreath-shell'. x - 1(<*2)-1[H]/2[U]-B x-B-x. Km x.
K: Hn LLL (where attested?). Matsumoto, Narada 1; Tappi, Aomori, Akita, Numazu,
Hattō, Hamada, Matsue, Izumo, Goka-mura, Wakamatsu 2; Sapporo, Hiroshima 0;
Hakata 2, ygr 1. Kōchi 2; Kōbe (Robb) 2/1:3; Ib sasae L2 = 3.5/7.

3.4   sazaki, (Mg) sasagi < saᵃ/₂akyi < *sa(n)saki. 'wren' (= miso-sazai). LLL -
x-x-x x-x-x. NS (93c [11:262-M] "fazakyi" → sazakyi) LLL; NS (T+ 60, kun)
ḶḶL ?= LLL. "Nr sazaki, Hn sasagi."

-          sazanami: see saᵃ/₂anami.

-          sazara, sazare: see saᵃ/₂ara, saᵃ/₂are.

2.3   sazi (< Ch .ts(r)ha-.žhye 'teaspoon'). 'spoon'. x - 1/2-2-B x-x-x.
Aomori, Sz 1. Hattō, Hamada, Matsue, Izumo 2. Ib H1 = 2.4. Earliest dictionary
citation 1180 Iroha-jirui-shō.

1.1   se (?< *se[y] < *sa-Ciₐdⱼ A or *[a]sa-Ciₐdⱼ A). 'shoal: rapids'.
H - 0-0-A A-A-x. Km (W) H-(H). Edo H. Hiroshima 1. Ōsaka, Ise 0; Ib H = 1.1.

?1.2   se < (*)so, ?< *se[y] < *so-Ci. 'back'. H - 1/0-2(/0[U])-A x-A-x. Km x.
    Edo sei HL. K: Edo HH/HL. Aomori, Narada, Hiroshima 1. Kt [U] 0 'back',
    2 'stature' (unrelated etymologically? cf. Okumura 1976b:220); Ōsaka, Ise 2; Kōchi
    (Kobayashi) 1; Ib F ← see F = 2.3. Cf. somuku, soru, sosisi, mimi*/zese;
    siri, usiro.

?1.3a   se (?< *ze, cf. e, < ?; ?< *so, cf. aso). 'older brother, beloved male'.
    x - 1-0-x x-x-x. NS (72c [11:208-M]) L(-H), (Okada) H; NS (T+ 55) F = L(-L);
    NS (T+ kun) R ?= H (or really R = LH?).

1.x   se, sei (?= /see/). 'shaggy hoof'. (?*R, LH) - x-x-x x-x-x. See Ch. 4, §7.

2.2x   sei < "sefi" (< ?). 'young sea-bass' (= seigo). HL - x-x-x x-x-x.

2.3   seki < sekyi (< ... ; see seku*). 'obstruction, barrier'. LL - 1-2-A
    x-x-x. Km x. Edo HL. Aomori, Sz 1. Ib F = 2.3.

2.3   seki < sekyi (< ... ; see seku*). 'cough'. x - 2-2-B B-(B)-(C). Km x.
    Aomori, Sz, Hattō, Hamada, Matsue, Izumo, Hiroshima 2; Goka-mura 1; Hakata 0,
    ygr 2 (=2.3). Ōsaka, Ise 2; Ib H1 = 2.2. Nk sahui B, Sr sakkwii B, and Yn suti
    C are quite irregular or unrelated; probably < syak(k)uri 'hiccup'.

3.5a   sekido < *sekiz.z (< ...) -n- twoi.i. 'a barrier (station/gate), a
    checkpoint'. LLH - 0-x-x x-x-x.

?2.1   seko < sekwo < *se1.9a (< ...) kwoi.i. 'beloved male; (female's)
    brother'. x - x-2-x x-x-x. NS (Okada) HH; NS (T 65) HH. Km (W) HH, LH, LL.

-         sema (NS) 'island': see sima.

2.2a   semi, [dial.] sebi ?< *senpi < *sanpi. 'cicada'. HL - 0-2-A x-(B)-(C).
    Hattō, Yamaguchi 2; Narada, Hamada, Matsue, Izumo, Goka-mura 0. Ib (formerly
    sebi) H1 = 2.2. Nk saasaa B, Sr simii-gwaa B; Yn san-san C. Shinsen-Jikyō sebi.

3.2x   semine < *se71.2 (< so) mi-ne72.1,72.2a (< ...). 'back ridge (of horse,
    ...)'. HHL - x-0-x x-x-x. Cf. setuka.

3.6   senaka < *so71.2 nakaz.4 (< ...). 'back (of body)'. LHH - 0-1-B x-x-x.
    Ongi LHH. 1700 Ōsaka LHH. Aomori 2 (expected); Sapporo, Tappi, Akita,
    Wakamatsu, Ōita 2; Narada 1; Hiroshima, Hida (= northern Gifu), Hattō,
    Hamada, Matsue, Izumo, Goka-mura, Hakata 0; Narada 1. Kōchi 1 (H, Kobayashi),
    0 (Doi 1952:35, Hattori 1973); Ib H = 3.1.

5.3 ?< 5.12 = 3.6|2.3   senakabone < senakaz.6 no fonez.z (< ...). 'backbone'.
    xHLxx - x-x-x x-x-x. Mr (Bm) HHHLL ?< *LHH(|)LL (otherwise the register is
    incongruent with the etymology).

4.7   senbei (< Ch .tsyen-'pyeng). 'rice crackers'. LLHH - 1(?<*2)-2-B x-B-x.
    Km x. Sz 1, Hata 2. Kōchi 2.

4.8   sendan < "semudamu" (< Ch .sen-.dhan). 'Japanese bead tree'. LHHH (Kn),
    RL (Ir) - 0-0-B x-x-x.

2.3   seri (?< *sori, ?< *sari). 'parsley'. Lx - 2-2-B x-x-x. NS (T 126) HH.
    Km x. Edo HL. K: Hn LL. Matsue, Izumo, Goka-mura 1; Aomori, Narada, Hattō,
    Hamada 2; Hakata 0, ygr 2 (= 2.3). Ib (rare) F = 2.3. (Also asara, NKD 1:228c.)

4.8   sesenagi, (JP) sesenage, sesenak/gi (< ?). '(the sound of) rapids
    (= seseragi); ditch, sewer; toilet'. LHHH - x-x-x x-x-x.

?3.4   sesimu (< ?). '(Paekche) Korean prince'. x - x-x-x x-x-x. NS (131a) LLx
    (?= *LLL).

?3.2x, ?3.7x   setuka < *se71.2(< so) tukaz.z. 'back ridge (of horse, ...)'.
    HHL (Kn) / LHL (Ir) - x-0-x x-x-x. Cf. semine.

1.1   si ?< *si[y] < *so-Ci. 'it; that; he'. x - x-x-x x-x-x. NS (79a [14:314-M],
    79c [14:338-M]) H(-H); NS (T+ 78; 80) H(-H), NS (T+ 41) L(-H).

1.1   si (< Ch .syey). 'poetry'. L (Ir) - 0-0-A x-x-x. Hiroshima 0. Ōsaka, Ise
    0; Ib H1 = 1.2.

?1.3x   *si. 'brush(wood), shrub' (?= si 'sorrel'). Cf. siba; si-garami 'fishweir; fence'.
?1.3x   *si. '(bird)': *see* sime. Cf. suzume.
1.3b   si. 'Rumex, sorrel, dock' (= gisigisi). LH - x-0-x x-x-x. NS (T+ kun) L.
   Wamyō-shō R (Cf. Ch. 4, §7). Cf. yamazi, imo*ᵃ*/ᵶi, oosi.
1.x   si. 'wind; direction': *see* sitomi; arasi; higasi, nisi; ? sakasima,
   sakasama; ti.
-          si = [i]siₛ.ₛₐ. 'rock' = iswo. NS (T+ kun) R ?= H (or really R = LH?).
*2.1   *siba, *sima < *sinpa 'while, period of time': *see* sibaraku, sibasi,
   sibasiba; sibayubari.
2.1   siba < *sinpa (?< *siₚ₍ₗ.ₛₚ₎ -n- paₗ.ₛ). 'turf'. HH/HL - 0/1-1[H]/0[U]-A
   x-(A)-x. Km x. Narada 1; Aomori, Sz, Matsue, Izumo 2; Hamada, Hattō, Goka-
   mura, Hiroshima 0. Ōsaka, Ise 1; Ib L = 2.4.
?2.3, ?2.4   siba < *sinpa (?< *siₚₗ.ₛ -n- paₗ.ₛ). 'firewood, brushwood, twigs'.
   LL (Kn) / L?H (Ir) - 0/1-1-B x-x-x. Km x. Edo LH. Sz 1; Ib L = 2.3.
?4.5, ?4.6   sibagaki < siba-kakyi < *sinpaₚₛ.ₛ,ₚₛ.₄ (< ...) kakiₛ.ₛₐ (< ...).
   'a twig fence'. x - 2-1[H]/3[U]-A x- x-x. NS (Okada) LLLL; NS (T+ 91) LLLH.
   K: Hn LLLH *(where attested?)*.
4.10   sibaraku < simara(-ku) ?< *sinpa-ra(-ku) (< ?). '(for) a while'. LHLL/LLxx
   - 2-1:3-B x-x-x. NS (108b) LHLL. Km (S) LHLL. K: Hn-Mr-Edo LHLL. Sz 2.
?3.1   sibasi < simasi < *sinpa-si. '(for) a while'. x - 2-1:3-A x-A[Lit.]-x.
   Km (W) LHH. Edo LHL.
4.1   sibasiba, simasima < *sinpaₛ.ₗ sinpaₛ.ₗ. 'frequently'. HHxx - 2-1:3-A/B
   x-x-x. Ongi HHxx. K: Km HHHH, Edo LHLL. Km (W) HHxx/HLxx/LHxx. Mr (W 18) LLLL.
5.2   sibayubari < (Mg) "sifa-yubari" < *si[n]paₛ.ₗ dunparisₗ.ₛ (< *duₗ.ₛₐ -n-
   par[a-C]iₐ). 'gonorrhea'. HHHHL (Zs) - x-4-x x-x-x. If the etymology is
   correct, we expect *sinpa; perhaps Mg "-f-" = -w- < -b-.
?2.4   sibe < ?*sibye < ?*sin-piCa (< ?). 'pistil; stamen'. LH - 1-2-B x-B-x.
?2.1, ?2.3   sibi < siᶠ/ʙi (< ?). 'tuna' *(fish)* (= maguro). HH - 1-1:3-x x-x-x.
   NS (Okada) LL; NS (T 87, 95) LH. Sz 1.
?2.3   sibu < *sinpu (?< sinpa < *si -n- pa): *see* sibukusa ('sorrel').
?2.4, ?2.3   sibu (?< *sinpuₚₛ.ₛ; ?< Ch s(r)yep 'astringent'). 'astringent
   (puckery) taste; water rust; (kuri no ~) inner skin of chestnut; (kaki ~)
   'persimmon juice'; ?*'persimmon'. LH - 2-2-B x-B-x. Km x. K: "Hn LF?" Aomori,
   Sz, Hattō, Hamada, Matsue, Izumo, Goka-mura 2. Ib F = 2.3. Cf. sibuₐₐⱼ ʙ;
   yamasibu = yamasimu.
3.1   sibuki ?< sifuki (< ?). 'Houttuynia cordata' (= dokudani). HHH - x-x-x.
4.11   sibukusa < *sinpuₚₛ.ₛ (?< *siₗ.ₛₚ -n- paₛ.ₛ 'Rumex leaf') kusaₛ.ₛ.
   'sorrel, Rumex japonicus' (= gisigisi). LLLx (Kn), LL?Hx (Ck), LLHL (Ir) -
   x-0-x x-x-x.
2.x (?2.4)   sida < *sinta (< ?). 'fern'. x - 1/0[H]-2-A x-x-x. Km (W) LH.
   Hattō 1/0; Hamada 0; Sz, Matsue, Izumo 2.
4.11   sidaraka < *sin[a]-tara -ka. 'drooping' *(adj-n)*. LLHL - x-x-x x-x-x.
?6.22   sidariyanagi < *sidariₚₛ.₄ - yanagiyₛ.ₗ < *sin[a]-tar[a-C]iₚʙ ?danaₚₛ.ₗ
   -n- ko̲-Ciₗ.ₛₐ. 'weeping willow'. LLLLxx - x-5-x x-x-x. Also sidareyanagi <
   *sin[a]-tara][C]i ⋯ (x - 4-5-B x-x-x). K: Hn LLLLHL *(inferred?)*.
4.5   sidatuki ?< *sida-tukyi < *sintaₛ.ₓ ₍ₚₛ.₄₎ (< ?) tuk[a-C]iʙ ('fern
   attach'). '(a kind of vine)' (= sensyoosi = yotiko). LLLL (Kn Hō-ka 137:6) -
   x-x-x x-x-x.
-          sidori: *see* sitori(gami), siᵗ/ᶻuori.
?4.6, ?4.11   sigarami < *siₚₗ.ₛ n[i] kara-m[a-C]iₚʙ. '(fish-)weir, fence'. x -
   0-0-x x-x-x. Km (W) LLLH, LLHL. Mr (W 18, 19) HHHL, (20) HHHx. K: Edo HHHHL.

2.5   sigi < sigyi < *sinki. 'snipe'. LH/LL - 1-1:3-x x-x-x. NS (Okada) LH.
NS (T 7) LH; (T+ kun) LH. Km x. K: Hn LF. (Kt 1:3 also in Ōhara 1951:418.)
Sz (rare) 1.

3.1   sigoto < *si (< *so-Ci_A) -n- ko̲to̲ɢ.ɕ. 'job'. x - 0-0-A x-A-x. Km x.
Aomori, Sz 0; Hattō 0/2. Ib H = 3.1.

3.7a   sigure (< ?). 'a shower (in late autumn or early winter)'. LHL - 0-0[H]/
2̲[U]-B x-x-x. Ib (rare) F = 3.4. K: "Hn HHH" (misprint?). Aomori, Sz 0. None of
the 12 etymologies in NKD seems convincing. Apparently the verb sigure- is a
later formation based on the noun. See also Yoshida 1979:87.

2.3   sii < sifyi < *sipi. 'chinquapin (tree)'. LL - 1-2-B x-B-x. NS (T+ kun) LL.
Aomori, Sz 1̲. Ib H1 = 2.2. The Tk 1̲ < *2 is due to monophthongization.

?2.1   [sii] < sif/b̲i 'tuna': see sibi.

3.2x   [siine] < sifine < sifyine < *sipi-ne ?< *sipi-naCi < *sip[a-C]i?A
na-Ci?₁.₁. 'lump, hump'. HHL - x-x-x x-x-x. Km x.

2.3   sika (?< *si[si no] ka LL-L|L). 'deer' (= ka). x - 0/2-2-B x-A-x.
NS (105b [11:237-K]) HL/LL. Km x. Hattō, Hamada 2; Matsue, Izumo 0; Goka-mura 1.
Ib F = 2.3. Nk siKaa A̲. Cf. oozika, saosika, meᵏ/ɢa.

2.3   sika (< si₁.₁ -ka 'that-wise' but register incongruent). 'so' (= sa adv).
LL - 2-2-(B) x-x-x. Km (W) LL. Mr (Bm) HL. K: Edo LH.

(3.7x/)3.5x = 2.3|ku   sikaku < si-kaɢ.ɕ -kuₐdⱼ ᵢₙf (H or F=HL). 'so'. (LHL/) LL(|)H
- x-x-x x-x-x. Cf. kaku.

3.4/3.5x = 2.3|mo   sika-mo < si-kaɢ.ɕ moₚcl (F=HL). 'moreover; and yet'.
LLL (Kn) / LLH (Kz) - (1[H]/)2-2-B x-x-x.

4.6   sikeito < sike? (< ?) itwoɢ.₄ (< ...). 'coarse silk thread from the outer
skin of the cocoon, used mostly as woof/weft'. LLLH - x-0/1-x x-x-x.

2.x   siki < si-kiy < [i]si?₂.₂ₐ kiy?₁.₃ₐ (< ?). 'stone fortress; festival site
surrounded by stones; Shiki (placename)'. x - 1/2-x-x x-x-x. Cf. momosiki.

3.1   sikii < sikyiwi: (1) < *siki bi[y] < *sik[a-C]i_A bᵘ/o̲-Ci[-Ci] ('spread
sit'); (2) < *sik[a-C]i_A bi₁.ₛb ('spread rush (plant))'; (3) < siki[m]iₐ.₁.
'threshold; seat'. HHH (Hoke-kyō tanji) - 0-0-A x-A-x. Aomori [šigie] 0. Ib H
= 3.1. Sr sici A.

4.1   sikimaki < sikyi makyi < *sik[a-C]i_A mak[a-C]i_A. 'one of the punishments
of Heaven: sowing seeds after another has sown (thereby disrupting ···)'.
HHHH - x-x-x x-x-x.

3.1   sikimi < sikyimyi < *siki(-)mi (?< *sik[a-C]_A mi?, but NKD treats siki
as a truncation of sikimi). 'threshold' (= sikii). HHH - x-1:3-x x-x-x.
Cf. tozikimi.

3.2a/b   sikimi < sikyimyi < *sikimi (< ?). 'star anise'. HHL (Kn) / HHH (Ck) -
0/3-1:3-x x-x-x.

3.1   sikiri < sikyiri < *sikir[a-C]i_A (< ...). 'frequent(ly), repeated(ly);
intent(ly), keen(ly)'. HHH - 0-0-A x-x-x. Edo HHH.

4.2   sikiriba < *sikyiri-ba < *sikiriₐ.₁₊A (< *so̲-Ci_A kir[a-C]i_B) -n-
paᵢ?₁.₂. 'black and white feathers joined to fletch an arrow (as a substitute
for the flecked feather of falcon or crested eagle)'. HHHL (Ir sigirifa) -
x-x-x x-x-x.

2.3   siko̲. 'being formidable; being ugly, despicable'. LL-··· - 2-2-x x-x-x.
NS (T+ kun) LL. See sikome, sikona.

?3.4, ?3.7x   sikome < siko̲ɢ.ɕ myeᵢ.ₛb (< *miCa ?= *mina). 'an ugly woman'
(= kokome). LLL (Kz) - 0-0/2-x x-x-x. NS (T+ kun) RHR ?= LH(|)H, ?= LH|R
(= LH|LR). K: Hn LHL (where attested?).

3.4   sikona < siko̲ɢ.ɕ na₁.₂. 'taboo (= real) name; my humble name; a sumō
wrestler's professional name; nickname'. LLL - 0/2-0/3-x x-x-x. Sz 0/2.

*2.1   *sima 'while, period of time': *see* siba.

?*2.2b   sima 'direction' (= sama): *see* sakasima, tatesi(ma), yokosi(ma).

2.3   sima. 'island; quarters, territory'. LL - 2-2-B B-B-B. NS (118b [14:148])
HL (kafara no sima); NS (Okada) LL (simakafara); NS (T 75, 109; T+ kun) LL,
(T+ 126) ᵬL ?= LL, (T 12, T+ 5 *[Takayama misprints "4" and interprets as HH],*
T+ 70) HL, (T+ 40) sima sima LL(|)LL. Km x. Edo HL. Ib F = 2.3. Cf. simeru;
Korean :syem, Paekche *syema (Toh 1981:29), thought to be the source of the
variant sema found in NS.

2.3   sima (?< sima*₂.₃*[-mono*₂.₃*] '(southern-)island [thing]'). 'stripe'. x -
2-2-B x-x-x. Sz, Narada, Hattō, Hamada, Matsue, Izumo, Goka-mura 2. Ib F = 2.3.

5.7 (?= 2.3|3.5)   simakawara < sima-kafara < *sima*₂.₃* kapara*₃.₁,₃.₂*.
? 'the island Kawara' = kawara no sima NS (118b [14:148-K]). x - x-x-x x-x-x.
NS (Okada) LL(|)LLH.

5.16   simatuᵗ/𝒹ori < *sima*₂.₃* -tu (-n-) tori*₂.₁*. 'island bird; (= u)
cormorant'. LLLHL (-d-) - x-x-x x-x-x.

2.3   sime < simey < *si(-)ma-Ci[-Ci]*₇ᵦ*. 'sacred (restricted) area; (= simenawa)
sacred rope'. LL - 2-2-B x-x-x. Narada, Hattō, Hamada, Matsue, Izumo 2.

?2.4 < ?3.6   sime < simey < *si-m[ur]ey < *si*₇₁.₃* mura-Ci[-Ci]*₄*. 'hawfinch,
grosbeak' *(bird)*. RH(?< LHH) - 1-2-x x-x-x. Km x. Variant hime.

?2.1   simi ?< *simiy < *simo-Ci-[Ci]*₄* (cf. simo). 'being cold; ice'. x - A-A-x
x-x-x.

2.1   simi < simyi < *sim[a-C]i*₄* (or *sima-Ci[-Ci]*₄*). 'stain; soaking in (or
what soaks in)'. x - A-A-A x-(A)-x. Ib H = 2.1. Sr sun A < *somi.

?2.2a   simi (< ?). 'clothes moth, bookworm, silverfish'. HL - 0-0-A x-x-x. Km x.

3.6   simizu < si-myidu ?< *si[y] myidu < *su[ma-C]i*ᵦ* mintu*₂.₁ᵦ* (< ...). 'clear
water'. LHH - 0-1:3[H](/2/1[U])- B x-x-x. Km (W) LHH. Yamaguchi 1; Aomori, Sz
2; Izumo 0.

?2.2a   simo < simwo (? si-mwo, cf. sita). 'below'. Hx (= *HL) - 2-2-A x-A-x.
Km (S) HL; (W) HL/HH. Edo HL. Narada ('south'), Hattō 0; Hamada, Goka-mura,
Hiroshima, Yamaguchi (Hiroto 1961:159) 2. Cf. kami 'above'.

2.3   simo (?< *simo, cf. simiru, simi *but register incongruent*). 'frost; cold
rain'. x - 2-2-B x-B-x. Km (W) LL. 1700 Ōsaka HL. K: Hn LL *(attested?)*.
Wakamatsu 1; Hakata 1 *(we expect 0)*, ygr 2; Narada, Hattō, Hamada, Matsue,
Izumo, Goka-mura, Hiroshima 2. Ib F = 2.3.

3.x   simobe < *simwo*₇₂.₂ₐ* (-)bye*₇₁.₃ₓ* (< ...). 'underlings, servants, slaves,
menials'. x - 0/3-0[H]/1[U]-B x-x-x. Edo HHH.

4.5   simodake (< ?): ~ furufu (Kn) 'shake off'. LLLL - x-x-x x-x-x.

4.5   simoguti < *simwo*₂.₂ₐ* -n- kutu-Ci*₂.₁*. 'back entrance'. LLLL - 0/2-x-x
x-x-x.

4.2   simoodo < simoudo < simofuto/simobito < *simwo*₇₂.₂ₐ* (-n-) pito*₂.₂ₐ*.
'servant; social inferior(s)'. HHHL - x-x-x x-x-x.

3.4   simoto (?< *si[gey]*ₐ𝒹ⱼ ᵦ* moto*₂.₃* 'luxuriant root', ?< *si*₁.₃ᵦ* moto*₂.₃*
'dock root'). 'whip, switch; twigs of bushes'. LLL - 3/0-2-x x-x-x. Km (W) LLL.

5.2   simotukata < *simwo*₂.₂ₐ* (< ...) -tu kata*₂.₂ᵦ*. 'below, downward(s)'.
HHHHL - x-x-x x-(A)-x. Sr simukata A.

3.4 = 2.3|1.3 simoyo < simo-ywo < *simo*₂.₃* dwo*₁.₃ₐ*. 'frosty night'. x - 2-2[U]/0[H]
-B x-x-x. Km (W) LL(|)L. K: "Km LHL" *(misprint?)*.

2.1   sina. 'quality; goods; step, level'. HH (Zs) / HL - 0-0-A A-A-x. Ongi HH.
NS (93a, 133b) HH. Km (W) HH(···). Narada, Hattō, Hamada, Matsue. Izumo 0. Ib H
= 2.1.

?2.1   sina (= sina-no-ki). 'Japanese linden'. x - 1-x-x x-x-x.

2.2a (?< 2.1) sina. 'coquetry'. x - 0/1/2-2-A x-x-x.

4.3   sinazina ‹ sina$_{2.1}$ n[i]$_{pcl}$ sina$_{2.1}$. 'of various qualities, varied' (adj-n). HHLL - 2-3-A x-x-x.

?2.4   -sine ‹ *[z]ina-Ci 'riceplant' (= ine): see katisine, kumasine, norisine, urusine.

?2.3, ?2.5   sino ‹ sinwo. '(a kind of) bamboo'. LL(/?HL) - 1/2-1:3-x x-x-x. Ib F = 2.3. NS (T+ kun) LH. Km x. (Cf. sinau.) Man'yō-shū has sinwo/sino.

?3.7b   sinobu ‹ sinwofu ‹ *sinwo(-)p[a]-u$_{?B}$ $_{pred}$. 'hare's-foot fern, Davallia mariesii' (= sinobugusa). x - 1/2-0-x x-x-x. Km (W) LHL.

5.11   sinobugusa ‹ sinwofu-kusa ‹ *sinwo-p[a-]u$_{?B}$ $_{attr}$ kusa$_{2.3}$. (1) 'a source of fond memories'; (2) 'hare's-foot fern, Davallia mariesii' (= sinobu); (3) 'polypody, Pleopeltis thunbergiana' (= noki-sinobu); (4) 'day lily, Hemerocallis fulva' (= wasuregusa). HHHxx (Kn -b-) / LHHHL (Zs -f-k-) - 3-4-x x-x-x. Km (W) LHHHL.

3.6   sinome ‹ *sinwo-mey ‹ *sinwo$_{?2.3,?2.5}$ ma-Ci$_{1.3a}$. 'a kind of bitter green bamboo shoot'. LHH - x-x-x x-x-x.

4.6, 4.7   sinonome ?‹ *sinwo$_{?2.3,?2.5}$ no mey$_{1.3a}$ (‹ ...). (?'bamboo sprouts' →) 'daybreak, dawn; dawn in the east'. x - 0-0-B x-x-x. Km (W) LLHH, LLLH. Mr (W 19) HHLx = *HHLL.

2.3   sio ‹ sifwo ‹ *sipwo. 'salt; tide'. LL - 2-2-B x-B-x. NS (T 41) LL. Edo HL. Ib sio/syoo F = 2.3.

3.6   siode ‹ sifode (‹ ?). 'a kind of saddle-rope'. LHH - 0-x-x x-x-x.

3.1   sioki ‹ *siokyi ‹ *si[y] okyi ‹ *so̲-[C]i$_A$ ok[a-C]i$_A$ ('do and put'). 'punishment'. x - 0-0-A x-x-x. Km x.

?3.6 ‹ 4.8   sioni ‹ siwoni (‹ Ch 'tsye-'ywan 'purple aster'). 'aster' (= si-on x - 1/0-0-x x-x-x). RHH - 1/0-0-x x-x-x. Km (W) LHH/HHH.

3.4   siose ‹ sifose ‹ sifwo-se ‹ *sipwo$_{2.3}$ se$_{1.1}$ (‹ ...). 'tide water/run/ flow'. x - x-x-x x-x-x. NS (Okada) LLL.

?2.3   sira(-) 'white' (= siro ‹ sirwo): see siraga, sirakami, sirami. Cf. sirakeru, sirageru; ? sir-u.

3.4   siraga ‹ sira-ka (Shinsen-Jikyō) ‹ *sira (-n-) ka ?‹ *sirwo$_{adj}$ $_B$ (-n-) ka$_{?1.1}$. 'white hair'. Narada, Hattō, Hamada, Matsue, Izumo, Goka-mura, Wakamatsu 2̲; Hakata (expected) 2, ygr O. Kōbe (Robb) 1:3; Ib H1 = 3.3. Sr siragi B ‹ *sira-ge.

4.5   siraginu ‹ sira-kinu ‹ *sira-kyinu ‹ *sira$_{?2.3}$ kinu$_{2.4}$. 'white silk'. LLLL - 0/3-3-x x-x-x. Zs metathesis (purely graphic?) → "siranuki".

5.16   sirahadake ‹ sirafada-ke ‹ *sira-fada$_{4.x}$ (‹ * sira$_{?2.3}$ panta$_{2.4}$) key$_{?1.1}$ (‹ ?). 'vitiligo, leucoderma'. LLLHL - x- x-x x-x-x.

4.5   sirahara ‹ sira-fara ‹ *sira$_{?2.3}$ para$_{2.3}$ ('white belly'). 'a kind of ailment' (characters: WHITE LIGHTNING). LLLL - x-x-x x-x-x. Cf. siratam¹/ₑ.

4.5   sirakami ‹ (*)sira-kamyi ‹ *sira$_{?2.3}$ kami$_{2.3}$ (‹ ...). 'white hair' (= sirokami = siraga). x - 2-x-x x-x-x. NS (114b) LLLL. Km x.

-       sirakinu: see siraginu.

4.5   sirakuti ?‹ *sira-kuti[y] ‹ *sira$_{2.3}$ kutu-Ci$_{2.1}$. 'Actinidia arguta' (= sarunasi). LLLL x-0-x x-x-x. Kn miswrites "-ke" for "-ti".

3.6   sirami (?‹ *sira$_{?2.5}$ mu-Ci$_{1.1}$ 'white body'; *sira$_{?2.5}$ no[mi]$_{2.3}$ (‹ ...) 'white flea'; ?‹ *sira- miy ‹ *sira$_{?2.5}$ mu[s]i$_{2.1}$ 'white insect'). 'louse'. LHH - 0-1-B B-B-C. Goka-mura 1; Narada, Hattō, Hamada, Matsue, Izumo, Hakata 0; Wakamatsu, NE Kyūshū 2̲; Aomori 2 (expected). Ib sirame L = 3.6. Yn can C.

4.5   sirataka ‹ sira$_{?2.5}$ taka$_{2.1}$. 'white hawk'. LLLL - x-3-x x-x-x.

4.5   siratama ‹ sira$_{?2.5}$ tama$_{2.3}$. 'white jewel; pearl'. LLLL - 0-0-x x-x-x. NS (Okada) LLLL; NS (T+ 92) LLLL.

4.9   siratam¹/ₑ ?‹ *sira$_{?2.5}$ [i]tamyi$_{3.4}$ (‹ itam[a-C]i$_B$). 'a sudden stomach-ache, an abdominal cramp/stitch'. LHLL - x-x-x x-x-x. Cf. sirahara.

4.5   siratuti ‹ sira*2.3* tuti*2.3*. 'white clay; potter's clay; white plaster'.
LLLL - 0/2-0[H]/1[U]/3[U]-B x-x-x.

2.3   siri ?‹ siri[y] ‹ *siro̲-Ci (cf. Matsumoto 1974:99) or ‹ *si[y]ri[y]
‹ *so̲-Ci -ro̲ -Ci. 'butt(ock), rear end'. LL - 2-2-B x- B-(x). NS (T 37. 38)
L̲H̲. K: Edo HL. Ib F = 2.3. Sr sirii B 'rear'; Yn cui C 'back-area', cu-bara A
'rear'. Cf. se, usiro.

4.6   siribone ‹ *siri*2.3* (‹ ...) -n- pone*2.3* (‹ ...). 'tail-bone'. LLLH -
0-x-x x-x-x.

?3.6, ?3.5x (?= 2.3|1.1) sirie ‹ siri[w]e ‹ siri-fye ‹ *siri*2.3* (‹ ...) piCa*1.x*.
'back, behind, the rear (direction)'. LHH (Kz) / xxH (Kn) - 0/2/3-0-x x-x-x.
NS (T+ kun) LL(|)R ?= LL|H. K: Hn LLF "?".

4.x   sirie-de ‹ sirifye-de ‹ sirifye*3.6, 3.5* (‹ ...) -de (‹ -n- ta-Ci*1.3a*).
'at the tail/back, behind'. x - x-x-x x-x-x. NS (T+ kun) sirifye-de ni
'(directs) from behind' HHH-L|H (incongruent).

4.5   sirigaki ‹ *siri-gakyi ‹ *siri*2.3* (‹ ...) -n- kak[a-C]i*B*. 'crupper'
(› sirigai x - 3/4-0-x x-x-x). LLLL - x-0-x x-x-x.

-        siri-he: *see* sirie.

4.8   siriomo ‹ siri*2.3* (‹ ...) omo*adj A* ('bottom heavy'). 'sluggish;
dysentery'. LHHH - 0-1-x x-x-x.

5.16   sirita^b/*mura ‹ *siri (‹ ...) tanpu*2.x* [a]ra*2.3*. 'the buttock' (= siri-
kobuta/-kobura/-tabu/-muta/-busa). LLLHL (-m-) - x-x-x x-x-x. Cf. mimi-tabu.

?*4.7   sirituto ‹ siri*2.3* (‹ ...) -tu two*1.1*. 'the back door; the door behind
(when one departs, cf. sitadati)'. ?*LL-H|H - x-x-x x-x-x.

2.1   siro. 'castle'. HH - 0-0-A x-A-x. Km x. Hiroshima 0. Ōsaka, Ise 0;
Ib H = 2.1.

2.1   siro̲. 'thing; material; substitute, price; unit of field width'. x - 2-0-x
x-A-x. K: Km HH *(attested?)*. Hiroshima 2. Ōsaka, Ise 0/2.

2.5   siro ‹ sirwo (?‹ *sir[a-]u*A* [ir]o*2.3* but *register incongruent*). 'white'.
x - 1-1:3-B B-B-B̲. Hattō, Hamada, Hiroshima, Hata 1; Izumo 1 *(we expect 2)*;
Matsue 2 *(expected reflex)*. Ōsaka, Ise, Kōchi 1:3; Ib L2 = 2.5. Km x. Nk siruu
LHL (?← B = LLH, ?← C = HLL); Sr siru B; Yn cuu-(mun). Cf. sira(-)*2.3*,
siro*adj B*, sir-u*A*; kuro : kura-, kuso : kusa-.

?4.5   sirokage ‹ *sirwo*adj B* kagey*2.3* (‹ ...). 'a horse color (fawn mixed with
white)'. LLxx - 0-x-x x-x-x.

4.7   siro^k/*gane ‹ sirwo-kane[y] ‹ *sirwo*adj B* (-n-) kana-Ci*2.1*. 'silver'.
LLHH - 0-1[H]/0[U]-B x-x-x. Km x. K: Edo HLLL. The -g- version is quite late
(cf. Komatsu 1977a:386-7).

7.21   siro^k/*ganezukuri ‹ sirokanedukuri ‹ *sirwokane*4.7* (‹ ...) -n- tuku-r[a-
C]i*B*. 'made of silver'. LLHxHHL = *LLHHHHL - 5-6-x x-x-x.

5.16   sironamari ‹ *sirwo*adj B* namari*3.7a*. 'lead'. LLLHL - 3-1:4-x x-x-x. Km x.

3.6   siroo ‹ siro-wo ‹ *sirwo*adj B* bo*1.3a*. 'whitebait, icefish' (= sira-uo).
LHH - x-x-x x-x-x.

4.x   sirooto ‹ sirouto ‹ *sirwo*adj B* pito*2.2a*. 'amateur, novice'. x - 1/2-2-B
x-x-x. Sz 2. Cf. kurooto.

6.22   sirotadamuki ‹ sirwo*adj B* tadamukyi*4.11,4.9* (‹ ...). 'white arms'.
x - x-x-x x-x-x. NS (73b [11:222-M]) LLLLHL; NS (T+ 58) LH|LHHH.

4.6   sirouri ‹ *sirwo*adj B* uri*3.4*. 'white muskmelon'. LLLH - 2-1:3-x x-x-x.

2.4   siru. 'juice'. LH - 1-1-B B-B-B̲. Km x. Edo LH. Ib L = 2.4. Nk siruu B;
Yn ciru B̲.

4.5   sirukayu ‹ *siru*2.4* ka-du*2.1*. 'rice gruel' (as contrasted with katagayu
'firm-cooked rice'). LLLL - x-x-x x-x-x.

4.1   sirumasi (‹ ?). 'portent'. x - x-x-x x-x-x. NS (110a) HHHH.

3.1   sirusi < *sirus[a-C]i_A. 'sign, token'. HHH - 0-0-A A-A-A. NS (97b) HHH.
Km (W) HHH. Edo HHH. Ib H = 3.1.

?3.4 < 4.10   sisai (< Ch 'tsyey-sey' 'finely detailed'). 'details, particulars;
circumstances; reasons'. RxL = *RLL (= *LHLL) - 0/1-1[H]/2[U]-A x-x-x.

2.3   sisi. 'flesh; animal'. LL - 1-2-A B-B-B. NS (75c, 115b [14:83L-K], 117b:
?83b) LL, (76a) Lx, (76c [14:135-M]) HL; NS (T 75, 117]) LL, (T 76) HH. Km x.
Edo HL. Sz, Hiroshima 1. Ōsaka, Ise 2; Ib H = 2.1. Ōra siisï (also long in ō
[= Okutake], ...); Nk sii B = sisii B; Sr sisi B. Yn cici B. Cf. sika.

-      sisi (< Ch .sriy-'tsyey). 'lion'. x - 1-2-A x-B-x. Hamada, Hiroshima 1;
Hattō, Matsue, Izumo, Goka-mura 2. Ōsaka, Ise 2; Ib H1 = 2.2. Nk sisi C =
siisaa C; Sr siisi B.

5.16   sisibisio < *sisi-biysifwo < *sisi_g.s -n- po-Ci[-Ci]_R sipwo_2.s. 'salted
chopped meat'. LLLHL - 3-1:4-x x-x-x.   See hisio_?s.1.

4.6   sisimura < sisi_g.s mura_g.1. 'a hunk of meat'. LLLL - 0-0-x x-x-x.

2.2a   sita (?= si-ta, cf. simo). 'below; (deep) inside, heart, mind'.
HL - 2/0-0-A A-A-C. NS (T 91) HL. Km (S,W) HL. Tk 2 only when modified but
Nagano 2 even unmodified (Kudō 1978:48-52). Hiroshima, Yamaguchi 2 (Hiroto
1961:159); Goka-mura, Hamada 2; Aomori, Narada, Hattō, Matsue, Izumo 0.
Ōsaka, Ise 0; Ib H1 = 2.2. Nk *s/hiCaa A; Yn Taara C < *sita-[pa]ra.

2.3   sita. 'tongue'. LL - 2-2-B B-B-B. Km (S) LL. Edo HL. Narada 0; Hiroshima
2. Ōsaka, Ise 2; Ib sita/hita F = 2.3. Sr sica B = şiba B; Yn Taa B.

3.1   sitabi, [sitai] = "sitafi" (?= sitawi) < sita-biy < *sita_g.2a -n-
p^u/oCi_1.3b. 'underground water-pipe; hollow of a Japanese harp'. x - x-0-x
x-x-x. NS (Okada) HHH, NS (T+ 69) LH-H.

4.11   sitabura < si[ri]-tab^b/mura_g.16 (< ...). 'the buttock'. LLHx = *LLHL -
x-x-x x-x-x.

4.6   sitadami < sitadamyi ?< *si-datami (metathesis) (?< *[i]si_g.2b -n-
tatam[a-C]i_A). 'periwinkle' (= kisago). LLLH - x-0-x x-x-x. NS (T+ 8) LLHH.
Km (S) LLLH.

3.x   sitade = sita^t/de < *sita_g.2a (-n-) ta-Ci_1.3a. 'below, beneath'. x - 0-0-A
x-x-x. Sz 0.

6.22   sitadeyubari < *sitade[y]_R (< *sita -n[a]-ta-Ci[-Ci]) yubari_3.6 (< *du_1.3a
-n- par[a-C]i_A). '(an ailment causing) urine drip'. LLLLHL - x-5-x x-x-x.

4.1   sitagura < *sita_g.2a -n- kura_g.2b. 'undersaddle, saddle pad'. HHHH - 0-x-x
x-x-x.

4.3   sitagutu < "sitakudu" (Zs, ?= sitagutu) < *sita_g.2a -n- kutu_g.s. 'under-
shoe pads; outdoor footgear' (> sitoozu). HHLL - 0-4-x x-x-x.

4.3   sitakubi < sita-kubyi < *sita_g.2a kunpi_g.1. 'jowl(s)'. HHLL - 0-4-x x-x-x.

3.6   sitami (?< *sita_g.2a mo-Ci_1.3b 'lower garment' but register incongruent).
'a bamboo basket round at the top and square at the bottom'. LHH - x-0-x x-x-x.
Cf. ii-sitami.

3.2x   sitamo < *sita_g.2a mo_1.3b. 'lower garment'. HHL - x-0-x x-x-x. Km x.

3.1   sitao < sita-wo < *sita_g.2a bo_1.1. 'earlier (deceased) husband' (cf.
uwao). HHH - x-0-x x-x-x.

4.5   sitatuki < *sita_g.s tuk[a-C]i_B. 'being tongue-tied'. LLLL - x-0-x x-x-x.

-      sitate: see sitade.

?5.10   sitatumiti < sita-tu-myiti < *sita_g.2a -tu miti_g.1 (< ...). '? the bottom
road, the low way'. x - x-x-x x-x-x. NS (122b) xxxHH, (Okada) LHHHH. Register
incongruent with etymology.

4.5   sitauti < *sita_g.s ut[a-C]i_B. 'clicking one's tongue'. LLLL - 3/4-4-B
x-x-x.

3.1   sitazi < sitadi < *sita*ₐ.ₑₐ di*ₗ.ₛₐ* (< Ch dhi'). 'groundwork'. x - 0-0-A
x-x-x. Km x. 1700 Ōsaka HLL. K: Hn HHH (where attested?).

4.1   sitazome < *sita-zomey < *sita*ₐ.ₑₐ* -n- soma-Ci[-Ci]ₐ. 'preparatory
dyeing; preliminary preparations, groundwork'. x - 0-0-x x-x-x. Km (W) HHHH.

4.8   sitodati ?< *si[ritu]to-dati < *siri*ₐ.ₛ* -tu two*ₗ.ₗ* -n- tat[a-C]i*ₑ*.
'(tying) a rope on the door to keep the departed spirit from coming back after
a funeral'. LHHx (Ck 122v:6 [Mochizuki: "121v:6 LHHH"]), xxxH (Kn Sō-chū 34) -
0-x-x x-x-x.

?3.6   sitodo < sitoto. '(a kind of bird)'. LHH - x-2-x x-x-x. Cf. Ch. 2, §2.

?3.6   sitogi (?< sitoki [Ōno]). 'rice cake offered to the gods'. xxH (-g-) -
0/2-0-x x-x-x. K: Hn LHH (attested?). Cf. Korean ttek < 'stek 'rice cake'.

?3.4   sitomi (?< *si*ₗ.ₓ* tom[a-C]iₐ 'wind stop'). 'awning'. LLL - 2/0-0-x x-x-x.
Km x. Edo HHL (K: Edo HHH mistaken?).

?3.4   sitone (< ?). 'square cushion; underquilt; sleeping place'. LLL - 0-0-B
x-x-x. Km x. 1700 Ōsaka HHL.

4.3   sitoozu < *sitoodu < sitaudu < "sita-kudu" (= sita-gutu) < *sita*ₐ.ₑₐ* -n-
kutu*ₐ.ₛ*). 'socks'. ⁁HxL (?= *HHLL) - x-x-x x-x-x. See sitagutu.

?3.4   sitori < sitwori: see sitorigami.

?4.6   sitorigami < sitworigamyi < *sitwori*?ₛ.₄* (< situ-wori*?*₊₄.₅ ?< si[ma*ₐ.ₛ*]
-tu bor[a-C]i*ₑ*) -n- kamiy (< *kamu-Ci). (god name). x - x-x-x x-x-x.
NS (T+ kun) LLL(|)LH.

?2.3   si*t*/ᵤu < si*t*/ᵈu < *situ[-wori] ?< *si[ma]-tu-[wori] < *sima*ₐ.ₛ* -tu bor[a-
C]i*ₑ* ('stripe weave'). 'shizu cloth (an ancient textile)'. x - 1-x-x x-x-x.
NS (T+ kun) situ-wori LL(|)LH.

4.11   si*t*/ᵤu-hata < si*t*/ᵈu (< ...) fata (< *pata*ₐ.ₑᵦ*). 'a loom for making shizu
cloth; shizu cloth'. x - 2-0-x x-x-x. NS (Okada) LLHL; NS (T+ 93) LLLL.

4.5   si*t*/ᵤumaki < si*t*/ᵈu*ₐ.ₛ* (< ...) makyi (< *mak[a-C]iₐ). 'cloth-entwined'.
x - 0-0-x x-x-x. NS (76a [14:121-M]) LLLL.

?4.5   si*t*/ᵤuori < situwori ?< *si[ma]-tu-[wori] < *sima*ₐ.ₛ* -tu bor[a-C]i*ₑ*
('stripe weave'). x - x-x-x x-x-x. NS (T+ kun) LL(|)LH. Cf. sitori(gami).

2.1   siwa < *siba. 'wrinkle'. HH - 0-0-A B-x-x. Km (W) HL/RL/HH(?). Eastern
Nagano 2 (Kudō 1978:147); Narada (syaa) 2; Hattō, Hamada, Matsue, Izumo,
Goka-mura 0. Ib H1 = 2.2. Nk siwaa B.

2.x   [siwa] < sifa < *sipa 'cough': see seku (Ch. 6), siwabuki.

4.11   siwabuki < sifabukyi < *sipa*ₐ.ₓ* -n- puk[a-C]i*ₑ*. 'cough(ing)' (= seki).
LLHL - 0/2-0-x x-x-x.

3.4   siwasu < sifasu < *sipasu (< ?). 'the 12th month; the last month of
winter'. x - 0-1[H]//2[U]-B x-x-x. NS (110b) LLL. Sz, Wakamatsu 0.

3.1   siwaza < *si[y] waza < *so-Ciₐ bansa*ₐ.ₑᵦ* ('doing deed'). 'act'. HHH -
0-0-A x-x-x. NS (134a) LHH. Km x. Edo HHH. 1700 Ōsaka HHL. Aomori (rare) 3/2;
Hakata 0 (we expect 2, ygr 0). Ib H = 3.1.

3.5x   sizaya < si[ri]-zaya < *siri*ₐ.ₛ* -n- sada*ₐ.₄* (< ...). 'a fur bag used to
protect the sheath of a sword'. LLH (Hoke-kyō tanji) - x-x-x x-x-x; siri-zaya
x - 0/4-x-x x-x-x.

2.4   sizi < sidi (< ?). 'a footstand for an ox-drawn carriage'. LH - 1-2-x
x-x-x.

?3.4   sizimi < *sinsi-m[a-C]i*ₑ*. 'corbicula' (= sizimigai). x - 0-0-B x-x-x.
Aomori 3; Sz 0. Ib H = 3.1. Nk siziimi A.

?5.2   sizimigai < sizimi-gafi < *sinsi-m[a-C]i -n- kapi*ₐ.ₛ*. 'corbicula'. HHHHL -
3-4-B x-x-x. Sz 4/0. Mg register incongruent with etymology.

4.1   siziraki ?< *sizira-kyi[nu] < *sinsi-ra*?₍ₛ.₁₎* kinu*ₐ.₄*. 'twill' (= sizira).
HHHH - x-0-x x-x-x.

?2.5   sizu < sidu < *sintu. 'poor, miserable'. x - 1-2-x x-x-x. Edo LF.

-      sizu(···): see situ.

3.7b   sizuka < siduka < *sintu-ka. 'quiet' (adj-n). LHL - 1-1:3-B B-B-x.
NS (99a) LHL. Km x. Edo LHL. Sz 1; Izumo 0 (Kobayashi).

?3.5b   sizuku < siduku < *sintuku (< ?). 'a drop (of liquid)'. x - 1[H]/3-2-B
x-x-x. Sz 2; Hattō, Hamada, Matsue, Izumo 3; Goka-mura 0.

-      sizumaki: see situmaki.

?1.1   so(-) 'arrow' (= sa-): see soya.

?1.2   so(-) 'back': see se.

1.x   -so < -swo 'ten': see miso, nanaso, yaso, ...

1.x   ··· so/su [dial.] 'thing/one/fact that ··· '. NKD examples of ··· so from
Shimane and Yamaguchi, the equivalent of Kyūshū ··· to (Hayata 1985:107-8).
Sr ··· si < ··· su; Sd wa-si 'mine', na-si 'yours', etc. Thorpe 242 associates
this doublet with -so/-su 'bird, animal' and also with the particle koso
'precisely', which he takes as something like 'this (very) thing', noting (243)
that "in Ōita this word remains kosu"; cf. NKD 8:203d. (Toyama, however, has
kosa for the particle, perhaps < *kos[o w]a.) Notice also the particle so/zo
'indeed' and so 'that' (also to < *to 'that'), which may be related.

1.x   -so/-su 'bird; animal': see -su.

1.1   so (< ?*zo). 'that' (= sore). H -1-0-(x) (x-x-A/B). NS (Okada) H.
Edo H. Yn uu A (H 1964) / B (H 1967). See soko, sono, sore, sotti. Cf. sa.

?1.1   so < swo. 'hemp; cloth' (= asa, o < wo). (?*H···) - x-x-x x-x-x.
Cf. suso, sode; osou 'wear'. Zdb has so for 'cloth' (cf. miso); Ōno has both
'cloth' and 'hemp' as "so" = either swo or unknown so. Cf. hiso, hahaso, sobo,
soma.

2.3   soba (< ?). 'wingèd spindle-tree (euonymus)' (= nisiki-gi). LL - x-x-x
x-x-x.

2.4   soba < *sonpa. 'beside'. LH - 1-1-B B-B-B. 1700 Ōsaka LH. Ib L = 2.4.
Nk subaa B; Yn suba B (H 1964:181b).

2.4   soba < *sonpa. 'slope, slant; corner, skirt hem; (a)side'. LH - 1-1-B
A-x-x. Km x. Cf. nazoe < nazofe 'slanting'; [dial.] naᵃ/zoeru 'cut slantwise'
?< *nan[a]ₚ₍₂.₃₎ - sopa-Ciₐ. (The register is probably incongruent for the
etymology *s[w]o -n- pa 'edge of cloth'.)

?2.5, ?2.4   soba < *sonpa (?< so (= ?) -n- paₗ.ₛ). 'buckwheat'. x - 1-1[H]/1:3[U]
-B B-A-x. NS (T +7) soba no LH L. Sz, Hakata 1; Tappi 'noodles' 2. Ib L = 2.4.
Nk subaa A. On the Kt 1:3 cf. Ōhara 1951:418. Mg has soba-mugi LLLH/LLLL.

2.x   soba/sowa < sofa < ?*sopa. 'cliff'. x - 1-x-x x-x-x. The -b- is "from Mr":
cf. soba-datu, sobieru.

2.4|2.4   soba-soba < *sonpaₛ.₄ sonpaₛ.₄. 'formal' (adj-n). LH|LH - x-x-x x-x-x.
(From 'corner'; cf. kado-baru.)

4.6   sobauri < *sonpaₚₛ.ₛ,ₛ.₄ uriₛ.₄ ('buckwheat melon'). 'cucumber' (= kyuuri).
LLLH - x-x-x x-x-x.

2.2b   sobi < sofi (< ?*swofyi) / swoni ?< *swonpi. 'kingfisher' (bird). HL -
x-2-x x-x-x. Km x.

2.3   sobi (< ?). 'swollen testicles'. LL - x-2-x x-x-x.

4.8   sobimame < sof[y]i-mame[y] < *so(n)piₛ.ₛb mamaCiₛ.ₛ ('kingfisher[-color]
bean'). 'peas' (= endoo). LLHH - x-x-x x-x-x.

?2.1   sobo < *sonpo. 'tree(s); [Iwate, Miyagi] name of a tree (= ryoobu)'.
HH-··· - x-x-x x-x-x. See sobo-koru; cf. soma, Korean 'swuph 'woods, forest'.

2.1   sode < swoᵗ/ae ?< *swoₚₗ.ₗ (-n-) ta-Ciₗ.ₛₐ ('cloth hand'), ? < *swo[paₐ]
(-n-) ta-Ciₗ.ₛₐ ('append hand'). 'sleeve'. HH - 0-0-A A-A-A. Km (S,W) HH.
1700 Ōsaka HH. Ib H = 2.1. Yn sudi A (Shibata 1959:117).

4.5   soegoto < sofekoto ?< [yo]sofe-ᵏ/ₑoto (< yosofey < *yosafey <) *do-sa-
pa-Ci[-Ci]ₐ (-n-) kotoₛ.ₛ. 'witticism; an apt metaphor'. LLLL - x-x-x x-x-x.

5.1   soeguruma < sofeguruma < *swofey-guruma < *swopa-Ci[-Ci]ₐ -n- kurumaₛ.₁.
'carriages lent to the attendants' (= hitoᵗ/ₐamai). HHHHH - x-4-x x-x-x.
K: Hn HHHHL (mistake?).

4.1   soemono < sofemono < *swofey-mono < *swopa-Ci[-Ci]ₐ monoₛ.ₛ. 'something
added, an extra, a lagniappe'. HHHH - 0-0-A x-x-x.

?3.6   soguki (< ?). '? (some kind of metal plate or fastener)'. Kn (Sō-jō 132:6)
LHx (?= *LHH) - x-x-x x-x-x.

3.1   sohuki (< sofuki) = sohoki < sofoki (< ?). 'the chest/breast area of a
horse or an ox'. HHH - x-0-x x-x-x.

2.1   soi < sofi < swofyi < *swop[a-C]iₐ. 'the steamed rice, malt, and water
that is added to the standing yeast base to brew rice wine' (= soe).
HH (sofi su 'add the ··· ') - x-x-x x-x-x.

4.1   soimono < sofimono < *swofyi-mono < *swop[a-C]i monoₛ.ₛ. 'something
added, an extra, a lagniappe' (= soemono). HHxx = *HHHH - x-x-x x-x-x.

?4.1   soiuma < sofim[u]ma < *swofyi-uma < *swop[a-C]iₐ umaₛ.ₛ. 'side horse,
reserve horse' (= soe-uma). HHxx ?= *HHHH - x-x-x x-x-x.

2.1   soko. 'bottom'. HH - 0-0-A A-A-A. Km (S,W) HH. 1700 Ōsaka HH. Goka-mura 2.
Ib H = 2.1. Yn sugu A (H 1964:71a). Cf. toko.

2.4   soko < so-koₛ.₁ (< ?*zo-ko). 'there, that place'. x -0-1-B x-x-x.
NS (70b, 76a) LH; NS (T 43) LL, (T 75) HH. Km (S,W) LH. Edo LH. Narada 0;
Hattō, Hamada 2; Matsue, Izumo 2/0; Goka-mura 1; Hakata 1, ygr 0. Ib L = 2.4.
The register is incongruent with so(-); cf. koko.

3.1   sokoi < sokofi < soko-fyi < *soko-fye < *sokoₛ.₁ piCaₗ.ₓ (?= *pina).
'the outer edges, the depths, deep inside'. x - x-x-x x-x-x. Km (W) HHH, LLL.

4.5   sokudoku < sokuᵗ/ₐoku (< Ch s(r)ok-dh(r)ok). 'elderberry; Sambucus
pendula; Ebulus chinensis' (= sokuzu). LLLL - 1/0-x-x x-x-x.

?2.1   soma < swoma. 'forested mountain, mountain forest/tree(s)'. x - 0/1-2-x
x-x-x. Km x. Cf. sobo, yama, ma; hiso, hahaso.

?4.4   somosomo < *soma-soma (cf. someruₐ). '(from) the beginning'. HLxx - 1-2-A
x-x-x. Km x. Mr (Bm) HLLL.

3.1   sonemi < sonemi (< sonem-ₚₐ/ₑ < ?). 'envy; hatred'. x - 3-0-B x-x-x.
Km (S) HHH.

2.2b   soni 'kingfisher': see sobi.

2.1   sono < soₗ.₁ -no (< ?*zoₗ.₁ -no). 'that ··· ' (adnoun). HH - 0-0-A A-A-A.
NS (71b, 71c, 112b) HH; NS (T+ 33, 48, 51, 83, 104) L-L. Km (S,W) HH.
Mr (Bm) HH. Ib H = 2.1. Yn unu A.

2.4   sono (< ?). 'garden'. LH - 1-2[H]/1[U]-A x-x-x. Km (S) LL. Hiroshima 1.
Ōsaka, Ise 2.

4.1   sonokami < sonoₛ.₁ kamyiₛ.₄ < *soₗ.₁ -no kamiₛ.₄. '(at) that time'.
HHHH - 0/3-2-x x-x-x. Km (S) HHLL. Mr (Bm) HHLL.

3.5x   sonou < sonofu < sonoₛ.₄ fuₗ.ₓ (< ...). 'garden'. LLH - 0/2-x-x x-x-x.

*2.1   soo < sɔɔ (Esopo) = "sau" (by analogy with koo < kɔɔ < kau < ka-[k]u).
'that way, like that [mesial]'. x - 0/1-0-A x-x-x. [H misprint for Kt (¯3").]
Ib H = 2.1. Attested Edo; earlier, sa and sika were used. Cf. so. to.

3.4   soobi < saubi (< Ch .dzhyang-.(m)bwey). 'rose'. x - 1-2-x x-x-x. Km (W)
LLL. Mr (W 19) HHL.

2.4   sora < swora. 'sky'. LH - 1-1-B x-(A)-x. NS (Okada) LH. Km (S) LH(-H);
(W) LH(-L) / LR (odd). Edo LH. Kōchi 1; Ib L = 2.4. Northern Okinawa (Dana.
Afuso) suura B (Kusakabe 1968:55); it is unclear whether Nk suraa C = Sr suura
B 'overhead branches' belongs here (cf. ura) as an older reflex than Sr [Lit.]
sura A 'sky'.

3.x   sorasi (?< *sworaₛ.₄ siₗ.₉ᵦ 'sky sorrel').   (1) 'Nothosmyrnium japonicum'
(= sawasorasi = kasamoti = koohon);   (2) 'asafetida' (= agi). x - x-x-x x-x-x.

2.1   sore < so̱-re < ?*zoₗ.ₗ [a]ra-Ciₛ.₉. 'that (one)'. HH - 0-0-A A-A-(x).
Km (S,W) HH. Mr (Bm) HH. 1700 Ōsaka HH. Ib H = 2.1. Sd quri A, Sr quri A (cf.
OJ ore 'you').

2.3   sori (?< Korean sa'li[p]). '?a twig gate'. LL - x-x-x x-x-x. Attested only
in Kn Mg?

?2.2b   sori (?< *sor[a-C]iᵦ 'warp'). 'sleigh'. x - 1-2-A x-x-x. Km x. Izumo,
Goka-mura 2; Sz, Hattō, Hamada, Matsue, Hiroshima 1. Ōsaka, Ise 2; Ib H1 = 2.2.

4.6 = 3.4(=2.3-no̱)|1.1   sosanoo < sosano-wo < susa-no wo < *susaₚ*ₛ.₉ no boₗ.ₗ.
'Susa-no-wo' (name). LLL(|)H - 3-x-x x-x-x.

?3.6   sosisi < *so̱ₗ.ₛ sisiₛ.₉. 'backbone flesh/meat'. LHx (?= *LHH) - x-x-x
x-x-x.

?3.6   sosoro (< ?). 'the spit-out remains of a hawk's meal'. LHx (?= *LHH) -
x-x-x x-x-x.

2.1   soti 'that way/direction': see sotti.

3.1   soti-ra < *so̱ₗ.ₗ tiₚₗ.ₗ [a]raₛ.₉₊ᵦ. 'that way/direction; you'.
x - (1/)3-1(soti 2̱[U])-A x-x-x.

2.4   soto (?< *so̱ₗ.ₛ twoₗ.ₗ 'back out'; ?< *so̱ₗ.ₛ -t[u]ₚ꜀ₗ o[mo]ₛ.₄ 'out side'
or 'back side'; ?< *zoto [Ch. 1, §31]). 'outside'. x - 1-1-B B-B-x. Km x.
1700 Ōsaka LH. Ib L = 2.4. Earliest attestation Mr. Cf. toₗ.ₗ < two 'outside'.

3.1 < 2.1 sotti < soti < *so̱ₗ.ₗ tiₚₗ.ₗ. 'that way/direction; you'. x -(1/)3-1(soti
2̱[U])-A x-x-x.

-       sowa: see soba.

2.3   so̱ya < *so̱-ₚₗ.ₗ daₗ.ₛ. 'battle arrow'. LL - 1-2-x x-x-x. Km x. (so =
sa[ti]; cf. sati-ya, satu-ya, ?iku-sa, Korean 'sal 'arrow').

3.6   so̱zo̱ro̱. 'in spite of oneself, unawares, involuntarily; unexpected,
excessive, unsatisfactory' (= suzuro, Mg LHH). x - 0-0[H]/1[U]-B x-x-x.
Cf. Korean su'sᵘ/ₒ'lwo.

?1.2 < 1.3b   su. 'sandbank'. L - 0/1-0-A x-x-x. Km (W) L(-H). Ib H = 1.1. Cf.
sunaₚₛ.ₗ.

1.3a   su. 'vinegar'. L - 1-1-B B-B-x. Km x. K: Edo LH. Ib L = 1.3.

1.3b   su. 'nest'. R - 1/0-0-B B-B-B. Km (W) H(-H). Edo H. Hattō, Hamada, Matsue,
Izumo, Okayama, Hiroshima 0; Aomori, Narada 1. Kōchi (Doi 1952:20), Ōsaka,
Ise 0; Ib H = 1.1. Yn cii B. A compound suu-ya (?*LHH) 'nest/den' occurs in
1116 Daijion-ji Sanzō-hōshi-den (Tsukishima 1969:396).

1.3b   su. 'reed screen, bamboo blind' (= sudareₛ.₅ₐ). R - x-x-(x) x-(x)-x. Km x.
(Edo mi-su HH.) Ib H = 1.1.

?1.3a   su- 'plain, simple, straight': see suasi, sude, suhizi, sunao; ? sugata,
? suge, ? suzi. Cf. sugu.

1.x   -su/-so (1) 'bird; insect': see karasu, hototogisu, uguisu, ... ;
kirigirisu, ... ; kizi, mozu. (2) 'animal': see mesu, osu. Etymology: ?<
su[ru] < *s[o̱]-uₐ ₚᵣₑ𝒹 'does = cries/is'. But Thorpe 242 argues convincingly
that this is the same etymon as ··· so/su 'thing/one that ··· '.

1.x   ··· su/so [dial.] 'thing/one that ··· ': see ··· so/su.

?3.4   suasi < su-ₚₗ.₃ₐ asiₛ.₉. 'bare/unshod foot, (being) barefoot'. LLx -
0̱[H]/1-1[U]/2[H]-B x-x-x.

?3.1   subaru < *sunparu (< *sunpa-r[a]-uₚ₄ 'bring many into one'). 'the
Pleiades'. HHx - 0[H]/2-0[H]/2[U]-A x-x-x. Cf. mi-sumaru 'necklace'.

?2.3, ?2.1, ?2.4 sube < subye < *su-n-pye ?< *s[o̱]-uₐ ₚᵣₑ𝒹 -n- piCaₗ.ₓ (or <
*su[ru] -n- pye < *s[o̱]-uruₐ ₐₜₜᵣ -n- piCaₗ.ₓ). 'means (to do)'. LL (Kn) / HH
(Kz) - 1/2-2[H]/1̱[U]-B x-x-x. Ib H1 = 2.1. NS (95a [11:65-K], 114a [14:43L-K])
LH. Km (W) LH/HH. Cf. subena.

3.3   subete < subey-te[y] (?< *sunpa-Ci[-Ci]ₐ ta-Ci[-Ci]ₐ ₐᵤₓ. 'all'. HLx -
1-1:3-A x-x-x. Km (S) HLL. Mr (Bm) HLL. Sz 2. Ib H1 = 3.3.

3.5a   sudare < *su-n-tare[y] < *su₁.₃ᵦ -n- tara-Ci[-Ci]ᵦ. 'reed screen'. LLH -
0-2-B x-B-C. Km x. Edo HLL. Sapporo, Akita 2; Aomori, Matsue, Izumo, NE Kyūshū,
Ōita 3; Narada, Hattō, Goka-mura, Wakamatsu, Hakata 0. Suzu 1 (we expect 1:3);
Toyama 1:3 (expected); Ib H1 = 3.3. Nk sidee B; Yn ndai C (H 1964:72a).

2.5   sude < su-de[y] < *su₂₁.₃ₐ -n- ta-Ci₁.₃ₐ. 'barehanded, empty-handed'.
x - 1/2-1:3-B x-x-x. Km x. Sz 2. Ib L2 = 2.5.

2.5, (3.7)   sude(-ni) = sunde ni (x - x-0-1) < ?*sumyi-te[y] (< ?*sum[a-C]iᵦ
ta-Ci[-Ci]ₐ ₐᵤₓ. 'already'. LH(-L) - 1-1:3-A x-x-x. NS (93a) LL-H. Km (S) LH-L.
Mr (Bm) LH-L.

2.1   sue < suwe (< ?). 'end'. HH - 0-0-A x-A-x. Ongi-m HL. NS (Okada) HH;
NS (T 89, T+ kun) LH. Km (S,W) HH. 1700 Ōsaka HH. K: Edo HH. Ib H = 2.1.
Sr şii A. Cf. e < ye 'branch', suwae, siri, suso.

?2.3   sue < suwe (< ?). 'porcelain, china(ware)' (= suemono). (LL-···) - 1-x-x.

3.2x   sue-he < suwe-fye < *suwe₂.₁ (< ?) ?piCa₁.ₓ. '(branch) tips, top (of a
plant)'. x - x-0-x x-x-x. NS (70b [11:51-M], 83c [17:123-M]) HHL; NS (T+ 43)
LHH, (T+ 97) LHL.

4.5   suemono < *suwe₂₂.₃ (< ?) mono₂.₃. 'porcelain, china(ware)'.
LLLL - 0/2-0-x x-x-x.

4.9(/4.8) sugadori < *sunka? -n- tori₂.₁. 'a bird: probably lark, quail, or dove'.
LHHL(/LHHH) - x-x-x x-x-x.

3.6   sugame < suga-mey < *sunka? ma-Ci₁.₃ₐ. 'squint (eye), strabismus'. LHH -
0/1-1-A x-x-x.

3.7b   sugao < sugafo < *su₂₁.₃ₐ -n- kapo₁.₁. 'unpainted/sober face'. x - 1-1:3-B
x-x-x. Wakamatsu 2. Earliest attestation JP.

3.5b   sugata < *su-₁.₃ₐ -n- kata₂.₂ᵦ. 'figure'. LLH - 1(<*2)-2-B B-A-x. Km (S)
LLH. Mr (Bm) HLL. Edo HLL. Sapporo, Numazu, Narada, Mino (= southern Gifu),
Hattō, Hamada, Goka-mura, Hiroshima, Wakamatsu, NE Kyūshū, Ōita 2; Hakata 2,
ygr 1; Aomori 2/3; Tappi, Akita, Matsue, Izumo 3. Ib F = 3.4. Nk siɡaaTa A.

?2.3   suge < sugey (< ?*sunka-Ci; < ?*su? -n- ko-Ci₁.₃ₐ < *sun? ko-Ci₁.₃ₐ with
the first part of unknown origin, perhaps a truncation of sumi?). 'sedge'.
x - 0-0[H]/2[U]-B x-x-x. K: Hn LL (attested?). Sz 0. Ib L = 2.4. Cf. hamasuge.
hamasuga-na.

2.1   sugi < sugiy < *sun? ko-Ci₁.₃ₐ. 'cedar, cryptomeria'. HH - 0-0-A B-A-x.
NS (Okada) HH. Km x. Ib H = 2.1. The first element, if not a truncation of
unknown origin, may be < Ch .s(y)ong 'pine'. Nk sizii A, Sr şizi A; on the
palatalization, see Ch. 1. §41.

?2.5   sugu < *sunku. 'straight; immediate'. x - 1-2[H]/1:3[U]-B x-B-x. Edo LF.
Sz 1. Ib L2 = 2.5. Cf. sugiruᵦ, sugosuᵦ; suzi₂.₄ su-₂₁.₃ₐ, muku₄. -ku (adj inf:
adverbial).

3.4   suhizi < sufyidi < *su-₁.₃ₐ pinti₂.₃. 'mud' (= uizi, hizi). LLL - x-0-x
x-x-x. NS (T+ kun) LLL.

5.2   suikazura < sufikadura < *sufyi-kadura < *sup[a-C]iₐ kan-tura₃.₂ (< ...).
'Japanese honeysuckle'. HHHHL - 3-4-x x-x-x.

2.1   suke < suke[-basira] < *suka-Ci[-Ci]ₐ. 'a support pillar'. HH - x-2-x
x-x-x.

2.x   suke < sukey (< ?). 'a large salmon' (cf. sake 'salmon'). x - x-x-x x-x-x.

2.1   suki < sukyi < *suk[a-C]iₐ. 'plow'. HH - 0-0-A A-x-x. Km x. Hiroshima 0.
Ōsaka, Ise 1; Ib H = 2.1.

4.5   sukimono < *sukyi-mono < *suk[a-C]iᵦ mono₂.₃. 'a dilettante: a lecherous
man'. x - 0-1-x x-x-x. Km (W) LLLL.

3.7b   sukosi < *sukwo-si*adj B (stem/pred)*. 'a little'. LHL - 2-1:3-A x-x-x. Km x.
Edo LHL. Sz, Hattō, Hamada, Matsue, Izumo 2; Goka-mura 0. Ib L2 = 3.5/7. Cf.
sukuna*adj B*.

4.10   sukosiki < *sukwosikyi < *sukwo-si-ki*adj B attr*. '(a) little; scant'
(quantity noun, adj-n). LHLL - x-1:3-x x-x-x. Km x. K: Hn LHLF (= LHL|F or
LH|LF).

?4.10   sukosiku < sukwosiku < *sukwo-si-ku*adj B inf*. 'a little, somewhat' *(adv)*.
x - x-x-x x-x-x.

4.11   sukoyaka, sukuyoka, sukuyaka < *suku-d*a*/*o*-ka. 'healthy' *(adj-n)*. LLHL -
2-4-B x-x-x. Km x. "Also sugoyaka in later *[= modern, post-1500]* times."

?3.1   sukumo (< ?). 'peat, turf; dried-up reeds/thatch, ... '. x - 0-x-x x-x-x.
Km x. Also sukubo? Cf. komo.

5.2   sukumomusi < sukumo*?3.1* (< ?) musi*2.1*. 'peat-bug'. HHHHL - x-1:3-x x-x-x.
-        sukuyaka, sukuyoka: *see* sukoyaka.

?3.1   sumai < sumafi < sumafyi < *sumap[a-C]i*?A*. 'wrestling' (= sumoo).
x - 2-2-x x-x-x. NS (128a [14:334-K]) "HLH" *mistake for HHH?*; (Okada) "also
HHH". K: Hn HHH.

3.4   sumai < sumafyi < *suma-p[a-C]i*B*. 'residence'. (x) - 1/2-2-B x-B-x. Km x.
Edo HHL. Aomori 2; Narada 3. The Tk 2 is due to monosyllabification (cf.
compounds N-zu¹mai < *sumai⁷) but the Tk 1 version is unexplained. Ib H1 = 3.3.

5.2   sumarogusa < *sumaro*?(3.1)* (< ?) -n- kusa*2.3*. 'a kind of asparagus' (=
kusa-sugi-kazura). HHHHL - x-x-x x-x-x.

5.6   sumasimono < *suma-s[a-C]i*B* mono*2.3* ('thing to be [constantly] laundered').
'a loincloth (fundoshi)'. LLLLL - x-0-x x-x-x.

5.6   sumera(-) < su*b*/*m*yera(-) < *sunpi*?* - [a]ra*2.3←B* ('divine existent').
'imperial': ~ mikoto (< ...) 'the emperor' x - x-x-x x-x-x: NS (116a
su["]fera··· ; 94a, 104b, 105a, 110b, 131a) HHH-HHH, (115b) xHH-HHH. Perhaps <
*sum[a-C]i*B* or *sum[a]-p[a-C]i*B* 'shining clear/unsullied' or just 'settling,
residing' (as of local god), despite the register.

4.1   sumeragi < su*b*/*m*yeragyi = sumerokyi < *sumyera*?3.1* o[ya]-*k*/*g*yi[myi] <
sunpi?* -[a]ra*2.3* oda*2.3* (-n-) kimi *2.1*. 'sovereign, emperor'. HHHH - 0-0-x
x-x-x. Km (W) HHHH, LLLL, LLHH; sumerakimi HHHHH.

2.3   sumi < sumyi < *sumi. 'charcoal; India ink'. LL - 2-2-B B-B-B. Km x. Edo
HL. Sapporo, Akita, Matsumoto, Numazu, Narada, Hattō, Hamada, Matsue, Izumo,
Goka-mura, Hiroshima, Ōita 2. Ōsaka, Ise 2; Ib F = 2.3. Nk simii B; Onna
suumii B; Yn hin C but also cin B (H 1964:71a). Cf. som-*A*/sim-*A* 'take dye' but
the register is incongruent; susu*2.3* 'soot', Korean swuch / swusk < *swuck
'charcoal'.

2.4   sumi < sumyi < *sumi. '(inside) corner'. LH - 1-1-B A-A-x. Km x. Izumo 2;
Matsue, Goka-mura, Hattō, Hamada, Narada, Hiroshima. Hata 1. Ōsaka, Ise.
Kōchi 1; Ib sumi/suma L = 2.4. Nk simii A.

5.16, 5.11 sumidagawa < *sumyida-gafa < *sumi-*t*/*d*a*2.x* -n- kapa*2.2a*. 'the Sumida
River' *(placename)*. x - 3-4-B x-x-x. Km (W) LLLHL, LHHHL, HHHxx.

3.7a   sumigi < *sumyi-*k*/*g*iy < *sumi*2.4* (-n-) ko-Ci*1.3a*. 'corner beam prop'.
LHL - 0-1-x x-x-x.

3.4   sumigo < *sumyi-*k*/*g*wo < *sumi*2.3* (-n-) kwo *1.3a*. 'a (char)coal basket'.
LLL - 0-x-x x-x-x.

3.4   sumika < sumyika < *sum[a-C]i*B* -ka*1.x* ('live place'). 'residence'. LLL -
1/2-2-B x-x-x. Km (S) LLL. Edo HHL. Aomori 1; Narada 3; Hakata 0 *(expected)*,
ygr 1. Ib H1 = 3.3.

4.5 = 2.3|2.3 sumikaki < *sumyi-kakyi < *sumi*2.3* kak[a-C]i*B* ('charcoal scrape').
'a charcoal hook'. LL(|)LL - 3/4-4-x x-x-x.

?4.5 = 2.3|2.3; ?4.11, ?4.9   suminawa < sumyi-nafa < *sumi*ε.ɜ* napa*ε.ɜ*. 'ink-cord'.
LL(|)LL / LLHL - 0/2-0-x x-x-x. NS (79c [14:337-M]) LHHL; NS (T+ 80) LL(|)LL.

?4.5   suminoe < sumyino̱ye̱ < *sumyi-no̱-yo̱ < *sum[a]C]i*ε* no do*ɐɟ B*.
'Suminoe' *(placename)* — since Heian called Sumiyoshi. x - 0/1-0-x x-x-x.
NS (97b [11:87-K]) LLL?L (LLL?F).

3.7a   sumire < sumyire (< ?*sumire[y] < *sumiraCi < ?). 'violet'. LHx - 0-1:3-B
x-x-x. K: Hn HHH "?". Aomori, Sz, Hattō, Hamada, Matsue, Izumo, Goka-mura,
Wakamatsu, Hakata 0. Ib L = 3.6.

4.1   sumisasi (JP) < sumizasi (Mg) < *sumi*ε.ɜ* (-n-) sas[a-C]i. 'a (bamboo)
carpenter's pen'. LLLL - x-x-x x-x-x.

-        sumisuri: *see* suzuri.

?4.6a, ?4.5   sumitubo < *sumyi-tufo < *sumi*ε.ɜ* tupo*ε.ɪɐ*. 'ink jar'. ?LLLF/?LLLL -
2/0-3-x x-x-x. K: Hn LLLL. *See* Ch. 4, §7.3.

4.11   sumiyaka ?< *sumyi-ya-ka < *sum[a-C]i*ε* -da-ka. 'swift; clear' *(adj-n)*.
LLHL - 2-4-B x-x-x. NS (101b) LLHL. Km (S) LLHL. K: Edo HLLL.

3.6 = 1.3|2.1   sumomo < su*ɐɟ B* momo*ε.ɪ* ('sour peach'). 'plum'. LHH - 0(?< *1)-1-B
x-x-x. Km x. Edo LHH (K: LLH *mistaken*). Hamada *(Hiroto-Ōhara corrigenda)*,
Goka-mura 1; Hakata 1,
ygr 0; Narada, Hattō, Matsue, Izumo 0. Ib L = 3.6.

3.1   sumoo < sumau < sumafu < *sumap[a]-*?ʌ*. 'wrestling'. HHH - 0-0-A (x)-(A)-x.
Km x. Aomori 2. Ib H = 3.1. Sr ʂima A.

3.7x   sumori < *su*ɪ.ɜb* mor[a-C]i*?ʙ*. 'nest-egg; a (person left on) guard'. LHL -
x-0/2-x x-x-x.

4.2   sumunori (?= /sunnori/ < ? - nori*ε.ɜ*). 'laver, amanori, purple seaweed'
(= murasaki-nori, murasaki). HHHL (Ir) - x-x-x x-x-x.

?2.1   suna ?< *su*?ɪ.ε* -na (?< *na*ɪ.ɜɐ*). 'sand'. x - 0-0-A A-A-A. Km x. Aomori,
Sz, Narada, Hattō, Hamada, Matsue, Izumo 0. The accent is 0/2 in dialects of
Shizuoka, Nagano, Yamanashi (K 1943) and 2 in parts of the Ida area of Gifu
(Okumura 1976c:289) — perhaps indicating 2.2a? Ib H = 2.1. Nk sinaa A;
Kunigami, Ōgimi (northern Okinawa) B; Yn cinan A (cf. Ch. 1, §52). Cf. sunago.

?3.1, (?3.4)   sunago < *suna-ᵏ/ᵍwo < *suna*?ε.ɪ* (-n-) kwo*ɪ.ɪ*. 'sand'. LLL (?= *HHH)
- 0-0-x x-x-x. Edo HHH. Cf. masago (= masunago), manago, isago, inago.

3.6   sunao < sunafo < *su-*?ɪ.ɜɐ* napo*?ε.ɜ*. 'straight(forward), naive, gentle'.
LHH - 1-1-A x-x-x. Km (W) LHH. Mr (Bm) LHH. Edo LHH. Aomori 2 *(expected)*; Sz 2.
Hattō, Hamada, Matsue, Izumo 0; Goka-mura 1/2. Ib L = 3.6.

?4.5   sunawati < sunafati (< ?). 'in other words, id est'. LLLL(/LHLL) - 2-1:3-A
x-x-x. Km (S) LLLL. Mr (Bm) HHHH. K: HHHH "Mr and since" *(misleading?)*.

5.16, 2.4|3.7 sundateru < "sumudateru" < *sum[yi]*ε.ɜ* n[i] tat[y]eru (< *tat[a-C]i*ʙ*
ar[a]-u*ʙ*. '? (⋯ that/what is) stood in a corner' *(adnoun?)*. LLLHL (Zs),
LH|LHL (Kn) - x-x-x x-x-x.

2.3   sune ?< *sune[y] < *sunaCi (?< *su-*?ɪ.ɜɐ* n[o̱ᴘᴄɪ p]anki*?ε.ɜ* or *su-*?ɪ.ɜɐ*
n[o̱]*ᴘᴄɪ* asi*ε.ɜ*. 'shank (lower leg)' (= hagi). x - 2-2-B x-B-C. 1700 Ōsaka HL.
Narada, Hattō, Hamada, Matsue, Izumo, Goka-mura 2. Ib F = 2.3. Nk sinii B; Yn
cini C. Cf. hagi, hiza.

1.3b-no̱|1.1 su-no-ko < *su*ɪ.ɜb* no̱ kwo*ɪ.ɪ*. 'narrow slat(s) of wood; drainboard; (=
sunoko-en) verandah'. R-L|H - 0/2/3-0-2 x-x-x. K: Hn "FL|H" must be a misprint.

2.3   suri. 'wicker basket, hamper'. LL - x-1-x x-x-x. Km x. Perhaps < su-[wo]ri
< *su*ɪ.ɜb* bor[a-C]i*ʙ* 'reed-screen weave'; are Sr suurii B 'medium-sized plate'
and Yn suri B 'plate' related?

4.6   surikuzu < suri-kudu < *sur[a-C]i*ʙ* kuntu*ε.ɜ* (?< *kunta). '(metal)
shavings'. LLLL - 0-3-x x-x-x.

?5.16   surituzumi < suri-tudumi < *sur[a-C]i*ʙ* tuntumi*₃.₁,₃.₄*. 'a kind of drum'.
LLLxx (?= *LLLHL) - 2-x-x x-x-x.

4.6 = 2.3|2.4   suriusu < *sur[a-C]i*ʙ* usu*ʙ.₄*. 'grinding mortar'. LL(|)LH - 3-3-x
x-x-x.

-    suro: *see* syuro.

3.1   surume (< ?). '(a kind of) cuttlefish; dried cuttlefish'. HHx/HxH = *HHH -
0-0-A x-x-x. Km x. Aomori, Sz 0; Goka-mura 1. Ib H = 3.1.

-    susanoo: *see* sosanoo.

2.3   susi < su-si*adj ʙ pred* ('it is sour'). 'sushi, vinegared rice'. LL - 1/2-
2-B x-B-x. Tk 1 "new" (K 1958), "old shitamachi [downtown Tk]" (Kudō 1979:78).
Narada, Hattō, Hamada, Matsue, Izumo, Goka-mura, Hiroshima (Okuda) 2. Ib F =
2.3.

2.1   suso < suswo (?< su[we]*ʙ.₁* swo*ʔ₁.₁* 'end cloth'). 'skirt bottom'.
HH - 0-0-A B-A-x. 1700 Ōsaka HH. Ib H = 2.1. Nk x; Sd suso(o) B; Sr susu A.

4.1   susotuke < *suswo-tukey < *suswo*ʙ.₁* (< ...) tuka-Ci[-Ci]*ʀ*. 'skirt-
attached': ~ no koromo '(a kind of garment)'. HHHH - x-x-x x-x-x.

?2.5, ?2.4   susu. 'soot'. LH - 1-1:3[H]/1[U]-B B-B-A. Km x. K: Hn LL "?".
Sz 1. Ib L2 = 2.5. Nk sisi C; Yn cici A (H 1964:183a). Cf. Korean swuch / swusk
< *swuck 'charcoal'; sumi.

4.10   susubana < *susu*ᵐⁱ* -n- pana*ʙ.₁*. 'snivel'. LHLL - x-1:3-x x-x-x.
Cf. susuru.

?3.6   susuki < susukyi < *susuki (< ?). 'eulalia, Miscanthus sinensis'. LHH -
0(?<*1)-0[H]/1[U]-B x-x-x. NS (110b [11:339-K]) HHH. Km x. 1700 Ōsaka LHH.
Aomori 2 *(we expect 1)*; Narada, Goka-mura 1; Hakata 1, ygr 0. Hattō, Hamada,
Matsue, Izumo, Wakamatsu 0. Ib H = 3.1.

3.4   suwae < sufae < "sufaye/sufawe" (?< *suwa-ye, cf. sue). 'a long straight
twig; a switch'. LLL - 0-0-x x-x-x.

2.4   suzi < *su*adj ʙ* -n- si*₁.₃ᵇ*. 'sour sorrel'. LH - x-x-x x-x-x.

2.4   suzi < sudi < *sunti (?< *su-*ʔ₁.₃ₐ* -n- ti*ʔ₁.₁*. ?< *sun[ku]*ʔ₂.ₐ* ti*ʔ₁.₁*).
'tendon, sinew'. LH - 1-1-B B-B-x. Km x. 1700 Ōsaka LH. Ib L = 2.4.
(K: "Hn LL ?" *wrong*.)

2.1   suzu < *sunsu. '(little) bell' (?< 'tin'; cf. kane 'metal; bell'). HH -
0-0-A B-x-x. Km x. Goka-mura 2. Toyama 2; Suzu 0; Ib H = 2.1. Nk x.

2.1   suzu < *sunsu. 'tin; tin flagon'. x - 0[H]/1[K]-0[H]/2[U]-A x-A-x. Km x.
Aomori, Sz 1. Ib H1 = 2.2.

4.2   suzu-ʰ/ᵇune (NKD -b-) < suzu-fune < *sunsu*ʙ.₁* puna-Ci*ʙ.₄*. 'bell-festooned
boat'. x - x-x-x x-x-x. NS (71c [11:189-M]) HHHL; NS (T+ 51) LHHｮ = LHHL.

3.1   suzuki < suzukyi < *sunsuki. 'perch, seabass' *(fish)*. HHH - 0-0-A x-x-x.
Km x. Aomori 2; Narada 1; Hakata 1 *(we expect 2)*, ygr 0. Ib H = 3.1.

3.7x   ? suzuki (< ?). ? 'a reed mat for raising silkworms' (= kaiko no su); cf.
sudare (tare-su), su-no-ko. Km (W Okada) LHL (Ch gloss THIN WORM).

3.6   suzume < suzumey < *sunsu-m[ur]ey < *sunsu mura-Ci[-Ci]*ʙ.₁*. 'sparrow'
(bird). LHH - 0(?<1)-1-B x-x-x. Km x. Aomori 1 *(we expect 2)*; Tappi, Akita,
Hattō, Goka-mura, Wakamatsu, Ōita 1; Hakata 1, ygr 0; Narada, Hamada, Izumo,
Hiroshima, Hida (= northern Gifu) 0; Sapporo 2. Ib L = 3.6. Cf. sime, -me.

5.12   suzumitaka (NKD) = suzumidaka (Mg) < suzume*ₐ.ₐ* (< ...) (-n-) taka*ʙ.₁*.
'female sparrow-hawk (tumi)'. LHHLL - x-x-x x-x-x.

3.4 < 4.5/4.6   suzuri < sumi-suri (LLLx) < *sumyi - sur[y]i < *sumi*ʙ.₄* sur[a-C]i*ʙ*.
'ink-slab'. (x) - 3-2-B x-B-x. Km x. Edo HHL. Aomori, Narada 0; Hattō, Hamada,
Matsue, Izumo 3. Ib F = 3.4.

3.6   suzuro = so̱zo̱ro̱ ('in spite of oneself, ... ' x - 0-0[H]/1[U]-B x-x-x).
LHH - 0-1-x x-x-x.

4.11   suzuᵃ/ᵤiro ?< suzu-siro (?< *sunsuᵤ.ᵢ sirwoᵤ.ᵤ 'tin white'). 'white radish
(= daikon); the (uncut) top of a child's hair'. LLHL - x-0-x x-x-x.

(1.1←) ?1.3b   sya < "siya" (< Ch .sra). 'silk gauze'. R (Zs, Wamyō-shō), LH (Ir).
HL (Kn) - 0-0-A x-x-x. Aomori "?1", Sz ("later") O. Ib F ← syaa F = 2.2.

?2.2b < 3.3   syako ?< siyako (?< Ch). 'squilla'. x - 1-2-A x-x-x.

?2.2b < 3.3   syako ?< siyako (?< Ch). 'partridge'. x - 1-2-A x-x-x.

?2.2b < 3.3   syako RL (Zs) = siyako LHL (Kn)   (< Ch .tšya-.ghyo). 'giant clam'.
      See §7.1. RL/LHL - 1-x-x x-x-x. Wamyō-shō RL (Numoto 1979:28).

2.3   syaku (< Ch tšyak). *(1)* 'foot(rule)'. x - 2-2-B x-B-x. *(2)* euphemism
for kotu (< Ch hwet) 'royal memorandum tablet'. LL - 1-0-x x-x-x. Ib F = 2.3.

2.4   syoo < syau < "siyau" (< Ch .tsrang/.sreng). 'a kind of harp or panpipe'.
LLH (Ck), R (Wamyō-shō) - 1-1-x x-x-x. (Kn Mg syau-no-⋯ LLH.)

?2.4, ?2.3   syoo < seu (?< Ch 'syew 'small' [Ōno]). 'small/male hawk' (= syoo-
aka). LH (Kn) / LL (Ck) - x-x-x x-x-x. Traditionally written as if from seₚₗ.₃ₐ
'older brother'.

3.x   syooto < seuto < se-fito < *seₗ.₃ₐ (< ...) pitoᵤ.₂ᵤ. 'a woman's brother
(by the same mother); a woman's sister; a brother'. x - 0-x-x x-x-x. Edo HHL.

3.1   syoozi < syauzi (< Ch tšyang'-'tsyey). 'shōji (translucent sliding
panel)'. x - 0-0-A A/B-x-x. Km x. Edo HHH. Ib H = 3.1. Nk x.

2.3   syubi < "siyubi" (< Ch 'tšyu-'m(b)ywey). 'fur-tipped scepter (of Buddhist
lecturer)'. LLL - x-2-x x-x-x. Wamyō-shō LL.

3.6   syuro = syuuro (< Ch .tsung-.lyo). 'hemp palm'. RH = LHH - 0/1[H]-0-A
x-A-x. Sz *(rare)* O. Ib syuro H = 2.1. See Ch. 4, §7.1.

3.1   syuuto < siuto < *sifuto < sifyito̱ < *siₚ pitoᵤ.₂ᵤ. 'father-in-law'.
HHH - 0-0-A x-A-x. Km x. Ib H = 3.1. Edo HHH.

4.1   syuutome < siutome < siuto-mye < *sifuto-mye < *sifyito̱-mye <
*si - pitoₛ.₁ miCaₗ.₉ᵦ (?= *mina). 'mother-in-law'. HHHH - 0-0-x x-x-x. Sz O.

?1.1   ta. 'who; someone' (= tare). H(/L) - 1-0-x A-A-A. NS (*see* tare) H; NS (T+
108 ta ga 'whose') L(-H). Km (W) H-(H) / L(-H) / L(-L). Edo H. Cf. taru. tare.

1.3a   ta(-) 'hand': *see* te. NS (T+ kun) ta-fyiro̱kasu L(|)LLHL, ta-fiy 'torch'
L(|)L.

1.3a   ta. 'ricefield'. L - 1-1-B B-B-B. NS (97a [11:77L-K]) L. Km (W) L. Edo R.
Ib L = 1.3.

2.4   taba < *tanpa. 'bunch'. x - 1-1-B A-x-x. Hattō, Hamada 2: Aomori, Matsue.
Izumo 2 *(expected)*; Sz, Goka-mura 1; Hakata 1(?/0). Ib L = 2.4.

3.x (?= *3.4)   tabari < *tanpari ?< *tanpa-r[a-C]i (verb unattested). 'bunch':
      see inatabari. Sr, Nk tabai B.

2.2b   tabi < tabyi < *tanpi. 'time, occasion'. HL - 2-2-A x-x-x. Km (S,W) HL.
Edo HL. Hakata 0 = tanbi 0, ygr 3. Ib H1 = 2.2. (?< *tam[aᵤ.₁ (no̱)] piₗ.ᵤ
'occasional day'; ?< *tam[aᵤ.₁ a]p[a-C]iᵦ)

2.2b   tabi < tabyi < *tanpi. 'journey' (?< 'occasion'). HL - 2-2-A B-A-A. Km (W)
HH-⋯ . 1700 Ōsaka HL. Matsue, Izumo 0; Narada, Hattō, Hamada, Hiroshima 2:
Hakata 0̱. Ōsaka, Ise, Toyama 2; Suzu 2 *(we expect 1:3)*; Ib H1 = 2.2. Nk tabii
A (cf. tanbi C 'occasion').

2.5   tabi < ?*tabyi < ?*tan-pyi (?< Ch .tan-.bhye 'single-skin'). 'socks; a
kind of shoe'. LH - 1-1:3-B B-B-x. Narada, Hattō, Hamada, Matsue, Goka-mura,
Hiroshima 1; Izumo 2. Kōbe (Robb) 1; Ōsaka, Ise 1:3; Ib L = 2.4. Sr taabi B /
tabi-.

4.1   tabibito < tabyi[fyi]to/*tabyibyito < *tanpi$_{2.2b}$ -n- pito$_{2.2a}$. 'traveler'.
HHHH - 0-0-A x-(A)-x. NS ta[¨]fyito HHH; (T+ 104) LFH. Sz 0. Sr tabi-nu-tcu A.

?2,4, ?2.3 tabo, tabu (< ?). 'chignon, bun (hair bundled at nape)'. x - 1-2-x x-x-x.
Km x. (Cf. Yoshida 1979:141).

-    -tabu: see mimi-tabu, sitabura, sirita^b/$_m$ura. (Cf. Yoshida 1979:132-51.)

3.4   tabusa < *ta$_{1.3a}$ -n- pusa$_{2.3}$. 'wrist' (= tekubi). LLL - 1/3-1:3-x x-x-x.

?3.4   tabute = tubute. 'pebble, stone (for throwing)'. LLx - x-x-x x-x-x.

?2.4, ?2.5 tada < *tanta. 'direct, ... ' (adv, adj-n). ?LH/?LF - 1-1-B x-(?A)-x.
NS (T+ 66) LH, (T+ 27, ?128 -t-) LL, (T+ 64) HF. Km (S,W) LH. Mr (Bm) LH. Edo
LF. K: "Hn and since LF" (misleading? cf. Kt). Ib L = 2.4. Perhaps < *ta$_{1.3a}$
n[i] ta$_{1.3a}$ 'hand to hand', but cf. derivatives tadasu, tada-si-: cf. sadameru.

4.11   tadaima < tada-ima < *tanta$_{?2.4,?2.5}$ ima$_{2.4}$. 'just now; (Sr) right away'.
LHLL - 2-1:3-B x-B-x. Km (S) LHLL. K: Edo LHLL.

?4.11, ?4.9 tadamuki < tadamukyi < *ta$_{1.3a}$ -n- ta-muki$_{*3.x}$ (< *ta$_{1.3a}$ muk[a-C]i$_A$).
'forearm' (cf. kaina 'upper arm'). L?HHL ("tatamugi") - x-x-x x-x-x. NS (108a
"tatamuki") LLHL, (Okada) LLLL; NS (T+ 58) LHHH.

?4.1, ?4.11 tadareme < *tadare[y]$_{3.1}$ - mey$_{1.3a}$ < *tantara-Ci[-Ci]$_A$ ma-Ci$_{1.3a}$.
'bleary/inflamed eye(s)'. HHHH (Kz tadara-) / LLHL (Kn) - 0/3-0[U]/1[H]-A
x-x-x.

3.4   tadati(-ni) (?< ta[t]i$_B$ n[i] tati$_B$ 'while standing' < tat[a-C]i$_B$ ··· ; ?<
tada$_{?2.4,?2.5}$ (< ...) ti$_{?1.1}$ 'straight way'). 'at once'. LLL - 1-1:3[H]/3[U]-B
x-(B)-x. Km (W) LLL. Mr (Bm) HHL. Sr taci-nama B. Cf. tatimati.

2.1   tade ?< *tade[y] < *tantaCi. 'knotweed'. HH - 0-0[H]/2[U]-B x-x-x. Km x.
Aomori (rare), Narada 2; Hakata 0. Ib (rare) L = 2.3.

3.2b   tadori < ta^t/$_d$ori < *ta$_{1.3a}$ (-n-) tori$_{2.1}$ ('paddy bird'). 'lapwing;
pewit' (= tageri). HHL - x-2-x x-x-x.

2.x   tae < tafey < *tapaCi. 'bark cloth'. x - 1-2-x x-x-x. NS (74b [14:25-M])
HH; NS (T 74) LH. Km x. Cf. tafe (naru) HH 'wonderfully skillful'; Polynesian
tapa (proto-Austronesian tambang); nigitae.

-    ta ga 'whose': see ta.

2.1   taga (< ?). 'hoop'. x - 2-0-A x-x-x. Km x. Aomori, Sz, Hattō, Hamada,
Matsue, Izumo 2. Ib F = 2.3. Cf. ta^k/$_g$a-ne[y]-$_B$, tago 'bucket' (?< *ta$_{1.3a}$ -n-
kwo$_{1.3a}$); taru 'vat'. Earliest attestation Edo? (Not in JP.)

4.11   tagaesi < tagafesi < *ta$_{1.3a}$ -n- kafyesi$_B$ (< kafyisi < kapis[a-C]i$_R$).
'arm-wrestling'. LLHL - x-x-x x-x-x.

3.6   tagai(-ni) < tagafyi < *tankap[a-C]i (?< *ta$_{1.3a}$ -n- kap[a-C]i$_A$). 'mutual;
reciprocal; opposite'. LHH(-H) - 0-1-B x-B-A. Km (S,W) LHH(-H). 1700 Ōsaka LHH.
K: Edo HHL(-L). Sz 0. Ib L = 3.6. Nk tagee-ni B. Yn -g- (instead of -ŋ-)
indicates the word is borrowed. Cf. tigai, tagui.

3.1   tagane < *ta$_{1.3a}$ -n- kana-Ci$_{2.1}$. 'cold chisel; spearhead, arrowhead'.
HHH - 0-0-B x-x-x. Register incongruent with etymology, but note Kg B.

4.8   tagataga < *tanka$_{?m1a}$ tanka (?< *ta[tu]$_B$ -n- ka). 'toddling'. LHHH - x-x-x
x-x-x.

?2.3   tago ?< *ta$_{1.3a}$ -n- kwo$_{1.3a}$ ('?field/?hand basket'). 'bucket; (= ko[y]e-
tago) "honey bucket" (for carrying human excrement used as manure)'.
x - 1/2-2[U]-x x-B-x. Sr taagu B.

3.5x   tagosi < *ta$_{1.3a}$ (-n-) kosi$_{2.2b}$. 'a kind of koshi riding platform'.
LLH (-k-) - x-2-x x-x-x.

-    tagosi < tagwosi < *ta$_{1.3a}$ -n- kwos[a-C]i$_A$. 'carrying over by hand'.
x - x-x-x x-x-x. NS (T+ 19) LHL.

3.4   tagui < tagufyi < *tankupi (?< *ta*1.3a* -n- kup[a-C]i*B*, cf. tagueru). 'sort,
kind'. LLL - 1/2/0-0-B x-x-x. NS (120a) LLH; NS (T+ 113) LLL. Mr (Bm) HHL. Edo
HHL. Aomori 2; Narada 1. Kōbe (Robb) 1:3/0; Ib *(rare)* F = 3.4. The Tk 2 (< *3)
version is due to monosyllabification. Cf. tagai.

2.3   tai < tafyi < *tapi. 'seabream' *(fish)*. LL - 1-2-B x-(A)-x. 1700 Ōsaka HL.
Aomori, Narada 1. The Tk 1 < *2 is due to monosyllabification; cf. Shimoda 2.
Ib F = 2.3. Is Sr taman A unrelated? Cf. Korean twomi.

-          tai < ta[w]i < ta-fiy < *ta*1.3a* po-Ci*1.3b*. 'torch'. x - x-x-x x-x-x.
NS (T+ kun) L(|)L. Sr tee B. Cf. taimatu.

4.x   taimatu < (*)tafiy-matu < *ta*1.3a* - po-Ci*1.3b* ('hand-fire') matu*B.x*.
'(pine) torch'.

3.5a   taira < tafyira < *ta*1.3a* pira*?B.2b* ('hand flat'). 'flat'. LLH -
0-1[H]/0[U]-A x-A-x. NS (T+ kun) LLH. Km x. Sz 0. Nk, Sr too A < *taw[ira] <
*tap[ira].

4.11   [tairaka] < ta[w]iraka < tafyiraka < *tapi-ra*adj-n 3.3a* -ka. 'flat'.
LLHx (= *LLHL) - x-x-x x-x-x.

2.1   taka(-) 'bamboo': *see* take.

2.1   taka. 'hawk'. HH - 0-0-A A-B-x. Km x. Ib H = 2.1. Nk taKaa B.

?2.3   taka (< *adj B*). 'height, high; amount, quantity'. x - 1/2-0-A x-x-x.
Hiroshima (Okuda) 1. Ib H1 = 2.2. *See* take; oka.

5.2   takabakari < *taka*B.1* -n- paka-r[a-C]i*B*. 'bamboo yardstick'. HHHHL - x-x-x
x-x-x.

3.5x   takabe < takabye < *taka*?B.3* -n- piCa*1.x* (?= *pina), or < *taka-mey <
-m[ura-Ci[-Ci]. 'teal, duckling' (= kogamo). LLH - x-x-x x-x-x. Km x.

3.x   takabe (< taka*?B.3* 'height' + ?). 'labracoglossa' *(fish)*. x - 0-x-x x-x-x.

5.2   takadanuki < *takadanukyi < *taka*B.1* -n- tanuki*?B.4* (< ta*1.3a* nuk[a-C]i*A*).
'falconer's glove'. HHHHL - x-x-x x-x-x.

4.5 = 2.3|2.3   takadono < *taka*adj B* -n- tono*B.3*. 'lofty mansion/tower'. LL(|)LL -
0-0-x x-x-. NS (98a) LL(|)LL.

4.2   takahara < taka-fara < *taka*B.1* para*B.3* (< *paru). 'bamboo grove'. HHHL -
x-x-x x-x-x.

3.6   takaki < taka-kiy < *taka*adj B* kiy*1.3a* (< ?) ('high fortress'). 'a
fortress built in a high place'. x - x-x-x x-x-x. NS (T+ 84) LHH. Km (W) LHH.

5.9 = 2.3|3.1   takamikura < taka-myikura < *taka*adj B* mi-kura*?B.1* (< ...). 'lofty
pavilion; imperial position/dignity'. x - 3-x-x x-x-x. NS (113a) LL(|)HHH.
(114a) LLxxx.

4.7 = 2.3|2.1   takamiya < taka-myiya < *taka*adj B* mi-da*B.1* (*mi-*?1.1* da*1.3b*).
'lofty palace; Takamiya *(placename)*'. x - 3-x-x x-x-x. NS (72c [11:201-M])
LL(|)HH, NS (T+ 54) LLHL.

4.1 = 2.1|2.1   takamura < *taka*B.1* mura*B.1*. 'bamboo grove/thicket'. HH(|)HH - x-0-x
x-x-x.

4.2   takanna < "takam[u]na" (Mg) < *taka*B.1* -n- na*1.3a*. 'bamboo shoot'. HHHL -
x-0-x x-x-x.

3.4   takara < *taka*adj B* [a]ra*B.3*. 'treasure'. LLL - 3-2-B B-B-B. Km x. Mr (Bm)
HHL. Edo HHL. Sapporo 2. Ib F = 3.4. Yn tagara(-munu) B (H 1964:71b).

3.6   takasa < taka*adj B* -sa. 'height'. LHH - 1/0-1-B (B)-(B)-(C). Aomori 2
(expected); Sapporo, Akita 2. Matsumoto, Numazu, Narada, Hattō. Goka-mura,
Hiroshima, Ōita 1; Hamada 1/0; Matsue, Izumo 0. Ib L2 = 3.5/7, L = 3.6.

?5.14, ?5.15, ?5.16 takasebune < taka-se*?B.2* (< taka*adj B* se*1.1* (< ...) 'high
shoals/rapids') -n- puna-Ci*B.4*. 'a shallow-bottomed boat'. LL?Hx - 4(/3[H])-
1:5[U]/1:4[H]-B x-x-x.

?3.6, ?3.7x   takasi ?< taka-[i]si < *taka*adj B* isi*?s.sa* ('high stones'). 'Takashi'
    (placename): ~ no fama 'Takashi beach (near Ōsaka)'. x - x-x-x x-x-x. Km (W)
    LHH, LHL.
2.1   take < takey < *taka-Ci. 'bamboo'. HH - 0-0-A B-A-A. NS (83c) HH; NS
    (T 97) HL = (T+ 97) FL. Km (W) HH-··· . Narada, Hattō, Hamada, Matsue, Izumo,
    Hiroshima, Hakata 0. Ib H = 2.1. Sd dehe(e) B; Nk daKii A; Kunigami, Ōgimi
    (northern Okinawa) B; Sr daki A; Yn tagi A. Forms with d- ?< *[ ] -n- take
    (see Ch. 1, §52). Cf. takahara, takamura, takanna.
2.3   take (?< *ta*1.sa* key*?1.1* (< *ka-Ci) 'field hair'; ?< taka- 'high [growth]'
    + -[C]i*suf*). 'mushroom' (= kinoko). LL - 0-2-x x-x-x.
2.3   take < takey < *taka*adj B* -Ci*suf*. 'height; stature'. x - 2-2-B x-x-x.
    1700 Ōsaka HL. Narada, Hattō, Hamada, Matsue, Izumo, Goka-mura, Hiroshima 2;
    Hakata 1, ygr 2. Ōsaka, Ise 2; Ib F = 2.3. Variant taki.
?2.3, ?2.4   take < takey (?< *taka*adj B* -Ci*suf*; ?< *tak[a n]ey < *taka*adj B*
    na-Ci*?1.1* 'tall peak'). 'mountain, peak'. x - 2-2-x x-B-x. NS (75c [14:118-M])
    LH(-H); NS (T 75) LL. Hiroshima (Okuda) 2. See mi-take.
?4.1, ?4.6   takenawa < takenafa ?< *takeynafa < *taka-Ci-na-pa-*B* (or perhaps
    *taka-Ci[-Ci]*B* napa*s.s*). 'at its height, in full swing' *(adj-n)*. LLLL/LLLH -
    0-0[U]/1[H]-A x-x-x.
2.1   taki < takyi (< ?, cf. tagir-u, tagitu). 'waterfall < rapids'. HH - 0-0-A
    A-B-B. 1700 Ōsaka HH. Hamada 2; Narada, Hattō, Matsue, Izumo, Goka-mura 0.
    Ib F = 2.3. Sr [Lit.] taci B. Yn tagi B.
2.3   taki < *tak[a*adj B*-C]i. 'height, stature'. x - x-2-x x-x-x. NS (116b) LL.
3.1   takigi < takyi-giy < *tak[a-C]i*A* -n- ko-Ci*1.sa*. 'firewood'. HHx - 0-0-A
    A-B-x. Km x. 1700 Ōsaka LHH. K: Hn HHH. Ib H = 3.1. Nk x; Sr tacizi B
    (sequential palatalization of *-gi?; see Ch. 1, §41).
2.3   tako < takwo. 'octopus'. LL - 1-2-B B-B-x. Km x. Narada 1; NE Kyūshū 2
    (H 1951:176); Hakata 0, ygr 1. Sd thoho B. The -kwo is imputed from phonograms
    used to write two placenames in the Man'yō-shū: takwo no sima (M 4011) and
    takwo no ura (M 4200). A third placename takwo no sakyi (M 4051) is written
    also as tagwo no sakyi (Tsuru and Moriyama).
2.3   tako. 'kite' (?< 'octopus'). x - 1-2-B x-(x)-x. Sz (= takko 1), Narada 1;
    Hakata 0, ygr 1. Ib F = 2.3. Sr mattakuu B.
4.6   ta-komura = ta-kubura.
2.3   taku (< thak): ~ no muma 'donkey' (= usagiuma). LL - x-x-x x-x-x.
4.6 = 1.3|3.5 ta-kubura < ta*1.sa* kwomura*s.4a/b*. 'the fleshy part of the arm'.
    x - x-0-x x-x-x. NS (76a [14:123-M]) L(|)LLH, (117a) Lxxx; NS (T+ 75 takufura)
    L(|)LLL.
4.2   takumamo (< ?). 'bulrush' (= tukumo = modern hutoi). HHHL - x-x-x x-x-x.
3.7x   takume: *see* toome 'entirely, ... '.
3.4   takumi < *takum[a-C]i (< *ta*1.sa* kuma-*B*). 'skill; artisan, carpenter'.
    LLL - 1/0-0-B x-x-x. NS (79b [14:316-M], 79c [14:337- M]) LLL, (120b) xLL;
    NS (T+ 78, 80) LLL. Mr (Bm 'skillful') HHL.
2.1   tama (ni/no). 'occasional'. (HH-···) - 0-0-B x-A-x. Sz, Hiroshima 0.
    Ōsaka, Ise 0; Ib H = 2.1. *See* tama-tama. Cf. tabi.
2.3   tama. 'jewel, (= madama = siratama) pearl; (something) beautiful; ball'.
    LL - 2-1[H]/2[U]-B B-B-x. NS (Okada) LL; NS (T 125) LL, (T+ 2) LF ?= LL, (T
    92) HL. Km (S,W) LL. Edo HL. Narada, Hattō, Hamada, Matsue, Izumo, Goka-mura,
    Hiroshima 2. Ōsaka, Ise 1/1:3; Ib L = 2.4, F = 2.3. Onna taamaa B.
?2.3   tama. 'spirit' (?< 'jewel'; ?< atama 'head'). (LL···) - 1-2-x x-x-x.
4.5   tamadare < tama-*t*/*d*are < *tama*s.s* (-n-) tara-Ci[-Ci]*B*. 'jewels on a
    string; a beautiful reed screen or bamboo blind (sudare)'. x - 0-0-x x-x-x.
    Km (W) LLLL.

3.7a   tamago < *tama₂.₃ -n- kwo₁.₁. 'egg'. x - 0/2-1:3-B B-B-x. Aomori, Narada,
Hamada, Goka-mura, Hata, Wakamatsu, NE Kyūshū, Hakata 2; Hattō, Matsue. Izumo
0. Kōchi 2 (Hattori 1973, Doi 1952:24). Ib L2 = 3.5/7. Ōno: use began in Mr.

4.5   tamagusi < *tama₂.₃ -n- kusi₂.₃. 'a sprig of sakaki (with pieces of white
paper attached) offered to the gods'. LLLL - 2-2-x x-x-x. Sz 3.

3.4   [tamai] < tamafi < *tamafyi < *tama-p[a-C]i₈. 'vomiting; spitting up'.
LLL - x-x-x x-x-x.

3.4   tamake < tama-key < *tama₂.₃ ka(-)Ci?₁.₂,?₁.₁ ('jewel tray'). 'food
container; rice tub'. x - x-x-x x-x-x. NS (Okada) LLL; NS (T+ 94) LLL.

?3.4a   tamaki < *ta₁.₃ₐ mak[a-C]i₄. 'arm ornament, elbow guard'. LLH/?LLF - 1-2-x
x-x-x. Ongi LLF. Km x. See Ch. 4, §7.3.

4.10   tamakizu < *tama-kyizu < *tama₂.₃ kinsu₂.₁. 'gem flaw'. LLHL - 2-x-x
x-x-x.

4.5   tamamaki < tama-makyi < *tama₂.₃ mak[a-C]i₄ 'jewel-entwined'. x - x-x-x
x-x-x. NS (76a [14:120-M]) LLLL; NS (T+ LHL.

4.5   tamamoi < tama-mofi < *tama₂.₃ mopi₂.₂ᵦ. 'jewel/beautiful water cup'.
x - x-x-x x-x-x. NS (Okada) LLLL.

5.3   tamarimizu < tamari-myidu < *tama-r[a-C]i₄ mintu₂.₁ₐ (< ...). 'stagnant
water'. HHHLL - 3-4-A x-A-x. Km x.

?4.5, ?4.6   tamasii < tamasifyi < *tama₂.₃ sipi?. 'spirit'. LLLL/LLLF - 1-2[H]/
3[U]-B x-B-x. NS (133a [14:425-K]) LLL?F, (127b [14:330-K]) LLLH. K: Edo HHLL.
Sz, Narada, Hamada, Matsue, Izumo 2; Hattō 3; Hakata 2, vgr 1.

?4.1 = 2.1|2.1 tamatama < tama₂.₁ tama₂.₁. 'occasional(ly)'. HHxx ?= HH(|)HH - 0-0-B
x-x-x. Km x. Sz 0.

4.11   tamazusa < tamadusa < tama-[a]dusa < *tama₂.₃ antusa₂.₄. 'a catalpa stick
carried by a messenger; a messenger; a message, a letter'. x - 2-2-x x-x-x.
Km (W) LLHL. K: Edo HHLL.

2.2a   tame < tamey < *tamaCi. 'benefit, sake; reason, cause'. HL - 2-2-A x-A-x.
Km (S) HL. Mr (Bm) HL. Edo HL. Ib H1 = 2.2. Cf. tamau₈ 'give' *but the register
is incongruent.*

3.4   tamesi ?< *ta-myesi₈ < *ta₁.₃ₐ miCa-s[a-C]i₈ ('let hand see'). 'trial;
precedent, example'. LLL - 3-0[H]/2[U]-B x-B-x. 1700 Ōsaka HHL. Ib F = 3.4.

?2.3   tami < tamyi (?< *ta₁.₃ₐ [o]mi₂.₃ (< ...) 'paddy minister'). 'subjects,
the people'. LL - 1-2-A x-x-x. NS (91b) LL. Km (W) LL. Edo HL. Hattō, Hamada,
Matsue, Izumo, Wakamatsu 1; Goka-mura 2.

3.4, 3.5b = 1.3|2.4 tamino < *ta-myino < *ta₁.₃ₐ mino₂.₄ (< ...). 'a straw rain-
cape to wear in ricefields': ~ no sima 'Tamino island' (in ancient Ōsaka).
x - 1-x-x x-x-x. Km (W) LLL, L(|)LH.

3.4, 3.5b tamizo < *tamyizo < *ta₁.₃ₐ minso₂.₁ₐ. 'irrigation ditch'. LLL (Kn). LLH
(Kz) - 1-x-x x-x-x.

3.4   tamoto < *ta-moto < *ta₁.₃ₐ moto₂.₃. 'sleeve'. x - 3-1:3-B B-B-x. Km x.
Edo HHL. Izumo 0 (Kobayashi), 3 (Hiroto and Ōhara); Hattō, Hamada. Matsue 3;
Hata 3. Kōchi 3 [> Kt *2] (Doi 1952:24). Ib F = 3.4.

2.1   tamu(-) = tamo(-): ~ no ki 'ash tree' (= toneriko). HH - x-x-x x-x-x.
Cf. ayame-tamu ('burnet').

2.1   tamu (< Ch .dham). 'sweet wine' (= Mg tamu no ofo-miki, Ir tamu no sake).
HH - x-x-x x-x-x.

?2.1   tamu (?< ta₁.₃ₐ mu[-Ci]₁.₁ 'field body'). *(mountain name).* x - x-x-x
x-x-x. NS (T+ kun) HH.

*3.x   *ta-muki: *see* tadamuki.

?3.2x = 2.1|1.3 tamuki, tamoki HHx ?= *HH(|)L 'ash tree' (Mg only?) = tannoki LLLL
(Ir) < tamu₂.₁ no ki₁.₃ₐ (< kiy < *ko-Ci).

3.5/3.6 (?< *3.4)   tamura ?= tamuro < tamurᵃ/ₒ₃.₄. 'encampment'. Km (W) LLH(-no) /
   LHH - x-x-x x-x-x.
3.4   tamure (< ?). 'mound, hillock'. LLL (Zs) / LLx (Kn) - x-0-x x-x-x.
   Cf. tumure.
3.4   tamuro < tamurᵃ/ₒ (?< *ta₁.₃ₐ muraₑ.₁ 'group of hands'). 'encampment'.
   LLL - 3/1/0-2[H]/0[U] x-x-x. Km x. Now used only as a bound verbal noun
   (tamuro-suru); Mkz has the accent oxytonic (3) but Mka has it atonic and lists
   the word as if it were a free noun, as does NHK.
4.3   tamuzake < tamusake < *tamuₑ.₁ (< Ch .dham) sakeyₑ.₁ (< saka-Ci).
   'sweet/delicious rice wine' = tamu no sake (Ir). HHLL - x-x-x x-x-x.
2.1   tana. 'shelf'. HH - 0-0-A A-A-A. NS (T+ kun) LL. Km (W) HH-. Ib H = 2.1.
2.4   tana(-) 'seed': see tane.
4.2 = 2.1|2.2   tanabata < *tanaₑ.₁ -n- pataₑ.₉ᵦ ('shelf loom'). 'weaving; weaver:
   loom; the Weaver (constellation)'. x - 0-0-A x-A-x. NS (Okada) HH(|)HL.
   Sz 4; Narada 0; Hakata (expected) 2, ygr 0.
?5.7   tanagokoro < *ta₁.₃ₐ -na- (?< no) kokoroₒ₃.₉ᵦ. 'the palm of the hand'.
   LLxxx / LxHLH (?= *LxLLH) = *LLLLH (-k-) - 3/5-4-A x-x-x. Km x. Mr (Bm) HHHHL.
   K: Hn LLLLL (attested?).
4.2   tanasisi < *tanaₑ.₁ sisiₑ.₉. 'membrane (between skin and meat)'. HHHL -
   x-x-x x-x-x.
4.11   tanasoko < *ta₁.₃ₐ -na- (?< no) sokoₑ.₁. 'the palm of the hand' (=
   tanagokoro, tanaura, tanauti). LLHL - 0-x-x x-x- x. NS (Okada) LL(|)HH;
   NS (T+ kun) LL(|)HH. Km x.
4.11   tanasue < tanasuwe < *ta₁.₃ₐ -na- (?< no) suweₑ.₁ (< ...). 'fingertips'.
   LLHL - x-x-x x-x-x. NS (T+ kun) LLLH. Km x.
5.16   tanatumono < *tanaₑ.₄ -tu monoₒ.₉. 'rice seed'. LLLHL - x-x-x x-x-x.
   NS (98b) LLLHL.
4.11   tanaura < *ta₁.₃ₐ -na- (?< no) uraₑ.₉. 'back of hand'. LLHL - x-x-x
   x-x-x. K: Edo HLLL.
2.4   tane < *tane[y] < *tana-Ci (?< *ta₁.₃ₐ na-Ci₁.₃ₐ 'paddy-field root').
   'seed (small?)'. LH - 1-1-B x-(B)-B. Km (W) LH. 1700 Ōsaka LH. Ib L = 2.4.
   Sr tani B 'penis', sani A 'seed'. Cf. sane.
?2.2b, ?2.5   tani 'tick': see dani.
2.3   tani. 'valley'. LL - 2-2-B x-B-x. NS (Okada) LL. Km (W) LL. Edo HL.
   Ib F = 2.3.
3.4   tanima < *tani₉.₃ maₐ₁.₁. 'valley' (= tani). x - 3/0-0-B x-x-x. Km x.
   Aomori 0; Narada 3. Ib F = 3.4.
3.7b   tanisi ?< *ta₁.₃ₐ n[o] isiₑₑ.₉ₐ ('paddy stone'). 'fresh-water snail'.
   x - 1-1:3-B x-(B)-x. Wakamatsu 1; Hattō 0/1; Hamada, Matsue, Izumo 0: Aomori.
   Sz, Yamaguchi 2. Dial. tanoisi, tanosi. (Sr taanna B < *ta-mina.)
4.11   tanogoi < tanogofyi < *ta₁.₃ₐ no(n)kop[a-C]iₑ. 'handkerchief' (= tenugui
   x - 0-0-B x-x-x). LLLHL - x-x-x x-x-x.
3.4   tanomi < tanomyi < *tanom[a-C]iₑ (< ...). 'request'. x - 3(/1[K])-0(/2[U])
   -B x-B-(B). NS (T+ 105) LLH. Km (W) LLL. Mr (Bm) HHL. Narada 3. Ib F = 3.4.
   Sr tanumi B, taᵃ/ᵣum- B; Yn tarum- B.
?3.4   tanuki < *tanukyi < *ta₁.₃ₐ nuk[a-C]iₐ. 'glove, gauntlet, wrist-band':
   see takadanuki.
3.7b   tanuki (< ?). 'raccoon-dog'. LHH - 1-1:3[H]/2[U,Ōhara 1932]-B B-x-x.
   Km x. Edo HLL. Narada, Goka-mura 1; Sapporo, Aomori, Akita, Hattō, eastern Mino
   (= SE Gifu), Ōita 2; Hakata 2, ygr 1. Hamada, Matsue, Izumo 0. Kōbe, Himeji 1:3
   (Ōhara 1932); Kōchi 2, younger 3 (Doi 1952:35); Wakayama 1:3 (Yukawa 1984:2:18);
   Toyama, Suzu 1:3 (we expect 1:2); Ib L2 = 3.5/7. Cf. tatake, mekoma; (m)unazi.

4.11   taoyaka < tawoyaka < *tabᵃ/oʒ.ʀ (B) -da-ka. 'pliant' (adj-n). LLHL - 2-4-B
x-x-x. Km x. Cf. tawamu, tameru.

4.5   taoyame, tawayame < tawoyamye, tawayamye < *tabᵃ/oʒ.ʀ (B) -da miCaᵒᵢ.ₐₕ
(?= *mina). 'a frail/gentle woman'. LLLL (-wo-) - 0-0-x x-x-x.

?2.5   tara. 'Aralia elata'. Hx - 1-1:3-A x-x-x. Km x. K: Hn HL "?". Aomori 2
(expected reflex). Cf. Sr taarasi B 'Magnolia obovata' (= hoonoki).

?2.5   tara. 'cod(fish)'. x - 1-1:3-A x-x-x. Izumo 0; Hattō, Hamada, Matsue,
Goka-mura, Sz 1; Hakata 0, ygr 1. Ib L2 = 2.5.

3.7a   tarai < tarafyi < *taᵢ.ₐₐ [a]ra-p[a-C]iₐ. 'washtub'. LHL - 0-1:3-B x-x-C.
Km x. Goka-mura, Ōita 1; Sapporo, Aomori (= tarɛ 2), Akita. Wakamatsu 2;
Hiroshima, Narada, Hattō, Hamada, Matsue, Izumo, Numazu, Hakata 0. Yn tarai C
(H 1964: 72a). Ib L2 = 3.5/7. Yoshida rejects the established etymology: "<
derived noun taraf-i" (see Ch. 6, [tarau]); cf. taru.

2.1   tare < *ta-re[y] < *taᵢᵢ.ᵢ [a]ra-Ciₐ.ₐ. 'who; someone' (> dare "from Edo").
HH - 1-0-A (A-A-A). Ongi (Iroha) tare-["]so HL-H. NS (70c [11:158-M], 75c
[14:118-M], 80a [14:338-M], 84b [17:127-M], 129b [14:383-K]) HH; NS (T 75. 80:
113; 97) HH, (T 93) LL, (T 44) LH. Km (S,W) HH, (W) LH. Mr (Bm) HH. Edo HH.
Narada 1; Hattō, Hamada, Matsue, Izumo 0. Sd tharu A; Sr [Lit.] taru A. See ta.

-         -tari (< *-t[u]ₚₑₗ ar[a-C]iʙ) 'person(s)': see -ri.

?2.3   taru. 'barrel, vat, cask'. x - 0(/2[Mkz,Hiroto-Ōhara])-2-B x-B-x. Km x.
Aomori, Hattō, Hamada, Goka-mura, NE Kyūshū 2; Hakata 0, ygr 2 (= 2.3). Sz.
Narada, Matsue, Izumo 0. Ib H1 = 2.2. Motoori Norinaga connected this word with
Koji-ki hodari 'wine vessel', a hapax, and said it was once "tari". but Yoshida
1979:210-2 rejects that and derives the noun from the verb taru; cf. tarai.
First attested 1268?

-         taru 'who': see tare, ta.

?3.5a   taruki < taru-kiy ("also tari-kiy") < *tar[a-C]iʙ / *tar[a]-uʙ ko-Ciᵢ.ₐₐ
('droop stick'). 'a kind of rafter (roof-support)'. LLH - 0-0[H]/2[U]-B x-x-x.
Aomori, Sz 2. Ib L2 = 3.5/7. Sr kici B < ?.

3.7b   tasika < *tasi-ka (?< *tas[a-C]iₐ -kaₛᵤᶠ < ... ; ?< *ta[da]siₐₑⱼʙ -kaₛᵤᶠ
< ...). 'certain, sure, ... ' (adj-n, adv). LHL - 1-1:3-B x-x-x. NS (121b) LLL.
Sz 1. Cf. tasi ni 'adequately; ... '.

-         ta-so < ta so 'who (is it)?': see ta, tare.

3.4   tasuke < tasukey < *tasuka-Ci[-Ci]ʙ (< ...). 'help, assistance'.
x - 3-0-B x-B-(B). Hamada 0; Narada, Hattō, Matsue, Izumo 3. Ib F = 3.4.

3.5a/b   tasuki < tasukyi ?< *taᵢ.ₐₐ suk[a-C]iᵢₐ ('hand follow'). ?< *tasukey
(dial. tasuke, tasuko) < *taᵢ.ₐₐ suka-Ci[-Ci]ₐ ('hand help'). 'sleeve-ties'.
LLH - 3/0-2[H,Ōhara 1932]/0[U]-B B-x-x. NS (T+ kun) LLL. Sapporo, Goka-mura,
Wakamatsu, NE Kyūshū, Ōita 1; Hakata 1, ygr 3/0; Aomori, Akita, Narada 2;
Hattō, Hamada, Matsue, Izumo, Hiroshima 0; Numazu 3. Nara 2: Ōsaka, Kōbe,
Himeji 1:3 (Ōhara 1932); Toyama 1:4 (we expect 1:3); Suzu 1:3 (expected):
Ib L2 = 3.5/7.

3.5x   tataᵏ/ɡe < tatakey (?< *tata[raᵒ.₄ no] keyᵒᵢ.ᵢ (< *ka-Ci) 'bellow fur'.
for its skin is used to make bellows). 'raccoon-dog (= tanuki); raccoon-dog
hairs used as the tip of a writing brush'. LLH - x-x-x x-x-x.

3.1   tatami < tatamyi < *tatam[a-C]iₐ (< ...). 'mat'. (H) - 0-0-A A-A-x.
NS (T+ 70a) HHH, (T+ 70b) HLH (mistake?). Km x. Edo HHH. Hakata 2 (expected).
ygr 0/3. Ib H = 3.1.

-         tatamugi: see tadamuki.

3.4   tatara (< *tata-ʙ [a]raₐₑ.ʒ 'stand thing'). 'foot-bellows'. LLL - 0-0-x
x-x-x. NS (T+ kun) LLL. Cf. tataᵏ/ɡe.

3.1 tatari < *tatar[a-C]i?ₐ (< ?). 'curse'. x - 1-0-0 x-B-x. NE Kyūshū 0. Hakata 0 *(we expect 2)*, ygr 1/3. Nk x; Sr tatari B may be borrowed (there is no verb, and the -r- is preserved).

3.5x/3.4 tatari (< ?). 'a kind of swift (yarn/skein winder)'. LLH (Zs) / LLL (Kn) x-0-x x-x-x.

5.7 tatarigata < tatarikata (< ?). *(1)* 'the stick running between the handle-shaft (torikubi) and the front strut (izari) of a karasuki plow'; *(2)* 'a truss on a pillar or beam'. *(1)* LLLLH, *(2)* LLLLx - x-x- x x-x-x.

4.11 = 2.3|2.2 tatasa(ma) < *tata-ₐ samaₐ.₂ᵦ. 'vertical, upright (position)'. LLHx ?= LL(|)HL - x-x-x x-x-x. Cf. tatasi(ma); yokosa(ma).

4.11 = 2.3|2.2 tatasi(ma) < *tata-ₐ simaₐ.₂ᵦ. 'vertical, upright' (= tatasama). LLxx ?= LL(|)HL - x-x-x x-x-x. Cf. yokosi(ma).

2.5 tate (?< *tate[y] < *tata-Ci[-Ci]ᵦ; ?< *ta[ti]-te[y] < *tat[a-C]iₐ ta-Ci[-Ci]ₐₐₓ; ?< tata[s]i < *tatasi(ma)₄.₁₁ < ...). 'upright, vertical'. x - 1-1:3-B A-x-x. Km x. Ib L2 = 2.5. Nk tatii B.

?2.4, ?2.5 tate (< *tate[y] < *tata-Ci. 'shield'. LH - 1-2-B x-x-x. NS (101b) LH. Edo LF. Sz, Hattō, Hamada 1; Aomori, Matsue, Izumo 2 *(expected)*. Ib H1 = 2.2. K: Hn-Edo LF. Cf. tata-namyi 'a line of shields' (NS kun-chū).

5.6 tateakasi < *tata-Ci[-Ci]ᵦ akasiₐ.₁ (< *aka-s[a-C]iₐ). 'standing torches'. LLLLL - x-1-x x-x-x. K: "Hn LLLHL" *(misprint?)*.

4.6 tateisi < *tateₐ.ₐ (< ...) isiₐ.₂ᵦ (or *tata-Ci[-Ci] isiₐ.₂ᵦ). 'upright stone'. LLLH - x-2-x x-x-x. Km x.

7.14 tatematurimono < tatematuri-mono < *tata-Ci[-Ci]ᵦ matur[a-C]iₐ monoₐ.₃. 'an offering (gift) to a superior; what a superior deigns to eat/wear/use'. LHHHHHH - x-1-x x-x-x.

2.3/2.4 *(or 2.5?)* tati < *tat[a-C]i. 'mansion, residence of a nobleman; a nobleman; a small fortress'. LL/LH - x-x-x x-x-x. Edo LF. Cf. tate.

2.3 tati (?< *tat[a-C]iᵦ). 'sword'. LL - 1-2-B x-B-x. NS (130a) LL; NS (T 20, 27) LL, (T 103) LH. Km x. Edo HL. Narada, Goka-mura, Hattō 2; Hamada, Wakamatsu, Hakata 1. Matsue, Izumo 0. Ib *(rare)* H1 = 2.2.

?2.4, ?2.3 ··· tati. 'group (of persons)': NS (122b [14:218-K]) kimi tati HH|LH. But cf. ookindati (2.3). Perhaps < *tat[a-C]iᵦ 'a stand (of ···)' (cf. kodati 'grove'); perhaps cognate with Korean 'tolh. Notice also OJ ··· dwoti 'companion(s), intimate(s); group of ··· ' (≠ doo-si < Ch), perhaps = *doti < *[tomo]doti < tomodati₄.₁ (< ...).

?2.4 tati < *taₐ.ₐₐ ti?₁.₁. 'paddy path' (= ta-miti, aze-miti). x - x-x-x x-x-x. NS (108b [14:310-K]) LH. Km (W) LH. *(Not in NKD.)*

4.8 tatibame ?< *tat[a-C]iᵦ -n- pama-Ci[-Ci]ₐ. 'leather sole for grass-woven footgear; leather-soled straw footgear'. LHHH - x-x-x x-x-x.

4.9 tatibana < tatiᶠ/ᵦana < *tati?₂.₄ (< ...) (-n-) panaₐ.₃. 'orange (blossom)'. LHLL - 2-1:3-B x-x-x. NS (T+ 125 -f-) HHHL. Km x. Sz 1. (Ōno: "OJ ᶠ/ᵦ".) Cf. karatati.

4.8 tatibare ?< *tat[a-C]iᵦ -n- para-Ci[-Ci]ₐ. '(a horse ailment)'. LHHH - x-B-x x-x-x.

5.7 tatibukuro < *tatiₐ.ₐ (?< *tat[a-C]iᵦ) -n- pukurwoₐ.₄. 'sword bag'. LLLLH - 3-4-x x-x-x.

3.x tatibu (< ?). '(a kind of small melon)' (= tatibu-uri). x - x-x-x x-x-x.

5.11 tatibu-uri < *tatibuₐ.ₓ uriₐ.₄. '(a kind of small melon)'. LHHHL - x-5-x x-x-x.

?5.9, ?5.14 tatidokoro < *tat[a-C]iᵦ -n- tokoroₐ.₁ₐ. 'where one is standing; on the spot'. LLHHₑ - 3-x-x x-x-x.

4.5   tatigami ‹ *tat[a-C]i₈ -n- kami₈.₃. ‘(a hair style)’ (= tategami x -
0(/2[H])-0-B x-x-x). LLLL - x-2-x x-x-x.

4.8   tatigare ‹ *tati-gare[y] ‹ *tat[a-C]i₈ -n- kara-Ci[-Ci]₄. ‘withering uncut
(in the field) or unpicked (on the vine)’. LHHH - 0-1-B x-B-x.

4.5   tatihaki ‹ *tati-fakyi ‹ *tati₈.₃ (‹ ...) pak[a-C]i₄. ‘wearing a sword;
a person wearing a sword’. x - x-2-x x-x-x. Km (W) LLLL.

?3.6 (?= 2.4|1.1)   tatii ‹ tati-wi ‹ *tat[a-C]i₈ bᵘ/₀-Ci[-Ci]. ‘standing and
sitting; simple activities’. x - 1/2-1:3-B x-x-x. Km (W) LHHHH, LHHHL, LLLxx
(= Okada LLLHL). Register incongruent with etymology.

4.10   tatimati(-ni) (?‹ *tat[a-C]i₈ mat[a-C]i₈ ‘while standing and expecting’).
‘at once’ (adv). LHLL(-L) - 0-1:3-B x-(x)-x. Km (S) LHLL. Mr (Bm) HHLL. Sr
taci-nama B. Cf. tadati-ni, tadaima.

6.2   tatimatigusa ‹ *tatimati₄.₁₀ (‹ ...) -n- kusa₈.₃ (‘instant [remedy]
grass’). ‘cranesbill, Geranium nepalense’ (= gennosyooko; niwayanagi). “HRHHHL”
= *HHHHHL - 4-x-x x-x-x. (Kn “.tati”-” = *’ta‘ti-.)

3.5x, 3.4   tatisi (no miti) ‹ *tatasi₃.₃(₊₄.₁₁) (the second vowel assimilated
to the third) ‹ *tata-₈ si(ma)₂.₂ᵦ. ‘longitudinal [= north-south] (road = tate
no miti)’. LLH(-H HH) (Zs), LLL(-L HH) (Kn) - x-x-x x-x-x.

3.4   tatoi ‹ tatofi (‘supposing/if’) = tatoe ‹ tatofey ‹ *tatopa-Ci[-Ci]₈.
‘example, simile’. LLL - 0/2-0-B x-B-x. Km (S) LLL. K: Mr HHL, Edo HHL/HHH.
Tk, Matsue, Izumo 2 due to monosyllabification; Hattō, Hamada 3.

2.1   tatu. ‘dragon’. HH - 0-0-A x-A-x. Km x. K: Hn-Km HH. Narada, Hiroshima 0;
Hakata 1 (expected). Ōsaka, Ise 0. Ib H = 2.1.

3.6   tatugi ?‹ tatuki ‹ *ta₁.₃ₐ tuk[a-C]i₈ (‘hand[le]-attached’). ‘a timber
ax’. LHH - x-x-x x-x-x.

4.11   tatukomo ‹ tatugomo ‹ *tat[a]-u₈ (-n-) komo₈.₁. ‘a mat wind-screen’.
LLHL - x-x-x x-x-x.

-        tatukuri: see tazukuri.

5.10, 5.11, ?5.16 tatutagawa ‹ tatuta-kafa ‹ *tatuta₈.ₓ (‹ tatu₈.₁ ta₁.₃ₐ ‘dragon
field’) -n- kapa₈.₂ₐ. ‘the Tatsuta River’ (placename). x - 3-1:4-A x-x-x. Km
(W) LHHHH, LHHHL, LLLxx (= Okada LLLHL). Register incongruent with etymology.

5.10   tatutayama ‹ *tatuta₈.ₓ (‹ tatu₈.₁ ta₁.₃ₐ ‘dragon field’) dama₈.₃. ‘Mount
Tatsuta’ (placename). Km (W) LHHHH. Register incongruent with etymology.

?4.1   tawagoto ‹ tafakoto ‹ *tapa- koto₈.₃. ‘jest, joke; silly act; prattle’.
x - A-A-x x-x-x. Cf. tawakeru, tawamureru, tawake, [tawasi].

6.1   tawamuregoto, tawaburegoto ‹ tafaᵇ/ₘure-goto ‹ *tapa-n-pura-Ci[-Ci]₄ -n-
koto₈.₃. ‘prank, (a bit of) mischief’. HHHHHH - 0-0-A x-x-x.

3.4   tawara ‹ “tafara” (?‹ *tapara; ?‹ *tabara; ?‹ *ta[bane]₈ wara₈.₄ ‹ ...).
‘bale’. LLx - 3-2-B x-B-B. Ib taara F = 3.4. Yn tara B. Km x.

4.5   tawayame: see taoyame.

3.7b (‹ 3.4)   tayori ‹ tayor₈-i ‹ *ta₁.₃ₐ dor[a-C]i₄. ‘aid, support, something to
rely on; news’. LHL - 1-1:3-A x-B-x. Km (W) LHL. Mr (Bm) LHL, Edo LHL. Izumo 2:
Aomori, Sz, Matsue 2/3; Akita 3; Wakamatsu 0; Narada, Hattō, Hamada, Goka-mura
1; Hakata 2/0, ygr 1. Ib L2 = 3.5/7.

-        ta-zo (= ta-so ‹ ta so) ‘who (is it)?’: see ta, tare.

?2.4, ?2.5   tazu ‹ tadu ‹ *tantu (?‹ *ta₁.₃ₐ -n- tu[ru]₈.₃ ‘paddy crane’).
‘crane’ (= turu). LH - 1-x-x x-x-x. Km LH.

3.6   tazuki(/tatugi/tatuki) ‹ ta-dukyi ‹ *ta₁.₃ₐ -n- tuk[a-C]i₈. ‘means,
resource’. x - 0/3-0-x x-x-x. Km (W) LHH, (LLH).

4.6 = 1.3|3.5 tazukuri ‹ ta-ᵗ/ᵈukuri ‹ (JP) ta-tukuri ‹ *ta₁.₃ₐ tuku-r[a-C]i₈.
‘making paddy fields; agriculture’. x - 2-3[U]/1:3[H]-B x-x-x.
NS (97a [11:77L-K]) L(|)LLH.

1.3a   te < *te[y] < *ta-Ci. 'hand'. L - 1-1-B B-B-B. NS (83a [17:116-M]) L(-H): NS (T+ 96) L(-L), (T+ 106, kun) H(-L). Km (S,W) L(-H). Edo R. Ib L = 1.3.

3.5b   teate < *ta-Ci*ı.ᴣₐ* ata-Ci[-Ci]*ₐ*. 'treatment, allowance, compensation'. x - 1-2-B x-x-x. Wakamatsu 1. Ib H1 = 3.3. Attested JP.

?3.4   tebiki < te-ᶠ/ᵇyikyi < *ta-Ci*ı.ᴣₐ* (-n-) pik[a-C]i*ₐ*. 'making paddy fields; agriculture'. x - 2-3[U]/1:3[H]-B x-x-x. NS (97a [11:77L-K]) L(|)LLH.

3.4   tebito < te-fyito̲ < *ta-Ci*ı.ᴣₐ* (-n-) pito*ᴣ.ᴣₐ*. 'skilled artisan'. x - x-x-x x-x-x. NS (121b) LLL.

3.5a   teboko < *ta-Ci*ı.ᴣₐ* -n- poko*ᴣ.ᴣ*. 'spear'. LLH - 0-x-x x-x-x. Km x.

3.4   tedate < *ta-Ci*ı.ᴣₐ* -n- tata-Ci[-Ci]*ᴮ*. 'steps, measures, actions'. LLx (Kz), LLL (Ir) - 1-2-B x-x-x.

3.5x   tedate < *ta-Ci*ı.ᴣₐ* -n- tate*ᴣᴣ.₄* (< ?). 'hand-shield'. LLH - x-2-x x-x-x.

3.4   tegara < *ta-Ci*ı.ᴣₐ* -n- kara*ᴣ.ᴣᵦ* ('hand characteristic'). 'feat; prowess'. x - 3-2-B x-B-x. Km x. 1700 Ōsaka HHL.

3.7b   tegasi < te[y]-kasi < *ta-Ci*ı.ᴣₐ* (-n-) kasi*ᴣ.ᴣ*. 'handcuffs, fetters, shackles'. LHL - 1-2-x x-x-x.

4.11   teguruma < *ta-Ci*ı.ᴣₐ* -n- kuruma*ᴣ.ı*. 'hand-cart'. LLHL - 2-3[U]/1:3[H]-B x-x-x.

3.4   temoto < *ta-Ci*ı.ᴣₐ* mo̲to*ᴣ.ᴣ*. 'at hand'. x - 3-2-B x-x-x. 1700 Ōsaka HHL. Kōbe (Robb) 1:3.

3.4   tenae < tenafe < *te[y]-nafe[y] < *ta-Ci*ı.ᴣₐ* napa(-)Ci[-Ci]*ᴮ*. 'loss of use of hand/arm'. LLL - x-x-x x-x-x.

3.4   teono < te-wono̲ < *ta-Ci*ı.ᴣₐ* bono*ᴣ.ᴣ*. 'adz'. LLL - 2/1-1-B x-(B)-x. Km x. Sr tiin B.

?2.2a   tera (?< Korean tyel). 'temple'. x - 2-2-A A-A-A. Km (S) HL. Mr (Bm) HL. Edo HL. Yn A (H 1964:71a). Aomori, Sz *(rare)* 0; Hakata 0, ygr 2. Ib H1 = 2.2.

5.2   teratutuki < *tera-tutukyi < *tera*ᴣ.ᴣₐ* tutuk[a-C]i*ₐ* (< ...). 'woodpecker'. HHHHL - x-4-x x-x-x. Km x.

3.4   tesiro (?< *ta-Ci*ı.ᴣₐ* siro*ᴣ.ı*). '(?) bracelet'. LLL - x-x-x x-x-x. Attested only in Mg?

3.1   tetere (?< *te-to̲ri < *ta-Ci*ı.ᴣₐ* to̲r[a-C]i 'hand hold' *but register incongruent*; ?< *tori*ᴣ.ı* tori*ᴣ.ı* 'birdie-birdie'). 'decoy bird' (= otori). HHH (Ir) - x-x-x x-x-x. Cf. tutu.

?4.10   tezukara < tedukara < *ta-Ci*ı.ᴣₐ* -n- -tu- kara*ᴣ.ᴣᵦ*. 'by oneself (unaided)'. LHxx (?= *LHLL) - 1-2-B x-x-x.

?4.11   tezukuri < tedukuri < *ta-Ci*ı.ᴣₐ* -n- tuku-r[a-C]i*ᴮ*. 'hand-made/-woven; handicraft'. LLHL - 2-3[U]/1:3[H]-B x-B-x. Sz 3.

1.x   -ti < ?*tiy (?< *tuCi, < *tu-Ci; ?< to[s]i). 'years': *see* hatati, misoti, yasozi. Earlier also counted things. Cf. -tu.

1.x   ti = si 'wind; direction': *see* hayati. Cf. koti 'east wind'.

?1.1   ti. 'road, path': *see* timata, tigai, kakezi, nozi, oozi, uzi; ? suzi; miti, oomiti; doti(-)ra.

1.1   ti. 'blood'. H - 0-0-A A-A-A. Km (S) H. Mr (Bm) H-H. Edo H. Ib H = 1.1.

?1.1   ti (?= 'blood'; ?< *ti[y] < *to̲-Ci; ?< *ti[y] < *tu-Ci). 'spirit; force'. x - x-x-x x-x-x. *See* mizuti; yamakagati; oti, oto(-); sati-/satu-ya.

?1.2   ti < *ti[y] < *tu-Ci. 'cogon (= thatching grass), Imperata cylindrica' (= tigaya). x - 1-2-x x-x-x. Km (W) ti-no fa-ni HL|HL. Mg (Sō-jō 37) tii. Cf. tu-bana 'thatch (cogon) ears' x - 0-1-x x-B-x, Sr çi-bana B, Gifu/Tottori tuibana. Cf. tigaya, asazi; timaki (Ib tumaki).

1.3a   ti ?< *ti[y] < *tu-Ci. 'milk'. *L - 1-1-x B-B-B. Km x. K: Hn LL "?". Sz 1. Sr cii B; Yn cii B. Cf. tu*ı.ᴣₐ* 'spit' (?= 'liquid', cf. mizu); titi*ᴣᴣ.₄*.

?1.3a   ti ?< *ti[y] < *to̲-Ci. 'esteemed male': *see* titi, ozi, oozi. NS (T+ 39) H.

1.3a   ti(-) ?< *ti[y] < *to̲-Ci (cf. to̲daru, sodaru, -so < -swo). 'thousand'.
L-··· - 1-x-x x-x-x. *See* ti-yo, yati-tabi.

1.x   [ti] < ti, tii (Shinsen-Jikyō) ?< *ti[y] < *tuCi (?= *tu[r]i 'fishing' <
*tur[a-C]i). 'fish hook'. x - x-x-x x-x-x.

3.7b   tido̲ri < *ti₁.₃ₐ -n- tori₂.₁ ('thousand birds'). 'plover' *(bird)*. LHL -
1-1:3-B x-B-x. NS (T+ 4) HHH. Km x. Hakata 1; Aomori, Sz 2. Ib L2 = 3.5/7.

3.1   tigai < tiga[w]i < tigaf[y]i < *ti₁.₁ -n- kap[a-C]i₄ ('road cross').
'difference, discrepancy'. (A) - 0-0-A x-x-(A). Aomori, Sz 2. Ib H = 3.1.
Not attested before Heian? Cf. tagai.

3.x   tigaya < *ti?₁.₂ (?< *tu-Ci) -n- kada₂.₄. 'cogon (= thatching grass),
Imperata cylindrica'. x - 1-2-x x-x-x.

?2.3   tigo < *ti₁.₃ₐ -n- kwo₁.₁ ('milk child'). 'baby'. x - 0/1-0[H]/2[U]-B
x-x-x. Sz *(rare)* 1.

3.1   tiguso < *ti?₁.₁ -n- kuswo₂.₃. 'dysentery'. HHH - x-x-x x-x-x.

3.1   tihaya < tifaya < [i]tifaya < *iti-paya. '(a kind of sleeve-tie)'. HHH -
x-0-x x-x-x.

-      tii: *see* ti 'cogon', 'fish hook'.

?3.1   tikai < tikafi < *tikafyi < *tikap[a-C]i₄ ?< *ti?₁.₁ kap[a-C]i₄. 'vow,
pledge'. x - 0/2(?<*3)-1[H]/0[U]-A x-x-x. Km (S) HHH. Mr (Bm) HHH. 1700 Ōsaka
HHH. Hamada 0/3; Sz, Hattō, Matsue, Izumo, Goka-mura 0.

3.3   tikara ?< *ti?₁.₁ kara₂.₂ᵦ ('spirit characteristic'). 'strength'. HLL -
3/0-2-A A-A-A. NS (127b) HLH ?= *HLL. Km (S) HLL. Mr (Bm) HLL. Edo HLL.
Matsumoto, Numazu, Narada 3; Hakata 2, ygr 3; Yamaguchi, Hiroshima, Hattō,
Hamada, western Mino (= SW Gifu) 2; Hida (= northern Gifu) 0/3; Sapporo, Tappi,
Aomori, Akita, Matsue, Izumo, Ōita 0; apparently no Tk-type has 1 (< *2). Ib
H1 = 3.3. Initial irregular in Yn sikara A, younger cikara A (H 1964:71b).

5.1   tikara-bito < tikara-fyito̲ < *tikara₃.₃ (< ...) (-n-) pito₂.₂ₐ.
'a mighty man'. x - x-x-x x-x-x. NS (109a) HHHHH.

5.2   tikaragawa < tikara-gafa < *tikara₃.₃ (< ...) -n- kapa₂.₃. '(a stirrup
strap)'. HHHHL - x-x-x x-x-x.

7.16   tikirikooburi (also tikirikanmuri, tikirikoomuri) < tikirikauburi (Mg)
< *tikiri? - kanburi₂ (< kagaf*/o̲ri < *kankapur[a-C]i₂). 'a head kerchief'.
LHHHHLL - x-5-x x-x-x.

3.1   timaki < *timakyi < *ti₁.₂ (< *tu-Ci) mak[a-C]i₄. 'leaf-wrapped rice
dumpling'. HHH - 0(/1[H])-0-A x-x-x. Mr (Bm) LHL. Narada 3; Hakata 1, ygr 0.
Ib tumaki H = 3.1.

3.1   timata < *ti?₁.₁ mata₂.₃. 'crossroads'. HHH - 0/1-0[H]/2[U]-A x-x-x.
Sz *(rare)* 0.

4.2   timegusa < *ti-mey - gusa < *ti?₁.₁ - ma-Ci₁.₃ₐ -n- kusa₂.₃ ('blood-eye
grass'). 'Patrinia' (= ominaesi). HHHL - x-x-x x-x-x.

2.1   tiri (?< *tir[a-C]i₄ 'scatter'). 'dust'. HH - 0/3-0-A A- A-x. NS (126a)
HH. Edo HH. Km (W) HH. Mr (Bm) HH. Narada, Hattō, Hamada, Matsue, Izumo 0.
Ib H = 2.1. Nk Cirii A.

2.5   tiri (< Ch dhi'-'lyey). 'geography'. x - 1-1:3-B A-x-x. Sz, Hiroshima 1.
Ōsaka, Ise 1:3; Ib H1 = 2.2.

2.x < 3.6 tis(y)a < tisa < *tiisa. 'lettuce'. RH (< *LHH) - 0-0-B x-B-x. Sr cisa-naa
B. Cf. kawatisanoki; oti; ti, timaki.

?2.4   titi. 'breasts; milk'. (x) - 2-1-B (x-x-x). Km x. Hiroshima 1; Tk accent
delay due to vowel unvoicing. Ib L = 2.4. The word looks to be a reduplication
(like mimi and momo), but it is unclear whether ti₁.₃ₐ (?< *tu-Ci) 'milk' is
the source, is itself a truncation of titi, or is unrelated. Cf. Korean 'cyec
'breasts; milk' (apparently not related to cec- 'get wet').

2.4   titi (?< *tiy-tiy < *to-Ci to-Ci). 'father'. LH - 2-1-B x-x-x. Km (W)
          LH(-H). Edo LH. Tk (and Hattō) 2 < *1 is due to vowel unvoicing (cf. Hiroto
          1961:160); Narada, Hamada, Goka-mura 1; Matsue, Izumo 2/1; Aomori (rare).
          Hata 0.

4.10   titiuma < titi-m[u]ma < *titiₐ.₄ (?< *to-Ci to-Ci) umaₐ.ₐ. 'stallion
          (male horse)'. LHLL - x-x-x x-x-x.

?3.4   titose < tiₐ.ₐₐ tose (?< tosiₐ.ₐ). 'a thousand years'. x - 0/1-1-x x-x-x.
          Km (W) HHH, LLL.

3.4   tiusi < tiuᵃ/zi < tiₐ.ₐₐ (< ...) usi/-uzi < *u(n)siₐ.ₐ. 'milk cow'.
          LLL (Kn -z-) - 1-2-x x-x-x.

?2.4   tizi < ti-di < *tiₐ.ₐₐ n[i] tiₐ.ₐₐ. 'thousands upon thousands'.
          LH - 1-2-A x-x-x. Km (W) LH(-H/L).

1.1   to < two. (1) 'door'; (2) 'place' (= to); (3) 'time, (~ ni) while':
          probably the same etymon. H - 0-0-A x-x-x. NS (83b [17:118-M]) H(-H); NS (T+ 41
          'gate') two no H-L, (T+ 96 'time') two ni H-H. Edo H. Cf. minato; tonaka.

?1.1   (-)to < (-)to. 'place' (= tokoro; = two).

?1.1   to 'ten': see too; -so.

1.1   to < two. 'outside' (= soto, which is attested only from Mr). H - x-0-x
          x-x-x. Km (W) to-no-fe HHH/HHL/HxL/LLH. NS (98b) H(-H).

1.3a   to < two. 'grindstone' (= to-isi x - 0-1:3-B x-B-x). L - 1-(x)/0[U]-x
          x-(x)-x. Km x. K: Hn LL, Edo LH. Km x. Narada, Hiroshima 1. Ōsaka 0; Ise 1.
          Sr tusi B (< *to-[i]si); Hakata toisi 0 (= 2.3). Cf. arato, mato; tome; toɑu.

?1.3b   to < *to (?< variant so). 'that'. L-(H···). See toni-kakuni. toᵃ/ₐama-
          kooᵃ/ₐama. Not attested before Hn.

1.x   to. 'footprint, trace': cf. to-myi < *toₐ.ₓ miC[a-C]iₐ 'game tracker;
          place with game tracks', ato < atwo. On /to/ and /two/, see Zdb.

1.x   ··· to (?< *toₐ.ₐₐ 'that'). 'thing/one/fact that ··· ': see ···so/su.

3.2a   tobari < *twoₐ.ₐ -n- par[a-C]iₐ ('door stretch'). 'curtain'. HHL - 0-0-A
          x-x-x.

?2.1, ?2.5   tobi < ?*tobyi < ?*tonpi (?< *tonp[a -C]iₐ 'fly'). 'kite (hen)'
          (bird). HH - 1/2-1:3-A x-x-x. Km x. Sz, Hakata 1. Ib L2 = 2.5. Cf. tonbiₐ.₇ₐ.
          (Ōno's "tobi" = tobyi is an artifact of his imprecise orthography, which
          lumps unknown Ci with known Cyi.)

6.2   tobinoogoto < tobinowo₍?₄.₁₎ -goto < tobiₐ.₁ (< ...) noₚₑₗ woₐ.ₐₐ
          (< *bo) -n- kotoₐ.₄ ('kite's tail harp'). 'a kind of harp'. HHHHL - x-1:6-x
          x-x-x.

3.1   [tobio] = tobiuo < tobiwo, tobi-iwo < *tonp[a-C]iₐ iwoₐ.₁ (< ...).
          'flying fish'. HHH - 2(/0[H])-3[U]/1:3[H]-A x-A-x. Sr tubuu A.

3.2b   tobira < *twobyira < *twoₐ.₁ -n- piraₐₐ.ₐₐ. '(panel/leaf of a) door'.
          HHL - 0-2[H]/0[U]-A x-x-x. Edo HHL. 1700 Ōsaka HLL. K: Hn-Km-Edo HHL.
          Sapporo, Aomori, Sz, Akita, Matsumoto, Numazu, Hattō, Hamada, Matsue,
          Hiroshima, Goka-mura, Ōita 0; Izumo 0/3. Kōchi 2; Toyama 2 (we expect 1:3);
          Suzu 2 (we expect 1); Ib L2 = 3.5/7.

3.2a   toboso < twoboso < *twoₐ.₁ -n- posoₐ.₁ ('door navel'). 'pivot: door'.
          HHL - 0-0-x x-x-x. Km (S) HHL. Mr (Bm) HHH. Edo LHH. 1700 Ōsaka HHL.

?2.5, ?2.4   toga < *tonka. 'blame, offence'. LH - 1-1[H]/1:3[U]-B x-B-x.
          Km (S) LH(-H). Mr (Bm) LH(-H) (Sakurai 1977:866b). Edo LH. On Kt 1:3 see also
          Ōhara 1951:418. Sakurai 1976:378 cites a Mr example (from Bumō-ki) of toga wo
          marked LH-L in contrast with naka ni (2.4) marked LH-H.

2.x   toga < twoga(-no-kiy = tuga-no-kiy) 'hemlock spruce': see tuga.

3.5x   togata < *toₐₐ.ₐ (< Ch 'tew) -n- kataₐ.ₐₐ. ('a box-shaped piece of wood
          ··· '). 'an architrave; the (square) piece of ground between the outer and
          inner gates of a castle' (Brinkley). LLH - x-0-x x-x-x.

2.3   toge < *two-gey < *two*adj* *ß* -n- ka-Ci*ʔı,ı* 'sharp hair'). 'thorn'. x -
2-2[H]/1:3[U]-B x-x-x. Km x. Sz, Hattō, Hamada, Matsue, Izumo 2; Goka-mura 1.
Ib F = 2.3.

?2.3   togi (< ?). 'solacing; nursing'. x - 1/2-2-x x-x-x. Km x. Cf. o-togi
x - 2/0-1[H]/1:3[U]-B x-x-x. Dial. toogi.

3.1   togura < *to[ri]*ß,ı* -n- kura*ß,ßb*. 'bird perch; birdhouse. henhouse'.
HHH - x-0-x x-x-x. Km x.

2.5   toi < tofi = tofiy < *to-ʔ pᵘ/₀Ci*ı,ßb*. 'water pipe'. x - 1-1:3-B x-B-A.
Sz, Hiroshima 1. Ōsaka, Ise 1:3; Kt toyu 1:3; Ib L2 = 2.5. Sr tii B; Yn cii A
(H 1964:64a). If 'pipe' is *poCi, perhaps *to- (= *to) is from *tu 'liquid'
(see ti 'milk', tu 'spit', mizu 'water'), with the first vowel assimilated to
the second.

3.2a   tokage ?< to[ri]-kage < *tori*ß,ı* kagey*ß,ß* (< ... 'bird shadow'): ?< *two*ı,ı*
kagey*ß,ß* (< ... 'door shadow'). 'lizard'. HHL - 0-1:3-A x-x-x. Km x. Yamaguchi.
western Mino (= SW Gifu), Hattō, Hamada 3 (as if 3.2b): Aomori 2; Hakata 2.
ygr 0. Sapporo, Tappi, Akita, Matsumoto, Numazu, Narada, Matsue, Izumo, Goka-
ura, Hiroshima, Ōita 0. Ib tokake L2 = 3.7. Dial. [Totsukawa etc.] torikage.

3.4   tokaki < *to*ʔı,ß* (< Ch 'tew) kakyi (< kak[a-C]i*ß*. 'grain-measure stick'.
LLL - 3-3-x x-x-x.

3.4 (?< *4.10) tokati (< Ch tho'-hhat). 'cloth of cotton blended with rabbit fur'.
RLL (?< *LHLL) - x-0-x x-x-x. Cf. kati.

?2.1, ?2.5   toki 'ibis' (bird): see tuki.

2.3   toki < tokyi < *toki. 'time'. LL - 2-2-B B-B-B. NS (96b, 126b) LL:
NS (T 125) LL; NS (T+ 68) tokyi tokyi 'tides' HHHH. Km (S.W) LL. Edo HL.
Ib F = 2.3.

3.1   tokiwa < tokyifa < *tok[o]*ʔß,ı* ipa*ß,ßb* ('eternal rock'). 'everlasting'.
HHH - 0-0-x x-x-x. Km (W) HHH. Edo HHH. Sz, Narada 0. Ib (placename) F = 3.4.

?3.5b   tokiyo < *tokyi-yo < *toki*ß,ß* do*ı,ı*. 'era'. LLH - 2-x-x x-x-x. Km x.

2.1   toko. 'bed, ... ; (kuruma no ~) the main frame of a cart (= kuruma-
bako)'. HH - 0-0-A x-A-x. Km (W) HH-··· . Edo HH. Ib H = 2.1.

?2.1   toko ··· . 'everlasting, eternal, unchanging': see tokomatu, tokonatu.
tokotowa, tokotukuni, tokoyo; tokiwa.

?4.2, ?4.1   tokomatu < *toko*ʔß,ı* matu*ß,ʻ*. 'evergreen fir'. x - x-x-x x-x-x.
NS (121b) HHxx (?= *HHHL), (Okada) HHHH.

?4.1, ?4.2   tokonatu < *toko*ʔß,ı* natu*ß,ßb*. 'eternal summer: (= nadesiko) wild
pink, Dianthus superbus'. HHxx - 0-0-A x-x-x. Km (W) HHxx/xxHH = *HHHH.
K: Hn-Km HHHH.

3.1a   tokoro. 'place'. HHH - 0/3-0-A x-A-x. NS (93a, ?107a, ?125a) LHH. (Okada)
HHH. Km (W) HHH. Mr (Bm) HHL. Edo HHL/(HHH). 1700 Ōsaka HHH. K: "Hn-Mr HHH, Edo
HHL." Aomori, Narada, Izumo 3; Hakata 0, ygr 3 (= 3.4). Matsue 0/3; Kurayoshi
(Tottori), Hattō 2; Hamada, Goka-mura 0. Ib H = 3.1. See §7.3.

5.2   tokosibari < *toko*ß,ı* sim[a]-par[a-C]i*ß*. 'the rope that ties the load box
of an oxcart to the frame'. HHHHL - x-4-x x-x-x.

4.2-ni   tokosie-ni < toko-sifey ni (< ?). 'everlastingly, forever'. x - 0-0-A
x-x-x. NS (T+ 68) HLLL. Mr (Bm) "HHHH-LL" (misprint?), HHHL-L. (Ōno suggests
< *toko*ʔß,ı* [i]si*ß,ßa* [u]fey*ß,ßa* 'top of eternal rock'.)

?4.1   tokotowa < tokotoba < *toko*ʔß,ı* tonpa (?= 'fly'*ʌ*). 'eternally. unchanging:
forever, always'. HHxx - x-x-x x- x-x. ("-ᵇ/*w*- from Km?") On the basis of
Man'yō-shū examples of tokofa (M 3436) and toko(-tu)-fana 'eternal blossoms'.
Tsuchihashi 1976:217 interprets tokotoba as a variant of *toko-tu-ba (or -fa?)
'eternal (evergreen) leaves' used metaphorically.

5.2 ?= 2.1-tu|2.2 tokotukuni < *toko?2.1 -tuPC1 kuni?2.1,?2.2a (< ...). 'the
eternal realm (= afterlife, death)'. HHHHL ?= HH-H(|)HL - x-x-x x-x-x.
NS (133a) HHHHL.

?3.1   tokoyo < *toko?2.1 do1.1. 'eternal. unchanging'. HHH - 0/2-0-x x-x-x. NS
(131b) "HLH" (?= HHH), (Okada) HHH; NS (T+ 32) "HLH" (?= HHH), (T+ 112) LHH.

3.5a (> ?4.6) tokuri (> tokkuri) (< ?). 'sake bottle'. x - 0-2-B x-x-x
(> x - 0-3-B x-x-x; Sz 3). Km x.

3.4   tokusa < *twokusa < *two1.3a (or adj B) kusa2.3. 'scouring rush'. LLL -
3-1:3[U]/2[H]-A x-x-x. Edo HHL. Aomori, Sz 1; Hattō, Hamada, Matsue, Izumo 3.

?2.1, ?2.2a toma (?< twoma, cf. Zdb). 'woven rain-cover for boat/hut'. HH - 0/1-2-x
x-x-x.

3.1   tomara < *two1.1 mara2.3 ('door penis'). 'pivot'. HHH - 0-0-x x-x-x.

3.1   tomari < *toma-r[a-C]i. 'lodging; anchorage'. HHH - 0-0-A A-A-A.
Ib H = 3.1.

3.1   tomaya (?< *twoma-ya < *twoma?2.1 da1.3b). 'a covered hut'. x - 0-0-A
x-x-x.

2.3   tome (?< *twomey, derived noun from infinitive *two-ma-Ci[-Ci]B of lost
verb 'sharpen it'). 'whetstone'. LL (Zs, Kn) - x-x-x x-x-x. (Not in NKD.)

2.1   tomi (?< Korean tyem-mi < Ch .n(d)rem-'m(b)ey; ?< Korean *two-mi
< Ch 'dhwo-'m(b)ey). 'glutinous (sticky) rice'. HH - x-x-x x-x-x. Attested
only in Mg? Cf. tomi-kusa 'riceplant; (= hinoki) cypress', which NKD analyzes
as 'rich (*twom[a-C]i?A) plant'.

2.1   tomi < twomyi < *twom[a-C]i?A. 'riches'. HH (Kz) - 1-2-A x-x-x. Sz. Narada.
Hattō, Hamada, Matsue, Izumo 1 (verb B); Goka-mura 2 (verb A). Ib H1 = 2.2.

2.1   tomo. 'companion'. HH - 1/2-2-A x-A-x. NS (T 12) HR = HH. Km (W) HL.
Mr (Bm) HH. Edo HL. Narada, Hamada 1; Aomori (rare), Hattō, Matsue, Izumo 2;
Goka-mura 0. Ib H1 = 2.2.

2.1   tomo(-ni). 'together'. HH(-H) - 0/1-0-A x-x-x. Km (W) HH-H. Edo HH.
Sz 0/1; Narada 1; Hattō, Hamada, Matsue, Izumo 2; Goka-mura 0. Ib H = 2.1.

2.3   tomo. 'stern of boat'. LL - 1/2-2-A x-B-x. Hattō, Hamada, Matsue, Izumo,
Goka-mura 2.

2.4   tomo (?< *ta1.3a omo2.4). 'an archer's left wrist-shield'. LH - 1/2-2-x
x-x-x.

4.1   tomobito < *tomo-f/byito < *tomo2.1 (-n-) pito2.2a. 'companion; friend'.
x - 0-0-x x-x-x. NS (124b) HHHH.

4.1   tomodati < *tomo2.1 -n- tati?2.4,?2.3. 'friend(s)'. HHHH - 0-0-A x-x-x.
Sz, Narada 0. Hakata 0 (we expect 2). Ib H = 4.1.

3.x   tomoe < tomo2.4 (< ...) we1.3a (< ... 'picture'). 'a comma-shaped whirl
design'. x - 0-0[H]/1:3[U]-A x-x-x.

3.x   [tomo-(h)e] < tomo-fe < *tomo2.3 fey1.1 (< *paCi). 'stern and prow'.
x - x-x-x x-x-x. Edo HLL.

4.1   tomogara < *tomo2.1 (-n-) kara2.2b. 'companion'. HHHH - 4/0-0-x x-x-x.
NS (111b, 124a) HHHH. Km (S) HHHH. On *-k/g-, see Ch. 2.

4.5 = 2.3|1.3 tomosibi < tomosibyi < *tonpo-s[a-C]i -n- po-Ci1.3b. 'torch'.
LLL(|)L - 3/0-4[H]/0[U]-A x-x-x. NS (127b) LLL(|)L. Mr (Bm) HHHL. Sz 4.

4.5 = 2.3|2.3 tomozuna < tomoduna < *tomo2.3 -n- tuna2.3. 'stern line on boat'
(opposite of hezuna < feyduna). LL(|)LL - 0-0-A x-x-x. Km x. K: Edo HHHH.

?3.4   tonae < tonafe < (*)twonafey < *two(-)na-pa-Ci[-Ci]?A/B. 'chant(ing).
call'. x - 3/2-0-(B) x-x-x. Km (S) LLL. K: Mr HHL.

?3.3   tonaka < two-naka < *two1.1 naka2.4 (< ...). 'the mouth of a strait/bay'.
x - x-x-x x-x-x. NS (T+ 41) HLL.

3.1   tonari < twonari < *twonar[a-C]i∆ < *twoɾ,ɾ nar[a-Cli*. 'neighbor'.
HHH - 0-0-A A-A-A. Ib H = 3.1.

3.7b   tonbi. 'kite (hen)' (bird) (= tobi). x - 1-1:3-B x-x-x. Km x. Aomori, Sz,
Narada, Hakata 1. Ib L = 3.6.

?3.6   tonbo (<?). 'dragonfly' (= enba, akizu). x - 0-1-B x-x-x. Aomori. Sz,
NE Kyūshū 1; Hakata 1, ygr 0.

?2.3   tone (?< tone[ri]₇₃.₄ < ...). 'an official; ... '. x - x-x-x x-x-x.

?3.4   toneri (?< ton[o fab]eri, see haber-u). 'chamberlain'. LLL - 1/0-0-x
x-x-x. NS (119a) LLL. Km x. Edo LHL. K: Hn LLH "?".

4.7 (?= 3.4|1.1)   toneriko (?< *toneri kwo). 'ash tree; (= hasibami) filbert'.
LLHH (?= LLH|H) - 0/3-0-2 x-x-x.

?1.3b-ni|2.2b-ni   toni-kakuni < to -ni kaku -ni. 'nonetheless. anyway, be that as
it may'. L-H|HL-H - 1-1:3-B x-x-x. K: Edo LH|HLL.

2.3   tono. 'building, residence, ... ; lord'. LL - 1-2-x x-(B)-x. NS (Okada) LL.
NS (T 16, 17]) HL. Km x. Edo HL. Ib H1 = 2.2. Sr tun(u)ci B < *tono-uti. qudun
B < *o-tono.

3.4   tonoi < tono-wi < *tono₂.₃ bᵘ/₀-Ci[-Ci]∆. 'night duty (in the palace)'.
LLL (Ir) - 0/3-0-x x-x-x. NS (127a) LLL. Edo LHL. K: "Hn HHH" (misprint?).

?2.2a   too < towo (?< tu - wo < *tu₇₁.₁ bo ₁.₃ₐ 'end of count'; cf. -so < -swo).
'ten'. x - 1-2-A (A/B)-A-A. Km x. Edo HL. 1700 Ōsaka HH. Tk 1 < *2: Shimoda 2
(K 1943); Nagano (Kudō 1978:14,42), Aomori 0: Sz 1/0. Ib H1 = 2.2.

?2.3   too < tafu < *tapu (< Ch thap). 'stupa'. x - 1-2-B x-x-x. Tk. Aomori,
Narada, Nagano, Hattō, Matsue, Izumo 1 due to monosyllabification; Shimoda
(K 1943), Hamada, Goka-mura, Hata 2. Ib F = 2.3. K: Hn LL (where attested?).

4.1   toobito < tofo-fyito < *topo₅ₐⱼ ∆ (-n-) pito₂.₂ₐ. 'a person with a long
life; a person from far away'. x - x-0-x x-x-x. NS (74a [11:302-M]) HHHH:
NS (T+ 62) HHHH.

?3.4, ?3.5b   tooge < tauge < ta-mukey(₇₃.₄) ('propitiatory offering to ensure a
safe journey') < *ta₁.₃ₐ muka-Ci[-Ci]∆ ('hand turn'). 'mountain pass'. ?LLL.
?LLH - 3-1-B x-x-x. Aomori 0; Hakata 0, ygr 3 (= 3.4); Narada, Hattō, Hamada,
Matsue, Izumo, Hata, NE Kyūshū 3; Goka-mura 1 (?< *0). Kōchi 3 (> Kt *2) (Doi
1952:24); Ib L = 3.6.

?3.1   tooka < towo₇₈.₂ₐ -ka₇₁.₃ₐ. 'ten days; tenth day of the month'. x - 0-0-x
A-A-x. NS (T+ 26) LHL. Hiroshima 0/3; Sz 3 (adv. 0). Ōsaka. Ise 0; Ib H = 3.1
(also adverbial). Sr tuka A.

?5.12   tookesyaku < tauk[u]wes[i]yaku (< Ch .thaw-.hwa žhyak). 'peach-blossom
stone = white stone with light pink dots'. LHHLx (= *LHHLL). See §7.1.

3.7x   toome (< *tɔɔme) < taume < ta[k]ume (< ?). 'entirely, exclusively,
wholeheartedly'. LHL - x-x-x x-x-x.

4.1   toosagi < tafusagi < tafusaki (< ?). 'loincloth, breechcloth (= fundoshi):
underpants, drawers (= sarumata)'. HHHH - x-3-x x-x-x. NS (128a) HHHH. For
etymologies, see Yoshida 1979:132:51; he reconstructs the word as tabusaki.

3.1 = 2.1-tu   too-tu ··· < tofo-tu < *topo -tu. 'distant': ~ oya (LL) 'ancestor'.
HH-H - x-x-x x-x-x.

4.x (?= 4.5)   toozimi < touzimi (< Ch .teng-.sim). 'lamp wick'. xLLL (?= *LLLL) -
0-1-x x-x-x. K: Hn LHHH (where attested?).

2.1   tora < twora. 'tiger'. HH - 0-0-A A-A-A. Km x. Edo HH. Ib H = 2.1. Yn tura
A (H 1964:71a).

2.1   tori. 'bird'. x - 0-0-A A-A-A. NS (83b [17:118-M, 119-M], 115b [14:83L-
K]) HH; NS (T 5; 12, 35, 96]) HH, (T 30, 31) LH. Km (W) HH. Mr (Bm) HH. Edo
HH. Ib H = 2.1. Yn tui A (H 1964:71a).

4.1   toriami < *tori$_{z.1}$ amyi$_{z.3}$ (< *am[a-C]i$_B$). 'bird net'. HHHH - 0-0-A
x-x-x. Km x.

5.2   toriawase < *tori-afase[y] < *tori$_{z.1}$ apa-sa-Ci[-Ci]$_R$. 'cockfight'.
HHHHL - 0-1-B x-x-x. Km x.

?3.5a, ?3.4   toride ?< tori-[i]de < *tor[a-C]i$_R$ inta-Ci[-Ci]$_R$. 'fort, stronghold'.
x - 0/3-0[U]/2[U]-B x-x-x. Hamada 0/3; Hattō, Matsue, Izumo 3: Goka-mura,
Wakamatsu 0. Attestations are rather late.

3.1   torii < tori-wi < *tori$_{z.1}$ b^u/$_o$-Ci[-Ci]$_A$ ('bird perch'). 'the gate of a
Shintō shrine'. x - 0-0-A A-A-x. Aomori (torie), Sz 0. Ib H = 3.1. Sr turi A.

3.4   toriko < *tworikwo < *twor[a-C]i$_R$ kwo$_{?(1.3a)}$. 'captive'. LLL - 3/0-2-A
x-x-x. Km x. Aomori (rare) 1; Hamada 2: Goka-mura 0; Narada, Hattō, Matsue,
Izumo 3; Hakata 1, ygr 3/0. Ib H = 1.1, older (rare) F = 3.4. (The kwo is said
to be 'cage, basket' rather than 'child'; why?)

3.1   tori^k/$_g$o < *tori$_{z.1}$ (-n-) kwo$_{1.3a}$. 'bird cage' (= tori-kago). HHH - x-0-x
x-x-x. Mg has -g-.

4.1   torikubi < torikufi (Mg) ?< *tori$_{z.1}$ kupi$_{z.1}$ ('bird stake'). 'the shaft
(handle) of a Chinese plow'. HHHH - x-0-x x-x-x. The register is incongruent
for the etymology *t(w)or[a-C]i$_R$ kupi$_{z.1}$ 'hold stake'.

?4.1   torisaka < tori$_{z.1}$ saka$_{z.3}$. 'cockscomb' (= tosaka). x - x-x-x x-x-x.

?6.2   torisaka-nori < tori-saka$_{4.1}$ (< ...) nori$_{?z.3}$. "Meristotheca papulosa,
a kind of seaweed' (= tosaka-nori x - 3-x-x x-x-x). HHHxxx - x-6-x x-x-x.
K: Hn HHHHHL.

?3.1   tosaka < to[ri]-saka < *tori$_{z.1}$ saka$_{z.3}$. 'cockscomb, crest'. HHx - 0-0-A
x-x-x. Sz, Hamada 0/3; Hattō, Matsue, Izumo, Goka-mura 0.

3.5x|4.1   to^a/$_z$ama - koo^a/$_z$ama < to-^{a}/$_z$ama$_{a.a}$ kau-^{a}/$_z$ama$_{4.1}$ < to$_{?1.3b}$ (-n-)
sama$_{?z.za}$ ka-[k]u$_{z.zb}$ (-n-) sama$_{?z.za}$ ('that-way this-way'). 'all directions'.
x - x-x-x x-x-x. NS (116b) LLH(|)HHHH.

*2.3   (-)tose < tose (?< tosi$_{z.3}$ with partially assimilated vowel; ?< *toso,
cf. Matsumoto 1974:100). ' ··· years'. See huta-tose.

2.3   tosi. 'year(s), age'. LL - 2-2-B B-B-B. NS (102a, 102b 'good harvest
year') LL. Km (W) LL. Edo HL. NE Kyūshū 0. Ib F = 2.3. Cf. -ti. Matsumoto
(1974:100) suggests *tosi[y] < *toso-Ci, with *toso > (-)tose secondary.

4.5 = 2.3|2.3   tosigoi < tosigofi < *tosi$_{z.3}$ -n- kop[a-C]i$_B$. 'harvest prayer'.
LL(|)LL - x-0-x x-x-x.

?2.1   toti. 'horse chestnut' (= toti-no-ki x - 1/3-4-A). x - 0/1-0-x x-x-x.
K: Hn HH (where attested?). Sz 0.

3.x   totoki (< ?; x - x-x-x x-x-x):
           (1) (= amazuta) 'Parthenocissus tricuspidata' (= tuta = natututa);
           (2) (= woka-totoki) 'bellflower, balloonflower' (= kikyoo);
           (3) 'Adenophora triphylla' (= turigane-ninzin);
           (4) 'dead/blind nettle' (= odoriko-soo).

3.3   totugi < *to$_{?1.1}$ tugyi$_{z.zb}$ (< *tunk[a-C]i$_A$). 'ten generations'. x - x-x-x
x-x-x. Km (W) HLL.

?4.1, ?4.2 = 2.1(=1.1-tu)|2.1/2.2   totukuni < twotu-kuni < *two$_{1.1}$ -tu$_{pc1}$
kuni$_{?z.1,?z.za}$ (< ...). 'distant land; outer province'. x - x-x-x x-x-x.

?6.3, ?6.4   totu-kuniguni < two$_{1.1}$ -tu$_{pc1}$ kuni-guni$_{?4.4}$ (< kuni$_{?z.1,?z.za}$ n[i]
kuni$_{?z.,?z.za}$ (< ...)). 'distant lands; the provinces outside the central
domain'. x - x-x-x x-x-x. NS (98b [11:95-K] H-H(|)H?LLL, (Okada) HHHHLL.

3.3 = 1.1|2.3   toyama < *two$_{1.1}$ dama$_{z.3}$. '(fringe mountains =) foothills'. x -
1-0/2-x x-x-x. Km (W) H(|)LL.

?2.3   toyo < *todo. 'rich'. x - x-x-x x-x-x. NS (107b, 112a) LL. Km (W) LL-···.
Edo HL.

?6.9 (= *6.10 = 2.3-no|3.1)   toyonoakari < toyo-no-akari < *todo₂.₃ no aka-r[a-
C]i₄. 'a banquet'. x - 1-x-x x-x-x. NS (107b) LLLLHH (?= *LL-L|HHH).

4.1/4.2   tozikimi < twozikyimyi < *two₁.₁ -n- siki-mi₃.₁ (< ...). 'threshold;
(kuruma no ~) a stretcher in a sedan-chair to lean on when bowing'. HHHH/HHHL
- x-3-x x-x-x.

?1.1   -tu (?< tu[-Ci], cf. -ti). '(number)'. Cf. too; particle -tu. See ikutu.
hitotu, hutatu, kokonotu, mi(t)tu, mu(t)tu, nanatu. ya(t)tu. yo(t)tu.

1.3a   tu. 'port, ferry'. L - 1-0-A x-x-x. NS (102a [11:140-K] L. Km x.

1.3a   tu. 'spit(tle)' (= tufaki = tubaki, tuba); ?'*liquid' (cf. mizu, ti).
L - 1-0-(x) (x)-(x)-x. Km x.

2.3 ?< 3.4   tuba (? truncation < tuba[ki]). 'spit'. x - 2/1-1-B x-B-B. Aomori. Sz
Hattō, Harada, Matsue, Izumo, Goka-mura, Hiroshima 2; Hakata 0 (expected). ygr
1. Ōsaka, Ise 2; Ib H = 2.1. Hateruma sïn. "Mr -w/b-: dial. -w-: Hn -w-, ?-f-."

?2.4, ?2.5 < 3.5x   tuba < tumyiba LLH, tumyifa ?< *tum[a-C]i₄ (-n-) pa?₁.₃ₕ ('pinch
blade'). 'sword-guard'. x - 1-1[H]/1:3[U]-B x-x-x. Km x. 1700 Ōsaka LH. Narada.
Hattō, Goka-mura 1; Hiroshima 1/2; Hamada 2; Matsue, Izumo 2 (= 2.4-5); Hakata
0, ygr 1. Ōsaka, Ise 1; Ib L = 2.4.

3.7x   tubaha < tuba-fa (< ?). 'earthenware jar'. LHL - x-x-x x-x-x.

5.16   tubaimomo < tuba[k]imomo < tubakyi-momo < *tunpaki₃.₇ₕ momo₂.₁.
'nectarine'. LLLHx (= *LLLHL) - 2(?<*3)-(1:3)-x x-x-x.

3.4   tubaki < tu-fakyi < *tu₁.₃ₐ pak[a-C]i₈. 'spit(tle)'. LLL - 3-2-x x-(B)-(B).
Km x. Hiroshima 3; Narada 3. Ōsaka, Ise 1:3; Ib (rare) L2 = 3.5/7. Sr çinpee B
(?< *tunpaki); Yn cubainti B (?< *tuba[k]i-buki). "Mr -w/b-; dialect -w-;
Hn -f-." See Ch. 2.

3.7a/b   tubaki < tubakyi < *tunpaki (?< Sino-Korean twong-poyk). 'camellia'.
LHL - 1-1:3-B x-B-x. Km x. 1700 Ōsaka LHL. Narada, Hamada, Goka-mura.
Hiroshima, Wakamatsu, Hakata, Ōita 1; Sapporo, Aomori, Akita, Hattō 2:
Numazu, Matsue, Izumo 0. Ōsaka, Ise 1:3; Ib L2 = 3.5/7.

4.x   tubakura (truncation) < tubakura[me]₈.₁₁ (< ...). 'swallow' (bird).
x - 0-1:3-x x-x-x.

5.11   tubakurame < *tunpa (?= tunpa[sa]₃.₂ₐ 'wing' but register incongruent; ?=
tunpa[ki₃.₄]₂.₃ 'spit') kura₈d₁ ₄ ('dark') -mey (< *m[ur]ey < *mura-Ci[-Ci])₄.
'swallow' (bird). LHHHL - 3/4-1:4-x x-x-x. Km x. Contracted to tubakura (JP)
and tubame (modern).

?3.6, ?3.7a/b < 5.11   tubame < tuba[kura]me₈.₁₁ (< ...). 'swallow' (bird).
x - 0-1-B x-x-x. Goka-mura, NE Kyūshū 1; Hattō 0/1; Izumo 2: Aomori 2
(expected); Hamada, Matsue, Yamaguchi 0; Hakata 1, ygr 0. Narada 0/3. Kōchi 1:3
(Doi 1952:23); Ib L2 = 3.5/7, L = 3.6. Toyama tuwame.

3.2a   tubasa < *tunpasa (< ?; cf. tob- < tonpa-₄ 'fly'). 'wing'. HHL -
0(/1[new])-1:3-B x-x-x. Km (S) HHL. Edo HHL. 1700 Ōsaka LHL. Kurayoshi
(Tottori), Narada, Hattō 1; Aomori, Akita 2; Matsumoto. Izumo 3; Goka-mura 0/1:
Hakata 2/1, ygr 0. Kōchi 2; Toyama 1:4 (we expect 1:3); Suzu 1:2 (we expect 1):
Ib L2 = 3.5/7. Cf. tobu₄ 'fly'; ture₂.₁ 'pair'; ha(- ne₂.₁)₂₁.₂ 'feather'.

2.3   tubi < ?*tubiy < *tunpᵘ/₀Ci. 'vulva'. LL - 2-x-2 x-A-B. Nk Cibii A,
Sr çibi A, Yn nbi (< tubi) B 'arse'.

?2.4a   tubi < tubiy < *tunpu-Ci. 'grain, granule' (= tubu). x - x-x-x x-x-x.

2.1a   tubo < tufo (?< *tupo; ?= tuwo < tu[b]o: "also tufu"). 'jar'. HF/HH -
0-0-A A-A-C. NS (T+ kun) tufu LL. Km (W) HH. Edo HH. Aomori, Narada, Hattō,
Hamada, Matsue, Izumo, Hiroshima, Hakata 0. Ib H = 2.1. Nk Cibuu A; Yn cibu C.
For the -f-, see Ch. 2, §1.2; on the accent, see Ch. 4, §7.3. Cf. utuwa.

?3.4   tubomi < *tunpo-m[a-C]i₂₄/ᵦ. 'bud'. x - 3-0-B x-B-x. Sz, Narada. Hattō,
Hamada, Matsue, Izumo, Hiroshima 3; Aomori 0; Goka-mura 1 (?< *0). Ōsaka 0:
Ise 1:3; Ib H = 3.1. See Ch. 4, Chart 6:1.

4.2   tubonage < *tufo-nagey (< ...). '(a game of) tossing arrows into a jar'.
HHHL - x-x-x x-x-x.
?3.1   tubone < tubo₂.₁ₐ (< ...) -ne₅ₐₑ (< *na-Ci). 'a temporarily
partitioned room; ... '. x - 0-0-x x-x-x. 1700 Ōsaka HHL.
4.2   tubouti < *tufo-uti (< ...). '(a game of) tossing arrows into a jar'.
HHHL - x-x-x x-x-x.
2.4   tubu < *tunpu. 'grain, granule'. HL - 1-1-B B-B-x. Narada, Hattō, Hamada,
Hiroshima 1; Matsue, Izumo 2. Wakamatsu 1. Ib L = 2.4. Sr çizi B ?< *tudi ?<
*tunbi.
-        [tubu] 'jar':   see tubo.
4.9   [tubu-husi] < tu(bu)busi (JP) < tuᶠ/ᵇu-fusi < *tunpu₂.₄ (-n-) pusi₂.₃ or
*tunpu₂.₄ pusi₂.₃ ('granule joint'). 'anklebone' (= tubunaᵏ/ᵧi, kuru-busi):
(Ryūkyū) 'knees' (= hiza). LHHL - x-0-x A-A-A. Sd tibuusyi/tibusy A < *tubusi:
Sr cinsi A 'knees, lap' (H 1967); Ikema (Miyako) cigusi; Kobama (Yaeyama)
cubusun A, Hateruma supusin; Yn nbuci A.
4.9   tubunaᵏ/ᵧi < *tunpu₂.₄ naᵏ/ᵧi₂ ('granule + ?'). 'anklebone' (= tubu-husi.
kuru-busi). LHHL - x-0-x x-x-x.
?3.6, ?3.7x tubune (< ?). 'servant'. LHx - x-x-x x-x-x.
5.11   tubunegusa < *tubune (< ?) (-n-) kusa₂.₃. 'Asarum nipponicum'
(= hutamaᵏ/ᵧami = kan-aoi). LHHHL - x-4-x x-x-x.
3.6   tubura < *tunpu-ra < *tunpu₂.₄ [a]ra₂.₃. 'rotund'. x - 0/1-1-B x-x-x.
NS (T+ kun) HLL. Km x.
3.6   tuburi < *tuᵇ/ₘuri < *tunpuri. 'grebe, dabchick' (bird) = kai-tuburi.
LHH (Ck) / HHH (Shinsen-Jikyō) - x-x-x x-x-x.
?3.4   tuburi 'head':   see tumuri.
?3.5b (?> 3.7b)   tubusa(-ni) ?< *tunpu₂.₄ sa[ma]₂₂.₂ₐ. 'complete; in detail'.
LLH(-L) - 1-1:3-B x-x-x. Km (S) HLL. Mr (Bm) HLL. Edo HLL.
?3.4   tubute ?< *tunpu₂.₄ ta-Ci₁.₃ₐ ('granule hand'). 'pebble, stone (for
throwing); stone-throwing, stoning'. x - 0/3-2-B x-x-x. Edo HHL. Sz (rare) 0.
Cf. tabute.
3.4   tudami (Mg) < "tutami" < *tu₁.₃ₐ (-n-) tam[a-C]i₈. LLL - x-x-x x-x-x.
'spitting up, regurgitating (by baby/dog)'.
2.4   tue < tuwe (?< *tubey < *tubaCi; ?< tu[k-ₐ su]we₂.₁ (< ... 'contact
end'); ?< tu[w]e < tu[k-i]ₐ e₂.₁ (?< ye[da]₂.₁ < ...) 'contact branch').
'rod, staff; measure of length (about 10 feet)'. LH - 1-1-B x-x-x. Km x. Edo
LH. Ib L = 2.4.
2.x   tuga = toga < twoga < *twonka. 'hemlock spruce'. x - 0/1/2-0-x x-x-x.
?2.1, ?2.3   tuge (< ?). 'boxtree'. x - 0-0-B x-x-x. Km x. K: Hn LL (attested?).
Sz 0. Ib F = 2.3.
2.1   tugi < tugyi < *tunk[a-C]i₄. 'patch'. x - 0-0-A x-x-x. Hakata 0, vgr 2 (=
2.3).
2.2x   tugi < tukiy < *tuku-Ci₂ₐ. 'tribute' (= mi-tugi). HL (~ no nuno) - x-x-x
x-x-x. Cf. tugunau (Ch. 2, §1.2).
2.2b   tugi < tugyi < *tunk[a-C]i₄. 'next'; (number of) generations'. HL - 2-2-A
x-x-x. Km (S) HL. Mr (Bm) HL. Edo HL. Hamada, Matsue. Izumo 1; Hakata 0. vgr 2
(= 2.3). Ib H1 = 2.2.
3.6   tugumi (< ?). 'thrush'; tugumi no i(f)ine 'Solanum lyratum' (= hiyodori-
zyoogo) (bird). LHH - 0-1:3-B x-x-x. Sz 2; Aomori 2, older 3 (we expect 1).
Ib F = 3.4.
4.5 < 5.6 = 2.3|3.4 tugumori, (metathesis) tumogori < *tu[kiy]-gomori / (*)tukiy-
komori < *tuku-Ci₂.₃ (-n-) koma-r[a-C]i₈. 'the last day of the month, the
interlune'. LLLL - 0-0[H]/4[U]-B x-x-x. NS (105a) tukumori LLLL. Mr (Bm) HHHL.
Sz (rare) 0.

2.5   tui(-ni) < "tufi" (= tuwi ?< *tu[w]i < *tu[k]iy < *tuku-Ci[-Ci]ᴿ 'exhaust'
— but M 4508 has tufyi, therefore < *tupi? — cf. tubiₛ.ₐ). '(at the) end.
final(ly)'. LF(|H) - 1-2[H]/1:3[U]- A x-x-(x). Km (S,W) LH(-L). Mr (Bm) LH(-L).
Edo LF. Ib tui-ni L2 = 3.5/7. (Yn cui C, see siri.)

3.1   tuide < *tu[g]yide < *tug[a-C]iₐ ta-Ci?₍₁.₃ₐ₎. 'order'. HHH - 0-0-A x-A-x.
Edo HHH. Hakata O (we expect 2 or 1). Ib H = 3.1. An early example of velar
elision tuide appears in Tosa-nikki. (The final element is 'hand' according to
Ōno; but it could be taken as the particle that is thought to derive from the
auxiliary infinitive te[y].)

4.1   tuigaki < tuikaki < tuki-kaki < *tukyi kakyi < *tuk[u-C]iₐ (< ?*tuk[a-C]i)
kakiₛ.ₛᵦ. 'a mud fence' (= tui[hi]zi). HHHH - 0-0-x x-x-x.

4.1   [tuihizi, tuiizi] > tuizi 'mud fence': see tuizi.

3.5x   tuisi (< Ch dhwey'-'tsyey). '(a ceremonial cake)'. LLH - x-x-x x-x-x.

?4.6, ?4.5 = 2.3|2.3   tuitati < tu[k]itati < *tukiy-tati < *tuku-Ciₛ.ₛ tat[a-C]iₙ.
'moonrise; first day of the month'. LLxx - 4-4-A x-B-x. Sz. Narada, Hattō,
Hamada, Matsue, Izumo 4; Goka-mura 0; Hakata 0, ygr 3 (?= 4.5). Mr (Bm) HHHL.
Sr çiitaci B.

3.1 < 4.1 tuizi < tuidi < *tui[w]idi < tuifidi < *tu[k]ifidi < *tukyi fyidi <
*tuk[u-C]iₐ (< ?*tuk[a-C]i) pintiₛ.ₛ. 'a mud fence' (= tuigaki). HHHH - 0-0-A
x-x-x. Edo HHH.

2.2b   tuka (?< *tuku-ₐ < ?*tuka-ₐ 'build'). 'mound'. HL - 2-2-A x-(x)-x. Km x.
Narada, Hattō, Hamada 2; Matsue, Izumo 2 (= 2.3). Ib (rare) F = 2.3.

2.3   tuka (?< *tuka-ᵦ 'attach', cf. tukamu < *tuka-m[a-]ᵦ 'grasp'). 'hilt'.
LL - 2-2-A x-B-x. Km x. Edo HL. Narada 2. Ib F = 2.3, L = 2.4.

?2.4, ?2.3 tuka (?< *tuka-ᵦ). 'bundle' (cf. tukane). LH-··· - x-x-x x-x-x.
Kn tuka-fasira LH-xxx.

3.1   tukai < tukafyi < *tuka-p[a-C]iₐ. 'errand; servant'. HHH - 0- 0-A x-A-B.
NS (113a) Hxx. Km (S,W) HHH. Edo HHH. Ib H = 3.1. Nk siKee A; Yn Kai B
(H 1964:72a).

?5.1, ?5.2 tukaibito < tukafi-bito < tukafyi-fyito < *tuka-p[a-C]iₛ.₁₄ₐ
pitoₛ.ₛₐ. 'servant, retainer (= tukaito); concubine; messenger'. x - 3-x-x
x-x-x.

4.1 < ?5.1, ?5.2 (< ...) tukaito < *tukafyi [fyi]to < *tuka-p[a-C]iₛ.₁₄ₐ pitoₛ.ₛₐ.
'servant, retainer'. x - x-x-x x-x-x. NS (109a) HHH.

3.4   tukane < *tuka -na-Ci[-Ci]ᵦ. 'bundle'. LLL - x-x-x x-x-x.

5.2   tukarigusa < *tuka-r[a-C]iₐ -n- kusaₛ.ₛ. 'Justicia gendarussa, water
willow' (= sinkyuu). HHHHL.

3.1   tukasa (< ?). 'elevated person/place; official'. HHH - 0/2-1:3-(?A)
x-x-x. NS (93a, 125b) HHH. Km (W) HHH.

?2.1, ?2.3 tuki < tukiy < *tuku-Ci. 'zelkova (tree)' (= keyaki). HH - 2-2-x
x-x-x. Km x. Hiroshima 2. Ōsaka, Ise 2. Cf. tukuyumi.

?2.1, ?2.5 tuki < tukyi (= toki ?< *twokyi < *twoki). 'ibis' (bird).
HH - 1-(1:3)-x x-x-x. Km x. Sz 1. Ib H1 = 2.2.

2.2x   tuki 'tribute': see tugi.

2.2b   tuki < tukyi < *tuki (?< *tuk[a-C]i, cf. *tunka-ₐ 'pour'). 'cup'.
HL - 2-2-x x-x-x. Km x.

2.3   tuki < tukiy < *tuku-Ci. 'moon'. LL (Ck) - 2-2-B B-B-B. NS (113b) LL.
Km (S,W) LL. Mr (Bm) HL. Edo HL. Goka-mura 0; Hattō. Hamada. Matsue, Izumo,
Hiroshima (etc.) 2. Toyama 1:3; Suzu 1; Ib F = 2.3. Kobama (Yaeyama) çïkui
(Ryūkyū-hōgen 9/10:82). Hateruma sï (cf. Ch. 1, §52). Yn Tii B.

4.5   tukigoro < tukigoro̱ = tukiy-goro < *tuku-Ciₛ.ₛ -n- koroₛ.ₛᵦ. 'these
several months now'. LLLL - x-x-x x-x-x. Km x.

4.11   tukigusa < *tukiy (< *tuku-Ci$_{2.3}$) -n- kusa$_{2.3}$. 'commelina' (= tuyukusa). "HLHL" ?= *LLHL - x-0-x x-x-x. Km (W) LLHL, HHHL, HLxx.

4.5   tukinami < *tukiy-namyi < *tuku-Ci$_{2.3}$ nam[a-C]i$_A$. 'every month'. "HLLL" ?= LLLL - 0-0-B x-x-x. Km x.

?3.5b   tukiyo < tuku[1]/$_n$-yo < tukyi/tuku ywo < *tuku(-Ci)$_{2.3}$ dwo$_{1.3a}$. 'moon(light); a bright name'. x - 2-2-B x-B-x. Km (W) xxH. 1700 Ōsaka HHL. Aomori <u>3</u>. Ib F = 2.3. Sr çicuu B.

?2.1, ?2.3   tuku 'zelkova': *see* tuki, tukuyumi.

?2.5   tuku 'owl': *see* zuku.

?3.1, ?3.2a   tukuba < tukufa < *tukupa (< ?). 'Tsukuba' (placename). x - 0/2-0-(B) x-x-x. NS (T+ 25) HHL.

4.1 ?= 3.1|1.1 tukuba-ne < tukufa-ne < *tukupa$_{?3.1}$ (< ?) ne$_{?1.1}$ (?< na-Ci). 'Tsukuba peak'. x - 0-0-x x-x-x. Km (W) HHH(|)H.

5.2   tukubayama < tukufa-yama < *tukupa$_{?3.1}$ (< ?) dama$_{2.3}$. 'Mount Tsukuba'. x - 0-x-x x-x-x. Km (W) HHHHL.

*3.1 < 4.1   tukuda: *see* tukurida.

3.1   tukue < tuku(w)e < tukuye (?< *tuku-de < ?). 'desk'. HHH - 0-0-A A-?A-x. Km x. Hakata 0 *(we expect 2)*. Ib H = 3.1. On why this is not from tukuwe, despite attested spellings, see Ōno's citations of early Heian data. The traditional etymology is < *tuk[a-C]i$_B$ suwe$_{2.1}$ (< ...) 'contact end'.

3.1   tukumo (< ?). 'bulrush' (= takumamo$_{4.2}$ = modern hutoi). HHH - x-1-x x-x-x.

3.4   tukura (< ?). 'young grey mullet (bora)' *(fish)*. LLL - x-0-x x-x-x.

4.1   tukurida, tuku[ri]da < *tuku-r[a-C]i$_B$ -n- ta$_{1.3a}$. 'fields that are under cultivation'. LLLL - x-0-x x-x-x.

?5.7a   tukurimizu < tukurimidu < *tukuri-myidu < *tuku-r[a-C]i$_B$ mintu$_{2.1a}$ (< ...). 'boiled (and cooled) water'. LLLLF - x- 4-x x-x-x. K: Hn LLLLL "?". See Ch. 4, §7.3.

-         tukuyo: *see* tukiyo.

4.x   tukuyumi < tuku-yumyi < *tuku$_{?2.1,?2.3}$ dumi$_{2.3}$. 'zelkova-wood bow'. x - x-x-x x-x-x. NS (T+ 28) HL|HH (incongruent).

2.1   tuma(-) 'claw': *see* tume. Cf. tumamu.

?2.2a   tuma. 'skirt; rim'. x - 2-2-A x-x-x. NS (T+ 96) LF (incongruent). Km x. Edo HL. Aomori, Goka-mura, Hattō, Hiroshima 2; Hamada, Hakata 0. Ib H1 = 2.2.

?2.2a   tuma. '(wife <) spouse'. HL - 1-2-A x-x-x. NS (82c [17:111-M]) HH, (Okada) HL; NS (T+ 87) LH, (T+ 94; 52; 69, 70) = HL, (T+ kun) LL. Edo HL. Aomori *(rare)* 0; Narada, Hamada, Hiroshima, Wakamatsu 1; Hakata 1 *(we expect 0)*. Hattō, Goka-mura 2. Ib H1 = 2.2.

?5.2   tumabarame < tumabarami *(last vowel partially assimilated to the preceding three vowels)* < *tuma$_{2.1}$ para-m[a-C]i$_B$. 'festering nails/hoof'. HHHxx - x-4-x x-x-x. K: Hn HHHHL.

5.16   tumabiraka < tuma^f/$_b$iraka, tubafiraka < *tubafyiraka (< ?*tunpa-(n)pira-ka or ?*tunp[u]$_{2.4}$ ap[a-C]i$_B$ -ra-ka). 'in clear detail'. LLLHL - 3-4-A x-x-x. Km x. Mr (Bm) HHHLL.

4.1   tumagoi < tumagwofiy < *tuma$_{2.2b}$ kwopo-Ci[-Ci]$_B$. 'conjugal love'. x - 0-0-x x-x-x. Km (W) HHHH.

4.1   tumagome < tumagomey < *tuma$_{2.2b}$ -n- koma-Ci[-Ci]$_B$. 'being confined (cohabitant) with spouse'. x - 0-x-x x-x-x. NS (T+ 1) HHHH. Km (W) HHHH.

4.1/4.2   tumairi < *tuma$_{2.1}$ ir[a-C]i$_A$. 'hoof disease'. HHHH (Zs) / HHHL (Kn) - x-0-x x-x-x.

2.1   tume < tumey < *tuma-ci. 'claw'. HH - 0-0-A A-A-A. Km x. Wakamatsu 2 (= 2.3, since this dialect regularly merges 2.2 with 2.1). Ib H = 2.1. Nk Cimii A; Kunigami, Ōgimi (northern Okinawa) B; Yn nmi A < *tumi (< tume).

4.6   tumeisi < *tumey-isi < *tuma-Ci[-Ci]*ᴮ* isi*₂.₂b*. 'rock pile' (= tumiisi).
LLLH - x-x-x x-x-x.

?2.1, ?2.2x   tumi. 'sparrow-hawk'. HH (Ck) - 1-2-x x-x-x. K: Hn HL *(where
attested?)*. Cf. suzumidaka.

2.4   tumi < tumyi < *tumi. 'sin'. LH - 1-1[H]/O̲[U]-B B-x-x. NS (106b, 107b) LH.
Km (S) LH. Edo LH. Izumo 2̲; Matsue 1/2̲. Kōbe (Robb) 2̲. Ib L = 2.4. Is Kt O̲[U]
a misprint? (The etymology < *tum[a-C]i*ₐ* is incongruent in register.)

3.5x   tumiba < tumyiba < *tum[a-C]i*ₐ* -n- pa*₇₁.₃b*. 'sword-guard' (> tuba). LLL -
x-x-x x-x-x. Register incongruent with etymology?

4.1   tumiisi < *tumyi-isi < *tum[a-C]i*ₐ* isi*₂.₂b*. 'rock pile; (= isizue) stone
foundation; a row of stones'. L̲L̲L̲H̲ - 0-0-A x-x-x. Cf. tumeisi.

3.1   tumori < *tumor[a-C]i (?< *tuma-ra-Ci*ₐ*). 'intention'. (H) - 0-0-A A-(A)-x.
Km (W) (H). Sz 2̲.

2.4   tumu. 'spindle'. x - 1-1-x x-x-x. Cf. tumugu. Hiroshima 1. Ōsaka 0̲; Ise 2̲.

3.4   tumure (< ?). 'a rise, a hillock'. LLL - x-0-x x-x-x. Cf. tamure.

?3.6   *tumuri 'grebe': *see* tuburi.

?3.4 < 3.7x   tumuri < *tuᵇ/**ᵐ**uri < *tunpuri (?< *tunpu*₂.₄* [a]r[a-C]i*ᴮ* 'round
thing'). 'head' (= atama, kasira). ⋯ |LHL - 3̲-0̲-B x-B-x. Narada tuburi 3̲.
Sr çiburu B (but Sd khamaatyi/khamaty B < *kamati, Yn minburu B).

?3.1, ?3.6   tumuzi < *tumu (?< *tunpu*₂.₄*) -n- si*₁.ₓ*. 'hair-whorl; whirlwind'.
HHH (Kn) / LHH (Ck) - 0-0-B̲ x-x-x. Km x.

5.3   tumuzikaze < *tumu-n-si*?₃.₁* (< ...) kansa-Ci*₂.₁*. 'whirlwind'. HHHLL -
3/5-4-B x-x-x. NS (101a [11:134-K]) HHHLL.

2.3   tuna. 'rope'. LL - 2-2-B B-B-B. Km x. Edo HL. Ib F = 2.3. Yn nna B <
*tuna. Cf. nawa.

2.3   (-)tuna 'horn' (= tuno): *see* mituna.

2.5   tune (?< *tu[ra]ne < *tura-na-Ci[-Ci]]*ₐ* *but register incongruent*; ?<
*tuna-Ci*₂.₃* 'rope', cf. Matsumoto 1974:95). 'longlasting, always'. LH/LF - 1-
1:3-B x-B-x. Ongi (Iroha) LH. NS (133a) tune-no LH-L 'common'. Km (S,W) LH(-L).
Edo LF. Sz 2. Ib L2 = 2.5. On Hn LF, see Ch. 4, §7.

2.3   tuno < tunwo. 'horn'. LL - 2-2-B B-B-B. NS (T+ 97) LL, (T+ 56) H̲H̲. Km x.
Edo HL. Ib F = 2.3. Sd tino(o) B; Onna tuunuu B; Yn nnun B < *tunon (for final
-n, see Ch. 1, §52).

4.6   tunouri < *tunwo*₂.₃* uri*₂.₄*. 'white muskmelon' (= modern sirouri). LLLH -
x-x-x x-x-x.

4.5 = 2.3|2.3 tunoyumi < tunwo-yumyi < *tunwo*₂.₃* dumi*₂.₃*. 'bow with bowstring nocks
made of horn'. LL(|)LL - x-4-x x-x-x.

?2.1, ?2.2a   tura. 'row, line'. HH - x-x-x x-x-x. NS (129a) HL. Km x.

?2.2a   tura 'vine': *see* turu. Cf. tuta.

2.3   tura. 'cheeks; face'. LL/H̲L̲ - 2-2-B B-B-B. Km x. Edo HL. Ib F = 2.3.

4.6   turabone < turafone (Mg) < *tura*₂.₃* (-n-) pone*₂.₃* (< ...). 'cheek bone'.
LLLH - 0-0-x x-x-x.

4.6   turazue < tura-duwe < *tura*₂.₃* -n- tuwe*₂.₄* (< ...). 'resting cheek on
hand' (= hozue). x - x-3-x x-x-x. Km (W) LLLH. Mr (W 20) LLLH. K: "Km LLLF".

2.1   ture < *ture[y] < *tura-Ci[-Ci]*ₐ*. 'companion'. x - A-A-A x-A-x. 1700
Ōsaka HH. Hiroshima (Okuda 270), Hamada, Hattō 2̲ (verb A). Ib H1 = 2.2.

2.1   turi < *tur[a-C]i*ₐ*. 'fishing'. HH - 0-0-A (A-A-A). Km (W) HH. Hiroshima
(Okuda 270) 2̲. Narada, Hattō, Hamada, Matsue, Izumo 0; Hakata 0̲ *(we expect 1,
ygr 0)*. Ib H = 2.1.

4.2   turibune < *tur[a-C]i*ₐ* -n- puna-Ci*₂.₄*. 'fishing boat'. HHHL - 0-0-A x-x-x.
Sz 0.

2.2a   turu < tura. 'vine'. (H) - 2-2[H]/1[U]-B x-A-A. Km x. Aomori (cira), Sz 0.
   Ōsaka, Ise 2; Ib H1 = 2.2. Yn cirun A < *turun (for final -n, see Ch. 1, §52).
2.2a   turu. '(bow)string'. HL - 2-2-B x-A-A. Km x. Edo HL. Aomori, Sz 0;
   Hiroshima 2. Ōsaka, Ise 2; Ib H1 = 2.2. Yn ciru A (H 1964:71a).
2.5   turu. 'crane' (bird). LH - 1-1:3-B A[new]-A-x. Km (W) LH. Edo LF.
   Hiroshima 1. Ōsaka, Ise 1:3; Ib L2 = 2.5. Nk Ciruu A.
4.5   turubami < turufamyi (?< *turu*g.*sb* pami*g.*s). 'acorn (= donguri); oak (=
   kunugi)'. LLL?L - 0-x-x x-x-x. Cf. hasibami.
3.2b   turube < *turubey < *turu-n-paCi < *tur[a-]u*A* -n- pa-Ci*g.g* ('hang jar').
   'well bucket'. HHL - 0-1:3-A x-(A)-(C). Km x. Yamaguchi, Narada, Hattō, Hamada
   3; Sapporo, Aomori, Akita, Matsumoto, Numazu, Hida (= northern Gifu), Matsue,
   Izumo, Hiroshima, Goka-mura, NE Kyūshū, Hakata, Ōita 0. Toyama 2 (we expect
   1:3); Suzu 1 (expected); Ib tubure H = 3.1. Sr çii A; Yn ciri C.
3.4   turugi < turu*k*/*g*yi < *turu(n)ki. 'sword'. LLL - 3-2-A (A)-(B)-(B). NS (T+
   kun) LLL. Mr (Bm) HHL. Edo HHL. Narada 1; Hattō, Hamada 3; Matsue, Izumo 2;
   Aomori, Wakamatsu 0; Goka-mura 0 (expected reflex). Ib F = 3.4. Sd 'uvula,
   penis'; Nk x; Sr çiruzi B 'cockspur'; Yn ciŋu B 'small knife/sword'. On -*k*/*g*-,
   see Ch. 2, §1.2.
4.10   tusidama < *tusi*?* (?< Ch; cf. zyuzu) -n- tama*g.g.* 'rosary beads; Job's-
   tears (plant)' (= zyuzu-dama). LHLL - x-x-x x-x-x. "Also zusi-dama."
3.2a/b   tusima < tu (= ?) sima*g.g.* 'Tsushima' (placename). HHL(-···) - 1/2-2[H]/
   1:3[U]-B x-x-x. Cf. next entry.
?4.3 < 3.2a/b|1.1   tusimem[u] HHLL = tusimeri "HHLH" (?= HHL|H) (Kn Butsu-ka moto
   124:4).   (1) ?< *tusima - ri (< Ch .1i):   (1a) ? 'a kind of pear (grown on
   Tsushima)', (1b) ? 'a shortnecked clam' (= Sino-Korean hap-li = Korean pacilak
   cwokay).   (2) ?< *tusima ami/ari: ? 'an ant (from Tsushima)'. Also tukiki?
2.2a   tuta. 'ivy; (= amazura) Parthenocissus tricuspidata (= natututa = totoki)'.
   HL - 2/0-2-A x-A-x. 1700 Ōsaka HL. NE Kyūshū (H 1951:174), Narada, Hakata 0;
   Hattō, Goka-mura 2; Hamada 0/2; Matsue, Izumo 0/2 (= 2.3). Ib F/H = 2.3/1. Cf.
   tura = turu 'vine'.
3.4   tutami: see tudami.
?4.8, ?4.7, ?4.1   tutegoto < tute-koto < *tuta-Ci[-Ci]*A* (-n-) koto*g.g.* 'rumor;
   (= kotozute) oral message'. x - x-x-x x-x-x. NS (118a) L?HHH or L?LHH, (Okada)
   HHHH; NS (T+ 128) LHHL. (We would expect HHHH.)
2.3   tuti. 'earth'. LL - 2-2-B x-x-x. Km (S,W) LL. Edo HL. Toyama 1:3; Suzu 1;
   Ib F = 2.3. If this is the first element in tuti-hanmyoo 'Cantharis', the
   synonym niwa-tu*t*/*z*u may indicate *tuti[y] < *tutu-Ci.
2.4 ?< *3.5   [tuti] < *tuti[y] < *tutu-Ci. 'hammer'. LH - 2-1-B B-x-x. Km x.
   Edo LH. Tk and Aomori 2 < *1 due to vowel unvoicing? Hakata 1, ygr 2. Ib L =
   2.4. Cf. kubu-tuti/-tutui, (*isi-tuti =) isi-tutui.
5.16   tutigaeru < tutigaferu < *tuti-gafyeru < *tuti*g.g* -n- ?kapiru*g.g.* 'toad,
   ranid'. LLLHL - 1-2-x x-x-x.
4.5   tutigura < *tuti*g.g* -n- kura*g.gb.* 'cellar'. LLLL - 0-0-x x-x-x.
4.6   tutihasi < tutifasi < *tuti*g.g* pasi*g.gb.* 'an earthen bridge'. LLLH - x-2-x
   x-x-x.
4.5   tutikure < *tuti*g.g* kure*g.x* (< ...). 'clod, lump of earth'. LLLL - 0/3-0-B
   x-x-x.
4.5 = 2.3|2.3   tutimuro < *tuti*g.g* murwo*g.g.* 'cellar'. LL(|)LL - 0-x-x x-x-x.
4.7   tutinabe < *tuti-nabey < *tuti*g.g* nanpaCi*g.g.* 'earthenware pot'. LLHH -
   0-0-x x-x-x. (On a sometime suspicion this may have been LLLF, see Sakurai
   1975:91-2.)

4.5   tutisuri < *tuti*ℬ.ℬ* sur[a-C]i*ℬ* ('[seabottom] earth rub'). 'the (fat)
underbelly of a fish'. LLLL - x-4-x x-x-x.

4.5   tuti*ᵗ*/ᵈara < *tuti*ℬ.ℬ* -n- tara*?ℬ.ℬ* ('earth aralia'). 'asparagus'.
LLLL - x-4-x x-x-x.

2.4   tuto < tutwo. 'straw-wrapped foodstuff; lunch-pack for a journey; a
souvenir gift (from a journey)'. x - 0/2-2-B x-B-x. Sz 2. Tk 2 < *1 due to
vowel unvoicing? K: Km "LH?". Cf. tutumu*ℬ*.

2.5   tuto (< *tutwo) (-ni) 'early (in the morning); from early on'. LH(-x) -
2(<*1)-2[H]/1:3[U]-A x-x-x. Cf. tutomete. K: Hn LHL "?".

?4.6   tutomete < *tutwomey te[y] < tutwo-ma-Ci[-Ci]*ℬ* ta-Ci[-Ci]*ₐᵤₓ ₐ*. 'morning'.
LLxx - x-2-x x-B-B. Irregular initial in Sr sutumiti B (hwitimiti B in H 1967).
Yn Tumuti B.

2.1   tutu. 'pipe, tube'. HH - 0/2-0-B A-x-x. Km x. Aomori 2; Narada, Hattō,
Hamada, Matsue, Izumo 0; Goka-mura 2. Ib H = 2.1.

?2.1   tutu (?< to-to < *to[ri]*ℬ.₁* to[ri]*ℬ.₁* 'birdie birdie'). 'wagtail (=
sekirei); swallow (= tubame); ? chick, baby bird (cf. tutuge)'. x - x-x-x
x-x-x. Cf. tetere.

(2.4)   [tutu] 'hammer': see [tuti].

3.1   tutuga < *tutunka < *tutum[a-C]i*?ₐ* (-)ka*₁.ₓ* ('hindrance place').
'illness'. HHH - 0-x-x x-x-x. Edo HHH.

3.2x   tutuge < *tutu*?ℬ.₁* -n- key*?₁.₁* (< ...). 'bird down'. HHL - x-x-x x-x-x.

3.4   tutumi < (*)tutumyi < *tutum[a-C]i*ₐ* (< ...). 'package, bundle'. LLL -
3-2-B x-B-x. Km x. Ib F = 3.4.

?3.1   tutumi < tutumyi < *tutum[a-C]i*?ₐ*. 'being hindered/blocked; handicap,
impairment, hindrance; mishap, accident'. x - x-x-x x-x-x. Cf. tutuga.

3.5a/b   tutumi < tutumyi (?< *tu[ti]*ℬ.ℬ* tum[a-C]i*ₐ* 'earth heap'). 'dike'. LLH -
3-2-B x-B-x. Km x. Hattō, Goka-mura 1; Hamada 0/1; Matsue, Izumo, Hiroshima 0;
Wakamatsu 3; Sz, Hakata 2. Ōsaka 1:3; Ise 3.

4.5   tutumono < *tutu-mono (?< *tutwo*ℬ.₄* mono*ℬ.ℬ*; ?< *tutu[ma-Ci]*ₐ* mono*ℬ.ℬ*
but the register is incongruent). ? 'bundle'. LLLL - x-x-x x-x-x. Attested
outside Mg? (Not in NKD.)

?3.3   tutuzi < *tutunsi (< ?). 'wisteria'. x - 2-2-A x-x-x. 1700 Ōsaka HLL.
Narada, Wakamatsu 1; Hamada, Goka-mura 0; Hattō, Matsue 0/2; Aomori, Sz, Izumo,
Hakata 2. Nara, Ōsaka, Kōbe, Himeji 1:3 (Ōhara 1932, who gives Kt as 3, perhaps
a misprint); Ib L2 = 3.5/7.

?4.10, ?4.5   tuwamono < tufamono < *tupamono (?= *tu? pa-mono*?*ℬ.₄* 'blade
instruments'; ?= *tupa? mono*ℬ.ℬ*, cf. tuba*?ℬ.₄,?ℬ.ℬ* 'hilt'). 'weapon(ry)'.
LHLL - 0-0-B x-x-x. NS (94b) LxLx, (122b) LLLL, (131b) LLLx. Sz 0.

6.13   tuwamonogura < tufamono-gura < *tupamono*₄.₁₀,?₄.ℬ* (< ...) -n- kura*ℬ.ℬ*
'armory'. LHHHHL - x-x-x x-x-x.

2.1   tuya < *tuda. 'gloss'. x - 0-0-A x-x-x. Km x. Narada, Hattō, Hamada,
Matsue, Izumo, Hiroshima 0; Goka-mura 2. Ōsaka, Ise 0; Ib H1 = 2.2.

2.5   tuyu < *tudu. 'dew'. LH - 1-0[H]/1:3[U]-B x-B-C. Km (S,W) LH(-L). Edo LF.
Aomori 2 (we expect 1; not pronounced /...yo/). Takamatsu 2. Onna tuuyu B; Yn
ciyu C (H 1964:71a). In the extended meaning 'broth, juice, sap' H has 1-2-B,
for 'rainy season' 0/1-0-A and other sources also give Tk 0 (Hiroto and Ōhara
have 0/2). For 'dew' Hattō, Hamada, Matsue, Izumo have 2; for 'rainy season' 0.
For 'dew' and 'broth' Hiroshima 1, for 'rainy season' 0. Sz 'sap' 1, 'rainy
season' 2. Toyama 1:3 (we expect 2); Suzu 1 (we expect 2); Ōsaka, Ise 'dew,
broth' 1:3; 'rainy season' Ōsaka 0, Ise 0/1:3; Ib 'dew' L2 = 2.5, 'rainy
season' H = 2.1.

2.1   tuzi < *tunsi. 'crossroads'. x - 0-0-A A-x-x. Km x. Sz 0.

2.1   tuzi (?< tu[mu]zi₇₃.₁ < ...). 'hair-whorl, kinky hair'. x - x-0-x x-x-x.

4.3 (< 5.3)   tuzikaze < tu[mu]zi-kaze₆.₃ (< ...). 'whirlwind'. HHLL - x-x-x x-x-x.

?3.1, ?3.4   tuzumi < tudumyi < *tuntumi (?< *tum[i]₇ₘₗₘ tumi₇ₘₗₘ 'boom boom!').
     'drum'. HHH - 3-2-B B-A-x. NS (T+ 33) HHL. Edo HHH. Narada 1; Hattō, Matsue,
     Izumo, Goka-mura 0; Hamada 3. Hakata 1 (we expect 2), ygr 0/3. Ib L = 3.6.
     Sr çiẓin A.

3.4   tuzumi < tudumi (< ?). 'wild mulberry, Morus bombycis' (= yamaguwa). LLL -
     x-x-x x-x-x. Attested only in Mg? Not in NKD.

3.5a   tuzura < tudura < *tuntura (?< tu[ra]₇₂.₂ᵦ n[i] tura₂.₂ᵦ 'vine upon vine'
     but register incongruent). 'strong vine(s), wicker; (= ~ kago) a wicker(work)
     hamper'. LLH - 0-2-B x-x-x. NS (T+ 20) HHH. 1700 Ōsaka HLL. Yamaguchi 0; Sz 1;
     Aomori, Izumo (Kobayashi) 3.

4.7   tuzurame < tudura-me[y] < *tuntura₂.₆ ma-ci₁.₃ₐ (? 'wicker eyes').
     'widened (surprised) eyes'. LLHH - x-x-x x-x-x.

3.5x   tuzusi < tudusi (< ?). 'ivy' (= tuta). LLH - x-x-x x-x-x. Attested only in
     Mg? Not in NKD. Perhaps a variant of (or a mistake for) tutuzi 'wisteria'?

1.3a   tya (< Ch .thra < .dhra). 'tea'. x - 0-1-B B-B-B. Narada x. Aomori, Hattō,
     Hamada, Matsue, Izumo 0. Ib L = 1.3. Attested 840.

3.x   tyoozu < teudu < te[y]-myidu < *ta-Ci₁.₃ₐ mintu₁.₁ₐ (< ...). 'ablution
     water'. x - 1-2-(B) x-B-x. Edo HLL. Sr cuuzi B.

1.x   u(-). 'above': see ude, ue, uwa-; ? uku.

1.2   u. 'cormorant'. H - 1-2-A x-x-x. Km x. K: Hn LL (misprint?). Narada, Hattō,
     Hamada, Hiroshima 1; Matsue, Izumo 0. Kōbe (Robb) 0; Ōsaka, Ise 2; Ib H1 = 1.2.
     Cf. ukawa (but register incongruent). Perhaps a truncation of u[wo₂.₁ nomi₈]
     'fish-swallower'?

?1.3a (> 1.2)   u (?< u[sagi]). '(sign of the) hare, rabbit'. x - 0-2-A x-x-x.
     K: Km LL (where attested?). Edo R. Sz 1; Hiroshima 0. Ōsaka, Ise 2; Ib H = 1.1.
     Cf. udati; uguti; uzi; ohagi.

2.2b   uba < *un₇ pa₇₁.₁. 'wet-nurse'. x - 1-2-A x-x-x. Km x. Sz (rare) 1.
     Ib H1 = 2.2. Cf. ui; oba.

3.2a   ubara: see ibara.

-          ubatama = nubatama.

2.1   ube < (m)ubey < *unpaCi (?< [u]n₁ₐₜⱼ 'yeah' -pa-Ci[-Ci]). 'indeed, quite
     so'. HH - 1-1-x x-x-x. NS (74c [11:305-M], 128b [14:359-K]) HH; NS (T+ 103,
     kun) HH, (T+ 63) LL.

2.3   ube (Stauntonia hexaphylla): see mube.

4.11   ubitai < ubitafi < ?*ubyitafyi (?< *u₇₁.₃ₐ -n- pitapi₃.₁ 'rabbit brow').
     '(a horse with) white-spotted forehead': ubitafi no muma. LLHL - 2-3-x x-x-x.

?2.5, ?2.1   ubu < *unpu (?< *um[a]-p[a]-u₄, ? variant of *um[a]-u₄). '(by) birth;
     naive'. x - 1-1:3[H]/2[U]-B x-(?A)-x. Km x. Aomori, Sz 1. Ib L2 = 2.5. (HH···
     in compounds.)

4.2   ubudono < *unpu₇₂.₄,₇₂.₁ (< ...) -n- tono₂.₃. 'parturition house' (=
     ubuya). x - x-x-x x-x-x. NS (97a) HH?HL.

?3.1   ubume < *ubu-mye < *unpu₇₂.₆,₇₂.₁ (< ...) miCa₁.₃ᵦ (?= *mina). 'midwife'.
     HHH - x-0-x x-x-x. Km x.

3.4   udati < *u₇₁.₃ₐ -n- tat[a-C]i₈ ('rabbit stand'). 'a short roof-beam
     support column on the top of a crossbeam'. LLx - 0-0-x x-x-x. NS (96b) LxL.
     K: Km LLL (attested?). Etymology with u[e] 'above' is incongruent in register.

2.3   ude < *u (= ?) -n- ta-Ci₁.₃ₐ. 'arm'. LL - 2-2-B A-B-B. Ongi LL. Km x.
1700 Ōsaka HL. Ib F = 2.3. Nk qudii B; Yn udi B (H 1964:71a, Shibata 1959:118).
Dial. uze, ure (cf. ure 'branch'). The etymology < *u[pa]-₇₂.₂ₐ ⋯ 'upper
limb') is incongruent in register.

2.3   udo = uto < *u(n)to. 'asparagus'. LL (Zs) / HH (Kn) / xL (Ck) - 1-2-B
x-x-x. Mr (Bm) HH. Aomori, Sz 1. Ib H1 = 2.2.

2.1   ue < ufey ?< *u[wo]₂.₁ pa-Ci₁.₁ ('fish jar'). 'weir, fish-trap'.
HH - 0-2-x x-x-x. Mr (Bm) HH.

?2.2a   ue < ufey < *upa-Ci. 'above, up'. HH / HL - 2/0-0-A A-A-(A). NS (77a:
[14:136-M], 83c, 84a [17:125-M], 115a) HL, (84b [17:128-M]) HL/RL; NS (T 116)
HL, (T 60, 76) HH, (T 97) LL. Km (S,W) HL. Mr (Bm) HH. Heike-mabushi (Edo) HL
but HH in sono ue (Okumura 1976:217). 1700 Ōsaka HL. Tk 2 only when modified
but Nagano 2 even unmodified (Kudō 1978:48-52); Hiroshima, Yamaguchi 2 (Hiroto
1961:159, but Hiroshima 0/2 in Terakawa 1944); Hamada, Goka-mura 2; Narada,
Hattō 0. Ib H1 = 2.2 (also modified). Yn uyabi A ?< *uwa-be.

3.1   ueki < uwe[y]-kiy < *[z]uba-Ci[-Ci]ₐ ko-Ci₁.₃ₐ. 'potted plant'. x - 0-0-A
x-x-x. Km (S) HHH. Sz 0. Ib H = 3.1.

2.3   uga < uka (< *uka[-Ci-]ʙ 'receive'). *'food received': ~ no mitama 'the
divine spirit of rice (and other cereals)'. LL-L|LHx (→ HHH) - x-x-x x-x-x.

3.1   ugai < ugafi < *unkap[a-C]iₐ < ?. 'gargle'. HHH - 0-0-A x-x-x. Ib H = 3.1.

3.2a   ugara: see ukara.

3.6 (> 2.1) ugoma, ogoma (> goma). 'sesame'. LHH/HHH - x-0-x x-B-x. See goma; cf.
Asayama 1943:426.

4.11   uguisu < ugufyisu < *unkupi-su (< ?). 'bush warbler'. LLHL - 2-3[H]/2[U]-B
A-B-x. Km (W) xLxx. Narada, Hattō, Hamada, Matsue, Goka-mura, Hata, Hakata 2;
Sz 3; Izumo 0. Kōchi 2 (Doi 1952:26); Kōbe (Robb) 1:3. Nk x. Dial. iguisu,
umuisu, umugisu.

5.6   uguromoti < *unkuromot[a-C]i (< ...). 'mole (rodent)' (= mogura). LLLLL -
x-x-x x-x-x. Km x. Variants uguramoti, ugura, ugoro, ...

?3.1, ?3.2x uguso ?= ugusa (last vowel partially assimilated to earlier vowels) <
*u₁.₂ -n- kusa₂.₃ ('cormorant grass'). (1) 'Glechoma hederacea' (= kakidoosi);
(2) 'Senecio campestris' (= sawa- [u]oguruma); (3) 'Sagiwa japonica (=
tumekusa); Trifolium repens (= sirotumekusa)'. HHx - x-x-x x-x-x.

3.6 (?= 1.3|2.1)   uguti < *u₁.₃ₐ -n- kutu-Ci₂.₁ ('rabbit mouth'). 'harelip, split
lip, cleft palate'. LHx ?= *L(|)HH - x-x-x x-x-x.

-          uhagi: see ohagi.

?2.1, ?2.2b   ui < ufi (?< u[mu]-fyi < *um[a-]uₐ pi₁.₂, or u[myi]-fyi < *um[a-C]iₐ
pi₁.₂ 'born day'). 'beginning, first (in one's life)'. x - 1-2-(A) x-(A)-x.
Km (W) HH.

?2.4   [ui] < uwi (< Ch hhyew'-hhywe.). 'saṃskṛta, life's course/vicissitudes'.
x - 1-x-x x-x-x. Ongi (Iroha) LH.

5.2   uiayumi < ufiayumi < *ufyi₇₂.₁ (< ...) ayumyiʙ (< ...). 'toddling,
taking one's first steps'. HHHHL - x-x-x x-x- x.

3.4   uizi < ufyidi < *u-pinti ?< *[s]u-₁.₃ₐ pinti₂.₃ (or < u[k]i-[fyi]di <
*uki₂.₂ₓ pinti₂.₃). 'mud'. LLL - x-x-x x-x-x. NS (100b) LLL; NS (T+ kun) LLL.
Cf. suhizi, hizi.

-          ? -uka (?> -[t]u - ka) 'day': see hatuka, hutuka, kokonoka, muika, yooka;
ka, ke, koyomi.

3.1   ukami < uka-myi < *uka(-)ₐ mi[Ca-Ci]ʙ. 'a spy; spying': ukami sú
'spies on'. HHH - x-x-x x-x-x. Cf. ukagau.

3.2a   u^k/ₑara < *u(m[i])-kara < *um[a-C]iₐ kara₂.ₓ (₂.₂ᵇ). 'clan, family,
kin(smen)'. HHL - 0/1-x-x x-x-x. NS (T+ kun) HHH.

4.1   ukareme < *ukare-mye < *uka-ra-Ci[-Ci]ₐ miCa₁.₃ᵦ (?= *mina). 'a female
     entertainer; a prostitute'. HHHH - 0/3-0-x x-x-x.

3.4   ukawa < u-kafa < *u₁.₂ kapa₂.₂ₐ. 'cormorant-fishing (river)'. x - x-x-x
     x-x-x. NS (116b [14:99L-K]) LLL.

2.1   uke < ukey < *uka-Ci[-Ciₐ. 'a float' (= uki). HH - x-x-x x-x-x.

?2.3   uke < ukey < *uka-Ci[-Ci]ᵦ. 'a grain container'. x - x-x-x x-x-x.
     NS (T+ kun) LL. Cf. uki.

?2.2x   uki (< ?). 'mud(dy place); bog'. HL (Ck) - x-x-x x-x-x. *See* uizi.

4.2   ukihasi < ukyi-fasi < *uk[a-C]iₐ pasi₂.₂ᵦ. 'floating bridge'.
     HHHL - 0/2-2-x x-x-x. Km (W) HHHH.

3.1   ukiᵏ/ɡi < ukyi-kiy < *uk[a-C]iₐ (-n-) ko̲-Ci₁.₃ₐ. 'raft, boat'.
     HHH - 0-0-x x-x-x.

?4.1, ?4.2, ?4.3 (= 2.1|2.3) ukikusa < ukyi-kusa < *uk[a-C]iₐ (-n-) kusa₂.₃.
     'floating plants/weeds; (= denzi-soo) Marsilea quadrifolia'. HHxx - x-0-x
     x-A-x. K: Hn HHHH, Edo HHHL. Sr qucigusa A.

2.3   uma (Hn/Km also m[u]ma = mma, originally perhaps just ma < Ch 'ma or
     Korean 'mol). 'horse'. LL - 2-2-B B-B-B. NS (79c [14:328-M], 117a) LL; NS (T+
     79) HL̲, (T+ 103) H᷂ ?= HL. Km (S) LL. Edo HL. Ib F = 2.3. Ikema, Uechi,
     Nakasuji (Miyako) nuuma; Kurojima, Taketomi (Yaeyama) nnma; Hateruma qman/nman
     (cf. Ch. 1, §52).

4.6   umabiru < m[u]ma-/uma-biru < *uma-byiru < *uma₂.₃ (-n-) piru₂.₅. 'giant
     leech'. LLLH - 0-x-x x-x-x.

4.6   umabiyu < *uma-byiyu < *uma₂.₃ (-n-) pidu₂.₄. 'purslane' (= suberi-hiyu).
     xLxx (Ck) ?= *LLLH - x-x-x x-x-x. Km x.

4.2   umaginu < m[u]ma-/uma-ginu < *uma-gyinu < *uma₂.₃ (-n-) kinu₂.₄. 'a girth
     cloth for a horse'. LLLH - x-3-x x-x-x.

5.16   umagitasi: *see* umakitasi.

?3.6(/7x) > 2.3   umago < m[u]mago ?< *umaₐdⱼ ᵦ -n- kwo₁.₁ (? 'worthy child').
     'grandchild' (> mago). (LHH-···) - x-0-x x-B-C. Km x. Sr qnmaga B; Yn maaɲu C.
     Cf. hatu-umago. (Etymology with *uma-ₐ 'birth' rejected; register incongruent.)

5.11   umago₃.₆-mei₂.₃/-oi₂.₁ (< ...). 'grand-niece/-nephew'. LHHHL - x-x-x
     x-x-x. Km x.

5.16   umagususi < m[u]ma-/uma-gususi < *uma₂.₃ -n- kususi₃.₆ (< ...). 'horse
     doctor'. xLLHL = *LLLHL - x-x-x x-x-x.

4.5   umaguwa < umagufa < *uma₂.₃ -n- kupa₂.₁. 'a kind of harrow/rake'. LLLL -
     0-x-x x-x-x.

5.16   umahadake < umafadake < *uma-fadakey < *uma₂.₃ pa(n)taka-Ci[-Ci]ᵦ. 'horse
     brush'. LLLHL(/HLLHL *mistake?*) - x-x-x x-x-x. NKD: umahatake.

4.9   umahito < uma-fyito̲ < *umaₐdⱼ ᵦ pito₂.₂ₐ. 'a worthy, a nobleman'.
     x - x-x-x x-x-x. NS (71a [11:172-M]) LHHL; NS (T+ 46) LHHL, (T+ 28a) HL᷂H,
     NS (T+ 28b) LL(|)HL.

?5.6, ?5.16   umahuʰ/ᵦuki < m[u]ma-/uma-buhuki < *uma₂.₃ (-n-) fufuki₂₃.₁ (< ...).
     'burdock' (= goboo). LLLLL (Ck) - x-4-x x-x-x. K: "Hn LLLHL".

3.4   umai < *umaₐdⱼ ᵦ i₁.₃ₐ. 'sweet sleep'. x - x-0-x x-x-x. NS (83b [17:118-
     M]) LL(|)L; NS (T+ 96) LL(|)L.

?5.6, ?5.16   umaikusa < *uma₂.₃ ikusa₂.₄. 'cavalry, horse-soldier(s)'. x - x-x-x
     x-x-x. NS (109a) LL(|)LLL, (123a) LLxHL; (Okada) LLLHL. Cf. katiikusa.

4.5 = 2.3|2.3 umakai < m[u]ma-/uma-kafi < uma-kafyi < *uma₂.₃ kap[a-C]iᵦ. 'groom,
     equerry'. L(|)LL - 2/3-1:4-x x-x-x. NS (78a [14:208W-M] LL(|)LL; NS (T+ kun)
     LL(|)LL.

3.4   umaki < m[u]ma-/uma-ki < *uma₂.₃ kiy₁.ₓ ('horse fortress' < ...). 'horse
     paddock'. LLL - x-x-x x-x-x.

5.16   uma^k/$_g$itasi (Kn), umakidasi (Ck). 'Eclipta prostrata' (= takasaburoo). LLLHL - x-x-x x-x-x. Also called tatarabi, unagitukami. The Mg forms may be a corruption of unagi-tukami 'eel-grasp', usually a name for Polygonum aestivum.

4.11   umasaku (< ?). 'feather cockscomb, Celosia argentea' (= amasaku = no-geitoo). LLHL - x-x-x x-x-x.

?5.14 (?= 3.4|3.2) umatunagi < uma-tunagyi < *uma$_{g.s}$ tu[ra]-na-n[a]-k[a-C]i. 'a horse depot'. LL(|)HHL (Kn -k-) - x-x-x x-x-x.

3.4 = 2.3|1.2 umaya < m[u]maya < *uma$_{g.s}$ da$_{1.9b}$. 'stable; barn'. LL(|)L - 0-0[H]/ 2[U]-x x-x-x. Km x. Edo HHL. Narada 3. Ib F = 3.4.

4.11 = 2.3|2.2 umazemi < m[u]ma-semi < *uma$_{g.s}$ (-n-) semi$_{g.8a}$ (< ...). 'giant cicada' (= kumazemi). LL(|)HL - 2-x-x x-x-x.

2.1   ume < m[u]mey (?< [m]mey < Ch .m(b)wey). 'plum'. HH - 0-0-A A-A-x. Km x. Ib H = 2.1.

2.3   umi < umyi < *um[a-C]i$_8$. 'pus; ooze'. (x) - 2-2-B B-B-x. Km x. Ib F = 2.3.

2.4   umi < umyi < *umi 'sea'. LH - 1-1-B B-B-(C). NS (T 68) HL, (T+ 8) LH. Km (W) LH. Edo LH. Matsue, Izumo 1/2; Hattō, Narada, Hamada, Hiroshima 1. Ōsaka, Ise 1; Ib L2 = 2.5. Yn nnaga C ?< *umi-naka.

?3.7a   umibe < umyi^f/$_b$ye < *umi$_{g.4}$ piCa$_{1.x}$ (?= *pina). 'seaside'. x - 3(/0[H])- 1:3-B x-x-x. Km (W) LHL, LHH, LLH. Sz 3.

?4.11   umigame < umyi-kamey < *umi$_{g.4}$ kamaCi$_{g.s}$. 'sea turtle'. "LH-LH" (Kn) ?= *LLHL (or LH|LF with later Kt version of kame as 2.5 < 2.3) - 0/2-0-x x-x-x. Sz 1/3.

4.6 = 2.3|2.4 umisiru < *umyi$_{g.s}$ siru$_{g.4}$ < *um[a-C]i$_8$ siru$_{g.4}$. 'pus'. LL(|)LH - 0/1-3-x x-x-x. Hoke-kyō tanji: umiziru.

4.1   umoregi < umore-giy < *umora-Ci[-Ci]$_A$ (< ...) ko̲-Ci$_{1.3a}$. 'lignite, bogwood; living in obscurity'. x - 0/3-0-A x-x-x. Km (W) mumore["]ki HHHH.

?3.1 = 4.1   umuki = umuki-na (< ?). 'barrenwort, Epimedium grandiflorum' (= ikari-soo). ?*HHH = HHHH - x-x-x x-x-x.

3.4   umuki (< ?). 'clam' (= hamaguri). LLL - x-x-x x-x-x.

?2.3, ?2.4 una (?< *u[pa]$_{g.8a}$ na$_{?1.3a}$ 'up(thrust) land', *register incongruent?*). *(1)* 'ridge': *see* une. *(2)* 'nape of neck; head' NS (Okada) LH: *see* unagami, unai, unazi; unadaku > inadaku > itadaku. Cf. unagu, unagasu, unazuku; una^t/$_d$e; unebi(yama), uneme, uzi.

?2.3   una(-) (?< *u[mi mi]na 'sea water'). 'sea'. NS (T+ 120) una kudari LL LHL. *See* unabara, una^t/$_d$e, ...

4.6   unabara < unafara ?< *u[mi$_{g.4}$ mi]na$_{?2.1}$ para$_{g.s}$ (< *paru) ('sea-water field', or *para-$_A$ 'spread'). 'the sea'. (-)LLLH - 0/2-0-x x-x-x. Cf. ao-unabara; wata.

4.9   unagami < una^k/$_g$ami < *una$_{?g.s}$ (-n-) kami$_{g.s}$ (< ...). 'mane (of horse)'. LHxx - x-B-x x-x-x. ? NS (100b [11:124-K]) LHLL.

3.6   unagi < munagyi < *(m)unanki. 'eel'. LHH - 0(?<1)-1-B B-B-(x). Km x. 1700 Ōsaka LHH. Narada, Goka-mura, Wakamatsu, Ōita 1; Aomori (*we expect 1*), Akita 2̲; Sapporo, Hiroshima, Hattō, Hamada, Matsue, Izumo, Hakata 0. Ib L = 3.6. Yn nada C (H 1964:72a) ?< *unagi-a (cf. Sr qoo-qnnazaa 'large blue snake'). Sr qnnazi puts proto *m- in doubt. Hateruma qnnan (cf. Ch. 1, §52).

3.4   unai < "unafi" = unawi < *unabi < *una-bi[y] < *una$_{?g.s}$ b^u/$_o$-Ci[-Ci]$_A$. 'hair hanging down (a child's) neck; a child'. LLL - 0-0-x x-x-x. Cf. unebi(-yama), uneme.

3.x   una^t/$_d$e < una-[i]de[y] < *una$_{g.s}$ inta-Ci[-Ci]$_B$. 'canal'. x - x-x-x x-x-x. Cf. oo-una^t/$_d$e.

3.4 unazi < una**ˢ/ᵤi** (Kn) < *una??.??.?? (-n-) si?. 'nape'. LLL - 0-0-B x-B/A-x. Km
(S) LLL. Mr (Bm) HLL. K: "Mr HHL" *(misprint?)*. Edo HHL. Narada 3. Ib F = 3.4.
Sr qnnazi B/A 'back seam of garment'. Perhaps si is 'back' (cf. siri, usiro) or
'bottom' (cf. sita, simo); or *s[unt]i > sudi > suzi 'sinew'; or *su[w]e 'end'
> *siy > si, cf. uzu 'hair-ornament'.

2.3 une < *une[y] < *una-Ci. 'ridge in field'. LL - 2-2-B x-x-x. Km x. Narada
2. Ib *(rare)* F = 2.3. Dial. (Iwate, Akita) nune. Perhaps from mune₂.₁ 'ridge
(of roof)' despite the register incongruity? Cf. mine.

?2.4 uni. 'sea-urchin' (= kaze). x - 1-2-B x-x-x. Km x. Aomori, Wakamatsu 1.
Ib H1 = 2.2. K: Hn HL *(attested?)*.

2.1 uo < uwo < iwo (?< *ibo; ?< *i[w]o < *iCo). 'fish'. HH - 0-0-A A-A-A.
NS (84a, 94b) HH; NS (T 97) LL. Km x. Edo HH. Narada yuo 0. Ib io H = 2.1.
Sr qiyu A.

?2.1 ura = ure 'branch, twig'.

2.3 ura. 'bay'. LL - 2-2-B x-x-x. Km (W) LL. Edo HL.

2.3 ura. 'reverse (side)'. LL - 2-2-B B-B-B. Km x. Yn ura B (H 1964:71a).

?2.4 ura. 'heart, mind'. x - x-2-2/0-x x-x-x. Km x. K: Hn LH or LF?

2.4 ura. 'divination, foretelling'. LH - x-x-x x-x-x. Km (W) LH.

4.5 uraguwa (no ki) < ura-gufa < ?*ura??.₁ -n- kupa??.??. 'mulberry-tree
(branch tips)'. x - x-x-x x-x-x. NS (73a [11:215-M, 11:216-M]) LLLL;
NS (T+ 56) LLHH. Register incongruent with etymology? Cf. uraguwasi*adj ?B*
'beautiful', uragasu*ₐ* 'delight'.

3.4 urami < uramiy ?< *ura??.₄ mo-Ci[-Ci]?A. 'regret; resentment'. LLL -
3-0[H]/2[U]-B x-B-B. Km (S) LLL. Edo HHL. Sapporo 0. Kōchi 1:3; Ib F = 3.4.
Yn urami B (H 1964:71b).

?2.1 ure ?< *ura-Ci, ?< *ura??.₁ ye??.₂ (< ...). 'branch, twig'. x - 2-2/0-x
x-x-x. Km (W) HH(-H). Cf. sue; mataburi.

3.4 [uree] < urefey < *urafey-*B* < *ura??.₄ [a]pa-Ci[-Ci]*B* or *ura??.₄ -pa-Ci[-
Ci]. 'grief'. LLL - (x-x-x x-x-x). Km (S) LLL. 1700 Ōsaka LHH. Modern uree <
urei < urefyi < *urafyi < *ura-p[a-C]i*B*.

2.4 (?< 2.5) uri. 'melon'. LH - 1-1-B B-B-B. Km x. Izumo 1/2. Ib H = 2.1. Nk qui B;
Yn ui B (H 1964:71a). Kg gui B (< ?).

4.6 uribae < uribafe < *uri-bafey < *uri₂.₄ -n- papaCi₂.₁. 'melon fly'. LLLH -
2-x-x x-x-x. Km x.

3.4 uroko < iroko (< ...). 'scale(s) on fish'. LLL - 0/1-2-B x-B-x. Km x. Sz,
Izumo 0; Hattō 1; Hamada, Matsue, Goka-mura, Yamaguchi, Wakamatsu 2; Aomori 3.
Sr qirici B. *See* iroko.

4.6 urokuzu < urokudu < irokudu < *irokuntu (< ?). 'scale(s) on fish' (=
uroko). x - 0/3-3-x x-x-x. Mr (Bm) HHLL.

2.x uru(-) 'moist, ... ': *see* urusi, urusine; urumu, uruosu, uruou, ...

3.7x urui < urufi (< ?). 'self-heal, Prunella vulgaris (= utubogusa); hosta,
plantain lily (= giboosi)'. LHL - x-x-x x-x-x.

3.1 urusi (?< *uru₂.ₓ si[ru]₂.₄ 'moist juice'). 'lacquer'. HHx - 0-0-A x-A-x.
Km x. Edo HHH. K: Hn-Edo HHH. NE Kyūshū 2; Goka-mura 1; Hakata 1, ygr 0;
Narada 0. Ib H = 3.1.

5.1 urusimuro < *urusi₃.₁ (< ...) murwo₂.₃. 'lacquerware drying room'.
HHHHH - x-x-x x-x-x.

4.6 urusine ?< *uru₂.ₓ [z]ina-Ci₂.₄. 'nonglutinous rice'. LLLH - x-x-x x-x-x.
Km x. Sz uru 1. *See* ine.

3.6   usagi < usagyi < usagyi / wosagyi (M 3529, Azuma?) < ?*[b]ᵘ/ₒsa(n)ki.
'rabbit, hare'. LHx - 0(?<1)-1-B B-B-B. K: Hn LHH. Km x. Southern Hiroshima,
eastern Tottori 0/1 (Hiroto 1961:166); Sapporo, Aomori *(we expect 1)*, Akita,
Matsue, Izumo 2; Wakamatsu, NE Kyūshū, Hakata 1; Matsumoto, Narada, Numazu,
Hida (= northern Gifu), Hiroshima, Yamaguchi, Hata 0. Ib (earlier osagi) L =
3.6. Hida osaki, Ōsumi usaki. On - ᵏ/ₒ- see Ch. 2. Cf. Koguryǒ *wusigam or
*(w)osagam and Miller 1971:116-8.

5.10   usagi(m)uma < uᵃ/ᵤzagim[u]ma < usagyi-(m)uma < *[b]ᵘ/ₒsa(n)ki₃.₆ uma₂.₃.
'donkey'. LHHHH - 3-1-x x-x-x. Ongi usagima LHHHH. Km x.

?5.2   usayuzuru < usa-yuduru < *usa-₂ₐ yumi-ᵗ/ₐuru (< ...). 'extra (= spare)
bowstring'. x - x-x-x x-x-x. NS (71a [11:173-M]) HHHxL; NS (T+ 46) Lₑ|LHL.
Cf. useru 'vanish', usinau 'lose'.

2.1   usi < usi/-uzi < *u(n)si. 'ox'. HH - 0-0-A A-A-A. Km x. Edo HH. Ib H =
2.1. See Ch. 2, §5.4.

?2.4   usi ?< *[n]usi₂₂.₄,₂₂.₆. 'sir, sire, esquire'. x - x-x-x x-x-x. NS (T+
kun) LH.

4.2   usikusa < usi₂.₁ kusa₂.₃. 'Andropogon brevifolius; (= niwa-yanagi)
Polygonum aviculare; (= senkyuu) Cnidium officinale'. HHHL - 0-x-x x-x-x.

6.1 = 2.1-no|3.1 usi-no-hitai < usi-no fitafi < *usi₂.₁ no ?pitapi₃.₁ ('ox brow').
(1) 'Juncus effusus' (= kohige);   *(2)* 'Ficus erecta' (= inubiwa);
(3) 'Persicaria/Polygonum thunbergii' (= mizo-soba). xx-H(|)HHH - x-x-x x-x-x.

3.4   usio < usifo < *u[mi]₂.₄ sipwo₂.₃. 'tide'. LLL - 0-0-B B-B-x. NS (100b)
LLL; NS (T+ 120) LLL. Km x. 1700 Ōsaka LHL. K: Hn HHH *(misprint?)*. Narada 3.
Ib H = 3.1, L = 3.4.

?3.7a/b   usiro. 'behind'. x - 0-1:3-B B-B-x. Ongi LLL. NS (129b — cf. 80b musiro
name?) LLH; NS (T+ 120) LLL. Km (S) LHL, (W) LLL. Mr (Bm) LHL. Edo LHL.
Sapporo, Aomori, Narada, western Mino (= SW Gifu), Hida (= northern Gifu),
Hattō, Hamada, Goka-mura, Hiroshima, Wakamatsu, NE Kyūshū, Hakata, Ōita 1;
Tappi, Akita, Matsue, Izumo 3. Ib L2 = 3.5/7. Sd qusyryo B *(we expect
qusyryu)*. Sr qusiru 'nape'. Ōno's etymology is *mu[-Ci]₁.₁ 'body' + a variant
of siri₂.₃ 'bottom'. Another possibility: *u[ra]₂.₃ siri₂.₃.

2.5   uso (< uto₂₂.ₓ = utu₂₂.₁ 'hollow', cf. utagau₄; ?< usu_ₐdⱼ ₐ 'thin' —
all incongruent in register?). 'lie, falsehood'. LH - 1-0[U]/1:3[H]-B x-x-x.
1700 Ōsaka HL. Narada 1; Aomori 2 *(expected)*; Sz, NE Kyūshū (H 1951:1765).
Hattō, Hamada, Goka-mura 2; Matsue, Izumo 2 *(expected reflex)*. Ib H1 = 2.2.

2.4   usu. 'mortar'. LH - 1-1-B B-B-C. NS (Okada) LH; NS (T 33) Lₑ ?= LH. Km x.
Ib L = 2.4. Sr quuşi B; Yn uci C. Cf. utu₂₂.₁ 'hollow'.

3.7x   usuba < *usu₂.₄ -n- pa₁.₃b. 'molar tooth'. LHL - 2-x-x x-x-x. Km x.

2.2a   uta (?< *uta-ᵦ < ?*buta-ᵦ *but register incongruent)*. 'song'. HL - 2-2-A
A-A-A. NS (T+ 102) HL. Km (W) HL. Edo HL. Aomori 0; Hattō, Hamada 2; Matsue,
Izumo 2 *(= 2.3)*; Goka-mura 0. Ib H1 = 2.2.

?5.2   utakakusa < *u₁.₂ - taka₂.₁ kusa₂.₃ ('cormorant-and-hawk grass'). 'Astilbe
congesta' (= toriasi-syooma). HLLLL (Ir) / HHHxx (Kn) = *HHHHL - x-x-x x-x-x.

4.1   utakata < utaᵏ/ₒata (< ?). 'surface bubbles, froth; ephemeral; for a
fleeting moment; (~ mo) perhaps, likely'. HHHH (Zs, -g-) - 0-0-A x-x-x.
Km (W) HHxx.

3.1 (?< *4.1)   utata < *uta-ᵦ [u]ta_ᵦ ('hit and hit' — *but register incongruent)*.
'more and more, increasingly'. HHH - 0/1-2-x x-x-x. Km (W) HHH.

?4.4   utatane < *utata₃.₁ na-Ci[-Ci]_ₐ. 'a catnap'. HLx - *HLL - x-x-x x-x-x.
Sz 0.

4.2   utazuki < uta-dukiy < *uta$_{2.2b}$ -n- tuku-Ci$_{2.2}$. 'offering a song (as one's tribute)'. x - x-x-x x-x-x. NS (Okada) HHHL.

?3.4   utena (< ?). 'an earthen mound/platform'. LLL - 0/1-1:3-x x-x-x. Edo HLL. Perhaps < *uta-na < uta-$_B$ na$_{?1.3a}$ 'hit earth'. Etymologies with ue < ufey$_{?2.2a}$ 'above' are incongruent in register. Cf. una^t/$_d$e.

2.2a(?/2.1)   uti < *uti[y] < *utu-Ci. (1) 'hollow': see utibora. (2) 'within, inside, among'. (3) 'home; (= ie) house'. (4) 'we/us; I/me'. HL - 2/0-2('home') /0('within')-A A-A-x. NS (96a, 98a, 98b, 115b [14:84-K]) HH; NS (T 62, 119]) HL, (T 28, 29) LL. Km x. Edo HL. Narada 0; Hiroshima, Yamaguchi 2 (Hiroto 1961:159). Ib H1 = 2.2 (also modified).

?2.4, ?2.5   uti 'game path': see uzi.

4.2   utibora < *uti[y]-bora < *utu-Ci$_{2.2a}$ -n- pora$_{?2.1}$. 'hollow'. HHHL - x-x-x x-x-x. Cf. utu(b)o. NKD has "utihora" but Mg has -b-.

?3.6, ?3.1   utigi: see uti^k/$_g$i.

4.8 < 6.13   utikake (truncation < utikake[-ginu]$_{6.13}$ < ...). 'a kind of long garment'. LHHH - 0-1-x x-(B)-x.

6.13   utikakeginu < utikake-^{k}/$_g$inu < *utikakey-^{k}/$_g$yinu < *ut[a-C]i$_B$ - kaka-Ci[-Ci]$_B$ (-n-) kinu$_{2.4}$. 'a kind of long garment'. LHHHHL - 5-1:5-x x-x-x. Km x.

?3.6, ?3.1   uti^k/$_g$i < utiki < *utikyi < *ut[a-C]i$_B$ (or *utu-Ci$_{2.2a}$) ki-[Ci]$_A$ / ki[Ca-Ci]$_A$. 'an undergarment'. LHH (Zs), HHx (Kn), HHH (Ir) - 0-0-x x-x-x.

5.10   utimidari < *ut[a-C]i$_B$ minta-r[a-C]i$_B$. ' ? ': ~ no fako (< *pakwo$_{1.3}$) 'a kind of fancy box'. LHHHHH - 0-1-x x-x-x.

4.1   utimiya < uti-myiya < *utu-Ci$_{2.2a}$ mi-da$_{2.1}$ (< mi-$_{?1.1}$ da$_{1.3b}$). 'inner palace' (= uti-tu-miya). x - x-x-x x-x-x. NS (96a) HHHH.

4.8   utinasi < *ut[a-C]i$_B$ na-s[a-C]i$_A$. 'making it (re)sound' (= utinarasi). LHHH - x-0-x x-x-x.

(?*3.1 <) 2.2|1.1   utito < uti-two < *utu-Ci$_{2.2a(?/2.1)}$ two$_{1.1}$. 'inside and out, inner and outer'. HL|H - 0-x-x x-x-x.

5.1 = 2.1-tu|2.1   utitu-kuni < *utu-Ci$_{2.2a(?/2.1)}$ -tu$_{pcl}$ kuni$_{?2.1, ?2.2a}$ (< ...). 'the Home provinces'. x - x-x-x x- x-x. NS (98b) HH-H|HH.

5.1 ?= 2.1-tu|2.1   utitu-miya < uti$_{2.2a(?/2.1)}$ -tu$_{pcl}$ myiya$_{2.1}$ < *utu-Ci$_{2.2a(?/2.1)}$ -tu mi-$_{?1.1}$ da$_{1.3b}$. 'the interior (hinder) palace'. x - x-x-x x-x-x.

3.4   utiwa < utifa < *utipa ?< *ut[a-C]i$_B$ pa$_{1.2}$. 'fan'. x - 2-2-B x-B-x. Km x. 1700 Ōsaka HHL. K: Hn LLL (where attested?). NE Kyūshū, Yamaguchi, Narada, Hattō, Matsue, Hiroshima 3; Hamada 2; Aomori, Izumo 0; Goka-mura 0 (expected reflex). Kōbe (Robb) 2/1:3; Ōsaka, Ise 2; Kōchi (Kobayashi) 1:3; Ib F = 3.4. Kg A according to Kobayashi but B according to Hirayama.

?2.x   uto (?< ut[u]o ···) 'empty; hollow' (= utu$_{?2.1}$). Cf. uso$_{2.5}$.

?2.1   utu(-). 'empty; complete(ly), total'. Cf. uti$_{2.2a}$; utuo$_{3.1}$, utubari$_{4.1}$, utugi$_{3.3}$, uturo$_{?3.6}$, utukeru$_{?A}$, utuwa$_{3.1}$; uto$_{2.x}$; uso$_{2.5}$.

4.1   utubari < utufari (?= utuwari) < *utu$_{?2.1}$ (-n-) pari$_{2.3}$. 'crossbeam'. HHHH - 0-0-x x-x-x. NS (96b) HHHH. JP -b-. NKD: "Till Hn -f-, later -b-."

-       utubo: see utuo.

3.3   utugi < *utugiy < *utu$_{?2.x}$ -n- ko-Ci$_{1.3a}$ ('hollow plant'). 'deutzia'. HLL - 0-2-x x-x-x. Km x.

4.2   utumomo, utimomo < *utu(-Ci)$_{2.2a}$ mwomwo$_{2.5}$. 'inside thigh(s)'. HHHL - 0/3-0-x x-x-x.

4.1   utumuro < *utu$_{?2.1}$ murwo$_{2.3}$. 'a shed with exit(s) plastered shut; a shed for giving birth'. HHHH - x-0-x x-x-x.

3.1   utuo/utubo ‹ utu[w]o ‹ utufo ‹ *utu$_{?2.1}$ -po$_?$, 'hollow'. HHH - 0-0-x x-x-(A). Edo HHH. Yn cibu A ‹ ?*[u]tubo. (Ōno: From late Hn till "Early Modern" [?= 1500] -w-; up till mid-Hn [?= 900] -f-, then -w-, "rarely -b-". See Ch. 2, §2.) Cf. utibora.

?3.6   uturo ‹ *utu$_{?2.x}$ -ro$_?$. 'hollow'. x - 0-0-B x-x-x. Kōbe (Robb) 1/0.

4.5   ututae(-ni) ‹ "ututafe(-ni)" ‹ uti-taye[y] (ni) ‹ *ut[a-C]i$_B$ tada-Ci[-Ci]$_R$. 'absolutely (not), (not) at all, ever'. LLLL(|H) - 0-x-x x-x-x.

3.5a   ututu (?‹ *utu$_{?2.1}$ [u]tu$_{?2.1}$). 'existent; consciousness, awareness; absentminded, dreamy'. LLH - 0/2-0[H]/2[U]-B x-x-x. Edo HLL.

3.1   utuwa ‹ utufa ‹ *utu-pa (?‹ *utu$_{2.x}$ pa$_{1.1}$, see he; ? variant ‹ *utu-po$_{3.1}$. see utuo). 'utensil, vessel'. HHH-··· - 0-0-B x-x-x. Sz 0/3. Ib F = 3.4. (Without -mono attested only from Edo.) Cf. tubo.

?5.2, ?5.1   utuwamono ‹ utufamono ‹ *utu-pa$_{2.1}$ mono$_{2.3}$. 'vessel, utensil'. HHHxx (?= *HHHHL) - 0-0-x x-x-x. NS (Okada) HHHHL. Mr (Bm) HHHHH.

?2.2a   uwa(-) ‹ ufa(-) ‹ *upa(-) 'above': see ue.

3.1   uwabe ‹ ufa-bye ‹ ?ufa-fye ‹ *upa$_{?2.2a}$ (-n-) piCa$_{1.x}$. 'surface, top'. x - 0-0-A x-A-x. Sz 0. Nk qwaabi HHL (= A). Sr qwaabi A.

3.1|2.4   uwaharaobi ‹ ufafara-obi (? reinterpreted ←) ufa$_{?2.2a}$ fara-obyi$_{4.6}$ ‹ *upa$_{?2.2a}$ para$_{2.3}$ ob[a-C]i$_B$. 'a kind of bellyband for a horse (in the Heian period)'. HHHH|LH - x-x-x x-x-x.

3.2a   uwami ‹ ufami ?‹ *ufa-miy ‹ *upa$_{?2.2a}$ mo-Ci$_{1.3b}$. 'an upper garment' (= uwamo = hirami). HHL - 0-0-x x-x-x.

3.2a   uwamo ‹ ufa-mo ‹ *upa$_{2.2a}$ mo$_{1.3b}$. 'an upper garment' (= uwami = hirami). HHL - 0-0-x x-x-x.

?4.1, ?4.2   uwanari ‹ ufanari ‹ *upa$_{?2.2a}$ nar[a-C]i$_B$. 'later/second wife'. "HLHH" ?= *HHHH (Kz) / HHHL (Kn) - 0-0-x x-x-x. K: Hn HHHH.

4.1   uwanuri ‹ ufa-nuri ‹ *upa$_{?2.2a}$ nur[a-C]i$_A$. 'plastering'. x - 0-0-A x-B-x. NS (96b) HHHH. Nk qwaanui C; Sr qwaanui B.

3.1   uwao ‹ "uwafu" (Mg) ‹ ufa-wo ‹ *upa$_{?2.2a}$ bo$_{1.1}$. 'later husband' (cf. sitao). "LLL" (Kn — must be a mistake for *HHH) - x-x-x x-x-x.

5.2   [uwasoi] ‹ ufa-osofi ‹ *ufa osofyi ‹ *upa$_{?2.2a}$ os[a-Ci]$_A$ op[a-C]i$_B$. 'an outer garment'. HHHHL - x-4-x x-x-x.

4.1   uwasiki ‹ ufasiki ‹ *ufa-sikyi ‹ *upa$_{?2.2a}$ sik[a-C]i$_A$. 'sheet, cover: saddle cover'. HHHH - 0-0-x x-x-x.

?2.2x, ?2.1   uya, wiya ?‹ *wiy-[y]a ‹ *b^u/$_o$-Ci[-Ci]$_A$ a([ra]-)$_B$ ('be/lead exist'). 'respect'. HL - x-x-x x-x-x. NS (108a) xH, (118a) HH. Cf. [iyabiru]. uyamau. [iyaiyasi-] = uyauyasi-.

2.2b   uzi ‹ udi ‹ *unti (?‹ *um[a-u/-Ci]$_A$ ti$_{?1.1}$). 'clan'. x - 1-2-A x-A-x. Km x. 1700 Ōsaka HL. Hiroshima 1. Ōsaka, Ise 2; Ib H1 = 2.2.

?2.3   uzi ‹ u^s/$_z$i ‹ *u(n)si (cf. musi). 'grub'. LL - 2(/1[H])-1:3[H]/1[U]-B x-B-x. Km x. Narada, Hattō, Hamada, Matsue, Izumo, Hiroshima 2. Kōbe (Robb), Ōsaka, Ise 2; Ib L2 = 2.5.

?2.4, ?2.5   uzi ‹ u^t/$_d$i ‹ *u$_{?1.3a}$ (-n-) ti$_{?1.1}$ 'rabbit path; [dial.] boar path, game run'. x - x-x-x x-x-x. ("By mistake, also utu.")

2.5   uzi ‹ udi ‹ *unti (?‹ *u$_{?1.3a}$ -n- ti$_{?1.1}$ 'rabbit path'; ?‹ *un[a]$_{?2.3,?2.4}$ ti$_{?1.1}$ 'ridge land'). 'Uji' (placename). x - 1-1:3-A x-x-x. NS (70a [11:45-M]) LH; NS (T 42) LH, (T 31, 43]) L̶F̶ ?= LH. Km (W) HL, LH. Edo LF.

3.4   uzina: see muzina.

4.11   uziyama ‹ udi-yama ‹ *unti$_{2.4}$ (‹ ...) dama$_{2.3}$. 'Mount Uji' (placename). x - 0-1-x x-x-x. Km (W) LLHL.

2.x   uzu ‹ udu ‹ *untu. 'precious' (～ no). x - x-x-x x-x-x. NS (T+ kun) LL. Cf. uzunau (Ch. 6).

?2.3, ?2.4 uzu < udu < *untu. 'eddy'. x - 1-2-B x-x-x. Hattō, Hakata 1; Hamada, Matsue, Izumo, Goka-mura 2. Ib H1 = 2.2.

2.3 uzu < *unsu (?< *un[a]?2.3 su[we]2.1, cf. unazi3.4). 'hair-ornament'. LL - 1-2-x x-x-x. NS (T 23) LH; (T+ kun) LH. Km x.

3.6 uzui < uzu-wi[y] < *unsu (= ?) bᵘ/ₒ-Ci[-Ci]ₐ. 'squatting quietly or steadily'. LHH - x-0-x x-x-x.

3.4 uzura < udura < *untura. 'quail' *(bird)*. LLL - 0- 0[U]/2[H]-B x-B-x. Km x. Edo HLL. Matsue, Izumo 3; Narada 0; Aomori 1; Hamada *(Hiroto and Ōhara corrigenda)* 0/1; Hattō 1; Goka-mura 1 (?< *0 *expected reflex*). Ib F = 3.4, H1 = 3.3.

1.3a ?< 2.3, ?< 2.4 wa < *ba[nu]. 'I/me' (= ware). x - 1-0-x B-B-(A/C). Ongi (Iroha) wa-ga H-H. NS wa-ga (70a [11:46-M], 72a [11:196-M, 11:199-M], 72b [11:200-M], 72c [11:208-M], 76a [14:122-M, 14:123-M], 76c [14:135-M], 79b [14:315-M], 83a [17:116-M], 84a [17:124-M, 17-126-M]) L-H; NS (T+ 75, 76, 96, 97) L-H, (T+ 5, 7, 14, 32, 42, 54, 55, 63, 67, 69, 70, 102) ʰH ?= L-H, (T+ 53) H-H. Km (S,W) L(-H). Edo R. Sd/Sr wan[u] B; Yn banu A 'we'(?), ban-ta C 'we', anu C 'I'. Mochizuki 1975:20-2 thinks wa may have been R (1.3b). Cf. wagimo, wagie.

1.3a wa < *ba. 'wheel, circle'. L - 1-1-B A-(x)-x. Km x. Ib L = 1.3. Nk waa A; Nk, Sr goo A must be a different etymon (but what?); cf. ooga 'spinning wheel'.

2.1 wabi < wabiy < *banpᵘ/ₒ-Ci[-Ci]ₐ. 'simple taste; apology'. (H) - 2/0-1/0-A x-A-x. Km (W) (H). Sz O. Ib *(rare)* ?L = 2.4. Sr wabi A 'surrender'. (The Tk and Kt "O" versions are for 'apology'.)

3.1/3.2x wabira (< ?). 'apricot leaves; (= gyooyoo) a crest with paired apricot leaves; a decorative medalion attached to a horse saddle'. HHH/HHL - x-x-x x-x-x. Not in NKD; is the word attested outside Mg?

?2.3 wada < *banta ?< *ba1.3a -n- to1.1 ('circle place', *last vowel assimilated to the first*), ?*ba1.3a -n- ta1.3a ('circle arm'). 'a bend (of land/shore); [dial.] an inlet, an arm of the sea; [dial.] a valley'. x - x-x-x x-x-x. Cf. kawawa.

- wa-ga: *see* wa ('I/me'). Ib L = 2.4.

?3.7b < ... wagie < wagyifye < *wa g[a] (y)ifye < *ba1.3a -n- kaᵖᶜˡ ?ipe2.3 (< ...). 'my home'. x - x-1:3-x x-x-x. NS (72c [11:201-M]) LHL; NS (T+ 21, 54) ʰHH.

3.7b < ... wagimo < wagyimwo < *wa g[a] (y)imwo < *ba1.3a -n-kaᵖᶜˡ imwo?2.4. 'my beloved (girl)'. x - 1-1:3-x x-x-x. NS (83b [17:120-M]) LHL; NS (T+ 96) LHH.

3.4 wakaᵏ/ᵍo < wakaᵃ/ᵤ-kwo/-gwo < *bakaₐdⱼ ᵦ (-n-) kwo1.1. 'baby, infant'. x - 2-x-x x-x-x. NS (118b) LLL. Cf. wakugo.

?3.5b wakame < *bakaₐdⱼ ᵦ me1.x (< ...). 'seaweed'. x - 2-2-B x-x-x. Sz. Wakamatsu 2; Aomori 3. Ib H1 = 3.3. Earliest attestation Edo.

3.4 wakare < *wakare[y] < *baka-ra-Ci[-Ci]ᵦ. 'separation; being separate'. x - 3-0[H]/2[U]-B x-B-(B). NS (131a [14:405W-K]) LLL. Km (S,W) LLL. Mr (W 18, 19) HHL. Edo HHL. Narada 1. Ōsaka, Kōbe 3; Ib L2 = 3.5/7.

4.5 wakataka < *bakaₐdⱼ ᵦ taka2.1. 'yearling hawk'. LLLL - 2-x-x x-x-x.

?2.5 ?< 2.3 wake < wakey < *baka-Ci[-Ci]ᵦ. 'distinguishing; meaning'. x - 1-1:3-B x-B-x. Km x. Matsue, Izumo 2; Hakata 1. Ib L2 = 2.5.

2.3 waki < wakyi < *bak[a-C]iᵦ. 'side'. LL - 2-2-B x-x-x. Km x. Edo HL. Ib F = 2.3.

2.3 waku < *baku (< ? — cf. wa). 'frame; a winding reel, a swift'. LL - 2-2-B B(/A)-B-x. Km x. Hiroshima 2. Ōsaka, Ise 2; Ib F = 2.3.

3.4 wakugo < wakugwo < *baku (= *bakaₐdⱼ ᵦ) -n- kwo1.1. 'youngster, boy'. x - x-2-x x-x-x. NS (Okada) LLL; NS (T+ 98) LLL, (T+ 95. 105) ʰLLL = LLL. Cf. wakago.

4.6 = 3.4(=2.3-no)|1.1   wakunoe ?< *waku-no-ey < *baku*g.s* no aCi*ı.ı*. 'a kind of
rowan tree, Sorbus alnifolia'. LLL(|)H - x-x-x x-x-x.

2.4   wana < *bana (?< *ba*ı.sa* na[pa]*g.s* 'circle rope'). 'trap'. LH/LL - 1-1-B
x-x-x. NS (T+ 7) sigi wana LH|LH. Km x. Ib L = 2.4. Cf. wanaku. (Sr yaama B.
Nk yamaa C, and Yn dama B must be a different etymon. Cf. yana.)

2.3   wani < *bani (< ?). 'crocodile; (= wani-zame) shark'. LL - 1-2-A x-x-x.
Km x. Narada, Matsue 1; Hattō, Hamada, Izumo, Goka-mura 2. Ib H1 = 2.2.

2.4   wara < *bara. 'straw'. LH - 1-1-B B-B-x. Km x. Edo LH. Narada, Hattō,
Hamada 1; Matsue, Izumo 2. Ib L = 2.4. Onna waaraa B.

3.5b   warabe < warafa-f/bye < ?*barapa*g.sb* mye*ı.sb* (< *miCa*ı.sb* ?= *mina).
'child' (< 'young wife'). LLx - 1-2-B x-B-x. Cf. warawa. (Etymology: see õno.)

3.4   warabi < warabyi < *baranpi (< ?). 'bracken'. LLL - 1-2-B x-B-x.
Km (W) LLL. Aomori 3; Narada 2 (= warubi 3); Sapporo, Matsumoto, Hiroshima 2:
Akita, Numazu, Hattō, Hamada, NE Kyūshū (H 1951:178), Õita 3; Matsue, Izumo 0;
Goka-mura 0 *(expected)*; Hakata 0 *(expected)*, ygr 1. Kōbe (Robb) 2/1:3; Ib H1 =
3.3, F = 3.4.

-          warabuta: *see* warooda.

4.6 (> 3.5a)   waragutu, warautu < *bara*g.4* -n- kutu*g.s*. 'straw sandals/boots'
(> waradu LLH > waradi > warazi). LLLH - 2/3-1:3-B x-x-x.

-          warahuda: *see* warooda.

?4.5 < 5.16 warahude < wara-fude < wara*g.4* - fu[mi]de*g.ı* < wara - fumyi-te <
*bara*g.4* pumi*g.sb* - ta-Ci*ı.sa*). 'a straw writing-brush'. LLLHL (warafumide) -
x-x-x x-x-x.

3.5b   warawa < warafa < *barapa. 'child'. LLH - 1-1:3-x x-(B)-x. 1700 Õsaka
warawa HLL, wappa LHH.

5.6   warawayami < warafa-yam[y]i < *barapa*g.sb* dam[a-C]i*ʔR*. 'intermittent
fever, ague'. LLLLL - x-x-x x-x-x.

3.5a < 4.6   warazi < waradu < waragutu < *bara*g.4* -n- kutu*g.s*. 'straw sandals or
boots'. LLH - 0-0-B x-(B)-x. Narada, Goka-mura 2; Aomori 2/3; Hakata 2, ygr 0.
Ib *(rare)* F = 3.4, waranzi F = 4.5.

2.4   ware < *ba*ı.sa* -re (< [a]ra-Ci*g.s*). 'I/me'. LH - 1-1-B (x-x-x). NS (74c
[11:305-M, 11:306-M], 83a [17:114-M, 17:116-M]) LH; NS (T 96; 110, 111) LH.
(T 12, 14, 28; T+ 63a, 63b) ¶H ?= LH. Km (S,W) LH(-H). Mr (Bm) LH. Edo LH.
1700 Õsaka ware-ra LHH. Aomori *(rare)*, Sz 1. Ib L = 2.4 ('you'), L2 = 2.5.

?3.2a   warigo (< ?). 'snowshoes' (= ka(n)ziki, [karehizi]). "HHR" ?= *HHL -
0-0-x x-x-x. Km x.

3.1   warihu < wari-fu < *bar[a-C]i*4* pu*ı.x* (< Ch .bhyu). 'chit, ticket'.
x - 0-0-x x-B-x. Mr (Bm) HHH. Sr waifu/wappu B.

4.5 = 2.3|2.3 waromono = warumono < *bar*u*/o *adj B* mono*g.s*. 'rascal'. LL(|)LL -
0-1-B x-x-x. Km x.

4.5   warooda < *war?ooda < wara[f]uda < warafuda / wara*f*/buta < *bara*g.4* (-n-)
puta*g.ı*. 'a kind of round seat-mat made of straw'. LLLL - x-1-x x-x-x.

?3.3   wasabi (< ?). 'horseradish'. HLL - 1(<*2)-2-B x-x-x. Km x. Hakata 1 (?<
*2); Narada, Hattō, Matsue, Izumo, Goka-mura 2; Hamada 0. Kōbe (Robb) 1:3;
Ib H1 = 3.3. Iwate masabi.

?2.4   wase < *wase[y] < *basa-Ci (< ?). 'early rice'. LH - 1-2-B x-x-x. Km x.
1700 Õsaka HL. Sz, Hattō, Hamada 1; Matsue, Izumo 2 *(expected reflex)*. Ib L2
= 2.5. (Cf. wasa-mono 'early produce', ...)

?2.2a   wasi < *basi. 'eagle'. LL - 0-2-A A-(B)-x. Km x. Hattō, Hamada, Matsue,
Izumo, Hiroshima 1; Aomori, Goka-mura 2. Õsaka, Ise 2; Ib H1 = 2.2. Cf.
kowasi.

?2.1   wata < *bata. 'sea'. HH-···· - 0/2-x-x x-x-x. Km (W) HH-/LH-/LL-··· .
Yaeyama (Taketomi, Hatoma) bata 'bay, sea'. Cf. watari. ("Modern also wada.")

2.3   wata < *bata. 'cotton'. LL - 2-2-B B-B-B. Km x. Ib F = 2.3.

2.3   wata < *bata. 'intestines, guts'. LL - 2-2-B B-B-B. Sz 2. Ib F = 2.3.
Onna waataa B; Yn bata B 'belly'.

4.1   watakusi (?< *ba₁.₃ₐ tuku-s[a-C]i?ₐ/ᵦ 'exhaust me' or 'I exhaust').
'private; I/me'. HHHH - 0-0-A x-x-x. NS (97a watakosi) HHHH, (129b) HHHL.
Km x. Mr (Bm) HHHH. 1700 Ōsaka wasi HH. Ib watasi H = 3.1. The register is
incongruent with the etymology given and also with that of Mochizuki 1971:21:
*wa -tu [a]ku si 'my place direction'.

3.1   watari < *bata-r[a-C]iₐ. 'crossover'. HHH - 0-0-A x-A-x. NS (70a [11:45-M,
11:48-M], 87b, 94b) HHH; NS (T+ 99) ᵽᵽH = HHH, (T+ 29, 30, 42, 43) HᵽLH.
Km (S,W) (H). Ib H = 3.1.

4.1   wataride < *bata-r[a-C]i₃.₁(←ₐ) -n- ta-Ci. 'ferry point' (= watari-
ₛ/ze). x - x-x-x x-x-x. NS (70a [11:48-M]) HHHH; NS (T+ 43) ᵽHH ?= HLHH.

5.2   watarimori < *bata-r[a-C]i₃.₁(←ₐ) mor[a-C]i?ᵦ. 'a ferry boatman' (=
watasimori). HHHHL - 4-x-x x-x-x. K: "Hn HHHH" (misprint?).

5.2   watasibune < *bata-s[a-C]i*₃.₁(←ₐ) -n- puna-Ci₂.₄. 'ferry boat'. HHHHL -
4-5[H]/1:4[U]-A x-B-x. Nk wataasibuni LLLHHL (= C). Sz 0.

5.2   watasimori < *bata-s[a-C]i*₃.₁(←ₐ) mor[a-C]i?ᵦ. 'ferry boatman'. HHHHL -
3-4[U]/1:4[H]-A x-x-x. Sz 0.

4.3   watatabi (< ?). (1) (= kinma) 'a kind of pepper (?= Piper longum, Korean
philpal)'; (2) (= matatabi) 'silvervine'. HHLL ('pepper') - x-x-x x-x-x.

4.3   wataᵗ/zumi < wadaᵗ/zumi < wata-tu-myi < *bata?₂.₁ -tuₚcₗ mi₁.₃ₐ.
'spirit/god of the sea'. HHLL - x-x-x x-x-x. NS (T+ kun) ᵽLLH (odd; oddly
glossed 'young child'). Km (W) HHHL, "HHLH" (?).

2.2b   waza < *bansa. 'trick, feat, ... '. HL - 2-2-A x-(x)-x. NS (127b, 133b)
HL. Km (W) HL/LL. Edo HL. Sz 2; Matsue, Izumo 2 (= 2.3). Ib H1 = 2.2.

4.1   wazawai < waza-fafyi < *bansa₂.₂b (-)pa-p[a-C]iᵦ₃ₐ ᵥ. 'misfortune,
disaster'. x - 0-0-x x-x-x. NS (111b) HHHH.

3.7b   wazuka(-ni) < waduka < *bantu-ka. 'little, scant'. LHL(|H) - 1-1:3-B
x-x-x. Km (S) LHL(|H). Mr (Bm) LHL(-L). Edo LHL. Ib L2 = 3.5/7.

1.1   ya(-) < *da. 'eight'. x - 1-2-(1[U])-A (A/B)-A-(A). See yae, ya(t)tu, yaso.

1.2   ya ?< *da. 'arrow'. L/H (?= HL = F) - 1-2-A A-A-x. NS (129b) L. Km x. Edo
F. K: Hn-Km-Edo HL. Sapporo, Aomori, Matsumoto, Hattō, Hamada, Matsue, Izumo,
Yamaguchi, Hata, Ōita 0; Akita, Numazu, Narada, Hiroshima 1. Kōchi, Hyōgo,
Toyama, Suzu 2; Ib H1 = 1.2. (Hiroto and Ōhara "Tk 0" must be a mistake or a
misprint.) Cf. iruₐ 'shoot'.

?1.3a; ?1.2 (= 2.2) ya < *da. 'spoke (of wheel)'. L, HL (yaa [Kn Sō-chū 90:6]) -
1-2-A x-x-x. Km x.

1.3b   ya < *da. 'building, house; roof (= yane)'. R - 1-0[H]/2[U]-B B-B-B.
Km (W) H(-H). Edo H. K: Hn LH, Km HH, Edo LH. Kt 0/2 is surprising in view of
yane 1. Ib L = 1.3. Yn daa B. Cf. ie, io; Ch. 1 §33, §45.

2.1   yabu < *danpu (?< *dam[a₂.₃ o]p[o-Ci]-uᵦ 'mountain grow'). 'bush,
thicket'. HH - 0-0-A x-x-x. Km (W) HH. Edo HH. Hakata 0 (we expect 1, ygr 0).
Ib H = 2.1.

4.2   yabuhara (< ?*yabuwara) < yabu-fara < *danpu₂.₁ para₂.₃. 'overgrown
field'. HHHL - 0-3-x x-x-x. NS (Okada) HHHL; NS (T+ 109, kun) HHHL. Km x.

4.5   yaburema < yabure[y]-ma < *da(-)npu(-)ra-Ci[-Ci]ᵦ ma (?= 'eye'₁.₃ₐ, ?=
'space'₁.₁). 'torn/decayed place' (= yabureme). x - x-x-x x-x-x. NS (99a) LLLL.
Cf. yarema.

?2.4, ?2.5   yado < yadwo < *da*1.3b* -n- two*1.1* ('roof door'). 'shelter. lodging'
(confused with yadori < *da t(w)or[a-C]i). x - 1-1-B B-B-x. Km (W) LH(-H).
1700 Ōsaka LH. Kōbe (Robb) 1:3/1/0. Ib L2 = 2.5. Sd yado(o) B 'door': Sr
yaadu/yadu B 'lodging'; Yn daadu A 'door' (H 1967:292). On Kt, cf. Ōhara
1951:417 "1:3 in some places".

3.4   yadori < yador-i*B* < *da*1.3b* t(w)or[a-C]i*B*. 'lodging(s)'. x - 0-0-x x-x-x.
Km (W) LLL. Edo HHL.

4.6   yadorigi < yadori-*k/g*i < *yadori*3.4←B* - *k/g*iy*1.3a* < *da*1.3b* t(w)or[a-C]i*B*
(-n-) ko-Ci*1.3a*. 'parasitic plant(s); mistletoe'. LLLH - 0/3-4[H]/1:4[U]-A
x-x-x.

2.2b   yae < yafye < *da*1.1* piCa*1.x*. 'eightfold'. x - 1[new]/2-2-A x-x-x. NS
(Okada) HL; NS (T 127) HH, (T 88, 90) LH. Km (W) HH/HL-⋯ . Edo HL. Aomori 1:
Narada 2. Ib H1 = 2.2.

4.2, 2.2|2.2, 4.4   yaegaki < yafegaki < yafye*2.2b* (< *da*1.1* piCa*1.x*) -gakyi
(< *-n- kaki*?2.2a* < ...). 'many-layered fence'. x - 3-x-x x-x-x. NS (T+ 57)
HHHL. Km (W) HHHL, "HHLH" (?).

5.4   yaemugura < yafemugura < yafye*2.2b* (< *da*1.1* piCa*1.x*) - mugura*?3.7a* (<
*munkura). 'overgrown weeds; a cleavers, goose grass, catchweed'. x - 3-4-x
x-x-x. Km (W) HHLLL.

3.2a   yagara < *da*1.2* -n- kara*2.2b*. 'arrow-shaft; (= awagara) cornet fish'.
HHL - 0-0-x x-x-x.

3.5x   yagata < ya-*k/g*ata < *da*1.3b* (-n-) kata*2.2b*. 'shelter on cart'. LLH -
x-x-x x-x-x.

?3.1   yagate (?< *yankate ?< *yam[i]-kata-[k]i < *dam[a-C]i*A* kata*ad? A* 'hard to
stop'). 'before long'. HHx - 0-1-A x-A-x. Km x. K: Edo HHH.

?2.4   yagi (?< Sino-Korean yang < Ch .yang 'sheep'). 'goat'. x - 1-0-B x-x-x.
Km x. Aomori, Sz, Narada, Hakata 1; Goka-mura 2. Kōbe (Robb) 2: Ib H1 = 2.2.

3.1   yagura < ya-*k/g*ura < *da*1.2* (-n-) kura*2.3*. 'attic storehouse for ("arrows"
=) weaponry; tower, turret, scaffolding'. HHH (-k-) - 0-0-B x-A-x. Edo HHH.
Hakata 0/1. Ib H = 3.1.

3.1   yagure < yakure < *yakure[y] < *ya*k*/gura*2.1* (< *da*1.2* (-n-) kura*2.3*)
i[ta]*2.4*. 'roofing boards (as for the conning tower on a medieval warship)'.
HHH - x-x-x x-x-x. (Not < ya*1.3b* 'building'; the register is incongruent.)

3.1   yahazu < ya-fazu < *da*1.2* pansu*2.1*. 'arrow-notch; nock'. HHH - 0-0-x x-x-x.

3.4   yahoti/yahotu < yafoti (Mg) (?< Ch 'ya-pywat 'night depart'). 'a
prostitute on the streets, a streetwalker'. LLL - x-x-x x-x-x.

2.1   ya-hu < *da*1.1* pu*?* (< pu[si]*2.3*). '(eight =) many joints/stitches in a
woven fence'. x - x-x-x x-x-x. NS (Okada) HH; NS (T 91) LH.

4.3   yaigari < ya[k]igari < *yakyi-gar[y]i < *dak[a-C]i*A* -n- kar[a-C]i*B*.
'fire-hunting'. HH?Lx (?= *HHLL) - x-x-x x-x-x.

4.1   yaigome: see ya[k]igome.

4.2   yaigusa < ya[k]i*k*/gusa < *yakyi-*k/g*usa < *dak[a-C]i*A* (-n-) kusa*2.3*.
'mugwort, artemisia' (= yomogi). HHHL (-k-) - 0-x-x x-x-x.

4.2   yaigusi < ya[k]igusi < *yakyi-gusi < *dak[a-C]i*A* (-n-) kusi*2.3*. 'skewer,
spit'. HHHL - 0-0/2-A x-x-x.

4.2   yaiisi: see yakiisi.

4.1   yaitoo < "yaitofu" < yaito < ya[k]ito < *yakyi-to < *dak[a-C]i to*?1.1*.
'moxibustion, moxacautery'. HHHH - 0-0-x x-x-x.

?2.3   yaka < *da*1.3b* -ka*1.x* ('house place'). 'house, mansion' (= yake).
x - x-x-x x-x-x.

3.4   yakara < *da*1.3b* kara*2.x*. 'family'. LLL - 1/3-0-x x-A-x. NS (131a) LLL.
Km (S) LLL. Edo HLL. Narada 1; Aomori (rare) 0. Ib (rare) H = 3.1. Nk x;
Sr "A" odd (cf. yaa B).

?3.1/3.4 yakaᵃ/ᵤu ?< *ya-kazu < *da₁.₉ᵦ kansu₈.₄ (< ...). 'house'. "HLH" (Kn) /
  HHH (Ck) / LLL (Kz, Wamyō-shō) - x-x-x x-x- x. Cf. Mochizuki 1971:20.
  Alternative etymology: *yaka₈.₃ (< *da₁.₉ᵦ -ka₁.ₓ) su₁.₉ᵦ 'house nest'.

?3.5a/b yakata < *da₁.₉ᵦ kata₈.₂ᵦ. 'shelter on boat; shelter on cart (= yagata):
  residence'. x - 0/1-0-B x-x-x. Km (W) LLH. Edo HLL.

?2.3 yake < yakey < *daka-Ci (< *da₁.₉ᵦ -ka₁.ₓ -Ci₉ᵤₜ). 'house, mansion' (=
  yaka). x - x-x-x x-x-x. See ooyake.

4.1 yakibata < yakifata < *yakyi-fata < *dak[a-C]i₄ (-n-) pata₈.₄. 'field-
  burning'. HHHH - 0-0-A x-x-x. Sz 0.

4.3 yakigane < *yakyi-gane[y] < *dak[a-C]i₄ -n- kana-Ci₈.₁. 'red-hot iron;
  branding-iron; brand(-mark); a needle for cauterizing boils'. HHLL - 0-0-x
  x-x-x.

4.1 yakigome < *yakyi-gomey < *dak[a-C]i₄ -n- komaCi₈.₃. 'roasted/toasted
  rice'. HHHH - 0-0-x x-x-x.

4.2 = 2.1|2.2 yakiisi < ya[k]iisi < *yakyi-isi < *dak[a-C]i₄ isi₈.₂ᵦ. 'heated
  stones, warming stones'. HH(|)HL - 0-x-x x-x-x.

3.5a yakko < yatukwo < *da₁.₉ᵦ -tu_ᵨᵧₗ kwo₁.₁. 'slave, vassal'. LHH - 0-0-B
  x-x-x. NS (113a) Lxx. Km (S) LHH. Edo HHH. 1700 Ōsaka LHL. Narada 0. Ib H =
  3.1.

3.7x yakuno (< ?). 'a kind of striped shell'. LHL (Kn) - x-x-x x-x. Not in NKD.

3.1 yakure: see yagure.

2.3 yama < *dama. 'mountain'. LL - 2-2-B B-B-B. NS (73c, 77b [14:155-M]) LL,
  (77b [14:154-M] mistake?) LH; NS (T 119) LL, (T 79; 22, 23; 71) HH; (T+ 12, 61,
  69, 79) LL, (T+ 77a, 77b) Hᵽ ?= LL, (T+ 77c, 77d) Hᵽ ?= HL, (T+ 22, 23, 71) HL.
  Km (W) LL. Mr (Bm) HL. Edo HL. Ib F = 2.3. Kin (northern Okinawa) yaamaa ?B
  (Kusakabe 1968:54).

4.10 yamabato < *yama-batwo < *dama₈.₃ -n- patwo₈.₃. 'turtledove'. LHLL - 0/3-
  0[H]/3[U]-B x-x-x.

4.11 yamabiko < yamabyikwo < *dama₈.₃ -n- pi-kwo?₈.₁. 'echo; the spirit of the
  mountain'. x - 0/2-0-B x-B-x. Km (W) LLHL. Sz 2.

4.11 < 5.16 yamabuki, yamabuhuki < yamabu(fu)kyi < *dama₈.₃ -n- pupuki?₈.₁
  (< ...). 'Kerria japonica, gloveflower; yellow; gold coin'. LLHL (yamabuki =
  yamabuhuki LLLHL) - 2-3[H]/2[U]-B x-x-x. Sz, Hakata 2. Kōbe (Robb) 1:3.

3.4 = 2.3|1.3 yamada < *dama₈.₃ -n- ta₁.₃ₐ. 'mountain ricefield; Yamada (place)'.
  x - 0-1-B x-B-x. NS (Okada) LL(|)L; NS (T+ 69) LLH. Km (W) LL(|)L. 1700 Ōsaka
  LHH.

4.9 yamadori < yama-ᵗ/ₐori < yama-dori < *dama₈.₃ (-n-) tori₈.₁. 'mountain
  birds/fowl; pheasants; (= Ezo-raityoo) hazel grouse'. LHHL (-t-) -
  2-2[U]/3[H]-B x-x-x. Sz 3; Hakata 2, ygr 3.

6.17 yamadori-kusa < yamadori₄.₉)< *dama₈.₃ -n- tori₈.₁) kusa₈.₃ = yamatori-
  gusa < yamatori₄.₉)< *dama₈.₃ tori₈.₁) -n- kusa₈.₃. 'barrenwort, Epimedium
  grandiflorum' (= ikari-soo). LLHHxx (-d-) ?= *LLHHHL - x-x-x x-x-x.

4.5 = 2.3|2.3 yamaemi < yamawemi < *yama wemyi < *dama₈.₃ bem[a-C]i₈.₃₊ᵣ (< ...
  'mountain smile'). 'Polygonatum falcatum' (= ooemi = emigusa = narukoyuri =
  amana). LL(|)LL - x-x-x x-x-x.

4.6 yamagaki < *dama₈.₃ -n- kaki₈.₁ (< ...). 'wild persimmon'. LLLH - 2-3-x
  x-x-x. Km (W) LLLH/"HLLH" (?= LLLH).

4.5 = 2.3|2.3 yamagami < *yama-gamiy < *dama₈.₃ -n- kamu-Ci₈.₃. 'the god of the
  mountain'. x - 0/2-x-x x-x-x. Km (W) LL(|)LL.

3.7x yamago < yama-ᵏ/ₒo < yama-ᵏ/ₒwo < *dama₈.₃ -n- kwo₁.₁. 'a mountain
  phantom/spirit/god'. LHL - 2-0-x x-x-x.

4.11   yamagusa < yama-ᵏ/ɢusa < *damaₛ.ₛ (-n-) kusaₛ.ₛ. 'mountain grass(es);
    ([Mg] = roodoku) Lycoctonum pseudolaeve (?= Justicia gendarussa ?= poisonous
    water willow)'. LLHL (-g-) - 2-x-x x-x-x.
4.5 = 2.3|2.3   yamaguwa < yamagufa < *damaₛ.ₛ -n- kupaₚₛ.ₛ. 'wild mulberry'. LL(|)LL
    - 0-x-x x-x-x. Km x. Toyama 1:4 (we expect 1:3); Suzu 1 (expected reflex).
3.7b (?< 3.4)   yamai < yamafyi < *dama-p[a-C]iₚₑ. 'illness'. LHL - 1-1:3-B x-B-(B).
    NS (103a) LLL, (133a) LHL. Km x. Mr (Bm) LHH-H. Edo LHL. K: Hn-Mr-Edo LHL.
    Sapporo, Akita, Matsue, Izumo 2; Numazu, Narada, Hida (= northern Gifu). Hattō.
    Hamada, Goka-mura, Hiroshima, Wakamatsu, Ōita 1. Aomori → yamε 2. Ib L2 =
    3.5/7. Sr yanmee B; Yn damun B 'ail'.
5.6 = 2.3|3.4   yamakagami < *yama - kagamyi < *damaₛ.ₛ kankamiₛ.₄ (< ... 'mountain
    mirror'). 'white lotus' (= byakuren). LL(|)LLL - x-x-x x-x-x.
?5.15, ?5.16   yamakagasi (?< *damaₛ.ₛ kankaₛ.ₛ [mu]siₛ.₁ 'mountain shadow/shining
    snake'; ? variant of yamakagati). 'grass snake, ring snake'. x - 3/5-4-x x-x-x.
5.15   yamakagati ?< *damaₛ.ₛ kankaₛ.ₛ tiₚₗ.₁ ('mountain shadow/shining spirit');
    ?< yamaₛ.ₛ kagatiₛ.₁ (< ... '[eyes like] mountain bladder-cherries'). 'a huge
    snake with red eyes'. LLHLL - x-x-x x-x-x.
5.8, 5.7, 5.14 yamakazura < yama-kadura < *damaₛ.ₛ -n- ka(n)turaₛ.₇ₐ (< ...). 'club
    moss, Lycopodium clavata (= hikage-no-kazura) or a head-dress made from it'.
    x - 3-x-x x-B-x. Km (W) LLLHH, LLLLH, LLHHL. Sr yamakanda B.
4.10   yamamomo < *damaₛ.ₛ momoₛ.₁. 'wild peach'. LLHL - 2-1:3-x x-B-x.
4.6   yamanasi < *damaₛ.ₛ nasiₚₛ.₂ₐ. 'wild pear'. LLLH - 2/0-3-x x-x-x.
?4.6   yamanobe < yamanobye (NS) < yama-no-fye < *damaₛ.ₛ no ?piCaₗ.ₓ (?=
    *pina). 'vicinity of the mountain, around the mountain' (= yamabe < yama-fye
    < ...); 'Yamanobe (placename)'. x - 0-0-x x-x-x. NS (79 [14:321-M]) LxLH-L;
    NS (T+ 79) LⱯLR ?= LLL(|)H. K: "Hn LLLF?"
5.x   yamanoimo < yama-ⁿᵒ/ₜᵤ-imo < *damaₛ.ₛ noₚₑₗ/-tuₚₑₗ imwoₛ.ₛ. 'Japanese
    yam'. LLHxx (-tu-) - 0/5-1:4-x x-(B)-x. K: Hn LLLLL (inferred?). Sz 5.
    Sr yamaqnmu B < yama-imo.
3.7x   yamaˢ/ᵤi < (Mg) yama-ˢ/ᵤi < *damaₛ.ₛ (-n-) siₗ.ₛₑ ('mountain sorrel').
    'Anemarrhena asphodeloides' (= hanasuge). LHL - x- 3-x x-x-x. Km (W) LLH, LLR.
    LHH. Mr (W 19) LHH.
4.6   yamasimu < *damaₛ.ₛ simuₚ (?< sibu < sinpuₚₛ.₄,ₚₛ.ₛ *'persimmon'). 'wild
    elm'; (?= yamasibu 'wild persimmon'). LLLH - x-x-x x-x-x.
4.5   yamasiro < yamasiro ?< yama[toₛ.ₛₑ u]siroₛ.₇ₐ/ₑ (< ...). 'Yamashiro'
    (placename). x - 0/2/3-0-B x-x-x. NS (72a [11:192-M], 72c [11:207-M]) LLLL;
    NS (T+ 55) LHLL, (T+ 52) HHLH
6.7   yamasirogawa < yamasiro-gafa < *yamasiro₄.ₛ (< ...) -n- kapaₛ.ₛₑ. 'the
    Yamashiro [= Kizu] River'. x - 4-x-x x-x-x. NS (72a [11:195-M, 72b [11:198-M]
    LLLLLL.
5.6 = 4.5|1.3   yamasirome < yamasiro-mye < *yamasiro₄.ₛ (< ...) miCaₗ.ₛₕ (?= *mina).
    'Yamashiro woman/women'. x - x-x-x x-x-x. NS (73a, 73b) LLLL(|)L; (T+ 57, 58)
    LLLL(|)"R" (?= H).
4.10   yamasuge < *yama-sugey < *damaₛ.ₛ sunka-Ciₛ.ₛ (< ...). 'wild sedge;
    Liriope platyphylla/graminifolia/spicata'. LHLL - 2-3-x x-x-x. Km x.
3.5b   yamato < *damato. 'Japan; Yamato'. (L) - 1-2-A x-B-x. NS (72b [11:200-M],
    74b [11:303-M], 74c [11:306-M], 75b [14:418-M], 76c [14:126W-M], 121b
    [14:200-K], 122b [14:218-K]) LLH; NS (T+ 62, 63, 84, 100) LLH, (T+ 75) HⱯH
    ?= LLH, (T+ 20) HLL, (T+ 15) LHⱯ ?= LHH. Sz 2.
6.11 = 3.5|3.1 [yamato-kooti] < yamatoₛ.ₛₕ kautiₛ.₁ < yamato ka[fa-u]ti <
    *damatoₛ.ₛₕ kapaₛ.ₛₕ utu-Ciₛ.ₛₑ. 'Yamato and Kawachi = (both) east and west'.
    LLH(|)HHH - x-x-x x-x-x.

?5.16 = 3.5|2.4/5   yamatokoto < (*)yamato-ᵏ/ₐoto < *damatoₐ.ₙₕ (-n-) kotoₐ.ₐ.
  'Japanese harp'. LLH|LH - 4-4-x x-x-x. Km x. K: Hn LLH|LF.
-        yamatori: see yamadori.
?5.14   yamatouta < (*)yamato - uta < *damatoₐ.ₐb utaₐ.ₐb. 'Japanese song'.
  LLHHL - 3-4-x x-x-x. Km (W) LLHLL, LLLHL, "HLHHL" (?).
-        yamatuimo: see yamanoimo.
4.5 = 2.3-tu|1.3   yamaᵗ/zumi < yama-tu-myi < *damaₐ.ₐ -tuₚₑₗ miₐₗ.ₐₐ. 'spirit/god
  of the mountain'. LL-L(|)L - x-x-x x-x-x.
5.16   yamaubara < *damaₐ.ₐ ?unparaₐ.ₐₐ. 'wild rose'. LLLHL - 3-x-x x-x-x. See
  ibara.
5.15 = 2.3|3.3 yamautugi < *yamaₐ.ₐ - utugiyₐ.ₐ < *damaₐ.ₐ utuₐₐ.ₓ -n- koCiₐₗ.ₐₐ).
  'Clerodendron trichotomum (= kusagi); bush honeysuckle (= Hakone-utugi)'.
  LL(|)HLL (Zs) - 3-4-x x-x-x.
-        yamazi: see yamasi.
-        yamazumi: see yamatumi.
2.3   yami < yamiy < *damᵘ/ₒCi. 'darkness'. LL - 2-2-B x-B-x. NS (116b) LL.
  Km x. Edo HL. Ib F = 2.3.
?3.1, ?3.2x yamome < (*)yamo-mye < *damoₐ miCaₐₗ.ₐb (?= *mina). 'widow; spinster'.
  HHH (Kz) / HHL (Kn) - 0-1[H]/0[U]-B x-x-x. NS (100a) HHᵗH (HHᵗF. HHᵗL). Km x.
  Aomori 2: Goka-mura 1; Narada, Hattō. Hamada, Matsue, Izumo 0. Ib 'widower' L
  = 3.6. Sd/Sr yagusami A; Yn dagusami A (why not -n- ?). Various etymologies
  are suggested. The most interesting: = yamu mye < *dam[a-]uₐ miCaₐₗ.ₐb (?=
  *mina) 'cease woman' with Azuma attributive -o for -u (see Ch. 7, §4), or
  o < *u by partial assimilation to the vowels of the other syllables.
?3.1   yamoo < yamo-wo < *damoₐ boₐ.ₗ. 'widower'. HHH (Kn, *miswritten* "kamowo") -
  0-0-x x-x-x. NS (100a) HHH. *See* yamome.
?3.7b, ?3.3   yamori < *daₐ.ₐb mor[a-C]iₐₐ ('building guard'). 'house-lizard.
  gecko'. x - 1-1:3-B x-x-x. NS (93a) HLL. Km x. Sz 2.
?2.4, ?2.5   yana < *dana. 'fishweir'. LH - 1-2-x x-x-x. NS (T+ kun) LH. Km x.
  Sz 1; Aomori 2 *(expected)*. Cf. Sr yaama B, Nk yamaa C, Yn dama B 'trap'.
3.1   yanagi < yanagiy < ?*danaₐₐ.ₗ -n- koCiₐₗ.ₐₐ. 'willow'. x - 0-0-A A-A-A.
  NS (Okada) HHL; NS (T+ 83) HLH. Km x. Mr (Bm) HHH. Edo HHH. K: Hn HHH
  (attested?). Hakata 1 *(we expect 2)*, ygr 0. Ib H = 3.1. Etymologies: ?< ya no
  kiy (< ...) 'arrow tree', ?< Ch 'yang 'willow'. Sr yanazi A (on the final
  syllable, see Ch. 1, §41).
4.2   yanagui < yanagufi ?< *ya-no kufyi < *daₐ.ₐ no kupiₐ.ₐb. 'quiver and
  arrows; arrow quiver for an honor guard'. HHHL - x-0-x x-x-x.
3.4   yanasu < *danaₐₐ.ₐ suₐₗ.ₐb. 'a weir blind (a reed screen used in a
  fishweir)'. LLL - x-0-x x-x-x. K: "Hn HHH" *misprint?*.
2.4   yane < *ya-ne[y] < *daₐ.ₐb na-Ciₐₗ.ₗ. 'roof'. x - 1-1-A x-x-x. Km x.
  Aomori 2 *(expected reflex)*; Sz, Narada, Hata, Hakata 1. Kōchi 1; Ib L = 2.4.
2.3   yani < *dani. 'resin'. x - 2-2-B x-B-x. Km x. K: Hn LL (where?). Narada 2:
  Hakata 1 *(we expect 0)*, ygr 2. Ib yari/yare F = 2.3.
3.6   [yanoe] < yano[w]e < ya-no-fe < ya-no [u]fe[y] < *daₐ.ₐb no upa-Ciₐ.ₐₐ.
  'roof-top, on the roof': yanofe-no koke 'roof-top moss' LHH-H LL - x-x-x x-B-x.
  Sr yaanuqwii B 'roof'.
3.4   yarema < ya[bu]remaₐ.ₐ (< ...). 'torn/decayed place' (= yaburema).
  x - 0/3-x-x x-B-x. NS (99a) LLL. Sr yarimii B.
2.1   yari < *dari (?< *dar[a-C]iₐ). 'spear'. x - 0-0-A x-A-x. Km x. Ib H = 2.1.
3.1   yasaki < yasakyi < *daₐ.ₐ sakiₐ.ₗ. 'arrowhead'. HHH - 0/1/3-0-A x-x-x.
  Goka-mura 0; Hattō, Hamada, Matsue, Izumo 3.

5.2   yasasugari ‹ ya-sasu kari ('dice that aim at eight') ‹ *da*ı.ı* sas[a]-u*ʙ*
kari*ɛ.ı*. '(name of an old game)'. HHHHL - x-x-x x-x-x. (Kn Sō-chū 42:4 has
intrusive -ke- before -ri, probably a scribal error.)

?2.4 (= 3.7b)   yasi (?= yaasi ‹ Ch .ya-'tsyey). 'palm tree'. RL (= LHL) (Ir) -
1-2-B x-B-x. Sz 1. Ib H1 = 2.2. Sr yaasi B.

5.1 (?= 3.1|2.1) yasimakuni ‹ ya-sima*?*3.1* (‹ *da*ı.ı* sima*ɛ.ɜ*) kuni*?2.1,?2.2a*
(‹ ...). 'the eight-island land'. x - x-x-x x-x-x. NS (82c [17:110-M])
HHH(|)HH, NS (T+ 96) HL*FLH.

3.4   yasiro ‹ *da*ı.ɜb* siro*ɛ.ı*. 'shrine'. LLL - 1-2-B x-x-x. Km x. Edo HHL.
1700 Ōsaka HLL. Aomori (rare) 3; Narada, Hattō 1; Hamada 1/3; Matsue 0/3;
Izumo 0; Goka-mura 0 (expected reflex). Ib H1 = 3.3, H = 3.1, F = 3.4.

4.2   yasiwago ‹ "yasifago" (= yasiwago) ‹ yasi[m]ago ‹ *yasi*?*2.1* (‹ *dasi
?= *das[a-C]i*A*, see yasinau) - magwo*ɛ.ɜ* (‹ *uma*adj ʙ* -n- kwo*ı.ı*). 'great-great-
grandchild'. HHHL - x-x-x x-x-x.

2.2b   yaso ‹ ya-swo ‹ *da*ı.ı* -swo*ı.x*. 'eighty'. HL (Kz) / xL (Kn) 1-2-x x-x-x.
NS (128b [14:360L-K]) RL. Km (W) HL-/HH- ··· .

2.2b|1.2 yaso-ba ‹ yaswo*ɛ.ɜb* - ba*ı.ɛ* ‹ *da*ı.ı* -swo*ı.x* -n- pa*ı.ɛ*. '(having)
eighty/many leaves, (being) eighty-/many-leafed'. x - x-x-x x-x-x; NS (72b
[11:197-M]) HL|H; NS (T+ 53) LHLL.

4.1   yasokage ‹ ya-swo*ɛ.ɜb* (‹ *da*ı.ı* -swo*ı.x*) kagey*ɛ.ɜ* (‹ *kanka-Ci ‹ ...)
('eighty [= vast] sunshine'). 'a spacious palace'. x - x-x-x x-x-x. NS (Okada)
HHHH; NS (T+ 102) LLLH.

4.3; 4.4 = 2.2|2.3   yasosima ‹ ya-swo*ɛ.ɜb* (‹ *da*ı.ı* -swo*ı.x*) sima*ɛ.ɜ*. '(eighty =)
many islands'. x - 0-x-x x-x-x. Km (W) HHLL; HL(|)LL. Mr (W 19) HLLL.

?5.5, ?5.2   yasotuzuki ‹ yaso-tuduki ‹ ya-swo*ɛ.ɜb* (‹ *da*ı.ı* -swo*ı.x*) tutukyi*ɜ.ı+A*
(?‹ *tu[gyi] - tukyi ‹ *tunk[a-C]i*A* tuk[a-C]i*ʙ*). 'long-continuing'. x - x-x-x
x-x-x. NS (128b [14:360L-K]) RLLLL, (Okada) HHHHL; (T+ kun) HHHHH.

?3.3, 3.2b   yasozi ‹ yaswo*ɛ.ɜb* - di*ı.x* ‹ *da*ı.ı* -swo*ı.x* -n- ti*ı.x* (‹ ...).
'eighty (years old)'. x - x-2-x x-x-x. Km (W) HLL, HHL.

3.4   yasumi ‹ yasumyi ‹ *dasu-m[a-C]i*ʙ*. 'rest'. (x) - 3-2-B x-B-x. Km x.
Aomori, Sz 3. Ib F = 2.3.

5.7   yasu-musiro ‹ *dasu*adj ʙ* musiro*ɜ.4*. 'a restful couch'. x - x-x-x x-x-x.
NS (74a [11:272-M]) LLLLH; NS (T+ 61) LLHH.

4.11   yasuraka ‹ *dasu*adj ʙ* -ra-ka. 'peaceful, happy, at ease' (adj-n).
x - 2-4-B x-x-x. NS (98a, 132b) LLHL.

3.1   yasuri ?‹ iya-suri ‹ *ida*?ɛ.ı* sur[a-C]i*ʙ*. 'file'. HHH - 0/3-0-A x-x-x.
Km x. Aomori, Sz, Hattō, Hamada, Matsue, Izumo, Goka-mura 0. Ib H = 3.1.

5.2   yatagarasu ‹ yata n[o] karasu ‹ *data*?ɛ.ı* ('big' ‹ *da*ı.ı* ata*ɛ.x* 'eight
spans') kara-su*ɜ.6*. 'a sacred (mythical) crow'. HHHHL (Ck -g-, Kn -k-) - 4-4-x
x-x-x.

4.2; 2.2 (= 1.1|1.3) | 2.2   yatikusa ‹ ya-ti*?ɛ.ɛ* kusa*ɛ.ɜb* ‹ *da*ı.ı* ti*ı.ɜa* kusa*ɛ.ɜb*.
'eight thousand (= many) kinds'. x - x-3-x x-x-x. Km (W) HHHL; H(|)L HL; LHHx.

4.1 = 1.1|3.1   ya-timata ‹ *da*ı.ı* ti-mata*ɜ.ı* (‹ ti*?ı.ı* mata*ɛ.ɜ*). 'a place where many
roads meet, a multiple intersection'. x - 2-x-x x-x-x. NS (Okada) H(|)HHH.

4.1; 2.2 (= 1.1|1.3) | 2.2   yati-tabi ‹ ya-ti*?ɛ.ɛ* tabyi*ɛ.ɜb* ‹ *da*ı.ı* ti*ı.ɜa*
tanpi*ɛ.ɛb*. 'eight thousand (= many) times'. x - 2/3-x-x x-x-x. Km (W) HHHH;
H(|)L|HL.

?3.1 ‹ 2.1   yattu ‹ ya-tu ‹ *da*ı.ı* -tu*?ı.ı*. 'eight'. x - 3-2[U]/3[H]-A (A/B-A-A).
Aomori 0; Narada 3. Ib H2 = 3.2.

2.1   yatu ‹ ya-tu ‹ *da*ı.ı* -tu*?ı.ı*. 'eight' (= yattu). HH - 2-2-x (A/B)-A-A.
Km x. Mr (Bm) HL. Nk yaaCi A, Sr yaaçi A, Yn daaci A.

2.3 yatu (< ya-tu[-ko]*s.sa* < ... 'slave'). 'damn guy; damn thing'. x - 1-2-A
x-x-x. Km x. Edo HL. Sz 1; Yamaguchi 2. Ib F = 2.3. The etymology makes 2.3
more likely than 2.2b; cf. Okumura 1981.

4.11 yatugare < yatukar*/ı < *yatuk[o*s.sa* w]are*s.4* (< *da*ı.sa* -tu*pcı* kwo*ı.ı*
ba*ı.sa* [a]ra[-C]i*s*). 'humble I/me'. LLHL - 0-0-x x-x-x. NS (91c, 92a, 95b,
120b) LLHL.

- yatuge = yatugi.

3.1 (?= 2.1|1.1) yatugi < yatu-giy < *da*ı.ı* -tu -n- kiy*sı.ı* (< ...). 'eight
(horses)'. NS (79c [14:322-M]) HHH ?= HH(|)H; NS (T+ 79) LLH. NKD: "Read
yatuge in the Maeda text"; Okada -ge.

3.5a yatuko: see yakko.

5.14 yatukorama < yatukwo*s.sa* (< *da*ı.sb* -tu kwo*ı.ı*) -ra-ma*suf* (?< *[a]ra*s.s*
ma*s*). 'slave, vassal'. x - x-x-x x-x-x. NS (92a, 132b) LLHHL, (92b) LLHHx:
(Okada) LLLLH.

6.2 yatumekabura < *yatumey*ss.ı* kabura*ss.ı* < *ya-tu*s.ı* (< *da*ı.ı* -tu*sı.x*)
ma-Ci*ı.sa* kanpu*s.ı* [a]ra*s.s*. 'a *kabura-ya* (= whistling arrow with a turnip-
shaped head) that has eight holes'. HHHHHL - x-1:6-x x-x-x.

4.11 yawaraka < yafara-ka < yafara*adj-n* (< *dapa*smtm* -ra) -ka. 'soft' *(adj-n)*.
LLHL - 3-4-B x-(x)-(x). Ongi LLHx. Km x. Mr (Bm) HLLL. K: "Edo HHLL?".
Sz 3. Yn daaran B (H 1964) / C (H 1967) 'is soft'. Tk accent borrowed from Kt?

?2.1 < 3.5b (?< 4.3) yaya (?< iya-iya < *ida*ss.ı* ida*ss.ı*, cf. iyo-iyo).
'slightly'. RH - 1-2-A x-x-x. Ib L = 2.4. K: Km-Edo HH. See §7.1. Cf. yooyaku.

3.1 yaziri < *da*ı.s* -n- siri*s.s*. 'arrowhead'. HHH - 0/1-0-A x-x-x. Mr (Bm)
HHH. Narada 0; Hakata 0, ygr 3 *(= 3.4)*. Ib F = 3.4.

1.1 yo(-) < *do. 'four' (= yon). x - 1-2-x (A/B)-A-(A). Km (W) H-··· .

1.1 yo < *do. 'world; generation' (perhaps < 'bamboo segment' but register
is incongruent). H - 0/1-1-A x-A-A. Ongi (Iroha) H. NS (74a [11:302-M], 97b,
120a, 123a [14:236-K]) H; NS (T+ 62) H, (T+ 5) ₣ = H, (T+ 102) ti yo L L.
Km (S,W) H(-H). Edo H. Aomori *(rare)*, Numazu, Narada, Hiroshima (Terakawa) 0;
Sapporo, Akita, Matumoto, Hiroshima [H], Wakamatsu, Ōita, 1. Kōchi, Ōsaka,
Hyōgo, Ise, Suzu 0; Toyama 1:2 *(expected reflex)*; Ib H = 1.1.

1.3a yo < *do. 'bamboo segment; interval'. L - 1-x-x x-x-x. Km (S,W) L(-x).
K: Km LL, Edo LH.

1.3a yo < ywo < *dwo. 'night' (= yoru). x - 1-1-B B-B-B. NS (116b) L(-H): NS
(T+ 26) "R" ?= H. Km (W) L(-H); (S) L. Mr (Bm) L(-H). Edo R. K: Km LL, Mr-Edo
LH. Ib L = 1.3. Yn duu B (H 1964:64a). *See* yoru, yoi.

3.2x (?= 1.1|2.2) yobito ("yohito" NKD, Ōno) < (*)yo-byito < *do*ı.ı* -n- pito*s.sn*.
'people (at large)'. x - x-x-x x-x-x. Km (W "name?") HHL. Mr (W 19) HHL.

3.5x yoboro: see yooro.

5.2 yobukodori < ywobukwo*sss.ı* -dori < *dwonp[a-]u*A* kwo*ı.ı* -n- tori*s.ı*
('whistle bird'). 'cuckoo or nightengale; a whistle (= yobuko-bue)'. HHHHL -
3-4-x x-x-x.

3.4 yodake < yo-dakey < *do*ı.sa* -n- taka-Ci*s.ı*. 'joined bamboo'. x - x-2-x
x-x-x. NS (83c [11:122-M]) LLL; NS + 97) LLL.

3.1 yodare, yodari < yotari < *do*s* tar[a-C]i*s*. 'drivel'. HHH - 0-0-A A-A-x.
Km x. Matsue 3; Izumo 0/3; Narada, Hattō, Hamada, Goka-mura 0. Ib yodare H =
3.1. (Mg yudari; Ōno says -t- in Hn, but the three citations in Mochizuki's
index are -d-.)

2.4 yodo < *donto. '(stagnant) pool in a river'. LH - 1-x-x x-x-x. Cf. yodomu.

4.5 yodogawa < yodo-gafa < *donto*s.4* -n- kapa*s.sb*. 'the Yodo(gawa) River'.
x - 0-0-A x-x-x. Km (W) LLLL.

3.7x   yodono < ywo-dono < *dwo*1.3a* -n- tono*2.3*. 'boudoir, bedchamber'. LHL -
        x-2-x x-x-x.

3.4   yogoro < *ywo-goro < *dwo*1.3a* -n- koro*2.2b*. 'many nights, every night;
        (during the) night'. LLL - 0/1-x-x x-x-x.

3.5x   yohoro: *see* yooro.

2.1   yoi < ywofyi(/yofyi) < *dwopi(?/dopi) ?< *dwo*1.3a* pi*1.2* (*but the register
        is incongruent*). 'evening'. HH - 0-0-B x- A-x. NS (Okada) HH; NS (T 65) HH.
        Edo HH. Narada, Hiroshima. Ōsaka, Ise 0; Ib H = 2.1. On the first vowel see
        Igarashi 13 n.1, Matsumoto 1974:139. Cf. koyoi.

?2.3/?2.4 < 2.1   yoki (?< yok[o-*k*/*g*ir]i < ... 'side cutting'). 'small ax'. HH -
        x-0[Kuno]-x x-B-x. Km x. Ōsaka [Makimura] 0; Sakawa 2. Sr yuuci B. Hida vooki.

3.1   yokka < *do*1.1* -ka*1.3*. 'four days'. x - 0-0-A A-A-(A). Narada 1; Hakata
        0, ygr 3 *(= 3.4)*. Ib H = 3.1. Yn duuga A 'four days from now'.

2.1   yoko < *doko. 'side'. (H) - 0-0-A x-A-x. Km x. Edo HH. Ib H = 2.1. OJ yoko
        attested only as 'horizontal' (adj-n).

4.1   yokogami < *yokogamyi < *doko*2.1* -n- kami*2.4* ('side top[-piece]').
        'wheel axle'. HHHH - x-0-x x-x-x.

4.1   yokosa(ma) < *doko*2.1* sama*2.2b*. 'sideways; wayward, wrongful'. HHHH -
        0-0-x x-x-x. Ongi HHHH. K: Edo HHHH. Cf. yokosi(ma); tatasa(ma); yokiru.

3.7x   yokosi (< ?). 'spleen'. LHL - x-x-x x-x-x.

4.1   yokosi(ma) < *doko*2.1* sima*2.2b*. 'sideways; wayward, wrongful'. HHHH -
        0-0-A x-x-x. NS (100b) HHHH. Mr (Bm) HHHH. Cf. yokosa(ma); tatasi(ma); yokiru.

2.1   yome ?< (*)yo-mye (Zdb) < *do*?* miCa*1.3b* (?= *mina). 'bride'. HH - 0-0-A
        A-A-A. Km x. Hakata 0(/1). Ib H = 2.1. Nk yumii A: Kunigami, Ōgimi (northern
        Okinawa) B.

5.4   yomezukae < yomedukafe < ?*yomye-dukafey < *yo-mye*2.1* (< ...) -n- tuka-
        pa-Ci[-Ci]*A*. 'a boudoir attendant, a lady-in-waiting; a servant accompanying a
        bride, a bridesmaid'. HHLLL - x-4-x x-x-x

?2.3   yomi < *yomiy < *domo-Ci. 'Hades, the land of the dead' (= yomo-tu-kuni).
        x - 1-2-x x-x-x. Zdb cites "yomiy" on the basis of yomo-tu-kuni; there are no
        phonograms for yomi before 900; cf. Kokugo-kokubun 407:4.

4.5, 4.6 yomibito < *yomyi-byito < *dom[a-C]i -n- pito*2.2a*. 'the composer of a
        poem/song; the poet'. x - 0/2-0[U]/1[H]-B x-x-x. Km (W) LLLL, LLLH.

?2.2b   yomo (?< yo-[o]mo < *do*1.1* omo*2.4* 'four sides'). 'all directions,
        everywhere'. x - 1-2-B x-A[Lit.]-x. NS (125a, 130b) HL. Km x. Mr (Bm) HL.

3.6   yomogi < yomogiy < *domo*?* -n- ko-Ci*1.3a*. 'mugwort'. LHH - 0-1-B x-x-x.
        Km x. Edo LHH. Aomori 2 *(we expect 1)*; Narada, Yamaguchi, Hattō. Hamada.
        Matsue, Izumo 0; Goka-mura 1; Hakata 1, ygr 3. Ib L = 3.6. Shinsen-Jikyō
        "[ifa-]yomugi". (Various etymologies have been suggested. but none are
        convincing. Perhaps < 'Hades plant'.)

?3.4   yomotu- < yomo-tu < *domo*2.3* -tu*pcl*: ～ kuni*?2.1,?2.2a* 'Hades, land of
        the dead' (= yomi)' NS (T+ kun) LLHL ?= LL-L|HL; ～ he(-gufyi) < fey(-gufyi) <
        pa-Ci?1.1* (-n- kup[a-C]i*B*) 'eating from hell's oven' NS (T+ kun) FHLLHF ?=
        LH(|)L(|)L HL (incongruencies); ～ hirasaka < fyira- saka < *pira*ad1 A* saka*2.3*
        'the slope before Hades' LHLFLHH ?= LH(|)L | HL|HH (odd).

5.16 (?= 2.3-tu|2.2) yomo-tu-kuni < *domo*2.3* -tu*pcl* kuni*?2.1,?2.2a* (< ...). 'Hades.
        land of the dead' (= yomi). LLLHL ?= LL-L|HL.

?2.1, ?2.4   yona(-) < *dona 'hulled rice': *see* yone.

?3.4   yonaka < ywo-naka < *dwo*1.3a* naka*2.4*. 'the middle of the night'.
        x - 3-2[U]/1:3[U]-B x-B-x. Aomori, Narada 3; Hakata 0. ygr 3 *(= 3.4)*.
        Ir F = 3.4. Sr yunaka B.

4.2   yonamusi < *yona-musi < *dona*s.1* musi*s.1*. 'rice weevil' (= kokuzoo-musi).
HHHL - x-x-x x-x-x.

?2.1|2.4) yona-yona < *ywo*1.3a* (< *dwo) na*pc1* iterated. 'every night'. Lxxxx (Kz) -
0/1-1:3[H]/1[U]-B x-x-x. NS (105a) LH-xx. Cf. Sr ··· -na (< n[i f]a) 'each'.

?2.1, ?2.4   yone < *yone[y] < *dona-Ci. 'hulled rice'. HH - 1-1-x x-x-x. Km x.
1700 Ōsaka HL. K: Hn-Edo HH. Cf. ine (LH). Cf. Hamada 1950:44-5.

3.1   yooka < yauka ?< *da(u)*1.1* -ka*?1.3a* ?< *daCu*?2.x* -ka*?1.3a* (?= *da*1.1* -tu
-ka*?1.3a*), ?< *da*1.1* -uka*?2.x* (?< *da*1.1* -[t]u -ka*1.3a*). 'eight days'.
x - 0-0-A B-A-x. Km x. Edo HHH. Ib H = 3.1. Hakata 0, ygr 3 (= 3.4). Nk x.

3.5x   yooro (yoboro, yohoro) < "yoforo" /yoworo/ < ?*doporo (< ?). 'the hollow
(crook) of the knee, the popliteal space (= hikagami); conscripted servants of
the court'. LLH - x-0-x x-x-x. NS (127a [14:301-K]) xxH.

5.16   yoorokubo < "yoforo"-kubo < ?*doporo*s.s* kunpo*?2.1*. 'the hollow of the
knee' (= yooro). x - x-x-x x-x-x. NS (111a [11:345-K]) LLLHL.

4.11   yooyaku < yauyaku < ya[k]uyaku < *daku-daku (iterated *[i]da*?2.1* -ku*suf*,
cf. yaya). 'gradually, slowly; finally, at last' (adv). LLHL - 0-1:3[U]/1:4[H]-
B x-x-x.

?3.6, ?3.5x   yorodo (< ?). 'a saury (fish)' (= sayori = hario). LHH (Kn), LLH (Ck)
- x-x-x x-x-x. Variant yorozu < yorodu.

3.1   yoroi < yorofyi < *dorop[a-C]i*A*. 'armor'. HHH - 0-0-A x-A-x. NS (130a)
HHx. Km x. Edo HHH. Sapporo 2. Hakata 0 (we expect 2). Ib H = 3.1.

?5.2   yoroigusa < yorofigusa < *yorofyi-gusa < *dorop[a-C]i*s.1←A* -n- kusa*s.s*
('armor grass'). 'Angelica dahurica' (= kasamoti = sawaudo). HHHxx (?= *HHHHL)
- x-x-x x-x-x.

4.5   yorotosi (scribal error for yorodu-tose?). 'many years'. x - x-x-x x-x-x.
NS (Okada) LLLL.

3.5x   yorozu < yorodu < *doron-tu (< ?). 'myriad, ten thousand; various, all
(kinds of); everything'. LLH-···, LLx - 0/1-0-x x-x-x. NS (102b [11:153-K])
LLH; NS (T+ 102) HHH. Mr (Bm) HLL. Edo HLL. Cf. -tu; yorosi-, yorokobu; Korean
yel < 'yelh 'ten', yele(s) < ye'leh 'many, various'.

?3.6, ?3.5x   yorozu < yorodu (< ?) = yorodo 'a saury (fish)' (= sayori = hario).
x - x-x-x x-x-x. Variant yorodo.

4.7 = 3.5|1.1 yorozuyo < yorozu-yo < *doron-tu*s.5x* (< ?) do*1.1*. 'myriad years/
generations; all eternity'. LLH(|)H - 3-0-x x-x-x. NS LLLL. Km (W) LLHL/xxxH.

2.5   yoru < yworu < *dwo*1.3a* -ru*?suf*. 'night(time)'. LH - 1-1:3-B B-B-B.
NS (100a) LH. Km (W) LH-(H). Mr (Bm) LH. Edo LH. Hakata 1. On Kt, cf. Ōhara
1951:217 "1 but in some places 1:3"; Ōsaka, Ise, Kōchi 1; Ib L = 2.4. Fukuoka
yooru. Nk yuruu B; Onna yuuruu B.

?3.2b   yorube < yoru-fye < *do-r[a]-u*A* piCa*1.x*. 'something/someone to depend
on'. x - 0(/3[K])-0-A x-x-x. Km (W) HHL. Mr (W 20) HHH. Cf. yosuga.

5.2   yosebasira < *yose[y]-basira < *do-sa-Ci[-Ci]*A* -n- pasira*s.5a*.
'a hitching/horse post'. HHHHL - x-4-x x-x-x.

?2.1   yosi < *do-s[a-C]i*A*. 'reason; gist; report'. HH - 1- 2[H]/1[U]-B x-x-x.
NS (112b) HH. Km (S,W) HH. Mr (Bm) HH. Edo HH/LH.

2.x   yosi (< ?). 'reed'. x - 1-1-x x-x-x. Km x. Aomori 1. Ib H = 2.1. (Appears
in Myōgo-ki. Said to be yo-si LH 'it is good' used to avoid asi 'reed', a
homophone of a-si 'it is bad'.)

3.5b   yosino < *yosi-nwo < *do-si*adj B pred* nwo*1.3a* ('it's nice, the field').
'Yoshino' (placename). x - 1/3-2-x x-x- x. NS (T+ 126) yesinwo HLH. Km (W) LLH.
Edo HLL.

5.9, 5.11 yosinogawa < *yosinwo-gafa < *yosi-nwo*ʒ.ₛ* (< ...) -n- kapa*ʒ.ₐ*. 'the
Yoshino River' *(placename)*. x - 3-4-x x-x-x. Km (W) LLHHH, LHHHL.

2.2b   yoso < *doso. 'outside'. x - 2-2-A x-A-x. Km (W) HL. Edo HL *(Okumura
lists as Ch)*. Ib H1 = 2.2. Cf. soto.

?3.4 < 4.5   yosoi (x - 2-0-A x-x-x) < yosofyi*ʒₑ* < yoso[fo]fyi*ₐ/ᵦ* < *doso*ʒ.ₑₕ*
opo-p[a-C]i*ᵦ*. 'armor' < 'array, dress, outfit'. LLLL - 0/3-0-A x-x-x.
NS (T+ 6) **FHF** ?= HHH. Km (S) LLLL. K: Edo HHHL. Sz 3/0. Cf. osoi.

4.5 > ?*3.4   yosooi: *see* yosoi.

2.4|2.4   yoso-yoso < *doso*ʒₘₜₘ* doso (?< *doso, cf. yosou). 'slowly, solemnly;
(mountains) rising majestically'. LH|LH - x-x-x x-x-x.

?3.2a   yosuga < yosu-ka < *do-s[a]-u*ₐ* ka*ₗ.ₓ*. 'a place to turn to (for help); a
means'. x - 0/1-0[H]/1:3[U]-A x-x-x. Km x. 1700 Ōsaka LHH. Cf. vorube.

3.7b   yotaka < *ywo-taka < *dwo*ₗ.ₛₐ* taka*ʒ.ₗ*. 'night-hawk'. LHL - 1-1:3-x x-x-x.

5.2   yoti-ozasi < yoti-wozasi < *yoti[y] wo-zasi < *dot*ᵘ*/*ₒ*-Ci[-Ci] bo*ₗ.ₛₐ*
sas[a-C]i*ᵦ*. 'sliced fish that is skewered and dried'. HHHHL (Ck -t-; *misspelled
hiti- in Kn*) - x-x-x x-x-x.

4.x < 3.2b   yottari < yotari < *do*ₗ.ₗ* -t[u]*ʒₗ.ₗ* ar[a-C]i*ʒ.ₛₑᵣ*. 'four people'.
x - 4-4-x x-x-x. NS (123c) HHL.

?3.1 < 2.1   yottu < yo-tu < *do*ₗ.ₗ* -tu*ʒₗ.ₗ*. 'four'. x - 3-2[U]/3[H,U*adv*]-A
(A/B-A-A). Km (W) HH-no. Mr (Bm) HL. Aomori 0; Narada 3; Hakata 2 *(expected)*.
ygr 3. Ib H2 = 3.2. Nk yuuCi HHL (= A).

2.1   yotu < yo-tu < *do*ₗ.ₗ* -tu*ʒₗ.ₗ*. 'four' (= yottu). x - 1[H]/2[K]-2-A
A/B-A-A. Sz 1. Ib H1 = 2.2. Yn duuci A.

4.2   yotuziro < *yo-tu*ʒ.ₛₐ* - zirwo < *do*ₗ.ₗ* -tu -n- sirwo*ʒ.ₛ*. 'a horse with
all four legs white from the knees down' (= asibuti). HHHL - 0-x-x x-x-x.

?2.4, ?2.5   yowa < yofa ?< *ywo-fa (Zdb, *inferred*) < *dwo*ₗ.ₛₐ* -pa*ʒ*. 'night'.
LH - 1-2[H]/1[U]-B x-x-x. Km (W) LH(-L). K: Km LF. ("An elegant word used in Hn
and Km." Cf. yoi.)

3.4   yowai < yofafi < *yo*ₗ.ₛₐ* fafyi*ᵦ* < *do pap[a-C]i. 'age'. LLx/xLL - 0/2-0-B
x-x-x. Ir LLL. Edo HHL.

5.2   yozi-ozasi < yodi-wozasi = yoti-ozasi. (Was the verb yoti[y]- confused
with yodi[y]-?)

1.3a   yu < *du. 'hot water'. L - 1-1-B B-B-B. Mg yu amu L(|)LH 'bathes'. Edo R.
Ib L = 1.3.

1.3b   yu (?< Ch yew', cf. yuzu). 'citron' (= yuzu). R (Ir) - x-2-x x-x-x.
Wamyō-shō R (Numoto 1979:30). Km x. K: Hn LH, Edo HL. JP "yu, yu-no-su".

-        yu(-) 'sacred': *see* i(-), [yuki].

3.6   yubari < yumari < *du*ₗ.ₛₐ* mar[a-C]i*ᵦ* (or *du*ₗ.ₛₐ* -n- par[a-C]i*ₐ*). 'urine'.
LHH - 0-0-x x-x-(x). Km x. K: Hn LHL *(misprint?)*.

?6.14   yubaribukuro < *yu*ᵇ*/*ₘ*ari-bukurwo < *du*ₗ.ₛₐ* mar[a-C]i*ᵦ* (or *du*ₗ.ₛₐ* -n-
par[a-C]i*ₐ* -n- pukurwo*ʒ.₄*. 'bladder'. LHxHLL (?= *LHHHLL) - x-x-x x-x-x.

2.3 < 3.4 yubi < *yubyi < (*)[o]yobyi < *odonpi*ʒ.₄* (?< *odo-n[a]-p[a-C]i < ... *but
register incongruent*). 'finger, toe'. LL - 2-2-B B-B-B. Edo HL. Hakata
(expected) 0, ygr 2. Ib F = 2.3. Sr qiibi B; Yn uyubi B.

4.6   yubimaki < *yubyi*ʒ.₃* - makyi*ₐ* < *oyobyi*ʒ.₄* - makyi*ₐ* < *odonpi*ʒ.₄* (< ...)
mak[a-C]i*ₐ*. 'ring' (= yubiwa). LLLH - x-1:4/4-x x-x-x.

4.x < 5.7 yubinuki < oyobi-nuki < oyobyi*ʒ.₄* nukyi*ʒ.ₗ* < ?* odonp[a-C]i*ₐ* nuk[a-C]i*ₐ*
('finger poke'). 'thimble'. x - 3/4-1:4-B x-x-x < LLLLH. Sz 4.

3.4/3.5x   yubune < yu-bune[y] < *du*ₗ.ₛₐ* -n- puna-Ci*ʒ.₄*. 'bath tub'. LLL/LLH -
1-1[U]/1:3[H]-B x-x-x. Ib L = 3.6.

?2.2b   yue < yuwe (< ?). 'reason'. HL - 2-2-x x-B-x. NS (79b. 95b) HL: NS (T+ 79)
   HH. Km (S) HL. Mr (Bm) HL. Edo HL. Ib H1 = 2.2. Nk yui C. Yuen is said to be a
   truncation of yue n[ari] or yue n[i nari], but it is more likely that "yuwe" is
   a truncation of yuen, a conflation (or reading pronunciation) of Ch .ywen.

2.3   yue < yuwe < yu [u]we[y] < *du₁.₃ₐ (z)uba-Ci[-Ci]₄ ('hot-water plant').
   'bath mistress (for nobleman's children)'. LL - x-x-x x-x-x. NS (T+ kun) HH.

3.4   yugake < yum[yi]-kakey < *dumi₂.₃ kaka-Ci[-Ci]ₐ. 'archer's glove'. LLL -
   3-0-x x-x-x.

2.5   yuge < *yu-gey < *du₁.₃ₐ -n- key?₁.₁ (< ?). 'steam'. x - 1-1:3-B B-x-B.
   Aomori 2 *(expected reflex)*. Nk x; Yn dugi B. Attested Edo.

?2.4   yugi < yukyi < *du(n)ki (?< *dum[i]₂.₃ k[aC]i?₁.₂). 'an arrow quiver'.
   LH (Ir -g-, Kn -k-) - 1-2-x x-x-x. NS (T+ kun) LL. Km x.

3.1   yuhata < yu[fi]-fata < *dup[a-C]i₄ pata₂.₂b. 'tie-dyeing; white-spotted
   (dappled) cloth or grass'. HHH - x-x-x x-x-x.

?2.3 < 3.7b   yu-hi < yu-fi[n] (= yuu-fin) (< Ch .yew-'bhyen). '(livestock)
   mating'. RL - x-x-x x-x-x.

4.1   yuiᵏ/ᵧura < yufi-kura < *yufyi-ᵏ/ᵧura < *dup[a-C]i₄ (-n-) kura₂.₂b.
   'a packhorse saddle'. HHHH - x-x-x x-x-x.

2.1   yuka < *duka. 'floor; (sleeping) platform'. HH - 0-0-A x-A-B. Km (S) HH.
   Aomori 2. Ib L = 2.3. Nk yuhwaa A; Yn duga B (H 1964:184a).

?3.5a < 5.15   yukata < yu-kata[bira]₅.₁₅ (< ...). 'an unlined bathrobe'. x - 0-2-B
   x-x-x. 1700 Ōsaka HLL. Aomori, Sz 3; Goka-mura, NE Kyūshū 2; Hakata 2; Narada 1;
   Hattō, Hamada, Matsue, Izumo 0. Ib F = 3.4.

5.15   yukatabira < yu-katabira < *yu₁.₃ₐ kata-byira₄.₅ < *du₁.₃ₐ kata?₂.₃ -n-
   pyira?₂.₂b. 'an unlined bathrobe'. LLHLL - x-x-x x-x-x. (Truncated to modern
   yukata.)

2.2a   yuki < yukyi < *duki. 'snow; (hail)'. x - 2-2-A A-A-A. Km (W) HL.
   Mr (Bm) HL. Edo HL. Aomori 0. Toyama 2; Suzu 1 *(we expect 1:3)*. Yn duti A.

-          [yuki] 'arrow quiver': *see* yugi.

-          [yuki] < yu-kiy < yu(-) (-)kiy ('sacred wine' < ...). 'Number-One land of
   grain tribute'. x - x-x-x x-x-x. NS (T+ kun) HH.

3.x   yukue < yuku-fe < yuku₂.₁ fye₁.ₓ (< ...). 'destination; whereabouts'.
   x - 0-0[H]/1:3[U]-A x-A[U]-x. Edo HHL. Sz 0. Ib H2 = 3.2.

4.1 = 2.1|2.1 yukusaki < yuku₂.₁ sakyi₂.₁ < *i-ₚᵣₑ uk[a]-u₄ saki₂.₁. 'destination;
   future'. HH(|)HH - 0-0-A x-x- x. Km (S) HHHL. Sz 0.

2.3   yume (?< i-mey < *i₁.₃ₐ ma-Ci₁.₃ₐ 'sleep eye'). 'dream'. LL - 2-2-B x-B-x.
   Mr (Bm) HL. Edo HL. Ib F = 2.3. Sr qimi B; Onna qiimii B.

?2.4   yume < yumey (< ?). '(not) ever' *(adv)*. LH - 1/2-2-B x-x-x. NS (T+ 70. 73)
   LL. Km (W) LH/LL. K: "Mr and since" HL. Ib F = 2.3.

2.3   yumi < yumyi < *dumi. 'bow (to shoot arrows)'. (x) - 2-2-B x-B-x. NS (70a
   [11:49-M], 70c [11:53-M], 101b [11:143-K]) LL. Km x. Edo HL. Ib F = 2.3. Onna
   yuumi ("? B").

5.7   yum[i]bukuro < (*)yumyi-bukurwo < *dumi₂.₃ (-n-) pukurwo₃.₄. 'bow-bag'.
   LLLLH - 3-4-x x-x-x. Km x.

4.6 (?= 2.3|2.4)   yumidame < yumyi-ᵗ/ᵤamey < *dumi₂.₃ tama-Ci[-Ci]?B. 'a bow-
   straightening device' (= yudame). LLLH ?= LL(|)LH - x-x-x x-x-x.

4.5 = 2.3|2.3 yumigake < *yumyi-kakey < *dumi₂.₃ kaka-Ci[-Ci]B. 'archer's glove' (=
   yugake). LL(|)LL - x-x-x x-x-x.

4.5   yumihari < *yumyi-fari < *dumi₂.₃ par[a-C]i₄. 'stringing a bow; a person
   who strings bows'. LLLL - x-0-x x-x-x.

?4.11, ?4.6 = 2.3|2.3   yumizuka < yumiduka < *yumyi-duka < *dumi*ᵣ.ᵣ* (-n-) tuka*ᵣ.ᵣ*.
   'bow-hilt'. LLHx (Ck, -t-) / LL?HL (Kn, -d-) - 0- 3-x x-x-x. K: Hn LL(|)LL.

?4.11, ?4.6   yumizuru < yumi*ᵗ/ᵈ*uru < *yumyi-*ᵗ/ᵈ*uru < *dumi*ᵣ.ᵣ* (-n-) turu*ᵣᵣ.ᵣₐ*.
   'bowstring'. LLHL - 0-3-x x-x-x. NS (134b [134b [14:436L-K]) LL?LH.

7.21   yumizurubukuro < yumi*ᵗ/ᵈ*urubukuro < (*)yumyi*ᵗ/ᵈ*uru*ᵣₐ.ᵢᵢ.ᵣₐ.ₑ* -bukurwo
   < *dumi*ᵣ.ᵣ* (-n-) turu*ᵣᵣ.ᵣₐ* -n- pukurwo*ᵣ.ₑ*. 'bowstring bag'. LLHHHHL - 5-x-x
   x-x-x.

4.5 = 1.3a-n*o*(=2.1)|2.3   [yunoawa] < ˮyu-no-afaˮ (= -awa) < *du*ᵢ.ᵣₐ* no aba*ᵣ.ᵣ*
   ('hot-water foam'). 'sulfur'. LL(|)LL - x-x-x x-x-x.

4.7   (? yunpazu =) ˮyumuhazuˮ < ˮyumufazuˮ < *dum[i]*ᵣ.ᵣ* pansu*ᵣ.ᵢ*. 'bowstring
   notch' (= yumi-hazu x-0-x). LLHH - x-x-x x-x-x. Km x.

3.6   yuoo 'sulfur': *see* ioo.

?2.1 < 3.6   yuri < yuri[y] < *duru-Ci (cf. Azuma sa-yuru no fana, M 4369).
   'lily'. RH (= LHH) - 0-0-A A-B-A. Ib H = 2.1. Nk yuri C. Yn duyu A. *See* §7.1.

4.1   yurugase < yuru*ᵏ/ᵍ*ase < *duru-(n[a]-)ka-sa-Ci[-Ci]*ᵣ*. 'neglected: (～ ni
   suru) neglect, slight'. x - 0-0-A - x-x-x. Cf. irukase. Register incongruent
   with etymology.

4.1/4.10   yusawari < yusa*ᵗ/ᵇ*ari < *dusa*ₘₜₐ* (-n-) par[a-C]i*ₐ*. 'a kind of swing'.
   HHHH (Ir, -f-) / LHLL (Kn, -b-) x-1:4-x x-x-x.

?2.4 < ?3.6   yusi (?< yuusi < *duusi; ?< isu). 'Distylium/Myloxylon racemosum,
   spinous evergreen' (= isu(-no-ki)). RH (= LHH) (1)-x-x x-x-x.

3.5x   yusuru ?< yu-siru < *du*ᵢ.ᵣₐ* siru*ᵣ.ₑ*. 'shampooing and combing the hair'.
   LLH - x-0-x x-x-x.

5.16   yusurubati < *yusuru*ᵣ.ᵣ* (< ...) -n- pati*ᵣ.ᵢ*. 'digger wasp (= anabati).
   so called because its hole resembles the yusuru-tuki, a shampoo jar'. LLLHL -
   x-x-x x-x-x.

3.7b   yutaka < *duta-ka. 'rich' *(adj-n)*. LHL - 1-1:3-B x-B-x. Km x. Hamada 1;
   Sz, Matsue, Izumo, Goka-mura 2; Hattō 3.

3.4   yutori < yu[mi]-tori < *yumyi-t(w)ori < *dumi*ᵣ.ᵣ* t(w)or[a-C]i*ᵣ*.
   'bowstring'. LLL - x-x-x x-x-x.

3.4   yuturi LLL (Zs) = yutori 'bowstring'.

2.1   yuu < yufu < *dupu (< ?). 'paper-mulberry fibers strewn (from the sakaki
   sacred tree as nusa offerings) on Shintō holidays'. HH - 1-2-x x-x-x.

?2.2a   yuu < yufu < *dupu. 'evening'. x - 0/1-2[H]/0[U]-A x-x-x.

?3.4, ?3.6, ?3.7x   yuube < yufube/yofube ?< *dupu*ᵣ.ᵣₐ* -n- ?piCa*ᵣ.ᵣ*. 'last night'.
   LHH (Ir) / LHL (Kz) / HHL (Kn; yofube Kn, Kz) - 3-1-B x-B-x. Edo HHL.
   1700 Ōsaka LHH. Matsumoto, Numazu 3; Aomori 1 *(we expect 2 unless it is*
   /···bi/); Sapporo, Akita, Hattō, Hamada,Izumo, Goka-mura. Wakamatsu, Ōita 1;
   Hakata 1, ygr 3; Matsue 0/1; Narada, Hiroshima 0. Kōchi 1 (H. Doi 1952:24);
   Kameyama 1:4; Toyama 1:2 *(= 3.6/3.1)*; Suzu 0 *(= 3.4/3.1)*: Ib L = 3.6.

6.2   yuutukedori(, yuudukedori, yuutugedori) < yufutuke-dori < *yufu tukey
   -d*o*ri < *dupu*ᵣ.ᵢ* tuka-Ci[-Ci]*ᵣ* -n- t*o*ri*ᵣ.ᵢ* ('bird with paper-mulberry fibers
   attached'). 'chicken (with cotton stuck on it)'. x - 4-5-x x-x-x. Km (W)
   HHHHHL.

5.2   yuwaizuna < yufafi-duna < *dupa-p[a-C]i*ₐ* -n- tuna*ᵣ.ᵣ*. 'a rope (to tie
   someone up with)'. x - x-x-x x-x-x. NS (128a) xxHxx, (Okada) HHHHL.

2.3 = 1.3|1.3   yuya < *du*ᵢ.ᵣₐ* da*ᵢ.ᵣᵦ*. 'bathhouse'. L(|)L - 1-1-x x-x-x.

2.2b   yuzu (?< Ch yew'-'tsyey). 'citron'. x - 1-2-A x-x-x. Km x. Izumo 2: Sz.
   Hattō, Hamada, Matsue 1. Ib ?F = 2.3, ?also H1 = 2.2. JP yu-no-su; cf. yu.

3.5a/b zakuro (< Ch nhyak-.lyew). 'pomegranate'. LLH - 1-2-B x-A-x. Km x.
Aomori, Sz, Narada, Goka-mura, Wakamatsu 1; Matsue. Izumo 0: Hamada 0/1; Numazu
2. Toyama 2 *(we expect 1:3)*; Suzu 1:4 *(we expect 1:3)*: Ib zyakuro H = 3.1.
Nk x; Sr zakura A.

3.4 zasiki < za-sikyi < *za$_{1,x}$ (< Ch dzhwa') sik[a-C]i$_A$. 'matted room'.
x - 3-2-B B-B-x. Km x. Edo HHL. Aomori, Sz, Narada. Hata 3. Kōchi 2 (Doi
1952:24).

2.4 ?< 2.5 zeni (< Ch .dzhyen). 'money'. LH - 1-1-B x-B-B. Km x. 1700 Ōsaka LH.
Izumo 2. Ib L = 2.4. Yn din B. Also seni; cf. kami-^{a}/$_z$eni.

4.11 zen(i)gasa < *zeni$_{g.4}$ (< Ch .dzhyen) (-n-) kasa$_{?g.1}$. 'athlete's-foot,
ringworm, fungus infection'. LLHL - x-x-x x-x-x. Km x.

4.6 zenigata < *zeni$_{g.4}$ (< Ch .dzhyen) (-n-) kata$_{g.gh}$. 'a coin shape/mold:
paper money'. LLLH - 0-0-x x-x-x.

4.10/4.11 zeniuti < *zeni$_{g.4}$ (< Ch .dzhyen) ut[a-C]i$_B$. 'a money-tossing game'.
LHLL (Kn) / LLHL (Ck) - 4-x-x x-x-x.

4.5 zenizura < zeni-^{t}/$_d$ura < *zeni$_{g.4}$ (< Ch .dzhyen) (-n-) tura$_A$ (cf. turanuku). 'a cord for stringing holed coins' (= zeni^a/$_z$asi). LLLL - x-x-x x-x-x.

1.1 zi < di (< Ch 'd(r)hye). 'hemorrhoids'. R - 0-0-A x-A-x. K: Hn LH "?".
Kn has di-no yamafi but also si-no yamafi (Mochizuki 1974:259b, 330a).
Wamyō-shō ti R; Ir ti H (Numoto 1979:28). Aomori, Sz, Hiroshima 0. Ōsaka,
Ise 0; Ib H = 1.1.

1.3a zi < di (< Ch dhi'). 'ground'. L - 1/0-1-B B-B-B. Km x. Aomori, Sz 0:
Hiroshima 1. Ōsaka, Ise 1; Ib L = 1.3.

1.3a zi < di (< Ch dzhyey'). 'written character'. L - 1-1-B B-B-B. Km x.
Aomori 0; Sz, Hiroshima 1. Ōsaka, Ise 1; Ib L = 1.3.

3.4 (?< *4.10) zisyaku (<Ch .dzhyey-zhyak). 'magnet; compass'. RLL (Zs, s-) (?<
*LHLL) - 1-2-A x-B-x. Hamada 1; Aomori, Sz, Hattō, Matsue, Izumo 2.

3.5a zoori < ^{a}/$_z$auri (< Ch 'tshaw-'li). 'straw sandals'. x - 0-0-B x-x-x.
Wamyō-shō LLH (Numoto 1979:27). Aomori, Sz, Hakata 1. Ib zyoori F = 3.4.

?2.5 zuku ?< [mimi]-zuku < *tuku. 'owl'. x - 1-1:3-x x-x-x. NS (97a [11:78-K])
LH. K: Hn LL. Cf. mimizuku, hukuroo.

4.10 zusidama < dusidama: *see* tusidama.

3.6 zyoodo < zyaudo < "ziyaudo" (< Ch .tsheng-.dhung). 'Chinese parasol tree'
(= aogiri). LLHH (= LHH) - x-x-x x-x-x

3.5x zyoogi < "defugi" (Kn), deugi (Ir) ?< *depu (< Ch dhep) -n- kiy (< *ko-
Ci$_{1.3a}$). 'a vertical stick attached to minimize the gap when the two wings of
a double gate or a sliding door are closed'. LLH - x-x-x x-x-x.

2.3 zyuzu (< Ch sriw'-.tšyu). 'rosary beads'. x - 0/2-2-B x-(B)-x. Edo HL.
Sz 2. Ib H = 2.1.

5.10. Supplementary list of nouns.

This list contains nouns which were earlier excluded because of limited data on the accent or for other reasons. They are not included in the statistical profiles.

-     [a] < [w]a < *ba. 'I/me'. NS (T+ 115, kun) a ga L(|)H.
-     [aga]: see [a].
-     agari = mo-[a]gari 'funeral': see honasi-agari.
-     [agi] < agyi (?< [w]a-g[a$_{2.4}$ k]yi[myi$_{2.1}$] 'my prince' or -gyi = -kyi$_{1.x}$ '([my] male'). 'you'. x - x-x-x x-x-x. NS (T+ 29, 35) LH.
- ?2.4   ago < agwo < *[w]agwo < *ba$_{1.3a}$ -n- kwo$_{1.1}$. 'my child; you'. x- 1-2-x x-x-x. NS (T 8, 10]) LH.
-     akadama < *aka$_{adj\ A}$ -n- tama$_{2.3}$ ('red jewel'). 'coral'. x - x-x-x x-x-x. NS (T+ 6) LLH[(register incongruent with etymology).
-     akagoma < akagwoma < *aka$_{adj\ A}$ -n- kwo-ma$_{2.1}$ (< ...). 'red pony'. x - x-x-x x-x-x. NS (T+ 128) LHHH (register incongruent with etymology).
-     amayo < *ama-ywo < *[z]ama$_{2.5}$ dwo$_{1.3a}$. 'rainy night'. x - 2-2-x x-x-x. 1700 Ōsaka HLL. Attested Hn.
-     aokaki < awo-kakyi < *abo$_{adj\ B}$ kaki$_{?2.2a}$ (< ...). 'green hedge'. x - x-x-x x-x-x. NS (T+ 22) LLLH.
-     aoni < awo-ni < *abo$_{adj\ B}$ ni$_{?1.3b}$. 'blue clay'. x - x-x-x x-x-x. NS (T+ 54) LLH.
-     arara ?< ara-[a]ra$_{?4.9}$ (< ...). 'sparse'. x - x-x-x x-x-x. NS (T+ 28) LHH.
-     [ario] < ariwo ?< *ar[a-C]i$_{B}$ bo$_{1.1}$ ('[existent =] veritable hill'). 'a (real) hill'. x - x-x-x x-x-x. NS (T+ 76) LHL.
-     asano < asa$_{adj\ A}$ nwo$_{1.3a}$ ('shallow moor'). x - x-x-x x-x-x. NS (T+ 110) L[H ?= LHH (register incongruent with etymology).
- 3.x   awazi < afadi < *apa$_{2.x}$ -n- ti$_{?1.1}$ ('road to Awa'). 'Awaji' (placename). x - 1-2-B x-x-x.
-     awazisima < afadi$_{3.x}$ (< ...) sima$_{2.3}$. 'Awaji Island' (placename). x - 3-4-B x-x-x. NS (T+ 40) LLH(|)LL.
-     azukisima < adukyi$_{3.2b}$ (< *antuki 'red bean') sima$_{2.3}$. 'Azuki-shima (= modern Shōdo-shima)' (placename). x x-x-x x-x-x. NS (T+ 50) LHH(|)LL.
-     -bi < -biy (? variant of miy < *mo-Ci[-Ci]$_{A}$). 'around, in the bend or vicinity of': fama-biy 'around the beach'; kafa-biy 'around the river, the river bend', cf. kafa-bye = kafa-no-bey/bye 'riverside', woka-biy 'around the hill'; yama-biy 'around the mountain', cf. yamanobye 'Mountainside' (placename) ?= yama-bye (name). Cf. (-)mi, (-)he. See Ch. 2, §3.5.3.
-     ⋯ da-ni < [ta]da$_{?2.4,?2.5}$ (< ...) ni. 'even'. NS (T+ 116) HL; (T+ 107, ["tani"] 127, kun) LH.
-     ⋯ dome: see tome.
-     ⋯ [doti] < ⋯ dwoti ?= *doti < *[tomo]doti (the third vowel assimilated to the first two vowels) < tomodati (< ...). 'companion(s), intimate(s); the group of ⋯ '. x - x-x-x x-x-x. NS (T+ 28) uma-fyito dwoti LL(|)HL LL, (T+ 28b) itwokwo dwoti LLL(|)LL.
-     ⋯ [e] < [w]e < fey < [u]fey (< *upa-Ci$_{2.2a}$. 'atop'. x - x-x-x x-x-x. NS (T+ 107) ifa no [u]fey ni LL L L H.
-     ebosi < ebo[u]si < ye-/yo-bo(u)si < yu (= i$_{*1.3a}$ 'sacred') bousi (< Ch m(b)au'-'tsyey 'hat'). 'a kind of ceremonial cap'. x - 0/1-1[U]/2[H]-B x-x-x. 1700 Ōsaka LHH.

- [esino] ‹ yesi-nwo ‹ yo̲si-nwo. 'Yoshino' *(placename)*. x - x-x-x x-x-x.
NS (T+ 126) myi - yesi-nwo H(|)HL|H.
- hagiri ‹ fa-giri ‹ *fa-gyiri ‹ *pa$_{1.3b}$ -n- kir[a-C]i$_B$. 'grinding one's
teeth'. x - 3-x-x x-x-x. 1700 Ōsaka LHL. First attested Edo.
- hahago ‹ fawago ‹ *fafa-gwo ‹ *papa$_{?2.1,?2.3,?2.4}$ -n- kwo$_{1.1}$. 'esteemed
mother'. x - 0/2-3[U]-x x-x-x. 1700 Ōsaka LHL. First attested Mr.
- hakaze ‹ fa-kaze ‹ *pa$_{?1.2}$ -n- kansa-Ci$_{2.1}$. 'wing-flapped breeze'.
x - 0/1-0[H]/2[U]-A x-x-x. 1700 Ōsaka LHH. First attested Km.
- [hama-bi] ‹ fama-biy: *see* -bi.
- harima ‹ farima ‹ *parima (‹ ?). 'Harima' *(placename)*. x - 1-2-A x-x-x.
NS (70 [11:159-M]) LLH. NS (T+ 45) HHL. K: Edo HLL.
- [haro-^{ʰ}/$_b$aro] ‹ farwo-farwo ‹ *parwo-parwo ?‹ *(the second vowel partially
assimilated to the first)* *paru-paru. 'far off'. x - x-x-x x-x-x. NS (T+ 109)
LH|LH. Cf. haruka.
- [hasa] ‹ fasa (no̲ yama) ‹ *pasa. 'Mt Fasa' *(placename)*. x - x-x-x x-x-x.
NS (T+ 71) H⌊.
- hasigo ‹ fasi-go ‹ *fasi-gwo ‹ *pasi$_{2.2b}$ -n- kwo$_{1.1}$. ladder. x - 0-3[U]/
1:3[H]-A x-(A)-x. 1700 Ōsaka LHL. Ib L2 = 3.5/7. Sr hasi A 'bridge'.
Not attested before Mr.
- hatade ‹ fatade ‹ *pata$_{2.1}$ -n- ta-Ci$_{1.3a}$. x - x-x-x x-x-x. 'edge, edging'.
NS (T+ 87) HL⌊ ?= HLL.
- hatune ‹ fatu-ne ‹ *pa$_{1.1}$ -tu$_{pcl}$ ne[y]$_{1.1}$ (‹*naCi ‹ ...). 'first cry
(crow/peep) of the year'. x - 0-0-A x-x-x. 1700 Ōsaka LHL. Attested Hn.
- hayamati ‹ fayamati ?‹ *pada$_{adj B}$ mati$_{2.2b}$. ?*(placename)*. x - x-x-x
x-x-x. NS (T+ 45) LLLH.
- hazue ‹ fa-zuwe ‹ *pa$_{1.2}$ -n- suwe$_{2.1}$ (‹ ?). 'leaf tip(s); descendants'.
x - 0-0-x x-x-x. 1700 Ōsaka LHL. Attested 10th century.
- [heguri] ‹ fyeguri ?‹ *fyi[r]a-guri ‹ *fyira-go[fo]ri ‹ *pira$_{adj A}$ -n-
ko̲pori$_{3.4}$. '(Mount) Heguri'. x - x-x-x x-x-x. NS (T+ 23) HLH.
- heita ‹ fe-ita ‹ *fey$_{1.1}$ (‹ *paCi) ita$_{2.4}$. 'the plank of a Japanese-type
boat' (= hutate). x - x-x-x x-x-x. 1700 Ōsaka HLL. First attested Edo.
?3.4   hibati ‹ fi-bati ‹ *fiy-bati ‹ *piy$_{1.3b}$ (‹ *po̲-Ci) -n- pati$_{2.3}$ (‹ ...).
'brazier, fire-pot'. x - 1-2-B x-B-x. 1700 Ōsaka HLL. Hakata 2, ygr 1. Ib F =
3.4. First attested Mr.
- higaki ‹ fi-gaki ‹ *fyi-gakyi ‹ *pi$_{1.3b}$ -n- kaki$_{?2.2a}$ (?‹ *kak[a-C]i$_A$).
'a fence woven of cypress laths'. x - 2-2-x x-x-x. 1700 Ōsaka HLL. Attested
10th century.
- hirakata ‹ fyirakata ‹ *pira$_{adj A}$ kata$_{2.2b}$. 'Hirakata' *(placename)*.
x - x-x-x x-x-x. ⌊HH⌊.
- hisakata ‹ fyisa-kata ‹ *pisa$_{?2.4,?2.5}$ kata$_{2.2b}$ or $_{adj A}$. 'eternal-shape'
(fixed epithet for heaven). x - x-x-x x-x-x. NS (T+ 59) ⌊H(|)HL. K: "perhaps
Hn HHHH, Km HHLL".
- hisigara ‹ fyisi-gara ‹ *pisi$_{2.1}$ -n- kara$_{2.2b}$. 'caltrop shell'. x - x-x-x
x-x-x. NS (T+ 36) ⌊HHL ?= HH(|)HL.
- hito-moto ‹ fyito̲-moto̲ ‹ *pito̲$_{?2.4,?2.3}$ mo̲to̲$_{2.3}$. 'one (plant)'. x - x-x-x
x-x-x. NS (T+ 36) LLHL.
- hitome ‹ fito-me ‹ fyito̲ (‹ *pito̲$_{2.2a}$) mey (‹ *ma-Ci$_{1.3a}$). 'the eyes of
men/others'. x - 0-0-x x-x-x. Km (W) HHx, xxH. Edo HHH. 1700 Ōsaka HHL.
- hiuti ‹ *fiy-uti ‹ *piy$_{1.3b}$ (‹ *po̲-Ci) ut[a-C]i$_B$. '(a flint for) striking
a fire'. x - 3-2-x x-x-x. 1700 Ōsaka HLL. K: Hn HHH (where attested?).
- honasi-agari ‹ fo-nasi agari ‹ *po na-si agar[a-C]i. 'secret funeral with
no fire'. x - x-x-x x-x-x. NS (T+ kun) L(|)LL(|)LHH.

- honemi < fone-mi < fone$_{2.3}$ (< ...) miy$_{1.1}$ (< mu-Ci). 'bones and flesh; body'. x - 1/2-0[H]/2[U]-B x-x-x. 1700 Ōsaka HLL. First attested Edo.

- honosusori < fo no suswori (< ...).'rising flames' (Ch 'fall' scribal mistake for 'rise'). x - x-x-x x-x-x. NS (T+ kun) L(|)L(|)LHH.

- [hotoriseri] < fotoriseri < fotori (< *potori$_{3.7a}$) seri$_{2.3+B}$ (< *ser[a-C]i$_B$ < ...). 'beach'. Zs xxLHL (characters "river beach" but Mochizuki omits the first). Cf. modern dial. seri 'end, edge, corner'.

- hotumakuni < fo (< *po$_{1.3b}$) -tu$_{pcl}$ ma-kuni$_{3.x}$ (< ma-$_{?1.1}$ kuni$_{?2.1a,?2.2a}$). 'true country of rich crops'. x - x-x-x x-x-x. NS (T+ kun) L(|)L(|)HHH.

- huname < funa-mye < *puna$_{2.4}$ miCa$_{1.3b}$ (< ...). 'crucian-carp woman' (= ?).

- [huru] < furu < *puru. 'Furu' (placename). x - x-x-x x-x-x. NS (T+ 94) HH.

- [huse] < fuse (?← se$_{1.1}$ [wo] fu$_B$ (< ...). 'passing shoals'. x - x-x-x x-x-x. NS (T+ kun) HH. Imitation of Chinese syntax? Cf. [hutu].

- hutomani < futwomani < *futwo$_{adj B}$ (< ...) mani$_{?2.1}$. 'scapulomancy'. x - x-x-x x-x-x. NS (T+ kun) HL|ℓH (incongruent).

- hutonorito < futwonoritwo < futwo$_{adj B}$ (< ...) nori-two. 'a mighty prayer'. x - x-x-x x-x-x. NS (T+ kun) HL|LHH (incongruent).

- [hutu] < fu-tu ?← tu$_{1.3a}$ [wo] fu[ru]$_{?B pred}$ (< *pa(-)Ci-u). 'passing port'. x - x-x-x x-x-x. NS (T+ kun) RL ?= H|L (or really R|L = HL|L). Imitation of Chinese syntax?

- [hutu] < futu < *putu (mimetic) 'swishing' (cf. hutu-ni): hutu no myi-tama (god name) x - x-x-x x-x-x. NS (T+ kun) HL(|)L|HHℓ.

- [ihurisahe] < ifuri-safye < *ipuri (< i$_{1.3a}$ pur[a-C]i$_A$ 'gallbladder-shaking') sap(y)e (last vowel partially assimilated to first) < sapi$_{?2.4,?2.1}$ ('spade'). 'a kind of spade'. x - x-x-x x-x-x. NS (T+ kun) LLL|ℓH.

- [ihuya] < ifu-ya < *ip[a$_A$]-u$_{attr}$ da$_{1.3b}$. ? 'a (tale-)teller'. x - x-x-x x-x-x. NS (T+ kun) LLL (incongruent).

- iki < ikyi < *iki. 'Iki (Island)' (placename). x - 1-2-A x-x-x. NS (T+ 99) HL.

- ikuri ?< (the last vowel partially assimilated to the first two) *ikure < *i[si]-kure$_{?4.1}$ (< ...). 'shoals'. x - x-x-x x-x-x. NS (T+ 41) HHL.

- [imaki] < ima-kiy < *ima$_{2.4}$ kiy$_{?1.3a}$ (< ?). 'Fort Ima' (placename). x - x-x-x x-x-x. NS (T+ 116) LℓH, (T+ 119) LLH.

- imoi < imo-wi < *imwo-wi[y] < *imwo$_{?2.4,?2.5}$ wi[y]$_A$ (< *b^u/$_o$-Ci). 'conjugal sex'. x - x-x-x x-x-x. 1700 Ōsaka HLL. First attested Edo.

- imose < imo$_{?2.4,?2.5}$ (< imwo) se$_{?1.3a}$ (< ...). 'wife and husband; sister and brother'. x - 1/0-0-x x-x-x. Km (W) LHH. 1700 Ōsaka LHH. Attested Hn.

- inamusiro < ina$_{2.4}$ musiro$_{3.4}$. 'ricestraw-mat' (fixed epithet). x - (3)-(4)-x x-x-x. NS (T+ 83) LLHLL. K: Hn LLLLH (where attested?).

- inasa (< ?). '(Mount) Inasa' (placename). x - (0)-x-x x-x-x. NS (T+ 12) LLL.

- ira-tu- (?← iro$_{?2.3,?2.2b}$ -tu$_{pcl}$ 'of the same mother'): ~ ko < kwo$_{1.1}$ 'esteemed male'; ~ me < mye$_{1.3a}$ (< ... 'esteemed female' NS (T+ kun) HL|H(|)H.

- iroka < *iro$_{2.3}$ ka$_{1.1}$. 'color and fragrance; sexy appearance; strong scent; appearance; complexion'. x - 2-2-B x-x-x. 1700 Ōsaka HLL. Attested 900s.

- isati ?< *i-swo$_{2.x}$ (< ...) ti$_{?1.2}$ (< *ti[y] < *tu-Ci) ('fifty cogons'). (name). x - x-x-x x-x-x (T+ 29) LHH.

- isikawa < isi-kafa < *isi$_{?2.2a}$ kapa$_{2.2b}$. 'stony river'. x - x-x-x x-x-x. NS (T+ 3) HHHH.

- isikoridome < isikori-dwomye < *isi-kori$_{4.x}$ (< *isi$_{?2.2a}$ kor[a-C]i$_{?A}$ 'stone-freeze') -n- twomye$_{2.x}$ (< ... glossed 'granny'). (goddess name). x - x-x-x x-x-x. NS (T+ kun) HLLL|HH.

-     isimura < *isi$_{?2.2a}$ mura$_{2.1}$. 'a heap of stones'. x - x-x-x x-x-x.
NS (T+ 19) LLHL.
-     [isomi] < iswo miy (M 3954, 3961) 'around the rock/beach'': _see_ -mi.
-     isu ?< iswo$_{2.1}$. 'rock'. x - x-x-x x-x-x. ? NS (T+ 7) isu kufasi 'the rock
is fine' _(epithet for whale)_ LL LLL (register incongruent with etymology).
-     isunokami < isunokamyi ?< *iswo$_{2.1}$ no kami$_{2.4}$ ('atop the rocks').
(placename). x - x-x-x x-x. NS (T+ 94) LLLHH (register incongruent).
-     itatwo < ita$_{2.4}$ two$_{1.1}$. 'plank door'. x - x-x-x x-x-x. NS (T+ 96) LLF.
-     [ituhe] < itufey < itu$_{2.3}$(?< i$_{*1.3a}$ -tu$_{pcl}$ fey$_{1.1}$ (< *pa-Ci). 'jar for
sacrificial wine'. x - x-x-x x-x-x. NS (T+ kun) LL(|)H.
-     iwakura < ifakura < *ipa$_{2.2b}$ kura$_{2.2b}$. 'firm seat'. x - x-x-x x-x-x.
NS (T+ kun) ama no ifakura LL(|)L HHHL.
3.1   iware < ifare < *ipa-ra-Ci[-Ci]$_A$. 'what is said; reason'. Hxx - 0-0-A
x-A-x.
-     iware < ifare (? = iware$_{3.1}$). _(name of a pond)_. NS (84a [17:125-M] HLL;
NS (T+ 97) HHH.
-     iyatiko (?< iya$_{?2.1}$ tika$_{adj B}$). _(adj-n)_ 'clear, manifest'. x - 0-0-x
x-x-x. NS (T+ kun) LLLH.
-     izumo < idumwo (< ?). 'Izumo' _(placename)_. x - 1-1:3-A x-x-x.
NS (T+ 1, 20) LHL. K: Mr-Edo HHH.
-     kaburi ?< *kabur[a-C]i$_B$ (< *kanpu$_{2.3}$ -ra-Ci). 'head'. x - 1/3-0-B x-x-x.
1700 Ōsaka LHH. First attested Edo.
-     kabusi < *kanpu-s[a-C]i$_B$. 'the cast (shape/looks) of the head or face'.
x - x-x-x x-x-x. NS (T+ kun) LLH.
-     kage-hime < kagey$_{2.5}$ (< ...) fyimye$_{2.2b}$ (< ...). ? 'princess of the
bright shadow'. x - x-x-x x-x-x. NS (T+ 92) HL|HL (register incongruent),
(T+ 94) LH(|)HH.
-     kagututi < _(2d vowel assimilated to 3d)_ *kagatuti < *kaga$_{2.5}$ -tu$_{pcl}$
ti$_{?1.1}$. 'spirit of light = god of fire'. x - x-x-x x-x-x. NS (T+ kun) FHHH.
-     kaguyama < *kank[a$_A$]-u$_{attr}$ dama$_{2.3}$. _(mountain name)_. x - 0-x-x x-x-x.
NS (T+ kun) FHHL ?= HHHL.
?2.1   [kai] < kafi < kafiy < *kap^u/$_o$Ci (< ?). 'Kai' _(placename)_. x - 1-2-x
x-x-x. NS (80a [14:340-M], 14:341-M] HH; NS (T+ 81) LH. K: "Hn-Km HH".
Hakata 1. Ib H2 = 2.2. The usual etymology (< kafyi 'valley') has incongruent
vowels; cf. Igarashi 49 n.4.
?3.1   kakera < kake[y]$_{2.1}$ (< *kaka-Ci[-Ci]$_A$) -ra (< *[a]ra$_{2.3+B}$). 'fragment,
shard, splinter' (= kake). x - 0-0-A x-(A)-x. Aomori 0. Ib F = 3.4. Sr kaki A.
-     kakimoto < kakyi-moto < *kaki$_{?2.2b}$ (< ...) moto$_{2.3}$. 'under the fence/
hedge'. x - x-x-x x-x-x. NS (T+ 13, 14) HL|HH (the second element is
incongruent with the etymology).
-     kakumiyadari < kakumyi-yadari ?< *kakumyi-yadori _(the next-to-last vowel
assimilated to preceding vowel)_ < kakumyi$_{*3.1}$ (< *kaku-m[a-C]i$_A$) yadori$_{3.4}$ (<
*da$_{1.3b}$ -n- t(w)ora-$_B$. ' ? '. x - x-x-x x-x-x. NS (T+ 49) HLHHH (odd pattern).
-     kakunomi < kakunomiy < ka[gufasi$_{adj A}$]-ku no miy$_{1.1}$. '(fragrant fruit =)
mandarin orange'. x - x-x-x x-x-x. NS (T+ kun) HL(|)L|H. (Also kaku no ko-no-
miy.)
-     [kamira] < kamyira < *ka$_{1.1}$ mira$_{2.3}$. '(smelly) leek'. x - x-x-x x-x-x.
NS (T+ 13) HHL.
-     kamugakari < *kamu$_{2.3}$ -n- kaka-r[a]-Ci$_B$. 'possession by a spirit'.
x - x-x-x x-x-x. NS (T+ kun) LH|LHL.
-     [kamuhosaki] < kamu-fosakyi < *kamu$_{2.3}$ posaka-$_B$. 'praying to the gods'.
x - x-x-x x-x-x. NS (T+ kun) HL|HHL.

-        kanaki < kana-kiy < *kana$_{2.1}$ k $\underline{o}$ -Ci$_{1.3a}$. 'crossbar for the door of a horse
stable'. x - x-x-x x-x-x. NS (T+ 115) HHH.

-        kanatwo < *kana two. 'entry gate with metal fittings'. x - x-x-x x-x-x.
NS (T+ 72) LLH.

-        karakaki < kara-kakyi < *kara$_{2.5}$ kaki$_{?2.2b}$ (< ...). 'Korean-style fence
(= mud wall)'. x - x-x-x x-x-x. NS (T+ 88) HL|HH (incongruent with etymology).

-        karama (NS T+ kun) LLL: kara-ma no fatakey 'Korea ··· (= ?) field'.

-        karano < *kara-nwo ?< *kara[-Ci]-$_A$ nwo$_{1.3a}$ ('parched moor') ← *karu$_{adj}$ $_{?A}$
nwo$_{1.3a}$ ('easy moor [to reach]'); on the etymological confusion see Tsuchihashi
1976:365). x - x-x-x x-x-x. NS (T+ 41) LLH (incongruent with etymology).

-        kariba < kari$_{?2.4<2.3}$ (< *kar[a-C]i$_{?B}$) ba$_{1.3a}$ (?< - n- pa, ...). 'hunting
place'. x - 0/3-0-x x-x-x. 1700 Ōsaka LHH. Not attested before Edo?

-        karu ?< *karu$_{adj}$ $_A$. (placename). x - x-x-x x-x-x. NS (T+ 71) karu wotomye
HL|HHH (second element incongruent).

-        [kata-huti] < kata-futi < *kata$_{?2.3}$ puti$_{2.4}$. 'side (= deep) pool'.
x - x-x-x x-x-x. HL|HH (the second element is incongruent with the etymology).

-        kataoka-yama < katawoka-yama < kata-woka$_{4.x}$ (< *kata$_{?2.3}$ woka$_{2.1}$ (< ...)
yama$_{2.3}$ (< *dama$_{2.3}$). (mountain name). x - x-x-x x-x-x. NS (T+ 104) HL|HL|HL
(incongruent with etymology).

-        katasiwa < katasifa < *kata$_{adj}$ $_A$ -si$_{pred}$ [i]pa$_{2.2b}$. 'hard rock'. x - x-x-x
x-x-x NS (T+ kun) LLLL (incongruent).

-        katatati < *kata$_{?2.3}$ tat[a-C]i$_B$ ('stand to one side'). ?= katai ('beggar;
leper'). x - x-x-x x-x-x. NS (T+ kun) LHHL.

-        (···) ka wa. (exclamatory particles). x - x-x-x x-x-x. NS (T+ kun) L(|)L.

-        [kawa-bi] < kafa-biy: see -bi.

-        [kawamatae] < kafa-mata (< *kapa$_{2.2b}$ mata$_{2.3}$) ye$_{?1.1}$ (< ...).
?(placename), ? 'inlet at river fork'. x - x-x-x x-x-x. NS (T+ 36) LHLL|H
(the initial register is incongruent with the etymology).

-        [kazuno] < kadunwo ?< *kadu[ra]-nwo < *kadura$_{2.2b}$ (< *kantura) nwo$_{1.3a}$.
(placename). x - x-x-x x-x-x. NS (T+ 34) LHH.

1.3a   [ke] < key ?(variant development) < *k $\underline{o}$ -Ci$_{1.3a}$ (> kiy > ki). 'tree(s)'.
NS (T+ kun) L. See mike.

-        kemi < kenmi (< ...). 'inspecting; inspector'. x - 0/1/2-2-x x-x-x.

?2.1, ?2 2   kena. 'Kena' (placename). NS (17:276-M kena n $\underline{o}$) HH-L, (T 98) HL.

-        kenmi < ken (< Ch 'ngiem) mi (< myi[y] < *mida-Ci$_B$) ('test look').
'inspecting; inspector'. x 0/1-x-x x-x-x. 1700 Ōsaka LHL.

?2.1   [kezu] < keydu (< ?). 'Kezu' (name). x - x-x-x x-x-x. NS (T 105) HH.

-        kitasi < kyitasi ?< *kitasi[-sifwo] < *kitas[a-C]i$_?$ sipwo$_{2.3}$. 'salt that
has been smoked black and hard (to rid it of bitterness)'. x - x-x-x x-x-x.
NS (T+ kun) LLH. On the putative verb *kitasu 'harden' (?< katasu), cf. kitai
and (Ch. 6) kitaeru.

?1.1   ko < kwo (?< Ch kho'). 'gown'. x - x-x-x x-x-x. NS (T+ kun) k $\underline{o}$ romo n $\underline{o}$
kwo HHH(|)L H.

-        kodati < *kwo-dati < *kwo$_{1.1}$ -n- tati$_{2.3}$ (?< tat[a-C]i$_B$). 'dagger'.
x - 1-1-x x-x-x. 1700 Ōsaka LHH. First attested Mr.

-        kogoe < *kwo-gowe < *kwo$_{1.1}$ -n- k $\underline{o}$ we[y]$_{2.3}$ (< *k $\underline{o}$ wa-Ci < ...). 'a low/
quiet voice'. x - 0-0-B x-(x)-x. Edo HHH. 1700 Ōsaka LHH. Sr gumaguti B.
First attested Mr.

-        k $\underline{o}$ g $\underline{o}$ to (< ?). ' ? '. x - x-x-x x-x-x. NS (T+ kun) k $\underline{o}$ g $\underline{o}$ to musu-fyi
HHH HHL 'spirit of ? '. Cf. k $\underline{o}$ tog $\underline{o}$ to; but perhaps k $\underline{o}$ g $\underline{o}$ is a reduplication
of ko[ù] < Ch .hyeng') + to$_{pcl}$.

-      [kohada] < kwofada (< ?). *(placename)*. x - x-x-x x-x-x. NS (T+ 37) HHH, (T+ 38) HLH (odd).
-      kokisi < k<u>o</u>kiy-si ?< *k<u>oko</u>-Ci$_{?2.3}$ -si$_{suf\ or\ pcl}$. 'lots, much/many'. x - x-x-x x-x-x. NS (T+ 7) LHL. Cf. kokono(-tu) 'nine'.
-      kokonoka < k<u>o</u>kono$_{?3.5}$ (< *k<u>oko</u>$_{2.3}$ no$_{pcl}$) -ka$_{?1.3a}$. 'nine days'. x - 4-4-x x-x-x. Sz 4. Hakata 0, ygr 0/4. Attested 1592.
-      kokono-yo < k<u>o</u>kono$_{?3.5}$ (< *k<u>oko</u>$_{?2.3}$ no$_{pcl}$) ywo (< *dwo$_{1.3a}$). 'nine nights'. x - x-x-x x-x-x. NS (T+ 26) LLLH.
-      ko-ra < kwo-ra < *kwo$_{1.1}$ [a]ra$_{*2.3+B}$. 'children; sons; lads'. x - 1-2-x (A)-(A)-(A). NS (T+ 67, 103) H(|)L, (T+ 9, 13, 14) HH. K: Hn HH.
-      [kosima-ko] < kwosima-kwo < *kwo-sima$_{?*3.1}$ (< *kwo-$_{1.1}$ sima$_{2.3}$ 'little island') + kwo$_{1.1}$ ('child'). *(name)*. x - x-x-x x-x-x. NS (T+ kun) HH█|H.
-      kosode < *kwo-swode < *kwo$_{1.1}$ swo^t/de$_{2.1}$ (< ...). 'a (small-sleeved) robe'. x - 0/1-2-x x-x-x. 1700 Ōsaka HLL. K: Edo HLL.
-      kotatu ?< Ch dial. version of 'hwa - thap(-'tsyey). 'a quilt-covered hearth'. x - 0-1-B x-x-x. 1700 Ōsaka LHH. First attested Mr.
-      k<u>o</u>t<u>o</u> *(adv)*. 'similarly, likewise'. x - x-x-x x-x-x. NS (T+ 67) HH. Cf. adjective goto-.
-      [kotodo] < k<u>o</u>t<u>o</u>-dwo < *k<u>oto</u>$_{?2.5}$ ('different') -n- two$_{1.x}$. 'a prayer to rid oneself of wife'. x - x-x-x x-x-x. NS (T+ kun) koto-["]two HH-H (the register is incongruent with the etymology).
-      k<u>o</u>t<u>o</u>g<u>o</u>t<u>o</u> < *k<u>oto</u>$_{2.3}$ n[i] k<u>oto</u>$_{2.3}$. 'everything, all'. (x) - 1-2-x x-x-x.
-      k<u>o</u>t<u>o</u>saka < *k<u>oto</u>$_{2.3}$ saka-$_A$. 'severing relations'. x - x-x-x x-x-x. NS (T+ kun) LL(|)HH.
-      [ku(h)i] < kufyi ?< *kup[a-C]i$_B$, ?< Ch 'khu-.bhye ('painful skin'). 'the itch; scabies; ringworm'. x - x-x-x x-x-x. NS (T+ kun) LL.
-      kukunoti < kuku$_{2.3}$ no ti$_{?1.1}$. 'god of plants/trees'. x - x-x-x x-x-x. NS (T+ kun) HHHL (register incongruent with etymology). Cf. kuki.
-      kumade < *kuma$_{2.3}$ -n- ta-Ci$_{1.3a}$ ('bear paw'). 'a (bamboo) rake'. x - 0/1-1:3-B x-x-x. Edo LHL. 1700 Ōsaka LHL.
-      kumade < *kuma$_{?2.3\ <\ 2.1}$ -n- te$_{1.3a}$ (< *ta-Ci). 'a preternatural world, the next world' or 'a place/road with many twists' (Ōno chooses the latter interpretation, and seems to treat te as < ti$_{1.1}$ 'road' rather than 'hand = direction'). x - x-x-x x-x-x. NS (T+ kun) H██.
-      [kumami] < kuma miy (M 886) 'around the corner, the bend': *see* -mi.
- ?2.3   kume < kumey < *kumaCi (< ?). 'Kume' *(surname)*. x - 1-x-x x-x-x. NS (T 7, 13, 14) LL.
-      kumoi < kumwo-wi < *kumwo$_{2.3}$ b█/$_o$-Ci[-Ci]$_A$ 'cloud[-seat]'. x - x-x-x x-x-x. NS (T+ 21) LL(|)H.
-      kurazi < *kura$_{2.3}$ -n- si[(-)ta$_{2.2a}$]. 'below the storehouse'. x - x-x-x x-x-x. NS (T+ kun) LLH.
-      kurazi < kuradi < *kuta-nti (?< *kura$_{2.3}$ m[i]ti, ?< *kura$_{2.3}$ -n- ti$_{?1.1}$). 'bridge to the storehouse'. x - x-x-x x-x-x. NS (T+ kun) HL|H.
- ?3.4   kurumi (?< kure$_{2.1}$ miy (< *mu-Ci) 'China fruit'; ?< kurwo$_{adj\ B}$ miy$_{1.1}$ 'black fruit'; ?< kuru[-Ci]$_{2.3}$ miy$_{1.1}$ 'chestnut fruit'). 'walnut'. x - 3/0-<u>1:3</u>[U]/2-B x-x-x. Aomori [kuruб̃i] 3. Ib F = 3.4. K: Hn LLL (attested?).
- ?3.4   kusanagi < kusa-nagyi < *kusa$_{2.3}$ nanku-Ci/nankwo-Ci$_{?A/B}$. 'mowing grass'. NS (T+ kun) kusa-nagyi no turugyi *(name of a sword)* L█HL LLL ?= LHH(|)L LLL.
-      kusimitama < kusi-myitama < ku-si$_{adj\ x}$ mi-tama$_{3.1}$. 'a spirit possessing wondrous powers'. x - x-x-x x-x-x. NS (T+ kun) LL H(|)L█.

-     kusizasi < *kusu-Ci*2.3* -n- sas[a-C]i*B*. 'skewering; staking, putting a stake into/through; staking claim to another's land'. x - 0/3-0-x x-x-x. NS (+ kun) HL|HH (incongruent).
-     kutuma (< ?). 'humpback' (= kuguse, segutu, kutuse, semusi). x - x-x-x x-x-x. NS (T+ kun) LHL ?= LHH.
-     kutuse (1124 text of Shinsen-Jikyō) < kutu (< ?) se*1.2* (< s*o*). 'humpback' (= segutu, kuguse, kutuma, semusi).
-     ⋯ made ?< mate < *ma (-n-) te[y] (< *ta-Ci*1.3a*) — see Ch. 2, §3.6. *(particle)*. x - 1-1-B x-(A)-x. NS (T+ kun) umasi made LLL HH.
-     [mahorama] < maforama < *ma-fwo (< *ma-*?1.1* pwo*1.3a* 'true grain') -ra (< *[a]ra*2.3+B* ma*1.1*. 'place of bountiful harvest' (= mafworoba K 31). x - x-x-x x-x-x. NS (T+ 22) LHHL.
-     [makurae] < makura[w]e < makura*3.5a/b* (< ...) fye*1.x* (< *piCa). 'at one's pillow/head'. x - x-x-x x-x-x. NS (T+ kun) LHL|H.
-     [makuzu-hara] < *makuzu-fara < *ma-kunsu*3.x* (< ma-*?1.1* kunsu*2.5* ('arrowroot field'). *(placename)*. x - x-x-x x-x-x. NS (T+ 128) LHHHL.
- ?2.1   mani. 'a magic spell, an incantation'. x - x-x-x x-x-x. *See* hutomani. Cf. mazi, Skt maṇḍala = mantra.
-     mari-ya < *mari*2.3* da*1.2*. 'a kind of arrow'. x - x-x-x x-x-x. NS (T+ 28) HHL (incongruent with etymology).
-     masaka, masakatu < *masa*2.5* kat[a*B*]-u. *(god name)* 'Correct-Victory' or 'Sure-Victor'. x - x-x-x x-x-x. NS (T+ kun) LHL, LHLL.
-     masakari < ma-*?1.1* sakari*3.1* (< *saka-r[a-C]i*A*). 'the very midst, right then'. x - x-x-x x-x-x. NS (T+ kun) LLHL (incongruent): myiru masakari ni, a poor translation of the Chinese phrase meaning 'in the instant that one looks back' (cf. Nakata); Ōno suggests masa-ka-ri 'true-place-direction' but that hardly helps.
-     [ma-soga] < ma-swoga < *ma-*?1.1* swonka*?2.4*. 'worthy Soga'. x - x-x-x x-x-x. NS (T+ 103) LHH.
-     matubara < *matu*2.4* -n- para*2.3*. 'pine field'. x - 2-2-x x-x-x. NS (T+ 28) LHHL.
-     [mayobiki] < maywo-byikyi < *madwo*?2.5* (< ...) -n- pik[a-C]i*A*. 'eyebrows painted in (after plucking)'. x - x-x-x x-x-x. NS (T+ kun) LH(|)HL.
-     mayuge < mayu*?2.5* -ge (< -n- key*?1.1* < *ka-Ci). 'eyebrow'. x - 1-1[U]/1:3[H]-B x-B-x. Sz 2. Nk x; Sr mayugii B. First attested Edo.
- ?2.1   mazi < *mansi ?< *man[i] si (< *seCi-[Ci]*A*). 'an incantation, a magic spell' (= mazi-mono/-waza). x - x-x-x x-x-x. Cf. mazinau; mazikoru < mazi-k*o*ru 'get spellbound (fascinated, bewitched)'; mani; Skt maṇḍala = mantra.
-     menuki < *mey (< *ma-Ci*1.3a* nukyi (< *nuk[a-C]i*B* 'gap pierce'). 'an ornamental piece of metal placed under the frapping of a sword-hilt'. x - 1/3-0-x x-x-x. 1700 Ōsaka HLL. Attested Ir.
-     meoto = meotto (JP) < *mye-woto < mye*1.3b* (< *miCa ?= mina) wotto*3.1* (< wofuto/wofyit*o* < *bo*1.1* pit*o*2.2a*). 'wife and husband'. x - 0-1-x x-x-x. 1700 Ōsaka LHH. First attested 12th century.
-     mezasi < *mey-zasi < *ma-Ci*1.3a* -n- sas[-aC]i*B*. 'a child's (forelock) haircut; a child'. x - 0-1-B x-x-x. Attested c. 900.
-     [mezurako] < meydura-kwo < meydura[-si-]*adj B* (< ...) kwo*1.1*. *(name)*. x - x-x-x x-x-x. NS (T+ 99) LHL|H.
-     [mi] < myi < [u]myi < *umi. 'sea; lake'. x - x-x-x x-x-x. NS (T+ 30, 31) afumyi no myi 'Lake Ōmi' LRH-L|H.

-       ... [mi] < miy < *mo-Ci[-Ci]ₐ. 'around, in the bend of ...': iswo miy 'around the rock/beach', kuma miy 'around the corner/bend', satwo miy 'around the village', suswo miy 'around the skirt of the mountain', ura miy 'around the bay'. Cf. -bi < -biy, (-)he < fye. *See* Ch. 2, §3.5.3.

-       [mibu] < myibu (< ?). ?'caretaker for a noble family's children'. x - x-x-x x-x-x. NS (T+ kun) HH.

-       miburi < *miy-buri < *miy$_{1.1}$ (< *mu-Ci) -n- pur[a-C]iₐ. 'gesture; stance, appearance'. x - 1/0-1[U]/0[H]-A x-x-x. 1700 Ōsaka HLL. First attested Edo.

-       migoto < *myi-goto < *myi[y]$_B$ (< *mida-Ci) -n- koto$_{2.3}$. 'a sight (worth seeing); splendid(ly)'. x - 1-2-B x-x-x. 1700 Ōsaka HLL. First attested Mr?

-       [miho] < myi-fo < *mi$_{?1.1}$ pwo$_{1.3a}$. 'three ears of grain'. x - x-x-x x-x-x. NS (T+ kun) HH.

-       [mikasio] < myi-ka$_{2.1}$ (< *mi-$_{?1.1}$ -ka $_{?1.3}$ sifo$_{2.3}$ (< sifwo < *sipwo). 'third-day tide'. x - x-x-x x-x-x. NS (T+ 45) HHHH.

?2.2   [mike] < myi-key ?< *mi$_{?1.1}$ ko-Ci$_{1.3a}$. 'tree(s)'. x - x-x-x x-x-x. NS (T 24) H# ?= HL.

-       mimata < myi-mata < *mi[na]$_{2.1}$ mata$_{2.3}$. 'fork(ing) of the water/stream' (= minamata). x - x-x-x x-x-x. NS (T+ kun) HH(|)L.

-       [mime] < myi-mye < *mi-$_{?1.1}$ (< ...) miCa$_{1.3a}$ (?= *mina). 'lady; empress; "probably the name of an island"'. x - x-x-x x-x-x. NS (T+ kun) #H = HH.

-       mimoro < myi-moro *(the last vowel assimilated to the preceding vowel)* < *mi- mori$_{2.1}$. '[wooded mountain] place where a god descends, sacred hill' = mi-muro < *mi-$_{?1.1}$ (< ...) murwo$_{2.3}$. x - x-x-x x-x-x. NS (T+ 97) HHH.

-       [minabe] < myi-na["]fey < *mi-$_{?1.1}$ nanpa-Ci-$_{2.5}$ (< ...). 'a deep round pottery bowl'. x - x-x-x x-x-x. NS (T+ kun) #-LH ?= H|LH.

-       misoka < *myi-swo$_{2.2b}$ ((< ...) -ka$_{?1.3a}$. 'thirty days; the last day of the month'. x - 0-0[H]/2[U]-A x-x-x. Sz 0.

-       [misumaru] < myi-sumaru = myi-subaru < *mi-$_{?1.1}$ sunpa-r[a]-uₐ. 'necklace'. x - x-(0)-x x-x-x. NS (T+ 2) HHHH, (T+ kun) HL#H ?= H|LLH.

-       [mimusu[w]i] < myi-musufyi: *see* musu[w]i.

?1.1   miti 'sea lion' (= asika). x - x-x-x x-x-x. NS (T+ kun) HH.

-       mituba < *myitu-ba < *mi$_{1.1}$ -tu?$_{1.1}$ -n- pa$_{1.2}$. 'three-leafed; lonewort, stone parsley'. x - 1-1-B x-x-x. Km (W) HHH. 1700 Ōsaka LHH.

-       [mitu-guri] < myitu-guri < *mi$^{⊥}$$_{?1.1}$ -tu?$_{1.1}$ -n- kuru-Ci$_{2.3}$. 'triple chestnut' *(epithet)*; cf. mikuri. x - x-x-x x-x-x. NS (T+ 35) HHHH.

-       miwa < myiwa < *miba. 'Miwa' *(placename)*. x - 1-x-x x-x-x. NS (T 16, 17) ## = ?.

-       miyake < *myi-yakey < *mi-$_{?1.1}$ daka-Ci$_{?2.3}$ (< ...). 'imperial field/ granary/granary-keeper'. x - x-x-x x-x-x. NS (T+ kun) #HH ?= HHH, HLL ?= H|LL.

-       [mizuwa] < myidu-fa < myitu-fa (?< mi -tu fa ?< *mi[na] tu pa < ... , ?< [a]myi -tu fa < *am[a-C]i$_B$ -tu pa, ?< [u]myi -tu fa < *umi$_{2.4}$ -tu pa). 'god of water/sea'. x - x-x-x x-x-x. NS (T+ kun) HLL. ~ no mye ?'Neptune's wife', ?'goddess of water/sea'.

-       [mogari] < m[o]-agari < *mo?$_{1.1}$ anka-r[a-C]iₐ. '(placing in) a temporary coffin (for the mourning period before entombment)' — also called arakiy < 'new fortress (= coffin)'. x - x-x-x x-x-x. Cf. [honasi-agari].

-       mogusa < *mo[ye$_{2.3}$] (< *moda-Ci-Ci$_B$) -n- kusa$_{2.3}$. 'mugwort (= yomogi); moxibustion powder'. x - 0/3-2-A x-x-x. 1700 Ōsaka HHL. Aomori 0. Ib H2 = 3.2. Cf. moyogi, moegi; moeru.

-       monosiro < mono-siro < *mono$_{2.3}$ siro$_{2.1}$. 'material, substance, stuff, ingredients'. x - x-x-x x-x-x. NS (T+ kun) #LHH = LL(|)HH.

-       morakumo < murakumwo *(first vowel partially assimilated to second)* < murakumwo < *mura(-)$_{2.1}$ kumwo$_{2.3}$. 'massed clouds'. x - x-x-x x-x-x. NS (T+ kun) HL|LH (odd).

-       moyura-ni < mo-yura ni < *mo-$_{pre}$ (?< *ma-$_{?1.1}$) dura$_A$ ni$_{pcl}$. 'tinkling (like jewels)'. x - x-x-x x-x-x. NS (T+ kun) HLL|H. *See* nunato.

-       [mugo[w]e] < mugwofye (< ?). ? *(name)*. x - x-x-x x-x-x. NS (T+ kun) HL|H.

-       [mukasakeru] < mukasakey- < *muka$_A$ saka-Ci-$_{?A}$. 'be off in the distance'. x - x-x-x x-x-x. NS (T+ 99) muka sakuru (attr.) HH|LHH.

-       muki < mukiy (< ?). 'mulberry'. Cf. Korean melwu < mel'Gwu 'wild grapes'.

-       murakumo < murakumwo < *mura(-)$_{2.1}$ kumwo$_{2.3}$. 'massed clouds'. x - x-x-x x-x-x. NS (T kun) HL|HL (odd). Variant morakumwo.

2.x   mure ?< *mura-Ci, ?< Korean *mwo'lih > :mwoyh > mey. 'mountain'. x - (1)-x-x x-x-x. *See* omure, ⋯ .

-       musu-hi < musu-fyi < *mus[a$_{?A}$]-u$_{attr}$ pi$_{1.x}$. 'generative spirit'. x - x-x-x x-x-x. NS (T+ kun) k̲o̲g̲o̲t̲o̲ musu-fyi HHH HLL; myi- musu-fyi H(|)HL(|)L.

-       mutuki ?< *mutu[byi$_A$ - tu]kiy$_{2.3}$ (< ...), ? < *mu$_{1.1}$ ('fruit') tukiy$_{2.3}$ (< *tuku-Ci 'month'). 'the first lunar month'. x - 1-2-A x-x-x. 1700 Ōsaka HLL. Attested Hn.

-       nabito < nabyit̲o̲ < *na$_{1.1}$ (-n-) pito$_{2.2a}$. 'you'. x - x-x-x x-x-x. NS (T+ kun) L(|)HL.

-       [nahitoyahamani] < nafyit̲o̲yafamani < *na$_{1.1}$ (-) pito$_{2.21}$ + ?. x - x-x-x x-x-x. NS (T+ kun) LLHLL̲F̲LH ? = LLH|L LL|H (*na-fyit̲o̲ ya faba [= fafa] ni 'you [being] like your mother', cf. Zdb 530a). The NS gloss is '[meaning] unknown'. Cf. nabito.

-       nakado < *naka-dwo < *naka$_{2.4}$ (< ...) -n- two$_{1.1}$. 'the door between'. x - 1-x-x x-x-x. 1700 Ōsaka HLL. First attested Mr.

-       nakai < naka-wi < *naka$_{2.4}$ wi[y]$_A$ (< *b^u/$_o$-Ci-Ci). 'parlormaid; ... '. x - x-x-x x-x-x. 1700 Ōsaka LHL. First attested Mr.

-       nakume < naku-mye < *nak[a$_A$]-u$_{attr}$. 'weeping woman'. x - x-x-x x-x-x. NS (T+ kun) LLR ?= LL|H (incongruent).

-       nanimo < *na$_{1.3x}$ n[o̲] imwo$_{?2.4,?2.5}$. 'you beloved woman' or 'my beloved woman' *(said by man)*. x - x-x-x x-x-x. Cf. nase.

-       nanorisomo < nan̲o̲ri-s̲o̲ (?< *na$_{1.2}$ - n̲o̲r[a-C]i$_A$ so (< Ch 'tsaw)) mo$_{?1.1}$. 'sargasso (seaweed)'. x - x-x-x x-x-x. NS (T+ kun HLHLL (odd). Variant *(second vowel assimilated to first)* nanari-s̲o̲.

-       [narabi-hama] < narabyi-fama < *naranp[a-C]i$_A$ (< ...) pama$_{2.3}$. ? 'Double Beach' *(placename)*. x - x-x-x x-x-x. NS (T+ 48) LLHHH.

-       nase < *na$_{1.3}$ se$_{?1.3a}$ (< ...). 'you beloved man' or 'my beloved man' *(said by woman)*. x - x-x-x x-x-x. NS (T+ kun) a-ga na-se 'you beloved man of mine' L(|)H L(|)H (last part odd); this example casts doubt on interpreting na- as 'my'. Cf. nanimo.

-       [nazu] < nadu < *nantu$_{?*2.3}$. 'brine-soaked'. x - x-x-x x-x-x. NS (T+ 41) nadu no LH(|)L. Cf. nazuku, nazusau.

-       nekaze < *ne[y]$_A$ (< *na-Ci) -n- kaze[y]$_{2.1}$ (< *kansa-Ci). 'a cold caught while asleep'. x - x-x-x x-x-x. 1700 Ōsaka HLL. First attested Edo.

1.x   ni < *ni[y] < *nu-Ci. 'jewel, gem'. *See* nuboko, nunato.

-       [nigihayahi] < nigyi-faya-fyi < *ninki$_{2.x}$ pada$_{adj\ B}$ pi$_{1.2}$. *(name)* 'Vigorous-Rapid-Sun' *(name)*. x - x-x-x x-x-x. NS (T+ kun) HH(|)LL-L.

-       nigite < nikyite < *niki$_{2.1}$ (?< *nikwo) ta-Ci$_{3.1a}$. 'rag (later paper) offerings strewn from branches at shrines'. x - x-x-x x-x-x. NS (T+ kun) LLH (incongruent). Nakata doubts that -te is a contraction of tafye 'bark-cloth'.

-     [niibari] ‹ [niwibari] ‹ nifyibari ‹ *nipi$_{2.1}$ -n- par[a-C]i$_B$ ('newly opened [well]'). *(placename).* x - x-x-x x-x-x. NS (T+ 25) HᵻHH = HHHH.
-     niki-mitama ‹ *nikyi myi-tama ‹ *niki$_{2.1}$ mi-$_{1.1}$ tama$_{2.3}$ (› mi-tama$_{3.1}$). 'gentle spirit'. x - x-x-x x-x-x (NS T+ kun) HHHLL = HH | H|LL.
-     nikita-tu ‹ nikyita tu ‹ *niki$_{2.1}$ ta$_{1.3a}$ tu$_{1.3a}$ ('gentle-field port'). *(placename).* x - x-x-x x-x-x. NS (T+ kun) HLL|H.
-     [nikode] ‹ nikwo-de ‹ *nikwo$_{?2.1}$ -n- ta-Ci$_{1.3a}$. 'soft hands'. x - x-x-x x-x-x. NS (T+ 108) HH(|)L.
-     nogami ‹ *nwo$_{1.3a}$ -n- kami$_{2.3}$. 'unkempt hair'. x - x-x-x x-x-x. 1700 Ōsaka LHH. First attested Edo.
-     ··· nomi ‹ nomiy ‹ ... . 'only'. NS (T+ 66) LH.
- ?3.1   norito ‹ noritwo ‹ nor[a-C]i$_A$ two$_{1.x}$. 'Shinto prayer'. x - 0-0-x x-x-x. *See* hutonorito.
-     notori ‹ no-tori ‹ *no$_{1.3b}$ tor[a-C]i$_B$. 'bear(ing) a burden'. x - x-x-x x-x-x.
- 1.x   nu(-). 'jewel': nu-Ci › ni[y] › ni. *See* nuboko, nunato.
-     [nuboko] ‹ nu-ᶠ/ᵇoko ‹ *nu$_{1.x}$ (-n-) poko$_{2.3}$. 'a bejeweled halberd'. x - x-x-x x-x-x.
-     nunato ‹ nuna-[o]to ‹ *nu$_{1.x}$ na$_{pc1}$ oto$_{2.2b}$. 'the sound of jewels, gem-like sound(s)': nunato mo mo-yura ni 'with even/also jewel-like music tinkling' x - x-x-x x-x-x; NS (T+ kun) LLH H HLL|H.
-     nunawa ‹ nunafa ?‹ *nu$_{1.3b}$ na$_{pc1}$ pa$_{1.2}$ ('marsh leaves'). 'water-shield, Brasenia purpurea/peltata'. x - x-x-x x-x-x. NS (T+ 36) LLL. K: "perhaps Hn LLL, Km HHL".
-     obasi ‹ wobasi ‹*wo-$_{?1.1}$ (‹ ...) -n- pasi$_{2.2b}$. 'little bridge'. *See* saobasi.
-     oguna ‹ woguna ‹ wo-$_{1.1}$ (‹ *bo 'male') + -guna (= ?). 'boy'. x - x-x-x x-x-x. NS (T+ kun) LHH (incongruent).
-     [oi-isi] ‹ ofiy-isi: *see* ooisi ‹ ofo-isi.
-     [okabe] ‹ woka-bye = woka-fye (M 9, 1751: semantograms). 'near the hill'. x - x-x-x x-x-x.
-     [okabi] ‹ woka-biy: *see* -bi.
-     okami ‹ okamyi (‹ ?). *(name of rainmaker god).* x - x-x-x x-x-x. NS (T+ kun) LHH.
-     okasaki ‹ wokasakyi ‹ woka$_{2.1}$ (‹ ...) sakyi (‹ *saki). 'promontory of a hill'. x - x-x-x x-x-x. NS (T+ kun) HH(|)HH.
-     oki-he ‹ okyi-fye ‹ *oki$_{2.3}$ piCa. 'offshore, (in) the offing'. x - x-x-x.
-     okime ‹ okyimey ‹ ... . *(name).* x - x-x-x x-x-x. NS (T+ 86) LLH.
-     oko ‹ wokwo (K 45) 'stupid': *see* uko.
-     omae ‹ [w]oma[w]e ‹ womafye ‹ wo-$_{?1.1}$ mafye (‹ ...). *(name).* x - x-x-x x-x-x. NS (T+ 72) LLH.
-     omoide ‹ omofyi-de ‹ omofyi$_{3.4}$ (‹ *omop[a-C]i$_B$) ide[y] (‹ *inta-Ci[-Ci]$_B$). 'a memory, remembrance'. LLHH (Zs), LLxL (Kn) - 0-0-x x-x-x.
-     omokururu-ni ‹ womo-kururu ni (‹ ?). *(mimetic)* 'rumbling along'. x - x-x-x x-x-x. NS (T+ kun) LL-HLL|ni.
-     omonoki ‹ omo-no-kiy ‹ *omo$_{2.x}$ no ko-Ci$_{1.3a}$ ('mother's tree'). *(placename).* x - x-x-x x-x-x. NS (T+ kun) HH-H(|)L.
-     omure ‹ wo-mure ‹ wo-$_{1.1}$ (‹ ...) mure$_{2.x}$ (‹ ...) ('little mountain'). *(placename).* x - x-x-x x-x-x. NS (T+ 116) LHH.
-     onabe ‹ wo-nabye ‹ wo-$_{?1.1}$ (‹ ...) nabye (= nabey ‹ ...). 'small pan'. x - x-x-x x-x-x. NS (T+ kun) L-LH (incongruent).

- onawa < wo-nafa< *bo_{?1.3b} napa_{2.3}. 'hemp rope; sisal'. x - x-x-x x-x-x.
1700 Ōsaka HLL. Attested 9th century.
- ooanamuti < ofoana-muti (= ofo[a]na-muti) < *opo_{adj B} ana_{2.3} muti_{2.x}
('esteemed great hole'). (god title). x - x-x-x x-x-x. (NS T+ kun) LL(|)LHHH.
- [oobako] < of_oba-kwo < *opo_{adj B} -n- pa_{1.2} kwo_{1.1} ('large-leaf child').
(name). x - x-x-x x-x-x. NS (T+ 100, 101) LHH(|)H.
- [oohirumenomuti] < ofofyirumye-no-muti < ofo_{2.4} (< *opo_{adj B}) fyiru-
mye_{3.1,3.2x} (< *piru_{2.2a} miCa_{1.3b}) no muti_{2.x} (?< *mutu-Ci) ('Great Daylight
Lady'). (goddess title). x - x-x-x x-x-x. NS (T+ kun) LHHL|H | L | HH.
- ooisi < ofoisi < ofo-isi < *opo_{adj B} isi_{2.2b}. 'large stone'. x - x-x-x
x-x-x. NS (T+ 8) LHHL. (The phonograms have also been interpreted as ofiy-isi.)
- ookara < ofokara < ofo kara < *opo_{adj B} kara_{2.5} ('great "Han"').
(placename). x - x-x-x x-x-x. NS(T+ kun) HHLL (incongruent).
- ookita < ofokyita (?< ofo-kyi ta_{1.3a}). (placename; ?= later ooita
'Ōita'). x - x-x-x x-x-x. NS (T+ kun) LHL(|)L.
- oomi < afumyi < *apumi . 'Ōmi' (placename). x - x-x-x x-x-x.
NS (T+ 30, 31, 86) LHH, (98) LLH.
- oomononusi < ofomono-nusi < ofo-mono_{4.5} (< *opo_{adj B} mono_{2.3})
nusi_{?2.4,?2.5}. (god name). x - x-x-x x-x-x. NS (T+ 15) LLLLL.
- oomuroya < ofo-murwoya < ofo_{adj B} (< *opo) murwo-ya_{3.x} (< *murwo_{2.3}
da_{1.3b}. 'large chamber, hall'. x - x-x-x x-x-x. NS (T+ 9) LL(|)HHH.
- oosaka < ofo-saka < *opo_{adj B} saka_{2.3}. 'Ōsaka' (placename). x - 0-0-A
x-x-x. NS (T+ 64) LLHH, (T+ 18) HL|HH (incongruent with etymology).
- ootati < ofo-tati < *opo_{adj B} tati_{2.3} (< ...). 'large sword'. x - x-x-x
x-x-x. NS (T+ 89) HL|LH ?← *LL|LH.
- oote < *ofo-te[y] < *opo_{adj B} ta-Ci_{1.3a}. 'the front of a fortress'.
x - 1-2-x x-x-x. 1700 Ōsaka HLL. K: Edo HLL. First attested Mr.
- ore (?< o[no]re_{?3.2x,?3.1} < ... , ?< [s]ore_{2.1} (< ... — cf. Ryūkyū
quri). 'you; (later) I/me'. x - (0)-0-A (x)-(x)-x. NS (T+ kun 'you') HH.
- osaka < *os[i]-saka < *osi_{?2.2x} saka_{2.3}. (placename, later Ossaka).
x - 1-x-x x-x-x. NS (T+ 9) LHH.
- osaka < wo-saka < wo-_{?1.1} (< ...) saka_{2.3}. 'small slope'. x - 1-x-x
x-x-x. NS (T+ 50) LLH.
- osao < [w]osa[w]o < wosafo ?< *wo-_{?1.1} safo (< sapo_{2.x} 'red clay').
(placename). x - x-x-x x-x-x. NS (94) LHL.
?2.2x   osi (< ?). 'Oshi' (placename). x - 1-x-x x-x-x. NS (T 106) HL. Cf. osaka.
- osinumi < osinumyi < *osi_{?2.2x} n[o] umi_{2.4}. 'Lake Oshi' (placename).
x - x-x-x x-x-x. NS (T+ 84) LL(|)LH.
- otakebi < wotakyebiy < wo-_{1.1} (< *bo) takye-biy_{?3.4←B} (< ...). 'a manly
show/shout, a war-cry (war-hoop), bravado'. x - x-x-x x-x-x. NS (T+ kun) LLHL,
LLLL (register incongruent).
- otode (?< ofotono < *opo_{adj B} tono_{2.3}). 'mansion; master'. x - 1/0-(1:3)-x
x-x-x. 1700 Ōsaka LHH. K: Edo 1:3. First attested 10th century.
- oto-tanabata < oto-_{2.3} tana-bata_{4.2} (< ...). '(lovely) weaver-maid'.
x - x-x-x x-x-x. NS (T+ 2) HL(|)LLLL.
- owari < wofari ?< *wo-_{?1.1} (< ...) par[a-C]i_{?B} ("small cultivation").
'Owari' (placename). x - x-x-x x-x-x. NS (T+ 27) LLH.
- oyazi < oya-di < *oda_{2.3} -n- ti[y]_{?1.3a} (< *to-Ci). 'father'. x - 0/1-2-B
x-x-x. 1700 Ōsaka HLL. First attested Edo.
- ozasa < wo-zasa < *wo_{?1.1} (?< *bo, ?< *[k]wo) -n- sasa_{2.1}. '(a kind of
small bamboo)'. x - 1-2-x x-x-x. 1700 Ōsaka HLL. Not attested before Mr?
- -ra (plural): see ko-ra, se-ra, sizue-ra, ...

-     sabaama < saba*ma* *2.x* ama*2.3*. 'noisy fisher(s)'. x - x-x-x x-x-x.
NS (T+ kun) HL|LL. Cf. sabameku = zawameku, sawagu.
-     sabae < sabafey < *sa-*?1.1* -n- papaCi*2.1*. '(buzzing) summer flies'.
x - x-(2)-x x-x-x. NS (T+ kun) HL*F* ?= HLL. K: Km HLL (where attested?).
-     ··· sae < safey < ··· . 'even ··· '. x - 1-2-x x-x-x. NS (T+ 99) HL.
-     sagiri < sa-giyri < *sa-*1.x* -n- kuCiri*2.1*. 'light fog, mist'. x - 0/2-0-x
x-x-x. NS (T+ kun) HHH.
-     sagume < sagu-mye ?< sagu[ru*A*] (< ?) mye*1.3a* (< *miCa) ('groping female').
(goddess name). x - x-x-x x-x-x. NS (T+ kun) HL|H.
-     sakabito < saka-byito < *saka*2.1* -n- pito*2.2a*. 'wine steward'.
x - x-x-x x-x-x. NS (T+ kun) HH(|)HL.
-     [sakae] < sakaye < *saka-*A* ye*1.2* (< ...). 'a luxuriant branch'.
NS (T+ 78) sakaye wo *F*LHL ?= HL|H|L.
-     sakamoto < saka-moto < *saka*2.3* moto*2.3*. 'bottom of the slope'.
x - (0)-x-x x-x-x. NS (T+ kun) LL(|)LL.
-     sakanokori < sakanokori < *saka*adj* *-si B* nokori*3.4* (< nokor[a-C]i*B*).
? 'wise/splendid bequest'. x - x-x-x x-x-x. NS (T+ kun) HH|LLH (first element
incongruent).
-     sami < sa-miy < sa-*?1.1* mu-Ci*1.1* ('true body'). 'blade'. x - x-x-x x-x-x.
NS (T+ 2) HL.
-     sanedoko < sa-*?1.1* ne-doko*3.2b* (< ...). 'bed'. x - x-x-x x-x-x.
NS (T+ 4) HHHH.
-     saobasi < sa-wobasi < sa-*?1.1* wo-basi*3.x* (<*wo-*?1.1* (< ...) -n-
pasi*2.2b*). 'little bridge'. x - x-x-x x-x-x. NS (T+ 24) H|LHH.
-     sasaragata < *sasara*3.7a, ?3.1* (< ...) -n- kata*2.2b*. 'small pattern'.
x - x-x-x x-x-x. NS (T+ 24) HLL|HL.
-     [satomi] < satwo miy (M 1243: semantograms): *see* -mi.
-     sawabe < *safabye < *safa (< *sapa*2.1*) -n- fye*1.x* (?< piCa ?= *pina).
'around a swamp'. x - 0/3-x-x x-x-x. 1700 Ōsaka HLL.
-     sayageri < sayagyeri ?< sayagyi ari (< *sada-n[a]-k[a-C]i*?B* ar[a-C]i*B*.
'murmur, rustle; noise'. x - x-x-x x-x-x. NS (T+ kun) HL(|)LH.
-     saya-saya < *sada-sada. *(mim)* 'rustling'. x - x-x-x x-x-x. NS (T+ 41).
-     saziki < sazuki < sazukyi < *sansuki ?= san (< Ch 'dzhryan 'frame')
suk[a-C]i*A* ('prop' cf. sukeru). '(temporary) stand, box, gallery, balcony'.
x - x-x-x x-x-x. NS (T+ kun) HHL.
-     segutu (Shinsen-Jikyō) ?< se*1.2* (< so) -n- kutu (< ?); ?← kutuse (< ...).
'humpback' (= kutuse, kutuma, kuguse, semusi). x - x-x-x x-x-x.
-     semusi < se*1.2* musi*1.1* ('back bug'). 'humpback' (= segutu, kutuse, kutuma,
kuguse). x - 0/3-1:3-A x-x-x.
-     serihu ?< seri*B* - [i]fu*A* (< ...), ?< seri*B* - [a]fu*B* (< ...). 'words,
lines'. x - 0/2-2[H]/1:3[U]-B x-x-x. 1700 Ōsaka LHL. First attested Edo.
-     seta ?< se*1.1* (< ...) ta*1.3a* ('shoal/rapids ricefield'). 'Seta'
(placename). x - 1/0-x-x x-x-x. NS (T+ 29, 30) *F*L.
- ?2.4   seto < setwo ?< se*adj* *x* (?< *sa*adj* *A* -Ci-) two*1.1*. 'narrow door'.
x - 1-(2)-x x-x-x. NS (T 3) LH. K: Hn LH.
- 4.1   si-kabane < *si (?< Ch; ?< si[ni] < *sin[a-C]i*B*) kabane*3.1* (< ...).
'corpse' (= kabane). x - 0-0-A x-x-x. Sz 0.
-     simada < *sima*2.3* -n- ta*1.3a*. 'the Shimada hair style'. x - 0[H]/1-0[H]/
1:3[U]-B x-x-x. (?) 1700 Ōsaka HLL.
-     [simami] < sima miy (M 3991): *see* -mi.
-     siose < si[w]o-se < sifwo-se < *sipwo*2.3* se*1.1* (< ...). 'tidal rapids'.
NS (T+ 87) LLH.

-     sirakasi ‹ sira(-)*2.3* kasi*?2.5‹2.3*. 'white oak'. x - x-x-x x-x-x.
NS (T+ 23) HHLL (incongruent).
-     sirikumenawa ‹ sirikumey-nafa ‹ siri-kumey (‹ *siri*2.3* + ?) napa*2.3*.
'sacred rope' (= simenawa). x - x-x-x x-x-x. LLLL(|)LL. The second element may
be ‹ *kumey- ‹ *kuma-Ci- = *kuma-*B* 'braid', though that derived stem seems to
be otherwise unattested.
-     sisikusiro̲ ‹ *sisi-kusi*?4.5* (‹ *sisi*2.3* kusi*2.3*) -ro̲*set*. 'a skewer of
boar-meat, boar-kebab'. NS (T+ 96) HHHHHH (incongruent).
-     sisiriko ‹ sisirikwo ‹ sisi*2.3* [i]ri (‹ *ir[a-C]i*A*) kwo*1.3a*. 'meat
basket'. x - x-x-x x-x-x. NS (T+ kun) LLLL.
-     sitanaki ‹ sita-nakyi ‹ *sita*2.2a* nak[a-C]i*A*. 'weeping to oneself'.
NS (T+ 69) HH|LH (second element incongruent), (T+ 71) LH|LH (incongruent).
-     sitorigami ‹ sitworigamyi ‹ *sitwori*?3.4* (‹ situ-wori*?*4.5* ?‹ si[ma*2.3*]
-tu*pcl* bor[a-C]i*B*) -n- kamiy*2.3* (‹ *kamu-Ci). (god name). x - x-x-x x-x-x.
NS (T+ kun) LLL(|)LH.
-     sizue-ra ‹ sidu-ye ‹ *si[ta*2.2a*] -n- -tu ye*?1.2* (‹ ...) -ra (‹ *[a]ra*B*).
'lower branches'. NS (T+ 35) LHH|L.
?2.4   soga ‹ swoga ‹ *swonka (‹ ?). (surname). x - 0-x-x x-x-x. NS (T 103) LH.
-     sokoi ‹ *soko̲*2.1* i (‹ Ch ye̲y'). 'underlying motive'. x - 0/2-0[U]/2[H]-A
x-x-x. Attested JP.
-     sonata ‹ *so̲*1.1* [-no̲ ka]ta*2.2b*. x -1/2-2-x x-x-x. 1700 Ōsaka HHL.
Attested 10th century.
-     subiki ‹ *su-byikyi ‹ *su-*?1.3a* -n- pik[a-C]i*A*. 'drawing an empty bow;
... '. x - 0/3-1-x x-x-x. 1700 Ōsaka LHL.
-     suga ‹ *sunka (?‹ *su-*1.3a* -ka*1.x* 'pure place'). (placename). x - x-x-x
x-x-x. NS (T+ kun) HL.
-     sugaru ‹ *sunkaru (‹ ?). 'mud dauber, digger wasp; deer'; (name).
x - 0/1-0-x x-x-x. Km (W) 'deer' HHH. NS (T+ kun) (name) LLH.
3.x   sukuna (‹ ?). (god name). NS (T+ 32) LHL.
-     sukune ?‹ sukun[a]*3.x* ye*?1.2* (‹ ... 'older sibling'), ?‹ *sukune[y]
‹ *sukuna-Ci*3.x*. 'sukune' (a title affixed to the names of ministers).
NS (T+ 29) LLH, (T+ 72) FLL.
-     [susomi] ‹ suswo miy (M 3985, with semantogram M 1758): see -mi.
-     susori ‹ suswori ?‹ su-*1.3a* swori (‹ *swor[a-C]i*B*). 'a rise, rising'.
x - x-x-x x-x-x. NS (T+ kun) fo̲ no̲ suswori L(|)L | LHH (god name).
Koji-ki suseri (o → e in assimilation to the environment /s···ri/).
-     susunomi ‹ susuno̲myi ?‹ susu-[ma-*A*] no̲*pcl* mi*1.3a* (? 'advancing spirit').
'raging, rampaging': susonomi-di ‹ ... -n- ti*1.x* (?‹ *tuCi ?= *turi). 'a wild(ly
jumping) fish-hook' (= sosuno-di) x - x-x-x x-x-x; NS (T+ kun) LLLHH.
-     [sutahe] ‹ sutafey ‹ *suta-[Ci-]*?A* pa-Ci*?1.1* ('discard door/hearth').
'coffin'. x - x-x-x x-x-x. (NS T+ kun) LLL (incongruent).
-     tabide ‹ *tabyi-de ‹ *tanpi*2.2b* n[i] [in]ta-Ci-Ci*B*. 'departure for a
journey'. x - 3-x-x x-x-x. 1700 Ōsaka LHH. First attested Edo.
-     tabizi ‹ tabi-di ‹ *tabyi-di ‹ *tanpi*2.2b* -n- ti*?1.1*. 'the path of a
journey'. x - 0/2-0-A x-x-x. 1700 Ōsaka LHL. First attested JP.
-     tagimati ‹ tagyima-ti ‹ *tankima (‹ ?) ti*?1.1*. 'the road to Tagima'.
x - x-x-x x-x-x. NS (T+ 64) HLLL.
-     tagosi ‹ ta-gwosi ‹ *ta*1.3a* -n- kwos[a-C]i*A*. 'passing on by hand, carrying
over'. x - x-x-x x-x-x. NS (T+ 19) LHL.
-     takabi ‹ takabyi: see takami ('sword handle').

- takahasi < taka-fasi < *taka*adj B* pasi*2.2b* ('tall bridge'). *(placename).*
x - x-x-x x-x-x. NS (T+ 94) LHHH (incongruent).
- takami < takamyi < *ta*1.3a* kami*2.4*. 'sword handle'. x - x-x-x x-x-x.
NS (T+ kun) LLF ?= L(|)LH. Also (Heian confusion) takabyi.
- takamuna-saka < taka-muna*?4.x* (< *taka*adj B* muna*2.2b*) saka*2.3*. 'the
breast/chest (of a supine body)'. LL(|)HH(|)FL ?= LL-HH | LL - x-x-x x-x-x.
- takuziri < ta-kuziri < *ta*1.3a* kuziri (< koziri < konsir[a-C]i*B*.
'a crudely scooped-out clay pot'. x - x-x-x x-x-x. NS (T+ kun) L-LHL.
- tanakami < ta-na-kamyi < *ta*1.3a* na*pcl* (? *assimilated* < n<u>o</u>) kami*2.4*
('field top'). *(placename).* x - x-x-x x-x-x. NS (T+ 31) L(|)L(|)LH.
- tatamikomo < tatamyi-kom<u>o</u> < *tatami*3.1* (< ...) kom<u>o</u>*2.1* 'straw matting'.
x - x-x-x x-x-x. NS (T+ 23) LLHHH (incongruent).
- tatanami < tatanamyi < *tata*?2.4,?2.5* nam[a-C]i*?A*. a line of shields'.
x - x-x-x x-x-x. NS (T+ kun) LLLH.
- tatisoba < tati-s<u>o</u>ba < *tat[a-C]i*B* s<u>o</u>npa*?2.5,?2.4* (< ...). 'standing
buckwheat'. x - x-x-x x-x-x. NS (T+ 7) LH|LH.
- tatukai < ta-tukafyi < *ta*1.3a* tukap[a-C]i*3.1←A*. 'supervisor (of the
far-off fields)'. x - x-x-x x-x-x. NS (T+ kun) LHLL.
- tatutu = tatudu < *tatu-[i]du < *tat[a-C]i*B* ind[a-Ci]-u*B pred*. 'a kind
of dance that involved standing up and then sitting down'. x - x-x-x x-x-x.
NS (T+ kun) LHH.
- tayu-ma (Tsuchihashi) = taye-ba (Ōno) < taye[y]-ba < *tada-Ci[-Ci] -n-
pa*pcl*. x - x-x-x x-x-x. NS (T+ 46) LL-F. Manuscripts differ on the second
character, but Ōno's interpretation seems better for the context.
- tazuna < ta-duna < *ta*1.3a* -n- tuna*2.3*. 'reins'. x - 0-2-B x-B-x.
Sr tanna B. Edo HHL. 1700 Ōsaka HHL. Attested Ir.
- tedori < *te[y]-dori < *ta-Ci*1.3a* -n- tor[a-C]i*B*. 'catching bare-handed;
capture; ... '. x -0/3-1[U]/2[H]-x x-x-x. 1700 Ōsaka HLL. First attested Mr.
- tegata < *te[y]-gata < *ta-Ci*1.3a*-n- kata*2.2b*. 'hand shape/print; bill,
note'. x - 0-1[H]/2[U]-B x-x-x. Edo HLL. 1700 Ōsaka HLL. First attested Edo.
- tihayahito < tifaya-fyit<u>o</u> < *ti*?1.1* pada*adj B* pit<u>o</u>*2.2a*. 'men quick of
spirit' (epithet for Uji). x - x-x-x x-x-x. NS (T+ 42, 43) LHL|HL (first
element incongruent?).
- tihiro ← ti[w]iro (JP) < ti-firo < *ti*1.3a* (?< *t<u>o</u>-Ci) ?piro. '1,000
fathoms; very long'. x - 1-0[H]/1[U]-A x-x-x. 1700 Ōsaka LHL. Attested NS.
- ti^k/gusa < ti-kusa < *ti*1.3a* (?< *t<u>o</u>-Ci) kusa*2.3*. 'many kinds, various'.
x - 1-1:3-x x-x-x. 1700 Ōsaka LHL. Attested early Hn.
- tin<u>o</u>ri < ti-n<u>o</u> [i]ri < *ti*?1.3a* (?< *ti[y] < t<u>o</u>-Ci) n<u>o</u>*1.3a* ir[a-C]i*A*
('a thousand arrowshafts enter'). 'a quiver with many arrows in it'.
x - x-x-x x-x-x. NS (T+ kun) LLL.
- tinu. 'black porgy (from the waters off Chinu, southern Izumi)'.
x - x-x-x x-x-x. NS (T+ kun) tinu *(read tinwo in Ōno 1953)* HH.
- tisuzi₁ < ti₁-sudi < *ti*1.1* sunti*2.4* (< ...). 'blood vessel, vein'.
x - 1[H]/0-2-A x-A-x. 1700 Ōsaka HLL. Sr ciişizi A. First attested Mr.
- tisuzi₂ < ti₂-sudi < *ti*1.3a* (?< *t<u>o</u>-Ci) sunti*2.4* (< ...). 'many tendons/
threads/hairs'. x - 1/2-x-x x-x-x. 1700 Ōsaka LHL. First attested Edo.
- titabi < *ti*1.3a* (?< *t<u>o</u>-Ci) tanpi*2.2b*. 'a thousand times; frequently'.
x - 1/2-2-x x-x-x. 1700 Ōsaka HLL. K: Edo LHL. Attested Hn.
- titihaha ← titi-fawa (JP) < titi fafa < *titi*2.4* (?< *t<u>o</u>-Ci t<u>o</u>-Ci)
papa*?2.1; ?2.3, ?2.4*. 'father and mother'. LH|LL (Kn), LH|LH (Ck) - 2-1:3-B
x-x-x.

-     ti^t/$_z$uka < *ti$_{1.3a}$ (?< *to-Ci) (-n-) tuka$_{?2.4, ?2.3}$. 'a thousand bunches; lots'. x - x-x-x x-x-x. 1700 Ōsaka LHL. First attested Edo.

2.3   tiyo < ti-yo < *ti$_{1.3a}$ (?< *to-Ci) do$_{1.1}$. 'a thousand years/generations'. x - 1-2-B x-x-x. NS (T 102) LL. K: Hn LL.

1.x   (-)to < two. 'words'. *See* norito, [kotodo], [tokoido]. Etymology unknown; cf. tou < twofu < *two(-)pa-$_A$; togou < togofu < *tokopa-.

2.x   tobe < twobye < *two$_{1.1}$ -n- fye$_{1.x}$ (?< *piCa) ('door vicinity'). 'Mr/Ms' *(title attached to name)*. Cf. [toe], tome; tozi.

-     todana < *two$_{1.1}$ -n- tana$_{2.1}$. 'cupboard, closet, wardrobe'. x - 0-0-A x-x-x. 1700 Ōsaka HHL. First attested Edo.

-     [toe] < [towe] < two-fye < *two$_{1.1}$ fye$_{1.3x}$ (?< *piCa (< 'door vicinity'). ? 'at the gate', ? 'wife'. x - x-x-x x-x-x. NS (T+ kun) HL. *Or is this* two[¨]fye = tobye?

-     [tohi-u] < twofyi-u < twofyi (written 'inquire' but perhaps a pun for 'rabbit-skin' < Ch tho' .bhye) u$_{?1.3a}$. 'Cuscuta japonica, a kind of dodder' (= ufona). NS (T+ kun) LLH. Cf. [uhona].

-     tokkuri (= tokuri). 'wine bottle'. x -0-3(=2)-B-x x-x-x. 1700 Ōsaka HLL. First attested Mr.

-     [tokobe] < toko[¨]fye (M 4331) < toko$_{2.1}$ (-n-) piCa$_{1.x}$. 'bedside' (= [tokonobe]). *See* Ch. 2, §3.5.3.

-     [tokoido] < [tokowido] < tokofyi-dwo < *tokop[a-C]i$_A$ -n- two$_{1.x}$. ? 'imprecation'. (Ōno: "togofyidwo".) Cf. togou.

-     [tokonobe] < toko-no-bye (K 34, M 904, M 3927) < *toko$_{2.1}$ no piCa$_{1.x}$. 'bedside' (= [tokobe]). *See* Ch. 2, §3.5.3.

2.x   tome < twomye < *two$_{1.1}$ miCa$_{1.3a}$ ('door woman'). ? (1) 'a woman, mistress of a house' (cf. tozi); (2) = tobe < twobye 'Mr/Ms' *(title attached to name)*. Cf. isikoridome.

-     tonoto < tono-two < *tono$_2$. two$_{1.1}$. 'palace gate'. x - x-x-x x-x-x. NS (T+ 16, 17) HL|H.

-     toriyama < tori-yama < *tori$_{2.1}$ dama$_{2.3}$ ('bird mountain'). *(name)*. x - x-x-x x-x-x. NS (T+ 52).

-     tozi < twozi < *two$_{1.1}$ n[u]si$_{2.4}$ ('house-owner'). 'the mistress (lady) of the house; lady, woman; wife'. x - x-x-x A-A-(A). NS (T+ kun) HH. Sd thudyi A, Sr tuzi A. Unclear whether Yn tun A is from this or from tuma.

-     tunosasi < tunwosasi < *tunwo$_{2.3}$ sas[a-C]i$_B$. x - x-x-x x-x-x. NS (T+ 84) LL$^\blacksquare$L.

-     tutuki < tutu-kiy < tutu$_{2.1}$ kiy$_{?1.3a}$ (< ?). *(placename)*. x - x-x-x x-x-x. NS (T+ 55) HHH.

?2.4   uda ?< *u$_{?1.3a}$ -n- ta$_{1.3a}$ ('rabbit field'). 'Uda' *(placename)*. x - 1-x-x x-x-x. NS (T 7) = LH.

-     [uhona] < ufona < *upona (?< *u$_{?1.3a}$ pwo$_{?1.2}$ na$_{1.3a}$ 'rabbit-top/-ear plant'). 'Cuscuta japonica, a kind of dodder' (= twofyi-u). NS (T+ kun) HHL. Cf. [tohi-u].

-     uka (= uke) 'food': uka no myi-tama 'spirit foods; rice' NS (T+ kun) HH(|)L LL$^\blacksquare$; uka no mye '(Food Woman =) goddess of rice' NS (T+ kun) LL(|)L L.

-     ukai < u-ka[w]i < u-kafyi < *u$_{1.2}$ kap[a-C]i$_B$. 'cormorant keeper'. x - x-x-x x-x-x. NS (T+ 12) HHH.

-     ukati ?< *uka-ta-Ci-[Ci]$_{?B}$ *(so glossed)*. *(name of a village, modern Ukashi)*. x - x-x-x x-x-x. NS (T+ kun) ukati no mura LHL(|)L HL.

?2.3   uke < ukey < *uka-Ci (?= *uka-Ci$_{2.3\leftarrow B}$ 'receipt'). '*food (cf. uka, ke$_{1.3a}$ 'meal'); 'grain container, rice basket' (cf. ke$_{?1.2, ?1.1}$). x - x-x-x x-x-x. NS (T+ kun) LL 'grain container'.

?3.4   ukei < uke[w]i < ukeyfyi < *uka-Ci-pa-Ci*ʙ* (or ...). 'praying (for prognostication), consulting the gods to resolve a dispute/rivalry'. x - x-x-x x-x-x. NS (T+ kun) ukeyfyi no myi-naka 'the (esteemed) midst of consulting the gods' HLH(|)L LLH (odd).

-         ukeigari < uke[w]igari < ukeyfyi-gari < ukeyfyi*?3.4* -gari (< *-n- kar[a-C]i*?ʙ*). 'resolving a dispute by seeing how the gods reward rival hunters'. x - x-x-x x-x-x. NS (T+ kun) LLꟼHL = LLL(|)HL.

-         ukemoti < ukey (<*uka-Ci[-Ci]*ʙ* mo̱t[a-C]i*ʙ*). 'receiving and keeping (food)': ukey-moti no̱ kamiy (T+ kun) HHHL(|)L LL (first element incongruent).

-         ukimizo (Mochizuki 80b) HL|HH (Ck 2:9b:5), probably better treated as two entries (the original text has a line break), as indicated by the accent pattern: uki*?2.2x* 'bog', mizo*2.1a* 'ditch'.

-         ukina < ukyi ('float', associated with u-kyi*adj attr* 'sad ... '; < *uk[a-C]i*A*) na*1.2*. 'ugly gossip'. x -0/2/1-1:3[U]/0-A x-x-x. 1700 Ōsaka LHL. Attested Hn.

-         ukine < *ukyi-ne[y] < *uk[a-C]i*A* na-Ci[-Ci]*A*. 'floating sleep; ... '. 1700 Ōsaka LHH. Attested Hn.

-         ukiyo < *u-kyi ywo ('sad world', later associated with 'floating world') < *u*adj ʙ* -ki*adj attr* dwo*1.3a*. 'bitter life; evanescent world'. x - 2/09(/2[K]) -0[H]/1[U]-A x-x-x. Edo LHH *(K: "Edo LLH" is a mistake)*. 1700 Ōsaka LHH.

-         ukizimari < ukyi-zimari ?< *ukyi-zima*?*4.1* (< *uk[a-C]i*2.1+A* -n- sima*2.3*) [a]ri (< *ar[a-C]i*ʙ*) ('float-island stuff'), ?< ukyi n[i] simari < *uk[a-C]i*2.1+A* ni*pcl* sima-r[a-C]i*ʙ* ('fix to a float'). 'a floating grass or sand plot'. x - x-x-x x-x-x. NS (T+ kun) ꟼHHꟼL ?= HHHHL.

-         uko < ukwo (= woko K 45). 'stupid'. x - x-x-x x-x-x. NS (T 36) LH.

-         umara (ni) < *uma*adj ʙ* -ra*suf* ni*pcl*. 'deliciously'. x - x-x-x x-x-x. NS (T+ 39) HLL|H; (T+ kun) HLL|H.

-         umasake < *uma-sakey < *uma*adj ʙ* saka-Ci*2.1*. 'delicious wine'. x - x-x-x x-x-x. NS (T+ 16, 17) Hꟼ|HL (incongruent).

2.1   umi < umyi < *um[a-C]i*A* ('birth'). *(placename)*. x - x-x-x x-x-x. NS (T+ kun) HH.

-         unebi < unebiy ?< *unabi[y] *(see* unai*3.4*)): ~ yama (< *dama*2.3*). *(placename)*. x - x-x-x x-x-x. NS (T+ 105) LLH|LL; NS (T+ kun) HHL|HL (incongruent).

-         uneme < une-mye < une (?< une[biy] < *unabi[y] *(see* unai*3.4*)) mye*1.3b* (< *miCa ?= *mina). 'court waitress'. x - 1-0-x x-x-x. NS (T+ kun) HL|H. Km (W) HHL. 1700 Ōsaka HHL.

-         [urami] < ura miy (M 3622; M 1799): *see* -mi.

-         uru(ke)zi < uru(key)-di ?< *uru-ka (= oro̱-ka*3.2b*) -n- ti*1.x* (?< *ti[y] < *tuCi (?= turi)). 'a no-good fish-hook'. x - x-x-x x-x-x. NS (T+ kun) LLLH.

?3.1   uruti ?< *uru-ti[ne] (Azuma?) = uru-sine (< ...). 'nonglutinous rice'. x - 0-0-A x-x-x. Sz 0 (= uru 1).

-         usa. *(placename)*. x - 1-x-x x-x-x. NS (T+ kun) HH.

-         utagaki < uta-gakyi ?< *uta*2.3b* -n- kaki*?2.2a* (?< *kak[a-C]i*A*) *(as glossed)*, ?< *uta*ʒb* -n- kak[apa-C]i (cf. Azuma kagafi ?< *kam[u] kap[a-C]i*A* or ?< ka-gafi < *ka[p[a-C]i*A*] n[i] kap[a-C]i*4*). 'a kind of party'. x - x-x-x x-x-x. NS (T+ kun) HL|HL.

-         utayomi < uta-yo̱myi < *uta*2.3b* do̱m[a-C]i*ʙ*. x - 0/2/3-4-A x-x-x. NS (T+ kun) HL|HH (last element odd).

-         [utuhagi] < utu-fagyi < *utu(-) *?2.1* pank[a-C]i*ʙ* (< *pa-n[a-]ka-Ci) 'completely stripping'. x - x-x-x x-x-x. NS (T+ kun) HL|HH

-         [utumasa]: *see* uzumasa.

- utumorimasa ?< *utu(-)₂₂.₁ mor[a-C]i_A masa₂.₅ ('completely heap true').
(name). x - x-x-x x-x-x. NS (T+ kun) HH|LH|LH (second element incongruent,
unless we disregard the Ch gloss and assume mor[a-C]i_B 'guard').

- utusiiwai < utusi-ifafyi < utu-si_adj ₂B ifafyi₂.₃ (< *ipap[a-C]i_B).
'a festival to induce a god to appear in immanent form'. x - x-x-x x-x-x.
NS (T+ kun) LLL|LHL.

- uwasa < ufasa ?< *upa₂.₂ₐ sa[ta₂.₃]. 'gossip'. x - 0-2-A x-x-x.
1700 Ōsaka HLL. Aomori, Sz 0; Hakata 0, (oldest) 2. Ib H1 = 3.3. Dial. iwasa,
wasa. First attested Mr.

- uwatukuni < *ufa-tu-kuni < *upa₂.₂ₐ -tu_pcl kuni₂₂.₁,₂₂.₂ₐ (< ...). 'the
upper world (= our world), as opposed to the nether world (= Hades)'. x - x-x-x
x-x-x. NS (T+ kun) ꟷLLHH = HH(|)L | HH.

- uzuhiko < udu-fyikwo < udu₂.ₓ (< *untu) fyikwo₂.₁ (< *pi₁.₂ kwo₁.₁)
('precious prince'). (name). x - x-x-x x-x-x. NS (T+ kun) LꟷLH.

- uzumasa < udumasa < utumasa ?< utu(-)₂₂.₁ masa₂.₅ ('completely true').
(name — family designation of the Hata, an early immigrant clan). x - 2-0-x
x-x-x. NS (T+ 112) HL|LH; NS (T+ kun) HH|LH.

- wagyimwokwo < wagyimwo₃.₇b (< *wa-g[a₂.₄] (y)imwo₂₂.₄ < *ba₁.₃ₐ -n- ka_pcl
imwo₂₂.₄) kwo₁.₁. 'my dear girl'. x - x-x-x x-x-x. NS (61) ꟷH|LH|H ?= LH|LH|H.

- wakakusa < *baka_adj B kusa₂.₃. 'young grass'. x - 2-0-x x-x-x. NS (T+ 117)
LHHꟷ.

- wakamiya < waka-myiya < waka_adj B (< *baka) myi-ya₂.₁ (< *mi-₂₁.₁ da₁.₃b).
'young prince'. x - x-x-x x-x-x. NS (T+ kun) LL(|)HH.

- [yagawae / yaga-hae] < yagafaye ?< *yagufaye < *da₁.₁ -n- kupa₂.₃ ye₂₁.₂
(< ...) ('eight/many mulberry branches'). 'vigorously flourishing/growing'.
x - x-x-x x-x-x. NS (T+ 57) LH|LH.

- yaiba < ya[k]i-ba < *yakyi-ba (< *dak[a-C]i)_A -n- pa₂₁.₃b. '(forged)
blade; sword'. x - 0-0[U]/2[H]-B x-x-x. 1700 Ōsaka LHH. Attested Ir.

- ya-kumo < ya kumwo < *da₁.₁ kumwo₂.₃. '(eight =) many clouds'. x - x-x-x
x-x-x. NS (T+ 1) HHH, (T+ 20) LHL.

- yamabe < yama-bye (K kun-chū, M 1516 heading) < *yama₂.₃ (< *dama)
-bye₁.ₓ (< -n- piCa). (name). Cf. yamanobe < yama-no̲-bye (NS 79) (placename).
See Ch. 2, §3.5.3.

- [yamabi] < yama-biy: see -bi.

- yama-dakamyi < *dama₂.₃ -n- taka_adj B -mi_suf. 'because the mountains are
high'. x - x-x-x x-x-x. NS (T+ 69) LL(|)HHL (last element incongruent).

- yamagawa < yama-gafa < *dama -n- kapa. 'mountain stream'. x - 0-0-x x-x-x.
NS (T+ 113) LL(|)LH.

- yaniwa < ya-nifa < *da₁.₃b nipa₂.₁. 'house site'. x - x-x-x x-x-x.
NS (T+ 34) HHL (register incongruent).

- yarara-ni < yara-ra ni < *dara_mis [a]ra₂.₃₊B. 'slapping, clapping,
briskly'. x - x-x-x x-x-x. NS (T+ kun) LLL(|)H.

- yatiyo < ya-ti₂.₂ (< *da₁.₁ ti₁.₃ₐ) yo̲₁.₁ (< *do̲). x - 2-2-x x-x-x.
1700 Ōsaka HLL. First attested Km.

- yatubo < ya₁.₂(?< *da) tubo₂.₁ₐ (< tufo ?< *tupo, ?= [tuwo] < *tubo).
'arrow target'. x - 1-0-x x-x-x. 1700 Ōsaka HLL. First attested Mr.

- ··· yo̲ < ... . 'hey ··· , O ··· '. NS (T+ 103) H.

- yoake < *ywo-ake[y] < *dwo₁.₃ₐ aka-ci[-Ci]_A. 'dawn(ing)'. x - 3-1-B
x-B[Lit.]-x. 1700 Ōsaka HLL. Attested Hn.

- yohuke < yofuke < *ywo-fuke[y] < *dwo₁.₃ₐ puka-Ci[-Ci]_B. 'late at night'.
x - 3-1-B x-x-x. Edo HLL. First attested Mr.

-      yokusu ‹ yok[o] usu. 'a flat-sided mortar'. x - x-x-x x-x-x. NS (T+ 39) HLL.
-      yomise ‹ *ywo (‹ *dwo$_{1.3a}$) myise[y]$_{2.3}$ (‹ *mi-sa-Ci[-Ci]$_B$). 'night shop'. x - 0-1-B x-x-x. 1700 Ōsaka LHH. First attested Edo.
-      yosami ‹ yosamyi ‹ ?. *(pond name)*. x - x-x-x x-x-x. NS (T+ 36) LHH.
-      yosazura ‹ yosa-dura ‹ yo-sa (*do$_{adj\ B}$ -sa$_{nominalizer}$) -dura (‹ *-n- tura$_{?2.2b}$) ('lucky arrowroot'). 'valerian' (?). x - x- x-x x-x-x. NS (T+ kun) ʔHLL ?= LHLL.
-      yosozura ‹ yoso-dura *(second vowel assimilated to first)* ‹ yosa-dura (‹ ...). 'valerian' (?). x - x-x-x x-x-x. NS (T+ kun) ʔLLL ?= LLLL.
- *1.3a   yu(-) (? ‹ i[m]u ‹ *im[a-$_{?B}$]-u$_{attr}$). 'sacred' = i(-): *see* yuki, yuniwa.
-      yumari ‹ *du$_{1.3a}$ mar[a-C]i$_B$. 'urinating'. x - x-x-x x-x-x. NS (T+ kun) LʔH = L(|)LH.
-      yuki ‹ yu-kiy ‹ yu-$_{*1.3a}$ (‹ ...) -ki$_{1.x}$ (?‹ kyi/kiy ‹ ···). '(sacred wine ›) Number-One land of grain tribute' (cf. suki).
-      yumiya ‹ yumyi$_{2.3}$ (‹ *dumi) ya$_{2.1}$ (?‹ *da). 'bow and arrow'. x - 2-2-B x-B-x. Edo HLL. 1700 Ōsaka HLL.
-      yumizu ‹ yu-midu ‹ *yu$_{1.3a}$ (‹ *du) myidu$_{2.1a}$ (‹ ...). 'hot water and cold'. x - 2-2-B x-x-x. 1700 Ōsaka LHH. K: "Edo LLH; historically Kt 1". Attested 10th century.
-      yuniwa ‹ yunifa ‹ yu(-)$_{*1.3a}$ nipa$_{2.1}$. 'sacred grounds'. x - x-x-x x-x-x. NS (T+ kun) HHL (incongruent).
- ?2.3   yura ‹ *dura. 'Yura' *(placename)*. x - 1-x-x x-x-x. NS (T 41) LL.
-      yura-ni ‹ *dura$_{mia}$ ni$_{pcl}$. 'tinkling (musically)'. x - x-x-x x-x-x. NS (T+ kun) LL-H.
-      yuuhi ‹ yufu-fyi ‹ *dupu$_{?2.2a}$ pi$_{1.2}$. 'evening sun'. x - 0-2-A x-x-x. Attested Nr.
-      yuuya: *see* i[h]uya.
- ?2.2b   zaru ‹ [i]zaru (‹ ?). 'bamboo basket'. x - 2-2-A x-x-x. Aomori 2. Ib H1 = 2.2. Dial. z(y)aru, izyaru.
-      zigami ‹ di-gami ‹ *di$_{1.3a}$ (‹ Ch <u>dhi</u>ʼ) -n- kami$_{2.3}$ (‹ ...). 'one's natural hair'. x - 0-1:3-x x-x-x. 1700 Ōsaka LHL. First attested Edo.

5.11. Accent classes of nouns.

In the lists of §5.11.1 the nouns studied in §5.9 are arranged for each accent class alphabetically by their modern shapes. Earlier shapes, attested or inferred, will be found in the entries of §5.9, where more detailed information is provided for each noun. Words known to be entirely of Chinese origin are preceded by "#". No indication is given whether the noun is believed to occur only in a particular period of earlier Japanese, is found only in later Japanese, or is attested throughout the history of the language. These are primarily finder lists; a number of adjectival nouns, adverbs, and adnouns are included, as well as the pure nouns that make up the bulk of the material. The accent classes are ordered by the number of syllables and the numerical designations presented in Chapter 4. It should be noted that the formulas for the accent pattern correspondences are model sets: particular exceptions for individual lexical items are explicitly marked in the entries of §5.9. Nouns of more than three syllables are assigned accent classes on the basis of the earliest philological attestation, so no dialect correspondences are arrayed for those classes. Statistical profiles of the data will be found in §5.11.2, followed by summary tables in §5.11.3 and §5.11.4.

5.11.1. List of nouns ordered by accent class.

<u>Nouns of one syllable</u> 1 = 1.1, 1.2, 1.3a, 1.3b, 1.3x; 1.x

<u>1.1</u> H(H) O-O-A A-A-A   Toyama 1:2

1.1	e ‹ ey 'hackberry'		1.1	ko 'child': 'egg'; 'silkworm'
?1.1	e ‹ ey 'perilla' (= e-goma)		1.1	ko- 'little'
1.1	e ‹ ye 'handle' (?‹ 'branch')		1.1	# ko 'arc'
?1.1	e ‹ ye 'inlet' (?‹ 'branch')		1.1	ko 'this'
?1.1	# ga 'moth'		1.1	ma 'room, space; *place' (cf. ba)
?1.1	ha(-) 'mother'		?1.1	ma(-) 'true, truth'
?1.1	ha(-) 'red; ? bright'		?1.1 ‹ 2.1	-me 'bird (‹ flock)'
1.1	ha 'jar'		?1.1	mi- 'water'
1.1	ha 'beginning, edge'		?1.1	mi- 'exalted, honored'
?1.1	he 'door(s), household(s)'		?1.1	mi(-) 'three'
?1.1	he 'oven'		1.1	mi 'body'
1.1	he 'jar, pot'		1.1	mi 'fruit'
1.1	he 'bow of ship'		?1.1	mo 'seaweed'
1.1	# hi 'monument'		?1.1	mo 'mourning; distress, misfortune'
1.1	ho 'sail'		?1.1	mu(-) 'six'
1.1	# i 'stomach' (= i-bukuro)		1.1	mu- 'fruit', 'body'
?1.1	i 'dam' (= iseki; see igui)		1.1	na 'you; I/me'
?1.2, ?1.1	i 'boar' (= i-no-sisi)		1.1	na (V-i so) 'don't (V)!'
1.1	ka 'mosquito'		?1.1	ne 'peak'
1.1	ka 'fragrance'		1.1	ne 'sound'
?1.1	(-)ka 'hair' (= ke)		?1.1, ?1.3x	*nu 'cloth'
?1.1	ke 'signs, appearance, feel'		1.1	o(-) 'male'
?1.1	ke 'hair'		?1.1	o- 'little'
?1.2, ?1.1	ke 'container (tray, box)'		1.1	o 'hill' (= oka)
1.1	ki 'onion' (= negi, cf nagi)		?1.3b, ?1.1	o 'cord'
1.1	ki 'vapor; spirit'		1.1	# ro 'oar'
?1.1	(-)ki 'counter (numeral auxiliary)'		?1.1 ‹ 1.3x	# ro 'hearth, fireplace'

?1.1   sa- *(prefix)* 'early (spring)'
?1.1   sa- *(prefix)* ?'true'
?1.1   ‡sa(-) ?'arrow'
1.1   se 'shoal'
1.1   si 'it; that; he'
1.1   si 'poetry'
?1.1   so(-) 'arrow' (= sa-): *see* soya
1.1   so 'that' (= sore)
?1.1   so 'hemp; cloth'
(1.1‹) ?1.3b   sya 'gauze'
?1.1   ta 'who; someone' (= tare)

?1.1   ti 'road, path'
1.1   ti 'blood'
?1.1   ti 'spirit; force'
1.1   to 'door'; 'place'; 'time'
?1.1   (-)to ‹ (-)to 'place'
?1.1   to 'ten': *see* too; -so
1.1   to 'outside'
?1.1   -tu '(number)'
1.1   ya(-) 'eight'
1.1   yo(-) 'four' (= yon)
1.1   yo 'world; generation'
1.1   ‡ zi ‹ di 'hemorrhoids'

1.2   H(L) O*-2-A A-A-A

*But 1 in Tōkyō-type dialects of Okayama, Tango, Tanba,
and western Hida, and in Totsukawa (K 1977:465).

1.2   a(-) 'that *(distal)*'.
?1.2   e 'branch'.
?1.2   e 'older [sibling]'.
?1.2   ha 'feather' (= hane)
1.2   ha 'leaf'
1.2   hi 'sun; day'
?1.2, ?1.1   i 'boar' (= i-no-sisi)
1.2   ka(-) 'that; this'
?1.2, ?1.1   ke 'container (tray, box)'
1.2   ki(-) ‹ kii (Mg) 'yellow; xanthic'
?1.2   ki 'fang' (= kiba)
1.2   ko(-) 'yellow': *see* ki

?1.2   mi '(sign of the) snake; ‡worm, insect'
1.2   na 'name; person
1.2   ne 'price'
?1.2   ne '(sign of the) rat'
(1.2)   ‡pu (?‹ ‡apu) = ‡pi 'day'
?1.2   se, so(-) 'back'
?1.2 ‹ 1.3b   su 'sandbank'
?1.2   ti 'cogon (= thatching grass)'
1.2   u 'cormorant'
(1.2) ‹ ?1.3a   u 'hare, rabbit'
1.2   ya 'arrow'
?1.3a; ?1.2 (= 2.2) ya 'spoke (of wheel)'

1.3a L(L) 1-1-B B-B-B   Toyama, Suzu 1:2

1.3a   ba
1.3a   ?‡ e 'picture'.
1.3a   [ha] 'place'
1.3a   he 'fart'
1.3a   hi 'ice; hail'
1.3a   hi 'blurred (purblind) vision'
1.3a   ho 'ear of grain'
1.3a   i 'well' (= i-do)
1.3a   i 'gallbladder'
?1.3a   i 'sleep'
‡1.3a   i(-) 'sacred'
1.3a   ka 'deer' (= sika)
?1.3a   (-)ka 'plate (to heap food on); utensil, jar'
?1.3a   (-)ka 'day'
?1.3a   ke 'days'

1.3a   ke 'meal'
?1.3a   ?‡ke- 'this' (= ko): *see* ‡ki-
1.3a   ke 'everyday, informal, private'
1.3a   ki 'tree'
?1.3a   ki 'pestle' (= kine)
?1.3a   ‡ki- 'this' (= ko): *see* kesa, kyoo
?1.3a   (-)ki ‹ kyi ‹ ‡ki 'inch'
?1.3a   ki 'enclosure, stockade, fortress'
1.3a   ko(-) 'tree': *see* ki
1.3a   ko 'flour' (= ko-na)
1.3a   ko 'basket' (= ka-go)
1.3a   ko 'sea-cucumber' (= nama-ko)
1.3a   ma(-) 'eye'
1.3a   me 'eye'
1.3a   me 'sprout'

?1.3a   mi 'god, spirit'
1.3a   mi 'winnower'
?1.3a < 2.4   mo
1.3a   na 'rape(weed); greens; side-dish food'
?1.3a   *na 'earth, ground; root'
?1.3a   *na 'inside' (= naka)
1.3a   ne 'root; ?*earth, ground'
1.3a   no 'arrow bamboo'
1.3a   no 'field'
1.3a   o 'tail'
?1.3a   sa(a) 'so'
?1.3a   se 'older brother, beloved male'
1.3a   su 'vinegar'
1.3a   su- 'plain, simple'
1.3a   ta(-) 'hand'
1.3a   ta 'ricefield'
1.3a   te 'hand'

1.3a   ti 'milk'
?1.3a   ti 'esteemed male'
1.3a   ti(-) 'thousand'
1.3a   to 'grindstone'
1.3a   tu 'port, ferry'
1.3a   tu 'spit(tle); ?*liquid'
1.3a   tya 'tea'
?1.3a (> 1.2) u '(sign of the) hare/rabbit'
1.3a ?< 2.3, ?< 2.4 wa 'I/me' (= ware)
1.3a   wa 'wheel, circle'
?1.3a; ?1.2 (= 2.2x) ya 'spoke (of wheel)'
1.3a   yo 'bamboo segment; interval'
1.3a   yo 'night'
1.3a   yu 'hot water'
1.3a   ‡ zi 'ground'
1.3a   ‡ zi 'written character'

....

1.3b L(H) ?1-?0-B B-B-B   Toyama, Suzu 1:2

The reasons for assigning hi 'fire' and ni 'load' to 1.3b and not 1.3a (the
residual category) are stated in Ch. 4, §7.1. Only seven of the words listed
are clearly preserved as free nouns in the modern dialects. Kyōto has "0" for
three (su 'reed screen', su 'nest', ya 'building'), "1" for two (hi 'fire', ni
'load'), and "2" for three (e 'bait', ha 'blade', ha 'tooth'). Tōkyō has "1"
for five (e 'bait', ha 'blade', hi 'fire', ni 'load', ya 'building') and "0"
for three (ha 'tooth', su 'reed screen', su 'nest' — the last "newly 1").

1.3b   a (= aa). 'oh!'
1.3b   e 'bait' (= esa).
1.3b   ‡ e 'epidemic' (= eyami).
1.3b   ‡ go 'the game of Go'.
?1.3b   ‡ go 'time; ··· '
?1.3b   ‡ go 'soybean mash'.
1.3b   ha 'tooth'
?1.3b   ha 'blade'
?1.3b   he 'the shed (= shedding device) of a loom'
1.3b   hi 'fire'
1.3b   hi 'water pipe' (= toi)
1.3b   hi 'cypress' (= hi-no-ki)
1.3b   hi 'shuttle'
?1.3b   ho 'prominent one/thing'
1.3b   ho- 'fire': see hi
1.3b   i 'rush' (plant).
(?1.3b >) 2.4 ‡ ka 'leather shoe'
1.3b   ke 'strange'
?1.3b   -me 'damn person'

1.3b   me 'female'
?1.3b   (-)mi 'garment'
1.3b   mo < *mo 'garment'
1.3b   ‡ na 'exorcism'
1.3b   na(-) ?= /nan/ < nan[i] 'wh(at)'
1.3b   ni 'load, burden'
?1.3b   ni 'earth; red (clay); beautiful; *odor'
?1.3b   no 'cloth; a length of cloth'
1.3b   nu 'marsh'
?1.3b   o 'hemp'
?1.3b, ?1.1   o 'cord'
1.3b   si 'Rumex, sorrel, dock' (= gisigisi)
1.3b   su 'reed screen'
1.3b   su 'nest'
(1.1<) ?1.3b ‡ sya 'silk gauze'
?1.3b   to 'that'
1.3b   ya 'building, house; roof (= yane)'
1.3b   ?‡ yu 'citron' (= yuzu)

....

<u>1.3x</u> (No evidence for <u>a</u> or <u>b</u>.)

?1.3x (-)be 'hereditary guild'	?1.3x < *2.3 -ra
?1.3x he(-) 'separate, apart'	?1.3x < *3.4 -re
1.x (?1.3x) ki(-) 'natural, unspoiled, pure'	?1.3x < *3.4 -ri
1.x (?1.3x) (-)ki 'brew'	?1.1 < 1.3x ‡ ro 'hearth, fireplace'
1.3x < 2.3 na(-) 'horse': *see* uma	?1.3x ‡ *si 'poetry'
?1.3x (-)mi(-) 'woman'	?1.3x *si 'brush(wood), shrub' (?= si 'sorrel')
?1.3x na 'you' (= nare)	?1.3x *si 'sparrow': *see* sime
?1.1,?1.3x *nu 'cloth'	

....

<u>1.x</u> (Insufficient data for assignment.)

1.x -be: *see* (-)he.	1.x (-)ku 'place'
1.x (-)he 'shore, boundary; vicinity; side, direction'	1.x me 'seaweed'
1.x (-)he 'layer'	1.x *na 'blade'
1.x hi '(divine) spirit, supernatural power'	1.x o- 'exalted' (honorific prefix)
1.x -(h)o 'hundred' (= momo)	1.x [-o] 'hundred'
1.x hu '(woven) stitch, mesh, weave, knit, knot'	1.x sa- *(prefix)*
1.x hu 'place where things grow'	1.x si 'wind; direction'
1.x ··· i 'fact (that); that (which)'	1.x -so 'ten(s)'
1.x ··· i 'niece/nephew'	1.x -su 'bird'
1.x (-)ka 'place'	1.x -su 'animal'
1.x ki 'coffin'	1.x -ti 'years'
1.x (?1.3x) ki(-) 'natural, unspoiled, pure'	1.x ti = si 'wind; direction'
1.x (?1.3x) (-)ki 'brew'	1.x [ti] 'fish hook'
1.x -ki(-) 'man, male'	1.x to 'footprint, trace'
1.x (-)ko 'place'	1.x u(-) 'above'

<u>Nouns of two syllables</u>

2 = 2.1, 2.2, 2.3, 2.4, 2.5; 2.x

<u>2.1</u> HH(H) O-O-A A-A-A   Toyama 1:2

     (Note: Nouns of type 2.1a are included here, but recapitulated below.)

*2.1 aa 'that way, like that'	2.1 ati (> atti) 'that way/direction'
2.1 ake 'red; ··· '	?2.1, ?2.3 aya 'Aya (···)'
2.1 aku 'lye'	2.1 azi 'flavor'.
2.1 ··· *aku. 'place/fact'	2.1 ‡ ban 'evening'
2.1 ame 'gluten'	2.1 ‡ bon 'tray'
?2.1 ami 'tiny shrimp'	2.1 ‡ boo < bou(?/bau) 'stick, club'
2.1 ane 'older sister'	?2.1 buta 'pig'
?2.1 ano < [k]a-no 'that ··· '	?2.2x, ?2.1 buti 'spots'
?2.1a ari 'ant'	2.1 dare 'who; someone'
2.1 (?) 2.4/5 asi 'reed'	?2.1 dobu 'gutter'

?2.1 ‹ 3.6   doko ‹ iduko/iduku 'where'
?2.1 ‹ 3.6   dore ‹ idure 'which one'
?2.1   dote 'embankment'
?2.1 ‹ 3.6   doti[-ra] ‹ iduti 'which way'
2.1   ebi 'shrimp'
2.1   eda 'branch, limb'
2.1   emi 'smile'
2.1   enu 'puppy-dog'
2.1 (?‹ 3.1) (?) 2.4)   gama 'bulrush'
2.1 ‹ 2.2b   gawa 'side'
?2.1 ‹ 3.6   goma ‹ ᵘ/ₒgoma 'sesame'
2.1   haba 'width'
?2.1   hade 'gaudy'
2.1   hae 'fly' (insect)
?2.1; ?2.3, ?2.4   haha 'mother'
2.1   hai 'ashes'
2.1   hako 'box'
2.1   hana 'nose'
?2.1   hana 'edge'
2.1   hane 'feather'
2.1   hani 'red clay'
?2.2b, ?2.1   hari 'cultivated land'
2.1   haˢ/zi 'edge'
2.1 ‹ 3.1 hasu 'lotus'
2.1   hasu 'aslant'
2.1   hata 'side, rim'
2.1   hata 'fin; fish'
?2.1a   hati 'bee'
2.1   hatu(-) 'first'
2.1   hazu 'arrow notch; expectation'
2.1   heso/hozo 'navel'
?2.1   heta 'calyx, stem (of fruit)'
2.1   hie 'barn-millet'
2.1   hige 'beard'
3.x ‹ 2.1 hiiki ‹ hiki 'popularity'
?2.1   (-)hiki (counter)
?2.1   hiko 'prince; male god'
2.1   hima 'gap; leisure'
2.1   himo 'cord'
?2.2b, ?2.1   hina 'remote place'
2.1   hira- (adj stem) 'flat, ordinary'
2.1   hire 'fin; scarf'
2.1 (?‹ *2.3) hiru 'garlic'
2.1   hisi 'water-chestnut, caltrop'
2.1   hitu 'lidded box'
?2.1   hiyo 'bulbul'
2.1   hiza 'lap; knee'
?2.1, ?2.4   hora 'cave'
2.1   hosi 'star'
2.1   hozo = heso 'navel'
2.1 ‹ 3.1 ‹ 4.1   huda 'card'
2.1 ‹ 3.1 hude 'brush'
2.1   hue 'whistle'
2.1   huka 'shark'

?2.1, ?2.3   huke 'dandruff'
?2.1   huki 'bog-rhubarb'
?2.1   husi 'brushwood; fence'
2.1   huta 'lid'
?2.1, ?2.2x   huta(-) 'two'
2.1   huzi 'wisteria'
2.1   ika 'cuttlefish'
?*2.1   ina 'neigh!' (sound of horse)
2.1   io 'fish': see uo
?2.1   isa 'whale' (= isana = kuzira)
?2.1   ise 'Ise' (placename)
2.1   iso 'beach; rock'
2.1   iya = iyo ('more and more; very')
?2.2x, ?2.1   iya 'respect' (= uya)
?2.1   iyo 'more and more; very'
2.1   kaba = kama/gama 'bulrush'
2.1   kabe 'wall'
2.1   [kabi/kai] 'sprout; (top of) ear of grain'
2.1   kabi 'mildew, mold'
2.1   kabu 'stump; (= kabura) turnip'
2.1   kago 'basket'
2.1   [kai] 'ear of grain': see [kabi/kai]
2.1   kai 'valley'
2.1   kai '(good) result, effect'
2.1   ‡ kai 'ascarid, roundworm'
2.1   kaki 'persimmon'
2.1   kama = kaba 'bulrush'
2.1   kama 'pot'
2.1   kamo 'woolen cloth'
2.1   kana(-) 'metal'
2.1   kana 'syllabary writing'
2.1   kane 'metal; bell'
2.1   kani 'crab'
2.1   kao 'face'
2.1   kari 'a kind of dice' (= tyobo).
2.1   kari 'temporary, ephemeral'
2.4 (?‹ *2.1) kari 'mowing; a "cut" of rice'
?2.1   kasa 'sore, ulcer'
2.1   kata(-) (adj stem) 'hard'
2.1   kaya 'mosquito net'
2.1   kayu 'gruel'
2.1   kaza(-) 'wind': see kaze
2.1   [kaza] (? 'wind') 'odor, scent'
2.1   kaze 'wind'
?2.1   kazi 'smith(ing)'
?2.1, ?2.2b   kazi 'paper mulberry'
?2.1   keba 'nap, shag'
2.1   ‡ kesa 'priest's robe'
2.1   kimi 'lord'
2.1   kiri 'paulownia'
2.1   kiri 'fog'
2.1 (‹ 3.1)   kizi 'pheasant'
2.1   kizu 'wound'
2.1   kobu 'metal tube ⋯ ' (= kamo)

2.1	koma 'pony'	
2.1	kono 'wild rice; rush-mat'	
2.1	kono 'this ··· '	
2.1	kore 'this one'	
?2.1, ?2.2a	koro 'time'	
?*2.1	koro 'self; (by) oneself; *body'	
2.1	kosi 'loins'	
2.1	kote 'gauntlet'	
2.1	koti () kotti) 'this way/direction'	
2.1	kubi 'neck'	
?2.1	kubo 'hollow'	
2.1 ?(*3.1	kuga 'nut-grass'	
2.1	kugi 'nail'	
2.1	kugu 'nut-grass'	
2.1	kuki 'mountainside cave; peak'	
?2.1 > ?2.3	kuma 'nook, corner; river bend'	
?2.1, ?2.2a	kuni 'country'	
2.1	kure 'end (of day/year)'	
?2.1	kure '(the state of Wu in ancient) China'	
2.1	kuti 'mouth'	
2.1	kuti 'hawk'	
2.1	kutu(-) 'mouth' (= kuti)	
2.1	kuwa 'hoe'	
*2.1	kuwa(-) 'heel'	
?2.1	maga 'disaster'	
2.1	mai 'dance'	
2.1	maki (?('true wood') 'firewood, brushwood'	
?2.1, ?2.2b	maki 'true wood; tree proper'	
2.1	mama 'as it is'	
2.1	mame 'sincere'	
?2.1	mana 'fish'	
2.1	mane 'mimicry'	
2.1	mara(-) 'rare'	
2.1	mare 'rare'	
2.1	maro (?(*maru) 'round'	
2.1	maru 'round (thing)'	
2.1	masu 'trout'	
2.1	mato 'target'	
2.1	mato 'fine grindstone'	
2.1	migi 'right'	
2.1	mike 'meal (offered to gods)'	
2.1	miki 'right': see migi	
2.1	miko 'prince'	
?2.1, ?2.2a	mina(-) 'water'	
2.2b ?(2.1a	mina 'all; everyone; everything'	
?2.1, ?2.2a	mine 'peak'	
?2.2a, ?2.1	mio 'channel'	
2.1	miso 'clothes, garment'	
2.1	miti 'road, path'	
?2.2x, ?2.1	mito 'port'	
2.1	miya 'shrine'	
?2.1a	mizo 'ditch'	
?2.1a	mizu 'water'	
2.1	moha 'seaweed'	

2.1	momi 'unhulled rice'	
?2.1	momi 'cloth rub-dyed solid red'	
2.1	momo 'peach'	
2.1	mori '(shrine) woods'	
?2.1	moro(-) 'various, several'	
2.1	moti 'holly; birdlime made from holly bark'	
2.1 (?(3.1)	moti (< motii) 'rice cake'	
2.1	mube 'indeed': see ube	
2.1	muda 'useless'	
2.1	muna(-) 'empty, vain'	
2.1	muna(-) 'ridge'	
2.1	mune 'ridge (of roof)'	
2.1	mune 'gist, purport'	
?2.1	mura 'mottle(s); motley'	
2.1	mura(-) '(being) a group/cluster/mass'	
2.1	mure 'flock'	
2.1	musi 'insect; *snake'	
?2.1	[muta] 'swamp, marshland; land'	
?2.1, ?2.2x	muyu(-) 'six'	
?2.1, ?2.3	nagi 'a kind of black pine'	
2.1	name 'diarrhea'	
2.1	nami 'you'	
2.1 (3.1	namu(-) 'you'	
2.1	nata 'ax'	
2.1 ((3.1)	nemu: nemu[ri]-no-ki 'silk tree'	
?2.1	neya 'boudoir'	
?2.1a	nie '···· new rice'	
2.1	nigi(-) 'soft'	
2.1	nii(-) 'new'	
?2.1/?2.4	niko(-) 'soft'	
2.1	nisi 'west'	
2.1	niwa 'garden'	
?2.1	nogi 'fishbone; awn'	
2.1	noki 'eaves'	
2.1 (3.1	nude (< nurude/nuride) 'sumac'	
2.1	nude < nute 'wooden bell'	
?2.1	nuka 'forehead'	
2.1	nuki 'woof, weft; brace'	
2.1	nuno 'cloth'	
2.1	nute (> nude) (nurite ((?) 'wooden bell'	
2.1	oba 'aunt'	
2.1	oi 'nephew'	
2.1	oka 'hill'	
2.1	ono 'self'	
2.1	ono '(small) field/moor'	
2.1	osi 'mandarin duck: lovebirds' (= osi-dori)	
2.1 (3.1	osi < o[o]si < o[f]usi '(deaf-)mute'	
?2.1	oti 'youthful/virile vigor'	
?2.2x, ?2.1	oti 'distant place, yon(der) way'	
2.1	ozi 'uncle'	
2.1	saba 'mackerel: ··· '	
2.1	sade 'scoop net'	
2.1	sagi 'heron'	
2.1	sai 'wild boar'	

?2.4, ?2.1   sai 'spade; (= ura-sai) sword'
2.1   saka(-) 'wine': see sake
2.1   saka(-) 'backward; opposite (direction)'
2.1   sake '(rice) wine, sake'
2.1   saki 'ahead'
2.1   saki 'tip; cape' (?< 'ahead')
?2.1, ?2.2a   *saki 'good luck (= sati), happiness'
?2.2a ?< 2.1   sama 'appearance'
2.1   same 'shark'
2.1   sara 'plate'
2.1   sasa 'bamboo-grass'
?2.1, ?2.3   sa-*/za 'small'
2.1   sasi 'maggot'
?2.1   sati 'luck, ··· '
2.1   sato 'village'
2.1   sawa 'swamp; valley'
?2.1, ?2.3   sa-za 'small' (= sa-sa)
?2.1   seko 'beloved male; ···'
*2.1   *siba, *sima 'while, period of time'
2.1   siba 'turf'
?2.1, ?2.3   sibi 'tuna'
?2.1   [sii] 'tuna' (= sibi)
*2.1   *sima 'while, period': see siba
?2.1   simi 'being cold; ice'
2.1   simi 'stain; soaking in (···)'
2.1   sina 'quality; goods; step, level'
?2.1   sina (= sina-no-ki) 'Japanese linden'
2.2a (?< 2.1) sina 'coquetry'
2.1   siro 'castle'
2.1   siro 'thing; material; ··· '
2.1   siwa 'wrinkle'
?2.1   sobo 'tree(s)'
2.1   sode 'sleeve'
2.1   soko 'bottom'
?2.1   soma 'wooded mountain'
2.1   sono 'that ··· '
*2.1   soo 'that way, like that'
2.1   sore 'that one'
2.1   sue 'end'
2.1   sugi 'cedar'
2.1   suke 'support pillar'
2.1   suki 'plow'
?2.1   suna 'sand'
2.1   suso 'skirt bottom'
2.1   suzu '(little) bell' (?< 'tin')
2.1   suzu 'tin; tin wine-vessel'
2.1   tade 'knotweed'
2.1   taga 'hoop'
2.1   taka(-) 'bamboo': see take
2.1   taka 'hawk'
2.1   take 'bamboo'
2.1   taki 'waterfall < rapids'
2.1   tama(-ni/-no) 'occasional'
2.1   tamu(-) = tamo(-): - no ki 'ash tree'

2.1   ‡ tamu 'sweet wine'
?2.1   tamu 'Mount Tamu' (placename)
2.1   tana 'shelf'
2.1   tare 'who; someone' (= dare)
2.1   tatu 'dragon'
2.1   tiri 'dust'
?2.1, ?2.5 tobi 'kite (hen)'
?2.1, ?2.5 toki 'ibis': see tuki
2.1   toko 'bed, ··· '
?2.1   toko ··· 'everlasting, unchanging'
?2.1, ?2.2a toma 'rain-cover'
2.1   tomi 'glutinous (sticky) rice'
2.1   tomi 'riches'
2.1   tomo 'companion'
2.1   tomo(-ni) 'together'
2.1   tora 'tiger'
2.1   tori 'bird'
?2.1   toti 'horse chestnut'
?2.1a   tubo 'jar'
?2.1, ?2.3 tuge 'boxtree'
2.1   tugi 'patch'
?2.1, ?2.3 tuki 'zelkova (tree)' (= keyaki)
?2.1, ?2.5 tuki (= toki) 'ibis' (bird)
2.1   tuma(-) 'claw'
2.1   tume 'claw'
?2.1, ?2.2x tumi 'sparrow-hawk'
?2.1, ?2.2a tura 'row, line'
2.1   ture 'companion'
2.1   turi 'fishing'
2.1   tutu 'pipe, tube'
?2.1   tutu 'wagtail; swallow; ··· '
2.1   tuya 'gloss'
2.1   tuzi 'crossroads'
2.1   tuzi 'hair-whorl, kinky hair'
2.1   ube 'indeed, quite so'
?2.5, ?2.1 ubu 'naive'
2.1   ue 'weir, fish-trap'
3.6 (> 2.1) ugoma, ogoma (> goma) 'sesame'
?2.1, ?2.2b ui 'beginning, first (in life)'
2.1   uke 'a float'
2.1   ume 'plum'
2.1   uo 'fish'
?2.1   ura = ure 'branch, twig'
?2.1   ure 'branch'
2.1   usi 'ox'
2.2a(?/2.1) uti 'hollow; within; home; ··· '
?2.1   utu(-) 'empty; total'
?2.2x, ?2.1 uya, [w]iya 'respect'
2.1   wabi 'simple taste; apology'
?2.1   wata 'sea'
2.1   yabu 'bush'
2.1   ya-hu 'many joints ··· '
2.1   yari 'spear'
2.1   ya-tu (> yattu) 'eight'

?2.1 < 3.5b (?< 4.3)   yaya 'slightly'   ?2.1, ?2.4   yone 'hulled rice'
2.1   yoi 'evening'   ?2.1   yosi 'reason, gist'
?2.3/?2.4 < 2.1   yoki 'hand-ax'   2.1   yotu (> yottu) 'four'
2.1   yoko 'side'   2.1   yuka 'floor'
2.1   yome 'bride'   ?2.1 < 3.6   yuri 'lily'
?2.1, ?2.4   yona(-) 'hulled rice'   2.1   yuu 'paper-mulberry fibers ··· '

2.1a HH < HF ?< *HLL = 3.3 (See Ch.4, §7.3 for more candidates. See also nusa.)

                    ?2.1a   ari 'ant'
                    ?2.1a   hati 'bee'
                    2.2b ?< 2.1a   mina 'all; everyone; everything'
                    ?2.1a   mizo 'ditch'
                    ?2.1a   mizu 'water'
                    ?2.1a   nie 'new rice'
                    ?2.1a   tubo 'jar'

2.2 = 2.2a, 2.2b, 2.2x

2.2a HL(L) < *HH(L) 0(/2)-2-A A-A-A   Toyama 2(-i/u), 1:3 (-e/a/o); Suzu 1:3

        (The "0/2" includes Tōkyō-type dialects. But, owing to the merger of 2.2 with
        2.1, "0" is irrelevant in NE Kyūshū, Ōita, Wakamatsu, Izumo, and Matsue.)

2.2a   ada, ata 'vain; foe'   2.2a   kita 'north'
2.2a   agi 'jaw, gill'   2.2a   kui 'stake'
2.2a   ara 'chaff, bran; offal'   ?2.1, ?2.2a   kuni 'country'
2.2a   aza 'birthmark'   2.2a   kuse 'habit'
2.2a   boro 'rag, scrap'   ?2.2a   kuti, guti 'yellow corvina' (fish)
?2.2a, ?2.3   era 'gills'   2.2a   mata 'again'
?2.2a < 2.3   hagi 'patch(ing)'   2.2a   mati 'field (sector/measure); town, market'
2.2a   hasi 'bridge, ladder'   2.2a   miki 'wine'
2.2a   hata 'flag'   2.2a   miki 'trunk'
2.2a   hata 'loom; cloth'   ?2.1, ?2.2a   mina(-) 'water'
2.2a   hiko 'great-grandson'   ?2.1, ?2.2a   mine 'peak'
2.2a   hito 'person'   ?2.2a, ?2.1   mio 'channel'
2.2a   hizi 'elbow'   ?2.2a   mori 'harpoon'
?2.2a < 3.6   hobo 'approximately'   2.2a   muna(-) 'breast'
2.2a   hodo 'interval, degree'   2.2a   mune 'breast'
?2.2a   ‡ hoo 'law, way'   ?2.2a   nasi 'pear'
2.2a   hoto: see hodo   2.2a   natu 'summer'
2.2a   huyu 'winter'   2.2a   nire 'yew'
2.2a   iwa 'crag'   ?2.2a < ?3.3   nizi 'rainbow'
?2.2a   kaki 'fence; hedge'   ?2.2a < ?3.3   nozi 'rainbow': see nizi
2.2a   kami 'paper'   2.2a   oto 'sound'
2.2a   kara 'shell; trunk; handle; character'   ?2.2a   ruri 'glass; ··· '
2.2a   kara 'empty' (< 'shell').   ?2.1, ?2.2a   ‡saki 'good luck (= sati), happiness'
2.2a   kata 'shape'   ?2.2a ?< 2.1   sama 'appearance'
2.2a   kawa 'river'; (Ryūkyū) 'well'   2.2a   semi, [dial.] sebi 'cicada'
2.2a   kazi 'rudder'

?2.2a   simi 'clothes moth, bookworm, silverfish'
?2.2a   simo 'below'
2.2a (?< 2.1) sina 'coquetry'
2.2a   sita 'below; (deep) inside, heart, mind'
2.2a   tame 'benefit, sake'
?2.2a   tera 'temple'
?2.1, ?2.2a toma 'rain-cover'
?2.2a   too 'ten'
?2.2a   tuma 'skirt; rim'
?2.2a   tuma '(wife <) spouse'
?2.1, ?2.2a tura 'row, line'

?2.2a   tura 'vine': see turu
2.2a   turu < tura 'vine'
2.2a   turu '(bow)string'
2.2a   tuta 'ivy; ··· '
?2.2a   ue 'above, up'
2.2a   uta 'song'
2.2a(?/2.1) uti 'hollow; within; home; ··· '
?2.2a   uwa(-) 'above'
?2.2a   wasi 'eagle'
2.2a   yuki 'snow'
?2.2a   yuu 'evening'

....

2.2b HL(L) 2-2-A A-A-A   Toyama 2(-i/u), 1:3 (-e/a/o); Suzu 1:3

2.2b   ago 'chin'
2.2b   are < [k]are 'that'
2.2b   aza 'village section'
2.2b   azi 'saurel' (fish)
?2.2b, ?2.5 dani 'tick' (insect)
?2.2b   ei 'ray' (fish)
2.2b   eri 'collar'
?2.2b   gawa 'side'
2.2b   ‡ gin 'silver'
2.2b   ‡ giri 'duty'
2.2b   haga 'bird snare'
?2.2b   hami 'viper'
?2.2b, ?2.1 hari 'cultivated land'
?2.2b < 2.3 haze 'goby' (fish)
?2.2b < 2.3 haze 'sumac'
2.2b   hemi 'a kind of honeysuckle'
2.2b   hime 'lady; princess'
?2.2b, ?2.1 hina 'remote place'
?2.2b   hina 'chick'
?2.2b   hira 'sheet; petal'
?2.2b   hiru 'daytime'
2.2b   hoo 'Magnolia hypoleuca'
2.2b   horo 'underwing feathers'
2.2b   hoya 'seasquirt'
2.2b   humi 'writings'
2.2b   iga 'bur'
(2.2b)   [ige] (JP) < iga 'bur; unhusked grain'
2.2b   ika(-ni) 'how'
?2.2b   ika(-)··· 'mighty' (? = ika 'how [much]')
?2.2b   iku- = ika- 'how (much); ? mighty'
?2.3, ?2.2b iro '(same) mother'
2.2b   isi 'stone'
?2.2b   ito 'extremely'
?2.2b   kado 'gate'
2.2b   kaku 'thus'
2.2b   kano 'that ··· '
2.x (?2.2b) kara 'clan, family' (?< 'trunk')
2.2b   kare 'he; that one (distal)'

2.2b   kasa 'quantity'
2.2b   kata 'direction'
2.2b   kata 'beach: lagoon'
?2.2b   kawa 'side, direction'
?2.1, ?2.2b kazi 'paper mulberry'
2.2b   kiba 'fang, tusk'
2.2b   ‡ kin 'gold; money'
?2.2b   koma 'cyprinodont'
2.2b   koo 'thus'
2.2b   kosi 'shoulder-borne riding platform'
2.2b   kosi 'story/level of a building'
2.2b   kura 'seat, saddle'
?2.2b   kusa 'seed, source; variety, sort'
?2.1, ?2.2b maki 'true wood; tree proper'
?2.2b   mana 'don't!'
2.2b   mari 'bowl'
?2.2b < 3.7b mazu 'first of all'
2.2b   mie 'Mie' (placename)
2.2b   mika 'large jar'
2.2b ?< 2.1a mina 'all; everyone; everything'
2.2b   mio 'grebe' (= nio)
2.2b   [mio] 'three hundred'
2.2b   miso 'thirty'
2.2b   mitu (> mittu) 'three'
2.2b   miwa 'wine offering'
2.2b   moi 'cup; water'
?2.2b   momi 'fir'
?2.2b   momi 'tree frog; flying squirrel'
2.2b < 3.3 mosi 'perchance'
?2.2b < 3.3 ‡ mozi < monzi 'writing, letters'
2.2b   mura 'village'
2.2b   mutu (> muttu) 'six'
?2.2b   nada 'rapids; rough sea'
?2.2b   nagi 'calm'
?2.2b   nara 'Nara'
2.2b   nio 'grebe' (bird)
2.2b   noma, nome, nomi 'caulking'
2.2b   nori 'law'

?2.2b   nue 'chimera; thrush' *(bird)*
2.2b   oma 'stallion'
?2.2b ‡ rati 'corral-fence'
?2.2b, ?2.3   sasi 'castle'
?*2.2b   sima 'direction' (= sama)
2.2b   sobi, soni 'kingfisher' *(bird)*
?2.2b ‹ 3.3   syako 'squilla'
?2.2b ‹ 3.3   syako 'partridge'
?2.2b ‹ 3.3   syako 'giant clam'
2.2b   tabi 'time, occasion'
2.2b   tabi 'journey' (?‹ 'occasion')
?2.2b, ?2.5   tani 'tick': *see* dani

2.2b   tugi 'next': (number of) generations'
2.2b   tuka 'mound'
2.2b   tuki 'cup'
2.2b   uba 'wet-nurse'
?2.1, ?2.2b   ui 'beginning, first (in life)'
2.2b   uzi 'clan'
2.2b   waza 'trick'
2.2b   yae 'eightfold'
2.2b   yaso 'eighty'
?2.2b   yomo 'everywhere'
2.2b   yoso 'outside'
?2.2b   yue 'reason'
2.2b   ?‡ yuzu 'citron'

2.2x (No evidence for a or b.)

?2.2x, ?2.1   buti 'spots'
2.2x   hata(-) 'twenty'
2.2x   hazu 'croton'
2.2x   hoya 'mistletoe' (= yadorigi)
?2.1, ?2.2x   huta 'two'
2.2x   ibi 'night heron'
?2.2x, ?2.1   iya 'respect': *see* uya
2.x (?2.2b)   kara 'clan, family' (?‹ 'trunk')
?2.2x, ?2.1   mito 'port'
2.2x ‹ 3.6   moda 'silence'
?2.1, ?2.2x   muyu(-) 'six'

2.2x   oda 'rice paddy'
?2.2x, ?2.1   oti 'distant place, yon(der) way'
2.2x   oti 'rape(weed)' (= abura-na)
2.2x   sei 'young sea-bass' (= seigo)
2.2x   tugi 'tribute' (= mi-tugi)
2.2x   tuki 'tribute': *see* tugi
?2.1, ?2.2x   tumi 'sparrow-hawk'
?2.2x   uki 'mud(dy place); bog'
?2.2x, ?2.1   uya, iya 'respect'
?1.3a; ?1.2 (= 2.2x) ya (= yaa) 'spoke (of wheel)'

2.3   LL(L) 2-2-B B-B-B   Toyama, Suzu 2(-i/u), 1:3 (-e/a/o)

?2.4 ‹ *2.3   ae 'feast'
?2.4 ?‹ 2.3   ai ‹ afyi 'meeting'
2.3   aka 'dirt'
?*2.3   aki 'barter, trade'
2.5 (?‹ 2.3)   ama(-) 'heaven'
2.3   ama 'fisher(woman)'
2.3   ami 'net'
2.3   ana 'hole'
*2.3   [a]ra 'what exists; ··· '
2.3   are 'barley flour stuck on rice cake'
2.3   asa 'hemp'
2.3   asi 'foot'
?2.4, ?2.3   aso 'my dear fellow'
2.3   asu 'morrow'
2.3   awa 'bubble, foam'
?2.1, ?2.3   aya 'Aya ··· '
2.3   aya ‹ *ada 'design'
2.3   aya ‹ *ada 'strange'
2.3   aze 'levee'
2.3   bara ‹ [i]bara 'rose'
2.3   ?‡ bati 'plectrum, drumstick'

?2.3   ‡ biwa 'lute'
2.3   buti(/muti) 'whip'
2.3   ‡ [dai] 'shroud; monk's robe'
2.3   ‡ desi 'apprentice'
2.3   ‡ doku 'poison'
2.3   doro 'mud'
?2.2a, ?2.3   era 'gills'
2.3   esa 'bait'
2.3   ‡ gaki 'hungry ghost; glutton'
?2.3   (-)gane 'material for'
2.3   gomi 'rubbish'
2.3   hae 'carp; dace' *(fish)*
?2.3 ‹ 3.7b   hagi 'shank (= lower leg)'
2.3   hagi 'bushclover, lespedeza'
?2.2a ‹ 2.3   hagi 'patch(ing)'
?2.1; ?2.3, ?2.4   haha 'mother'
2.3   haka 'grave'
2.3   haka 'alloted amount; aim; progress'
2.3   hake 'brush'
2.3   hama 'beach'
2.3   hami 'Phlomis umbrosa'

2.3	hami 'eating; ··· '
2.3	hana 'flower, blossom'
2.3	hara 'field'
2.3	hara 'belly'
2.3	hare 'fair weather'
2.3	hari 'crossbeam'
?2.3	has°/u 'carp'
2.3	hate 'end; limits'
2.3	hati 'bowl, pot'
2.3	hato 'pigeon'
?2.3	haya 'dace, carp' *(fish)*
?2.2b < 2.3	haze 'goby' *(fish)*
?2.2b < 2.3	haze 'sumac'
2.3	hazi 'shame'
?2.3	hedo 'vomit'
2.3	heo 'falcon foot-cord'
2.3	heri 'rim, brink'
2.3	heta 'clumsy, unskillful'
2.3	heya 'a room'
2.3	hibi 'skin cracks'
2.3	hida 'pleat'
?2.3	hiki 'toad'
2.3	hime 'oven-cooked rice'
?2.3	hio 'whitebait' *(fish)*
2.3	hiro 'fathom'
2.1 (?< *2.3)	hiru 'garlic'
2.3	hiso 'ceiling rafters'
?2.4, ?2.3	hito(-) 'one'
2.3	hizi 'mud'
?2.3	hogu 'wastepaper'
2.3	hoho 'cheek': *see* hoo
2.3	hoko 'halberd'
2.3	hone 'bone'
?2.3	hono(-) 'faint, slight'
2.3	hoo, hoho 'cheek(s)'
2.3	hori 'ditch'
?2.3	hoto 'vagina'
?2.1, ?2.3	huke 'dandruff'
2.3	‡ huku 'clothes'
2.3	huro 'bath'
2.3	husa 'bunch'
2.3	husi 'bamboo joint'
2.3	huzi '(Mount) Fuji'
2.3	ie 'house'
2.3	ii 'cooked rice'
2.3	ike '(fish)pond'
2.3	ik/ɡe 'a rush-woven lunchbox'
2.3 (?= 1.3|1.3)	ime (= yume)
2.3	imo 'yam'
2.3	inu 'dog'
2.3	io 'hut' (= iori)
2.3	io 'five hundred'

2.3	ira 'thorn, spine'
2.3	iro 'color'
?2.3, ?2.2b	iro '(same) mother'
?2.3	itu(-) 'five'
?2.3	itu(-) 'sacred'
?*2.3	kabu 'head'
2.3	kae 'cypress; nutmeg'
?2.3, ?2.4	kage '"deer hair" (horse color)'
2.3	kagi 'key; hook'
2.3	kai 'shell; (=kaigo) egg, eggshell; spoon
?2.4/5 < 2.3	kaki 'oyster'
2.3	kame 'tortoise'
2.3	kame 'jar'
2.3	kami 'god; (= naru kami) thunder'
2.3	kami 'hair (on head')'
2.3	kamo 'metal tube ··· : metal ring ··· '
?2.5 < 2.3	kamo '(wild) duck'
2.3	kamu(-) 'god'
?2.3	*kana(-) 'one'
2.3 > 3.4	kana (> kanna) '(carpenter's) plane'
2.3	kare 'the reason'
?2.4 < 2.3	kari 'hunting'
?2.3	kase 'shackles': 'skein frame/reel'
2.3	kasi 'shackles'
?2.5 < 2.3	kasi 'oak'
?2.3	kata(-) 'one side (of two), ··· '
2.3	kate 'provisions'
2.3	kati 'victory'
2.3	‡ kati, katin 'rough wool cloth: ··· '
2.3	kawa 'skin, fur'
?2.3	kaya 'Japanese nutmeg'
2.3	kega 'mishap'
?2.3, ?2.4	kego 'lunchbox'
2.3	kera 'mole cricket'
?2.3	kida 'cut, notch'
?2.3 (< 1.3a)	kii 'the land of Kii'
2.3	‡ kiku 'chrysanthemum'
2.3	kimo 'liver'
2.3	kisa 'grain (of wood)'
2.3	kisa 'ark shell'
?2.3	*kisa(-) 'shaving, scraping'
2.3	kisi 'cliff; shore'
?2.3	kisi '(Paekche) Korean lord'
2.3	kiwa 'brink'
?2.3	kiza 'cut, notch'
?2.5, ?2.3	kobu 'gnarl, lump'
2.3	koe 'fertilizer'
2.3	koga 'barrel, vat, tub; bucket'
2.3	koge 'scorched (thing)'
?2.3 < 3.7	‡ ko-hi 'sore throat'
?2.3	[koi] 'sore throat': *see* ko-hi
2.3	koi 'love'

2.3	koke 'moss'		2.3	mek/ga 'female deer'
2.3	koma 'Koguryŏ (Kokwulye), ··· '		2.3	mesi 'food, rice'
2.3	koma '(toy spinning) top'		2.3	mesu 'female animal'
(*2.3)	koma(-) 'small, fine'		2.3	mimi 'ear'
2.3	kome 'hulled rice'		2.3	mina 'snail' (= nina)
2.3	kome 'ray (fish) (= ei); ··· '		?*2.3	*mina (?= *mi-na) 'woman'
2.3	komi 'paddy flooding'		2.3	mira = nira 'leek'
2.3	komo 'wild rice; straw matting'		2.3	mise 'shop, display'
?2.3, ?2.4	kona 'flour'		?2.3	[mita] 'earth; (dry) land'
?2.3	koni ··· 'big, great'		2.3	‡ miti 'honey' = mitu
2.3	kose 'eczema'		2.3	‡ mitu 'honey'
?2.3	kosi 'Koshi' (placename)		2.3	mono 'hundred'
?2.3	koti 'east (wind)'		2.3	mono, -mono 'thing'
2.3	koto 'fact, thing; words, saying'		2.3	moto 'root; under; original'
2.3	koya 'hut, shed'		2.3	mozi 'crepe; muslin, sackcloth'
2.3	kudo 'oven (smoke-hole)'		2.3	mozi 'a weight of silk or cotton'
2.3	kui 'green caterpillar' (= imomusi)		2.3	mube 'Stauntonia hexaphylla'
2.3	kuki 'stalk'		2.3	muro 'room, shed'
?2.1 > ?2.3	kuma 'nook, corner; river bend'		2.3	musi 'ramie, Chinese silk plant'
2.3	kuma 'bear'		2.3	muti/buti/huti 'whip'
2.3	kumi 'set'		2.3	‡ myaku 'pulse, vein'
2.3	kumo 'cloud'		2.3 (?< 2.5)	nae 'seedling'
2.3	kura 'storehouse'		2.3	nage 'throwing'
2.3	kure 'plank, stave'		?2.1, ?2.3	nagi 'a kind of black pine'
2.x (?2.3)	kure 'lump, clod'		2.3	nagi 'pickerelweed'
2.3	kuri 'chestnut'		2.3	nami 'wave'
?2.5, ?2.3	kuro 'black'		2.3	nana(-) 'seven'
2.3	kuru(-) 'chestnut': see kuri		2.3	nara 'Japanese oak'
2.3	kusa 'grass'		2.3	nari 'shape'
2.3	kusa 'eczema'		2.3	nawa 'rope'
2.3	kusi 'comb'		2.3	nawa(-) 'seedling' (= nae)
2.3	kusi 'skewer'		?2.3, ?2.5	neko 'cat'
?2.3	kusi 'elixir'		2.3	neri 'tempering'
2.3	kuso 'dung'		2.3	nezi 'screw'
2.3	kutu 'shoes'		?2.3	nibe 'croaker (fish); fishglue'
2.3	kuwa 'mulberry'		2.3	nige ? 'cud'
?2.3, ?2.4	kuzi 'lottery (chance)'		2.3	‡ niku 'meat'
2.3	mago 'grandchild'		2.3	‡ niku 'a wool mattress/blanket'
?2.3	mai 'offering, gift'		2.3	nina < *mina 'snail'
2.3	‡ maku 'curtain'		2.3	nira 'leek'
2.3	mame 'bean'		2.3	nobe 'stretching; ··· '
2.3	mara '(evil;) penis'		2.3	nomi 'flea'
2.3	mari 'ball'		2.3	‡ noo 'shroud; monk's robe'
?2.3	maru 'chamberpot' (= o-maru)		?2.3	nora 'brambles; moors, fields'
2.3	mase 'rough-woven fence'		2.3	nora(-) 'wild; laziness; scoundrel'
?2.4, ?2.3	masi 'monkey'		?2.3	nori 'seaweed'
2.3	masu 'measure'		2.3	nori 'paste; starch'
2.3	mata 'crotch'		2.3	nosi 'noshi; iron'
2.3	mate 'razor-clam'		2.3	noti 'later'
2.3	mei 'niece'		?2.3	nuka 'bran'
?2.3	meri 'diminishing'		2.3	numa 'marsh'

?2.3, ?2.4   nusa 'paper offering'
2.3   nuta 'mud; bouillabaisse'
?2.3   ogi 'reed; sugarcane'
2.3   oi 'being old; old person'
2.3   oi 'a wooden back-pack'
2.3   oki 'offshore'
?2.3   oku 'interior'
2.3   omi 'minister'
2.3   oni 'ogre'
2.3   ono 'pickax'
2.3   oo(-) *(adj stem)* 'big, much'
?2.3   ori 'cage'
?2.3   oso 'otter'
2.3   osu 'male animal'
?2.3   oto(-) 'lower, lesser, younger'
?2.3   oto(-) ? 'young adult'; 'yester-'
2.3   oya 'parent'
?1.3x < *2.3   -ra 'thing; some; (plural)'
2.3   ‡ roo 'wax'
2.3   sabi 'rust'
?2.3, ?2.4   saga 'omen'
?2.3   sage 'lowering'
2.3   saka 'slope; (= sakai) boundary'
2.3   saka (= to[ri]-saka) 'cockscomb, crest'
2.3   sake 'owl'
?2.3, ?2.5   sake 'salmon'
?2.3   sane '(large) seed, core'
2.3   sao 'pole'
?2.1, ?2.3   sa-s/za 'small'
?2.2b, ?2.3   sasi 'castle'
2.3   ‡ sata 'tidings'
?2.1, ?2.3   sa-za 'small' (= sa-sa)
2.3   ‡ sazi 'spoon'
2.3   seki 'obstruction, barrier'
2.3   seki 'cough'
2.3   seri 'parsley'
?2.3, ?2.4   siba 'firewood, brushwood'
?2.1, ?2.3   sibi 'tuna'
?2.3   sibu: *see* sibukusa ('sorrel')
?2.4, ?2.3   sibu 'astringent taste; ··· '
2.3   sii 'chinquapin (tree)'
2.3   sika 'deer' (= ka)
2.3   sika 'so'
?2.3   siko 'formidable; ugly'
2.3   sima 'island; quarters, territory'
2.3   sima 'stripe'
2.3   sime 'sacred territory; sacred rope'
2.3   simo 'frost; cold rain'
?2.3, ?2.5   simo '(a kind of) bamboo'
2.3   sio 'salt; tide'
?2.3   sira(-) 'white' (= siro < sirwo)
2.3   siri 'buttocks'

2.3   sisi 'flesh; animal'
2.3   sita 'tongue'
?2.3   sit/zu 'shizu cloth'
2.3   soba 'winge'd spindle-tree'
2.3   sobi 'swollen testicles'
2.3   sori '? twig gate'
?2.3   sori 'sleigh'
2.3   soya 'battle arrow'
?2.3, ?2.4   sube 'means'
?2.3   sue 'porcelain'
2.3   suge 'sedge'
2.3   sumi 'charcoal; ink'
2.3   sune 'shank'
2.3   suri 'wicker basket'
2.3   susi 'sushi'
2.3   ‡ syaku 'footrule; royal tablet'
?2.4, ?2.3   ‡ syoo 'small/male hawk'
2.3   ‡ syubi 'fur-tipped scepter'
?2.4, ?2.3 tabo, tabu (< ?) 'back-hair'
?2.3   tago '"honey bucket"'
2.3   tai 'seabream'
?2.3   taka 'height, high; amount, quantity'
2.3   take 'mushroom' (= kinoko)
2.3   take 'height; stature'
?2.3, ?2.4   take 'mountain, peak'
2.3   taki 'height, stature'
2.3   tako 'octopus'
2.3   tako 'kite' (?< 'octopus')
2.3   ‡ taku: - no muma 'donkey' (= usagiuma)
2.3   tama 'jewel; ball; beautiful'
?2.3   tama 'spirit'
?2.3   tami 'people'
?2.3   tani 'valley'
?2.3   taru 'barrel, vat, cask'
2.3/2.4 *(or 2.5?)* tati 'mansion; fortress'
2.3   tati 'sword'
?2.4, ?2.3 ··· tati 'group (of persons)'
?2.3   tigo 'baby'
2.3   toge 'thorn'
?2.3   togi 'solacing'
2.3   toki 'time'
2.3   tome 'whetstone'
2.3   tomo 'stern of boat'
?2.3   tone 'official; ··· '
2.3   tono 'building; lord'
?2.3   ‡ too 'stupa'
*2.3   (-)tose '··· years'
2.3   tosi 'year(s); age'
?2.3   toyo 'rich'
2.3 ?< 3.4   tuba (?< tuba[ki]) 'spit'
2.3   tubi 'vulva'
?2.1, ?2.3   tuge 'boxtree'

2.3	tuka 'hilt'		?2.3	wada 'bend: inlet; valley'
?2.4, ?2.3	tuka 'bundle'		?2.5 ?< 2.3	wake 'distinguishing; meaning'
?2.1, ?2.3	tuki 'zelkova (tree)'		2.3	waki 'side'
2.3	tuki 'moon'		2.3	waku 'frame'
2.3	tuna 'rope'		2.3	wani 'crocodile; shark'
2.3	(-)tuna 'horn': see mituna		2.3	wata 'cotton'
2.3	tuno 'horn'		2.3	wata 'intestines, guts'
2.3	tura 'cheeks; face'		?2.3	yaka 'house, mansion'
2.3	tuti 'earth'		?2.3	yake 'house, mansion'
2.3	ube = mube 'Stauntonia hexaphylla'		2.3	yama 'mountain'
2.3	ude 'arm'		2.3	yami 'darkness'
2.3	udo = uto 'asparagus'		2.3	yani 'resin'
2.3	uga *'food received'		?2.3	yatu 'damn guy; damn thing'
?2.3	uke 'grain container'		?2.3/?2.4 < 2.1	yoki 'handax'
2.3	uma 'horse'		?2.3	yomi 'Hades'
2.3	umi 'pus; ooze'		2.3 < 3.4	yubi < oyobi 'finger, toe'
?2.3, ?2.4	una 'ridge; nape of neck; head'		2.3	yue 'bath mistress ···'
?2.3	una 'sea': see unabara, ...		?2.3 < 3.7b ‡	yu-hi 'mating'
2.3	une 'ridge in field'		2.3	yume 'dream'
2.3	ura 'bay'		2.3	yumi 'bow (to shoot arrows)'
2.3	ura 'reverse (side)'		4.5 = 2.3	yumigake 'archer's glove'
?2.3	uzi 'grub'		2.3 = 1.3|1.3	yuya 'bathhouse'
?2.3, ?2.4	uzu 'eddy'		2.3	‡ zyuzu 'rosary beads'
2.3	uzu 'hair-ornament'			

....

2.4 LH(H) 1-1-B B-B-C   Toyama, Suzu 1:2

?2.4 < *2.3	ae		2.4	hasi 'chopsticks'
?2.4 ?< 2.3	ai 'meeting'		2.4	hata '(dry) field'
?2.4	ama 'nun'		2.4	hera 'moldboard'
?2.4	amo = omo 'mother'		?2.4	hii 'baby's pubic area'
2.4	ani ?< [n]ani 'how possibly?!'		?2.4 ?< 3.6	hime = sime 'hawfinch' (bird)
2.4	are < [w]are (< ...) 'I/me'		?2.4, ?2.5	hisa 'longlasting'
2.1 (?) 2.4/5)	asi 'reed'		?2.4	hita(-) 'straight'
?2.4, ?2.3	aso 'my dear fellow'		?2.4, ?2.3	hito(-) 'one'
2.4	ato 'footprint'		?2.4, ?2.5	hiyu 'amaranthus'
?2.5 < 2.4	awa 'millet'		?2.4	hizu 'salmon head-bone'
2.4	‡ baka = hakka 'mint'		2.4	hoka 'other'
2.4	beni 'rouge'		?2.1, ?2.4	hora 'cave'
2.4 < 3.7b	‡ biwa 'loquat'		2.4	huna(-) 'boat'
2.1 (?< 3.1) (?) 2.4)	gama		2.4	hune 'boat'
2.4	geta 'clogs'		?2.4	huti 'rim; cliff'
2.4	geta 'square': see keta		2.4	iki 'breath'
2.4	hada 'skin, flesh'		?2.4, ?2.5	ima 'now'
?2.1; ?2.3, ?2.4	haha 'mother'		?2.4, ?2.5	imo 'male's sister: beloved girl'
?2.4 < ?3.6	hara 'trumpet (horn)'		2.4	ina(-) 'riceplant'
2.4	hari 'needle'		2.4	ina 'nay; disagreement'
2.4	hari 'black alder'		2.4	ine 'riceplant'

2.4   isa: *see* iza
2.4   ita 'board'
2.4   iti 'market'
2.4   ito 'thread'
?2.4, ?2.5   itu 'when; sometime'
2.4   iza 'well ··· : hey'
(?1.3b >) 2.4 ‡ ka < kwa < "kuwa" 'leather shoe'
2.4   kado 'corner'
?2.3, ?2.4   kage '"deer hair" = a horse color'
2.4   kai 'paddle'
2.4   kake 'cock; fowl'
2.4   kako 'belt buckle'
2.4   kama 'sickle'
2.4   kami 'above'
2.4   kari 'barb of a fish-hook'
2.4 (?< *2.1) kari 'mowing; a "cut" of rice'
?2.4 < 2.3   kari 'hunting'
?2.4   kari 'wild goose'
2.4   kasa 'umbrella'
?2.4, ?2.5   ka^s/$_z$e, [dial.] gaze 'sea-urchin' (= uni)
2.4   kasu 'dregs'
2.4   kata 'shoulder'
?2.4   kati 'walking'
2.4   kaya 'thatch'
?2.4, ?2.5   kaze 'sea-urchin': *see* kase
2.4   kazo 'father'
2.4   kazu 'number'
?2.3, ?2.4   kego 'lunchbox'
2.4   kesa 'this morning'
2.4   keta 'rafter, beam; lath, slat; row'
2.4   keta, geta 'square'
?2.4   kibi 'Kibi' *(placename)*
2.4 < ?2.5   kinu 'silk; garment'
2.4   kiri 'awl'
2.4   koko 'here'
?2.3, ?2.4   kona 'flour'
2.4 < 3.5 ‡ kozi < konzi 'scarf'
2.4   kozo 'last year/night'
2.4   kuda 'tube, pipe, ···'
?2.4 < 3.6 ‡ kuko 'Chinese matrimony vine'
2.4   kuri 'black clay' (= kuri-tuti)
?2.4   kusu(-) 'medicine' (?= 'camphor')
?2.3, ?2.4   kuzi 'lottery (chance)'
2.4   kuzu 'trash'
?2.4, ?2.5   kyoo 'today'
2.4 < 3.5 mada < imada '(not) yet'
?2.4   maro '(male name, name-suffix); I/me'
?2.4, ?2.3   masi 'monkey'
2.4   matu 'pine'
?2.4 < ?3.5   medo 'Sericea lespedeza; divining sticks'
2.4   mino 'raincape'
2.4   miru 'a kind of seaweed'
2.4   miso 'beanpaste'

?2.4   mizu 'vigorous; virtue: good omen'
?2.4, ?2.5   mozu 'shrike' *(bird)*
2.4 (?< 2.5) mugi 'barley'
?2.4, ?2.5   nai 'earthquake'
2.4   naka 'inside'
2.4   nani 'what: something'
?2.4, ?2.5   nao 'straight; ... : better'
?2.5, ?2.4   nare 'you'
?2.1/?2.4   niko(-) 'soft'
?2.4, ?2.5   nobe 'field'
?2.4, ?2.5   nobi 'wild fire'
2.4 < 3.5 nodo 'throat'
2.4   nomi 'chisel'
?2.4   nosi = nozi 'aster'
?2.3, ?2.4   nusa 'paper/cloth offering'
?2.4, ?2.5   nusi 'owner'
2.4   nuu 'marsh' LH (= nu R)
2.4   obi 'belt'
2.x (?2.4)   omo 'mother'
2.4   omo 'surface: face' (= omo-te)
?2.4, ?2.5   osa 'yarn guide'
?2.4, ?2.5   osa 'elder, leader, chief'
?2.4, ?2.5   osa 'interpreting; interpreter'
?2.3, ?2.4   saga 'omen'
?2.4   saga 'characteristic: fate, ... '
?2.4, ?2.1   sai 'spade: (= ura-sai) sword'
?2.4   ‡ sai 'rhinoceros'
?2.4   sawa(-) *mimetic*
2.4   saya 'sheath'
?2.4   saya 'pod; legume' (?= 'sheath')
?2.3, ?2.4   siba 'firewood, brushwood'
?2.4   sibe 'pistil; stamen'
?2.4, ?2.3   sibu 'astringent taste; ... '
2.x (?2.4)   sida 'fern'
?2.4 < ?3.6   sime 'hawfinch' *(bird)*
?2.4   -sine 'riceplant' (= ine)
2.4   siru 'juice, broth'
2.4   sizi 'footstand for ox carriage'
2.4   soba 'beside'
2.4   soba 'slope; corner, hem; (a)side'
?2.5, ?2.4   soba 'buckwheat'
2.4   soko 'there'
2.4   sono 'garden'
2.4   sora 'garden'
2.4   soto 'outside'
?2.4, ?2.1, ?2.3   sube 'means'
2.4   sumi '(inside) corner'
?2.5, ?2.4   susu 'soot'
2.4   suzi 'tendon, sinew'
2.4   ‡ syoo 'a kind of harp or panpipe'
?2.4, ?2.3 ‡ syoo 'small/male hawk' (= syoo-taka)
2.4   taba 'bunch'
?2.4, ?2.5   tada 'direct'

?2.3, ?2.4   take 'mountain, peak'
2.4   tana(-) 'seed'
2.4   tane 'seed'
?2.4, ?2.5 tate 'shield'
2.3/2.4 (or 2.5?)   tati 'mansion; fortress'
?2.4, ?2.3 ··· tati 'group (of persons)'
?2.4   tati 'paddy path'
?2.4, ?2.5   tazu 'crane'
?2.4   titi 'breasts; milk'
2.4   titi 'father'
?2.4   tizi 'thousands'
?2.5, ?2.4   toga 'blame, offence'
2.4   tomo 'an archer's left wrist-shield'
?2.4, ?2.5 < 3.5   tuba 'sword-guard'
?2.4a   tubi 'grain, granule' (= tubu)
2.4   tubu 'grain, granule'
2.4   tue 'staff'
?2.4, ?2.3   tuka 'bundle'
2.4   tumi 'sin'
2.4   tumu 'spindle'
2.4   *tuti 'hammer'
2.4   tuto 'straw-wrapped ··· '
?2.4   ‡ [ui] 'life's course/vicissitudes'
2.4   umi 'sea'
?2.3, ?2.4 una 'ridge; nape of neck; head'
?2.4   uni 'sea-urchin'
?2.4   ura 'heart, mind'

2.4   ura 'divination, foretelling'
2.4 (?< 2.5) uri 'melon'
?2.4   usi 'sir'
2.4   usu 'mortar'
?2.4, ?2.5   uti 'game path': see uzi
?2.4, ?2.5   uzi 'rabbit path; game path'
?2.3, ?2.4   uzu 'eddy'
1.3a ?< 2.3, ?< 2.4 wa 'I/me' (= ware)
2.4   wana 'trap'
2.4   wara 'straw'
2.4   ware 'I/me'
?2.4   wase 'early rice'
?2.4, ?2.5   yado 'lodgings'
?2.4   yagi 'goat'
?2.4, ?2.5   yana 'fishweir'
2.4   yane 'roof'
?2.4 (?= 3.7b)   ‡ yasi (?= yaasi) 'palm tree'
2.4   yodo 'pool'
?2.3/?2.4 < 2.1   yoki 'handax'
?2.1, ?2.4   yona(-) 'hulled rice'
?2.1, ?2.4   yone 'hulled rice'
?2.4, ?2.5   yowa 'night'
?2.4   yugi 'arrow quiver'
?2.4   yume '(not) ever'
?2.4 < ?3.6   yusi
2.4 ?< 2.5   ‡ zeni

2.5   LH(L) 1-1:3-B B-B-C   Toyama 2(-i/u), 1:3(-e/a/o); Suzu 2(-i/u), 1(-e/a/o)

2.5   abu < amu(?/abu) 'gadfly'
2.5   ai < awi 'indigo'
?2.5 < 2.1   aka 'red'
2.5   aki 'autumn'
2.5   ama(-) 'rain'
2.5 (?< 2.3) ama(-) 'heaven'
2.5   ame 'rain'
2.5   ame 'heaven'
?2.5   ani 'older brother'
2.5   ao 'blue'
2.5   ara(-) 'new'
2.5   asa 'morning'
2.5   ase 'sweat'
?2.5 < 2.4   awa 'millet'
2.5   ayu 'sweetfish'
?2.5   ‡ boke 'Japanese quince': see moke
?2.5   buto 'gadfly'
?2.5   buy°/u 'gadfly'
?2.2b, ?2.5   dani 'tick' (insect)
2.5   hamo 'eel'
2.5   haru 'spring(time)

?2.5   haya 'early; already'
2.5 ?< 3.6   hebi 'snake'
?2.5   hine 'late rice'
2.5   hiru 'leech'
?2.4, ?2.5   hisa 'longlasting'
?2.5   hiwa 'siskin' (bird)
?2.4, ?2.5   hiyu 'amaranthus'
?2.5   hora 'trumpet(-shell)'
?2.5   hugu 'blowfish'
2.5   huna 'crucian carp' (fish)
?2.5   hutu-ni 'with a slice: all'
2.5 < 3.5 ibo 'rice grain; wart'
2.5   ido 'well'
?2.4, ?2.5   ima 'now'
?2.4, ?2.5   imo 'male's sister; beloved girl'
?2.4, ?2.5   itu 'when; sometime'
?2.5 < 3.2a   kaba 'birch'
2.5   kaga(-) 'shade; light'
2.5   kage 'shade; light'
?2.5 < 2.3   kaki 'oyster'
?2.5   kako 'rower'

?2.5 < 2.3	kamo '(wild) duck' *(bird)*
2.5	kara 'Han': = Imna (= Mimana); ···
?2.4, ?2.5	kas/ze 'sea-urchin' (= uni)
?2.5 < 2.3	kasi 'oak'
?[2.5] < 3.7b	katu < katuu 'moreover'
?2.5	kaya 'Imna (= Mimana)'
?2.4, ?2.5	kaze 'sea-urchin': *see* kase
2.5	kibi, kimi 'millet'
2.5	kido 'wicket'
?2.5	kimi = kibi 'millet'
2.4 < ?2.5	kinu 'silk; garment'
?2.5, ?2.3	kobu 'gnarl, lump'
2.5 < 3.7b	kobu < konbu 'seaweed'
2.5	koe 'voice'
2.5	koi 'carp'
2.5	koto 'harp'
?2.5	koto 'different; special'
2.5	kowa(-) 'voice': *see* koe
2.5	kumo 'spider'
?2.5, ?2.3	kuro 'black'
2.5	kuzu 'arrowroot'
?2.4, ?2.5	kyoo 'today'
2.5	mado 'window, opening'
2.5	mae 'front'
2.5	masa(-ni) 'truly'
?2.5	mati 'sewn-in strip (in hakama etc.)'
?2.5	mato 'round'
?2.5	mayu 'eyebrow; cocoon'
?2.5	medo 'aim; needle eye'
?2.5	‡ moke = boke 'Japanese quince'
2.5	moko: *see* muko
?2.5	momo 'thigh(s)'
?2.5	moya 'haze, mist'
?2.4, ?2.5	mozu 'shrike'
2.4 (?< 2.5)	mugi 'barley'
?2.5	muko 'bridegroom'
?2.5	muku 'yew; grey sparling'
?2.5	muku 'shaggy'
2.5	nabe 'pan'
2.3 (?< 2.5)	nae 'seedling'
?2.4, ?2.5	nai 'earthquake'
2.5	nama 'raw'
?2.4, ?2.5	nao 'straight; ··· ; better'
?2.5, ?2.4	nare 'you'
2.5	nasu 'eggplant'
2.3 (?< 2.5)	nawa(-) 'seedling': *see* nae
?2.5 < ?3.7b	nazo 'riddle'
2.5	negi 'onion'
?2.3, ?2.5	neko 'cat'
?2.4, ?2.5	nobe 'field'
?2.4, ?2.5	nobi 'wild fire'
2.5	noko 'saw'
?2.4, ?2.5	nusi 'owner'

?2.5	oba < o[fo]-ba 'grandmother; old woman'
2.5	oke 'bucket'
?2.5	omo 'important'
?2.4, ?2.5	osa 'yarn guide'
?2.4, ?2.5	osa 'elder, leader, chief'
?2.4, ?2.5	osa 'interpreting; interpreter'
?2.3, ?2.5	sake 'salmon'
2.5	sara(-ni) 'new(ly)'
2.5	saru 'monkey'
2.5	sigi 'snipe'
?2.3, ?2.5	sino 'a kind of bamboo'
2.5	siro 'white'
?2.5	sizu 'poor, miserable'
?2.5, ?2.4	soba 'buckwheat'
2.5	sude 'barehanded'
2.5, (3.7)	sude(-ni) = sunde-ni 'already'
?2.5, ?2.4	susu 'soot'
2.5	tabi 'socks: a kind of shoe'
?2.4, ?2.5	tada 'direct'
?2.2b, ?2.5	tani = dani 'tick'
?2.5	tara 'Aralia elata'
?2.5	tara 'cod(fish)'
2.5	tate 'upright, vertical'
?2.4, ?2.5	tate 'shield'
2.3/2.4 *(or 2.5?)*	tati 'mansion; fortress'
?2.4, ?2.5	tazu 'crane'
2.5	‡ tiri 'geography'
?2.1, ?2.5	tobi 'kite (hen)' *(bird)*
?2.5, ?2.4	toga 'blame, offence'
2.5	toi 'water pipe'
?2.1, ?2.5	toki = tuki 'ibis' *(bird)*
?2.4, ?2.5 < 3.5	tuba 'sword-guard'
2.5	tui(-ni) '(at the) end'
?2.1, ?2.5	tuki = toki 'ibis' *(bird)*
?2.5	tuku 'owl': *see* zuku
2.5	tune 'always'
2.5	turu 'crane'
2.5	tuto(-ni) 'early (in the morning)'
2.5	tuyu 'dew'
?2.5, ?2.1	ubu 'naive'
2.4 (?< 2.5)	uri 'melon'
2.5	uso 'lie'
?2.4, ?2.5	uti 'game path': *see* uzi
?2.4, ?2.5	uzi 'rabbit path; game path'
2.5	uzi 'Uji' *(placename)*
?2.5 ?< 2.3	wake 'distinguishing; meaning'
?2.4, ?2.5	yado 'lodgings, shelter'
?2.4, ?2.5	yana 'fishweir'
2.5	yoru 'night'
?2.4, ?2.5	yowa 'night'
2.5	yuge 'steam'
2.4 ?< 2.5	zeni
2.5	zuku 'owl'

2.x (Inadequate data for assignment to specific patterns.)

2.x	‡ baba 'horserace ground'
2.x	bora 'mullet' *(fish)*
2.x	bira 'handbill'
?2.x	dono 'which ··· '
2.x (?‡2.3)	hae 'south (wind)'
2.x	hei 'wall'
2.x	hena 'mud, earth'
2.x	[hio] 'paper mulberry'
2.x	iso 'fifty'
2.x	[ito] 'young, lovable; beloved child'
2.x	ito(-) 'interval': *see* itoma; itonamu
2.x (?2.2b)	kara 'clan, family' (?< 'trunk')
2.x ?< 3.6	ki^s/$_z$a 'elephant'
2.x	kiso 'last night'
2.x	(-)koro 'lump': *see* isi-koro
2.x (?2.3)	kure 'lump, clod'
2.x	kusi '"wondrous elixir" = rice wine'
2.x	kuzu 'aboriginal peoples (of Japan)'
2.x	‡matu 'fire, torch' (?< 'pine' 2.4)
2.x	mige 'ox/sheep stomach'

2.x < 3.6	moda 'silence'
2.x	-muti = -muzi 'esteemed and beloved ··· '
2.x	-muzi < -muti 'esteemed and beloved ··· '
2.x	nigi 'lively'
2.x	nozi 'a road through the moor(s)'
2.x	ogo 'a kind of reddish seaweed'
2.x (?2.4)	omo 'mother'
2.x	sayo 'night'
2.x (?2.4)	sida 'fern'
2.x	siki 'stone fortress: ··· '
2.x	[siwa] 'cough'
2.x	soba/sowa 'cliff'
2.x	tae 'bark cloth'
2.x < 3.6	tis(y)a < tisa < ‡tiisa 'lettuce'
2.x	toga 'hemlock spruce'
2.x	tuga = toga 'hemlock spruce'
?2.x	? -uka (?< -[t]u - ka) 'day'
2.x	uru(-) 'moist, ··· '
?2.x	uto 'empty, hollow'
2.x	uzu 'precious'
2.x	yosi 'reed'

Nouns of three syllables
_____

3 = 3.1, 3.2, 3.4, 3.5a, 3.5b, 3.5a/b, 3.6, 3.7a, 3.7b, 3.7a/b, 3.7x; 3.x

3.1 HHH(H) 0-0-A A-A-A   Toyama 1:2
___

   (Note: The few examples that may be 3.1a are recapitulated at the end.)

3.1	abara 'ribs'
3.1	abara 'sparse; gazebo'
3.1	adana: *see* azana
3.1	agito 'jaw(s), gill(s)'
?3.1	akama 'bulrush'
?3.1, ?3.2x	akana 'red turnip'
?3.1, ?3.2x	akane 'madder'
3.1	akari 'light'
3.1	akasi 'light'
3.1	akubi 'yawn'
3.1	akuta 'dirt'
3.1	amagi 'licorice'
?3.1	ama[h]i = amani ('clematis')
3.1	amana *(plant names)*
3.1	amani 'clematis'
3.1	aoi 'hollyhock'
3.1	arare 'hail'
3.1	arata 'wild/rough field'
3.1	arato 'rough grindstone'
3.1 (= 2.1|1.1)	asase 'river shallows'
?3.6, ?3.1	asaza 'water fringe'

?3.5x (?‡3.1	asazi 'low-stemmed cogon'
?3.1, ?3.3	asibe 'where reeds grow'
3.1	asii 'Arthraxon hispidus'
3.1	atai 'value'
3.1	atara 'alas; regrettably'
?3.2b < 3.1	atari 'vicinity'
3.1	ati-ra 'yon way'
3.1 < 2.1	atti < ati 'yon way'
?3.1	azami 'thistle'
3.1	azana (= adana) 'alias; falsehood'
3.1 < 4.1	aziro 'rough-woven mat'
3.1	azuti 'archery target mound'
?3.1	dotira 'which way'
?3.1 < 3.7b	dotti 'which way'
?3.1	ebisu 'Ainu'
?3.1	eburi 'hoe'
?3.1, ?3.2x, ?3.3	enba 'dragonfly'
3.1	enoko 'puppy-dog'
3.1	eturi 'roof/wall underlay'
2.1 (?< 3.1) (?) 2.4)	gama 'bulrush'
3.1	hadate: *see* hatate

?3.1   hahako 'Artemesia keiskiana'
3.1   hahaso 'oak'
3.1   hanazi 'nosebleed'
3.1   haniwa 'burial objects'
3.1   haori 'coat'
3.1   ha^t/$_ч$ate 'brink, limit'
3.1   hatisu 'lotus' (> hasu 2.1)
3.1   hatuka 'twenty days'
?3.1, ?3.4   hatuko 'descendants'
3.1   hazime 'beginning'
?3.1   henoko 'testicle; penis'
?3.1   hesaki 'bow of boat'
3.1   hetima 'snake gourd'
3.1   hideri 'drought'
3.1   hikage 'shady place'
3.1   hikite 'doorknob'
3.1   hirada 'flatbottomed boat'
?3.1   hirade 'offertory bowl'
3.1   hirage 'ordinary'
3.1   hiraka 'plate'
3.1   hirate 'hand clap'
3.1, 3.2x hirume 'Day(light) Female'
3.1   hisame 'hail; sleet'
3.1   hisasi 'eaves'
?3.1   hisio 'a kind of beanpaste'
3.1   hitai 'forehead'
3.1   hitira 'a kind of rice cake'
3.1   hitomi 'pupil of eye'
3.1   hitoya 'jail'
3.1   hitugi 'coffin'
3.1   hitugi 'the Imperial Dignity; ··· '
3.1   hituzi 'sheep'
3.1   hituzi 'sprouting (anew, ···)'
3.1   hiyoko 'chicken'
3.1   hiyori 'good weather'
?3.5a/b, ?3.1 hizume 'hoof'
3.1   hokora 'shrine'
3.1   hokori 'dust'
(?3.1) < 4.5   horike 'man-made pond'
3.1   hosozi = hozoti 'ripe melon'
3.1   hozoti 'ripe melon'
3.1   hozuna 'halyard'
?3.1   [huhuki] 'bog-rhubarb'
3.1   hukura 'swelling; holly'
3.1 > 2.1 [humida] > huda 'card'
3.1 > 2.1 [humide] > hude 'brush'
?3.1, ?3.4   humoto 'foot of mountain'
3.1   hunori 'funori (glue plant)'
3.1   hurui 'sieve'
3.1   hutuka 'two days'
3.1   huyugi 'Welsh onion'
3.1   huzina 'dandelion'

?3.1, ?3.2x   hyuuga 'turning toward the sun'
3.1   igata 'matrix'
3.1   igisu 'a kind of seaweed'
3.1   ikada 'raft'
3.1   ikao = ikaho 'Ika(h)o' (placename)
3.1   ikari 'anchor'
?3.1   inago 'sand'
3.1   inaka 'country(side)'
3.1   inoko 'wild boar'
3.1   iome 'fish eye'
3.4 (> 3.1)   iori 'hut'
3.1   iruka 'dolphin'
3.1   isago 'sand'
3.1   isami 'bravery'
?3.1   isana 'whale'
3.1   isari 'plowshare'
?3.1   isuka 'grossbeak' (bird)
3.1   iwao 'crag'
3.1   iware 'reason'
3.1   iwasi 'sardine' (fish)
3.1   iwaya 'grotto'
3.1   kabane 'corpse'
?3.1   kabura 'turnip; arrow whistle'
?3.1   kadobi 'gate fire'
3.1   kadoya 'gate-house'
3.1   kagari 'bonfire'
?3.1   kagati 'bladder/ground cherry'
3.1 < 4.2 kaizi 'commuting route'
?3.1, ?3.4   kakina 'Arthraxon hispidus'
?3.1   kakine 'fence'
3.1   kakiwa 'steadfast rock'
3.1   kamado 'oven'
4.1 (> 3.1)   kamudati = kandati 'malt, yeast'
3.1   kanae 'tripod kettle'
?3.1   kanagu 'metal fixture'
3.1   kaname 'pivot'
?3.2b, ?3.1   kanata 'that way/direction'
3.1   kaori 'fragrance'
3.1   karada 'body'
3.1   kasumi 'mist'
3.1   katami 'keepsake'
3.1   katane 'carbuncle'
3.1   katati 'shape'
3.1 (< *4.1)   katori 'tight-woven cloth'
3.1   katuo 'bonito'
3.1   katura 'judas-tree' (= oka^t/$_z$ura)
3.1   kawana 'edible river-weeds'
?3.1 (< *4.1), ?3.2 kawara 'riverbed'
3.5 (?< ?3.1, ?3.2) kawara 'Kawara', 'the River'
3.1 (< *4.1)   kawawa 'river bend'
3.1   kawaya 'toilet'
3.1   kazari 'ornament'

3.1   kemuri, keburi 'smoke'
3.1 > 2.1 kigisu > kigisi > kizi 'pheasant'
3.1   kihada 'cork-tree'
3.1   kimono 'garment'
?3.1, ?3.2x   kitai 'fish/meat dried whole'
?3.1, ?3.4   kizuna 'fetter, leash'
3.1   kodomo 'child'
3.1   kogai 'sericulture'
3.1   kogame 'a small tortoise; ···'
?3.1   kogame 'a little jar (?)'
3.1   koguso 'silkworm excrement'
3.1   kohagi 'small bushclover'
?3.1   komatu 'small pine'
?3.1, ?3.2x   komira 'leek'
3.1   konami 'first wife'
3.1   konori 'male sparrow-hawk' (bird)
3.1   koono 'small ax'
3.1   koori 'ice'
3.1 < 4.1 koozi 'malt, yeast'
3.1   koromo 'gown'
3.1   kosame 'fine rain'
3.1 = 1.1|2.1 kosuzu 'little bells'
3.1   koti-ra 'this way'
3.1   kotori 'bird'
3.1   kotosi 'this year'
3.1 < 2.1 kotti < koti 'this way'
?3.1, ?3.5x   kotuo 'shark'
3.1   kousi 'calf'
3.1   koyama 'hill'
3.1   koyoi 'tonight'
3.1   kozaru 'little monkey'
3.1 = 1.1|2.3 kozima 'little island'
3.1   kozuno 'ox-horn tip bone'
3.1   kubote 'offertory basket'
3.1   kudari 'descent'
2.1 ?< *3.1   kuga 'dry land'
3.1   ǂ kugo, kuugo 'harp'
?3.1   kuguse 'rickets'
3.1   kuize 'stick'
3.1, 3.2   kurabu 'Kurabu' (placename)
3.1   kurai 'position'
3.1   kuruma 'car(t)'
3.1   kusari 'chain'
3.1   kutuwa 'bridle bit'
3.1   madara 'spots'
3.1   magari 'a kind of cake'
?3.1   mamusi 'viper'
3.1 (?< 4.x)   manago 'sand'
?3.1 (?<4.x)   masago 'sand'
?3.4, ?3.1   masaki 'Euonymus japonicus'
3.1   maturi 'festival'

?3.1   mayumi 'euonymus, spindletree'
?3.1, ?3.4   menoto 'wet-nurse'
3.x (?= 3.1)   migiri = migi 'right (hand)'
3.1   migiwa 'water-edge'
3.1   mikado 'emperor'
3.1   mikage 'image, soul'
3.1   mikata 'ally'
3.1   mikawa 'Mikawa' (placename)
3.1   mikka 'three days'
3.1   mikoto 'lord/god; prince'
?3.1   mikura 'the emperor's seat/position'
3.1   mikura 'the Treasury'
?3.1   mikuri, miguri 'bur reed'
3.1   mikusa 'aquatic plants'
3.1   mimaya 'stable'
?3.1   mimoto 'where the divine/noble is'
3.1 (?3.1a)   minami 'south'
3.1   minato 'port'
3.1   misago 'osprey' (bird)
3.1   misao 'fidelity'
3.1   misora 'sky'
3.1   mitake 'peak'
3.1   mitama 'spirit'
?3.4,?3.1 mitani 'valley'
3.1   mitose 'three years'
?3.1   mitugi 'tribute'
3.1   miyako 'capital'
3.1   miyama 'deep mountains'
3.1   mizore 'sleet'
3.1   mizuha 'god of water'
3.1   mizuti 'sea serpent'
?3.1   mizuto 'floodgate'
?3.1   mosio 'seaweed salt'
3.1   mosoro 'thin sake; unrefined sake'
3.1   motii 'rice cake' (> moti 2.1)
3.1   muika 'six days'
3.1   mukai 'opposite'
3.1 (?3.1a)   mukasi 'yore'
3.1   mukuro 'body; ···'
3.1   munagi = unagi 'eel'
3.1   murado 'kidney; heart'
3.1   murazi '(a rank title)'
3.1   musuko 'son'
3.1   namae 'name'
2.1 < 3.1 namu(-) 'you'
3.1   na-muzi: see nanzi
3.1   nanzi 'you'
3.1   naori 'wave upon wave'
3.1   natume 'jujube'
3.1   nazasi 'designation'
3.1   ne^b/muri 'sleepiness': 'silk tree'

3.1   negoto 'sleep-talking'
3.1   nemuri: *see* ne^b/_muri
?3.2x, ?3.1 nigime 'seaweed'
3.1   nikawa 'glue'
?3.1   niwabi 'yard torch'
3.1   niwaso 'spurge'
3.1   nobori 'climb'
3.1   noosa: noosa-noosa 'to one's utmost'
3.1   nozomi 'view, hope'
?3.1   nuride 'sumac': *see* nurude
3.1   nurite 'wooden bell': *see* nute
?3.1(> 2.1) nurude, nuride (> nude) 'sumac'
3.1   odate 'small shield'
3.1   odori 'dance'
3.4 *(?= 3.1)* odori 'male bird, ··· '
?3.1   okibi 'blazing fire'
?3.1   okubi 'belch'
?3.1   omoni 'heavy burden'
3.1/3.4   omosi 'weight'
3.1   onora 'we/us; you'
?3.2x, 3.1 onore 'self'
3.1   oosi 'whole; wholly'
3.1 > 2.1 oosi > osi '(deaf-)mute'
3.1   osoi 'cover; ··· '
3.1   osui 'outer garment'
3.4 *(= 3.1?)*   otori 'male bird; soldier'
3.1 (?< 3.1a) otto 'husband'
3.1   owari 'end'
(3.1<) 3.5a ‡ rakuda 'camel'
3.1   ‡ renizi 'lattice-work' (= renzi)
?3.4, ?3.1 sakaki 'sacred tree'
3.1   sakan 'flourishing'
3.1   sakana 'fish'
3.1   sakari 'prospering'
3.2a (> 3.1) sakura 'cherry'
3.1   samomo 'early peach; ··· '
3.1   sanae 'rice sprouts'
3.1   sarai 'rake'
?3.6, ?3.1 sasage 'cowpea'
?3.7a, ?3.1 sa^s/_zara 'small'
?3.7a, ?3.1 sa^s/_zare 'small'
3.1   satori 'enlightenment'
3.1   sawari 'hindrance'
?3.1   sibasi < simasi 'a while'
3.1   sibuki 'Houyttuynia cordata'
3.1   sigoto 'job'
3.1   sikii 'threshold; seat'
3.1   sikimi 'threshold'
3.1   sikiri 'frequently'
3.1   sioki 'punishment'
3.1   sirusi 'sign, token'

3.1   sitabi 'underground water-pipe; ··· '
3.1   sitao 'earlier husband'
3.1   sitazi 'groundwork'
3.1   siwaza 'act'
3.1   sokoi 'outer edges; depths'
3.1   sonemi 'envy'
3.1   soti-ra 'that way'
3.1 < 2.1 sotti < soti 'that way'
?3.1   subaru 'Pleiades'
?3.1   sukumo 'peat'
?3.1   sumai 'wrestling'
?3.1   sumera(-) 'imperial'
3.1   sumoo 'wrestling'
?3.1, ?3.4 sunago 'sand'
3.1   surume 'dried cuttlefish'
3.1   suzuki 'perch, seabass' *(fish)*
3.1   ‡ syoozi 'shōji'
3.1   syuuto 'father-in-law'
3.1   tagane 'cold chisel; ··· '
3.1   takigi 'firewood'
3.1   tatami 'mat'
3.1   tatari 'curse'
3.1   tetere 'decoy bird'
3.1   tigai 'difference'
3.1   tiguso 'dysentery'
3.1   tihaya 'a kind of sleeve-tie'
?3.1   tikai 'pledge'
3.1   timaki 'leaf-wrapped rice dumpling'
3.1   timata 'crossroads'
3.1   [tobio] = tobiuo 'flying fish'
3.1   togura 'bird perch'
3.1   tokiwa 'everlasting'
3.1a   tokoro 'place'
?3.1   tokoyo 'eternal'
3.1   tomara 'pivot'
3.1   tomari 'lodging'
3.1   tomaya 'covered hut'
3.1   tonari 'neighbor'
?3.1   tooka 'ten days'
3.1 = 2.1-tu too-tu ··· 'distant'
3.1   torii 'shrine gate'
3.1   tori^k/_go 'bird cage'
?3.1   tosaka 'cockscomb'
?3.1   tubone 'temporarily partitioned room'
3.1   tuide 'order'
3.1 < 4.1 tuizi 'mud fence'
3.1   tukai 'errand'
3.1   tukasa 'elevation; official'
?3.1, ?3.2a tukuba 'Tsukuba' *(placename)*
‡3.1 < 4.1 tukuda < tukurida 'cultivated field'
3.1   tukue 'desk'

3.1	tukumo 'bulrush'	
3.1	tumori 'intention'	
?3.1, ?3.6	tumuzi 'whirlwind'	
3.1	tutuga 'illness'	
?3.1	tutumi 'hindrance, handicap, impairment'	
?3.1, ?3.4	tuzumi 'drum'	
?3.1	ubume 'midwife'	
3.1	ueki 'potted plant'	
3.1	ugai 'gargle'	
?3.1, ?3.2x	uguso ?= ugusa (plant name)	
3.1	ukami 'spy'	
3.1	uki^k/ɡ i 'raft, boat'	
?3.1 = 4.1	umuki = umuki-na 'barrenwort'	
3.1	urusi 'lacquer'	
3.1 (< *4.1)	utata 'more and more'	
?3.6, ?3.1	utigi: see uti^k/ɡ i	
?3.6, ?3.1	uti^k/ɡ i 'undergarment'	
(?*3.1 <) 2.2|1.1	utito 'inside and outside'	
3.1	utuo/utubo 'hollow'	
3.1	utuwa 'utensil'	
?3.1	uwabe 'surface'	
3.1	uwao 'later husband'	
3.1/3.2x	wabira 'apricot leaves; ··· '	

3.1	waribu 'chit'
3.1	watari 'crossover'
?3.1	yagate 'before long'
3.1	yagura 'tower'
3.1	yagure 'roofing boards'
3.1	yahazu 'arrow-notch, nock'
?3.1/3.4	yaka^s/ᵤ u 'house'
3.1	yakure: see yagure
?3.1, ?3.2x	yamome 'widow'
?3.1	yamoo 'widower'
3.1	yanagi 'willow'
3.1	yasaki 'arrowhead'
3.1	yasuri 'file'
?3.1 < 2.1	yattu < ya-tu 'eight'
3.1 (?= 2.1|1.1)	yatugi 'eight (horses)'
3.1	yaziri 'arrowhead'
3.1	yodare, yodari 'drivel'
3.1	yokka 'four days'
3.1	yooka 'eight days'
3.1	yoroi 'armor'
?3.1 < 2.1	yottu < yotu 'four'
3.1	yuhata 'tie-dyeing'

3.1a HHH < HHF ?< *HHHL   (See Ch. 4, §7.3.)

3.1 (?3.1a)	minami 'south'
3.1 (?3.1a)	mukasi 'yore'
3.1 (?< 3.1a)	otto 'husband'
3.1a	tokoro 'place'

3.2 = 3.2a, 3.2b, 3.2a/b, 3.2x

3.2a HHL(L) < *HHH(L) 0-1:3-A A-A-(C)*   Suzu 1

*For Yonaguni only mukade and umago are attested; monaka is A, as are
hutari and hutatu. Kyōto has 0 for quite a few of the 3.2a nouns,
and also for a number of the 3.2b and 3.2x nouns.

3.2a	aka^k/ᵍ o 'baby'
3.2a	akaza 'Chenopodium album'
3.2a	enoki 'hackberry'
?3.2a	hagusa 'paddy weeds, tare'
3.2a	hanage 'nostril hairs'
3.2a	hanagi 'ox nose-ring'
?3.2a	hiziki 'wooden brace'
3.2a	hogeta 'sailyard, boom'
3.2a	huyuge 'winter fur'
3.2a	ibara 'thorn, bramble'

3.2a	iwane 'rock'
3.2a > ?2.5	[kaniwa] 'birch'
3.2a	kasiwa 'oak'
3.2a	katami 'bamboo basket'
?3.7x, ?3.2a	katano 'Katano' (placename)
3.2a < 4x	kibisu 'heel'
3.2a	kigawa 'orange peel'
3.2a	kohone, koohone 'candock'
?3.2a	konata 'this way/direction, here'
3.2a < 4.x	kubisu, kufisu = kibisu 'heel'

?3.2a	midori 'green'		3.2a	toboso 'pivot; door'
?3.2a	misok/gi 'ablution'		3.2a	tokage 'lizard'
?3.2a, ?3.7b	monaka 'very midst'		3.2a	tubasa 'wing'
3.2a	mubara: *see* ibara		?3.1, ?3.2a	tukuba 'Tsukuba' *(placename)*
3.2a	mukade 'centipede'		3.2a	ubara: *see* ibara
3.2a	nikoge 'down(y hair)'		3.2a	uk/gara 'clan'
3.2a	odoro 'bush, thicket'		3.2a	uwami, uwamo 'upper garment'
3.2a	okera 'Atractylodes japonica'		?3.2a	warigo 'snowshoes'
3.2a () 3.1)	sakura 'cherry'		3.2a	yagara 'arrow-shaft'
?3.2a	sanagi 'chrysalis, pupa'		?3.2a	yosuga 'means'
3.2a	tobari 'curtain'			

3.2b　HHL(L)　3(/0)-2-A　A-A-(A)*　　　　Toyama 1:3; Suzu 1

　　　*For Yonaguni only hutari, hutatu, huguri, and nagori are attested.

3.2b	aida 'interval'		3.2b	mamugi 'wheat'
?3.2b, ?3.3	anata ⟨ kanata 'over there'		?3.2b	mikosi 'palanquin'
3.2b	arame 'Eisenia bicyclis'		?3.2b ⟨ 2.2b	mittu ⟨ mitu 'three'
?3.2b ⟨ 3.1	atari 'vicinity'		?3.2b	mukoo 'yonder'
3.2b	azuki 'red bean'		?3.2b	musume 'daughter'
?3.2b	ekubo 'dimple'		?3.2b	muttu 'six'
3.2b ⟨ 4.2	higasi 'east'		?3.2b, ?3.4	nagori 'aftertraces, memory'
3.2b	huguri 'testicles; scrotum'		?3.2b	namako 'sea-cucumber'
?3.7a/b = 2.4|1.3; ?3.2b inaba 'Inaba' *(place)*			3.2b ⟨ 4.2	nedoko 'sleeping place, alcove'
?3.2b, ?3.1	kanata 'over there'		3.2b	onna ⟨ "wom[u]na" ⟨ womyina 'woman'
3.2b	kawabe 'riverside'		3.2b	oroka 'trifling; stupid'
3.2b	kazura 'vine, creeper'		3.2b	tadori 'lapwing; pewit' *(bird)*
3.2b	kenuki 'tweezers'		3.2b	tobira 'door'
?3.4, ?3.2b	kinoo 'yesterday'		3.2b	turube 'well-bucket'
?3.2b	koozo 'paper mulberry'		?3.3, 3.2b	yasozi 'eighty'
3.2b	kubiki 'crosspiece ⋯ '		?3.2b	yorube 'something to depend on'
?3.2b, ?3.3	kusyami 'sneeze'		4.x ⟨ 3.2b	yottari ⟨ yotari 'four people'
3.2b	magusa 'forage'			

3.2a/b　(Evidence for both <u>a</u> and <u>b</u>.)

3.2a/b	hutae 'double, twofold'
3.2a/b	hutari 'two people'
3.2a/b	hutatu 'two'
3.2a/b	sikimi 'star anise'
3.2a/b	tusima 'Tsushima'

3.2x (No evidence for assignment to either a or b.)

?3.1, ?3.2x   akana 'red turnip'
?3.1, ?3.2x   akane 'madder'
?3.2x   asika 'sea lion, hairseal'
3.2x   azika 'woven basket'
3.2x   emisi 'Ainu'
?3.1, ?3.2x, ?3.3   enba 'dragonfly'
3.2x   enisu 'pagoda tree'
3.2x   hanizi 'sumac'
3.2x   hatae 'handle/shaft of spear'
3.2x   hirab/mi 'a kind of garment'
3.1, 3.2x   hirume 'Day(light) Female' (god name)
3.2x   horosi 'Solanum lyratum'
?3.3 < 4.3, ?3.2x < 4.2   hubako 'box for letters'
?3.1, ?3.2x   hyuuga 'Hyūga' (placename)
?3.2x   igui 'support stakes ··· '
3.2x   iroe 'inlaying color'
3.2x   kakiho 'fence (top)'
3.2x (> ?2.4) kaniwa (> kaba) 'birch'
?3.1 (< *4.1), ?3.2x   kawara 'riverbed'
3.5 (?< ?3.1, ?3.2x) kawara 'Kawara', 'the River'
?3.1, ?3.2x   kitai 'fish/meat dried whole'
?3.1, ?3.2x   komira 'leek'
3.2x   kowasi 'small eagle'
3.2x   kubosa 'profit'
3.1, 3.2x   kurabu 'Kurabu' (placename)

3.2x = 2.1|1.3 kutuko 'feed-basket ··· '
?3.2x, ?3.3   kuzika 'fanged roe deer'
3.2x   marera 'being few/rare'
3.2x   migara 'small insect in well water'
3.2x   mimana(-no-kuni) 'Imna, Mimana'
*3.2x   minari 'appearance, attire'
3.2x   mitari 'three people'
3.2x   mituna = mituno 'three-horn(ed)'
?3.2x   mooto 'nobleman'
3.2x   nayosi 'grey mullet fingerling' (fish)
?3.2x, ?3.1   nigime 'a kind of seaweed'
?3.3, ?3.2x   onoko 'boy, man'
?3.2x, 3.1   onore 'self'
3.2x   sakeku 'safely'
3.2x   semine 'back ridge'
3.2x, ?3.7x   setuka 'back ridge'
3.2x   [siine] 'lump, hump'
3.2x   sitamo 'lower garment'
?3.2x = 2.1|1.3 tamuki, tamoki 'ash tree'
3.2x   tutuge 'bird down'
?3.1, ?3.2x   uguso ?= ugusa (plant names)
3.1/3.2x   wabira 'apricot leaves: ··· '
?3.1, ?3.2x   yamome 'widow'
3.2x (?= 1.1|2.2)   yobito 'people'

···

3.3   HLL(L) 1(<*2)-2-A A-A-A   Toyama, Suzu 1:3

Note: Tōkyō retains 2 for komugi and tutuzi. Most of the
Tōkyō-type dialects have 2 as the regular reflex for 3.3.

3.3   adasi < atasi 'other; vain, empty'
?3.7a ?< 3.3   akebi 'Akebia quinata'
?3.2b, ?3.3   anata < kanata 'over there'
?3.1, ?3.3   asibe 'where reeds grow'
3.3   awabi 'abalone'
?3.1, ?3.2x, ?3.3   enba 'dragonfly'
?3.3   hatati 'twenty years'
?3.3   hinata 'sunny place'
3.3   horo-ha 'underwing feathers'
?3.3 < 4.3, ?3.2x < 4.2   hubako 'box for letters'
3.3   ikura 'how much'
?3.3   kamina 'hermit crab'
3.3   kasiko 'there'
3.3   kasuga 'Kasuga' (placename)
3.3   katak/gi 'pattern board'
3.3   ‡ kazami 'a kind of garment'

3.3   kobiru 'wild leek: garlic'
3.3   kogane 'gold'
3.3   kokaze 'slight breeze'
3.3   komiti 'alley'
3.3   komugi 'wheat'
?3.3   kusabi 'wedge'
?3.2b, ?3.3   kusyami 'sneeze'
3.3   kutune = kitune₃.₆ 'fox'
?3.2x, ?3.3   kuzika 'fanged roe deer'
3.3   misaki 'promontory'
3.3   miziro 'white-grained'
3.3 (< 4.3) mohara 'exclusively'
3.3   mohaya 'already'
?3.3   ‡ monzi 'writing, letters'
2.2b < 3.3   mosi 'perchance'
?3.3, ?3.4   mottomo < motomo 'sensible; most'

?2.2b < 3.3 ‡ mozi < monzi 'writing, letters'   3.3   tikara 'strength'
?2.2a < ?3.3 nizi 'rainbow'   3.3   ?tonaka 'the mouth of a strait/bay'
?2.2a < ?3.3 nozi 'rainbow': *see* nizi   3.3   totugi 'ten generations'
?3.3, ?3.7   ogiro 'vast'   3.3 = 1.1|2.3 toyama 'foothills'
?3.3, ?3.2x onoko 'boy; man'   ?3.3   tutuzi 'wisteria'
?3.4, ?3.3   sarak/ge 'shallow jar'   3.3   utugi 'deutzia'
?2.2b < 3.3 syako 'squilla'   ?3.3   wasabi 'horseradish'
?2.2b < 3.3 syako 'partridge'   ?3.7b, ?3.3 yamori 'gecko'
?2.2b < 3.3 syako 'giant clam'   ?3.3, 3.2b   yasozi 'eighty'

....

<u>3.4</u>   LLL(L) 3-2(<3)-B B-B-B   Kōchi 3; Toyama 1:3(-i/u), 1:4(-e/a/o); Suzu 0

3.4   abumi 'stirrup'   3.4   hadake 'brush'; 'psoriasis'
3.4   agata 'rural land'   3.4   hakama 'man's skirt'
3.4   agoe 'bird's claw'   3.4   hakari '(weighing) scales'
?3.4   ahiru 'duck'   ?3.4 ‡ hakase (= hakusi) 'expert'
?3.4   aima 'interval'   3.4   hanada 'dark blue'
3.4   akit/da 'autumn fields'   3.4   hanami 'flower viewing'
3.4   amari 'excess'   3.4   hanasi 'talk'
?3.4 (= 2.3|1.3) aona 'greens; turnip'   3.4 (= 2.3|1.3) harame 'pregnant woman'
3.4   aori 'mudguards'   3.4   haruhi 'spring day'
?3.4a   aoto 'blue(-gray) grindstone'   3.4   hasami 'scissors'
?3.4   arasi 'storm'   ?3.4/?3.7a hatake 'psoriasis'
?3.4   arata 'new'   ?3.1, ?3.4 hatuko 'descendants'
3.4   arika 'location'   3.4   hayasi 'forest'
3.4   ario 'hill'   3.4   hayati 'wind storm'
3.4   asaka 'Asaka' *(placename)*   *3.4 < ?*4.5 hayato 'the Hayato (people)'
?3.4, ?3.5x asake 'dawn'   3.4   hazama 'gap, valley'
?3.4   asari 'fishing, clamming; ··· '   3.4 < 4.5 hazuma 'bareback horse'
3.4   aseb/mo 'heat rash'   3.4   hibiki 'echo'
3.4/3.5x asida 'clogs'   3.4   hidame 'pleat'
3.4   asio 'hawk jess'   3.4   hikari 'flash, light'
?3.4   asita 'tomorrow'   3.4   hikiri 'fire stick'
3.4   atama 'head'   ?3.4   himusi 'moth'
3.4   atiki ' ? '   ?3.4a   hirome 'seaweed'
3.4   atori 'mountain finch' *(bird)*   3.4   hitaki 'burning fires'
3.4   awaki 'a tree ··· '   3.4   hitao 'straight hills'
3.5b ?< 3.4 aware 'sympathy, pity'   ?3.4   hitati 'Hitachi' *(placename)*
3.4   awase 'lined garment'   ?3.4   hiziki 'a kind of seaweed'
3.4   awata 'kneecap'   ?3.4   hok/gusi 'a post-hole digger'
?3.4 (?= 2.3|1.3) ayabe 'the Aya (guild)'   ?3.4   hokuso 'tinder'
?3.4, ?3.6   ayame 'design; sweetflag'   3.4   horie 'canal'
?3.4, ?3.7b azuma 'Azuma' *(placename)*   ?3.4   hosoki 'Japanese pepper-tree'
3.4   azusa 'catalpa'   3.4   hotoke 'Buddha'
?3.4 ‡ basyoo 'banana'   3.4   hotue 'top branches'
3.4 (?< 4.10) edati 'conscripted labor; war'   3.4   hukuro 'bag'
?3.4, ?3.5b ekaki 'artist'   ?3.4   huk/gusi 'a post-hole digger'
3.4 < 4.10 eyami 'epidemic'   ?3.1, ?3.4 humoto 'foot of mountain'
3.4   hadae 'flesh'   3.4   hunani 'cargo'

3.4   hunayu 'bilge'
3.4   huroba 'bathroom'
3.4   husuma 'fusuma; bedding'
3.4   ibiki 'snore'
3.4   iei '(staying at) home'
3.4   iibo 'rice grain; wart'
?3.4   ikaga 'how'
3.4   ikesu 'fish crawl'
3.4   ikusa 'battle'
3.4   imina 'taboo name'
3.4   imoi 'purifying oneself; ··· '
3.4   imo^{s}/$_{z}$i 'yam stalks'
3.4   inagi 'drying pole'
3.4   inori 'prayer'
3.4 (> 3.1)   iori 'hut'
3.4   iriko 'dried sea-cucumber'
?3.4   iroko (> uroko) 'gills'
3.4   irori 'bonito stock (broth)'
3.4/3.5x itabi 'fig'
?3.4   itade 'wounded hand'
3.4   itado 'plank door'
3.4   itai 'plank well'
3.4   itami 'pain'
3.4   itati 'weasel'
?3.4   itaya 'shingle roof'
?3.4   itii 'Japanese yew'
3.4   itoma 'leisure'
3.4   ituka 'five days'
?3.5b, ?3.4   itutu 'five'
?3.7a ?< 3.4 izumi 'spring'
?3.4   kabati 'cheekbone'
3.4   kabuti 'bitter orange; nutmeg'
3.4   kagami 'mirror'
?3.4   kagiri 'limit'
3.4/3.5 kaigo 'egg'
3.4   kaina 'Arthraxon hispidus'
?3.1, ?3.4   kakina 'Arthraxon hispidus'
?3.4   kamati: see kabati
3.4 < 2.3 kanna < kana '(carpenter's) plane'
3.4 < 4.x karei 'dried rice ··· for a journey'
±3.4   karite 'provisions': see kate
3.4   kasira 'head; chief'
?3.4   kasuri 'splashed pattern'
3.4   kataki 'enemy'
?3.4   katami 'one side of the body'
3.4   katana 'sword'
3.4   katane 'sleeping on one side; ··· '
3.4   [kawabe] 'skin layer'
3.4   kawara 'tile'
3.4   kazasi 'hair-ornament'

3.4 = 4.5 kaziki = kanziki 'a kind of snowshoe'
3.4   kemono 'animal'
3.4   kikugi 'peg; wooden stopper'
?3.4, ?3.2b   kinoo 'yesterday'
?4.6 (> 3.4)   kinuita 'fulling block'
3.4   kisage 'scraper, ··· '
?3.1, ?3.4   kizuna 'fetter, leash'
3.4   kobusi 'fist'
3.4   ko-hizi 'mud'
3.4   kokisi 'king (of Paekche Korea)'
3.4   kokome 'ugly woman'
3.4   kokuwa 'a wooden hoe'
?3.4   kokuwa 'Actinidia arguta' (= sarunasi)
3.4   konata 'well-developed riceland (paddy)'
3.4   koori 'district, county'
3.4   kosuki 'all-wood spade'
3.4   kotoba 'word'
3.4   kotoi 'sturdy ox'
3.4   [kotoo] 'harp string'
3.4   kotori 'bodyguard to the emperor; ··· '
3.4   kotozi 'harp bridge'
3.4   koyomi 'calendar'
3.4   ‡ koziki 'beggar'
3.4   koziri 'chape'
3.4   kozue 'twig'
3.4   kudara 'Paekche (Korea)'
3.4   kuina 'mud hen' *(bird)*
3.4   kukumi 'holding in mouth; ··· '
3.4   kunegi '? thread-winder stick'
3.4   kunugi 'oak'
3.4   kuriya 'kitchen'
3.4   kuromi 'blackness; ···; octopus ink'
3.4   kuromi 'dark meat/fish'
3.4   kusaya 'grass hut; hay barn'
3.4   kutuo 'shoestring'
3.4   mabusi 'hunter's blind'
?3.4   mamori 'amulet'
3.4   maneki 'loom treadle'
3.4   masai 'sharp sword'
?3.4, ?3.1   masaki 'Euonymus japonicus'
3.7b(/3.4)   medori 'hen'
3.4   mekoma 'raccoon-dog'
3.7 < 3.4 = 1.3|2.3 mekuso 'eye discharge'
3.4   ‡ menoo 'agate'
?3.1, ?3.4   menoto 'wet-nurse'
?3.4   mesii 'blind, sightless'
3.4   meuma 'mare'
3.4   meyani 'eye discharge'
3.4   migiri 'eave-trough stones/tiles; ··· '
3.4   mimono 'something worth seeing; ··· '

?3.4, ?3.1   mitani 'valley'
3.4   momizi 'autumn colors'
3.4   moromi 'unrefined sake/soy'
3.4   motai 'sake jar'
3.4   motoi 'basis'
?3.3, ?3.4   mottomo 'sensible; most'
3.4   musiro 'straw mat'
3.4   muzina 'badger; ··· '
3.4   nagae 'long handle'
3.4   nagame 'view'
3.4   nagare 'flow, stream'
3.4   nageki 'lament'
3.4   nagisa 'beach'
?3.2b, ?3.4   nagori 'aftertraces, memory'
?3.4, ?3.7a   nakago 'center'
3.4   nakama 'companion'
3.4   namasu 'raw-fish salad'
3.4   namazu 'catfish'
?3.4, ?3.5x   nanae 'seven layers'
3.4   naname, (Hn /) nanome 'aslant'
3.4   naniwa 'Naniwa' (= Ōsaka)
3.4   nanoka, nanuka 'seven days'
?3.4   naobi 'restoring regularity ··· '
3.4   narai 'custom'
3.4   nawate 'footpath between ricefields'
3.4   nazuki 'brain; head'
3.4   nebiru 'wild rocambole'
3.4   negai 'request'
3.4   nemoto 'root'
3.4   nigori 'muddiness'
3.4   nikibi 'pimple'
3.4   nioi 'odor; red, beautiful'
3.4 = 1.3|2.3 nogai 'pasturing animals'
3.4   nomusi, nomuzi 'field insects; ··· '
3.4   norane 'shrewmouse'
?3.4   nosaki 'first crop of the year'
3.4   nuime 'seam'
3.4   nukae 'beefsteak plant'
3.4   obisi 'the small of the back'
3.4   obusa 'bird's tail spread out'
3.4 (= 3.1?) odori 'male bird, ··· '
?3.4   ogase 'skein'
3.4 = 2.3|1.3; 3.5x, 3.6 okitu 'Okitsu' (placename)
3.4   oko^a/_zi 'stingfish'
?3.4, ?3.5x, ?3.6 okute 'late rice'
3.4   omoi 'thought'
3.1/3.4   omosi 'weight'
3.4   omote 'surface'
3.4 (4.5 = 3.4|3.4 omoto 'august presence'
?3.4   onibi 'fox fire'

3.4 = 2.3|1.3 onote '(Great-)Ax-Hand' (name)
3.4   ooga 'spinning wheel'
3.4   oogi 'fan'
3.4   ooi 'cover'
3.4 = 2.3|1.3 ooi 'bulrush' (= huto-i)
3.4   oo^k/_ɡo 'shoulder-pole'
3.4   oon- 'exalted'
3.7x, 3.4 = 2.3|1.3 oone 'white radish'
3.4 = 2.3|1.3 oowa 'big wheel'
3.4   osore 'fear'
3.4   otoko 'male; young man'
3.4 (= 3.1?) otori 'male bird; ··· '
3.4 > 2.3   oyobi () yubi) 'finger'
3.4 (4.11   oyoso (o[f]oyoso 'roughly'
3.4   ozasi 'fish dried on skewer'
?1.3x (*3.4 -re (suffix)
?1.3x (*3.4 -ri (suffix)
4.5 ()3.4)   ‡ ringo 'apple'
3.4   sadame 'decision; rule'
3.4   sagari 'a wide-brimmed pot ··· '
3.4   sakai 'boundary'
?3.4, ?3.1   sakaki 'sacred tree'
3.4   sakeme 'crevice'
3.4   sakide 'skin-cracked hands'
3.4   sakuri 'hiccup'
?3.5x, ?3.4   sakuzu 'bath-soap powder ··· '
?3.4, ?3.5x   saoge 'small fine hairs'
?3.4, ?3.3   sara^k/_ɡe 'a shallow jar'
3.4   sasagi 'wren' (= sazaki)
3.4   sasimi 'sliced raw fish'
3.4   sasue 'a utensil ··· '
?3.4   ‡ satoo 'sugar'
3.4   sazaki, (Mg) sasagi 'wren' (bird)
?3.4   sesimu 'Korean prince'
3.4/3.5x = 2.3|mo sika-mo 'moreover; and yet'
?3.4, ?3.7x   sikome 'ugly woman'
3.4   simoto 'whip'
3.4 = 2.3|1.3 simoyo 'frosty night'
3.4   siose 'tidewater'
3.4   siraga 'white hair'
?3.4 (4.10   ‡ sisai 'details'
?3.4   sitomi 'awning'
?3.4   sitone 'underquilt'
?3.4   sitori (god name)
3.4   siwasu 'lunar December'
?3.4   sizimi 'corbicula'
3.4   ‡ soobi 'rose'
3.4   suhizi 'mud'
3.4   sumai 'residence'
3.4   sumigo 'coal basket'

3.4   sumika 'residence'
3.4   suwae 'twig, switch'
3.4 < 4.5/4.6 suzuri 'ink-slab'
3.x (?= *3.4) tabari 'bunch'
3.4   tabusa 'wrist'
?3.4   tabute = tubute 'stone(-throwing)'
3.4   tadati(-ni) 'at once'
3.4   tagui 'sort, kind'
3.4   takara 'treasure'
3.4   takumi 'carpenter; skill(ful)'
3.4   [tamai] 'vomiting'
3.4   tamake 'splendid dinnerware'
?3.4a   tamaki 'arm ornament'
3.4   tamesi 'trial'
3.4, 3.5b = 1.3|2.4 tamino 'rain-cape'
3.4, 3.5b tamizo 'irrigation ditch'
3.4   tamoto 'sleeve'
3.5/3.6 (?< *3.4) tamura ?= tamuro 'encampment'
3.4   tamure 'mound, hillock'
3.4   tamuro 'encampment'
3.4   tanima 'valley' (= tani)
3.4   tanomi 'request'
?3.4   tanuki 'glove; wrist-band'
3.4   tasuke 'help'
3.4   tatara 'foot-bellows'
3.5x/3.4   tatari 'a swift (yarn/skein winder)'
3.5x, 3.4 tatisi (no miti) 'longitudinal'
3.4   tatoi = tatoe 'example'
3.4   tawara 'bale'
3.7b (< 3.4) tayori 'something to rely on'
?3.4   tebiki 'guiding'
3.4   tebito 'skilled artisan'
3.4   tegara 'feat'
3.4   temoto 'at hand'
3.4   tenae 'loss of use of hand/arm'
3.4   teono 'handax'
3.4   tesiro 'bracelet'
?3.4   titose 'a thousand years'
3.4   tiusi 'milk cow'
3.4   tokaki 'grain-measure stick'
3.4 < 4.10 ‡ tokati 'cotton-and-rabbit cloth'
3.4   tokusa 'scouring rush'
?3.4   tonae 'chant'
?3.4   toneri 'chamberlain'
3.4   tonoi 'night duty'
?3.4, ?3.5b tooge 'mountain pass'
?3.5a, ?3.4 toride 'fort'
3.4   toriko 'captive'
3.4   tubaki 'spit(tle)'
?3.4   tubomi 'bud'
?3.4   tuburi 'head': see tumuri
?3.4   tubute = tabute 'stone(-throwing)'

3.4   tudami 'spitting up'
3.4   tukane 'bundle'
3.4   tukura 'young grey mullet' (fish)
3.4   tumure 'rise, hillock'
?3.4 < 3.7 tumuri 'head'
3.4   turugi 'sword'
3.4   tutami = tudami 'spitting up'
3.4   tutumi 'package, bundle'
?3.1, ?3.4 tuzumi 'drum'
3.4   tuzumi 'wild mulberry, Morus bombycis'
3.4   udati 'a short roof-beam support column'
3.4   uizi 'mud'
3.4   ukawa 'cormorant-fishing'
3.4   umai 'sweet sleep'
3.4   umaki 'horse paddock'
3.4 = 2.3|1.2 umaya 'barn'
3.4   umuki 'clam' (= hamaguri)
3.4   unai 'child('s neck hair)'
3.4   unazi 'nape'
3.4   urami 'regret'
3.4   [uree] 'grief'
3.4   uroko < iroko 'scale(s) on fish'
3.4   usio 'tide'
?3.4   utena 'earthen mound'
3.4   utiwa 'fan'
3.4   uzina = muzina 'badger; ··· '
3.4   uzura 'quail' (bird)
3.4   waka^k/_g o 'baby'
3.4   wakare 'separation'
3.4   wakugo 'youngster'
3.4   warabi 'bracken'
3.4   yadori 'lodgings'
3.4   yahoti/yahotu 'streetwalker prostitute'
3.4   yakara 'family'
?3.1/3.4   yaka^s/_z u 'house'
3.4 = 2.3|1.3 yamada 'mountain ricefield'
3.7b (?< 3.4) yamai 'illness'
3.4   yanasu 'a weir blind'
3.4   yarema 'torn/decayed place'
3.4   yasiro 'shrine'
3.4   yasumi 'rest'
3.4   yodake 'joined bamboo'
3.4   yogoro 'many nights'
?3.4   yonaka 'middle of the night'
?3.4 < 4.5 yosoi 'armor'
3.4   yowai 'age'
3.4/3.5x   yubune 'bathtub'
3.4   yugake 'archer's glove'
3.4   yutori 'bowstring'
?3.4, ?3.6, ?3.7x yuube 'last night'
3.4   ‡ zasiki 'matted room'
3.4 < 4.10 ‡ zisyaku 'magnet; compass'

3.4a LLL < LLF ?< *LLHL   (See Ch. 4, §7.3.)

?3.6, ?3.4a   akitu 'dragonfly'   ?3.4a   himizu 'ice water'
?3.4a   aoto 'blue(-gray) grindstone'   ?3.4a   konzu 'broth from boiling rice'
?3.4a   hirome 'seaweed'   ?3.4a   tamaki 'arm ornament'

....

3.5 = 3.5a, 3.5b, 3.5a/b, 3.5x

<u>3.5a</u> LLH(H) 0-2-B B-B-B   Toyama, Suzu 1:3

3.5a   agura 'high seat; cross-legged'   ?3.5a   ona^a/_zi(-ku/-to) 'same'
?3.5a, ?3.6   ariso 'rocky shore'   (3.1<) 3.5a ‡ rakuda 'camel'
3.5a   asuka 'morning fragrance'   3.5a   sekido 'barrier'
3.5a   hasita 'fragment'   3.5a   taira 'flat'
3.5a = 2.3|1.1 hirose 'wide shallows'   ?3.5a   taruki 'rafter'
2.5 < 3.5a ibo 'rice grain; wart'   3.5a   teboko 'spear'
3.5a   ideya 'well; nay; ··· ' *(interj)*   3.5a (> ?4.6) tokuri (> tokkuri) 'bottle'
3.5a   iraka 'roof tile (ridge)'   ?3.5a, ?3.4   toride 'fort'
?3.5a   kakasi 'scarecrow'   3.5a   tuzura 'wicker'
3.5a   keyaki 'zelkova'   3.5a   ututu 'existent: ··· '
?3.5a   ‡ kibone 'lower jawbone'   3.5a < 4.6   warazi < waragutu 'straw sandals'
?3.5a   nakaba 'middle; half'   3.5a   yakko 'slave'
?3.5a   natane 'rape(weed)' (= abura-na)   3.5a   yatuko: *see* yakko
3.5a   nazuna 'shepherd's purse'   ?3.5a < 5.15 yukata < yu-kata[bira] 'bathrobe'

....

<u>3.5b</u> LLH(H) < *LLH(L) 1(<2)-2-B B-B-B   Toyama, Suzu 1:3

Note: There are problems with the Tōkyō accent of the items marked "*". The
Tōkyō forms of hosozi, itoko, itutu, kokoro, nanatu, obone, tokiyo, and (3.5a/b
hirome retain "2" rather than moving the locus back to "1", as the other 3.5b
nouns do; hitoi and hitoe are similar but the locus may be the result of
unvoicing the first vowel. Kyuuri goes back to ki-u'ri or ki'-uri, probably
the former for it follows the modern compound rules; western Mino (= SW Gifu)
attests both patterns. The Tōkyō-type dialects show sporadic irregularities
in the accent of 3.5b nouns; for example, the usual reflex in Goka-mura is "2"
but "<u>1</u>" is found in hibasi, hotaru, kagami, kyuuri, and makura.

3.5b   amata 'extremely'   3.5b   * itoko 'cousin'
3.5b   aruzi 'owner'   ?3.5b, ?3.4 * itutu 'five'
3.5b   asahi 'morning sun'   3.5b   kagura 'sacred music'
3.5b ?< 3.4 aware 'sympathy'   3.5b < 4.6   karei < kar[a]ei 'flatfish'
?3.4, ?3.5b ekaki 'artist'   ?3.5b, ?3.7b katami 'upper torso ··· '
3.5b   haegi 'rafter'   3.5b   kinoko 'mushroom'
3.5b   hibasi 'firetongs'   ?3.5b   * kokoro 'heart'
3.5b   * [hitoi] 'one day'   3.5b   konomi 'fruit'
?3.5b < ?4.7, ?4.6 * hosozi 'narrow road'   ?3.5b< 4.11   konzu 'rice broth'
3.5b   hotaru 'firefly'   3.5b   kosiki 'steamer'
3.5b   imada '(not) yet'   3.5b   ‡ kumotu 'offering'
3.5b   inoti 'life'   ?3.5b   * kyuuri 'cucumber'

3.5b   nanako 'eye'
?3.5b   matuge 'eyelash(es)'
3.5b   megane 'eyeglasses'
3.5b   mutuki 'diapers'
?3.5b < *4/6 nagame < naga-ame 'a long rain'
3.5b   namida 'tear(s)'
?3.5b   * nanatu 'seven'
3.5b   nasubi 'eggplant'
3.5b   nimotu 'baggage'
3.5b   nisiki 'brocade'
3.5b   nodati 'dagger'
3.5b   * obone 'tailbone'
?3.5b   ooi 'large well'
3.5b   oomi 'Ōmi' (placename)
3.5b   oozi 'father's father; old man'
3.5b   oroᵗ/zi 'huge serpent'
3.5b   ‡ saisi 'hairdress decoration'
3.5b   ‡ sango 'coral'

?3.5b   sazae, sazai 'wreath shell'
?3.5b   * sizuku 'drop'
3.5b   sugata 'figure'
3.4, 3.5b = 1.3|2.4 tamino 'rain-cape'
3.4, 3.5b tamizo 'irrigation ditch'
3.5/3.6 (?< *3.4) tamura ?= tamuro 'encampment'
3.5b   teate 'treatment, ··· '
?3.5b   * tokiyo 'era'
?3.4, ?3.5b tooge 'mountain pass'
?3.5b (?) 3.7b) tubusa(-ni) 'complete, in detail'
3.5b   tukiyo 'moon(light)'
?3.5b   wakame 'seaweed'
3.5b   warabe 'child'
3.5b   warawa 'child'
3.5b   yamato 'Yamato; Japan'
?2.1 < 3.5b (?< 4.3) yaya 'slightly'
3.5b   yosino 'Yoshino' (placename)

3.5a/b (Evidence for assignment to both a and b.)

3.5a/b   abura 'oil'
3.5a/b   hasira 'pillar'
3.5a/b   hinoki 'cypress'
?3.5a/b, ?3.1 hizume 'hoof'
3.5a/b   hooki 'broom'
3.5a/b   kaina 'upper arm'
3.5a/b   kodati 'grove'
3.5a/b   komura / kobura 'calf of leg'

3.5a/b   kugui 'swan'
3.5a/b   kugutu 'puppet'
3.5a/b   makura 'pillow'
3.5a/b   nasake 'sentiment'
3.5a/b   tasuki 'sleeve-ties'
3.5a/b   tutumi 'dike'
?3.5a/b   yakata 'shelter; residence'
3.5a/b   zakuro 'pomegranate'

3.5x (No evidence for assignment to a or b.)

?3.4, ?3.5x asake 'dawn'
?3.5x < ?*3.1 asazi 'low-stemmed cogon'
3.4/3.5x asida 'clogs'
3.5x/3.6 gugusa < kukusa 'honey locust'
3.5x (= 2.3|1.1) hamamo 'beach seaweed'
?3.5x   hanima 'clay horse'
3.5x   hasiha 'pyramid-shaped gemstone'
3.5x   higure 'cypress plank'
?3.5x   hiiru 'moth(s)'
3.5x < 4.x hinizu 'icewater'
3.5x   hobara 'swim (= air) bladder'
?3.5x   hotogi 'jug'
3.5x   husube 'skin blemishes'
3.5x   iine 'cooked rice'
?3.5x   ikuha 'archery target'
3.4/3.5x itabi 'fig'
3.5x   kaeru 'two-year-old hawk'
3.5x   kagami (< ?). 'Metaplexis japonica'

3.4/3.5x kaigo 'egg'
3.5x   kakezi 'stony mountain road'
3.5x   kasumo 'freckle'
3.5x (?< ?3.1, ?3.2) kawara 'Kawara', 'the River'
3.5x   komura 'a stand of trees, a grove'
3.5x   konzi 'kerchief'
3.5x   kosizi 'the Koshi road'
3.5x   kozake (Mg), kosake 'overnight brew'
?3.1, ?3.5x kotuo 'shark'
3.5x/3.6 kuᵗ/dani 'a plant, ··· '
?2.4 < ?3.5x medo 'Sericea lespedeza; ···'
3.5x   moᵏ/gosi 'casket room'
3.5x   moto[h]e 'bottom-side'
?3.4, ?3.5x nanae 'seven layers'
?3.5x   nanaso 'seventy'
2.4 < 3.5x nodo 'throat'
3.5x   obune 'little boat'
3.4; 3.5x, 3.6 okitu 'Okitsu' (placename)

?3.4, ?3.5x, ?3.6   okute 'late rice'
3.5x   onbe 'new-rice festival'
3.5x   oosi 'rhubarb'
3.5x   sakugi 'wood for a royal memorandum tablet'
?3.5x, ?3.4   sakuzu 'bath-soap powder ··· '
?3.4, ?3.5x   saoge 'small fine hairs'
3.5x   sayomi 'fine-woven cloth'
(3.7x/)3.5x = 2.3|ku   sikaku 'so'
3.4/3.5x = 2.3|mo sika-mo 'moreover; and yet'
?3.5x (= 2.3|1), ?3.6   sirie 'back, ··· '
3.5x   sizaya 'sword-sheath bag'
3.5x   tagosi 'riding platform'
3.5x   takabe 'teal, duckling' (= kogamo)
3.5x   tata^k/$_g$e 'raccoon-dog (hairs)'
3.5x/3.4   tatari 'a kind of swift (yarn/skein winder)'
3.5x, 3.4   tatisi 'longitudinal'

3.5x   tedate 'hand-shield'
3.5x   togata 'architrave; ··· '
3.5x(|4.1) to^a/$_z$ama: - koo^a/$_z$ama 'all ways'
3.5x   tuisi '(a ceremonial cake)'
3.5x > ?2.4, ?2.5 tumiba > tuba 'sword-guard'
3.5x   tuzusi 'ivy'
3.5x   yagata 'shelter on cart'
3.5x   yoboro = yooro 'hollow of knee'
3.5x   yohoro = yooro 'hollow of knee'
3.5x   yooro 'hollow of knee'
?3.6, ?3.5x   yorodo 'saury'
3.5x   yorozu 'saury'
3.4/3.5x   yubune 'bathtub'
3.5x   yusuru 'shampooing ··· '
3.5x   zyoogi 'a vertical stick ··· '

<u>3.6</u>   LHH(H) 0(?<1)-1-B B-B-(C)*   Toyama, Suzu 1:2

> *Although usagi, the noun often chosen to represent 3.6, is A in
> Yonaguni, a number of the other entries are C: hadaka, karasu,
> sirami, ? yubari. For the Tōkyō reflex, a number of the words have
> 1 in Tōkyō-type dialects, and Tōkyō itself has 1 for a few words,
> such as karasu and sunao. We will consider the reflex regular if
> Tōkyō has 0, 1, or 0/1.

?3.6, ?3.5b   akitu 'dragonfly'
?3.7a, ?3.6   akome 'middle garment'
?3.5a, ?3.6   ariso 'rocky shore'
?3.6, ?3.1   asaza 'water fringe'
?3.4, ?3.6   ayame 'design; sweetflag'
3.6   dan-go 'dumpling'
3.5x/3.6 gugusa (Mg) < kukusa 'honey locust'
3.6   hadaka 'naked'
3.6   hadasi 'barefoot'
3.6   ‡ hahuni '(rice-)powder ··· '
?2.4 < ?3.6   hara 'trumpet (horn)'
3.6   haraka 'croaker' (fish)
3.6   ‡ haseo 'banana'
3.6   hasike 'barge'
2.5 ?< 3.6   hebi 'snake'
?3.6   hemaki 'falcon's foot-cord reel'
3.6   hibari 'skylark' (bird)
3.6   hidari 'left'
?2.4 ?< 3.6   hime = sime 'hawfinch' (bird)
3.6   hinoe '3d of the Ten Heaven's Stems'
3.6   hirosa 'width'
3.6   hisago 'gourd'
3.6   hisaku: see his(y)aku
?3.6   hisiko 'anchovy'

?3.6   ‡ hisui 'kingfisher (fish); jade'
3.5   his(y)aku 'ladle'
?2.2a < 3.6   hobo 'approximately'
?3.6, ?3.7x   hososi '(?) stake, door-stop'
3.6   hukube 'gourd'
3.6   hukube 'blowfish'
?3.6   hunato 'crossroads (god)'
3.6   ioo 'sulfur'
3.6   irara 'thorns; nettle; vetch'
?3.6, ?3.7x   irori 'hearth'
3.6   izuko 'where'
3.6   izure 'which one; ··· '
3.6   kaburo 'a hair-style; bald; treeless'
3.6 < 4.1 kaede 'maple'
3.6   kaeru 'frog' (= kawazu)
?3.6   kakato 'heel'
3.6   kamome 'seagull'
3.6   karasu 'crow'
3.6   katae 'one of a pair; a part, half; ··· '
3.6   katae 'the branch(es) on one side'
?3.6   katate 'one hand'
3.6   kawazu 'frog'
3.6   kirara 'mica, isinglass'
2.x ?< 3.6   ki^a/$_z$a 'elephant'

3.6   kitune 'fox'
3.6   kiuta 'pestler's song'
3.6   kohada 'tree bark'
?3.6   komai 'lath'
3.6   ‡ konisi 'coriander'
?3.6, ?3.7a/b koobe 'head'
3.6   kubiti 'a (rat-)trap'
3.5x/3.6 kut/dani 'a plant ··· '
?2.4 ‹ 3.6   ‡ kuko 'Chinese matrimony vine'
?3.6   kunat/do = hunato 'crossroads (god)'
3.6   kurara 'Sophora angustifolia'
3.6   kururi 'double-headed arrow'
3.6   kusabu 'hedgehog'
3.6   kusagi (tree names)
3.6   kususi 'doctor'
?3.6   maguro 'tuna' (fish)
3.6   makoto 'truth'
3.6   mimizu 'earthworm'
3.6   [miizu] = mi[m]izu 'earthworm'
?3.6   mizura 'an ancient hair-style'
2.2x ‹ 3.6   moda 'silence'
3.6   mukago, (Mg) nukago 'brood bud'
?3.6   nagara 'Nagara' (placename)
3.6   nagasa 'length'
3.6   namai 'arrowhead (plant)'
3.6   neziro 'white-rooted'
3.6   nezumi 'rat'
3.6   nigana 'lettuce; gentian'
3.6   nozeri 'wild parsley; angelica'
3.6   nukago: see mukago
3.6   ogoma = ugoma 'sesame'
3.6   okina 'old man'
3.4 = 2.3|1.3; 3.5x, 3.6 okitu 'Okitsu' (placename)
?3.4, ?3.5x, ?3.6 okute 'late rice'
?3.6   omina 'old woman, gammer'
3.6   onna ‹ "om[u]na" ‹ omyina 'old woman, gammer'
3.7a, 3.6 onoe 'mountain top'
3.6   oyako 'parent and child'
3.6   oziro 'white-tailed'
3.6   ‡ rokuro 'pulley, windlass'
?3.6 ‹ 4.8 ‡ ruban 'pagoda roof'
?3.6, ?3.1 sasage 'cowpea'
?3.6   sasame 'grasses ··· '
3.6   sasibu 'Vaccinium bracteatum'
?3.6, ?3.7a/b sasori 'scorpion'
3.6   senaka 'back'
?2.4 ‹ ?3.6 sime 'a kind of sparrow'
3.6   simizu 'clear water'
3.6   sinome 'a kind of bitter green bamboo shoot'
3.6   siode 'a kind of saddle-rope'
?3.6 ‹ 4.8 ‡ sioni 'aster'

3.6   sirami 'louse'
?3.6, ?3.5x (= 2.3|1)   sirie 'back; ··· '
3.6   siroo 'whitebait, icefish'
3.6   sitami 'bamboo basket ··· '
?3.6   sitodo '(a kind of bird)'
?3.6   sitogi 'rice cake offered to gods'
?3.6   sosisi 'backbone flesh/meat'
?3.6   sosoro 'spit-out hawk's meal'
3.6   sozoro 'involuntarily; ··· '
3.6   sugame 'squint'
3.6   sumomo 'plum'
3.6   sunao 'straight, naive'
?3.6   susuki 'eulalia'
3.6   suzume 'sparrow' (bird)
3.6   suzuro = sozoro 'involuntarily; ··· '
3.6   ‡ syuro = syuuro 'hemp palm'
3.6   tagai(-ni) 'mutual; reciprocal'
3.6   takaki 'fortress in high place'
3.6   takasa 'height'
?3.6, ?3.7x   takasi 'Takashi' (placename)
3.5/3.6 (?‹ ‡3.4)   tamura ?= tamuro 'encampment'
?3.6 (?= 2.4|1.1) tatii 'standing and sitting'
3.6   tatugi 'timber ax'
3.6   tazuki(/tatugi/tatuki) 'means, resource'
2.x ‹ 3.6 tis(y)a ‹ tisa ‹ ‡tiisa 'lettuce'
?3.6   tonbo 'dragonfly'
?3.6, ?3.7a/b ‹ 5.11   tubame 'swallow' (bird)
?3.6, ?3.7x tubune (‹ ?) 'servant'
3.6   tubura 'rotund'
3.6   tuburi 'greve, dabchick' (bird)
3.6   tugumi 'thrush' (bird)
?3.6   ‡tumuri 'grebe' (bird): see tuburi
?3.1, ?3.6   tumuzi 'whirlwind'
3.6 (› 2.1) ugoma, ogoma (› goma) 'sesame'
3.6 (?= 1.3|2.1) uguti 'cleft palate, split lip'
?3.6(/7x) › 2.3   umago 'grand-child' (› mago)
3.6   unagi 'eel'
3.6   usagi 'rabbit'
?3.6, ?3.1   utik/gi 'undergarment'
?3.6   uturo 'hollow'
3.6   uzui 'squatting quietly/steadily'
3.6   [yanoe] 'roof-top'
3.6   yomogi 'mugwort'
?3.6, ?3.5x   yorodo 'saury' (fish)
?3.6, ?3.5x   yorozu 'saury' (fish)
3.6   yubari 'urine'
3.6   yuoo = ioo 'sulfur'
?2.1 ‹ 3.6   yuri 'lily'
?2.4 ‹ ?3.6   yusi 'spinous evergreen'
?3.4, ?3.6, ?3.7x   yuube 'last night'
3.6   ‡ zyoodo 'Chinese parasol tree' (= aogiri)

3.7 = 3.7a, 3.7b, 3.7a/b, 3.7x

<u>3.7a</u> LHL(L) < *LHH(L) 0-1:3-B B-B-C   Toyama 1:4(-i/u), 1:3(-e/a/o); Suzu 1

3.7a ?< 3.3	akebi 'Akebia quinata'	
??3.7a, ?3.6	akome 'middle garment'	
?3.7a	awai 'border (area); ··· '	
3.7a	ayui 'cord ··· '	
3.7a	ebira 'arrow quill'	
3.7a < 4.9 (= 2.3|2.2)	habaki 'leggings'	
3.7a	hatago 'travel pack of provisions; ··· '	
?3.4/?3.7a	hatake 'psoriasis; ··· '	
3.7a	hotori 'vicinity'	
3.7a	itibi 'Indian mallow'	
?3.7a	ituki 'sacred grove'	
?3.7a ?< 3.4	izumi '(well)spring'	
3.7a	kariko 'beater'	
3.7a	katai 'beggar'	
3.7a	katura/kazura 'head-dress'	
3.7a	kodama 'tree-spirit; echo'	
3.7a	kusuri 'drug'	
3.7a	magusa 'lintel'	

?3.7a	mogura 'mole'
?3.7a	mugura 'creepers'
?3.7a	mukuge 'shaggy'
?3.4, ?3.7a	nakago 'center'
3.7a	namari 'lead'
?3.7a	ninuri 'varnishing with red'
3.7a, 3.6	onoe 'mountain top'
3.7a	ooi 'medic, bur(r)/snail clover'
3.7a	otome 'female, maiden'
3.7a	otori 'decoy'
?3.7a, ?3.1	sa^s/z ara 'small'
?3.7a, ?3.1	sa^s/z are 'small'
3.7a	sigure 'shower'
3.7a	sumigi 'corner beam prop'
3.7a	sumire 'violet'
3.7a	tamago 'egg'
3.7a	tarai 'washtub'
?3.7a	umibe 'seaside'

<u>3.7b</u> LHL(L) 1-1:3-B B-B-C   Toyama 1:4(-i/u), 1:3(-e/a/o); Suzu 1

?3.4, ?3.7b	azuma 'Azuma' *(placename)*
2.4 < 3.7b	‡ biwa 'loquat'
?2.3 < 3.7b	hagi 'shank (= lower leg)'
3.7b	haruka(-ni) 'way distant'
3.7b	hisoka 'secret'
3.7b	hitori 'one person'
3.7b	hitotu 'one'
3.7b	hiyaka 'cold'
3.7b	ho^k/g usi 'a bonfire stake/post'
3.7b	honoka 'faint'
3.7b	ikutu 'how many'
3.7b = ?2.4/5	1.3	ituka 'sometime'
3.7b	izuti 'which way'
3.7b	kabuto 'helmet'
3.7b	kaiko 'silkworm'
3.7b	kasuka 'dim'
?3.5b, ?3.7b	katami 'upper torso ··· '
?[2.5] < 3.7b	katu < katuu 'moreover'
3.7b	kedasi 'probably; perhaps'
3.7b	komaka 'fine'
3.7b > 2.5	konbu > kobu 'seaweed'
3.7b	kuboka 'hollow'
3.7b	mabuta 'eyelid'
3.7b	madoka 'round'
3.7b	magaki 'rough-woven fence'
?2.2b < 3.7b	mazu 'first of all'
3.7b(/3.4)	medori 'hen'
?3.7b < 3.4 = 1.3	2.3	mekuso 'eye discharge'
?3.7b (> 2.2b?)	minna 'all; everyone; everything'

?3.2a, ?3.7b	monaka 'very midst'
3.7b	musiro 'rather'
?3.7b, ?3.4	naname, nanome 'aslant'
?2.5 < ?3.7b	nazo = nanzo = na[a]-so 'why; riddle
3.7b	niwaka 'sudden'
3.7b	nohara, nobara, noppara 'field'
3.7b	nowaki 'autumn typhoon'
3.7b	otona 'adult'
3.7b	sayaka 'clear, bright'
?3.7b	sinobu 'hare's-foot fern'
3.7b	sizuka 'quiet'
3.7b	sukosi 'a little'
3.7b	tanisi 'fresh-water snail'
3.7b	tanuki 'raccoon-dog'
3.7b	tasika 'certain'
3.7b (< 3.4)	tayori 'something to rely on'
3.7b	tegasi 'handcuffs'
3.7b	tidori 'plover' *(bird)*
3.7b	tonbi 'kite (hen)' *(bird)*
?3.5b (?) 3.7b)	tubusa(-ni) 'complete; in detail'
?3.7b < ...	wagie 'my house'
3.7b < ...	wagimo 'my beloved (girl)'
3.7b	wazuka(-ni) 'scant'
3.7b (?< 3.4)	yamai 'illness'
?3.7b, ?3.3	yamori 'gecko'
?2.4 (= 3.7b) ‡ yasi (?= yaasi) 'palm tree'
3.7b	yotaka 'night hawk'
?2.3 < 3.7b	‡ yu-hi '(livestock) mating'
3.7b	yutaka 'rich'

3.7a/b (Evidence for both a and b.)

3.7a/b arawa 'overt'
3.7a/b hatake 'field'
3.7a/b hiziri 'saint'
?3.7a/b = 2.4|1.3; ?3.2b inaba 'Inaba' *(placename)*
3.7a/b itigo 'strawberry'
3.7a/b karasi 'mustard'
3.7a/b kisai 'empress'
?3.6, ?3.7a/b koobe 'head'
?3.7a/b kurage 'jellyfish'
?3.7a/b kuzira 'whale'
?3.7a/b nobiru 'wild leek'
3.7a/b nubiru = nobiru 'wild leek'
?3.6, ?3.7a/b sasori 'scorpion'
3.7a/b tubaki 'camellia'
?3.6, ?3.7a/b < 5.11 tubame 'swallow' *(bird)*
?3.7a/b usiro 'behind'

....

3.7x (No evidence for assignment to a or b.)

3.7x hario 'saury' *(fish)*
3.7x hinoo 'Hinoo' *(placename)*
?3.7x (?= 2.4|1.3) hitoyo 'one night'
3.7x [hiyase] 'a partial eclipse of the sun'
?3.6, ?3.7x hososi '(?) stake, door-stop'
3.7x hukuge 'chick/baby down'
3.7x hunako 'boatman'
?3.6, ?3.7x irori 'hearth'
3.7x itori 'five people'
?3.7x, ?3.2a katano 'Katano' *(placename)*
?2.3 < 3.7x ‡ ko-hi 'sore throat'
3.7x mekura 'blind, sightless'
3.7x (?= 2.4|1.3) mirume 'a kind of seaweed'
3.7x mizuo 'stirrup strap'
3.7x = 1.3|2.2 mo$^s/_z$ ita 'underwear'
3.7x namomi 'cocklebur'
?3.7x, ?3.3 ogiro 'vast'
?3.7x omura 'Omura' *(placename)*
3.7x, 3.4 = 2.3|1.3 oone 'white radish'
?3.2x, ?3.7x setuka 'back ridge'
(3.7x/)3.5x = 2.3|ku sikaku 'so'
?3.4, ?3.7x sikome 'ugly woman'
3.7x sumori 'nest-egg; ··· '
3.7x ? suzuki 'reed mat for raising silkworms'
?3.6, ?3.7x takasi 'Takashi' *(placename)*
3.7x takume > toome 'entirely, ··· '
3.7x toome 'entirely, ··· '
3.7x tubaha 'earthenware jar'
?3.6, ?3.7x tubune (< ?) 'servant'
?3.4 < 3.7x tumuri 'head'
3.6(/7x) > 2.3 umago 'grand-child'
3.7x urui 'selfheal, hosta'
3.7x usuba 'molar tooth'
3.7x yakuno 'a kind of striped shell'
3.7x yamago 'mountain phantom'
3.7x yama$^s/_z$ i 'Anemarrhena asphedoloides'
3.7x yodono 'boudoir'
3.7x yokosi 'spleen'
?3.4, ?3.6, ?3.7x yuube 'last night'

....

3.x (Insufficient data for assignment to a specific class.)

3.x abata 'pockmark'
3.x asoko 'over there'
3.x < 2.1 hiiki < hiki 'popularity'
4.x < 3.x hiimago < himago 'great-grandchild'
3.x horosi 'hives, nettle rash'
3.x < 4.11 huigo 'bellows'
3.x huruya 'old house'
3.x kakehi, kakei 'drain-pipe'
?3.x < ?4.x kizaya 'animal shed'
3.x kokoti 'feeling'
3.x kusaba 'leaf of grass'
3.x kusiro 'bracelet'
3.x kutiba 'dead leaves'
3.x (?= 3.1) migiri = migi 'right (hand)'
3.x misoti 'thirty'
3.x moegi 'yellowish green'
3.x moyogi 'yellowish green'
3.x nakara 'middle'
3.x < 4.9 = 2.4|2.2 nazure 'why'
4.x < 3.x ninniku, "also niniku" 'garlic'
3.x ohagi/uhagi 'aster, starwort'
3.x < 4.7 / 4.6 omiki '(offertory) wine'
3.x oote 'front gate (of castle)'
3.x ooya 'big arrow'

3.x   oozi 'main road, highway'
3.x   oruku = koni-oruku 'Korean queen'
3.x   simobe 'underlings, menials'
3.x   sita^t/d e 'below, beneath'
3.x   syooto 'woman's brother; ··· '
3.x (?= *3.4) tabari 'bunch'
3.x   takabe 'labracoglossa' (fish)
*3.x   *ta-muki: see tadamuki

3.x   tatibu '(a kind of small melon)'
3.x   tigaya 'cogon'
3.x   tomoe 'comma-shaped whirl design'
3.x   [tomo-(h)e] 'stern and prow'
3.x   totoki (plant names)
3.x   tyoozu 'ablution water'
3.x   una^t/d e 'canal'
3.x   yukue 'destination; whereabouts'

Nouns of four syllables

4 = 4.1 — 4.11; 4.x

4.1 HHHH

4.1   abaraya
4.1   adabara, atabara
4.1   adabana
4.1   agebari
4.1   ainiku
4.1 (= 2.1|2.1)   akagane
4.1   akagari
4.1   akasama(-ni)
4.1   akatuki
4.1   akebono
?4.1   ameu^s/z xi
4.1 > 3.1 amu^s/z iro > aziro
?4.1   amututi ?= antuti
?4.1   aoguro
4.1   arak/g ane
4.1   aramoto
4.1   aratama
?4.1, ?4.2   arizuka
4.1 (= 2.1-tu|1.1)   asatuki
4.1   asi^h/b iki
4.1   asizuno
4.1   [aziroi]
4.1   butiuma
4.1   ebisune
?4.1; ?4.5   haha-kata
?4.2, ?4.1   hahakuri
4.1   hahakuso
4.1   hakimono
4.1   harimati
4.1   hasi^t/d ate
4.1   hataasi
4.1   hatabari
4.1   hatahoko
4.1   hatamono
?4.1   hataori
?4.1   hazikami

4.1   himorogi
4.1   hinasaki
4.11   hinezumi
4.1   hirabari
4.1   hirazima
4.1 (= 2.1|2.1)   hirusaki
4.1   hitodomo
4.1   hitogoto
4.1   hitokazu
4.1   hitokusa
4.1   hizatuki
4.1   hodozura
4.1   horaana
?4.1   hosodono
4.1   hunadoko
4.1/4.2 hunzuki
4.1   husizuke
4.1   hutamata
4.1   hutatose
4.1   hutokoro
4.1   huyukawa
4.2, 4.1 huzigawa
4.1   ii^t/d oyo
?4.1   ika-hodo
4.1   ikarii
4.1   ikazuti
4.1(?/4.3)   irehimo
?4.1   iriai
4.1   irukase
4.1   i^s/z arai
?4.1   isibai
?4.1   isikoro
?4.1   isikure
4.1   isimoti
4.1   isizue
4.1   itazura

4.1   iwamuro
4.1 < 3.6 [kaerude, kairude] > kaede
4.1   kamaboko
4.1 (> 3.1)   kamudati = kandati
4.1   kanagaki
4.1   kanakuso
?4.2,?4.1 kanamari
?4.1, ?4.5   karakusa
4.1   kari^k/g omo
4.1 = 2.1|2.1 karimiya
4.1   kariyosu
4.1   kasabuta
4.1   kasiwade
4.1   katabami
4.1   katazake
3.1 < *4.1 katori < *kat[a]-ori
4.1   katuragi, kazuragi
4.1   kawa^k/g una
4.1   kawanaka
?4.1   kawa-^s/z iri
4.1   kawazoi
4.1   kayaribi
4.1   kazakiri
4.1   kedamono
4.1/4.3 kienba
4.1   komozuno
?4.2, ?4.1 (= 2.1|2.1,|2.2) konogoro
(4.5|)4.1   (to^s/z ama) - koo^s/z ama
4.1   koro-oi
4.1 = 2.1|2.1 koru-moha
?4.1   kozyuuto
?4.1   kubizuna
4.1   kurabone
4.1   kutiwaki
4.1   kutubami
4.x (?4.1)   kuwabira

?4.1	nagagoto	4.1	ogatama	4.1	toosagi
?4.2, ?4.1	namatiti	4.1 < ?*5.1	oharano	4.1	toriami
4.1	namayumi	4.1 = 1.1|3.1	oka^t/$_z$ura	4.1	torikubi
?4.1, ?4.1	naroodo	?4.1	onname	?4.1	torisaka
?4.1	nasunago	?4.3 (?< *4.1)	onoono	?4.1, ?4.2	totukuni
4.1 ?< *4.5	natumuro	4.1	orimono	4.1/4.2	tozikimi
4.1	nikohana	4.1	osouma	4.1	tuigaki
4.1	nimasaka	4.1	otikata	4.1 > 3.1 [tui(-h)izi] > tuizi	
4.1	nina-ai	4.1	saiwai	4.1 < ?5.1, ?5.2 (< ···) tukaito	
4.1	ninamata	4.1	sakasama	4.1 ?= 3.1|1.1 tukuba-ne	
4.1	ninamoto	4.1	sakasima	4.1	tukurida, tuku[ri]da
4.1	ninasibo	4.1	saosika	4.1	tumagoi
4.1	ninasita	?4.1	sa^s/$_z$a-nami	4.1	tumagome
4.1	ninas^s/$_z$oko	4.1	satobito	4.1/4.2	tumairi
4.1	nisasagi	?4.1	sawaudo	4.1	tumiisi
?4.1, ?4.2	miso-hagi	4.1	sayodoko	?4.8, ?4.7, ?4.1	tutegoto
4.1	nitumata	?4.1, ?4.2	sayonaka	4.1	ukareme
?4.1a	niyabito	4.1	sibasiba, simasima	?4.1, ?4.2, ?4.3 (= 2.1|2.3) ukikusa	
4.1	nizuai	4.1	sikimaki	4.1	umoregi
?4.1/4.2	nizukaki 'paddle'	4.1	sirumasi	4.1	umuki-na
4.1, 4.2	nizu^k/$_g$uki	4.1	sitagura	4.1	utakata
4.1	nizutuki	4.1	sitazome	4.1	utimiya
4.1	noe^k/$_g$ui	4.1	siziraki	4.1	utubari
4.1	morobito	4.1	soemono	4.1	utumuro
4.1 = 2.1|2.1	moromoro (-no)	4.1	soimono	?4.1, ?4.2	uwanari
?4.1	motinawa	?4.1	soiuma	4.1	uwanuri
?4.1	munabone	4.1	sonokami	4.1	uwasiki
4.1	murasame	4.1	sumeragi	4.1	watakusi
4.1 = 2.3|2.3	nagakusa	4.1	sumisasi	4.1	wataride
?4.5, ?4.1	namu-^{t}/$_d$ati	4.1	susotuke	4.1	wazawai
4.1	natumusi	4.1	syuutome	4.1	yaigome = ya[k]igome
4.1	negigoto	4.1	tabibito	4.1	yaitoo
4.1	nigitae	?4.1, ?4.11	tadareme	4.1	yakibata
?4.1, ?4.2	niiname	4.1 = 2.1|2.1	takamura	4.1	yakigome
?4.1, ?4.2	niodori	?4.1, ?4.6	takenawa	4.1	yasokage
?4.1, ?A|3.6	ni(-)omoi	4.1 = 2.1|2.1	tamatama	4.1 = 1.1|3.1	ya-timata
4.1	nisigawa	4.1 = 2.3|2.2	tatasi(ma)	4.1; 2.2	2.2	yati-tabi
4.1/4.2	niwakusa	?4.1	tawagoto	4.1	yokogami
4.1	niwatori	4.1	tawayame: *see* taoyame	4.1	yokosa(ma)
4.1	norigoto	?4.2, ?4.1	tokomatu	4.1	yokosi(ma)
4.1	notogoto	?4.1, ?4.2	tokonatu	4.1	yonamusi
4.1	nubatama	?4.1	tokotowa	4.1	yui^k/$_g$ura
4.1	nukagaki	4.1	tomobito	4.1 = 2.1|2.1	yukusaki
4.1	nukagami	4.1	tomodati	4.1	yurugase
4.1	nunobiki	4.1	tomogara	4.1/4.10	yusawari
4.1, 4.2	obayasi	4.1	toobito		

··

4.1a HHHH < HHHF ?< *HHHHL = 5.2 (See Ch. 4, §7.3.)

?4.1a   niyabito

4.2 HHHL

4.2 = 2.1|2.2 amazura	4.2 iwagumi	?4.2 < ?5.2 mizubuki
?4.2, ?4.11 aomusi	?4.2 izumai	?4.1/4.2 mizukaki
?4.2 aoyagi	?4.2 kadomori	4.1, 4.2 mizu^k/$_g$uki
4.2 = 2.1|2.2 araoda	3.1 < 4.2 kaizi	?4.2 moronari
?4.2; ?4.3 = 2.1|2.3 arikusa	4.2 kami^s/$_z$eni	4.2 morotomo
?4.2, ?4.1 arizuka	4.2 kanabasi	?4.2 motiawa
4.2 = 2.1|2.2 asigaki	4.2 kanabata	4.2 [mukatuo]
4.2 asinawa	?4.2, ?4.1 kanamari	4.2 musasabi
4.2 asiwata	4.2 kananabe	?4.2 naginata
4.2 ebisume	4.2 kanazue	4.2 nanariso
4.2 emigusa	4.2 kanazuti	3.2b < 4.2 nedoko
4.2 essai	4.2 kanbase/kaobase	?4.1, ?4.2 niiname
4.2 haetori	4.2 kanbata	?4.1, ?4.2 niodori
?4.2, ?4.1 hahakuri	4.2 karuisi	4.1/4.2 niwakusa
4.2 hakomono	4.2 kasiyone	4.2 niwa-tuzu/-tutu
4.2 hanahada	4.2 kawabune	4.2 nokizuke
4.2 hanazura	4.2 kawagiri	4.2 nunoobi
4.2 hanegaki	?4.2 kawahone	4.1, 4.2 obayasi
4.2 hiedori	4.2 kayoizi	4.2 osikawa
3.2b < 4.2 higasi	4.2 kazitori	4.2 otonai
4.2 higurasi	4.2 kona^k/$_g$aki	4.2 sadatami
4.2 hikiobi	?4.2, ?4.1 = 2.1|2.2,2.1 konogoro	4.2 saigusa
?4.2 hikobosi	4.2 = 2.1|2.2 konokata	4.2 sakazuki
4.2/4.3 himematu	?4.2 kooyobi	?4.2, ?4.5; ?4.1 saoyama
4.2 hinatume	4.2 kosibone	?4.2, ?4.5 sarayama
4.2 hiranabe	4.2 kubikase	4.2 sasaguri
4.2 hisakaki	4.2 kunimagi	?4.1, ?4.2 sayonaka
4.2 hitosasi	?4.2; ?4.11 kurutuhi	4.2 sikiriba
4.2 hiyodori = hiedori	4.2 kutibase	4.2 simoodo
4.2 hiziita	4.2 kutibasi	4.2 sumunori
4.2 hizimaki	4.2 kutibiru	4.2 suzu-^{h}/$_b$une
4.2 hobasira	4.2 kutibuto	4.2 takahara
4.2 hohodori	4.2 kutihibi	4.2 takanna
?4.2 hosodati	4.2 kutisubo	4.2 takumamo
4.2 [hotodori]	4.2(/4.1) kutitori	4.2 tanabata 'weaver: ··· '
4.2 huehuki	4.2 kuwayugi	4.2 tanasisi
?4.3, ?4.2 humibako	4.2 makayaki	4.2 timegusa
?4.3, ?4.2 [hunbako]	4.2 makiita	?4.2, ?4.1 tokomatu
4.1/4.2 hunzuki	4.2 makikusa	?4.1, ?4.2 tokonatu
4.2 hutatabi	4.2 mamahaha	4.2-ni tokosie-ni
?4.2 hutomugi	?4.2, ?4.1 mamatiti	?4.1, ?4.2 totukuni
4.2 huyukusa	4.2 manaita	4.1/4.2 tozikimi
4.2, 4.1 huzigawa	?4.1, ?4.2 maroodo	4.2 tubonage
4.2 ibokai	4.2 maru^u/$_o$-musi	4.2 tubouti
4.2 inemuri	4.2 masurao	4.1/4.2 tumairi
4.2 inisie	4.2 mimidare	4.2 turibune
4.2 iotori	4.2 minasigo	4.2 ubudono
4.2 iozuki	?4.1, ?4.2 miso-hagi	4.2 ukihasi
4.2 isibasi	4.2 miso^k/$_g$ake	4.2 umaginu
4.2 iwabasi	4.2 mitegura	?4.1, ?4.2, ?4.3 = 2.1|2.3 ukikusa
4.2 iwagoke	4.2 mitosagi	4.2 usikusa

4.2	utazuki	4.2, 2.2|2.2, 4.4 yaegaki	4.2	yanagui
4.2	utibora	4.2 yaigusa ‹ ya[k]igusa	4.2	yasiwago
4.2	utumono, utimono	4.2 yaigusi ‹ ya[k]igusi	4.2; 2.2 (= 1.1|1.3) | 2.2 yatikusa
?4.1, ?4.2	uwanari	4.2 yaiisi = yakiisi	4.2	yonamusi
4.2	yabuhara	4.2 = 2.1|2.2 yakiisi	4.2	yotuziro

4.3 HHLL

?4.3 aosaba	4.3 iyo-iyo	4.3 nayo^{t}dake
4.3 arabako	?4.3 kasugai	?4.3 (?‹ *4.1) onoono
?4.2; ?4.3 (= 2.1|2.3) arikusa	4.3 katagayu	?4.3 sasagane
4.3 hatukari	4.3 kawagane	4.3 sinazina
4.3 = 2.1 | 2.3 hatusimo	4.3 kawatake	4.3 sitagutu
4.2/4.3 himematu	4.1/4.3 kienba	4.3 sitakubi
4.3 himemiko	4.3 konasubi	4.3 sitoozu
4.3 hiragane	?4.3, ?2.1|2.4 konokami	4.3 tamuzake
?4.3, ?4.2 humibako	?4.3 kumaguma	4.3 (‹ 5.3) tuzikaze
4.3 humibitu	4.3 kurenai	?4.1, ?4.2, ?4.3 (= 2.1|2.3) ukikusa
?4.3, ?4.2 [hunbako]	4.3 kuretake	4.3 watatabi
4.3 inoasi	4.3 masumasu	4.3 wata^t/$_z$umi
4.1(?/4.3) irehimo	4.3 mati-mati 'varied'	4.3 yaigari ‹ ya[k]igari
4.3 isigane	4.3 mikabati	4.3 yakigane
4.3 isigani	4.3 mizu^k/$_g$ane	4.3; 4.4 = 2.2|2.3 yasosima
?*4.3 *isi-tuti	4.3 mizukara	?2.1 ‹ 3.5b (?‹ 4.3) yaya
?4.3 iya-iya	3.3 (‹ 4.3) mohara	

4.4 HLLL

4.4 (= 2.2-no 1.3) isinoti	?4.4 = 1.1|3.1 okemono	?4.4 utatane
?4.4 kuniguni	?4.4 otodosi	4.2, 2.2|2.2, 4.4 yaegaki
?4.4 ‹ 2.2|2.2 matamata	?4.4 ototoi	4.3; 4.4 = 2.2|2.3 yasosima
4.4 mis/$_z$akari	?4.4 oto^t/$_d$osi	
4.4 mitokoro	?4.4 somosomo	

4.5 LLLL

4.5 aemono	4.5 (= 2.3|2.3) atumono	4.5 hanatumi
?4.5 akinai	4.5 (= 2.3|2.3) awasio	4.5 haneuma
4.5 amagumo	4.5 azumatu	4.5 harakara
4.5 (= 2.3|2.3) anadama	4.5 (=3.4|1.3) azumaya	4.5 harawata
?4.5 anziti, anzitu	4.5 ehasito	4.5 hayabusa
4.5 aobie	4.5 › 3.4 [hadauma] › hazuma	?*4.5 › *3.4 haya[hi]to › hayato
4.5 arisama	?4.1; ?4.5 haha-kata	4.5 = 3.4|1.3 hitakiya
(6.23 =) 4.5|2.5 asidaka-gumo	4.5 hamabisi	4.5 ‡ hitiriki
4.5 asimaki	?4.5, ?4.6 hamasuge	?4.5, ?4.10 hitomura
?4.7, ?4.5 asinabe	?4.5 hanabira	4.5 hizikimo
4.5 asinae	4.5 = 2.3|2.3 hanabusa	4.5 hiziriko
4.5 asiwake	4.5 hanagane	4.5 hokotori

4.5/4.6	hoosuke
(?3.1) < 4.5	horike
4.5	hosi-uo
?4.5	hotondo
4.5	hukatumi
4.5/4.11	hukuroo
4.5	hunabata
?4.5	hunadana
4.5	iebato
4.5	iiue
4.5	ikenie
(?4.5)	ikioi: *see* ikiou (Ch. 6).
?4.5, ?4.6, ?4.11	imogara
4.5	imooto
4.5	inabana
?4.5	ina^k/$_g$usa
4.5	inamura
4.5	inazuka
?4.5	inazumi
?4.5	itazuki
4.5	itigura
?4.5	izayoi
4.5	kakurega
4.5	kamasisi
4.5	kamebara
4.5	kamigaki 'hair pin'
4.5	kamigaki 'banner'
?4.5	kaminari
4.5 = 3.4|1.3	kaminone
4.5	kamitoki
4.5	kamizori = kamisori
4.5	kannie
4.5	kanniwa
4.6/4.5	kanzasi
4.5 = 3.4	kanziki = kaziki'
4.11, 4.5	karahagi
4.5	karakumi
4.5	karakuni
?4.1, ?4.5	karakusa
4.5	karamomo
4.5	karamusi
4.5	karatati
4.5/4.11	karazake
4.5	[karehizi]
4.5	kasamoti
?4.5, ?4.6, ?4.11	kasatori
4.5	kasumomi
4.5	[katabio]
4.5	katabira
4.5	katakoi
?4.5 (= 2.3|2.3)	katatoki
4.5	katigata
4.5	kayaziri
?4.5	ki^h/$_b$atisu
4.5	kirikui
4.5	kirimimi
4.5	kokenori
4.5/4.6	komabue
4.5	komoriku
4.5 (?= 3.4)	‡ konnyaku
4.5	konosiro
4.5	koogai
4.5	kooketi
?4.5	kotobuki
4.5	kotogami
4.5	kotowaza
4.5	kudamono
4.5	kuimono
4.5	ku^k/$_g$atati
?4.5	kukutati
4.5	kuma^t/$_d$aka
4.5	kuminawa
4.5	kurituti
4.5	kurogane
4.5 (?= 2.3|2.3)	kurokusa
4.5	kurotori
4.5 (?= 2.3|2.3)	kurotuti
4.x (?4.5)	kuru-busi
4.5	kurukusa
?4.5	kusabira
?4.5, ?4.10	kusamura
4.5	kusotobi
4.5	kutinawa
4.5	kutubako
4.5	kutubiki
4.5 = 3.4|1.3	kuwasime
?4.5	mainai
?4.5	makabura
4.5	masakari
4.5	mataburi
4.1 ?< *4.5	matumuro
4.5	mayuzumi
4.5	midarao(-no uma)
4.5	mimikuso
4.5	mimisii
4.5	minowata
4.5	‡ mokurani, mokuran
4.5	[monohami]
?4.5	motoara
4.5	motodori
4.5	mozizuri
4.5	muginawa
?4.5	murotumi
4.5	musimono
4.5	nagahito
?4.5	nagatati
?4.5	nakayama
4.5	namazii
?4.5, ?4.1	namu-^{t}/$_d$ati
4.5 = 3.4(|)1.3, ?4.6	naniwazu
4.5	nariwai
4.5	nawasaba
?4.5, ?4.6	nigatake
4.5	niguruma
4.5	nitutuzi
4.5	noasobi
4.5	nokogiri
4.5	[nuikinu]
4.5 = 2.3|2.3	nuimono
4.5, 4.6	numamizu
?4.11, ?4.5	nusubito
4.5 = 1.1|3.4	ogawara
4.5 = 2.3|2.3	oikake
4.5	omogai
3.4 < 4.5 = 2.3|2.3	omoto < o[f]o-moto
4.5 = 2.3|2.3	onmono < "om[u]mono"
4.5	oodaka = ootaka
4.5	oodake
4.5	oodoko
4.5	ooemi
4.5	oogame
4.5	oogane
4.5, 4.7	ookawa
4.5	ookaze
4.5	ookubi
4.5	oomira
4.5	oomiti
4.5(/4.11)	oomune
4.5	oo^t/$_d$aka
4.11 (?4.5 = 2.3|2.3)	ootono
4.5	ootori
4.5	ootubo
?4.5, ?4.9	ooyake
4.5 = 2.3|2.3	oozika
4.5	otooto
4.5 (>3.4)	‡ ringo < riukou
4.5	saizue
?4.2, ?4.5; ??4.1	saoyama
?4.2, ?4.5	sarayama
?4.5	sasigusi
?4.7, ?4.5, ?4.11	sasunabe
?4.5, ?4.6	sibagaki
4.5	sidatuki

4.5 simodake	4.5 tamadare	4.5 = 2.3|2.3 umakai
4.5 simoguti	4.5 tamagusi	4.5 uraguwa
4.5 siraginu	4.5 tamamaki	4.5 ututae(-ni)
4.5 sirahara	4.5 tamamoi	4.5 wakataka
4.5 sirakami	?4.5, ?4.6 tamasii	?4.5 < 5.16 warahude
4.5 sirakuti	4.5 taoyame, tawayame	4.5 = 2.3|2.3 waromono = warumono
4.5 sirataka	4.5 tatigami	4.5 warooda
4.5 siratama	4.5 tatihaki	4.5 yaburema
4.5 siratuti	4.5 = 2.3|1.3 tomosibi	4.5 = 2.3|2.3 yamadori
4.5 sirigaki	4.5 = 2.3|2.3 tomozuna	4.5 = 2.3|2.3 yamaemi
?4.5 sirokage	4.x (?= 4.5) toozimi	4.5 = 2.3|2.3 yamagami
4.5 sirukayu	4.5 = 2.3|2.3 tosigoi	4.5 = 2.3|2.3 yamaguwa
4.5 sitatuki	4.5 < 5.6 = 2.3|3.4 tugumori	4.5 yamasiro
4.5 sitauti	?4.6, ?4.5 = 2.3|2.3 tuitati	4.5 = 2.3-tu|1.3 yamaᵗ/zumi
4.5 siᵗ/ḍumaki	4.5 tukigoro	4.5 yodogawa
4.5 soegoto	4.5 tukinami	4.5, 4.6 yomibito
4.5 ‡ sokudoku	4.5 = 2.3|2.3 tunoyumi	4.5 yorotosi
4.5 suemono	4.5 turubami	4.5 < ?3.4 [yosooi] > yosoi
4.5 sukimono	4.5 tutigura	4.5 = 2.3 yumigake
4.5 = 2.3|2.3 sumikaki	4.5 tutikure	4.5 yumihari
?4.5 = 2.3|2.3; ?4.11, ?4.9 suminawa	4.5 = 2.3|2.3 tutimuro	4.5 = 1.3a-no(=2.1)|2.3 [yunoawa]
4.5 suminoe	4.5 tutisuri	4.5 zenizura
4.5/4.6 > 3.4 sumi-suri > suzuri	4.5 tutiᵗ/ḍara	
4.6 < 5.16; ?4.5 sumitubo	4.5 tutumono	
?4.5 sunawati	?4.10, ?4.5 tuwamono	
4.5 = 2.3|2.3 takadono	4.5 umaguwa	

4.6 LLLH

4.6 abukuma	?4.6a hasitubo	4.6 karakagi
4.6 aezuki	(2.1|)4.6 (hatu-)hanazome	4.6 karakoto
4.6 aisiru	4.6 hizisame	4.6 karanasi
4.6 aimuko	4.5/4.6 hoosuke	4.6 karasao
4.6 akindo, akyuudo	4.6 hosokuzu	4.6 karauri
4.6 amaginu	?4.7, ?4.6 hosomiti	4.6 karausu
?4.6 aouri	4.6 hukagutu	3.5b < 4.6 karei < kar[a]e[f]i
?4.6 asatte	4.6, ?4.11 ikigusa	4.6 kariginu
?4.6 asazuma	?4.5, ?4.6, ?4.11 imogara	?4.5, ?4.6, ?4.11 kasatori
?4.6a asemizo	4.6 inabune	4.6 kasezue
?4.6a asemizu	4.6 inatubi	4.6 (= 2.3|2.4) katasumi
4.6 asiato	4.6 [irokuzu]	4.6 katawara
4.6 asiginu	4.6 itosuzi	4.6 katindo = katim[u]do
4.6 hakikuzu	4.6 kaidako	4.6 katisine
4.6 hamaguri	4.6 kakehasi	4.6 katuuri
4.6 (= 2.3|2.4) hama-hai	4.6 kamouri	4.6 kawaginu
?4.5, ?4.6 hamasuge	4.6 kannagi	4.6 kinugasa
4.6 haramaki	4.6/4.5 kanzasi	?4.6 (> 3.4) kinuita
4.6 (= 2.3|2.4) haraobi	4.6 (> 3.5b) kar[a]ei (= karei)	4.5/4.6 komabue
4.6 harusame	4.6 kara-ᵏ/ginu	4.6 kotozute

4.6	kozigata	4.6	ooani	4.6	tateisi
?*4.6	kubutati	4.6/4.7	oobako	4.6 = 1.3|3.5	tazukuri
4.6	kumasine	4.6	oogasa	3.5a (> ?4.6) tokuri (> tokkuri)	
4.6	kumikaki	?4.6	oohara	?4.6, ?4.5 = 2.3|2.3	tuitati
4.6	kurodai	4.6	ook/ɡuti	4.6	tumeisi
4.5, 4.6	kurokami	4.6/4.7	[oomiki]	4.6	tunouri
4.6	kuromugi	4.6	oomiya	4.6	turabone
4.6	kutugata	4.6/4.7 = 2.3|2.1	oonie	4.6	turazue
?4.6a	maedare	4.6	oon-ma	4.6	tutihasi
4.6 ?= 3.4 (= 2.3-no)	1.1 mamenoha	4.6	oon-zo	?4.6	tutomete
4.6	marazaya	4.6	oowasi	4.6	umabiru
4.6; ?4.9 = 2.4	2.2 mayuage	4.6 = 2.3	2.4 saotori	4.6	umabiyu
4.6 = 2.3 (= 1.3-no)	2.4 menomae	?4.5, ?4.6	sibagaki	4.6 = 2.3|2.4	umisiru
4.6	minis/zese	?4.6, ?4.11	sigarami	4.6	unabara 'the sea'
4.6	mimi-tabu/-tabi	4.6	sikeito	4.6	uribae
4.6	mitubati	4.6, 4.7	sinonome	4.6	urokuzu
?4.6	mizugaki	4.6	siribone	4.6	urusine
?4.6	[mizukaki]: see mizugaki	4.6	sirouri	4.6 = 3.4|1.1	wakunoe
4.6	mugikasu	4.6	sisimura	4.6 (> 3.5a) waragutu, warautu	
4.5 = 3.4(	)1.3, ?4.6 naniwazu	4.6	sitadami	3.5a < 4.6	warazi
4.6	neriito	?4.6	sitorigami	4.6	yadorigi
?4.5, ?4.6 nigatake	4.6	sobauri	4.6	yamagaki
4.6	nodobue	4.5/4.6 > 3.4 suzuri < sumi-suri	4.6	yamanasi
4.6	norisine	?4.6a; ?4.5	sumitubo	?4.6	yamanobe
4.6	nosigata	4.6	surikuzu	4.6	yamasimu
4.5, 4.6	numamizu	4.6 = 2.3	2.4 suriusu	4.5, 4.6	yomibito
4.6	obasima	?4.1, ?4.6	takenawa	4.6	yubimaki
4.6	obikawa	?4.1, ?4.6	takenawa	4.6 (?= 2.3|2.4) yumidame	
4.6	obitori	4.6 ta-komura = ta-kubura	?4.11, ?4.6 = 2.3	2.3 yumizuka	
4.6	obukuro	4.6 = 1.3	3.5 ta-kubura	?4.11, ?4.6	yumizuru
4.6	omozura	?4.5, ?4.6	tamasii	4.6 zenigata	

···

4.6a LLLH < LLLF ?< *LLLHL = 5.16   (See Ch. 4, §7.3.)

?4.6a	asemizo
?4.6a	asemizu
?4.6a	hasitubo
?4.6a, ?3.6	maedare
?4.6a, ?4.5	sumitubo

···

4.7 LLHH

4.7	agemaki	?4.7, ?4.5	asinabe	?4.7, ?4.6	hosomiti
4.7	aiyome	4.7	azimame	4.7	isibusi
4.7	amabiko	?4.7	[haman(i)si, hamazi]	4.7 = 2.3|2.1 kandomo < kamudomo	
?4.7	aobuti	4.7	haya-h/bune	4.7	karakago
4.7	arahito	4.7	himetone	4.7	karakura
4.7 (= 2.3	2.1) asanuno	4.7 = 2.3	2.1 hokosaki	4.8, 4.7, 4.11 karasaki	

4.7 (= 2.3|2.1) kata-naki	?4.7 (?= 2.3|2.1) ook/ɡimi	4.7 sasinabe
4.7 ‡ kitikoo	?4.7, ?4.9 oomae	?4.7, ?4.5, ?4.11 sasunabe
4.7 komeª/zaki	4.6/4.7 [oomiki]	4.7 ‡ senbei
4.7 konosita	4.7 oomoto	4.6, 4.7 sinonome
4.7 koorogi	4.7 = 2.3|2.1 oonbe	?4.7 (< ...) sirituto
4.7 kowadaka	4.6/4.7 = 2.3|2.1 oonie	4.7 sirok/ɡane
4.7 (?= 2.3|2.1) kurokoma	4.7 (= 2.3|2.1), 4.8 oosawa	4.7 = 2.3|2.1 takamiya
4.7 motizuki	4.7 = 2.3|2.1 ooyome	?4.7 (?= 3.4|1.1) toneriko
4.7 noramame	4.7 (= 2.3|2.1) / 4.11 oozume	?4.8, ?4.7, ?4.1 tutegoto
4.7 = 1.3a-tu|2.1 notutori	4.7 otoyome	4.7 tutinabe
4.6/4.7 oobako	4.7 = 2.3|2.1 samukaze	4.7 tuzurame
4.5/4.7 ookawa	4.7 sanebuto	4.7 = 3.5x|1.1 yorozuyo
		4.7 (? yunpazu =) "yumuhazu"

4.8 LHHH

?4.8, ?4.9 ariake	?4.8 nanbito	4.8 siriomo
4.8 aruiwa	4.8 nanigoto	4.8 sitodati
?4.8 azisai	4.8 nanimono	4.8 sobimame
4.8 basyooba	4.8 oobune	4.9(/4.8) sugadori
4.8 eozi	?4.8, ?4.11 oomono	4.8 tagataga
4.8 (?= 3.6|1.2) haseoba	4.7 (= 2.3|2.1), 4.8 oosawa	4.8 tatibame
4.8 kaigane	?4.8 ‡ rindoo	4.8 tatibare
4.8, 4.7, 4.11 karasaki	?3.6 < 4.8 ‡ ruban	4.8 tatigare
4.8 = 3.6 (= 2.4-ga|1.1) karigane	4.8 ‡ ryuutan	?4.8, ?4.7, ?4.1 tutegoto
4.8 kasugome	4.8 ‡ sendan	4.8 < 6.13 utikake
4.8 kinuginu	4.8 sesenagi	4.8 utinasi
?4.8 kusudama	?3.6 < 4.8 ‡ sioni	

4.9   LHHL

?4.9 araara	4.9 karyuudo	4.9 siratami/e
?4.9 araragi	4.9, 4.10 kaseyama	4.9(/4.8) sugadori
?4.8, ?4.9 ariake	4.6; ?4.9 = 2.4|2.2 mayuage	?4.5 (= 2.3|2.3); ?4.11, ?4.9 suminawa
4.9 > 3.7a [hagi-haki] > habaki	?4.9 < 5.11 medogusa	?4.11, ?4.9 tadamuki
4.9 hokodati	4.9 murasaki	4.9 tatibana
4.9(/4.11) hoozuki	3.x < 4.9 = 2.4|2.2 nazure < nan[i]-sure	4.9 [tubu-husi] < tububusi (JP)
4.9 inaguki	?4.7, ?4.9 oomae	4.9 tubunak/ɡi
4.9 = 2.4|2.2 [inakui]	?4.5, ?4.9 ooyake	4.9 umahito
4.9 itadori	?4.9 otogai	4.9 unagami 'mane (of horse)'
4.9 kageroo	?4.9 ‡ saibara	4.9 yamadori

4.10 LHLL

4.10	anagati	4.10	kawamusi	4.10	susubana
4.10	atakamo	4.10 / 2.4|2.4	kotosara	4.10	tamakizu
4.10 ‡	gyooyoo	4.10 (?= 2.5|2.3)	kototae (ni)	4.10	tatimati(-ni)
4.10	haitaka	?4.5, ?4.10	kusamura	?4.10	tezukara
?4.10	hasibami	4.10	kusunoki	4.10	titiuma
4.10	hasitaka	4.10	kuwamayu	3.4 ?< *4.10 ‡	tokati
4.10 (?= 2.4|2.3)	hitomozi	?4.10	maborosi	4.10	tusidama
?4.5, ?4.10	hitomura	4.10	nadesiko	?4.10, ?4.5	tuwamono
?4.10	ienire	4.10	namekuzi	4.10	yamabato
?4.10	ikubaku	4.10	nemugoro, nengoro	4.10	yamamomo
4.10	insaki	?4.10 (?= 2.4|2.3)	omodaka	4.10	yamasuge
4.10	kare-koti	4.10	orihusi	4.1/4.10	yusawari
4.10	kasabiru	4.10	sibaraku < simara(-ku)	4.10/4.11	zeniuti
4.10	kasasagi, kasasaki	?3.4 < 4.10 ‡	sisai	3.4 ?< *4.10 ‡	zisyaku
4.10	kasesaba	4.10	sukosiki	4.10	zusidama: *see* tusidama
4.9, 4.10	kaseyama	4.10	sukosiku		

4.11 LLHL

4.11	ainbe	4.5/4.11	hukuroo	4.11	mame^t/$_z$uki
4.11	akaraka	4.11	ikaruga	4.11	mameyaka
4.11	akiraka	?4.6, ?4.11	ikigusa	4.11	manabuta
4.11	amadori	?4.11	imaniti	4.11	manaziri
4.11	amagoi	?4.5, ?4.6, ?4.11	imogara	4.11	matuyama
4.11	amasaku	?4.11	inazuma	4.11	mawatasi
4.11	anahira	4.11	iyoyoka	4.11	me-haziki
4.11	anaura	4.11	kakenawa	4.11	mezuraka
4.11	aohaka	4.11 (?= 2.3|2.2)	kaminaga	?4.11	minizuku
?4.2, ?4.11	aomusi	4.11 = 2.3|2.2	kanzemi	4.11	miyabika
4.11	aonori	4.11, 4.5	karahagi	4.11	monosi^k/$_g$i
4.11	aoyaka	4.11	[karaoi]	4.11	mugigara
4.11	asabaka	4.8, 4.7, 4.11	karasaki	4.11	nabiyaka
4.11	asagao	4.5/4.11	karazake	4.11	nadaraka
4.11	asibuti	?4.5, ?4.6, ?4.11	kasatori	4.11	nagatuki
4.11	asigas^i/$_e$, asikas^i/$_e$	4.11	katasaki	4.11	nakagoro
4.11	atataka	4.11	katugime	4.11	naka-hi^t/$_d$a
4.11	awagara	4.11	kayaguki	4.11	nameraka
4.11	azayaka	4.11	kisaragi	4.11	nawazemi
4.11	hanayaka	4.11	kitakisu	4.11	nigiraka
4.11	hinezumi	4.11	kokonotu	4.11	nigiyaka
4.11	hiomusi	4.11	komayaka	?4.11, ?4.5	nusubito
4.11	hitaburu	4.11 > ?3.5b	komizu > konzu	4.11	obaoba
4.11 = ?3.4a-ni	hitoe-ni	4.11	koomori	4.11	odaika
4.11 (?= 2.3|2.2b)	hitokusa	?4.2: ?4.11	kurutuhi	4.11	ogimusi
4.11	hitotue	4.11	kusomusi	4.11	ogosoka
4.11	hitoyori	4.11	madaraka	?4.11	okuyama
4.11	hogaraka	4.11	madoyaka	4.11	omeasi
4.9(/4.11)	hoozuki	4.11	makunagi	4.11	omemusi
4.11	[hukigawa] > huigo	4.11	mamegara	?4.11	oodati

?4.11	ookami
4.11	oomizi
?4.8, ?4.11	oomono
4.5(/4.11)	oomune
?4.11	oooba
4.11	ooroka
4.11 (?4.5 = 2.3|2.3)	ootono
?4.11 = 2.3|2.2 (> 3.4)	ooyoso
4.7 (= 2.3|2.1) / 4.11	oozume
4.11	orosoka
4.11	oto-ozi
?4.7, ?4.5, ?4.11	sasunabe
4.11	sibukusa
4.11	sidaraka
?4.6, ?4.11	sigarami
4.11	sitabura
4.11	sit/zu-hata
4.11	siwabuki
4.11	sukoyaka

?4.5 = 2.3|2.3; ?4.11, ?4.9	suminawa
4.11	sumiyaka
4.11	suzus/ziro
4.11	tadaima
?4.11, ?4.9	tadamuki
?4.1, ?4.11	tadareme
4.11	tagaesi
4.11	[tairaka]
4.11	tamazusa
4.11	tanasoko
4.11	tanasue
4.11	tanaura
4.11	tanogoi
4.11	taoyaka
4.11 = 2.3|2.2	tatasa(ma)
4.11 = 2.3|2.2	tatasi(ma)
4.11	tatukomo
4.11	teguruma
?4.11	tezukuri

4.11	tukigusa
4.11	ubitai
4.11	uguisu
4.11	umasaku
4.11 = 2.3|2.2	umazemi
?4.11	umigame
4.11	uziyama
4.11	yamabiko
4.11 < 5.16	yamabuki, yamabuhuki
4.11	yamagusa
4.11	yasuraka
4.11	yatugare
4.11	yawaraka
4.11	yooyaku
?4.11, ?4.6 = 2.3|2.3	yumizuka
?4.11, ?4.6	yumizuru
4.11	zen(i)gasa
4.10/4.11	zeniuti

4.x

4.x	[aikui]
4.x < 3.x	hiimago
4.x < *5.x	hiiragi
4.x	isasaka
3.4 < 4.x	karei 'dried rice ····'
4.x	katakuna
4.x	‡ kengozi
?3.x < ?4.x	kizaya
4.x	kuroodo
4.x	kurooto

4.x (?4.5)	kuru-busi
4.x < 5.16	kusamoti
4.x (?4.1)	kuwabira
3.1 (?< 4.x)	manago
?3.1 (?<4.x)	masago
4.x	mimiaka
3.1 (< 4.x)	motii
4.x	mukudori
4.x	mukuinu
4.x = 5.16	‡ mukurezi = muku-renizi

4.x < 3.x	ninniku, "also niniku"
4.x	ookata
4.x	sirie-de
4.x	sirooto
4.x	taimatu
4.x (?= 4.5)	‡ toozimi
4.x	tubakura < tubakura(me)
4.x	tukuyumi
4.x < 3.2b	yottari
4.x < 5.7	yubinuki

Nouns of five syllables

5 = 5.1 — 5.16; 5.x

5.1 HHHHH

5.1	abarabone
?5.1, ?5.2	akahadaka
?5.1	aotuzura
5.1	ayahatori
5.1	hataori-me
?5.1, ?5.2	hatusigure
?5.1, ?5.2	hazukuroi
5.1	hitotonari
5.1/5.2	hugurizuki
5.1	ikarizuna
5.2, 5.1; 5.16	kamiyagawa
5.1	kanat/zunai

5.1, 5.2	komatunagi
5.2, 5.1	kurabuyama
5.1	kuretuzumi
5.1	kurumazaki
5.1	maturigoto
5.1	mikotomoti
5.1	mikotonori
5.1	mitugimono
5.1	niwatutori
4.1 < ?*5.1	oharano (?< *ooharano)
5.1	onozukara
5.1	oroka-oi

5.1	osimazuki
5.1 = 2.1-tu|2.2	saituk/goro
5.1 ?= 3.1|2.1	sas/zara-nami
5.1 ?= 3.1|2.1	sas/zare-nami
5.1	soeguruma
5.1	tikara-bito
?5.1, ?5.2	tukaibito
5.+	urusimuro
5.1 = 2.1-tu|2.1	utitu-kuni
5.1 ?= 2.1-tu|2.1	utitu-miya
5.1 (?= 3.1|2.1)	yasimakuni

5.2 HHHHL

5.2 (= 2.1|3.2)	akaazuki	5.2	kanabukusi	5.2	saka-abura
?5.1,?5.2	akahadaka	5.2	kanahodasi	5.2	sakayomoi
5.2	akamagusa	?5.2: ?2.1|3.1	kaokatati	5.2	sakibarai
?5.2, ?5.7	aogaeru	5.2	kasadokoro	5.2	sanekazura
5.2	asazihara	5.2	katagaeri	5.2 ?= 3.1|2.2 sa^s/$_z$are-isi	
5.2	ebikazura	5.2	katuomusi	?5.2	sawasorasi
5.2	enokogusa	5.2	kawanagusa	5.2	sibayubari
5.2	haeharai	5.2	kawanegusa	5.2	simotukata
5.2	hanabasira	5.2	kawayanagi	?5.2	sizimigai
5.2	hanagenuki	5.2	kaza-ha^h/$_b$orosi	5.2	suikazura
?5.1, ?5.2	hatusigure	?5.2, ?5.11	kirigirisu	5.2	sukumomusi
?5.1, ?5.2	hazukuroi	5.2	kizudokoro	5.2	sumarogusa
?5.16, ?5.2	hikiyomogi	5.1, 5.2	komatunagi	5.2	takabakari
5.2	hime^k/$_g$omatsu	5.2	komobuturo	5.2	takadanuki
5.2	hirasirage	5.2	kosiguruma	5.2	teratutuki
5.2	hitaibiro	5.2	kubiooi	5.2	tikaragawa
5.2	hitogasira	5.2, 5.1	kurabuyama	5.2	tokosibari
5.2	hito-^{t}/$_d$amai	5.2	kure-hatori	5.2 ?= 2.1-tu|2.2	tokotukuni
5.2	hituzigusa	5.2	kutisakira	5.2	toriawase
5.2	hizakabura	5.2	kutuwazura	?5.1, ?5.2	tukaibito
5.2	hoogasiwa	5.2	madaramaku	5.2	tukarigusa
5.1/5.2	hugurizuki	5.2	madarauri	5.2	tukubayama
5.2	humizukue	5.2	maruganae	?5.2	tumabarame
5.2	hutagokoro	5.2 = 3.1|2.2	masakizura	5.2	uiayumi
5.2	hutama^k/$_g$ami	5.2	mikadomori	?5.2	usayuzuru
5.2	huzibakama	5.2	mike-tu-mono	?5.2	utakakusa
5.2	huzigoromo	5.2 = 2.1|3.2	mitikurabe	?5.2, ?5.1	utuwamono
5.2	isanatori	5.2	miyatukogi	5.2	[uwasoi] < ufa-osofi
5.2	isidatami	?4.2 < ?5.2	mizubuki < mizu-hubuki	5.2	watarimori
5.2	isihaziki	?5.2	mutuoyobi	5.2	watasibune
5.2	iwa^k/$_g$usuri	5.2 = 2.1|3.2	niimagusa	5.2	watasimori
5.2	iwatutuzi	5.2	niwatazumi	5.2	yasasugari
5.2	iya-itoko	5.2	niwazakura	?5.5, ?5.2	yasotuzuki
5.2	kabanegusa	5.2	nukikaburi	5.2	yatagarasu
5.2	kaburaeri	5.2	okatotoki	5.2	yobukodori
5.2	kakitubana	?5.2	ominaesi, omina^b/$_m$esi	?5.2	yoroigusa
5.2	kakitubata	5.2	onna-domo	5.2	yosebasira
5.2	kakumagusa	5.2	osuigane	5.2	yo^t/$_z$i-ozasi
5.2, 5.1: 5.16	kamiyagawa	5.2	osumedori	5.2	yuwaizuna

5.3 HHHLL

5.3	akaenba	5.3	magarikane	5.3	tamarimizu
5.3	akakagati	5.3	mikawamizu	5.3	tumuzikaze
5.3	iwasimizu	5.3	mizukuroi		
5.3	kawarafuzi	5.3 ?< 5.12 = 3.6|2.3	senakabone		

5.4 HHLLL

5.4	arakazime	5.4	niwatutori
?5.16; ?5.4, ?5.9	asakayama	5.4	yaemugura
5.4 = 2.1|3.4	hutatamura	5.4	yomezukae
5.4	niwanoai		

....

5.5 HLLLL

5.5	ikumidake
?5.5, ?5.2	yasotuzuki

....

5.6 LLLLL

5.6	aburazuno	5.16/5.6	kawagoromo	5.6 = 3.4|2.3	osamemono
?5.6	aburimono	?5.6	kezuribana	5.6	saenokami
?5.6	akitusima	5.6	kokorobae	5.6, 5.7	sagarigoke
5.6 (= 3.4|2.3)	azusayumi	5.6, 5.7, ?5.16	kokorogae	5.6	tateakasi
5.6	hakarigoto	5.6	kokorozasi	4.5 < 5.6 = 2.3|3.4	tugumori
5.16, 5.6	hamahukura	5.6 (= 3.4|2.3)	koyosimono	5.6	uguromoti
5.6 (= 3.4|2.4)	haraegoto	5.6	namidatari	?5.6, ?5.16	umahuʰ/ᵇuki
5.6	hitotubiru	5.6	nigorizake	?5.6, ?5.16	umaikusa
5.6	inaturubi	5.6	nikimibana	5.6	warawayamai
5.6	iwaiuta	5.6	nioiuma	5.6 = 2.3|3.4	yamakagami
5.6 = 3.4|2.3	kaerigoto	5.6 = 3.4|2.3	nokorimono	5.6 = 4.5|1.3	yamasirome
5.6	kareituke	5.6/5.16	ooziozi		

....

5.7 LLLLH

5.7	aburaᵗ/ᵤᵤki	5.7	komatuzura	5.7	okosigome
?5.2, ?5.7	aogaeru	?5.7, ?5.8	kosiabura	5.7	ooozi
5.7	hirumusiro	?5.7, ?5.7 (?= 3.4|2.5)	kudara-goto	5.7 > 4.x	oyobinuki > yubinuki
5.7	hisaku-gata	5.7	kumatuzura	5.6, 5.7	sagarigoke
5.7	hitoeginu	5.7	kusobukuro	5.7 (?= 2.3|3.5)	simakawara
5.7	inatabari	?5.7	kusokazura	?5.7	tanagokoro
5.7	itatihaze	5.7	mizikaginu	5.7	tatarigata
5.7	itayagai	5.7	namaenoki	5.7	tatibukuro
?5.7	karigoromo	?5.7	nokogiriba	5.8, 5.7, 5.14	yamakazura
5.7	kokorobuto	5.7 = 3.4|2.4	nokorisine	5.7	yasu-musiro
5.6, 5.7, ?5.16	kokorogae	5.7	obibukuro	5.7	yum[i]bukuro

....

5.7a LLLLF ?< *LLLLHL = 6.22   (See Ch. 4, §7.3.)

?5.7a   tukurimizu

5.8 LLLHH

?5.8 (= 2.3|3.6) hananigana	5.8 narihisago	5.8, 5.10 oon-koto
5.8 ikusabune	5.8 = 2.3|3.6 nigahisago	5.8 rokurogana
?5.7, ?5.8 kosiabura	5.8, 5.16 ooaraki	5.8, 5.7, 5.14 yamakazura
5.8 nakago-gati	5.8 oomi-hune	

5.9 LLHHH

?5.16; ?5.14, ?5.9 asakayama	?5.14; ?5.9 oniyarai	5.9 = 2.3|3.1 takamikura
5.16; 5.14; 5.10, 5.9 asukagawa	5.9 (?= 2.3|3.1) oomi-fune	?5.9, ?5.14 tatidokoro
5.9 iyasibito	5.9 = 2.3|3.1 ootakara	5.9, 5.11 yosinogawa
5.9 kasikigate	5.9 = 2.3|3.1 ootuzumi	

5.10 LHHHH

?5.16; 5.14; 5.10, 5.9 asukagawa	5.8, 5.10 oon-koto	5.10 usagi(m)uma
?5.11, ?5.10 iku-hisasa	?5.10 sitatumiti	5.10 utimidari
5.10 katatagai	5.10, 5.11, ?5.16 tatutagawa	
5.x (?5.10) mukuge-inu	5.10 tatutayama	

5.11 LHHHL

5.11 asaborake	5.11 katunegusa	5.10, 5.11, ?5.16 tatutagawa
5.11 ayamegusa	?5.2, ?5.11 kirigirisu	5.11 > ?3.6, ?3.7a/b tubakurame
?5.11 himekagami	?4.9 < 5.11 medogusa	5.11 tubunegusa
?5.11, ?5.10 iku-hisasa	5.11 oonemusi	5.11 umago-mei/-oi
5.11 itikomame	5.11 sinobugusa	5.9, 5.11 yosinogawa
5.11/5.12 karasumugi	5.16, 5.11 sumidagawa	
5.11 karasuuri	5.11 tatibu-uri	

5.12 LHHLL

5.12   ayametamu
5.11/5.12 karasumugi
5.3 ?< 5.12 senakabone
5.12   suzumitaka
?5.12 ‡ tookesyaku

5.13 LHLLL

?5.13   harugasumi
5.13   [komakunegi]

....

5.14 LLHHL

?5.16; ?5.14, ?5.9 asakayama	?5.16; ?5.14 kudara-humi	?5.9, ?5.14 tatidokoro
?5.16; 5.14; 5.10, 5.9 asukagawa	?5.14; ?5.9 oniyarai	?5.14 (?= 3.4|3.2) umatunagi
?5.14, ?5.16 hitokasane	5.14 oo-una^t/ₐe	5.8, 5.7, 5.14 yamakazura
5.15, 5.14 komurasaki	?5.14, ?5.15, ?5.16 takasebune	?5.14 yamatouta
		5.14 yatukorama

....

5.15 LLHLL

5.15 = 3.5|2.3 kokorogimo	5.15 = 2.3|3.3 oozikara (NKD:"ootikara")	5.15 = 2.3|3.3 yamautugi
5.15, 5.14 (= 1.3|4.9) komurasaki	?5.14, ?5.15, ?5.16 takasebune	5.15 yukatabira
5.15 kuromanako	?5.15, ?5.16 yamakagasi	
5.15 oosazaki	5.15 yamakagati	

....

5.16 LLLHL

5.16 abumizuri	5.16 hototogisu	5.16 katiikusa
5.16 aburabiki	?5.16 hukami-^{k}/ₒusa	5.16/5.6 kawagoromo
5.16 aburawata	5.16 hunayakata	?5.16 kitunegusa
5.16 ai-tutuzi	5.16 hunayamoi	?5.16 kokorobase
5.16 amagaeru	5.16 ibomusi = ibomusiri	5.6, 5.7, ?5.16 kokorogae
5.16 = 2.3-no|2.2 amanogawa	5.16 iisitami	5.16 kotodomori
5.16 amasidari	5.16 ikisudama	?5.16 =3.4|2.2; ?5.14 kudara-humi
5.16 amazakume, amasakume	5.16 ikusagimi	5.16 kusainagi
5.16 [arakazura]	5.16 imeawase	4.x < 5.16 kusamoti < kusamotii
?5.16 asabayaka	5.16 inabikari	5.16 kusomayumi
5.16 asakasiwa	5.16 itatigusa	5.16 kuzukazura
?5.16; ?5.4, ?5.9 asakayama	5.16 kagamikake	?4.6 < 5.16 maedare
5.16 asiganae	5.16 kakuremiti	5.16 me-no-warabe/-warafa
5.16; 5.14; 5.10, 5.9 asukagawa	5.2, 5.1; 5.16 kamiyagawa	5.16 mimigusari
5.16 eyamigusa	5.16 kannazuki	5.16 mimihutagi
5.16 haimayumi	5.16 kara^h/ᵦakari	4.11 miyabika
5.16 hamaakana	5.16 karasuhe^b/ₘi	5.16 = 3.4|2.2 mooke-kimi
5.16, 5.6 hamahukura	5.16 karayatuko	5.16 mugisukui
5.16 hamasasage	5.16 kasiragasa	4.x = 5.16 ⌀ mukurezi = muku-renizi
5.16 hamasugana	5.16 katakasiki	5.16 nana-tokoro
?5.16, ?5.2 hikiyomogi	5.16 katakuzure	5.16 nenasigusa
?5.14, ?5.16 hitokasane	5.16 kataomote	5.16 nisikihebi
5.16 hitokusari	5.16 katasigiri	5.16 numigusuri
5.16 hookiboosi	?5.16 katatukata	5.16 obisibari

5.16	okinabito	5.16	sironamari	5.16	umagususi
5.16	okinagusa	5.16	sisibisio	5.16	umahadake
5.8, 5.16	ooaraki	5.16, 5.11	sumidagawa	?5.6, ?5.16	umahu^h/$_b$uki
5.16	oonaobi	5.16, 2.4|3.7	sundateru	?5.16	umaikusa
5.16	oon-kutu	?5.16	surituzumi	?4.5 < 5.16	warabude
5.16	oooyobi	?5.14, ?5.15, ?5.16	takasebune	5.16 > 4.11	yamabuhuki > yamabuki
5.6/5.16	ooziozi	5.16	tanatumono	?5.15, ?5.16	yamakagasi
5.16	‡ sakunanza	5.10, 5.11, ?5.16	tatutagawa	?5.16 = 3.5|2.4/5	yamatokoto
5.16	saruogase	5.16	tubaimono	5.16	yamaubara
5.16	simatu^t/$_d$ori	5.16	tumabiraka	5.16 (?= 2.3-tu|2.2)	yomo-tu-kuni
5.16	sirahadake	5.16	tutigaeru	5.16	yoorokubo
5.16	sirita^b/$_m$ura	5.16	uma^k/$_g$itasi, umakidasi	5.16	yusurubati

5.x

5.x	aezukuri	5.x (?5.10)	mukuge-inu
4.x < ‡5.x	hiiragi	5.x	yamanoimo
5.x	i-no-huguri		

Nouns of six syllables

6 = 6.1 — 6.23, 6.x

6.1 HHHHHH

6.1, 6.2	hosotanigawa	6.1	tawamuregoto, tawaburegoto
6.1, 6.2	mizukukiburi	6.1	usi-no-hitai
6.1 = 3.1|3.1	noborikudari		

6.2 HHHHHL

?6.2	adasi-^{k}/$_g$okoro	6.2	kawarayomogi	6.2	tatimatigusa
?6.2	ae-/abe-tatibana	6.2	koromozutumi	6.2	tobinoogoto
6.2	ebisugusuri	6.2	mikado-ogami	?6.2	torisaka-nori
6.2	hazikamiuo	6.2	minasikogusa	6.2	yatumekabura
6.1, 6.2	hosotanigawa	6.1, 6.2	mizukukiburi	6.2	yuutukedori
6.2	kaburaminizu	6.2	sawaararagi		
6.2	kaku-bakari	?6.2	sawahiyodori		

6.3 HHHHLL

6.3	agekasugai	?6.3	minizukara
6.3	asiharagani	6.3	niwakunaburi
6.3	kawatisanoki	?6.3, ?6.4	totu-kuniguni
6.3 (?= 4.2|1.3x)	kurazukuri-be		

?6.4 HHHLLL

?6.3, ?6.4   totu-kuniguni

....

?6.5 HHLLLL: ---

....

?6.6 HLLLLL: ---

....

6.7 LLLLLL

?6.7, ?6.22   ikuhadokoro
6.7   yamasirogawa

....

?6.8 LLLLLH: ---

....

?6.9 LLLLHH

?6.9, ?6.22   netamasigao
?6.9 (= *6.10 = 2.3-no|3.1)   toyonoakari

....

6.10 LLLHHH

6.10 = 2.3-tu|3.1   ama-tu-hitugi
6.10   kamiokosi-na
6.10   oon-husuma
?6.10   oon-takara
?6.9 (= *6.10 = 2.3-no|3.1)   toyonoakari

....

?6.11 LLHHHH

6.11 = 3.5|3.1 [yamato-kooti]

....

?6.12 LHHHHH

6.13/6.12 (= 3.6|3.1)   hisikoiwasi
?6.12, ?6.22   makabura-ᵗ/ₔaka

....

<u>6.13</u> LHHHHL

6.13/6.12 (= 3.6|3.1)   hisikoiwasi
6.13   tuwamonogura
6.13   utikakeginu

....

?6.14 LHHHLL

?6.14   yubaribukuro

....

?6.15 LHHLLL: ---

....

?6.16 LHLLLL

6.16   yamabuhuki: *see* yamabuki

....

<u>6.17</u> LLHHHL

?6.17, ?6.20 oon-yamai
6.17   ooyakegoto
6.17   yamadori-kusa

....

?6.18 LLHHLL

?6.18 = 4.7(=2.3|2.1)|2.3   ookindati

....

?6.19 LLHLLL: ---

....

<u>6.20</u> LLLHHL

6.20 = 3.4 (= 2.3-no)|1.3 kaminoyagara
6.20   oomitegura
?6.17, ?6.20 oon-yamai

....

6.21 LLLHLL

6.21	anahazikami	?6.21	ikusaguruma	6.21	miranonegusa
6.21	hayahito-gusa	6.21	imozyuutome	6.21	nenasikazura
6.21	hita-omo^b/_muki	6.21	kata-minasigo	6.21	omoharakara

6.22 LLLLHL

6.22	abumigawara	6.22	kokoromadoi	6.22	onnakazura
?5.1b ‹ 6.22	amazakume	6.22	komuragaeri	6.22	otoko-ª/_zakari
?6.7, ?6.22	ikuhadokoro	6.22	kugutumawasi	6.22	sagaribusube
6.22	kamikirimusi	?6.12, ?6.22	makabura-ᵗ/_daka	?6.22	sidariyanagi
6.22	kanonigegusa	?6.22	[moe-hazikami]	6.22	sirotadamuki
6.22	karasunameri	?6.9, ?6.22	netamasigao	6.22	sitadeyubari
?6.22	katasiro-gusa	6.22	omohahakuso		

6.23 LLLLLH

6.23 (=4.5|2.5) ‹ 4.5-no|2.4   asidaka-gumo
6.23   katawarabone
6.23   kugutumawasi

6.x

6.x   makurakotoba

Nouns of seven syllables

7 = 7.1 — 7.32, 7.x

?7.1 HHHHHHH: ---.

7.2 HHHHHHL

7.2   amakutinezumi
7.2   kawakumatuzura

7.3 HHHHHLL

7.3   karasukutinawa

```
7.4 HHHHLLL: ---.
7.5 HHHLLLL: ---.
7.6 HHLLLLL: ---.
7.7 HLLLLLL: ---.
7.8 LLLLLLL: ---.
7.9 LLLLLLH: ---.
```

....

?7.10 LLLHHHH

```
?7.10 = 3.4|4.1    itatihazikami
?7.10    oon-atumono
```

....

<u>**7.11**</u> **LLLLHHH**

```
7.11    ooutadokoro
```

....

```
7.12 LLLHHHH: ---.
7.13 LLHHHHH: ---.
```

....

<u>**7.14**</u> **LHHHHHH**

```
7.14    tatematurimono
```

....

```
7.15 LHHHHHL: ---.
```

....

<u>**7.16**</u> **LHHHHLL**

```
7.16    tikirikooburi (tikirikanmuri, tikirikoomuri) < tikirikauburi
```

....

```
7.17 LHHHLLL: ---.
7.18 LHHLLLL: ---.
7.19 LHLLLLL: ---.
7.20 LLHHHHH: ---.
```

....

7.21 LLHHHL

7.21	**ooziga-huguri: LLHH(|)HHL**
7.21	**siro^k/ɠanezukuri**
7.21	**yumizurubukuro**

7.22 LLHHHLL: ---.
7.23 LLHHLLL: ---.
7.24 LLHLLLL: ---.
7.25 LLLHHHH: ---.
7.26 LLLHHHL: ---.
7.27 LLLHHLL: ---.
7.28 LLLHLLL: ---.
7.29 LLLLHHH: ---.

7.30 LLLLHLL

7.30	**inaoosedori**
7.30	**kutukutuboosi**

7.31 LLLLLHL: ---.
7.32 LLLLLLH: ---.

7.x

7.x	**oooziozi**

5.11.2. Statistical profiles of noun accent classes.

Below are tables which show the populations of the accent classes to which the nouns of §5.9 have been assigned. Many nouns are counted more than once, because variant forms or accentuations are listed as separate entries in the count list. The totals are therefore somewhat inflated (in particular for the longer entries) but the ratios of the accent classes do not appear to be skewed by that. Counts are given for words known to be of Chinese origin ("< Ch") and for questioned assignments ("?" preceding the formula designating the type). The column "?" does not include entries counted in the preceding column ("Ch") that happen also to be questioned; it includes items with the notations "?<" and "?/". The three columns on the right give the number of entries excluding the Chinese borrowings, the questioned assignments, or both.

Type	Entries	"Ch"	"?"	-"Ch"	-"?"	-"Ch,?"
ONE-SYLLABLE						
1.1	77	7	38	70	39	32
1.2	24	0	12	0	12	12
1.3	115	11	44	104	69	60
1.3a	63	3	18	60	45	42
1.3b	37	6	14	31	23	17
1.3x	15	2	12	13	3	1
1.x	30	0	0	30	30	30
TOTAL	246	18	96	204	150	134
A (1.1, 1.2)	101	7	50	70	51	44
B (1.3)	115	11	44	104	69	60
TOTAL	216	18	94	174	120	104
Unknown	30	0	0	30	30	30
Atonic (1.1, 1.3a)	140	10	56	130	84	74
Tonic (1.2, 1.3b)	61	6	26	31	35	29
TOTAL	201	16	82	161	119	103
Unknown (1.3x, 1.x)	45	2	12	43	13	31

Type	Entries	"Ch"	"?"	-"Ch"	-"?"	-"Ch,?"
TWO-SYLLABLE						
2.1	356	6	111	350	245	239
2.1a	7	7	7	7	7	7
2.2	195	6	78	189	117	111
2.2a	74	1	30	73	44	43
2.2b	101	5	38	96	63	58
2.2x	20	0	10	20	10	10
2.3	399	27	108	372	291	264
2.4	201	11	100	190	101	90
2.5	148	3	83	145	65	62
2.x	41	1	2	40	39	38
TOTAL	1,340	54	482	1,286	858	804
A (2.1-2)	551	12	189	539	362	350
B (2.3-5	748	41	291	707	457	416
TOTAL	1,299	53	480	1,246	819	766
Unknown (2.x)	41	1	2	40	39	38
Atonic* (2.1, 2.3)	755	33	219	722	536	503
Tonic (2.2, 2.4-5)	544	20	261	524	283	263
TOTAL	1,299	53	480	1,246	819	766
Unknown (2.x)	41	1	2	40	39	38

*This includes the seven entries of 2.1a with 2.1.

Type	Entries	"Ch"	"?"	-"Ch"	-"?"	-"Ch,?"
THREE-SYLLABLE						
3.1	395	4	95	391	300	296
3.1a	4	0	0	4	4	4
3.2	130	0	50	130	80	80
3.2a	41	0	11	41	30	30
3.2b	35	0	20	35	15	15
3.2a/b	5	0	0	5	5	5
3.2x	49	0	19	49	30	30
3.3	50	0	20	50	30	30
3.4	377	11	91	366	286	275
3.4a	6	0	6	6	0	0
3.5	170	5	43	165	127	122
3.5a	28	2	9	26	19	17
3.5b	59	3	17	56	42	39
3.5a/b	16	0	2	16	14	14
3.5x	67	0	15	67	52	52
3.6	150	10	48	140	102	92
3.7	150	4	42	146	108	104
3.7a	37	0	13	37	24	24
3.7b	58	3	10	55	48	45
3.7a/b	16	0	8	16	8	8
3.7x	39	1	11	38	28	27
3.x	40	0	1	40	39	39
TOTAL	1,462	34	390	1,428	1,072	1,038
A (3.1-3)	575	4	165	571	410	406
B (3.4-7)	847	30	224	817	623	593
TOTAL	1,422	34	389	1,388	1,033	999
Unknown (3.x)	40	0	1	40	39	39
Atonic (3.1, 3.4)	772	15	186	757	586	571
Tonic (the rest)	650	19	203	631	447	428
TOTAL	1,422	34	389	1,388	1,033	999
Unknown (3.x)	40	0	1	40	39	39

Type	Entries	"Ch"		"?"		-"Ch"		-"?"		-"Ch,?"	
FOUR-SYLLABLE											
4.1	245	0		53		245		192		192	
4.1a			1		0		1		1	0		0
4.2	168	0		34		168		134		134	
4.3	50	0		13		50		37		37	
4.4	13	0		8		13		5		5	
4.5	263	5		50		258		213		208	
4.6	152	0		29		152		123		123	
4.6a			5		0		5		5	0		0
4.7	55	2		9		53		46		44	
4.8	35	5		7		30		28		23	
4.9	30	1		11		29		19		18	
4.10	47	4		11		43		36		32	
4.11	146	0		34		146		112		112	
4.x	30	3		3		27		27		24	
TOTAL	1,234	20		262		1,214		972		952	

A (4.1-4)	476	0	108	476	368	368
B (4.5-11	728	17	151	711	577	560
TOTAL	1,204	17	259	1,187	945	928

Unknown (4.x)	30	3	3	27	27	24

Atonic (4.1, 4.5)	508	5	103	504	405	400
Tonic (the rest)	696	12	156	683	540	528
TOTAL	1,204	17	259	1,187	945	928

Unknown (4.x)	30	3	3	27	27	24

Type	Entries	"Ch"	"?"	-"Ch"	-"?"	-"Ch,?"
FIVE-SYLLABLE						
5.1	35	0	6	35	29	29
5 2	117	0	19	117	98	98
5.3	10	0	0	10	10	10
5.4	7	0	1	7	6	6
5.5	2	0	1	2	1	1
5.6	35	0	5	35	30	30
5.7	33	0	8	33	25	25
5.8	11	0	2	11	9	9
5.9	11	0	3	11	8	8
5.10	10	0	3	10	7	7
5.11	19	0	3	19	16	16
5.12	5	1	2	4	3	2
5.13	2	0	1	2	1	1
5.14	13	0	8	13	5	5
5.15	10	0	2	10	8	8
5.16	109	1	17	108	92	91
5.x	5	0	0	5	5	5
TOTAL	434	2	81	432	353	351
A (5.1-5)	171	0	27	171	144	144
B (5.6-16	258	2	54	256	204	202
TOTAL	429	2	81	427	348	346
Unknown (5.x)	5	0	0	5	5	5
Atonic (5.1, 5.6)	70	0	11	70	69	59
Tonic (the rest)	359	2	70	357	289	287
TOTAL	429	2	81	403	348	346
Unknown (5.x)	5	0	0	5	5	5

Type	Entries	"Ch"	"?"	-"Ch"	-"?"	-"Ch,?"
SIX-SYLLABLE						
6.1	5	0	0	5	5	5
6 2	19	0	4	19	15	15
6.3	7	0	2	7	5	5
6.4	1	0	1	1	0	0
6.6	0	0	0	0	0	0
6.6	0	0	0	0	0	0
6.7	2	0	1	2	1	1
6.8	0	0	0	0	0	0
6.9	2	0	2	2	0	0
6.10	5	0	1	5	4	4
6.11	1	0	0	1	1	1
6.12	2	0	1	2	1	1
6.13	3	0	0	3	3	3
6.14	1	0	1	13	0	0
6.15	0	0	0	0	0	0
6.16	0	0	0	0	0	0
6.17	3	0	1	3	2	2
6.18	1	0	1	1	0	0
6.19	0	0	0	0	0	0
6.20	3	0	1	3	2	2
6.21	9	0	1	9	8	8
6.22	20	0	6	20	14	14
6.23	3	0	0	3	3	3
6.x	1	0	0	1	1	1
TOTAL	88	0	23	88	65	65
A (6.1-6)	32	0	7	32	25	25
B (6.7-23	55	0	16	55	39	39
TOTAL	87	0	23	87	64	64
Unknown (6.x)	1	0	0	1	1	1
Atonic (6.1, 6.7)	7	0	1	7	6	6
Tonic (the rest)	80	0	22	80	58	58
TOTAL	87	0	23	87	64	64
Unknown (6.x)	1	0	0	1	1	1

Type	Entries	"Ch"	"?"	-"Ch"	-"?"	-"Ch,?"
SEVEN-SYLLABLE						
7.1	0	0	0	0	0	0
7 2	2	0	0	2	2	2
7.3	1	0	0	1	1	1
...						
7.10	2	0	2	2	0	0
7.11	1	0	0	1	1	1
...						
7.14	1	0	0	1	1	1
...						
7.16	1	0	0	1	1	1
...						
7.21	3	0	0	3	3	3
...						
7.30	2	0	0	3	3	3
...						
7.x	1	0	0	1	1	1
TOTAL	14	0	2	14	12	12
A (7.1-9)	3	0	0	3	3	3
B (7.10-)	10	0	2	10	8	8
TOTAL	13	0	2	13	11	11
Unknown (7.x)	1	0	0	1	1	1
Atonic (7.1, 7.8)	0	0	0	0	0	0
Tonic (the rest)	13	0	2	13	11	11
TOTAL	13	0	2	13	11	11
Unknown (7.x)	1	0	0	1	1	1

5.11.3. Summary table of statistical profiles.

The figures exclude items unassigned to accent classes ("N.x"). The count for each class is followed by its percentage of the shapes included in the relevant larger group.

	O v e r a l l			Without Ch or "?"		
1.1	77	.36		32	.31	
1.2	24	.11		12	.12	
1.3	115	.53		60	.58	
1.3a		63	.55		42	.70
1.3b		37	.32		17	.28
1.3x		15	.13		1	.02
TOTAL	216	= .05		104 = .03		
2.1	356	.27		239	.31	
2.1a		7	.02		7	.03
2.2	195	.15		111	.14	
2.2a		74	.38		43	.39
2.2b		101	.52		58	.52
2.2x		20	.10		10	.09
2.3	399	.31		264	.34	
2.4	201	.15		90	.12	
2.5	148	.11		62	.08	
TOTAL	1,299	= .28		767 = .21		
3.1	395	.28		296	.30	
3.1a		4	.01		4	.01
3.2	130	.09		80	.08	
3.2a		41	.32		30	.38
3.2b		35	.27		15	.19
2.2a/b		5	.04		5	.06
3.2x		49	.38		30	.38
3.3	50	.04		30	.03	
3.4	377	.27		275	.28	
3.4a		6	.02		0	.00
3.5	170	.12		122	.12	
3.5a		28	.16		17	.14
3.5b		59	.35		39	.32
3.5a/b		16	.09		14	.11
3.5x		67	.39		52	.43
3.6	150	.11		92	.09	
3.7	150	.11		104	.10	
3.7a		37	.25		24	.23
3.7b		58	.39		45	.43
3.7a/b		16	.11		8	.08
3.7x		39	.26		27	.26
TOTAL	1,420	= .31		999 = .28		

	O v e r a l l				Without Ch or "?"	
4.1	245		.20		192	.20
4.1a		1		.00	0	.00
4.2	168		.14		134	.14
4.3	50		.04		37	.04
4.4	13		.01		5	.01
4.5	263		.22		213	.23
4.6	152		.13		123	.13
4.6a		5		.03	0	.00
4.7	55		.05		46	.05
4.8	35		.03		28	.03
4.9	30		.02		19	.02
4.10	47		.04		36	.04
4.11	146		.12		112	.12
TOTAL	1,204 = .26				945 = .26	

5.1	35	.08	29	.08
5.2	117	.27	98	.28
5.3	10	.02	10	.03
5.4	7	.02	6	.02
5.5	2	.00	1	.00
5.6	35	.08	30	.09
5.7	33	.08	25	.07
5.8	11	.03	9	.03
5.9	11	.03	8	.02
5.10	10	.02	7	.02
5.11	19	.04	16	.05
5.12	5	.01	2	.01
5.13	2	.00	1	.00
5.14	13	.03	5	.01
5.15	10	.02	8	.02
5.16	109	.25	91	.26
TOTAL	429 = .09		346 = .10	

     O v e r a l l   Without Ch or "?"

6.1	5	.06		5	.08
6.2	19	.22		15	.23
6.3	7	.08		5	.08
6.4	1	.01		0	.00
6.5	0	.00		0	.00
6.6	0	.00		0	.00
6.7	2	.02		1	.02
6.8	0	.00		0	.00
6.9	2	.02		0	.00
6.10	5	.06		4	.06
6.11	1	.01		1	.02
6.12	2	.02		1	.02
6.13	3	.03		3	.05
6.14	1	.01		0	.00
6.15	0	.00		0	.00
6.16	0	.00		0	.00
6.17	3	.03		2	.03
6.18	1	.01		0	.00
6.19	0	.00		0	.00
6.20	3	.03		2	.03
6.21	9	.10		8	.13
6.22	20	.23		14	.22
6.23	3	.03		3	.05
TOTAL	87 = .02			64 = .02	

7.1	0	.00		0	.00
7.2	2	.15		2	.18
7.3	1	.08		1	.09
. . .					
7.10	2	.15		0	.00
7.11	1	.08		1	.09
. . .					
7.14	1	.08		1	.09
. . .					
7.16	1	.08		1	.09
. . .					
7.21	3	.23		3	.27
. . .					
7.30	2	.15		2	.18
TOTAL	13 = .00			11 = .00	

TOTAL   4,655   3,263

5.11.4. Summary table of register and tonicity.

Excluding only unassigned items (?N.x"):

Syll.	Total	N.x	-N.x	A		B		Atonic		Tonic	
1	246	30	216	101		115		140		61*	
					.47		.53		.65		.28
2	1,338	41	1,299	551		748		755		542	
					.42		.58		.58		.42
3	1,462	40	1,422	575		847		772		650	
					.40		.60		.54		.46
4	1,234	30	1,204	476		728		508		694	
					.40		.60		.42		.58
5	434	5	429	171		258		70		359	
					.40		.60		.16		.84
6	88	1	87	32		55		7		80	
					.37		.63		.08		.92
7	14	1	13	3		10		0		13	
					.23		.77		.00		1.00
TOTAL	4,818	148	4,670	1,909		2,761		2,252		2,403	
					.41		.59		.48		.51*

*This excludes the 15 items of 1.3x (= .07).

Also excluding Chinese borrowings ("< Ch") and questioned assignments ("?"):

Syll.	Total	N.x	-N.x	A		B		Atonic		Tonic	
1	134	30	104	44		60		74		29*	
					.42		.58		.71		.28*
2	804	38	766	350		416		503		263	
					.46		.54		.66		.34
3	1,038	39	999	406		593		571		428	
					.41		.59		.57		.43
4	952	24	928	368		560		400		540	
					.40		.60		.43		.57
5	351	5	346	144		202		59		287	
					.42		.58		.17		.83
6	65	1	64	25		39		6		58	
					.39		.61		.09		.90
7	12	1	11	3		8		0		11	
					.27		.73		.00		1.00
TOTAL	3,356	138	3,218	1,340		1,878		1,613		1,604*	
					.40		.60		.48		.52

*This excludes one item of 1.3x.

Chapter 6. Verbs.

6.0. Introduction.

The heart of this chapter is a list of about 2200 verbs. The list is a fairly extensive inventory of the verb stems of historic Japanese, compiled primarily to enable the reconstruction of the accentual register for each stem. Omitted are a fair number of the verbs of Old Japanese which failed to survive into the Heian and later periods. Included are a certain number of compound verbs, which were mostly pronounced as two-word phrases before around A.D. 1300; also, phrases that are often treated as single lexical entities in studies of Japanese word formation. Although most of the entry verbs persist into the modern language, we have included certain stems which have not survived but are well attested from earlier periods, especially when they seem relevant to our study of accentual registers or shed light on the etymology of the other stems.

6.1. Verb stems; conjugations; notational devices.

Our model of the Japanese verb takes as its point of departure the structure STEM + ENDING. In accordance with the conventional practice, as found in Nihon-Kokugo-Daijiten (NKD), each entry starts with the "dictionary" form of the modern verb, the finite "imperfect" or "nonpast", which ends in ···-u or ···^{i}/$_e$-ru in the modern standard language. The verbs of earlier and later Japanese alike divide into CONJUGATIONS according to the specification of just how the endings are attached to particular sets of stems. The two basic conjugations are often referred to as CONSONANT stems and VOWEL stems, and that is because we assume that the underlying form of the stem ends in a consonant in the one conjugation and in a front vowel (i or e) in the other. The vowel stems are traditionally subcategorized by whether the vowel is /i/ ("upper" in the kana chart) or /e/ ("lower") and by whether they follow the ending-selection option of what were originally polysyllabic ("bigrade") or monosyllabic ("monograde") stems. In addition there are a few common verbs with relatively minor irregularities and at least two (sinu 'die', inu 'depart') which are hybrid in conjugation. Suzuki Kazuhiko 1977 ("Bunpō no utsuri-kawari", Nihongo-kōza 6:197-242) cites statistics for the older stems:

720	quadrigrade (*yo-dan*)	···C-
200	lower bigrade (*simo - ni-dan*)	···e-
40	upper bigrade (*kami - ni-dan*)	···i-
20	upper monograde (*kami - iti-dan*)	(C)i-
2	hybrid	inu, sinu
1	irregular upper bigrade (*ka-hen*)	kuru
1	irregular upper bigrade (*sa-hen*)	suru
1	lower monograde (*simo - iti-dan*)	ker-u < keru*
4	irregular quadrigrade	ari, [w]ori, haberi, imasokari

> *But keru 'kick' was lower bigrade until about A.D. 1100 (and quadrigrade ker-u from the middle of the nineteenth century).

The "irregularity" of the last group lies in the use by literary Japanese of the
infinitive (-i) in most of the situations that call for the predicative finite (-u);
this can be treated as a syntactic peculiarity, rather than an irregularity of the
morphology.

Our list includes a fair number of verbs which are not attested for early
periods; and some of these, despite our reconstructions of the shapes they might
have had a thousand years ago, are known to have come into being as clearly later
innovations. The finite forms of the vowel-stem verbs are simplified in the modern
language by attaching -ru to the stem, which is identical to the infinitive. In
literary Japanese, that is true for the monosyllabic vowel stems (such as miru 'see'
and keru 'kick') but the polysyllabic vowel stems suppress the final vowel ···e- or
···i- and attach -u for the "predicative" finite form and -uru for the "attributive"
(adnominal) finite: oti 'fall' (infinitive), saru otu 'monkeys fall', oturu saru
'falling monkeys'; nige 'flee' (infinitive), saru nigu 'monkeys flee', niguru saru
'fleeing monkeys'. In Old Japanese two polysyllabic vowel stems (arabi- 'rage' and
isati- 'weep') act like monosyllabic stems, but the former also enjoyed the expected
conjugation (which is thought to be older) and the latter probably incorporated a
monosyllabic stem of unknown origin. Also in Old Japanese the monograde stem wi[y]-
'be' sometimes appears in the predicative form wu; that indicates either the bigrade
conjugation wu(ru) / wi[y], despite the monosyllabicity of the stem, or perhaps a
contraction w[i-r]u.

For each entry we attempt to present a series of successively earlier versions,
either attested or reconstructed; the unattested forms are preceded by an asterisk.
(Notice that the asterisk does not in itself imply a particular period for which the
unattested form is adduced, though the nature of the following notation may well
preclude periods later than a certain time.) The notations are to be interpreted in
accordance with discussions in other parts of this book. Brackets enclose ellipses
that lead to contracted forms. If the entire verb form is in brackets, that means
the form as such does not survive into the modern mainstream of the language as
attested by the entries of NKD. Notably, this device is used when we cite those
bigrade verbs that fell into disuse before the modern analogical ···e-ru and ···i-ru
forms replaced the earlier forms with ····-uru, so that the shapes cited in brackets
are what would have developed if the verb had survived the restructuring of forms.
According to Okumura 1968 the general restructuring of the polysyllabic vowel stems
to the modern monograde (*iti-dan*) conjugation did not begin before the Muromachi
period; but Kokugo-gaku dai-jiten cites a few cases from somewhat earlier: sabiru
1190, manabiru 1192, hedateru 1203, yabureru 1213, saka[f]eru and kana[f]eru 1216.
According to Okumura the upper bigrade verbs, being considerably fewer in number,
were the first to be restructured, and that is why the modern dialects rarely show
a trace of the earlier grammar for the ···-u(ru) → ···i-ru verbs, though the lower
bigrade verbs preserve earlier forms ····-uru / ····-ey in certain of the peripheral
dialects, especially those of Kyūshū. Other observations made by Okumura 1968
include the fact that the few shorter verbs (deru, neru, heru) were restructured
earlier than the longer verbs and the related fact that the bound auxiliaries which
make the causatives and passives (→ modern -saseru and -rareru) preserved the
earlier forms till later than the lower bigrade stems of free verbs did; that this
restructuring took place before the hybrid sinu(ru) / sini 'die' was regularized as
a quadrigrade (consonant-stem) verb, as is evidenced by the persistence of sinuru
in modern dialects; and that the two modern Kansai quadrigrade auxiliaries -sasu
and -naharu came directly from the predicative forms of -sasu(ru) and -nasaru(ru)
without passing through the monograde stage of -saseru and -nasareru. Restructuring
of the bigrade verbs appears to have started in the east; Rodriguez noted that ageru

and motomeru were the usual versions in 16th-century versions in the Kantō area but
they were used by only some of the inhabitants of Kyōto, most of whom said aguru
and motomuru for these verbs. Fossilized relics of the bigrade conjugation survive
in a few adnouns of modern Japanese: akuru (hi) 'next (day)', arayuru 'all kinds
of', iwayuru 'so-called'.

The segmental notations are to be interpreted according to the descriptions for
various periods that were given earlier in this work. Notice in particular that what
is written as an intervocalic "-f-" was probably never pronounced as the voiceless
fricative implied by that letter: during the later stages, from around A.D. 1100,
the sound was [-w-] and earlier it was the [-b-] allophone of the phoneme /p/, at a
period when the ancestor of the modern -b- was prenasalized [-mb-], which we have
interpreted as /-np-/. We assume that the earliest ancestor of the historic w- was
pronounced b- and that the historic y- was earlier pronounced either d- (as our
notation implies) or as a palatalized version of that, possibly affricated to [dž],
at a time when the ancestor of modern -d- was prenasalized [-nd-], which is to be
interpreted as /-nt-/. There is no ambiguity in these notations, provided the reader
keeps in mind the relative chronology of the particular stage that is under current
consideration.

6.2. Verb endings.

The endings are reconstructed as follows. The infinitive ending is treated as
-Ci, with an underlying initial consonant that probably was the voiced velar stop [g]
or a fricative version thereof, though there is no internal evidence to keep us
from positing the simpler -yi or just -i. The finite endings are reconstructed as -u
(or -Cu) for the predicative and -uru (or -Curu) for the attributive, though I think
that these endings are perhaps reductions from a more complex structure that is made
up of infinitive (or root) + auxiliary. The substitution of the attributive for the
expected predicative form of the short monograde stems, such as miru 'see' < myi-ru
instead of *myuu < *myi-u, is left unexplained; Ōno Tōru 1978:209 hypothesizes a
kind of "hiatus filler" (i.e. epenthetic) -r-.

The subjunctive ending is simply the verb root (or stem) itself with its final
underlying vowel (see below), which otherwise drops when not followed by a formant
(= a suffix other than an ending). By historic times, however, the prevalent form
of the quadrigrade stems, CVCVa-, was analogically extended so that the vowel -a-
either became a part of the auxiliaries (-amu, -anu, -asu, -aru/-ayu) or perhaps
achieved the status of a separate morpheme, a formant in its own right.

Notice that our notation for the infinitive ···C[a-C]i implies that the first
of two adjacent vowels dropped and then the initial consonant of the ending was
automatically suppressed. This took place only where our notational hyphen marks a
word-final suffix, as it does in -Ci and -(C)u, and not when the hyphen marks a nonfinal suffix or auxiliary, for in those cases the two vowels form a diphthong which
is in due course monosyllabified: ···Ca-Ci- > ···Cey-. My reluctance to write -Cu
for -u despite -Ci for -i owes to a belief that -u and -uru are reductions from
more complex structures that involve the ellipsis of more than a single segment. In
all cases the ellipted consonant here written as C was probably a voiced velar stop
[g] that became a fricative, softened to a [y], and eventually vanished. We assume
that the earliest periods of Japanese did not permit adjacent vowels within a word.
The notation ···[-Ci] for the ancestor of a vowel-stem infinitive implies that the
entire ending is ellipted, but at least a few of the monosyllabic stems retained a
trace in the form of vowel length, as attested by their accentuations. What has
sometimes been called "first-syllable reduplication with nigori" is here treated as

the truncation of a structure V₁-infinitive V₁ with the infinitive followed by a
marker -n- or -n[i]-, rather than as the "stuttering" that is implied by the other
interpretation.

Our underlying *···Ca-, as in *noma- 'drink', is the subjunctive form to which
various auxiliaries are attached, such as -mu (presumptive), -nu (negative), etc.
(Cf. Mabuchi 1972.) The infinitive nom-i and finite nom-u result from obligatorily
dropping the final underlying vowel before an ending and then automatically
suppressing the initial consonant, if any, that begins the ending: *nom[a-C]i;
*nom[a]-u or perhaps *nom[a-C]u. The imperative ending (OJ -ye) and the provisional-
concessive (OJ -ey / -ure[y]) are reduced forms of more complex structures: the
infinitive attaches a particle to form the imperative (-Ci a), and the provisional-
concessive consists of the attributive (-uru, reduced to -[ur]u after a consonant)
in its primordial root form (-ura- / -[ur]a-) followed by the bound noun i 'fact,
thing, one, ... '. (This means that the expressions aruˈi-wa and aˈre-ba are taken
as manifestations — created at different times, to be sure — of the very same
constituents.) For the imperative, however, Hattori 1981 reconstructs proto-Japanese
/-e/ on the basis of the correspondence of Amami (e.g. Shodon) nonpalatal -Ci with
Old Japanese -Cye.

6.3. Complex verb stems.

A complex verb stem results from prefixing to a verb some other element, such
as a noun. There are several types, as shown below.

Prefix + Verb

    i- noru 'pray'; ...
    do- naru 'yell, roar'; ...
    sa- neru 'sleep', sa- suru 'rub; pat', sa- wataru 'go across'; ...
    ...

These prefixes were probably independent adverbs at an earlier period. The separate
accentuation of i(-) as 1.1 (high atonic) can be detected in a few of the markings
of the Maeda text of Nihon-Shoki, as listed by Ishizuka: ī kyirazu (70b [11:53-M])
'without cutting', ī tworamu to (70b [11:50-M]) 'to take'. Stems showing a reduced
form of i- include iku/yuku, yokosu, yuturu, and perhaps yusugu.

Adjective, Adjectival Noun, or Adverb + Verb

    nageku < *naga - iku 'sigh; lament'
    wakagaeru < *waka n[i] kaer- (< ...) 'be rejuvenated'
    tikazuku < *tika -n- tuk- 'draw near, approach'
    ...

Mimetic + Verb

    ina - naku 'neigh'
    kaka - naku 'caw, crow, croak'
    sobo - huru 'drizzle'
    u - naru 'groan'
    u - taku 'roar'
    ...

Noun + Verb

These can be treated as lexical reductions of sentences; the noun itself functions
as subject or object, or plays some other role in valence with the verb: tuti - kau
'cultivate land', ... Some of the verbs appear in "nigoried" form with a modern
voiced initial that reflects the earlier prenasalization; except for analogical
cases this probably represents an earlier marker -n-, in some compounds clearly a
reduction of ni or no, but sometimes of obscure origin:

saki - datu 'go ahead' < *saki n[i] tat··· 'ahead stand'
hara - datu 'get angry' < *para n[o] tat··· 'belly stand'
kokoro - zasu 'aspire to' < *kokoro -n- sas··· 'heart point'

The formation is not always transparent, for the noun may appear in altered form
(especially truncated) and the verb may turn up in a variant shape.

Many examples of Noun + Verb are carried by dictionaries as single lexical
entries, as if "compound verbs", but they are given accentuations in Myōgi-shō
that indicate two words (= phrases):

sú kúfu (not *sukúfu), mé afásu (*meafásu); me físigu (*mefísigu), me fúsagu
(*mefúsagu); te narásu (*tenarásu), te árafu (*teárafu); tī haku (*tīhaku);

yubi sasú (*yubisasú), kami ótu (*kamiótu), asi kíru (*asikíru), asi tatú
(*asitatú), ana fóru (*anafóru), tuti fúru (*tutifúru), fara fukúru (*farafukúru);
kaze fúku (*kazefúku), īsi nagu (*īsinagu), kāfa amú (*kāfaamú), sake sitamu
(*sakesitamu); kokorō okósu (*kokorookósu).

The *onbin* phenomena (Ch. 3) may be independent, for the "word juncture" here
merely demarcates an accent phrase: "tumuzaku" ?= tūn zaku < tumi saku.

But there are also examples of Noun + Verb treated as a single word in Myōgi-shō:

kufatatu (*kufa tatú), fanafīru (*fana fīru); farabáfu (*fara fafú),
? sakiTatu (*sakī tatú); obisīmu (*obī sīmu).

And for some examples you cannot tell, at least in the citation form, because the
results would come out the same way in either case:

te( )utú, yu( )amú, ki( )kirú, fedo( )tuku; kutī( )susugu, koromo( )kīsu.

Perhaps ki( )tuku, yu( )bīku, ... , and fi mómu '(?) throw the shuttle' (Kn Butsu-ka
moto 61:6) belong here.

Attested both ways: namidatu = nami tatú, kusagīru = kusa kirú (cf. Komatsu
1977a:380-2); mé maku = memaku. A problem case: ? ti( )siboru 'stanch blood' (Kn)
should be tī sibóru if two words, tisibóru if one word. And in some cases the
lexicalization is incomplete: kokoro-mīru (*kokorō miru, *kokoromīru).

Verb Infinitive + Verb (V-i V)

Modern compound verbs were usually pronounced as two words in the Heian period and earlier; the infinitive carried a separate accent even when the function of the second verb was reduced to that of an auxiliary: hikiiru < f̄iki [w]īru 'lead', uketamawaru < uke tamafaru 'humbly receive/listen/hear'. The minor juncture to which we attribute the separate accentuation apparently persisted for some time after the tightening of the morphological ties between the two verbs by nigori (earlier: insertion of the -n- marker) or the reductions and assimilations called *onbin* (Ch.3): osaeru < ōs[i] afu 'restrain', nottoru < no[ri] torū 'conform'.

A list of Myōgi-shō examples of V-i V arranged by shape types:

A+A		yufi tunagu	tatematuri īru
		tobi noforu *(unmarked)*	
A+B	sofi fusu	īfi wosamu	
	osi utu	sube atumu	
	f̄iki saku	ōsi fakaru	
	yufi tuku	ōsi firaku	
	nuki [i]du	(= *firaku)	
B+B	sasi kufu	kufi nikumu	sasi sirizoku	tutome hagemasu
	nomi faku	tati sizumu	uke tamafaru	
	nage utu	sasi fasamu		
	kami famu	sasi firasu		
	seme toru	sasi kakusu		
B+A	nage sutu	kufi tukusu	tati motoforu	itami wononoku
	sasi ōku	nomi tukusu		
	ide masu	fusi afugu		
	tome sīri	nosi tatamu		
		tori fisigu		
		sasi nozoku		
		kaki konasu		

Examples of iterated V₁-i V₁: kare karu 'freeze to death', sasi sasu, saki saku; kubiri kubir-u, tasuke tasuku, ...

The verb in some of these complex verb structures may be a "bound verb" that does not occur except attached to something: (-)meku 'gives the appearance of' is usually attached to a noun or a mimetic; and it likely goes back to a derivative made up of mi- 'look' and the formant -ka-, discussed below.

6.4. Verb roots and formants.

Most verbs in our list may appear to be "simplex" stems at first glance, but a closer inspection reveals that many of these stems consist of a ROOT, the ultimate simplex, and one or more derivational FORMANTS. Some of the roots occur as nouns, adverbs, adjectival nouns, adjectives, or mimetics; others are bound, and occur only with the formants attached. Often a particular formation is obscured by various reductions and assimilations. The majority of the older Japanese stems ended in a consonant, according to the statistics cited above, but our model calls for each of these stems to have an underlying final vowel, usually but not always -a. This -a can be regarded as the "neutral vowel" of earlier Japanese; it appears at the end of a consonant stem whenever a formant (or another root) is attached, unless the final underlying phoneme is one of the other vowels: i, u, o, (C)wo. The most common of the formants is -Ci-, which we assume originally had an initial consonant, probably the voiced velar stop [g] or a fricative version thereof; by historic times the weakened consonant dropped, leaving two vowels nakedly juxtaposed, and they coalesced into a diphthong, which then finally monophthongized. That is why in the modern language certain pairs of stems seem somewhat obscure in their surface relationship:

>   tomaru ‹ tomara- ‹ toma-ra- 'stop'
>   tomeru ‹ tomey- ‹ toma-Ci- 'stop it'
>
>   tukiru ‹ tukiy- ‹ tuku-Ci- 'get exhausted'
>   tukusu ‹ tukusa- ‹ tuku-sa- 'exhaust'
>
>   okiru ‹ okiy- ‹ oko-Ci- 'arise'
>   okosu ‹ okosa- ‹ oko-sa- 'rouse'

Most examples of an underlying vowel o or u echo the preceding vowel, as can be seen in the examples above, so that we speculate that the vowel is perhaps the result of assimilation from an earlier final /a/, and in some cases we can find etymological evidence for that vowel. Perhaps we would do well to assume that all cases of root-final vowel were originally /a/, which functioned as a kind of epenthetic vowel that we might simply ignore in our etymological comparisons. But caution is in order, for there is also the possibility that the "wastepaper basket" category of final -a may be the result of a merger into the neutral vowel of some distinctions that are now lost to us but might be recovered through comparative evidence. In any event, for the purposes of this study we will infer the final underlying vowel on the basis of the internal evidence discovered for each root.

The formants, or certain strings of them, may once have been independent roots, something like our "bound verbs". They appear singly and in strings of from one to four formants, though there are relatively few examples of the longer strings. In §7 you will find a list of the formants arranged according to the modern strings that result, with most of those examples from the verb list in §6 that incorporate each formant string. That is followed in §8 by a study of the occurrence of formants in strings and a list of the approximate populations of the most common formant strings in our list of verbs. Although it is often quite obscure just what a given formant

contributes to the meaning of a particular stem, the three most common formants
clearly have to do with transitivity: -sa- creates "exoactive" stems (transitive or
causative), -ra- "endoactive" stems (intransitive or passive), and -Ci- reverses the
polarity of transitivity inherent in the root. For an attempt to find meanings for
the other formants, see Unger. The formant -sa- was freely used in older Japanese as
an auxiliary of subject-exaltation ('deign to do') but our study will not list all
the examples of V-sa- 'deign to V', with a few exceptions (such as nasu 'deign to
sleep'), nor is this -sa- cited or counted in the discussion of formants.

6.5. Citations.

In Myōgi-shō and most other dictionaries the verbs are normally cited in the
predicative form, so that it is unclear whether the reference is to a consonant stem
or a vowel stem when both exist: "woru" (with the attributive woru) could be 'breaks
it' (later oru) or, with the attributive woruru (later oreru), 'it breaks' (later
oreru). In general we will assume that the Myōgi-shō citation refers to both such
stems, when they are known to exist, but when one or the other is less likely we
will put it in parentheses. It should be borne in mind that a few of the accentual
notations in the dictionaries may be artificial; for example, the verb neyasu
(Myōgi-shō B´) does not survive in the modern dialects, yet Umegaki (in NKD) gives
a modern Kyōto version 0 (high atonic), the appropriate development from "Edo HLL".
Certain of the data on accent class are perhaps misprints or mistakes, e.g. Kyōto A
(Hirayama) for sike 'bad weather', the derived noun of sikeru. Throughout, the
notation "A" refers to the category of high atonic or the appropriate modern reflex,
both for verb stem and for the noun derived from the infinitive (when one exists);
Similarly, "B" refers to the category of low atonic or to the appropriate modern
reflex, but since both the Tōkyō and the Kyōto dialects have lost the category,
the regular patterns for the dissyllabic nouns is Tōkyō oxytonic (oo⁻¹) and Kyōto
prototonic (ō⁻¹o), so that Kyōto .ōbī (.obi-ga) 'girdle' is irregular. On the
many accentual irregularities among the infinitive-derived nouns, see Chapter 4.
    Verb stems (and adjective stems) are essentially indigenous, for there are very
few that were taken from older Chinese or from modern foreign languages. Words with
a verbal meaning are typically borrowed as nouns which can be predicated as if verbs
by attaching the auxiliary suru 'do'. These words can be called verbal nouns (or
nominal verbs). Verbal nouns taken from a single Chinese morpheme, rather than a
binom (two-morpheme compound), are mostly bound and cannot be separated from suru;
the more common of these usually reduce suru to -su and conjugate just like the
indigenous verb stems that end in ···s-. Free verbal nouns, including Chinese-origin
binoms, can be separated from the verbalizer, can be used independently of it as
predicate adjuncts (such as subject or object), and can be predicated by a copular
expression; they also permit suru to be replaced by nasa¹ru 'deign to do' and itasu
'(humbly) do'. Following is a list of verb stems, some obsolete, that have been
directly created from Chinese loan elements through the years.

Vowel stems

dooke- < *dau-ke[y] 'jest' (= dooke suru)
gebi- < *ge[y] -(n-)pi 'be vulgar, low(class)'
taizi- < tai-di 'exterminate'

Consonant stems

soozok- < sauzok- < *saṳ-zok(u)/syok(u) 'wear formal attire'
kozik- 'beg' < kot(u)-zik(i) 'beggar (monk)'
ryoor- < reur- 'cook', from ryoori < reu-ri taken as infinitive

Consonant stems with formant

-m[a]-

rikim- < rik(i) 'endeavor'
mokurom- < mok(u)-ro[n] 'plan'

-r[a]-

daber-u < da-be[n] 'chatter'
gyuuzir-u < giu-zi ('ox ear') 'lead, boss'
(The stem yazir- 'jeer, heckle' does not belong here.)

Modern foreignisms have supplied a few verb stems by attaching the formant -r[a]-:

azir- 'agitate'
demor- 'demonstrate' < de'mo = demo[nsutore'esyon]
sabor- 'cut class' < French sabotage
posyar- 'collapse', said to be a metathesis < sya'ppo 'felt hat' < French chapeau

Several such stems may be preserving an original -r- < -l-:

dabur- 'double'
negur- 'neglect, disregard [an insignificant fraction]'
dopper- 'fail' (obsolete student slang) < German doppeln
gebar- 'engage in strong-arm tactics' < geba'ruto < German Gewalt
haikar- 'put on airs' < haikara 'high collar = classy'

Modern examples tend to be slangy and some are too ephemeral to make it into the dictionaries: sobar- 'eat buckwheat noodles', takur- 'take a taxi' (as opposed to tekur- 'foot it' from a mimetic teku-teku), ··· .

6.6. List of Verb Stems.

B   abaku < *anpaka- (< ?). 'disclose; open up'. B - B-A-B x-x-x. Ib B.

B   "abanewasu" (NKD) = awanewasu (= amanewasu 'extend widely/pervasively').

A   abareru < abare[y]- < *anpara-Ci- 'rampage, rage'. (x) - A-A-A x-B-x.
Ib A. Nk abaarin A; Sr qamar- B. Cf. amara(-ya), ara, ara*adj A*.

?B   abiru < amiy-/ama- (NS 112a) < *anpu-(Ci-) ?< *anpa- *(the second vowel
assimilated to the labial)*. 'bathe oneself in'. B - A-B-A A-A-x. NS (112a) B.
Edo B. Narada A. Ib B. Nk qamiirun A; Sr amir- A. The accent is incongruent
with abiseru. Cf. amusu.

A   abiseru (Edo) = a^b/**m**use[y]- = a^b/**m**usu. 'douse with'. x - A[NKD]/B[H]-A-A
x-x-x. Hattō, Hamada B. The accent is incongruent with [amiru] > abiru.

-        aburasu, abureru: *see* ahureru.

B´   aburu < *anpura- ?< *a[tu]*adj B* n[i] pura-*?B*. 'roast'. B´ - B-A-B x-B-x.
Edo B. K: "Hn B´?, B?; Km LLH, Edo HLL". Ib B. Nk anbin B, Sr qanzun B (neg.
andan) < *abur-. Cf. abura*s,sa*.

A   abusu < *anpu(-)sa-. 'let remain, leave; discard'. A - A-x-x x-x-x.
Mg u̅ti̅ a̅bu̅su̅. Cf. abureru = ahureru, amasu.

?B   abusu < amusu < *anpu-sa- (?< *anpa-sa- with vowel assimilation to /m/).
'douse with'. x - x-x-x x-x-x. Cf. abiru.

-        adamu: *see* atamu.

?A/B   aegu < awe^k/**g**u (Mr) < afeku (Hn) < afeyku (Nr) < *apa*(?)B* - ika-*B*. 'gasp,
pant'. A - B-A-B x-(x)-x. Km x. Mr (Bm) B. Shinsen-Jikyō afaku. Cf. awaremu;
is *apa mimetic? 〚 aegi A - B-A-x x-(B)-x. Sr qeezi B 'calling' ?< aegi.

?A   aeru < aye[y]- < *ada-Ci-. 'fall, spill, drip' (vi.): appears in modern
dialects of Kyūshū as ayuru/a[y]e; cf. ayasu. A - x-x-x x-x-x. According to
Miyara (1930:12b) the Kobama (Yaeyama) dialect verb abirun '(fruit) falls,
(tooth) falls out, (milk or pus) drips/oozes out' is cognate; but the -b-
is hard to explain. I suspect the Kobama verb is a semantic extension of the
reflex of ahureru 'overflow'.

B   aeru < aye[y]- < *ada-Ci-. 'be similar' (= ayakaru). B - B-B-x x-x-x.
NS (T+ kun) aye LH.

B   [aeru] < afey- < *apa-Ci-. 'endure; dare, boldly do'. (B) - B-B-x x-x-x.
〚 ae(-)te 'boldly'. LL|H 1-1:3-A̲ x-x-x. Km (W) B. Mr (Bm) B. Edo B.

B   aeru < afey- < *apa-Ci-. 'dress (vegetables etc. with condiments etc.)'.
(B) - B-B-B x-B-x. NS (Okada) B. Ib B. Nk qeerun B; Sr qeer- B.

A   aeru < afey- < *apa*adj B* -Ci-. 'lose flavor, go flat, grow stale' (treated
by NKD within the entry above). x - x-x-x A-A-x. Sd qahweer- A; Sr qahweer- A.
The register is incongruent with the etymology.

B   agaku < *a[si]*s,s* -n- kaka-*B*. 'paw (the air); struggle, strive; show
spirit, work energetically; advance'. B - B-A-A̲ x-B-x. Nk qagaaCun B; Sr qagak-
B 'work (hard); advance'. 〚 agaki x - 1/3-A-A x-x-x.

?B   agameru < agamey- < *anka-ma-Ci-. 'respect, revere, worship'. B - B-A-A̲
x-B-x. Narada B. NS (Okada) B. Km (S) B. Edo B. Ib B. Nk qagaameerun A̲ =
qagaamin B; Sr qagamir- B. Cf. agaru, despite register incongruity.

?B   aganau < aganafu ?< *akanafu ?< *aka-na-pa- (cf. agau, akinau). 'expiate,
atone/pay for; buy'. x - B-A-A x-(B)-x. Nk x; Sr qaganeer- B (?< aganafey-)
'economize'. 〚 aganai x - 3/0-A-A x-B-x.

A   agaru < *anka-ra-. 'rise'. A - A-A-A x-A-x. NS (Okada) A. Nk qagaarun A;
qagar- A. 〚 agari x - 0-0-A x-A-x. NS (T+ kun) agari ﬁHL = HHL. Km (S) A.
Edo A. Ib A. Nk, Sr agai A.

B agau < agafu (Hn) < akafu < *akapa- (= *aka-pa-, cf. akyi₇₂.₉ < *ak[a-C]i 'commerce'; ?< *aki₇₂.₉ kapa-ₐ). 'expiate, atone/pay for; buy'. B - B-A-x x-x-x.

A ageru < agey- < *anka-Ci-. 'raise'. A - A-A-A x-A-x. NS (98a [11:92-K]) A. Km (W) A. Mr (Bm) A (Sakurai 1977:848a). Edo A. Ib A. Nk qagiirun, Sr qagir- A.

A ageturau < ageturafu (?< *agey turafu < *anka-Ci[-Ci]ₐ tura-pa-₇). 'discuss, argue (the merits of), criticize'. A - B-A-A x-x-x.

A agitou < agyitofu (? agi top- < *anki₂.₂ᵦ topa-ₐ; ?< agito₃.₁ -pa- < *anki-to -pa-). 'work the jaws, (fish) breathe'. A - B-A-x x-x-x.

A [ahudokoᵇ/ₘu] < afudokomu < *apuntokonpa- (< ?). 'leapfrog, straddle-jump' (= afudofumu, afudukumu). A - x-x-x x-x-x.

?A/B [ahurasu] < *aburasu < *anpu-ra-sa-. 'let it overflow'. x - x-x-x x-x-x. Nk qanbasun A < *anba[ra]su; Sr qandas- < *anburas-.

?A/B ahureru < abure- (Mg) = abure[y]- < *anpu(-)ra-Ci-. 'overflow'. A - B-A-A x-A-x. Mr (Bm) B. Narada B; Matsue, Izumo A. Ib B. Nk qanbin (qanbir-) A, Sr qandir- A < *a(n)bur-. Cf. abusu, abiru, amaru; hahuru.

?A aidamu < afyidamu < *apinta₃.₂ᵦ -ma-. 'take a break, rest'. x - x-x-x x-x-x. Mg xxHL (?= HHHL = A); Ir "afidamu" (da marked high and low) is odd.

B akareru < [w]akare[y]- (< ...). 'get divided (up); get separated/weaned'. x - B-x-x x-?B-x. NS (109a [11:315-K]) B. Nk x; Sr qakarir- ?B (cf. akatu). (Ōno takes this as < *ak[u] are- 'place be separated'.)

A akaru < *akaₐdⱼ ₐ -ra-. 'get bright/red'. x - x-x-x x-x-x. [] akari x - A-A-A x-x-x. NS (107b [11:277-K] ?LHH; NS (T+ 35) akareru LLHL.

A akasu < *akaₐ-sa- ('red, bright' ₐdⱼ ₐ or 'open' ᵥ₁.). 'spend (night); reveal, prove, explain, clarify, enlighten'. x - A/B-A-A x-A-x. Km (S) A. Mr (Bm) A. Edo A. Narada A. Ib A. Nk haKaasun A; Sr qakas- A. [] akasi 'evidence, proof'. x - A-A-A x-x-x.

?A/B akasu < *aka-sa-. 'weary, satiate' (vt.). x - B-A-A̲ x-x-x (Kg mistake? — cf. akiru).

B [akasu] < akatu < [w]akatu < *baka-ta-: see akatu.

B akatu < [w]akatu < *baka-ta-. 'divide it (up); separate, wean'. B - x-A-x x-(x)-x. NS (129a) B. Km x. Sr qakas- B. Cf. akareru.

A akeru < akey- < *aka-Ci-. 'open it; get bright'. (A) - A-A-A (A)-A-A. NS (83b [17:120-M]) A; NS (T+ 96) akeynikyeri LLHH. Km (W) A. Edo A. Ib A. Sd hwee(r)yum A, weheeyum A; Nk haKiirun A; Sr qakir- A.

?B akinau < akyinafu < *aki₇₂.₉ -na-pa-(< *ak[a-C]i ···). 'deal in, sell'. B - B-A-A̲ x-(B)-x. [] akinai B - 2/3-2-A x-B-x. Nk haCinee B; Sr qacinee B.

B akirameru < akyiramey- < *aki(-)ra -ma-Ci-. 'make it bright/clear; clear one's heart or mind; resign oneself to'. B - B-A-B x-x-x. Matsue, Izumo A. Ib A̲. [] akirame x - 3/4/0-A-B x-x-x. (Unger: *aka-ra with a > i analogical.)

A akireru < akire[y]- (< ?). 'be amazed/shocked'. x - A-A-A x-x-x. Ib A.

B akiru < aku < *aka- 'get satiated/weary'. (B) - B-B-B x-B-x. Edo B. Hattō A̲/B. Nk qaCi-... B; Sr qac(i)-... B. [] aki x - 2-A[H]/2-B x-x-x.

B (<B+A) aki-tariru < aki-ᵗ/dₐru < *akyi - taru < *ak[a-C]iᵦ tar[a-C]i-ₐ. 'be content' [usually negative]. B (LL-xx) - B-B-B x-x-x.

A akogareru < akugare[y]- (< ?). 'yearn (for); admire'. x - A/B[H]-A-A x-x-x. Hattō B. Km (W) A. Ib A. [] akogare x - A-A-A x-x-x. (Ōno takes this as *aku -n- kara-Ci- 'be separated from the place'.)

A aku < *aka-. 'open' (vi.). x - A-A-A x-A-x. Km x. Edo A. Ib A. Nk haCun A; Sr qak- A. [] aki x - A-A-A x-x-x. (Unger connects this with saku < *zaka-.)

B aku < *aka-. 'get satiated/weary' (→ akiru). B - B-B-B x-B-x. Km (W) ak- B. Ib B. *See* akiru.

A   amaeru < amaye[y]- < *ama*adj A* -da-Ci-. 'seek favor'. x - A/B-A-A x-x-x.
Ib A. Nk qameerun A. 〇 amae x - A[NKD]-x-x x-x-x. Cf. amayakasu.

?A   amanau < amanafu < *ama*?adj A* -na-pa-. 'cooperate, be nice/friendly to'.
A - B-x-x x-x-x. NS (103a [11:162-K] A.

B   amanewasu < amanefasu < *amane*adj B* -pa-sa- (< ...). 'extend widely or
pervasively'. B - x-x-x x-x-x. Cf. awanewasu.

B   amaru < *ama-ra-. 'be excessive, too much; remain (left over)'. B - B-A-B
x-B-B. NS (94a: <u>momo amarī</u> 'over 100', Okada) B. Km (S) B. Edo B. Ib B.
Nk qamaarun B; Sr qamar- B. 〇 amari B - B-1:3-B x-B-x; o-amari x - 2-1:4-B
x-x-x. NS (T+ 41) LLL. Izumo <u>A</u>/B (verb B); Goka-mura 1 (verb B). See Ch. 5.
Cf. amasu, ahureru.

B   amasu < *ama-sa-. 'let remain'. B - B-A-B x-B-x. Ib B. Nk qamaasun B;
Sr amas- B. Cf. amaru; abusu.

A   amayakasu < *ama*adj A* -da-ka-sa-. 'indulge, pamper'. x - A/B-A-A x-x-x.
Hattō, Hamada, Matsue, Izumo A. Ib A. Nk qameerasun A. 〇 amayakasi x - A-x-x
x-x-x. Cf. amaeru.

-          [amiru] < amiy-: *see* abiru.

A   [amiseru]: *see* abiseru.

-          [amu] 'bathe oneself in' (NS): *see* abiru.

B   amu < *ama-. 'knit'. B - B-B-B x-x-B. Ib B. Nase B; Nk qamin (qam-) B;
Sr x (→ kum- B); Yn (nmun B < kum- =) amun B (H 1967:72a). 〇 ami 'net'. B -
B-2-B x-B-B. Nase qami B; Nk qamii B; Sr qami B; Yn an B.

?B   amusu < *anpu-sa- (?< *anpa-sa- *with assimilation of the second vowel to
the labial consonant*). 'douse with'. x - x-x-x x-x-x. Cf. abusu, abiru.

?A/B   anadoru < anaduru ?< *ana - n[i]*adv/intj* t*ª/ₒ*ra-?. 'despise'. A - B-A-B
x-x-x. NS (134a) A. 〇 anadori x - 3/4/0-A-B x-x-x.

B   anaguru < *ana*g.s* -n- kura-*B*. 'seek (as groping in a hole for)'. B - x-x-x
x-x-x.

?B   ananau < ananafu ?< *a[si*g.s*] ninafu*B* (< ...). 'help, assist'. (x) - x-x-x
x-x-x. 〇 ananai 'helping; a foothold'. LLHx (Ch 'hemp prop', see NKD) - x-x-x.

?A   aogu < afugu < *apunka- (< ?). 'look up at/to; solicit; rise up'. A -
B-A-B x-x-x. Km (S) A; ?(W) B. Edo (A/)B. Ib B.

B   aogu < afugu < *apunka- < *apu-n[a]-ka- (cf. aoru). 'fan'. B - B-A-B
x-B-x. Km (S) B. Edo B. Ib B. Nk qoozun B; Sr qoog- B. 〇 oogi < aogi (< ...)
B - B-2-B B-B-x. Nk, Sr qoozi B.

?A/B   aoru < afuru < *apu-ra-. 'flap, fan; incite'. x - B-A-A x-x-x. Ib B.
〇 aori x - B-A-A x-x-x.

?A   arabiru < arabi[y]- < arabiy-/arabyi- < ara-biy- < *ara*adj A* -npª/ₒCi-
(?< -n[a]-pa-Ci-). 'act wild, rampage, rage'. x - x-x-x x-x-x. Originally
bigrade conjugation arabu(ru), but in Koji-ki sometimes treated as monograde
arabiyru/arabyiru even though not a monosyllabic stem (similar: isatiru);
cf. Ōno Tōru 1978:291.

?B   aragau < aragafu < *ara-n[a]-ka-pa- (cf. arasou). 'dispute, argue; wager'.
B - B-A-x x-x-x.

?B   arakeru < arakey- < *ara-ka-Ci-. (vi.) 'get scattered; [later] get rough,
boisterous'; (vt.) 'open (a road); leave a space/gap'. B - B-x-x x-x-x.
Note that the adjective ara- 'rough; coarse' is A.

?B   arasou < araswofu < *ara-swopa-. 'dispute, argue over'. B - B-A-A x-B-x.
〇 arasoi x - 3/0-A-A x-B-x. NS (T+ 38) araswofazu LLHHH. Ib B. Cf. isou. Mr (Bm)
<u>arasofi</u>. Hattō, Matsue 3; Hamada 4/0; Izumo <u>A</u> (verb B); Goka-mura 1 (verb A).

A   arasu < *ara*adj A* -sa-. 'devastate, ravage'. A - A-A-A x-A-x. Edo A. Ib A.
Nk qaraasun A; Sr qaras- A. Cf. arasi (Ch. 5).

B   aratamaru ‹ *ara-ta*ɜ.ₐ* -ma-ra- (‹ ...). 'get renewed; get modified, improved; become formal, ceremonious'. (B) - B-A-B x-B-x. Mg aratafaru (?= aratabaru). Ib B. Nk qaraatamaarun B; Sr qaratamar- B.

B   aratameru ‹ *ara-ta*ɜ.ₐ* -ma-Ci- (‹ ...). 'renew, renovate; alter, improve; inspect, examine'. B - B-A-B x-B-x. Ib B. Nk qaraatami(i)run B; Sr qaratamir- B.

A   arau ‹ arafu ‹ *ara-pa- (‹ ?). 'wash'. A - A-A-A A-A-A. Mr (Bm) A. Edo A. Ib A. Nk qaren A; Sr qarayun A (neg. qaraan) ‹ *araw- ‹ *araf-; Yn qarun A. Cf. sarau, sarasu; arata, sara (Ch. 5).

?B   arawareru ‹ arafare[y]- ‹ *ara-pa*ɜ.₇* -ra-Ci-. 'appear'. B - B-A-A x-B-x. Km (S,W) B. Ib B. Nk qaraawarirun B; Sr qarawarir- B. ◻ araware x - 3/4-A-A x-x-x. Cf. aru, areru; arawa (Ch. 5).

?B   arawasu ‹ arafasu ‹ *ara-pa*ɜ.₇* -sa-. 'express, indicate, show; author'. B - B-A-A x-B-x. Km (S) B. Mr (Bm) HHL-L (= B). Ib B. Nk qaraawasun B; Sr qarawas- B. Cf. aru, areru; arawa (Ch. 5).

?A   [arebiru] ‹ arebiy- ‹ *ara-Ci-ₐ -np*ᵐ*/₀Ci- (‹ ...), ?‹ *arabiy- (‹ ... ; *second vowel partially assimilated to third*). 'rage, be wild'. x - x-x-x x-x-x.

A   areru ‹ are[y]- ‹ *ara*ₐdⱼ A* -Ci-. 'rage, run wild; get devastated, go to ruin/waste'. A - A-A-A B̲-A-x. Km (W) A. Edo A. Ib A. Nk qariirun A; Sr qarir- A. ◻ are x - A-A-A x-x-x.

?B   [areru] ‹ are[y]- ‹ *ara-Ci-. 'be separate(d), distant'. x - x-x-x x-x-x. Cf. arakeru, [kareru].

B   [areru] ‹ are[y]- ‹ *ara-Ci-. 'appear (= arawareru); be born'. x - x-x-x x-x-x. Cf. aru; arawa (Ch. 5).

B   aru ‹ *ara- (?= *a-ra-). 'be'. B - B-B-B B-B-C̲. NS (105b [11:239-K]) B. NS (T+) B: aramu LLH (86), aramey LLH (82), arazu LLH (49); ari to̲ LH(|)L (6), LHH (96); ari-kyi to̲ LH-L(|)L (117), arikyeri LHHH (6), arikyemey LHLL (48), arise-ba LHH-H (27); are ya LH(|)L (28 '[how] be there?!'). Km (S,W) B. Mr (Bm) B. Edo B. Ib B. Nk, Sr qan B.

B´ ‹ B+A   aruku/ariku ‹ ari yuku/iku ‹ *ar[a-C]i*ᵦ* i-uka-ₐ. 'walk'. B´ - B-B-B B-B-B. NS (114b) LHH. Edo (ariku) B´. In B´ (= L). Sd akkyum B; Nk qaqCun HHLL; Sr qatcum (qakk-) B; Yn aigun B. Cf. saruku/sariku.

?   [asameru] ‹ asame[y]- ‹ *asa(-)ma(-)Ci- (‹ ?). 'admonish (= isameru)'. x - x-x-x x-x-x.

?A   asamu ‹ *asa*ɜdⱼ A* -ma-. 'be astonished/surprised; think it astonishing; despise'. x - A/B-A-x x-x-x. From Edo also azamu. Cf. asamasi*ɜdⱼ ?*.

B   asaru ‹ *asa-ra-. 'scavenge, forage, hunt, fish for'. B - A/B-A-B x-B-x. NS (Okada) B. Nk hasaarun B; Sr qasar- B. ◻ asari x - A-A-B x-x-x. Cf. isaru; Middle Korean :az- ‹ a'zo- ‹ *a'sV- 'grab'; asa*ɜ.ɜ* 'morning = breakfast'.

?A/B   aseru ‹ ase[y]- ‹ *asa*ɜdⱼ A* -Ci-. 'get shallow; fade, discolor'. x - A/B-B-A x-x-x. Hiroshima A. Ōsaka, Ib B; Ise A. Cf. useru.

B   aser-u ?‹ *ase*ɜ.ɜ* -ra-; ?‹ a[fi*ᵦ* -] ser-*ᵦ* (cf. ser-u, seku; isogu). 'fret over; be hasty, impatient, overzealous'. x - B-A-B x-(A̲)-x. Ib B. Nk hasiigaCun A̲, Sr qasigak- A̲ (?‹ *ase kak- 'sweat', but ase is B).

?A/B   asirau ‹ asirafu ‹ a[e]sirau ‹ afesirafu ‹ *afey*?ɜ.ₐ‹ɜ.ɜ* sirafu ‹ *apa-Ci[-Ci]*ᵦ* sira-*ᵦ*(a)pa-. 'treat, handle, manage'. x - B-A-B x-A̲-x. Nk x. ◻ asirai x - 3/0-A[U]/2-B x-x-x.

A   asobu ‹ aswobu ‹ *a(-)swonpa- (cf. sobaeru). 'play'. A - A-B̲-A A-A-A. NS (112a, 115a) A; NS (87) aswobyi LLH, (76) aswobasi-si LLLL-H. Km x. Mr (Bm) A. Edo A. NE Kyūshū B̲. Ōsaka, Kameyama, Hyōgo, Suzu B̲; Kōchi [H], Ib A — but Kindaichi 1942:169 has Kōchi a̲sobu (misprint?) and Takamatsu aso̲bu. Nk hasiibin A; Sr qaşib- A; Yn qanbun A. ◻ asobi A - A-B-A x-A-x. NE Kyūshū B̲.

A   ataeru ‹ atafey- ‹ *ata-pa-Ci-. 'present, give'. A - A-A-A x-x-x.
Km (S) A. Mr (Bm) ··· <u>atafu</u> (Sakurai 1977:848a). Edo A. Ib A.

A   at/ₐamu ‹ *a(n)taₐ.ₓₐ -ma-. 'regard as enemy, hate'. A - x-x-x x-x-x.

A   atanau ‹ atanafu ‹ *ata-na-pa-. 'harm, injure'. x - x-x-x x-x-x.
NS (134b) A. Also -d- "from 1700s"; JP x.

A   atarasigaru₁ ‹ atarasiₐdⱼ ₐ (‹ ...) -n- k[ey]ₗ.ₗ ara-ₑ. 'regret'.
A - x-x-x x-x-x.

B   atarasigaru₂ ‹ atarasiₐdⱼ ₑ (‹ ...) -n- k[ey]ₗ.ₗ ara-ₑ. 'take pride in
what is new, seek novelty'. x - B-A-x x-x-x. Earliest attestation Meiji?

A   ataru ‹ *ata-ra-. 'hit, touch; face; be equal/equivalent (to); apply
(to)'. A - A-A-A x-A-A. NS (113a, 134a) A. Km (W) A. Mr (Bm) A. Edo A. Ib A.
Nk haTaarun A; Sr qatar- A. ⬚ atari x - A-A-A x-x-x; 'vicinity' HHL [Hoke-kyō
tanji] - 1-2-A x-(A)-x.

B   atatamaru ‹ *ata - tama-ra- ‹ *atuₐdⱼ ₑ ‹ tama-ra-ₐ. 'get warm'. B - B-A-B
x-x-x. Note: Sr nuku-tamar- A supports the etymology. On the assimilation of
the second vowel, cf. the placename ata-mi 'Warm Sea'.

B   atatameru ‹ atatame[y]- ‹ *ata - tama-Ci- ‹ *atuₐdⱼ ₑ tama-Ci- ₐ. 'warm
it, make it warm'. B - B-A-B x-x-x.

A   atau ‹ atafu ‹ *ata-pa-. 'be suitable, possible'. A - A/B-A-x x-x-x.
NS (87) atafanu <u>LHHH</u>. ⬚ atai ‹ atafyi ‹ *ata-p[a-C]i 'value, price'. A - A-A-A
x-x-x.

A   ategau ‹ ategafu ?‹ *ata-Ci-n[a]-ka-pa-, ?‹ ate[y] n[i] kafu ‹ *ata-Ci[-
Ci]ₐ ni kapa-ₐ. 'apply, put; fit; allot, allow, provide'. x - A(B[H,NHK])-A-A
x-x-x. Mr (Bm) A. Ib A. ⬚ ategai x - A-A-A x-x-x.

A   ateru ‹ ate[y]- ‹ *ata-Ci-. 'apply; hit; guess; succeed; assign'. A -
A-A-A x-A-(A). Edo A. Ib A. Nk haTiirun A; Sr qatir- A; Yn ('compare') atirun A
(H 1967:432a). ⬚ ate A - A-A-A A-A-<u>B</u> A-A-x. NS (128a) A. Nk haTii A; Sr qati A.

?B   [atoeru] ‹ atofey- ‹ *at(w)o-pa-Ci-. 'invite; propose marriage;
(= aturaeru) order'. x - B-x-x x-x-x. NS (Okada) B.

A   [atueru] ‹ atuye[y]- ‹ *a(n)tuₐdⱼ ₐ ˈillˈ -da-Ci-. '(illness) get worse'
(= atusireru). x - x-x-x x-x-x.

A   atukau ‹ atukafu ?‹ *atuₐdⱼ ₐ ˈcordialˈ -ka-pa-; ?‹ a-ₚᵣₑ (‹ ?) tuka-pa-ₐ.
'treat; entertain; manage; handle, use'. x - A/B-A-A A-A-x. ⬚ atukai x - A-2-A
x-x-x.

?A   atukau ‹ atukafu ‹ *atuₐdⱼ ₑ ˈhotˈ -ka-pa-. 'suffer heat; flush (in
consternation)'. A - x-x-x x-x-x. NS (114a) A. Ib A. Nk haCiKaan/haCiKeen A;
Sr qaçikayun A (neg. qaçikaran/qaçikaan) ‹ *atukar-/*atukaw- ‹ *atukaf-.
But the register of the adjective atu- is B.

B   atumaru ‹ *a(-ₚᵣₑ?) tumaₑ-ra-. 'gather (come together), collect, crowd,
assemble'. B - B-A-B x-B-x. NS (113b) B. Km (S) B. Mr (Bm) A. Hattō <u>A</u>. Ib B.
Nk haCiman B; Sr qaçimar- B [new]. ⬚ atumari x - 3/4-A-B x-x-x. Goka-mura 1
(‹ A). Nk haCimai B. The etymology *atuₐdⱼ ₐ ˈthickˈ -ma-ra- is incongruent
with the register, but it would help explain dialect variants with -b- for -m-
as *atu-n[a]-pa-ra- (› atubaru) and *atu-n[a]-pa-Ci- (› atuberu).

B   atumeru ‹ *a(-ₚᵣₑ?) tuma-Ci-ₑ (cf. tudou). 'gather/collect them; focus,
concentrate'. B - B-A-B B-B-B. Edo B. Hattō <u>A</u>. Ib B. Sd qatmiyum B; Nk haCimin
(haCimir-) B; Sr qaçimir- B [new]. *See* atumaru.

B   aturaeru ‹ atᵃ/ₒrafey- ‹ *at(w)o-ra-pa-Ci-. '(custom-)order'. B - B-A-B
x-B-x. ⬚ aturae x - 3/4[NKD]-A[U]/4[H]-B x-B-x. Cf. [atoeru].

A   [atusireru] ‹ atusire[y]- ‹ *atuₐdⱼ ₐ sira-Ci-ₐ. '(illness) get worse'.
x - x-x-x x-x-x. NS (133a) A.

B   au < afu < *apa-. 'meet; fit, agree'. B - B-B-B x-B-x. NS (Okada) B.
NS (T+) B: afamu ka mo LLL(|)L(|)H (52), afamu to zo LLH(|)H(|)L (89); afa-na
LL-L; afyi LH (93), LF = LH (37, 40); afu ya LH(|)L (82), LHH 64); afey ya mo
LH(|)L(|)L. Km (S,W) B. Edo B. Ib B. Nk aarun B = qoorun B, Sr qaar- B
restructured from *aw- < *af-.

B   awanewasu ("afanefasu" Kn Mg) = amanewasu. 'extend widely or pervasively'.
B - x-x-x x-x-x. NKD has "abanewasu" but there is no evidence for -b- rather
than -w-.

?A/B   awaremu < afare^b/_u < *apare[y]*intj* (< apa-ra-Ci[-Ci]*B inf*) -n[a]-pa- (or
-ma-). 'pity'. A - B-A-B x-x-x. Mr (Bm) A.

B   awaseru < afase[y]- < *apa-sa-Ci-. 'bring together, unite; mix'. B - B-A-B
x-B-x. Edo B'. Ib B. Nk qaasun B; Sr qaas- B. [] awase x - B-A-B x-(B)-x. NS
(118a) B. Edo HHL.

A   awatasu < "afatasu" (Ck) ?= afa^t/_dasu ?< *apa*adj A* -(n)ta-sa-.
? 'treat lightly, make light of'. A - x-x-x x-x-x.

A   awateru < "afa^t/_de[y]-" (Mg): (1) 'be diluted/weak' < *apa*adj A*
-(n)ta(-)Ci-; (2) 'get confused, flustered, nervous; rush' (?< *aba*z.s*
-nta(-)Ci- *but register is incongruent*). A - A-A-A x-A-x. Edo A. Ib A. Nk
qawaatin A; Sr awatir- A. It is unclear whether these are two stems or one.
[] awate x - A-x-x x-x-x.

A   ayabumu ?< *ada*z.s* -npu(-)ma-; ?< *ada*z.s* -n[i] puma-*A*; ?< ayafumu <
*ada-pu*adj A* -ma-. 'feel anxiety over; suspect'. A - B-A-A x-x-x. Ib A.
[] ayabumi x - 3/4-A-A x-x-. The adjective ayau- < ayafu- < *ada-pu- is A, but
both aya*z.s* and the adjective aya-si- < *ada-si- are B.

?A/B   ayakaru < *ada - kara- ('similar borrow' or 'design borrow'?). 'be favored
with similar good luck'. B - B-A-A x-A-x. Ib A. Nk qayaakan B; Sr qayakaar- A.

B   ayamaru < *ada*?adj-si B* -ma-ra-. 'err, mistake; apologize'. B - B-A-B
x-B-x. Ib B. Nk x; Sr qayamar- B. [] ayamari (B) - 3/4-A-B x-B-x.
Nk qayaama(r)ii B; Sr qayamai B. Is Mg ayamari the infinitive?

B   ayamatu < *ada*?adj-si B* -ma-ta-. 'err, mistake'. B - B-A-B x-x-x.
[] ayamati (B) - 3/4-A-B x-B-x. NS (128a [14:334L-K] B. Nk qayaamaCi B; Sr
qayamaci B. Is Mg ayamati the infinitive?

B   ayasigaru < *ayasi*adj B* (< *ada-si) -g[e] (< *-n- key*1.1*) ar[a]-*B*. 'think
it strange; suspect, distrust'. x - B-A-x x-x-x.

?A/B   ayasimu < ayasi^b/_u < *ada-si*adj B* -n[a]-pa-. 'doubt, suspect; wonder,
marvel'. B - B-A-A x-x-x. Ib A. Nk qayaasimin A. [] ayasimi x - 4/0-A-x x-x-x.
Mr (Bm) A. Attested in 1186 as ayasime[y]- (KggD 972a).

?A   ayasu < *ada-sa-. 'drop, spill, shed'. x - x-x-x x-x-x. Cf. aeru.

?B   ayasu < aya (< *ada*z.s*) [na]su (< *na-sa-*B*) ('handle skillfully' B-x-x).
'fondle, humor, pacify'. x B-A-A x-x-x. Ib B. Examples date from Edo.

?A/B   ayaturu ?< *aya-t(w)oru < *ada*z.s* t(w)ora-*B*. 'manipulate, work'. B - B-A-A
x-x-x. [] ayaturi x - 3/4/0[NHK]-A-x x-x-x.

?B   ayugu, ayuku < *adu(n)ka- (< ?;cf. asi*z.s*); ? same as next verb; ? < a[ri]
yuku < *ar[a-C]i i-uka- (cf. aruku). 'walk' (= ayumu). x - B-A-x x-x-x.
K: Km B (*where attested?*)

?B   ayugu < ayuku < aywoku < *adwoka- (< ?; cf. asi*z.s*). 'shake, move'.
x - B-x-x x-x-x.

B   ayumu ?< *ayom- < *a[si]*z.s* doma-*B*; ?< a[s]i*z.s* [f]umu*A* (< *puma-). 'step,
walk'. B - B-A-B x-B-x. Edo B. Sakawa B (Clarke 150), as if Mg were *ayumu;
influenced by synonym aruku? Ib B. [] ayumi x - B-A-B x-x-x. 1700 Ōsaka HHL.

?A   azaeru < azafey- < *ansa*z.sb* -pa-Ci- (or [a]pa-Ci-*B*). 'entwine; cross
(one's legs, etc.)'. A - B-x-x x-x-x. Km x. But azawaru is (mostly) Mg B.

A   azaker-u ?< *ansa₂.₂b key₇₁.₁ (< ?) -ra-. 'deride'. A - B-A-A x-x-x.
Sapporo, Akita, Izumo, Goka-mura A; Matsumoto, Numazu, Hattō, Matsue,
Hiroshima, Ōita B; Hamada A/B. Km (S) A. Cf. azawarau.
◍ azakeri x - B-A-A x-x-x.

A   azamuku < *ansa₂.₂b muka-ₐ. 'deceive, dupe'. A - B-A-A x-A-x.
NS (116a [14:99L-K]) A. Km (W) A, (W[17]) B. Nk x; Sr qazamuk- A.

B   azareru < azare[y]- (< ?). '(meat) spoil'. B - A/B-A-x x-x-x.
NS (95a) B. Km (W) B.

A   azawarau < azawarafu < *ansa₂.₂b bara-pa-. 'deride'. A - A[NHK]/B-A-A
x-x-x. Km x. ◍ azawarai x - 3(/A[H,NHK])-x-x x-B-x.

?B   azawaru < azafaru < *ansa₂.₂b -pa-ra (or [a]paᵦ-ra-). 'get entwined, be
crossed'. (A/)B - B-A-x x-x-x. NS (83b [17:117-M]) B. But azaeru is Mg A.

A   aziwau < adifafu < *anti₂.₁ (-)papa-ᵦₐₐ ᵥ. 'taste'. A - A/B-A-A x-x-x.
Hattō, Hamada B. Ib A. ◍ aziwai < adifafi (< ...) A - 3/0-A-A x-A-x. Nk x;
Sr qaziwee A. (Unger: < *adi [i]fafu 'celebrate the taste'.)

B   azukaru < adukaru < *antuka-ra-. 'take/receive in trust; participate/share
in'. B - B-A-B B-B-x. NS (93a) B. Ib B. Nk qaziKan B; Sr qazikar- B. ◍ azukari
x - 3/4-A-B x-x-x. Nk qaziKai B.

B   azukeru < adukey- < *antuka-Ci-. 'give/leave in trust'. x - B-A-B x-B-x.
Mr (Bm) B. Edo B. Ib B. Nk qaziKin B; Sr qazikir- B. ◍ azuke x - B-A-B x-x-x.

B   bakeru < bakey- < *npaka-Ci- (< ?). 'transform oneself (into); disguise
oneself (as)'. B [Ir] - B-B-B x-B[new]-x. Nk x; Sr bakir- [new]. ◍ bake
'means, method, technique'. B - x-x-x x-x-x.

?A/B   barasu < *npara-sa- (< ?). 'reveal, lay bare, expose; dismantle, disjoint;
sell off, sell cheap'. x - B-B-A x-x-x. Ib B. Cf. bara-bara.

?A/B   bareru < *npara-Ci- (< ?). 'have it exposed; get disarrayed or dismantled;
fail'. x - B-B-A x-x-x. Cf. abareru; awareru; wareru (Komatsu 1981:110).

B   bau < bafu = [u]bau (seize by force). B - x-x-x x-B-x. Nk boorun B; boor-
B = qnbayun (qnbar-) A [Lit.].

?B   bokeru < boke[y]- [Ir] / fokey- < *(n)po(-)ka-Ci- ?< *(n)po[po](-)ka-Ci-;
?< bo[ya]ke- (< *poda-ka-Ci-). 'dote; get dim/blurred'. B - B-B-A̱ x-x-x.
Hattō, Hamada, Goka-mura B; Matsue, Izumo A̱. Ib B. Cf. hookeru, horeru.

?A/B   boyakeru ?< *foyake[y]- < *poda-ka-Ci-. 'get dim/blurred, fade'. x - B-A-A
x-x-x. Matsue, Izumo A; Hattō, Hamada B. Ib A.

B   butu = utu 'hit'. x - B-B-B x-x-x.

(B+B)   butukaru < bu[ti]-tukaru < *but[a-C]iᵦ tuka-ra-ᵦ. 'run into/against';
collide (with); face'. x - A-B-B x-x-x. Ib B´ (= L). (Nk huqCaarun B is from
*uti-kakar-.)

(B+B)   butukeru < bu[ti]-tukey- < *but[a-C]iᵦ tuka-Ci-ᵦ. 'hurl, throw; strike,
knock, bump'. x - A-B-B x-x-x. (Nk huqCaKirun B is from *uti-kake-.)

?A/B   daber-u < *dabe[n] (< Ch .dha-'bhyen) -ra-. 'chatter'. x - B-A-A x-x-x.

?A   daku 'embrace': (x - A-A-A x-A-x; Narada A; Ib Ḇ) = idaku (A - B-A-A
x-x-x; Ib A). Nk daCun A; Sr dak- A. Attested as daku 1169.

?B´   damaru ?< *[mo]damaru < *mo(n)ta₂.₂<₃.₆ -ma-ra- (cf. namaru). 'hush, be
silent'. x - B-B-B x-A̱-x. Ib B´ (= L). Nk damaarun B; Sr damar- A. ◍ damari x -
B-x-x x-x-x. Cf. domoru.

?A/B   damasu ?< *dama-s- ('strike dumb') < *[mo]damasu < *mo(n)ta₂.₂<₃.₆ -ma-sa-.
'cheat, swindle, deceive'. x - B-A-B x-A-A. Ib B. Nk damaasun A; Sr damas- A.
◍ damasi x - B-A-B x-x-x.

B   dasu 'put out' (x - B-B-B x-B-x; Edo B) = idasu (B - B-A-x B-B-x). The
initial d- is attested from 1188 (KggD 972a). ◊ dasi x - B-2-B x-x-x.
B < B+B   dekiru < [i]de ki- < *inta-Ci-[Ci]ℬ k[o̱-C]iℬ. 'get produced; be done/made;
can do'. x - B-A-B x-B-x. Hattō, Goka-mura B; Hamada, Matsue, Izumo A. Ib A. Nk
ᵈ/ᵣiKirun B, Sr dikir- B. Dial. dekeru. ◊ deki 'make; yield' x - A-A-B x-x-x;
'ready-made (< deki[ai]); this year's fish (< deki[uo])' x - 1-x-x x-x-x.
B   deru 'emerge; come/go out; leave' (x - B-B-B x-x-x) = ideru (B - B-B-x
B-B-x). Ib B. ◊ de x - A̱-A̱-B x-x-x.
A   dokeru < doke[y]- ?< *ntoka-Ci- (= nokeru). 'remove, get it out of the
way'. x - A-A-A x-A-x. Nk duKiirun A; Sr dukir- A.
A   doku ?< *ntoka- (= noku). 'get out of the way, step aside'. x - A-A-A
x-A-x. Nk duCun A; Sr duk- A.
B   domoru ?< *damaru?ℬA (< ...); ?< [*ko̱to̱ ₂.₃] -n- tomaruA (< ... , second
vowel assimilated to the first). 'stammer'. x - B-A-B x-x-x. Ib B. ◊ domori
x - 1-1:3-B x-x-x. Matsue B; Hamada A; Izumo 2; Hattō 1.
B   donaru < do-ₚᵣₑ nar- ?< it(w)oₐdᵥ ?₂.₂ᵦ nara-ₐ. 'yell, roar'. x - B-A-B
x-x-x. Ib A.
?A/B   doyasu < doyaₘᵢₐ -s- < *ntoda -sa-. 'hit (on the back); roar at'.
x - B-A-B x-x-x.
-          doyogu: see toyoku.
?A/B   doyomeku < *doyo - myeku < *ntodo̱ₘᵢₐ miCa-ka-ᵦₐd ᵥ. 'resound'. x - B-A-A
x-x-x. ◊ doyomeki x - A-A-A x-x-x. Cf. doyomu, toyomu.
B   doyomeru < doyome- (Hn) < to̱yomey- < *to̱do̱ ₘᵢₐ -ma-Ci-. 'make it
resound' (= doyo-mekasu). B [Ir] - B-A-x x-x-x. Km (W) B, (Okada) A̱.
B   doyomosu < to̱yomosu < *toyomasu < *to̱do̱ -ma-sa-. 'make it resound'
(= doyomeru). x - B-A-x x-x-x. NS (Okada) B. NS (T+ 110, kun) to̱yomosazu
LLLHH, to̱yomosuₐₜₜᵣ LLLL.
B   doyomu (Hn) < to̱yomu < *to̱do̱ₘᵢₐ -ma-. 'resound' (= doyo-meku).
B [Ir] - B-A-x x-x-x. NS (83b [17:119-M]) B. NS (T+) to̱yomyi (91) LLH;
to̱yo̱muₚᵣₑd (73) HHL, (96) HLH (? mistake for LLH). Km (W) B.

B   egaku < wegaku < we - kaku < *weₗ.₃ₐ (< ...) kaka-ℬ. 'draw (a picture)'.
B - B-A-B x-x-x. NS (Okada) B. Ib B. ◊ egaki x - B-2-B x-B-x. Nk iihacii B;
Sr iikaci B.
B   eguru < weguru ?< weri - kuru < *ber[a-C]iℬ (< ...) kura-ℬ. 'gouge;
scoop, pick'. x - B-A-B x-B-x. Km x. Nk (?) wagurun B; Sr wiigur- B.
A   emau < wemafu < *bema-pa- (< ...). 'keep smiling'. x - x-x-x x-x-x.
A   emu < wemu < *bema- (?< *boma-; ?< *ba[ra]-ma-, cf. warau, eraku).
'smile; laugh'. A - B-B-x x-x-x. Km (S) B. K: Km A (misprint?). Edo A.
◊ emi x - 1/2-2[U]/A[H]-A x-x-x. Mr (Bm) A. (Modern accents artificial?)
Cf. mi-we si (NS 118b).
B´   erabu < eraᵇ/ₘu < eyrafu ?< *yoraᵇ/ₘu (Hachijō yoramu, NKD 3:241a) <
*dora-(n[a])-pa- . 'choose'. B´ - B-A-B x-B-B. Mr (Bm) B. Edo (-ᵇ/ₘ-) B. Ib B.
Nk qiraabin B; Sr qirab- B. ◊ erabi x - B-x-x x-x-x. If eyrafu (Shinsen-Jikyō)
is not an error, it must be the result of palatal metathesis and/or vowel
assimilation (to the palatal).
?A   eraku < weraku < *bera-ka- (?< *bara-ka-). 'laugh with joy'. x - x-x-x
x-x-x. NS (116a) A. Cf. warau, emu; wera-wera.
?B   eru < e[y]- < *a-Ci- (cf. aru 'have'). 'get'. B - B-A-A x-B-x. NS (102a
[11:147-K], 102b [11:154-K]) B. Km (S): ū (< ú), ē < é) but e̱n̄ < e̱mu = B.
Ōsaka, Ise A. Ib (rare) B. Nk yun B; Sr iir- B; Kabira (Yaeyama) (i)irun.
Thorpe (290) would includeᵧn irun A 'borrow'; see [iraeru].

B   er-u < (Nr) eyr-u ?< (*)yoru (see erabu) < *dora-. 'choose'. x - B-B-B
x-x-x. Is yoru unattested before Edo?

B   er-u < wer- < *bera- (?< *baCira-, ?< *bara-, ?< *bora-). 'carve'.
B - B-B-x x-x-x. Edo B. Cf. horu.

-        [eru] < we- < [u]we- (< ...). 'hunger, thirst': see ueru.

?A   ewarau < wewarafu < *we[myi] - warafu < *bem[a-C]i_A (< ...) bara-pa-_A.
'laugh out loud'. HHHx [Kz] / LHHx [Kn] - x-x-x x-x-x.

B   ganbaru < *gan (?< Ch ngan' 'eyeball') para-_A. 'try hard; hold firm;
persist'. x - B-A-B x-x-x. Ib A. [] ganbari x - 4/0-A-B x-x-x.

A   garameku < gara - myeku < *nkara_mim miCa-Ca-_bed v. 'rattle'. A [Ir (HHHL)]
- x-x-x x-x-x.

A/B   gomakasu ?< goma (< Ch < Skt homa 'esoteric rite of cedar-stick burning',
x - 0-0-B x-x-x) -ka-sa-. 'cheat; misrepresent; tamper with'. x - B-A-A x-x-x.
Ib A, B. [] gomakasi x - 3/4/0-A-A x-x-x.

?A/B   guzuru < guduru < *(n)kuntu_?mim (cf. kuzu 2.4) -ra-. 'grumble, fret'.
x - B-A-A x-x-x.

A   habakaru < fabakaru (?< *panpa(-)ka-ra; ?< *pa[ka-ra-Ci]_B n[i] paka-ra-_B).
'be afraid of, shrink from; spread'. A - A/B-A-A x-A-x. NS (106b) A; NS (T+
128) fa["]fakaru LLHH. Hamada B; Hattō, Matsue, Izumo A. Nk pabaaKan A ('work
hard'); Sr habakar- A ('expand one's work'). [] habakari x - A-A-A x-x-x. Mr
(Bm) A.

B   [habaku] < *fabaku ?< *pa[ka -n-] paka-; ?< *panpa_2.3 -ka-. 'advance, make
progress' (= hakadoru). x - x-x-x x-x-x. Nk x; Sr pabak- B.

?A/B   habamu < fabamu < *panpama- (?< *pam[a-C]i pama-, or ?< *pa[ma-Ci] n[i]
pama-). 'obstruct, hinder'. A - B-A-A x-x-x. Cf. kobamu; hameru.

B   haber-u < fam[u]ber- < *fambyer- < *panp[a-C]i ara- < *pa[pa-Ci]_B n[i]
p[apa-C]i_B ara-_B. 'serve; humbly do'. B - B-A-x x-x-x. NS (127a [14:301-K]) B.

?A/B   habikoru < fabikoru < fabyikoru (?< *pa[pa-Ci]_B n[i] papa-_B) kora-_B.
'spread, thrive, overgrow' (= hobikoru). A (Ck) / B (Kn, Zs) - B-A-A x-x-x.

?A/B   habukeru < fabuke[y]- < *panpuka-Ci- (< ?). 'get excluded, omitted,
curtailed, reduced'. (A) - B-A-B x-x-x.

?A/B   habuku < fabuku < *panpuka- (< ?). 'exclude, omit; curtail, reduce'.
A - B-A-B x-x-x. Ib (rare) A.

B´   haburu < faburu < ?fa_f/buru < *panpura- (< ?). 'bury' (= hoomuru). B´ -
B-x-x x-x-x. [] haburi x - x-x-x x-x-x. NS (125a) B; NS (T+ 70) faburi LLH.

-        haburu = hahuru = hooru ('throw; neglect').

?A/B   ha_d/takaru < fa_d/takaru < *pa(n)taka-ra- (< ?). 'get exposed, bared,
opened up'. x - A/B-A-A x-A-x. Nk paTaaKaan A; Sr hatakar- A. Cf. hada_2.4,
hadaka_3.6, ak-_A.

B   hadakeru < fadakey- < *pantaka-Ci-. 'rub, brush'. B [Ir] - x-x-x x-x-x.
Cf. hake, uma-hadake.

B   [haeru] < fafey- < *papa-Ci- (? *pa-pa-Ci-; see hau). 'stretch it out; let
it stretch/creep/crawl'. B - x-x-x x-x-x. NS (T+ 36) fafeykyeku HLLL. Nk peerun
B, Sr hweer- B 'stretch (a line)'.

B   haeru < faye[y]- < *pada-Ci-. 'bud, proliferate, grow; shine'. x - B-B-B
x-x-x. NS (T+ kun) faye 'bud' LH. K ('shine') Km B (where attested?) Ib B.
Does 'shine' have a separate etymology?

B   hagasu < fagasu/fagatu < *panka-sa-/-ta-. 'peel off, strip' (= hagu).
x - B-A-B x-B-x. Ib B. Nk pagaasun B; Sr hagas- B. Cf. hanasu = hanatu.

B   hagemasu < fagemasu ?< *fageymasu < *panka-Ci-ma-sa- (< ?). 'encourage,
inspire'. Ib B. B - B-A-B x-x-x. 〇 hagemasi x - 4/0-A-B x-x-x (Tk O Mkz only).

B   hagemu < *fageymu < *panka-Ci-ma-. 'spur oneself; strive, labor'.
B - B-A-B x-(B)-x. Ongi B. Ib B. Sr hamar- B (< ?). 〇 hagemi x - B-A-B x-x-x.
Cf. hagesi*adj B*.

A   hageru < fage[y]- < *panka-Ci-. 'put arrow to bowstring'. A - A-B̲-A
x-x-x. Edo A.

B   hageru < fage[y]- < ?*pa(n)ka-ci-. 'get stripped/bald'. x - B-B-B x-B-B.
Ib B. Nk pagirun B; Sr hagir- B.

A   hagu < fagu < *panka- (?= *pa-n[a-]ka-, cf. hameru). 'attach, insert;
fletch, feather an arrow'. A - A-B̲-A x-x-x.

?A   hagu < fagu < *panka-. 'patch; join boards together; build (a boat)';
(same etymon?) 'distribute'. x - A-B-A (A)-(A)-x. Nk pazun B; Sr hag- A.
〇 hagi x - A-2-A x-x-x.

?B   hagu < fagu < (Nr) ?faᵏ/₉u < *pa-(n[a-])ka- (?< *pa*1.3* 'blade'). 'peel
off; strip'. B - B-A[H]/B[U]-B x-B-B. Ib B.

A   hagukumu < fagukumu < *pa*1.2* -n- kuku-ma-*B* ('feather wrap'). 'sit/brood
over, foster'. A - B-A-A x-x-x.

?B   hagurakasu < fagurakasu < *pankura-ka-sa- (<?). 'parry, dodge'.
x - A/B-A-B x-x-x.

B   hagureru < fagure[y]- < *pankura-Ci- (< ?). 'lose (sight of) companions or
gear; miss doing'. x - B-A-B x-B-x. Nk x; Sr hangwir- B 'come undone'.

-      hahaku: *see* hawaku.

-      hahuru: *see* haburu, hohuru, hooru.

?   hahuru < fafuru(/fafure[y]-) < *papura-. 'flood'. Cf. ahureru.

A   hahuru < fafuru < *pa*?1.2* pura-*A*. 'fly up'. A - x-A-x x-x-x.
B´ = B+A hair-u < fa[fi] ir- (or faf[i] ir-, or fafi [i]r-) < *pap[a-C]i*B* ira-*A*.
'enter'. x - B-B-B x-x-B [H 1967:407b — borrowed?]. Km x. Ib B´ (= L).

B   hakadoru < fakadoru < *paka*2.3* -n- t(w)ora-*B*. 'advance, make progress'.
x - B-A-B x-B-x. Nk x; Sr hakadur- B [new?]. Km x.

?B   hakarau < fakarau < *paka-ra-pa-. 'arrange, manage, contrive'.
?A/B - B-A-B x-B-x. Nk paKaaren B; Sr hakarayun B (neg. hakararan/hakaraan) <
fakarar-/fakaraw- < *fakaraf-. 〇 hakarai x - 3/0-A-B x-B-x. Nk paKarai B [new]
= paKaaree B; Sr hakaree B.

?B   [hakareru] < fakare[y]- < *paka-ra-Ci-. 'separate' (= wakareru).
x - x-x-x x-x-x.

B   hakaru < fakaru < *paka*2.3* -ra-. 'measure, calculate; consult (with);
plan, strive for'. B - B-A-B x-B-B. Ongi-m B. NS (105a, 118a) B. Km (S) B.
Edo B. Ib B. Nk pa(Ka)arun B; Sr hakar- B. 〇 hakari LHL - B-A(but 1:3 as
'scales')-B x-x-x. Nk pa(Ka)i B; Sr hakai B.

?A   [hakasu] < fakasu < *paka-sa-. 'deign to wear'. x - x-x-x x-x-x.
〇 [hakasi] < fakasi 'one's sword': myi-fakasi (NS T+ kun) H|LLH (odd).

B   hakeru < fake[y]- < *paka-Ci-. 'flow/drain off; sell well'. x - B-B-B
x-x-x. 〇 hake x - B-2-B x-x-x.

?A   hakeru < fakey- < *paka-Ci-. 'have/let someone wear'. A - A-A-B x-A-x.
NS (T+ 27) fakeymasi wo L̲L̲L̲L̲(|)H. Nk paKiirun A; Sr hakir- A.

A   hakobu < fakwobu < *pakwonpa- (?< *pakwo*2.1* -n[a]-pa-). 'convey,
transport, carry'. A - A-A-A x-x-x. Ongi-m A. Ib A. 〇 hakobi x - A-A-A x-x-x.
(Yoshida: *paka- 'wear'.)

?A   haku ‹ faku ‹ *paka-. ‘slip (something) on, wear’. A - A-A-B x-A-x.
NS (Okada) A. NS (T+ 89) fakyi HH, (20) fakyeru LLL. Edo A. Ib A. Nk paCun A;
Sr hak- A.

B   haku ‹ faku ‹ *paka-. ‘spit out’; ‘sweep’ (Ir; cf. hawaku). B - B-B-B
B-B-B. Km (S) B. Nk paCun B; Sr hak- B. Ib B.

A   hamaru ‹ famaru ‹ *pama-ra-. ‘get/slip/fall into; fit’. x - A-A-A x-B̲-x.
Goka-mura B̲. Nk x; Sr hamar- B̲ “new?”.

A   hameru ‹ famey- ‹ *pama-Ci- (?‹ *pa-ma-, cf. hagu A). ‘insert; put/wear
on one’s fingers; entrap’. A - A-A-A B̲-x-x. Goka-mura B̲. Ib B̲. Nk x.
◻ hame ‘panel; situation, predicament’. x - 2-2[H]/A[U]-A x-x-x.

B   hamu ‹ famu ‹ *pama- (?= *pa₁.₃ᵦ “tooth” -ma-, cf. Yoshida 1979:85).
‘eat’. B - (B)-(B)-(A) x-x-x. Edo B. ◻ hami ‘bridle bit; (Sr) feed’ LL -
1̲/2/2-B x-B-x. Cf. hami-dasu/-deru ‘protrude, bulge’.

(A)   [hanahiru] ‹ fanafiru ‹ fanafiy- ‹ *pana₂.₁ pᵘ/₂Ci-. ‘sneeze’. A - x-x-x
x-(A+B)-A. Nk panaa A Pyun B; Sr hana A hwir- A.

B   [hanarasu] ‹ *fanarasu ‹ *pana-ra-sa-. ‘separate, alienate, ... ’ (=
hanasu). x - x-x-x x-x-x. Nk panaarasun B.

B   hanareru ‹ fanare[y]- ‹ *pana-ra-Ci-. ‘get separate(d), distant’.
B - B-A-B x-B-B. Km (S,W) B. Ib B. Nk panaarin B; Sr hanarir- B. ◻ hanare x -
1/3-A[U]/1:3[H]-B x-B-x. Nk panaarii B; Sr hanari B.

?A   [hanaru] ‹ fanaru ‹ *pana₇₂.₁ -ra-. [dial.] ‘begin’ (vi.).

?B   [hanaru] ‹ fanaru (Azuma) ‹ *pana-ra- = hanareru.

B   hanasu = hanatu ‹ fanatu ‹ *pana-ta-. ‘separate, alienate; release; utter,
speak’. B - B-A-B B-B-B. NS (129b) B. Km (S) B. Edo B. Ib B. Nk panaasun B;
Sr hanas- B; Yn hanan B. ◻ hanasi x - B-2-B B-B-B. Nk panaasii B; Sr hanasi B;
Yn hanasi B. Cf. hagasu.

?A   haneru ‹ *fane[y]- ‹ *pana₇₂.₁ -Ci-. [dial.] = hazimeru (‘begin it’).

?B   haneru ‹ fane[y]- ‹ *pana-Ci-. ‘jump’ (vi.), ‘flip; splash, hit; exclude,
eliminate’ (vt.). B - B-B-A̲ x-B-x. Edo B. Ib A̲. Nk panirun B; hanir- B.
◻ hane x - B-2-A x-B-x. Nk pani C. Cf. hanareru, hanasu.

B   hanikamu ?‹ fayugamu [Ir B] ‹ *pa₁.₃ᵦ n[i] dunkama (see yugamu). ‘teeth
grow crooked; bare one’s teeth; be shy, bashful’. (Reanalyzed as ha-ni-kam-
‘bite at the teeth’? Not in JP.) (B) - B-A-B x-x-x. ◻ hanikami x - 4/0-A-B
x-x-x.

B   harabau ‹ farabafu ‹ *para₂.₃ n[i] papa-ᵦ. ‘crawl on one’s belly’.
B - x-x-x x-x-x. ◻ harabai x - 0/2-1-B x-x-x.

B   haradatu ‹ faradatu ‹ *para₂.₃ -n- tata-ᵦ. ‘get angry’. x - B-A-B x-x-x.
◻ haradati x - 4/0-A-B-x-x-x.

B   [haraeru] ‹ farafey- ‹ *para-pa-Ci-. ‘pray away disasters and sins’.
(?B) - B-A-(?B) x-x-x. ◻ harae B (LLL) - 2-x-x x-x-x.

B   haramu ‹ faramu ‹ *para₂.₃ -ma- (‘belly’, note that hareru ‘swell’ is A).
‘get pregnant; get filled/swollen with’. B - B-A-B x-x-x. NS (116a) A̲. Ib B.
Nk paraamin B.

A   harasu ‹ farasu ‹ *para-sa-. ‘make it swell’. x - A-A-A x-x-x.

?B   harasu ‹ farasu ‹ *para-sa-. ‘clear, dispel’. x - B-A-A̲ x-B-x. Ib B.
Nk paraasun B.

B´   harau ‹ farafu ‹ *para-pa- (cf. hareru). ‘sweep, clear; remove; pay’.
B´ - B-A-B x-B-x. NS (Okada) B (?= B´). NS (T+ kun) farafu LLH, osi farafyi LL
L̲L. Km (S,W) B. Mr (Bm) B. K: “Hn LLF” (= B), but most Mg citations, including
the only Zs example, are B´. Nk paren B; Sr harayun B (neg. haraan) ‹ *faraw- ‹
*faraf-. ◻ harai x - 2(?/0) - A[H]/2[U]-B x-B-x. Hattō, Hamada B (3); Matsue,
Izumo 2.

A   hareru < fare[y]- < *para-Ci-. 'swell'. A - A-A-A x-A-x. Nk pariirun A;
Sr harir- A. 〇 hare x - A-A-A x-x-x. Ib A.

B   hareru < fare[y]- < *para-Ci-. 'get clear, open up'. B - B-B-B x-B-B.
NS (Okada) B. Km (S,W) B. Edo B. Ib B. 〇 hare x - 1/2-2[U]/1:3[H]-B x-x-x.
Edo HL, Hattō, Izumo, Goka-mura B (2); Matsue 1/2, Hamada 1. Nk parirun B;
Sr harir- B; Yn harirun B. Cf. harau; haru; haruku. Perhaps *para- < *paru-
with the second vowel assimilating to the first.

A   haru < faru < *para- (? *pa-ra-; cf. hayu, haeru). 'stretch/paste it'. A -
A-A-A x-A-A. NS (T+ 3) fari HH, (7) faru HL. Edo A. Ib A. Nk pan A; Sr har- A.

B   haru < faru < *para- (?< *paru-). 'open ground, clear land (for
cultivation)'. B - x-x-x x-x-x. Cf. haruku, hareru; hara.

B   [haru] ?< *pa[si]ra- 'run' (Ryūkyū): see hasir-u. But Thorpe 248
suggests an opposite sort of derivation: *pa[ra]-si ir- > hasir-u.

?B   harukasu < farukasu < *paru-ka-sa-. 'make it clear' (= harasu).

?B   [harukeru] < faruke[y]- < *paru-ka-Ci-. 'make it clear/bright'. x - x-x-x
x-x-x.

?B   haruku < faruku < *paru-ka-. 'clear up, open up, get bright; open it up,
dispel'. x - x-x-x x-x-x. Cf. hareru, harau; haru 'spring'.

B   hasamaru < fazamaru (JP) <*pa(n)sa-ma-ra-. 'get inserted, be put/caught
between, get nipped'. B - B-A-B x-x-x. Ib B. Nk pasaaman B.

B   hasameru < fazame[y]- (JP) < *pa(n)sa-ma-Ci-. 'insert; ... ' (= hasamu).
(B) - x-x-x x-x-x.

B   hasamu < fasamu / ?*fazamu < *pa(n)sa-ma-. 'insert; put/catch between;
nip'. B - B-A-B x-B-x. Edo B. Ib B. Nk pasaamin (pasaam-) B; Sr hasam- B.
〇 hasami 'scissors'. B - B-1:3-B B-B-x. Sapporo 2. Ōsaka, Kōbe 1:3/2.
Kōchi, Sakawa 2. Nk pasaamii B; Sr hasan B. Cf. haseru; hazama.

B   [hasasageru] < fasasagey-: ?< *pasa-sa-n[a-]ka-Ci- 'make it run/gallop';
?< *pasa-sa[-Ci]ʙ [a]nka-Ci-ᴀ 'make it gallop up'. x - x-x-x x-x-x.

?B   haseru < fase[y]- < *pasa-Ci-. 'run'. B - B-B-A x-x-x. Km (S) B.
Mr (Bm) B. Edo B.

B   haseru < fase[y]-/*faze[y]- < *pa(n)sa-Ci-. 'insert; put/catch between;
nip' (= hasamu). (B) - x-x-x x-x-x.

B   hasirakasu < fasirakasu < *pasira-ka-sa- ?< *pas[a-C]i-ra-ka-sa-. 'make it
run/gallop'. x - x-x-x x-x-x.

B   hasir-u < fasir-u < *pasira- ?< *pas[a-C]i-ra- (cf. haseru). 'run'.
B - B-A-B x-(B)-x. Ongi-m B. NS (126b) B. Km (W) B. Edo B. Ib B. Nk pan B;
Sr har- B (?< *pa[si-]r-) 'run; flow'. Cf. wasir-u. 〇 hasiri 'first (supply)
of the season; kitchen sink'. x - B-A[H]/1:3[U]-B x-x-x. Thorpe 248 suggests
the etymology *parasi ir- (= *para-s[a-C]iʙ ir-ᴀ); cf. haru.

B   *hasu < *fasu < *pasa- 'run': see haseru, hasir-u, [hasaseru],
[hasasageru].

A   hatagakureru < fatagakure[y]- < *pata?ᵉ.₁ -n- kakura-Ci-ʙᴀ. 'be partly
concealed, be half hidden'. A - x-A-x x-x-x. Cf. hasita.

-        hatakaru, hatakeru: see hadakaru, hadakeru.

B   hataku < faᵗ/ᵈaku < *pa(n)taka-. 'dust, beat, slap'. B [Ir] - B-A-B x-x-x.
Ib B. 〇 hataki 'duster; dusting' x - B-1:3-B x-x-x.

A   hatameku < fata-meku (< *-myeku) < *pata?ₘᵢₐ or ?ₑ.₂ᵦ "flag" miCa-ka-ᵦᵤᵈ v.
flutter, flap; resound; flare up'. A - B-A-A x-x-x.

A   hataraku < fataraku < *pataraka- ?< *pata-ra-ka-. 'work'. x - A-A-A A-A-A.
Mr (Bm) A. Ib A. Nk pataaraCun A; Sr hatarak- A. 〇 hataraki x - A-A-A x-x-x.
Nk pataaraCi A; Sr hataraci A. Cf. hataru, hatasu, hateru.

B   hataru < fataru < *patara- ?< *pata-ra-. 'demand, exact, tax,levy'.
B - x-A-x x-x-x. Cf. hataraku, hatasu, hateru.

B   hatasu < fatasu < *pata-sa-. 'accomplish, fulfill'. B - B-A-A x-x-x.
(Kg A incongruent with hateru B.) NS (Okada) B; NS (T+ 89) fatasi te mo
LLH(|)F(|)L. Mr (Bm) B. Ib A, B.

B   hateru < fate[y]- < *pata-Ci-. 'reach the end; anchor'. x - B-B-B x-B-x.
NS (T+ 123) fate te LH(|)H. Edo B. Nk x; Sr hatir- B. [] hate 'the end; the
limits'. x - B-A-B x-B-x. Km (W) B. Nk patii B; Sr hati B. K: Edo HLL
(attested?). Cf. haʰ/ᵈate.

B   hatureru < fature[y]- < *patu(-)ra-Ci- (< ?). 'ravel, fray' (vi.,
= hotureru, hogureru). B - B-A-x x-x-x. Km (W) B.

B   haturu < faturu < *patu(-)ra-. 'remove the skin; pare/whittle down' (vt.).
B - B-A-x x-x-x. [] haturi 'skinning; paring down; a garment come unsewn, get
frayed'. B - x-x-x x-x-x.

-          (-) hau < (-) fafu: see (-) wau.

B   hau < fafu < *papa- (?< *pa-pa-, cf. *pa-Ci-) fey- 'elapse, pass',
*pa-ra- 'stretch'). 'crawl, creep'. B - B-B-B x-B-B. NS (76b) B; NS (T+ 75)
fafu LH. Km (W) B. Edo B. Ib B. Nk poorun B, Sr hoor- B restructured from *faw-
< *faf-. Cf. haeru.

B   hawaku/habaku < fafaku < *pa[ka-Ci]ᴮ (n[i]) paka-ᴮ. 'sweep'. x - x-x-x
x-B-x. Nk pooCun B; Sr hook- B. [] hawaki LLH - 0/1-0-x x-x-x > hooki (0/1-2-B
x-B-x) 'broom' ?3.5a/b (?< *3.4). Nk pooCii B; Sr hooci B. (NKD etymology with
ha 'feather' is bad because that is 1.1 = A.)

B   hayamaru < fayamaru < *pada-ma-ra-. 'be hasty/rash; be early'. x - B-A-B
x-x-x. Nk peeman (peemar-) B. [] hayamari x - x-x-x x-(B)-x.
Nk peemai B; Sr hayami-gutu.

B   hayameru < fayaᵇ/ₘey- < *pada-ma-Ci-. 'hasten/quicken it'. B - B-A-B
x-B-x. Edo B. Nk peemin (peemir-) B; Sr hayamir- B.

B   hayaru < fayaru < *pada-ra-. 'become popular/prevalent, flourish'; (Nk)
'become early' (cf. hayamaru). x - B-A-B x-B-x. Ib B. Nk peerun B; Sr hweer- B.
[] hayari 'fad; prevalence'. x - B-A-B x-B-x. Edo B. Sr hweei B.

B   hayasu < fayasu < *pada-sa-. 'grow (beard); musically accompany, beat
time'. x - B-A-B x-B-x. Edo B. Ib B. Sr hwees- B. Cf. haeru. [] hayasi x - B-B-B
x-x-x. Nk peesii B; Sr hweesi B.

B   hayugamu: see hanikamu.

?B   hazeru < *faze[y]- < *pansa-Ci- (< ?). 'burst open; split, crinkle'.
x - B-B-A x-x-x. Cf. haneru, haziku.

B   hazikeru < fazike[y]- < *pansika-Ci- (< ?). 'burst/split/ spring open'
(vi.). (B) - B-A-B B-x-x.

B   haziku < faziku < *pansika- (< ?). 'flip, snap; repel'. B - B-A-B x-B-x.
Ib B. Sr hancun (hank-) B. Cf. haneru, hazeru. [] haziki x - 1/3-1:3/1[U]-B
x-x-x.

A   hazimaru < fazimaru < *pansima-ra- < *pan[a]-si(-)ma-ra-. 'begin' (vi.).
x - A-A-A x-A-x. Ib A. [] hazimari x - A-A-A x-x-x. Cf. hana₇₂.₁, haˢ/ᵤi₂.₁ <
*pa(n)si.

A   hazimeru < fazimey- < *pansima-Ci- < *pan[a]-si(-)ma-Ci-. 'begin it'.
A - A-A-A x-A-A. NS (Okada, mistake?) B. Km (S,W) A. Mr (Bm) A. Edo A. Ib A.
[] hazime A - A-A-A x-A-x. Km (S) A. Mr (Bm) A. Edo A. Goka-mura 1 (verb A).

B   hazirau < fadirafu < fadi[y]rafu < *pantu-Ci-ra-pa-. 'feel shy, bashful'.
x - B-A-B x-x-x. [] hazirai x - 3/0-A-B x-x-x.

B   haziru < fadi[y]- < *pantu-Ci-. 'feel shame, be ashamed'. B - B-B-B x-x-x.
Km (W) B. Edo B. Ib B. [] hazi 'shame'. B - B-2-B x-x-x. NS (133b) B. Nk pazii
B; Sr hazi B. Cf. hazu-ka-siₐ𝒹ⱼ ᴮ.

B   hazukasimeru < fadukasimey- < *pantu-ka-siₐ𝒹ⱼ ᴮ -ma-Ci-. 'shame, disgrace,
humiliate'. B - B-A-B x-x-x. [] hazukasime x - A/B-A-B x-x-x (cf. RGJ 884:3).

A   hazumu < fadumu < *pantu-ma- (< ?). 'bounce, spring, (re)bound' (vi.);
'splurge (spend big) on' (vt.). x - A-A-A x-x-x. Edo A. Ib A.
[] hazumi 'moment(um), force'. x - A-A-A x-x-x.

A   hazureru < fadure[y]- < *pantu-ra-Ci-. 'get disconnected/separated/loose;
fail, miss; deviate (from), run counter (to)'. A - A-A-A x-A-x. Edo A. Ib B.
Nk panzin A; Sr handir- A. [] hazure x - A-A-A x-x-x.

A   hazusu < fadusu < *pantu-sa-. 'disconnect, remove, unfasten; miss, let it
go by; avoid, dodge'. A - A-A-A x-A-x. Edo A. Ib A. Nk pansun A; Sr hans- A;
Kobama (Yaeyama) panzun.

?B   hedataru < fyedataru ?< *piCa (?= *pina₂.₂ᵦ) -n- tataₑ-ra-. 'be apart,
distant'. x B-A-A x-B-x. Nk x; Sr hwidatar- B. Cf. [hidamaru]; [henaru].
[] hedatari 'gap, gulf'. x - A/B-A-A x-x-x.

?B   hedateru < fyedate[y]- ?< *piCa (?= *pina₂.₂ᵦ) -n- tata-Ci-ᵦ. 'set apart,
separate; alienate'. B - B-A-A x-B-B. Mr (Bm) B. Edo B. Ib B. Nk pidaaTin B;
Sr hwidatir- B. Cf. [hidameru]; [henaru]. [] hedate 'partition, gap, distance'.
x - B-A-A x-B-x. Edo HHL. Nk pidaatii B; Sr hwidati B.

-     hedatu < fyedatu < *piCa (?= *pina₂.₂ᵦ) -n- tata-ᵦ. = hedataru.

B   hegu < fegu < ?*feygu < *pa-Ci-n[a]-ka-; ?< *fyegu < *piCa-n[a]-ka-.
'pare/peel/strip down' (= hagasu = hagu). B - B-B-B x-B-x. Ib B. Nk pizun B;
Sr hwig- B. Cf. hezuru, her-u; [hieru]; hagu.

B   [henarasu] < *fyenarasu < *piCa (-)na-ra-sa-. 'shrink/lessen it'. x -
x-x-x x-x-x. Nk pinaarasun B.

?B   [henaru] < fyenaru < *piCa (?= *pina₂.₂ᵦ) nara- 'be apart'. x - x-x-x
x-x-x. Attested Man'yō-shū.

B   [henaru] < *fyenaru < *piCa (-)na-ra-. 'shrink, get less' (= her-u).
x - x-x-x x-x-x. Sd hyinaa(r)yum A; Nk pin (pir-) A = pinaarun A =; Sr hwir- A
= hwinar- A; Yn hinnarun A. Narada A. On *fye < *piCa 'a little' (Nk q¹/ᵤqPi C,
Sr qihwi B) cf. Thorpe; see hegu, hezuru.

B   [hen¹/ₒgeru] < *fey-n¹/ₒgey- < *pa(-)Ci[-Ci]₇ᵦ nonka-Ci-₇ᵦ. 'run away,
escape'. x - x-x-x x-B-B. Nk (hee)pinigin B; Sr hwingir- B; Yn hingirun B.
There is a transitive version Nk pinigasun B, Sr hwingiras- B 'let escape'.

A   herasu < ferasu ?< *pa(-)Ci-ra-sa-; ?< *fe[na]ras- < *fyenaras- <
'shrink/lessen it'. x - A-A-A x-(x)-x. First attested JP.

?B   heru < fey- < *pa(-)Ci-. 'pass' (vi.). B - B-A[H]/B[U]-A x-A-x.
NS (100a) fénu, (70c, 84a — set epithets) fu̅. NS (T+ 44, 56, kun) fu "R" ?= H
(or really R = LH?), (97) H; (78 nominalized attr) HL. Km (S) fe(-te); (W) B,
but inf A. Mr (Bm) furu, fe-te. Nk x. Cf. he₇₁.₃ᵦ 'the shed of a loom'.

A   her-u < fer-u ?< *feyr- ?< *pa(-)Ci-ra- (cf. hegu); ?< *fe[nar]- < fyenar-
< *piCa (-)na-ra. 'shrink, become less; humble oneself' (vi.). Attested Hn
('humble oneself'). A - A-A-A A-A-(A). Ib A. Sd hyinaa(r)yum A; Nk pin (pir-) A
= pinaarun A; Sr hwir- A = hwinar- A; Yn hinnarun A. Narada A. [] heri x -
A-A-A x-x-x.

A   hesu < fyesu ?< *piCasa- (< ?); ?< *pi-₇ osa-ₐ. 'push, force' (= osu).
A [Ir] - x-A/B-x x-x-x. Narada (used instead of osu) A.

A   hesu < fesu < ?*feysu ?< *paCi-sa-. 'reduce, curtail; humble oneself'
(= herasu). A - A-x-x x-x-x.

?A/B   heturau < feturafu ?< *pe-tura-pa-; ?< *feyturafu < *paCi-tura-pa- (cf.
her-u). 'flatter'. B - B-A-A x-x-x. [] heturai x - 3-A-A x-x-x. On the
etymology see Kōza Nihon-go no goi 11 (Goshi 3):213-5.

?A/B   hezuru < feturu ?< *feyturu ?< *pa-Ci - tura-; ?< *piCa - tura-.
'pave/whittle down; pilfer'. x - A/B-A-A x-x-x. Cf. hegu, hagu; henaru.

A   [hibaru] < fibaru (< ?). 'demolish'. A - x-x-x x-x-x. (Attested Mg, Ir.)

B   hibikasu < *fyibyikasu < *pinpika-sa- (< ...). 'make it echo/resound'.
x - B-A-B x-x-x. Km (S) B.

B   hibiku < fyibyiku ?< *pinpi ?ᴍᵢᴍ(-)ka-; ?< *pi[ka] ?ᴍᵢᴍ -n- pika-.
'(re)sound; echo'. B - B-A-B x-B-x. Ongi B. Km (W) B. Edo B. Ib B. Nk x.
◊ hibiki B - B-1-B x-B[new]-x. Km (S) B.

-        hibiraku: see hiiraku.

A   hidaku < fidaku < *pinta(-)ka-. 'crush'. A - x-x-x x-x-x. (NKD x.)
Cf. hisigu, hisagu.

B   [hidamaru] < *fyidamaru ?< *pinta-ma-ra-. 'get separated, be put at a
distance'. x - x-x-x x-B-x. Nk x; Sr hwizamar- B.

B   [hidameru] < *fyidame[y]- ?< *pinta-ma-Ci-. 'separate, put at a distance;
put in a pleat'. x - x-x-x x-B-x. Nk Pizaamin B; Sr hwizamir- B. ◊ [hidame]
LLL - x-x-x x-B-x. Nk x; Sr hwidami B.

?A   [hidaru] < fitaru < fyiᵗ/ₐaru < *piₗ.₂ (-n-) ta-ra-ₐ ('days suffice').
'mature'. x - x-x-x x-x-x.

?A   [hidasu] < fidasu < fyiᵗ/ₐasu < *piₗ.₂ (-n-) ta-sa-ₐ ('make the days
suffice'). 'nurture, raise'. x - x-x-x x-x-x.

A   hider-u < fyider-u < *piₗ.₂ -n- tera-ᴮ (< ... 'sun shine'). 'have a
drought'. (A - A/B-A-A x-A-x.) See hideri (Ch. 5).

B   hieru < fiye- < *fyiye[y]- < *piₗ.₃ₐ -da-Ci-. 'get cold'. x - B-B-B x-x-x.
Ib B. ◊ hie x - B-2-B x-B-x. Cf. hiyasu.

?A   [hieru] < fi[y]e [Mg] < fiywe[y]- ?< *pᵐ/₂Ci-baCi-. 'scrape, slice thin'.
NS (T+ 7) fiywe[y]-ne HH-L 'I want you to slice'. Cf. hegu, hagu; her-u; waku;
? hogu. (The NKD entry is hiu.)

B   higamu < figamu < *fyigamu ?< *pinaₐ.₂ᵦ -ka-ma-; ?< *pinka-ma- (?<
*pi-muka-ma-). 'get biased, prejudiced, (mentally) warped'. B - B-A-B x-x-x.
Hamada, Sapporo, Akita, Wakamatsu A̲. Mr (Bm) B. Ib B. ◊ higami x - B-A-B x-x-x.
Cf. higa < figa 'wrong, twisted' (adjectival noun), Korean pi(-s)-.

B   [higoru] < figoru < *piₗ.₃ₐ -n- kora-ₐ ('ice freeze'). 'get cold' (=
hieru). x - x-x-x x-B-x. Nk Pizurun B; Sr hwizuyun B < hwizuri- < fig(y)ur-i <
figur(u)- (> hwizuru-ₐdⱼ ᴮ 'cold'). ◊ [higori] x - x-x-x x-B-x. Nk Pizui B,
Sr hwizui B < fig(y)ur-i < *pi -n- kor[a-C]i. Cf. [hi-]ₐdⱼ ᴮ, Sd hyiguruₐdⱼ ᴮ,
Nk Pizu(u)rusenₐdⱼ ᴮ, Sr hwizuru-ₐdⱼ ᴮ 'cold'.

?A   hihiku < fyifyiku < *pipi-ka-. 'smart, tingle; be pungent'. x - x-x-x
x-x-x. NS (T+ 14) kuti - byifyiku HH(|)HHL (fyifyiku in Koji-ki).

?A/B   hiideru < fi[y]de- < *poₐ₁.₂ᵦ inta-Ci-ᴮ ('the best emerge'). 'excel'.
A - B-A-A x-x-x. Mg f̄īd̲u̲ (?= f̄īīd̲u̲).

-        [hiiku]: see hihiku.

A   hiiragu [NKD] = fibiraku [Mg] < fifiraku [Mg] < *pipi-ra-ka-. 'smart
with pain'. A - x-A-x x-A-x.

A   hiir-u < fifir-u < *fyifyir- < *pi[ra] - pira (mimetic, or noun 'petal'
?2.2b). 'flutter up'. A - x-(A)-x x-x-x. Cf. hiiru < fifiru 'moth'; hirugaer-u.

A   hikaeru < *fyikafey- < *pika-pa-Ci-(or *pik[a-C]i apa-Ci-). 'hold back
(restrain) from; wait; jot/write down'. A - A[H]/B-A-A x-A-x. Edo B̲. Matsue,
Izumo A. Mg f̄īka̲f̲u (?< f̄īki af̲e-). Nk pikeerun A; Sr hwikeer- A.
◊ hikae x - 2/3/0-A-A x-x-x.

B   hikaru < fyikaru < *pikaₐᵢ -ra-. 'shine'. B - B-A-B B-B-x. NS (119a) B.
Km (S) B. Edo B. Ib B. Nk piKaarun B = piCaarun B; Sr hwicar- B. ◊ hikari
'light'. B - B-2-B x-B-x. NS (6) ₤LH = LLH. Mr (Bm) HHL. Nk piCai B; Sr
hwikari B = hwiCai B.

A   hikeru < fike[y]- < *pika-Ci-. '(school/office) close'. (A) - A-A-A x-x-x.
  [] hike 'closing; defeat; loss'. x - A-A-A x-x-x.

A+A   hikiireru < fiki ireru < fyikyi*A* ire-*A* < *pik[a-C]i*A* ira-Ci-*A*. 'pull in'.
  NS (T+ kun) fyikyi ire [LHH = HL|HH; (T+ 21) fyikyi-[i]re [LH = HL|H.

A+A   hikiiru < fiki wiru < fyikyi*A* wi[y]-*A* < *pik[a-C]i*A* u/*o*-Ci-*A*. 'lead'.
  A+A - B-A-A x-x-x. NS (129a) A+A. Mg HL|HL.

A   [hikobaeru] < fikobaye[y]- < *fyikwo*2.2* -baye[y]- < *pi kwo -n- pada-Ci-*B*
  ('grandsons proliferate'). 'sprout (anew — after being cut)'. A - (x-x-)x
  x-x-x. [] hikobae (x) - A-A-x x-x-x.

A   hikozurau < fyiko̱durafu < *piko̱-*A* -n- tura-pa-*?*. 'pull, grasp'. A - x-A-x
  x-x-x. Dial. hikozuru, hikozir-u.

A   hiku < fyiku < *pika-/*piko̱- (cf. hikozurau). 'pull, ...' (vt.); 'withdraw,
  retreat, subside' (vi.). A - A-A-A A-A-A. NS (Okada) A. NS (T+ 41) fyiku ya
  HH(|)L, (111) fyikyi [i]re te [L-H-H = HL(|)H(|)H. Edo A. Ib A. Yn Kun A.
  [] hiki A-A-A x-x-x. Cf. (-)hiki (counter).

?A/B   himeru < *fyimey- < *pi-ma-Ci- (?< *pi[so]-ma-Ci-). x - B-B-A x-x-x.
  'conceal'.

A   [hinaraberu] < fyinarabey- < *pi*1.2* na(ra)npa-Ci-*A*. 'pass time, let the
  days go by' (= kenaraberu). x - x-x-x x-x-x.

B   hiner-u < finer-u ?< *fyiner-u < *pi(-)nera- (< ?). 'twist; pinch'.
  B - B-A-B x-B-x. Ib B. Nk pinirun B; Sr hwinir- B. [] hineri x - B-A-B x-x-x.

B   hirakeru < fyirakey- < *pira-ka-Ci-. 'get opened up, ... '. (B) - B-A-B
  x-A̱-x. Km (S) B. Ib B. Nk PiraaKin B; Sr hurakir-B = hwirakir- B.

B   hiraku < fyiraku < *pira-ka-. 'open'. B - B-A-B x-A̱/B-x. NS (83a
  [17:114-M]) B. NS (T+ 96) osi fyirakyi HL LLH. Km (S) B. Mr (Bm) ?B. Edo B.
  Ib B. Nk PiraaCun B; Sr hurak- A̱ = hwirak- B.

?A/B   hirameku < *fyira-myeku < *pira*mim* - miCa-ka-*bnd* *v*. 'flash; flutter'.
  B - B-A-A x-x-x. Ib B. [] hirameki x - 3/4/0-A-A x-x-x. Cf. hiromeku.

-        hirau: *see* hirou. Cf. irou = irau.

-        hiriu (< firifu): *see* hirou.

A (?< *B) hirogaru < firogaru < *fyirogaru < *piro̱*adj B* -n[a]-ka-Ci- (or:
  *fyiro̱gey ar- < *piro̱ -n- key ara-*B*?). 'spread out, extend'. A - A-A-A x-A-x.
  Ib A. Nk Piruugan A = Pyuugan A; Sr hwirugar- A. [] hirogari x - A-A-A x-x-x.

A (?< *B) hirogeru < firoge- < *fyiro̱gey- < *piro̱*adj B* -n[a-]ka-Ci- (or:
  *fyiro̱gey ar- < *piro̱ -n- key ara-*B*?). 'spread/extend/widen it'. x - A-A-A
  x-A-x. Edo A. Ib A. Nk Piruugin A = Pyuugin A; Sr hwirugir- A.

B   hiromaru < fyiro̱maru < *piro̱*adj B* -ma-ra-. 'spread, get propagated or
  circulated'. B - B-A̱-A̱ x-B-x. Km (S,W) B. Hamada A/B; Hattō, Matsue, Izumo B.
  Ib A. Nk Piru(u)man B = Pyuuman A̱; Sr hwirumar- B. (Kg A̱ is incongruent with
  hiromeru Kg B.)

?A/B   [hiromeku] < firomeku < *fyira-myeku < *pira*mim* - miCa-ka-*bnd* *v*. 'flash;
  flutter' (= hirameku). B - x-x-x x-x-x. NS (119a) A. Not in NKD.

B   hiromeru < fyiro̱mey- < *piro̱*adj B* -ma-Ci-. 'spread (extend, diffuse) it'.
  B - B-A-B x-B-x. Ib B. Nk Piru(u)min A̱ = Pyuumin A̱; Sr hwirumir- B.

?B   hiroru < fyiro̱ru < *piro̱*adj B* -ra-. 'be widespread'. x - x-x-x x-x-x.

A   hirou, hirau [dissimilation? - or, back-formation? > Tappi hurar- (Clarke
  84)] < fyir*2*/*1*fu- < *pir*2*/*1*(-)pa- 'pick up'. A - A[U]/B[H]-A A-A-x. NS (100a)
  <u>firo̱wazu</u>. Km (W) A. Mr (Bm) A. Edo A. Kt A also in in K 1942:169; Ib A.
  Sd hyiryaa(r)yum A; Nk puruurun A, Sr hwirir- A = hwirayun A (neg. hwiraan) <
  *firaw- < *firaf-. Cf irou = irau.

B   hiru < fiy- < *po-Ci-. 'get dry'. x - B-B-B B?-B-B. NS (T+ kun) fu "R" ?= H (or really R = LH?). Km (W) B. Edo B. Sd hyaa(r)yum B 'suffer drought'; Nk Pyun (Pyur-) B; Sr hwir- B; Yn cirun B. Hagiwara (Tsuzuku 1941:179) lacks this verb, replacing it by hoseru, which occurs in various dialects (see NKD).

A   hiru < *fiy- < *pᵘ/₀Ci-. 'winnow'. A - x-x-x x-x-x. Km (W "?") A. Cf. noun (*)fiy (hypothesized from a Koji-ki placename) = miy < *mᵘ/₀Ci₁.₃ₐ.

B   hiru < fiy- < *pᵘ/₀Ci-. 'sneeze'. x - B-x-x x-B-x. Km (W) A/B. Cf. hanahiru, hir-u, he.

B   hir-u < fir-u < *fiyr-u < *pᵘ/₀Ci-ra-. 'expel/eject from the body': he ~ 'fart', kuso ~ 'shit'; (= hiru) hana ~   'sneeze'. (B) - B-B-x x-B-x. Nk Pyun B; Sr hwir- B. Cf. hiru, he. Unattested in OJ; Zdb takes the stem as a development from hiru 'sneeze'.

?A/B   hirugaer-u < firugafyer-u < ?*fyiru-gafyer-u < ?*piro̲ -n- kapi- ra- (or *pira - ⋯ with vowel-height assimilation of the second syllable to the first). 'turn over; flutter'. B - B-A-A x-x-x.

?A/B   hirugaesu < firugaf[y]esu < ?*piro̲ -n- kapi-sa- (or *pira - ⋯). 'turn it about, reverse; wave/fly it'. B - B-x-x x-x-x.

B   hirumu < firumu (< ?). 'get paralyzed; lose heart; flinch, wince'. B - B-A-B x-x-x. Edo B. Ib B. Cf. sibireru.

-          [hisageru] < fisageru = hissageru.

A   hisagu < fisaᵏ/ₒu < *fyisaku < *pisaka-. 'sell'. A - A/B-A-x x-x-x.

?A   hisagu (?< *fyisaku < *pi[ka-Ci]ₐ saka-ᵦ). 'crush' (= hisigu). x - x-A-x x-x-x.

?A   hisigeru < fisiᵏ/ₒe- < *fyisikey- < *fyi[kyi] sikey- < *pik[a-C]iₐ sika- (?< saka-₇ᵦ with assimilation to preceding vowel). 'crush' (= hisigu). x - B-A-A x-x-x. Kg incongruent with hisigu.

?A   hisigu < fisigu < fisiku < ?*fyisiku < *fyi[kyi] siku < *pik[a-C]iₐ sika- (?< saka-₇ᵦ with assimilation to the preceding vowel). 'crush; (mey̲ ~) close (the eyes)'. A - B-A-B x-A-x. Kg incongruent with hisigeru. Nk x; Sr hwiig- A. Cf. hidaku.

B   hisomaru < fisomaru < ?*fyiso̲maru < *piso̲-ma-ra-. 'lurk, lie concealed; be hushed'. x - B-A-x x-x-x.

B   hisomeru < fisomey- < ?*fyiso̲mu < ?*piso̲-ma-. 'lurk, lie concealed', vi. (= hisomaru); 'wrinkle (eyebrows) in frown/scowl', vt. B (vt.) - A/B-A-B x-x-x. ▯ hisomi x - B-x-x x-x-x.

A   hissageru < "fisage-" = fissage- < fyik[yi]ₐ - sagey-ᵦ < *pik[a-C]iₐ sanka-Ci-ᵦ. 'carry/have in hand'. A - B-A[U]/B[H]-A x-A-x. Mg HHL(/HLL). Nk Pissagirun A; Sr hwisagir- A. ▯ hissage x - A-x-x x-x-x.

B   hitaku < fitaku < *fiy-taku < *po̲-Ci₁.₃ᵦ taka-ₐ. 'burn a fire'. B - (x)-(x)-x x-x-x. ▯ hitaki 'burning a fire; fireplace'. B - 3-2-x x-x-x.

?A   hitaru 'mature': see hidaru.

B   hitaru < fitaru < ?*fyitaru < *pita-ra-. 'get soaked (in)' = [hitiru]. x - A/B-A-B x-x-x. Edo B.

B   hitasu < fitasu < ?*fyitasu < *pita-sa-. 'soak it (in)'. B - A/B-A-B x-x-x. Edo B. Ib B. ▯ hitasi x - B-A-B x-x-x. Cf. [hitiru], hitaru.

B   [hitatakeru] < fitatake[y]- (< ?). 'mix, confuse; get mixed/confused'. B - x-A-x x-x-x. Mr (Bm) A.

B   [hitiru] < fiti[y]- (Hn) < fit- (Nr) < *fyit- < *pita-. 'get soaked (in)' = hitaru. x - x-x-x x-x-x. Km (W) B.

B   hitokorou < *fito-korofu/?-korobu ?< *fyito̲-kurabu < *pito̲₇₈.₄ kura-n[a]-pa-ₐ. 'line up equally/uniformly'. B - x-x-x x-x-x. Cf. hitosii, kuraberu.

B   [hitu] = [hitiru] 'get soaked' (< fitu < *fyit- < *pita-). Cf. hitaru.

B   hiyakasu < fiyakasu < *fyiyakasu < *pida-ka-sa-. 'poke fun at; browse'.
x - B-A-B x-x-x. Ib B. ◻ hiyakasi x - 3/4-A-B x-x-x.

B   hiyasu < fiyasu < *fyiyasu < *pi*1.3a* -da-sa-. 'cool it, make it cold'.
x - B-B-B x-x-x. Ib B. Cf. hieru.

B   [hiyu]: 1. *see* hieru. 2. *fyiyu < *pi*1.3a* -da- 'get cold': Mg fi[y]ī̲
(< *pid[a-C]i) su̲yu̲re̲ru '? (stuff) that is chilled and soured, cold pickles'.

?A/B   hizamazuku < fyiza-maduku < *pinsa*2.1* mantuka- (?< *man[ka-Ci-Ci]*A* tuka-*B*)
'kneel'. A - B-A-B x-x-x.

?B   [hizutu] < fyidutu < *pint[i*72.3* "*mud*"] uta-*B*. 'get wet/muddy'. x - x-x-x
x-x-x. Cf. hitiru < fiti[y]- < fit- < ?*fyit- < *pita- ; hizi < fyidi.

B   hobikoru < fobyiko̲ru ?< *fabyiko̲ru (< ...) *with the first vowel
assimilated to the labial consonants*. 'spread, thrive, overgrow' (= habikoru).
B - x-x-x x-x-x.

B´   [hoburu] < foburu (Mg) < fofuru (Nr) < *po(n)pa-ra ?< *pa(n)pa-ra-.
'slaughter' (= hohuru). B´ - B-A-A x-x-x.

A   hodaru < fodaru < *ponta-ra- (?< *panta-ra- < *pam[a-(Ci-)]*A* ta-ra-*A*; ?<
*p[inp]o*2.1* -n- tara-*A*, cf. Yoshida 1979.147). 'get shackled'. A x-x-x x-x-x.

?A/B   hodasu < fodasu < *ponta-sa- (?< *panta-sa- < *pam[a-(Ci-)]*A* ta-sa-*A*;
?< *p[inp]o*2.1* -n- ta-sa-*A*. 'shackle'. A - B-A-x x-x-x. Km (W) A.
◻ hodasi A - A/B-A-x x-x-x. Note: The verb is first attested in 892, the noun
in 934. But the noun fumodasi occurs in M 3886 and that has prompted two
etymological theories: *(1)* f[um]odasi > fodasi, *(2)* fum[i-f]odasi > fumodasi.
Neither necessarily implies that the verb is a secondary formation.

-        hodobasir-u: *see* hotobasir-u.

B   hodokeru < fodoke- < *fodo̲key- ?< *pon[o]*(2.3)* to̲ka-Ci-*B* ('come slightly
undone'). 'come loose, get undone/untied'. x - B-A-B x-?B-x. Km x. Ib B.
Nk puTuKin B; Sr hutungwir- B ?< *fotoki fogure-. ◻ hodoke x - x-x-x x-x-x.
Nk puTuKii B; Sr hutungwi B.

A   hodokoru < fodoko̲ru < *pontoko̲-ra- (?< *ponto-ka-ra-). 'spread out,
proliferate'. x - x-x-x x-x-x. Cf. hodokosu.

A   hodokosu < fodoko̲su < *pontoko̲-sa- (?< *ponto-ka-sa-). 'give in charity;
do, perform, carry out'. A - A/B̲-A-A x-x-x. Km (S,W) A. Hattō, Hamada B;
Matsue, Izumo A. Ib A. ◻ hodokosi 'alms'. x - A/B̲- A-A x-x-x. Cf. hodokoru.

B   hodoku < fodo̲ku ?< *pon[o]*(2.3)* to̲ka-B̲ ('slightly undo'). 'loosen,
untie'. x - B-A-B x-B-x. Km x. Ib B. Nk puTuCun B, Sr hutuk- B < *fotok- <
*po[no] to̲ka-.

B   hoeru < foye[y]- < *podaCi-. 'bark; roar, cry'. B - B-B-B (B)-(B)-x.
Km (S,W) B. Ib B. Sd beeyum B; Nk buirun B; Sr qabir- B; cf. ibaeru.

-        hogasu < *fogasu ?< *fagasu < *panka-sa-. 'open up (a hole)'. x - x-x-x
x-A-x. Nk pugaasun A; Sr hugas- A.

?B   [hogau] < fokafu < *fwokafu < *pwoka-pa-. 'pray; felicitate'. x - x-x-x
x-x-x. ◻ hogai < fokafyi LLH- (K "LLL-" = B) - A̲-A̲-x x-x-x. Cf. hogu.

A   hogeru < *foge[y]- ?< *fagey- < *panka-Ci-. [Kyūshū] '(a hole) open up'.
x - x-x-x x-A-x. Nk pugiirun A; Sr hugir- A. Cf. hogasu, hagasu; hogureru.

?B   hogu < fwoku < *pwoka- 'pray'. x - B-x-x x-x-x. NS (Okada) A̲. NS (T+ 32)
fokyi HH = A̲. Cf. hosaku.

?B   hogureru < fogure[y]- ?< (*)fagure[y]- < *panka-ra-Ci-. 'come undone/
untied/loose; fray'. x - B-A-B x-x-x. Cf. hogeru, hogusu, hagasu, hokorobu.

?B   hogusu < fog°/u̲su ?< (*)fagasu < *panka-sa-. 'undo, untie, unsew, unravel,
disentangle'. x - B-A-A̲ x-x-x. Ib A, B. Kg A̲ is incongruent with hogureru Kg B.

B   hohoemu < fofo-wemu < *popo*2.3* bema-*A* (?< *boma-). 'smile'. (B) - B-A-A̲
x-x-x. ◻ hohoemi x - 3/4/0-A-A x-x-x.

-        hohomu, hohomau: *see* huhumu.

B´   hohuru = [hoburu] < (Mg) foburu < (Nr) fofuru < *po(n)pura-. 'slaughter'.
B´ - B-A-<u>A</u> x-x-x. Cf. hoomuru, hooru.

-        hokau: *see* [hogau].

B   hokorobu = hokorobiru < fokorobi[y]- < f<u>o</u>korob- (Nr consonant-stem) ?<
*fo<u>k</u>/_gurab- < *po(n)ku-ra-n[a]-pa- (?< *panka-···). 'come unsewn, come apart
at the seams'. B - B-A-B x-x-x. Matsue, Izumo <u>A</u>; Hattō, Hamada B. Ib B.
◍ hokorobi B - 3/4/0-A-B x-x-x. Matsue, Izumo <u>A</u>; Hattō, Hamada B.

?A/B   hokorou < fokorofu < *fokorafu < *pokora-pa-. 'be proud of oneself'.
x - x-x-x x-x-x.

A   hokoru < fokoru < *pokora- ?< *pwo?1.3a kora-?A ('grain harden [into
ear]') →) 'take pride in, boast of'. A - B-A-A x-A-x. Mr (Bm) A. Hamada A/B;
Hattō, Matsue, Izumo A. Ib A. Nk, Sr hukur- A [Lit., Archaic] 'rejoice'.
◍ hokori x - A/B-A-A x-x-x. Hamada A/B; Hattō. Matsue, Izumo A. Matsumoto
1974:124 derives this from hoku 'pray': ? < *p<u>o</u>ko-r-a- < *p<u>o</u>ka-ra- (*with the
second vowel assimilated to the first*). Cf. hokorasi*adj* ?.

?B   hoku > hogu 'pray': *see* hogu.

B   [homareru] = homerareru (regular passive x - B-B-B x-x-x) 'get honored':
*fomare[y]- < *poma-ra-Ci- (?< *pwo-ma-ra-Ci-). ◍ homare B - A/B-2-A x-x-x.
1700 Ōsaka HHL. Wakamatsu A (verb x).

A   homeku < fomeku < fo-myeku < *po?ala miCa-ka-aux B. 'rustle'.
A (Ck ?b-) - x-x-x x-x-x. Mochizuki has Ck "b-" but that is not evident in the
photo reproduction of the text.

B   homeru < fomey- < *poma-Ci- (?< * pwo?1.2 -ma-Ci-, Mochizuki 1971:25).
'praise, honor'. B - B-B-B x-B-B. NS (98a, 99b, 100b, 119b) B. Km (S) B.
Mr (Bm) B. Edo B. Ib B. Nk pumirun B; Sr humir- B. ◍ home x - B-2-B x-x-x.

-        [honamotu]: fonamotu xxLH (Kn Butsu-ka moto 56:3, Mochizuki 490a) 'lightly
hold, finger' is perhaps a variant/error for fono 'slightly' + motu 'hold'.

B   honogiku < fonogiku < *fono-gyiku < *po-no?2.3 -n- kika- A. 'dimly/faintly
hear'. LHHx [Ir] (?= *LLHL, ?= *L[L]-H|Hx *fono [ni] kiku) - x-x-x x-x-x.

B   honomekasu < fonomekasu < *fono-myekasu < *pono(2.3) miCa-ka-sa-bnd v.
'hint, insinuate'. x - B-A-<u>A</u> x-x-x. Ib B.

B   honomeku < fonomeku < *fono-myeku < *pono2.3 miCa-ka-bnd v. 'glimmer'.
x - B-A-x x-x-x. ◍ honomeki x - 3/4-x-x x-x-x. Cf. honoka.

B   [hookeru] < fofoke[y]-/bofoke[y]- < *(n)popo(-)ka-Ci-. 'dote' (= bokeru).
B - x-x-x x-x-x.

-        hooburu = hoomuru 'bury'.

B   hoomuru < fɔɔmuru (JP) < faumuru < fauburu (Mg) < ?fa*f*/ьuru < *pa(n)pura-.
'bury'. Cf. [haburu] = hahuru; hooru. B - B-A-A x-A[Lit.]-x.

A   hooru < fafuru < *papura- (?= pa(n)pura- 'bury'). 'throw, fling; neglect'.
A - A-A-A x-A-x. Ib horu A. Nk poorun A, Sr hoor- A 'spill, scatter'.
Cf. hoburu, hohuru, haburu.

A   horeru < fore[y]- < *pora-Ci-. 'love; (= boreru = bokeru) dote'.
A - A-A[U]/B[H]-A x-A-x. NS (Okada) A. Ib A. Nk puriirun A 'go mad, lose
one's senses'; Sr hurir- A 'love, get infatuated; go mad'.

A   horobiru < forobiy- < *poronpo-Ci- < ?*poronpa-Ci- (*see* horobosu). 'go to
ruin'. A - A/B-A-A x-A-x. Mr (Bm) A. Edo A(/B). Hattō, Hamada, Matsue, Izumo A.
Ib horobu A. Nk puruubin (puruub-) A, Sr hurub- A < *poronpa- (cf. horobosu).

A   horobosu < forobosu < *poronpo-sa- < ?*poronpa-sa- (*with the third vowel
assimilated to the fourth, cf. Nk, Sr*). 'ruin, destroy'. A - A/B-A-A x-A-x.
Hattō, Hamada, Matsue, Izumo A. Nk puruubasun A, Sr hurubas- A ?< *poronpa-sa-.

A   [horobu]: *see* horobiru (Ib, Nk, Sr).

?A   horu < foru < *pora- (? *pwora-, cf. ho-si*adj B*). 'desire'. x - x-x-x
x-x-x. NS (T+ 123) fori, (92) LH. Cf. horeru.

B   horu < foru < *pora- (?< *pwora-). 'watch' (= moru): see mamoru.

B   horu < foru < *pora-. 'dig; carve'. B - B-B-B B-B-B. Km (S) B. Edo B.
Ib B. Nk pun (pur-) B; Sr hur- B. [] hori B - B-2-B x-x-x.

?B   hosaku < fosaku < *posaka- (?= *posa-ka, *po-saka-, *po-sa-ka-). 'pray'.
x - x-x-x x-x-x. NS (T+ kun) kamu fosakyi fosakyi-kyi HL|HLL|HLL-L. Cf. hogu.

?B   hosaku < fosaku < *posa-ka-. 'protect against' (= husegu). x - x-x-x x-x-x.

?B   hosaku = hozaku ('speak, prate'). x - B-A-x x-x-x.

?B   hoseku < foseku < fosaku (the second vowel partially assimilated to the
first) < *posa-ka-. 'protect against' (= husegu). x - x-x-x x-x-x.

B   hoseru [dial.] < fose[y]- < *po-sa-Ci-. 'get dry' (= hiru). x - x-x-x
x-x-x. See hiru, hosu.

B   hosigaru < *fosi*adj B* (< posi < ...) -g[e] (< -n- key*1.1*) ara-*B*. 'think
it desirable, desire'. x - B-A-x x-x-x. Ib B. Attested 10th century.

?B   hosokeru < fosoke[y]- < *fosakey- (the second vowel assimilated to the
first) < *posa-ka-Ci-. 'protect against' (= hosoku = husegu). x - x-x-x x-x-x.

?B   hosoku < fosoku < *fosaku (the second vowel assimilated to the first)
< *posa-ka-. 'protect against' (= husegu). x - x-x-x x-x-x. NS (100b) B.

B   hosoru < fosoru < *fos*o*ru < *pos*o adj B* -ra-. 'get slender/thin/slim;
dwindle'. x - B-A-B x-x-x.

B   hosu < fosu < *p*o*-sa-. 'dry it'. B - B-B-B x-B-x. Km (W) B. Ib B. Nk
pusun B; Sr hus- B. Cf. hiru.

A+B   hos-suru < fossu(ru) < fori su(ru) < *por[a-C]i*?A* su(ru)*A* (< ...).
'desire'. f̄o[s]su - A/B-B-B x-x-x.

B   hoter-u < foter-u < *p*o*1.3b tera-*B* (< ...). 'feel hot, flush'. x - B-A-B
x-x-x. Izumo A; Hattō, Hamada, Matsue, Goka-mura B. Ib B. [] hoteri x - B-A-B.

?A   hotobasir-u < fodofasir-u/fotobasir-u < *poto*?sis* -n- pasira- *B*. 'leap,
spring; gush, spurt'. A - B-A-A x-x-x.

?A   hotobiru < fotobiy- < *potonp*o*-Ci- (< ?). 'swell/bloat (with water),
soak'. x - A/B-x-x x-x-x. Ib A.

?B   hotoboru < "fotoforu" (?= fotoboru) < *f*o* to*b*/*sis*oru ('fire blaze') <
*p*o*1.3a tonpo-ra-*B*. 'get heated, fervent, angry'. ?B - x-x-x x-x-x.
[] hotobori 'lingering heat/fervor'. x - 4/0-A-A x-x-x.

A   hotobosu < fotobosu < *potonp*o*-sa- (< ?). 'swell it up (with water); soak
it'. A - x-x-x x-x-x.

B   hotureru < foture[y]- < fature[y]- < *patu(-)ra-Ci- (<?). 'ravel, fray'
(vi.) (= hatureru, hogureru). x - B-A-*A* x-x-x. [] hoture x - B-A-B x-x-x.
Kg verb accent incongruent with that of derived noun (mistake?).

?B   hozaku < fosaku < *posaka- (?< *po[ka-Ci] saka- 'pray(er) rip'). 'prate,
speak; congratulate; curse'. x - B-A-x x-x-x.

B   hubuku < fufuku ?< *pu[ka-Ci]*B* (n[i]) puka-*B*. 'heavily blow/rain/snow'.
B - B-A-B x-x-x. Ib B. [] hubuki x - 1-2-B x-x-x. Hamada B; Hattō, Matsue,
Izumo A.

B   hueru < fu(y)e- < *fuye[y]- < *puda-Ci-. 'increase, mount up, swell;
proliferate'. x - B-B-B x-x-x. Km x. Ib B. Not attested before Mr? Cf. huyasu.

-        huhuku: see hubuku.

B   huhumu = hu[h]umu < fu[f]umu < *pupum- < *pukuma- (the second consonant
assimilated to the first). 'hold in mouth, comprise (= hukumu); (buds)
proliferate'. B - x-A-x x-x-x. Ongi (fuumu) B. Km (W) B. Azuma fufumar-
= fufumyer- < fufumyi ar- < *pupum[a-C]i ara-. Azuma fofomu, fofomaru.

B   hukameru < fukamey- < *puka*adj B* -ma-Ci-. 'make it deep'. x - B-A-x x-x-x.
K: Km B (attested?). Ib B.

B   hukasu ‹ fukasu: *(1)* ‹ *puka*ₛ-sa- 'puff, smoke', *(2)* 'steam';
(3) ‹ *puka*ₐₐⱼ ₚ -sa- 'let the night grow late' (three etyma). x - B-A-B x-x-x.
Ib ('steam') B. Nk pukaasun B, Sr hukaas- B 'boil (water)'. ◌ fukasi '(rice)
steamer, steaming' x - B-A-B x-x-x.

B   hukeru ‹ fukey- ‹ *puka*ₐₐⱼ ₚ -Ci- 'deepen; get late, grow old';
‹ *puka*ₛ-Ci- 'get steamed'. x - B-B-B x-B-x. Hoke-kyō tanji B. Edo B. Ib B.
Nk x; Sr [Lit.] hukir- B 'get late'.

B   huker-u ‹ fuker- ‹ *fukeyr- ‹ *puka*ₐₐⱼ ₚ -Ci-ra- (or perhaps *puka[-Ci]*ₚ
ira-ₐ). 'get addicted'. B - B-A-B x-x-x. Ib B.

A   huku ‹ fuku ‹ *puka-. 'wipe'. x - A-A-A B̲-A-x. Ib A. Nk x; Sr huk- A
(H 1967:462).

?A   huku ‹ fuku ‹ *puka-. 'cover, thatch'. A - A(/B"new")-A-B̲- x-A-x.
? NS (96b "maku" = huku) A. Hattō, Hamada, Matsue, Izumo A. Ib A. Nk puCun A;
Sr huk- A.

B   huku ‹ fuku ‹ ?*puku- ‹ *puka- *(the second vowel assimilated to the first,
as also in hukureru, hukumu, ...)*. 'blow; emit'. B - B-B-B̲ B-B-B.
NS (87a, 87b) B. NS (T+ 97, 98b) LH, (98a) H̲H̲. NS (T+ kun) fukyi uturu
LL(|)LLH̲. Km (W) B. Edo B. Ib B; Nk puCun B; Sr huk- B; Yn Kun B.

?A   huku ‹ fuku ‹ *puka-. 'brandish, wield' (= huru, huruu). x - x-x-x x-x-x.
NS (T+ kun) [sirifye-de ni] fuku 'direct [from behind]' HL.

B   hukumeru ‹ fukumey- ‹ *puku-ma-Ci-. 'include'. (B) - B-A-B x-x-x.

B   hukumu ‹ fukumu ‹ *puku-ma-. 'hold (in mouth); bear (in mind); comprise,
contain; imply'. B - B-A-B x-(B)-x. NS (Okada) HLH ?= *LLH = B. Km (S) B, (W)
fufum- B. Mr (Bm) B. Ib B. Nk kuKuumin (kuKum-) B, Sr kukunun (kukum-) B *(first
consonant assimilated to the second?)*. ◌ hukumi 'implication' x - B-A-B x-x-x.
Cf. huhumu, kukumu.

A   hukuramasu ‹ fukuramasu ‹ *puku-ra-ma-sa-. 'swell (expand, inflate) it'.
x - x-x-x x-x-x. Ib A.

A   hukuramu ‹ fukuramu ‹ *puku-ra-ma-. 'swell, bulge' (= hukureru). A - A-A-A
x-x-x. Ib A. ◌ hukurami x - A-A-A x-x-x.

A   hukureru ‹ fukure[y]- ‹ *puku-ra-Ci-. 'swell, bulge (= hukuramu); sulk'.
A - A-A-A A-A-A. Ib A. Nk puqKin (puqKir-) A; Sr huqkwir- A = huukee(ri)r- A;
Yn Kurirun A. ◌ hukure 'scab'. x - A-A-A x-x-x. Cf. hukura.

A   humu ‹ fumu ‹ *puma-. 'step/tread on'. A - A-A-A x-x-x. NS (T+ kun) fumyi
narasu 'smooth by stomping' HH LLL. Ongi A. Km (S,W) A. Mr (Bm) A. Edo A. Ib A.

B   hurasu ‹ furasu ‹ *pura-sa-. 'let/make it rain'. x - B-A-B x-x-x.

?B   hureru ‹ fure[y]- ‹ *pura-Ci-. 'touch; announce; mention'. B - A-B-A x-B-x
NS (Okada) B. NS (T+ 69 ··· koso ···) fure, (41) fure tatu HH LH. Km (W) B.
Edo B. Nk x; Sr hurir- B. ◌ hure x - A[H]/B[U]-A[H]/2[U]-B x-B-x. Nk purii B;
Sr huri B. ◌◌ o-hure 'official communication'. x - 2/3-1[H]/1:3[U]-B x-x-x.

?B   [huriru] ‹ furi[y]- ‹ *puru*ₐₐⱼ ₚ -Ci-. 'get old'. x - x-x-x x-x-x.
Km (W) B.

A   huru ‹ furu ‹ *puru- (cf. huruu). 'wave, shake; wield'. A - A-A-A x-A-x.
NS (T+ 101) furasu HLL, (100) furasu mo HLL|H. Km (W) A. Edo A. Ib A. Nk pun
(pur-) A; Sr A. ◌ huri x - A-A-A x-(A)-x. As postadnominal ('pretense') 2 in
Tōkyō and Hiroshima.

B   huru ‹ furu ‹ *pu-ra-. 'rain; fall down'. B - B-B-B B-B-B. Km (S,W) B. Edo
B. Ib B. Nk pun (pur-) B; Sr hur- B. Cf. huku; husu, huseru; hurasu; neᵇ/ₘuru.

?B   huru ‹ furu ‹ *pura-. 'touch' (= hureru). (B) - x-x-x x-x-x.

A   hurueru ‹ furufey- ‹ *puru-pa-Ci-. 'tremble, ... '. (A) - A-A-A x-A-x. Km
(S) A. Ib A. Nk puruuurun B; Sr hurir- A. ◌ hurue x - A-A-A x-A-x. Nk purii B̲;
Sr hurii A.

B   [hurumasu] < furumasu < *puru_{adj} _B -ma-sa-. 'make it old' (= hurusu).
x - x-x-x x-B-x. Sr hurumas- B.

A   hurumau < furumafu < *puru-ma-pa-. 'behave (expansively), carry on
activities, do; treat, entertain'. A - B-A-A x-x-x. [] hurumai A - 2/3/0-A-A
x-x-x.

B   hurumeku < furu-m[y]eku < *puru_{adj} _B miCa-ka-_{bad} _v. 'look oldish'.
x - B-x-x x-x-x.

B   [hurumu] < furumu < *puru_{adj} _B -ma-. 'get old'. x - x-x-x x-B-x.
Sr hurunun (hurum-) B.

?B   hurusu < furusu < *puru_{adj} _B -sa-. 'make it old'. x - x-x-x x-x-x.
Cf. [huriru].

A   huruu < furufu < *puru-pa-. 'shake/wield it; sift, sieve'. A - A-A-A
x-x-x. Ongi A. Edo A. Ib A. Nk quurun A < ?. [] hurui x - A-A-A x-x-x.

A   huruwasu < furufasu < *puru-pa-sa-. 'let/make it shake or tremble'.
x - A-A-A x-x-x. Ib A.

A   husagaru < fusagaru ?< futagaru < *puta-n[a]-ka-ra-. 'be obstructed, get
closed (clogged, stopped, choked) up; be fully occupied'. A - A-A-A x-x-x.
Ib A. Nk pusaagan A. Cf. hutagaru.

A   husagu < fusagu ?< futagu < *puta-n[a]-ka-. 'obstruct, close (clog, stop,
choke) it up; mope'. A - A-A-A x-A-x. Ongi A. Edo A. Ib A. Nk pusaazun B
'endure; cope'. Sr husag- A. Cf. hutagu. [] husagi x - A-A-A x-x-x. Nk pusaazii
B 'coping, tiding over'.

B   husanaru < fusanaru < *pusa_{g.s} -na-ra-. 'form a bunch, bunch out'.
B - x-x-x x-x-x.

B   [husaneru] < fusane[y]- < *pusa_{g.s} -na-Ci-. 'bunch them (together), make
into a bunch'. B - x-A-x x-x-x. Mr (Bm) B.

?A   husau < fusafu < *pusa(-)pa-. 'suit, be suitable'. x - B-x-x x-A-x.
Nk x; Sr husaar- A, husayun A (neg. husaran/husaan) < *fusaw- < *fusaf-.
Cf. husawasi_{adj} _{?A}.

?B   husegu < fuseku ("until Nanboku-chō" = 1336-92) < *pusa-Ci-ka- (or *pusa-
ka- *with the second vowel partially assimilated toward the height of the first
vowel*). 'protect/defend against, ward off'. B - B-A-A x-B-x. NS (123b) B.
Edo (-k-) B. Narada B. Ib B. Nk pusizun B; Sr husig- B. Old variants foseku,
fosoku, fosaku. Cf. hutagu. [] husegi x - B-A-A x-x-x.

B   huseru < fuse[y]- < *pu(-)sa-Ci-. 'lie/lay down' (originally vt.).
(B) - B-B-B x-x-x. Km (W) B. Edo B. Ib B. [] huse x - B-2[U]/1:3[H]-B x-x-x.

B   husu < fusu < *pu(-)sa-. 'lie down'. B - B-B-B x-x-x. NS (75c [14:118-M])
B. NS (T+ 75) fusu to LL(|)H. Km (W) B. Edo B. Ib B.

B   husuberu < fusube[y]- ?< kusubey- *(k- assimilated > p- before /u/?)*
(< ...). '(make it) smoke, fumigate'. B - x-x-x x-x-x.

B   husuboru < fusuboru ?< kusub^u/_oru *(k- assimilated > p- before /u/?)*
(< ...). 'get smoky/sooty'. B - x-x-x x-x-x.

A   hutagaru < futagaru < *puta_{g.1} -n[a]-ka-ra-. 'be lidded, tight, stopped
up' (= husagaru). A - A-x-x x-x-x.

A   hutageru < futagey- < *puta_{g.1} -n[a]-ka-Ci-. 'put a lid on, stop up'.
x - A-x-x x-x-x.

A   hutagu < futagu < *puta_{g.1} -n[a]-ka-. 'put a lid on, stop up'. x - A-x-x
x-x-x.

B   hutoru < futoru < *futworu < putwo_{adj} _B -ra-. 'get fat'. B - B-A-B
x-(B)-x. Ib B. Nk x; Sr buteer-, muteer- B (< ?).

B   hutukumu < futukumu < *putuku(-)ma-. 'get angry'. B x-x-x x-x-x.
Cf. futu(-)ku ni 'everything'. (NKD: "Also huzukumu. Accent history: Kt A.")

-       huumu: *see* huhumu = hu[h]umu.
B   huyasu < fuyasu < *puda-sa-. 'increase, multiply, propagate'. x - B-A-B
x-x-x. Km x. Earliest attestation Mr? Cf. hueru.

?A   ibaeru < ibaye[y]- ?< *iboye[y]- < *in[a]₇ₛ.₁ poda-Ci-ᵦ. 'neigh'.
A - B-A-x x-x-x.
B   ibaru < wibaru < *wi₁.ₛ (< Ch hhywey') -n- para-ᵦ. 'swagger'. x - B-A-B
x-B[new]-x. Hamada, Goka-mura A̱; Hattō, Matsue, Izumo B. Ib B. Nk qibaarun A̱;
Sr qibar- B (new: notice the glottal initial).
?B   ibukaru < iᶠ/ᵇukaru (Hn) < ifukaru < *ipukaₐdⱼ-ₛ₁ ᵦ -ra-. 'be curious; be
indignant'. B - B-A-A x-x-x. Km (W) B. (Zdb derives this from i[kyi]ₛ.₄ fuk-ᵦ
'blow breath'.)
B   ibuku < ?i-fuku < i[kyi]ₛ.₄ fukuᵦ < *ik[a-C]iᵦ puka-ᵦ. 'breathe'.
x - B-x-x x-x-x. NS (Okada) B. NS (T+ kun) i-fukyi LLL.
?A/B   iburu < *inpu-ra- (< ?). 'smolder, be smoky'. x - B-A-A x-x-x. Ib B.
◊ iburi x - B-x-x x-x-x.
B   [ibusemu] < *ibuseₐdⱼ ᵦ (< ?) -ma-. 'feel glum, be melancholy'. x - x-x-x
x-x-x. Attested in Man'yō-shū.
?A/B   ibusu < *inpu-sa- (< ?). 'smoke, fumigate'. x - B-A-A x-x-x.
◊ ibusi x - A/B-A-A x-x-x.
A   idaku < idaku/m[u]daku (Mg, cf. tamudaku) < *(m)iydaku < *m[uC]idaku =
mu[Ci]daku < *mu-Ci₁.₁ taka-₇ᵦ (or *i-ₚᵣₑ m[u-Ci]₁.₁ taka-₇ᵦ?). 'embrace'.
A - B-A-A x-x-x. NS (91b u[¨]taki̱) A. Km (S) A. ◊ idaki 'girth'. x - x-x-x
x-x-x. NS (110a [11:332-K]) ···LLL. Later daku x - A-A-A x-A-x; Wakamatsu Ḇ.
B   idasu < *inta-sa-. 'put out'. B - B-A-x B-B-x. Km (S,W) B. Edo B.
Nk qizaasun B; Sr qnzas- B. K: Mr-Edo HLL. Later dasu x - B-B-B x-B-x.
B   [ideru] < ide[y]- < *inta-Ci-. 'emerge, come/go out'; (vt.) 'express;
produce; read'. B - B-B-x B-B-x. NS (96a, 103b, 104a, 104b, 106b, 108b, 114a,
125b [14:283-K]) B. NS (T+ 16) ide te LHᴴ ?= LH(|)H, (102) ide HH; (114) [i]de
H; (97a) [i]de te L(|)L, (97b) ᴵ(|)L. K (S,W) B. Edo B. Nk qizirun B; Sr qnzir-
B; Yn tundirun A < *tobi ide- (< ... 'fly out', Thorpe 291). Later → deru
x - B-B-B x-x-x. ◊ ide x - x-x-x x-x-x.
?B   idomu < *intoma- (< ?). 'challenge; attack'. B - B-A-A x-x-x. Ib B.
◊ idomi x - B-x-x x-x-x.
?A   [ieru] < iye[y]- < *i-da-Ci- 'get shot'. x - x-x-x x-x-x. NS (T+ 9) iyu
HL. *See* iru.
?B   ieru < iye[y]- < *ida-Ci- (?< *i (= yo)ₐdⱼ ᵦ "good" -da-Ci-). 'heal, get
well' (vi.). B - B-B-A x-x-x. Ib B. Cf. iyasu.
-       igoku: *see* ugoku.
-       i-huku: *see* ibuku.
A   ikaru < *ika-ra-. 'get angry'. A - A("old")/B-A-A x-x-x.
NS (109b mey wo ikarasi te[y]) A. Mr (Bm) A. Edo A. Narada, Wakamatsu B.
Ib (*rare*) A. ◊ ikari A - A/B-A-A x-x-x. Edo A.
B   ikasu < *ika-sa-. 'give life to; keep alive, let live; make the best use
of'. x - B-A-B x-B-x. Ib B. Nk x; Sr qikas- B.
B+B   ikedoru < ikeydoru < *ika-Ci[-Ci]ᵦ -n- t(w)ora-ᵦ. 'capture alive'. x -
A/B-A[U]/B[H]-B x-x-x. Hattō A. ◊ ikedori x - 4/0-A[U]/B(1)[H]-B x-B-x. Hattō
(verb A), Matsue 3; Hamada, Izumo 4. Sr qicidui B < *ik(y)edori, *ikidori.
B   ikeru < ikey- < *ika-Ci-. 'give life to' (= ikasu). (B) - B-B-B x-B-x.
Nk x; Sr qicir- B.
B   ikidooru < ikyidoforu < *iki₅.₄ -n- topo-ra-ᵦ. 'get indignant/resentful'.
B - B-A-B x-x-x. ◊ ikidoori x - A/B-A-B x-x-x.

B   ikigomu < *ikyigomu < *iki₂.₄ -n- koma-ᵦ. 'be filled with enthusiasm or
spirit'. x - B-A-B x-x-x. 🛛 ikigomi x - 3/4/0-A-B x-x-x.

?B   ikiou < ikifofu < *ikyi-fofu < *iki₂.₄ [o]po-pa-ᵦ (or [o]p[o]-opo-)
or < *ikifafu < *iki₂.₄ -pa-pa-. 'show spirit; prosper, flourish' (cf. kiou).
x - x-x-x x-x-x. 🛛 ikioi 'force, vigor, impulse'. B - 3-3-B x-B-x. NS (112b)
B. Nk (h)iCiui B; Sr qicui B.

B   ikiru < iku "till Km" — but Heike has it also as consonant stem (Okumura
1981:270, cf.271) < *ika-. 'live'. (B) - B-B-B B-B-x. NS (95b, 124b) B.
Km (W) B. Edo B. Ib B. Nk hiCun B = hiCiCun B, Sr qicik- < *ik[i]-ik-.
🛛 iki 'fresh' x - B-B-A x-x-x; 'breath' LH - 1-B-B B-B-C. NS LH. Km (W) LH.
Nk qici C̲, Sr qiici B 'breath'.

B   ikizuku < ikyiduku < *iki₂.₄ -n- tuka-ₐ ('breath poke'). 'breathe; pant,
breathe with difficulty'. B - B-B-x x-x-x. Azuma ikuduku.

?B   [ikoeru] < ikofey- < *ikopa-Ci- (< ...). 'let one relax'. B - x-x-x
x-x-x. NS (97b, ?115a) B.

?B   ikou < ikofu < *ikopa- ?< *iki₂.₄ opa-ₐ 'pursue breath' or *iki₂.₄ opo-
[Ci-]ᵦ 'breath grow'; ?< *yokof- < *dokopa- (?< *doko₂.₁ -pa-, cf. Thorpe 320).
'relax'; (= [ikoeru]) 'let one relax'. B - B-A-A x-B-B. NS (115a) B. Nk yuhumin
(yuhum-) B = yuhurun B, Sr yukur- B restructured < *yukuw-; Yn dugun B. Thorpe
(319) reconstructs Ryūkyūan *yokow- and calls attention to the Kyūshū yoku(u).
Perhaps yokou < ikou, the first vowel assimilated to the second.
🛛 ikoi 'recreation'. x - 3/0-A-A x-B-x. Nk (x); Sr yukui B.

A   ikuu < ikufu < *i[-Ci]?ₐ kupa-ᵦ (?< *i[-Ci]?ₐ kapa-ₐ). 'shoot arrows,
engage in archery'. x - x-x-x x-x-x. Cf. ikuha (?3.5); iru (further etymology).

?B   imasimeru < ima-simey- < *ima-?ᵦ sima-Ci-ᵦₐᵈ ᵥ ('make shun'?). 'admonish'.
B - A/B-A-A x-x-x. Km (S) B. Mr (Bm) A. Nk qimaasimirun B. 🛛 imasime B -
4/0[NHK]-A-A x-B-x. Nk qimaasimii B; Sr qimasimi B.

B   imasu ?< *i-ₚᵣₑ masa-ₐ. 'deign to be/stay; deign to have; deign to go/
come'. B - B-A-x x-x-x. NS (76a) B; NS (T+ 32) imasu LLH.

?B   imu < *ima-. 'shun'. B - B-B-A x-x-x. NS (Okada) B. 🛛 imi x - B-2-x x-B-x.
Nk qimii B; Sr qimi B.

B´   imuku ?< *i-muke[y]- (< ?). 'pour a (ceremonial) cup (and place it)'.
B´ - x-x-x x-x-x.

B   [inabiru] < inaᵇ/ₘiy- < *ina₂.₄ -npᵃ/₀Ci- (?< -n[a]-pa-Ci-). 'refuse'.
B - B-A-x x-x-x. NS (93a) inafi HLL (odd).

B   [inabu] < *ina -n[a]-pa-. 'deny, decline, refuse'. B - B-A-x x-x-x. Edo
(inamu) B. Attested NS.

A   inaku: see ina-[na]ku.

B   inamu = inabu < *ina -n[a]-pa-. 'deny, decline, refuse'. Edo B. Attested
10th century.

A   ina-[na]ku < *inaₘₜₘ naka-ₐ. 'neigh'. A - A/B-A-A x-x-x. 🛛 inanaki x -
A/B-A-A x-x-x. Cf. ibaeru. Ibaraki ibanaku is a blend of ibaeru + [ina-]naku.

B   ineru < ine[y]- < i₁.₃ [wo] ne[y]-ₐ (< *na-Ci-). 'sleep' (> neru,
attested Nr as nu(-ru) / ne[y]-). B - B-B-x x-x-x. NS (T+ 5) wi ne-si H H-H.
Km (W) B.

B   inoru < *i-ₚᵣₑ nora-ₐ. 'pray'. B - B-A-B x-B[new]-x. Edo B. Ib B.
🛛 inori B - B-A[H]/2[U]-B x-x-x. Edo HHL.

A*   inu < ini[y]-/in- < *inᵐ/₀-Ci-/*ina-. 'depart, pass/go away'. A - A-A-A
x-(A)-x. Km (W) A. Edo A. Sr qnzi A (< *ini-te), suppletive gerund (and its
derivatives) in paradigm of qicun (qik-) < *ik- 'go'. Cf. sinu (same etymon?).
  *But perhaps A´ or irregular; see Ch. 4, §8.2, (3). Ib H̲1̲ (like oru 'be').

B   ioru < iforu < *ipo₂.₃ -ra-. 'lodge in a hut'. (B) - B-x-x x-x-x.
🛛 iori B - A-A-A x-x-x.

?B   iradatu < *ira*g.s* -n- tata-*ß* ('thorn stand'). 'get irritated/exasperated'.
x - B-A[U]/B[H]-B x-x-x. Ib B. 〇 iradati x - A-A-B x-x-x.

A   [iraeru] < irafey- < *ira-pa-Ci-. 'borrow'. x - x-x-x x-(A)-(A).
Nk iren A, Sr qirayun A (neg. qiraan) < *iraf- < *ira-pa-; Yn irun A (?<
*ira-; cf. iramirun A 'lend'), but Thorpe 290 takes this as from 'get' [eru].
Cf. irasu, [irau].

B   [iraeru] < irafey- < *ira(-)pa-Ci-. 'respond'. B - B-A-x x-B-x.
Nk qireerun B; Sr qireer- B.

A   irasu < *ira-sa-. 'lend'. A [Ir] - x-A-x x-A-(A). Nk qiraasun A; Sr
qiraas- A < *irawas- < *irafas- < *ira-pa-sa-; Yn iramirun A ?< *ira-me- <
*ira-ma-Ci-.

A   irau < irafu < irofu < *iro(-)pa-. 'touch, tamper with; concern/trouble
oneself with'. x - x-A-x x-x-x. Cf. hirau < firafu/firofu.

A   [irau] < irafu < *ira-pa-. 'borrow'. See Sr forms under [iraeru], [irasu].

A   ireru < ire[y]- < *ira-Ci-. 'put in'. A - A-A-A x-A-x. NS (91b [11:8-K],
101a, 103b, 106a) A. NS (T+ 111) fyikyi [i]re te 〄L H H. Edo A. Ib A.
Nk qinrun A; Sr qirir- A.

B   irodoru < irod(w)oru < *iro*g.s* -n- t(w)ora-*ß*. 'color'. B - B-A-B x-x-x.
Km (W) B. Mr (Bm) B. 〇 irodori x - 3/4/0-A-B x-B-x. Km (W) B. Mr (Bm) B.

?B   iroeru < irofe[y]- < *iro*g.s* -pa-Ci-. 'color it'. A [Ir, Hoke-kyō tanji]
- B-A-x x-x-x. 〇 iroe HHL (Zs) - x-x-x x-x-x.

A   irou = irau < irafu < irofu < *iro(-)pa-. 'touch, tamper with'. A (Kn
[Hō-chū 49:1]) - B-x-x x-x-x. Cf. izir-u, hirou.

?B   irou < irofu < *iro -pa-. 'become resplendent with color'.
A [Ir, Hoke-kyō tanji] - B-A-x x-x-x. K: "Hn A?"

B   irozuku < iroduku < *iro*g.s* -n- tuka-*ß*. 'take on color, get colored
(tinged)'. x - B-A-B x-x-x. Km (W) B. Ib B.

A   iru < wi- < *wi[y]- < *b*ᵐ*/*ₒ*-Ci-. 'be; sit'. A - A-A-A A-A-(A).
NS (Okada) A. NS (T+ 113, 123) wi te H(|)H; (35) wi - garasi 'wither it by
perching on it' 〄HLL ?= H(|)HLL. Km (W) A. Edo A. Hiroshima [Terakawa] B;
Narada, Hattō, Hamada, Matsue, Izumo, Goka-mura A; Ōsaka, Ise A. Nk yun A,
Sr ir- A 'sit'; Yn nturun ?< *witte wori womu (Thorpe 329). Cf. oru < *bo(-)ra-

?A   iru < i- = *iy[a]- < *i-*pre* da*ı.ı* "arrow". 'shoot'. A - B-A-A B-B-x.
NS (101b: i tofosu, 117b: matī i te) i < *īi "B" = A, (101b [143-K]) A.
Hiroshima B. Ōsaka, Ise A. Ib B. Nk qin B; Sr qir- B. (Modern Tk > ir-u.)
Cf. ieru < iye[y]- < *ida-Ci- 'get shot'; ya < *da 'arrow' 1.2. (No immediate
connection with yumi 'bow'.) Our etymology presumes that 'shoot' is derived
from 'arrow', but 'arrow' may be a truncation of the stem *iya-.

?A   iru < i- (< ?). 'cast metal'. A - B-A-A x-x-x. Ib (rare) B.

A   iru < wi- < *wi[y]- < *b*ᵐ*/*ₒ*-Ci-. 'lead' (?< 'sit'). A x-x-x x-x-x. NS (T+
113) wi-nikyemu HHL|H. Edo A. Cf. hikkiru, tuzuiru.

A   ir-u < *ira- (?= *yira- < *dira- [cf. Korean tul-]; initial *yi and i are
neutralized in attested Japanese). 'enter; need'. A - A-A-A A-A-A. NS (73b, 83a
[17:114-M], 97a [11:78-K, 11:80-K]. 101a, 115b) A. NS (T+ 9) iri wori to mo
HL|LH L-L, (96) iri masi HL LH, (57) iri LH. Km (S) A. Mr (Bm) A. Hiroshima
[Terakawa] B; Hattō, Hamada, Matsue, Izumo, Goka-mura A. Ib A. Nk qin A.

B   ir-u < *ira-. 'roast'. B - B-B-B x-B-x. Ib B. Nk qiriCun B, Sr qirik- B <
*iri- + ?. 〇 iri x - B-2-x x-x-x.

B   isabu < "izafu, isa*f*/*ₘ*u" (Mg) < *isanpa- < *isa-n[a]-pa-. 'scold'.
B - x-A-x x-x-x. Cf. isameru.

-         [isaeru] < "isafe[y]-" (= /isawe/) 'admonish': see isameru.

B   isakau < isakafu < *isa-ka-pa-. 'scold; argue'. B - B-A-x x-x-x.
〇 isakai x - A-A-B x-x-x.

?A/B   isameru < isabe[y]-, "isaᶠ/ₘe[y]-" < *isanpa-Ci- < *isa-n[a]-pa-Ci-.
'admonish'. B - A/B-A-A x-A-x. NS (Okada) B. Km (S) A. Mr (Bm) A. Edo A.
Nk qisaamin (qisaamir-) B; Sr qisamir- A < *isame- 'stimulate, spur on'.
Nr also asamey-? Cf. isabu. ▯ isame x - A/B-A-B x-x-x. Mr (Bm) A.

?A/B   isamu < *isama- (?< isa₈.₄ -ma-; ?< *i[ki₈.₄ su]samu₄). 'show spirit,
prance'. A - A/B-A-B x-x-x. Edo A. Narada, Wakamatsu B. Ib A. Kg B incongruent
with isameru A. ▯ isami x - A-A-x x-(A)-x. NS (101b) A. Sr qisami-tat- A.

A   isaru < izaru (?< *i[bo₈.₁ a]sa-ra-ᴮ). 'fish'. x - A/B-(A)-(A) x-(B)-x.
▯ isari x - A/B-A-(A) x-B-x. Km (W) A. Nk qizai A; Sr qiẓai B̲. On relating
earlier izar- and asar- see Miller 1980:198-9.

B   isatiru < isadi[y]- < isati- (Nr) < *isa₈.₄ (-)ti-₍₇. 'weep'. B - x-A-x
x-x-x. NS (101a, 104b, 128b, 130b) B. Km x. Zs Mg has (naki -) isad̄uru ···
(attributive) but Koji-ki has isatiru, differing both in the voicing of the
stop and in the conjugation type (cf. Ōno Tōru 1978:292), which seems to have
been originally upper monograde even though it apparently did not have a
monosyllabic stem (cf. arabiru).

B   isogu < iswogu < *iswoₐdⱼ-ₛ₁ ?ᴮ -n[a]-ka-. 'rush; vie to get ahead'. B -
B-A-B B-B-B. NS (96a) B, (Okada) HLH (?= *LLH = B). Edo B. Ib B. Nk qisuuzun B;
Sr qisug- B. ▯ isogi x - B-A-B x-B-x. Nk x; Sr qisuzi B.

B   isou < isofu < *iswoₐdⱼ-ₛ₁ ?ᴮ -pa-. 'vie to get ahead'. B [Ir] - x-x-x
x-x-x. Cf. isogu.

A   itadaku ?< inadaku/unadaku [dial.] < *una [i]daku (< ...). 'get crowned,
wear on head/top; humbly receive'. A - A-A-A x-x-x. Ib A. ▯ itadaki 'crown,
peak'. A - A-A-A x-x-x. Km (S) A.

B   itameru < itamey- < *itaₐdⱼ ᴮ -ma-Ci-. B - B-A-B x-x-x. 'hurt, afflict'
(vt.). Km (S) B. Edo B. Ib B. Nk hiCaamin (hiCaamir-) B.

B   itamu < *itaₐdⱼ ᴮ -ma-. 'get hurt/damaged/spoiled'. B - B-A-B x-B-x.
Km (S) B. Edo B. ▯ itami B - B-A-x x-x-x; Izumo A̲. Mr (Bm) HHL. Edo HHH. Ib B.
Nk hiCaamin (hiCaam-) B; Sr itam- B. Cf. itamasiₐdⱼ ᴮ, itawasiₐdⱼ ᴮ; NS also
itabu (NKD 2:114b) < *ita-n[a]-pa-.

A   itaru < *ita-ra-. 'reach, get/come to'. A - A/B-A-A x-(A)-x. Ongi-m A.
NS (Okada) A. Km (S,W) A. Mr (Bm) A. Edo A. Narada, Wakamatsu B̲. ▯ itari
'utmost limit'. x - A/B-A-A x-x-x; Km (S) A; Mr (Bm) HHL; Edo HHH. Ib A. Nk x;
Sr qitarir- A (< *itare- < *ita-ra-Ci-) 'reach (the heart/secret of an art)'.

A   itasu < *ita-sa-. 'bring (about), cause; do'. A - A/B-A-A x-x-x.
Km (S) A. Edo A(/B). Ib A.

?A/B   itawaru < itafaru < *itaₐdⱼ ᴮ -pa-ra. 'fall ill; go to trouble, work hard;
show compassion; care for, rear'. B - B-A-A x-x-x. Hattō, Hamada, Matsue,
Izumo B. Ib B. ▯ itawari x - 3/4/0-A-A x-x-x.

?B   itazuku < itatuku (till Mr - but Hn "-ᵗ/ᵈuku"?) < *itaₐdⱼ ᴮ (-n-) tuka-ᴮ
(or *itam[yi]ᴮ tukuᴮ < *itaₐdⱼ ᴮ -m[a-C]iᴮ tuka-ᴮ). 'fall ill; go to trouble,
work hard'. (B) - A/B-x-x x-x-x. Cf. itaᵗ/ᵈukafasiₐdⱼ ᴮ.

?B   itonamu < itonaᵇ/ₘu < *itwo₊₈.₉ nama-?ₐ (?nanpa-) ('array time').
'perform, conduct, carry on'. B - B-A-A x-x-x. ▯ itonami 'business'. x -
3/4/0-A-A x-B[Lit.]-x. Cf. itoma, [naᵇ/ₘeru].

?B   itou < itofu < *ito(-)pa- ?< *itaₐdⱼ ᴮ -pa- (the second vowel assimilated
to the labial consonant). 'hate, loathe; grudge, spare oneself'. B - B-A-A
x-B-x. Km (W) B. Mr (Bm) B. Edo B. Nk hituurun B, Sr qitur- B restructured <
*itow- < *itof-. ▯ itoi x - 3/4-x-x x-x-x.

B   ituku < *i₊₁.₃ₐ tuku-ᴮ. 'purify oneself for a sacred service; hold dear,
treasure'. B - B-x-x x-x-x. ▯ ituki x - A/B-A-x x-x-x; NS (83c [11:261-M])
LHL, NS (T+ 60) LHL. Cf. ituku-siₐdⱼ ᴮ.

A/B   itukusimu < *itukusi$_{adj\ B}$ (< ...) -ma-. 'love; pity'. x - B-A-A x-x-x.
Km x. Mr (Bm) A. ⬚ itukusimi x - 0/4-A-x x-x-x. Cf. utukusibiru.

B   ituwaru < itufar- < *utu-far- < *utu$_{?s.x}$ para-$_A$ ('hollow stretch', cf.
utuo, ? uso). 'falsify, lie; feign'. B - B-A-B x-x-x. Km (W) B / LLHH.
Mr (Bm) HHLL = B.Ib B. ⬚ ituwari x - 4/0-A-B x-x-x.

A   iu < ifu < *ipa-. 'say'. A - A-A-A A-A-x. NS (73a, 73b, 79b, 98a, 100a,
117a, 130b, 133a) A. NS (T+ 70) ifamey HHL, (58) LLL; (96) ifazu te LH**𝕰**; (6)
ifey do LH(|)H, (11) ifey do mo HL|H(|)L; ifyi-si L**𝕰**; ifyese koso (unusual
form) LHH(|)LL; (99) [i]fu koto so H LH(|)H. Km (S,W) A. Mr (Bm) A. Edo A.
Ib A. Nk yun A; Sr qyun A.

B   iwamu < ifamu < *ipama- (?= *ipa$_{s.sb}$ -ma-). 'throng, gather, assemble,
cluster together; be filled'. x - x-x-x x-x-x. NS (111b, 112a, 134b) B.

B   iwau < ifafu < *ipapa- (< ?). 'congratulate, celebrate'. B - B-A-B x-x-x.
Edo B. Ib B. ⬚ iwai x - 3-A[H]/2[U]-B x-B-x. NS (T+ kun) LHL (ōno, but some
texts have LLL). Nk (-)yuuee B; Sr yuuwee = qiwee B. Unger would derive this
verb from *ipa- 'say' but that stem is A.

A   [iyabiru] < wiyabiy- < *wiya$_{?s.s,?s.1}$ (< ...) -np^u/$_o$Ci- (?< -n[a]-pa-Ci-).
'show respect'. x - x-x-x x-x-x. NS (116a [14:88-K] A.

-           iyamau < wiyamafu: see uyamau.

?B   iyasu < *ida-sa-. 'cure, heal' (vt.). B - B-A-A̲ x-x-x. Ib B. Cf. ieru.

A   iyodatu < *iyo$_{s.1}$ n[i] tata-$_{B}$. '(hairs) bristle'. x - x-0-x x-x-x.
Km (S) A. Also yodatu.

?A/B   izanau < izanafu < *i^s/$_z$a$_{s.4}$ (< ?) -na-pa-. 'entice; invite'. B - B-A-A
x-x-x. Km (W) B. Mr (Bm) izanofu HHLL = B. ⬚ izanai B - A/B-A-x x-x-x.

?A/B   izaru < wizaru < *wi[y] (< b^u/$_o$Ci[-Ci]) n[i] sara-$_{?A}$. 'crawl (on one's
knees); sit'. x - A/B-A-B x-x-x. Km (W) A. ⬚ izari x - A-A[H]/B[U]-B x-x-x.

-           izaru 'fish': see isaru.

?B   izayou (from Km) < *isayofu < isaywofu < ?*i^s/$_z$a $_{s.4}$ (< ?) dwopa-$_{bsd\ v.}$
'waver, hesitate; drift'. x - B-A-x x-x-x. ⬚ izayoi x - A-A-A x-x-x.

?A   izimeru < idimey- < *inti-ma-Ci-. 'tease, torment'; (= izir-u) 'finger,
fumble with'. x - A-A-A x-x-x. Ib B̲. Register incongruent with izir-u.

?B   izir-u < idir-u < *inti-ra-. 'finger, fumble/tamper with, touch; tease;
importune'. x - B-A-B x-x-x. Register incongruent with izimeru.

B   kabau < kabafu < *kanpapa- (< ?). 'shelter, protect'. x - B-A-B x-x-x.
Ib A̲. Cf. tabau.

A   kabiru < kabi- < *kabiy- < *kanp^u/$_o$-Ci- 'mildew, mold'. A - A-A-A x-x-x.
⬚ kabi 'mold' (x) - A-A-A x-B̲-x; Nk haabui B, Sr kaabui B (?< ka[f]a- b^u/$_o$ri
'skin - ?'). Is the verb a late formation derived from the noun?

-          [kabu] 'smell/scent it': see kagu.

A   kabureru < kabure[y]- < *kanpura-Ci- (< ?). 'be touched; get infected'.
x - A-A-A x-x-x. Hamada, Izumo B̲; Hattō, Matsue A. Ib B̲.

B´   kaburu < *kanpu$_{s.s}$ -ra-. 'put/wear on one's head'. B´(/B) - B-A-B x-B-x.
Ib B´ (= L). Nk ^{k}/$_ʌ$anbin B. ⬚ kaburi 'head'. x - 1/3(/0[H])-A-B x-(x)-x. Edo
HHL. Sr kanmui B 'hat', kaabui B 'shaking head in denial'. Cf. kabuto, koomuru.

B   kabuseru, kabusu < kabuse[y]-/kabus- < *kanpu$_{s.s}$ -sa(-Ci)-. 'cover with'.
x - B-A-B x-B-x. Ib B. Nk hansin B, Sr kansir- B restructured < *kabuse-.

B   kadamu < katamu < *ka(n)ta-ma- (< ?). 'deceive'. B [Ir] - x-A-x x-x-x.
Cf. kadama$_{adj-si\ B}$.

B < B+B   kaerimiru < kafyeri myi- < kafyiri myi- < *kapi-r[a-C]i_B mi-/miCa-_B.
    'look back, take into consideration'. B - B-A-B x-x-x.

B < B+B   kaeriutu < kafyeri ut- < kafyiri ut- < *kapi-r[a-C]i_B (b)uta-_B. 'revenge'.
    B - x-x-x x-x-x.

A   kaeru < kafey- < *kapa-Ci-. 'change it'. A - A-A-A A-A-x.
    NS (111b) kafenu (= B) — mistake? Km (W) A. Edo A. Sd kheeyum A; Nk heerun A;
    Sr keeyun A. [] kae x - A-A-A x-(B)-x. Sr keeii B = keeruu B (both odd).

x   [kaeru] < kafey- < *kapa-Ci-. 'assent; allow'. This occurs only in the
    negative kafeyzu < kafeyni (*kapa-Ci n[a-C]i) su(ru) > gaenzu(ru) 'assent', but
    the earlier negative was forgotten by c. 1200 and gaenzezu was newly created.

?A   [kaeru] < kaye[y-] < *ka(-)da-Ci-. 'get apart' = kare[y]- < *ka(-)ra-Ci.
    x - x-x-x x-x-x.

B   kaer-u < kafyer-u < (Azuma) kafyir-u < *kapi-ra-. 'return' (vi.).
    B - B-A-B x-B-B. NS (93b) B. Km (S,W) B. Mr (Bm) B. Edo B. Ib B. Nk keerun B.
    [] kaeri x - B-A-B x-B-x. Nk keerii B.

B   kaesau < kafesafu < *kafyesafu < *kafyisafu < *kapi-sa-pa-. 'overturn; do
    repeatedly; look back, reconsider; question; refute; decline'. B - x-A-x x-x-x.

B   kaesu < kafyesu < *kafyisu (cf. kaer-u) < *kapi-sa-. 'return it'. B -
    B-A-B x-B-x. Km (W) B. Edo B. Ib B. Nk keesun B. [] kaesi x - B-A[H]/2-B x-B-x.
    Nk keesii B.

-          kagahuru: see koomuru.

A   kagamaru ?< *kan-kama-ra- < *kam[a]-kama-ra- or *kam[a-Ci] kama-ra-.
    'be bent/inclined'. A - A/B-A-A x-A-x. Nk x; Sr kagamar- A.

A   kagameru < kagamey- ?< *kan-kama-Ci- < *kam[a]-kama-Ci- or *kam[a-Ci]
    kama-Ci-. 'bend/incline it'. A - A/B-A-A x-x-x. Edo A. Ib A.

B   kagamiru < *kagamyiru < *kanka_B,_B mi-/miCa-_B. 'see it mirrored; consider
    with (follow) model/precedent; (gods) see clearly'. B - x-x-x x-x-x.
    Cf. kagami_9,_4.

A   kagamu ?< *kan-kama- < *kam[a]-kama- < *kam[a-Ci] kama-. 'stoop; crouch'.
    A - A-A-A x-(x)-x. Ib A. (Sr: see kagamaru.) Also kogomu, kugumu. Cf. ogamu.

?B=1.3|A   [kaganaberu] < kaganabey- < *ka_1,_9 -n- ka_1,_9 nanpa-Ci-_?A. 'count the
    days'. x - x-x-x x-x-x. NS (T+ 26) kaganafey te LH HH(|)F.

?B   kagaru < kakaru (Mg) (< ?). 'cross-stitch, darn'. B - A-A-B x-x-x.
    NS (119a) B. [] kagari x - A-x-x x-x-x.

A   kagayaku < kakayaku (JP) < kaka?_mim -da-ka-. 'shine, glisten'. A -
    A[H]/B-A-A x-x-x. Ongi-m ?A (HHLL). NS (Okada) B. [] kagayaki x - 3/4-A-A x-x-x.

?B   kagayou < kagaywofu < *kanka_B,_9 (< ...) dwopa-_bnd _v ('light/shadow
    waver'). 'twinkle'. x - x-x-x x-x-x.

?A/B   kager-u < *kageyr-u < *kanka-Ci_B,_9 (< ...) -ra-. 'get obscured/dark'.
    x - B-A-A x-x-x. Ib B. [] kageri x - B-x-x x-x-x.

B   kagir-u < kagyir-u ?< *ka_?1,_9 -n- kira-_B ('day cut'), or ?<
    *kan[a]_?*9,_9 kira-_B ('one cut'). 'limit'. B - B-A-B x-x-x. Mr (Bm) B. Edo B.
    Ib B. [] kagiri B - 1/3-A[H]/2[U]-B A-B-x. NS LHL. Km (W) LLL/LHL. Edo HHL.
    Nk kazirii B.

?B   [kagir-u] < kagyir-u ?< *kan[a]_9,_9 kira-_mim ('one glitter'), or ?< kager-u
    (< ...). 'glimmer'. x - x-x-x x-x-x. Cf kageroo.

A   kagu < *kanka- ?< *ka_1,_1 m[u]ka-_A (?< *npuka-), ?< *ka_1,_1 -n[a]-ka-,
    ?< kab- (labial assimilated to initial velar) < *kanpa-. A - A-A[U]/B[H]-A
    A-(A)-x. 'smell'. Hiroshima A/B. Ōsaka, Ise, Ib A. Sd khabyum A; Kikai hab-;
    Nakijin hamin A; Miyako, Yaeyama kab-. [] kagi x - A-x-x (A)-(A)-x. Sr kaẓa A
    ?< *kan[pa-]sa(-). Cf. Nk hazaa A 'stench' vs. habaa A 'aroma'.

B´   kakaeru ‹ kakafey- ‹ *kaka(-)pa-Ci-. 'hold in arms; keep, retain'.
B´ - A/B-B-B x-(B)-x. Narada, Hamada, Matsue, Izumo B; Hattō A. Ib B´ (= L).
Sr kakee-hwicee B 'interrelatedly' ?‹ *kakafe-fikake. ▯ kakae 'armful;
employee' x - A-B-B x-x-x. Cf. kakawaru, kakaru.

?B´‹B+A   kakageru ‹ kakagey- ?‹ *kaki - agey- ‹ *kak[a-C]i_ß anka-Ci-_A. 'put up,
hoist, display'. x - A/B-A[H]/B[U,O]-A x-x-x. Edo B´. (Yoshida's etymology
would amount to *kaka_ß-n[a]-ka-Ci-, cf. kakeru.)

A   kakanaku ‹ *ka-ka_ßia naka-_A. 'caw, crow, croak'. A - x-A-x x-x-x.

B   kakaru ‹ *kaka-ra-. 'hang, ... ' (vi.). B - B-A-B B-B-x. Km (S,W) B. Edo B.
Ib B. Nk kakarun/haarun B. ▯ kakari x - 1-1:3-B B-x-x; Hattō, Hamada, Matsue,
Izumo 3; Wakamatsu 1.

B   [kakaru] ‹ kak[u] aru ‹ *ka-ku_ß.ßb ara-_ß. 'be thus' → 'such ··· '.
x - B-B-x x-x-x. Edo HLL. Attested Man'yō-shū.

?A/B   kakawaru ‹ kakafaru ‹ *kaka(-)pa-ra-. 'be concerned (in)'. x - A/B-B-B
x-A-x. Mr (Bm) B´. Hattō, Hamada, Matsue, Izumo B. ▯ kakawari 'relation,
connection' x - A/B-B-B x-A-x. Cf. kakaeru, kakaru.

A   kakeru ‹ kakey- ‹ *kaka-Ci-. 'be lacking; get damaged, (partly) break'.
(A) - A-A-A x-A-x. Mr (Bm) A. Edo A. Ib kageru A. Nk haKiirun A 'be lacking' ≠
hagiirun A 'be absent (from one's seat)'; Sr kagir- A 'be lacking/absent' ≠
kakir- A 'get damaged/broken'. ▯ kake 'fragment' (= kake-ra) x - O-O-A x-A-x.

B   kakeru ‹ kakey- ‹ *kaka-Ci-. 'hang it, ... ; wager; run' (How many
etyma?). B - B-B-B x-B-B. NS (79c [14:337-M], 80a [14:338-M]) B. NS T+ 80)
kakey-si LL-H; (80) kakeymu yo LLH(|)H. Km (W) B. Edo B. Ib B. Nk haKirun B
'hang it; wager'. ▯ kake x - B-2-B x-B-x. Nk kaaKii B.

?A   kaker-u ‹ kakeyr-u ‹ *kakaCira- (‹ ?). 'soar'. A - B-B-B x-x-x.
NS (73c [11:261-M]) A. NS (T+60) HHL. Km (W) A. Edo B.

A   kakomu ‹ ka_k/_ßomu ‹ kakumu (the second vowel partially assimilated to the
first) ‹ *kaku-ma-. 'enclose, surround'. A - A-A-A x-x-x. Ongi A. Km (S) A.
Edo A. Ib B. ▯ kakomi x - A-A-A x-x-x.

?A/B   kakotu (‹ ?). 'offer a pretext for an excuse; grumble' (= kakotukeru).
A - B-A-A x-x-x.

A   kakou ‹ kakofu ‹ kakufu (the second vowel partially assimilated to the
first) ‹ *kaku-pa-. 'enclose; store, preserve'. A - A-A-A x-A-x. Nk _k/_ßaKuurun A
Ib A. ▯ kakoi 'fence, enclosure; storage' x - A-A-A x-A-x. Nk haKui A.

A   kaku ‹ *kaka-. 'lack it'. A - A-A[U]/B[H]-A x-A-x. Nk haCun A ('lack,
break, partly ruin'), hazun A. Not attested before Hn; cf. kakeru.

B   kaku ‹ *kaka-. 'write, draw; scratch; stroke'. B - B-B-B B-B-B. NS (T+ 41)
kakyi LH. Km (W) B. Mr (Bm) B. Edo B. Ib B. Nk haCun B.

B   kaku ‹ *kaka-. 'hang it (= kakeru); shoulder/carry; put it together'.
(B) - B-B-x x-B-x. NS (T+ 90) kakamey ["]to mo HHL(|)L(|)L; (90) kakanu HHL;
(78) kakyi te LH(|)ℓ. Edo B. Tk, Kt 'carry'; Nk haCun B = Sr kacun (kak-) B
'put it together'.

?B   kakumau ‹ kakumafu ‹ *kaku-ma-pa-. 'shelter, hide, give refuge to'.
x - B-A[H]/B[U]-A x-x-x. Ib B. Should be proto A if from kakum-; but cf.
kakureru, kakusu.

*B   *kakumeru 'hide (vi.)': see kakureru (Nakijin form).

-         kakumu: see kakomu.

B   [kakurasu] ‹ *kaku-ra-sa-. 'hide/conceal it' (= kakusu). x - x-x-x x-B-x.
Sr kwakkwas- B ‹ *kakuras-.

B´   kakureru ‹ kakure[y]-/kakur- ‹ *kaku-ra-(Ci-). 'hide' (vi.). B´ - B-B-B
x-B-x. NS (94b) B´, (122b) B, Km (W) B/B´. Edo B. Narada B. Kōchi A; Ib B´
(= L). Nk haKumin B (?‹ *kakume- ‹ *kaku-ma-Ci-) = haKur_ª/_ın B = haqKun B;
Sr kakkwir- B ‹ *kakure-.

B´   kakusu ‹ *kaku-sa-. 'hide/conceal it'. B´ - B-B-B x-B-x. Ongi B´.
NS (130a) B´, (Okada) B´/B. Km (W) B/B´, (S) B. Edo B. Ib B´ (= L).
Nk haKu(u)sun B; Sr kakus- B. [] kakusi x - B-A[H]/1:3[U]-B x-B-x.

-        kakuu ‹ kakufu: see kakou.

B   kamaeru ‹ kamafey- ‹ *kama(-)pa-Ci-. 'set up; assume (a posture)'.
B - B-A-B x-?B-x. Edo B. Ib B. Nk kameerun B; Sr kameer- B 'pick up; seek'.
[] kamae 'structure' x - 1/2/3-2-B x-A-x. Nk kamee B.

?A/B   kamakeru ‹ kamakey- ?‹ *kama(-)ka-Ci-. 'be struck with admiration, be
impressed'. x - A/B-A-x x-x-x.

B   kamau ‹ kamafu ‹ *kama-pa-. 'be concerned (with)'. B - B-A-B x-A-x. Ib A.
Nk kamuurun A, kamin A; Sr kamayun A (neg. kamaan), kamuyun A (neg. kamuran)
‹ *kamar-/kamor- restructured from *kamaf-.

B   kami-sabiru, [kansabiru] ‹ kam[u]sabiy- ‹ *kamu[-Ci]₂.₃ sanpᵘ/₂-Ci-bnd v
(‹ ...). 'act godly'. x - B-x-x x-x-x.

?A/B   kamosu ?‹ *kamasu (the second vowel assimilated to the preceding labial)
‹ *kama-sa-. 'brew'. x - B-A-A x-x-x.

?A   kamu ‹ *kama- 'blow (nose)'. A - A-A-B x-(B)-x. Ib A. (The Mg high dot is
missing on the third syllable of fana kamu HH HL in Mochizuki's index.)

B   kamu ‹ *kama-. 'chew, bite, eat; (= kamosu) brew'. B - B-B-B B-B-B.
NS (T+ 15) kamyi-si HL(|)L, (39) kamyeru LLL, (33) kamyi-kyemu LL-L(|)H,
(33) kamyi-kyemey ka mo LL-L-L(|)L(|)H; (kun) kamu LH. Mr (Bm) B. Edo B. Ib B.

?B   kanaderu ‹ kanade[y]- ‹ ?*ka[ki] nade[y]- ‹ *kak[a-C]iₐ nanta-Ci-ₐ. 'dance
moving one's hands; grasp (a whip etc.), play (a harp etc.)'. B - B-A-A x-x-x.
Narada A. Ib B.

?B   kanaeru ‹ kanafey- ‹ *kana₇₂.₃ "one" -pa-Ci-. 'make it suitable/possible;
grant (a request)'. (B) - B-A-A x-x-x. Hattō, Hamada, Matsue, Izumo B. Ib B.

A   kanasimu ‹ (Hn) kanasiᵇ/ₘu ‹ (Nr) kanasibiy- ‹ *kana-siₐdⱼ ₐ -npᵘ/₂Ci-.
'grieve'. A - B-A-A x-x-x. NS (104a, 109b) A. Km (S) A. Mr (Bm) A. Akita,
Hattō, Matsue, Izumo, Ōita A; Hamada B. Ib B. [] kanasimi x - 3/4/0-A-x x-x-x.
Km (W) A. Hattō, Hamada, Matsue, Izumo A.

?B   kanau ‹ kanafu ‹ *kana₇₂.₃ "one" -pa-. 'be a match (for); be suitable
(for); be possible (for), be realized'. B - B-A-A x-B-x. Mr (Bm) B. Edo B.
Hattō, Hamada, Matsue, Izumo B. Ib B. Nk kanaawan B = kanaarun B = kaneen B.

B   kaneru ‹ kane[y]- ‹ *kana₇₂.₃ "one" -Ci-. 'combine, unite; cannot'.
B - B-B-A x-B-x. NS (82c [17:111-M]) A. NS (T+ 96) kane te HⁱF(|)F. Km (W) B,
(Okada) A. Mr (Bm) B. Edo B but A as auxiliary (Okumura 1981:220, 271).
Ib (rare) B. Nk kanirun B. Yoshida 1979:47 claims this verb was earlier a
consonant stem; if so, kanu ‹ *kana-. Cf. kateru.

B   kangaeru ‹ "kam[u]gafe[y]-" ?‹ *kanka₂.₅ -pa-Ci- (cf. kagami₃.₄);
?‹ *kan (‹ Ch kam' 'reckon') kapa-Ci-ₐ. 'think'. B - B-A-B B-B-B. Mr (Bm) B.
Nk kangeerun LLHHHL (?= A; we expect LLLLHL for B). Ib B. [] kangae x - 3-4-B
x-B-x. NS (107b, 112b, 116b) B. Nk kangee B.

B   kanguru ‹ kan (‹ Ch kham') kuru-ₐ (?‹ *kura-) ('reel one's intuitions').
'surmise hidden motives, have one's suspicions'. x - B-B[U]-x x-x-x.
[] kanguri x - A/B-x-x x-x-x. No examples before Edo?

?A/B   kanzuku ‹ *kanduku ‹ *kan (‹ Ch kam' 'reckon' or 'kam 'feeling') tuka-ₐ.
'come to a suspicion/realization'. x - B-A-A x-x-x.

A   kaoru ‹ "kaforu/kaboru" (Mg) = kaworu ‹ *ka₁.₁ bora-ₐ ('vapor/smoke/odor
bend [= swirl up]'). 'be fragrant, emit odor'. A - A-A-A x-x-x. Ongi A. Ib A.
[] kaori A - A-A-A x-x-x. Km x. Mr (Bm) A. Goka-mura 1 (verb x).

?B   *karabu ‹ *kara-n[a]-pa-. 'entwine' (= karameru). See utukarabu =
uturakau.

B   karageru < karage[y]- ?< kara[myi] agey- < *kara(-)m[a-C]i*ₛ* anka-Ci-*ₐ*.
'tie/tuck up'. B - B-A-B x-B-x. Ib B. Nk hayaagin B; Sr kanagir- B.

?A/B   karakau < karakafu < karakapa- (< ?). 'tease, make fun of'. x - B-A-A
x-x-x.

?B   karamaru < *kara(-)ma-ra-. 'wind/twist itself around, get entangled'.
x - B-A-A x-B?-x. Ib B.

B   karameru < karame[y]- < *kara-ma-Ci-. 'entwine, entangle'. B - B-A-A
x-B-x. NS (Okada) B. Edo B. Nk karaamin B; Sr karamir- B. Cf. utukarabu.

?B   karamu < *kara-ma-. 'tangle; get entwined/entangled'. B - B-A-A x-(B)-x.
Ib B. Nk haraamaCun B, Sr karamacun B < *kara[?mi]-mak-.

A   karasu < *kara-sa-. 'blight, kill, make/let wither'. x - A-A-A x-A-x.
NS (T+ 35) wi - garasi 'make it wither by perching on it' *FHLL ?= H(|)HLL.
Ib A. Nk haraasun A. Cf. kareru; korosu.

A   kareru < kare[y]- < *kara-Ci-. 'wither; get dry/parched, get hoarse'.
A - A-A-A x-A-A. Km (W) A. Edo A. Ib A. Nk hariirun A.

A   [kareru] < kare[y]- < *kara-Ci-. 'get far apart (distant); cease'.
x - x-A-x x-x-x. Km (W) A. Cf. wakareru, akareru; [kaeru] < kaye[y]-.

A   kariru (from mid-Edo) < karu < *ka-ra-. 'borrow'. A - A-A-A x-(A)-x.

A   karomeru < karome[y]- < *karumey- (the second vowel partially assimilated
to the first) < *karu*ₐdⱼ A* -ma-Ci-. 'make it light (in weight); slight,
treat lightly'. A - x-x-x x-x-x.

A   karomu < *karumu (the second vowel partially assimilated to the first) <
*karu*ₐdⱼ A* -ma-. 'get lightened, get light (in weight)'. A - x-x-x x-x-x. Ib A.

A   karu < *kara-. 'mow; cut'. A - A-A-A x-A-A. Km (W) A. Nk han A.

A   karu < *ka-ra-. 'borrow' (= kariru). A - A-A-A x-A-x. Km (W) A. Nk kan B
(= qiren A; Yn irun A, cf. irau). [] kari (x) - A-A-A x-A-x. Nk x; Sr kai A.
Cf. kasu.

?B   karu < *kara-. 'hunt; drive'. B - A/B-A-A x-x-x. Ongi B. Km (S) A, (W)
B/?A. Mr (Bm) A. Edo B. Hiroshima B. Ōsaka A/B; Ise B; Ib A. [] kari LH (like
inf.) - 1-A[H]/2[U]-A x-x-x. Izumo 2; Hamada 1/0; Hattō, Matsue, Goka-mura 1.

?A   kasabaru < *kasa*₇₂.₂b* -n[a]-pa-ra-. 'be bulky; be piled up' (= kasanaru).
x - B̲-A-A x-B̲-x. Matsue, Izumo A; Hamada A/B̲; Hattō B. Ib A. Nk kasaaban A;
Sr kasabar- B̲ (the register is incongruent with kasabir- A).

?A   kasaberu < *kasabey- < *kasa*₇₂.₂b* -n[a]-pa-Ci-. 'make it bulky, pile it
up' (= kasaneru). x - x-x-x x-A-x. Nk kasaabin A; Sr kasabir- A.

?A   kasamu < *kasa*₇₂.₂b* -ma-. 'increase, mount in volume' (vi.). x - A/B̲-A-A
x-B̲-x. Mr (Bm) A. Nk kasaamin B̲.

A   kasanaru < *kasa*₇₂.₂b* -na-ra-. 'grow in bulk'. A - A-A-A x-x-x. Ib A.

A   kasaneru < kasane[y]- < *kasa*₇₂.₂b* -na-Ci-. 'pile it up; layer it'.
A - A-A-A x-x-x. Km (S) A. Mr (Bm) kasanete HHLL = A. Edo A. Ib A.
[] kasane 'pile, layer' A - A-A-x x-x-x.

B   kasegu < *kase-n[a]-ka- (< ?). 'work, earn (by work)'. x - B-A-B x-x-x.
Ib B. [] kasegi x - 1/3-A-B x-x-x.

?A/B   kasigeru < kasige[y]- < *kasinka-Ci- (< ?). 'tilt it'. x - B-A-A x-x-x.
Not attested before Edo. Cf. katamukeru; Sr şiikur- B 'totter, ... '.

B   kasigu < kasiku ("till Mr") < *kasika-. 'cook'. B - B-A-x x-x-x.
NS (98a, 98b, 99b) B. Ib B.

B   kasikomaru < kasikwomaru < *kasikwo*ₐdⱼ B* -ma-ra-. 'be in awe, humble
oneself'. B - B-A-B x-x-x. NS (103a, 108a) B. Ib B.

B   kasikomu < kasikwomu < *kasikwo*ₐdⱼ B* -ma-. 'be in awe, fear'. x - x-x-x
x-x-x. NS (76c [14:135-M]) B. NS (T+ 102) kasikwomyi te LLHH(|)*F*. Km (W) B.

B   kasizuku ‹ kasiduku ?‹ *kasi[kwo] n[i] tuka-ᵦ. ‘look after, guard and
nurture; wait in attendance upon’. x - B-A-x x-x-x. Mr (Bm) HHLL = B.
◊ kasizuki LHHx - x-x-x x-x-x. Mg kasiduki seraru.

B   [kasobu]/kasou ‹ kaswobu ‹ *kaswo-n[a]-pa- (‹ ?). ‘steal; ? graze, skim
(past)’; cf. kasumu, kasumeru. B - x-x-x x-x-x. Kn Mg “kazofu” (?= kasobu) LLH.

A   kasu ‹ *ka-sa-. ‘lend’. A - A-A-A (A)-(A)-x. Km (W) A. Ib A. Sd kharaasyum
A; Nk karaasun A = qiraasun A; Sr karas- A. ◊ kasi x - A-A-A x-x-x. Cf. kariru.

A   kasu ‹ *kasa-. ‘soak in water; polish rice (by rinsing)’. A - B̲-B̲-x x-x-x.
Tk/Kt accents must be artificial; the verb is obsolete. Cf. kasi-yone 4.2.

B   kasudoru ?‹ *kasuₛ.₄ -n- t(w)ora-ᵦ. ‘purify (= take away the dregs)’.
LLHL [Ir] - x-x-x x-x-x. Attested in any other texts?

?A/B   kasumeru ‹ kasumey- ‹ *kasuma-Ci- (‹ ...). ‘steal (= kasumu); graze, skim
(past)’. A - A/B-A-B x-x-x. NS (Okada) A. Narada B. Ib (rare) A. Cf. kasobu.

?A/B   kasumu ‹ ?kasuᶠ/ᵤu ‹ *kasu-(n[a]-)pa-. ‘steal; ?graze, skim (past)’.
x - A/B-x-x x-x-x. NS (111a) A, or is that kasumeru? Cf. kaswo- keyₐdⱼ ?ₐ =
kasu-kaₐdⱼ-ᵣ.

A   kasumu ‹ *kasu-ma-. ‘be hazy; get misty/dim’. x - A-A-A/B x-x-x.
Edo A. Goka-mura A/B. Ib H. ◊ kasumi A - A-A-A/B x-x-x. Sapporo 2; Narada B̲.
Cf. kaswo-keyₐdⱼ A = kasu-kaₐdⱼ-ᵣ.

?A/B   kasuru ?‹ *kasu-ra-, ?‹ *ka-sura-. ‘graze’. x - B-A-x x-x-x. Cf. kasumu,
kasumeru, kosuru, suru, kasu-ka, kasobu.

B   kataᵇ/ᵤukeru ‹ *kataᵇ/ᵤukey- ‹ *kataₛ.₃ -muka-Ci-ₐ (?‹ *npuka-Ci-ₐ).
‘slant/tilt it’. x - B-A-B x-B-x. Ib (-b-) B. Nk haTanKin B.

B   kataᵇ/ᵤuku ‹ *kataₛ.₃ muka-ₐ (?‹ *npuka-ₐ). ‘be inclined, slant, tilt’.
x - B-A-B x-B-x. Km (S) B. Ib (-b-) B. Nk haTanCun B. ◊ katamuki x - 3/4/0-A-B
x-B-x.

A   katadoru ‹ *kataₛ.₂ᵦ -n- t(w)ora-ᵦ. ‘model after, copy, assume the shape
of’. A - B-A-A x-x-x.

A   katamaru ‹ *kataₐdⱼ A -ma-ra-. ‘get hard; bunch together’. x - A-A-A x-A-x.
Km (W) A. Ib A. Nk haTaaman A. ◊ katamari x - A-A-A x-A-x. Nk haTaamai A.

A   katameru ‹ katamey- ‹ *kataₐdⱼ A -ma-Ci-. ‘make it hard; lump/mass them
together’. A - A-A-A x-A-x. NS (108b) A. Edo A. Ib A. Nk haTaamin A.
◊ katame x - A-A-A x-A-x. Nk x; Sr katami A ‘oath of love’.

B   ?[katameru] ‘shoulder’: see katugu (Nk, Sr, Yaeyama).

-        katamu: see kadamu; see katameru.

-        katamukeru: see katabukeru.

-        katamuku: see katabuku.

A   katanaru ‹ *kataₐdⱼ A -na-ra-. ‘summarize’ (= kataneru). A - x-x-x x-x-x.

A   katanasu ‹ *kataₐdⱼ A -na-sa-. ‘summarize’ (= kataneru). A - x-x-x x-x-x.
Only Mg attests this verb. ◊ katanasi (an old court ritual) A - x-x-x x-x-x.

A   kataneru ‹ katane[y- ‹ *kataₐdⱼ A -na-Ci-. ‘summarize; lump/bunch them
together’ (= katanasu). x - x-x-x x-x-x.

B   katanugu ‹ kata - nuku ‹ *kataₛ.₄ nuka-ᵦ. ‘bare a shoulder’. B - B-(B)-x
x-x-x. Kt [U] “.kata̅‿nugu” ?= .kata̅ | .nugu̅.

A   katarau ‹ katarafu ‹ *kata(-)ra-pa-. ‘talk together’. A - B-A-A x-A-x.
Nk katareerun A. ◊ katarai x - 3/0-A-A x-A-x. Nk kataaree A.

A   kataru ‹ *kata(-)ra-. ‘tell’. A - A-A-A x-A-x. NS (119b) A. Km (S) A.
Edo A. Narada B̲. Ib A. Nk kataarun A. ◊ katari x - A-A-A x-x-x. NS (78b) A.
NS (T+ kun) HLH̅ (? mistake for HHH). It is often assumed that *kata is a
variant of kotoₛ.₃ ‘words’ but the registers are incongruent; perhaps
kataₛ.₂ᵦ ‘shape, form’ would be better. The meaning ‘deceive, swindle,
defraud’ dates from the Edo period; katari ‘fraud’ 1700 Ōsaka HLL.

A   katasu ‹ *kata*adj* A -sa-. ‘forge, temper’. A [Ir] - x-x-x x-x-x.
Cf. kitaeru, kitameru.

?B   katatu ?‹ *kata*2.3* -ta- (“single out”). ‘honor, favor’. x - x-x-x x-x-x.

B   katayoru ‹ *kata*2.3* d̲o̲-ra-*A*. ‘lean; be partial’. x - B-A-B x-x-x. Ib B.
◊ katayori x - 3/4/0-A-B x-x-x.

B   katazukeru ‹ katadukey- ‹ *kata*2.3* n[i] tuka-Ci-*B*. ‘shape/tidy up; put in
order, settle, deal with’; earlier also ‘get it to stick to one side’. B -
B-A-B x-B-x. Ib B. Nk haTaaziKirun B. ◊ katazuke x - A[H]/B[NKD]-3[H]-B x-x-x.

B   katazuku ‹ kataduku ‹ *kata*2.3* n[i] tuka-*B*. ‘be (put) in order; be dealt
with, settled’; earlier also ‘stick to one side’. B - B-A-B x-x-x. Ib B.

B   kateru ‹ kate[y]- ‹ *kata*2.3* -Ci- (?‘make [into] one’). ‘join, unite; mix;
blend, join; add (in)’ (vt.). x - B-A-x x-(B)-x. NS (T+ 19) katemu H? ?= HL|H.
Nk x; Sr katir- B ‘use as a side dish (to go with rice)’. Cf. ···-gatera ‹
-gateri ‘incidental to ···’, ···-gate ni ‘mixed with ···’.

B   kateru ‹ kate[y]- ‹ *kata-Ci-. (‘get vanquished’ =) ‘can be done’ (after
verb infinitive). (B) - x-x-x x-x-x. Cf. katu; kaneru.

B   katu ‹ *kata-. ‘win’. B - B-B-B B-B-B. Edo B. Ib B. Nk kaCun B.
◊ kati B - B-A[H]/2[U]-B x-B-x.

B   katu ‹ *kata-. ‘pound/hull (rice)’ (= tuku). (B) - x-x-x x-x-x.
Cf. katisine, katigata.

-        katugeru: see kazukeru.

-        katugu: see kazuku.

B   katugu ‹ (*)katagu ‹ *kata*2.4* -n[a]-ka-. ‘shoulder, carry it on one’s
shoulder’. x - B-A-B x-(B)-x. NS (Okada) B. Ib katagu B. Nk haTaamin B; Sr
katamir- B; Yaeyama katami(ru)n (?‹ *katame-r- ‹ *katamey- ‹ *kata*2.4* -ma-Ci-).

A   kau ‹ kafu ‹ *kapa-. ‘buy, exchange; cross, intersect’. A - A-A-A B̲-A-A.
Km (W) A(/B). Ib A. Nase B̲; Sd khoo(r)yum B̲; Nk hoorun A (HHHL); Sr koor- A.
◊ kai ‘valley’ A - 1-x-x x-x-x.

?B   kau ‹ kafu ‹ *kapa-. ‘raise (animals)’. B - B-B-A̲ x-(B)-x. NS (T+ 115)
LH. Km (W) B. Edo B. Ib B. Sr karayun B (neg. karaan) ‹ *karaf- (cf. dialect
karau ‘bear on one’s back’).

-        kau ‘assent’: see [kaeru].

?B   kawakasu ‹ *kaba-ka-sa-. ‘make it dry’. x - B-A-A̲ x-(B)-x. Ib B.

?B   *kawakeru ‘get/make dry’: see kawaku, [kawarageru].

?B   kawaku ‹ *kaba-ka-. ‘get dry’. B - B-A-A̲ x-(B)-x. Hyōgo A, Suzu, Kōchi B.
Ib B. Nk haaCun (‹ *kawak-) = haaraCun (?‹ *kawarak- ‹ *kaba-ra-ka-); ‘get/be
thirsty’ Nk haaKin B = Sr kaakir- B ‹ kawake-. Cf. kawaragu, [kawarageru],
kareru. ◊ kawaki x - B-A-A x-x-x.

?B   [kawaragasu] ‹ kawarakasu ‹ *kaba-ra-ka-sa-. ‘make it dry’.
Nk haaraKa(a)sun A (‹ *kawarakas- ‹ *kaba-ra-ka-sa-) = haaraKirun A.

?B   [kawarageru] ‹ kawarake- ‹ *kawarakey- ‹ *kaba-ra-ka-Ci-. ‘make it dry’
(= kawakasu, kawarakasu). x - B-x-x x-x-x. Nk haaraKirun A.

?B   kawaragu (JP) ‹ kawaraku ‹ *kaba-ra-ka-. ‘get dry’ (= kawaku). x - B-x-x
B-A̲-A̲. Sd khoorakyun B; Nk haaraCun A̲; Sr kaarak- A̲; Yn karagun A̲.

A   kawaru ‹ kafaru ‹ *kapa-ra-. ‘change; be substituted (for)’ (vi.).
A - A-A-A B̲-A-A. NS (126b) B̲. Km (W) A. Mr (Bm) A. Edo A. Ib A. Sd seems not
to be a mistake; Nase B̲ (H 1967:388b) — cf. kau ‘buy, ... ’. Nk kawaarun A.
Kg listed as B̲ for kawari-au and kawasu. ◊ kawari x - A-A-A x-A-x.

?A   kawasu ‹ kafasu ‹ *kapa-sa-. ‘exchange’. x - A-A-B̲ x-x-x. Nk kawaasun A.
Kg incongruent with kawaru.

?A   kayoru ‹ *ka*2.1* - d̲o̲ra-*A* (‘yon approach’ — cf. ka-yori kaku-yor- ‘run
thither and hither = hither and thither’). ‘approach’. x - x-x-x x-x-x.

A   kayou < kaywofu / (Azuma) kayufu < *ka(-)dwopa-. 'go regularly, commute; go back and forth'. A - A-A-A x-?A[Lit.]-x. Ib A. Nk ᵏ/ₕayuurun A. NS (95a, 114a, 121a) A. Edo A. 〖 kayoi x - A-A-A x-<u>B</u>-x. 1700 Ōsaka HHL. Nk x.

A   kayowasu < kaywofasu < *ka(-)dwopa-sa-. 'send, convey'. A - A-A-x x-x-x.

A   kazaru < *kansa(-)ra-. 'adorn'. A - A-A-A x-A-x. NS (96b[11:76-K) A. Km (S) A. Mr (Bm) A. Edo A. Akita <u>B</u>. Ib A. Nk kazaarun A. 〖 kazari A - A-A-A x-A-x. Akita <u>B</u>; Goka-mura 1. Nk kazai A; Sr kaẕai A.

?A   kazasu < kam[iₛ.ₛ ni] sasu (< *sasa-ₑ). 'put into the hair as adornment; adorn'. x - A-A-A x-x-x. Km (W) A. Ought to be B, but perhaps influenced by kazaru. 〖 kazasi B - A-A-A x-x-x.

?A   kazasu < kam[yiₛ.₄ ni] sasu (< sasa-ₑ). 'hold above/over, shelter with'. x - A-A-A x-x-x. Mr (Bm) B (Sakurai 1977:855a). Ought to be B.

A   kazikamu ?< *kasikamu < *kasi(-)ka-ma-. 'get numb/weak, wither'. x - A-A-A x-x-x.

?A   kazikeru < kasikeru < kasikey- < *kasi(-)ka-Ci-. 'get numb/weak' (= kazikamu). A -<u>B</u>-A-x x-x-x.

B   kazir-u < *kansira- ?< *kam[i]-sira- < *kam[a-C]iₑ sira-ₐ (or sura-ₑ). 'gnaw'. x - B-A-B x-(B)-x. Ib B. Sr kakazir- B (with partial reduplication).

B   kazoeru < kazwofey- < *kan[a]ₛₛ.ₛ swopa-Ci-ₑ. 'count'. B - B-A-B x-B-x. NS (115a) B. Ib B. Nk x. Yoshida derives this from kaz[u]ₛ.₄ + suffix; Ōno from kazuₛ.₄ apa-ₑ. There are examples of kazufey- in Genji and later.

-      [kazuer-u] ' ? ': Mochizuki 148a kazuferu LHHL but the space in Myōgi-shō (Kn Hō-ka 111:8) indicates two words: kazu fer-u LH | HL ?'shrink in number'.

B   kazukeru < kadukey- < *kantuka-Ci- < *kan[pu]ₛₛ.ₛ tuka-Ci-ₐ. 'completely cover/submerge someone's head'. B - B-A-x x-x-x. Km (W) B. Edo B. "Hn and later katugeru."

B   kazuku < kaduku < *kantuka- < *kan[pu]ₛₛ.ₛ tuka-ₐ. 'duck one's head in water; completely cover one's head'. B - B-A-x x-x-x. NS (T+ 30, 31) kadukuₐₜₜᵣ LHL; (29) kadukyi se-na LHL ₣H. Km (W) B. Edo B. "Hn and later katugu." 〖 kazuki 'shawl' x - 1/0-A-x x-x-x. 1700 Ōsaka LHL.

B   kazuraku < kaduraku < *ka(n)turaₛₛ.₇ₑ -ka- < *kami - tura -ka-. 'attach/wear as hair ornament'. x - x-x-x x-x-x.

?A/B   kebadatu < *key-baₛₛ.₁ (< ...) -n- tata-ₑ. 'get nappy, fluffy'. x - B-A-A x-x-x.

B´   kegareru < kegare[y]- < *kenkaₛ.ₛ -ra-Ci-. 'get soiled, besmirched'. B´ - A/B-A-B x-B-x. Ib B. Nk x; Sr cigarir- B (the palatalization unexplained). 〖 kegare x - A/B-2-B x-x-x.

B´   kegasu < *kenka -sa-. 'soil, besmirch'. B´ - B-A-B x-x-x. Edo B.

A   kemuru < keburu (?< *keyburu < ?*kᵃ/₀Cinpu-ra- < ?). 'smoke = emit smoke'. x - A-A-A x-A-x. Edo A. Nk kibuurⁱ/ₘn A. Ib keburu (but kemuri) A. 〖 kemuri A - A-A-A x-A-(A). Km (S) A. Mr (Bm) A. Nk kibuusi A; Sr cimuri A [Lit.] = kibusi A. Yn kibunci A (< ?). Cf. keᵇ/ₘu = keᵇ/ₘuri; keᵇ/ₘuri; keᵇ/ₘu-taₛₐⱼ ₐ.

B   [kenaraberu] < keynarabey- < *ka-Ciₗ.ₛₑ na(ra)npa-Ci-ₐ. 'pass the time, let the days go by' (= hinaraberu). x - x-x-x x-x-x.

?A   kenasu < *kenasa- (< ?). 'disparage, denounce, condemn'. x - A[U]/B[U]-B x-x-x.

A   [keru] < key- < *ka(-)Ci-. 'get extinguished, vanish' (= kieru). Cf. ketu. x - x-x-x x-x-x.

B   ker-u ("late Edo") < keru < "kuweru" = /kweru/ < koye[y] / kuwe[y] (/ kuye[y]-) < *kuba-Ci- (?/kᵥCa-Ci-). 'kick'. A/B - B-<u>A</u>-B B-B-B. NS (T+ kun) kuwe fararakasu 'scatter by kicking' LH HHHHL. Km x. Kn Mg A, but mari koyu 'kick ball' (Kn) is LL|LH (2.3 + B); not lexicalized, for that would be *LLH|L. Kōchi, Ib <u>A</u>. Nk kin B. Cf. [koeru].

A   [kesu] < kyesu < *kiCa-sa-. 'make wear, clothe'. x - x-x-x x-x-x. (The
etymology *ki aras- 'cause to be wearing' is doubtful; in Old Japanese the
stative auxiliary would have preceded the 'wear' verb.)   See kiru.

A   kesu < *kyesu < *ki[C]a-sa- (? metathesis < *kaCi-sa-). 'extinguish'.
A - A-A-A A-A-x. Ongi A. Km (S) kiyasu A, (W) kesu A. Ib A. Narada keyasu A.
Sd kyaasyun A; Nk Ceesun A; Sr caas- A. Attested from Hn; earlier keytu.
Cf. kieru.

A   ketu (a late Hn example in 1218 Uji-shūi-monogatari [KggD 973b]) < keytu
< *ka(-)Ci-ta-. 'extinguish, make vanish' (> kesu from Km). x - x-x-x x-x-x.
Cf. keru, kieru.

A   kezuru < keduru < keyduru (< ?). A - A-A-A x-x-A. 'shave, whittle'.
Mr (Bm) A, but B in one text (Sakurai 1977:857b). Edo A. Hamada B. Ib A.
Nk kiziirun A. Yn kindun A.

?B´   kezuru < keduru < keyduru (< ?). 'comb'. B´ - A-A-B x-x-x.

?A/B   kibamu < *kiy (< kᵘ/₀-Ciₗ.ₛ) -n[a]-pa-ma-. 'turn yellow'. A - B-A-A
x-x-x. Ib A.

A   kieru < kiye[y]- < *ki[C]a-[C]i- (? metathesis < *kaCi-Ci). 'vanish, get
extinguished, go out/off'. A - A-A-A A-A-x. NS (110b) A. Km (W) A. Edo A. Ib A.
Sd kyiiyun A; Nk Ceerun A; Sr caayun (caar-) A < *kiyar-. Cf. keru; kesu, ketu

A   kikoeru < kyikoye[y]- < *kiko-da-Ci-. 'get heard'. A - A-A-A x-A-(A).
NS (81b, 81c, 92a, 105b) A. NS (T+ 82) kyikoyezu aramey HHHH LLH; (112)
kyikoye HHH; (82) kyikoye te na HHHH(|)F(|)L; (109) kyikoyuru HHHH, (kun)
LHHH (? mistake for HHHH); (37) kyikoyesika do HLHLHH (odd). Km (S,W) A.
Mr (Bm) A. Edo A. Ib A. Nk ʰ/ₛikaarin A < *kikare-; Sr cikwiir- A; Yn Karirun A
< *kikare-.

A   [kikosu] < *kyiko-sa-. 'deign to say/eat/drink; deign to do as a favor'.
x - x-x-x x-x-x. Cf. kiku. NS (Okada) A. NS (T+ 56) kyikosanu HHL|H, (39)
kyikosi HLL. Edo A.

A   kiku < kyiku < *kiko-. 'hear'. A - A-A-A A-A-A. NS (74b [11:303-M],
74c [11:306-M]) A. NS (75) kyikasi te HHL(|)F, (63) kyikazu HHH, (96) kyikyi
te HH(|)H. Km (S,W) A. Edo A. Ib A. Nk h/siCun < *kik-; Yn Kun A. Cf. kikosu,
kikoeru. ◻ kiki x - A-A-A x-x-x.

A   kimaru ?< ki[wa]maru < kyi[fa]maru < *ki[pa]-ma-ra-. 'be decided/settled'.
x - A-A-A x-(x)-x. Goka-mura B (but kimeru A). Ib B (but kimeru A).
Nk kimaarun B = Cibaaman B < *kiwamar-; Sr ciwamar- B < *kiwamar-. (No
examples before 1400s?) ◻ kimari x - A-B-A x-x-x: o-kimari 2-1[H]/3[U]-B x-x-x.

A   kimeru ?< ki[wa]me- < kyi[fa]mey- < *ki[pa]-ma-Ci-ₛ. 'decide; [JP] scold'.
x - A-A-A x-(x)-x. Goka-mura A (but kimaru B). Ib A (but kimaru B).
Nk kimi(i)run B = Cibaamin < *kiwame-; Sr ciwamir- B < *kiwame-. (No examples
before 1400s?)

?B   kiou < kyifofu ?< *ikyi [o]fofu < *ikiₛ.₄ opo-pa-ʙ (or [o]po-op[o]-);
or < *ikifafu < *ikiₛ.₄ -pa-pa-. 'strive (harder); compete'. B - B-A-A x-x-x.
Ongi-m B (LHH). Km (S) B. Cf. kisou.

?A/B   kirameku ?< *kyira - myeku < *kiraₘₗₘ miCa-ka-ᵦₐₔ v. 'glitter'. x - B-A-A
x-x-x.

B   kirasu < kyirasu (<*kira-sa-. 'run/sell out of'. x - B-A-B x-B-x.
Nk Ciraasun B.

A   kirasu < kiyrasu < *kᵘ/₀Cira-sa- but probably *kuCira-sa-. 'cause to
fog/cloud up'. x - x-x-x x-x-x. Cf. kiriₛ.ₗ.

A   kirau < kyirafu < *kira-pa-. 'dislike'. A - A-A-A x-A-x. Mr (Bm) A. Edo A.
Ib A. Nk x. Incongruent with kir-uₛ 'cut'. ◻ kirai x - A-A-A x-A-x. Sr ciree A
'thing one mustn't do'.

B   kireru ‹ kyire[y]- ‹ *kira-Ci-. ‘can cut = be sharp; get cut; run (be
sold) out'. (B) - B-B-B B-B-x. Nk Cirirun B. ◻ kire 'piece, cut; cloth'.
x - B-2-B x-B-x. Nk Cirii B.

A   kiru ‹ kyi- ‹ *ki-/*kiCa-. ‘put on (clothes), wear'. A - A-A-A A-A-A.
NS (71b, 94a kyi··· ‹ *k̄īi) "B" = A. NS (T+ 81) kyiseba HHH, (27) kyisemasi wo
LH-LL(|)L, (49) kyi te L̲ ̲(̲|̲)̲E̲. Km (S,W) A. Edo A. Goka-mura B̲. Ib A. Nk Cun A.
Cf. [kesu] ‹ kyesu ‹ *kiCa-sa- ‘make wear, clothe'. For more, see kiseru.

A   kir-u ‹ kiyru ‹ *kuCira- (see Ch. 5 kiri₂.₁). ‘fog up, get foggy'.
x - x-x-x x-x-x. Cf. minegirau. ◻ kiri ‘fog' A - A-A-A A-A-A; Km (S) A.
Nk cirii A. Hachijō kuri. Thorpe (288-9) suggests an etymology kiy (‹ *kuCi)
‘fog' + ira- ‘enter', with the simple noun surviving only in Miyako: Uechi
kïï, Nakasuji (Tarama) cïï.

B   kir-u ‹ kyir-u ‹ *kira-. ‘cut'. B - B-B-B x-B-B. Ongi B. NS (97a) B.
NS (T+ kun) kyiri LH. Km (S,W) B. Mr (Bm) ?B. Edo B. Ib B. Nk Cin B; Yn cun B.
◻ kiri x - B-2-A̲ x-x-x. (Kg may be a mistake; the compounds are all B.)

?B   kir-u ‹ kyir-u ‹ *kira-. ‘make fire by friction'. x - x-x-x x-x-x.
The derived noun may be kiri ‘awl' (2.3 = B).

B   [kisageru] ‹ kyisagey- ‹ *kisa -n[a]-ka-Ci-. ‘shave metal or stone'.
x - x-x-x x-x-x. ◻ kisage B - A̲-x-x x-x-x.

A   kiseru ‹ kyise[y]- ‹ *ki-sa-Ci-. ‘dress someone; let wear'. x - A-A-A
x-A-x. NS (Okada) A. Edo A. Ib A. Nk husiir- A ‹ *kusir-; Sr kusir- A: the -u-
is unexplained, but Serafim suggests ‹ *ko-sa-Ci- (cf. koromo ‘gown' ‹ koro-mo
‘wear-garment') implying that ki- ‘wear' is restructured from the infinitive of
*ko- (see Ch. 5 koromo).

?A+A   kisesu ‹ kyisesu ?‹ *ki[-Ci] se-sa- (?‹ so-sa-). ‘? deign to wear'.
x - x-x-x x-x-x.

B   kisimu ?‹ *kyisimu ‹ *kisi━━ -ma-. ‘creak, squeak'. x - B-A-B x-x-x.
◻ kisimi x - B-A-B x-x-x.

B   [kisirou] ‹ kisirofu ‹ *kyisirofu ‹ *kisir[i -] ofu ‹ *kisir[a-Ci]ʙ opa-ₐ;
or ‹ *kyisirafu (vowel assimilated to labial consonant) ‹ *kisir[a-C]iʙ apa-ₐ.
‘vie/struggle with each other'. B x-x-x x-x-x.

B   kisir-u ?‹ *kyisir-u ‹ *kisi━━ -ra-. ‘creak, rasp'. B - B-A-B x-x-x. Ib B.

?A/B   kisou ‹ kisofu ?‹ *kyiswofu (not attested for Nr) ‹ *[i]ki₂.₄ [i]swo-pa-ʙ.
‘vie, compete'. Cf. kiou, isou; kisirou; arasou. x - B-A-A x-x-x. Ib (rare) A.

?A   kitaeru ‹ (kitafey-) ‹ kitaf- ‹ *kyitaf- ‹ *kita-pa- ?‹ *kataₐ𝒹ⱼ ₐ -pa-.
‘forge, temper, drill, train'. A - B-A-A x-x-x. Hattō B; Hamada, Matsue, Izumo,
NE Kyūshū A. Ib A. ◻ kitafi ‘fish/meat dried whole' HHH/HHL - x-x-x x-x-x.
Cf. kitameru, katasu.

?A   [kitamasu] ‹ kyitamasu ‹ *kita-ma-sa- ?‹ *kataₐ𝒹ⱼ ʙ -ma-sa-. ‘deign to
punish, chastise'. NS (Okada) B̲. NS (T+ 112) kyitamasu mo LLLL(|)H.
Cf. kitameru, katameru.

?A   [kitameru] ‹ kyitame[y]-/kyitam- ‹ *kita-ma-(Ci-) ?‹ *kataₐ𝒹ⱼ ₐ -ma-(Ci-).
‘punish, chastise'. x - x-x-x x-x-x. Cf. katameru.

?A   [kitamu] = kitameru ‘punish, chastise'. x - x-x-x x-x-x.

A ‹ B+A   kitaru ‹ k[i]l̄ī itaru (‹ ...). ‘come'. A - A/B-A-x x-x-x.
Km (S) A. Mr (Bm) A. Edo A. Cf. Kindaichi 1973:80b.

A   *kitasu ?‹ katasu ‹ *kataₐ𝒹ⱼ ₐ -sa-. ‘harden it'. ◻ kitasi (cf. Nakata).
Cf. kitaeru; kitai.

A ‹ B+A   kitasu ‹ k[i]l̄ī itasu (‹ ...). ‘bring'. A - B-A-A x-x-x. Ib A.

B   kiwamaru ‹ kyifamaru ‹ *kipa₂.₃ -ma-ra-. ‘come to an end, reach an extreme';
(Nk, Sr) ‘be decided'. B - B-A-B x-B-x. Nk cibaaman B̲ ‹ *kiwamar-, or ciwamar- B̲
‹ *kiwamar-. ◻ kiwamari x - B-A-B x-x-x; Km (S) B.

B   kiwameru < kyifame[y]- < *kipaₑ.₃ -ma-Ci-. 'carry to the extreme; attain
(the extremity of)'; (Nk, Sr) = kimeru 'decide'. B - B-A-B x-B-x. NS (124b) B.
Km (S) B. Edo B. Ib B. Nk Cibaamin < *kiwame-; Sr ciwamir- B < *kiwame-.

B   [kiwamu] < *kyifamu < *kipaₑ.₃ -ma-. 'come to an end, reach an extreme' (=
kiwamaru). x - x-x-x x-x-x. ▯ kiwami 'limit, extreme' x - B(/A[H])-A-B x-x-x.

B   [kiwaru] < kyifaru < *kipaₑ.₃ -ra-. 'come to an end, wear out'. x - x-x-x
x-x-x.

B   kiwatu (Mg "kifatu") < *kipaₑ.₃ -ta-. ?'pare down'; ?= kiwaru.
-          kiyasu: see kesu.
B   kiyomaru < *kyiywomaru (<*kidwoₐdⱼ ᴮ -ma-ra-. 'become pure, purify
oneself'. x - x-x-x x-x-x.

B   kiyomawaru < kyiywomafaru < *kidwoₐdⱼ ᴮ -ma-pa-ra-. 'purify oneself'.
B - x-x-x x-x-x.

B   kiyomeru < kyiywomey- < *kidwoₐdⱼ ᴮ -ma-Ci-. 'purify, cleanse'. B - B-A-B
x-x-x. Ib B. ▯ kiyome x - B-A-B x-x-x. Cf. Sr curasan B 'beautiful; pure' <
*kiyo-ra-sa a-.

A   kizamu < *kinsaₑ.₃ -ma-. 'cut/chop fine; carve'. A - A-A-A x-A-x.
NS (127a) A. Edo A. Nk kizaamin A. ▯ kizami x - A-A-A x-x-x.

A   kizasu < *kiₗ.ₗ (< ...) -n- sasa-ᴮ. 'show signs of; sprout'. A - A/B-A-A
x-x-x. ▯ kizasi 'symptom; omen; sprouting' x - A-A-A x-x-x.

?1.3 + A   kizuku < kiduku: (1) < kyiduku < *kiₗ.₃ₐ -n- tuku-ₐ (or perhaps, as in
Tsuchihashi 1972:331, tuka-ᴮ) 'make (or pound?) with a pounder'; (2) < kituku
(Mg) < *kiy-tuku < *kiy₉₁.₃ (< ?) tuku-ₐ 'build (a fortress)'. B′ (?< 1.3+A) -
B-A-A x-x-x. Edo B̲.

?A/B   kobamu ?< ko̲[fa-fa]bamu ('strong-obstruct') ?< *ko̲paₐdⱼ ᴮ panpama-₇ₐ/ᴮ.
'oppose, resist; refuse'. A [Ir] - B-A-A x-x-x. Cf. habamu.

A   kobiru < kwobiy- < *kwoₗ.ₗ -npᵘ/₂Ci- (?< -n[a]-pa-Ci-). 'flatter'.
A - A-A-A x-x-x. ▯ kobi 'flattery'. A - 1/2-2-A x-x-x. (The register leads
us to reject etymologies based on *kwopo̲-ᴮ 'love'.)

A   kobomeku < *kobo-myeku < *konpoₘᵢₘ miCa-ka-ᵦₐd v. 'creak, squeak; gurgle;
cough'. A (=HHHL) [Ir] - x-A-x x-x-x.

B   koboreru < kobore[y]- < kofore[y]- < *ko(?n)po-ra-Ci-. 'fall, drop, be
scattered; (= kowareru) be shattered, broken'. B - B-A-B x-B-x. Ib B. Nk koorin
B = Sr kuurir- B < *kofore- 'be broken; fall to ruin'. Cf. kowareru. ▯ kobore
x - B(o-ko˥bore)-A-B x-B-x. Sr kuuri(-ẕeewee) B '(fortune out of) disaster'.

B   kobosu < *konpo-sa- (< ?). 'spill; grumble; (= kobotu) shatter it'.
B - B-A-B x-x-x. Ib B. Nk Koosun/Konsun B = Sr kuusyun B 'destroy, break'
(cf. kowasu). ▯ kobosi x - B-A/1:3-x x-x-x.

B   kobotu < kofotu (Mr) < *kopo-ta-. 'shatter it' (= kowasu), later confused
with kobosu 'spill it'. B - B-A-x x-B-x. Sr kuus- B < *kofos- 'take apart;
tear down'. K : Edo HLL.

A   koburu ?< *ko̲[wa]-buru < *ko̲wa (< ... , see koe) -n- pura-ᵦ. 'clamor'.
A [Ir] - x-x-x x-x-x.

B′   koburu ?= kaburu. ? 'put on head'. B′ (LHx = *LHL) - x-x-x x-x-x.

?A/B, ?B′ kodawaru < kodafaru < *kontapara- (< ?). 'show prejudice (against) or
opposition (to)'. x - A/B-B-A x-x-x. Ib B′ (= L). ▯ kodawari x - 3/4/0-B-A
x-x-x.

A   koeru < kwoye[y]- < *kwo-da-Ci-. 'pass over; exceed'. A - A-A-A x-A-x.
Ongi (Iroha) B̲; Ongi-m A. NS (74a, 126a) A. NS (T+ 119) kwoye te HH(|)H,
(61) kwoyure-ba HHH(|)L. Km (S,W) A. Edo A. NE Kyūshū, Hamada B̲. Ib A.
Nk huirun A; Sr kwiir- A.

B   koeru < kwoye[y]- < *kwo*adj B* -da-Ci-. 'grow fertile; get fat'. x - B-B-B x-B-x. Nk Kweerun B; Sr kweer- B. 〚 koe x - B-2-B x-B-x. Ib B. Nk Kwee C̲; Sr kwee B. Cf. koyasu.

?B   [koeru] < koye[y]- < *koda-Ci-. 'freeze, get frozen'. x - x-x-x x-x-x. Cf. [koiru], *koyasu, *koyosu, koru.

B   [koeru] < koye[y]- / kuwe[y]- (?/ kuye[y]-) < *kuba-Ci- (?/ *kuCa-Ci-). 'kick': see ker-u.

?B   [kogarasu] < *kwogarasu < *kwonka-ra-sa-. 'burn, scorch' (= kogasu). x - x-x-x x-A̲-x. Nk kugaarasun B; Sr kugaras- A̲.

?B´   kogareru < kwogare[y]- < *kwonka-ra-Ci-. 'be burning (= passionate, yearning)'. B´ - B-A-A̲ x-A̲-x. Km (S) B. Edo B. Nk kugaarin B; Sr kugarir- A̲.

?B´   kogasu < *kwogasu < *kwonka-sa-. 'burn, scorch; yearn for'. B´ - B-A-A x-x-x. Ib B. Cf. kogeru, kogareru, [kogarasu].

B   kogeru < *kwogey- < *kwonka-Ci-. 'get scorched'. x - B-B-A x-x-x. Ib B. 〚 koge x - B-1:3-A x-x-x; o-koge 2-1:3-B x-x-x.

?A/B   kogoeru < kogofe[y]- < *ko[pa-Ci] n[i] kopa-Ci-. 'freeze (= get frozen)'. x - A/B-A-B x-x-x. Hattō B; Hamada, Matsue, Izumo A. Cf. kogoru; kooru; koru, [koiru].

A   kogomu ?< *kon-kom- < *kom[a]-koma- or *kom[a-Ci] koma-. 'stoop; crouch' (= kagamu). x - A-A-A x-x-x.

A   kogoru < *konko-ra- (?< *ko̲[ra-Ci] n[i] ko̲ra-; ?< *ko[fori] n[i] ko[fo]ru < *ko[pa-ra-Ci] n[i] ko[pa]-ra-). 'freeze = get frozen'. 〚 kogori x - A-A-x x-x-x. Cf. kogoeru.

B   ko̲gu < *ko̲nka-. 'row'. B - B-B-B B-B-B. Km (W) B. Edo B. Ib B. Nk huzun B; Sr kuuzun (kuug-) B.

B   kogu (JP, Ib) 'thresh, strip' = koku.

B   koiru < kwofiy- ← *kwopo̲-Ci- 'love'. B - B-B-x x-x-x. NS (T+ 123) kwofiymu mo LLH(|)L. Km (S,W) B. Edo B. This began to be replaced by kou sometime in Mr, though it persisted beside the newer assignment of conjugation. 〚 koi x - 1-2-B x-B-x. Nk kui C̲ [Lit.]; Sr kui B [Lit.].

?B   koiru = "koyu" < ko̲yi[y]- (?< *ko̲ye[y]- < *ko̲da-Ci-). 'lie flat'. x - x-x-x B-x-x. NS (114a) A. Sd kheeyum (?< koyaru; ? < koyi [w]oru). Nk x. K: Hn LF (where attested?). Cf. koyaru, koyasu.

?B   [koiru] < koyi[y]- < *kodo-Ci- (?< *koda-Ci- with vowel assimilation). 'freeze (= get frozen)'. (B?)- x-x-x x-x-x. Is Mg ko̅i - ta̅ru̅ to̅bi̅ '(?) cold kite (bird)' an example? Cf. koyoru; [koeru] < koye[y]-; kogoru, kogoeru, koru.

-       [kokaru]: see kokeru.

?A   kokasu < *koka-sa- (< ?). 'topple, make it tumble'. x - B̲-x-x x-x-x. Ib A.

?A   kokeru < kokey- < *koka-Ci- (< ?). 'tumble; roll'. Wakayama kokaru < *koka-ra-. x - B̲-A-x x-x-x. NS (Okada) A. Cf. kuki, kukeru.

B   kokoroeru < kokoroe- < ko̲ko̲ro̲*3.B(?b)* e[y]-*B* (< *a-Ci-*B*). 'understand, know'. x - B-A-B x-x-x. Mr (Bm) B. Nk kuKu(u)rin B; ? Sr kukuriyun B 'notice, take care'. 〚 kokoroe x - 3/4-4-B x-B-x. The Tōkyō oxytonic is from NHK; H has an atonic version (misprint for oxytonic?). Matsue, Izumo A̲. Nk x; Sr kukurii B.

B   kokoromiru < ko̲ko̲ro̲ myiru < *ko̲ko̲ro̲*3.B(?b)* mi/miCa-*B*. B - B-A-B x-x-x. 'try'. Ib B. Nk kuKu(u)rumin B. 〚 kokoromi B - 3/4/0-A-B x-B-x. Matsue, Izumo A̲; Hattō, Hamada B. Sr kukurumi B.

B   kokorozasu < *ko̲ko̲ro̲*3.B(?b)* -n- sasa-*B*. 'aspire to'. x - B-A-B x-x-x. Izumo A̲. 〚 kokorozasi x - A̲/B-A/4[U]-B x-B-x. Km (S) B. Hattō B; Hamada, Matsue, Izumo A̲. Sr kukuruzasi B.

B   koku, kogu (JP) < kwoku < *kwoka-. 'excrete, expel (from body); (= igoku,
koki-tukeru) thresh. strip'. B - B-B-(B) x-x-x. NS (118b [14:157-K]) B. Km (W
"?") B. Narada B. Ib kogu B. Nk s¹/ᵤzun B 'thresh' is from sog-.

B   komanuku (< ?). 'fold one's arms'. B - B-A-B x-x-x.

B   komaru (JP) < *koma-ra-. 'get put inside; be inside'. x - x-x-x x-B-x.
See komoru.

B   komaru ?< *koma-ra-. 'be distressed/perplexed'. x - B-A-B x-x-x. Ib B.
Nk kumaarun B. (Same as preceding — 'boxed in'?)

B   komeru < komey < *koma-Ci-. 'put in; include'. B - B-B-B x-B-x. Km (W) B.
Edo B. Ib B. Nk humirun B; Sr kumir- B. Variant [komiru].

B   [komiru] < komiy- < *komo-Ci- < *koma-Ci- *(the second vowel assimilated to
the labial nasal and/or the first vowel)*. 'put in; include' (= komeru).
(B) - x-x-x x-(B)-x.

B   komoru < komaru *(the second vowel assimilated to the labial nasal and/or
the first vowel)* < *koma-ra-. 'be confined; be filled (with)'. B - B-A-B
x-(B)-x. NS (Okada) B. NS (T+ 105) komoraserikyemu LᴾHHLL ?= LLLHHLL,
(22) komoreru HHHH. Edo B. Ib B. Nk kumurun B, humaarun B (< *komar-); Sr
kumar- B (< *komar-). ◫ komori x - B-A-x x-x-x. Edo HHL.

B   komu < kwomu < kwoma- ?< *kwoₐdⱼ ᴮ "ˢᵃᵗᵘʳᵃᵗᵉᵈ" -ma-. 'get flooded'.
x - x-x-x x-x-x. ◫ komi x - x-x-x x-x-x. NS (100b [11:126-K]) B.

B   komu < *koma-. 'be crowded; be elaborate; intricate'; (in compounds)
'enter'. (B) - B-B-B x-x-x. Ib B. ◫ komi x - B-2-A̱ x-x-x. Kg mistake?

A   konareru < konare[y]- < *kona-ra-Ci-. 'be digested; mature'. x - A(/Ḇ[H])-
A-A x-x-x. Hamada A/Ḇ; Hattō, Matsue, Izumo A. ◫ konare x - A-A-A x-x-x. If
kwona-ta 'well-developed riceland' has the etymology suggested in Zdb and NKD,
this stem would be *kwona- ··· , but the register is incongruent.

A   konasu < *kona-sa-. 'grind; digest; handle', (Nk, Sr) 'trample, pulverize,
plow (up)'. (A) - A-A-A x-A-x. Kn Mg: kak̄i̱ k̄onas̱u (B+A). Nk kunasyun A,
Sr kunas- A. ◫ konasi 'one's carriage/behavior'. x - A/B-A-A x-x-x.

?B   koneru < kone[y]- < ?*kona-Ci- (< ?). 'knead'. x - B-B-A x-x-x.

B   konomu < *konoma- (< ?). 'like, be fond of'. B - B-A-B x-x-x.
NS (117b) HLL, (Okada) HLH (?= *LLH = B). Ib B. ◫ konomi x - B-2-B x-x-x.

B   koomuru < kauburu < kagafᵘ/ₒru < *kankapura- (< ?). 'incur, sustain'.
B - B-A-B x-A̱-x. ◫ koomuri < kauburi B - x-x-x x-x-x. Cf. kaburu, kamuru.

A (?< B)   kooru < koforu < *kofar- < *kopaₐdⱼ ᴮ "ʰᵃʳᵈ" -ra-. 'freeze = get frozen'.
A - A-A-A A-Ḇ-x. Km (W) A. Edo A. NKD 7:65b Tk "B" must be a misprint. Ib A.
Nk huPaarun Ḇ = Sr kuhwar- B (< *kopa-ra-) 'get hard/frozen; awaken'.
◫ koori 'ice' x - A-A-x Ḇ-A-x; Sr kuuri A new? Cf. koru; kogoru, kogoeru,
kooru, [koiru].

?B´   koraeru < korafey- < *ko̱ra-pa-Ci-. 'endure; restrain'. x - B-B-B x-B-x.
Edo B. Ib B´ (= L). Sr kuneyun B (the -n- is unexplained, as is the opposite
case of the -r- in tarum- < *tanom- 'request').

B   korasimeru < korasimey- < *ko̱ra-₇ᴮ simey-₇ (< ?). 'chastise' (= korasu).
x - B-A-B x-x-x. Ib B.

?A/B   korasu < *ko̱ra-sa-. 'freeze/harden it; concentrate it, condense it'.
A [Ir] - B-A-B x-x-x. Km (S) A. Ib *(rare)* B. Cf. koyasu.

B   korasu, korosu < *ko̱ra-sa-. 'chastise' (= korasimeru). B - B-A-B x-x-x.
Km (S) korosu B. Ib *(rare)* B.

B   koriru < kori[y]- < *ko̱ro-Ci- < *ko̱ra-Ci- *(the second vowel assimilated
to the first)*. 'learn by experience'. B [Ir] - B-B-B x-x-x. Km (W) B. Ib B.

A   korobasu < *koro -n[a]-pa-sa-. 'roll it; knock/throw down'. x - A-A-A
x-x-x. Nk Kuru(u)basun A.

A   korobu < *koro -n[a]-pa-. 'roll; tumble'. x - A-A-A x-A-A. Edo A. Ib A.
Nk Kuruubin A; Sr kurubun A.
A   korogaru < *koro -n[a]-ka-ra-. 'roll; tumble'. x - A-A-A x-x-x. Ib A.
A   korogasu < *koro -n[a]-ka-sa-. 'roll it, make it roll/tumble'. x - A-A-A
x-x-x. Ib A. Nk Kuruugasun A.
A   korogeru < *koro -n[a]-ka-Ci-. 'roll; tumble' (= korogaru). x - A-A-A
x-x-x. Ib korokeru A. Nk Kugeerun B̲.
A   [korogu] = korogaru 'roll; tumble': Nk Kuruuzun A.
A   kororoku < *koro-[ko]ro -ka-. 'bark (in hoarse voice); neigh (= inanaku);
chirp (cf. koorogi)'. HHxx (= A) - x-x-x x-x-x. Incongruent with koorogi.
A   korosu < *korosa- (?< *kora-sa-, the second vowel assimilated to the
first; ?< koro[ba]su). 'kill'. A - A-A-A A-A-A. NS (127a) A. Edo A(/B̲). Ib A.
Nk kuru(u)sun A; Sr kurus- A; Yn kurun A.
B   korosu < *kora-sa-. 'chastise' (= korasu). B - x-x-x x-x-x. Km (S) B.
-          korou < *korofu ('compare'): see hitokoru.
?B   korou < korofu < *kora-pa- (the second vowel assimilated to the first
and/or to the following labial). 'scold'. x - x-x-x x-x-x. ◻ koroi: NS (T+
kun) korofyi HLL. Cf. korosu < korasu.
?A   koru < *kora-. 'harden, get stiff, freeze (cf. kareru); get absorbed
(in/by)'. A - B-B-A x-x-x. Km (W) ?B. Ib B. ◻ kori x - 2-2-A x-x-x. Cf. kooru,
kogoeru; [koiru], [koeru], *koyasu, *koyosu.
B   koru < *ko₁.ₛₐ -ra-. 'cut/chop wood' (= ki-koru). B [Ir] - B-B-x x-x-x.
(The etymology denies that the stem is related to kar- or kir- 'cut'.)
?B   koru < *kora-. 'rebuke'. x - x-x-x x-x-x.
?A   kosikakeru < kosikakey- < *kosi₂.₁ kaka-Ci-ᵦ. 'sit'. x - B-A[U]/B[H]-A
x-x-x. ◻ kosikake x - 3/4-2[U]/1:4[H]-A x-x-x. Hattō, Hamada, Matsue, Izumo A.
A   kosiraeru < kosirafey- < *kosirapa-Ci- (?< *ko₁.₁ sira₄-pa-Ci- 'make know
it this [= my] way'). 'sweettalk, cajole, contrive; concoct, make'. A - A-A-A
x-A-x. Ongi A. Km (S) A. Ib (also kosaeru, kossyaeru) A. Nk kusireerun A,
Sr kusireer- A 'cut up (meat/fish for cooking)'. ◻ kosirae x - A-A[U]/4[H]-A
x-ẋ-x. In older Hagiwara (Tsuzuku 1941:188) the verb is a consonant stem:
kosirau < *kosirapa-.
A   kosu < kwosu < *kwo-sa- (cf. koeru). 'send/cross over (vt./vi.); filter'.
x - A-A-A x-A-x. NS (T+ 19) kwosa-ba HL|H, (19) kwosi HL. Km (W) A. Ib A. Nk
kusun A.
B   kosuru (?< kwo₁.₃ₐ sura-ᵦ, cf. Thorpe 322). 'rub'. x - B-A-B B-x-x.
Ib A̲, B. Cf. kasuru < *kasu-ra-, suru < *sura- / soru < *sora-.
?B′   kotaeru < kotafey- < *koto apaₛ-Ci-. 'answer'. B - B-B-B x-B-x.
NS (95b) B. Km (S) B. Mr (Bm) B. Edo B. Nk x; Sr kuteer- B. ◻ kotae x - 2/3-
1:3-B x-(x)-x. NS (106a) B. Km (W) B. Ōsaka, Kōbe 3;Ib B. Sr qiree-kute'e B
(with a secondary accent) 'response'.
-          kotobuku = kotohogu.
B   kotohogu < kotofoku < *koto₂.₃ pwoka-?ᵦ. 'felicitate; congratulate'.
x - B-A-B x-x-x. ◻ kotohogi < kotofokyi (< ...) 'congratulations; gift'.
x - 2-2-B x-B-x. Nk x; Sr kutubuci B.
-          kotonaru: see koto (Ch. 5).
B   kotowaru < *koto₂.₃ bara-₄. 'reject, decline'. B - B-A-B x-B-x. Hattō A̲;
Hamada, Matsue, Izumo B. Ib B. Ib B. Nk kuTuwan B; Sr kutuwar- B.
◻ kotowari x - 3/4-A-B x-x-x. NS (121a, 127a, 133a) B. Hattō A; Hamada, Matsue,
Izumo B. Goka-mura 2. Nk kuTuwai B.
B <2.3+A kotoyoseru < kotoyose[y]- < *koto₂.₃ do-sa-Ci-₄. 'verbally collaborate'.
x - A/B-A-x x-x-x.

B   kotozukeru ‹ kotozuke[y]- ‹ *ko̲to̲z.з -n- tuka-Ci-ʙ. 'send as a message'.
x - B-A-B x-(x)-x. Sr tuẕikir- B (truncation?). ◰ kotozuke x - 4/0-A-B x-(x)-x.
Sr tuẕiki B.

B   kou ‹ (*ko[w]iru ‹) kwofi[y]- ‹ *kwopo̲-Ci-. 'love'. x - B-B[U]-(B) x-(B)-x
Km (S,W) B. ◰ koi B - 2/3-2-B x-B-x; Tk 2 in NKD only. Nk kui C̲, Sr kui B
borrowed?

B   kou ‹ ko̲fu ‹*ko̲pa-. 'beg'. B - B-B-B x-B-x. NS (T+ 7) ko̲fasaba LLHH.
Edo B. Sr kuur- B 'ask for a wife'. ◰ koi x - 2/3-x-x x-x-x.

?B   kowagaru ‹ kofagaru ‹ *ko̲pa sdj ʙ -g[e] (‹ -n- key₁,₁) ara-ʙ. 'fear'.
x - B-A-x x-x-x. Ib B. Attested 10th century.

B   kowareru ‹ kofare[y]- ‹ ?*kofore[y]- ‹ ?*kopo-ra-Ci-. x - B-A-B x-(x)-x.
'break = get broken/ruined'. Ib B. Sr kuurir- B ‹ *kofore-: see koboreru.
◰ koware x - B-A-B x-x-x.

B   kowaru ‹ kofaru ‹ *ko̲pa-ra-. 'get hard; freeze'. x - x-x-x x-B-x.
Nk huPaarun B, Sr kuhwar- B 'get hard/frozen; have a falling out; awaken,
be unable to sleep'. Cf. kowa- ‹ ko̲fa- ‹ *ko̲pa sdj ʙ 'fearsome; hard; [Sr]
incompatible'; kooru.

B   kowasu ‹ kofasu ‹ ?*kofosu ‹ ?*kopo-sa-. 'break/ruin it'. x - B-A-B x-B-x.
Ib B. Cf. kobosu.

?B   ko̲yaru ‹ *ko̲da-ra-. 'lie flat'. Cf. koiru, koyasu. x - x-x-x x-x-x.

?B, ?B´ ko̲yasu ‹ *ko̲da-sa-. 'deign to lie flat'. x - x-x-x x-x-x.
NS (Okada) B´. NS (T+ 104a) ko̲yaseru HHHH, (104b) HHHL. Km (W) B. Cf. koiru.

B   koyasu ‹ *kwoyasu ‹ *kwo sdj ʙ -da-sa-. 'fertilize; fatten, enrich'.
B - B-A-B x-x-x. Ib B. Nk Kweesun B. Cf. koeru. ◰ koyasi x - B-2-B x-x-x.

?B   *koyasu ‹ *koda-sa-. 'make it harden/congeal/freeze' (= koyosu). x - x-x-x
x-x-x. Cf. nikoyasu = nikoyosu; [koeru]; korasu.

?B   *koyosu ‹ *kodo-sa- ‹ *koda-sa- (the second vowel assimilated to the
first). 'make it harden/congeal/freeze'. Cf. koyosimono, nikoyosu; [koeru];
korosu.

B   kozireru ‹ konzire[y]- ‹ *konsira-Ci-. 'get wrenched'. x - B-A[U]/B[H]-B
x-x-x. Ib B.

B   koziru (‹ "kozi[y]-") ?‹ *kodi[y]- (NKD) ‹ *kont u/o̲-Ci-; ‹ *kons u/o̲-Ci-.
'dig/root out' (cf. ne-koziru). B - x-x-x x-x-x. (› kuziru › kuzir-u 'pick,
scoop').

B   kozir-u ‹ *konsira-. 'wrench, gouge'. x - B-A[U]/B[H]-B x-x-x.

?A   kozoru ?‹ *kom[i]-soru ?‹ *kom[a-C]iʙ soro-?ʙ. 'join them all together'.
A - B-A-x x-x-x. Gerund → adverb kozotte 'altogether': x - 2-2-B x-x-x.
Mg register incongruent with etymology.

B   kubaru ‹ *kunpa-ra- ?‹ *kum[a]-pa-ra-. 'share, distribute; allocate'.
B - B-A-B x-B-x. NS (111a) B. Ib A. Nk kubaarun B; Sr kubar- B. ◰ kubari x -
B-A-B x-x-x. Cf. kumaru.

A   kuberu ‹ kubey- ‹ *kunpa-Ci- ?‹ *kum[a]-pa-Ci-. 'fuel/stoke with'.
x - A/B-A-A x-x-x. Hattō, Hamada B; Izumo A/B; Matsue A. ? Nk qubi(i)run A
(≠ aburu for that is Nk anbin B, Sr qabur-/qand- B).

?A   kubireru ‹ kubire[y]- ‹ *kunpiз.₁ -ra-Ci-. 'be constricted; hang oneself'.
A - A-A/B[U]-A x-A-x. Hattō, Hamada B; Izumo A/B; Matsue A. Ib (rare) B.

?A   kubir-u ‹ *kunpiз.₁ -ra-. 'strangle; tie, truss, bind'. A - A-A/B[U]-A
x-A-x. Sr kunzun (kund-) A ‹ *kubir-.

A   kubomu ‹ *kunpoз.₁ -ma-. 'become hollow'. A - A-A-A x-x-x. Km (S) A.
Ib A̲. Nk Kubuumin A. ◰ kubomi x - A-A-A x-A-x.

B   kudakeru < kudakey- < *kunta(-)ka-Ci-. 'get broken, be shattered'. (B) -
B-A-B x-B-x. Ib B. Nk Kudaakin B; Sr kudakir- B. ◖ kudake x - 3-x-x x-x-x.
Nk KudaKii B 'crushed rice/beans'.

B   kudaku < *kunta(-)ka-. 'break, shatter'. B - B-A-B x-A-x. Ongi B. Edo B.
Hyōgo A; Suzu, Kōchi B. Ib B. Nk KudaaCun B; Sr kudak- A (cf. kudakeru). Cf.
kuzu, kuzusu; kuyasu; kudakudasi_adj_ B, kudokudosi_adj_ B, kudo_adj_ ?.

A   kudaru < *kunta-ra-. 'descend, go/come down'. A - A-A-A x-x-x. Km (S,W) A.
Edo A. Ib A. ◖ kudari x - A-A-A x-A-x. Is Mg HHL the infinitive? NS (T+ 120)
sifo no kudari LL(|)L HHH, una-kudari LL LHL (Tsuchihashi: infinitives).

?A   kudasaru < *kunta-sa-ra-. 'give (me/us)'. x - B-A-A x-x-x.

A   kudasu < *kunta-sa-. 'lower; defeat'. A - A[K]/B[H]-A-A x-A-x. Edo A.
Nk x. Cf. kutasu. ◖ kudasi x - A[K]-A-x x-A-x. NS (T+ 45) LH?. Edo HHH.

?A/B   kudatu (from late Hn) < (Nr) kutatu < *kuta-ta-. 'deteriorate'. x - x-x-x
x-x-x. Km (W) A/B, (Okada) A.

B   kudoku ?< *kunto_adj_ B -ka- ?< *ku[ti]_2.1_ n[i] toka-_B_. 'grumble, complain;
plead, beseech; convince'. x - B-A-x x-x-x. Edo B. Ib B. Attested 13th century.

?B   [kueru] < kuye[y]- 'kick': see ker-u.

B   kugir-u ?< *kugyir-u < *ku (< Ch .kyu) n[i] kira-_B_. 'mark off, partition,
punctuate'. x - B-A[U]/B-B x-x-x. Ib B. ◖ kugiri x - A/B-A[H]/1[U]-B x-x-x.

A   kugumaru (= se ~) 'stoop, crouch': ?< *kun-kuma-ra- ?< *kum[a]-kuma-ra-;
?< *kum[a-Ci] kuma-ra-, ?< *ku[ma-Ci] n[i] kuma-ra-. A - x-x-x x-x-x.

A   kugumeru = kogomeru = kagameru 'stoop; crouch': kugumey- ?< *kun-kumey- ?<
*kum[a]-kuma-Ci-, ?< *kum[a-Ci] kuma-Ci-, ?< *ku[ma-Ci] n[i] kuma-. x - x-x-x.

B   kugumoru < kukumoru ?< *kukumaru < *kuku-ma-ra-. 'get wrapped/tied up,
... '. B - B-A-x x-A-x. Nk x; Sr kukumur- A '(flowers) bud'.

A   kugumu (JP) = kogomu = kagamu (stoop; crouch): < *kunkuma- ?< *kum[a]-
uma-; ?< *kum[a-Ci] kuma-; ?< *ku[ma-Ci] n[i] kuma-. x - x-x-x x-x-x.
Cf. uzukumaru; kuguse.

B   kuguru < ku^k^/_g_uru (Hn) < kukuru < *kuku-ra-. 'dart/crawl through;
dive; evade'. B - B-A-B x-x-x. Km (W) B. ◖ kuguri x - B-A-B x-x-x.
NS (T+ kun) kukuri no myiya LHH L ?L.

B   kuiru < kuyi[y]- < *kuyo-Ci- (cf. kuyo-kuyo) < *kuya-Ci- (the second vowel
partially assimilated to first, cf. kuyamu) < *kuda-Ci-. 'regret'. B - B-B-B
x-x-x. Km (S) B. Edo B. ◖ kui x -2/3-B[H]2[U]-B x-x-x. NS (T) LL. Km (W) B.

?A   kukeru < kukey- (< ?). 'blindstitch'. x - A-A-B x-A-x. Nk kuKuurun A,
Sr kukur- A (also = kukuru). Cf. kokeru. ◖ kuke - A-A-B x-x-x.

?B   kuku < *kuku-. 'dart through' (= kuguru). x - x-x-x x-x-x.

B   kukumoru: see kugumoru.

B   kukumu < *kuku-ma-. 'wrap/tie it up'. x - B-x-x x-x-x. Cf. hagukumu; kuki.

B   kukumu < *kukuma- ?< *puku-ma- (the first consonant assimilated to the
second). 'hold in the mouth' (= hukumu). B - B-A-x x-B-x. Sr kukunun (kukum-) B.

A   kukuru < *kuku-ra-. 'tie up, bundle, fasten'. x - A-A-A x-A-x. Edo A.
Ib A. Nk kuKuurun A; Sr kukur- A (also = kukeru). ◖ kukuri x - A-A-A x-A-x.
Cf. kukumu, kuki.

B   kukuru 'dart/crawl through; dive; evade': see kuguru.

?B   kumaru < *kuma-ra-. 'share'. x - x-x-x x-x-x. Cf. kubaru. Mg has kumaru A
with the Ch character 'go mad' but that must be a different etymon — what?

B   kumoru < kumworu < *kumwo_2.5_ -ra-. 'get cloudy'. B - B-A-B x-B-x.
Mr (Bm) B. Edo B. Hyōgo, Suzu A; Kōchi, Ib B. Nk kumurun B; Sr kumur- B.
◖ kumori x - B-2-B x-B-x. Ōsaka, Kōbe 3.

A   kumu < *kuma-. 'dip, scoop up'. A - A-A-A x-A-A. Mr (Bm) A. Edo A. Ib A.
Nk Kumin A; Sr kum- A.

B   kumu < *kuma-. 'braid; assemble it; ... '. B - B-B-B x-B-x. Edo B. Ib B.
Nk Kumin B; Sr kum- B. ∏ kumi 'set' B - B-2-B x-B-x.

-        *kunabaru, *kunaberu: see [kurabaru], kuraberu (Nk, Sr forms).

B   kuner-u (?< kunner-u) ?< *ku[ri -]ner- < *kur[a-C]iᴮ ner-ᴮ (< ...). 'turn
and twist, be crooked/zigzag; wind, meander; (= suneru) sulk'. (x) - B-A-B
x-x-x. Cf. kunner-u.

B   kunner-u ?< *kur[i]-ner- < *kur[a-C]i ner- (< ...). 'take offense, sulk'.
xxHL (= *LLHL = B) - x-x-x x-x-x. See kuner-u.

A   [kurabaru] < *kura-n[a]-pa-ra-. 'line up (for comparison), vie, contest;
equal'. x - x-x-x x-A-x. Nk Kuraaban A; Sr kunabar- A.

A   kuraberu < kurabey- < *kura-n[a]-pa-Ci-. 'compare'. A [Hoke-kyō tanji] -
A-A-A x-A-x. Km (W) A. Ib A. Nk Kunaabin A; Sr kurabir-/kunabir- A.

A   kuramasu < kuraₐdⱼ ₐ -ma-sa-. 'darken, obscure it; swindle, hoodwink'.
A - A/B-A-A. x-x-x. Hattō, Hamada, Matsue, Izumo A.

A   kuramu < *kuraₐdⱼ ₐ -ma-. 'get dark/obscured'. x - A-A-A x-x-x. Hattō,
Hamada, Matsue, Izumo A. Nk Kuraamin A.

A   kurasu < *kuraₐdⱼ ₐ -sa- ('make dark'). 'live; see the day(s) through'.
x - A-A-A A-A-x. Km (W) A. Ib A. Nk Kuraasun B 'live', A 'let it get dark/late'
∏ kurasi A - A-A-A x-A-x. Mg HHH, HHL, HHx. Km (W) A.

A   kurau < kurafu < *kurapa- (< ?). 'eat, drink; receive'. A - A/B-A-A
x-A-x. Mr (Bm) A. Ib A. Nk Kwan A; Sr kwayun A 'eat; win at gambling' (neg.
kwaan) < *kuraf-. Register incongruent with kuu; perhaps kuti < *kutu-Ciₐ.₁
'mouth', truncated and lenited (kut- > kur-), was attached to *apa-ᴮ 'meet'?

A   kureru < kure[y]- < *kuraₐdⱼ ₐ -Ci-. 'get dark; come to an end'. A - A-A-A
x-(x)-x. Km (W) A. Edo A. Ib A. Nk Kuirun A. Sr yukkwir- A ?< *yoru kure- 'day
ends', yukkwasyun A ?< *yoru kuras- 'end the day'. ∏ kure A - A-A-A x-x-x.

A   kureru < kure[y]- (< ?; ?< ku[da]re[y]- < *ku[nta]-raᴮ-Ci-). 'give
(me/us)'. x - A-A-A A-A-x. Ib A. Nk Kiirun A; Sr kwir- A; Yaeyama hiyoorun
(Miyara 1930:92b); Hateruma hirun, Yn hiyun (Thorpe 290).

B   kuromeru < *kurwomey- < *kurwoₐdⱼ ᴮ -ma-Ci-. 'make black'. B - B-x-x x-x-x.

B   kuromu < *kurwomu < *kurwoₐdⱼ ᴮ -ma-. 'get black'. B - B-x-x x-B-x.
Sr kurunun (kurum-) B. Cf. kuro-miₐ.₄ 'squid ink', treated as adj + suffix.

B   kuru < *kuru- (cf. kurumu, kuruu, kuru-si-) ?< kura- (the second vowel
early assimilated to the first). 'wind, reel'. B - B-B-B x-B-x. NS (36) kuri
LH. Km (W) B.

B   kuru (ki-, ko-) < *ko- / Azuma ke- (?). 'come'. B - B-B-B B-B-B.
NS (70a [11:46-M] komu LH; 73b [11:220-M] kyi R (= LH); 83c [17:121-M] kuru
LH) B. NS (T+ 42) komu LH, (70) komu zo HL(|)L; (114 'not come') konu LL;
(91 'if come') koba HL; (32 'came') kosi L-L; (12 'please come') kone L-H,
(3) H-H; (92 'is come') kyi wiru H HH, (99) 'come and reach') kyi [i]taru H
ꟓH, (9 'though come in and stay') kyi iri wori to-mo H LL LH(|)L-L, (57) kyi
iri (mawi kure) H LH (LL LH); (87, 97, 117) kuru LH; (57) kure LH; (85) ku rasi
mo L LL(|)H, (65) ku [?¨]fey-kyi H H-H. Km (W) B, but infinitive kī < ki-ī.
Ib B. Nk sun B (attr kuruu B, inf cii C / sii... B). Cf. ko 'this'.
Paradigmatic forms (cf. suru 'do'):
     infinitive *ko-[C]i > kyi > ki; Azuma kye (kye-ni te M 4337) unexplained.
     imperative *ko-[C]i > koi, or *ko-[Ci] (or just ko) i/yo > (later) koi.
     future   *ko-mu (the later ko-yoo is an analogic blend, Ch. 3).
     predicative *k[o]-u > ku.
     attributive *k[o]-uru > kuru.

?A/B kurumaru < *kuru-ma-ra-. 'be bundled/wrapped up'. x - B-A-A x-x-x.

?A/B kurumeru < kurumey- < *kuru-ma-Ci-. 'wrap it up' (= kurumu < *kuru-ma-). x - A[H]/B-A-A x-x-x. Hattō A; Matsue, Izumo A/B; Hamada B. Ib kurumu B.

?A/B kurumu < *kuru-ma-. 'wrap it up'. x - B-A-A x-x-x.

B kurusimeru < kurusimey- < kurusi^b/$_m$ey- < *kuru-si$_{adj\ B}$ -n[a]-pa-Ci-. 'make one suffer'. (B) - B-A-B x-x-x. Hattō A; Hamada, Matsue, Izumo B. Ib B.

B kurusimu < kurusi^b/$_m$ey- < *kuru-si$_{adj\ B}$ -n[a]-pa-Ci-. 'suffer'. (B) - B-A-B x-B[new]-x. Hattō A; Hamada, Matsue, Izumo B. Ib B. Nk kurusimin B, Sr kurusim- B [new].

B kuruu < kurufu < *kuru-pa-. 'go mad'. B - B-A-B x-x-x. Ib B. ▯ kurui x - 2/3-A-B x-x-x.

B / 2.3+B kusagir-u < kusakir-u < *kusa$_{2.3}$ kira-$_B$. 'weed out, remove (weeds)'. LLHL (-g-) / LL|LH (-k-) x-x-x x-x-x. Also → HHHL (Kn) with specialized meaning? (Cf. Komatsu 1977a:382.)

B kusarasu < *kusa$_{adj\ B}$ -ra-sa-. 'spoil it, let it rot'. x - B-A-B x-x-x.

A kusaru < *kusara- (< ?). 'link'. A - x-x-x x-A-x. Nk x. ▯ kusari 'chain' A - A-A-A x-A-x. Nk kusaari A; Sr kusai A.

B kusaru / kusareru < kusar- / kusare[y]- < *kusa$_{adj\ B}$ -ra-(Ci-). 'spoil, rot'. x - B-A-B B-B-B. NS (99a [11:98-K]) B. Km (B). Ib B. The Ryūkyū forms (Sd khsareyum B, Nk kusaarin B, Sr kusarir- B, Yn carirun B < [ku]sarir-) are restructured from *kusare[y]-. ▯ kusari x - B-A-B x- x-x. Cf. kutiru, kuso.

?A/B kusasu < *kusa$_{adj\ B}$ -sa-. 'disparage; (= kusarasu) spoil it, let it rot'. x - A/B-A-B x-x-x. Cf. kutasu, kusaru.

2.3 + B kuso-hir-u < kuswo$_{2.3}$ fir-u$_B$ (< *fi[y]r- < *p^w/$_o$Ci-ra-). 'defecate'. LLLL [Ir] (= *LL|LH). x - x-x-x x-x-x. ▯ kusofiri LLLL: - no yamafi 'diarrhea; dysentery'.

2.3 + B kuso-maru < kuswo maru < *kuswo$_{2.3}$ mara-$_B$. 'defecate'. LL|LH - B-x-x x-(x)-x. NS (T+ kun) LL|LH. Nk kusuu$_B$ man$_B$; Sr kusu$_B$ mar-$_B$.

B kusuberu < kusubey- < *kusunpa-Ci- (< ?). '(make it) smoke, fumigate'. (x) - B-A-B x-x-x. Cf. husuberu.

B kusuburu < *kusunpura- < *kusunpa-ra- *(the third vowel assimilated to the first two)* (< ?). 'get smoky/sooty; smolder'. Ib (-b^u/$_o$-) B. ▯ kusuburi x - A/B[Mkz]-A-B x-x-x.

A kusuguru < *kusunkura- (< ?). 'tickle'. x - A-A-A x-A-x. ▯ kusuguri x - A-A-A x-x-x.

B kusuneru < kusune[y]- < *kusunaCi- (< ?). 'pilfer, filch; deceive, conceal'. x - B-A-B x-x-x.

A [kusunuku] < *kusu$_{2.3}$ nuka-$_{?A}$. 'skewer'. A - x-x-x x-x-x. The register is incongruent with the etymology. Attested early Hn.

B kutabireru < kutabire[y]- < *kutanpiraCi- (< ?). 'get tired'. x - B-A-B x-B-x. Ib A, B. Nk kuTanrin, Sr kutandir- B < *kutabirer- (← *kutabire-). ▯ kutabire x - 3/4-A-B x-B-x. Izumo A (verb B). Nk kuTandi(i) B; Sr kutandi B.

B kutaru < *kuta-ra-. 'spoil, rot' (= kusaru). x - x-x-x x-x-x.

?A/B kutasu < *kuta-sa-. 'make/let it rot' (= kusasu). A - B-A-x x-B-x. Nk kuTaasun B; Sr kutas- B. NKD "modern also kudasu": cf. kudasu A. Cf. kutiru.

?A <2.1+B kutihisomu < kuti[y] fisomu < *kutu-Ci$_{2.1}$?piso-ma-. 'scowl'. A (Kz), 2.1+B (Kn) - x-x-x x-x-x.

B kutiru < *kuti[y]- < *kutu-Ci- < *kuta-Ci- *(the second vowel assimilated to the first)*. 'rot'. B - A/B-B-B x-B-x. Edo B. Ib B. Sr kucun (kut-) B < *kuta-. Cf. kutaru, kutasu.

\- kuti-sasi tudou < *kuti[y] (< *kutu-Ci$_{2.1}$) sasi-tudofu (< *sas[a-C]i$_B$ tuntwopa-$_{?B}$. 'clamor together'. HHHH HLH (Kn) = HH|LH LLH (Kz) - x-x-x x-x-x.

?A/B   kutugaer-u ‹ kutugafyer-u ?‹ *kutu₂.₁ -n- kapi-ra-ᵦ ('mouth return').
       'get overturned, be overthrown, capsize'. A - B-A-B x-x-x.
?A/B   kutugaesu ‹ kutugafyesu ?‹ *kutu₂.₁ -n- kapi-sa-ᵦ ('mouth return')
       'overturn, overthrow, capsize it'. A - B-A-B x-x-x.
B = 2.3+A kutuoru ?‹ *kutu₂.₃ ora-ₐ. 'weave footgear'. LL(|)HL (Kn) - x-x-x x-x-x.
?A/B   kuturogu ‹ *kuturonka- (‹ ?). 'relax'. A - B-A-B x-A-x.
       Nk x; Sr kuçirug- A. ▯ kuturogi x - 3/4/0-A-B x-A-x.
B   kuu ‹ kufu ‹ *kupa-. 'eat'. B - B-B-B x-B-x. NS (Okada) B. NS (T+ 75)
       kufyi LH. Edo B. Ib B. Nk Kwan B, Sr kuur- B restructured ‹ *kuf-. ▯ kui x -
       1/2-x-x x-x-x. (Because of register differences of kurau and kuti, both A, we
       do not further analyze this stem as *ku-pa-.)
B   kuu ‹ "kufu" (? ‹ *kupa-, cf. kuwaeru, taguu; ?‹ ku[m]a-). 'make (a
       nest)'. B - x-x-x x-x-x. See sukuu ‹ su kufu 'roost'.
?A/B   kuwa^d/ₜateru ("-t- till Mr" [Ōno]) ‹ kufa-tate[y]- ‹ *kupa₇(₂.₁) tata-Ci-ᵦ
       ('stand hoe' — cf. kuwabira). 'plan, attempt; put (one's feet) tiptoe'.
       A - B-A[U]/B[H]-B x-x-x. Matsue, Izumo A; Hattō, Hamada B.
       ▯ kuwadate x - 2/3/0-A[U]/B[H]-B x-x-x.
?B´   kuwaeru ‹ kufafey- ‹ *kupa-pa-Ci-. 'add; inflict'. B - A/B-B-B x-B[Lit.]-x
       Km (S) B. Edo B. Hattō, Hamada, Matsue, Izumo B. Ib A.
B´   kuwawaru ‹ kufafaru ‹ *kupa-pa-ra-. 'be added; participate; grow'.
       x - A/B-B-B x-x-x. Km (W) B. Hattō, Hamada, Matsue, Izumo B.
B   kuyamu ‹ *kuda-ma-. 'regret; lament'. x - B-A-B x-B-x. Ib B. Nk B.
       ▯ kuyami x - B-A-B x-B-x. Matsue A (verb B). Cf. kuiru.
?B   kuyasu ‹ *kuda-sa-. 'crush' (= kuzusu, kudaku). x - x-x-x x-x-x.
?A/B   kuzikeru ‹ kuzikey- ‹ *kunsi-ka-Ci-. 'get sprained or dislocated'.
       A - B-A-B x-x-x. Ib B.
?A/B   kuziku ‹ *kunsi-ka-. 'sprain, dislocate'. A - B-A-B x-x-x. Narada, Matsue,
       Goka-mura A; Hattō, Hamada B. Ib B. Cf. kozir-u.
B   kuzir-u ‹ kuzi- ‹ kozi- (‹ ...). 'pick, scoop': see koziru. B - B-A-x
       x-B-x. Nk x. ▯ kuziri B - B-A-x x-x-x.
B   [kuzurasu] ‹ *kudurasu ‹ *kuntu -ra-sa- ?‹ *kunta -ra-sa-. 'destroy'.
       x - x-x-x x-B-x. Nk Kᵘ/ₒnzasun B; Sr kundasyun B ‹ *kuduras- 'cancel'.
B   kuzureru ‹ *kudure[y]- ‹ *kuntu₂.₄ -ra-Ci- ?‹ *kunta -ra-Ci- (cf. kudaku).
       'collapse [into rubble]'. B - B-A-B x-B-x. NS (101a) B. Matsue, Izumo A;
       Goka-mura A (expected); Hattō, Hamada B. Ib B. Nk Kᵘ/ₒnzin B; Sr kundir- B
       ‹ *kudurer- 'get rubbed out, be cancelled' is restructured from *kudure-;
       kuzurir- B is probably a (restructured) borrowing. Cf. [kueru] ‹ kuye[y]-.
       ▯ kuzure x - B-A-B x-x-x.
B   kuzusu ‹ kudusu ‹ *kuntu₂.₄ -sa- ?‹ *kunta -sa- (cf. kudaku). 'destroy,
       demolish, break'. B - B-A-B (B?)-(B)-x. Hyōgo, Suzu, Kōchi A. Matsue, Izumo,
       Goka-mura A; Hattō, Hamada B. Ib B. Sr kuẓis- B (borrowed?); see [kuzurasu].

B   mabaru ‹ *ma₁.₃ₐ (-n-) para-ₐ. 'look at'. B - x-x-x x-x-x.
B   mabataku ‹ *ma₁.₃ₐ (-n-) pa(n)taka-ᵦ (cf. hataku). 'wink, blink'.
       x - B-A-B x-x-x. ▯ mabataki x - 2-3-B x-x-x.
A   [mabirokeru] ‹ mabiroke[y]- ‹ *ma-byirokey- ‹ *ma₁.₁ n[i] piro_ₐdⱼ ᵦ
       -ka-Ci-. 'totally disrobe'. A - x-x-x x-x-x.
?A   madasu ‹ *mantasa- (‹ ?). 'give, send'. ?A - x-x-x x-x-x. Mg m̄adasu,
       tate m̄adasu. (? ‹ maturi-dasu ‹ ...)
?A/B   ma^d/ₜataku ‹ *ma₁.₃ₐ (-n-) tataka-ᵦ (‹ ...). 'wink, blink, flicker'.
       B - B-A-A x-x-x. Mg -d-, JP -^d/ₜ-. ▯ matataki x - 2-A-A x-x-x; Tk 2, Mkz 4.

?A/B   madoromu ?< *ma$_{1.3a}$ (-n-) toroma- ?< *tora-ma- or (cf. toro^b/$_m$osu) *tora-
n[a]-pa- *(the second vowel assimilated to the first)*. 'doze off'. x - B-A-A
x-x-x. ⓪ madoromi x - A-A-A x-x-x.

?B   madou < matofu < *matopa-. 'get bewildered'. B - B-A-A x-x-B. NS (Okada) B.
Km (W) B. Mr (Bm) B. Edo B. Ib *(rare)* B. Yn madurun B (?< mayou). ⓪ madoi x -
2-A-A x-x-x.

?B   madowasu < matofasu < *matopa-sa-. 'bewilder'. x - B-A-A x-x-x.
(Sr mangwasyun A < *maguras-, cf. magureru.)

?B   magaeru < *magafey- < *ma$_{1.3a}$ -n- kapa-Ci-$_A$. 'confuse, fool the eye'.
(B) - x-x-x x-x-x.

A   magaru < *manka-ra- (cf. maga$_{2.1}$). 'bend, turn' (vi.). A - A-A-A A-A-x.
Ib B̲. Nk magaarun A; Sr magar- A; Hateruma man^k/$_g$arun. ⓪ magari x - A-A-A x-A-x.

?B   magau < magafu < *ma$_{1.3a}$ -n- kapa-$_A$ ('eye exchange'). 'get mixed (up),
be confused (with); resemble'. B - B-A-A x-x-x. Km (W) B. ⓪ magai x - 3/0-A-A
x-x-x. Km (W) B.

A   mageru < magey- < *manka-Ci- (cf. maga$_{2.1}$). 'bend it'. A - A-A-A A-A-x.
Edo A. Ib B̲. Nk magi(i)run A; Sr magir- A. ⓪ mage 'topknot'. A - A-A-A x-A-x.

(B)   magirau (Myōgo-ki) = magireru.

B   magireru < magire[y]- ?< *ma-giyre[y]- < *ma$_{1.3a}$ -n- k^u/$_o$Cira-Ci- ('eyes
fog'). 'be confused (with); be indistinguishable; get diverted'. x - B-A-B
x-x-x. Km (B). Edo B. Ib B. ⓪ magire x - B-A-B x-A̲-x. Edo HHL. Sr mazirir- A
< *magire-. Cf. magirawasi$_{adj}$ $_B$.

?A   magu < *manka-. 'pursue, seek'. x - x-x-x x-x-x. Cf. kunimagi.

B   magureru < magure[y]- < *ma$_{1.3a}$ -n- kura-Ci- $_A$ ('eyes get dark'). 'get
dizzy, faint'. x - B-A[U]-(B) x-A̲-x. Sr mangwir- A̲.
⓪ magure B - 1/3-A[U]/B[H]-B x-A̲-x. Sr mangwi A̲.

-         mai(-) < mawi(-): *see* *mau.

?B´<?B+A [maideru] < mawide[y]- < *mawi ide[y]- < *mab[a-C]i inta-Ci-. 'humbly
go/come'. x - x-x-x x-x-x. *See* mooderu.

?B   mainau < mafyinafu < *mapi$_{2.x}$-na-pa-. 'bribe'. x - B-x-x x-x-x.
⓪ mainai < mafyinafyi B - A-A-x x-x-x. The noun mai < mafyi$_{2.x}$ 'gift,
offering' may be derived from a verb infinitive *map[a-C]i; cf. tamau.

?B   ?*mairu: *see* *mau.

B´<?B+A   mair-u < mawiru < *mawi ir-u < *mab[a-C]i$_{?B}$ ira-$_A$. 'humbly go/come'.
B´ - B-B-B x-(x)-x. Edo B´. Tk 1<2. Ib B´ (= L). Sr mooyun B 'deign to go/come'
probably has a different etymology, perhaps < *mi-wofar-.

?B´<?B+A [maitaru] < mawitaru < *mawi itaru < *mab[a-C]i$_{?B}$ ita-ra-$_A$. 'humbly
reach/arrive'. x - x-x-x x-x-x.

B   makanau < makanafu < *maka-na-pa-. 'provide (food), supply, pay for;
prepare, do in advance'. x - B-A-B x-x-x. NS (113b) B. Ib A, B.
⓪ makanai x - 2/0-2[H]/3[U]-B x-B-x.

B´   makaru < *makara-. 'humbly go/come (to report)'. B´ - (B-A-A) x-x-x.
Kz Mg Rxx/LHL (see Mochizuki 1973:50). NS (93a LHL) B´. Km (W) B. Edo B´.

A   makasu < *maka-sa-. 'vanquish'. x - A-A-A x-A[H 1967:450b]-x. Izumo B̲
(but makeru A). Nk makaasun A.

?B   makasu = makaseru < makase[y]- < *maka-sa-Ci-. 'entrust'. B - B-A-A x-x-x.
Km (S) B. Mr (Bm) B. Edo B. Ib A, B. Nk makaasun A.

A   makeru < makey- < *maka-Ci-. 'be vanquished'. A - A-A-A x-A-A.
NS (T+ kun) [ugara] makey-zi [HHH] 𝄐H𝄐 ?= HL|H. Edo A. Ib A. Nk maKiirun A;
Sr makir- A. ⓪ make x - A-A-A x-A-x.

?A   [makeru] < makey- < *maka-Ci-. 'make one withdraw'. x - x-x-x x-x-x.

?B   [makeru] < makey- < *maka-Ci-. 'appoint one'. x - x-x-x x-x-x. Cf. makaru.

?B   [makeru] < *maka-Ci- (?< *ma[ta-Ci*ß* u]ka-Ci-*ß*). 'prepare'. x - x-x-x
x-x-x. Cf. mookeru.

A   maku < *maka-. 'roll it; use as a pillow (= makuraku); embrace one's wife'
A - A-A-A (A)-A-A. NS (73b [11:222-M], 82c [17:111-M], 83a [17:116-M], 106b
[11:256-K] A. NS (T+ 58) makazukyeba k*oso* LHHLL(|)LL; (20) ᴪH, (96) ᴪL; (37)
maku LL. Mr (Bm) A. Edo A. Ib A. Nk maCun A; Sr mak- A.
◻ maki 1-A[U]/2[H]-A (A)-A-x. Mr (Bm) A. Nk x; Sr maci A. Cf. makura.

A   [maku] < *maka-. 'withdraw, retreat'. x - x-x-x x-x-x.

B   [maku] < *maka-. 'entrust' (= makaseru). x - x-x-x x-x-x.

B   maku < *maka-. 'sow (seed)'. B - B-B-B x-B-B. Ib B. Nk maCun B; Sr mak- B.

B   makuraku < *makura*s.5a/b* (< ...) -ka-. 'use as a pillow'. x - x-x-x x-x-x.

A   makureru < makure[y]- < *ma[ka-Ci]*A* kura-Ci-*ß*. 'get rolled/turned up'.
x - A-A-A x-x-x. Ib A.

A   makuru < *ma[ki -] kuru < *mak[a-C]i*A* kura-*ß*. 'roll, tuck up'. x - A-A-A
x-x-x. Ib A. Nk maqKun **B**. Cf. mekuru.

B   mamieru < mamiye[y]- < *ma-myiye[y]- < *ma*1.3a* mi-da-Ci-*ß* (or miCa-Ci-*ß*).
'have an audience (with)'. B - B-A-**A** x-x-x.

?A   mamireru < mamire[y]- (< ?). 'be covered/smeared (with)'. A - B-A-A x-x-x.
◻ mamire x - x-x-x x-x-x.

?B   mamoru < ma**b**/**◾**oru/maforu, mamworu < *ma*1.3a* mora-/pora-*?ß* ('eye watch').
'guard'. B - B-A-**A** x-B-x. Ongi B. Km (S) B. Mr (Bm) ?B. Edo (-**b**/**◾**-) B. Ib B.
Nk mamurun B. ◻ mamori x - B-A-**A** x-B-x. Km (W) B. Wakamatsu **A**. Nk mamui B.

A   manabu < (*manabiru <) manabiy- < *mana-np**◾**/**◦**Ci- (?< -n[a]-pa-Ci-).
'learn; emulate'. A - A-A-A x-x-x. Edo A. Ib A. Attested as manabi- in 1187
(KggD 972a). ◻ manabi x - A-A-A x-x-x. Cf. mane, maneru.

?A   manebu < (*manebiru <) manebiy- ?< *mana-Ci[-Ci]*A* -np**◾**/**◦**Ci- (?< -n[a]-
pa-Ci-). 'mimic; report exactly'. x - A-x-x x-x-x. ◻ manebi x - A-x-x x-x-x.
Nk meebi A (< *ma[n]ibi); Sr neebi A.

A   manegir-u < *mane-gyir- < *mana-Ci[-Ci]*2.1a* n[i] kira-*ß*. 'model/pattern
after, imitate'. A - x-A-x x-x-x.

B   maneku < *maneka- (< ?). 'beckon, invite'. B - B-A-A x-B[Lit.]-x. Edo B.
Ib B. Sr man**i**/**◾**cun (manik-) B. ◻ maneki x - B-A-A x-x-x.

A   maneru < mane[y]- < *mana-Ci-. 'mimic'. x - A-A-A A-x-x. Hattō, Hamada,
Goka-mura **B**; Matsue, Izumo A. Ib **B**. ◻ mane x - A-A[U]/2[H]-A x-B-x. Matsue,
Izumo, Goka-mura A. Nk x; Sr mani A. Cf. manabu, manebu.

B   manu**k**/**ɡ**areru < manu**k**/**ɡ**are[y]- < manogare[y]- < *ma*1.3a* nonka-ra-Ci-*ß'*.
'escape, be saved (from)'. B - B-A-B x-x-x. Km (S) B. Mr (Bm) B.

A   marobasu < marobasu < *maro*s.1* -n[a]-pa-sa-. 'cause to roll/tumble'.
A - A-x-x x-x-x.

A   marobu < marobu < *maro*s.1* -n[a]-pa-. 'roll, tumble'. A - A-A-x x-x-x.
NS (114a) A. Hachijō marubu 'die'. Cf. korobu ("from Km").

A   maro**k**/**ɡ**ar(er)u < marokaru/marokare[y]- < *maro*s.1* -ka-ra-(Ci-). 'form a
lump or mass'. x - x-x-x x-x-x.

A   maro**k**/**ɡ**asu < marokasu < *maro*s.1* -ka-sa-. 'lump it (make it into a lump)'.
x - x-A-x x-x-x.

B   maru < *mara- (or perhaps *-n-para-). 'void (feces/urine); (kuso ~)
defecate; urinate'. B - x-x-x x-B-x. NS yu-mari L-ᴪH =? L|LH 'urinating'.
Nk man B; Sr mar- B. Fukuoka baru/maru. Cf. maru*?2.3*, yubari*s.6*; mor- 'leak';
Korean malyew- 'feel an urge to urinate or defecate'.

A   marumaru < *maru*s.1* -ma-ra-. 'become round'. x - A-A-A x-(x)-x.

A   marumeru < marumey- < *maru*s.1* -ma-Ci-. 'make it round'. x - A-A-A x-A-x.
Ib A. Nk maru(u)min A.

A   marumu < *maru$_{2.1}$ -ma-. 'become round' (= marumaru). x - x-x-x x-A-x.
Sr marunun (marum-) A.
A   masaguru ?< *ma$_{1.1}$ sagur-$_A$ (< ?). 'grope'. A - B-A-A x-x-x.
A   masaru < *masa-ra-. 'excel, surpass'. A - A/B-A-A x-A-x. Km (W) A. Edo A.
Wakamatsu B. Ib B. Nk masaarun A.
A   [maseru] < mase[y]- < *ma-sa-Ci-. 'get/invite someone to deign to
sit/go/come'. x - x-x-x x-x-x.
?A+A   masimasu < masi-masu < *mas[a-C]i$_A$ masa-$_A$ (iteration). 'deign to be'.
HHLx, xHLx, HHxx - B-A-x x-x-x. K: Edo HLLL.   See masu.
A   masu < *masa-. 'increase (vi./vt.); excel'. A - A-A[U]/B[H]-A x-x-x.
Km (S,W) A, Edo A. Kōchi, Ib A. ◻ masi x - A-A-A x-A-x.
A   masu < *ma-sa- (< ?). 'deign to be/stay; deign to go/come'. A - B-x-x
x-x-x. NS (91a masimas-, 94a, 95b, 103b, 112b [14:11L-K but 14:11-K mi-n̄e
mas̄eru has mistakes in both parts], 114a, 124b) A. NS (T+ 96) masi L̲H̲;
(102) masu LL.
B   matagaru < *mata$_{2.3}$ -n[a]-ka-ra-. 'get astride/astraddle; extend (over),
span' (vi.). B - B-A-B x-x-x. Ib B.
?B=2.3+A matagoeru < mata-koye[y]- < *mata$_{2.3}$ kwoda-Ci-$_A$. 'bestride'. x - x-x-x
x-x-x. NS (95a) ?B = 2.3+A.
B   matagu < *mata$_{2.3}$ -n[a]-ka-. 'bestride, straddle'. x - B-A-B x-x-x. Ib B.
-        matataku: see madataku.
B   matigaeru < matigafey- < *ma$_{1.3a}$ tinkapa-Ci-$_A$ (< *ti$_{?1.1}$ -n- kapa-Ci-$_A$).
'mistake; blunder'. x - B-A-B x-B-x. Ib A. Nk maCige(eru)n B; Sr macigeer- B.
B   matigau < matigafu < *ma$_{1.3a}$ tinkapa-$_A$ (< *ti$_{?1.1}$ -n- kapa-$_A$). 'be
wrong/mistaken'. x - B-A-B x-B-x. Ib A. Nk maCiga(aru)n B; Sr macigar- B.
◻ matigai x - 3-A-B x-B-x. Nk maCigai B. The first element must be 'eye', not
'room, space, interval' (despite the traditional orthography), for otherwise
the register would be incongruent.
A   matomaru < *mato(-)ma-ra-. 'be settled; get into order, take shape; be
brought together, united'. x - A-A-A x-A-x. Hattō, Hamada, Matsue, Izumo B.
Ib A. ◻ matomari x - A-A-A x-x-x. Hattō, Hamada, Matsue B; Izumo A/B.
Cf. matou, matuwaru.
A   matomeru < matome[y]- < *mato(-)ma-Ci-. 'settle; put into order, arrange;
put together, unite, consolidate'. x - A-A-A x-A-x. Hattō, Hamada, Matsue,
Izumo B. Ib A. ◻ matome x - A-A-A x-x-x. Cf. matou, matuwaru.
A   matou < matofu < *mato-pa-. 'wrap around; put on, wear'. A - A/B-A-A
x-x-x. Edo A/B. Cf. matuu. ◻ matoi 'foreman's standard' x - A-A-A x-x-x.
A   matowaru < matofaru < *mato-pa-ra-. 'coil (round), wreathe' (= matuwaru).
x - B-x-x x-x-x. Tk artificial?
A   matowasu < matofasu < *mato-pa-sa-. 'entwine'. x - B-x-x x-x-x. Tōkyō
accent artificial?
B   matu < *mata-. 'wait, expect'. B - B-B-B B-B-B. NS (76a [14:122-M], 76b
[14:122-M], 117b) B. NS (T+ 75) matu t̲o̲ LLL = LL(|)L, (7) matu ya HH(|)H.
Km (S,W) B. Edo B. Ib B. Nk maCun B; Sr mat- B. Unger has *matu- because of
maturu, but that verb is A and therefore must be unrelated in etymology.
A   maturau < maturafu < *matura-pa-. 'wait upon'. x - x-x-x x-x-x.
NS (76b) A. NS (T+ 75) maturafu HLLL. K: Hn A, Kt A.
A   [maturoeru] < maturo̲fey- < maturafey- < *matura-pa-Ci-. 'have/let
one serve'. x - x-x-x x-x-x.
A   [maturou] < maturwofu < maturafu < *matura-pa- (< ...). 'serve, be in
service'. x - x-x-x x-x-x.

A   maturu < *matura- (?< *ma*1.1* *"place"* tura-*A*). 'celebrate a festival;
offer up; deign to eat/drink'. A - A/B-A-A x-A-A. NS (124b) A. NS (T+ 102)
maturamu LLLH, (78) maturamu to LLLH|L; (32) maturi ko-si LHH L-L; (102)
maturu ꬲLL ?= LLL. Km (S) A. Edo A. Narada, Hattō, Hamada, Matsue, Izumo,
NE Kyūshū A; Goka-mura B. Ib A. Nk x. ꬲ maturi A - A/B-A-A x-A-x. Narada
(etc.) A. Nk maCii A.

A   matuu < matufu < *matu-pa-. 'put on, wear' (= matou). A - x-A-x x-x-x.

A   matuwaru < matufaru < *matu-pa-ra-. 'coil (round), wreathe'. A - B-A-A
x-(?A)-x. Km (S,W) A. Ib *(rare)* A. Sr maçibur- A. Cf. matowaru, matowasu.

A   mau < mafu < *mapa- (?= *ma-pa-, cf. *mo-Ci- > miy-). 'whirl; dance'. A -
A-A-A x-A-x. NS (Okada) A. NS (T+ 57) LL. Edo A. Ib A. Nk moorun A; Sr moor- A.
ꬲ mai (A) - A-A-A x-A-x. Km (W) A. Nk moi A; Sr mooi A. Cf. hurumau, uyamau.

?B   ?*mau < *mafu < *mapa-. 'offer, give': *see* mai, mainau; mookeru, mookaru.

?B   *mau < *mawu < *maba-. 'humbly do/be': occurs only in the infinitive mawi
< *mab[a-C]i, as in mawi kure (Koji-ki and NS), mawi komu (M), mawi te[y]-mu
(Bussokuseki 8); NS mawi- → mau-. *See* maideru, maitaru, mair-u; mooderu;
moosu. Perhaps mawi is better treated as mawi[y] < *mab**ᵘ**/₂-Ci[-Ci]. NS (93b)
maū-kó["]su 'not yet come [back]'; (73b) mawī-kuré; (93b) mau-kéri 'has come';
(113b) maū-susum[u] (= susum[i]) tē 'advanced'; (119b) maū-nofara[se] 'go up';
(126b) maū-kerū 'who had come'.

A   mawaru < mafaru < *mapa-ra-. 'go/turn round; revolve, rotate'. x - A-A-A
x-A-x. Edo A. Ib maaru A. Nk maarun A; Sr maar- A. ꬲ mawari x - A-2-A A-A-x.
Nk x. ꬲꬲ o-mawari 3-1:3-B x-x-x. Edo A.

A   mawasu < mafasu < *mapa-sa-. 'turn it round; send round; forward; hand it
on'. x - A-A-A x-A-x. Edo A. Ib maasu A. Nk maasun A; Sr maas- A.

-          mawi(-), ?mawi[y]-: *see* *mau.

?B   mayou < may**ʷᵒ**/ᵤfu < *ma*1.3a* dwopa-*bad* **v** ('eye waver'). 'get frayed; get
bewildered' (later confused with madou). B - B-A-A x-(B)-B. Mr (Bm) B. Edo B.
Ib B. Nk mayurun B; Sr mayaas- B (= mayowasu); Yn madurun B (?< madow-).
ꬲ mayoi x - B-A-A x-x-x. Nk mayui B.

B   mazaru < *mansa-ra- ?< *mansi-ra- *(the second vowel assimilated to the
first)*; ?< maz[e] ar- (< ...). 'get/be mixed' (vi.). x - B-A-B x-(x)-x.
Ib B. Nk mazaarun B; Sr mazirir- B < *mazire-. Cf. mazeru, mazir-u. Komatsu
1981:81 says mazaru is a Meiji creation to replace mazir-u for phonesthetic
reasons; but Nakijin has not only a reflex of mazar- but also the transitive
mazaasun B < *mazas-.

B   mazeru < maze[y]- < ?*mansa-Ci-; ?< (maz[if]ey- <) *mansi-pa-Ci- *(the
second vowel assimilated to the first)*. 'mix' (vt.). x - B-B-B (B)-B-x. Ib B.
Sd matyryeyun (?< *matire- < *mazire-); Nk manKin B, manzin B; Sr mazir- B
(= mankir- A): see mazir-u. Cf. mazaru.

?B   mazieru < mazife[y]- < *mansi-pa-Ci-. 'mix (= mazeru); cross; exchange'
(vt.). B - B-A-A x-x-x. NS (112a) B. Km (S) B. Ib B.

A   mazinau < mazinafu < *mansi*(?2.1)* -na-pa-. 'charm'. A - A/B-A-A x-x-x.
ꬲ mazinai x - 3/0-A-A x-x-x. Hattō, Hamada, Matsue, Izumo A; Goka-mura 1.

B   mazirogu < maziroku < *ma*1.3a* -n- siroka-*B* (?< *sirwo-ka-). 'blink'.
B - B-A-x x-x-x. ꬲ mazirogi x - A/B-A-A - x-x-x.

B   mazir-u < *mansi-ra-. 'get mixed' (vi.). B - B-A-B x-x-x. Edo B. Ib B.
Nk mancun B; Sr mancun (mank-) B and mankiyun (mankir-) A are probably <
*mansi[-ra]-ki-; cf. wasureru, Thorpe 306.

?B   maziwaru < mazifaru < *mansi-pa-ra-. 'mingle' (vi.). B - B-A-<u>A</u> B-B-x.
Km (S) B. NE Kyūshū <u>A</u>. Nk x; Sr maziwar- B 'socialize' borrowed?
[] maziwari x - 3/4/0-A-<u>A</u> x-B-x. Hattō <u>A</u>; Hamada, Matsue, Izumo B;
Goka-mura 1. Nk maziwai B. Is Mg <u>mazifari</u> the infinitive?

B   mederu < meyde[y]- (?< *ma-Ci -n[a]-ta-Ci-, cf. megumu_B, [megu]_{adj B}).
'appreciate, like'. B - B-B-x x-x-x. NS (T+ 67) meydezu LH<u>L</u>; (67) meyde-ba
LH-L; (67) meyde LH; (67)meyduru LHL. Km (W) B. Edo B. Cf. medeta_{adj B,}
mezurasi_{adj B}.

?A/B   megeru < mege[y] < *menka-Ci- (< ?). 'collapse, get smashed/broken;
succumb, surrender; decline in health/spirit'. x - B-A[H]/B[U]-A x-x-x.

?A/B   megu < *menka- (< ?). 'smash, crush, break'. x - x-x-x x-x-x. Cf. Korean
mwunu- 'demolish'.

?B´   megumu < meygumu ?< *meygu_{adj B} (?< *ma-Ci_{1.3a} n[i]ku_{adj B}) -ma-. 'love;
bestow; bless'. B´ - A/B-A-A x-x-x. NS (102b, 134a) B. Edo B. Narada A/B;
Hattō A; Hamada, Matsue, Izumo B. Ib B. [] megumi x - A-A-A x-B[Lit.]-x. NS
(91a, 92a) B. Nk x.

A   megurasu < meygurasu ?< *ma[pa-C]i_A -n- kura-sa-_B. 'enclose/surround with;
... '. A - A-<u>B</u>[new]-A x-A-x. Ib (rare) A, B. NS (110a) A. Nk miguraasun A;
Sr miguras-/mingwas- A.

A   meguru < meyguru ?< *ma[pa-C]i_A -n- kura_B-. 'go/turn round; surround'.
A - A-A-A x-A-A. Ongi A. NS (115a) A. Km (S) A. Edo A. Ib A. Nk miguurun A;
Sr migur-/mingwir- A. Yn (H 1967:399a, 1964:186b) A. [] meguri x - x-A-x x- A-x.
Note: Yoshida derives this from mey < *ma-Ci_{1.3a} but the register (B) is wrong.
Unger takes it to be a lexicalized mey- (instead of the expected *miy-) <
*m<u>o</u>-Ci- with a root *m<u>o</u>- 'turn' found also in mogoyou, motooru/motoosu, and
perhaps motoru (all A); he also includes mom- 'rub' (A) and momit- 'leaves turn
color' but the latter has the wrong register (B). In support of the etymology
suggested here are mawaru and mawasu (A), with similar meanings.

1.3a + A   mehisigu < mey_{1.3a} (< *ma-Ci) fisigu_{?A} (< fisiku < ...). 'close one's
eyes'. L|HHL x-x-x x-x-x.

-    mekari utu < mey-kari utu ?< *ma-Ci_{1.3a} kar[a-C]i_{?B} uta-_B ('hit with eye-
hunt'). 'look askance at'. LLH|LH x-x-x x-x-x.

(B)   (-) meku < myeku < *miCa_B-ka- 'show signs of being; look to be'.

A   mekuru < *meykuru < *ma[ka-C]i_A kura-_B. 'turn over/up; tear off'.
x - A-A-A x-x-x. Ib A. Cf. makuru.

1.3b+A   me-maku < mye-maku < *miCa_{1.3b} maka-_A. 'take a wife, get married' (≠ 'seek
a wife' with magu). RHx (Kn), <u>HHL</u> (Kz) - x-x-x x-x-x.

?B   mer-u < mera- (?< Ch <u>myat</u>, by way of Sino-Korean myel; ?< (n)pera-,
cf. her-u). 'diminish, weaken' (vi.). x - x-x-x x-x-x. [] meri x - 2/0-1-x x-x-x.

B   mesu < myesu < *miCa-sa-. '(deign to see >) do, wear, eat, ... '.
B - B-B-B x-B-x. Ongi B. NS (92b, 93b, 102b, 103a, 103b, 120a) B. Edo B. Narada
A [Lit.]. Sr miṣeen B (?< *mesi-ofari-). [] mesi 'food' x - B-2-B B-x-x.

B   mezamasu < *meyzamasu < *ma-Ci _{1.3a} (-n-) sama-sa-_B. 'rouse, wake someone
up'. x - B-A-B x-x-x.

B   mezameru < *meyzamey- < *ma-Ci_{1.3a} (-n-) sama-Ci-_B. 'wake up' (vi.).
x - B-A-B x-x-x. Ib B. [] mezame x - B-A-B x-x-x.

B   mezasu < *meyzasu < *ma-Ci_{1.3a} (-n-) sasa-_B. 'aim'. x - B-A-B x-x-x.
Ib B. Not attested before Mr. [] mezasi x - B-x-x x-x-x.

B   midarakasu (JP) < *minta-ra-ka-sa-. 'disorder, disturb' (= midasu).
x - x-x-x x-B-x. Sr nzarakas- B < *midarakas-.

B   midareru < myidare[y]- < *minta-ra-Ci-. 'fall in disorder; be disturbed,
chaotic; be corrupt'. B - B-A-B x-B-x. Km (W) B. Edo B. Ib A. Nk midaarin B,
(concrete things) mizyaarin B, ('get snarled') zaarin B; Sr nzarir- B.
◌ midare x - B-A-B x-B-x. Edo HHL. Cf. midara*adj-B* x - 1/0-A-A x-x-x.

B   midaru < myidaru < *minta-ra-. '(put/throw into) disorder), disturb,
corrupt' (vt.), replaced by midasu "from chūsei" (i.e., sometime after 1200).
B - B-A-x x-x-x. Km (W) B. Edo (midar-/midare-) B. ◌ midari B - 1-A[H]/B[U]-A
x-x-x. Mr (Bm) LHH.

B   midasu < myidasu < *minta-sa-. 'disorder, disturb, corrupt', replacing
midaru "from chūsei" (i.e., sometime after 1200). x - B-A-B x-x-x. Ib A.
Cf. midarakasu.

B   mieru < myiye[y]- < *mi-da-Ci- or *miCa-Ci- (?= *mida-Ci-). 'get seen'.
B - B-B-B x-B-x. NS (126a) B. NS (T+ 86) myiyezu ka mo aramu LHE H(|)L LLH;
myiyene-ba HHH-H (Ōno), LHH-H (Tsuchihashi, Aiso); (34, 87, 101) myiyu LH.
Km (W) B. Mr (Bm) B. Edo B. Ib B. Nk miirun B.

A   migaku (?< *myigaku < *m[om]i-kaku < *mom[a-C]i*A* kaka-*B*; ?< *min[a]*2.1*
kaka-*B*). 'polish'. A - A-A-A x-A-x. Mr (Bm) A. Edo A. Ib A. Nk migaacun B;
Sr nzas- A < *miga[ka]s-. ◌ migaki x - A-A-A x-x-x.

?A   migomoru < *miy-gomoru < *mu-Ci*1.1* (-n-) koma-ra-*B*. 'get pregnant'.
x - B-A-A x-x-x.

?B   [mimisiu] < myimyi-sifu < *mimi*2.3* sipa-*?A*. 'go deaf'. (B) - x-x-x x-x-x.
◌ [mimisii] < mimisifi LLLL - x-x-x x-x-x. Cf. Miyako min-s[ï]p[ï]sa 'deaf
person'.

?A   minagirau < myinagiyrafu < *mina*?2.1* (-n-) k*a*/*o*Cira-pa-. '(a cloud of)
spray arise'. x - x-x-x x-x-x. This verb occurs only in M 1401, where it is
written with semantograms.

?A(/B)   minagirau < myinagyirafu < *mina*?2.1* (-n-) kira-pa- *B*. 'keep overflowing'.
x - x-x-x x-x-x. NS (T+ 118) myinagyirafyi tutu HL|HLL LL.

?A(?B)   minagir-u < myinagyir-u < *mina*?2.1* (-n-) kira-*B*. 'overflow'. A - B-A-B
x-x-x.

A   minoru < *miyno- < *mu-Ci*1.1* nora-*A* ('ride, be borne' — or ?< *nara-
'become'). 'bear fruit'. x - A/B-A-A x-x-x. Matsue A; Hattō, Hamada, Izumo,
Goka-mura B.

A   miobiku < myiwobyiku < *mi-bo*?2.2b/2.1* (< ...) -n- pika-*A*. 'row with the
current'. (A) - x-x-x x-x-x. ◌ miobiki A - x-x-x x-x-x.

?A   [miru] < miy- < *mo-Ci-. 'turn'. x - x-x-x x-x-x. Cf. meguru, motooru,
motoosu, motoru, modoru, modosu; mau; [tamiru], [i-tamiru]. ◌ (···)mi 'around,
the bend of ···'. Cf. -bi.

B   miru < myi- < *mi-/miCa-. 'see'. B - B-B-B B-B-B. Ongi (Iroha) B.
NS (72c [11:208-M], 84a [17:124-M], 98a, 99b, 101a) B. NS (T+) myire-ba (34)
LH-H, (87) LL-L, (55, 102) HH-L; myi ga fosi (54) H(|)H LL, (84) H(|)H HH;
(115) myituramu ka H(|)LLL|H(|)H, (40) myi-turu mono H(|)HL|HL. NS (T+ kun)
myiru masakari ni HH LLHL|H. Km (S,W) B. Edo B. Nk myun B; Sr nuun/nnzun (neg.
nndan) B. Cf. mesu < myesu < *miCa-sa- 'deign to see' (= misu < *mi-sa-).

B   miseru < myise[y]- < *mi-sa-Ci-. 'show'. x - B-B-B x-B-x. NS (102b, 119a)
B. NS (T+ 97) myise-ba LH-H. Km (S,W) B. Mr (Bm) B. Edo B. Ib B. Nk misi(i)run
B. ◌ mise x - B-2-B x-x-x. Cf. mesu.

A   misogu < *miy-[so]sogu < *mu-Ci*1.1* sosoka-*A*. 'wash (as religious
purification)'. (A - A-A-A) x-x-x. ◌ misogi A - A-A-A x-x-x.

B   mitasu < *myitasu < *mita-sa-, but Nr and Hn use miteru. 'fill, supply,
satisfy'. x - B-A-B x-B-x. Nk miKaasyun B 'fill', miCaasun B 'close the door';
Sr mitas- B = micir- B (< mite[y]-). Cf. miteru; mitiru.

x   mitasu (< ?). 'deign to go/come'. x - x-x-x x-x-x.

B   miteru < myite[y]- < *mita-Ci-. 'fill it' (= mitasu). (B) - x-x-x x-B-x.
Edo B. Nk micirun B; Sr micir- B; the -c- is due to the preceding palatal
syllable: miciy··· < mitir-y··· < miter-y··· restructured from mite-.

A   mitibiku < myitibyiku < *miti₂.₁ -n- pika-ₐ. 'guide, lead'. A - B-A-A
x-B[Lit.]-x. Hattō, Hamada, Matsue, Izumo B. Ib A. ⬚ mitibiki x - B-A-A x-x-x.

B   mitiru < miti- ("from Km" — but still a consonant stem in Heike-mabushi,
Okumura 1981:270) ← mit- < myit- < *mita-. 'get full'. (B) - B-B-B x-(B)-x.
Km (S,W) B. Edo B. Ib B. Nk miCun B; Sr micun (mit-) B < mity··· < mit-i ··· .
Cf. miteru, mitasu, mitu. Mg mit̄eri < *mit[y]eri < *mit[a-C]i ar[a-C]i.

A < B+?   mitomeru < myiī tomey- ('see stop', Ōno) or myiī tomey- ('see seek',
Ōtsuki) (< ...). 'recognize, acknowledge; judge'. x - A-A[U]/B[H]-B x-x-x.
Hattō A; NE Kyūshū, Hamada, Matsue, Izumo B; Goka-mura 1/A. Ib A. Nk miTumin B.
⬚ mitome x - A[U]/B[H]-B x-x-x. Hattō, Hamada, Matsue, Izumo A.

B   mitu < myitu < *mita-. 'get full' (→ mitiru from Km). B - (B-B-B) x-B-x.
See mitiru. Cf. miteru, mitasu.

?A/B   [miyabiru] < myiyabiy- < *mi-da₂.₁ -npᵘ/₂Ci- (?< -n[a]-pa-Ci-).
'be urban, elegant'. x - B-x-x x-x-x. ⬚ miyabi x - A-A-x x-x-x. NS (91b) A.

?A/B   miyakobiru < myiyakwo-biy- < *mida-kwo₂.₁ -npᵘ/₂Ci- (?< -n[a]-pa-Ci-).
'be cosmopolitan'. x - B-x-x x-x-x.

-        [mizuwasasu]: mizuwasasu LHxxxx (Kn Sō-chū 136:4), mituwasasu LLLLH (Ck
3:92, misprinted as "3:91" in Mochizuki 519a) = mizufa-sasu 'get very old' <
mizufa (?*LHL, cf. usuba) < myidu₂.₄ fa₁.₃b < *mi(n)tu pa 'felicitous tooth;
tooth growing back in an old person; getting old, an old person' + *sasa-ᵦ.

?A   mizuku < myiduku < *min[a]₂.₁ tuka-?ₐ. 'get soaked (in water)'. x - B̲-A-x
x-x-x. NS (Okada) A. NS (T+ 95) myiduku HHH.

1.1 + B   mizuku < miduku < *miy-duku < *mu-Ci₁.₁ n[i] tuka-ᵦ ('adhere to one's
body/self'). 'get skilled, proficient'. HLxx = *H[H]-LH - x-x-x x-x-x. Is the
contracted form attested only by Mg?

?A/B   modaeru < modaye[y]- < *montadaCi- (< ?; cf. mogaku, mogoyou, [miru] <
miy-). 'writhe, agonize'. ?A [Ir] - B-A-A x-x-x. Edo A. Hattō B; Hamada,
Matsue A; Izumo A/B. ⬚ modae x - 2/3-A-A x-x-x.

2.2 + A   modasu < moda su < *mo(n)ta?ₐdᵥ so̲-ₐ (*see* suru). 'keep silent, not
speak'. HL|F, HL|H, [Ir] RL|L - x-x-x x-x-x. Km (S) modasite HLLL. Edo HLL.

B   modoku < *montoka- (< ?). 'imitate; censure, reproach'. ?B - B-x-x x-A̲-x.
⬚ modoki x - B-x-x x-x-x. Cf. modokasiₐdⱼ ᵦ.

A   modorokasu < *montoro-ka-sa-. 'make it speckled or spotted; confuse'.
A - x-A-x x-x-x.

A   modorokeru < modorokey- < *montoro-ka-Ci-. 'make it speckled/spotted;
confuse' (= modorokasu). x - x-x-x x-x-x.

A   modoroku < *montoro-ka-. 'become speckled/spotted; get confused';
(Nk, Sr) 'be confused/hesitant (as from failing eyesight)'. A - x-x-x x-A-x.
(modoro = madara₃.₁ 'spot')

B   modoru < *monto̲-ra- (see mozir-u); other ideas: ?< *moto-ra-; ?< *mo̲-
(cf. [miru] < miy-) tora- (cf. Korean :twol- 'turn') or *mo̲- ara- *(the second
vowel assimilated to the first)* < *mo̲- [i]ta-ra-. 'return, go back; revert'.
B - B-A-B x-A̲-B. Ib B. Nk mudurun B; Sr mudur- A̲ [accent mistaken?].
⬚ modori x - B-A-B x-x-x. Nk, Sr mudui B.

B   modosu < *monto̲-sa- (see mozir-u); other ideas: ?< moto-sa-; ?< *mo̲-
to[ra]-sa- or < *mo̲- tasa- *(second vowel assimilated to the first)* < *mo̲-
[i]ta-sa-. 'return it; put/send it back; vomit'. x - B-A-B x-B-x. Edo B. Ib B.
Nk mudusun B, Sr mudus- B.

A   moeru < mwoye[y]- < *mwoda-Ci-. 'burn' (vi.). A - A-A-A A-A-A. Km (S,W) A.
    Ib A. Sd mii(r)yum A; Nk muirun A; Sr meer- A. [] moe x - A-A-A x-x-x.
?(A/)B   moeru < moye[y]- < *moda-Ci- (cf. moyasu), or meye[y]- (the first vowel
    assimilated to the second) < *maCi₁.₉ₐ -da-Ci. 'sprout'. B - A-A-A x-B-x. Ib A.
    Nk muirun B; Sr miir- B. Cf. moyoosu, ?[moiru]. [] moe [dial.] 'sprout'.
?(A/)B   mogaku ?< *monka-ka- < *monkoₘ₁ₘ -ka- (cf. mogoyou); ?< mom[i]-kaku <
    *mom[a-Ci]ₐ kaka-ₐ. 'writhe, struggle, flounder'. x - B-A-A x-x-x. Cf. modaeru.
?B   mogaku < *monka-ka-. 'pluck; wrench/tear off, wrest' (= mogu). x - x-x-x.
?B   mogeru < moge[y]- < *monka-Ci-. 'get wrenched/torn off, be plucked'.
    (B) - B-A[H]/B[U]-A x-x-x. Ib B. Nk mugirun B.
A   mogoyou < mogoyofu < *monkoₘ₁ₘ dwopa-ₐₐₐ v. 'wriggle/wiggle along; snake'.
    A - x-x-x x-x-x. NS (Okada) B. Cf. mogo-mogo = mogu-mogu; ugo-meku; [miru] <
    miy-; mogaku, modaeru.
?B   mogu < *monka-. 'pluck; wrench/tear off, wrest'. B - B-A[H]/B[U]-A x-(x)-
    x. Mg (Kn) -k-. Ib B. Nk muzun B; Sr muink- < *mori-mug- B. (Nk mun B ← mur-
    < mor-.) Cf. mogaku, moru.
B   moguru < *monkura- (< ?, cf. kukuru). 'dive'. x - B-A-B x-x-x. Izumo A.
    Ib A, B. [] moguri 1-1:3-B x-x-x.
x   ?[moiru] < mo[y]i[y]- (?< *modo-Ci- < *moda-Ci-). 'bud' (= moeru). We have
    but one example, and Zdb (751a) is dubious about it: mo[y]i - tutu (M 4111).
B   mokuromu < *mokuro[n] (< Ch myuk-.lwen) -ma-. 'plan, envisage'.
    x - B-A[H]/A´[U]-B x-B-x. Nk muKurumin B; Sr mukurum- B. Is Umegaki's Kyōto
    mokuromu a mistake? [] mokuromi x - A/B-A-B x-B-x. Nk mukurumii B; Sr mukurumi B.
B   [momiziru, momizu] < momidi- < momyitu < *momi₉₂.₁ -ta-. '(leaves) turn
    color'. B - x-A-x x-x-x. Km (W) B. Edo (A/)B. [] momizi x - 1-2-B x-A-x. The
    etymology is incongruent in register.
?B   [momodaru] < *mwomwo₉.₉ -n- tara-ₐ ('hundred suffice'). 'be amply provided'
    Cf. [sodaru], [todaru], [tidaru].
A   momu < *moma-. 'rub (with both hands), massage'. A - A-A-A A-A-A. Edo A.
    Ib A. Nk mumin B; Sr mum-. [] momi 'cloth rub-dyed solid red' x - 1-A-x x-x-x.
B=2.3+A   monoiu < mono(-)ifu < *mono₉.₉ ipa-ₐ. 'speak'. LL(|)HL - 2(monoˈiu)-
    2(moˈnoiu)-x x-x-x. Nk x. [] monoii 'speech; dispute; objection'.
    x - 3-3[U]/4[H]-B x-B-x. Nk, Sr munuqii B.
B   monukeru < monuke[y]- ?< *mo₁.₉ₑ nuka-Ci-ₐ. 'shed (its skin); escape'.
    B - B-x-x x-x-x.
?B´<?B+B   mooderu < maude[y]- < *mawi[y]ₑ ide[y]-ₑ < *ma-bᵐ/₂-Ci[-Ci] inta-Ci-.
    'humbly go out (to worship), visit a temple'. B´ - A[Mkz]/B-A[U]/B[H]-B x-x-x.
    NS (118a, 132b) B´. Edo B.
B   mookaru < mɔɔkaru < maukaru ?< *ma[fyi]₉.₉ ukaruₑ < ?*map[a-C]i uka-ra-ₑ.
    'profit'. x - B-A-B x-x-x.
B   mookeru < mɔɔke- < mauke[y]- ?< *ma[fyi]₉.₉ ukey-ₑ < *map[a-C]i uka-Ci-ₑ.
    'gain as profit'. B-A-B x-B-x. Ib B. Nk mooKin B; Sr mookir- B.
    [] mooke x - B-2-B x-B-x. NS (134a) B. Edo HHL. Nk mooKi B; Sr mooki B.
B   mookeru < mɔɔke- < mauke[y]- ?< *ma[fyi]₉.₉ ukey-ₑ <
    *ma[ti]ₑ ukey-ₑ < *mat[a-C]iₑ uka-Ci-ₑ. 'prepare, set up'. B - B-A-B x-x-x.
    Edo B. Ib B. Cf. [makeru]. Both verbs mookeru are usually regarded as a single
    etymon and that is often treated as an "extension" of makey-.
B   moosu < mɔɔsu < mausu < mawosu < *mawasu (the second vowel assimilated
    to the labial w) < *maba-sa-; ?< mawi[y]₉ₑ (< ...) osa-ₐ, ?< *ma(-)bᵐ/₂-sa-
    ('make it humbly be'). 'humbly say'. B - B-A-B x-B-x. NS (104a; 96a, 106b;
    110a) B. NS (T+ 55) mono mawosu ₣L HL₣. Km (S,W) B. Mr (Bm) B. Edo B. Ib B.
    Nk x; Sr (inf) moosi-... B. See *mau.

B´   morasu ‹ *mora-sa-. 'let leak; vent, express; disclose; omit'. B´ - B-A-B
x-x-x. Km x. Ib B. Nk muraasun B.

A   morau ‹ morafu ‹ *morapa- (?= *mora-pa- 'keep heaping up'). 'receive'.
A - A-A-A x-x-x. Ib A. [] morai x - A-A-A x-x-x. Nk x.

?B   morau ‹ morafu ‹ *mora-pa-. 'watchfully await'. x - x-x-x x-x-x.

B   moreru ‹ more[y]- = moru ‹ *mora-. 'leak'. B - B-B-B x-B-x. NS (99a
[11:100L-K]) B. Km (S,W) B. Edo B. Ib B. Nk mun B; Sr mur- B. [] more = mori
x - B-2-B x-x-x.

A   moru ‹ *mora-. 'heap/pile up, dish out/up (food), administer (drugs);
grow thick/dense'. A - A-A-A x-A-x. NS (Okada) A. NS (T+ 94) mori HH. Ib A. Nk
murun A; Sr mur- A. [] mori 'a helping, measure'. x - A-A-A x-x-x. Cf. mori₂.₁.

?B   moru ‹ *mora- (?*mwora-, cf. mamoru). 'guard'. x - B-A-(B) x-A-x. Km (W)
B. Sr muyun (mur-) A. [] mori x - 1-A[U]/B[H](as 'baby-sitter' 1:3)-B x-B-x.
The verb is obsolete except as "dialect".

B   moru ‹ *mora-. 'pluck; wrench/tear off, wrest' (= mogu): see NKD.
x - x-x-x x-B-x. Nk murun B; Sr mur- B ‹ *mor-.

B   moru 'leak': see moreru.

B´   motageru ‹ mot[i]-agey- ‹ *mot[a-C]i anka-Ci-ₐ. 'lift, raise'.
B´ - A/B-A[H]/B[U]-B x-B-x. Nk muCaagin B; Sr mucagir- B ‹ *moti-age-.
[] motage x - x-x-x x-x-x. Nk muCaagi B.

B   motasu ‹ *mota-sa-. 'give, let one have' (= motaseru). x - B-A-B x-x-x.
Nk mutaasun B.

B+B   moteamasu ‹ mote[y] amasu ‹ *mota-Ci[-Ci] ama-sa-ᵦ. 'have too much or
too many'. x - A/B-B-B x-B-x. Nk x. [] motamasi [NKD] x - A-B-x x-B-x. Nk x.

B+A   moteasobu ‹ mote[y] aswobu ‹ *mota-Ci[-Ci] a(-)swonpa-ₐ. 'play with/on,
trifle with'. B+A - A/B-B-B x-B-x. Nk muTaabin B; Sr mutab- B. [] moteasobi
[NKD] x - A-B-x x-x-x.

B+B   motehayasu ‹ mote[y] fayasu ‹ *mota-Ci[-Ci]ᵦ pada-sa-ᵦ. 'extol, praise,
laud; value, treasure'. x - A/B-B-B x-x-x.

B   motenasu ‹ mote[y] nasu ‹ *mota-Ci[-Ci]ᵦ na-sa- ᵦ. 'treat hospitably,
entertain'. x - A/B-B-B x-x-x. Hamada B; Hattō, Matsue, Izumo A. Nk mutinasun B.
[] motenasi x - A-B-B x-x-x. Nk mutinasii B.

B   moteru ‹ mote[y]- ‹ *mota-Ci-. 'be warmly received, be popular'. x - B-B-B
x-x-x. Ib B. Nk muTirun B.

B+A   motiiru ‹ motiwi- ‹ moti wi[y]- ‹ *mot[a-C]i bᵘ/₀-Ci-. 'use'.
B´ (= B+A) - A/B-B-B x-x-x. Ib B´ (= L).

B   motomeru ‹ motomey- ‹ *motomaCi- (‹ ?). 'seek, pursue; desire; request'.
B - B-A-B x-B[Lit.]-x. Ongi B. Mr (Bm) B. Edo B. Ib B. Nk mutumin B; Sr
mutumir- B [Lit.]. Cf. tomeru. [] motome x - B-A-B x-x-x.

A   motooru ‹ motoforu ‹ *motopora-(?‹ *mo-ₐ topo-ra-ₐ). 'turn round'.
A - x-A-x x-x-x. NS (115a) A. NS (T+ 8) motofori HHHL, motoforu HHHH. Cf. [miru]
‹ miy- ‹ *mo-Ci-. (Etymologies with moto₂.₃ are incongruent in register.)

A   motoosu ‹ motofosu ‹ *motoposa- (?‹ *mo-?ₐ topo-sa-ₐ). 'turn; return'.
NS (T+ 32) HLLL. [] [motoosi] ‹ motofosi (‹ ...) HHHH (Zs), HHxx (Kn) - x-(O)-x
x-x-x. Cf. miru ‹ miy- ‹ *mo-Ci-.

?A/B   motoru ‹ motᵗ/ₐoru ‹ *mo(n)tora- ?‹ *moto[fo]r- ‹ *motopora- (?‹ *mo-ₐ
topo-ra-ₐ). 'deviate, run counter (to)'. x - B-A-A x-A-x. Nk x; Sr mudur- A.
Cf. modoru, [miru].

B   motozuku ‹ motoduku ‹ *moto₂.₃ n[i] tuka-ᵦ. 'be based (on)'. B - B-A-B
x-x-x. Ib B.

A   *motu ‹ *mota-. 'stick, adhere'. Cf. moti, moti-moti 'sticky'; mota-mota
'sluggish', (Sado) 'sticky'; motureru; mutubu; mutturi, muttiri; beta-beta.

B   motu < *mota-. 'hold, have'. B - B-B-B B-B-B. NS (73a, 73b, 94b) B. NS
(T+) moti (9) LH, (39, 57, 58) HL. Km (S,W) B. Mr (Bm) ?B. Edo B. Ib B. Nk
muCun B; Sr mut- B (Sr also means 'swell up', cf. mukumu). [] moti x - B-2-B
x-x-x. Cf. moteru.

A   motureru < moture[y]- < *motura-Ci- (?< *mot[a-Ci]ᴀ tura-Ci-ᴀ). 'get
entangled'. x - A/B-A-A x-A-x. Hattō, Hamada, Matsue, Izumo A. Nk x.
[] moture x - A/B-A-A x-A-x.

A   moyasu < *mwoyasu < *mwoda-sa-. 'burn (a fire)' (vt.). x - A-A-A x-A- x.
Ib A. Nk moosun A; Sr mees- A. Cf. moeru.

?A/B   moyasu < *moda-sa-, or (the first vowel assimilated to the labial initial)
< *meyasu < *maCi-da-sa-. 'make it sprout'. (B) - A/B-x-x x-x-x.
[] moyasi x - A/B-A[U]/2[H]-B x-x-x. Cf. moeru.

?A/B   moyau < moyafu < *moda-pa-. (1) 'tie boats together'. (2) 'people gather
for an event' (cf. moyoosu). x - A/B-A-x x-x-x.

?A/B   moyoosu < moyofosu ?< *moyafasu < *modapa-sa-. 'hold (a meeting/party);
arouse, provoke'. B - A/B-A-A x-A-x. Km (S) B. Ib B. Nk x; Sr muyuus- A.
[] moyoosi 'meeting, social function; auspices; urge'. x - A-A-A x-A-x. Nk x;
Sr muyuusi A. Matsumoto 1974:124 derives the verb from moeru 'sprout': ?<
*moye-fasu < *moda[-C]i-pa-sa-.

B   mozir-u < modir-u < *monti-ra- (/ *monti[y]- < *monto̲-Ci-). 'twist'.
B - B-A-A̲ x-B-B. Sr mudir- B < *mude- (lack of palatalization) < *mode[y]- <
*monto̲-Ci-. Yn mudirun B. Cf. nezir-u < nedi[y]-; modoru, modosu; mozi-zuri.
[] moziri x - B-A-A̲ x-x-x; mozi (= mozi-ori) 'crepe' B - B-x-x x-x-x.

-          mubau: see ubau.

A   mudaku < *mu[-Ci]ₗ.ₗ taka-?ʙ. 'embrace'. A - x-x-x x-x-x. Cf. tamudaku;
idaku < *miydaku (or *i-miydaku?) < *mu-Ciₗ.ₗ taka-ʙ.

A   mukaeru < mukafey- < *muka-pa-Ci-. 'welcome, greet'. (A) - A-A-A x-A-x.
Km (S) A. Edo A. Ib A. Nk muKeerun A; Sr nkeer- A. [] mukae x - A-A-A x-x-x.
Edo A. Nk muKee A; Sr qu-nkee B < *o-mukafe.

?A   muka-tamu < *mukaₘᵢₘ₍?<ᴀ₎ tama-ʙ. 'vomit'. x - x-x-x x-x-x.

A   mukau < mukafu < *muka-pa- (?< *npuka-pa-). 'face, be opposite (to),
confront'. A - A-A-A x-A-x. NS (Okada) A. NS (T+ 27) mukafyeru HLHL (? mistake
for HHHL). Km (S) A. Mr (Bm) A. Edo A. Nk muKaarun A = muKeen A; Sr nkayun A
(neg. nkaan). [] mukai x - A-2/A[U]-A x-A-x. Km (W) A. Edo A. Nk muKee A;
Sr mukee A.

A   mukeru < mukey- < *muka-Ci- (?< *npuka-Ci-). 'direct toward' (vt.).
x - A-A-A x-A-x. Edo A. Ib A. Nk muKiirun A; Sr nkir- A.

A   mukeru < mukey- < *muka-Ci-. 'get peeled' (vi.). x - A-A-A x-A-x. Ib A.
Nk muKiirun A; Sr nkir- A.

A   muku < *muka- (?< *npuka-). 'turn toward, face' (vi.). x - A-A-A x-x-x.
NS (T+ 100, 101) mukyi te HL(|)H. Edo A. Matsue, Izumo B̲; Hattō, Hamada,
Goka-mura A. Ib A. Nk muCun A; Sr x (see mukau). [] muki x - 1-1:3-A x-x-x.
Nk, Sr x (see mukai). Cf. [mukatuo] in Ch. 5.

A   muku < *muka-. 'peel, pare, skin'. x - A-A-A x-A-x. Matsue, Izumo B̲;
Hattō, Hamada, Goka-mura A. Ib mugu A. Nk muCun A; Sr ncun A (neg. nkan) ←
nk- < *muk-.

A/B   mukuiru < "mukuwi-, mukufi-" = muku(w)i- < mukuyi[y]- ?(verbalization) <
muku-(y)i < *muk[a-]uᴀ iₗ.ₓ ('that which one faces' [Ōno]). 'reward; requite;
revenge'. A - A/B-A-B x-x-x. Mg mukuyu A. Narada, Hamada B; Hattō, Matsue,
Izumo A. Ib A. [] mukui (see etymology) x - A/B-A-B x-A-x. Edo A. NE Kyūshū A.
Nk, Sr mukui A probably borrowed. Only the noun is attested for Nara period
and that without phonograms.

?A/B   mukumu < *muku_sis_ -ma-. 'swell/puff up'. x - A/B-A-A̲ x-B-x. ⬚ mukumi x - A/B-A-B̲ x-B-x. Nk muKuumin A; Sr mukum- B. Kg register incongruent between verb and noun; mistake in one or the other?

-      mukuu < "mukufu", variant (JP) < mukuiru. Edo A.

A   muneutu < *muna-Ci_2.2b_ uta-_B_. 'beat one's breast (in anguish)'. HHxx (= *HHHL) (Kn) - x-x-x x-x-x.

A   muragaru < *mura_2.1_ -n[a]-ka-ra- (or *mura_A_-n[a]-ka-ra-). 'flock/throng together'. A - B̲-A-A x-x-x. Hattō, Hamada, Matsue, Izumo A. Ib A.

A   mureru < mure[y]- < *mura-Ci-. 'gather, cluster, flock'. x - B̲-A-x x-A-x. Km (W) A. NKD 19:122d has the Kt accent "A", but it is "B" in the "Accent History" note of the adjacent column. Nk buriirun A (and burii-Ku B 'a cluster'), Sr buri- A < *bure- 'gathered, clustered' imply *npura-Ci-. ⬚ mure x - B̲-A-A x-x-x.

B   mureru < mure[y]- < *[u]mu-ra-Ci- (?< *[u]npu-ra-Ci-). 'get steamed'. x - B-B-B x-B-x. Nk quburin B; Sr qnburir- B < *unbure-. Perhaps the initial *u represents an assimilation of the prefix i-. Cf. musu.

A   musaboru < *musa_adv/adj_ ? -n- pora-_?A_. 'covet; indulge in'. A - B̲-A-A x-x-x.

A   musebu < muse^b/_u < musefu (Nr) < *mu(-)sa-Ci-(n[a-])pa-. 'be choked, get stifled'. A-A-A x-x-x. Ib (rare) A.

?A   museru < muse[y]- < *mu(-)sa-Ci-. 'be choked, get stifled'. A/B̲ - A-B̲-A x-x-x. Nk musiirun A. ⬚ muse x - A-x-x x-x-x. Nk x.

?A/B   musibamu < *musi_2.1_ -n- pama-_B_. 'get worm-eaten'. x - B-A-A x-x-x.

A   musikamu < *musi_2.1_ kama-_B_. '(insect) bite'. A - x-x-x x-x-x.

A   musir-u < *musira- (< ?). 'pluck'. A - A-A-A x-A-x. Ib A. Nk musiirun A; Sr musir- A.

?A   musu < *mu-sa-. '(grass/moss) grow, proliferate; *come into being'. Cf. musu-me_3.3_, musu-ko_3.1_; umu_A_.

B   musu < *[u]mu-sa- (?< *[u]npu-sa-). 'steam'. B - B-B-B x-B-x. Kn Mg umosu, Shinsen-Jikyō and modern dialects umusu (see NKD). Ib B. Nk qubusun B; Sr qnbus- B < *unbus-. Perhaps the initial *u represents an assimilation of the prefix i-. Cf. mureru.

A   musubooreru < musubofore[y]- < *musunpopora-Ci- ?< *musunpa-pa-ra-Ci- (with vowel assimilations). 'get snarled up, ... '. A - x-A-x x-x-x.

A   musuboreru < musubore[y]- < *musunpora-Ci- ?< *musunpa-ra-Ci- (with vowel assimilation). 'get tied/knotted tight; feel dejected'. x - A-A-x x-x-x.

A   musubu < *musunpa- (< ?). 'tie, knot, fasten'. A - A-A-A B̲-A-x. NS (84a) A, (Okada) B̲. NS (T+) musubyi (93) HL|H, (97) HLL. Km (W) A. Edo A. Ib A. Nk musuubin A; Sr musub- A. ⬚ musubi x - A-A-A x-(B̲)-x; o-musubi x - 2-1:4-B x-B-x. Nk musuubi A = musubii C̲; Sr musubii B 'contract; ... '.

?A/B   mutiutu < *nputi_2.3_ uta-_B_. 'whip'. B - B-A-A x-x-x. The etymology favors B; Kg irregular (as also for the noun muti).

A   mutu^b/_u < *mutu -n[a]-pa- = [mutubiru] < mutu-biy- < *mutu -np^u/_o_Ci- (?< -n[a]-pa-Ci-). 'show affection, act friendly, be intimate'. A - A-A-x x-x-x. ⬚ mutubi x - A-A-x x-x-x. Cf. mutu-goto, mutumazi_adj A_; *motu.

A   muzukaru (Tk), mutukaru (Kt) < *mutu(-)ka_adj-si A_-ra-. 'be vexed'. (A) - A-A-x x-x-x. Ib (-z-) B. Cf. muzu-muzu_sis_; muzukasi_adj A_.

A   ?muzukeru, mutukeru < mutuke[y]- < *mutu(-)ka_adj-si A_ -Ci-. 'feel it to be vexing'. x - x-x-x x-x-x.

?B   [na^b/_aru] < *nanpa-ra-. 'hide oneself' (= nabu). x - x-x-x x-x-x. Cf. [yokona^b/_aru], namaru.

?A   [naᵇ/ₘeru] < naᵇ/ₘey- < *nanpa-Ci- ?< *nam[a]-pa-Ci- (but see namu for an alternative etymology). 'line them up'. x - x-x-x x-x-x. Km (W) A. Nk namiirun A (vi./vt.).

?B   [naberu] < nabey- < nab[ik]ey- < *nam[a-Ci] pika-Ci-. 'cause to bend/yield/flutter'. x - x-x-x x-x-x. Nk nabenCun B.

-        [*naber-u] 'slip, slide': see namer-u.

B   nabikasu < nabyikasu < *nanpika-sa- < *nam[a-Ci]? pikaₐ-sa-. 'make it bend/yield/flutter; subdue, conquer'. B - B-A-x x-x-x.

B   nabikau < nabikafu < *nabyikafu < *nanpika-pa- < *nam[a-Ci]? pikaₐ-pa-. 'keep bending/yielding/fluttering'. x - x-x-x x-x-x.

B   nabikeru < nabyikey- < *nanpika-Ci- < *nam[a-Ci]? pikaₐ-Ci-. 'make it bend/yield/flutter' (= nabikasu). B - B-x-x x-x-x.

B   nabiku < nabyiku < *nanpika- < *nam[a-Ci]? pika-ₐ. 'bend, yield, flutter'. B - B-A-B x-B-x. NS (Okada) B. NS (T+ 83) nabyikyi LHH. Edo B. Ib B. Nk B.

?   nabu < *nanpa- (?< *nama-pa-). 'hide (oneself)' (= nabaru, namaru). x - x-x-x x-x-x.

B   *nabu < *nanpu 'torment': see (-)namu, naburu, sainamu.

B   naburu < *nanpura- ?< *nanpu-ra- (cf. sainamu). 'tease, ridicule, torment' B - B-A-B x-(B)-x. Ib B. Sr nabakur- B < ?. [] naburi x - B-x-x x-x-x.

B   nadameru < nadamey- < *nanta-ma-Ci-. 'soothe, placate'. B - B-A-B x-x-x. Edo B. Matsue A̲; Izumo A̲/B. Ib B. Cf. naderu.

B   nadareru < nadare[y]- < *nantara-Ci- ?< *nan[ᵃ/₀]-tara-Ci-. 'slope'. x - B-A-B x-x-x. [] nadare 'slope; avalanche'. x - A/B-2-B x-x-x. Matsue, Izumo, Goka-mura, Wakamatsu A̲; Hattō, Hamada B. Cf. naname/nanome, nazoe 'aslant'.

B   nadasu < *nanta-sa-. 'deign to pat/stroke'. x - x-x-x x-x-x. NS (T+ 74) nadasu mo LLL(|)H.

B   naderu < nade[y]- < *nanta-Ci-. 'pat, stroke'. B - B-B-B B-B-B. NS (Okada) B. Km (S, Okada W) B. Mr (Bm) B. Edo B. Ib B. Nk nadirun B; Sr nadir- B. Cf. kanaderu; nadaraka 'smooth'.

B   naegu < nafegu < *nafeygu < *napa(-)Ci-n[a]-ka-. 'limp'. B - x-A-x x-B-x. Nk meezun B (meeg- ?< *m[p]eenk- < *n[a]pa-[C]i-n[a]-ka-); Sr neezun (neeg-) B < *nafeg-(< ...). Cf. naeru.

?B   [naeru] < nafe[y]- < *napa(-)Ci-. 'lose free movement of hand or leg; go lame, limp'. x - x-x-x x-x-x. Cf. naegu, tenae, asinae; naeru < naye[y-.

B   naeru < naye[y]- (but later confused with nafey-) < *nada-Ci- < *nadwo-Ci- (the second vowel assimilated to the first). 'lose its starch, soften; wither'. B - B-B-B x-B-x. Nk neerun B; Sr neer- B. Cf. nayo- < naywo-; nayamu.

B   nagameru < nagame[y]- < *nankaᵦ ma-Ci-₁.₃ₐ (verbalized) or < *naga-myi- (the third vowel partially assimilated to the first two vowels) < ... . 'gaze at'. x - B-A-B x-B-x. Km (W) B. Ib B. Nk nagaamin B; Sr nagamir- B. [] nagame x - B-2-B x-B-x. Km (W) B. Nk nagaami B; Sr nagami B.

B   [nagameru] < nagamey- < *nankaₐdⱼ ᵦ -ma-Ci-. 'prolong voice; recite'. x - B-x-x x-x-x. Edo B. Attested 10th century.

?A/B   nagaraeru < nagarafey- < *nanka-ra-pa-Ci-. 'live on/long'. x - B-A-A x-A[Lit.]-x. Km (W) A/B. Sr [Lit.] nagarayun A (neg. nagaraan) < *nagaraf- < *nanka-ra-pa-.

B   nagareru < nagare[y]- < *nanka-ra-Ci-. 'flow'. B - B-A-B B-B-B. NS (83c nagare for nagare?; 94b) B. NS (T+ 97) nagare LHH. Km (S,W) B. Edo B. Ib B. Nk nagaarin B; Sr nagarir- B; Yn narirun B. [] nagare 'stream'. x - B-2-B x-B-x. Ōsaka, Kōbe 3. Mr (Bm) HHL. Nk nagaarii B; Sr nagari B. Edo HHL. [][] o-nagare 'suspension, abandonment; shared cup'. x - 2-1-B x- x-x. Cf. nagaₐdⱼ ᵦ 'long'.

B   nagasu < *nanka-sa-. 'let flow; float it'. x - B-A-B x-B-x. Km (S) B. Edo
B. Ib B. Nk nagaasun B = nagaarasun B; Sr nagas- B. [] nagasi x - 1/3-2-B x-B-x.
Nk nagaasii B; Sr nagasi B 'summer shower'.

B   nageku < nageyku < *naga-iku < *nanka*adj B* ika-*B* ('long breathe').
'sigh; lament, deplore'. B - B-A-B x-x-x. NS (84a [17:126-M], 84b, 124a) B.
NS (T+ 116) nageykamu LLLH, (97) nageyku LLH. Km (S,W) B. Edo B. Ib B.
[] nageki x - B-A-B x-x-x. Km (S,W) LLL. Edo HHL. Ōsaka, Kōbe 3.

B   nageru < nagey- < *nanka*adj B* -Ci- (cf. Hattori 1933:68). 'throw;
throw away, abandon'. B - B-B-B B-B-B. NS (101a, 103b) B. Km (S) B. Mr (Bm)
?B. Edo B. Ib B. Nk nagirun B; Sr nagir- B. [] nage x - B-2-B x-x-x.

?A/B   [nagiru] < nagiy- (probably < *nagu-Ci-) < *nankwo-Ci-. 'become calm'
(> nagu). x - x-x-x x-x-x. Cf. nagomu, nagusam(er)u, nago-yaka; [nikomu],
[nikibiru]; niko(-), nigi(-).

?A/B   nagomu < nagwomu < *nankwo-ma-. 'calm down'. x - B-A-A x-x-x.

?A/B   nagu < *nankwo-/nanku- (cf. nagomu, nagusameru). (vt.) 'mow'; (vi.,
replacing nagiy-) 'become calm'. x - B-B-A x-x-x. Km (W) B.
[] nagi < nagyi ?< *nank[u-C]i. x - B-2-A x-x-x. Hattō 1/B.

B   nagureru < nagure[y]- ?< *nankura-Ci-. 'get off the path; go to ruin;
get dissipated'. x - x-x-x x-x-x.

B   naguru < *nankura- (< ?). 'beat, hit'. x - B-A-B x-x-x. Ib B.

A   nagusameru < nagusamey- < *nanku-sa-ma-Ci-. 'comfort, solace; amuse,
distract, entertain'. x - A/B-A-A x-A-x. Km (W) A. Hattō <u>B</u>; Hamada, Matsue,
Izumo A. Nk nagu(u)samirun A; Sr nagusamir- A. [] nagusame x - A/<u>B</u>-A-A x-A-x;
Hattō, Hamada, Matsue, Izumo A. Nk naguusami A (LHHLL); Sr nagusami A.

A   nagusamu < *nanku-sa-ma-. (vi.) 'get calm/relieved; relax, enjoy oneself';
(vt.) 'calm/refresh (one's spirit); dally, toy with'. x - A/<u>B</u>-A-A x-A-x.
Nk naguusamin A; Sr nagusamir- A. [] nagusami x - A-A-A x-A-x. Nk naguusami A
(LHHLL); Sr nagusami A.

A   naku < *na(-)ka-. 'cry'. A - A-A-A A-A-A. NS (83b, 95a [11:65-K] na̅[k]i
···) A. NS (T+ 71) nakaba <u>LHL</u>; (94) nakyi sofoti LL LL̸; (71) naku*pred* HH,
(69) naku*attr* <u>LH</u>, (96) naku nari LL LL. Km (S,W) A. Edo A. Ib A. Nk naCun A;
Sr nak- A. [] naki x - A-A-A x-x-x. Cf. naru, nasu; ne.

-        nakusu < *na̅a̅-k̅u̅ | s̅u̅ (< *na*adj B* -ku so*A*-u.). 'lose'. x - A-A-A x-x-x.
NS (Okada) B.

?A/B   namakeru < namake[y]- < *nama*g.s* -ka-Ci-. 'be lazy; neglect, shirk'.
x - B-A-A x-x-x. Ib A. Nk namaaKin B. Cf. [namareru].

B   namameku < *nama*g.s* - myeku (< *miCa*g*-ka-*bnd v*). 'be charming, voluptuous,
fascinating'. B - B-A-B x-x-x.

B   [namareru] < *namare[y]- < *nama*g.s* -ra-Ci-. 'get dull'. x - x-x-x x-B-x.
Nk namaarin B; Sr namarir- B 'get dull; shirk'.

?B   namaru = nabaru 'hide (oneself)'. x - x-x-x x-x-x.

B   namaru < *nama*g.s* -ra-. 'get dull'. x - B-A-B x-(x)-x. Ib B. *See*
[namareru]. Cf. nama-kura 'dull'.

B   namaru < *namara- < ?< *napa-ra-. 'speak in dialect. corrupt one's
speech'. x - B-A-B x-x-x. Mr (Bm) B. Ib B. [] namari 'dialect'. x - B-2-B x-x-x.
Mr (Bm) HLL (Sakurai 1977:868a; K "Mr HHL" misprint?). Cf. [yokona*b*/■aru].

-        [nameru] 'line them up': *see* na*b*/■eru.

B   nameru < namey- < *nama-Ci-. 'lick'. B - B-B-B x-B[H 1967:448]-B. Ongi B.
Km (S) B. Ib B. Nk namirun B = nanbin B.

?B   namer-u < *namyer-u (/*nabyer-u) < *namiCa-ra- / *nanpiCa-ra-. 'slip,
slide; be slippery'. LHH (Kn) ?= *LLH - x-x-x x-x-x. Yaeyama (Ishigaki)
nabutcirun. Cf. nameraka, [name]*adj B*, [nabero]*adj*; nadaraka, naderu < *nanta-Ci-.

B   namida-gumu ‹ (“namuda-···” = /nanda-···/) ‹ namyita-gumu ‹ *namita₉.₅ᵦ
-n- kuma-₇₍ₐ₎. ‘get tearful, shed tears’. B - B-A-B x-x-x. Ib B.

B   namidatu ‹ *namyidatu ‹ *nami₈.₉ (-n-) tata-ᵦ. ‘waves rise; sea swell’.
B - B-A-B x-x-x.

?A   namu ‹ *nama-. (vi.) ‘line up’; (vt.) ‘line them up’ (= nameru). x - x-x-x
x-x-x. Edo A. ◻ nami ‘average’ x - A-A-A x-A-x. Km (W) A. Nk namii A.
(Cf. nami₈.₉ ‘wave’.) Cf. naᵇ/₌eru, narabu, naraberu; tinamu. Perhaps namu
and naᵇ/₌eru are truncations from *nara-n[a]- pa- ‘make them smooth/even’
(cf. narasu).

B   (-)namu ‹ *nanpu- (cf. naburu) ‘torment’:   see sainamu.

B   ? [namu] = nabiku ‘bend, yield, flutter’. (Only one example, from the
Man’yō-shū, and that is inferred.)

A   nanoru ‹ *na₁.₉ nora-ₐ. ‘call oneself, give/state one’s name (as)’. x -
A/Ḇ-A-A x-A-x. NS (126b) A. Edo A. Ib A. Nk x. ◻ nanori x - A-Ḇ-A x-A-x. Nk x.

B   *naoᵇ/₌u ‹ *napoₐdⱼ ᵦ -n[a]-pa-. ‘restore regularity or fortune’.
x - x-x-x x-x-x. ◻ naobi: see Ch. 5.

B   naoru ‹ *naforu ‹ *napoₐdⱼ ᵦ -ra-. ‘get well/better; recover, be mended
or restored’. x - B-A-B x-B-B. Edo B. Ib B. Nk noorun B; Sr noor- B.
◻ naori x - B-A-B x-x-x.

B   naosu ‹ nafosu ‹ *napoₐdⱼ ᵦ -sa-. ‘mend, repair, cure, restore; improve,
do over, convert’. x - B-A-B x-B-x. Km (S) B. Edo B. Ib B. Nk noosun B; Sr
noos- B. ◻ naosi LLL/LHL - B-A-B x-x-x.

A   naraberu ‹ narabey- ?‹ *na(ra)npa-Ci- (with infixed -ra-) ?‹ *nama-pa-Ci-;
?‹ *nara-[na]npa-Ci- (for an alternative etymology see namu). ‘line them up’.
A - A-A-A A-A-A. NS (71a, 71b, 71b) A. NS (T+ 47) narabeymu ₣LLH,
(48) narabeymu to̱ ko̱so̱ ₣LLH|L(|)LL, (48) narabey te mo ga mo HLL(|)₣(|)L|H(|)₣
(all odd). Mr (Bm) A. Edo A. Ib A. Nk naraabin (naraabir-) B; Sr narabir- B.
Cf. naᵇ/₌eru, kenaraberu; kuraberu.

A   narabu ?‹ *na(ra)npa- (with infixed -ra-) ?‹ *nama-pa-; ?‹ *nara[na]npa-
(‘smooth line’, but for an alternative etymology see namu). ‘line up’ (vi.).
A - A-A-A A-A-A. NS (T+ 40) narabyi ₣LH (odd). Km (W) A. Edo A. Ib A.
Nk naraabin (naraab-) B; Sr narab- B. ◻ narabi A - A-A-A x-A-x. Mr (Bm) A.
Edo A. Nk naraabi A; Sr narabi A. Cf. namu.

A   narasu ‹ *na(-)ra-sa-. ‘sound/ring it’. A - A-A-A x-A-x. Ib A. Nk naraasun
A; Sr naras- A.

B   narasu ‹ *nara-sa-. ‘tame, train, accustom, inure; smooth, level’.
B - A[U]/Ḇ[H]-B x-B-x. NS (108a) B. NS (T+ kun) fumyi narasu HH LLL ‘smooth by
stomping’. Km (W) B. Ib B. Nk naraasun B, naras- B. ◻ narasi ‘average’. B -
1-A-B x-x-x. Nk naraasi B (‘training’); Sr narasi B.

B   narau ‹ narafu ‹ *nara-pa-. ‘learn; imitate; copy’. B - B-A-B x-B-B.
Ongi B. Km (W) B. Edo B. Ib B. Nk naren B; Sr naraayun (neg. naraan) B;
Yn narun B. ◻ narai x -2-A-B x-B-x. Ōsaka, Kōbe 3. Km (S) B. Edo HHL.
Nk, Sr naree B.

B   narawasu ‹ narafasu ‹ *nara-pa-sa-. ‘train; teach’. (B) - B-A-B x-B-x.
Km (W) B. Nk naraasun B; Sr naraas- B. ◻ narawasi ‘custom, usage’.
x - A̱/B-A-B x-B-x. Nk naraawasii B; Sr naraasi B.

B   nareru ‹ nare[y]- ‹ *nara-Ci-. ‘get habituated (accustomed, familiar);
become tame; mature’. B - B-B-B B-B-B. Edo A̱/B. Ib B. Nk narirun B; Sr narir- B.
◻ nare ‘practice, experience’. x - B-2-B x-Ḇ-x. Nk narii B; Sr nari B (= naree
B, cf. narai).

B   *nariwau ‹ *narifafu ‹ *nar[a-C]iᵦ (-)papa-ᵦₙd ᵥ. See nariwai (Ch. 5).

A   naru ‹ *na(-)ra-. 'sound, ring'. A - A-A-A A-A-A. Edo A. Ib A. Nk nan A;
Sr nar- A. ⬚ nari x - A/B[H]-A x-x-x. Cf. naku, ne.

B   naru ‹ ni ar- ‹ *ni ar[a]-ʙ. (copula = essive particle + existential
auxiliary). B - B-B-B (x)-(x)-(x). NS (T+) naraba (92) LLH, (103) HLL; (47,
48) narabeymu LLLH; narazu (15, 32) LLH; nari (65) HH; naruₐₜₜᵣ (84, 116) LH,
(40) ⬚L = LL.

B   naru ‹ *na-ra-. 'become; come into being; fruit be borne'. B - B-B-B
B-B-B. NS (95a, 100b [11:124-K], 123b, 126a) B. NS (T+ 104) narikyemye ya
LHLHH ?= LH|LH(|)H; (125) narere [?‥]to̲ mo LHH|L|H. Ib B. Nk nan B; Sr nar- B.
⬚ nari: 'shape' x - B-2-B x-B-x; 'bearing fruit' x - B-A[H]/B[U]-B x-B-x.
NS (118b) B. Km (W) B. Nk, Sr nai B. Cf. nasu.

A   nasu ‹ *na-sa-. 'deign to sleep'; (= nekasu) 'put to sleep'. x - x-x-x
x-x-x. Cf. neru.

A   nasu ‹ *naᵃ/₀-sa-. 'make resemble, liken to; (which is) like ‥·'. x - x-x-x
x-x-x. NS (T+ 57) LL. Azuma nosu. Cf. niru, niseru; particles na, no̲, ni.

A   nasu ‹ *na(-)sa-. 'make resound' (= narasu). A - x-x-x x-x-x. Mg (tudumi
wo) n̄asi̲ t̄e. NS (Okada) A. NS (T+ 97) LL. Cf. naru, ne; naku.

B   nasu ‹ *na-sa- (cf. naru). 'make, do; give birth to'. B - B-B-B B-B-(B).
NS (T+ 15) nasuₐₜₜᵣ LL. Km (S,W) B. Edo B. Ib B. Nk nasun B; Sr nas- B; Yn nan,
naan ('give birth to').

?A/B   nasuru ‹ *na(-)sura- ?‹ *n[ur]a-ₐ sura-ʙ. 'rub, smear'. x - B-A-A x-B-x.
Nk nasirun B; Sr naṣir- B. Cf. suru; nuru.

B   natukeru ‹ *natukey- ?‹ *na[re[y]]-tukey- ‹ *nara-Ci[-Ci]ʙ tuka-Ci-ʙ.
'win the affection of; tame, domesticate'. B - B-A-A̲ x-x-x.

B   natuku ?‹ *na[re[y]]-tuk- ‹ *nara-Ci[-Ci]ʙ tuka-ʙ. 'become familiar
(with), get attached (to), be fond (of)'. B - B-A-A̲ x-x-x. Kōchi B; Ib A̲.
Cf. Sr naçikasyan B ‹ *natukasi- 'sad'.

B   nau ‹ nafu ‹ *napa-. 'twist, plait, weave (into rope)'. B - B-B-B x-B-x.
Nk noorun B, Sr noor- B: restructured from naw- ‹ naf-. Cf. nawa; nuu.

B   nayamasu ‹ *nada-ma-sa- (?‹ *nadwo-ma-sa-). 'trouble, cause to suffer'.
B - B-A-B x-x-x. Ongi-m B. Ib B.

B   nayameru ‹ nayame[y]- ‹ *nadama-Ci- (?‹ *nadwo-ma-Ci-). 'trouble, cause to
suffer' (= nayamasu). B - B-A-x x-x-x.

B   nayamu ‹ *nada-ma- (?‹ *nadwo-ma-~; cf. Azuma nayum-, nayo- ‹ *nadwo-).
'suffer, be troubled (with)'. B - B-A-B x-x-x. NS (Okada) B. Edo B. 1700 Ōsaka
HLL. Ib B. ⬚ nayami x - B-A-B x-x-x. Cf. naeru.

B   nayasu ‹ *nada-sa- ‹ *nado-sa- (second vowel assimilated to the first).
'soften/temper it'. x - B-x-x x-x-x. Cf. neyasu, nayo-, naeru.

?B   nazimu ?‹ na[re]-simu ‹ *nara-Ci[-Ci]ʙ sima-ₐ. 'get familiar/intimate'.
x - B-A-A̲ x-x-x. Ib A̲, B. ⬚ nazimi x - B-2-A x-x-x. The etymology is supported
by Shimane nazyomu ?‹ na[re]-somu.

B   nazir-u ‹ *nansira- (?‹ *non[o]sira-). 'rebuke'. B - B-A-B x-x-x.
Mr (Bm) B. Ib B.

A   nazoraeru ‹ nazᵘ/₀rafey-, (Nr) naswofey- ‹ *naswo(ra)pa-Ci- (‹ ...).
'liken; imitate, copy'. A - B̲-A-A x-x-x. Mr (Bm) B. Cf. nasu/nosu; nazoru.

A   nazorau ‹ nazᵘ/₀rafu, (Nr) ?*naswofu ‹ *naswo(ra)pa- ?‹ *nam[a-C]i?ₐ
s[w]opa-ₐ (with -ra- later infixed). 'be like'. A - x-A-x x-x-x.

?A/B   nazoru (?‹ *naswaru ‹ *naswo-ra-; ? truncation ‹ nazora[f]e[y]-). 'trace
(a model); imitate, mimic'. x - B̲-A-A x-x-x. Cf. nasu/nosu.

?A   nazukeru ‹ nadukey- ‹ *naᵢ.ₛ (-n-) tuka-Ci-ʙ. 'name'. A - B̲-A-A x-x-x.
Km (S) A. Edo A. ⬚ nazuke x - B̲-A-A x-B̲-x. Nk naasiKi A (HHLL); Sr naaʒikii B̲
(but naa A).

?B   nazumu < nadumu < *nantuma- (?= *nantu-ma-, cf. nazusau). 'bog down,
be impeded; be distressed; cling/adhere (to)'. B - B-A-A x-x-x.
NS (71c) ?B (na̲dumyi̲ for nadumy̅i̅?). NS (T+ 51) nadumyi ꞵHH ?= LHH.

?B   nazusau < nadusafu < *nantusapa- (?= nantu-sa-pa-, cf. nazumu; ?= *nantu-
sapa-ₐ, cf.sawaru). 'float around (water-logged)'; 'get familiar/intimate'
(it is unclear whether these meanings have a common source). x - x-x-x x-x-x.

B   nebaru < *nenpa■■ -ra- (<?). 'be sticky; persevere'. x - B-A-B x-x-x.
Ib B. ◖ nebari x - B-A-B x-x-x. Or, the mimetic could perhaps be viewed as a
truncation (from the infinitive-derived noun) and the verb stem taken to be
*na-Ciₗ.₃ₐ -n- para-ₐ 'root stick'.

A   neburu 'sleep': see nemuru.

B´   neburu ?< *neᵇ/■uru < *nampuru (the first vowel partially assimilated to
the second — or, for some reason, was independently raised) < *nam[a-Ci(Ci)]ᵦ
pura-₇ᵦ ('lick touch'). 'lick' (= nameru). B´ - B-A-x x-x-x. Km (S) B̲.
Cf. Sr nanduruₐ𝒹𝒿 ᵦ ?< *nabururu- 'slippery'; nameru, nameraka.

?B   nedaru < *na-Ciₗ.₃ₐ (-n-) ta-ra-ₐ. 'be firmly rooted'. x - x-x-x x-x-x.

?A/B   nedaru ?< *ne[giy -] taru < *nenk[u-C]iₐ (< ...) ta-ra-ₐ ('request be
sufficient'); ?< ne (-n-) taru < *na-Ciₗ.₃ₐ (-n-) ta- ra-ₐ ('be firmly rooted,
i.e. insistent'). 'importune, ask for, solicit, wheedle'. x - A/B-A-B x-x-x.

B´   negau < negafu < neg[ir]afu (< ...). 'request, pray for, desire'.
B´ - B-A-B x-x-B. Km (S,W) B. Edo B. Ib B. Nk nigaarun B = nigen B; Sr nigayun
(neg. nigaan) B; Yn niŋun B. ◖ negai x - 2-A[H]/2[U]-B x-x-B. NS (129a) B.
Ōsaka, Kōbe 3. Hamada 3; Hattō, Matsue, Izumo 2; Goka-mura 1/0. Nk, Sr nigee B.
Cf. negu, incongruent in register?

A   negirau < negirafu < *negiyrafu < *nenkᵘ/₀-Ci-ra-pa- < *nanku/nankwo
-Ci-ra-pa- 'solace; appreciate (work)'. L̲H̲H̲L̲ (?= *HHHL) - A-A-x x-x-x.

A   [negiru] < negiy- < *nenkᵘ/₀-Ci- < *nanku/nankwo -Ci- (or restructured
← *na-Ciₐ-n[a]-ka- with negu as basic, cf. Matsumoto 1974:97; naru, nasu).
'appease; solace; pray'. A - x-x-x x-x-x x-x-x. Cf. negu, negau.

A   negu < neg- ?< neg[iy-], ?< *na-Ci-n[a]-ka-. 'request, pray for'.
A - x-B̲-x x-x-x.

A   nekasu < *na-Ci-ka-sa-. 'put to sleep; lay down'. x - A-A-A x-x-x.

A   nemuru < neᵇ/■uru < *na-Ciₐ (n[i]) - pu-ra-₇ᵦ. 'sleep'. A - A-A-A A-A-A.
Hattō B̲. Ib A. Nk ninbin A; Sr ninzun (nind-) A; Yn nindun A: < *nebur-.
◖ nemuri x - A-A-A x-x-x. Km (S) A. Hattō B̲.

A   nerau < nerafu (< ?). 'aim at'. x - A-A-A x-x-x. Edo A. Hata B̲; Kōchi B̲
(both Doi 1952:30). NS (79 — ?; Tsuchihashi has -derafu) HL|H.
◖ nerai x - A-A-A x-x-x. Goka-mura 1. Cf. niramu.

B   nereru < nere[y]- (?< *ne[y]re[y]- < *nay[a]re[y]- < *nada-ra-Ci- <
*nado-ra-Ci-, the second vowel assimilated to the first). 'get softened;
mellow'. (B) - B-B-B x-x-x.

A   neru < ne[y]- < *na-Ci-. 'lie down, sleep'. x - A-A-A x-x-x. NS (83b
[17:118-M]) A. NS (T+ 66) ꞵH H = HH(|)H; (5, 96) ne-si H-H; (38) ne-si-ku wo
si zo̲ ꞵLLHLH = H-L-L|H(|)L|H; (25) ne-turu H-HL; (110) ne-sika-do̲ H-HL-L.
Km (W̅) A. ◖ ne x - A-A-A x-x-x. Cf. nasu < *na-sa-; nemuru.

B   ner-u (?< *ne[y]r-u < *nay[a]r-u < *nada-ra- < *nado-ra, the second vowel
assimilated to the first). 'knead; temper; train'. B - B-B-B x-B-x. Mr (Bm) B.
Edo B. Ib B. Nk nin B; Sr niir- B. ◖ neri B - B-2-B x-x-x. Cf. neyasu (B´),
nayasu, nayo-, naeru, niragu.

B   netamu < netaₐ𝒹𝒿 ᵦ (< ...) -ma-. 'envy'. B - B-A-B x-x-x. Mr (Bm) B.
Ib B. Nk niTaamin B [new]. ◖ netami x - A̲/B-A-B x-x-x. Hattō, Hamada, Matsue,
Izumo B. (Ōno's etymology 'the name hurts' is incongruent in register.)

?B´   neyasu ?< nayasu < *nada-sa- < *nado-sa- *(the second vowel assimilated to the first)*. 'knead, temper'. B´/B - x-A[U]-x x-x-x. Ongi B. Mr (Bm) B. Cf. nayasu, naeru, nayo-, ner-u. K: Edo HLL.

B   nezikeru < nedike[y]- < *nedi[y]- (< *nentᵘ/o̩-Ci- < ?) -ka-Ci-. 'get twisted, screwed; be crooked, perverse'. x - B-A[U]/B[H, *misprint?*]-B x-x-x. ⫴ nezike x - B-x-x x-x-x.

B   nezir-u < nedi- (JP) < *nedi[y]- < *nentᵘ/o̩-Ci- (< ?). 'twist, screw'. x - B-B-B x-B-x. Nk x. ⫴ nezi 'screw'. x - B-2-B x-B-x. Edo B. Nk x; Sr niziri B.

A+B   niau < niafu < *ni[-Ci]ₐ apa-ᴮ. (vi.) 'be suitable (for), befit'. x - B-A-A x-A-x. Km x. Ib A. Sr nawar- A, nioor- A, noor- A. ⫴ niai x - A-A-A x-A-x. Sr nawai A.

B   niburu < *ninpuₐdⱼ ᴮ -ra-. 'get dull, blunted'. x - B-A-B x-x-x. Ib B.

A   nieru < niye[y]- < ni(y)e[y] (epenthesis) < *niCa-Ci-. 'get boiled'. A - A-A-A A-A-x. Ib A. Sd nyiiyun A; Nk niirun A; Sr niir- A.

A   nigamu < nikamu < *nikama- (< ?). 'feel disgruntled; get wrinkled'. A - x-A-x x-x-x. (Etymologically confused with nigaₐdⱼ ᴮ 'bitter'?)

B   nigasu < *ninka-sa- (?< *nonka-sa-). 'let go/escape' (= nogasu). x - B-A-B x-x-x. Ib B.

?B   nigeᵏ/ɡamu < *nigeₛ.₃ (< ...) kama-ᴮ. 'ruminate (chew cud)'. x - x-x-x x-x-x. Variant nirekamu.

B   nigeru < nigey- < *ninka-Ci- (?< *nonka-Ci-). 'escape, flee'. B - B-B-B x-x-x. NS (76c [14:135-M], 107a, 109a, 109b, 126b) B. NS (T+ 76) LH. Km (W) B. Edo B. Ib B. ⫴ nige ?B - B-2-B x-x-x. Cf. nogareru B´.

?B   [nigioeru] < nigyifofey- < *nigifafey- *(the third vowel assimilated to the labial consonants)* < *ninki-pa-pa-Ci-. 'enrich'. x - x-x-x x-x-x.

A   nigir-u < nigyiru < *ninki(-)ra- (< ?). 'grasp, seize'. A - A-A-A x-A-x. Ongi A. Edo A. Ib A. Nk niziirun A; Sr nizir- A. ⫴ nigiri x - A-A-A x-x-x. (Yoshida relates nigir-u to nigiwau, but the register is incongruent.)

B   nigiwau < nigyifafu < *ni(n)ki (-)papa-. 'be prosperous, crowded, lively'. ⫴ nigiwai 'prosperity; bustle'. B - 3-A-B x-x-x. Cf. (-)wau.

B   nigorasu < *ni(n)ko̩-ra-sa-. 'dirty/muddy/obscure it'. B - B-A-B x-B-x. Nk mingasun B; Sr mingwas- B < *minguras- < *ninguras- (< ...).

B   nigoru < *ni(n)ko̩-ra- (perhaps *ni?₁.₃ ko̩ra-?ₐ 'dirt congeal'). 'get muddy'. B - B-A-B x-(B)-x. Mr (Bm) B. Ib B. Nk mingin B; Sr mingwir- B < *mingur- < *ningur- < ... . ⫴ nigori B - B-2-B x-(B)-x. Nk mingii B; Sr mingwi B < *mingur- < *ninguri < ... .

B   nigosu < *ni(n)ko̩-sa (perhaps *ni?₁.₃ ko̩[ra]?ₐ-sa- 'make dirt congeal'). 'muddy it'. x - B-A-B x-x-x. Ib B.

A   nikoyosu (Mg) / nikoyasu < *ni[-Ci]ₐ (kodo- ←) koda?ᴮ-sa-. 'let it boil and congeal'. A - x-x-x x-x-x.

B   nikumareru < nikumare[y]- < *niku-ma-ᴮ (< ...) -ra-Ci-. 'be hated'. B - B-A-B x-x-x.

B   nikumu < *nikuₐdⱼ ᴮ -ma-. 'hate'. B - B-A-B x-B-x. Mr (Bm) B. Edo B. Ib B. Nk niKuumin B; Sr nikum- B. ⫴ nikumi x - B-A-x x-?B-x. Mr (Bm) A̲. Nk niKuumi B, Sr nikun B 'pimple' < *nikumi (= nikibi).

?B   ninau < ninafu < *ni₁.₉ᵦ (< ...) -na-pa-. 'shoulder; bear, carry (on one's shoulder)'. B - B-A-A̲ x-x-x. Km (S) A̲. Mr (Bm) B. Ib B.

B   [nioeru] < nifofey- < *nipo-pa-Ci-. 'color/dye it (red or beautiful)'. x - x-x-x x-x-x.

B   [nioeru] < nifoye[y]- < *nipo-da-Ci-. 'become red/beautiful'. x - x-x-x x-x-x.

B   niou < nifofu < *nipopa- < *ni?₁.₃ [o]po-pa-ʙ (or, < *nifafu < *ni₁.₃ₐ
-pa-pa-). 'get red; shine beautifully; be fragrant'. B - B-A-B x-x-x. Ongi
(Iroha) B. Mr (Bm) B. Edo B. Matsue, Izumo, A̲. Ib B. ◊ nioi x -2-2-B x-x-x.
Km (W) B. Mr (Bm) B. Edo HHL. Matsue, Izumo A̲; Goka-mura 1 (verb B).

B   [niowasu] < nifofasu < *ni?₁.₃ [o]po-pa-sa-ʙ (or, < *nifafasu < *ni₁.₃ₐ
-pa-pa-sa-). 'make it red/beautiful/fragrant, color/scent it'. x - B-A-B x-x-x.
Ib B.

B   niragu < ?*niraku < *nira(n)ka- (< ?; cf. ner-u). 'temper metal; stammer'.
B - B-A-x x-x-x.

B   niramu < *nira-ma-. 'glare at; watch'. B - B-A-B x-x-x. Mr (Bm) B. Edo B.
Ib B. ◊ nirami x - B-A-B x-x-x. Cf. nerau.

A   niru < ni-/?*niCa-. 'resemble'. A - A-A-A A-A-A. Km (S,W) A. Mr (Bm) A. Ib
A. Sr nir- A; Nk naarun A, Sr nawar-/n(i)oor- A < *ni-aw- (< *ni[Ci]/niC[a-Ci]ₐ
apa-ʙ.)

A   niru < ni-/*niCa- (cf. niyasu, nieru). 'boil'. x - A-A-A A-A-A.

A   niseru < nise[y]- < *ni-sa-Ci-. 'make resemble; imitate; forge'. A -
A[U]/B̲[H]-A x-A-x. (Is Kt [H] a mistake?) Sr nisir- A; Nk naarasun A <
*ni-awas- (see niru).

?A   nituku < *ni[-i]ₐ (< ni-Ci) tuka-ʙ. 'closely resemble, harmonize (with)'.
x - B-A-x x-x-x. Attested Man'yō-shū. Cf. nitukawasiₐdⱼ ?A, nitukorasiₐdⱼ ?A.

A   niyou (JP) < niyofu < ?*niyobu < *nido?ₘᵢₐ -(n[a]-)pa-; ?< *ni-ywobu <
*ni?ₘᵢₐ - dwonpa-ₐ. 'groan, moan'. A - x-x-x x-x-x. Other possibilities:
*ne₁.₁ ywob-ₐ; *n[ak ₐ-]i/n[ar ₐ-]i ywob-ₐ.

B   nizir-u < *ninsira- (<?). 'crawl; edge forward (on one's knees or
crouching)'. B - B-A-(B) x-x-x. Zs Mg: f̄umi nizi[t] t̄e.
◊ niziri (x) - B-x-x x-x-x.

B   nobasu < *nonpa-sa-. 'extend, lengthen, defer'. x - B-A-B x-B-x. Edo B.
Ib B. Nk nubaasyun B; Sr nubas- B.

B   noberu < nobey- < *nonpa-Ci-. 'spread/extend it; set forth, state'.
B - B-B-B x-B-x. Km (S) B. Edo B. Ib B. Nk nubirun B (vt./vi.); Sr nubir- B.
◊ nobe x - B-2-B x-(B)-x. Nk nubii B; Sr nubi B ?< *nobe, ?< *nobi.

B   nobiru < nobiy- < *nonpo̲-Ci- (cf. noboru) ?< *nonpa-Ci- (the second vowel
assimilated to the first). 'extend, lengthen, spread, grow; be postponed'.
B - B-B-B x-B-x. NS (126a). Ongi B. Km (Okada W) B. Edo B. Ib B. Nk nubin B;
Sr nub- B < *nob- (< *nonpa-). ◊ nobi B - B-2-B x-(B)-x. Nk nubi C̲; Sr nubi B
?< *nobi, ?< *nobe.

A   noboru < (Nr) no̲fo̲ru < *no̲po̲-ra-. 'rise, climb'. A - A-A-A x-A-x.
NS (72a [11:196-M], 72b [11:199-M], 76c [14:135-M], 83c, 87a, 87b, 115a, 117b,
119b) A. NS (T+) no̲fori (53, 54, 60) LLH, (97) LLL; no̲fori-si (76) LLH-H;
no̲foreru (18) HHHH; no̲foru (98) LLL; no̲fore-ba LLH-H (43, 54). Km (S,W) A.
Edo A. Ib A. Nk nubuurun A; Sr nubur- A̲. ◊ nobori A - A-A-A x-A-x. Edo A.
Nk, Sr nubui A. On -b- < -f-, see Ch. 2.

A   noboseru < nobose[y]- < no̲fose[y]- < *no̲po̲-sa-Ci-. 'send upstream; raise;
have it (blood/excitement) rise'. x - A-A-A x-A-x. Edo A. Nk nubuusin A,
Sr nubusir- A. ◊ nobose x - A-A-A x-A-x. Nk nubuusi A; Sr nubusi A.

B   [nobu] < *nonpa- 'extend': see nobiru (Nk, Sr forms).

B′   nogareru < nogare[y]- < *nonka-ra-Ci-. 'flee, escape' (= nigeru).
B′ - B-A-B x-x-x. Edo B.

B′   [nogaru] < *nonka-ra-. 'flee, escape' (= nogareru = nigeru). (B′) - x-x-x
x-B-x. Nk nugaarun B, Sr nugaar- B < *nogaar- < *nonka-ra-. Note: Nk nugiirun
A, Sr nugir- A 'flee' < *nuge-, with an extended meaning of nugeru 'slip off/
away, be removed'.

?B   nogasu < *nonka-sa-. 'let escape' (= nigasu). x - B-A-B x-A-x.
Nk nugaasun A (≠ nugaasun B, see nukasu), Sr nugas- A < *nogas-.

?A   ?[*nogeru] < *nonka-Ci-. 'flee, escape' (= nogaru = nogareru). x - x-x-x
x-A-x. Nk nugiirun A; Sr nugir- A. The register suggests these may be
irregular reflexes of nukeru or nokeru in a semantic extension.

-           nogou: see nuguu.

A   nokeru < noke[y]- < *noka-Ci- (?< *noko-Ci-. 'remove, put out of the way;
exclude'. x - A-A-A x-A-x. Edo A. Hamada B. Nk nuKiirun A; Sr nukir- A.
Cf. dokeru; oku; noku; [*nogeru].

B   nokoru < *noko-ra-. 'remain, be left'. B - B-A-B x-B-B. Km (W) B.
Mr (Bm) B. Edo (A/)B. Ib B. Nk no(ho)orun B; Sr nukur- B. ◻ nokori B - B-2-B
x-B-x. Edo A (HHH), incongruent with nokosu. Nk nohoi B; Sr nukui B.

?B   nokosu < *noko-sa-. 'leave it (behind/over)'. B - B-A-A x-B-x.
Km (S) B. Mr (Bm) B. Edo B, cf. nokoru. Ib B. Nk no(ho)osun B; Sr nukus- B.
Is Kg a misprint? (Cf. nokoru B.)

A   noku < *noko-. (vi.) 'get out of the way, step aside'; (vt.) 'leave it
(= nokosu); remove, exclude (= nozoku)'. x - A-A-A x-A-x. Nk nuCun A; Sr nuk-
A. Cf. noki₂.₁ 'eaves'; doku, oku; nokeru.

B   nomasu < *noma-sa-. 'deign to drink; make/let drink'. x - B-A[U]/B[H]-B
x-x-x.

B   nomer-u < *nomera- (< ?). 'stumble, fall (forward)'. x - B-A[U]/B[H]-A
x-x-x. Cf. nomesu, numer-u; sober-u, suber-u, subesu.

B   nomesu < *nome-sa- (<?). 'make someone slip (fall down); cheat; eat lots
(plentifully)'; V-i ~ 'do completely'. x - B-A-x x-x-x.

?A   nomu < *no-ma-. 'pray'. Cf. tanomu, (i)nomu. x - x-x-x x-x-x.
NS (T+ kun) nomu HH 'kowtow, pray with head down'.

B   nomu < *noma-. 'drink; swallow'. B - B-B-B B-B-B. Edo B. Ib B. Nk numin B;
Sr num- B.

A   nonosir-u < *nonosira- (< ?). 'revile, denounce, reproach'. A - B-A-A
x-x-x. ◻ nonosiri x - A/B-A-A x-x-x. Tk A/B [NKD], A [H]. Cf. nazir-u.

?A   norou < norofu ?< *no(-)ra-pa- (the second vowel assimilated to the
first). 'curse'. (A) - B-A-A x-(x)-x. Nk nuren A, Sr nurayun A (neg. nuraan)
'scold' < *noraf-. ◻ noroi x - 2/0-A-A x-x-x.

A   noru 'declare, say'; noru 'scold': < *no(-)ra-. A - x-x-x x-x-x.
NS (Okada) A. NS (T+ 64) norazu LHE, (64) norupred LL. Cf. inoru, no-tabu,
nori, nanoru; nomu, tanomu.

A   noru < *no-ra-. 'ride; mount; be borne/carried; be recorded (written)'.
A - A-A-A A-A-A. Edo A. Ib A. Nk nun A; Sr nur- A. Cf. noseru; ni₁.₃ᵦ 'load'
(register incongruent).

A   noseru < nose[y] < *no-sa-Ci-. 'let ride; carry, load; place (on);
record'. (x) - A-A-A x-A-x. NS (94a) A. Edo A. Ib A. Nk nusiirun A; Sr
nusir- A. ◻ nose x - x-x-x x-x-x. Nk nusii A, nusi A.

A   nosu < *no-sa-. 'make resemble' (= niseru), the Azuma version of nasu.
x - x-x-x x-x-x.

?B   nosu < *no(-)sa-. 'stretch/flatten it (= nobasu); iron it; extend, go
far'. B - B-A[H]/B[U]-A/B x-x-x. Ib B. ◻ nosi x 2-2-B x-B-x. Nk x. H gives Kg
A for the meaning 'stretch it', B for 'iron it'.

A+B   no-tabu < no[ri] tabu < *nor[a-C]i₄ tam[a]-pa-ᵦ. 'deign to say'.
H|LH   - x-x-x x-x-x.

A+B   notamau < notamafu < *no[ri -] tamafu < *nor[a-C]i₄ tama-pa-ᵦ. 'say'.
H[x]-LLH - B-A-x x-x-x. Mg no̱ tafu̱/b[u] aku, NS (93b) no̱ tamafu (or, in both,
/not t···/); Mr (Bm) notamafaku.

A+B   nottoru < no[t]-toru < *nori-t(w)oru < *nor[a-C]i_A t(w)ora-_B.
'conform to, follow; imitate, model after'. H[L]-LH - B-A-A x-x-x.
Mg no toru = not toru.

A   nozoku < *nonso-ka- (?< *non - so 'eye do', cf. nozomu). 'peek, peer'.
x - A-A-A x-x-x. Edo A. Ib A. ◻ nozoki x - A-A-A x-x-x.

B   nozoku < *nonso-ka-. 'exclude, remove'. B - A-A-A x-x-x. Km (S) B.
K: Mr HLL. Wakamatsu A.

A   nozomu < *nonso-ma- (?< *non - so 'eye do', cf. nozoku, Korean 'nwun
'eye'). 'hope/wish for; look for/to; look over'. A - A/B[new]-A-A x-A-x. NS
(98a, 99b) A. Mr (Bm) A. Edo A. Hamada B. Ib A, B. Nk nuzuumin A; Sr nuzum- A.
◻ nozomi A - A/B-A-A x-A-x. Km (S) A. Hamada B. Nk nuʐuumi A; Sr nuʐumi A.

B   nugeru < nuge- < *nukey- < *nuka-Ci-. '(clothing) come off, be taken off',
(Ryūkyū) 'get removed, be taken off/out'. (B) - B-B-B x-B-x. Ib B.
Nk nugi(i)run B; Sr nugir- B.

B   nugu < (Nr) nuku < *nuka-. 'remove (clothing)'; (Ryūkyū) 'remove, take off
or out'. B - B-B-B x-B-B. Km (W) B. Edo B. Narada nuku B. Ib B. Nk nuzun B;
Sr nug- B.

B   nuguu < "nugufu" < nogofu < *no(n)kopa-. 'wipe'. B - B-A-B x-B-x.
Km (S) nogof- B. Mr (Bm) nogof- B. Ib nogou B. Nk nugurun B; Sr nugur- B
(restructured from *nogof-).

A   nukaru < *nukara- (< ?). 'get muddy'. x - A-A-A x-x-A. Yn ngarun A 'get
wet'.

A   nukaru < *nuka-ra-. 'blunder'. x - A-A-A x-x-x. ◻ nukari x - A-A-A x-x-x.

A   nukasu < *nuka-sa-. 'omit'. x - A-A-B x-x-x. Nk nugaasun B ≠ nugaasun A
'let escape'.

A   nukeru < nuke[y]- < *nuka-Ci-. 'be removed'. (A) - A-A-A x-(x)-x.
NS (125b nuke i["]te) A. Ib A. See *[nogeru], nugeru.

A+B   nukinderu < *nuk[a-C]i_A inta-Ci-_B. 'excel, stand out, be select'. B-A-B
x-B-x. Mg nuki de- < nukyi ide[y]-. Nk nuCiizin A; Sr nugiqnzir- B.
See nuku_?A, nugu_B.

?A   nuku < *nuka-. 'remove, omit, extract; pierce; poke'. A - A-A-B x-(A)-
(A). NS (Okada) A. NS (T+ 89) nukazu to-mo LHH(|)H-H; nuku_attr LH. Km (W) A.
Edo A. Hata B (Doi 1952:29); Ōita B. Ib A. Nk nuCun A 'pierce'. ◻ nuki x -
2-A[U]/2-B x-A-x. Km (W) A ('woof'). Nk nuCii A, Sr nuci A 'rafter'.

B(<?A)   nuku < *nuka-. 'remove (clothing)' > nugu_B. x - x-x-x x-x-x. See nugu.

B   numer-u < *nume-ra- (< ?). 'slip, slide; be slippery; cheat; eat lots
(plentifully)'. x - B-A-x x-x-x. ◻ numeri 'slime; sliminess; oiliness;
slippery' x - B-A-x x-x-x.

A   nurasu < *nura-sa-. 'wet it'. A - A-A-A x-A-x. Km (W) A. Edo A. Ib A.
Nk daasun A, Sr ndas- A < *nuras-.

A   nureru < nure[y]- < *nura-Ci-. 'get wet; come undone/loose'. A - A-A-A
x-A-x. NS (104a) A. Km (W) A. Edo A. Ib A. Nk diirun A; Sr ndir- A.

A   nuru < *nura-. 'paint, smear'. A - A-A-A x-A-x. Mr (Bm) A. Edo A. Ib A.
Nk nurun A, Sr nur- A (neg. nuran) < *nur- (why do we not get the *ndu- that
the reflex of nureru leads us to expect?). ◻ nuri x - A-A-A x-x-x.

B   [nurukeru] < nuruke[y]- < *nuru_adj B -ka-Ci-. 'get tepid/warm' (=
nurumu). x - x-x-x x-x-x. Nk nuruKin B.

B   nurumeru < nurume[y]- < *nuru_adj B -ma-Ci-. 'make it tepid/warm'.
x - B-A-B x-B-x. Nk nurumin B (nurumir-); Sr nurumir- B.

B   nurumu < *nuru_adj B -ma-. 'get tepid/warm'. x - B-A-B x-B-x. Ib B. Nk
nurumin B (nurum-); Sr nurum- B (why not *ndum-?). Cf. nuruma-yu 'tepid water'.

B   nusumu < *nusuma- (?< *nusu-ma-; ?< *nu[ki -] sumu <*nuk[a-C]i?ₐ suma-ʙ;
     ?< *nu[ki - ka]sumu < ... [Yoshida]). 'steal'. B - B-A-B x-B-B. NS (T+ 18)
     nusumaku LLHH. Mr (Bm) B. Edo B. Ib B. Nk nusimin B (nusim-); Sr nusum- B.
     [] nusumi B - B-A-B x-x-x. Cf. nusubito.
B   nuu < nufu < *nupa- (?← *napa-, see nau). 'sew'. B - B-B-B (B)-B-B. Ib B.
     Sd, Nk, Sr noor- B ?< *naw- < *napa-. [] nui x - 2/3-2[U]-x x-x-x.
?B/B´   obasu < *onpa-sa-. 'deign to gird/wear'. x - x-x-x x-x-x. NS (Okada) B/B´.
     NS (T+ 97) obaseru LLHH.
A   obieru < obyiye[y]- < *onpi-da-Ci-. 'take fright (at)'. A - A/B-A-A x-A-x.
     Edo A. Nk x; Sr qnbiir- A ?< *ubi··· . Cf. obiyakasu. [] obie x - A/B-x-x x-x-x.
     (Unger reconstructs *onpo- and relates that to oboreru 'drown'; even if the
     semantic fit were better, it would be easier to derive the latter from the
     former, by way of vowel assimilation.)
B´   obiku < *obi[fi]ku < *obyi fyiku < *onp[a-C]iʙ pik[a-C]iₐ. 'gird;
     inveigle'. LHx = *LH(|)L - B-A-x x-x-x. Later orthography has the neutralized
     "wo-" for the surviving meaning 'inveigle', which Ōno etymologizes to include
     the infinitive woki 'invite'. I assume (as does, tacitly, NKD) that the two
     meanings form a single etymon, but there appear to be no textual examples of
     'gird' and Myōgi-shō has only that gloss.
B   obiru < obi- < (Nr) ob- < *onpa-. 'gird; be girt with, wear'.
     (B) - A/B-B-A x-x-x. Narada A. (Kg A misprint? Cf. obi.) [] obi < obyi <
     *onp[a-C]i. 'girdle'. LH - 2-1-B B-B-x. Hamada, Matsue 2. Ib (rare) B. Nk qubii
     B 'barrel hoop'; Sr quubi B 'girdle'.
B   [obisimeru] < obi-sime[y]- < *obyiₛ.₄ (< onp[a-C]iʙ sima-Ci-ʙ. 'tie (or
     tighten) a belt, gird'. B - x-x-x x-x-x.
A   obiyakasu < *obyiyakasu < *onpi-da-ka-sa-. 'frighten, intimidate,
     threaten'. (A) - B-A-A x-x-x. Hattō, Matsue, Izumo A; Hamada B. Cf. obieru.
B   oboeru (< *oboye[y]- < *onpo-da-Ci- ?< *om[o]po-da-Ci-) < omofoye[y]-
     < *omo-po-da-Ci- < *omo-pa-da-Ci-. 'remember, learn, know'. B - B-A-B x-B-B.
     NS (128b, 130b omofoye[¨]su) B. NS (T+ 118) omofoyuru ka mo LHHHH(|)L|H. Km (W)
     omofoye-te) A. Mr (Bm) B. Edo B. Ib B. Nk qubi(i)run B; Sr qubir- B. Cf. omou.
     (The annotations on a ninth-century text include both oboye[y] and omofoye[y];
     see KggD 958a.) [] oboe x - 2/3- A[U]/2[H]-B x-B-x. Nk qubii B; Sr qubi B.
A   [oboosu] < obofosu < *onpopo-sa- < *onpo-pa-sa-. 'make drown, drown
     someone'. x - x-x-x x-x-x. Cf. oboreru.
A   oboreru < obo[fo]re- < obofore[y]- < *onpopo-ra-Ci- < *onpo-pa-ra-Ci-.
     'drown'. A - A/B-A-A x-A-x. Km (S) A. Ib A. Nk qabunkin A, Sr qnbukkwir- A < ?.
     Ongi (ofoforu) A.
?B/?B´   obosu < om[o]fosu < *om[o]posu < *omopo-sa- < *omo-pa-sa-. 'deign to
     think' (= obosi-mesu). x - B-B-B x-x-x. NS (95b [11:68-K]) B; (127a) ?B;
     (114a, Okada) B´. Edo B´.
?A   obotor(er)u < obotor(e[y])- ?< ofotor(e[y])- < *o(n)po(-) tora-(Ci-).
     'get strewn/disheveled'. (?A) - x-x-x x-x-x.
B   obu (Nr) 'gird; wear': see obiru.
?B   obusaru < *onpu-sa-ra- (?< *onpa-sa-ra-). 'ride piggyback'. x - B-B-A
     x-x-x. Ib (rare) B.
?B   obuu < obufu < *onpu-pa- (?< *onpa-pa-). 'carry piggyback'. x - B-B-A
     x-x-x. Ib oburu B.
A   odateru < odate[y]- ?< *o[si] -n- tate[y]- < *os[a-C]iₐ (-n-) tata-Ci-ʙ.
     'instigate; flatter'. x - A/B[H]-A-A x-x-x. Ib A. [] odate x - A-A-A x-x-x.
A   odokasu < *ontо-ka-sa-. 'threaten, menace'. x - A-A-A x-x-x. Ib A.
     [] odokasi x - A-A-A x-x-x. Nk qudu(u)kasun A. Cf. oziru, odosu.

(A/)B   [odokasu] (< ?). '? *cause to fool around'. x - x-x-x x-x-x. Nk qudukasun
B 'cause a loss (at trade)'.

A/B   odokeru < odoke[y]- (< ?). 'fool around; jest'. x - A/B[H]-A-A x-(B?)-x.
Hattō B, Hamada A/B. ? Nk quduKin B, Sr qudukir- B 'lose money (at trade)'.
[] odoke x - A-A-x x-x-x. Nk qudukii B 'loss of money (at trade)'. Etymologies
in NKD derive the verb from the noun and that from several possible sources,
including *o[fo] - toke[y] < *opo_adj_B toka-Ci[-Ci]_B 'big loosening', which
would make the register B.

?B   odorokasu < *odorakasu < *onto-ra-ka-sa-. 'surprise'. B - B-A-A x-x-x.
Km (S) B. Mr (Bm) B. Ib A. Nk qudurukaasun B. Cf. odoroku.

?B   odoroku < *odoraku < *onto-ra-ka-. 'get surprised (startled); be horror-
struck'. B - B-A-A B-B-B. NS (125a) B. Mr (Bm) B. Ib A. Nk quduruCun; Sr
quduruk- B. [] odoroki x - 3/4-A-A x-x-x.

A   odoru < wodoru < *bontora- (<?). 'jump/fly up; dance'. A - A-A-A A-A-A.
NS (101b[11:135-K]) A. Edo A. Ib A. Nk x; Sr udur- A; Yn budurun A (H 1967:
404b). Cf. ozuku. [] odori x - A-A-A x-A-A. Nk udui B; Sr udui A; Yn budui A.

A   odosu < *onto-sa-. 'intimidate'. A - A-A-A x-x-x. Nk quduusun A. Ib A.
[] odosi x - A-A-A x-x-x.

A   oeru < wofey- < *bo(-)pa-Ci-. 'end it'. A - A-A-A x-x-x. Km (S) A.
Hattō A/B. Ib A. Cf. owaru; o_1.3a_ (register incongruent).

?   [oeru] < woye[y]- < *boda-Ci- ?< *bo_?1.1_ -da-Ci-. 'get weak(ened), be
enfeebled'. x - x-x-x x-x-x.

B´   ogamu < wogamu ?< *wo [ka]gamu < *bo_1.3a_ kankama-_A_ ('tail crouch' =
'bow'). 'worship'. B´ - B-A-B x-B-B. Ib B. Nk qugaamin B *(the glottal initial
is unexpected)*; Sr ugam- B. [] ogami x - x-x-x x-x-x. Nk qugaami B 'shrine';
Sr ugami B 'supplication'.

A+A   oginau, oginuu < (Hn) oki nufu ('place and sew') < *okyi nufu < *ok[a-C]i_A_
nupa-_B_. 'make up for; supply; supplement'. A (= A+A) - B-A-A x-A-x. Mr (Bm) A.
Ib B. Nk quziinan A = quziinen A; Sr ('nurture') quzinayun A (neg. quzinaan).
[] oginai x - 3/4/0-A-A x-x-x. Nk quziinai A = quziinee A (LHHLL).

B   ogoku ?< *(first vowel assimilated to the second)* ugok- < *unk^u/_osia_ -ka-.
'change position, move' (= ugoku). B - x-A-x x-x-x.

A   ogoru < *onko-ra- (?< *anka-ra- 'rise'). 'get proud, be arrogant; be
extravagant; give as a treat, treat one to'. A - A-A-A x-A-x. Km (W) A. Edo A.
Nk quguurun A; qugur- A. [] ogori x - A-A-A x-x-x. Nk qugui A.

?B   oiru < *oyi[y]- < *odo-Ci- ?< *oda-Ci- *(the second vowel assimilated
to the first)*. 'age, get old'. B - B-A[H]/B[U]-A x-B-B. Km (W) B.
Nk quirun B; Sr qwiir- B. [] oi x - 1/0-A[H]/2[U]-B x-x-x. Km (W) B. Edo B.
Cf. oyosu; oya. (Unger relates this stem to oyobu, but that is A.)

B   [oiru] < ofiy- < *opo_adj_B_ -Ci-. 'grow, get bigger'. x - B-B-x x-B-x.
NS (T+ kun) LH. Km (S,W) B. Narada B. Ib *(rare)* B. Nk quirun A; Sr qwiir- B.

A   okasu < wokasu < *boka-sa-. 'commit; violate; assault; invade; defy; risk,
venture'. A - A/B-A-A x-x-x. Ongi A. Mr (Bm) A. Ib A.

B   okiru < okiy- < *oko-Ci-. 'arise'. x - B-B-B B-B-B. NS (Okada) B.
NS (T+ 83) okiy LH. Km (W) B. Edo B. Ib B. Sd hwiiyum B = qwihiiyum B;
Nk huKirun B; Sr qukir- B.

A   okonau < okonafu < *oko-na-pa-. 'act; do, perform'. A - A-A-A x-A-x. Ib B.
Nk x. [] okonai x - A-A-A x-A-x. NS (T+ 65) LLHF. Nk huKuunee A; Sr qukunee A.

?B   okoru < *oko-ra-. 'arise, occur, happen; originate; get angry'.
B - B-A-A x-B-x. Km (S,W) B. Mr (Bm) B. Ib B. Nk hukuurin B; Sr qukur- B.
[] okori x - B-A-A x-x-x.

?A   okosu (late Mr) < okose[y]- < *okosa-Ci- (?< *oku-sa-Ci-, cf. okuru).
'send here' (= yokosu). x - x-x-x x-x-x. Km (W) A.

B   okosu < *oko-sa-. 'raise; begin; arouse; revive; kindle'. B - B-A-A/B
(B)-B-(B). Mr (Bm) B. Edo B. Ib B. Nk huKu(u)sun B = huusun B; Sr qukus-.

A   okotaru < *oko(-)tara- (< ?). 'shirk'. A - A/B-A-A x-A-x. NE Kyūshū A.
Nk x. ◻ okotari x - A-A-A x-x-x. Note: Unger etymologizes < *okwotar- < *oku-_A_
tara-_B_ 'put-dangle', cf. okureru. Yoshida: < *oki-tar- *(the second vowel
presumably assimilated to the first)* < *okyi tara- < *ok[u-C]i_A_ tara-_A_.

A   okoturu < wokoturu < *bokotura- (< ?). 'deceive; flatter, court favor'.
A - x-A-x x-x-x. Cf. wakaturu, [oku] < woku 'invite'.

A   oku < *oku- (cf. okuru). 'put'. A - A-A-A x-A-x. NS (76b, 127a [14:302-K])
A. NS (T+ 75) okamu LLH, (120) okyi te ka HL|H(|)H. Km (S,W) A. Mr (Bm) A. Edo
A. Dialects of Shizuoka, Nagano, Yamanashi B. Ib A. Nk huCun A; Sr quk- A.

?A   [oku] < woku < *boka-. 'invite'. x - x-x-x x-x-x. Cf. okoturu, wakaturu.

A   okureru < *oku-ra-Ci-. 'be late, lag'. A - A-A-A x-A-x. NS (122a) A.
Edo A. Ib A. Nk huKuurin A; Sr qukurir- A. ◻ okure x - A-A-A x-x-x.

A   okuru < *oku-ra-. 'send; see off, escort; pass (time); present, bestow'.
A - A-A-A A-A-A. NS (117a) A. Edo A. Ib A. Nk huKuurun A; Sr qukur- A.
◻ okuri x - A-A-A x-x-x. Edo HHH. (Nk quuKui C is a reflex of o-okuri.)
Cf. okosu 'send here'; okureru.

?B   omeru < omey- ?< *omaCi-. 'fear'. x - x-x-x x-x-x. Cf. ome-asi, ome-musi.

B   omo^b/_m_uku < *omo_B.4_ muka-_A_ (?< *npuka-_A_). 'face; direct one's course
(toward); grow, tend (toward)'. B - B-A-A x-x-x. Km (S) B. Mr (Bm) B.
◻ omomuki B - 3/4/0-A-A x-B-x. Mr (Bm) B.

B   omoner-u < *omo_B.4_ ner-_B_ (see ner-u) ('knead face'). 'flatter'.
B - B-A-A x-x-x.

B   [omooeru] < omofo[y]e-: *see* oboeru.

B   [omoosu] < omofosu < *omopo-sa- < *omo-pa-sa- *(with vowel assimilation)*.
'deign to think'. x - x-x-x x-x-x. NS (105a) B.

A   omoru < *omo_adj A_ -ra-. 'become heavy/serious'. x - 0-0-x x-x-x. Edo A.
Attested Hn (also NS but not phonetically). ◻ omori x - A-A-A x-x-x.

B   omou < omofu < *omo-pa-. 'think, feel'. B - B-B-B x-B-x. NS (70b, 105b,
127b [14:330-K]) B. NS (T+) omofanaku ni (93) LLLLL(|)H, [o]mofanaku ni (117)
LLLL(|)H; omofyi (43)L_m_H = LLH; omofu_pred_ (89) LLH; [o]mofu_attr_ (52) HH;
[o]mofey-do (43) _m_HH = [L]LH(|)H. Km (S,W) B. Mr (Bm) B. Edo B. Nk qumin B;
Sr qumir- B. ◻ omoi 'thought'. B - 2-2-B x-B-x. Edo HHL. Matsue, Izumo 2;
Narada, Hattō, Hamada 3. Ib B. Nk, Sr qumui B. Cf. obosu; omo_B.8_ 'important',
omo_B.4_ 'surface, face'; omo_adj B_ 'heavy'; o[p]o_adj B_ 'big'.

B   [omowaeru] < omofafey- < *omo-pa-pa-Ci-. 'fully consider, think through'.
x - x-x-x x-x-x.

A   ononoku < wononoku < *bononoka- < *bono-[bo]no-ka- (= *bana-[ba]na-ka).
'shudder, tremble'. A - A-A-A x-x-x. Cf. wananaku.

B   ooseru < ofose[y]- < ... (?= next entry). 'complete, achieve'.
x - B-A-x x-x-x.

B   ooseru < ofose[y]- < ?*ofwose[y]- = ofuse[y]- (Azuma) < *opu-sa-Ci-.
'burden/charge with' (= owaseru, owasu); 'command'; 'deign to tell/say'
(= ooserareru > ossyaru). B - B-A-x x-B-x. NS (98b, 99b, 103b) B. Km x.
Mr (Bm) B. Edo B. Nk x. ◻ oose (LxL =) B - A-1-B x-B-x. Edo HHL. Nk x;
Sr qwiisi B.

B   oosu < ofosu < *opo_adj B_ -sa-. 'grow (plants/hair); rear (children)'.
x - x-x-x x-x-x.

-         ootor(er)u: *see* oboto(re)ru.

?B   ootoru < ofotoru < *opo-*ᴮ* tora-*ᴮ* ('cover take'). 'get (en)tangled'.
x - x-x-x x-x-x. Cf. obotoreru; NKD treats these as the same etymon, but Zdb
is more cautious.

B   oou < ofofu < *opo-pa-. 'cover'. B - A̲/B[K]-A-A̲ x-x-x. NS (91b [11:8-K]),
106a, 119a) B. Km x. Mr (Bm) B. Edo B. 〚 ooi B - 2/3-2-A x-x-x.
The source of Nk husuurun A, Sr qusur- A 'cover' is osou; cf. osaeru.

A   orabu < *oranpa- < ?*ora-n[a]-pa-. 'wail, yell'. x - x-x-x x-x-x. NS (95a
[11:65-K], 114a [14:43-K]) A. Ib A, B̲. Nakijin wurabin A. (Yoshida treats ora
as interjection. Cf. Korean :wul- ?< *wu'tu- 'cry', Japanese oto*ᴸ.ᴬᵇ* 'sound'.)

B   oreru < wore[y]- < *bora-Ci-. (vi.) 'break (= be broken); yield; turn
(to the right/left)'. (B) - B-B-B x-B-x. Nk urirun B; Sr uurir- B < *wore-.

B   oriru < ori[y]- < *oro-Ci-. 'descend; alight'. B - B-B-B B-B-B. Edo B.
Ib B. Nk qurirun B; Sr qurir- B. Cf. orosu; otiru.

B   orogamu < worogamu ?< *woro*(?ᴸ.ᵃ/ᴸ.ᵇ)* [ka]gam-*ᴮ* < *bo*₁.₃ₐ* -ra kan-kama-
(< ... 'tail crouch'). 'bow in obeisance'. x - x-x-x x-x-x.
NS (Okada) B. NS (T+ 102) worogamyi te LHHH(|)F̲. Cf. ogamu, kagamu.

B   orokeru < orokey < *oro(-)ka-Ci-. 'be indistinct, vague; get dazed or
inattentive'. B - x-x-x x-x-x. NS (Okada) B. Cf. oroka 'stupid'.

A   orosu < *ora-sa- (second vowel assimilates to first). 'deign to weave'.
x - x-x-x x-x-x.

B   orosu < *oro-sa-. 'lower, drop; sell wholesale'. B - B-A-B x-B-x. NS
(126b) B. Km (W) B. Edo B. Ib B. Nk qurusun B; Sr qurus- B. 〚 orosi x - 1/3-2-B
x-x-x. Km (W) LLL. Ōsaka, Kōbe 3. Cf. oriru; otosu.

A   oru < *ora-. 'weave'. A - (A[K]/)B̲-A[U]/B̲[H]-B̲ x-A-A. NS (73c, 106b) A.
NS (T+ 59) oru*ₐₜₜᵣ* LL. Km (W) A. Narada, Hattō, Hamada, Matsue, Izumo A. Ib A.
Nk qun A; Sr qur- A. 〚 ori A[H]/B̲-A[U]/2[H]-A x-x-x. Hiroshima B̲ (Okuda 270).

?A´   oru < wor- < *bo(-)ra- ?< *bᵘ/₂- ara- (or w͡i ar- < *bᵘ/₂-Ci ara-). 'be'.
A - B-A[H]/A´[U]-A A-A-A. NS (T+ 9) iri wori to̲-mo HLLHLL = HL|LH(|)L(|)L.
Km (W) A. Tk A/B according to Mkz, Hiroto and Ōhara; western Mino (= SW Gifu)
B (Okumura 1976:184), Hiroshima B (Terakawa); Okayama A (?< *B, Mushiaki 29);
Hattō, Hamada, Matsue, Izumo, Goka-mura A; Hata A (Doi 1952:29); NE Kyūshū A.
Sakawa A´/o̅ru). Nk un B; Sr un B (neg. uran) < *wo(r)- B.

B   oru < woru < *bora-. 'bend, fold, break'. B - B-B-B x-B-B. Km (W) B.
Edo B. Ib B. Nk un B; Sr uur- B. 〚 ori x = B-2-B x-B-x. Km (W) LH.
Edo LH(/HL). (Nk -ui;) Sr uui B.

A+B   osaeru < osafe[y]- < *osi afe[y]- < *os[a-C]i*ᴬ* apa-Ci-*ᴮ*. 'restrain,
suppress, control, check'. Mg o̅safu̅ / o̅safu - B-A-A x-(A)-x. Km (S), Mr (Bm)
o̅saete. Edo B. Hattō, Hamada B; Matsue, Izumo A. Ib A. Sr qusuyun A (negative
qusuran) < *osor- restructured from *osof- < *osaf- ; cf. causative qusaasyun
< *osafas-, passive qusaariyun < *osafare- 'be attacked, get pressed down';
Nk husaasun A < *osafas-. Cf. osou. 〚 osae x - 2/3-A-A x-x-x.

B   osamaru < wosamaru < *bosa-ma-ra-. 'be at peace, ... '. B - B-A-B x-B-x.
Ib B. Nk usaaman B; Sr usamar- B. 〚 osamari B - 3/4/0-A-B x-x-x.

B   osameru < wosamey- < *bosa-ma-Ci-. 'obtain, collect; restore; pursue,
study; subdue, rule'. B - B-A-B x-B-x. NS (107b, 110b) B; (134a, *mistake?*) HLH.
Km (S,W) B. Mr (Bm) B. Ib B. Nk usaamin B; Sr usamir- B.
〚 osame x - A̲[H,NHK]/B[NKD]-A-B x-x-x. NS (112a) B.

A+B   [osau] < osafu < *os[a-C]i*ᴬ* apa-*ᴮ*. 'restrain, ... ': *see* osou, osaeru (Sr).

A   osieru < wosife[y]- < *bosipa-Ci- (< ?). 'teach, inform, tell'. A - A-A-A
x-x-x. Cf. osowaru. 〚 osie x - A-A-A x-A-x. Mr (Bm) A. Ib A. Nk x; Sr qusii A
must be borrowed (because of the glottal initial).

B   osimu < wosimu < *bo-si_adj_ _B_ -ma-. 'spare, grudge; regret; prize, value'.
B - B-A-B x-x-x. Km (S,W) B. Edo B. Ib B.

B   osoreru < osore[y]- (< *oso-ra-Ci-) / osori[y]- (< *osoro-Ci- <
*oso-ra-Ci-) / osor- (< *oso-ra-). 'fear, dread; be apprehensive'. B - B-A-B
x-B-x. Edo B. Nk husurin B; Sr ('honor, exalt') qusurir- B. [] osore x - B-2-B
x-B-x. Mr (Bm) A. Edo HHL. Nk x; Sr qusuri B. Note that *o(n)so- = *o(n)to-
'fear'; cf. odosu, oziru, odo-odo/(ozu-ozu <) odu-odu, odoroku; o*/*orosi_adj_ _B_.

A   osou < osofu < *os[i -]ofu < *os[a-Ci]_A_ opa- _A_. 'attack; (sup)press;
cover'. A - A/B-A-A x-(A)-x. Edo _B_. Nk husuurun A 'cover', Sr qusuyun A
'cover, suppress' < *osor- restructured < *osof- < *osaf- (see osaeru).
[] osoi x - x-x-x x-x-x (see Ch. 5).

A   osowaru < wosofaru ?< *wosifaru (second vowel assimilated to the first) <
*bosipa-ra- (< ?). 'be taught'. x - A-A-x x-x-x. Ib A. First attested Edo.

A   osu < *osa-. 'push; infer; recommend'. A - A-A-A x-A-A. NS (83a, 105b) A.
NS (T+) osi fyirakey (96) HL LLH, osi - byiraka-ne LL-HLH-H (odd); osi -
farafyi (kun) LL-LLF; osi - ter-u_attr_ (48) LLFL ?= LLHL; osi waku (kun) HLFH
= HL|LH; osu (kun) HL. Km (W) A. Edo A. Ib A. Nk husun A; Sr qus- A. Cf. hesu.
[] osi x - A-A-A x-x-x. Note: Unger has *oso- because of osou (but this can be
explained as truncated V + op-), osoreru (but a different etymology seems
better), and oso-butu 'push and move' (perhaps the second vowel assimilated to
the first vowel and/or to the following labial).

?A   osu < wosu < *bosa- (< ?). '(*take possession of →) deign to control or
rule; deign to eat/drink; deign to wear'. x - x-x-x x-x-x. NS (T+ 'drink')
wose_imper_ (39) HH, (32) HF. Cf. osikawa, sirosimesu. (Perhaps *bo-sa-, related
to *bo-ra- 'be'? Cf. Yoshida 1979:59.)

B+A   otiiru < oti[y] ir-u < *oto-Ci[-Ci]_B_ ira-_A_. 'fall (into)'. (B´) - A/B-B-B
x-x-x. Mg LHL / LH(|)HL.

B   otiru < oti[y]- < *oto-Ci-. 'fall'. B - B-B-B B-B-B. NS (Okada) B. NS (73)
oti-nikyi to LH-HL|H. Km (W) B. Edo B. Ib B. Nk huTirun B; Sr qutir- B.
[] oti x - B-2-A x-B-x. Cf. otosu; oriru.

?   otiru < woti[y]- < *boto-Ci-. 'be young and vigorous'. x - x-x-x x-x-x.
B´ < B+A otir-u LHL (Mg) = otiir-u.

?A   otonau < otonafu < *oto_2.2b_ -na-pa-. 'make a noise'. x - B-A-x x-x-x.
[] otonai x - x-x-x x-x-x. NS HHHL.

?B   otoroeru < otorofe[y]- < *otorofe[y]- < *otorafe[y]- < *oto-ra-pa-Ci-.
'get weak(ened), decline'. B - B-A-B x-A-x. Ib B. Nk huTuurin A; Sr quturir- A.
[] otoroe x - 3/4-A[U]/4[H,U]-B x-x-x.

?B   otoru < *oto-ra-. 'be inferior, fall behind'. B - B-A-A x-A["new?"]-x.
Hattō, Hamada, Matsue, Izumo A. Ib B. Cf. otosu, otiru.

B   otosu < *oto-sa-. 'drop it'. B - B-A-B x-B-B. Edo B. Ib B. Nk quTusun B;
Sr qutus- B; Yn utun B. Cf. otiru, orosu.

A   otozureru < otodure[y]- < *oto_2.2b_ -n- tura-Ci-_A_. 'make a sound, speak;
visit; inquire by letter'. x - A/B-A-A x-x-x. Km (W) A. Izumo A/B; Hattō,
Hamada, Matsue B. [] otozure x - 4/0[NHK]- A-A x-x-x.

A   ou < ofu < *opa-. 'pursue'. A - A-A-A x-A-A. Edo A. Ib A. Nk quurun A,
Sr quur- A < *oor- restructured from *of-.

?B   ou < ofu < *opu- (see ooseru). 'bear'. B - A/B[Mkz,Hiroto-Ōhara]-B-A
x-B-x. NS (76c [11:126W-M) ofamu to HL|H(|)H. NS (T+ 29) ofazu fa LHH(|)H.
Edo B. Hattō, Hamada, Matsue, Izumo, Goka-mura B. Ib B. Nk quurun B,
Sr quur- B < *oor- restructured from *of-. K: Hn A/B; Km, Edo B.

?B   ou < ofu < *opo-. 'cover'. x - x-x-x x-x-x. Cf. ootoru, oou, osou.

B   ou < ofiy- < *opo_adj_ _B_-Ci 'grow': see [oiru]. Perhaps also of- < *opo-
as consonant stem; cf. [owaru].

A   owaru < wofaru < *bo(-)-pa-ra-. A - A-A-A x-A-x. NS (95a [11:63-K) w̄ōf̄i =
wofa<u>ri</u> indicates *wofu < *bo(-)-pa-. Km (S) A. Edo A. Ib A. Nk q(a)waarun A,
Sr quwar- A is probably borrowed (glottal initial). Cf. oeru; o*1.3a* (register
incongruent). [] owari A - A-A-A x-<u>B</u>-x. Goka-mura 1 (verb A). Nk qwai A, Sr
quwai <u>B</u> (probably a borrowing).

B   [owaru] < ofaru ··· (Azuma) = of[yi] aru < *op[o-Ci]*B* ara-*B*. 'grow'.
x - x-x-x x-x-x.

?A/B   owasu < "ofasu" (a late replacement for ooseru). 'burden with' (= owaseru,
the regular causative of ou). x - A/B-A-A x-x-x. Cf. ooseru.

?   oyasu < woyasu < *boda-sa-. 'weaken, enfeeble'. x - x-x-x x-x-x.
Cf. [oeru].

A   oy<u>o</u>bu < *od<u>o</u>-n[a]-pa- ?< *oda-n[a]-pa- (the second vowel assimilated to
the first). 'reach; equal'. A - A-A-A x-A-x. NS (106a) A. Km (S) A. Mr (Bm) A.
Edo A. Ib A. Nk quyuubin A; Sr quyub- A. [] oyobi x - 1/0-1-A x-x-x. Mr (Bm) A.
Cf. oyobi*3.4* > yubi*2.3* 'finger'.

A   oy<u>o</u>bosu < *od<u>o</u>npo-sa- < *od<u>o</u>-n[a]-pa-sa- ?< *oda -n[a]-pa-sa-. 'make it
reach'. A - A/<u>B</u>-A-A x-x-x.

B   oyogu < *odonka- < ?. 'swim'. B - B-A-B B-B-B. Edo B. Ib B. Sd qwiigyum B;
Sr qwiizun (qwiig-) B; Yn uŋun B. [] oyogi x - B-A-B (B)-B-(B). Sr qwiizi B.

?B   oy<u>o</u>su < *od<u>o</u>-sa- (?< *oda-sa-). '(an esteemed person) get old'. B - x-x-x
x-x-x. Attested only in Mg (Kn: sō-ka 133:1)? Cf. oy<u>o</u>si-wo 'old man' (M 804),
usually taken to be an adjective oy<u>o</u>si[-si] as predicative (or stem) + noun.

A   ozikeru < odike[y]- < *odi[y]-key- < *ont<u>o</u>-Ci-ka-Ci-. 'take fright, fear'.
x - A/<u>B</u>[H]-A-A x-x-x. Hattō <u>B</u>; Hamada, Matsue, Izumo A. [] ozike x - A-A-A
x-x-x.

A+A   oziononoku < odi[y] wononoku < *ont<u>o</u>-Ci[-Ci]*?A* bononoka-*A* (< ...).
'shake with fear'. HL|HHHL x-x-x x-x-x.

?A   oziru < odi[y]- < *ont<u>o</u>-Ci-. 'fear'. A - <u>B</u>-A-A x-A-x. Nk quziirun A,
Sr quzir- A. Cf. odokasu, odosu, odoroku; osoreru.

?A   [ozomu] (JP) ?< *o(n)so-ma-. 'be surprised/startled; fear'. x - x-x-x
x-x-x. Cf. osoreru, oziru.

A   [ozuku] < woduku < *bontuka- (< ?). 'prance, bounce, frisk about'.
A - x-A-x x-x-x. Cf. odoru.

B   sabakeru < sabake[y]- < *sanpaka-Ci- (< ?). 'get sold; get worldly-wise'.
x - B-A-B x-B-x. Sr sabakir-.

B   sabaku < *sanpaka- (< ?). 'judge; sell'. B - B-A-B x-B-x. Ib B. Nk
sabaaKun B; Sr sabak- B. [] sabaki x - 1/3-A[U]/2[H]-B x-x-x. Nk sabaaKui B.

A   sabiraku (?< *sanpiraka- < ?; ?< *pas[a-C]i-ra-ka- with metathesis and
voicing of -p-). 'run'. HHxx - x-x-x x-x-x. Note that the Chinese character
this verb glosses has the phonetic .sam 'three'; one conceivable etymology
would be *san pas[a-C]i-r[a-u] aku (= "san to iu hasir-u koto").

B   sabireru < sabiyre[y]- < *sanpu-Ci-ra-Ci-. 'deteriorate, get desolate; be
rustic'. x - A/B-A[H]/B[U]-B x-B-x. Ib B. Nk sabirin B; Sr sabirir- B.

B   sabiru < sabiy- < *sanpu-Ci-. 'get desolate, old, rusty, faded'. x - B-B-B
x-x-x. Ib B. [] sabi 'rust'. B - B-2-B x-B-x. Cf. sabi*2.3* 'loneliness'
(x - B-2-<u>A</u> x-x-x); sab^u/1-si*adj B* 'desolate, lonely'.

x   ··· sabiru < ··· sabiy- < *sanp^u/<u>o</u>-Ci- ?< *sa-n[a]-pa-Ci-, ?< *sama*?2.2a*
-pa-Ci-. 'act as (appropriate for) ··· '. x - x-x-x x-x-x. See kami-sabiru.

-        saburau: see samurau.

B   sadamaru < *santama-ra- ?< *santa-ma-ra-. 'be decided, settled'. B - B-A-B
x-x-x. Nk sadaaman B. (Unger derives this stem from *sam[a]₇₂.₂ₐ tama-ra-ₐ but
the register is incongruent.)

B   sadameru < sadamey- < *santama-Ci- ?< *santa-ma-Ci-. 'decide (on);
prescribe'. B - B-A-B x-B-x. Km (S,W) B. Mr (Bm) B. Edo B. Ib B. Nk sadaamin B;
Sr sadamir- B. ◖ sadame x - B-2-B x-B-x. Edo HHL. Nk sadaamii B; Sr sadami B.

A   saegir-u < (Mg) saigir-u < saigir-u / *sakyi-gyir-u < *sa[k]iₓ.₁ -n-
kira-ᵦ. 'intercept, interrupt'. A - B̲-A-A x-x-x. Confused with saeru?

A   saeru < safey- < *sapa-Ci-. 'obstruct, bother'. A - x-x-x x-x-x. Km (S) A.
Cf. sawaru (vi.); saegir-u. ◖ sae A - x-x-x x-x-x.

?B   saeru < saye[y]- < *sada-Ci- (?< *sa-da-Ci-). 'get clear/bright; get cold'.
B - B-B-A̲ x-x-x. Ib B. ◖ sae x - B-2-A x-x-x. Cf. sayakeₐdⱼ ᵦ; sayayaka;
sayameru; samasu, sameru; samuₐdⱼ ᵦ.

A   saezuru < saf•/₁duru < safyiduru < ?*sapiₘᵢₘ -n- tura-ₐ. 'sing, chirp,
twitter; prattle'. A - B̲-A-A x-x-x. ◖ saezuri A - B̲-A-A x-x-x.

B´   sagaru < *sanka-ra-. 'descend, go/come down, sink, abate; hang down'.
B´ [Ir] - B-A-B x-B-x. Edo B. Ib B. Nk sagaarun B; Sr sagar- B.
◖ sagari x - 1/3(o-sagari 2)-A[H,U]/2[U]/1:3[U]-B x-B-x. Nk, Sr sagai B.

A   sagasu ?< sagu[ra]su (< ...). 'seek'. x - A-A-A x-A-x. Edo A.
Nk sageesun A, Sr sagees- A ?< *sagwees- < *saguras-.

A   sagasu (< ?). 'spread out (to dry in the sun)'. A - x-A-x x-x-x.

B   sageru < sage[y]- < *sanka-Ci-. 'lower; let it hang down; carry by hand;
... '. x - B-A̲[U]/B-B x-B-x. Km (S) B. Edo B. Hattō, Hamada, Matsue, Izumo,
Goka-mura B but A̲ meaning 'carry by hand'. Nk sagirun B; Sr sagir- B.
◖ sage x - B-2-B x-B-x. Nk x.

?A   sagukumu < ?*sa[ka-Ci]ₐ -n- ku[ma-Ciₐ] kuma-ₐ. 'push (waves) apart'.
x - x-x-x x-x-x. Cf. sakumu, saku; kuku.

?A   sagumoru < sagumworu ?< *sa-ₚᵣₑ -n- kumwo-ra-ᵦ, ?< *sam[a₇₂.₂ₐ] kumwoₓ.₅
-ra-. 'get cloudy'. x - x-x-x x-x-x.

A   saguru (< ?). 'search/grope for'. A - A/B̲[new]-A-A x-A-x. Ongi A.
Km (W) A. Mr (Bm) A. Edo A. Hata B̲. Kōchi B̲ (Doi 1952:30); Ib A. Nk saguurun
A, Sr sagur- A. Cf. sagasu. ◖ saguri x - A/B-A-A x-x-x. Nk, Sr sagui A.

A   saidatu < sa(k)yi-datu < *sakiₓ.₁ n[i] tata-ᵦ. 'go ahead, precede'.
x - x-x-x x-x-x. NS (107a) A.

-          saigir-u: see saegir-u.

A=2.1+A   saimaᵏ/ᵤuru < sa[k]iₓ.₁ makuruₐ (< ...). 'forestall, arrive ahead (of
others), anticipate'. HH(|)HHL [Ir (-g-)] - x-x-x x-x-x.

?B   sainamu < sa[k]inamu ?< *sak[a-C]iᵦ nanpu-ᵦ (cf. naburu). 'torment,
reproach'. B - B-A-A̲ x-x-x.

A   saiwaeru (= [sakiwaeru]) < sa[ky]i-fafe[y]- < *saki (< *sak[a-C]iₐ)
(-)papa-Ci-. 'bring good fortune to'. x - x-x-x x-x-x. NS (92b) A.

?A   saiwau (= sakiwau) < saifafu < sa[k]yi-fafu < *saki (?< *sak[a-C]iₐ)
(-)papa-. 'be fortunate'. x - x-x-x x-x-x. ◖ saiwai A - A-A-B x-A-x. Km (S) A.

-          saizuru: see saezuru.

?A   sakadatu < *sakaₓ.₁ -n- tata-ᵦ. 'stand on end, bristle'. x - B̲-A-A x-x-x.

?A   sakaeru < sakaye[y]- < *saka-da-Ci-. 'prosper'. A - B̲-A-A x-A̲-x. Ib A.
NS (Okada) A. NS (T+ 53) sakayuru LHHH. Km (W) A. Edo A. Hattō, Hamada B̲;
Matsue, Izumo A. Nk ꜱaKeerun A; Sr ꜱakeer- A. ◖ ꜱakae x-2/0-A-A x-x-x.
NS (72a [11:196-M], 79a [14:313-M "fakaye" for sakaye]) A.

?A   sakaeru < sakafey- < *sakaₓ.₁ -pa-Ci-. 'oppose; reverse; (= sakau) turn
one's back on'. A - x-A-x x-x-x. Edo A.

A   sakanoboru ‹ (Nr) saka-n<u>o</u>f<u>o</u>ru ‹ saka*_{s.1}* n<u>o</u>p<u>o</u>-ra-*_A*. 'go upstream; go back
in time'. A - A(/<u>B</u>[H])-A-<u>B</u> x-x-x. Km (W) A. NS (100b) A, (104a, mistake?)
HHLH··· . Ib <u>B</u>. On -b- from -f-, see Ch. 2.

?A   sakarau ‹ sakarafu ‹ *saka*_{s.1}* -ra-pa-. 'run counter (to), oppose'.
x - <u>B</u>-A-A x-x-x. Hattō, Hamada, Matsue, Izumo <u>B</u>. Ib <u>B</u>.

A   sakaru ‹ *saka-ra-. 'flourish'. x - A-A-A x-A-x. Km (W) A. Nk x; Sr sakar-
A (= sakeer- A). 🛛 sakari A - A-A-A x-x-x. Ongi A. Mr (Bm) A. Edo A.

A   sakaru ‹ *saka-ra-. 'get distant, apart'. A - x-A-x x-x-x. NS (105a) A;
NS (T+ 3) HHH. Km (W) A. Cf. sakeru.

?A   sakaru ‹ *saka*_{s.1}* -ra-. 'turn one's back on' (= sakau). x - x-x-x x-x-x.

B   [sakasigaru] ‹ *sakasi*_{adj B}* (‹ ...) -g[e] (‹ -n- key*_{1.1}*) ara-*_s*. 'act
wise(ly), show acumen'. x - x-x-x x-x-x. Attested 10th century.

?A   sakau ‹ sakafu ‹ *saka*_{s.1}* -pa-. 'turn one's back on'. A - x-A-x x-x-x.
Edo A.

B   sakau ‹ sakafu ‹ *saka*_{s.3}* -pa-. 'set a boundary, delimit'. B - x-A-x
x-x-x. 🛛 sakai B -2(‹*3)-2-B B-B-B. NS (107b) B.

2.1+A   [sakeageru] ‹ sakey agey- ‹ *saka-Ci*_{s.1}* anka-Ci[-Ci]*_A*. 'strain rice wine'
(= sakesitamu). HH(|)HL = 2.1+A - x-x-x x-x-x.

?A/B   sakebu ‹ sakyebu ‹ *sak[y]i yeb- ‹ *sakyi ywob- ‹ *sak[a-C]i*_{?B}* dwonpa-*_A*.
'yell, shout, cry, yell; advocate'. A - B-A-B x-x-x. Km (S) A. Edo A. Hata A;
Wakamatsu B. Kōchi A (Doi 1952:31); Ib (rare) A. Northern Honshū sakabu
assimilates the second vowel to the first, or perhaps simply retains the root-
final vowel of the first stem. 🛛 sakebi x - B-A[H]/2[U]-B x-x-x. Ōsaka, Kōbe 3.

?A   sakeru ‹ sakey- ‹ *saka-Ci-. 'put apart, put at a distance, separate;
send/drive/keep away; avoid'. A - <u>B</u>-A[U]/<u>B</u>-A x-x-x. NS (Okada) A. NS (T+ 66)
sakey te HH(|)H; (99) muka sakuru HH <u>LHH</u>. Km (S,W) A. Hattō, Hamada, Matsue,
Izumo <u>B</u>. Ib <u>B</u>. Cf. toozakeru, sokeru.

?B   sakeru ‹ sakey- ‹ *saka-Ci-. 'get ripped, split'. B - B-B-<u>A</u> B-B-B.
NS (T+ 108) HH<u>F</u>-L. Nk saKirun B; Sr sakir- B. We leave unexplained the word
sakiy-de 'rough(-skinned) hands' (?‹ *sakey-de).

2.1+B   sakesitamu ‹ sakey sitamu ‹ *saka-Ci*_{s.1}* sita-ma-*_s*. 'strain rice wine' (=
[sakeageru]). HHLLL (Ck) ?= *HH|LLH - x-x-x x-x-x.

?A   sakidateru ‹ sakyidate[y]- ‹ *saki*_{s.1}* n[i] tata-*_s*. 'give precedence to'.
x - <u>B</u>-A-x x-x-x. NS (T+ kun) sakyi [ ]taturu HL|LHH.

?A   sakidatu ‹ sakyidatu ‹ *saki*_{s.1}* n[i] tata-*_s*. 'go ahead, precede'.
<u>B</u>(?) - <u>B</u>-A-A x-<u>B</u>-x. NS (126b) A. Km (S) A. Ib A. 🛛 sakidati x - A-A-x x-A-x.

A   [sakiwaeru] ‹ sakyifafey- ‹ *sak[a-C]i*_A* (-) papa-Ci-. 'bring good fortune
to'. x - <u>B</u>-x-x x-x-x. Cf. saiwaeru.

A   sakiwau ‹ sakyifafu ‹ *sak[a-C]i*_A* (-) papa-. 'flourish'. x - <u>B</u>-x-x x-x-x.
Cf. saiwau.

?A   saku ‹ *saka-. 'bloom; [figuratively] (surf-)waves break'. A - A-A-<u>B</u>
x-A-A. NS (Okada) A. NS (T+ 35) sakaba HLL; (114) sakyi [i]de k<u>o</u>nu HH H LL;
(96) saku*_{pred in epithet}* HL; (114) sakey [¨]to-mo HL(|)L-L. Km (W) A. Edo A.
Sapporo, Matsue, Izumo, Ōita, NE Kyūshū, Wakamatsu <u>B</u>. Akita, Matsumoto, Numazu,
Hattō, Hamada, Goka-mura, Hiroshima A. Ib A. Nk saCun A; Sr sak- A. Unger
relates saku to aku, with a reconstructed root that we would write *[z]aka-.

A   saku ‹ *saka-. 'separate, part, put at a distance, send away' (= sakeru).
A - x-B(?)-x x-x-x. Cf. sakaru, sakeru, soku; kotosaka 'severing relations'.

?B   saku ‹ *saka- (cf. sakeru) / *saku- (cf. sakumu). 'rip it, split it'.
B - B-B-<u>A</u> B-B-B. NS (T+ kun) ifa saku HH <u>F</u>H = HH|LH. Ongi B. Km (S) B.
Ib B. Nk saCun B; Sr sak- B.

?B   sakumu < *sakuma- (?= *saku-ma-). 'push one's way through (mountains, rocks, trees)'. Cf. Sd saku(u) B 'valley' = sako [dial., see NKD].

B   sakuru < *sakura- (?< *sa[ka-Ci]_B kura-_B). 'scoop up (dirt/water); dig a ditch; get choked up, sob'. B - x-A-x x-B-x. Nk saKurun B, Sr sakur- B 'scratch (the skin with a sharp object)'. [] sakuri B - x-x-x x-B-x. Nk x; Sr sakui B 'a scratch'.

B   [samaru] < *sama-ra-: see sameru (Nk, Sr forms).

B   samasu < *sama-sa- (?< *sama-sa-, ?< *sa-npa-sa- < *sa-n[a]-pa-sa-). 'cool it; rouse, awaken; sober'. x - B-A-B x-B-x. Ib B. Nk samaasun B; Sr samas- B. Cf. sameru; samu_adj B; saeru.

A   samatageru < samatagey- < *samatanka-Ci-(<?, cf. sawaru). 'hinder, hamper, disturb'. A - A/B-A-A x-A-x. NS (103a) A. Mr (Bm) A. Hamada B. Nk samaadagirun A; Sr samatagir- A. There is one example of samatag- as a consonant stem (see Zdb). [] samatage x - 3/4/0-A-A x-A-x. Mr (Bm) A.

A   samayou < samayofu < *sa(-)ma_?2.2a dwopa-_bnd v ('appearance/direction waver'). 'wander, roam, prowl'. x - B-A-A x-x-x. Ib B.

A   [samayou] < "samaywofu" = samaywo[b]u < *sa(-)ma_?2.2a dwonpa-_A. 'wail in complaint or accusation'. A - x-x-x x-x-x.

A   sameku < *sa-myeku < *sa_mia miCa-ka-_bnd v. 'be noisy' (= sawa-meku). A - x-x-x x-x-x.

B   sameru < samey- < *sama-Ci- (?< *sa-ma-Ci, ?< *sa-npa-Ci- < *sa-n[a]-pa-Ci-). 'get cool, abate; wake up, get sober/undeceived; fade'. B - B-B-B x-B-B. Km (S) B. Edo B. Ib B. Nk samirun B, Sr samir- B < *same- (< *sama-Ci-) = Nk samaarun B, Sr samar- B < *sama-ra-. Cf. samasu; samu_adj B; saeru.

A   samurau < sa^b/_murafu < samorafu < *sa-_pre mora-pa-_?B. 'serve, wait on' (> saurau > sɔɔroo > sooroo). A - B-x-x x-x-x. NS (121a) A. Mr (Bm) ?B. The form with -b- is Heian and later. Ōno treats sa- as the mesial deictic. [] samurai x - A-A-A x-A-x.

?A   [saneru] < sane[y]- < *sa-_pre na-Ci-_A. 'sleep'. x - x-x-x x-x-x.

A   saraeru < sarafey-/saraf- < *sara-pa(-Ci)-. 'review, rehearse'. x - A-A-A x-x-x. Ib B. Sr sareer- A < sarafe- 'dredge, clean' (= sarau).

A   sarasu < *sara-sa-. 'bleach; expose'. A - A-A-A x-A-x. Ib A. Nk saraasun A; Sr saras- A. [] sarasi x - A-A-A x-x-x.

A   sarau < sarafu < *sara-pa-. 'clean, dredge; (= saraeru) review, rehearse; snatch away, abduct'. x - A-A-A x-(A)-x. See saraeru. [] sarai 'cleaning, ... ; rake, pitchfork'. A - A-A(but 1:3 as 'rake')-x x-(x)-x.

?A   sareru < sare[y]-/sara- < *sara[-Ci]-. 'get bleached; get exposed'. x - x-x-x x-A-x. Nk sariirun A; Sr sarir- A.

?A   saru < *sara-. 'depart'; also (OJ) 'move (forward)' and (= sari-yuku/ -ku[ru]) '(a time) come, come around'. A - A/B-A[U]/B[H]-A x-x-x. NS (95a, 123b, 126b, 134b) A. Km (S,W) A. Mr (Bm) A. Edo A. Narada B [Lit.]; Wakamatsu, Hattō, Hamada, Goka-mura B; Matsue, Izumo A.

?A   saru 'get bleached/exposed': see sareru.

?A+A   saruku/sariku [dial.] < sari yuku/iku < *sar[a-C]i_?A yuka-/ika-_A. 'walk around, walk'. NKD cites Kyūshū, Shikoku, and Wakayama for saruku. It gives sariku "< sari ku[ru]" ('come'), with Kyūshū variants saiku and sareku. Cf. aruku/ariku.

?B´   sasaeru < sasafe[y]- < *sas[i] - afey- < *sas[a-C]i_B apa-Ci-_B. 'support, prop'. B´ - A/B-B-A x-x-x. Km x. Narada, Hamada B; Hattō, Matsue, Izumo A. Ib B´ (= L). [] sasae x - 3/4/0-1-A x-x-x.

?B´   sasagasu < *sasanka-sa- < *sas[a-Ci]_B anka-sa-_A. 'deign to present'. x - x-x-x x-x-x.

?B´   sasageru < sasagey- < *sasanka-Ci- < *sas[a-Ci]*B* anka-Ci-*A*. 'hold up,
offer'. B´ - A-A[H]/B[U]-A x-x-x. Edo B´.

?A/B   sasameku < *saya-myeku < *sasa*mi* miCa-ka-*bnd v*. 'murmur, whisper,
rustle'. x - B-A-A x-x-x.

?B   sasaru < *sasa-ra-. 'be stuck/embedded'. x - B-A-A x-x-x. Ib B.
Cf. sasareru x - B-B-B x-B-x.

?A/B   sasayaku < *sasa*mi* -da-ka-. 'whisper'. B - A/B-A-A x-x-x. Ib A, (B).
Cf. sasameku, sosoyaku. [] sasayaki x - A/B[K]-A-A x-x-x.

B+A   sasiyoru < sasi - yoru < *sas[a-C]i*B* do̲ra- *A*. 'get close'. LHxx - A/B-x-x
x-x-x.

A   sasou < sasofu/sasufu < ?*saswopa- (< ?). 'entice, tempt, invite'.
A - A-A[H]/B̲[U]-A x-x-x. Ib A. The Kt version from NKD may well be a misprint;
but sasoi-dasu is also given as B, despite sasoi-awasu/-awaseru A.
[] sasoi x - A-A-A x-x-x.

B   sasu < *sasa-. 'point to; prick; insert; ... '. B - B-B-B B-B-x.
NS (130a) B. NS (T+ 36) sasikyeku H̲LLL; (23) sase*imper*. Km (S,W) B. Mr (Bm) B.
Edo B. Ib B. Nk sasun B; Sr sas- B. [] sasi B - B-2-B x-x-x.

A   sasurau < sasuraf-/sasurafey- < *sasurapa-[Ci-] (<?). 'wander, roam'.
A - B-A-A x-x-x. [] sasurai x - A/B[K]-A-A x-x-x.

A   sasuru < *sa-*pre* sura-*A*. 'rub; pat'. x - A-A-A x-x-x. Hattō A/B̲.

A   satoru < *satworu < *satwo*adj A* -ra-. 'realize, awaken to; be
enlightened'. A - A/B̲[new]-A-A x-S-x. Mr (Bm) A. Edo A. Narada B̲; Matsue,
Izumo, Goka-mura A; Hattō, Hamada A/B̲. Ib A. Nk saTuurun A; Sr satur- A.
[] satori A - A-A-A x-x-x. NS (91b, 95b, 109b,133a) A. Mr (Bm) A.
The adjective ('wise') is assumed to be the prefix sa- + two- 'sharp'.

A   satosu < *satwosu < *satwo*adj A* -sa-. 'admonish'. A - A/B̲-A-A x-x-x.
Narada B̲; Hattō, Hamada A/B̲; Matsue, Izumo, Goka-mura A. Ib Ā. Nk satuusun A
[new]. [] satosi A - A-A-A x-x-x.

?A/B   sawagu < (Nr) sawaku < *saba*mi*-ka-. 'clamor, make noise, fuss'. B - B-A-A
x-A-x. NS (Okada) B. Km (W) B. Edo B. Ib B. Nk sawaazun A; Sr sawag- A.
[] sawagi x - 1-2-A x-x-x.

A   sawaru < safaru < *sapa-ra-. 'hinder, hamper, affect; touch, feel' (vi.).
A - A-A-A A-A-x. Ib A. Nk sa(wa)arun A; Sr saar- A. Cf. saeru. [] sawari A -
A-A-A x-A-x. Mr (Bm) A. Nk, Sr sawai A 'sickness'.

-          sawasu < "safasu" (< ?). 'remove the astringency (of persimmon juice);
bleach; lightly lacquer'. x - A/B-A-x x-x-x. First attested Edo. Shimane awasu.

?A   sawataru < *sa-*pre* bata-ra-*A*. 'go across'. x - x-x-x x-x-x.

?B   sayagu < *sada*mi* -n[a]-ka-. 'rustle'. x - B-A-x x-x-x. Km (W) B.

?B   [sayameru] < sayamey- < *sada-ma-Ci-. 'clean/purify it'. x - x-x-x x-x-x.
Cf. saeru.

?   [sayaru] < *sada(-)ra-. 'obstruct; get trapped, caught, entangled'.
x - x-x-x x-x-x. NS (T+ 7) sayarazu HHL̲F, sayari HHL. Cf. sawaru, saeru.

?A/B   sazameku < *saza-myeku < *sansa*mi* miCa-ka-*bnd v*. 'make an uproar'.
x - B-A-A x-x-x. [] sazameki x - A/B-A-A x-x-x.

?A/B   sazukaru < sadukaru ?< *sam[a]-tukar- < *sama*7z.2a* tuka-ra-*B*; ?< *sag[ey]-
tukar- < *sanka-Ci[-Ci]*B* tuka-ra-*B*. 'be gifted/blessed with; be taught'.
x - B-A-B x-A-x. Nk x; Sr sazakar- A *(second vowel assimilated to first)*.

?A/B   sazukeru < sadukey- ?< *sam[a]-tukey- < *sama*7z.2a* tuka-Ci-*B*; ?< *sag[ey]-
tukey- < *sanka-Ci[-Ci]*B* tuka-Ci-*B*. 'grant, award; teach'. A - B-A-B x-A-x.
NS (127b: sa̅[¨]tu̲ku) ?A; (Okada) A. Edo B. Ib B. Nk x; Sr sazakir- A *(the
second vowel assimilated to the first)*.

B   sebamaru < *saCinpa*adj B* (< ...) -ma-ra-). 'get narrow'. x - B-A-B x-x-x.
Cf. semaru, semeru, subomu, subomeru, subomaru, suberu; sibomu; Sr siba- B =
sema- (?< *sa-inpa- 'small-narrow', cf. Sr qiba-'narrow').
B   sebameru < *saCinpa*adj B* -ma-Ci-). 'make it narrow'. x - B-A-B x-x-x.
Ib B. Nk sibaamin B.
?B   sebaru [dial.] = semaru.
?B   sebir-u < *senpu-ra- (< ?). 'importune' (= segamu). x - B-A-x x-x-x.
?B   seburu < *senpu-ra- (< ?). 'importune' (= segamu). x - x-x-x x-x-x.
B   segamu ?< se (-n-) kamu < *so*1,2* (-n-) kama-*B* ('back bite'). 'importune,
pester; scold'. x - B-A-B x-x-x. Ib B. Sr sicimin (syun) B < ?. Also seb¹/ᵘr-.
A   segukumaru < sekugumaru *(syllable metathesis)* < *se (<*so*1,2*) kunkuma-ra-*A*
(< ...). 'hunch (up/over)'. A - B-A-x x-x-x. Mg H(|)HHHL 'have a hunched back'.
B   sekasu < *seka-sa- (< ...). 'rush it, urge on'. x - B-A-B x-x-x. Ib B.
B   seku (?< *saku < *saka-; ?< *soku < *soka-). 'obstruct, check'. B - B-B-B
x-x-x. Km (W) B. Edo B. Ib B. ⌽ seki 'barrier; dam'. B - 1-2-A̲ x-x-x.
B   seku ?< seku 'obstruct'; ?< *si[f]a[bu]k- < OJ sifa-buk- < *sipa*2,x* -n-
puka-*B*. 'cough'. x - B-B-B x-x-x. sek[y]i - age[y]- 'cough up' attested Hn.
⌽ seki x - B-2-B A[new]/B-(?B)-(C). Sd syekyi A̲ = syeehe B. Nk sahui B,
Sr sakkwii B (?< *sakurii = Tk sya˩kkuri 'hiccup'). Northern Honshū, Saga
siyabuki; Nagasaki siwabuki.
B   seku < *seka- (< ?, cf. ser-u, isogu). 'hurry; (= sekasu) make hurry,
rush'. x - B-B-B x-x-x. Km (W) (A/)B. K: Hn, Km B. Ib B.
?B   semaru < seb/ᴍaru < *saCinpa*adj B* (< ...) -ra-. 'get narrow; impend, draw
near; press for; force'. B(?/B´) - B-A-B x-x-x. Km (S) B. Ib B. Mg sefasaru B
(?< *se[n]pa-sa-ra-) suggests there may have been a stem *seb/ᴍa-sa-.
?B   semegu < semeᵏ/ɢu < *seb/ᴍeᵏ/ɢ- < *saCinpa*adj B* (< ...) -Ci-(n[a]-)ka-.
'quarrel, struggle (with each other); maltreat, molest, persecute'.
B/B´ - B-A-x x-x-x. Cf. semeru.
B   semeru < semey- < *seb/ᴍey- < *saCinpa*adj B* (< ...) -Ci-. 'attack;
blame'. B - B-B-B x-B-x. Ongi B. NS (99a) B; (Okada) A̲. Km (Okada W) B. Edo B.
Ib B. Nk simirun B; Sr simir- B. ⌽ seme B - B-2-B x-x-x. Edo HL. Cf. semegu.
?A/B   seou < seofu < *se*1,2* (< *so̲) opu-*?B*. 'carry on one's back, bear'.
x - B-A-A x-x-x.
B   ser-u (?< se[ma]r-u; ?< *sera- < ?). 'narrow the gap; press for quick
action; [dial.] hurry, rush'. x - B-B-x x-x-x.
B   ser-u < *sera- (< ?). 'compete'. x - B-B-B x-x-x. ⌽ seri x - B-2-B x-x-x.
B   sesekamu ?< *se - se (< *so*1,2* - so*1,2*) kama-*B* ('back back bite'). 'scold,
rebuke'. B - x-A[U]-x x-x-x. Cf. segamu. (Ōno "sesegamu", but Mg has only -k-.)
A   [sesu] < *se-sa- (?< *so-sa-). 'deign to do'. *See* suru.
A   ? sibaru (?< *sinpa-ra-, ?< *so-Ci*A* -n- para-*A*). 'do repeatedly or
continually'. A (Ck) - x-x-x x-x-x. Attested only in Ck Mg? Cf. siba-siba.
B   sibaru < *sinpara- < *sim[a]-pa-ra- (cf. simeru). 'bind, tie, restrict'.
B - B-A-B x-B[Lit.]-x. NS (T+ kun) twori sibaru LH|LLH. Hyōgo A; Suzu, Kōchi,
Ib B. Nk x.
B   sibireru < sibire[y]- < *sinpi(-)ra(-)Ci- (< ?). 'get numb'. x - B-A-B
x-x-x. Hattō, Matsue A̲; Hamada, Izumo B. Ib B. ⌽ sibire x - B-A[U]/1:3-B
x-x-x. Hattō, Izumo A̲; Matsue A̲/B; Hamada 1. Cf. [siiru].
A   sibomu < *sinpo(-)ma- ?< *sinpa-ma- (?< senpa-ma- < *sonpa-ma-). 'wither,
shrivel'. A - A-A-A x-x-x. Km (S) A. Ib subomu A. Nk sibu(u)min B̲.
Cf. sebamaru, sebameru; tubomu.
B   siboru < *sinpo(-)ra- (< ?). 'wring, squeeze'. B - B-A-B x-B-x. Km (W) B.
Ib B. ⌽ sibori x - B-A[U]/1:3-B x-x-x. Nk s¹/ᵤburun B; Sr sibur- B. Cf. siromu.

B   sibukasu < ?*sinpu*adj B* -ka-sa-. 'slowly advance'. B - x-x-x x-x-x.
No text examples.

B   siburu < ?*sinpu*adj B* -ra-. 'falter, hesitate'. B - B-A-x x-x-x.

B   sidaku < si*t*/*d*aku < sitaku ?< *sita-ka-. 'devastate, lay waste; trample'.
x - B-x-x x-x-x. Km (W) B.

?B   sidaru < *sin[a]-tara*B*-. 'droop/hang (down)'. (B) - x-x-x x-x-x.
NS (T+ kun) LHH.

?A   [sideru] < *sin[a]-tara*B*-Ci-. x - x-x-x x-x-x. Mg sidari-yanagi B 'weeping
willow'; sidayaka, sinayaka B 'pliant, lissome'.

-          siedakeru/sietageru: *see* siitageru.

B   sigaramu < *si*1.3* n[i] kara-ma-*?B*. 'entwine, entangle; construct a weir'.
x - x-x-x x-x-x. [] sigarami x - A-A-x x-x-x. Km (W) LLLH, LLHL. Mr (W 18, 19)
HHHL, (20) HHHx. K: Edo HHHL.

B   siger-u < sigeyr-u < *sinka-Ci-ra-. 'grow thick/dense'. ?B-B-A-B x-x-x.
Cf. sige*adj B*.

A+B   sigoku < *si[y] (< *so-Ci*A* 'do') -n- kwoka-*B*. 'draw or squeeze through
one's hands'. x - B-A-B x-x-x. [] sigoki x - A/B-A[H]/1:3[U]-B x-x-x.

?B   [siiru] < sifi[y]- < *sip*u*/*o*Ci-. 'lose the function of a sensory organ'
(= siu). x - x-x-x x-x-x. Cf. sibireru.

?B   siiru < sifi[y]- < sip*u*/*o*Ci- (< ?). 'force, compel; slander, falsely
accuse'. B - B-A-B B-B-x. Km (W) B. Ib *(rare)* B. Nk siirun B; Sr siir- B.
[] sii LH (Ck, "sii") - x-x-x x-x-x.

?A   siitageru < sifitage- < (Hn) sifetage-/sifedake- < sifetake[y]- (< ?;
cf. siiru). 'oppress'. A - B̲-A-A x-x-x.

A+B   sikakeru < si-kakey- < *si[y] (< *so-Ci*A*) kaka-Ci-*B*. 'start, set out, set
to'. x - A-A-A x-A-x. Ib A. Nk siKaaKin A; Sr sikakir- A. [] sikake 'device,
contrivance'. x - A-A-A x-A-x. Nk siKaaKi A; Sr sikaki A.

A   sikameru < sikame[y]- < *sikama-Ci- (< ?). 'make (one's face) scowl,
frown, grimace, pucker (up)'. x - A-A-A x-x-x. Ib A,

A   sikamu < *sikama- (< ?). 'get wrinkled; wrinkle up, pucker'. x - A-x-x
x-x-x. Cf. hazikami.

?A/B   sikaru < *sikara- ?< *sikka (< situ-ka < Ch chet-.ha) -ra-. 'scold'.
x - A/B-A-B x-x-x. Goka-mura B; Hattō, Hamada, Matsue, Izumo A. Ib A.
[] sikari x - A-A-B x-x-x.

(B)   [sikaru] < sikar- < *si-ka*2.3* [a]ra-*B*. 'be so'. B - B-A-B x-x-x.
Mr (Bm) B. Edo HLL.

B   sikeru < sike[y]- (< ?). 'be damp, wet, humid'. x - B-B-B x-(B)-x.
Nk simiKin B; Sr simikeer- B. [] sike 'heavy weather, dull season'. x - B-
A̲/2[U]-B x-x-x. Aomori A̲. Probably < si[meyri -]key = sikke = sikki (< Ch
tsyet-khyey') 'humidity'; *see* simer-u, simesu. The adjective stem sikye-si-
'? dirty' is probably not related.

A+A   sikiiru < siki wiru < sikyi wi[y]- < *sik[a-C]i*A* b*u*/*o*-Ci[-Ci]*A*. 'spread
it and sit'. HL|HL - x-x-x x-x-x.

A   sikir-u < sikyir-u (?< *sikyer-u < *sik-i ar- < *sik[a-C]i*A* ara-*B*; ?<
*siki-[i]ru < sik[a-C]i*A* ira-*A*; ?< *siki -ra- < *sik[a-C]i*A* -ra-). 'continue
(one after another), be uninterrupted'. x - B̲-A-x x-x-x.
[] sikiri (ni) A - A-A-A x-x-x. Edo A.

A+B   sikir-u < si[y]-kyir-u < *so-Ci*A* "do" kira-*B*. 'partition'. x - B-A-A
x-x-x. [] sikiri x - B-A-A x-x-x.

A+?A   sikoru < si[y]-koru < *so-Ci*A* "do" k̲ora-*?A*. 'get stiff, harden'.
x - A/B-A-A x-x-x. [] sikori x - A-A-A x-x-x.

B   sikoziru < sik̲odi[y]- ?< *si[y] - kont*u*/*o*-Ci- (< *so-Ci*A* "do" ···).
'falsely report' [Ōno]; '(ailment) fail to get cured' [NKD]. B - x-x-x x-x-x.

A   siku < *sika-. 'spread it (out); control, rule'. A - A-A-A x-A-x.
Km (S) A. Edo A. Nk ˢ/ʰiCun A; Sr sik- A.

A   siku < *sika-. 'pile up, continue without a break (cf. sikir-u); grow
dense, proliferate (cf. siger-u)'. A - x-B[U]-x x-x-x. Km (W) A.

A   siku < *sika-. 'reach, catch up (with), be equal (to)'. A - A-B-x x-x-x.
NS (T+ 52) sikye*imper* LL. Edo B.

B   simaru < *sima-ra- (cf. sibaru). 'be shut, tight, firm; shut it tight'.
x - B-A-B x-x-x. Nk simaarun B. ▯ simari x - 1-A[H]/1-B x-B-x. Hamada 1;
Hattō, Matsue, Izumo B. Nk simaarii B; Sr ('doorstop') simari B.

?A/B   simau < simafu < *sima-pa-. 'finish; put away; close up'. x - A-A-B x-x-x.
Ib A. ▯ simai x - A-A-A x-x-x. 1700 Ōsaka HLL. (Traditionally: < *si[y]ₐ (<
sǫ-Ci) -ma-pa- or *si[y]ₐ (< sǫ-Ci) mapa-ₐ.)

?   (-)simeru < *(-)simey- (< ?, perhaps *sǫ-Ci-ma-Ci-). 'cause (to do)'.
x - x-x-x x-A-x. Nk simiirun A; Sr simir- A. For the accent of verbs with this
auxiliary, see Ch. 4, p.*60*.

?B   simeru < *simey- < *sima(-)Ci- (< ?). 'mark out as one's territory;
occupy, take possession of'. B - B-B-A̱ x-x-x. Ib B. Cf. sima*ɜ.ɜ*. ▯ sime 'holy
territory, restricted area; (= simenawa) sacred rope'. B - B-2-B x-x-x.

B   simeru < sime[y]- < *sima-Ci-. 'tie up, tighten, strangle; add up; shut,
close'. B - B-B-B x-B-x. Ib B. Nk simiirun B; Sr simir- B. ▯ sime x - B-2-B
x-B-x. Nk x.

(?A/)B   simer-u < *simeyr- < *sima-Ci-ra-. 'get damp'. x - A̱-A-B (B)-B-x.
Hiroshima (Okuda 280), Hata (Doi 1952:30), Hamada, Izumo, Goka-mura B; Hattō,
Matsue A̱. Kōchi B. Sr simir- B could be either < *simer- or < *sime- but
simi-keeyun (see sikeru) indicates < *sime- < *sima-Ci- (without -ra-).
▯ simeri x - A̱-A-B x-x-x; o-simeri A̱-4[U]/1[H]-B. Hattō, Hamada B; Matsue,
Izumo A̱.

(?A/)B   simesu < *simeys- < *sima-Ci-sa-. 'dampen/wet it'. x - A̱-A-B x-x-x.
▯ simesi x - A̱-x-x x-B-x.

A+B   simesu < si[y] myesu < *sǫ-Ciₐ "*do*" miCa-sa-ᵦ. 'show, indicate'. HL|F -
A/B-A-A x-x-x. Km (S) HL(|)L. Edo HLL. Hattō, Hamada, Matsue, Izumo, Goka-mura
B. Ib ᵀq(rare) B, ▯ simesi x - A/B-A-A x-x-x. The Mg accent indicates the
etymology s̄ime s̄u, according to K (see Ch. 4, §8.2); cf. Seki 1977:73.

A   simiru < simi[y]- < simey- < *sima-Ci-. 'permeate, soak'. A [Ir] - A-A-A
x-(A)-x. Nk suumin A; Sr suunun (suum-) A ?< *som-. Cf. simu; somu, someru,
somaru. Ib A. ▯ simi x - A-A-A x-(A)-x. Sr sun A < *somi.

A   simiru < simi[y]- ?< *simo-Ci- (cf. simo*ɜ.ɜ* despite the incongruent
register). 'freeze'. A - A-A-A x-x-x. ▯ simi x - A-A-x x-x-x.

A   simu < *sima-. 'get soaked, be permeated' (cf. somu = somaru). A [Ir] -
x-x-x x-x-x. Km (W) A. ▯ simi x - A-A-A x-(A)-x. Sr sun A < *somi.

?A/B   sinadareru < *sina-?ᵦ tara-Ci-ᵦ. 'droop'. x - B-A-A x-x-x. Cf. sideru,
sidaru, sinau.

?B   sinaeru < sinafey- < *sina-pa-Ci-. 'bend, be pliant/pliable' (= sinau).
B - x-x-x x-x-x.

?B   [sinaeru] < sinaye[y]- < *sina-da-Ci-. 'droop, wither'. x - x-x-x x-x-x.

?B   [sinameru] < siname[y]- < *sina-ma-Ci-. 'wrap to conceal, shroud'.
x - x-x-x x-x-x.

?B   sinau < sinafu < *sina-pa-. 'bend, be pliant/pliable'. B - B-A-A̱ x-x-x.
Ib *(rare)* B.

?A   sinobu < sinobiy- ?< *sinǫ -npᵘ/ǫCi- (?< -n[a]-pa-Ci-). 'endure, bear,
suffer; hide'. Cf. sinogu. A - A/Ḇ-A-Ḇ x-A-x. Km (S,W) A. Edo A. Wakamatsu A.
Ib A. Sr sinub- A < *sinob- *(next entry)*. ▯ sinobi 'spy; incognito' x - x-A-x
x-A-x.

?B   sinobu ‹ sinwofu ‹ *sinwo(-)pa-. 'fondly recall'. (B) - A/B̲-A-B̲ x-x-x.
Mg sinobu-gusa. NS (105a) A. Edo A. Nk sinuubin A. [] sinobi x - x-x-x x-x-x.
Nk sinuubi B [Lit.]. Form confused with 'endure' in later times (cf. Sr form in
the preceding entry).

B   sinogu ‹ sinwogu ‹ *sinwo -n[a]-ka-. 'endure, stand; find shelter from;
surpass'. B - B-A-B x-B-x. Km (W) B. Edo B. Ib B. Nk sinu(u)zun B; Sr sinug- B.
[] sinogi x - 1/3-A-B x-x-x. Cf. sinobu.

A*   sinu ‹ sini[y]-/sin- (hybrid conjugation) 'die': ?‹ *si - ini[y]-/in- ‹
*si[yi] inᵘ/o̲-Ci-/ina-, with a verb *si- ?‹ *siy- ‹ *so̲(-)Ci- 'die' (cf. sosu
= sise[y]- 'kill', Korean ci- 'die, wilt; pass by/away'); ?‹ *sinᵘ/o̲-Ci-/sina-
(?‹ *zinᵘ/o̲-Ci-/zina-, cf. inu). A - A-A-A A-A-A. NS (80a, 107a, 109a
[11:319-K], 109b [11:322-K], 131a, 134a) A. NS (T+ 81) sinamasi HL|HH.
Km (W) A. Edo A. Nk sinun A; Sr sin- A; Yn nnirun A ‹ *sinir-, restructured ‹
*sini-; or (Thorpe 165) ‹ *siner-. Cf. inu (same etymon?).
 *But perhaps A´ or irregular — see Ch. 4, §8.2, (3). Yet Ib H (unlike inu).

?A/B   sioreru ‹ siwore[y]- ?‹ *si-bora-Ci-; ?‹ *siware[y]- ‹ *siba-ra-Ci-.
'droop'. x - A-A-B̲ x-x-x. Km (W) B (?). Ib B. Unger treats si- as a prefix,
Yoshida treats it as the noun si[si]ɢ.ɢ 'flesh'; why not the infinitive si[y] ‹
*so̲-Ci_A 'do' (cf. sikoru)?

B   siotareru ‹ sifotare[y]- ‹ *sipwoɢ.ɢ tara-Ci-ʙ. 'clothes drip (from tide,
rain, ...); be wet with tears; cry, weep'. B - A̲/B-A-x x-x-x.

B   siraberu ‹ sirabey- ‹ *sira-n[a]-pa-Ci-. 'investigate; inspect, check;
interrogate'. B - B-A-B x-B-B. Nk siraabin B; Sr sirabir- B. [] sirabe B -
B-A[H]/2[U]-B x-B-x. Km (W) B. Ōsaka, Kōbe 3. Ib B. Nk siraabii B; Sr sirabi B.

B   sirageru ‹ sirage[y]- ‹ *sira-n[a]-ka-Ci-. 'polish rice'. B - B-x-x x-B-B.
Narada B. Nk siraagin B; Sr siragir- B; Yn caɲirun B.

?B   sirakeru ‹ sirakey- ‹ *sira-ka-Ci-. 'get white'. x - B-A-A̲ x-x-x. Ib B.

A   siraseru ‹ sirase[y]- ‹ *sira_A-sa-Ci-. 'inform'. (In the modern language
this can be treated as the regular causative conversion.) x - A-A-A x-A-x.
Ib A. Nk siraasun A; Sr siras- A ‹ *siras- (‹ *sira-sa- without -Ci-).
[] sirase x - A-A-A x-A-x.

?A   (-)sirau ‹ sirafu ?‹ *sira-pa-_A (?‹ *sir[a]-_A apa-ʙ). 'do mutually or
respectively'. See a[e]sirau, ...

A   sireru ‹ *sira-Ci-. (1) 'get known; can know; let know, inform';
(2) 'be preoccupied, absorbed, possessed; be a dolt'. A - A-A-A x-x-x.

B   [siriutageru] ‹ siriutage[y]- ‹ siriɢ.ɢ ut[i]-age[y]- (‹ *ut[a-C]iʙ
anka-Ci-_A). 'sit, squat'. B - x-x-x x-x-x.

B   sirizokeru ‹ sirizokey- ‹ *siriɢ.ɢ -n- so̲ka-Ci-?. 'repel, expel;
reject, spurn'. B - B-A-B x-(B)-x. Nk x; Sr sizirakas- B ‹ ?.

B   sirizoku ‹ *siriɢ.ɢ -n- so̲ka-?. 'retreat; withdraw; retire'. B - B-A-B
x-(B)-x. Nk siizun B; Sr s̜izik- B ‹ *suzik- ‹ ?.

B   siromu ‹ *siroma- (‹ ?). 'squeeze' (= siboru). B - x-x-x x-x-x.

?A+B   sirosimesu 'deign to know/rule': NS (94a) HHL|LH··· (= A+B); Mg LHL|xx.
Zdb has "siro̲simyesu" but NKD treats sirosimesu as a Hn variant of Nr sirasi-
myesu (‹ *sira-s[a-C]i_A miCa-sa-ʙ) and says there are no certain cases of Nr
sirosi-··· . If the single Mg accent example is not a mistake, it may be
evidence that the infinitive sirosi B´ itself derives from a compound verb,
perhaps siri wos- ‹ *sir[a-C]i_A bosa-₍?A/B₎. No other accent data available.

A   sir-u ‹ *sira-. 'know; rule, hold sway over, possess' (different etyma?).
A - A-A-A A-A-A. NS (73b, 91b, 94a, 95a [11:65-K], 114a [14:43L-K]) A.
NS (T+) sirazu (kun) HL̲E = (111) HL|H, sirazu mo (111) HL|H(|)H, sirazu to̲-mo
LLH(|)H-H; sirani (18) HL|H, (36) LLH; siri-nu [?¨]fey-myi (71) LHL|L-H.
Km (S,W) A. Edo A. Ib A. Nk sin A; Sr sir- A; Yn cun A.

A   sirusu < *sirusa- (< ?). 'mark, write'. A - A-A-A x-x-x. Ongi A. Edo A.
Hattō, Hamada B; Matsue, Izumo A. Ib A. [] sirusi A - A-A-A A-A-A. NS (97b) A.
Km (W) A. Edo A. Hattō, Hamada, Matsue, Izumo A. Nk siruusi A; Sr sirusi A.

B   si**/z**aru ?< *si[ri]**2.3** (-n-) sara-**?A**. 'fall back; retreat'. B - B-A-x
x-x-x. Mg -s-. ?NS (Okada) A.

A   [siseru] < sise[y]- ?< *si-sa-Ci- (?< *siy-sa-Ci- < *s**o**Ci-sa-Ci-) *or*
*si[na]-sa-Ci-. 'kill'. (Also sosu, so-sutey-.) x - x-x-x x-x-x.
NS (T+ 18) sisemu t**o** H**F**HL ?= HL|H|L. But si-seru N 'dead N' is the attributive
form of the literary perfect of si-suru 'die' with the verbal noun si 'death'
(?< si[ni], ?< Ch).

B   [sitaderu] < sitade[y] = < *sita-n[a]-ta-Ci-. 'let it drip, pour it'.
B - x-A-x x-x-x. ("Also sitate[y]-.")

A   sitagaeru < sitagafey- < *sita**2.2a** n[i] kapa-Ci-**A** *or* *sita**2.2a** -n[a]-ka-
pa-Ci-. 'make follow/obey'. A - A/**B**-A-A x-x-x.

A   sitagau < sitagafu < *sita**2.2a** n[i] kapa-**A** *or* *sita**2.2a** -n[a]-ka-pa-.
A - A/**B**-A-A x-A-x. Ongi-m A. NS (91b, 104b, 124a, 131b, 134a) A. Km (S) A.
Mr (Bm) sitagofu A. Hattō, Hamada, Matsue, Izumo, NE Kyūshū A. Ib A. Nk x.

B   sitamu < *sita-ma-. 'let it drip'. B - B-A-x x-x-x.

B   sitataru < sitadaru (till 1600) < *sita-n[a]-ta-ra- (cf. sitaderu,
sitamu). 'drip'. B - B-A-B x-x-x. Nk siTaaTan **A** = siTaarun **A**. [] sitatari x -
3/4/0-A-B x-x-x. (The etymology < *sita**2.2a** n[i] tara-**B** 'hang down' is
incongruent in register.)

-          [sitateru]: *see* [sidateru].

A   sitau < sitafu < *sita**2.2a** -pa-. 'love; follow'. A - A/**B**-A-A x-x-x.
Km (W) A. Mr (Bm) sitofu A. Edo A. Matsumoto, Numazu, Narada, Hattō,
Goka-mura **B**; Hamada, Matsue, Izumo A/**B**. Ib A. Cf. sitasi**adj B**.

B   [sitomu] < sitoma- < ? (cf. toma). 'cover or shield against rain or
waves'. x - x-x-x x-x-x. Edo B.

A+B   situkeru < si-tukey- < *si[y] (< *s**o**-Ci**A**) tuka-Ci-**B**. 'impart, teach
(manners, ...), train'. x - B-A-A x-A-x. Nk siCiiKin A; Sr siçikir- A.
[] situke x - A-A-A x-A-x.

B   situraeru = siturau < (siturafey-/) siturafu ?< *si[y] (< *s**o**-Ci**A** "**do**")
tu[ku]-ra-pa-**B** ('do mend', *see* tukurou). 'prepare; repair'. B - B-A-x x-x-x.
But the etymology implies incongruent register. Cf. -turau.

?A   siu < sifu < *sipa-. 'lose the function of a sensory organ'. x - x-x-x
x-x-x. Cf. mimi-siu; [siiru]; namazii; ? siine.

B   siwabuku < sifabuku < *sipanpuka- < *sipa (*'phlegm') -n- puka-**B** ('emit').
'cough'. B - B-A-x x-x-x. [] siwabuki B - 2/0-B-x x-x-x. Northern Honshū, Saga
siyabuki; Nagasaki siwabuki. *See* seku.

A   siwameru < siwame[y]- < *siba**2.1** -ma-Ci-. 'wrinkle it'. A - **B**-x-x x-x-x.

A   siwamu < *siba**2.1** -ma-. 'get wrinkled'. A - **B**-x-x x-x-x.

?A/B   siwaru ?< *siba-ra-. 'droop, go limp; have a griping stomachache; feel
empty in the stomach, be hungry'. x - B-x-x x-x-x. Cf. siwamu; sioreru.

-          sizaru: *see* si**/z**aru.

B   sizimaru < *sinsi-ma-ra- (> tizimaru). 'shrink; lose heart'. B - x-A[U]-x
x-x-x. Ib B.

B   sizimau < sizimafu < *sinsi-ma-pa-. 'be stalled/stuck (= unable to move),
be at a standstill (an impasse)'. x - x-x-x x-x-x.

B   sizimeru < sizimey- < *sinsi-ma-Ci-. 'shrink it'. B - x-x-x x-x-x.

B   sizimu < *sinsi-ma- (> tizimu). 'shrink' (vi.). B - x-x-x x-x-x. Cf.
sizimi 'corbicula'. But Ōno says this stem is a reduplication: sim[i]-sim-
(thus < *sim[a-Ci] - sima-); cf. Takahashi, Nihon Bungaku Kenkyū 31:23 (1971).
Cf. tizimu.

?A   [sizukasu] < sidukasu < *sintu-ka-sa-. 'sink it'. x - x-x-x x-x-x.
Nk sinKasun A < *sin[tu]-ka-sa-.

?A   sizuku < siduku < *sintu-ka-. 'sink' (vi.). x - x-x-x x-x-x. Nk sinCun
(sink-) A. Cf. sizumu.

?B   sizumaru < sidumaru < *sintu-ma-ra-. 'calm down, subside'. B - B-A-A̲
x-(B)-x. Ib A. Nk siziiman A̲.

A   sizumeru < sidumey- < *sintu-ma-Ci-. 'sink it'. A - A-A-A x-x-x. Edo A.
Ib A. Nk siziimin A = sinKasun A (< *sin[tu]-ka-sa-).

?B   sizumeru < sidumey- < *sintu-ma-Ci-. 'soothe; calm (one's nerves); quell,
suppress'. B - B-A-x x-B-x. Edo B. Ib B. Nk siziimin A̲; Sr sizumir- B 'tidy
up' < *sidyume- (second syllable palatalized in assimilation to the first) <
*sidume- (cf. siẓika B < *sizu-ka < sidu-ka).

A   sizumu < sidumu < *sintu-ma-. 'sink' (vi.). A - A-A-A A-A-x. Km (W) A.
Mr (Bm) A. Edo A. NE Kyūshū B̲. Ib A. Sr siẓim- A.

B   sizumu < sidumu < *sintu-ma-. 'calm' (vi./vt. = sizumaru/sizumeru).
x - x-x-x x-x-x.

B   sobadatu < soba-t/datu < *sonpa₂.₄ tata-ʙ. 'soar high; be acrimonious'.
B - B-A-A̲ x-x-x. Cf. sobieru, soba/sowa.

?   sobaeru [dial.] < sobafe- < swobaf- < *swonpa-pa-. 'frolic; flirt, dally'.
x - x-x-x x-x-x. Cf. asobu.

B   sobameru < sobamey- < *swonpa₂.₄ -ma-Ci-. 'make (one's eyes) look askance,
(me o ~) look askance; make it face sideways; slant it; bother, disturb'.
B - B-A-x x-x-x.

B   sobamu < *sonpa₂.₄ -ma-. 'face sideways; show displeasure or resentment;
be slanted/biased'. B - B-A-x x-x-x.

?B   sober-u < *sonp[y]er- < *sonpa₂.₄ -Ci-ra-. 'sprawl'; [dial.] 'tumble, fall
down/over'. x - x-x-x x-x-x. Cf. suber-u; nomer-u, nomesu, numer-u.

?A/B   sobieru < sobiye[y]- < *sobyiye[y]- < *sonpi-da-Ci-; or < *sobaye[y]- (/a/
assimilated to the following /y/) < *sonpa₂.ₓ -da-Ci (cf. soba-datu). 'tower,
soar'. x - B-A-A x-x-x. Cf. sobik(er)u.

?A/B   [sobikeru] = sobiku < *sobyik(ey)- < *sonpi-ka-(Ci-). 'soar' (= sobieru).
A [Kz] / B´ [Kn] - x-A-x x-x-x. Cf. sobadatu.

?A/B   sobiyakasu < *sobyiyakasu < *sonpi-da-ka-sa-; or < *sobayakasu (/a/
assimilated to the following /y/) < *sonpa₂.ₓ -da-ka-sa-, cf. soba-datu).
'raise (one's shoulders)'. x - B-A-A x-x-x.

?A/B   sobo-huru < sofo-furu < *sopo∎ₗ∎ pura-ʙ. 'drizzle'. x - B-A-A x-x-x.

?A   sobokoru < *sobo-koru < *sonpo?₂.₁ ko-ra-ʙ (< *ko₁.₃ₐ -ra-). 'fell trees'.
HHxx (?= *HHHH or *HH|LH) - x-x-x x-x-x.

?A   sobotu < "so[f]odu" < sofotu = sobotiru < soboti[y]- < sofod-/sofodi[y]-
?< *sopo (-n-) tᵘ/₀Ci-*?ʙ. 'get drenched'. x - B-A-x x-x-x. NS (Okada) A.
NS (T+ 94) sofoti LLⱇ = LLH. Km (W) A.

?   [sodaru] < *sontara- < ?*son - tara-ₐ ('*hand enough'), ?< *son[apa-Ci]ʙ
taras-ₐ. 'be fully arrayed/supplied'. x - x-x-x x-x-x. Cf. sodataku, sonaeru,
sonau, Korean 'swon 'hand'. But Unger says this is so 'ten' + tara- 'enough';
cf. ti-daru, momo-daru. There is also todaru; Ōno and Yoshida treat the to- as
a variant of ti 'thousand' (= ti-daru).

B   sodateru < sodate[y]- ?< *sudate[y]- ('make leave nest') < *su₁.₃ᵦ -n-
tata-Ci-ʙ. 'rear, raise'. x - B-A-B B-B-B. Edo B. Ib B. Nk sudaatin B; Sr
sudatir- B.

B   sodatu ?< sudatu ('leave nest') < *su₁.₃ᵦ -n- tata-ʙ. 'grow up, be
reared/raised'. x - B-A-B (x)-B-(B). Ib B. Nk sudaaCun (sudaak-) B; Sr sudat-
B. 〚 sodati x - B-2-B x-B-x. Nk sudaaCi B; Sr sudati B.

A   soeru < sofey- < *s[w]opa-Ci-. 'attach/add it'. (A) - A-A-A A-A-x.
NS (120a) A. Km (W) A/B. Edo A. Ib A. Sd siiyum A; Nk siirun A; Sr ŝiir- A.
[] soe x - A-A-x x-x-x.

?B   sogeru < sogey- < *sonka-Ci- (?< *so_-n[a]-ka-Ci-, cf. soru).
'get chopped/split; get reduced; get hollow(-cheeked)'. B - B-A-x x-B-x.
Nk x; Sr sugir- B < *soge-.

?B   sogu < *sonka- (?< *so_-n[a]-ka-, cf. soru). 'chop/split off; diminish'.
B - B-B-A x-(B)-x. Ib B. Nk s¹/ᵤzun (s¹/ᵤg-) B. (Sr hwizun B: see hegu.)
[] sogi x - 1/2(= sogi-i¹ta)-x-x x-x-x. "Anciently -k-": if so, why the -g- in
Sr sugir- (cf. sogeru)? Cf. saku.

?   [sokeru] < so_key- < *so_ka-Ci-. 'make distant; stay away from'. x - x-x-x
x-x-x. Cf. sirizokeru, sakeru.

B   sokonau < sokonafu < *soko-na-pa- (< ?). 'harm, spoil'. B - B-A-A x-B-x.
NS (Okada) B). Mr (Bm) B. Izumo A. Nk x.

?   so_ku < *so_ka- (?< *so_₁.₂ "back" -ka-). 'get distant, recede'. x - x-x-x
x-x-x. Cf. sirizoku, (i)saku. Another etymology: < *so_ku- on the basis of the
transitive sokusu < *soku-sa- found in myi[yi] sokus[y]i 'looks distantly at'
(M 3362) but there is doubt about the identity of this verb (Zdb 703c).

A   so_maru < *so_ma-ra-. 'get dyed/tinted/imbued (with)'. (A) - A-A-A x-x-x.
Ib A. Nk sumaarun A.

A   someru < so_mey- < *so_ma-Ci-. 'dye, color, imbue; set in, begin'. A - A-A-A
x-A-A. Km (W) A. Mr (Bm) A. Edo A. Ib A. Nk sumiirun A; Sr sumir- A.
Cf. simiru. [] some x - A-A-A x-A-x. Nk sumii A, Sr sumi A < *some.

A   somu < *so_ma-. 'get dyed' (= somaru). A - x-x-x x-A-x. Nk sumin, Sr sum-
A < *som-. Cf. simu.

B   somukeru < so_mukey- < *so₁.₂ muka-Ci-ₐ. 'avert, turn (face/eyes) away'.
B/B´ - B-A-B x-x-x. Register incongruent?

B   somuku < *so₁.₂ muka-ₐ. 'turn one's back (on); go against, violate;
rebel' (vi.). B/B´ - B-A-B x-B-x. Km (S,W) B. Mr (Bm) B. Edo B. Sr sumucun
(sumuk-) B < *somuk- (why not > *suncun?). Register incongruent with etymology?

B   sonaeru < so_nafey- < *so_napa-Ci- (?< *son₂.ₓ apa-Ci-ʙ or *sona₂.ₓ
-pa-Ci-). 'furnish with, provide'. B - B-A-B x-(x)-x. Mr (Bm) sonofu B. Ib B.
Sr: see sonawaru. [] sonae x - 2/3-A[U]/2[H]-B x-x-x.

?A   sonaru ?< sona[fa]ruʙ (< ···). ? 'be well endowed/qualified (for)'.
?A - x-x-x x-x-x. Only attestation Mg?

B   sonau < swonafu (but /swo/ is anomalous, cf. so_nafey-) ?< *so_nafu
< *so_napa- (?< *son₂.ₓ apa-ʙ or *sona₂.ₓ -pa- with '*hand', cf. sorou, sodaru,
Korean 'swon). (?)'be fully arrayed or supplied'. B - x-x-x x-x-x.

B   sonawaru < sonafaru < *so_napa-ra- (?< *son₂.ₓ apaʙ-ra-, ?< *sona₂.ₓ
-pa-ra-). 'be furnished/provided/endowed with, be well qualified (for)'.
B - B-A-B x-A-x. Nk sunaawan A 'be arrayed'; Sr sunawar- A.
[] sonawari x - x-x-x x-B-x. Nk sunaawai A; Sr sunawai B. (Cf. sonae.)

B   [sonawareru] < sonafare[y]- < *so_napa-ra-Ci- (< ...) = sonawaru.
See NKD 12:418a.

?A/B   so_nemu (< ?). 'envy'. A - B-A-B x-x-x. NS (124b) A. Edo A/B.
[] sonemi x - B-A-B x-x-x. Km (S) A. Yoshida derives this from so₁.₂ "back"
ne[ta]m-ʙ; see netamu.

B   sonuku ?< *so₁.₂ nuka-ₐ ('bare the back' — incongruent in register but
cf. somuku). 'quarrel' (= semegu). B - x-x-x x-x-x. Only attestation Mg?

?B   sorasu < *sora-sa-. 'bend, warp; avert, divert'. x - B-A[U]/B[H]-A x-x-x.
Ib B.

?B   soreru < *sora-Ci-. 'swerve, turn aside, diverge, go astray'. (B) - B-B-A
x-x-x. Ib B.

?B   soroeru < sorofey- < *soro(-)pa-Ci-. 'arrange; make them uniform/even;
complete, get all of'. x - B-A-B x-x-x. Edo B. (Nk suraasun B, Sr suraas- B <
*sorowas-.) Cf. sonaeru.

?B   sorou < sorofu < *soro(-)pa-. 'be complete/assembled; be uniform/regular'.
x - B-A-B x-B-x. Ib B. Nk suriirun B; Sr surir- B. Hokekyō-tanji sorobu.
Cf. kozoru.] soroi x - 2/3-1:3-B x-B-x. Nk sur{ᵘ}/ᵢi B; Sr surii B.

?B   soru < *sora- (?< *so [wo]r- < *so₁.₂ bora-ʙ 'back bend'). 'be curved,
bent; warp, bend (vi.)'. x - B-B-A x-x-x. Ib B.] sori x - B-2-A x-x-x.

B   soru < *sora-. 'shave'. B - B-B-B x-B-B. Edo B. Ib B. Cf. suru 'rub'.

?B   soru < sworu < *swora-. 'rise/loom high'. x - x-x-x x-x-x. Cf. fo no
suswori (NS T+ kun) L L LHH 'rising flames'; sosoru; sobadatu; sora.

?A/B   sosir-u (< ?). 'slander, blame'. A - B-A-A x-B-x. Hata (Doi 1952:31),
Hamada, Matsue, Izumo A; Hattō, Goka-mura B. Kōchi A (Doi 1952:31). Nk x.
] sosiri x - B-A-A x-B-x. Nk x.

A   sosogu < (till 1600s) sosoku (= sosoku, cf. mina-sosoku) < *soso?ₘᵢₘ
-ka-. 'pour' (vi./vt.). A - A/B-A-A x-x-x. Ongi A. NS (Okada) A. NS (T+ 95)
myina sosoku HL LLH. Km (S) A. Mr (Bm) B. Hattō B; Hamada, Matsue, Izumo,
Goka-mura A.] sosogi x - A-A-A x-x-x. Cf. misogi.

A   sosogu < susugu < susuku (Nr) < ?*susu?ₘᵢₘ -ka-. 'rinse, wash'.
A - A/B-A-A x-x-x. Ib sosoku B.

?   sosogu < *swoswoku < *swoswo?ₘᵢₘ -ka-. 'ruffle'. x - x-x-x x-x-x.
] sosogi x - A-A-A x-x-x. Cf. misogi. Cf. sosokkasiₐdⱼ ?.

?   sosomeku < *soso-myeku < *sosoₘᵢₘ miCa-ka-ᵦₙₐ ᵥ. 'fidget; (= sosoyaku =
sasayaku) whisper'. x - B-x-x x-x-x. ("Also zozo-.")

?   sosoru (< ?). 'arouse, excite, stimulate'. x - A/B-A-A x-x-x.
] sosori x - A/B-A-A x-x-x.

?   sosoru < sosoru < *sosora- (< ?); ?< *swo[ra-Ci] swora-. 'soar, loom'
(= sosori-tatu). x - (A/B-A-A) x-x-x. NKD treats this as the same etymon found
in the entry above ('arouse').

B   sosoyaku < *sosoₘᵢₘ -da-ka-. 'whisper'. B - x-A-x x-x-x. (Ōno: "modern
also sosoyagu".) Cf. sosomeku, sasayaku, soyomeku.

B   sosu < *sosa- ?< *so-sa-. 'kill' (= sise[y]-). B - x-x-x x-x-x. Cf. sinu.

A   sou < sofu < *s[w]opa- (cf. kazoeru, soi). 'follow'. A - A-A[U]/ B[H]-A
A-A-A. Km (S) A. Edo A. Narada A(/B"Lit."). Kōchi A (Doi 1932-3:30, which
wrongly has Tk B); Ib A. Nk x; Sr suuyun A (neg. suuran) < *suura- has been
restructured from "literary" suyun A (neg. suwan) < *sofa-. Cf soeru, sowaru.
] soi A - A-A[U]-x x-x-x. NS (T+ 83) swofyi H{ᵉ} = HH; (cf. Nakata).

A   sowaru < sofaru < *s[w]opa-ra-. 'add/append itself' (vi.). x - A-A-x
x-x-x. Km (W) A. Perhaps also (*)swofor- with assimilated vowel; see Zdb.

?A/B   soyogu < *sodoₘᵢₘ -n[a]-ka-. 'rustle, stir, sway'. x - B-A-A x-A-x.
Km (W) B. Nk suzun A; Sr sug- A.] soyogi x - B-A-A x-x-x.

B   soyomeku < *soyo-myeku < *sodoₘᵢₘ miCa-ka-ᵦₙₐ ᵥ. 'rustle, stir, sway'.
x - B-x-x x-x-x.

?A   *subaru < *sunpa-ra-. 'many become one' (= sumaru). x - x-x-x x-x-x. Cf.
suberu; myi-subaru = myi-sumaru (NS T+ 2) H-HHH 'necklace'; subaru 'Pleiades'.

?B   subaru < *sunpa-ra-. 'get narrow; shrink'. x - x-x-x x-x-x. Cf. subomu,
semaru.

B   suberakasu < *sunpe-ra-ka-sa- (< ?). 'let it slip'. x - B-A-B x-B-x.
Sr şindakas- B < *suburakas- < *suberakas- (the second vowel assimilated to
the first). Cf. subesu.

B   suberasu < *sunpe-ra-sa- (< ?). 'let it slip'. x - B-A-B x-x-x.
Nk sinrasun B < *suburas- < *suberas-.

?A   suberu ‹ subey- ‹ *sunpa-Ci-. 'bring many into one, amass; control'.
A - B-A[H]/B[U]-A x-x-x. NS (134a, Okada) B. Edo A. Hattō, Hamada, Matsue,
Izumo B. Cf. *subaru, *sumaru, *sumeru.

?B   suberu ‹ subey- ‹ *sunpa-Ci-. 'make it narrow'. x - x-x-x x-x-x.
Cf. subaru, subomaru, subomeru, subomu, suboru; sibomu; sebaru = semaru,
semeru, sebamaru, sebameru.

B   suber-u ‹ *sunpe-ra- (‹ ?). 'slip, slide'; 'lower a bamboo blind' (cf.
su[dare]). x - B-A-B x-B-x. Edo B. Ib B. Nk sinrin B, Sr şindir- ‹ *subur-
‹ *suber- *(the second vowel assimilated to the first)*. Dialect zumer-u. Cf.
subesu, subekko*adj B*, sube-sube; numer-u, nomer-u.

B   subesu ‹ *sunpe-sa- (‹ ?). 'let it slip (off/down)'. x - x-x-x x-x-x.
Cf. suberakasu, suberasu; nomesu.

A   subomaru ‹ *sunpo*adj B* -ma-ra- ?‹ *sunpa-ma-ra- *(with partial vowel
assimilation, cf. subaru)*. 'get narrow, contract'. x - A/B[new]-A-A x-x-x.
Cf. suberu (and the words listed there).

A   subomeru ‹ subomey- ‹ *sunpo*adj B* -ma-Ci- ?‹ *sunpa-ma-Ci- *(with partial
vowel assimilation)*. 'make it narrow, close it up'. x - A/B[new]-A-B x-x-x.
Ib A. (Is Kg a misprint? Cf. subomaru.) Cf. suberu (and the words listed there).

A   subomu ‹ *sunpo*adj B* -ma- ?‹ *sunpa-ma- *(with partial vowel assimilation,
cf. subaru)*. 'get narrow, contract' (= subomaru). x - A/B[new]-A-A x-x-x.
◻ subomi x - A-x-x x-x-x. Cf. kuti-subo; suberu (and the words listed there).

?A   suboru ‹ *sunpo*adj B* -ra- ?‹ *sunpa-ra-. 'get narrow, shrink' (= subaru);
[dial.] 'decline, droop' (= sioreru). x - x-x-x x-x-x.

B   sudaku ‹ *su*1.3b* n[i] taka-*A*. 'swarm (noisily)'. x - B-A-B x-x-x.

B   [sudamu] ‹ *sunta-ma-. 'cool oneself'. x - x-x-x x-B-x. Nk sidaamin B;
Sr şidam- B; Shitoke sudamyui; Kabira sïdamun. Cf. [suda(si)-]*adj B*.

B   sudatu ‹ *su*1.3b* -n- tata-*B*. 'leave the nest, become independent'.
x - B-A-B x-x-x. Ib B. ◻ sudati x - A/B-A-B x-x-x. Cf. sodatu.

A   sueru ‹ suwe[y]- ‹ *suba-Ci- ‹ *zuba-Ci-. 'set it up; seat, place'.
Ib A. (A) - A-A-A x-x-x. Edo A. *See* suwaru, uwaru, ueru.

B   sueru ‹ suye[y]- ‹ *su*1.3a* -da-Ci-. 'turn sour, spoil'. x - B-B-B x-B-x.
For Kyōto, U has literary B but modern A; misprint? Cf. suyuru. Nk siirun B,
Sr şiir- B ‹ *suye- or *suyur-.

?A   sugareru ‹ sugare[y]-/sugar- ?‹ *sunka-ra-(Ci-); ?‹ su[we]*2.1* - n-
kare[y]*A*. 'wither, fade, shrivel'. x - A/B-A-x x-x-x.

A   [sugareru] ‹ *sugare[y]- ‹ *sunka-ra-Ci-. 'air oneself, cool oneself with
air'. x - x-x-x x-A-x. Nk sugaarin A, Sr sugarir- A restructured ‹ *sugare-.
Cf. [sugasu], sugasugasi-*adj ?A*.

?A   sugaru ‹ *sunka-ra-. 'cling (to); depend (on)'. A - A/B[new]-A-B x-A-x. Km
(W) A. Hattō, Hamada, Matsue, Izumo A. Nk sigaarun A; Sr sigar- A. Cf. sugeru.

A   [sugasu] ‹ *sunka-sa-. 'ventilate, cool with air'. x - x-x-x x-A-x.
Nk sugaasun A; Sr sugas- A. Cf. [sugareru], sugasugasi*adj ?A*.

?A   sugau ‹ sugafu ?‹ *sunka(-)pa-. 'line up; match, equal; go crisscross,
just miss meeting, be discrepant'. x - x-x-x x-x-x. Cf. suku (= tugu).

A   sugeru ‹ sugey- ‹ *sunka-Ci-. 'tie (a thong), attach (a cord), fasten into
a hole'. A - A-A-A x-A-x. Km (W) A. Cf. sugaru.

B   sugiru ‹ sugiy- ‹ *sunku-Ci-. 'pass by; exceed; elapse'. B - B-B-B B-B-x.
NS (72b [11:200-M], 95b, 96a [11:73-K], 121b [14:195-K]) B. NS (T+) sugiy
(85, 94) LH, (54) ⌐L ?= LL; sugiy te (25, 31) LH⌐ ?= LH(|)H. Km (W) B. Edo B.
Ib B. Nk siziirun B, Sr sizir- B ‹ *sugir-. ◻ sugi x - B-x-x x-x-x.

?A/B   sugosu < sugwosu = sugusu < *sunku-sa-. 'pass/spend (time); get through; overdo'. B - B-A-A x-A-x. Km (W) B. Edo B. Ib B. Nk x; Sr şigus- A. Must be B, despite Kg and Sr.

?A/B   sugureru < sugure[y]- < *sunku(-)ra-Ci- (cf. sugiru). 'excel'. (A) - B-A-A x-A-x. NS (126a) A. Km (S) A. Edo A. Narada, Hattō, Hamada B; Matsue, Izumo A. Ib B. Kg register incongruent with suguru. Nk suguurin A and Sr sugurir- A either retained the first syllable (not > *şi) or restored it under the influence of the second vowel.

?A/B   suguru < *sunku(-)ra- (cf. sugiru). 'select'. A - B-A-B x-x-x. Edo A/B. Kg register incongruent with sugureru.

B   suguru < *sunku-ra-. 'pass by; exceed' (= sugiru). x - B-B-x x-x-x.

A   sukasu < *suka-sa-. 'space; make transparent'. A - A-A-A x-x-x. Km x. Mr (Bm) A.

?B   sukasu < sukas-/sukase[y]- < *suka-sa-(Ci-). 'coax, cajole, persuade; deceive (a woman)'. x - A-A-A x-B-x. Nk sikaasun B; Sr şikas- B < *sukas-.

A   sukeru < sukey- < *suka-Ci-. 'help' (= tasukeru). x - A-A-A x-?A-x. NS (T+ 12) sukey ni ko-ne ⌐LHLH = HL|H | L-H. Ib A. Nk sikiirun A, Sr şikir- A < *suke- 'set in place; start boiling/cooking preparations'. Cf. sukuu. ⌂ suke 'support pillar'. HHx - x-2-x x-x-x.

A   suku < *suka-. 'plow; slice (thin); comb'. A - A-A-A x-A-x. Km (W 'plow') A. Nk ˢ/ʰiCun A, Sr şik- A 'enter/lift from below; comb'. ⌂ suki 'a plow'. A - A-A-A A-x-x. Hiroshima A. Ōsaka, Ise 1.

A   suku < *suka-. 'become empty; be transparent; have a gap'. A - A-A-A x-x-x. ⌂ suki 'gap'. x - A-A-A x-x-x.

A   suku < *suka-. 'make paper; make a net'. x - A-A-A x-A-x. Nk x; Sr şik- A.

?A   suku ?< *suku- < ?*suka-. 'scoop, dip, ladle' (= sukuu). x - x-x-x x-x-x.

B   suku < *suka-. 'like'. x - B-B-B B-B-x. Edo B. Nk ˢ/ʰiCun B; Sr şik- B. ⌂ suki x - B-1-B x-B-x. Nk ˢ/ʰiCii B; Sr şici B.

B   suku < *suka-. 'eat, drink, ingest' (?< 'like' = relish'). B [Hoke-kyō tanji] - x-x-x x-x-x.

?A   suku < *suka-. 'follow immediately' (= tugu). x - x-x-x x-x-x. Cf. tasuki.

A   sukumeru < sukumey- < *sukuma-Ci-. 'crouch (one's body); make (one's body) small, shrink; duck (one's head)'. A - A/B-A-x x-x-x. Nk siKu(u)min A.

A   sukumu < *sukuma- (< ?). 'crouch'. A - A/B-A-A x-A-x. Ib A. Nk siKuumin A, Sr sukum- A (su < *şi assimilated to next vowel) < *sukum-.

A   sukuu < sukufu < *suku-pa- (? *suka-pa- (the second vowel assimilated to the first). 'rescue; scoop' — unclear whether two etyma or one. A - A-A-A x-A-x. NS (112b) A. Km (S) A. Mr (Bm) A. Edo A. Ib A. Nk s¹/ᵤKuurun A, Sr sukur- A (su < *şi) < *sukur-. ⌂ sukui x - A-A-A x-A-x.

1.3+B   sukuu < su kufu < *su₁.₃ᵦ kupa-ᵦ. 'roost; make nest'. R|LH - B-A-B x-x-x.

?A   *sumaru = subaru 'many become one'. Cf. myi-subaru = myi-sumaru 'necklace'.

B   sumasu < *suma-sa-. 'conclude, finish; settle, pay; make do (with); cleanse, wash, launder; make it clear, clarify; strain (one's ears); act composed'. B - B-A-B x-B-x. Ib B. Nk simaasun B; Sr şimas- B.

B   sumau < sumafu < *suma-pa-. 'reside'. B - B-A-B x-x-x. Km (W) B. Edo B. ⌂ sumai x -1/2-2-B x-B-x. Edo HHL. Nk x.

?A   sumau < sumafu < *sumapa- (< ?). 'wrestle'. x - B[NKD]-x-x x-x-x. But as noun: A - A-A-A x-A-x. NS (128a sumafi) HLH (?= *HHL or *HHH = A). Nk simaa B, Sr şima A < *suma. ⌂ sumai x - 2-2-x x-x-x. NS (128a [14:334-K]) "HLH" — ?mistake for HHH (Okada "also HHH"). K: Hn HHH.

?A   *sumeru = suberu 'make many into one'.

B   sumu < *suma- (?= *su*1.3b* -ma-, cf. Yoshida 1979:85). 'live, reside; end;
become clear' (< 'settle'). B - B-B-B x-B-B. Km (W) A/B (?). Edo B. Ib B. Nk
simin B; Sr şim- B. 〗 sumi 'end'. x - B-2-B x-x-x.

B   sunadoru < *suna [see below] (-n-) t(w)ora-*B*. 'catch fish or collect
shellfish'. (B) - B-A-x x-x-x. 〗 sunadori B - A̲/B-A-x x-x-x. On suna: ?=
suna*?2.1* 'sand'; ?= *suna = tuna*2.3* 'line' (Unger); ?< *su*?1.2<1.3b* 'sandbank'
na*1.3a* 'fish' (Yoshida). Ck Mg has also sunatoru LLLH but that should be LLHL
unless it is to be taken as 2.3 noun + B verb; perhaps this supports Yoshida's
etymology (or Unger's).

B   suneru < sune[y]- (< ?). x - B-B-B x-x-x. 'pout'.

B   sureru < sure[y]- < *sura-Ci-. 'rub against each other; chafe'.
(B) - B-B-B x-?B-x. Ib B. Sr şirir- B < *sure- 'get past the appointed time'.

A   suru (si-, se-, *so-) < *so̲- (/ *se-). 'do'. A - A-A-A A-A-x. NS (passim,
e.g. 114a [14:43L-K]) A. NS (T+ 11) sezu HH, (29) se-na 𝔽H ?= H-H, (111) se-si
fyito̲ no̲ HH 𝔽L(|)L, (96) si-te L̲H̲; (18) su mo L(|)𝔽 ?= L|H. Ongi (Iroha) A.
Km (S,W) A. Ib A. Nk A sun; Sr syun A; Yn kirun A, irun B (< ?).

Paradigmatic forms *(cf. kuru 'come')*:
   infinitive   *so̲-Ci > si[y] or *s[o̲-C]i > si.
   imperative   *so̲ i/yo̲ > se yo̲, se (i); *s[o̲-C]i ro̲ > si ro̲; na V-[C]i so̲.
   future   *so̲-mu > se-mu. Later si-yoo < syoo < sye[m]u < semu (Ch. 3).
   predicative *so̲-u > su.
   attributive *so̲-uru > suru.

B   suru < *sura-. 'rub; grind; print; pick one's pocket'. B - B-B-B x-B-x.
Edo B. Ib B. Nk sin B; Sr şir- B. 〗 suri: 'printing; rubbing' x - B-2-B x-x-x;
'pickpocket' x - 1-2-B x-x-x.

?A   susameru < susame[y]- < ?*susa-ma-Ci-. 'take to, like; keep one's distance
from'. (A) - x-x-x x-x-x. Km (W) B̲.

A   susamu, susabu (from Hn) < (Nr) susabiy- < *susa*?bnd n* -np*ª*/o̲Ci-
(?< -n[a]-pa-Ci-). 'grow wild/undisciplined'. A - A-A-A x-x-x. Matsue B̲. Ib A.
〗 susami, susabi 'pastime, diversion'. A - A-A-x x-x-x. The adjective susamazi-
is B.

-    su*ª*/z̲aru = si*ª*/z̲aru.

?B   susu ?< *susu- (cf. susu*2.5*). 'get sooty' (= susukeru). x - x-x-x x-x-x.

A   susugu < (Nr) susuku < ?*susu*ªiª* -ka-. 'wash, rinse'. A - A-A-A x-A-x. Edo
A. Ib A. Nk x; Sr [Lit.] şişizun (şişig-) A < *susug-.

A   susumeru < susumey- < *susuma-Ci- (< ?). 'advance it, put forward,
promote, hasten; encourage, exhort; offer'. (A) - A-A-A x-A-x. NS (113b) A.
Km (S) A. Edo A. Ib A. Nk x. 〗 susume x - A-A-A x-x-x.

A   susumu < *susuma- (< ?; perhaps *susu-ma-, cf. suu-suu 'smoothly').
'advance, go forward, ... '. A - A-A-A x-A-x. NS (120b) A. Mr (Bm) A. Edo A.
Ib A. 〗 susumi x - A-A-A x-x-x.

(A) susurou < susurofu < *susurafu < *susu(-)ra-pa-. 'keep slurping'.
x - x-x-x x-x-x.

A   susuru ?< *susu -ra-; ?< *su[fi -]su[fi] -ra- (cf. suu). 'slurp, sip
(noisily)'. A - A-A-A A-A-x. Hattō B̲. Ib A. Nk x; Sr şişir- A. Cf. susubana.

?A   sutarasu < *suta-ra-sa-. 'sully, denigrate'. x - x-x-x x-x-x.
Nk siTaarasun B̲.

?A   sutareru < sutare[y]- < *suta-ra-Ci- ?< *zuta-ra-Ci-. 'get disused,
obsolete'. (A) - A-A-B̲ x-B̲-x. Hattō, Hamada A; Matsue, Izumo B̲. Ib A.
Nk siTaarin B̲, Sr şitarir- B̲ < *sutare-.

?A   sutaru < *suta-ra- ?< *zuta-ra-. 'get disused, obsolete'. A - A-A-B̲ x-x-x.
〗 sutari x - A-A-B̲ x-x-x.

A   suteru < sute[y]- < *suta-Ci- ?< *zuta-Ci- (cf. [uteru], useru, sutaru).
'discard, abandon, throw away'. A - A-A[U]/B[H]-A A-A-x. Km (S,W) A. Mr (Bm) A.
Edo A. Hattō, Hamada, Matsue, Izumo A. Hyōgo, Toyama, Suzu, Kōchi, Ib A;
K 1942:169 has Kt A. Some of the Kg compounds are B. Nk (also 'lose, drop,
spill; divorce') siTiirun A, Sr şitir- A < *suter-.

A   suu < sufu < *supa-. 'suck; inhale; absorb'. A - A-A-A (x)-A-x. Ongi A.
Sapporo B. (Sd sis[i]yum A, cf. susuru.) Ib A. Nk suurun A, Sr suur- A (< *suw-
< *suf-) = Nk sipuurun A, Sr şipuyur- A < *sup-.

A   suwaru < *suba-ra- < *zuba-ra-. 'sit'. x - A-A-A x-x-x. Ib A.
◯ suwari x - A-A-A x-x-x. Cf. sueru; uwaru; ueru.

B   suyuru, [dial.] suyaru < *sudara- (the second vowel assimilated to the
first) < *su₁.₃ₐ -da-ra-. 'get sour'(= sueru). B - x-x-x x-B-x.
Mg fi[y]ī suyureru 'chilled and soured' (attributive perfect).
NS (99a [11:98-K]) B. Nk siirun B, Sr şiir- B < *suye- or *suyur-.

B   suzumu < *sunsu_adj-si B_ -ma-. 'cool oneself'. x - B-A-B x-x-x.
◯ suzumi x - B-A[H]/2[U]-B x-x-x. Cf. sudamu.

B   [tabaeru] < tabaye[y]- < *tanpa₂.₄ -da-Ci-. 'bundle, bunch, sheave'.
x - x-x-x x-B-x. Nk tabaarun B, Sr tabar- B < tabar-. Cf. NKD 13:153a.
A   tabakaru ?< *tan[a]₂.₁ paka(-)ra-_B_. 'plan, consider; dupe, manipulate,
cheat'. A - B-A-A x-x-x. Cf. tabakeru = tobokeru.
?A/B   tabakeru < tabake[y]- (< ?). 'feign ignorance' (= tobokeru). x - x-x-x
x-x-x.
B   tabaneru < tabane[y]- < *tanpa₂.₄ -na-Ci-. 'bundle'. B - B-A-A x-(B)-x.
Ib B. ◯ tabane x - A/B-A-x x-(B)-x. Wakamatsu A (verb x). Nk tabaanin B 'bundle
(into a sheaf)'. Cf. tabaeru.
?B   tabaru < *tanpa-ra- ?< *tam[a]-pa-ra. 'humbly receive', [later] 'give
(to me/us)'. x - x-x-x x-(B)-x. Nk taboori B (LLLH) 'please', Sr taboor- B <
*tabawar- < *tanpa-pa-ra- ?< *tam[a]-pa-pa-ra-. Cf. tamawaru.
A   tabau < tabafu < *tanpa(-)pa- (?< *tama-pa-). 'protect (= kabau B); save,
preserve, keep (= tamotu A); cover'. A - x-x-x (B)-(A)-x. Sd thaboo(r)yum B
'save'. Nk tabuurun A; Sr tabur- A < *tabor-. Cf. tameru A.
?B   taberu < *tam[a]fe[y]- < *tama-pa-Ci-. 'eat; give'. x - B-B-A x-A-x.
NS (T+ kun) ka tabu H LL 'give incense'. Ib B. Nk x; Sr tabir- [Lit.] 'give'.
?A/B   tabidatu < tabyi-datu < *tanpi₂.₂ᵦ -n- tata-_B_. 'set off on a journey'.
x - B-A-A x-x-x. ◯ tabidati x - A/B-A-A x-B-x. Nk tabidaCii B, Sr tabidaci B
(but Nk tabii A, Sr tabi A).
?B   tabu < *tam[a]-pa-. 'deign to give'. x - x-x-x x-x-x. Edo B. See tamau,
tamawaru, no-tabu.
A   taburakasu, taburokasu (Mg with the third vowel partially assimilated to
the second) < *tanpura-ka-sa-. 'madden; confuse, deceive'. A - B-A-A x-x-x.
Km x. Mr (Bm) A.
A   tabureru < tabure[y]- < *tanpura-Ci- (< ?). 'go mad, get confused, lose
one's senses'. A - x-x-x x-x-x. Ongi A. Km x.
-          [tadaneru]: tadanureba LLLHL (Hoke-kyō tanji, Mochizuki 343a) is probably
a scribal error for tadunureba 'upon inquiry', but it could be a variant with
the second vowel assimilated to the first.
A   tadareru < tadare[y]- < *tantara-Ci- (< ?). 'get inflamed'. A - A(/B[H])-
A-A x-A-x. Ongi-m A. Narada A. Ib A. Nk x; Sr tadarir- A. ◯ tadare x - A-A-A
x-A-x. Nk x; Sr tadari A. Cf. tadare-me.

B   tadasu ?< *tanta*adj-s1 B* -sa-, ?< *tanta*₂₂.₄* -sa-. 'correct; question,
probe; verify'. B - B-A-B x-B-x. Mr (Bm) B. Ib B. Nk tadaasun B; Sr tadas- B.
?A/B   tadayou < tadaywofu (Igarashi = Zdb tadayofu) < *tanta*₂₂.₄* - dwopa-*bad v*
'drift'. A - B-A-B x-x-x.
?A/B   tadayowasu < tadayofasu < *tadaywofasu < *tanta*₂₂.₄* - dwopa-sa-*bad v*.
'set/carry adrift'. A - B-A-B x-x-x.
?A   taderu < tade[y]- ?< *tanta-Ci-. 'poultice, foment'. A(/B[Lit.])-A-x
x-A-x. Nk x; Sr tadir- A. Cf. tadareru A.
?A/B   tadoru < tadworu < *tantwora- ?< *ta*₁.₃ₐ* n[i] twora-*B* 'take by hand' (if
so, then B); ?< *tantwo*ₐₗₐ* -ra- (cf. tado-tado = tadu-tadu(si-)). 'follow,
trace; grope one's way'. x - B-A-A x-x-x. Nk tadurun B. Km (W) B.
B   taeru < tafe[y]- < *tapa-Ci-. 'endure, withstand; block, intercept'.
B - B-B-B x-x-x. Km (S) B. Edo B. Ib B.
B   taeru < taye[y]- < *tada-Ci-. '(come to an) end'. B - B-B-B x-B-x.
NS (71a [11:173-M], 126a) B. Km (S,W) B. Edo B. Ib B. Nk teerun B; Sr teer- B.
Cf. tayasu; tuieru.
B   tagaeru < tagafey- < *ta*₁.₃ₐ* -n- kapa-Ci-*A*. 'break (a promise), violate'.
(B) - B-A-A x-x-x. Edo B. Nk tage(eru)n B. ◊ tagae x - 2/3-x-x x-x-x. Edo HHL.
-        tagaesu: *see* tagayasu.
?B   taganeru < takaneru < takane[y]- < *taka-na-Ci-. 'bundle together'.
x - B-A-x x-x-x. Cf. takaru; tabaneru.
B   tagau < tagafu < *ta*₁.₃ₐ* -n- kapa-*A* ('hand cross'). 'differ; deviate
(from), violate'. B - B-A-x x-B-x. Mr (Bm) B. Edo B. Nk tagaarun B, Sr tagayun
B (neg. tagaan) < *tagaw-. ◊ tagai (> 'mutual, reciprocal') LHH - A-B-B x-B-A.
Km (S,W) LHH. Nk tagee-ni B; Sr tagee(-ni) B. Yn tagai-ni is probably borrowed:
it has an oral [g] where we expect the nasal [ŋ].
?B   tagayasu < tagayesu < taga[f]yesu < *tagafyisu < *ta*₁.₃ₐ* -n- kapi-sa-*B*.
'till, cultivate'. x - B-A-A x-B-x. Narada A. Ib A, B. Nk x; Sr tagees- B =
kees- B < *kafes-.
B   [tageru] < tagey- < *tanka-Ci- (< ?; cf. taberu, tamau). '(let one) eat
or drink'. x - x-A-x x-x-x. NS (Okada) B. NS (T+ 107) tagey te LH(|)F = LH|H;
(kun) tagey LH.
?A   tagir-u < *ta*ᵏ*/*ɡ*yiru < *ta(n)ki-ra-. 'seethe, boil, foam'. x - B-A-A
x-A-x. Nk tazirun A = tanzun (tag-) B; Sr tazir- A. ◊ tagiri x - B-x-x x-x-x.
Cf. tagitu; taki*₂.₁*.
A   tagitu < ta*ᵏ*/*ɡ*yitu < *ta(n)ki-ta-. 'flow rapidly; seethe'. x - x-x-x
x-x-x. Km (W) A. Cf. tagir-u; taki *₂.₁*.
-        tagu: *see* tageru.
B   tagueru < tagufey- < *ta*₁.₃ₐ* -n- kupa-Ci-*B*. 'line up, bring together;
let/make accompany; imitate; compare'. x - B-x-x x-x-x. NS (T+ 28) tagufey LHL.
?B   taguru = (Mg) takuru < *ta*₁.₃ₐ* (-n-) kura-*B*. 'pull/draw/reel in'.
B - B-A-A x-B-x. Nk taguurun B; Sr tagur- B. Hattō B; Hamada, Matsue, Izumo,
Goka-mura A. Ib A.
B   taguru ?< *tam[i] kuru < *tam[a-C]i*B* kura-*B*. 'vomit, spit up, cough up'.
x - x-x-x x-x-x.
B   taguu < tagufu < *ta*₁.₃ₐ* -n- kupa-*B*. 'line up, come together, accompany;
be suitable'. B - B-A-x x-x-x. NS (71c [11:181-M]) B. NS (T+ 113) tagufyi LLL,
(50) tagufyi te zo LHH(|)F(|)H; (113) tagufyeru LLHH. Km (W) B. Edo B.
◊ tagui B - 1/2/0-A-B x-x-x. Km (S) B. K: Mr HHL.
A   tairageru < tafyiragey- < *ta(-)pira*₃.₅ₐ (adj-B)* -n[a]-ka-Ci-. 'flatten,
smooth; subdue; totally consume'. A - B-A-A x-x-x. The register is incongruent
with the etymology.

A   tairagu < tafyiragu < *ta(-)piras.₅ₐ ₍ₐdⱼ₋ₐ₎ -n[a]-ka-. 'get flat; become
peaceful'. A - B-A-x x-x-x. The register is incongruent with the etymology.

B   [takabiru]/takabu < takabiy-/takab- < *takaₐdⱼ ᵦ - npᵐ/₂Ci-
(?< -n[a]-pa-Ci-)/-n[a]-pa-. 'be proud'. B - x-x-x x-x-x. Nk takaabin B,
takkabin A, takaabun A; Sr takabir- A. (Zdb: conjugation unclear. Unger
chooses the consonant-stem conjugation, Yoshida the vowel-stem.)

A   (-)takaru < *taka -ra- 'be high': attested in kwo-dakaru (Nr) < *kwo -n-
taka-ra- 'be elevated'. x - x-x-x x-x-x.

A   takaru < (Nr) takare[y]- < *taka(-)ra-Ci-. 'swarm, flock, gather; rob;
cadge'. x - A-A-A x-A-x. Sr takarir- (< takare-). Cf. sudaku.

?B   [takebiru] < takyebiy- ?< *takyeₐdⱼ ᵦ -npᵐ/₂Ci- (?< -n[a]-pa-Ci-).
'act roughly / fiercely / oppressively; display bravado'. x - x-x-x x-x-x.
Cf. otakebi.

A   takeru < takey- < *taka-Ci-. 'get boiled/cooked'. (A) - A-A-A x-x-x. Ib A.

?B   takeru < takey- < *takaₐdⱼ ᵦ -Ci-. 'be advanced (in time/skill); excel'.
B - B-B-A x-x-x. Mg take(?), take-tari, take-nu B; cf. takenawa.

?A/B   taker-u ?< *takyer-u < *takyeₐdⱼ ᵦ -ra-. 'rage; roar; get excited; show
spirit/courage'. x - B-A-A x-x-x. NS (130a) B; NS (T) 'brave man' takyeru (20)
LLL, (kun) LHH.

A   taku < *taka-. A - A-A-A x-A-x. 'burn it; boil/cook it'. Km (S) A. Edo A.
Ib A. Nk taCun A; Sr tak- A.

?B   ?*taku < *taka = *ta₁.₃ₐ -ka-. 'embrace': see mudaku, idaku; tamudaku.

?   taku < *taka-: (1) 'comb (one's hair) up into a bun'; (2) 'row hard';
(3) 'pull a net in/up'; (4) 'handle a horse with rein'. x - x-x-x x-x-x.

A   *taku < *taka-. 'swarm': see sudaku, takaru.

B   takumu < *ta₁.₃ₐ kuma-ᵦ. 'plan, devise'. B - B-A-x x-B-x. Nk takumin B;
Sr takum- B. K: Km B (where attested? W,S x). ▯ takumi 'skill; carpenter'.
B - 1/O-A-B x-x-x. NS (79b [14:316-M], 79c[14:337-M], 120b [14:186-K]) B.
Mr (Bm) HHL. Nk x. Cf. takuramu.

B   [takuraberu] < ta-kurabey- < *ta₁.₃ₐ kura-n[a]-pa-Ci-ₐ. 'compare'.
B - x-A-x x-x-x.

B   takuramu < takurama- (?< *takura-ma-, cf. taguru; ?< *ta₁.₃ₐ kuma-ᵦ with
-ra- infixed). 'scheme, plan, contrive, design'. x - B-A-B x-(B)-x.
Dial. (Tottori, Shimane, Sado, ...) takunamu. ▯ takurami x - A/B-A-B x-x-x.

?A/B   takuwaeru < takufafey- < *takupapa-Ci-: (1) if B, < *ta₁.₃ₐ kupa-pa-Ci-;
(2) if A, < *ta[ma]ₐ - kupa-pa-Ci-ᵦ. 'store, save' (= takuwau). A - x-x-x
x-x-x.

?A/B   [takuwau] < takufafu < *takupapa-. 'store, save' (= takuwaeru). A - x-x-x
x-x-x.

A   tamaru < *tama-ra-. (vi.) 'accumulate, collect, stand, stay'. (A) - A-A-A
x-A-x. NS (T+ 36) tamaruₐₜₜᵣ LLL. Km (W) A. Ib A. Nk tamaarun A; Sr tamar- A.
Cf. tumoru. ▯ tamari x - A-A-A x-A-x. Nk x; Sr tamai A.

B   [tamaru] < *tama-ra-. (vi.) 'bend, be bent'. x - x-x-x x-B-x. Nk tamaarun
B; Sr tamar- B. ▯ tamari x - x-x-x x-x-x. Nk tamai B. Cf. tameru; tawameru,
tawamu.

B   tamau < tamafu < *tama-pa-. 'give'. x - B-A-x x-B-x. NS (92a, 93a, 94a,
95a, 96a, 99b, 102b, 103b, 104b, 105a, 106b, 108b, 112a, 112b, 116b, 117b,
132a, 134a) B. Km (S) B. Mr (Bm) B. Edo B. Ib (rare) B. (For Sr taboor- B, see
tabaru.) Cf. tabaru, tabu. Yoshida would derive tamau from ta- ₁.₃ₐ 'hand' +
mafyi 'offering to gods' (cf. mainau).

B   tamau < *tamafu < *tama-pa-. 'vomit'. x - x-x-x x-x-x. ▯ [tamai] < tamafi
< *tamafyi < *tamap[a-C]i. B - x-x-x x-x-x.

B   tamawaru < tamafaru ?< *tama-pa-ra-. 'humbly receive, be given'; (from
c. 1200) 'deign to give'. x - B-A-B x-x-x. NS (Okada "taufaru") B.
Cf. tabaru, tabu, taberu; [toobaru].

?A/B   tamerau < tamerafu < *tamerapa- (< ?). 'hesitate, waver'. Ib B.
⟨⟩ tamerai x - A-A-A x-x-x.

A   tameru < tame[y]- < *tama-Ci-. 'accumulate, let accumulate, amass, save'.
x - A-A-A x-A-x. Km (W) A. Ib A. Nk tamiirun A; Sr tamir- A. Cf. tabau.

?B   tameru < tamey- < *tama-Ci-. 'bend it'. B - B-A-A x-B-x. Nk tamirun B,
Sr tamir- B. Cf. tamaru; tawameru, tawamu; taoyaka.

B   tamesu ?< *ta-myesu < *ta₁.₃ₐ miCa-sa-ᵦ ('let hand see'). 'try'. x - B-A-B
x-B-x. Edo A. Ib B. Nk tamisun B; Sr tamis- B. ⟨⟩ tamesi 'trial, example'. B -
B-A[H]/2[U]-B x-B-x. Nk tamisii B (adv.); Sr tamisi B.

?B   [tamiru] < tamiy- ?< *ta₁.₃ₐ mo-Ci-?A ('hand turn'). 'go round, turn'.
x - x-x-x x-x-x. Also: i-tamiy-, with prefix. ⟨⟩ tami → ···-dami (< -n- tamiy)
'approximate extent, (round) about ··· '.

?A/B   tamotu ?< *ta[mey] motu < *tama-Ci[-Ci]ₐ mota-; ?< *ta₁.₃ₐ mota-ᵦ
('hand hold', the traditional etymology). 'protect, preserve'. A - B-A-B x-B-x.
NS (121a, 130a) A. Km x. Wakamatsu B. Nk tamuCun B; Sr tamut- B. Cf. tameru A.

B   tamu < *tama-. 'vomit, spit up'. x - x-x-x x-x-x.   See tamau B, mukatamu,
tudami.

B   tamudaku < *ta₁.₃ₐ mudakuₐ (< ...). 'clasp one's hands'. B - x-x-x x-x-x.

B   tamukau < tamukafu < *ta₁.₃ₐ muka-pa-ₐ. 'oppose'. x - x-x-x x-x-x.
NS (116b [14:105L-K] [ta]mukafi) B; NS (T+ 11) tamukafyi mo sezu LLLL(|)L HH.

B   tamukeru < tamukey- < *ta₁.₃ₐ muka-Ci-ₐ. 'offer, pay as a tribute'.
(B) - B-A-B x-x-x. Km (W) B. ⟨⟩ tamuke x - B-A-B x-x-x.

A   tanabiku < tanabyiku (?< *tana₂.₁ -n- pika-ₐ; ?< *ta[na]-nabiku < *tana₂.₁
nam[a-Ci]ᵦ - pik[a]-ₐ). 'spread out (over), hang over'. A - B-A-A x-A-x.
Km (W) A/B.

A   [tanabiru] < tana-bi[y]- < *tana₂.₁ -npᵘ/₂Ci- (?< -n[a]-pa-Ci-).
'be extravagant'. A - x-x-x x-x-x.

B   [tanomeru] < tanomey- < *ta₁.₃ₐ noma-Ci-?A. (?) 'lead a person to look to
one (for help)'. (B) - x-x-x x-x-x.

B   tanomu < *ta₁.₃ₐ noma-?A ('hand pray'). 'request; entrust; hire, engage'.
B - B-A-B x-B-B. Km (W) B. Edo B. Nk taⁿ/ᵣumin B; Sr taⁿ/ᵣum- B; Yn tarumun B.
⟨⟩ tanomi x - 1/3-A/2[U]-B x-B-x. NS (T+ 105) tanomyi ka mo LLH(|)H(|)Ɫ.
Km (W) B. Mr (Bm) HHL. Ib B. Nk tanumii B; Sr tanumi B.

B   tanosiᵇ/ᵤ < *tanwosi-ᵇ/ᵤ < *tanwosiₐdⱼ ᵦ -n[a]-pa-. 'enjoy'. B - B-A-B
x-B-x. Hamada, Izumo B; Hattō, Matsue A. Ib B. Nk taⁿ/ᵣusimin B; Sr tanusim- B.
⟨⟩ tanosimi B - 3/4/0-A-x x-B-x. Nk tanusimii B; Sr tanusimi B. Km (S) B. Hattō,
Matsue, Izumo A; Hamada B; Goka-mura 1.

B´   taoreru < tafure[y]- < *tapu-ra-Ci-. 'fall down, collapse; succumb; go to
ruin'. B´ - B-A-B x-B-x. Km (S) B ("tafar-, tafur-"). Edo B. Ib B. Nk toorin B;
Sr toorir- B. ⟨⟩ taore x - B-x-x x-x-x. Cf. taosu.

B   taoru < taworu < *ta₁.₃ₐ bora-ᵦ ('hand bend'). 'bend it'. x - B-A-B x-x-x.
Km (W) A.

B´   taosu < tafusu < *tapu-sa-. 'bring/throw down, topple; overthrow, defeat'.
(?B´) - B-A-B x-B-x. Edo B. Ib B. Nk toosun B; Sr toos- B.

?A   [taraeru] < *tarafey- < *ta-ra-pa-Ci-. 'add, complete'. x - x-x-x x-B-x.
Nk tare(eru)n B; Sr tareer- B < tarafe-.

B   tarasu < *tara-sa-. 'let it hang down; let it drip/drop'. x - B-A-B x-B-x.
Ib B. Nk taraasun B; Sr taras- B.

?B   tarasu ?< torasu (< ...). [dial.] 'give'.

?A   [tarau] ⟨ tarafu ⟨ *tara-pa-. 'be complete(ly supplied or equipped)'.
x - x-x-x x-x-x. *See* [taraeru].

?A   [tarawasu] ⟨ tarafasu ⟨ *tara-pa-sa-. (vt.) 'complete'; (vi.) 'deign to be
completely supplied/equipped'. x - x-x-x x-x-x.

B   tareru ⟨ tare[y]- ⟨ *tara-Ci-. 'hang down, droop; drip'. B - B-B-B x-B-x.
NS (84a) B. NS (T+) tare (89, 93) LL, (97) LH. Km (S,W) B. Mr (Bm) B. Edo B.
Ib B. Nk tarirun B; Sr tarir- B. Also taru; cf. tarasu. ⓪ tare x - B-2-B x-x-x.

A   taru ⟨ taru ⟨ *ta-ra-. 'suffice'. x - A-A-A x-A-x. NS (72b) A. Km (W) A.
Mr (Bm) A. Edo A. Ib A. Nk tan A; Sr ta(ri)r- A. Cf. tasu; tatau, tataeru.

A   taru: *see* tariru.

B   taru ⟨ *tara-. 'hang down, droop; drip'. B - B-x-x x-x-x. Km (S) B. Edo B.
See tareru; cf. tarasu.

?B   tarumu ⟨ *taru*adj B* -ma-. 'slacken, sag, relax'. x - A̲-A-B x-x-x.
⓪ tarumi x - A̲-A-B x-x-x. Also d- (*ntaru-).

B   tasikameru ⟨ tasikame[y]- ⟨ *tasi-ka*3.7b* (⟨ ...) -ma-Ci-. 'ascertain,
confirm'. x - B-A-B x-B-x. Ib A, B. Nk tasi(i)kamirun B; Sr tasikamir- B.
⓪ tasikame x - A̲-A-B x-x-x.

B   tasinameru ⟨ tasinamey- ⟨ *tasinama-Ci-(⟨ ?). 'make suffer; reprove,
reproach'. (B) - B-A/B[U](misprint?)-B x-x-x.

B   tasinamu ⟨ *tasinama- (⟨ ?). 'suffer (hardship); be sober, prudent,
discreet'; [later] 'relish, like'. B - B-A-B x-x-x. Ongi-m B. ⓪ tasinami
'taste; prudence; accomplishments; toilette'. x - 3/4/0-A-B x-B-x.

A   tasu ⟨ *ta-sa-. 'add'. A - A-A-A A-x-x. Ib A. Nk tasun A. ⓪ tasi x - A-A-B̲
x-A-x. Kg misprint? Nk tasii A; Sr tasi A (for the Sr verb see [taraeru]).
Cf. taru; tatau, tateru. Not attested before Heian.

B   tasukaru ⟨ *ta*1.3a* suka-ra-*A*. 'be saved/helped'. (B) - B-A-B x-x-x. Ib B.

B   tasukeru ⟨ tasukey- ⟨ *ta*1.3a* suka-Ci-*A*. 'help; save'. B - B-A-B x-B-B.
NS (Okada) B. Km (S) B. Mr (Bm) B. Edo B. Ib B. Nk tasiKin B; Sr tasikir- B.
⓪ tasuke B - B-A-B x-B-x. Mr (Bm) HHL. Hamada A̲ (verb B). Nk tasiKii B;
Sr tasiki B. Cf. sukuu, sukeru.

?A/B   tataeru ⟨ tatafey- ⟨ *tata-pa-Ci- (?= *ta-ta-pa-Ci-). 'fill with; fill
with praise'. (B) - A/B-A[U]/B[H]-A x-x-x. Ongi B, Ongi-m B. Km (S) t̄atafe.
Mr (Bm) B´ (= LHH). Edo A(/B). Ib A. Narada, Hamada B; Hattō, Matsue, Izumo A.
Cf. tatau; taru, tasu.

(?A/)B   tatakau ⟨ tatakafu ⟨ *tataka-pa- (*see* tataku). 'fight'. B - A̲-A-A̲ x-A̲-x.
Ongi B. NS (124b, 129bv) B. NS (T+ 12) tatakafey-ba LLHL|H. Hattō B.
Nk taTaaKan A̲ [new]; Sr tatakayun A̲ (neg. tatakaan/tatakaran). Modern register
incongruities are unexplained. ⓪ tatakai x - A̲-A-A̲ x-A̲-x. Ib A. Nk tatakai A
[new]; Sr tatakee A.

B   tataku ?⟨ *ta*1.3a* tuka-*A* ('hand poke', *the second vowel assimilated to the
first*). 'strike, beat, tap; mince'. B - B-A-B x-B-B. NS (83b [17:117-M] B.
Km (S) B. Edo B. Suzu, Kōchi, Ib B; Hyōgo A. Nk taTaaCun B; Sr tatak- B.
⓪ tataki x - B-1:3-B x-x-x.

A   tatamaru ⟨ *tatama-ra- (⟨ ...). 'pile up, get involved or intricate';
(= todokooru) [dial.] 'get delayed/slowed; stay undrained or undigested, get
clogged up'. (A) - A-A-(x) (x)-A-x. Nk x; Sr tatamar- A 'get clogged up'.
⓪ tatamari x - A-x-x x-x-x.

A   tatamu ?⟨ *tatama- 'fold (up)': *(1)* ?⟨ *ta[ma]*A*- tama*A*- (cf. tamaru,
tameru); *(2)* ?⟨ *tata*B*-ma- (Unger: 'cut' — but surely 'stand' was intended,
cf. tataneru); *(3)* ?⟨ *ta*1.3a* ta*1.3a* - ma- ('hand hand' [Yoshida]). A - A-A-A
A-x-x. Edo A. Ib (also tatomu) A. Nk taTaamin A = taKuuubin A; Sr takub- A ⟨ ?.
⓪ tatami A - A-A-A A-A-x. NS HHH. Edo A. Nk tatan A = tataami A; Sr tatan A.
Cf. tataneru, tatanawar(er)u. Dial. tatomu probably assimilated the second

vowel to the labial nasal, but cf. tomaru : tomeru and tamaru : tameru. The register is incongruent for etymologies (2) and (3).

A tatanawareru < tatanafare[y]- = tatanawaru < tatanafaru: < *tatana-pa-ra-(Ci-) (< *tata(-)na-, *see* tataneru). 'get folded/piled up'. A - x-x-x x-x-x.

?A tatanazuku < tatanaduku < *tata(-)na-*?A* (-n-) tuka-*B* (*see* tataneru). 'pile (them/it) up'. x - x-x-x x-x-x. NS (T+ 22) LLL(|)HH.

?A [tataneru] < tatane[y]- 'fold/pile up': *(1)* ?< *tatame[y]-*A* *(nasal assimilated to apicality of stops)* < *tatama-Ci-; *(2)* ?< *tata-na-Ci-*B* ('stand' [Unger]); *(3)* ?< *ta*ɪ. sa* ta*ɪ.sa* -na-Ci- ('hand hand' Yoshida). x - x-x-x x-x-x. Register is incongruent for etymologies (2) and (3).

?A tataru < *tatara- (< ?). 'curse, haunt, torment'. A - B̲-A-A x-x-x. Km (W) B̲. Hattō, Hamada, Goka-mura B̲; Matsue, Izumo A. Ib A. ⬚ tatari x - 2-A-A x-B̲-x. NE Kyūshū A. Sr tatari B̲ (borrowed?; no verb).

B tatasu < *tata-sa-. 'deign to stand'. x - x-x-x x-x-x. NS (T+ 75) tatase-ba LLH(|)L; (75, 101, kun) tatasi LLH; (74) tatasi te LLH(|)H; (32, 102) tatasu LLL.

B tatau < tatafu < *tatapa- (?< *tata-pa-). 'get (brim-)full, overflow'. B - x-x-x x-x-x. Km x. Mr (Bm) B´. Etymology with ta- (cf. taru, tasu) incongruent in register.

B tatazumu < tata*ᵇ/z*umu < *tata-*B* (-n-) suma-*B*. 'stand still; linger, loiter'. B - B-A-B x-x-x.

B+?A tatemadasu < tate[y] madasu/madaseru < *tata-Ci[-Ci]*B* manta(-)sa-(Ci-)*?A*. 'give, send'. LH|HHL (Kz) - x-x-x x-x-x. Kz Mg tat̲e̲ mad̲a̲s̲u̲; Kn Mg "tat̲e̲m̲a̲d̲a̲s̲u̲" looks like a mistake.

B+A tatematuru < tate[y] maturu < *tata-Ci[-Ci]*B* matura-*A*. 'offer (up); do respectfully'. Mg tat̲e̲ mat̲u̲r̲u̲ - A/B-B-B x-x-x. NS (101b, 103a, 103a, 108b, 119a) B+A. Mr (Bm)) LH|HHH (= B+A).

B tateru < tate[y]- < *tata-Ci-. 'erect, stand' (vt.). B - B-B-B A̲-B-B. NS (70a [11:49-M], 71a [11:173-M], 94b [11:54-K], 121a [14:193L-K]) B. NS (T+ 33) tate te L̲H̲H̲ ?= LH(|)H; taturu (46) LHH. Km (S,W) B. Mr (Bm) B. Edo B. Ib B. Nk tatiirun B; Sr tatir- B. *See also* sakidateru. ⬚ tate: *(1)* 'shield' LH - 1̲-2-B x-x-x. *(2)* 'vertical' x - 2-1̲:3̲-B x-B̲-x; Hattō, Hamada 1̲; Matsue, Izumo 2 (= B); Nk tatii B; Sr tati B. (NKD 13:101c:5 misprints "KYŌ-a̲" for "HYŌ-a̲".)

B tatoeru < tatofey-/tatof- < *tatopa-(Ci-) (< ?). 'compare, liken'. B - B-A-B x-B̲-x. Mr (Bm) B. Edo B. Ib B. Nk tatuurun B, Sr tatur- B < *tator- restructured from *tatow- < *tatof-. ⬚ tatoe < tatofe[y] = tatoi < tatofyi. (B) - B-A[H]/2-B x-B̲-x. Km (S) B. Nk, Sr tatui B < *tatori restructured from *tatowi < *tatofi.

A [tattobiru/tootobiru] < tafutwobiy- < *taputwo*adj A* -np*ᵐ/ₐ*Ci-(?< *-n[a]-pa-Ci-). 'value, esteem, honor, revere'. A - B̲-A-x x-x-x.

A tattobu/tootobu < tattomu (JP) / tootomu < tafutwomu < *taputwo*adj A* -ma-. 'value, esteem, honor, revere'. A - B̲- A-A x-A-x. Km (S) A. Hattō, Hamada B̲; Matsue, Izumo A. Nk x; the -tt- of Sr tattub- A suggests that it is borrowed.

B tatu < *tata-. 'stand, be built; leave; (time) pass, elapse'. B - B-B-B B-B-B. NS (72a [11:196-M], 74b [14:26-M], 76a [14:121W-M, 14:123-M], 98a [11:91-K], 124b [14:257-K], 126a [14:283-K]) B. NS (T+) tataba (116) LLL; tateri (87) L̲H̲H; tateru (108, kun) LHH; tati (72b, 83, 97) LH, (53, 72a) LL; tati s̲o̲ba n̲o̲ (7 'standing buckwheat') LH|LH(|)L; tati ku mo (21) LL L(|)H; tati te (89) LH(|)H̲ = (100) LH(|)H; tatu (1, 20, 41) LH. Km (S,W) B. Edo B. Ib B. Nk taCun B; Sr tat- B. ⬚ tati 'mansion, ... ' LL/LH - x-x-x x-x-x; 'nature, temperament' x - 1̲-1̲:3̲-B x-x-x.

B   tatu < *tata-. 'cut off, sever; abstain from; exterminate'. B - B-B-B
B-B-B. Km (S) B. ⬚ tati 'sword'. B - 1-2-B x-B-x. Hattō B (2), Hamada 1;
Matsue, Izumo A. Ib B. Cf. taeru, tayasu.

?A/B   tawakeru < tafakey- < *tapa-ka-Ci-. 'fool around; misbehave, engage in
adultery'. x - B-A-A x-x-x. ⬚ tawake 'tomfoolery'. x - B-1:3-A x-x-x.

?A/B   tawameru < tawamey- < *taba-ma-Ci-. 'bend it, make it bend'. A - B-A-A
x-x-x. Cf. tameru; taoyaka.

?A/B   tawamu < *taba-ma- (cf. tawawa). 'bend, be bent, yield'. A - B-A-A x-x-x.
Hamada B; Hattō, Matsue, Izumo, Goka-mura A. Cf. tameru, tawameru, [toomu];
taoyaka.

A   tawamureru < tafaᵇ/ᴍure[y]- < *tapa-n-pura-Ci-. 'frolic, romp, dally'.
A - B-A-A x-x-x. ⬚ tawaᵇ/ᴍure A - A/B-A-A x-B[Lit.]-x. Sr [Lit.] tawahuri B
(?< *tapa-pura-Ci-). Cf. tawareru, tawakeru.

A   [tawareru] < tafare[y] < *tapa-ra-Ci-. 'romp, frolic, dally'. x - x-A-x
x-x-x. Km (W) A. Cf. tafa-siₐdⱼ ₐ 'profligate'.

B   (-)tawaru < (-)tafaru < *tapa-ra- 'be blocked': see yokotawaru. Cf. taeru.

B   tayasu < *tada-sa-. 'end it; put an end to it; let it come to an end'.
x - B-A-B x-B-x. Nk teesun B 'waste'; Sr tees- B 'end it; waste'. Cf. taeru;
tuiyasu.

?A/B   tayoru < *tayoru < *taₗ.₃ₐ dora-ₐ. 'rely (on); resort (to)'. x - B-A-A
x-x-x. Ib B. Nk tayurun B. ⬚ tayori LHL - 1-1:3-A x-B-x. Mr (Bm) LHL. Edo LHL.
Hattō, Hamada, Goka-mura 1; Matsue 2/3; Akita 3; Izumo 2. Nk, Sr tayui B.
(For the verb Sr uses taⁿ/ᵣum- < *tanom-.)

B   tayumeru < tayumey- < *taduma-Ci- (< ...). 'cause to flag / slacken'.
(B) - x-x-x x-x-x.

B   tayumu < *taduma- (? < *taₗ.₃ₐ du[ru]-ma-ᵦ). 'flag, slacken one's
efforts'. B - B-A-B x-x-x. Ib (rare) B.

B   tazuneru < tadune[y]- < *tantuna-Ci- (< ?). 'seek; ask, inquire; visit'.
B - B-A-B B-B-x. Km (S) B. Edo B. Ib B. Nk tazunin/tannin B; Sr tannir-/
taẓunir-/taẓinir- B. ⬚ tazune x - 3-x-x x-x-x. Edo HHL.

?A/B   tazusaeru < tadusafe- < *tantwusapa-Ci-(< ?). 'have in hand/company'.
B - A/B-A-A x-x-x.

?A/B   tazusawaru < tadusafaru < *tantusapa-ra- (< ?). 'have a hand (in),
participate; go in company; go (= be connected) with'. B - A/B-A-A x-x-x.

?A/B   tazusau < tadusafu < *tantusapa- (< ?). 'go in company; be relevant (to),
go (= be connected) with'. (B) - x-x-x x-x-x.

B   ? [tedateru] < tedate[y]- < *ta-Ciₗ.₃ₐ -n- tata-Ci-ᵦ. 'take steps (measures,
action)'. x - x-x-x x-x-x. ⬚ tedate B - 2-2-B x-x-x.

B   temadoru/*tematoru < *ta-Ciₗ.₃ₐ - maₗ.₁ (-n-) t(w)ora-ᵦ. 'take time, be
delayed'. x - B-A-B x-x-x. ⬚ tematori 'piecework(er)' x - 3/4/0-3(ᵗ/ₐ)-x
x-B-x. Nk, Sr tima-tuyaa B < *tema-tori -aₛᵤբ.

B   temaneku < *ta-Ciₗ.₃ₐ maneka-ᵦ (< ?). 'beckon'. x - B-A-B x-x-x.
⬚ temaneki x - 2-3-B x-B-x. Sr ti(i)manuci/tiimanici B.

?B   terasau < terasafu < *tera-sa-pa- (< ?; see ter-u). 'show clearly'.
x - x-x-x x-x-x.

?B´   terasu < *tera-sa- (< ?; see ter-u). 'shine on, illuminate; compare it
(with)'. B/B´ - B-A-B x-(A)-x. Km (S) B. Mr (Bm) B. Edo B. Sapporo, Numazu A.
Ib B. Nk tiraasun B; Sr tiracagar- A < *tira[si]kyagar- (palatal spread from
third syllable to fourth) < *terasi-kagar-.

?B´   terau < terafu < *tera-pa- (< ?; see ter-u). 'show off; pretend, affect'.
B´ - B-A-A x-x-x. NS (Okada) B. NS (T+ 79) fyitо-derafu (phonograms also taken
as -nerafu) ꬲLHLH = HL | HL|H. ⬚ terai x - 2/0-A-A x-x-x.

?B   terawasu < terafasu < *tera-pa-sa-. 'sell by showing'. x - x-x-x x-x-x.

B   tereru < *tere[y]- < *tera-ᵦ (< ...) -Ci-. x - B-B-A̲ x-x-x. 'be/feel embarrassed, awkward'. Earliest attestation Edo. Ib B. ◻ tere x - B-x-x x-x-x.

B   ter-u < *tera- ?< *to(-)ra- (cf. tomosu, tomoru) 'shine': ?< Azuma twor-; ?< *te[y]ra- < *ta-Ci-ra- (cf. hotaru); ?< *tira- 'scatter [rays]' (cf. kesu : kieru); ?< te[n] (< Ch .thyen) -ra-. B - B-B-B x-B-x. NS (T+ 48) osi ter-uₐₜₜᵣ LL ꟼH = LH. Ongi B. Edo B. Ib B. Nk tin B; Sr tir- B. ◻ teri x - B-2-B x-x-x.

?A/B   tetudau < tetudafu < *te-dutafu (metathesis) < *ta-Ciₗ.₃ₐ (-n-) tuta-pa-ₐ. 'help, assist'. x - B-A-A x-x-x. Ib (also tettau) B. ◻ tetudai x - 3-2-A x-x-x. Tk 3 < 4, cf. o-teˈtudai < *tetudaiˈ.

?A/B   tibasir-u < *tiₗ.ₗ -n- pasira-ᵦ (< ...). 'get bloodshot'. x - B-A-A x-x-x.

B   tibiru < tibi[y]- < *tinpᵘ/₂Ci- (?< *ti[ti] -npᵘ/₂-Ci-). 'get mastitis'. B - x-x-x x-x-x.

?A/B   tibir-u (late Edo) < tibiru < tibi[y]- < *tinpᵘ/₂Ci- (< ?). 'get worn down/out'. x - A/B-A(/B[Lit.U])-A x-x-x.

?B   [tidaru] (NS semantograms) < tiₗ.₃ₐ (?< *tiy < *to̲-Ci) -n- tara-ₐ. 'be fully arrayed/supplied'. x - x-x-x x-x-x. Cf. [to̲daru], [sodaru], [momodaru].

A   tigaeru < tigafey- < ?*tiₗ.ₗ -n- kapa-Ci-ₐ. 'alter; mistake; ... '. A - A-A-A x-x-x. Edo A.

A   tigau < tigafu < ?*tiₗ.ₗ -n- kapa-ₐ ('road cross'). 'be different, differ'. A - A-A-A x-A-A. Mr (Bm) A. Numazu B̲. Kōchi, Ib A. Nk Cigaarun A; Sr cigaar- A; Yn cigai··· A (H 1967:388). Cf. matigau; tagau. Tigau is newer than tagau; they differ in register. ◻ tigai x - A-A-A x-x-x.

?A/B   tigir-u < tigyir-u ?< *tiₗ.ₗ -n- kira-ᵦ ('blood/spirit cut'). 'pledge'. A - B-A-B x-(x?)-x. NS (113b) A. Edo B. ◻ tigiri LHL - A/B-A-B x-A-x. Edo HHL. Nk Ciziiri A [new]; Sr ciziri A.

?B   tigir-u ?< *tegyir-u < *ta-Ciₗ.₃ₐ -n- kira-ᵦ; ?< *[ta]ti-gyir- < *tat[a-C]iᵦ -n- kira-ᵦ. 'tear off, pluck'. x - B-A-B x-x-x.

A   tikau < tikafu ?< *tiₗ.ₗ kapa-ₐ ('exchange blood/spirit'). 'vow, swear, pledge'. A - A/B̲-A-A x-x-x. Hattō A/B̲-A x-x-x. Km (S) A. Mr (Bm) A. Hattō, Matsue, Izumo, (automatically) Goka-mura A; Hamada A/B̲. Ib A.

B   tikazukeru < tikadukey- < *tikaₐdⱼ ᵦ -n- tuka-Ci-ᵦ. 'bring it near'. B - B-A-B x-B-x. Nk x; Sr cikaȥikir- B.

B   tikazuku < tikaduku < *tikaₐdⱼ ᵦ -n- tuka-ᵦ. 'draw near, approach'. B - B-A-B x-B-x. NS (126a) B. Mr (Bm) B. Ib B. Nk x; Sr cikaȥik- B. ◻ tikazuki x - A/B̲-A-B x-x-x.

?A   tinamu < *tiₗ.ₗ ('road?, 'blood'?) nama-₂ₐ (?*nanpa-). 'be connected (with)'. x - B̲-A-A x-x-x. Km (S) A. Wakamatsu B̲. ◻ tinami A - 1/3/0-A-A x-x-x. Mr (Bm) A. The 1218 notation "tinafini" (KggD 973b) attests a variant, tinabi.

1.1+A(=A)   tinuru < *tiₗ.ₗ nura-ₐ. 'stain one's blade with blood (= kill in battle)'. H(|)HL - x-x-x x-x-x.

A   tirakaru < *tira-ka-ra-. 'get scattered'. x - A-A-A x-x-x. Ib A. Nk CiraaKan A; Sr x. (The NKD attestations are late.) Cf. torokeru.

A   tirakasu < *tira-ka-sa-. 'scatter them'. x - A-A-A x-A-x. Ib A. Nk CiraaKasun A; Sr cirakas- A. Attested Hn.

A   tirasu < *tira-sa-. 'scatter, strew'. x - A-A-A x-A-x. NS (104a) A. Km (W) A. Edo A/B. Ib A. Nk Ciraasun A; Sr ciras- A 'dry up a boil (= disperse the liquid)'. Cf. tirakasu.

A   tiribameru < tiribame[y]- < *tir[a-C]iₐ -n- pama-Ci-ₐ. 'inlay'. A - B-A-A x-x-x. Mr (Bm) B̲.

?B   ?*[tiru] < *ti[y]- < *tᵘ/₀Ci- (? = tu-Ci-, cf. tiiₗ.₃ₐ, tuₗ.₃ₐ, mizuₗ.ₗₐ). *'get wet'. See subotu = subotiru.

A   tir-u < *tira-. 'scatter, get scattered' (vi.). A - A-A-A x-A-x. Ongi
(Iroha) B̲. Km (S,W) A. Mr (Bm) A. Edo A. Ib A. Nk Cin A; Sr cirir- A ?< *cire-
< *tira-Ci-. 🛇 tiri 'dust'. A - A-A-A x-A-x. Km (S,W) A. Cf. ter-u.

B   titibomu (< ?). 'break out with measles'. B - x-x-x x-x-x.

B   titihakuru < titifakuru (< ?). 'break out with measles'. B - x-x-x x-x-x.

?A   [tiwaeru] < tifafey- < *ti₁.₁ (-)papa-Ci-. 'divine spirits protect and
help'. x - x-x-x x-x-x.

?A   [tiwau] < tifafu < *ti₁.₁ (-)papa-. 'display spiritual power'. x - x-x-x
x-x-x.

A   tizimaru < tidimaru ?< sizimar- < *sinsi-ma-ra-. 'shrink' (vi.). x - A-A-A
x-x-x. Nk Cizi(i)man A.

A   tizimeru < tidime[y]- ?< sizime[y]- < *sinsi-ma-Ci-. 'shrink it'.
(A) - A-A-A x-B̲-x. Ib A. Nk Cizi(i)min A; Sr cizimir- B. Cf. tuzumeru.

A   tizimu < tidimu ?< sizimu < *sinsi-ma-. 'shrink' (vi.) = tizimaru.
(A) - A-A-A x-A-x. Hattō A/B̲. Ib A. 🛇 tizimi x - A-A-A x-B-x. Nk Ciziimi A
[new], Sr cizimi B 'crepe'. See sizimu. Cf. Takahashi 1971.

A   tobasir-u ?< *tob[i - f]asir- < *tonp[a-C]i pasira-ʙ (< ...); ?<
*tobas[i] - ir- < *tonpa-s[a-C]iₐ iraₐ-ₐ. 'splash' (= tobi-tir-u). A - B̲-x-x
x-x-x. 🛇 tobasiri x - A/B̲-x-x x-x-x.

A   tobasu < *tonpa-sa-. 'let/make it fly; skip over, omit'. x - A-A-A x-A-A.
Ib A. Nk tubaasun A; Sr tubas- A; Yn tuban A.

?A(/B)   tobokeru < toboke[y]- (< ?). 'feign ignorance; look blank; dote'.
x - B-A-A x-x-x. Hattō, Hamada, Matsue, Izumo A. Ib A. Also tabakeru.

-        toboru, tobosu: see tomoru, tomosu.

A   tobu < *tonpa- (?< *tona-pa-, cf. tonakaru). 'fly; skip; jump'.
A - A-A-A A-A-A. NS (73c [11:261-M], 97a [11:78-K, 11:80-K], 125b) A.
NS (T+ 60) tobyi HH. Km (S,W) A. Edo A. Ib A. Nk tubin A; Sr tub- A.

-        toburau: see tomurau.

?A/B   todaeru < todafe[y]- < *tontapa-Ci- ?< *tom[a]-ₐ (?= toma-[Ci]ₐ) tapa-Ci-ₐ.
'cease, come to a halt'. x - B-A-B x-A[new?]-x. Km x. Nk x; Sr tudeer- A =
tudeek- A (?< *todafe ok-).

?   [todaru] (Koji-ki text) = [sodaru] 'be fully arrayed/supplied'.

B   todokeru < todoke[y]- < *tonto-ka-Ci- (< ?). 'deliver, forward; report'.
x - B-A-B x-B-x. Ib B. Nk tuduKin B; Sr tudukir-B. 🛇 todoke x - B-2-B x-B-x.
Nk tuduKii B; Sr tuduki B.

A   todokooru < todokoforu < *tonto-kopora- (< *-kopara-). 'stagnate; be
delayed, fall behind (in arrears)'. A - A/B̲-A-A x-A-x. Mr (Bm) A.
Nk x; Sr tudukuur- B. 🛇 todokoori x - A-A-A x-A-x. Nk x; Sr tudukuui B.
Cf. tatamaru, todomaru, tooru.

B   todoku < todoku/toduku < *tonto-ka- (?< *ton- tuka-, ?< ton- twoka-).
'reach; arrive'. x - B-A-B x-B-B[H 1967:403b]. Ib B. Nk tuducun B; Sr tuduk- B.

A   todomaru < *tontoma-ra- ?< *tom[a]-toma-ra- (?= *toma-[Ci]ₐ toma-ra-ₐ).
'come to a halt, stop; stay; be limited'. A - A-A/B̲-A-A x-A[Lit./new]-x.
NS (103b, 128a) A, (121a) B̲. Km (S) A. Mr (Bm) A. Hamada A/B̲; Hattō, Matsue,
Izumo B̲. Nk tuduuman A; Sr tudumar- A [Lit./new]. Cf. tatamaru, todokooru.

A   todomeku < *todo-myeku < *tontoₘₐ miCa-ka-ᵇⁿᵈ v. 'rumble' (= todoroku).
A - x-x-x x-x-x.

?A/B   todomeru < todomey- < *tontoma-Ci- ?< *tom[a]-toma-Ci- (?= toma[-Ci]ₐ
toma-Ci-ₐ). 'put a stop to; restrict oneself to'. A - B-A-A x-x-x. Km (S,W) A.
Edo A. Narada, Matsue, Izumo, Hattō, Hamada B. Ib (rare) B. Nk tudumin B;
Sr tudumir- B. 🛇 todome 'coup de gṟace, decisive blow' x - B-A-B x-x-x.
(Kg B may be a misprint; the verb is A).

-      [todomiru] < todomiy- < *tontomo-Ci- *(the third vowel assimilated to the
first two)* < *tontoma-Ci- (< ...). 'stop it' (= todomeru).

-      todomoru *(the third vowel assimilated to the first two)* = todomaru.

A   todorokasu < *tonto-ro_mis -ka-sa-. 'let it roar/rumble/throb'. x - B-A-A
x-x-x. [] todoroki x - B-A-A x-x-x.

B   todoroku < *tonto-ro_mis -ka-. 'roar, rumble; throb'. A - B-A-A x-x-x.
Nk tuduuruCun B [rare].

B   togameru < togamey- < *tonka_?s.s -ma-Ci-. 'find fault with'. B - B-A-B
x-B-x. Km (W) B. Edo B. Ib B. Nk tugaamin B; Sr tugamir- B. [] togame x - B-A-B
x-B-x. 1700 Ōsaka HHL. Nk tugaamii B; Sr tugami B.

B   togarasu < *twogarasu < *two_adj s -n[a]-ka-ra-sa-. 'sharpen (to a point);
pout'. x - B-A-B x-B-x. Nk tugaarasun B; Sr tugaras- B.

B   togaru < *twogaru < *two_adj s -n[a]-ka-ra-. 'be pointed, tapered, sharp'.
B - B-A-B x-B-x. Hattō, Matsue, Izumo, Goka-mura A; Hamada B. Ib tongaru B.
Nk tugaarun B; Sr tugar- B.

B   togeru < togey- < *tonkaCi- (<?). 'attain'. B - B-B-A x-B-x. Km (W "?") B.
Edo B. Ib B. Sr tuzir- B ?< togi(r)- (< ?).

A   togou < (Mg) togofu < tokofu < *tokopa- (?< *twop[a-Ci]_?A kopa-_s 'inquire,
beg'). 'imprecate, (ask gods to) curse'. A - x-x-x x-x-x.

B   togu < twogu < *two_adj s -n[a]-ka-. 'whet, sharpen; polish; wash (rice)'.
B - B-B-B x-B-B. Ib B. Ib B. Nk tuzun B; Sr tug- B.

B   tokasu < *toka-sa- (? < *to[ra]-ka-sa-). 'melt/dissolve it; comb'.
x - B-A-B x-B-x. Ib B. Ib B. Nk tukaasun B; Sr tukas- B.

B   tokeru < tokey- < *toka-Ci- (? < *to[ra]-ka-Ci-). 'come untied/loose, be
solved; get melted/dissolved'. (B) - B-B-B x-B-B. Km (W) B. Ib B. Nk tuKirun B;
Sr tukir- B.

B   toku < *toka- (? contraction < *to[ra]-ka-). 'untie, solve; melt,
dissolve; explain, persuade, preach'. B - B-B-B x-x-x. NS (Okada) B. NS (127)
tokane-["]fa LLH(|)L; (66) tokyi HH. Km (S,W) B. Mr (Bm) B. Edo B.
(Unger reconstructed *toko- on the basis of hodokoru and hodokosu, but those
can be explained as assimilation to the first vowel.)

B   [toku] < twoku 'arrive' (= tuku). x - x-x-x x-x-x.

B   tomaeru < *tomafey- < *toma-pa-Ci-. [Shuri] 'pursue, seek; pick up';
[dial.] 'catch, seize'. x - x-x-x x-B-x. Sr tumeer- B < *tomafe-.

A   tomaru < *toma-ra-. 'stop; anchor; lodge'. x - A-A-A x-A-A. NS (104a) A.
Ib A. Nk tumaarun A; Sr tumar- A. [] tomari A - A-A-A x-A-x. Nk, Sr tumai A.

A   tomeru < tomey- < *toma-Ci-. 'stop it, fasten, curb, detain; lodge,
shelter, put up for the night'. x - A-A-A x-A-x. Nk tumirun A; Sr tumir- A.
[] tome A - x-x-x x-x-x.

B   tomeru < tomey- < toma-Ci-. 'pursue, seek out'. B - x-x-x x-B-x.
Km (W) B. Mr (Bm) B [misprint in Hattori 1942:146? — cf. Sakurai 1977:867b].
Nk tumeerun B; Sr tumeer- B (also 'pick up'). Cf. tomaeru; tome-yuku; motomeru;
mitomeru. [] tome x - A-x-x x-x-x.

A   tomonaeru < tomonafey- < *tomo_s.s -na-pa-Ci-. 'let accompany, bring
along'. A - B-A-A x-x-x.

A   tomonau < tomonafu < *tomo_s.s -na-pa-. (vi.) 'accompany, go (with);
take along'. A - B-A-A x-x-x. Ib B.

B   tomoru, toboru < *tonpo-ra- (?< ... ; *see* tobosu). (vi.) 'burn, be lit/
alight'. (x) - A["old"]/B-A-B x-B-x. Hattō, Hamada, Matsue, Izumo, Goka-mura
B. Nk tubuuruun B; Sr tubur- B. Cf. hotoboru.

-      tomoru = todomoru = todomaru. (Also tumaru?)

B   tomosu, tobosu < *tonpo-sa-. 'burn (a light)'. B - A["old"]/B-A-B x-x-x.
NS (Okada B). Edo B. Hattō, Hamada, Matsue, Izumo B. Nk tubuusun B; Sr tubus- B
(?< ter- 'shine' + *mo-[da-] > moya-.)

?A   tomu < twomu < *twoma- (but Ōno Tōru 1978:48 rejects twomu in favor of
*tomu, "cf. toyo"). 'be rich; abound (in)'. x - B-B-A x-x-x. Goka-mura A. K: Km
A (attested?). Cf. tumu A; toyo*adj-s*. 〇 tomi A[Kz] - 1-2-A x-x-x. (Goka-mura 1.)

A   tomurau < to^b/**urafu < *tonpurapa- (<?): -m- 'condole, mourn for', -b-
'inquire, visit'. A - A[Mkz,Hiroto-Ōhara]/B-A-A x-x-x. Km (S,W) A. Mr (Bm)
tomorofu A (with vowel assimilations). Hattō, Hamada, Matsue, Izumo B.
〇 tomurai 'mourning' x - A-A-x x-x-x; toburai 'visit' x - A-x-x x-x-x.

?A/B   tonaeru < twonafey- < *two(-)na-pa(-)Ci- (cf. tou). 'chant, cry, call out,
advocate'. A - B-A-B x-x-x. Km (S) A. Mr (Bm) B. Edo (A/)B.
〇 tonae x - 2/3-A-x x-x-x. Km (S) B (incongruent with verb). Mr (Bm) HHH.

?A   tonakaru ?< *tona-ka-ra-. 'jump up'. x - x-x-x x-x-x. Cf. tobu; ? agaru.

A   tonaru < twonar- ?< *two*1.1* nara-*s* (or -na-ra-). 'be adjacent, neighbor
(on), abut'. x - A/B-A-x x-x-x. 〇 tonari A - A-A-A A-A-x. Nk, Sr tunai A.
Only the noun is attested for the Nara period; Ōno suggests the verb is
derived from the noun.

B   [toobaru] < taubaru < *tanparu < *tam[a]para- (= *tama-pa-ra-). 'humbly
receive'. x - x-x-x x-x-x. See tamawaru.

B   [toobaru] < taubaru < *tanparu < *tan[ku]pa-ra- (vi. of taguu). 'are
similar, resemble each other'. x - x-x-x x-x-x. NS (114b, 116b) B. The
etymology follows Ōno; NKD derives this verb from the other toobaru.

?A/B   [toomu] < towomu < *tobo-ma-. 'bend, be bent, yield' (= tawamu). x - x-x-x

?   [toorau] < toworafu < *tobo-ra-pa-. 'swell, roll'. x - x-x-x x-x-x. Azuma
towerafu.

B   tooru < toforu < *topo*adj A* -ra-. 'pass by/through'. B - B-A-B B-B-x. NS
(Okada) B. NS (T+ kun) toforu LLH; (107, kun) toforase*imper* LLLL. Edo B. Tk
1<2. Ib B. Nk tuurun B; Sr tuur- B. 〇 toori x - B-A[U]/2[H]-B x-B-x. Nk tui C;
Sr tuui B. The register is incongruent with the etymology.

B   toosu < tofosu < *topo*adj A* -sa-. 'let pass by/through'. B - B-A-B x-B-x.
NS (101b, 130a) B. Km (W) B. Edo B. Tk 1<2. Ib B. Nk tuusun B; Sr tuus- B.
〇 toosi x - B-1:3[H]/2[U]-B x-(x)-x. Nk tuusi B; ? Sr tuusi-nu-mii B 'outhouse
hole'. The register is incongruent with the etymology.

-          tooto^b/**u: see tattobu.

?B´   toraeru < torafey- < *tor[i] afey- < *t(w)or[a-C]i*s* apa-Ci-*s* (or <
*t(w)ora-pa-Ci-). 'capture'. B´ - B-B-A x-x-x. NS (129a) B´. NS (T+ 32)
torafey-tu HHH-H. Km x. Edo B´. Ib B´ (= L).

-          torakasu, torakeru: see torokasu, torokeru.

B   toraseru/torasu < torase[y]-/toras- < *t(w)ora-sa-(Ci-). 'give, let one
have'. x - B-B-B (x)-B-(B). ?NS (71c [11:189, 190-M]) B. Nk turaasun B; Sr
turas- B; Yn turan B.

B   torasu < *t(w)ora-sa-. 'deign to take'. x - x-x-x x-x-x. NS (T+ 60)
torasa-ne HLHL (odd); (108) torasu mo ya LLL(|)L(|)H; torase*imper* LLL ?= LLH.

?B´   torawareru < torafare[y]- < *t(w)ora-pa-ra-Ci-. 'get captured'. B´ - B-B-A
x-x-x. 〇 toraware x - A/B-B-A x-x-x.

?A   toro^b/**osu < *tora^n/**asu (the second vowel assimilated to the first) <
*tora-n[a]-pa-sa-. 'melt (?); temper (metal) [NKD]'. A (-m-) - x-x-x x-x-x.
Km x. Cf. torokasu.

?B   torokasu < torakasu (the second vowel assimilated to the first) <
*tora-ka-sa-. 'melt it; scatter them'. B - A/B-A-A x-x-x. Cf. tokasu,
toro^b/**osu; tirakasu.

?B   torokeru ‹ (Mr, Hn) torake[y]- ‹ *tora-ka-Ci-. (vi.) 'melt, dissolve; get infatuated; disappear; scatter'. B - A̲/B-A-A̲ x-x-x. Cf. tokasu, toro^b/ₘosu; tirakasu.

‥   toromosu: *see* torobosu.

B   toru ‹ t(v)oru ‹ *t(w)ora-. 'take; ... '. B - B-B-B B-B-B.
NS (83a [17:117-M], 93c [11:262-M], 106a [11:239-K], 128a [14:334-K]) B.
NS (T+ 108) toramey LLH; (35) tori HH; (kun) twori sibaru LH(|)LLH.
Km (S,W) B. Mr (Bm) B. Edo B. Ib B. Nk tun B; Sr tur- B.

?A/B   totir-u (‹ ?). 'fumble'. x - B-A-A x-x-x. (? Edo slang, cf. Mr toti-meku 'be confused, dazed' with toti of uncertain origin.)

B   totonoeru ‹ totonofey- ‹ (*)totonafey- *(the third vowel assimilated to the first two)* ‹ *toto-na-pa-Ci-. 'arrange, put in order, prepare; procure'.
B - B-A-A̲ x-x-x. NS (97a) B. Ib B. *See* totonou.

B   totonooru ‹ totonoforu ‹ *totonofaru *(the fourth vowel assimilated to the first three)* ‹ *totonafaru *(the third vowel assimilated to the first two)* ‹ *toto-na-pa-ra-. 'be arranged, settled, prepared, in order' (= totonou).
B - x-x-x x-x-x.

B   totonou ‹ totonofu ‹ (*)totonafu *(the third vowel assimilated to the first two)* ‹ *toto-na-pa-. 'be arranged, settled, prepared, in order; (= totonoeru) arrange, order'. (Ōno: "Originally it was vt. but with the later formation of totonoeru it became vi." But why is the Shuri form intransitive?) B - B-A-A̲ x-B-x. NS (124a) B. Mr (Bm) B. Nk x; Sr tutunar-/tutuna[w]- B. Ōno says toto is to-to 'that and that'; Yoshida says it is a variant of 'hand and hand' (i.e. ta - ta); Unger takes it as a back formation (from what?).

B+B   tottuku ‹ tor[i -] tuku ‹ *t(w)or[a-C]iᵦ tuka-ᵦ. 'approach; possess, take possession of, obsess'. x - A/B-B-A̲ x-x-x. ⬚ tottuki 'approach; beginning, onset'. x - A-B-A̲ x-x-x.

?A   totugu ?‹ *two₁.₁ ('gate' [= 'vulva']) tunka-ₐ. 'marry a man, become a wife'. A - B̲-A-A x-x-x. Ib B. ⬚ totugi A - x-x-x x-x-x.

?A   tou ‹ twofu ‹ *two(-)pa- (cf. tonaeru). 'inquire, ask; accuse; visit'.
A - A/B̲-A-B̲ x-A-x. NS (74c [11:305-M], 107b, 112b, 116b) A. NS (T+ 64) twofey-ba HH(|)L. Km (W) A. Mr (Bm) A. Edo A. Narada B̲ [Lit.]. Ib A. Nk tuurun A; Sr tuur- A. ⬚ toi x - A-A-B̲ x-x-x.

?A   [towasu] ‹ twofasu ‹ *two(-)pa-sa-. 'deign to inquire, ask'. x - x-x-x x-x-x. NS (T+ 63) twofasu na 'ah you ask [me]' HLₚL = HLL(|)L.

?B   toyoku ‹ *todoₘ₁ₘ -ka-. 'resound; loudly say'. x - B-x-x x-x-x. Also doyogu (*ntodo -n[a]-ka-). Cf. todoroku, toyomu.

–   toyomosu: *see* doyomosu.

–   toyomu: *see* doyomu.

A   tozasu ‹ (Hn) tosasu ‹ *two₁.₁ sasa-ᵦ. 'shut/close it'. (A) - A/B̲-A-A x-x-x. Ib B. ⬚ tozasi HHL (only one citation) / HHx - A-A-x x-x-x.

B   toziru ‹ todi[y]- ?‹ *tontoCi- (‹ ?). 'shut/close it; sew/stitch up, bind'. B - B-B-B x-B-x. Km (S) B. Mr (Bm) B. Edo B. Hattō, Hamada, Matsue, Izumo, Goka-mura A̲. Ib B. Nk x; Sr tudir- B ‹ *todi-. ⬚ tozi LH - B-2-x x-x-x. (Is Mg writing the infinitive instead of the noun?) Cf. todomeru, todokooru; todo 'at last'.

(B)   tubaku/tuwaku ‹ tufaku ‹ *tu₁.₃ₐ paka-ᵦ. 'spit'. x - x-x-x x-x-x.
See tubaki (Ch. 5).

?A/B   tubomaru ‹ *tunpo-ma-ra-. 'get narrow'. x - A[K]/B[H]-A-A x-x-x. Ib *(rare)* A. Cf. tubomu.

A   tubomeru ‹ tubome[y]- ‹ *tunpo-ma-Ci-. 'make it narrow'. x - A-A-A x-x-x.

?A/B   tubomu < *tunpo-ma-. 'get narrow, close up'. x - A/B-A-A x-<u>B</u>-x.
Nk Cibuumin A [new]; Sr cibum- <u>B</u>. 〖 tubomi 'a bud (about to open)'. x - B-A-<u>B</u>
x-<u>B</u>-x. Nk Cibuumi A [new]; Sr cibumi <u>B</u>. (Kg incongruent with verb.)

A   tubureru < tubure[y]- < *tunpu-ra-Ci-. 'get crushed, collapse'.
(?A) - A-A-A x-(x)-x. Narada A. Ib A. Nk x; Sr sipirir- A (< ?).

?A   tuburu, tumuru < *tunpura- (< ?). 'shut (one's eyes)'. x - A-A-A x-x-x.

A   tubusu < *tunpu-sa-. 'crush, demolish, ruin'. x - A-A-A x-x-x.
〖 tubusi x - A-A-A x-x-x.

?A/B   tubuyaku < *tunpu-da-ka-. 'mutter, grumble'. x - B-A-A x-x-x. Ib B´ (= L).
〖 tubuyaki x - A/B-A-A x-x-x.

?B   tudoeru < *tudwofey- < *tuntwopa-Ci- (< ...). 'bring them together'.
(B) - B-x-x x-x-x.

?B   tudou < tudwofu < *tuntwopa- (?< *tum[i] - twopa- < *tum[a-C]i_A twopa-_?A).
'gather, come together'. B - B-x-x x-x-x. Ib (rare) B. 〖 tudoi x - 2/0-A-A
x-x-x. Ōno's etymology: < tudu '(granule →) star' af-.

A   tugaeru < tugafey- < *tunka-pa-Ci- (?< ...). 'put arrow to bow; firmly
promise'. x - A(/B[H])-A-A x-x-x. Cf. tugau.

A   tugaru < *tunka-ra- (?< ...). 'join/piece/sew/chain it on' (vt.); (= i-
tugaru) 'continue, be a continuation, help complete' (vi.). x - x-x-x x-A-x.
NS (108a) A. Nk x; Sr çigaar- A 'work by shifts'. 〖 tugari x - A/<u>B</u>-x-x x-A-x.
Sr çigaai 'shift work'.

A   tugau < tugafu < *tunka-pa- (?< ...). (vi./vt.) 'pair, couple, mate
(them); keep passing down (an inheritance)'. x - A-A-x x-x-x. Edo A.
Clearly attested in 1186 (KggD 972a). Cf. tugaeru.

A   tugeru < tugey- < *tunka-Ci- (?< ...). 'tell, let one know, pass on
(information)'. A - A-A-A x-A-x. Km (S,W) A. Edo A. Ib (rare) A. Nk x; Sr
çigir- A. 〖 tuge x - x-A-x x-A[Lit.]-x. Km (S) A. Nk x; Sr çigi [Lit.] A.

A   tugu < *tunka- (?< *tu[ra]-n[a]-ka-, cf. tunagu). (vt.) 'pour'; (vi.)
'succeed, be next' (unclear whether one or two etyma). A - A-A-A A-A-A.
NS (71a [11:173-M], 98b [11:95-K]) A. NS (T+ 46) tugamu ni HHH(|)H; (19) tugyi
n<u>o</u>fore-ba HH HLHH (? mistake for HHHH). Km (W) A (vi.). Edo A (vi.). Ib A.
Nk Cizun A; Sr çig- A. 〖 tugi: (1) 'next' HL - B-2-A x-x-x; Km (S) HL; Mr (Bm)
HL; Hattō <u>B</u>; Hamada, Matsue, Izumo 1. (2) 'patch' x - A-A-A x-x-x.

?B   tugumu < (Hn) tukumu < *tuku-ma- (?< *tuku-n[a]-pa-). 'shut one's mouth;
fasten tight'. B - B-A-<u>A</u> x-B-x. Nk Cigumin B; Sr çigum- B. Cf. [tukuu] =
tukubu.

?A/B   tugunau < tugunafu < tukunafu = tukunofu (which partially assimilated the
third vowel) < *tuku_8.2 -na-pa- . 'compensate for; expiate'. (B) - B-A-A x-x-x.
〖 tugunai x - 3/0-A-A x-x-x. Cf. tugi < tukiy < *tuku-Ci 'tribute'(= mi-tugi).

?A/B   tugunou < (Mr) tugunofu < tukunofu < *tukunafu < *tuku_8.2 -na-pa-.
'compensate for; expiate'. B - B-A-x x-x-x.

A   tuibamu < tuifamu < tu[k]i famu < *tuk[a-C]i_A pama-_B. 'peck at'. A - B-A-A
x-x-x. Mg HxHx/HLxx.

A   [tuideru] < tuide[y]- < *tu[g]-i [i]de[y]- < *tunk[a-C]i inta-Ci-.
'order, put in order'. A - x-A-x x-x-x. Edo A. 〖 tuide A - A-A-A x-x-x.

A   tuieru < tufiye[y]- ?< *tufyiye[y]- < *tupida-Ci-. 'be spent, wasted,
routed'. A - A/<u>B</u>-A-A x-x-x. Ongi A. (Sr teeyun B < *taye-: see taeru.)
Cf. taeru; tuiyasu; tui-ni.

A   tuiyasu < tufiyasu < *tufyiyasu < *tupida-sa-. 'spend, waste'. A - A/<u>B</u>-A-A
x-x-x. Ib A. (Nk teesun B, Sr tees- B < *tayas-: see tayasu.)

A   tukaeru < tukafey- < *tuka-pa-Ci-: *(1)* 'be used' (A) - A-A-A x-x-x;
(2) 'serve' (vi.) x - A/B[new]-A-A x-x-x. NS (79b [14:315-M]) A. NS (T+ 102)
HLH *(odd)*, (78) LLL. Km (W) A(/B´). Edo A. Ib A. ⬚ tukae x - x-x-x x-x-x.
NS (127a [14:301-K] A.

A/B   tukaeru < tukafey- < *tuka-pa-Ci-. 'get obstructed/choked'. x - B-B-A
x-A-x. Ib A. Nk x; Sr çikeer- A. ⬚ tukae x - 2/3-1-A x-A-x. Nk x; Sr çikee A.

B   tukamaeru < tukamafe[y]- < *tuka-ma-pa-Ci-. 'catch; arrest'. x - B-B-B
x-x-x. Ib B´ (= L).

B   tukamaru < *tuka-ma-ra-. 'be caught; cling (hold on) to'. x - B-B-B x-x-x.
Ib B´ (= L).

A+A   tukamaturu < tukam[u]-maturu(HHH), tukau-maturu < tukafe[y] maturu <
*tuka-pa-Ci[-Ci] matu-ra-. 'humbly do'. HL|HHL - B-A[U]/B[H]-B x-x-x. NS (102b)
HH|HHL, (Okada — attributive) HH|HHH.

B   tukamu < *tuka-ma-. 'grasp'. B - B-A[U]]/B[H]-B x-B-B. Edo B. Ib B. Nk
siKaamin B; Sr çikam- B; Yn Kamun B. ⬚ tukami x - B-A-x x-x-x.

B   tukaneru < tukane[y]- < *tuka-na-Ci-. 'bundle (them into one)'. B - B-A-A̱
x-x-x. Km x. Mr (Bm) tukanete HHLL = A. K: Km LLLH *(where attested?)*
⬚ tukane B - x-x-x x-x-x. Km (W) B.

B   tukarasu < *tukara-sa- (? < *tuku-ra-sa-). 'make one weary'. x - B-A-x
x-x-x. Cf. tukareru; tukiru, tukusu.

?B´   tukareru < tukare[y]- < *tukaraCi- (?< *tuka-ra-Ci-). 'get weary'.
B´ - B-A-A x-A-x. Ongi B´. Edo A. NE Kyūshū A. Ib A. Nk siKaarin A; Sr
çikarir- A. Cf. tukarasu; tukiru, tukusu. ⬚ tukare x - B-2-A x-x-x. NE
Kyūshū A. Nk sikaari A [new].

A   tukaru < *tuka-ra-. 'get soaked'. x - A-A-A x-A-x. Km x. Nk siKaarun A;
Sr çikar- A.

B   tukaru < *tuka-ra-. [dial.] 'be attached, ... ' (= tuku). x - x-x-x x-B-x.
Nk siKaarun B; Sr çikar- B.

A   tukasadoru < *tukasaₐ.ₗ -n- t(w)ora-ᵦ. 'rule'. A - B-A-A x-x-x. Mr (Bm) A.

A   tukasu < *tuka-sa-. 'soak it' (= tukeru). x - x-x-x x-x-x.

B   tukasu ?< *tukusu < *tuku-sa-. 'exhaust'. x - x-x-x x-x-x.

A   tukau < tukafu < *tuka-pa-. 'use; employ; send (as messenger)'. A - A-A-A
x-A-A. NS (96a, 98b, 99b, 101b, 110b, 111a) A. Km (W) A. Edo A. Ib A. Nk siKen
A, Sr çikar- A; Yn Kun A. ⬚ tukai A - A-A-A x-A-x. NS (113a) A. Km (S,W) A.
Edo A. Nk siKee A; Sr çikee A.

A   tukawasu < tukafasu < *tuka-pa-sa-. 'deign to use; employ, dispatch'.
A - A/Ḇ[H,NHK]-A-A x-x-x. NS (93b [11:27-K], 120b [14:180W-K], 127a [14:307-
K]) A. NS (T+ 103) tukafasu rasi-kyi HLHL LHH *(odd)*.

A   tukeru < tukey- < *tuka-Ci-. 'soak it'. (?A) - A-A-A x-A-x. Ib A. Nk
siKiirun A; Sr çikir- A. NS (102a [11:146-K]) A. Narada Ḇ.

B   tukeru < tukey- < *tuka-Ci-. 'attach it, ... '. ?B - B-B-B x-B-x.
NS (108a [11:289-K]) B. NS (T+ 115) tukey LL. Km (W) B. Edo B. Nk siKiirun B;
Sr çikir- B. ⬚ tuke x - B-2-B x-x-x.

?A/B   tukiru < tukiy- < *tuku-Ci- (?< *tuka-Ci-). 'get exhausted'. B - A/B-B-B
x-x-x. NS (79a [14:314-M]) A. Km (S) A. Edo A. NE Kyūshū, Wakamatsu B. Ib B.

B   [tukiru] < tukiy- ← tukey- < *tuka-Ci-. 'attach it, ... '. x - x-x-x
x-x-x. NS (T+ 102) LH.

A   tuku < *tuka-. 'poke, thrust; spit out'. A - A-A-A x-A-A. NS (109a) A.
Km (W) A. Sapporo, Numazu Ḇ. Ib A. Nk ˢ/ʰiCun A; Sr çik- A; Yn Kun A.
⬚ tuki x - A-A-A x-x-x.

A   tuku < *tuku- (cf. tukuru, tukurou) < ? *tuka-. 'build' (= kizuku).
A - A-A-x x-x-x. NS (T+ 36) HL. Edo A.

A   tuku < *tuka-. (vi.) 'soak, get soaked' (= tukaru). A - A-A-<u>B</u> x-x-x.
Cf. mizuku.

?A   tuku ?< *tuku-. 'give, supply'. x - x-x-x x-x-x. Cf. tugunau.

B   tuku < *tuka-. 'arrive (= twoku); be attached; come in contact, touch,
reach; ... '. B - B-B-B <u>A</u>-B-x. NS (T+ 75) tukyi-tu LH-L. Km (W) B ('be
attached'). Edo B ('be attached'). Ib B. Nk ^s/ʜiCun B; Sr çik- B. Cf. tukaru,
tukeru. [] tuki 'attendant' x - B-A-B x-x-x.

B   tuku < *tuka-. 'pound, husk'. B - B-B-B x-B-<u>C</u>. Ib B. Nk ^s/ʜiCun B; Sr
cicun B [H 1967:461] = çicun (çik-); Yn sikun <u>C</u>.

?B   tukubu [NKD] = "tukufu" (?< *tuku-pa-; ?< tuku[m]u < *tuku-ma- ?<
*tuku-n[a]-pa-). 'shut (one's mouth)'. x - x-x-x x-x-x. Cf. tugumu.

B   tukurou < tukurofu [no direct evidence for -rwo-] < *tukurafu (the third
vowel partially assimilated to the first two) < *tuku-ra-pa-. 'repair, mend;
adjust'. B - B-A-B x-B-x. NS (100a, 120a) B. Nk siqKun B (siqKur-);
Sr çukuri(i)r- B < *çikuriir- < *tukurof(e)-. Cf. situraeru = siturau.
[] tukuroi x - 3-4-B x-x-x.

B   tukuru < *tuku-ra-. 'make'. B - B-A[U]/B[H]-B x-B-B. NS (79a [14:314-M],
83c, 97a [11:77L-K], 100a [11:117-K], 115b [14:27-K] B. NS (T+) tukuri (97)
LLH, (39, 41) <u>HHL</u>, (69) <u>HHH</u>; tukuru_{pred} (1) LLL, tukuru_{attr} (78) LHH. Km (W) B.
Mr (Bm) B. Edo B. Ib B. Nk siKoorun A; Sr çukur- < *çikur- < *tukur-; Yn Kurun
B. [] tukuri B - B-2-B x-x-x.

?A/B   tukusu < *tuku-sa- (cf. tukiru) — but, in view of tukareru, tukarasu, and
tukasu (= tukusu), perhaps *tuku- < *tuka- (the second vowel assimilated to the
first). 'exhaust; render service, work'. A - B-A-A x-A-x. Ongi A. NS (133a
[14:426-K]) A. Km (S) A. Mr (Bm) A. Edo (A/)B. Narada, Hattō, Hamada, Matsue,
Izumo, Wakamatsu B. Ib B. Nk x; Sr çikus- A.

?B   [tukuu] < "tukufu": see tukubu.

A   tumabiku < tuma-fyiku < *tuma_{2.1} pika-_A. 'strum, snap one's fingers'.
[] tumabiki x - A-A-A x-x-x.

A   tumadatu < *tuma _{2.1} -n- tata-_B. 'stand tiptoe'. x - B-A-A x-x-x.

A   tumamu < *tuma-ma- (or < *tuma_{2.1} -ma-). 'pinch, hold in one's fingers'.
x - A-A-A x-x-x. [] tumami x - A-A[U]/1:3[H]-A x-x-x.

B   tumaru < *tuma-ra-. 'get clogged, jammed; get shortened, shrink'.
x - B-A-B x-B-B. Ib B. Nk ('shrink') Cimaarun B; çimar- B.

?A   tumazuku < tumaduku < *tuma_{2.1} -n- tuka-_A. 'stumble, trip'. A - A-A-<u>B</u>
x-x-x. Hattō, Hamada, Matsue, Izumo <u>B</u>. Ib A, <u>B</u>. [] tumazuki x - A-A-<u>B</u> x-x-x.

B   tumeru < tumey- < *tuma-Ci-. 'cram; shorten, curtail; (= tameru)
accumulate'. x - B-B-B x-B-x. Km (W) (A/)B. Nk Cimirun B; Sr çimir- B. Ib B.
[] tume x - 2-1/2-x x-x-x; NS (T 'bridgehead') LL. Cf. tameru, tamaru; tumu,
tumoru (all register A).

?B   tumer-u < *tumeyr-u < ?*tunpa-Ci_{2.1} -ra- (but register is incongruent).
'pinch' (= tuner-u, tumu). x - B-A-B x-x-x.

B   tuminaeru = tuminau < tumyinafey-/tumyinafu < *tumi_{2.4} -na-pa-(Ci-).
'punish'. B - x-x-x x-x-x.

A   tumoru < *tumo-ra- ?< *tuma-ra- (second vowel partially assimilated to
the first). (vi.) 'accumulate, get piled up'; (vt.) 'estimate'. A - A/<u>B</u>-A-A
x-A-x. Km (W) A. NE Kyūshū A; Wakamatsu <u>B</u>. Ib A. Nk Cimuurun A; Sr çimur- A.
[] tumori x - A-A-A (x)-A-x.

A   tumu < *tuma-. 'amass; accumulate' (vi.). A - A-A-A x-A-A. NS (127a
[14:302-K]) A. Nk Cimin A; Sr çim- A (both vi. and [= çimir- B] vt.).

A   tumu < *tuma-. 'pinch, pluck' (= tuner-u). A - A-A-A x-B[Lit.]-x. NS (T+)
tumyi ni '(so as) to pick/pluck' (35a) HH(|)H, (35b Ōno's phonograms) HL(|)H.
Km (W) A. Ib A. Nk Cimin A; Sr [Lit.] çim- A. Cf. tumeru, tume.

B   tumu < *tuma-. 'be obstructed (ahead); come to the end; get congested,
crowded, crammed; be fine-meshed; get checkmated'. x - B-B-A x-(A)-x.

B   tumugu < *tumu₂.₄ -n[a]-ka-. 'spin, make into yarn'. B - B-A-B x-B-x. Ib
B. Nk Cinzun B; Sr çing- B < *tum[u]g- = çinag- B < *tunag-. 〚 tumugi 'pongee'.
B - A/B-A[U]/1:3[H]-B x-B-x. Sr çimuzi B (not *çinzi) < *tumugi, borrowed?

A   tunagaru ?< *tu[ra]-na-n[a]-ka-ra-. 'be connected/related'. x - A-A-A
x-(x)-x. Ib A. Sr çirugar- A < *turugar- < *turagar- (the second vowel
assimilated to the first) < *tura-n[a]-ka-ra-. 〚 tunagari x - A-A-A x-x-x.

A   tunageru < tunage[y]- ?< *tu[ra]-na-n[a]-ka-Ci-. 'join, link'. A - A-x-x
x-A-x. Nk Ciruugin A, Sr çirugir- A < *turuge- < *turage- (the second vowel
assimilated to the first) < *tura-n[a]-ka-Ci-.

A   tunagu ?< *tu[ra]-na-n[a]-ka-. 'tie, fasten, connect; track, trail,
pursue'. A - A-A-A x-A-x. NS (T+ 13) tunagyi te LLHꟻ ?= LLH(|)H; (117) tunagu
LLH. Ib A. Nk Cinaazun A = Ciruuzun A; Sr çirug- A < *turug- < *turag- (second
vowel assimilated to the first) < *tura-n[a]-ka-. 〚 tunagi x - A-A-A x-x-x.

B   tuner-u (< ?; cf. tunoru, tumer-u). 'pinch, nip'. x - B-A-B x-x-x.
Perhaps < tumer-u (the nasal assimilated in articulatory place to the
apical stop); cf. tumu A (but the register is incongruent).

?B   tunoru < *tunora- (< ?; perhaps < *tumo-ra-, the nasal assimilated in
articulatory place to the apical stop). (vt.) 'collect, raise (funds)'; (vi.)
'grow violent/intense'. B - B-A-A x-x-x. Mr (Bm) A. Ib A.

A+B   tunzaku < "tumu-zaku" (Mg) = tum[i] saku < *tum[a-C]i₄ saka-₄. 'rend,
cut, pierce'. HL|LH - B-A-A x-x-x.

?   *turagaru = tunagaru. x - x-x-x x-A-x.

?   *turageru = tunageru. x - x-x-x x-A-x.

?A   turanaru < *tura-na-ra-. 'stand in a row, be linked (strung out)'. A -
B-B-A x-x-x. Km (S) A.

A   turaneru < turane[y]- < *tura-na-Ci-. 'put in a row, link'. A - A/B-A-A
x-x-x. Km (S) A. Edo A.

?A   turanuku < *tura-?₄ nuka-?ₐ. 'pierce, penetrate; attain'. A - A/B-A-A
x-x-x. Km (S) A. Edo A.

?   -turau < -turafu < *(-)tura-pa- ?< *(-)twora-pa-. See ageturau, heturau,
hikozurau, ? situraeru = siturau.

A   tureru < ture[y]- < *tura-Ci-. 'bring as company'. x - A-A-A x-A-x. Edo A.
Nk Ciriirun A (= soorun A); Sr çirir- A (= soor- A < *sowe- < *sofe-, see
soeru).

A   turu < *tura-. 'hang; suspend; fish for; entice'. x - A-A-A x-A-A.
Km (W) A. Ib A. Nk x; Sr çir- A; Yn cirun A. 〚 turi A - A-A-A x-x-x. Okuda
270 gives the Hiroshima noun as B.

B   turuᵇ/ₘu < *turunpa- (?< *turu-n[a]-pa- < *tura-n[a]-pa-, the second
vowel assimilated to the first). 'mate'. B - B-A-x x-B-x. Kz Mg RLH/LLH
(cf. Mochizuki 1973:50). Nk Ciruubin B; Sr çirub- B. 〚 turuᵇ/ₘi B - x-A-x
x-x-x. Nk Ciruubi B.

A   turusu < *turu-sa- ?< *tura-sa- (second vowel assimilated to the first).
'suspend'. x - A-A-A x-x-x. Hattō, Goka-mura B; Hamada, Matsue, Izumo A. Ib A.

A   tutaeru < tutafey- < *tuta-pa-Ci-. 'transmit, convey, tell'.
A - A/B[U]-A[U]/B[H]-A x-A-x. NS (Okada) B. Edo A. Mr (Bm) A. Narada,
Hattō, Hamada, Matsue, Izumo A. Nk x; Sr çiteer- A. 〚 tutae x - A/B-2-x
x-A-x. Ib A. Nk x; Sr çitee A.

A   tutau < tutafu < *tuta-pa-. 'go/follow along'. A - A-A-A x-x-x.
◫ tutai x - x-x-x x-x-x. (?< tuta₂.₂ₐ 'ivy', Matsumoto 1974:102.)

A   tutawaru < tutafaru < *tuta-pa-ra-. 'be transmitted'. (x) - A-A[U]/B[H]-A
x-A-x. Ib A. ◫ tutawari x - A-x-x x-x-x.

A   tuteru < tute[y]- < *tuta-Ci-. 'transmit' (= tute-yaru). x - x-x-x x-x-x.
Km (W) A. ◫ tute x - B-1:3[U]-x x-x-x. Edo HL.

B   tutikau < tutikafu < *tuti₂.₉ kapa-ᵦ. 'cultivate'. x - B-A-B x-x-x.

B   tutomeru < tutwomey- < *tutwo?₂.₅ -ma-Ci-. 'endeavor, work, serve'.
B - B-A-B x-B-x. NS (117a) B, (Okada) A̲. Nk siTumin B; Sr çitumir- B.
◫ tutome B - B-2-B x-B-x. Goka-mura 1/0. Ōsaka, Kōbe 3. Ib B. Nk siTumii B;
Sr çitumi B. Cf. tuto-ni, tutomete.

?A/B   tutuku < *tutuka- ?< *tu[ka-]ₐ tuka-ₐ (Unger); ?< *tutu -ka- (Yoshida,
Ōno). 'peck; nudge, poke; needle, incite'. x - B-A-A x-B-x. Ib B. Nk hiCiCun B;
Sr çiçik- B.

?A/B   tutumaru (?= todomaru). 'be prolonged'. A (Zs) / B (Ck) - x-x-x x-x-x.

?B   tutumeku < *tutu-myeku < *tutuₘᵢₘ miCa-ka-ᵦₐₐ v. 'murmur, whisper'.
x - x-x-x x-x-x. Cf. tutuyaku.

B   tutumu < *tutuma- ?= *tutu -ma- < *tutwo -ma-. 'wrap; cover, enshroud'.
B - B-A-B x-B-B. Km (W) (A/)B. Edo B. Ib B. Nk hiCiimin B; Sr çiçim- B; Yn
Kumun B. ◫ tutumi 'package; restraining, repressing one's emotions'. B - B-2-B
x-B-x. Ōsaka, Kōbe 3. (Unger connects tutumu with tum- and tumor- but the
register is incongruent.) Note that Mg also has tutu-mono₄.₉ 'package'.

B   tutumu < *tutuma- (< ?). 'be hindered, blocked; be cautious or prudent (to
avoid harm); be afflicted/injured'. ◫ tutumi < tutumyi 'hindrance; affliction'.
B - x-x-x x-x-x. Cf. tutuga(-nai) = tutumi nasi 'is unafflicted or unharmed =
is healthy/safe'.

?A   tutusimu < *tutu(-)sima-. 'be careful, cautious, prudent, discreet'.
(A/)B - B-A-B x-A-x. NS (Okada) A. Hattō A; Matsue A/B; Hamada, Izumo B. Ib A.
K: Edo A. ◫ tutusimi x - A/B-A-B.

B   tutuyaku < *tutuₘᵢₘ -da-ka-. 'murmur, whisper' (= tutumeku). B - x-x-x
x-x-x. (Ōno: "From Edo also tuduyaku.")

-          tuwaku = tubaku/tuwaku.

A   tuwaru < tufaru < *tupara- (<?). 'bud; ripen; get morning-sickness (from
pregnancy)'. ◫ tuwari A - A-A-B̲ x-x-x.

B   tuzuiru < tudu-wiru < tudu-wi[y]- < *tuntu-₍ᵦ₎ bᵘ/₂-Ci-. '(a heavy thing)
be sunk to the bottom'. B - x-x-x x-x-x.

A   tuzukeru < tuduke- < tutukey- ?< tu[gyi] tukey- < *tunk[a-C]iₐ tuka-Ci-ᵦ.
'continue it'. (A) - A-A-A x-A-A. Ib A. Nk x; Sr çizikir- A (H 1967:397); Yn
cidikirun A. ◫ tuzuke x - A-x-x x-x-x.

A   tuzuku < tuduku < (Nr) tutuku ?< tu[gyi] tuk- < *tunk[a-C]iₐ tuka-ᵦ.
'continue, go on; be adjacent, adjoin'. A - A-A-A A-B̲-(A). Edo A. Ib A.
Nk Cizi(i)Cun A; Sr çiʒik- B (borrowed?). ◫ tuzuki (A̲) - A-A-A x-x-x.
NS (128b [14:360L-K]) ···LLL (? LLF). Goka-mura 1 (? truncation < 1:3 = A).
Nk Ciziiki A [new].

?A/B   tuzumaru < tudumaru ?< *tuntuma-ra- < *tum[a(···)]-tuma-ra-; ?< *tizimaru
(< ...). (vi.) 'shrink; be condensed'. B - B-A-A̲ x-x-x. Cf. tizimu.

?B   tuzumeru < tudume[y]- ?< *tuntuma-Ci- < *tum[a(···)]-ᵦ tuma-Ci-ᵦ.
contract, condense, shorten it'. B - A̲/B-A-A̲ x-x-x. Cf. tizimeru.

B   tuzuru < tuduru < *tuntura- ?< *tu[ra]-n-tura-. 'spell; compose, write;
bind'. B - A̲/B-A-B x-x-x. Mr (Bm) B. Wakamatsu A̲. Ib A̲. ◫ tuzuri x - A/B-2-B
x-x-x. Km (W) B. Cf. tuzura, tura₂.₂ₐ.

B   tuzusir-u < tudusir-u < *tuntusira- (< ?). 'mouth (a little at a time),
mumble'. B - x-A-x x-x-x.

B   tuzuu < tudufu < *tuntu-pa-. 'be stuck to (stagnate on) the bottom'.
B - x-x-x x-x-x. Cf. tuzuiru.

?A/B   tyakasu (< ?). 'mock at'. x - B-A-A x-x-x.

?B   ubau < ubafu ?< *unpapa-; ?< uti-farafu < *ut[a-C]i_B para-pa-_B'.
'seize by force, rob one of'. B (m[u]bafu) - B-A-A x-A-x. Ongi (m[u]bafu) B.
Hata A (Doi 1952:31). Kōchi A (Doi 1952:31); Ib A. Nk boorun B, Sr boor- B
restructured from *baw- < *[u]baf-; Sr [Lit.] qnbayun (neg. qnbaan) A < *ubaw-
< *ubaf-. Cf. bau.

?A   ubenamu < ubeynamu < *un(-)pa(-)Ci_{2.1} -na-ma- ?< *un(-)pa(-)Ci -na-pa-
(but NKD assumes the opposite). 'comply'. x - x-x-x x-x-x.

A   ubenau < [m]ubeynafu < *un(-)pa(-)Ci -na-pa-. 'agree, assent, comply'.
A - B-A-x x-x-x.

-         uderu: see yuderu.

A   ueru < uwe[y]- < *[z]uba-Ci-. 'plant; raise, grow'. A - A-A[U]/B[H]-A
A-A-A. NS (T+ 14) uwe-si HH-H. Km (W) A. Mg (Bm) A. Edo A. Ib A. Sd qwiiyum A;
Nk quirun B; Sr qwiir- A; Yn birun A. Hattori 1942:169 has Kt A. Hyōgo,
Toyama, Suzu, Kōchi A. Cf. uwaru; sueru, suwaru.

B   ueru < uwe[y]- < *uba-Ci-. 'hunger; starve, (mizu ni ~) thirst'. B -
B-B-A x-(B)-(B). NS (Okada) B. NS (T+ 12) [u]we-nu L-H; (104) [u]we te H(|)E.
Km (W) B. Mr (Bm) B. Ib (rare) A. Nk ugaarin B, Sr ugarir- B < *u[we] + ?.
|] ue x - 1/2-2-A x-(B)-(B). Mr (Bm) LH. Nk ugaarii B; Sr ugari B.

?B   ugatu < (Hn) u^k/_gatu < (Nr) ukatu < *uka-ta-. 'dig, bore; (= haku) wear'.
B - B-A-A x-x-x.

A   ugau < ugafu < *unkapa- (< ?). 'gargle'. A - x-x-x x-x-x.
|] ugai A - A-A-A x-x-x.

?B   [ugeru] < (Hn) u^k/_ge- < (Nr) ukey- < *uka-Ci-. 'get worn hollow/through;
get tattered; (scab) wear/come off'. x - x-x-x x-x-x. Cf. ugatu.

B   ugokasu, igokasu < *unk^u/_omim -ka-sa-. 'move it'. B - B-A-B x-x-x.
NS (110a) B. Km (S) B. Ib igokasu B. Nk qeekasun B.

B   ugoku, igoku < *unk^u/_omim -ka-. (vi.) 'move'. B - B-A-B x-(B)-(B).
NS (Okada) B. Km (S) B. Mr (Bm) B. Ib B. Nk qeecun B; Sr qnzuk- B = qwiik- B.
Cf. ugoku, ugomeku. |] ugoki x - B-A-B x-x-x.   Note: The igoku version is
probably just a variant of the mimetic, but it might reflect the prefix i- .
I am uncertain just what to make of the Ryūkyū forms that reflect *uyuk-
(Thorpe 308), such as Sr qwiik- B 'move, sway' and Yn uigun B. Miyako forms
with initial m- (Ikema muyuk-) may have metathesized the nasal of *unko and
assimilated it to the labial vowel. Or, they have perhaps incorporated mu(Ci)
'body' (> mi[y]_{1.1}); cf. Sr qnzuk- B 'fidget, move one's body', though that
might be from *igok- rather than *mi uyuk-, for which the register would be
incongruent.

?A/B   ugomeku < *ugo-myeku < *unk^u/_omim miCa-ka-_bnd v. 'wriggle, squirm'.
x - B-A-A x-x-x.

B   ugomoru = ugomotu ?< *unk^u/_o[ro]mim - mota-_B (or ?< *unk^u/_omim -ma-ra-/
-ma-ta- with vowel assimilations). '(earth) bulge up'. B - x-A-x x-x-x.
Cf. ugoromotu.

B   ugonawaru < ugonafaru < *unk^u/_omim -na-pa-ra-. 'crowd together'. x - x-x-x
x-x-x. NS (132b [14:420L-K]) B.

?A/B   ugotuku < *unk^u/_omim tuka-_B. 'wiggle, swarm'. x - x-x-x x-x-x.
Cf. ugutuku.

B   uguromotu ?< *unkᵘ/ₒ[ro]ₘₗₘ - mota-ᵦ (or ?< -ma-ta-, *the second vowel
assimilated to the preceding labial). '(earth) bulge up'. x - x-x-x x-x-x.
▯ uguromoti: *(1)* '(earth) bulging up' x - x-x-x x-x-x; *(2)* 'mole *(rodent)*'
B - x-x-x x-x-x (= mogura; variants ugura, ugoro, ugurᵃ/ₒmoti).

A   ugutuku < *unkᵘ/ₒₘₗₘ tuka-ᵦ. A - x-A-x x-x-x. 'gallop; talk fast'.
Km (S) B̲. Cf. ugotuku.

A   ukabaseru < ukabase[y]- < *uka-n[a]-pa-sa-Ci-. 'let it float, let it rise
to the surface'. x - A-A-A x-x-x. NS (101a) A.

A   ukaberu < ukaᵇ/ₘey- < *uka-n[a]-pa-Ci-. 'float it, let it float'. A -
A-A-A A-A[new?]-x. Km (S) A. Edo A. Ib A. Nk huKaabin A; Sr qukabir- A [new?].

A   ukabu < ukaᵇ/ₘu < *uka-n[a]-pa-. (vi.) 'float'. A - A-A-A A-A[new?]-x.
Km (S,W) A. Mr (Bm) A. Edo A. Ib A. Nk huKaabin A; Sr qukab- A [new?].

A   ukagau < ukagafu < (Nr) ukakafu ?< *uka-ₐ kapa-ₐ ('float [= furtive]
exchange'). 'peep through, spy, watch, infer; visit, inquire, hear'. A - A-A-A
x-A-x. NS (116b) A. Mr (Bm) A. Ib A. Nk huKaagan A; Sr qukagayun A (neg.
qukagaan or qukagaran). ▯ ukagai x - A-A[U]/4[H]-A x-x-x. Mr (Bm) HHHL.
Cf. uka-nerau, uka-mi.

A   ukareru < ukare[y]- < *uka-ra-Ci-. 'float, get afloat'. A - A-A-A x-x-x.
Edo A.

A   ukasu < *uka-sa-. 'float it, let it float'. (?A) - A-A-A x-x-x.

?B   ukatu: *see* ugatu. Cf. ukeru.

A   ukeru < ukey- < *uka-Ci-. 'float it, let it float' (= ukaberu, ukasu).
(A) - A-A-x x-A-x. ▯ uke 'fishing float' (= uki). A - x-x-x x-A-x. Ib A.
Nk huKii A; Sr quki A < *uke.

?B   ukeru < ukey- < *uka-Ci-. '(a hole) open up, be bored'. x - x-x-x x-x-x.
Cf. ukatu; [ugeru], ugatu.

B   ukeru < ukey- < *uka-Ci-. 'receive'. B - B-B-B B-B-x. NS (91b, 103b) B.
Km (S) B. Mr (Bm) B. Edo B. Ib B. Nk huKirun B; Sr qukir- B. ▯ uke x - B-2-B
x-x-x. Cf. uga < uka.

B+B   uketamawaru < uke-tamafaru < ukey tamafaru < *uka-Ci[-Ci]ᵦ tanpa-pa-ra-ᵦ.
'humbly receive/listen/hear'. B+B [Ir] - A/B-B-B x-x-x.

B   ukeu < ukeyfu < *uka-Ciᵦ-pa- (or *uka-Ci[-Ci]ᵦ [i]pa-ₐ). 'pray (for
prognostication), consult the gods to resolve a dispute/rivalry; fulfill (or
look for fulfillment of) a prognostication'. x - B-x-x x-x-x.

A   uku < *uka-. 'float'. (A) - A-A-A x-A-x. NS (94b [11:44-K, 11:47-K],
101b [11:135-K]) A. Km (W) A. Edo A. Narada A. Nk huCun A; Sr quk- A.
▯ uki x - A-A-A x-x-. (Sr quki A < *uke.)

A   umareru < umare[y]- < *uma-ra-Ci-. 'get born'. A - A-A-A x-A-A. Ib A.
Nk qmaarin A; Sr qnmarir- A; Yn maarun A. ▯ umare A-2-A x-A-x.

A   umaru < *uma-ra-. 'get buried; get filled up'. x - A-B̲-A x-x-x.
Cf. uzumaru, umoreru.

A   [umau] < umafu < *uma-pa-. 'give birth repeatedly'. x - x-x-x x-x-x.
Cf. ubu.

A   umawaru < umafaru < *uma-pa-ra-. 'proliferate'. x - x-x-x x-x-x.
NS (130b "m̄umafar-") A.

-        umeku = wameku.

A   umeru < umey- < *uma-Ci-. 'bury; fill up, plug (a gap)'. A - A-B̲-A x-A-x.
Edo A. Ib A. Nk qubeerun A, Sr qnbeer- 'pour cold water in (in order to lower
the temperature of hot water)'.

A   umoreru < umore[y]- < *umora-Ci- ?< *uma-ra-Ci- *(the second vowel
assimilated to the preceding labial)*. 'get buried'. x - A-B̲-A x-x-x. Ib A.
Cf. uzumoreru, umoregi.

A   umu < *uma- (?< *ma-, cf. musu). 'give birth to'. A - A-A-A x-x-x.
NS (97a) A. Edo A. Kun[i]naka (Yamanashi), Chiba, Akita, Sapporo B̲. Ib B̲.
Replaced by nasu in many dialects (including Sr, and earlier Chiba).
〗 umi x - A-A-A x-x-x. NS (128b) ūmi-no-ko and (133a, 133b) ūmi-no k̄o are
lexicalized. Cf. ubu.

A   umu < *uma-. 'bury' (= umeru). A - x-x-x x-x-x.

B   umu < *uma-. 'spin yarn' (= tumugu). B - B-B-x x-x-x. NS (97a [11:77L-K])
B. Km x. Nk qumin B.

B   umu < *uma-. 'fester; get ripe'. B - B-B-B B-B-x. Mg, Hoke-kyō tanji umi-
ª/ziru LLLH. Ib B. Sd qumuyun B 'ripen'; Nk qumin B; Sr qnnun B (neg. qnman)
< *um-. Cf. ureru. 〗 umi (B) - B-2-B B-B-x. Nk qumii B; Sr qnmi B.

B   umu < *uma- < *uadj B -ma-. 'get bored, weary'. B - B-B-B x-x-x.

B   unadareru < unadare[y]- < *una?2.3,?2.4 -n- tara-Ci-B̲. 'hang one's head'.
x - A/B-A-x x-x-x. Edo A. Ib B.

?B   unagasu < *una?2.3 -n[a]-ka-sa-. 'bend the neck; urge, press'.
B - A̲/B-A-B x-x-x. NS (Okada) B. NS (T+ 2) unagaseru LLHHL ?= LLHHL.

?B   unagu < *una2.3 -n[a]-ka-. 'hang around one's neck'. x - x-x-x x-x-x.
Cf. unazi.

B   unaru < *uɐⁱɐ na(-)ra-A. 'groan'. x - B-A-B x-x-x. Cf. utaku.
〗 unari x - B-A-B x-x-x.

?B   unazuku < unaduku < *una2.3 -n- tuka-A. 'nod, bow head'. ?B - A̲/B-A-B
x-x-x. Ib B.

B   uner-u ?< *una-Ci-ra-. 'meander, wind, undulate'. x - B-A-B x-x-x.
〗 uneri x - B-A-B x-x-x.

?A/B   urabureru < urabure[y]- < *ura?2.4 -n- pura-Ci-?B. 'lose support/power;
droop in despair'. x - A/B-A-x x-x-x.

B   [uraeru] < urawe- < urafey- < *ura2.4 -pa-Ci-. 'divinate, foretell'.
x - x-x-x x-x-x. ("From Edo also urabe-.")

?B   uragasu < *ura?2.4 -n[a]-ka-sa-. 'delight'. x - x-x-x x-x-x.

?B   urageru < *urage- < *ura?2.4 -n[a]-ka-Ci-. 'be elated, delighted'.
x - x-x-x x-x-x. Cf. uresi-adj B.

B   uragir-u < uragyir-u < *ura2.3 -n- kira-B. 'betray'. x - B-A-B x-x-x.
Ir B. 〗 uragiri x - 3/4/0-A-B x-x-x.

B   uramu < uramiy-/(?)uram- < *ura?2.4 -mª/o-Ci- *(the third vowel
assimilated to the labial nasal)* < *ura -ma-(Ci-), from which the modern
conjugation could be directly derived (cf. uramesiadj B), bypassing the Nara
form; but perhaps < *ura?2.4 mo-Ci-?A ('heart turn'), or < *urab/ɱiy- <
*ura2.4 -npª/oCi-. 'resent; regret'. B - B-A-B x-B-x. Edo (urami-) B. Ib B.
Nk quraamin B; Sr quram- B. 〗 urami x - B-A[H]/2[U]-B x-B-x. Km (S) B. Edo
HHL. Sapporo A̲. Kōchi 1:3. Nk qurami B; Sr quraamii B.

B   uranau < uranafu < *ura2.4 -na-pa-. 'divine, foretell'. B - B-A-B x-x-x.
Ib B.〗 uranai x - 3-A-B x-B-x.

B   urayamu < *ura?2.4 dama-?B. 'envy'. B - B-A-B x-x-x. Ib B.

B   ureeru < urefey- < *urafey- *(the second vowel assimilated to the third
and partially to the first)* < *ura?2.4 [a]pa-Ci-B (or *ura?2.4 -pa-Ci-). 'grieve
for; be troubled or anxious about'. B - B-A[H]/B[U]-B x-(B)-x. Ongi B. Edo
(A/)B. Ib B. 〗 uree (> "urei") B - A̲[H]/2-A[H]/1[U]-B x-B-x. Nk x; Sr qurii B.

A   ureru < ure[y]- < *ura-Ci-. 'get sold, find a ready market'. (A) - A-A-A
x-A-x. Nk quriirun B; Sr qurir- A.

?B   ureru < ure[y]- < *ura-Ci-. 'ripen, get ripe'. x - B-B-A x-x-x. Ib A̲.

A   uru < *ura-. 'sell'. A - A-A-A A-A-A. Nk qun A; Sr qur- A. 〗 uri x -
A-A-A x-x-x. Ib A.

?B   [urueru] < urufey- < *uru-pa-Ci-. 'make it wet'. B - B-A-x x-x-x.

?B   urumu < *uru-ma-. 'get wet, moist'. B - B-A-A̲ x-x-x. Ib B.

?B   uruosu < *urufosu *(the third vowel partially assimilated to the first two vowels and/or to the preceding labial)* < *urufasu < *uru-pa-sa-. 'moisten/wet it; profit/enrich one'. B - B-A-A̲ x-x-x.

?B   uruou < urufofu *(the third vowel partially assimilated to the first two vowels and/or to the preceding labial)* < ?*urufafu < *uru-pa-pa- (or < *uru-p[a-Ci] opa-). 'get damp, moist; receive benefits/profit, get enriched (by)'. B - B-A-A̲ x-x-x. Mr (Bm) B. Ib B. [] uruoi B - 3/0-A-A x-B-x. Km (S) B.

?   [urutaeru] < urutafe[y]- < *uru(-)tapa-Ci- ?< *ura₇₈.₄ - tapa-Ci-ₐ (cf. ureeru). 'sue; appeal; complain of' (> uttaeru). x - x-x-x x-x-x.

?B   uruu < urufu < *uru-pa-. 'get wet' (= uruou). B - B-A-x x-x-x. Cf. uruwasi*adj B*.

?A   useru < use[y]- < *usa-Ci- (?< *zusa-Ci-). 'vanish'. A - A/B̲-B̲-A x-x-x. NS (126b; also 124b, 131b mi̅ - 'die'). NS (T+ 83) usezu HHH. Edo A. Ib A. The Tōkyō "A/" is from NKD, Mkz. Cf. usinau, suteru, [uteru]; but also aseru < *asa-Ci- 'fade' : *usu-Ci- 'vanish' and asa*adj A* 'shallow' : usu*adj A* 'thin').

?A   usinau < usinafu < *usi-napa- ?< *us[a-C]i -na-pa- (with the infinitive-derived noun *usi < *usa- ?< *zusa-). 'lose'. ?A - A-A-A x-A-x. NS (107a) A. Km (S) A. Ib A. Nk husiinan A; Sr qusinayun A (neg. usinaan) < *usinaw- < *usinaf-. Cf. useru. (Alternatively, ?< *usa-napa- with partial assimilation of the second vowel to the first.)

B   uso^b/ₑuku < *uso₂.₅ muka-ₐ (?< *npuka-). 'whistle, howl, brag'. B - B-A-B x-x-x. Ōno's ambiguous "so" represents the unknown value of the vowel, not /swo/; there is no phonogram evidence. (An alternative etymology: < *uso₂.₅ puka-ₑ 'falsehood blow', with the nasal version unaccounted for.)

B   usomu (?truncation < usomuku; ?< *uso₂.₅ -ma-). 'whistle, howl, brag' (= usobuku). B - x-x-x x-x-x.

-         *usu- < *usa- (?< *zusa-). 'lose' (= usinau): *see* useru; suteru, [uteru].

A   usuragu < *usu*adj A* -ra-n[a]-ka-. 'get thin or pale; abate'. A - A/B̲-A-A x-x-x. Hattō, Hamada, Matsue, Izumo A.

A   usureru < usure[y]- < *usu*adj A* -ra-Ci-. 'get thin or pale; abate'. x - A/B̲-A-A x-x-x. Ib B.

A   utagau < utagafu < *uto/utu₇₈.₁ n[i] kapa-ₐ ('buy it as hollow', cf. utuo₉.₁). 'doubt; suspect; distrust'. A - A/B̲-A-A x-A-A. NS (92b, 112b) A. Km (S) A. Ib A. Nk huTaagan A = huTaage(eru)n A; Sr qutagar- A. [] utagai A - A-A-A x-A-x. Goka-mura 1.

?A   utaku < *u*ᵗⁱˢ* taka-ₐ *"boil"*. 'roar (in anger)'. x - x-A-x x-x-x. Cf. unaru. [] utaki x - x-A-x x-x-x. NS (76c [14:135-M]) A. NS (T+ 76) utakyi HLH (? mistake for HHH).

A   utau < utafu < *uta₂.₂b -pa-. 'sing'. A - A-A-A A-A-(A). Edo A. NS (T+ 33) utafyi tutu LL|HH = LLH(|)HH. Nk huTaarun A = huTen A; Sr qutayun A (neg. qutaan) < *utaw- < *utaf-. [] utai x - A-A-A x-x-x.

?A   [uteru] < ute[y]- < *uta-Ci- (?< *zuta-Ci-). 'discard, throw away, abandon' (= suteru). ?B - x-B̲-x x-x-x. Cf. useru.

B   uteru < ute[y]- < *uta-Ci-. 'be struck down'. (B) - B-B-B x-x-x. Edo B. Attested 13th century.

?A   [utobiru] < uto^b/ₑi- < utwobiy- < *utwo*adj A* -np*ⁿ*/ₒCi- (?< -n[a]-pa-Ci-). 'be aloof'. x - x-x-x x-x-x.

?A   uto^b/ₑeru < utwobey- < *utwo*adj A* -n[a]-pa-Ci-. 'make one shun/neglect, alienate'. x - x-x-x x-x-x.

?A   uto^b/ᴇu < *utwobu < *utwo*adj A* -n[a]-pa-. 'shun, neglect'. x - B̲-A-x
x-x-x. Km (W) ?A/B.

?A/B   uttaeru < ur[u]-tafey- < *uru(-)tapa-Ci-. 'sue; appeal; complain of'.
B - A/B-A-B x-A-x. Nk quqTeerun A; Sr qutteerun A. ◊ uttae B - A-4-B x-A-x.
Nk quqTee A; Sr quttai A is odd. Zs Mg has "u." with the entering tone (lower-
right dot) and that is to be taken as /ut-(t···)/.

B   utu < *uta- (?< *buta-). 'hit; ... '. B - B-B-B B-B-B.
NS (73a [11:218-M, 11:219-M], 73b [11:221-M], 95a [14:65-K], 120b [14:183- K],
123b [14:240-K], 127a [14:302-K]) B. NS (T+) uti kyitamasu mo (112) HH̲
LLLL(|)H, uti watasu (57) LL(|)F̲LL; uti te ((8, 9, 14) LHF̲ ?= LH(|)H, (13)
LLF̲ ?= LL(|)H; uti-si (57) LH-L. Km (W) B. Edo B. Ib B. Nk huCun B; Sr qut- B.

?B   utubuseru < utubuse[y]- < *utu*2.1* n[i] pu(-)sa-Ci-*в*. 'lay it face/top side
down'; (= utubusu) 'lie prone (face down)'. B - A̲/B-A-B x-x-x.

?B   utubusu < *utu*?2.1* n[i] pu(-)sa-. 'lie prone (face down)'. B - A̲/B-A-B
x-x-x. ◊ utubusi x - A̲-A-B x-x-x.

?A   utukeru < utuke- (JP) < utukey- < *utu*?2.x* -ka-Ci-. 'get empty'. x - A-x-x
x-x-x.

-       utukarabu: *see* uturakau.

B   [utukusibiru] < utukusibiy- < *utuku-si*adj в* -np^u/ǫCi- (?< -n[a]-pa-Ci-).
'show love/affection for, cherish'. B - B-A-x x-x-x. NS (91a) B. Cf. itukusimu.
◊ utukusibi B - A̲-A-x x-x-x.

?B   utumukeru < utumuke[y]- < *utu*2.x* muka-Ci-*A*. 'face it down, ... '. x -
A̲/B[K]-A-B x-B-x. Sr quçginkir- B (*see* utumuku). ◊ utumuke x - A̲-A-B x-x-x.

?B   utumuku < *utu*?2.x* muka-. 'face down; (= utumukeru) face it down'.
x - A̲/B-A-B x-A̲-x. NE Kyūshū B. Nk huqCi-nCun B (LLH-LLL). The accent of
Sr quçgincun (quçgink-) A̲ is a puzzle; Sr quçgi B is the gerund (< *uti-te)
of 'hit'. ◊ utumuki x - A̲-A-B x-x-x.

B   uturakau < "uturakafu" = uturaka[¨]fu (Maeda NS) *metathesis* ← utukarabu
< *uti-karabu < *ut[a-C]i*в* kara-n[a]-pa-*B* (= kara-ma-Ci-*в* > karameru
'entwine'). 'clasp hands'. x - x-x-x x-x-x. NS (115b [14:83L-K]) B.

B   uturou < uturo̲fu (*the third vowel partially assimilated to the first two*)
< *uturafu < *utu-ra-pa-. 'change, shift'. ?B - B-A-x x-x-x. Km (W) B.

B   uturu < *utu-ra-. (vi.) 'move, change; be reflected; match; (picture) get
taken'. B - B-A-B x-B-x. NS (T+ kun) fukyi uturu LL LLH. Edo B. Ib B. Nk
huCirun B; Sr quçir- B. ◊ uturi x - B-A-B x-B-x. Nk x; Sr quçiri B (*retained
-r- is odd*). OJ yuturu is probably < *i-uturu with prefix i-; cf. yuku, yokosu.

B   utusu < *utu-sa-. 'move/transfer/divert it; reflect it, copy/photograph
it'. B - B-A-B x-B-x. Km (S,W) B. Edo B. Ib B. Nk huCisun B; Sr quçus- B,
perhaps assimilated from the expected *-çi-.

?A   [ututeru] < utute[y]- < *ut[i]-uta-Ci- < *ut[a-Ci]*?A* uta-Ci-*?A* (?<
*zuta-Ci zuta-Ci-). 'discard'. x - x-x-x x-x-x.

A   uwaru < *[z]uba-ra-. 'get planted'. A - A-A[U]/B[H]-A x-(A)-x.
Sr qwaa(ri)r- A 'get an erection'. Cf. suwaru, sueru; ueru.

A   uyamau < uya-/wiya-mafu < *wiy-[y]a*?2.2x,?2.1* -mafu < *b^u/ǫ-Ci a(-) -ma-
pa-. 'respect, honor, esteem'. A - B-A-A x-A-x. Hattō, Matsue, Izumo A; Hamada
B. Nk quyaaman A = quyaame(eru)n A; Sr quyamayun A (neg. quyamaan/quyamaran) <
*uyamaw-/*uyamar- < *uyamaf-. ◊ uyamai x - A-A-A x-x-x.

B   uzuku < uduku < *untuka- (< ?). 'ache, smart, tingle'. x - B-A-B x-(x)-x.
◊ uzuki x - B-x-x x-x-x. K: Hn HHL (*where attested?*).

B   uzukumaru < ?*unsu - kuma-ra- (no Hn evidence for *udu). 'squat, crouch'.
B - A̲[U]/B-A-A̲ x-x-x. Ib B. Cf. kugumu; uzui.

B   uzumaku < udumaku < *untu*₂.₃,₂.₄* maka-*ₐ*. 'whirl'. x - B-A-B x-x-x.
◌ uzumaki x - 2-2-B x-x-x.

?A   uzumaru < udumaru < *untuma-ra-. 'get buried; get filled up'. A - A-B̲-A
x-B̲-x. Ib B̲. Nk quzuuman A; Sr quʒumur- B (assimilation from expected *-ʒi-) <
*udumor- (?< *udumar-).

?A   uzumeru < udumey- < *untuma-Ci-. 'bury; fill up'. A - A-B̲-A x-x-x.
Ongi-m A. Ib B̲. Nk quzuumin A.

?A   uzumoreru < udumore[y]- *(the third vowel assimilated to the first two*
vowels and/or the preceding labial) < *untuma-ra-Ci-. 'get buried'. x - A-B̲-A
x-A-x. Ib A. Sr quʒumurir- A (assimilation from expected *-ʒi-) < *udumore-
(?< *udumare-).

A   [uzumu] < udumu < *untuma- (?< *um[a]-*₂ₐ* tuma-*ₐ*). 'bury' (= uzumeru).
A - x-x-x x-A-x. Edo A. Sr quʒum- A < *uʒim- < *udum-. There is a late
example in 1218 Uji-shūi-monogatari (KggD 973b), and a much later one in
Heike-mabushi (Okumura 1981:271).

?   uzunau < udunafu < *untu*₂.ₓ* -na-pa-. 'value, prize'. x - x-x-x x-x-x.

?   uzunou < udunofu *(the third vowel partially assimilated to the first two)*
< udunafu < *untu*₂.ₓ* -na-pa-. 'value, prize'. x - x-x-x x-x-x.

B   uzuwaku < uduwaku < *untu (w)aku < *untu*₂.₃* [m]aka-*ₐ*. 'whirl, swirl' (=
uzumaku). B - x-A-x x-x-x.

A   wabiru < wabiy- < ?*banpu-Ci- (cf. waburreru); < ?*ba-np\ᵘ/₂Ci- (cf.
wazurau). 'be embarrassed or disappointed; apologize for; feel lonely/bereft'.
A - A-B̲-A x-x-x. Km (W) A. Hattō, Izumo B̲; Hamada, Matsue, Goka-mura A. Ib B̲.
◌ wabi x - A-A[U]/B[H]-A x-x-x.

A   [wabureru] < wabure[y]- ?< *banpu-ra-Ci- (cf. wabiru); ?< *ba-n[a]-pura-
Ci- (cf. wazurau). 'be disappointed/discouraged' (NKD "= wabiiru"). x - x-x-x
x-x-x.

?A/B   wadakamaru ?< *banta*₂.₃* (< ...) ka[nka]ma-ra-*ₐ* (< ...). 'be coiled up;
lurk (in one's mind)'. B - A/B-A-A x-x-x. ◌ wadakamari x - A-A-A x-x-x.

?A/B   waganeru < wagane[y]- < *banka-na-Ci-. 'bend (into a circle/ring)'.
A - B-A-x x-x-x.

?A   wageru < wage[y]- < *banka-Ci- (variant < *manka-Ci-, *see* mageru). 'bend
(into a circle/ring)'. A - A-A-x x-x-x. If the noun wa*₁.₃ₐ* is a direct part of
the etymology, the register should be B. ◌ wage 'topknot'. x - A-x-x x-x-x.
Not attested before Edo (cf. mage).

B   wakaeru < wakaye[y]- < *baka*ₐдⱼ ʙ* -da-Ci-. 'become young (rejuvenated)'.
x - x-x-x x-x-x. Km (W) B.

B   wakagaer-u < *wakagafyer- < *baka*ₐдⱼ ʙ* n[i] kapi-ra-*ʙ*. 'get rejuvenated'.
x - B-B-B x-B-x. Nk wahaageerun B; Sr wakageer- B. (Not attested before Edo.
Cf. wakaeru.) ◌ wakagaeri x - A-B-B x-x-x.

B   wakareru < wakare[y]- < *baka-ra-Ci-. 'get divided/separate, diverge'.
B - B-A-B x-B-x. NS (118b, 126b, 132a) B. Km (W) B. Ib B. Nk wa\ᵏ/ₕaarin B,
wakkin B; Sr wakarir- B.

B   wakaru < *baka-ra-. 'be clear(ly understood); (come to) understand, know,
realize, appreciate'. (B) - B-A-B x-B-x. Ib B. Nk wahaarun B; Sr wakar- B.
◌ wakari x - B-A-B x-x-x.

A   wakasu < *baka-sa-. 'boil/melt it'. A - A-A-A x-A[new?]-A. Ib A. Nk
wakaasun A; Sr wakas- A [new?]; Yn bagan A.

B   [wakasu] < *baka-sa-. (vt.) 'divide, separate, share' (= wakatu). x -
x-x-x x-B-x. Nk wa\ᵏ/ₕaasun B; Sr wakas- B; Yn bagan B. (Cf. hanasu = hanatu.)

B   wakatu < *baka-ta-. (vt.) 'divide, separate, share'. B - B-A-B x-x-x.
Km (S) B. Mr (Bm) B. Edo B. Ib B.

A   wakaturu < *bakatura- (< ?). 'deceive'. A - x-x-x x-x-x. Cf. okoturu.
[] wakaturi (Kn Mg wagaturi) A - x-A-x x-x-x.

B   wakayagu < *baka*adj B* -da-n[a]-ka-. 'feel (more) youthful, feel renewed
(rejuvenated)'. x - B-A-B x-x-x.

B   wakeru < wakey- < *baka-Ci-. (vt.) 'divide; split up; distinguish;
distribute'. (B) - B-B-B x-B-x. Edo B. Ib B. Nk waKiirun B; Sr wakir- B.
[] wake x - 1/2-1:3-B x-B-x. Nk wakii B; Sr waki B.

B   wakibasamu < wakyibasamu < *baki*ɛ.ɜ* n[i] pasa-ma-*B*. 'hold/clutch under
one's arm'. B - B-A-x x-x-x.

B   wakimaeru < wakimafe- < *wakyimafey- < *bak[a-C]i*B* mapa-Ci-*A*. 'discern,
discriminate, understand'. B - B-A-B x-x-x. [] wakimae x - 3-A/4-B x-x-x.

A   waku < *baka-. (vi.) 'boil, seethe; gush, well up'. A - A-A-A x-A-x. Ib A.
Nk waCun A; Sr wak- A. [] waki x - A-A-A x-x-x.

B   waku < *baka-. 'divide it' (= wakeru, wakatu). B - x-B-x x-B-x. Km (W) B.
Edo B. Nk waCun B; Sr wak- B. Cf. aki, akinau, agau; sabaku; Sr waciee < *waki-
afi 'meaning'. (Register incongruent with waru.)

B   wameku < *wa-myeku < *ba*ᵐⁱᵃ* miCa-ka-*bᵃᵈ v*. 'cry, scream, shriek'.
x - B-A-B x-x-x. Hamada A̲. Ib B.

B   wanaku < *bana*ɛ.ɟ* -ka-. 'tie (around) the neck, strangle'.
x - x-x-x x-x-x. NS (109a, 116b) B.

A   wananaku < *bananaka- < *bana-[b]ana*ᵐⁱᵃ* -ka-. 'shudder, quiver' (=
ononoku). A - B̲-A-A x-x-x. Km (S) A. [] wananaki x - 3/4-A-B x-x-x.

A   warau < warafu < *bara-pa- ('keep splitting'). 'laugh'. A - A-A-A A-A-A.
Edo A. Ib A. Nk waren A; Sr warayun A (neg. waraan) < *waraw- < *waraf-;
Yn barun A. [] warai x - A-A-A x-x-x. Cf. emu.

A   wareru < ware[y]- < *bara-Ci-. (vi.) 'split (be broken) in two'.
(A) - A-A-A x-A-x. Km (W) A. Ib A. Nk wariirun A. [] ware x - A-A-A x-A-x.
Nk warii A; Sr wari A.

A   waru < *bara-. (vt.) 'split, break, halve'. A - A-A-A x-A-A. Edo A. Ib A.
[] wari x - A-A-A x-x-x. (Register incongruent with waku.)

B   wasir-u < *basi-ra-. 'run, rush ahead'. B - x-x-x x-x-x.
NS (77b [14:155-M]) B. Cf. hasir-u.

B   [wasiseru] < wasise[y]- < *basi-sa-Ci-. 'make/let run'. x - x-x-x x-x-x.
NS (T+ 69) wasise*ᵢₙf* FH = LLH.

A   wasureru < wasure[y]- < *basura-Ci- (?< *basi-ra-Ci-). 'forget'. A - A-A-A
A-A-A. NS (T+ 14) wasurezu HFHH = HHHH. Km (S,W) A. Edo A. Ib A. Nk waqsin A;
Sr waşir- A; Yn bacirun A — or are these from wasur-? There are Miyako forms
with -ki- (?< *basi[-ra]-ki-); see Thorpe 289 and cf. mazir-u and mazeru.

A   [wasuru] < *basura- (?< *basira-). 'forget' (= wasureru). A - x-x-x x-x-x.
?NS (Okada) A. NS (T+ 5) wasurazi FHHH = HHHH, (119) wasurayu masizi LLLH LHH.

A   [watarasu] < *bata-ra-sa-. 'deign to cross over; ... '. x - x-x-x x-x-x.
NS (T+ 2) FLLL ?= LLLL.

A   watarau < watarafu < *bata-ra-pa-. 'cross over; maintain oneself, make a
living'. A - x-x-x x-x-x. NS (108a) A. Km x.

A   wataru < *bata-ra-. 'cross (over); span; get transferred, get imported'.
A - A-A-A x-A-A. NS (Okada) A. NS (T+ 106) wataramu to LLLH(|)L; (28) watari
FLH ?= LLH; (119) wataru to̲-mo LLL(|)L(|)H. Km (S,W) A. Mr (Bm) A. Edo A.
Ib A. Nk wataarun A; Sr watar- A. [] watari A - A-A-x x-B̲-x. NS (70a[11:45-M],
11:48-M], 87b, 94b) A. Nk x; Sr watai B̲.

A   watasu < *bata-sa-. 'pass/take over; hand over, transfer, give; build
over/across'. A - A-A-A A-A-x. NS (73a [11:219-M], 102a) A. NS (T+ 3) watasi
ℓLH ?= LLH; (57) uti watasu LL ℓLL = LL LLL. Km (S) A. Edo A. Ib A.
Nk wataasun A; Sr watas- A. ⬚ watasi x - A-A-A x-x-x.

-        (-)wau < (-)fafu < *(-)papa- (?= *-pa-pa-; ?< 'creep'). Bound verb: *see*
aziwau, *nariwau, nigiwau, sakiwau, tiwau.

A   wazurau < wadurafu < *banturapa- ?= *ba-n[a]-tura-pa- (cf. wabiru,
wabureru). 'worry; have trouble with (an ailment)'. A - A/B-A-A x-A-x. Hattō,
Hamada, Matsue, Izumo A. Nk wacaaren A; Sr waCarayun A (neg. wacaraan) <
*wacaraw- (?< *waçiraw- < *waturaf-). ⬚ wazurai A - A-A-A x-A-x. Goka-mura 1.
Nk waCaaree A; Sr wacaree A < wacarai (?< *waçirawi < *waturafi).

A   wazurawasu < wadurafasu < *banturapa-sa- ?= *ba-n[a]-tura-pa-sa-. 'vex,
trouble, bother'. x - A/B-A-A x-x-x. Hattō, Hamada B; Izumo A/B; Matsue A.

?B´   yabureru < yabure[y]- < *da(-)npu(-)ra-Ci-. 'get torn/burst, be worn out/
through'. B - B-B-B x-B-x. NS (134a) B. Edo B. Ib B. Nk yanbin (yanbir-) B,
Sr yandir- B < *yabure- = Nk yarirun B, Sr yarir- B < *yare-. ⬚ yabure x -
B-1:3-B x-(B)-x. Ōsaka, Kōbe 1:3/3. Nk yanbii B, Sr yandi/yaburi B = Nk yarii
B, Sr yari B < *yare.

?B´   yaburu < *da(-)npu-ra-. (vt.) 'tear, rip, break; thwart'. B - B-B-B x-B-B.
Edo B. Ib B. Nk yanbin (yamb-) B = yan (yar-) B; Sr yanzun (yand-) B < *yabur-
'break' (V-i yanzun 'unsuccessfully V' = yayun ← yar-) B; Yn danburan B.

B   yabusagaru < yafusagaru < *yafyisagaru < *dapisa*adj (B)* -n[a]-ka-ra-.
'be stingy'. B - x-x-x x-x-x.

B   yadoru < *da*1.3b* -n- t(w)ora-*B*. 'lodge, take shelter'. B - B-A-A x-B-x.
Edo B. Ib B. ⬚ yadori (B) - A-A-x x-x-x. Km (W) B. Edo HHL. A different
etymology, *dato-ra- from *da -n- to > *yado 'house place' (≠ yadwo 'house
door'), is offered by Matsumoto 1976:78, who argues that the transitive form
yados- (< *dato-sa) is hard to explain from the other etymology.

A   yakeru < yakey- < *daka-Ci-. 'get burned/roasted'. A - A-A-A x-A-A. Edo A.
Ib A. Nk yaKiirun A; Sr yakir- A. ⬚ yake x - A/2[H,NKD]-A[U]/1:3[H]-B x-x-x.

A   yaku < *daka-. 'burn/roast it'. A - A-A-A x-?A-A. NS (Okada) A. Km (S,W)
A. NS (T+ 41) yakyi LH, (107) yaku HL. Mr (Bm) ?B. Edo A. Ib A. Nk yaCun A; Sr
"B" may be a misprint (cf. H 1967:468 "A", yakeru). ⬚ yaki x - A-A-A x-x-x.

B+B   [yama-husu] < yama-fusu ?< dama*?B* pusa-*B*, ?< yama[fyi] fusu < *dama-p[a-
C]i*?B* pusa-*B*; ?< yami-fusu *(the second vowel assimilated to the first)* < *yamyi
fusu < *dam[a-C]i pusa-. 'lie ill'. LH|LH - x-x-x x-x-x.

?B   yamau < yamafu < *dama-pa-. 'keep being ill'. (B) - x-x-x x-x-x.
⬚ yamai LHL - 1-1:3-B x-B-(B). NS (103a) LLL, (133a) LHL. Km x. Mr (Bm) LHH|H.
Edo LHL. K: Hn-Km-Mr LHL. Sapporo, Akita, Matsue, Izumo 2; Numazu, Narada, Hida
(= northern Gifu), Hattō, Hamada, Goka-mura, Hiroshima, Ōita, Wakamatsu 1.
Nk, Sr yanmee B. Because the verb is not attested early it is sometimes assumed
to be a back formation, but the noun is most easily explained as derived from
the verb infinitive. Cf. yamu.

A   yameru < yamey- < *dama-Ci-. 'stop/quit it'. (A) - A-A-A x-A-A. NS (98b,
110a) A. NS (T+ 72) yameymu HLL. Km (S) A. Ib A. Nk yamiirun A; Sr yamir- A.
⬚ yame x - A-A-A x-x-x.

?A   yamou < yamofu (= yamau). 'be ill'. A (ȳamoferu ⋯ 'ill') - x-x-x x-x-x.

A   yamu < *dama-. (vi.) 'stop, cease'. A - A-A-A x-A-x. NS (T+ 8, 9, 13, 14)
yamamu HHH. Km (S,W) A. Mr (Bm) A. Edo A. Sapporo, Akita B. Ib A. Nk yamin A;
Sr yam- A.

?B   yamu ‹ *dama-. ‘ail; fall ill’. B - B-A̲[H]/B[U]-A̲ x-B-B. Ib B. Nk yamin B;
Sr yam- B; Yn damun B. Cf. yami₂.₃ ‘darkness’; yamai, yamau.

A   yarau ‹ yarafu ‹ *dara-pa- (‘keep sending’). ‘dispel, chase away;
dispatch, eat/drink up’. A (= HHL) - x-A-x x-x-x.

B   [yareru] ‹ ya[bu]reru ‹ *danpura-Ci-. ‘get torn/burst, be worn out’.
x - x-x-x x-B-x. Ib B. Nk yarirun B; Sr yarir- B. ◊ yare (= yabure) x - B-
A[H]/2[U]-B x-B-x. NS (91) yaremu LLH. Nk yarii B; Sr yari B. Cf. yarema.

A   yaru ‹ *dara-. ‘send; give; do’. A - A-A-A x-(A)-x. NS (114a, 121a [14:
190-K] A. Km (S,W) A. Mr (Bm) A. Edo A. Ib A. Sr yaras- A. Cf. yari₂.₁ ‘spear’.

A   [yaru] ‹ ya[bu]ru ‹ *danpura-. ‘tear, rip, break’. x - x-x-x x-B-(B).
Nk yan (yar-) B; Sr yayun (yar-) B; Yn dan-dan B.

A   yaseru ‹ yase[y]- ?‹ *dasa-Ci-. ?‹ i-ₚᵣₑ ase[y]-₍A/B ((‹ asa_adj A -Ci-).
‘get thin, lose weight’. A - A-A-A (B̲?)-A-x. Ongi A. Ib A. Sd yee(r)yum B;
Nk (x); Sr yaşir- A. Cf. yatureru. ◊ yase x - A-A-A x-x-x.

A   yasinau ‹ yasinafu ‹ *yasi-na-pa- (?‹ *das[a-C]i -na-pa-, assuming a verb
*yasu- ‹ *dasa- with infinitive-derived noun; or *yasu-···, with palatalization
of the second syllable in assimilation to the palatal initial of the first).
‘nurture, bring up, foster’. A - A/B-A-A x-A-x. NS (70c [11:158-M], 71a
[11:160-M]) A. NS (T+ 44, 45) yasinafamu LHLHH (odd). Ib A. Nk yasiinan A,
yasiinen A; Sr yasinayun A (neg. yasinaan/yasinaran) ‹ yasinaw-/yasinar- ‹
*yasinaf-. ◊ yasinai x - A-A-A x-(A)-x.

B   yasumaru ‹ *dasu_adj B -ma-ra-. ‘be rested, at ease; feel relieved’.
x - B-A-B x-B-x. Nk yasimarin B; Sr yaşimar- B.

B   yasumeru ‹ yasumey- ‹ *dasu_adj B -ma-Ci-. ‘put at ease; relieve; (Nk, Sr)
cheapen’. (B) - B-A-B x-B-x. Ib B. Nk yasimin (yasimir-) B; Sr yaşimir- B.

B   yasumu ‹ *dasu_adj B -ma-. ‘rest; sleep; (Nk, Sr) become cheap(er)’. B -
B-A-B x-B-x. NS (105b) B. Km (S) B. Ib B. Nk yasimin (yasim-) B; Sr yaşim- B.
◊ yasumi x - B-2-B x-B-x.

A   yasuraeru ‹ yasurafe[y]- ‹ *dasu_adj B -ra-pa-Ci-. ‘let relax’.
(A) - x-x-x x-x-x. Km (W) A.

A   yasurau ‹ yasurafu ‹ *dasu_adj B -ra-pa-. ‘let relax’.
(A) - x-x-x x-x-x. Km (W) A.

B   yatou ‹ yatofu (?‹ *ya twofu ‘house ask’ ‹ *da₁.₃ᵦ twopa-₍A). ‘hire,
engage’. B - B-A-A B-B-x. Ib B. Nk yatuurun B; Sr yatur- B.
◊ yatoi x - 2-A[U]/1:3[H]-A x-x-x.

B   yatureru ‹ yature[y]- ‹ *datu-ra-Ci-. ‘get shabby; get emaciated/gaunt’.
B - B-A-B x-A̲-x. Ib A̲. Nk yaCiirin A; Sr yaçirir- A ‘get emaciated; disguise
oneself’. ◊ yature x - B-A[U]/2[H]-B x-x-x. Cf. yaseru.

B   yatusu ‹ *datu-sa-. ‘dress (oneself) shabbily; disguise oneself, ... ’.
B - B-A-B x-x-x. Edo B. Ib A̲.

?A/B   yawarageru ‹ yafaraᵏ/ᵨey- ‹ yafara_adJ-ₐ (‹ *dapa-ra ‹ *dapa_sis -ra)
-(n[a]-)ka-Ci-. ‘soften it’. (A) - A[Mkz,Hiroto-Ōhara]/B-A-B x-A-x. Hattō,
Matsue A; Izumo A/B; Hamada B. Sr -k-.

?A/B   yawaragu ‹ yafaraᵏ/ᵨu ‹ yafara_adJ-ₐ (‹ *dapa-ra ‹ *dapa_sis -ra)
-(n[a]-)ka-. ‘get soft, soften’. A - B-A-B x-A-x. Hattō,
Hamada B, Matsue, Izumo A. Nk yaPaaraCun A; Sr yahwarak- A.

A   yobau ‹ ywobafu ‹ *dwonpa-pa-. ‘keep calling’. A - x-A-x x-x-x.
NS (114a) A. Km (W) A(/B).

B   yobau ‹ ywobafu ‹ *dwonpapa- (‹ ?). ‘seek bride’. B - x-A-x x-x-x.
◊ yobai (B) - 2-A-x x-x-x. (It is unclear why yobau is B; there are problems
of vowel or register with all the etymologies that have been suggested.)

?A/B   yobawaru ‹ yobafaru ?‹ *ywobafaru ‹ *dwonpa-pa-ra-. 'yell'. x - B-A-A
x-x-x. ◻ yobawari x - A-x-x x-x-x.

A   yobu ‹ ywobu ‹ *dwonpa-. 'call (out); summon; invite; name'. A - A-A-A
A-A-x. Ongi A. NS (95b) A. Km (W) A. Ib A. Nk yubin A; Sr yub- A. ◻ yobi x -
A-A-A x-x-x. Cf. sakebu; yomu.

A   yodatu ‹ [i]yodatu ‹ *iyo₂.₉ n[i] tata-ᴮ. '(hairs) bristle'. x - x-(A)-x
x-x-x. Edo A. Attested 14th century.

A   [yodawaru] ‹ yodafaru ?‹ *donta-pa-ra, ?‹ *yoda[rⁱ/e]₃.₁ (‹ yo-tari ‹
*do? tar[a-C]i-ᴮ 'drivel') + far- (‹ *para- ᴀ 'stretch'). 'smear'. HHLx (Kn
Hō-chū 67:4) - x-x-x x-x-x.

B   [yodomaru] ‹ yodomar- ‹ *donto₂.₄ -ma-ra-. 'stagnate, be stagnant'
(= yodomu). x - x-x-x x-x-x. Nk yudumarun B.

B   [yodomeru] ‹ yodome[y]- ‹ *donto₂.₄ -ma-Ci-. 'make/let it stagnate'.
(B) - x-x-x x-B-x. Nk yudumin B; Sr yudumir- B.

?B   yodomu ‹ *donto₂.₄ -ma-. 'stagnate, be stagnant; stammer'. B - B-A-A
x-B-x. Km (W) B. ◻ yodomi B - A/B-A-A x-x-x.

?A   yogir-u (Mr) ‹ yokir-u ?‹ *yokiyr-u ‹ *doko₂.₁ ira-ᴀ. 'go/pass by, go
across'. A - B-A-A x-x-x. Hattō, Hamada B; Matsue, Izumo A. Cf. yokeru,
[yokiru].

A   yogoreru ‹ yogore[y]- ‹ *donko-ra-Ci-. 'get dirty'. x - A-A-A x-A-x.
Ib A. Nk yuguurin A; yugurir- A. ◻ yogore x - A-A[U]/2[H]-A x-A-x. Nk yuguuri
A; Sr yuguri A. Cf. nigoru.

A   yogosu ‹ *donko-sa-. 'make it dirty, soil it'. x - A-A-A x-A-x. Ib A.
Nk yuguusun A; Sr yugus- A. ◻ yogosi x - A-A-A x-x-x. Cf. nigosu.

B   yokeru ‹ yoke[y]- (-g- 1450-1750 [Ōno]) ?‹ *dok[o₂.₁ i]ra-Ci-ᴀ. 'avoid,
dodge' (= [yokiru]). B - B-B-B x-x-x. Edo (-g-) B. Ib B. Cf. nokeru, dokeru.

B   [yokiru] ‹ yokiy- ?‹ *doko₂.₁ i[ra-]ᴀ ('enter side'). 'avoid'. B - x-x-x
x-x-x. Hn also yoku. Cf. noku, doku. Etymology incongruent in register. Only
example: yokiy-di (M 1226) 'by-pass'.

?A/B   yokogir-u ‹ (*)yokogyir-u ‹ *doko₂.₁ -n- kira-ᴮ. 'cross, traverse'.
x - B-A-A x-x-x. Ib A.

?A/B   yokosu ?‹ yo[ri]ᴀ okosu?ᴀ (‹ ...); ?‹ *i-pre okosu?ᴀ (‹ ...). 'send
(here)'. x - B-A-A x-x-x. Ib A. Earliest attestation Edo? See okosu.

?   yokosu ‹ *doko-sa-. 'slander'. x - x-x-x x-x-x.

?A   yokotaeru ‹ yokotafey- ‹ *doko₂.₁ tapa-Ci-ᴮ. 'lay/place down'. A - B-A-A
x-A-x. Hamada B; Hattō, Matsue, Izumo A. Nk x; Sr yukuteer- A.

?A   yokotawaru ‹ yokotafaru ‹ *doko₂.₁ tapa-ra-ᴮ. 'lie down'. A - B-A-A
x-x-x. Hamada B; Hattō, Matsue, Izumo A. Ib A.

B   [yokou] ‹ *dokopa-. 'rest': see ikou (but perhaps a separate etymon).

B   yoku ‹ *doko-. 'avoid' (= yokiru, yokeru). B - x-x-x x-x-x. Cf. noku,
doku.

B   yomeru ‹ yome[y]- ‹ *doma-Ci-. 'get read'. (B) - B-B-B x-x-x. Ib B.

B   yomigaer-u ‹ yomiy₂.₉ (ni) kafyer-ᴮ ('return from Hades') ‹ *domo-Ci
kapi-ra-ᴮ. 'return to life, revive'. B - A/B-B-B x-x-x.

B   yomu ‹ *doma-. 'read; [Ryūkyū] count, chat'. B - B-B-B B-B-B. NS (Okada)
B. Km (W) B. Edo B. Ib B. Nk yumin B; Sr yum- B. ◻ yomi x - B-2-B x-x-x.
Cf. yobu.

B   yoreru ‹ yore[y]- ‹ *dora-Ci-. 'get twisted'. x - B-B-B x-x-x. Ib B.

A   yorobou ‹ yorofofu ‹ *doropopa- (?‹*doro₌₁₌ -pa-pa-). 'toss about; get
warped'. x - x-x-x x-x-x. NS (73a [11:216-M]) A. NS (T+ 56) yorofofyi HLLH (odd,

B   yorokobu < yorokobiy- < *doro(-)ko(-)np^a/₂Ci- (?< -n[a]-pa-Ci-). 'rejoice'.
B - B-A-B B-B-x. NS (125b) B. Mr (Bm) B. Nk yuruKubin B; Sr yurukub- B. Ib B.
The bigrade conjugation is attested as late as 1172 (KggD 971a). ▯ yorokobi
'joy'. B - 3/4/0-A-B x-B-x. NS B. Km (S,W) B. Nk yuruuKubi B; Sr yurukubi B.
Cf. yorosi-/yorasi- adj B.

?A/B   yoromeku < *yoro - myeku < *doro mia miCa-ka-bnd v. 'stagger, totter;
have an adulterous affair'. x - B-A-A x-x-x. ▯ yoromeki x - A-A-A x-x-x.

A   yorou < yorofu ?< *yorafu (the second vowel assimilated to the first) <
*dora-pa-. 'wear (put on) armor'. x - B-x-x x-x-x. ▯ yoroi A - A-A-A x-A-x.
Edo A.

A   yoru < yoru < *do-ra-. 'approach; gather; rely (be based) on, be due to'.
A - A-A-A x-A-A. NS (73a [11:215-M], 105a) A. NS (72) yorane HLF = HLL;
(3) yori HH; (68) yoruattr LL; (56) yoru masizi-kyi HH LHHH; (4) yore-do mo
FHHH = HH(|)H(|)H. Km (S,W) A ('rely on'), Mr (Bm) A ('approach'). Edo A.
Ib A. Nk yun A; Sr yur- A. ▯ yori 'a gathering' x - A-A-B x-x-x. Cf. yoseru,
yosoru, yosu.

A   yoru < *dora-. 'sway' (= yuru). A - x-x-x x-x-x. NS (T+ 91) yori FL = HL.
B   yoru < *dora-. 'twist'. x - B-B-B x-x-x. Km (W) B. (Okada) A. Ib B.
▯ yori x - B-2-B x-x-x.
B   yoru < *dora-. 'select'. x - B-B-B x-x-x. Ib B. Not attested before Edo?
See erabu, er-u.

A   yoseru < yose[y]- < *do-sa-Ci-. 'bring it near; ... '. x - A-A-A A-A-x. Km
(W) A. Edo A. Ib A. Nk yusiirun A; Sr yusir- A. Azuma yese[y]-. Cf. yoru, yosu.
?A/B   yosoeru < yosofey- < *doso-pa-Ci-. 'liken, compare'. x - A/B-A-x x-x-x.
B   yosonooru < yosonoforu < ? yoso-noforu < *doso?mia nopo-ra-A.
'go/whirl round and round'. B - x-x-x x-x-x.
?A/B   yosoou (second vowel assimilated to the first) < *doso₂.₂b opo-pa-B (or
< *yosofafu < *doso (-)papa-bnd v). 'dress/adorn/equip oneself; feign'.
x - B-A-A x-x-x. ▯ yosooi B -3/0-A-A 1-x-x. Km (S) B.
?A   yosoru < *yosaru (second vowel assimilated to the first)< *do-sa-ra-.
(vi.) 'approach, come up (to)'. x - x-x-x x-x-x. (= yoru; cf. yoseru.)
?B   yosou < yoso[o]u (< yosofofu < *doso₂.₂b opo-pa-B). 'dress/adorn/equip
oneself; dish up food'. B - A[H]/B-A-A x-x-x. Ib B. ▯ yosoi B - 2-A-A x-x-x.
A   yosu < *do-sa-. 'bring it near (= yoseru); entrust/leave (a matter) to'.
A - A-A-x x-x-x. NS (129a [14:363L-K]) A. NS (T+ 3) yosi HH. Cf. yoru.
B   yosu (< ?). 'stop it'. x - B-A[U]/B[H]-B x-A?-x. Ib B. First attested
Edo?

A   yotiru < yoti[y]- < *dot^a/₂-Ci-. 'skewer and dry': see yoti-ozasi (Ch. 5).
x - x-x-x x-x-x. Shinsen-Jikyō has yotimu '[that which is] to be skewered and
dried', with future -mu.

B   you < /ye[w]u/ < /e[w]u/ < /we[w]u/ = wefu < *bepa- (< *bopa-). 'get
drunk/intoxicated'. B - B-B-B x-B-B. Ongi B. Ib B. Nk uirun B; Sr wiir- B. Yn
birun B. ▯ yoi x - 1/2-2-B x-B-x. Ongi (Iroha) B. Hattō, Hamada, Goka-mura 2;
Matsue, Izumo 1. Nk ui B; Sr wii B.

-        [(-)you] < (-)ywofu < *dwopa-. 'waver': see izayou, kagayou, ?kayou,
?kayowasu, mayou, mogoyou, samayou, tadayou.

B   yowamaru < *ywowamaru < *dwobaadj B -ma-ra-. 'grow weak' (= yowamu).
x - B-A-B x-x-x. Nk yooman B. Ib B.

B   yowameru < *ywowamey- < *dwobaadj B -ma-Ci-. 'weaken (= make one weak)'.
x - B-A-B x-x-x. Nk yoomin B.

B   yowaru < *ywowaru < *dwoba*adj B* -ra-. 'grow weak'. x - B-A-B x-x-x. Edo B.
Nk yoorun B, Sr yoor- B < *yowar-. Ib B.

B   yozireru < yozire[y]- < *donti-ra-Ci-. 'get twisted, contorted'. x - B-B-B
x-x-x.

B   yozir-u < yodir- < *donti-ra-. 'twist, contort'. x - B-B-B x-x-x. Ib B.

?A   yoziru < yodi[y]- < *dont*u*/ₑ-Ci-. 'grab and pull; cling; scramble up';
? 'skewer and dry' (cf. yoᵗ/zi-ozasi). A - B-B-x x-x-x.

B´/B   yubiku < *yu-byiku < *du*ı.ₛ* -n- pika-*A*. 'boil'. L(|)HL / LLH [Ir] - B-A-x
x-x-x.

?A/B   yudaneru < yudane[y]- < *dunta(-)na-Ci-. 'entrust with; devote oneself
to'. x - B-A-A x-x-x. NS (113b, 132a) A.

B   yuderu, uderu < (y)ude[y]- < *du*ı.ₛₑ* [i]nta-Ci-*ʙ*. 'boil it'. B (?= 1.3+B)
- B-B-B x-B-x. Ib ideru B. Nk yudirun B; Sr yudir- B.

A   yugameru < yugame[y]- < yu[re - ka]gamey- < *dura-Ci[-Ci]*A* kan-kama-Ci-*A*
(< ...). 'warp/bend/distort it'. A/*B*-A-A x-A-x. Nk yugaamin (yugaamir-) A;
Sr yugamir- A. (We are tempted to relate yumi 'bow' but that is 2.3 = B. *See
also* hanikamu.)

A   yugamu < yu[re - ka]gamu < *dura-Ci[-Ci]*A* kan-kama-*A*(< ...). 'get warped,
bent, distorted'. A - A/*B*-A-A x-A-x. Ib igamu A. Nk yugaamin (yugaam-) A;
Sr yugam- A. 〇 yugami x - A/*B*-A-A x-A-x.

A   yuku: *see* iku.

A   yuragu < yuraku < *dura-ka-. 'swing, sway, shake; rattle, clink, tinkle'.
x - A/*B*-A-A x-x-x. NS (T+ 85) yuraku mo y*o* HLL(|)H(|)*ᴸ*.

A   [yurareru] < yurare[y]- < *dura-ra-Ci-. 'sway[ing emerge]'. x - x-x-x
x-x-x. Edo A. Not attested before 1700.

A   yureru < yure[y]- < *dura-Ci-. (vi.) 'sway; shake, vibrate'. A - A-A-A
x-x-x. Izumo *B*; Goka-mura A/*B*. Ib A. Cf. yuru. 〇 yure x - A-A-A x-x-x.

B   [yureru] < yure[y] ← yuri[y]- < *duru*adj B* -Ci-. 'be forgiven'. Attested
Edo. *See* yuriru.

B   [yuriru] < yuri[y]- < *duru*adj B* -Ci-. 'be forgiven'. x - x-x-x x-x-x.
Edo B. Attested 13th century. Also [yureru].

A   yuru < *dura-. (vi./vt.) 'sway; shake, vibrate'. x - A-A-x x-x-x. Edo A.
Ib A. Nk yun (yur-) A. Cf. yusuru.

A   yurugasu < *duru-n[a]-ka-sa- (?< *dura-n[a]-ka-sa-, *the second vowel
assimilated to the first*). 'make it shake (waver, vacillate)'. A/*B*-A-A x-x-x.
Also yurugase[y]- < *···-sa-Ci-?

A   yurugu < *duru-n[a]-ka- (?< *dura-n[a]-ka-, *the second vowel assimilated
to the first*). 'shake, waver, vacillate; be negligent'.
A [Hoke-kyō tanji] - A/*B*-A-A x-x-x.

B   [yurukeru] < *duru-ka-Ci-. 'come loose; relax' (= yurumu). x - x-x-x
x-x-x. Nk yuruKin B.

B   yurumeru < yurube- < yurufey- ?< *duru*adj B* -ma-/-pa-Ci-; ?<
*duru*adj B* -(n[a]-)pa-Ci-. 'loosen it'. B - B-A-B x-B-x. Izumo *A*/B. Ib B.
Nk yurumin B; Sr yurumir- B.

B   yurumu < yurubu < yurufu ?< *duru*adj B* -ma-/-pa-; ?< *duru*adj B*
-(n[a]-)pa-. 'relax'. B - B-A-B x-x-x. Ib B. Nk yurumin (yurum-) B.

B   yurusu < *duru*adj B* -sa-. 'allow; forgive'. B - B-A-B x-B-B. NS (103b
[11:172-K, 11:182-K]. NS (T+ 88) yuruse t*o* ya LHH(|)H(|)L. Mr (Bm) B. Edo B.
Ib B. Nk yurus- B; Sr yurus- B; Yn yunun B. 〇 yurusi B - B-A[H]/2[U]-B x-B-x.
Mr (Bm) HHL. Izumo *A*/B. Nk yurusii B; Sr yurii B < *yurusi 'permission; leave;
holiday'.

A   yusugu ?< *dusunka- (< ?); ?< i-*pre* usunka- (= ?). 'wash out, rinse'.
x - A-A-A x-A-x. Ib A. Nk yus¹¹/ᵤᵤzun A; Sr yuşig- A. ◊ yusugi x - A-A-A x-x-x.
Cf. susugu. Dial. usugu, isugu.

A   yusuru < *dusura- (< ?). (vi./vt.) 'shake, rock; extort'. A - A-A-A x-x-x.
◊ yusuri x - A-A-A x-x-x. Cf. yuru.

-   yuturu: *see* uturu.

A   yuu < yufu < *dupa-. 'tie (up)'. A - A-A-A x-A-x. Km (W) A. Edo A. Ib A.
Nk yuurun A, Sr yuur- A restructured from *yuw- < *yuf-.

A   yuu 'say': *see* iu.

?A   yuwaeru < yufafe[y]- < *dupa-pa-Ci-. 'tie (up)'. A - B̲-A-A x-x-x. Hattō,
Hamada B̲; Matsue, Izumo A. Ib A.

?A, A+A yuwau < yufafu < *dupa-pa-. 'tie up (bind) tight'. HL|H[L] (Zs, Kn) / HHH
(Kn) x-A-x x-x-x.

B   yuwau 'celebrate': *see* iwau.

A   yuzuru < yuduru < *duntu(-)ra- (< ?). 'yield, concede'. A - A-A-A x-A-A.
Ongi A. Mr (Bm) A. Edo A. Ib A. Nk yuziirun A; Sr yuzir- A; Yn dudirun A.
◊ yuzuri x - A-A-A x-A-x. Sr yuẓiri A (anomalous -r-?). Cf. yudaneru.

?A/B zawameku < *ˢ/ẓawa - myeku, (Nr) saba-myeku < *(n)sabaₘᵢₘ / sanpa?ₘᵢₘ
miCa-ka-*bnd v*. 'murmur, buzz, clamor'. x - B-A-A x-x-x. Ib A. ◊ zawameki x -
A/B-A-A x-x-x. Cf. sawagu. The zawa- version is not attested before Edo.

?A/B zirasu < ?*nsira-sa- (< ?). 'irritate'. x - B-A-A x-x-x. Ib B. Earliest
examples Edo.

?A/B zireru ?< *nsira-Ci-. 'get irritated/frustrated'. x - B-B-A x-x-x. Earliest
examples Edo. ◊ zire x - B-x-x x-x-x.

?A/B zurasu < *n-?*pre* sura-sa-*в*. 'slip/shift/slide it (out of place). x - B-A-A
x-x-x.

?A/B zureru < zure[y]- < *n-?*pre* sura-Ci-*в*. (vi.) 'slip (out of place)'.
x - B-A[U]/B[H]-A x-x-x. Ib B. ◊ zure 'discrepancy, lag' x - B-2-A x-x-x.

6.7. List of Verb Formant Strings.

-bamu ‹ *-n[a]-pa-ma-. kibamu.
-baru ‹ *-n[a]-pa-ra-. kasabaru; ?mabaru.
-baseru ‹ *-n[a]-pa-sa-Ci-. ukabaseru.
-basu ‹ *-n[a]-pa-sa-. korobasu, marobasu.
-beru: ‹ -bey- ‹ *-n[a]-pa-Ci-. kasaberu, kuraberu, naraberu, siraberu,
    [takuraberu].
        ‹ -ᵇ/ₘey- ‹ *-n[a]-pa-Ci-. isameru, ukaberu, utoᵇ/ₘeru.
-biru ‹ -biy- ‹ *-npᵘ/ₒCi- ?‹ *-n[a]-pa-Ci-. arabiru, [inabiru], [iyabiru],
    kanasimu ‹ kanasibiru, kobiru, manabiru/manabu, ?manebiru/manebu, [miyabiru],
    miyakobiru, [mutubiru], ? ··· sabiru, sinobu ‹ sinobi[y]- 'endure', susamu ‹
    susabiy-, [takabiru]/takabu, [takebiru], [tanabiru], [tattobiru/tootobiru],
    [utobiru], [utukusibiru], ?wabiru, ?yorokobu ‹ yorokobi[y]-.
-bosu ‹ *-npo-sa- ‹ *-n[a]-pa-sa-. oyobosu.
-ᵇ/ₘosu ‹ *-npo-sa- ‹ *-n[a]-pa-sa-. toroᵇ/ₘosu.
-bu ‹ -fu ‹ *-pa-. sinobu 'fondly recall'.
-bu ‹ *-n[a]-pa-. *karabu, [kasobu], korobu, marobu, ?narabu, orabu, oyobu,
    takabu/[takabiru].
-ᵇ/ₘu ‹ *-n[a]-pa-. awaremu, erabu, isabu, ?madoromu, mutubu, ukabu.
-deru ‹ *-n[a]-ta-Ci-. mederu. *See also* -teru.
-ebu ‹ -ebiy- ‹ *···a-Ci-npᵘ/ₒCi- ?‹ *···a-Ci-n[a]-pa-Ci-. manebu. Cf. -sebu.
    -egau ‹ -eygafu ‹ *···a-Ci-n[a]-ka-pa-. ategau.
-egu ‹ -eyku ‹ *···a-Ci-ka-. ?husegu.
-egu ‹ -eyᵏ/ₘ ‹ *···a-Ci-(n[a]-)ka-. naegu, ?negu, semegu.
-ekasu ‹ -eykasu ‹ *···a-Ci-ka-sa-. nekasu.
-emu ‹ -eymu ‹ *···a-Ci-ma-. hagemu.
-eru₁ ‹ -ye[y]- ‹ *-da-Ci-. amaeru, [atueru], haeru, hieru, [ieru] 'get shot',
    kikoeru, koeru 'pass over', koeru 'grow fertile; get fat', mamieru, ?mieru,
    [nioeru] 'get red', obieru, oboeru, ?[oeru] 'get weak', sakaeru 'prosper',
    [sinaeru] 'droop', sobieru, sueru 'turn sour', [tabaeru], wakaeru.
-eru₂ ‹ -fey- ‹ *-pa-Ci-. ataeru, [atoeru], aturaeru, azaeru, ?[haeru], [haraeru],
    hikaeru, hurueru, [iraeru]₁,₂, iroeru, ?kakaeru, ?kamaeru, kanaeru, ?kangaeru,
    koraeru, kosiraeru, ?kuberu, kuwaeru, mazieru, mukaeru, [nioeru] 'dye red',
    ?oeru 'end', [omowaeru], saeru 'obstruct', sakaeru 'oppose', saraeru, sinaeru
    'bend', ?sonaeru, ?soroeru, taberu, takuwaeru, tataeru, tatoeru/tatou,
    [tomaeru], ?toraeru, tugaeru, tukaeru₁,₂, [uraeru], ?ureeru, yosoeru, yuwaeru.
-eru₃ ‹ -ey- ‹ *···a-Ci-. abareru, aeru₁₋₅, ageru, akeru, areru, aseru, atumeru,
    [atusireru], ?awateru, azukeru, bakeru, bareru, butukeru, ?dokeru, eru,
    habukeru, hadakeru, [haeru], hageru₁,₂, hakeru₁,₂, hameru, haneru₁,₂,
    hareru₁,₂, haseru₁,₂, hatagakureru, hateru, hazeru, hazikeru, hedataru, ?heru,
    hiideru, hikeru, hissageru, ?hodokeru, hogeru, homeru, horeru, hueru, hukeru,
    hureru, [ideru], ieru 'heal', ikeru, [ikoeru], ireru, ineru, kabureru, kaeru
    'change it', [kaeru] 'assent', ?[kaeru] 'get apart', kakageru, kakeru₁,₂,
    kanaderu, kaneru, karageru, kareru, [kareru], kasigeru, kasumeru, katamukeru,
    katazukeru, kateru₁,₂, kazukeru, kazoeru, ?[keru] 'get extinguished', ker-u ‹
    keru 'kick', kieru, kireru, [koeru] 'freeze', kogeru, kogoeru, kokeru, komeru,
    kozireru, kuberu, [kueru], kureru, kusuberu, kuwadateru, mageru, magireru,
    [maideru], makeru, makureru, maneru, ?mazeru, ?megeru, mezameru, ?mieru,
    miteru, mitomeru, moeru₁,₂, mogeru, monukeru, mooderu, moreru, moteasobu,
    moteru, ?motureru, mukeru₁,₂, mureru 'flock', nadareru, naderu, naeru₁,₂,
    nageru, nareru, natukeru, nazukeru, neru, nieru, nigeru, nokeru (?‹ ···ₒ-Ci-),

nugeru, nukeru, nukinderu, nureru, odateru, oreru, osieru, otozureru, sabakeru,
saeru 'get cold', sageru, sakeru₁,₂, samatageru, sameru, sareru, sasageru,
sazukeru, semeru, [sideru], sikakeru, sikameru, simeru tie up', ?simeru
'occupy', sinadareru, siotareru, sireru, [siriutageru], sirizokeru, situkeru,
?sodateru, soeru, sogeru, [sokeru], someru, somukeru, soreru, suberu 'make it
narrow', sueru 'set it up', sugeru, sukeru, sukumeru, sureru, susumeru, suteru,
tabureru, tadareru, taderu, taeru 'endure', taeru 'come to an end', [tageru],
takeru₁,₂, tameru₁,₂, tamukeru, [tanomeru], tareru, tasinameru, tasukeru,
tateru, tatoeru, tayumeru, tazuneru, tazusaeru, tigaeru, tikazukeru,
tiribameru, todomeru, tokeru, tomeru, tudoeru, tugeru, [tuideru], tuieru,
tukareru, tukeru₁,₂, tumeru, tureru, tuteru, tuzukeru, uderu, ueru₁,₂, [ugeru],
ukeru₁,₂,₃, umeru, urabureru, ureru₁,₂, [urutaeru], useru, uttaeru, utumukeru,
uzumeru, wageru, wakeru, wakimaeru, wareru, yakeru, yameru, yabureru, [yareru],
yaseru, yokotaeru, yomeru, yoreru, yuderu, yugameru, yureru, zireru, zureru.

-er-u ‹ -eyr-u ‹ *···a-Ci-ra-. ?huker-u, ?namer-u, siger-u, simer-u, ?uner-u.

-esu ‹ -eysu ‹ *···a-Ci-sa-. simesu 'dampen it'.

-eu ‹ -eyfu ‹ *···a-Ci-pa-. ukeu.

?-gaeru ‹ -gafey- ‹ *-n[a]-ka-pa-Ci-. ?sitagaeru.

-garasu ‹ *-na-ka-ra-sa-. togarasu.

-garu₁ ‹ *-n[a]-ka-ra-. husagaru, hutagaru, korogaru, matagaru, muragaru, togaru,
    tunagaru, yabusagaru.

-garu₂ ‹ -g[e] (‹ *-n- key₁.₁) ara-ʙ. atarasigaru₁,₂, ayasigaru, hosigaru,
    [sakasigaru], kowagaru.

-gasu ‹ *-n[a]-ka-sa-. korogasu, unagasu, uragasu, yurugasu.

-gau ‹ -gafu ‹ *-n[a]-ka-pa-. aragau, sitagau. *See also* -egau; ?-gaeru.

-geru ‹ -gey- ‹ *-n[a]-ka-Ci-. hirogeru, hutageru, [kisageru], korogeru, sirageru,
    ?sogeru, tairageru, tunageru, urageru.

-geru ‹ -ᵍ/ₖey- ‹ *-(n[a]-)ka-Ci-. yawarageru.

-gu ‹ *-n[a]-ka-. aogu, doyogu (= toyoku), husagu, hutagu, isogu, ?kagu, kasegu,
    katugu, matagu, sayagu, sinogu, ?sogu, soyogu, tairagu, togu, ?tugu, tumugu,
    tunagu, unagu, yurugu. *See also* -egu; -ragu, -yagu; [negiru].

-gu ‹ -ku ‹ *-ka-. ?husegu, sawagu, sosogu₁,₂,₃, susugu, yuragu. *See also* -egu.

-gu ‹ -ᵏ/gu ‹ *-(n[a]-)ka-. yawaragu.

-ikeru ‹ -i[y]keyru ‹ *···o̱-Ci-ka-Ci-. ozikeru.

-iru ‹ -iy- ‹ *···ᵘ/o̱-Ci-:

   u: abiru, haziru, [huriru], kutiru (‹ a), ?[nagiru] (?‹ wo), sabiru,
   sugiru, tukiru, ?wabiru.

   o̱: hiru, ?horobiru (?‹ a), hotobiru, koiru 'love', [komiru] (?‹ a), koriru (?‹
   a), kuiru (‹ a), miru 'turn', [mozir-u](/*moziru), nobiru (?‹ a), oiru 'age'
   (?‹ a), [oiru] 'grow', okiru, oriru, osori- (= osoreru), otiru 'fall', otiru
   'be young and vigorous', oziru, ?[tamiru], [todomiru]. Cf. nokeru; uramu.

   ᵘ/o̱: iru 'be', iru 'lead', kami-sabiru, koziru, motiiru, [negiru], (nezir-u ‹)
   nediru, ?simiru 'freeze', ?sinu, ?tibiru, tuzuiru, uramu/urami-, ?wabiru,
   yotiru, yoziru. Cf. oru 'be', sobotu.

-kamu ‹ *-ka-ma-. ?kazikamu.

-karu ‹ *-ka-ra-. marokaru, ?muzukaru, tirakaru, ?tonakaru. Cf. ayakaru.

-kareru ‹ *-ka-ra-Ci-. maroᵏ/gareru.

-kasu ‹ *-ka-sa-. gomakasu, hagurakasu, harukasu, hasirakasu, ?hibikasu, hiyakasu,
    kawakasu, marokasu, modorokasu, odokasu, sibukasu, taburakasu, tirakasu,
    todorokasu, ?tokasu, torokasu/torakasu, ugokasu. *See also* -ekasu, -rakasu,
    -rokasu, -yakasu; (-)mekasu; -gasu.

-kau ‹ -kafu ‹ *-ka-pa-. atukau₁,₂, isakau; ?ukagau.

-keru < -key- < *-ka-Ci-. arakeru, ?bokeru, boyakeru, [harukeru], hirakeru,
    ?[hookeru], hosokeru, ?kamakeru, ?kazikeru, ?kudakeru, kuzikeru, [mabirokeru],
    modorokeru, [makeru] 'prepare', namakeru, nezikeru, ?orokeru, ozikeru,
    sirakeru, tawakeru, todokeru, ?tokeru, torokeru/torakeru, utukeru, [yurukeru].
    See also -geru, -rageru.
-kosu < -kasu < *-ka-sa-. ?hodokosu, torokosu = todorokasu.
-ku < *-ka-. eraku, haruku, ?hibiku, hiraku, hosaku, hoseku, hosoku, kawaku,
    kazuraku, kororoku, ?kudaku, kuziku, makuraku, modoroku, mogaku₁,₂, ?naku,
    nozoku₁,₂, ononoku, sizuku, [sobikeru] = sobiku, ?soku, todoku, todoroku, ?toku
    toyoku, ?tutuku, ugoku, wanaku, wananaku. *See also* (-)meku; -gu.
-maeru < -mafey- < *-ma-pa-Ci-. tomaeru, tukamaeru. Cf. wakimaeru.
-mareru < *-ma-ra-Ci-. ?homareru, nikumareru.
-maru < *-ma-ra-. aratamaru, atatamaru, atumaru, ayamaru, ?damaru, hasamaru,
    hayamaru, ?hazimaru, hiromaru, hisomaru, kasikomaru, ?kasanaru, ?kasumeru,
    katamaru, ?kimaru, kiwamaru, kiyomaru, kurumaru, marumaru, ?matomaru, osamaru,
    sadamaru, sebamaru, sizimaru, sizumaru, subomaru, tizimaru, tubomaru, tukamaru,
    yasumaru, [yodomaru], yowamaru.
-masu < *-ma-sa-. ?damasu, hagemasu, [kitamasu], kuramasu, nayamasu, doyomosu <
    toyomosu < *toyamasu.
-matu < *-ma-ta-. ayamatu, ?ugomotu, ?uguromotu.
-mau < -mafu < *-ma-pa-. hurumau, kakumau, sizimau, uyamau.
-mawaru < -mafaru < *-ma-pa-ra-. kiyomawaru.
(-)mekasu < *(-)myekasu < *miCa-ka-sa-. honomekasu.
(-)meku < *(-)myeku < *miCa-ka- (bound verb). doyomeku, garameku, hatameku,
    hirameku, [hiromeku], homeku, honomeku, hurumeku, kirameku, kobomeku, namameku,
    sameku, sasameku, sazameku, sosomeku, soyomeku, todomeku, tutumeku, ugomeku,
    wameku, yoromeku, zawameku.
-meru < -mey- < *-ma-Ci-. agameru, akirameru, aratameru, atatameru, doyomeru,
    hasameru, hayameru, ?hazimeru, hazukasimeru, himeru, hiromeru, ?hisomeru,
    ?homeru, hukameru, hukumeru, itameru, izimeru, karameru, karomeru, katameru,
    kimeru, [kitameru[, kiwameru, kiyomeru, kuromeru, kurumeru, marumeru,
    ?matomeru, nadameru, [nagameru] 'prolong voice', nagusameru, nayameru,
    nurumeru, osameru, sadameru, sebameru, ?(-)simeru, [sinameru], siwameru,
    sizimeru, sizumeru₁,₂, sobameru, ?susameru, tasikameru, tawameru, tizimeru,
    togameru, tubomeru, tutomeru, yasumeru, [yodomeru], yowameru.
-meru < -■/ᵬey- < *-n[a]-pa-Ci-. *See* -beru.
-meru < -fey- ?< *-(n[a]-)pa-Ci-. yurumeru.
?-moru < -maru < *-ma-ra-. kugumoru.
-mu < *-ma-. aidamu, asamu, aᵗ/ᵈamu, ?ayabumu, doyomu, haramu, hasamu, hazumu,
    higamu, hisomu (> hisomeru), hukumu, [hurumu], ?hutukumu, [ibusemu], itamu,
    itukusimu, kadamu, kakomu, karamu, karomu, kasamu, kasikomu, kasumu, ?kisimu,
    [kitamu], [kiwamu], kizamu, ?komu 'get flooded', kubomu, kukumu, kuramu, kuromu
    kuyamu, ?madoromu, marumu, megumu, mokuromu, mukumu, nagomu, nayamu, nikumu,
    niramu, nomu 'pray', nozomu, nurumu, osimu, sibomu, sitamu, siwamu, sizimu,
    sizumu₁,₂, sobamu, subomu, suzumu, ?tatamu, tumamu, ?tutumu, urumu, ?usomu,
    yasumu, yodomu. *See also* -bamu, -emu, -ramu, -samu; tukubu.
-mu < -ᵇ/■u < *-n[a]-pa-. *See* -ᵇ/■u.
-mu < -fu ?< *-(n[a]-)pa-. yurumu.
-naeru < -nafey- < *-na-pa-Ci-. tomonaeru, ?tonaeru, tuminaeru = tuminau.
    See also -noeru.
-namu < *-na-ma-. ubenamu. *See also* itonamu; -nau.

-naru < *-na-ra-. husanaru, kasanaru, katanaru, ?tonaru, turanaru.
-nasu < *-na-sa-. katanasu.
-nau < -nafu < *-na-pa-. aganau, akinau, amanau, atanau, izanau, mainau, makanau, mazinau, ninau, okonau, otonau, sokonau, tomonau, tugunau, (tuminaeru =) tuminau, ubenau, uranau, usinau, uzunau, yasinau. Cf. -namu.
-nawaru < -nafaru < *-na-pa-ra-. ugonawaru.
-neru < -ne[y]- < *-na-Ci-. [husaneru], kasaneru, kataneru, tabaneru, taganeru, ?[tataneru], tukaneru, turaneru, waganeru, ?yudaneru.
-noeru < -nofey- < *-na-fey- < *-na-pa-Ci-. totonoeru.
-nooru < -noforu < *-nofaru < *-na-pa-ra-. totonooru.
-nou < -nofu < *-nafu < *-na-pa-. totonou, tugunou, uzunou.
-osu < -fosu < *-fasu < *-pa-sa-. [oboosu], obosu, [omoosu], uruosu.
-ou < -fofu < *-fafu- < *-pa-pa- (or < *opo-pa-, or *op[o]-opo-, or *-p[a-Ci] opa-). ikiou, ?kiou, niou, ?uruou, yosoou.
-owasu < -fofasu < *-fafasu < *-pa-pa-sa- (or < *opo-pa-sa-, or *-p[a-Ci] opa-). [niowasu].
-raeru < -rafey- < *-ra-pa-Ci-. aturaeru, nagaraeru, [taraeru], yasuraeru.
-rageru = -rakeru < -rakey- < *-ra-ka-Ci-. [kawarageru]. Cf. tairageru.
-ragu = -raku < *-ra-ka-. hiiragu, kawaragu.
-ragu < *-ra-n[a]-ka-. usuragu.
-rakasu <*-ra-ka-sa-. midarakasu, suberakasu. (Cf. hagurakasu.)
-rakeru: see -rageru.
-raku < *-ra-ka-. (hiiragu =) [hiiraku], ?sabiraku.
-ramasu < *-ra-ma-sa-. hukuramasu.
-ramu < *-ra-ma-. hukuramu.
-rasu < *-ra-sa-. [kogarasu], kusarasu, [kuzurasu], ?narasu 'sound it', nigorasu, suberasu
-rau < -rafu < *-ra-pa-., hakarau, hazirau, ?katarau, sakarau, watarau, yasurau.
-reru < -re[y]- < *-ra-Ci-. ?abureru, akareru, [hakareru], hanareru, ?hatureru, hazureru, ?hogureru, [homareru], ?hotureru, hukureru, kakureru, kegareru, koboreru, kogareru, konareru, ?kowareru, kubireru, kusareru, kuzureru, maro^k/gareru, midareru, mureru 'get steamed', musubo(o)reru, nagareru, [namareru], nareru, nogareru, oboreru, okureru, osoreru, sabireru, ?sioreru, [sonawareru], ?sugureru, sutareru, ?(takaru <) takare[y]-, taoreru, [tawareru], tubureru, ?tukareru, ukareru, umareru, ?umoreru, usureru, ?uzumoreru, ?[wabureru], wakareru, ?wasureru, yatureru, yogoreru, yozireru.
    See also -kareru, -mareru, -wareru.
-roeru < -rofey- < *-rafey- < *-ra-pa-Ci-. otoroeru.
-roku < *-raku < *-ra-ka-. odoroku.
-rokasu < *-rakasu < *-ra-ka-sa-. odorokasu. Cf. todorokasu, torokasu.
-rou < -rofu < *-rafu < *-ra-pa-. norou, ?susurou, tukurou, uturou.
-ru < *-ra-. agaru, akaru, amaru, aoru, asaru, ataru, ?azaker-u, azukaru, butukaru, daber-u, guzuru, hakaru, hamaru, hayaru, hedataru, hikaru, hiroru, hir-u, hitaru, ?hoburu, hosoru, hutoru, ibukaru, iburu, ikaru, ioru, itaru, izir-u, kaburu, kaer-u, kager-u, kakaru, (kariru <) karu, kawaru, kisir-u, [kiwaru], kogoru, komaru, komoru, kooru, koru 'cut wood', kowaru, koyaru, ?kubaru, kubir-u, kudaru, kugumaru, kuguru, kukuru, kumaru, kumoru, kutaru, magaru, masaru, mawaru, mazaru, mazir-u, midaru, ?modoru, mozir-u, nabaru, namaru₁,₂, naoru, ?naru 'sound', naru 'become', ?ner-u, niburu, nigoru, noboru, ?nogasu, nokoru, nomer-u, ?noru 'declare', noru 'mount, ride', nukaru 'blunder', numer-u, ogoru, okoru, okuru, osoru (= osoreru), otoru, sagaru, sakaru₁,₂,

sasaru, satoru, sawaru, sebiru, seburu, semaru, ?siboru, siburu, simaru,
?siwaru, sober-u, somaru, sowaru, subaru, suber-u, suboru, sugaru, suguru
'pass by', ?suguru 'select', susuru, sutaru, suwaru, tabaru, tagir-u, (-)takaru
?taker-u, tamaru$_{1,2}$, (tariru <) taru, tasukaru, ?ter-u, toboru/tomoru, todomaru
tomaru, tukamaturu, tukaru$_{1,2}$, tukuru, tumaru, tumoru, umaru, uturu, uwaru,
uzumaru, wakaru, wasir-u, wataru, yaburu, yoru 'approach', yowaru, yozir-u.
See also -baru, -er-u, -garu, -karu, -maru, -naru, -saru, -yaru.
-sageru < -sagey- < *-sa-n[a]-ka-Ci-. [hasasageru], [kisageru].
-samu < *-sa-ma-. nagusamu.
-saru < *-sa-ra-. kudasaru, obusaru.
-sau < -safu < *-sa-pa-. kaesau, terasau.
-sebu < *-se[y]bu < *-sa-Ci-n[a]-pa-. ?musebu.
-seru < -se[y]- < *-sa-Ci-. awaseru, hoseru [dialect], ?huseru, kabuseru, kiseru,
    kotoyoseru, makaseru, [maseru], miseru, ?museru, niseru, noboseru, noseru,
    okosu < okose[y]- 'send here', ooseru, siraseru, [siseru], sukasu/sukase[y]-,
    toraseru, [wasiseru], yoseru. *See also* -baseru.
-simeru: < *-si$_{adj}$-ma-Ci-. hazukasimeru.
         < -si^{b}/$_{■}$ey- < *-si$_{adj}$-n[a]-pa-Ci-. kurusimeru.
-simu < -si^{b}/$_{■}$u < *-si$_{adj}$-n[a]-pa-. ayasimu, ?itukusimu, kurusimu, osimu,
    tanosimu.
-soru < *-saru < *-sa-ra-. yosoru.
-su < *-sa-. abusu, akasu$_{1,2}$, amasu, amusu, arasu, awatasu, ayasu, barasu, doyasu,
    harasu$_{1,2}$, hatasu, hayasu, hazusu, ?hesu, hibikasu, hirugaesu, hitasu,
    hodasu, ?hodokosu, hogasu, ?hogusu, horobosu, hotobosu, hosu, hukasu, hurasu,
    hurusu, huyasu, ibusu, idasu, ikasu, irasu, itasu, iyasu, kabusu, kaesu,
    [kakurasu], kakusu, ?kamosu, karasu, kasu, katasu, kawasu, kegasu, [kesu],
    kesu, [kikosu], kirasu$_{1,2}$, kisesu, kobosu, kogasu, kokasu, konasu, korasu,
    korosu, kosu, kowasu, koyasu 'deign to lie flat', *koyasu 'make it harden',
    *koyosu, kudasu, kurasu, kusasu, kutasu, kuyasu, kuzusu, madowasu, makasu, masu
    'deign to be', mawasu, mesu, megurasu, mezamasu, midasu, mitasu, modosu, moosu,
    morasu, motasu, motenasu, moyasu, moyoosu, musu$_{1,2}$, nabikasu, nagasu, naosu,
    narasu 'tame', nasu 'deign to sleep', nasu 'make resemble', ?nasu 'make it
    resound', nayasu, neyasu, nigasu, nigosu, nikoyosu, nobasu, nogasu, nokosu,
    nomasu, nomesu, nosu, nukasu, nurasu, obasu, [oboosu], obosu, odosu, okasu,
    okosu, [omoosu], oosu, orosu$_{1,2}$, otosu, oyasu, oyosu, samasu, sarasu, sasagasu,
    satosu, sekasu, simesu 'show', [sesu], (? sokusu), sorasu, ?sosu, subesu,
    sugosu, sukasu, sumasu, tadasu, taosu, tarasu, tasu, tayasu, terasu, tirasu,
    tobasu, tokasu, tomosu/tobosu, toosu, torasu, tubusu, tuiyasu, tukarasu,
    ?tukasu 'exhaust', tukasu 'soak it', tukusu, turusu, ukasu, utusu, wakasu
    'boil', [wakasu] 'divide', watasu, yatusu, yogosu, yokosu 'slander', yosu,
    yurusu, zirasu, zurasu.   *See also* -bosu, -esu, -gasu, -kasu, -masu, -nasu,
    -osu, -rasu, -rokasu, -wasu, -yasu, -yowasu; -sau.
-su/-tu < -tu < *-ta-. hagasu, hanasu.
-taru < -daru < *-n[a]-ta-ra-. sitataru.
-teru < -de[y]- < *-n[a]-ta-Ci. [sitateru]. Cf. -deru.
-tu < *-ta-. akatu, hagasu (= fagasu/fagatu), (hanasu =) hanatu, ?katatu, ketu,
    kiwatu, kobotu, kudatu, [momiziru, momizu] < momyitu, tagitu, ugatu, wakatu.
    See also -matu.
-u < -[w]u < -fu < *-pa-. ?agitou, agau, ?arau, atau, azawaru, emau, harau,
    ?heturau, [hogau], hokorou, huruu, irau, [irau], irou, isou, ?itou, kakou,
    kamau, kanau, [kasobu]/kasou, kirau, kitaeru < kitaf-, korou, kuruu, matou,
    maturau, matuu, minagirau, ?morau 'receive', morau 'watchfully await', mukau,
    nabikau, narau, ?norou, obuu, omou, oou, sakau$_{1,2}$, sarau, simau, sinau, sitau,

sobaeru < sobaf-, ?sonau, ?sorou, ?sugau, sukuu, sumau 'reside', ?tabau, tabu
< tamau 'give', tamau₁,₂, [tarau], tatakau, terau, ?tou, tugau, tukau, -turau,
tutau, tuzu, [umau], uruu, utau, warau, yamau, yarau, yobau, yorou, yuwau.
See also -bu, -gau, -kau, -mau, -nau: (-)wau.

-(w)au *(bound verb)* < *(-)fafu < *(-)papa- (?= *-pa-pa-; ?< 'creep'). aziwau,
*nariwau, nigiwau, sakiwau, [tiwau].

-yakasu < *-da-ka-sa. amayakasu.

-yaku < *-da-ka-. kagayaku, sasayaku, sosoyaku, tubuyaku, tutuyaku.

-yaru < *-da-ra-. suyuru < suyaru. Cf. -eru.

-yasu < *-da-sa-. hiyasu, koyasu 'fertilize'.

(-)you < (-)ywofu < *dwopa- (bound verb 'waver'). izayou, kagayou, ?kayou, mayou,
mogoyou, samayou, tadayou.

(-)yowasu < (-)ywofasu < *dwopa-sa-. ?kayowasu, tadayowasu.

-yu < *-da-. [hiyu].

6.8. Distribution of Formants.

When we look at the occurrence of individual formants in strings, we find the
common formants in several positions, as shown by the following chart.

Position:	first	second	third	fourth
	-sa-	-sa-	-sa-	-sa-
	-Ci-	-Ci-	-Ci-	-Ci-
	-ra-	-ra-	-ra-	
	-pa-	-pa-	-pa-	
	-ma-	-ma-		
	-ta-	-ta-		
	-ka-	-ka-		
	-na-			
	-n[a]-*			
	-da-			
	10	7	4	2

*Also, perhaps -na-n[a]-: see tunagaru, tunageru, tunagu.

If all possible strings occurred, including those repeating the same formant, we
would expect:

10		one-formant strings
10 x 7 =	70	two-formant strings
70 x 4 =	280	three-formant strings
280 x 2 =	560	four-formant strings
	910	total number of possible strings

But there are, in fact, limitations. There are few two-formant strings for -n[a]-,
and not many of the longer strings for other formants. In the list of actually
occurring strings we find:

10	one-formant strings
38	two-formant strings
27	three-formant strings
7	four-formant strings
92	total number of occurring strings

And some of the occurring strings are limited, at least in our list, to one or two
examples.

The approximate shape-populations of formant strings in the list of verbs can
be displayed in four groups according to size; the 22 most populous groups are
ranked below:

Group	Rank	String	Number of verb stems
I	1.	···a-Ci-	227 (with ···ᵐ/₉-Ci 271)
	2.	-sa-	171
	3.	-ra-	137
II	4.	-pa-	68
	5.	-ma-	62
	6.	-ma-Ci-	56
	7.	-ra-Ci-	50
	8.	···ᵐ/₉-Ci-	44
	9.	-pa-Ci-	42
III	10.	-ka-	32
	11.	-ma-ra-	31
	12.	-n[a]-pa-Ci-	28
	13.	-ka-Ci-	24
	14.	-sa-Ci-	21
	15-16.	-na-pa-	20
		-n[a]-ka-	20
	17.	-da-Ci-	19
	18.	-ka-sa-	17
IV	19.	-n[a]-pa-	14
	20.	-na-Ci-	10
	21.	-n[a]-ka-Ci-	9
	22.	-n[a]-ka-ra-	8
	···	···	···
	···	···	···

6.9. Supplementary List of Verbs.

Below are listed additional verbs, for many of which we have little accentual information; where the notation would be x - x-x-x x-x-x it is simply omitted, and the accent categories in the left column are based on etymological inferences. Also included are a few verbs which were omitted from the main list for various reasons, such as lateness of attestation.

?B   [akatuku] ‹ *aka*2.3* tuka-*B*. 'get tainted'.

?B   [anayumu] ‹ *a[si*2.3*] nadu-ma- (?= nazumu ‹ *nantu-ma-). 'limp' (Azuma?).

?B   [aratu] ‹ *ara-ta-. 'separate, put at a distance'. NS (T+ 40) arati-si LLH-L.

B   asebamu ‹ *ase*2.3* (‹ ?) -n[a]-pa-ma-. 'get sweaty'. x - B-B-B x-x-x. Ib B. Attested Edo.

B   asegumu ‹ *ase *2.3* (‹?) -n- kuma-*A*. 'get sweaty'. x - x-x-x x-B-x. Sr qasigum- B. Attested 1254.

-      [*asu] ‹ *asa- (?‹ asa*adj A*). ? 'be(come) shallow'. NS (T+ 32) asazu LHH (? mistake for HHH). Or is asazu the result of assimilation (by the second vowel to the first) ‹ asezu?

?B   ayanasu ‹ *ada*2.3* na-sa-*B*. 'make beautiful patterns; manipulate skilfully; cheat out of, swindle'; [? mistake for ayasu] 'spill'. Earliest example JP.

B   damakasu ?‹ *[mo]damakasu ('strike dumb') ‹ *mo(n)ta*2.2‹3.6* -ma-ka-sa-. 'cheat, swindle, deceive'. x - B-A-B x-x-x. Ib B. Attested Edo.

?B   [hagatu] ‹ fagatu ‹ *panka-ta-. 'break, destroy'. NS (T+ kun) fiy fagatu "R" (?= H) LLL 'breaks the water pipe'. Cf. [hanatu].

?A   [hahuku] ‹ fafuku ‹ *pa*1.2* puka-*B*. 'ruffle feathers'.

?B   [hanatu] ‹ fanatu ‹ *pan[k]a-ta-. 'break, destroy' (= [hagatu]). NS (T+ kun) fanatu LLH.

?B   [harakaru] ‹ farakaru ‹ *para-ka-ra-. 'make it clear' (= [harukeru]).

?A   [hararakasu] ‹ fararakasu ‹ *para-[pa]ra*mia* -ka-sa-. 'scatter them, disperse'. NS (T+ kun) kuwe fararakasu LH HHHHL 'scatter by kicking'.

?B   [haraku] ‹ faraku ‹ *para-ka-. 'clear up, open up, get bright' (= haruku). NS (T+ kun) farakyi LLH.

?   [hetuku] ‹ fyetuku ‹ *piCa*1.x* tuka-*B*. 'follow the shoreline'.

?B   [hirokasu] ‹ fyirokasu ‹ *piro (?= *pira*mia*) -ka-sa-. 'wave (one's hand)'. NS (T+ kun) ta fyirokasu L(|)LLHL.

?A   [hisikeru] ‹ fyisikey- ‹ *pi*1.2* sikey-*B* (‹ ...). 'the sun darken' (?).

?B   [huhogomoru] ‹ fufogomoru ?‹ *(the second vowel assimilated to third and fourth vowels)* *fufugomoru ‹ *fufum[yi]-komoru ‹ *pupum[a-C]i*B* (‹ ...) komora-*B* (‹ koma-ra-). 'be still in bloom'. NS (T+ 35) HHHHH.

A/B   huyakeru ‹ fukaye[y]- ‹ *puda-ka-Ci-. 'bloat, swell'. x - B-A-A x-x-x. Ib A. Attested Meiji.

?B   ibusemu ‹ *inpuse-*adj B* (‹ ?) -ma-. 'feel glum'.

?A   [igaer-u] ‹ igafyer-u ?‹ *i-*pre* -n- kapi-ra-*B* *(but this prefix does not usually take -n-)*, ?‹ *in[i] kafyeru ‹ *in[a-C]i*A* kapi-ra-*B* ('depart and return'). 'come back'. NS (70) HHHH.

?   [ihamu] ‹ ifamu ‹ *i-*pre* pama-[ra-*A*]. 'become full, crowded'.

?   [ihau] ‹ i-fafu ‹ *i-*pre* papa-*B*. 'crawl'. NS (T+ 8) H|LH.

?   [iki*k*/*g*imu] ‹ ikyikimu (? = *ikyigyimu) ‹ *iki(n)kima- (‹ ?; Yoshida "iki-iki -ma-"). 'menace (with snarling face)'.

?   [ikir-u] < i-kyir-u < *i-*pre* kira-*в*. 'cut'. NS (T+ 43) i-kyiramu to LHLHL
(odd), i-kyirazu so LHLHL *(odd)*.

?   [isiku] < i-siku < *i-*pre* sika-*A*. 'catch up, overtake'. NS (T+ 52) i-sikyi
LLH, i-sikye*imper* LLL.

?   isobau < i-swobafu < *i-*pre* swonpa-pa-*?*. 'frolic; flirt, dally'.

?B   [itaburu] < *ita*adj в* -n- pura-*A*. 'shake hard' (vi., Edo also vt.).

?   [itoru] < *i-t(w)oru < *i-*pre* t(w)ora-*в*. 'take'. NS (T+ 43) i-tworamu to
LHLHL *(odd)*.

?   [itugaru] < *i-*pre* tunka-ra-*A*. (vi.) 'join on'.

?B   [iwakeru] < iwakey- < *i-*pre* baka*adj в* -Ci-. 'act immature, childish'.
Attested 11th century. Cf. iwakena*adj в*.

?   [iwamu] < i-famu < *i-*pre* pama-*A* (cf. hamaru). 'throng, swarm, gather'.
NS (T+ kun) ifamyi (-) wi LLHL 'encamp'.

?   [iwatarasu] < i-watarasu < *i-*pre* bata-ra-sa-. 'deign to cross over'.
NS (T+ 3) H̄E̱L̄E̱H ?= H-HHHH; (24) i-watarasu mo L̄E̱HLHH ?= L|HHLH(|)H *(mistake?)*.

B   iyagaru < *ida 'nay' -gar- < *g[e] (< -n- key) ar[a]-*в*. 'dislike'.
x - B-A-A̱ x-x-x. Ib B. Attested Edo.

?   [iyuku] < i-yuku < *i-*pre* yuk- (< *i-*pre* uka-*A*) — *but this may be an
artificial way of looking at the etymology; perhaps the -y- is epenthetic and
the derivation is:* i-yuku < i-[y]uku < *i- uka-. 'go'. NS (T+) i-yukyi (12)
H(|)HL, (128) H(|)HH.

?B   kaburu < *kanpura- < *kam[a-(Ci)]*в* pura-*?в*. 'gnaw, nibble'.

?B   [kabusu] < *kanpu*x?2.в* -sa-. 'lean/incline one's head'.
◫ kabusi 'the shape/looks of one's head': NS (T+ kun) LLH.

?   [kaganaberu] < kaga-nabey- < *ka*?1.в* n[i] ka*1.в* nanpa-Ci-*A*. 'line up
day upon day'. NS (T+ 26) LHHH̄E̱ = LH(|)HH(|)H.

?   [kadoeru] < kadofey- = [kadou] < kadofu < *kanto-pa(-Ci)- (< ?). 'entice,
abduct'. Cf. kadamu < katamu.

?B   [kainuku] ?< *kaCi*в.4* nuka-*?A* ?< ka[k]i-nuku < *kak[a-C]i*в* nuka-*?A*. 'poke
out'.

B   kakuru < *kaku-ra-. 'hide'. NS (102) kakuri masu LHH(|)LL; (86) myi-yama -
gakuri te (< *mi- dama n[i] kaku-r[a-C]i t[a-C]i) E̱H̱E̱HLH(|)H ?= H-HH LLH|H.

B   [kam(u)biru] < kam(u)biy- < *kamu*в.в* -n[a]-pa-Ci-. 'become godly/divine;
grow old'.

?B   kasir-u, [dial.] kazir-u (< ?). 'curse' (vi.). ◫ kasiri: NS (T+ kun) i-tu
no kasiri LL L LLL.

?B   [katayaku] < *kata*в.4* daka-*A* ('shoulder burn'). 'prognosticate by burning
deer shoulder bones or tortoise shells'.

?A   [kikamu] < *kiykamu < *k*в*/*o*-Ci*1.в* kama-*в*. 'gnash teeth'.

?A   [*kitasu] < *kyitasu (?< *katasu < *kata*adj A* -sa-). 'harden'. Cf. kitaeru,
kitai. ◫ kitasi < kyitasi 'hard salt' (cf. Nakata).

?B   kodaru < *ko*1.в* -n- tara-*A*/tara-*в* ('tree suffice/droop'). 'grow lush'.

?A   [komu] < kwomu < *kwo*1.1* -ma-. 'hatch'. NS (62, 63) kwomu to HH(|)H.

A   [kosizukurau] < kosi-dukurafu < *kosi*в.1* -n- tukura-pa-*в* (→ tukurofu).
'gird one's loins, gird oneself'. NS (T+ 106) HH(|)HHLL.

?B   [kotodateru] < *koto*в.в* -n- tata-Ci-*в*. 'explicitly state'.

?B   [kotodatu] < *koto*в.в* -n- tata-*в*. 'do something special; get married'.

?B   [kototou] < kototofu < *koto*в.в* t(w)opa-*?A*. 'exchange words'.

?B   [kozutau] < kodutafu < *ko*1.в* -n- tuta-pa-*A*. 'flit from branch to branch'.

?   [kuna*k*/*gu*]: *see* ma*k*/*gu*na*k*/*gi*.

?B [kuruosu] < kurufosu < *kurufasu < *kuru-pa-sa-. 'madden, drive one mad, frenzy'. NS (T+ 32) kurufosi HLHL (odd).

? [kusibiru] < kusi-biy- < kusi*adj* (?<*kusu-Ci-) -np^u/$_o$Ci- (?< (-n[a]-pa-Ci-). 'appear marvelous, wondrous'.

?A/B kutabaru < *kuta-n[a]-pa-ra-. 'get enfeebled, enervated, exhausted; die; [dial.] rest, sleep'. A - B-A-A x-x-x. Ib A. Cf. kutabireru.

? [kutatu] < *kutata- (?*ku-tata-). 'time dwindle (wear away), get late'. Cf. yogutatu, tatu.

? [makaseru] < makase[y]- < *maka-sa-Ci- (< ?). 'irrigate'.

?B [makatu] < *ma$_{1.3a}$ kata-$_B$. 'stare down'.

- [mamorau] < ma^b/$_m$ora[f]u < mamworafu < *ma$_{1.3a}$ mora-/pora-$_{?B}$ -pa-. 'keep watching, keep an eye on'. NS (12) mamorafyi LLLL.

?A mazikoru < *mansi$_{?2.1}$ kora-$_{?A}$. 'be bewitched/cursed'. Cf. mazinai.

?B [mekareru] < meykare[y]- < *ma-Ci$_{1.3a}$ kara-Ci-$_A$. 'be far from sight'.

?B [menaraberu] < mey narabey- < *ma-Ci$_{1.3a}$ na(ra)npa-Ci-$_A$. 'pass many eyes; scrutinize'.

?A [mizukau] < myidukafu < *mintu$_{2.1}$ kapa-$_B$. 'water (animals), provide water for'.

? moru < *mo(-)ra-. 'snatch, wrest, pluck' (= mogu). Attested 1212.

?A [munawakeru] < munawakey- < *muna$_{2.2b}$ baka-Ci-$_A$. 'push (thrust oneself) through with one's chest'.

B namesu ?< *nameys- < *nama-Ci-sa-. 'tan (leather), taw'. x - B-A-B x-x-x. Ib B. Attested Meiji. Cf. namer-u, nameraka.

?B [nebau] < nebafu < *na-Ci$_{1.3a}$ -n- papa-$_B$. 'get rooted'.

? [nikibiru] < nikyibiy- < *niki$_{?2.1}$ -np^u/$_o$Ci- (?< -n[a]-pa-Ci-). 'become calm/docile'. Also nikimu.

? [nikimu] < *niki$_{?2.1}$-ma-. 'become calm/docile' (= [nikibiru]).

? [nikomu] < nikwomu < *nikwo-ma-. 'become calm' (= nagomu).

?A [nukatuku] < *nuka$_{2.1}$ tuka-$_A$ ('forehead poke'). 'bow one's head'.

?B [okumaeru] < okumafey- < *okumapaCi- (?= oku-ma-pa-Ci- [Unger]; ?= okumakeru < okumakey- < *oku$_{?2.3}$ maka-Ci-$_{?B}$). 'anticipate, prepare for the future'.

?B [okumakeru] < okumakey- < *oku$_{?2.3}$ maka-Ci-$_{?B}$. 'anticipate, prepare for the future'.

?B [omokatu] < *omo$_{2.4}$ kata-$_B$. 'face and overcome'.

?B [ooku] < ofoku (?< *opo$_{adj}$ $_B$ -ka-). 'covet food'.

?A [osoburau] < osoburafu < *osobura-pa ?< *osa-bura-pa < *osa-$_A$ -n- pura-pa-. 'keep shaking and rattling it'.

?A [osoburu] ?< *osa-buru (second vowel assimilated to first) < *osa-$_A$ -n- pura-$_A$. 'shake and rattle it'.

? sabameku < sabamyeku ← *sawa-myeku < *saba$_{mim}$ miCa-ka-$_{bnd\ v}$. 'murmur, buzz, clamor' (cf. zawameku); 'criticize, fault-find'. NS (T+ kun) HL|HH.

? [saobiku] < sawobyiku ?< *sa-$_{pre}$ bo$_{?1.3b}$ "cord" -n- pika-$_A$. 'lead a horse'.

?A [sitabaferu] < sitafafey- < *sita$_{2.2a}$ (-n-) papa-Ci-$_B$. 'harbor secret thoughts'.

? [sitau] < sitafu < *sitapa- (< ?). 'get/glow red'.

B sokoneru < *sokone[y]- < *soko-na-pa-Ci- (< ?). 'harm, spoil' (= sokonau). x - B-A-A x-x-x. Ib B. Attested Edo.

? [sukobiru] < su-kobi[y]- < *su-$_{pre}$ kwobiy-$_A$ (< ...). 'act impertinent'. (NKD: "Also zu-.")

?A [susobiku] < suswobyiku < *suswo$_{2.1}$ -n- pika-$_A$ 'drag a skirt, draw a train'.

B   susukeru < susuke[y]- < *susu$_{?2.5,?2.4}$ -ka-Ci-. 'get sooty'. x - A̲/B-A-B
x-x-x. Hattō, Hamada, Matsue, Izumo, Goka-mura B. Ib A̲. Attested 10th century.

?B   [tabasamu] < *ta$_{1.3a}$ -n- pasa-ma-$_B$. 'clutch, grasp between one's hands'.

B   takamaru < *taka$_{adj\ B}$ -ma-ra-. 'get high'. x - B-A-B x-x-x. Ib A̲.
Attested Meiji.

B   takameru < *taka$_{adj\ B}$ -ma-Ci-. 'heighten it'. x - B-A-B x-x-x. Ib B.
Attested Meiji.

?   [tasareru] < ta-sare[y]- < *ta$_{1.3a}$ sara-$_{?a}$-Ci-. 'take leave, depart'.
NS (T+ 40) LHH.

?B   [tazukuru] < tadukuru < *ta$_{1.3}$ -n- tuku-ra-$_B$. ?'don, put on, wear'.
NS (T+ 106) tadukuri LHHL.

A   tirabaru < *tira-n[a]-pa-ra. 'scatter, litter' (vi.). x - A-A-A x-x-x.
Ib A. Attestation recent.

?A   [tiwaku] < *ti$_{?1.1}$ baka-$_A$. 'blaze a trail'.

A   tizikamu < tidikamu ?< *sizikamu < *sinsi-ka-ma-. 'shrink, flinch, be
stunned'. x - A-A-A x-x-x. Ib A. Attested Edo. Cf. kazikeru.

A   tizireru < tidire[y]- ?< *sinsi-ra-Ci-, ?< *ti[ra-$_A$] n[i] tira-Ci-.
'get curled, frizzy; wrinkle; shrink'. x - A-A-A x-x-x. Nk CiCirun A; Sr x.
[] tizire x - A-A-A x-x-x. Attested Meiji.

?   [tonameru] < tonamey- ?< *[a]two$_{2.4}$ nama-Ci-$_{?A}$ (= nampa-Ci- ?< nam[a]-pa-
Ci-) [Yoshida], ?< *tona-ma-Ci- (cf. tonakaru, tobu) [Unger]. 'go around in
order'.

A   [tubakumu] ?< *tunpa (?< *tuk[a-C]i$_A$ -n- pa$_{1.1}$ 'collide edge', cf. Yoshida
193) kuma-$_B$. 'stick out, project, protrude'. A - x-x-x x-x-x.

?B   [tubutatu] < *tunpu$_{2.4}$ tata-$_B$. 'grow/come into grain'.

?A   [tumatou] < tumadofu < *tuma$_{?2.2a}$ -n- t(w)opa-$_A$. 'propose marriage'.

?A   [turanameru] < *tura$_{?2.1,?2.2a}$ nama-Ci-$_{?A}$ (= nampa-Ci- ?< nam[a]-pa-Ci-).
'line up'.

?B´   tuttuku ?< tuktuk- + infix. 'peck; poke' (= tutuku). x - B-A[U]/B[H]-A̲
x-x-x. Attested Meiji.

B   tuyomaru < *tuyomar- < *tudo$_{adj\ B}$ -ma-ra-. 'get strong(er)'. x - B-A-x
x-B-x. Sr cuumar- B. Attestations recent.

B   tuyomeru < *tuyome[y]- < *tudo$_{adj\ B}$ -ma-Ci-. 'strengthen'. x - B-A-B
x-B-x. Ib B. Sr cuumir- B. Attested Edo.

A   unuboreru < *unubore[y]- < onobore[y]- < *ono$_{2.1}$ n[i] pora-Ci-$_A$. 'be
vain, conceited'. x - A-A-A x-x-x. Ib B̲. Attested Meiji.

?A   [uragareru] < uragare[y]- < *ura$_{?2.1}$ -n- kara-Ci-$_A$. 'wither (at the
branch)'.

?B   [urasabiru] < urasabiy- < *ura$_{?2.4}$ sanpu-Ci-$_B$. 'feel desolate/lonely
(at heart)'.

?B   [uresibiru] < uresibiy- < *uresi-$_{adj\ B}$ (< ...) -np^u/$_o$Ci- (?< -n[a]-pa-
Ci-). 'feel joyful'.

A   utaguru < *uto/utu$_{?2.1}$ n[i] kura-$_B$ ('reel it as hollow'). 'doubt,
suspect'. x - A-A-A x-x-x. Ib A. Attested Edo. Cf. utagau.

?A   [yasasu] < *da$_{1.2}$ sasa-$_B$. 'notch an arrow'.

?   yawasu < yafasu < *dapa$_{adj\ a}$ -sa-. 'soften, pacify, quell'.

?B   yayamu < ya[mi] yamu < *da[ma-Ci]$_{?B}$ dama-$_{?B}$. 'be troubled'.

?B   [yogutatu] < ywogutatu < *dwo$_{1.3a}$ -n- kutata-$_?$. 'night deepen, get to
be late at night'.

?A   [yokona^b/$_m$aru] < y̲o̲k̲o̲-na^b/$_m$aru < *d̲o̲k̲o̲$_{2.1}$ nanpa-ra-$_B$. 'corrupt one's
speech, speak in dialect'. NS (T+ kun) FHHFL = HHHHL.

?   [yuturu] < *i-$_{pre}$ utu-ra-$_B$. (vi.) 'move, change; (time) pass'.

Chapter 7. Adjectives.

7.0. Introduction.

In this chapter we first consider the characteristics that distinguish the inflected adjective (*keiyō-shi*) from other parts of speech. The paradigmatic forms of historic Japanese are shown as developments of simple agglutinative structures, which consist of the adjective stem with one of three suffixes attached: -ku, -sa, and (of lesser consequence) -myi. Consideration is then given to the attributive and predicative forms (§7.3); an attempt is made to show that these may have been secondary developments. We examine (§7.4) the implications of certain striking parallels between modern dialect forms used in the southern Izu islands and those attested for the eastern ("Azuma") dialect of Old Japanese, with respect to the verb as well as the adjective. A survey of the syntactic patterns displayed by the adjective stem (§7.5) is followed by a description of the derivational structures found within adjective stems (§7.6). A brief discussion of the accentuation (§7) is followed by three lists: the main list of adjective stems (§7.8) and two additional lists. The first supplementary list (§7.9) contains those stems which were not attested before 1500; the second (§7.10) contains early stems on which we have no accent information. The lists are extensive, but not exhaustive. A few stems that are late in attestation or lacking in adequate accent information are included in the main list for various special reasons.

7.1. Characterizing the adjective.

Tradition divides the Japanese lexicon into two major parts: uninflected words (*taigen*), loosely called "nouns", and inflected words (*yōgen*). The latter group includes verbs (*dōshi*) and predicable adjectives (*keiyō-shi*). The noun is said to be uninflected because the stem itself is free: it can occur without an attached particle. It is true that examples of certain subclasses, such as that of "pure nouns" (those that can serve as subject or object), are typically found marked by one of the postpositional particles, a group that includes the essives (objective ni and subjective to), which attach the auxiliary ar- 'be' to form the copular expressions, but the nouns are also found alone. Other subclasses, such as certain kinds of adverbs, seldom if ever carry a closely attached particle; a word of that sort comprises an independent phrase in itself. The stems of uninflected words often enter into compounds without attachments; common types are noun + noun, noun + verb stem, and noun + adjective stem. In the absence of prosodic or collocational clues, it is not always clear whether a given structure is lexicalized or is to be treated as a syntactic phrase that contains an ellipted or unexpressed particle. Sometimes the particle is incorporated, often in reduced and disguised form. That is how we account for the phenomenon of rendaku (sequential voicing): this compound-marking device, characterized by voicing and nasality, is treated as an old particle -n-, sometimes clearly a truncation of n[i] and sometimes perhaps a shortening of n[o], though the prehistory of particular instances is often hard to discern.

Verb stems as such are only rarely found as the first member of a compound; instead, a paradigmatic form we call the "infinitive" (*ren'yō-kei*) is used. This form is typically made with a suffix -i, which we reconstruct as earlier *-Ci, with a disappearing consonant that was probably a voiced velar fricative or stop. When the consonant became a glide and then disappeared, the vowel left behind was then incorporated into the preceding vowel of certain stems that were the prototypes of the modern "vowel-stem conjugations": the *ichi-dan* 'monograde' type, which were mostly monosyllabic stems, and the polysyllabic *ni-dan* 'bigrade' type, the stems of most of which already incorporated a formant. These verbs are sometimes referred to as the "···eru/···iru" verbs; for each of them the stem and the infinitive are now identical. In the modern language the infinitive of the verb is like a noun in two ways. It is sometimes used independently, serving as a connective or conjunctive form ('do and'), a somewhat stiff substitute for the gerund V-te (< V-i te); and it is the form to which the particles of focus or emphasis are attached: V-i wa/mo/sae/koso + auxiliary si- 'do'. The verb infinitive is also the usual form in which the verb enters into compounds and through which it derives lexical nouns.

The modern adjective is like the verb in attaching endings to mark syntactic function, aspect, and mood; the form corresponding to V-i is A-ku, the adjective infinitive, and that is the form to which you attach the particles of focus: A-ku wa/mo/sae/koso + auxiliary ar- 'be'. But that is not the form that enters into compounds; instead, the adjective stem itself is used. In at least this respect, the adjective is like the noun. The adjective stem is not so free as the noun (you don't name things with it), but it is more independent than the verb stem. We have found evidence to suggest that verb stems may have been independent at some prehistoric time. From these observations we surmise three stages of evolution. First, the verbs began to require that some sort of particle be tacked on, and then gradually the attachment got stickier so that the stem and the particle (now an "ending") formed a single word, often with morphophonemic adjustments where the stem is joined to the ending. Later on, the adjective followed a similar path, requiring the addition of endings such as -ku or -sa and creating various paradigmatic forms by attaching the auxiliary ar- 'be', with the resulting phrases compressed into single words. In some of the dialects of later Japanese, such as those of Okinawa, nouns attach particles rather closely, and some postpositions (especially the focus marker ya = wa) require morphophonemic adjustments that make them seem more like inflectional endings.

The largest class in the lexicon is that of the nouns, and they comprise an open-ended class. For it is as nouns that foreign words are borrowed, regardless of their grammar and meaning in the language from which they are taken; and it is as nouns that new terms are concocted from native sources, as well. The list of verb stems and adjective stems grows only by the creation of new compounds made up of old stems. There are exceptions, such as the verb daburu 'doubles' and recently the adjective naui 'now-ish, uptodate' from English, but such ventures are rare or ephemeral and usually carry slangy overtones. Stems of Chinese origin: (si)kaku-'rectangular'; dialect sindo- 'weary' < sindoo < sin-roo 'bitter work' or 'heart work' (exact etymology uncertain); Edo-period mendo- = mendo(o)kusa- 'troublesome', syoosi- 'comical; pitiful', seturo(o)-si- (also setura-si-) 'hasty, pressed/pressing' (?< setu-ra[f]u 'season-wax'); and u- 'gloomy', an Old Japanese adjective stem that has survived in the abstract-noun form u-sa 'gloom' (identification with the Chinese etymon may be wrong). In general, when the new word bears a typically verbal or adjectival meaning, it is borrowed into the subclasses we call "verbal nouns" and "adjectival nouns". Verbal nouns are predicated by using the auxiliary suru and adjectival nouns are predicated by using the copular expressions that are derived from ni/to + ar-. Many of the adjectival nouns (such as sizuka 'quiet') are limited in their independence and typically they are found followed by a copular form (sizuka ni/na/de ···); for that reason, traditional Japanese grammar has put them with the inflected words, setting up a category called "adjectival verbs" (keiyō-dōshi). The verbal nouns are traditionally regarded as compounds of N + si-'do' and get no special mention. (For new terms I would suggest keiyō-meishi and dō-meishi, or mei-keiyōshi 'nominal adjectives' and mei-dōshi 'nominal verbs'.) It must be borne in mind that some of the verbal nouns, especially single morphemes of Chinese origin, are bound; they cannot be separated from the auxiliary even by a particle of focus, but instead add the particle to the infinitive of the attached

auxiliary: yaku-si wa/mo (suru) '(does) translate'. These bound verbal nouns are
appropriately entered into the lexicon as verb stems. Few if any of the adjectival
nouns are similarly bound; most of them will sometimes appear independently, in one
structure or another. Martin 1975 did not recognize a category of "bound adjectival
nouns" corresponding to "bound verbal nouns".

7.2. Paradigmatic forms.

In modern Japanese the predicated adjective, like any predication, is directly
adnominalized by placing it (and any adjuncts it carries) in front of the noun to be
modified. The unmarked situation ("imperfect" or "nonpast") calls for the finite
ending -i, which corresponds to the verb ending -(r)u. The verb and adjective
predications of modern Japanese go back to adnominalized forms in earlier Japanese,
and the ending -i is a shortening of -ki, the "attributive" (= adnominal) ending of
the adjective paradigm in classical Japanese, which had a different ending -si for
the "predicative" (= sentence-final) form. The predicative forms fell into disuse
during the Kamakura and Muromachi periods, when colloquial preference turned to
predications that were simply the direct (zero-marked) nominalizations which had
originated in the kakari-musubi phenomenon of Heian and Nara times, whereby most
sentential particles (such as emphatic zo and interrogative ka) were preposed from
the logical position at the end of the sentence, leaving intact the appropriately
adnominalized form of the adjective or verb that these particles called for because
they were originally a kind of nominalization: "It's indeed a fact that ⋯ "; "It's
a question of ⋯ ".
        Most of the paradigmatic forms of the modern adjective are obvious contractions
of the infinitive -ku + the auxiliary ar- 'be', and the attributive and predicative
forms of that "secondary paradigm" were used parallel to the shorter forms: the
attributive -ku aru ⟩ -karu, and the predicative -ku ari ⟩ -kari, with the auxiliary
infinitive that normally replaces the expected predicative form which coincides in
shape with the attributive (aru). This structure can be found uncontracted even
today when focus or emphasis is applied to the adjective itself: -ku wa/mo aru
corresponds to the unfocused -i (= -kari ← -ku ari). For the negative form of the
auxiliary the modern language has replaced the classical forms aranu/arazu with the
adjective na-i 'is nonexistent, is lacking'; the unfocused modern negative -ku nai
replaces the classical -karanu/-karazu ⟨ -ku aranu/arazu. The formal (or "polite")
version -ku arimasen[u] retains the older formation, in its attributive form, with
the last syllable reduced to the nasal mora.
        In the Ryūkyūs there are similar formations deriving from -ku ar-, such as
Miyako takakaz ⟨ taka-k[u] a[r]i and its emphatic version takaftu az ⟨ taka-k[u] zo
a[r]i. Predicative forms ending in -ka, probably ⟨ *-k[u] a[ri], are found not only
in Ryūkyū dialects (Shodon thahaakha ⟨ taka-ka 'it is high'), but also in parts of
Kyūshū, as well: yo-ka 'it's good; OK'. But the common pattern in the Ryūkyūs is to
contract forms of a structure that consists of the nominalizing -sa + the auxiliary
a(r)-. That structure is unattested in Old Japanese and later forms of the written
language; nor does it occur in modern dialects outside the Ryūkyūs. Even there, the
structures corresponding to standard -ku nai and -ku naru/suru generally use the
infinitive -ku. But there are dialects also using -sa, as in the speech of Kikai,
where the form of the negative conversion freely varies between -ku nee and -sa nee,
and the mutative conversions are similar: -ku/-sa nayui 'becomes' (= -ku naru),
-ku/-sa sun 'makes it be' (= -ku suru). Even simple adverbializations can use the
-sa form: pëësa turi 'take it quickly!' (Ryūkyū-hōgen 4:99b). We are reminded that
the noun particle sa, which in dialects of northeastern Honshū corresponds to e or
ni, also appears in the mutative conversions, as in the Aomori examples of N sa naru

'become N' (Zhs 1:64, cf. Martin 1975b:49). In some of those northeastern dialects
the morpheme representing the adjective infinitive is treated as a postadnominal
(= syntactically bound) noun, as in Aomori A-i ku (= standard A-ku, cf. Martin
1975b:49). That structure is also found in Akita (Kindaichi 1977:69), where what
corresponds to aka-ku (naru) '(becomes) red' is pronounced agægu (?= /akayku/) and
is a reflex of aka-i ku; Akita even uses the postadnominal ku (phonetically -gu)
after a verb, V-ru ku naru corresponding to standard V-ru yoo ni naru 'gets so that
one does V'. The grammatical similarities of (-)ku, (-)sa, and ⋯ ni are striking.
It is to be noted that such structures as A-ku ni (RGJ 398 n.6) and A-sa ni (RGJ
910-1) are found both in modern dialects and in literary attestations; these result
from the adverbialization of predicated nominalizations.

Although the Ryūkyū -sa a(r)- forms are usually contracted, on Okinoerabu and
Ie-jima the auxiliary is clearly set apart — by an initial glottal according to
Hirayama 1966:181b but written with the apostrophe in Zhs 11; on Ie-jima there are
focused forms -sa du qa- (< *-sa zo ar- = -ku mo ar-) and -saa qar- (< *-sa [w]a ar-
= -ku wa ar-). Ie-jima also seems to have a form -sanu (?< -sa no, ?← -sa ni)
'because of being': Nyanma icunaasanu yankai icyaii 'I am busy just now, so I'll go
home' (Zhs 11:105). This is similar to the standard A-sa ni 'out of a feeling of
being A' (RGJ 910-1), and may be identical in origin.

Moreover, there are two dialects (Isen and Hetono) on Tokunoshima that attach
the auxiliary ar- directly to the adjective stem (Hirayama 1966:226, 229), perhaps
a further attestation to the independent nature of the stem.

In the Chūgoku area (Hiroshima etc.) all the monosyllabic adjective stems have
incorporated the ending -[k]i into the stem (Shin Nihongo-kōza 3:213): ko- → koi-
'saturated', su- → sui- 'sour', oo- → oi- 'much/many', too- → toi- 'far'. Special
cases: yo- → e-/yo- 'good' (ee 'is good' < yo-[k]i, ee/yoo 'well' < yo-[k]u), na-
→ ne-/na- 'lacking' (nɛɛ 'is lacking' < na-[k]i, nee/noo 'without' < na-[k]u).

7.3. Early structures.

The adjective stems of Old Japanese attached the endings -ku, -sa, and -myi
(< *-mi). All three seem to have been nominalizations of one sort or another, and
lexicalized derivations from each can be found in modern standard Japanese, though
only -sa is a productive nominalizer. In Old Japanese, clearcut lexicalizations are
hard to find. One example is sigeymyi 'thicket', but most such derived nouns (e.g.
fukami 'depths' and asami 'shallows') are first attested in Heian literature. Almost
all Old Japanese examples of -sa are direct predications: imwo ga kanasisa (M 3727)
'the dear girl [is] so adorable!', fyito no tomosisa (M 863) 'the people [are] so
few!'. These examples are very similar to some of the common Ryūkyū structures.
Lexicalizations with -ku are relatively few and late in attestation, but ofoku no
mono 'lots of things' occurs in Genji. In the modern language -ku (infinitive and
adverbializer) and -sa (abstract lexical nominalizer) are productive, but -mi is
not. The ending -ku attaches only to the stems of adjectives, but -sa and -mi can be
attached to adjectival nouns, as well: sinken-sa, sinken-mi 'earnestness'. In Old
Japanese the -myi form was used in these structures:
   (1) N wo A-myi 'because N is A': kokoro wo yuramyi (K 108) 'because your heart
is slack'; FYITO-MEY wo ofomyi (M 207) 'because there are many eyes'; izamyi no
yama wo TAKA-myi ka mo (M 44) 'for Mount Izami is so high'.
   (2) N [wo] A-myi 'N is A and so': utakyi kasikwomyi (K 99) 'because the roar is
awesome'; ...; yama takamyi kafa tofosirosi (M 324) 'its mountains are high and
(or: and so) its rivers are mighty'.
   (3) N-A-myi < *N -n- A-myi 'N is A and so': yama-dakamyi (K 79) 'the mountain
being high (therefore)'.

(4) (N wo) A-myi to 'deeming (N) to be A': yama wo sagasi-myi to (K 70) 'thinking the mountain steep'; TUKAFYI nokeyre[y]-ba uresi-myi to (M 3957) 'delighted that the messenger was left'; kyefu dani mo kotodofyi semu to wosi-myi tutu (M 4408) 'while thinking it would be valuable to have a conversation this very day'.

(5) (N wo) A-myi su/omofu 'deem (N) to be A': (··· koso ···) urufasi-myi sure[y] (M 4088) '(precisely ···) finds it beautiful'; ··· koto wo namo katazikeynamyi iswosi-myi omofosimasu (Senmyō 52) 'deigns to appreciate as unworthy but energetic the deed of ··· '.

We do not know where the three suffixes -ku, -sa, and -myi came from. The infinitive -ku is probably related somehow to an old nominalization that is best described as a bound noun *aku attached to truncated forms of the attributive: kataraku (M 852) 'what it tells (is ···)' ← katar[u] aku, nageykaku (M 4008) 'the wailing' ← nageyk[u] aku; oyuraku (M 3246) 'getting old' ← oyur[u] aku, suraku (NS 18a) ← sur[u] aku 'doing (= thinking, intending)'. The bound noun also attaches to the adjective attributive: ukyeku turakyeku (M 897) 'what is sad, what is trying' ← u-kyi aku tura-kyi aku. We might speculate that -ku itself is a truncation of *aku, but I think it likelier that the bound noun consists of a[r]- 'be' + -ku, not a truncation of araku 'what is' (M 809, 3919, ...) ← ar[u] aku for that would leave the a- to be explained, but a direct attachment of -ku to the root *a- which seems to underlie the historic stem ar- < *a(-)ra-. Notice also the suffix (or bound noun) -ra 'quantity; group', which I take as a truncation of *ara 'what exists', a direct use of the stem *a(-)ra- as a noun. (The reconstruction of *aku, which originated with Ōno Susumu, is rejected by many scholars in Japan who prefer to leave what they call "ku-gohō" raggedly unexplained; but I think Ōno is essentially right, though I would carry the derivation a step further, as above.)

The suffix -sa is thought to be etymologically related to sama 'appearance; direction', as is the dialect particle sa 'to' (= e or ni), but it is unclear whether -sa is a truncation of the dissyllable or whether sama contains a suffix, perhaps ma 'room; place' used in Ryūkyū deictics such as Sr ku-ma 'here'. And the suffix -sa may, of course, be quite unrelated to the noun sama.

The suffix -myi < *-mi may have originated as the infinitive (< *-ma-[C]i) from a bound verb stem *-ma- that serves as a formant in the stems of a number of the verbs that today end in ···mu or, with an additional formant (*-ma-Ci- > -mey-), ···meru. Not many stems with this formant are attested for Old Japanese, and it is unclear whether there would have been a contrast between, say, N [wo] kurwo-myi 'N is black and so' and N kurwomyi 'N becomes black (and)', for the verb kuromu < *kurwomu 'become black' is not attested before the Heian period. I am not sure whether a contrast may be shown in the two passages tabyi wo kurusi-myi (M 3674) 'because the journey is painful' and mataba kurusimyi (M 3998) 'if I wait I suffer'; is the last verb a sentence-final infinitive, an infinitive-derived noun, or the A-myi structure? And wosi-myi tutu (M 4408) in the example given earlier could be taken as the transitive verb wosimu 'regret; prize', but clear attestations of that verb are not found before the eleventh century. Arguing for a verbal interpretation of A-myi is the fact that the accusative particle is used, as if N wo A-mu meant 'treats N as A'; yet most of the ···mu verbs are intransitive, and the transitive counterparts (···mey- < *-ma-Ci-) have an extra formant: yasum- < *yasu-ma- 'become at ease', yasumey- < *yasu-ma-Ci- 'put at ease'. There are exceptions, such as wosim- < *wosi-ma- 'regret; prize'. We presume that the A-myi form could be made for any adjective, even though many of the expected forms remain unattested, but that the verbs derived by suffixing the formant *-ma- to an adjective stem were pretty much limited to the ones we find attested or surviving; that seems to be the best argument against simply identifying that this -myi as the infinitive of the formant.

There is another possibility, not necessarily in conflict: the auxiliary -mu < *ma-
which attaches to the verb stem, as in yukamu 'I will go'. And, as Yoshida points
out, the V-i - myi that corresponds to the modern representative form (V-tari) could
perhaps be accounted for as the infinitive of that auxiliary, here attached to the
infinitive rather than to the stem. Zdb derives V-i - myi from the infinitive of
myi-ru 'see', myi < *mi-[Ci], attempting to justify that with an interpretation of
the meaning that I find unconvincing.

7.4. Attributive and predicative forms.

In addition to -ku, -sa, and -myi, Old Japanese also had the endings -kyi for
the attributive and -si for the predicative. These endings have been the subject of
discussion for a number of reasons. The predicative -si dropped out of existence,
except in literary relics, with the spread of the attributive-final sentence that
replaced the earlier predicative-marked sentence starting sometime in the 1300s. The
attributive form of the adjective, marked with the ending -ki which sporadically was
weakening and eliding its velar stop (> -[k]i) even in the Heian period, became the
dominant form both for sentences that were adnominalized and those that were not.
In the modern dialects of the Ryūkyūs there is little evidence for either of these
two endings. We might presume that forms like the adnoun represented by Sr ii (A)
'good' developed like the corresponding main-island forms: yo-kyi > yo-[k]i > yoi >
*yei > (y)ee > (y)ii. But there are two other possibilities. Perhaps the form,
despite the fact that its reflexes are widely found in the Ryūkyūs, was borrowed
from main-island dialects. And perhaps it was an indigenous lengthening of *ye- (<
yo-) to yee with later raising to (y)ii; in that case, the form is simply the stem
itself, used adnominally as the Ryūkyū dialects rather freely use other adjective
stems. But is there evidence that -k[y]i existed earlier in Ryūkyū speech? Perhaps.
Hokama 1971 ("Okinawa hōgen keiyō-shi no shi-teki hensen", Okinawa no gengo-shi 101-
200 [it was originally published 1970 in Gendai Gengo-gaku], cites three omoro
examples of uki 'big' < ofo-kyi and one of wakai 'young' < waka-[k]yi, and from
tablets erected 1501-1624 two examples of A-si (na-si 'is nonexistent' and suzu-si
'is cool'), all of which are probably borrowed. The Chinese work Ryūkyū kan yakugo
(early 15th century) has two examples of A-si: nagasi 'long' and misinasi 'short'.
But these examples are out of place with the other adjectives cited, all of which
end in -san. Ryūkyū Kanwa-shū (?1600-) carries a single example, kibisi-ki 'strict'
(Nakamatsu 154). The 1711 Okinawan dictionary Konkōken-shū lists three adjectives
with -ki forms (natukasiki 'nostalgic', mesamasiki 'eye-opening', kitanaki 'dirty')
and two with -[k]i (warui mono 'bad thing', yofi [= yo(w)i] mono 'good thing').
These are surely either borrowings or imitations of the main-island forms, literary
and colloquial, respectively. Among the kumi-odori (written and performed since
1719) there are a number of forms with -si (some used attributively, some used
predicatively) and a few examples of -ki and -[k]i. All of these appear to be the
result of main-island influences; the -ki forms are surely the result of knowing the
literary language, which artificially preserved the grammar of the 12th century.
The Ryūka (1795, 1798, 1802) have a few examples of the predicative -si and of the
attributive -ki, but no examples of -[k]i. Chamberlain (1895) noted only ii 'good'
and miẓirasii munu 'rare thing'; Okinawa-go jiten (86 n.16) cites miẓirasii hanasi
'a rare story' and quturusii ninẓin 'a frightful person' with the note that they are
"emotional or emphatic" compared to the normal -saru forms. So the case is weak for
indigenous A-ki and A-si in the southern islands. The few examples are probably
borrowings from main-island dialects or imitations of literary Japanese.

There are a number of peculiarities about the endings -kyi and -si. They would
appear to be complementary in syntactic function, yet there is evidence that the

"attributive" and "predicative" functions were not always clearly marked in Old
Japanese. Verb stems, for example, used the same shape for the categories in the
case of consonant-ending stems and monosyllabic vowel-ending stems, differentiating
-u from -uru only in the case of the polysyllabic vowel stems, virtually all of
which contain a derivational suffix *-Ci-. (For the Type-A verbs the late-Heian
accentual notations differentiated the two forms: N $\overline{yuku}$ 'N goes', $\overline{yuku}$ N 'N who
goes'. But the HH pattern represents a secondary atonicization, as pointed out in
Ch. 4.) And there are examples of variation in the use of the forms that seem to
indicate they were to some extent rivals, each competing for both functions, rather
than partners in complementary distribution. This evidence was mentioned in Martin
1967:260 n.24 and used to justify the seemingly audacious etymologies proposed
there: contractions of *-k[u ar]-i > -k(y)i and *-s[a ar]-i > -si. Roy A. Miller
and John Street, seeking Altaic cognates for these two morphemes, have expressed
skepticism about the evidence, claiming that Martin was misled by a secondary
source, which (they say) misinterpreted remarks in the original study of Yamada
1954. Their argument is that the numerous examples of A-si N are to be accounted for
not as the haplological predicative A-si[-si] but as the simple stem, forming a
compound noun. That sounds plausible, and it is indeed what Yamada thought, but it
is wrong. To begin with, there is accentual evidence that in the Heian period the
expressions were pronounced as two phrases, not as a single word: yorosi | mye $\overline{wo}$
(NS 82c [17:112-M, 113-M]) 'a fine woman', kufasi | mye $\overline{wo}$ (NS 82c [112-M]) 'a
comely woman'; presumably sakasi mye wo (K 2) 'a wise woman' was similarly phrased.
Secondly, even within genuinely lexicalized compounds with the structure A-si - N,
there are examples of adjective stems which did not contain the formant -si-:
yosi-nwo (M 4099, 4100) 'Yoshino (= Good-Moor, a placename)' ← yo- 'good', and
compounds with ne-nasi 'is rootless' such as nenasi-gusa 'duckweed' and nenasi-
kadura 'dodder' (both first attested in the Heian period) ← na- 'be lacking'; the
kun-chū glosses of Nihon-Shoki include ika-si fyi 'mighty day', ika-si foko 'mighty
halberd', and kata-s[i] ifa 'hard rock'. There are also lexicalizations which derive
from V-u N where we would expect V-ru N: izumi '(well-)spring' < idu-myi (not *iduru
myi) ← idu myi[du] 'it emerges, water' and not *iduru myidu 'water that emerges';
yosu-ka (M 1382, Bussokuseki 18) 'a (place to) hold' may be a similar example.
Thirdly, there are examples of A-kyi where we would expect the predicative. Sansom
103 suggests that these "can perhaps be accounted for on metrical grounds", citing
the passage tafutwoku uresikyi (M 4273) 'is sacred and delightful', in which the
haplological predicative uresi[si] would give a line of only six instead of the
required seven syllables if the string -ku u- is run together as one syllable, as
was usual under the prosodic rules. (This must be what Sansom had in mind as his
"metrical grounds", which were left unstated.) Fourthly, although fwosi-kyi was the
normal form of fwosi- 'desirous/desired' when adnominalized, the expressions V-yi
ga fwosi 'desire to V' were always adnominalized as fwosi; the only examples are
with the verbs myi- 'see' and ar- 'be': myi[y] ga fwosi kuni (K 59) 'the (home)land
I want to see', ARI ga f[w]osi SUMYI-YOKYI SATWO no ARAraku WO SI MO (M 1059)
'Alas the desolation of the comfortable village where ⋯ and where I want to be!'.
One interpretation of urufasi to (K 81) is as a direct nominalization 'with my
beloved [I slept ⋯]', i.e. urufasi[si] = urufasi-kyi fyito, but Tsuchihashi may
be right in taking the meaning as 'thinking her lovely [I slept ⋯]'.

   We have used the term "haplological" to refer to the predicative of adjective
stems containing the formant -si-, which typically marks subjective adjectives
referring to emotional states or psychological reactions, often involving cathexis
whereby the affected person psychologically projects the emotion onto an affective
object, which can function as a grammatical subject. We take the sentence-final

uresi 'is delighted/delightful' as a shortening of uresi[-si] or ure[si]-si: the stuttered syllable is reduced to a single enunciation, and that reduction seems to have been obligatory. Full forms with ···si-si are attested from late-Heian and early-Kamakura times, but these are surely analogical reformulations rather than relics: asi-si 'it is bad' is attested in 1219 (KggD 974a) and there are numerous examples of A-si-si in a 1309 text of Heike-monogatari (id. 979a). Some scholars have etymologically identified the predicative ending -si with the derivational formant -si-. There are other elements to which the formant could perhaps be more convincingly related, such as the emphatic particle si and the infinitive si ‹ *s[o-C]i 'do; deem'.

    Among the infinitive-attached auxiliaries of Literary Japanese there is a perfect which has the predicative form -kyi and the attributive form -si, just the opposite of the paired suffixes for the adjective. Notice that the forms meaning 'did' are si-kyi and, irregularly, se-si.) For consonant verb stems ending in the sibilant the attributive forms were originally regular: korosi-si koto. But in the artificial literary language used in modern times, i.e. for the past five hundred years, the forms are usually written ···se-si, perhaps by analogy with se-si; forms like korose-si were "permitted" variants in Meiji prescriptive grammar. Cf. NKD 5:469b. Examples of ···si-si are uncommon, but a few can be cited from the orthographic renditions in Zdb: MYESI-si MYI-OTO nari (Fuju-monkō), MASI-si TEN-WAU (Senmyō 4). There is an example in the prefatory text of K 93 (itadura ni sakari o sugusi-si koto 'you have passed your prime years in vain') and K 99 contains the phonogram attestation of at least one occurrence and possibly two (the first word being a fixed epithet): yasumyisi-si wa ga ofo-kyimyi no aswobasi-s sisi 'the beast trifled with [= shot] by our great lord who is ruling-in-peace'. There is no consensus as to whether the two perfect forms, which are complementary in their syntactic distribution, are to be identified with the adjective endings or whether they come from some other source, such as the infinitives kyi ‹ *k[o-C]i 'come' and si ‹ *s[o-C]i 'do', or perhaps s[ar]i ‹ *sar[a-C]i 'leave'. If they are identified with the adjective endings, the largely opposite distribution of function may be fallout from an earlier competition by each form for both functions. There are a few examples of V-i-si where would expect V-i-kyi, as pointed out by Yoshida 1973:158: wa ga futari ne[y]-si (K 19, M 109) 'we slept as a pair', wa ga nusumafyi-si (M 2832) 'I kept stealing [long periods of time]'; and perhaps (w)a ga kwofiy somey-si (M 642 written in semantograms but the final character may represent a simultaneous phonogram) 'I began to fall in love' and imey ni myiye[y] ko-si (M 633 if the final character is taken as a phonogram) 'came to be seen in a dream'. Yoshida explains such examples as a direct nominalization with exclamatory meaning, almost as if a sentential particle were present; if so, these examples may represent rather early precursors for the "rentai-dome" (predication by means of a direct nominalization) of Heian and Kamakura days that led to the demise of the predicative form. Despite the repeated claims of Miller and Street, it seems highly unlikely that the expression tofotofosi Kwosi no kuni (K 2) 'the far-off land of Koshi' contains a compound noun. But what we may have, instead, is the use of the simple stem to modify a noun without necessarily compressing the resulting phrases into a compound noun; there are parallels in the Ryūkyū patterns. We do not know whether examples like awo yama (K 2) 'green mountain', two mey (K 18, 19) 'sharp eyes', and ye wotokwo (Koji-ki text) 'a fine man' were compounds in Old Japanese or not, though the rendaku of examples like aka-dama (K 8) 'red jewel (= coral)' might be taken to indicate lexicalization. Yet, rendaku as such does not necessarily make a compound; see below, §5, and compare the remarks in Ch. 4 on phrasal junctures that surface despite morphophonemic reductions. In any event there is no rendaku found in the expressions onazi kuni nari (M 4073) 'it is the same country' and oyazi tokyifa ni

(M 4006) 'with the same permanence' where we would expect onazi-kyi and oyazi-kyi;
despite Yamada, it makes no more sense to call these compounds than to consider
modern onazi kuni 'the same country' a single lexeme. In many instances, the chosen
adjective is a fixed epithet, and in Old Japanese it appears to have been common to
use the inverted syntax Predicative + Noun for such epithets, whether adjectives or
verbs, with the appropriate interpretation a convoluted 'it is/does, the N' rather
than a straightforward 'the N that is/does …':
   ka-gufasi fana-tatibana fa (K 44) 'the "it-is-fragrant" flowering orange'.
   awo-ni yosi Nara wo sugiy (K 59) 'went beyond "its blue clay is good" Nara'.
The adjective form in the first example is metrically irregular (four syllables);
the expected attributive ka-gufasikyi would be regular, as would an untruncated ka-
gufasi[si]. The first phrase of the second example is metrically regular (five
syllables) and is clearly a predicative, since the stem yo- does not contain the
formant -si-. Certain expressions such as kanasi im[w]o wo (M 3577) 'dear girl',
utukusi im[w]o ga (NS 114) 'lovely girl', utukusi fafa ni (M 4392) 'to the lovely
mother' may have been stereotypes of similar origin. Let's examine some examples of
vowel-stem verbs. The forms are cited with final "[ ]" rather than "[ru]", so as not
to prejudge whether they represent a contracted version of the attributive, as some
scholars have suggested, or are genuinely predicative; the parenthesized number
after the translation indicates whether the meter of the phrase as given is regular
(5 or 7 syllables) or irregular.
   nayu[ ] TAKEY no (M 420) 'the "it-bends" bamboo' (5).
   iyu[ ] sisi wo (NS 117) 'the "it-gets-shot" deer' (5) = IYU[ ] SISI wo (M 3874, in
which the predicative 'gets shot' is inferred for the semantogram 'shoot' because of
the NS passage and the meter).
   swora myitu[ ] Yamato no kuni ni (K 72) 'to the land of "it-fills-the-sky" Yamato'
(4,7); cf. SWORA myitu[ ] Yamato no KUNI FA (M 1) and, regularizing the meter,
SWORA ni MYITU YAMATO wo (M 29).
The semantogram writing of the verb in the following examples cannot explicitly
attest the predicative form, but that is the form usually assumed in order to make
the meter regular:
   NAGU[ ] YA si omofoyu (M 3345) 'is deemed verily the "it-is-flung" arrow' (7).
   NAGARU[ ] SAKYITA no KAFA NO SE ni (M 4156) 'in the rapids of the "it-flows"
      river Sakita" (7, 5).
   TABYI WAKARU[ ] dwoti (M 4252) 'those going on separate journeys' (7).
The last example is not a fixed epithet, but it comes from one of the Azuma dialect
poems, and they offer a variety of examples that are not epithets:
   kafyiri (= kafyeri) ku[ ] mate ni (M 4339, M 4350) 'until I come back'.
   ta ka kyi-nu[ ] (M 4387) 'who has come?' (4) — attributive expected because of
the preposed interrogative particle.
   nakyi-si zo [o]mofayu[ ] (M 4357) 'appears to have wept' (7) — attributive
expected because of the preposed emphatic particle.
   akey-nu[ ] sida kuru (M 4357) 'there comes the time that it has dawned' (7).
Yoshida 1973:495 says that the suffix for the attributive vowel verb (V-ru) got to
be part of the system only gradually during the Nara period, and he claims that the
perfect auxiliary (V-yi) nu/nuru usually appeared without the -ru even when the
attributive is called for, using that as an argument against Ōno's reconstruction
of V-r[u a]ku to account for the nominalization we have mentioned: "because -nuraku
WAS used". But the non-dialect poems fail to substantiate Yoshida's claim, as can
be seen in his own examples on p.585 of the attributives TIRI-NUru (M 120 — the
explicit -ru is missing from one manuscript), MYITI-nuru (M 1144), and yadori-nuru
(3693). Yoshida neglects to offer any Old Japanese examples of V-yi - nuraku, nor
have I noticed any; do they really exist?

7.5. Attributive forms in eastern dialects.

Literary Japanese does not distinguish attributive and predicative forms for the consonant-stem verbs, with the seeming exception of the stem ar- 'be' and of verbs derived from that stem, which substitutes the infinitive (ari) in most of the syntactic environments where we would expect the predicative (aru). But in the dialects of Hachijō-jima, in the southern Izu islands, the two forms are different, even for consonant-stem verbs. The predicative ends in -u, but the attributive ends in -o. We cite examples from Zhs 7: iko toki (24) 'when one goes'; hanaso hodo (232) 'the more I talk'; yoru no usuguraku naro zibun ni (225) 'at the time of evening it gets to be twilight'; aro ga (184, 216, 229) 'is but', aro zya (183) 'is the case that it is' (= aru no da); ... . Sometimes the -o is lengthened: ··· te yoo hito no (188) 'a person called ···' (= to iu hito ga); katagoo tokoro de mo (204) 'even when shouldering it' (= katugu tokoro de mo); sitoo koto ga (184) 'what one did' (?= sita[ru] koto ga). To be sure, there are examples of the -u attributive in the same texts, but they are probably due to the influence of outside dialects: toru toki wa (180) 'when I take it'; un no aru hito ga (182) 'a person who has luck', kasi no aru wake zya na si (210) 'it doesn't mean I have sweets'; ato n naru sito wa (211) 'those people who get behind'; iku nara (185) 'if one is to go'; yobu hito wa (203) 'the person calling'; ... . Moreover, the Hachijō dialects extend the -o attributive even to vowel-stem verbs: dero ga (217) 'goes (out) but'. With the exception of that example — and compare gakkau i deyo kotau sya 'if one goes off to school' (= gakkoo e deru koto o siya/sureba) — after /i/ or /e/ the expected -ro seems to be -yo: niyo mo (233) 'cooking too' (= niru no mo); tabesaseyo hito mo na si (231) 'they have no one who will feed them'; and even ato de iyo sito no (234) 'people who enter later' (= ato de [ha]ir-u hito ga), though that ought to be a consonant stem. (But Iitomi Yokiichi 1959 has -ro for verbs of these types.) The attributive form of suru is syo(o): ··· syo toki (180) 'when I do'; syo nte (196) 'since it does (= is) [like that]'; syo ni wa (235) 'in doing it'; syo ga (181, 182) = syoo ga (181, 234) 'does but', oyo wa ga taisetu ni syo ga yoke dayaa (185) 'it's better for us to take good care of our parents' (= oya o ware ga taisetu ni suru no ga ii no desu). Iitomi lists both su and suru for the predicative; good examples of predicative forms are hard to find in the texts: sogon su to wa (229) 'doing/being that way' (= soo suru to; sogon < so[no] go[to] n[i] = sono gotoku).

The Hachijō dialects also have an attributive form for the adjective, and it ends in -ke: tiisake kodomo (231) 'a little child'; nekkoke toki (180, 186, 204) 'when I was tiny'; yoke sake (217) 'good sake', tenki ga yoke nte (190) 'since the weather's good', yoke ga (217, 219) 'it's good but'; waruke n yotte (207) 'because it's bad'; yowake hito ga (188) 'a weak person'; okkanake mityo (189) 'a fearsome road' (= okkanai miti o); akaruke yonte (214) 'since it is bright'; mezurasike hito (219) 'a rare person'; atuke toki ni (226) 'when it is hot'; usugurake toki kara (226) 'from the time it is dusky'; yoku tuyoke mon (228) 'quite strong'; ha[y]ake sito wa ··· nagake sito wa (230 [n.20 says the first -ke "sounds much like -ku"]) 'people who are fast ··· people who take a long time'; hayake hoo de mo naku osoke hoo de (229) 'not early but late'; ... . Gemination occurs in nakke ga (219) 'is lacking but' (= nai ga). The form used for sentence-final predication ends in -kya or -kyaa: uresikya (220) 'is delighted', kowakyaa (235) 'it is trying'. Gemination occurs in nakkya (akaku nakkya 'is not red' 24) and yokkya (210) 'that's all right'; and also apparently in V-i-takkya 'wants to V' (Hirayama 1965:199b). The rule seems to be: -ke and -kya geminate when attached to a monosyllabic adjective stem.

What is of special interest in the Hachijō attributive forms is that they are similar to forms that are attested for the eastern dialect of Old Japanese. We know

something about this dialect from the 230 "Azuma" songs of volume 14 of the Man'yō-
shū (M 3348-3597); from the 93 (of 224) songs of Volume 20 (M 4293-4516) that are
attributed to "sakimori", border-guards sent from eastern Japan to Kyūshū; and also
from the Hitachi-fudoki. In the eastern dialect the predicative form of consonant-
stem verbs ended in -Cu, as in the language of Nara, but the attributive ended in
-Cwo: yukwo sakyi ni (M 4385) 'ahead (toward which we go)'; tatwo tuku no (M 3476)
'the moon that rises'; sifobune no fey kwoswo siranamyi (M 4389) 'the whitecaps
that the prow of the ("tide-boat" =) seafarer ship crosses over'; af[w]o sida mo
(3479) 'even when we meet', faf[w]o mamey no (M 4352) 'creeping beans'; nwozi
arafarwo made mo (M 3414) 'even till the rainbow appears'; okyi ni sum[w]o wo-gamo
no mokoro (M 3527) 'like a little duck that lives offshore'; kwo-ro ga osokyi
no arwo koso ye si mo (M 3509) 'having the lad late turns out to be good' — cf.
the noun arwozi (M 4498) = aruzi 'master, owner' < aru n[u]si. There are exceptions:
yukyi ka mo furaru (M 3351) 'snow has fallen' (furaru = fureru < furi aru), where
we would expect *ywokyi ka mo furarwo, matching the forms found in furwo ywokyi no
(M 3423) 'the snow that falls' and awo YAGIY no fararwo kafa-two ni (M 3546) 'at the
river ferry where the green willows are stretched' (fararwo = fareru < fari aru).

Moreover, the early easterners used -ke for the adjective attributive. In terms
of the phonograms of Old Japanese this was sometimes written -kye, sometimes -key.
Fukuda Yōsuke believes that the eastern dialect did not distinguish the two kinds
of front-vowel syllables, but like modern Japanese just had Ce and Ci instead of Cye
≠ Cey and Cyi ≠ Ciy. There is other evidence that the eastern dialect may not have
had to cope with some of the situations which led to the formation of Cey and Ciy:
simple tuku is used for 'moon' (M 3476) where the central dialect used tukiy <
*[tukui] < *tuku-Ci. Examples of the old eastern -ke, here spelled out -kye or -key
according to the phonograms: kanasikye se-ro ni (M 3548) 'to the beloved fellow',
kanasikye wo okyi te (M 3551) 'abandoning the loved one', aze ··· kanasikye (M 3517)
'why [so dearly] beloved?'; asikey fyito nari (M 4382) 'is a bad person'; nagakey
ko no ywo wo (M 4394) 'this night that is long'. To be sure, forms with -kyi also
are attested in the eastern songs: kanasikyi kwo-ro ga (M 3351) 'beloved lad';
nagakyi faru-fyi mo (M 4020) 'the long spring days too'. These are perhaps, like
some of the exceptional forms in modern Hachijō speech, the result of influence
from other dialects.

The resemblance between the Hachijō attributive forms and those attested for
the Nara-period dialect of eastern Japan has not escaped the attention of Japanese
linguists, who generally take the position that the A-ke and V-o forms of the modern
dialect must be a continuation of the early forms. What does this mean about proto-
Japanese? Hattori (1976:26-8) thinks the earliest attributive must have been A-ke
and V-o; in these attributive endings, he says, the non-eastern dialects early in
their prehistory raised -ke to -kyi, and similarly raised V-o to V-u, so that it
merged with the shape of the predicative. We have mentioned the likelihood that the
eastern dialect had only one variety for each of the two front syllables Ce and Ci.
What about Cwo ≠ Co? There are a number of Azuma words with Cwo that correspond to
non-eastern forms with Cu: ywokyi (M 3423) = yukyi 'snow', nwozi (M 3414) = nuzi
'rainbow' (but for doubts about the interpretation nwo, see Zdb 553-4), ...
Within the mainstream of the language there are a few doublets with Cu/Cwo, such as
the traversal/ablative particle yu/ywo(ri), and some of the Azuma forms won out over
the central versions: modern sugosu maintains the vowel of Azuma sugwosu rather than
that of the usual OJ sugusu 'let pass beyond'. But in general Cwo and Cu were kept
distinct. There are a fair number of native nouns ending in Cu: amu (K 98)
'gadfly', faru (M 815) 'spring', fuyu (M 4003) 'winter', fyiru (K 3) 'daytime',

fyiru (NS 35) 'garlic', asu (M 3510) 'tomorrow', masu (on a tablet from Heizei palace) 'trout' (but masu 'measure' is not phonetically attested until the Wamyō-shō), matu (M 4501) 'pine', natu (M 4011) 'summer', ... ; inu 'dog' is written in a semantogram in M 3278 and was not attested phonetically before the Heian period, and similar examples are kasu 'dregs', kazu 'number', and fitu 'large lidded box'; aku 'lye' was first attested in the Heian period. There are monosyllabic nouns like su 'nest' (M 892) and (variously attested) su 'sand(bar)' and tu 'boat-mooring place'; the phonetic attestations of su 'vinegar' and 'weir' and of yu 'hot water' and u 'cormorant' are Heian. Also, there are adverbs like itu (M 804) 'when' and madu (M 818) 'first of all', adjective stems that end in ···Cu- such as samu- 'cold', yasu- 'easy', niku- 'hateful', and the counter -tu found in numbers. None of these words appear with Cwo. It would seem that Cu was distinguished from Cwo in both dialects of Old Japanese, though there were competing variants for a few words. But there is a distinct likelihood that Cwo and Co diverged from a single prehistoric vowel (Co), as we observed in Ch. 1. On the other hand, we have taken both Cye and Cey back to dissyllabic origins, Cye < Cia < Ci[C]a and ey < Cai < Ca[C]i. Was the putatively proto-Japanese *-ke also diphthongal in origin? If so, both the eastern -ke[y] and the central -kyi could be explained as competing ways of contracting -ku ari: -k[u] a[r]-yi > -key, -k[u ar]-yi > -kyi. (For A-ku/-kyi Ōno Tōru 1978:297-8 reconstructs "< *ko/-key" for A-ku/-kyi and connects both with ko 'this'; he also relates A-si "< *-se" with so 'that'.) What about the verb forms? In Ch. 6 it was suggested that the finite ending -u had been formed by incorporating the stem of an auxiliary such as wor- ?< *bo(-)ra- (or ?< wi[y] ar- < *b^u/$_o$-Ci ara-) and wi[y]- ?< *b^u/$_o$-Ci-, two verbs meaning 'be, stay' with likely cognates in Altaic languages. Perhaps there were two versions of this contraction, only one of which survived in the non-eastern dialect, while the eastern dialect assigned separate functions to the -Co and to the -Cu, as in modern Hachijō.

Finally, it should be borne in mind that many historic dialects of Japanese during the past thousand years show difficulties in keeping mid and high vowels distinct. The Azuma variant kafyir- reflects the etymological composition of that verb stem ('return') better than the central version kafyer-; see Ch. 6. The noun sima 'island' appears in NS in a variant form sema, which is usually attributed to influence of an earlier version of the Korean syem 'island' (Ch. 5). Whatever the relationship with the Korean word, which Lee Ki-Moon reconstructs with a high vowel /i/ that later "broke" to /ye/, the NS sema may be an early dialect variant; if the noun is etymologically related to the verb stem simey- < *sima-Ci 'occupy', as is suggested by the fact that it has been used to mean 'quarters, territory', the sima version better reflects the original shape. A number of the eastern dialects today have trouble distinguishing /i/ from /e/, especially in non-initial syllables. And "wenoko" = (y)enoko 'puppy' is attested from the Muromachi period on; the mid vowel of the first syllable, however, may be the result of partial assimilation to the following two vowels, assuming that the immediate source is i[nu]-no-ko. The variant ooke- = ooki- 'big' is found in a number of dialects of western and central Honshū and (Toguchi 1974:119) Kyūshū, but it must be a relatively late assimilation of -ki- to the mid vowel quality of the other moras of the stem. Incidentally, this stem is perhaps the only example where the colloquial language retains a trace of the velar stop for the ending -ki. How did that come about? The attributive form owo-ki (< *ofo-kyi) often appeared as a predicated direct nominalization owoki nari 'it's a big one' or 'it's [a fact] that it is big'. The form was reinterpreted in late Heian and Kamakura times as an adjectival noun with the attributive (w)owoki na[ru] and the infinitive (w)owoki ni. Then in the Muromachi period there was a back-formation by which the adjective ending -[k]i, now bereft of its velar, was attached to the adjectival noun, leading to the forms that are found in the 1603

Japanese-Portuguese dictionary: vôqina (= wooki na) and vôqi ni (= wooki ni) with
the same meaning as vôqij (= wookii) and vôqiǔ (= wookyuu) 'big'. With a narrowing
of meaning, the original stem ofo- persists as vouoi (= wowoi) and vouô (= wowoo)
'much, many', leading to the modern forms o(ꜛ)oi and o(ꜛ)oo = o(ꜛ)oku.

7.6. Syntactic patterns of adjective stems.

When Old Japanese adjectives were used in situations calling for the expected
"predicative" form, as in the typical sentence-final environment, they usually
attached the ending -si; the double -si-si that resulted for stems carrying the
formant -si- was reduced to a single /si/. Occasionally we find sentences ending in
-sa, such as MYIRE[Y]-BA KANASI-sa (M 1442) 'seeing the child ⋯ is endearing'.
If the surface sentence ends in -kyi, it is because the attributive is called for by
a preposed particle of focus or emphasis; at a slightly deeper level of analysis, the
the adjectival sentence is to be regarded as adnominalized to that particle, and a
similar analysis applies to verbal sentences under the same circumstances. More
often, the -kyi form is used to modify a noun; the ending is used to adnominalize
the clause, whether that consists of a single adjective or an adjective carrying
adjuncts (subjects, adverbials, etc.). The most frequent situation is that of a lone
adjective, with no adjuncts; and the most common way to adnominalize the adjective
to the noun is by using the -kyi ending. But there are other structures that let an
adjective modify a noun. Some of these structures have been treated traditionally as
"compound nouns", on the basis of their accentual phrasing in later Japanese, as
well as the tightness of the modification, which is imputed from the fact that the
adjective carries no adjuncts or modifiers of its own. At the earliest stages of the
language, such structures seem to have been more productive and were probably spoken
as separate "words". Here we will treat together both the structures that were later
considered compound nouns and those regarded as syntactic formations.

The common way for a noun to modify another noun was N no N. This structure
was reduced to N -n- N, with the marker -n- historically reflected in the voiced
nasality we call nigori, and that is one source of the phenomenon called rendaku
'sequential voicing' or 'compound nigori'. (Another source is N n[i] N. And rendaku
occurs also with some of the N-V and N-A compounds.) But the nigori that represents
the -n- was preserved only before obstruents (p-, t-, k-, s-); the reflex was zero
before nasals, vowels, y- and w-. And in some cases, the adnominal marker dropped
before obstruents, too. Shorter structures with N (-) N are usually treated as
lexicalized compound nouns (and given the appropriate accentual patterns), even
though their formation is productive, and the degree of lexicalization varies.
Moreover, certain strings of N (-) N (- ⋯), especially the longer ones, are given
phrasings that indicate a casual ellipsis of the marker [no], which can readily be
inserted. These three surface structures are also found for adjective stems when
modifying nouns: A no N, A -n- N, and (in OJ the most common) A (-) N. Such cases
are usually treated by the grammarians as keijō-gen ("attributionals") that happen
also to be adjective stems, just as some adjective stems happen also to be nouns
(e.g. color names). As keijō-gen they are like adjectival nouns, but they are
adnominalized by attaching no instead of naru; and some occur also as adverbs, for
they are directly adverbialized without the ni that usually marks the adverbialized
adjectival noun. Not all of the keijō-gen are also adjective stems; there is no
*toyo-si 'is rich' to go with toyo 'rich' as in toyo myi-kyi (K 6) 'luxurious wine',
TOYO NO AKARI (M 4266) '[the rich blush of inebriation of] a party at the palace',
and (directly adverbial) toyo fwokyi (K 40) 'richly blessing'. Examples of the
modification structures:

(1) A no̱ N (cf. Ōno Tōru 1978:62, 64).

oso̱ no̱ MYIYABIY (-) WO (M 126) '[belated =] stupid dandy'. As adverb: oso̱ faya mo na wo ko̱so̱ matamey (M 3493) 'I will await you whether early or late'.

to̱fo̱ no̱ kuni (M 3688) 'the distant land (of Shilla)'; cf. (3).

(2) A -n- N.

asa - zinwo (- fara) (K 36) '(field of) low bamboo', asa - di (- fara) (K 112) '(field of) low reeds'; cf. asa nwo (NS 110) 'shallow field'.

aka - gwoma (M 804, NS 128) 'red pony'.

taka - gaya (M 3497) 'tall cogon'.

ofo - bune (M 326) 'big ship'.

(3) A (-) N.

huzi no̱ taka (-) ne no̱ (M 3358) 'the high peak of Fuji', taka kiy (K 10) 'high fortress'. As adverb: taka yuku ya (K 68) 'he goes on high (Prince Faya-busa-wake)', taka fyikaru fyi no myi-kwo (K 72) 'Prince of the high-shining Sun', taka terasu FYI NO̱ MYI-KWO (M 45) 'the Sun Prince who deigns to shine on high'. The noun-like nature of taka '(on) high' is confirmed by examples like taka tu to̱ri (Norito) 'birds on high' with the locative-genitive marker tu, and iya taka ni iya fyiro̱ ni (Norito) '(prospers) ever higher ever wider'.

fyiro̱ FASI wo (M 3538) 'the wide bridge'. As adverb: myiya-basira fyiro̱ siri tate (Norito) 'broadly establishes domain over the palace pillars'.

futwo no̱rito̱-goto̱ (M 4031) 'the mighty words of prayer'. As adverb: myiya-basira futwo siri (K text) 'mightily reigns over the palace pillars'.

two ama (K 28) 'sharp sickle', two mey (K 18, 19) 'sharp eyes'.

ywo no̱ to̱fo̱ fyito̱ (NS 62) 'a person who has lived since the distant past'; cf. to̱fo̱ tu fyito̱ (M 857, 3947) '[being far-off like] a distant person', to̱fo̱ no̱ kuni (M 3688) 'the distant land (of Shilla)'. As adverb: iya to̱fo̱ so̱kyi-nu (some read this as ··· zokyi-nu) (M 3389) 'got farther and farther distant'.

naga fyito̱ (K 74) 'long-lived person', naga kwofiy sezu fa (M 864) 'not loving for long'; cf. mwomwo naga ni i fa nasamu wo (K 3) taken as either 'will sleep [a hundred =] a long time' or 'sleeps with outstretched thighs'.

ofo̱ kafara (K 37) 'big river', ofo̱ kyimyi (K 29, ...) 'great prince'. There is probably a variant of the stem yo- 'good' in the expressions ye woto-kwo 'a fine lad' and ye woto-mye 'a fine lass' (Koji-ki text). The directly adverbial use of ita- 'painful' occurs in ita naka-ba (K 84) 'weeps hard'. Compare the direct adverbial use of goto̱- in kaku no̱ goto̱ (K 98) 'like thus', etc.

In parts of the Ryūkyūs the adjective stem is rather freely adnominalized by positioning it in front of a noun. Although rendaku is common, and usual for the shorter phrases, there are various exceptions. The prosodic marking and shape types often indicate two words rather than a compound, even when rendaku is present. Some examples from Shodon, where the stems either apocopate or extend the final vowel: hyigur midi m 'cold water too', kwahaa/khataa myithyaa 'hard earth', yur qubyi m 'a loose sash too', kharuu qyisyi m 'light stone too', huruu syimoti m 'an old book too'; sii kuniibu m 'a sour tangerine too', hyiryuu byiya m 'a wide room too', nuk byiya m 'a warm room too', nyigyaa gusuryi m 'bitter medicine too', quhuu banusi m 'a large sweet potato too', qumusyryii hanasyi m 'an amusing story too'.

Dialects of the southern Ryūkyūs, such as those of Miyako, often adnominalize the adjective stem by attaching nu (the reflex of the marker no̱), but first they reduplicate the stem, lengthening the last vowel of the first rendition: takaa-taka nu yama 'a tall mountain'. But they also use shorter structures of adjective stem + noun (cf. Hirayama 1967:134b). The reduplication occurs in other structures: akaa-aka paz 'it is probably red', akaa-aka du sz 'makes it red' (< aka-aka zo suru).

Reduplication of the adjective stem is not uncommon in lexicalizations found in other parts of Japan; the modern standard language uses a number of adjectives with the structure reduplicated stem + -si-. Old Japanese attests tofo-tofo-si 'it is far distant', which is assumed to contain the formant -si-, even though the word occurs only once and in a place where the form might be taken as the predicative -si without the formant; the reason for assuming the formant is that there are said to be "many such reduplications", yet phonetically written attestations of such forms apparently do not occur before the Heian period, so that the presumption of a real formant in the OJ form is extrapolated back from later evidence. Another example of the reduplicated adjective stem: taka-taka ni (M 4107), in which the reduplication is indicated by ditto marks, so it could have been pronounced taka-daka ni. Reflexes found in the Japanese-Portuguese dictionary show that the 16th-century pronunciation was -d- for both taka-daka ("tacadacato") and to(w)odo(w)osi- ("touodouoxij"). Although the OJ phonograms indicate -t- for tofo-tofo-si-, the orthography was perhaps cavalier toward rendaku in some of the reduplicated forms.

In modern Japanese the adjective stem sometimes occurs alone, as a kind of interjection (cf. RGJ 399): O kowa! 'Oh, scary!'; Aa ita! 'Ouch, it hurts!'; O samu! 'Brr, it's cold!'. And in Ōsaka, it is said, even desideratives are so used: A nomi-ta! 'Gee, I'm thirsty!'. (Wakayama has the usual -ta-i for the affirmative desiderative, but -ta' na-i/na-katta; this may be a truncation of -ta[-ku] na-. Cf. AA Kenkyū-jo tsūshin 50:2, 6.) The use of stem in exclamations is probably quite ancient, for Kogo-shūi (807) reports that there were "old expressions" ana omosiro 'what fun!', ana tanosi 'goody-goody!', and ana sayake 'how cool!'. An attestation: ana myiniku 'ugh, ugly!' (NS kun-chū). Man'yō-shū offers several examples of the exclamatory ana A-si used as an anticipatory predication, with the statement of a condition delayed, as if it were an afterthought: ana ikidukasi afyi wakare[y]-na-ba (M 1454) 'how oppressive! — if we must part', ana ikidukasi myizu fyisa ni si te[y] 'how oppressive! — letting it be long without seeing one', ana tadutadusi fitori sa-nure[y]-ba 'how desolate! [like a lone *tadu* crane in the field of reeds: *a pun is involved*] — if I sleep alone'. These could be treated as examples of the predicative -si, but because of the examples from Kogo-shūi cited above, they are usually taken to be the stem without the formant. An example found in Myōgi-shō (Kn sō-jō 78:4): ana yukasi 'how tasteful!'. In the Man'yō-shū there appear to be no examples of the exclamatory use of OJ adjective stems without the formant -si-.

In §179 of A Handbook of Colloquial Japanese (p. 122 of the 4th edition, 1907), Chamberlain cites as colloquial "such emphatic locutions as" Samu-sa wa samu-si 'It *is* cold' and Kura-sa wa kura-si 'It *is* dark'. I have seen no other reference to this structure, but I am told that it can be found in Heike-monogatari.

7.7. Structures forming adjective stems.

Most adjective stems of one or two syllables are single morphemes, but longer
stems often consist of two or more elements. While the etymological structure of
some of the longer stems is not always clear, valid examples can be found that will
illustrate a number of types. There are compounds of free stems such as these:

$A_1 - A_2$: atu(k)kurusi- 'stuffy', hosonaga- 'long and slender', kosu(k)kara-
'stingy and shrewd', ...

$A_1 -n- A_2$: akaguro- < aka -n- kurwo 'reddish black', amazuppa- 'sweet-and-sour',
warugasiko- 'sly, cunning', ...

$A_1 - A_1$: Except for the Ryūkyū structures earlier described, adjective stems
that are reduplicated always attach the formant -si- (see below).

N - A: hodotika- 'nearby', kagirina- 'boundless, unlimited', kokorona- 'heartless;
thoughtless', kokoroyo- 'pleasant, delightful', omosiro- 'interesting, amusing',
siokara- 'salty', soraosorosi- 'apprehensive', ...

N -n- A: haraguro- 'blackhearted, wicked', kiwado- 'risky; extreme', kokoroboso-
'helpless', kusabuka- 'grassy', kutigitana- 'abusive, gluttonous', mezato- 'sharp-
eyed', usirogura- 'shady, dubious', ...

Structures of V-yi - A are mostly productive, e.g. the desiderative V-yi - ta-. Each
such structure contains the stem of an auxiliary adjective. A similar treatment is
accorded (V-a) - na- 'not V'; in later Japanese the negative auxiliary conjugates as
an adjective but it was originally a verb stem, for which we have a few relics of
the infinitive (V-a) ni, as well as the attributive (V-a) nu. There are several
bound adjectives, derived from somewhat obscure structures: -bayu- (-hayu-, -wayu-);
-gamasi-; -gawasi-; -(t)tarasi-. Two quasi-free adjectives, goto- 'like' and rasi-
'apparent, seeming', attach freely to noun phrases and nominalized sentences, among
other uses.

Many longer adjectives consist of a simple stem (adjective, noun, or verb) + a
formative suffix or "formant" (F); a few appear to enjoy a string of two formants.
Some of the formants, including the one that is most used (-si-), are of obscure
origin; others, such as -na- and -(k)ko- and -ppo- are probably reductions from
simple stems. The formants are sometimes attached to reduplicated stems and other
complex formations. Examples:

A + F: mazusi- 'poor, meager'; arappo- 'rough', tikasi- 'intimate, close',
yasuppo- 'cheap', ...

A + F - F: abunakkasi- 'doubtful', ? komakasi- 'fine, detailed'.

$A_1 - A_1 + F$: araarasi- 'rough', naganagasi- 'quite long', niganigasi- 'bitter;
disgusting, scandalous', omoomosi- 'serious, grave, solemn', tadotadosi- 'unsteady;
insecure; uncertain', utoutosi- 'aloof, alien(ated), distant', wakawakasi- 'young',
yowayowasi- 'weak', ...

$A_1 -n- A_1 + F$: huruburusi- 'very old/stale', karugarusi- 'frivolous; rash',
sirozirosi- 'white, bright, interesting', takedakesi- 'brave', ...

N + F: abura(k)ko- 'oily', otonasi- 'gentle, good; mature, wise'; iroppo- 'sexy,
erotic', ...

$N_1 - N_1 + F$: kadokadosi- 'full of angles; testy, crabby', kotogotosi- <
kotokotosi- 'pompous, ostentatious', magamagasi- 'ominous', memesi- 'feminine',
yosoyososi- 'standoffish, distant, cool', ... Under this type we can perhaps put
examples of reduplicated Chinese morpheme + F (bibisi- 'beautiful', dokudokusi-
'venomous', ...) and reduplicated mimetic + F (kirakirasi- 'bright; splendid,
resplendent', ...).

N₁ -n- N₁ + F: hakabakasi- 'expeditious, speedy; active; satisfactory', hanabanasi- 'glorious, splendid', hukubukusi- 'happy and prosperous-looking', sorazorasi- 'feigned', ... (all dating from Edo).
   V + F: isamasi- 'brave', isogasi- 'busy', nayamasi- 'melancholy', utagawasi- 'doubtful, suspicious', yorokobasi- 'delightful, welcome'; imasi- 'vexing', ...
   V + F - F: ? hazukasi- 'shy, embarrassed', isogawasi- 'busy', itawasi- 'painful', nayamasi- 'melancholy', ...
   V₁ - V₁ + F: imaimasi- 'vexing', ? ... .
   V-yi₁ - V-yi₁ + F: narenaresi- 'familiar', ...
   V-yi₁ -n- V-yi₁ + F: harebaresi- clear, bright, cheery', saezaesi- 'clear, bright, cheerful', ...
   N - V + F: okuyukasi- 'modest', ? ... .
   N -n- V + F: haradatasi- 'provoking, aggravating, maddening'; [ikidoorosi-] 'indignant, resentful', ...
   V-yi -n- A + F: matidoosi- 'impatiently awaited', ...

   We will refer to several adjective stems that occur in N - A or N -n- A compounds as "quasi-formants" because their meaning is often attenuated: -buka- (occasionally also -huka-) 'deep with', -daka- 'high with (respect to)', ? -ganasi- 'sad (with respect to)', -gara- 'piquant, spiced (with)', -gata- 'hard (with respect to)', -guwasi- 'fine (with respect to)', -kurusi- (also -kkurusi- and -gurusi-) 'onerous (with respect to)', -kusa- (sometimes -gusa-) 'smelling of', -na- 'deficient/unpleasant (with respect to)', -zuyo- 'strong (with respect to)'. Some stems have an attached prefix. We know the etymology of some of the prefixes; others are obscure. A number of nouns or adverbs that retain their basic meanings will be referred to as "quasi-prefixes". These are not always easy to differentiate from the other group.
   Below are listed examples of the various formative elements. The stems are alphabetically arrayed in three groups, according to the three lists in §7.8, §7.9, and §7.10. The groups are separated by semicolons, except for the formant -si-, where indentation is used and a count is given for each group; the individual stems are separated by commas.

FORMANTS:

   -betta-. ---; hira-betta-; ---. But perhaps the lone example is from
      *pira n[i] pi[r]a -ta-, or from *pira n[i] pira ita-.
   -botta- ?< *[o]npo (or *-n- [o]po𝑎𝑑𝐽 𝐵) -ta-. ---; atu-, hare-; ---.
   -ka-si-. ---; abunakkasi- < abuna- (< ...) -ka -si-, ? komakasi-; ---.
      Several examples of ···kasi-, probably including the last, are to be
      treated as adjectival noun (< ···-ka) + -si-.
   -ke- < -key- < -ka -Ci-. ? [isasake-], nodoke-; [sayake-], [tairake-],
      [tawake-]; [akirake-], [haruke-], [kasoke-], [keyake-], [sizuke-],
      [sumiyake-], [tuyuke-], [yutake-]; ---.
   -(k)ko- < *kwo𝑎𝑑𝐽 𝐵. abura(k)ko-; hiya(k)ko-, hosokko-, madarukko-,
      maru(k)ko-, natukko-, nebakko-, situ(k)ko-, subekko-, tyoroko-,
      yani(k)ko-; ---.
   -ko-si- < *kwo𝑎𝑑𝐽 𝐵 -si-. ---; yayakosi-; ---.
   -na-₁ < na𝑎𝑑𝐽 'un[pleasantly] ··· '. abuna-, ozina-; adokena-, egetuna-,
   okkana-, ? sigana-; [iwakena-], [ogirona-]. See also -si-na-. Cf. -na-₂
      (quasi-formant, N + na𝑎𝑑𝐽 𝐵); V-a - na-.
   -ne- < -na- -Ci-. [amane-]; ---; ---.

-ppo- ‹ *opo_adj B. ---; adappo-, akippo-, arappo-, awareppo-, egarappo-,
      gutippo-, hokorippo-, honeppo-, igarappo-, iroppo-, karuppo-, kizappo-,
      kuroppo-, mizuppo-, museppo-, netuppo-, okorippo-, rikutuppo-, simeppo-,
      siroppo-, tuyappo-, tuyuppo-, utagurippo-, wasureppo-, yasuppo-, zokuppo-;
      ... .
 -si-. This is the major adjective-stem formant, found in 247 stems. (See also
      -ka-si-, -ko-si-, -wa-si-, and -zi-; a few of those appear also here.
      Cf. -bosi-, -gamasi-, -ganasi-, -gurusi-; yakamasi-.)
         [akarasi-], araarasi-, asamasi-, atarasi- A 'precious/regrettable',
      atarasi- B 'new', [atukawasi-], awaawasi-, ayasi-, bibisi-, gyoogyoosi-,
      [haebaesi-], [hanahadasi-], harebaresi-, hazukasi-, hisasi-, [hi^a/$_z$ukasi-]
      hitosi-, hohoemasi-, hosi-, [huruburusi-], hurumekasi-, husawasi-,
      ibukasi-, ikamesi-, [imasi-] 'present, immediate', imaimasi-, iradatasi-,
      irairasi-, isamasi-, [isi-], isogasi-, [isukasi-], itamasi-, itizirusi-,
      itowasi-, [itukusi-], [iyaiyasi-], iyasi-, kadamasi-, kadokadosi-,
      kagayakasi-, kaigaisi-, kanasi-, karugarusi-, [katakunasi-], kegarawasi-,
      ketatamasi-, kewasi-, kibisi-, [kirakirasi-], koisi-, konomasi-, koogoosi-
      ? kosu-, kotogotosi-, kudakudasi-, kuruosi- ‹ kuruwasi-, kurusi-,
      [kususi-], kuwasi-, kuyasi-, ? mabusi-, madasi-, magamagasi-, magirawasi-,
      [makirawasi-], mamemamesi-, [masasi-], matidoosi-, mazusi-, memesi-,
      mezamasi-, mezurasi-, misuborasi-, madasi-, monoganasi-, monoguruosi-,
      monomonosi-, monosabisi-, munasi-, mutumazi- ‹ mutumasi-, muzukasi- =
      mutukasi-, naganagasi-, nagekawasi- = nagekasi-, nagoriosi-, namamekasi-,
      namasi-, namanamasi-, namidagumasi-, [naonaosi-], narenaresi-, natukasi-,
      nayamasi-, negawasi-, netamasi-, niganigasi-, [niisi-], obosi-, [odaisi-],
      [odasi-], okuyukasi-, omoomosi-, omowasi-, [onazi-] ‹ ona^a/$_z$i, oosi-,
      orokasi-, osi-, osorosi-, [dial.] otorosi-, otonasi-, sabisi-, [dial.]
      samisi-, sa^b/$_m$usi-, [sagasi-], samosi-, sawagasi- (‹ ?sawakasi-),
      sebasebasi-, sewa^a/$_z$ewasi-, sewasi-, sirozirosi-, sitasi-, soozoosi-,
      soraosorosi-, [sugasi-], sugasugasi-, [sukosi-], susamazi- ‹ susama^a/$_z$i-,
      suzusi-, tadasi-, tadotadosi- (= tadutadusi-), takedakesi-, takumasi-,
      tanomosi-, [toodoosi-], tumasi-, tutumasi-, uiuisi-, uraganasi-, uramesi-,
      urayamasi-, uresi-, [uruwasi-], utagawasi-, utomasi-, uyauyasi-, wabisi-,
      wakawakasi-, wazurawasi-, yamasi-, yasasi-, yatuyatusi-, yorokobasi-,
      yorosi-, yosoyososi-, yowayowasi-, yukasi-, yuyusi-. (158)
         abunakkasi-, aikurusi-, bakabakasi-, dokudokusi-, hakabakasi-, hokorasi-
      hukubukusi-, hutebutesi-, imasi- 'vexing', itaitasi-, ? izirasi-,
      kebakebasi-, kihazukasi-, kimuzukasi-, kisokutadasi-, kizewasi-,
      komagomasi-, komakasi-, kudokudosi-, kudarasi-, matasi-, meatarasi-,
      memagurusi-, memesi-, mendo(o)si-, mimiatarasi-, mizumizusi-, modokasi-,
      monomezurasi-, munagurusi-, niawasi-, nikunikusi-, norowasi-, nozomasi-,
      oisi-, okasi-, orimetadasi-, ozomasi-, reireisi-, saezaesi-, samuzamusi-,
      sema(k)kurusi-, sese(k)komasi-, sorazorasi-, sosokkasi-, sowasowasi-,
      subarasi-, tikasi-, togetogesi-, tuyatuyasi-, tyootyoosi-, uttoosi-,
      zuuzuuusi-. (58)
         [hokasi-], [ikidoorosi-], [ikizuk^a/$_u$si-], [isaosi-], [isosi-],
      [itaburasi-], [itukasi-], [ituituasi-], [kesi-], [kirawasi-], [kogosi-],
      [kokidasi-], [kokorokoisi-], [kumagumasi-], [monokoisi-], [nitasi-],
      [niwasi-], [okokosi-], [omoiganasi-], [omoigurusi-], [osaosasi-],
      [oyosi-], [sitaemasi-], [tagitagisi-] = [taidaisi-], [tawasi-],
      [tokizi-], ? [umugasi-], [uragoisi-], [utusi-], [waiwaisi-]. (31)
 -si-na-. sewasina-; ---; ---.

-ta- < *[i]ta*adj B* ('hurting' → 'extremely'). kemuta- < kebuta-, medeta-,
  kusugutta- < kusuguri-ta-, kutihabatta-, nemuta- (= nemurita- = nemu-),
  omota-, ? tumeta-, ? usirometa-, yabotta-; hirata-, ziretta-; ---.
  See also -betta-, -botta-. Cf. [koita-], [ureta-]; V-i - ta-; itaru.
-wa-si- < -fa-si- < *-pa-si-. ikagawasi-, imawasi-, isogawasi-, itawasi-,
  [itazukawasi-], [kakarawasi-], [kusubasi-], [midarigawasi-], nagekawasi-,
  nigiwasi-, nitukawasi-, [oboosi-] (?< *onpo-pa-si-), [tatawasi-],
  [urewasi-]; ikaga(wa)si-; ---. But a number of adjective stems that end
  ···wasi- are from verb stems ···awa- < ···apa-: norowasi-, kizukawasi-,
  kuruwasi-, niawasi-, ...
-zi-₁ ?< -si-, ?< -n[i]-si- ?< n[i-Ci] -si- ('resemblant'). onazi- ('same' ?=
  *on**o** - zi- 'like self') = oyazi-; ---; ---. Also, Old Japanese N - zi-
  'like N, virtually/almost N', as in omo - zi-ki fito 'a person almost a
  sibling (with the same mother)' (Senmyō 25 [misinterpreted by Igarashi?]),
  ware - zi-ku 'like me' (M 4280), and N - zi - mon**o** 'one like N, a sort-of
  N, virtually an N; an N'.
-zi-₂ ?< -n[i]-si- ?< (-)ni (< n[a-C]i) si (negative: 'un-'). ---; ---;
  tokizi-. Cf. Old Japanese masizi- > mazi- 'probably not' (> mai).
  Note: The Edo adjective himozi- 'hungry', while treated by lexicographers
  as a "-zi-" stem, contains neither this formant nor the preceding.
-Ci-. [kusi-] < *kusiy- < *kusu-Ci-. [se-] ?< *sa*adj ?A* -Ci-, [sige-] <
  *sinka-Ci-; ---; ---. See -ke-, -ne-.

QUASI-FORMANTS

-buka- < *-n- puka*adj B*.   ---; kebuka-, kobuka-, kusabuka-, nasakebuka-,
  nebuka-; enryobuka-, kangaebuka-, sianbuka-, siryobuka-, syuunenbuka-,
  tutusimibuka-, tyuuibuka-, utagaibuka-, utaguribuka-, yoozinbuka-,
  zihibuka-, zyasuibuka-, zyatibuka-; ---. See -huka-.
-daka- < *-n- taka*adj B*. kedaka-, nadaka-, [nakadaka-]; kandaka-,
  kanzyoodaka-, keisandaka-, monomidaka-, sorobandaka-; [kasadaka-].
  Cf. kodaka- (prefix + adjective).
-ganasi- < *-n- kanasi*adj A*. monoganasi-, uraganasi-; [omoiganasi-]; ---.
-gara- < *-n- kara*adj A*. egara-; setigara-; ---. Cf. dadagara-.
-gata- < *-n- kata*adj A*. girigata-, kutigata-, tegata-; bakagata-,
  ? monogata-; ---.
-gurusi-: see -kurusi-.
-gusa- < *-n- kusa*adj B*. namagusa-; tinamagusa-, waru**k**/gusa-; ---. See -kusa-.
-guwasi- < *-n- kupasi*adj B* (< ...). [uraguwasi-]; ---; [hanaguwasi-],
  [maguwasi-], [naguwasi-].
-huka- = -**h**/buka- < *(-n-) puka*adj B*. oku**h**/buka-, tumi**h**/buka-, yoku**h**/buka-;
  ---; ---. See -buka-.
-kurusi-, -kkurusi-, -gurusi- (< kurusi*adj B* < ...). ---; aikurusi-,
  atu(k)kurusi-, ikigurusi-, kata(k)kurusi- (also katagurusi- NKD),
  kokorogurusi-, mimigurusi-, musakurusi-, omo(k)kurusi-/omogurusi-,
  munagurusi-, musakurusi-, sema(k)kurusi-; [omoigurusi-].
  (But memagurusi- < memagirasi- < ... .) Cf. V-i - gurusi-.
-kusa- < kusa*adj B*. akakusa-, hurukusa-; ahookusa-, aokusa-, bakakusa-,
  batakusa-, dorokusa-, hankakusa-, hinatakusa-, hitokusa-, hotokekusa-,
  hunbetukusa-, inakakusa-, inkikusa-, isokusa-, kabikusa-, ketikusa-,
  kinakusa-, kogekusa-, makkookusa-, mendo(o)kusa-, mizukusa-, norokusa-,
  nukamisokusa-, otokokusa-, sakekusa-, sinkikusa-, sirootokusa-,
  sitimendo(o)kusa-, syarakusa-, syoobenkusa-, terekusa-, titikusa-,

torokusa-, tutikusa-, usankusa-, waru^k/ɡusa-, zimankusa-, zyukusikusa-;
---.

-na-₂ (N + na_adj _B). aena-, azikena- = azikina-, hakana-, hatesina-, kagirina-,
katazikena-, kitana-, kokoromotona-, kokorona-, menbokuna-, nanigokorona-,
narabina-, nasakena-, nigena-, obotukana-, osana-, otonagena-, sarigena-,
sidokena-, sikatana-, [subena-], sugena-, tayorina-, ? turena-, tutugana-,
warina-, yarukatana-, yarusena-, yosina-. zyutuna- = zutina-/zutuna-;
akkena-, daizina-₁, ? darasina-, ganzena-, hugaina-, mittomona-, nanigena-,
nibena-, omoigakena-, otonagena-, setuna-, sokkena-, syozaina-, tawaina-,
wakena-, ? yogina-, yondokorona-, zoosana-, zyosaina-; [mot̲o̲na-],
? [tasina-], [tunena-], [uramot̲o̲na-], [uyana-].

-zuyo- ‹ *-n- tuy̲o̲- _adj _B (‹ ...). kokorozuyo-; gamanzuyo-, kizuyo-,
nebarizuyo-, nezuyo-, rinkizuyo-, sinbo(o)zuyo-, tezuyo-, tikarazuyo-; ---

BOUND ADJECTIVES:

-bayu-, -hayu-, -wayu- ‹ (-n-) fayu_adj _?B (‹ * pad[a-Ci]-_B -u). [siwawayu-];
kosobayu-, mabayu-, omo^h/ɓayu-; kawai-.

-gamasi- ?‹ *-n[a]-ka-ma-si-; ?‹ *-n kama*_adj _B -si-.   haregamasi-,
hazigamasi-, hitogamasi-, kagotogamasi-, kasigamasi- = kasikamasi- (JP)
‹ *ka[ma]si-gamasi-, nezikegamasi-, okogamasi-, wazatogamasi-;
atetukegamasi-, benkaigamasi-, hihyoogamasi-, hunbetugamasi-,
iiketugamasi-, ikengamasi-, kokkeigamasi-, kyoohakugamasi-, mendoogamasi-,
midarigamasi-, mirengamasi-, monogamasi-, ongamasi-, onkisegamasi-,
ositukegamasi-, sasidegamasi-, tumiegamasi-, utayomigamasi-;   ---.
Cf. atukamasi-, yakamasi-, namidagumasi-.

-gawasi- ‹ -gafasi- ?‹ -n[a]-ka-pa-si-. [midarigawasi-], for which Genji also
has a "Chinesey" version rau (= raů/ran ‹ Ch) -gafasi-; ---; ---.

-(t)tarasi- ?‹ *tara-_B -si-, ?‹ *tara-_A -si-.   ---; busyoottarasi-,
mizimettarasi-, mugotarasi-, naga(t)tarasi-, nikutarasi-, sukebeettarasi-,
zimantarasi-; ---.

QUASI-FREE ADJECTIVES:

got̲o̲- ‹ *-n- k̲o̲t̲o̲. 'like'. Mg goto- HL-. NS (76b [14:126-MW]) goto HH.
Km (W) HL-. Mr (Bm) HL-.

rasi- ‹ *[a]ra-_B -si-. 'apparent, seeming'. airasi-, ? suborasi-; ahorasi-,
bakarasi-, hunbeturasi-, iyarasi-, ? izirasi-, kawairasi-, kitanarasi-,
kodomorasi-, kudarasi-, mottairasi-, mottomorasi-, nikurasi-, ningenrasi-,
[nitukorasi-], onnarasi-, otokorasi-, sikatume-/sikatube-/sikazume-rasi-,
siorasi-, sisairasi-, taisoorasi-, usanrasi-, wazatorasi-, zimanrasi-; ---

AUXILIARY ADJECTIVES:

(V-i) - ta- ‹ *[i]ta_adj _B. 'desiring (to V), tending to (V)'.

(V-i) - bosi- ‹ *-n- posi_adj _B (‹ ...). 'desiring (to V)'. (Cf. mebosi-.) This
formation, widespread in the Ryūkyūs, has the same meaning as the
following OJ expressions:
V-a-ma-ku fosi-, which became Heian V-a-ma[k]u-[fo]si = -mausi,
V-a-ma[ku]-fosi- = -amafosi-, V-a-ma[ku]-[fo]si- = -amasi-.
V-i ga fosi-, with OJ attestations for two verbs: ari ga fosi- 'want
to be' (M 1059), myi ga fosi- 'want to see' (K 59; M 324, 910,
1047, 2327, 3985, 4111, 4112, 4170); and in Heian (981 Kinkafu)
sumyi ga fosi- 'want to reside'.

V-i fosi- attested only as reading of semantograms in kyi fosi
('wear' M 1311); perhaps this should be read kyi ga fosi?

(V-i) - gata- < *-n- kata*adj A*. 'difficult (to V)'; Sr -gatana-. arigata-,
egata-, sarigata-, taegata-; dosigata-, iigata-, kokoroegata-,
osaegata-, oyobigata-, sigata-, yamigata-; ---.

(V-i) - gurusi- < *-n- kurusi*adj B* (< ...). 'difficult (to V)'; Sr - gurisi-.
migurusi-, kikigurusi-; negurusi-; ... .

(V-i) - niku-. 'difficult (to V)'. miniku-, siniku-. Cf. turaniku-.

(V-i) - yasu- < *dasu*adj B*. 'easy (to V)'. miyasu-; kanziyasu-, kiyasu- 'easy
to wear'; [keyasu-]. Cf. kiyasu- 'congenial', kayasu-, tayasu-.

(V-i) - yo- < *do*adj B*. 'good (to V); easy (to V)'. ---; miyo-; ---.

(V-i) - zura- < - dura- < *-n- tura*adj A*. 'difficult (to V)'. Examples *(not in
the lists)*: kikizura-, mizura-, yomizura-, (Sr) *ikizura-.

AUXILIARY VERB (> ADJECTIVE):

(Va) - na- 'not (V)'. ---; kudarana-, tumarana-, yarikirena-; ---.
Note: This is the root of a defective verb with the attributive nu
and the old infinitive (Va) - ni. The adjective *na*B* derives from it,
as do the modern verb negatives. (Va-na-i may be restructured from
Va-nawe < Va - naf[y]e < *na-pa-Ci, infinitive of the Azuma negative
auxiliary verb. There is no evidence for *Va-na-ki or *V-ana-si.)

PREFIXES:

dada-. ---; dadabiro-/dadappiro-, dadagara-, dadaguro-; ---.

do(o)-, don-. 'utter(ly), extreme(ly)', often pejorative. ---; dekka- <
do-ika-, dogitu-; ---.

do-su-. ---; dosuguro-; ---.

hi-. ---; higosu-, hiyowa-; ---. Cf. hidaru-.

ike- ?< ikey < *ika-Ci[-Ci]*B*, ?< yo-kei (< Ch). 'unpleasantly, excessively'.
---; ikeatazikena-, ikeatukamasi-, ikesituko-, ikesukana-, ikeurusa-,
ikezuuzuusi-; ---.

ita-. ? [itazukawasi-]; ---; ---.

iti-. [iti^h/ᵦaya-], ? itizirusi-; ---; ---.

ka-. kaboso-, kaguro-, kayowa-; ---; [kaao-].

ko- < kwo(-). 'somewhat, rather; quite'. kodaka-, komuzukasi-, kozakasi-;
kogitana-, konikurasi-, koppido-, kourusa-, koyakamasi-, kozuraniku-; ---.

ma-, maC-, man-. 'truly, really'. ---; maatarasi-, makkuro-, manmaru-,
massiro-; ---.

mi- < myi-. 'exalted' (honorific). *Usually attached to noun; are there examples
with adjectives?*

o- < oo- < o[f]o- < *opo*adj B*. 'great; big'. oisi- < o-; ---; ---. Also
used as an honorific prefix: o-medeta-, o-samu-.

o- < wo- (< *bo-*?1.1*). 'slight(ly)'. ogura-; ---; ---.

sa-. ? sakasi-; ---; [sadoo-]. Sr sa- A/B.

siti-. ---; sitikudo-, sitimendo(o)kusa-, sitimu^t/ᵤukasi-; ---.

su-. ?sugena-; subasi(k)ko-, subaya-; ---. Cf. do-su-.

ta- (≠ 'hand', cf. sa-). ? tatto-/tooto-, [tayowa-]; ---; [tadoo-].

QUASI-PREFIXES:

baka- < baka*2.x* 'fool(ish)', 'stupid(ly)'. ---; bakabakasi-, bakadaka-,
bakagata-, bakakusa-, bakaooki-; ---.

hono- < fono- < *po-no*2.3*. 'slightly'. ---; honoakaru-, honogura-; ---.

horo-. 'slightly'. ---; horoniga-; ---.
hyoro-. 'slightly'. ---; hyoronaga-; ---.
koto- ‹ koto$_{2.3}$ 'fact'. ---; kotoatarasi-; ---.
kuti- ‹ kuti$_{2.1}$ (‹ ...) 'mouth'. kutigata-, kutigitana-, kutisagana-;
     kutihabatta-, kutiosi-, kuti-sabisi-/-zamisi-, kutiyakamasi-; ---.
ma- ‹ *ma[-Ci]$_{1.3a}$ 'eye'. mabayu-, mabusi-, magirawasi-, [makirawasi-]; ---;
     [maguwasi-].
me- ‹ mey ‹ *ma-Ci$_{1.3a}$ 'eye'. mezamasi-, mezato-; meatarasi-, memagurusi-;
     ---.
mimi- ‹ myimyi ‹ *mimi$_{2.3}$ 'ear'. ---; mimidoo-, mimi^t/$_d$ika-, mimizato-; ---.
     Cf. mimi-gurusi-.
mono- ‹ mono$_{2.3}$ 'thing' › 'somehow, in some (vague, ill-defined) way, vaguely'.
     monoganasi-, [monogura-], monoguruosi-, monosabisi-, monosugo-,
     [monosusamazi-], monou-; monogata-, monogamasi-, monomezurasi-; monokoisi-
nama- ‹ nama$_{2.3}$ 'raw'. namagusa-; namaatataka-, namanuru-, namayasasi-; ---.
sora- ‹ swora$_{2.4}$ 'sky'. soraosorosi-; ---; ---.
ta- ‹ *te[y] ‹ *ta[-Ci]$_{1.3a}$ 'hand'. takumasi-; ? tawaina-; ---.
te- ‹ *te[y] ‹ *ta-Ci$_{1.3a}$ 'hand'. tebasika- = tebasiko-, tebiro-, tegata-,
     tegowa-, teita-; teara-, tebaya-, tegowa-, tehido-, tekibisi-,
     tettoribaya-; ---.
ura- ‹ ura$_{2.4}$ 'mind, heart'. uraganasi-, [uraguwasi-], urawaka-, urayamasi-,
     uresi- ?‹ *ur[a] ye-, [ureta-] ‹ ure[y]ta- ‹ *ura ita-, urusa- ?‹ *urasa-
     ‹ *ura sa- or ?‹ *ur[a] u-sa, [uruwasi-] ‹ urufasi- ?‹ ura fasi (‹ *pasi);
     ---; [uragoisi-], [uramotona-], [ureta-] ‹ *ura [i]ta-.
uso- = usu-. 'somewhat, slightly'. ---; usosamu-; ---.
usu- ‹ usu$_{adj}$ $_A$ ('thin'). 'somewhat, slightly'. usugura-; usuaka-, usuakaru-,
     usuao-, usugitana-, usu^k/$_g$imiwaru-; ---.

SUFFIXES:

-ka. Forms adjectival nouns. Cf. -ra-ka, -ya-ka; adjective formant -ke-.
-ke ‹ -kye (M vol. 14, all instances) / -key (M vol. 20, most instances)
     [Azuma] = -ki.
-ki ‹ -kyi ‹ *-ki. Attributive (= adnominal).
-ku. Infinitive (= nominal/adverbial).
-sa. Abstract nominal ("-ness").
-si. Predicative.
-mi ‹ -myi ‹ *-mi. Putative/causative nominalization ('deeming it A').
-ra (?‹ *[a]ra-$_B$). Forms adjectival nouns.
-ra-ka. Forms adjectival nouns.
-ya. Forms adjectival nouns.
-ya-ka. Forms adjectival nouns.

7.8. Accentuation of adjective stems.

Like the verb stems, the adjective stems have just two basic accentual types; the predictable patterns of the paradigmatic forms are quite similar for adjectives and for verbs. Kyōto speakers of the 11th century put high pitch on the stem of an adjective of Type A and low pitch on an attached ending. They did just the opposite for adjectives of Type B; there were a few complications involving metathesis of locus (see Ch. 4), and the locus was often lost altogether in adnominal structures, which were smoothed to atonic high or low. But with the general erosion of the low atonic that took place in the 1300s (see Ch. 4), the initial syllables of both types became high and the difference between the two types came to be marked by the locus of the pitch fall: in Type A the fall is at the end of the stem, so that the ending is low, as in Kōchi a̅ka̲i̲ 'is red'; in Type B the fall is normally on the last syllable of the stem, as in Kōchi ta̅ka̲i̲ 'is high'. But the old initial low pitch is retained in the contracted forms of the -[k]u infinitive: Kōchi ta̅ko̅o̲ < ta̲ka̲-ku̲ (< *ta̲ka̲-k̅u̅). Wakayama is like Kōchi, and so was Kyōto in the Muromachi period. But later Kyōto merged the B stems into the accent class of the A stems, so that a̅ka̲-i̲ and t̅a̅ka̲-i̲ carry identical tunes, as do a̲ko̅o̲ (= Kōchi a̅ko̅o̲ < a̅ka̲-ku̲) and ta̲ko̅o̲. Ōsaka, Ise, Suzu, and Toyama are like Kyōto; they have only one accent type for adjectives, and that is the historic descendent of the A type. A small group of longer stems, however, still retain the old initial low register in Kyōto, as we see in the data offered by Hirayama and by Umegaki; these two sources are in accord on about 30 such stems, but disagree on almost as many. We will treat the longer "B" stems that still retain the old initial low as a class of exceptions and mark them for Kyōto as "B!". Some 30 stems are so indicated by both Hirayama and Umegaki:

> dosigata-, hadasamu-, ikigurusi-, kogekusa-, matidoosi-, menbokuna-, mittomona-, sarigena-, sasidegamasi-, taegata-, tayorina-, tumiᵇ/ᵦuka-, usirogura-, usirometa-, yogina-; ahorasi-, endoo-, gigotina-, makkuro-, nanigena-, negurusi-, nukamisokusa-, oisi-, otonagena-, setigara-, sinbo(o)zuyo-, titikusa-, warugasiko-, zoosana-, zyasuibuka-.

Hirayama shows low register "B!" in 20 other stems that are "B" for Umegaki:

> darasina-, matidoosi-, musiatu-, sarigata-; amasuppa- , gutippo-, kinakusa-, kizappo-, manmaru-, massiro-, museppo-, namaatataka-, oisi-, sokkena-, syozaina-, tawaina-, usosamu-, zihibuka-, zoosana-, zyosaina-.

Hirayama also has "B!" for kimariwaru-, which Umegaki renders as a phrase 1 | 1:3. Umegaki has "B!" for three stems that are "B" in Hirayama: kandaka-, yabotta-, maaru- ('round'); he has "B/B!" for three stems that Hirayama gives as "B": tebaya-, negurusi-, nukamiso-kusa-. And Umegaki has "B!" for four that are not listed in Hirayama: neba-, taisoorasi-, yosina-, wakena-. The monosyllabic stems na- and yo- and the obsolete dissyllabic stem [isi-] also retained the low register, according to our sources, so they too are marked "B!" for Kyōto. We might wonder why the other two monosyllabic stems differ; ko- 'saturated' is pronounced with a long vowel k̅o̅o̲-i̲ (cf. Kobayashi 131), and perhaps the same is true of su- 'sour' (? s̅u̅u̲-i̲). In Sakawa and Kōchi e̅e̲ = y̲o̲-i̲ 'is good' is low-initial, but n̅a̲-i̲ 'lacks' is high-initial; data are unavailable for the other two monosyllabic stems.

In Tōkyō-type dialects, too, the old distinction of types A and B have been difficult to maintain for the adjective stems. In Tōkyō itself the distinction is maintained, but a number of the longer A-type stems, such as yorosii and muzukasii, have gravitated toward the B group. And in Nagoya the two types have completely fallen together (as Type B), a predictable merger that has undoubtedly taken place elsewhere (and independently) in dialects of this type; the same merger has been confirmed for Hagiwara and Okayama. In modern Tōkyō speech a number of perturbating factors have actually led to a proliferation of sub-classes of Type B (see Martin 1967). The stem-final locus that is found in the imperfect of the Type-B adjectives is normally anticipated (i.e. moved back) by one syllable in the infinitive, the gerund, and the past (taꞌkaku, taꞌkakute, taꞌkakatta), but for a number of these adjectives you will often hear the stem-final locus retained: akudoꞌku, akudoꞌkute, akudoꞌkatta. Many of the affected stems are longish and sound as if they might be compounds or carry suffixes: omosiroꞌku < omosiꞌroku. There are shorter stems that behave the same way except for the infinitive, perhaps because it is shorter: nibuꞌkute, nibuꞌkatta; niꞌbuku. But when a one-syllable particle is attached to the infinitive, the pattern of the phrase is like that of the gerund: nibuꞌku wa/mo. Compare the infinitive of a Type-A stem: akaku naꞌru 'gets red', akakuꞌ/akaꞌku mo naꞌru 'gets red too' (the perfect is only akaꞌkatta). There appear to be quite a few variations in accentuating adjective forms in contemporary Tōkyō; some are in the direction of simplification, others tend to complicate the system. A given speaker may be following an unstable set of rules, with free variants for paradigmatic forms of certain groups of adjectives.

Because of the merger of Type-B and Type-A stems, Kyōto data in the following lists (except for the "B!" stems) can be ignored as irrelevant. Unfortunately, adequate data from a dialect such as that of Kōchi or Wakayama are not available. The patterns for those dialects, however, can often be safely imputed from the historical information given, and to some extent from the patterns in Kagoshima and the Ryūkyūs, though caution is well advised in extrapolating from those patterns, especially with reference to longer or less common stems.

7.9. List of Adjective Stems.

Note: As entry headings the adjective stems are listed with a final hyphen, but in
etymological formulas the hyphen will usually be seen only after a verb stem or
root, a prefix, or a formant; the formants (-si-, -ta-, -ppo-, ...) are normally
written with hyphens on both sides, as is the marker -n-. Longer stems marked "B"
begin with the high register in modern Kyōto (with a fall to low within the stem)
but some stems retain the old low register, and attestations of these are marked
"B!". The notation " ... " means that further etymological information is available,
and some of it can be found elsewhere in this book; "⋯" is used instead of writing
out obvious elements such as reduplications. Abbreviations: adj = adjective; adj-n =
adjectival noun; adn = adnoun; adv = adverb; attr = attributive; bnd = bound, inf =
infinitive; mim = mimetic; pcl = particle; pre = prefix; suf = suffix; vn = verbal
noun.

?A abuna- ‹ abu- (?‹ a[ya]bu- = ayafu- ‹ ...) -na-. ‘dangerous’. x - B-B-A B-A-x.
   Narada, Hata, NE Kyūshū A. Kōchi A. Sd qapne- B (borrowed?); Nk qab(u)unasen A,
   qangasen A; Sr qabunasyan A (= qukaasyan B, see okasi-), qabunee tukuru ‘a
   dangerous place’. Earliest attestation Mr? Cf. ayau-. ayasi-.

- abura(k)ko- ‹ abura₂.₉ (‹ ...) kwo_adj B. ‘oily’. x - B-B-B x-x-x. Nk qanra-
   zuusen B (‹ abura tuyo-); Yn anda-butan (Takahashi 1977).

B aena- ‹ ae₂.₉ (‹ aye (JP) ‹ *awe ‹ afe ‹ apa-Ci[-Ci]_B) na_adj B. ‘tragic, sad;
   frail, transient’. x - B-/B![H]/B[U]-B.

- airasi- ‹ ai (‹ Ch ay’) rasi (‹ [a]ra-_B -si-). Earliest attestation Mr.
   ‘lovely’. x - B-B-A x-B-x. Sr qeerasi- B.

A aka- (?‹ aka-_A). ‘red; bright’. A - A-B-A A-A-A. Edo A. Sapporo, Akita,
   Matsumoto, Numazu, Narada, Hattō, Hamada, Matsue, Izumo, Hiroshima, Hata,
   Ōita, NE Kyūshū A. Kōchi A. Nk ʰ/qaKaasen.

- akaguro- ‹ aka_adj A -n- kurwo_adj B. ‘reddish black’. x - A/B-B-A x-x-x. Attested
   Hn.

- akakusa- ‹ aka₂.₉ (‹ ...) kusa_adj B. ‘dirty-smelling’. x - B-B-x x-x-x. Earliest
   attestation Mr.

A [akarasi-] ‹ aka-ra_adj-n -si-. ‘poignant’. x - x-x-x x-x-x. Ir LHHH (?= *HHHH).

A ama- ‘sweet’. A - A-B-A A-A-A. Km (S) A. Sapporo B̲; Akita, Matsumoto, Numazu,
   Narada, Hattō, Hamada, Matsue, Izumo, Hiroshima, Hata, Ōita, Kyūshū A.
   Kōchi A. Nk qamaasen A.

B [amane-] ‹ *ama-na-Ci- ‹ ? (cf. amata; amaru, amasu; ame). ‘extensive’.
   B - x-x-x x-x-x. Km (S) B. Mg "aᶠ/■ane-si" LxL-H, aᵇ/■ane-si LLL-H. Adverb
   amane-ku LLH-L - 3[H]/4-0[H]/4[U]-B x-x-x. Also OJ samane- (?‹ s[a]-_pre, ?‹
   *zamane- [Ch. 1, §31]) and mane-, perhaps a truncation, unless amane- itself
   is a truncation of samane- (?= sa-mane-).

B ao- ‹ awo- ‹ *abo₂.₉ (‹ ?*zabo̲ [Ch. 1, §31]). ‘blue, green’. B - B-B-B
   A-A-(A)/B. NS (T+ kun) LL = B. Km (S) B. Narada, Hattō, Hamada, Matsue, Izumo,
   Hata, NE Kyūshū B. Kōchi A̲ (Doi 1952:32). Sd qoo- A; Nk qoosen A ‘unripe,
   unseasoned’; Sr qoo- A; Yn au-cici A (H 1969), aun B (H 1964). Yaeyama (Sonai)
   abossadaru ← abo-(s)sa du (‹ *zo) aru.

A ara- ‘rough; (Yn) new’. A - A-B-A A-A-B. NS (123b [14:239-K]) A. Km (W) A/B.
   Mr (Bm) A. Edo A/B. Sapporo B̲; Akita, Matsumoto, Numazu, Narada, Hattō,
   Hamada, Matsue, Izumo, Hiroshima, Ōita A. Nk qaraasen A. Cf. arata, sara.

- araarasi- ‹ ara_adj B ⋯ -si-. ‘rough’. x - B-B-A x-x-x. Cf. araara₄.₉.

B arigata- ‹ ari (‹ *ar[a-C]i_B) -n- kata_adj A. ‘welcome; obliged’. x - B-B-B x-x-x.
   Sr qarigatee kutu (borrowed?). Attested in Man'yō-shū.

A   asa- 'shallow'. A - A-B-A A-A-A. Km (S,W) A. Edo A. Sapporo, Akita, Matsumoto,
     Numazu, Narada, Hattō, Hamada, Matsue, Izumo, Hiroshima, Ōita, NE Kyūshū A.
     Kōchi A. Nk qassen (HHLL =) A; Sr qassan A = qasasan B.

?   asaguro- ‹ asa*adj A* -n- kurwo*adj B*. 'light(ly) black'. x - A/B-B-B x-x-x.
     Attested 1300s.

?   asamasi- ‹ asama-*?A* (‹ asa*adj A* -ma-) -si-. 'disgusting'. x - B-B-B x-A-x.
     Nk hasaamasen B. K: "Edo HHHLL".

B   [asi-] 'bad'. B - x-x-x x-x-x. NS (109b [11:321-K], 111b [11:354-K] asiki LLL;
     127b [14:326-K]) asiku LLL. Km (W) B. Edo B.

A   atarasi- ‹ ataraз.1 (?‹ *atara-*A*) -si-. 'precious; regrettable'. A [Ir] - x-x-x
     B-A-x. NS (79c [14:337-M] 'much-to-be-regretted') A. NS (T+ 80) atarasi-kyi
     ⌷LLL-H (odd). Cf. atarasigaru (Zs) 'regret'. Nk haTaarasen A.

B   atarasi- ?‹ arata-si- (metathesis) ‹ arata*adj-n* з.4 (?‹ *zara-ta) -si-. 'new'.
     B - B-B-B (B)-(A)-x. Ir A. Cf. ara-.

B   atataka- ‹ atataka4.11 *adj-n* ‹ *ata-[a]ta- (‹ atu*adj B* ···) -ka. 'warm'.
     (B) - B-B-B x-x-x. Mg atatake- B, atataka (nari).

A   atu- 'thick; cordial'. A - A-B-A A-A-A. Edo A. Sapporo, Akita, Matsumoto, Numazu,
     Narada, Hattō, Hamada, Matsue, Izumo, Hiroshima, Ōita A. Kōchi, Sakawa A. Sd
     qaty(i)- A; Nk haCiisen A; Sr qaçi- A; Yn acan A. In many Amami and Okinawa
     dialects and in Taketomi the forms go back to *ati- with a different final
     vowel from *atu- 'hot'. Cf. Thorpe 339.

B   atu- 'hot'. B - B-B-B B-x-B/C. Edo B. Sapporo, Akita, Matsumoto, Numazu, Narada,
     Hattō, Hamada, Matsue, Izumo, Hiroshima, Ōita, NE Kyūshū B. Kōchi, Sakawa B.
     Sd qati- B; Nk haCisen B; Sr qaçi- B, Yn acan B (H 1964) / C (H 1967) ‹ *atu-
     san. Hateruma acahan ‹ *atu-sa-san (cf. Thorpe 298).

A   [atukawasi-] ‹ atukafasi- ‹ *atukapa-*A* (‹ ...) -si-. 'struggling to cope'.
     A - x-x-x x-x-x.

B   awa- ‹ afa- ‹ *apa-. 'thin, insipid, bland'. B - B-B-B x-B-x. Narada ("uncommon")
     B. Nk haPaasen B, Sr qahwa-san B 'insipid, bland'.

?   awatadasi- ‹ (JP) awatatasi- (?‹ *abaз.з tata-*в* 'foam stand'; ?‹ awate-*A* ‹ ...).
     'restless'. x - B-B-A x-x-x. K: "Edo B".

?B awaawasi- ‹ afaafasi- ‹ *apa*adj B* ··· -si-. 'pale; light; superficial'. x - B-x-x
     x-x-x.

B   ayasi- ‹ aya-si- ‹ *ada-[Ci-*?A* 'fall'] -si-. 'doubtful'. B - A-B-A x-A-A.
     NS (116b [14:101-K]) ayasiki LLLL. Km (S,W) B. Edo A/B. Narada, NE Kyūshū B.
     Sakawa A. Nk qayaasen A, Sr qayassan A 'untrustworthy, dangerous'. Cf. ayau-,
     abuna-; aeru, ayasu.

A   ayau- ‹ ayafu- ‹ *aya-pu- ‹ *ada-[Ci*?A* 'fall'] -pu- (?‹ *-po- ‹ *[o]po*adj B*).
     'dangerous'. A - A/B-B-A x-x-x. Cf. ayasi-, abuna-; aeru, ayasu.

B   [azarake-] (‹ ?). 'fresh'. B - x-x-x x-x-x. Cf. atarasi-, arata, sara, ara-.

B   azikina- ‹ adikina- ‹ adiз.1 (‹ *anti) ki1.1 (?‹ kiy) na*adj B*. 'wearisome'.
     B - B-B-A x-x-x.

?   bibisi- ‹ *bi (‹ Ch mbyey') ··· -si-. 'beautiful'. x - B-B-A x-x-x. From 900s.

B   [e-] ‹ ye- (= yo- ‹ ...). 'good'. See yo-.

?   egara- ‹ wegara- ‹ we[gu]*adj B* (‹ ...) kara*adj A*. 'acrid, pungent'.
     x - (A/B)-x-x x-x-x. Dial. igara-.

B   egata- ‹ *e[y]*в* (‹ *a-Ci[-Ci]) -n- kata*adj A*. 'hard to obtain/experience'.
     x - B-B-A x-x-x.

B   egu- ‹ wegu- ‹ weguз.x (‹ ?; a kind of sedge, Eleocharis kuroguwai). 'acrid,
     pungent; cold, heartless'. B - B-B-x B-B-x. Nk (ui)goosen B 'itchy'; Sd yiigoo-
     B 'itchy, scratchy'; Sr wiigoo- B 'acrid; itchy' ‹ *wegu a[ra-]. A variant
     "wego-" (the second vowel partially assimilated to the first) is not attested
     until Edo. The noun occurs in Man'yō-shū; the adjective first appears in Mg.

- girigata- ‹ giri*2.2b* (‹ ...) -n- kata-*adj A*. 'punctilious'. x - B-B-A x-x-x.
  Earliest attestation Mr.
- gyoogyoosi- ‹ geu-geu (‹ Ch ?; see NKD) -si-. 'exaggerated'. x - B-B-B x-x-x.
  Earliest attestation Mr.
- hadasamu- ‹ fadasamu- ‹ *panta*2.4* sanpu*adj B* (‹ ...). 'chilly'. x - B-B!-B x-x-x.
- [haebaesi-] ‹ faye[y] (‹ *pada-Ci-[Ci]*B*) -n- ··· -si-. 'radiant, brilliant'.
  x - B-x-x x-x-x.
- *hagayu- (Ryūkyū) ‹ *pankayu- (‹ ? + kayu*adj B* ‹ ...). 'dirty; ugly'. Sd hagoo-
  B 'ugly, hateful'; Nk pᵘ/ₒgoosen B = pagoosen 'dirty, itchy'; Sr hagoo- B
  'dirty'. Thorpe suggests that the first element may represent 'skin' (?‹
  *[ka]pa); there are also forms with paçi- and paşi- which require explanation.
- B hagesi- ‹ fagesi- (?‹ *fagey-si- ‹ *panka- [cf. hagemu] -si; ?‹ *pa[da]*adj B*
  -n- key*?1.1*). 'severe; extreme; frequent'. B - B-B-B x-x-x. Edo B. Narada,
  NE Kyūshū B.
- [haka-] ‹ faka ‹ *paka*2.3*. 'expeditious, speedy; active; satisfactory'.
  x - x-x-x x-x-x. Single attestation in Shiki-shō (1477).
- B hakana- ‹ fakana- ‹ *paka*2.3* na*adj B*. 'inconstant'. B - B-B-B x-x-x. Km (W) A.
  K: "Edo HLL-L".
- B [hanahadasi-] ‹ fanafada*4.2* (‹ ...) -si-. 'extreme'. B - B-B-A x-x-x.
- B haradatasi- ‹ faradatasi- ‹ *paradata-*B*(‹ *para*2.3* -n- tata-*B*) -si-. 'provoking,
  aggravating, maddening'. x - B-B-B x-x-x.
- B haraguro- ‹ farakuro- (JP) ‹ *para*2.3* (-n-) kurwo*adj B*. 'blackhearted, wicked'.
  x - B-B-B x-x-x. Attested 10th century.
- B harebaresi- ‹ farebaresi- ‹ fare[y] (‹ *para-Ci[-Ci]*B*) -n- ··· -si-. 'clear,
  bright, cheery'. x - B-B-B x-x-x.
- B haregamasi- ‹ faregamasi- ‹ fare*2.3* (‹ ...) -gamasi- (‹ ...). 'ostentatious,
  showy, gala'. x - B-B-B x-x-x. Attested 1288.
- A [hasi-] ‹ fasi- ‹ *pasi-. 'lovable, precious, beautiful'. x - x-x-x x-x-x.
  NS (83b [17:119-M]) fasikyeku mo HHHL-L. NS (T+ 21) fasi-kyi yosi LL-H H-L.
  Cf. kuwasi-.
- hasitana- ‹ fasita*3.5a* (‹ *pasita) -na-. 'vulgar; fragmentary'. x - B-B!-B x-x-x.
- B hatesina- ‹ fatesi-na- ‹ fatesi*3.x* (‹ fate[y]*2.3* ‹ *pata-Ci[-Ci]) -si*?pcl* na*adj B*.
  'boundless, unlimited'. x - B-B-B x-x-x. Hattō, Hamada,Matsue, Izumo B.
- B haya- ‹ faya- ‹ *pada-. 'quick; early'. B - B-B-B B-B-C. NS (70a [11:45-M])
  fayakyemu LLHL. NS (T+ 75) faya-ku LH-L, (67) fayaku fa LL-L(|)L; (42)
  fayakyemu HLLH *(odd)*. Km (S,W) B. Edo B. Sapporo, Akita, Matsumoto, Numazu,
  Narada, Hattō, Hamada, Matsue, Izumo, Hiroshima, Hata, Ōita, NE Kyūshū B.
  Kōchi, Sakawa B. Sd hwee- B; Kikai pëë B; Nk peesen B; Sr hweesan B;
  Miyako (Sawata, Kerima, Yonaha) pyaa- (‹ *paya-).
- [hayu-] ‹ *fayu- ‹ *pad[a-Ci-]*B* -u. 'shining, radiant, bright, brilliant'.
  x - x-x-x x-x-x. *See* [siwawayu-], syoppa-, suppa-; kosobayu-, mabayu-; kawai-.
- B hazigamasi- ‹ fadi*2.3* (‹ *panti[y] ‹ *pantu-Ci[-Ci]*B*) -gamasi- (‹ ...).
  'shamefaced'. x - x-x-x x-x-x.
- B hazukasi- ‹ *fadukasi- ‹ *pantu[-Ci]-*B* -ka -si-. 'shy, embarrassed'. B - B-B-B
  x-B-x. Hattō, Hamada, Matsue, Izumo B. Okinawa: Nk paziKasen B; Sr hazikasyan
  B; Ō pazika-han, Kushi hwadukwa-han, Onna pazoko-hon.
- B [hi-] ‹ *fyi- ‹ *pi-. x - x-x-x (B)-B-C. 'cold'. x - x-x-x x-B-x. Sd hyigur(u)- B
  ‹ figor(u) ‹ *pi*1.3a* *(or adj B)* -n- koru (‹ *kora-u); Nk piisen B; Sr hwizuru-
  (‹ figuru ‹ figoru ‹ ...) B = hwii-san B; Miyako pzguroo-pzguru ‹ *piguru-;
  Yn hii- C 'cold'. Sr şiibii- B 'chilly' ‹ *su- -n- pi-. Yn hiragi-san B 'cool',
  hiragintai B 'cold' ‹ *pi [a]ra- -n- key. Cf. hi*1.3a*, hiyasu, hieru; [hisi-],
  [hiya-]. Thorpe 273 would reconstruct *peye for the Ryūkyū forms; in that case
  *pi- would be merely a truncation of *pida- (› [hiya-]).

B hiku- < fiku-/fiki- < Nr fiki*sds* < *fyikiy < *pik^u/$_o$Ci. 'low'. x - B-B-B B-B-C.
   Edo B. Sapporo, Akita, Matsumoto, Numazu, Narada, Hattō, Hamada, Matsue,
   Izumo, Hiroshima, Ōita, NE Kyūshū B. Kōchi, Sakawa B. Kikai pityaa-sai B;
   Nk piKusen B; Kobama piko-; Yn Kw-an C < *piku-.

A hira- < fira*sds* < fyira < *pira*?2.2b*. 'flat'. x - x-x-x A-A-x. Sd hyiryaa- A;
   Nk x; Sr hwira- A. Attested 1477.

B hiro- < fyiro- < *piro-. 'wide, broad, vast'. B - B-B-B B-B-A/C. NS (T+ kun)
   fyiro-kyi ▮HL ?= LH-L. Km (S) B. Mr (Bm) hiro-si LH-L / HL-L. Edo B. Narada,
   Hattō, Hamada, Matsue, Izumo, Hata, NE Kyūshū B. Kōchi B. Nk Piru(u)sen B;
   Miyako pssu- < *piro-; Kobama pisoo- < *piro-; Yn ca-an, ca-ru A (H 1964) / C
   (H 1967) < *piro-.

B hisasi- < fyisasi- < fyisa*?2.4* (< *pisa) -si-. 'long-lasting'. B - B-B-B x-x-x.
   NS (120a [14:177-K], 125b [14:271-K]). Km (S,W) B. Mr (Bm) fisa-si HL-L (K:
   "HH-L"). Edo (A/)B. Narada, Hattō, Hamada, Matsue, Izumo B. (Sd, Nk, Sr use
   the stem nagee- ?< naga-[w]i- 'long-stay'.)

B [hisi-] < *fyisi- < *pi*adj B* -si-. 'cold'. x - x-x-x x-x-x. In addition to Miyako
   forms such as Ōra pisikan, Thorpe (273) cites Yn hican < *pi-si-sa··· as an
   equivalent of Yn hii-san C; notice also Miyako Hirara psyaa-/psii-psi < *pisi-.
   Cf. [hi-], [hiya-].

B *hisu- (Ryūkyū) 'thin': see hoso-.

B [hi^s/$_z$ukasi-] < fizukasi- < *pinsu-ka*adj-s* (< ?) -si-. 'stupid; loud(-mouthed),
   noisy'. B - x-x-x x-x-x. Cf. [isukasi-].

- hitogamasi- < fito*2.2a* (< *pito) -gamasi- (< ...). 'proper (for a person),
   refined, genteel'. x - B-x-x x-x-x. Attested 11th century.

B hitosi- < fitosi- < *fyito*?2.4,?2.3* -si-. 'equal'. B - B-B-B x-x-x. Km (S) B.
   Mr (BM) HLL(-L) (K: "HHL-L"). Sapporo, Akita, Matsumoto, Numazu, Narada, Hattō,
   Hamada, Matsue, Izumo, Hiroshima, Ōita B. Kōchi B.

B [hiya-] < fiya- (JP) < *pida (?< *pi*1.3a* -da-). 'cold'. Occurs in many dialects,
   including Kōchi (Hattori 1973:38) hiyai 2 = B. Cf. [hi-], [hisi-], , hi*1.3a*,
   hieru, hiyasu.

- hodotika- < fodotika- < *po(n)two*2.2a* (< ...) tika*adj B*. 'nearby'. x - B-B-A
   x-x-x. Attested 1300s.

- hodotoo- < fodotofo- < *po(n)two*2.2a* (< ...) topo*adj A*. 'far (from), distant,
   distanced'. x - A/B-B-A x-x-x. Earliest attestation late Mr.

? hokorasi- < fokorasi- < *pokora-$_A$ -si-. 'prideful; (Sd) happy; (Sr) delighted,
   delightful'. x - B-B-A B-A-x. Sd hoorasyi- B; Nk x; Sr [Lit.] hukurasyan A;
   Miyako pkarasz-pkaras < *pukarasi-. Attested 905.

B hosi- < fosi- < fwosi- < *pwosi- < *po[ra]-$_B$ -si-. 'desired'. B - B-B-B B-B-x.
   Mg fosi[k]i mama (ni). NS (72b [11:200-M]); 105a [11:224-K]) B. Mr (Bm) hosi-i
   mama HL-L LL. Hattō, Hamada, Matsue, Izumo. Nk puqsen B. The etymology implies
   contraction from *pora-si- but no such adjective is attested; perhaps the verb
   and the adjective derived separately from a root *po- → *po-ra-, → *po-si-.

B hoso- < foso- < *poso-. 'slender'. B - B-B-B x-x-x. NS (Okada) B. Edo B. Narada,
   Hattō, Hamada, Matsue, Izumo, Hata B. Kōchi B. Thorpe 339 reconstructs a proto-
   Ryūkyūan stem *pisu/pesu 'thin' (Sd hyisi- B, Nk pisisen/piqsen B, Sr hwisi- B,
   Yn hican C) which he posits as cognate with *poso- (?< *posu- with the second
   vowel assimilated to the first); cf. usu-.

B huka- < fuka- < *puka-. 'deep'. B - B-B-B B-B-B/C. Edo B. Km (S) B. Mr (Bm) fukasi LH-L. Sapporo, Matsumoto, Numazu, Narada, Hattō, Hamada, Matsue, Izumo,
   Hiroshima, Ōita, NE Kyūshū B. Nk puKaasen B; Yn Kan B (H 1964) / C (H 1967).

B huru- < furu- < *puru-. 'old'. B - B-B-B B-B-B. Km (W) B. Edo B. Sapporo, Akita,
   Matsumoto, Numazu, Narada, Hattō, Hamada, Matsue, Izumo, Hiroshima, Ōita,
   NE Kyūshū B. Nk puru(u)sen B; Miyako fuzz-fuz < *furu-; Kobama huro-han;
   Yn huru-cici B.

B huruburusi- < furuburusi- < *puru*adj B* -n- ··· -si-. 'very old/stale'. x - x-x-x
   x-x-x.

B hurukusa- < furukusa- < *puru*adj B* kusa*adj B*. 'old, stale'. x - B-B-B x-x-x.
   Attested 12th century.

B hurumekasi- < furumeka-*B* (< *puru*adj B* - miCa-ka-*bnd v*) - si-. 'oldish'. x - B-x-
   x x-x-x. Attested Hn.

?A husawasi- < fusafasi- < *pusa(-)pa-*?B* -si-. 'suitable'. x - B-B-A x-x-x. Attested
   10th century.

B huto- < futo- < futwo- < *putwo-. 'big (in girth), fat'. B - B-B-B x-x-x. Edo B.
   Narada, Hattō, Hamada, Matsue, Izumo B. Are Nk -butaa 'big one', Sr buta-,
   Miyako vda- (etc.) 'fat' somehow related to this stem? (See also buta*2.1*.)

- ?[iba-] < *inpa-. 'narrow; small'. *See* sema-.

B ibukasi- < ifukasi- < *ipuka (< ?) -si-. 'curious; dubious'. B - B-B-A x-x-x.
   Cf. ibukaru.

B [ibuse-] < *inpuse- (< ?). 'glum, melancholy; anxious, worried; unpleasant,
   disliked; shabby, squalid'. x - x-x-x x-x-x. Km B. Edo B. Cf. ibusemu.

B ika-. 'mighty; big, much'. x - x-x-x x-x-x. NS (T+ kun) ika-si HLL, HHL. Narada
   ('big') B. This adjective is obsolete except as dialect. Cf. deka- < do-ika-
   'huge'; ika 'how', iku- 'how many/much'.

- ikamesi- < ika*adj B* me (?< *mye < myiye[y] < *mida-Ci[-Ci]*B*) -si-. 'awesome; huge;
   severe; dreadful'. x - B-B-A x-x-x.

B [imadasi-]. *See* [madasi-].

- [imasi-] < *ima*?2.4,?2.5* -si-. 'present, immediate'. x - x-x-x x-x-x. Attested:
   imasi-ku and imasi-kiy (Senmyō 31), which is perhaps a mistake for the expected
   *imasi-kyi, if not some other (unknown) formation.

- imaimasi- < *ima-*B* ··· -si-. 'vexing'. x - B-B-B x-x-x. K: "Edo B". From 1000s.

B imawasi- < imafasi- < ima-*B* -pa-si-. 'ominous; odious'. x - B-B-B x-x-x.

B iradatasi- < *iradata-*B* (< ...) -si-. 'exasperating'. x - B-x-x x-x-x. Attested
   1275.

B [irairasi-] < ira*2.3* ··· -si-. 'irritating, irritated'. x - B-x-x x-x-x. Attested
   Ir, JP. The modern iraira is a subjective adjectival noun and an adverb.

B [irana-] < ira*2.3* -na- (< na*adj B* 'un[pleasantly] thorny'). 'extreme(ly tough,
   rough, sharp); onerous'. x - x-x-x x-x-x. NS (70b [11:52-M]) B; NS (T+ 43)
   iranakyeku LL*E*LL = LLLLL.

? isagiyo- (?< *isam[i]-kiyo- < *isami*3.1* (< *isa-m[a-C]i*?A/B*) kyiywo*adj B*.
   'gallant, manly'. A - B-B-B x-x-x. Tk 3/B (NKD, but K "B").

- [isaka-] ?< *isa-ka- (cf. isasake-, isasaka, isago). 'little (= not much), few,
   scant'. x - x-x-x x-x-C. Yn sagan C < *isaka-an; Kobama isyakahan, Hateruma
   isyagahan, Taketomi isyaasan.

- isamasi- < *isama- (< *isa-ma-*?A/B*) -si-. 'brave'. x - B-B-A x-x-x. Attested
   1300s.

B [isasake-] < isasakey- < isasaka*4.x* (< ...) -Ci-. 'trifling, petty'. x - x-x-x
   x-x-x. NS (124b [11:52-M]) B. Kikai qisaa- 'few, little'.

B [isi-] < yesi- < ye*adj x* (< yo*adj B* < ...) -si-. 'good, splendid; delicious,
   ... '. x - (B-B!-x) x-x-x. (The stem is obsolete, though the NKD entry might
   suggest it is not.) Cf. oisi-.

B isogasi- < *iswoga-*B* (< *iswo-n[a]-ka-) -si-. 'busy'. (B) - B-B-B x-x-x.
   B isogawasi- < isogafasi- < *iswoga-*B* -pa-si-. 'busy'. B - x-x-x x-x-x.

? [isukasi-] ?< isuka*?3.1* ('crossbeak [bird]') -si-. 'stupid; loud(-mouthed),
   noisy'. x - x-x-x x-x-x. Attested NS. Cf. [hi*s/z*ukasi-].

B ita- 'painful; extreme'. B - B-B-B x-B-x. Km (W 'extreme') B. Edo B. Narada,
   Hattō, Hamada, Matsue, Izumo B. Nk hiCaasen B, Sr qica-san B 'pathetic;
   painful'. Cf. itamu; itaru, itasu (register incongruent); ita*adv* (= ito).

B   itamasi- < *itama-*B* ((< *ita*adj B* -ma-) -si-. 'pathetic; painful'.x - B-B-B x-x-x.
    K: "Edo B". Attested 1238.

B   itawasi- < itafasi- < *ita*adj B* -pa-si-. 'pitiful'. B - B-B-B x-x-x.

B   [itazukawasi-] < ita*t*/*d*ukafasi- (Nr) < *ita-*t*/*d*uka-*?B* (< ...) -pa-si-. 'busy'.
    B - x-x-x x-x-x. Mg -*t*/*d*u-.

B   [iti*h*/*b*aya-] < itifaya- < *iti-*pre* pada*adj B*. 'quick, smart, keen-witted'.
    x - B-B-x x-x-x. Brinkley 1896 (overlooked by NKD) has iti*h*/*b*ayaku.

B   itizirusi- ((< itiziru -si-) < itiziru- < itisiru (JP) < iti-sirwo < iti*adv*
    sirwo*2.8*. 'striking'. B - B-B-A̲ x-x-x.

A   itokena-, itokina- < *itwo*2.x* key*?1.1*/ki[?y]*1.1* -na- (< na*adj B*). 'young,
    immature'. A - x-x-x x-x-x. Km (W) A.

?B ito(o)si- < it*o̲*fosi- ?< itafasi- (< ...). 'tough, unpleasant; pitiful; lovable,
    cute'. x - B-B-A x-x-x. Edo HHHL-L.

?B itowasi- < itofasi- < *it*o̲*(-)pa-*? B* (< ...) -si-. 'hateful, detestable,
    disagreeable'. x - B-B-x x-x-x.

B   [itukusi-] ?< itukasi- < *ituka-*B* (< ...) -si-. 'miraculous, marvelous,
    wonderful'; (= utukusi-) 'beautiful'. B - (B)-x-x x-x-x. Cf. [kusi-].

B   [iyaiyasi-] < wiyawiyasi- < wiya/uya*?8.8,?8.1* (?< *wiy-[y]a < ...) ··· -si-.
    'deferential, respectful' (= uyauyasi-). B - x-x-x x-x-x.

?B iyasi- < iya (< *ida 'nay') -si-. 'vile; miserable; greedy, hungry'. B - A/B-B-A
    B-x-C. Km (S) A. Mr (Bm) A. Edo A. Tappi, Narada, NE Kyūshū B. Sakawa B.
    Nk qiyaasen A 'inadequate', yaasen B 'hungry'; Miyako yaasz-yaas ?< *(i)yasi-
    'hungry', Yn daasa- 'hungry'. Cf. NS iya̅si-fito̅ (113a [14:28-K]).

B   izato- ?< i*1.3a* -n- satwo*adj B*. 'quick to awaken'. x - B-x-x x-x-x. Earliest
    attestation 10th century. Cf. yosato-.

?A kaboso- < *ka-*pre* -n- pos*o̲*adj B*. 'slender, delicate'. x - A/B-B-A x-x-x.

B   [kadamasi-] (JP) < ka*t*/*d*amasi- < *ka(n)tama-*B* -si-. 'crooked, perverse'.
    B - x-x-x x-x-x.

-   kadokadosi- < kadwo*?8.8b* ··· -si-. 'full of angles; testy, crabby'. x - B-B-x
    x-x-x.

B   kagayakasi- < kakayakasi- (Hepburn 1886) < *kakayaka-*B* (< ...) -si-. 'brilliant;
    red-faced (with shame)'. x - B-B-A x-x-x.

B   kagirina- < kagyiri*8.4* (< ...) na*adj B*. 'boundless, unlimited'. x - B-B-B x-x-x.
    (NKD "Kt 2" must be a misprint.)

?B kaguro- < kagurwo- < *ka-*pre* -n- kurwo*adj B*. 'black'. x - B-B-x x-x-x. Hepburn
    1868 "kakuro-".

A   kaguwasi-.   *See* koobasi-.

B   kaigaisi- < kafigafisi- ?< *kafyi (< *kap[a-C]i*A*) -n- ··· -si-. 'gallant'.
    x - B-B-B x-x-x. K: "Edo B".

?B *kama- (?< *kama-*B* 'chew, bite, gnaw'). 'noisy'. *See* atukamasi-, kamakamasi-,
    kama*b*/*m*isusi-, kamabisi-, kasigamasi-, kasimasi-; yakamasi-; -gamasi-.

?B kamabisi- [dial., NKD 5:109a]. 'noisy'. x - x-x-x x-x-x.

B   kama*b*/*m*isusi- < kamabisu-(si-) < *kama*adj ?B* -npisu- (< ?). 'noisy'. B - x-x-x
    x-x-x.

A   kanasi- < *kana- (?= kana-[Ci-]*B*) -si-. 'sad; (Ryūkyū) cute, lovable; (OJ)
    beloved, dear'. A - A/B-B-A B-A-x. NS (T+ 43) L*F*HLL = L̲L̲H̲L̲L̲. Km (S,W) A.
    Sapporo, Matsumoto, Numazu, Narada, Hiroshima B; Sapporo, Akita, Hattō, Hamada,
    Matsue, Izumo, Hata, Ōita, NE Kyūshū A. Kōchi A[Doi]/B[H]; Sakawa A.
    Nk hanaasen A. On the etymology cf. Ōno Tōru 1978:299.

A   kanbasi-.   *See* koobasi-/kanbasi-.

B   kara- 'spicy, salty'. B - B-B-B B-B-x. Mg B (except Kn Sō-ka 56:8 "A").
    NS (Okada) B. Edo B. Narada, Hattō, Hamada, Matsue, Izumo B; NE Kyūshū A.
    Nk haraasen B.

A   karu- 'lightweight'. A - A-B-A B̲-A-A. Mr (Bm) karo- A (with partial assimilation
     of the second vowel to the first). Edo A. Sapporo B̲; Akita, Matsumoto, Numazu,
     Narada, Hattō, Hamada, Matsue, Izumo, Hiroshima, Hata, Ōita A. Kōchi A. Kikai
     gas-sai, gak-ku; Nk karuusen A; Sr kassan (abstract) / gassan (concrete) A.

?   karugarusi- < karu*adj A* -n- ··· -si-. 'frivolous; rash'. x - B-B-A x-x-x.

    ? kasigamasi-, kasikamasi- (JP) < *ka[ma]si-gamasi- < *kama*?adj B* -si- -gamasi-
     (< ...). 'noisy'. A - B-B-x x-x-x. Km (W) B. Cf. kasimasi-.

B   kasiko- < kasikwo- 'awesome; wise'. B - B-B-A̲ x-x-x. NS (71a [11:160-M]; 71b
     [11:176-M]; 110a [11:330-K]). NS (T+ 45) kasikwo-ku to̲ mo LLH-L|H(|)Ɛ̲; (47)
     kasikwo-kyi ro̲ ka mo HLH-L|H(|)H(|)Ɛ̲ (odd); (76) kasikwo-myi HLH-H (odd). In
     JP also adjectival noun; cf. kasiko ni 'wisely' (Esopo 417). Cf. kasikomu.

?   kasimasi- < *kasi-[ka]masi- < ka[ma]si-kamasi- < *kama*?adj B* -si-. 'noisy,
     annoying'. x - B-B-A x-B-(A). Nk kasiimasen A; Yaeyama kasamasaan, ngamasaan;
     Yn kaçima-san A.

A   kata-. 'hard'. A - A-B-A A-A-x. NS (79b [14:314-M], 93a[11:19-K]) kataku HHL;
     121a [14:191L-K]) kata[k]i HHL. NS (T+ 78) kata-ku LL̲-L̲. Km (S,W) A. Mr (Bm) A.
     Edo A. Sapporo B̲; Akita, Matsumoto, Numazu, Narada, Hattō, Hamada, Matsue,
     Izumo, Hiroshima, Hata, Ōita, NE Kyūshū A. Kōchi, Sakawa A. Nk hataasen A
     'saturated; dense'; Sr kata- A 'sturdy; sure; saturated', cf. kuhwa- B 'strong'
     (see kowai).

-   [katakunasi-] < katakuna*adj-B* (< ...) -si-. 'obstinate'. ?B - B-B-x x-x-x.
     Mg LHHHL ?= *LLLHL.

-   [katana-]. See kitana-.

?   katazikena- < katazike (< ?) na*adj B*. 'unworthy; grateful'. x - B-B-B x-x-x.
     Km (S) A.

?   kawai- < kawayu- < kafayu- ?< kaf[o-f]ayu- < *kapo*2.1* padu*adj x* ('radiant-faced').
     'cute'. x - B-B-A B-x-x. Narada, Hattō, Hamada, Matsue, Izumo, NE Kyūshū B.
     Sd khawayi- B (borrowed?).

?   kayowa- < *ka-*pre* ywowa*adj B* (< *dwoba). 'weak, feeble'. x - B-B-A x-x-x.

B   kayu- < *kadu-. 'itchy'. B - B-B-B x-x-(C). Narada, NE Kyūshū B. Kikai kayoo-sai;
     Yn kyan C ?< *kayu-an (H 1967) = byuuŋan (Miyara 1930), Taketomi byuusan,
     Hatoma byuuwan (< ?). The stem occurs as koo- or kau- (< ka[y]u-) in a number
     of the Ryūkyū dialects; but in others 'itchy' is expressed by *wegu*adj B*
     a[ra-*B*] 'acrid', as in Sd yigoo- B 'itchy' and Sr wigoo- 'itchy; acrid' (see
     egu-). The stem koo- also occurs in a Ryūkyū stem 'dirty'; see *hagayu-.

?   kayasu- < ka-*pre* yasu*adj B* (< *dasu). 'easy'. x - x-x-x x-x-x.

-   kebuka- < *key*?1.1* (< *ka-Ci) -n- puka*adj B*. 'hairy, hirsute'. x - A/B-B-A x-x-x.

-   kedaka- < ketaka- (JP) < *key*1.1* (< ...) taka*adj B*. 'noble'. x - B-B-A x-x-x.

B   kegarawasi- < kegarafasi- < *kenka*2.3* -ra-pa-*(B)* -si-. 'soiled, disgusting'.
     B - B-B-B x-x-x. For kegara[f]u, see NKD 7:155c; cf. kegareru.

A   kemu-, kebu- < ke*b*/*m*u (= ke*b*/*m*uri*3.1* < ...). 'smoky'. x - A-B-A B̲-A-x.
     Sd khib(u)- B̲; Nk kibuusen A; Sr kibu- A; Miyako kivv-kiv < *kibu-.

A   kemuta- < kebuta- (?< *keybu-ta- < ?*k*ª/*o*Cinpu-ta- < ?). 'smoky'. x - A/B̲-B-A
     x-x-x.

-   ketatamasi- ?< *key*1.1* (< ...) tatama-*A* (< ...) -si-. 'shrill'. x - B-B-A x-x-x.
     Hattō, Hamada, Matsue, Izumo B. Attested 1275. Hepburn 1868 "ketadamasi-"
     (? dialect). Also attested as ketatasi-, perhaps a contraction.

-   keuto-. See kyooto-.

B   kewasi- < kefasi- < *kyifa-si- < *kipa*2.3* -si-. 'steep; fierce; strict'.
     x - B-B-B x-A̲-x. Hattō, Hamada, Matsue, Izumo B. Sr ciwasi- A̲.

B   kibisi- < kibi(?/kibu) (< ?) -si-. 'strict; tight(ly arrayed)'. B - B-B-A̲ x-x-x.
     Mr (Bm) kibisi-ku HLL-L. Narada B. Nk x. Sr cibis-san A *(borrowed?)* = ciwa-syan
     A (< *kipa-si-).

? kikigurusi- < kyikyi-gurusi- < *kik[a-C]i*A* -n- kurusi*adj B* (< ...). 'hard (or
   unpleasant) to hear'. x - B-B-A x-x-x.

B [kirakirasi-] < *kyirakyirasi- < *kira*sis* ··· -si-. 'bright, glittering; splendid,
   resplendent'. B - B-B-x x-x-x.

? kitana- ?< *kata*s.sb* na*adj B*. 'dirty'. (A) - B-B-B B-B-x. Mg katan̄asi 'ugly'.
   K: "Edo HHL-". Hattō, Hamada, Matsue, Izumo, NE Kyūshū B. Nk x; Sr citana-san.
   Attested (kitana-) NS.

- kitu- 'tight; strict; severe; extreme; striking'. x - A-B-A x-x-x. Nk kuCi-sen B,
   see kurusi-; Sr ciwa-syan A, *see* kibisi-. Kobama tyoo- ?< *[ki]tu-. Earliest
   attestation Mr.

B kiwado- < kifado- < *kyifadwo- < *kipa*s.s* -n- two*adj B*. 'risky; extreme'.
   x - B-B-B x-x-x. Attested 1220.

B kiwamarina- < kyifamari*4.6* (< *kipamar[a-C]i*B* < *kipa*s.s* -ma-ra- -Ci) na*adj B*.
   'endless, boundless'. x - B-B-B x-x-x. Attested 10th century.

B kiyo- < kyiywo- < *kidwo-. 'pure'. B - B-B-B x-(B)-(B). Km (W) A/B. Edo B.
   Narada B. Sd khuraa- B (? < k[iy]o-ra-); Nk suraasen B, Sr cura-san B 'pretty'
   < kiyo-ra-.

?A [ko-] < kwo(-)*1.1*. 'small, little; young'. x - x-x-x x-A-x. Nk huusen A; Sr kuu-
   A. Cf. koma(ka)-.

? ko- < kwo- 'saturated'. ?A - B-B-B x-x-x. Km (W) A/B. Edo B. Tappi ko'e B;
   Narada B. Kt "ko-" = koo- B. Nk kuusen A; Naha kuu-san. (Shuri uses kata-san,
   see kata-.) Cf. koyasu, koeru.

B kobuka- < *ko*1.3a*-n- puka*adj B*. 'bosky, woodsy'. x - B-B-x x-x-x. Attested 11th
   century.

- kodaka- < ko-*pre* (< *kwo*1.1*) -n- taka*adj B*. 'rather high/tall'. x - B-B-A x-x-x.
   (Kt "A [H]" must be a misprint.) Attested 11th century.

B koisi- < kwofiysi-/kwof(w)osi- < *kwopo-Ci-*B* -si-. 'beloved'. B - B-B-B x-x-x.
   Edo (A/)B. Narada, Hattō, Hamada, Matsue, Izumo B.

B kokoroboso- < *kokoro*?s.sb* -n- poso*adj B*. 'helpless'. x - B-B-B x-x-x.
   Attested 10th century.

B kokoromotona- ?< kokoromoto*s.x* (< kokoro*?s.sb* moto*s.s*) na*adj B*, ?<
   kokoro*?s.sb* motona*adj ?B* (< *moto*s.s* na*adj B*). 'apprehensive, insecure,
   unreliable'. x - B-B-B x-B-x. K: "Edo B". Attested 10th century.
   Cf. [uramotona-] (§7.11).

B kokorona- < *kokoro*?s.sb* na*adj B*. 'heartless; thoughtless'.
   x - B-B-B x-x-x. Attested 11th century.

B kokorou- < *kokoro*?s.sb* u*adj B*. 'sad-hearted'. x - B-(B)-x x-x-x. K: "Edo
   HHHH-L" (= A). Attested 10th century.

B kokoroyo- < *kokoroyo- < *kokoro*?s.sb* do*adj B*. 'pleasant, delightful'.
   B - B-B-B x-x-x. Km (S) B. K: "Edo A".

B kokoroyowa- < *kokoro*?s.sb* ywowa*adj B* (< *dwoba). 'fainthearted'. x - B-B-x
   x-x-x. K: "Edo B".

B kokorozuyo- < *kokoro*?s.sb* -n- tudo*adj B*. 'heartening'. x - B-B-B x-x-x.
   Attested 10th century.

B kokotiyo- < kokoti*s.1* (< ...) yo*adj B* (< *do). 'comfortable, pleasant'.
   x - B-B-A x-x-x. Attested 11th century.

- komuzukasi- < ko-mu*t*/*d*ukasi- < ko-*pre* (< *kwo*1.1*) mutukasi*adj A* (< ...).
   'troublesome, finicky, querulous, difficult (to please)'. x - A/B-B-A x-x-x.
   Earliest attestation Mr.

B konomasi- < *konoma-*B* (< ?) -si-. 'desirable, pleasant'. x - B-B-B x-x-x.
   Attested 11th century.

A koobasi-/kanbasi- < kaubasi- (< ?*ka[g]uwasi-) < kagufasi- < *ka$_{1.1}$ -n-
    kupasi$_{adj B}$ (< ...). 'savory, fragrant'. A - A/B-B-A B-B-x.
    NS (T+ 35) ka-gufasi L(|)HHHH. Sd khabaa(syi)- B optionally omits the last
    syllable (this may be a truncation but cf. sidaa(syi)- 'cool'); Nk habaasen A;
    Sr kabasyan A; Miyako kabasz-kabas < *kabasi-.
B koogoosi- < kaugausi- < *ka[m]u$_{2.3}$ -n- ka[m]u$_{2.3}$ -si-. 'holy'. x - B-B-B x-x-x.
    Attested 10th century.
?B [koosi-] < kwofusi- (Azuma) = kwofosi- (< ...). 'beloved'. See koisi-.
B kotogotosi- < kotokotosi- (JP) *koto$_{2.3}$ (-n-) ··· -si-. 'pompous, ostentatious'.
    x - B-B-B x-x-x.
B kowa- < kofa- < *kopa-. 'strong; hard; fearful'. B - B-B-B B-B-C. Edo B. Narada
    B 'strong; fearful'. Kikai huba- < *kuba- (< *koba-) 'hard'; Sd kwahaa- B
    'hard', Nk huPaasen B, Sr khuwa-san B 'hard'; Miyako kupaa-kupa < *kupa-;
    Kobama koo- < kowa- 'hard'; Yn kwan C.
- kozakasi- < ko-$_{pre}$ (< *kwo$_{1.1}$) -n- sakasi$_{adj B}$ (< ...). 'brash; crafty; sharp-
    witted'. Attested 1252.
A [kubo-] < *kunpo$_{?2.1}$. 'hollow, sunken, concave'. x - (A/B)-x-x x-x-x. Edo A.
    Attested 1220.
B kudakudasi- < *kunta ··· -si- (cf. kudaku). 'overly complicated, overmeticulous,
    fussy'. B - B-A-B x-x-x. Cf. kudokudosi-.
A kura- 'dark'. A - A-B-A A-A-(A). Km (W) A. Edo A. Sapporo B; Akita, Matsumoto,
    Numazu, Narada, Hattō, Hamada, Matsue, Izumo, Hiroshima, Ōita, NE Kyūshū A.
    Kōchi, Sakawa A. Nk Kuraasen A; Yn dwaṅ A (?< kura-).
B kuro- < kurwo-. 'black'. B - B-B-B B-B-(A). Edo B. Sapporo, Akita, Matsumoto,
    Numazu, Narada, Hattō, Hamada, Matsue, Izumo, Hiroshima, Ōita, NE Kyūshū B.
    Nk Kuru(u)sen B; Miyako ffu- < *kuro-; Kobama hoo- < *kuro-; Yn kurasadaru A
    (H 1967 - mistake?), kurusadaru (Nakamoto 1976) < kuru-sa du (< zo) aru.
    Cf. kuro$_{?2.5,?2.3}$; kuri$_{2.4}$; kura$_{adj A}$.
B kuruosi-, kuruwasi- < kuruf°/$_{a}$si- < *kurupa- (< ...) -si-. 'mad'. x - B-B-B
    x-x-x. Attested 1079.
B kurusi- < kuru- (?< *kur[a-]$_B$ -u; ?< kuru[-pa]-$_B$, cf. kuruu) -si-. 'painful'.
    B - B-B-B x-x-A. NS (112b [11:361-K]) LLHL. Km (W) B. Edo B. Narada, NE
    Kyūshū B. Sd V-i - gurusyi- 'hard to V'; Nk kuCisen B; Sr kurisyan B,
    kuçisyan B (?both < *kurusi-); Yn kuçisan A. On the etymology cf. Ōno Tōru
    1978:299.
B kusa- 'stinking'. B - B-B-B B-B-(A). Narada, Hattō, Hamada, Matsue, Izumo B.
    Kikai ssa- < *kusa-; Nk kusaasen B; Yn can A ?< *kusa-. Cf. kusaru; kuso.
B kusabuka- < *kusa$_{2.3}$ -n- puka$_{adj B}$. 'grassy'. x - B-B-B x-x-x. Attested 11th
    century.
? [kusi-] < *kusiy- < *kusu-Ci-. 'marvelous, wondrous, mysterious'. x - x-x-x
    x-x-x. Cf. [kususi-], [kusubiru]. Ōno Tōru (1978:300) takes this stem to be
    a contraction of ku[su]-si-.
? [kusubasi-] < *kusu-n-pa-si-. 'strange, unusual'. x - x-x-x x-x-x.
? [kususi-] < *kusu-si-. 'marvelous, wondrous, mysterious; unusual, rare'.
    B - x-x-x x-x-x.
A kutigata- < kuti$_{1.1}$ -n- kata$_{adj A}$. 'close-mouthed, tight-lipped; assertive'.
    x - A/B-B-A x-x-x. Attested 11th century.
? kutigitana- < kuti$_{2.1}$ -n- kitana$_{adj B}$ (< ...). 'abusive; gluttonous'. x - B-B-A
    x-x-x. Attested 13th century.
? kutisagana- < kuti$_{2.1}$ sagana$_{adj B}$ (< ...). 'gossipy, scandalous, slanderous'.
    x - B-B-A x-x-x. Attested 11th century.
?B [kuusi-] < kufusi- (Azuma) = kwofusi- (Azuma) = kwofosi- (< ...). 'beloved'.
    See koisi-.

B kuwasi- < kufasi- < *kupa- -si-, ?< *kwo- pasi- (cf. [hasi-]). 'fine, detailed;
   beautiful'. B - B-B-B x-x-x. Sapporo, Akita, Matsumoto, Numazu, Narada, Hattō,
   Hamada, Matsue, Izumo, Hiroshima, Ōita B. Kōchi, Sakawa B. Tsuchihashi 1976:23⁊
   and Ōno Tōru 1978:299: < kufa- (< *kupa-ʙ) 'eat(able)' → 'desirable'.

B kuyasi- < kuya- (< *kuda-) -si-. 'vexing; regrettable'. x - B-B-B x-x-x. Narada,
   NE Kyūshū B. Attested in Koji-ki, Man'yō-shū. Cf. kuyamu, kuiru.

B mabayu- < *ma₁.ₛₐ -n- padu*adj ʙ. x - B-B-B x-x-x. 'brilliant, dazzling'. Hattō,
   Hamada, Matsue, Izumo B. Attested 11th century.

B madasi- < [i]madasi- < imadaₛ.ₛ₆ (< ...) -si-. 'too soon/early, premature,
   unripe'. B - x-x-x x-x-x.

- magamagasi- < *mankaᵣₛ.₁ ··· -si-. 'ominous'. x - B-x-x x-x-x. NKD does not give
   the colloquial form but Brinkley 1896 has it.

B magirawasi- < magirafasi- ?< *ma₁.ₛₐ -n- kᵘ/₂Cira-pa-ʙ -si-. 'equivocal, vague,
   confusing'. x - B-B-B x-x-x. Cf. [makirawasi-].

?B [makirawasi-] < makyirafasi- < *ma₁.ₛₐ kirapa- (?< kira-pa- ₐ, ?< kira-ʙ -pa-)
   -si-. 'dazzling'. x - x-x-x x-x-x. This Man'yō-shū word is usually taken to
   be the OJ ancestor of magirawasi-.

- mamemamesi- < *mamey (?< *ma-ᵣ₁.₁ ma-Ci₁.ₛₐ) ··· -si-. 'faithful'. x - B-B-B
   x-x-x. Attested 10th century.

A maru- < maruₛ.₁ (< maro < ...). 'round'. x - A-B-A A-A-(x). Hattō, Hamada,
   Matsue, Izumo, Hata, NE Kyūshū A. Kōchi A. Nk marusen B; Sr maru- A; Kobama
   maro-han; Yn marunka A. Attested 10th century as maro-, Mr as maru-.

B [masasi-] < masaadj-ʙ ₂.ₛ -si-. 'true, sure, real'. B - x-x-x x-B-x. Mr (Bm)
   masasi-ku HLL-L. Nk masaasen B; Sr masasi- B 'wonder-working'.

- [maso-]. '? correct, proper' (?= mata-). x - x-x-x x-x-x. NS (T+ 23) masokyemu
   LLLH.

A [mata-] 'complete, perfect'. A - x-x-x x-x-x. NS (121b [14:195L-K]) A. Mr (Bm)
   mata-si HL-L.

- matidoosi- < matidofo(-si)- < *mat[a-C]iʙ -n- topoadj ₐ. 'impatiently awaited'.
   x - B-B!-B x-x-x. Earliest attestation Mr.

? mazika- < maᵗ/ₐika- < *ma₁.₁ (-n-) tikaadj ʙ. 'nearby'. x - B-B-A x-x-x. Attested
   (matika-) in Man'yō-shū.

B mazu- < madu- < *mantu-. 'poor; unpalatable; awkward'. (B) - B-B-A̲ x-x-x. Hattō,
   Hamada, Matsue, Izumo B. Apparently not attested before Edo, yet the derivative
   mazusi- is attested 10th century.

B mazusi- < madusi- < *mantuadj ʙ -si-. 'poor, meager'. B - B-B-B x-x-x. Hattō,
   Hamada, Matsue, Izumo, NE Kyūshū B.

B medeta- < meyde[y]-ʙ (< ...) -ta- (< [i]taadj ʙ). 'auspicious'. B - B-B-B x-x-x.
   Narada, Hattō, Hamada, Matsue, Izumo, NE Kyūshū B.

B [megu-] < meygu- < *ma-Ci₁.ₛₐ (-n-) n[i]kuadj ʙ. 'pitiful, painful to look at;
   (terribly) cute'. B - x-x-x x-x-x. Cf. [kokorogu-].

- memesi- < *mye (< miCa < ...) ··· -si-. 'feminine; effeminate'. x - B-B-A x-x-x.
   Hattō, Hamada, Matsue, Izumo B. Attested 10th century.

- menbokuna- < men-bokuᵣ₄.₆ (< Ch myan'-m(b)wok) naadj ʙ. 'ashamed'. x - B-B!-B
   x-x-x. Attested 10th century.

- mezamasi- < me-ᵃ/ᵤzamasi- < mey (< ma-Ci₁.ₛₐ) (-n-) sama-[sa-ʙ] -si- ('eye-
   wakening'). 'striking, eye-catching'. x - B-B-B x-x-x. Attested 11th century.

B mezato- < mey (< *ma-Ci₁.ₛₐ) -n- satoadj ʙ (< ...). 'sharp-eyed'. x - B-B-B
   x-x-x. Earliest attestation Mr.

B mezurasi- < meydurasi- < meydura- (= meyd[ey-ʙ < ...] -ura-attr root) -si-.
   'splendid; rare'. B - B-B-B x-B-x. NS (T+ kun) meydurasi[-si] L̲H̲H̲H̲. Km (W) B.
   Nk miẓirasen B 'rare; strange'; Sr mindasyan B = miẓirasyan B.

B [midarigawasi-] < midarigafasi- < myidarigafasi- < *minta-r[a-C]i$_B$ -n[a]-ka-pa-
si-. 'disorderly'. B - (B)-(B)-x x-x-x. Cf. midarigamasi-.

B migurusi- < *myigurusi- < *mi[-Ci]$_B$ -n- kurusi$_{adj B}$ (< ...). 'ugly'. x - B-B-B
x-B-x. Km x. Edo HHHL- (= B). Nk miiguruusen B 'hard to look at'; Sr mii-
gurisi- B < mi-gurusi- (< ...); Miyako mzgii-mzgi < *mi-g[ur]i- (< ...).
Attested Ir, JP.

- mii- 'new': see nii-.

- mimizika- < mimi^t/$_d$ika- < *mimi$_{2.3}$ (-n-) tika$_{adj B}$. 'near (one's ear); intimate'.
x - B-x-x x-x-x. Attested 11th century.

B miniku- < myiniku- < *mi[-Ci]$_B$ niku$_{adj B}$. 'ugly; hard to look at'. B - B-B-B
x-x-x. NS (T+ kun) ana myi-niku ‖H HHH.

- misuborasi- ?< mi (< miy < *mu-Ci$_{1.1}$) suborasi$_{adj}$ (< ...). 'shabby'. x - A/B-B-B
x-x-x. Earliest attestation Mr.

- miyasu- < *mi[-Ci]$_B$ dasu$_{adj B}$. 'easy/nice to look at'. x - A/B-B-B x-B-x.
Nk miiyassen B. Attested 10th century.

B mizika- < *minsika- (< ?). 'short'. B - B-B-B x-x-x. NS (133a [14:424-K]) B.
Narada (-zi-/-di-), Hattō, Hamada, Matsue, Izumo, NE Kyūshū B.

B modokasi- < *montoka-$_B$ (< ?) -si-. 'irritating; reproachable'. x - B-B-A x-x-x.
Attested 10th century.

B monoganasi- < *mono$_{2.3}$ -n- kanasi$_{adj A}$ (< ...). 'rather sad'. x - A/B-B-B x-x-x.
Attested in Man'yō-shū.

B [monogura-] < *mono$_{2.3}$ -n- kura$_{adj A}$. 'rather dark, dusky'. x - (B)-x-x x-x-x.
Attested 10th century.

B monoguruosi- < monokurufosi- < *mono$_{2.3}$ -n- kurufosi$_{adj B}$ (< kuruf°/$_a$si < ...).
'mad'. x - B-B-B x-x-x. Attested 10th century.

B monosabisi- < *mono$_{2.3}$ sabisi$_{adj B}$ (< ...). 'rather lonely'. x - A/B-B-B x-x-x.
Attested 10th century.

B monomonosi- < *mono$_{2.3}$ ⋯ -si-. 'magnificent, imposing, elaborate, showy'.
x - B-B-B x-x-x. Attested 10th century.

B monosugo- < *mono$_{2.3}$ sunko$_{adj B}$. 'awful'. x - B-B-B x-x-x. Hattō, Hamada,
Matsue, Izumo B. Earliest attestation Mr.

B [monosusama^s/$_{zi}$-] < *mono$_{2.3}$ susama^s/$_{zi adj B}$. 'drab, dull, dismal; (= monosugo-)
dreadful'. x - (B)-x-x x-x-x. Attested 11th century.

B monou- < *mono$_{2.3}$ u$_{adj B}$. 'sad, melancholy'. B (?= 2.3 | B)- B-B-B x-x-x.
Km (S,W) B. K: "Edo B". Attested 10th century.

B moro-. 'fragile'. B - B-B-A x-x-x. Narada, Hattō, Hamada, Matsue, Izumo B.

- mottaina- < mot-tai (< Ch mwot-they') na$_{adj B}$. 'impious; wasteful'. x - B-B-B
x-x-x. Attested 13th century.

A munasi- < muna- (?< mu[-Ci]$_{1.1}$ na$_{adj B}$) -si-. 'empty'. A - A/B-B-A x-(A)-x. Km
(S,W) A. Mr (Bm) muna-si HL-L (= B). Edo A. Sapporo, Akita, Matsumoto, Numazu,
Narada, Hiroshima, Ōita B. Kōchi B. Nk naa- A, Sr nna A 'empty' ? < *muna(-).

?B musa- 'dirty; sullied; vulgar'. x - B-B-A x-x-x. Hattō, Hamada, Matsue, Izumo B.
Earliest attestation Mr.

A mutumazi- < mutumasi- (JP) < mutu^b/$_{ma}$-$_A$ (< *mutu -n[a]- -pa-) -si-. 'intimate'.
A - B-B-A x-x-x. Km (W) A.

A muzukasi-, mutukasi- < mutu(-)ka (?< mutu$_{ai a}$ -ka) -si-. 'difficult, vexing'.
A - A/B-B-A B-x-A. Sd mutkasy(i)- B; Nk muCiiKasen A; Sr muçikasyan A;
Yn muçikaçan A.

B na- 'lacking, non-existent'. B - B-B!-B (B)-(B)-x. NS (79c [14:322-M]; 79c
[14:338-M]) B; NS (T+ kun: fonasi-agari) na-si L-L; (T+ 20, 79) ‖L = H-L;
(80) nakyeba ‖HL = LHL; (7) nakyeku wo ‖LHH ?= LLH(|)H. Km (S,W) na-si L-H,
na-ku H-L. Mr (Bm) na-si/-[s]i L-L. Edo B. Narada B; Hata B. Kōchi, Sakawa,
Suzu, Toyama 2 (= B). Sd neem/nee B; Sr neenu B.

- [*nabe-] < *nabye-/namye- < *nanpiCa-. 'slippery'. Taketomi nabu-san < nabu-sa
  (< *nabi-, with last vowel assimilated to the labial, < *nabe-) an (< ...).
- [nabero-] < *nabyero-(/*namyero-) < *nanpiCa*adj* -ro- (< ?). 'slippery'. x - x-x-x
  B-B-B. Sd napryoosan B < *napiro-sa an; Nk nanburuusen B; Sr nandurusan B <
  *nabiru-ru-san (< ...); Yn nabiran B < *nabir[u]-an; Hatoma nabura(s)san.
  Hateruma nahukahan (Miyara 1930) must be from nabu- (< *nabi- < *nabe- < ...)
  -ka-sa an (< ...), if not a mistake for naburahan. The *-ro- perhaps should be
  *-rwo-, or (if the vowel has partially assimilated to the preceding mid vowel)
  *-ru-. (Is this a truncation of *aro, Azuma attributive < [a]ra-*B* 'be'?)
  Cf. nameraka*adj-B* *4.11*.
- nadaka- < *na*1.2* -n- taka*adj B*. 'famed, famous, (highly) reputed'.
  x - B-B-A x-(A)-x. Sr nadakee-mun A (borrowed?). Attested 10th century.
B naga- < *nanka-. 'long'. B - B-B-A̲ B-B-C. NS (79b [14:315-M]) B. NS (T+ 78) naga-
  ku mo ga to̲ ꟼHLHLL = LHL|H(|)L(|)L. Km (S) B. Edo B. Sapporo, Akita, Matsumoto,
  Numazu, Narada, Hattō, Hamada, Matsue, Izumo, Hiroshima, Hata, Ōita, NE Kyūshū
  B. Kōchi, Sakawa B. Nk nagaasen B; Yn naan C. Sd, Sr nagee- B 'longlasting'
  and Sr nagee B 'for a long time' are probably from naga wi[y]- 'long stay'.
?B naganagasi- < *nanka-*B* ··· -si-. 'quite long'. x - B-B-x x-x-x. Cf. naganaga*adv*
  x - 0/3-2-B-x-x-x.
B nagekawasi- = nagekasi- (JP) < *nageyka(fa)si- < *nanka-ika-*B*) -(pa)-si-.
  'deplorable'. x - B-B-B x-x-x.
?B nago- < nagu- < *nanku-. 'calm, quiet, peaceful'. x - x-x-x x-x-x. K: "Km B".
? nagoriosi- < nagori*?3.2b, ?3.4* (< ...) wosi*adj B* (< ...). 'reluctant to leave'.
  x - B-B-B x-x-x.
- [nakadaka-] < *naka*2.4* -n- taka*adj B*. 'having a high center, convex; having a
  straight (shapely) nose'. x - x-x-x x-x-x. Attested 11th century.
B namagusa- < *nama*2.5* -n- kusa*adj B*. 'fishy(-smelling)'. B - B-B-A x-x-x. Hattō,
  Hamada, Matsue B; Izumo A/B. Nk namaagusaasen B.
B namamekasi- < *namamyeka- (< *nama*2.5* miCa-ka-*bnd v*) -si-. 'coquettish'.
  x - B-B-B x-x-x.
B namasi- < nama*2.5* -si-. 'fresh'. x - B-B-B x-x-x. (Now obsolete except dialect.)
  B namanamasi- < nama*2.5* ··· -si-. 'fresh, vivid'. x - B-B-B x-x-x.
B [name-] < namye-(/*nabye-) < *nanpiCa- (< ?). < *nami-Ca- (< ?). 'unceremonious;
  *smooth; *slippery'. B - x-x-x x-x-x. Taketomi nabu-san 'slippery': *see*
  [*nabe-]. Cf. nameraka, namer-u; [nabero-].
- [*namero-] < *nanpiCa-ro- 'slippery': *see* [nabero-].
B namidagumasi- < namyitagumasi- < namyitaguma-*B* (< *namita*3.5b* -n- kuma-*?A*) -si-.
  'tearful'. x - B-B-B x-x-x. NS (Okada) B. NS (T+ 55) namidagumasi mo ꟼꟼLHLLꟼ
  ?= LLLHLL(|)H.
B nanigokorona- < *nani-gokoro (< nani*2.4* -n- ko̲ko̲ro̲*?3.5b*) na*adj B*. 'indifferent,
  unconcerned; naive, innocent'. x - B-x-x x-x-x.
B [nao-] < nafo- < *napo. 'straight; orderly; honest, proper'. B - x-x-x x-x-x.
?B [naonaosi-] < nafonafosi- < *napo*adj B* ··· -si-. 'very ordinary, orderly,
  humdrum; dull, inferior, base; honest, proper'. x - x-x-x x-x-x.
?A narabina- < narabyi*3.1* (< naranp[a-C]i*A* < ...) na*adj B*. 'unparalleled'.
  x - B-B-A x-x-x. K: "Edo B". Attested 10th century.
- narenaresi- < nare[y] (< *nara-Ci-*B*) ··· -si-. 'familiar'. x - B-B-B x-x-x.
B nasakebuka- < *nasake*3.5* (< ...) -n- puka*adj B*. 'compassionate, kindhearted'.
  x - B-B-B x-x-x.
B nasakena- < nasake*3.5* (< ...) na*adj B*. 'thoughtless, unfeeling'.
  x - B-B-B x-x-x. K:"Edo HLLL-" (?= HLL|L-).
B natukasi- < natuka-*B* (< ...) -si-. 'yearned-for; [Ryūkyū] sad'. B - B-B-A x-B-B.
  Km (S) B. Hattō, Hamada, Matsue, Izumo B. Nk naCikasen B, Sr naçikasan B 'sad'.

B   nayamasi- < *nada-ma-ʙ (< ...) -si-. 'melancholy'. B - B-B-B x-x-x. Hattō,
      Hamada, Matsue, Izumo B.
?B neba- < *nenpaʙɪʙ (< ?). 'sticky'. x - B-B![U]-x x-x-x. Attested 1477.
B   nebuka- < *neɪ.₃ₐ (< *na-Ci-[Ci]) -n- pukaₐdⱼ ʙ. 'deep-rooted'. x - B-B-B x-x-x.
B   negawasi- < negafasi- < negafa-ʙ (< ...) -si-. 'desirable'. x - B-B-B x-x-x.
-   nemu- < neᵇ/ₘu[ri-ta]- < *neᵇ/ₘuriʙ (< ...) -ta- (< [i]taₐdⱼ ʙ). 'sleepy'.
      x - A-B-A x-x-x. Earliest attestation Edo.
-   nemuta- < neᵇ/ₘu[ri]-ta- < *neᵇ/ₘuriʙ (< ...) -ta- (< [i]taₐdⱼ ʙ). 'sleepy'.
      Earliest attestation Mr?
B   [neta-] ?< *na-Ci ita- ('root/nature hurt'). 'envious'. x - (B)-x-x x-B-x.
      Km (W) B. Nk nitaasen B 'odious; envious'; Sr niita- B 'reproachful,
      chagrined'; Yn nita-san 'envious' (Miyara 1930). Cf. netamu.
B   netamasi- < netama-ʙ (< ...) -si-. 'enviable'. (B) - B-B-B x-x-x. The stem is
      attested by Mg in netamasi-gafo.
B   nezikegamasi- < nedikeₛ.₁ (< nedike[y] < *nentᵘ/₀-Ci - ka-Ci[-Ci]ʙ) -gamasi-
      (< ...). 'perverse, twisted, crooked'. x - x-x-x x-x-x. Attested 11th century.
B   nibu- < *ninpu-. 'dull; slow, late'. B - B-B-B B-B-C. Narada B. Sd nyibu- B
      'dull'; Nk niisen B 'slow'; Sr nii- B 'slow; unsavory, insipid'; Yn ninsa(a)n C.
      Taketomi nyussan, nuusan; Hatoma niihan.
B   niga- < *ninka-. 'bitter'. B - B-B-B B-B-(C). Narada, Hattō, Hamada, Matsue,
      Izumo, NE Kyūshū B. Hachijō-jima miga-. Kikai niya- (< *nigya- < *niga);
      Nk zaasen B; Sr nza-san B (< *nigya- < *niga-); Yn ndan C < *niga-an 'salty'.
B   niganigasi- < *ninkaₐdⱼ ʙ ⋯ -si-. 'bitter; disgusting, scandalous'. x - B-B-B
      x-x-x. Attested 13th century.
?   nigena- < ni-geₑ.ₓ (< *ni[-Ci]ₐ (< ...) -n- keyɪ.₁) naₐdⱼ ʙ. 'unsuitable'.
      x - B-B-x x-x-x.
B   nigiwasi- < nigifasi- < *ni(n)ki -pa-si-. 'bustling'. x - B-B-B x-x-x. Attested
      Ir. Cf. nigiwau, nigiyaka.
?A [*nii-] < *nifyi- < *nipi (?< *nip[a-C]i). 'new'. (A) - x-x-x A-A-x. Nk miisen A
      [new]. Old Japanese has only the adnoun nifyi (Mg HH), but the stem is
      conjugated in Sd myii- A and Sr mii- A ?< *mipi- < *nipi- (with nasal initial
      assimilated to the labial of the second syllable). The reconstruction *n- is
      nicely supported by Hateruma neesyan and perhaps Ie-jima niisyan though the
      latter may be secondary (mi- → ni-), in accordance with an unusual rule of
      assimilation in that dialect. Miyako mizz-miz ?< *mii-. Cf. [niwasi-], niwa-ka.
?A [niisi-] < nifyisi- < *nipiₐdₙ -si-. 'new'. x - x-x-x x-x-x. Obsolete except as
      dialect. Cf. [*nii-], [niwasi-], niwa-ka.
B   niku- 'hateful'. x - B-B-B x-B[Lit.]-x. Km (W) A(/B). Km (W) A/B. Edo B. Hattō,
      Hamada, Matsue, Izumo B. Nk niKusen B. (Sr usually mikkwa-san B ?< *mikura-;
      cf. mikkwa B < *mikura < mekura 'blind'.) Attested in Man'yō-shū.
?A nitukawasi- < nitukafasi- < ni[-Ci]ₐ tuka-ʙ -pa-si-. 'suitable, becoming' (=
      niawasi-). x - B-B-A x-x-x. Attested 10th century.
B   [nodoke-] < *nodokey- < *nodokaₐdⱼ-ₙ (< *nₒntₒ?ₐdᵥ -ka) -Ci-. 'quiet, serene,
      untroubled'. x - x-x-x x-x-x. Km (W) B. Attested 11th century.
?B noro-. 'slow'. x - B-B-A x-B-x. Hattō, Hamada, Matsue, Izumo B. Nk x.
      Cf. nuru-, oso-.
B   nuru-. 'tepid, lukewarm'; (= noro-) 'slow'. x - B-B-B B-B-x. Hattō, Hamada,
      Matsue, Izumo B. Nk nurusen B 'tepid'.
-   obitadasi-, (JP) obitatasi- (< ?). 'extreme, extraordinary; huge; extremely many;
      noisy'. x - B-B-A x-x-x. K: "Edo HHHHL-" (= B). This adjective is said to have
      been a popular male colloquialism in Middle Japanese.
?A [oboobosi-] < *onpo-onpo-si-. 'dim; insecure, uneasy; aloof, distant, cool'.
      x - x-x-x x-x-x. Cf. [oboosi-]. Attested 11th century.

?A [oboosi-] < obofosi- < oᶠ/ᵦfosi- < *onpo-po-si- (?< *onpo-pa-si-). 'vague,
   unclear, dim, gloomy, murky'. x - x-x-x x-x-x. Cf. obotukana-; oboreru,
   [oboosu]; ? oomaka, ooyoso.

B obosi- < om[o]fosi- < *om[o]po- (< *omo-pa-ᵦ) -si-. 'appearing to be'. x - B-B-A
   x-x-x. Edo B.

- obotukana- < ofotukana- < *onpo tuka(ᵦ) naₐdⱼ ᵦ. 'uncertain, doubtful, weak'.
   x - A/B-B-A x-x-x. K: "Edo B". Attested in Man'yō-shū.

?B [odaisi-] < odafyisi- < odafyiₐdₙ ?< *onta-pi (< ?) -si-. 'calm, quiet, peaceful'
   x - x-x-x x-x-x. Cf. odasi-, odayaka; on (< Ch), taira. Attested 869.

?B [odasi-] < oda-si- < *onta -si-. 'calm, quiet, peaceful'. Edo B. Cf. [odaisi-],
   odaika, odayaka; on (< Ch), taira. Attested 10th century.

- ogura- < wogura- < *boₚᵣₑ ?₁.₁ -n- kuraₐdⱼ ₐ. 'darkish, dusky'. x - A/B-B-x
   x-x-x. Attested 883.

B okasi- < wokasi- ?< *bokaₐ/baka -si- (cf. waka-/oko-turu); ?< *boka-ₐ -si-
   ('inviting, attractive, interesting'). 'strange, funny'. x - B-B-B B-B-C. Edo
   B. Hattō, Hamada, Matsue, Izumo, Hata, NE Kyūshū B. Kōchi B. Sd hwaasy(i)- B;
   Nk wahaasen B; Sr ukasyan B; Yn bagasan C. Attested 10th century.

- okogamasi- < *wokoₐdⱼ-ₙ ₓ (< *boko 'stupid') -gamasi- (< ...). 'ridiculous'.
   x - B-B-A x-x-x. Attested 10th century.

- okuʰ/ᵦuka- < okuᶠ/ᵦuka- < *okuₐ.₃ (-n-) pukaₐdⱼ ᵦ. 'deep, profound, recondite'.
   x - B-B-B x-x-x. Attested 11th century.

- okuyukasi- < oku?₂.₃ yuka-ᵦ (/ ika-ₐ < *i-ₚᵣₑ uka-ₐ) -si-. 'modest'. x - B-B-B
   x-x-x. Attested 11th century.

A omo- (?< *onpo-/*inpo-). 'heavy'. A - A-B-A A-A-(A/B). Km (W) A. Mr (Bm) A. Edo
   A. Sapporo B̲; Akita, Matsumoto, Numazu, Narada, Hattō, Hamada, Matsue, Izumo,
   Hiroshima, Ōita, NE Kyūshū A. Kōchi A. Sd qub(u)- A; Okinawa: Igei nbo-hon,
   Kushi and Onna qibo-han, Yabu oboo-hain, Nk qubu(u)sen A; Sr qnbu-san A;
   Miyako ivv-iv < *ibu-; Yaeyama issaan = nbusaan; Taketomi ii-san; Yn in-san A
   (H 1967) / B (H 1964, misprint?).

- omoʰ/ᵦayu- < omoᶠ/ᵦayu- < *omoₐ.₄ (-n-) paduⱼₐdⱼ ₓ). 'embarrassed; flushed (with
   embarrassment)'. x - B-B-A x-x-x. K: "Edo B". Earliest attestation Mr.

A omoomosi- < omoₐ ··· -si-. 'serious, grave, solemn'. x - B-B-A x-x-x. From 900s.

B omosiro- < omosirwo- < omoₐ.₄ sirwoₐdⱼ ᵦ. 'interesting, amusing'. B - B-B-A
   B-B-x. Hattō, Hamada, Matsue, Izumo B. Nk qumusiruusen B = qumusen B, Sr
   qumusiru-san B = qumus-san B. Okinawa also uses a reflex of o- iro-ke, as
   found in Nk quuruKiisen B and Sr qwiirᵘ/₁iki- B. K: "Edo HHHL-" (= B).

- [omota-] < omoₐdⱼ ₐ (?< *onpo) -ta- (< [i]taₐdⱼ ᵦ). 'heavy'. x - A/B[H]-B-A
   x-x-x. Hattō, Hamada, Matsue, Izumo, NE Kyūshū A. One example of obota- in
   NKD. Dial. obota-, obuta-, ubuta-. Attested 12th century.

- omowasi- < omofasi- < *omo-pa-ᵦ -si-. 'satisfactory, desirable'. x - B-B-B x-x-x.
   Attested 10th century.

B [onazi-] < onaᵇ/ᵢzi < *ona (? → ono 'self') -si-. 'same'. B - (A)-x-x (A)-x-x.
   NS (96a [11:71-K]) onasi LLL. Km (S) B. Edo B. Sd qunadyi / qunasy ··· A. As
   adjective this word is obsolete (→ onazi adnoun). Cf. oyazi-.

B oo- < ofo- < *opo-. 'much, many; great, big'. B - B-B-B B-B-x. Km (S) LH-L,
   (W) LL-H / LH-L. Mr (Bm) B. Edo B. Sapporo, Akita, Matsumoto, Numazu, Narada,
   Hiroshima, Ōita, NE Kyūshū B. Sd (qu)huu- B; Nk huPoosen B; Sr quhu- B;
   Miyako upu-, upoo- 'big'; Yn ubusaan (Miyara 1930). JP "vouoi" = wowoi (< ofo-
   [k]i), "voûô = wowoo (< ofo-[k]u).

B ooki- < ofok[y]iₐdⱼ ₙ < *opoₐdⱼ ᵦ -kiₐₜₜᵣ. 'big'. (x) - B-B-A x-x-x. Narada B
   (but usually ika- B); Hattō, Hamada, Matsue, Izumo A̲. Kikai qubï-sai B;
   Nk huPiisen B; Sr quhwisen B. The earliest attestation as an adjective is
   Muromachi. As an adjectival noun: Mg ofokī̲ (narī̲), Km (S,W) ofokī̲ (ni̲ / naru).
   Cf. ooi-ni 1-2-A x-x-x.

B   oosi- ‹ wowosi- ‹ *bo₁.₁ ··· -si-. 'manly, brave'. x - B-B-A x-x-x. Attested NS.

-   orokasi- ‹ *oro-ka𝘢𝘥𝘫-𝘮 𝘴.𝟸𝘣 -si-. 'stupid'. x - B-B-B x-x-x. Attested Km.

B   osana- ‹ wosana-, (JP) wosanasi- ‹ *bosa₇₂.₄ na𝘢𝘥𝘫 𝘣 (-si-). 'juvenile'.
      B - B-B-A x-x-x. K: "Edo B".

B   osi- ‹ wosi- ‹ wo-₇₁.₁ ('little' ‹ ...) -si-. 'regrettable; lovable, cute'.
      x - B-B-B x-x-x. NS (79c [14:322-M]) B. NS (79) wosikyeku mo L̤HHL = LLH-H(|)L.
      Km (W) B. Edo B. Narada, Hattō, Hamada, Matsue, Izumo, NE Kyūshū B.

A   oso̲-. 'slow'. A - A-B-A x-A-x. NS(126b [14:285L-K]) A. Km (W) A. Edo A. Tappi
      oso'e B̲; Sapporo B̲; Akita, Matsumoto, Numazu, Narada, Hattō, Hamada, Matsue,
      Izumo, Hiroshima, Ōita, NE Kyūshū A. Kōchi A. Nk x; Sr qus̲i-san A.

B   osorosi-, [dial.] otorosi- ‹ *oso̲ro- (‹ oso̲-ra-) -si-. 'horrible'. B - B-B-B
      (B)-B-x. Sd quthur(u)- / quthur(a)- B; Nk huTuurusen B; Kikai qutus-sai,
      uturu(si)-ku; Sr quturusyan B; Miyako uturusz-uturus ‹ *uturusi-. Cf. osoreru.

B   otonasi- ‹ otona𝘢.₇𝘣 (‹ ...) -si-. 'gentle, good; mature, wise'. x - B-B-B
      B-B["new?"]-x. Hattō, Hamada, Matsue, Izumo B. Nk huTunasen B [new]. Attested
      11th century.

-   [oyazi-] ?‹ *oda-si- (‹ ?). 'same' (= onazi). x - x-x-x x-x-x. NS (T+ 125) oyazi
      LHH. Ōno Tōru 1978:302: "‹ oya 'parent'".

A   [ozina-] ‹ wodina- ‹ wodi (‹ ?) -na-. 'inept, clumsy, ignorant; feeble, weak'.
      A - x-x-x x-x-x. NS (117b [14:131-K], 14-391L-K) A (Okada takes the first as
      "woti-", the second as "wodi-").

?A [sa-]. 'narrow (= [se-]); small'. A [Ir] - x-x-x x-x-x.

B   sabisi-, [dial.] samisi-, saᵇ/𝗺usi- ‹ *saᵇ/𝗺iysi- ‹ *sanpu(-Ci₂.₃) -si-.
      'lonesome'. x - B-B-B x-B-x. Edo B. Narada, Hattō, Hamada, Matsue, Izumo,
      NE Kyūshū B. Nk sabisen B; Sr sabis-san B; Miyako sabsz-sabs ‹ *sab(i)si-.
      Attested 10th century.

B   sagana- ‹ saga₇₂.₃,₇₂.₄ (?‹ Ch syang') -na- (‹ na𝘢𝘥𝘫 𝘣). 'bad, evil(-minded);
      noisy, talky, gossipy'. x - B-x-x x-x-x. Attested 11th century.

B   [sagasi-] ‹ saga𝘢𝘥𝘫-𝘮 ?‹ sa𝘢𝘥𝘫 𝘈 -n- ka₁.ₓ 'narrow place', ?‹ *sanka[-ra/Ci]-𝘣
      'descend', cf.Ōno Tōru 1978:299) -si- . 'steep'. B - x-x-x x-x-x. NS (73c
      [11:271-M], 122b [14:222-K]) B. NS (T+ 61) sagasi-kyi HHH-H. Km (S) A̲. Edo B.

B   sakasi- ?‹ saka (?= saka₂.₃ 'boundary', ?= saka-𝘣), ?‹ sa-𝘱𝘳𝘦 kasi[kwo𝘢𝘥𝘫 𝘣].
      'wise, shrewd'. B - B-B-A x-x-x. NS (91a [11:4-K]) B. Km (W) B. Cf. NS (T+ kun)
      saka no̲ko̲ri HH LHH '(?) wise/splendid bequest'.

-   samosi- ‹ samo[n] ‹ s(y)a-mon ('ascetic' ‹ Ch ‹ Skt śramaṇa) -si-. 'squalid,
      sordid, mean'. x - B-B-A x-x-x. Earliest attestation Mr.

B   samu-, [dial.] sabu- ‹ *sanpu- (?‹ *sa-npa- ‹ *sa-n[a]-pa-). 'cold'. B - B-B-B
      x-x-x. Km (W) B. Edo B. Narada sabu- B; Hattō, Hamada, Matsue, Izumo, Hata, NE
      Kyūshū B. Kōchi B. Cf. samasu, sameru; saeru, [sayake-].

-   sarigata- ‹ *sar[a-C]i𝘣 -n- kata𝘢𝘥𝘫 𝘈. 'hard to avoid/decline'. x - B-B![H]/B[U]-
      A x-x-x. Attested 11th century.

-   sarigena- ‹ sarige𝘢𝘥𝘫-𝘮 ‹ sa-[a]ri (‹ sa₁.₃𝘢 (?‹ s[ika]) ar[a-C]i𝘣) -n- key₁.₁
      (‹ ...) na𝘢𝘥𝘫 𝘣. 'nonchalant, unconcerned'. x - B-B!-A x-x-x. From 1000s.

?A sato- ‹ (*)satwo- (?‹ *sa-𝘱𝘳𝘦 two𝘢𝘥𝘫 𝘣). 'smart, wise'. A - B-B-A x-x-x.

B   sawagasi- (‹ ?sawakasi-) ‹ sawaga- ‹ sawaka-𝘣 (‹ *saba-ka-) -si-. 'noisy,
      clamorous'. B - B-B-A x-x-x. Mg safakasi (Kn Butsu-jō 85:3), not listed by
      Mochizuki. Mr (Bm) A.

B   [sayake-] ‹ sayakey- ‹ *sada-ka𝘢𝘥𝘫-𝘮 𝘴.₇𝘣 (‹ ...) -Ci-. 'cool; clear, pure'.
      B - B-B-x x-x-x.

?   [se-] ?‹ *sa𝘢𝘥𝘫 ?𝘈 -Ci-. 'narrow' (= [sa-]). x - x-x-x x-x-x. Attested
      11th century.

B   sebasebasi- ‹ seba- = sema𝘢𝘥𝘫 𝘣 (‹ ...) ··· -si-. 'quite narrow'. B - x-x-x
      x-x-x.

B   sema-, [dial.] seba- < *saCinpa- ?< *sa-Ci*adj x* -n(-)pa*1.3a* ('place'), ?< *sa-
    Ci*adj x* -n[a]-pa-, ?< *sa*adj A* inpa*?*adj*. 'narrow'. B - B-B-B x-B-C. Mg seba- B.
    Edo seba- B. Narada, Hattō, Hamada, Matsue, Izumo, NE Kyūshū B. Nk qibaasen B,
    sibaasen B; Sr qiba-san B (concrete), siba-san B (abstract); Yaeyama siba-saan
    (Ishigaki, Hateruma) ibasaan (Hateruma also syubasaan), Kobama qiba- = (Miyara
    1930) siba-; Miyako siba- (Kerima), sipa- (Ōgami), iba- (Sawata, Yonaha);
    Yn siban C.
-   senkatana- < se-mu (< *so-mu*A*) kata*2.2b* na*adj B*. 'inevitable, unavoidable'.
    x - B-B-B x-x-x. Attested 11th century.
-   sewa*a*/*z*ewasi- < sefasefasi- < *sepa (< ?) ⋯ -si-. 'busy'. x - x-x-x x-x-x.
    Attested 1178.
-   sewasi- < sefasi- < *sepa (< ?) -si-. 'busy'. x - B-B-B x-x-x. Attested 1178.
-   sewasina- < sefasi-na- < *sepa (<?) -si-na-. 'busy'. x - B-B-B x-x-x. From 1100s.
B   sibu- ?< sibu*?2.4,?2.3* (< ...); ?< *sinpu- (<?), whence the noun. 'astringent,
    tart, puckery'. B - B-B-B A-B-x. Narada, Hattō, Hamada, Matsue, Izumo B.
    Nk sibusen B. I am puzzled by the citation "Yn bwaan" (Thorpe 262) from Miyara
    1930, for I have been unable to find the word in that or any other source;
    Thorpe takes the form as probably a mistake for (unfound) Pwaan < *sibu-an.
    Cf. siburu; sibu.
B   sibuto- ?< sifi[y] (< *sip*u*/*o*Ci-[Ci]*?A*) futwo*adj B* (< *putwo). 'stubborn'. x -
    B-B-B x-x-x. Cf. Sr sipu- A 'sturdy', Sr sippa B 'stubborn (one)'. Attested Mr.
B   sidokena- < sidoke (< ?) na*adj B*. 'disorderly; slovenly; irresolute'. x - B-B-x
    x-x-x. K: "Edo B". Earliest attestation 10th century.
B   [sige-] < *sinka-Ci-. 'luxuriant, profuse, dense'. B - x-x-x x-x-x. Km (W) B.
    Edo B. Cf. siger-u.
-   sikatana- < si*k*/*g*atana- < *si-*k*/*g*ata (< si[y]*A* (< *so-Ci) (-n-) kata*2.2b*)
    na*adj B*. 'inevitable, unavoidable'. x - B-B-A x-x-x. Earliest attestation Mr.
-   siniku- < si*A* (< *s[o-C]i) niku*adj B*. 'hard to do'. x - B-B-A x-x-x.
B   siokara- < sifokara- < sifwo*2.3* (< *sipwo) kara*adj A*. 'salty'. x - B-B-B x-B-x.
    Nk siPuKaraasen B = suuKaraasen B; Sr sipukara-san B. Attested Kn Mg.
B   siro- < sirwo*2.5*. 'white'. B - B-B-B B-B-x. Km (S,W) B. Edo B. Sapporo, Akita,
    Matsumoto, Numazu, Narada, Hattō, Hamada, Matsue, Izumo, Hiroshima, Ōita,
    NE Kyūshū B. Kōchi, Sakawa B. Nk siru(u)sen B; Miyako ssu- < *siro-; Kobama
    soo- < *siro-, but Thorpe 348 has Kobama sïsohaan "(< *sïsugasa-")".
B   sirozirosi- < sirwo*2.5* -n- sirwo*2.5* -si-. 'white, bright, interesting'. B - B-B-x
    x-x-x.
-   [siru-] < siru-/ziru- [dial.] ?< siru*2.4*. 'watery, soupy; sticky, muddy'.
    x - x-x-x x-x-x. Attested 1275.
A   [siru-] (?< sira-*A* -u, ?< sirwo*adj B*). 'clear, distinct; just as predicted or
    anticipated'. A - x-x-x x-x-x. NS (T+ 65) siru-si mo LL-L(|)L.
B   sitasi- < sita[wa]si- < sitafasi- < *sitapa-*A* (< *sita*2.2a* -pa-) -si-.
    'intimate'. B - B-B-B x-x-x. Edo A(/B). Sapporo, Akita, Matsumoto, Numazu,
    Narada, Hattō, Hamada, Matsue, Izumo, Hiroshima, Ōita, NE Kyūshū B. Kōchi B.
    Register incongruent with etymology.
B   [siwawayu-] < sifafayu- < sifofayu- < *sipwo*2.3* padu*adj B* (< ...). 'salty'.
    B - x-x-x x-x-x. Mg sifafayu- = sifofayu-.
-   soozoosi- ?< *sauzau (?< sawa-zawa < *saba*mim* -n- saba*mim*) -si-, ?< souzou [as
    indicated by JP spelling] (< soű < Ch .tshong 'hasten' -n- ⋯) -si-. 'noisy'.
    x - B-B-B x-x-x. Earliest attestation Mr.
B   soraosorosi- < swora*2.4* osorosi*adj B* (< ...). 'apprehensive'. x - B-B[H]-B x-x-x.
    For Kt, Umegaki has 1 | 0 (odd?). Earliest attestation Mr.
B   su- < su*1.3a*. 'sour'. B - B-B-B B-B-(C). Sd sii- B; Nk siisen B; Sr şii- B;
    Yn cyan C (< ?); Miyako svv-sv < *su-.

- [subena-] < sube(-)na- < subye (< ...) na*adj B*. 'helpless, unavoidable'.
  ?LLLH, ?LH|LH (Zs) / HLxx (Kn) - x-x-x x-x-x.
?B suborasi- ?< subo (< *sunpo < ?) rasi (< *[a]ra-*B* -si-), ?< subora-*B* (< *sunpo-
   ra- ?< *sunpa-ra-) -si-. 'poor, shabby'. x - x-x-x x-x-x. Cf. misuborasi-.
B [suda(si)-] < *sunta (< ?) (-si-). 'cool'. x - x-x-x B-B-x. Sd sidaa(syi)- B;
   Nk sidaasen B; Sr şida- B; Yn ndasaan (Miyara 1930:274). Sr şiibii- B 'chilly'
   = prefix şii- (< *su-) + hwii- < *pii-; *see* [hi-]. The ambivalent Sd form is
   like Sd khabaa(syi-) B 'fragrant'. Cf. [sudamu], sugasugasi-; samu-.
?A [sugasi-] < *sunka (< ?) -si-. 'fresh'. x - x-x-x x-x-x. Attested: sugasi mye
   'innocent girl' (K 65). Cf. sugasugasi-, suda(si)-, [sugasu].
?A sugasugasi- < *sunka (< ?) ··· -si-. 'refreshing'. x - B-B-A x-x-x. Attested in
   Koji-ki. Cf. sugasi-, [suda(si)-], [sugasu].
- sugena- < suge (?< su-*1.3a* -n- key*?1.1*) na*adj B*. 'curt'. x - B-B-B x-x-x.
   Attested 10th century.
B sugo- < *sunko- (< ?). 'awful'. x - B-B-A x-x-x. Edo B. Narada B. From 900s.
B [sukosi-] < sukwosi- < *sukwo -si- (cf. sukuna-). 'little'. (B) - (B)-(B)-(A)
   x-x-x. Edo LHL(-). Only attested forms: sukwosi-ku (infinitive), sukwosi-k[y]i
   (attributive), sukwosi (stem used as adverb).
B sukuna- < *suku (?< *sukwo, cf. [sukosi-]) -na- (< na*adj B*). 'little (= not
   much); few'. B - B-B-B x-x-x. K: "Edo B". Narada B.
?B susamazi- < susama*s*/*z*i- ?< *susama-*A* (< ...) -si-; ?< *s[am]u*adj B* sama-[Ci-/sa-]
   -si-. 'dreadful; terribly cold'. B - B-B-A x-x-x. Cf. susamu; samu-, suzusi-;
   sameru, samasu.
?B susudo- ?< surudo*adj ?B* (< ...). 'sharp-minded, shrewd, spirited'. x - B-B-x
   x-x-x. K: "Edo HHL" (= B). Earliest attestation Mr.
B suzusi- < *su -n- su (?< s[am]u*adj B* -n- s[am]u*adj B*) -si-. 'cool'. B - B-B-B
   x-x-x. NS (Okada) B. Km (S,W) B. Sapporo, Akita, Matsumoto, Narada, Hiroshima,
   Ōita B. Kōchi B.
B tadasi- < *tanta*2.4* -si-. 'correct'. B - B-B-B x-x-x. Km (W) B. Mr (Bm) B.
   Edo (A/)B. Sapporo, Akita, Matsumoto, Numazu, Narada, Hattō, Hamada, Matsue,
   Izumo, Hiroshima, Ōita, NE Kyūshū B. Kōchi B.
- tadotadosi- = tadutadusi- ?< *tantwo*mia* ··· -si- (cf. tadoru). 'unsteady;
   insecure; uncertain'. x - B-B-A x-x-x. Attested 11th century.
- taegata- < *taye[y] (< *tada-Ci[-Ci]) -n- kata*adj A*. 'hard to bear'. x - B-B!-B
   x-x-x. Attested 11th century.
B [tairake-] < tafyirakey- < tafyiraka*adj-n 4.11* (< tafyira*adj-n 3.5a* -ka < ...)
   -Ci-. 'safe, without mishap'. B - x-x-x x-x-x.
B taka- 'high, tall'. B - B-B-B B-B-C. NS (125b [14:283-K]). NS (T+ 7) taka kiy ni
   LL L(|)H. Km (S,W) B. Edo B. Sapporo, Akita, Matsumoto, Numazu, Narada, Hattō,
   Hamada, Matsue, Izumo, Hiroshima, Ōita, NE Kyūshū B. Kōchi, Sakawa B. Nk taasen
   B = taKaasen B; Yn tagan C.
B [take-] < takye- (< ?). 'brave'. B - x-x-x x-x-x. NS (127b [14:328-K; 109a
   [11:313-K]) B. Km (W) B. Edo B.
?B takedakesi- < takye*adj B* (< ?) -n- ··· -si-. 'brave'. x - B-B-A x-x-x. Not
   attested before Mr.
B takumasi- < takuma-*B* (< *ta*1.3a* kuma-*B*) -si-. 'stout; stalwart, bold'. B - B-B-A
   x-x-x. K: "Edo B".
B tanomi*s*/*z*ukuna- < *tanomi*3.4* (< ...) sukuna*adj B* (< ...). 'forlorn, helpless,
   hopeless'. x - B-B-x x-x-x. JP -z-. Attested 11th century.
B tanomosi- < *tanomasi- < tano͡ma-*B* (< *ta*1.3a* no͡ma- *?A*) -si-. 'trusty'. x - B-B-B
   x-x-x. Hattō, Hamada, Matsue, Izumo B. Attested 797.
B tanosi- < tanwosi- (< ?). 'enjoyable'. B - B-B-B x-x-x. Km (W) B. Narada, Hata,
   NE Kyūshū B. Kōchi A (Doi 1952:32).

- taru- 'tired': *see* daru-.
A tatto-/tooto- < tafutwo- < *taputwo- (?< ta-*pre* putwo*adj B*). 'exalted, sacred'.
   A - B-B-A x-x-x. NS (T+ 6) tafutwo-ku <u>LHH-H</u>. Mg tafuto- A. K: "Edo A". Hamada,
   Matsue A; Sapporo, Akita, Matsumoto, Numazu, Hattō, Izumo, Hiroshima, NE
   Kyūshū B. Kōchi B; Sakawa A.
A tayasu- < *ta-*pre* dasu*adj B*. 'easy'. A - A/B-B-B x-x-x. Km (S) A. Mr (Bm) B.
- tayorina- < tayori*9.7b<3.4* (< *tad<u>or</u>[a-C]i*B* < *ta*1.3a* d<u>or</u>[a-C]i*A* na*adj B*.
   'forlorn'. x - B-B!-A x-x-x. Attested 10th century.
B tayu-. 'tired'. x - x-x-x x-x-x. Km (W) B. *See* (taru- =) daru-.
- [tazutazusi-] < tadutadu-si-. *See* tadotadosi-.
- tebiro- < *te (< *ta-Ci*1.3a*) -n- piro*adj B*. 'extensive, wide'. Attested Mr.
- tegata- < *te (< *ta-Ci*1.3a*) -n- kata*adj A*. 'steady, solid, reliable'. x - B-B-B
   x-x-x.
B tegowa- < tegofa- < *te*1.3a* (< *ta-Ci) -n- k<u>op</u>a*adj B*. x - A[H]/B-B-B x-x-x.
   Earliest attestation Mr.
- teita- < *te (< *ta-Ci*1.3a*) ita*adj B*. 'severe, serious'. x - B-B-B x-x-x. From Mr.
B tiisa-/tittya- < tifyisa- < *tipi-sa-. 'little, small'. B - B-B-A x-x-x.
   K: "Km B" (where attested? S,W x), "Edo B". Narada B. Cf. titto < ti-to, tyottc
   < tyo-to, tyoi(-to); sa*adj ?A*, -sa*nominalizer*.
B tika- 'near'. B - B-B-B B-B-C. Km (W) B. Edo B. Sapporo, Akita, Matsumoto, Numazu
   Narada, Hattō, Hamada, Matsue, Izumo, Hiroshima, Ōita, NE Kyūshū B. Kōchi B.
   Nk hiCaasen B; Sr cica-/cika-san B; Yn Ta-an C < *tika-.
?B tobosi-, tom<u>o</u>si- < *t<u>onp</u>osi- (< ?). 'poor; yearning; envious'. B - A/B-B-A x-x-x.
   Mg tomosi- B. Narada B.
B [to-] < two-. 'sharp; swift; early'. B - x-x-x x-x-x. NS (101b [11:135-K]) to-ku
   R-L. Km (W) to-ku H-L. Edo B.
A too- < t<u>of</u>o- < *t<u>op</u>o-. 'far, distant'. A - A-B-A A-A-x. NS (125a [14:270L-K];
   132a [14:418-K]) A. Km (S) A. Mr (Bm) A. Edo A/B. Sapporo, Akita, Matsumoto,
   Numazu, Narada, Hamada, Matsue, Izumo, Ōita, NE Kyūshū A; Hattō, Hiroshima <u>B</u>.
   Kōchi, Sakawa A. Nk tuusen B; Sr tuusan A. (The "f<u>o</u>" is attested in the
   reduplicated derivative t<u>of</u>o-t<u>of</u>o-si-.)
- [toodoosi-] (JP) < t<u>of</u>ot<u>of</u>osi- (Koji-ki) < *t<u>op</u>o*adj A* ··· -si-. 'distant'.
   x - x-x-x x-x-x.
B toro-. 'slow, easy-going; slow-burning'. x - B-x-x x-x-x. Attested 1275.
   Cf. noro-; toro-bi 'slow fire'.
- tumasi- < tuma-*A* -si-. 'frugal'. x - B-B-A x-x-x. Attested 1477.
- tumeta- ?< *tume-[i]ta- < tumey*2.1* (< *tuma-Ci) ita*adj B*. 'cold'. x - B-B-A
   x-x-x. Narada, Hattō, Hamada, Matsue, Izumo, NE Kyūshū A. Attested 10th century
- [tumiegamasi-] < tumi*2.4* (< tumyi < *tumi) e[y]-*B* (< *a-Ci[-Ci]) -gamasi- (< ...).
   'looking sinful/guilty'. x - x-x-x x-x-x. The word occurs in Genji (Kōjien).
B tumi*h*/*b*uka- < tumyi*2.4* (< *tumi) (-n-) fuka*adj B* (< *puka). 'sinful'. x - B-B!-B
   x-x-x. Attested 11th century.
A tura- 'tough'. x - A/B-B-A x-x-x. Edo A. Narada, Hattō, Hamada, Matsue, Izumo A.
   Attested NS.
B turena- (?< *tura*2.3* na*adj B*). 'pitiless, unkind'. x - B-B-A B-B-x. Sd thurinaa-
   B 'lonely'; Nk x (cf. huiTuruusen 'lonely'); Sr çirina- B. Attested in the
   Man'yō-shū.
A tutana- (< ?). 'inferior; clumsy, awkward, inept'. A - B-B-A x-x-x.
B tutugana- < tutuga*3.1* (< ...) na*adj B*. 'without mishap or hindrance, safe(ly)'.
   x - B-A/B[U]-B x-x-x. For Kyōto, Hirayama has "5" = 3.1[|]B. Attested
   11th century.
- tutumasi- < tutuma-*B* (< ...) -si-. 'modest'. x - B-B-B x-x-x. Hattō, Hamada,
   Matsue, Izumo B. Attested 10th century.

B tuyo- < tuy<u>o</u>- < *tud<u>o</u>-. 'strong'. B - B-B-B B-B-C. NS (109a [11:313-K]) B.
   Edo B. Sapporo, Akita, Matsumoto, Numazu, Narada, Hattō, Hamada, Matsue,
   Izumo, Hiroshima, Ōita, NE Kyūshū B. Sd tyuu- B; Nk Cuusen B; Sr cuu-san B;
   Kobama tyoo-; Yn su-san C (→ swa(a)n 'bitter', cf. Thorpe 336) < *tuyusa-an.
   The "y<u>o</u>" follows Zdb but the examples cited are from texts which did not
   distinguish y<u>o</u> from ywo, and Igarashi leaves it an indeterminate "yo".

?B [u-]. 'sad; unhappy; [earlier] unpleasant, troublesome'. x - (A)-(B)-x x-x-x.
   Km (W) A. Edo B. Attested in Man'yō-shū.

- uiuisi- < "ufiufisi-" = uwiuwisi- (with intercalated -w-) < *u[k]iu[k]i-si- <
   *uk[a-C]i$_A$ ··· -si-. 'naive'. x - B-B-A x-x-x. Attested 10th century.

B uma- (?< nma- < *ma-). 'proficient; delicious; sweet; worthy'. B - B-B-<u>A</u> B-B-C.
   Mg muma- (= nma-) B. NS (Okada) B; NS (T+ kun) uma-si LL-L. Narada, Hattō,
   Hamada, Matsue, Izumo B. Sd maa- B; Nk qmaasen B; Sr maa-san B; Yn maan C.
   Cf. ama$_{adj}$ $_A$.

? uraganasi- < ura$_{2.4}$ -n- kanasi$_{adj}$ $_A$ (< ...). 'sad(-hearted)'. x - A[K]/B-B-B
   x-x-x. Attested in Man'yō-shū.

B [uraguwasi-] < ura-gufasi- < *ura$_{?2.4}$ -n- kupasi$_{adj}$ $_B$ (< ...). '(strikingly)
   beautiful'. x - x-x-x x-x-x. NS (77b [14:156-M]) B. NS (T+ 77) uragufasi LLLLL.
   Attested in Man'yō-shū.

B uramesi- < uramyesi- ?< *uramiCa- < (last two syllables metathesized) *urama-Ci-$_B$
   (< ...) -si-, ? (third vowel partially assimilated to the second) < *urami$_{2.4}$
   (< ...) -si-. 'rueful'. x - B-B-B x-x-x. Hattō, Hamada, Matsue, Izumo B.
   On the problem posed by /mye/ cf. Matsumoto 1974:115, [sike-], and [sikome-].

B urawaka- < *ura$_{2.4}$ baka$_{adj}$ $_B$. 'youthful'. x - B-B-B x-x-x. Attested 10th century.

B urayamasi- < urayama-$_B$ (< *ura$_{?2.4}$ dama-$_{?B}$) -si-. 'enviable; envious'. x - B-B-B
   x-(B)-(B). Hattō, Hamada, Matsue, Izumo B. Nk qurenmasen B; Sr qureemasan B;
   Yn uramisan B. Attested 11th century.

B uresi- ?< *ur[a]$_{?2.4}$ ye$_{adj}$ $_x$ (< y<u>o</u> < *d<u>o</u>$_{adj}$ $_B$) -si-. 'joyful'. x - B-B-B x-B-x.
   K: "Hn, Km B" (where attested?). Edo A/B. Narada, Hattō, Hamada, Matsue, Izumo,
   NE Kyūshū B. Nk quqsen B; Sr qussyan B. Attested in Man'yō-shū.

?B [ureta-] < ure[y]ta- < *ura$_{?2.4}$ ita$_{adj}$ $_B$. 'rueful; hateful'. x - (B)-x-x x-x-x.
   NS (T+ kun) ureta-kyi ka ya LLL-H L H.

B [urewasi-] < urefasi- < *ura-Ci-$_B$ -pa-si-. 'deplorable'. B - x-x-x x-x-x.
   Km (W) B.

B urusa- ?< *urasa- < *ura$_{?2.4}$ sa$_{adj}$ $_A$ [Ōno], ?< *ur[a]$_{2.4}$ u$_{adj}$ $_{?B}$ -sa. 'noisy,
   annoying'. x - B-B-A B-x-x. NE Kyūshū B. Attested 11th century.

B [uruwasi-] < urufasi- (earliest example of -w- < -f-) ?< urufa-$_{?B}$ (< *uru-pa-)
   -si-, ? (second vowel assimilated to the first) < ura$_{?2.4}$ fasi$_{adj}$ (< *pasi).
   'beautiful'. B - B-B-A x-x-x. NS (91a [11:5-K], 128b [14:353-K]) B. NS (T+ 22)
   urufasi LHHH (odd), (38) urufasi-myi LLLL-L.

- usirogura- < usiro$_{?3.7a/b}$ -n- kura$_{adj}$ $_A$. 'shady, dubious'. x - A/B-B!-B x-x-x.
   Earliest attestation Mr.

B usirometa- ?< usiro-me (< usiro$_{?3.7a/b}$ ma-Ci$_{1.3a}$) [i]ta$_{adj}$ $_B$. 'shady, dubious'.
   x - B-B!-B x-x-x. Km (W) B. K: "Edo HHHHH-L" (= A). Attested 10th century.

A usu-. 'thin'. A - A-B-A B-B-x. NS (Okada) A. Km (W) A. Edo A. Sapporo <u>B</u>; Akita,
   Matsumoto, Numazu, Narada, Hattō, Hamada, Matsue, Izumo, Hiroshima, Ōita,
   NE Kyūshū A. Kōchi, Sakawa A. Sd qusuu- B (borrowed?) / qus(i)- B; Nk x;
   Sr qu$_s$i-san B = hwis[i]-san B, see hoso-.

A utagawasi- < utagafasi- < utagafa-$_A$ (< ...) -si-. 'doubtful, suspicious'.
   x - A/B-B-A x-x-x. K: "Edo B". Attested early Hn.

? utayomigamasi- < utayomi$_{(4.x)}$ (< *uta$_{2.2b}$ d<u>o</u>m[a-C]i$_B$) -gamasi- (< ...). 'having
   the air of a poet'. x - x-x-x x-x-x.

A uto- < utwo-. 'distant, alien'. A - B-B-A x-x-x. Edo A. Cf. too-.

?A utomasi- < utoma-_A (< utwo_{adj A} -ma-) -si-. 'unpleasant, offensive'. x - B-B-x
    x-x-x. Attested 10th century.

? utoutosi- < *utwo ··· -si-. 'aloof, alien(ated), distant'. x - B-x-x x-x-x.
    Attested Ir.

B utukusi- (< ?). 'beautiful'. B - B-B-B x-x-x. K: "Edo B". Cf. itukusi-.

B uyauyasi- < uya/[w]iya (?< *wiy-[y]a < ...) ··· -si-. 'deferential, respectful'.
    B - B-B-x x-x-x. Mr (Bm) A.

?A [uzihaya-] < udifaya- < *unti (< ? — perhaps < *muti_{2.3} 'whip') pada_{adj B}.
    'critical, precarious, dangerous'. A - x-x-x x-x-x.

?A uzutaka- < u^t/_dutaka < *u(n)tu (< ?) taka_{adj B}. 'piled high'. A (Zs -d-, Kn -t-)
    - B-B-B x-x-x. K: Edo B. Cf. uzumeru.

B wabisi- < wabiysi- < *banp^u/_o-Ci-_A -si-. 'forlorn'. x - B-B-A x-x-x. Km (W) B.
    Attested in Man'yō-shū.

B waka- < *baka (?< *baku, cf. waku-kwo/-gwo). 'young'. B - B-B-B B-B-C. Edo B.
    Narada, Hattō, Hamada, Matsue, Izumo, NE Kyūshū B. Nk wahaasen B; Yn bagan C.

B wakawakasi- < *baka_{adj B} ··· -si-. 'young'. x - B-B-B x-x-x.

?A warina- < wari (< *bar[a-C]i_{2.1<A}) na_{adj B}. 'incomprehensible, unfathomable,
    beyond comprehension'. x - x-x-x x-x-x. Km (W) A.

B waru- ?< *baru-. 'inferior; bad'. B - B-B-B B-B-C. Mg waro- B. Narada, NE
    Kyūshū B. Sr was-san B; Kikai was-sai, waru-ku; Nk waqsen B; Miyako bazz-baz
    < *baru-; Yn bara-san C. This word is not found in OJ (cf. asi-). Hn attests
    both waru- and waro-; the latter was more common but it is probably from waru-,
    with the second vowel partially assimilated to the first.

- [wazatogamasi-] < waza-to (< *bansa_{2.2b} to_{pcl}) -gamasi- (< ...). 'deliberate,
    forced'. x - (B)-x-x x-x-x. Attested 11th century.

A wazurawasi- < wadurafa-_A (< ...) -si-. 'troublesome, vexing'. A - A/B-B-A x-x-x.
    K: "Km B" (where attested? S,W x).

?B [yabusa-] ?< *dabusa; ?< yafusa- (< ...). 'stingy'. x - x-x-x x-x-x. Mr yabusa-
    ka_{adj-n}. Cf. [yausa-].

?B [yaisa-] < yafyisa- < *dapi(-)sa (< ?). 'stingy'. x - x-x-x x-x-x. Cf. [yausa-],
    [yabusa-], yabusagaru; sa- 'narrow'.

B [yaiyaisi-] 'deferential, respectful' (= [iyaiyasi-] = uyauyasi-): <u>yawiyawisi</u>
    (Zs) — perhaps a scribal error for wiyawiyasi. B - x-x-x x-x-x.

B yamasi- < yama-_B (< *dama-) -si-. 'ill; upset, uneasy; ashamed'. B - B-B-A x-x-x.
    Mg yamasi LLL, LHx. Hattō, Hamada, Matsue, Izumo B.

- yarukatana- < yaru (< *dar[a]-_A -u_{attr}) kata_{2.2b} na_{adj B}. 'heartbroken,
    mortified; inevitable'. x - B-B-x x-x-x.

- yarusena- < yaru (< *dar[a]-_A -u_{attr}) se_{1.1} (< ...) na_{adj B}. 'cheerless'.
    x - B-B-B x-x-x. Earliest attestation Mr.

A yasasi- ?< *dasa[-Ci_A 'shrink'], (?< *yasusi- < *dasu_{adj B} -si- but register is
    incongruent, so probably just a semantic extension). 'gentle, amiable; easy'.
    A - A-B-A B-x-C. Edo A(/B). Narada, Hattō, Hamada, Matsue, Izumo A. Nk x;
    Yn daçan C.

B yasu- < *dasu-. 'easy, cheap'. B - B-B-B B-B-x. NS (Okada) B. NS (T+ 69) yasu-ku
    LH-L. Edo B. Narada, Hattō, Hamada, Matsue, Izumo B. Nk yaqsen B; Sr yas-san B
    < yaşi- < yasu- 'cheap'.

- yatuyatusi- < *datu ··· -si-. 'much emaciated, gaunt, haggard'. B - x-x-x x-x-x.

?B [yausa] < yafusa- < *dapusa- (?< *dapisa). 'stingy'. B - x-x-x x-x-x.

? [yawa-] ?< *daba-. 'hungry'. x - x-x-x x-x-x. Zdb treats this as yafa-, but NKD,
    Ōno, and Nakata all have -w-. Cf. yowa-, yawaraka(-).

B yo- ‹ yo̲- ‹ *do̲-. 'good'. B - B-B!-B B-(B)-x. NS (71c [11:179-M]) yo-ku R-H;
   (119b [14:175-K]) yo-ki L-L, (92a [11:12-K], 92b [11:16-K]) yo-ki L-H. NS (T+
   21, 54) yo̲-si "R"-L ?= HL; yo̲-ku mo arazu "R"-L ₤ LLH; yo-kyi (47) "R"-L ?=
   H-L, (50) "R"-H ?= H-H; (35) ye na (‹ yo̲-[ky]i na, ?‹ yo̲ na) "R" ₤ ?= H(|)H.
   Km (S) yo-ku H-L; Km (W) yo-si/-ki L-H, yo-ku/-mi H-L. Narada B; Hata B. Kt ii
   1 = yoi 1, yoo 2 = yoku 2; Kōchi yoi 1, yoku 2 = yoo 2; Sakawa 1. Sd yii-/yu-/
   yit- B; Nk x (yutasen B, cf. yuta-ka*adj-n*); Sr yukaru B 'good', yuu ‹ *yo-ku B
   'well; often', ii(-) A 'good ···' (→ yuta-syan B). Cf. Sin-e chep-hay (Shingo-
   shōkai 1676): yey.i tyen.ki.ni (10:15v), tyen.ki.mwo ywo.kwu (10:16u).

B yoku^h/ᵦuka- ‹ yoku (‹ Ch yok) (-n-) fuka*adj B* (‹ *puka). 'greedy'. x - B-B-B
   x-x-x. Earliest attestation Mr.

B yorokobasi- ‹ yorokoba-*A* (‹ ...) -si-. 'delightful, welcome'. x - B-B-B x-x-x.
   Attested NS.

A yorosi- ‹ yo̲rosi- ‹ yo̲rasi- ‹ *do̲ra-*A* -si-. 'satisfactory'. A - A/B-B-A x-x-x.
   NS (77b [14:154-M]) A. NS (T+ 40) yo̲rosi-kyi HHL|H. Mr (Bm) HHL-. Narada, Hattō
   A; Hamada, Matsue, Izumo B. Cf. yorokobu. On etymology cf. Ōno Tōru 1978:299.

- yosina- ‹ yo̲si*?2.1* (‹ *do̲s[a-C]i*A*) na*adj B*. 'groundless, senseless'. x - B-B!-x
   x-x-x. K:"Hn HH|LF" (= HH|LH-), "Edo B".

? yosoyososi- ‹ yo̲so*2.2b* (‹ *do̲so) ··· -si-. 'standoffish, distant, cool'.
   x - B-B-A x-x-x. Attested 11th century.

B yowa- (‹ "yofa-" = /yowa-/) ‹ ywowa- ‹ *dwoba-. 'weak'. B - B-B-B B-B-C.
   NS (117b [14:131-K]) yowaku LHL. Edo B. Sapporo, Akita, Matsumoto, Numazu,
   Narada, Hattō, Hamada, Matsue, Izumo, Hiroshima, Ōita, NE Kyūshū B. Kōchi B.
   Nk yoosen B; Sr yoo-san B; Kobama yoo- ‹ *yowa-; Yn duwan C.

- yowayowasi- ‹ ywowa*adj B* (‹ *dwoba) ··· -si-. 'weak'. x - B- B-B x-x-x. Hattō,
   Hamada, Matsue, Izumo B. Attested 13th century.

?A yukasi- ‹ yuka-*A* (‹ ...) -si-. 'tasteful'. x - B(/A[Hiroto])-B-A x-x-x. Hattō,
   Hamada, Matsue, Izumo B. Attested 11th century. Cf. okuyukasi-.

?B yura- ‹ *dura-. 'lenient, generous'; (= yuru-) 'loose'. x - x-x-x x-x-C.
   Yn durankai C 'loose'. Attested in Koji-ki: ko̲ko̲ro̲ wo yura-myi 'because of a
   generous heart' (K 108).

B yuru- ‹ yuru*adj-n* ‹ *duru ?‹ *dura *(the second vowel assimilated to the first)*.
   'loose, slack; lenient, generous'. B - B-B-B B-B-(x). Narada B. Nk yurusen B;
   Kobama yurun; Yn durankai C.

? yuyusi- ‹ yu-yu (‹ ?) -si-. 'serious, grave'. x - B-B-A x-x-x. K: "Km B" *(where
   attested?)*. Edo (A/)B. Attested in Koji-ki.

- zyutuna- (attested Mr) ‹ zyutu (‹ Ch dž ̣ywet) na*adj B*; = zutina/zutuna- (Hn) ‹
   zut^i/ᵤ (‹ Ch dž ̣ywet) na*adj B*. 'lacking technique/means'. x - B-x-x x-x-x.

7.10. Supplementary list 1: newer adjective stems.

This list contains stems first attested in 1500 or later. Most of these stems are
unattested for the Ryūkyū dialects; the accent formulas have been simplified by
omitting the second set "x-x-x" when no Ryūkyū data were available. And "x - " for
Myōgi-shō has been omitted throughout. Stems noted "x-x-x" for Tōkyō, Kyōto, and
Kagoshima are obsolete, though some survive in dialects.

Attested   Stem

Edo   abunakkasi- < abuna- (< ...) -ka -si-. 'doubtful'. B-B-A.

Edo   adappo- < ada (< *anta₂.₂ᵦ) -po- (< *[o]po_adj ᵦ). 'coquettish'. B-B-A.

Edo   adokena- < adoke (< ?) -na-. 'innocent'. B-B-A.

Edo   ahookusa- < afoo (< afau (1/2-1:3-A < ?) kusa_adj ᵦ. 'stupid'. B-x-x.

Edo   ahorasi- < afo[o] (< afau (1/2-1:3-A < ?) rasi (< *[a]ra-ᵦ -si-).
    'stupid'. B-B!-A.

Edo   aikurusi- < ai (< Ch gay') kurusi_adj ᵦ (< ...). 'lovely, charming'.
    B-B-B.

Edo   akaru- (?< akaru < *aka-ra-ₐ -u). 'light, bright'. A-B-A. Tappi, Narada,
    NE Kyūshū A.

Edo   akippo- < aki₂.₃ (< akyi < ak[a-C]iᵦ) -po- (< *[o]po_adj ᵦ). 'inconstant'.
    B-B-B.

Edo   akkena- < akke (< ake[y]₂.₁ < aka-Ci-[Ci]ₐ) na_adj ᵦ. 'unsatisfying'.
    B-B-B.

Edo   akudo- < aku (< Ch gak 'bad') -do- (< -n- two_adj ᵦ). 'gaudy'. B-B-B.

Edo   ama-(t)taru-, -daru- < ama_adj ₐ taru_adj (< ...). 'sweet'. A-B-A. But
    taru- may be a truncation; perhaps < *tar[a-Ci-ᵦ] -u 'droops' (→ 'drippingly
    sweet') or < *tar[a-ₐ] -u_pred 'suffices'.

Recent   amazuppa- < ama_adj ₐ -n- suppa_adj ᵦ (< ...). 'sweet-and-sour'.
    A/B-B![H]/B[U]-A.

Recent   aoguro- ← awo-guro_adj-ᵦ HHxx (Mg) < *abo₂.₅ (< ...) -n- kurwo?₂.₅. 'ashen'.
    A[K]/B-B-B.

Edo   aokusa- < awo (< *abo₂.₅) kusa_adj ᵦ. 'unripe'. B-B-B.

Edo   aoziro-, aosiro- (Hepburn 1867) ← awo (< *abo₂.₅) -n- sirwo₂.₅. 'pale'.
    A/B-B-B.

Edo   arappo- < ara_adj ₐ -ppo- (< *[o]po_adj ᵦ). 'rough'. A/B-B-A.

Edo   atubotta- ?< atu_adj ₐ -bo(t)ta- (?= [o]mo-ta-_adj ₐ). 'thick'. A/B-B-A.

Edo   atukamasi- (?< atu_adj ₐ + ?; cf. yakamasi-, -gamasi-). 'impudent; noisy,
    annoying'. B-B-A.

Edo   atetukegamasi- < atetuke(₄.₂) (< ate[y]-tuke[y] < ata-Ci[-Ci]ₐ tuka-Ci[-
    Ci]ᵦ) -gamasi- (< ...). 'insinuating, sarcastic'. x-x-x.

Edo   atu(k)kurusi- < atu_adj ᵦ kurusi_adj ᵦ (< ...). 'stuffy'. B-B-B.

Edo   awareppo- < aware₃.₅ᵦ ?<₃.₄ (< ...) -ppo- (< *[o]po_adj ᵦ). 'plaintive,
    pitiful'. B-B-x.

Edo   azato- ?< asato- ?< asa_adj ₐ -to(?pcl). 'small-minded, shallow, petty'.
    B-B-x.

Edo   bakabakasi- < baka(₂.₃) (< ?) ... -si-. 'stupid'. B-B-B.

Recent   bakadaka- < baka(₂.₃) (< ?) -n- taka_adj ᵦ. 'outrageously expensive'.
    B[Mkz]-x-x.

Edo   bakagata- < baka(₂.₃) (< ?) -n- kata_adj. 'damned hard'. A/B-x-x.

Edo   bakakusa- < baka*(2.3)* (< ?) kusa*adj B*. 'awfully stupid'. B-B-B.
Recent   bakaooki- < baka*(2.3)* (< ?) ooki*adj B* (< ...). 'ridiculously big'. B-B-x.
Edo   bakarasi- < baka*(2.3)* rasi (< *[a]ra-*B* -si-). 'stupid'. A[H]/B-B-B.
Recent   batakusa- < bata(a) kusa*adj B*. 'buttery(-smelling); occident-mimicking'.
          B-B-A.
Edo   benkaigamasi- < ben-kai (< Ch 'bhyen-'kay') -gamasi- (< ...).
          'apologetic'. x-x-x.
Edo   boro- (?< boro*2.2a*). 'lucrative, profitable'. B-B-A.
Recent   busyoottarasi- < bu-syoo (< bu-syau < bu-syaǔ < Ch :pyew-.tsyeng) -tarasi-
          (< ...). 'lazy'. B-B-B.
Edo   dadabiro-, dadappiro- < dada-*pre* (< ?) (-n-/-T-) fyiro*adj B* (< *piro).
          'excessively wide, overly spacious'. A/B-B-A.
Recent   dadagara- [dial.] < dada-*pre* (< ?) -n- kara*adj A*. 'too spicy, oversalted'.
          x-x-x.
Recent   dadaguro- < dada-*pre* (< ?) -n- kurwo*adj B*. 'unduly (dreadfully) black'.
          x-x-x.
Edo   daizina- < dai-zi (< Ch dhay'-dzhryey') na*adj B*. 'inconsequential,
          unimportant'. B-x-x.
Edo   daizina- < daizi-na (< dai-zi*adj-n* (< Ch dhay'-dzhryey') n[i] a[ru] (<
          ara-*B* -u*attr*). '(quite) important'. x-x-x. NKD takes the formant -na- as a
          simple intensifier.
Edo   darasina- ?< *(metathesis)* sidara (< ?) na*adj B*. 'sloppy'. B-B!-A.
Edo   daru- < taru- (Hepburn), tayu- (Man'yō-shū) (?< *tara-*B* -u 'droop').
          'languid; tired'. B-B-B B-B-x. Hattō, Hamada, Matsue, Izumo B. Nk darusen B.
Edo   de(k)ka- < do-*pre* ika*adj B*. 'huge, enormous'. B-B-B.
Edo   dogitu- < do-*pre* (-n-) kitu*adj B* (< ...). 'very strict/tight'. A/B-B-B.
Edo   dokudokusi- < doku*2.3* (< Ch dhok) ⋯ -si-. 'gross'. B-B-B.
Edo   donkusa- < don (< ?) kusa*adj B*. 'sluggish, stupid'. B-x-x. Cf. torokusa-.
Edo   dorokusa- < doro*2.3* (< *ntoro) kusa*adj B*. 'muddy(-smelling)'. B-B-B.
Edo   dosigata- < do*bsd vb* (< Ch dho') si (< so-Ci*A*) -n- kata*adj A*.
          'irredeemable, incorrigible'. B-B!-A.
Meiji   dosuguro- < do-su-*pre* -n- kurwo*adj B*. 'very black'. A/B-B-A.
Meiji   egarappo- < wegara- (< ...) -ppo- (< [o]po*adj B*). 'acrid, pungent'.
          B-B-A. Dial. igarappo-.
Recent   egetuna- < egetu (< ?) -na-. 'brazen, offensive'. B-B-A.
Edo   endoo- < en (< Ch .ywen') (-n-) tofo*adj A* (< *topo). 'late in getting
          married'. B-B!-B.
Edo   enryobuka- < en-ryo (< Ch .hhywen-lyo') -n- fuka*adj B* (< *puka).
          'reserved, demure, modest, bashful'. B-B-x.
Edo   era- (< ?). 'great, eminent; much, many'. B-B-A. Narada, Hattō, Hamada,
          Matsue, Izumo, Hata, NE Kyūshū B. Kōchi A (Doi 1952:32). NKD offers a variety
          of intriguing etymologies.
Edo   gamanzuyo- < ga-man (< Ch 'nga-'m(b)wan) (-n-) tuyo*adj B*. 'patient, stoic;
          proud, heroic'. B-B-B.
Edo   ganzena- < gwan-ze (< Ch .ngwan-'zhye) na*adj B*. 'naive'. B-B-A.
Edo   gigotina- < gikoti-na < gigotu-/gikotu-/kigotu-na- < gikotu (< ?) -na-.
          'clumsy'. B-B!-A.
1898   gotu- < gotu*ala*. 'tough, rough'. B-B-A.
Edo   gutippo- < gu-ti (< Ch .ngu-.threy) -ppo- (< *[o]po*adj B*). 'querulous,
          peevish'. B-B-B.
Edo   hagayu- < fa*1.3b* (< *pa) -n- kayu*adj B* ("teeth itchy"). 'impatient'. B-B-B.

Edo   hakabakasi- < fakabakasi- < *paka*ₛ.ₛ* -n- ··· -si-. 'expeditious, speedy;
           active; satisfactory'. B-B-B.
Edo   hanabanasi- < fanabanasi- < *pana*ₛ.ₛ* -n- pana*ₛ.ₛ* -si-. 'glorious,
           splendid'. B-B-x.
Recent   hankakusa- < han-ka (< Ch pwan'-'kha) kusa*adj B*. 'stupid, worthless;
           uppity'. B-x-x.
Edo   harebotta- < farebotta- < fare[y]*ₛ.₁* (< *para-Ci[-Ci]*ₐ*) -botta- (< ...).
           'swollen'. A/B-B-A.
Edo   hasika- < fasika- ?< *pasi-ka (< ... 'awn'). 'itchy, annoying; quick-
           witted, shrewd'. x-x-x.
Edo   hasi(k)ko- < fasi(k)ko- (?< *pasi-ko = pasi-ka 'awn'). 'itchy, annoying;
           quick-witted, shrewd'. B-B-B. Cf. tebasiko-.
Edo   hidaru- < fidaru- (< ?). 'hungry'. B-B-B. (This word appears in many
           dialects. The etymology is uncertain, but it probably includes daru-.)
Edo   hido- < fido- < fi-do[o] < fi-dau (< Ch .pywey-dhaw'). 'severe'. B-B-A.
           Hattō, Matsue, Izumo B; Hamada A.
Edo   higosu- < figosu- < *fi-*pre* (< ...) -n- kosu*adj B* (< ...). 'very sly,
           cunning'. x-x-x.
Meiji   hihyoogamasi- < fi-fyau (< Ch .bhey-.bhyeng) -gamasi- (< ...).
           'cavilling, faultfinding'. x-x-x.
Edo   himozi- ← fimozi < fi[daru*adj B*] (< ...) mo(n)zi*ₚₛ.ₛ* (< ...).
           'hungry'. B-B-B. Cf. hidaru-.
Edo   hinatakusa- < finata*ₛ.ₛ* (< ...) kusa*adj B*. '(smelling) sun-bleached;
           farmerish'. B-B-x.
Recent   hirabetta- < *firabetta- < fyira*adj A* -betta- (< ...). 'flat'. A[K]/B-B-A.
Edo   hirata- < fira-ta- < *fyira-ta- < *pira*ₚₛ.ₛb* -ta-. 'flat'. A-B-A. Hattō,
           Hamada, Matsue, Izumo A. Kobama pirataan.
Edo   hitokusa- < fito*ₛ.ₛₐ* (< *pito) kusa*adj B*. 'smelling of (the presence of)
           people; (all too) human'. B-B-x.
Recent   hitonatu(k)ko- < hito*ₛ.ₛₐ* (< ...) natu(k)ko*adj B* (< ...). 'affable,
           amiable'. B-B-A.
Edo   hiya(k)ko- < fyiya*B* (< ...) -(k)ko- (< kwo*adj B*). 'chilly'. B-B-x. Also
           hyakko-. Tappi syakkoe B < hyakkoi. Cf. hieru.
Edo   hiyowa- < fiyowa- < *fi-*pre* (< ...) yowa*adj B* (< ywowa < *dwopa). 'weak,
           sickly'. A/B-B-A.
Edo   hodoyo- < fodo-yo- < fotwo*ₛ.ₛₐ* (< ...) yo*adj B* (< *do). 'moderate;
           proper'. B-B-A.
Recent   hohoemasi- < *fofo-wemasi- < fofo-wema-*B* (< ...) -si-. 'smile-provoking,
           amusing, pleasant'. B-A-x.
Recent   hokorippo- < fokori*ₛ.₁* (< ...) -ppo- (< *[o]po*adj B*). 'dusty'. A/B-B-A.
Edo   honeppo- < fone*ₛ.ₛ* (< ...) -ppo- (< *[o]po*adj B*). 'bony'. B-x-x.
Meiji   honoakaru- < fono-akaru- < *po-no*ₛ.ₛ* akaru*adj B* (< ...). A[H]/B-B-B.
Edo   honogura- < fono-gura- < *po-no*ₛ.ₛ* (-n-) kura*adj A*. 'darkish'. A/B-B-B.
           K: "Edo A".
?Recent   horoniga- < foro (? = fono < *pono) niga*adj B* (< *ninka). 'bitterish,
           slightly bitter'. A/B-B-A.
1868   hosokko- < foso*adj B* (< *poso) -kko- (< kwo*adj B*). 'very slender, quite
           thin'. B-B-x.
Edo   hosonaga- < fosonaga- (JP) ← foso-naga*adj B* < *poso*adj B* nanka*adj B*.
           'long and slender, slim'. A/B-B-B.
Edo   hotokekusa- < foto̲key*ₛ.₄* (<...) kusa*adj B*. 'Buddhistic, religiose'. B-x-x.

Edo   hugaina- < fugaina- < fu (?< Ch pu' 'vital organ, guts')) -n- kafyi$_{2.1}$
(< *kap[a-C]i$_A$) na$_{adj B}$. 'pluckless'. B-B-A. Tk also (syntactic reduction) 1.

Meiji   hukubukusi- < fukubukusi- < fuku (< Ch pyuk) -n- ⋯ -si-. 'happy and
prosperous (looking)'. B-B-B.

Edo   hunbetugamasi- < fun-betu (< Ch .pywen-bhyet) -gamasi- (< ...). 'prudent-
seeming'. B-x-x.

Edo   hunbetukusa- < fun-betu (< Ch .pywen-bhyet) kusa$_{adj B}$. 'prudent-seeming'.
B-B-B.

Edo   hunbeturasi- < fun-betu (< Ch .pywen-bhyet) rasi (< *[a]ra-$_B$ -si-).
'prudent-seeming'. B-x-x.

Edo   hutebutesi- < futebutesi- < *futobuto (< *putwo$_{adj B}$ -n- putwo) -si-.
'impudent'. B-B-B.

Recent   hyakko- 'chilly': see hiya(k)ko-.

Edo   hyoronaga- < fyoro$_{mim}$ (?< *pyoro) naga- (< *nanka). 'slender'. A/B-B-A.

Recent   igarappo- < egarappo$_{adj B}$ (< ...). 'acrid, pungent'. B-B-A.

Edo   igitanai- < i$_{1.3a}$ -n- kitana$_{adj B}$ (< ...). 'sleepy-headed; sloppy-
sleeping'. B-x-x.

Recent   iigata- < ifi$_A$ (< *ip[a-C]i) -n- kata$_{adj B}$. 'hard to say, unexpressible'.
x-x-x.

Recent   iiketugamasi- < ii-ketu[gari] (< ifi$_{inf}$ (< *ip[a-C]i$_A$) ketu⋯) -gamasi-
(< ...). 'foul-mouthed, sharp-tongued'. x-x-x.

Edo   ikaga(wa)si- < ikaga(fa)si- < ika-ga$_{3.4}$ (< ika$_{2.2b}$ n[i] ka) (-pa)-si-.
'questionable'. B-B-A.

Edo   ikatu- < (JP) ikatu$_{adj-n}$ (?< *ika$_{adj B}$ tu[ra$_{adj A}$]). 'hard, rough,
severe'. A/B[K]-B-A.

Edo   ikeatazikena- < ike-$_{pre}$ atazikena$_{adj B}$ (< ...). 'terribly stingy'. B-x-x.

Edo   ikeatukamasi- < ike-$_{pre}$ atukamasi$_{adj B}$ (< ...). 'terribly brazen'. B-x-x.

Edo   ikengamasi- < i-ken (< Ch qyey'-ken') -gamasi- (< ...). 'opinionated,
preachy'. B-B-A.

Edo   ikesituko- < ike-$_{pre}$ situko$_{adj B}$ (< ...). 'awfully obtrusive'. B-x-x.

Edo   ikesukana- < ike-$_{pre}$ sukana$_{adj B}$ (< suka-$_B$ na-$_{aux}$). 'most unpleasant, much
disliked'. B-x-x.

Edo   ikeurusa- < ike-$_{pre}$ urusa$_{adj B}$ (< ...). 'most annoying'. B-x-x.

Edo   ikezuuzuusi- < ike-$_{pre}$ zuuzuusi$_{adj B}$. 'terribly brazen'. B-x-x.

Recent   ikigurusi- < *ikyi (< iki$_{2.4}$ < *ik[a-C]i$_B$) -n- kurusi$_{adj B}$ (< ...).
'stifling'. B-B!-B. (Sr qicizira-san < *iki-zura- < -dura-.)

Edo   [imasi-] < *ima-$_B$ -si-. 'worrisome, vexing'. x-x-x.

Edo   inakakusa- < inaka$_{3.1}$ (< winaka < *bina(-)ka) kusa$_{adj B}$. 'rustic,
countryfied, farmerish'. B-B-A.

Meiji   inkikusa- < in-ki (< Ch 'qyen'-khyey') kusa$_{adj B}$. 'gloomy'. B-B-x.

Meiji   iroppo- < *iro$_{2.3}$ -ppo- (< [o]po$_{adj B}$). 'sexy, erotic'. B-B-B.

Edo   itaitasi- < ita$_{adj B}$ ⋯ -si-. 'pathetic'. B-B-B.

Edo   iyarasi- < iya (< *ida 'nay') -rasi- (< *[a]ra-$_B$ -si-). 'nasty'. B-B-A̲.

Edo   izi^k/$_g$itana- < i-di (< Ch qyey'-dhiy') (-n-) kitana$_{adj B}$ (< ...).
'gluttonous, greedy, voracious'. B-B-A.

Edo   izirasi- < idirasi- ?< *i-di (< Ch qyey'-dhiy') rasi- (< [a]ra-$_B$ -si-),
?< *idira-si- < *intira-$_B$ -si-. 'spiteful'. B-B-A.

Edo   kabikusa- < kabiy$_{2.1}$ (< ...) kusa$_{adj B}$. 'moldy, musty'. A/B-B-A.

Edo   kaidaru- < kainadaru- < kaina$_{3.5a/b}$ (< ...) daru$_{adj B}$ (< ...). '(arm-
tired =) bone-weary, languid, listless'. x-x-x.

Edo (JP)   kanakusa- < *kana[-Ci]$_{2.1}$ kusa$_{adj B}$. 'metallic-smelling'. B-B-x.

Meiji   kandaka- < kan (← kau < Ch kap "A = high musical tone") -n- taka$_{adj B}$.
'shrill'. B-B-A.

Meiji   kangaebuka- < kangafe[y]*4.5* (< ...) -n- fuka*adj B* (< *puka). 'thoughtful,
    prudent; deep-thinking'. B-B-B. Cf. Sr qumiibuka- B < *omoibuka-.
1886   kanziyasu- < kan-zi (< kan (< Ch 'kam) si[y]*A* (< *so̲-Ci)) yasu*adj B* (<
    *dasu). 'sensitive'. B-B-A.
Edo   kanzyoodaka- < kan-dyau (< kan-dyaɷ < Ch kham'-dh(y)eng') -n- taka*adj B*.
    'money-minded, penny-pinching'. B-B-A.
Recent   karuppo- < karu*adj A* -ppo- (< *[o]po̲*adj B*). 'light(weight), easy'. x-x-x.
Edo   kata(k)kurusi- ?< kata (= ?) kurusi*adj B* (< ...). 'formal, stiff,
    ceremonious'. B-B-A. ("Also -gurusi-" NKD.)
Edo   kattaru- = kaidaru-.
Edo   kawairasi- < kawai*adj B* (< ...) rasi- (< *[a]ra-*B* -si-). 'cute, charming'.
    B-B-A.
Edo   kebakebasi- ?< kewakewasi- < kefakefasi- ?< *kyifakyifa-si- < *kipa*2.3* ···
    -si-. 'showy'. B-B-A.
Meiji   kedaru- < ke*?1.1* (< *key < ?) daru*adj B* (< ...). 'listless'. A/B-B-A.
?Recent   keisandaka- < kei-san (< Ch key'-'swan') -n- taka*adj B*. 'money-minded,
    stingy'. B-x-x.
Meiji   ketikusa- < keti*(2.x)* (< ?) kusa*adj B*. 'stingy, mean'. B-B-A.
Edo   kihazukasi- < ki*1.1* (?< *kiy) fadukasi*adj B* (< ...). 'embarrassed'. B-B-A.
Meiji   kiiro- < kiiro*adj-n* < ki*1.2* (< *kⁿ/o̲-Ci) iro*2.3*. 'yellow'. A-B-A x-(A)-A.
    Hattō, Hamada, Matsue, Izumo A. Sr ciiru A; Yn kiru-cici A. (Unattested as an
    adjective before Brinkley 1896?)
Edo   kimariwaru- < kimari*3.2* (< *kimar[a-C]i*A* < ...) waru*adj B* (< *baru). 'ill
    at ease, nervous, abashed'. B-B![H]-A. For Kt, Umegaki has 1 | 1:3.
Edo   kimazu- < kimadu- < ki*1.1* (?< *kiy) madu*adj B* (< ...). 'unpleasant,
    disagreeable'. A/B-B-A.
Edo   kimiwaru- < ki-mi (< Ch khyey'-m(b)ywey') waru*adj B* (< ...). 'weird,
    ghastly, sinister'. B-B-x. Cf. usuᵏ/ɡimiwaru-.
Edo   kimuzukasi- < ki*1.1* (?< *kiy) muᵗ/ɑukasi*adj B* (< ...). 'hard to please'.
    A/B-B-A.
Edo   kinakusa- < kina (< ?) kusa*adj B*. 'scorched-smelling, smoldering'.
    B-B![H]/B[U]-A.
Meiji   kisokutadasi- < ki-soku (< Ch .khywey-tsok) tadasi*adj B* (< ...). 'regular,
    orderly'. B-B-A.
Edo   kitanarasi- < kitana*adj B* (< ...) rasi (< *[a]ra-*B* -si-). 'dirty'. B-B-B.
Recent   kiyasu- < ki*1.1* (?< *kiy) yasu*adj B* (< *dasu). 'congenial, relaxed, easy
    (company)'. B-B-A.
Recent   kiyasu- < kyi[yi]*A* (< *ki-Ci) yasu*adj B* (< *dasu). 'easy to wear,
    comfortable'. B-B-A.
Recent   kizappo- < kiza*2.3* (< *kinsa) -ppo- (< [o]po̲*adj B*). 'affected; gaudy'.
    B-B![H]/B[U]-A.
Meiji   kizewasi- < ki*1.1* (?< *kiy) sefasi*adj B* (< ...). 'restless'. B-B-A.
Edo   kizukawasi- < kidukafa-si- < *kiduka-pa-*B* (< ki*1.1* tuka-pa-*B*) -si-.
    'worrisome'. B-B-A.
Edo   kizuyo- < ki-duyo- < ki*1.1* (?< *kiy) -n- tuyo̲*adj B*. 'strong-hearted;
    heartening'. B-B-A.
Edo   kodomorasi- < kodomo*3.1* (< ...) rasi (< *[a]ra-*B* -si-). 'childlike;
    childish'. B-B-A.
Meiji   kogekusa- < koge*2.3* (< *kwogey < kwonka-Ci[-Ci]*B*) kusa*adj B*. 'burnt-
    smelling'. B-B!-A.
Edo   kogitana- < ko-*pre* (< *kwo*1.1*) -n- kitana*adj B* (< ...). 'rather dirty'.
    A/B-B-A.

Edo   kokkeigamasi- < kot[u]-kei (< Ch <u>kwet-'key</u>) -gamasi- (< ...). 'comical, droll'. x-x-x.

Recent   kokoroegata- < kokoroe[y]ₐ (< ...) -n- kataₐdⱼ ᵦ. 'hard to understand, incomprehensible'. x-x-x.

Edo   kokorogurusi- < *k<u>okoro</u>₇ₛ.₅ᵦ -n- kurusiₐdⱼ ᵦ. 'regretful, painful'. B-B-B. K: "Edo B".

Edo   koma- < *kwo₇ₐdⱼ ₐ -ma-. 'small, fine'. x-x-x B-B-B. Sd khumaa- B 'modest; detailed' and gumaa- B; Nk gumaa-sen B, Sr guma-san B 'small, fine' (? < n-koma-); Sonai (Yaeyama) guumai; Yn kuma-san C 'fine' (H 1967:489), guman C 'small' (H 1964:181). Attested JP; Edo attests an adjectival noun komai na ?= koma-[k]i na, cf. o[f]o-ki na. Register incongruent with etymology?

Edo   komagomasi- < *komaₐdⱼ (< ...) -n- ⋯ -si-. 'very fine, minute, petty, picayune'. B-x-x.

Edo   komaka- < kwomakaₐdⱼ₋ₐ ₃.₇ᵦ < kwo-maₐdⱼ ₇ᵦ (< ...) -ka. 'fine'. B-B-A. Narada, Hattō, Hamada, Matsue, Izumo B. Mg k<u>omaka</u> (nari). The incongruity of register is perhaps due to the canonical accentuation of adjectival nouns with the suffix -ka.

Edo   komakasi- < kwomakaₐdⱼ₋ₐ ₃.₇ᵦ (< ...) -si-. 'fine, detailed'. x-x-x.

Edo   konikurasi- < ko-pre (< *kwo₁.₁) nikurasiₐdⱼ ᵦ (< ...). 'quite hateful'. B-B-x.

Recent   koppido- < ko-pre (< *kwo₁.₁) fidoₐdⱼ ᵦ (< ...). 'quite horrible/severe'. B-B-B.

Edo   kosoba- < kosobai- < kosobayu- (< ...). 'itchy'. x-x-x. Sakawa A.

Edo   kosobai(i)-, kosobayu- < *koso₇ₘₗₘ -n- padu⋆ₐdⱼ ᵦ (< ...). 'ticklish'. B-B-A.

Edo   kosu- ?< *kwoₐdⱼ ᵦ suₐdⱼ ᵦ (< ...), ?< *kwoₐdⱼ ᵦ -si-. 'cunning; stingy, small'. B-B-A.

Recent   kosu(k)kara- < kosuₐdⱼ ᵦ (< ...) karaₐdⱼ ₐ. 'stingy and shrewd'. B-B-A.

Edo   kotoatarasi- < k<u>oto</u>₂.₃ atarasiₐdⱼ ᵦ (< ...). 'new, unusual, especial'. B-B-B.

Edo   kourusa- < ko-pre (< *kwo₁.₁) urusaₐdⱼ ᵦ (< ...). 'rather annoying'. B-B-A.

Edo   kowarasi- < kofarasi- < *k<u>opa</u>ₐdⱼ ᵦ rasi (< *[a]ra-ᵦ -si-). 'frightening, awful'. x-x-x.

Edo   koyakamasi- < ko-pre (< *kwo₁.₁) yakamasiₐdⱼ ᵦ (< ...). 'fussy, finicky, picky, captious'. A/B-B-A.

Edo   kozuraniku- < ko-pre (< *kwo₁.₁) -n- turanikuₐdⱼ ᵦ (< ...). 'quite ugly of face'. B-B-x.

Edo   kudarana- < kudara-ₐ na-ₐᵤₓ ('not descend' < ...). 'worthless'. A-B-A.

Edo   kudarasi- < *kunta [a]ra-ᵦ -si-. 'overly complicated, overmeticulous, fussy' (= kudakudasi-). x-x-x.

Edo   kudo- (?< kuda- < *kunta). 'garrulous, wordy; fussy'. B-B-A. Hattō, Hamada, Matsue, Izumo B. Cf. kudakudasi- = kudokudosi-; kudaku.

Edo   kudokudosi- = kudakudasi-. B-B-x.

Meiji   kuroppo- < kurwo₂.₅ -ppo- (< *[o]poₐdⱼ ᵦ). 'black'. B-B-B.

Edo   kusugutta- < kusuguri-ta- < *kusunkar[a-C]iᵦ (< ?) -ta- (< itaₐdⱼ ᵦ). 'ticklish'. A(/B[NHK])-B-A.

Edo   kuti- (?< kuti₁.₁). 'full, satiated'. A(/B[K])-B[H]/B![U]-B.

Edo   kutihabatta- < kuti-haba (< kuti₂.₁ panpa₂.₁) -tta- (< [i]taₐdⱼ ᵦ). 'talking big'. A/B-B-A.

Edo   kutiosi- < kuti₁.₁ wosiₐdⱼ ₐ (< ...). 'chagrined, disappointed'. B-B-A.

Edo   kuti-sabisi-/-zamisi- < kuti*1.1* sabisi*adj B* (< ...). 'wanting to put
    something in one's mouth, craving food (without being hungry)'. B-x-x.
Edo   kutiyakamasi- < kuti*1.1* yakamasi*adj B* (< ...). 'nagging, faultfinding,
    carping'. A/B-B-A x-A-x. Nk x; Sr kuciyagamasi- A.
Meiji   kyoohakugamasi- < kefu-haku (< Ch <u>hyep-pak</u>) -gamasi- (< ...).
    'threatening, intimidating'. B-x-x.
Edo   kyooto- < ke-uto- < key*?1.1* (< ?) utwo*adj A*. 'alienated, disaffected;
    dismal; lonely; weird; (easily) startled; extreme'. x-x-x.
Edo   maatarasi- < ma-*pre* atarasi*adj B* (< ...). 'quite new'. B-B-A.
Edo   mabusi- ?< *mab[ay]u-si- < *ma*1.3a* -n- padu*adj B* -si-. 'dazzling'. B-B-B.
    Hattō, Hamada, Matsue, Izumo B.
Edo   madaru- < ma*1.1* daru*adj B* (< ...). 'sluggish'. B-B-x.
Meiji   madarukko- < madaru*adj* (< ...) -kko- (< kwo*adj B*). 'sluggish'. B-B-A.
Edo   makkookusa- < makkoo (< matu-kau < Ch <u>m(b)wat-.hyang</u>) kusa*adj B*. 'smelling
    of incense/religion'. B-B[H]/B![U]-B.
Meiji   makkuro- < maC-*pre* kurwo*adj B*. 'jet-black'. B-B!-A. Cf. Sr makkuuru A.
Meiji   manmaru- < man-*pre* maru*adj A*. 'perfectly round'. A-B![H]/B[U]-A.
1867   manuru- < ma*1.1* nuru*adj B*. 'tardy, slow'. B-B-A.
Recent   maru(k)ko- < maru*2.1* -ko- (< kwo*adj B*). 'ever so round'. B-B-A.
Edo   massiro- < maC-*pre* sirwo*adj B*. 'snow-white'. B-B![H]/B[U]-A.
    Cf. Sr massiira A.
1868   matasi- < mata-*B* -si-. 'long-waiting, impatient, eager(ly expecting)'.
    x-x-x.
Recent   matiko- ?< *mati[ra]- (< *ma*1.3a* tira-*A*) -ko- (< kwo*adj B*). [dial.]
    'dazzling, brilliant'. x-x-x. Tappi matikoe B.
Edo   mawaridoo- < mafari-dofo- < *mapar[a-C]i*A* -n- <u>topo</u>*adj A*. 'roundabout'.
    B-x-x.
Edo   mawari(k)kudo- < mafari-kudo- < *mapar[a-C]i*A* (kudo- < kuda- <) kunta*adj ?*.
    'roundabout'. B-B-A.
Meiji   meatarasi- < mey*1.3a* (< *ma-Ci) atarasi*adj B* (< ...). 'new (to one's
    eyes), unusual, rare'. A/B-B-B.
Meiji   mebosi- (< *mey-bosi- < *ma-Ci*1.3a* -n- posi*adj B*). 'outstanding,
    valuable'. B-B-B.
Edo   memagurusi- < memagirasi- < mey*1.3b* (< ma-Ci) magira[fa]si*adj B* (< ...).
    'dizzy, dizzying'. B-B-B.
Edo   memesi- < mye*1.3b* (< ...) ··· -si-. 'feminine; effeminate'. B-B-A.
Edo   mendo- < mendoo < (JP) mendɔɔ < mendau < *me[y]da[k]u < *ma-Ci*1.3a* -n-
    taku (< ?). 'troublesome, bothersome'. B-x-x.
Meiji   mendoogamasi- < mendoo (< ... *(above)*) -gamasi- (< ...). 'troublesome'.
    x-x-x. Attested Brinkley 1896:334b.
Edo   mendo(o)kusa- < mendoo (< ... *(above)*) kusa*adj B*. 'troublesome,
    bothersome'. B-B-B.
Edo   mendo(o)si- < mendoo (< ... *(above)*) -si-. 'troublesome, bothersome'.
    B-x-x.
Meiji   midarigamasi- < midari (< *minta-r[a-C]i*B*) -gamasi- (< ...). 'disorderly'
    (= midarigawasi-). B-1|B-x.
Meiji   mimiatarasi- < mimi*2.3* (< ...) atarasi*adj B* (< ...). 'fresh (to the ear),
    newsy'. B-B-B.
Edo   mimidoo- < mimidofo- < *mimi*2.3* -n- <u>topo</u>*adj A*. 'hard of hearing; hard to
    comprehend; distantly past'. B-B-x. JP -douoi = -dowoi.
Edo   mimitti- (< ?). 'stingy'. B-B-A.
Meiji   mimizato- < *mimi*2.3* -n- satwo*adj ?A* (< ...). 'sharp-eared'. B-x-x.

Meiji mirengamasi- < mi-ren (< Ch m(b)ywey'-lyen') -gamasi- (< ...).
 'regretful, irresolute'. B-B-B.
Edo mittomona- < mitomona- (JP) < mitoo (< mi-ta[k]u < myi[-Ci]*B* ta*aux adj*
 -ku*inf*) mo*pcl* na*adj B*. 'indecent'. B-B!-B. Sr miitoon neen.
Edo miyo- < *mi[-Ci]*B* do*adj B*. 'not bad to look at; easy to see'. B-B-B.
Recent mizimettarasi- < mizime*adj-n 3.x* -(t)tarasi- (< ...). 'miserable,
 wretched'. B-x-x.
Edo mizukusa- < midu*1.1a* (< ...) kusa*adj B*. 'watery; unfriendly'. A/B-B-A.
1868 mizumizusi- < midumidusi- < *myidu-myidu-si- < *mintu*2.1a* (< ...) ···
 -si-. 'young and fresh'. B-B-A.
Edo mizuppo- < midu*2.1a* (< ...) -ppo- (< [o]po*adj B*). 'watery'. A/B-B-A.
 Hattō, Hamada, Izumo B; Matsue A [corrections list].
Edo monogamasi- < mono*2.3* -gamasi- (< ...). 'pompous, ostentatious'. x-x-x.
Edo monogata- < mono*2.3* -n- kata*adj A*. 'honest, sound'. B-B-B.
Meiji monomezurasi- < mono*2.3* medurasi*adj B* (< ...). 'unusual, rare'. A/B-B-B.
Edo monomidaka- < *monomi*(3.4)* (< mono*2.3* mi[Ca]-Ci*B*) -n- taka*adj B*.
 'curiosity-seeking, curious'. B-B-B.
Edo mottairasi- < mot[i]-tai (< Ch m(b)ywet-'they) rasi (< *[a]ra-*B* -si-).
 'pompous, haughty'. B-B-x.
Edo mottomorasi- < mottomo*?3.3,?3.4* (< ...) rasi (< *[a]ra-*B* -si-).
 'plausible, reasonable'. B-B-A.
Edo mugo- (< ?). 'cruel'. B-B-A. Hattō, Hamada, Matsue, Izumo B.
Edo mugotarasi- < mugo*adj B* (< ...) -tarasi- (< ...). 'cruel, atrocious'.
 B-B-A.
Edo munagurusi- < muna*2.2b* -n- kurusi*adj B* (< ...). 'oppressed (in the
 chest)'. B-B-A.
Edo musakurusi- < musa*adj* kurusi*adj B* (< ...). 'filthy'. B-B-A.
Edo museppo- < muse*?2.1* (< musa-Ci[-Ci]*?A*) -ppo- (< *[o]po*adj B*). 'stifling,
 choking'. A[K]/B-B![H]/B[U]-A.
Edo musiatu- < musi*2.3* (< [u]mus[a-C]i*B* < ...) atu*adj B*. 'sultry'.
 B-B![H]/B[U]-A.
?Recent muzugayu- < muzu*mim* -n- kayu*adj B* (< ...). 'itchy, crawly'. A/B-B-A.
Recent nagapposo- < naga*adj B* (< *nanka) -T- hoso*adj B* (< foso < *poso).
 'slender; narrow' (= hosonaga-). B-B-A.
1659 naga(t)tarasi- < naga*adj B* (< *nanka) -(t)tarasi- (< ...). 'terribly long'.
 B-B-A.
Meiji namaatataka- < nama*2.5* atataka*adj B* (< ...). 'rather warm'.
 A/B-B![H]/B[U]-A.
Edo namanuru- < nama*2.5* nuru*adj B*. 'lukewarm'. B-B-A.
Recent namattiro- = namaziro-.
Edo namayasasi- < nama*2.5* yasasi*adj A* (< ...). 'easy, simple'. A/B-B-A.
 Tk also (syntactic reduction) 1.
Meiji namaziro- < *nama*2.5* -n- siro*adj B* (< sirwo*2.5*). 'rather white'. A/B-x-x.
1867 nanigena- < nani-ge (< nani*2.4* key*1.1* < ...) na*adj B*. B-B!-B.
Meiji natukko- ?< *natuk[i]ko- < natuk[a-C]i*B* -ko- (< kwo*adj B*). 'affectionate,
 amiable'. B-B-A.
Recent nebakko- < neba*adj B* (< ...) -kko- (< kwo*adj B*). 'sticky'. B-B-x.
Meiji nebarizuyo- < nebari*3.4* (< *nenpa-r[a-C]i*B*) -n- tuyo*adj B*. 'tenacious;
 sturdy'. B-B-B.
Edo negurusi- < *ne[y]*A* (< naCi[-Ci]) -n- kurusi*adj B* (< ...). 'hard to
 sleep, wakeful'. B-B[H]/B![U]-A.

Edo   netu- ?< ne[ba]tu[k]i*A* < *nenpa*mim* (< ?) tuka-*B*. 'sticky, persistent, obtrusive'. B-B-x.

Recent   netuppo- < netu (< Ch nhyet) -ppo- (< *[o]po*adj B*). 'feverish'. B-B-x.

Edo   nezuyo- < *ne[y]*1.3a* (< na-Ci) -n- tuyo*adj B* (< tudo). 'strong-rooted; stubborn'. B-B-B.

Edo   niawasi- < niafa- (< *ni[-Ci]*A* apa-*B*) -si-. 'suitable, becoming' (= nitukawasi-). B-B-A x-A-x. Sr nawaasi- A.

Edo   nibena- < nibe*2.3* (< ?) na*adj B* ('lack fishglue'). 'brusque, curt'. B-x-x.

Edo   niginigisi- < *nigyi (< *ni(n)ki) ··· -si-. 'bustling, lively'. B-B-x.

Edo   nikunikusi- < niku*adj B* ··· -si-. 'hateful'. B-B-B.

Edo   nikurasi- < *niku*adj B* rasi (< [a]ra*B* -si-). 'hateful'. B-B-B.

1868   nikutarasi- < niku*adj B* -tarasi- (< ...). 'hateful'. B-B-B.

Recent   ningenrasi- < nin-gen (< Ch .nhyen-.k(y)an) rasi (< *[a]ra-*B* -si-). 'human-worthy, like a (true) human being'. B-x-x.

Edo   [nitukorasi-] ?< *nitukurasi- (the third vowel partially assimilated to the fourth) < nituku*A* (< *ni[-i]*A* tuka-*B* -u) rasi- (< *[a]ra-*B* -si-). 'highly suitable/becoming; very similar, closely resemblant'. x-x-x.

Edo   nobuto- < *no*1.3a* ('arrow bamboo') -n- putwo*adj B*. 'brazen, impudent; loud-voiced'. B-x-x.

Edo   norokusa- < noro*adj B* kusa*adj B*. 'terribly slow, sluggish'. B-x-x.

Meiji   norowasi- < norofasi- < norofa-*B* (< ...) -si-. 'cursed/cursing, damn(ed), damnable, execrable'. B-B-A.

Edo   nozomasi- < *nonso-ma-*A* -si-. 'desirable'. B-B-A. Attested JP.

Edo   nukamisokusa- < nuka-miso*4.x* (< ...) kusa*adj B*. 'smelling of salted rice-bean paste'. B-B[H]/B![U]-B.

Edo   nuku-. 'warm'. x-x-x B-B-C. Nk nukusen B. Dial. noko-, niku-. Attested JP.

Edo   oisi- < o- (< *opo*adj B*) isi*adj B* (< yesi- < yosi- < *do*adj B* -si-). 'delicious'. A/B[H]-B![H]/B[U]-B. NE Kyūshū A.

Edo   okkana- < okka (< ?) -na-. 'frightened; exaggerated'. B-B-A.

Meiji   okorippo- < okori*?3.4* (< oko-r[a-C]i*?B*) -ppo- (?< *[o]po*adj B*). 'quick-tempered, testy'. B-B-A.

Edo   omoigakena- < omof[y]igake[y]*5.6* (< *omop[a-C]i*B* -n- kaka-Ci[-Ci]*B*) na*adj B*. 'unexpected'. B-B-B.

Meiji   omo(k)kurusi-, omogurusi- < omo*adj A* (-n-/-T-) kurusi*adj B* (< ...). 'oppressed, gloomy; awkward'. B-B-A.

Edo   ongamasi- < on (< Ch .gen) -gamasi- (< ...). 'imposing (obligations on others), assuming (others are obliged), obligating'. x-x-x.

Edo   onkisegamasi- < on (< Ch .gen) kyise[y] (< *ki-sa-Ci[-Ci]*A*) -gamasi- (< ...). 'imposing (obligations on others), obligating'. x-x-x.

Meiji   onnarasi- < onna*3.2b* (< ...) rasi (< *[a]ra-*B* -si-). 'womanly'. B-B-A.

Edo   orimetadasi- < wori-me (3-2-B < *bor[a-C]i*B* ma-Ci*1.3a*) tadasi*adj B* (< ...). B-B-B.

Recent   osaegata- < *osafey (< osa-pa-Ci[-Ci]*A*) -n- kata*adj B*. 'uncontrollable, irresistible'. x-x-x.

Edo   ositukegamasi- < osituke*4.1* (< *os[a-C]i*A* tuka-Ci[-Ci]*B*) -gamasi- (< ...). 'inconsiderate, pushy'. B-B-A.

Edo   otokokusa- < wotoko*3.4* (< ...) kusa*adj B*. 'masculine(-smelling)'. x-x-x.

Edo   otokorasi- < wotoko*3.4* (< wotokwo < *boto*2.3* kwo*1.1*) rasi (< *[a]ra-*B* -si-). 'manly'. B-B-B. Earliest attestation JP.

Edo   otomasi- < (the first vowel assimilated to the second) utomasi*adj* (< ...). 'unpleasant, cruel; pitiful'. x-x-x.

Edo   otonagena- ‹ otona-ge (‹ otona*3.7b* (‹ ...) -n- key*1.1*) na*adj B*.
          'childish, unbecoming a grownup'. B-B!-B.
Recent   oyobigata- ‹ oyob[y]i*A* (‹ *d̲o̲np[a-C]i) -n- kata*adj B*. 'hard to reach,
          unattainable'. B-x-x.
Edo   ozomasi- (‹ ozoma- JP 'be awakened/startled; fear') ‹ o(n)so-ma-*?A* -si.
          'strong-willed, severe, harsh, fearsome; stupid'. B-x-x x-B-x. Nk husuumasen B,
          Sr qusumusi- B 'terrible; startling'.
Meiji   reireisi- ‹ rei (‹ Ch ˈlyey) ··· -si-. 'ostentatious'. B-B-A x-B-x. Nk x;
          Sr riris-san B.
Edo   rikutuppo- ‹ ri-kutu (‹ Ch ˈlyey-khywet) -ppo- (‹ *[o]p̲o̲*adj B*).
          'argumentative'. B-B-A.
Edo   rinkibuka- ‹ *rin-ki (‹ Ch lyenˈ-khyeyˈ) -n- puka*adj B*. 'jealous'. B-x-x.
Edo   rinkizuyo- ‹ *rin-ki (‹ Ch lyenˈ-khyeyˈ) -n- tuy̲o̲*adj B*. 'jealous'. B-x-x.
Edo   saezaesi- ‹ saye[y]*B* (‹ *sada-Ci-[Ci]) -n- ··· -si-. '(crystal-)clear;
          bright(-spirited), cheerful'. B-x-x.
Edo   sakekusa- ‹ sake[y]*2.1* (‹ ...) kusa*adj B*. 'winey(-smelling)'. A/B-B-A
          x-x-x. Nk saKi(i)Kusasen B.
Edo   saku- ‹ *sak[a]-*B* -u). 'lighthearted, good-humored; (wood) easily split;
          (Sr) fragile, frail'. B-B-x x-B-x. Hattō A; Hamada, Matsue, Izumo B. Nk
          sakusen B, Sr saku- B: opposite of Nk siPuusen A 'fibrous, tough', Sr sipu- A
          'sturdy, strong, tenacious' (‹ ?).
Recent   samuzamusi- ‹ samu*adj B* (‹ ...) -n- ··· -si-. 'very cold; meager'. B-x-x.
Edo   sasidegamasi- ‹ saside*?3.4* (‹ *sasa-Ci*B* [i]nta-Ci[-Ci]*B*) -gamasi- (‹ ...).
          'impertinent'. B-B!-B.
Meiji   sema(k)kurusi- ‹ sema*adj B* (‹ ...) kurusi*adj B* (‹ ...). 'constricted,
          cramped'. B-B-B.
Edo   sese(k)komasi- ‹ se*adj x* ··· komasi- (?‹ koma[ka]-si-, ?‹ koma-*B* -si-).
          'narrow, cramped'. B-B-A.
Edo   setigara- ‹ se-ti*2.x* (‹ Ch šyeyˈ-tryeyˈ) -n- kara*adj A*. 'hard to live'.
          B-B!-A.
Edo   setuna- ‹ setu*2.x* (‹ Ch tshet) na*adj B* 'painful (either physically or
          emotionally); considerate, kind'. B-B-A. JP syetnai.
Recent   sianbuka- ‹ *si-an (‹ Ch .syeyˈ-qanˈ) -n- fuka*adj B* (‹ *puka).
          'thoughtful'. B-x-x.
Edo   sigana- (?‹ sagana-*B* ‹ ...). 'poor, wretched, unfortunate'. B-B-x.
Recent   sigata- ‹ *si*A* (‹ *s̲o̲-Ci) -n- kata*adj A*. 'hard to do': myoozyoo sigata-
          'indescribable', ... x-x-x. Cf. dosigata-.
Recent   sikaku- ‹ si-kaku*adj B* (‹ Ch syeyˈ-kak). 'square'. B-B-B. Not attested as
          an adjective before the 20th century.
Meiji   sikatume-/sikatube-/sikazume-rasi- ‹ (bnd n. ‹ ?) rasi (‹ *[a]ra-*B* -si-).
          'formal, solemn'. B-B-A.
1886   simeppo- ‹ simeri*3.4* ‹ *simeyr-i ‹ *sima-Ci-r[a-C]i*B* -ppo- (‹ [o]p̲o̲*adj B*).
          'damp'. A/B-B-B.
1752   sinbo(o)zuyo- ‹ sin-boo (‹ sin-bau ‹ Ch .syen-ˈbhaw) -n- tuy̲o̲*adj B*.
          'patient, long-suffering'. B-B!-B.
Edo   sindo- ?‹ sindo[o] ‹ sin-roo (‹ Ch .syem-.lawˈ). 'trying, tough; tired,
          (body-)weary'. B-x-x.
Edo   sinkikusa- ‹ sin-ki (‹ Ch .syen-khyeyˈ) kusa*adj B*. 'depressed; fretful;
          irritated, irritating'. B-B-B.
Edo   siorasi- ‹ siworasi- ?‹ siwora- (‹ ... , cf. sioreru*?A/B*), ?‹ siwo (‹?)
          rasi (‹ [a]ra*B* -si-). 'modest; elegant; lovable'. B-B-B x-B-x. Sr syuuraa-/
          syura-syan.

1921   sirootokusa- < sirooto$_{4.x}$ (< ...) kusa$_{adj}$ $_B$. 'amateurish'. B-B-B.

Edo   siroppo- < siro (< sirwo$_{2.5}$) -ppo- (< *[o]po$_{adj}$ $_B$). 'white; amateurish'.
            B-B-B.

Recent   siryobuka- < si-ryo (< Ch .syey'-lyo') -n- fuka$_{adj}$ $_B$ (< *puka).
            'prudent, judicious'. B-B-A.

Edo   sisairasi- < si-sai (< Ch 'tsyey-sey') rasi (< *[a]ra-$_B$ -si-).
            'pedantic; self-important'. B-x-x.

Edo   sitataru- < sita$_{2.3}$ taru$_{adj}$ $_x$. 'cloying, too sweet'. A/B-B-x.

Edo   sitikudo- < siti-$_{pre}$ kudo$_{adj}$ $_B$ (< ...). 'very tedious'. B-B-x.

Meiji   sitimendo(o)kusa- < siti-$_{pre}$ mendo(o)kusa$_{adj}$ $_B$ (< ...). 'extremely
            troublesome'. B-B-B.

Edo   sitimu^t/ᵈukasi- < siti-$_{pre}$ mu^t/ᵈukasi$_{adj}$ $_A$ (< ...). 'very difficult or
            troublesome'. B-B-B.

Edo   situ(k)ko- ?< situ (< Ch tšep) -(k)ko- (< kwo$_{adj}$ $_B$). 'obtrusive (in color,
            taste, smell); stubborn, vexing'. B-B-B.

Edo   siwa- (< ?). 'stingy'. B-B-B. Iwate dial. sippa- may be evidence for <
            sifa- < *sipa-.

Recent   siwa- (< ?). 'firm, sturdy; stubborn, obstinate'. x-x-x.

Meiji   sokkena- < sokke (?< *su-$_{pre}$ $_{?1.3a}$ ke$_{?1.1}$ < ...) na$_{adj}$ $_B$.
            'inconsiderate'. B-B![H]/B[U]-A.

Edo   sorazorasi- < *swora$_{2.4}$ -n- swora$_{2.4}$ -si-. 'feigned'. B-B-B.

Recent   sorobandaka- < *soroban$_{4.x}$ (< ...) -n- taka$_{adj}$ $_B$. 'stingy, money-minded'.
            B-x-x.

Edo   sosokkasi- < *swoswoka-$_?$ -si-. 'careless'. B-B-A.

Recent   sowasowasi- < "sofa" = sowa$_{mim}$ ... -si-. 'restless, fidgety'. x-x-x.

Edo   subarasi- ?< *sunpa-ra-$_B$ ('be unified/concentrated', cf. suberu) -si-.
            '(extreme, terrible →) magnificent'. B-B-B.

1886   subasi(k)ko- < *su-$_{pre}$ $_{?1.3a}$ -n- pasi-kwo$_{adj}$ $_B$. 'nimble; ?shrewd'. x-x-x.

Edo   subaya- < *su-$_{pre}$ $_{?1.3a}$ -n- pada$_{adj}$ $_B$. 'swift'. B-B-B.

Meiji   subekko- < subeko- < *sunpe (< ?) -ko- (< kwo$_{adj}$ $_B$). 'slippery'. B-B-B.
            Cf. suber-u$_B$, sube-sube$_{adv}$.

Recent   sueosorosi- < suwe$_{2.1}$ (< ?) osorosi$_{adj}$ $_B$ (< ...). 'ominous'. B-B-A.

Edo   suetanomosi- < suwe$_{2.1}$ (< ?) tanomosi$_{adj}$ $_B$ (< ...). 'promising, hopeful'.
            B-B-x.

Recent   suitarasi- < suita (< *su[k]i-ta[ri] < suk[a-C]i$_B$ te < ...) ar[a-C]i$_B$)
            rasi (< *[a]ra-$_B$ -si-). 'liked, likeable'. B-B-x.

Recent   sukebeettarasi- < sukebee$_{adj-n}$ $_{4.x}$ (< *suki-bee < ...) -ttarasi- (< ...).
            'lecherous'. B-x-x.

1872   suppa- < *su-fayu- < su$_{1.3a}$ fayu$_{*adj}$ (< *padu, see [siwawayu-]). 'sour'.
            B-B-B. Kikai subee-.

Edo   surudo- < surudo$_{adj-n}$ $_{?B}$ < *suru (< ?) -n- two$_{adj}$ $_B$. 'sharp; extreme;
            unfeeling, cold'. B-B-A. Earlier this was an adjectival noun: Mg surudo nari
            (Kn), surudo nari (Zs); JP surudo na.

Edo   syarakusa- < syara$_{(2.x)}$ (?< sara-$_{?A}$) kusa$_{adj}$ $_B$. 'foppish, trendy; cheeky,
            impertinent'. B-B-x.

Edo   syoobenkusa- < seu-ben (< Ch 'syew-.bhyen') kusa$_{adj}$ $_B$. 'urine-smelling;
            diaperish, babyish, immature'. B-x-x.

Edo   syoppa- < sifo-fayu- < sifwo$_{2.3}$ (< *sipwo) fayu$_{*adj}$ (< *padu, see
            [siwawayu-]). 'salty'. B-B-B.

Edo   syozaina- < syo-zai (< Ch 'sryo-'dzhay') na$_{adj}$ $_B$. 'low(ly) in position;
            bored'. B-B![H]/B[U]-A.

Edo   syuunenbuka- ‹ syuu-nen (‹ Ch tšyep-n(d)yem˙) (-n-) fuka*adj B* (‹ *puka). 'tenacious; vindictive'. B-B-A.

Edo   taisoorasi- ‹ tai-sou (‹ tai-soǘ ‹ Ch dhay˙-.dzheng) rasi (‹ *[a]ra-*B* -si-). 'exaggerated; pompous'. B-B![U]-x.

Edo   taru-. 'sweet'. x-x-x. See NKD 13:223b (darui, 4); sitataru-. This may be a truncation of ama(t)taru-/-daru-, but cf. Korean tal- ‹ tol-.

Edo   tawaina- ‹ ta(w)ai (?‹ *ta*1.3a* ap[a-C]i*B*) na*adj B*. 'absurd; frivolous; inconsequential; easy'. B-B![H]/B[U]. Tk also (by syntactic reduction) prototonic.

Edo   [tawake-] ‹ *tafakey- ‹ *tapa-ka-Ci-. 'jesting, joking; bawdy'. x-x-x. Cf. [tawasi-], tawakeru, tawamureru, tawagoto.

Edo   teara- ‹ *te (‹ *ta-Ci*1.3a*) ara*adj A*. 'rough, harsh'. A/B-B-B.

Edo   tebasika- ‹ *te*1.3a* (‹ *ta-Ci) -n- pasika*adj B* (‹ ...). 'quick, agile' (= tebasiko-). x-x-x.

Edo   tebasiko- ‹ *te*1.3a* -n- pasiko*adj B* (‹ ...). 'quick, agile'. B-B-x.

Edo   tebaya- ‹ *te*1.3a* (‹ *ta-Ci) -n- paya*adj B*. 'nimble, quick, agile'. B-B(/B![U])-B x-B-x.

Edo   tehido- ‹ te*1.3a* (‹ *ta-Ci) fido*adj B* (‹ ...). 'rough, harsh'. B-B-B.

Edo   tekibisi- ‹ *te (‹ *ta-Ci*1.3a*) kibisi*adj B* (‹ ...). 'severe, cruel'. A[K]/B-B-B.

Recent   terekusa- ‹ tere*2.3* (‹ tera-Ci[-Ci]*B* ‹ ...) kusa*adj B*. 'embarrassed'. B-B-A.

Edo   tettoribaya- ‹ tettori*bnd n* (‹ *te*1.3a* (‹ ta-Ci) tor[a-C]i*B*) -n- faya*adj B* (‹ *paya). 'prompt'. B-B-B.

Meiji   tikarazuyo- ‹ tikara*3.3* -n- tuyo*adj B*. 'forceful, reassuring'. B-B-A. Nk siKaarazuusen A.

Edo   tikasi- ‹ *tika*adj B* -si-. 'intimate, close'. B-B-B.

Edo   tinamagusa- ‹ ti*1.1* namagusa*adj B* (‹ ...). 'bloody-smelling; atrocious'. B-B-A.

Edo   titikusa- ‹ titi*2.4* (‹ ...) kusa*adj B*. 'milky-smelling; babyish'. B-B!-A.

Meiji   togetogesi- ‹ toge*2.3* (‹ ...) ⋯ -si-. 'stinging'. B-B-B.

Edo   torokusa- ‹ toro*adj B* kusa*adj B*. 'sluggish, stupid'. B-x-x.

Edo   tumarana- ‹ tuma-ra-*B* na-*aux*. 'boring, dull; ... '. 3-4-B.

Edo   turaniku- ‹ tura*2.3* niku*adj B*. 'ugly(-faced)'. B-B-B.

Edo   tutikusa- ‹ tuti*2.3* kusa*adj B*. 'earthy(-smelling)'. B-B-B.

1678   tutusimibuka- ‹ tutusimi*?4.1* (‹ *tutu(-)sim[a-C]i*?A*) -n- fuka*adj B* (‹ *puka). 'circumspect, prudent'. B-B-B.

Meiji   tuyappo- ‹ tuya*2.1* (‹ *tuda) -ppo- (‹ *[o]po*adj B*). 'glossy; romantic, amorous, love-involved'. A/B-B-A.

Recent   tuyatuyasi- ‹ tuya*2.1* (‹ *tuda) ⋯ -si-. 'glossy'. B-x-x.

1886   tuyuppo- ‹ tuyu*2.5* (‹?) -ppo- (‹ *[o]po*adj B*). 'dewy'. B-B-A.

Recent   tyootyoosi- ‹ tefutefusi- ‹ tefu-tefu ‹ Ch tyep-tyep) -si-. 'talkative, garrulous, loquacious; expansive, proud; fickle'. B-x-x.

Edo   tyoro- ‹ tyoro*mim*. 'worthless; stupid; feeble, flimsy, a pushover'. B-B-x.

Edo   tyoroko- ‹ tyoro*adj B* -ko- (‹ *kwo*adj B*). 'feeble, flimsy, little'. x-x-x.

Meiji   tyuuibuka- ‹ tyuu-i (‹ Ch tšyu˙-qyey˙) -n- fuka*adj B* (‹ *puka). 'cautious, careful'. B-B-A.

Edo   usankusa- ‹ u-san (‹ Ch .hho-san˙) kusa*adj B*. 'suspicious, suspect, doubtful'. B-B-A.

Edo   usanrasi- ‹ u-san (‹ Ch .hho-san˙) rasi (‹ *[a]ra-*B* -si-). 'suspicious, suspect, doubtful'. x-x-x.

Edo   usosamu- < *usu*adj A* sanpu*adj B* (< ...). 'somewhat cold'. B-B![H]/B[U]-B.

Edo   usuaka- < usu*adj A* aka*adj A*. 'light red'. A/B-B-A.

Meiji   usuakaru- < usu*adj A* akaru*adj B* (< ...). 'somewhat bright'. A/B-B-A.

Edo   usuao- < usu*adj B* awo*adj B* (< ...). 'pale blue'. A/B-B-A.

Edo   usugitana- < *usu*adj B* -n- kitana*adj B* (< ...). 'somewhat dirty'. A/B-B-A.

Edo   usugura- < *usu*adj A* -n- kura*adj A*. 'dim'. A/B-B-A x-A-x. Tappi, Hattō, Hamada, Matsue, Izumo A.

Meiji   usu*k*/*g*imiwaru- < usu*adj A* kimiwaru*adj B* (< ...). 'weird, eerie, uncanny'. B-B-A.

Meiji   usurasamu- < usu-ra*adj-n* samu*adj B* (< ...). 'rather cold'. A/B-B-A.

Edo   utagaibuka- < utagaf[y]i*4.1* (< ...) -n- fuka*adj B* (< *puka). 'doubtful'. B-B-A.

Edo   utaguribuka- < utaguri*4.1* (< utagur[a-C]i*A* < ...) -n- fuka*adj B* (< *puka). 'doubtful'. B-B-A.

?Edo   utagurippo- < utaguri*4.2* (< utagur[a-C]i*A*) -ppo- (< *[o]po*adj B*). 'doubtful'. B-B-A.

Edo   uttoosi- < ut-tau (< Ch ywet-.dhaw) -si-. 'gloomy'. B-B-B.

Edo   wakena- < wake*72.5 ?<2.3* (< wakey < *baka-Ci[-Ci]*B*) na*adj B*. 'very easy'. B-B![U]-x.

Edo   warugasiko- < waru*adj B* (< ...) -n- kasiko*adj B* (< ...). 'sly, cunning, crafty, wily'. B-B!-B.

Edo   waru*k*/*g*usa- < waru*adj B* (-n-) kusa*adj B*. 'malodorous, bad-smelling'. B-x-x. Brinkley 1896 -k-; Kindaichi and Ikeda -g-.

Meiji   wasureppo- < wasure*s.1* (< *basura-Ci*B*) -ppo- (< *[o]po*adj B*. 'forgetful'. A/B-B-A.

Meiji   wazatorasi- < waza-to (< *bansa*2.2b* to*pcl*) rasi (< *[a]ra-*B* -si-). 'deliberate, forced'. B-B-A.

Edo   yabotta- < yabo (1-1:3-A ?< yabu*2.1* < ?) -(t)ta- (< *[i]ta*adj B*). 'uncouth'. B-B[H]/B![U]-A.

Edo   yakamasi- < [i]ya*72.1* (< *ida) kamasi*adj* (< *kama*×adj ?B* -si-). 'noisy'. B-B-B x-A-x. Nk yagaamasen A; Sr yagamasyan A; Yaeyama yagamasaan. Cf. kamakamasi-.

Recent   yamigata- < yami*B* (< *dam[a-C]i) -n- kata*adj B*. 'hard to stop, uncontrollable, irresistible'. x-x-x.

Edo   yani(k)ko- < yani*2.3* (< *dani) -kko- (< kwo*adj B*). 'gummy, resinous; tenacious'. B-B-B.

Recent   yarikirena- < yari (< *dar[a-C]i*A*) kyire[y]- (< *kiraCi-*B* < ...) na-*aux*. 'unbearable'. 4-B-A.

Edo   yasuppo- < yasu*adj B* (< *dasu) -ppo- (< *[o]po*adj B*). 'cheap'. B-B-B.

Edo   [yawa-] < yafa- < *dapa-. 'soft'. x-x-x.

Edo   yawaraka- < yafara-ka*adj-n* < yafa-ra (< *dapa*adj/?nln* -ra) -ka. 'soft'. B-B-B x-(B)-(B). Nk yapaarasen B; Sr yahwara-san B; Miyako (Sawata) yaparagi-; Kobama yahwaran; Yn daan B (H 1964) = daaran C (H 1967). As an adjective not attested before Edo; earlier this was an adjectival noun: Mg yafaraka (nari).

Meiji   yayakosi- < *[i]ya[i]ya*4.3* -ko- (< kwo*adj B*) -si-. 'complicated, difficult'. B-B-A. Hattō, Hamada, Matsue, Izumo B.

Edo   yogina- < yogi (?< Ch .yo-.ngye 'excess law/measure') na*adj B*. 'unavoidable, urgent'. B-B!-B. Tk also (syntactic reduction) 1/2.

Edo   yondokorona- < yori-dokoro (< *dor[a-C]i*A* -n- tokoro*3.1a*) na*adj B*. 'unavoidable, urgent'. B-B[H]/B![U]-B.

1471   yoozinbuka- < yoozin (< you-zin < you-sin < Ch yong'-.syem) (-n-) fuka*adj B* (< *puka). 'careful, cautious'. B-B-B.

Edo   yozato- < *ywo*1.3a* (< *dwo) -n- satwo*adj B* (< ...). 'quick to awaken, vigilant'. B-x-x.

Edo   zihibuka- < zi-fi (< Ch <u>tsiy'-.pywi</u>) -n- fuka*adj B* (< *puka). 'merciful'. B-B![H]/B[U]-A.

Edo   zimankusa- < zi-man (< Ch <u>dzhiy'-'m(b)wan</u>) kusa*adj B*. 'prideful'. x-x-x.

Edo   zimanrasi- < zi-man (< Ch <u>dzhiy'-'m(b)wan</u>) rasi (< *[a]ra-*B* -si-). 'prideful; self-important'. B-x-x.

Recent   zimantarasi- < zi-man (< Ch <u>dzhiy'-'m(b)wan</u>) -tarasi- (< ...). 'prideful'. B-1|B-x.

Edo   ziretta- < zire[y]-*?A/B* (?< *nsira-Ci-) -(t)ta- (< *[i]ta*adj B*). 'irritating'. B-B-A.

Edo   zizimusa- < didi (< ?) musa*adj ?*. 'filthy'.

Meiji   zokuppo- < zoku (< Ch <u>zhyok</u>) -ppo- (< *[o]p<u>o</u>*adj B*). 'lowbrow, popular, common'. B-B-A.

Edo   zoosana- < zoo-sa (< zau-sa < Ch <u>'dzhaw'-tsa'/tsak</u>) na*adj B*. 'easy, simple'. B-B!-B.

Edo   zubuto- < *dubuto- (?< *ntunpu*sia* putwo*adj B*). 'imperturbable, cool-headed; bold, brazen'. B-B-B. Cf. nobutwo-, zuuzuusi-.

Edo   zuru- ? < *(second vowel assimilated to the first)* zure[y]-*?A/B* (< ...). 'sly'. B-B-A. Hata B. Kōchi <u>A</u> (Doi 1952:32).

Edo   zuuzuusi- < duuduusi- ?< *du[b]u*sia* (< *ntunpu) ··· -si-. 'impudent'. B-B-B.

Meiji   zyasuibuka- < *zya-sui (< Ch <u>.zhya-.tšyuy</u>) -n- fuka*adj B* (< *puka). 'distrustful, suspicious'. B-B!-A.

Edo   zyatibuka- < *zya-ti (< Ch <u>.zhya-trye'</u>) -n- fuka*adj B* (< *puka). 'wily, cunning'. B-x-x.

Edo   zyosaina- < zyo-sai (< Ch <u>.nhyo'-.dzhay</u>) na*adj B*. 'adroit; tactful'. B-B![H]/B[U]-A.

Edo   zyukusikusa- < zyuku-si (< Ch <u>nhyet-'dzrhyey</u>) kusa*adj B*. '(a drinker's breath) smelling like a ripe persimmon'. B-B-x.

7.11. Supplementary list 2: older stems lacking accent attestations.

- [akirake-] < akyirakey- < *akiraka*adj-n* 4.11 (< ak[a-C]i *A* -ra-ka) -Ci-. 'evident, unmistakable; clear, pure'.

?B [hanaguwasi-] < fana-gufasi- < *pana*2.3* -n- kupasi*adj B* (< ...). 'flowery, florid, fine-blossoming, lovely-flowered'. NS (T+ 67) LFHLL = LHHLL.

- [haruke-] < farukey- < *paruka*adj-n* 3.7b -Ci-. 'distant'.

?B [hokasi-] < fokasi- < *poka*2.4* -si-. 'different, unusual, alien'.

?B [ikidoorosi-] < ikyidoforosi- < *ikidoporosi- < *ikidoporasi- < *ikidopora- (< *iki*2.4* topo-ra-*B*) -si-. 'indignant, resentful'. NS (T+ 29) ikyidoforosi mo HHHHH-L|H.

?B [ikizuk**a**/**u**si-] < ikyiduk**a**/**u**si- < ikiduka- (< *iki*2.4* -n- tuka-*A*) -si-. 'hard to breathe, stifling/stifled'.

?B [isaosi-] < isawosi- < isawo (?< isa-wo < *isa*2.4* bo*1.1*) -si-. 'brave; diligent, industrious'.

?B [isosi-] < iswosi- < *iswo-si-. 'hustling, energetic, industrious, diligent'. NS (T+ kun) LLH (? → noun). Cf. isogu, isou.

?B [itaburasi-] < itabura-*?B* (< ...) -si-. 'upset, distraught, shaken'.

?B [ituitusi-] ?< itu(-)*?2.3* ··· -si-. 'awesome'.

?B [itukasi-] < ituka-*B* -si-. 'solemn, imposing, splendid, sacred'. Cf. itukusi-.

- [iwakena-] < iwake[y]*?2.3* (< iwakey-*B* < *i-*pre* baka*adj B* -Ci-) -na-. 'immature, childish'.

- [iyana-] < wiyana-. *See* [uyana-].

- [kaao-] < kaawo- < *ka-*pre* abo*adj B* (< ...). 'green'.

- [kagotogamasi-] < kagoto*(3.x)* (< ka (< ?) -n- koto) -gamasi- (< ...). 'grumbling'.

B [kakarawasi-] < kakarafasi- < *kaka-ra-*B* -pa-si-. 'easily (en)snared'.

- [kasadaka-] < *kasa*2.2b* -n- taka*adj B*. 'large (in quantity, bulk, number); arrogant; grandiose'. Attested 10th century.

?A [kasoke-] < kaswokey- ?< *(the second vowel partially assimilated to the others)* *kasukey- < kasu-ka*adj-n* 3.7b -Ci-. 'faint (sound or color)'. The accentuation of kasu-ka is canonical. Cf. kasumu.

- [kenaga-] < key-naga- < key*?1.3a* (< *ka-Ci) naga*adj B* (<*nanka). 'days being long/many, being a long time'.

- [kaoyo-] < kafoyo- < *kapo*2.1* do*adj B*. 'fair-faced'.

- [kesi-] < kyesi- < kye*adj-n 1.3b* (< *kiCa) -si-. 'queer, bad, untrustworthy; terrible, grave'.

?B [keyake-] < ke-yakey- < *kye-yakey- < kye*adj-n 1.3b* (< *kiCa) -ya-ka (< *-da-ka). 'extremely different, queer, bad; outstanding, noble; clear'.

- [keyasu-] < key*A* (< *kaCi[-Ci]) yasu*adj B* (< *dasu). 'easily vanishing; evanescent, momentary'.

?A [kirawasi-] < kyirafasi- < *kirapa-*A* -si-. 'disliked, hateful'.

- [kogosi-] < kogosi- ?< ko n[i] ko (< ?) -si-. 'rugged(ly precipitous)'.

?B [koita-] < kwofiyta- < kwofiy*2.3* (< *kwopo-Ci[-Ci]*B*) [i]ta*adj B*. 'love-smitten'. Attested M 130.

- [kokidasi-] < kokiydasi- < kokiyda (< *kokoCida) = kokoda 'lots, much/many', cf. kokoba[ku] 'so terribly') -si-. 'very important'.

?B [kokorogu-] < kokoro-gu- ?< *kokoro*3.5(?b)* n[i]ku*adj B*. 'distressing, trying'. Attested in Man'yō-shū.

?B [kokorokoisi-] < kokoro*3.5(?b)* kwofiysi*adj B* (< *kwopo-Ci*B* -si-). 'enchanting, fetching, lovely'.

?A [kumagumasi-] < kumaguma*?4.3* (< kuma*?2.3<2.1* n[i] kuma) -si-. 'labyrinthine; dark; luxuriant, thick (growth), ramified; with many secrets'.

?B [maguwasi-] ‹ ma-gufasi- ‹ *ma$_{1.3a}$ -n- kupasi$_{adj}$ $_B$ (‹ ...). 'eye-pleasing, good-looking'.

?B [monokoisi-] ‹ *mono-kwof^{iy}/$_o$si- (M 67, semantograms) ‹ *mono$_{2.3}$ kwofiysi/ kwof(w)osi$_{adj}$ $_B$ (‹ *kwopo-Ci-$_B$ -si-). 'beloved'. Now obsolete.

?B [motona-] ‹ *moto$_{2.3}$ na$_{adj}$ $_B$. 'unrestrained, indiscriminate; groundless, unreasonable'. Attested only as stem used adverbially, but cf. [uramotona-] and perhaps kokoromotona-.

- [naguwasi-] ‹ na-gufasi- ‹ *na$_{1.2}$ -n- kupasi$_{adj}$ $_B$ (‹ ...). 'well-named'.

- [niguro-] ‹ ni-gurwo- ‹ *ni$_{?1.3b}$ -n- kurwo$_{adj}$ $_B$. 'dirt-black'.

- [niko-] ‹ nikwo-. 'soft'.

- [nitasi-] ‹ nita-si- (‹ ?). 'damp, moist, humid' (Izumo-fudoki).

- [niwasi-] ‹ nifasi- ‹ *nipa -si-. 'sudden' (nifasi-ku M 4389). Cf. niwaka, [*nii-], [niisi-].

- [ogirona-] ‹ ogyiro$_{adj-n}$ $_{?3.3,?3.7}$ (‹ *onkiro ‹ ?) -na-. 'vast'.

- [okokosi-], [okookosi-], [okosi-] (‹ ?). 'great, formidable, powerful'. Ōno treats this as ogoogosi- and relates it to ogosoka and ogoru.

?B [omoiganasi-] ‹ omofyi-ganasi- ‹ *omop[a-C]i$_{3.4←B}$ -n- kanasi$_{adj}$ $_A$ (‹ ...). 'saddening, depressing, unpleasant to think about'.

?B [omoigurusi-] ‹ omofyi-gurusi- ‹ *omop[a-C]i$_{3.4←B}$ -n- kurusi$_{adj}$ $_B$ (‹ ...). 'regrettable, painful, distressing' (= kokorogurusi-).

?B [osaosasi-] ‹ wosawosasi- ‹ *bosa$_{?2.4,?2.5}$ ('elder') ⋯ -si-. 'outstanding, splendid'.

?B [oyosi-] ‹ oyosi- ‹ *oyo[-Ci-$_B$] (‹ *odo ?‹ *oda, cf. oya) -si-. 'old, aged'. The stem is attested in oyosi wo (M 804) 'old man'.

- [sadoo-] ‹ sadofo- ‹ *sa-$_{pre}$ -n- topo$_{adj}$ $_B$. 'far away'.

- [sike-] ‹ sikye- ?‹ *sikiCa- ‹ (metathesis of last two syllables) *sika-Ci- (‹ ?). 'dirty'. On the /kye/ cf. Matsumoto 1974:115, [sikome-], uramesi-.

- [sikome-] ‹ sikomey- ‹ *sikomaCi- ?‹ (metathesis of the last two syllables) *sikyomiCa- ‹ *siko$_{adn}$ miCa (? = mina 'woman'). 'dirty, soiled, impure'. NS (T+ kun) sikomey-kyi HLL-L. On /mey/ ← /mye/ cf. uramesi-, [sike-].

- [sitaemasi-] ‹ sitawemasi- ‹ sita$_{2.2a}$ wema-$_B$ ('smile underneath') -si-. 'smiling to oneself, delighted at heart'.

- [sizuke-] ‹ sidukey- ‹ *sintu-ka$_{adj-n}$ $_{3.7b}$ -Ci-. 'quiet, still'.

- [sumiyake-] ‹ sum^u/$_i$yakey- ‹ sumiyaka$_{adj-n}$ $_{4.11}$ (‹ ...) -Ci-. 'hasty, speedy'.

- [tadoo-] ‹ tadofo- ‹ *ta-$_{pre}$ -n- topo$_{adj}$ $_A$. 'far away'.

- [tagitagisi-]. See taidaisi-.

- [taidaisi-] (Hn) ‹ tagyitagyisi- ‹ *tanki (‹ ?) ⋯ -si-. 'bumpy, hard to walk (on); bad, inconvenient, objectionable'.

- [tasina-] ?‹ tasi$_{2.1}$ (‹ *tas[a-C]i$_A$) na$_{adj}$ $_B$. 'hard (to bear); poor, wanting, impoverished'.

?B [tatawasi-] ‹ tatafasi- ‹ *tata-$_B$ -pa-si-. 'full (time); formidable; strict, stern, severe'.

- [tawasi-] ‹ tafasi- ‹ *tapa-si-. 'bawdy, licentious'. Cf. tawake-, tawagoto, tawakeru, tawamureru.

- [tayowa-] ‹ ta-ywowa- ‹ *ta-$_{pre}$ dwoba$_{adj}$ $_B$. 'weak, feeble'.

- [tokizi-] ‹ tokyi-zi- ‹ *toki$_{2.3}$ n[i] (‹ n[a-C]i$_{aux}$ $_{inf}$) -si-. 'untimely, unseasonable; all the time (regardless of season)'.

- [toonaga-] ‹ tofo-naga- ‹ *topo$_{adj}$ $_A$ nanka$_{adj}$ $_B$. 'very distant; eternal'.

- [tuda-] ‹ ?. Meaning unknown. Perhaps a metathesis of tutana- › *tun[a]ta.

- [tunena-] ‹ tune$_{2.5}$ (‹ ...) na$_{adj}$ $_B$. 'inconstant, unstable, evanescent, changeable'.

?B [tuyuke-] ‹ tuyu$_{2.5}$ (‹ *tudu) -ka-Ci-. 'dewy; tearful'. The Mkz entry ("B") is a poetic archaism.

- [ukasi-] (< ?). 'sly, cunning'. NS (T+ kun) ukasi[-si] LH-H.
- [umugasi-] (Nr) ?< *umag[uf]asi- (< *uma$_{adj\ B}$ -n- kupasi$_{adj\ B}$); ?< *omomuka-$_B$
   (< ...) -si-, for which the later (Hn) omokasi- would be a surviving
   intermediate form, less aberrant than the Nr version. 'delightful'.
?B [uragoisi-] < ura-gwof$^{iy}/_o$si-/-gwof(w)osi- < *ura$_{2.4}$ kwopo̲-Ci-si$_{adj\ B}$ (< ...).
   'loving, heart-smitten'.
?B [uramoto̲na-] < ura$_{2.4}$ moto̲na$_{adj\ B}$ (< ...). 'long-waiting; depressed'.
   ?B [ureta-] < *ure[y]ta- < *ura$_{2.4}$ ita$_{adj\ B}$. 'disliked, distressing, deplorable'.
- [utadanosi-] < utadanwosi- (K 41) = utadanusi- (S 33) < uta[ta]$_{3.1}$ -n-
   tanwosi$_{adj\ B}$ (< ...). 'utterly delightful'.
- [utusi-] < utu (< ?) -si-. 'immanent, real; true'. NS (T+ kun) utusi[-si] LLL,
   utusi-kyi HLHL (odd). Cf. ututu$_{adj-n}$ (?< utu-utu).
- [uyana-] < uya/wiya$_{2.2x,?2.1}$ (< ...) na$_{adj\ B}$. 'discourteous'.
- [waiwaisi-] < wa[k]iwa[k]i-si- < *bak[a-C]i$_A$ ⋯ -si-. 'clear(ly delineated),
   distinct'.
- [yutake-] < yuta-key- < *duta-ka$_{adj-n\ 3.7b}$ -Ci-. 'rich'.

Bibliography

AA Kenkyū-jo tsūshin [journal]

Aiso Teizō. 1962. Kiki-kayō zen-chūshaku. (Yūsei-dō)

Akinaga Kazue. 1957. "Akusento kara bunpō e: hinshi no benbetsu ni tsuite",
-----. 1960. "Yaeyama-hōgen ichini-onsetsu meishi no akusento no keikō", Kgg 121-5.
  Kokugogaku-kenkyū (16.8?=) 37:12-31.
-----. 1966. "Sanagi akusento no teiki suru mono", Kokubungaku-kenkyū 33:74-88.
-----. 1967. "Edo-akusento kara Tōkyō-akusento e", Kokugo-to-kokubungaku 44:131-46.
-----. 1968. "Akusento shūtoku hōsoku", Appendix to Kindaichi 1968.
-----. 1972, 1974. Kokin-waka-shū shōten-bon no kenkyū. 2 vols. (Waseda)
-----. 1977a. "Hatsuon no utsuri-kawari", Nihon-go no rekishi = Nihongo-kōza
  6:77-114. (Taishū-kan)
-----. 1977b. Tōkyō-akusento dai ichi-ji chōsa hōkoku. (Privately published;
  1957 ms, results of survey made in 1953-5.)
-----. 1977c. "MATSUBARA to YANAGIHARA: hagyō-tenko o chūshin ni",
  Kgg 111:62-77.

Aoki Haruo. 1974. "Reconstruction and reality: a case of Japanese vowels", Acta
  Linguistica Hafniensia 15:1:101-11.

Arisaka Hideyo. 1955. Jōdai-on'in kō. (Sansei-dō)

Asayama Nobuya. 1943. "Kokugo no kashira-onsetsu ni okeru dakuon ni tsuite",
  Kokugo-to-kokubungaku 20(:5-16-26=):422-32.

Ashworth, David. 1977. "Historical perspective on voicing and gerund in Japanese",
  Papers In Japanese Linguistics 5:27-40.

Brinkley, F., et al. 1896. An unabridged Japanese-English dictionary. (Sansei-dō)

Bussokuseki-no-uta. c.753. The clearest photographic reproduction is in the plates
  of Kizaki Aikichi 1972: Dai-Nihon kinseki-shi, vol. 6 (Rekishi-tosho-sha). The
  text is most accessible in Kariya Ekisai (ed. by Yamada Yoshio) 1968 reproduction
  of 1912: Kokyō ibun (Sensei-sha). Elaborately studied by Miller 1975.

Chamberlain, B.H. 1888. A handbook of colloquial Japanese.
-----. 1895. Essay in aid of a grammar and dictionary of the Luchuan language.

Clarke, Hugh D.B. 1973. The phonology of three Japanese dialects. University of
  Sydney dissertation.

Doi Shigetoshi. 1952. "Kokugo hōgen akusento no hikaku-kōsatsu (Tōkyō, Hata,
  Kōchi)", Kōchi-daigaku kyōikugaku-bu hōkoku 2:19-35.
-----. 1958. Tosa-kotoba. Kōchi (Kōchi shiritsu shimin tosho-kan)

Doi Tadao, ed. 1957. Nihon-go no rekishi. Revised edition. (Shibun-dō)

Endō Kunimoto. 1966. "Rendaku-go no yure", Kokugo-kokubun 35:5:68-77.
-----. 1969. "Gairai-go akusento no seikaku", Kōka-kiyō 7:68-84 (1969:11).
-----. 1971. "Gotō-on no seikaku", Kokugo-kokubun (40:7=)443:30-41.
-----. 1974. "Kyoshō-ten/Kyosei-ten to dakuon", Kokugo-kokubun (43:3=)475:35-48.
-----. 1977. "Dakuon genka-ishiki: gotō no sei-daku o koto ni suru nijū-go o
  taishō ni", Kokugo-kokubun (46:4=)512:222-34.

Folkman, E.A. 1953. Slovar´ yaponskikh imeniy i familiy. Moscow.

Fujii Nobuo. 1944. "Koji-ki ni okeru shisei no chūki ni tsuite",
  Kokugo-to-kokubungaku 21:2:23-32.

Fujiwara Yoichi. 1938. "Kansai sho-hōgen no akusento", Kokugo-kokubun 12:7:33-58,
  8:56-89.
-----. 1972. "Hōgen no gaku o mezashite", Hōgen kenkyū sōsho 1:3-195.

Fukuda Yoshisuke. 1965. Nara-jidai tōgoku-hōgen no kenkyū. (Kazama-shobō)

Genkai = Ōtsuki Fumihiko 1889-91 *(4-vol. dictionary)*

Haguenauer, Charles. 1956. Origines de la civilisation japonaise. Paris (Imprimerie Nationale).

Hamada Atsushi. 1945. "Sokuon enkaku kō", Kokugo-kokubun 14:10:1-15.

-----. 1950. "Kodai-kokugo ni okeru sonyū-teki shion", Jinbun-kenkyū 1:7:41-64.

-----. 1951. "Chōon", Jinbun-kenkyū 2:375:405, 489-504.

-----. 1952. "Hatsuon to dakuon to no sōkan-sei no mondai", Kokugo-kokubun (21:3:18-32=)212:198-212.

-----. 1960. "Rendaku to renjō: dōka no mondai", Kokugo-kokubun (29:10=)314:1-16.

-----. 1964. "Onbin: hatsu-onbin to u-onbin to no kōshō", Kokugo-kokubun (23:3:1-17 =) 235:127-43.

-----. 1970. Chōsen shiryō ni yoru Nihon-go kenkyū. (Iwanami-shoten)

-----. 1971. "Sei-daku", Kokugo-kokubun (40:11=)447:40-51.

-----. 1977. "Kokugo-shi no sho-mondai", Kokugo-kokubun (46:5=)513.578-96.

Haraguchi, Shosuke. 1977. The tone pattern of Japanese: an autosegmental theory of tonology. (Kaitaku-sha)

Harima-fudoki. c.716. (Cited from Zdb.)

Hateruma no hōgen. Ryūkyū-hōgen kinkyū chōsa 2, Okinawa-ken bunka-zai chōsa hōkoku-sho 3. 1975. (Okinawa-ken kyōiku-iinkai)

Hattori Shirō. 1928-30. "Mie-ken Kameyama-machi chihō no nionsetsu-meishi ni tsuite", Onsei-gakkai kaihō 11:11, 12:11, 14:6-7, 17/18:5.

-----. 1931-3. "Kokugo sho-hōgen no akusento gaikan I-VI": Hōgen 1:11-33, 170-80, 245-61; 2:77-88, 148-56; 3:406-19.

-----. 1932. "'Ryūkyū-go' to 'kokugo' to no on'in-hōsoku I-III", Hōgen 2:516-31, 580-603, 750-55.

-----. 1933. Akusento to hōgen. Kokugo-kagaku-kōza 7. (Meiji-shoin)

-----. 1937. "Genshi-Nihongo no nionsetsu-meishi no akusento", Hōgen 7:372-421.

-----. 1942. "Bumō-ki no kenkyū", Nihon-hōgen-gakkai hen 1942:125-59.

-----. 1951. "Genshi-Nihongo no akusento", Terakawa et al. 1951:45-65.

-----. 1960. "'Bunsetsu' to akusento", Gengo-gaku no hōhō 328-46.

-----. 1961. "Prosodeme, syllable structure, and laryngeal phonemes", ICU Summer Institute in Linguistics Bulletin 1. Reprinted in Nihon no Gengo-gaku 2:186-218 (Taishū-kan 1980).

-----. 1964. Ainu hōgen jiten. (Iwanami-shoten)

-----. 1968. "Nihon-go no Ryūkyū-hōgen ni tsuite", Bungaku 36:1: - . [Repr. Hokama 1972:46-64.]

-----. 1970. "Hōgen-kugaku-ron shūken-ron to kisogoi-tōkeigaku", Gengo no kagaku 2:1-12.

-----. 1972. "Akusento-so to wa nani? ... ", Gengo no Kagaku 4:1-61.

-----. 1973. "Japanese dialects", Current Trends in Linguistics 11:368-400.

-----. 1976a. "Ryūkyū-hōgen to hondo-hōgen", Okinawa no Reimei 7-55. (Okinawa Bunka-kyōkai)

-----. 1976b. "Jōdai-Nihongo no boin-taikei to boin-chōwa", [Gekkan-]Gengo 1976:2-13.

-----. 1977. "Ryūkyū-hōgen dōshi 'shūshi-kei' no tsūji-teki henka", Gengo-kenkyū 72:19-28.

-----. 1978. "Hachijō-jima hōgen ni tsuite", Kotoba no uchū 3:11.

-----. 1978-9. "Nihon-sōgo ni tsuite 1-22", [Gekkan-]Gengo 1978-9.

-----. 1981. "Shibata-kun no Nara-jidai Nihon-go hachi-boin onso setsu o baku-su", [Gekkan-]Gengo 10:2:85-9.

-----. 1983. "Hashimoto Shinkichi sensei no gakuon", Kgg 133:1-14.

Hayata Teruhiro. 1971. "Accent in Old Kyoto and some modern Japanese dialects",
  Gengo no Kagaku 4:139-80.
-----. 1977a. "Seisei-akusento-ron", Iwanami Kōza Nihon-go 5:323-60.
-----. 1977b. "Nihon-go no on'in to rizumu", Dentō-to-gendai 45:41-9.
-----. 1978. "Go-seichō hōgen: Sanagi-jima to Manabe-shima no akusento",
  Kyūshū-daigaku Bungaku-bu Bungaku-kenkyū 75:29-38.
-----. 1985. Hakata-hōgen no akusento keitai-ron. (Fukuoka: Kyūshū-daigaku)
Hepburn, J.C. 1867; (rev. ed.) 1886. A Japanese and English dictionary. London.
Hinomizu, Ken. 1979. "Compounding and voicing in Japanese", Sophia Linguistica
  5:104-10.
Hirayama Teruo. 1951a. Kyūshū-hōgen onchō no kenkyū. (Gakkai-no-shishin - sha)
-----. 1951b. "Hokkaidō-hōgen no onchō", Onsei-gakkai kaihō 78:10-5.
-----. 1953. "Nihon hōgen-on no kenkyū to onchō-shiryō", [Tōkyō-]Toritsu-daigaku
  Jinbun-gakuhō 9:93-122.
-----. 1955. "Gengo-tō no onchō-taikei seiritsu to sono kaishaku",
  Kokugo-to-kokubungaku 32:12:44-57.
-----. 1957a. Nihon-go onchō no kenkyū. (Meiji-shoin)
-----. 1957b. "Shikoku-hōgen no akusento-taikei to sono keifu", Onsei no kenkyū
  8:239-62.
-----. 1960. Zenkoku akusento jiten. (Tōkyō-dō)
-----. 1964. Ryūkyū Yonaguni-hōgen no kenkyū. (Tōkyō-dō)
-----. 1965. Izu-shotō hōgen no kenkyū. (Meiji-shoin)
-----. 1966. Ryūkyū-hōgen no sōgō-teki kenkyū. (Meiji-shoin)
-----. 1967. Ryūkyū Sakishima-hōgen no sōgō-teki kenkyū. (Meiji-shoin)
-----. 1968a. Satsunan-shotō no sōgō-teki kenkyū. (Meiji-shoin)
-----. 1968b. Nihon no hōgen. (Kōdan-sha)
-----. 1971. "Nihon-go akusento no shōrai", Kindaichi hakase beiju kinen ronshū
  435-51.
-----. 1979. "Gengo-tō Nara-ken Totsukawa hōgen no seikaku", Gengo-kenkyū 76:29-73.
  76:29-73.
Hiroto Atushi. 1961. "Chūgoku-chihō no akusento", Onsei no kenkyū 9:155-68.
Hiroto Atsushi and Ōhara Takamichi. 1953. San'in-chihō no akusento. Matsue (Hōkō-sha)
Hiroto Atsushi and Yatomi Kumaichirō. 1963. Shimane-ken hōgen jiten. Matsue
  (Shimane-ken hōgen gakkai)
Hn = Heian period: 784-1185.
Hōgen-gaku gaisetsu: *see* Kokugo-gakkai 1962; 1968.
Hōgen-gaku kōza (= Tōjō 1961) 2, 3
Hōgen kenkyū sōsho (Fujiwara Yoichi, ed.) 1 (1972), 3 (1974), 4 (1977).
  (Miyai-shoten)
Hōgen to hyōjun-go (Ōishi Hatsutarō and Uemura Yukio, ed.) 1975. (Chikuma-shobō)
Hōjō Misao. 1951. Zenkoku hōgen jiten. (Tōkyō-dō)
-----. 1955. Bunrui hōgen jiten. (Tōkyō-dō)
Hōjō Tadao. 1951. "Jōdai tokushu-kanazukai ni okeru 'o'-retsu no sho-mondai",
  Onsei no kenkyū 7:75-95.
-----. 1966. Jōdai tōgoku-hōgen no kenkyū. (Nippon gakujutsu-shinkōkai)
Hokama Shuzen. 1972. Okinawa bunka ronsō 5: gengo-hen. (Heibon-sha)
Honzō-wamyō. 901-23. (Cited from Zdb.)
?Hoshika ?Shūichi/?Sōichi. 1932. "Dakuten no seiritsu ni tsuite",
  Kokugo-to-kokubungaku 9(:12:87-9=):2132-43.
Igarashi Jin'ichi. 1969. Jōdai-kanazukai jiten. (Shōgak[u]-kan)
Iha Fuyū. 1931. "Kaitō-shokoku-ki fusai no ko-ryūkyū-go ni tsuite",
  Kokugo-to-kokubungaku 8:3:233-42. Reprinted in Hokama 1972:388-95.

Iitomi Yokiichi 1959. "Hachijō-jima hōgen no gohō", Kotoba no kenkyū = KKK 1:215-32

Ikeda Kaname. 1942. "Kinki-akusento keishiki-kan no mondai: 'zansō-kan' [gradual-level view] ni tsuite" = Nihon-hōgen-gakkai hen 1942:196-228.

Ikuta Sanae. 1951. "Kinki akusento-ken henkyō-chiku no akusento ni tsuite" = Terakawa et al. 1951:255-346.

Ikegami Teizō. 1949. "Gochū no hagyō-on", Kokugo-kokubun 18:1:45-57.

Inokuchi Yūichi and Horii Reiichi. 1972. Kyōto-go isō no chōsa kenkyū. Tōkyō-dō)

Inoue Fumio. 1968. "Tōhoku-hōgen no shion-taikei", Gengo-kenkyū 52:80-98.

Inukai Takashi. 1978. "Jōdai tokushu-kanazukai no hōkai-katei to Koji-ki no
o, si, ho no kana", Kokugo-kokubun 529:21-38.

Ishizuka Harumichi. 1977. "Maeda-bon Nihon-Shoki Insei-ki ten (honbun-henpo)",
Hokkaidō-daigaku bungaku-bu kiyō 26:1:69-136.

-----. 1978. "Maeda-bon Nihon-Shoki Insei-ki no shōten", Kokugo-gakkai Shōwa 53-nen shunki taikai yōshi 52-5.

Itoi Kan'ichi. 1984. "Ōita-ken nai 2-titen no hōgen ni okeru zagyoo-on,
dagyoo-on", Gendai hōgen-gaku no kadai 2:101-22.

Iwanami Kōza Nihon-go 5: On'in (1977); 11: Hōgen (1977).

Jinrui-kagaku [journal]

JP = Japanese-Portuguese dictionary: Vocabulario da lingoa de Iapam. 1603, 1604.

Jugaku Akiko. 1979. Kurashi no Kyō-kotoba. (Asahi-sensho 140)

Kindaichi Haruhiko 1958.

Koji-ki songs, cited by number according to the order in Philippi. For most of
the songs the numbers in Ōno differ by one digit.

Kamei Takashi. 1960. "Zaitō-ki no 'hongō ha-zi on' ni kan-suru kaishaku",
Kgg 40:126-31.

-----. 1969. "Kōgo no kan'yō no chōshō ni tsuki, sono hakkutsu to hyōka",
Kgg 76:1-16.

-----. 1975. "How did the sparrow twitter in ancient Japanese?",
Hitotsubashi Journal of Arts and Sciences 16:1:1-10.

Kawabata Yoshiaki. 1966. "Meishi no katsuyō", Kokugo-kokubun (35:5=)381.133-52.

Kawakami Shin. 1973. "Dōshi kara no tensei-meishi no akusento", Imaizumi hakase
koki-kinen kokugo-gaku ronsō 55-70. (Ōfū-sha)

Kawamoto Takao. 1976. "Nihon-go no dōshi katsuyō taikei no seiritsu to kigen",
[Kikan] Jinrui-gaku 7:1:105-27.

Kenkyusha = Kenkyusha's new Japanese-English dictionary. Fourth edition, 1954.

Kgg = Kokugo-gaku (journal)

KggD = Kokugo-gakkai 1980: Kokugo-gaku dai-jiten.

KggJ = Kokugo-gakkai 1955: Kokugo-gaku jiten.

Kgkb = Kokugo-kokubun [journal]

Khg = Kyūshū-hōgen-gakkai 1969.

Kibe Nobuko. 1983. "Fuzoku-go no akusento ni tsuite", Kgg 134:23-42.

Kida Akiyoshi. 1978. "Dakuon-shi tekiyō", (Sakakura Atsuyoshi hakase kanreki kinen)
Ronshū: Nihon-Bungaku Nihon-go 1:285-306.

-----. 1979. "Rendaku to akusento", Kokugo-kokubungaku (48:3=)535:51-64.

Kikuta Kirō. 1966. "Seidaku-henka no ichi-yōin", [Tōhoku-daigaku] Kokugogaku-kenkyū 6:41-9.

Kim Chin-Wu (Cinwu) and Toh Soo-Hee (To Swuhuy). 1980. "Rule reordering in Middle
Korean phonology", Language Research (Ehak yenkwu) 16:75-86.

Kim Wanjin. 1957. "Chep-hay sin-e ey se uy Ilpon-e censa ey tay-ha.ye", Sewul tay-hak.kyo Mun.li-tay hakpo V-2. Repr.1971, Kwuk.e um.wun cheykyey uy yenkwu,
Sekang tay-hak.kyo inmun yenkwu cenkan 4:199-215, English summary 238-40.

Kindaichi Haruhiko. 1942. "Bumō-ki no kenkyū, zokuchō" = Nihon-hōgen-gakkai hen 1942:162-93.

-----. 1943(-4?). "Shizuoka, Yamanashi, Nagano-ken - ka no akusento", Onsei-gakkai kaihō 72:3:9-11, 10; 74:5:11-5, 19.

-----. 1944. "Ruiju - Myōgi-shō ni hodokosareta seifū ni tsuite", [Hashimoto hakase kanreki kinen] Kokugo-gaku ronshū 182-217. (Iwanami-shoten)

-----. 1947. "Konkōmyōsaishōō-kyō ongi ni mieru isshu no Man'yō - kana-zukai ni tsuite", Kokugo-to-kokubungaku 24:11:33-48.

-----. 1951a. "Nihon-go no akusento", Kōza Gendai Kokugo-gaku 2:67-94.

-----. 1951b. "Nihon shishō/shisei kogi" = Terakawa et al. 1951:629-708.

-----. 1953. "Kokugo akusento-shi no kenkyū ga nan ni yaku-datu ka", [Kindaichi hakase kanreki kinen] Gengo-minzoku-ronsō 329-54. (Sansei-dō)

-----. 1954. "Tōzai ryō-akusento no chigai ga dekiru made", Bungaku 22:8:63-84. Reprinted with additional notes in Kindaichi 1975:49-81. English transl. Bailey, Papers of the CIC Far Eastern Language Institute 1963 (Ann Arbor 1964) 89-112.

-----. 1955a. "Kodai-akusento kara kindai-akusento e", Kgg 22:15-29.

-----. 1955b. "Kinki chūō-bu no akusento oboegaki", Tōjō Misao sensei koki-shukuga ronbun-shū 323-45.

-----. 1958a. Meikai Nihon-go akusento jiten. (Sansei-dō)

-----. 1958b. "Tōkyō-akusento no tokuchō wa nani ka", Gengo-seikatsu 1958:8:58-68.

-----. 1959. "Heikyoku no onsei", Onsei-gakkai kaihō 99:12-16, 19; 101:11-13, 10.

-----. 1960a. "Hyōshō-karu no ten ni tsuite", Kgg 41:115-21.

-----. 1960b. "Kokugo no akusento no jidai-teki hensen", Kokugo-to-kokubungaku 37:10:28-46.

-----. 1963. [English version of 1954a]

-----. 1964a. Shiza-Kōshiki no kenkyū. (Sansei-dō)

-----. 1964b. "Tōzai-akusento hassei no mondai-ten", Kgg 58:10-22.

-----. 1967a. "Tōgoku-hōgen no rekishi o kangaeru", Kgg 69:40-50.

-----. 1967b; 1972. Nihon-go on'in no kenkyū. (Tōkyō-dō)

-----. 1971. "On'in-henka kara akusento-henka e", Kindaichi hakase beiju kinen ronshū 956-29 [sic].

-----. 1972. Nihon-go on'in no kenkyū. (Tōkyō-dō)

-----. 1973. "Kyoshō-ten/Kyosei-ten de hajimaru goi ni tsuite", Kgg 93:74-80.

-----. 1974. Kokugo-akusento no shi-teki kenkyū. (Hanawa-shobō)

-----. 1975. Nihon no hōgen: akusento no hensen to sono jissō. (Kyōiku-shuppan)

-----. 1976. "Rendaku no kai", Sophia Linguistica 2:1-22.

-----. 1977a. "Akusento no bunpu to hensen", Iwanami Kōza Nihon-go 11: Hōgen.

-----. 1977b. Nihon-go hōgen no kenkyū . (Tōkyō-dō)

-----. 1981. [revised ed. of 1968a]

-----. 1982. Review of Okumura 1981. Kgg 131:82-9.

-----. 1984a. "Hōkō-kan ni yoru Heian-chō akusento [The pitch accent of the Heian era]", Sophia Linguistica 17:24-36.

-----. 1984b. "Nihon-go sogo no akusento to Ryūkyū-go", Sophia Linguistica 17:3-25.

----- and Ikeda Yasaburō. 1978. Gakken Kokugo dai-jiten. (Gakushū-kenkyū-sya)

Kindaichi Kyōsuke. 1935. [Zōho] Kokugo on'in-ron. (Tōkō-shoin)

-----. 1952. Jikai. (Sansei-dō)

Kinka-fū. 891. (Cited from Zdb, Aiso.)

Kishida Takeo. 1976. "Boin /-a/ no shōmetsu o tomonau on'in-tenkan ni tsuite", [Saeki Umetomo hakase kiju kinen] Kokugo-gaku ronshū 25-48. (Hyōgen-sha)

Kitahara Yasuo. 1967. "Keiyō-shi no u-onbin - sono bunpu kara seiritu no katei saguru", Kgkb (36:8=)396.19-36.

KKK = Kokuritsu Kokugo Kenkyūjo. 1953. Hōkoku 5: Chiiki-shakai no gengo-seikatsu.
Km = Kamakura period: 1185-1340.
Kobayashi Akemi. 1981. "Ennin no kijutsu suru Sansukuritto onsetsu 'ca' no onka:
    kyū-seiki NIhon-go Sui-on no kokoromi", Ōsaka Gaikokugo-Daigaku Gakuhō 52:63-80.
Kobayashi, Chieko Oyama. 1975. Japanese dialects: phonology and reconstruction
    of the proto-accentual system. Cornell Univ. dissertation. (UM 75-24,207)
Kōjien = Shinmura 1955
Koji-ki. 712. See Aiso; Maruyama; Nihon koten bungaku zenshū; Tsuchihashi.
Kokugo-gakkai. 1955. Kokugo-gaku jiten. (Tōkyō-sō) = KggJ
-----. 1962; 1968. Hōgen-gaku gaisetsu. (Musashino-shoin)
-----. 1980. Kokugo-gaku dai-jiten. (Tōkyō-dō) = KggD
Kokugo-kokubun [journal]
Kokuritsu Kokugo Kenkyū-jo. 1963. Okinawa-go jiten. (Ōkura-shō)
Komatsu Hideo. 1957. "Wa-kun ni hodokosareta hyōshyō-kei no shōten", Kgg 29:17-36.
-----. 1959-60. "Heian-makki Kinai-hōgen no onchō-taikei 1, 2", Kgg 39:49-74,
    40:55-81. (= Komatsu 1971:562-646).
-----. 1971. Nihon seichō-shi ronkō. (Kazama-shoin)
-----. 1973. Kokugoshi-gaku kiso-ron. (Kasama sōsho 35)
-----. 1974. "Jōtō-gata meishi sonzai no riron-teki konkyo", Bungaku 42:644-51.
-----. 1975. "Onbin kinō kō", Kgg 101:1-16.
-----. 1977a. "Akusento no hensen", Iwanami Kōza Nihon-go 5:362-410.
-----. 1977b. "Jōtō-gata meishi sonpi-ron no kiketsu", Kgg 109.16-25.
-----. 1981. Nihon-go no on'in. Nihon-go no sekai 7. (Chūō-Kōron-sha)
Kōtai-jingū gishiki-chō. 804. (Cited from Zdb.)
Kōza Kokugo-shi: 1 (Nihongo-shi sōron, Matsumura Akira, ed.) 1977; 2 (On'in-shi
    moji-shi, Nakata Norio, ed.) 1972. (Taishū-kan)
Kōza Nihon-go no goi 11 (Goshi 3).
Kudō Rikio. 1978. Futatsu no akusento: Nagano-ken no kotoba to kyōtsū-go. Nagano
    (Ginka-shobō)
-----. 1973. "Jōdai keiyō-shi gokan no yōhō ni tsuite", Kokugo-kokubun
    (42:7=)467:1-14.
Kuno Makoto. 1984. "Kyōto-shi hōgen no on'in", Gendai hōgen-gaku no kadai 2:71-99.
Kuranaka Susumu. 1975. Jōdai Nihon-go on'in no ichi-kenkyū. Kōbe Gakujutsu sōsho 4.
Kurashima Sesshō. 1983. "Kasiradaka-kei akusento o megutte", Kgg 133:109-11.
Kusakabe Fumio. 1968. "Okinawa hokubu hōgen akusento chōsa goi ni tsuite",
    Gengo-kenkyū 52:33-57.
Kyūshū-hōgen-gakkai. 1969. Kyūshū-hōgen no kiso-teki kenkyū. (Kazama-shobō)
Lange, R.A. 1973. The phonology of eighth-century Japanese. (Sophia University)
Language [journal of the Linguistic Society of America]
Lee Ki-Moon ['Yi Kimun]. 1959. "On the breaking of *i in Korean", Aseya Yenkwu
    2:2:131-8.
-----. 1980. "Ewen swucey", Kim Hyengkyu paksa songswu kinyem ¹nonchong 431-9.
Lessing, Ferdinand D., et al. 1960. Mongolian-English Dictionary. Berkeley
    (University of California Press).
Lewin, Bruno. 1959; 2d ed. 1975. Abriss der Japanischen grammatik. Wiesbaden.
Lyman, Benjamin Smith. 1894. "Change from surd to sonant in Japanese compounds",
    Oriental Club of Philadelphia.
Man'yō-shū poems cited by number from Tsuru and Moriyama 1975.
Mabuchi Kazuo. 1957. "Koji-ki no SI O HO no kana", Kgg 31:61-90.
-----. 1959. "Jōdai, chūko ni okeru sa-gyō tōon [= kasira-on] no onka",
    Kokugo-to-kokubungaku 36:1:60-7.
-----. 1971. Jōdai no kotoba. (Shibun-dō)

-----. 1973. "Man'yō-shū no on'in", Man'yōshū-kōza 3:161-86.

-----. 1976. "Kokugo no 'boin'", [Saeki Umetomo hakase kiju kinen] Kokugo-gaku ronshū 1-23. (Hyōgen-sha)

Maeda Isamu. 1949. Ōsaka-ben no kenkyū. (Ōsaka: Asahi-shinbun-sha)

-----. 1953. "Ōsaka-akusento no fukugō-hōsoku: yon-onsetsu mukatsuyō-go no baai", Kinki-hōgen 19:9-17.

Maeda Tomiyoshi. 1966. "Kodai ni okeru kokugo-akusento-kan", [Tōhoku-daigaku] Kokugogaku-kenkyū 6:50-61.

Maeda Tomiyoshi. 1967. "Kinsei ni okeru kokugo-akusento kan", Kgg 71:1-12.

Makimura Shiyō. 1956. Ōsaka hōgen jiten. Ōsaka (Sugimoto-shoten)

Martin, Samuel E. 1952. Morphophonemics of standard colloquial Japanese. Baltimore (Linguistic Society of America).

-----. 1967. "On the accent of Japanese adjectives", Language 43:246-77.

-----. 1968. "On the forms of Japanese adjectives", Glossa 2:46-69.

-----. 1970a. "Junctural cues to ellipsis in Japanese", Studies in General and Oriental Linguistics (Jakobson and Kawamoto, ed.) 429-46. Tōkyō (TEC Co.).

-----. 1970b. "Shodon: a dialect of the northern Ryukyus", Journal of the American Oriental Society 90:97-139.

-----. 1975a. "Problems in establishing the prehistorical relationships of Korean and Japanese", Proceedings of the International Symposium Commemorating the 30th Anniversary of Korean Liberation 149-72. Seoul (National Academy of Sciences).

-----. 1975b. A Reference Grammar of Japanese. New Haven (Yale University Press).

-----. 1978. "On comparing the accentual patterns of Korean and Japanese", Nwun-moy He Wung paksa hwankap kinyem nonmun-cip 563-79. Seoul (SNU Press).

-----. 1981. "The nature of accentual distinctions in earlier Japanese", Proceedings from the first Nordic Symposium in Japanology 84-105 (Occasional Papers No. 3, East Asian Institute, University of Oslo).

Maruyama Jirō. 1965. Hyōchū kundoku Koji-ki. (Yoshikawa Kōbun-kan)

Mase Yoshio. 1977 . "Tōzai ryō-hōgen no tairitsu", Iwanami Kōza Nihon-go 11:235-89.

Mathias, G.B. 1973. "On the modification of certain proto Korean-Japanese reconstructions", Papers In Japanese Linguistics 2:31-47.

-----. 1977. "Statistical skewing in the phonological canon of Old Japanese", paper presented at the Symposium on Historical Relationships of Japanese and Korean, 1977 Linguistic Institute, Honolulu.

Matsumoto Katsumi. 1974. "Kodai Nihon-go boin-soshiki kō: nai-teki saiken no kokoromi", Kanazawa-daigaku hō-bungakubu ronshū: bungaku-hen 22:83-152.

-----. 1976. "Man'yō-gana no o-retsu kō-otsu ni tsuite", [Gekkan-]Gengo 5:11:72-80.

-----. 1977. "Nihon-go no boin-soshiki", [Gekkan-]Gengo 6:6:15-25.

-----. 1984. "Gengo-shi no saiken to gengo-huhen", Gengo-kenkyū 86:5-32.

Matsumoto Takashi. 1965. "Magyō-on bagyō-on kōtai-genshō no keikō", Kokugogaku-kenkyū 5:8:52-65.

McCawley, James D. 1968. The phonological component of a grammar of Japanese. (Mouton)

-----. 1977. "Accent in Japanese", Studies in Stress and Accent (Larry Hyman, ed.), Southern California Occasional Papers in Linguistics 4:261-301.

Mg = (Ruiju -) Myōgi-shō. 1081 (and later). Cited mostly from Mochizuki 1974.

Miller, Roy Andrew. 1967. The Japanese Language. Chicago (Univ. of Chicago Press).

-----. 1971. Japanese and the other Altaic languages. Chicago (U. of Chicago Press).

-----. 1975. 'The Footprints of the Buddha': An eighth-century Old Japanese poetic sequence. New Haven (American Oriental Society).

-----. 1979. "Some Old Paekche fragments", Journal of Korean Studies 1:3-69.

-----. 1980. Origins of the Japanese language. (University of Washington Press)

Minami Fujio. 1956. "Myōgi-shō jidai no Kyōto-hōgen ni okeru ni-ji yodan-katsuyō dōshi no akusento", Kgg 27:69-80.

-----. 1975. "Tōkai no hōgen", Hōgen to Hyōjun-go (Ōishi and Uemura, eds).

Miyaji Yutaka. 1966. "Dōon-go no akusento", Kokugo-kokubun 35:6:454-63.

Miyajima Hiroshi. 1944. Heian-jidai chūki izen no ha-gyō shion", Kokugo-kokubun 40:2:17-42.

Miyajima Tatsuo. 1961. "Boin no musei-ka wa itsu kara atta ka", Kgg 45:38-48.

Miyara Tōsō. 1930. Yaeyama goi. (Tōyō-bunko)

-----. 1954. Fūdo to kotoba. (Iwasaki-shoten)

Mka = Meikai Nihon-go akusento jiten (= Kindaichi 1958).

Mkz = Shin Meikai kokugo jiten. (Sansei-dō 1972)

Mochizuki Ikuko [mistakenly called "Yūko" on back cover of Kgg 93]: undated references are to 1974a.

-----. 1971. "Gogi to gochō to gogen to no kankei: kyosei/kyoshō no taigen to sono hasei-go ni okeru", Tokiwa Joshi-tanki-daigaku kiyo 4:17-30.

-----. 1972. "Dai ichi-onsetsu no seichō-itchi no hōsoku ni tai-suru hitotsu no utagai: gokan kyoshō no keiyō-shi no baai o chūshin ni", Kgg 90:18-9.

-----. 1973. "Jōshō-chō ichi-onsetsu no joshi no heichō-ka: joshi *ni* no gochō no sai-kentō", Tokiwa Joshi-tanki-daigaku kiyō 6:31-58.

-----. 1974a. Ruiju - Myōgi-shō yonshu-shōten tsuki wakun shūsei. (Kasama-shoin)

-----. 1974b. "Jōshō-chō ichi-onsetsu no joshi no heichō-ka — joshi *ni* no gochō ni sai-kentō". Tokiwa joshi tan[ki]-dai[gaku] kiyō 6:   -   .

-----. 1975. "Shōten no seichō-nintei no hōhō: Ruiju - Myōgi-shō no dai ni-rui dōshi shūshi-kei gomatsu no shōten o chūshin ni", Kgg 102:31-49.

Morishige Satoshi. 1975. "Jōdai tokushu-kanazukai to wa nani ka", Man'yō 89:1-47.

-----. 1984. Jōdai tokushu-kana ongi. (Izumi-shoin)

Morita Takeshi. 1977. "Nippo-jisho no mieru goon renketsu jō no ichi-keikō", Kgg 108:20-32.

Mr = Muromachi period: 1336-1600.

Murayama Shichirō. 1954. "Kodai-Nihongo no ni-san no on'in-genshō ni tsuite", Kgg 17:79-90.

-----. 1978. Nihon-go keitō no tankyū. (Taishū-kan)

Muroyama Toshiaki. 1969. "Akusento no yama no ikō suru mono: Tottori-ken Kurayoshi-shi hōgen no baai", Kgkb (38:4=)417:44-56.

Mushiaki Kichijirō. 1954. Okayama-ken no akusento (sono ichi). Okayama (San'yō tosho shuppan KK)

Nakagawa Yoshio. 1966. "Rendaku, rensei (kashō) no keifu", Kokugo-kokubun 35(:6):302-14.

-----. 1978. "Rendaku kansei", Kokugo-kokubun (47:3=)523:34-56, 524:41-58.

Nakai Yukihiro. 1984. "Manabe-shiki akusento ni tsuite", Gengo-kenkyū 86:69-105.

Nakamatsu Takeo. 1983. Okinawa no hōgen. (Ōfū-sha)

Nakamoto Masachie. 1976. Ryūkyū-hōgen on'in no kenkyū. (Hōsei-daigaku shuppan)

-----. 1983. Ryūkyū goi shi no kenkyū. (San'ichi-shobō)

Nakasone Seizen. 1983. Okinawa Nakijin-hōgen jiten. (Kadokawa-shoten)

Nakata Norio. 1983. Kogo dai-jiten. (Shōgak[u]-kan)

NHK = Nippon-hōsō-kyōkai. 1966. Nihon-go hatsuon akusento jiten.

-----. 1967-72. Zenkoku hōgen shiryō. 11 vols.

Nihon Bungaku Ronkyū [journal]

Nihon-hōgen-gakkai hen. 1942. Nihon-go no akusento. (Chūō-kōron)

Nihon koten bungaku zenshū 1: Koji-ki, Jōdai-kayō. Edited by Ogihara Asao and Kōnosu Hayao. 1973. (Shōgak[u]-kan)

Nihon-Shoki. 720. (Cited from Ōno Susumu 1953. Cf. Aiso, Tsuchihashi.)

Nishimiya Kazutami. 1970. Nihon jōdai no bunshō to hyōki. (Kazama-shobō)
NKD = Nihon-kokugo-daijiten. 20 vols. 1972-6. (Shōgak[u]-kan)
Nr = Nara period: 710-841.
NS = Nihon-Shoki songs, cited by number from Ōno 1953..
Numoto Katsuaki. 1973. "Kan-on no rendaku", Kokugo-kokubun (42:12=)472:26-43.
-----. 1976. "Go-on no seichō-taikei ni tsuite", Kgg 107:1-15.
-----. 1979. "Heian-jidai ni okeru nichijō-kango no akusento", Kokugo-kokubun
   (48:6=)538:25-40.
Ogawa Takeo. 1942. "Kinki-akusento ni okeru jōge (otsu) gata seishitsu" =
   Nihon-hōgen-gakkai hen 1942:229-56.
Ogura Shinpei. 1910. "Lyman-si no rendaku-ron", Kokugakuin-zasshi 16:695-708, 863-77.
-----. 1920. "Kokugo no rendaku-on", Kokugo Chōsen-go no tame 270-95.
   (Keijō = Seoul) Utsuboya-shoten. Repr. 1974 Ogura Shinpei chosaku-shū 4:280-305.
Ōhara ?Hidetsugu. 1937. "Akusento tsuki hōgen-bunrei no jakkan", Hōgen 7:53-80,
   156-79. [Kinki and Chūgoku dialects]
Ōhara Takamichi. 1932-3. "Kamigata-kotoba no akusento", Kokugo-kyōiku 17:6:75-9.
-----. 1942. "Ruiju - Myōgi-shō no akusento to sho-hōgen akusento to no taiō-kankei
   (shu to shite san-onsetsu meishi ni tsuite)" = Nihon-hōgen-gakkai hen 1942:50-122.
-----. 1951a. "Kinki-akusento ni okeru jōge-gata meishi no kō-rui otsu-rui no
   betsu no hassei ni kan-suru ichi-kōsatsu" = Terakawa et al. 1951:415-52.
-----. 1951b. "Koji-ki ni chūki sareta akusento ni tsuite no shiken 1, 2",
   Onsei-gakkai kaihō 77:10-15, 10; 78:1-4, 15.
Okada ?Shōko (?Hisako/?Naoko). 1956. "Nihon-shoki no akusento to Kokin-Kunten-shō
   no akusento", Joshidai-bungaku 8:51-69; 9:1-56.
Okinawa-go jiten [Shimabukuro Seibin, Higa Shunchō]. KKK Shiryō-shū 5. 1963.
Okuda Kunio. 1975. Accentual systems in the Japanese dialects: a generative
   approach. (Bunka Hyoron Publishing Co.)
Okumura Mitsuo. 1952. "Jion no rendaku ni tsuite", Kokugo-kokubun (21:5:9-22=)
   214:327-40.
-----. 1955. "Tōzai akusento bunri no jiki", Kokugo-kokubun (24:12:34-44=)
   256:784-94.
-----. 1957. "Go-on no seichō-taikei", Kunten-go to kunten-shiryō 8:1-11 = 308-18.
-----. 1958. "On'in to akusento: akusento-kenkyū no igi", Kokugo-kokubun (27:9:1-
   16=) 289.507-22.
-----. 1961a. "Kango no akusento", Kokugo-kokubun (30:1=) 317:1-16.
-----. 1961b. "Go-on seichō no ichi-seikaku", Kunten-go to kunten-shiryō 18:17-32
   (= 88-102).
-----. 1962. "Iwayuru Kan Go-on no seichō ni tsuite", Kokugo-kokubun (31:1=)329:1-16.
-----. 1963. "Kango no akusento — akusento kara goi-ron e", Kgg 55:36-53.
-----. 1964. "Kango akusento no ichi-seikaku", Kokugo-kokubun (33:2=)354:48-68.
-----. 1966a. "Kango akusento shōkō — Sankan-bon Iroha-jirui-shō o chūshin
   to shite", Kunten-go to kunten-shiryō 32:102-17.
-----. 1966b. "Ji no keitai-ron - teki seikaku", Kokugo-kokubun 25(:9):539-43.
-----. 1968. "Sa-gyō i-onbin no shōchō", Kokugo-kokubun (37:1=)401:34-48.
-----. 1969. "Kokugo-shi to hōgen kenkyū", [Kokubungaku] Kaishaku to kanshō
   34:8:24-45.
-----. 1972. "Kodai no on'in: 7. Akusento no shi-teki kōsatsu", Kōza Kokugo-shi
   2:139-74 (Nakata Norio, ed.). (Taishū-kan)
-----. 1974. "Sho-hōgen akusento bunpa no jiki : kango no akusento no kenkyū",
   Hōgen kenkyū sōsho 3:1-38.
-----. 1975a. "Heikyoku-fuhon to fuzoku-go no akusento", [Kyūshū-daigaku] Gobun-
   kenkyū 39/40:88-101.

-----. 1975b. "Heikyoku-fuhon ni han'ei shita dōshi no akusento", Bungaku-kenkyū 72:735-67.

-----. 1975c. "Kinki-hōgen", Shin Nihongo-kōza 3:147-77.

-----. 1976a. "Kokugogaku-shiryō to shite mita Heikyoku-fuhon: fuki to akusento to no sōkan-sei o chūshin ni", Kokugo-kokubun 46:210-21.

-----. 1976b. "Heikyoku-fuhon to katsuyō-go no akusento: zyodō-shi o chūshin ni", [Ōtsubo Heiji kyōju taikan kinen] Kokugo-shi ronkō 335-61. (Hyōgen-sha)

-----. 1976c. Gifu-ken hōgen no kenkyū. (Taishū-shobō)

-----. 1981. Heikyoku-fuhon no kenkyū. (Ōfū-sha)

Omodaka Hisataka et al. (Asami Tetsu, Ikegami Teizō, Ide Itaru, Itō Hiroshi, Kawabata Yoshiaki, Kinoshita Masatoshi, Kojima Noriyuki, Sakakura Atsuyoshi, Satake Akihiro, Nishimiya Kazutami, and Hashimoto Shirō). 1967. Jidai-betsu kokugo dai-jiten: jōdai-hen. (Sansei-dō)

O'Neill, P.G. Japanese names. (Weatherhill)

Ōno = Ōno Susumu et al. 1974.

Ōno Susumu. 1950. "Kanazukai no kigen ni tsuite", Kokugo-to-kokubungaku 27:12:1-20.

-----. 1953. Jōdai kanazukai no kenkyū. (Iwanami-shoten)

-----. 1977. "On'in no hensen (1)", Iwanami Kōza Nihon-go 5:148-219.

-----. 1978. Nihon-go no bunpō o kangaeru, 175-212: "Dōshi katsuyō-kei no kigen". (Iwanami-shoten)

Ōno Susumu et al. (Satake Akihiro, Maeda Kingorō). 1974. Iwanami Kogo-jiten (Iwanami-shoten)

Ōno Tōru: unspecified references are to 1962.

Ōno Tōru. 1957. Nihon-go no sakugen/sogen-teki kenkyū.

-----. 1962. Man'yō-gana no kenkyū. (Meiji-shoin)

-----. 1978. Zoku Man'yō-gana no kenkyū. (Meiji-shoin)

Ōshima Ichirō et al. 1980. Hachijō-jima hōgen no kenkyū. (Toritsu-daigaku Kokugo-gaku Kenkyūshitsu)

Otsu Yukio. 1980. "Some aspects of rendaku in Japanese and related phenomena", Theoretical Issues in Japanese Linguistics = MIT Working Papers in Linguistics Cf. Vance 1980b.

Ōtsuki Fumihiko. 1889-91. Genkai *(4-vol. dictionary)*.

-----. 1959. Shin-Genkai. (Nihon-shoin)

Philippi, Donald. 1968. Koji-ki, translated with an introduction and notes. (University of Tokyo Press)

Ramsey, Samuel Robert. 1978. "The old Kyoto dialect and the historical development of Japanese accent", Harvard Journal of Asiatic Studies 39:1:57-75.

-----. 1982. "Language change in Japan", Journal of Japanese Studies 8:99-131.

Ramstedt, G.J. 1935. Kalmückisches Wörterbuch. (Helsinki: Suomalais-Ugirlainen Seura

RGJ = Martin 1975b.

Rodriguez, Ioão. 1604-8. Arte da lingoa de Iapam. Nagasaki.

Ryō-no-shūge. 718. (Cited from Zdb.)

Ryūkyū-hōgen [journal (Ryū-dai Ryūkyū-hōgen kenkyū kurabu)]

SA = Shūkan-Asahi

Sakai Kiyonari. 1971. "Akusento-keishiki to onsetsu-keishiki to no sōkan-sei", Onsei-gakkai kaihō 137:8-10.

Sakakura Atsuyoshi, ed. 1976. Kokugo-gaku gaisetsu. (Yūsei-dō)

Sakamoto Kiyoe. 1983. "Chikamatsu jōruri fuhon ni han'ei shita 17-seiki-matsu Ōsaka akusento", Kgg 133:25-36.

Sakuma Ei. 1972. Nihonjin no sei. (Rokugei-shobō)

Sakuma Kanae. 1929. Nihon-onsei-gaku. [53: "Akusento no suberi oyobi heiban-ka" 602-21]. (Kyōbun-sha)

Sakurai Shigeharu. 1958a. "Fukugō-meishi no akusento-hōsoku", Kgg 33:56-78.
   (= Sakurai 1975:142-82)
-----. 1958b. "Joshi *no* no akusento: Wa-Kan ryōgo e no setsuzoku no shi-teki
   kōsatsu", Kokugakuin-zasshi 59:9:1-15. (= Sakurai 1976:280-306)
-----. 1959a. "Kango akusento no kokugo-ka", Kokugakuin-zasshi 60:9:26-45.
-----. 1959b. "San-kan - bon Iroha-jirui-shō shosai no akusento: keiyō-shi *sa*-hen
   dōshi ni tsuite", Kokugakuin-zasshi 60:4:39-47.
-----. 1960a. "Heian-Insei jidai ni okeru 'fukugō-meishi'", Kokugo-to-kokubungaku
   37:7:58-73.
-----. 1960b. "Shiza-Kōshiki shosai no akusento: shi-teki ichi, bunsetsu-katsuyō
   no hōsoku nado", Kokugakuin-zasshi 61:4:59-81.
-----. 1961a. "Akusento-shiryō to shite no shōmyō 1, 2", Kgg 44:34-51, 45:29-37.
-----. 1961b. "Koji-ki no shisei-chūki shiken", Kokugakuin-zasshi 62:11/12:11-26.
-----. 1962a. "Kaisō no jodō-shi 'ki' to rentai-kei 'si': akusento-shi kara mita
   katsuyō-kei no seiritsu", Kokugo-kenkyū 14:1-28.
-----. 1962b. "Shingon-shū 'Shōmyō' bokufu no keifu to sono akusento", Kgg 51:44-52.
-----. 1962c. "Kodai-Nihongo no keiyō-shi no kōzō", Kokugo-kokubun
   (31:8=)336:1-31.
-----. 1962d. "Kodai-Nihongo no 'gotoshi' ni tsuite: sono rekishi to go-kōzō",
   Kokugakuin-zasshi 63:6:76-93.
-----. 1963. "'Rongi' no senritsu ni han'ei shita Muromachi-jidai shoki no akusento-
   taikei", Kokugo-kokubun (32:5=) 345:1-32. (= Sakurai 1976:132-79)
-----. 1964. "Nihon-Shoki ko-shahon shosai no akusento", Rikkyō-daigaku
   Nihon-Bungaku 13:25-37.
-----. 1965a. "Keiyō-shi no katsuyō-kei no seiritsu ni tsuite: toku ni akusento-
   keitai o chūshin to shite", Kokugakuin-zasshi 66:8:31-51.
-----. 1965b. "Keiyō-shi onbin no hōgen-bunpu to sono kaishaku: onbin to akusento",
   Nihon-bungaku-ronkyū 24:82-92.
-----. 1965c. "Joshi akusento no shi-teki kōsatsu", Kokugo-kokubun (34:2=) 366:36-62.
   (= Sakurai 1975:183-225)
-----. 1966a. "Keiyō-shi onbin no ichi-kōsatsu", Rikkyō-daigaku Nihon-bungaku 16:2-9.
-----. 1966b. "Keiyō-shi onbin kō: hassei no yōin", Kokugakuin-zasshi 67:10:45-57.
-----. 1966c. "On'in-shi shiryō to shite no Bumō-ki: chūki no bunrui to kentō: 1,2",
   Kokugo-kokubun (36:3=)390:35-57; (36:4=)391:15-49. (= Sakurai 1975:81-103)
-----. 1966d. "Iwayuru Heian-akusento no ichi-mondai: nionsetsu-meishi dai yon-rui
   to dai go-rui no betsu ni tsuite", Kokugo-kokubun (35:1=) 377:32-46.
   (= Sakurai 1975:104-28)
-----. 1966e. "Nionsetsu-meishi no ruibetsu ni tsuite", Bungaku-gogaku 40:80-3.
-----. 1967. "Chūsei Kyōto-hōgen no onsetsu-kōzō: sono shirabiimu-teki seikaku ni
   tsuite", Bungaku-gogaku 46:81-92.
-----. 1968. "Kodai-Nihongo no onsetsu-kōzō ni tsuite: sono tokushitsu
   to kaishaku", Kokugakuin-zasshi 69:8:28-41.
-----. 1970. "Jōdai no akusento", [Gekkan-]Bunpō 3:1:72-8.
   (= "Nara-jidai no akusento", Sakurai 1975:52-65).
-----. 1972. "(Heian-Insei-jidai ni okeru) Wago no rendaku ni tsuite:
   Kanchi-in - bon Myōgi-shō ni okeru", Kokugo-kokubun (41:6=)454:1-19, 56.
-----. 1973. "(Heian-Insei-jidai ni okeru) Nihon-go no bion ni tsuite: Kanchi-in -
   bon Myōgi-shō o chūshin to shite", Kokugo-kokubun (42:12=)472:1-25.
-----. 1974. "'Jōtō' gata meishi no sonpi o megutte", Bungaku 42:(2:96-103=)210-7.
-----. 1975. Kodai kokugo akusento-shi ronkō. (Ōfū-sha)
-----. 1976. Chūsei kokugo akusento-shi ronkō. (Ōfū-sha)
-----. 1977. [Shingi-shingon-shū den] Bumō-ki no kokugo-gaku - teki kenkyū. (Ōfū-sha)

-----. 1978a. "Historical aspects of the melody of the Japanese language",
   Descriptive and Applied Linguistics = Bulletin of the ICU Summer Institute in
   Linguistics 11:31-51.

-----. 1978b. Nihon-go no senritsu. (Sōbun-sha)

-----. 1979. "Nihon-go no senritsu-shi kara mita joshi no mondai — bukkyō-ongaku o
   chūshin to shite", [Tanabe hakase koki kinen] Kokugo joshi jodō-shi ronkō 249-65.
   (Ōfū-sha)

-----. 1984. Chūsei Kyōto akusento no shi-teki kenkyū. (Ōfū-sha)

Sandness, Karen. 1986 ms. "The pronunciation of the s-initial syllables in the Nara
   period: a critical look at Arisaka's and Mabuchi's theories".

Sansom, George. 1928. An historical grammar of Japanese. (Oxford)

Sasaki Takashi. 1973. "Heian-makki ni okeru 'jō-tō' gata meishi no sonpi ni tsuite",
   Bungaku 41(:8):919-22.

Satō Eisaku. 1985. "Kagawa-ken Ibuki-jima hōgen no akusento-taikei o kangaeru",
   Kgg 140:(31-44)=89-102.

Satō Kiyoji, ed. 1973. Kokugo-shi. 2 vols. (Ōfū-sha)

-----. 1977. Kokugo-gaku kenkyū jiten. (Meiji-shoin)

-----. 1979. "Nihon-go ni okeru sei-daku no kigen", [Gekkan-]Gengo 8:1:28-37.

Sato, Paul Tosio. 1975 ms. "Apophony in Japanese, Korean and the Altaic languages".

Seki Kazuo. 1977. Kokugo fukugō-dōshi no kenkyū. (Kasama-shoin)

Senoo Shūko. 1966. "Kagawa-ken Ibuki-jima no akusento", Kokugo-kenkyū 22:22-3.

Serafim, Leon A. 1977. "The relationship of pre-Japanese and proto-Japanese", paper
   presented at the Symposium on Historical Relationships of Japanese and Korean,
   1977 Linguistic Institute, Honolulu.

-----. 1984. Shodon: the prehistory of a northern Ryukyuan dialect of Japanese.
   Yale University dissertation.

Shibata Takeshi. 1955. "Nihon-go no aksuento taikei" (Kgg 21), repr 1980: Nihon no
   gengo-gaku 2:404-42.

-----. 1958. Nihon no hōgen. (Iwanami-shoten)

-----. 1959. "Ryūkyū Yonaguni-tō [NKD: Yonakuni-jima] hōgen no on'in",
   Kotoba no kenkyū (KKK ronshū 1) 103-20.

-----. 1965. Kotoba no shakai-gaku. NHK Bukkusu 22.

-----. 1971. "Yonaguni-hōgen ni kan-suru jakkan no hōkoku",
   Kindaichi hakase beiju kinen ronshū 928-12 [sic].

-----. 1977. Gendai Nihon-go. (Asahi-shinbun-sha)

-----. 1980. Repr. of Shibata 1955.

-----. 1981. "Amami-Ōshima sho-hōgen ni okeru o-retsu kō-rui to otsu-rui no
   kubetsu", Jinrui-kagaku 33:41-59.

-----. 1984. Amami-Ōshima no kotoba: bunpu kara rekishi e. (Akiyama-shobō)

Shibata Takeshi and Fukushima Chitsuko. 1981. Izumo Iishi-gun chūō-bu gengo-chizu.
   (Saitama: Shibata)

Shibata Takeshi and Mitsuishi Yasuko. 1979. "Historical relationship between
   Nara-period Old Japanese and the dialect of Shiba, Kakeroma, Amami Islands",
   Explorations in Linguistics: Papers in Honor of Kazuko Inoue 484-93.

Shin-Genkai = Ōtsuki 1959

Shin Meikai kokugo jiten. 1972. Compiled by Kindaichi Kyōsuke, Kindaichi Haruhiko,
   Kenbō Hidetoshi, Shibata Takeshi, Yamada Tadao. (Sansei-dō)

Shinmura Izuru. 1955. Kōjien. (Iwanami-shoten)

Shin Nihongo-kōza 3: Gendai no Nihon-go no onsei to hōgen. 1975. (Sekibun-sha)

Shinsen-Jikyō. 898-901. (Cited from Zdb.)

Shirota Shun. 1977. "Tokushu-kanazukai oretsu-on no irei", Kgg 111:11-24.

Shoki = Nihon-Shoki. Shoki kun-chū (phonogram reading notes in the Kanbun prose
  of Nihon-Shoki) cited from Ōno 1953.
Shoku-Nihongi. 794-7. Contains 62 Senmyō, written 697-789, partly in phonograms.
Shōsoin-[ko]monjo (Komonjo) = Shōsoin kana-monjo. 702--. See Zdb 879b.
Sin Swukcwu [et al.]. 1501. Haytong ceykwuk ki, pulok: eum pen.yak (= Kaitō-shokoku-
  ki, furoku: goon hon'yaku). Date from colophon; photoplates in Tōjō 1969.
Skillend, W.E. 1956. The vocabulary of the Manyoosyuu. Cambridge University
  dissertation.
Soeda Kenjirō. 1975. "Fukuoka-ken hokubu-chihō no hōgen-akusento", I: [Kyūshū-
  daigaku] Gobun-kenkyū 39/40:57-67; II: Yamaguchi-daigaku Bungakkai-shi 26:45-67.
Starostin, S. 1975. "K voprosu o rekonstruktsii prayaponskoy fonologicheskoy
  sistemy", Ocherki po fonologii vostochnykh yazykov 271-80. (Moscow)
Suzuki Kazuhiko. 1977. "Bunpō no utsuri-kawari", Nihongo-kōza 6:197-242.
Suzuki Makio. 1952. "Hokkaidō Okushiri-tō hōgen no akusento ni tsuite",
  Onsei-gakkai kaihō 79:22-9.
Suzuki Yutaka. 1984. "Nihon-Shoki Jindai-kan no shōten", Kokugo-gaku 136:13-23.
Syromyatnikov, N.A. 1972. Drevneyaponskiy yazyk. (Moscow: Nauka).
-----. 1973. "O perelome glasnykh i i í v yaponskom yazyke", Voprosy
  yaponskogo filologii (Izd. Moskovskogo universiteta) 2:106-19.
Tai Nobuyuki. 1968. Gogen o saguru: kokugo on'in-ron no kōsei. Toyonaka
  (Sakura-shoin).
Tajiri Eizō. 1975. "Tokara-rettō (Nakanoshima, Tairashima) no akusento to goi",
  [Kyūshū-daigaku] Gobun-kenkyū 39/40:46-55.
Takahashi Hiroyuki. 1971. "Gokei no henka to kōbi ni tsuite — 'sizimu' kara
  'tizimu' e", Nihon Bungaku Ronkyū 31:22-30.
Takahashi Toshizō. 1977. "Okinawa-ken Yaeyama-yun Yonaguni-chō no hōgen no
  seikatsu-goi", Hōgen kenkyū sōsho 4:159-217.
Takamatsu Masao. 1969. "*Bei* kō", Kokugo-kokubun (38:7=)419:28-39.
Takayama Michiaki. 1981. "Gen'on seichō kara mita Nihon-Shoki on-gana hyōki shiron",
  [Kyūshū-daigaku] Gobun-kenkyū 51:13-20+charts.
-----. 1982. "Shoki kayō on-gana to gen'on seichō", [Kyūshū-daigaku] Bunken-tankyū
  10:1-6.
-----. 1983. "Shoki kayō nionsetsu-meishi no hyōki ni tsuite — akusento gorui
  to no kanren o megutte", [Kyūshū=daigaku] Bunken-tankyū 12:47-55.
-----. 1984. "Nihon-Shoki no on-gana to sono gen'on seichō ni tsuite — jōdai
  akusento to no sōkan-sei o kangaeru", Kindaichi Haruhiko hakase koki-kinen
  ronbun-shū 1:45-69.
Takeda Yūkichi. 1956-7. Man'yō-shū zen=chūshaku. 14 vols. (Kadokawa-shoten)
Terakawa Kishio and Kusaka Miyoshi. 1944. Hyōjun Nihon-go hatsuon dai-jiten.
Terakawa Kishio, Kindaichi Haruhiko, Inagaki Masayuki, eds. 1951. Kokugo akusento
  ronsō. (Hōsei-daigaku shuppan-kyoku)
Thorpe, Maner L. 1983. Ryūkyūan Language History. Univ. of Southern California diss.
Ting Pang-hsin. 1975. "A new interpretation of the even and oblique tones",
  BIHP (Academia Sinica) 47:1:1-15.
-----. 1983. "Some aspects of tonal development in Chinese dialects",
  CAAAL 21:115-30.
Toguchi Shigemi. 1974. "Ōita-ken Ōita-shi Ō-aza Tsurusaki hōgen wabu-onsei no
  kenkyū", Hōgen kenkyū sōsho 3:91-144.
Toh Soo-hee [= To Swuhuy]. 1981. "The Paekche language", Chōsen-gakuhō 98:21-32.
Tōjō Misao. 1951. Zenkoku hōgen jiten. (Tōkyō-dō)
-----, ed. 1953. Nihon-hōgen-gaku. (Yoshikawa Kōbun-kan)

-----. 1954. Bunrui hōgen jiten. (Tōkyō-dō)

-----, ed. 1961. Hōgen-gaku kōza. 4 vols. (Tōkyō-dō)

-----. 1969. Nantō-hōgen shiryō. (Tōkō-shoin)

Tokugawa Munemasa. 1972. "Towards a family tree for accent in Japanese dialects"
   (translated by J.D. McCawley), Papers In Japanese Linguistics 1:301-20.

Toyama Eiji. 1968. "*Ha*-gyō yodan katsuyō dōshi onbin-kei ni tsuite", Kindai-go
   kenkyū 2:235-55.

Tsuchihashi Yutaka. 1972. Kodai-kayō zen-chūshaku: Koji-ki hen. (Kadokawa-shoten)

-----. 1976. Kodai-kayō zen-chūshaku: Nihon-Shoki hen. (Kadokawa-shoten)

Tsukishima Hiroshi. 1951. "Jōben - bon Shūi-waka-shū shosai no akusento ni tsuite",
   Terakawa et al. 1951:107-78 .

-----. 1963. "Dakuten no kigen", (Tōkyō-daigaku kyōyō-gakubu jinbun-kagaku-ka
   kiyō 30 =) Kokubungaku-kanbungaku 9:283-325.

-----. 1969. Heian-jidai-go shinron. (Tōkyō-daigaku)

-----. 1977. Kokugo no rekishi. (Tōkyō-daigaku shuppan-kai)

Tsuru Hisashi and Moriyama Takashi. 1975. Man'yō-shū. 2d ed. (Ōfū-sha)

Tsuzuku Tsuneo. 1941. "Hida Hagiwara hōgen ni okeru dōshi to keiyō-shi to no
   katsuyō", Hōgen-kenkyū 4:177-205.

-----. 1951. "Dōshi no ren'yō-kei to akusento", Terakawa et al. 1951:385-412.

-----. 1968. "*au, ou* kara *o:* e", Kindai-go kenkyū 2:353-71.

-----. 1970. "Hondo hōgen no on'in-kenkyū", Hōgen kenkyū no mondai-ten 45-66.

-----. 1971. "Tōzai ryō-hōgen no tigai wa dō-shite dekita ka", Gengo-seikatsu
   1971:6:50-60.

Uemura Yukio. 1959. "Ryūkyū sho-hōgen ni okeru ichini-onsetsu meishi no akusento no
   gaikan", Kotoba no kenkyū (KKK ronshū 1) 121-40.

Uji-shūi-monogatari. c.1215. (Cited from Yoshida 1973.)

Umegaki Minoru. 1946. Kyō-kotoba. (Takagiri-shoin)

-----. 1957. "Ōsaka-hōgen henka no keikō", Kinki-hōgen sōsho 6:39-52.

-----. 1958. "Akusento henka katei no jittai (shiryō-hen)", Tezukayama-gakuin
   Tanki-daigaku kenkyū-nenpō 6:1-33.

-----. 1959. "Akusento henka katei no jittai (riron-hen)", Tezukayama-gakuin
   Tanki-daigaku kenkyū-nenpō 7:1-22.

-----. 1962. Kinki-hōgen no sōgō-teki kenkyū. (Sansei-dō)

-----. 1963. "Onchō-sai to sono hōsoku: Kyōto-shi hōgen o rei to shite",
   Kokugo-kenkyū 15:17-65.

Unger, J.M. 1975a. Studies in early Japanese morphophonemics. Yale University
   dissertation. Reproduced, University of Indiana 1977.

-----. 1957b. "A note on Kō-type O-ending syllables in Old Japanese", Journal of
   the Association of Teachers of Japanese 10:201-8.

-----. 1977a. "Intuition and rigor: more on o-ending syllables in Old Japanese",
   Papers In Japanese Linguistics 5:377-92.

-----. 1977b. "Some new ideas of proto-Japanese", paper presented at the Symposium
   on Historical Relationships of Japanese and Korean, 1977 Linguistics Institute,
   Honolulu.

-----. 1977c. Reproduction of Unger 1975a.

----- and Tomita, Yōko Itō. 1983. "The classification of Old Japanese adjectives",
   Papers in East Asian Linguistics (University of Hawaii) 1:52-65.

Urushibara Naomichi. 1979. "Man'yō-shū ni okeru joshi 'ba' no onka ni tsuite",
   [Tanabe hakase koki kinen] Kokugo joshi jodō-shi ronkō 87-104. (Ōfū-sha)

Uwano Zendō. 1975. "Akusento-so no benbetsu-teki tokuchō", Gengo no Kagaku 6:23-84.

-----. 1976a. "Hirosaki-akusento to kyōzō-kankei", Hirosaki-daigaku Gakuen-dayori
   35:4-5.

-----. 1976b. "Narada no akusento-so no shozoku-goi", Hirosaki-daigaku jinbungaku-bu Bun-Kei Ronsō [Studies in the Humanities ...] 11:3:1-32.

-----. 1976c. Review of Kindaichi 1974. Gengo-kenkyū 69:36-56.

-----. 1977a. "Narada-hōgen no kiso-goi (1)", Hirosaki-daigaku jinbungaku-bu Bun-Kei Ronsō [Studies in the Humanities ...] 12:3:1-13.

-----. 1977b. "Nihon-go no akusento", Iwanami Kōza Nihon-go 5:281-321.

-----. 1978. "Akusento no kojin-sa o meguru kenkyū gaikan", Gengo-seikatsu 320:48-59.

-----. 1982. "Kanazawa-hōgen no meishi no akusento: akusento taikei to shozoku goi", Kokugo-kenkyū 45:1-31 [horizontal].

-----. 1982-3. "Akusento-chōsa goi yō sankō shiryō: taigen hen (1), (2)", Azia Ahurika Bunpō Kenkyū 1982:3:95-224, 1983:3:91-236. (Extensive lists of accent patterns of Uwano's native dialect, Shizukuishi in Iwate.)

-----. 1983. "Kanazawa-hōgen ni okeru akusento to goon no kankei", Nihon-kai Bunka 1983:3:01-043.

-----. 1984a. "Aomori-shi no akusento-so no shozoku goi", Nihon-kai Bunka 1984:3:1-42.

-----. 1984b. "Rui no sōgō to shiki-hozon: Oki no fukugō-meishi no akusento", Kokugo-kenkyū 47:1-53.

----- and Nitta Tetsuo. 1983. "Kanazawa-hōgen no 5-mōra meishi no akusento shiryō", Kanazawa-daigaku Nihonkai-iki Kenkyū-jo hōkoku 15:71-107.

-----. 1985. "Kagawa-ken Ibuki-jima hōgen no akusento", Nihon Gakushi-in kiyō 40:2:75-179.

Vance, Timothy J. 1979. "Nonsense-word experiments in phonology and their application to Rendaku in Japanese", University of Chicago dissertation.

-----. 1980a. "Particle deletion and accent in Aomori Japanese", Chicago Linguistics Circle 16:365-70.

-----. 1980b. "[Otsu:] 'Some aspects of rendaku in Japanese and related phenomena': comments on", Theoretical Issues in Japanese Linguistics = MIT Working Papers in Linguistics 2: 229-36.

-----. 1980c. "The psychological status of a constraint on Japanese consonant alternation", Linguistics 18:245-67.

-----. 1982. "On the origin of voicing alternation in Japanese consonants", Journal of the American Oriental Society 102:333-41.

-----. 1987. An introduction to Japanese phonology. SUNY Press.

Wada Minoru. 1942. "Kinki-akusento ni okeru meishi no fukugō-keitai", Onsei-gakkai kaihō 71:10-3.

-----. 1943. "Fukugō-go akusento no kōbu-seiso to shite mita ni-onsetsu - meishi", Hōgen-kenkyū 7:1-26.

-----. 1944. "Kinki-akusento: 'Neko to Shōzō to Futari no Onna' o rei ni", Kokugo-bunka 4:1:42-56; 4:2:45-56.

-----. 1952. "Koji-ki no sei no chū", Kokugo-to-kokubungaku 29:6:50-61.

-----. 1959. "Kansai-akusento no inshō", Onsei-gakkai kaihō 99:17-9.

-----. 1962. "Akusento", Hōgen-gaku gaisetsu 162-208. (Musashino-shoin)

-----. 1966a. "Daiichi-ji akusento no hakken: Ibuki-jima", Kokugo-kenkyū 22:24-8.

-----. 1966b. "Nihaku-meishi itsutsu no rui o itsutsu ni ii-wakeru akusento", Gengo-kenkyū 50:128-30.

-----. 1969. "Ji no akusento", Kokugo-kenkyū 29:1-20.

Wamyō-shō = Wamyō-ruiju-shō. 931-8. (Cited from Zdb.)

Watanabe Fumio. 1957. "Kyōtsū-go to Yamanashi-ken - ka no akusento no sōi", Onsei no kenkyū 9:181-94.

Wenck, Günther. 1954. "Über die Entdeckung und systematisierung der japanischen Konjugation", Nachrichten der Gesellschaft für Natur- und Völkerkunde Ostasiens 76: - .

-----. 1959. Japanische Phonetik, Band IV: Erscheinungen und Probleme des
   japanischen Lautwandels. (Wiesbaden: Harrassowitz)
-----. 1967-7. "On the reconstruction of a proto-Japanese verb inflection system",
   Papers In Japanese Linguistics 5:393-407.
-----. 1968. "An early corollary of initial voicing as a means of Japanese word
   formation", Papers of the CIC Far Eastern Language Institute, Ann Arbor 1967
   (published 1968), 99-105.
Whitman, John B. 1984. "Old Japanese vowel distinctions and accent classes",
   Conference on Japanese and Korean Linguistics, Harvard University.
-----. 1985. The phonological basis for the comparison of Japanese and Korean.
   Harvard University dissertation.
Yamada Yoshio. 1954. Nara-chō bunpō-shi. (Hōbun-kan)
Yamagata-ken hōgen kenkyū-kai. 1970. Yamagata-ken hōgen jiten.
Yamaguchi Yoshinori. 1974. "Kodai Nihon-go ni okeru gotō-shion no datsuraku",
   Kgg 98:1-15.
-----. 1979. "Kodai-go no shion-kōtai ni kan-suru ni-san no mondai" [abstract],
   Kgg 116:77.
Yamaguchi Yukihiro. 1962. "Keihan akusento no kata no yōso", Onsei-gakkai kaihō
   110:21-4.
-----. 1976. "Minami-Kinki akusento kyokusho-hōgen no seiritsu", Kokugo-kenkyū
   39:1-40 (horizontal).
Yamana Kunio. 1951. "Totsugawa [= Totsukawa] onchō", Onsei no kenkyū 7:191-201.
-----. 1965. "Awaji no akusento", Onsei no kenkyū 11:241-63.
Yasuda Akira. 1974. "Ha-gyō tenko-on no shūhen: ho no baai",
   Bungaku 42(:11:86-105=):1332-51.
-----. 1977. "Chōsen shiryō ni okeru hyōki no mondai", Kgg 108:33-46.
-----. 1980. Chōsen shiryō to chūsei kokugo. (Kasama sōsho 147)
Yoshida Kanehiko. 1971. Gendai-go jo-dōshi no shi-teki kenkyū. (Meiji-shoin)
-----. 1973. Jōdai-go jodō-shi no shi-teki kenkyū. (Meiji-shoin)
-----. 1976. Nihon-go gogen-gaku no hōhō. (Taishū-kan)
-----. 1979. Kodai-Nihongo o saguru. (Kadokawa sensho 102)
Yoshimachi Yoshio. 1932. "Iwayuru Totsukawa-akusento no ichirei: Kinki-chihō ni
   okeru tokui naru ichi-hōgen", Hōgen 2(:2):604-19.
Yoshitake, S. 1929. "The history of the Japanese particle I", Bulletin of the
   School of Oriental and African Studies 5:889-95.
Yukawa Yasutoshi. 1984. "Wakayama hōgen akusento kō: (1) dōshi o chūshin ni,
   (2) meishi o chūshin ni", AA Gengo Bunka Kenkyū-jo tsūshin 50:1-6, 51:18-23.
Zdb = Omodaka et al. 1967.
Zhs = Zenkoku hōgen shiryō (= NHK 1967-71).

adv = adverb 825

adverb(s) 24; [no nigori on verb] 95; [+ adj] 99; [predicable] 107; 182; [with
   suppressed final accent] 150; [oxytonic/atonic alternants] 260; [+ verb] 668; 801

adverbial conversion 99 ◊ adverbialization(s) 94 803; [of nominalizations] 804

affricated palatalization 55 ◊ affricate(s) 5 7 16 18 23 33 34 66

affrication 17; [in Shuri, now palatalized] 56; [s and z in OJ?] 86; [of -tu]) 124

agglutination of -ku 127 ◊ -(a)hi [Korean suffix] 65

ai 3 4 76 ◊ ai > ee 2 ◊ ai > [ɛ] 43 ◊ ai > [æ:] 47

/ai/ or /ee/ (reconstructed by Hattori for ancestor of OJ non-palatal "ey") 253

-ai > -ey 58; ...a-i < *...a-Ci 265

A-i daro'o, A-i de aro'o/arimasyo'o 129 ◊ A-i ku [Aomori] = standard A-ku 804

Ainu 64 83 ◊ ?*A-karimasyo'o [not encountered] 129 ◊ A-karo'o ← A-ku aro'o 129

A-ke (Hachijō attributive) 811

A-ki (attributive) 37 170; [and retrospective V-i-ki] 127; see A-kyi

Akō [Hyōgo] (HL-L for B verbs) 198; (lacks register distinctions) 361

*aku [bound noun] 134 805

A-ku (adjective infinitive) 802; [lexicalized examples few and late] 804

A-[k]u [velar elision not so early or widespread as for A-si-ku] 127

A-ku/-kyi "< *-ko/-key" [Ōno Tōru] 812

A-ku a'ri (intensive or explicit form) 37; A-ku aro'o → A-karo'o 129

A-[k]u + na'ru/suru, + -te 128 ◊ A-ku ni 804 ◊ A-ku to mo 108

A-ku wa/mo/sae/koso + auxiliary ar- 'be' 802

A-kyi where predicative (A-si) is expected 807; see A-ki

all-low atonic phrases [Ōsaka?] 345; see also low flat tune

allomorph [unique] 9 81 ◊ allophone(s) 17 25 34 55 59

"alpha-switch" rule [for Tōkyō compound verb accent] 207

Altaic 57 427 807 812 ◊ Altaicists 83

altered forms of verb infinitive in 16th century (before -te, -ta, -tu) 124

altered [accent] pattern with particle deletion [Aomori] 19

alternation 1; [Ca with Cey in paired verbs] 62; [disguised] 62; [/e/ with /o/] 68;
   [h- with p-] 8; [kane⁻ with kana-] 49; [s and r] 34; [s- and zero] 35;
   [š (+ -i) and s] 7; [t and r] 34; [tš (+ -i) and ts (+ -u) and t] 7

alveolar ridge 34 ◊ always-low particles 168 ◊ amalgamation with gerund 206

Amami [separate development for "yi" = Type One i] 52

ambiguous: accent 349; citation forms 672

ambivalent phonogram(s) 84 85 116; [even/rising] 349

ambivalent (consonant/vowel) stems of a hybrid conjugation 201

A-mi su(ru) > A-n-zu(ru) 26 ◊ A-myi 804 805

-amu [earlier form of presumptive] 37 38 129 667; -a'[m]u 45

an = [a~] 142 ◊ -an [as a surviving form of presumptive -amu] 37

-AN "with an adjectival noun for second element" 228

-(a)n- [bound negative auxiliary verb] 111

ana A-si (exclamatory) used as an anticipatory predication 815

analogical: reformation [of presumptive] 37; restorations 44; reformulations 808

analogy 17 33 59; [with do'ko accounts for d- in da're etc.] 81; [specific] 114 125
   (of syoo < semu to account for all vowel-stem presumptives) 130, (of syoo
   conflated to siyoo responsible for hortative -yoo?) 130 253 358

ancestor of Old Japanese and Okinawan 53

ancestral form [of -f- persisting down to modern Shuri] 12

ancestral language [accent classes posited for] 162 163; [accent reconstruction] 246

ancient: compound 145; Greeks 3; vowel distinctions [evidence from dialects] 52

animal names 29; [with voiced initials] 88; [with Wakayama double-low accent] 169

anomalies of accent 145 213
anomalous: final falls [dynamic register C?] 264; final nasal 83; (accent) markings 145; (accent) patterns [Kyōto paradigmatic forms] 158; rise [Mg 'loquat'] 165; sets [of correspondences] 49
A no̱ N 813 814
-anu 667 ◻ -an-[y]i si[y] ⟩ -azi, -an-[y]i su ⟩ -azu 111
Aomori [extends initial automatic low] 141; [no accent retreat for polysyllabic vowel stems + -t···] 206; [oxytonic noun accent retained before /no/] 256; [merges 2.3 with 2.2] 256
apheretic form 36 107 107
apical pairs t/d and s/z palatalized before OJ -(y)i 86
apostrophe 2 3 44 ◻ appare [always -p-?] 12
ar- 'be' (aux) [with ni and to̱ forms copula] 801; [with A-ku or A-sa makes adjective paradigmatic forms] 802; [aux attached directly to adj stem] 804; [⟨ *a(-)ra-] 805; ['be'] 807; [inf substituted for predicative] 810
arabi- 'rage' (OJ monograde/bigrade) 666
aranu/arazu [replaced by na-i in modern Japanese] 803 ◻ "archaism" 77
ari [verb infinitive used for predicative] 665; see also ar[y]i
a[r]iku (= aruku) [retreat of locus in parts of Yamanashi] 355
Arisaka's Law 58 59 66
articulation [determined by following C] 2; [not in contrast] 5; [single] 34; [distinctive place of] 72; [of final vowel in Chinese loans ending in -t] 73
articulatory: difficulty 33; parameters [of vowels] 67; point 72
artifact [of the analysis/analyst] 144 231 345
artificial: readings 24 144; dictionary notations 672; literary language 808
aru [morphologically "true" predicative before mazi] 132; [B but Yonaguni A´] 282
-aru/-ayu 667 ◻ aruk- 'walk' 154 ◻ ar[y]i 'stay' [used as intensive prefix] 95
asa 2.5 'morning' [truncation of *asam?] 266; [Korean cognate has final -m] 361
A-sa A-si ("emphatic locution") 815 ◻ A-saa qar-, A-sa du qa- [Ie-jima] 804
A-sa ni 'out of a feeling of being A' 804; A-sanu 'because of being' [Ie-jima] 804
A-si [adjective predicative] 37; [Hn-Km accent] 170; 806; "⟨ *-se" [Ōno Tōru] 812
A-si N ?= Asi-N (compound) 807
A-si-ki [late?]; A-si-ku [→ A-si-u]; A-si[-si] (used for attrib) 127; A-si-si 808
aspect (marked by endings on verb and adjective) 802
aspirated: affricate in Nakijin [rare, Nakasone "ç"] 363; allophone of voiceless consonant before e o a 55; and unaspirated consonants 25 55 121 262; consonants [Shodon] written Ch- 83; stops 121
aspiration suppression 132 ◻ assent [grunt of] 107
assignment of: ko'o or o'tu status 50; pitch pattern to a word 138; pitch patterns in Tōkyō 138; verb stem to accent type 202; words to original accent classes 162
assimilated Chinese loanwords 130
assimilation [in place of articulation] 2; [of u to s] 7; [of initial vowel to voicelessness of next consonant] 10; [of high vowel to create long vowel] 26; [of -rV- to nasal] 35; [consonant] 37; [unusual] 42; [progressive] 43; [idiosyncratic] 54; [palatal] 57; [of nasal left by vowel elision] 72; [of /r/ in manner and place] 72; [of obstruent to voicing of surrounding vowels] 85; [of vowel to vowels of surrounding syllables 96; [triggered by loss of juncture before -te] 121; [dental] 122 132; [vowel] 128; [of /oo/ in tongue height to preceding /i/] 130; [oral] 132; [partial, to voiceless consonant of preceding syllable] 133; [of /a/ to palatal quality of preceding /y/] 137; [of verb accent to that of homophone] 356; rule [in Ie-jima] 837 ◻ assimilations 210
asterisk "*" 121; [used to transcribe character ZYOO] 245; 666 ◻ -asu 667

borrowing [indicated by voiced-obstruent initial] 30; [as explanation for OJ /e/]
  58; [by Tōkyō from Kyōto] 127; [from another dialect, to account for sporadic
  irregularity] 264 ▯ borrowings 1; [from Chinese] 30; 55; *see also* loans, loanwords
-bosi- [auxiliary adjective] 820 ▯ -bosu, -ᵇ/ₘosu 790
botanical names (well represented in 2.5) 361 ▯ -botta- [adjective-stem formant] 817
bound [verbal nouns] 26 203 802 803; [auxiliary] 35 47 104 211; 59; [morpheme
  haka] 69; [verb (negative)] 111, [in complex structures] 670; [morphemes (Chinese)
  114, 230; [Greek and Latin elements in English] 229; [loanmorphs] 229; [noun i] 66
  [adjectival nouns] 803; [adjectives] 816 820
boundaries [morphophonemic] 3; [underlying] 4; [etymological, morphemic] 25; [within
  "nigori"] 25; [morpholexical] 76; [Middle Korean, retained after elision] 82; 138
bracketed y posited as underlying segment 51
brackets enclose: explicitly phonetic notation; ellipted/optional elements 86 130;
  suppressed/cancelled junctures 139; ellipses or nonsurviving forms 666
"breaking" [of Korean vowel *i to *ye] 68
bu- 'not, un-' (prefix) 229 324 ▯ -bu 32 790 ▯ -ᵇ/ₘu ‹ *-n[a]-pa- 790
Buddhist [term] 29; [names] 30 ▯ -buka- (also -huka-) 'deep with' 817 819
Bumō-ki 78 118 198; [Muromachi accent] 200 205; [HL-L for B verbs] 198; 343 344
Bungo [Ōita] distinguishes 2.3 from 2.1/2 but before /no/ only 257
Bussokuseki-no-uta 32 78 87 100 105 107 109 111 112 119
Buzen [Fukuoka] distinguishes 2.3 from 2.1/2 but before /no/ only 257
-b- verbs [Nase-Kominato reflexes]) 14
[-b-] version of intervocalic labial 80 ▯ -bVr- › -nd- [Okinawa] 80
bwo [syllable lacking in Koji-ki and NS] 36 119
C- (Yonaguni tense deaspirated affricate [ts-]) 25 39 81
C = (1) any consonant (as distinct from V = vowel) 81; (2) an obstruent unspecified
  as to voiced vs. voiceless; (3) an unspecified consonant (as hiatus-filler in
  derivational forms 36; (4) the [usual] unaspirated palatal affricate in Nakijin
  [written for Nakasone's "c"] 363; (5) Yonaguni tense deaspirated affricate [ts] 25
  39 81; (6) a third register in Nakijin and Yonaguni (reflex of the low tonic) 246
c [representing the affricates] 17; [palatal stop] 33, (earlier "s"?) 34
*c- [voiceless affricate reconstructed by Unger for most OJ s-] 34 66
"c" of Shuri palatalized (= cy) 366 ▯ "ç" of Shuri formerly unpalatalized (= c) 366
"ç" (Hirayama for Yonaguni) rewritten as "c" 366
C accent type [Nakijin and Yonaguni reflex of 2.4 and 2.5] 177
*···Ca- verb subjunctive form 668
Ca alternating with Cey in paired verbs 62 ▯ CaC stems paired with C-ey- 51
CaCo uncommon 58
···Ca-Ci- › ···Cey- 667 ▯ ···C[a-C]i quadrigrade verb infinitive 667
Cambodian [Khmer] 115 ▯ cancellation of loci [after first in phrase occurs] 141
canonical accent pattern(s) 203 209 346 ▯ canonical shape(s) 66 139 219; (CVki) 358
canonical types [to account for locus assignment with -T-] 345
Cantonese 45; [changed-tone marker] 169; [tones proliferated] 266
Cao as source of Cwo? 58 ▯ capital cities 11
capital letters [to represent initials sensitive to sei-daku distinction] 84
case marker [Korean] 64
casual ellipsis 99: of marker [no] in certain strings of N (-) N (-...) 813
casual reductions 38 ▯ cathexis 807 ▯ *Cau [as source of Cwo?] 58
causative [Korean] 64; [V-as-] 65; [auxiliary attached to subjunctive -a] 131 352;
  [gerunds in JP] 126; [A or B like underlying stem] 204; [absorbed into Kyōto Type
  A] 205; [older rules for younger Tōkyō too] 207; [Tōkyō accent same type as verb
  stem] 206; 666

Cye [OJ *ko'o*-type syllable] 52 54 57; [all the result of compressions?] 62; [< *Ce
(Unger often must assume)] 66; [< Cia] 58, [< C(y)i-a] 62; [< Cya] 50; ["neutral"
version of mid front vowel?] 54; [relatively rare] 62; [three sources] 62; 86
Cye ≠ Cey 81; [distinction lost before Myōgi-shō] 215 ▯ Cye < Cia < Ci[C]a 812
Cyi [OJ *ko'o*-type syllable] 52 86 ▯ Cyi ≠ Ciy 81; [distinction lost before Mg] 215
Cyo [unneeded in OJ] 51; Cyo(o) syllable type 129; Cyu [unneeded in OJ] 51
CyV (*kai-yo'o'on* syllables) [lacking in OJ] 64; [contraction of native
dissyllables] 72; [in Chinese loanmorphs, compressed or conflated?] 83
Czech [predictable accent developed out of more complex system?] 266
"D" [rising register (not needed for historical frame of reference?)] 265
*d- (or "*j-") [ancestor of initial y-] 20 36 57 366
d- [= ¨t- and ¨s-] 34; [borrowing, truncation, "special"] 30; [and n-] 32; 79; (of
da're) 391; [Yonaguni] 19 20
d 6 20; [after T] 76; [and z] 17 34; [and y] 19; [for -t-] 21; [for -n] 30
-d- 25; [and -n-] 32; [and -r- confused] 34; [prenasalized, Shikoku] 21; [> -y-] 20;
[devoiced in Hagiwara verb forms?] 133; [< prenasalized -nd- = /-nt-/] 667
-~d- (nasality on vowel) for -¨t- 21 ▯ ···d- [no such verb stems] 17
/da/ = ¨ta and ¨sa [Izu-Ōshima] 34 ▯ [da] = "za" [Aden] 34
da' [copula] 19; [Aomori forms] 19; [drops before daroo/desyoo] 129
δa = za [Toshima, Narada] 33 ▯ *-da- [verb formant] > -y- 35
*-da-Ci- > -ye[y]- [formant string = OJ bound auxiliary] 35 796
dada- [adjective-stem prefix] 821 ▯ [da'] daro'(o)/desyo'(o) 129
-daka- 'high with (respect to)' 817 819
dake 'only' (particle) [Ōsaka low] 170; [Kōchi and Kyōto "unaccented"] 171
DAKU (¨) 84; [contiguous to nasal syllable?] 85; [on initial syllable that was
earlier SEI] 88; [marks moved to upper right of kana] 118
dakuon ([syllables with] voiced obstruents) 20 23 27 35; [restrictions on initial
occurrence] 35; [and seion written with different characters in OJ] 116; [(in
Heian) distinguished from seion] 116
dakuon-ka 85 ▯ dakuo'n-ten [often neglected] 116; (= dakuten⁻) 118 190
DAKU sounds 84; [prenasalized through most of OJ period] 86
DAKU syllable(s) 29; [corresponding to SEI of OJ] 85; [contiguous to nasal] 85; [as
repeat of SEI] 85; [with DAKU that must be after 1600 (because JP has SEI)] 92;
[from contraction of nasal + SEI] 112; [marked with paired circles (1035)] 118;
[which were always DAKU] 118; [as morphophonemic variants of SEI syllables] 118
dakuten = dakuten⁻ = dakuo'n-ten 116 118 190
dani 'even' [particle] 104; (low in early-Edo Kyōto)] 170
daro'(o) after finite forms (= tentative) 129
data sources 78; [for earlier accent (chronology)] 342 ▯ date for proto-Japanese 53
da'tta daro(o)/desyo(o) 129 ▯ -dde < -gi-te or -bi-te [Hachijō] 125
/de/ = ¨te and ¨se [Izu-Ōshima] 34 ▯ [de] = ze [Aden] 34
de [syllable] 76; [to write OJ initial ye?] 51
de [copula gerund; Kyōto accent] 171 ▯ de' [Aomori forms] 19
... de: *see* V-a de ▯ δe = ze [Toshima, Narada] 33 ▯ /dea/ (= da' copula) [dial.] 19
deapicalization 33 ▯ deaspirated versions [of Ryūkyū stops] 25
de' a(r···) 19 ▯ decrescendo-crescendo effect 3
de 'emerge' [infinitive] A < B [Kyōto] 354 ▯ defective verb (root na- 'not') 821
degree of lexicalization [of compound nouns] 219 ▯ deictic(s) 20 36; [Ryūkyū] 805
delabialization [of F] before /o/ and /e/ (and /i/?) 11 ▯ delabialized [o] < [wo] 79
delayed voice onset for voiceless consonant before e o a 55
deleted copula in Aomori 19 ▯ delimiters [= "restrictives"] 30
de'-mo [particle; set off by juncture for emphasis (Tōkyō)] 172

du- 23 ⫿ [du] = "zu" [Aden] 34; [lacks affrication in dialects] 16
/du/ ("tu) different from /zu/ ("su) 17 ⫿ du [dzu] transcription for JP citations 86
du [emphatic particle in Ryūkyūs (Okinawa > ru) < unlenited zo] 71 110
du > dɨ 56 ⫿ ðu = zu [Narada] 33 ⫿ -du- (not always the value of BEAN) 87
dvandva [= coordinative] compounds 99 ⫿ [dᵥ] as ancestor of initial y-? 20 366
/dwo/ ≠ /to/ 58 ⫿ (-)dwoti [OJ pluralizer] 65
dy- 23 ⫿ dyads of nasal + oral 25 ⫿ dya˺ [dža] (= da˺ copula) [dialect] 19
dynamic register ("C" [falling]) 264; (also "D" [rising]?) 265
ᵈz 5 6; 33 34; [after T] 76
ᵈž 34; [after T] 76 ⫿ dž 33 34; [for proto-Japanese *d- (> y-)] 20 366
-[ᵈž]- alternating with -[ž]- 34 ⫿ dže [innovative] 16; for "de" 18
ᵈzɨ 16 76 16 ⫿ [dzɨ] [Kōchi] = earlier "tu, [various dialects] = "su 16
ᵈži [syllable] 16 76
[dži] = "ti [Kōchi], [Narada (affricated)] 16; [various dialects] = "si 16
džo 16 ⫿ [džɔ:] written "jŏ" [JP] 123 ⫿ džu 16 ⫿ -dzu [JP] 124
e- [phonograms for] 19; [and ye- fell together as ye- (mid Heian)] 130
e(-) 'can(not ···)' distinguished from ye- [in kana of 935] 83
E [Mathias notation for sensitive vowel of unattested or unknown type] 50
ë [for OJ Type B vowel (= -ey)] 50 ⫿ é [Mathias notation for Type A vowel] 50
*ə [Hattori] as source of OJ "ö" = Co 68 ⫿ ɛ < ai 43
*e [Hattori] > OJ central dialect /i/ = Cyi 68
e (type-neutral, unknown, or merged vowel) [two kinds neutralized after dentals] 49;
   50; [mostly < ey] 57; 58; [and i (merger of all varieties in Okinawa, Yonaguni)]
   52; [earlier Ryūkyu] 55, [preserved in Aka and Keruma] 52; [all cases go back to
   diphthongs?] 58; [Ryūkyū raising of] 122
/e/ [after epenthetic palatal glide] 15; [end of paired verb stem] 48; [in first
   syllable] 48; [low frequency] 48; [two kinds in OJ velar and labial syllables] 48,
   [two kinds of underlying] 49; [in proto-Japanese?] 53 58 68; [weak distribution
   for both OJ types explained] 58; [> /o/?], [> /i/?] 68; [alternating with /o/] 68;
   [and /ye/ merged as ye] 79; [written "ye" (JP)] 79
[e] < proto-Japanese ···oCi 53 ⫿ [e] < [ye] [by 1775 (earlier in east?)] 79
   (')e [and (')ye merged as ye early Heian] 19 51 83; [two kinds] 49; [< [e] (Zdb
   line on right)] 50; [< [ye] (Zdb line on left)] 50; 66
e₁ [ye] ≠ e₂ [e] 49 ⫿ e ≠ ye, e ≠ we 79 ⫿ e 'get' 42
e < fe 'to' (particle) 168; (Hn-Km accent) 170; [low] (Kyōto] 158 171, (early-Edo
   Kyōto, Ōsaka) 170, (Kōchi, Wakayama) 171; [1.3 not 1.1?] 347; 803
-e row of syllabary 83 ⫿ -e < -i [partially assimilated to preceding vowel] 70
-e [Shodon] < OJ -ey after velar preceded by OJ low vowel 54 ⫿ -e see V-e
/-e/ Hattori reconstruction of proto-Japanese imperative 668
···e infinitives [explanation] 131 ⫿ ···e- adjective stems 128
e > i [Ryūkyū] 25, (except Aka and Keruma) 52; e > (y)i 53
e > o after labial consonant 69 ⫿ earlier forms [of Chinese] 5
earlier juncture [to account for "pre-accent" of particles] 144
earlier pattern [of accent for an irregular word] preserved by related dialects 163
earlier phonetic value of Chinese tones [uncertain] 167
early attestations 51 51
early Chinese [loans] 35 72 73 165
early colloquial (Go-on) versions of Chinese loans [tone system preserved in initial
   syllable] 184
early Edo 158 170 203 343; [Kyōto] 205, (low particles) 170, (accent for B verbs of
   3 or 4 syllables [like Kōchi]) 205, (reflexes of /no/-attachment rule) 260
early Heian 77 ⫿ early Kamakura 210 343 ⫿ Early Middle Japanese 77
early spellings 81 ⫿ early voiced initials 30

f- [dating uncertain] 12; [Hankul transcription] 23; [bilabial through most of OJ
   period?] 84; [syllables with single circle (hudaku˺-ten)] 118
f [labiodental (Matsue, Miyako)] 12
-f- (= "h") [change to -w- started before Nara?] 12; [Hankul transcription] 23;
   [pronounced -w- before dropping between vowels] 37; [of kofor- 'freeze', spurious?]
   43; [of kufosa 'profit'] 87
"-f-" [major source of modern -w-] 12; [never voiceless fricative?] 366 667
FØ [Uwano notation for Ibuki-jima 2.3] 166
Fa [innovative] 76 ◊ Fa [for ha (Iwate ...)] 12 ◊ fa ≠ -wa 79
fa [initial written with Hankul "light p"] 11
fa (focus particle) 104; fā [Heian] (examples) 347; faa [Mg underlying] 359
fall and rise within a "syllable" (= mora) [dialects which have] 147
fall of pitch [inherent] 5; [from high to low] (usual realization of locus) 138,
   (Shuri) 139; [within a "syllable" = mora] (dialects which have)] 147, (represented
   by ˋ on vowel] 138; [persists for Kyōto oxytonic final syllable before juncture,
   heard as low on attached particle] 147; [of Tōkyō oxytonic may persist with heavy
   syllables] 148; [as manifestation of register] 161; [on last mora of Kyōto 2.5
   nouns in isolation (developed later?)] 168
fall register [Ibuki-jima (Uwano)] 166
false analogy 6 ◊ false etymology 13 ◊ false rendaku [after Vu not from nasal] 28
familiar: notation "s-" 36; verbs [majority Tōkyō tonic] 202 ◊ familiar words 3
family names [accent] 347 ◊ fa mo [particle string] 105 ◊ fast [speech] 3 185
fatas- 'complete, accomplish', fate[y]- 'reach completion' 51
fa ya, fa yo [particle string] 105
Fe [innovative] 76 ◊ Fe = se [Yamagata] 33
Fe for he [older Izumo] 8; [older Yamaguchi] 8 33; [northern Honshū dialects] 12
fe [Collado], [initial written with Hankul "light ph"] 11
-fe ≠ -we 79 ◊ "-fe" pronounced -we in late Heian and -ye by Muromachi 89
features of contour that cross word-length classes 179
feeling of "markedness" about initial voiced sounds 30
female personal names [accent] 347
fey ≠ fye 79 ◊ (fey/)fye 'direction/vicinity' 101 ◊ Fi [innovative] 76
fi [Collado], [Hankul phi; initial written with Hankul "light p"] 11
-fi ≠ -wi 79 ◊ fia (= /fya/) [Collado] 11
final /a/ in combining forms of nouns that end in /e/ 48
final accent [only when particle attached] 141; [suppressed (Tōkyō; Kōchi)] 148
final close (= high) vowel [attached to Chinese loans by the Japanese borrowers] 73
final fall [for 2.2a, 3.1a] 186; [as conditioned allophone of high pitch] 190;
   [adj attributive Hn-Kamakura -kì = -kíi] 190 217; [from compressing two syllables
   ("F" < "HL")?] 265; [in Wakayama as semantic marker] 361
final-fall words predominantly end in high vowels (-i, -u) 190
final high vowel [probably nasal] supplied for Chinese words ending in -ŋ 73
final high vowels (i u) going back to Chinese -ŋ -y -w -p 45
final long vowel 178
final low of 3-syllable [or longer] stem metathesized with high of ending 204
final modern high vowels [in Ryūkyūs] that come from earlier mid vowels 248
final nasal [in a few earlier nouns?] 74; [anomalous] 83; [in southern Ryūkyūs] 361
final /o/ or /u/ in combining forms of nouns that end in /i/ 49
final velar nasal of Chinese morphemes 26 45 73
final vowel [not pronounced c. 1500 in -tu of Chinese loanmorphs] 73; [reconstructed
   for basic forms of consonant stems of Old Japanese] 131
final vowel close (i u) or not [correlates with accent patterns in dialects] 166

front-vowel syllables [two kinds not distinguished in eastern OJ?] 811
frozen compound 44
Fu 1; [also hu] 76; [Iwate ...] 12 [] [Fʉ] before voiceless consonant 12
fu [initial written with Hankul "light p"], [Hankul hwu] 11
-fu ≠ -u 79 [] ···[f]-u ending 44
Fujiwara Sadaie/Teika 78 174 342 343 358 [] Fujiwara Tameie 83
Fujitani Nariakira 131 344 [] "fukúda" [JP] attempt to write [fukúda] 123
Fukuoka [2.3 and 2.2 merged with 2.1 as LH(-L); 2.4 and 2.5 as HL] 256; [oxytonic
    noun accent of 2.1/2/3 cancelled before /no/] 256
"Fukuoka city" like Ōita distinguishes 2.3 from 2.1/2 but before /no/ only 256
functional load [of opposition between syllables so and zo (low)] 110; [of
    sei-daku distinction in non-Chinese vocabulary (low)] 116
furigana 133 [] further compounding [does not affect accent pattern] 234
future [= presumptive] ending (V-amu) 38 65; *see* presumptive
fwo ≠ fo 57 [] fye [particle] 104 [] fye(/fey) 'direction/vicinity' [OJ] 101
fyikyi 'pull' as intensive prefix [common only Heian and later] 95
-G- ([γ], Middle Korean) 5
g- [in proto-Japanese?] 20 36; [borrowing, truncation, "special"] 30; 79
g [in contrast with ḡ = ŋ] 7; [two kinds as single phoneme] 7; [for -k- (Iki,
    ...)] 21; [after T] 76
ğ of Turkish 37 [] [˜g] for -g- [sporadic (Shima, Makurazaki)] 21
ḡ = [ŋ] 1 6 7; [in mimetic reduplications] 5; [with no oral reflex] 7; [dropped
    between vowels] 7; [epenthetic] 20; [for -g- (northeast)] 21
-g- [dropped between vowels] 7; [for -k- (northeast)] 7 21; [replaced by glottal
    stop] 7; [epenthetic] 20; [later] 20; [prenasalized (Shikoku)] 21; [Yonaguni] 25;
    [of koogen = kooken⁻ 'efficacy'] 28
-ḡ- 25; [later] 20; [for -ˈk-] 21; expanded to -nḡ- [-ŋ:ŋ-] 81
-g- [OJ] doublet forms? 92 [] -g- stems 133 [] ga [syllable] 76; [Kudaka] 10
ga (particle) [genitive-nominative marker] 104; [written as "ka"] 109; [marking
    subject of subordinate clause in Man'yō-shū] 119; 163 168; [early-Edo high after
    high, low after low] 170; [had rise? (Mochizuki)] 170; [Kyōto, Kōchi "unaccented"]
    171; [Mg tonic particle (switches pitch from preceding syllable)?] 173; [Hn-Km
    accent ga] 214; [NS high] 348
ga 'but' [Tōkyō accent] 152; [no juncture in Hagiwara] 153; [in Kyōto preceded by
    juncture after Type-A imperfect only] 156
-gaeru < -gafey- 791 [] -gamasi- [bound adjective] 816 820
ga-na [desiderative] 104 [] -ganasi- 'sad (with respect to)' 817 819
ga-ni [particle (Hn-Km accent)] 170 [] -gara- 'piquant, spiced (with)' 817 819
-garasu < *-na-ka-ra-sa- 791 [] 'garlic' [words for] 53 54
-garu₁ < *-n[a]-ka-ra- 791 [] -garu₂ < -g[e] (< *-n- key₁,₁) ara-ᵦ 791
-gasu < *-n[a]-ka-sa- 791 [] -gata 'model' or 'shape' (quasi-free) 233
-gata- 'hard (with respect to)' 817 819; 'difficult (to V)' [aux adj] 821
-gatana- [Shuri] 'difficult (to V)' [aux adj] 821
-ḡateni 'unable' < V-i n[i] kate- 26
-gau < -gafu < *-n[a]-ka-pa- 791 [] -gawasi- < -gafasi- [bound adjective] 816 820
geminate -tt- [attempt to preserve voiceless allophone?] 125
geminated -n, -t 75 [] geminated vowels 13
geminates [written for long vowels] 3; [Korean] 23; [simplification] 37; [to write
    initial tense consonants of Yonaguni and Nakijin] 81
geminate vowels [in adjective -[k]u forms] 127; [from joining morphemes] 349
gemination 2; [of -m-, -n-, and rarely -t-] 75; [in eastern dialects] 134; [in
    Hachijō nakke < na-ke = na-[k]i 'is lacking'] 810

he'i = he'i(-sei) = hyo'o(-syoo) 'even (tone)' [low pitch] 167 181
Heian = Heian‾ [period] (Hn) 2 10 12 20 24 26 31 32 38; [vowel system] 43; 45;
  [velar elision] 71; [orthographic variants] 72; 77; 85 93 95 110 116 119 121
  125 129 130 132 134; [sources for accent] 167; [notations] 174, (of accent) 167,
  (many do not differentiate 2.5 from 2.4) 185; [texts] 174; [markings (of ue, sita,
  uti, hito) as 2.2] 186; 190 210; 215; [dialect] 216; [attestations] 229; 217 346
Heian accents with final high-fall of pitch for adjective forms 127
Heian and later evidence for SEI-DAKU distinctions 84
Heian hiragana orthography failed to indicate SEI-DAKU distinctions 87
Heike-mabushi 203; [early-Edo Kyōto accent] 205; 343 360 361
Heike-monogatari 78 343 815
Heike-seisetsu = Heike-mabushi 254 343; (Heike-shōsetsu) 361
Hepburn (romanization) ["fu", "shi"] 19 ▯ -hh- 142
HHL [Ōsaka nouns] = HLL [Kyōto] 158 259; HHL → HHH(-L) [Kyōto] 360
HHLH [Mg gerunds] = HHL|H 244
hi- (adj-stem prefix) 821 ▯ hi(-) 'non-' (prefix; pseudo adnoun; free noun) 229 319
hi = [hi], [çi] 6; (Iwate ...) 12; (replaced by ši) 1 18; (Fi in dialects) 11; 76
hi = .hi‾ 'fire' [Kyōto] 228 307 349
hi 'sun; day' [1.2 despite Mg irregular marking] 350
hi 'day' [Tōkyō atonic only when unmodified, yet 1.2] 186 ▯ -hi- [Korean formant] 64
hiatus filler 36; [epenthetic -r-] 667
Hideo < fide-wo 'excellent male' 13; Hide-yo < fide-[w]o 15
high (pitch) [represented with a line above the syllable] 138; [nondistinctive in
  Kyōto] 143, (except when it ends at a locus before low) 155; [on final mora of
  Kyōto low atonic words disappears after suppressed juncture] 149; [after Kyōto
  initial low never more than one syllable] 157; [particles that attached high] 170;
  [before locus in low-register tonic word] 143; [prototonic not so high as other
  Tōkyō tonic types] 345; [on next-to-last syllable of Kagoshima Type A] 834
high atonic (nouns [velar elision in]) 133; (Kyōto four-mora words favor) 227
high front vowel [Ie-jima] < *i or *e 42; [non-palatal(izing)] 122
high front vowels [Ryūkyū evidence for ancient distinctions] 53
high-low contour [in Chinese binoms] 184
high-low distinctions of pitch accent [marking by early Japanese scholars] 84
high-low-high tunes [of Narada] 146
high/low pitch shown by upper/lower marks on left of kana 118
"high plateau" of Tōkyō [Tōkyō-type dialects which lack] 152
high register [stems] 133; [phrases] 143; [Ibuki-jima (Uwano)] 166; [with no
  accentual locus (2.1, 3.1, 4.1, etc.)] 251; Nakijin/Yonaguni "A"] 262
high vowel (= close vowel: i u) [dropped between voiceless consonants (Yonaguni)]
  25; [from final velar nasal] 26; 76
high vowel i [(as infinitive) losing syllabicity before -te] 125
hih··· 5 ▯ hi'-hi 'baboon' 6 ▯ hįki [verb infinitive] 8 ▯ hima‾ 'free time' 6
hiragana 4 23 24; [connotations of] 30; [spelling] 45; ["N"] 75; 87 116
Hirayama [accent notation] (Kagoshima) 139, (Kyōto) 145; see also H
Hirosaki ("mirror image" accent) 145 146; [phonetic redefinition of locus] 246
Hiroshima [no locus on second mora of heavy syllable] 144 ▯ hiss 34
historical change (of "-h-" to -w-) 12
historical development [of DAKU for older SEI] 85; [of accent patterns] 341
historical difference [of one-mora vs. two-mora nouns] 139
historically misleading [descriptions of hortative ending] 129; [explanations] 131
historical processes [deriving -oo different from those deriving -u] 129
historical process led oxytonic accent [of Kyōto] to retreat in longer phrases? 158

historical spelling 9 17 23 24; [connotations of] 30; 33 37 38 45 48 82; ["ha"] 87
historical traces [of "h" and "w" medially] masked by vowel crasis or contraction 12
historic Japanese 44 ◊ hi̯T = hi̯ki 8 ◊ Hitachi-fudoki 78 811 ◊ H-L of Type 1.2 180
HLH [Mg gerunds] = HL|H 244; HLHL [modern dialects, one H always nondistinctive] 350
*HL(L)H [unusual within a (Heian-attested) word] 350
Hn = Heian period (c. 800-1200) 85 372 ◊ ho- (combining form of .hi⁻ 'fire') 228
ho [syllable] 11; [devoiced before k or s] 76 ◊ Hōbutu-shū (1221) 75
hodo 'as much as' (particle) [early-Edo high after high, low after low] 170; [Ōsaka
   low] 170 171; [Kyōto, Kōchi unaccented] 171
Hōjō-ki 75 78 ◊ hoka 'save' (particle) [always low in Kyōto] 158
Hokkaidō [does not cancel oxytonic noun accent before /no/] 256
Hoke-kyō tanji 78 80 118 167 342 ◊ homogeneity of [OJ] orthography 84
homonymous surface patterns of accent 371 ◊ homophone 6 9, [clash] 126 346
homorganic [nonsyllabic vowel extension] 2 ◊ hondaku⁻¹-ten 118
hono- < fono- 'slightly' [quasi-prefix] 821
honorific prefix: mi- < myi- [no nigori] 102 107 230; o- 230
honorific: sama 121; title 33; V-as- 65 ◊ Honzō-wamyō (918) 78 181
hook mark (⁷) 5 ◊ horizontally paired circles 118
hortative 17 129 131; hortative-tentative (= presumptive) 37
horo- 'slightly' [quasi-prefix] 822
hu- 'not' (prefix) 229 320 ◊ hu [syllable] 1 11; [Fu for many Tōkyō speakers] 12; 76
hudaku⁻¹-ten 118 ◊ huh··· 5 ◊ -huka- = -ᵇ/ᵇuka- 'deep with' 817 819
humble verb mausi > mɔɔsi > mo⁷osi 'say/do' 45 ◊ Humō-ki = Bumō-ki 344
"···huru" for "···yuru" 42 ◊ hush 6; hushing [did not precede syncope?] 124, 132
(husi-)ha⁷kase [chanting guides] 174
/hw/ = [F] 13 ◊ hw- [Hankul] 11 23 ◊ hwV common in Ryūkyūs 72
hy- [replaced by š-] 1, 11 ◊ hybrid conjugation/verbs 32 201 665
hyo⁷o = hyo⁷o(-syoo) = he⁷i(-sei) 'even (tone)' [low pitch] 167
hyo⁷o-kei/he⁷i-kei = hyo⁷o-syoo/he⁷i-sei [no] karu 'even-tone light' = to⁷o(-syoo/
   -sei) 'East (tone)' [fall?] 172
hyoosyoo-/heisei-kei = hyo⁷o-syoo /he⁷i-sei no karu 350 ◊ hypercorrected 4
hyphen 2; [separates rearticulated vowels] 3; [shows boundary between syllables or
   morphemes] 3; [within a morpheme] 3; [in etymological formulas] 825
hypothetical: addition(s) to Old Kyōto accent patterns [by Hattori (3.5a)] 180, [by
   Hayata (2.2a and 3.2a)] 180, [by McCawley (3.7a)] 180; intermediate forms 121
hypothetical (and unpronounced) -W in Sino-Korean words [with Chinese Vu = -Vw] 11
"hypothetical" form (izen-kei): here called provisional-concessive
hyoro- 'slightly' [quasi-prefix] 822 ◊ "H x" 228
i- [dropped (leaving voiced initial)] 29
i- 'shoot (an arrow)' (not "*[y]i-" or "*i[y]-") 52; (A → B, tonic in Tōkyō) 354
i(-) verb prefix 70 94; [given separate accentuation] 668; [in reduced form y-] 668
I [Mathias notation for sensitive vowel of unattested or unknown type] 50
i (type-neutral, unknown, or merged vowel) [as diphthongal extension] 2; 5; [when
   fully voiced] 6; [after t] 17; [(y)i] 19; [< e] 25; [interdental fricatives
   before] 33; [at end of verb stem paired with stem ending /uC/ or /oC/] 48; [two
   kinds of underlying] 49, (neutralized after dentals) 49; 50 52; [and e (merger of
   all varieties in Okinawa and Yonaguni)] 52; [central allophone in Shodon] 55;
   [< i or e (Ryūkyū)] 55; [elided, leaving N or T] 72; 76; [and yi not distinguished
   in proto-Japanese] 122; [written for Ryūkyū non-palatal(izing) high front vowel]
   122; [devoicing in verb gerund] 124; [losing syllabicity before -te] 125;
   [adjective stems that end in] 135; [that later "broke" to /ye/] 812; [difficult
   for some eastern dialects to distinguish from /e/]) 812

infinitive 7 8; [e or i] 15; 17; [VN-ǯi] 17; [ši 'do'] 17; ending -i- 18; [of old
    negative auxiliary] 26; [of hybrid conjugation] 32; [Kansai] 37 44; 45 51; [of
    lower bigrade stem myise[y]- 'show'] 54; [eliding stem-final *a] 62; (verb ending
    -i or -[i]) 121; [for consonant stems had short vowel ···C-i] 121; [for vowel
    stems] 125, (pronounced with long vowel?) 121; 151 191; [accent preserved in old-
    fashioned Tōkyō accentuation of compound verbs] 207; (as V-'[y]i) 191; [marked by
    pitch change (11th-century Kyōto)] 211; [modern Kyōto locus heard only when
    something is attached] 211; [before juncture at end of phrase (as substitute for
    gerund)] 211; [honorific o- prefixed (atonic)] 232; [substituting for predicative
    finite (-u)] 666; (= ren'yō-kei) 801; 802
infinitive and gerund 'te separated by juncture 191
infinitive-attached auxiliaries 808
infinitive-derived noun(s) 35; [with velar elision] 126; 191; [accent if from tonic
    infinitive more than two syllables long] 207; [honorific o- prefixed] 230-232;
    [as simplex even when derived from compound verb] 234; [B stems → Kyōto A] 274;
    [Goka-mura atonic: many pronounced prototonic] 370; [irregularities of accent] 672
infinitive-derived nouns [listed as "2.1" but qualifying for "?2.1a"] 188, [as "3.1"
    but qualifying for "?3.1a"] 187; ["B" include 3.4 (Kōchi HHL)] 258
infinitive ending -i [lost its syllabicity before -te] 125; [absorbed after vowel
    stem] 126 155; [Kyōto attaches high to B stem, low to A] 155; [as -Ci] 667
infinitive -[k]u of adjective 127
infinitive of: bound neg aux -(a)n- 111; perfect aux (V-i) tu[ru] 191; "third"
    type verb (B´, 11th century LHL) 198
infinitive (or root) + auxiliary [reduced to make predicative and attributive] 667
infinitive + semu = /syemu/ > /syeu/ > /syoo/ as explanation for hortatives 130
infinitives and derived nouns of four or more syllables [accent] 291
infinitives (monosyllabic = one-syllable) 197
infinitives of: Type A stems 156; A and B stems both Kyōto oxytonic (but phrase-
    final locus moves left) 212; atonic stems [oxytonic accent often cancelled] 355;
infinitive + -te 121; [juncture lost] 125; [syllabicity of i lost] 125
infix 8; [expressive] 80; [intensive] 81
inflected: adjective (= keiyō-shi) 801; forms [contracted] 62, [broken into two
    phrases] 356; stems 151; words (= yōgen) 801 ◌ inflection 45
influence [on Kinki accentuations] of other dialects (especially Tōkyō) 219
inherent: basic accent ["tonic" words] 160; fall of pitch 5
initial accent [= prototonic] 141; [acquired by -t··· forms of auxiliary o̅k̅u̅
    after atonic gerunds] 210
initial automatic low [of Tōkyō first mora, extended in Aomori] 141
initial consonants [mimetic sets] 5; [sporadic dropping] 42; [of particles] 119
initial DAKU syllables [OJ largely lacks] 93
initial elision [sporadic] 36 ◌ initial fall of pitch 185 ◌ initial fortition 20
initial glottal in Nakijin and Shuri 73 ◌ initial h- [Greek] 3; [prothetic] 10
initial-high Chinese loans with "rising" tone 184
initial high (pitch) [in Kyōto] 143; [in Narada always nondistinctive (like initial
    low in Tōkyō)] 146; [falls to low in Ryūkūs and southern Kyūshū] 205;
    [nondistinctive in Nozaki a̅m̅e̅ g̅a̅ but distinctive in k̅a̅s̅a̅ g̅a̅] 254
initial low [in Kyōto always distinctive, in Tōkyō automatic] 143; [of Kyōto as
    special case of locus] 143; [register treated as different from locus] 144; [of
    Kyōto Type B verb stem continues till ending is attached] 155; [string raised to
    modern Kyōto high in a number of longer double-low words] 249; [in Tōkyō
    nondistinctive] 256; [in Tōkyō not so low as Kyōto initial low] 345
initial mp- [Hankul] 22 ◌ initial o- 38

irregularity of cross-dialect correspondence of compound nouns 219
irregularly cancelled accent of oxytonic infinitive of atonic verb [after ni in
  Tōkyō purpose expressions] 210
irregular quadrigrade verbs 665 ◻ irregular reflexes [Goka-mura] 370
irregular upper bigrade [(*ka-hen*) verb kuru] 665; [(*sa-hen*) verb suru] 665
irregular verb stems 665
-iru ⟨ -iy- ⟨ *⋯ᵐ/₂-Ci- 791 ◻ -iru/-i monograde conjugation 126
isati- 'weep' (OJ monograde) 666
Ise (from Terakawa and Kusaka 1944) 369 ◻ Ise-monogatari 78 134
Ishizuka Harumichi 211 ◻ iˈsi 2.2b (beginning Kyōto compounds that are B) 220
isolated areas with [-g-] in northeastern Honshū 7
isolated citations of Myōgi-shō (mostly 2.5 = 2.4: low-high) 168
isolated pockets in southern Nara [accent like Tōkyō] 255
isolated verb forms 152 ◻ ita- [adjective-stem prefix] 821
-iˈ-ta [Kyōto] with accent delayed one mora when i is absorbed into contraction 155
italics 1; italic *k t* = Yonaguni -K- -T- 25
itasu '(humbly) do' (for suru in predicating free verbal nouns) 672
⋯i-te [gerund of vowel stem] 121
iterate 5 ◻ iterated V₁-i V₁ 670 ◻ iterative nigori 85 87; 109 92
iti- [adjective-stem prefix] 821 ◻ Itō-machi in Shizuoka 211
Itoshima-gun [Fukuoka] 2.3 ≠ 2.1/2 but before /no/ only 257
itte from iki-te 'going' 125 ◻ ⋯i-u ⟩ ⋯yuu 127
iy [⟨ oy or uy] 50 52 63 64; [Ryūkyū reflexes] 52; [phonetic source] 52 64
-iy [OJ] ⟩ Shodon -i [ɨ] 54
-iy 52; [treated as "-wi" by Unger] 57; [all compressions of -oi and -ui] 58; [few
  root-internal] 63; [nouns from verb inf with -u or -o in root] 64; [ɨy] 67
⋯i-yoo forms developed in east? 131 ◻ *izen-kei* = provisional-concessive 133 668
Izumo [no accent retreat for polysyllabic vowel stems before -t⋯ endings] 206;
  [merges 2.1 with 2.2 as LH(-H) and keeps 2.3 as oxytonic LH(-L)] 256; [does not
  cancel oxytonic noun accent before /no/] 256; [data] 368; [accent notations] 369
"j-" (Okinawa-go jiten) changed to "y-" 366 ◻ *j- (or *d-) ⟩ y- 57; -j- ⟩ -y- 20
Japanese: babytalk 33; grammarians 77 86 130; lexicographers 28; linguists 3 17 119
  363; philologists 12; scholars 73, [early] 84
Japanese-English dictionary [Hepburn] 28 ◻ Japanese-Korean glossary 2
Japanese pluralizers tati and (-)dwoti [Korean cognate for] 65
Japanese-Portuguese dictionary = JP = Vocabulario da lingoa de Iapam 4 11 27 28 42
  44 45 69 73 74 78 79 81 85 104 115; [citations normalized in transcription] 86
  120; 122 126 127 132 133 813
Japan-made *kokuji* "BOW-ONE" (variant of HEAVEN?) 97
je [to write initial ye of OJ?] 51; "je" for modern /ze/ [JP] 79
Jikyō = [Shinsen-]Jikyō (892) 71 78 92 98 100 102 104 120 167 181 342
"jŏ" [JP] = [dʒɔ:] 123 ◻ Jōben: [Jōben - bon] Shūi[-waka]-shū 343
Jōgū-ki 97 ◻ Jōgū-Shōtoku - hōō - teᵉ/ₐisetsu 78
JP = Japanese-Portuguese dictionary (1603-4): Vocabulario da lingoa de Iapam 372
juncture 3 5 33 44; [after word with basic accent] 76; [auxiliary separated from
  infinitive by] 121; [before gerund ending -te] 121, (retained; dropped) 125;
  [between two atonic phrases (clearly heard in Shuri)] 139; 147; [persists between
  tonic words (Tōkyō-type dialects)] 149; [persists between low-register words
  (Kyōto)] 149; [may drop after suppressing final accent] 150; [cancelling final
  accent of gerund of Tōkyō atonic stem before dropping] 154; [before Kyōto
  particles] 156, (before ni in purpose expressions) 156; [setting off Tōkyō
  dissyllabic enclitics for emphasis] 172; 191; [dropping] 209

ka-na [particle string] 104

kana (syllabic phonograms) [symbols for "h-"] 12; [Gang of Four] 16; 49; ["mu"] 75; ["o" first used for "wo" in 883] 79; ["o" and "wo" to show pitch of merged syllable [wo]] 79; [with "-tu"] 73; ["wo" in official orthography] 79; [mostly ignored sei-daku] 85; 113; [used only for particles etc.] 116; [with tone marks] 118; [reading note] 137

kana spelling/orthography 4 18 43; [misleading on CyV and CwV) 72; [for nasal vowels (-i, -u, or nothing)] 73; [ignored long vowel for gerunds?] 121; ["-u" to spell -[k]u] 127; ["u" representing nasal -m- or -ũ-] 132; 137

kana-ma'ziri writing 116

Kana-mozi-zukai Ken-syuku-ryoo-ko [= *tidimi-sizimi - suzumi-tudumi*] syuu 16

kana-written words with no accent indications [in Myōgi-shō] 85 ◊ Kanbun texts 471

Kanchi-in [- bon] Myōgi-shō (Kn) 167 342 ◊ Kan'ei-bon [text of Man'yō-shū] 111

kane 'metal' < kane[y] < *kana-Ci 266 ◊ "Kango" 248

kanguru 'surmise hidden motives' [Kyōto B (Umegaki)] 199 ◊ Kang Wuseng 11 22

kanji [giving false etymology] 220

kannoo⁻ 'response' < kan-oũ 'response' [spelled kannou in 1185] 75

Kan-on [accent] 248 ◊ Kansai [adjective] 44; [version of copula] 80

Kantō area settled by migrants from Kyūshū? 177

Kantō-type pattern for velar-final verb stem 124 ◊ kan-ži' 'feel' (infinitive) 17

*kapaa 'skin' and 'river' [Hattori] 253 ◊ kappa [Greek] = Yonaguni -K- 25

kara [particle] 104; [Hn-Km accent kara] 170; [Kōchi unaccented; Wakayama low] 171; ['···-ru kara (Tōkyō)] 152

-kara [bound element in compounds] 100

-kareru < *-ka-ra-Ci-, -karu < *-ka-ra- 791 ◊ -ka-sa- 796

ka-si 'indeed' (particle string) 104; [early-Edo low] 170

-ka-si- [adjective-stem formant] 817

kasite as two syllables [khašte] though three moras? 124 ◊ -kasu < *-ka-sa- 791

kata- 'hard' attached as auxiliary to verb infinitive [obligatory nigori] 99

katakana [connotations of] 30; ["N" probably a variant of "ni"] 75; 116 119

kau- < kaw' without a nasal final [first syllable of koɔgen = kooken⁻] 28

ka'u [notation] 'buys' 44 ◊ -kau < -kafu < *-ka-pa- 791 ◊ kaze⁻ 'wind' 5

Kazu-(')o, Kazu-ho = Kazu-wo ('Number [One]) male') 13

Kazusa (province; DAKU initials prenasalized?] 109

ke [syllable] 6; [palatalized in Toyama] 18; 76

ke as /kye/ [evidence from kana spellings] 137

-ke [Hachijō ending for adjective attributive] 810

-ke < -kye / -key [Azuma] = -ki [adjective attributive] 811 822

-ke [and -kya geminate after monosyllabic adjective stem (Hachijō)] 810; [raised to -kyi in non-eastern OJ adjective attributive] 811

*-ke (?*proto-J attributive) diphthongal in origin 812

-ke- < -key- < -ka -Ci- [adjective-stem formant] 817 ◊ Keichū 78 125 246 343

keijō-gen ("attributionals") 813 ◊ keiyō-meishi ('adjectival noun') 802

-keku nominalization of retrospective 127 ◊ kenkyuu-zyo'⁻ 'research institute' 120

keru 'kick' lower bigrade > ker-u quadrigrade 665 666

-keru < -key- < *-ka-Ci- 792 ◊ "keu" = kyoo [kana spellings] 137

ke'wa'i⁻) 'signs' [etymology] 13 ◊ key ≠ kye 79

key 'tree(s)' as OJ variant reduction of ko-Ci (> kiy) 68

-key- [derivative suffix (making adjective stems)] 51 134

-key or -kye written for eastern OJ adj attributive 811 ◊ -key ?< -k[u] a[r]-yi 812

Kg = Kagoshima 372 ◊ KggD = Kokugo-gaku dai-jiten 372

-khi- [Korean formant] 64 ◊ Khmer [Cambodian] 115

ki [syllable] 17 76; [Shuri reflex distinguished from that of ke by affricated
   palatalization] 55 ◊ ki- 'this'? 69
.ki⁻ 'tree, wood' [Kyōto] 228; [as first element of noun compounds] 306; 359
k̄ī < k̄ī-i 'wear', < ki-ī 'come' infinitive [Kyōto] 354
-ki- (in Miyako verb forms) 783; (Korean formant) 64
-ki < -kyi [adjective attributive (= adnominal)] [loosely attached] 127;
   [-kì = -k̄īi (Hn-Km)] 217, 347; [separate phrase] 357; 803; [Ryūkyū examples] 806;
   [trace of -k- retained in stem ooki-] 812; 822
-[k]i [adjective attributive with velar elision] 45 79 126 127; [elision in all
   dialects except Hachijō] 127; 134; [incorporated into monosyllabic adjective stems]
   804; [sporadic in Heian] 806; [Ryūkyū examples] 806; [general in 1200s?] 357
Kii (placename) < kiy (< *ko-Ci) 'tree(s)' 71
ki-ka⁷e⁷ru 'change (clothes)' lexicalized to kiŋa⁷e⁷ru (c. 1960) 115
Kikai velar nasal 21 ◊ -[⁷]kin 'money' (suffix) [Tōkyō] 233
Kindaichi [2.5 ≠ 2.4] 171; [treatment of "pre-accent"] 144
ki(ni) 'because' [particle; Kōchi low] 171 ◊ Kinkai-[waka-]shū (1213) 133
Kinki dialects 143; [other than Kyōto] 157; [with double-low words differing from
   Kyōto versions] 185; [regular compound-verb accent for -masu] 211; [trend toward
   high atonic for four-mora words] 227; [accent remarkably stable] 255
kin roles [terms for] 6 ◊ ki⁷nsei 'modern' contrasted with ko⁷dai 'ancient' 77
kinterms with long vowels 71 ◊ Kishū - bon Man'yō-shū 119
-ki-te > -tte [Hachijō] 125 ◊ ···[k]i-te [verb gerund] 37
kiy ≠ kyi 79 ◊ kiy 'tree' [rendaku form -giy] as a suffix in OJ nouns 53
*kiy [for first syllable of kiba 'fang'] < *kuCi not *koCi 53
-kiy 'wine' in compounds 102
kk- [to write unaspirated velar stop of Yonaguni and Nakijin] 81 ◊ -kk- 2 142
"K.K." 113 ◊ -(k)ko- [adjective formant] 816 817
K kun(-chū) = phonogram translation notes in Koji-ki 372
-kkurusi- = -kurusi- = -gurusi- 'onerous (with respect to)' 817
Km = Kamakura period 365 ◊ Kn = Kanchi-in text of Myōgi-shō 372
ko- < kwo(-) [adj-stem prefix] 821 ◊ ko- (?< *kwo-) / ka- 'slightly' 69
ko-, ko(T)- 'little' [prefix] 8 229 310 ◊ ko- 'thick(ly saturated)' (adj stem) 216
ko- 'day' 69 ◊ ko-, ko(-) 'tree' 59 228 ◊ ko⁷- , ko- 'come' 36 59 69
ko-, ko [proximal deictic 'this'] 36; [connected with A-ku/-kyi?] 812
ko (S ko = S ka 'whether S') 69
-ko 'place' 69 ◊ -ko/-ŋo [diminutive] 115 ◊ Kōbō-daishi = Kūkai 118
Kōchi [anomalies of verb form accent] 158; [B´ verbs LH-H] 198; [Type B verbs
   HL-L] 198; [retains "B" category for verb stems, like Muromachi and early-Edo
   Kyōto] 205; [infinitive-derived nouns from original B verbs; only last syllable
   low] 212; [atonicization before /no/ for 2.2, 2.3, (Kobayashi) 3.4] 258
Kōchi-type pronunciation [of 2.5 nouns comes from suppressing low in isolation]1180
ko⁷dai, kodai-go⁻ = Early Middle Japanese = "classical" Japanese (Heian period) 77
ko⁷go = "older Japanese", "obsolete", "archaism" 77 ◊ Kogo-shūi (807) 78 88 815
Koji-ki 49 57 65 74; (= Ki SPEECH radical) 78; 100 105 106 107; (mo ≠ mwo)
   108; 110 111 112 119 127 253 342 542
Kojiki-den 78; [gave essence of Lyman's Law] 93
Kokin-kunten-shō = [Kokin - [waka-shū]] Kunten-shō 171
Kokin mokuroku-shō [confused -m and -n] 75
Kokin-shū = Kokin[-waka]-shū 78 118 134 342 ◊ [Kokin[-waka-shū]] Kunten-shō 78 343
kokugogaku [the field of] 125 ◊ kokuji 97
Komatsu dialect [2.5 ≠ 2.4] 171 [long first syllables H:L in reflexes of 2.2 and
   2.3 with final high vowel] 248

labial: glide 13 15; initial [p- > f- by 842?] 12, 59; lenition [stages of] 37; onset of [we] 79; pronunciation of "h-" (before i, e, ya) 11; semivowel -w- 57; fricative [before palatal syllables] 11, [used for sibilant, Yamagata] 33; syllables Fi and Fe 12; vocalization 122 132

labiality 5; [of f- (erosion of)] 11 ▯ labialization a > o 54

labiodental version [of bilabial fricative] in dialects 12

lagging articulation of rounded vowel 13

language change [recurrent types rather than universal trends] 266

languages [other than Japanese] 1

laryngeal voiced fricative [lenition of Middle Korean stops] 82

last high syllable 5 ▯ last low mora BEFORE a high [Narada locus] 145

last mora of low atonic word automatically high in Kyōto 143

late Heian 73 77 148 348; ["Insei"] 32; late mid Heian 77

late Muromachi 343 ▯ Late Middle Japanese 77 119 ▯ Latin [elements in English] 229

lax [Type B vowel] 50 ▯ left-shift in Kyōto? 255

length of Kyōto oxytonic final syllable [curtailed before juncture, suppressed before particle] 147

length of Kagoshima phrase [determines phonetic manifestations of accent] 140

lengthened monosyllables 349; [kaa as abbreviation of ka-yo'o⁻ 'Tuesday'] 72

lengthened vowel [in Shuri] 139; *see* long vowels, vowel lengthening

lengthening [of hiss (in -ss-)] 142; [of hush (in -ssy-)] 142; [of pharyngal breathiness (in -hh-)] 142; [of vowel of basically one-mora words in Shuri] 134; *see also* elongation, long vowels, vowel lengthening.

lengthening of final syllables in Yonamine [secondary] 253

lengthening of last vowel of reduplicating adj stem in Ryūkyūs 814

lengthening of monosyllabic infinitives of verbs 357

lengthening of monosyllables [automatic] 64; [attested 794] 71; 72 349

lengthening of short monosyllabic first morpheme of Chinese binom 220

lengthening of vowel [compensatory, after dropping reduced nasal syllable]? 122

lengthenings and shortenings of Shodon [secondary] 253

lenition(s) [-b- to -w-] 12; [voiced stops (initial)] 20; 34; [*-b- > -w-] 36; [labial] 37; [-m- to -w-] 38; [du to ru in Okinawa] 71; [-d- to -r- (early in Ryūkyū 'who') and 'what'] 71; [-k- (in Chiba) between back vowel and front or high vowel] 81; [F to subminimal phoneme of juncture] 82; 210

lexicalization(s) [of delimiters] 30; [of nasal grunt] 73; 95 101; [ellipsis of ga/no without] 96; [of ki-ka'e'ru 'change (clothes)' to kiŋa'e'ru (c.1960)] 115; [of N-tu N] 103; [of Numeral-tu-N 103]; [of mitukeru (old because younger speakers lack tonic variant)] 214; [with respect to accent] 214; [of compound verbs (Tōkyō) 354; 357; [from syntactic reduction] 359; [incomplete] 669; [of A-ku] 804

lexicalized compounds [inherit simple accent reflexes] 219

lexicalized structure vs. syntactic phrase 801

lexical: reductions of sentences 669; restructuring of morphemes 59; variants [with compression] 363 ▯ lexicographers 120 121 ▯ lexicon 138

LH [Mg 2.4/5] attached /no/ as L 260 ▯ LH˦ [Tōkyō, Hiroshima] = H˦L [Kyōto] 338

L-H of Type 1.3 180

LHH / LLH [early Edo free variation?], LHH > LLH [Kyōto before Ōsaka?] 360

LH-H [Matsue] 176 ▯ *LH-H with an "original" 2.4-no [why not attested?] 174

LHL [1700 Ōsaka] ← HHH (similar cases in modern dialects?) 360 ▯ LH-L [Matsue] 176

"light" entering tone 190; "light" syllables (one mora) 141

linguists 25 34 168 180 162 169 ▯ linguist's device 10 ▯ [Lit.] = literary 372

literacy [spread of] 125; [preventing oxytonic length compression?] 147

... masi: *see* V-a masi 〚 masi- 132 〚 masizi- > mazi- 'probably not' (> mai) 819
-⁻maˈsu [polite auxiliary (the old predicative), contraction of -marasu(ru)] 131
-masu < *-ma-sa- 792 〚 -⁻masuˈreba provisional of polite auxiliary 131
-⁻masuˈru [attributive of polite auxilary sometimes used in adnominalizations] 131
-masyoo = -⁻masyoˈo < -mase-u < -mase-mu 47 129 131
/mateni/ as "older form" of made ni? 112
Matsue (from Hiroto and Ōhara 1955) 368; [accent notations] 369
ˈmatu > maˈtu 'pine' 2.4 [Tōkyō] 254 〚 -matu < *-ma-ta- 792
-mau < -mafu < *-ma-pa- 792 〚 -mawaru < -mafaru < *-ma-pa-ra- 792 〚 *maw[aya] 71
mazi < *mazi[-si] [predicative of aux adj] 132 〚 ma[z]i, ma[zi]i > maˈi 132
mazi-ki [attributive], mazi-[k]i (Muromachi); mazi-ku [infinitive] 132
-■b- [Aomori] 21 〚 [m:be] pronunciation of ubey/mubey? 107
McCawley's "long" nouns 160 〚 me- < mey 'eye' [quasi-prefix] 822
me [syllable] 76; (as /mye/ [evidence from kana spellings]) 137
me > mi but mi > ni [Ie-jima] 483 〚 me < mye (?< myina < *mi-na) 'woman' 474
.me⁻ 'eye' [Kyōto] 228; [as first element in compound nouns] 305
meaning difference between forms with -Co/-Cwo and those with -Ca 59
medial: *dakuon* 20; gemination of -m, -n, -t 75; voiced obstruents as reductions
   of nasal syllable 30; -y- 19 〚 mei-dōshi 'nominal verbs' 802
Meiji (= Meˈizi 77): prescriptive grammar 808; restoration 125
mei-keiyōshi 'nominal adjectives' 802 〚 (-)mekasu < *(-)myekasu < *miCa-ka-sa- 792
(-)meku < *(-)myeku < *miCa-ka- (bound verb) 670 792
"meδ" = myoo [Portuguese spellings] 137 〚 merged predicative-attributive form 133
merger(s) 44; [obscuring earlier situation] 162; [of accent classes (except Ibuki-
   jima] 166; [of B stems into A (Goka-mura; Kyōto)] 203; [of accent types in modern
   dialects] 247; [2.3 with 2.1 in parts of Shikoku], [2.3 with 2.2] 254; [of low
   atonic classes into Kyōto high tonic] 358 〚 merging of vowels [crasis] 37
-meru 32; -meru < -fey- ?< *-(n[a]-)pa-Ci-, -meru < -mey- < *-ma-Ci- 792; <
   -■/ʙey- < *-n[a]-pa-Ci-: *see* -beru 792 〚 mesial [deictic] 36
mesotonic [locus elsewhere than start or end of word] 141 〚 metaphor 36
metathesis 63 71; [of initial consonants] 88; [of high and low on last two
   syllables] 216; [of pitch of -zu with that of last syllable of subjunctive] 351;
   [of final low of 3-syllable stem with basic high of ending] 352; 553 673 749 767
   781; [of locus] 823; 826; [of syllables] 843; 847 861
"metrical grounds" for attr A-kyi used in place of haplological pred Asi[-si] 807
"meu" = myoo [kana spellings] 137 〚 ? *mey 'plum' 72
Mg = Myōgi-shō = Ruiju Myōgi-shō 85 104 372 〚 mi- > ni- [Ie-jima] 42
mi- < myi- 'exalted' (honorific prefix, usually attached to noun) 230; 821
mi- 'not yet, un-·····en' (prefix) 230; [Kyōto accent] 328 〚 mi- 'see' 670
mi [for ni] 42; [< mi or me] 56 〚 mi 'see' [inf] A < B [Kyōto] 354
-mi < -myi < *-mi [adjective putative/causative nominalization ('deeming it A') =
   circumstantial] 26 51; (-'m[y]i) 215 216 216; 801 804; [not productive for
   modern adj] 804; [etymology] 805; 822 〚 -[m]i- 38
mid and high vowels [not always kept distinct in dialects] 812
mid front vowel(s) [Amami correspondences with OJ] 54; [OJ common type = -ey] 62;
   [proto-Japanese /e/]? 68
Middle Chinese 5 24 26 37 45; [tones of loanwords] 364 〚 Middle Japanese 75
Middle Korean 5; [z] 23; [-s- (genitive marker)] 36; [Chinese loans] 45; 65 82
mid vowels [Ryūkyū raising of] 52 25 〚 mim = mimetic element/adverb/etymon 372 825
"Mima Miyoshi" area (from western Kagawa to Tokushima, 2.1/3) 261
mimetic(s) 1 2; [reduplications] 5, (Tōkyō prototonic) 347; [with p-] 6 7;
   [adverbs] 13; 14 29 30 55; [variants] 69; 71 72; [+ verb] 668

monosyllabic nouns [lengthened in Kyōto, Shuri] 59; [modern three accent types must
    go back to four] 180; [with other than going tone were short-vowel?] 181;
    [with going tone were heavy syllables with long vowels?] 181; [with going-tone dot
    in upper-right corner (= rise)] 182; [over 60 percent atonic if we distinguish
    1.3a as low atonic] 251; [lengthened to two moras in Nakijin] 263; 359
monosyllabic parallel to 2.5? (fa 'tooth' as *LH-L) 350
monosyllabic particle [Kagoshima] 140
monosyllabic stems retaining a trace of infinitive ending as vowel length 667
monosyllabic ("monograde") vowel stems 665 666
monosyllabification 37 253; monosyllabified diphthongs 667
monosyllable accent types [three-way division preceded Tōkyō-Kyōto split] 346
monosyllable(s) [automatic lengthening of] 59 64; [Cwo] 59; [Co] 59; [Cey] 62; 161;
    [Kagoshima] 205; [not long in Mr? Hn long but short with particle?] 359
moo 'already' < mɔɔ < *maw[aya] < ma-faya < mo-faya (?< ma-faya) 71
mood (marked by endings on verb and adjective) 802
moosu 'humbly say' 126 〗 moppara [always -p-?] 12
mora [strings] 4; [subsyllabic] 74; [boundary] 139; [in heavy syllables] 142
morpheme(s) [and groups of morphemes] 1; [division] 4; 5; [containing b ḡ d z ž] 6;
    [native] 7 8; [Chinese origin] 10 26 28 29 45; 52; 59; [shunning *rendaku*] 114
morpheme boundary [within long vowel] 3; 7; [morphemic boundaries) 25; [before -u
    44; 76; [between two one-mora syllables reduced to a heavy syllable] 142;
    [indicated by Tōkyō locus on second of two like vowels 367
morpheme-initial allophones 84 〗 morpheme-internal 9; [-w-] 13
morpheme differentiation accent role weakened by loss of initial low string 360
morpheme shapes of Old Japanese 84 〗 morpholexical boundaries 76
morphological choice [in selection of formant for derived stem] 32
morphologically distinct markers [source of Ryūkyū finite endings -n -m -r] 35
morphologically "true" predicative of existential verb aru 132
morphological structure of verb forms 17
morphophonemic: analogies 120; boundaries not heard at surface level 3; confusion
    between atonic and oxytonic patterns 264; distinction between Kōchi low atonic and
    oxytonic 147; evidence [underlying -y- and -w-] 42, [for OJ vowel distinctions]
    49; level 157; notation [responsible for compound-noun accent exceptions?] 234;
    phenomena 255, (equating initial low with low of locus) 143; [peculiarity of last
    syllable of noun (= oxytonic accent)] 180; rules [for verb gerund] 37
morphophonemic adjustment(s) [at syllable boundaries] 75; [analogy] 63; [alternate
    shape] 59; [alternations] 52; [common to all dialects] 52; 261; [where stem is
    joined to ending] 802
-moru < -maru < *-ma-ra- 792 〗 mos [modern Korean] analogical restructuring 354
Mōtan-shichin-shō 261 343 358 〗 Motoori Norinaga 78 93 125 344 542
mp [Hankul, syllable-embedded digraph] 22
mp- [Hankul] = b- 22 23; [mistakenly written as "pph-"] 80
Mr = Muromachi period (1378-1573) 85 372
mu- 'lacking, un-, -less' (prefix) 230 325; mu as free noun 230
mu = [m:] 'uh-huh' 107 〗 "mu" [for the merged N] 75
mu [syllable] 76, [< mu or mo (Ryūkyū)] 56 〗 [m]u 42 〗 (m)u- [not all prothetic] 72
-mu presumptive 32; ["-n" in 1216 Hōjō-ki] 75; [+ su(ru) 'do'] 130; [attached
    directly to stem] 131, (of ···e verbs)? 131; [incorporated in etymology of
    masi-] 132; [written "-N"] 137; [with A-stems (mostly) atonicizes accent] 351; 668
-mu < *-ma- [verb formant], < -fu ?< *-(n[a]-)pa-, < -ᵇ/ₘu < *-n[a]-pa- 792
···mu verbs [mostly intransitive] 805 〗 mubafu = ubaᵓu 'seize' [Myōgi-shō] 81
mubey 'quite true' 107 〗 (m)ubey 'quite true' 72 〗 muf··· 107

*muina/moina > miyna 63 〇 Murasaki Shikibu's diary = Murasaki-Shikibu-nikki 78 127
Muromachi (= Muro˥mati‾) [period] 5 11 16 43; [distinctions of ɔ: and o:] 43; 44 75;
    [earlier and later halves] 77; 85 101 115 119 130 132 158; [B´ verbs LH-H, B
    verbs HL-L] 198; [accent of B verbs of 3 or 4 syllables like Kōchi] 205; 217; 255
Musashi [placename] anciently muzasi? 88 〇 mutative conversions 803
-mu to su 137; ···mu-to-su(ru) > ···n - su(ru) and ···u - zu(ru) 130
mutukasii/muzukasii 'is difficult' 113
mV > nV before dental 42 〇 mVf [rare sequences] 107 〇 mwo ≠ mo 79
*-my- [in gerunds] 122 〇 myaku 'pulse' compression of earlier miyaku? 83
*···myd··· [in gerunds] 122
mye 'woman' [from myi-na 'female-person'?] 62; (as prefix) 'female' 102
myi- [honorific prefix, no nigori] 102 107 〇 myi- 'see' 807
-myi > -mi [adj putative/causative nominalization = circumstantial]: -mi 26 51;
    (-'m[y]i) 215 216; 801; [not productive for modern adj] 804; [etymology] 805; 822
(-)myina (?< *mi-na) 'woman': see me, mye, onna (< womyina)
Myōgi-shō (Mg) = [Ruiju -] Myōgi-shō 26 69 70 71 78 81 83 85 [marks distinguishing
    'silkworm' from 'egg, shell'] 104; [notations in which rendaku affects second
    syllable] 115; 118 120 121; [uncommon pattern rise-low (for biwa 'loquat'] 165;
    167; 172; 174; [notations (confirming tones indicated by phonogram pairs)] 175;
    176; [accent patterns] 180; ["even" or "going" tone for Chinese loans not -p -t -k]
    184; 190 191 192; [verb forms] 192; 198 200; [differs from proto language in
    assigning verbs to accent types] 202; 203 205 210 234 243 246 258 259 342 349 350;
    [attestations of later compounds as two words] 367
Myōgo-ki 13 78 343 〇 *myuu < *myi-u → myi-ru > miru 'see' 667
N = (1) noun; (2) unspecified nasal; (3) nasal mora/syllable
N [written just "n"] 2, [Okinawan] 366; [before vowel or y] 2; [lacking in OJ?] 64;
    [word-final to pronounce Chinese words ending in -n or -m] 73; 76; 79
-N 25; [part of colloquial language by 1200] 125; [neutralized -m and -n] 130
"-N" was written to represent colloquial version of -mu 137
-N- (hatu˥on) [little evidence in OJ] 64; 73 146
n- [> m- before rounded vowel] 42; [left by elision of i or u (> N)] 72
n [alternating with y] 19; [alternating with r] 34
-n (aberrant [d] for) 30 〇 -n and -m [confused/distinguished] 75 130
-n [Chinese words] 73, (taken into J as -ni/-nu) 75, (written with katakana "i" or
    "ni") 75, (Shinran also used for -t) 73; [= Hateruma -ŋ] 74; [geminated] 75;
    [unwritten in non-Chinese words in 1221] 75; [for -ri in sakan 'flourishing'] 35;
    [stops nondistinctively voiced after] 122; [reduced from -nV] 184
-n [Hateruma (reduction from -na?); south Ryūkyū accretion?] 74
-n [Ryūkyū finite ending] 35
-n- [Aomori] 25; [alternating with -d-] 32; [and -t-] 32; [for -r- (Shuri)] 35; [as
    reduction of ni or no; as obscure] 669
-n- [allomorph of intensive infix (-N/T-)] (elided) 62; 81
-n- marker (genitive = adnominalizer) 367; [nigoried form of verb in lexical
    reductions] 669; 801; [reflected in nigori (voiced nasality)] 813
-n- or -n[i]- marker between iterated verb stems 668
[ŋ] 1 7; [for -g- (Iki, etc.)]] 21; [in Ryūkyūs] 21; see also ḡ, velar nasal
-ŋ [> -i/-u] 73; [for -ru in main-island dialects] 35
-ŋ- [no evidence proto-J distinguished it from -nk-] 32; [Ryūkyū] 7, [Yonaguni] 25
na- 'lacking, nonexistent', 'not' (negative auxiliary [(V-a -) na-]) 42 816
/na/ [Azuma] = /ra/ 35 〇 [n]a 42 〇 na 'name' [1.2 despite Mg irregular marking] 350
na 'you see' (sentence particle) [early-Edo low] 170
na = na˥ '(which) is' (copula attributive) 19; [replaced by da (Aomori)] 19; 32 171

na (particle [?= copula attributive]) 367 733
na [old prohibitive adverb (na V-i so̲)] 42 489
na [of V-a na] used to express desires [OJ] 66
-na/-ne 74 ⫝ -na- 'not' (negative auxiliary [V-a - na-]) 42 816
-na-₁ < na𝑎𝑑𝑗 'un[pleasantly] ... ' (adj-stem formant) 817
-na-₂ (N + na𝑎𝑑𝑗 ʙ) [adj-stem quasi-formant] 820
-n[a]- (few formant strings) 795 ⫝ -na-Ci- 796
*nadu < *na-do < *na-zo 'what' [Ryūkyū] 71 ⫝ -naeru < -nafey- < *-na-pa-Ci- 792
-naf- 90; -nafye [Azuma] = standard OJ -ne[y] (izen-kei of neg aux) 106
Nagano [oxytonic noun accent cancellation?] 256 ⫝ Nagasaki 257 ⫝ nagiy 'calm' 64
Nagoya [use of -[k]u] 128; [no accent retreat for polysyllabic vowel stems before
    -t··· endings] 206; [expression of purpose V-i ni iku 'go to V' run together as
    complex atonic phrase] 210; [tradition of Ogino Chiichi (reciting Heike)] 361;
    [Type A adjectives merged with Type B] 823
nagusam- 63 ⫝ nagwo(-ya-ka) secondary development from /nagu/? 63
-naharu (modern Kansai quadrigrade) < predicative form of -nasaru(ru) 666
na-i 'is nonexistent, lacking' 803 ⫝ -ŋa˥isya 'company' 114
-n[a]-ka-, -n[a]-ka-Ci- 796 ⫝ "Nakada" 113 119
-n[a]-ka-ra- 796 ⫝ Nakasone Seizen 363
Nakata = Nakata Norio et al.: Kogo dai-jiten (1983) 372
Nakijin [derived noun and infinitive have same accent] 211; [three registers A B C]
    246; [forms from Nakasone 1984 (with notational adjustments)] 366
nama- 'raw' [quasi-prefix] 822
name(s) [male; surname(s)] 13 35; [plants and animals] 29; [Indic Buddhist] 30;
    [province] 30; [phonograms of] 57; 113; [female] 134; [accent] 347
namu [OJ particle] 66; ["nan" in 1216 Hōjō-ki] 75 ⫝ -namu < *-na-ma- 792
N-A-myi < *N -n- A-myi 'N is A and so' [OJ] 804
nan- 'how many' 27 ⫝ -na-n[a]-: see tunagaru, tunageru, tunagu 795
Nanboku-chō period [1336-92] 89
nando 'or something, ... ' (particle) [early-Edo low; also ··· nan̄do] 170
nani + emphatic particle 110 ⫝ -na-pa-, -n[a]-pa-, -n[a]-pa-Ci- 796
nara 'if it be' [particle = copula provisional; Kyōto low] 171
Nara = Na˥ra [period] (Nr) 2 12 32 49 53 66 77 85 116 121 131 215 245
Narada [locus at end of last low mora, BEFORE a high] 145; [locus a point ofrise
    not fall] 146; [locus same as Tōkyō's in position but different in realization]
    146; [phonetic redefinition of locus] 246; [an unusual Tōkyō-type dialect] 256;
    [cancels oxytonic noun accent before /no/] 256; [data from Uwano 1976] 368;
    [accent notations represent reflexes of Tōkyō despite tune differences] 368
Narada type accent system [locus at syllable before high = last low syllable] 146
nari̲ / nar̄i̲ (free variants?) [particle = copula (Hn-Km accent)] 170
*naru 'what' [Ryūkyū] < *nadu < *na-do < *na-zo 71
na˥ru after A-[ku] ('become A') 128 ⫝ -naru < *-na-ra- 793
nasal [mora N] 2; [prolongation of vowel] 2; [prothetic] 2; 7; [before voiced dental
    or velar obstruent (Kobama)] 21; [vowels, semivowels] 27; [-rV- assimilated to
    following] 35; [before elided vowel (assimilated to next phoneme)] 72; [final in
    earlier Japanese?] 74; [onset of a dakuon syllable (< -nC-)] 74; [anomalous
    final] 83; [dental, elided?] 122; [Chinese verbal nouns ending in] 130;
    [elongation of vowel] 142
nasal ḡ = [ŋ] [in mimetic reduplications] 5; 6; [with no oral reflex] 7
nasal-initial syllable [reduced] 30
nasality [reduction to simple] 29; [gradual disappearance from DAKU sounds after OJ
    period] 86; [(of nasal vowel) dropped but vowel quality remained] 130

nasal + oral 25; nasals [SEI syllables contiguous to] 85
nasal syllable [DAKU syllable contiguous to] 85
nasal versions of DAKU syllables 85
nasal vowel [Portuguese] 123; [in -(a)û < -(a)mu] 129
-nasareru [not present in development of Kansai -naharu] 666
nasaʼru 'deign to do' [for suru in predicating free verbal nouns] 672
N-A structures [from N ni A] 98; [mostly from N ga/no A] 98
-nasu < *-na-sa- 793
native compound nouns [*rendaku* marking of] 28 ◊ native morphemes 7 8
native nouns of susceptible shape types that have never shown *rendaku* 114
native words 30 44; [reducing final nasal syllables to N] 73; [-p- ("f") > -w-] 73
-nau < -nafu < *-na-pa- 793
na V-i so 'don't V!' 24 42 489; [na] V-i <u>so</u> 'don't V!' 170
-nawaru < -nafaru < *-na-pa-ra- 793
···n-b··· [for modern ···n-p···] 28 ◊ ···ˉnbeʼ(e) < be-[k]i [dialect] 132
-n.cwu [Hankul] 23 ◊ -ᵐd- [Wakayama] 21 ◊ -nd- < *-nb- [Shuri] 22
nd [for -d- (observed by Rodriguez)] 22; [*nd to account for nasal of Ryūkyū taŋ
   'who' (< ta-do < ta-zo)] 71
ᵐda [Aomori copula] 19 ◊ N [daʼ] daroʼ(o)/desyoʼ(o) 'it is probably N' 129
N daroʼo/desyoʼo replaced by N de aroʼo/arimasyoʼo 129
N daʼtta daro(o)/desyo(o) 'it was probably N' 129
-nde < -gi-te or -bi-te [one dialect of Hachijō] 125 ◊ ···nde 20
N de aroʼo/arimasyoʼo [uncontracted structure] 129
[ᵐdʰ] before /u/ [Sakawa] 21
[ᵐdz], [ᵐdᶻ] before /u/ [Sakawa] 21
ne [syllable] 76; [palatalized in Toyama] 18 ◊ -ne/-na 74
-ne- < -na- -Ci- [adjective-stem formant] 817 ◊ necessity ('must') 132
negative 7 17; [ending -azu] 23; [(V-a -) na-] 42; [forms of verb] 25; [infinitive]
   26; [V-anu] 65; [of verb] 701
negative adverb mo:t 'not possibly' [Korean] 203
negative attributive [written "-nu"] 137; [Hn-Km accent] 170
negative auxiliary [(V-a -) na-] 42, [V-anu] 65; [-(a)n- (bound)] 111; [attached
   directly to stem] 131; [attaches to subjunctive] 352; [originally verb stem, later
   conjugated as adjective] 816
negative conversion 803 ◊ negative forms V-a-zu and V-a-zi 111
negative prefixes [are productive] 229; [Kyōto accent of compounds] 319
negative structure corresponding to hortative 132
"NE Kyūshū" = Shirakawa (of Miyako in Fukuoka) [from Hirayama 1951a:172-85] 368
nen 'you see' (sentence particle) [Kyōto low] 171
-neru < -ne[y]- < *-na-Ci- 793
neutralization [of juncture distinction] 3; [of oxytonic and atonic in Tōkyō] 168
neutralized: distinctions in Nakijin 363; environment 55; phonetic distinction 49;
   vowel pairs [actual pronunciation] 49, 50
new: close vowels [from earlier mid vowels] 55; (= "back") formation 154; terms
   from native sources (typically nouns) 802; verb stems ending ···k- not being
   created 126; w- syllables 38
N fa m<u>o</u>, N fa ya, N fa y<u>o</u> 105
ng for -g- (observed by Rodriguez) 22 ◊ -ⁱᵍg- [Wakayama] 21
ngk ("ng" = [ŋ]) [Hankul] syllable-embedded digraph 22
NHK = Nippon-Hōsō-Kyōkai: Nihon-go hatsuon akusento jiten (1966) 372
ni [syllable] 76; [< ni or ne] 56; [for mi] 42
[n]i (initial) 42 ◊ ··· [n]i (in Kansai dialects) 80 ◊ ni 'load' [Kyōto LH] 349

ni (particle) ['(in order) to' after Type-A infinitive (accent exceptional)] 153;
   168; [Hn-Km accent n̄ī] 170, [had rise niī (Mochizuki)] 170, [Mg atonic (pitch of
   preceding syllable continues)] 173, [high in NS commentary] 171; [early-Edo high
   after high, low after low] 171; [Kyōto "unaccented"] 171; 367 733 803
⋯ ni [essive (grammatical similarities with (-)ku and (-)sa)] 804
-ni infinitive of neg aux (V-a - ni 'not doing V') [incorporated in -zi?] 132; 816
-n[i]- [in combinations of nouns with verb or adjective] 26
-ŋi [expected from -gi replaced by -di (Yonaguni)] 81; [Yonaguni only from -ŋe (=
   Tōkyō ge-/-ŋe)?] 118
n[iˀ] aˀ[ri] contracted to naˀ 19 〕 Nichiren (1222-82) 16 44
nicknames [with double-low accent in Wakayama] 169
ni-dan 'bigrade' verb stems (polysyllabic; most incorporate a formant) 352 801
ni fa [particle string] 104 244 〕 niffon 'Japan' (Collado) 23
nigori 85; [iterative] 85; [within morphemes] 89; [process vacuous when second
   morpheme has -b- -d- -z- -g-] 93, [vacuous before initial DAKU or m n y w r] 93;
   95; [marks casually omitted] 109; [mark no more than a reminder] 113; [device
   activated by analogy] 113; [marks (history)] 118; 190; [across minor juncture]
   670; [preserved only before obstruents] 813
"nigoried" form of verb (in lexical reductions of sentences) 669
nigori form of si-(ru) 'does' 17
Nihon-gi = Nihon-Shoki 78 342; Nihon-gi shi-ki [NS commentaries] 343
Nihon Kan-yakugo = Rìběn Guān-yuèyǔ 78 〕 Nihon koten bungaku zenshū 1 105
Nihon-Shoki (= Nihon-gi = Ki THREAD radical) 78; [songs] 81; 84 94 98 100 105
   106 107 108 110 112; [kun-chū] 85 92; 127 167 170 171 175 185 211 342 290 348;
   [Maeda text] 348; (Okada) [verb forms marked LLL-H with no metathesis] 352
Nihon-Shoki commentaries = Nihon-gi shi-ki 343 343
ni-hwon [Hankul] ?= niffon 'Japan' 23
Niigata [accent retreat] 206
-niku- 'difficult (to V)' [auxiliary adjective] 821
ni.pphwon [Hankul] ?= niffon 'Japan' 23 〕 ni si[y]-te[y] fa 104
nissei = nissyoo "entering" tone [lower-right dot] 190: no karu 'the "light"
   entering tone' = toku-sei/-syoo [slightly raised lower-right dot] 190
ni-te ⟩ de = niˀ-te ⟩ deˀ [copula gerund] 20 112 〕 niˀ-te aˀ[ri] 19
⋯ni-te ⟩ ⋯nde [verb gerund] 20 〕 ⋯ŋi-te ⟩ ⋯si-te [Hagiwara] 133
⋯ ni wa [Tōkyō] 152
/nk/ 25; nk- 29; -nk- (modern) = [ŋk] 142; (proto-J, no evidence -ŋ- distinctive) 32
/-nk-/ became -g- or -ḡ- = [ŋ] 32
NKD = Nihon kokugo dai-jiten (1972-6) 372 666 〕 Nmaˀ [replaced by umaˀ?] 2
-nn- ⟨ -nˀ- 75 〕 N-¨N 26
N (-) N [usually treated as lexicalized compound nouns] 813
N | N structures in which juncture is suppressed limited to elliptical N [no] | N 367
N-N compounds [with no semantic correlation to account for nigori] 100
N -n- A 816 〕 N ni fa 104 〕 N ni si[y]-te[y] fa 104
N n[i] N [coordinative compound] 26; [one source of rendaku] 813
N [ni] taˀt-u → N-¨tat-u 26 〕 N [ni] tateˀ-ru → N-¨tate-ru 27
N [ni] tukeˀ-ru → N-¨tuke-ru 27 〕 N -n- N (as reduction of N no N) 813
N-no-bey/-bye 'direction/vicinity of N' 101
N [no/ḡa] A-i 26 〕 N [no/ḡa] simi-ru 26
N [no/ḡa] tuˀk-u → N-¨tuk-u 27
N no N 103 813 〕 N -n- -tu N, N -n- -tu [N] 368
N -n- V + Formant [comprising adjective stem] 817
⋯nnwo [Hankul] = nwo = particle noˀ 'of' 23

no [suppletive attributive form of copula] 19; [Kyōto accent] 171
no (bound noun, nominalizer) [tonic in Tōkyō-type dialects, juncture implied] 155
no ← no no 'the one of ··· ' [Wakayama low] 171
no = no̠ (particle) [N no̠ N] 103; [neutralizes Narada oxytonic and atonic nouns] 145;
  [neutralizes Tōkyō oxytonic and atonic polysyllables] 168; [Hn-Km accent high
  after high, low after low] 170; [had rise? (Mochizuki)] 170; [stickier than most
  particles] 172; [Mg atonic (continues pitch of preceding syllable)] 173; 174; 367;
  [and nasu = Azuma nosu] 733
-n[o]- [in combinations of noun with verb or adjective] 26
/no/-attachment rule [creates an atonic phrase] 259; [(enclitic mirrors register)
  lost sometime between 1200 and 1500?] 260
-noeru < -nofey- < *-na-fey- < *-na-pa-Ci- 793
/no/ [Old Kyōto low after low, high after high (but low after 2.4/5, 3.5)] 259
no̠ko̠ [root 'remain'] 67 ◊ nom-i 'drink' infinitive < *nom[a-C]i 668
no̠mi̠ (particle) [Hn-Km accent] 170
nominalization(s) 104 804 805; [of verb with -ku] 127
nominal verbs = verbal nouns 672 ◊ nominative case marker i [Korean] 64
nom-u finite (imperfect) < *nom[a]-u or *nom[a-C]u 668
"N" *onbin* 125 ◊ non-dialect songs 110
nondistinctive: high [on last syllable of Kagoshima atonic phrase] 140, [on last
  syllable of Kyōto 2.4 and 3.6] 247; lowering of initial syllable [Tōkyō] 362;
  semivowel onset 36; rise 155
nondistinctively aspirated stops [initial before proto-Japanese nonhigh vowels] 121
nondistinctively voiced stops [after -n in proto-Japanese] 122
nonfinal [N] 2 ◊ nonfinal suffix 667 ◊ nonlabial pronunciation of hu 1
no no → no 'the one of ··· ' [Wakayama low] 171
nonpalatal -Ci [Amami imperative] 668
nonpalatal front vowels [origin as diphthongs] 50
nonpalatalized d- of Yonaguni 51
non-palatal(izing) high front vowel [in Ryūkyūs] 122
nonpalatal or labiovelar quality for Type Two front vowels 49
nonpalatal-type front vowels [of OJ] written as Ciy and Cey 50
nonpalatal vowel ···iy [eventually merged with palatal vowel ···yi 53
nonpast or imperfect form (-ru or -[r]u) 151 665
nonsyllabic: mora 2; oral obstruent 2; voiceless i̠ 6; vowel extension 2
-nooru < -noforu < *-nofaru < *-na-pa-ra- 793 ◊ Norinaga = Motoori Norinaga 78 344
normal allophone 59; normal phrasing [retaining junctures] 141
northeastern Kyūshū distinguishes 2.3 from 2.1/2 but only before /no/ 257
northern Okinawa [three accent types (A B C)] 262 ◊ nosu [Azuma] = nasu 733
notation [accent] 5; 20; ["*z-" or "*[z]-" used for (s)-] 36; [-ey : -ye] 67;
  [-iy : -yi (advantage)] 67; [of Shodon dialect] 83; [for Kyōto accent] 270
notational conventions 57
notations [providing information on SEI-DAKU and accent] 85; [in chanting guides]
  174; [for earlier forms] 666 ◊ ···-n[o]-to̠ri > -(n)dori 'fowl' 102
N [o] tuke¹-ru → N-"tuke-ru 27 ◊ -nou < -nofu < *-nafu < *-na-pa- 793
noun compounds [of OJ with and without nigori] 99; [Tōkyō accentuation rules similar
  to those of Kyōto] 160; [accent locus determined by second member] 222
noun + infinitive or noun + infinitive-derived noun [not always clear which] 214
noun + particle ni¹ 26 ◊ "nouns" (uninflected words) 801
noun [prefixed to verb] 668
nouns [that usually have nigori in OJ compounds] 101; ["tonic" types deceptively
  preponderant] 161; [open-ended class, largest class in lexicon] 802

nouns derived from: compound-verb infinitives [atonic, same register as compound]
  213; verb infinitives 98, [accent] 212 370; N [ ] V-yi with unclear underlying
  structures 98
nouns ending in /a/ that never show final /e/ 48
nouns ending in /e/ [but /a/ in compounds] 48, [and always /e/] 48
nouns ending in /i/ [but /o/ or /u/ in compounds] 49, [and always /i/] 49
nouns of two and three syllables [over 60 percent atonic] 251
noun stems ending in ···ey 265 ⬚ noun suffix *-gi [diminutive or vacuous?] 64
noun + verb 669; noun + verb infinitive [same rules as noun + noun] 160
/np/ 25 ⬚ np- 29 ⬚ *np- [initial] 32 ⬚ -np- (modern) = [mp] 142
-np- (proto-Japanese) [distinct from -m-] 32; [should have yielded -b-] 32
···n-p··· competing with ···n-b··· (in the 1500s) 28
-n-pa 29 ⬚ Nr = Nara period (c. 700-800) 85 372
/ns/ 25; */Ns/ or */s/ [proto-Japanese for "disappearing s"?] 66 ⬚ ns- 29
-n.s- [Hankul] = -z- 23
NS = Nihon-Shoki (from Ishizuka 1977) 372
NS (Okada) = Okada 1956 (where accent differs from Ishizuka 1977) 365 372
NS (Sakurai) = Sakurai 1964 (where accent differs from Ishizuka 1977) 365
NS (T) = Takayama 1983 (Nihon-Shoki accents as reflected in phonograms) 365 373
NS (T+) = Nihon-Shoki (Martin's additions/emendations to Takayama) 365 373
N sa naru 'become N' [Aomori] 803 ⬚ N-¨simi-ru 26
N si zo̲ , N so̲, N so̲ mo ya 110 ⬚ ···n - su(ru) 130
/nt/ 25 ⬚ nt [Hankul] syllable-embedded digraph 22 ⬚ nt- [Hankul] 23 29
-nt- = [nt] 142; /-nt-/ (proto-Japanese) [became -d- in all cases] 32
-N/T- [intensive infix] 81
N-¨tate-ru 27; N-¨tat-u 26; N-¨tuke-ru 27; N-¨tuk-u 27
N -tu -n- 368; N -tu [N] 367; N -tu N [usually no nigori] 103, 367; N -tu -n- N 368
nu [syllable] 76; [< nu or no] 56 ⬚ [n]u 42
-nu (negative attributive) [attached directly to stem] 131; [some Type A verbs
  atonicized the form] 351; 668; (= V-a - nu) 816; 821
nuclear vowels [earlier only four?] 58
nuku B (= nugu 'remove' [Narada]), confused with nugu [Kagoshima] 282
number of [accent] phrase types in Kyōto nearly double that in Tōkyō 142
number-noun phrases 107
Numeral: -n- -ti ; -n- -tu; -ti (?< -tu-Ci or ?< to[s]i) 368
Numeral -tu: -n- N 368; -N 103; -tu, -tu N 368
numerical code [to designate accent class] 162 179
-nuraku = V-yi - nuraku 809 ⬚ nu(ru) [perfective auxiliary] 35
nV > mV before labial or velar 42; nV > n [final in a few noun]? 74
N-V compound(s) 88; [with later nigori] 98
nVf [in just a few words] 107 ⬚ -Nw- 42 ⬚ nwo [Hankul] = particle no˺ 'of' 23
N wo A-mu [?= 'treats N as A'] 805
N wo A-myi 'because N is A' [OJ] 804 805; N [wo] A-myi 'N is A and so' [OJ] 804
N wo si zo̲, N wo si zo̲ mo̲ 110 ⬚ N [wo] V 96
*-ny- [in gerunds] 122 ⬚ *···nyd··· [in gerunds] 122
N yuku 'N goes' vs. yuku N 'N who goes' [late-Heian, with secondary atonicization
  of the attributive] 807
N ywo fa, N ywori fa 104
*[nz] to account for nasal of Ryūkyū taŋ 'who' [< ta-zo] 71
-n.z- [Hankul] = -z- 23
N - zi- 'like N, virtually/almost N' [adjective-stem formant] 819
N - zi - mono̲ 'one like N, a sort-of N, virtually an N; an N' 819

N zo̱ 110

O = (1) Ōhara Hidetsugu's data for Ōsaka-Kōbe and Akashi-Himeji (in Ōhara 1937) 274;
    (2) Mathias notation for sensitive vowel of unattested or unknown type 50

o- (honorific prefix) [accent] 230-232; (< oo- < o[f]o- 'great; big') 821; o-AN
    [regularly low atonic; exceptions] 232

o- < wo- 'slight(ly)' [as adjective-stem prefix] 821

o < wo (particle) 168; [early-Edo high after high, low after low] 170

o [type-neutral, unknown, or merged vowel] 13; [words with o where -m- > -b- and
    later -b- > -m-] 32; [for both "wo" and "o"] 38; [two kinds neutralized after
    labials other than m and later after m] 49; [syllable, two kinds?] 49; 50;
    [preserved unraised in Aka and Keruma] 52; [vowel in earlier Ryūkyūan] 55;
    [retained by Shodon for Co in non-initial syllable] 56; [of uncertain value] 57;
    [two kinds put in opposition] 59; 76

o₁ ≠ o₂ 49; o ≠ wo 79

(')o syllable [two kinds reconstructed by Mabuchi] 49; [OJ] 57; [acquiring prothetic
    w-] 38, [and (')wo merged as wo] 59 79 83, [spelled "vo-" = wo- in JP] 123; ([o] <
    [wo] developed in 1700s) 79

"o" (kana): used for "wo" (883) 79; used for "even-tone" (low) syllable [wo̱] 175

o (transcription of Middle Korean obsolete vowel, unrounded [ɔ]) 5

[o] (Korean rounded mid back vowel, for Middle Korean transcribed "wo") 5

*o (Hattori) [for OJ /u/ corresponding to earlier-Shuri */o/]

ó (Mathias notation for type-neutralized vowel) 50

o̱, ö (notation for OJ Type B vowel) 50 53 ◊ ö [front rounded] < oi 43

"ö" (= Co̱) or u corresponding to earlier-Shuri */o/ or */u/ 68

"ŏ" represents ɔɔ < au [JP] 123; "ŏ" represents oo < ou [JP] 123

[o:] (Muromachi Kyōto) [< ou] 43; [sloppy or fast-speech pronunciation] 44

[ɔ] (as value of Cwo? [Shibata]) 82

[ɔ:] (Muromachi Kyōto) [< au] 43; [sloppy or fast-speech pronunciation] 44

-o [neutral, unknown, or later vowel] 86; [mostly < -o̱] 57; [row of syllabary] 83

-o [Shodon] (< o̱) 57, (corresponding to standard -u) 57; [Tokunoshima] 56

-o [Hachijō ending for verb attributive] 810

-o [raised to -u in non-eastern OJ verb attributive, merging with predicative] 811

-o < -oo [presumptive] 38

obligatory: dropping of da⁷ before daro⁷o/desyo⁷o 129; haplology of *mazi[-si] 132;
    nigori 96 97 98 99; rule [for colloquial Muromachi pronunciation] 75

obsolete: adjective form be-mi < bey-myi 137; adjectives ending in ···(y)e- 128;
    Korean sounds 5; verb modasu 'keep silent' 203; words (= ko⁷go) 77

obstruence 5 ◊ obstruent [devoiced because of secondary devoicing of syllable in
    Kobama] 21, [voiced initial] 29; 813

o̱Ci 64 ◊ "ŏe" spelled "Ohye" 15 ◊ ofo [written "ouo" by JP] 45

oi [> ee] 2; [within morpheme] 3; 4 76; [> ö] 43 ◊ o[ ]i [verb infinitive] 8

-oi > -iy 58 ◊ ···oi without notation of elided consonant 83

···o̱Ci [> iy] 52; [merged with ···uCi > ···iy] 53

/oC̱/ stems paired with final-i stems 48

Ogawa [thinks 2.5 is a secondary development] 171 ◊ Ogino Chiichi [kengyō] 254 343

Ōhara [thinks 2.5 later developed, perhaps late Heian] 171

"ohu" (historical spelling for long vowel of inuoomono) 363

oi 'the old' [B accent despite A for verb 'get old'] 211

o̱ita or ōita (Tōkyō-type dialects with either) 153

Ōita [accent pattern common matrix for Kyūshū and Ryūkyūs?] 176; [hypothesis on
    origin of Ryūkyū accent (Thorpe rejects)] 177; [preserves distinctive 2.3] 254;
    [distinguishes 2.3 from 2.1/2 but before /no/ only] 256

oite[˺] | iru˺ > oite iru˺ > oiteru˺, oite˺ta, oite˺ wa/mo [|] ita˺ [Tōkyō] 154

OJ = Old Japanese

Okayama [permits locus on second mora of heavy syllable] 144; [segmental phonology has no influence on locus] 146; [1.1 ≠ 1.3; in some areas 1.2 joins 1.1, in others 1.3] 346; [Type A adjectives merged with Type B] 824

Okinawa 52 80 165; *see also* Ryūkyū 〚 Okinawa-go jiten 139

Okinawan [Hankul transcriptions of] 22; [copula yan ⟨ ya a-] 80; [reflexes of nuku and nugu overlap in meaning] 213

···o-[k]u monophthongized [JP] 45 〚 Okuda = Okuda Kunio 1971 373

older: compounds 159; Japanese 35 77; "older" Tōkyō pattern of "1" for modern "0" i Type 3.6 words 182; older Tōkyō speakers [polarity-reversing rule for accentuating compound verbs] 207

Old Kyōto [dialect] 52 167 252 255

Old Japanese [o··· in of- 'pursue'] 10; 19; [stem] 20; 24; 33 34; [Azuma] 35; 36; [orthography] 48; [vowel distinctions despite neutralization] 49; [data on two kinds of o-] 50; [phonograms] 50; [vowels] 50; 52 53; [doublet] 57 58; 82 85; [orthography (SEI vs. DAKU)] 84; [sei-daku distinctions (differing from later)] 84; [citations] 86; 110 131; [adjectives] 804 813

old manuscripts (*ko-sya˺hon*) of Nihon-Shoki 167 〚 Old Turkish 514

-omai = -mai after consonant-final stem [dialect] 132

omission of nigori marks [casual] 109 〚 omoro 806; Omoro-sōshi 78

on = [o˜] 142 〚 onazi (for onazi-kyi) 'same' 808

onbin = onbin⁻ 37 121; [the term] 125; [phenomena] 126, (examples of compression) 363, (independent of accentuation?) 669; [reductions (faster articulatory stance?) 360, (and assimilations across minor juncture) 670

onda [JP attempt to write (with ˜o-")?] 123

one-mora morpheme [lengthened] 72; one-mora morphemes which are never lengthened 139

one-mora noun [lengthening] 64 71

one-mora nouns [of Tōkyō are two-mora words in Shuri] 139; [in Kyōto long] 180

one-mora phrases [lacking in Shuri] 139

one-mora syllable(s) 2; [+ T, + N, + vowel extension; with initial voiceless consonant (devoicing)] 76

one-syllable: *see also* monosyllable(s), monosyllabic

one-syllable atonic phrase [Kagoshima, apparently no rise of pitch] 140

one-syllable infinitives 197; [of atonic stems (oxytonic accent before -te?)] 207

one-syllable nouns [at least three proto accent classes: 1.1, 1.2, 1.3] 162; [in isolation all long in Kyōto; also in Old Kyōto?] 244

one-syllable particle [after Kyōto monosyllabic noun] tends to lengthen also 180

one-syllable phrases [did not exist in Old Kyōto with a few possible exceptions] 244

one-syllable words [Kagoshima locus heard as fall within that syllable (ȯ)] 140

Ongi = [Shōreki-bon] Konkōmyōsaishōō-kyo ongi (Text; Komatsu's index) 78 373

Ongi-m = Man'yō-gana in Ongi [assumed to reflect the accent] 373

Ongi-n = inserted notes in Ongi 373

Ongyoku-gyokuenshū (1727) [distinguished ɔ: from o:] 44; 78

Ōno = Ōno Susumu [notation] 89, [romanization] 90, [dieresis as default] 366; [etymologies) 373; [reconstruction of V-r[u a]ku) 809

Ōno Tōru 96; 107

onset [consonant /n/] 2; [vowel] 3; [of low pitch] (always distinctive in Kyōto) 143, (in a high-register word is a cue for the locus) 250

on-yomi (phonogram) 35

oo [two syllables] 3; 4; [two kinds] 43; [and /ɔɔ/ confused] 44; 76; (= [o:]) 142

/oo/ reconstructed [by Hattori] for ancestor of OJ *koo*-type ˜o" [= (C)wo] 253

oo < ɔɔ (< ...) 46; oo < o[w]o < ofo or owo [now written "oo"] 45 46
oo < ou [≠ ɔɔ < au] 43; [merged with ɔɔ < au] 44; [< *oũ, < ...] 46
oo- 'big' (as prefix) [accent] 229 308
ɔɔ < au 43; [merged with oo < ou] 44; [< awa, < awa < afa] 46; [JP writes "ŏ-"] 123
-ɔɔ > -oo (> -o) [presumptive; attested as -a(w)u] 37; 38; 129
ɔŏda [JP attempt to write with "o-"?] 123 ▯ /oo-o/ reduced to just /oo/ 4
opaque compounds [lexicalized so they resemble single morphemes] 84
open-ended class of "preaccentuated suffixes" 160
open long [ɛ:] (Nagano) 43; open vowel [= low vowel] 45
opposition [phonological] 6 67; [of voiced vs. unvoiced obstruent] 5
optionally voiced stops [between vowels in proto-Japanese] 122
oral (nasal +) 25; oral assimilation 132; oral elongation of vowel [in same
    position] 142, [with higher glide (ai oi ui; ei; au)] 142
oral g [in mimetic reduplications] 5; 6; [with no nasal reflex] 7; [Yonaguni -g-
    corresponds to OJ -k-] 93
ordered phonetic developments [for gerund] 121 ▯ original accent classes 162
original -m- distinct from -np- 32
original -ŋ- distinct from -nk-? [no evidence] 32 ▯ original sibilant *s- 36
orthographic: "h" and "w" 12; "hi"? 19; (m)u = mu- even before a nasal? 73;
    notation with phonetic implications 50; omission of "r" syllables [attested from
    935] 72; retention of boundaries after elision 82; "-w-" [few instances] 13;
    underdifferentiation [of sei-daku] 104
orthography [OJ] 48; [OJ, questions of homogeneity] 84; [kana] 85; [conventional in
    discussing sei-daku distinctions] 86; 139; [failed to show distinctive voicing
    until late] 130; [used for Yonaguni forms] 366
oru < woru 'be' [Ryūkyū reflexes A] 282; [Nagoya and Tōkyō accent type B result of
    Kinki phonetic influence?] 353; [earlier not used in east (iru used instead)] 353
Ōsaka [prototonic HL(L) atonicized to HH(H) before the particle /no/ only when HL
    corresponds to Tōkyō oxytonic] 257; [rule of prototonic noun atonicization before
    /no/ not limited to nouns that were low atonic?] 258; 369
-osu < -fosu < *-fasu < *-pa-sa- 793 ▯ os[y]i 'push' [used as intensive prefix] 95
oT = o[ ]i [verb infinitive] 8 ▯ o'to > oto' 'sound' 2.2 [Tōkyō] 254
Ōtsuki = Ōtsuki Fumihiko [etymologies cited from NKD or Daigenkai] 373
o'tu type o- 50 ▯ otu'-rui Cǫ [reflected as -u in Shodon] 57
otu'-rui high front vowel -iy 63
"ou" [diphthongal version] 44; [a device to write "oo"] 45
ou > oo [o:] (Izumo) 43, (Kyōto completed by 1450?) 44
[ou] as Muromachi "clear version" of [o:] 44
/ou/ surviving 44; in modern Kyōto omou 'think' [restored?] 125
o'u replaced by oo 4 ▯ ···o-u > ···oo 127
···p- > ···f- > ···w- > ···[w]- [verb stems] 127
-ou < -fofu < *-fafu- < *-pa-pa- (or ...) 793
overarticulated pronunciations 5 ▯ overly slow "reading pronunciations" 171
overt: accent [of a word with fall of pitch in Tōkyō] 152; juncture [following Tōkyō
    polysyllable + no'] 168; marking [of atonic words] 5
Owari [preserves oxytonic accent of infinitive of atonic stem before -te, -ta] 206
-owasu < -fofasu < *-fafasu < *-pa-pa-sa- (or ...) 793
owo [written "ouo" by JP] 45 ▯ oyazi (for oyazi-kyi) 'same' 808
oxytonic = final basic accent 141; [Tōkyō] = all words of more than one syllable
    with locus on last 256
oxytonic accent: basic to finite forms of atonic verbs 356; cancelled (delayed?)
    when particle attached to Izumo final i or u 356

oxytonic accent of infinitive [of atonic consonant stems, treatment before -te] 207;
  [of atonic stem cancelled before -te in Tōkyō but survives in Totsukawa, Owari,
  Gifu, Hata] 206; [before -te preserved in suspensive use but not before auxiliary]
  207; [retained in compound verb in Tōkyō-type dialects] 208
oxytonic accent of verb forms [often cancelled because no particle is attached] 355
oxytonic/atonic alternants of adverbs 260
oxytonic final syllable in Kyōto [underlyingly long?] 147
oxytonic forms of atonic verbs [all traces lost in Izumo?] 356
oxytonic infinitives (like the stems) simply atonic? 355
oxytonic noun accent cancellation rule 256
oxytonic nouns [of Tōkyō] 143; [Kyōto treatment in isolation] 150, (before juncture)
  157; [of Kyōto (= "double-low") mostly dissyllabic] 158; [two-syllable of Tōkyō]
  163; [few long ones in Tōkyō] 363
oxytonic nouns and adverbs of Tōkyō cancel final locus before juncture 260
oxytonic nouns [Tōkyō] cancel final locus before enclitic /no/ 256
oxytonic varying with retracted oxytonic [Tōkyō nouns of 4 or more syllables] 178
oxytonic words [neutralized with atonic except before particles other than /no/
  (Narada)] 145; [become Tōkyō atonic when juncture drops after suppressing final
  accent] 150; [in Kyōto limited to phrases that begin with low pitch] 157; [of
  Tōkyō; some A, some B in Kagoshima] 163
¨P = b 86
p- [relics of] 9; [coexisted with F- throughout] 11; [basic (left by elision of
  vowel) > T] 72; [after T] 76
"-p" (in formulas) = a one-mora atonic particle attached without juncture 243
-p [Chinese] 66 73; [> -u] 45
-p- [Hankul] 23; [in Nakijin 'soft') 14; > "f" > -w- 37 73, [Ryūkyū cases?] 80
-pa [counter for bundles] 9 ▯ -pa-, -pa-Ci- 796 ▯ Paekche [= Kudara] 68 401 467
paired stem [for upper bigrade verb] that ends in u or o̱ 63
pairs of phonograms used to mark tone as high or low 175
pairs of verbs [relationship obscured by Kyōto accentuation] 355
palatal assimilation 43; [progressive] 54 57 66
palatal glide [in 16th-century Kyōto] 15; [of ye] 79; [epenthetic] 82
palatal /i/ [original] 53
palatality [of syllable] 54; [realized as voiced glide -y-] 126
palatalization 17; [of sibilant before /e/ as well as /i/] 18; [Cyi in Okinawa] 52;
  [kyi in Shuri] 52; [affricated] 56; 63; [dental or velar initials] 66; [of t/d
  and s/z only after -yi and -iy fell together?] 86
palatalized t 18
palatalized reflex of earlier -g- in Shuri ('cedar') 53, ('nail' and 'rabbit'] 93
palatal mid vowel [origin as diphthong in at least some words] 50
palatal onglide in syllable [ye] (Zdb line on left) 50
palatal quality [Type One front vowels] 49; [of original Cyi, found in consonant] 52
palatal "smear" more prevalent earlier? 66
palatal fricative [voiceless] 126 ▯ palatal stop 33 34 ▯ palatal syllables 11
palatal-type front vowels [of OJ] treated as /Cyi/ and /Cye/ (Zdb line on right) 50
palatal version(s) [sibilant] 17; [te, ne, ke (Toyama)] 18
palatal vocalization 122 132 ▯ palatal vowel ···yi 53
paradigm [of deictics] 20; [verb] 125 ▯ paradigmatic endings 151
paradigmatic form to which honorific o- attaches [adj, any; verb, infinitive] 232
paradigmatic forms [Ryūkyū] 83; [of Kyōto verbs that are basically oxytonic] 157,
  (before juncture suppress both length and fall) 148; [pitch patterns predictable
  given stem information] 151; [pitch patterns obtained by rules working from two
  basic types] 161; [and phrase accent types (differences from Kindaichi)] 359

prehistoric: contraction 87; version of Arisaka's Law 59
pre-Japanese 34 36; pre-modern [Japanese = ko'go] 77
prenasal (position) 109, (drip) 112 ◊ prenasalization [order in which lost] 25
prenasalized 20, (consonants) 24, (stops) 25; (obstruents) 25 29 31
prenasalized oral ([ŋg] or [ᴺg]) 7
preposed particle [interrogative] 352; [of focus or emphasis] 813
presence or absence of locus in an ending 191
preservation of velar in -ku [correlated with unrounded articulation of /u/?] 134
presumptive (= future; hortative; tentative) [of hybrid conjugation] 32; 37; [ending
   -a-mu › -a[m]u › -ɔɔ › -oo (› -o)] 38
presumptive auxiliary -mu 32; ["-n" in 1216 Hōjō-ki] 75; [attached directly to stem]
   131, (of ···e verbs?) 131; [incorporated in etymology of masi-] 132; [written
   "-N"] 137; [with A-stems (mostly) atonicizes accent] 351; 668
presumptive V-(a)mu 129 131; [adnominalized 1500s and earlier (with no change)] 131
prevailing-type accent pattern 201 ◊ primary [voicing] 28 ◊ primitive long vowels 45
problematic: correspondences (short infinitives and derived nouns) 279; *g- 36
processes to account for gerund forms 122
productive [accent] rules for a Kyōto compound of two free nouns 159
progressive assimilation 18 43; [palatal] 54 57 66
prohibitive adverb na (V-i so) 42 ◊ prohibitive command 24
prohibitive use of masi- (negative counterpart of permissive be-si) 132
proliferation of adjectives 127
prolongation [of vowel] 2 ◊ prolonged consonant 2
pronoun forms [coexistent] 126
pronunciation [JP attempt to write initial /ɔ/] 123; [of 16th century (preserved in
   idiom with -tu form)] 124
pronunciations: [ši] and [tši] or [tʸi] 18; [tu] and [du] 17; of Old Kyōto 167
proper names [accent assignment rules] 219
prosodic: adjustment 174; factors [to account for Hankul geminate spellings] 23
prothetic: "h-" 10; nasal 2 72; w- [picked up by initial o] 38; y- [picked up by
   merged e-] 38, [of ye- 'get' retained in yuru [JP] 133
proto language 201
proto-Japanese 18 20 25 29 34 35 37 53 55 60 84 121 192 218 255 356
proto-Japanese accent [types for nouns] 179; [verbs] 191; [patterns different from
   11th-century Kyōto?] 245; [reconstruction] 246; [pitch patterns] 246; [phonetic
   nature of initial register] 247
proto-Japanese: accentuation (vowel length as factor) 64; adjective [just stem] 127
   attributive forms 811; /c-/ (Unger reconstructs for most OJ s-) 66; *d- (or *j-) =
   OJ y- 51; /e/? 53; internal /p/ 37; ···ₒCi 53; phonology [assumptions about] 121;
   varieties with voiceless -t- and -k- 25; vowels [five?] 58, [four?] 67, (Hattori's
   elaborate scheme) 68
proto-Japanese-Ryūkyūan *e 68 ◊ proto phoneme 36
proto-Ryūkyū(an) 68 80 ◊ proto *s- [as reconstructed by Unger] 34
proto-syllable *bwo (ko'o-type "bo") 36
proto system earlier than extant notations of 11th and 12th centuries 162
prototonic [Tōkyō words ("1" in Mkz)] 141; [Tōkyō two-syllable noun] 163; [heavy
   syllables of Tōkyō/Hiroshima with accent on second mora in other dialects] 169
prototonic: accents freely maintained in Tōkyō gerunds etc. 209; high [not so high
   as in other Tōkyō tonic types] 345; locus of Tōkyō adjectival noun often retained
   in honorific o- form 232; nouns [Ōsaka; only some correspond to Tōkyō oxytonics]
   258; patterns of Tōkyō felt slightly "odd" 347
proto-vowel *e 53 ◊ province names 30

repeated shifts of locus [frequent and independent in dialects] 246; [required to account for later forms] 253

representative -tari 124 ▯ -reru ‹ -re[y]- ‹ *-ra-Ci- 793

restorations [analogical] 44 ▯ restrictives 114

restructuring [of monosyllabic nouns with Cwo] 59; [of morphemes] 59; [of polysyllabic vowel stems to monograde] 666; [of bigrade verbs] 666

retention of accent of gerund of atonic stem before -t··· forms of iru 'be' with the i- elided 210

retreat of accent in polysyllabic vowel stems before -t··· endings 206

retrospective attributive (V-i)-si [originally = adjective predicative -si?] 127

retrospective (V-i)-ki is predicative except in -keku 127

reversal of pitch level [in attaching particle] 172

"reverse nigori" in English 113

reverse tonicity 170; [of first infinitive in compound verb (older Tōkyō)] 356

reversion to low pitch in double-low accent patterns 250; [right after change to high] 250; [nondistinctive if distinctiveness pinned on initial vowel] 251

-re[y] ‹ *-ra-Ci- [OJ bound auxiliary] 35 ▯ rhetorical effect 107

ri [syllable] 76; [‹ ri or re] 56

Rìběn Guān-yuèyǔ (= Nihon Kan-yakugo) 18 22 78; ▯ riddle 11

right shift [of locus (Tōkyō)] 144, (operated on both 2.2 and 2.3 › 2.2) 254

-rim- › -Nm-, -rin- › -Nn- 72

"riŏ" [JP] to be taken as /riɔɔ/ or as /ryɔɔ/? 123

rise [and fall within syllables (evidence for additional proto accent types)] 162; [as two-mora sequence of low + high] 184; [gentle, at end of Shuri atonic phrase] 139; [gentle, to the last high-pitched syllable (Aomori)] 141; [within a syllable (represented by ′)] 138; [words not limited to attested "going" tone?] 184; [in low atonic words being eliminated in Ōsaka?] 345

rise after fall [unusual pattern if juncture of gerund V-i | t̄e is ignored] 244

"rise-fall" = "double-low" [2.5, 3.7] 174

rise from low to high became automatic [in Kyōto, Tōkyō] 218

rise-high contour [in Chinese binoms] 183

rises and falls the transient result of compression and conflation? 265

'rising (tone)' [high pitch] = zyo⌐o(-syoo/-sei) 167

Rodriguez 22 **44** 78 79 123 343 666

-roeru ‹ -rofey- ‹ *-rafey- ‹ *-ra-pa-Ci- 793

-rokasu ‹ *-rakasu ‹ *-ra-ka-sa- 793 ▯ -roku ‹ *-raku ‹ *-ra-ka- 793

romanization [romanized spellings of Portuguese missionaries] 15, ["xe" = [še] 19; [of OJ vowels] 50; [forces decision on voiced vs. voiceless] 113

Rongo [Kōzan-ji text] 133 ▯ root(s) [verb] 35 67 671 ▯ root-internal -iy [rare] 63

-rou ‹ -rofu ‹ *-rafu ‹ *-ra-pa- 793

rounded versus unrounded [vowels] 67

rounded version of /u/ 2; [rounding often weak] 2; [only when unvoiced] 7

ru [syllable] 76; [‹ ru or ro] 56 ▯ ru and i [as separate syllables in rui] 2

ru [Okinawa] ‹ du ‹ zo [emphatic particle] 71 110

-ru (verb imperfect/nonpst ending) 35; [→ -u after consonant (yom-ru → yom-u)] 129; [attaches high in Kyōto] 155; [-ru⌐ explains kak̄u ḡa 'writes but'] 155; [···i/e-ru] 665 ▯ -ru ‹ *-ra- 793 ▯ -(r)u (vb imperfect/nonpast ending) 803

rui = word types comprising phrase accent patterns (*gun*) 243

Ruiju-koshū text [of Nihon-Shoki] 105 119

[Ruiju -] Myōgi-shō (Mg) 78 85 167 342; *see* Myōgi-shō

rule that neutralized the 2.4-5 distinction before /no/ only 174

rule [Sakurai's, for accent of /no/-attachment] 260

rules 6 28; [assigning accent patterns] 138; [for cancellation of loci in Tōkyō (can
   be complicated)] 141; [for accentuating compound nouns] 162
rules of compound-noun accentuation [exemplified in Myōgi-shō] 234
rules of locus [work from end of compound] 233
rules of register assignment [work from beginning of compound] 233
-rum- ⟩ -Nm-, -run- ⟩ -Nn- 72
-rV- assimilated to following nasal 35; -rVb- ⟩ -nd- [Okinawa, before 1700?] 80
[Ryōshūge →] Ryō no shūge 78 100 〚 Ryūka (1795, 1798, 1802) 806
Ryūkyū(s) 8; [erosion of labial quality] 12; [koo 'river'] 12; [nonpalatal ≠ palatal
   si, ti] 18; [verb gerunds -tši] 18; [finite endings] 35; [words without s-] 36;
   [mesial deictic] 36; [reflexes of OJ iy] 52; [morphological data for dating proto-
   Japanese] 53; [/u/ ⟨ u or o] 55; [vowel raisings favor treating Cwo as -ɔ]? 83;
   [paradigmatic forms (of pronoun)] 83; [formations from -ku ar-] 803; [adjective
   structures] 804; [evidence for adj attributive ending (not much in modern)] 806
Ryūkyūan 104; [developments for gerund forms] 121
Ryūkyū dialects [other than Shuri] 12 139; 14 16 36 49 159; [without aspiration
   distinction] 55; [first-person pronoun forms incorporate marker n[u] ⟨ no?] 83;
   [with interesting accent classes] 177; [with third register "C" (as reflex of low
   tonic accent)] 264
Ryūkyū Kanwa-shū (?1600⁻) 806 〚 Ryūkyū kan yakugo (early 15th century) 806
S (1) = Shiza-kōshiki (Kamakura accent, Kindaichi 1964a) 365 373; (2) a sibilant
   unmarked whether s or z 〚 ̈S, ̈s = z 34 86 117
s- 25; [⟩ z- (in auxiliary for verbal nouns)] 26; [quality] 33; [in contrast with
   θ (Kudaka)] 33; [affricate] 33; [replaced by affricate in babytalk] 33;
   [alternating with zero] 35; [stable] 36
(s)- [as relic of genitive marker] 36; [as variant of OJ particle (-)tu] 36
s [alternation with š] 7; [before -yV and -i] 17; [Kyōto] 33; [deapicalization
   (s-swallowing)] 33; [alternation with t] 33; [unaspirated tci] 33; [articulatory
   difficulty] 33; [and r] 34 43; [corresponding to Korean c/t/s] 66; [after T] 76;
   [nondistinctively affricated in OJ?] 86
/s/ [proto-Japanese] 34, (competing versions?) 34, (sibilant?) 36, (affricate?] 66;
   [original disappeared with no written trace?] 81
"s" of Shuri palatalized (= sy) 366; "ş" of Shuri formerly unpalatalized (= s) 366
-s- [written with Korean geminate] 23; [of combining forms] 35
-s- [Hankul] = [Japanese] -s- or -z- 23; [Middle Korean genitive marker] 36
š 1 7 17; [allophone of s (Yonaguni)] 25; [articulatory difficulty] 33;
   [lacking] 33; [as ancestor of s-] 34; [after T] 76
š₁ [alternates with ž] ≠ š₂ (also pronounced ç) [alternates with b(i)] 6
š- for hy- 1 〚 s : ᵈz 5 〚 s : z 6 〚 sa [Yonaguni reflex] 33 〚 ̈sa = za 34
ša [for hya] 1 76; [as /sya/] 17; [as ancestor of "sa"] 34
sa- (adjective-stem prefix) [induces nigori] 101; 821
sa- 'small' 35; [proto-J root (Unger); why not *c-?] 66
sa(-) 'that' [mesial deictic] 36 69; sa ⟩ soo 'like that'? 71
sa [noun particle] 'to' (= e or ni) 803 805
(-)sa [grammatical similarities with (-)ku and ⋯ ni] 804
-sa [adjective abstract nominalizer ('-ness')] 51 215 216 217 801 804; [OJ almost
   all direct predications] 804; [etymology] 805; [ending a sentence] 813; 822
-sa- [formant] 67; [makes "exoactive" stems (transitive or causative)] 672 796
-sa- as auxiliary of subject-exaltation 672
-sa + a(r)- 215 803 804; *-s[a ar]-i ⟩ -si ? 807 〚 -sa-Ci- 796
sae ⟨ safey 'even' (particle) [?⟨ swofey] 69 83; [Hn-Km sa[f]e] 170; [early-Edo
   low] 170; [Kōchi low] 171; [Tōkyō saˡe set off by juncture for emphasis] 172

stop(s) [not necessarily heard by Koreans writing ph- for "h-"] 11; [pronunciation
    of ancestor of -w-] 13; [in proto-Japanese] 121; [intervocalic] 122;
    [nondistinctively aspirated] 121; [nondistinctively voiced] 122; [optionally
    voiced between vowels] 122; [unvoiced] 122; [shortening] 132
stretch of Kyōto high pitch may be of any length only in high-register word 143
stretch of Tōkyō high pitch extends to locus 141 ◊ string between junctures 139
strings [(of syllables) not found in OJ morphemes] 58; [of VV, lacking in OJ] 64
"strong": consonants [in eastern dialects], vowels [in western dialects] 134
structural: considerations 180; interpretation [of OJ vowel distinctions] 50
structure of infinitive + auxiliary [separate phrasing till after 1200] 192
structure of syllable and syllable string 83 ◊ s/t variants [explained by *c?] 66
su- [adjective-stem prefix] 821 ◊ su- 'sour' 216
su [< so] 25; [Yonaguni reflex] 33; [> si = sɨ (Shodon)] 56; [> *sɨ > şi (Okinawa,
    by early 1800s)] 80 ◊ [su] and/or [se] > [si] 18
[su] < tu (but not tu < to)[Yonaguni] 33 ◊ ¨su = zu ([ǰu] in Narada) 16
šu [for hyu] 1; [as ancestor of "su"] 34
su 'nest' [Kyōto LH; earlier *LH-H?] 349 ◊ su 'reed screen' [Kyōto LH] 349
su = su(ru) 26 ◊ -su (from suru) conjugated like indigenous verb stems ···s- 672
-su < *-sa- 794 ◊ -su < -tu < *-ta- 794
-su (of wo-su, m[y]e-su) related to suffix in bird names? 102
sub-classes of adjectives of Type B in Tōkyō 824
subject [unmarked in OJ main clause] 119; [of hortative is first-person] 129
subject-exaltation (honorific) auxiliary [attaches to subjunctive] 352
subjective adjectives 807 ◊ subjective essive (= adverbial) 24, (= particle toˀ) 130
subjunctive (-a) 65 131; (ending [V-a ?= verb root or stem itself]) 191 352 667
subjunctive: of hybrid conjugation 32; form(s) 182, [attested accents not too
    consistent] 351; + na (= V-a na) used to express desires [OJ] 66
subordination [of first noun to second in compound] 26 ◊ substandard speech 17 44
subsyllabic mora(s) [earlier] 5; [nasal mora N] 72; [oral (obstruent) mora T] 72;
    [none in OJ] 74; [from final high vowel after velar elision] 127; [-N] 130
suf = suffix 825
suffix(es) 8; [Chinese loanmorphs used as] 28; [inflectional] 51; [diminutive] 58;
    59; [*···-gi] 62; [incorporated to make nagwo- from nagu-?] 63; [Korean -(a)ki,
    -(a)hi, etc.] 65; [-a derives nouns?] 65; -[g]i- 67; [of Chinese origin] 114;
    [diminutive (-ko/-ŋo)] 115; [term used for Chinese elements as second element
    of compound] 233; [incorporated into 2.5 nouns?] 361; [non-segmental?] 361
suffix for the attributive vowel verb (V-ru) gradually acquired? 809
suffix: -maro 35; -Tpoˀ- 14 (see -ppo-); -zyami [Amami], -zyan [Okinawa] 29
suffixes and suffixed particles with DAKU initials [etymologically SEI] 93
suffixes optionally atonicizing or preaccentuating 233
sugosu maintains vowel of Azuma sugwosu 811
sugusu 'let pass beyond' [OJ] preserved as the Azuma version sugwosu 63 811
suppletive attributive form [of copula] 19
suppressed juncture 150 157 367
suppressing initial consonant of verb ending (after dropping stem-final vowel) 668
suppression [of final high vowels] 4; [of final vowel of "-tu" in texts of 16th and
    17th century] 73; [of final high vowels ignored in spelling Kagoshima forms] 139
sura [particle] 104
surface [contrasts] 5; [level] 3, (of OJ) 51; [neutralization] 49; [adjustments
    (that cause a juncture to drop in Tōkyō)] 152; [cancellation of underlying
    juncture after verb adnominalized to noun] 153; [manifestation of accent pattern
    of Type-A verb past (in Nagoya etc.) coinciding with that for Type-B verbs] 153

T = (1) a dental stop unmarked whether t or d; (2) the tense unaspirated dental stop
of Nakijin and Yonaguni 〗 ¨T, ¨t = d 34 86
(T) = NS (T) 373; (T+) = NS (T+) 373 〗 (T+ kun) = NS (T+ kun) 373
t- 25; [in contrast with [θ] (Kudaka)] 33; [(left by elision of vowel) > T] 72;
[Yonaguni slightly aspirated; replaced by s- before original u and i] 25
[θ] 33; [for s or h < s (Kyōto)] 33; [= s- or t- (Kudaka)] 33
/t/ [Aomori (voiceless after voiceless vowel, -n-, -T-)] 25; [Shodon, automatically
replaced by /th/ when vowel is devoiced] 54; /t/, /ts/, /s/ once in contrast? 81
t [tša and tši treated as /tya/ and /ti/] 17; [affricates automatically before a
high vowel] 17; [palatalized before i] 17; [(Ryūkyū) affricated to [ts] before
original i] 17; [alternating with y] 19; [alternating with s] 33; [and r] 34
-t [Chinese loans] 66, [Chinese words] 73; [back at least to early Kamakura] 73;
[pronunciations (in Chinese borrowings) original?] 73; [written with same notation
as -n (by Shinran)] 73; [geminated] 75; [in Chinese loanwords] 190; [geminated] 75
-T [part of colloquial by 1200] 125; [in modern Korean, verb stems only] 354
(-)T [written as gemination] 2; [often left unwritten] 75; [written as "tu" after
/u/, otherwise as "ti" in 1234] 75; [written with kana "tu" occasionally but
usually left unmarked] 75; 76 79; [indicated by "entering-tone" mark (in Myōgi-shō
verbs)] 83 〗 ···T reduction of ···tu or ···ti 8
-T- (*soku ʼon⌐) [Aomori] 25; [Yonaguni] 25; [lacking in OJ?] 64; [word-final to
pronounce Chinese words ending in -n or -m] 73; 144 146; [formed one syllable with
preceding mora till Muromachi?] 345; [(Wakayama) treated as low except when
between two highs] 345 〗 -T- [intensive infix] 8; -T/N- 259
-t- [written with Korean geminate] 23; [Yonaguni voiceless and tensely deaspirated]
25; [of proto-Japanese preserved] 25
-t··· forms [contracted from -t[e] a[r]- attach to Type-A stem infinitive as
low] 156; [reduced from attachments to the infinitive] 155
-t··· → -d··· [no examples of counters] 27
¨ta = da 34 〗 θa = sa [Toshima, Narada] 33
ta- ʻhand' [quasi-prefix (combining form of te ʻhand')] 228 822
ta- [adj-stem prefix] 821 〗 ta(-) ʻmany' (prefix) 229 〗 ta(-) ʻother' (prefix) 229
-ta [perfect form of verb] 122; (from earlier -t[e] a[r-]) 151
-ta- [adjective-stem formant] 819; [auxiliary adjective] 820
-ta [da]roʼo 129 〗 *tadu < *ta-do < ta-zo ʻwho' [Ryūkyū (→ taru)] 71
tag translations 139 〗 *tagi rather *taki for proto-Japanese ʻwaterfall'? 118
Taigen-shō 11 〗 Taisyoo⁻ 77
Takamatsu [LHL for B´ verb stems] 198; [merges high and low three-syllable atonic
nouns (3.1/4)] 261; [2.1/3 "HH", "LH", "both LH and HH"] 261
Takayama Michiaki's discovery 175 〗 *taki proto-Japanese ʻwaterfall' or *tagi? 118
Tanabe [LH-H for B´ verbs, HL-L for B verbs] 198
-taʼ na-i/-katta [Wakayama] truncation of -ta[-ku] na-? 815
T'ang period 84 〗 [¨]tani = dani ʻeven' 104 〗 Tappi [north Honshū] (Clarke 1973) 368
-tarasi- = -(t)tarasi- [bound adjective] 820
-tari [representative, same meaning as earlier -tu] 124
taru ʻwho' [Ryūkyū] < *tadu < *ta-do < ta-zo 71 〗 -taru < -daru < *-n[a]-ta-ra- 794
tati [pluralizer] 65 〗 tau [Greek] = Yonaguni -T- 25
tautosyllabic: clusters [Hankul] 23; syllable-initial ngk- [Hankul] 22
ta-zo ʻwho' 71 〗 [tci] = si [Yonaguni (result of fortition)] 33
te [syllable] 6; [palatalized (Toyama)] 18; [as tey at underlying level] 51; 76
¨te = de 34 〗 θe = se [Toshima, Narada] 33
/te/ [(? =ˮtye") and /tey/, no morpheme-initial contrast?] 51; 112; [no indication
of affrication, Portuguese did not write "che"] 137

"tonic Type A" verb stems (← Type B of three or more syllables) [Kōchi, Tanabe, Akō, Shingū]) from the stems of "atonic Type A" [merged in Kyōto] 353
tonic types [number equal to number of syllables in phrase but some little used] 252
tonic verbs (Type B) of Hagiwara elide stem-final s in gerunds 133
tonic words [Kagoshima locus on penultimate] 140 ▯ toosu 'let pass' 126
to'o(-syoo/-sei) '"east" (tone)' [fall?] 172 350
to'o-ten '"east" dot' (slightly raised, lower left corner) 185
/to/ phonograms in Nihon-Shoki 108 ▯ Tosa-nikki 78 83 554
Tosho-ryō [- bon] Myōgi-shō 167 ▯ tossyori for tosiyori 'oldster' 75
Totsugawa = Totsukawa 120; [oxytonic infinitive of atonic stem before -te, -ta] 206
to'u [notation] 'inquires' 44
Toyama [LH-L for verbs of all three types] 198; [data from Hirayama 1960] 369
Toyoda [city] 119, (changed to "Toyota") 120; [family] 119
Toyogawa [river] 120 ▯ Toyohara Sumiaki 11 ▯ Toyokawa [city (Aichi)] 120
"Toyota" 119; TO-YO-TA, TO-YO-"TA 120
-Tp- 42; -Tpanaši (deˀ) '(leaving) just as it is' [suffix] 8
trace(s): of earlier vowel distinctions [in quality of adjacent consonants] 52; of palatal or nonpalatal vowel [left behind in consonant] 5
traditional: Chinese tones of Man'yō-gana phonograms 175; etymologies 199; identification of e(-) 'can(not ···)' with infinitive 'get' 83; Japanese grammar 802; kana spelling [of "-h-" or "-w-" not always reliable] 12; orthography 28 42; philology of China 84; pronunciations 2; values for tones [in China] 167, [of Chinese readings in Japan] 167 248; view of OJ vowel distinctions 50
tradition for Kan-on accent just opposite that for Go-on 248
transcription(s) [broadly phonetic] 1; [of prothetic nasal] 2; [Hankul] 18; 44
transitive/intransitive forms 64
transitivity [derivational suffix or formant] 51 672 ▯ transivity-paired verbs 41
translations [tag] 139
traversal/ablative particle yu/ywo(ri) 811 ▯ triangle [Hankul] = z 23
trisyllabic Type-A imperfects [Takamatsu unexpectedly lowers first syllable] 345
trisyllabic verb accent types merge (independently) in Kyōto and Takamatsu 345
true compound [unlike syntactic reduction] ignores accent of first member 160
"true" predicative of existential verb aru [before mazi] 132
truncation(s) 6 29; [indicated by voiced-obstruent initial] 30; 35 43 59 71 74 88; [leaving DAKU initials] 93; [characterized by double-low accent in Wakayama] 169; [nouns of 2.5] 361; 546 559 565 579 668; (n[i]) 801; 805 815 825 833 836 846
ts- = babytalk s- 33 ▯ ts : z 6 ▯ [ts], [tˢ] for "s" 34, [proto-Japanese?] 66
[ts-] > [s-] first with -i and then -u? 81 ▯ t(s/š) after T 76
[tš] [articulatory difficulty] 33; [Spanish] 33; [earlier sound of "s"?] 34
tš : ž 6 ▯ [tš] = s- [Hachijō] 33 ▯ tsa [syllable] 17; [innovative] 76
tša [interpreted as /cya/] 17; [as ancestor of "sa"] 34; 76
-tsan = -san [title] 33 ▯ -[tšaru] < -t[e]yaru < -te yaru 'does as a favor' 38
tse 17; [innovative] 76 ▯ tše [for "te"] 18; [innovative] 76
tši 17; [interpreted as /ti/] 17; 76 ▯ -tši [Tsushima gerund] 121
tsɨ 76; [tsɨ] treated as /tu/ 17 ▯ [tsɨu] 18
tso 17; [innovative] 76 ▯ tšo [as ancestor of "so"] 34; 76
-[tšoku] < -t[e]yoku < -te[y]oku < -te oku 'does for now/later' 38
-tsu [Tsushima gerund] 121; [JP] 124 ▯ tšu [syllable] 76
t- syllables with single circle (hudakuˀ-ten) 118
[ᵗθ] = s- or t- [Kudaka] 33
tt- [to write initial tense dental stop of Yonaguni and Nakijin] 81
-tt- 2 75 142 ▯ -(t)tarasi- [bound adjective] 816 820
-tte < -ki-te or -si-te [Hachijō], < -pi-te [only in east], < -ri-te, < -ti-te 125

*u-ri [expected for Ryūkyū quri] 36 ▯ u(ru) 'get' [analogical] 42 ▯ "···uru" 42
-uru (or -Curu = verb attributive ending) [forms surviving in modern dialects] 133;
   ["attributive" finite of vowel verbs (literary)] 666; [reduction from more
   complex structure] 667; (reduced to -[ur]u after consonant) 668
-uru/-e [lower bigrade conjugation] 126; [simplified later than -uru/-i] 133
-uru/-i [upper] bigrade conjugation 126; [simplified earlier than -uru/-e] 133
usagi 'rabbit' [velar voiced?] 93; LHH > LLH [1700 Ōsaka LHH > LLH] 360; [Kyōto low
   atonic treated as ꜜusagi] 143, [final high nondistinctive] 261
usii (= usui) not ušii 2 ▯ uso- = usu- 'somewhat, slightly' [quasi-prefix] 822
uti- 'hit and' (intensifies) 204 ▯ Utsubo-monogatari 78 120
uttaeru 'sues' [-T- indicated by entering tone] 190
ut[y]i 'hit' [as intensive prefix] 95 204
uu = [u:] or after sibilant [ɨ:] 4 76 142
uu < u-u; uu < *uꟲ; uu < u-ku; uu < u(w)-u < uf-u 46
*uutu [expected for Ryūkyū quutu] 36
-u versions [of -f- verb-stems] restored in modern Kyōto (except yuu 'say')] 127
uweru 'plants' [Shingū, Wakayama] 15
"U x" = no Umegaki data 228 ▯ [üy] earlier pronunciation of -iy 67
"Uyeda" [romanized spelling] 15 ▯ uyeru 'plants' [Tanabe, Wakayama] 15
···u - zu(ru) 130
v, vb = verb 373 ▯ v [labiodental voiced fricative (Miyako)] 12
v [uniquely used by Miyara for initial of Yonaguni 'bucket'] 9
V = verb; = vowel (vs. C = consonant); V = β [bilabial voiced fricative] 1
[V:] treated as two syllables while vowel + -T- formed one syllable? 345
Va [innovative syllable] 76 ▯ V-a [subjunctive] 191
V-a-ba 'if V' 105 106; [developed later than V-ey-ba?] 119; [disappeared after 1600]
   119; [from V-a-m[u] fa?] 119; V-a ba (Hn-Km accent)] 170
V-a-ba ≠ V-ey-ba distinction survives in Ryūkyūs 119
vacillation in spellings [for Japanese "h-"] of 1492 Korean Ilopha 11
V-a-de as substitute for V-azu te[y] 111; V-a de 'not doing' [Hn-Km accent] 170
"vague" (aimai) accent systems [from recent loss of distinctive patterns] 146
V-a-ma-ku fosi- (became Heian V-a-ma[k]u-[fo]si = -mausi) 820
V-a-ma[ku]-fosi- = -amafosi-, V-a-ma[ku]-[fo]si- = -amasi- 820
V-a masi [bound auxiliary (Hn-Km accent)] 170
V-(a)mu (presumptive) 65 129; [originally like presumptive + su(ru) 'intend to'] 130
V-a-m[u] fa source of V-a-ba? 119 ▯ V-a-mu to so, V-a-mu to zo, V-a-mu zo 110
V-a na [desires, OJ] 66 ▯ V-a - na- 'not V' 42 816 821
Va-na-i restructured from Va-nawe? 821
V-anai yoꜜ 'I won't do it!' 132 ▯ V-anai yoꜜo ni siyoo 'let's not do it' 132
*Va-na-ki, *V-a-na-si [no evidence they ever existed] 821
Va-nawe < Va - naf[y]e < *na-pa-Ci (infinitive of Azuma negative auxiliary verb) 821
V-a ne [desires (OJ)] 66
V-a - ni [relic of infinitive of negative auxiliary] 816 821 ▯ V-an[i] su 26
*V-an-[y]i te[y] [unattested] 111
V-a - nu [attributive of negative auxiliary] 25 65 816 ▯ V-are[y]- passive 65
variant [accentuations] 5; [reductions] 30 43; [copula forms] 32; [versions of
   syllables] 76; [versions of words with more than one accent pattern] 86;
   [pronunciations] 112; [versions of common vocabulary unnoticed] 120; [Kinki
   accents] 219
variations in accentuating adjective forms in contemporary Tōkyō 824
variants [unattested except in Hankul] 24; [of honorific title] 33; [of gerund] 121
variation of compressed and conflated forms for Chinese CyV and CwV 83

verb stems ending in: /a/ 15; ···ey- from *···a-gi- 65; "morphophonemic w" 13;
  /i/ [few attested for presumptive forms] 137; /m/ [longer] 123; sibilant
  (attributive of perfective originally regular -si) 808; ···žir- 17
verb stems of Type B of three or more syllables kept distinct from A though becoming
  high-initial [Kōchi, Tanabe, Akō, Shingū] 353
verbs with ···e infinitives [explanation for] 131
vertically paired circles 118 ◊ ···Ve-ru 15
V-ey-ba 'V and so/then' 105; [with phonograms ambivalently ma or ba] 105 106
V-ey-do 'V but' 108 109
V-ey-do mo 108 109, contracted to V-ey-do? 119; V-ey-do [mo] 108
vi = intransitive verb 373 ◊ Vi [innovative syllable] 76
Vi (= vowel + i): [···Vi-] 15; [going back to velar nasal] 27; [Vi ≠ Vyi not
  distinguished in modern language] 39; 41; [interpreted as Vyi (OJ)] 64
Vï = vowel + ï 27
V-i (= verb + infinitive -[y]i): - bosi- 'desiring (to V)' (V-i ga fosi-) 820;
  - gata-, - gatana- [Shuri], - gurusi-, - gurisi- [Shuri] 'difficult (to V)';
  - niku- 'difficult (to V)'; - yo- 'good (to V); easy (to V)'; - zura- ‹ - dura-
  'difficult (to V)' (auxiliary adjectives) 819 821
V-i-kaeru 'change V-ing; change the N that one V-s' 115
(V-i)-ki retrospective [predicative except in -keku] 127
(V-i)-si of retrospective attributive [originally the same as the adj pred -si?] 127
V-i - myi [OJ] = modern V-tari (representative) 806
V-i nagara [particle (Hn-Km accent)] 170
[V-i]-n-pa 29 ◊ ···Vi-ru 15 ◊ V-i-si for V-i-kyi (examples) 808
V-i - ta- 'desiring (to V), tending to (V)' [auxiliary adjective] 820
V-i-takkya 'wants to V' [Hachijō sentence-final] 810
V-i te (gerund), V-i tutu (particle) [Hn-Km accent] 170
V-i V [separate accentuations (Heian)] 210; [list of Myōgi-shō examples] 670
V-i wa/mo/sae/koso + auxiliary si- 'do' 802
VN, vn = verbal noun 825
Vn = vowel + -n (treated as two syllables while vowel + -T- formed one?) 345
VN-zɨ(ru), VN-žiru 17
Vo = vowel + o 39 ◊ Vo [innovative syllable] 76
V-o [Hachijō attributive] a continuation of proto-Japanese forms? 811
vocabulary [older] 45 ◊ vocalization [labial, palatal] 122
voiced initial that reflects the earlier prenasalization 669
voiced stops [after -n in proto-Japanese] 122
voiced velar stop or fricative (probable value of -C- in -Ci) 667
voiced allophones [for obstruents] 25
voiced obstruent(s) [vs. unvoiced] 6; 29 35; [after -n- intensive infix] 81
voiced affricates [dži] and [dzɨ] = ¨si and ¨su [in dialects] 16
voiced affricates vs. voiced fricatives [maintained in Chep-hay sin-e] 21
voiced (bi)labial fricative [β] 7; [for OJ -f-?] 37
voiced fricative neutralizing lenited velar and labial stops of Middle Korean 82
voiced initials (from dropping initial syllable) [traditional] 29; [early] 30
voiced interdental fricative 16
voiced stop(s) 19; [as proto-J initials] 20; [transcribed with Hankul digraphs] 22
voiced sounds between vowels 20
voiced (DAKU) syllables = syllables with distinctively voiced initials 29
voiced velar fricative [γ] in place of [ŋ] 7 ◊ voiced velar stop [proto-J?] 20
voiceless [vs. voiced] 84
voiceless affricate *c- [reconstructed by Unger] 34 ◊ voiceless allophone 125

vowel-stem verbs [infinitives ···e-i, ···i-i?] 121; [juncture slower to disappear] 121; [in modern language] 666; [predicatives used for attributive] 809
vowel structure of Old Japanese 57
vowel system [of Kametsu] similar to that of Shodon 55
vowel unvoicing 5 ◊ vowel variation in related words 69
V-r[u a]ku 809 ◊ V-ru ku naru [Akita] = V-ru yoo ni naru 804
V-ru ⁻ma⁊i 132 ◊ V-ru⁊ ni 92 ◊ V-ru⁊ no o yameyoo 132 ◊ V-ru -tu N 368
V-sa- 'deign to V' 672 ◊ V-u so̱ 110
vt = transitive verb 373 ◊ V-te V ‹ V-[y]i te[y] V 93
V-u to̱ mo̱ 108 ◊ V -tu N 368 ◊ /VtunV/ › /VtnV/ in dialects 74
Vu = vowel + u [going back to velar nasal] 27; [not from nasal] 28; 39 40
Vu [innovative] 76 ◊ Vɡ 27
V-u N for V-uru N in lexicalizations 807 ◊ V-u na (earlier na V-i so̱) 'don't' 471
V-(ur)'ey (-ba/-do) [provisional-concessive (*izen-kei*) form] 191
VV [as single syllable] 4; [lacking in OJ] 64 ◊ V-V ‹ VCV in proto-J 37 ◊ V-VT 2
V-'[y]i + a → V-'ye › V-'e imperative 'do!' 191
V-yi - A [mostly productive] 816 ◊ Vy[¹/ₑ s]uru 41
V-yi ga fwosi 'desire to V' always adnominalized as fwosi 807
V-yi - gata-, V-yi - gata ni 'difficult to V' 94
V-yi - gate[y]n[y]i 'unable to V' 94
V-yi kane[y] / kanu(ru) 'cannot V' [written ga- in Azuma songs only] 94
V-yi kate[y] / katu(ru) 'can V' 94
V-yi - N with nigori 104 ◊ V-yi -n- A + Formant [comprising adjective stem] 817
V-yi - nuraku [are there OJ examples?] 809
V-yi₁ -n- V-yi₁ + Formant [comprising adjective stem] 817
V-yi - ta- 816 ◊ V-yi te[y] zo̱ 110
V-yi - V (single compound verb), V-[y]i V 93
V-yi₁ - V-yi₁ + Formant [comprising adjective stem] 817
V-(y)oo to suru [any subject permitted] 129
···Vy-u[ru] [literary] 15 41
W = Kokin-waka-shū shōten-bon (mostly Kamakura accent; from Akinaga 1974) 365
...W- = "wari[-chū]" = interlinear note (in Ishizuka's NS references) 373
w- [tightened into b- in southern Ryūkyūs] 20; [as nondistinctive] 36; [in /we/] 38; [syllables, new] 38; [words once pronounced with distinctive] 38; [initial] 57
w- ‹ (*)b- 20 36 57 667 ◊ w 5; (before a) 7; [never distinctive] 44 ◊ w··· 9
"-w-" [artificial; introduced from orthography for tokotowa] 87
-w- (sound of "-f-" from c. 1100) 667 ◊ -[w]- expected for morpheme-internal -h- 87
-w- [of iti-wa 'one bird'] 9; [from -p-, early Heian?] 12; [elision] 12; [for "-h-"] 12; [modern, with voiceless ancestor] 12; [proper] 13; [verbs (Nase-Kominato reflexes)] 14; [OJ evidence for] 14; [‹ *-b-] 20; [later within certain morphemes] 20; [‹ -f- (‹ -p-)] 37 42 44, (before dropping between vowels) 37; [often ignored even before /a/] 39; [underlying] 42; [of Cwo] 57; [not articulated in loanmorphs ⁻kwi, kwe, kwen, gwen"?] 72; [Ryūkyū cases from *-p-?] 80
···w··· after -n- allomorph of intensive infix 81
-W [in Sino-Korean words (with Chinese Vu = -Vw)] 11
-W- [earlier Korean (probably bilabial voiced fricative β)] 5 11
wa [initial] 10 76; [Kudaka] 10; [only w-syllable in Tōkyō] 13 ◊ w(a) 9; [w]a 42
wa ‹ fa (particle) [with Kyōto verb inf] 158; [low after Kyōto B inf (unpredictable from N wa)] 158 168; [Hn-Km wa (‹ fa 170 [had rise? (Mochizuki)] 170; [early-Edo high after high, low after low] 170; ··· ◊ wa⁊ ◊ [insistent] 172
wabiy 'simple taste; apology' 64 ◊ wa ga myi [OJ dial.] = wa ga mye 'my wife' 119
wa ga written with phonogram ADD instead of CONGRATULATE 119

words [in Tōkyō] 152; [without a basic accent (no inherent fall of pitch) are
  "atonic"] 160; [attested both low-initial and high-initial (= initial rise?)] 184
words borrowed from Chinese: *see* loanwords [Chinese]
words for 'father' and 'mother' 6 ◊ words lacking [tone] marks in Mg 85
words with DAKU syllable earlier and SEI later 86
words with more than one accent pattern 86
word types (*rui*) 243 ◊ word types and phrase types [accent] 297
word [accent] patterns and phrase patterns 243 ◊ [w]ori 665
"woru" (attributive woru > oru) 'breaks it', (woruru → oreru) 'it breaks' 672
wo si zo̲, wo si zo̲ mo̲ 110
"woW" [Hankul spelling] 45 ◊ written: Japanese 93; standards [influence of] 2
*···wt··· < *···pyt··· [in gerunds] 122
wu 5; [as distinct from u] 10 56; [< wo] 56 ◊ wu = (')u [no OJ distinction] 52
wu [Hankul (in Iroha poem)] = /u/ 11 ◊ wu 'is' (OJ predicative for wi[y]-) 666
-(w)u 40 ◊ ?wu(ru) / wi[y] 'be' (OJ) 666 ◊ Wwu = u [syllable in Iroha poem] 11
x = unknown (data unavailable or lacking; etymon missing) 364 373; [in accent
  pattern schema] the syllable lacks a mark in the attestation 365
"xe" [še] for modern /se/ [JP] 79
y- [z used for] 19; [tightened into d- in southern Ryūkyūs] 20; [with d- and n-] 32;
  [nondistinctive] 36; [in "ye" palatal glide? nonpalatalized d-?] 51; [initial] 57
y- [< *d- (or *j-)] 20 667 ◊ y- [initial lacking in Yonaguni] 19; [prothetic] 133
y- [reduced form of verb prefix i-] 668
/y/ [as dropping after a consonant (yom-yoo → yomoo, yom-ru → yom-u)] 129
y [ž used for] 19; [alternating with d and/or t] 19; [alternating with n] 19; [in
  -yoo alternant of presumptive after vowel stems] 37
-y- [epenthetic(ally inserted)] 15 38 82 129
-y- [in etymon ni[y]- 'boil'] 15; [distinct from -d- (Yonaguni)] 19; [within certain
  morphemes later] 20; [and -n- as variants] 32; [underlying] 42; [or -r- in OJ verb
  stems] 35; [in literary forms] 42; [in second syllable (Shodon)] 57; [as extension
  of palatal quality of preceding i] 82; [from weakened palatal spirant] 126
···y··· after -n- allomorph of intensive infix 81
ya [initial, OJ] 51; [syllable] 76 ◊ ya = wa (focus marker) 802
ya 'and' (particle) [Kyōto low] 158; [Hn-Km ȳa, early-Edo low] 170; [Kōchi,
  Wakayama low] 171 ◊ ya 'hey' (particle) [early-Edo low] 170
ya = ya˦ 'is' (= da˦ copula predicative) [dialect] 19; [Kyōto low] 158 171;
  [Wakayama low] 171
ya 'question' (particle) [early-Edo] 170 ◊ -ya [suffix: forms adjectival nouns] 822
yaa (< ...) 46 ◊ Yaeyama [separate development for Cyi] 52
*ya-ka > yauka > yɔɔka > yooka 'eight days' 71
-ya-ka [suffix: forms adjectival nouns] 241 822 ◊ -yakasu < *-da-ka-sa 795
yaki (infinitive-derived noun) [beginning Kyōto compounds that are B] 221
-yaku < *-da-ka- 795 ◊ ya[k]u-yaku > ya[k]u-ya[k]u > yooyoo 'eventually' 71
Yale romanization [of Korean] 5 11 ◊ yama-bye 101
Yamaguchi [permits locus on second mora of heavy syllable] 144; [does not cancel
  oxytonic noun accent before /no/] 256; [merges 2.3 with 2.2 as oxytonic] 256
Yamato 53 ◊ yan < ya a- [Okinawan copula] 80 ◊ -yan = -san [title] 33
Yanagita Kunio's surname miswritten as Yanagida 119 ◊ Yán Shī-gǔ 118
*yap > yafu > yau > yɔɔ > yoo [does not occur] 47
yara 'and the like' (particle) [Kōchi low] 158 171; [Kyōto low] 171
-yaru < *-da-ra- 795 ◊ yasu- 'easy (to do)' [auxiliary adjective] 821
-yasu < *-da-sa- 795 ◊ yatta 'was' (copula perfect) [Kyōto low] 158 171
*yaw > yau > yɔɔ > yoo [does not occur] 47 ◊ *···yd··· [in gerunds] 122

ye- [not distinguished from e] 15; [e- merging with] 19; [phonograms for] 19;
  [syllable within morphemes] 51; [in some words must be underlying yey] 51; [(OJ,
  initial syllable) > Shodon yi-] 54
(y)e- words lacking 51 ▯ "ye" for modern /e/ [JP] 79 ▯ ye [innovative] 76
[ye] (> [e] by 1775, earlier in east?) 79; (after -N) 79; (in modern dialects) 79;
  (value of merged /e/ and /ye/) 79
[ye] pronounced [ze] in Gifu 18 ▯ /ye/ and /e/ merged as [ye] 79
/ye/ and /yey/ [no morpheme-initial contrast in OJ] 51
-ye [OJ postconsonantal] 57; [norm for -e row of syllabary?] 83
-ye [(OJ) > Shodon -i = ɨ (but syllable ye- > yi-)] 54
-ye [imperative ending (OJ)] 668
···(y)e- adjectives [survived till 1600] 128
yee < (y)εε (< yai < ya-ki, < yai < -ai) 47
yep > yefu > yeu > you > yoo 47 ▯ y[e s]uru 42
···(y)e-u > ···yoo [16th-century presumptives] 127 131
yew > yeu > you > yoo 47
/yey/ and /ye/ [no morpheme-initial contrast in OJ] 51
-ye[y]- < *-da-Ci- [OJ bound auxiliary] 35 790 ▯ ygr = younger speakers 373
yi- [Shodon] < ye- 54
yi [syllable not distinguished from i] 15; [written for nondistinctive yi/i] 122
yi = (')i [no OJ distinction] 52 ▯ yi [i] 52
*yi ≠ *iy [no distinction in OJ] 52 ▯ (y)i [ǰi used for] 19
-yi (OJ) [> Shodon -yi] 54; [treated as norm (= "i") by Unger] 57
-yi = -Ci 667
-yi and -iy [fell together around 800, but before 700 after apicals] 86
-(y)i- spelled for -fi- 82 ▯ Yn = Yonaguni 373 ▯ yo- 'good' 216
yo [initial, OJ] 51; [syllable] 76; yo [ko'o-otu distinction?] 57
yo 'generation; bamboo segment' [OJ; unexceptional?] 58
yo (sentence particle) [early-Edo, Kōchi low] 171; yò = yōo 347
-yo for -ro in Hachijō attibutive of verb stems ending in i or e 810
-yo shortened form of -yoo [hortative] 129
-yo- 'good (to V); easy (to V)' [auxiliary adjective] 821
yǒ··· 'meet' in compounds after infinitive [Esopo] 123
yo-dan [conjugation] 7; [verbs (= consonant stems)] 154; 352
yo[ ]i [verb infinitive] 8 ▯ yo-ka (= yori) 'than' (particle) [Ōsaka low] 170
yo[k]u > yoo [Kansai] 83 ▯ yon- 'four' 27
Yonaguni [velar nasal] 21; [notation] 81; [derived noun and infinitive have same
  accent] 211; [three registers A B C] 246 262; [uniquely A´ for reflex of aru] 282;
  [forms (mostly from Hirayama 1964 and 1967) 366
yoo < you < *yoᵤ, < you < (y)eu (< ...) 47
yoo < yɔɔ < yau < *yaᵤ 47
-yoo [alternant of presumptive after vowel stems] 37; [as hortative] 129, (basic
  form) 129, (→ -oo after consonant) 129; [example of conflation] 363
/-yoo/ rather than /-yɔɔ/ for 16th-century hortative ending 130
yoo V-an 'can't very well V' [Kansai] 83
yooyoo ?< ya[k]u-ya[k]u < ya[k]u-yaku 'eventually'; ?< yaya = iyoiyo 71
yori 'than; from' (particle) [Kyōto low] 158 171; 168; [Hn-Km yòri after LOW, yori
  after HIGH] 170, [Mg 'yori (tonic particle (switches pitch from preceding
  syllable)?] 173, [last syllable always low; basic shape yorii?] 173, [treated as
  falling yóri = yòori by Sakurai] 170 348; [early-Edo, Kōchi low] 171
yori-mo 'even than' (particle string) [Ōsaka low] 170
Yoshida = Yoshida Kanehiko 373 ▯ yoT = yo[ ]i [verb infinitive] 8

yotu-ḡana⁻ 16; [distinctions not maintained in Ryūkyūs] 16
(-)you < (-)ywofu < *dwopa- (bound verb 'waver') 795
younger speakers 2; [Tōkyō] (make all compound verbs tonic, have few longish atonic
    verbs except passives and causatives) 207
yow- < [w]ew- 'get intoxicated' 79 ◻ (-)yowasu < (-)ywofasu < *dwopa-sa- 795
yo(w)-u < (y)ew-u < (w)ew-u < wef-u 47
···yt··· < ···çt··· < ···št···) 122
yu- 'sacred' [no nigori] 102 ◻ yu [(Ryūkyū) < yu or yo] 56 76
yu [initial, OJ] 51 ◻ [y]u 42 ◻ -yu < *-da- 795 ◻ ···yu(ru) 42
yu/ywo(ri) traversal/ablative particle 811 ◻ yuu (< ... 46
ywo 'night' ≠ yo 'generation; bamboo segment' 59
[ywo] for Old Japanese [Unger deems implausible] 58
ywo fa 104 ◻ ywori fa 104
z 6; [substitutes for ᵈz internally] 6; [Hankul transcription = voiced sibilant]
    22; 25; [nondistinctively affricated before at least some vowels of OJ] 86
/z/ 23; [alternating with /d/] 34
[z] [z or ž = ˝t] 17; [for y- (Fukushima)] 19; [articulatory difficulty] 33
z- [borrowing, truncation, "special"] 30; [ᵈz after juncture] 33; 79
*z- 36 36; [voicing questioned] 36 ◻ "*z-" or "*[z]" used for (s)- 36
˝z˝ of Shuri palatalized (= zy), "ʐ" formerly unpalatalized 366
-[z]- alternating with [ᵈz]- 34 ◻ -z- [ambiguously represented by Hankul s] 23 25
[˜z] (Shima, sporadic) 21 ◻ [˜ᵈz] = -z- (northeastern Honshū, southern Kinki) 21
ž 6 6; [for y] 19; [= ˝t] 17; [articulatory difficulty] 33; [as ancestor of z-] 34
-[ž]- alternating with -[ᵈž]- 34 ◻ ··· zaru: see V-a zaru
Zdb = Omodaka et al. 1967: Jidai-betsu kokugo dai-jiten, jōdai-hen 373
ze [= dže] 18; [modern syllable] 19; written "ie" or "je" [JP] 79
[ze] in eastern Japan noted by Rodriguez 79
[že] = ze [distribution correlated with ye] 18; [Toyama] 18; 19
zero (before -i and -u) alternating with w (before a) 7
zero initial (') = vowel onset 10 57
zero (vowel beginning) [before -i and -u] 7; [alternating with -w-] 13; 20;
    [alternating with s-] 35
Zhāng Shǒujié 118 ◻ zi [ži] transcription for JP citations 86
-zi 'will not' [?< -n[i] - si] 104 132
-zi-₁ [adjective-stem formant], -zi-₂ (negative 'un-') [adj-stem formant] 819
-zi- of auxiliary mazi- [same as -zi 'will not'?] 132
zɨ (as well as za zo ze initial and medial) 16 ◻ zɨ (Kōchi) = earlier ˝su 16
ži (Kōchi) = earlier ˝si = zi 16; [Narada] 16 33; [for (y)i] 19
zo = zo [emphatic particle ('indeed')] 24 71 104; [as DAKU variant] 110; [as
    single shape] 110; [voiced initial in Ryūkyū reflexes too] 110; [Kyōto low?] 158;
    [Hn-Km accent] 170, [treated as falling zǒ by Sakurai] 170; [early-Edo low] 170
zo/so > so(/zo) > zo [emphatic particle] 110
zonzimase˥n (A-ku +), zonzima˥su (A-[k]u +) 127
zoological names (in Type 2.5) 361 ◻ Zs = Zusho-ryō text of Myōgi-shō 373
-zu [< -n-su] 68; 104; [in Koji-ki] 111; [methathesis of pitch with that of last
    syllable of subjunctive] 351
-zura- < - dura- 'difficult (to do)' [auxiliary adjective] 821
-zu(ru) > -ziru 26
··· zu(ru) [after Chinese verbal noun ending in nasals] 130; [presumptive +] 130
Zusho-ryō [- bon] Myōgi-shō = Tosho-ryō [- bon] Myōgi-shō 167 172 192 342
-zuyo- 'strong (with respect to)' 817 820
zwo [syllable lacking in Koji-ki and NS] 119

zya [copula] 80 ▯ -zyami suffix [Amami] 29
-zya-mono and -zya-hito/-bito 'person who is ⋯ ' 80 ▯ -zyan suffix [Okinawa] 29
zyo- 'female' [compounds mostly high in Kyōto but B in Kagoshima] 229 315
-zyo⌐ (with no retreat) / -zyo (atonicizing) 'place' 233
zyo⌐o = zyo⌐o(-syoo/-sei) 'rising (tone)' [high pitch] 167
zyo⌐odai (= Nara period) 77; zyoodai-go⁻ = Old Japanese (Nara period) 77
(zyo⌐odai) tokusyu-kanazu⌐kai 'special kana spelling (of the Nara Period)' 50
zyo⌐o-sei = zyo⌐o(-syoo/-sei) 'rising (tone)' [high pitch] 167
(-⁻)zyuu⁻ 'all through (a time/place)' 28

List of Chinese Phonograms

The mnemonic tag is followed is followed by the usual reading assigned each
of the phonograms discussed. A few semantograms are given, without readings.

加	ADD	ka	儒	CONFUCIANIST	zu
怒	ANGER	nwo/nu	賀	CONGRATULATE	ga(/ka)
孺	BABY	zu	句	COUPLET	ku
豆	BEAN	tu/du	涅	DAUB	de
勾	BENT	ku	妣	DEAD-MOTHER	byi
破	BOIL(/EAT)	zo̲	魔	DEVIL	ba/ma
弓	BOW-ONE	te	難	DIFFICULT	na
彌	BOW-YOU	byi/myi	升	DIPPER/MEASURE	two
破	BREAK	fa	溝	DITCH	ko
都	CAPITAL	tu	倍	DOUBLE	fey
子	CHILD/si	—	婁	DRAG	ru
氐	CLAN-ONE	te	珥	EAR-ORNAMENT	zi
涅	CLAY	de	我	EGO	ga
登	CLIMB	to	耐	ENDURE	do̲/de
比	COMPARE	fyi	委	ENTRUST	wi

等	EQUAL(/GROUP)	t<u>o</u>
齊	EQUAL/Rad.210	se
每	EVERY	mey
薇	EVIL	fey
存	EXIST	z<u>o</u>
望	EXPECT	mo
太	FAT	da
毘	(FIELD-)HELP	fyi/byi
滿	FILL	ma(n)
麼	FINE/QUERY	ba/ma
跡	FOOTPRINT/seki	t<u>o</u>
曾	FORMERLY	s<u>o</u>
與	GIVE	y<u>o</u>
施	GIVE ALMS	si
婆	GRANNY	ba
俱	GROUP	ku
天	HEAVEN	te(n)
高	HIGH	k<u>o</u>
馱	HORSE LOAD	ta/da
餓	HUNGER	ga
兒	INFANT/ni	—
保	KEEP	fo

刀	KNIFE	two
知	KNOW	ti
提	LIFT	de
多	MANY	ta
符	MARK	fu
荷	MINT	ka
苔	MOSS	t<u>o</u>
母	MOTHER	mo
泥	MUD	de(/ne/di)
浣	MUDDY WATER	wa
茸	MUSHROOM	zi
叙	NARRATE	z<u>o</u>
須	NECESSARILY	su
無	NOT	mu
古	OLD	kwo
㢠	PCL (RUN-WEST)	d<u>o</u>
所	PLACE	s<u>o</u>
圖	PLAN	two
鋤	PLOW	z<u>o</u>
磨	POLISH	ba/ma
有	POSSESS/yuu	—
序	PREFACE	z<u>o</u>

奈	PRESS	na
拖	PULL	ta/da
受	RECEIVE	zu
騰	RISE	t<u>o</u>
摩	RUB	ma
稜	RUGGED MAJESTY	ro
士	SCHOLAR	zi
見	SEE/ken	—
舍	SHED	sa
射	SHOOT	za
閉	SHUT	fey
杼	SHUTTLE	d<u>o</u>
寐	SLEEP	byi
播	SOW	fa
鏄	SPEAR-TANG	z<u>o</u>
在	STAY/zai	—

磋	STONE-DISCREPANCY	sa
止	STOP	t<u>o</u>
藏	STORE	za
層	STRATUM	s<u>o</u>
那	THAT/WHAT	na
薄	THIN	(ba)/fa
思	THINK	si
縻	TIE	ba/ma
度	TIMES	dwo
具	TOOL	gu
題	TOPIC	te
瀰	WATER-BOW-YOU	myi
浚	WATER-LITTLE-WOMAN	sa
波	WAVE	fa
何	WHAT	ga
煩	WORRY	f<u>o</u>